292

# Campbell-Walsh UROLOGY

EDITORS

## Louis R. Kavoussi, MD

Chairman
The Arthur Smith Institute for Urology
North Shore-Long Island Jewish Health System
Manhasset, New York
Professor of Urology
New York University School of Medicine
New York, New York

## Andrew C. Novick, MD

Chairman
Glickman Urological Institute
Cleveland Clinic Foundation
Professor of Surgery
Cleveland Clinic Lerner College of Medicine of
Case Western Reserve University
Cleveland, Ohio

## Alan W. Partin, MD, PhD

David Hall McConnell Professor and Director
James Buchanan Brady Urological Institute
Johns Hopkins Medical Institutions
Baltimore, Maryland

## Craig A. Peters, MD

John E. Cole Professor of Urology
University of Virginia
Charlottesville, Virginia

# Campbell-Walsh
# UROLOGY

**NINTH EDITION**

EDITOR-IN-CHIEF

**Alan J. Wein, MD, PhD(Hon)**
Professor and Chair
Division of Urology
University of Pennsylvania School of Medicine
Chief of Urology
University of Pennsylvania Medical Center
Philadelphia, Pennsylvania

**Volume 2**

SAUNDERS

ELSEVIER

# SAUNDERS
ELSEVIER

1600 John F. Kennedy Blvd.
Ste 1800
Philadelphia, PA 19103-2899

CAMPBELL-WALSH UROLOGY

ISBN 13: 978-0-7216-0798-6
ISBN 10: 0-7216-0798-5
E-dition ISBN 13: 978-1-4160-2966-3
ISBN 10: 1-4160-2966-4
International Edition ISBN 13: 978-0-8089-2353-4
ISBN 10: 0-8089-2353-6

---

### Notice

Knowledge and best practice in this field are constantly changing. As new research and experience broaden our knowledge, changes in practice, treatment, and drug therapy may become necessary or appropriate. Readers are advised to check the most current information provided (i) on procedures featured or (ii) by the manufacturer of each product to be administered, to verify the recommended dose or formula, the method and duration of administration, and contraindications. It is the responsibility of the practitioner, relying on his or her own experience and knowledge of the patient, to make diagnoses, to determine dosages and the best treatment for each individual patient, and to take all appropriate safety precautions. To the fullest extent of the law, neither the publisher nor the editors assume any liability for any injury and/or damage to persons or property arising out of or related to any use of the material contained in this book.

Note that the term ESWL has been trademarked by Dornier MedTech in the United States. The generic term for extracorporial shock wave lithotripsy is SWL. As the use of ESWL has become part of the vernacular of urology, some of the authors have elected to use this term in their chapters.

The Publisher

---

**Library of Congress Cataloging-in-Publication Data**

Campbell-Walsh urology.—9th ed. / editor-in-chief, Alan J. Wein; editors, Louis R. Kavoussi . . . [et al.].
   p. ; cm.
  Rev. ed. of: Campbell's urology / editor-in-chief, Patrick C. Walsh; editors, Alan B. Retik . . . [et al.]. 8th ed. ©2002.
  Includes bibliographical references and index.
  ISBN 0-7216-0798-5 (set)
    1. Urology.  I. Campbell, Meredith F. (Meredith Fairfax).  II. Wein, Alan J.  III. Kavoussi, Louis R.  IV. Campbell's urology.  V. Title: Urology.
  [DNLM:  1. Urogenital Diseases.  2. Urology—methods. WJ 100 c192 2007]
RC871.C33 2007
616.6—dc22
                                 2006041807

*Acquisitions Editor:* Rebecca Schmidt Gaertner
*Developmental Editor:* Anne Snyder
*Publishing Services Manager:* Tina Rebane
*Project Manager:* Norm Stellander
*Design Direction:* Ellen Zanolle

Printed in China
Last digit is the print number: 9  8  7  6  5  4  3  2  1

*To our families, our teachers, and our residents, all of whom have suffered our behavior in various ways and are responsible for our ability to do what we do.*

# CONTRIBUTORS

**Paul Abrams, MD, FRCS**
Professor of Urology,
Bristol Urological Institute,
Southmead Hospital,
Bristol, United Kingdom
*Overactive Bladder*

**Mark C. Adams, MD**
Professor, Division of Pediatric Urology,
Vanderbilt Children's Hospital,
Vanderbilt University Medical Center,
Nashville, Tennessee
*Urinary Tract Reconstruction in Children*

**Mohamad E. Allaf, MD**
Assistant Professor,
James Buchanan Brady Urological Institute,
Johns Hopkins Medical Institutions,
Baltimore, Maryland
*Diagnosis and Staging of Prostate Cancer*

**J. Kyle Anderson, MD**
Assistant Professor,
Department of Urologic Surgery,
Veterans Affairs Medical Center,
University of Minnesota Medical School,
Minneapolis, Minnesota
*Surgical Anatomy of the Retroperitoneum, Adrenals, Kidneys, and Ureters*

**Karl-Erik Andersson, MD, PhD**
Professor, Lund University;
Head Physician, Clinical Chemistry and Pharmacology,
Lund University Hospital,
Lund, Sweden
*Pharmacologic Management of Storage and Emptying Failure*

**Kenneth W. Angermeier, MD**
Associate Professor,
Prosthetic Surgery and Genitourethral Reconstruction,
Glickman Urological Institute,
Cleveland Clinic Foundation,
Cleveland, Ohio
*Surgery of Penile and Urethral Carcinoma*

**Rodney A. Appell, MD**
Professor, Scott Department of Urology,
Baylor College of Medicine;
F. Bantley Scott Chair in Urology,
St. Luke's Episcopal Hospital,
Houston, Texas
*Injection Therapy for Urinary Incontinence*

**Dean G. Assimos, MD**
Professor,
Division of Surgical Sciences,
Head, Section of Endourology and Nephrolithasis,
Department of Urology,
Wake Forest University School of Medicine,
Winston-Salem, North Carolina
*Pathophysiology of Urinary Tract Obstruction*

**Anthony Atala, MD**
W. Boyce Professor and Chair,
Department of Urology,
Wake Forest University School of Medicine;
Director, Wake Forest Institute for Regenerative Medicine,
Winston-Salem, North Carolina
*Tissue Engineering and Cell Therapy: Perspectives for Urology*

**Darius J. Bägli, MDCM, FRCSC, FAAP, FACS**
Associate Professor of Surgery,
Institute of Medical Science,
University of Toronto;
Director of Urology Research,
Research Institute,
The Hospital for Sick Children,
Toronto, Ontario, Canada
*Reflux and Megaureter*

**John M. Barry, MD**
Professor of Surgery,
Head, Division of Urology and Renal Transplantation,
The Oregon Health & Science University School
    of Medicine;
Staff Surgeon, Doernbecher Children's Hospital,
Portland, Oregon
*Renal Transplantation*

**Georg Bartsch, MD**
Professor and Chairman,
Department of Urology,
Medical University of Innsbruck,
Innsbruck, Austria
*Surgery of Testicular Tumors*

**Stuart B. Bauer, MD**
Professor of Surgery (Urology),
Harvard Medical School;
Senior Associate in Urology,
Children's Hospital,
Boston, Massachusetts
*Anomalies of the Upper Urinary Tract*
*Voiding Dysfunction in Children: Non-Neurogenic and Neurogenic*

**Clair J. Beard, MD**
Assistant Professor, Harvard Medical School;
Vice-Chair, Division of Radiation Oncology,
Dana-Farber Cancer Institute,
Brigham and Women's Hospital,
Boston, Massachusetts
*Radiation Therapy for Prostate Cancer*

**Arie S. Belldegrun, MD, FACS**
Professor of Urology,
Chief, Division of Urologic Oncology,
Roy and Carol Doumani Chair in Urologic Oncology,
David Geffen School of Medicine,
University of California, Los Angeles,
Los Angeles, California
*Cryotherapy for Prostate Cancer*

**Mark F. Bellinger, MD**
Professor of Urology,
Children's Hospital of Pittsburgh,
University of Pittsburgh Medical Center,
Pittsburgh, Pennsylvania
*Abnormalities of the Testes and Scrotum and
Their Surgical Management*

**Mitchell C. Benson, MD**
George F. Cahill Professor and Chairman,
J. Bently Squier Urological Clinic,
Columbia University Medical Center,
New York, New York
*Cutaneous Continent Urinary Diversion*

**Sam B. Bhayani, MD**
Assistant Professor of Surgery,
Department of Urology,
Washington University School of Medicine,
St. Louis, Missouri
*Urinary Tract Imaging: Basic Principles*

**Jay T. Bishoff, MD**
Associate Clinical Professor of Surgery,
University of Texas Health Science Center,
San Antonio, Texas;
Director,
Endourology Section,
Wilford Hall Medical Center,
Lackland AFB, Texas
*Laparoscopic Surgery of the Kidney*

**Jerry G. Blaivas, MD**
Clinical Professor of Urology,
Weill Medical College of Cornell University;
Attending,
New York-Presbyterian Hospital,
Lenox Hill Hospital,
New York, New York
*Urinary Incontinence: Epidemiology, Pathophysiology,
Evaluation, and Management Overview*

**Jon D. Blumenfeld, MD**
Associate Professor of Medicine,
Weill Medical College of Cornell University;
Director of Hypertension,
Director of The Susan R. Knafel Polycystic Kidney
    Disease Center,
The Rogosin Institute;
Associate Attending Physician,
New York-Presbyterian Hospital,
New York, New York
*Pathophysiology, Evaluation, and Medical Management
of Adrenal Disorders*

**Michael L. Blute, MD**
Professor of Urology,
Mayo Medical School;
Chairman, Department of Urology,
Mayo Clinic,
Rochester, Minnesota
*Surgery of the Adrenal Glands*

**Joseph G. Borer, MD**
Assistant Professor of Surgery,
Department of Urology,
Harvard Medical School;
Assistant in Urology,
Children's Hospital Boston,
Boston, Massachusetts
*Hypospadias*

**George J. Bosl, MD**
Chairman, Department of Medicine,
Patrick M. Byrne Chair in Clinical Oncology,
Memorial Sloan-Kettering Cancer Center,
New York, New York
*Surgery of Testicular Tumors*

**Charles B. Brendler, MD**
Professor and Chief, Section of Urology,
University of Chicago School of Medicine,
Chicago, Illinois
*Evaluation of the Urologic Patient: History, Physical
Examination, and Urinalysis*

**Gregory A. Broderick, MD**
Professor of Urology,
Mayo Medical School,
Mayo Clinic,
Jacksonville, Florida
*Evaluation and Nonsurgical Management of Erectile
Dysfunction and Premature Ejaculation*

**James D. Brooks, MD**
Associate Professor,
Department of Urology,
Stanford University Medical Center,
Stanford, California
*Anatomy of the Lower Urinary Tract and Male Genitalia*

**Ronald M. Bukowski, MD**
Professor of Medicine,
Cleveland Clinic Lerner College of Medicine of
　Case Western Reserve University;
Director, Experimental Therapeutics,
Cleveland Clinic Foundation,
Cleveland, Ohio
　*Renal Tumors*

**Arthur L. Burnett, MD**
Professor of Urology, Cellular and Molecular Biology,
Johns Hopkins University School of Medicine;
Staff Urologist, The Johns Hopkins Hospital,
Baltimore, Maryland
　*Priapism*

**Jeffrey A. Cadeddu, MD**
Associate Professor,
Clinical Center for Minimally Invasive Urologic
　Cancer Treatment;
Department of Urology,
University of Texas Southwestern Medical Center,
Dallas, Texas
　*Surgical Anatomy of the Retroperitoneum, Adrenals,*
　*Kidneys, and Ureters*

**Anthony A. Caldamone, MD, MMS, FAAP, FACS**
Professor of Surgery and Pediatrics,
Department of Urology,
Brown University School of Medicine;
Head of Pediatric Urology,
Hasbro Children's Hospital,
Providence, Rhode Island
　*Prune Belly Syndrome*

**Steven C. Campbell, MD, PhD**
Professor of Surgery,
Cleveland Clinic Lerner College of Medicine of
　Case Western Reserve University;
Section of Urological Oncology,
Glickman Urological Institute,
Cleveland Clinic Foundation,
Cleveland, Ohio
　*Renal Tumors*
　*Non–Muscle-Invasive Bladder Cancer (Ta, T1, and CIS)*

**Douglas A. Canning, MD**
Professor of Urology,
University of Pennsylvania School of Medicine;
Director, Division of Urology,
Children's Hospital of Philadelphia,
Philadelphia, Pennsylvania
　*Evaluation of the Pediatric Urology Patient*

**Michael Carducci, MD**
Associate Professor of Oncology and Urology,
Johns Hopkins University School of Medicine;
Staff Physician, The Sidney Kimmel Comprehensive Cancer
　Center at Johns Hopkins,
Baltimore, Maryland
　*Treatment of Hormone-Refractory Prostate Cancer*

**Michael C. Carr, MD, PhD**
Associate Professor of Surgery in Urology,
University of Pennsylvania School of Medicine;
Attending Surgeon, Pediatric Urology,
Children's Hospital of Philadelphia,
Philadelphia, Pennsylvania
　*Anomalies and Surgery of the Ureteropelvic Junction in*
　*Children*

**Peter R. Carroll, MD**
Professor and Chair,
Department of Urology,
University of California, San Francisco, School of Medicine;
Surgeon in Chief, Comprehensive Cancer Center,
University of California, San Francisco, Cancer Center,
San Francisco, California
　*Treatment of Locally Advanced Prostate Cancer*

**H. Ballentine Carter, MD**
Professor of Urology and Oncology,
James Buchanan Brady Urological Institute,
Johns Hopkins Medical Institutions,
Baltimore, Maryland
　*Basic Instrumentation and Cystoscopy*
　*Diagnosis and Staging of Prostate Cancer*

**Anthony J. Casale, MD**
Professor and Chairman,
Department of Urology,
University of Louisville;
Chief of Urology,
Kosair Children's Hospital,
Louisville, Kentucky
　*Posterior Urethral Valves and Other Urethral Anomalies*

**William J. Catalona, MD**
Professor of Urology,
Feinberg School of Medicine,
Northwestern University;
Director, Clinical Prostate Cancer Program,
Robert H. Lurie Comprehensive Cancer Center,
Northwestern Memorial Hospital,
Chicago, Illinois
　*Definitive Therapy for Localized Prostate Cancer—*
　*An Overview*

**David Y. Chan, MD**
Assistant Professor of Urology and Pathology,
Director of Outpatient Urology,
James Buchanan Brady Urological Institute,
Johns Hopkins Medical Institutions,
Baltimore, Maryland
　*Basic Instrumentation and Cystoscopy*

**Michael B. Chancellor, MD**
Professor of Urology,
McGowan Institute of Regenerative Medicine,
University of Pittsburgh School of Medicine,
Pittsburgh, Pennsylvania
　*Physiology and Pharmacology of the Bladder and Urethra*

**C. R. Chapple, BSc, MD, FRCS (Urol)**
Professor of Urology (Hon),
Sheffield Hallam University;
Consultant Urological Surgeon,
Royal Hallamshire Hospital,
Sheffield, United Kingdom
*Retropubic Suspension Surgery for Incontinence in Women*

**Robert L. Chevalier, MD**
Benjamin Armistead Shepherd Professor and Chair,
Department of Pediatrics,
University of Virginia;
Pediatrician-In-Chief,
University of Virginia Medical School,
Charlottesville, Virginia
*Renal Function in the Fetus, Neonate, and Child*
*Congenital Urinary Obstruction: Pathophysiology*

**Ben H. Chew, MD, MSc, FRCSC**
Assistant Professor of Urology,
University of British Columbia,
Vancouver, British Columbia, Canada
*Ureteroscopy and Retrograde Ureteral Access*

**George K. Chow, MD**
Assistant Professor,
Department of Urology,
The Mayo Clinic,
Rochester, Minnesota
*Surgery of the Adrenal Glands*

**Ralph V. Clayman, MD**
Professor of Urology,
University of California, Irvine, Medical Center;
Chair of the Department of Urology,
University of California, Irvine, School of Medicine,
Orange, California
*Basics of Laparoscopic Urologic Surgery*

**Craig V. Comiter, MD**
Associate Professor of Surgery/Urology,
Instructor of Obstetrics and Gynecology,
University of Arizona;
Chief, Section of Urology,
Director, Urology Residency,
University of Arizona Health Sciences Center,
Tucson, Arizona
*Surgical Treatment of Male Sphincteric Urinary Incontinence: The Male Perineal Sling and Artificial Urinary Sphincter*

**Michael J. Conlin, MD**
Associate Professor of Surgery,
Director, Minimally Invasive Urologic Surgery,
Division of Urology and Renal Transplantation,
The Oregon Health & Science University School of Medicine,
Portland, Oregon
*Renal Transplantation*

**Juanita Crook, MD**
Associate Professor of Radiation Oncology,
University of Toronto;
Radiation Oncologist,
University Health Network,
Princess Margaret Hospital,
Toronto, Ontario, Canada
*Radiation Therapy for Prostate Cancer*

**Douglas M. Dahl, MD**
Assistant Professor of Surgery,
Department of Urology,
Harvard Medical School;
Assistant in Urology,
Massachusetts General Hospital,
Boston, Massachusetts
*Use of Intestinal Segments in Urinary Diversion*

**Anthony V. D'Amico, MD, PhD**
Professor of Radiation Oncology,
Harvard Medical School;
Professor and Chief of Genitourinary Radiation Oncology,
Dana-Farber Cancer Institute,
Brigham and Women's Hospital,
Boston, Massachusetts
*Radiation Therapy for Prostate Cancer*

**John W. Davis, MD**
Assistant Professor of Urology,
University of Texas MD Anderson Cancer Center,
Houston, Texas
*Tumors of the Penis*

**John D. Denstedt, MD, FRCSC**
Professor of Urology,
Chairman, Department of Surgery,
Schulich School of Medicine and Dentistry,
The University of Western Ontario,
London, Ontario, Canada
*Ureteroscopy and Retrograde Ureteral Access*

**Theodore L. DeWeese, MD, PhD**
Professor of Oncology,
Johns Hopkins University School of Medicine;
Radiation Oncologist-in-Chief,
Department of Radiation Oncology and Molecular
   Radiation Science,
Johns Hopkins Medical Institutions,
Baltimore, Maryland
*Radiation Therapy for Prostate Cancer*

**David A. Diamond, MD**
Associate Professor of Surgery,
Department of Urology,
Harvard Medical School;
Associate in Urology,
Children's Hospital,
Boston, Massachusetts
*Sexual Differentiation: Normal and Abnormal*

**Roger R. Dmochowski, MD, FACS**
Professor,
Department of Urologic Surgery,
Vanderbilt University Medical Center,
Nashville, Tennessee
  *Tension-Free Vaginal Tape Procedures*

**Steven G. Docimo, MD**
Professor of Urology,
Vice Chairman of Urology,
University of Pittsburgh School of Medicine;
Director of Urology,
Division of Pediatric Urology,
Children's Hospital of Pittsburgh,
Pittsburgh, Pennsylvania
  *Pediatric Endourology and Laparoscopy*

**Marcus Drake, DM, MA**
Consultant Urological Surgeon,
Bristol Urological Institute,
Southmead Hospital,
Bristol, United Kingdom
  *Overactive Bladder*

**James A. Eastham, MD**
Associate Professor,
Department of Urology,
Memorial Sloan-Kettering Cancer Center,
New York, New York
  *Expectant Management of Prostate Cancer*

**Louis Eichel, MD**
Clinical Associate Professor of Urology,
University of Rochester School of
    Medicine and Dentistry;
Director of Minimally Invasive Surgery,
Center for Urology,
Rochester, New York
  *Basics of Laparoscopic Urologic Surgery*

**Mario A. Eisenberger, MD**
R. Dale Hughes Professor of Oncology and Urology,
The Sidney Kimmel Comprehensive Cancer Center at
    Johns Hopkins,
Johns Hopkins University School of Medicine,
Baltimore, Maryland
  *Treatment of Hormone-Refractory Prostate Cancer*

**Alaa El-Ghoneimi, MD, PhD**
Professor of Pediatric Surgery,
University of Paris;
Senior Surgeon,
Hospital Robert Debré,
Paris, France
  *Anomalies and Surgery of the Ureteropelvic Junction
  in Children*

**Jack S. Elder, MD**
Professor and Vice Chairman,
Department of Urology,
Case Western Reserve University School of Medicine;
Division of Pediatric Urology,
Children's Hospital,
Cleveland, Ohio
  *Abnormalities of the Genitalia in Boys and
  Their Surgical Management*

**Jonathan I. Epstein, MD**
Professor of Pathology, Urology, and Oncology,
The Reinhard Professor of Urologic Pathology,
Johns Hopkins University School of Medicine;
Director of Surgical Pathology,
Johns Hopkins Medical Institutions,
Baltimore, Maryland
  *Pathology of Prostatic Neoplasia*

**Andrew P. Evan, PhD**
Chancellor's Professor,
Department of Anatomy and Cell Biology,
Indiana University School of Medicine,
Indianapolis, Indiana
  *Surgical Management of Upper Urinary Tract Calculi*

**Robert L. Fairchild, PhD**
Professor of Pathology,
Case Western Reserve University School of Medicine;
Staff, Department of Immunology,
Cleveland Clinic Foundation,
Cleveland, Ohio
  *Basic Principles of Immunology*

**Amr Fergany, MD, MB, BCh**
Staff, Section of Urologic Oncology,
Section of Laparoscopic Surgery and Robotics,
Glickman Urological Institute,
Cleveland Clinic Foundation,
Cleveland, Ohio
  *Renovascular Hypertension and Ischemic Nephropathy*

**James H. Finke, PhD**
Professor of Molecular Medicine,
Cleveland Clinic Lerner College of Medicine of
    Case Western Reserve University;
Staff, Department of Immunology,
Cleveland Clinic Foundation,
Cleveland, Ohio
  *Basic Principles of Immunology*

**John M. Fitzpatrick, MCh, FRCSI, FRCS(Glas), FRCS**
Professor and Chairman,
Department of Surgery,
University College, Dublin;
Professor of Surgery and Consultant Urologist,
Mater Misericordiae University Hospital,
Dublin, Ireland
  *Minimally Invasive and Endoscopic Management
  of Benign Prostatic Hyperplasia*

**Robert C. Flanigan, MD**
Albert J. Jr. and Claire R. Speh Professor and Chair,
Department of Urology,
Stritch School of Medicine,
Loyola University;
Chair of the Department of Urology,
Loyola University Medical Center,
Maywood, Illinois
*Urothelial Tumors of the Upper Urinary Tract*

**Stuart M. Flechner, MD**
Professor of Urology,
Cleveland Clinic Lerner College of Medicine of
  Case Western Reserve University;
Director of Clinical Research,
Section of Renal Transplantation,
Glickman Urological Institute,
Cleveland Clinic Foundation,
Cleveland, Ohio
*Basic Principles of Immunology*

**Tara Frenkl, MD, MPH**
Assistant Professor of Urology,
Director, Female Urology and Reconstructive Surgery,
Robert Wood Johnson Medical School,
The University of Medicine and Dentistry of New Jersey,
New Brunswick, New Jersey
*Sexually Transmitted Diseases*

**Dominic Frimberger, MD**
Assistant Professor of Urology,
University of Oklahoma Health Sciences Center;
Pediatric Urologist,
Children's Hospital of Oklahoma,
Oklahoma City, Oklahoma
*Bladder Anomalies in Children*

**John P. Gearhart, MD**
Professor of Pediatric Urology,
Johns Hopkins University School of Medicine;
Chief of Pediatric Urology,
The Johns Hopkins Hospital,
Baltimore, Maryland
*Exstrophy-Epispadias Complex*

**Glenn S. Gerber, MD**
Associate Professor,
Department of Surgery (Urology),
University of Chicago School of Medicine,
Chicago, Illinois
*Evaluation of the Urologic Patient: History, Physical
Examination, and Urinalysis*

**Inderbir S. Gill, MD, MCh**
Professor of Surgery,
Head, Section of Laparoscopic and Robotic Urology,
Glickman Urological Institute,
Cleveland Clinic Foundation,
Cleveland, Ohio
*Laparoscopic Surgery of the Urinary Bladder*

**Kenneth I. Glassberg, MD**
Professor of Urology,
Columbia University College of Physicians and Surgeons;
Director, Division of Pediatric Urology,
Morgan Stanley Children's Hospital of
  New York-Presbyterian,
New York, New York
*Renal Dysgenesis and Cystic Disease of the Kidney*

**David A. Goldfarb, MD**
Head, Section of Renal Transplantation,
Glickman Urological Institute,
Cleveland Clinic Foundation,
Cleveland, Ohio
*Etiology, Pathogenesis, and Management of Renal Failure*

**Irwin Goldstein, MD**
Editor-In-Chief,
The Journal of Sexual Medicine,
Milton, Massachusetts
*Urologic Management of Women With
Sexual Health Concerns*

**Marc Goldstein, MD, FACS**
Professor of Urology and Reproductive Medicine,
Surgeon-In-Chief, Male Reproductive Medicine and Surgery,
Executive Director, Men's Service Center,
Cornell Institute for Reproductive Medicine,
Weill Medical College of Cornell University;
Senior Scientist, Center for Biomedical Research,
The Population Council,
New York, New York
*Male Reproductive Physiology
Surgery of the Scrotum and Seminal Vesicles*

**Leonard G. Gomella, MD**
Professor and Chairman,
Department of Urology,
Jefferson Medical College;
Director,
Jefferson Prostate Diagnostic Center,
Kimmel Cancer Center,
Thomas Jefferson University Hospital,
Philadelphia, Pennsylvania
*Ultrasonography and Biopsy of the Prostate*

**Mark L. Gonzalgo, MD, PhD**
Associate Professor of Urology and Oncology,
Johns Hopkins Medical Center,
Baltimore, Maryland
*Management of Invasive and Metastatic Bladder Cancer*

**Richard W. Grady, MD**
Associate Professor of Urology,
The University of Washington School of Medicine;
Director, Clinical Research,
Children's Hospital & Regional Medical Center,
Seattle, Washington
*Surgical Techniques for One-Stage Reconstruction of
the Exstrophy-Epispadias Complex*

**Matthew B. Gretzer, MD**
Assistant Professor of Clinical Surgery,
Department of Surgery/Urology,
University of Arizona Health Science Center,
Tucson, Arizona
  *Prostate Cancer Tumor Markers*

**Mantu Gupta, MD**
Associate Professor,
Columbia University College of Physicians and Surgeons;
Director of Endourology, and Director of
  Kidney Stone Center,
Columbia University Medical Center New York-
  Presbyterian Hospital,
New York, New York
  *Percutaneous Management of the Upper Urinary Tract*

**Ethan J. Halpern, MD**
Professor of Radiology and Urology,
Jefferson Prostate Diagnostic Center,
Thomas Jefferson University,
Philadelphia, Pennsylvania
  *Ultrasonography and Biopsy of the Prostate*

**Misop Han, MD, MS**
Assistant Professor,
Department of Urology,
James Buchanan Brady Urological Institute,
Johns Hopkins Medical Institutions,
Baltimore, Maryland
  *Retropubic and Suprapubic Open Prostatectomy*
  *Definitive Therapy for Localized Prostate Cancer—*
  *An Overview*

**Philip M. Hanno, MD, MPH**
Professor of Urology,
University of Pennsylvania School of Medicine;
Medical Director, Department of Clinical Effectiveness
  and Quality Improvement,
University of Pennsylvania Health System,
Philadelphia, Pennsylvania
  *Painful Bladder Syndrome/Interstitial Cystitis and*
  *Related Disorders*

**Matthew P. Hardy, PhD**
Professor, Department of Urology,
Weill Medical College of Cornell University;
Member, Population Council,
The Rockefeller University,
New York, New York
  *Male Reproductive Physiology*

**David M. Hartke, MD**
Resident Physician,
Department of Urology,
University Hospitals of Cleveland;
Case Western Reserve University School of Medicine,
Cleveland, Ohio
  *Radical Perineal Prostatectomy*

**Jeremy P. W. Heaton, MD, FRCSC, FACS**
Professor of Urology,
Assistant Professor Pharmacology and Toxicology,
Queen's University,
Kingston, Ontario, Canada
  *Androgen Deficiency in the Aging Male*

**Sender Herschorn, BSc, MDCM, FRCSC**
Professor and Chairman, Division of Urology,
Martin Barkin Chair in Urological Research,
University of Toronto;
Attending Urologist,
Director, Urodynamics Unit,
Sunnybrook Health Sciences Centre,
Toronto, Ontario, Canada
  *Vaginal Reconstructive Surgery for Sphincteric*
  *Incontinence and Prolapse*

**Khai-Linh V. Ho, MD**
Endourology Fellow,
Mayo Clinic,
Rochester, Minnesota
  *Lower Urinary Tract Calculi*

**Thomas H. S. Hsu, MD**
Assistant Professor of Urology,
Director of Laparoscopic and Minimally
  Invasive Surgery,
Department of Urology, Stanford University
  School of Medicine;
Director of Laparoscopic, Robotic, and Minimally
  Invasive Urologic Surgery,
Stanford University Medical Center,
Stanford, California
  *Management of Upper Urinary Tract Obstruction*

**Mark Hurwitz, MD**
Assistant Professor,
Harvard Medical School;
Director, Regional Program Development,
Department of Radiation Oncology,
Dana-Farber/Brigham and Women's Cancer Center,
Boston, Massachusetts
  *Radiation Therapy for Prostate Cancer*

**Douglas Husmann, MD**
Professor of Urology,
Vice Chairman,
Department of Urology,
Mayo Clinic,
Rochester, Minnesota
  *Pediatric Genitourinary Trauma*

**Jonathan P. Jarow, MD**
Professor of Urology,
James Buchanan Brady Urological Institute,
Johns Hopkins Medical Institutions,
Baltimore, Maryland
  *Male Infertility*

**Thomas W. Jarrett, MD**
Professor of Urology,
Chairman, Department of Urology,
George Washington University,
Washington, DC
*Management of Urothelial Tumors of the Renal Pelvis*

**Christopher W. Johnson, MD**
Clinical Instructor of Urology,
Weill Medical College of Cornell University,
New York, New York;
Assistant Attending,
North Shore-Long Island Jewish Health System,
Manhasset, and St. Francis Hospital, Roslyn, New York
*Tuberculosis and Parasitic and Fungal Infections of
the Genitourinary System*

**Warren D. Johnson, Jr., MD**
B. H. Kean Professor of Tropical Medicine,
Chief, Division of Internal Medicine and Infectious Diseases,
Weill Medical College of Cornell University;
Attending Physician,
New York-Presbyterian Hospital, Cornell Campus,
New York, New York
*Tuberculosis and Parasitic and Fungal Infections of
the Genitourinary System*

**Deborah P. Jones, MD**
Associate Professor of Pediatrics,
University of Tennessee Health Science Center;
Attending, Le Bonheur Children's Medical Center,
Children's Foundation Research Center,
Memphis, Tennessee
*Renal Disease in Childhood*

**J. Stephen Jones, MD, FACS**
Associate Professor of Surgery (Urology),
Vice Chairman, Glickman Urological Institute,
Cleveland Clinic Lerner College of Medicine of
    Case Western Reserve University,
Cleveland Clinic Foundation,
Cleveland, Ohio
*Non–Muscle-Invasive Bladder Cancer (Ta, T1, and CIS)*

**Gerald H. Jordan, MD, FACS, FAAP**
Professor of Urology,
Eastern Virginia Medical School,
Norfolk, Virgina
*Peyronie's Disease*
*Surgery of the Penis and Urethra*

**Mark L. Jordan, MD**
Harris L. Willits Professor and Chief,
Division of Urology,
University of Medicine and Dentistry of New Jersey,
New Jersey Medical School;
Chief of Urology, University Hospital,
Newark, New Jersey
*Renal Transplantation*

**David B. Joseph, MD**
Professor of Surgery,
University of Alabama at Birmingham;
Chief of Pediatric Urology,
The Children's Hospital of Alabama,
Birmingham, Alabama
*Urinary Tract Reconstruction in Children*

**John N. Kabalin, MD**
Adjunct Assistant Professor of Surgery,
Section of Urologic Surgery,
University of Nebraska College of Medicine,
Omaha, Nebraska;
Regional West Medical Center,
Scottsbluff, Nebraska
*Surgical Anatomy of the Retroperitoneum, Adrenals,
Kidneys, and Ureters*

**Martin Kaefer, MD**
Associate Professor, Indiana University,
Riley Hospital for Children,
Indianapolis, Indiana
*Surgical Management of Intersexuality, Cloacal
Malformation, and Other Abnormalities of the
Genitalia in Girls*

**Irving Kaplan, MD**
Assistant Professor of Radiation Oncology,
Harvard Medical School;
Radiation Oncologist,
Beth Israel Deaconess Medical Center,
Boston, Massachusetts
*Radiation Therapy for Prostate Cancer*

**Louis R. Kavoussi, MD**
Chairman, The Arthur Smith Institute for Urology,
North Shore-Long Island Jewish Health System,
Manhasset, New York;
Professor of Urology,
New York University School of Medicine,
New York, New York
*Laparoscopic Surgery of the Kidney*

**Mohit Khera, MD, MBA, MPH**
Fellow, Division of Male Reproductive Medicine
    and Surgery,
Scott Department of Urology,
Baylor College of Medicine,
Houston, Texas
*Surgical Management of Male Infertility*

**Antoine Khoury, MD, FRCSC, FAAP**
Chief of Urology,
Senior Associate Scientist,
The Hospital for Sick Children;
Professor of Surgery,
The University of Toronto,
Toronto, Ontario, Canada
*Reflux and Megaureter*

**Adam S. Kibel, MD**
Associate Professor, Division of Urologic Surgery,
Washington University School of Medicine,
St. Louis, Missouri
*Molecular Genetics and Cancer Biology*

**Roger Kirby, MD, FRCS**
Professor and Director, The Prostate Centre;
Visiting Professor, St. George's Hospital,
Institute of Urology,
London, United Kingdom
*Evaluation and Nonsurgical Management of Benign
Prostatic Hyperplasia*

**Eric A. Klein, MD**
Professor of Surgery,
Cleveland Clinic Lerner College of Medicine of
Case Western Reserve University;
Head, Section of Urologic Oncology,
Glickman Urological Institute,
Cleveland Clinic Foundation,
Cleveland, Ohio
*Epidemiology, Etiology, and Prevention of Prostate Cancer*

**John N. Krieger, MD**
Professor of Urology,
University of Washington School of Medicine;
Chief of Surgical Urology,
VA Puget Sound Health Care System,
Seattle, Washington
*Urological Implications of AIDS and HIV Infection*

**Bradley P. Kropp, MD**
Professor of Urology,
University of Oklahoma Health Science Center;
Chief, Pediatric Urology,
Children's Hospital of Oklahoma,
Oklahoma City, Oklahoma
*Bladder Anomalies in Children*

**John S. Lam, MD**
Clinical Instructor in Urology,
David Geffen School of Medicine,
University of California, Los Angeles;
Attending Urologist,
University of California, Los Angeles, Medical Center,
Los Angeles, California
*Cryotherapy for Prostate Cancer*

**Herbert Lepor, MD**
Professor and Martin Spatz Chair,
Department of Urology,
New York University School of Medicine;
Chief of Urology,
New York University Medical Center,
New York, New York
*Evaluation and Nonsurgical Management of Benign
Prostatic Hyperplasia*

**Ronald W. Lewis, MD**
Witherington Chair in Urology,
Professor of Surgery (Urology) and Physiology,
and Chief of Urology,
Medical College of Georgia,
Augusta, Georgia
*Vascular Surgery for Erectile Dysfunction*

**James E. Lingeman, MD**
Director of Research,
Methodist Hospital Institute for Kidney Stone Disease;
Volunteer Clinical Professor,
Department of Urology,
Indiana University School of Medicine,
Indianapolis, Indiana
*Surgical Management of Upper Urinary Tract Calculi*

**Richard E. Link, MD, PhD**
Associate Professor of Urology,
Director, Division of Endourology and Minimally
Invasive Surgery,
Scott Department of Urology,
Baylor College of Medicine,
Houston, Texas
*Cutaneous Diseases of the External Genitalia*

**Larry I. Lipshultz, MD**
Professor of Urology,
Scott Department of Urology,
Lester and Sue Smith Chair in Reproductive Medicine,
Chief, Division of Male Reproductive Medicine
and Surgery,
Baylor College of Medicine,
Houston, Texas
*Surgical Management of Male Infertility*

**Mark S. Litwin, MD, MPH**
Professor of Urology and Health Services,
David Geffen School of Medicine,
University of California, Los Angeles;
University of California, Los Angeles, School of
Public Health,
Los Angeles, California
*Outcomes Research*

**Yair Lotan, MD**
Assistant Professor,
Department of Urology,
University of Texas Southwestern Medical Center;
Attending,
Parkland Health and Hospital Systems,
Zale Lipshy University Medical Center,
Veterans Affairs Medical Center,
Dallas, Texas
*Urinary Lithiasis: Etiology, Epidemiology,
and Pathogenesis*

**Tom F. Lue, MD**
Professor and Vice Chair,
Emil Tanagho Endowed Chair,
Department of Urology,
University of California School of Medicine, San Francisco,
San Francisco, California
*Physiology of Penile Erection and Pathophysiology of
Erectile Dysfunction*
*Evaluation and Nonsurgical Management of
Erectile Dysfunction and Premature Ejaculation*

**Donald F. Lynch, Jr., MD**
Professor and Chairman,
Department of Urology,
Professor of Obstetrics and Gynecology,
Eastern Virginia School of Medicine;
Urologic Oncologist,
Sentara Hospitals;
Consultant Urologist,
Jones Institute for Reproductive Medicine,
Norfolk, Virginia
*Tumors of the Penis*

**Michael Marberger, MD, FRCS(Ed)**
Professor and Chairman,
Department of Urology,
Medical University of Vienna,
Vienna, Austria
*Ablative Therapy of Renal Tumors*

**Fray F. Marshall, MD**
Professor and Chairman,
Department of Urology,
Emory University School of Medicine,
Atlanta, Georgia
*Surgery of Bladder Cancer*

**Brian R. Matlaga, MD, MPH**
Assistant Professor of Urology,
Johns Hopkins University School of Medicine;
Director of Stone Disease,
Johns Hopkins Bayview Medical Center,
Baltimore, Maryland
*Surgical Management of Upper Urinary Tract Calculi*

**Ranjiv Mathews, MD**
Associate Professor of Pediatric Urology,
James Buchanan Brady Urological Institute,
Johns Hopkins Medical Institutions,
Baltimore, Maryland
*Exstrophy-Epispadias Complex*

**Julian Mauermann, MD**
Senior Resident,
Department of Urology,
Medical University of Vienna,
Vienna, Austria
*Ablative Therapy of Renal Tumors*

**Sarah J. McAleer, MD**
Chief Resident, Department of Urology,
Brigham and Women's Hospital,
Boston, Massachusetts
*Tuberculosis and Parasitic and Fungal Infections of the
Genitourinary System*

**Jack W. McAninch, MD**
Professor of Urological Surgery,
Department of Urology,
University of California, San Francisco, School of Medicine;
Chief of Urology, San Francisco General Hospital,
San Francisco, California
*Renal and Ureteral Trauma*

**John D. McConnell, MD**
Professor of Urology, Department of Urology,
Executive Vice-President for Health Systems Affairs,
University of Texas Southwestern Medical Center,
Dallas, Texas
*Benign Prostatic Hyperplasia: Etiology, Pathophysiology,
Epidemiology, and Natural History*

**W. Scott McDougal, AB, MD, MA(Hon)**
Walter S. Kerr, Jr. Professor of Urology,
Harvard Medical School;
Chief of Urology, Massachusetts General Hospital,
Boston, Massachusetts
*Use of Intestinal Segments in Urinary Diversion*

**Elspeth M. McDougall, MD, FRCSC**
Professor of Urology,
Irvine Medical Center,
University of California, Irvine,
Irvine, California
*Basics of Laparoscopic Urologic Surgery*
*Percutaneous Management of the Upper Urinary Tract*

**Edward J. McGuire, MD**
Professor, Department of Urology,
University of Michigan,
Ann Arbor, Michigan
*Pubovaginal Sling*

**James M. McKiernan, MD**
Assistant Professor, Department of Urology,
Herbert Irving Comprehensive Cancer Center,
Columbia University;
Assistant Attending Urologist,
New York-Presbyterian Hospital,
New York, New York
*Cutaneous Continent Urinary Diversion*

**Alan W. McMahon, MD**
Associate Professor, Department of Medicine,
Division of Nephrology and Transplant Immunology,
University of Alberta,
Edmonton, Alberta, Canada
*Renal Physiology and Pathophysiology*

**Maxwell V. Meng, MD**
Assistant Professor,
Department of Urology,
University of California, San Francisco,
San Francisco, California
*Treatment of Locally Advanced Prostate Cancer*

**Edward M. Messing, MD**
W. W. Scott Professor,
Chairman, Department of Urology,
Professor of Pathology and Oncology,
University of Rochester School of Medicine and Dentistry,
Rochester, New York
*Urothelial Tumors of the Bladder*

**Michael E. Mitchell, MD**
Professor and Chief of Pediatric Urology,
University of Washington School of Medicine,
Children's Hospital & Regional Medical Center,
Seattle, Washington
*Surgical Techniques for One-Stage Reconstruction of the Exstrophy-Epispadias Complex*

**Drogo K. Montague, MD**
Professor of Surgery,
Cleveland Clinic Lerner College of Medicine of
  Case Western Reserve University;
Head, Section of Prosthetic Surgery and
  Genitourethral Reconstruction,
Glickman Urological Institute,
Cleveland Clinic Foundation,
Cleveland, Ohio
*Prosthetic Surgery for Erectile Dysfunction*

**Alvaro Morales, MD, FRCSC, FACS**
Emeritus Professor,
Queen's University;
Director, Center for Advanced Urological Research,
Kingston General Hospital,
Kingston, Ontario, Canada
*Androgen Deficiency in the Aging Male*

**Allen F. Morey, MD**
Clinical Associate Professor of Urology,
University of Texas Health Science Center;
Chief, Urology Service,
Brooke Army Medical Center,
San Antonio, Texas
*Genital and Lower Urinary Tract Trauma*

**John Morley, MB, BCh**
Dammert Professor of Gerontology,
  and Director of Geriatrics, St. Louis University Medical
  Center;
Director of GRECC, St. Louis Veterans Affairs Hospital,
  St. Louis, Missouri
*Androgen Deficiency in the Aging Male*

**Michael J. Morris, MD**
Assistant Member,
Memorial Sloan-Kettering Cancer Center;
Instructor in Medicine,
Weill Medical College of Cornell University;
Assistant Attending Physician,
Memorial Hospital for Cancer and Allied Diseases,
New York, New York
*The Clinical State of the Rising PSA Level after Definitive Local Therapy: A Practical Approach*

**M. Louis Moy, MD**
Assistant Professor,
Division of Urology,
University of Pennsylvania Medical School;
University of Pennsylvania Health System,
Philadelphia, Pennsylvania
*Additional Therapies for Storage and Emptying Failure*

**Ricardo Munarriz, MD**
Assistant Professor of Urology,
Boston University School of Medicine,
Boston, Massachusetts
*Vascular Surgery for Erectile Dysfunction*

**Stephen Y. Nakada, MD**
Professor of Surgery,
University of Wisconsin School of Medicine and
  Public Health;
Chairman of Urology,
University of Wisconsin Hospital and Clinics,
Madison, Wisconsin
*Management of Upper Urinary Tract Obstruction*

**Joseph V. Nally, Jr., MD**
Staff, Department of Nephrology and Hypertension,
Cleveland Clinic Foundation,
Cleveland, Ohio
*Etiology, Pathogenesis, and Management of Renal Failure*

**Joel B. Nelson, MD**
Frederic N. Schwentker Professor,
Chair, Department of Urology,
University of Pittsburgh School of Medicine;
Chairman of Urology,
University of Pittsburgh Medical Center;
Co-Chair, Prostate and Urological Diseases Program,
University of Pittsburgh Cancer Institute,
Pittsburgh, Pennsylvania
*Hormone Therapy for Prostate Cancer*

**Michael T. Nguyen, MD**
Fellow, Pediatric Urology,
The Children's Hospital of Philadelphia,
Philadelphia, Pennsylvania
*Evaluation of the Pediatric Urology Patient*

**J. Curtis Nickel, MD**
Professor of Urology, Queen's University;
Staff Urologist, Department of Urology,
Kingston General Hospital,
Kingston, Ontario, Canada
*Inflammatory Conditions of the Male Genitourinary
Tract: Prostatitis and Related Conditions, Orchitis,
and Epididymitis*

**Peter T. Nieh, MD**
Assistant Professor, Department of Urology,
Emory University School of Medicine,
Atlanta, Georgia
*Surgery of Bladder Cancer*

**Victor W. Nitti, MD**
Associate Professor and Vice-Chairman,
Department of Urology,
New York University School of Medicine;
Attending Physician,
New York University Hospitals Center,
New York, New York
*Urinary Incontinence: Epidemiology, Pathophysiology,
Evaluation, and Management Overview*

**H. Norman Noe, MD**
Professor of Urology,
Chief, Pediatric Urology,
University of Tennessee,
Saint Jude's Children's Research Hospital,
Memphis, Tennessee
*Renal Disease in Childhood*

**Andrew C. Novick, MD**
Chairman, Glickman Urological Institute,
Cleveland Clinic Foundation;
Professor of Surgery,
Cleveland Clinic Lerner College of Medicine of
    Case Western Reserve University,
Cleveland, Ohio
*Renovascular Hypertension and Ischemic Nephropathy
Renal Tumors
Open Surgery of the Kidney*

**Seung-June Oh, MD, PhD**
Associate Professor, Department of Urology,
Seoul National University Hospital,
Seoul National University College of Medicine,
Seoul, Korea
*Pubovaginal Sling*

**Carl A. Olsson, MD**
John K. Lattimer Professor and Chairman Emeritus,
Columbia University College of Physicians and Surgeons;
Attending, New York-Presbyterian Hospital,
New York, New York
*Cutaneous Continent Urinary Diversion*

**Michael C. Ost, MD**
Fellow, Endourology and Laparoscopy,
Institute of Urology,
North Shore-Long Island Jewish Medical Center,
New Hyde Park, New York
*Percutaneous Management of the Upper Urinary Tract*

**Vernon M. Pais Jr., MD**
Assistant Professor,
Department of Surgery,
Division of Urology,
University of Kentucky School of Medicine;
University of Kentucky Medical Center,
Lexington, Kentucky
*Pathophysiology of Urinary Tract Obstruction*

**John M. Park, MD**
Associate Professor of Urology,
University of Michigan Medical School;
Chief of Pediatric Urology,
University of Michigan Health System,
Ann Arbor, Michigan
*Normal Development of the Urogenital System*

**Alan W. Partin, MD, PhD**
David Hall McConnell Professor and Director,
James Buchanan Brady Urological Institute,
Johns Hopkins Medical Institutions,
Baltimore, Maryland
*Retropubic and Suprapubic Open Prostatectomy
Prostate Cancer Tumor Markers
Diagnosis and Staging of Prostate Cancer
Anatomic Radical Retropubic Prostatectomy*

**Christopher K. Payne, MD**
Associate Professor of Urology,
Director,
Female Urology and Neurourology,
Stanford University Medical School,
Stanford, California
*Conservative Managment of Urinary Incontinence:
Behavioral and Pelvic Floor Therapy, Urethral and
Pelvic Devices*

**Margaret S. Pearle, MD, PhD**
Professor of Urology and Internal Medicine,
University of Texas Southwestern Medical Center,
Dallas, Texas
*Urinary Lithiasis: Etiology, Epidemiology, and Pathogenesis*

**Craig A. Peters, MD**
John E. Cole Professor of Urology,
University of Virginia,
Charlottesville, Virgina
*Congenital Urinary Obstruction: Pathophysiology
Perinatal Urology
Pediatric Endourology and Laparoscopy*

**Andrew C. Peterson, MD, FACS**
Assistant Professor of Surgery,
Uniformed Services University of the Health Sciences,
Bethesda, Maryland;
Program Director,
Urology Residency,
Madigan Army Medical Center,
Tacoma, Washington
  *Urodynamic and Videourodynamic Evaluation of
  Voiding Dysfunction*

**Curtis A. Pettaway, MD**
Associate Professor of Urology, and
  Associate Professor of Cancer Biology,
Department of Urology,
University of Texas MD Anderson Cancer Center,
Houston, Texas
  *Tumors of the Penis*

**Paul K. Pietrow, MD**
Director of Minimally Invasive Surgery,
Hudson Valley Urology,
Poughkeepsie, New York
  *Evaluation and Medical Management of Urinary Lithiasis*

**Louis L. Pisters, MD**
Associate Professor of Urology,
Department of Urology,
University of Texas MD Anderson Cancer Center,
Houston, Texas
  *Cryotherapy for Prostate Cancer*

**Elizabeth A. Platz, ScD, MPH**
Associate Professor,
Department of Epidemiology,
Johns Hopkins Bloomberg School of Public Health,
Johns Hopkins Medical Institutions,
Baltimore, Maryland
  *Epidemiology, Etiology, and Prevention of Prostate Cancer*

**Jeannette Potts, MD**
Senior Clinical Instructor,
Department of Family Medicine,
Cleveland Clinic Lerner College of Medicine of
  Case Western Reserve University;
Staff Physician,
Glickman Urological Institute,
Cleveland Clinic Foundation,
Cleveland, Ohio
  *Sexually Transmitted Diseases*

**Glenn M. Preminger, MD**
Professor of Urologic Surgery,
Duke University Medical Center,
Durham, North Carolina
  *Evaluation and Medical Management of Urinary Lithiasis*

**Raymond R. Rackley, MD**
Professor of Surgery (Urology),
Cleveland Clinic Lerner College of Medicine of
  Case Western Reserve University,
Co-Head, Section of Female Urology and Voiding
  Dysfunction,
The Glickman Urological Institute,
Cleveland Clinic Foundation,
Cleveland, Ohio
  *Electrical Stimulation for Storage and Emptying Disorders*

**John R. Ramey, MD**
Jefferson Prostate Diagnostic Center,
Departments of Urology and Radiology,
Kimmel Cancer Center,
Thomas Jefferson University,
Philadelphia, Pennsylvania
  *Ultrasonography and Biopsy of the Prostate*

**Robert E. Reiter, MD**
Professor of Urology,
Member, Molecular Biology Institute,
Associate Director,
Prostate Cancer Program,
Geffen School of Medicine,
University of California, Los Angeles,
Los Angeles, California
  *Molecular Genetics and Cancer Biology*

**Neil M. Resnick, MD**
Professor of Medicine,
Chief, Division of Gerontology and Geriatric Medicine,
Director, University of Pittsburgh Institute on Aging,
University of Pittsburgh and University of Pittsburgh
  Medical Center,
Pittsburgh, Pennsylvania
  *Geriatric Incontinence and Voiding Dysfunction*

**Martin I. Resnick, MD**
Lester Persky Professor and Chair,
Department of Urology,
Cleveland Clinic Lerner College of Medicine of
  Case Western Reserve University,
Cleveland Clinic Foundation,
Cleveland, Ohio
  *Radical Perineal Prostatectomy*

**Alan B. Retik, MD**
Professor of Surgery (Urology),
Harvard Medical School;
Chief, Department of Urology,
Children's Hospital,
Boston, Massachusetts
  *Ectopic Ureter, Ureterocele, and Other Anomalies of
  the Ureter*
  *Hypospadias*

**Jerome P. Richie, MD**
Elliot C. Cutler Professor of Urologic Surgery,
Chairman, Harvard Program in Urology,
Harvard Medical School,
Brigham and Women's Hospital,
Boston, Massachusetts
*Neoplasms of the Testis*

**Richard Rink, MD**
Professor, Indiana University,
Riley Hospital for Children,
Indianapolis, Indiana
*Surgical Management of Intersexuality, Cloacal
Malformation, and Other Abnormalities of the
Genitalia in Girls*

**Michael L. Ritchey, MD**
Professor of Urology,
Mayo Clinic College of Medicine,
Phoenix, Arizona
*Pediatric Urologic Oncology*

**Ronald Rodriguez, MD, PhD**
Associate Professor of Urology, Medical Oncology, Radiation
    Oncology, Cellular and Molecular Medicine,
Johns Hopkins University School of Medicine,
Baltimore, Maryland
*Molecular Biology, Endocrinology, and Physiology of the
Prostate and Seminal Vesicles*

**Claus G. Roehrborn, MD**
Professor and Chairman, Department of Urology,
University of Texas Southwestern Medical Center,
Dallas, Texas
*Benign Prostatic Hyperplasia: Etiology, Pathophysiology,
Epidemiology, and Natural History*

**Jonathan A. Roth, MD**
Assistant Professor of Urology and Pediatrics,
Temple University Children's Hospital,
Temple University,
Philadelphia, Pennsylvania
*Renal Function in the Fetus, Neonate, and Child*

**Eric S. Rovner, MD**
Associate Professor of Urology,
Department of Urology,
Medical University of South Carolina,
Charleston, South Carolina
*Urinary Tract Fistula*
*Bladder and Urethral Diverticula*

**Thomas A. Rozanski, MD**
Professor, Department of Urology,
The University of Texas Health Science Center;
Chief, Medical Operations,
University Hospital,
San Antonio, Texas
*Genital and Lower Urinary Tract Trauma*

**Arthur I. Sagalowsky, MD**
Professor of Urology and Surgery,
Chief of Urologic Oncology,
Dr. Paul Peters Chair in Urology in Memory of Rumsey
    and Louis Strickland,
The University of Texas Health Science Center,
Dallas, Texas
*Management of Urothelial Tumors of the Renal Pelvis
and Ureter*

**Jay I. Sandlow, MD**
Associate Professor and Vice-Chair,
Department of Urology,
Medical College of Wisconsin;
Director of Andrology and Male Infertility,
Froedtert Memorial Lutheran Hospital,
Milwaukee, Wisconsin
*Surgery of the Scrotum and Seminal Vesicles*

**Richard A. Santucci, MD**
Associate Professor and Chief of Urology,
Wayne State University School of Medicine,
Detroit, Michigan
*Renal and Ureteral Trauma*

**Peter T. Scardino, MD**
Chair, Department of Surgery,
Head, Prostate Cancer Program,
Memorial Sloan-Kettering Cancer Center,
New York, New York
*Expectant Management of Prostate Cancer*

**Harriette Scarpero, MD**
Assistant Professor,
Department of Urologic Surgery,
Vanderbilt University Medical Center,
Nashville, Tennessee
*Tension-Free Vaginal Tape Procedures*

**Anthony J. Schaeffer, MD**
Herman L. Kretschmer Professor and Chair,
Department of Urology,
Northwestern University Feinberg School of Medicine;
Chief of Urology,
Northwestern Memorial Hospital,
Chicago, Illinois
*Infections of the Urinary Tract*

**Edward M. Schaeffer, MD, PhD**
Department of Urology,
James Buchanan Brady Urological Institute,
Johns Hopkins Medical Institutions,
Baltimore, Maryland
*Infections of the Urinary Tract*

**Howard I. Scher, MD**
Professor of Medicine,
Weill Medical College of Cornell University;
Member, Department of Medicine,
Memorial Sloan-Kettering Cancer Center;
Attending Physician,
Memorial Hospital for Cancer and Allied Diseases,
New York, New York
*The Clinical State of the Rising PSA Level after Definitive
Local Therapy: A Practical Approach*

**Peter N. Schlegel, MD**
Professor and Chairman,
Department of Urology,
Professor of Reproductive Medicine,
Weill Medical College of Cornell University;
Staff Scientist, The Population Council;
Urologist-in-Chief, New York-Presbyterian Hospital;
Associate Physician, Rockefeller University Hospital,
New York, New York
*Male Reproductive Physiology*

**Steven M. Schlossberg, MD**
Professor, Eastern Virginia Medical School,
Norfolk, Virginia
*Surgery of the Penis and Urethra*

**Richard N. Schlussel, MD**
Assistant Professor, Department of Urology,
Columbia University;
Assistant Professor, Division of Pediatric Urology,
Morgan Stanley Children's Hospital of New York-
    Presbyterian,
Columbia University Medical Center,
New York, New York
*Ectopic Ureter, Ureterocele, and Other Anomalies of
the Ureter*

**Francis X. Schneck, MD**
Associate Professor of Urology,
Children's Hospital of Pittsburgh,
University of Pittsburgh Medical Center,
Pittsburgh, Pennsylvania
*Abnormalities of the Testes and Scrotum and
Their Surgical Management*

**Mark P. Schoenberg, MD**
Professor of Urology and Oncology,
Director of Urologic Oncology,
James Buchanan Brady Urological Institute,
Johns Hopkins Medical Institutions,
Baltimore, Maryland
*Management of Invasive and Metastatic Bladder Cancer*

**Martin J. Schreiber, Jr., MD**
Chairman,
Department of Nephrology and Hypertension,
Cleveland Clinic Foundation,
Cleveland, Ohio
*Etiology, Pathogenesis, and Management of Renal Failure*

**Joseph W. Segura, MD**
Consultant in Urology,
Carl Rosen Professor of Urology,
Department of Urology,
The Mayo Clinic,
Rochester, Minnesota
*Lower Urinary Tract Calculi*

**Jay B. Shah, MD**
Chief Resident,
Columbia College of Physicians and Surgeons;
Department of Urology,
Columbia University Medical Center,
New York, New York
*Percutaneous Management of the Upper Urinary Tract*

**Robert C. Shamberger, MD**
Robert E. Gross Professor of Surgery,
Harvard Medical School;
Chief of Surgery, Children's Hospital,
Boston, Massachusetts
*Pediatric Urologic Oncology*

**David S. Sharp, MD**
Fellow, Department of Urology,
Memorial Sloan-Kettering Cancer Center,
New York, New York
*Surgery of Penile and Urethral Carcinoma*

**Joel Sheinfeld, MD**
Vice-Chairman, Department of Urology,
Memorial Sloan-Kettering Cancer Center,
New York, New York
*Surgery of Testicular Tumors*

**Linda M. Dairiki Shortliffe, MD**
Professor and Chair, Department of Urology,
Stanford University School of Medicine;
Chief of Pediatric Urology,
Stanford Hospital and Clinics,
Lucile Salter Packard Children's Hospital,
Stanford, California
*Infection and Inflammation of the Pediatric
Genitourinary Tract*

**Daniel A. Shoskes, MD, FRCSC**
Professor of Surgery, Cleveland Clinic Lerner College of
    Medicine of Case Western Reserve University;
Urologist, Glickman Urological Institute,
Cleveland Clinic Foundation,
Cleveland, Ohio
*Renal Physiology and Pathophysiology*

**Cary L. Siegel, MD**
Associate Professor of Radiology,
Division of Diagnostic Radiology,
Mallinckrodt Institute of Radiology,
Washington University School of Medicine,
St. Louis, Missouri
*Urinary Tract Imaging: Basic Principles*

**Mark Sigman, MD**
Associate Professor of Surgery (Urology),
Brown University,
Providence, Rhode Island
*Male Infertility*

**Jennifer D.Y. Sihoe, MD, BMBS(Nottm),**
**FRCSEd(Paed), FHKAM(Surg)**
Specialist in Pediatric Surgery,
Division of Pediatric Surgery and Pediatric Urology,
The Chinese University of Hong Kong,
Prince of Wales Hospital,
Hong Kong, China
*Voiding Dysfunction in Children: Non-Neurogenic and*
*Neurogenic*

**Donald G. Skinner, MD**
Professor and Chair,
Department of Urology,
Keck School of Medicine of the University of Southern
    California, Norris Cancer Center,
Los Angeles, California
*Orthotopic Urinary Diversion*

**Arthur D. Smith, MD**
Professor, Department of Urology,
Albert Einstein School of Medicine,
New York, New York;
Chairman Emeritus, Department of Urology,
North Shore-Long Island Jewish Medical Center,
New Hyde Park, New York
*Percutaneous Management of the Upper Urinary Tract*

**Joseph A. Smith, Jr., MD**
Professor,
Department of Urologic Surgery,
Vanderbilt University School of Medicine,
Vanderbilt University Medical Center,
Nashville, Tennessee
*Laparoscopic and Robotic-Assisted Laparoscopic Radical*
*Prostatectomy and Pelvic Lymphadenectomy*

**Jonathan Starkman, MD**
Clinical Instructor,
Department of Urologic Surgery,
Vanderbilt University Medical Center,
Nashville, Tennessee
*Tension-Free Vaginal Tape Procedures*

**David R. Staskin, MD**
Director, Section of Voiding Dysfunction,
Female Urology and Urodynamics,
New York Hospital-Cornell;
Associate Professor, Urology and Obstetrics and Gynecology,
Weill Medical College of Cornell University,
New York, New York
*Surgical Treatment of Male Sphincteric Urinary*
*Incontinence: The Male Perineal Sling and Artificial*
*Urinary Sphincter*

**Graeme S. Steele, MD**
Assistant Professor of Surgery,
Harvard Medical School;
Urologist, Brigham and Women's Hospital,
Boston, Massachusetts
*Neoplasms of the Testis*

**John P. Stein, MD**
Associate Professor in Urology,
Keck School of Medicine of the University of Southern
    California, Norris Cancer Center,
Los Angeles, California
*Orthotopic Urinary Diversion*

**John T. Stoffel, MD**
Assistant Professor of Urology,
Tufts University School of Medicine,
Boston, Massachusetts;
Senior Staff Urologist, Department of Urology,
Lahey Clinic Medical Center,
Burlington, Massachusetts
*Pubovaginal Sling*

**Jack W. Strandhoy, PhD**
Professor, Department of Physiology and Pharmacology,
Wake Forest University School of Medicine,
Winston-Salem, North Carolina
*Pathophysiology of Urinary Tract Obstruction*

**Stevan B. Streem, MD (*deceased*)**
Head, Section of Stone Disease and Endourology,
Glickman Urological Institute,
Cleveland Clinic Foundation,
Cleveland, Ohio
*Management of Upper Urinary Tract Obstruction*

**Li-Ming Su, MD**
Associate Professor of Urology,
Director of Laparoscopic and Robotic Urologic Surgery,
James Buchanan Brady Urological Institute,
Johns Hopkins Medical Institutions,
Baltimore, Maryland
*Laparoscopic and Robotic-Assisted Laparoscopic Radical*
*Prostatectomy and Pelvic Lymphadenectomy*

**Anthony J. Thomas, Jr., MD**
Head, Section of Male Infertility,
Glickman Urological Institute,
Cleveland Clinic Foundation,
Cleveland, Ohio
*Surgical Management of Male Infertility*

**Ian M. Thompson, MD**
Glenda and Gary Woods Distinguished Chair in
    Genitourinary Oncology,
Henry B. and Edna Smith Dielman Memorial Chair in
    Urologic Science,
The University of Texas Health Science Center,
San Antonio, Texas
*Epidemiology, Etiology, and Prevention of Prostate Cancer*

**Sandip P. Vasavada, MD**
Associate Professor of Surgery (Urology),
Cleveland Clinic Lerner College of Medicine of
  Case Western Reserve University;
Co-Head, Section of Female Urology and
  Voiding Dysfunction,
Glickman Urological Institute,
Cleveland Clinic Foundation,
Cleveland, Ohio
  *Electrical Stimulation for Storage and Emptying Disorders*

**E. Darracott Vaughan, Jr., MD**
James J. Colt Professor and Chairman Emeritus of Urology,
Weill Medical College of Cornell University,
New York-Presbyterian Hospital,
New York, New York
  *Pathophysiology, Evaluation, and Medical Management of
  Adrenal Disorders*

**Robert W. Veltri, PhD**
Associate Professor,
Department of Urology
Johns Hopkins University School of Medicine,
Baltimore, Maryland
  *Molecular Biology, Endocrinology, and Physiology of the
  Prostate and Seminal Vesicles*

**Patrick C. Walsh, MD**
University Distinguished Service Professor of Urology,
James Buchanan Brady Urological Institute,
Johns Hopkins Medical Institutions,
Baltimore, Maryland
  *Anatomic Radical Retropubic Prostatectomy*

**George D. Webster, MD**
Professor of Urologic Surgery,
Department of Urology,
Duke University Medical Center,
Durham, North Carolina
  *Urodynamic and Videourodynamic Evaluation of
  Voiding Dysfunction*

**Alan J. Wein, MD, PhD(Hon)**
Professor and Chair,
Division of Urology,
University of Pennsylvania School of Medicine;
Chief of Urology,
University of Pennsylvania Medical Center,
Philadelphia, Pennsylvania
  *Pathophysiology and Classification of Voiding Dysfunction
  Lower Urinary Tract Dysfunction in Neurologic Injury
  and Disease
  Pharmacologic Management of Storage and
  Emptying Failure
  Additional Therapies for Storage and Emptying Failure*

**Robert M. Weiss, MD**
Donald Guthrie Professor and Chief,
Section of Urology,
Yale University School of Medicine,
New Haven, Connecticut
  *Physiology and Pharmacology of the Renal Pelvis and Ureter*

**Howard N. Winfield, MD, FRCS**
Professor, Department of Urology,
Director, Laparoscopy and Minimally Invasive Surgery,
The University of Iowa Hospitals and Clinics,
University of Iowa,
Iowa City, Iowa
*Surgery of the Scrotum and Seminal Vesicles*

**J. Christian Winters, MD**
Clinical Associate Professor,
Louisiana State University Health Sciences Center;
Vice-Chairman and Director of Female Urology and
  Voiding Dysfunction,
Ochsner Clinic Foundation,
New Orleans, Louisiana
  *Injection Therapy for Urinary Incontinence*

**John R. Woodard, MD**
Formerly: Clinical Professor of Urology,
Director of Pediatric Urology,
Emory University School of Medicine;
Formerly: Chief of Urology,
Henrietta Egleston Hospital for Children,
Atlanta, Georgia
  *Prune Belly Syndrome*

**Subbarao V. Yalla, MD**
Professor of Surgery (Urology),
Harvard Medical School;
Chief, Urology Division,
Boston Veterans Affairs Medical Center,
Boston, Massachusetts
  *Geriatric Incontinence and Voiding Dysfunction*

**C. K. Yeung, MBBS, MD, FRCSE, FRCSG, FRACS, FACS,
FHKAM(Surg), DCH(Lond)**
Clinical Professor in Pediatric Surgery and
  Pediatric Urology,
Chinese University of Hong Kong,
Prince of Wales Hospital,
Hong Kong, China
  *Voiding Dysfunction in Children: Non-Neurogenic
  and Neurogenic*

**Naoki Yoshimura, MD, PhD**
Associate Professor of Urology and Pharmacology,
University of Pittsburgh School of Medicine,
Pittsburgh, Pennsylvania
  *Physiology and Pharmacology of the Bladder and Urethra*

# PREFACE

For each discipline in medicine and surgery, there is generally an acknowledged authoritative text, otherwise known as "the bible." For virtually every urologist in current practice, *Campbell's Urology* has had that distinction. The text, first published in 1954 with Meredith Campbell as its sole editor, has seen the editor-in-chief position pass to J. Hartwell Harrison, and then to Patrick Walsh. Under Dr. Walsh's leadership as editor-in-chief for the past 20 years (4 editions), *Campbell's Urology* has changed as much as the field itself—in virtually every way possible except for its preeminence. The current editorial board felt strongly that Pat's contributions to urologic education through his continuing improvements and innovations to *Campbell's* should be recognized in perpetuity by renaming the text in his honor; thus the new title—*Campbell-Walsh Urology.*

Aside from the name, the 9th edition is quite different from its predecessors, continuing the tradition of a constant evolution paralleling the changing nature of the field and its relevant pertinent information. We have changed the editorial board and increased it by one. Louis Kavoussi, Andrew Novick, Alan Partin, and Craig Peters all have moved up from their associate editor positions. From the standpoint of organization, Volume 1 now covers anatomy; molecular and cellular biology, including tissue engineering; the essentials of clinical decision-making; the basics of instrumentation, endoscopy, and laparoscopy; infection and inflammation; male reproductive function and dysfunction; and sexual function and dysfunction in both men and women. Volume 2 covers all aspects of the upper urinary tract and adrenal, including physiology, obstruction, trauma, stone disease, and neoplasia. Volume 3 includes all topics related to lower urinary tract function and dysfunction, including calculi; trauma, bladder, and prostate disease; and all aspects of urine transport, storage, and emptying. Volume 4 remains a 900-page textbook of pediatric urology. There are 24 totally new chapters; an additional 19 chapters have new authors; and the remaining 89 chapters have all undergone substantial revision. All chapters contain the latest concepts, data, and controversies. Illustrations, algorithms (extensively used), and tables are now in color, as are clinical photographs. Extensive highlighting is utilized, as well as key point boxes. The complete reference list is now online and bound on a CD; a list of suggested key references appears at the end of each chapter. An **e**-dition includes a fully searchable online version with downloadable images (for powerpoint, papers, etc.) and video clips of the key portions of certain procedures, and it will include weekly content updates (summaries of key journal articles in all areas) for the life of the edition. The *Review*, with questions, answers, and explanations, will continue as a separate publication.

Each of us is grateful for the opportunity to be a part of the continuing tradition of *Campbell-Walsh Urology* and wish to express our immense appreciation to all of our superb authors and to those at Elsevier who facilitated our efforts in bringing the 9th edition to publication: Rebecca Schmidt Gaertner, Senior Acquisitions Editor, and Anne Snyder, Senior Developmental Editor.

ALAN J. WEIN, MD, PhD (Hon)
For the Editors

# CONTENTS

## VOLUME 1

### SECTION I
### ANATOMY .......................... 1

**1** Surgical Anatomy of the Retroperitoneum, Adrenals, Kidneys, and Ureters ................ 3
J. KYLE ANDERSON, MD • JOHN N. KABALIN, MD
JEFFREY A. CADEDDU, MD

The Retroperitoneum   3
The Adrenal Glands   19
The Kidneys   24
The Ureters   32

**2** Anatomy of the Lower Urinary Tract and Male Genitalia ................................. 38
JAMES D. BROOKS, MD

Bony Pelvis   38
Anterior Abdominal Wall   38
Soft Tissues of the Pelvis   43
Pelvic Circulation   46
Pelvic Innervation   52
Pelvic Viscera   56
Perineum   68

### SECTION II
### CLINICAL DECISION-MAKING .......... 79

**3** Evaluation of the Urologic Patient: History, Physical Examination, and Urinalysis .......... 81
GLENN S. GERBER, MD • CHARLES B. BRENDLER, MD

History   81
Physical Examination   89
Urinalysis   95
Summary   109

**4** Urinary Tract Imaging: Basic Principles ........ 111
SAM B. BHAYANI, MD • CARY L. SIEGEL, MD

Conventional Radiography   111
Ultrasound   119
Computed Tomography   127
Magnetic Resonance Imaging   135
Nuclear Scintigraphy   139

**5** Outcomes Research ...................... 144
MARK S. LITWIN, MD, MPH

Access to Care   144
Costs of Care   144

Quality of Care   147
Health-Related Quality of Life   149
Future Implications   156

### SECTION III
### BASICS OF UROLOGIC SURGERY ........ 159

**6** Basic Instrumentation and Cystoscopy ........ 161
H. BALLENTINE CARTER, MD • DAVID Y. CHAN, MD

Urethral Catheterization   161
Urethral Dilatation   165
Cystourethroscopy   166
Retrograde Pyelography   169

**7** Basics of Laparoscopic Urologic Surgery ........ 171
LOUIS EICHEL, MD • ELSPETH M. McDOUGALL, MD
RALPH V. CLAYMAN, MD

History of Laparoscopy in Urologic Surgery   171
Preoperative Patient Management   174
In the Operating Room   176
Performing the Procedure   178
Postoperative Patient Management   198
Physiologic Considerations in the Adult   199
Troubleshooting in Laparoscopic Surgery   203
Limitations and Advantages of Transperitoneal vs. Extraperitoneal Approach to the Flank and Pelvis   219
Summary   220

### SECTION IV
### INFECTIONS AND INFLAMMATION ...... 221

**8** Infections of the Urinary Tract ................ 223
ANTHONY J. SCHAEFFER, MD
EDWARD M. SCHAEFFER, MD, PhD

Definitions   223
Incidence and Epidemiology   225
Pathogenesis   227
Clinical Manifestations   238
Imaging Techniques   242
Principles of Antimicrobial Therapy   243
Antimicrobial Prophylaxis for Common Urologic Procedures   250
Bladder Infections   254
Kidney Infections   265
Bacteremia, Sepsis, and Septic Shock   287
Bacteriuria in Pregnancy   289
Bacteriuria in the Elderly   293
Catheter-Associated Bacteriuria   296

Management of UTI in Patients with Spinal Cord
Injury  297
Funguria  299
Other Infections  301

**9**  Inflammatory Conditions of the Male
Genitourinary Tract: Prostatitis and Related
Conditions, Orchitis, and Epididymitis  . . . . . . . .304
J. CURTIS NICKEL, MD

Prostatitis  304
Related Conditions  326

**10**  Painful Bladder Syndrome/Interstitial Cystitis
and Related Disorders  . . . . . . . . . . . . . . . . . . . . . .330
PHILIP M. HANNO, MD, MPH

Historical Perspective  330
Definition  331
Epidemiology  333
Etiology  337
Pathology  349
Diagnosis  351
Clinical Symptom Scales  354
Assessing Treatment Results  355
Conservative Therapy  358
Oral Therapy  359
Intravesical and Intradetrusor Therapy  362
Neuromodulation  364
Hydrodistention  365
Surgical Therapy  366
Principles of Management  368
Urethral Syndrome  368

**11**  Sexually Transmitted Diseases  . . . . . . . . . . . . . . . .371
TARA FRENKL, MD, MPH • JEANNETTE POTTS, MD

Epidemiology and Trends  372
Genital Ulcers  372
Herpes Simplex Virus Infection  373
Chancroid  374
Syphilis  375
Lymphogranuloma Venereum  377
Chlamydia Trachomatis Infection  378
Gonorrhea  379
Trichomoniasis  380
Genital Warts  380
Molluscum Contagiosum  382
Scabies  383
Pediculosis Pubis  383
Overview of Other Sexually Associated Infections  384

**12**  Urologic Implications of AIDS and HIV
Infection  . . . . . . . . . . . . . . . . . . . . . . . . . . . . . . . .386
JOHN N. KRIEGER, MD

HIV/AIDS Epidemiology  386
HIV Virology and Targets for Antiviral Therapy  388
Pathogenesis of HIV Infection Tests to Diagnose and
Monitor HIV Infection: What the Urologist Should
Know  393

Urologic Manifestations of HIV Infection  394
Occupational Risks for HIV Infection in Urology  400
Antiretroviral Therapy  401

**13**  Cutaneous Diseases of the External Genitalia  . . . .405
RICHARD E. LINK, MD, PhD

Introduction to Basic Dermatology  405
Dermatologic Therapy  406
Allergic Dermatitis  407
Papulosquamous Disorders  410
Vesicobullous Disorders  415
Noninfectious Ulcers  417
Infections and Infestations  419
Neoplastic Conditions  426
Benign Cutaneous Disorders Specific to the Male
Genitalia  430
Common Miscellaneous Cutaneous Disorders  431

**14**  Tuberculosis and Parasitic and Fungal
Infections of the Genitourinary System  . . . . . . . .436
SARAH J. McALEER, MD • CHRISTOPHER W. JOHNSON, MD
WARREN D. JOHNSON, Jr., MD

Genitourinary Tuberculosis  436
Parasitic Diseases of the Genitourinary System  448
Fungal Diseases of the Genitourinary System  459

**SECTION V**
MOLECULAR AND CELLULAR
BIOLOGY  . . . . . . . . . . . . . . . . . . . . . . . . . . . . . .471

**15**  Basic Principles of Immunology  . . . . . . . . . . . . . . .473
STUART M. FLECHNER, MD • JAMES H. FINKE, PhD
ROBERT L. FAIRCHILD, PhD

Innate and Adaptive Immunity  473
Immunoresponsive Cell Populations  475
Cell Surface Activation  478
Cell Signal Transduction  482
T-Cell Activation and Effector Function  484
Apoptosis-Programmed Cell Death  488
Lymphocyte Tolerance  490
Adhesion Molecules and Control of Lymphocyte
Trafficking  492
Chemokines and Peripheral Tissue Recruitment of
Leukocytes  494
Tumor Immunology  495
Immunity to Infections  500
Molecular Immunology  502

**16**  Molecular Genetics and Cancer Biology  . . . . . . . .507
ADAM S. KIBEL, MD • ROBERT E. REITER, MD

DNA  507
Dysregulation  513
Inherited Susceptibility to Cancer  515
The Cell Cycle  520
DNA Repair  526
Apoptosis  529

Telomerase   533
Stem Cells and Cancer   534
Cellular Signaling   535
Receptors and the Cell Surface   538
Viruses   541
Angiogenesis   542
Mouse Models of Malignancy   545
Molecular Diagnosis in Oncology   547
Rational Drug Development   550
Gene Therapy   551

**17**  Tissue Engineering and Cell Therapy:
Perspectives for Urology . . . . . . . . . . . . . . . . . . . . .553
ANTHONY ATALA, MD

Tissue Engineering: Strategies for Tissue
Reconstitution   554
Biomaterials for Genitourinary Tissue Engineering   554
Vascularization   556
Tissue Engineering of Urologic Structures   557
Other Applications of Genitourinary Tissue
Engineering   566
Summary   573

**SECTION VI**
**REPRODUCTIVE AND SEXUAL**
**FUNCTION** . . . . . . . . . . . . . . . . . . . . . . . . . .575

**18**  Male Reproductive Physiology . . . . . . . . . . . . . . .577
PETER N. SCHLEGEL, MD · MATTHEW P. HARDY, PhD
MARC GOLDSTEIN, MD

The Male Reproductive Axis   577
Testis   581
Epididymis   596
Spermatozoa   604
Ductus Vas Deferens   606
Summary   607

**19**  Male Infertility . . . . . . . . . . . . . . . . . . . . . . . . . .609
MARK SIGMAN, MD · JONATHAN P. JAROW, MD

History   610
The Evaluation of the Female Partner   611
Physical Examination   613
Initial Basic Laboratory Evaluation   614
Diagnostic Algorithms Based on the Initial Evaluation   619
Additional Testing   623
Treatment Overview   634
Diagnostic Categories   635
Assisted Reproductive Techniques   650

**20**  Surgical Management of Male Infertility . . . . . . . .654
LARRY I. LIPSHULTZ, MD · ANTHONY J. THOMAS, Jr., MD
MOHIT KHERA, MD, MBA, MPH

Diagnostic Procedures   655
Procedures to Improve Sperm Production   658
Procedures to Improve Sperm Delivery   665
Sperm Retrieval   699

Surgical Management of Ejaculatory Duct Obstruction   706
Treatment of Anatomic, Congenital, and Organic Causes of
Infertility   713
Genetic Abnormalities Related to Azoospermia   716
In Vitro Fertilization with Intracytoplasmic Sperm
Injection   716

**21**  Physiology of Penile Erection and
Pathophysiology of Erectile Dysfunction . . . . . . . .718
TOM F. LUE, MD

Physiology of Penile Erection   718
Pathophysiology of Erectile Dysfunction   738
Perspectives   748

**22**  Evaluation and Nonsurgical Management of
Erectile Dysfunction and Premature
Ejaculation . . . . . . . . . . . . . . . . . . . . . . . . . . . .750
TOM F. LUE, MD · GREGORY A. BRODERICK, MD

Patient-Centered Evaluation   750
Evaluation of the Complex Patient   757
Nonsurgical Management of Erectile Dysfunction   768
Future Research   783
Premature Ejaculation   784

**23**  Prosthetic Surgery for Erectile Dysfunction . . . . . .788
DROGO K. MONTAGUE, MD

Types of Prostheses   788
Preoperative Patient-Partner Counseling   788
Surgical Approaches   790
AMS 700 Ultrex Inflatable Penile Prosthesis Implantation
by the Transverse Penoscrotal Approach   790
Postoperative Care   795
Complications   795
Penile Prosthesis Implantation in Special Cases   798
Results   800

**24**  Vascular Surgery for Erectile Dysfunction . . . . . . .802
RONALD W. LEWIS, MD · RICARDO MUNARRIZ, MD

A History and Review of Vascular Erectile Dysfunction
Surgery   802
Counseling of the Patient for Vascular Erectile Dysfunction
Surgery   803
Penile Arterial Reconstruction (Penile
Revascularization)   803
Penile Venous Surgery   812

**25**  Peyronie's Disease . . . . . . . . . . . . . . . . . . . . . . .818
GERALD H. JORDAN, MD, FACS, FAAP

Anatomic Considerations and Etiologic Factors   819
Pathophysiology and Natural History   822
Symptoms   824
Evaluation of the Patient   825
Management   826

**26**  Priapism . . . . . . . . . . . . . . . . . . . . . . . . . . . . . .839
ARTHUR L. BURNETT, MD

Definition   839
Epidemiology   839

Etiology 840
Natural History 841
Pathology 841
Pathophysiology 842
Classification 843
Diagnosis 844
Treatment 845
Summary 849

**27**   Androgen Deficiency in the Aging Male . . . . . . . . .850
ALVARO MORALES, MD, FRCSC, FACS
JOHN MORLEY, MB, BCh
JEREMY P. W. HEATON, MD, FRCSC, FACS

Definition 850
Historical Perspective 850
Epidemiology of Hypogonadism in Aging 851
Physiologic Principles 851
Diagnosis 853
Treatment of Symptomatic Late-Onset Hypogonadism 857
Recommendations and Guidelines 860

**28**   Urologic Management of Women with Sexual
Health Concerns . . . . . . . . . . . . . . . . . . . . . . . .863
IRWIN GOLDSTEIN, MD

Classification and Epidemiology 864
Diagnosis 865
Treatment 875
Summary 889

**SECTION VII**
**MALE GENITALIA** . . . . . . . . . . . . . . . . . . . . .891

**29**   Neoplasms of the Testis . . . . . . . . . . . . . . . . . . .893
JEROME P. RICHIE, MD • GRAEME S. STEELE, MD

Germ Cell Tumors 893
Clinical Staging 903
Extragonadal Germ Cell Tumors 924
Other Testicular Neoplasms 925
Tumors of Testicular Adnexa 932

**30**   Surgery of Testicular Tumors . . . . . . . . . . . . . . . .936
JOEL SHEINFELD, MD • GEORG BARTSCH, MD
GEORGE J. BOSL, MD

Management of the Primary Tumor 936
Staging 938
The Retroperitoneum and Germ Cell Tumors 938
Retroperitoneal Lymph Node Dissection 940
Surgery for High-Stage Germ Cell Tumors 950
Nonseminomatous Germ Cell Tumors 950
Seminoma 956
Fertility in Advanced Germ Cell Tumors 957

**31**   Tumors of the Penis . . . . . . . . . . . . . . . . . . . . . .959
CURTIS A. PETTAWAY, MD • DONALD F. LYNCH, Jr., MD
JOHN W. DAVIS, MD

Benign Lesions 959
Premalignant Cutaneous Lesions 960
Virus-Related Dermatologic Lesions 961
Buschke-Löwenstein Tumor (Verrucous Carcinoma, Giant
Condyloma Acuminatum) 963
Squamous Cell Carcinoma 964
Surgical Management of the Primary Tumor 972
Treatment of the Inguinal Nodes 974
Radiation Therapy 984
Chemotherapy 987
Nonsquamous Malignant Neoplasms 989

**32**   Surgery of Penile and Urethral Carcinoma . . . . . .993
DAVID S. SHARP, MD • KENNETH W. ANGERMEIER, MD

Penile Cancer 993
Male Urethral Cancer 1011
Female Urethral Cancer 1018

**33**   Surgery of the Penis and Urethra . . . . . . . . . . . .1023
GERALD H. JORDAN, MD, FACS, FAAP
STEVEN M. SCHLOSSBERG, MD

Principles of Reconstructive Surgery 1023
Selected Processes 1040
Penetrating Trauma to the Penis 1049
Urethral Stricture Disease 1054
Distraction Injuries of the Urethra 1075
Vesicourethral Distraction Defects 1084
Complex Fistulas of the Posterior Urethra 1086
Curvatures of the Penis 1087
Total Penile Reconstruction 1092
Female-to-Male Transsexualism 1096

**34**   Surgery of the Scrotum and Seminal Vesicles . . .1098
JAY I. SANDLOW, MD • HOWARD N. WINFIELD, MD
MARC GOLDSTEIN, MD

Scrotum 1098
Seminal Vesicles 1109

# VOLUME 2

**SECTION VIII**
**RENAL PHYSIOLOGY AND**
**PATHOPHYSIOLOGY** . . . . . . . . . . . . . . . . .1129

**35**   Renal Physiology and Pathophysiology . . . . . . . .1131
DANIEL A. SHOSKES, MD, FRCSC • ALAN W. McMAHON, MD

Renal Physiology 1131
Renal Pathophysiology 1146

**36** Renovascular Hypertension and Ischemic Nephropathy ..............................1156
ANDREW C. NOVICK, MD • AMR FERGANY, MD

Historical Background   1156
Definitions   1157
Pathology and Natural History   1157
Physiology of the Renin-Angiotensin-Aldosterone System   1161
Pathophysiology of Renovascular Hypertension   1164
Human Correlates of Experimental Renovascular Hypertension   1165
Pathophysiology of Ischemic Nephropathy   1165
Clinical Features of Renovascular Hypertension   1166
Clinical Features of Ischemic Nephropathy   1167
Diagnostic Evaluation   1168
Cost-Effective Approach for Diagnosis   1173
Selection of Patients for Surgical or Endovascular Therapy   1173
Surgical Revascularization   1174
Percutaneous Transluminal Angioplasty   1180
Endovascular Stenting   1184
Other Renal Artery Diseases   1187

### SECTION IX
## UPPER URINARY TRACT OBSTRUCTION AND TRAUMA .......................1193

**37** Pathophysiology of Urinary Tract Obstruction ...............................1195
VERNON M. PAIS, Jr., MD • JACK W. STRANDHOY, PhD
DEAN G. ASSIMOS, MD

Prevalence of the Problem   1195
Global Renal Functional Changes   1195
Pathologic Changes of Obstruction   1207
General Issues in Management of Patients   1208
Selected Extrinsic Causes of Ureteral Obstruction   1215

**38** Management of Upper Urinary Tract Obstruction .............................1227
THOMAS H. S. HSU, MD • STEVAN B. STREEM, MD
STEPHEN Y. NAKADA, MD

Ureteropelvic Junction Obstruction   1227
Retrocaval Ureter   1253
Ureteral Stricture Disease   1255
Ureteroenteric Anastomotic Stricture   1267
Retroperitoneal Fibrosis   1270

**39** Renal and Ureteral Trauma .................1274
JACK W. McANINCH, MD • RICHARD A. SANTUCCI, MD

Renal Injuries   1274
Ureteral Injuries   1282

### SECTION X
## RENAL FAILURE AND TRANSPLANTATION ...................1293

**40** Renal Transplantation .......................1295
JOHN M. BARRY, MD • MARK L. JORDAN, MD
MICHAEL J. CONLIN, MD

End-Stage Renal Disease   1295
History of Human Renal Transplantation   1296
Selection and Preparation of Kidney Transplant Recipients   1297
Donor Selection, Preparation, and Surgery   1301
Kidney Preservation   1306
Recipient Selection for Deceased Donor Kidney Transplants   1308
Preoperative Assessment   1309
Preparation of Kidney Graft   1309
Recipient Operation   1309
Postoperative Care   1312
Renal Allograft Rejection   1314
Problems   1318
Summary   1324

**41** Etiology, Pathogenesis, and Management of Renal Failure .........................1325
DAVID A. GOLDFARB, MD • JOSEPH V. NALLY, Jr., MD
MARTIN J. SCHREIBER, Jr., MD

Acute Renal Failure   1325
Acute Tubular Necrosis   1329
Clinical Approach to the Differential Diagnosis of Acute Renal Failure   1333
Management of Acute Renal Failure   1335
Chronic Renal Failure   1341

### SECTION XI
## URINARY LITHIASIS AND ENDOUROLOGY ....................1361

**42** Urinary Lithiasis: Etiology, Epidemiology, and Pathogenesis ...........................1363
MARGARET S. PEARLE, MD, PhD • YAIR LOTAN, MD

Epidemiology of Renal Calculi   1363
Physicochemistry   1365
Mineral Metabolism   1371
Pathogenesis of Upper Urinary Tract Calculi   1373

**43** Evaluation and Medical Management of Urinary Lithiasis .........................1393
PAUL K. PIETROW, MD • GLENN M. PREMINGER, MD

Diagnostic Evaluation of Nephrolithiasis   1393
Classification of Nephrolithiasis and Diagnostic Criteria   1401
Use of Stone Analysis to Determine Metabolic Abnormalities   1408

The Economics of Metabolic Evaluation    1409
Conservative Medical Management    1411
Selective Medical Therapy for Nephrolithiasis    1415
Miscellaneous Scenarios    1427
Summary    1429

**44**    Surgical Management of Upper Urinary
Tract Calculi . . . . . . . . . . . . . . . . . . . . . . . . . . .1431
JAMES E. LINGEMAN, MD · BRIAN R. MATLAGA, MD, MPH
ANDREW P. EVAN, PhD

Historical Overview    1431
Renal Calculi    1434
Ureteral Calculi    1450
Urinary Calculi During Pregnancy    1456
Stone Removal: Surgical Techniques and
Technology    1458

**45**    Ureteroscopy and Retrograde Ureteral Access . . .1508
BEN H. CHEW, MD, MSc, FRCSC
JOHN D. DENSTEDT, MD, FRCSC

Indications for Ureteroscopy and Retrograde
Access    1508
Equipment Necessary for Ureteroscopy and
Retrograde Access    1508
Step-By-Step Ureteroscopy in the Treatment of
Ureteronephrolithiasis    1514
Is Routine Stenting Necessary Following
Ureteroscopy    1516
Ureteral Stents and Biomaterials    1517
Postoperative Care    1518
Results of Ureteroscopy for Treatment of Ureteral
Stones    1518
Ureteroscopy in Special Cases    1519
Retrograde Ureteroscopic Treatment of Ureteral
Strictures    1521
Ureteroscopic Management of Upper Tract Transitional
Cell Carcinoma    1522
Complications of Ureteroscopy    1524
Conclusions    1525

**46**    Percutaneous Management of the Upper
Urinary Tract . . . . . . . . . . . . . . . . . . . . . . . . .1526
MANTU GUPTA, MD · MICHAEL C. OST, MD
JAY B. SHAH, MD · ELSPETH M. McDOUGALL, MD
ARTHUR D. SMITH, MD

Indications for Percutaneous Nephrostomy    1526
Pertinent Renal Anatomy    1527
Imaging Modalities for Percutaneous Access    1530
Retrograde and Retrograde-Assisted Percutaneous Renal
Access    1534
Technical Aspects of Percutaneous Entry    1535
Dilation of the Nephrostomy Tract    1541
Complications of Percutaneous Renal Surgery    1544
Percutaneous Procedures of the Upper Urinary
Tract    1549
Nephrostomy Drainage    1557
Future Directions    1562

**SECTION XII**
**NEOPLASMS OF THE UPPER**
**URINARY TRACT** . . . . . . . . . . . . . . . . . . . . . . .1565

**47**    Renal Tumors . . . . . . . . . . . . . . . . . . . . . . . . . .1567
STEVEN C. CAMPBELL, MD, PhD · ANDREW C. NOVICK, MD
RONALD M. BUKOWSKI, MD

Historical Considerations    1567
Classification    1568
Radiographic Evaluation of Renal Masses    1569
Benign Renal Tumors    1575
Renal Cell Carcinoma    1582
Treatment of Localized Renal Cell Carcinoma    1608
Treatment of Locally Advanced Renal Cell Carcinoma    1619
Treatment of Metastatic Renal Cell Carcinoma    1623
Other Malignant Renal Tumors    1632

**48**    Urothelial Tumors of the Upper Urinary
Tract . . . . . . . . . . . . . . . . . . . . . . . . . . . . . . . .1638
ROBERT C. FLANIGAN, MD

Basic and Clinical Biology    1638
Epidemiology    1638
Natural History    1639
Pathology    1641
Prognostic Factors    1643
Diagnosis    1644
Staging    1647
Treatment    1647

**49**    Management of Urothelial Tumors of the
Renal Pelvis and Ureter . . . . . . . . . . . . . . . . . . . .1653
ARTHUR I. SAGALOWSKY, MD · THOMAS W. JARRETT, MD

Open Nephron-Sparing Surgery for Renal Pelvis
Tumors: Pyelotomy and Tumor Ablation and Partial
Nephrectomy    1656
Open Radical Nephroureterectomy    1657
Laparoscopic Radical Nephroureterectomy    1664
Open Segmental Ureterectomy    1667
Endoscopic Treatment    1672
Isolated Upper Tract Cytologic Abnormality Or Urinary
Marker    1680
Adjuvant Therapy    1681
Follow-Up    1682
Treatment of Metastatic Disease    1684

**50**    Open Surgery of the Kidney . . . . . . . . . . . . . . . . .1686
ANDREW C. NOVICK, MD

Historical Aspects    1686
Surgical Anatomy    1686
Preoperative Preparation    1688
Intraoperative Renal Ischemia    1689
Surgical Approaches to the Kidney    1691
Simple Nephrectomy    1703
Radical Nephrectomy    1707
Partial Nephrectomy for Malignant Disease    1720
Partial Nephrectomy for Benign Disease    1731

Renal Arterial Reconstruction    1733
Indications for Treatment    1733
Preoperative Considerations    1734
Aortorenal Bypass    1734
Alternative Bypass Techniques    1737
Postoperative Care    1748
Clinical Results    1748
Complications    1749
Miscellaneous Renal Operations    1753

**51**    Laparoscopic Surgery of the Kidney . . . . . . . . . .1759
JAY T. BISHOFF, MD · LOUIS R. KAVOUSSI, MD

Historical Overview    1759
Patient Evaluation and Preparation    1759
Surgical Approaches    1761
Simple Nephrectomy    1761
Renal Biopsy    1770
Renal Cystic Disease    1772
Nephropexy    1776
Pyelolithotomy and Ureterolithotomy    1776
Calceal Diverticulectomy    1778
Laparoscopy for Renal Malignancy    1778
Transperitoneal Radical Nephrectomy    1781
Retroperitoneal Radical Nephrectomy    1788
Hand-Assisted Radical Nephrectomy    1791
Nephron-Sparing Surgery    1799
Laparoscopic Ablative Techniques    1804
Complications of Laparoscopic Renal Surgery    1807
Summary    1808

**52**    Ablative Therapy of Renal Tumors . . . . . . . . . . .1810
MICHAEL MARBERGER, MD, FRCS(Ed)
JULIAN MAUERMANN, MD

Rationale for Energy Ablative Therapy    1810
Defining Successful Ablation    1811
Cryoablation    1811
Radiofrequency Ablation    1814
Microwave Ablation    1816
Interstitial Laser Coagulation    1817
High-Intensity Focused Ultrasound    1817
Radiosurgery    1818
Conclusion    1818

**SECTION XIII**
**THE ADRENALS** . . . . . . . . . . . . . . . . . . . . .**1819**

**53**    Pathophysiology, Evaluation, and Medical
Management of Adrenal Disorders . . . . . . . . . . .1821
E. DARRACOTT VAUGHAN, Jr., MD
JON D. BLUMENFELD, MD

Historical Background    1821
Anatomy, Histology, and Embryology    1822
Adrenal Physiology    1824
Cushing's Syndrome    1830
Adrenal Carcinoma    1837

Adrenal Oncocytoma    1842
Adrenal Cysts    1843
Adrenal Insufficiency    1843
Primary Hyperaldosteronism    1846
Pheochromocytoma    1857
Malignant Pheochromocytoma    1861

**54**    Surgery of the Adrenal Glands . . . . . . . . . . . . . .1868
GEORGE K. CHOW, MD · MICHAEL L. BLUTE, MD

History    1868
Surgical Anatomy    1869
Clinical Indications and Selection of Patients    1869
Preoperative Management    1871
Open Adrenalectomy    1871
Laparoscopic Adrenalectomy    1876
Hand-Assisted Surgery    1878
Robotic Surgery    1884
Intraoperative Ultrasonography    1884
Postoperative Management    1884
Outpatient and Short-Stay Laparoscopic
Adrenalectomy    1884
Outcomes    1885
Complications    1885
Special Considerations    1887
Nonsurgical Alternatives    1887

# VOLUME 3

**SECTION XIV**
**URINE TRANSPORT, STORAGE, AND**
**EMPTYING** . . . . . . . . . . . . . . . . . . . . . . . . . .**1889**

**55**    Physiology and Pharmacology of the Renal
Pelvis and Ureter . . . . . . . . . . . . . . . . . . . . . . .1891
ROBERT M. WEISS, MD

Cellular Anatomy    1891
Development of the Ureter    1891
Electrical Activity    1892
Contractile Activity    1897
Mechanical Properties    1902
Role of the Nervous System in Ureteral Function    1903
Urine Transport    1907
Pathologic Processes Affecting Ureteral Function    1910
Effect of Age on Ureteral Function    1916
Effect of Pregnancy on Ureteral Function    1918
Effect of Drugs on the Ureter    1918

**56**    Physiology and Pharmacology of the Bladder
and Urethra . . . . . . . . . . . . . . . . . . . . . . . . . . .1922
NAOKI YOSHIMURA, MD, PhD
MICHAEL B. CHANCELLOR, MD

Relevant Anatomy and Biomechanics    1923
The Urinary Bladder    1926

The Urethra   1935
Neural Control of the Lower Urinary Tract   1937
Pharmacology   1948
Mechanisms of Detrusor Overactivity   1966
Summary   1970
Future Research   1971

**57  Pathophysiology and Classification of
       Voiding Dysfunction** . . . . . . . . . . . . . . . . . . . . . .1973
ALAN J. WEIN, MD

Normal Lower Urinary Tract Function: Overview   1973
Mechanisms Underlying the Two Phases of Function:
Overview   1974
The Micturition Cycle: Simplification and Overview   1976
Abnormalities of Filling/Storage and Emptying/Voiding:
Overview of Pathophysiology   1976
Classification Systems   1978

**58  Urodynamic and Videourodynamic Evaluation
       of Voiding Dysfunction** . . . . . . . . . . . . . . . . . . . .1986
ANDREW C. PETERSON, MD  ·  GEORGE D. WEBSTER, MD

Indications   1986
Preparation of Patients and Precautions   1987
Urodynamic Equipment   1988
Conducting the Urodynamic Evaluation   1990
Ambulatory Urodynamics   2008
Urodynamic Analysis and Interpretation   2009

**59  Lower Urinary Tract Dysfunction in
       Neurologic Injury and Disease** . . . . . . . . . . . . . .2011
ALAN J. WEIN, MD

Objectives   2011
General Patterns of Neuropathic/Voiding Functions   2012
Disease at or above the Brain Stem   2014
Diseases Primarily Involving the Spinal Cord   2019
Disease Distal to the Spinal Cord   2031
Miscellaneous Neurologic Diseases Causing Voiding
Dysfunction   2035
Miscellaneous Conditions Definitely, Probably, or Possibly
Related to Neuromuscular Dysfunction   2037
Other Conditions   2043
Treatment of Neurogenic Lower Urinary Tract Dysfunction:
Overview   2044

**60  Urinary Incontinence: Epidemiology,
       Pathophysiology, Evaluation, and Management
       Overview** . . . . . . . . . . . . . . . . . . . . . . . . . . . . . . .2046
VICTOR W. NITTI, MD  ·  JERRY G. BLAIVAS, MD

Definition and Classification of Urinary Incontinence   2046
Epidemology of Urinary Incontinence   2047
Continence and the Physiology of Micturition   2049
Etiology and Pathophysiology of Urinary
Incontinence   2053
Diagnostic Evaluation   2059
Urinary Incontinence Treatment Overview   2070

**61  Overactive Bladder** . . . . . . . . . . . . . . . . . . . . . . . .2079
PAUL ABRAMS, MD  ·  MARCUS DRAKE, DM, MA

Etiology   2079
Prevalence   2081
Clinical Assessment   2082
Distinguishing Overactive Bladder from Painful Bladder
Syndrome   2084
Urodynamic Confirmation of Detrusor Overactivity   2085
Management   2089

**62  Pharmacologic Management of Storage
       and Emptying Failure** . . . . . . . . . . . . . . . . . . . . .2091
KARL-ERIK ANDERSSON, MD, PhD  ·  ALAN J. WEIN, MD

Pharmacologic Therapy to Facilitate Bladder Filling and
Urine Storage   2091
Pharmacologic Therapy to Facilitate Bladder
Emptying   2114

**63  Conservative Management of Urinary Incontinence:
       Behavioral and Pelvic Floor Therapy,
       Urethral and Pelvic Devices** . . . . . . . . . . . . . . . .2124
CHRISTOPHER K. PAYNE, MD

General Considerations   2124
The Tools of Conservative Therapy   2126
Concept of "Therapeutic Package"   2130
Pelvic Floor Rehabilitation   2130
Devices   2136
Practical Approach to Treatment   2140
Summary   2146

**64  Electrical Stimulation for Storage and
       Emptying Disorders** . . . . . . . . . . . . . . . . . . . . . .2147
SANDIP P. VASAVADA, MD  ·  RAYMOND R. RACKLEY, MD

History of Electrical Stimulation   2147
Neurophysiology of Electrical Stimulation for Storage
and Emptying Disorders   2148
Electrical Stimulation and Storage Disorders   2151
Electrical Stimulation for Emptying Disorders   2163
Future Research and Conclusions   2167

**65  Retropubic Suspension Surgery for Incontinence in
       Women** . . . . . . . . . . . . . . . . . . . . . . . . . . . . . . . . .2168
C. R. CHAPPLE, BSc, MD, FRCS(Urol)

Therapeutic Options   2168
Choice of Surgical Technique   2169
Assessing Outcomes of Therapy   2170
Indications for Retropubic Repair   2172
General Technical Issues   2174
Marshall-Marchetti-Krantz Procedure   2174
Burch Colposuspension   2176
Paravaginal Repair   2178
Vagino-Obturator Shelf Repair   2180
Laparoscopic Retropubic Suspension   2180
Complications of Retropubic Repairs   2182
Comparisons Between Incontinence Procedures   2184

**66** Vaginal Reconstructive Surgery for Sphincteric Incontinence and Prolapse ...................2187
SENDER HERSCHORN, BSc, MDCM, FRCSC

Epidemiology of Urinary Incontinence, Anal Incontinence, and Pelvic Organ Prolapse   2187
Anatomy of Pelvic Floor, Supporting Structures, and Pathophysiology of Pelvic Organ Prolapse   2190
Pelvic Organ Prolapse   2198
Vaginal Surgery for Stress Incontinence   2212
Vaginal Surgery for Prolapse   2215

**67** Pubovaginal Sling ........................2234
SEUNG-JUNE OH, MD • JOHN T. STOFFEL, MD
EDWARD J. McGUIRE, MD

Brief Historical Note   2234
Specific Indications for Fascial Slings   2234
Sling Materials   2237
Evaluation of Patients for Slings   2238
Operative Procedure   2243
Modifications of the Standard Sling   2244
Postoperative Care   2245
Complications and Problems   2245
Outcome Studies   2246

**68** Tension-Free Vaginal Tape Procedures ........2251
ROGER DMOCHOWSKI, MD, FACS
HARRIETTE SCARPERO, MD • JONATHAN STARKMAN, MD

The Tension-Free Vaginal Tape Procedure   2251
Transobturator Slings   2266

**69** Injection Therapy for Urinary Incontinence ....2272
RODNEY A. APPELL, MD • J. CHRISTIAN WINTERS, MD

Patient Selection   2272
Injectable Materials   2273
Intraurethral Injection Techniques   2275
Postoperative Care   2280
Efficacy of Injectable Treatment   2280
Complications   2283
Safety   2284
Present and Future of Injectables in Urinary Incontinence   2285

**70** Additional Therapies for Storage and Emptying Failure ........................2288
M. LOUIS MOY, MD • ALAN J. WEIN, MD

To Facilitate Bladder Filling/Urine Storage   2288
To Facilitate Bladder Emptying   2298
Summary   2304

**71** Geriatric Incontinence and Voiding Dysfunction ............................2305
NEIL M. RESNICK, MD • SUBBARAO V. YALLA, MD

The Impact of Age on Incontinence   2305
Causes of Transient Incontinence   2306
Established Incontinence   2309

Diagnostic Approach   2311
Therapy   2314
Summary   2320

**72** Urinary Tract Fistula ......................2322
ERIC S. ROVNER, MD

General Considerations   2322
Urogynecologic Fistula   2323
Uroenteric Fistula   2351
Urovascular Fistula   2357
Other Urinary Tract Fistulas   2359

**73** Bladder and Urethral Diverticula ............2361
ERIC S. ROVNER, MD

Bladder Diverticula   2361
Female Urethral Diverticula   2372

**74** Surgical Treatment of Male Sphincteric Urinary Incontinence: The Male Perineal Sling and Artificial Urinary Sphincter ........2391
DAVID R. STASKIN, MD • CRAIG V. COMITER, MD

General Indications   2391
Prosthetics for Male Incontinence   2392
Male Perineal Sling   2393
Artificial Urinary Sphincter   2396
Summary   2403

**SECTION XV**
**BLADDER; LOWER GENITOURINARY**
**CALCULI AND TRAUMA ................2405**

**75** Urothelial Tumors of the Bladder ............2407
EDWARD M. MESSING, MD

Basic and Clinical Biology   2407
Epidemiology   2407
Etiology and Risk Factors   2410
Pathology   2417
Urothelial Carcinoma   2418
Origin and Patterns of Dissemination of Urothelial Carcinoma   2423
Natural History   2426
Prognostic Indicators   2427
Diagnosis   2430
Early Detection   2432
Staging   2438
Prevention   2441
Nonurothelial Tumors of the Bladder   2444
Nonepithelial Bladder Tumors   2445

**76** Non–Muscle-Invasive Bladder Cancer (Ta, T1, and CIS) ........................2447
J. STEPHEN JONES, MD • STEVEN C. CAMPBELL, MD, PhD

Staging   2447
Endoscopic Surgical Management   2450

Immunotherapy   2455
Intravesical Chemotherapy   2458
Management of Refractory Disease   2460
Surveillance   2462

**77**   Management of Invasive and Metastatic
Bladder Cancer . . . . . . . . . . . . . . . . . . . . . .2468
MARK P. SCHOENBERG, MD • MARK L. GONZALGO, MD, PhD

Clinical Presentation, Diagnosis, and Evaluation   2468
Axial Imaging   2469
Radical Cystectomy for Invasive Bladder Cancer   2469
Adjuncts to Standard Surgical Therapy   2473
Alternatives to Standard Therapy   2474
Management of Metastatic Bladder Cancer   2476
Local Salvage and Palliative Therapy   2478
Molecular Markers and Invasive and Advanced Bladder
Cancer   2478
Summary   2478

**78**   Surgery of Bladder Cancer . . . . . . . . . . . . . . . .2479
PETER T. NIEH, MD • FRAY F. MARSHALL, MD

Transurethral Resection of Bladder Tumors   2479
Surgical Approaches   2483
Radical Cystectomy in the Male   2483
Urethrectomy   2489
Radical Cystectomy in the Female   2493
Simple Cystectomy   2501
Partial Cystectomy   2503

**79**   Laparoscopic Surgery of the Urinary Bladder  . . .2506
INDERBIR S. GILL, MD, MCh

Laparoscopic Ureteral Reimplantation   2506
Seminal Vesicle Cysts   2507
Boari Flap   2509
Laparoscopic Bladder Diverticulectomy   2511
Vesicovaginal Fistula   2512
Laparoscopic Enterocystoplasty   2512
Laparoscopic Partial Cystectomy   2515
Laparoscopic Radical Cystectomy and Urinary
Diversion   2516

**80**   Use of Intestinal Segments in Urinary
Diversion . . . . . . . . . . . . . . . . . . . . . . . . . . . .2534
DOUGLAS M. DAHL, MD • W. SCOTT McDOUGAL, MD

Surgical Anatomy   2534
Selecting the Segment of Intestine   2536
Bowel Preparation   2537
Intestinal Anastomoses   2540
Ureterointestinal Anastomoses   2554
Renal Deterioration   2563
Urinary Diversion   2564
Metabolic and Neuromechanical Problems of Urinary
Intestinal Diversion   2570
Summary   2578

**81**   Cutaneous Continent Urinary Diversion . . . . . . .2579
MITCHELL C. BENSON, MD • JAMES M. McKIERNAN, MD
CARL A. OLSSON, MD

General Considerations   2579
Continent Urinary Diversion   2582
Quality of Life Assessments   2606
Variations in Operative Technique   2606
Summary   2611

**82**   Orthotopic Urinary Diversion . . . . . . . . . . . . . . .2613
JOHN P. STEIN, MD • DONALD G. SKINNER, MD

Evolution of Urinary Diversion   2613
Principles of Continent Urinary Diversion   2515
Selection of Patients   2617
Continence Mechanism in Patients Undergoing Orthotopic
Diversion   2618
Continence Preservation   2619
Urethral and Pelvic Recurrence in Patients with Bladder
Cancer after Cystectomy   2623
Previous Pelvic Radiotherapy   2629
Orthotopic Diversion and the Need to Prevent Reflux   2630
Techniques of Orthotopic Bladder Substitutes   2633
Results of Orthotopic Substitutes   2642
Use of Absorbable Stapling Techniques in Orthotopic
Substitutes   2645
Quality of Life After Urinary Diversion   2645
Summary   2647

**83**   Genital and Lower Urinary Tract Trauma . . . . . .2649
ALLEN F. MOREY, MD • THOMAS A. ROZANSKI, MD

Injuries to the External Genitalia   2649
Bladder Injuries   2655
Urethral Injuries   2658

**84**   Lower Urinary Tract Calculi . . . . . . . . . . . . . . . .2663
KHAI-LINH V. HO, MD • JOSEPH W. SEGURA, MD

Bladder Calculi   2663
Calculi of Prostatic and Seminal Vesicles   2670
Urethral Calculi   2670
Preputial Calculi   2672

**SECTION XVI**
**PROSTATE** . . . . . . . . . . . . . . . . . . . . . . . . . . .**2675**

**85**   Molecular Biology, Endocrinology, and
Physiology of the Prostate and Seminal
Vesicles . . . . . . . . . . . . . . . . . . . . . . . . . . . . . .2677
ROBERT VELTRI, PhD • RONALD RODRIGUEZ, MD, PhD

Development and Cell Biology   2678
Endocrine Control of Prostate Growth   2684
Regulation of Prostate Growth by Steroids and Protein
Growth Factors   2689
Regulation of Prostate Growth at the Molecular Level:
Steroid Receptors   2696

Growth Factors and Growth Suppressors   2705
Regulation of Prostate Growth: Balance of Cell Replication and Cell Death   2711
Prominent, Nonpeptide Components of Prostatic Secretions   2715
Prostatic Secretory Proteins   2718
Coagulation and Liquefaction of Semen   2725
Prostatic Secretions and Drug Transport   2725

**86  Benign Prostatic Hyperplasia: Etiology, Pathophysiology, Epidemiology, and Natural History** .........................2727
CLAUS G. ROEHRBORN, MD · JOHN D. McCONNELL, MD

Etiology and Pathophysiology   2727
Epidemiology and Natural History   2738

**87  Evaluation and Nonsurgical Management of Benign Prostatic Hyperplasia** ..............2766
ROGER KIRBY, MD · HERBERT LEPOR, MD

Diagnosis   2767
Assessing the Effectiveness and Safety of Medical Therapy for Benign Prostatic Hyperplasia   2773
Medical Therapy for Benign Prostatic Hyperplasia   2776
Therapy with α-Adrenergic Blockers   2777
Androgen Suppression as a Treatment Option   2788
Combination Therapy   2793
Aromatase Inhibitors   2797
Phytotherapy   2797
Future Strategies for Drug Development in Benign Prostatic Hyperplasia   2801

**88  Minimally Invasive and Endoscopic Management of Benign Prostatic Hyperplasia** ...........................2803
JOHN M. FITZPATRICK, MCh, FRCSI, FRCS(Glas), FRCS

Intraprostatic Stents   2804
Transurethral Needle Ablation of the Prostate   2809
Transurethral Microwave Therapy   2813
Lasers   2820
Transurethral Resection of the Prostate   2829
Transurethral Vaporization of the Prostate   2838
Transurethral Incision of the Prostate   2841
Other Technologies   2842
Conclusions   2843

**89  Retropubic and Suprapubic Open Prostatectomy** ..........................2845
MISOP HAN, MD, MS · ALAN W. PARTIN, MD, PhD

Overview   2845
Indications for Open Prostatectomy   2846
Preoperative Evaluation   2846
Operating Day Preparation   2847
Surgical Technique   2847
Postoperative Management   2851
Complications   2852
Summary   2852

**90  Epidemiology, Etiology, and Prevention of Prostate Cancer** ........................2854
ERIC A. KLEIN, MD · ELIZABETH A. PLATZ, ScD, MPH
IAN M. THOMPSON, MD

Epidemiology   2854
Risk Factors   2857
Etiology and Molecular Genetics   2863
Chemoprevention   2867
Summary   2871

**91  Pathology of Prostatic Neoplasia** .............2874
JONATHAN I. EPSTEIN, MD

Prostatic Intraepithelial Neoplasia   2874
Adenocarcinoma   2875
Subtypes of Prostate Adenocarcinoma   2880

**92  Ultrasonography and Biopsy of the Prostate** ....2883
JOHN R. RAMEY, MD · ETHAN J. HALPERN, MD
LEONARD G. GOMELLA, MD

Ultrasonographic Anatomy of the Prostate   2883
Gray-Scale Transrectal Ultrasonography (Trus)   2885
Prostate Biopsy Techniques and Outcomes   2887
Advanced Ultrasonographic Techniques for Prostate Imaging   2892

**93  Prostate Cancer Tumor Markers** ..............2896
MATTHEW B. GRETZER, MD · ALAN W. PARTIN, MD, PhD

Kallikrein Tumor Markers   2897
Prostate Specific Membrane Antigen   2907
Molecular Biology and Discovery of Serum Biomarkers for Prostate Cancer   2908
Conclusion   2910

**94  Diagnosis and Staging of Prostate Cancer** ......2912
H. BALLENTINE CARTER, MD · MOHAMAD E. ALLAF, MD
ALAN W. PARTIN, MD, PhD

Detection of Prostate Cancer   2912
Diagnostic Modalities   2915
Guidelines for Early Detection of Prostate Cancer   2923
Staging of Prostate Cancer   2925

**95  Definitive Therapy for Localized Prostate Cancer—An Overview** ....................2932
WILLIAM J. CATALONA, MD · MISOP HAN, MD

Background   2932
Conservative Management   2933
Radical Prostatectomy   2934
Radiation Therapy   2938
Other Treatments   2943
Recommendations for Treatment by Patient Risk Groups   2945

**96  Expectant Management of Prostate Cancer** .....2947
JAMES A. EASTHAM, MD · PETER T. SCARDINO, MD

"Watchful Waiting" Versus Active Surveillance with Selective Delayed Definitive Therapy   2947

Watchful Waiting 2948
Watchful Waiting Versus Treatment 2949
Identifying Men with "Low-Risk" Prostate Cancer 2950
Active Surveillance with Selective Delayed Definitive Therapy 2951
Summary 2955

**97** Anatomic Radical Retropubic Prostatectomy . . . .2956
PATRICK C. WALSH, MD • ALAN W. PARTIN, MD, PhD

Surgical Anatomy 2956
Surgical Technique 2959
Postoperative Management 2972
Complications 2972
Surgical Modifications to Classic Anatomic Radical Prostatectomy 2974
Salvage Radical Prostatectomy 2977
Summary 2978

**98** Radical Perineal Prostatectomy . . . . . . . . . . . . . .2979
DAVID M. HARTKE, MD • MARTIN I. RESNICK, MD

Selection of Patients 2979
Preoperative Care 2980
Position 2980
Exposure of the Prostate 2980
Nerve-Sparing Dissection 2981
Vesicourethral Anastomosis 2982
Closure 2983
Postoperative Care 2983
Pathologic Outcomes 2983
Morbidity 2983
Summary 2984

**99** Laparoscopic and Robotic-Assisted Laparoscopic Radical Prostatectomy and Pelvic Lymphadenectomy . . . . . . . . . . . . . . . . . . . . . .2985
LI-MING SU, MD • JOSEPH A. SMITH, Jr., MD

Laparoscopic and Robotic-Assisted Laparoscopic Radical Prostatectomy 2985
Laparoscopic Pelvic Lymph Node Dissection 3002
Summary 3004

**100** Radiation Therapy for Prostate Cancer . . . . . . . .3006
ANTHONY V. D'AMICO, MD, PhD • JUANITA CROOK, MD
CLAIR J. BEARD, MD • THEODORE L. DEWEESE, MD, PhD
MARK HURWITZ, MD • IRVING KAPLAN, MD

Historical Perspective 3006
Localized Disease 3006
Treatment: Cancer Control and Quality of Life 3014

**101** Cryotherapy for Prostate Cancer . . . . . . . . . . . . .3032
JOHN S. LAM, MD • LOUIS L. PISTERS, MD
ARIE S. BELLDEGRUN, MD, FACS

History of Cryotherapy 3032
Cryobiology 3034

Technical Improvements in Cryotherapy Equipment 3037
Patient Selection 3039
Surgical Technique 3040
Patient Follow-Up 3045
Outcomes After Primary Cryotherapy 3045
Outcomes After Salvage Cryotherapy 3047
Management of Local Recurrence After Cryotherapy 3048
Adjunctive Therapy 3049
Complications 3049
Quality of Life After Cryotherapy 3050
Costs of Cryotherapy 3051
Future Directions 3052

**102** Treatment of Locally Advanced Prostate Cancer . . . . . . . . . . . . . . . . . . . . . . . . . . . . . . . . .3053
MAXWELL V. MENG, MD • PETER R. CARROLL, MD

Definition 3053
Trends in Incidence and Treatment 3055
Natural History 3056
Radical Prostatectomy 3057
Radiation Therapy 3063
Androgen Deprivation and Its Timing 3065
Management of Delayed Sequelae 3067
Clinical Trials 3068

**103** The Clinical State of the Rising PSA Level after Definitive Local Therapy: A Practical Approach . . . . . . . . . . . . . . . . . . . . . . . . . . . . . . . .3069
MICHAEL J. MORRIS, MD • HOWARD I. SCHER, MD

When does a Patient Occupy the Clinical State of a Rising PSA Level? 3070
Radiographic and Other Tests to Determine Whether the Rising PSA Level Signifies Localized Disease, Metastatic Disease, or Both 3071
Models to Predict Local Versus Systemic Recurrence and to Predict for Survival 3072
Treatment Strategies for the Patient with a Rising PSA Level 3076
Summary 3080

**104** Hormone Therapy for Prostate Cancer . . . . . . . .3082
JOEL B. NELSON, MD

Historic Overview of Hormone Therapy for Prostate Cancer 3082
Molecular Biology of Androgen Axis 3083
Sources of Androgen 3084
Mechanisms of Androgen Axis Blockade 3085
Response to Androgen Blockade 3088
General Complications of Androgen Ablation 3089
Combination Therapy 3091
Timing of Therapy 3095
Economic Considerations 3099
The Future of Hormone Therapy 3099

**105** Treatment of Hormone-Refractory Prostate
Cancer ...................................3101
MARIO A. EISENBERGER, MD · MICHAEL CARDUCCI, MD

Clinical Considerations   3102
Experience with Cytotoxic Chemotherapy   3105
Palliative Management of Patients with Hormone-Refractory
Prostate Cancer   3112
Novel Approaches   3114

# VOLUME 4

## SECTION XVII
PEDIATRIC UROLOGY ................3119

**106** Normal Development of the Urogenital
System ...................................3121
JOHN M. PARK, MD

Kidney Development   3121
Bladder and Ureter Development   3131
Genital Development   3136

**107** Renal Function in the Fetus, Neonate,
and Child ...............................3149
ROBERT L. CHEVALIER, MD · JONATHAN A. ROTH, MD

Anatomic Stages of Development   3149
Functional Development in the Fetus   3149
Evaluation of Fetal Renal Function   3150
Postnatal Functional Development   3151
Evaluation of Renal Function in the Infant and Child   3153
Hormonal Control of Renal Function During
Development   3157
The Functional Response of the Developing Kidneys to
Malformation or Injury   3159
Summary   3162

**108** Congenital Urinary Obstruction:
Pathophysiology .........................3163
CRAIG A. PETERS, MD · ROBERT L. CHEVALIER, MD

Introduction   3163
Patterns of Congenital Obstructive Nephropathy   3165
Patterns of Effect Growth   3166
Differentiation   3168
Fibrosis   3169
Functional Integration   3171
Reversal of Congenital Renal Obstruction   3172
Human Relevance   3173

**109** Perinatal Urology .......................3176
CRAIG A. PETERS, MD

Fetal Diagnosis   3176
Pathophysiology of Congenital Obstruction   3185
Management of Fetal Uropathies   3186
Postnatal Evaluation and Management   3189

Neonatal Urologic Emergencies   3194
Specific Diagnoses   3196

**110** Evaluation of the Pediatric Urology Patient ....3198
DOUGLAS A. CANNING, MD · MICHAEL T. NGUYEN, MD

Triage of the Pediatric Urologic Patient   3198
The Pediatric Urology Office Visit   3204
Summary   3216

**111** Renal Disease in Childhood ................3217
H. NORMAN NOE, MD · DEBORAH P. JONES, MD

Hematuria   3217
Proteinuria   3219
Nephrolithiasis   3221
Renal Parenchymal Diseases Common in Childhood   3225
Renal Tubular Disorders   3228
Nephrogenic Diabetes Insipidus   3229
Care of the Child with Chronic Renal Insufficiency
and End-Stage Renal Disease   3229
Summary   3230

**112** Infection and Inflammation of the Pediatric
Genitourinary Tract ......................3232
LINDA M. DAIRIKI SHORTLIFFE, MD

Epidemiology of Pediatric Urinary Tract Infections   3232
Pathogenesis of Urinary Tract Infection in Children   3234
Diagnosis of Urinary Tract Infection   3242
Management of Pediatric Urinary Tract Infections   3246
Prophylactic Antimicrobial Agents   3249
Imaging Evaluation   3252
Specific Imaging Techniques   3254
Sequelae of Urinary Tract Infection   3256
Management of Special Urinary Tract Infections and
Common Associated Problems   3261
Other Genitourinary Tract Infections and Syndromes   3263
Genitourinary Tract and Nosocomial Infections   3266
Bacteriologic Ecology and Antimicrobial Resistance   3266
Considerations in Treating Children with Urinary Tract
Infection   3267

**113** Anomalies of the Upper Urinary Tract .........3269
STUART B. BAUER, MD

Anomalies of Number   3269
Anomalies of Ascent   3278
Anomalies of Form and Fusion   3283
Anomalies of Rotation   3291
Anomalies of Renal Vasculature   3292
Anomalies of the Collecting System   3297

**114** Renal Dysgenesis and Cystic Disease of the
Kidney ..................................3305
KENNETH I. GLASSBERG, MD

Molecular Genetics   3305
Renal Agenesis   3307
Dysplasia   3307
Hypoplasia and Hypodysplasia   3310

Cystic Disease   3313
Autosomal Recessive ("Infantile") Polycystic Kidney Disease   3315
Autosomal Dominant ("Adult") Polycystic Disease   3318
Juvenile Nephronophthisis/Medullary Cystic Disease Complex   3326
Congenital Nephrosis   3328
Familial Hypoplastic Glomerulocystic Kidney Disease (Cortical Microcystic Disease)   3329
Multiple Malformation Syndromes with Renal Cysts   3329
Multicystic Dysplastic Kidney   3334
Benign Multilocular Cyst (Cystic Nephroma)   3339
Simple Cysts   3343
Medullary Sponge Kidney   3348
Sporadic Glomerulocystic Kidney Disease   3350
Acquired Renal Cystic Disease   3351
Calyceal Diverticulum (Pyelogenic Cyst)   3354
Parapelvic and Renal Sinus Cysts   3354

**115**   Anomalies and Surgery of the Ureteropelvic Junction in Children . . . . . . . . . . . . . . . . . . . . . .3359
MICHAEL C. CARR, MD, PhD · ALAA EL-GHONEIMI, MD

Evidence   3359
Etiology   3359
Symptoms/Presentation   3362
Diagnosis   3363
Surgical Repair   3370
Outcome   3380
Summary   3380

**116**   Ectopic Ureter, Ureterocele, and Other Anomalies of the Ureter . . . . . . . . . . . . . . . . . . .3383
RICHARD N. SCHLUSSEL, MD · ALAN B. RETIK, MD

Terminology   3383
Embryology   3384
Anomalies of Termination   3387
Anomalies of Structure   3397
Anomalies of Number   3413
Anomalies of Position   3417

**117**   Reflux and Megaureter . . . . . . . . . . . . . . . . . . . .3423
ANTOINE KHOURY, MD, FRCSC, FAAP
DARIUS J. BÄGLI, MDCM, FRCSC, FACS

Introduction   3423
Historical Perspective   3423
Demographics   3424
Inheritance and Genetics   3425
Embryology of the Uterovesical Junction   3426
Functional Anatomy of the Antireflux Mechanism   3427
Etiology of Vesicoureteral Reflux   3428
Lower Urinary Tract Infection and Reflux   3429
Grading of Reflux   3430
Diagnosis and Evaluation of Vesicoureteral Reflux   3431
Assessment of the Lower Urinary Tract   3432
Assessment of the Upper Urinary Tract   3435
Cortical Defects   3436

Associated Anomalies and Conditions   3441
Natural History and Management   3445
Surgical Management   3450
Complications of Ureteral Reimplantation   3460
Endoscopic Treatment of Vesicoureteral Reflux   3462
Laparoscopy as Applied to Correction of Reflux   3466
Megaureter   3467

**118**   Prune Belly Syndrome . . . . . . . . . . . . . . . . . . . .3482
ANTHONY A. CALDAMONE, MD · JOHN R. WOODARD, MD

Genetics   3482
Embryology   3482
Clinical Features of Prune Belly Syndrome   3483
Presentation   3487
Evaluation and Management   3489
Long-Term Outlook   3493

**119**   Exstrophy-Epispadias Complex . . . . . . . . . . . . .3497
JOHN P. GEARHART, MD · RANJIV MATHEWS, MD

The Exstrophy-Epispadias Complex   3497
Classic Bladder Exstrophy   3500
Surgical Reconstruction of Bladder Exstrophy   3508
Other Modern Approaches to Exstrophy Reconstruction   3517
Modern Staged Repair of Exstrophy: Outcomes and Results   3530
Other Exstrophy Repairs: Outcomes   3534
Exstrophy Reconstruction Failures   3535
Cloacal Exstrophy   3538
Surgical Reconstruction of Cloacal Exstrophy   3541
Long-Term Issues in Cloacal Exstrophy   3544
Epispadias   3544
Sexual Function and Fertility in the Exstrophy Patient   3550
Long-Term Adjustment Issues   3553

**120**   Surgical Techniques for One-Stage Reconstruction of the Exstrophy-Epispadias Complex . . . . . . . . . . . . . . . . . . . . . . . . . . . . . .3554
RICHARD W. GRADY, MD · MICHAEL E. MITCHELL, MD

Background   3554
Complete Primary Exstrophy Repair   3555
Results   3569
Summary   3571

**121**   Bladder Anomalies in Children . . . . . . . . . . . . .3573
DOMINIC FRIMBERGER, MD · BRADLEY P. KROPP, MD, FAAP

Bladder and Urachal Development   3573
Classification of Bladder Anomalies   3574
Summary   3582

**122**   Posterior Urethral Valves and Other Urethral Anomalies . . . . . . . . . . . . . . . . . . . . . . . . . . . . . .3583
ANTHONY J. CASALE, MD

Posterior Urethral Valves   3583
Valve Bladder Syndrome   3596

Antenatal Diagnosis and Management  3598
Prognostic Indicators of Renal Function  3598
Transplantation in Valve Patients  3599
Anterior Urethral Valves  3599
Congenital Urethral Stricture  3600
Urethral Polyps  3601
Urethral Duplication  3601

**123** Voiding Dysfunction in Children:
Non-Neurogenic and Neurogenic . . . . . . . . . . . . .3604
C. K. YEUNG, MD · JENNIFER D. Y. SIHOE, MD
STUART B. BAUER, MD

*Non-Neuropathic Dysfunction of Lower*
*Urinary Tract  3604*
C. K. YEUNG, MD · JENNIFER D. Y. SIHOE, MD

Normal Bladder Function in Infants and Children  3605
Epidemiology and Classification of Non-Neuropathic
Bladder-Sphincter Dysfunction in Children  3609
Bladder-Sphincter Dysfunction During Bladder Filling  3611
Bladder-Sphincter Dysfunction During Bladder
Emptying  3612
Dysfunctional Elimination Syndrome, Constipation, and
Bladder Dysfunction  3613
Relationship Between Bladder-Sphincter Dysfunction,
Vesicoureteral Reflux, and Recurrent Urinary Tract
Infections  3614
Evaluation of Non-Neuropathic Bladder-Sphincter
Dysfunction  3614
Mamagement of Non-Neuropathic Bladder-Sphincter
Dysfunction  3618
Nocturnal Enuresis  3621
Summary  3624

*Neuropathic Dysfunction of the Lower*
*Urinary Tract  3625*
STUART B. BAUER, MD

Urodynamic Evaluation  3625
Neurospinal Dysraphisms  3628
Central Nervous System Insults  3648

**124** Urinary Tract Reconstruction in Children . . . . .3656
MARK C. ADAMS, MD · DAVID B. JOSEPH, MD

The "Functional" Urinary Tract  3657
Evaluation of the Patient  3659
Preparation of the Patient  3660
Antireflux  3661
Bladder Neck Reconstruction  3664
Augmentation Cystoplasty  3672
Continent Urinary Diversion  3691
Continence Mechanisms and Catheterizable
Segments  3693
Antegrade Continence Enemas  3700
Urinary Undiversion  3701
Summary  3702

**125** Hypospadias . . . . . . . . . . . . . . . . . . . . . . . . . . . .3703
JOSEPH G. BORER, MD · ALAN B. RETIK, MD

Development  3704
Etiology  3706
Epidemiology  3708
Associated Findings  3709
Special Considerations: Preoperative  3710
Historical Aspects of Hypospadias Repair  3712
General Principles of Hypospadias Repair  3712
Special Considerations: Perioperative  3718
Intraoperative Algorithm  3720
Primary Hypospadias Repair  3722
Complications  3738
Reoperative Hypospadias Repair  3740
Long-Term Follow-Up  3742
Current Trends  3743
Future Concepts  3743
Summary  3743

**126** Abnormalities of the Genitalia in Boys and
Their Surgical Management . . . . . . . . . . . . . . . . .3745
JACK S. ELDER, MD

Normal Genitalia and Association with Other
Abnormalities  3745
Male Genital Anomalies  3746

**127** Abnormalities of the Testes and Scrotum
and Their Surgical Management . . . . . . . . . . . . . .3761
FRANCIS X. SCHNECK, MD · MARK F. BELLINGER, MD

Testicular Embryology and Normal Descent  3761
The Undescended Testis  3763
Hernias and Hydroceles  3787
Acute Scrotum  3790
Variocele  3794
Congenital Anomalies of the Vas Deferens, Seminal Vesicles,
and Epididymis  3797

**128** Sexual Differentiation: Normal and
Abnormal . . . . . . . . . . . . . . . . . . . . . . . . . . . . . .3799
DAVID A. DIAMOND, MD

Normal Sexual Differentiation  3799
Abnormal Sexual Differentiation  3808
Evaluation and Management of the Newborn With
Ambiguous Genitalia  3827

**129** Surgical Management of Intersexuality, Cloacal
Malformation, and Other Abnormalities of the
Genitalia in Girls . . . . . . . . . . . . . . . . . . . . . . . .3830
RICHARD RINK, MD · MARTIN KAEFER, MD

Female Reproductive and Caudal Embryology  3830
Structural Anomalies of the Female Internal
Genitalia  3832
Classification of Urogenital Sinus and Cloacal
Anomalies  3846

Surgical Reconstruction of Intersex Conditions and
Urogenital Sinus    3853
Surgical Reconstruction for Cloacal Malformations    3865
Summary    3869

**130**    Pediatric Urologic Oncology . . . . . . . . . . . . . . . .3870
MICHAEL L. RITCHEY, MD  ·  ROBERT C. SHAMBERGER, MD

Neuroblastoma    3870
Genitourinary Rhabdomyosarcoma    3878
Wilms' Tumor    3885
Other Renal Tumors    3898
Testicular Tumors    3900

**131**    Pediatric Endourology and Laparoscopy . . . . . . .3907
STEVEN G. DOCIMO, MD  ·  CRAIG A. PETERS, MD

Pediatric Endourology    3907
Pediatric Laparoscopy    3914
Summary    3928

**132**    Pediatric Genitourinary Trauma  . . . . . . . . . . . . .3929
DOUGLAS HUSMANN, MD

Similarities and Differences in Evaluating Pediatric Versus
Adult Traumatic Injuries    3929
Radiographic and Endoscopic Assessment and Treatment of
Upper Tract Genitourinary Injuries    3930
Management of Renal Trauma    3932
Renal Vascular Injuries    3935
Trauma-Induced Renal Vascular Hypertension    3935
Ureteropelvic Junction Disruption    3936
Ureteral Trauma    3937
Bladder Injuries    3938
Urethral Injuries    3939
Penile Injuries    3944
Scrotal/Vulvar and Testicular Trauma    3945

Index    i

# SECTION VIII

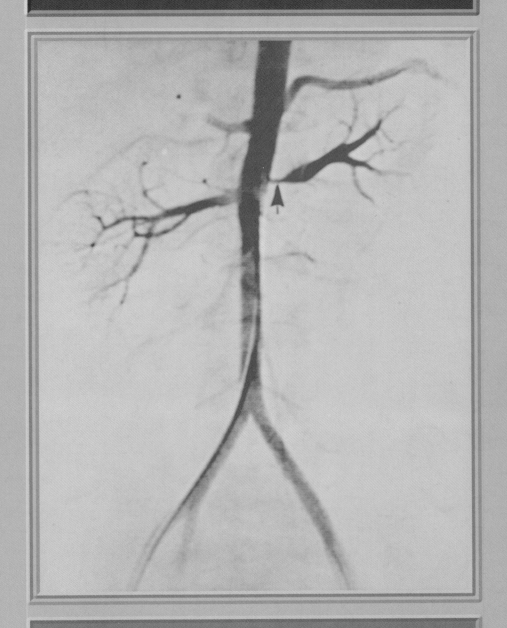

# RENAL PHYSIOLOGY AND PATHOPHYSIOLOGY

# Renal Physiology and Pathophysiology

## DANIEL A. SHOSKES, MD, FRCSC • ALAN W. McMAHON, MD

RENAL PHYSIOLOGY

RENAL PATHOPHYSIOLOGY

Renal physiology affects the urologic care of patients in numerous ways. These can include the pathophysiology of surgical disease (renal tubular acidosis, malignant paraneoplastic syndromes), the modification of surgical technique (ischemia reperfusion injury and intrarenal surgery), and iatrogenic complications of surgery (hyponatremia, metabolic complications of urinary diversions). The purpose of this chapter is not to turn urologists into nephrologists but rather to provide a firm fundamental knowledge of renal physiology and pathophysiology to provide the foundation for specific urologic conditions and therapies.

# RENAL PHYSIOLOGY
## Vascular (Renal Blood Flow and Glomerular Filtration Rate)

### Renal Blood Flow

Renal blood flow (RBF) is regulated by changes in vascular resistance of all the arteries up to and including the efferent arteriole, which in turn is regulated by a variety of neurohormonal signals (see later).

Blood enters the kidney through the renal arteries and divides into progressively smaller arteries (interlobar, arcuate, and interlobular arteries) until it enters the glomerular capillary through the afferent arteriole. A portion of the plasma that enters the glomerulus is filtered across the glomerular membrane; this is called the *filtration fraction*. The rest of the blood exits the glomerular capillary through the efferent arteriole. In nephrons located in the renal cortex, these capillaries travel in close proximity to the tubules and modulate solute and water reabsorption. In juxtamedullary nephrons (located deeper in the medulla), the efferent arterioles branch out to form vasa recta, which participate in the countercurrent mechanism through which urine is highly concentrated and body water conserved (see later discussion).

Under normal resting conditions, RBF is 20% of total cardiac output. Total blood flow is different for men and women, averaging 982 ± 184 mL/min in women and 1209 ± 256 mL/min in men (Dworkin and Brenner, 2004). Renal plasma flow (RPF) is slightly less, averaging 592 mL/min in women and 659 mL/min in men, and varies with hematocrit (RPF = RBF × [1 − Hct]). RBF is not evenly distributed to all parts of the kidney. Flow to the outer cortex is two to three times greater than that to the inner cortex, which in turn is two to four times greater than that to the medulla (Dworkin and Brenner, 2004).

### Determinants of Glomerular Filtration

**The most important function of the kidney is the process of glomerular filtration.** Through the passive ultrafiltration of plasma across the glomerular membrane, the kidney is able to regulate total body salt and water content and electrolyte composition and eliminate waste products of protein metabolism.

The process of filtration is analogous to fluid movement across any capillary wall and is governed by Starling's forces. **The glomerular filtration rate (GFR) is thus determined by both hydraulic and oncotic pressure differences between the glomerular capillary and Bowman's space as well as by the permeability of the glomerular membrane:**

$$\text{GFR} = \text{LpS} - (\Delta \text{hydrostatic pressure} - \Delta \text{oncotic pressure})$$

where Lp = glomerular permeability and S = glomerular surface area.

The rate at which filtration occurs within an individual nephron is termed the single-nephron GFR (SN-GFR). A more relevant measurement is that of total GFR, which is the sum of all SN-GFR and is expressed in milliliters per minute. **GFR is thus a reflection of overall renal function.** Alterations in GFR can occur either with alterations in any aspect of Starling's forces or through a change in RPF.

1. *Transglomerular (hydraulic) pressure (TGP)*—the most significant determinant of GFR is the TGP. Although systemic arterial pressures affect TGP, the glomerular capillary is unique in that it is interposed between two arterioles (the afferent and efferent arterioles) and can thus regulate intraglomerular capillary pressure (IGP) independent of systemic pressures through changes in afferent and efferent arteriolar tone. Under normal circumstances, the pressure within Bowman's space is essentially zero, and only in conditions of urinary

obstruction does the pressure increase to clinically significant levels. Thus, the TGP = IGP.

2. *Renal plasma flow*—increases in RPF lead to increases in GFR. Although the filtration fraction cannot exceed 20% under normal circumstances, an increase in RPF leads to an increase in absolute GFR.

3. *Glomerular permeability*—generally, an increase in permeability does not lead to an increase in GFR, as the glomerulus is already at maximal permeability for water and other relevant solutes. It may, however, lead to increased filtration of larger molecules not normally filtered, such as albumin. Reductions in permeability or in glomerular surface area can lead to reductions in GFR.

4. *Oncotic pressure*—the least relevant of all the variables. Under normal circumstances, plasma proteins are not filtered across the glomerular membrane and so oncotic pressure within Bowman's space is essentially zero.

### Regulation of Glomerular Filtration Rate

**Under normal circumstances, GFR is tightly maintained at a relatively constant level despite large fluctuations in systemic arterial pressures and RBF.** This is accomplished through the processes of autoregulation and tubuloglomerular feedback.

1. *Autoregulation*—with increases in mean arterial pressure (MAP), afferent arteriolar tone increases to minimize increases in IGP. Similarly, with reductions in MAP, afferent arteriolar tone decreases to allow increased flow into the glomerulus to maintain IGP, thus maintaining GFR. Autoregulation of IGP is effective to an MAP of about 70 mm Hg; below that, reductions in MAP lead to similar reductions in GFR, and below an MAP of 40 mm Hg, filtration ceases. The mechanism by which autoregulation is achieved is not well understood. It is probably mediated through myogenic stretch receptors in the afferent arteriole wall, possibly mediated by ATP (Schnermann and Levine, 2003), but angiotensin II is also involved with more severe fluctuations.

2. *Tubuloglomerular feedback (TGF)*—tubular ultrafiltrate flow rates are monitored by cells in the macula densa. If SN-GFR increases, delivery of $Na^+$ and $Cl^-$ to the distal tubule also increases. This increased $Cl^-$ delivery triggers a response through the macula densa that ultimately leads to an increase in afferent arteriolar tone and subsequent decrease in RPF, thus returning SN-GFR (and tubular flow) back to baseline (Schnermann et al, 1998). Thus, TGF can be thought of as a mechanism to minimize salt and water losses through regulation of GFR. The mediators of this response are not well understood, but it seems that angiotensin II plays a permissive role in TGF. Both adenosine and thromboxane can cause afferent arteriolar vasoconstriction and have been implicated in TGF. Nitric oxide (NO) (Schnermann and Levine, 2003) is also believed to be important, particularly in minimizing TGF in the setting of increased NaCl intake.

Under abnormal conditions, however, neurohumoral responses become more important. With significant reductions in effective circulating volume, both norepinephrine and angiotensin II play an important role in maintaining GFR

through arteriolar vasoconstriction, often at the expense of reduced RPF. It should also be noted that renal prostaglandins (PGs) and NO offset afferent arteriolar vasoconstriction, so that arteriolar tone is a balance between the vasoconstrictive and vasodilatory effects of the aforementioned hormones. Inhibition of PG synthesis (by administration of nonsteroidal anti-inflammatory drugs), particularly in states of high angiotensin II production, can lead to severe vasoconstriction and acute reduction in GFR. In contrast, norepinephrine and angiotensin II levels are diminished in states of volume expansion, whereas dopamine and atrial natriuretic peptide (ANP) levels are increased to facilitate an increase in RPF (dopamine) and natriuresis (ANP), thus returning volume status back to normal.

### Clinical Assessment of Glomerular Filtration Rate

Unfortunately, GFR cannot be measured directly. It can, however, be estimated by a variety of methods, some more accurate (but usually more cumbersome) than others.

**Renal Clearance.** **The best estimate of GFR can be obtained by measuring the rate of clearance of a given substance from the plasma.** However, in order to be accurate, the substance to be measured must meet certain criteria. It must:

- Be able to achieve a stable plasma concentration,
- Be freely filtered across the glomerulus,
- Not be secreted, reabsorbed, synthesized, or otherwise metabolized by the renal tubules, and
- Not be affected by any other means of removal from the plasma.

If all these criteria are met,

$$\text{Filtered X} = \text{excreted X}$$

and because

$$\text{Filtered X} = \text{GFR} \times \text{plasma [X]}$$

and

$$\text{Excreted X} = \text{urine [X]} \times \text{urine volume (in mL/unit time)}$$

we can now see that

$$\text{GFR} \times \text{P[X]} = \text{U[X]} \times \text{urine volume}$$

$$\text{GFR} = \text{U[X]} \times \text{urine volume/P[X]}$$

This is called the *clearance* of a substance and reflects the amount of plasma that is completely cleared of the substance per unit time. A number of substances have been used clinically to estimate GFR.

1. *Inulin.* Inulin is a fructose polysaccharide that meets the requirements, and inulin clearance is thought to be the best measure of GFR. However, inulin is not clinically useful as it is difficult to administer (requires an intravenous infusion of inulin) and difficult to measure.

2. *Radiolabeled compounds.* These include iothalamate and diethylenetriaminepentaacetic acid (DTPA). These clearances are also very accurate but are again limited in clinical use by their cost and availability (Perrone et al, 1990).

3. *Creatinine.* **The most widely used estimate of GFR is the 24-hour creatinine clearance (CrCl)** (Levey, 1990).

It utilizes endogenous creatinine, which is produced at a constant rate. The rate of production varies from individual to individual, but for a single individual daily variability is less than 10%. It has the advantage of being easy to perform (no intravenous infusion), is relatively cheap, and is readily available. However, it is less accurate than inulin clearance, as some creatinine is cleared from plasma through proximal tubular secretion; thus, a CrCl overestimates true GFR, on average, by 10% to 20%. This becomes even more important as GFR declines, as tubular secretion increases in response to increasing serum creatinine levels and may contribute up to 35% of all creatinine removal at GFR levels of 40 to 80 mL/min (Shemesh et al, 1985). **At best, then, the CrCl should be considered the "upper limit" of the true GFR.**

**Plasma Markers.** An even simpler method to estimate GFR is with the use of plasma levels of substances that can be used as surrogate markers of GFR. To be useful, the substance must fulfill the preceding criteria. Three such substances have been utilized:

1. *Plasma creatinine (PCr),* **the most widely used plasma marker of GFR.** Although creatinine production is constant within an individual from day to day, there is marked variation in production rates between individuals. The absolute rate depends upon muscle mass, which in turn is influenced by age, sex, and body mass. Thus, **there is no single "normal" PCr that reflects a "normal" GFR; it must be individualized for every person.** This can be accomplished through mathematical manipulation (see later). However, the relationship of PCr to GFR is relatively constant (Fig. 35–1), and changes in PCr can be used to predict corresponding changes in GFR. As a general rule, every 50% reduction in GFR results in a doubling of PCr. There are limitations to the use of the PCr that should be noted:
   • As GFR falls, tubular secretion of creatinine increases and PCr may not change noticeably until there has been a significant drop in GFR (Shemesh et al, 1985).
   • Creatinine production may increase in states of increased muscle breakdown (e.g., rhabdomyolysis) or with increased dietary protein intake or supplementation and lead to an underestimation of true GFR.

   • Creatinine production may decrease with liver cirrhosis, leading to an overestimation of true GFR.
2. *Plasma urea,* another widely used plasma marker. Urea production and excretion are highly variable, influenced by such things as dehydration, high-protein diets, and increased tissue breakdown. As a result, it is a much less reliable marker of GFR than is the PCr and should not be used as the sole determinant.
3. *Plasma cystatin C,* an endogenous protein found in all nucleated cells. It has a constant rate of production unaffected by diet, and clearance is not influenced by tubular functions (Filler et al, 2005). This test is not widely available at present but is likely to replace PCr as the standard test in GFR assessment.

**Mathematical Correction.** **A number of mathematical formulas have been developed to improve the accuracy of the PCr estimation of GFR** (National Kidney Foundation, 2002). The two most widely used are the Cockcroft-Gault and modification of diet in renal disease (MDRD) formulas.

1. *Cockcroft-Gault,* originally developed from data collected from individuals with normal renal function, is a simple formula to estimate CrCl (not GFR) that corrects for age, sex, and body mass (IBW, ideal body weight) (Cockcroft and Gault, 1976). The formula is

$$CrCl = \frac{\{[(140-age)\times(IBW\ in\ kg)]}{[PCr(mg/dL)\times72]\}}\times0.85\,(women)$$

It has the advantage of being very simple, but it is not as accurate as other methods when renal function is impaired.
2. *MDRD formulas,* a series of formulas derived from data collected for patients with severe renal impairment, are more complex but more accurate than the Cockcroft-Gault formula. The simplest estimate of GFR is the four-variable equation (PCr, age, sex, and ethnicity) (Manjunath et al, 2001):

$$GFR = 186 \times (PCr)^{-1.154} \times (age)^{-0.203}$$
$$\times (0.742\ if\ female) \times (1.210\ if\ African\ American)$$

In summary, the GFR is analogous to renal function. Total GFR is a summation of all SN-GFR values (which in turn are determined primarily by TGP and the glomerular permeability of the individual nephrons), and it is usually tightly regulated. **A GFR estimate should be obtained for all patients with renal impairment (rather than a PCr alone), and the recommended method is through the use of the four-variable MDRD formula or Cockcroft-Gault formula.**

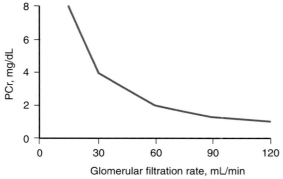

**Figure 35–1.** Relationship between serum creatinine and creatinine clearance. PCr, plasma creatinine.

---

## KEY POINTS: RENAL BLOOD FLOW AND GLOMERULAR FILTRATION RATE

■ GFR reflects total renal function.

■ GFR can be approximated by creatinine clearance.

■ Formulas based on patient's age, weight, and serum creatinine can best estimate GFR.

# Hormonal

## Control of Renal Vascular Tone

Vascular tone of the renal vessels, the net balance of vasoconstrictive and vasodilatory forces, is key to the maintenance of RBF, GFR, tubular renal function, and systemic blood pressure. **There is a complex network of hormones and vasoactive substances with both direct and indirect effects resulting in a system that is pleiotropic and redundant.** Although much has been learned from animal models about the function of individual molecules, the complexity of the total system can lead to unexpected outcomes when individual pathways are manipulated pharmacologically. A summary of substances known to affect vascular tone is given in Table 35–1.

### Vasoconstrictors

*Angiotensin II.* Angiotensin II is a potent vasoconstrictor. In the kidney, there is a more pronounced constrictive effect on the efferent than the afferent arteriole because of inhibition of angiotensin II actions in the afferent arteriole by nitric oxide and prostaglandin (Arima, 2003). Elevated levels of angiotensin II are important for maintaining GFR in pathologic conditions that reduce RBF (e.g., renal artery stenosis, dietary sodium restriction). The classical effects of angiotensin II (vasoconstriction, aldosterone release, sodium retention) are mediated by the AT1 receptor (Kaschina and Unger, 2003). The AT2 receptor, however, may cause intrarenal dilation and be protective against renal ischemic injury (Carey, 2005).

| Table 35–1. **Vasoactive Substances That Control Renal Artery Tone** |
| --- |
| *Vasoconstriction* |
| Angiotensin II |
| Norepinephrine |
| Vasopressin |
| Endothelin |
| Atrial natriuretic peptide |
| *Vasodilation* |
| Nitric oxide |
| Carbon monoxide |
| Prostaglandin E$_2$ |
| Acetylcholine |
| Serotonin/bradykinin |
| Glucocorticoids |

*Norepinephrine.* Norepinephrine vasoconstricts all the major vascular beds in the kidney, mediated through the $\alpha_1$ receptor. In patients who receive norepinephrine as a pressor agent in the presence of systemic vasodilation, renal function is preserved and may actually improve (Albanese et al, 2004).

*Endothelin.* **Endothelin is the most potent vasoconstrictor yet identified.** There are three isoforms, with ET-1 being the most fully described. An endothelin precursor (big ET-1; 39 amino acids) is cleaved to ET-1 (21 amino acids) by an endothelin converting enzyme found on the endothelial cell membrane. The endothelin receptors are subclassified into ET(A), which are purely vasoconstrictive, and ET(B). The ET(B) receptors may cause either vasodilation, by stimulating the release of nitric oxide from endothelial cells, or vasoconstriction of vascular smooth muscle cells (Fellner and Arendshorst, 2004). ET-1 release is stimulated by angiotensin II, antidiuretic hormone, thrombin, cytokines, reactive oxygen species, and shearing forces acting on the vascular endothelium. ET-1 release is inhibited by nitric oxide as well as by prostacyclin and ANP. Blockade of the ET(A) receptor can reduce the renal vasoconstriction seen in such ischemic conditions as ureteral obstruction (Bhangdia et al, 2003).

ET-1 has a number of other actions besides vasoconstriction. ET-1 stimulates aldosterone secretion, produces positive inotropy and chronotropy in the heart, decreases RBF and GFR, and releases ANP. **Despite reduction in RBF, sodium excretion is increased,** suggesting that ET may be responsible for maintaining sodium balance when the renin-angiotensin system is depressed (Perez del Villar et al, 2005). Medullary blood flow is preserved in the presence of endothelin-induced vasoconstriction, which may explain the relative stimulation of tubular functions (Evans et al, 2004).

*Vasopressin.* Vasopressin acts directly on blood vessels through the vasopressin V1 receptor but does not directly change RBF at low doses (Malay et al, 2004). Vasopressin does potentiate the vasoconstrictive effects of norepinephrine (Segarra et al, 2002) and can induce renal ischemia at high doses. **At the low doses typically employed in the management of septic shock, renal function is preserved** (Holmes et al, 2001).

*Atrial Natriuretic Peptide.* ANP is a vasoactive hormone synthesized primarily by the atria in response to stretching, such as that which occurs during physiologic levels of volume expansion (Fig. 35–2). **The primary actions of ANP on the**

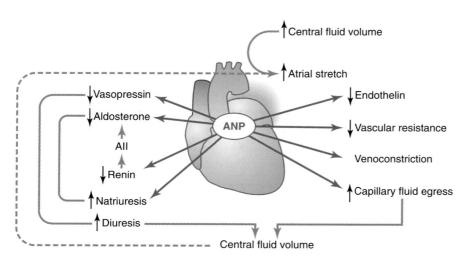

**Figure 35–2.** Schematic representation of the fundamental biologic processes of atrial natriuretic peptide (ANP). AII, angiotensin II.

**kidney are increased GFR and natriuresis.** ANP can increase GFR without a change in RBF (Sward et al, 2005) by the combination of afferent arteriolar vasodilatation and efferent arteriolar vasoconstriction. In addition, ANP dilates vessels that have been preconstricted by norepinephrine, angiotensin II, or vasopressin. ANP production increases during bilateral obstructive uropathy, which may be one mechanism of preserving GFR (Kim et al, 2002).

ANP increases natriuresis through increased GFR, decreased renin, and decreased aldosterone production (Laragh, 1985). Clinically, however, infusion of low-dose ANP during surgery increases water and electrolyte excretion without measured systemic changes in cortisol, angiotensin II, or aldosterone (Koda et al, 2005). This approach has also been used to prevent ischemic renal damage in high-risk cardiac surgery (Sward et al, 2004).

### Vasodilators

*Nitric Oxide.* Nitric oxide (NO) is a highly reactive gas that participates in multiple physiologic and pathophysiologic reactions in the body. **NO is synthesized from the reaction between arginine, NADPH, and oxygen to produce citrulline, NADP, water, and NO.** This reaction is catalyzed by a family of enzymes called nitric oxide synthase (NOS). Although all NOS enzymes catalyze the same reaction, they differ in distribution, expression, and stimuli. Neuronal NOS (nNOS, NOS-1) and endothelial NOS (eNOS, NOS-3) are constitutively expressed and iNOS (NOS-2) is inducible. **eNOS is found in the vascular endothelium, and the NO produced there plays a key role in vasodilation and vascular remodeling** (Rudic et al, 1998). eNOS expression is stimulated by shear stress through activation of the tyrosine kinase c-Src (Davis et al, 2004), by heat shock protein 90 (Harris et al, 2003), by oxidant stress (Cai et al, 2001), and by vascular mediators such as bradykinin, serotonin, adenosine, ADP/ATP, histamine, and thrombin (Arnal et al, 1999).

After its formation by vascular endothelial cells, NO diffuses to vascular smooth muscle cells, where it activates soluble guanylyl cyclase (sGC), producing guanosine 3′,5′-cyclic monophosphate (cGMP). Subsequently, cGMP activates both cGMP- and adenosine 3′,5′-cyclic monophosphate (cAMP)-dependent protein kinases (PKG and PKA, respectively), leading to smooth muscle relaxation. eNOS blockade increases renal vascular resistance and decreases the glomerular ultrafiltration coefficient (Gabbai, 2001). NO also helps maintain vascular integrity, with increased expression being linked to decreased neointimal formation and medial thickening (Kawashima et al, 2001). Indeed, the degenerative changes seen in chronic allograft nephropathy related to cyclosporine use can be mitigated by increased nitric oxide expression (Chander et al, 2005). Increased eNOS activity is also associated with protection from renal ischemia-reperfusion injury (Shoskes et al, 1997).

Whereas raised local levels of NO from eNOS can be beneficial to renal function, induction of iNOS and overproduction of NO from inflammatory cells can be deleterious. In the presence of free oxygen radicals at the site of inflammation, NO can interact with reactive oxygen species to form peroxynitrite, which induces protein damage by formation of nitrotyrosine. Increased iNOS has been related to damage from nitrotyrosine in glomerular disease (Trachtman, 2004), lupus nephritis (Takeda et al, 2004), and chronic transplant

rejection (Albrecht et al, 2002). Increased iNOS activity has direct renal effects as well, including upregulation of sodium and bicarbonate tubular transport (Wang, 2002).

*Carbon Monoxide.* Carbon monoxide (CO) gas is another reactive diffusible mediator with multiple effects throughout the body and especially in the kidney. **Heme oxygenase (HO), an essential enzyme in heme catabolism, catalyzes the rate-limiting step in heme degradation, resulting in the formation of iron, carbon monoxide, and biliverdin** (Hill-Kapturczak et al, 2002). Biliverdin is subsequently converted to bilirubin by biliverdin reductase. HO is expressed in two forms, constitutive HO-2 and inducible HO-1. Increased CO production produces vasodilation in the kidney and can counteract catecholamine-induced vasoconstriction (Mustafa and Johns, 2001). In particular, both HO-1 and HO-2 are highly expressed in the medulla and help maintain renal medullary blood flow (Zou et al, 2000). In cirrhosis, decreased renal expression of HO-1 is linked to renal dysfunction (Miyazono et al, 2002). CO also regulates sodium transport in the loop of Henle, with HO-2 blockade inhibiting sodium excretion (Wang et al, 2003) and stimulation increasing natriuresis and diuresis (Rodriguez et al, 2003).

**The other primary effect of CO in the kidney is renoprotection from oxidant injury.** CO has documented anti-inflammatory, antioxidant, and cytoprotective actions (Sikorski et al, 2004). Indeed, a patient with a genetic HO-1 deficiency had significant tubular and vascular endothelial injury (Ohta et al, 2000). Increased CO is protective against ischemia-reperfusion injury in native and transplant kidneys (Nakao et al, 2005). Induction of HO-1 through agents such as bioflavonoids protects against tubular damage and improves renal transplant function (Shoskes et al, 2005).

### KEY POINTS: HORMONAL

- Multiple chemical mediators act on renal vascular tone, which controls renal blood flow.
- Endothelin is the most potent vasoconstrictor.
- Nitric oxide and carbon monoxide are potent vasodilators.

### Erythropoiesis

Red blood cell (RBC) production is a tightly regulated process. Basal RBC production is roughly 10 RBCs/hr, but this rate can be greatly increased during times of anemia or hypoxia. The kidney is the major organ involved in this process and is responsible for monitoring RBC levels and increasing RBC output through the production of the hormone erythropoietin.

**Erythroid Progenitor Cells.** Mature RBCs are produced from a small pool of multipotent progenitor cells (Suda et al, 1984), which in turn are derived from the fetal liver. The earliest committed cell is the erythroid burst-forming unit (BFU-E), which, under appropriate stimulation, divides to produce erythroid colony-forming units (CFU-Es). Further differentiation leads to the production of proerythroblasts, reticulocytes, and ultimately (after extrusion of the nucleus) mature RBCs. The entire process requires about 2 weeks.

**Erythropoietin.** Maturation of the BFU-E and CFU-E depends on the appropriate growth factors. The most important of these factors is erythropoietin (EPO). The kidney is responsible for the majority of EPO production (90%), and the liver may contribute a smaller amount (10%). Kidney-derived EPO is produced by a subpopulation of interstitial fibroblasts and possibly proximal tubular cells in response to decreased $O_2$ tension.

EPO-deficient mice die in utero with a marked reduction in erythropoiesis (Munugalavadla and Kapur, 2005). Additional growth factors such as interleukin 3, granulocyte-macrophage colony-stimulating factor, stem cell factor, activin, insulin-like growth factor I (IGF-I), and possibly hepatic growth factor act synergistically with EPO to reduce apoptosis and thus promote proliferation of erythroid cells (Muta and Krantz, 1993).

EPO has also been shown to have effects outside the bone marrow. EPO receptors have been demonstrated in kidney, brain, retina, heart, skeletal muscle, and endothelial cells (Juul et al, 1998). In the kidney, pretreatment with high-dose EPO has been shown to reduce ischemia-reperfusion injury in an animal model related to decreased apoptosis (Patel et al, 2004).

**Regulation of Erythropoietin Production and Erythropoiesis.** Production of EPO, and hence erythropoiesis, is closely associated with circulating $O_2$ tension. Under hypoxic conditions, the alpha subunit of the regulatory protein hypoxia-inducible factor-1 (HIF-1) is exposed (Wang et al, 1995). Binding of HIF-1 alpha with HIF-1 beta, hepatic nuclear factor 4 (HNF-4), and p300 turns on erythropoietin transcription (Arany et al, 1996). When the hypoxia has been corrected, HIF-1 alpha is ubiquinated and rapidly degraded by proteosomes, thus shutting down erythropoietin production. There is also in vitro evidence that hypoxia itself may directly increase erythropoiesis through HIF-1–mediated increases in autocrine motility factor production and subsequent decrease in apoptosis (Mikami et al, 2005).

In states of chronic inflammation, erythropoiesis is decreased. Apoptosis of erythroid progenitor cells occurs in the presence of the tumor-associated antigen RCAS1, which is also produced by macrophages under inflammatory conditions (Suehiro et al, 2005).

Erythropoiesis is also decreased in most forms of chronic renal failure, and subsequently anemia is common in the later stages of the disease. This is due to decreased EPO levels as a result of a reduction in the number of functional EPO-producing cells within the kidney. Recombinant human erythropoietin (rHuEPO) has been shown to be an effective treatment for this type of anemia.

### Bone Mineral Regulation

Normal regulation of bone mineralization, through maintenance of serum calcium and phosphorus levels, is achieved through the actions of vitamin D and parathyroid hormone (PTH). The actions of both hormones are exerted largely through the kidney (Fig. 35–3).

**Vitamin D Regulation.** **The kidney plays an important role in the regulation of vitamin D activity.** The major source of

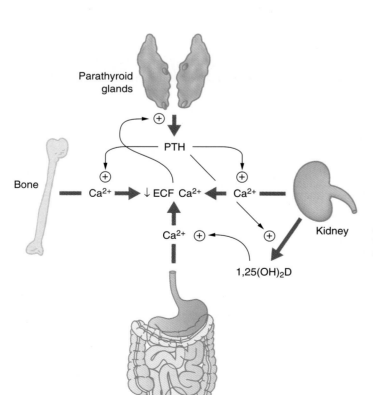

**Figure 35–3.** Effects of vitamin D and parathyroid hormone (PTH) on calcium homeostasis. EFC, extracellular fluid. (From Yu SLY: Renal transport of calcium, magnesium, and phosphate. In Brenner BM [ed]: Brenner and Rector's The Kidney, 7th ed. Philadelphia, WB Saunders, 2004, p 536.)

vitamin D is dermal synthesis of the precursor compound cholecalciferol (vitamin $D_3$) or dietary intake of vitamin $D_3$-fortified foods. Vitamin $D_3$ has minimal biologic activity and requires two hydroxylations to become active. The first hydroxylation occurs in the liver through the action of 25-hydroxylase to form 25-hydroxycholecalciferol (calcidiol). The calcidiol molecule is bound to vitamin D binding protein and transported to the kidney, where it is filtered and reabsorbed by renal tubular cells. A second hydroxylation occurs within the tubular cell. Because these cells contain both $1\alpha$-hydroxylase and $24\alpha$-hydroxylase, hydroxylation produces either inactive 24,25-dihydroxycholecalciferol or 1,25-dihydroxycholecalciferol (calcitriol), which is the biologically active form and 100 times more potent than calcidiol. Calcitriol production is regulated by calcidiol levels as well as $1\alpha$-hydroxylase levels. These are in turn determined by PTH and plasma phosphate levels (which increase enzyme activity) and serum calcitriol levels (which decrease enzyme activity) (Portale et al, 1989). However, unregulated calcitriol synthesis can occur in macrophages in granulomatous conditions such as sarcoidosis and tuberculosis and in prostate epithelial and cancer cells (Young et al, 2004).

**Vitamin D Activity.** Calcitriol functions through a single intracellular vitamin D receptor (VDR) to regulate gene transcription (Lowe et al, 1992). Its primary function is the maintenance of serum calcium and phosphorus levels. The four main target organs are the intestine (increases intestinal absorption of calcium and, to a lesser extent, phosphorus), the bones (regulates osteoblast activity and, in combination with PTH, allows osteoclast activation and bone resorption), the kidney (increases reabsorption of calcium), and the parathyroid gland (suppresses PTH release). Evidence suggests that both calcidiol and calcitriol may also function as antiproliferative agents. Prostate epithelial and cancer cells demonstrate VDR, and vitamin D may suppress the growth of these cells, especially in combination with androgens (Tuohimaa et al, 2005).

**In summary, vitamin D contributes to normal bone mineralization by maintaining normal serum calcium and phosphorus levels through increased intestinal absorption of calcium and phosphorus and increased renal reabsorption of calcium.**

**Parathyroid Hormone Regulation.** Synthesis, secretion, and degradation of PTH are influenced directly by serum calcium levels through calcium-sensing receptors located on parathyroid cells. During periods of hypocalcemia, PTH synthesis and secretion are increased and degradation is decreased. The opposite occurs during hypercalcemia. In addition, calcitriol has a suppressive effect on PTH synthesis and parathyroid cell proliferation that is mediated through VDRs located on the surface of parathyroid cells. Hyperphosphatemia also directly stimulates PTH release, primarily in advanced renal insufficiency. Finally, other cations such as magnesium and aluminum have slight stimulatory effects, probably mediated through the calcium-sensing receptors.

**Parathyroid Hormone Activity.** PTH exerts its activity through PTH/PTH-related protein (PTHrP) receptors, which are localized primarily to the kidneys and bone.

*Bone.* The effect of PTH on bone metabolism depends upon its administration; if given continuously, it stimulates

bone resorption and increases serum calcium and phosphorus levels. Given intermittently, it leads to increased bone formation and mineral density.

*Kidney.* The renal effects of PTH are threefold. First, it increases active calcium reabsorption at the level of the distal tubule (Friedman and Gesek, 1993). Second, it decreases phosphate reabsorption in the proximal convoluted tubule (and the distal tubule, to a lesser degree) through its action on the sodium-phosphorus cotransporter (Pfister et al, 1997). Third, it stimulates calcitriol production by increasing $1\alpha$-hydoxylase levels while decreasing $24\alpha$-hydroxylase levels (Broadus et al, 1980).

**In summary, PTH functions to maintain normal serum calcium and phosphorus levels by increasing bone resorption, increasing renal reabsorption of calium and excretion of phosphorus, and stimulating production of calcitriol.**

### Antidiuretic Hormone

Antidiuretic hormone (ADH), or arginine vasopressin as it is called in humans, is a polypeptide secreted by the posterior pituitary gland. It functions to maintain serum osmolality and volume through the regulation of free water excretion in the kidney.

**ADH Actions. ADH increases the passive reabsorption of water at the level of the collecting duct.** Through interaction with the V2 receptor, it facilitates the insertion of preformed water channels known as aquaporin 2 (AQP-2) into the luminal membrane of the principal cells (Agre et al, 2002). This allows luminal water to enter the cell and then diffuse back into the systemic circulation through the basolateral membrane of the cell (Fig. 35–4). ADH increases urea reabsorption in the medullary collecting tubule through specific urea transporters, which helps maintain the high interstitial osmolality required for water reabsorption. ADH also increases systemic vascular resistance through interaction with the V1 receptor; this is of minor physiologic importance. Other effects of ADH include increased sodium reabsorption and potassium excretion, increased prostaglandin synthesis, increased adrenocorticotropic hormone secretion (through V3 receptors), and release of both factor VIII and von Willebrand's factor from vascular endothelium.

**Control of ADH Secretion. There are two major stimuli for ADH release, hyperosmolality and decreased effective circulating volume (ECV),** as well as a number of less common factors (Table 35–2).

**Table 35–2. Physiologic and Pathologic Factors Affecting the Release of Antidiuretic Hormone**

| *Stimuli* | *Inhibitors* |
| --- | --- |
| Hyperosmolality | Hypo-osmolality |
| Hypovolemia | Hypervolemia |
| Stress (e.g., pain) | Ethanol |
| Nausea | Phenytoin |
| Pregnancy | |
| Hypoglycemia | |
| Nicotine | |
| Morphine | |
| Other drugs | |

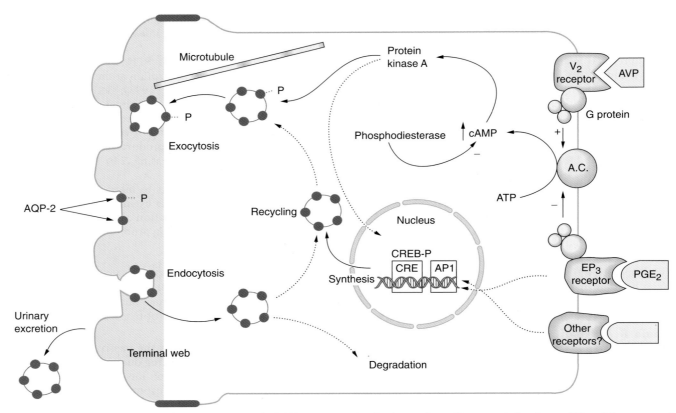

**Figure 35–4.** Action of antidiuretic hormone on aquaporin (AQP) transport. AC, adenylate cyclase; AP1, transcription factor; AVP, arginine vasopressin; cAMP, cyclic adenosine monophosphate; CRE, cAMP response element; CREB-P, CRE binding protein; EP3, prostaglandin receptor; PGE₂, prostaglandin E₂. (From Brown D, Nielsen S: The cell biology of vasopressin action. In Brenner BM [ed]: Brenner and Rector's The Kidney, 7th ed. Philadelphia, WB Saunders, 2004, p 574.)

*Hyperosmolality.* The major extracellular osmole is sodium, so for practical purposes ADH release is governed by changes in serum sodium concentrations. Serum osmolality is monitored by osmoreceptors in the hypothalamus, and changes as little as 1% are enough to affect ADH release (Robertson, 1987).

*Decreased Effective Circulating Volume.* Circulating volume is monitored by pressure (baro) receptors in the carotid sinus, which stimulate ADH release in response to reductions in ECV. These receptors are much less sensitive than the osmoreceptors, and ADH release is not affected until there is a noticeable drop in MAPs (usually around 10% to 15% blood volume loss) and after other vasoconstrictive hormones such as renin and norepinephrine have been activated.

*Other Stimuli.* A number of other factors can increase ADH secretion (see Table 35–2). Nausea and pain are probably the most clinically relevant, and as a result postsurgical hyponatremia related to excessive ADH release is a potentially life-threatening problem.

**When both decreased ECV and hyponatremia coexist, the pressure receptors usually override the osmoreceptors and prevent the inhibition of ADH secretion that is usually seen with hyponatremia** (Baylis, 1987). This is clinically relevant in conditions of decreased ECV and hyponatremia such as congestive heart failure in which ADH secretion persists despite significant hyponatremia.

## Renal Tubular Function

### Basic Functions

The renal tubule has two basic functions: *reabsorption* (transport of substances from lumen to blood) and *secretion* (transport of substances from blood to lumen). Transport can involve one of two pathways, either *transcellular* (across the luminal and basolateral membrane) or *paracellular* (between cells) (Fig. 35–5). **Each section of the tubule (Fig. 35–6) is specialized to facilitate absorption and secretion of certain substances through a variety of transport mechanisms.**

### Proximal Convoluted Tubule

**The proximal convoluted tubule (PCT) is responsible for reabsorption of 60% of the glomerular filtrate**. Under normal circumstances it reabsorbs 65% of the filtered sodium, potassium, and calcium; 80% of filtered phosphate, water, and bicarbonate; and 100% of filtered glucose and amino acids (Moe et al, 2004). The PCT is able to increase or decrease reabsorption in response to changes in GFR in order to maintain constant reabsorptive fractions through the process of *glomerulotubular balance*. The majority of this is accomplished by the early (S1 and S2) segments of the PCT. The later (S3) segment is responsible for secretion of numerous drugs and toxins that are too large, or protein bound, to be filtered. As well, the PCT is responsible for the generation of ammonia from glutamine, necessary for urinary acidification.

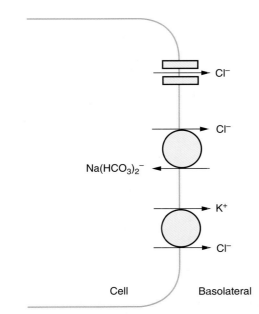

**Figure 35–5.** Example of transcellular transport between the tubule cell and the basolateral membrane. (From Moe OW, Baum M, Berry CA, Rector FC Jr: Renal transport of glucose, amino acids, sodium, chloride, and water. In Brenner BM [ed]: Brenner and Rector's The Kidney, 7th ed. Philadelphia, WB Saunders, 2004, p 425.)

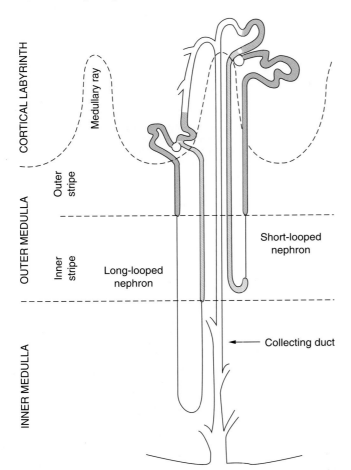

**Figure 35–6.** Organization of the renal tubule. (From Knepper MA, Gamba F: Urine concentration and dilution. In Brenner BM [ed]: Brenner and Rector's The Kidney, 7th ed. Philadelphia, WB Saunders, 2004, p 601.)

**Sodium.** The majority of sodium reabsorption occurs in the PCT and occurs through both secondary active and passive mechanisms (Fig. 35–7).

1. *Secondary active reabsorption*—luminal $Na^+$ moves passively into tubular cells; this movement, however, is driven by osmotic and electrochemical gradients between the luminal and intracellular environments established by the energy-requiring sodium-potassium adenosine triphosphatase ($Na^+,K^+$-ATPase) located in the basolateral cell membrane. There is an active exchange of three intracellular $Na^+$ for two extracellular $K^+$ ions, which keeps the intracellular sodium concentration low and the cell interior negative with respect to the lumen. This is called *secondary passive reabsorption*. $Na^+$ then enters the cell through coupled transport with other solutes (see later) or in exchange for $H^+$ through an $Na^+/H^+$ antiporter. The activity of this transporter is under neurohormonal regulation and can be influenced by angiotensin II, norepinephrine, and dopamine to either increase or decrease $Na^+$ reabsorption in response to changes in ECV.

2. *Passive reabsorption*—this occurs when $Na^+$ moves paracellularly into the intercellular space. It is mediated through $Cl^-$ transport across the paracellular pathway, which creates an electrochemical gradient favoring $Na^+$ movement out of the lumen into the intercellular space.

In summary, then, one can see that sodium is the most significant solute for the PCT for three reasons:

- It is the only solute that is actively reabsorbed (through the basolaterally located $Na^+,K^+$-ATPase pump).
- All other solutes are passively reabsorbed through $Na^+$ coupled transport.
- Early reabsorption of $Na^+$ (as well as other solutes) creates an osmotic gradient that facilitates passive reabsorption of water.

**Potassium.** The majority of potassium reabsorption occurs by the paracellular route. It is largely dependent on sodium and fluid movement, as potassium reabsorption parallels that of water and sodium.

**Bicarbonate. The majority of filtered bicarbonate (90%) is reclaimed in the PCT.** There is no upper limit to bicarbonate reabsorption; in states of volume depletion and increased proximal reabsorption of $Na^+$, bicarbonate reabsorption continues even in the presence of significant alkalemia (Moe et al, 2004). Bicarbonate is not transported across PCT cells; its reabsorption is dependent upon $H^+$ secretion by the $Na^+/H^+$ antiporter. Within the lumen, bicarbonate combines with $H^+$ to form $H_2O$ and $CO_2$, which can diffuse intracellularly and be converted back to $H^+$ and bicarbonate and subsequently secreted through the basolateral membrane by an $Na^+$ coupled transporter and returned to the circulation. Both these reactions are catalyzed by carbonic anhydrase (Fig. 35–8).

**Water. Water reabsorption in the PCT is a passive process, driven by the reabsorption of other solutes and the subsequent osmotic gradient that develops between the lumen and intercellular space.** The majority of water reabsorption occurs in the late PCT. As with $Na^+$ movement, water can also move either transcellularly or paracellularly. Transcellular movement accounts for 80% of water reabsorption and occurs through the specialized water channel aquaporin-1 (AQP-1)

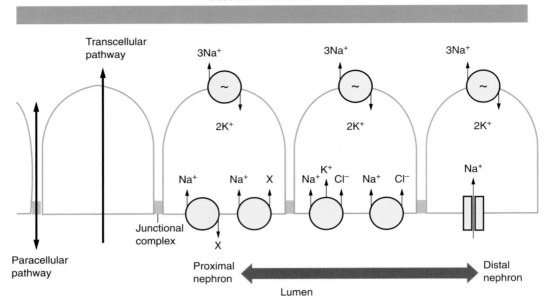

**Figure 35–7.** Mechanisms of sodium reabsorption in the proximal tubule. (From Moe OW, Baum M, Berry CA, Rector FC Jr: Renal transport of glucose, amino acids, sodium, chloride, and water. In Brenner BM [ed]: Brenner and Rector's The Kidney, 7th ed. Philadelphia, WB Saunders, 2004, p 414.)

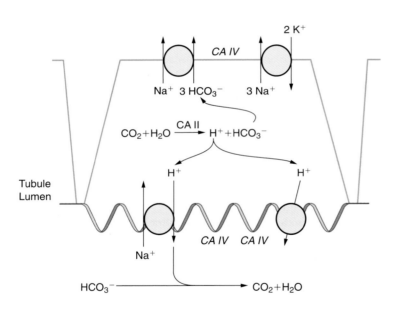

**Figure 35–8.** Reabsorption of bicarbonate in the renal tubule. CA, carbonic anhydrase. (From Hamm LL: Renal acidification mechanisms. In Brenner BM [ed]: Brenner and Rector's The Kidney, 7th ed. Philadelphia, WB Saunders, 2004, p 500.)

(Agre et al, 2002). Paracellular movement accounts for only 20% of water reabsorption and occurs across the tight junctions between cells.

**Glucose.** Glucose reabsorption is driven by passive Na+ reabsorption. In the early (S1 and S2) PCT, this occurs through a high-capacity, low-affinity Na+/glucose transporter called SGLT-2 (Moe et al, 2004). In the later (S3) segment of the PCT, reabsorption occurs through a low-capacity, high-affinity 2Na+/glucose transporter (also found in intestine) called SGLT-1. Intracellular glucose is then transported out of the cell through the basolateral membrane by the facilitative transporter GLUT-2. At normal plasma glucose levels, all filtered glucose is reabsorbed. **However, if plasma levels exceed 200 mg%, the filtered load exceeds the reabsorptive threshold and urinary glucose is detected** (Fig. 35–9).

**Proteins and Amino Acids.** Amino acid transport is very complex. As a rule, there are separate transporters for the basic, acidic, and neutral amino acids, and most are Na dependent. There are a few amino acids that have specialized transporters, and some are Na independent. Larger proteins are usually catabolized by brush border peptidases and reabsorbed as amino acids; some, however, enter the cell through carrier-mediated endocytosis.

**Phosphate.** About 85% to 90% of filtered phosphate is reabsorbed, primarily in the PCT. Phosphate reabsorption occurs through an Na+/phosphate cotransporter. The activity of this transporter is regulated by both plasma phosphate levels and PTH levels (Fig. 35–10).

**Calcium.** Most calcium reabsorption occurs in the late S2 segment and early S3 segment of the PCT. It is a passive process, driven by the lumen (+) potential difference (PD). Calcium movement occurs by the paracellular route, through the specific calcium channel claudin 2 (Amasheh et al, 2002), located in the tight junctions. It is also possible that there is a small amount of active calcium reabsorption in the late S3 segment, but this is poorly characterized (Fig. 35–11).

**Magnesium.** About 15% of filtered magnesium is reabsorbed in the PCT, but the mechanism is poorly understood (Konrad et al, 2004).

## Loop of Henle

The loop of Henle consists of four segments: the thin descending limb (DLH), the thin ascending limb (ALH), the medullary thick ascending limb (mTALH), and the cortical thick ascending limb (cTALH). It receives the 40% of ultrafiltrate not reabsorbed by the PCT. **Each segment of the loop of Henle has specific functions related to fluid, electrolyte, and acid-base balance, but the major function of the loop as a whole is to reabsorb 25% to 30% of the filtered Na⁺ and to reabsorb NaCl in excess of water in order to establish an extremely concentrated medullary interstitium, necessary for the excretion of a concentrated final urine.** The loop of Henle, like the PCT, is also controlled by glomerulotubular balance, which maintains a consistent ultrafiltrate delivered to the collecting ducts (Fig. 35–12).

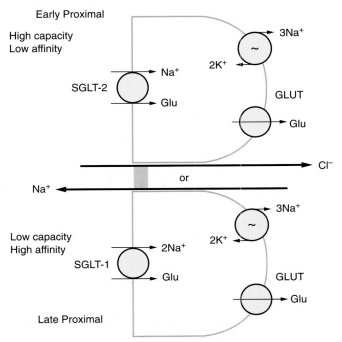

**Figure 35–9.** Absorption of glucose by the renal tubule. (From Moe OW, Baum M, Berry CA, Rector FC Jr: Renal transport of glucose, amino acids, sodium, chloride, and water. In Brenner BM [ed]: Brenner and Rector's The Kidney, 7th ed. Philadelphia, WB Saunders, 2004, p 417.)

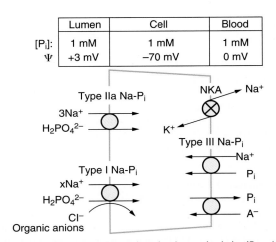

**Figure 35–10.** Absorption of phosphate by the renal tubule. (From Yu SLY: Renal transport of calcium, magnesium, and phosphate. In Brenner BM [ed]: Brenner and Rector's The Kidney, 7th ed. Philadelphia, WB Saunders, 2004, p 555.)

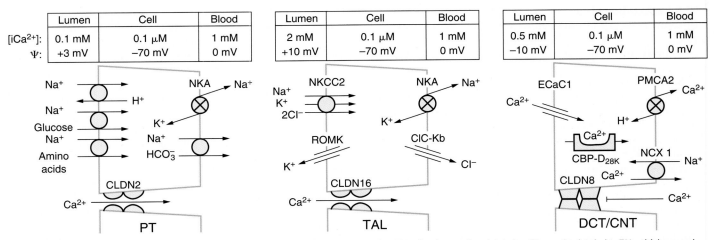

**Figure 35–11.** Absorption of calcium by the renal tubule. CNT, connecting tubule; DCT, distal convoluted tubule; PT, proximal tubule; TAL, thick ascending limb. (From Yu SLY: Renal transport of calcium, magnesium, and phosphate. In Brenner BM [ed]: Brenner and Rector's The Kidney, 7th ed. Philadelphia, WB Saunders, 2004, p 538.)

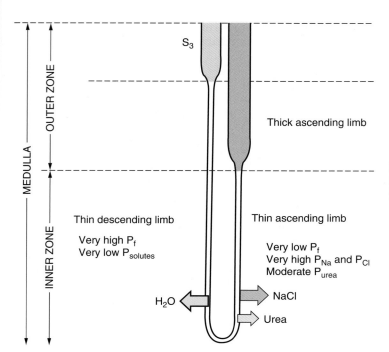

**Figure 35–12.** Anatomy of the loop of Henle. (From Moe OW, Baum M, Berry CA, Rector FC Jr: Renal transport of glucose, amino acids, sodium, chloride, and water. In Brenner BM [ed]: Brenner and Rector's The Kidney, 7th ed. Philadelphia, WB Saunders, 2004, p 431.)

**Thin Descending Limb.** The DLH consists of the segment of the nephron between the end of the PCT (S3 segment) and the bottom of the loop. Cortical nephrons, in general, have a short DLH and juxtaglomerular nephrons have a longer DLH. There is little active transport of any kind within the DLH, but it has high water permeability because of abundant expression of AQP-1 (Agre et al, 2002).

**Thin Ascending Limb.** The ALH begins at the loop and continues up to the thick ascending limb. The ALH is of variable length; cortical nephrons may have very little ALH. As with the DLH, there is no active transport of solutes. However, unlike the DLH, the ALH is water impermeable. There is high permeability for NaCl as well as urea, and reabsorption of these solutes occurs passively along an osmotic gradient as their luminal concentrations are quite high as a result of water removal during transit through the DLH.

**Thick Ascending Limb.** The TALH is far more active in terms of solute reabsorption than either thin limb. Water reabsorption, however, is negligible as this segment of the loop is entirely impermeable to water because of the lack of aquaporins.

*Sodium, Potassium, and Chloride.* The TALH reabsorbs 25% to 30% of the sodium filtered across the glomerulus. This is primarily through the secondary active process driven by basolateral Na$^+$,K$^+$-ATPase pumps that keep the intracellular sodium concentration low. Na$^+$ is transported transcellularly by an Na$^+$/K$^+$/2Cl$^-$ (NKCC2) transporter located in the apical membrane. Once inside the cell, Cl$^-$ is pumped out across the basolateral membrane by a Cl$^-$/K$^+$ cotransporter, which helps keep the intracellular chloride concentration low. K$^+$, however, preferentially exits the cell back through the apical membrane K channel ROMK and reenters the tubular lumen, where it can interact once again with the NKCC2 transporter. **This K$^+$ recycling is important; without it, sodium reabsorption would be limited by the luminal potassium concentration,** which is much lower than either sodium or chloride concentrations. By recycling K$^+$, the tubule is able to reabsorb sodium independent of potassium. A secondary benefit of this process is to help establish a lumen (+) PD, which helps facilitate paracellular transport of a variety of cations, including sodium (Fig. 35–13).

The NKCC2 transporter is the site of action of loop diuretics. These drugs bind to the Cl$^-$ receptor and interfere with normal transporter action, resulting in decreased NaCl reabsorption and subsequent diuresis.

**Sodium reabsorption along the TAHL, in the absence of water reabsorption, is critical to the formation of the interstitial concentration gradient.** This gradient is essential to subsequent urinary concentrating ability in the collecting duct. It also creates a progressively more hypotonic ultrafiltrate, which is important for water diuresis to occur (see later).

*Calcium and Magnesium.* About 15% of the filtered calcium is reabsorbed in the TALH. Reabsorption is passively driven by the lumen (+) PD by the paracellular route, facilitated by the calcium channel paracellin 1 (also known as claudin 16). Magnesium reabsorption (60% to 70%) also occurs in the TALH in a similar manner (Konrad et al, 2004). Inhibition of the NKCC2 transporter with loop diuretics induces renal calcium and magnesium wasting because of dissipation of the lumen (+) PD.

*Bicarbonate.* The TALH also reabsorbs 10% to 20% of the filtered bicarbonate, mainly through H$^+$ secretion through the Na$^+$/H$^+$ exchanger. Water reabsorption occurring in the DLH increases bicarbonate reabsorption by increasing luminal bicarbonate concentrations.

*Countercurrent Mechanism.* A critical function of the kidney is the preservation of body water; this is accomplished through the osmotic reabsorption of solute free water in the collecting tubule (see later) and the excretion of urine that is hyperosmolar with respect to plasma. Human kidneys can produce a urine concentration up to 1200 mOsm/kg. **In order**

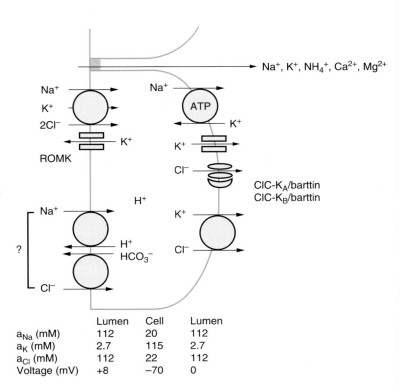

**Figure 35–13.** Paracellular transport of cations in the thick ascending limb. ROMK, renal outer medullary potassium channel. (From Moe OW, Baum M, Berry CA, Rector FC Jr: Renal transport of glucose, amino acids, sodium, chloride, and water. In Brenner BM [ed]: Brenner and Rector's The Kidney, 7th ed. Philadelphia, WB Saunders, 2004, p 433.)

|  | Lumen | Cell | Lumen |
|---|---|---|---|
| $a_{Na}$ (mM) | 112 | 20 | 112 |
| $a_K$ (mM) | 2.7 | 115 | 2.7 |
| $a_{Cl}$ (mM) | 112 | 22 | 112 |
| Voltage (mV) | +8 | −70 | 0 |

to achieve this degree of urinary concentration, the kidney must be able to generate an interstitial osmotic gradient of similar degree. Through the process of *countercurrent multiplication*, the loop of Henle is able to produce an interstitial osmotic gradient ranging from 285 mOsm/kg (isosmotic with plasma) in the outer medulla to 1200 mosmol/kg in the inner medulla. The basic steps of countercurrent multiplication are as follows:

1. Medullary interstitium is made hyperosmolar by the reabsorption of NaCl (in the absence of water reabsorption) in the ascending limbs of the loop of Henle.
2. Because of the hairpin (*countercurrent*) configuration of the loop, the concentration of the luminal fluid can be progressively increased (*multiplied*) to as much as 1200 mosmol/kg (Fig. 35–14). This allows the interstitial osmolarity to increase to similar levels.
3. In the presence of ADH, urea diffuses from the medullary collecting tubule into the interstitium, increasing the interstitial osmolarity even further (Yang and Bankir, 2005). This has a secondary benefit of increasing water reabsorption in the DLH, thus increasing luminal sodium and chloride concentrations in the ascending limbs and making step 1 even more efficient (Fig. 35–15).
4. Because of the high interstitial osmolality, water is passively reabsorbed in the medullary collecting tubule (in the presence of ADH). This could potentially lead to dilution of the interstitium. To minimize this effect, the volume of ultrafiltrate is minimized through water reabsorption in the cortical collecting tubule. Also, the vasa recta are arranged in a similar hairpin loop that allows water removal but minimizes removal of interstitial solutes (Pallone et al, 2003).

OSMOLALITY (mOsm/kg H₂O)

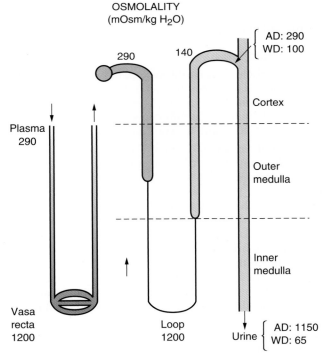

**Figure 35–14.** Countercurrent mechanism in the renal tubule. AD, antidiuresis; WD, water diuresis. (From Knepper MA, Gamba F: Urine Concentration and Dilution. In Brenner BM [ed]: Brenner and Rector's The Kidney, 7th ed. Philadelphia, WB Saunders, 2004, p 604.)

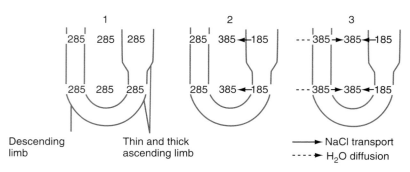

**Figure 35–15.** Role of active NaCl transport in initiating countercurrent multiplication. In step 1, at time zero, the fluid in the descending and ascending limbs and the interstitium is isosmotic to plasma. In step 2, NaCl is transported out of the ascending limb into the interstitium to a gradient of 200 mosmol/kg. In step 3, the fluid in the descending limb equilibrates osmotically with the hyperosmotic interstitium, primarily by water movement out of the tubule. Dilution of the interstitium by this water movement is prevented by continued NaCl transport out of the ascending limb. The result is the creation of an osmotic gradient between the ascending limb and the relatively hyperosmotic descending limb and interstitium.

The osmotic gradient can be disturbed in certain clinical conditions. Increased medullary blood flow (as seen with osmotic diuresis) increases removal of interstitial solutes through the vasa recta and leads to a lower interstitial osmolality. As well, prolonged use of loop diuretics prevents the transport of NaCl in the ascending limb of the loop of Henle, necessary for the ongoing maintenance of the interstitial hyperosmolality; hence, a prolonged water diuresis may be seen after discontinuation of the drug, until the gradient can be reestablished.

***Tamm-Horsfall Mucoprotein.*** The TALH is also the site of secretion of Tamm-Horsfall mucoprotein, or uromodulin. It is clinically important as it forms the matrix of all urinary casts. It has been shown to be important in the prevention of urinary tract infections. It has also been implicated in the pathogenesis of cast nephropathy, medullary cystic renal disease, and familial juvenile hyperuricemic nephropathy.

## Distal Tubule

The distal tubule is primarily involved in sodium and calcium reabsorption. There may be some capacity for $H^+$ and $K^+$ secretion, but the importance of this is unknown. The distal tubule can be subdivided into two sections, the distal convoluted tubule (DCT) and the connecting tubule.

**Sodium and Chloride.** The DCT reabsorbs another 5% to 10% of the sodium filtered through the glomerulus. As in the TALH, it is a secondary active process driven by basolateral $Na^+,K^+$-ATPase pumps that occurs in the absence of water reabsorption. $Na^+$ is reabsorbed electroneutrally with $Cl^-$ through an $Na^+/Cl^-$ (NCC) cotransporter, which can be inhibited with the thiazide diuretics. In addition, there may be some $Na^+$ reabsorption through the $Na^+/H^+$ exchange transporter in the luminal membrane. It should be noted that $Na^+$ reabsorption in the DCT is regulated by luminal sodium concentration and not by hormonal influences. **Hence, anything that increases delivery of $Na^+$ to the DCT leads to increased $Na^+$ reabsorption in the section of the tubule.** One clinical example would be the use of loop diuretics. By inhibiting the NKCC2 transporter in the TALH, $Na^+$ delivery increases to the DCT. In response, there is usually a marked increase in $Na^+$ reabsorption that may significantly diminish the diuretic response achieved with the loop diuretic. Such a response may be minimized by concomitant use of a thiazide diuretic.

The connecting segment can also reabsorb sodium but does so under the influence of aldosterone in a fashion similar to that of the principal cells of the cortical collecting tubule.

**Calcium. The DCT accounts for 10% to 15% of calcium reabsorption.** Unlike that in either the PCT or loop of Henle, calcium reabsorption in the DCT is independent of $Na^+$ reabsorption. Calcium enters the cell through the luminal calcium channel $ECaC_1$ and binds to the intracellular binding protein calbindin $D_{28}$ (Loffing and Kaissling, 2003). In this way, free intracellular calcium concentration is kept low, thus facilitating inward movement of calcium. Extrusion from the cell occurs through the basolateral membrane by either a $Ca^{2+}/H^+$ (PMCA) or $Na^+/Ca^+$ (NCX) exchanger (Loffing and Kaissling, 2003). In contrast to the situation in the PCT or loop of Henle, movement of calcium by the paracellular route is inhibited by the presence of the protein claudin 8, which markedly decreases calcium permeability through tight junctions.

Calcium reabsorption is regulated in this region by the actions of PTH and, to a lesser degree, calcitriol (vitamin D). PTH increases calcium reabsorption, possibly through alterations in intracellular voltage as a result of increased $Cl^-$ flux through the basolateral membrane. Calcitriol is thought to increase the number of $ECaC_1$ channels and increase calbindin production, both of which would increase calcium reabsorption.

**Magnesium.** Five percent to 10% of filtered magnesium is actively reabsorbed in the DT by the transcellular route. This probably occurs through the luminal magnesium channel TRPM6 (Voets et al, 2004) and is driven by a basolateral Na-Mg pump that generates an Mg gradient favoring inward flow of Mg.

## Collecting Tubule

The collecting tubule consists of two parts, the cortical collecting tubule (CCT) and the medullary collecting tubule (MCT). Although the more proximal portions of the nephron are designed for bulk reabsorption of ultrafiltrate, the collecting tubules are responsible for the final qualitative changes in ultrafiltrate composition in response to dietary intake.

## Cortical Collecting Tubule

The CCT consists of two distinct cell types, each with distinct functions. Principal cells (65%) are generally involved in NaCl reabsorption, and intercalated cells (35%) are mostly involved with acid secretion. Both are also involved in K regulation as well.

### Principal Cells

***Sodium, Potassium, and Chloride.*** Sodium reabsorption occurs passively through the luminal Na channel ENaC rather than through a cotransporter system (Loffing and Kaissling,

2003). Basolateral $Na^+,K^+$-ATPase pumps keep intracellular sodium concentration low, facilitating inward movement of sodium. Movement of sodium intracellularly, without an accompanying anion, creates a lumen (−) PD that results in either passive paracellular movement of Cl out of the lumen or secretion of intracellular K into the lumen in order to restore electroneutrality. Sodium reabsorption is regulated in the CCT primarily by aldosterone, which increases the number of open ENaCs. Blockade of the Na channel by the diuretic amiloride leads to reduced Na reabsorption as well as K secretion, as the electrochemical gradient is eliminated and thus the driving force for K secretion is abolished (Fig. 35–16). Prostaglandin $E_2$ also seems to inhibit Na reabsorption, and reduction of $PGE_2$ by nonsteroidal anti-inflammatory drugs leads to sodium retention.

K secretion in the CCT depends not only on aldosterone-sensitive inward Na movement but also on luminal flow rates. When flow decreases in the tubular lumen, the local intraluminal potassium concentration increases and minimizes the favorable potassium gradient, thus minimizing secretion. This can be partially offset by the actions of ADH, which increase potassium secretion possibly by the insertion of new K channels in the luminal membrane or by increased Na reabsorption (Wang, 1995). **Thus, any condition that leads to decreased luminal flow rates, or increased aldosterone production, can lead to reduced potassium excretion.**

*Water.* The water permeability of the CCT is low in the basal state. However, it can be greatly increased in the presence of ADH. This is due to the insertion of preformed AQP-2 water channels into the luminal membrane (Agre et al, 2002), which allows water to be passively reabsorbed and equilibrate with the cortical interstitium through basolateral AQP-3 and AQP-4 channels. This is important for the development of a highly concentrated final urine, as it decreases the volume of ultrafiltrate delivered to the MCT, where most of the final concentration of urine occurs (Knepper et al, 1994) (Fig. 35–17).

**Intercalated Cells.** There are two different types of intercalated cells, with different functions: type A intercalated cells, involved mostly with $H^+$ secretion; and type B intercalated cells, involved mostly with bicarbonate secretion.

*Hydrogen and Bicarbonate.* **In both cell types, intracellular $H_2O$, under the influence of carbonic anhydrase, is combined with $CO_2$ to produce $H^+$ and $HCO_3^-$.** As well, in both cell types, the $H^+$ and $HCO_3^-$ are secreted out of the cell through similar transporters. What is different is the location of the transporters.

Type A intercalated cells have both $H^+$-ATPase and $H^+,K^+$-ATPase pumps located on the luminal membrane, which facilitate $H^+$ secretion into the tubular lumen. Bicarbonate is transported back to the systemic circulation through an $HCO_3^-/Cl^-$ transporter on the basolateral side of the cell. The net effect is acidification of the urine and subsequent increase in extracellular pH. As expected, this process is stimulated under conditions of acidemia. Aldosterone seems to have a permissive effect on this, probably through actions on the $H^+$-ATPase pump, as increased urine $H^+$ loss and subsequent systemic alkalosis are seen in conditions of hyperaldosteronism.

Type B intercalated cells have similar transporters, but they have reversed polarity. That is, the $H^+$-ATPase pumps are located on the basolateral side of the cell, and the $HCO_3^-/Cl^-$ transporters are localized to the luminal membrane. The result of this is net loss of bicarbonate and a decrease in systemic pH. This is necessary in states of alkalemia and thus functions to lower systemic bicarbonate.

*Potassium.* Although there is normally net secretion of potassium in the CCT, there is the potential for potassium reabsorption through the $H^+,K^+$-ATPase. This becomes more relevant in states of potassium depletion, when the activity of these pumps is increased. **Although this may help correct systemic hypokalemia, it is often at the expense of increased $H^+$ secretion and resultant systemic alkalosis.**

## Medullary Collecting Tubule

The MCT is divided into the outer MCT (oMCT) and inner MCT (iMCT). Both segments contain cells similar to the principal cells and intercalated cells found in the CCT; hence, the handling of sodium, potassium, hydrogen ion, and bicarbonate is very similar. The main functional difference lies with the MCT's water and urea permeabilities and thus its ability to concentrate the urine to levels far above that of plasma.

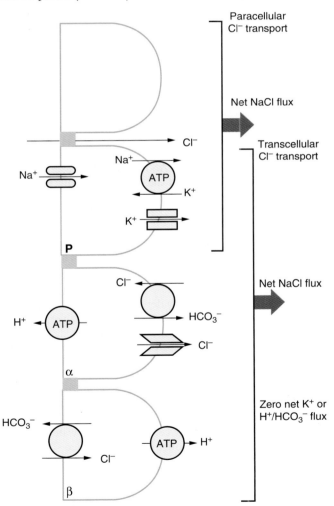

**Figure 35–16.** Effect of blockade of the Na channel by the diuretic amiloride. (From Moe OW, Baum M, Berry CA, Rector FC Jr: Renal transport of glucose, amino acids, sodium, chloride, and water. In Brenner BM [ed]: Brenner and Rector's The Kidney, 7th ed. Philadelphia, WB Saunders, 2004, p 439.)

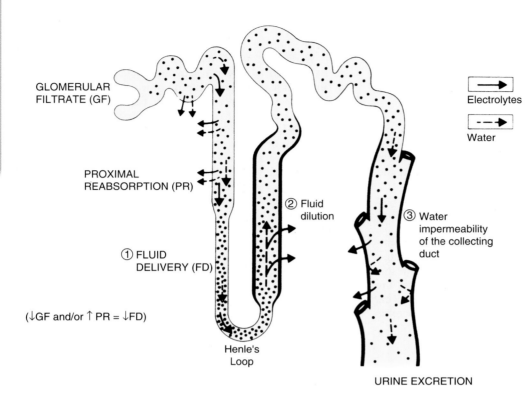

**Figure 35–17.** The components of the normal urine dilution mechanisms. (Redrawn from Berl T, Schrier RW: Water metabolism and the hypoosmolar syndrome. In Brenner BM, Stein JH [eds]: Sodium and Water Homeostasis. New York, Churchill Livingstone, 1978, pp 1-23.)

**Water and Urea.** The MCT is relatively impermeable to water in the basal state, but under the influence of ADH, permeability increases in both the iMCT and oMCT through the insertion of AQP-2 water channels. This allows water to move out of the tubule into the hyperosmolar interstitium and urine concentration to occur. Equally important to this process is urea. The oMCT is relatively impermeable to urea, both in the basal state and under ADH stimulation. In contrast, the iMCT has a high basal permeability for urea, largely because of specific urea transporters (UT-A1 and UT-A3) located on the basolateral cell membrane as well as, to a lesser extent, the luminal membrane. Short-term regulation is under the influence of ADH, which can increase urea permeability as much as fourfold through an increased number of UTs. Longer term regulation can be affected by protein intake. **This allows a high concentration of urea to develop in the interstitium, thus sustaining the osmotic gradient that is responsible for water reabsorption and ultimately urinary concentration** (Yang and Bankir, 2005).

## KEY POINTS: RENAL TUBULAR FUNCTION

- The nephron has different functional segments that control homeostasis.

- Most resorption of bicarbonate and ions occurs in the proximal tubule.

- The architecture of the loop of Henle allows a highly hypertonic interstitium to develop, which is key to maximal urinary concentration.

**Sodium.** As mentioned earlier, Na reabsorption in the MCT is similar to that occurring within principal cells in the CCT. However, it has been shown the Na reabsorption is diminished in the MCT under conditions of volume expansion. This is due in part to the actions of ANP, which decreases Na reabsorption in the iMCT but not the oMCT. This effect seems to be due to a reduction in the number of open Na channels in the luminal membrane.

## RENAL PATHOPHYSIOLOGY
## Sodium and Water Imbalances

Imbalances of sodium and water are often poorly managed and understood by clinicians despite the mechanisms and appropriate therapy being quite well documented. **The most consistent clinical misconception is that sodium concentration reflects total body sodium content.** Because sodium is primarily extracellular, the serum concentration reflects water balance. Therefore, hyponatremia can occur in the presence of total body sodium excess, and hypernatremia can occur with sodium deficits. For an imbalance to occur, there has to be an imbalance between sodium and water that the normal mechanisms of response have not handled. **Therefore, the way to approach serum sodium abnormalities is to determine the water status of the patient and then to determine why the normal compensatory mechanisms have failed** (Fig. 35–18).

### Hyponatremia

By definition, hyponatremia exists if there is a water excess relative to extracellular sodium that has not been handled by the

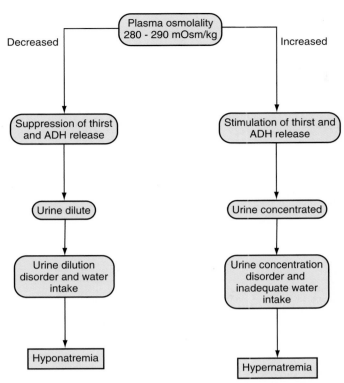

**Figure 35–18.** Flowchart illustrating the development of disorders of water metabolism. ADH, antidiuretic hormone.

normal compensatory mechanisms of thirst suppression and decreased ADH release, leading to a serum sodium less than 135 mEq/L. Hyponatremia is seldom symptomatic unless severe (<120 mEq/L), but when severe or of sudden onset it can produce seizures, altered mental state, coma, and death. Most commonly hyponatremia occurs because the kidney is unable to excrete urine that is free from solutes (Mallie et al, 1997). **To calculate the amount of water excreted or retained by the kidney, it is useful to consider that urine has two components: one that contains all of the solute in an isotonic solution (termed $C_{osm}$, or osmolar clearance) and another that contains only solute-free water (termed $C_{H_2O}$ or free water clearance).** The total urine volume (V) (e.g., liters per day) is the sum of $C_{osm}$ and $C_{H_2O}$:

$$V = C_{osm} + C_{H_2O}.$$

When the urine is hypo-osmotic to plasma, $C_{H_2O}$ is a positive value.

**Hyponatremia occurs when one or more of these requirements are not fulfilled, such as when GFR is reduced, when diuretics impair NaCl reabsorption, or when vasopressin is in excess (e.g., syndrome of inappropriate ADH secretion).** If water intake exceeds the kidney's capacity to form solute-free water (>10 to 20 L/day), hyponatremia also occurs. This abnormality in solute-free water clearance in hyponatremic patients is reflected by the failure to excrete maximally dilute urine ($U_{osm} = 100$ mOsm/kg).

The diagnosis of hyponatremia is made by measurement of serum electrolytes. There are several conditions in which a low

serum sodium is misleading, however. The reported laboratory value is usually in terms of sodium per volume of plasma rather than water. If large molecules such as lipids or protein are present in large quantities, they decrease the amount of water in a given volume of plasma, but these molecules contribute little to plasma osmolality. **What is truly important is the amount of osmotically active solute per volume of water.** Pseudohyponatremia is most commonly seen with abnormal elevations of serum lipids or glucose. For every 1 g/dL increase in triglycerides, measured sodium is decreased by 2 mEq/L, and for every 100 mg/dL of glucose, measured sodium is decreased by 1.6 mEq/L.

**The approach, therefore, to a patient with true hyponatremia begins with an assessment of volume status** (Fig. 35–19). Clinical features such as skin turgor, orthostatic hypotension, jugular venous distention, ascites, and respiratory crackles can all be helpful in this decision. Patients who are clinically hypovolemic by definition have a sodium deficit greater than their water deficit. The appropriate renal response would be to excrete urine that is hypo-osmotic with a high $C_{H_2O}$. Therefore, if the urine is not hypo-osmotic, the etiology is related to the kidney. Measuring the urinary sodium ($U_{Na}$) is a useful surrogate for urinary osmolality. A hypovolemic patient with an appropriately low $U_{Na}$ (<20) has extrarenal sodium losses such as from trauma, vomiting, diarrhea, burns, or third spacing. In a hypovolemic patient with an inappropriately high $U_{Na}$ of greater than 20, a renal source should be suspected, such as diuretic excess, osmotic diuresis, renal tubular acidosis, or mineralocorticoid deficiency. If the hyponatremic patient is hypervolemic, total body sodium can be low, normal, or high. A high $U_{Na}$ of greater than 20 would point to renal failure. A low $U_{Na}$ of less than 20 would suggest heart failure, cirrhosis, or nephrotic syndrome.

A patient who is euvolemic would have low or normal total body sodium. The differential diagnosis would include glucocorticoid deficiency, hypothyroidism, stress, and the syndrome of inappropriate antidiuretic hormone secretion (SIADH). **SIADH is a syndrome triggered by release of ADH through a mechanism other than low blood volume or high plasma osmolality, associated with increased aquaporin expression in the kidney** (Kwon et al, 2001). The most common causes of SIADH are brain infections and surgery, neoplasm, and drug side effects (Table 35–3). Pharmacologic antagonists that can be used to treat patients with SIADH include lithium and demeclocycline. Lithium inhibits vasopressin action both proximal and distal to cAMP formation in the collecting duct (Miller, 1994). Demeclocycline, in doses ranging from 600 to 1200 mg/day, induces vasopressin-resistant diabetes insipidus that corrects the serum sodium within 1 to 2 weeks (Goh, 2004).

**Therapy of hyponatremia is directed at both the cause of the condition and the water imbalance itself** (Fig. 35–20). Patients with acute severe hyponatremia symptomatic with confusion, convulsions, or coma should undergo fluid restriction plus administration of hypertonic (3%) saline (about 1 mL/kg/hr). Fluid overload is unlikely as long as fluid is restricted but may be further reduced by simultaneous administration of a loop diuretic such as furosemide (which causes excretion of hypotonic fluid equivalent to half-normal saline). The serum sodium concentration should be raised no more

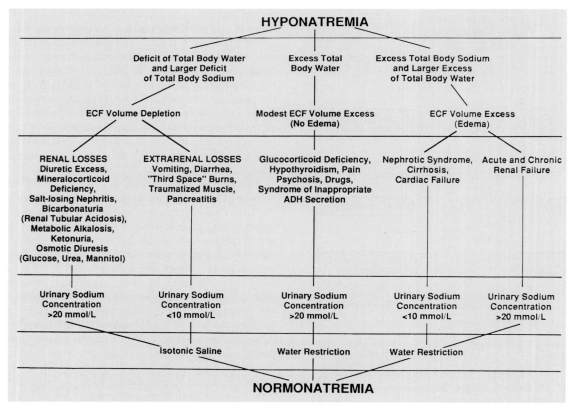

**Figure 35–19.** Clinical approach to patient with hyponatremia. ADH, antidiuretic hormone; ECF, extracellular fluid. (From Berl T, Anderson RJ, McDonald KM, Schrier RW: Clinical disorders of water metabolism. Kidney Int 1976;10:117-132.)

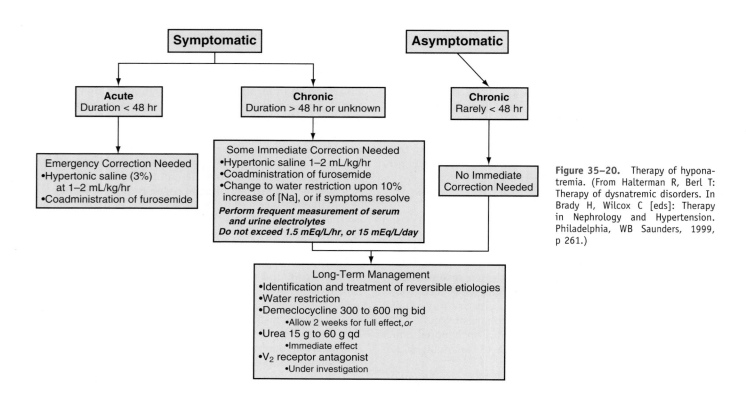

**Figure 35–20.** Therapy of hyponatremia. (From Halterman R, Berl T: Therapy of dysnatremic disorders. In Brady H, Wilcox C [eds]: Therapy in Nephrology and Hypertension. Philadelphia, WB Saunders, 1999, p 261.)

| Table 35-3. Disorders Associated with the Syndrome of Inappropriate Antidiuretic Hormone Secretion | | |
|---|---|---|
| Carcinomas | Pulmonary Disorders | Central Nervous System Disorders |
| Bronchogenic | Pneumonia (viral, bacterial) | Encephalitis (bacterial, viral) |
| Duodenum | | Meningitis (viral, bacterial, |
| Pancreas | Pulmonary abscess | tubercular, fungal) |
| Thymoma | | Head trauma |
| Ureter | Tuberculosis | Guillain-Barré syndrome |
| Lymphomas | Aspergillosis | Subarachnoid hemorrhage |
| Ewing's sarcoma | Positive pressure breathing | Subdural hematoma |
| | | Cerebellar or cerebral atrophy |
| Mesothelioma | Asthma | Cavernous sinus thrombosis |
| Bladder | Pneumothorax | Hydrocephalus |
| Prostatic | Cystic fibrosis | Shy-Drager syndrome |
| | | Rocky Mountain spotted fever |
| | | Delirium tremens |
| | | Olfactory neuroblastoma |
| | | Hypothalamic sarcoidosis |
| | | Multiple sclerosis |

Adapted from Levi M, Berl T: Water metabolism. In Gonick HC (ed): Current Nephrology (1983-1984), vol 9, Chicago, Year Book Medical, 1986.

than 25 mEq/L in the first 48 hours, at a rate of no more than 2 mEq/L/hr, and the target goal should be 120 to 125 mEq/L. Total sodium deficit to reach this point can be calculated as

$$(\text{Volume of distribution}) \times \text{body weight (kg)} \times (125 - \text{plasma [Na]})$$

where volume of distribution is 0.5 for men and 0.6 for women.

If the hyponatremia is severe but chronic, the rate of correction should not exceed 8 to 12 mmol/L/day, or a cerebral demyelination syndrome may occur (Martin, 2004). Therefore, the rate of correction should be slower (0.5 to 1 mEq/L/hr). During acute intervention for severe hyponatremia, frequent electrolyte measurements and reassessment of the patient are required. Aggressive therapy should be discontinued when the serum sodium concentration is raised 10% or symptoms subside. At that point, water restriction and reversal of underlying causes should suffice. This is also the best approach for therapy of asymptomatic hyponatremia. Obviously, patients with associated hypovolemia should have this corrected with the appropriate volume of normal saline.

## Hypernatremia

The underlying problem of hypernatremia is a disorder of urine concentration with inadequate water intake (Adrogue and Madias, 2000). **Again, in hypernatremia it is the water balance that matters and total body sodium can be high, normal, or even low.** Symptoms are nonspecific and overlap those seen in hyponatremia, with the early occurrence of restlessness, nausea, and vomiting that can progress to tremor, lethargy, and coma. Indeed, mortality is higher in hypernatremia than in most other electrolyte disorders. **Most patients with an intact thirst mechanism and free access to water can prevent hypernatremia,** and the condition is more common at the extremes of age.

The approach to a patient with hypernatremia again begins with an assessment of fluid status (Fig. 35-21). Hypovolemia is common and may be due to renal causes that fail to concentrate the urine adequately (loop diuretics, postobstructive diuresis) or extrarenal water loss such as seen with burns, diarrhea, or fistulas. Patients with hypervolemia have a metabolic or iatrogenic reason for high sodium in excess of the elevated total body water. Causes include Cushing's syndrome, primary hyperaldosteronism, and excessive exogenous sodium (orally or intravenously). Patients who are euvolemic may have renal or extrarenal losses that may be caused by diabetes insipidus, an impairment in renal concentrating ability related to lack of central production (neurogenic), or impaired renal response (nephrogenic).

In neurogenic diabetes insipidus, vasopressin deficiency is most commonly caused by destruction of the neurohypophysis. To produce symptomatic polyuria, 80% to 90% of the neurosecretory neurons must be destroyed at or above the level of the infundibulum. As a consequence of the reduced vasopressin level, the kidney excretes a high volume of dilute urine. This leads to a reduction in total body water, a rise in total body osmolality, and thus hypernatremia. The related cellular dehydration stimulates thirst. Compensatory water intake decreases plasma osmolality (and $Na^+$ concentration) toward normal, but they stabilize at the threshold level for thirst, which is slightly above normal. **As in all forms of diabetes insipidus, the ability of the kidney to concentrate the urine maximally in response to vasopressin is also impaired in neurogenic diabetes insipidus. This abnormality occurs because the medullary osmotic gradient is reduced by the high urine flow.** In nephrogenic diabetes insipidus, secretion of vasopressin by the neurohypophysis is normal, but renal responsiveness to the hormone is attenuated or absent and urinary concentrating ability is impaired (Sasaki, 2004). Several different mutations of the aquaporin gene have been identified that contribute to the pathogenesis of this disorder (Leung et al, 2005).

**Therapy of hypernatremia is directed at fluid deficit, water replacement, and reversal of underlying causes.** Hypovolemia should be initially corrected with half-normal saline. If the patient is awake and not symptomatic, oral hydration with water is sufficient. Otherwise, intravenous therapy should be started with the goal of slowly lowering plasma osmolality at no more than 2 mOsm/L/hr to avoid cerebral edema. The water deficit can be calculated as

$$(\text{Volume of distribution}) \times \text{body weight (kg)} \times ((\text{plasma [Na]}/140) - 1)$$

where again the volume of distribution is 0.5 for men and 0.6 for women.

For patients with central diabetes insipidus, desmopressin, a synthetic exogenous vasopressin, can be given intranasally. For nephrogenic diabetes insipidus, the underlying cause (lithium, hypercalcemia) should be treated. If polyuria persists while the kidney recovers, therapy includes modest sodium restriction, thiazide diuretics, and nonsteroidal anti-inflammatory drugs (Pattaragarn and Alon, 2003).

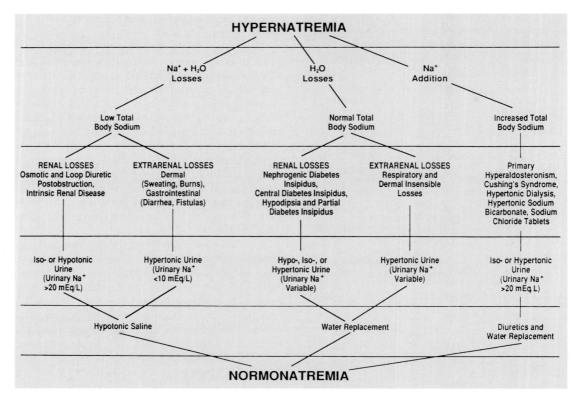

**Figure 35–21.** Clinical approach to patient with hypernatremia. (From Berl T, Anderson RJ, McDonald KM, Schrier RW: Clinical disorders of water metabolism. Kidney Int 1976;10:117-132.)

## KEY POINTS: SODIUM AND WATER IMBALANCES

- Serum sodium represents sodium concentration, *not* total body sodium.

- The best tools to determine the cause of a sodium disorder are the history, volume status, and urinary sodium.

- Severe sodium deficit or excess must be corrected slowly.

## Potassium Imbalances

Potassium is primarily an intracellular ion, and serum levels do not represent total body content in disease states. Because neuromuscular excitability is closely linked to serum potassium levels, extremes of low or high values can lead to cardiac arrhythmias and death. The body responds to changes in potassium intake and levels by controlling urinary excretion and by changing the balance between intracellular and extracellular stores. **Urinary excretion can be increased in the kidney through increased aldosterone, a high sodium load in the distal tubule, and acidosis. Potassium is driven into the cells by insulin, bicarbonate, and β-agonists.**

### Hypokalemia

The most common causes of hypokalemia are increased losses through the gastrointestinal (GI) tract or urine and increased intracellular shift of potassium in response to alkalosis (mnemonic: aLKalosis = low $K^+$). The most common iatrogenic causes are diuretics, laxatives, amphotericin, theophylline, and postobstructive diuresis. Metabolic causes include conditions associated with elevated aldosterone such as adrenal adenoma, Cushing's syndrome, and adrenal carcinoma. The patient may have no symptoms or present with signs and symptoms of the underlying condition (e.g., hypertension). Severe hypokalemia may produce tachycardia, heart block, and ST depression. Therapy is directed at correction of the underlying cause and oral or parenteral potassium supplementation. In general, intravenous potassium replacement should not exceed 40 mEq per hour.

### Hyperkalemia

Hyperkalemia usually reflects decreased renal excretion of potassium or a shift out of cells into the extracellular space (usually by acidosis). A compromised excretory capacity can be further exacerbated by GI bleeding or hemolysis. The most common causes (Table 35–4) are renal failure, drugs (potassium-sparing diuretics, lithium, digoxin, angiotensin-converting enzyme inhibitors), chronic acidosis (e.g., renal tubular acidosis type 4), and hypoaldosteronism. Hemolysis of the drawn blood sample can falsely elevate serum potassium, and therefore an unexpectedly high value in a patient

## Table 35-4. Etiology of Hyperkalemia

*Factitious*

Laboratory error
Pseudohyperkalemia: in vitro hemolysis, thrombocytosis, leukocytosis

*Increased Input*

Exogenous: diet, salt substitutes
Endogenous: hemolysis, Gl bleeding, catabolic states, crush injury, tumor lysis

*Renal Failure*

Acute: especially tubulointerstitial disease
Chronic: GFR <15-20 mL/min

*Impaired Renin-Aldosterone Axis*

Addison's disease
Congenital adrenal enzyme deficiencies (e.g., corticosterone methyl oxidase deficiency)
Drug induced: heparin, prostaglandin inhibitors, ACE inhibitors, pentamidine, $\beta$ blockers
Hyporeninemic hypoaldosteronism
Primary hypoaldosteronism (normal renin)

*Primary Renal Tubular Potassium Secretory Defect*

Sickle-cell disease
Systemic lupus erythematosus
Postrenal transplantation
Obstructive uropathy
Tubulointerstitial renal disease
Pseudohypoaldosteronism
Hyperkalemic distal renal tubular acidosis

*Inhibitors of Tubular Secretion*

Diuretics: amiloride, spironolactone, triamterene
Cyclosporine
Lithium
Digitalis

*Abnormal Potassium Distribution*

Metabolic acidosis
Insulin deficiency
Hypertonicity (e.g., hyerglycemia)
Aldosterone deficiency
$\beta$-Adrenergic receptor blockade
$\alpha$-Adrenergic receptor agonist
Exercise
Periodic paralysis
Digitalis
Succinylcholine

ACE, angiotensin-converting enzyme; GFR, glomerular filtration rate; Gl, gastrointestinal.
Adapted from Rastegar A, DeFronzo RA: Disorders of potassium metabolism associated with renal disease. In Schrier RW, Gottschalk CW (eds): Diseases of the Kidney, 5th ed. Boston, Little, Brown, 1992, pp 1645-2661.

with no symptoms, risk factors, or electrocardiographic (ECG) changes should be checked with a redrawn sample pending aggressive therapy. The classical ECG changes include a short QT interval, peaked T waves, and ultimately ventricular arrhythmias.

Need for therapy is determined by the degree of elevation of potassium, the acuteness of elevation, and the presence of ECG changes. Mild hyperkalemia without ECG changes requires only dietary restriction and reversal of underlying causes. ECG changes require emergency therapy: intravenous calcium gluconate (to protect the heart) and a cocktail of drugs to drive the potassium into the cell including sodium bicarbonate, insulin (given with glucose to avoid hypo-

glycemia), and nebulized albuterol (especially if there is a delay in gaining intravenous access). Therapy to increase intracellular potassium must be coupled with therapy to remove potassium stores, or the hyperkalemia will recur when infusions stop. Potassium-binding exchange resins (sodium polystyrene sulfonate [Kayexalate], calcium polystyrene sulfonate [Resonium]) can be used for this purpose orally or by enema. Finally, hemodialysis can remove extracellular potassium most quickly and completely.

### KEY POINTS: POTASSIUM IMBALANCES

- Potassium is primarily intracellular.

- Serum potassium levels reflect total body potassium as well as the equilibrium between intra- and extracellular potassium.

- Alkalosis produces a low serum potassium.

## Acid-Base Metabolism

Although the hydrogen ion ($H^+$) is present in miniscule concentrations in the extracellular fluid compared with other common ions in the body, its primary importance is reflected by the multiple mechanisms that exist to control its concentration within a tight range. The reason is that small alterations in $H^+$ concentration have large effects on the relative concentrations of other conjugate bases and acids of all the weak electrolytes. At neutral body pH, most biologically active molecules are in their charged state and can be trapped more effectively within cells to perform their functions. Furthermore, pH determines the net charge of proteins, which influences protein conformation and enzyme binding characteristics. Outside normal blood pH (7.35 to 7.46), severe metabolic problems occur.

In order to maintain pH, the body has to deal with the daily production of acid. There is a large production of acid by the metabolism of carbohydrates and fats, largely in the form of carbon dioxide, approximately 15,000 mmol/day. $CO_2$ is not an acid in the classical sense of the Brønsted-Lowry theory (Kildeberg, 1983) because it is not capable of donating an $H^+$ to a base. $CO_2$ can be considered a "volatile" acid because it is easily converted into $H_2CO_3$, carbonic acid:

$$H^+ + HCO_3^- \rightleftharpoons H_2CO_3 \rightleftharpoons H_2O + CO_2$$

Each molecule of $CO_2$ excreted by the lungs results from the reaction of one molecule of bicarbonate with one molecule of $H^+$. The $H^+$ remains in the body as $H_2O$. The metabolism of ingested proteins into amino acids is another source of acid production, estimated as between 50 and 100 mEq of $H^+$ per day (sulfate from the three sulfur-containing amino acids, phosphate from phosphoproteins). Because these acids cannot be excreted by the lungs, they are considered "fixed" and must be excreted by the kidneys.

The body therefore has three primary mechanisms to handle physiologic and pathophysiologic acid loads: buffers in the blood, $CO_2$ excretion by the lungs, and $H^+$ excretion by

$HCO_3$ metabolism in the kidneys (Vasuvattakul et al, 1992). The immediate response to an acid load is buffering. A buffer is simply a mixture of a weak acid and its conjugate base or a weak base and its conjugate acid that resists changes in pH when another acid or base is added. The key buffers in the blood are $HCO_3$ for metabolic acids and hemoglobin for $CO_2$. Within the cell, proteins and phosphates, which are found in higher concentrations than in the blood, become important as well. In the extracellular fluid, $HCO_3$ is responsible for about 80% of buffering. Changes in pH are governed by the Henderson-Hasselbalch equation, which generally is

$$pH = pKa + \log base/acid$$

When specifically formulated for the bicarbonate system, it becomes

$$pH = 6.1 + \log HCO_3^-/0.03 \times pCO_2$$

In general, optimal buffering occurs within 1.0 pH unit of the pKa. Therefore, the pKa value of 6.1 of bicarbonate buffer does not appear to be the most efficient for maintaining the pH 7.4 that is required for normal homeostasis. **The bicarbonate buffer system is effective despite having a low pKa because the body also controls $pCO_2$.**

Excretion of $CO_2$ by the lungs can occur rapidly and change both blood and intracellular pH. Elevated $pCO_2$ is detected by central and peripheral chemoreceptors which increase respiratory rate, leading to increased alveolar ventilation. Respiratory compensation in response to a pure metabolic acidosis cannot reduce $CO_2$ to below 10 mm Hg and is therefore unable to maintain pH in the setting of a large acid load.

Although most of the daily acid production is volatile and therefore excreted by the lungs, the kidneys must excrete the fixed acid and in doing so also reabsorb most of the filtered bicarbonate so that efficient extracellular buffering can be maintained. A healthy individual, with a GFR of 180 L/day and a plasma $[HCO_3^-]$ of 24 mEq/L, filters 4300 mEq of $HCO_3^-$ daily from the glomerulus into the proximal tubule. Of this filtered load, less than 0.1% normally appears in the urine. **The bulk of the filtered bicarbonate is reclaimed in the proximal nephron, with approximately 80% of the filtered $HCO_3^-$ reabsorbed within the proximal convoluted tubule.** In the tubular urine, $H^+$ and $HCO_3^-$ are formed from $CO_2$ and $H_2O$ in a reaction catalyzed by carbonic anhydrase (Kaunisto et al, 2002). The $H^+$ is returned to the tubular urine through two mechanisms: an $Na^+$-$H^+$ pump (antiporter) and a direct $H^+$-ATPase proton pump. The net result is reabsorption of $NaHCO_3$ into the interstitial fluid and secretion of $H^+$ into the proximal collecting duct urine. Note that the use of a carbonic anhydrase inhibitor such as acetazolamide reduces $HCO_3$ reabsorption and increases excretion of $Na^+$ and water, resulting in a weak diuretic effect (Puscas et al, 1999). The reabsorption of $HCO_3$ does not result in net excretion of $H^+$ from the body; however, the proximal tubular reabsorption of $HCO_3$ is essential to preserving acid-base balance. The primary factors that increase $HCO_3$ reabsorption are arterial $pCO_2$, $HCO_3$ concentration in the lumen, luminal flow rate, and angiotensin II (de Mello-Aires and Malnic, 2002).

The remainder of the filtered bicarbonate is reabsorbed in the distal nephron by a mechanism independent of carbonic anhydrase. In the distal tubule, further $H^+$ is secreted through the production of titratable acid, usually by buffering with phosphate. The term *titratable acidity* refers to the quantity of NaOH required to titrate urine back to a pH of 7.40, which is similar to that of blood. Other buffers, such as uric acid (pKa, 5.75) and creatinine (pKa, 4.97), contribute to the titratable acidity but only to a minor extent. $H^+$ is also secreted through the production of ammonium ion ($NH_4^+$). $NH_4$ is produced from glutamine, primarily by proximal tubular cells (Michoudet et al, 1994). Because of its high pKa (about 9.2), it is present almost exclusively as the $NH_4^+$ ion. Ammonium excretion can increase significantly during systemic acidosis (Nagami, 2004), which is the key mechanism for secreting excess $H^+$ because at very low urinary pH titratable acid cannot increase much (unless other ions such as ketoanions are being produced).

Regulation of $H^+$ secretion occurs through multiple biochemical and hormonal actions upon the preceding system. **Volume depletion** leads to Na retention and enhanced $HCO_3$ absorption, with a net loss of $H^+$. **Elevated $pCO_2$** as seen in chronic respiratory acidosis (see later) leads to a renal response of increased $H^+$ secretion. **Reduced GFR** reduces the amount of filtered $HCO_3$, leading to increased $H^+$ excretion. **High aldosterone levels** indirectly increase $H^+$ excretion by increasing $Na^+$ absorption. **Low potassium and low chloride** increase $HCO_3$ reabsorption and can maintain chronic metabolic alkalosis.

## Acid-Base Disorders

Those of us outside the fields of nephrology and anesthesia encounter acid-base disorders less commonly and are often intimidated by the process of working through the appropriate diagnosis. Nevertheless, when the terminology and basic equations are understood, the process is simple and, in many ways, mechanical (Corey, 2005). Common misconceptions begin with definition of terms. **The actual pH disturbance is an "emia" and the disease causing it is an "osis."** Acidemia refers strictly to a low arterial blood pH, less than 7.36. **Alkalemia** is a blood pH greater than 7.44. **Acidosis** is an abnormal condition or process that would lower arterial pH if no other condition was present, and **alkalosis** is a condition that would raise pH. **The basic information required to diagnose an acid-base disturbance is a history, physical, serum electrolytes, and arterial blood gas.** If the acid-base disorder is caused by a respiratory problem, the $pCO_2$ moves in the opposite direction to the pH (Madias and Adrogue, 2003). If caused by a metabolic (renal) disorder, the $HCO_3$ moves in the same direction as the pH. In every disorder, there should be an attempt by the other acid-handling mechanism to compensate for the change. For instance, chronic loss of bicarbonate from the kidney causing a metabolic acidosis (low pH and low $HCO_3$) should lead to increased ventilation to try to excrete the excess acid through the lung, leading to a lower $pCO_2$ (respiratory compensation). In **simple** acid-base disorders, there is one mechanism causing the acid disturbance with an appropriate compensation. In **mixed** disorders, the clue to multiple mechanisms comes from significant under- or overcompensation. Although formulas have been developed to predict appropriate compensation for each disorder, visual nomograms are more practically used at the bedside.

## Metabolic Acidosis

In metabolic acidosis, loss of bicarbonate leads to systemic acidemia, which produces a low arterial pH and low serum $HCO_3$. The appropriate compensation is increased respiration leading to a reduced $pCO_2$. In general, the expected degree of $pCO_2$ reduction is calculated as

$$\text{Expected } pCO_2 = 1.5 \times [HCO_3^-] + 8 \pm 2$$

This bicarbonate loss can be direct or from secondary effects of other ions. The presence of active ions that are not measured in routine blood work can be detected by the anion gap. The anion gap is defined as the difference between the levels of routinely measured cations ($Na^+$) and anions ($Cl^-$ and $CO_2$) in blood:

$$\text{Anion gap} = Na^+ - (Cl^- + HCO_3^-) = 140 - (105 + 24) = 11$$

The normal range is 9 to 14 mEq/L. The predominant unmeasured anions include albumin and phosphate. The major unmeasured cations include calcium, magnesium, and gamma globulins. If the anion gap is elevated in a patient with metabolic acidosis, the condition occurs because acids that do not contain chloride are present in the blood. The most common are ketones (diabetic ketoacidosis), lactate (lactic acidosis), and drug intoxication (methanol, aspirin) (Levraut and Grimaud, 2003).

Metabolic acidosis with a normal anion gap is caused by direct bicarbonate loss through the gut or kidney or by the addition of exogenous acid that is buffered by bicarbonate (Table 35–5). The patient's history can give major clues to the diagnosis, involving either GI loss (vomiting, diarrhea, fistula), drug use (acetazolamide), or previous surgery (ileal conduit). Serum potassium can be a further clue to etiology. Low potassium is associated with loss through the GI tract or renal tubular acidosis because renin is stimulated from the

---

### Table 35–5. Hyperchloremic Metabolic Acidosis (Normal Anion Gap)

*Acid Loads*

Ammonium chloride
Hyperalimentation
Ketoacidosis with renal ketone loss

*Bicarbonate Losses*

Diarrhea
Pancreatic, biliary, or small bowel drainage
Ureterosigmoidostomy
Drugs
   Cholestyramine
   Calcium chloride
   Magnesium sulfate
Posthypocapnia

*Defects in Renal Acidification*

Proximal: decreased $HCO_3^-$ reclamation
Distal: decreased net acid excretion
   Primary mineralocorticoid deficiency
   Hyperreninemic hypoaldosteronism
   Mineralocorticoid-resistant hyperkalemia

*Dilutional*

Adapted from Cogan MG, Rector FC Jr: Acid-base disorders. In Brenner BM, Rector FC (eds): The Kidney, 4th ed. Philadelphia, WB Saunders, 1991, pp 737-804.

---

volume contraction. In acidosis associated with severe renal dysfunction, potassium is often elevated.

## Renal Tubular Acidosis

**Renal tubular acidosis (RTA) is a family of syndromes of metabolic acidosis resulting from defects in tubular H secretion and urinary acidification.** They are classified according to the mechanism of the defect, and each type has different clinical manifestations. RTA type 1 is the most common form and the most clinically significant to the urologist. It has also been called classical RTA and distal RTA. The old classification of RTA type 3 is now recognized as a type 1 variant. The underlying problem is failure of $H^+$ secretion in the distal nephron, which can be congenital or acquired. Associated disorders include autoimmune diseases (thyroiditis), toxic nephropathy, and chronic ureteral obstruction. **The hallmark is a hyperchloremic metabolic acidosis with a high urinary pH (>5.5) in the presence of persistently low serum $HCO_3$.** If no metabolic acidosis is present but the condition is still suspected, acid loading with ammonium chloride decreases the serum $HCO_3$ while maintaining a high urine pH. Volume contraction from sodium loss is common, which leads to secondary hyperaldosteronism and hypokalemia. These patients often develop recurrent renal stones composed of calcium phosphate. The most likely contributing factor is low urinary citrate coupled with a high urinary pH and hypercalciuria. Treatment with sodium bicarbonate can alkalinize the urine, correct the sodium defect, lower aldosterone, and raise the potassium. Potassium citrate can augment the urinary citrate levels and inhibit stone formation (Domrongkitchaiporn et al, 2002).

**Type 2 RTA, also called proximal, is caused by failure of bicarbonate reabsorption in the proximal tubule** (Igarashi et al, 2002). The mechanisms of $H^+$ secretion in the distal tubule are overwhelmed, resulting in $HCO_3$ loss in the urine. The bicarbonate is replaced in the circulation by $Cl^-$, resulting in hyperchloremia. Increased sodium delivery to the distal tubule increases aldosterone secretion, resulting in hypokalemia. Ultimately, a new steady state is reached in which serum $HCO_3^-$ is decreased, and, hence, the filtered load, distal delivery, and urinary excretion of $HCO_3^-$ are all reduced. **The acidosis is self-limited because acid production and excretion are equivalent at this reduced pH; the plasma $HCO_3^-$ remains at 15 to 20 mEq/L.** Because urinary citrate levels are not reduced, stone formation does not occur despite increased urinary calcium. This condition is more common in children, and it can lead to growth retardation and metabolic bone disease (Roth and Chan, 2001). Oral supplementation with $NaHCO_3$ can correct the condition but can lead to further hypokalemia, and potassium supplements may also be required. As an interesting aside (and possible memory aid), it was suggested that Dickens' character of Tiny Tim was based on a child with type 2 RTA (growth retardation, osteomalacia), which was reversed when Mr. Scrooge paid for his therapy (sodium bicarbonate).

Type 4 RTA is due to impairment of cation exchange in the distal tubule with reduced secretion of both $H^+$ and $K^+$. It is due to aldosterone deficiency or resistance. **The unique feature compared with other RTAs is hyperkalemia.** Patients often have associated azotemia and hypertension. Because the distal tubule $H^+$ pump functions normally, patients are able to

**SECTION VIII**

**Table 35-6. Differential Diagnosis of Metabolic Alkalosis**

| Measurement | Saline Responsive | Normotensive: Saline Unresponsive | Hypertensive: Saline Unresponsive |
|---|---|---|---|
| Urinary [Cl⁻] | <15 mEq/L | >15 mEq/L | >15 mEq/L |
| Blood pressure | Normal | Normal | Increased |
| Differential diagnosis | Vomiting | Diuretics | Primary mineralocorticoid excess |
|  | Nasogastric suction | Bartter's magnesium deficiency |  |

Adapted from Alpern RJ, Emmett M, Seldin DW: Metabolic alkalosis. In Seldin DW, Giebisch G (eds): The Kidney: Physiology and Pathophysiology, 2nd ed. New York, Raven, 1992, pp 2733-2758.

decrease urine pH to less than 5.5 in response to the acidosis. Urinary citrate may be normal or low, but renal dysfunction reduces secretion of calcium and uric acid, and stones do not form (Uribarri et al, 1994). Therapy is typically directed at controlling the hyperkalemia.

## Metabolic Alkalosis

**In metabolic alkalosis, the pH is high (alkalemia) and the HCO₃ high (mirrors pH in primary metabolic disorder)** (Khanna and Kurtzman, 2001). The appropriate respiratory compensation is reduced ventilation with increased $pCO_2$. The expected degree of respiratory compensation can be estimated by

Expected $pCO_2$ = 6 mm Hg per 10 mEq/L increase in $HCO_3$

An exogenous alkali load is usually rapidly excreted into the urine by the kidney, and other mechanisms are required to maintain the disorder. Maintenance of the alkalosis requires a process that greatly impairs the kidney's ability to excrete bicarbonate and prevent the return of the elevated plasma level to normal. Chloride deficiency leads to the kidney reabsorbing more bicarbonate anion than usual because there is not sufficient chloride anion present to maintain electroneutrality. This condition is reversed with fluid and chloride. Consequently, metabolic alkalosis is most conveniently classified as chloride responsive and chloride resistant.

The most common chloride-responsive conditions are GI loss (vomiting, nasogastric drainage, laxative abuse) and kidney loss (diuretics). These make up over 90% of clinical cases of metabolic alkalosis (Table 35–6). Volume contraction in these conditions stimulates aldosterone production and distal secretion of H⁺ and K⁺. **Thus, there may be a paradoxical aciduria, which persists until volume is replaced.** Chloride-resistant metabolic alkalosis is associated with potassium loss resulting from mineralocorticoid excess. It is associated with volume expansion and high urinary chloride levels, which can aid in the diagnosis. Common causes are hyperaldosteronism (primary or secondary), Cushing's syndrome, diuretics, and congenital conditions such Bartter's syndrome (hyperplasia of the juxtaglomerular apparatus).

## Respiratory Acidosis

In respiratory acidosis, pH is low (acidemia) and $pCO_2$ is high because of inadequate respiration (Epstein and Singh, 2001). The anticipated compensatory response is increased $HCO_3$:

Acute: Expected $HCO_3$ = 1 mEq/L for each 10 mm Hg $pCO_2$

Chronic: Expected $HCO_3$ = 3.5 mEq/L for each
10 mm Hg $pCO_2$

Elevated $pCO_2$ can be caused by increased production of $CO_2$, decreased ventilation, and increased $CO_2$ in the inspired air. Because increased production is usually handled quickly by increased respiration and $CO_2$ does not vary except in ventilated patients, the most common cause is decreased ventilation. This can be due to central depression of respiration (e.g., opiates, trauma, cervical cord trauma), chest cavity problems (e.g., pneumothorax, pulmonary edema), upper airway obstruction, or an iatrogenic cause (insufficient ventilation). Because $CO_2$ readily diffuses across all cellular membranes, marked elevation can severely interfere with intracellular metabolism. Clinical effects of elevated $pCO_2$, which are separate from acidosis per se, include elevated intracranial pressure, tachycardia, central depression, and eventually coma and death.

## Respiratory Alkalosis

In respiratory alkalosis, pH is high (alkalemia) because of a low $pCO_2$. This is due to hyperventilation (Foster et al, 2001). The appropriate compensatory response is a lowering of $HCO_3$ by the following expected amounts:

Acute: Expected $HCO_3$ = 2 mEq/L for each 10 mm Hg $pCO_2$

Chronic: Expected $HCO_3$ = 5 mEq/L for each
10 mm Hg $pCO_2$

Common causes of hyperventilation that can lead to respiratory alkalosis are fever, pain, anxiety, septicemia, head trauma, pulmonary embolism, and iatrogenic (excessive mechanical ventilation). Neurologic symptoms such as paresthesia and tetany may occur. Therapy is directed at improving oxygenation and ventilation.

## KEY POINTS: ACID-BASE

- Physiologic chemical reactions require a narrow range of serum pH.

- Acid is excreted through the lungs and the kidney.

- Type 1 RTA (distal) is the only type associated with renal stones.

- In acid-base disorders, determine first whether the kidney ($HCO_3$) or lungs ($pCO_2$) are responsible for the primary disorder, then determine whether the compensatory response is appropriate.

# SUGGESTED READINGS

Agre P, King LS, Yasui M, et al: Aquaporin water channels—From atomic structure to clinical medicine. J Physiol 2002;542:3-16.

Cockcroft DW, Gault MH: Prediction of creatinine clearance from serum creatinine. Nephron 1976;16:31-41.

Corey HE: Bench-to-bedside review: Fundamental principles of acid-base physiology. Crit Care 2005;9:184-192.

Delles C, Klingbeil AU, Schneider MP, et al: The role of nitric oxide in the regulation of glomerular haemodynamics in humans. Nephrol Dial Transplant 2004;19:1392-1397.

Goh KP: Management of hyponatremia. Am Fam Physician 2004;69:2387-2394.

Hill-Kapturczak N, Chang SH, Agarwal A: Heme oxygenase and the kidney. DNA Cell Biol 2002;21:307-321.

Kaschina E, Unger T: Angiotensin AT1/AT2 receptors: Regulation, signalling and function. Blood Press 2003;12:70-88.

Khanna A, Kurtzman NA: Metabolic alkalosis. Respir Care 2001;46:354-365.

Lariviere R, Lebel M: Endothelin-1 in chronic renal failure and hypertension. Can J Physiol Pharmacol 2003;81:607-621.

Levraut J, Grimaud D: Treatment of metabolic acidosis. Curr Opin Crit Care 2003;9:260-265.

Madias NE, Adrogue HJ: Cross-talk between two organs: How the kidney responds to disruption of acid-base balance by the lung. Nephron Physiol 2003;93:61-66.

Miller M: Inappropriate antidiuretic hormone secretion. Curr Ther Endocrinol Metab 1994;5:186-189.

Robertson GL: Physiology of ADH secretion. Kidney Int Suppl 1987;21:S20-S26.

Roth KS, Chan JC: Renal tubular acidosis: A new look at an old problem. Clin Pediatr (Phila) 2001;40:533-543.

Sasaki S: Nephrogenic diabetes insipidus: Update of genetic and clinical aspects. Nephrol Dial Transplant 2004;19:1351-1353.

Schnermann J, Traynor T, Yang T, et al: Tubuloglomerular feedback: New concepts and developments. Kidney Int Suppl 1998;67:S40-S45.

Shemesh O, Golbetz H, Kriss JP, Myers BD: Limitations of creatinine as a filtration marker in glomerulopathic patients. Kidney Int 1985;28:830-838.

Shoskes DA, Xie Y, Gonzalez-Cadavid NF: Nitric oxide synthase activity in renal ischemia-reperfusion injury in the rat: Implications for renal transplantation. Transplantation 1997;63:495-500.

Wang T: Role of iNOS and eNOS in modulating proximal tubule transport and acid-base balance. Am J Physiol 2002;283:F658-F662.

Yeates KE, Singer M, Morton AR: Salt and water: A simple approach to hyponatremia. CMAJ 2004;170:365-369.

# 36 Renovascular Hypertension and Ischemic Nephropathy

ANDREW C. NOVICK, MD • AMR FERGANY, MD

HISTORICAL BACKGROUND

DEFINITIONS

PATHOLOGY AND NATURAL HISTORY

PHYSIOLOGY OF THE RENIN-ANGIOTENSIN-ALDOSTERONE SYSTEM

PATHOPHYSIOLOGY OF RENOVASCULAR HYPERTENSION

HUMAN CORRELATES OF EXPERIMENTAL RENOVASCULAR HYPERTENSION

PATHOPHYSIOLOGY OF ISCHEMIC NEPHROPATHY

CLINICAL FEATURES OF RENOVASCULAR HYPERTENSION

CLINICAL FEATURES OF ISCHEMIC NEPHROPATHY

DIAGNOSTIC EVALUATION

COST-EFFECTIVE APPROACH FOR DIAGNOSIS

SELECTION OF PATIENTS FOR SURGICAL OR ENDOVASCULAR THERAPY

SURGICAL REVASCULARIZATION

PERCUTANEOUS TRANSLUMINAL ANGIOPLASTY

ENDOVASCULAR STENTING

OTHER RENAL ARTERY DISEASES

## HISTORICAL BACKGROUND

Richard Bright, Physician Extraordinary to the Queen of England, was the first to associate proteinuria, fullness and hardness of the pulse, and dropsy with "hardening of the kidneys" (Bright, 1827). In 1856, Traube, from an analysis of pulse tracings, suggested that the abnormality might be high blood pressure, and Mohomed (1874) demonstrated "high tension in the arterial system" in association with renal disease.

The critical experimental work was the discovery of renin by Tigerstedt and Bergemann (1898), who noted an increase in arterial blood pressure in rabbits injected with a saline renal extract. They reasoned that the renal extract contained a pressor substance and coined the term *renin*. However, the significance of their work was not recognized until the critical experiments by Goldblatt and colleagues (1934), who produced diastolic hypertension in dogs by clamping the main renal arteries and corrected the hypertension by clamp removal.

Soon thereafter, Butler (1937) reported the first reversal of hypertension after nephrectomy in a patient with a small "pyelonephritic kidney"; 1 year later, Leadbetter and Burkland (1938) reported another cure of hypertension in a child with pathologic signs of a renal arterial lesion.

These clinical observations were paralleled by laboratory investigation, and in 1940, Page and Helmer and Braun-Menendez and associates independently reported that renin itself was not a pressor substance but acted as an enzyme to release a pressor peptide, now called *angiotensin*, from a circulating plasma globulin. Goormaghtigh and Grimson (1939), who had previously described the juxtaglomerular cells, described increased granularity of these cells in both animals and humans with renal hypertension and postulated that these cells were secreting excessive amounts of renin.

There followed an aggressive but disappointing clinical experience with nephrectomy for cure of hypertension in patients with unilateral renal disease. This experience led to the search for a way of proving that a renal lesion was actually causing the hypertension. Smith (1948), reviewing the literature, reported relief of hypertension in only 19% of 200 patients whose elevated blood pressure was thought to result from unilateral renal disease. Thus, it became apparent that even if pressor mechanisms did underlie some forms of renal hypertension, there were no ways to measure them.

This challenge led to studies of the effect of renal artery constriction on renal function. **In dogs, renal artery constriction resulted in a marked decrease in sodium and water excretion from the affected kidney** (Blake et al, 1950; Pitts and Duggan, 1950). In 1964, Howard and Connor used these observations to develop a differential renal function test based on bilateral ureteral catheterization to identify the "ischemic kidney."

Another major advance was the development of translumbar aortography and the demonstration of its value in visualizing renal arterial lesions (Smith et al, 1982). By 1957, the first large series of studies of patients with renal arterial lesions was reported (Poutasse and Dustan, 1957).

In addition, interest in what would become known as the *renin-angiotensin-aldosterone system* (RAAS) was emerging as new discoveries were made. Accordingly, it was determined that there were two forms of angiotensin (Skeggs et al, 1954), and angiotensin was sequenced and synthesized (Bumpus et al, 1957). These critical advances led to an accurate radioim-munoassay for angiotensin, the development of angiotensin analogs, and angiotensin-converting enzyme (ACE) inhibitors, all major tools now used to identify the patient with renovascular hypertension (RVH). More recently, the presence of a family of angiotensin receptors has been clarified (Kang et al, 1994; Goodfriend et al, 1996).

It is now recognized that the RAAS is a critical integrated system regulating not only blood pressure, sodium balance, and potassium balance but also regional blood flow and, in particular, the glomerular filtration rate (GFR) (Gunning et al, 1996; Laragh and Blumenfeld, 1996). Moreover, there is an expanding body of literature implicating angiotensin II in cell proliferation and interstitial fibrosis (Mai et al, 1993; Eng et al, 1994; Stoll et al, 1995; Egido, 1996; Gunning et al, 1996).

## DEFINITIONS
## Hypertension

As strange as it may seem, it has been difficult to establish a precise definition of *hypertension*. The problem was best stated by Sir George Pickering, who wrote that "there is no dividing line. The relationship between arterial blood pressure and mortality is quantitative; the higher the pressure the worse the prognosis" (Pickering and Pickering, 1995; Pickering et al, 1996). Indeed, cumulative data obtained from insurance companies have validated this point. **Untreated blood pressure in excess of 140/90 mm Hg is associated with excess mortality, and diastolic pressures below 70 mm Hg are optimal** (Lew, 1973). For operational purposes, the World Health Organization has defined hypertension in adults as a systolic pressure greater than 160 mm Hg or a diastolic pressure greater than 95 mm Hg or both. In addition, consistent elevation of blood pressure should be established with repeated readings before evaluation is instituted. In children, there is a rise in blood pressure with age; an upper normal limit of 130/80 mm Hg is reached by 12 to 15 years of age.

## Renal Arterial Disease versus Renovascular Hypertension

The development of arteriography provided an accurate means of identifying renal arterial disease and heralded the advent of renal arterial vascular repair, which renewed enthusiasm for surgical management of the disease. However, it soon became apparent that normotensive patients undergoing arteriography for other reasons often had renal arterial disease (Eyler et al, 1962), especially those with arteriosclerotic disease (Wilms et al, 1990), and autopsy figures supported the

radiologic findings (Holley et al, 1964). Accordingly, **the finding of renal arterial disease alone is not sufficient justification to warrant correction in a hypertensive patient. The lesion must be functionally significant** (i.e., it must reduce blood flow by an amount sufficient to activate renin release, initiating RVH). Hence, a practical definition of RVH is hypertension resulting from a renal arterial lesion that is relieved by correction of the offending lesion or removal of the kidney.

## PATHOLOGY AND NATURAL HISTORY

**The two major pathologic entities that cause renal arterial disease are atherosclerosis (ASO) and fibrous dysplasia (FD).** The Cleveland Clinic group has emphasized the importance of the various distinct histologic patterns, identifiable by angiographic techniques, that have predictable natural histories (Schreiber et al, 1984, 1989; Novick et al, 1994). Their classification is shown in Table 36–1.

## Atherosclerosis

**Approximately 70% of all renovascular lesions are caused by atherosclerosis** (Novick et al, 1996). This disease may be limited to the renal artery but more commonly is a manifestation of generalized ASO, involving the abdominal aorta and coronary, cerebral, and lower extremity vessels. Atherosclerotic stenosis usually occurs in the proximal 2 cm of the renal artery, and distal arterial or branch involvement is distinctly uncommon. Owing to the proximal location of these lesions, oblique aortic views are often needed to visualize adequately the area of stenosis. The lesion involves the intima of the artery and, in two thirds of the cases, arises as an eccentric

---

**Table 36–1.  Classification and Natural History of Renovascular Disease**

**Atherosclerosis:** Proximal intimal plaques. Seen predominantly in males and usually in older age groups. Progressive in about 40% of patients; may dissect or thrombose. May involve renal arteries only or may involve carotid and coronary arteries, aorta, and other vessels.

   **Intimal fibroplasia:** Collagenous disease involving intima; seen in children and young adults. Progressive; may dissect. May involve other vessels.

   **True fibromuscular hyperplasia:** Diffusely involves media. Seen in children and young adults. Progressive. Radiographically indistinguishable from intimal fibroplasia. Very rare.

   **Medial fibroplasia:** Series of collagenous rings involving media of main renal artery, often extending into branches. Usually seen in women in their 30s and 40s. Produces typical "string of beads" pattern in angiography. Does not dissect, thrombose, or rupture, and seldom progresses after 40 years of age. May involve other vessels.

   **Perimedial (subadventitial) fibroplasia:** Dense collagenous collar involving media, just beneath adventitia of vessel. Tightly stenotic, with extensive collateral circulation on angiography. Seen mostly in women ("girlie disease"). Progressive. Involves renal arteries only.

   **Miscellaneous:** Renal artery aneurysms, middle aortic syndrome, periarterial fibrosis, and post-traumatic intimal or medial disease. Variable in location and obstruction; occurs in diverse clinical settings.

From Stewart BH, Dustan HP, Kiser WS, et al: Correlation of angiography and natural history in evaluation of patients with renovascular hypertension. J Urol 1970;104;231.

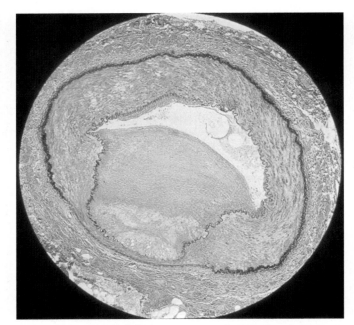

**Figure 36-1.** Histopathologic appearance of eccentric atherosclerotic plaque causing renal artery stenosis.

| Table 36-2. **Natural History of Atherosclerotic Renal Artery Sclerosis** | | | |
|---|---|---|---|
| | Patients (N) | Progression of Obstruction (%) | Complete Occlusion (%) |
| Wollenweber et al, 1968 | 30 | 63 | NA |
| Stewart et al, 1970 | 39 | 36 | 8 |
| Schreiber et al, 1984 | 85 | 44 | 16 |
| Zucchelli et al, 1987 | 36 | 40 | NA |
| Tollefson and Ernst, 1991 | 48 | 53 | 9 |
| Zierler et al, 1994 | 80 | 42 | 11 |

NA, not available.

plaque (Fig. 36-1); in the remainder, the vessel is circumferentially involved, with narrowing of the lumen and destruction of the intima. Dissecting hematomas frequently complicate this disease, sometimes resulting in thrombosis of the entire vessel.

The natural history of atherosclerotic renal artery disease has been studied by obtaining sequential abdominal aortography or duplex ultrasound scanning in patients with documented renal artery lesions who have been treated medically (Table 36-2). The largest of these studies have shown that **progressive arterial obstruction occurs in 42% to 53% of patients with atherosclerotic renal artery disease, often within the first 2 years of radiographic follow-up. The incidence of progression to complete renal artery occlusion in these studies has ranged from 9% to 16%, and this has occurred more often in arteries that initially showed high degrees of stenosis.**

In a study at the Cleveland Clinic (Schreiber et al, 1984), we reviewed the natural history of atherosclerotic renal artery stenosis (ARAS) in 85 patients who were observed with sequential renal angiograms obtained 3 to 172 months after an initial diagnostic angiogram. Progressive obstruction of the renal artery related to ASO occurred in 37 patients (44%), including 14 (16%) in whom such progression eventuated in complete occlusion of the involved renal artery. In patients in whom progressive disease developed, it occurred primarily within the first 2 years of angiographic follow-up. The rate of progression of ARAS correlated directly with the degree of stenosis on the initial angiogram. The majority of renal arteries with mild (50%) or moderate (50% to 75%) stenosis on the initial angiogram were unchanged on follow-up angiograms. In contrast, 39% of renal arteries with more than 75% stenosis on the initial angiogram progressed to complete occlusion. Other studies have since validated this observation that **progression to 100% occlusion occurs more often and**

more rapidly in renal arteries that are initially involved with a high degree (>75%) of stenosis (Tollefson and Ernst, 1991; Zierler et al, 1994).

Clinical follow-up of patients in our study also revealed that significantly more patients with progressive disease developed deterioration of overall renal function compared with patients with stable disease. Interestingly, **serial blood pressure control** was equivalent in these two groups, indicating that blood pressure is not a useful clinical marker for progressive ARAS.

These natural history data clearly show that **atherosclerotic renal artery disease progresses in many patients and that loss of functioning renal parenchyma is a common sequela of such progression.** It is now further appreciated that progressive atherosclerotic renal artery obstruction can eventuate in end-stage renal disease (ESRD). The typical occurrence of ESRD is in older patients with generalized ASO who are not candidates for transplantation and whose prognosis on chronic dialysis is poor in terms of both the quality of life and longevity. In an early study, we identified 25 patients in whom ESRD was clearly a consequence of advanced atherosclerotic renal artery disease (Novick, 1994b). Seventeen of these patients were maintained with chronic dialysis, and of these, 13 died within 1 year (mean survival 8.7 months). The causes of death on dialysis were myocardial infarction (6), infection (2), gastrointestinal bleeding (1), ruptured aortic aneurysm (1), mesenteric infarct (1), cardiogenic shock (1), and cerebrovascular accident (1). In a subsequent study, Mailloux and colleagues (1988) analyzed the survival of patients started on dialysis from 1970 to 1985 according to the primary renal diagnosis. Patients with renovascular disease as the cause of ESRD had the poorest survival, with a 27-month median survival time and a 12% 5-year survival rate. In another study in which 51 patients with bilateral ARAS were observed for 52 months, 12% of the patients progressed to ESRD, and an average rate of decline of GFR of 4 mL/min/yr was noted (Baboolal et al, 1998). A crude mortality rate of 45% was reported. These data further highlight that ESRD from atherosclerotic renal artery disease does not respond well to renal replacement therapy.

The exact incidence of ESRD caused by atherosclerotic renal artery disease in the United States is not known. Fatica and coauthors (2001) reported an increase in incidence of renovascular disease (RVD) as a cause for ESRD in patients starting dialysis treatment. This increase was from 1.4% to 2.1%, with an annual increase of 12%. This information was derived from the recorded diagnosis of these patients in the U.S. Renal Data System database, and the disease was not specifically searched for. No increase in mortality on dialysis was found in these patients when compared with other etiologies of ESRD.

van Ampting and associates (2003) reported a 27% incidence of significant renal artery stenosis (RAS) in 49 patients older than 45 years starting dialysis when investigated using computed tomography angiography (CTA).

Uzu and coworkers (2002) reported a higher (50%) incidence in 44 patients with ESRD studied by magnetic resonance angiography when additional vascular disease (cerebral, coronary, or peripheral) was also diagnosed.

In a report from England, Scoble and colleagues (1989) prospectively performed renal arteriography in all new patients with ESRD during an 18-month period. Atherosclerotic renal artery disease was the cause of ESRD in 6% of all patients and in 14% of patients older than 50 years. Approximately 300,000 patients in the United States are currently being maintained with chronic dialysis. Their median age is older than 60 years, and a majority have evidence of generalized ASO obliterans. **Although the exact number of patients with ESRD caused by atherosclerotic renal artery disease is not known, based on the data previously described, there appear to be several thousand patients in this category.**

## Intimal Fibroplasia

**Primary intimal fibroplasia occurs in children and in young adults and constitutes approximately 10% of the total number of fibrous lesions.** This lesion is characterized by a circumferential accumulation of collagen inside the internal elastic lamina (Fig. 36–2). Disruption and duplication of the elastica interna occur more often in younger patients, with dissecting hematomas as a complication in many patients. The possibility of ASO as a cause of renal artery disease in this group can be excluded histologically by the absence of lipid demonstrable with special staining techniques. Intimal fibroplasia with complicating medial dissection is characterized pathologically by large dissecting channels in the outer half of the media. These lesions are thought to develop because of defects in the internal elastica with resultant medial dissection and aneurysmal dilatation.

**Angiography in primary intimal fibroplasia reveals a smooth, fairly focal stenosis, usually involving the proximal or midportion of the vessel or its branches** (Fig. 36–3). Dissecting hematomas may distort the area of the stenosis. With nonoperative management, progressive renal artery obstruction and ischemic atrophy of the involved kidney invariably occur. Severe intimal fibroplasia may subsequently develop de novo in the contralateral renal artery. Although primary intimal fibroplasia most commonly affects the renal arteries, it may also occur as a generalized disorder with concomitant involvement of carotid, upper and lower extremity, and mesenteric vessels.

## Medial Fibroplasia

**Medial fibroplasia is the most common of the fibrous lesions, constituting 75% to 80% of the total number. It tends to occur in women between the ages of 25 and 50 years**

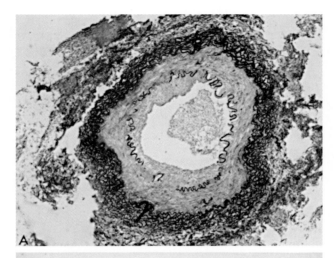

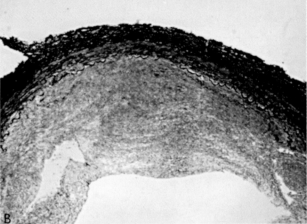

**Figure 36–2. A,** Photomicrograph of a cross section demonstrates intimal fibroplasia with focal fragmentation and partial absence of the elastica interna. **B,** Photomicrograph of a cross section demonstrates severe renal arterial intimal fibroplasia with a dense cuff of intimal collagen apposed to the luminal surface of a partially disrupted elastica interna. A small recannulized channel is noted in the lower left. (From Novick AC: Renal vascular hypertension in children. In Kelalis PP, King LR, Belman AB [eds]: Clinical Pediatric Urology. Philadelphia, WB Saunders, 1984.)

**and often involves both renal arteries.** It may involve other vessels in the body, most notably the carotid, mesenteric, and iliac arteries. Microscopically, the internal elastic membrane is focally and variably thinned and lost. Within the alternating thickened areas, much of the muscle is replaced by collagen, hence the term *medial fibroplasia*. In other areas, thinning of the media occurs to the point of complete loss, and microaneurysms can be seen as saccules lined by only the external elastica. In extreme cases, giant aneurysms may be found in association with medial fibroplasia.

**Angiographically, medial fibroplasia demonstrates a typical "string of beads" appearance involving the distal two thirds of the main renal artery and branches** (Fig. 36–4). The areas of stenosis are often overshadowed by contrast medium in the microaneurysms, making the degree of actual stenosis difficult to assess. The aneurysms themselves are greater in diameter than the normal renal artery proximal to the disease, and extreme collateral circulation is absent. These are

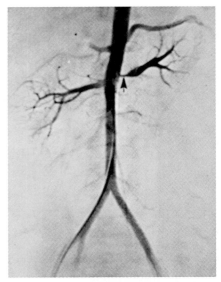

**Figure 36–3.** Aortogram of a 6-year-old boy demonstrates proximal left renal artery stenosis *(arrow)* from intimal fibroplasia. (From Novick AC: Renal vascular hypertension in children. In Kelalis PP, King LR, Belman AB [eds]: Clinical Pediatric Urology. Philadelphia, WB Saunders, 1984.)

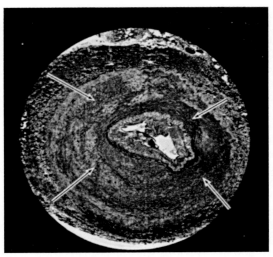

**Figure 36–5.** Cross section of the main renal artery in a girl with perimedial fibroplasia demonstrates a dense collagenous collar *(arrows)* involving the outer media of the vessel, which causes a severe progressive stenosis. (From Novick AC: Renal vascular hypertension in children. In Kelalis PP, King LR, Belman AB [eds]: Clinical Pediatric Urology. Philadelphia, WB Saunders, 1984.)

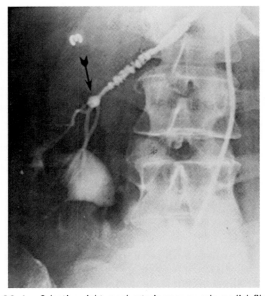

**Figure 36–4.** Selective right renal arteriogram reveals medial fibroplasia involving the main renal artery with typical "string of beads" appearance. (From Novick AC: Renal vascular hypertension in children. In Kelalis PP, King LR, Belman AB [eds]: Clinical Pediatric Urology. Philadelphia, WB Saunders, 1984.)

important features in differentiating the lesion from perimedial fibroplasia. Schreiber and colleagues (1984) studied the natural history of renal artery disease related to medial fibroplasia in 66 patients who were observed with serial angiography. Progressive RAS occurred in 22 patients (33%), and, contrary to an earlier report, this occurrence was no different whether patients were older or younger than 40 years. Significantly, there were no cases of progression to total arterial occlusion in this group. Also, clinical follow-up revealed that serial decreases in either overall renal function or the size of the involved kidney seldom occurred in patients with progressive medial fibroplasia, suggesting that the risk of losing renal function is relatively small in patients with this disease who are managed medically.

## Perimedial Fibroplasia

**Perimedial fibroplasia occurs predominantly in young women between the ages of 15 and 30 years and has therefore been referred to, rather crudely, as *girlie disease.*** It constitutes about 10% to 15% of the total number of fibrous lesions and occurs only in the renal artery. This is a tightly stenotic lesion that, pathologically, consists of a collar of dense collagen enveloping the renal artery for variable lengths and thicknesses. The collagen is deposited in the outer border of the media, usually replaces a considerable portion of the media, and may replace it completely in some areas (Fig. 36–5). Islands of smooth muscle are occasionally seen trapped within the collagenous ring. Special stains show that the lesion is confined within the external elastic lamina and contained in all cases by intact adventitial connective tissue. The arterial lumen may be further compromised by a process of secondary intimal fibroplasia. It has been suggested that this secondary thickening of the intima is related to slowing of blood flow through a narrowed arterial segment, with resultant platelet and fibrin deposition and subsequent fibrous organization.

**The arteriogram in perimedial fibroplasia may give the appearance of arterial beading, but careful observation shows that the caliber of the normal segment of the vessel is not exceeded by the "bead"** (Fig. 36–6). This fact, along with the frequent occurrence of extensive collateral circulation, differentiates this lesion angiographically from that of medial fibroplasia. Perimedial fibroplasia produces severe stenosis, and, although complicating thrombosis or dissection is

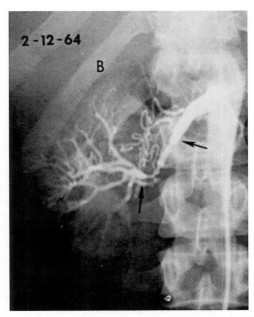

**Figure 36–6.** Renal arteriogram in a patient with perimedial fibroplasia shows slightly irregular yet severe stenosis of the midrenal artery *(arrows)* associated with extensive collateral circulation to the kidney. The small size of the arterial irregularities and the presence of collateral circulation distinguish this lesion radiographically from medial fibroplasia. (From Novick AC: Renal vascular hypertension in children. In Kelalis PP, King LR, Belman AB [eds]: Clinical Pediatric Urology. Philadelphia, WB Saunders, 1984.)

relatively uncommon, progressive obstruction with ischemic renal atrophy occurs in almost all patients managed nonoperatively.

## Fibromuscular Hyperplasia

**Fibromuscular hyperplasia is an extremely rare disease, constituting only 2% to 3% of fibrous lesions, and tends to occur in children and young adults.** This is the only renal arterial disease in which true hyperplasia of the smooth muscle cells is present. The renal artery shows a concentric thickening of its wall with a mixture of proliferating smooth muscle and fibrous tissue in variable quantity. Angiographically, fibromuscular hyperplasia arises as a smooth stenosis of the renal artery or its branches and, from a radiographic standpoint, may be indistinguishable from intimal fibroplasia. Most patients with this disease have developed progressive vascular obstruction when observed with serial angiographic studies.

## PHYSIOLOGY OF THE RENIN-ANGIOTENSIN-ALDOSTERONE SYSTEM

The RAAS plays a fundamental role in maintaining arterial blood pressure as well as extracellular volume. The system is composed of a series of proteins and peptides that react in a cascade, ultimately resulting in a widespread series of actions. Local renin-angiotensin systems are widely present in several organ systems and exert numerous local actions. **The main**

components of the system are angiotensinogen, renin, ACE, and various angiotensins, most important among which is angiotensin II (AII). AII is a powerful vasoconstrictor that increases peripheral vascular resistance to raise blood pressure. In addition, AII stimulates sodium reabsorption directly and through stimulation of aldosterone synthesis. The primary role of the RAAS is to maintain tissue perfusion, especially in cases of hypovolemia.

**The basic cascade involves conversion of angiotensinogen to angiotensin I (AI) through the action of renin.** This is the rate-limiting step for the entire system, and, accordingly, control of renin release regulates the activity of the whole system. ACE then acts on AI to produce AII, which exerts a wide variety of immediate and delayed actions on the vascular system and kidneys as well as stimulates production of aldosterone from the adrenal cortex. In healthy subjects with normal dietary sodium intake, the RAAS probably plays little role in day-to-day blood pressure control. Several disease states, however, activate the RAAS. True hypovolemia or hypotension is the physiologic stimulus for AII secretion. Inappropriate activation of the RAAS occurs in cases of perceived hypovolemia such as RAS, congestive heart failure, or advanced hepatic disease, leading to hypertension, inappropriate salt and fluid retention, or both.

## Angiotensinogen

Angiotensinogen is a 452-amino-acid protein and is the source of all angiotensins (Kageyama et al, 1984). It is formed as preangiotensinogen and loses the signal peptide as it becomes secreted from the cell as angiotensinogen. It functions as a serine protease inhibitor (serpin) similar to $\alpha_1$-antitrypsin and antithrombin III, with which it shares some structural homology (Carrell et al, 1987). It is present in plasma in two forms, a smaller (52- to 60-kD) predominant molecule and a larger (450- to 500-kD) molecule that increases in pregnancy and after estrogen treatment (Tewksbury and Dart, 1982). The larger form is probably composed of the smaller molecule bound to other plasma proteins. Renin acts on the smaller form of angiotensinogen preferentially, cleaving AI off the larger molecule. Renin reacts with much less affinity with the larger form, also forming AI.

**The liver is the primary site of synthesis of angiotensinogen, which is not stored but secreted directly after production.** Angiotensinogen messenger RNA (mRNA) is widely present in several tissues that are regulated by local renin-angiotensin systems, including the central nervous system (CNS), kidney, adrenal, heart, and leukocytes (Dzau et al, 1987). Several hormones stimulate angiotensinogen synthesis by the liver, including estrogens and glucocorticoids. Stressful stimuli such as infection or tissue injury also increase plasma angiotensinogen levels (Hoj Nielsen and Knudsen, 1987). Feedback control through the RAAS is also present, with AII increasing and renin decreasing plasma levels of angiotensinogen.

## Renin

Renin is a single-polypeptide-chain aspartyl protease that is secreted from the juxtaglomerular cells of the afferent arteriole. **The kidney is the major site of renin production,** although renin mRNA is found in several other tissues where a local renin-angiotensin system functions. It is produced as pre-prorenin, and both active renin and prorenin are secreted (Atlas et al, 1980). The function of circulating prorenin is not clear, and it does not appear that prorenin is transformed to active renin in the circulation (Sealey et al, 1977). The action of renin is very specific, restricted to cleavage of a single bond, separating AI from angiotensinogen. Because renin controls the rate-limiting step of the RAAS, control of renin secretion regulates the activity of the RAAS. Several mechanisms affect the secretion of renin, as described in the following sections:

### A—Macula Densa Mechanism

The macula densa region of the thick ascending loop of Henle comes in close proximity to the juxtaglomerular cells and influences renin release. **Reduction of distal tubule salt delivery stimulates renin secretion and vice versa.** Although sodium was initially thought to be responsible for this action, it now appears that the signal for macula densa–controlled renin release is the alteration of tubular chloride concentration (Lorenz et al, 1990).

### B—Baroreceptor Mechanism

The juxtaglomerular cells of the afferent arteriole act as their own baroreceptors by responding directly to stretch of the afferent arteriole (Tobian et al, 1959). **Diminished cell stretch as a result of renal hypoperfusion hyperpolarizes the juxtaglomerular cells, resulting in decreased intracellular calcium and increased renin release.**

### C—Neural Mechanism

**The juxtaglomerular cells are richly innervated by β-adrenergic sympathetic nerve fibers. Stimulation of these β-adrenergic nerves leads to increased renin secretion** (Keeton and Campbell, 1980). Dopamine is also stimulatory to renin release, although the limited number of dopaminergic nerve endings results in a much smaller role (Mizoguchi et al, 1983). Renal nerve stimulation is the mechanism through which renin release is increased as a result of exercise and tilting.

### D—Endocrine and Paracrine Mechanisms

Several local and systemic hormones affect the rate of renin secretion. Foremost among these are prostaglandins. **Prostaglandin E$_2$ and I$_2$ (prostacyclin) as well as exogenously administered arachidonic acid stimulate renin secretion** (Franco-Saenz et al, 1980; Whorton et al, 1980). This prostaglandin effect is independent of the other mechanisms controlling renin release. AII inhibits renin release as a feedback mechanism. Other inhibitors of renin release include endothelin, vasopressin, and atrial natriuretic peptide.

### E—Intracellular Mechanisms

**Agents that increase adenylate cyclase activity increase the secretion of renin, including β-adrenergic agonists, prostaglandin E$_2$,** prostaglandin I$_2$, dopamine, histamine, and parathyroid hormone. This is because cyclic AMP is an important second messenger in renin release. Intracellular calcium concentrations are also important in controlling renin release.

AII, vasopressin, and adenosine increase intracellular calcium levels and inhibit renin secretion through their effect on intracellular calcium levels.

## Angiotensin-Converting Enzyme

ACE is a zinc-containing single-chain glycoprotein enzyme. It is also known as *kininase II* and is a dipeptidyl carboxypeptidase (Ehlers and Riordan, 1989). It splits two amino acids off the carboxy terminus of AI to form AII and, at the same time, functions in the kallikrein-kinin system by inactivating bradykinin. ACE is found in a wide variety of organs, where it is primarily expressed on endothelial, epithelial, and neuroepithelial cells. A high concentration of ACE is found in the kidney, ileum, duodenum, and uterus (Lieberman and Sastre, 1983). **Although pulmonary endothelial ACE was presumed to be the major site of ACE activity for the systemic RAAS, it is now believed that peripheral sites might play an equal role.** The majority of circulating ACE originates from endothelial cells and macrophages.

ACE is expressed in several tissues where local renin-angiotensin systems function. Renal ACE is localized to the glomerular endothelial cells and the proximal tubule brush border, where it might play a role in cleaving filtered protein for reabsorption (Danilov et al, 1987). Within the CNS, ACE is found in several locations, where it functions in the local renin-angiotensin system. This local CNS renin-angiotensin system is thought to have dipsogenic and hypertensive effects as well as to stimulate vasopressin secretion (Strittmatter and Snyder, 1987). Adrenal ACE is found predominantly in the medulla, where it is thought to stimulate catecholamine secretion (Peach et al, 1971). ACE is abundantly found in the testes and prostate, in the Leydig cells, as well as in cytoplasmic droplets in sperm (Pandey et al, 1984; Yotsumoto et al, 1984). In the female reproductive tract, ACE is found in follicular and fallopian tube oocytes (Brentjens et al, 1986). The precise role of ACE in the reproductive system has not been elucidated. Several hormones and disease states affect the level and activity of ACE. Corticosteroids as well as thyroid hormones stimulate ACE activity (Friedland et al, 1978; Smallridge et al, 1983). The serum ACE level is increased in silicosis, primary biliary cirrhosis, and sarcoidosis (Studdy et al, 1983). As mentioned previously, **ACE is not the rate-limiting step in the RAAS cascade, so changes in serum ACE levels do not directly affect the activity of the systemic RAAS (circulating AII levels).**

In addition to ACE, several angiotensinases act in the RAAS to lesser degrees. The physiologic contribution of these enzymes to the function of the RAAS is not clear. Most of these enzymes are present in body tissues such as the kidney. Among these are aminopeptidase A and angiotensinase A, B, and C. Nonspecific angiotensinases hydrolyze AII and angiotensin III (AIII), inactivating them rapidly.

## Angiotensin II

The role of the RAAS in the control of blood pressure and extracellular volume is carried out through the integration of a variety of actions performed by AII. Vasoconstriction and the release of aldosterone occur immediately and are of short duration, supporting the role of AII in maintaining tissue perfusion in hypovolemia. Other actions such as vascular growth and ventricular hypertrophy are slower in onset and longer in duration, lasting for several days or weeks.

## Effect of Angiotensin II on Glomerular Circulation

**One of the most important actions of AII is the autoregulation of the GFR in response to changes in renal perfusion. These are effected through changes in vascular resistance as well as mesangial cell tone.** AII causes a marked increase in efferent arteriolar resistance in cases of renal hypoperfusion but does not affect afferent arteriolar resistance unless there is an increase in renal perfusion pressure. The result of this disproportionate increase in efferent over afferent resistance is an increase in capillary hydraulic pressure, and subsequently in filtration pressure, maintaining the GFR in the presence of decreased renal perfusion (Hall et al, 1977). It is through inhibition of this action that ACE inhibitors result in a decrease in GFR in cases of RAS. This effect of AII on the glomerular circulation is thought to be mediated through differential induction of vasodilatory prostaglandins from the afferent and efferent vessels (Hura and Kunau, 1988).

In addition to its effects on the glomerular vessels, AII directly results in mesangial cell contraction, leading to a decrease in the filtration coefficient of the glomerulus (Blantz et al, 1976).

## Tubular Effects of Angiotensin II

AII-induced increases in the filtration fraction lead to an increase in the oncotic pressure in the postglomerular vessels. This leads to an increase in fluid reabsorption in the proximal tubules. AII receptors are also present on the proximal tubule brush border and basolateral sides, and AII is produced in large amounts locally within the proximal tubules. AII is present within the proximal renal tubule in much higher concentration than in the plasma (Seikaly et al, 1990). **The effect of AII on sodium reabsorption is bimodal; physiologic concentrations of AII stimulate sodium reabsorption in the proximal tubule, whereas higher concentrations inhibit sodium transport** (Harris and Young, 1977).

## Medullary Effects

AII decreases medullary blood flow, leading to increased medullary hypertonicity and concentration of urine (Arendshorst and Finn, 1977).

## Vascular Effects

**AII raises blood pressure by increasing peripheral vascular resistance through a direct effect on vascular smooth muscle cells, causing them to contract.** Medium-sized and small arteries are more responsive to AII than large vessels. Contraction occurs mainly in the vessels of the kidney, skin, mesentery, coronary arteries, and brain. Vessels of the lung and skeletal muscle are less responsive to AII. In addition to vasoconstriction, AII stimulates vascular smooth muscle cell growth, leading to a hypertrophic response (Geisterfer et al, 1988).

## Adrenal Effects

**AII acts directly on the adrenal glomerulosa cells to stimulate aldosterone secretion.** This is accomplished through increased desmolase activity and increased conversion of corticosterone to aldosterone (Aguilera, 1993). This augments the salt reabsorptive actions of AII to conserve sodium.

## Central Nervous System Renin-Angiotensin-Aldosterone System

The CNS is affected mainly by the local renin-angiotensin system, but high circulating levels of AII may also affect CNS function. Central AII results in an increase in blood pressure as well as increased drinking and salt appetite (Sweet et al, 1971; Fitzsimons, 1980). Central AII also leads to increased secretion of corticotropin, prolactin, luteinizing hormone, oxytocin, and vasopressin (Unger et al, 1988).

## Gonadal Renin-Angiotensin-Aldosterone System

Gonadal RAAS is present in both the testis and the ovary. The function of testicular RAAS is not clear; in the ovary, RAAS may play a role in oocyte maturation.

## Angiotensin II Receptor Subtypes

**Nonpeptide receptor antagonists have provided definite proof of at least two major angiotensin receptor subtypes, named AT1 and AT2.** Both receptors are polypeptides containing 360 amino acids spanning the cell membrane several times. They are functionally distinct with a sequence homology of 30%. The gene for the AT1 receptor is located on chromosome 3, and the gene for the AT2 receptor is located on the X chromosome (Goodfriend et al, 1996). AT1 receptors are blocked by DuP 753 (losartan), and AT2 receptors are blocked by tetrahydroimidazopyridines such as PD 123177. AT1 receptors have a higher affinity for AII than AIII, but AT2 receptors bind both AII and AIII equally. AT1 receptors have been further subtyped into two isoforms, AT1A and AT1B, although the function of the subtypes is not clear.

The AT1A receptor is expressed in the liver, kidney, aorta, uterus, adrenals, ovary, spleen, and lung as well as in the hypothalamus. The AT1B receptor is expressed in the pituitary, adrenal, kidney, uterus, and liver and is absent in the heart, brain, and spleen. In fetal life, the AT2 receptor is widely present in the adrenal, kidney, liver, skin, tongue, and brain. In the adult, this distribution becomes restricted to the adrenals, uterus, ovary, heart, and some nuclei in the brain.

In the kidneys, AT1 receptors are located predominantly in the glomeruli and tubulointerstitium, whereas AT2 receptors are located in the large cortical blood vessels (Goldfarb et al, 1994).

**Almost all the vascular effects of AII, including vasoconstriction, aldosterone release, and β-adrenergic stimulation, are mediated by the AT1 receptor** (Timmermans et al, 1992). The development of AT1 receptor antagonists (e.g., losartan) has produced a new class of drugs as well as an effective tool for blocking the RAAS in a variety of disease states including hypertension as well as modulating cardiac and renal injury responses to disease.

**The function of the AT2 receptor has not been fully defined;** however, it may act in a manner antagonistic to the AT1 receptor, especially in the cardiovascular system, where it exerts antiproliferative, antihypertrophic, and proapoptotic functions (Horiuchi et al, 1999). AT2 receptors are also believed to play a crucial role during gestational growth and development, mainly because of the widespread distribution of these receptors in most body tissues during fetal life. Reexpression of these receptors in adult life occurs as a response to vascular injury or inflammation (Horiuchi et al, 1999).

The signal transduction mechanism initiated by binding of AII to the AT1 receptor has been well described; however, the signal transduction mechanism for the AT2 receptor is not yet known. Binding of AII to the AT1 receptor leads to the dissociation of subunits of a guanine nucleotide–binding protein, which activates phospholipase C to generate diacylglycerol and inositol triphosphate. Inositol triphosphate releases calcium from the endoplasmic reticulum, and AII also increases calcium entry through the cell membrane. The intracellular calcium as well as diacylglycerol activate protein kinase C and other enzymes that phosphorylate protein and ultimately regulate the specific cellular function induced by AII (Goodfriend et al, 1996).

## Other Angiotensins

The parent peptide of the angiotensin family is the decapeptide AI. Several other peptides are formed within the RAAS, some of which have weak activity compared with AII and some of which have undetermined activity. As previously mentioned, AII (also called angiotensin 1-8) is the major active peptide in the system; it is an octapeptide formed by the removal of terminal histidine and leucine from the carboxy terminus of AI. AIII (or angiotensin 2-8) is similar to AII but lacks the aspartyl amino acid at the amino end of the polypeptide chain. It can be formed from AII or directly from AI. Angiotensin 1-7 lacks the three amino acids at the carboxy terminus of AI and has undetermined receptor activity. AIV is a hexapeptide lacking the two terminal amino acids at both ends of the AI polypeptide chain (Goodfriend et al, 1996).

The actions of angiotensin 1-7 have been defined. It appears to be formed from AI directly by a different enzyme than ACE, called neprilysin. ACE inhibitors thus increase the levels of circulating angiotensin 1-7. It acts in an opposing fashion to AII, producing vasodilatation and natriuresis, and also has antiproliferative effects on vascular smooth muscle (Chappell and Ferrario, 1999).

## PATHOPHYSIOLOGY OF RENOVASCULAR HYPERTENSION

**The classical experiments on RVH were performed by Goldblatt and colleagues** (1934), who demonstrated that hypertension could be produced by constricting the renal artery in the dog. Two models of experimental Goldblatt hypertension are described: the two-kidney, one-clip (2K,1C) model, in which one renal artery is clipped and the contralateral kidney is in place and normal, and the one-kidney, one-clip (1K,1C)

model, in which one renal artery is clipped and the contralateral kidney is removed. RVH results in both models, but the evolution and the pathophysiologic mechanisms are different. These models provide the basis for understanding the mechanism and evolution of RVH in humans.

## Two-Kidney, One-Clip Model

In the two-kidney, one-clip model, the renal artery to one kidney is clipped, resulting in ischemia of the clipped kidney. The RAAS is activated as a result of renal hypoperfusion, resulting in generalized vasoconstriction and systemic hypertension. The adrenal cortex is also stimulated, resulting in secondary hyperaldosteronism and promoting sodium retention by the stenotic kidney. This is the early phase of RVH and is totally mediated by high circulating levels of AII. The normal contralateral kidney is subjected to higher than normal perfusion pressure and reacts by suppression of renin secretion as well as "pressure" natriuresis, excreting higher than normal levels of sodium and water. Renal vein renin (RVR) from the normal kidney is equal to the arterial value, indicating no secretion by the kidney. In this manner, both kidneys work against each other, with the normal kidney preventing the systemic blood pressure and sodium content from reaching levels high enough to suppress renin release from the stenotic kidney.

**In brief, the two-kidney, one-clip model is characterized by the unilateral release of renin from the ischemic kidney accompanied by contralateral suppression of renin release from the normal kidney, sodium retention by the stenotic kidney, and excretion by the contralateral kidney; euvolemia; and hypertension dependent on AII-induced vasoconstriction. Accordingly, unclipping of the ischemic kidney, ACE inhibitors, or AII antagonists result in a marked decrease in blood pressure.**

## One-Kidney, One-Clip Model

In the one-kidney, one-clip model, one renal artery is clipped and the contralateral kidney is removed. The solitary ischemic kidney secretes renin, activating the RAAS and resulting in systemic hypertension. Owing to the absence of the normal contralateral kidney, pressure natriuresis does not occur, and the stenotic kidney avidly conserves sodium and fluid, producing volume expansion. The elevation of blood pressure, sodium retention, and volume expansion gradually suppress renin release from the ischemic kidney. Accordingly, although the *generating* mechanism of hypertension is similar in both models, **hypertension in the one-kidney, one-clip model is largely *maintained*** by volume and sodium excess, in the presence of normal circulating AII levels. ACE inhibitors or AII antagonists do not result in a marked decrease of blood pressure. Under conditions of sodium depletion, hypertension once again becomes dependent on AII, with a marked response to ACE inhibition.

In addition, both models do not remain static but rather pass through an acute phase, a transitional phase, and then a final chronic phase (Table 36–3). In cases of two-kidney, one-clip hypertension, after several days or weeks a chronic phase is eventually reached in which unclipping of the stenotic kidney fails to normalize blood pressure. In this chronic phase,

| Table 36-3. **Phases of Experimental Renovascular Hypertension** |
| --- |
| *Acute Phase* |
| Renin dependence |
| *Transitional Phase* |
| Progressive volume and sodium retention |
| Gradual onset of secondary hyperaldosteronism |
| Thirst |
| Progressive suppression of renin secretion |
| Progressive decline of contralateral natriuresis |
| *Chronic Phase* |
| Volume expansion |
| Suppressed renin secretion |
| Systemic vasoconstriction |
| Increased sensitivity to angiotensin II |
| Increased vasopressin secretion |
| Increased sympathetic activity |
| Structural vessel wall changes |
| Development of contralateral nephrosclerosis |

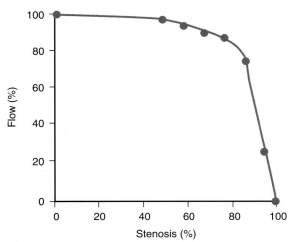

**Figure 36–7.** Relationship between renal artery stenosis and renal blood flow.

the elevated perfusion pressure as well as high levels of AII have resulted in widespread arteriolar damage to the contralateral kidney. The excretory function (natriuresis) of the contralateral kidney declines, resulting in extracellular volume expansion, a decrease in circulating AII levels, and the gradual development of a "volume-dependent" type of hypertension. ACE inhibition or removal of the stenotic kidney fails to cure the hypertension in this phase of the disease unless sodium depletion is instituted. Systemic vasoconstriction continues to play a role in maintaining hypertension in the chronic phase, with increased sensitivity to AII, increased vasopressin secretion, and increased sympathetic nervous system activity.

## HUMAN CORRELATES OF EXPERIMENTAL RENOVASCULAR HYPERTENSION

The situation in cases of human RVH is not as simple as the experimental models, but **in most cases human unilateral RAS resembles the two-kidney, one-clip model.** A similar sequence of events ensues, with activation of the RAAS resulting in hypertension and secondary hyperaldosteronism, sometimes resulting in hypokalemia. Relief of the stenotic lesion by revascularization or nephrectomy has a higher chance of amelioration of hypertension if carried out before the development of a chronic phase in which parenchymal damage in the contralateral kidney maintains the blood pressure elevation.

**Bilateral renal artery stenosis in humans does not clearly follow either experimental model but rather is a mixed picture with some characteristics of each.** In this respect, a beneficial blood pressure response is seen with ACE inhibition, indicating overactivity of the RAAS, and there is also evidence of volume expansion with frequent pulmonary edema as well as diuresis after revascularization. Different reasons for this mixed picture are possible, mainly owing to the asymmetrical development of RAS, starting with unilateral disease and progressing to bilateral disease. Undetermined renal parenchymal damage may occur to the contralateral normal kidney before the onset of bilateral disease as well. Volume

overload would then be exacerbated by the development of bilateral disease.

**The one-kidney, one-clip model clinically resembles cases of stenosis to a solitary functioning kidney, unilateral renal artery stenosis with parenchymal damage to the contralateral kidney (nephrosclerosis or atheroembolism), and transplant renal artery stenosis.**

## PATHOPHYSIOLOGY OF ISCHEMIC NEPHROPATHY

**In addition to RVH, a second, equally important phenomenon resulting from renal artery stenosis is deterioration of renal function, termed** *ischemic nephropathy* (IN). This is a clinical syndrome that occurs through different pathophysiologic mechanisms, is distinct from RVH, and can occur in the absence of elevated blood pressure.

**IN is the result of chronic hypoperfusion of the total functioning renal mass. This occurs in the setting of bilateral severe stenosis or stenosis to a functionally or anatomically solitary kidney.** The pathophysiology of renal injury as a result of chronic ischemia is poorly understood. This injury is not simply cell death related to a lack of oxygen and nutrients because the oxygen demand of the kidney never exceeds the supply. Experiments studying the effects of acute renal ischemia do not lend themselves to the explanation of chronic ischemic injury. For ischemic injury to occur, the reduction in renal blood flow needs to exceed the compensatory ability of the kidneys. Renal autoregulation fails to maintain the GFR when renal perfusion decreases below 70 to 80 mm Hg. This occurs when the luminal diameter of the renal artery is stenosed by more than 70% of the original size. At this point, the stenosis becomes hemodynamically significant, resulting in a gradual deterioration of the GFR with an accompanying rise in the serum creatinine level (Fig. 36-7).

**Critical reduction of renal blood flow results in IN without affecting renal viability because renal blood flow is severalfold higher than blood flow to other organs such as the liver or heart.** This flow rate far exceeds the needs of the kidney for oxygenation but is necessary to drive glomerular filtration. It is estimated that the kidney needs only about 10% of its blood flow to maintain its oxygen requirement. Under conditions of chronic ischemia, collateral circulation to the kidney develops from the adrenal, lumbar, and ureteric vascular beds and can sustain renal viability even in cases of complete occlusion of the renal artery.

**Reduction of renal blood flow activates the RAAS to produce angiotensin II, which maintains glomerular capillary hydrostatic pressure (and GFR) through efferent arteriolar vasoconstriction.** Reduction of renal blood flow also leads to redistribution of blood within the kidney and diminished cortical blood flow to prevent medullary anoxia.

The cellular mechanisms by which a decrease in renal size and IN develop are not well understood. Several mechanisms play a role, including vascular mediators (endothelin, thromboxane, prostacyclin, and nitric oxide), calcium accumulation in or ATP depletion of the ischemic cells, production of oxygen free radicals, or disruption of cellular membrane polarity (Textor, 1994). The exact role played by each of these mechanisms is not well defined. The action of repetitive cycles of hypoperfusion may allow renal injury to continue before repair is complete, whereas a disturbance in cellular repair processes may hinder recovery between these episodes (Textor, 1996). The point at (or mechanism through) which these changes become irreversible after relief of renal ischemia is even more poorly understood.

Although the exact mechanisms through which chronic ischemic injury of the kidneys occur are not clear, the resulting structural changes within the chronically ischemic kidney have been well identified. Tubular changes are usually most prominent, in the form of patchy tubular necrosis and atrophy. Glomeruli decrease in size with wrinkling of the glomerular tuft and thickening of Bowman's capsule. Localized or global glomerular sclerosis is also seen. Hypercellularity of the juxtaglomerular apparatus is commonly seen. Blood vessels show the effects of comorbid conditions, such as essential hypertension, diabetes, and hyperlipidemia, with arteriolar thickening and hyalinosis.

## Atheroembolism (Cholesterol Embolism)

**Renal cholesterol embolism occurs most commonly in older hypertensive patients, with severe abdominal aortic ASO as the most common associated underlying cause, and contributes significantly to renal dysfunction in cases of IN** (Vidt et al, 1989). Atheroembolism can occur spontaneously but more commonly follows manipulation of the atherosclerotic aorta by surgery, angiography, or the use of thrombolytic agents. In a review of 221 cases of cholesterol embolism, 69% were spontaneous, and an inciting event precipitated embolism in 31%. Renal manifestations were present in 50% of cases, and the mortality rate was 81% (Fine et al, 1987).

Atheromatous fragments lodged in blood vessels are highly thrombogenic, leading to occlusion of the vessels in which they lodge, and at the same time an inflammatory reaction and fibrosis are incited. Cholesterol crystals can remain histologically detectable in blood vessels for up to 9 months after the event. Diagnosis of atheroembolism is made by examina-

tion of biopsy samples from the affected tissue, most commonly skin, muscle, or kidney. Cholesterol microemboli are seen within the renal vasculature (needle-shaped cholesterol crystals, which appear birefringent on frozen section and are dissolved by the solvents used in permanent sections leaving empty cholesterol clefts) and generally portend a poorer prognosis. In a study of 44 patients from the Cleveland Clinic, findings reflective of atheroembolism were identified on intraoperative biopsy of 16 patients (36%) at the time of open surgical renal revascularization. Patients with atheroembolism had a significantly decreased 5-year survival (54% versus 85%) compared with patients who did not exhibit histologic evidence of atheroembolism. Patients with atheroembolism had a significantly higher incidence of postoperative atherosclerotic complications as well as renal and renovascular complications (Krishnamurthi et al, 1999).

The organs most commonly affected by atheroembolism are the kidney, spleen, pancreas, and gastrointestinal tract. Virtually all organs can be affected, however, leading to multisystem organ disease. Cutaneous manifestations are the most common extrarenal manifestation, in the form of livedo reticularis (lacy bluish discoloration affecting the lower extremities), digital cyanosis or gangrene, ulceration, or subcutaneous nodules. Retinal emboli (Hollenhorst's plaque) can occur, leading to visual symptoms, or can be silent.

**Renal affection takes the form of deteriorating renal function, usually after a precipitating event. Decline of renal function can vary in severity from mild to rapid acute renal failure.** Gradual improvement in renal function occurs after the event, but recurrent episodes lead to progressive loss of renal function with time (Siemons et al, 1987). Symptoms of renal involvement are usually absent, but new-onset hypertension or worsening of preexisting hypertension may occur.

A preventive approach to atheroembolism entails avoiding unnecessary or rough manipulation of atherosclerotic vessels as well as avoiding prolonged anticoagulation in patients at risk for developing atheroemboli. **Management of cholesterol embolism is supportive, with removal of the inciting trauma if present, cessation of anticoagulation, control of hypertension, and institution of renal replacement therapy as needed.** Increased awareness of this condition has led to early diagnosis and institution of aggressive supportive care, resulting in a decline in mortality from the disease. A 1999 study of intensive multiorgan support for 67 patients reported a mortality rate of only 16%, with 32% of the survivors requiring long-term dialysis therapy (Belenfant et al, 1999).

## CLINICAL FEATURES OF RENOVASCULAR HYPERTENSION

Although RVH is the most common correctable cause of secondary hypertension (with the exception of hypertension related to oral contraceptive use), the prevalence of RVH is probably less than 1% for patients with mild or moderate hypertension (Lewin et al, 1985). For this reason, before subjecting patients to numerous diagnostic procedures that are potentially invasive and costly, enough clinical suspicion needs to be generated to prevent unnecessary investigations of patients with essential hypertension. Patients with RAS may also present with renal impairment (IN) in the presence or absence of RVH.

## Clinical Clues

Symptoms suggestive of RVH are rare, with the exception of flank pain related to segmental infarction or arterial dissection and generalized nonspecific symptoms in cases of Takayasu's arteritis. The clinical course of hypertension, however, may be suggestive of a renovascular cause.

**The age at presentation is a clue. The onset of hypertension before the age of 30 years or after the age of 55 years is more commonly associated with renovascular disease, typically FD in young patients and ASO in those older than 55 years.** In the Cooperative Study for Renovascular Hypertension, the average age at the onset of essential hypertension was 35 years; for hypertension secondary to FD, the average age of onset was 33 years, and for atherosclerotic renal artery stenosis (ASO-RAS), the average age of onset was 46 years (Maxwell et al, 1972).

**A family history of hypertension** suggests essential hypertension, although there are reports of familial fibromuscular disease of the renal arteries, especially in females (Major et al, 1977; Pannier-Moreau et al, 1997).

**Sudden onset and shorter duration of hypertension** are usually associated with RVH; they may also be associated with a better chance of cure after treatment.

**Hypertension that is difficult to control** with two or three medications is more likely to be associated with renovascular disease. A sudden increase in severity or difficulty of control of previous mild or well-controlled hypertension is also suggestive of the development of RVH on top of preexisting essential hypertension.

**Accelerated, malignant hypertension or hypertensive crises** are more frequently associated with RVH than essential hypertension (Simon et al, 1972).

**Hypertension associated with episodes of pulmonary edema, evidence of generalized atherosclerotic disease, or gradual impairment of renal function** is also suggestive of RVH.

**Smoking** is a risk factor for developing atherosclerotic disease. In a retrospective study comparing patients with documented RVH with patients with essential hypertension, 88% of patients with ASO-RAS were smokers, compared with 42% of patients with essential hypertension. Patients with FD also showed a higher incidence of smoking (71%) (Nicholson et al, 1983).

On physical examination, clues suggestive of RVH include severe hypertension, the presence of an upper abdominal or epigastric bruit (with both systolic and diastolic components), severe hypertensive retinopathy (grade III or IV), and evidence of generalized ASO.

## Laboratory Investigations

The presence of mild *proteinuria* is not uncommon in RVH; however, nephrotic-range proteinuria has also been described with RVH (Kumar and Shapiro, 1980; Chen et al, 1995) and has been reversed by renal revascularization (Zimbler et al, 1987). Apart from renal artery disease, proteinuria

may be the result of coexisting disease such as diabetes or glomerulosclerosis.

**Azotemia** in the presence of generalized ASO with or without the presence of hypertension is strongly suggestive of a renal arterial cause.

**Hypokalemia** (serum potassium level 3.4 mEq/L) especially in the absence of diuretic use is strongly suggestive of RVH resulting in secondary hyperaldosteronism. In the Cooperative Study for Renovascular Hypertension, 16% of patients with RVH were found to have hypokalemia (Maxwell et al, 1972).

## CLINICAL FEATURES OF ISCHEMIC NEPHROPATHY
### Epidemiologic Considerations

**Epidemiologic studies indicate that atherosclerotic renal artery disease is quite common in patients with generalized atherosclerosis obliterans, regardless of whether RVH is present.** These studies have involved renal angiography in patients with a documented abdominal aortic aneurysm, aorto-occlusive disease, or lower extremity occlusive disease. In such patients, the overall incidence of ARAS has ranged from 31% to 61%, with significant (>50%) ARAS present in 14% to 42% of patients (Table 36–4). In a detailed study by Olin and colleagues (1990), significant ARAS was present in 41 of 108 patients (38%) with an abdominal aortic aneurysm, 7 of 21 patients (33%) with aorto-occlusive disease, and 74 of 189 patients (39%) with lower extremity occlusive disease.

Other studies have evaluated the prevalence of atherosclerotic renal artery disease in patients with coronary artery disease by obtaining abdominal aortography at the time of coronary angiography. Vetrovec and colleagues (1989) noted significant (>50%) ARAS in 22 of 76 patients (29%) with coronary artery disease. In a much larger study, Harding and associates (1992) found significant (>50%) ARAS in 164 of 817 patients (20%) with coronary artery disease. In the latter study, the prevalence of significant ARAS was greater in patients with more severe coronary artery disease; significant ARAS was present in 29% of patients with three-vessel disease and in 39% of patients with left-main disease. More recently, the Mayo Clinic group (Rihal et al, 2002) reported a 19% incidence of greater than 50% stenosis, 7% greater than 70% stenosis, and 3.7% bilateral stenosis in 297 hypertensive

**Table 36–4. Prevalence of Atherosclerotic Renal Artery Stenosis in Patients with Peripheral Vascular Disease**

| Study | Patients (N) | No. with 50% ARAS | No. with >50% ARAS |
|---|---|---|---|
| Choudhri et al, 1990 | 100 | 17(17%) | 42 (42%) |
| Wilms et al, 1990 | 100 | NA | 22 (22%) |
| Olin et al, 1990 | 318 | 71 (22%) | 122 (38%) |
| Salmon & Brown, 1990 | 374 | 64 (17%) | 52 (14%) |
| Swartbol et al, 1992 | 450 | 117 (26%) | 104 (23%) |
| Valentine et al, 1993 | 98 | 36 (37%) | 24 (24%) |
| Missouris et al, 1994 | 127 | 22 (17%) | 35 (28%) |

ARAS, atherosclerotic renal artery stenosis; NA, not available.

patients undergoing coronary angiography. Similar results were reported by Aqel and colleagues (2003) in a smaller group of 90 veterans with hypertension. A 16% incidence of severe stenosis and 6% incidence of bilateral disease was reported in this study. None of these studies reported an increase in complications related to the addition of abdominal angiography to coronary angiography. This would present a logical rationale for screening the renal arteries in patients with risk factors such as peripheral vascular disease, renal insufficiency, and hypertension.

In a large population-based study of nonselected subjects, Hansen and colleagues (2002) screened 870 patients for RAS using duplex ultrasonography. An overall prevalence of 6.8% was noted, with 12% having bilateral disease, and stenosis was associated with hypertension, advancing age, and elevated low-density lipoprotein.

**Another study has shown an increased prevalence of ARAS in patients with diabetes mellitus.** Sawicki and colleagues (1991) evaluated 5194 consecutive autopsy protocols from patients who died between 1980 and 1988. Significant (>50%) ARAS was present in 4.3% of all patients but in 8.3% of all diabetic patients; all but one of the latter had type 2 diabetes mellitus. Bilateral ARAS was found in 30% of the nondiabetic patients with ARAS but in 43% of diabetic patients with ARAS. These data suggest that the presence of type 2 diabetes increases the risk of ARAS and that the latter is more likely to involve both kidneys.

These studies show that **ARAS is commonly present in patients with generalized atherosclerosis, particularly those with peripheral vascular disease or coronary artery disease. Although hypertension is also commonly present in such older patients with ARAS, it is far more likely to be idiopathic (essential) than renovascular in origin. Therefore, the prevalence of anatomic ARAS is much greater than that of atherosclerotic RVH.**

## Screening and Diagnosis

The screening of patients for atherosclerotic renal artery disease is based in part on an early study by Gifford and associates (1965). These investigators found that in 53 of 75 older patients (71%) with unilateral renal atrophy, the renal atrophy was caused by stenosing atherosclerotic renal artery disease. Of equal importance was the finding that 22 of these 53 patients (42%) also had unsuspected atherosclerotic renal artery disease involving the opposite, normal-sized kidney. Subsequently, Lawrie and associates (1980) reviewed 40 patients with renal atrophy caused by total arterial occlusion and noted contralateral ARAS in 31 patients (78%). **These observations underscore the high incidence of renal artery disease, often bilateral, in patients with generalized atherosclerosis and diminished renal size. The additional finding of even mild azotemia in this setting further enhances the likelihood that underlying large vessel occlusive disease is present.**

Harding and associates (1992) evaluated clinical variables associated with ARAS in a study of 1235 patients undergoing simultaneous cardiac catheterization and abdominal aortography. **A multivariate logistic-regression analysis identified the following five risk factors as strongly predictive of significant ARAS: higher age, coronary artery disease, a history**

of congestive heart failure, female gender, and peripheral vascular disease. An elevated serum creatinine level was also predictive of ARAS by univariate logistic-regression analysis. Hypertension was not helpful in identifying patients with ARAS.

**Another important clinical clue to the presence of significant ARAS is the development of progressive azotemia after medical control of the blood pressure in patients with significant hypertension.** This problem strongly suggests the presence of perfusion-dependent renal function related to significant underlying renal artery obstruction (Textor et al, 1983). In addition to reducing flow across a stenotic renal artery by lowering the systemic blood pressure, antihypertensive medications can impair renal function in such patients through other mechanisms. β-Adrenergic blockers produce a fall in cardiac output, which may occasionally diminish effective renal plasma flow and the GFR. ACE inhibitors can lead to deterioration of renal function through loss of efferent arteriolar vasoconstrictor tone in the kidney (Hricik et al, 1983).

Finally, **atherosclerotic renal artery disease should also be suspected in older patients with renal insufficiency and no obvious cause for the latter.** Corradi and associates (1993) obtained renal angiography in 51 consecutive patients with the following criteria: age older than 60 years, creatinine clearance less than 50 mL/min, no analgesic abuse, proteinuria less than 1 g/day, clinical signs of generalized ASO, and no biochemical or radiographic findings indicative of glomerulopathy, diabetic nephropathy, polycystic disease, obstructive nephropathy, or pyelonephritis. Angiographic studies revealed significant RAS in 29 patients (56.8%); RAS was present bilaterally in 10 patients (19.6%) and unilaterally in 19 patients (37.2%).

The studies described indicate that clinical screening for atherosclerotic renal artery disease is appropriate in older patients with most or all of the following features: (1) evidence of generalized ASO; (2) a decrease in the size of one or both kidneys; (3) renal insufficiency, even of a mild extent, particularly in patients with no obvious underlying cause; (4) the development of progressive azotemia after restoration of normotension with medical antihypertensive therapy; (5) coronary artery disease; (6) a history of congestive heart failure; and (7) peripheral vascular disease. It should be emphasized that **patients with atherosclerotic renal artery disease may or may not have significant hypertension, and this should not influence the decision to investigate the patient for this disease.**

## DIAGNOSTIC EVALUATION

Several noninvasive studies are available to diagnose RAS. Most of these studies are intended for hypertensive patients, aiming to identify patients with a renovascular cause of hypertension. Among these studies are rapid-sequence intravenous (IV) urography, ultrasonography, peripheral renin activity assays, captopril testing, and radionuclide renal scanning (with and without ACE inhibition). A variety of modern noninvasive tests have become available and have largely superseded the previously mentioned tests; these are duplex ultrasonography (DUS), magnetic resonance angiography (MRA), and computed tomography angiography (CTA). These tests offer anatomic information only, with no functional information. **The definitive diagnosis of RAS, however, is documented by angiographic study of the aorta and renal vessels, which remains the "gold standard" against which all other diagnostic modalities are compared.**

Diagnostic evaluation for patients presenting with suspected RVH differs from that for patients presenting with suspected IN. **For patients with suspected RVH, a number of tests are available for functional diagnosis of RVH. These tests (plasma renin activity [PRA], captopril test, captopril renography, and RVR assays) diagnose hyperactivity of the RAAS but provide no anatomic information regarding the offending arterial lesion.** Captopril renography and RVR assays can localize the ischemic kidney as well. Anatomic delineation of the arterial lesion guides the treatment decisions and is obtained by intra-arterial angiography. A variety of noninvasive anatomic studies (DUS, MRA, and spiral CTA) can be used before angiography in cases in which clinical suspicion of RVH is not confirmed by functional tests.

The pathophysiology of RVH is different and distinct from that of IN. The diagnostic evaluation of patients with suspected IN is hampered by the lack of functional tests and the inability to determine conclusively that an anatomic lesion in the renal artery is responsible for impairment of renal function. Noninvasive anatomic testing is used to confirm a clinical suspicion of RAS, which is definitively diagnosed by intra-arterial angiography. Stabilization or improvement of renal function after revascularization remains the final proof of the cause, provided that ischemic damage to the kidney has not become irreversible.

## Intravenous Urogram

Until better methods were developed, a modification of the standard IV urogram, called the hypertensive, rapid-sequence, or minute-sequence urogram, was used as a screening test for RVH. Several findings are suggestive of RVH, including a delayed appearance of contrast material in the calyces of the affected kidney (most important), disparity of renal size of more than 1.5 cm (most common finding), delayed hyperconcentration of contrast material within the affected collecting system, retention of contrast material in a nonobstructed collecting system, and notching of the pelvicalyceal system by collateral vessels.

**The poor sensitivity and specificity of the rapid-sequence urogram and the development of multiple other more sensitive diagnostic tests have led to the discontinuation of its use for diagnosing renovascular disease.**

## Peripheral Plasma Renin Activity

Measurement of peripheral PRA is a functional test designed to diagnose overactivity of the RAAS. Originally intended as a screening test for RVH, it provides no anatomic information and has no value for diagnosing IN. In order to obtain meaningful results from this test, all antihypertensive medications should be discontinued for 2 weeks, and the PRA should be indexed to the sodium intake. Blood should be collected at noon after 4 hours of the patient's ambulation. When the test is standardized as mentioned, a sensitivity and specificity of 80% and 84%, respectively, can be expected (Pickering et al, 1984).

**Important limitations of this test have restricted its general use. Sixteen percent of patients with essential hypertension have elevated PRA, whereas up to 20% of patients with RVH have normal PRA** (Brunner et al, 1972). In addition, discontinuation of all antihypertensive medication in a population of patients with severe, sometimes life-threatening hypertension is not generally feasible.

## Captopril Test

**Measurement of peripheral PRA before and after an oral dose of captopril is called the *captopril test*.** This is a functional test of RVH that does not provide anatomic information. The test is based on the observation that after the administration of ACE inhibitors, patients with RVH show a higher reactionary rise of PRA than patients with essential hypertension (Case and Laragh, 1979). Patients may continue to take $\beta$ blockers, but all diuretics and ACE inhibitors need to be discontinued for at least 1 week before the test. A normal- or high-salt diet is needed. Blood should be drawn with the patient in the same position before and after captopril administration, after measurements of blood pressure are stable. An oral dose of 25 mg of captopril is used, and blood is drawn again 1 hour after the dose.

Criteria for a positive test are the presence of all the following: postcaptopril PRA greater than 12 ng/mL/hr, an absolute increase in PRA greater than 10 ng/mL/hr, and a 400% increase in baseline PRA (150% increase if the baseline PRA was more than 3 ng/mL/hr) (Muller et al, 1986). The test is generally safe, with the main risk being an excessive fall of blood pressure in hyperreninemic patients who are also volume depleted. Overall sensitivity is about 74% and specificity is around 89% (Pickering et al, 1996). **The test is not reliable in patients who are azotemic, nor is it sufficiently accurate for use in children** (Gauthier et al, 1991).

**The low sensitivity of the captopril test makes it not suitable for use as a general screening test for RVH.** The major strength of the captopril test is its accuracy in excluding RVH, especially in patients with low clinical suspicion. The high negative predictive value (approximately 95%) of captopril testing has been confirmed in several studies (Gosse et al, 1989; Svetkey et al, 1989; Frederickson et al, 1990).

## Renal Vein Renins

**The primary criterion for the functional diagnosis of RVH is hypersecretion of renin from the ischemic kidney combined with contralateral suppression of renin secretion.** Calculation of net renin secretion from any kidney is performed by subtracting the renin value in the arterial blood to the kidney (inflow) from the renin value in the venous blood from the kidney (outflow). Because renin values in both the aorta and the inferior vena cava (IVC) are the same, IVC renin is used instead of aortic renin (Sealey et al, 1973). RVR assays are useful for localizing the ischemic kidney in unilateral RAS as well as the more ischemic kidney in bilateral cases. A moderate sodium intake should be maintained at the time of the sampling, which is usually performed with the patient in the supine position. Blood samples from both renal veins as well as from the IVC are obtained.

Hypersecretion of renin from the ischemic kidney (>50% of PRA) confirms the diagnosis of RVH. Contralateral suppression of renin secretion (renal vein − IVC renin = 0) indicates an appropriate response of the normal contralateral kidney to the elevated blood pressure and predicts a cure of hypertension after revascularization. Increasing severity of stenosis reduces blood flow to the ischemic kidney, resulting in an increased RVR increment (after subtracting IVC renin) higher than 50% of the total peripheral PRA (Vaughan et al, 1973). In patients with high PRA and RVR failing to show an increment above 50% from both kidneys, sampling from segmental renal veins may be performed to localize the segment of kidney responsible for hypersecretion of renin (Schambelan et al, 1974). Administration of captopril results in accentuation of renin secretion from the ischemic kidney (similar to the captopril test), resulting in increased accuracy in diagnosing RVH (Simon and Coleman, 1994). This is particularly useful when RVR values are equivocal, in cases of branch stenosis, and in cases of coexisting hypertension or renal disease.

## Captopril Renography

**Radionuclide renography without ACE inhibition has limited use for the functional or anatomic diagnosis of renovascular disease. The physiologic principle of captopril renography is the loss of preferential vasoconstriction of the efferent arteriole that is mediated by AII and maintains the glomerular pressure gradient in cases of RAS. This loss of postglomerular pressure results in a decreased GFR of the kidney distal to the stenosis, which is measured noninvasively by radionuclide renography.**

The study is performed in well-hydrated patients with liberal salt intake. ACE inhibitors are discontinued for 3 to 5 days before the study, but other antihypertensives may be continued (Setaro et al, 1991). Oral hydration is continued on the day of the procedure. Oral captopril (25 to 50 mg) is usually used, although IV enalapril (0.04 mg/kg) can be used as well (Sfakianakis and Sfakianakis, 1988). The captopril renogram is obtained 1 hour after the captopril dose. The use of furosemide has also been suggested to improve the accuracy of ACE renography (Erbsloh-Moller et al, 1991).

Considerable debate continues around the optimal radionuclide agent to use for captopril renography. The most commonly used agents are technetium 99m ($^{99m}$Tc) diethylenetriaminepentaacetic acid (DTPA) and orthoiodohippurate (OIH) I 131, with the addition of $^{99m}$Tc mercaptoacetyltriglycine (MAG3). The imaging characteristics of $^{99m}$Tc compounds are better than those of iodine 131 ($^{131}$I) compounds. On the other hand, OIH and MAG3 are excreted by both glomerular filtration and tubular secretion, whereas DTPA is excreted by glomerular filtration only, making it less optimal for patients with renal dysfunction. To date, $^{99m}$Tc-MAG3 has shown the best results for captopril renography, especially in patients with impaired renal function (Dondi, 1991). Studies have shown that $^{99m}$Tc ethylenedicysteine (EC) can be used as an imaging agent for captopril renography to diagnose RVH and predict the outcome of revascularization (Ugur et al, 1999).

Captopril renographic diagnostic criteria have not been well standardized. The following are the criteria suggested by the Consensus Panel on Captopril Renography (Nally et al, 1991). Two categories of information are used: asymmetry of renal size and function, as suggested by the scintigraphic images, and specific captopril-induced changes in the renogram. These changes on the postcaptopril renogram include a delayed time to maximal activity (>11 minutes), significant asymmetry of peak activity of each kidney, marked cortical retention of radionuclide, and a marked decrease in the GFR of the ipsilateral kidney. For radionuclides with tubular excretion ($^{131}$I-OIH and $^{99m}$Tc-MAG3), the ratio of 20-minute counts to peak counts can also be used. Normally less than 0.3, a 0.15 change is considered significant. A small poorly functioning (30%) kidney that shows no change after ACE inhibition, as well as bilateral symmetrical change after ACE inhibition, is considered to be moderately indicative of RVH (Taylor et al, 1998).

The use of AT1 receptor antagonists for hypertension does not preclude the use of captopril renography as a diagnostic test. In a study comparing captopril renography in patients using AT1 receptor antagonists and hypertensive control subjects, Picciotto and colleagues (2003) found equally accurate results in both groups.

**Overall, the sensitivity of captopril renography appears to be approximately 90% to 93%, and the specificity approximately 93% to 98%** (if the test is used in patients with a strong clinical suspicion). More important, captopril renography is predictive of a cure or improvement in blood pressure after revascularization in 80% to 90% of cases (Nally, 1996). The presence of bilateral RAS, RAS to a solitary kidney, or impaired renal function (serum creatinine level >2.5 to 3 mg/dL) decreases the accuracy of captopril renography.

## Duplex Ultrasonography

DUS of the renal arteries is a noninvasive anatomic study that has shown an excellent ability to diagnose RAS. It combines the use of real-time B-mode renal ultrasonography with color-coded pulsed Doppler to obtain blood flow velocities within the major abdominal vessels. Flow velocity at the renal hilum and inside the renal parenchyma can be measured as well. **The basis for diagnosing renal artery stenosis is the altered flow pattern distal to the stenosis, with a turbulent jet during systole and a decrease in diastolic flow.** Measurements are obtained at the proximal main renal artery using a standardized angle of incidence, and several indices as well as waveform analysis are used to diagnose stenosis. More than 180 cm/sec **peak systolic velocity (PSV) in the renal artery** is indicative of RAS (normal renal PSV averages 100 ± 25 cm/sec). PSV has been found to be the most important single indicator of RAS (Miralles et al, 1996). The ratio of the renal PSV to the aortic PSV (renal PSV/aortic PSV) is called the *renal aortic ratio* (RAR). A ratio of 3.5 or more indicates severe (>60%) stenosis. The use of the RAR is not possible in cases of aortic occlusive or aneurysmal disease because of the abnormal aortic flow patterns in these situations. Measurement of the flow patterns within the distal hilar renal artery branches as well as within the parenchyma can be analyzed to provide indices indicative of arterial stenosis or increased renovascular resistance (Nazzal et al, 1997; Riehl et al, 1997). These indices (acceleration time, acceleration index, resistive index) have not proved as universally reliable as the aforementioned (PSV, RAR) measurement. Intraluminal ultrasonography has also been used to measure flow rate directly within the renal artery (van der Hulst et al, 1996; Chavan et al, 1998), and this has been useful to evaluate the flow rate before and after angioplasty (Savader et al, 1998).

**Diagnostic categories obtained by DUS include normal, mild stenosis (60%), severe stenosis (>60%), and technically unsatisfactory study (unable to visualize the renal arteries).** Renal artery occlusion is indirectly diagnosed by the findings of a small kidney and the inability to detect a renal artery flow pattern.

**DUS offers significant advantages as a diagnostic tool for RAS. It is noninvasive, uses portable equipment that is relatively inexpensive and widely available, does not use iodinated contrast material, and has no effect on renal function. Azotemia does not affect the results of the study, and no discontinuation of antihypertensive medications is required.**

The main disadvantage of DUS is its dependence on operator skill, with less reliable results obtained from less experienced vascular laboratories. In obese patients and patients with a great deal of bowel gas, the renal arteries may be difficult to visualize. Accessory renal arteries are difficult to visualize, and occluded renal arteries cannot be diagnosed with certainty. Finally, DUS offers anatomic data with no indication of the functional significance of the lesion.

In a prospective study comparing DUS with angiography in 102 patients, DUS was found to have a sensitivity and specificity of 98%, correctly identifying the lesions in 182 of 187 arteries with different degrees of stenosis (Olin et al, 1995). In another prospective study involving 41 patients, DUS (compared with angiography) revealed a sensitivity of 95% and a specificity of 90% (Strandness, 1994). In a more recent prospective study evaluating 53 patients with both DUS and angiography, a DUS sensitivity of only 75% was reported, with 103 (of 112) arteries and 12 (of 16) stenoses detected by DUS. Specificity for detecting RAS was 100% (Mollo et al, 1997).

In a study using slightly different diagnostic criteria (PSV > 210 cm/sec) and evaluating 46 patients, the sensitivity and specificity of DUS were 89.5% and 90.7%, respectively. Of note is that in the same study, only 23 patients were hypertensive, and captopril renography was positive in only 5 cases (Miralles et al, 1993). The superior utility of DUS over captopril renography reported in this study was not validated in a later study prospectively comparing both DUS and captopril renography with angiography in 28 patients. After 11 (of 45) renal arteries were excluded from the study because no Doppler signal could be obtained, the accuracy of both diagnostic modalities was comparable, with a sensitivity and specificity for DUS and captopril renography of 78% and 81%, and 83% and 81%, respectively (Kaplan-Pavlovcic and Nadja, 1998).

Continuous developments in equipment and techniques of DUS are occurring and promise increased accuracy and utility. Among these developments are the use of power Doppler imaging, three-dimensional imaging, harmonic imaging, and ultrasonic contrast agents. Power Doppler imaging is more sensitive, especially in the detection of low flow rates (Murphy and Rubin, 1997). Three-dimensional imaging uses computer technology to produce a three-dimensional image of the region of interest. Harmonic imaging also improves the imaging of structures that might be moving, such as the proximal renal arteries. The use of biodegradable microbubbles in the circulation increases the echogenicity and enhances the visualization of the renal vessels (Missouris et al, 1996).

## Magnetic Resonance Angiography

MRA is a modern noninvasive anatomic diagnostic modality that has become available for diagnosing RAS. The techniques used for MRA are time of flight and phase contrast. Gadolinium DTPA enhances the blood signal, resulting in improved images of the aorta and the proximal renal arteries. **MRA has the advantage of being noninvasive, not using radiation, having a low technical failure rate, and not using iodinated contrast material, which latter factor makes the technique suitable for use in patients with renal insufficiency** (Ghantous et al, 1999). Multiple projections can be obtained, and the morphology of the kidney can be evaluated as well. Functional information, including individual renal blood flow and GFR, can also be obtained (Grist, 1994).

**MRA provides an image quality that is inferior to that of angiographic images. Only the proximal parts of the main renal arteries are visualized without the ability to image the distal arterial tree. MRA is contraindicated in patients with magnetic implants and claustrophobia,** and it uses sophisticated, expensive equipment that might not be widely available.

MRA was compared with intra-arterial angiography in 103 patients, all of whom had both studies performed. When MRA was used, all main renal arteries and 31 of 33 accessory renal arteries were visualized, and 61 of 65 stenoses were diagnosed and graded correctly. The overall sensitivity was 93% and the specificity was 90% (Hany et al, 1998). Another study evaluated 62 patients with both MRA and angiography (Thornton et al, 1999). MRA had a sensitivity of 88% and a specificity of 98% and visualized 93% of all the arteries seen on angiography. The reproducibility of interpretation and interobserver variability of MRA were found to be comparable to those of conventional angiography in 54 patients who underwent both diagnostic procedures (Gilfeather et al, 1999).

A prospective study compared gadolinium-enhanced MRA with color DUS in 45 patients, and the results of both examinations were referenced to angiography in all cases (De Cobelli et al, 2000). Of 13 accessory renal arteries detected by digital subtraction angiography (DSA), 12 were detected by MRA and only 3 were detected by DUS. The sensitivity and specificity of MRA were 94% and 91% for diagnosing all degrees of stenosis, whereas the sensitivity and specificity of DUS were 71% and 76%. For the detection of stenoses of more than 50%, the corresponding values were 93% and 95% for MRA, compared with 93% and 89% for DUS. Another group (Leung et al, 1999) compared the two modalities (and referenced results to DSA studies) and reported similar results, with slightly better sensitivity and specificity for MRA (90% and 86%) compared with DUS (81% and 87%). This study also confirmed the superior ability of MRA over DUS in detecting accessory renal arteries (96% versus 5%). MRA was more sensitive in detecting RAS related to ASO than in detecting RAS caused by FD, according to this study; this could be related to the more distal nature of most FD lesions. MRA can also diagnose renal artery aneurysms, and is useful to follow the size of renal artery aneurysms over time, although aneurysms distal to the primary branches of the renal artery are not well visualized on MRA (Browne et al, 2004).

Improving techniques and increasing experience with MRA continue to increase its accuracy and utility. The use of time-resolved imaging to decrease artifacts, decrease venous overlap, and improve spatial resolution and contrast enhancement has been reported (van Hoe et al, 2000). Gadolinium has been administered intra-arterially in vitro in an attempt to improve visualization of blood vessels (Omary et al, 1999). The multiecho gradient echo technique for three-dimensional MRA has been reported to produce high vessel-to-background contrast with decreased bowel-related artifact (Papachristopoulos et al, 1999).

## Computed Tomography Angiography

The availability of spiral CT technology with rapid acquisition time has made possible imaging of the renal arteries. Scanning through the area of the renal arteries using thin (2-mm) slices during the arterial phase of contrast material injection is performed while the patient holds a single breath. Three-dimensional reconstruction of the axial image is then carried out, showing the abdominal aorta with its main branches. Atherosclerotic disease affecting the aorta and the renal arteries can be visualized, as well as renal morphology and parenchymal lesions. **Spiral CTA lacks the ability to define disease distal to the main stem renal artery, and a relatively large volume of IV iodinated contrast material is required to perform the study;** however, CTA might offer the advantages over MRA of cost, convenience, and widespread availability (Prokop, 1998).

Comparison between CTA and DSA in 82 patients revealed a sensitivity and specificity of 96% and 99%, respectively, for hemodynamically significant stenosis, with only 1 stenosis (of 34) missed on CTA. Thirty-three accessory renal arteries were visualized in this study, as well as 5 adrenal masses (Wittenberg et al, 1999). In another study evaluating 50 patients with suspected RAS, CTA showed a sensitivity of 90% and a specificity of 97% and demonstrated 27 of 28 accessory renal arteries (Kim et al, 1998). Modern CT technology can also be utilized to perform virtual endoscopy, which can be helpful for evaluating renal artery stenoses and positioning arterial stents (Neri et al, 2000). Multiple detector-row CTA is a new method of CTA that also promises more accurate depiction of the renal and other visceral arteries (Pannu and Fishman, 2002; Fleischmann, 2003).

In order to clarify the various limitations of noninvasive imaging modalities in respect to accessory renal arteries as well as proximal branches of the renal artery, a study compared DUS, CTA, and MRA with angiography. The points of comparison were the ability to evaluate accessory renal arteries and proximal branches. Fifty-six patients underwent angiography; of those patients, 45 underwent DUS, 52 underwent CTA, and 28 underwent MRA. When angiography was used, 28 accessory renal arteries as well as 21 proximal (>2 cm from the aorta) renal artery branches were visualized. DUS depicted 21% of the accessory arteries and 0% of the proximal branches. MRA depicted 73% of the accessory arteries (and four additional arteries not seen on angiography) and 0% of the proximal branches. CTA depicted 92% of the accessory arteries and 76% of the proximal branches. Although

experience with modalities differs among institutions, this study offers an interesting comparison of the limitations of these techniques (Halpern et al, 1999).

In a more recent study comparing MRA against CTA with intra-arterial DSA as the reference standard, there was no significant difference in the accuracy of both MRA and CTA, with sensitivity around 92% and specificity around 99% for both modalities. Acceptance by patients was also measured and estimated to be best for CTA, although the time consumed for reconstruction of the images was most in CTA (Willmann et al, 2003).

## Contrast Arteriography

**Intra-arterial angiography remains the gold standard for diagnosing renal artery disease, and it is the test against which the results of other tests are compared.** The availability of modern interventional techniques (angioplasty and arterial stents) has allowed angiography to become a combined diagnostic and therapeutic procedure. However, for several reasons, angiography is not suitable for use as a preliminary screening tool for all patients suspected of having RAS. It is an expensive test that cannot be done on an outpatient basis. It is also an invasive test utilizing ionizing radiation and requiring arterial puncture, manipulation of arterial catheters, and injection of iodinated contrast material.

Complications of arterial puncture and manipulation include bleeding, hematoma, dissection, thrombosis, and distal embolization of atherosclerotic plaque as well as cholesterol embolization. The use of iodinated contrast material carries the risk of allergic reaction and volume overload. The contrast load also leads to a transient impairment of renal function, especially in patients with preexisting renal insufficiency and in diabetic patients. Several advances in the field of angiography have been directed at decreasing side effects from iodinated contrast material. These advances include decreasing the contrast load through digital postprocessing as well as the use of contrast agents with decreased nephrotoxicity such as carbon dioxide or gadodiamide (Spinosa et al, 1999).

Conventional angiography uses conventional cut film and large volumes of contrast material as well as larger catheters to deliver the contrast volume. The advent of DSA has allowed reduction of the contrast load with a concomitant reduction in catheter size. Although the spatial resolution of DSA is lower than that of conventional angiography, the contrast resolution of DSA is superior. The ability to subtract bone and soft tissue with DSA is an important advantage, making DSA the most commonly used technique today.

Early in the development of digital techniques, it was suggested that IV studies (IV-DSA) would be accurate and supersede the arterial approach (Wilms et al, 1986). The attraction of visualizing the renal arteries angiographically with an outpatient procedure was not realized, however. Several disadvantages led to the gradual abandonment of IV-DSA in favor of intra-arterial studies. These disadvantages include the need for a large contrast material volume, the frequent need for central venous catheters to deliver this large volume, poor image quality owing to overlying visceral arteries, frequent uninterpretable studies, and poor opacification, especially in elderly patients or those with cardiac dysfunction (Buonocore et al, 1981; Smith et al, 1982).

**Carbon dioxide has been introduced as a contrast agent for intra-arterial injection in an effort to reduce contrast nephrotoxicity from iodinated contrast material.** An injected bolus of carbon dioxide displaces blood from the vessels to be imaged and provides sufficient contrast for adequate imaging using DSA technology and postprocessing enhancement. The injected carbon dioxide is cleared by the lungs without deleterious effects. Carbon dioxide has no effect on renal function, making it an ideal agent for use in patients with renal insufficiency. It is nonallergenic, is cheap, and presents no problems with fluid overload. Smaller, softer arterial catheters can be used for injection, minimizing trauma to the arterial walls. This technique can also provide information that is not visualized using standard iodinated contrast material, including small arteriovenous shunts, small tumor vessels, and minute amounts of arterial bleeding (Hawkins et al, 1994).

In a prospective study comparing carbon dioxide angiography with standard contrast arteriography in 100 patients, the overall accuracy of carbon dioxide DSA was 97% (Schreier et al, 1996). Carbon dioxide DSA was successfully used for guiding angioplasty and renal artery stenting in 17 patients in another study with only one transient rise in the serum creatinine level (Caridi et al, 1999). Similarly, no cases of contrast nephropathy were reported in a study employing carbon dioxide DSA as the main imaging technique for patients with renal impairment (Fitridge et al, 1999). Carbon dioxide renal angiography has been used safely in children (Kriss et al, 1997). Although carbon dioxide is generally regarded as a benign contrast medium, a case of fatal complications (rhabdomyolysis and intestinal infarction) after carbon dioxide angiography has been reported (Rundback et al, 1997).

Ailawadi and colleagues (2003) evaluated the use of gadolinium as a contrast agent for intra-arterial angiography in patients with renal insufficiency and found it to be safe and adequate for imaging the renal arteries as well as first- and second-order branches. No comparison with conventional contrast angiography was performed, but this might be an option to decrease nephrotoxic side effects of angiography.

## COST-EFFECTIVE APPROACH FOR DIAGNOSIS

The diagnostic approach for patients with RAS should be tailored according to the predominant clinical picture; that is, patients with IN should be worked up differently from patients with hypertension as the presenting clinical problem. As mentioned previously, **patients with IN constitute the majority of patients presenting for treatment today, may not have hypertension as part of the clinical picture, and cannot be diagnosed by functional testing. In these patients, an anatomic diagnosis is pursued directly.** Patients with a strong suspicion of renal arterial disease should probably undergo intra-arterial angiography (iodinated contrast material or carbon dioxide) directly. Patients with mild or moderate suspicion of having RAS should undergo a noninvasive anatomic test (DUS, MRA, or CTA). The choice of diagnostic procedure depends on the patient's level of renal function (azotemic patients more suitable for DUS than CTA) as well as the experience with the various modalities at different centers. Positive

findings on noninvasive testing should lead to definitive confirmation of the lesion and therapeutic planning through intra-arterial angiography. Negative findings on these tests should be interpreted with understanding of the limitations of each technique and should lead to further noninvasive testing if technical factors are suspected or to no further testing if a technically perfect study is clearly negative in a patient with minimal clinical suspicion.

**Patients with suspected RVH present a different diagnostic challenge. Functional evaluation of the RAAS is possible and is usually performed as a first step in the diagnosis before anatomic diagnosis.** The steps used to screen and select patients for further study differ according to different centers and have changed over the years, mainly owing to the introduction of reliable noninvasive anatomic imaging techniques.

Patients should be stratified according to the clinical findings suspicious for RVH into patients with low, moderate, and high suspicion. Like patients with IN, patients with a high suspicion for RVH are probably best served by performing angiography directly. Negative findings on other studies would not prevent these patients from progressing to angiography in any case. In bilateral cases, RVR assays can be used to localize the more ischemic side.

Patients with low or moderate suspicion of RVH are more problematic. In these cases, it is probably reasonable to perform captopril renography as a preliminary test. A positive test should be followed by further testing, preferably definitive diagnosis through angiography. Patients with low clinical suspicion and a technically satisfactory negative study should not be subjected to further testing. Technically unsatisfactory studies should probably be followed by a noninvasive test of a different type (e.g., DUS). These tests (DUS, MRA, or CTA) provide no functional information or prediction of cure after intervention. To date, anatomic confirmation of the disease and treatment planning still require intra-arterial angiography.

**The role of renin assays has decreased significantly since the 1980s.** Few centers use the captopril test to exclude patients from having RVH because of its consistently high negative predictive value. RVR assays are rarely used to diagnose RVH before a noninvasive test indicates the anatomic presence of stenosis; their role has focused on localizing the more ischemic kidney in bilateral cases.

## SELECTION OF PATIENTS FOR SURGICAL OR ENDOVASCULAR THERAPY
### Renovascular Hypertension

In patients with RVH secondary to FD, the decision for intervention (surgery or angioplasty) is guided by the specific type of disease as determined by angiographic findings and the associated natural history (Novick et al, 1996). **Medical management of hypertension is the preferred initial treatment for patients with medial fibroplasia because loss of renal function from progressive obstruction is uncommon with this disease. Interventive treatment** in the latter category is reserved for patients whose blood pressure is difficult to control with multiple drugs. Conversely, RAS secondary to intimal or perimedial fibroplasia generally progresses and often eventuates in ischemic renal atrophy. Furthermore, these lesions tend to occur in younger patients and to cause hypertension that is extremely difficult to control. Early interventional therapy in these patients is therefore indicated both to preserve renal function and to minimize the need for long-term antihypertensive medication.

In selecting patients with FD for surgical renal revascularization, the efficacy of percutaneous transluminal angioplasty (PTA) must also be considered. **The results of angioplasty for FD of the main renal artery have been excellent** and equal to those obtained with surgical revascularization; therefore, angioplasty is the initial treatment of choice in such cases. However, as many as 30% of patients with FD have branch renal arterial involvement, which increases the technical difficulty of, and often precludes, angioplasty. Therefore, surgical renal revascularization is the primary interventional treatment in this category.

**In patients with atherosclerotic RVH, more vigorous attempts at medical management are warranted** because these patients are older and often have extrarenal vascular disease. Therefore, multiple-drug regimens that control the blood pressure are often the preferred approach. Indeed, the advent of new β-blocking agents and converting enzyme inhibitors has enhanced the efficacy of medical antihypertensive therapy. Intervention with surgery or endovascular therapy is best reserved for patients whose hypertension cannot be adequately controlled or when renal function is threatened by advanced vascular disease (Novick et al, 1996).

## Ischemic Nephropathy

### Anatomic Severity and Extent of Renal Artery Disease

**After angiographic diagnosis of ARAS,** and with knowledge of the natural history of this disease, one can identify the patients in whom such disease poses a significant threat to overall renal function. This designation applies to patients with high-grade (>75%) arterial stenosis affecting their entire renal mass, namely, where such stenosis is present bilaterally or involves a solitary kidney (Fig. 36–8). In these patients, the risk of complete renal arterial occlusion is significant, and if this occurs, the clinical outcome is a critical decrease in functioning renal mass with resulting renal failure. Intervention to restore normal renal arterial blood flow is indicated in such patients for the purpose of preserving renal function. In a study from the Cleveland Clinic (Novick et al, 1987), surgical revascularization for preservation of renal function was performed in 161 patients with ARAS bilaterally or in a solitary kidney. Postoperatively, renal function was improved in 93 patients (58%), stable in 50 patients (31%), and deteriorated in only 18 patients (11%).

**The benefit of undertaking revascularization for the preservation of renal function in patients with unilateral ARAS and an unobstructed contralateral renal artery is not established.** If the contralateral kidney is anatomically and functionally normal, revascularization for this purpose is clearly not warranted. If the opposite kidney is functioning but involved with some type of parenchymal disorder, revascularization of the ischemic kidney may benefit some

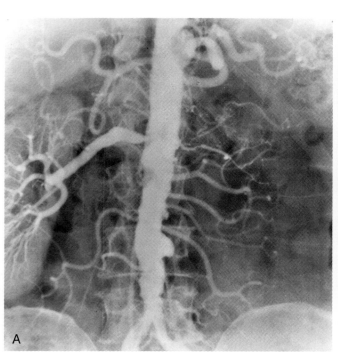
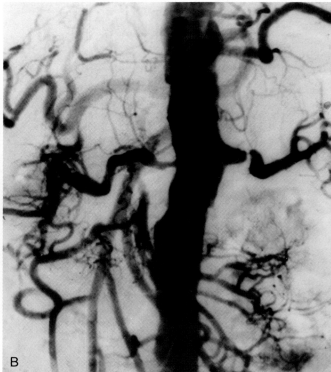

**Figure 36–8.** Atherosclerotic renal artery disease poses the greatest threat to overall renal function in patients with high-grade arterial stenosis to a solitary (right) kidney (**A**) and bilateral high-grade renal artery stenosis (**B**), as demonstrated on these abdominal aortograms.

patients, but specific indications for this approach are not well defined. Dean and associates (1991) reviewed the renal functional outcome after surgical revascularization in 53 patients with IN. The postoperative estimated GFR was improved significantly in 41 patients treated for bilateral ARAS but was unaltered in 12 patients with unilateral ARAS.

**Complete occlusion of the renal artery most often eventuates in irreversible ischemic damage of the involved kidney. However, in some patients with gradual arterial occlusion, the viability of the kidney can be maintained through the development of a collateral arterial supply** (Morris et al, 1956; Zinman and Libertino, 1977; Schefft et al, 1980). Helpful clinical clues suggesting renal salvability in such cases include (1) angiographic demonstration of retrograde filling of the distal renal arterial tree by collateral vessels on the side of total arterial occlusion (Fig. 36–9), (2) a renal biopsy showing well-preserved glomeruli, (3) kidney size greater than 9 cm, and (4) function of the involved kidney on isotope renography or IV pyelography. When such criteria are present, restoration of normal renal arterial flow can lead to recovery of renal function.

### Level of Renal Function

**In general, revascularization to preserve renal function in patients with ARAS is most likely to be beneficial in those who have not yet sustained severe, permanent impairment of overall renal function.** In a study from the Cleveland Clinic (Bedoya et al, 1989), we evaluated the effect of baseline renal function on the outcome of surgical revascularization in elderly patients with ARAS. The majority of these patients had preoperative serum creatinine levels of less than 3 mg/dL; postoperative renal function was stable or improved in 89% of patients in this category.

**Revascularization to preserve renal function is generally not worthwhile in patients with severe azotemia (serum creatinine level >4 mg/dL)** because advanced underlying renal parenchymal disease is inevitably present and obviates improvement in renal function with restored perfusion. This

observation has been recorded by several groups including our own (Mercier et al, 1990; Chaikof et al, 1994). Severe nephrosclerosis is the most common form of renal parenchymal disease in such patients; however, renal cholesterol embolization may be an additional complicating feature (Fig. 36–10) (Vidt et al, 1989). In patients with atherosclerotic ischemic renal disease and a serum creatinine level greater than 4 mg/dL, our policy is to perform a renal biopsy to evaluate the severity of renal parenchymal involvement from one or both of these disorders.

Some patients present with severe impairment of overall renal function that has developed acutely after the initiation of medical antihypertensive therapy (Hricik et al, 1983; Textor et al, 1983). Such rapidly progressive renal insufficiency may be a manifestation of perfusion-dependent renal function related to underlying ARAS. If this problem is detected promptly, renal function often improves after discontinuation of the offending antihypertensive medications. Intervention to relieve renal arterial obstruction can prevent permanent renal damage in patients with this type of severe acute renal insufficiency.

**In addition to the absolute level of renal function, the rate of decline in overall renal function is an important determinant of the outcome after intervention in atherosclerotic ischemic renal disease.** In a study by Dean and associates (1991), patients with a rapid rate of deterioration in estimated GFR during the 6 months preceding surgical revascularization achieved the greatest benefit in terms of postoperative improvement of estimated GFR. Unfortunately, their data precluded definition of a critical rate of decline in estimated GFR that would predict retrieval of renal function by revascularization. Nevertheless, rapid deterioration of overall renal function in association with ARAS suggests a strong possibility of retrieval of function by intervention to restore normal renal arterial flow.

**Occasional patients with ESRD from IN have been encountered in whom renal function has been salvable with revascularization** (Wasser et al, 1981; Kaylor et al, 1989). The basis for this has been the presence of chronic bilateral total renal arterial occlusion in which, fortuitously, the viability of one or both kidneys has been maintained through collateral vascular supply. In such cases, revascularization can yield dramatic recovery of renal function (Fig. 36–11). Unfortunately, this clinical presentation is rare, and a less favorable outcome

### ISCHEMIC NEPHROPATHY

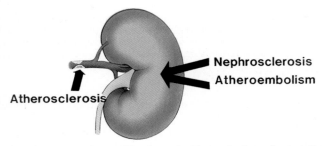

**Figure 36–10.** Patients with atherosclerotic renal artery disease often have renal parenchymal involvement with varied degrees of nephrosclerosis or atheroembolic disease.

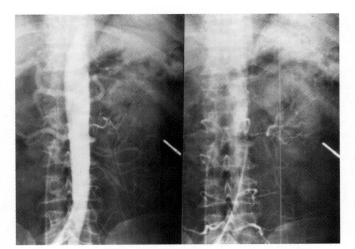

**Figure 36–9.** Abdominal aortograms reveal complete occlusion of the left renal artery *(left)* with filling of the distal renal artery branches from an extensive collateral supply on delayed film *(right)*.

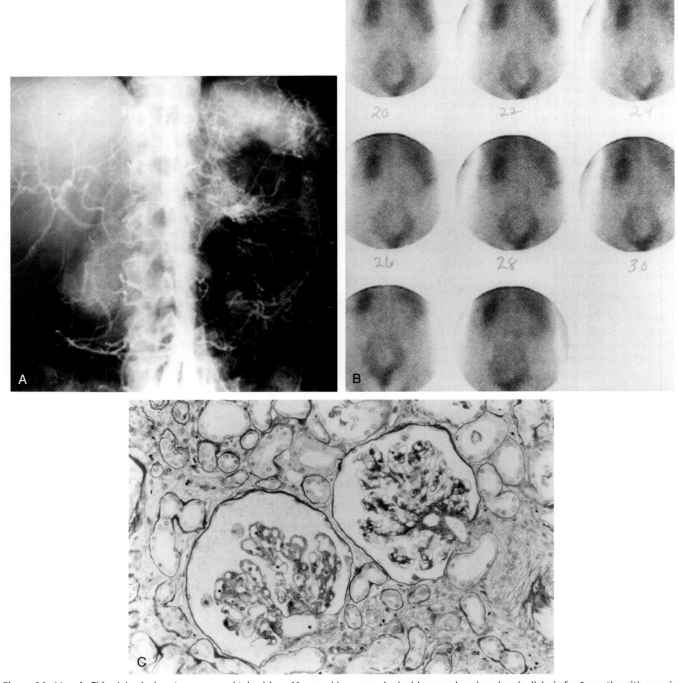

**Figure 36–11.** **A,** This abdominal aortogram was obtained in a 60-year-old woman who had been undergoing chronic dialysis for 9 months with no urine output. The aortogram shows complete bilateral renal artery occlusion with evidence of collateral vascular supply to the left kidney. **B,** Technetium renal scan confirms blood flow to the left kidney *(left)* from collateral supply. **C,** Left renal biopsy shows hypoperfused but viable glomerular tissue, indicating a salvageable kidney. Left renal revascularization led to recovery of renal function and discontinuation of dialysis in this patient.

of bilateral arterial occlusion on renal viability is far more common.

We reported nine patients with ESRD caused by atherosclerotic renal artery occlusion who underwent surgical revascularization with subsequent recovery of renal function (Kaylor et al, 1989). The duration of dialysis preoperatively ranged from 1 to 13 months. In all cases, renal viability was being maintained by collateral vascular supply. Postoperatively, renal function improved immediately, and no patient required subsequent dialysis. Excellent overall rehabilitation was achieved in all patients. Six patients were alive at a mean interval of 4 years postoperatively and with satisfactory renal function (mean serum creatinine level of 2.7 mg/dL). Three patients died at a mean interval of 6.8 years postoperatively, and they all maintained satisfactory renal function (mean serum creatinine level of 3 mg/dL) until death. Although some patients with ESRD caused by atherosclerotic arterial occlusion can be salvaged in this manner, in most such cases irreversible loss of renal function has occurred. Therefore, the most effective approach is to relieve arterial obstruction before the development of ESRD.

Finally, it is important to emphasize that **patients with ESRD and ARAS without complete occlusion are not appropriate candidates for revascularization to restore function.** In such cases, main renal arterial blood flow is preserved, albeit at a reduced level, yet the supplied renal parenchyma is without function. The basis for this is the presence of severe unalterable parenchymal damage that precludes recovery of renal function with improved perfusion.

### Renal Histopathology

Evaluation of renal histopathology can help to determine the presence of salvable renal function in selected patients with atherosclerotic renal ischemic disease. **In patients with ARAS and severe existing impairment of overall renal function (serum creatinine level >4 mg/dL),** renal biopsy findings can help to predict whether revascularization is likely to forestall further progressive renal insufficiency. In patients with atherosclerotic renal artery occlusion, renal biopsy findings can indicate whether the involved kidney is viable and functionally salvageable on the basis of collateral vascular supply. The two predominant morphologic lesions in such patients are arteriolar nephrosclerosis and atheroembolic renal disease, with the former more often encountered. Both these diagnoses can be established on a frozen section histopathologic examination, and, therefore, the renal biopsy can be done at the same time as surgical revascularization, if the biopsy findings are favorable. In patients with arteriolar nephrosclerosis, the most important favorable criterion is histologic evidence that a majority of examined glomeruli are intact and viable (Zinman et al, 1977; Schefft et al, 1980). Histologic findings of tubular atrophy, interstitial fibrosis, and arteriolar sclerosis are of lesser importance and do not necessarily preclude recovery of renal function; these findings may merely reflect the histologic changes of chronic reversible renal ischemia. However, the finding of widespread glomerular hyalinization indicates irreversible ischemic renal injury that obviates any benefit from relief of renal arterial obstruction (Fig. 36–12A). The finding of extensive atheroembolic disease would also preclude renal revascularization (see Fig. 36–12B). With respect to the technique for renal biopsy in such patients, a more representative specimen of renal tissue is obtained with an open surgical wedge biopsy than with a closed needle biopsy.

## SURGICAL REVASCULARIZATION
### Preoperative Preparation

When surgical revascularization is indicated for renal artery disease, it is important to define accurately the general medical condition of the patient because this will determine the risk of undertaking a major vascular operation. Most patients with

renal arterial FD are young and otherwise healthy, and the operative risk is minimal in this group (Novick, 1994a). **In patients with atherosclerotic renovascular disease, the preoperative evaluation should include a thorough search for coronary artery disease because this has been the leading cause of operative death after surgical revascularization.** In our program, in addition to a careful history, a physical examination, and an ECG, a thallium cardiac stress test is done on all operative candidates in this category. If any of these assessments suggest the presence of coronary artery disease, our policy is to perform coronary cineangiography and left-sided ventriculography. Myocardial revascularization is recommended for patients with significant correctable coronary artery disease before renal revascularization (Novick et al, 1981).

**Cerebrovascular accident has also been a significant cause of death after renal revascularization in patients with atherosclerosis,** albeit a less common complication than myocardial infarction. The approach to patients whose history or examination suggests extracranial cerebrovascular disease is analogous to that employed for patients with suspected coronary artery disease. In such patients, carotid arteriography is obtained preoperatively, and if significant occlusive disease is found, endarterectomy is recommended before renal revascularization (Novick et al, 1981).

In patients with generalized ASO and renal artery disease, cardiac function is often compromised to various degrees. In these patients, hypertension increases the workload on the left ventricle, which decreases cardiac reserve and renders the heart less efficient. In addition to having an impaired myocardium, these patients often have a decreased intravascular volume because of prior treatment with diuretic agents. These patients can benefit from a careful hemodynamic assessment in an intensive care unit for 12 to 24 hours before surgical revascularization. In the intensive care unit, Swan-Ganz arterial and urethral catheters are placed for measurement of blood pressure, pulmonary capillary wedge pressure, pulmonary artery pressure, cardiac output, total peripheral resistance, and urinary output. While these parameters are being monitored, IV vasodilators can be administered to control the blood pressure and decrease the cardiac afterload while the intravascular space is carefully expanded with isotonic fluid. Afterload reduction and fluid repletion in this manner optimize perioperative cardiac function by increasing cardiac output and decreasing cardiac work. This approach can enhance the safety of surgical renal revascularization in patients with generalized ASO.

## Operative Techniques

Advances in both surgical renovascular reconstruction and medical antihypertensive therapy have limited the role of total or partial nephrectomy in the management of patients with renal artery disease. These operations are only occasionally indicated in patients with severe arteriolar nephrosclerosis, severe renal atrophy, uncorrectable renovascular lesions, and renal infarction.

A variety of surgical revascularization techniques are available for treating patients with significant renal artery disease. **Aortorenal bypass with a free graft of autogenous**

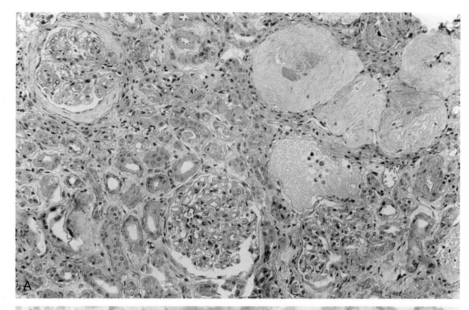

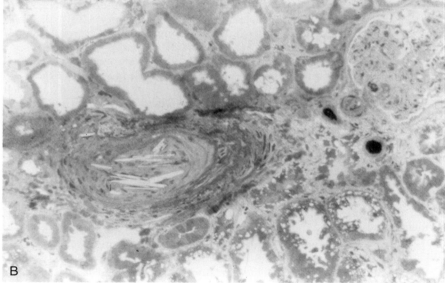

**Figure 36–12.** **A,** Light microscopic findings on biopsy of a kidney with total arterial occlusion demonstrate extensive glomerular hyalinization, which precludes any benefit from revascularization. **B,** Biopsy of a kidney in another patient demonstrates atheroembolic disease.

**hypogastric artery or saphenous vein remains a popular method in patients with a healthy abdominal aorta.** Polytetrafluoroethylene aortorenal bypass grafts have been successfully employed by some authors, usually when an autogenous graft is not available. Renal endarterectomy also continues to be utilized occasionally to treat atherosclerotic renal artery disease. Patients with complex branch renal artery lesions are managed with extracorporeal microvascular reconstruction and autotransplantation.

In older patients, **severe atherosclerosis of the abdominal aorta may render an aortorenal bypass or endarterectomy technically difficult and potentially hazardous to perform.** In such cases, several authors prefer alternative surgical approaches that allow renal revascularization to be safely and effectively accomplished while avoiding operation on a badly diseased aorta. The most effective alternative bypass techniques have been a splenorenal bypass for left renal revascu-

larization and a hepatorenal bypass for right renal revascularization. The absence of occlusive disease involving the origin of the celiac artery is an important prerequisite for these operations. A 1995 study indicated the presence of significant celiac artery stenosis in 50% or more of patients with ARAS (Fergany et al, 1995). This information underscores the importance of obtaining preoperative lateral aortography to evaluate the celiac artery origin in patients who are being considered for hepatorenal or splenorenal bypass.

**Use of the supraceliac or lower thoracic aorta for renal revascularization is a more recent surgical alternative in patients with significant atherosclerosis of the abdominal aorta and its major visceral branches.** The supraceliac aorta is often relatively disease free in such patients and can be used to achieve renovascular reconstruction with an interposition saphenous vein graft. Simultaneous aortic replacement and renal revascularization have been associated with an increased risk of operative mortality, and this approach is best reserved for patients with a fixed indication for aortic replacement such as a significant aortic aneurysm or symptomatic aortoiliac occlusive disease.

## Results

Reports from several centers indicate that the techniques described previously for surgical renovascular reconstruction can be safely performed with a high technical success rate. **Patients with FD are usually otherwise healthy, and operative morbidity and mortality after revascularization in this group have been minimal** (Novick et al, 1987; Hansen et al, 1992). Operative mortality rates of 2.1% (Novick et al, 1987), 3.1% (Hansen et al, 1992), 3.4% (Bredenberg et al, 1992), and 6.1% (Libertino et al, 1992) have been reported after surgical revascularization in patients with atherosclerotic renal artery disease. An increased risk of operative mortality has been observed with bilateral simultaneous renal revascularization (Hallett et al, 1987) or when renal revascularization is performed in conjunction with another major vascular operation such as aortic replacement (Lawrie et al, 1989). Most studies have indicated a high technical success rate for surgical vascular reconstruction with postoperative thrombosis or stenosis rates of less than 10% (Novick et al, 1987; Van Bockel et al, 1987; Libertino et al, 1992).

In a retrospective study from the Cleveland Clinic, Tsoukas and colleagues (2001) evaluated the results of simultaneous aortic and renal revascularization and reported a 13% postoperative mortality rate for bilateral renal revascularization versus 7% for patients with unilateral renal revascularization when both are performed simultaneously with aortic replacement. The 5-year survival rate for patients with preoperative serum creatinine greater than 2 mg/dL was 53% compared with 85% for patients with lower creatinine. The authors recommend adjunctive use of endovascular techniques to decrease the magnitude of the surgical procedure for patients with concomitant aortic and bilateral renal artery atherosclerotic disease.

**In evaluating the results of surgical revascularization for RVH,** most studies have considered patients to be cured if the blood pressure is 140/90 mm Hg or less postoperatively. Patients have been considered to be improved if they have either shown a reduction in diastolic pressure of 10 to 15 mm Hg or more or become normotensive with medication. Failures have been those who have not qualified for either of the aforementioned categories. The results of surgical treatment for RVH vary according to the underlying pathologic diagnosis. In patients with FD, 50% to 60% are cured, 30% to 40% are improved, and the failure rate is less than 10% (Novick et al, 1987; Hansen et al, 1992). In patients undergoing revascularization for atherosclerotic RVH (Table 36–5), the failure rate is approximately the same; however, fewer patients are cured and more patients are improved postoperatively. The explanation for this is that RVH is often superimposed on existing essential hypertension in older patients. A study by Van Bockel and colleagues (1987) highlighted the excellent long-term results after reconstructive surgery for atherosclerotic RVH; with a mean follow-up of 8.9 years, postoperative hypertension was cured or improved in 83 of 105 patients (79%).

### Table 36–5. Results of Surgical Revascularization for Atherosclerotic Renovascular Hypertension

| Series | Patients (N) | No. Cured | No. Improved | No. Failed |
|---|---|---|---|---|
| Van Bockel et al, 1987 | 105 | 19 (18%) | 64 (61%) | 22 (21%) |
| Novick et al, 1987 | 180 | 55 (31%) | 110 (61%) | 15 (8%) |
| Libertino et al, 1988 | 86 | 38 (44%) | 44 (51%) | 4 (5%) |
| Hansen et al, 1992 | 152 | 22 (15%) | 116 (75%) | 14 (10%) |

### Table 36–6. Results of Surgical Revascularization for Atherosclerotic Ischemic Nephropathy

| Series | Patients (N) | No. Improved | No. Stable | No. Deteriorated |
|---|---|---|---|---|
| Novick et al, 1987 | 161 | 93 (58%) | 50 (31%) | 18 (11%) |
| Hallett et al, 1987 | 91 | 20 (22%) | 48 (53%) | 23 (25%) |
| Hansen et al, 1992 | 70 | 34 (49%) | 25 (36%) | 11 (15%) |
| Bredenberg et al, 1992 | 40 | 22 (55%) | 10 (25%) | 8 (20%) |
| Libertino et al, 1992 | 91 | 45 (49%) | 31 (35%) | 15 (16%) |

During the past 15 years, **more centers have been performing surgical revascularization to preserve renal function in patients with high-grade atherosclerotic arterial occlusive disease affecting both kidneys or a solitary kidney.** These are generally older patients with diffuse ASO, ostial renal artery lesions, and varied degrees of renal functional impairment. Studies from several centers (Table 36–6) have indicated improvement or stabilization of renal function postoperatively in 75% to 89% of patients. Considering the significant risks of progressive occlusive disease and renal failure that have been associated with medical management of such patients, these results demonstrate a favorable influence of revascularization on the natural history of untreated atherosclerotic renal artery disease.

We have reviewed the contemporary experience at the Cleveland Clinic with surgical renal revascularization employing an extra-anatomic bypass operation between 1980 and 1992 (Fergany et al, 1995). A total of 175 operations were done including hepatorenal bypass ($n = 59$), splenorenal bypass ($n = 54$), iliorenal bypass ($n = 37$), thoracic aortorenal bypass ($n = 23$), renal autotransplantation ($n = 1$), and superior mesenterorenal bypass ($n = 1$). There were five operative deaths (2.9%) and seven cases of postoperative graft thrombosis (4%). All patients with poorly controlled hypertension were cured or improved postoperatively. Among patients with IN, postoperative renal function improved in 35%, remained stable in 47%, and deteriorated in 18%. These extra-anatomic techniques have become an important component of the surgical armamentarium for ARAS.

In another study, we analyzed long-term clinical outcomes and survival after surgical revascularization for ARAS in 222 patients treated from 1974 to 1987 at the Cleveland Clinic (Steinbach et al, 1997). The indications for surgical revascularization were treatment of hypertension in 60 patients, preservation of renal function in 12 patients, and both control of hypertension and preservation of renal function in 148 patients. The mean postoperative follow-up interval was 7.4 years.

In this study, there were five operative deaths (2.2%) and postoperative thrombosis or stenosis of the repaired renal artery occurred in 16 patients (7.3%). Long-term improvement or stabilization of renal function was achieved in 71.3% of patients. Actuarial 5- and 10-year survivals for the entire series from the time of revascularization were 81% and 53%, respectively. The expected 5- and 10-year survivals for a comparable healthy population are 89% and 77%, respectively. Using a multivariate analysis, factors correlating with diminished long-term survival were age older than 60 years ($P$ = .002), coronary artery disease ($P$ = .031), and previous vascular operations ($P$ = .001). These data support the long-term therapeutic efficacy of surgical revascularization in patients with ARAS. The merits of newer forms of therapy, such as PTA and endovascular stenting, must ultimately be weighed against these results.

Cherr and colleagues (2002) reported on the results of surgical revascularization in 500 patients with atherosclerotic renal artery disease from 1987 to 1999. Unilateral surgery was performed in 40%, bilateral in 60%, and combined aortic and renal surgery in 41%. Mortality rate was 4.6% overall. Hypertension was cured, improved, and unchanged in 12%, 73%, and 15%, respectively. Renal function was improved in 43%, unchanged in 47%, and deteriorated in 10%.

The results of renal autotransplantation for RAS caused by various pathologies (fibromuscular dysplasia [FMD], ASO, and Takayasu's arteritis) were reported by Chiche and coauthors (2003). Results of surgery were better in the FMD patients, with early or delayed nephrectomy performed in five of eight patients with ASO. Hypertension was cured or improved in 96% of patients with FMD and 89% of patients with Takayasu's disease.

## Secondary Renal Revascularization

Relatively few reports have addressed the management of patients with recurrent RAS after failed surgical revascularization or PTA. For patients in the latter category, repeated PTA may be attempted; however, ultimately, many of these patients require surgical revascularization. **There has been controversy concerning whether the prior performance of PTA increases the technical difficulty or compromises the outcome of surgical renal revascularization.** A report by Dean and associates (1987) indicated that the task of arterial reconstruction may be rendered more complicated by a perivascular inflammatory response induced by PTA. Reports from McCann and colleagues (1988) and Martinez and coworkers (1990) found that surgical revascularization is not more technically difficult after PTA than when done primarily and that the same satisfactory results can be achieved. The latter study comprised 53 patients treated surgically after failed PTA for RAS. Three patients underwent nephrectomy because of the finding of a nonviable kidney at operation. Successful surgical revascularization was achieved in all the remaining 50 patients. The authors noted no significant fibrosis or inflammation around the previously dilated renal artery. PTA necessitated the performance of a more complicated revascularization operation in only one patient. These data indicate that if the kidney is viable at operation, prior performance of PTA does not increase the technical difficulty of surgical renovascular reconstruction.

**Recurrent renal artery stenosis after surgical revascularization is typically a late complication, occurring weeks, months, or even years postoperatively.** If the involved kidney is functionally salvable, another attempt to restore normal renal arterial flow is indicated. There has been scant experience with PTA or stenting in this setting; however, this is an appropriate initial approach for focal stenotic lesions. Secondary surgical revascularization has constituted the predominant reported approach, and this may be technically complicated (Stanley et al, 1985; Erturk et al, 1989). Reoperation often entails dissection in a surgical field obliterated by fibrous scar tissue, and it is most efficacious to employ a secondary reconstructive technique that avoids the site of previous surgery. In patients with recurrent RAS after an abdominal aortorenal bypass, alternative approaches that may be used for secondary revascularization include hepatorenal bypass, splenorenal bypass, thoracic aortorenal bypass, iliorenal bypass, and renal autotransplantation.

## PERCUTANEOUS TRANSLUMINAL ANGIOPLASTY

Percutaneous dilatation of arterial stenoses (angioplasty) was originally introduced by Dotter and Judkins in 1964; however, their technique of using coaxial catheters of increasing diameter was limited to the femoral and popliteal arteries and did not gain wide acceptance. It was the development of the balloon catheter by Gruntzig and colleagues in 1978 that permitted the widespread use of angioplasty for dilatation of the renal, coronary, and almost all other visceral arteries. Numerous modifications have been made to the original technique since its introduction, and there are currently several approaches to performing renal PTA.

## Technique

All angioplasty techniques require a high-quality angiogram before dilatation in order to delineate the lesion accurately and allow assessment of proper equipment needs and approach. A proper-sized balloon should be selected to correspond to the original diameter of the renal artery as measured on the angiogram. Because there is 15% to 20% magnification on the angiogram, the result is the intentional overdilatation of the renal artery by 1 mm. Progress of angioplasty is monitored as the balloon inflates, and a postdilatation angiogram is obtained to assess the results and diagnose complications. PTA should be performed only when a skilled vascular surgeon is immediately available in case inadvertent occlusion or disruption of the renal artery creates a surgical emergency.

The original Gruntzig coaxial technique utilizes a No. 8 or 9 Fr renal guiding catheter through which a No. 4.3 or 4.5 Fr balloon catheter is passed over a guide wire traversing the stenotic segment through a femoral arterial puncture. In selected circumstances, an axillary approach may be used. Modification of the original technique and balloon catheters have allowed the use of a No. 5 Fr femoral artery puncture through which a No. 5 Fr diagnostic catheter is passed to the renal artery using the Seldinger technique. After the lesion is negotiated with an appropriate guide wire, the diagnostic catheter is exchanged with a No. 5 Fr balloon catheter and the angioplasty is performed (Tegtmeyer et al, 1980).

## Mechanism

**The principal mechanism through which the increase in arterial diameter after PTA occurs in cases of ASO is fracture of the atherosclerotic plaque. Stretching of the arterial wall with tearing of the media and adventitia also occurs** but contributes to a smaller degree in cases of ASO than in FD. This stretching effect probably occurs after the atherosclerotic plaque is fractured and becomes more pronounced with increasing plaque circumference and a decrease in the uninvolved area of the vessel wall.

## Complications

Renal angioplasty is a complex and technically demanding procedure that should be performed only by skilled interventional radiologists to prevent the occurrence of potentially serious complications. The complications of PTA include those of standard angiography (complications related to arterial puncture and to the use of iodinated contrast material) as well as specific complications related to manipulation of the renal arteries. **Transient deterioration of renal function is the most frequently occurring complication and is related to the contrast load delivered during the procedure.** Adequate hydration, minimizing the volume of contrast material, separating the diagnostic procedure from the PTA (by several days), and possibly the use of carbon dioxide or nonnephrotoxic contrast agents may decrease the incidence of this complication.

**Technical mishaps during PTA may lead to an intimal dissection or even thrombosis of the renal artery.** A small intimal flap is usually inconsequential, healing without sequelae. A larger flap compromising blood flow is usually managed by placing an arterial stent across the dissection. Thrombosis

of the renal artery can be managed by injecting a thrombolytic agent through the renal artery or by emergency surgery. Rupture of the renal artery, a rare complication, is also managed by emergency surgery after reinflation of the balloon catheter to control retroperitoneal hemorrhage. Overall, the complication rate can be expected to be 5% to 10%.

## Fibrous Dysplasia

Several studies have reported the results of PTA for blood pressure in cases of FD. Cure of hypertension is usually defined as a diastolic blood pressure of 90 mm Hg or less with no antihypertensive medication. Improvement of hypertension is usually defined as either a decrease in diastolic pressure of 15 mm Hg or a diastolic pressure of 90 mm Hg or less with a decrease in the antihypertensive medication needed to maintain normal blood pressure. Standardization of the results of these studies is difficult for several reasons. Several definitions are not uniform, including *significant stenosis* (varying from >50% to >80% of the original lumen) and technical success (defined as no stenosis or insignificant residual stenosis). Measures of success are also variable, with most studies relying on clinical parameters (blood pressure response) as the measure of success. Follow-up angiographic studies are rarely available. In addition, most studies combine ASO and FD patients, and sometimes results or complication rates are not referred specifically to one of the disease groups. Further complicating the interpretation of results is the reporting of results per patient in some studies and per lesion in others. The results of these studies are summarized in Table 36–7. Data per patient are used and represent primary procedures only.

**Overall, PTA is usually performed in cases of FD without stent placement and has become the primary modality of treatment for these lesions. With the use of modern equipment and increasing experience with the technique, technical success has been more than 90%** in most modern studies. A beneficial blood pressure response, that is, cure of hypertension or improvement in blood pressure control, can be expected in more than 80% and up to 100% of cases (Fig. 36–13). The incidence of major complications (when reported for FD patients alone) was 6% or less. At short to moderate follow-up intervals, restenosis of the treated artery was reported in up to one third of cases; however, most of these

| Table 36–7. **Results of Angioplasty in Fibrous Dysplasia** | | | | | | | | |
|---|---|---|---|---|---|---|---|---|
| *Study* | *Technical Success* | *Follow-up* | *Cured* | *Improved* | *Failed* | *Restenosis* | *Major Complications* | *Minor Complications* |
| Sos et al, 1983 | 87% | 16 mo | 52% | 29% | 19% | | 6% | 0 |
| Martin et al, 1985 | 82% | 16 mo | 25% | 60% | 15% | | 11%* | 19%* |
| Greminger et al, 1989 | 88% | 20 mo | 41% | 47% | 12% | 20% | 6% | 0 |
| Klinge et al, 1989 | 90% | | 35% | 50% | 15% | | 12%* | 23%* |
| Tegtmeyer et al, 1991 | 100% | 39 mo | 39% | 59% | 2% | 10% | 2% | 14% |
| Plouin et al, 1993 | | 9 mo | | | | 12% | 0 | 10% |
| Losinno et al, 1994 | 95% | 6 mo | 57% | 22% | 21% | | | |
| Jensen et al, 1995 | 97% | 12 mo | 39% | 47% | 14% | 7% | 3% | 12% |
| Bonelli et al, 1995 | 88.6% | 43 mo | 22% | 63% | 15% | 5.7% | 11.5% | 10% |
| Klow et al, 1998 | 98% | 12 mo | 25% | 63% | 29% | 33% | 0 | 0 |
| De Fraissinette et al, 2003 | 94% | 39 mo | 14% | 74% | 12% | 7% | 2% | 9% |

*Combined results for atherosclerosis and fibromuscular dysplasia cases in the study.

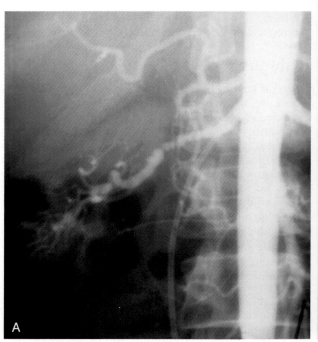 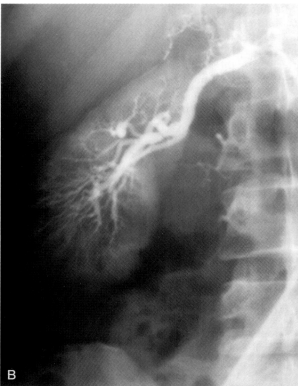

**Figure 36–13.** **A,** Right renal arteriogram shows medial fibroplasia causing stenosis of the main renal artery. **B,** After percutaneous transluminal angioplasty, the arteriogram shows relief of right renal artery stenosis.

cases have been successfully redilated. Rare reports describe the use of renal artery stents for resistant fibrous lesions (Joffre et al, 1992; Imamura et al, 1998); however, these are usually not needed for this form of RAS.

## Atherosclerotic Renal Artery Stenosis

The pattern of arterial disease in cases of ASO is different from that in FD. **Renal artery stenosis in cases of ASO is usually bilateral and ostial or very proximal in the main renal artery. In most ostial cases, this represents encroachment of the atherosclerotic plaque in the abdominal aorta on the origin of the renal artery rather than primary renal artery disease.** The patients affected by atherosclerotic RAS are also different from patients with FD of the renal arteries. Patients with ASO are generally older and have a number of comorbid medical conditions as well as generalized ASO affecting the coronary or carotid arteries or the peripheral vascular tree. Associated essential hypertension and nephrosclerosis are usually present. All the previously mentioned factors, as well as the propensity for atheroembolism in patients with generalized ASO, make PTA for ASO-RAS less successful and associated with higher morbidity (and some mortality) than in cases of FD. The presence of renal insufficiency or borderline renal function in a significant percentage of patients leads to an increased incidence of contrast nephrotoxicity as well.

The results of PTA for blood pressure in cases of RVH secondary to ASO are summarized in Table 36–8. Because of the previous factors, **the cure rate is lower than that for FD, com-** monly **around 15%, and less in cases with bilateral PTA.** Failure to improve the blood pressure occurs in 15% to 85% in the reported series. Technical success at the time of angioplasty varies from 57% to 92% (Fig. 36–14) and is lower in cases in which separate results for ostial stenosis are reported (62% to 72%). Restenosis rates of 8% to 22%, and as high as 68% in some earlier series, are reported. Restenosis of ostial lesions is higher, reaching 35%, although more recent studies of ostial angioplasty show improved results (Eldrup-Jorgensen et al, 1995; Hoffman et al, 1998). Major complications requiring surgical intervention are reported in 5% to 24% of cases, and a mortality rate of 1% to 2% is also generally reported. More recent reports tend to show higher rates of technical success and lower complication rates (Martin et al, 1986), reflecting improved equipment and increasing expertise (Table 36–9); however, major complications and mortality rates reflect the fact that PTA is a serious procedure with significant attendant risks in this population of patients. Renal artery stents are an adjunct to renal PTA that has been developed to improve the results obtained in ASO patients (see later).

With the advent of newer, more potent antihypertensive medication as well as the increasing awareness of IN as a cause of renal failure, renal revascularization in patients with ASO is increasingly being performed with the intent of preserving or improving renal function rather than the intent of curing RVH. **Several studies have reported the results of PTA for renal function in patients with ASO-RAS** (Table 36–10). Clinical benefit is defined as an improvement in renal

## Table 36–8.    Results of Angioplasty on Blood Pressure in Atherosclerosis Patients

| Study | No. of Patients | Follow-up | Cured (%) | Improved (%) | Failed (%) |
|---|---|---|---|---|---|
| Sos et al, 1983 | 51 | 16 mo | 17 (unilateral) | 30 | 53 |
| | | | 10 (bilateral) | 5 | 86 |
| Tegtmeyer et al, 1991 | 75 | 24 mo | 23 | 71 | 6 |
| Martin et al, 1995 | 77 | 16 mo | 15 | 50 | 35 |
| Hayes et al, 1988 | 55 | 13 mo | | 26[†] | |
| Canzanello et al, 1989 | 100 | 22 mo | * | 72 (unilateral) | 28 |
| | | | | 45 (bilateral) | 55 |
| Klinge et al, 1989 | 134 | | * | 92 | 8 |
| Plouin et al, 1993 | 59 | 9 mo | | | |
| Losinno et al, 1994 | 153 | | 12 | 51 | 37 |
| Eldrup-Jorgensen et al, 1995 | 52 | 16 mo | * | 36 | 63 |
| Jensen et al, 1995 | 107 | 12 mo | 15 | 49 | 36 |
| Bonelli et al, 1995 | 190 | 33 mo | 8 | 62 | 30 |
| Karagiannis et al, 1995 | 62 | 39 mo | 15 | 40 | 45 |
| Klow et al, 1998 | 295 | 61 mo | 5 | 59 | 36 |

*Combined with improved results as "benefit" result.
[†]Clinical benefit: cured or improved blood pressure or renal function.

## Table 36–9.    Technical Success, Restenosis, and Complications of Angioplasty in Atherosclerosis Patients

| Study | Technical Success | Restenosis | Major Complications* | Minor Complications | Mortality |
|---|---|---|---|---|---|
| Sos et al, 1983 | 57% | | 10% | 6% | 0 |
| Tegtmeyer et al, 1984 | 94% | 15%[†] | | | |
| Martin et al, 1986 | 88% | | 11%[†] | 19%[†] | 0 |
| Hayes et al, 1988 | 69% | 68% | 24% | 7% | 7% |
| Klinge et al, 1989 | 74% | 22% | 12%* | 23%* | 2% |
| Canzanello et al, 1989 | 73% | 14% | 7% | 8% | 2% |
| | 62% ostial | | | | |
| Greminger et al, 1989 | 88% | | 5% | 3% | 0 |
| Weibull et al, 1993 | 83% | 25% | 17% | 48% | 0 |
| Plouin et al, 1993 | | 19% | 0 | 7% | 0 |
| | | 35% ostial | | | |
| Losinno et al, 1994 | 95% | | 5% | 5% | 0 |
| Bonelli et al, 1995 | 82% | 8% | 22.5% | 15% | 2.2% |
| Jensen et al, 1995 | 82% nonostial | 15% | 5% | 3% | 1% |
| | 72% ostial | | | | |
| Karagiannis et al, 1995 | 72% | | | | |
| Eldrup-Jorgensen et al, 1995 | 92% | 11% | 5% | | 2% |
| Von Knorring et al, 1996 | 76%[†] | 8%[†] | | 15%[‡] | |
| Hoffman et al, 1998 | 58% ostial only | 27% | 17% | | 4% |
| Klow et al, 1998 | 92% | 43% | 3% | 4.2% | 1% |

*Includes emergency surgery and mortality.
[†]Combined results for atherosclerosis and fibromuscular dysplasia groups in the study.
[‡]Combined major and minor complications.

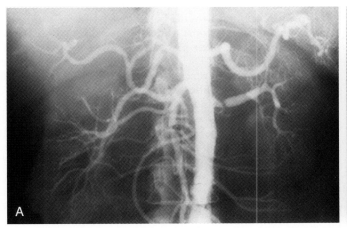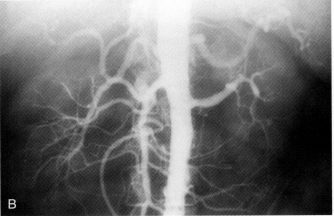

**Figure 36–14.**  **A,** Aortography shows high-grade left renal artery stenosis from nonostial atherosclerotic plaque. **B,** After percutaneous transluminal angioplasty, aortography shows relief of left renal artery stenosis.

**Table 36–10. Results of Angioplasty on Renal Function in Atherosclerosis Patients**

| Study | Follow-up | Improved (%) | Stable (%) | Worse (%) |
|---|---|---|---|---|
| Martin et al, 1988* | 16 mo | 43 | | |
| Hayes et al, 1988 | 13 mo | | 26[†] | 74 |
| Jensen et al, 1995 | 12 mo | | 74[‡] | 26 |
| Karagiannis et al, 1995 | 39 mo | 15 | 33 | 52 |
| Zuccala et al, 1996 | 37 mo | 40 | 50 | 10 |
| Paulsen et al, 1999 | 104 mo | 23 | 56 | 21 |

*Study population with impaired renal function (creatinine >1.7 mg/dL), no report of stable renal function.
[†]Clinical benefit: cured or improved blood pressure or renal function.
[‡]Combined with improved results as "benefit" result.

function or a stabilization of renal function, in view of the steadily progressive decline in renal function associated with IN. With technically successful angioplasty, improvement can be expected in 15% to 43% of cases and stabilization of renal function in 26% to 50% of cases. The remaining cases continue to suffer a decline in renal function. Although a mean follow-up of more than 100 months was achieved in one of these studies (Paulsen et al, 1999), follow-up for the rest of the studies is generally short to intermediate, ranging from 1 to 3 years. Percutaneous revascularization has also been reported to be successful in improving blood pressure control and renal function in a diabetic subset of ASO patients (Zuccala et al, 1998).

## Inflammatory Renal Artery Stenosis

**Takayasu's arteritis is one of the causes of RAS in children and accounts for a majority of cases of RAS in South and East Asian countries.** In the absence of active disease or inflammation, angioplasty has been performed to relieve RVH as well as to prevent renal loss. In a series of 24 patients aged 5 to 16 years, all with inactive disease, technically successful dilatation was achieved in 92%, with a restenosis rate of 20% after a mean of 33 months of follow-up, and these were successfully redilated. Half the children in this study were cured of hypertension, and the other half were improved. No complications were specifically reported in this study (Sharma et al, 1996). In a slightly larger group of 31 children (age range 5 to 14 years) in which less importance was given to the presence of active disease, technical success was possible in 87% of cases, with a restenosis rate of 26% at a mean follow-up of 23 months. Thirty-one percent of the patients were cured, 61% improved, and 8% failed clinically. One acute occlusion of the renal artery was reported; it was successfully redilated (Tyagi et al, 1997).

These excellent results were not duplicated in a smaller Canadian study of six patients in which only one patient obtained clinical benefit and the remaining five patients proceeded to surgical autotransplantation (D'Souza et al, 1998). All these studies were in agreement that long stenoses starting at the ostium of the renal artery were much less likely to have a successful result with PTA.

Management of RAS secondary to Takayasu's disease in adults with PTA has also been successful (Dong et al, 1987; Deyu et al, 1998; Sharma et al, 1998). Technical success was obtained in more than 80% of patients in these studies, with overall clinical benefit in the range of 85%.

## Children

**RAS in children is caused by a variety of arterial diseases, including FD, middle aortic syndrome, and neurofibromatosis.** In Asian countries, a significant proportion of RAS in children is also caused by aortoarteritis (Takayasu's disease). The main limitation to performing PTA in children was the lack of suitably small-sized equipment. With modern angiographic techniques and digital imaging, PTA has been reported in several studies and is becoming a primary mode of management for children with RVH. The largest series reporting on PTA for treatment of FD in children comprises 16 children, 12 of whom were diagnosed with FD. Three patients required a secondary PTA. Overall, nine patients were cured and two were improved; in five patients, the treatment failed, and four of these were treated surgically. The PTA failed in all three patients with multiple stenoses in this study (none had FD). There were no reports of complications in this study (Courtel et al, 1998).

Reports of smaller studies of PTA in children with FD also demonstrate the technical success and beneficial blood pressure response obtained with this treatment modality (Lund et al, 1984; Millan et al, 1985; Chevalier et al, 1987; Simunic et al, 1990). Angioplasty has been successfully used in very young children, with reports of 18-, 15-, and even 9-month-old children being treated using small coronary angioplasty equipment (Hofbeck et al, 1998; Lee et al, 1999; Liang et al, 1999).

## ENDOVASCULAR STENTING

With increasing experience with PTA, limitations of the technique, especially in regard to atherosclerotic lesions, have become well recognized. These limitations involve mainly ostial lesions that represent engulfment of the renal ostium in aortic plaque. These cases represent a significant percentage of ASO-RAS cases, and elastic recoil of the plaque leads to poor initial results and frequent restenosis. **Renal artery stents are an adjunct to PTA that was introduced in an effort to oppose this recoil force and provide better results for angioplasty, especially in ostial lesions. Almost all renal artery stents in the literature have been placed to treat ASO of the renal arteries** (estimated at 97%), with many fewer stents placed in cases of FD, transplant renal arteries, and other miscellaneous renal arterial abnormalities (Rees, 1999).

Arterial stents are radiopaque, expandable metallic wire mesh tubes that have been widely used in the peripheral vascular system. Experience in other parts of the vascular as well as the biliary tree has led to the use of stents in the renal artery, although none are specifically approved by the U.S. Food and Drug Administration for use in the renal artery. Different stents are currently available and include the Palmaz, Strecker, Wallstent, and Nitinol stents. Stent expansion either is spontaneous on extrusion from a delivery catheter (self-expandable) or occurs on inflation of a balloon on which the stent is preloaded (balloon expandable).

## Technique

Several techniques for stent placement in the renal artery have been developed. It is essential in all cases to obtain a high-quality angiographic study (immediately before stent placement at the same sitting or separately) in order to delineate the lesion precisely and assess balloon and stent length and diameter. The stent used should be long enough to traverse the entire lesion, taking into consideration shortening of the stent with expansion. Excessive length beyond the lesion is undesirable because the presence of the stent may excite an intimal hyperplastic reaction, placing healthy segments of the vessel at risk. This might also obstruct a site suitable for later bypass surgery. In cases of ostial lesions, the stent should be placed to protrude 1 to 2 mm into the aortic lumen to prevent restenosis caused by recoil of the aortic plaque.

## Indications

Current indications for stent placement are poor immediate results during PTA as well as restenosis after PTA. Stents are also used to treat angioplasty complications (artery dissection and intimal flaps) and have markedly reduced the incidence of emergency surgery for these complications. **"Primary" stent placement is becoming increasingly popular in cases of RAS in which PTA alone is unlikely to be successful (ostial lesions).**

## Results

The results of several studies reporting on endovascular stent placement in the renal arteries are summarized in Tables 36–11 and 36–12. Most of the published experience in the renal arteries has been described using the Palmaz stent. With the exception of two of the earliest studies using Strecker stents and Wallstents, **the reported technical success for stent placement has consistently been above 95%** and in most studies has been 99% or 100% (Fig. 36–15). With short to moderate follow-up intervals, restenosis of the renal artery after stent placement has ranged from 6% to 38%. A single early study (Wilms et al, 1991) reported a 71% restenosis rate; however, most larger contemporary series average a restenosis rate of 15% to 20%. Restenosis commonly occurs within the stent owing to a hyperplastic intimal reaction. In other cases, an intimal lining about 1 mm thick covers the luminal surface of the stent. Renal arteries that are dilated and stented to a luminal diameter of less than 6 mm are more likely to develop restenosis.

**The blood pressure response to renal revascularization by PTA and stenting is shown in Table 36–11.** The low cure rates (31% at most) reflect the pathophysiologic nature of atherosclerotic renal artery disease in which anatomic stenosis is frequently associated with concomitant essential hypertension and renal parenchymal damage, precluding a simple pathologic explanation for hypertension. Revascularization for preservation of renal function has become the focus of intervention in cases of ASO-RAS. The result of renal artery stent placement (for renal function preservation or improvement) in various studies is shown in Table 36–12. Because of the progressive nature of renal dysfunction related to ASO, a clinical benefit is defined as improvement or stabilization (halt of decline) of renal function after revascularization. Improvement in renal function was achieved in 13% to 60% of cases, and stabilization was achieved in 24% to 75% of cases, with the remaining cases continuing to have progressive dysfunction.

Perhaps the clearest situation of IN is RAS to a solitary kidney, and it is in these patients that the effect of revascularization on renal function can be most clearly identified. In a study of 21 such patients, an improvement in the serum creatinine level was obtained after stent placement in 42% of cases and stabilization in 29% of cases. Within the group of improved patients were four who were relieved of dialysis dependence. These results were associated with a major complication rate of 19% including a single early (and another late) procedure-related mortality (Shannon et al, 1998).

In the only prospective study comparing PTA alone versus PTA with stenting in ostial ASO, a total of 85 patients were randomly assigned to either treatment group. Technical success was higher in the stented group (88% versus 57%), and

| Table 36–11. Renal Artery Stents: Blood Pressure Results | | | |
|---|---|---|---|
| *Study* | *Cured (%)* | *Improved (%)* | *Same (%)* |
| Hennequin et al, 1994 | 14 | 86 | 0 |
| Raynaud et al, 1994 | 6 | 45 | 49 |
| MacLeod et al, 1995 | 0 | 44 | 56 |
| Van de Ven et al, 1995 | 0 | 75 | 25 |
| Iannone et al, 1996 | 4 | 35 | 61 |
| Henry et al, 1996 | 18 | 57 | 25 |
| White et al, 1997 | | 76* | 24 |
| Blum et al, 1997 | 16 | 62 | 22 |
| Boisclair et al, 1997 | 6 | 61 | 33 |
| Dorros et al, 1998 | 1 | 42 | 57 |
| Tuttle et al, 1998 | 0 | 55 | 45 |
| Fiala et al, 1998 | 0 | 53 | 47 |
| Rodriguez-Lopez et al, 1999 | 13 | 55 | 32 |
| Burket et al, 2000 | | 71* | 29 |
| Sivamurthy et al, 2004 | | 52* | 48 |
| Zeller et al, 2004 | | 46* | 54 |

*Combined "clinical benefit" rate.

| Table 36–12. Renal Artery Stents: Renal Function Results | | | |
|---|---|---|---|
| *Study* | *Improved (%)* | *Stable (%)* | *Worse (%)* |
| Rees and Snead, 1994 | 37 | 37 | 26 |
| Iannone et al, 1996 | 36 | 46 | 18 |
| White et al, 1997 | 20 | 75 | 5 |
| Harden et al, 1997 | 34 | 34 | 32 |
| Dorros et al, 1998 | | 75* | 25 |
| Tuttle et al, 1998 | 13 | 76 | 11 |
| Fiala et al, 1998 | 33 | 62 | 5 |
| Rundback et al, 1998 | 29 | 71 | 0 |
| Rodriguez-Lopez et al, 1999 | | 95 | 5 |
| Burket et al, 2000 | 43 | 24 | 33 |
| Perkovic et al, 2001 | 8 | 57 | 35 |
| Sivamurthy et al, 2004 | | 87* | 13 |
| Zeller et al, 2004 | 34 | 39 | 27 |

*Combined "clinical benefit" rate.

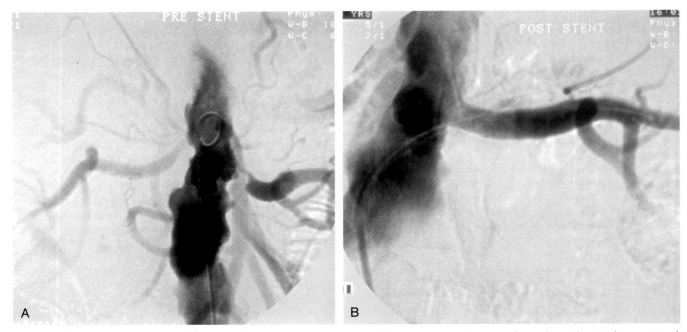

**Figure 36–15.** **A,** Aortography shows high-grade left renal artery stenosis from ostial atherosclerotic plaque. **B,** After endovascular stenting, aortography shows relief of left renal artery stenosis.

patency at 6 months was 75% for patients in the stent group versus 29% for PTA alone. In patients with successful primary procedures, restenosis occurred in 14% of the patients with stents and in 48% of patients with PTA alone. Stenting for immediate or late failure of PTA was required in 12 (of 42) patients in the PTA group. **This study reflects the overall higher success of PTA with stenting in treating ostial ASO when compared with PTA alone and probably also justifies the increasing trend to perform primary stenting in these cases to avoid exposing patients to a secondary procedure** (Van de Ven et al, 1999).

Several studies addressed the factors affecting outcome after stenting and recommended selecting patients for interventional treatment on the basis of their findings: Kennedy (2003) and Zeller (2003) and their colleagues reported that baseline renal insufficiency correlates with decreased survival and increased adverse events after renal artery stenting. In Zeller's study, the 5-year survival rate was 30% for patients with creatinine more than 2.5 mg/dL versus 95% for patients with creatinine less than 1.2 mg/dL. Major causes of death were cardiac events, cerebral events, and malignancy.

Perkovic and associates (2002) studied several parameters for patients undergoing renal artery stenting and reported baseline renal impairment, older age (>70), and diabetes as predictors of a poor outcome. ACE inhibitor therapy after stenting appeared to improve outcome in this series.

## Complications

**Complications of renal artery stent placement are similar to those of renal PTA, with the added complications of stent delivery.** The incidence of access site complications is higher because of the larger arterial puncture needed. The incidence of intimal injury and dissection is lower than that of PTA

| Table 36–13. | **Complications of Renal Artery Stents** | | |
|---|---|---|---|
| *Study* | *Major\* (%)* | *Minor (%)* | *Mortality[†] (%)* |
| MacLeod et al, 1995 | 10 | 31 | 3 |
| Iannone et al, 1996 | 20 | 28 | 3 |
| Henry et al, 1996 | 2 | 0 | 0 |
| White et al, 1997 | 2 | 8 | 0 |
| Blum et al, 1997 | 0 | 4 | 0 |
| Boisclair et al, 1997 | 21 | 12 | 0 |
| Harden et al, 1997 | 13 | 10 | 3 |
| Dorros et al, 1998 | 1 | 14 | 1 |
| Tuttle et al, 1998 | 4 | 19 | 0 |
| Fiala et al, 1998 | 5 | 24 | 0 |
| Rundback et al, 1998 | 9 | 0 | 4 |
| Rodriguez-Lopez et al, 1999 | 3 | 7 | 3 |
| Burket et al, 2000 | 1 | 4 | |
| Perkovic et al, 2001 | 7 | 6 | 0.5 |
| Sivamurthy et al, 2004 | 4 | 14 | 0.7 |

\*Including mortality and emergency surgery.
[†]Procedure-related mortality only.

because stent placement in itself is a treatment for these complications. A higher incidence of contrast nephrotoxicity owing to a larger contrast load is noted, but the increasing use of carbon dioxide as a contrast agent may decrease the incidence of this complication. The literature has rare reports of endovascular infection from renal artery stents, resolving after conservative therapy with IV antibiotics (Gordon et al, 1996) or progressing to form mycotic aneurysms of the aorta and renal artery necessitating major excision and vascular reconstructive surgery (Deitch et al, 1998).

Major complications (including death) are reported in 0% to 20% of cases (Table 36–13). Minor complications are reported in 0% to 40% of cases. Mortality directly related to the procedure is reported in almost all large series, in the range of 3%. This attests to the fact that PTA with stent placement is not a benign procedure and is associated with definite risk. In a review of complications of stent placement in 50 patients, a complication rate of 20% was noted, 10% of patients suffered major complications, and a 10% rate of cholesterol embolism was reported (Beek et al, 1997).

Proper selection of patients for endovascular intervention in cases of ASO-RAS should be a careful process that takes into account the patient's chances of a successful outcome. This process should be as rigorous as selection of patients for open surgery in order to minimize morbidity and poor outcomes from endovascular intervention.

**Complications of PTA with stenting were not found to be significantly different from those of PTA alone in a prospective study comparing both procedures.** Specifically, bleeding-related complications were 19% in both groups, cholesterol embolism was 10% in both groups, and access site pseudoaneurysm and renal artery injury were slightly higher with stent placement (7% versus 5%). Transient deterioration of renal function from contrast nephrotoxicity was noted in 24% of patients undergoing PTA and 21% of patients undergoing PTA with stent placement (Van de Ven et al, 1999).

## OTHER RENAL ARTERY DISEASES
### Renal Arterial Aneurysms

**A renal arterial aneurysm is a localized dilatation of the main renal artery or its branches or both caused by weakening of the elastic tissue and media of the arterial wall.** The estimated incidence of such lesions in the general population ranges from 0.09% to 0.3%. Renal arterial aneurysms may be clinically significant because of a causative relation to hypertension, associated local symptoms, or the risk of catastrophic rupture in certain situations (Novick, 1982). According to the classification of Poutasse (1975), there are four basic types of renal artery aneurysms: saccular, fusiform, dissecting, and intrarenal (Fig. 36–16).

**Saccular aneurysms** are the most common type and constitute about 75% of renal artery aneurysms. They generally occur at the bifurcation of the renal artery, perhaps owing to an inherent weakness in the wall of the artery at this point. Because of this location, branch arterial involvement is common. The incidence of bilateral or multiple aneurysms or both is approximately 25%. These aneurysms may become involved with secondary atherosclerotic degeneration or intramural calcification or both. Incompletely calcified aneurysms may become soft, thin, and ulcerated between zones of calcification, predisposing to rupture. In addition to rupturing spontaneously, saccular aneurysms may erode into the renal vein or into the renal pelvis. Mural thrombus formation may also occur within saccular aneurysms, occasionally leading to peripheral renal embolization.

**Fusiform aneurysms** occur as a uniform dilatation of an entire segment of the renal artery to as much as three to four times its normal diameter. These aneurysms range in length from 1 to 3 cm and are generally not calcified. They are typically found in young hypertensive patients with stenosing fibrous renal arterial disease. The fusiform aneurysm is actually a poststenotic dilatation and can involve either the main renal artery or its branches. The major complication of this lesion is thrombosis of the involved arterial segment from progressive proximal stenosing vascular disease.

**A dissecting aneurysm** results from a tear in the internal elastic membrane of the renal artery, and as blood flows through the opening, the intima is separated from the remainder of the arterial wall. In some patients, the dissection may reenter the lumen distally to preserve renal function. In other cases, arterial thrombosis with renal infarction or rupture with hemorrhage may occur. Dissecting aneurysms are most often complications of renal arterial involvement with ASO, intimal fibroplasia, or perimedial fibroplasia. Less commonly, such an aneurysm may occur as an extension of a dissecting aortic aneurysm.

**Intrarenal arterial aneurysms** are of mixed origin and may be congenital, post-traumatic, iatrogenic, neoplastic, or associated with polyarteritis nodosa. They are usually saccular or fusiform and may or may not be calcified. Intrarenal aneurysms constitute approximately 17% of all renal arterial aneurysms, and they do have a propensity for rupture. Intrarenal aneurysms that occur after blunt trauma or closed renal biopsy occasionally resolve spontaneously with expectant management.

In general, the diagnosis of renal arterial aneurysm should be considered when ringlike calcification in or near the renal hilum is found on a plain abdominal radiograph. These calcifications occur in about 50% of cases. **The majority of renal arterial aneurysms are small and asymptomatic.** The most common clinical manifestations are hypertension, subcostal or flank pain, hematuria, an abdominal bruit, and, rarely, a palpable pulsating mass. RVH is reported to occur in 15% to 75% of patients and may be due to turbulent flow within an aneurysm, associated arterial stenosis, dissection, arteriovenous fistula formation, thromboembolism, or compression of adjacent arterial branches by a large aneurysm. Complications of renal arterial aneurysms include peripheral dissection, arterial thrombosis with renal infarction, emboli arising from mural thrombus within an aneurysm, obstructive uropathy, erosion into a vein with formation of an arteriovenous fistula, and spontaneous rupture with hemorrhage. Factors that appear to predispose to aneurysmal rupture include absent or incomplete calcification, aneurysmal size greater than 2 cm in diameter, coexisting hypertension, and pregnancy.

A small (2-cm) well-calcified renal arterial aneurysm in an asymptomatic normotensive patient does not require operative intervention. These aneurysms can be followed with serial plain abdominal radiographs to detect any change in size. Surgical removal is indicated for renal arterial aneurysms, regardless of size, in (1) aneurysm causing renal ischemia and hypertension, (2) dissecting aneurysm, (3) aneurysm associated with local symptoms such as flank pain or hematuria, (4) aneurysm occurring in a woman of childbearing age who is likely to conceive, (5) aneurysm occurring with functionally significant renal arterial stenosis, (6) aneurysm with radiographic evidence of expansion on serial radiographs, or (7) aneurysm containing a thrombus detectable on angiography with evidence of distal embolization.

When none of these criteria are present, small (2-cm) asymptomatic noncalcified or incompletely calcified aneurysms can be managed nonoperatively. Such patients should be observed periodically with serial CT or magnetic

SECTION VIII

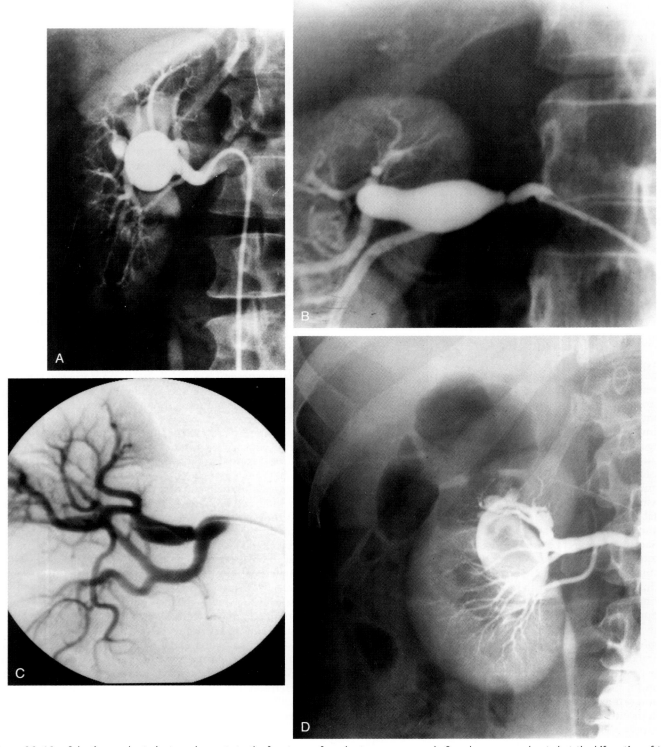

**Figure 36–16.** Selective renal arteriograms demonstrate the four types of renal artery aneurysms. **A,** Saccular aneurysm located at the bifurcation of the main renal artery. **B,** Fusiform aneurysm distal to a stenotic lesion of the main renal artery. **C,** Dissecting aneurysm involving a renal artery branch. **D,** Intrarenal aneurysm.

resonance imaging (MRI) studies to document the size of the aneurysm. It is not possible to define rigidly indications for operative intervention in asymptomatic patients with aneurysms greater than 2 cm in diameter and with none of the previous criteria. The available data would seem to support surgical excision if these aneurysms are not calcified throughout or are intrarenal because of the increased tendency to rupture in these settings.

In the largest series of renal artery surgery reported in the recent literature (Henke et al, 2001), a total of 121 patients underwent surgical repair. Eight unplanned nephrectomies were necessary resulting in the need for permanent dialysis in one patient, no perioperative mortality was encountered, and all but two reconstructions remained patent at follow-up.

In a retrospective review of surgical repair of renal artery aneurysms in 94 patients, Pfeiffer and colleagues (2003) encountered one postoperative mortality (in an emergency repair secondary to aneurysm rupture), an overall morbidity of 17%, and a primary success rate of 97%.

English and colleagues (2004) reported their results of surgical repair of 72 renal artery aneurysms of varying etiology over a 16-year period. One aneurysm only was deemed not reconstructable, and nephrectomy was performed. One operative mortality was encountered, and 12% of patients had significant perioperative morbidity, with 96% of repairs maintaining patency at 48 months.

A significant body of literature (almost all case reports) has accumulated over the last few years reporting successful endovascular management of renal artery aneurysms as well as dissection of the renal artery. In the case of renal artery aneurysms, two methods of endovascular treatment are reported. The first involves embolization of the aneurysm (usually with coils) to occlude it without disrupting the renal blood flow (Halloul et al, 2000; Karkos et al, 2000; Mounayer et al, 2000; Tshomba et al, 2002; Lupattelli et al, 2003). The second method involves placing an arterial stent in the renal artery or the branch where the aneurysm originates, thereby maintaining flow through the stent and effectively excluding the aneurysm (Tan et al, 2001; Bruce and Kuan, 2002; Pershad and Heuser, 2004). Stenting the renal artery across an aneurysm has also been described as a successful and rapid method of dealing with ruptured renal artery aneurysm (Schneidereit et al, 2003). Dissection of the renal artery can be managed endovascularly as well by placing a renal artery stent through the area of dissection to keep the lumen patent and keep the dissected intima immobilized against the outer layers of the artery (Bilge et al, 2003).

## Renal Arteriovenous Fistula

**Renal arteriovenous fistulas are relatively uncommon lesions that are generally discovered during the course of angiographic evaluation for suspected renal or renovascular disease. There are three categories of renal arteriovenous fistulas:** congenital, idiopathic, and acquired (Tynes et al, 1970; Novick, 1982).

**Congenital fistulas** have a cirsoid or angiomatous configuration with multiple communications between arteries and veins. They are usually supplied by a renal arterial branch of normal caliber. The angiographic appearance is one of multiple, small interconnecting arterial and venous channels with

impaired distal renal parenchymal vascularity and early filling of the renal vein. They constitute 22% to 25% of all renal arteriovenous fistulas, occur equally in both sexes, and generally do not become manifest until adult life.

**Idiopathic fistulas** are single, are not cirsoid, and have no apparent cause. They constitute only 3% to 5% of all renal arteriovenous fistulas. These lesions are called *idiopathic* because their angiographic appearance is similar to that of acquired arteriovenous fistulas, but their origin is unclear.

**Acquired fistulas** are the most common type, accounting for 70% to 75% of all renal arteriovenous fistulas. On angiography they appear as solitary communications between an artery and a vein. By far the most common cause is iatrogenic trauma resulting from needle biopsy of the kidney (Fig. 36–17). Other causes include renal carcinoma, blunt or penetrating renal trauma, inflammation, and renal surgery such as nephrectomy, partial nephrectomy, or nephrolithotomy.

The clinical manifestations of a renal arteriovenous fistula depend on the size of the fistula. **Approximately 75% of patients have an abdominal bruit,** which is usually loud, high pitched, and continuous with systolic accentuation. Congestive heart failure, cardiomegaly, and diastolic hypertension are observed in 50% of patients. Hematuria is present in about one third of cases, tachycardia is occasionally found, and a palpable flank mass from spontaneous rupture is rarely encountered.

The management of a patient with a renal arteriovenous fistula depends on the cause of the fistula and the associated clinical manifestations. For patients with renal carcinoma, immediate nephrectomy is obviously indicated. **Approximately 70% of fistulas occurring after needle biopsy of the**

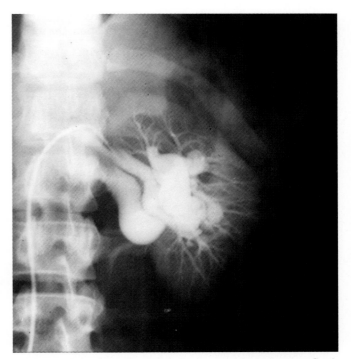

**Figure 36–17.** Left renal arteriogram shows renal arteriovenous fistula with early filling of the renal vein. This patient had previously undergone needle biopsy of the left kidney.

kidney close spontaneously within 18 months. A smaller number of fistulas diagnosed immediately after renal trauma have also resolved spontaneously. Therefore, in the absence of significant related symptoms, expectant management is appropriate initially in these cases.

Treatment of renal arteriovenous fistulas is indicated for patients who have hypertension, heart failure, severe hematuria, serial angiographic evidence of an expanding lesion, rupture, or progressive renal failure. When specific therapy of these lesions is indicated, renal-sparing procedures should be employed whenever possible.

Transcatheter angiographic occlusion is a nonsurgical therapeutic alternative that has been employed primarily in treating patients with postbiopsy fistulas, in which the arteriovenous connecting vessels are usually small. More recently, transcatheter occlusion of congenital or idiopathic fistulas with a stainless steel coil has also been performed.

Various operations have been employed in the surgical treatment of renal arteriovenous fistulas. Most congenital or cirsoid fistulas have been managed with total or partial nephrectomy because of the difficulty of completely excising the many small communicating vessels. In patients with idiopathic or acquired fistulas, a single communication between the artery and the vein is characteristically present, and surgical obliteration of the fistula with preservation of the involved kidney is more often possible.

## Renal Artery Thrombosis or Embolism

Thromboembolic disorders of the renal artery can arise as fulminant clinical syndromes that threaten life or may be entirely asymptomatic and detected only at postmortem examination (Hoxie and Coggins, 1940; Schoenbaum et al, 1971). The various causes of acute renal artery thrombosis or embolism are listed in Table 36–14. The term *paradoxical embolism* refers to a clot originating in the venous circulation that gains

---

Table 36–14. **Causes of Renal Arterial Thrombosis and Embolism**

*Renal Artery Thrombosis*
Blunt or penetrating trauma
Aortic or renal artery angiography
Atherosclerosis of aorta or renal artery
Fibrous dysplasia of renal artery
Polycythemia vera
Umbilical artery catheterization in neonates
Inflammation of renal artery
Syphilis
Polyarteritis
Thromboangiitis obliterans

*Renal Artery Embolism*
Bacterial endocarditis
Aseptic cardiac valvular vegetations
Open heart surgery
Atrial fibrillation
Saccular renal artery aneurysm
Cardiac tumor
Acute myocardial infarction
Ventricular aneurysm
"Paradoxical" embolism

---

entrance to the systemic arterial circulation through an intracardiac septal defect.

Renal arterial thrombosis commonly involves the proximal or middle third of the main renal artery, whereas renal arterial embolization generally involves peripheral arterial branches. Acute arterial occlusion is more common on the left side because of the more acute angle between the left renal artery and the aorta. Post-traumatic renal arterial occlusion is also more common on the left side, presumably because of the acute angulation of the shorter left renal artery at its aortic junction, which predisposes to intimal disruption with deceleration of the mobile kidney.

The clinical symptomatology in these disorders is extremely varied. Bilateral acute renal arterial occlusion arises with rapidly progressing oliguric renal failure, whereas chronic occlusion of a single renal artery may be unnoticed because of the development of collateral circulation. The most common symptoms, when present, are dull aching abdominal or flank pain often associated with nausea, vomiting, and fever. Other findings include hypertension, albuminuria, microscopic hematuria, leukocytosis, and elevation of serum lactate dehydrogenase levels.

Patients with unilateral renal arterial embolic occlusion generally have serious underlying extrarenal disease and are best managed nonoperatively with systemic anticoagulation or by percutaneous transcatheter thromboembolectomy (Millan et al, 1978; Hamilton, 1996). Patients with unilateral traumatic renal arterial thrombosis also often have severe associated injuries, and the results of vascular reconstruction are generally unsatisfactory unless this is undertaken within several hours of the time of injury. Surgical treatment in these cases is generally ill advised when a normal contralateral kidney is present. Percutaneous intra-arterial infusion of a fibrinolytic agent such as streptokinase now offers a nonoperative approach to the management of acute renal arterial thrombosis (Hamilton, 1996).

Renovascular reconstruction is generally indicated when renal artery thrombosis or embolism occurs bilaterally or in a solitary kidney. Alternatively, if angiographic and isotopic studies in such cases demonstrate an extensive collateral vascular supply maintaining renal viability, an initial therapeutic trial with one of the previously mentioned nonoperative approaches may be worthwhile.

## Neurofibromatosis

Neurofibromatosis affecting the renal arteries is a congenital hereditary disorder characterized by café-au-lait cutaneous pigmentation, cutaneous neurofibromas, tumors of the CNS, skeletal disorders, and occasional gigantism (Grad and Rance, 1972; Tilford and Kelsch, 1973). Hypertension in patients with neurofibromatosis is most often due to RAS; less commonly, this may be the result of an associated pheochromocytoma or aortic coarctation. Vascular abnormality occurs in the kidneys, heart, and gastrointestinal tract and consists of fibrosis and thickening of the intima, proliferation of neural tissue within the arterial wall, perivascular nodular proliferations, and occasional aneurysmal dilatation. In the kidney, arterial stenosis usually occurs at the origin or in the proximal third of the main renal artery, and the angiographic appearance may be indistinguishable from that of intimal fibroplasia. Considering the young age of these patients, renal revascularization is generally the treatment of choice for associated RVH.

## Middle Aortic Syndrome

**The middle aortic syndrome is a rare disorder, occurring in children or young adults, characterized by nonspecific stenosing arteritis affecting the aorta and its major branches including the renal arteries** (Fig. 36–18). This is thought to be a form of Takayasu's disease, and an autoimmune pathogenesis is suspected (Kaufman, 1973). This disease can extensively involve the subdiaphragmatic aorta or, in some cases, may spare the aorta and involve primarily the renal or splanchnic vessels. The natural history is not well understood because most cases are diagnosed when the disease has already resulted in significant renal arterial stenosis in young good-risk patients, necessitating early revascularization. Because the inflammatory process generally does not extend to involve the iliac arteries, renal autotransplantation is the surgical treatment of choice.

## Extrinsic Obstruction

Extrinsic obstruction of the renal artery has been observed but is extremely rare (Silver and Clements, 1976). Neural tissue, musculocutaneous fibers, and diaphragmatic crura have been suggested as etiologic factors contributing to this process. Other possible causes of extrinsic perivascular fibrosis include inflammation, trauma, tumor, and prior radiation.

## Page's Kidney

In 1934, Page (1939) produced a renin-dependent model of hypertension by wrapping a dog kidney in cellophane. Hypertension could be reversed by removing the cellophane wrap or the kidney. **The clinical equivalent of this hypertensive model is the kidney compressed by a subcapsular or perirenal process causing renal ischemia, inducing unilateral hypersecretion of renin and contralateral suppression.** Causes of the perinephric process include blunt trauma, closed renal biopsy, anticoagulation, and hemorrhage from a tumor.

The diagnosis of Page's kidney depends on the presence of either a surrounding hematoma or an encasing fibrous pseudocapsule. Imaging with ultrasonography, CT, or MRI localizes the hematoma or fibrous capsule.

The treatment of Page's kidney aims to preserve renal function and cure hypertension. Medical antihypertensive therapy and observation, percutaneous evacuation of the perirenal hematoma, open drainage of the hematoma, and nephrectomy have all been used (Suffrin, 1975).

Some cases of acute Page's kidney with new-onset hypertension have resolved spontaneously. A hematoma may reabsorb, relieving the parenchymal compression without forming an adhesive fibrotic pseudocapsule. Treatment with medical antihypertensive therapy can control the blood pressure until the hematoma resolves. If the hematoma does not resolve, it may be drained percutaneously or surgically.

## Renal Parenchymal Disease

Renin-mediated hypertension may be secondary to a variety of renal parenchymal diseases. The incidence of hypertension in patients with chronic pyelonephritis is approximately 5% to 10%. The mechanism of renin-mediated hypertension in such kidneys with segmental scars is ischemia of the relatively normal renal cortex in proximity to areas of interstitial fibrosis, within which are small vessels with intimal thickening. Other renal disorders that may cause hypertension include hydronephrosis, congenital hypoplasia or dysplasia, segmental hypoplasia (Ask-Upmark kidney), vesicoureteral reflux, renal cell carcinoma, benign cyst, Wilms' tumor, radiation nephritis, and juxtaglomerular cell tumor.

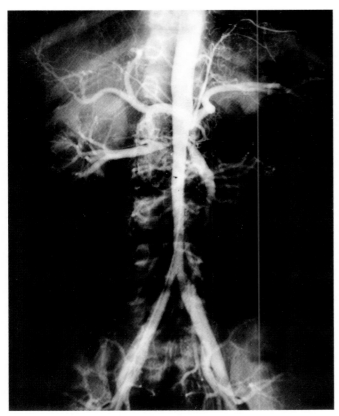

**Figure 36–18.** Aortography in a child with the middle aortic syndrome shows hypoplasia of the abdominal aorta and right renal artery stenosis.

### SUGGESTED READINGS

Case DB, Laragh JH: Reactive hyperreninemia in renovascular hypertension after angiotensin blockage with saralasin or converting enzyme inhibitor. Ann Intern Med 1979;91:153-160.

Fergany A, Kolettis P, Novick AC: The contemporary role of extra-anatomical surgical renal revascularization in patients with atherosclerotic renal artery disease. J Urol 1995;153:1798-1802.

Hansen KJ, Edwards MS, Craven TE, et al: Prevalence of renovascular disease in the elderly: A population-based study. J Vasc Surg 2002;36:443-451.

Kaylor W, Novick AC, Ziegelbaum M, et al: Reversal of end-stage renal failure with surgical revascularization in patients with atherosclerotic renal artery occlusion. J Urol 1989;141:486-488.

Lawrie GM, Morris GC, Claeser DH, DeBakey ME: Renovascular reconstruction: Factors affecting long-term prognosis in 919 patients followed up in 31 years. Am J Cardiol 1989;63:1085-1092.

Novick AC, Scoble J, Hamilton G (eds): Renal Vascular Disease. London, WB Saunders, 1996.

Novick AC, Straffon RA, Stewart BH, et al: Diminished operative morbidity and mortality following revascularization for atherosclerotic renovascular disease. JAMA 1981;246:749-753.

Novick AC, Ziegelbaum M, Vidt DG, et al: Trends in surgical revascularization for renal artery disease: Ten years' experience. JAMA 1987;257:498-501.

Olin JW, Melia M, Young JR, et al: Prevalence of atherosclerotic renal artery stenosis in patients with atherosclerosis elsewhere. Am J Med 1990;188:46-51.

Schreiber MJ, Pohl MA, Novick AC: The natural history of atherosclerotic and fibrous renal artery disease. Urol Clin North Am 1984;11:383.

Steinbach F, Novick AC, Campbell S, Dykstra D: Long-term survival after surgical revascularization for atherosclerotic renal artery disease. J Urol 1997;158:38-41.

Taylor AT Jr, Fletcher JW, Nally JV Jr, et al: Procedure guideline for diagnosis of renovascular hypertension. Society of Nuclear Medicine. J Nucl Med 1998;39:1297-1302.

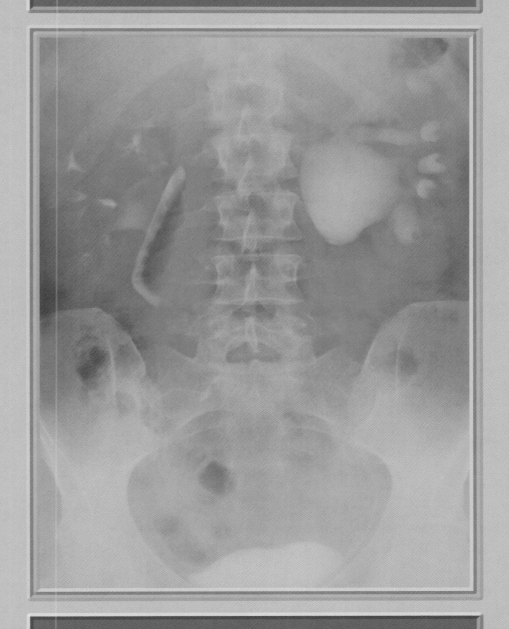

# UPPER URINARY TRACT OBSTRUCTION AND TRAUMA

# 37 Pathophysiology of Urinary Tract Obstruction

VERNON M. PAIS JR., MD • JACK W. STRANDHOY, PHD • DEAN G. ASSIMOS, MD

PREVALENCE OF THE PROBLEM

GLOBAL RENAL FUNCTIONAL CHANGES

PATHOLOGIC CHANGES OF OBSTRUCTION

GENERAL ISSUES IN MANAGEMENT OF PATIENTS

SELECTED EXTRINSIC CAUSES OF URETERAL OBSTRUCTION

Obstruction of the urinary tract can occur during fetal development, childhood, or adulthood. The point of obstruction can be as proximal as the calyces and as distal as the urethral meatus. The cause of obstruction may be congenital or acquired and benign or malignant. The impact of the obstruction is influenced by the extent or degree of obstruction (partial or compete, unilateral or bilateral), its chronicity (acute or chronic), the baseline condition of the kidneys, the potential for recovery, and the presence of other mitigating factors such as urinary infection. These may ultimately lead to permanent renal damage, which may result in limiting the excretion of metabolic wastes and altering water and electrolyte balance.

Certain terms utilized in this chapter as descriptors of this process need to be defined from the outset. *Hydronephrosis* is the dilation of the renal pelvis or calyces. It may be associated with obstruction but may be present in the absence of obstruction. *Obstructive uropathy* refers to the functional or anatomic obstruction of urinary flow at any level of the urinary tract. *Obstructive nephropathy* is present when the obstruction causes functional or anatomic renal damage.

## PREVALENCE OF THE PROBLEM

The prevalence of urinary tract obstruction is best estimated from autopsy series. In a series of 59,064 autopsies performed on individuals ranging from neonates to geriatric subjects, hydronephrosis was reported in 3.1% (Bell,1950). There were no gender differences in this series until the age of 20 years. However, hydronephrosis was more prevalent in women in the

20- to 60-year interval. The latter was attributed to pregnancy and development of gynecologic malignancies. It was more prevalent in males after age 60 years because of prostatic diseases. Hydronephrosis has been reported to be present in 2% to 2.5% of children subjected to autopsy (Campbell, 1970; Tan et al, 1994). It is somewhat more prevalent in boys, and the majority of cases were in subjects younger than 1 year. The aforementioned prevalences are most likely an underestimate of obstructive events, as temporary bouts of obstruction such as those induced by prior pregnancy or stone episodes were not captured.

The pathophysiology of obstructive nephropathy is discussed in detail in the beginning of this chapter to provide a platform for understanding the clinical ramifications of this process, some of which are detailed in later sections that focus on unique causes of obstructive uropathy. The mechanisms of obstructive nephropathy are unveiled at genetic, molecular, cellular, glomerular, renal tubular, whole kidney, and systemic levels. The impact of obstruction on the fetal and developing kidney is not emphasized as this is covered in other sections of this book. A list of possible causes of obstructive nephropathy is provided in Table 37–1.

## GLOBAL RENAL FUNCTIONAL CHANGES
### Glomerular Filtration, Renal Blood Flow, Collecting System Pressure

There are many functional changes in the kidney associated with obstructive uropathy that affect renal hemodynamic variables and glomerular filtration. These are influenced by the extent and severity of obstruction, whether the obstruction is unilateral or bilateral, and whether the obstruction currently persists or has been relieved. A brief discussion of the determinants of glomerular filtration is in order to understand the interrelationships between changes in renal hemodynamics and alterations in the glomerular filtration rate (GFR) during and after obstruction. Factors influencing GFR are expressed in the following equation:

$$GFR = K_f (P_{GC} - P_T - \pi_{GC})$$

$K_f$ is a glomerular ultrafiltration coefficient related to the surface area and permeability of the capillary membrane. $P_{GC}$ is the glomerular capillary pressure, which is influenced by

### Table 37–1. Possible Causes of Obstructive Nephropathy

| | |
|---|---|
| *Renal* | |
| Congenital | Polycystic kidney |
| | Renal cyst |
| | Fibrous obstruction at ureteropelvic junction |
| | Peripelvic cyst |
| | Aberrant vessel at ureteropelvic junction |
| Neoplastic | Wilms' tumor |
| | Renal cell carcinoma |
| | Transitional cell carcinoma of the renal pelvis |
| | Multiple myeloma |
| Inflammatory | Tuberculosis |
| | *Echinococcus* infection |
| Metabolic | Calculi |
| Miscellaneous | Sloughed papillae |
| | Trauma |
| | Renal artery aneurysm |
| *Ureter* | |
| Congenital | Stricture |
| | Ureterocele |
| | Ureterovesical reflux |
| | Ureteral valve |
| | Ectopic kidney |
| | Retrocaval ureter |
| | Prune-belly syndrome |
| Neoplastic | Primary carcinoma of ureter |
| | Metastatic carcinoma |
| Inflammatory | Tuberculosis |
| | Schistosomiasis |
| | Abscess |
| | Ureteritis cystica |
| | Endometriosis |
| Miscellaneous | Retroperitoneal fibrosis |
| | Pelvic lipomatosis |
| | Aortic aneurysm |
| | Radiation therapy |
| | Lymphocele |
| | Trauma |
| | Urinoma |
| | Pregnancy |
| *Bladder and Urethra* | |
| Congenital | Posterior urethral valve |
| | Phimosis |
| | Urethral stricture |
| | Hypospadias and epispadias |
| | Hydrocolpos |
| Neoplastic | Bladder carcinoma |
| | Prostate carcinoma |
| | Carcinoma of urethra |
| | Carcinoma of penis |
| Inflammatory | Prostatitis |
| | Paraurethral abscess |
| Miscellaneous | Benign prostatic hypertrophy |
| | Neurogenic bladder |

renal plasma flow and the resistances of the afferent and efferent arterioles. The hydraulic pressure driving fluid into Bowman's space is resisted by the hydraulic pressure of fluid in the tubule ($P_T$) and also the increasing oncotic pressure ($\pi$) of the proteins remaining in higher concentration in the late glomerular capillary and efferent arteriolar blood. Although filtered fluid is not completely free of small proteins, for practical purposes, its oncotic pressure is negligible. The net pressure determining glomerular filtration is referred to as the ultrafiltration pressure ($P_{UF}$) and is derived from ($P_{GC} - P_T - \pi_{GC}$). $P_{GC}$ is also influenced by renal plasma flow (RPF). RPF depends upon the renal perfusion pressure and intrarenal resistance to flow, the latter primarily mediated by the resistances in the afferent and efferent arterioles. The aforementioned relationships are depicted in the following equation:

$$RPF = \frac{(aortic\ pressure - renal\ venous\ pressure)}{renal\ vascular\ resistance}$$

Thus, constriction of the afferent or efferent arteriole or both would reduce RPF. Constriction of the afferent arteriole results in a decrease of $P_{GC}$ and GFR, whereas an increase in efferent arteriolar resistance increases $P_{GC.}$ Whole kidney GFR depends upon factors regulating perfusion of each glomerulus and also upon the percentage of glomeruli actually filtering. For each glomerulus, the single-nephron glomerular filtration rate (SNGFR) is determined by the previously mentioned GFR equation. Obstruction can transiently or permanently alter GFR and some or all of the determinants of GFR.

The results of animal experiments are used here to profile the hemodynamic, renal, and systemic responses of renal obstruction. The limitations of animal models including the potential for a species-specific response must be taken into consideration when making analogies or comparisons with humans.

## Hemodynamic Changes with Unilateral Ureteral Occlusion

There are differences between unilateral ureteral obstruction (UUO) and bilateral obstruction (BUO) that have been characterized in animal models. These include hemodynamic patterns and other factors that influence GFR. Renal blood flow (RBF) was assessed in the classical studies characterizing hemodynamic differences. In some, RBF was measured directly with various types of flow probes, and in others it was determined indirectly by measuring RPF using secretory markers and indexing this to hematocrit. A number of vasoactive substances are thought to play a role in the changes in RBF and GFR occurring with both models of obstruction. The timing of changes in intrarenal concentrations of vasoconstrictors and vasodilators during the course of obstruction and the release of obstruction is poorly understood. The varying hemodynamic patterns during the time course of obstruction may be due to a combination of vasoactive hormones synthesized and released at different rates, physical damage to glomerular and tubular units, and extrarenal compensatory mechanisms.

**Animal experiments have demonstrated a triphasic pattern of RBF and ureteral pressure changes in UUO that differs from BUO or unilateral obstruction of a solitary kidney** (Fig. 37–1). With UUO, RBF increases during the first 1 to 2 hours and is accompanied by a high $P_T$ and collecting system pressure because of the obstruction. In a second phase lasting 3 to 4 hours, these pressure parameters remain elevated but RBF begins to decline. A third phase beginning about 5 hours after obstruction is characterized by a further decline in RBF, now paralleled by a decrease in $P_T$ and collecting system pressure. These changes are explained by physical alterations in flow dynamics within the kidney and are modified by changes in the biochemical and hormonal milieu regulating renal resistance.

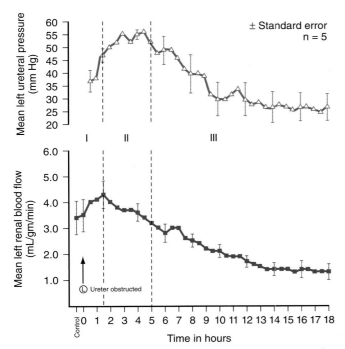

**Figure 37–1.** Triphasic relationship between ipsilateral renal blood flow and left ureteral pressure during 18 hours of left-sided occlusion. The three phases are designated by Roman numerals and separated by vertical dashed lines. In phase I, renal blood flow and ureteral pressure rise together. In phase II, the left renal blood flow begins to decline and ureteral pressure remains elevated and, in fact, continues to rise. In phase III, the left renal blood flow and ureteral pressure decline together. (From Moody TE, Vaughn ED Jr, Gillenwater JY: Relationship between renal blood flow and ureteral pressure during 18 hours of total unilateral urethral occlusion. Implications for changing sites of increased renal resistance. Invest Urol 1975;13:246-251.)

In the first phase of UUO, the increase in $P_T$ would logically be expected to reduce GFR greatly. However, this is counterbalanced by an increase in RBF related to afferent arteriolar vasodilation (Vaughan et al, 1970), which limits the fall in GFR because $P_{GC}$ rises. This hyperemic response has been attributed to stimulation of the tubuloglomerular feedback mechanism that relaxes the afferent arterioles as a consequence of decreased sodium delivery to the macula densa (Wright and Briggs, 1979), changes in interstitial pressure within the kidney (Vaughan et al, 1971; Francisco et al, 1980), or the release of vasodilators such as prostanoids like prostaglandin $E_2$ ($PGE_2$) (Allen et al, 1978). There are various lines of evidence supporting the role of prostaglandin involvement. Frøkiær and Sørensen (1995) demonstrated an increase in $PGE_2$ excretion in the urine from the contralateral kidney after UUO. In addition, studies have shown that the increase in $PGE_2$ and the vasodilation of the obstructed kidney could be blocked by indomethacin, a prostaglandin synthesis inhibitor (Allen et al, 1978; Blackshear and Wathen, 1978; Gaudio et al, 1980). Nitric oxide (NO) may also contribute to the early renal vasodilation in UUO. The kidney contains nitric oxide synthases that are both constitutive (endothelial and neuronal isoforms) and inducible (iNOS). In obstructed kidneys from rabbits and rodents, iNOS increases (Salvemini et al, 1994; Miyajima et al, 2001). Furthermore, Lanzone and

colleagues (1995) showed that administration of the NOS inhibitor $N^{\omega}$-monomethyl-L-arginine (L-NMMA) before UUO attenuated the early rise in RBF and that the renal vasodilation returned when L-NMMA was discontinued. **Thus, it is likely that both $PGE_2$ and NO contribute to the net renal vasodilation that occurs early following UUO.**

After this initial phase of several hours, GFR and RBF progressively decline in UUO (Jaenike, 1972; Harris and Yarger, 1974; Dal Canton et al, 1980). In contrast to the early rise in $P_T$ in the initial phases of UUO, this parameter and RBF both decline 12 to 24 hours after obstruction. This is best explained by an increase in afferent arteriolar resistance ($R_{aff}$) that occurs. At this time, there are also shifts in regional blood flow in the kidney with large portions of the cortical vascular bed not perfused or underperfused (Harris and Yarger, 1974; Gaudio et al, 1980). A shift in RBF from the outer cortex to more juxtamedullary regions was reported by Yarger and Griffith (1974) in dogs with UUO. **Thus, reduced whole kidney GFR at this stage of obstruction is due not only to reduced perfusion of individual glomeruli related to afferent vasoconstriction and reduced $P_{GC}$ but also to global reduction in filtration related to no perfusion or underperfusion of many glomeruli** (Arendshorst et al, 1974).

Vasoconstrictors appear to play a role in the reduction in RBF after UUO. There is evidence that the renin-angiotensin system is activated during UUO because during the first phase of UUO renal vein renin levels increase (Moody et al, 1975; Yarger et al, 1980) even though there is a net renal vasodilation at this time. **Infusion of the angiotensin-converting enzyme (ACE) inhibitor captopril attenuates the declines in RBF and GFR in UUO, suggesting that angiotensin II is an important mediator of the preglomerular vasoconstriction occurring during the second and third phases of UUO** (Ichikawa et al, 1985).

Other vasoconstrictors also appear to be involved in the reduction of RBF with UUO. Thromboxane $A_2$ ($TXA_2$) is also thought to be an influential postobstructive vasoconstrictor that contributes to the continued reduction in GFR and RBF. Administration of $TXA_2$ synthesis inhibitors to the obstructed kidney limits the reduction in RBF and GFR (Klotman et al, 1986; Loo et al, 1987; Purkerson and Klahr, 1989). $TXA_2$ may be generated in the kidney itself, perhaps in glomeruli (Yanigasawa et al, 1990), but synthesis from macrophages migrating to the kidney during obstruction is another potential source of this vasoconstrictor (Schreiner et al, 1988; Harris et al, 1989).

Endothelin is another endogenous vasoconstrictor thought to participate in these events, although perhaps later in the established phase of UUO and after release of the obstruction. Administration of endothelin antagonists limits the reduction of RBF and GFR in rats during and after release of UUO (Syed et al, 1998; Bhangdia et al, 1998; Colon et al, 2000). Furthermore, endothelin excretion is increased in the targeted kidney after release of UUO in swine but not in the contralateral renal unit (Kelleher et al, 1992).

The kidney's response to the release of UUO depends on the duration and extent of obstruction and is also species specific. Many models of UUO use complete obstruction of the ureter for 24 hours before release. After release of 24-hour UUO, the GFR is initially 50% of normal in dogs and less than 25% of normal in rats, accompanied by greatly reduced RBF.

There are also regional differences within the kidney. Harris and Yarger (1974) showed a marked decrease in perfusion of the superficial cortex accompanied by an increase in juxtamedullary glomerular perfusion after release of 24 hours of UUO in rats. Tubuloglomerular feedback may play a role these responses (Tanner, 1985). Some of the mediators of the hemodynamic changes in the kidney following release of the obstruction may be different from those involved in the earlier phases.

## Hemodynamic Changes with Bilateral Ureteral Occlusion

The changes with BUO or obstruction of a solitary kidney are different. **In contrast to the early robust renal vasodilation with UUO, there is a modest increase in RBF with BUO lasting approximately 90 minutes followed by a prolonged and profound decrease in RBF that is greater than that found with UUO** (Gulmi et al, 1995). Reyes and Klahr (1992) found that an NO synthesis antagonist caused a further decline in RBF and GFR compared with control values, suggesting that NO helps maintain renal hemodynamics in early BUO. Other potential vasodilators, such as platelet-activating factor, have been postulated to contribute to renal hemodynamic changes with BUO. Reyes and Klahr (1991) showed in rats that when vasoconstrictors such as $TXA_2$ were blocked, endogenous or exogenous intrarenal PAF vasodilation contributed to the preservation of RBF and GFR. The earlier and more profound decrease in RBF with BUO may be contributed to by increased renal nerve stimulation that initiates vasoconstriction related to increased renorenal reflex activity (Francisco et al, 1980; Ma et al, 2002). Endothelin may also contribute to these responses in BUO. The administration of an endothelin antibody to rats with BUO was reported to attenuate the decreases in GFR and RPF (Reyes and Klahr, 1992). Angiotensin II and $TXA_2$ are also probably involved in the changes occurring with BUO. The administration of inhibitors of either of these vasoconstrictors to rats prior to BUO resulted in improved postobstructive GFR and RPF as compared with when they were administered at the time of release of obstruction (Purkerson and Klahr, 1989).

The intrarenal distribution of blood flow is quite different with BUO than with models of UUO. Jaenike (1972) used microspheres to show that 55% of the RBF perfused the cortical nephrons while the innermost zones received only 14% of the flow in rats after BUO. Similarly, Solez and associates (1976) showed a 92% decrease in inner medullary plasma flow with 18 hours of BUO in rats. **Thus, the shift seen with UUO of blood flow from outer to inner cortex is the opposite with BUO.**

Ureteral pressure is higher with BUO than with UUO. Although in both cases ureteral and tubular pressure is increased for the first 4 to 5 hours, the ureteral pressure remains elevated for at least 24 hours with BUO, whereas it begins to decline and approaches preocclusion pressures by 24 hours with UUO. The prolonged elevation in intratubular pressure contributes to the profound decrease in SNGFR and whole kidney GFR. Micropuncture studies (Yarger et al, 1972; Dal Canton et al, 1980) in which intratubular pressure is measured directly have demonstrated that it remains elevated

in rats after 24 hours of BUO in comparison with pressure normalization in animals after 24 hours of UUO. Ureteral pressure remains high because BUO passes through a phase of preglomerular vasodilation and then a prolonged postglomerular vasoconstriction. This explains the persistent elevation in ureteral pressure in spite of a decrease in RBF and increase in renal resistance. In contrast, in UUO the initial preglomerular dilation and short-lived postglomerular vasoconstriction are followed by a more prolonged preglomerular vasoconstriction that tempers elevations in $P_{GC}$ and hence in $P_T$. **This difference between the two pathophysiologic conditions has been hypothesized to be due to an accumulation of vasoactive substances in BUO that could contribute to preglomerular vasodilation and postglomerular vasoconstriction. Such substances would not accumulate in UUO as they would be excreted by the contralateral kidney. Atrial natriuretic peptide (ANP) appears to be one of these substances** (Purkerson et al, 1989). With excretory ability abrogated, BUO increases intravascular volume, as evidenced by an increase in pulmonary capillary wedge pressure and body weight, which serves as the stimulus for secretion of ANP. ANP increases afferent arteriolar dilation and efferent arteriolar vasoconstriction, thus increasing $P_{GC}$. It also decreases the sensitivity of tubuloglomerular feedback, inhibits release of renin, and increases $K_f$ (Fried et al, 1987; Brenner et al, 1990; Cogan, 1990).

Glomerular filtration and RBF remain depressed after release of BUO. This is due to persistent vasoconstriction of the afferent arteriole (Jaenike, 1972; Moody et al, 1977). The decrease in RBF in the renal medulla remains more prominent than in the cortex (Solez et al, 1976). Tubuloglomerular feedback does not appear to contribute to this response as it does with UUO (Tanner, 1985). Urine flow and sodium excretion are increased after release of BUO. ANP appears to play a prominent role in this response based on its natriuretic properties and those previously reviewed. It may also have a protective effect. Ryndin and associates (2005) reported that the administration of ANP or phosphoramidon, an inhibitor of ANP degradation, to rats with BUO resulted in improved GFR and a more brisk diuresis and natriuresis after release of obstruction.

In summary, both UUO and BUO involve increases in renal vascular resistances and increases in ureteral pressures. However, the timing and regulation of these changes differ (Fig. 37–2). With UUO, early renal vasodilation primarily mediated by prostaglandins and NO is followed by prolonged vasoconstriction and normalization of intratubular-ureteral pressure as the contralateral kidney contributes to fluid balance. With BUO, little early vasodilation is seen and vasoconstriction is more profound. When the obstruction is released, the postobstructive diuresis is much greater with BUO because volume expansion, urea and other osmolytes, and secreted ANP contribute to a profound diuresis and natriuresis.

## Partial Ureteral Occlusion

Although most models of urinary tract obstruction study complete obstruction over a fixed time interval such as 24 hours, many clinical conditions involve partial obstruction over varying times. Partial obstruction models often involve

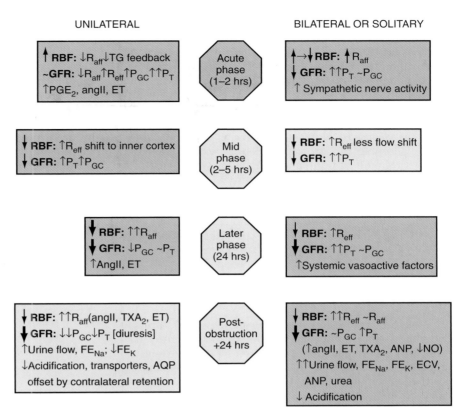

**Figure 37-2.** Summary of the functional changes during and following ureteral obstruction. Symbols and abbreviations indicate $\uparrow\downarrow$, increases and decreases; $\sim$, little change; angII, angiotensin II; ANP, atrial natriuretic peptide; AQP, aquaporin; ECV, extracellular volume; ET, endothelin; FE, fractional excretion; NO, nitric oxide; $P_{GC}$, glomerular capillary hydraulic pressure; $P_T$, proximal tubular hydraulic pressure; $PGE_2$, prostaglandin $E_2$; $R_{aff}$, afferent arteriolar resistance; $R_{eff}$, efferent arteriolar resistance; RBF, renal blood flow; TG feedback, tubuloglomerular feedback; $TXA_2$, thromboxane $A_2$.

perinatal obstruction because renal growth and differentiation may be affected as well as hemodynamics and excretion. In many cases, the changes in renal hemodynamics and in tubular function are similar to those induced by more acute, complete models of obstruction but develop more slowly. In other cases, such as perinatal models of obstruction either before or shortly after birth, an animal such as a rat is still in a period of nephrogenesis. **Consequently, formation of glomeruli and tubules may be compromised so that irreversible changes occur without total loss of kidney function.**

Recovery of renal function in adult animals with partial obstruction has been studied as a potential guideline for clinical treatment. Leahy and coworkers (1989) studied dogs in which partial UUO with stents was studied for up to 60 days. Reversibility of renal function was estimated by creatinine clearance. Renal function became normal in dogs partially obstructed for 14 days. Animals partially obstructed for 28 days recovered 31% of function, and those partially obstructed for 60 days recovered only 8% of function. Casts of the microvasculature showed arteriolar constriction, supporting the concept that postobstructive renal dysfunction is influenced by vascular responses.

Much less is known about the roles of vasoactive or inflammatory mediators in the partial ureteral obstruction model. As with acute occlusive models, administration of indomethacin or meclofenamate, both prostaglandin synthetase inhibitors, decreases GFR and increases arteriolar resistance (Ichikawa and Brenner, 1979) so that changes in eicosanoids are implicated in partial obstruction responses. Several investigators have shown that the renin-angiotensin-aldosterone axis is activated with partial obstruction, including studies in

the fetus. Gobet and colleagues (1999) studied fetal sheep in utero and showed that partial obstruction of the bladder outlet increased renin messenger RNA (mRNA) after 2 weeks and increased the expression of renal $AT_2$ receptors as well as the mRNA for transforming growth factor $\beta$ (TGF-$\beta$), a mediator of fibrosis.

One could hypothesize that changes in angiotensin II may be responsible for much of the hemodynamic, fibrotic, and apoptotic changes in neonatal animals with partial obstruction, as has been shown in more acute models. Beharrie and coworkers (2004) examined weanling male rats that had been subjected to a partial UUO. The partial obstruction led to proteinuria, hyperuricemia, and increased solute excretion primarily from the unaffected contralateral kidney. A parallel group of rats treated with the ACE inhibitor enalapril was protected from these changes. This suggests that angiotensin is involved with functional tubular changes as well. Eskild-Jensen and colleagues (2002) examined partial UUO for up to 24 weeks in young, postnatal pigs. The number of glomeruli was 28% less in the obstructed kidney, yet function was just transiently reduced by the occlusion. **Thus, partial neonatal obstruction can impair nephrogenesis independently of renal functional decline and these changes may depend upon species, stage of renal development, or degree of occlusion.** More work is needed to define the variables.

Various methods have been used to create partial obstruction. The models for preparing partial ureteral occlusions fall into three main categories. Intraluminal stents or catheters of varying sizes have been placed in the ureters of sheep (Abu-Zidan et al, 1999) and in dogs (Ryan and Fitzpatrick, 1987; Leahy et al, 1989) to restrict flow. In rats, or in growing animals, many investigators have used the technique of Ulm and Miller (1962), which involves splitting the psoas muscle longitudinally to form a groove into which the ureter is placed. This method has a potential advantage of increased constriction in proportion to the growth of the animal. Beharrie and colleagues (2004) used such a technique in young male weanling rats. A major problem with studies involving partial obstruction is the ability to determine reproducibly and accurately the degree of obstruction induced with these techniques. Thornhill and associates (2005) devised a method in neonatal rat pups of ligating a ureter along with a wire of a calibrated diameter that was then removed to make a partial and graded constriction of one ureter. When ureteral diameter was reduced by 70% to 75%, renal growth and number of glomeruli were reduced and fibrosis and pelvic dilation were proportionally increased. GFR was reduced by 80% after 28 days of partial UUO. Such models may offer new opportunities to model the clinical condition reproducibly.

## Egress of Urine from the Kidney

Although the normal flow of urine from the kidney through the urinary tract is compromised with obstruction, urine may still egress from the kidney. An example of this is extravasation at the calyceal fornix (pyelosinus) that occurs with acute obstruction, typically ureteral stones (Stenberg et al, 1988). Extravasation of urine into the venous (pyelovenous) and lymphatic system (pyelolymphatic) may also occur in this setting. In chronic obstruction, fluid is thought to exit into the renal venous system.

## Effects of Obstruction on Tubular Function

Obstruction of one or both kidneys can have profound effects on sodium, potassium, and hydrogen excretion and mechanisms of urinary concentration and dilution. In the case of UUO, relatively normal function of the nonobstructed kidney partially offsets the reduced ability of the postobstructive kidney to reabsorb solutes and water. **Postobstructive diuresis, something that is commonly encountered after reversal of BUO, occurs uncommonly after release of UUO, probably as a consequence of the contralateral renal unit's functional capacities.** The eventual correction of abnormal renal excretory function depends upon the degree and duration of obstruction.

Changes in tubule function after correction of UUO related to ureteropelvic junction or ureteral obstruction were characterized in 10 patients by Gillenwater and colleagues (1975). The mean period of obstruction in these cases was 12 months and the range was from days to years. Functions of the normal and obstructed kidney were evaluated 1 week after relief of the obstruction. The GFR in the obstructed kidney was significantly less than that in the nonobstructed kidney (24 versus 60 mL/min), and the urine osmolality, osmolar clearance, and fractional free water clearance were all significantly less in the postobstructed kidney. The similar osmolar clearances (volume of urine required to excrete urinary solute isosmotically) relative to GFR of the previously obstructed and unobstructed kidneys indicate that there is a true concentrat-

ing defect in the obstructed kidneys 1 week after relief of obstruction.

## Urinary Concentrating Ability

**Normal urine concentrating ability requires a hypertonic medullary interstitial gradient because of active salt reabsorption from the thick ascending limb of Henle, urea back flux from the inner medullary collecting duct, and water permeability of the collecting duct mediated by vasopressin and aquaporin water channels.** Obstructive nephropathy can disrupt some or all of these mechanisms and lead to deficits in urinary concentration. A brief review of the normal concentrating mechanisms is provided to facilitate understanding the effects of obstruction.

In normal physiology, AVP is secreted into the bloodstream from the posterior pituitary gland in response to increased serum osmolality or a reduction in effective circulating volume. Arginine vasopressin binds to the V2 vasopressin receptor located on the basolateral surfaces of the collecting duct cells. This promotes G protein signaling, resulting in generation of cyclic adenosine monophosphate (cAMP). Generation of cAMP in turn activates protein kinase A, which stimulates the fusion of cytoplasmic vesicles containing aquaporin 2 (AQP2) with the apical membranes of the collecting duct cells. The fusion causes the normally water tight membrane to become water permeable. This promotes transcellular absorption of water through the AQP2 channels, which is transported through aquaporin 3 (AQP3) and aquaporin 4 (AQP4) channels located in the basolateral cell membrane into the interstitium. This sequence of events is driven by the osmotic gradient of sodium (Knoers, 2005). Another aquaporin, aquaporin 1 (AQP1), is abundant in renal proximal tubules, the thin descending limb of Henle, and the descending vasa recta in the kidney. It promotes urinary concentration through the countercurrent multiplier by facilitating water transport from the descending limb of Henle into the interstitium (King et al, 2001).

The onset of concentration defects may develop soon after obstruction. Jaenike and Bray (1960) demonstrated a concentrating defect in the unilaterally obstructed kidney after only 6 minutes of ureteral obstruction. Development of vasopressin resistance has been hypothesized as a mechanism of this occurrence. However, various studies have demonstrated conflicting results concerning whether vasopressin resistance is present. Vascular changes may play a role. Even after only 18 hours of UUO, Solez and colleagues (1976) found a decrease in inner medullary plasma flow that increased when the occlusion was released. Necrosis of both the inner and outer medullae was present, indicating that ischemia may contribute to the development of a concentrating defect.

Evidence from Li and coworkers (2001) demonstrated that the polyuria following the release of BUO correlates with a decreased expression of the aquaporin water channels AQP1, AQP2, and AQP3 in rats. Release of obstruction resulted in polyuria that gradually decreased over a 30-day period, even though urinary concentrating capacity remained significantly impaired. Expression of AQP2 and AQP3 became normal by 30 days after release, but the expression of AQP1 remained decreased. **Thus, dysregulation of aquaporin water channels in the proximal tubule, thin descending loop, and collecting** duct may contribute to the long-term polyuria and impaired concentrating capacity of obstructive nephropathy.

## Sodium Transport

A decrease in sodium transport in the nephron appears to play an additional prominent role in the decreased ability of the postobstructed kidney to concentrate and dilute urine. When UUO is released after an occlusion period of 24 hours, total urine excretion is normal to modestly increased despite increased fractional excretion of sodium ($FE_{Na}$) in the previously obstructed kidney. This is attributed to the contralateral kidney compensating for the sodium losses of its mate. However, with BUO, sodium and water excretions may be quite robust after release of obstruction. The $FE_{Na}$ may be increased to as much as 20 times normal in this setting (Zeidel and Pirtskhalaishvili, 2004). **Although ANP appears to play a role in sodium diuresis after release of BUO, it is unlikely to affect sodium transport defects associated with UUO.** The latter is most likely due to selective cell membrane changes in the nephron that reduce the number and effectiveness of sodium transporters. Such changes may also occur with BUO.

In spite of differential quantitative responses between UUO and BUO after release of the obstruction, the reabsorption defects in segmental nephron $Na^+$ transport are similar. Micropuncture studies of kidneys from animals have been undertaken to assess these responses. These studies demonstrate normal to modestly enhanced isotonic volume flux ($J_v$) in superficial proximal convoluted tubules after release of UUO or BUO. On the other hand, sodium delivery to the loop of Henle in juxtamedullary nephrons and to the first accessible portion of the inner medullary collecting duct is substantially increased after release of both UUO and BUO, indicative of reduced sodium transport. Sonnenberg and Wilson (1976) even found evidence for net addition of sodium throughout the medullary collecting duct, which further contributed to an increased $FE_{Na}$. However, this was more prominent with BUO in their rat model.

Studies in isolated perfused nephron segments have also provided knowledge about the impact of obstruction at the level of the nephron. They have shown normal isotonic reabsorption in the superficial proximal convoluted tubules from animals with either UUO or BUO, whereas $J_v$ in proximal straight tubules from juxtamedullary nephrons was demonstrated to be impaired (Hanley and Davidson, 1982). Similarly, chloride reabsorption and transport-dependent oxygen consumption ($QO_2$) from the medullary thick ascending limb of Henle's loop (MTAL) were severely impaired (Hanley and Davidson, 1982; Hwang et al, 1993a).

Cell suspensions from nephron segments have been used to assess the effects of obstruction at a cellular level. Active transport of $Na^+$ across cell membranes requires apical entry through selective $Na^+$ transporters or channels and basolateral exit driven by sodium-potassium adenosine triphosphatase ($Na^+,K^+$-ATPase). Furthermore, adequate adenosine triphosphate (ATP) must be generated to drive these primary transport steps. Hwang and associates (1993c) showed that the amount and activity of the apical $Na^+$, $K^+$, $2Cl^-$ cotransporter and bumetanide binding sites were reduced in cells isolated from the MTAL derived from obstructed rabbit kidneys. Basolateral transport is also affected in that ouabain-sensitive

oxygen consumption, an index of $Na^+,K^+$-ATPase activity, has been shown to be reduced in cell suspensions from obstructed kidneys (Hwang et al, 1993a). A marked decrease in amiloride-sensitive oxygen consumption and $Na^+$ entry in isolated cells from the inner medullary collecting ducts of obstructed rabbit kidneys reflects reduced activity of the apical Na channel (ENaC). In addition, ouabain-sensitive transport as measured by oxygen consumption and ATPase activity was shown to be reduced in cells from this portion of the nephron harvested from obstructed kidneys (Hwang et al, 1993c). Because cell suspension studies indicate that ATP generation is not the rate-limiting step underlying sodium transport dysfunction in this setting, the evidence points to downregulation of sodium transporters. This may be due to translational factors (reduction in mRNA for transporter synthesis) or post-translational processing of receptor proteins (Hwang et al, 1993c).

The signals responsible for downregulation of transporter activity with obstruction have not been clearly defined, but a number have been hypothesized. Stasis of tubular fluid flow may be one of the signals. When urine flow is obstructed, upstream $Na^+$ delivery to apical cell membranes slows so that the transmembrane gradient is reduced. This could then serve as the signal for the downregulation of transporter activity or expression resulting in reduced active $Na^+$ transport across the basolateral cell membrane (Zeidel, 1993). Several studies indicate that this is a feasible mechanism. For example, ouabain-sensitive $Na^+,K^+$-ATPase activity is reduced in MTAL and collecting duct cells when mineralocorticoid activity is controlled and chronic furosemide or amiloride is given to reduce $Na^+$ entry into tubule cells (Petty et al, 1981; Grossman and Hebert, 1988). Additional studies have explored this concept in established cell lines. When A6 cells, an established line of collecting duct cells, are grown on a permeable substrate, $Na^+$ influx across the apical membrane through the ENaC $Na^+$ channel occurs. When $Na^+$ entry was blocked, this induced a decreased expression of the β-subunit of the epithelial sodium channel in the apical membrane (Rokaw et al, 1996). Ischemia has also been proposed as a signal in this setting, where ischemia that accompanies the reduced perfusion of the kidney with obstruction can also be a mediator of reduced transporter expression. The reduction in major renal sodium transporters reported with ischemic models of renal failure supports this concept (Kwon et al, 2000). Other proposed downstream signals include changes in renal interstitial pressure and local generation of natriuretic substances. **Thus, substrate delivery may be a regulatory step in the expression of sodium and possibly other transporters.**

Intrarenal and extrarenal substances and hormones can also modulate sodium transport. The milieu of influential hormones may be substantially different between UUO and BUO. A number of investigators have shown that obstruction markedly increases the endogenous production of $PGE_2$ in the renal medulla. Furthermore, supraphysiologic concentrations of $PGE_2$ are well known to produce natriuresis (Strandhoy et al, 1974), and studies in isolated tubules and cell suspensions show that $PGE_2$ inhibits Na reabsorption in the MTAL and throughout the collecting duct (CD). One mechanism of this natriuretic response may be that $PGE_2$ reduces the amount of $Na^+,K^+$-ATPase at the basolateral membrane (Marver and Bernabe, 1992). $PGE_2$ can also inhibit the tubular effects of vasopressin (Zook and Strandhoy, 1980), thereby contributing to the free water loss from the post-UUO kidney. The influence of other substances and hormones in the post-obstructed UUO kidney is counterbalanced or minimized by the contralateral renal unit.

Extracellular fluid volume may be greatly expanded with BUO. When the BUO is relieved, both intrarenal and extrarenal factors greatly enhance salt and water excretion so that a postobstructive diuresis is often seen. The normal physiologic consequences of extracellular fluid volume expansion ensue. These include a downregulation of sympathetic tone and the secretion of aldosterone and manifestation of the effects of ANP and probably other natriuretic factors. Levels of ANP are significantly elevated following BUO but not UUO (Purkerson and Klahr, 1989). The direct and indirect consequences of increased ANP levels include partial support of glomerular filtration, reduction of renin secretion and effects of angiotensin on transport, reduced aldosterone secretion, and direct inhibition of Na transport in the collecting duct (Brenner et al, 1990). Furthermore, BUO results in the accumulation of osmotic substances such as urea that can contribute to salt and water loss when the obstruction is relieved (Harris and Yarger, 1975, 1977). **Thus, the $FE_{Na}$ following relief of BUO is typically greater than that after UUO because BUO causes retention of Na, water, urea nitrogen, and other osmolar substances and increased production of ANP, all of which stimulate a profound natriuresis.**

## Potassium Transport

Obstruction has a complex impact on renal potassium handling, depending upon the type of obstruction. Harris and Yarger (1975) reported that there is a decrease in $K^+$ excretion, in proportion to the decrease in GFR, after release of a 24-hour period of UUO. This may be partially due to reduced delivery of Na to the distal nephron and a low volume flow rate that would minimize the transmembrane gradient for $K^+$ secretion. Other investigations indicate that there is also an intrinsic defect in $K^+$ secretion after relief of UUO (Thirakomen et al, 1976). In contrast, $K^+$ excretion increases in parallel with Na excretion with the relief of BUO. Micropuncture studies in rats showed that proximal reabsorption of $K^+$ remains unchanged whereas secretion in the collecting duct is increased following release of BUO. This may be due to the massive increases in $Na^+$ and water delivery to the collecting duct acting as stimuli to secretion and also to the presence of high levels of ANP that can stimulate $K^+$ secretion in the distal nephron (Sonnenberg and Wilson, 1976).

## Hydrogen Ion Transport and Urinary Acidification

**Obstruction causes a deficit in urinary acidification that has been demonstrated in human subjects as well as animal models.** The cumulative evidence indicates that the major acidification defect is in the distal nephron. Release of obstruction does not result in increased bicarbonate excretion, indicating that bicarbonate reclamation in the proximal tubule remains intact. In contrast, urinary pH does not decrease after an acid load, which is indicative of a distal nephron acidification defect, most likely related to defective

$H^+$ transport in the collecting duct. A number of causes for the lack of acidification have been proposed including defects in $H^+$-ATPase or $H^+,K^+$-ATPase, $Cl^-/HCO_3^-$ exchange, a back leak of protons into the renal interstitium, or failure to generate a satisfactory transluminal electrical gradient. Obstruction has been demonstrated to decrease the expression of $H^+$-ATPase in the apical membrane of the intercalated cells of the collecting duct. However, the extent of this apical transporter decrease was too small to explain the significant acidification defects that develop. Therefore, other mechanisms are also likely to play a role in the development of this acidification defect (Purcell et al, 1991). Valles and Manucha (2000) showed that the decrease in $H^+$-ATPase with UUO depends upon an increase in iNOS, which, in turn, appears to be regulated by angiotensin II. Thus, recovery of $H^+$-ATPase activity in the inner medullary collecting duct of obstructed kidneys by losartan treatment may be related to a decrease in angiotensin-stimulated iNOS activity.

In the proximal tubule, glutamine uptake and oxidation and ammonia generation are diminished after release of obstruction. This has an impact on acid elimination in that a greater proportion of $H^+$ is buffered as titratable acid. Because phosphate excretion may be compromised and binding of protons to phosphate has a limited capacity, the net result may be a lower urinary pH related to unbuffered protons in spite of a net decrease in total $H^+$ secretion.

## Effects of Obstruction on Anion and Other Cation Transport

The effects on phosphate reabsorption after the release of obstruction vary depending upon whether it was bilateral or unilateral. When BUO is released, accumulated phosphate is rapidly excreted in proportion to sodium (Beck, 1979). Conversely, a decrease in phosphate excretion and a net retention occur with release of UUO. Weinreb and colleagues (1982) showed that the decrease in the fractional excretion of phosphate following release of UUO in dogs produced no change in the transport of phosphate across brush border membrane vesicles. A reduced filtered load in the previously obstructed renal unit may stimulate increased phosphate reabsorption. Westenfelder and coauthors (1998) reported findings supporting the latter. They demonstrated that the increased reabsorption of phosphate after release of UUO in rats is due to a generalized increase in proximal tubular sodium reabsorption, a process linked to a reduction in GFR. They noted that this was linked to increased cotransport of phosphate and glucose with sodium.

Other cation excretion is also induced by obstruction. **Magnesium excretion is markedly increased after the release of either UUO or BUO.** The increase most likely results from compromised transport in the thick limb of Henle related to ischemia. This causes decreased influx of $Na^+$, $K^+$, and $Cl^-$ by the cotransporter and reduced back flux of $K^+$ across the apical membrane. It attenuates the positive luminal transepithelial voltage that normally drives the paracellular flux of both magnesium and calcium from lumen to basolateral membrane. The result is reduced passive reabsorption of $Mg^{2+}$ and $Ca^{2+}$ from the loop of Henle. However, calcium excretion may be increased or decreased, which depends to a degree on the type of obstruction and the species. Although $Mg^{2+}$ and $Ca^{2+}$ are handled similarly in the thick limb of Henle's loop, calcium handling in the early distal tubule differs. Beaumont and coworkers (1989) demonstrated that the thiazide-inhibitable sodium-chloride cotransporter is rapidly downregulated during ischemia such as may accompany ureteral occlusion. Blocking influx of $Na^+$ and $Cl^-$ through this transporter hyperpolarizes the cells in the distal nephron, thereby increasing calcium reabsorption (Gesek and Friedman, 1992). Thus, disruption of transport in areas of the nephron where $Ca^{2+}$ and $Mg^{2+}$ are differentially transported may account for varying effects of obstruction on their net transport and excretion.

Organic anions and cations are transported by the renal tubules as substrates of metabolism and as a mechanism of drug elimination. In rats, BUO decreases the renal clearance of *p*-aminohippurate (PAH), a prototypical substrate for the organic anion transporter 1 (OAT-1). Although secretion of PAH was reduced, the reduction did not correlate with a decrease in OAT-1 abundance or with cortical blood flow. It is postulated that decreased $Na^+,K^+$-ATPase activity, which provides the primary active transport to which OAT-1 is coupled, explains the decrease in PAH transport. In addition to the implications for drug transport and excretion with obstruction, this indicates that PAH clearance without measurement of extraction is an inaccurate index of RPF in postobstructed kidneys (Villar et al, 2004).

## Effect of Obstruction on the Excretion of Peptides and Proteins

Some peptides and small proteins are normally filtered by the glomerulus and readily absorbed in the nephron. Some enzymes and proteins such as Tamm-Horsfall protein and aquaporins may normally be secreted into the tubular fluid. Obstruction can exaggerate or disrupt the excretion of these proteins and peptides. Some changes simply represent alterations in transport, whereas others are due to tubular damage and remodeling.

Monocyte chemoattractant protein 1 is a mediator of the inflammatory process accompanying obstruction in the kidney. Its excretion in the urine after UUO increases (Stephan et al, 2002) and has been considered an index of tubular damage. Conversely, epidermal growth factor (EGF) excretion, the renal cortical and outer medullary concentration of pre-pro-EGF, and excretion of Tamm-Horsfall protein (Storch et al, 1992) all decrease with obstruction. Urinary enzymes thought to be derived from the proximal tubule such as alkaline phosphatase, γ-glutamyltransferase, *N*-acetyl-β-D-glucosaminidase, and leucine aminopeptidase have been reported to be elevated in patients with obstructed kidneys (Carr et al, 1994). However, such increases in enzymuria have been reported to be either biphasic, occurring only in the early stages of obstruction, or absent in animal models of partial or total ureteral obstruction (Everaert et al, 1998).

In summary, major changes occur with the ability of the kidney to concentrate the urine because of downregulation of transporters and aquaporin water channels. These defects are enduring and correct slowly with time. Sodium excretion is greater after relief of bilateral obstruction because extracellular volume is expanded and ANP directly affects

transport and glomerular filtration. Potassium and phosphate excretions follow changes in sodium; they are decreased with UUO because of altered transporters and postobstructive retention and increased transiently with BUO in parallel with the massive natriuresis. Obstruction causes a deficit in urinary acidification that has been demonstrated in humans and in animals. Magnesium excretion is increased in both models, but calcium handling is more complex. Changes in peptide excretion reflect mediators and markers of renal damage.

## Metabolic Determinants of Ion Transport

An overview of the normal metabolic processes linked to ion transport provides a foundation for the understanding of changes that occur with obstruction. The myriad of transporters involved in maintaining cellular homeostasis and electrolyte balance is integrated longitudinally and vertically within the nephron. Families of ion-translocating ATPases mediate primary and secondary transport and are fueled by the availability and synthesis of ATP. In addition to providing energy for ion pumps, the adenine nucleotides can directly influence ATP-sensitive $K^+$ channels that link the activity of the sodium pump with the leak of potassium in some of the nephron segments such as the thick ascending limb of Henle and the collecting duct.

Although there is considerable variability between nephron segments and even between species in the normal physiologic substrate for ATP generation in nephron segments, a few generalizations can be made. Aerobic glycolysis in several cell types including renal tubules links ATP generation to increased activity of $Na^+,K^+$-ATPase, $QO_2$ and ATP, and primary active transport of ions. In normal physiology, the renal cortex has a high rate of aerobic metabolism indicative of fatty acid oxidation and a low content of glycogen. Proximal tubules have relatively little glycolytic capacity and depend upon aerobic mitochondrial metabolism for ATP synthesis from substrates such as ketone bodies, fatty acids, glutamine, and lactate (Uchida and Endou, 1988; Ruegg and Mandel, 1990). Metabolism even varies along the length of the proximal tubule. For example, the proximal convoluted tubule cannot utilize glucose to support oxidative metabolism but the proximal straight tubules can.

The medullary and cortical regions of the thick ascending limb of Henle possess abundant mitochondria and high $QO_2$. Substantial energy reserve allows increased transport associated with glomerulotubular balance. This nephron segment and those downstream have the capability of aerobic and anaerobic glycolysis, which results in lactate accumulation and increased glycogen content (Abodeely and Lee, 1971; Cohen, 1979; Bagnasco et al, 1985). Compared with the proximal tubule, the medullary thick ascending loop of Henle has a greater capacity for anaerobic glycolysis but still requires ATP production from mitochondrial oxidative phosphorylation to maintain active $Na^+$ transport.

In addition to its role as a fuel for metabolism and transport, ATP and its metabolites can serve as regulators of solute transport such as the ATP-sensitive $K^+$ channels previously mentioned and activation of purinergic P2 receptors within the kidney that modulate solute transport (Schwiebert and Kishore, 2001).

Although substrate availability for energy production related to transport is not generally rate limiting under physiologic conditions (Guder and Schmidt, 1976), some parts of the kidney such as the thick ascending limb of Henle are located in areas where there is a tenuous balance between oxygen supply and demand. Consequently, these parts of the nephron are more susceptible to hypoxic injury and associated transport dysfunction. Therefore, in addition to downregulation of the transport proteins themselves with obstruction, the energy sources for transport function are at risk.

**Renal obstruction provokes a number of changes in the metabolic cascade. There is a shift from oxidative metabolism to anaerobic respiration. This shift results in a reduction of renal ATP levels, an increase in amounts of adenosine diphosphate (ADP) and adenosine monophosphate (AMP), and an increase in the renal lactate-to-pyruvate ratio** (Stecker et al, 1971; Middleton et al, 1977; Nito et al, 1978; Klahr et al, 1986).

## Cellular and Molecular Changes Leading to Fibrosis

**Urinary tract obstruction leads to progressive and eventually permanent changes in the structure of the kidney including the development of tubulointerstitial fibrosis, tubular atrophy and apoptosis, and interstitial inflammation.** A number of cytokines and growth factors have been shown to play roles in these events, among which the most prominent include TGF-β, angiotensin II, nuclear factor κB (NFκB), and tumor necrosis factor α (TNF-α). Some are produced directly from the renal tubular and interstitial cells; others are generated from infiltrating macrophages.

Tubulointerstitial fibrosis develops as a consequence of extracellular matrix being synthesized and deposited at a greater rate than it is degraded. A family of enzymes known as matrix metalloproteinases (MMPs) that includes collagenase normally cleaves and degrades the collagenous and noncollagenous components of the extracellular matrix. **Obstruction increases the synthesis of tissue inhibitors of metalloproteinases (TIMPs) that reduce MMP activity, resulting in the accumulation of extracellular matrix.** Infiltrating macrophages stimulate TGF-β synthesis, and this growth factor increases TIMP production, thus reducing collagen turnover. Macrophages also produce other cytokines and growth factors such as interleukin 2, interleukin 6, fibroblast growth factor, and platelet-derived growth factor (PDGF) that appear to contribute to this inflammatory and fibrotic process. Active TGF-β binds directly to its type 2 receptor, which subsequently activates and phosphorylates the type 1 TGF-β receptor. Both of these receptors have been shown to be upregulated in rats with UUO, in both the obstructed and contralateral renal units. This may be a factor in the hypertrophic response sometimes seen in the non-obstructed kidney (Sutaria et al, 1998). The activated type 1 TGF-β receptor subsequently phosphorylates SMAD (mobile transcription factors with a name derived from related genes in C. elegans (Sma) and drosophila (MAD)) proteins. A heteromeric complex of SMAD proteins translocates to the nucleus, where it interacts with transcription factors to regulate gene transcription (Wamsley-Davis et al, 2004) and stimulates tubulointerstitial fibrosis (Fukasawa et al, 2004). Stimulation of TGF-β furthermore stimulates the JNK1 (C-Jun N-terminal protein kinase 1) pathway, which targets the activation of c-Jun and activates transcription factor 2, which are critical components in activating fibronectin production. Increased mRNA expression of TGF-β is seen as early as 10 hours after obstruction and increases for 4 days (Walton et al, 1992; Diamond et al, 1994). The increase occurs primarily in medullary tubules and the interstitium and is less prominent in cortical tubules or glomeruli. Furthermore, TGF-β interacts with other profibrotic growth factors such as EGF and angiotensin II (Kaneto et al, 1993; Ishidoya et al, 1995; Chevalier et al, 1998).

Angiotensin II upregulates the expression of TGF-β1 in UUO, whereas ACE inhibitors or angiotensin receptor blockers diminish TGF-β1 expression and reduce tubulointerstitial fibrosis. This effect and increases in TNF-α and NFκB promoted by activation of the renin-angiotensin axis underscore the importance of this system in the obstructive process. Angiotensin II exerts its biologic effect through both AT1 and AT2 receptors, although in adult mammals the AT1 receptors predominate and account for most of the known effects of the peptide. With UUO, a significant rise in both renal angiotensin II content and AT1 receptor expression is found (Misseri et al, 2004). Nephron angiotensin receptors are found in areas of the kidney where the peptide is known to have its greatest biologic effect: the proximal tubule, the thick ascending limb of Henle, and the glomerulus (Sechi et al, 1992; Meister et al, 1993). The importance of this pathway has been shown in a murine AT1a receptor knockout model in which the mice have significantly less collagen expression and deposition, interstitial volume, and extent of obstruction-induced renal fibrosis (Morrissey and Klahr, 1998a). Angiotensin II activates the transcription factor NFκB, which in turn increases the expression of several chemokines and cytokines involved with the fibrotic process. The NFκB also upregulates the expression of the angiotensinogen gene and thereby provides a positive feedback for further angiotensin II production (Morrissey and Klahr, 1998b). The intimate link between angiotensin and NFκB was demonstrated in a study in which enalapril, an ACE inhibitor, reduced the levels of NFκB and fibrosis in a model of renal obstruction (Morrissey and Klahr, 1997).

The release of TNF-α, a potent inflammatory cytokine, is also stimulated by angiotensin, especially in the first few hours of renal obstruction. It can upregulate its own expression as well as that of other inflammatory mediators such as interleukin 1, platelet-activating factor, nitric oxide, eicosanoids, and cell adhesion molecules. Although macrophages are a major source of TNF-α, renal tubular cells are also capable of producing it and become the predominant source of TNF-α after renal injury. Its role in renal inflammation and fibrosis is supported by studies in mice with knockout deletions of the two types of TNF receptors having less fibrosis.

**Although the events leading to fibrosis are thought to be initiated by increased angiotensin II, other profibrotic factors appear to play a significant role because inhibition of angiotensin synthesis by ACE inhibitors or antagonism of the AT$_1$ receptors blunts but does not completely abolish the fibrotic process** (Kaneto et al, 1993; Ishidoya et al, 1995; Pimental et al, 1995).

## Cellular and Molecular Mechanisms Leading to Tubular Cell Death

Besides inflammation and fibrosis of the kidney, renal obstruction produces atrophy and cell death. The major mechanism by which tubular cells die is apoptosis, a process that is normally involved in postnatal development and tissue renewal in adults. The process can be triggered by both intrinsic and extrinsic factors and results in degradation and condensation of the nucleus. The cells are further degraded into apoptotic bodies, which are eventually phagocytized by healthy cells without inducing inflammation. When rat kidneys are obstructed, renal tubular cell apoptosis begins in about 4 days and peaks after 15 days, with interstitial cell apoptosis continuing for the duration of obstruction (Choi et al, 2000). Glomerular cells appear to be resistant to obstruction-induced apoptosis.

Cysteinyl aspartate–specific proteinases (caspases) are known to mediate apoptotic cell death in obstructed kidneys (Hengartner, 2000; Truong et al, 2001). This family of 12 enzymes can be categorized into three main groups: initiators, effectors, and cytokine processors. Two distinct pathways of caspase activity are involved. One pathway involves activation of membrane death receptors by extrinsic binding of TNF-α to its receptor. A second pathway involves intrinsic stress signals that result in mitochondrial release of proapoptotic proteins such as cytochrome *c*. The two pathways converge to activate effector caspases, which cleave nuclear and cytoplasmic components, resulting in condensation of nuclear material and cell death. Truong and colleagues (2001) showed that all of the caspases increased with renal obstruction and that their levels paralleled renal cell apoptosis. Caspases 3 and 8 best correlated with renal cell apoptosis and appear to be central to this process (Choi et al, 2000; Truong et al, 2001).

In contrast to the defined role of angiotensin II in obstruction-induced renal fibrosis, its involvement in renal cell apoptosis is less clear. In mice with a knockout deletion of the AT2 receptor, there is a decreased degree of obstruction-induced apoptosis. However, these receptors are normally downregulated in the adult kidney, and their role in normal function and pathophysiologic responses is uncertain in the mature kidney. Enalapril pretreatment has been shown by one group of investigators to reduce apoptosis in the early phases of renal obstruction (Truong et al, 1998), but others have reported conflicting results.

**TNF-α can be a directly cytotoxic cytokine that can induce apoptosis in addition to its role in renal inflammation.** When TNF-α binds to its receptor, TNFR1, an associated death domain (TRADD) binds to the TNFR1 and activates several signaling pathways. When coupled to a Fas-associated death domain, it triggers caspase 8 activation, which is pivotal to apoptosis. Alternatively, the TNFR1-TRADD complex can activate NFκB, which can have both pro- and antiapoptotic activity depending upon the cellular milieu. Increased amounts of TNF-α and its receptors have been demonstrated in rat models of obstruction (Tartaglia et al, 1991; Kaneto et al, 1996; Choi et al, 2000) along with other components of this cascade. These findings suggest an important role for TNF-α in apoptosis after obstruction.

**In summary, obstruction of normal ureteral outflow results in biochemical, immunologic, hemodynamic, and** functional changes. It stimulates a cascade in which elevated levels of angiotensin II, cytokines, and growth factors lead to cellular inflammation, increased net matrix formation, tubulointerstitial fibrosis, and tubular cell apoptosis. Many of the mediators are intrinsic to the renal tubular cells, whereas others are contributed by fibroblasts and by migrating macrophages (Fig. 37–3).

## Experimental Treatment Approaches to Attenuate Renal Fibrosis and Functional Impairment

The aforementioned cascade of events points to many possible avenues to attenuate renal damage associated with obstruction. Experimental strategies to attenuate these noxious responses are reviewed.

Wamsley-Davis and colleagues (2004) administered the ACE inhibitor enalapril, AT1 antagonists losartan or candesartan, or vehicle for up to 52 days to male rats with UUO. Candesartan inhibited the rise in JNK1 activity, losartan attenuated it, and enalapril did not affect it. Candesartan also reduced SMAD2 protein activation while attenuating the chronic tubulointerstitial fibrotic injury in obstructed kidneys and preserved renal mass. The apparent differences between candesartan, losartan, and enalapril may be dose or delivery related in that the AT1 antagonists were continuously infused by minipumps, whereas enalapril was added to the drinking water and dose-response relationships were not examined. In another study in which oral enalapril was studied in rats with UUO, enalapril accelerated the reversal of interstitial expansion after the release of obstruction.

Manucha and colleagues (2004) showed that losartan prevented the development of renal fibrosis and kept interstitial volume and TGF-β mRNA expression near control levels. Furthermore, these investigators implicated the well-known interactions between angiotensin II and activation of NOS isoforms and cyclooxygenase 2 (COX-2) in the inflammatory process. Whereas UUO increased iNOS in the obstructed renal medulla and increased neuronal NOS (nNOS) and endothelial NOS (eNOS) in the cortex, losartan treatment downregulated iNOS and nNOS with unchanged levels of eNOS. In addition, obstruction increased COX-2 expression in the obstructed renal cortex. It, too, was decreased by losartan treatment. **These studies suggest an important role of angiotensin-mediated profibrotic and apoptotic events occurring with renal obstruction that can be reduced with currently available inhibitors of angiotensin synthesis or receptor blockade.**

The known association of aldosterone and cardiac fibrosis prompted investigators to assess whether the administration of an aldosterone antagonist could attenuate the renal fibrosis generated with obstruction. Trachtman and coworkers (2004) examined this in a rat model of UUO. Whereas 1 week of obstruction produced minimal parenchymal damage, 2 weeks of obstruction produced renal fibrosis, which was significantly reduced by administration of the aldosterone antagonist spironolactone without raising serum potassium or aldosterone concentrations.

Nitric oxide synthases are known to be double-edged swords in the processes of tissue perfusion and tissue inflammation. Obstruction increases inducible, neuronal, and

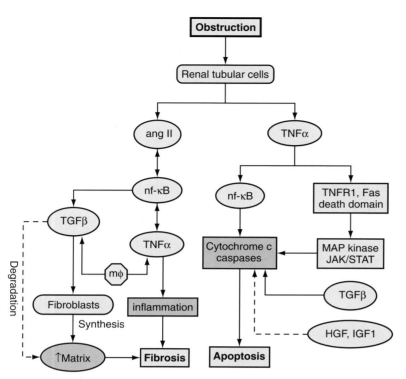

**Figure 37-3.** Summary of major pathways leading to tubulointerstitial fibrosis and tubular apoptosis as a consequence of ureteral obstruction. Membrane proteins and regulators are discussed in the text. ang II, angiotensin II; HGF, human growth factor; IGF, insulin-like growth factor; JAK/STAT, Janus kinase/signal transducers and activators of transcription; mϕ, macrophages; MAP, mitogen-activated protein; nf-κB, nuclear factor κB; TGF, transforming growth factor; TNF, tumor necrosis factor; TNFR1, tumor necrosis factor receptor 1.

endothelial NOS and high concentrations of NO can result in peroxynitrite production. Administration of L-arginine by infusion or even by oral administration prevents the upregulation of iNOS, blunts the increase in renal interstitial volume, and attenuates the infiltration of the renal parenchyma by macrophages in rats with obstructed kidneys (Ito et al, 2004b; Klahr and Morrissey, 2004).

Klahr and Morrissey (2003) showed that bone morphogenic protein 7, a structural relative of TGF-β, was effective in preventing the tubulointerstitial changes and accelerating the return of renal function in a rat model of obstruction. They demonstrated that this agent inhibited apoptosis. This group also reported that the administration of hepatocyte growth factor has similar beneficial effects and proposed that it works by suppressing expression of TGF-β and PDGF. Pirfenidone, a drug that purportedly inhibits collagen synthesis, downregulates production of multiple cytokines and blocks fibroblast proliferation. It may be another candidate to attenuate obstruction-induced renal injury and facilitate renal remodeling (Lasky, 2004).

Although the results of the preliminary studies are encouraging, these agents should not be prescribed to patients for this purpose at this time. Their safety and efficacy first need to be established through carefully designed and controlled clinical studies.

## Compensatory Renal Growth

Compensatory renal growth of the unobstructed kidney was first described by Hinman (1943). This phenomenon has been subsequently demonstrated in a number of other animal models of UUO (Taki et al, 1983; Peters et al, 1993). There is evidence that it occurs in the human fetus. An increase in con-

tralateral renal volume has been detected ultrasonographically when hydronephrosis or unilateral renal agenesis is present (Mandell et al, 1993).

The mechanisms and nature of this growth are influenced by several factors including age and degree and duration of obstruction. Both hyperplastic and hypertrophic compensatory growth have been demonstrated (Dicker and Shirley, 1973; Castle and McDougal, 1984; Peters et al, 1993). Compensatory growth was demonstrated to decrease progressively with increasing age at which the obstruction occurred in animal models (Taki et al, 1983). **Studies of humans subjected to nephrectomy, a functional surrogate for obstruction, have demonstrated that a reduction in renal compensatory growth occurs with increasing age** (Edgren et al, 1976). Animal experiments have also demonstrated that compensatory growth is directly proportional to the duration of obstruction (Chevalier et al, 1999). Compensatory growth is less prominent with partial than with total UUO (Chevalier and Kaiser, 1984; Eskild-Jensen et al, 2001). **While the kidney enlarges, an increase in the number of nephrons or glomeruli does not occur** (Peters et al, 1993). However, an increase in the length of the proximal tubule has been described (Moller, 1988).

Insulin-like growth factor I (IGF-I), a mitogenic and anabolic peptide, may play a role in compensatory renal growth after obstruction. There is both animal and clinical evidence for its role. In rats, mean renal IGF-I is significantly elevated in the normal kidney compared with the contralateral 7-day obstructed kidney (Serel et al, 2000). Inferences can also be made from nephrectomy performed in animals and humans. Renal IGF-I mRNA levels are increased in immature rats previously subjected to nephrectomy (Mulroney et al, 1991). Significant increases in serum IGF-I have been demonstrated in humans after donor nephrectomy and peak 6 months after the procedure. Serum IGF-I was positively correlated with increases in renal volume demonstrated on serial postoperative imaging (Nam and Chang, 1999). It has also been demonstrated that the expression of IGF-I may be age dependent. Although renal IGF-I mRNA levels were found to be elevated after nephrectomy in immature rats, this did not occur in adult rats (Mulroney et al, 1991). Exogenous IGF-1 can attenuate renal injury from obstruction (Chevalier et al, 2000).

The presence of compensatory growth in infants has been considered by some as an indicator that contralateral hydronephrosis is functionally significant (Koff and Peller, 1995). However, this approach has been challenged by others (Brandel et al, 1996). In addition, it was demonstrated that functional deterioration occurred in a rat model of partial UUO before compensatory growth developed in the contralateral renal unit. This implies that there may be a risk for functional renal loss if one utilizes only compensatory growth as an indication of correction of obstruction (Wen et al, 1999).

## Renal Recovery after Obstruction

The duration of obstruction has a significant influence on renal functional recovery. **When acute, complete ureteral obstruction is promptly relieved, full recovery of global GFR can occur.** In the rat model, after 3 days of UUO, GFR and RBF were reduced to less than 10% of their baseline values. Both returned to their baseline within 14 days of relief of obstruction (Ito et al, 2004a). Bander and colleagues (1985) also noted complete return of GFR by 14 days after 24 hours of acute UUO, although they noted that the recovery was heterogeneous at the nephron level. Studying SNGFR, they found that approximately 15% of superficial and juxtamedullary nephrons were permanently lost, but hyperfiltration of the remaining nephrons allowed maintenance of whole kidney GFR. **Longer periods of complete ureteral obstruction are associated with diminished return of GFR.** Kerr (1954) reported that in dogs with complete UUO for 7 days, GFR 1 hour after relief of obstruction was 25% of the preligation GFR. GFR was then followed over time to assess the degree and time course of renal recovery. Maximal recovery was 58% of baseline, and this occurred within 57 days. Similar studies were conducted by Vaughan and Gillenwater (1971), who demonstrated that there was full functional renal recovery at 2 weeks after a 7-day period of UUO in dogs. This result declined to 70% recovery of GFR after 14 days of UUO, 30% after 4 weeks of UUO, and no recovery after 6 weeks of UUO.

The fate of the human kidney after prolonged periods of obstruction is less well defined and may be unpredictable. Functional recovery has been reported after a 150-day period of UUO (Shapiro and Bennett, 1976). Permanent reductions in GFR may occur after UUO or BUO in humans. However, there may be a differential pattern of recovery after BUO in adults. Jones and associates (1988) described two phases of functional improvement: an initial phase during the first 2 weeks after relief of obstruction when tubular function improved and a later phase occurring over the next 10 weeks when GFR gradually improved. Patients with BUO or obstruction of a solitary kidney may also be at risk for unique sequelae such as chronic urinary acidification and concentrating defects (Berlyne, 1961).

Other factors influence functional return. Factors that have a positive influence on functional recovery include a smaller degree of obstruction, greater compliance of the collecting system, and presence of pyelolymphatic backflow (Shokeir et al, 2002). Conversely, older age and decreased renal cortical thickness are predictors of diminished recovery of renal function (Lutaif et al, 2003).

Nuclear renography may help predict functional recovery. An assessment of functioning cortex with such imaging is the best predictor. For example, **dimercaptosuccinic acid (DMSA), a cortical agent, has been shown to be superior to tubular selective agents such as diethylenetriaminepentaacetic acid (DTPA) or mercaptoacetyltriglycine (MAG3) for the prediction of renal recovery.** This was demonstrated in a prospective study in children undergoing pyeloplasty or ureteral reimplantation for ureterovesical junction obstruction (Thompson and Gough, 2001). It was postulated that DMSA better defines functional cortex and is less affected by the dilated collecting system and dilution by undrained urine. Similarly, when the tubular agent *ortho*-iodohippurate was utilized, whole kidney activity was less predictive than the cortical phase (Kalika et al, 1981).

**Renal recovery after relief of obstruction is affected by the duration of obstruction, degree of obstruction, patient's age, and baseline renal function. Cortical phase nuclear renograms may offer accurate prediction of the capacity of the kidney to recover after reversal of the obstruction.**

## PATHOLOGIC CHANGES OF OBSTRUCTION

Distinct gross and microscopic pathologic changes may occur with obstruction of the upper urinary tract. These may be affected by the presence of infection, duration of obstruction, and intra- versus extrarenal localization of the renal pelvis.

## Gross Pathologic Findings

The gross pathologic changes occurring in the kidney have been characterized in animal models and parallel those in humans. Hodson and colleagues (1969) performed unilateral ureteral ligation in a porcine model and described pathologic changes in both kidneys over several time points. Dilation of the pelvis and ureter and blunting of the papillary tips were present in the obstructed kidney at 42 hours after obstruction and the weight of this renal unit was heavier. Pelviureteric dilation and weight further increased and the parenchyma became edematous in the obstructed kidney at 7 days. The cortex remained slightly enlarged, and there was increased calyceal dilatation at 12 days in this renal unit; at 21 and 28 days, the external renal dimensions of both kidneys were similar. However, the cortex and medullary tissue in the obstructed kidney were diffusely thinned. Ladefoged and Djurhuus (1976) evaluated partial and complete obstruction in a porcine model. **They found that totally obstructed kidneys were enlarged, had a cystic appearance, and weighed less than the contralateral renal unit 6 weeks after obstruction. However, such gross differences in appearance were not present at this interval in the partially obstructed kidneys.**

## Microscopic Pathologic Findings

Light microscopic changes reported in the aforementioned porcine model at 42 hours after obstruction included lymphatic dilation, interstitial edema, and tubular and glomerular preservation. Collecting duct and tubular dilatation was prominent by 7 days. In addition, further interstitial edema, widening of Bowman's space, tubular basement membrane thickening, cell flattening, and cytoplasmic hyalinization were demonstrated. Papillary tip necrosis, regional tubular destruction, and inflammatory cell response were noted at 12 days (Hodson et al, 1969). Interstitial fibrosis and thickening of the tubular basement membranes were reported at 16 days after obstruction in a mouse model (Sharma et al, 1993). The inner cortex demonstrated severe tubular loss, proliferation of fibroblasts, and collagen deposition 3 weeks after obstruction in the porcine kidney. Cortical thinning and development of glomerular crescents were present at the 3- to 4-week interval in this model (Hodson et al, 1969). **Widespread glomerular collapse and tubular atrophy, interstitial fibrosis, and proliferation of connective tissue in the collecting system were reported at 5 to 6 weeks after obstruction in the porcine model** (Ladefoged and Djurhuus, 1976). Similar findings are noted in the chronically obstructed human kidney (Figs. 37–4 to 37–6).

## Electron Microscopic Pathologic Findings

Electron microscopic (EM) studies have confirmed the aforementioned light microscopic findings, including the presence of tubular atrophy, glomerular collapse, and renal pelvic smooth muscle atrophy at 5 to 6 weeks after obstruction (Fig. 37–7). Electron microscopic studies have also demonstrated other changes including the development of a cell-poor stroma composed of elastic and collagen fibers in the renal interstitium and obstructed portions of the collecting system (Ladefoged and Djurhuus, 1976). Collagen and elastin are

normal components of the collecting system but are more prominent and have structural changes with obstruction (Gosling and Dixon, 1978; Murakumo et al, 1997).

## GENERAL ISSUES IN MANAGEMENT OF PATIENTS
## Diagnostic Imaging

As the clinical signs and symptoms of obstructive uropathy are so widely variable, prompt and accurate diagnosis is dependent upon appropriate imaging. The practicing urologist should be well versed in the diagnostic imaging modalities currently available as well as their relative advantages, limitations, and appropriate modifications. An overview of current imaging techniques, with an emphasis on recent modifications, is presented here.

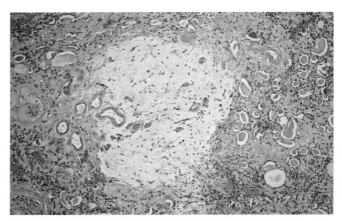

**Figure 37–5.** Sections of deep cortex and outer medulla from a patient with chronic obstructive uropathy. Obsolescent glomerulus (left edge) and pool of extravasated Tamm-Horsfall protein (center) are seen. Hematoxylin and eosin stain; original magnification, ×25. (Courtesy of Dr. Sami Iskandar.)

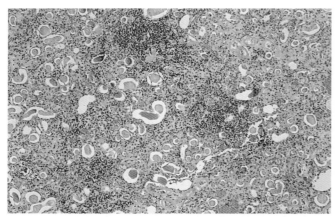

**Figure 37–4.** Sections of deep cortex and outer medulla from a patient with chronic obstructive uropathy. Tubules demonstrate thyroidization-type atrophy interspersed with mononuclear inflammatory infiltrate. Hematoxylin and eosin stain; original magnification, ×25. (Courtesy of Dr. Sami Iskandar.)

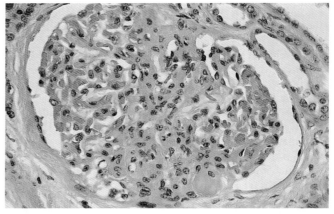

**Figure 37–6.** Sections of deep cortex and outer medulla from a patient with chronic obstructive uropathy. Glomerulus with segmental tuft sclerosis (center) and hyalinosis is seen. Hematoxylin and eosin stain; original magnification, ×100. (Courtesy of Dr. Sami Iskandar.)

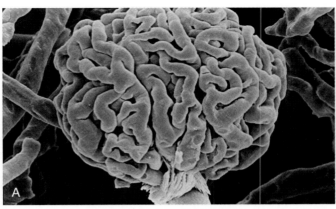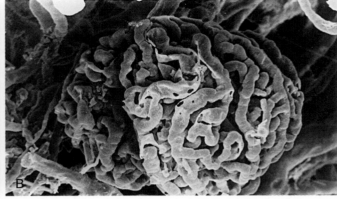

**Figure 37–7.** **A,** Scanning electron microscopic appearance of a normal glomerular cast (×390). **B,** Appearance of a glomerular microvascular cast after obstruction shows capillary collapse and irregularity (×390). (**A** and **B,** from Leahy AL, Ryan PC, McEntee GM, et al: Renal injury and recovery in partial ureteric obstruction. J Urol 1989;142:199-203.)

## Ultrasonography

Renal ultrasonography is a mainstay in the evaluation of suspected urinary tract obstruction. Although it is primarily an anatomic study, Doppler modifications may add a functional component. **There is no associated ionizing radiation, and it is thus considered safe in pediatric and pregnant patients. Because there is no need for iodinated contrast material, ultrasonography can be utilized in those with azotemia or contrast allergy.** As it remains relatively inexpensive and widely available, ultrasonography is often a first-line investigation.

Renal parenchymal thickness can be measured readily, and cortical thinning may be indicative of chronic obstruction. The renal pelvis and calyces can be imaged, and dilatation is readily identifiable. **Caution in interpretation must be exercised, however, in that hydronephrosis is an anatomic as opposed to a functional diagnosis. Specifically, caliectasis and pelviectasis both may exist in an unobstructed system.** Functional inferences cannot be presumed from static images. For instance, the hydronephrosis of vesicoureteral reflux may not be obstructive. In addition, renal sinus cysts can be misinterpreted as hydronephrosis. Conversely, early in acute obstruction, hydronephrosis may not be prominent, and the presence of an intrarenal collecting system or dehydration may lead to false-negative interpretations. **A prospective study of ultrasonography in obstruction by Laing and colleagues (1985) revealed a 35% false-negative rate in acute obstruction, underscoring the need to correlate the clinical picture carefully with the radiologic findings.**

**Doppler ultrasonography allows measurement of the renal resistive index (RI), which has been used to assess for obstruction. The RI is defined as peak systolic velocity (PSV) minus the end-diastolic velocity (EDV) divided by the PSV.** Several groups have assessed its ability to diagnose obstruction, but its utility has yet to be fully established. Platt and coworkers (1991) have suggested 0.7 as the upper limit of normal, with values greater than 0.7 reflecting elevated resistance to blood flow and thus suggesting obstructive uropathy. They subsequently reported their experience using this modality in 23 patients with acute unilateral obstruction. Three patients had false-negative studies, two of whom had

pyelosinus extravasation and one of whom had been obstructed for less than 5 hours. They concluded that Doppler determination of RI was a valuable adjunct to routine sonographic evaluation of urinary tract obstruction (Platt et al, 1993). Conversely, others have found the sensitivity inadequate for the detection of obstruction. Tublin and associates (1994) reported that of 32 patients with colic, 12 of 19 patients with obstruction had normal RI and 5 of 13 without obstruction had abnormal RIs.

One factor that may account for the dichotomy between such studies is the degree of obstruction. Chen and colleagues (1993) evaluated 27 patients with suspected obstruction by both Doppler ultrasonography and intravenous pyelography. Overall, utilizing an RI of 0.7 as the critical value, the sensitivity was only 52%. However, when correlated with degree of obstruction on intravenous pyelography, RI was shown to differentiate the kidneys with mild obstruction from those with severe obstruction. In those with mild obstruction, the mean RI was only 0.64, whereas in those with severe obstruction the mean RI was 0.74, and the sensitivity of an RI greater than 0.70 for significant obstruction was 93.3%. Fung and coauthors (1994) also assessed this modality for evaluating obstruction. They measured RI in nine patients undergoing Whitaker testing for grade 3 or 4 hydronephrosis and reported that RI directly correlated with renal pelvic pressure. They determined that when renal perfusion pressures were normal RI was less than 0.82. Major pitfalls in many of the studies assessing this modality have been the inconsistent definition of obstruction and degree of obstruction. **Although the presence of hydronephrosis associated with an abnormally elevated RI may be indicative of the severity of obstruction, it is important to recognize these limitations and use other clinical information and renal functional assessment for treatment planning.**

## Excretory Urography

Long considered the "gold standard" for the evaluation of the upper urinary tract, excretory urography (EXU) has been gradually supplanted by other modalities for many of its prior indications. Nevertheless, it provides both anatomic and functional information, underscoring its utility. **Acute urinary** obstruction may be inferred from the *functional* abnormality of a delayed nephrogram and pyelogram on the affected side or sides. Delayed images may then ultimately reveal the *anatomic* level of obstruction and perhaps causation. In addition, other signs may be present that may indicate chronicity of obstruction such as parenchymal thinning, extreme calyceal blunting, and ureteral tortuosity.

As the imaging is dependent upon glomerular filtration and renal concentration of the contrast medium, the utility of EXU is limited in those with renal insufficiency. Furthermore, the risk of contrast nephropathy increases with increasing serum creatinine. EXU, therefore, should not be performed in subjects with renal insufficiency, those who are at higher risk for developing contrast-induced nephropathy, or those with history of contrast allergy. Radiation exposure limits its utility in pregnancy, although abbreviated protocols have been established (Zagoria and Tung, 1997).

### Retrograde Pyelography

Retrograde pyelography accurately defines ureteral and collecting system anatomy, including the location of an obstructive lesion and its extent. It should be considered in those who have renal insufficiency or have other risks for receiving intravenous iodinated contrast material. It may also be used in cases in which anatomy is not sufficiently defined with other imaging studies. In essence, a loopogram is another form of retrograde pyelography and may be useful in evaluating patients with cutaneous urinary diversion when obstruction is suspected.

### Antegrade Pyelography

This technique may be helpful when other imaging studies do not adequately define collecting system or ureteral anatomy and when retrograde pyelography is not technically feasible.

### Whitaker Test

**First described by Whitaker in 1973, this study involves measurement of renal pelvic pressure during infusion of either saline or contrast material into the collecting system through a percutaneous needle or nephrostomy at a fixed rate of 10 mL/min.** A catheter is placed in the bladder to monitor intravesical pressure, which is subtracted from the measured collecting system pressures to calculate the "true pressure" within the pelvis. **A true intrapelvic pressure of less than 15 cm $H_2O$ is considered normal, greater than 22 cm $H_2O$ indicative of obstruction, and between 15 and 22 cm $H_2O$ indeterminate.** Although its reliability to detect obstruction and differentiate degree of obstruction has been established in animal models (Ryan et al, 1989), the clinical utility of this test has been advocated by some and questioned by others. For example, one group reported that it was a valid test to confirm ureteral obstruction after renal transplantation (Kashi et al, 1993). However, others have reported a sensitivity and specificity of only 79% and 50% in this setting (Sperling et al, 2000).

Other concerns regarding potential shortcomings of the Whitaker test have been noted. Mortensen and colleagues (1983) reported wide variation in pelvic pressures in a normal porcine model, questioning the definition of a "normal" study. It has also been noted that a small, noncompliant obstructed system may give rise to a more rapid increase in pressure than a large, dilated obstructed system (Wahlin et al, 2001). Modifications have been suggested to overcome this pitfall. Individualized infusion rates based on maximum physiologic urine output have been advocated by some (Fung et al, 1995). Wahlin and colleagues (2001) proposed measuring flow as a function of pressure over a range of physiologic pressures. Resistance was then calculated and used to categorize responses as nonobstructed, indeterminate, or obstructed. They found that the major benefit of this modification was that it allowed identification of obstruction in some patients categorized as indeterminate with the standard Whitaker test. These noted discordant results and the invasiveness of the study reflect the Whitaker test's limited applicability in contemporary clinical practice.

### Nuclear Renography

Nuclear renography is a useful, noninvasive test for evaluating patients with suspected obstruction. **It provides a functional assessment without exposure to iodinated contrast material.** Radiopharmaceuticals for renography are selected on the basis of the function to be studied. The glomerular agent Tc 99m DTPA and the tubular agent Tc 99m MAG3 are most commonly used in the evaluation of obstruction. All radiopharmaceutical tracers are administered intravenously, and their uptake and subsequent clearance can then be evaluated and quantitated scintigraphically. From these data, relative renal function can be calculated. Obstruction can be assessed by measuring the clearance curves, either from a visual assessment of the pattern or from calculation of the half-time (time at which 50% of the radiopharmaceutical is eliminated from the collecting system). **By convention, a half-time less than 10 minutes is considered normal, greater than 20 minutes is considered obstructed, and between 10 and 20 minutes is equivocal.** Tracer clearance can be spuriously delayed because of renal insufficiency and the presence of vesicoureteral reflux, and some have suggested that renal immaturity in neonates may generate false-positive studies (Karam et al, 2003).

In order to detect obstruction, a high-flow state may be necessary. Patients therefore should be well hydrated to prevent misinterpretation related to low-flow states. Theoretically, bladder catheterization should be performed to maintain low intravesical pressure. However, in clinical practice this is utilized only in certain cases such as suspected lower urinary tract obstruction, vesicoureteral reflux, neurogenic or noncompliant bladder, or low-lying, pelvic kidneys from which the renal signal may be obscured by intravesical radiopharmaceutical (Karam et al, 2003). The diuretic renogram is a modification designed to maximize flow and potentially distinguish truly obstructed collecting systems from those that are dilated but unobstructed. Because a given patient's response to the diuretic may be affected by the patient's baseline renal function, adjustments may need to be made on the basis of creatinine clearance (Upsdell et al, 1988).

As classically described, the diuretic, typically furosemide (F), is administered 20 minutes after the tracer to induce a brisk diuresis (F +20 study). Others have suggested alteration of diuretic timing to coincide with tracer administration (F +0) or precede it by 15 minutes (F −15). English and colleagues (1987) recognized that some patients with a partial obstruction may eliminate the tracer in the 20 minutes before the induction of diuresis using the standard, F +20 sequence. To address this, they advocated administration of diuretic 15 minutes before injection of the radiopharmaceutical (F −15) so that initial tracer clearance could be studied during the period of maximal diuresis. Thirty-five renal units with hydronephrosis having equivocal or normal standard (F +20) diuretic renograms were evaluated by English and colleagues using the F −15 sequence. Utilizing contralateral normal kidneys for comparison, they selected a clearance half-time less than 5 minutes as normal, greater than 10 minutes as obstructed, and between 5 and 10 minutes as equivocal. With these criteria, 13 of the kidneys were demonstrated to be obstructed and 18 were shown to be unobstructed. Only four kidneys remained in the equivocal range, underscoring the utility of this modified approach. This has also been confirmed in a crossover designed study demonstrating that **although an F +20 study is reliable when obstruction is demonstrated, both the F −15 and F +0 sequences can induce obstructed patterns in previously equivocal cases** (Turkolmez et al, 2004).

## Computed Tomography and Magnetic Resonance Imaging

Cross-sectional imaging, provided by computed tomography (CT) and magnetic resonance imaging (MRI), generates greater anatomic definition of abdominal and retroperitoneal anatomy than EXU or ultrasonography. In the previous edition of this textbook, unenhanced helical CT was described as an alternative to EXU. Over the brief elapsed time, because of its speed, safety, and accuracy, this modality has now replaced EXU as an initial imaging study in those with suspected ureteral obstruction, especially in an acute setting such as stone-induced colic. In their landmark study, Smith and coauthors (1995) demonstrated the efficacy of unenhanced helical or spiral CT in the evaluation of possible ureteral obstruction, prospectively comparing it with EXU in 20 patients presenting with acute flank pain. Obstruction was identified by EXU and CT in 12 patients. In these 12 patients, the ureteral calculus was identified in 11 with CT and only 5 with EXU. In the last remaining patient with obstruction, multiple high-attenuating pelvic clips obscured definitive identification of a calculus, although a dilated ureter could be traced down to the level of these clips. **In the detection of ureteral calculi, CT has a sensitivity of 97%, specificity of 96%, and overall accuracy of 97%** (Smith et al, 1996b). **At this time, CT is the most accurate radiologic study for the diagnosis of ureteral calculi.**

CT directly demonstrates calculi classically considered radiolucent when evaluated by plain radiography, including uric acid, xanthine, dihydroxyadenine, and many drug-induced stones. Exceptions, however, are calculi composed of protease inhibitors, which are not visualized by CT (Gentle et al, 1997). Secondary CT signs of obstruction such as ureteral dilatation, nephromegaly, perinephric stranding, or fluid can facilitate the diagnosis of acute obstruction. These signs have been reported to have a positive predictive value of 99% and negative predictive value of 95% for identification of acute ureteral obstruction (Smith et al, 1996a). This is also an excellent study for evaluating patients suspected of having chronic obstruction who have renal insufficiency or other contrast risks.

Contrast-enhanced spiral CT has also been advocated for the evaluation of patients with chronic obstructive uropathy and normal serum creatinine. In addition to the aforementioned anatomic details afforded by noncontrast CT, functional evaluation including calculation of differential GFR is possible. Abo El-Ghar and colleagues (2004) compared contrast-enhanced CT with EXU and nuclear renography in 65 patients. **CT had significantly improved sensitivity for identification of the cause of obstruction compared with EXU.** Furthermore, they reported an excellent correlation between isotope and CT estimated GFR. Multiphasic helical CT has also been shown to be useful in surgical planning for ureteropelvic junction obstruction, with sensitivity for detection of crossing vessel of 97%, specificity of 92%, and overall accuracy of 96% (El-Nahas et al, 2004).

The role of magnetic resonance urography (MRU) is still being defined (Rothpearl et al, 1995). **Although this study accurately identifies hydroureteronephrosis, a limitation is its inability to demonstrate either calculi or the ureteral anatomy of unobstructed systems.** The latter can be overcome with the administration of diuretics, which facilitates imaging of the nonobstructed collecting system and ureters. Diuretic MRU thus has utility for assessing patients with obstruction. A prospective study compared it with EXU in patients with ureteral obstruction (Karabacakoglu et al, 2004). The accuracy of diuretic MRU for detection of obstruction was demonstrated to be 93% in those with obstructing stones and 100% in those with obstruction related to strictures or congenital anomalies, whereas the accuracy of EXU was 96% and 55%, respectively. The incorporation of intravenous administration of gadopentetate-DTPA has allowed a dynamic, functional assessment of the collecting system that correlates well with diuretic renal scintigraphy yet provides far greater anatomic detail than nuclear studies. Differential GFR can be assessed with postimaging processing, and contrast washout can be measured to calculate renal clearance, differentiating dilated systems from obstructed systems (Rohrschneider et al, 2002; Chu et al, 2004). Cost, availability, time for acquisition of images, and need for sedation in pediatric patients have all been cited as possible limitations of this technique, but the superior anatomic detail, functional assessment, elimination of risk of contrast-induced nephropathy, and lack of ionizing radiation make this an attractive option that is likely to continue to evolve. **The absence of ionizing radiation has allowed its utilization in the assessment of pregnant patients with flank pain and hydronephrosis, which is further explored in the discussion of hydronephrosis of pregnancy later in this chapter.**

## Hypertension

Ureteral obstruction that is symptomatic, accompanied by fever, complicated by an undrained infection, or determined to be high grade, bilateral, or inducing renal failure warrants immediate drainage of the affected renal unit. The indications for the relief of urinary tract obstruction are outlined in Table 37–2.

Hypertension can be precipitated by ureteral obstruction and is a well-recognized sequela of BUO or obstruction of a solitary kidney. Vaughan and Gillenwater (1973) noted hypertension in 17 of 22 patients with BUO, which was corrected in

**Table 37–2. Indications to Relieve Obstruction**

| Unilateral Obstruction | Bilateral Obstruction |
| --- | --- |
| Pain unrelieved by analgesics | Same as for UUO or |
| Signs and symptoms of sepsis | Elevated BUN and creatinine |
| Persistent nausea and vomiting | Signs and symptoms of uremia |
| High-grade obstruction | Hyperkalemia |

BUN, blood urea nitrogen; UUO, unilateral ureteral obstruction.

15 subjects upon relief of BUO. This response has also been demonstrated in pregnant patients with BUO (Satin et al, 1993). Patients with BUO are typically volume overloaded. Gulmi and colleagues (1989) measured ANP and plasma renin activity (PRA) in nine patients with BUO before and after relief of obstruction and compared them with those of age-matched control subjects. ANP was significantly increased in the BUO group prior to relief and progressively returned to normal after drainage. Conversely, PRA was depressed prior to relief of BUO. These findings are suggestive of a volume-mediated mechanism for hypertension in BUO. Hypertension is significantly less common, however, with UUO (Vaughan and Sosa, 1995). In contrast to the BUO model, in UUO the contralateral, unobstructed kidney compensates and eliminates excess volume and solutes. Renin activation and resultant angiotensin II generation have been demonstrated in animal models of UUO and may be the mechanism by which new-onset hypertension occurs in this setting. Pain may be another contributing factor (el-Dahr et al, 1993). **In summation, there is a good chance of reversal of new-onset hypertension with relief of BUO but this is less likely with UUO.**

## Renal Drainage

Minimally invasive endourologic and interventional radiologic techniques allow prompt drainage of the obstructed kidney. These measures may allow temporary drainage until a definitive procedure is performed or, in some circumstances, may be a permanent form of management. Urine specimens for urinalysis and culture should be obtained from the obstructed renal unit at the time of relief of obstruction when infection is suspected. Antibiotic therapy is started if these tests are indicative of infection or there are clinical signs and symptoms of infection.

The relative merits of indwelling ureteral stents and percutaneous nephrostomy tubes have been evaluated by several groups. Indwelling stents obviate the need for external collection devices but are associated with bothersome voiding symptoms. In spite of this, prospective studies have demonstrated that there is no statistically significant difference in health-related quality of life (Joshi et al, 2001; Mokhmalji et al, 2001). The choice of drainage ultimately depends on the clinical setting. If the patient has an uncorrectable coagulopathy or platelet abnormality, ureteral stenting is indicated. There does not appear to be a significant advantage of either approach in those requiring drainage for stone-related problems (Pearle et al, 1998; Mokhmalji et al, 2001). **Ureteral stenting may not be as effective for treating patients with extrinsic ureteral obstruction.** Docimo and

Dewolf (1989) reported a mean 43% failure rate in ureteral stents placed for extrinsic ureteral obstruction, the majority related to malignancy. This was subsequently confirmed in a prospective study evaluating success rates for retrograde ureteral stenting (Yossepowitch et al, 2001). Initial retrograde access failed in 27% of patients with extrinsic ureteral obstruction, compared with only 6% of those with intrinsic obstruction. At 3-month follow-up, 56.4% of stents placed for ureteral obstruction had failed. Of note, on multivariate analysis, stent diameter did not predict risk of stent failure. Chung and colleagues (2004) similarly identified an overall 42% rate of stent failure in patients with extrinsic obstruction of the ureter and additionally noted that 43% of those failures occurred within 6 days of the initial placement. **A diagnosis of cancer, metastatic disease requiring chemotherapy or radiation, and renal insufficiency were predictors of stent failure in this series.** Some have advocated the placement of two parallel ureteral stents to provide better drainage as an alternative to percutaneous nephrostomy (Liu and Hrebinko, 1998). **Closer monitoring for stent failure should thus be considered in patients with extrinsic ureteral obstruction** (Ku et al, 2004).

Compared with percutaneous nephrostomy placement, stent placement typically requires greater x-ray exposure (Mokhmalji et al, 2001). This may be of concern in pregnant patients, particularly early in gestation when the fetus is most sensitive to radiation effects (McAleer and Loughlin, 2004). Ultrasound-guided ureteral stent placement is a described option in this setting (Jarrard et al, 1993). Another issue in this cohort is acceleration of stent encrustation, which may be due to increased calcium excretion during pregnancy (Goldfarb et al, 1989). Nephrostomy tube drainage is an option for pregnant patients if this problem arises (Denstedt and Razvi, 1992). Percutaneous nephrostomy should be strongly considered if pyonephrosis is suspected. However, if it is not suspected and thick, purulent fluid is obtained from the kidney at ureteral stenting, placement of a large-diameter stent is recommended. If this does not provide satisfactory drainage, percutaneous nephrostomy should be performed.

## Choice of Surgical Intervention

After the acute obstruction has been addressed, definitive management is based upon the cause of the obstruction, the functional recovery of the affected kidney and the condition of its counterpart, and the patient's age and medical status. Endoscopic, open, or laparoscopic ablative and reconstructive procedures may all be utilized. Indications and pertinent preoperative, intraoperative, and postoperative considerations are discussed elsewhere in this text. The threshold of differential renal function for which reconstruction may be preferable to nephrectomy, although still debated, has been proposed to be between 15% to 20% (Thompson and Gough, 2001). The decision to remove a kidney should be made only after the affected kidney has been adequately drained for a sufficient period of time, 6 to 8 weeks based on the results of animal experimentation (Kerr, 1954). Split renal function can be assessed by measuring creatinine or inulin clearance (both surrogates of glomerular filtration) directly from bilateral nephrostomy tubes or a nephrostomy tube and an indwelling urethral catheter when there is complete UUO and the other renal unit is not obstructed. However, nuclear imaging techniques are more commonly utilized to assess renal function in this setting.

A less than 10% contribution to global renal function has been proposed as the threshold for nephrectomy. Another criterion has been the ability of the affected renal unit to provide sufficient function to prevent dialysis dependence if the contralateral kidney were removed. These criteria were not generated by prospective study but by clinical inference from functional reconstructive outcomes. For example, renal units with less than 10% renogram-derived differential function in children have been shown to derive no benefit from reconstruction (Dhillon, 1998). In addition, GFR of less than 10 mL/min/1.73 $m^2$ in the affected kidney successfully predicted renal function that did not stabilize or improve after surgical correction of obstruction in adults (Khalaf et al, 2004). The decision to proceed with nephrectomy in a patient with significant global renal insufficiency, however, should not be based solely on the aforementioned criteria as this could hasten dialysis dependence and dramatically affect quality of life. The patient may prefer life with a stent or percutaneous nephrostomy.

## Pain Management

A time-honored, first-line therapy in the management of renal colic has been parenteral administration of narcotic analgesics. Nonsteroidal anti-inflammatory drugs (NSAIDs), however, have assumed an increasing role in the acute management algorithm. Both classes of medication may be administered parenterally or orally. Narcotics have a rapid onset of analgesia but may promote nausea and emesis, cause excessive sedation, and have a potential for abuse. NSAIDs are nonopioid analgesics that, unlike narcotics, target the inflammatory basis of pain. Prostaglandins, generated from arachidonic acid metabolism mediated by both *iso* forms of cyclooxygenase, potentiate pain receptors. Therefore, inhibition of prostaglandin synthesis prevents this potentiation of nociceptors (Mense, 1983).

Increases in collecting system pressure and ureteral wall tension are proposed mechanisms of renal colic (Holmlund, 1983). Primate models reveal that distention-mediated activation of renal pelvis mechanoreceptors results in spinothalamic (pain pathway) C fiber excitation. The mean threshold pressure to elicit this primate response was 32 mm Hg. This is similar to the 30 mmHg proposed threshold for evoking pain in humans (Ammons, 1992). Interventions that reduce collecting system pressure should theoretically reduce pain.

NSAIDs have been demonstrated to reduce collecting system pressure. Pretreatment with indomethacin significantly blunted the rise in pelvic pressure and RBF in pigs with UUO (Frokiaer et al, 1993). Indomethacin administered 30 minutes after UUO reduced an already elevated renal pelvic pressure by approximately 30% in rats (Sjodin et al, 1982). A study of four different NSAIDs in dogs with acute obstruction showed 25% to 58% reductions in renal pelvic pressure after administration of these drugs, which were most pronounced after the first dose (Gasparich and Mayo, 1986). A concomitant reduction in RBF induced by NSAIDs is thought to be one of the mechanisms for decreasing collecting system pressure. This has been demonstrated in a canine model of UUO

in which the administration of ketorolac, an NSAID, induced prompt reduction in both RBF and intrapelvic pressure (Perlmutter et al, 1993). A second potential mechanism involves regulation of aquaporin water channels. COX-2 expression is upregulated in the obstructed ureter (Nakada et al, 2002). There is also a downregulation of AQP2 water channels associated with this COX-2 induction, and this promotes diuresis after obstruction is relieved. Rats treated with a COX-2 inhibitor during obstruction had only a 28% reduction of AQP2, attenuating the diuresis occurring after release of UUO (Cheng et al, 2004).

The utility of NSAIDs for managing renal colic was demonstrated in a meta-analytic study of 20 trials comparing NSAIDs with opioids in 1613 patients. A greater reduction in pain score, less need for "rescue" analgesia, and less emesis occurred in the NSAID cohort (Holdgate and Pollock, 2004).

The choice of pain management should be based on the patient's clinical profile. **NSAIDs should not be utilized in patients with renal insufficiency as this could be exacerbated by the induced reduction in RBF.** COX-1 inhibitors should not be administered to patients at risk for gastrointestinal bleeding or when optimal platelet function is needed. Although COX-2 inhibitors are attractive on a pathophysiologic basis, the market withdrawal of some COX-2 inhibitors related to increased risk of cardiac morbidity underscores the need for prospective trials to assess their long-term safety in managing patients with renal colic. Although opioid-derived agents have untoward side effects, they provide excellent analgesia and are still considered front-line drugs for colic management. They are certainly effective as initial analgesic therapy and can also be used to rescue those whose pain is not controlled adequately with NSAIDs or as an adjunct to NSAID therapy.

## Postobstructive Diuresis

### Mechanisms

**Following the relief of urinary tract obstruction, postobstructive diuresis, a period of significant polyuria, may ensue.** Urine outputs of 200 mL/hr or greater may be encountered. Although this occurs mainly after relief of BUO or obstruction of a solitary kidney, it can rarely occur when there is a normal, contralateral kidney (Schlossberg and Vaughan, 1984). The diuresis is typically a normal physiologic response to the volume expansion and solute accumulation occurring during obstruction. Sodium, urea, and free water are eliminated and the diuresis subsides after solute and fluid homeostasis is achieved. With the return of homeostasis, the period of diuresis ends (Loo and Vaughan, 1985).

However, a "pathologic" postobstructive diuresis may ensue, characterized by inappropriate renal handling of water or solutes, or both. It is due to a number of mechanisms previously reviewed in this chapter, including a derangement of the medullary solute gradient and a number of altered signaling and transport pathways. Downregulation of sodium transporters with subsequent impaired sodium reabsorption in the thick ascending limb of Henle prevents maintenance of the medullary interstitial solute gradient promoting a continued diuresis (Rokaw et al, 1996). The increased endogenous production and altered regulation of ANP induce a saline diuresis (Kim et al, 2001b). In addition, other natriuretic peptides such as the *Dendroaspis* natriuretic peptide may play a role (Kim et al, 2002). Pathologic postobstructive diuresis is also marked by poor responsiveness of the collecting duct to ADH. This is thought to be due to a downregulation of aquaporin water channels in this segment of the nephron and perhaps in the proximal tubule, which has been demonstrated in experimental models of UUO and BUO (Nielsen and Agre, 1995; Frokiaer et al, 1996; Kim et al, 2001a; Li et al, 2003c).

Various reasons have been proposed for the rare occurrence of postobstructive diuresis with release of UUO and a normal contralateral kidney. GFR may be atypically preserved in the setting of distal tubular damage, such that the kidney filters a normal volume but there is limited free water reabsorption. Alternatively, a pronounced aquaporin channel defect may be present, causing diminished free water absorption in this setting (Schlossberg and Vaughan, 1984; Li et al, 2003c).

## Clinical Management of Postobstructive Diuresis

**The majority of patients do not demonstrate a clinically significant postobstructive diuresis following relief of urinary tract obstruction. Those who are susceptible to this phenomenon typically have signs of fluid overload including edema, congestive heart failure, or hypertension** (Loo and Vaughan, 1985). The most common clinical setting is release of urinary retention. A catheter should be placed to drain the bladder rapidly in those with urinary retention. There is no role for gradual bladder decompression, as this has not been demonstrated to limit hematuria or the risk of postobstructive diuresis (Nyman et al, 1997).

**Subjects in whom BUO or UUO in a solitary kidney is relieved should be monitored for a postobstructive diuresis.** Serum electrolytes, magnesium, blood urea nitrogen (BUN), and creatinine should be checked. The intensity of monitoring depends on presence of risk factors for postobstructive diuresis and the subject's mental status, renal function, and electrolyte status. Those with normal renal function and electrolytes, no evidence of fluid overload, and who are mentally alert should have their vital signs and urine output monitored. They are allowed free access to oral fluids, and if they do not manifest signs of a postobstructive diuresis they can be discharged and return later for further urologic evaluation and care. If they show signs of a postobstructive diuresis but are alert, able to consume fluids, and have normal vital signs, observation is continued and the patients may consume fluids as desired. **This is a physiologic diuresis in the majority of cases that resolves when free water and excess solutes are eliminated.** Serum electrolytes, BUN, magnesium, and creatinine are checked daily until the diuresis resolves. If patients have signs of fluid overload, azotemia, or poor cognitive function or if hypotension or other indicators of hypovolemia develop, more intense monitoring should be instituted. Vital signs and urine output are checked more frequently. Electrolytes, BUN, magnesium, and creatinine are assessed every 12 hours and more frequently if necessary. Urinary osmolarity should be checked in this setting. Hypo-osmolar urine is indicative of a primary water diuresis as opposed to a solute diuresis. Of note, an initial solute diuresis may convert to a pathologic water diuresis, underscoring the need for obtaining a baseline urine osmolarity and continued monitoring of this parameter.

**The clinically stable patient with good cognitive function should be given free access to oral fluids.** Intravenous fluids should probably not be administered as this may prolong the period of diuresis. However, there may be a theoretical role for maintenance of volume expansion in this setting. Gulmi and associates (1995) demonstrated improved GFR in dogs undergoing volume expansion just prior to relief of BUO. This is linked to increased generation of ANP and the salutary effects of this peptide on RBF and GFR. A clinical trial is needed to determine whether this would facilitate recovery of GFR in humans.

Those with poor cognitive function should receive intravenous hydration but below the normal maintenance amounts. The majority of this group also have a self-limiting physiologic diuresis. On rare occasions a pathologic diuresis develops and the patients can become hypovolemic because of excess water loss; they can develop electrolyte abnormalities as a result of the former or salt and potassium losses, or both. These patients warrant the most intense monitoring and require careful electrolyte and fluid replacement, initially by an intravenous route. Assessing urinary output, vital signs, and both urinary and serum electrolytes facilitates prescribing the optimal amount and type of fluids to be administered. We have seen very few such cases at our medical center, and the diuresis resolved with time. Some patients have salt wasting associated with hyponatremia and hyperkalemia mimicking adrenal insufficiency. This has been reported to occur mainly in children (Melzi et al, 1995). It is thought to be due to tubular resistance to aldosterone, and supporting evidence for this is the significantly increased serum aldosterone levels reported in these cases. The underlying cause may be a reduction in aldosterone receptors (Kuhnle et al, 1993).

## Experimental Modulation of Postobstructive Diuresis

Animal and cell culture experiments demonstrate the potential of pharmacologically attenuating postobstructive diuresis. Ureteral obstruction induces expression of COX-2 in collecting duct cells (Guan et al, 1997). Evidence suggests that the downregulation of AQP2 receptors is mediated by COX-2. Administration of COX-2 inhibitors prevented the downregulation of AQP2 and significantly diminished postobstructive diuresis in rats with BUO (Cheng et al, 2004). In addition, with ureteral obstruction, there is blunted cAMP generation in response to vasopressin (Kim et al, 2001a). Vasopressin-induced, cAMP-mediated pathways induce phosphorylation and subsequent membrane insertion of AQP2 (Nishimoto et al, 1999; Van Balkom et al, 2002). A cAMP-independent, cyclic guanosine monophosphate (cGMP) pathway has been demonstrated in both in vitro and in vivo models to allow membrane insertion of AQP2 (Bouley et al, 2000). Acute exposure to the phosphodiesterase type 5 inhibitor sildenafil citrate elevated intracellular cGMP and has been shown to facilitate collecting duct accumulation of AQP2 (Bouley et al, 2005). **Although such data are suggestive that postobstructive diuresis can be manipulated pharmacologically, it is unclear whether such manipulation would be ultimately beneficial or harmful.**

# SELECTED EXTRINSIC CAUSES OF URETERAL OBSTRUCTION

A plethora of intraperitoneal and extraperitoneal disease processes may ultimately result in ureteral obstruction. Hydronephrosis, either symptomatic or incidental, may thus be the initial presentation of these conditions. Herein, selected extrinsic causes of ureteral obstruction are reviewed.

## Retroperitoneal Fibrosis

Retroperitoneal fibrosis is an uncommon condition in which a predominantly inflammatory mass envelops and potentially obstructs retroperitoneal structures including either or both ureters. The initial report is now attributed to Albarran (1905), although idiopathic retroperitoneal fibrosis has had the eponym Ormond's disease after that author's description and definition of this clinical entity in 1948 (Albarran, 1905; Ormond, 1948). Of the two patients Ormond initially described, one had progressive renal deterioration and ultimately expired, whereas the other underwent exploration and ureterolysis without subsequent signs or symptoms of recurrent ureteral obstruction during the ensuing 12 years, underscoring the need to recognize and address this process (Ormond, 1960).

**Grossly, retroperitoneal fibrosis appears as a fibrous, whitish plaque encasing the aorta, inferior vena cava, and their major branches, and the ureters, other retroperitoneal structures, and at times intraperitoneal structures including the gastrointestinal tract.** Its longitudinal axis usually extends from the renal hilum to the pelvic brim, but it may extend into pelvis and mediastinum.

The development of retroperitoneal fibrosis is hypothesized to take place in two phases. The initial phase is thought to be inflammatory, histologically characterized by abundant plasma cells, lymphocytes, macrophages, and eosinophils. An autoimmune response has been proposed to incite this phase. Leakage of ceroid, a complex lipoprotein, originating from atheromatous plaques in the aorta has been hypothesized to induce an autoimmune antigenic response and generate a local inflammation leading to varying degrees of fibrosis (Baker, 2003). The second phase is characterized as a fibrotic maturation with the development of homogeneous fibrous tissue with limited cellularity.

The incidence of retroperitoneal fibrosis has been estimated to be 1 in 200,000 (Debruyne et al, 1982). There is a 3:1 male-to-female ratio, and the mean age at onset is 50 years (Wu et al, 2002). Numerous medications have been associated with the development of retroperitoneal fibrosis and are listed in Table 37–3, along with other etiologies of this process. A definitive etiology of retroperitoneal fibrosis is found in only 30% of cases (Koep et al, 1977). The term "idiopathic retroperitoneal fibrosis" should be used only when an inciting etiology is not defined. **An underlying malignancy should always be considered, as one is reported to be present in 8% to 10% of such cases** (Amis, 1991).

Patients usually have nonspecific symptoms, which may include back, abdominal, or flank pain, weight loss, anorexia, and malaise. Signs can be similarly nonspecific and include hypertension in 50%, fever, and lower extremity edema. Because of its insidious nature, many patients do not present until later in the course of the disease, manifesting with signs or symptoms attributable to ureteral or vascular obstruction (Amis, 1991). Reported laboratory abnormalities are nonspecific and include an elevated erythrocyte sedimentation rate in 80% to 90%, elevated serum creatinine, hypergammaglobulinemia, and normochromic, normocytic anemia (Monev, 2002).

Before the advent of cross-sectional imaging, radiologic diagnosis relied upon imaging not the disease process itself but its secondary effects on the ureters. The classic radiologic findings included medial deviation of extrinsically compressed ureters with hydronephrosis. Medial deviation is a nonspecific finding as it has been demonstrated in up to 18%

| Table 37–3.  **Suspected Causes of Retroperitoneal Fibrosis** | |
|---|---|
| *Drugs* | *Hemorrhage* |
| Methysergide | Abdominal and pelvic surgery |
| Hydralazine | Ruptured viscera |
| Reserpine | Henoch-Schönlein purpura with hemorrhage |
| Haloperidol | |
| LSD | *Periarteritis* |
| Methyldopa | Aortic or iliac artery aneurysm |
| β Blockers | Inflammatory response to advanced atherosclerosis |
| Ergotamine alkaloids | Collagen vascular disease |
| Phenacetin | |
| Amphetamines | *Infection* |
| *Chemicals* | Gonorrhea |
| | Tuberculosis |
| Avitene | Chronic UTI |
| Methyl methacrylate | Syphilis |
| Talcum powder | |
| | *Radiation Injury* |
| *Retroperitoneal Tumors* | *Other* |
| *Inflammatory Processes* | |
| | Sarcoidosis |
| Ascending lymphangitis | Biliary tract disease |
| Chronic inflammatory bowel disease | Endometriosis |

LSD, lysergic acid diethylamide; UTI, urinary tract infection.

of normal subjects (Saldino and Palubinskas, 1972). Hydronephrosis is typically demonstrated on ultrasonography, and there may also be a smooth, well-demarcated, hypoechoic mass anterior to the lumbar or sacral spine (Amis, 1991). Retrograde pyelography typically demonstrates hydronephrosis, with medially deviated and segmentally narrowed ureters without filling defects (Fig. 37–8). Currently, cross-sectional imaging with CT or MRI is the modality of choice for evaluating patients with suspected retroperitoneal fibrosis. Both modalities have been demonstrated to delineate accurately the extent of the disease when correlated with surgical exploration (Mulligan et al, 1989). **CT typically reveals a well-demarcated retroperitoneal mass, isodense with muscle on unenhanced studies** (Fig. 37–9) (Vivas et al, 2000). Variable degrees of contrast enhancement may be seen, typically more pronounced earlier in the course of the disease when the presumably more immature plaque has increased vascularity (Amis, 1991). Some have advocated noncontrast multidetector CT imaging combined with antegrade CT pyelography for evaluation as it can define the fibrotic process and the level and degree of ureteral obstruction without administration of intravenous contrast material (Ghersin et al, 2004). However, the invasive nature of this diagnostic approach limits its applicability.

MRI offers cross-sectional and multiplanar evaluation of the retroperitoneal fibrosis plaque (Fig. 37–10). **Theoretically, MRI allows superior soft tissue discrimination and can more accurately distinguish the plaque from the great vessels than unenhanced CT.** In addition, the disease can be followed without the radiation exposure of repeated CT (Burn et al, 2002). Typically, T1-weighted images of the lesion reveal low to medium signal intensity (hypointense compared with muscle); T2-weighted imaging is variable. Low T2 signal intensity has been correlated with mature plaque (Mulligan et al, 1989). High signal intensity on T2-weighted images suggests increased water content and hypercellularity and may represent either inflammatory edema in a benign plaque or an underlying malignant process (Amis, 1991; Burn et al, 2002). With gadolinium administration, variable enhancement of the plaque may be seen, with greater degree of enhancement in the more acute phases of the disease process. Enhancement ratios can be calculated with dynamic gadolinium enhance-

ment, and investigators have used these ratios to assess disease activity and monitor treatment responses (Burn et al, 2002).

**If there is evidence of obstructive uropathy at presentation, therapy should be first directed at its correction.** This may be accomplished with internalized ureteral stents but percutaneous nephrostomy may be necessary if stenting is not possible or ineffective. **Biopsy to exclude malignancy should be performed next. This can be attempted percutaneously with CT, MRI, or ultrasound guidance.** If this is not technically possible or the tissue obtained is inadequate, an open surgical or laparoscopic biopsy is recommended with

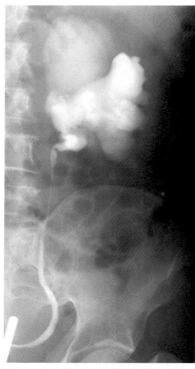

**Figure 37–8.** Retrograde pyelogram performed in a patient with retroperitoneal fibrosis. Note evenly narrowed midureteral segment with proximal hydronephrosis. (Courtesy of Dr. Ronald Zagoria.)

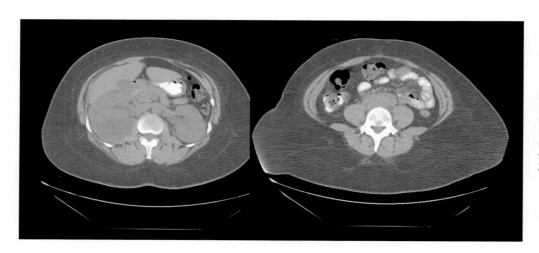

**Figure 37–9.** Unenhanced computed tomography performed in a patient with retroperitoneal fibrosis. Note hydronephrosis and soft tissue mass indistinguishable from the great vessels. (Courtesy of Dr. Ronald Zagoria.)

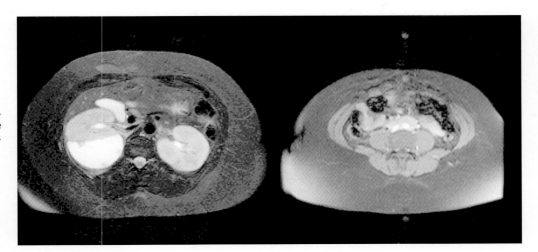

**Figure 37–10.** Unenhanced magnetic resonance imaging from the same patient as in Figure 37–9. (Courtesy of Dr. Ronald Zagoria.)

concomitant ureterolysis if malignancy is not suspected on frozen section analysis. If the percutaneous biopsy demonstrates findings compatible with retroperitoneal fibrosis, possible inciting medications should be discontinued.

**The potential morbidity of ureterolysis, accurate image-guided biopsy techniques, and more sensitive cross-sectional imaging studies for diagnosis and follow-up have made medical therapy the preferred approach in this setting. However, it should be noted that there have been no randomized prospective studies addressing the merits of initial medical therapy versus a surgical approach.** Patients should be informed about the side effects of the proposed medical therapy and the risk of disease progression or undiagnosed malignancy. Medical therapy has been directed to address the presumed autoimmune and inflammatory components of retroperitoneal fibrosis.

**The administration of corticosteroids has been used for primary therapy.** Although many steroid regimens have been described, appropriate dosing schedules and duration of therapy have not been clearly established. The sequence suggested by Kardar and colleagues (2002) has been demonstrated to be effective after long-term follow-up. Their algorithm for adults consists of prednisolone administered at an oral dose of 60 mg on alternate days for 2 months, tapered to 5 mg daily over the next 2 months. The latter dose is continued for a total duration of 2 years. Of the 11 patients who completed this regimen at a median follow-up of 63 months, 9 maintained a good response, 1 required ureterolysis, and 1 recurred but responded to reinitiation of therapy.

**Tamoxifen, a nonsteroidal antiestrogen, has also been used for primary treatment.** It is thought to alter TGF-β, potentially limiting fibrosis. There have been scattered case reports documenting successful outcomes with tamoxifen therapy but no published series. The most commonly reported dose was 20 mg/day, and duration of therapy varied (Loffeld and Van Weel, 1993; Al Rabi et al, 2002). Successful combination therapy using a tapered steroid regimen and daily tamoxifen has also been described (Tziomalos et al, 2004).

**Aggressive immunotherapy has also been used as primary therapy for those afflicted with retroperitoneal fibrosis.** Marcolongo and colleagues (2004) reported 26 patients who

were treated with a 6-month course of prednisone, combined with either 6 months of cyclophosphamide or 1 year of azathioprine. Severe adverse effects in the cyclophosphamide group included death in one, sepsis in one, and severe leukopenia in two patients. In the azathioprine group, activation of hepatitis, pancreatitis, and oral candidiasis developed. All surviving patients had disease resolution, although seven required a second course of treatment.

**Ureterolysis is undertaken if medical therapy fails or if the patient is not a candidate for medical therapy.** Traditionally, this has been done by an open surgical approach, but successful laparoscopic ureterolysis has been reported and may be a feasible option for selected patients. Bilateral ureterolysis is recommended, even in the setting of unilateral disease, as the disease typically progresses to involve the contralateral side. The ureteral dissection should begin in a region free of disease, and care must be taken to avoid devascularization of the ureter. A biopsy of the fibrotic area should be repeated to limit the risk of sampling error associated with percutaneous biopsy. Several strategies have been employed to prevent recurrent ureteral involvement in the fibrotic process. **The ureter may be displaced to a lateral position, brought to an intraperitoneal location by closing the peritoneum behind it, or wrapped within a sleeve of omentum. One method has not been definitively demonstrated to generate superior results** (Barbalias and Liatsikos, 1999). If it is determined intraoperatively that ureterolysis is not technically possible, alternatives include ileal ureter replacement, autotransplantation, chronic ureteral stenting, or nephrostomy tube drainage.

It has been suggested that ureteral stents can generally be removed 6 to 8 weeks after ureterolysis (Varkarakis and Jarrett, 2005). Some have advocated postoperative steroid therapy to expedite disease resolution or prevent recurrence, but there is limited experience with this approach (Varkarakis and Jarrett, 2005).

There is limited published information on the results of ureterolysis; 66% to 100% success rates were reported for small series. The best success rates were reported by Elashry and colleagues (1996); 100% for seven laparoscopic and 100% six open surgical procedures. Alexopoulos and associates (1987), however, noted only 66% long-term success with ureterolysis combined with postoperative steroid administration in six patients with severe retroperitoneal fibrosis. Of note, one of their patients failed 16 years after surgery and became dialysis dependent. **Long-term follow-up in those subjected to medical or surgical therapy is warranted.** Serial cross-sectional imaging should be obtained to assess for disease recurrence, progression, or findings suggestive of malignancy. Renal function should also be monitored.

## Pelvic Lipomatosis

**Pelvic lipomatosis is a rare, benign condition marked by exuberant pelvic overgrowth of nonmalignant but infiltrative adipose tissue.** Engels first described the condition in 1959, and it has been the subject of several reviews and many case reports in the interim. The largest review to date comprised 130 patients, of whom the mean age at presentation was 48 years. Racial and gender differences were noted, with 67% of the patients black and 33% white; there was an 18:1 male-to-female ratio (Heyns, 1991).

The etiology of this disorder is unknown. Obesity has been proposed to play a role, as radiographic improvement and worsening have been noted in response to weight loss and gain (Sacks et al, 1975). In addition, obesity has been noted in over one half of the patients afflicted (Heyns, 1991). However, if pelvic lipomatosis were simply a manifestation of obesity, its observed frequency should be far greater (Morretin and Wilson, 1971). The reported occurrence of pelvic lipomatosis in two brothers raises the possibility of an underlying genetic etiology (Tong et al, 2002). An abnormality in the chromatin-regulating high mobility group A (HMGA) proteins has been implicated as a possible causative factor in pelvic lipomatosis, as transgenic mice with truncated HMGA developed pelvic lipomatosis (Fedele et al, 2001).

**Approximately one half of patients present with lower urinary tract symptoms and one quarter with bowel symptoms, typically constipation.** Suprapubic, back, flank, or perineal discomfort can also be an initial clinical manifestation. The nonspecific nature of these symptoms may result in a significant delay in diagnosis (Heyns, 1991). **Physical findings may include a suprapubic mass, a high-riding prostate, and an indistinct pelvic mass.** Hypertension has been reported in as many as one third of patients (Klein et al 1988; Heyns, 1991).

There are various radiologic signs of pelvic lipomatosis. On plain film, increased pelvic lucency may be noted (Fig. 37–11). **On excretory urography, the bladder characteristically assumes a pear or gourd shape, extrinsically compressed and elongated, and the bladder base is frequently elevated** (Fig. 37–12). Hydroureteronephrosis may be seen (Heyns, 1991). CT is quite helpful in establishing the diagnosis as it readily demonstrates pelvic fat (Fig. 37–13). Extrinsic compression of the rectum may also be demonstrated (Susmano and Dolin, 1979). Liposarcoma should be suspected if there is tissue heterogeneity, areas of positive attenuation coefficients, enhancement with contrast, and poor margination (Andac et al, 2003). MRI can also be used to make the diagnosis as it permits characterization of fat deposits (Demas et al, 1988).

**Evaluation should include cystoscopy, as some form of proliferative cystitis has been found in 75% of patients including cystitis glandularis in up to 40%** (Heyns, 1991).

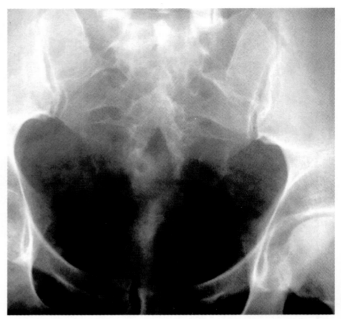

**Figure 37–11.** Plain film of pelvis in a patient with pelvic lipomatosis. Note increased pelvic lucency. (Courtesy of Dr. Ronald Zagoria.)

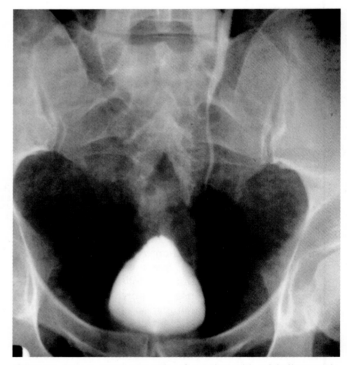

**Figure 37–12.** Excretory urography of a patient with pelvic lipomatosis. Note classic pear-shaped bladder with increased surrounding pelvic lucency. (Courtesy of Dr. Ronald Zagoria.)

Continued cystoscopic surveillance is recommended in those with cystitis glandularis as there have been reports of the development of adenocarcinoma of the bladder in this cohort (Sozen et al, 2004). **Elongation of the prostatic urethra, elevation of the bladder neck, and pelvic fixation may impair**

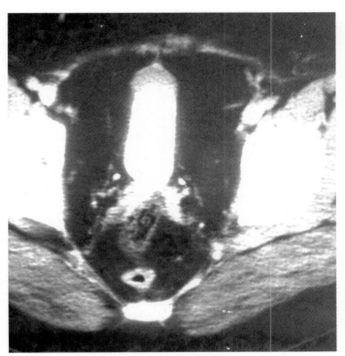

**Figure 37-13.** Computed tomography cystogram of a patient with pelvic lipomatosis. Note narrowed bladder and increased pelvic fat in perivesical and perirectal spaces. (Courtesy of Dr. Ronald Zagoria.)

**cystoscopic access to the bladder.** In Heyns' review (1991) of 72 patients in whom cystoscopy was attempted, evaluation of the bladder was difficult in 24% and impossible in 18%. Hence, flexible cystoscopy may be required if anatomic distortion precludes rigid cystoscopy.

Klein and associates (1988) suggested that there are two clinically separate groups of patients. The first is composed of young, stocky men with irritative lower urinary tract symptoms, vague pelvic complaints, hypertension, and proliferative cystitis. This group may be more susceptible to developing progressive ureteral obstruction. The second group includes older men with incidentally discovered pelvic lipomatosis who are reported to have a more indolent course. Others have not found age to affect disease progression (Heyns, 1991). **Nevertheless, there is agreement that in light of the potential for progressive ureteral obstruction, long-term follow-up is mandated.** Overall, 39% of patients in Klein's series ultimately required operative intervention for upper tract obstruction.

Surgical options in patients with obstructive uropathy secondary to pelvic lipomatosis include ureteral stenting, percutaneous nephrostomy, ureteral reimplantation, and urinary diversion. Pelvic exploration should be approached cautiously, as there is obliteration of normal anatomic planes and increased vascularity within the fatty mass.

## Obstetric and Gynecologic

### Pregnancy

**Hydronephrosis develops commonly during pregnancy, the reported occurrence varying between 43% and 100%** (Faundes et al, 1998). This wide variability is due to the utilization of different definitions of hydronephrosis. The right kidney becomes hydronephrotic two to three times more commonly than the left (Cietak and Newton 1985; Faundes et al, 1998). Hydronephrosis may initially manifest in the first trimester, and it increasingly develops through pregnancy (Au et al, 1985; Loughlin, 1997). This progression was also reported in a large prospective study by Faundes and colleagues (1998), who found that hydronephrosis was present in 15%, 20%, and 50% of women during the first, second, and third trimesters, respectively . The degree of hydronephrosis also increased over time. Hydronephrosis has been demonstrated to be more common during a first-time pregnancy (Erickson et al, 1979). The maximal calyceal diameters during pregnancy over time were measured by Faundes and associates (1998). These parameters are provided (Table 37–4), as they may be useful when evaluating patients with hydronephrosis during pregnancy. After delivery, hydronephrosis gradually resolves. **Approximately one third of patients may have persistent hydronephrosis during the first postpartum week, but it resolves in the majority within 6 weeks** (Cietak and Newton, 1985).

Two etiologies for hydronephrosis of pregnancy have been postulated, one hormonal and one mechanical. The 10% to 15% incidence of observed first-trimester ureteral dilatation, occurring before the uterus reaches the pelvic brim, supports a nonmechanical mechanism. Progesterone, a hormone in more abundance during pregnancy, has been hypothesized to promote ureteral dilatation and subsequent development of hydronephrosis (Faundes et al, 1988). The increased incidence and degree of hydronephrosis after the 20th week of gestation, a time when the uterus is large enough to compress the ureters extrinsically, supports a mechanical etiology. The significantly lower incidence of left-sided hydronephrosis also supports this hypothesis (Cietak and Newton, 1985). However, it is quite plausible that both mechanisms play a role.

Hydronephrosis of pregnancy is usually clinically silent. However, some with hydronephrosis of pregnancy may experience flank pain or develop pyelonephritis or renal failure. Renal ultrasonography should be undertaken in this setting. **The typical ultrasonographic findings of this entity are hydroureteronephrosis extending to the pelvic brim. When ureteral dilation extends below this, a different etiology of obstruction such as a ureteral stone should be considered.** If the latter is suspected, limited IVU is a diagnostic option. However, MRI is now another consideration. **Magnetic resonance urography has been advocated by some as a noninvasive, nonradiating method of assessing those with hydronephrosis of pregnancy. The presence of hydroureter below the pelvic brim is readily apparent on high-resolution T2 sequences, and filling defects representing stones or soft tissue may be seen** (Spencer et al, 2004). In addition, MRI has proved useful in identifying other causes of acute abdominal pain in pregnancy, including appendicitis, ovarian torsion, and adrenal hemorrhage (Birchard et al, 2005).

The majority of patients with symptomatic hydronephrosis of pregnancy can be managed with conservative measures such as intravenous hydration, analgesics, and antibiotic therapy when clinically indicated. However, placement of ureteral stents may be necessary when these measures are unsuccessful, especially with signs of sepsis or compromised renal function. **Rapid stent encrustation may be problematic**

**Table 37–4. Observed and Adjusted Percentiles of Maximal Caliceal Diameter (mm) of Right and Left Kidneys According to Gestational Age**

| Gestational Age (wk) | Observed Percentiles | | | | Adjusted Percentiles | | | |
|---|---|---|---|---|---|---|---|---|
| | Right | | | Left | Right | | | Left |
| | 50th | 75th | 90th | 90th | 50th | 75th | 90th | 90th |
| 4–6 | 0.0 | 3.0 | 5.0 | 2.1 | 1.4 | 2.4 | 3.4 | 0.1 |
| 7–8 | 0.0 | 0.0 | 5.0 | 0.0 | 0.3 | 3.2 | 4.5 | 2.2 |
| 9–10 | 0.0 | 0.0 | 4.0 | 0.0 | 1.2 | 4.0 | 5.7 | 3.5 |
| 11–12 | 0.0 | 5.0 | 7.0 | 6.0 | 2.0 | 4.9 | 7.0 | 4.5 |
| 13–14 | 0.0 | 5.8 | 8.0 | 6.9 | 2.7 | 5.7 | 8.4 | 5.3 |
| 15–16 | 0.0 | 1.0 | 8.9 | 4.9 | 3.0 | 6.7 | 9.8 | 6.0 |
| 17–18 | 5.0 | 9.5 | 12.0 | 8.8 | 3.7 | 7.6 | 11.2 | 6.6 |
| 19–20 | 0.0 | 8.0 | 11.0 | 7.7 | 4.2 | 8.6 | 2.6 | 7.1 |
| 21–22 | 5.0 | 9.0 | 13.8 | 6.8 | 4.6 | 9.6 | 13.9 | 7.1 |
| 23–24 | 8.0 | 12.0 | 15.0 | 8.2 | 4.9 | 10.5 | 15.1 | 7.9 |
| 25–26 | 7.0 | 13.0 | 16.7 | 8.0 | 5.3 | 11.4 | 16.2 | 8.2 |
| 27–28 | 7.0 | 13.0 | 21.0 | 9.0 | 5.6 | 12.2 | 17.2 | 8.4 |
| 29–30 | 7.0 | 11.0 | 16.0 | 9.0 | 5.9 | 13.0 | 18.0 | 8.6 |
| 31–32 | 8.0 | 15.5 | 19.4 | 8.2 | 6.1 | 13.7 | 18.7 | 8.7 |
| 33–34 | 4.5 | 13.0 | 20.5 | 8.5 | 6.4 | 14.3 | 19.3 | 8.8 |
| 35–36 | 6.0 | 15.0 | 19.0 | 8.0 | 6.6 | 14.8 | 19.7 | 8.9 |
| 37–38 | 5.0 | 14.0 | 20.4 | 8.0 | 6.8 | 15.2 | 19.8 | 8.9 |
| 39–42 | 7.0 | 14.0 | 17.0 | 9.2 | 7.1 | 15.5 | 19.8 | 8.7 |

as urinary calcium excretion increases during pregnancy (Goldfarb et al, 1989). This may necessitate more frequent stent changes. Percutaneous nephrostomy is an alternative if this occurs, and it is also a consideration if pyonephrosis is suspected.

## Benign Pelvic Abnormalities

**Tubo-ovarian Abscess.** Pelvic inflammatory disease (PID) is a common problem, affecting 10% of women during their lifetime. **Tubo-ovarian abscess, occurring in approximately 15% of those afflicted with PID, may cause extrinsic ureteral obstruction** (Aral et al, 1991). This process may be demonstrated with ultrasonography, CT, or MRI. Ureteral obstruction may resolve with antibiotic therapy or transvaginal drainage of the abscess. However, an open surgical or laparoscopic intervention may be required to drain or excise the involved ovary and fallopian tube if the aforementioned measures are unsuccessful. Placement of an internalized ureteral stent or percutaneous nephrostomy should be considered if high-grade renal obstruction or urosepsis is suspected. Stent or nephrostomy tube removal is undertaken after the inflammatory process has resolved. Follow-up renal imaging is recommended as some patients have persistent obstruction.

**Endometriosis.** Endometriosis is defined as the presence of functional endometrial tissue in an ectopic site. Although endometriosis is usually confined to the ovaries, uterosacral ligaments, and cul-de-sac, it has been documented in almost every organ system in the body (Jubanyik and Comite, 1997). It may affect 10% to 20% of women of reproductive age, with a peak incidence in the mid-20s (Eskenazi and Warner, 1997). There is no relationship of endometriosis to race or socioeconomic status.

**Endometriosis of the urinary tract is predominantly found in the bladder, accounting for 70% to 80% of the cases. The ureter may be involved in 15% to 20% of the** urinary tract cases (Williams, 1975). Involvement may be either intrinsic or extrinsic. Intrinsic endometriosis is characterized by endometrial glands and stroma within the lamina propria, tunica muscularis, or ureteral lumen; extrinsic endometriosis is localized within periureteral tissue. Eighty percent of ureteral endometriosis is extrinsic and primarily involves the distal ureter (Klein and Cattolica, 1979). The left side is more often affected, and bilateral disease has been reported in up to 23% of cases (Antonelli et al, 2004).

Classic symptoms and signs of urinary tract endometriosis include cyclical flank pain, dysuria, urgency, urinary tract infection, and hematuria (Jubanyik and Comite, 1997). Patients with intrinsic endometriosis experience these symptoms more than those with extrinsic disease. **Notably, a significant portion of patients with ureteral endometriosis do not have genitourinary symptoms.** For example, in one series ureteral obstruction was silent in approximately 40% of those with severe ureteral endometriosis (Antonelli et al, 2004). Furthermore, silent loss of renal function has been reported in 25% to 43% of patients with ureteral endometriosis, which may result in total loss of function of the affected kidney (Watanabe et al, 2004). Historically, up to one third of kidneys affected by ureteral endometriosis were lost (Klein and Cattolica, 1979).

**Because a large percentage of patients with ureteral endometriosis can have asymptomatic obstruction of the kidney with a loss of renal function, it has been recommended to image the upper urinary tract in all patients with pelvic endometriosis.** Initial imaging may be done with ultrasonography as a noninvasive test to look for hydroureteronephrosis. An EXU may be a better test when the index of suspicion for ureteral involvement is high. Pyelographic findings of intrinsic disease include ureteral filling defects, whereas smooth strictured ureteral segments are seen with extrinsic disease (Stebbing and Notley, 1995). Retrograde ureteropyelography, CT, and MRI may help to ascertain the exact location and volume of the disease and may provide valuable information for planning treatment.

Treatment has several goals: (1) preservation of renal function, (2) management of the ongoing disease process, (3) maintenance of the patient's fertility, and (4) relief of the patient's symptoms with the least invasive methods available.

**If renal function is normal and there is minimal to mild hydronephrosis with no functional obstruction as determined by radionuclide renal scanning, hormone therapy may be prescribed.** Ovarian hormonal ablation with gonadotropin-releasing hormone agonists has been utilized with success in some series. Rivlin and associates (1990) described three patients treated with leuprolide acetate for 6 to 9 months. One patient had BUO, and two had UUO. The obstruction resolved in the patient with BUO and in one of the patients with UUO. The failure occurred in the patient with intrinsic ureteral disease.

Hormonal therapy is not as effective for patients with extensive endometriosis as reflected by high treatment failure and recurrence rates (Lam et al, 1992).

Surgical intervention is the treatment of choice for most patients with significant hydroureteronephrosis and periureteral disease. If the patient does not desire future pregnancy, treatment is total abdominal hysterectomy and bilateral salpingo-oophorectomy. If pregnancy is desired, lesser extirpative procedures can be performed, such as unilateral oophorectomy. Ureterolysis may correct ureteral obstruction in those with extrinsic disease. If laparoscopic ureterolysis is undertaken, a transperitoneal approach is preferable in that it allows a superior assessment of endometrial implants on the peritoneum overlying the ureter (Watanabe et al, 2004). When intrinsic disease is present or in cases in which ureterolysis fails or is unlikely to work, distal ureterectomy with reimplantation is reported to have excellent long-term results with regard to renal preservation (Antonelli et al, 2004).

**Ovarian Remnants.** **The ovarian remnant syndrome results from residual, viable ovarian tissue after bilateral salpingo-oophorectomy.** Although uncommon, it is a recognized complication of a technically difficult oophorectomy, most typically in those with endometriosis, PID, or prior abdominal and pelvic surgery (Lafferty et al, 1996). Ovarian remnants may be quite large, up to 10 cm, and may be present in the normal ovarian bed but may be located in other areas as a consequence of dissemination and implantation occurring during surgery (Lafferty et al, 1996). **Mass effect or a localized fibrosis may cause extrinsic ureteral obstruction.** This process may be demonstrated with ultrasonography, CT or MRI (Klutke et al, 1993).

**Treatment is usually surgical excision of the mass and ureterolysis.** Preoperative ureteral stenting may be considered if there is high-grade obstruction or as an aid to intraoperative identification of the ureter, although the latter has not been reported to be necessary by some investigators (Lafferty et al, 1996). Medical management of ureteral obstruction is an option for poor surgical candidates. Successful resolution of the mass and hydronephrosis have been reported with leuprolide acetate therapy. However, chronic medical therapy may be required to prevent recurrence (Koch et al, 1994).

**Mass Lesions of the Uterus and Ovaries.** Other benign lesions of the uterus and ovary may become large enough to cause extrinsic ureteral obstruction. These include uterine fibroids, ovarian cysts, and ovarian fibromas. **Uterine fibroids, the most common tumor of the upper female genital tract, are also the most common, benign gynecologic neoplasm causing ureteral obstruction** (Greenberg and Kazamel, 1995). The most common site of extrinsic ureteral obstruction is at the pelvic brim. Surgical resection or ablation of the leiomyomas should be considered in this setting.

## Vascular Causes of Ureteral Obstruction

The ureters course adjacent to vascular structures and as a consequence may be affected by various vascular disease processes and anomalies that may result in their obstruction. An overview of several of these entities is subsequently provided.

### Arterial Causes of Obstruction

**Abdominal Aortic Aneurysm.** **Clinical signs and symptoms of ureteral obstruction may be the initial manifestation of an abdominal aortic aneurysm (AAA)** (Labardini and Ratliff, 1967). The obstruction may be due to a mass effect or localized inflammation (Pennell et al, 1985).

Currently, CT scanning is most frequently utilized to evaluate patients with an AAA that may demonstrate associated hydronephrosis (Fig. 37–14A and B). Ureteral findings associated with AAA vary. The ureters may be pushed laterally on both sides, or one side may deviate laterally while the opposite side is drawn medially within the perianeurysmal inflammation, or both may be medially deviated. Some have noted that lateral deviation of the ureter with AAA is usually not associated with obstruction (Labardini and Ratliff, 1967). **The medial deviation of the ureter associated with the desmoplastic reaction of inflammatory aneurysms (IAAA), however, carries a more significant risk of ureteral obstruction.** Although IAAA represents only between 4% and 15% of AAAs, the associated retroperitoneal desmoplastic reaction significantly increases the risk of ureteral obstruction, which has been reported in 21% of this cohort (Pennell et al, 1985; Arroyo et al, 2003).

At one time ureterolysis was routinely performed during repair of IAAA associated with ureteral obstruction. However, this practice has generally been abandoned as obstruction commonly resolves without ureterolysis. Placement of internalized ureteral stents is commonly undertaken prior to aneurysm repair. Ureteral obstruction has been reported to resolve in 80% of patients managed with this approach (Arroyo et al, 2003). Some have advocated endovascular repair of the IAAA in this setting (Nevelsteen et al, 1999). Internalized ureteral stents are inserted prior to endovascular graft placement and are removed when it is thought that the associated fibrosis has resolved. A 50% resolution of ureteral obstruction has been reported with this approach (Rehring et al, 2001; Deleersnijder et al, 2002). Patients with IAAA treated with open surgery or an endovascular approach warrant close monitoring for development of recurrent or de novo ureteral obstruction, as delayed ureteral obstruction has been reported to occur (Simons et al, 2002; Jetty and Barber, 2004; Lambie et al, 2004).

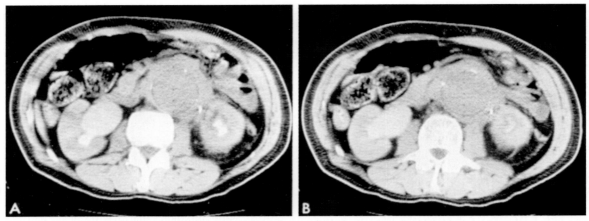

**Figure 37–14.** **A** and **B,** Computed tomography scans demonstrate extensive retroperitoneal fibrosis associated with aneurysm of the abdominal aorta.

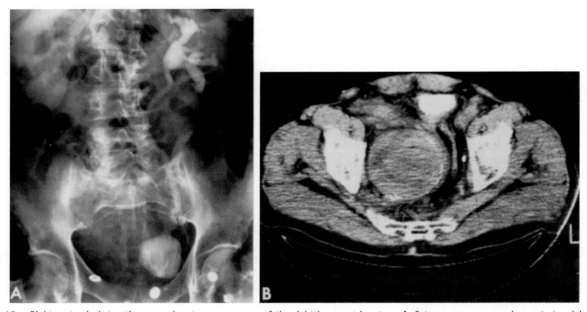

**Figure 37–15.** Right ureteral obstruction secondary to an aneurysm of the right hypogastric artery. **A,** Intravenous urogram demonstrates delayed visualization of the right kidney and marked deviation of the urinary bladder. **B,** Computed tomography scan demonstrates a large aneurysm. Note calcification of the wall.

**Iliac Artery Aneurysms.** Iliac artery aneurysms can cause ureteral obstruction. This has been reported in 35% of those with common iliac artery aneurysms and 19% of those involving the internal iliac artery. **An iliac artery aneurysm should be suspected if a pulsatile mass is palpated on rectal examination** (Marino et al, 1987). The diagnosis can be made with various imaging studies including ultrasonography, MRI, and CT (Fig. 37–15A and B). Ureteral obstruction may be due to extrinsic compression or localized inflammation (Mineta et al, 2004).

Treatment options for common iliac artery aneurysms in the setting of ureteral obstruction include ureterolysis, aneurysm resection and graft placement, or endovascular graft placement. Options for obstructing internal iliac artery aneurysms include open surgical ligation and ureterolysis or initial endovascular occlusion and subse-quent retrograde placement of an iliac artery endovascular graft. Internalized ureteral stents are typically placed before these procedures and are removed 6 to 8 weeks later. These patients need to be observed closely to determine whether ureteral obstruction resolves or recurs. If it recurs, management options include chronic internalized ureteral stenting, ureterolysis, or ureteral reconstruction (Marino et al, 1987).

An additional cause of ureteral obstruction is the retroiliac ureter (Corbus et al, 1960). Treatment of the ureteral obstruction involves transection of the ureter and transposition to the normal, anterior position. Other genitourinary abnormalities are associated with this condition, including renal hypoplasia, vesicoureteral reflux, ureteral ectopia, ectopic vas deferens, hypospadias, bifid scrotum, hypoplastic or duplex uterus, and hydrometrocolpos (Nguyen et al, 1989; Katz and Meirow,

1993). **Therefore, a search for other genitourinary abnormalities should be undertaken in patients with retroiliac ureter.**

**Ureteral Obstruction after Vascular Graft Placement.** Hydronephrosis may occur in up to 10% to 20% of patients after aortic bypass graft surgery (Goldenberg et al, 1988; Schein and Saadia, 1991). There are several possible causes for this problem. Mechanical obstruction of the ureter may be due to graft placement anterior to the ureter, which is readily identified on axial imaging (Bouterie and Harbach, 1979). However, this is the cause in the minority of cases. Other possible etiologies include ureteral entrapment in perigraft fibrosis, ureteral devascularization, unidentified ureteral ligation, and ureteral compression from a postoperative pseudoaneurysm (Sant et al, 1983). Symptoms and signs of ureteral obstruction in this setting arise typically in the first postoperative year and include flank pain, anorexia, hypertension, anuria, and renal failure or insufficiency. A minority may remain asymptomatic or manifest delayed symptoms.

The management approach to this problem varies. **If hydronephrosis is demonstrated early in the postoperative period and renal function is not compromised, close observation is initially indicated as hydronephrosis resolves spontaneously in the majority of cases** (Goldenberg et al, 1988). Temporary internalized ureteral stent placement or percutaneous nephrostomy drainage may be required for those with renal impairment or severe symptoms while awaiting spontaneous resolution. If ureteral obstruction does not resolve spontaneously and the graft is placed anteriorly, transposition of the ureter and vascular graft should be a consideration. In order to reduce the risk of graft infection, however, it has been suggested that the vascular graft, rather than the ureter, should be transected and repositioned (Bouterie and Harbach, 1979). A trial of steroid or tamoxifen therapy, similar to that employed for retroperitoneal fibrosis, may be considered if persistent ureteral obstruction is ascribed to perigraft fibrosis. Although success has been reported with such regimens, careful follow-up is mandatory as delayed treatment failure has been reported (Huben and Schellhammer, 1981; Baskerville and Browse, 1987; Jetty and Barber, 2004). Ureterolysis and ileal ureter substitution if the former is not feasible are considerations if medical therapy is not successful. Chronic ureteral stenting may be required in those who are not candidates for the aforementioned procedures (Sant et al, 1983; Matlaga et al, 2003).

### Venous Causes of Obstruction

**Puerperal Ovarian Vein Thrombophlebitis.** Ureteral obstruction has been ascribed to a mechanical effect from a dilated ovarian vein, a condition called "ovarian vein syndrome." The clinical relevance of this entity has since been questioned and discounted (Dure-Smith, 1979). **However, ovarian vein pathology has been documented to be the cause of ureteral obstruction in the postpartum period. Puerperal ovarian vein thrombophlebitis, a rare but well-documented postpartum condition, has been reported to cause ureteral obstruction** (Dure-Smith, 1979; Brown et al, 1999). Although more common on the right, it may occur in either or both ovarian veins. The associated signs and symptoms are often nonspecific but include abdominal or flank pain and fever,

usually beginning 2 to 3 days after birth. On physical examination, abdominal tenderness and guarding may be elicited. A tender indurated adnexal mass may be discerned in 50% of patients (Toland et al, 1993). CT or MRI can detect this condition and the associated ureteral obstruction (Twicker et al, 1997).

**The majority of patients respond to conservative measures, including antibiotic therapy** (Brown et al, 1999). Internalized ureteral stent placement may also be required for management of ureteral obstruction and symptoms (Toland et al, 1993). Laparoscopic or open surgical ureterolysis and ovarian vein resection are undertaken if ureteral obstruction persists (Almeida et al, 2003).

**Testicular Vein Thrombophlebitis.** Thrombophlebitis of the left testicular vein causing extrinsic obstruction of the left ureter has been reported (Kretkowski and Shah, 1977). Although the patient presented with the clinical picture of ureteropelvic junction obstruction, surgical exploration revealed a dilated and thrombosed left testicular vein impinging upon the proximal ureter. Ureterolysis and excision of the thrombosed vein eradicated the obstruction. A similar event could also occur on the right side (Meyer et al, 1992).

**Circumcaval Ureter.** Obstruction of the ureter has been described in association with an anomalous course posterior, medial, anterior, and finally lateral to the inferior vena cava (IVC) (Bateson and Atkinson, 1969). This course may lead to extrinsic obstruction of the ureter. Although commonly referred to as circumcaval or retrocaval ureter, a more appropriate term may be preureteral vena cava as it is due to a congenital abnormality in development of the vena cava. The term retrocaval is now primarily used to describe ureters that simply knuckle behind the IVC and reemerge laterally.

Formation of the infrahepatic vena cava is based upon the development and regression of three pairs of embryonic veins: the posterior cardinal, the supracardinal, and the subcardinal. It is postulated that the normally developed IVC results from persistence of the right subcardinal vein suprarenally and the right supracardinal infrarenally. The posterior cardinal veins persist as the common iliac veins (Bass et al, 2000). The anastomosis between the right subcardinal and supracardinal vein crosses anterior to the fetal ureter. In normal development, this connection regresses and the supracardinal vein persists as the infrarenal IVC. The prevailing theory of the development of this anomaly is that the subcardinal vein persists as the infrarenal IVC, thus crossing anterior to the midportion of the ureter and resulting in its circumcaval course (Schulman, 1997). Others have suggested that the persistence of the posterior cardinal vein as the infrarenal cava is responsible for this anomaly. However, failure of the supracardinal vein to develop into the infrarenal IVC is common to both theories (Bass et al, 2000) (Fig. 37–16A to C).

The reported incidence of circumcaval ureter is approximately 1 in 1100. There is a 2.8-fold male predominance (Lutin et al, 1988). Symptomatic patients typically present in the third or fourth decade of life (Zhang et al, 1990). **This vascular anomaly is not always associated with ureteral obstruction** (Crosse et al, 1975). The majority involve the right ureter, although left-sided circumcaval ureter has been reported in association with a duplicated IVC and in association with situs inversus (Watanabe et al, 1991; Rubinstein

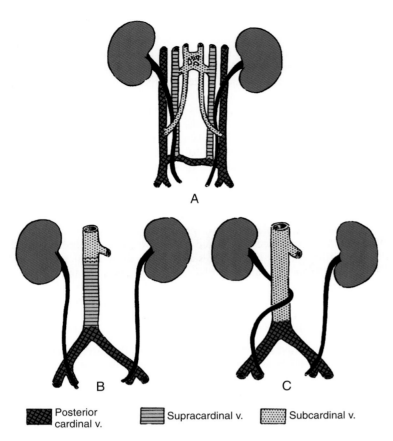

**Figure 37–16.** Relationship between the development of the infrarenal portion of the inferior vena cava and the retrocaval ureter. **A,** Primitive condition with the ureter winding among three cardinal veins. **B,** Usual method of formation of the vena cava from the right subcardinal vein (dorsal to ureter). **C,** Main portion of the vena cava formed from the subcardinal vein. (From Hollinshead WH: Anatomy for Surgeons, vol 2, 2nd ed. New York, Harper & Row, 1971.)

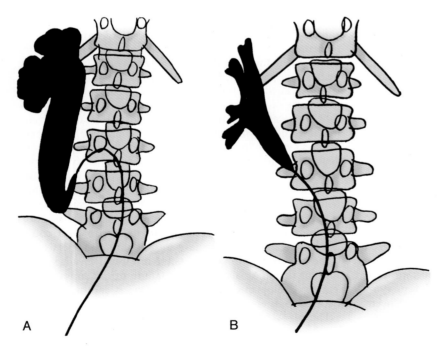

**Figure 37–17.** **A,** Diagram illustrating the radiologic features of the type 1 circumcaval ureter. **B,** Diagram illustrating the radiologic features of the type 2 circumcaval ureter. (**A** and **B,** from Bateson EM, Atkinson D: Circumcaval ureter: A new classification. Clin Radiol 1969;20: 173-177.)

et al, 1999). Other genitourinary anomalies may be present. Circumcaval right ureter with a retrocaval horseshoe isthmus has been reported (Knutson and Hawas, 2004).

Circumcaval ureter has been classified using different parameters based on IVU or retrograde pyelographic findings.

Bateson and Atkinson (1969) classified a ureter with an S-shaped, fish hook, or shepherd's crook appearance as type I (Fig. 37–17A). The ureter typically overlies or is medial to the lower lumbar vertebral processes and eventually crosses anterior to the iliac vessels, where it then assumes a normal distal course in this setting. A less angulated "sickle-shaped" ureteral deformity is classified as type II (Fig. 37–17B). The point of maximal obstruction in type I is lateral to the lateral margin of the IVC and is associated with a greater degree of hydronephrosis than type II, in which the point of obstruction is at the lateral border of the IVC (Bateson and Atkinson, 1969). Another classification scheme is based on the level of obstruction; type I crosses at the level of the third lumbar vertebra and type II crosses at the level of the ureteropelvic junction. The latter may be confused with ureteropelvic junction obstruction (Kenawi and Williams, 1976). The obstruction has been attributed to extrinsic compression of the ureter by the IVC, its lumbar or gonadal branches, or the psoas muscle. However, an intrinsic ureteral abnormality may be contributory as histologic studies of involved ureteral segments have demonstrated fibrotic changes (Kumar and Bhandar, 1985).

Abdominal and flank pain, recurrent urinary tract infection, and hypertension are some of the initial symptoms and signs. A number of cases are now discovered on imaging studies performed to evaluate patients with nonurologic problems (Belis and Milam, 1980; Sener, 1993). The diagnosis should be suspected when the aforementioned pyelographic findings are present (Fig. 37–18A to C). The diagnosis can be confirmed with CT and MRI (Fig. 37–19A and B). Diuretic renography is used to confirm the presence and determine the functional impact of obstruction.

**Treatment is undertaken only in the presence of obstruction.** The ureter is divided proximally and at the distal point from which it emerges lateral to the IVC. A spatulated ureteroureterostomy is performed. This has been performed by open, laparoscopic, and retroperitoneoscopic approaches and is best dictated by the surgeon's experience (Polascik and Chen, 1998; Gupta et al, 2001).

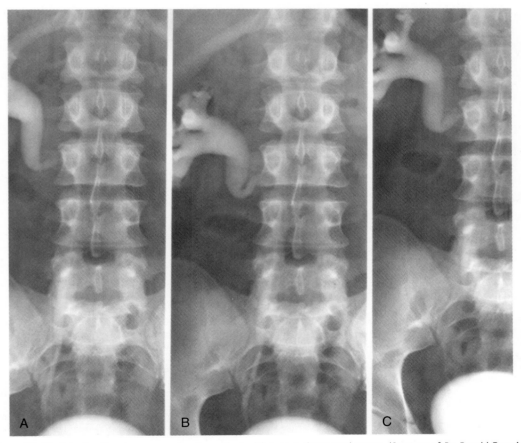

**Figure 37–18. A to C.**    Excretory urography of a patient with type 1 circumcaval ureter. (Courtesy of Dr. Ronald Zagoria.)

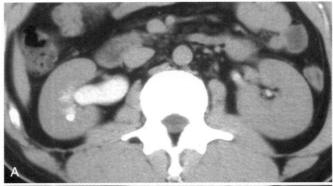

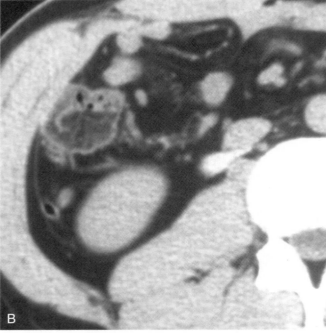

**Figure 37–19. A,** Contrast enhanced computed tomography of a patient with circumcaval ureter. Note mild right-sided hydronephrosis. **B,** Lower section from same study and patient. Note ureter traversing posterior to inferior vena cava. (**A** and **B,** courtesy of Dr. Ronald Zagoria.)

## KEY POINTS

- Ureteral obstruction leads to renal inflammation, increased extracellular matrix formation, tubulointerstitial fibrosis, and apoptosis of renal tubule cells.

- Unilateral and bilateral ureteral obstructions differ in the patterns of hemodynamic and ureteral pressure changes. Massive postobstructive diuresis occurs primarily with BUO.

- Ureteral obstruction causes persistent decreases in concentrating ability, urinary acidification, and electrolyte transport.

- Key mediators of obstructive uropathy that are potentially amenable to current pharmacotherapy include angiotensin II, TGF-β, TNF-α, nitric oxide, thromboxane, and endothelin.

- Recovery of renal function after the correction of obstruction is adversely affected by increasing duration and degree of obstruction, increasing age of the patient, and decreasing collecting system compliance.

- Nuclear renography provides reliable functional information, and cross-sectional imaging provides reproducible and reliable anatomic delineation.

- Drainage of the obstructed system is the first step in management in cases of threatened functional impairment or infection. Definitive management of the underlying pathology may then be considered as dictated by the disease process.

- Hydronephrosis of pregnancy is a common finding with overall predictable patterns.

## SUGGESTED READINGS

Chevalier RL: Molecular and cellular pathophysiology of obstructive nephropathy. Pediatr Nephrol 1999;13:612-619.

Dhillon HK: Prenatally diagnosed hydronephrosis: The Great Ormond Street experience. Br J Urol 1998;81(Suppl 2):39-44.

Faundes A, Bricola-Filho M, Pinto e Silva JL: Dilatation of the urinary tract during pregnancy: Proposal of a curve of maximal caliceal diameter by gestational age. Am J Obstet Gynecol 1998;178:1082-1086.

Harris RH, Yarger WE: Renal function after release of unilateral ureteral obstruction in rats. Am J Physiol 1974;227:806-815.

Heyns CF: Pelvic lipomatosis: A review of its diagnosis and management. J Urol 1991;146:267-273.

Hodson CJ, Craven JD, Lewis DG, et al: Experimental obstructive nephropathy in the pig. Br J Urol 1969;41(Suppl 41):21-35.

Kerr WS: Effect of complete ureteral obstruction for one week on kidney function. J Appl Physiol 1954;6:762-772.

Klahr S, Morrissey J: Obstructive nephropathy and renal fibrosis. Am J Physiol 2002;283:F861-F875.

Li C, Wang W, Kwon TH, et al: Altered expression of major renal Na transporters with bilateral ureteral obstruction and release of obstruction. Am J Physiol 2003;285:F889-F901.

Misseri R, Rink RC, Meldrum DR, et al: Research review: Inflammatory mediators and growth factors in obstructive renal injury. J Surg Res 2004;119:149-159.

Varkarakis IM, Jarrett TW: Retroperitoneal fibrosis. AUA Update Series 24, Lesson 3, 2005.

Vaughan ED, Gillenwater JY: Recovery following complete chronic unilateral ureteral occlusion: Functional, radiographic, and pathologic alterations. J Urol 1971;106:27-35.

Wamsley-Davis A, Padda R, Truong LD, et al: AT1A-mediated activation of kidney JNK1 and SMAD2 in obstructive uropathy: Preservation of kidney tissue mass using candesartan. Am J Physiol 2004;287:F474-F480.

Zagoria R, Tung G: Genitourinary Radiology; the Requisites. St. Louis, Mosby, 1997.

# 38 Management of Upper Urinary Tract Obstruction

THOMAS H.S. HSU, MD • STEVAN B. STREEM, MD* •
STEPHEN Y. NAKADA, MD

---

**URETEROPELVIC JUNCTION OBSTRUCTION**

**RETROCAVAL URETER**

**URETERAL STRICTURE DISEASE**

**URETEROENTERIC ANASTOMOTIC STRICTURE**

**RETROPERITONEAL FIBROSIS**

---

Technologic advances have significantly improved both the diagnostic and therapeutic alternatives available in the contemporary management of upper urinary tract obstruction. The obstructive processes can be congenital to iatrogenic, and the cause of obstruction may not be immediately evident. Furthermore, making the diagnosis of obstruction can also be a challenge.

The treatments of upper tract obstruction range from ureteral stent placement to complex open surgery involving ileal interposition or autotransplantation. Myriad skills are required for total surgical management of upper urinary tract obstruction. Not surprisingly, laparoscopy is now featured prominently in the management of upper urinary tract obstruction. As a result of the wide array of available treatments, the practicing urologist must have an understanding of the indications and risks of all the options.

This chapter provides a contemporary, state-of-the-art presentation of the major management strategies for patients with upper urinary tract obstruction. The chapter is organized by the anatomic location of obstruction. The etiology, diagnosis, indications for intervention, risks, and therapeutic options (including endoscopic, laparoscopic, and open approaches) are thoroughly reviewed.

## URETEROPELVIC JUNCTION OBSTRUCTION

The diagnosis of "ureteropelvic junction (UPJ) obstruction" results in a functionally significant impairment of urinary transport from the renal pelvis to the ureter. Although most

*Deceased.

cases are probably congenital, the problem may not become clinically apparent until much later in life (Jacobs et al, 1979). Acquired conditions such as stone disease, postoperative or inflammatory stricture, or urothelial neoplasm may also present clinically as symptoms and signs of obstruction at the UPJ level. Similarly, extrinsic obstruction can occur at this level as well. The focus in this section is primarily on the diagnosis and treatment of "congenital" UPJ obstruction, although these techniques may be applied to the management of certain acquired conditions, in particular urinary stones.

### Pathogenesis

**Congenital UPJ obstruction most often results from intrinsic disease. A frequently found defect is the presence of an aperistaltic segment of the ureter, perhaps similar to that found in primary obstructive megaureter.** In these cases, histopathologic studies reveal that the spiral musculature normally present has been replaced by abnormal longitudinal muscle bundles or fibrous tissue (Allen, 1970; Foote et al, 1970; Hanna et al, 1976; Gosling and Dixon, 1978). This results in failure to develop a normal peristaltic wave for propagation of urine from the renal pelvis to the ureter. Recognition that this type of segmental defect is often responsible for UPJ obstruction is of utmost importance clinically because such ureters may appear grossly normal at the time of surgery, and, in fact, may often be calibrated to 14 Fr or greater. Further investigations in the etiology of UPJ obstruction have shown decreased interstitial cells of Cajal at the UPJ in children (Solari et al, 2003). In addition, the cytokine produced in the urothelium has also been proposed to exacerbate UPJ obstruction (Chiou et al, 2005). Other experimental studies have implicated transforming growth factor-β, epidermal growth factor expression, nitric oxide, and neuropeptide Y in UPJ stenosis (Knerr et al, 2001; Yang et al, 2003). A less frequent intrinsic cause of congenital UPJ obstruction is true ureteral stricture. Such congenital ureteral strictures are most frequently found at the UPJ, although they may be located at sites anywhere along the lumbar ureter. Abnormalities of ureteral musculature have been implicated as electron microscopy has demonstrated excessive collagen deposition at the site of the stricture (Hanna et al, 1976).

Intrinsic obstruction at the UPJ may also result from kinks or valves produced by infoldings of the ureteral mucosa and musculature (Maizels and Stephens, 1980). In these cases, the obstruction may actually be at the level of the proximal ureter. This phenomenon appears to result from retention or exaggeration of congenital folds normally found in the ureter of developing fetuses. In some of these cases, the defects are bridged by ureteral adventitia. Grossly, this can manifest as external bands or adhesions that appear to be causing the obstruction. In fact, Johnston and coworkers, in 1977, reported that lysis of external adhesions can at times reestablish flow without pyeloplasty. In the majority of cases, however, these bands or adhesions are likely to be a secondary phenomenon associated with intrinsic obstruction, so that operative pyeloplasty would generally be most effective. The presence of these kinks, valves, bands, or adhesions may also produce angulation of the ureter at the lower margin of the renal pelvis in such a manner that, as the pelvis dilates anteriorly and inferiorly, the ureteral insertion is carried further proximally. In these cases, the most dependent portion of the pelvis is inadequately drained and the apparent "high insertion" of the ureteral ostium is actually a secondary phenomenon (Kelalis, 1976). In at least some cases, however, the high insertion itself is likely the primary obstructing lesion, because this phenomenon is found more frequently in the presence of renal ectopia or fusion anomalies (Zincke et al, 1974; Das and Amar, 1984). As such, a high insertion can have implications in the subsequent surgical management, particularly endourologic approaches.

**Significant controversy persists regarding the potential role of "aberrant" vessels in the etiology of UPJ obstruction.** Significant crossing vessels have been noted in as many as 40% of cases of UPJ obstruction but as little as 20% of cases of normal kidneys (Quillin et al, 1996; Zeltser et al, 2004). Although these lower pole vessels have often been referred to as aberrant, these segmental vessels, which may be branches from the main renal artery or arise directly from the aorta, are usually normal variants (Stephens, 1982). In some patients, these lower pole vessels cross the ureter posteriorly and truly have an aberrant course. Regardless, it is unlikely that the associated vessel alone is causing the primary obstruction (Hanna, 1978). In fact, the true etiology is an intrinsic lesion at the UPJ or proximal ureter that causes dilatation and ballooning of the renal pelvis over the polar or aberrant vessel. Recent studies using three-dimensional multidetector row computed tomography (CT) demonstrated that the precise location of crossing vessels did not correspond to the obstructive transition point in patients with UPJ obstruction (Lawler et al, 2005). In contrast, one group found improvement in patients undergoing only ligation of crossing vessels (Keeley et al, 1996). **Regardless, the presence of crossing vessels most certainly has a detrimental effect on the success rates of minimally invasive treatments of UPJ obstruction, in particular endopyelotomy** (Van Cangh et al, 1994, Nakada et al, 1998). UPJ obstruction with concomitant anatomic anomalies such as horseshoe kidney and pelvic kidney also present further surgical challenges. Preoperative spiral CT angiographic studies are very useful in these patients to identify crossing vessels and to aid in surgical planning (Pozniak and Nakada, 1997).

UPJ obstruction may also result from acquired lesions. In children, vesicoureteral reflux can lead to upper tract dilatation with subsequent elongation, tortuosity, and kinking of the ureter. In some cases, these changes may only mimic the radiographic findings of true UPJ obstruction. However, true UPJ obstruction may definitely coexist with vesicoureteral reflux, although it may be difficult to determine whether the anomalies are merely coincident or whether the upper tract ureteral obstruction has resulted from the reflux (Lebowitz and Johan, 1982). Diuretic renography is most helpful for differentiating between UPJ obstruction and reflux.

Other acquired causes of obstruction at the UPJ include benign tumors such as fibroepithelial polyps (Berger et al, 1982; Macksood et al, 1985), urothelial malignancy, stone disease, and postinflammatory or postoperative scarring or ischemia. For these acquired diseases, the techniques discussed in this section may be useful adjuncts for management of the obstruction as long as the primary problem is also addressed where appropriate. For instance, fibroepithelial polyps can be managed using retrograde ureteroscopy and holmium laser excision (Lam et al, 2003a).

## Patient Presentation and Diagnostic Studies

UPJ obstruction, although most often a congenital problem, can present clinically at any time of life. Historically, the most common presentation in neonates and infants was the finding of a palpable flank mass. However, **the current widespread use of maternal, prenatal ultrasonography has led to a dramatic increase in the number of asymptomatic newborns being diagnosed with hydronephrosis, many of whom are subsequently found to have UPJ obstruction** (Bernstein et al, 1988; Wolpert et al, 1989). A fraction of cases may also be found during evaluation of azotemia, which may result from bilateral obstruction in a functionally or anatomically solitary kidney. UPJ obstruction may also be incidentally found during studies performed to evaluate unrelated anomalies such as congenital heart disease (Roth and Gonzales, 1983). In older children or adults, intermittent abdominal or flank pain, at times associated with nausea or vomiting, is a frequent presenting symptom. Hematuria, either spontaneous or associated with otherwise relatively minor trauma, may also be an initial symptom. Laboratory findings of microhematuria, pyuria, or frank urinary tract infection might also bring an otherwise asymptomatic patient to the urologist. Rarely, hypertension may be a presenting finding (Riehle and Vaughan, 1981). **Radiographic studies should be performed with a goal of determining both the anatomic site and the functional significance of an apparent obstruction.** Excretory urography remains a reasonable first-line option for radiographic diagnosis. Classically, findings on the affected side include delay in function associated with a dilated pelvicalyceal symptom (Fig. 38–1). If the ureter is visualized, it should be of normal caliber. In some patients, symptoms may be intermittent and intravenous pyelography between painful episodes may be normal. In such cases, the study should be repeated during an acute episode when the patient is symptomatic (Nesbit, 1956). In some, provocative testing with diuretic urogram may allow accurate diagnosis. The patient should be well hydrated and the study then performed by injecting furosemide, 0.3 to 0.5 mg/kg, intravenously at the time of intravenous urography (Malek, 1983) (Fig. 38–2).

Ultrasonography has also maintained an important role in diagnosis. Although it is a valuable initial diagnostic study

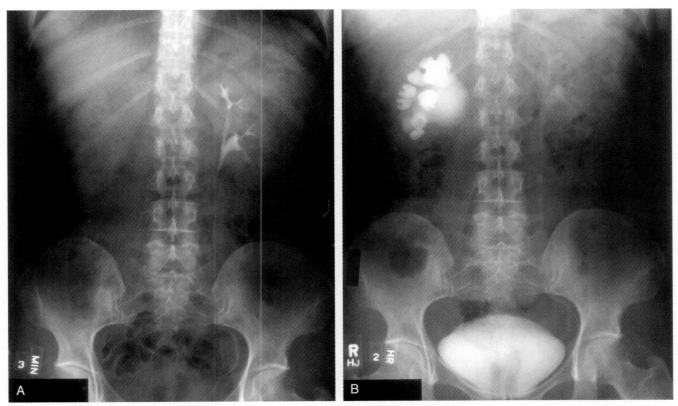

**Figure 38–1.** Intravenous urogram in a female with right flank pain reveals delay in function (**A**) and moderate hydronephrosis on the right to the level of the ureteropelvic junction (UPJ) (**B**), consistent with UPJ obstruction.

under any circumstances in which overall renal function is inadequate to give intravenous contrast, ultrasonography may also be performed in any patient in whom an initial intravenous urogram reveals nonvisualization of the affected collecting system to differentiate ureteral obstruction from alternate causes of nonvisualization. Despite this, CT is now the first imaging technique generally obtained for any patient presenting with acute flank pain (Fielding et al, 1997; Dalrymple et al, 1998; Vieweg et al, 1998) (Fig. 38–3). Both ultrasonography and CT also have a role in differentiating acquired causes of obstruction such as radiolucent calculi or urothelial tumors. **In neonates and infants, the diagnosis of UPJ obstruction has generally been suggested either by routine performance of maternal ultrasonography or by the finding of a flank mass. In either setting, renal ultrasonography is usually the first radiographic study performed. Ideally, ultrasonography should be able to visualize dilatation of the collecting system, to help differentiate UPJ obstruction from multicystic kidney, and to help determine the level of obstruction.** UPJ obstruction and multicystic kidneys should, in fact, be distinguishable in the majority of cases by ultrasound alone. With UPJ obstruction, the pelvis is visualized as a large, medial sonolucent area surrounded by smaller, rounded sonolucent structures representing dilated calyces. At times, dilated calyces will be seen connecting to the pelvis via dilated infundibula.

Occasionally, a solid-appearing renal cortex can be seen surrounding the sonolucent areas or separating the dilated

calyces. In contrast, the cysts of multicystic kidneys are visualized as various-sized sonolucent areas in random distribution. Although the cysts may be connected, this is rarely visualized sonographically. Furthermore, little solid tissue is seen and that which is present has a random distribution among the cysts. Rarely, a large, centrally located cyst may cause confusion in the diagnosis (King et al, 1984a). In this setting, nuclear renography should be performed. Specifically, a technetium 99m–labeled diethylenetriaminepentaacetic acid ($^{99m}$Tc-DTPA) scan allows differentiation of these two entities. Multicystic kidneys rarely reveal concentration of this isotope. When uptake is seen, the areas of functioning tissue are initially discrete and are usually medial to the bulk of the mass, which itself remains a "cold" area. In contrast, neonatal kidneys with UPJ obstruction generally exhibit good concentration of the isotope. Furthermore, even with severe obstruction in which only a cortical rim remains, uptake of the isotope will be seen peripherally in the cortex, again helping to differentiate this from multicystic kidney (King et al, 1984a).

Diuretic renography is effective in predicting recoverability of function in cases in which intravenous urography has revealed nonvisualization. Diuretic renography allows quantification of the degree of obstruction and can help differentiate the level of obstruction. Today, $^{99m}$Tc-MAG3 is the preferred isotope because of favorable imaging and dosimetry considerations over $^{99m}$Tc-DTPA or radioiodinated Hippuran (Roarke and Sandler, 1998). **Presently, diuretic renography is**

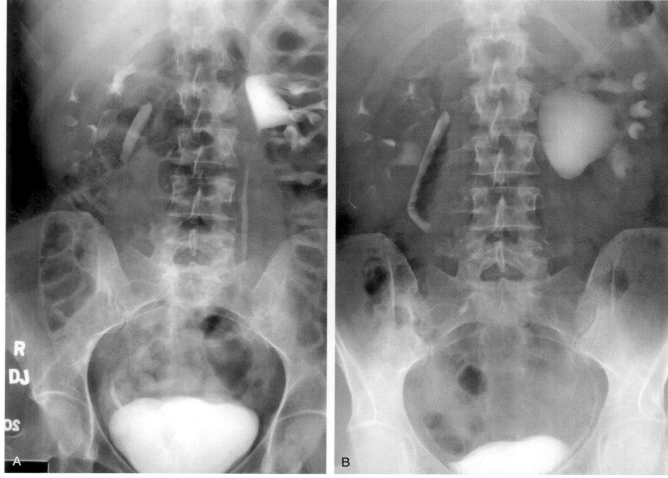

**Figure 38–2.** **A,** This patient with intermittent left flank pain underwent intravenous urography. The calyces are sharp bilaterally without evidence of obstruction. However, there is a "box-shaped" pelvis on the left side, which may be associated with intermittent obstruction. **B,** This intravenous urogram in the same patient was performed along with injection of intravenous furosemide, which brought out the obvious left-sided UPJ obstruction. The patient's symptoms were subsequently relieved with a left pyeloplasty.

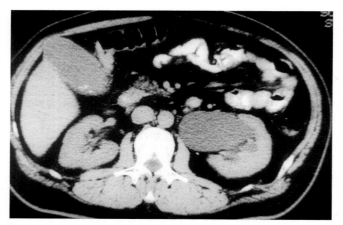

**Figure 38–3.** Noncontrast CT scan performed as the initial radiographic study in a patient presenting with left flank pain revealed hydronephrosis to the level of the UPJ. No calculus was visualized, and a presumed diagnosis of UPJ obstruction was considered. The diagnosis proved correct on subsequent radiographic studies.

a commonly utilized study for diagnosing both UPJ and ureteral obstruction, because it provides quantitative data regarding differential renal function and obstruction, even in hydronephrotic renal units. Diuretic renography is non-invasive and readily available in most medical centers. It ideally can be used to follow patients for functional loss, but it is most effective when a standard protocol is used. The diuretic is given 20 minutes into the study to allow time for filling of the collecting system. One study found diuretic renography to be useful in children to rule out concomitant UPJ obstruction with associated high-grade reflux (Stauss et al, 2003). There is evidence that the diuretic renography using $^{99m}$Tc-MAG3 is a most accurate study for patients with UPJ obstruction after therapeutic intervention (Niemczyk et al, 1999) (Fig. 38–4).

The diagnosis of UPJ obstruction can generally be made with a high degree of certainty based on the clinical presentation and the results of any one or more of the imaging studies already cited. It is preferable to have a combination of anatomic and functional studies, such as retrograde pyelography and diuretic renography, to best plan therapy. Retrograde

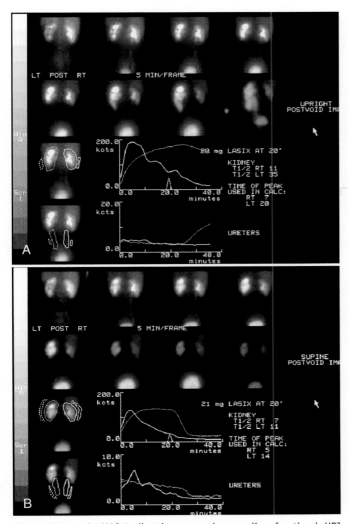

**Figure 38–4.** **A,** MAG-3 diuretic renography revealing functional UPJ obstruction of the left kidney, with a half-life greater than 35 minutes. **B,** Follow-up MAG-3 diuretic renography reveals normal drainage of the left kidney after successful laparoscopic pyeloplasty.

lecting system, placement of a percutaneous nephrostomy tube allows access for dynamic pressure perfusion studies. First described by Whitaker in 1973, the renal pelvis is continuously perfused at 10 mL/min with normal saline solution or dilute radiographic contrast solution under fluoroscopic control. Renal pelvic pressure is monitored during the infusion, and the pressure gradient across the UPJ is determined. During the infusion, the bladder is continuously drained with an indwelling catheter to prevent transmission of intravesical pressures. Renal pelvic pressure ranging up to 12 to 15 cm H$_2$O during this infusion suggests a nonobstructed system. In contrast, pressures in excess of 15 to 22 cm H$_2$O are highly suggestive of a functional obstruction. Pressures between these extremes may be nondiagnostic (O'Reilly, 1986).

Although pressure perfusion studies can often provide valuable information regarding the functional significance of an apparent obstruction, these studies can at times be inaccurate. This inaccuracy may be a result of variations in renal pelvic anatomy and compliance (Koff et al, 1986) or positional variations (Ellis et al, 1995). As such, there remains an important role for the urologist as a diagnostician to collate the clinical presentation and results of all diagnostic studies performed to recommend appropriate clinical intervention.

## Indications and Options for Intervention

**Contemporary indications for intervention for UPJ obstruction include the presence of symptoms associated with the obstruction, impairment of overall renal function or progressive impairment of ipsilateral function, development of stones or infection, or, rarely, causal hypertension.** The primary goal of intervention is relief of symptoms and preservation or improvement of renal function. Traditionally, such intervention should be a reconstructive procedure aimed at restoring nonobstructed urinary flow. This is especially true for neonates, infants, or children in whom early repair is desirable, because these patients will have the best chance for improvement in renal function after relief of obstruction (Bejjani and Belman, 1982; Roth and Gonzales, 1983; Wolpert et al, 1989). However, timing of the repair in neonates remains controversial (DiSandro and Kogan, 1998; Koff, 1998, 2000; Hanna, 2000; Shokeir and Nijman, 2000), mostly because of difficulty in defining those kidneys truly at risk for functional obstruction. In a prospective study of 104 neonates with primary unilateral hydronephrosis suspected of being caused by UPJ obstruction, after a mean follow-up of 21 months only 7 (7%) required pyeloplasty for functional obstruction, defined as a progression of hydronephrosis or a 10% reduction in differential glomerular filtration rate on serial ultrasonography and diuretic renography (Koff and Campbell, 1994). All treated patients had a return of renal function to predetermination levels, supporting selective nonoperative management of neonatal hydronephrosis.

**UPJ obstruction may not become apparent until middle age or later** (Jacobs et al, 1979). Occasionally, if the patient is asymptomatic and the physiologic significance of the obstruction seems indeterminate, careful observation with serial follow-up studies may be appropriate, typically using diuretic renography. However, the majority of affected patients may

pyelography thus retains a role for confirmation of the diagnosis and for demonstration of the exact site and nature of obstruction before repair. In most cases this study is performed at the time of the planned operative intervention to avoid the risk of introducing infection in the face of obstruction. However, retrograde pyelography is indicated emergently whenever the UPJ obstruction requires acute decompression, such as in the setting of infection or compromised renal function. **In cases in which cystoscopic retrograde manipulation has been unsuccessful or may be hazardous, particularly in neonates or infants, placement of a percutaneous nephrostomy is an excellent alternative. This allows the performance of antegrade studies that will help define the nature and exact anatomic site of obstruction.** It also allows decompression of the system in cases of associated infection or compromised renal function and allows assessment of recoverability of renal function after decompression. **When there remains some doubt as to the clinical significance of a dilated col-**

ultimately benefit from reconstructive intervention (Jacobs et al, 1979; Clark and Malek, 1987; O'Reilly, 1989). **When intervention is indicated, the procedure of choice has historically been open operative repair of the UPJ, usually dismembered pyeloplasty. However, less invasive endourologic approaches have gained a proven role as an initial procedure of choice in many centers** (Brannen et al, 1988; Motola et al, 1993a; Kletscher et al, 1995; Cohen et al, 1996; Nadler et al, 1996; Thomas et al, 1996; Tawfiek et al, 1998; Lechevallier et al, 1999; Gerber and Kim, 2000; Nakada, 2000; Conlin, 2002). **Most recently, laparoscopic pyeloplasty has gained acceptance in centers with laparoscopic expertise.** Yet despite the availability of various minimally invasive procedures for UPJ obstruction, one survey showed many academic urologists still perform a significant number of open pyeloplasties (Marcovich et al, 2003).

Although success rates with most endourologic techniques have not proven to be comparable with those of open or laparoscopic pyeloplasty, it has been suggested that the success rates may be significantly improved with careful patient selection. In an important prospective study, Van Cangh and associates (1994) achieved an overall success rate for endopyelotomy of 73%. However, these investigators found the presence of crossing vessels to be a major determinant of outcome (42% success rate in the setting of a crossing vessel vs. 86% success without a crossing vessel). Furthermore, when endopyelotomy was applied to patients with "a high degree of obstruction," the success rate was only 60% compared with an 81% success rate for those patients with "low-grade" obstruction. When patients with both a crossing vessel and a high degree of obstruction were excluded from analysis, the success rate improved to 95%, which is comparable with that of open pyeloplasty. However, other studies have suggested a less important role for these factors in regard to their impact on a successful outcome (Gupta et al, 1997; Danuser et al, 1998; Nakada et al, 1998).

Although the indications for intervention for UPJ obstruction are similar regardless of technique, it is critical to discuss the risks and benefits of all available options with patients. As such, each patient should be advised individually based on all the anatomic and functional information available preoperatively. In this setting, many patients will opt for a minimally invasive approach, even with the understanding that success rates may be lower or secondary intervention may become necessary. As a result of studies linking crossing vessels to hindered endourologic successes, there is increased interest in intraoperative management of the UPJ and crossing vessel by either an open or laparoscopic approach (Conlin, 2002). **Therefore, for "secondary" UPJ obstruction, it is reasonable to recommend an open or laparoscopic approach to any patient who has failed primary endourologic management and an endourologic approach to those who have failed open or laparoscopic repair.** The results of endourologic management in this setting were generally excellent (Jabbour et al, 1998).

Rarely, nephrectomy may be the procedure of choice. Indications for nephrectomy as primary therapy include diminished function or nonfunction of the involved renal moiety and a normal contralateral kidney based on radiographic and nuclear studies. These patients may be symptomatic with urinary tract infections or pain. In such cases, ultrasonography or CT is generally performed and will reveal only a thin shell of parenchyma remaining. **Renography can provide quantitative measures of renal function, and generally kidneys with less than 15% differential function are nonsalvageable in adults.** If the potential for salvageability of function is still unclear, an internal stent or percutaneous nephrostomy may be placed for temporary relief of obstruction and then renal function studies subsequently repeated. Nephrectomy may also be considered for patients in whom the obstruction has led to extensive stone disease with chronic infection and significant loss of function in the presence of a normal contralateral kidney. Removal of the kidney may also be chosen over reconstruction for patients in whom repeated attempts at repair have already failed and in whom further intervention would therefore be extremely complicated. This option should be considered only when the contralateral kidney is essentially normal.

## Options for Intervention

### Endourologic Management

Open operative intervention for UPJ obstruction has historically provided a widely patent, dependently positioned, well-funneled UPJ. In addition, the option to reduce the size of the renal pelvis is readily available with this approach. Although the procedure has stood the test of time with a published success rate of 95%, several less invasive alternatives to standard operative reconstruction are available (Clark and Malek, 1987). **The advantages of endourologic approaches include a significantly reduced hospital stay and postoperative recovery. However, the success rate does not approach that of standard open or laparoscopic pyeloplasty. Furthermore, whereas open or laparoscopic operative intervention can be applied to almost any anatomic variation of UPJ obstruction, consideration of any of the less invasive alternatives requires that the surgeon take into account the degree of hydronephrosis, ipsilateral renal function, concomitant calculi, and, possibly, the presence of crossing vessels.** Of note, Albani and colleagues (2004) reported contemporary long-term results with various endopyelotomy approaches to have a success rate of 67%, with the majority of failures in the first 32 months.

Endourologic management of UPJ obstruction was introduced by Ramsay and colleagues in 1984 as a "percutaneous pyelolysis" and then popularized in the United States by Badlani and coworkers (1986), who coined the term *endopyelotomy*. **Although various nuances in the technique have been described** (Korth et al, 1988; Van Cangh et al, 1989; Ono et al, 1992), **the basic concept is constant and involves a full-thickness incision through the obstructing proximal ureter, from the ureteral lumen out to the peripelvic and periureteral fat.** A stent is placed across the incision and left to heal, based on the original work of Davis in 1943, who performed an "intubated ureterotomy" to repair UPJ obstruction. Subsequently, alternative techniques utilizing a retrograde approach to the UPJ were developed. The retrograde techniques available today include a "hot-wire" cutting balloon, which incises the UPJ under fluoroscopic control, and the ureteroscopic approach, typically utilizing the holmium laser to incise the UPJ under direct visual control. Finally, hybrid approaches, such as the percutaneous endopyeloplasty, have also been reported (Desai et al, 2004).

### Percutaneous Antegrade Endopyelotomy

*Indications and Contraindications.* The indications to intervene for any patient with UPJ obstruction include the presence of symptoms, progressive or overall impairment of renal function, development of upper tract stones or infection, or, rarely, causal hypertension. Historically, a percutaneous approach for definitive management of UPJ obstruction was offered only to those patients undergoing percutaneous removal of associated stones or to those who had previously failed open pyeloplasty. However, encouraging results ultimately led many centers to offer percutaneous endopyelotomy as primary therapy for almost any patient with UPJ obstruction. **Even today, with several alternative minimally invasive options available including laparoscopy, a percutaneous approach is most appropriate for those patients with concomitant pyelocalyceal stones, which can then be managed simultaneously. Contraindications to a percutaneous endopyelotomy are similar to the contraindications to any endourologic approach and include a long segment (>2 cm) of obstruction, active infection, or untreated coagulopathy.** Whereas the impact of crossing vessels is controversial, the mere presence of crossing vessels is not a contraindication to an endopyelotomy (Motola et al, 1993a; Nakada et al, 1998;

Lam et al, 2003b). However, significant entanglement of the UPJ by crossing vessels can occasionally be identified and this may render any endourologic approach unsuccessful. When such entanglement is suggested by intravenous or retrograde pyelography (Fig. 38–5), it can be reliably verified using three-dimensional helical CT (Kumon et al, 1997).

*Patient Preparation.* Patients undergoing a percutaneous endopyelotomy undergo preoperative evaluation and preparation as if they were undergoing any percutaneous, laparoscopic, or open renal intervention. The evaluation includes an assessment for any comorbidity that may increase the risk of anesthesia. Sterile urine should be ensured at the time of definitive intervention. If upper tract infection cannot be cleared because of obstruction, temporization should be accomplished using internal stenting or percutaneous nephrostomy drainage alone. The patient should be counseled as to the risks and benefits of the procedure, and in particular the fact that the success rate of any endourologic approach, including percutaneous endopyelotomy, may be less than that of operative intervention. Patients should also be counseled of the risk of bleeding requiring transfusion, urinary leak, drainage-related complications, and hydropneumothorax, particularly if upper pole access is utilized.

*Technique.* **An endopyelotomy cannot be performed safely by any route until access across the UPJ is established.** This can be accomplished in a retrograde fashion cystoscopi-

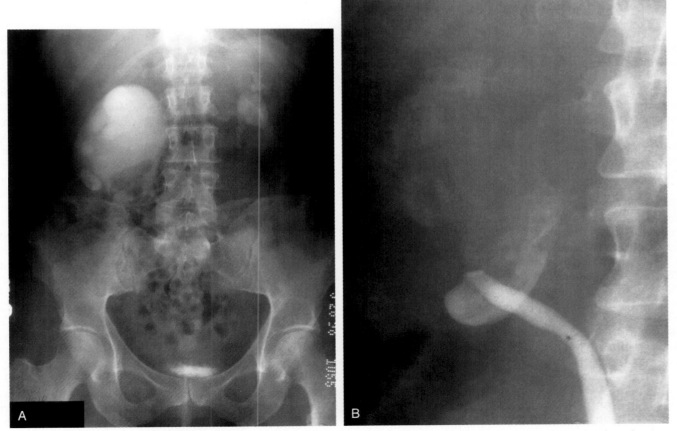

**Figure 38–5.    A,** Intravenous pyelogram (IVP) reveals apparent right UPJ obstruction in this woman with right flank pain. **B,** Retrograde study suggests entanglement at the UPJ by crossing vessels. This was subsequently proved with three-dimensional CT angiography.

cally or in an antegrade manner percutaneously. For retrograde access, the UPJ can almost always be traversed utilizing a hydrophilic wire passed through an open-end catheter. Once the hydrophilic wire is successfully positioned in the pyelocalyceal system, the open-end catheter is advanced over it into the renal pelvis. The wire can then be withdrawn so that contrast material can be injected through the open-end catheter to guide subsequent percutaneous access.

With the patient in the prone position, the site for percutaneous access is chosen to allow straightforward access to the UPJ. Generally, a midposterior or superolateral calyx is chosen, although, occasionally, an inferolateral calyx may be utilized. Typically, the UPJ can be intubated in an antegrade fashion when the tract is initially established with fluoroscopic control. Alternatively, once the tract is dilated and nephroscopy is performed, a wire can again be passed in a retrograde fashion through the open-end catheter and grasped from above, so that through-and-through access is reestablished. In either case, as soon as access is obtained with one wire, an introducing catheter is utilized to pass a second wire as a "safety wire," so that a working and a safety wire are now both in place. At this point, percutaneous access is complete and the endopyelotomy may be performed.

In the original descriptions of the technique both from the Institute of Urology in London (Ramsay et al, 1984) and from Long Island Jewish Hospital in New York (Badlani et al, 1986), the endopyelotomy was performed using a cold knife technique under direct vision. With one or two wires in place across the UPJ, a direct vision "endopyelotome" is utilized. This hook-shaped cold knife may be used to completely incise the UPJ in a full-thickness manner, from the ureteral lumen to periureteral and peripelvic fat (Fig. 38–6). **Rigorous anatomic studies have shown the incision should generally be made laterally, because this is the location devoid of crossing vessels** (Sampaio, 1993). However, in cases of high insertion, the incision should instead "marsupialize" the proximal ureter into the renal pelvis, such that an anterior or posterior incision may be required (Fig. 38–7). When such incisions are done under direct vision, any crossing vessel can be directly visualized and avoided. In addition to the endopyelotome, the holmium laser or the cutting balloon catheter may also be utilized to perform an antegrade endopyelotomy.

Once the incision is complete, stenting is accomplished. There is no consensus as to the optimal stent size or duration for endopyelotomy, and a 14/7 Fr endopyelotomy stent may be passed in an antegrade fashion with the larger diameter end of the stent positioned across the UPJ. In some cases, especially when the patient has not been pre-stented, passage of this large-caliber stent may be difficult. In those instances, a No. 10/7 Fr endopyelotomy stent or even a standard No. 8 Fr internal stent may be utilized without compromising the ultimate outcome. Once proper positioning of the stent is determined fluoroscopically, any remaining safety wires are withdrawn. One group showed no difference between larger and standard stents in a porcine study of endopyelotomies (Moon et al, 1995). Alternatively, Danuser and colleagues (2001) demonstrated improved success rates using a modified No. 27 Fr stent after percutaneous endopyelotomy at nearly 2 years follow-up.

Whereas a "tubeless" percutaneous endopyelotomy is advocated by some authors (Bellman et al, 1997), our preference is to leave a nephrostomy tube indwelling for 24 to 48 hours, at which time a nephrostogram is performed to ensure proper positioning of a patent stent. The nephrostomy tube may then be removed, with or without a brief trial of clamping.

There is an alternative modification of percutaneous endopyelotomy utilizing a "stent first/hot knife" technique (Savage and Streem, 2000). We have found it advantageous at this point to pass a stent before performing the actual endopyelotomy incision. Having the stent in place at the outset of the procedure obviates concern about avulsing the UPJ during placement of a stent after the UPJ has already been incised. Additionally, we have found that placement of the stent before making the incision serves to better define the UPJ itself, thus allowing a more precise incision. The UPJ and proximal ureter can then often be seen to bulge into the renal pelvis, such that the subsequent endopyelotomy is equivalent to a ureteral meatotomy at the ureterovesical junction.

Once the stent is in place, the hot knife, the cold knife, or the holmium laser is used to marsupialize the proximal ureter into the renal pelvis. In the setting of a high insertion, the incision can often be extended to the dependent portion of the renal pelvis under direct vision, bridging the gap between the lateral wall of the ureter and the medial wall of the pelvis, across the periureteral and peripelvic fat. Once the incision is complete, the stent is already in place and nephrostomy drainage is instituted for 24 to 48 hours.

***Simultaneous Percutaneous Nephrolithotomy/Endopyelotomy.*** **Percutaneous management is particularly favorable when the UPJ obstruction is associated with upper tract stone disease, because the stones can be managed concomitantly.** In such cases, percutaneous access is again established with a wire across the UPJ. The stone should be removed before the endopyelotomy, so that stone fragments do not migrate into the peripyeloureteral tissue, as can happen if the endopyelotomy is performed first. Otherwise, localized obstruction may result from fibrosis or granuloma formation (Giddens et al, 2000; Streem, 2000). The urologist must take care to ensure that the UPJ obstruction is not a result of edema from the concomitant stone disease, in particular with stone disease in the renal pelvis. In this circumstance, initial management of the stone percutaneously and subsequent radiographic assessment of the UPJ once the stone has been removed is most prudent. In addition, if a nephrostomy tube is retained, a Whitaker test is straightforward and definitive to assess for persistent obstruction. Conversely, UPJ obstruction and solitary lower pole calculi do not represent a dilemma regarding UPJ edema and combined percutaneous management remains most efficient. Alternatively, laparoscopic pyeloplasty and concomitant stone removal is also effective for these patients.

***Postoperative Care.*** Avoidance of strenuous activity for 8 to 10 days after the procedure is recommended. The optimal time course for post-endopyelotomy stent placement has yet to be determined, although 2 to 4 weeks' duration has proven successful (Mandhani et al, 2003). Although the need for prophylactic antibiotics while the stent is indwelling is not literature based, our practice is to utilize a daily suppressive dose. Once the stent is removed, the patient returns 1 month later for clinical follow-up and radiographic evaluation. This generally includes a history, physical examination, urinalysis, and diuretic renography. If the patient remains asymptomatic and

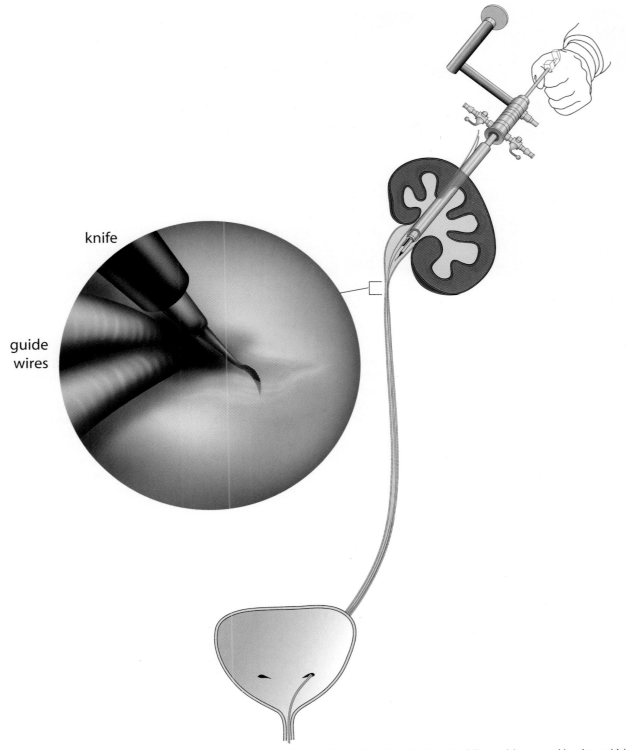

knife

guide
wires

**Figure 38–6.**   Percutaneous nephroscopic view of "cold knife" endopyelotomy *(inset)*. The line of incision is delineated by two guide wires, which have been passed across the UPJ in an antegrade fashion through a superior calyx using a rigid nephroscope through a No. 30 Fr sheath. The lateral incision is performed under direct visual control.

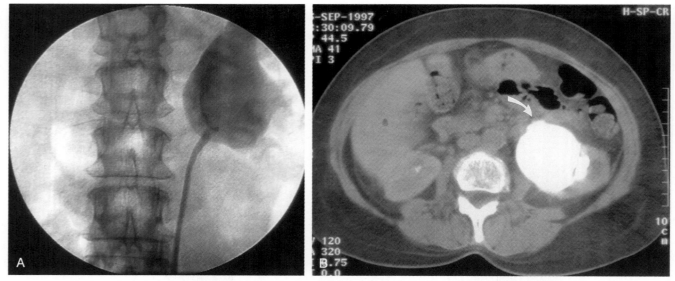

**Figure 38–7.** **A,** Retrograde study in this patient with left UPJ obstruction reveals a "high insertion" of the left ureter. **B,** CT scan in the same patient reveals the ureter inserting on the anatomically anterior aspect of the renal pelvis. A marsupializing incision must be made in a true posterior direction from the ureter into the renal pelvis.

the diuretic renography reveals normal drainage (normal half-life), reevaluation is performed at 6 months and then at 12-month intervals for up to 3 years. Most studies have shown that the majority of endopyelotomy failures occur within the first 24 months, but failures can appear up to 32 months postoperatively (Nadler et al, 1996; Albani et al, 2004).

*Results.* The immediate and long-term results of percutaneous endopyelotomy are well established. Although percutaneous endopyelotomy compares favorably with open operative pyeloplasty in terms of postoperative pain, length of hospital stay, and return to prehospitalization activities (Karlin et al, 1988; Brooks et al, 1995), retrograde endopyelotomy and laparoscopy also offer favorable convalescence.

Gerber and Lyon, in 1994, reviewed the outcome of percutaneous endopyelotomy in 672 patients reported from 12 centers and found a success rate ranging from 57% to 100% (mean, 73.5%) at follow-up ranging from 2 to 96 months. Currently, success rates approaching 85% to 90% are being reported at experienced centers, with little difference in outcome noted in those patients undergoing the procedure for primary versus secondary UPJ obstruction (Motola et al, 1993a; Kletscher et al, 1995; Shalhav et al, 1998). Of note, Knudsen and colleagues (2004) reported long-term results in 80 patients using the cold knife and holmium laser for antegrade endopyelotomy, with 55-month follow-up. This series had a success rate of 67%, slightly lower than otherwise reported.

When percutaneous endopyelotomy does fail, several options exist, including a retrograde endopyelotomy, repeat percutaneous endopyelotomy, or laparoscopic or open operative intervention. **There is a role for spiral CT angiography in failed endopyelotomy to rule out a crossing vessel. If a significant vessel is found, repeat endopyelotomy is generally not recommended** (Nakada, 2000). **As such, operative intervention is generally offered to any patient who has failed an endourologic approach. In this setting, the results**

**of laparoscopic or open intervention will not be compromised** (Motola et al, 1993b; Gupta et al, 1997; Conlin, 2002).

*Complications.* **The complications associated with percutaneous endopyelotomy are analogous to those associated with percutaneous nephrolithotomy** (Badlani et al, 1988; Weiss et al, 1988; Cassis et al, 1991; Malden et al, 1992; Bellman, 1996), **and hemorrhage is a risk of any percutaneous procedure, including endopyelotomy.** However, because in patients with UPJ obstruction the renal parenchyma is generally thinner than that associated with a normal kidney, and because the collecting system is dilated, this risk may be different than that in the general population of stone patients undergoing percutaneous manipulation. Treatment of hemorrhage in this setting is generally conservative to start, and this includes bed rest, hydration, and transfusion as necessary. The nephrostomy tube should not be irrigated acutely. Rather, it is preferable to allow the pyelocalyceal system to tamponade the bleeding. When continued bleeding does not respond to these conservative measures, the next step is selective angiographic embolization. **Generally, the urologist should have a low threshold to proceeding to angiography to minimize the need for transfusion and potential exploration. Successful angiographic embolization often obviates the need for operative "exploration" that can lead to nephrectomy.**

Infection is a risk of any urinary tract manipulation, including percutaneous endopyelotomy, and all attempts should be made to sterilize the urinary tract before the procedure. Whereas the role of prophylactic antibiotics at the outset of the procedure in the setting of a sterile urine is unproven, most urologists give a second-generation cephalosporin "on call" to the procedure. Consideration should be given to the use of prophylactic antibiotics while the endopyelotomy stent is indwelling for the month after the procedure, especially in women who are more prone to bacteriuria.

Persistent obstruction is rare in the early postoperative period because of the internal stent. Occasionally, the stent can be obstructed from blood clots, and continued nephrostomy drainage for a few days typically allows the problem to resolve spontaneously.

**"Cautery Wire Balloon" Endopyelotomy.** Use of a cautery wire balloon for management of UPJ obstruction was first reported in a clinical series by Chandhoke and associates in 1993. The original device included as its essential elements a No. 7 Fr catheter on which was mounted an 8-mm balloon with a 150-μm-wide, 2.8-cm-long electrosurgical cutting wire. Use of this device gained rapid acceptance by many clinicians because standard cystoscopic techniques and real-time fluoroscopy are all that is needed for its use. Furthermore, the technique is readily mastered with a relatively short "learning curve" because advanced ureteroscopic skills are not necessary.

*Indications and Contraindications.* **As for any treatment of UPJ obstruction, the indications to intervene include associated symptoms, progressive or overall impairment of renal function, development of upper tract infection, or, rarely, causal hypertension. As for any endourologic approach, contraindications to this technique include a stricture greater than 2 cm. A more specific contraindication to this particular procedure is the associated presence of upper tract stones, because this approach does not allow their simultaneous management.** An area of ongoing controversy is the potential presence of crossing vessels. Because the procedure is guided fluoroscopically, such vessels may increase the risk of hemorrhage after activation of the cautery wire balloon. As such, some authors recommend preoperative imaging for such vessels with relatively noninvasive techniques such as CT or three-dimensional CT angiography (Fig. 38–8) (Streem and Geisinger, 1995; Quillin et al, 1996; Herts et al, 1999). Others, however, suggest that the risk of such bleeding is negligible as long as the incision is made in a true lateral or anatomically posterolateral position, because vessels crossing in that region are rare (Nakada et al, 1998; Nakada, 2000; Sampaio and Favorito, 1993).

*Technique.* The procedure begins with a retrograde pyelogram under fluoroscopic control, with C-arm imaging generally recommended to easily allow oblique views. During the retrograde study, the anatomy at the UPJ is completely defined (Fig. 38–9). At this point, a stiff, nonconducting guide wire is passed in a retrograde fashion across the UPJ and coiled within the pyelocalyceal system. The cautery wire balloon catheter is then passed with the cutting wire positioned laterally. The renal pelvis should be drained via the cautery wire balloon catheter and filled with dilute contrast material since the contrast medium or the retained urine may act as an electrolyte solution and inhibit activation of the cutting balloon. At this point, the 3-mL low-profile balloon is partially inflated. In general, a waist will be visualized to ensure proper positioning across the UPJ. C-arm fluoroscopy should also be used at this point to make sure the cutting wire is positioned appropriately.

The hot-wire electrocautery incision is then performed. The low-profile balloon is filled with another 1 to 2 cm of dilute contrast medium as 75 W of pure cutting current is applied to the cautery balloon wire for 2 to 3 seconds. During

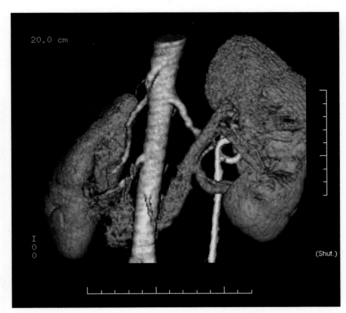

**Figure 38–8.** Spiral CT angiography with three-dimensional reconstruction clearly identifies an accessory lower pole crossing vessels at the level of the UPJ in a patient with UPJ obstruction. This case was managed successfully with laparoscopic pyeloplasty.

this time, the waist should be seen to resolve. If it does not, the procedure can be repeated once; multiple activations should be avoided. During deflation, extravasation of contrast material may often be identified at the incision site. If not, contrast agent can be reinjected to ensure extravasation is seen. If no extravasation is identified, ureteroscopy can be performed to ensure that an adequate incision has been made. Use of a ureteral access sheath allows rapid ureteroscopic access to the UPJ.

The cautery wire balloon catheter is now withdrawn completely, with a wire still in place across the UPJ. Completion of the procedure now requires ureteral stent placement. A Foley catheter is left in place initially to assess for bleeding and to minimize reflux through the stent.

*Postoperative Care.* At most centers, the patient is observed in an outpatient surgical area for 12 to 24 hours and the Foley catheter removed the morning after the procedure if the urine has grossly cleared. As previously noted, optimal stent duration remains unproven, although 4 weeks is common. Follow-up then generally involves an office evaluation 1 month later that includes diuretic renography. If the patient remains asymptomatic and if the half-life from the diuretic renography proves no obstruction, reevaluation is performed at 6- or 12-month intervals as necessary for 3 years.

*Results.* In their initial study, Chandhoke and associates (1993b) reported a 67% rate of complete resolution of symptoms and 85% improvement in radiographic appearance after hot wire balloon endopyelotomy. In a subsequent multicenter study, Preminger and colleagues (1997) reported an initial "patency" rate of 77% at a mean follow-up of 7.8 months. More recently, longer-term follow-up has become available. In 1999, Lechevallier and his associates in France defined success as both subjective and objective improvement and achieved this result in 75% of their patients followed for a median of

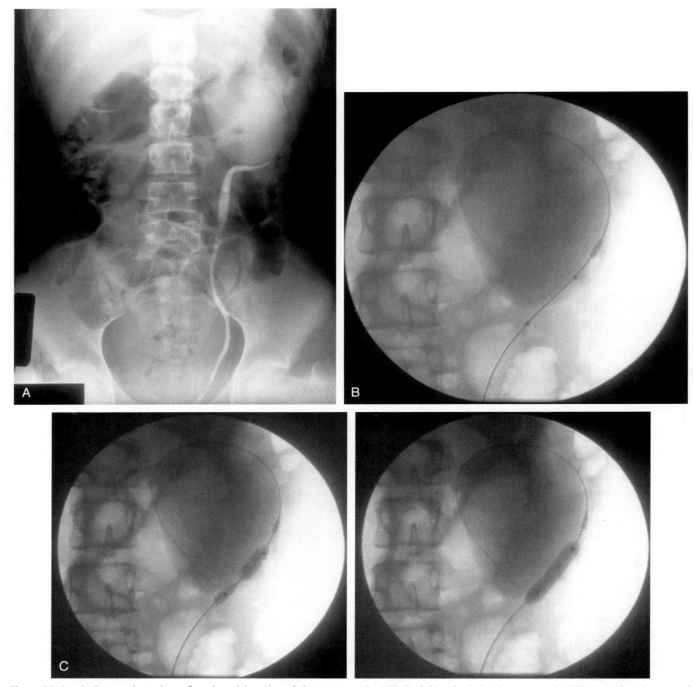

**Figure 38–9. A,** Retrograde study confirms lateral insertion of the ureter on the UPJ. **B,** Guide wire is in place across the UPJ. Note that the ureteral insertion is still lateral. **C,** *Left:* Fluoroscopic view of a balloon partially inflated before application of electrocurrent through the cutting wire. Note the "waist" at the UPJ. *Right:* After application of current and complete balloon inflation, the waist disappears.

2 years. Nadler and associates (1996) were able to reevaluate 28 patients 2 or more years after cautery wire balloon endopyelotomy. With a mean follow-up of 32.5 months, subjective improvement was noted in 61% of patients and 81% had a patent UPJ based on diuretic renography or Whitaker testing. In their study, all failures occurred within 1 year of treatment, and this early time to failure has been noted in other endopyelotomy studies. More recent studies have demonstrated lower

success rates than these initial series (32% to 63%) and perhaps that high-grade hydronephrosis has a negative impact on success (Sampaio and Favorito, 1993; Albani et al, 2004; Sofras et al, 2004).

*Complications.* **The major complications associated with cautery wire balloon incision are hemorrhagic. Whereas injury to crossing vessels has been reported using the cutting balloon catheter, strict adherence to lateral incision**

**principles minimizes this risk** (Streem and Geisinger, 1995; Wagner et al, 1996). In addition, although some believe crossing vessels hinder success rates primarily, others believe hemorrhage is a real concern (Aslan and Preminger, 1998). Appropriate management includes arteriography to delineate the site of arterial injury and subsequent embolization. In a review of their complications with this procedure, Schwartz and Stoller (1999) reported lower pole accessory arterial injuries in three patients and ovarian vein laceration in another, who ultimately required nephrectomy. These authors also summarized other reported complications of the procedure, which have included ureteral avulsion, stent-related problems, and detachment of the cutting wire. Failure of balloon inflation has also been reported (McGuire and English, 1997).

**Ureteroscopic Endopyelotomy.** A ureteroscopic approach to endopyelotomy was first suggested in 1985 when Bagley and colleagues reported a combined percutaneous and flexible ureteroscopic procedure approach for management of an "obliterated" UPJ. Subsequently, Inglis and Tolley (1986) reported a ureteroscopic "pyelolysis" for UPJ obstruction. Shortly thereafter, Clayman and coworkers (1990) reported an initial experience in a small number of patients performing ureteroscopic endopyelotomy with a No. 3 or 5 Fr cutting electrode passed under direct vision using large, rigid or flexible ureteroscopes. In that series, however, a No. 8 Fr nephrostomy tube was placed at the outset of the procedure and left indwelling for at least 48 hours. As such, that series still represented a "combined" endourologic approach to endopyelotomy. Stents were routinely left in place for 6 to 8 weeks, after which diagnostic studies were performed. With a mean follow-up approaching 1 year, a success rate of 81% was achieved in 16 patients. However, two patients developed distal ureteral strictures probably resulting from the larger-diameter rigid instrumentation.

Thomas and associates (1996) subsequently reported their experience with ureteroscopic endopyelotomy. Again, only relatively larger-diameter ureteroscopic instrumentation was available such that preoperative stent placement was routine and some male patients required perineal urethrostomy. The endopyelotomy incision itself was performed with either cold knife or electrocautery attachments to the ureteroscope. The authors achieved a success rate of approximately 90%, although nephrectomy was ultimately performed in two patients, in one of whom it was done urgently for bleeding.

Advances in instrumentation and technique now allow a ureteroscopic approach to be performed reliably at a single setting (Conlin and Bagley, 1998), and this is now considered the standard. **The main advantage of a ureteroscopic approach is that it allows direct visualization of the UPJ and assurance of a properly situated, full-thickness endopyelotomy.** Another advantage of the ureteroscopic approach is a decrease in cost compared with the use of the cautery wire balloon, assuming ureteroscopic equipment and electroincision or holmium laser is already available. Gettman and associates (2003) found that the retrograde ureteroscopic endopyelotomy was more cost effective than hot wire cutting balloon endopyelotomy, antegrade endopyelotomy, and pyeloplasty for treating UPJ obstruction when taking into account treatment failures.

***Indications and Contraindications.*** **The indications and contraindications to a ureteroscopic endopyelotomy include functionally significant obstruction, as defined earlier. Contraindications include relatively long areas of obstruction and upper tract stones, which are best managed simultaneously with alternative approaches, usually percutaneously or laparoscopically.** Another consideration is that in patients with significant hydronephrosis there is evidence that an antegrade endopyelotomy may be more efficacious (Lam et al, 2003b).

***Technique.*** The instrument that allows the most straightforward retrograde access to the UPJ, as well as providing an effective working channel, is a small caliber (<7 Fr) semirigid ureteroscope. In women, the UPJ can often be reached with a No. 6.9 Fr semirigid ureteroscope. In men, typically small caliber (<7.5 Fr) actively deflecting flexible ureteroscopes are utilized, and today with availability of improved ureteral access sheaths and improved flexible ureteroscopes, many retrograde endopyelotomies are done using the flexible ureteroscope.

General anesthesia is used to minimize patient movement during ureteroscopy and the subsequent incision of the UPJ. In preparation for the endopyelotomy, a retrograde pyelogram is performed under fluoroscopic control at the outset of the procedure. A hydrophilic guide wire is passed cystoscopically under fluoroscopic control and coiled in the pyelocalyceal system. The cystoscope is then withdrawn and exchanged for the semirigid ureteroscope. The ureteroscope is passed alongside the guide wire to the level of the UPJ (Fig. 38–10). If the distal ureter is too narrow to allow easy passage of the ureteroscope, the intramural ureter can be dilated using a 5-mm balloon or a No. 9 or 10 Fr "introducing" catheter. If the ureter is still too narrow at any point to easily accommodate the ureteroscope, then an internal stent is placed and the procedure is postponed for 5 to 10 days to allow "passive" ureteral dilatation.

Once the UPJ is reached with the ureteroscope, the renal pelvis is drained to facilitate movement across the UPJ during the incision. When using a semirigid ureteroscope, the 200- or 365-μm holmium laser fiber is inserted through the working channel as the ureteroscope is positioned at the proximal extent of the UPJ or in the renal pelvis itself. At a setting of 0.8 to 1.2 J and a frequency of 10 to 15 Hz, the UPJ is incised, usually in a posterolateral direction, while the ureteroscope is withdrawn back down across the UPJ. This procedure is repeated and the incision gradually deepened to extend into the peripelvic and periureteral retroperitoneal space. Because this is done gradually and under direct vision, any visualized vessels, and thus potentially significant bleeding, are usually avoided.

The incision is carried caudally into normal ureteral tissue, until the UPJ is widely patent. Injection of contrast material through the ureteroscope can demonstrate extravasation and confirm an adequate depth of incision, although this is generally not necessary because the entire procedure has been performed under direct vision. Balloon dilation up to size No. 24 Fr can also be performed to complete the incision. If any small bleeding points are visualized ureteroscopically, they can be treated by defocusing the holmium laser. Similarly, the balloon can be reinflated to allow tamponade for 10 minutes to see if the bleeding will subside. The ureteroscope is then

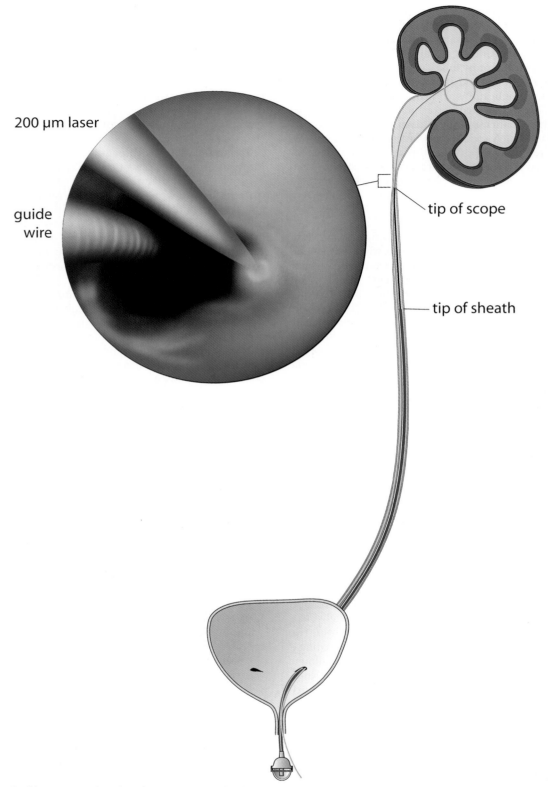

**Figure 38–10.** Flexible ureteroscopic endopyelotomy using holmium laser demonstrating endoscopic view of the UPJ *(inset)*. A safety wire is in place, and the ureteroscope is passed through a ureteral access sheath as a lateral incision is being made under endoscopic view, using holmium laser fiber. A properly sited, complete incision is straightforward with this direct visualization technique.

withdrawn from the ureter while the safety wire is left in place in the renal pelvis for subsequent passage of a stent. Experimental studies have shown that dilation with a No. 36 Fr balloon alone can create linear incisions in the UPJ (Pearle et al, 1994). **Although retrograde balloon dilation alone has been reported for treatment of UPJ obstruction, most recent long-term follow-up studies have shown a diminishing success rate over time, as low as 42%** (McClinton et al, 1993; Webber et al, 1997).

When flexible ureteroscopy is used, a ureteral access sheath is quite useful. The sheath allows for rapid transfer of the ureteroscope for assessment of the UPJ. Once the flexible ureteroscope is passed to the UPJ, a 200-μm holmium fiber is placed through the working channel and the UPJ incised in the appropriate location, as suggested by the radiographic studies.

Once the ureteroscope has been removed, a stent is advanced over the remaining wire using fluoroscopic guidance. A Foley catheter is left indwelling, again to obviate the risk of reflux and extravasation at the site of the endopyelotomy incision and to rapidly identify any significant bleeding. Diuretic renography is performed 4 weeks after stent removal to assess results. Clinical and radiographic follow-up is then continued at 6- to 12-month intervals for 24 to 32 months.

*Results.* Biyani and colleagues (1997) described their initial experience with a ureteroscopic approach using holmium laser energy. With a mean follow-up of just over 12 months, they achieved a success rate of 87.5% in a small group of patients. One patient developed a urinoma, which was managed conservatively. In 1998, Renner and coworkers reported a larger series of patients undergoing ureteroscopic laser endopyelotomy. By using a semirigid ureteroscope, the UPJ was incised at a posterolateral location unless vessels were visualized in that area, in which case a contralateral incision was made. Tawfiek and associates (1998) reported the Jefferson Medical College experience with ureteroscopic endopyelotomy. They combined endoluminal ultrasound with their ureteroscopic approach to definitively identify crossing vessels or a ureteropelvic septum, which is present in patients with high-inserting ureters. They believed this helped them definitively site their endopyelotomy incision. Different modalities were used for the endopyelotomy itself, including electrocautery and holmium laser. An 87.5% success rate was achieved in 32 patients. There were no significant bleeding complications, and all patients were discharged within 24 hours of the procedure.

**Gerber and Kim** (2000) **and Matin and associates** (2003) **reported contemporary experiences with ureteroscopic holmium laser endopyelotomy, demonstrating success rates of 70% to 80% with follow-up to 5 years.** Improved results were reported by Conlin (2002) (91% success rates) with retrograde endopyelotomy in patients when culling patients with crossing vessels greater than 4 mm using preoperative ultrasonography. Giddens and Grasso (2000) also published excellent results when culling patients with anterior and posterior crossing vessels from retrograde endopyelotomy using endoluminal ultrasound. To date, the use of endoluminal ultrasound to identify crossing vessels has been controversial, and although it may play a role in preoperative decision-making, similar data can be obtained using the less invasive spiral CT angiography. Yet despite this additional information, the best

endopyelotomy success rates still lag behind those of open or laparoscopic pyeloplasty.

*Complications.* Complications of this approach have diminished in frequency and severity with the refinement of ureteroscopic instrumentation and the introduction of small-caliber holmium laser fibers. Postprocedural ureteral strictures are rare in contemporary series, and angiographic embolization or nephrectomy is rare using the retrograde approach. Most complications are minor and relate primarily to urinary leak, stent migration, and infection (Tawfiek et al, 1998; Gerber and Kim, 2000). As more long-term follow-up becomes available, the complication rates may evolve.

## KEY POINTS: ENDOUROLOGIC MANAGEMENT OF UPJ OBSTRUCTION

- Contemporary indications for intervention for UPJ obstruction include the presence of symptoms associated with the obstruction, impairment of overall renal function or progressive impairment of ipsilateral function, development of stones or infection, or, rarely, causal hypertension.

- When intervention is indicated, the procedure of choice has historically been open operative repair of the UPJ, usually dismembered pyeloplasty. However, endopyelotomy has gained a proven role as an initial procedure of choice in many centers.

- The advantages of endourologic approaches include a significantly reduced hospital stay and postoperative recovery. However, the success rate does not approach that of standard open or laparoscopic pyeloplasty. Furthermore, whereas open or laparoscopic operative intervention can be applied to almost any anatomic variation of UPJ obstruction, consideration of any of the less invasive alternatives requires that the surgeon take into account the degree of hydronephrosis, ipsilateral renal function, concomitant calculi, and, possibly, the presence of crossing vessels.

- Generally, the urologist should have a low threshold to proceeding to angiography in patients with bleeding after endopyelotomy to minimize the need for transfusion and potential exploration. Successful angiographic embolization often obviates the need for operative "exploration" that can lead to nephrectomy.

### Open Operative Intervention

**General Surgical Principles.** Several types of surgical incisions have been utilized for a pyeloplasty in the management of UPJ obstruction. An anterior extraperitoneal approach is chosen by some because it allows surgical repair with minimal mobilization of the pelvis and proximal ureter. Alternatively, a posterior lumbotomy provides direct exposure to the UPJ and again allows repair with minimal mobilization of the surrounding structures. Like the anterior extraperitoneal approach, posterior lumbotomy is best suited to relatively thin patients without previous ipsilateral surgery. Our preference for most patients undergoing primary surgical repair of UPJ obstruction is an extraperitoneal flank approach. This incision may be subcostal but usually is performed through the bed of the 12th rib or carried anteriorly off its tip. The extraperitoneal flank approach is advantageous in that it is familiar to all urologists and provides excellent exposure without regard to body habitus. In the presence of other renal anomalies associated with the UPJ, such as horseshoe or pelvic kidney, anterior extraperitoneal approaches are often preferable, although laparoscopic management may be considered in this setting.

**Before the definitive surgical management, drainage of a kidney with UPJ obstruction is recommended only in select circumstances, including infection associated with the obstruction or azotemia resulting from obstruction in a solitary kidney or bilateral disease.** Procedural drainage may be of value in the uncommon scenario of severe, unrelenting pain requiring emergent relief of obstruction. For any of these situations, such drainage can be achieved by placement of an internal ureteral stent or a percutaneous nephrostomy tube.

**The clinical indications for placement of stents or nephrostomy tubes intraoperatively remain controversial and vary among the urologists.** For adults, our preference is for routine placement of a soft, inert, self-retaining internal ureteral stent, which is removed 4 to 6 weeks postoperatively. Such stents in adults can be easily removed in an outpatient office setting under local anesthesia. Routine use of internal ureteral stents offers several advantages, especially in the early postoperative period. Such practice appears to decrease the amount and length of time of urinary extravasation at the surgical repair site, thereby decreasing the risk of secondary fibrosis. Decreased urinary extravasation also allows earlier removal of external drains. For the uncomplicated pyeloplasty in adult patients, there appears to be no advantage to using both a nephrostomy tube and a stent, because this may result in a prolonged hospital stay and an increased incidence of infection (Wollin et al, 1989). Instead, nephrostomy tubes may be reserved for complicated procedures such as those required for secondary UPJ obstruction or those associated with active inflammation. However, if a percutaneous nephrostomy tube had been placed preoperatively, it is generally left in place to allow proximal diversion and access for antegrade radiographic studies during the postoperative period.

Although the use of internal stents and nephrostomy tubes remains somewhat controversial, provision of external drainage from the site of surgical repair is absolutely necessary. Such external drainage may be achieved with a Penrose or closed suction drain placed near, but not on, the suture line and brought out through a separate stab incision. This practice helps to minimize the risk of urinoma formation leading to possible disruption of the suture line, scarring, or sepsis.

**Historical Notes.** The historical aspects of UPJ repair were previously examined by Kay in 1989 and by Schaeffer and Grayhack in 1986. The first reconstructive procedure was performed by Trendelenburg in 1886; however, the patient died of postoperative complications. In 1891, Kuster divided the ureter and reanastomosed it to the renal pelvis, thus apparently performing the first successful dismembered pyeloplasty. Kuster's technique, however, was prone to recurrent stricture. In 1892, Fenzer applied the Heineke-Mikulicz principle to UPJ

repair. This surgical technique involves transverse closure of a longitudinal incision. However, this technique can cause shortening of the suture line on one side, resulting in buckling or kinking of the UPJ with recurrent obstruction. In 1916, Schwyzer introduced the YV-pyeloplasty, which was subsequently modified by Foley in 1937. However, this technique was best applied to high ureteral insertions and was essentially unsuitable when the UPJ itself was already in a dependent position. Later on, flap techniques were developed that were more universally applicable, including the spiral flap of Culp and DeWeerd (1951) and the vertical flap of Scardino and Prince (1953). Thompson and associates (1969) reported the use of a renal capsular flap for complex cases in which an adequate amount of renal pelvis is not available for repair.

In 1949, Nesbit followed the principle of Kuster's dismembered procedure and further modified it by creating an elliptical anastomosis to decrease the likelihood of stricture formation at the site of repair. Also in 1949, Anderson and Hynes described their modifications of this dismembered technique that involved anastomosis of the spatulated ureter to a projection of the lower aspect of the pelvis after a redundant portion was excised. Use of healing by secondary intention was also investigated in the similar time period. The techniques of intubated ureterotomy were popularized by Davis in 1943, but they had been previously described by Fiori in 1905, Albarran in 1909, and Keyes in 1915.

Although a variety of techniques have been described for the management of UPJ obstruction, several basic principles must always be applied to maximize the success of surgical repair. **For any procedure, the resultant anastomosis should be widely patent and completed in a watertight fashion without tension. In addition, the reconstructed UPJ should allow a funnel-shaped transition between the pelvis and the ureter that is in a position of dependent drainage.**

### Dismembered Pyeloplasty

*Indications.* **At present, a dismembered pyeloplasty is preferred by most urologists in the surgical repair of UPJ obstruction because this procedure is almost universally applicable to the different clinical scenarios.** This approach can be used regardless of whether the ureteral insertion is high on the pelvis or already dependent. It also permits reduction of a redundant pelvis or straightening of a tortuous proximal ureter. Furthermore, **anterior or posterior transposition of the UPJ can be achieved when the obstruction is due to accessory or aberrant lower pole vessels.** In addition, unlike the flap techniques, **only a dismembered pyeloplasty allows complete excision of the anatomically or functionally abnormal UPJ itself. It is important to note that a dismembered pyeloplasty is not well suited to UPJ obstruction associated with lengthy or multiple proximal ureteral strictures or to patients in whom the UPJ obstruction is associated with a small, relatively inaccessible intrarenal pelvis.**

*Technique.* Surgical exposure to the UPJ is achieved by first identifying the proximal ureter in the retroperitoneum. The proximal ureter is then dissected cephalad to the renal pelvis, leaving a large amount of periureteral tissue to preserve the ureteral blood supply. A marking stitch of fine suture is then placed on the lateral aspect of the proximal ureter, below the level of the obstruction, to facilitate proper orientation for the subsequent repair. In a similar fashion, the medial and lateral aspects of the dependent portion of the renal pelvis are marked with traction sutures (Fig. 38–11*A*). The UPJ tissue is excised, and the proximal ureter is then spatulated on its lateral aspect. The apex of this lateral, spatulated aspect of the proximal ureter is brought to the inferior border of the renal pelvis, whereas the medial side of the ureter is brought to the superior aspect (see Fig. 38–11*B*). The anastomosis is then performed with fine interrupted or running absorbable sutures, placed full thickness through the ureteral and renal pelvic walls in a watertight manner (see Fig. 38–11*C*). As discussed earlier, our preference for adult patients is to routinely perform the anastomosis over an internal ureteral stent, which is left indwelling.

If the renal pelvis is exceptionally redundant, a "reduction" pyeloplasty can be performed by excising the redundant portion of the pelvis (Fig. 38–12). The cephalad aspect of the pelvis is then closed with running absorbable sutures down to the dependent portion, which will subsequently be anastomosed to the ureter. In the event that aberrant or accessory lower pole vessels are found in association with the UPJ obstruction, a dismembered pyeloplasty allows transposition of the UPJ in relation to these vessels (Fig. 38–13).

***Results.*** The overall success of open dismembered pyeloplasty has been very favorable in the literature. In a retrospective review, Persky and coworkers (1977) noted that none of their 109 dismembered pyeloplasties for UPJ obstruction required subsequent nephrectomy. In another retrospective review involving 111 patients with UPJ obstruction undergo-

ing open surgical repair over a 15-year-period, Clark and Malek (1987) found 95% success in resolution of clinical symptoms and 91% success in decompression of pelvicalyceal system on urography after one surgical repair. Of the 111 patients with open pyeloplasty, 95 (86%) patients underwent dismembered pyeloplasty. Examining the functional outcomes based on the split-function analysis from preoperative and postoperative renal scans, O'Reilly (1989) found that open Anderson-Hynes dismembered pyeloplasty arrests functional deterioration in almost every case and improves function significantly in the majority in 26 consecutive patients with UPJ obstruction.

### Flap Procedures

***Foley YV-Plasty.*** **The Foley YV-plasty was originally designed for repair of a UPJ obstruction secondary to a high ureteral insertion.** Like other flap techniques, however, its use has generally been replaced by the more versatile dismembered pyeloplasty. Like other flap techniques, the Foley YV-plasty is specifically contraindicated when transposition of lower pole vessels is necessary. In situations requiring concomitant reduction of redundant renal pelvis, this technique is also of little value.

In Foley YV-plasty, the renal pelvis and proximal ureter are first exposed and a widely based triangular or V-shaped flap is outlined with methylene blue or fine stay sutures. The base of the V is positioned on the dependent, medial aspect of the ipsilateral renal pelvis and the apex at the UPJ. The incision from

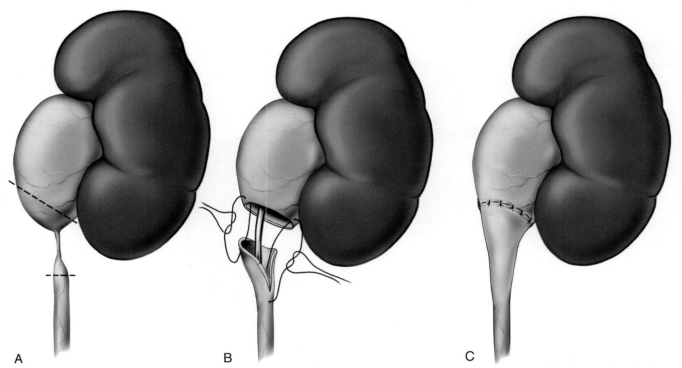

**Figure 38–11.** **A,** Traction sutures are placed on the medial and lateral aspects of the dependent portion of the renal pelvis in preparation for dismembered pyeloplasty. A traction suture is also placed on the lateral aspect of the proximal ureter, below the level of obstruction. This will help maintain proper orientation for the subsequent repair. **B,** The UPJ is excised. The proximal ureter is spatulated on its lateral aspect. The apex of this lateral, spatulated aspect of the ureter is then brought to the inferior border of the pelvis while the medial side of the ureter is brought to the superior edge of the pelvis. **C,** Anastomosis is then performed with fine interrupted or running absorbable sutures placed full thickness through the ureteral and renal pelvis walls in a watertight fashion. In general, we prefer to leave an indwelling internal stent for adult patients. The stent is removed 4 to 6 weeks later.

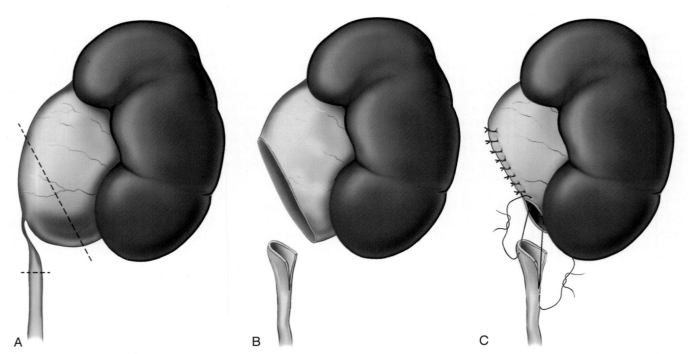

**Figure 38–12.** **A,** For large or redundant renal pelves, a reduction pyeloplasty is performed by excising the redundant portion between traction sutures. **B,** The cephalad aspect of the pelvis is then closed with running absorbable suture down to the dependent portion. **C,** The dependent aspect of the pelvis is then anastomosed to the proximal ureter.

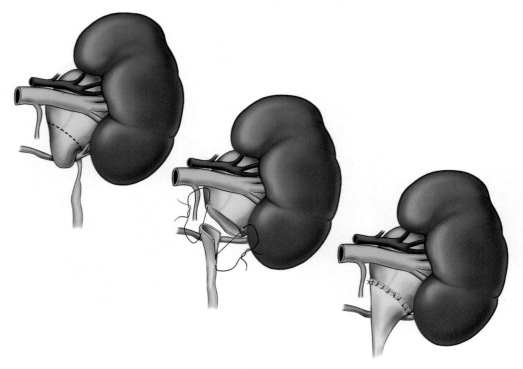

**Figure 38–13.** When aberrant or accessory lower pole vessels are found in association with the UPJ obstruction, a dismembered pyeloplasty allows transposition of the UPJ in relation to the vessels.

the apex of the flap (the stem of the Y) will then be performed along the lateral aspect of the proximal ureter. The surgical incision in the ureter should be long enough to completely traverse the area of stenosis and extend for several millimeters into the normal-caliber ureter (Fig. 38–14A). The renal pelvic flap and ureterotomy are then created. A fine scalpel blade is

used for the initial pelvic incision, after which a Potts or a fine Metzenbaum scissors is used to complete the flap and ureterotomy (see Fig. 38–14B). An internal ureteral stent is now placed and the repair performed over it. First, the apex of the pelvic flap is approximated to the apex (inferior aspect) of the ureterotomy incision using fine absorbable suture. The

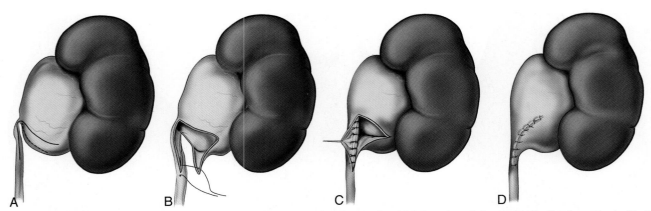

**Figure 38–14.** **A,** Foley YV-plasty is best applied to a UPJ obstruction associated with a high insertion of the ureter. The flap is outlined with tissue marker or stay sutures. The base of the V is positioned on the dependent, medial aspect of the renal pelvis and the apex at the UPJ. The incision from the apex of the flap, which represents the stem of the Y, is then carried along the lateral aspect of the proximal ureter well into an area of normal caliber. **B,** The flap is developed with fine scissors. The apex of the pelvic flap is then brought to the most inferior aspect of the ureterotomy incision. **C,** The posterior walls are then approximated using interrupted or running fine absorbable suture. **D,** The anastomosis is completed with approximation of the anterior walls of the pelvic flap and ureterotomy.

posterior walls are then approximated using fine interrupted or running suture (see Fig. 38–14C). Interrupted technique is likely to minimize pursing or buckling of the suture line as well as local tissue ischemia. Anastomosis of the anterior walls is then performed, thereby completing the surgical repair (see Fig. 38–14D).

*Culp-DeWeerd Spiral Flap.* The Culp-DeWeerd spiral flap is generally best suited for large, readily accessible extrarenal pelves in which the ureteral insertion is already in a dependent, oblique position. Although most of these patients are also good candidates for a standard or reduction dismembered pyeloplasty, the spiral flap may be of significant value when both UPJ obstruction and a relatively long segment of proximal ureteral narrowing or stricture occur in the same setting.

The spiral flap is first outlined with a broad base positioned obliquely on the dependent aspect of the renal pelvis. To maximize preservation of the flap blood supply, the base is placed in a position anatomically lateral to the UPJ, that is, between the ureteral insertion and the renal parenchyma. The pelvic flap itself may be spiraled posteriorly to anteriorly or vice versa. In either case, the anatomically medial line of incision (farthest from the parenchyma) is carried down the proximal ureter, completely traversing through the obstructed segment (Fig. 38–15A). Appropriate placement of the apex of the flap is determined by the length of flap needed. This, in turn, depends on the length of proximal ureter to be bridged. The longer the flap required, the farther away the apex will be from the base. However, to preserve vascular integrity of the flap, the ratio of flap length to width should not be greater than 3:1. In general, the outline of the flap should be made longer than what may initially be perceived as necessary because the flap will shrink once the pelvis is incised. If the flap is found to be too long, excess length can be reduced by trimming back the apex, thereby preserving its blood supply. Once the flap is created, the apex is rotated down to the most inferior aspect of the ureterotomy (see Fig. 38–15B). The anastomosis with fine absorbable sutures is subsequently performed over an internal stent (see Fig. 38–15C).

*Scardino-Prince Vertical Flap.* The Scardino-Prince vertical flap technique generally has limited clinical application, because it may be used appropriately only when a dependent UPJ is situated at the medial margin of a large, square ("box-shaped") extrarenal pelvis (Fig. 38–16A). Its use in most instances has been replaced by a standard dismembered pyeloplasty, although the vertical flap may be preferable for relatively long areas of proximal ureteral narrowing. **The vertical flap technique generally cannot produce as long a flap as the spiral flap.**

The Scardino-Prince vertical flap is similar to the spiral flap technique except that the base of the flap is positioned more horizontally on the dependent aspect of the renal pelvis, between the UPJ and the renal parenchyma. The flap itself is created by straight incisions converging from the base vertically to the apex on either the anterior or the posterior aspects of the renal pelvis. The site of the apex and the length of the flap are determined by the length of proximal ureter to be bridged. The medial incision is carried down the proximal ureter, completely traversing through the stenotic area and into normal-caliber ureter, using fine scissors (see Fig. 38–16B). The apex of the flap is then rotated down and approximated to the most inferior aspect of the ureterotomy. Finally, the flap is closed with interrupted or running fine absorbable sutures (see Fig. 38–16C).

### Intubated Ureterotomy

*Indications.* The Davis intubated ureterotomy, which is very rarely used today, was developed for surgical repair of lengthy or multiple ureteral strictures. If these strictures are found in association with UPJ obstruction, the intubated ureterotomy may be combined with any of the standard pyeloplasty procedures. However, in such situations, the intubated ureterotomy would be best combined with a spiral flap procedure. Compared with the vertical flap, the spiral flap can be made longer, which allows more of the strictured area to be bridged by a pelvic flap, thereby leaving a shorter area to rely on healing by "secondary intention." In fact, in this specific clinical setting, any flap technique would be preferable to a

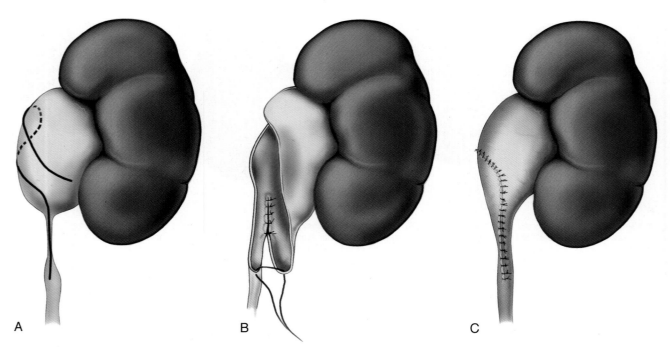

A          B          C

**Figure 38-15.** **A,** Spiral flap may be indicated for relatively long areas of proximal ureteral obstruction when the UPJ is already in a dependent position. The spiral flap is outlined with the base situated obliquely on the dependent aspect of the renal pelvis. The base of the flap is positioned anatomically lateral to the UPJ, between the ureteral insertion and the renal parenchyma. The flap is spiraled posteriorly to anteriorly or vice versa. The anatomically medial line of incision is carried down completely through the obstructed proximal ureteral segment into normal-caliber ureter. The site of the apex for the flap is determined by the length of flap required to bridge the obstruction. The longer the segment of proximal ureteral obstruction, the further away is the apex, because this will make the flap longer. However, to preserve vascular integrity to the flap, the ratio of flap length-to-width should not exceed 3:1. **B,** Once the flap is developed, the apex is rotated down to the most inferior aspect of the ureterotomy. **C,** The anastomosis is then completed, usually over an internal stent, again utilizing fine absorbable sutures.

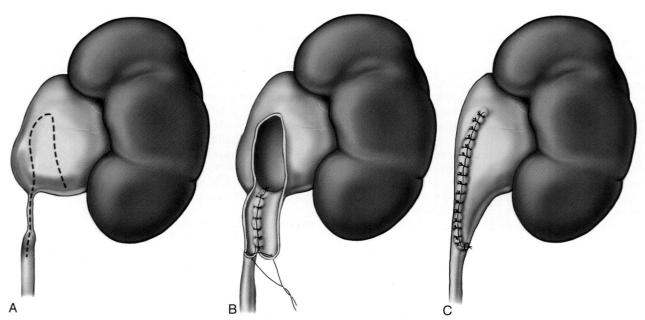

A          B          C

**Figure 38-16.** **A,** Vertical flap technique may be utilized when a dependent UPJ is situated at the medial margin of a large, box-shaped extrarenal pelvis. In contrast to the spiral flap, the base of the vertical flap is situated more horizontally on the dependent aspect of the renal pelvis, between the UPJ and the renal parenchyma. The flap itself is formed by two straight incisions converging from the base vertically up to the apex on either the anterior or the posterior aspect of the renal pelvis. As for the spiral flap, the position of the apex determines the length of the flap, which should be a function of the length of proximal ureter to be bridged. The medial incision of the flap is carried down the proximal ureter completely through the strictured area into normal-caliber ureter. **B,** The apex of the flap is rotated down to the most inferior aspect of the ureterotomy. **C,** The flap is then closed by approximating the edges with interrupted or running fine absorbable sutures.

dismembered repair, at least in regard to preservation of blood supply and subsequent healing.

*Technique.* A flap is outlined as described previously, with the ureterotomy to be made completely through the long, strictured area (Fig. 38–17A). The flap is then created, with minimal dissection of the ureter to preserve its blood supply. Unlike the uncomplicated pyeloplasties, these cases require routine nephrostomy tube drainage to prevent postoperative formation of a urinoma. Nephrostomy drainage in these cases also allows access for subsequent antegrade radiographic studies during the postoperative period.

Based on the original description, the ureteral intubation is achieved with a stenting catheter that is placed across the stenotic area to the distal ureter or bladder. Proximally, it is brought out through the renal cortex alongside a nephrostomy tube. Currently, most urologists use a self-retaining, soft, inert, internal ureteral stent instead. The apex of the flap is brought over the stent as far down as possible on the ureterotomy, and the flap is closed with either interrupted or running absorbable suture (see Fig. 38–17B). The distal aspect of the ureterotomy is then left open for secondary healing via ureteral regeneration (see Fig. 38–17C).

An antegrade nephrostogram is usually obtained 6 weeks after the surgery. If there is no extravasation, the ureteral stent is removed cystoscopically and an antegrade radiographic study is repeated. When ureteral patency without extravasa-

tion is ensured with such study, the nephrostomy tube is clamped and subsequently removed.

## Ureterocalycostomy

*Indications.* Ureterocalycostomy may be used as a primary reconstructive procedure whenever a UPJ obstruction or proximal ureteral stricture is associated with a relatively small intrarenal pelvis (Fig. 38–18A). When the UPJ is associated with rotational anomalies such as horseshoe kidney (Levitt et al, 1981), ureterocalycostomy may be useful to provide completely dependent drainage. Furthermore, ureterocalycostomy is a well-accepted salvage technique for the failed pyeloplasty (Ross et al, 1990).

*Technique.* The ureter is first identified in the retroperitoneum and dissected proximally with a generous amount of periureteral tissue. For secondary procedures, however, extensive scarring may preclude adequate identification and dissection of the renal pelvis itself (see Fig. 38–18B). The kidney is then mobilized to gain access to the lower pole. An important technical point in ureterocalycostomy is that the parenchyma overlying the lower pole calyx must be resected rather than simply incised, because a simple nephrotomy may lead to a secondary stricture (Couvelaire et al, 1964).

The proximal ureter is first spatulated laterally, and the ureterocalyceal anastomosis is completed over an internal stent. Leaving an indwelling nephrostomy tube should also be

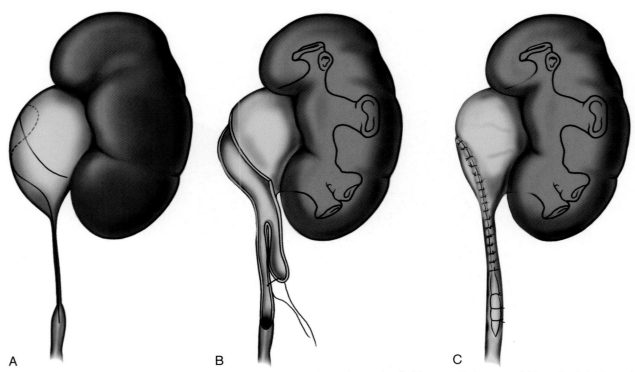

A                                B                                C

**Figure 38–17.** **A,** Intubated ureterotomy may be of value when a UPJ obstruction is associated with extremely long or multiple ureteral strictures. A spiral flap is outlined and developed as described in Figure 38-15. The ureterotomy incision will be carried completely through the long strictured areas or through each of the multiple areas of stricture. **B,** The flap is developed, taking care to use minimal dissection of the ureter to preserve its blood supply. In contrast to uncomplicated repairs, nephrostomy tube drainage is utilized routinely. A self-retaining, soft, inert internal ureteral stent is then placed and positioned proximally in the renal pelvis or lower infundibulum and distally in the bladder. The apex of the flap is then brought as far down as possible over the stent on the ureterotomy, and the flap is closed with interrupted or running absorbable suture. **C,** The distal aspect of the ureterotomy is left open to heal secondarily by ureteral regeneration. A few fine absorbable sutures may be loosely placed to keep the sides of the ureter in apposition to the stent.

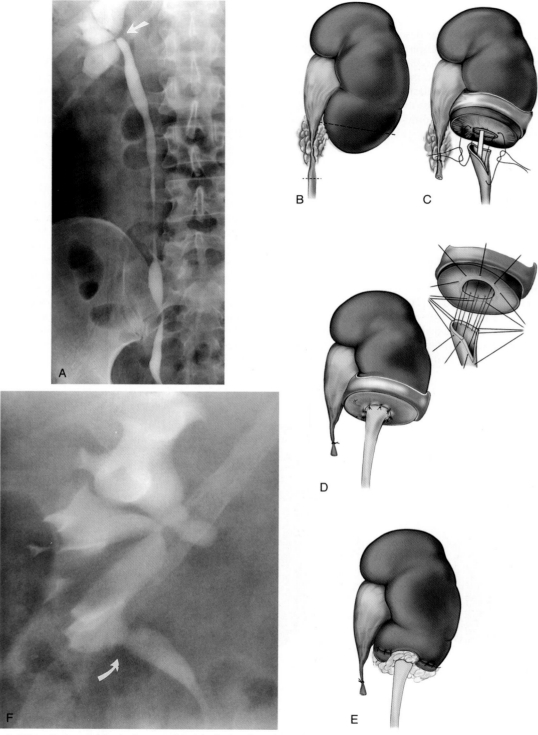

**Figure 38–18.** **A,** This patient complained of progressive right flank pain and was found on this retrograde study to have a UPJ obstruction *(arrow)* associated with a small intrarenal pelvis. This situation may be best managed with a ureterocalycostomy. **B,** The ureter is identified in the retroperitoneum and dissected proximally as far as possible. The kidney is mobilized as much as necessary to gain access to the lower pole and to subsequently perform the anastomosis without tension. A lower pole nephrectomy is performed, removing as much parenchyma as necessary to widely expose a dilated lower pole calyx. **C,** The proximal ureter is spatulated laterally. The anastomosis should subsequently be performed over an internal stent, and consideration should also be given to leaving a nephrostomy tube. The initial sutures are placed at the apex of the ureteral spatulation and the lateral wall of the calyx with a second suture placed 180 degrees from that. **D,** Anastomosis is then completed in a "open" fashion, placing each suture circumferentially *(inset)* but not securing them down until the anastomosis has been completed. **E,** The renal capsule is closed over the cut surface of the parenchyma whenever possible. However, the capsule should not be closed near the anastomosis itself because that may compromise the lumen by extrinsic compression. Instead, the anastomosis should be protected with a graft of perinephric fat or a peritoneal or omental flap. **F,** Intravenous urogram 2 months after right ureterocalycostomy reveals a widely patent ureterocalyceal anastomosis at the lower pole *(arrow)*.

considered in these cases. The first suture is placed at the apex of the ureteral spatulation and lateral wall of the calyx, and the second suture is placed 180 degrees apart. The remainder of the anastomosis is then performed utilizing an interrupted "open" suture technique. That is, each suture placed is left untied until the final one is in place (see Fig. 38–18C). This method seems to provide a more accurate anastomosis under direct vision. When the full set of circumferential sutures has been placed, the sutures are secured down together (see Fig. 38–18D). The renal capsule is closed over the cut surface of the parenchyma if possible. However, such closure should not be close enough to the anastomosis itself to cause extrinsic compression on the anastomosis. Instead, the anastomosis should be covered with perinephric fat or a peritoneal or omental flap (see Fig. 38–18E). A follow-up urogram is generally obtained at 1 month after the ureteral stent extraction (see Fig. 38–18F).

**"Salvage" Procedures.**  Failed open pyeloplasty is a challenging problem that is usually best managed initially using an endourologic approach. In some cases, such approach may not be applicable. In these cases, successful reconstruction can at times be achieved utilizing one of the flap or dismembered techniques already described. The secondary open operative reconstruction may be significantly aided by the placement of a ureteral catheter to aid intraoperative identification and dissection of the ureter and renal pelvis. In these situations there is often a relatively long length of proximal ureteral stenosis to repair and wide mobilization of the kidney and ureter is generally a necessity. This helps to bridge the area of stenosis and allows a tension-free secondary pyeloplasty.

Several other options are available for these secondary and often complex repairs. These surgical alternatives include those generally available for any extensive ureteral problem, such as ileoureteral replacement and autotransplantation with a Boari flap pyelovesicostomy. For cases in which function of the involved kidney is already significantly compromised and the contralateral kidney is normal, nephrectomy can be considered.

**Postoperative Care and Management of Complications.**  In general, external drains are advanced and removed 24 to 48 hours after urinary drainage has ceased. When internal stents have been placed, they remain in situ for 4 to 6 weeks. If a nephrostomy tube is present, a nephrostogram is obtained generally 7 to 10 days postoperatively, or even later for particularly complicated repairs. When that study demonstrates a patent anastomosis without obstruction or extravasation, the tube is clamped for 12 to 24 hours and removed if there is no flank pain, fever, or leakage around the tube.

If an internal stent had not been left indwelling and urinary drainage persists after 7 to 10 days, or recurs after the external drain has been removed, retrograde studies should be obtained and an attempt made to pass an internal stent. The problem then generally resolves immediately, and, again, the internal stent is removed 1 month later. If an attempt at passing an internal stent is unsuccessful, a percutaneous nephrostomy is placed and then managed as if it had been left intraoperatively. If drainage persists despite nephrostomy tube placement, an internal or internal/external stent should be placed in an antegrade fashion. At times, despite appropriate use of stents, drains, and nephrostomy tubes, urinary extrava-

sation will result in urinoma formation. This is best managed with direct percutaneous drainage of the fluid collection, utilizing ultrasound or CT guidance.

Standard follow-up of the functional result is accomplished with a urogram or renogram obtained approximately 4 weeks postoperatively or 4 weeks after any stents or nephrostomy tubes have been removed. More urgent evaluation is indicated if the patient becomes symptomatic. Compared with preoperative studies, radiographic evaluation at this time should show improvement in the degree of hydronephrosis. If a question remains as to the functional significance of any residual calycectasis, further evaluation can be performed using intravenous urography, diuretic renography, or retrograde pyelogram as outlined earlier in the chapter.

> ### KEY POINTS: OPEN OPERATIVE INTERVENTION OF UPJ OBSTRUCTION
>
> ■ Dismembered pyeloplasty can be applied to high ureteral insertion, redundant renal pelvis, and/or crossing vessels. It also allows excision of abnormal UPJ itself. It is the most versatile form of pyeloplasty. However, it is not well suited for lengthy or multiple proximal ureteral strictures or small, relatively inaccessible intrarenal pelvis.
>
> ■ Flap procedures can be useful in situations involving a relatively long segment of ureteral narrowing or stricture. Of the various flap procedures, a spiral flap can bridge a strictured or narrow area of longer length. The flap procedures are not appropriate in the setting of crossing vessels.
>
> ■ Ureterocalycostomy may be used for UPJ obstruction or proximal ureteral stricture associated with a relatively small intrarenal pelvis. It may also be used as a salvage technique for the failed pyeloplasty.

### Laparoscopic Operative Intervention

**Laparoscopic Pyeloplasty.**  Laparoscopic approach to pyeloplasty was first introduced in 1993 by Schuessler and associates and has been developed worldwide as a viable minimally invasive alternative to open pyeloplasty and endopyelotomy. Relative to both open pyeloplasty and endopyelotomy, laparoscopic pyeloplasty is associated with greater technical complexity and a steeper learning curve. **In the hands of the experienced laparoscopic surgeons, it has been shown to provide lower patient morbidity, shorter hospitalization, and faster convalescence, with the reported success rates matching those of open pyeloplasty (90% or higher).** Following the similar surgical principles of anatomic dissection and repair used in open pyeloplasty, laparoscopic pyeloplasty has been shown to provide the success rates surpassing those of endopyelotomy by 10% to 30%.

*Indications and Contraindications.*  **The indications and contraindications for a laparoscopic repair are similar to those for either an endourologic or an open operative procedure. Indications to intervene include the presence of** clinical symptoms of UPJ obstruction, the progressive impairment of renal function, and the development of ipsilateral upper tract calculi or infection. Cases requiring the transposition of crossing vessels obstructing the UPJ or the size reduction for massively dilated renal pelvis are suitable for the laparoscopic approach. **Absolute contraindications to intervene include the presence of uncorrected coagulopathy, the absence of adequate treatment of active urinary tract infection, and the presence of cardiopulmonary compromise unsuitable for surgery. The objective of the laparoscopic surgery is to provide a tension-free, watertight repair with a funnel-shaped drainage product to relieve clinical symptoms and to preserve renal function.**

*Techniques.* Four laparoscopic techniques for pyeloplasty have been described in the literature, including the standard transperitoneal approach, retroperitoneal approach, anterior extraperitoneal approach, and robotic-assisted approach. For each approach, a dismembered Andersen-Hynes pyeloplasty, which is preferred by most surgeons, or one of the non-dismembered methods such as YV-plasty and flap pyeloplasty (Culp-DeWeerd) analogous to those described for the open pyeloplasty can be used.

*Transperitoneal Laparoscopic Approach.* The initial transperitoneal approach to laparoscopic pyeloplasty was first described by Schuessler and associates (1993) and Kavoussi and Peters (1993), and **this approach has been the most widely used laparoscopic method because of its associated large working space and familiar anatomy.** Prior to the laparoscopic portion of the procedure, cystoscopy with retrograde pyelography is performed to define the anatomy and confirm the diagnosis, followed by placement of a ureteral stent and a urethral Foley catheter. The patient is placed in a 45-degree lateral decubitus position, and access to the peritoneal cavity is obtained via either the Veress needle or the Hassan access technique. Three to five laparoscopic ports are placed after the creation of $CO_2$ pneumoperitoneum. Typically, the umbilical port is for the laparoscope use. After medial mobilization of the colon, the ureter is identified and dissected in the cephalad direction to achieve mobilization of the ipsilateral proximal ureter, UPJ, and renal pelvis (Fig. 38–19*A*). Extensive dissection of the ureter and excessive electrocautery use in close proximity to the ureter should be avoided to minimize injury to its vascular supply. At this time, the anatomy of the proximal ureter, renal pelvis, and nearby vasculature are carefully examined to determine the etiology of the UPJ obstruction and the appropriate type of surgical repair. The general methods and principles of various types of surgical repair for laparoscopic pyeloplasty are identical to those described for open pyeloplasty. If dismembered pyeloplasty is to be performed, which is suitable for the presence of crossing vessels, the renal pelvis is first transected circumferentially above the UPJ and the lateral aspect of the proximal ureter is spatulated (see Fig. 38–19*B*). The renal pelvis and proximal ureter are then transposed to the opposite side of the crossing vessel, if such vessel is present, and the ureteropelvic anastomosis is then completed with intracorporeal suturing techniques (see Fig. 38–19*C* and *D*). In the presence of redundant renal pelvis, reduction pelvioplasty may be performed by excising redundant renal pelvic tissue and closing the pyelotomy. The actual laparoscopic suturing maneuver can be accomplished either free-hand or with a semi-automated

device (EndoStitch, U.S. Surgical Inc., Norwalk, CT). Either continuous running or simple interrupted suturing method may be used in the dismembered laparoscopic pyeloplasty, typically with 4-0 absorbable suture. A surgical drain is placed after the completion of the anastomosis, and one of the trocar sites is typically utilized as the drain exit site.

*Retroperitoneal Laparoscopic Approach.* The initial retroperitoneoscopic approach to pyeloplasty was first reported by Janetschek and colleagues (1996). Cystoscopy with retrograde pyelography and ureteral stent placement is first performed as described previously. For the retroperitoneal approach, the patient is usually positioned in a flank position with the use of flexion and elevation of the kidney rest of the operating table. By following the Hassan access technique to enter the retroperitoneum, a retroperitoneal working space can be created with balloon dilation. After creation of a $CO_2$ pneumoretroperitoneum, three to four laparoscopic ports are used to perform the laparoscopic pyeloplasty. The ureter is usually identified early in the procedure, and the dissection, mobilization, and UPJ repair steps are identical to those described for the transperitoneal approach (Fig. 38–20).

*Anterior Extraperitoneal Laparoscopic Approach.* The anterior extraperitoneal laparoscopic approach to pyeloplasty was first described by Hsu and Presti (2003). Cystoscopy with retrograde pyelography and ureteral stent placement are first performed as described previously. For the anterior extraperitoneal approach, the patient is placed in a 45-degree lateral decubitus position. Access to the preperitoneal space is obtained using open surgical techniques via a 10-mm incision, after which a large preperitoneal space is created with balloon dilation. After $CO_2$ insufflation and placement of four ports, the boundary between the retroperitoneal fat and peritoneal sac is identified and developed, allowing medial mobilization of the peritoneal sac containing the bowel contents en bloc. Subsequently, full exposure of the anterior aspects of the retroperitoneal structures including the ipsilateral ureter and kidney is attained. The proximal ureter, UPJ, and renal pelvis are identified, dissected, mobilized, and repaired as in transperitoneal laparoscopic pyeloplasty. The entire procedure is completed in an extraperitoneal manner. A surgical drain is placed at the end of the procedure.

*Robotic-Assisted Laparoscopic Approach.* The robotic-assisted laparoscopic pyeloplasty in the experimental setting was first reported by Sung and coworkers (1999). Its feasibility was subsequently confirmed with worldwide clinical application in recent years. Typically, the procedure is performed in a transperitoneal manner providing a larger working space for the robotic arms. After the initial laparoscopic access and trocar placement, the robotic system is placed in close proximity to the operating table and the robotic arms are attached to the laparoscope and specifically designed laparoscopic instruments. The surgeon at the console operates via the control of the robotic arms, while the assistant remains at the bedside and performs suction, retraction, exchange of laparoscopic instruments, suture needle introduction, and removal. The general surgical steps are identical to those described for non–robotic-assisted laparoscopic pyeloplasty.

***Postoperative Care and Complications.*** Typically, a clear liquid diet is initiated on postoperative day 1 and advanced rapidly. Perioperative prophylactic antibiotic coverage is maintained. The Foley catheter is usually removed after 24 to

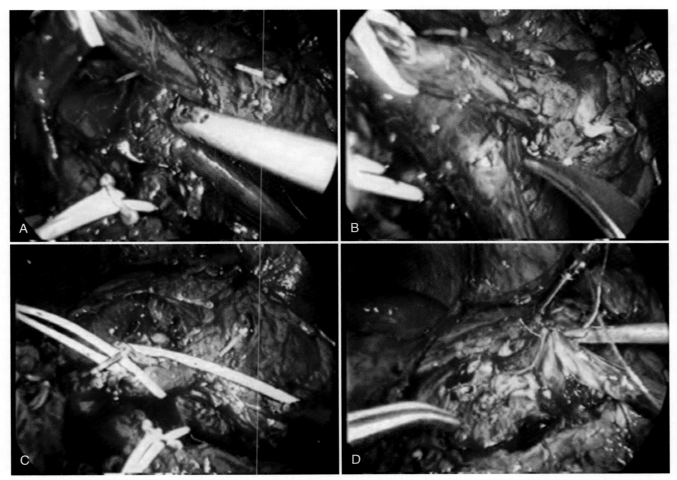

**Figure 38–19.** **A,** Transperitoneoscopic view of a patient with left pyeloplasty. The patient's head is to the left. Note the proximal ureter is sandwiched between an anterior crossing lower pole renal artery (wrapped with white vessel loop and retracted upward) and a posterior crossing lower pole vessel (wrapped with white vessel loop). The suction-irrigator tip points at the left UPJ. **B,** The left proximal ureter is being transected with laparoscopic scissors, revealing the preplaced ureteral stent within the ureteral lumen. **C,** The ureteral stent is transposed anterior to the anteriorly crossing vessel after circumferential transection of the proximal left ureter. **D,** Ureteropelvic anastomosis is completed with intracorporeal suturing techniques.

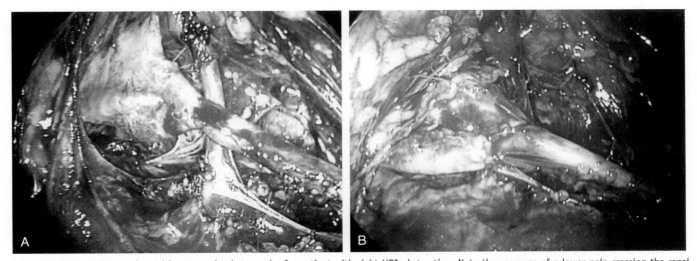

**Figure 38–20.** **A,** Retroperitoneal laparoscopic photograph of a patient with right UPJ obstruction. Note the presence of a lower pole crossing the renal vessel anterior to the UPJ. **B,** Intraoperative view of completed ureteropelvic anastomosis after retroperitoneal laparoscopic dismembered pyeloplasty.

36 hours, and the surgical drain is removed before hospital discharge if the drain output remains negligible. If the drain output increases after the Foley catheter removal, the Foley catheter should be replaced for 7 days to eliminate urinary reflux along the stent in the treated ureter and decrease urinary extravasation at the ureteropelvic anastomosis. The ureteral stent is typically removed 4 to 6 weeks later in an outpatient setting, and follow-up including the use of imaging studies such as diuretic renal scan is performed as for any open pyeloplasty. Most of the complications of laparoscopic pyeloplasty are similar to those of general laparoscopic procedures, including colonic injury, hemorrhage, ileus, pneumonia, congestive heart failure, thrombophlebitis, and urinoma formation. In the first 100 cases of laparoscopic pyeloplasty performed at Johns Hopkins Medical Institutions (Jarrett et al, 2002), such complications occurred in 12% of the patients. A typical postoperative appearance of a laparoscopic pyeloplasty patient is illustrated in Figure 38-21.

***Results.*** Most of the published laparoscopic pyeloplasty reports have utilized the classic Andersen-Hynes dismembered technique, because most laparoscopic surgeons attempt to duplicate the well-established principles of open surgery (Janetschek et al, 2000; Eden et al, 2001; Soulie et al, 2001; Jarrett et al, 2002; Turk et al, 2002). The overwhelming majority of the patients in these recent series had primary laparoscopic pyeloplasties, and the mean operative times are in the range of 119 to 252 minutes. In experienced hands, the entire procedure can be consistently performed in less than 3.5 hours (Jarrett et al, 2002), reflecting greater confidence in intracorporeal suturing and knot-tying. Perioperative complication rates are low, ranging from 2% to 12%, demonstrating the safety of the laparoscopic procedure. Open conversion rates are also low, less than 5%. Furthermore, blood transfusion risks are low, being limited to anecdotal reports. Postoperative analgesic use is generally minimal. Mean length of hospital stay ranges from 2.6 to 4.5 days, and such average has decreased to 3.8 days in the series reported since 2000. With mean follow-up times of 14 to 26 months, the rates of surgical success (defined as durable clinical and/or radiographic success) reach the range of 87% to 99%, with the majority of contemporary series reporting success rates of greater than 95%. For the patients who fail laparoscopic pyeloplasty, most cases can be well managed with endoscopic intervention such as endopyelotomy, with success rates of approximately 70% (Varkarakis et al, 2004). Additional current concerns for the robotic-assisted laparoscopic pyeloplasty include cost, limited instrumentation, and need for experienced bedside laparoscopic assistance (Peschel et al, 2004).

No prospective randomized trial has been successfully completed to compare laparoscopic with open pyeloplasty to date. The unwillingness of the patients to undergo randomization due to the different levels of perceived invasiveness appears to be the most significant barrier to completing such studies. In a retrospective study, Bauer and colleagues (1999) compared 42 laparoscopic pyeloplasties and 35 open pyeloplasties. With a minimal follow-up of 12 months for each of the patients, the two groups were found to be equivalent in pain relief (90% vs. 91%, respectively) and relief of obstruction (98% vs. 94%, respectively). In another retrospective study, Soulie and associates (2001) examined 26 laparoscopic pyeloplasties and 28 open pyeloplasties. The two groups were found to be equivalent in mean operating time (165 vs. 145 minutes, respectively), mean blood loss (92 vs. 84 mL, respectively), perioperative complication rate (11.5% vs. 14.3%, respectively), mean hospital stay (4.5 days vs. 5.5 days, respectively), and radiologic success (89% vs. 89%, respectively). However, more laparoscopic patients were found to have return to normal activity by postoperative day 15 (90% vs. 70%, respectively). In a third retrospective study, Klingler and colleagues (2003) compared 40 laparoscopic pyeloplasties with 15 open pyeloplasties. In this series, the laparoscopic group was found to have lower mean postoperative visual analog scale score (day 1, 3.5 vs. 5.4; day 5, 0.9 vs. 3.1) and shorter mean hospital stay (5.9 vs. 13.4 days).

Primary UPJ obstruction associated with renal anomalies such as horseshoe kidneys and pelvic kidneys has also been managed with laparoscopic pyeloplasty safely and successfully (Janetschek et al, 1996; Hsu and Presti, 2003; Bove et al, 2004). Furthermore, secondary UPJ obstruction has similarly been managed with success. In a retrospective review, Sundaram and colleagues (2003) identified 36 cases of laparoscopic transperitoneal pyeloplasty for secondary UPJ obstruction, mostly following failed retrograde or antegrade endopyelotomies. Mean operative time was 6.2 hours, longer than the reported times associated with primary UPJ obstruction. Open conversion was necessary in 1 patient, and postoperative complication occurred in 8 patients. With a mean follow-up of 21.8 months, the overall success rate of a greater than 50% decrease in pain, a patent UPJ, and stable or improved function of the affected renal unit was 83% (30 of 36 patients).

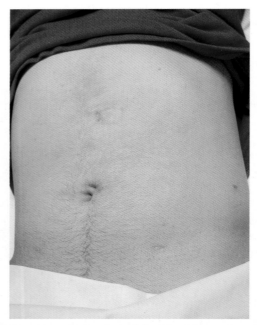

**Figure 38–21.** Postoperative photograph of the abdomen of a patient with left-sided laparoscopic dismembered pyeloplasty. Note the four small scars from the laparoscopic procedure.

## Special Situations of Laparoscopic Management of UPJ Obstruction

*Laparoscopic Ureterocalicostomy.* The clinical experience with laparoscopic ureterocalicostomy has been limited to one report to date. Gill and colleagues (2004) successfully performed laparoscopic ureterocalicostomy in two patients with UPJ obstruction associated with small renal pelvis and dilated lower pole calix. In both patients, a double-J ureteral stent was first placed into the ipsilateral ureter cystoscopically. With the patient in a 45- to 60-degree flank position, a transperitoneal approach using three or four ports was used to gain access to the ipsilateral renal unit laparoscopically. A circular rim of the tip of the thin lower pole renal parenchyma was identified and excised. The UPJ was transected, followed by ligation of the renal pelvic opening. The ureter was spatulated laterally, and end-to-end ureterocaliceal anastomosis with mucosa-to-mucosa apposition over the pre-placed double-J stent was performed with free-hand intracorporeal suturing and knot-tying techniques. The general reconstructive principles are identical to those of open ureterocalicostomy described previously, including the need to achieve tension-free, watertight, dependent drainage. Intravenous indigo carmine was administered to confirm no significant anastomotic leak. A Jackson-Pratt drain was then placed at the end of the laparoscopic procedure.

*Laparoscopic Pyeloplasty with Concomitant Pyelolithotomy.* Presence of calculi in the setting of UPJ obstruction can be managed laparoscopically with success. In a retrospective review, Ramakumar and colleagues (2002) reported 20 cases of laparoscopic pyeloplasty with concomitant extraction of renal stones through the pyelotomy site under laparoscopic guidance. In the series, extraction of the caliceal stones was facilitated by the use of flexible cystoscope introduced through a 10- to 12-mm port site. At a mean follow-up of 3 months, 90% of patients were stone free and 90% of patients had a patent UPJ radiographically.

*Laparoscopic Dismembered Tubularized Flap Pyeloplasty.* Presence of a significant upper ureteral defect after the excision of UPJ stricture may also be managed laparoscopically with success. Kaouk and coworkers (2002) described a case of laparoscopic pyeloplasty for secondary UPJ obstruction, in which a 3-cm upper ureteral defect was found after excision of the long stricture. By using a four-port transperitoneal approach, a wide-base renal pelvic flap was created and tubularized to bridge the defect, using intracorporeal freehand suturing techniques. At a 2-month follow-up, excretory urography and diuretic renal scan confirmed a widely patent upper ureter.

*Laparoscopic Calicovesicostomy.* Presence of a large-capacity bladder in the setting of UPJ obstruction associated with a low-lying obstructed renal unit can be managed successfully using an unconventional laparoscopic reconstructive strategy. Hsu and associates (2005) described a case of laparoscopic management of UPJ obstruction involving a horseshoe kidney with a unilateral hydronephrotic yet functioning lower pole moiety, ipsilateral ureteral duplication with high bifurcation, and complex anomalous renal vasculature. Rather than performing tedious anatomic dissection and complex ureteral reconstruction in such scenarios as required in conventional laparoscopic pyeloplasty, a nephrotomy was created at the most dependent portion of the hydronephrotic lower pole

moiety and then laparoscopically anastomosed to the bladder dome vesicostomy using intracorporeal freehand suturing and knot-tying techniques. At the 4-month follow-up, patent calicovesicostomy was confirmed endoscopically and clinically.

---

### KEY POINTS: LAPAROSCOPIC OPERATIVE INTERVENTION

■ Transperitoneal laparoscopic approach is the most widely used method due to its associated large working space and familiar anatomy.

■ Retroperitoneal laparoscopic approach and anterior extraperitoneal approach rely on creation of a working space using manual or balloon dilation.

■ Laparoscopic management of UPJ obstruction has been shown to provide low perioperative complication rates, short hospital stay, and success rates over 95% in experienced hands.

---

## RETROCAVAL URETER
## Etiology and Diagnosis

**Retrocaval ureter is a rare congenital urologic anomaly. It occurs as a consequence of the persistence of the posterior cardinal veins during embryologic development** (Considine, 1966). Its presence should be suspected with the finding of a characteristic S-shaped deformity on intravenous or retrograde pyelography (Fig. 38–22*A*). Today, a definitive diagnosis can be made noninvasively utilizing three-dimensional CT (see Fig. 38–22*B*) (Pienkny et al, 1999). Procedural intervention is indicated in the presence of functionally significant obstruction leading to pain or renal function deterioration.

## Operative Intervention

### Open Surgical Management

**The standard repair of retrocaval ureter is open surgical pyelopyelostomy.** In this procedure, the ureter, dilated renal pelvis, and inferior vena cava are identified and dissected using the standard open surgical techniques. The dilated renal pelvis is then transected, following which the ureter is transposed to its normal anatomic position anterior to the vena cava (Fig. 38–23). Pyelopyelostomy is then performed circumferentially with absorbable sutures in a tension-free, watertight manner. A surgical drain and internal ureteral stent are typically used.

### Laparoscopic Surgical Management

Retrocaval ureter has been managed successfully with the laparoscopic approach in the clinical setting as shown by a series of sporadic case reports in recent years (Baba et al, 1994; Matsuda et al, 1996; Polascik and Chen, 1998; Salomon et al, 1999; Gupta et al, 2001; Ramalingam and Selvarajan, 2003). Either a transperitoneal or a retroperitoneal approach may be used laparoscopically. A double-J ureteral stent is first placed into the ipsilateral ureter cystoscopically. After transperitoneal or retroperitoneal laparoscopic access, the ipsilateral ureter is identified and mobilized off the inferior vena cava. The ureter

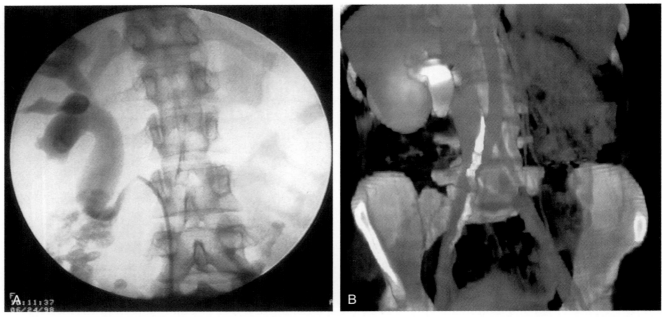

**Figure 38–22.** **A,** Retrograde pyelography in a patient with right-sided hydronephrosis. This study reveals a typical S-shaped deformity secondary to the ureter coursing laterally to medially posterior to the inferior vena cava. **B,** Three-dimensional spiral CT demonstrates the presence of a retrocaval ureter.

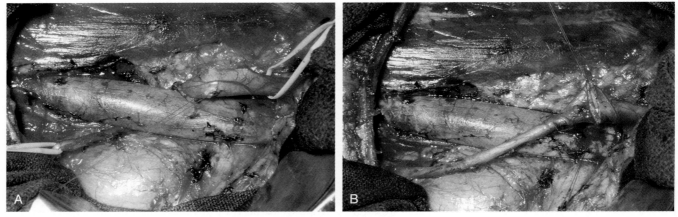

**Figure 38–23.** **A,** Intraoperative photograph of a patient with retrocaval ureter undergoing surgical repair via a retroperitoneal flank approach. Right side of the photograph represents the cephalad direction. Note the dilated proximal right ureter passing behind the inferior vena cava. **B,** Right ureteropelvic anastomosis has been completed after transection of the right renal pelvis and transposition of the ureter anterior to the inferior vena cava.

is then divided at the most distal segment of the dilated ureter. Redundant segment of dilated proximal ureter and stenotic segment of ureter are excised if present. The ureteral ends are positioned anterolateral to the vena cava, spatulated for 1.5 to 2 cm on opposite ends, and then anastomosed with absorbable sutures using intracorporeal suturing techniques over the stent. Tension-free, watertight anastomosis is the objective. A surgical drain is then left in place before formal laparoscopic exit. The surgical drain is typically removed within a few days postoperatively, and the ureteral stent is removed in 4 to 6 weeks. **The overall clinical results of the laparoscopic repair in the literature have been favorable, providing minimal postoperative patient morbidity, short convalescence, and anastomotic patency on short-term radiographic follow-up.**

## KEY POINTS: RETROCAVAL URETER

- Retrocaval ureter results from the persistence of the posterior cardinal veins.

- Retrocaval ureter can be diagnosed using intravenous or retrograde pyelography or three-dimensional CT.

- Procedural intervention is indicated in the presence of functionally significant obstruction, and both open and laparoscopic approaches can be successfully applied.

| Table 38-1. **Etiology of Ureteral Stricture** |
| --- |
| Malignancy (e.g., transitional cell carcinoma, cervical) |
| Ureteral calculus |
| Radiation |
| Ischemia/trauma due to surgical dissection |
| Periureteral fibrosis due to abdominal aortic aneurysm or endometriosis |
| Endoscopic instrumentation |
| Infection (e.g., tuberculosis) |
| Idiopathic |

# URETERAL STRICTURE DISEASE
## Etiology

Common causes of ureteral stricture formation include ischemia, surgical and nonsurgical trauma, periureteral fibrosis, malignancy, or a congenital disorder (Table 38–1). **Proper evaluation and treatment of a ureteral stricture is essential to preserve renal function and rule out the presence of malignancy.** Although the classic radiographic presentation of a transitional cell carcinoma of the ureter is a radiolucent filling defect within the lumen with the characteristic goblet sign, it may appear as a benign stricture. In addition, metastatic tumors such as cervical, prostate, ovarian, breast, and colon cancer may appear as a ureteral stricture (Lau et al, 1998). Although the incidence of ureteral strictures in the general population is unknown, it is clear that the **presence of ureteral calculi and associated treatment of stones are risk factors.** Roberts and colleagues (1998) evaluated 21 patients with impacted ureteral stones and found that impaction for more than 2 months' duration was associated with a 24% incidence of stricture formation. Any ureteral instrumentation can lead to the development of a ureteral stricture. As advances in ureteroscopic technology have provided smaller, more flexible instruments with better optics, these endoscopic procedures have become less traumatic and are now associated with a long-term complication rate of less than 1% (Harmon et al, 1997). Other causes of benign ureteral strictures include radiation; abdominal aortic aneurysm; infections, such as tuberculosis and schistosomiasis; endometriosis; and trauma, including iatrogenic injury from previous abdominal or pelvic surgery (El Abd et al, 1996; Lacquet et al, 1997; Ramanathan et al, 1998; Oh et al, 2000). Patients with presumed idiopathic ureteral strictures should be evaluated utilizing CT to rule out the presence of an intrinsic ureteral malignancy or a lesion causing extrinsic compression.

## Diagnostic Studies and Indications for Intervention

**An intravenous pyelogram and retrograde pyelogram reliably define the location and length of the ureteral stricture.** Subsequent ureteroscopy with biopsy or barbotage should be performed in any patient for whom the etiology of the stricture is not certain. Endoluminal ultrasound is an alternate approach that allows one to characterize a stricture and guide therapy, although it is not commonly utilized (Grasso et al, 1999). Diuretic renography will provide differential renal function and evaluate the renal unit for functional obstruc-

tion. **It is critical to assess the renal unit for function before starting treatment, because endourologic therapies generally require 25% function of the ipsilateral moiety to have reasonable success rates** (Wolf et al, 1997). Once a ureteral stricture is diagnosed, indications for intervention include the need to rule out malignancy, compromised renal function, recurrent pyelonephritis, and pain associated with functional obstruction.

## Endourologic Options for Intervention
### Ureteral Stent Placement

Ureteral stent placement is effective acutely in treating most ureteral strictures, in particular intrinsic ureteral strictures. Generally, select intrinsic ureteral strictures can be managed with endoscopic options, but cases of extrinsic ureteral compression are better suited to percutaneous drainage or surgical management. In cases in which the patient is not a candidate for definitive repair, or has a poor prognosis, chronic stent placement with periodic stent changes may be considered. **The use of chronic stent placement must be guarded, particularly when treating ureteral obstruction from extrinsic compression, because in many cases adequate drainage is short lived** (Docimo and Dewolf, 1989; Chung et al, 2004). Some urologists have placed two stents to maintain ureteral patency in cases in which a single stent did not provide adequate drainage (Yohannes et al, 2001).

### Retrograde Balloon Dilation

Retrograde dilatation of ureteral strictures has historically been part of the urologic armamentarium. The technique was rarely definitive and usually required repeated dilatations on a regular basis. In the early 1980s, angiographic and vascular balloons were introduced into urologic practice, and the technique of balloon dilatation with temporary internal stenting became an accepted mode of treatment (Banner et al, 1983; Finnerty et al, 1984).

**As for any patient with a ureteral stricture, the indications to intervene include functionally significant obstruction. Contraindications to this approach include active infection or a stricture longer than 2 cm, because dilatation alone will rarely be successful in this setting.**

A retrograde approach is indicated whenever access across the strictured area is easily accomplished using transurethral techniques. The procedure generally begins with a retrograde pyelogram performed under fluoroscopic control to precisely delineate the site and length of stricture. A floppy-tipped guide wire is passed in a retrograde fashion across the strictured area and coiled proximally in the pyelocalyceal system. This is most easily accomplished by passing an open-end catheter up to the level of the stricture to use as a guide for the hydrophilic or floppy-tipped wire. Passage of the open-end catheter through the strictured area over the wire will then aid subsequent passage of a balloon catheter. Techniques for bypassing difficult areas of obstruction have been described in detail (Mata et al, 1994).

At this point, the open-end catheter is withdrawn and replaced with a high-pressure, 4-cm-long, 5- to 8-mm balloon. Under fluoroscopic control, the balloon catheter is positioned across the strictured area with proper position ensured by visualization of radiopaque markers at the tip of the balloon. Balloon inflation is then begun, and a waist will be visualized at the strictured area that will disappear with progressive balloon inflation (Fig. 38–24). After 10 minutes of tamponade, the balloon is deflated and withdrawn. A guide wire is still in place, and this is used to pass an internal stent, which is left indwelling for 2 to 4 weeks. Follow-up radiographic studies including intravenous urography, ultrasonography, or diuretic renography, are generally performed approximately 1 month after stent extraction and at 6- to 12-month intervals thereafter.

Occasionally, access across the involved area cannot be obtained using fluoroscopic control alone. In such cases, direct ureteroscopic visualization can aid initial passage of the guide wire and the procedure can be continued as described. Alternatively, a low-profile balloon can be passed through the ureteroscope and the stricture dilated under direct vision.

### Antegrade Balloon Dilation

At times, retrograde access across a strictured area is impossible. In such cases, access can be obtained using an antegrade approach and fluoroscopic control (Mitty et al, 1983; Banner and Pollack, 1984), with or without direct antegrade ureteroscopic visualization (De Jonge et al, 1986). **Percutaneous nephrostomy drainage is established, and, in cases associated with infection or compromised renal function, percutaneous drainage alone is instituted to allow resolution of**

**infection and return to baseline renal function.** Once that is accomplished, the percutaneous tract is used for access for a fluoroscopically or ureteroscopically guided approach. The procedure is then analogous to a retrograde approach. Under fluoroscopic guidance, an antegrade contrast agent study is used to definitively define the site and length of the stricture. A floppy-tipped guide or glide wire is passed antegrade across the level of obstruction, following which a balloon catheter is passed; and the balloon is progressively inflated until the waist disappears. The balloon catheter is withdrawn over a wire and replaced with an internal stent, and a nephrostomy tube is also left indwelling. A follow-up nephrostogram is obtained within 24 to 48 hours to ensure proper positioning of a functional internal stent, and, at that time, the nephrostomy tube can be removed. Alternatively, access can be maintained by the use of an internal/external stent, which can be capped to allow internal drainage.

**Results.** Initial reports of retrograde and antegrade balloon dilatation of ureteral strictures suggested that results were better when the stricture was anastomotic and of relatively short duration and length (King et al, 1984b; Chang et al, 1987; Netto et al, 1990). **Goldfischer and Gerber (1997) reviewed the literature in regard to results of balloon dilatation of ureteral strictures and found reported success rates ranging from 50% to 76%. In that review, the best results were obtained in patients with iatrogenic, nonanastomotic strictures such as those following ureteroscopic instrumen-**

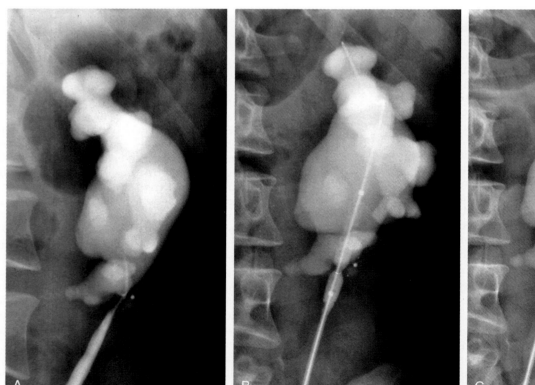
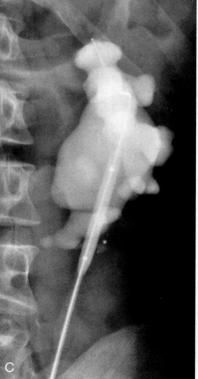

**Figure 38–24.**  **A,** Retrograde study confirms a short stricture at the level of the UPJ in this patient with a horseshoe kidney who was referred after failed ureteroscopic management of a ureteral calculus impacted at that level. **B,** The stricture has been traversed with a guide wire, over which a high-pressure balloon has been passed. A waist is evident at the level of the stricture during initial balloon inflation. **C,** Balloon inflation and stricture dilatation are complete with disappearance of the waist.

tation. In that setting, a success rate of 85% was achieved compared with a rate of 50% for anastomotic strictures. Alternatively, Ravery and associates (1998) found a 40% success rate utilizing retrograde balloon dilation in treating inflammatory ureteral strictures at 16 months follow-up. Richter and coworkers (2000) reviewed their results with balloon dilatation in 114 patients with a minimal 2-year follow-up. As in other series, balloon dilatation was more successful for patients with relatively short strictures. In addition, these authors noted the significance of an intact vascular supply on the success of this procedure. For longer ureteral strictures and those associated with compromised vascular supply, an incisional approach (endoureterotomy) was recommended as a more successful endourologic alternative to balloon dilatation. Of note, in experimental models, balloon dilation created longitudinal incisions similar to endoureterotomy, possibly explaining some of the success seen using balloon dilation in ureteral strictures (Nakada et al, 1996).

## Endoureterotomy

Endoluminal ureteral incision is a logical extension of balloon dilatation for "minimally invasive" management of ureteral strictures. As for balloon dilatation, access to and across the strictured area can be obtained in a retrograde or antegrade fashion, although a retrograde approach is preferable whenever possible because it is less invasive. The procedure is performed under direct vision using ureteroscopic control, or it can be guided fluoroscopically using the hot wire cutting balloon catheter. Generally, radiographic follow-up using diuretic renography is recommended for up to 3 years to detect most late failures (Wolf et al, 1997).

**Retrograde Ureteroscopic Approach.** A retrograde study is performed under fluoroscopic control at the outset of the procedure. Whenever possible, a floppy-tipped guide wire or hydrophilic glide wire is passed across the level of obstruction, as outlined earlier. If a wire cannot be passed across the stric-

tured area using fluoroscopic control alone, a semirigid or flexible ureteroscope is passed to the level of obstruction and the guide wire advanced through the ureteroscope across the involved area under direct vision. The ureteroscope is then withdrawn, but a safety wire is always left in place across the stricture. The ureteroscope is then reintroduced and passed alongside the guide wire to the level of obstruction.

**The position for the endoureterotomy incision is chosen as a function of the level of the ureter involved. In general, lower ureteral strictures are incised in an anteromedial direction, taking care to stay away from the iliac vessels. In contrast, upper ureteral strictures are incised laterally or posterolaterally, again away from the great vessels** (Meretyk et al, 1992) (Fig. 38–25).

The ureterotomy incision itself can be performed using a cold knife (Schneider et al, 1991; Yamada et al, 1995), a cutting electrode (Conlin et al, 1996), or a holmium laser (Fig. 38–26). In all cases, the incision is made from the ureteral lumen out to periureteral fat in a full-thickness fashion. Proximally and distally, the endoureterotomy should encompass 2 to 3 mm of normal ureteral tissue. In certain instances, the stricture must be balloon dilated to gain access across the stricture. Similarly, the strictures may be balloon dilated after endoincision, to enlarge the incision. Once the endoureterotomy incision is complete, the remaining guide wire is used to pass an internal stent. In general, the larger diameter stents should be considered, because larger stents (12 Fr) have been associated with improved results in some series (Hwang et al, 1996; Wolf et al, 1997). Similarly, Wolf and associates (1997) found benefit in the injection of triamcinolone ureteroscopically after endoureterotomy. Corticosteroids and other biologic response modifiers may have a role in the future in managing select strictures.

**Cautery Wire Balloon Incision.** Cautery wire balloon incision has been used for ureteral strictures in the same manner as it has for UPJ obstruction. The procedure requires safety

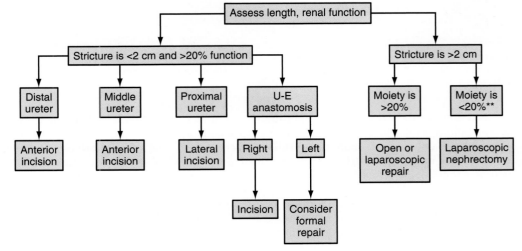

OPTIMAL THERAPY FOR BENIGN URETERAL STRICTURES*

**Figure 38–25.** Algorithm for management of benign ureteral and ureteroenteric stricture disease.

*Consider balloon if transplant on immunosuppression
**Pediatric and younger patients may warrant repair

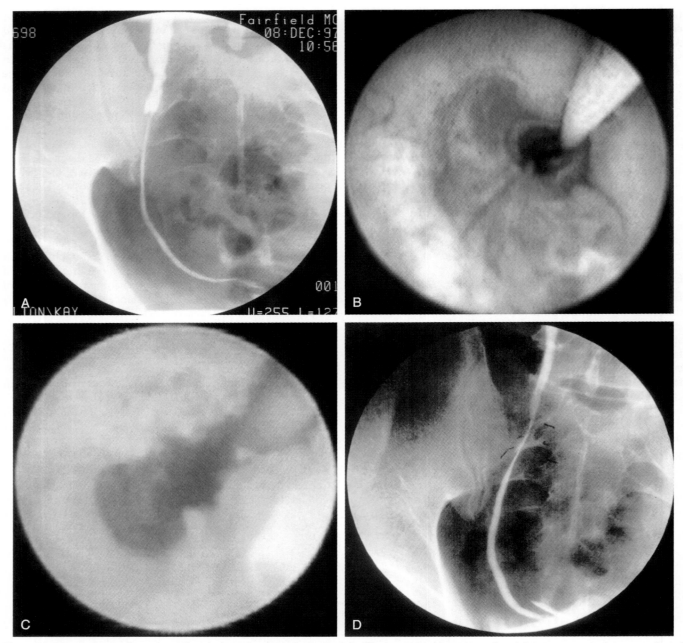

**Figure 38–26.** **A,** Antegrade study confirms hydronephrosis at the level of the iliac ureter in this patient referred for management after a complicated open ureterolithotomy. **B,** Ureteroscopic view confirms a tight ureteral stricture. **C,** Ureteral lumen is widely patent after holmium laser endoureterotomy. **D,** Follow-up ureterogram confirms resolution of the stricture.

wire access across the strictured area and is performed under fluoroscopic control. The cautery wire balloon is passed in a retrograde or antegrade fashion and positioned across the stricture using radiopaque markers. In the proximal ureter the incision should be posterolateral, whereas in the distal ureter an anteromedial incision is used. **Fluoroscopically guided cautery wire balloon incision should not be used in close proximity to the great vessels, such as at the iliac level of the ureter.** As for any form of endourologic management, success utilizing this technique depends on the length and vascularity of the involved segment (Chandhoke et al, 1993b; Cohen et al, 1996; Wolf et al, 1997).

**Antegrade Approach.** When direct visual ureteroscopic access to the strictured area cannot be accomplished in a retrograde fashion, an antegrade approach may be used. Nephrostomy tube drainage is instituted and any associated infection or compromised renal function is allowed to resolve prior to definitive incision. The percutaneous tract is dilated to a size large enough to allow a working sheath through which a flexible ureteroscope is passed. The procedure is then performed in a fashion analogous to a retrograde approach. A safety wire should be in place at all times alongside the ureteroscope, across the obstructed area and coiled distally in the bladder.

**Combined Retrograde/Antegrade Approach.** Rarely, a ureteral stricture is associated with an area of complete ureteral obliteration across which a wire cannot be passed to allow subsequent balloon dilatation or ureteroscopic endoureterotomy. In such cases, a combined retrograde/antegrade approach has been described (Cardella et al, 1985; Conlin et al, 1996; Beaghler et al, 1997; Knowles et al, 2001). The obstructed area is defined radiographically with a simultaneous antegrade and retrograde pyelogram. Ureteroscopes are passed simultaneously in both a retrograde and an antegrade manner, and the two opposing ureteral ends are localized under fluoroscopic guidance. A working guide wire is then passed from one end of the ureter, through and through to the other lumen, utilizing a combination of fluoroscopic and direct visual control. For completely obliterated ureteral segments, this is most easily accomplished using the stiff end of a guide wire passed through a semirigid ureteroscope via the retrograde approach, although when a semirigid ureteroscope cannot be placed, a flexible ureteroscope or even an open-end ureteral catheter can be used to stabilize the wire from above or below. A "cut to the light" technique can be helpful in this setting. The ureteral segments are aligned as closely as possible under endoscopic and fluoroscopic guidance and with the light source to one of the ureteroscopes turned off. The light from the opposite ureteroscope is then used to aid incisional restoration of urinary continuity. The strictured area is then recannulated using the stiff end of a guide wire, a small electrocautery electrode, or a holmium laser. Once through-and-through control is obtained with a guide wire, a stent is passed and left in place for 8 to 10 weeks. As for other endourologic approaches to ureteral strictures, success rates are inversely related to the length of the strictured area. **Although success rates may be uncertain, internalization of urinary flow, even when dependent on long-term stent placement, can be a quality-of-life advantage for certain high-risk patients.** Knowles and associates (2001) reported a 90% patency rate in 10 patients treating obliterated distal ureteral segments using cautery wire balloon incision at 36 months follow-up, 3 of whom required the combined approach.

## Surgical Repair

Before any surgical repair, it is essential to conduct careful evaluation of the nature, location, and length of the ureteral stricture. Preoperative assessment typically includes an intravenous pyelogram (or antegrade nephrostogram) and a retrograde pyelogram if indicated. Other studies such as a nuclear medicine renogram to assess renal function and ureteroscopy, ureteral barbotage, or brushing to rule out carcinoma should be individualized. Based on such information, the appropriate surgical procedure can then be planned for the patient (Table 38–2).

### Open Ureteroureterostomy

**A short defect involving the upper ureter or midureter, either in the form of stricture or as a consequence of recent injury, is most appropriate for ureteroureterostomy.** On the other hand, a lower ureteral stricture is usually best managed by ureteroneocystostomy with or without a psoas hitch or Boari flap. In the transplant setting, a donor ureteral stricture

### KEY POINTS: ENDOUROLOGIC MANAGEMENT OF URETERAL STRICTURE

- Proper evaluation and treatment of a ureteral stricture is essential to preserve renal function and rule out the presence of malignancy. It is critical to assess the renal unit for function before starting treatment, because endourologic therapies generally require 25% function of the ipsilateral moiety to have reasonable success rates.

- The use of chronic stent placement for ureteral obstruction must be guarded, particularly when treating ureteral obstruction from extrinsic compression, because in many cases adequate drainage is short lived.

- As for any patient with a ureteral stricture, the indications to intervene include functionally significant obstruction. Contraindications to this approach include active infection or a stricture longer than 2 cm.

- The position for the endoureterotomy incision is chosen as a function of the level of the ureter involved. In general, lower ureteral strictures are incised in an anteromedial direction, taking care to stay away from the iliac vessels. In contrast, upper ureteral strictures are incised laterally or posterolaterally, again away from the great vessels.

**Table 38–2. Bridging Various Ureteral Defect Lengths with Different Reconstructive Surgical Techniques**

| Technique | Ureteral Defect Length (cm) |
|---|---|
| Ureteroureterostomy | 2-3 |
| Ureteroneocystostomy | 4-5 |
| Psoas hitch | 6-10 |
| Boari flap | 12-15 |
| Renal descensus | 5-8 |

may be managed by a ureteroureterostomy to a healthy, native ureter. Because tension on the anastomosis almost always leads to stricture formation, only short defects should be managed by end-to-end ureteroureterostomy. Determination of whether enough ureteral mobility can be achieved to allow tension-free ureteroureterostomy usually cannot be made until the time of surgery.

The choice of surgical incision depends on the level of the ureteral stricture. A flank incision is appropriate for the upper ureter. A Gibson or a lower midline incision is suitable for the middle and lower ureter. If the patient has sustained an iatrogenic ureteral injury from a previous surgery performed through a Pfannenstiel incision, the same incision may be used for the ureteral reconstruction. In such a situation, proximal ureteral dissection may be difficult through the Pfannenstiel incision, requiring cephalad extension of the lateral portion of the incision in a "hockey stick" fashion.

Extraperitoneal dissection is usually performed except in cases of transperitoneal surgical ureteral injury.

After surgical incision, the retroperitoneal space is developed as the peritoneum is mobilized and retracted medially. Frequently, the ureter can be easily identified as it crosses the iliac vessels. A Penrose drain or vessel loop may be placed around the ureter to facilitate its atraumatic handling. Direct handling of the ureter with forceps should be minimized. Care should be taken to preserve its adventitia, which loosely attaches the blood supply to the ureter.

During ureteral dissection and mobilization, enough mobility must be achieved to avoid tension after the excision of the diseased ureter. With a gunshot injury, devitalized tissue and an adjacent segment of normal-appearing ureter should be excised to eliminate late ischemia and stricture formation from the blast effect. Once both ends of the ureter have been adequately trimmed to healthy areas, mobilized, and correctly oriented, they are spatulated for 5 to 6 mm. Spatulation is performed for both ureteral segments at 180 degrees apart. If a grossly dilated ureter is involved, it may be transected obliquely and not spatulated in order to match the circumference of the nondilated segment. A fine, absorbable suture is placed in the corner of one ureteral segment and the apex

of the other, and the two ends of the suture are tied outside the ureteral lumen. The opposite corner and apex are similarly sutured and approximated. The anastomosis may then be completed by running these two sutures continuously and tying them to each other or in an interrupted fashion (Fig. 38–27). A double-J ureteral stent should be placed before completion of the anastomotic closure. Observation of reflux of methylene blue irrigant from the bladder to the ureterotomy can be used to verify the appropriate placement of the distal stent in the bladder. Retroperitoneal fat or omentum may be used to cover the anastomosis. A surgical drain is placed, and a Foley catheter is generally left indwelling for 1 to 2 days. The surgical drain may be removed if there is minimal output for 24 to 48 hours. If the surgical procedure is not performed entirely in a retroperitoneal manner, it is important to determine the nature of the fluid from the surgical drain, which can be achieved by checking the creatinine level of the fluid. If there is no urinary extravasation, the drain can then be removed. The double-J ureteral stent is removed endoscopically, usually 4 to 6 weeks postoperatively.

The success rate for a tension-free, watertight ureteroureterostomy is high, well over 90% (Carlton et al, 1969; Guiter et al, 1985). If a urinary fistula is suspected, a plain

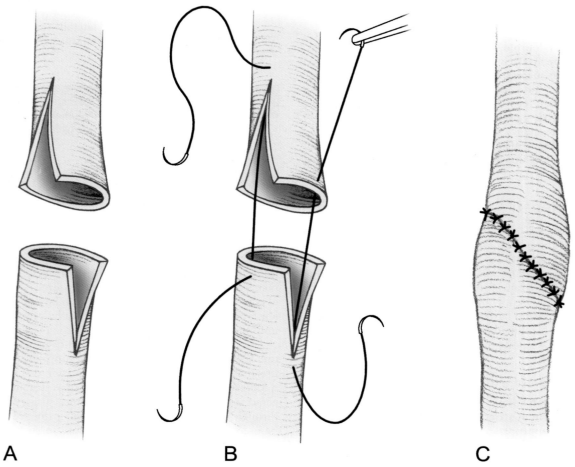

**A**      **B**      **C**

**Figure 38–27.** **A,** Spatulated ureteral ends. **B,** Placement of sutures. **C,** End-to-end ureteroureterostomy.

abdominal radiograph should first be obtained to verify the position of the double-J stent. The proximity of a drain to the anastomosis should also be checked because it may exacerbate a leak. Suction should be stopped if a suction drain device is used, because straight drainage may facilitate closure of the ureteral leakage site. Reflux from voiding or bladder spasms may also contribute to prolonged urinary extravasation, and such problems can be managed by Foley catheter drainage and anticholinergics. Prolonged urinary leakage from the anastomosis may require the placement of a nephrostomy tube for proximal urinary diversion.

### Laparoscopic Ureteroureterostomy

A laparoscopic approach may be offered to patients with ureteral stricture disease. Nezhat and colleagues (1992) first reported laparoscopic management of an obstructed ureter due to endometriosis. In this case, ureteroureterostomy was performed laparoscopically over a ureteral stent after resection of the obstructed ureteral site. In their more recent retrospective review involving eight laparoscopic ureteroureterostomy patients, seven were found to have patent anastomosis with relatively short follow-up, ranging from 2 to 6 months (Nezhat et al, 1998). The overall clinical experience in laparoscopic ureteroureterostomy is limited worldwide. However, in the hands of experienced laparoscopic surgeons, it appears to be a viable minimally invasive approach applicable to almost any patient with a relatively short area of obstruction.

### Open Ureteroneocystostomy

Ureteroneocystostomy to manage vesicoureteral reflux is covered elsewhere in this text. Ureteroneocystostomy without a psoas hitch or Boari flap in an adult is appropriate for injury or obstruction affecting the distal 3 to 4 cm of the ureter. A lower midline, Pfannenstiel, or Gibson incision may be used, and the extraperitoneal approach is generally more preferable. After surgical incision, the ureter is usually identified as it crosses the iliac vessels, dissected distally, and transected at the level of the obstruction. After adequate proximal ureteral mobilization, direct ureteroneocystostomy is performed only if a tension-free anastomosis is possible. Otherwise, a psoas hitch or Boari flap should be used as an adjunct. A direct, nontunneled anastomosis may be performed if postoperative reflux is acceptable. Otherwise, a submucosal tunnel is created for antireflux anastomosis. A double-J stent and surgical drain are used as described for ureteroureterostomy (see earlier).

The issue of refluxing versus antirefluxing anastomosis in ureteroneocystostomy in adults has been examined previously. **In a retrospective review of adult patients with ureteroneocystostomy, no significant difference in the preservation of renal function or risk of stenosis was identified in the refluxing versus antirefluxing procedures** (Stefanovic et al, 1991). However, it is unclear if a nonrefluxing anastomosis decreases the risk of pyelonephritis in an adult patient.

### Laparoscopic Ureteroneocystostomy

Successful laparoscopic application to ureteroneocystostomy has been reported by several investigators (Ehrlich et al, 1993; Reddy and Evans, 1994; Yohannes et al, 2001). In the management of distal ureteral stricture, laparoscopic ureteroneo-

cystostomy is usually performed transperitoneally incorporating intracorporeal suturing techniques. Ureteral stenting is typically used postoperatively as in open surgery. The overall clinical experience for laparoscopic management of distal ureteral strictures is limited in the literature. However, the clinical outcomes have been reported to be favorable and comparable to those of open surgical data while providing minimal postoperative morbidity as in many other laparoscopic urologic procedures.

### Open Psoas Hitch

The psoas hitch is an effective method to bridge a defect of the lower third of the ureter. However, a ureteral defect extending proximal to the pelvic brim usually requires more than a psoas hitch alone. Indications include distal ureteral stricture, injury, and failed ureteroneocystostomy (Prout and Koontz, 1970; Ehrlich et al, 1978; Rodo Salas et al, 1991). A psoas hitch may also be used in conjunction with other maneuvers such as a transureteroureterostomy in more complicated urinary tract reconstruction. **Generally, a small, contracted bladder with limited mobility is considered as a contraindication.** In addition to the preoperative radiographic and endoscopic evaluation described previously, urodynamic studies may provide information regarding detrusor capacity and compliance before the surgery. Bladder outlet obstruction or neurogenic dysfunction, if present, needs to be treated preoperatively.

To gain access to the distal ureter, a Pfannenstiel or lower midline incision is usually used. Extraperitoneal approach is preferred, if possible. In such a scenario, the space of Retzius is developed and the bladder mobilized by freeing its peritoneal attachments and dividing the vas deferens or round ligament. With traction, the ipsilateral dome of the bladder should be able to reach the level proximal to the iliac vessels. **Additional mobility can be achieved by dividing the contralateral superior vesical artery.** The ipsilateral ureter is identified as it crosses the iliac vessels, mobilized, and divided just above the diseased segment. An anterior cystotomy, generally created in a vertical or oblique fashion, is frequently made to facilitate manual displacement of the bladder toward the ipsilateral ureter. The ureter is delivered into the lumen of the bladder at the ipsilateral superolateral aspect of the dome, followed by the tension-free anastomosis with or without a submucosal tunnel. **The ipsilateral bladder dome is secured to the psoas minor tendon or the psoas major muscle using several absorbable sutures. Care should be taken to avoid injury to the genitofemoral nerve and the femoral nerve in the vicinity when placing these sutures.** Alternatively, psoas fixation may be performed before ureteroneocystostomy. A double-J stent is used usually, followed by closure of cystotomy with absorbable sutures (Fig. 38–28).

Relative to simple ureteroneocystostomy, psoas hitch can provide an additional 5 cm of length. Relative to the Boari flap, the advantages of psoas hitch include increased technical simplicity and decreased risk for vascular compromise and voiding difficulties. The success rate of ureteroneocystostomy with a psoas hitch is over 85% in both adults and children based on recent reports (Mathews and Marshall, 1997; Ahn and Loughlin, 2001). Complications occur uncommonly but have included urinary fistula, ureteral obstruction, bowel injury, iliac vein injury, and urosepsis (Fig. 38–29).

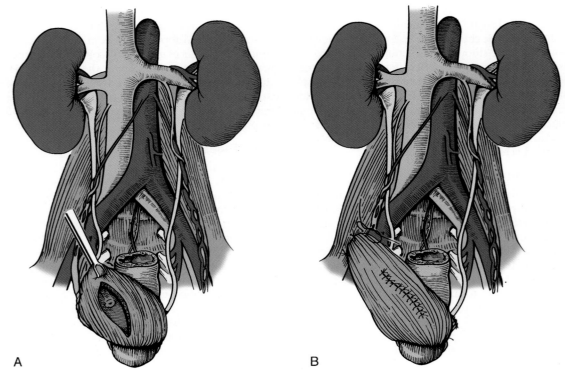

**Figure 38–28.** **A,** In psoas hitch, an anterior cystotomy is performed after bladder mobilization. **B,** The bladder dome is fixed to the ipsilateral psoas tendon, and the ureteral reimplantation is completed in a tension-free manner.

## Laparoscopic Psoas Hitch

Ureteroneocystostomy with psoas hitch has been performed laparoscopically with success (Nezhat et al, 2004). Preoperative ureteral stenting is generally performed, and the procedure is typically completed via the transperitoneal approach. Overall, the clinical experience with such a procedure is quite limited in the literature. However, based on the short-term and intermediate-term follow-up data to date, the clinical outcomes appear to be satisfactory and equivalent in experienced hands.

## Open Boari Flap

When the diseased ureteral segment is too long or when ureteral mobility is too limited to perform a tension-free ureteroureterostomy, a Boari flap may be a useful alternative. Boari first described the use of this technique in the canine model in 1894. **A Boari flap can be constructed to bridge a 10- to 15-cm ureteral defect, and a spiraled bladder flap can reach the renal pelvis in some circumstances, especially on the right side.** As in a psoas hitch, evaluation of bladder function should be performed preoperatively in addition to the ureteral evaluation. Bladder outlet obstruction and neurogenic dysfunction, if present, should be addressed preoperatively. **A small bladder capacity is likely to be associated with difficult or inadequate Boari flap creation, warranting consideration of alternative methods in the preoperative surgical planning.**

In the Boari flap procedure, a Pfannenstiel incision may be used at the time of surgery, although a midline incision is preferred and allows easier access to the upper ureter. The bladder

is mobilized from its peritoneal attachments, and the umbilical ligaments are divided. The contralateral bladder pedicle is divided and ligated, allowing greater mobility toward the ipsilateral ureter, and the ipsilateral bladder pedicle including the superior vesical artery is preserved. The affected ureter is carefully mobilized, with care being taken to preserve its blood supply. The diseased segment is then excised. After the identification of the ipsilateral superior vesical artery or one of its branches, a posterolateral bladder flap is outlined based on this vascular supply. The flap continues obliquely across the anterior bladder wall, with the base of the flap being at least 4 cm in width and the tip of the flap being at least 3 cm in width. The flap length should equal the estimated ureteral defect plus an addition of 3 to 4 cm if a nonrefluxing anastomosis is planned. Furthermore, the ratio of flap length to base width should not be greater than 3:1 to help minimize flap ischemia.

After bladder flap creation, the distal end of the flap is pexed to the psoas minor tendon or psoas major muscle with several absorbable sutures. The ureter is delivered through a small opening created in the posterior flap, and a tension-free mucosa-to-mucosa refluxing anastomosis is performed after spatulation of the distal ureteral end. Alternatively, a nonrefluxing tunneled anastomosis can be used. The flap is then tubularized anteriorly and closed using absorbable suture. Furthermore, the ureteral adventitia may be secured to the distal aspect of the flap and then the base of the flap may be secured to the psoas (Fig. 38–30).

The number of reported patients treated with a Boari flap is small, yet the results are good if a well-vascularized flap is used (Ockerblad, 1947; Scott and Greenberg, 1972;

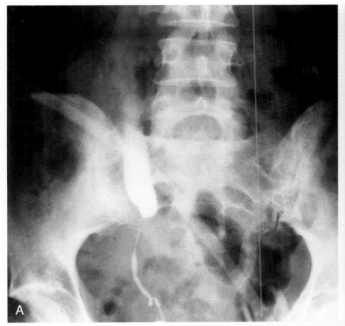

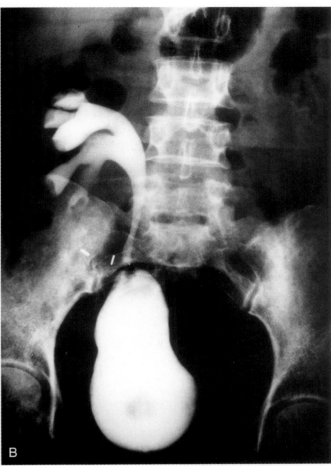

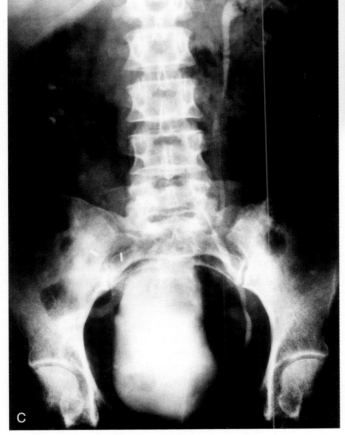

**Figure 38–29.** A female patient presented with right distal ureteral stricture. **A,** Preoperative retrograde pyelogram shows ureteral dilation proximal to the stricture site. **B** and **C,** Postoperative voiding cystourethrogram and IVP following a psoas hitch procedure.

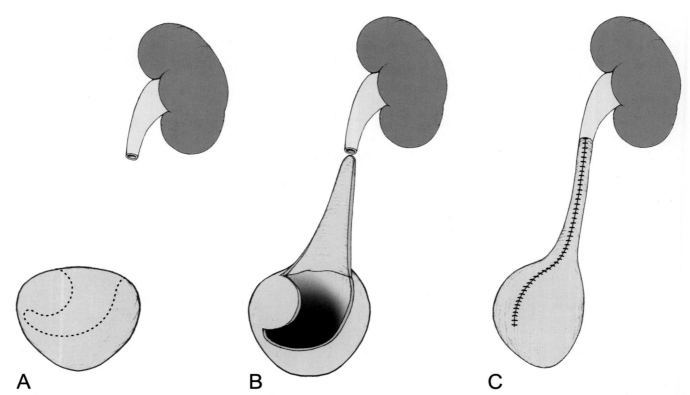

**A**      **B**      **C**

**Figure 38–30.** **A,** In Boari flap, the intended flap is first marked on the anterior and lateral aspects of the mobilized bladder. **B,** The flap is created, ensuring good vascular supply. **C,** Ureteroneocystostomy is completed, with the longitudinal bladder tube closure.

Thompson and Ross, 1974; Middleton, 1980; Benson et al, 1990; Motiwala et al, 1990) (Fig. 38–31). The most common complication is clearly recurrent stricture formation, resulting from either ischemia or excessive tension on the anastomosis. Rare pseudodiverticulum has also been reported (Berzeg et al, 2003).

## Laparoscopic Boari Flap

Laparoscopic Boari flap has been uncommonly yet successfully performed in the clinical setting. Kavoussi and colleagues reported three successful cases for distal ureteral obstruction, in which a transperitoneal approach was used (Fugita et al, 2001). Following the same principles in open surgery, the bladder flap was created and anastomosed to the ureteral end over a stent in a tension-free, watertight manner. Operative time ranged from 120 to 330 minutes, and blood loss ranged from 400 to 600 mL. Two patients were discharged home within 3 days postoperatively whereas 1 patient was hospitalized for 13 days for *Clostridium difficile* colitis. With a follow-up of over 6 months there was radiographically demonstrated patency of the anastomosis. In this report the information of the length of distal ureteral stricture was not available. However, in the clinical experience of one of the authors (T.H.), ureteral loss of 8 to 12 cm can be comfortably bridged with Boari flap in the laparoscopic setting, as in open surgery.

## Renal Descensus

Renal mobilization, which was originally described by Popescu in 1964, can provide additional length to bridge a defect in the upper ureter or decrease tension on a ureteral repair (Harada et al, 1964; Passerini-Glazel et al, 1994). A transperitoneal, subcostal, midline, or paramedian incision may be used to gain access to the kidney and the appropriate level of the ureter. After entry to Gerota's fascia, the kidney is completely mobilized and rotated inferiorly and medially on its vascular pedicle. The lower pole of the kidney is then secured to the retroperitoneal muscle using several absorbable sutures. Up to 8 cm of additional length may be gained using this technique. In such cases, the renal vessels, especially the renal vein, limit the extent to which the kidney can be mobilized. As a solution, the technique for division of the renal vein with reanastomosis more inferiorly to the inferior vena cava may be performed but rarely applied clinically.

## Intubated Ureterotomy

The Davis intubated ureterotomy has been described previously in this chapter. Because of the development of more effective surgical treatment alternatives, this procedure is described primarily for historical interest. An intubated ureterotomy is generally used for a ureteral stricture too long for conventional ureteroureterostomy or ureteroneocystostomy and has been performed to treat stricture up to 10 to 12 cm in length. An innovative modification to this procedure has incorporated a buccal mucosal patch graft in a small number of patients with good results (Naude, 1999).

## Transureteroureterostomy

The initial clinical application of transureteroureterostomy was described by Higgins in 1934. In the management of ureteral stricture, this procedure may be used when ureteral

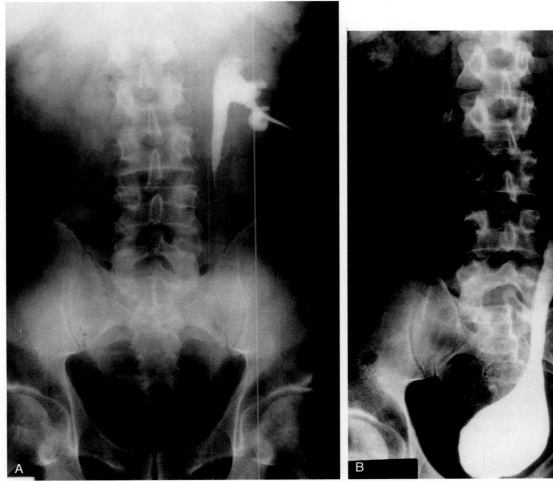
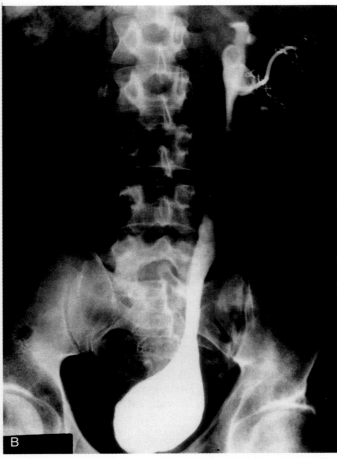

**Figure 38–31.** **A,** Preoperative nephrostogram of a patient with left proximal ureteral injury after aortobifemoral bypass surgery. **B,** Postoperative voiding cystourethrogram after a Boari flap procedure.

length is insufficient for anastomosis to the bladder (Brannan, 1975). **The only absolute contraindication is insufficient length of the donor ureter to reach the contralateral recipient ureter in a tension-free manner. However, any disease process that may affect both ureters represents a relative contraindication. Absolute contraindications include the presence of a diseased recipient ureter or a donor ureter of inadequate length. Relative contraindications include history of nephrolithiasis, retroperitoneal fibrosis, urothelial malignancy, chronic pyelonephritis, and abdominopelvic radiation. Reflux to the recipient ureter, if present, needs to be identified and corrected simultaneously.** Therefore, a voiding cystogram should be performed preoperatively, in addition to the other imaging and endoscopic studies previously described for thorough evaluation of both ureters.

In performing a transureteroureterostomy, a midline, transperitoneal approach is used to gain access to both ureters. After medial colonic mobilization, the affected ureter is mobilized, preserving the adventitia with the ureteral blood supply, and divided just proximal to the level of obstruction. The contralateral colon is medially mobilized. Only the portion of

recipient ureter needed for the anastomosis is exposed, which is generally 5 cm proximal to the level of division of the affected ureter. A tunnel under the sigmoid colon mesentery is created proximal to the inferior mesenteric artery to avoid ureteral tethering by this vessel, after which the donor ureter is then brought through the tunnel to the recipient side. Mobilization of the recipient ureter should be minimized to help preserve the integrity of its vascular supply. An anteromedial ureterotomy is made in the recipient ureter, which is then anastomosed to the spatulated donor ureteral end in a tension-free, watertight manner using either interrupted or running absorbable sutures. A double-J ureteral stent is usually passed from the donor renal pelvis, through the anastomosis and into the bladder. A second ureteral stent may also be placed throughout the length of the recipient ureter if the ureter is found to be adequately large in diameter.

The clinical success of transureteroureterostomy has been demonstrated by multiple investigators. Hendren and Hensle (1980) reported 75 cases of pediatric transureteroureterostomy without compromising a single recipient kidney. Hodges and associates (1980) reported a similar success in a large group of children and adults. However, two patients required revision due to ureteral kinking by the inferior mesenteric artery. The successful application of transureteroureterostomy was further confirmed more recently by Pesce and colleagues (2001). In two other recent studies, nephrectomy for ureteral stenosis was found to be rarely necessary (Mure et al, 2000; Sugarbaker et al, 2003). Laparoscopic transureteroureterostomy has not been demonstrated in the human setting thus far.

## Open Ileal Ureteral Substitution

Surgical management of long length of ureteral defect or loss, especially the proximal ureter, is particularly challenging (Benson et al, 1990). Reconstruction of the ureter with tissue lined with urothelium is most preferable because urothelium is not absorptive and is resistant to the inflammatory and potentially carcinogenic effects of urine (Harzmann et al, 1986). Incorporation of other tissue in ureteral repair is, therefore, reserved for situations in which a defect cannot be bridged by other methods or the bladder is unsuitable for reconstruction. In such a scenario, ileal interposition has been demonstrated to be a satisfactory option for very complicated ureteral reconstruction. On the other hand, the appendix and fallopian tube have been found to be unreliable ureteral substitutes.

Shoemaker reported the first ileal ureter in a woman with tuberculous involvement of the urinary tract in 1909. Later, the metabolic and physiologic effects of the ileal ureter have been investigated in the canine model (Hinman and Oppenheimer, 1958; Martinez et al, 1965). When an isoperistaltic segment of ileum is directly anastomosed to the bladder, reflux and renal pelvic pressure increase are generally seen only during voiding. The retrograde transmission of intravesical pressure is dependent on the length of ileum segment used in interposition and the voiding pressure. In patients with ileal segments longer than 15 cm, Waldner and colleagues (1999) found no reflux into the renal pelvis in a report involving 19 cases of ileal ureter with refluxing ileovesical anastomosis. Comparing dogs with tapered versus nontapered ileal segments, Waters and coworkers (1981) found no difference in renal perfusion pressure or metabolic derangements.

A large clinical experience in ileal ureter involving 89 patients was reported by Boxer and associates (1979). Only 12% of patients with normal preoperative renal function developed significant metabolic problems postoperatively, and preoperative renal function was identified to be an important prognostic factor. In a separate study, nearly half of those with a serum creatinine value of greater than 2 mg/dL developed hyperchloremic metabolic acidosis, requiring conversion to a conduit (Koch and McDougal, 1985). In the same study, patients with bladder dysfunction also experienced more complications. There are no sufficient clinical data to establish the superiority of a tapered segment, a nonrefluxing anastomosis, or a shorter, segmental replacement over a standard ileal substitution (Waters et al, 1981). **Given the above, the general contraindications to an ileal ureteral substitution are baseline renal insufficiency with a serum creatinine value of greater than 2 mg/dL, bladder dysfunction or outlet obstruction, inflammatory bowel disease, or radiation enteritis.**

Before the surgical procedure, a full mechanical and antibiotic bowel preparation is often used. A long midline incision is made. The ipsilateral colon is mobilized medially, and the affected ureter is dissected proximally to the level of healthy tissue. The proximal anastomosis may be performed at the level of the renal pelvis if the entire upper ureter is unhealthy. The length of the ureteral defect is measured, and an appropriate segment of distal ileum is chosen. The segment should be at least 15 cm away from the ileocecal valve, and adequate blood supply should be confirmed before harvesting. The mesentery is usually divided more extensively than with a standard ileal conduit to provide greater mobility. Occasionally, a segment of colon may be more accessible than ileum and is harvested using the similar surgical principles. **In the presence of a scarred or intrarenal pelvis, ileocalycostomy may be performed** (McQuitty et al, 1995). In this circumstance, excision of a piece of lower pole renal parenchymal tissue is helpful in preventing stenosis at the anastomosis, as in a typical ureterocalicostomy. After bowel division, the distal end of the ileal segment is marked for orientation and bowel-to-bowel continuity is reestablished. A small window is made in the colonic mesentery, through which the segment of ileum is delivered laterally. Alternatively, the cecum and ascending colon can be reflected superiorly to avoid mesenteric window creation in performing right ureteral reconstruction. The orientation of the ileal segment is checked to ensure isoperistalsis, and the anastomoses are performed at the level of the renal pelvis or lower pole calyx and at the bladder (Fig. 38–32). Bilateral ileal ureteral substitution may be achieved by using a longer segment that travels intraperitoneally from one kidney to the other and then to the bladder. An alternative is to use two separate bowel segments.

Perioperative complications associated with ileal ureter include early urinary extravasation or urinoma formation and obstruction from edema, a mucus plug, or a kink in the segment. Ischemic necrosis of the ileal segment may occur and should be considered if signs of an acute abdomen are present. Significant electrolyte abnormalities and renal insufficiency are unusual if preoperative renal function is normal. **Patients with worsening metabolic abnormalities associated with a progressively dilating ileal ureter should be evaluated for vesicourethral dysfunction. Furthermore, malignancy arising from an ileal ureter segment has been reported in four cases in the literature** (Austen and Kalble, 2004), **and it is recommended that regular endoscopic examination should be performed starting at the third postoperative year for early detection of such malignancy.** However, Matiaga and colleagues (2003) have confirmed the safety and reliability of ileal ureter creation for complex ureteral stricture/loss in 18 patients with a mean follow-up of 18.6 months. This conclusion was further supported by Bonfig and associates (2004) in another contemporary series involving 43 patients with a mean follow-up of 40.8 months.

## Laparoscopic Ileal Ureteral Substitution

The clinical experience in laparoscopic ileal ureteral substitution is limited worldwide, yet this procedure appears to hold significant promise. Gill and coworkers (2000) reported successful laparoscopic ileal ureter replacement using a transperitoneal, three-port approach. The entire procedure, including free-hand suturing and knot-tying, was performed using the intracorporeal laparoscopic technique. Although the operative procedure was relatively long at 8 hours, there was minimal

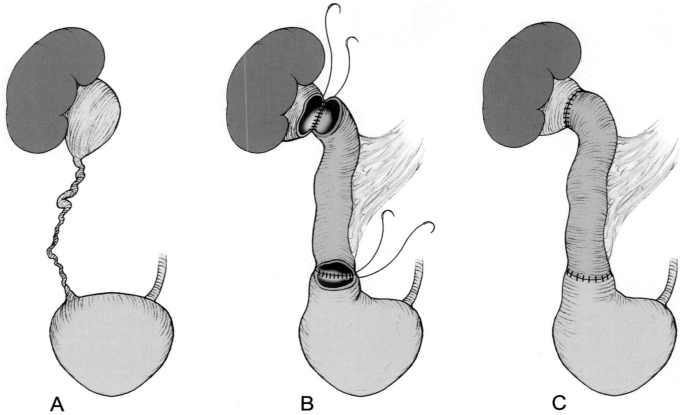

**Figure 38–32.    A,** In ileal ureteral substitution, the affected ureter is first identified and dissected, which is followed by removal of the diseased portion. **B,** A piece of ileum is brought through the colonic mesentery to bridge the renal pelvis and the bladder. **C,** Both proximal and distal anastomoses are completed in a full-thickness, watertight, tension-free manner.

postoperative morbidity and a short hospital stay (of 4 days) as in most other laparoscopic procedures.

### Autotransplantation

In 1963, Hardy performed the first autotransplantation for a patient with proximal ureteral injury. Since then, clinical autotransplantation has been performed for a variety of problems, including extensive ureteral loss or stricture (Hardy, 1963; Novick and Stewart, 1981; Chuang et al, 1999; Wotkowicz and Libertino, 2004). Generally, autotransplant is considered when the contralateral kidney is absent or poorly functioning or when other methods for ureteral substitution or repair are not feasible. The kidney is harvested with maximal vessel length as in a typical live donor nephrectomy for allotransplantation, and the renal vessels are anastomosed to the iliac vessels to reestablish renal perfusion. A healthy segment of the proximal ureter is anastomosed to the bladder (Bodie et al, 1986). Alternatively, the ipsilateral renal pelvis may be anastomosed directly to the bladder (Kennelly et al, 1993).

Recently, laparoscopy has been successfully incorporated in autotransplantation for severe ureteral loss. Nephrectomy can be performed laparoscopically as in any typical laparoscopic donor nephrectomy, followed by renal graft retrieval, bench preparation, and autotransplantation in the ipsilateral iliac fossa via a Gibson incision using the standard open surgical techniques (Fabrizio et al, 2000; Meng et al, 2003; Bluebond-

Langner et al, 2004). The use of laparoscopy in autotransplantation has been shown to provide reduced postoperative analgesic need and faster recovery because a large open upper abdominal or flank incision for renal harvest is avoided. Laparoscopic nephrectomy in autotransplantation is most commonly performed transperitoneally. However, retroperitoneal approach for such purpose has been applied successfully by Gill and colleagues (2000).

## URETEROENTERIC ANASTOMOTIC STRICTURE
### Incidence and Etiology

Several factors determine the incidence of stricture formation at the anastomosis of the ureter and intestine at the time of urinary diversion. The longest follow-up data available are for urinary conduits, in which the stricture rate is between 4% and 8% and more common on the left (Schmidt et al, 1973; Skinner et al, 1980). Factors potentially influencing outcome in this population include the technique used for ureteral dissection, the segment of bowel used for the diversion, and the type of anastomosis performed. Because ureteral ischemia is central to the etiology of ureteroenteric strictures, careful attention to dissection is necessary to prevent complications. The ureteral blood supply runs parallel to the ureter in the adventitia. Although ureteral mobilization is necessary to approximate the ureter and bowel and prevent tension on the anastomosis, stripping the ureter of its surrounding adventitia can lead to distal ureteral ischemia and stricture formation. **When performing an ileal conduit, the left ureter is brought underneath the sigmoid mesentery just overlying the aorta. The additional length and dissection needed on the left and the possibility of angulation around the inferior mesenteric artery may lead to a higher incidence of stricture formation on the left** (Mansson et al, 1989).

Much controversy exists over the choice of bowel segment employed for conduit diversion. One theoretical advantage to the use of colon is the feasibility of performing a nonrefluxing anastomosis. However, the reported incidence of renal deterioration with a nonrefluxing versus a refluxing uretero-colonic anastomosis has been mixed, and there does not appear to be a clear advantage with respect to renal function and colonization to a nonrefluxing anastomosis. The issues influencing stricture formation in continent urinary diversions become even more complex, owing to the variety of bowel segments, reservoir configurations, and types of anas-

tomoses available for reconstruction. **The reported rate of ureteroenteric anastomotic stricture after continent diversion is 4% to 25%, with the majority presenting within the first 2 years** (Lugagne et al, 1997; Weijerman et al, 1998). Despite the paucity of randomized studies, there is a growing body of evidence in the literature that the risk of obstruction with a nonrefluxing anastomosis is significantly higher than that of a refluxing anastomosis. Pantuck and associates (2000) compared 60 nonrefluxing ureteroenteric anastomoses with 56 direct, refluxing anastomoses and found the long-term stricture rate to be 13% and 1.7%, respectively. With a mean follow-up of 41 months, there was no significant difference in the two groups with respect to hydronephrosis, pyelonephritis, nephrolithiasis, or renal insufficiency. Similarly, Roth and colleagues (1996) found a greater than fivefold increase in ureteral strictures in the group undergoing a nonrefluxing anastomosis. Their data also indicated that the risk of obstruction was unrelated to surgical expertise.

Studer and coworkers (1995) have reported a randomized study evaluating a nonrefluxing versus a refluxing anastomosis into an isoperistaltic afferent ileal limb. Thirteen percent of nonrefluxing anastomoses resulted in stricture formation, as compared with 3% of refluxing anastomoses. Although there is no clear evidence that reflux into an adult kidney is detrimental, it is clear that obstruction is quite harmful to renal function. These studies and others support the use of a refluxing anastomosis in low-pressure continent reservoirs.

## Evaluation

A minimally invasive means of screening the upper tracts in patients who have undergone any type of urinary diversion is a renal ultrasound. In addition, patients with renal colic, recurrent urinary tract infection, or loss of renal function will require evaluation. In patients with hydronephrosis on ultrasound, an intravenous pyelogram and contrast study of the conduit or reservoir will provide information on the length and location of the stricture. If a stone or recurrent tumor is suggested, CT or MRI may be helpful. Diuretic renography is indicated in patients with chronic hydronephrosis to assess differential renal function and to confirm the presence of functional obstruction. If hydronephrosis is present but renal function is insufficient for intravenous urography or renography, placement of a nephrostomy tube and performance of an antegrade nephrostogram is both diagnostic and therapeutic. This approach is also useful before endoscopic intervention and clarifies stricture length, which aids in surgical planning.

## Indications for Intervention

Not all patients with urinary diversion and hydronephrosis require intervention. **Most patients with a long-term urinary conduit will have an element of chronic hydronephrosis that is not secondary to obstruction. In this population, a decrease in renal function or loss of reflux on a routine loop-o-gram should prompt diuretic renography to quantitatively assess for functional obstruction.** Indications for intervention in patients with diversions and hydronephrosis include pain, infection, and renal insufficiency associated with functional obstruction. Although recurrence of transitional cell carcinoma at the level of the anastomosis is uncommon, the radiographic picture of an irregular mass at the level of the stricture and the rapid progression of obstruction and loss of renal function should prompt further evaluation and intervention (Tsuji et al, 1996).

A particularly challenging subset of patients includes those undergoing urinary diversion as part of a pelvic exenteration for gynecologic malignancy. Penalver and coworkers (1998) reported on 66 patients, 95% of who had undergone previous pelvic irradiation. Early and late complications at the ureteroenteric anastomosis were 22% and 10%, respectively. Eighty-five percent of their postoperative complications were managed successfully by conservative measures such as percutaneous nephrostomy.

## Endourologic Management

Endourologic management of ureteroenteric strictures has evolved in a manner analogous to that for ureteral stricture disease. Whereas the initial procedures involved simple balloon dilatation and stent placement, unsatisfactory results led to incisional techniques using electrocautery, and more recently, lasers were applied utilizing both fluoroscopic and direct endoscopic control. The present-day state-of-the-art incisional technique for endoureterotomy includes small-caliber flexible ureteroscopic instrumentation along with holmium laser incision (Siegel et al, 1982; Muench et al, 1987; Cornud et al, 1992; Delvecchio et al, 2000; Laven et al, 2001, 2003).

**Endourologic management of ureteroenteric or uretero- colic strictures, unlike the management of ureteral strictures, favors antegrade management.** As such, endourologic procedures typically begin with antegrade percutaneous access. Simple percutaneous drainage is continued to allow relief of any associated infection- or obstruction-related renal dysfunction. Once the patient is clinically stable, fluoroscopic control is utilized to pass a guide wire in an antegrade fashion across the anastomotic stricture, over which a balloon catheter can be positioned and inflated until the waist disappears. Stents are a routine part of the endourologic management, and these are generally inserted in this same antegrade fashion. However, because of difficulty with mucus plugging of stents in this setting, many centers routinely utilize an internal/external stent, which can be easily flushed or changed over a wire. In addition, retrograde looposcopic access can be combined with percutaneous access and antegrade passage of a wire. With through-and-through control, the anastomosis can be visualized fluoroscopically or, preferably, with direct ureteroscopic, looposcopic, or trans-stomascopic visualization. Any number of procedures can then be utilized for the dilatation itself, including balloon dilatation alone, electroincision with an electrode or hot wire cutting balloon, or holmium laser incision. In all cases, a stent is placed, usually for 4 to 8 weeks.

Balloon dilatation of ureteroenteric strictures was one of the first endourologic forms of management used, and fortunately long-term results are available. Notably, short-term reports using high-pressure balloon dilation have demonstrated success rates as high as 61% (Ravery et al, 1998). Alternatively, Shapiro and colleagues (1988) reported balloon dilatation for 37 benign ureteroenteric strictures in 29 patients. Only 6 (16%) were considered to have a successful result at least 1 year after interventional treatment, and repeat

dilatations were often required to maintain ureteral patency. Similarly, Kwak and coworkers (1995) achieved an overall success rate of less than 30% at 9 months for patients undergoing antegrade balloon dilatation of ureteroenteric strictures. More recently, DiMarco and associates (2001) reported a 5% three-year success rate in 52 balloon dilations of ureteroenteric anastomotic strictures.

Results of cautery wire balloon incision have also been reported in patients treated for ureteroenteric strictures (Lin et al, 1999). For benign strictures, a stent-free long-term patency was achieved in only 30% of patients. Meretyk and colleagues (1991) reviewed the long-term results of endourologic management of ureteroenteric anastomotic strictures at Washington University. In that study, 15 patients with 19 ureteroenteric strictures were followed for an average of 2.5 years. An antegrade approach was used most frequently and was usually combined with electroincision. A 57% long-term stent-free patency rate was achieved, even with follow-up longer than 2 years. **Whereas long-term patency of most endoscopic procedures seems to be in the range of 50%, such approaches are still used preferentially as the initial intervention, reserving open operative management for those patients failing endourologic intervention** (Kramolowsky et al, 1987, 1988).

Cornud and associates (1996) reported their long-term results with percutaneous electroincision of ureterointestinal anastomotic strictures and specifically compared the results of fluoroscopic and endoscopic guidance. Twenty-seven patients were followed for longer than 1 year after stent removal, and an overall patency rate of 71% was reported. These investigators found better results when direct endoscopic control was combined with fluoroscopic guidance, compared with fluoroscopic guidance alone. In that report, right common iliac artery damage was reported during electroincision in one patient who had the procedure performed under fluoroscopic guidance alone. As a result, direct visual approaches have been favored for the management of ureteroenteric or ureterocolic anastomotic strictures, and the holmium laser has proven to be an excellent incisional tool. Endoureterotomy is typically performed antegrade, and success rates ranging from 50% to 80% have been reported (Singal et al, 1997; Laven et al, 2001; Watterson et al, 2002). These reports suggest the left side is more resistant to management, because the majority of the failures occurred on the left side in one series (Laven et al, 2003). **When considering endoscopic incision of a left ureteroenteric stricture, the risk of hemorrhage is a consideration because the sigmoid mesentery can be in close proximity. This, taken with the lower success rates of all endoscopic approaches on the left side, supports serious consideration to open repair when treating left ureteroenteric strictures.**

## Open Intervention

**Open surgical management of ureterointestinal strictures is technically challenging and associated with a longer recovery than endoscopic options but is often necessary due to the low success rates of less invasive alternatives, in particular balloon dilatation** (DiMarco et al, 2001). When undertaking open repair, it is optimal to sterilize the urine and prepare the bowel preoperatively. If a cutaneous stoma is present, it is prepared into the field and the conduit or reservoir is drained with a Foley catheter during the procedure. Placement of a nephrostomy tube and ureteral stent is helpful. Through a midline incision, the conduit or reservoir is identified and preserved, the colon is reflected medially, and the proximal, dilated ureter is identified and traced down to the area of the previous anastomosis. Care is taken to preserve the adventitia and associated blood supply. If enough ureteral length is available, the ureter can be transected proximal to the stricture, spatulated, and anastomosed to a convenient area of the bowel. If the dissection is particularly difficult, there may be significant trauma to the conduit or reservoir, requiring major revision. In addition, insufficient ureteral length may require an additional segment of bowel to interpose between the ureter and the reservoir. The anastomosis is carried out over a No. 7 Fr stent, and a drain is left in situ. The stent remains for 4 to 6 weeks. Good long-term success rates have been reported with open repair, as high as 80% (Laven et al, 2003). As expected, strictures longer than 1 cm were more likely to recur and the left side had lower success rates (DiMarco et al, 2001; Laven et al, 2003) Major complications were encountered in 11% of cases in one series (DiMarco et al, 2001).

## KEY POINTS: URETEROENTERIC STRICTURES

- Whereas long-term patency of most endourologic procedures for ureteroenteric strictures seems to be in the range of 50%, such approaches are still used preferentially as the initial intervention, reserving open operative management for those patients failing endourologic intervention.

- When considering endoscopic incision of a left ureteroenteric stricture, the risk of hemorrhage is a consideration because the sigmoid mesentery can be in close proximity. This, taken with the lower success rates of all endoscopic approaches on the left side, supports serious consideration to open repair when treating left ureteroenteric strictures.

- Good long-term success rates have been reported with open repair, as high as 80%. As expected, strictures longer than 1 cm were more likely to recur and the left side had lower success rates.

## RETROPERITONEAL FIBROSIS
### Presentation and Etiology

**Retroperitoneal fibrosis (RPF) is typically characterized by the presence of an inflammatory, fibrotic process in the retroperitoneum causing compression of the retroperitoneal structures including the ureters.** RPF most commonly affects patients who are 40 to 60 years of age. However, more than 30 cases of RPF have been reported in patients younger than 18 years of age (van Bommel, 2002). RPF cases have a male predominance, with a male-to-female ratio of 2 to 3:1. The true incidence is unknown but has been estimated to be 1:200,000 to 1:500,000 per year.

**The retroperitoneal fibrotic mass generally centers around the distal aorta at L4-L5 and wraps around the ureters, leading to hydronephrosis via extrinsic compression on the ureters or interference with ureteral peristalsis** (Lepor and Walsh, 1979; Koep and Zuidema, 1987). In most patients, the presenting symptom is pain in the lower back and/or flank. The pain, which is typically dull, noncolicky, and unchanged with posture, may radiate to the lower abdomen or groin. Furthermore, the pain is often relieved by aspirin rather than narcotics. Other symptoms include weight loss, anorexia, nausea, generalized malaise, fever, hypertension, and oliguria/anuria. The mass may compress the inferior vena cava, resulting in deep venous thrombosis and lower extremity edema (Rhee et al, 1994). The mass may extend proximally to the renal hilum and encase the renal vein, resulting in renal vein hypertension and subsequent gross hematuria (Powell et al, 2000). Aortic obstruction and involvement of the mediastinum, the biliary system, the mesentery, and the kidney itself are rare (Tripodi et al, 1998; Azuma et al, 1999; Dejaco et al, 1999; Klisnick et al, 1999). Distal extension to the bifurcation of the iliac vessels may occur, and extension to spermatic cord with scrotal involvement has been reported (Palmer and Rosenthal, 1999; Schulte-Baukloh et al, 1999). Duration of symptoms before diagnosis is usually 4 to 6 months, and approximately half of the patients present with fibrosis that has caused significant ureteral obstruction and symptoms secondary to uremia.

**In approximately 70% of the cases, the disease is idiopathic.** However, there is evidence that idiopathic RPF may be related to an immune-mediated periaortitis. Ceroid, a complex polymer of oxidized lipids and protein found in atherosclerotic plaques, has been suggested as the antigen initiating the inflammatory response (Parums et al, 1991). Indeed, a higher incidence of aortic aneurysms has been identified in patients with RPF recently (Breems et al, 2000).

**RPF usually presents as an isolated disease entity.** However, it may present as part of multifocal fibrosclerosis, a rare syndrome characterized by fibrosis involving multiple organ systems. In such a scenario, the clinical presentation may include RPF, sclerosing mediastinitis, sclerosing cholangitis, orbital pseudotumor, and Riedel's thyroiditis (Dehner and Coffin, 1998; Özgen and Cila, 2000). The pathogenesis of these disorders is unknown but appears to be autoimmune.

Among the 30% of RPF patients who have an identifiable cause, **drugs such as methysergide (Sansert) and other ergot alkaloids are most commonly associated with RPF.** β-Adrenergic blockers and phenacetin have also been implicated. The exact pathophysiology of drug-induced RPF remains unknown. Other causes of RPF include malignancies such as lymphoma, the most common malignancy in RPF cases, and multiple myeloma, carcinoid, pancreatic cancer, prostate cancer, and sarcoma (Webb and Dawson-Edwards, 1967; Usher et al, 1977). Radiation therapy for retroperitoneal malignancy is also known to produce a residual fibrotic mass leading to secondary ureteral obstruction. Abdominal aortic aneurysm may cause significant retroperitoneal inflammatory reaction, leading to fibrosis and ureteral obstruction. In addition, infectious causes such as tuberculosis, *Actinomyces,* gonorrhea, or schistosomiasis have been suggested in the pathogenesis of RPF.

Association of RPF with membranous glomerulonephritis has also been documented in the literature (Mercadal et al, 2000; Shirota et al, 2002). The exact etiology remains unclear, although the association has been speculated to be secondary to an unknown antigen triggering a systemic immune response that leads to RPF. Association of RPF with ankylosing spondylitis and Wegener's granulomatosis have also been reported, further suggesting an underlying immune etiology in some patients (Izzedine et al, 2002; LeBlanc et al, 2002).

Pathologically, the typical gross appearance of RPF is that of a smooth, flat, tan-colored, dense mass enveloping the surrounding retroperitoneal structures. It is also known to invade the ureter or psoas muscle. Histologically, the appearance of RPF is that of a nonspecific inflammatory process that varies with stage of the disease. Early in the disease, affected tissue consists mainly of collagen bundles with capillary proliferation and inflammatory cells including lymphocytes, plasma cells, and fibroblasts. In the later stage, the mass becomes relatively acellular and avascular, consisting of sheets of hypocellular collagen. RPF secondary to malignancy is often histologically indistinguishable from idiopathic RPF, and it can be identified only based on the demonstration of small islands of tumor cells within the fibrotic mass.

## Evaluation

**In most RPF patients, the clinical symptoms are generally nonspecific and physical examination is usually unrevealing. Laboratory evaluation may reveal an elevated erythrocyte sedimentation rate, moderate leukocytosis, anemia, and variable renal insufficiency with associated electrolyte abnormalities.** If the overall renal function is normal, an intravenous pyelogram (IVP) or CT with contrast medium enhancement may be performed. Typical IVP findings include hydronephrosis with medial deviation of the proximal ureter and midureter and a smoothly tapered ureter at the level of obstruction. Urinary obstruction is usually bilateral, but unilateral cases have been described. Uncommonly, there are patients with symptoms of urinary obstruction but very little hydronephrosis on imaging. CT typically reveals hydronephrosis associated with a well-delineated retroperitoneal soft tissue mass enveloping the great vessels and the ureters (Fig. 38–33). If the patient has significant renal impairment, a retrograde pyelogram may be performed, demon-strating similar findings as in IVP. In the radiographic evaluation of RPF, MRI can also be helpful, because the mass has characteristic T1- and T2-weighted images. If a kidney is suspected to be nonfunctioning, a radioisotope renogram needs to be considered to determine differential renal function because it may affect surgical planning. Representative biopsies of the mass need to be obtained percutaneously or at the time of open or laparoscopic ureterolysis to rule out malignancy and allow one to proceed with treatment for RPF.

## Management

### Initial Management

The initial management of RPF depends on the patient's clinical status. Patients with hydronephrosis and uremia should be emergently decompressed by either percutaneous nephrostomy or indwelling ureteral stents. The advantages to placing ureteral stents include the opportunity to perform retrograde pyelograms to evaluate the anatomy and the convenience of internal drainage. Interestingly, ureteral stent placement is usually not difficult to perform in the setting of ureteral obstruction due to RPF. In a critically ill patient with electrolyte abnormalities and little or no urine output, nephrostomy tube placement can be performed at the bedside with local anesthesia. **After renal decompression, the patient needs to be monitored closely for postobstructive diuresis, renal function status, and appropriate replacement of fluids and electrolytes.**

After the initial management, an attempt to search for the etiology of RPF should be made. Methysergide or any other potentially inciting drug, if identified, should be discontinued. Although most patients with malignant RPF have a prior history of malignancy, a thorough search for occult malignancy with careful application of imaging studies is necessary. Biopsy to rule out malignancy, performed percutaneously or at the time of ureterolysis to provide long-term relief of obstruction, needs to be considered. However, some believe that in patients with classic radiographic features on MRI or CT, no lymphadenopathy, and no history of prior malignancy, a biopsy is not essential before medical therapy.

### Medical Management

**Once the diagnosis of idiopathic RPF is made, the most common primary medical management has been corticosteroid therapy.** Although there has been no large clinical series because the disease entity is uncommon, there are approximately 140 cases of idiopathic RPF treated with corticosteroids that resulted in about an 80% clinical response in the medical literature, including having a decrease in size of the mass and improvement in ureteral obstruction or inferior vena cava compression (Kearney et al, 1976; Baker et al, 1987; Adam et al, 1998; Higgins et al, 1998, van Bommel, 2002). The characteristic clinical response to corticosteroid therapy includes resolution of pain and constitutional symptoms within days after treatment, a rapid fall of erythrocyte sedimentation rate, and diuresis. Dose and duration of corticosteroid therapy varied considerably in the literature, but most therapies were of 6 months or greater in duration. Chronic corticosteroid therapy up to 2 years has been shown to provide significant improvement in clinical symptoms and regression of retroperitoneal mass in one recent report involving 12

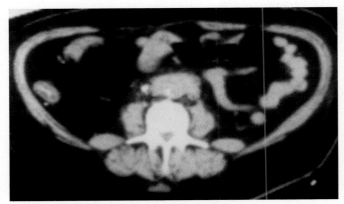

**Figure 38–33.** Typical CT findings of retroperitoneal fibrosis. The study demonstrates the presence of a homogeneous mass obliterating the outline of the great vessels at the lower lumbar area. Note the placement of a stent in the right ureter.

patients (Kardar et al, 2002). Although corticosteroids do not reverse the established fibrosis, further inflammatory reaction and fibrosis with their associated symptomatology and sequelae may be minimized. Therefore, it appears that patients who have the evidence of active inflammation—manifested by increased erythrocyte sedimentation rate, leukocytosis, or active inflammation on a biopsy—are more likely to respond to corticosteroid therapy.

In addition to corticosteroids, several other immunosuppressive agents have been described to provide benefit in idiopathic RPF in isolated case reports, including azathioprine, cyclophosphamide, cyclosporine, and mycophenolate mofetil (Wagenknecht and Hardy, 1981; McDougall and MacDonell, 1991; Grotz et al, 1998; Marzano et al, 2001). Medroxyprogesterone acetate, progesterone, and particularly tamoxifen, a nonsteroidal antiestrogen, have been found to be beneficial in idiopathic RPF in several case reports (Clark et al, 1991; Benson and Baum, 1993; Al-Musawi et al, 1998; Dedeoglu et al, 2000; Puce et al 2000). The exact mechanisms of action of these medications are unclear, but they are believed to inhibit fibroblastic proliferation leading to clinical response.

## Surgical Management: Open Ureterolysis

A ureterolysis may be performed open surgically or laparoscopically, although open surgery has been considered as the standard (Lindell and Lehtonen, 1988; Elashry et al, 1996). It is performed with concomitant biopsy of the mass in patients with an unclear diagnosis as the definitive initial treatment or in those who fail medical therapy. **When open surgery is performed, a midline, transperitoneal abdominal incision is made to allow access to both ureters.** Placement of ureteral catheters or stents before the abdominal incision is advisable to facilitate identification and dissection of the ureters. **Although hydronephrosis may be unilateral on preoperative assessment, the process is generally bilateral, requiring bilateral ureterolysis.** After medial mobilization of the ascending and descending colon, deep biopsies of the mass should be obtained for frozen and permanent section to rule out malignancy. Dissection should begin at the distal, nondilated ureteral segment to avoid injury to the thin, dilated proximal segment. A right-angle clamp can be placed between the ureter and the retroperitoneal mass along the course of the ureter, and the fibrotic tissue is then incised above the clamp. This is repeated throughout the length of the entrapped ureter, using both blunt and sharp dissection techniques to free the affected ureter from its fibrous bed. The ureteral wall may become quite thin at times after the dissection. An inadvertent ureterotomy should be closed with absorbable suture. Ureteral excision with ureteroureterostomy is usually unnecessary.

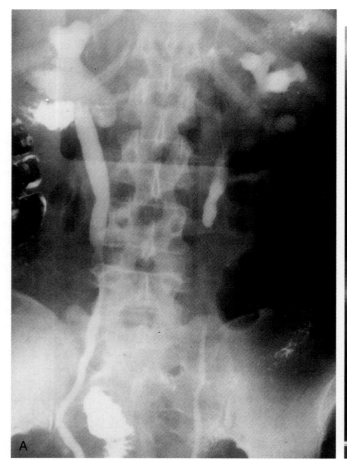 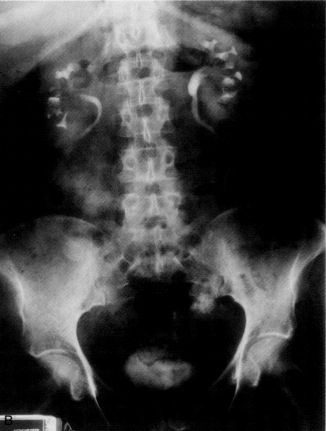

**Figure 38–34.** **A,** Preoperative IVP of a patient with idiopathic retroperitoneal fibrosis shows bilateral hydronephrosis with medial deviation of the ureters. **B,** Postoperative IVP of the same patient after surgical ureterolysis with intraperitoneal omental wrapping.

After bilateral ureterolysis, the ureters should be repositioned and protected from further fibrous entrapment. Several surgical options are available. One option is to retract the ureters laterally and secure the overlying peritoneum medially to the psoas muscle to maintain the ureters in this location. Another option is to close the peritoneum behind the ureters so that the ureters may be displaced anteriorly into the peritoneal cavity (Tresidder et al, 1972). It is important not to obstruct the ureter in the closure of the peritoneum at the ureteral hiatus. In a report on a group of patients with idiopathic RPF undergoing intraperitoneal placement of the ureters or lateral retroperitoneal placement of the ureters, no difference in the radiologic or clinical outcome was found (Barbalias and Liatsikos,1999). In the setting of extensive RPF, a more definitive approach is to surround the ureters with omentum and reposition them within the peritoneal cavity (Carini et al, 1982). To perform the omental wrap, the omentum is first mobilized from its attachment to the transverse colon, followed by its division along its midline with ligation of the small omental vessels up to the gastric attachment. The short gastric vessels are then divided and ligated at the level of the stomach wall, after which the two halves of the omentum can be retracted laterally based on the right and left gastroepiploic arteries. The entire length of the ureter can be surrounded by omental tissue, which is tacked in place with absorbable sutures (Fig. 38–34). The omentum provides protection of the ureter against recurrent extrinsic compression and vascularity to a potentially ischemic ureter. Corticosteroid therapy may be used postoperatively in an attempt to prevent recurrent upper tract and venous compression. If no ureterotomy occurs during ureterolysis, the previously placed stents may be removed shortly after surgery.

If ureterolysis is impossible to perform due to extensive periureteral fibrosis, renal autotransplantation may be performed if the ipsilateral renal unit demonstrates satisfactory function (Penalver et al, 2001). If no significant renal function can be recovered after an adequate time period of decompression in the presence of the satisfactory contralateral renal function, nephrectomy may be considered.

## Surgical Management: Laparoscopic Ureterolysis

The first laparoscopic ureterolysis was reported by Kavoussi and Clayman in 1992. Subsequent success with such technique was confirmed by others (Puppo et al, 1994). In a more recent report, Kavoussi and colleagues described their experience with laparoscopic ureterolysis in 13 patients, including bilateral procedure in 7 and unilateral procedure in 6 (Fugita et al, 2002). Preoperative stent placement was performed in all cases before laparoscopy. For each ureter, the laparoscopic procedure was performed using a transperitoneal four-port approach. After incision of the posterior peritoneum and mobilization of the colon, the affected ureter was dissected free from the retroperitoneal fibrotic tissue. Multiple frozen-section biopsies of the periureteral tissue were obtained to rule out malignancy. The edge of the posterior peritoneum was reapproximated to the side wall underneath the ureter to intraperitonealize the ureter. Laparoscopic ureterolysis was completed successfully in 11 (85%) of cases, with 2 (15%) open conversions due to iliac vein injury (in 1 patient) and marked fibrosis (in 1 patient). Mean operative time was 381 minutes for bilateral procedures and 192 minutes for unilateral procedures. Mean use of parenteral analgesics was 59 mg of morphine sulfate equivalent. Mean hospital stay was 4 days. Postoperative complications occurred in 4 (30%) patients, including epididymitis, umbilical port erythema, prolonged ileus, and urinary retention. Pathology showed fibrous tissue with lymphocytes, plasma cells, macrophages, and fibroblast proliferation in all cases. At a mean follow-up of 30 months, upper tract imaging such as intravenous urography or renal scan showed lack of obstruction in 92% (12) of the patients.

## KEY POINTS: RETROPERITONEAL FIBROSIS

- Retroperitoneal fibrotic mass generally centers around the distal aorta at L4-L5 and wraps around the ureters, leading to hydronephrosis via extrinsic compression on the ureters or interference with ureteral peristalsis. In most cases, the disease is idiopathic. Drugs such as methysergide and other ergot alkaloids are most commonly associated with RPF.

- RPF symptoms and signs are usually nonspecific. Laboratory evaluation may show an elevated erythrocyte sedimentation rate, moderate leukocytosis, anemia, and variable renal insufficiency associated with electrolyte abnormalities.

- Initial management of RPF in the presence of hydronephrosis and uremia includes emergent decompression by percutaneous nephrostomy or indwelling ureteral stents. After decompression, the patient needs to be monitored closely for postobstructive diuresis.

- The most common primary medical management of idiopathic RPF has been corticosteroid therapy.

- In surgical bilateral ureterolysis, the ureters need to be protected by intraperitonealization or omental wrapping. Both open and laparoscopic techniques may be applied successfully. If ureterolysis is impossible to perform, renal autotransplantation may be performed.

## SUGGESTED READINGS

Anderson JC, Hynes W: Retrocaval ureter: A case diagnosed preoperatively and treated successfully by a plastic operation. Br J Urol 1949;21:209.

Boxer RJ, Fritzsche P, Skinner DG, et al: Replacement of the ureter by small intestine: Clinical application and results of the ileal ureter in 89 patients. J Urol 1979;121:728.

Carini M, Selli C, Rizzo M, et al: Surgical treatment of retroperitoneal fibrosis with omentoplasty. Surgery 1982;91:137.

Foley FEB: New plastic operation for stricture at the ureteropelvic junction. J Urol 1937;38:643.

Jarrett TW, Chan DY, Charambura TC, et al: Laparoscopic pyeloplasty: The first 100 cases. J Urol 2002;167:1253.

Ockerblad NF: Reimplantation of the ureter into the bladder by a flap method. J Urol 1947;57:845.

Turner-Warwick RT, Worth PHL: The psoas bladder-hitch procedure for the replacement of the lower third of the ureter. Br J Urol 1969;41:701.

# 39 Renal and Ureteral Trauma

JACK W. McANINCH, MD • RICHARD A. SANTUCCI, MD

---

**RENAL INJURIES**

**URETERAL INJURIES**

---

Traumatic injury is a leading national and international health problem. In the United States, 1 of every 14 deaths—over 150,000 per year—results from trauma (Baker et al, 1992). Indeed, in young people, trauma results in more deaths between ages 1 and 37 years than any other cause. Violence alone claims 50,000 lives annually, and more than 2.2 million in the United States suffer injuries from assaults each year. With the development of trauma care systems and centers, death rates from major injuries have declined significantly over the past 20 years (Kivioj et al, 1990).

The initial evaluation and resuscitation of the injured patient are done by the emergency room physician and the trauma surgeon, but it is important that the involved urologist understand the mechanism of injury, its extent, the methods used in the initial resuscitation process, and their success rates. Individuals who survive the immediate impact of the initial trauma can often be resuscitated in the field. Immediate transport to a trauma center where complete evaluation and care can be provided is essential.

The first hour of care after a major injury is extremely important and requires rapid assessment of the injuries and resuscitation based on priorities established by the American College of Surgeons' Acute Trauma Life Support Program. The mnemonic "ABCDE" defines these priorities in order of importance: A, airway with cervical spine protection; B, breathing; C, circulation and control of external bleeding; D, disability or neurologic status; E, exposure (undress) and environment (temperature control) (American College of Surgeons Committee on Trauma, 1997).

The best care provided to a polytrauma patient comes from a well-organized team of specialists, most often led by a surgeon experienced in trauma care. As approximately 10% of injuries involve the genitourinary tract—with the kidney being the most commonly injured organ—the urologist is a valued team member because of the experienced care he or she can provide for these special types of injuries.

## RENAL INJURIES
## Presentation

Of all injuries to the genitourinary system, injuries to the kidney from external trauma are the most common. It is essential to obtain as many details of the injury as possible; for example, depending on whether the cause is blunt or penetrating trauma, the approach to evaluation and management is quite different.

**Blunt renal injuries most often come from motor vehicle accidents, falls from heights, and assaults. Perhaps the most important information to obtain in the history of the injury is the extent of deceleration involved.** Rapid deceleration can cause vascular damage to the renal vessels, resulting in renal artery thrombosis, renal vein disruption, or renal pedicle avulsion. In high-velocity-impact trauma, multiple-organ injury is likely to be associated.

**Penetrating renal injuries most often come from gunshot and stab wounds.** The gunshot to the upper abdomen or lower chest should alert the physician to renal injury; of all patients sustaining renal trauma in a large reported series, renal gunshot wounds occurred in approximately 4.0% (McAninch et al, 1993). **Important factors in assessing a gunshot wound initially are weapon characteristics and bullet ballistics.** Bullet velocity has the greatest effect on soft tissue damage, as noted in the equation:

$$KE = \frac{mass \times V^2}{2 \times G}$$

where KE = kinetic energy, V = velocity, and G = gravity.

Whether the preceding equation reflects tissue damage precisely is controversial; however, high-velocity weapons clearly cause extensive soft tissue damage (Santucci and Chang, 2004). The greater the bullet velocity, the larger the temporary cavity created, indicating the extent of soft tissue stretch and destruction (Hutton and Rich, 1996). Handguns generally are considered low-velocity weapons (<2000 ft/sec), with numerous types of weapons in between.

Stab wounds usually result from assaults or self-inflicted injuries. The upper abdomen, flank, and lower chest are entry sites commonly resulting in renal injury. Should the weapon be recovered, its dimensions should be inspected carefully because the length and width give valuable information on its penetrating and destructive characteristics.

Physical examination must be complete and should detail all body systems. If the patient is conscious, history can be taken during the examination. In the case of polytrauma, rapid resuscitation should be under way. Immobilization of the cervical spine is necessary in blunt trauma until radiography confirms that it is intact. The abdomen, chest, and back must be examined; fractures of the lower ribs and upper lumbar and lower thoracic vertebrae are associated with renal injuries. Gunshot wounds can be misleading. Often small entrance wounds do not reveal the massive destruction within the body. Exit wounds are frequently much larger, but a bullet seldom takes a direct path from entrance to exit. Soft tissue and bone can alter the bullet's course; should the bullet fragment, secondary missiles are created, often resulting in multiple exit sites. When radiographs are taken of the chest and abdomen, it is useful to place a small metallic object such as a paper clip at entrance and exit sites to define these locations on the films.

## Hematuria

**Hematuria is the best indicator of traumatic urinary system injury.** The presence of microscopic (>5 red blood cells/high-power field [RBCs/HPF] or positive dipstick finding) or gross hematuria is characteristic. **However, the degree of hematuria and the severity of the renal injury do not correlate consistently**: in up to 36% of renal vascular injuries from blunt trauma, hematuria is absent (Cass, 1989). Also, gross hematuria has been observed with renal contusions, although it is more likely to be associated with a significant renal parenchymal injury. Microscopic hematuria may be present in a wide range of significant renal injuries, including vascular and parenchymal lacerations. In patients with blunt trauma, if shock (systolic blood pressure <90 mm Hg) is noted with microscopic hematuria, the incidence of significant renal injuries increases (Nicolaisen et al, 1985; Mee et al, 1989; Miller and McAninch, 1995). In addition, hematuria has been used as a predictor of intra-abdominal organ injury after blunt trauma (Knudson et al, 1992).

We use the first aliquot of urine obtained either by catheterization or by voiding to determine the presence of hematuria. Later urine samples are often diluted by diuresis from resuscitation fluids, resulting in an underestimation or absence of hematuria.

Visible blood of any degree in the urine is regarded as gross hematuria. Microscopic hematuria can be detected by dipstick analysis or microanalysis. The dipstick method is rapid and has a sensitivity and specificity for detection of microhematuria of more than 97%, even though a poor correlation with actual urinalysis was noted in a study by Chandhoke and McAninch (1988).

## Classification

Numerous classifications of renal injuries exist, but the most widely used and accepted classification (Table 39–1; Fig. 39–1) was developed by the American Association for the Surgery of Trauma's Organ Injury Scaling Committee (Moore et al, 1989). The increasing use of contrast-enhanced computed tomography (CT) has provided anatomic detail that facilitates very accurate grading of renal injuries (Bretan et al, 1986). In contrast, excretory urography (intravenous pyelography [IVP]) is less sensitive and much less specific.

Grading scales of all injuries have ambiguities, and the grading of renal injuries is no exception. Grades I through III can be clearly established with appropriate studies, but grades IV and V have areas of overlap; for example, vascular and parenchymal injuries can be present in both. In grade IV injuries to the parenchyma, the scale notes that a laceration extends through the parenchyma and into the collecting system. Vascular injury in grade IV refers to main renal artery thrombosis with contained hemorrhage, implying an intimal

### Table 39-1. American Association for the Surgery of Trauma Organ Injury Severity Scale for the Kidney*

| Grade[†] | Type | Description |
|---|---|---|
| I | Contusion | Microscopic or gross hematuria, urologic studies normal |
| | Hematoma | Subcapsular, nonexpanding without parenchymal laceration |
| II | Hematoma | Nonexpanding perirenal hematoma confined to renal retroperitoneum |
| | Laceration | <1 cm parenchymal depth of renal cortex without urinary extravasation |
| III | Laceration | >1 cm parenchymal depth of renal cortex without collecting system rupture or urinary extravasation |
| IV | Laceration | Parenchymal laceration extending through renal cortex, medulla, and collecting system |
| | Vascular | Main renal artery or vein injury with contained hemorrhage |
| V | Laceration | Completely shattered kidney |
| | Vascular | Avulsion of renal hilum, devascularizing the kidney |

*Data drawn from Moore EE, Shackford SR, Pachter HL, et al: Organ injury scaling: Spleen, liver, and kidney. J Trauma 1989;29:1664-1666.
[†]Advance one grade for bilateral injuries up to grade III.

flap dissection from blunt trauma, and to main renal vein injury with contained hemorrhage. In addition, segmental renal artery or vein injury is included in grade IV.

Grade V parenchymal injuries are referred to as "shattered kidney," suggesting multiple grade IV–type lacerations, but some authors have used grade V classification to report more than one laceration of any parenchymal depth. Grade V injuries also include renal pedicle avulsion.

Even with these minor variations in reporting, the classification system has established a common scale by which injuries can be identified at disparate centers according to the extent of damage, and it has worked well (Santucci et al, 2001).

## Staging

Staging of renal injuries refers to the use of appropriate imaging studies to define the extent of injury. Combining these findings with information gleaned at history and physical examination provides maximal guidance for management decisions.

### Indications for Renal Imaging

As already stated, hematuria is the best indicator of renal injury, and most authors accept 5 RBCs/HPF as a significant level. However, when this was used in the past as the sole indication for renal imaging, IVP and other studies found a low incidence of renal abnormalities. This prompted an extensive study, based at San Francisco General Hospital, evaluating indications for radiographic imaging in a prospective manner. This study has been ongoing for more than 25 years and at least three reports have updated the findings (Nicolaisen et al, 1985; Mee et al, 1989; Miller and McAninch, 1995). Figure 39–2 provides the results of the study for adult blunt renal trauma.

Based on information from this study, **all blunt trauma patients with gross hematuria and patients with microscopic hematuria and shock (systolic blood pressure**

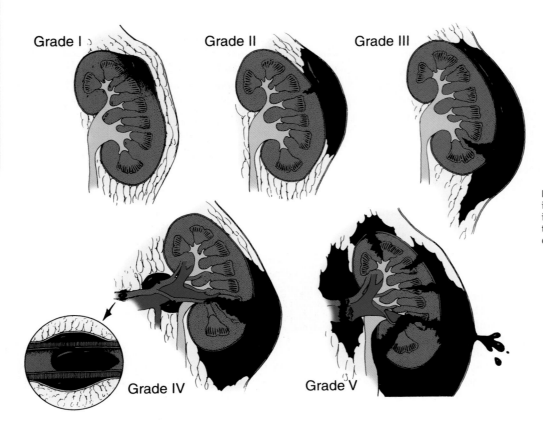

Grade I Grade II Grade III

Grade IV Grade V

**Figure 39–1.** Classification of renal injuries by grade (based on the organ injury scale of the American Association for the Surgery of Trauma [based on Moore et al, 1989]).

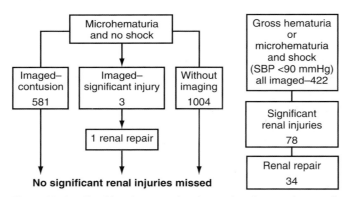

Microhematuria and no shock

Imaged– contusion
581

Imaged– significant injury
3

Without imaging
1004

1 renal repair

**No significant renal injuries missed**

Gross hematuria or microhematuria and shock (SBP <90 mmHg) all imaged–422

Significant renal injuries
78

Renal repair
34

**Figure 39–2.** Algorithm demonstrating the results of our study on radiographic assessment of renal injuries. In adults with blunt trauma, imaging studies may be performed selectively. SBP, systolic blood pressure. (From Miller KS, McAninch JW: Radiographic assessment of renal trauma. Our 15-year experience. J Urol 1995;154:352-355.)

**< 90 mm Hg any time during evaluation and resuscitation) should undergo renal imaging, usually CT with intravenous contrast.**

Patients with microscopic hematuria without shock can be observed clinically without imaging studies. As noted by Miller and McAninch (1995), such patients rarely have a significant injury (<0.0016%). However, should one suspect any possible renal injury on the basis of history or examination, imaging should be performed; for example, patients sustaining blunt trauma from rapid deceleration (i.e., head-on or

high-speed motor vehicle accidents or falls from great heights) are at risk for vascular injury, which can occur in the absence of microscopic hematuria.

**Penetrating injuries with any degree of hematuria should be imaged.** In a report by Carroll and McAninch (1985), 27 of 50 patients with penetrating renal trauma had microscopic hematuria. Three of these had 0 to 3 RBCs/HPF and one of the three had a renal pedicle injury. The presence of shock, the degree of hematuria, the location of the entry wound, and the type of injury do not permit reliable discrimination among categories.

Pediatric patients (younger than 18 years) sustaining blunt renal trauma must be carefully evaluated for hematuria. Brown and colleagues (1998a) noted that children are at greater risk for renal trauma than adults after blunt abdominal injury. Morey and associates (1996) reported no significant renal injuries in 185 children when less than 50 RBCs/HPF were noted on microscopic examination of the urine. Children have a high catecholamine output after trauma, which maintains blood pressure until approximately 50% of blood volume has been lost. Therefore, shock is not a useful criterion in children to determine whether imaging studies should be performed. For pediatric patients, liberal use of studies should be considered (Buckley and McAninch, 2004).

## Imaging Studies

**The preferred imaging study for renal trauma is contrast-enhanced CT** (Bretan et al, 1986; Federle et al, 1987). Highly sensitive and specific, CT provides the most definitive staging information: parenchymal lacerations are clearly defined; extravasation of contrast-enhanced urine can easily be detected (Fig. 39–3); associated injuries to the bowel, pancreas, liver, spleen, and other organs can be identified; and the degree of retroperitoneal bleeding can be assessed by the size and dimensions of the retroperitoneal hematoma. Lack of uptake of contrast material in the parenchyma suggests arterial injury.

Currently, spiral CT is being used in many centers to evaluate renal injuries (Brown et al, 1998b). Although the rapidity of the study—2 to 3 minutes—is advantageous for demonstrating arterial and venous injuries, it is a major disadvantage in renal parenchymal injuries: contrast material has not had time to be excreted into the parenchyma and collecting system adequately; and parenchymal lacerations and urinary extravasation cannot be detected reliably. Repeated scanning of the kidneys 10 minutes after injection of contrast material demonstrates parenchymal and most collecting system injuries with great accuracy.

Findings on CT that suggest major injury are (1) medial hematoma, suggesting vascular injury; (2) medial urinary extravasation, suggesting renal pelvis or ureteropelvic junction avulsion injury; and (3) lack of contrast enhancement of the parenchyma, suggesting arterial injury.

One major limitation of CT is the inability to define a renal venous injury adequately. With normal arterial perfusion, the parenchyma appears normal and the collecting system may contain contrast material. A medial hematoma accompanying the preceding findings strongly suggests a venous injury.

**Excretory urography has been used for years to evaluate urinary system injuries, but it has largely been replaced by CT. The exception is "single-shot" intraoperative IVP.** The indications are uncommon, but when the surgeon encounters an unexpected retroperitoneal hematoma surrounding a kidney during abdominal exploration, the study can provide essential information. The technique is key to gaining important information and minimizing the time involved: only *a single film* is taken 10 minutes after intravenous injection (IV push) of 2 mL/kg of contrast material. If findings are not normal or near normal, the kidney should be explored to complete the staging of the injury and reconstruct any abnormality found.

Morey and coworkers (1999) have reported their experience with single-shot intraoperative IVP for the immediate management of renal injuries; in 50 patients, the film quality was adequate to avoid renal exploration in 32%. This report supports the value of this intraoperative imaging technique when done properly.

Arteriography is largely used to define arterial injuries suspected on CT or to localize arterial bleeding that can be controlled by embolization.

Sonography is being used with greater frequency in the immediate evaluation of injuries. It confirms the presence of two kidneys and can easily define any retroperitoneal hematoma. The study cannot clearly delineate parenchymal lacerations or vascular or collecting system injuries and cannot accurately detect urinary extravasation in the acute injury. With the advent of power Doppler, perhaps in the future more functional information will be obtainable in the acute injury phase.

## Nonoperative Management

Significant injuries (grades II to V) are found in only 5.4% of renal trauma cases (Miller and McAninch, 1995). A hemodynamically stable patient with an injury well staged by CT can usually be managed without renal exploration; indeed, 98% of blunt renal injuries can be managed nonoperatively. Grade IV and V injuries more often require surgical exploration, but even these high-grade injuries can be managed without renal operation if carefully staged and selected (Fig. 39–4) (Santucci and McAninch, 2000; Santucci et al, 2004).

Penetrating trauma from gunshot or stab wounds to the kidney can be managed nonoperatively if carefully staged with CT. In our experience, 55% of renal stab wounds and 24% of gunshot wounds were appropriately managed nonoperatively in carefully selected patients with well-staged injuries (McAninch et al, 1991).

Patients with high-grade injuries (grades III to V) selected for nonoperative management should be observed closely with serial hematocrit readings and abdominal CT scans. Should bleeding persist or delayed bleeding occur, angiographic studies with embolization of bleeding vessels often suffice and obviate surgical intervention.

Endovascular stents have been used with reported success during angiography in patients with renal artery thrombosis occurring from intimal flaps (Goodman et al, 1998). Longer term follow-up and more cases are needed to determine whether this will be a successful management approach.

### Isolated Renal Injuries

Approximately 80% to 90% of renal injuries have major associated organ injury that can affect the choice of renal injury management. The isolated renal injury, without significant associated injuries, occurs more commonly from blunt trauma and in most circumstances can be managed nonoperatively. The exception is major grade V vascular pedicle avulsion injuries.

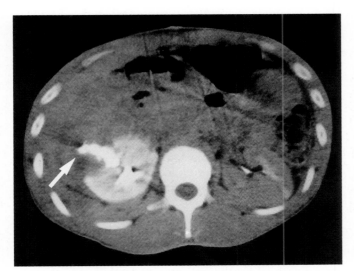

**Figure 39–3.** Computed tomographic scan of a right renal stab wound (grade IV), demonstrating extensive urinary extravasation and large retroperitoneal hematoma.

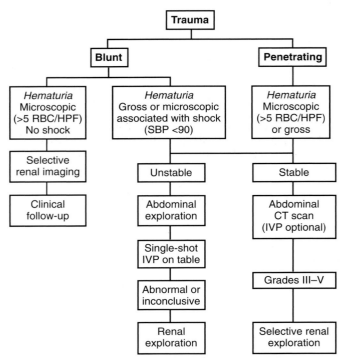

**Figure 39–4.** Flow chart for adult renal injuries to serve as a guide for decision-making. CT, computed tomography; IVP, intravenous pyelography; RBC/HPF, red blood cells per high-power field; SBP, systolic blood pressure.

Isolated renal injuries with parenchymal lacerations and even segmental arterial injury can have active bleeding well controlled by angiographic embolization. Interventional radiology skills and techniques allow selective embolization of even the smallest parenchymal vessels with maximal preservation of functioning parenchyma. However, one must recognize that renal vessels are end-arteries, and any selective vessel embolization results in tissue death peripheral to the embolized site.

Patients with grade IV parenchymal lacerations who have well-contained hematomas can be observed expectantly. They should be closely monitored for bleeding, with vital signs, serial hematocrit readings, and pulse rates. If urinary extravasation is present, serial renal CT scanning should be instituted. If significant urinary extravasation persists beyond 48 hours, placement of an internal ureteral stent for drainage often prevents prolongation of the extravasation and decreases the chance of perirenal urinoma formation.

If nonoperative management is selected for a patient with gross hematuria whose injury has been well staged with appropriate imaging, hospital admission and bed rest are required. Once the gross hematuria clears, ambulation is allowed; should gross hematuria recur, bed rest is reinstated. Ambulation without any sequelae allows hospital discharge with close clinical follow-up.

## Operative Management

Indications for renal exploration after trauma can be separated into absolute and relative (McAninch et al, 1991). **Absolute indications include evidence of persistent renal bleeding, expanding perirenal hematoma, and pulsatile perirenal hematoma** (see Fig. 39–4). **Relative indications include urinary extravasation, nonviable tissue, delayed diagnosis of arterial injury, segmental arterial injury, and incomplete staging.**

Urinary extravasation alone from a grade IV parenchymal laceration or forniceal rupture can be managed nonoperatively with an expectation of spontaneous resolution in 87.1% of patients (Matthews et al, 1997). Should nonviable tissue constitute more than 20% in association with a parenchymal laceration or urinary extravasation or both, the potential for complications greatly increases and the choice of nonoperative management can be questioned (Husmann and Morris, 1990). Very often a combination of relative indications necessitates renal exploration (McAninch et al, 1991).

Segmental renal artery injury with an associated renal laceration results in a substantial amount of nonviable tissue (usually >20%), and such injuries usually resolve more quickly with surgical reconstruction and tissue removal. This approach often avoids the high complication rate noted when this group is observed without renal exploration (Husmann et al, 1993).

Incomplete staging is an important concern when determining whether renal exploration is needed. When the patient's critical condition necessitates surgical intervention before appropriate imaging studies and renal injury is obvious (manifested by perirenal hematoma or hematuria), single-shot intraoperative IVP should be done (see earlier). If findings are not normal, renal exploration provides the opportunity to complete the staging process and reconstruct a significant injury. Our experience in exploring over 200 renal units suggests that this approach is safe, without renal loss, and provides the opportunity to reconstruct high-grade injuries and prevent complications in the postoperative period.

### Renal Exploration

**Surgical exploration of the acutely injured kidney is best done by a transabdominal approach, which allows complete inspection of intra-abdominal organs and bowel.** In some reported series of penetrating injuries, associated organ injury has been noted to be as high as 94% (McAninch et al, 1993). Injuries to the great vessels, liver, spleen, pancreas, and bowel can be identified and stabilized if necessary before renal exploration.

The surgical approach to renal exploration is shown in Figure 39–5 (McAninch and Carroll, 1989). The renal vessels are isolated before exploration to provide the immediate capability to occlude them if massive bleeding should ensue when Gerota's fascia is opened (Scott and Selzman, 1966). The transverse colon is lifted superiorly onto the chest, and the small bowel is lifted superiorly and to the right. This exposes the midretroperitoneum. An incision is made over the aorta in the retroperitoneum just superior to the inferior mesenteric artery. The incision is extended superiorly to the ligament of Treitz. Exposure of the anterior surface of the aorta is accomplished and followed superiorly to the left renal vein, which crosses the aorta anteriorly. With a vessel loop controlling the vein, the anatomic relationships of the right and left renal arteries as they leave the aorta provide the ability to isolate and secure these structures with vessel loops. The right renal vein can be secured through this incision; if this proves difficult,

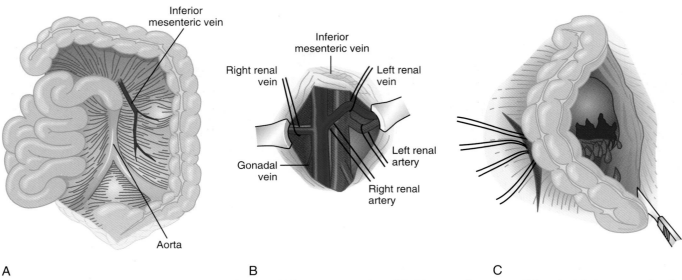

**Figure 39–5.** The surgical approach to the renal vessels and kidney: **A,** retroperitoneal incision over the aorta medial to the inferior mesenteric vein; **B,** anatomic relationships of the renal vessels; **C,** retroperitoneal incision lateral to the colon, exposing the kidney.

reflecting the second portion of the duodenum provides excellent exposure to the vein.

Large hematomas may extend over the aorta and obscure the landmarks for the planned initial retroperitoneal incision. In such instances, the inferior mesenteric vein can be used as an anatomic guide for an appropriate incision. By making the retroperitoneal incision just medial to the inferior mesenteric vein and dissecting through the hematoma, the anterior surface of the aorta can be identified and followed superiorly to the crossing left renal vein.

The kidney is exposed by incising the peritoneum lateral to the colon, followed by mobilization off Gerota's fascia. This maneuver often requires release of the splenic (left) or hepatic (right) attachments of the colon. Gerota's fascia is then opened and the kidney with injury is completely dissected from the surrounding hematoma. Should troublesome bleeding develop, the previously isolated vessels can be temporarily occluded with a vascular clamp or a vessel loop tourniquet.

**Is Early Vessel Isolation Necessary?** Renal bleeding is a major cause of nephrectomy in renal trauma. **Obtaining early vascular control before opening Gerota's fascia can decrease renal loss**: in a comparative series, the total nephrectomy rate was reduced from 56% to 18% (McAninch and Carroll, 1982). Carroll and coauthors (1989), evaluating the use of early vascular control, reported the need to occlude the vessels in 12% of renal explorations. In a series of 133 renal units in which early vessel isolation and control before opening Gerota's fascia was achieved in all, McAninch and associates (1991) reported a renal salvage rate of 88.7%.

The need for early vascular control has been questioned. Corriere and colleagues (1991) reported a series of renal units in which vascular control was obtained only if needed after opening Gerota's fascia. In this group, the total nephrectomy rate was 37.1%. Atala and coworkers (1991) reported a similar group of patients with a total nephrectomy rate of 36.2%. On the whole, the currently available data support an improved renal salvage rate with early vascular control.

## Renal Reconstruction

**The principles of renal reconstruction after trauma include complete renal exposure, débridement of nonviable tissue, hemostasis by individual suture ligation of bleeding vessels, watertight closure of the collecting system, and coverage or approximation of the parenchymal defect** (Fig. 39–6).

Renorrhaphy denotes repair of a parenchymal laceration. The technique, illustrated in Figure 39–7, involves complete exposure of the kidney, débridement of nonviable tissue, hemostasis obtained with absorbable 4-0 chromic sutures on bleeding vessels (the addition of hemostatic agents may also be helpful), closure of the collecting system, and approximation of the margins of the laceration (3-0 absorbable suture) with the use of renal capsule and absorbable gelatin (Gelfoam) bolster.

When polar injuries cannot be reconstructed, a partial nephrectomy should be done and all nonviable tissue removed, hemostasis obtained, and the collecting system closed. The open parenchyma should then be covered when possible by a pedicle flap of omentum (see Fig. 39–6). With its rich vascular and lymphatic supply, omentum promotes wound healing and decreases the risk of delayed bleeding and urinary extravasation. Should it not be available, the use of absorbable mesh, peritoneal graft, or retroperitoneal fat has been successful.

In a high percentage of major renal injuries, intra-abdominal structures are also injured, the liver and spleen being the most common. Injuries to the colon, pancreas, and stomach also occur frequently, and in previous years total nephrectomy was suggested because of the high complication rate with attempted renal salvage. However, in our hands renal repair in these injuries has been successful with minimal complications (Rosen and McAninch, 1994; Wessells and McAninch, 1996). Drains should be used liberally in these repairs.

**Renovascular Injuries.** Vascular repair requires occlusion of the involved vessel with vascular clamps. The perforated main renal vessels injured by penetrating trauma can be repaired with 5-0 nonabsorbable vascular suture (Fig. 39–8). Main

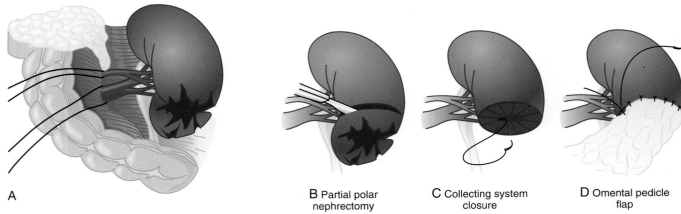

A

**B** Partial polar
nephrectomy

**C** Collecting system
closure

**D** Omental pedicle
flap

**Figure 39–6.** Technique for partial nephrectomy: **A,** total renal exposure; **B,** sharp removal of nonviable tissue; **C,** hemostasis obtained and collecting system closed; **D,** defect covered.

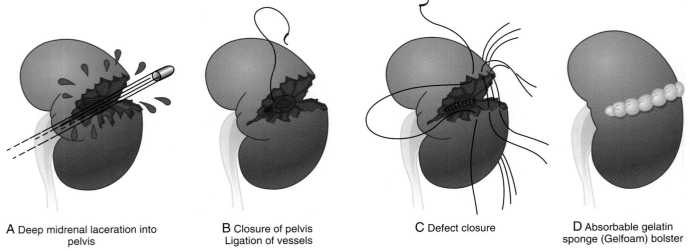

**A** Deep midrenal laceration into
pelvis

**B** Closure of pelvis
Ligation of vessels

**C** Defect closure

**D** Absorbable gelatin
sponge (Gelfoam) bolster

**Figure 39–7.** Technique for renorrhaphy: **A,** typical injury in midportion of kidney; **B,** débridement, hemostasis, and collecting system closure; **C,** approximation of parenchymal margins; **D,** sutures tied over gelatin sponge bolster.

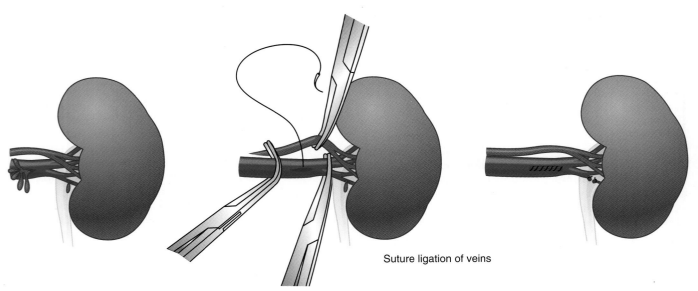

Suture ligation of veins

**Figure 39–8.** Vascular injuries. *Left,* Venous injuries may occur in the main renal vein or the segmental branches. *Middle,* Repair of main renal vein. *Right,* Ligation of segmental branch can be done safely.

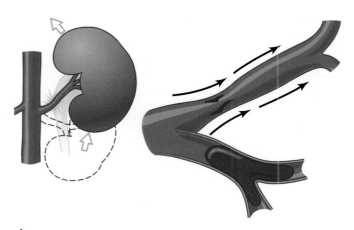

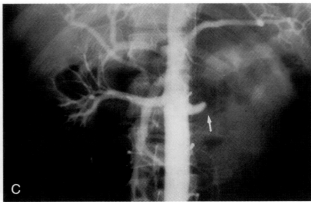

A

**Figure 39–9.** **A,** Movement of the kidney from blunt trauma (deceleration injury) causes stretch on the renal artery, resulting in rupture of the arterial intima and formation of a thrombus. **B,** Computed tomography of a left kidney with renal artery thrombosis, demonstrating lack of contrast material perfusion to the kidney. **C,** Arteriography demonstrating complete occlusion of the left renal artery secondary to thrombus formation.

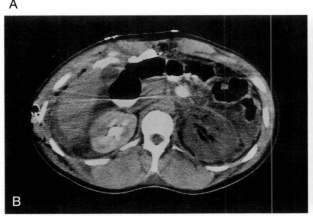

renal artery thrombosis from blunt trauma occurs secondary to deceleration injuries. The mobility of the kidney results in stretch on the renal artery, which in turn causes the arterial intima, low in elastic fibers, to disrupt; the consequent thrombus occludes the vessel, rendering the kidney ischemic (Fig. 39–9). Prompt diagnosis by CT or angiography should lead to immediate renal exploration in the appropriate candidate in an attempt to salvage the kidney.

Case reports of successful renal revascularization through the use of endovascular stents during angiography offer a new and perhaps promising approach to the problem of blunt trauma renal artery thrombosis caused by the intimal flap (Inoue et al, 2004). The great disadvantage of this approach has been the inability to effect anticoagulation, as this patient typically has bleeding from other organ injury. Attempts at surgical repair of renal artery thrombosis by a variety of techniques have largely failed.

**With delayed diagnosis (>8 hours), the kidney typically cannot be salvaged** (Cass, 1989). With a 15-year experience, Haas and coworkers (1998) have reported that surgical revascularization was seldom successful in renal artery thrombosis and at least 43% of their patients with repairs developed hypertension. Hypertension was also common in those observed nonoperatively. When repair is attempted in renal artery thrombosis, the area of injury (noted by a visible contusion on the vessel) should be excised and a replacement graft done, preferably with hypogastric or splenic artery. Many patients with renal vascular injury are critically injured, with

numerous associated organ injuries; time constraints thus limit attempts at vascular repair and a nephrectomy must be done.

Segmental renal arterial injuries result in ischemic infarction to a segment of the kidney. These should be observed nonoperatively when diagnosed unless associated with a parenchymal laceration. Should the laceration with infarction be greater than 20% of the parenchyma, careful consideration should be given to surgical correction.

Injuries to the main renal vein require repair with fine vascular suture (5-0) (see Fig. 39–8). Partial occlusion of the vein is ideal for repair, but in some instances total occlusion with vascular clamps is necessary; if so, temporary occlusion of the renal artery is necessary.

Segmental venous injuries are best managed by ligation of the vessel. This can be done because of the collateral venous circulation of the kidney.

### Damage Control

Coburn (2002) has noted the benefit of damage control to improve renal salvage. The wound and area around the injured kidney are packed with laparotomy pads to control bleeding with a planned return in 24 hours to explore and evaluate the extent of injury. This approach is commonly used by trauma surgeons in patients with extensive injuries and has long been used by general surgeons. It may well be useful in managing complex renal injuries to avoid total nephrectomy.

## Indications for Nephrectomy

The ability to reconstruct an injured kidney depends on numerous factors. The unstable patient, with low body temperature and poor coagulation, cannot risk an attempt at renal repair if a normal contralateral kidney is present. As noted earlier, damage control (packing the wound to control bleeding and attempting to correct metabolic and coagulation abnormalities) with a plan to return for corrective surgery within 24 hours provides an option in management. Total nephrectomy would be indicated immediately in extensive renal injuries when the patient's life would be threatened by attempted renal repair. When Nash and colleagues (1995) examined the reasons for nephrectomy in patients with renal injuries, 77% required removal because of the extent of parenchymal, vascular, or combined injury and the remaining 23% required nephrectomy in otherwise reconstructable kidneys because of hemodynamic instability.

## Complications

Persistent urinary extravasation can result in urinoma, perinephric infection, and renal loss. These patients are initially administered systemic antibiotics and carefully observed with appropriate antibiotics. In a high percentage, the extravasation resolves spontaneously (Matthews et al, 1997). Should it persist, placement of an internal ureteral stent often corrects the problem. A nonoperative approach with careful observation usually results in a functional renal unit.

Delayed renal bleeding can potentially occur several weeks after injury but usually occurs within 21 days. The initial management is bed rest and hydration. Should the bleeding persist, angiography can often localize the bleeding vessel and embolization can often gain control.

Perinephric abscess rarely occurs after renal injury, but persistent urinary extravasation and urinoma are the typical precursors. Percutaneous drainage offers a good initial method of management, followed by surgical drainage if necessary.

Hypertension is seldom noted in the early postinjury period (Monstrey et al, 1989), but postinjury blood pressure measurements are not obtained consistently, as patients often do not return for follow-up evaluation. The basic mechanisms for arterial hypertension as a complication of trauma are (1) renal vascular injury, leading to stenosis or occlusion of the main renal artery or one of its branches; (2) compression of the renal parenchyma with extravasated blood or urine; and (3) post-trauma arteriovenous fistula. In these instances, the renin-angiotensin axis is stimulated by partial renal ischemia, resulting in hypertension (Goldblatt et al, 1934; Crosgrove et al, 1973).

## URETERAL INJURIES
## Etiology

### External Trauma

Ureteral injuries (Table 39–2) after external violence are rare, occurring in less than 4% of cases of penetrating trauma and less than 1% of cases of blunt trauma. During wartime in the past century, 3% to 15% of urologic injuries have involved the ureter, with an average of 5% over reports from World War II

**Table 39–2. American Association for the Surgery of Trauma Organ Injury Severity Scale for the Ureter***

| Grade[†] | Type | Description |
|---|---|---|
| I | Hematoma | Contusion or hematoma without devascularization |
| II | Laceration | <50% transection |
| III | Laceration | ≥50% transection |
| IV | Laceration | Complete transection with <2 cm devascularization |
| V | Laceration | Avulsion with >2 cm devascularization |

*From Moore EE, Cogbill TH, Jurkovich GJ, et al: Organ injury scaling. III: Chest wall, abdominal vascular, ureter, bladder, and urethra. J Trauma 1992;33:337-339.
[†]Advance one grade for bilateral up to grade III.

up to modern conflicts (Busch et al, 1967; Selikowitz, 1977; Marekovic et al, 1997). In the nonmilitary setting, a similar incidence of ureteral injuries is caused by civilian gunshot injuries. **These patients often have significant associated injuries and a devastating degree of mortality that approaches one third** (Medina et al, 1998). Associated visceral injury is common, predominantly small (39% to 65%) and large (28% to 33%) bowel perforation (Presti et al, 1989; Campbell et al, 1992; Medina et al, 1998). A significant percentage (10% to 28%) (Presti et al, 1989; Medina et al, 1998) of patients with ureteral injuries also have associated renal injuries. A smaller percentage (5%) have associated bladder injuries (Medina et al, 1998).

The mechanism by which bullets injure the ureter is thought to be similar to the mechanism by which they injure analogous structures such as blood vessels, that is, not only by direct transection but by disruption of the delicate intramural blood supply and subsequent necrosis. In experimental models, such microvascular damage has been found as far away as 2 cm from the point of transection (Amato et al, 1970). This finding provides experimental support for the technique of débriding the ureter back to a bleeding edge after bullet injury to remove tissue that may have invisible microvascular damage. Some authors have even advocated injection of intravenous fluorescein and examination of the ureter by Wood's lamp to ensure viability (Gill and McRoberts, 1992); however, we have not found published evidence to support this technique.

Whereas penetrating trauma imparts a large degree of energy over a small area (as in the course of a bullet), **blunt trauma patients with ureteral injuries are subject to extreme force applied over the entire body. The great degree of energy imparted to the victim is associated with such uncommon injuries as fractured lumbar processes** (Evans and Smith, 1976) **and thoracolumbar spinal dislocation** (Campbell et al, 1992). The presence of these injuries in the blunt trauma patient should always increase the level of suspicion for ureteral injury.

Penetrating trauma victims with any degree of hematuria or a wound pattern that suggests the possibility of genitourinary injury should be imaged. Blunt trauma patients with gross hematuria or microhematuria plus hypotension, a history of significant deceleration, or significant associated injuries should be imaged (Mee and McAninch, 1989). A history of rapid deceleration was found in 100% of patients with ureteropelvic junction (UPJ) injury in one small series (Boone et al, 1993).

The rare entity of UPJ disruption consequent to blunt trauma is often missed because the patients do not always exhibit hematuria, and the injury is difficult to palpate during intraoperative manual examination (Boone et al, 1993). Because of this, we recommend abdominal CT with contrast and delayed images whenever possible (Mulligan et al, 1998) or, if time does not permit, an intraoperative "one-shot" pyelogram (2 mL/kg intravenous contrast material given 10 minutes before flat plate abdomen radiograph). Typically, UPJ disruption is associated with an unusual pattern of either medial contrast extravasation (Kenney et al, 1987) (Fig. 39–10) or a "circumrenal" contrast extravasation (Kawashima et al, 1997).

## Surgical Injury

Ureteral injuries can occur after a multitude of surgical procedures but largely result from surgeries in the pelvis (such as hysterectomy) and retroperitoneum (such as major vascular replacement). One report, which reviewed 13 previously published studies, concluded that **hysterectomy was responsible for the majority (54%) of surgical ureteral injuries. Next most common was colorectal surgery (14%), followed by pelvic surgery such as ovarian tumor removal and transabdominal urethropexy (8%), followed lastly by abdominal vascular surgery (6%)** (St Lezin and Stoller, 1991). One series reported that repeat cesarean section can also result in a large number of ureteral injuries, in this case up to 23% of the reported ureteral injuries at one hospital (Ghali et al, 1999). The total incidence of ureteral injury after gynecologic surgery is reported to be between 0.5% and 1.5%, and after abdominoperineal colon resection it ranges from 0.3% to 5.7% (St Lezin and Stoller, 1991). Open urologic procedures, because they often occur in proximity to the ureters, were also responsible for a significant number (21%) of reported ureteral injuries in one series (Selzman and Spirnak, 1996).

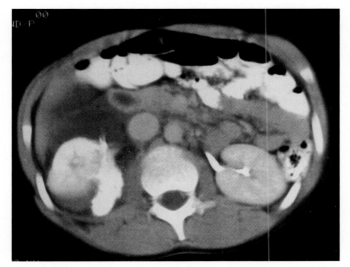

**Figure 39–10.** Computed tomography showing right medial extravasation of contrast material in a patient with a renal pelvis laceration.

**Intraoperative ureteral manipulation resulting in subsequent hydronephrosis is common after aortoiliac and aortofemoral bypass surgery (12% to 20%), but the course is benign in most** (St Lezin and Stoller, 1991). Symptomatic ureteral stenosis, usually delayed in presentation by months, occurs in only 1% to 2% of these patients (St Lezin and Stoller, 1991; Adams et al, 1992). This is in contrast to the experience of patients who suffer ureteral injury during pelvic surgery such as sigmoidectomy or hysterectomy: without treatment, most of these patients are immediately symptomatic, suffer lasting complications, or require reconstructive surgery or nephrectomy (St Lezin and Stoller, 1991).

In patients undergoing intra-abdominal vascular surgery, risk factors for surgical injury of the ureter include reoperation, placement of a vascular graft anterior to the ureter (Adams et al, 1992), and large dilated arterial aneurysms that cause retroperitoneal inflammation that can involve the ureter. The majority (up to 85%) of surgical injuries to the ureter after vascular procedures are not recognized immediately (Adams et al, 1992). When symptoms of ureteral injury are present, they include flank pain (36% to 90%), fever, ileus, abdominal distention, and urinary fistula (St Lezin and Stoller, 1991; Adams et al, 1992).

Since the inception of laparoscopic surgery in the 1960s, ureteral injuries have resulted during these procedures, although they were not widely reported until the early 1970s (Grainger et al, 1990). At first, laparoscopy was developed and perfected only for gynecologic indications, but the explosion of laparoscopy into other surgical specialties has meant that the incidence of ureteral injury after minimally invasive surgery has likewise skyrocketed. At one center, the incidence of ureteral injuries from laparoscopy went from 0% of all reported ureteral injuries in the early 1980s to 25% of all the reported ureteral injuries only 5 years later (Assimos et al, 1994). Currently, the reported rate of ureteral injury during laparoscopic surgery varies between 0.5% (experienced surgeons) and 14% (inexperienced surgeons) after laparoscopic hysterectomy cases, for example (Harkki-Siren et al, 1999; Cosson et al, 2001).

A large percentage of ureteral injuries after gynecologic laparoscopy occur during electrosurgical or laser-assisted lysis of endometriosis (Grainger et al, 1990). There are probably three reasons for this: (1) endometrioma can involve the ureter either extrinsically or intrinsically; (2) long-standing endometriosis can cause intraperitoneal adhesion, making ureteral visualization difficult (Ribeiro et al, 1999); and (3) the disease can deviate the ureters medially away from their normal anatomic position (Nackley and Yeko, 2000). A significant number of ureteral injuries also occur during tubal ligation, even when bipolar cautery is used (Grainger et al, 1990). The incidence of ureteral injury after laparoscopic hysterectomy severe enough to cause ureteral obstruction was 3.4% in a series of 118 patients (Ribeiro et al, 1999); however, in larger series with much higher numbers of patients and presumably more experienced surgeons, the rate was a more reasonable 1% (Harkki-Siren et al, 1999).

**In contradistinction to open operation, where at least one third of ureteral injuries are recognized immediately** (Rodriguez and Payne, 2001), **fewer injuries to the ureter are immediately identified after laparoscopy** (Grainger et al, 1990). **Therefore, during laparoscopy, a high index of suspi-**

cion for ureteral injury is required. Postoperatively, patients must be monitored for fever, peritonitis, and leukocytosis (Grainger et al, 1990), which herald the potential for missed ureteral injury. A smaller number of patients with missed ureteral injury present with hematuria or a pelvic mass representing urinoma (Grainger et al, 1990).

**Avoidance of ureteral injury is predicated on intimate knowledge of its location, especially its relation to the uterine and ovarian arteries, if those structures are going to be ligated, as in a hysterectomy** (Fig. 39–11). Visualization of the ureter in the area of the ureterosacral ligaments is thought to be especially difficult, and special care must be taken in this area (Grainger et al, 1990). It is axiomatic that ureteral injury is more likely in cases of uncontrolled bleeding, and adequate intraoperative hemostasis and surgical exposure should further decrease these injuries, even in high-risk cases. Intraoperative hydration or diuretic administration may enhance ureteral visualization and potentially further decrease the risk of injury. Preoperative ureteral stenting can be used to ease identification of the ureter in high-risk cases; however, published data in the gynecologic and colectomy population show that, although it may increase intraoperative *recognition* of ureteral injury, it may not actually decrease ureteral injuries (Leff et al, 1982; Bothwell et al, 1994; Kuno et al, 1998). Ureteral stents are not without complications: the rate of anuria after ureteral stent removal has been reported between 1% and 5% (Leff et al, 1982; Sheikh and Khubchandani, 1990; Kyzer and Gordon, 1994), and the rate of iatrogenic ureteral

injury during stent placement 1% (Bothwell et al, 1994). One study showed that stents may even increase rather than reduce the chance of intraoperative injury (Dowling et al, 1986). Ureteral stents cannot be placed on one side in 13% of cases, and total failure to place either catheter can occur in 2% (Bothwell et al, 1994) Fiberoptic catheters have been used with good effect (Ben-Hur and Phipps, 2000), although rare complications of ureteral edema and obstruction have been reported after their use (Chahin et al, 2002). Finally, some authors recommend injection of 5 to 10 mL of intravenous indigo carmine dye followed by cystoscopy to ensure patency of the ureters after laparoscopic hysterectomy. When this technique was used in 118 patients undergoing laparoscopic hysterectomy, 4 of 4 cases of ureteral occlusion were identified immediately (mostly caused by suture ligation) and repaired immediately without complications (Ribeiro et al, 1999).

### Ureteroscopic Injury

Ever since Kaufman first reported ureteral injury after rigid ureteroscopy in 1984, countless ureteral injuries have resulted from this common procedure. For example, Huffman (1989) reported an explosion of ureteral injuries after ureteroscopy became widely used in the late 1980s. Improvements in equipment and operator experience subsequently decreased the rate of ureteral perforation to a stable average of 7% in the 1990s (range 0% to 28%) (Huffman, 1989). More recent expert series have a perforation rate of 1% to 5% (Schuster et al, 2001), of which 0.2% require open surgery (Butler et al, 2004). One factor cited as a cause of ureteral injury during ureteroscopy was persistence of stone basket attempts after recognition of ureteral tear. Current recommendations are to stop the procedure and place a ureteral stent when ureteral perforations are identified (Chang and Marshall, 1987). The wide use of the holmium:yttrium-aluminum-garnet (Ho:YAG) laser to fragment larger stones before basket manipulation is attempted should further decrease the potential for this complication (Bagley et al, 2004). It is also recommended to perform ureteroscopy alongside or over a wire placed up into the renal pelvis (Chang and Marshall, 1987; Flam et al, 1988), although some experts no longer use a safety wire during routine flexible ureteroscopy (Bratslavsky and Moran, 2004). This wire facilitates not only safe ureteroscopy but also placement of a ureteral stent later in the case if necessary. **Factors associated with higher complication rates during ureteroscopy were longer surgery times, treatment of renal calculi, surgeon inexperience, and previous irradiation** (Huffman, 1989; Schuster et al, 2001). During stone fragmentation attempts, electrohydraulic lithotripsy is associated with the highest risk of ureteral injury, followed by the neodymium:YAG (Nd:YAG) laser and finally by the Ho:YAG laser (Johnson and Pearle, 2004). Factors that are thought to protect against ureteral injury are smaller ureteroscopes (Flam et al, 1988; Huffman, 1989) and flexible ureteroscopes (Huffman, 1989).

## Diagnosis

### Gunshot and Stab Wounds

**Incidence of Hematuria.** Because many (25% to 45%) cases of ureteral injury after violence do not demonstrate even

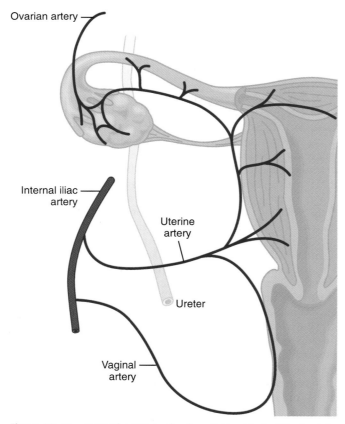

**Figure 39–11.** Ureteral anatomy showing relationship to fallopian tube and uterine artery.

Ovarian artery

Internal iliac artery

Uterine artery

Ureter

Vaginal artery

microscopic hematuria (Presti et al, 1989; Campbell et al, 1992; Brandes et al, 1994; Palmer et al, 1999), a high index of suspicion is required in cases of potential ureteral injury after penetrating trauma. Attention to the course of the bullet or knife and wide use of imaging may decrease the rate of delayed appreciation of these wounds.

**Intraoperative Recognition.** In an analysis of five previously published reports concerning ureteral injury from external violence, Armenakas (1999) noted that 93% of injuries were recognized promptly, including 57% that were identified intraoperatively. We and others (Brandes et al, 1994; Medina et al, 1998) make every attempt to diagnose these injuries during exploratory laparotomy, which is required in 80% to 100% of cases involving the population of patients most at risk for ureteral injury (Pitts and Peterson, 1981; Palmer et al, 1983; Campbell et al, 1992). Intraoperative detection requires a high degree of suspicion, but there is evidence that specific vigilance for ureteral injuries may decrease the incidence of missed injuries (McGinty and Mendez, 1977). The trajectory of the knife or missile must be carefully examined during laparotomy and ureteral exploration undertaken in all cases of potential injury. Liberal use of preoperative diagnostic tools (urinalysis, IVP, CT), even if imperfect, is helpful.

Vigilance for delayed presentation of ureteral injuries also allows detection of injuries missed on presentation. Fever, leukocytosis, and local peritoneal irritation are the most common signs and symptoms of missed ureteral injury and should always prompt CT examination. In contrast to acute injuries, "missed" injuries that are discovered more than 48 hours after injury are best delineated with retrograde ureterography.

*Methylene Blue.* If a ureter or renal pelvis injury is suspected intraoperatively, 1 to 2 mL of methylene blue dye can be injected into the renal pelvis with a 27-gauge needle to confirm the diagnosis. Care must be taken not to inject excessive dye as it can spill and stain local tissues, making determination of the source of leak impossible.

### Imaging Studies

*Excretory Urography.* Ureteral injuries after external violence, unlike renal injuries, are difficult to detect with the usual array of diagnostic tools: preoperative urinalysis, CT scan, and intraoperative one-shot IVP. IVP is often unhelpful, proving nondiagnostic 33% to 100% of the time (Palmer et al, 1983; Presti et al, 1989; Campbell et al, 1992; Brandes et al, 1994; Azimuddin et al, 1998); however, in the absence of a better test, we still recommend intraoperative one-shot pyelography together with intraoperative inspection to detect ureteral injuries. When IVP abnormalities *are* found, obvious contrast extravasation can sometimes be seen (Fig. 39–12). However, IVP findings are often subtle and nonspecific, for example, delayed function, ureteral dilation, and ureteral deviation. Insensitivity of these usual diagnostic tools is one of the reasons why delay of detection occurs in a surprising 8% to 20% of cases (Presti et al, 1989; Brandes et al, 1994; Palmer et al, 1999).

*Computed Tomography.* CT is used increasingly in the evaluation of the trauma patient and, although it appears promising in detecting ureteral injuries (Kawashima et al, 2001), there are few published data to assess its accuracy to date (Kenney et al, 1987; Townsend and DeFalco, 1995).

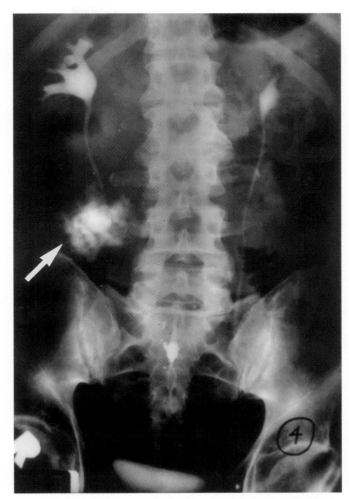

**Figure 39–12.** Excretory urography demonstrating extravasation in the upper right ureter consequent to stab wound. Note lack of contrast *(arrow)* in the ureter below the site of injury, indicating complete ureteral transection.

Reports of the utility of CT in ureteral trauma are still limited to small numbers of cases.

Ureteral injuries can be difficult to diagnose on CT. If the urinary extravasation from the ureteral injury is contained by Gerota's fascia, the extent of medial leakage can be very small, obscuring the diagnosis (Kenney et al, 1987). It is also known that ureteral injuries often manifest with absence of contrast in the ureter on delayed images. This underscores the absolute necessity of tracing both ureters throughout their entire course on CT scans obtained to evaluate urogenital injuries (Townsend and DeFalco, 1995). In addition, because modern helical CT scanners can obtain images before intravenous contrast dye is excreted in the urine, delayed images must be obtained (5 to 20 minutes after contrast injection) to allow contrast material to extravasate from the injured collecting system, renal pelvis, or ureter (Brown et al, 1998; Mulligan et al, 1998; Kawashima et al, 2001). Because ureteral injuries are often detected late, periureteral urinoma seen on delayed CT scans may be diagnostic (Gayer et al, 2002).

In reported series, all patients with significant ureteropelvic laceration, for instance, had either medial extravasation of contrast material or nonopacification of the ipsilateral ureter on CT (Kenney et al, 1987; Kawashima et al, 2001). Such findings should always raise suspicion for ureteral injury.

*Retrograde Ureterography.* Retrograde ureterograms are used in some centers as a primary diagnostic technique to detect acute ureteral injuries (Campbell et al, 1992); however, we tend to use noninvasive methods such as one-shot IVP and CT scan or to make the diagnosis intraoperatively when feasible. Retrograde ureterography is used, however, to delineate the extent of ureteral injury seen on CT scan or IVP if further clinical information is needed. Retrograde ureterography is most commonly used to diagnose missed ureteral injuries, as it allows the simultaneous placement of a ureteral stent if possible.

*Antegrade Ureterography.* Antegrade ureterography is seldom used in our practice. In cases in which ureteral injury is discovered, we most often plan retrograde ureterography and stent placement or open repair. If retrograde stent placement is not possible (usually secondary to a large gap in the two ends of the transected ureter), we use anterograde ureterography and stent placement at the time of percutaneous nephrostomy placement (Toporoff et al, 1992).

## Management (Fig. 39–13)
### External Trauma
#### Contusion

*Ureteroureterostomy.* Ureteral contusions, although the most "minor" of ureteral injuries, often heal with stricture or breakdown later if microvascular injury results in ureteral necrosis. **Severe or large areas of contusion should be treated with excision of the damaged area and ureteroureterostomy.**

Following certain general principles of ureteral surgery increases the success rate of this delicate surgery. Repair of the

ureter must be meticulous (Fig. 39–14). Ureteral blood supply is tenuous, and a sequela of imperfect repair can be urine leakage that can result in the patient's debility, nephrectomy, and in rare cases even death. Principles of management of the injured ureter are as follows:

1. Mobilize the injured ureter carefully, sparing the adventitia widely, so as not to devascularize the ureter.
2. Débride the ureter liberally until edges bleed, especially in high-velocity gunshot wounds.
3. Repair ureters with spatulated, tension-free, stented (Palmer et al, 1983), watertight anastomosis; use optical magnification and retroperitoneal drainage afterward.
4. Consider omental interposition to isolate the repair when possible.

Ureteroureterostomy, or so-called end-to-end repair, is used in injuries to the upper two thirds of the ureter. It is required commonly, up to 32% of the time in large series (Presti et al, 1989; Elliott and McAninch, 2003), and has a reported success rate as high as 90% (Carlton et al, 1971). Complications after ureteroureterostomy, usually urine leakage, occur 10% to 24% of the time (Bright and Peters, 1977a; Pitts and Peterson, 1981; Presti et al, 1989; Campbell et al, 1992; Velmahos et al, 1996; Medina et al, 1998). Other acute complications include abscess and fistula. Chronic complications, usually comprising ureteral stenosis, are less common, involving approximately 5% (Palmer et al, 1999) to 12% (Velmahos et al, 1996) of patients. Interestingly, some authors report prolonged leakage of urine from the drain in patients with ureteral injury after external violence who underwent repair but otherwise did well. Steers and colleagues (1985) reported that most of their patients had persistent drainage (averaging 12 days) from the retroperitoneal Penrose drain after repair. This has not been our experience, but this observation might prompt watchful waiting in such patients who leak persistently after repair.

Management of dehiscence by percutaneous nephrostomy placement and ureteral catheter placement for at least 6 weeks has been reported in small studies, with a surprisingly good success rate (83% [Toporoff et al, 1992] to 88% [Lang, 1984]). Other authors have recommended stenting for a longer period, up to 8 weeks (Steers et al, 1985).

Rarely, acute nephrectomy is required to treat ureteral injury after external violence. Reasons for nephrectomy include associated severe visceral injuries (although damage control without nephrectomy is probably preferable acutely) or severe associated injury to the ipsilateral kidney when renal repair is not possible (McGinty and Mendez, 1977; Gill and McRoberts, 1992). Delayed nephrectomy may be required, because of poor renal function (which can sometimes be seen after delayed recognition of an obstructing ureteral injury), severe panureteral injury when ileal ureter or other reconstruction is impossible, or persistent ureteral fistula (especially vascular fistula) despite previous intervention (Ghali et al, 1999).

*Internal Stenting.* Minor ureteral contusions can be treated with stent placement. Caution must be exercised, however, as minor-appearing ureteral contusions may stricture later or break down secondary to unappreciated microvascular damage to the ureter. When in doubt, the injured portion of the ureter should be débrided and ureteroureterostomy used to repair the injury.

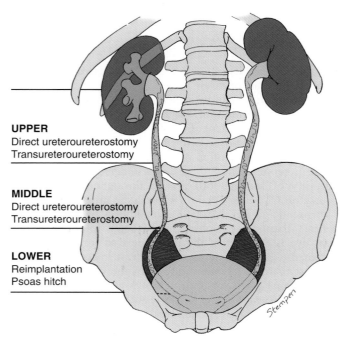

**UPPER**
Direct ureteroureterostomy
Transureteroureterostomy

**MIDDLE**
Direct ureteroureterostomy
Transureteroureterostomy

**LOWER**
Reimplantation
Psoas hitch

**Figure 39–13.** Suggested management options for ureteral injuries at different levels.

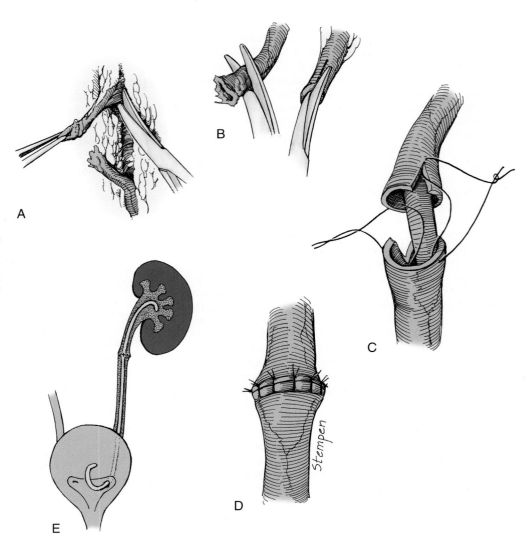

**Figure 39–14.** Technique of ureteroureterostomy after traumatic disruption: **A,** injury site definition by ureteral mobilization; **B,** débridement of margins and spatulation; **C,** stent placement; **D,** approximation with 5-0 absorbable suture; **E,** final result.

## Upper Ureteral Injuries

*Ureteroureterostomy.* Ureteral avulsion from the renal pelvis, or very proximal ureteral injury, can be managed by reimplantation of the ureter directly into the renal pelvis. The principles of repair include spatulation, lack of tension, stenting, postoperative drainage, and a watertight anastomosis with fine nonreactive absorbable suture. Although the majority of these injuries are treated by open surgery (especially when not discovered immediately), laparoscopic repair of ureteral injuries is increasingly common in the literature (Tulikangas et al, 2001). Laparoscopic pyeloplasty in the absence of trauma is now quite common (Eden et al, 2004), and this procedure might mature into laparoscopic repair of traumatic UPJ avulsion in the future. Rarely, ureterocalycostomy, in which the ureteral stump is sewn end to side into an exposed renal calyx, can also be used where there is profound damage to the renal pelvis and UPJ (Matlaga et al, 2005).

*Autotransplantation.* Autotransplantation of the kidney has been used after profound ureteral loss or after multiple attempts at ureteral repair have failed. Renal units are sometimes lost after autotransplantation, occurring in 2 of 24 (8%) kidneys in one series (Bodie et al, 1986). The nephrectomy portion of the autotransplantation has been performed with laparoscopic techniques (Fabrizio et al, 2000; Meng et al, 2003).

*Bowel Interposition.* Delayed ureteral repairs, especially when a very long segment of ureter is destroyed, can also be performed by creation of a ureteral conduit out of ileum, much in the same way that an ileal conduit is constructed to drain the urine after cystectomy. Success rates for ileal replacement of the ureter have been reported to be 81% (Boxer et al, 1979; Verduyckt et al, 2002) to 100% (Bonfig et al, 2004; Matlaga et al, 2003). Some have used the Monti procedure, in which short segments of small or large bowel are formed into a long thin tube successfully in ureteral reconstruction (Ubrig et al, 2001; Ali-el-Dein and Ghoneim, 2003). The use of appendix has also been reported (Jang et al, 2002). Although most practitioners create a wide-open, refluxing, ileal replacement of the ureter, it appears that significant clinical reflux is not a problem (Waldner et al, 1999). Ileal interposition is not suggested for acute repair of ureteral injury but rather would be used in delayed or staged repairs.

## Midureteral Injuries

*Ureteroureterostomy: Transureteroureterostomy.* A rarely used (Presti et al, 1989) but often (90% to 97%) successful (Rainwater et al, 1991; Sugarbaker et al, 2003) technique in adults is transureteroureterostomy. (Pediatric series show a lower success rate of 70% [Mure et al, 2000].) This form of repair involves bringing the injured ureter across the midline and anastomosing it end to side into the uninjured ureter and is most often performed as a secondary or delayed procedure. It might also be mandated in some cases of middle or distal ureteral injury, where ureteroureterostomy or bladder flap/hitch repair is impossible (usually because of severe bladder scarring, a congenitally small bladder, or a very long segment of missing ureter). However, transureteroureterostomy leaves the patient and urologist with some vexing problems postoperatively. The injured ureter becomes difficult to intubate or image with ureteroscopy through the bladder—ureteral access needs to be provided by a nephrostomy placed on the injured side. Some authors feel this operation is contraindicated in patients with a history of urothelial cancer or calculi, although this information is seldom available to the operating trauma surgeon. Caution is mandated in performing this procedure as it involves surgery on the uninjured, contralateral ureter with the theoretical risk of converting unilateral ureteral injury into (iatrogenic) bilateral ureteral injury. Instead of transureteroureterostomy, we have preferred either ileal ureter or ureteroureterostomy with renal mobilization if necessary.

## Lower Ureteral Injuries

*Ureteroneocystostomy.* Ureteroneocystostomy is used to repair distal ureteral injuries that occur so close to the bladder that the bladder does not need to be brought up to the ureteral stump with a psoas hitch or Boari procedure. Principles of ureteroneocystostomy include creation of a submucosal tunnel for a nonrefluxing ureteral repair, usually a tunnel that is at least three times longer than the ureter is wide. A new ureteral orifice is constructed with the use of interrupted 6-0 monofilament absorbable sutures in a watertight and nonobstructing fashion. The repair should be stented postoperatively.

In some cases, a refluxing nontunneled anastomosis can be considered if ureteral length is insufficient for tunneling or if tunneling is thought by the surgeon to increase the risk of ureteral stenosis. Refluxing uretero-neobladder (Minervini et al, 2005) and uretero–ileal loop (Wiesner and Thuroff, 2004) anastomoses show no increase in complications related to urine reflux, although these populations of patients are different from the average trauma population and reports do not address whether ureteral implantation into the native bladder is equally safe. Further study is needed to resolve this issue.

*Psoas Bladder Hitch.* The psoas hitch procedure is a mainstay in the treatment of injuries to the lower third of the ureter and has a high success rate, from 95% to 100% (Middleton, 1980; Riedmiller et al, 1984; Ahn and Loughlin, 2001). It is preferred to ureteroureterostomy in this area because the tenuous independent blood supply might not survive transection.

*Boari Flap.* Injuries to the lower two thirds of the ureter with long ureteral defects (too long to be bridged by bringing the bladder up in the psoas hitch procedure) can be managed with a Boari flap or a transureteroureterostomy. In this case, a pedicle of bladder is swung cephalad and tabularized to bridge the gap to the injured ureter. The procedure is time consuming, however, and some have questioned its usefulness in the acute setting. The procedure is not commonly performed, but authors report a high success rate (Benson et al, 1990). Laparoscopic Boari flap has been described by one center of laparoscopic excellence (Fugita et al, 2001).

**Partial Transection.** Primary repair of a partial transection is used in the majority of ureteral injuries, up to 58% of the time in one large series (Presti et al, 1989). It must be limited to low-velocity gunshot wounds or stab wounds. Principles of primary repair involve spatulated, watertight closure under optical magnification, with interrupted or running 5-0 or 6-0 absorbable monofilament such as Maxon (polyglyconate) or Dexon (polyglycolic acid). The ureteral injury is closed by converting a longitudinal laceration into a transverse one so as not to narrow the ureteral lumen (Heineke-Mikulicz procedure). An internal stent and retroperitoneal drain are placed.

**Damage Control.** In cases of ureteral injury after external violence, it is sometimes necessary to treat the injured ureter by deferring definitive treatment until later. This is usually because the patient is too unstable to tolerate the operative time required to complete the repair (Cass, 1983). Some have suggested that in cases of severe hemorrhagic shock, uncontrollable intraoperative bleeding, or severe colon injury (especially those requiring colectomy), ureteral repair should be avoided in favor of nephrectomy or staged repair (Velmahos et al, 1996).

There are four options for damage control in ureteral injuries: (1) do nothing, but plan a reoperation when the patient is more stable, usually within 24 hours; (2) place a ureteral stent and do nothing else; (3) exteriorize the ureter; or (4) tie off the ureter and plan percutaneous nephrostomy (Hirshberg et al, 1994). In most cases of planned staged repair, we tie off the damaged ureter, using long silk ties to aid the dissection of the ureteral stump during the second-stage repair. The kidney is then drained percutaneously. We advocate percutaneous placement of a nephrostomy tube, either by the surgeon just postoperatively or later by interventional radiology specialists. We have found that intraoperative open nephrostomy placement can be too time consuming in these unstable patients. Other authors have advocated placing an 8 French feeding tube into the ureter and exteriorizing it until definitive repair can be completed (Gill and McRoberts, 1992).

## Surgical Injury

**Ligation.** Ligation of the ureter should be treated by removal of the ligature and observation of the ureter for viability. If viability is in question, ureteroureterostomy or ureteral reimplantation should be performed (Assimos et al, 1994). Placement of a ureteral stent, either by opening the bladder or by immediate cystoscopic placement, is highly advised.

## Transection

*Immediate Recognition.* Ureteral injuries that occur during vascular graft surgery are a special case. Intraoperative management of these injuries is debated and can uncommonly include nephrectomy, if the patient has an adequately functioning contralateral kidney, versus primary uretero-ureterostomy with isolation of the repair with omentum (Adams et al, 1992). Nephrectomy in cases of ureteral injury is controversial and should be considered only in limited situations, usually involving prosthetic graft surgery. The argument for nephrectomy is that, although it is a radical solution, it avoids the potential for postoperative urine leakage around an aortic or iliac vascular graft, which can be potentially fatal (Schapira et al, 1981). Nephrectomy must be performed with caution, however, as the mortality rate from renal failure in routine aortic aneurysmectomy is 3% and climbs to 12% in patients with a ruptured aneurysm (Schapira et al, 1981). The argument for repair also cites the risk of postoperative renal insufficiency after nephrectomy in this population. Although an accurate assessment of the complication rate after repair of ureteral injuries that occur during vascular surgery is not available, the risk of breakdown of ureteral repair after other surgeries has been reported to be 8% (Ghali et al, 1999) to 40% (Spirnak et al, 1989). In one small reported series, breakdown resulted in nephrectomy in two of two patients (Spirnak et al, 1989). We recommend careful repair of the ureteral injury, reserving nephrectomy for patients who develop urine leakage postoperatively.

Immediately discovered injuries after nonaortic surgery are largely treated in the same way delineated previously for ureteral injury after external violence. Most lacerations can be treated with ureteroureterostomy, although additional maneuvers such as omental wrapping of the repair or placement of an ipsilateral nephrostomy tube have been advocated to decrease the potential for urine leakage or breakdown of the repair (Adams et al, 1992). Although not yet commonly done, laparoscopic (Nezhat and Nezhat, 1992) and ureteroscopic (Tsai et al, 2000) ureteroureterostomies for operative ureteral injuries have been reported.

***Delayed Recognition.*** Intraoperative recognition of ureteral injuries occurs in approximately 34% of patients undergoing open operation (Ghali et al, 1999) and sometimes in none of those undergoing laparoscopy (Grainger et al, 1990). Delayed diagnosis of ureteral injury is most often (66% [Ghali et al, 1999] to 76% [Grainger et al, 1990]) achieved by CT pyelography, IVP, or retrograde ureterography (Grainger et al, 1990). Patients present with a variety of signs and symptoms: anuria (5 of 35 patients, most with bilateral injury), urogenital fistula (4 of 35 patients), persistent pain or fever (3 of 35 patients), urinary leakage from the wound (3 of 35 patients), hydronephrosis (1 of 35 patients), and hematuria (1 of 35 patients) (Ghali et al, 1999). Some authors have cited a triad of fever, leukocytosis, and generalized peritoneal signs as being most diagnostic for missed ureteral injury (Medina et al, 1998). Repair of these delayed-recognition injuries is controversial. Some advocate immediate attempt at placement of a double-J ureteral stent (Bright and Peters, 1977b), but this is possible in only 20% (Ghali et al, 1999; Oh et al, 2000) to 50% (Cormio et al, 1993). When stent placement is possible, some authors have reported an ultimate success rate as high as 73% without the need for open surgery (Dowling et al, 1986). Usually, failure to place a stent is due to complete obstruction of the ureter or to too long a gap (Cormio et al, 1993). Some authors have suggested that stenting be avoided in patients who have had multiple pelvic operations, radiation therapy, or significant previous ureteral surgery, as they suffer

high rates of failure (Chang and Marshall, 1987). The time required for stenting has never been studied in a randomized, prospective, double-blind fashion, but some authors recommend at least 6 weeks (Selzman and Spirnak, 1996). Some authors had a 100% success rate in treating late ureteral complications with a ureteral stent for 3 months (Cormio et al, 1993). Other authors reported much less satisfactory results with stenting: in a series of ureteral injuries after laparoscopy that were recognized late (3 to 33 days after surgery), all ultimately required open repair (Oh et al, 2000).

Although some suggest stent placement as the first line of therapy for ureteral injuries with delayed recognition, others recommend that these injuries be repaired in an open fashion as soon as possible. These authors cite low complication rates, which can be as low as in repair of injuries that are recognized immediately (Witters et al, 1986; Ghali et al, 1999). However, delayed diagnosis of ureteral injury itself increases the complication rate of the repair significantly (Selzman and Spirnak, 1996), from 10% to 40% in one series (Campbell et al, 1992), and some have advocated late repair (6 weeks) to allow maximal resolution of perioperative inflammation (Cangiano and deKernion, 1988).

We attempt retrograde placement of a ureteral stent in most cases of delayed recognition of ureteral injury. If stent placement is achieved, open repair is required only in patients with persistent leakage or ureteral stricture (Dowling et al, 1986; Cormio et al, 1993). In cases in which we cannot place a retrograde ureteral stent, we usually place a nephrostomy tube and make a gentle attempt at anterograde stenting of the injury. If this fails, we place a nephrostomy tube and wait 7 to 14 days to reattempt anterograde ureteral stenting. Ureteral balloon catheters, which stop urine from traveling down the ureter, may be required if simple stenting does not eliminate associated urine leakage or urinoma. If the ureter ultimately cannot be stented, we believe the safest approach is to allow at least 6 weeks for complete healing of the wounds, then attempt open repair. Some have reported the requirement for even longer ureteral drainage in some specialized cases, such as in the presence of ureteroenteric fistula (Bright and Peters, 1977b). We recognize that some experts in the field repair these injuries whenever they are discovered, with seemingly good results (Bright and Peters, 1977b; Flynn et al, 1979; Blandy et al, 1991; Oh et al, 2000).

Some authors have advocated treating postinjury ureteral stenosis endoscopically with either balloon dilation (Richter et al, 2000) or laser incision (Singal et al, 1997; Patel and Newman, 2004). Others have used endoluminal stents for ureteral obstruction after injury with good results in very limited numbers of patients (Yohannes et al, 2001). We personally have had poor results after endoscopic dilation and incision techniques in the long, devascularized, postinjury or postoperative ureteral strictures that seem to dominate our practice, although we often try them in short strictures before open repair is contemplated. Metal endoluminal stents must be considered experimental until large series validate their use.

## Ureteroscopy Injury

**Avulsion.** Ureteral avulsion during ureteroscopy is treated in the same manner as ureteral injuries after open or laparoscopic surgery, as detailed in the previous section.

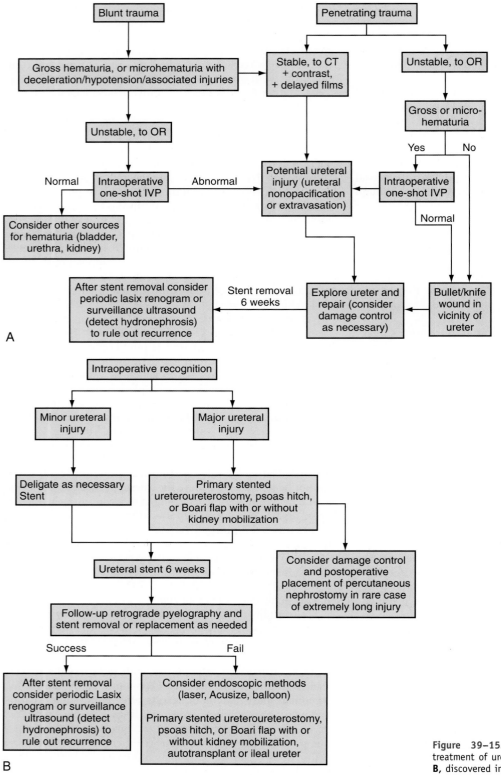

**Figure 39–15.** Algorithms for the diagnosis and treatment of ureteral injuries: **A,** from external violence; **B,** discovered intraoperatively.

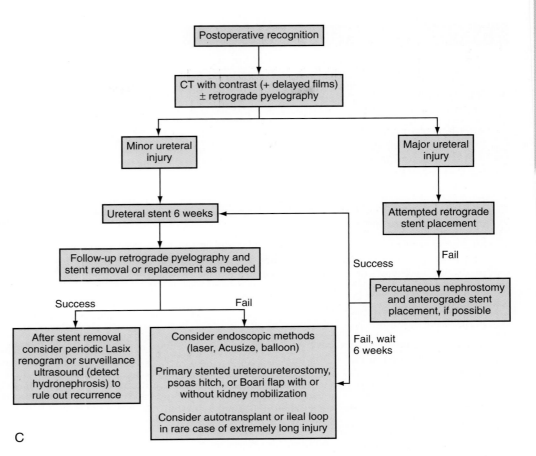

**Figure 39–15, cont'd** **C,** discovered postoperatively. CT, computed tomography; IVP, intravenous pyelography; OR, operating room.

**Perforation.** **Ureteral perforation can be treated by ureteral stenting, usually with no subsequent complications** (Flam et al, 1988; Huffman, 1989). The safest approach is to avoid injury by performing ureteroscopy over a ureteral guide wire. The next safest approach is to use a second ureteral "safety wire" that is always in place during ureteroscopy and facilitates ureteral stent placement in the presence of problems. We recognize that some expert centers do not use a ureteral guide wire during ureteroscopy and that some no longer use a safety wire (Bratslavsky and Moran, 2004), but we believe that a safety wire is most prudent for the majority of practitioners. (Fig. 39–15).

## KEY POINTS: URETERAL TRAUMA

Ureteral injuries must be carefully searched for, or they will be missed.

- Intraoperatively, surgically expose and inspect the ureter when necessary:

  After penetrating injury, use CT scan and intraoperative one-shot IVP liberally.
  After penetrating injury, determine the course of the knife or bullet tract to ensure that the ureter is not at risk.

- If delayed recognition is suspected, use retrograde pyelography aggressively.

  Successful repair of ureteral injuries, whether from external violence or surgical misadventure, is predicated on the use of well-vascularized tissue.

- Ureteral viability must be ensured by interval removal of nonviable segment before ureteroureterostomy.

- Tenuously viable distal ureter is bypassed by sewing the bladder to the uninjured proximal ureteral stump.

- Upper ureteral injuries can be removed and the ureter reimplanted into the renal pelvis after renal mobilization.

  Avoidance of iatrogenic ureteral injury is of utmost importance.

- Safe ureteroscopy practices should be followed, including limiting ureteroscopy times, use of safety wires, and use of guide wires.

- Periureteral surgery should be undertaken with constant knowledge of its course.

## SUGGESTED READINGS

American College of Surgeons Committee on Trauma: Advanced Trauma Life Support for Doctors. Chicago, American College of Surgeons, 1997.

Brandes S, Coburn M, Armenakas NA, McAninch JW: Diagnosis and management of ureteric injury: An evidence-based analysis. BJU Int 2004;94:277-289.

Bretan PN Jr, McAninch JW, Federle MP, Jeffrey RB Jr: Computerized tomographic staging of renal trauma: 85 consecutive cases. J Urol 1986;136:561-565.

Buckley JC, McAninch JW: Pediatric renal injuries: Management guidelines from a 25-year experience. J Urol 2004;172:687-690.

Carroll PR, Klosterman P, McAninch JW: Early vascular control for renal trauma: A critical review. J Urol 1989;141:826-828.

Chandhoke PS, McAninch JW: Detection and significance of microscopic hematuria in patients with blunt renal trauma. J Urol 1988;140:16-18.

Coburn M: Damage control surgery for urologic trauma: An evolving management strategy. J Urol 2002;160:13.

McAninch JW: Surgery for renal trauma. In Novick AC, Pontes ES, Streem SB (eds): Stewart's Operative Urology, 2nd ed. Baltimore, Williams & Wilkins, 1989, pp 234-239.

Miller KS, McAninch JW: Radiographic assessment of renal trauma: Our 15-year experience. J Urol 1995;154:352-355.

Moore EE, Shackford SR, Pachter HL, et al: Organ injury scaling: Spleen, liver, and kidney. J Trauma 1989;29:1664-1666.

Morey AL, McAninch JW, Tiller BK, et al: Single shot intraoperative excretory urography for the immediate evaluation of renal trauma. J Urol 1999;161:1088-1092.

Presti JC Jr, Carroll PR, McAninch JW: Ureteral and renal pelvic injuries from external trauma: Diagnosis and management. J Trauma 1989;29:370-374.

Santucci RA, McAninch JW: Diagnosis and management of renal trauma: Past, present and future. J Am Coll Surg 2000;191:443-451.

Santucci RA, Wessells H, Bartsch G, et al: Evaluation and management of renal injuries: A consensus statement of renal trauma. BJU Int 2004;94:27-32.

Selzman AA, Spirnak JP: Iatrogenic ureteral injuries: A 20-year experience in treating 165 injuries. J Urol 1996;155:878.

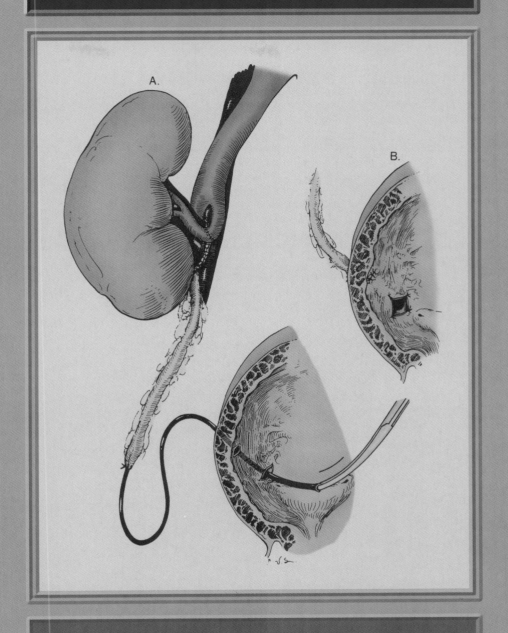

# 40 Renal Transplantation

JOHN M. BARRY, MD • MARK L. JORDAN, MD •
MICHAEL J. CONLIN, MD

END-STAGE RENAL DISEASE

HISTORY OF HUMAN RENAL TRANSPLANTATION

SELECTION AND PREPARATION OF KIDNEY
TRANSPLANT RECIPIENTS

DONOR SELECTION, PREPARATION, AND SURGERY

KIDNEY PRESERVATION

RECIPIENT SELECTION FOR DECEASED DONOR
KIDNEY TRANSPLANTS

PREOPERATIVE ASSESSMENT

PREPARATION OF KIDNEY GRAFT

RECIPIENT OPERATION

POSTOPERATIVE CARE

RENAL ALLOGRAFT REJECTION

PROBLEMS

SUMMARY

**Kidney transplantation is the pioneer discipline in solid organ transplantation, and the relationship between transplant surgeon and nephrologist has served as a model for multidisciplinary team care.**

Each renal transplantation operation is a study of pelvic anatomy, each deceased donor nephrectomy is a study of intraperitoneal and retroperitoneal anatomy, and each living donor nephrectomy is a surgical procedure on a kidney, procedures that are decreasing in frequency because of the development of nonoperative methods of treating renal stones and obstruction. Nowhere in urology must the principles of urinary tract reconstruction and infection control be more rigorously applied than in the immunosuppressed kidney transplant recipient. Understanding the molecular mechanisms of antigen-lymphocyte interactions in transplantation should provide insights into other disease processes such as cancer and infection. Renal preservation principles are often applied to parenchyma-sparing renal operations and to complex renovascular reconstruction procedures. As more renal transplantations are performed, more of these patients are likely to present to the practicing urologist for evaluation and preparation of the urinary tract for transplantation and for the care of urologic problems after transplantation, which may or may not be related to the transplantation surgery or to the consequences of immunosuppression.

## END-STAGE RENAL DISEASE
### Incidence and Prevalence

The estimated number of patients starting renal replacement therapy each year for end-stage renal disease (ESRD) in the United States is about 335 per million population (U.S. Renal Data System [USRDS], 2004). The median age of these new ESRD patients is 65 years. Both the prevalence and the incidence of ESRD are more common in elderly than in young patients, in men than in women, and in African Americans, Hispanics, and Native Americans than in whites. Diabetes mellitus is the most frequent cause of ESRD, followed in order by hypertension and glomerulonephritis. Diabetes is especially common among Native Americans, and hypertension is disproportionately high among African Americans. The incidence of ESRD is greater than that for any urologic malignancy except prostate cancer, and more patients die annually of ESRD than from any urologic malignancy (USRDS, 2004: Hoyert et al, 2005; Jemal et al, 2005).

### Treatment Options

The purposes of renal replacement therapy are to prolong and to maintain the quality of life. **The treatment or treatments that are chosen for an individual patient are those that will allow the longest extension of useful life.** Renal replacement therapy is now considered to be a right in the United States and most other developed countries. Permanent renal failure in adults is commonly defined as an irreversible glomerular filtration rate of less than 10 mL/min or a serum creatinine level of greater than 8 mg/dL (United Network for Organ Sharing [UNOS], 1994). Patients with symptomatic uremia, especially children and diabetic adults, are considered on an individual basis as meeting criteria for permanent renal failure. A reasonable goal for ESRD treatment programs is the transplantation of all patients in whom the risk is equal to or less than that of remaining on maintenance dialysis. Renal transplantation is the preferred method of therapy for most patients with ESRD because it is more cost effective and allows a return to a more normal lifestyle than maintenance dialysis does. A recent quality of life year (QALY) cost analysis strongly favored transplantation over dialysis (Mendeloff et al, 2004). The number of patients listed for kidney transplantation continues to expand disproportionately to the number of kidney transplantations performed annually. There are currently more than 60,000 patients waiting for deceased donor kidney transplants, and with about 9500 deceased donor kidney transplants performed annually, there are nearly seven times as many ESRD patients waiting as there will be deceased donor kidneys available in the coming year. Despite this obvious disparity, the number of deceased donor kidney transplants has increased only 22% over the past 10 years, and this is mostly due to the use of expanded criteria kidney transplants (Organ Procurement and Transplant Network [OPTN], 2005). The inadequate supply of deceased donor kidneys is one of the factors that has influenced the increase in the number of living donor kidney transplants by 120% in the past decade. The increase in living renal donation has been further facilitated by the widespread adoption of minimally invasive donor nephrectomy techniques, the increased use of living, biologically unrelated renal donors, and the development of protocols for transplantation across alloantibody barriers, including ABO blood group incompatibility. Xenotransplantation and tissue engineering are fields of research for the continuing problem of inadequate supply of transplantable organs.

In-center hemodialysis is the predominant form of therapy for adults with ESRD. In the United States, it accounts for more than one half of all treated ESRD patients (USRDS, 2004). Transplantation, however, is the predominant mode of care for patients younger than 20 years. About 10% of ESRD patients are treated with chronic peritoneal dialysis. A desire for self-care, a long distance from a hemodialysis unit, difficulties with hemodialysis therapy, serious cardiac disease, diabetes mellitus, and small stature are characteristics of patients especially suited for peritoneal dialysis. Unsuitable characteristics of patients for chronic peritoneal dialysis are considered to be obesity, hernias, poor hygiene, inflammatory bowel disease, and obliterated peritoneal space (Nicholson and White, 2001).

The advantages of living related donor renal transplantation compared with deceased donor renal transplantation are better probabilities of graft survivals, less recipient morbidity, specific planning of the operation to allow preemptive transplantation or limitation of the waiting time on dialysis, and partial alleviation of the insufficient supply of deceased donor kidneys. **The timing of preemptive renal transplantation must be such that the patient does not have months to years of usable function in the failing native kidneys.** Objections to transplantation before dialysis are that the procedure removes the experience of dialysis so that the advantages of transplantation are not appreciated and that of concern that a preemptive deceased donor kidney transplantation means that a patient has been unfairly advantaged over patients already on dialysis, some of whom have been waiting a long time for a kidney graft.

When compared with adults with ESRD, children are more likely to receive chronic peritoneal dialysis and they are more likely to undergo renal transplantation (USRDS, 2004). There

is a relatively greater availability of parental kidney donors, and children receive preferential points when they are listed for deceased kidney transplantation. **Special problems in children with ESRD include growth failure, poor nutrition, and psychiatric problems.** They often suffer from a cycle of depression, anxiety, and loss of self-esteem, and these problems can result in family stress and divorce (National Institutes of Health [NIH] Consensus Development Conference, 1993). The development of recombinant growth hormone has made possible the treatment of short stature in pediatric patients with chronic renal failure and after renal transplantation (Fine, 1997). Nutritional supplementation can be done by nasogastric feeding tube or button gastrostomy.

## Results of Treatment

**Data from the USRDS indicate that survival after renal transplantation is significantly better than that of patients treated with dialysis** (USRDS, 2004). Although this may simply mean that healthier patients are more likely to undergo a transplant, more controlled analyses have indicated a significantly reduced mortality risk for renal transplant recipients when compared with acceptable transplantation candidates waiting on dialysis (Meire-Kriesche et al, 2002). Regardless of whether the treatment modality is dialysis or transplantation, the major causes of death are, in order, heart disease, sepsis, and stroke (USRDS, 2004).

The survival of kidney grafts has steadily improved, and those for the current era are quite remarkable (Table 40–1).

## HISTORY OF HUMAN RENAL TRANSPLANTATION

The history of renal transplantation illustrates the successful combination of the fields of surgery, medicine, immunology, and government. Carrel established the modern method of vascular suturing at the turn of the 20th century, and he was awarded the Nobel Prize in 1912 for his work on organ grafting (Hamilton, 2001). In 1933, the first human renal allograft was performed by Voronoy in the Ukraine (Hamilton and Reid, 1984). The recipient was a 26-year-old woman who had attempted suicide by ingesting mercuric chloride. The donor was a 66-year-old man whose kidney was removed 6 hours

**Table 40–1. Kidney Transplant Survival Rates for Primary Transplants Done 1998-2002**

| Donor | No. | 5 Year (%) | Half-Life (Yr)* |
|---|---|---|---|
| HLA-identical sibling | 2,189 | 87 | 29 |
| One-haplotype sibling | 3,584 | 81 | 19 |
| Spouse | 2,803 | 78 | 18 |
| Other biologically unrelated | 3,094 | 78 | 18 |
| Deceased | 34,208 | 66 | 10 |
| Standard criteria | 28,440 | 70 | 11 |
| Expanded criteria | 5,223 | 52 | 7 |

HLA, human leukocyte antigen.
*Half-life is projected for those kidney transplants surviving the first year.
Data from Cecka JM: The OPTN/UNOS renal transplant registry 2003. In Cecka JM, Terasaki PI (eds): Clinical Transplants 2003. Los Angeles, UCLA Immunogenetics Center, 2004, pp 2-3.

after death. Under local anesthesia, the renal vessels were anastomosed to the femoral vessels and a cutaneous ureterostomy was performed. A small amount of blood-stained urine appeared, but the patient died 48 hours after the procedure.

The first long-term success with human renal allografting, in which the patient survived for over a year, occurred in Boston in 1954, when a kidney from one twin was transplanted into the other, who had ESRD (Murray et al, 1955). In 1958, the first histocompatibility antigen was described. Radiation was used for immunosuppression in 1959, azathioprine became available for human use in 1951, and corticosteroids became part of a standard immunosuppression regimen with azathioprine in 1962 (Goodwin et al, 1963). In the same year, the first use of tissue matching to select donor-recipient pairs was done. The direct crossmatch between donor lymphocytes and recipient serum was introduced in 1966, and heterologous antilymphocyte serum was used as an immunosuppressant in human renal transplantation.

In the late 1960s, human renal preservation over 24 hours became possible with either pulsatile machine perfusion (Belzer et al, 1967) or simple cold storage after flushing with an ice-cold intracellular electrolyte solution (Collins et al, 1969). The beneficial effect of blood transfusions was described by Opelz and colleagues in 1973, and this led to immunologic conditioning with blood products for both deceased and living donor renal transplants. Donor-specific blood transfusions eventually became part of standardized pretransplantation immunologic conditioning protocols for living donor renal transplantation (Salvatierra et al, 1980). In the cyclosporine era, the beneficial effects of random blood transfusions and donor-specific blood transfusion protocols have been difficult to establish, and transfusion protocols have been associated with donor-specific sensitization and the transmission of viral illnesses. For these reasons, pretransplantation transfusion protocols are no longer routinely prescribed.

**Medicare co-insurance for ESRD patients was passed into law in 1972 and instituted in 1973. This removed a significant impediment to renal transplantation in the United States.** In the mid 1970s, brain-death laws were passed. This allowed organ retrieval from beating-heart deceased donors, reduced warm ischemia time, and improved the quality of deceased donor kidney grafts. The first clinical trials of cyclosporine were reported by Calne and colleagues in 1978, and this was followed 3 years later by reports of the successful use of a monoclonal antibody for the treatment of renal allograft rejection in humans (Cosimi et al, 1981). In 1984, Congress passed the National Transplant Act, which authorized a national organ-sharing system and grants for organ procurement. The University of Wisconsin (UW) solution, introduced in the late 1980s, provided one solution for the preservation of all transplantable abdominal organs, including kidneys (Belzer and Southard, 1988). Recombinant erythropoietin became available in 1989, and this significantly improved the quality of life for maintenance dialysis patients and reduced the need for blood transfusions (Carpenter, 1990). This has decreased the risk of virally transmitted infections and the risk of the development of anti-human leukocyte antigen (HLA) antibodies in potential kidney transplant recipients. Thirty-six years after the first long-term success of human-to-human kidney transplantation, Joseph E. Murray

received the Nobel Prize in Medicine in 1990 for his pioneering work in renal transplantation.

Laparoscopic donor nephrectomy was introduced in 1995 to reduce disincentives for living donor nephrectomy (Schulam et al, 1996; Pradel et al, 2003).

The last decade has witnessed the development of novel immunosuppressive agents as well as approaches to graft tolerance that may allow reduction and, in some cases, complete discontinuation of chronic immunosuppressive agents (Matthews et al, 2003; Starzl et al, 2003).

# SELECTION AND PREPARATION OF KIDNEY TRANSPLANT RECIPIENTS

The pretransplantation evaluation is a multidisciplinary process that is performed well in advance of the renal transplantation operation and immunosuppression. **The purposes of the evaluation are generally considered to be to diagnose the primary renal disease and its risk of recurrence in the kidney graft and to rule out active invasive infection, a high probability of operative mortality, noncompliance, active malignancy, and unsuitable conditions for technical success** (Barry, 2001; Kasiske et al, 2001).

## Preliminary Screening

The process of evaluating the transplantation candidate is initiated by identifying the presence or absence of the risk factors at the top of the algorithm in Figure 40–1. Candidates with a history of substance abuse must have unannounced drug screens with negative results before continuing the process. Candidates with morbid obesity, defined as greater than 100 pounds over desirable body weight or a body mass index of greater than 35, must demonstrate weight reduction before continuing the process because of the risks associated with renal transplantation in obese patients (Glanton et al, 2003; Meier-Kriesche et al, 2003). Gastric bypass surgery may be an option to prepare dialysis-dependent morbidly obese patients for transplantation (Alexander et al, 2004). Candidates considered to be at risk for noncompliance must demonstrate contract satisfaction, for example, a hemodialysis-dependent patient may be required to maintain his or her serum phosphorus level less than or equal to 6 mg/dL, predialysis serum potassium level less than or equal to 6 mmol/L, and interdialytic weight gain less than or equal to 3 kg for 3 months. It is recommended that patients older than age 50 years or with a history of coronary artery disease, cardiac symptoms, or insulin-dependent diabetes mellitus undergo stress cardiac testing with further diagnosis and treatment of significant cardiac disease before proceeding with the rest of the algorithm (Lewis et al, 2002).

## Kidney Disease Recurrence

**Patients with focal segmental glomerulosclerosis, hemolytic-uremic syndrome, and primary oxalosis should be counseled about the significant probability of disease recurrence and the risk of secondary graft failure** (Cameron, 1993; Jamieson, 1998; First and Peddi, 1999; Hariharan et al, 1999). Patients with a high risk of recurrent focal segmental

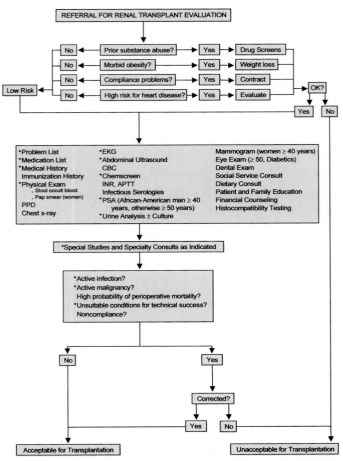

**Figure 40–1.** Algorithm for the evaluation of renal transplantation candidates. Circumstances may change the order in which data are obtained. APTT, activated partial thromboplastin time; CBC, complete blood cell count; EKG, electrocardiogram; INR, International Normalized Ratio; PPD, purified protein derivative (tuberculin skin test); PSA, prostate-specific antigen; PT, prothrombin time. *Asterisks* indicate items of special significance for the urologist. (From Barry JM: Current status of renal transplantation: Patient evaluations and outcomes. Urol Clin North Am 2001;28:677.)

glomerulosclerosis are those younger than 15 years of age, those who have a rapidly progressive course, and those with mesangial proliferation on biopsy of the native kidneys. If a first transplant has failed because of recurrent focal segmental glomerulosclerosis, the risk of recurrence in a second transplant approaches 80%. Hemolytic-uremic syndrome is a relatively common cause of ESRD in children, and recurrence has been associated with cyclosporine immunosuppression. Oxalosis can rapidly recur in a kidney graft, and this disease is probably best treated with combined liver and kidney transplantation to correct both the metabolic defect and the renal failure. The ESRD of renal amyloidosis, cystinosis, and Fabry's disease is potentially treatable with renal transplantation despite significant recurrence rates.

Diabetes mellitus and IgA nephropathy are examples of diseases that commonly recur in the transplanted kidney but rarely result in graft failure.

Autosomal dominant polycystic kidney disease (ADPKD), renal dysplasia, and Alport's syndrome without anti-glomerular basement membrane antibodies are examples of renal diseases that do not recur in the transplanted kidney.

## Infection

**Infections must be detected and treated before transplantation or prevented with immunizations.**

Potential sources of dental sepsis must be treated. Dialysis access sites must be clear of infection. Pulmonary infections or tuberculin skin test conversions require treatment before immunosuppression. Reasonable indications for pretransplantation cholecystectomy are considered to be symptomatic cholecystitis, multiple small gallstones, and cholelithiasis with gallbladder wall thickening. Segmental colectomy is reasonable for patients with recurrent diverticulitis because of the morbidity and mortality of bowel perforation in the immunosuppressed kidney transplant recipient (Salem et al, 2004). Diabetic foot ulcers must be healed before transplantation, and urinary tract infection should be inactive at the time of engraftment.

Serologic testing for cytomegalovirus (CMV) is important because this disease is a major cause of morbidity in immunosuppressed patients (Kaye, 1999). Patients who are seropositive for herpes simplex virus or who have a history of oral or genital herpes simplex or shingles need antiviral therapy during intense immunosuppression. Epstein-Barr virus titers are determined in children; and for the Epstein-Barr virus–seronegative child, a kidney from an Epstein-Barr virus–seronegative donor is preferred to reduce the risk of a post-transplantation lymphoproliferative disorder (Birkeland et al, 1999), the most common new malignancy in pediatric organ transplant recipients (Penn, 1998). Recipient human immune deficiency virus (HIV) infection has been considered to be a contraindication to renal transplantation, but successful outcomes have been reported in HIV-positive patients who have had low viral loads and sufficient CD4 T-cell counts (Stock et al, 2003). Chronic active hepatitis is a major cause of mortality in the late post-transplantation period. The treatment of chronic, active hepatitis B and C is evolving (Simon, 1999), and patients with active hepatitis C infection may benefit from antiviral therapy before transplantation (Mahmoud et al, 2005).

Corticosteroids enhance viral replication, and these infections should be inactive at the time of transplantation. Unless the patient is protected by antibody development after infection or prior immunizations, the following immunizations are given to transplantation candidates: hepatitis A, hepatitis B, pneumococcus, diphtheria, tetanus, pertussis, polio, varicella, measles, mumps, and rubella.

## Active Malignancy

**To reduce the risk of cancer recurrence, a waiting time of 2 to 5 cancer-free years from the time of the last cancer treatment is recommended for patients who have had invasive malignancies** (Kasiske et al, 2001). Shorter intervals from cancer treatment to transplantation are generally accepted for patients who have had low-grade, noninvasive cancers. The application of cancer progression algorithms to recommend cancer-free intervals before transplantation may be helpful in individual cases (Secin et al, 2004). Cholecystectomy is recommended for transplantation candidates with gallbladder polyps greater than 1 cm in diameter because of the risk of malignancy (Boulton and Adams, 1997).

## High Probability of Perioperative Morbidity or Mortality

**Heart disease is the predominant cause of death after renal transplantation** (USRDS, 2004), and it is common for kidney transplantation candidates with a history of cardiac disease, cerebrovascular disease, or diabetes mellitus or who are older than 50 years to undergo a cardiac performance evaluation. Further testing and treatment are based on the results of a screening evaluation. Cerebrovascular disease, peptic ulcer disease, and significant pulmonary disease must be detected and treated. For example, patients with ADPKD and headaches or a family history of stroke should be screened for cerebral aneurysms. Cigarette smoking increases the risks of surgery, post-transplantation malignancy, cardiovascular disease, and renal allograft loss (Sung et al, 2001). It must be stopped before transplantation in patients who already have clinical evidence of vasculopathy or cardiopulmonary disease.

## Noncompliance

Compliance issues are extremely important in the long-term management of kidney transplant recipients. Transplantation candidates with chemical dependency need to have an objectively documented drug- or alcohol-free period of at least 6 months before transplantation (Kasiske et al, 2001). Financial and psychosocial consultations are necessary to identify and correct problems that could result in noncompliance, for example, the lack of funds to pay for maintenance immunosuppressants or a mental handicap that could prevent the recipient from following a post-transplantation treatment plan.

## Unsuitable Conditions for Technical Success

Evaluations of the vascular system and the urinary tract are necessary to identify problems that need to be corrected before transplantation or addressed at the time of transplantation.

Patients with symptoms and signs of lower extremity arterial disease or a history of abdominal or pelvic vascular surgery need to undergo a diagnostic evaluation to be certain that revascularization of a kidney graft is possible. Vascular screening with Doppler flow studies is recommended for the indications listed in Table 40–2. If significant arteriosclerosis or venous disease is detected, it may be necessary to perform angiography to select alternative sites, such as the aorta or splenic artery, for renal revascularization, or to plan corrective vascular surgery before renal transplantation.

**Thrombosis is a significant cause of kidney transplant loss, especially in children** (Singh et al, 1997). Renal transplantation patients at risk for graft thrombosis are those with previous vascular access thrombosis, previous venous thrombosis, antiphospholipid antibodies, and previous large vein renal transplant thrombosis (DeLoughery, 2004). A hypercoagulable state can occur in the nephrotic syndrome with urinary loss of the natural anticoagulants antithrombin III, protein C, and protein S. Hyperhomocysteinemia is common in ESRD, and it has been associated with thrombophilia (Levey et al, 1998). Antiphospholipid antibodies are found in 30% to 50% of patients with systemic lupus erythematosus, a systemic cause of ESRD. Patients can be evaluated with the activated protein C–resistant ratio (factor V Leiden mutation), protein C activity, protein S activity, antithrombin III activity, homocysteine level, prothrombin gene mutation, and antiphospholipid antibodies (DeLoughery, 2004; Irish, 2004). It is reasonable to screen for thrombophilia when a patient is admitted for renal transplantation, to administer low-dose heparin intraoperatively to all recipients, and to continue low-molecular-weight heparin therapy until the results of the thrombophilia panel are known. Based on the thrombophilia panel results, a decision can be made about intermediate- or long-term anticoagulation with low-molecular-weight heparin or warfarin.

**The purposes of the urologic evaluation are to determine the suitability of the urinary bladder or its substitute for urinary tract reconstruction and to determine the necessity for removal of the native kidneys before or at the time of renal transplantation.** The urologic evaluation includes a history for urologic disease and operations on the urinary tract; a physical examination, including the location of scars, abdominal catheters, and stomas that may interfere with transplantation; urinalysis; urine or bladder wash culturing; and ultrasonography of the abdomen and pelvis to include a postvoid bladder image, the kidneys, and the gallbladder. Further study of the urinary tract is indicated for a history of urologic abnormalities, nonglomerular hematuria, single-

**Table 40–2. Recommendations for Doppler Flow Studies in Renal Transplant Candidates**

| | | Areas Studied | |
| --- | --- | --- | --- |
| Indications | Carotids | Aorta and Iliac Arteries, Splenic and Renal Arteries, Lower Extremity Arteries | Pelvic Veins, Inferior Vena Cava |
| Cerebrovascular symptoms or bruits | × | | |
| Lower extremity claudication or bruits | | × | |
| Extensive aortoiliac calcifications or bruits | | × | |
| Prior bilateral renal transplants | | × | × |
| Prior abdominal vascular surgery | | × | × |
| Prior abdominal radiation | | × | × |
| Prior pelvic venous thrombosis | | | × |

Modified from Barry JM: Current status of renal transplantation: Patient evaluations and outcomes. Urol Clin North Am 2001;28:677.

**Table 40-3. Indications for Additional Urologic Studies in Renal Transplant Candidates**

| Studies | Indications |
|---|---|
| Voiding cystourethrogram ± urodynamics | Voiding dysfunction, history of pyelonephritis or reflux, inconclusive ultrasonography |
| Cystoscopy | Suspected lower urinary tract cancer or planned invasive prostate therapy |
| Retrograde pyelography | Planned orthotopic renal transplantation or inconclusive ultrasonography |
| Renal CT scan | Inconclusive ultrasonography for stone or mass, autosomal dominant polycystic kidney disease to accurately size kidneys |
| Urine or bladder wash cytology | Prior cyclophosphamide therapy or significant irritative voiding symptoms |
| Bladder biopsy | Suspected bladder fibrosis or cancer |
| Retrograde loopogram | Intestinal conduit |
| Retrograde pouchogram | Intestinal or gastric reservoir |

Modified from Barry JM: Current status of renal transplantation: Patient evaluations and outcomes. Urol Clin North Am 2001;28;677

**Table 40-4. Indications for Pretransplant Nephrectomy**

Renal stones not cleared by minimally invasive techniques or lithotripsy
Solid renal tumors with or without acquired renal cystic disease
Polycystic kidneys that are symptomatic, extend below the iliac crest, have been infected, or have solid tumors
Persistent antiglomerular basement membrane antibody levels
Significant proteinuria not controlled with medical nephrectomy or angioablation
Recurrent pyelonephritis
Grade 4 or 5 hydronephrosis

organism bacteriuria, calculi, hydronephrosis, ADPKD, significant bladder residual urine, or inconclusive preliminary imaging studies (Table 40-3). The anuric patient will need to be queried about bladder function that was present before urine production ceased. In chronic peritoneal dialysis patients, ultrasound examination of the bladder may overestimate residual urine.

An ESRD patient with upper urinary tract diversion may have a bladder that is acceptable for transplantation, especially if the original reason for diversion was vesicoureteral reflux. **A defunctionalized bladder usually regains normal volume within weeks of transplantation.** It is advisable that transplantation candidates with small, contracted bladders who have had multiple lower urinary tract operations undergo bladder biopsy. If fibrosis is extensive on histologic examination and the bladder cannot be coaxed into becoming a low-pressure reservoir with bladder cycling, autoaugmentation or augmentation cystoplasty can be done before renal transplantation or afterward if satisfactory bladder function does not return within a few months (Barry, 2004). Functionalized augmentation is preferable to dry augmentation because it permits continence and bladder compliance to be documented before transplantation (Gonzales, 1997). A urothelium-lined augmentation is best because mucus does not have to be rinsed from the bladder on a regular basis. Advantages of gastrocystoplasty over enterocystoplasty are the lack of metabolic acidosis and significant mucus with the former. Disadvantages of gastrocystoplasty are the frequency-urgency syndrome due to acid from gastric mucosa and recalcitrant metabolic alkalosis. Patients with augmented bladders usually require clean intermittent catheterization after transplantation, and the patient should be trained in this technique well in advance of the transplantation procedure. **Clean intermittent self-catheterization has been used successfully in transplant recipients for more than 2 decades for patients with neuropathic bladders or transient bladder outlet obstruction** (Schneidman et al, 1984).

Cyclophosphamide is commonly used to treat immune complex glomerulonephritis, and a bladder wash for cytologic examination is recommended for patients with prior cyclophosphamide therapy because of its reported association with transitional cell carcinoma (Radis et al, 1995).

Renal transplants into intestinal conduits or continent intestinal pouches have been successful (Hatch et al, 2001; Surange et al, 2003). The pouches require frequent irrigations before transplantation to remove mucus and to maintain pouch volume.

Men with obstructing prostates whose voiding problems cannot be managed successfully with medical therapy are candidates for prostatectomy or transurethral incision of the bladder neck and prostate before or after transplantation. **Sometimes, it is possible to treat both hypertension and bladder outlet obstruction with one of the less specific α-adrenergic blocking agents, such as doxazosin or prazosin.** It is preferable to avoid surgical treatment of bladder outlet obstruction in the oligoanuric renal transplant candidate until after transplantation because of the risk of bladder neck contracture or prostatic fossa obliteration. If bladder outlet surgery is done pretransplant in the oligoanuric patient, it is advisable to place a suprapubic cystostomy at the time of bladder outlet surgery to allow the patient to instill sterile water and void daily until the operative site has healed, usually 6 weeks, or to have the patient perform daily intermittent self-catheterization, fill the bladder, and then void.

The generally accepted indications for pretransplantation nephrectomy are outlined in Table 40-4. Renal calculi can be managed by minimally invasive techniques, and severe proteinuria can be managed by renal infarction. **The incidence of renal cell carcinoma is more common in patients with acquired renal cystic disease and in transplant recipients than in the general population,** and nephrectomy is indicated for solid renal tumors (MacDougall et al, 1990). If a polycystic kidney extends below the iliac crest, it is best removed to allow room for a kidney transplant. Pretransplantation nephrectomy is usually performed 6 weeks before transplantation or active wait-listing for deceased donor renal transplantation to allow wound healing and the detection and treatment of surgical complications. It is common to perform kidney removal at the time of renal transplantation in children. It is common to do preliminary nephrectomies in adults, especially when the patient is to be listed for deceased donor renal transplantation, when recurrent pyelonephritis has been noted, or when difficult nephrectomy with possible adjacent organ injury is anticipated. Bilateral nephrectomies for ADPKD at the time of renal transplantation have been reported (Glassman et al, 2000). We reserve this option for ADPKD patients who are undergoing living donor renal transplantation. The use of synthetic erythropoietin has reduced the effects of anemia while the patient awaits transplantation. Although laparoscopic or retroperitoneoscopic nephrectomies are becoming more commonly performed in these patients, bilateral vertical lumbotomies are quickly performed and well tolerated by patients with small kidneys undergoing nephrectomy (Freed, 1976). An open flank approach is often used when a kidney is too large to be removed by a vertical lumbotomy or a laparoscopic technique. The open abdominal approach is used when the kidneys are too large to remove with a minimally invasive technique, or when additional procedures, such as total ureterectomy, intestinal conduit removal, augmentation cystoplasty, the creation of a continent intestinal pouch, or the kidney transplantation are to be done at the same time.

Impotence is a significant problem in men with ESRD, and potency improves in a significant proportion of men after transplantation. Contributing factors to erectile dysfunction in ESRD are the accelerated arteriosclerosis associated with dialysis, hyperprolactinemia with secondary testosterone deficiency, side effects from antihypertensive drugs, and a poor self-image. **If penile prosthesis surgery is necessary before renal transplantation, a device that has no prevesical reservoir is recommended because a prevesical reservoir can interfere with urinary tract reconstruction and be mistaken for the urinary bladder until the reservoir has been accidentally incised.**

# DONOR SELECTION, PREPARATION, AND SURGERY

**The basic criteria for a renal donor are an absence of renal disease, an absence of active infection, and an absence of transmissible malignancy.** Whether the kidney is removed from a living donor or a deceased donor, the surgical goals are to minimize warm ischemia time, to preserve renal vessels, and to preserve ureteral blood supply. In the deceased donor, it is also necessary to obtain histocompatibility specimens.

## Living Donor

On the basis of the preoperative evaluation, one must be able to assure the living donor of nearly normal renal function after unilateral nephrectomy. On evaluation, if one of the potential donor's kidneys is better than the other, the better kidney is left with the donor (Murray and Harrison, 1963). It is preferable to use the right kidney from women who may become pregnant because hydronephrosis of pregnancy and pyelonephritis of pregnancy occur predominantly in that kidney (Stevens, 1933; Monga, 1998). An algorithm for the evaluation of a living renal donor is presented in Figure 40–2. Circumstances may change the order in which data are obtained. A living renal donor is considered to be unsuitable when one of the following is present: significant mental dysfunction, significant renal disease, high risk of perioperative mortality or morbidity, and significant transmissible disease. ABO incompatibility and a positive crossmatch between donor lymphocytes and recipient serum were usually considered to be contraindications to directed living renal donation, but protocols are evolving to deal with these issues (Warren et al, 2004). Serologic testing is performed for human immunodeficiency virus (HIV) and human T-lymphoproliferative virus type 1 (HTLV-1) infection, hepatitis, CMV infection, and syphilis. Some programs also screen for Epstein-Barr virus (Bia et al, 1995), especially when the recipient is a child. Diabetes mellitus is excluded in the donor by determining that the casual or random plasma glucose level is less than 200 mg/dL; the fasting plasma glucose level is less than 125 mg/dL; or after a 75-g glucose load, the 2-hour plasma glucose level is less than 200 mg/dL (Report of the Expert Committee on the Diagnosis and Classification of Diabetes Mellitus, 1997). Abdominal ultrasonography can be performed to exclude donors with significant renal abnormalities and to detect incidental intra-abdominal abnormalities. Diagnostic imaging techniques for living renal donors are compared in Table 40–5. Three-dimensional CT angiography without and with intravenous contrast material followed by

| Table 40–5. Rank Order of Renal Imaging Techniques for Living Renal Donors | | | |
|---|---|---|---|
| | **Imaging Techniques** | | |
| | **3D Helical CT Angiogram with and without Intravenous Contrast** | **Intravenous Urogram + Arteriogram** | **Magnetic Resonance Imaging + Intravenous Gadolinium** |
| Stone detection | 1 | 2 | 3 |
| Mass detection | 1 | 3 | 2 |
| Collecting system definition | 1.5 | 1.5 | 3 |
| No. of arteries | 2.5 | 1 | 2.5 |
| No. of veins | 1.5 | 3 | 1.5 |
| Patient morbidity | 1 | 3 | 2 |
| Total | 8.5 | 13.5 | 14 |
| Rank | 1 | 2 | 3 |

1 = best

Data from Pozniak MA, Lee FT: Computerized tomographic angiography in the preoperative evaluation of potential renal transplant donors. Curr Opin Urol 1999;9:165 and Tsuda K, et al: Helical CT angiography of living donors: Comparison with 3D Fourier transformation phase contrast MRA. J Comput Assist Tomogr 1998;22:186.

SECTION X

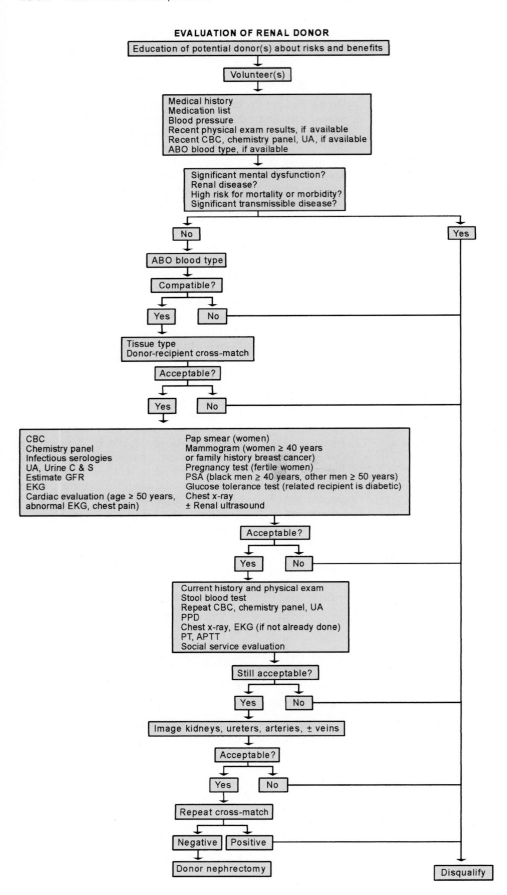

**Figure 40–2.** Algorithm for the evaluation of living renal donors. APTT, activated partial thromboplastin time; CBC, complete blood count; C & S, culture and sensitivity; EKG, electrocardiogram; GFR, glomerular filtration rate; PPD, tuberculin skin test; PSA, prostate-specific antigen; PT, prothrombin time; UA, urinalysis.

plain radiography of the abdomen has been widely accepted because it satisfactorily excludes stone disease, demonstrates renal and vascular anatomy, and defines the urinary collecting system, all with minimal donor morbidity and at reasonable expense (Tsuda et al, 1998; Pozniak and Lee, 1999).

Hyperfiltration injury has not been a significant problem for living renal donors. Endogenous creatinine clearance rapidly approaches 70% to 80% of the preoperative level, and this has been shown to be sustained for more than 10 years (Najarian et al, 1992). The development of late hypertension is nearly the same as for the general population, and the development of proteinuria is negligible (Steckler et al, 1990; Kasiske et al, 1995). The mortality of kidney donation has been estimated to be 0.02% (Matas et al, 2003), the risk of a potentially life-threatening or permanently debilitating complication has been estimated to be 0.23%, and there are isolated reports of ESRD developing in renal donors (Bia et al, 1995). **The short- and long-term risks of living donor nephrectomy are generally considered to be low enough, and the probability of successful graft outcome high enough, to make the risks acceptable for fully informed donors.**

Live donor nephrectomy can be performed either as an open or laparoscopically assisted procedure. Open live donor nephrectomy (ODN) is usually performed through a flank incision with a rib-resecting (Marchioro et al, 1964) or supracostal approach (Barry and Hodges, 1974), or by an anterior extraperitoneal incision (Jones et al, 1999). Laparoscopic donor nephrectomy (LDN) has become the preferred technique for live donor nephrectomy at most transplant centers in the United States (Ratner et al, 1999; Jacobs et al, 2004), and a retroperitoneoscopic approach for either kidney has been described (Yang et al, 2001). Regardless of the technique of living donor nephrectomy, diuresis is promoted by intravenous fluids, mannitol infusion, and loop of Henle diuretics. Overnight hydration of the living donor is unnecessary. It is common to prepare the LDN candidate with a clear liquid diet and a laxative the day before surgery.

Regardless of the technique, the upper pole of the kidney is usually mobilized early in the procedure, diuresis is confirmed by transecting the ureter and observing urine flow before interrupting renal circulation, and care is taken to preserve ureteral blood supply. A hand-assisted laparoscopic left donor nephrectomy is described in detail in Figure 40–3. General anesthesia is used. Epidural analgesia for pain management is optional. Nitrous oxide inhalation is avoided to prevent bowel distention. Intravenous fluids and mannitol are used to prevent oliguria associated with pneumoperitoneum. Right laparoscopic hand-assisted donor nephrectomy is slightly different from left donor nephrectomy. Positions of the monitor, surgical team, and patient and incision and trocar placements are the mirror images of those described for the left-sided procedure. However, the telescope is used through the right lower quadrant trocar, the left hand is placed through the hand assist device, and the upper trocar is used for working instruments operated with the surgeon's right hand. An additional 5-mm trocar is placed in the subxiphoid region through which a locking grasper can be placed for liver retraction. This grasper is used to lift the liver craniad, which is then clamped to the body wall. The remainder of the procedure is the same as for left nephrectomy, except for management of the renal vein. After clipping or stapling and dividing the renal artery, the renal vein is stapled with the Endo TA device placed through the upper trocar, across the renal vein, and flush with the inferior vena cava. The vein is incised with endoscopic scissors just beyond this staple line. Although it is not possible to obtain a small cuff of vena cava with this technique, the length of vein is usually adequate. It is unnecessary to administer and reverse heparin during ODN, but this is commonly done during laparoscopic donor nephrectomy because the renal vessels are sometimes divided between rows of vascular staples that must be removed after renal extraction and before core cooling is initiated by renal artery infusion of an ice-cold kidney preservation solution. The kidney is then taken in an ice bath into the recipient's operating room or cold-stored until the time of transplantation if that procedure is delayed. (See "Preparation of Kidney Graft.")

The reported advantages of LDN when compared with historical cases of ODN have been decreased analgesic requirement, decreased length of hospital stay, and an earlier return to work. The disadvantages have been reported to be increased operating time, donor surgeon preference for the left kidney, an increased need for special equipment, a longer warm ischemia time, and delayed graft function (Jacobs et al, 2004; Barry, 2005). Although initial renal transplant function may be somewhat slower to recover after LDN, and single center longer-term results are not significantly different from those of ODN (Goel et al, 2004; Tooher et al, 2004), registry data have indicated that 3-year kidney transplant survivals and projected half-lives of kidney transplants significantly favor the ODN flank approach over the LDN approach (Cecka, 2003). This difference in favor of ODN has been documented with the transplantation of adult kidneys into children (Troppman et al, 2005). Although LDN for right kidneys was initially associated with poorer results due to thrombosis of the shorter right renal vein, further experience with this technique has resulted in results equivalent to those reported for left LDN (Posselt et al, 2004). Emerging randomized trials of ODN versus LDN have reported equivalent renal transplant outcomes (Simforoosh et al, 2005).

## Deceased Donor

The declaration of brain death is the responsibility of the potential deceased organ donor's physician.

**The criteria for an ideal deceased kidney donor are normal renal function, no hypertension requiring treatment, no diabetes mellitus, no malignancy other than a primary brain tumor or treated superficial skin cancer, no generalized viral or bacterial infection, acceptable urinalysis, age between 6 and 50 years, and negative assays for syphilis, hepatitis, HIV, and human T-lymphoproliferative virus.** Exceptions are made in an effort to expand the donor pool, resulting in the adoption of the "expanded criteria donor" (ECD). ECDs are defined as donors older than 60 years or donors 51 to 59 years old with any two of the following risk factors: cerebrovascular death, hypertension, and serum creatinine level greater than 1.5 mg/dL (Cecka, 2004). Blood is cultured if the donor has been hospitalized for more than 72 hours. ECD kidney transplant survival rates and those from donors younger than the age of 6 years and older than the age of 50 years are significantly inferior to those from ideal deceased donor kidney transplants (Cecka, 2003). The poorer

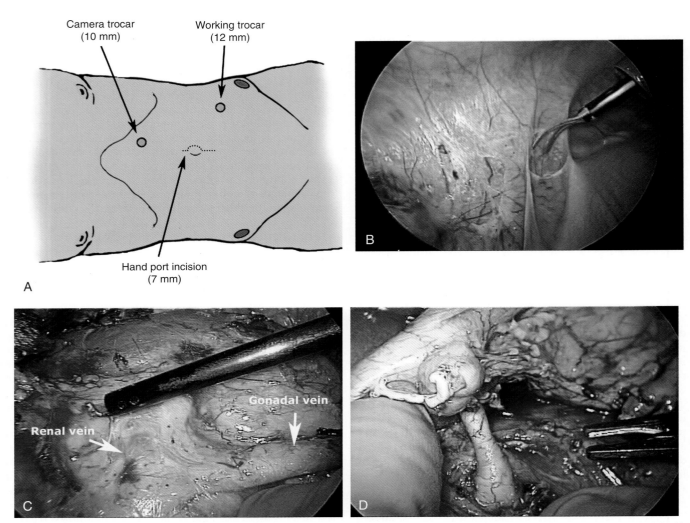

**Figure 40–3.** Hand assisted laparoscopic left donor nephrectomy. **A,** The patient is placed in a modified right lateral decubitus position with the left side elevated approximately 45 degrees with a large gel roll. The table is partially flexed; it is unnecessary to raise the kidney rest. The patient's left arm is placed in a sling and all extremities are padded. The patient is secured to the table with 2-inch cloth tape just below the anterior superior iliac spines. This will permit rotation of the table during the procedure. The monitors are placed on the left side of the patient, across from the surgeons. The nurse assistant generally stands opposite the surgeons on the patient's left. Following the skin preparation and draping, a 7-cm periumbilical, midline incision is made. The peritoneum is opened under direct vision. A hand assist device that will allow room on the abdomen for placement of two trocars is placed in the incision. A trocar is inserted directly through the hand assist device. The abdomen is insufflated to 15 mm Hg. A 10-mm 30-degree telescope that will be used throughout the procedure is first used through this trocar in the hand assist device. A 12-mm trocar is inserted under direct vision into the left lower quadrant (LLQ) at the lateral border of the rectus muscle. This trocar must be 12 mm to allow passage of the endoscopic stapling device. The telescope is removed from the trocar in the hand assist device and inserted into the LLQ trocar, and the trocar in the hand assist device is removed. A second trocar (10-12 mm) is placed in the subcostal area (LUQ) just lateral to the midline. Occasionally, a third trocar (5 mm) will be placed in the midaxillary line for lateral retraction. The left laparoscopic donor nephrectomy is performed with the telescope in the LUQ trocar, the left hand in the hand assist device, and the right hand using the working instruments through the LLQ trocar. **B,** The first step is the reflection of the colon and spleen from the level of the iliac vessels to above the spleen. Anteromedial traction of the left colon will keep the tissue to be divided under tension. The first layer of tissue encountered, the peritoneum, is divided with either scissors or hook electrocautery. A combination hook, suction, and irrigation device will enable the surgeon to quickly switch between sharp dissection with hook cautery and blunt dissection with the suction probe. Anterior and medial retraction of the colon with the left hand is critical for identification of the plane between the mesentery and Gerota's fascia. Once the peritoneum is incised, the colon can be reflected primarily with blunt dissection. The splenocolic ligament is left intact, and the plane of dissection is carried lateral to the spleen to allow the spleen to drop medially. Care is taken when reflecting the colon to avoid injury to the bowel or its mesentery. At this point in the procedure, the table is rotated toward the surgeon to place the patient in a more lateral decubitus position, so gravity will aid with retraction of the intestines. **C,** The next step is exposure of the gonadal and renal veins. This is generally easily done after complete reflection of the left colon. Hook electrocautery is used to clean the surface of the gonadal vein to its insertion in the renal vein. The renal vein is dissected, and its branches (gonadal, lumbar, and adrenal veins) are freed in the process. A 10-mm laparoscopic right angle dissector is useful for dissection of these branches. The branches of the renal vein are divided with either clips, vascular staples, or a feedback controlled vessel sealing bipolar device. These bipolar devices will seal and divide vessels up to 7 mm in diameter. Avoidance of clips on the branches of the renal vein will diminish the chance of an endoscopic vascular stapler misfire due to a clip in the jaws of the stapling device. **D,** After division of the lumbar vein, the renal artery is visible posterior to the renal vein. Be careful when dissecting in the renal hilum area because there are frequently more than one lumbar vein, and these lumbar veins are difficult to identify on preoperative CT scan because they do not reliably fill with contrast medium. The tissue surrounding the artery is divided with the hook electrocautery. Once the proper plane is entered immediately adjacent to the renal artery, the emancipated artery will spring free of the surrounding tissues. All of the tissue surrounding the artery and between the artery and vein must be divided. Cautery is generally sufficient. *Continued*

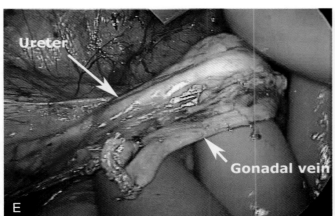
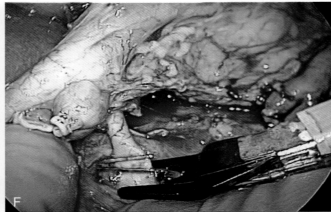

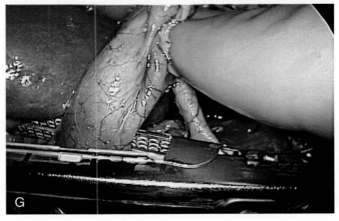

**Figure 40–3, cont'd.** **E,** The ureter is prepared by blunt dissection and hook electrocautery. It may be necessary to leave the gonadal vein attached to the ureter to preserve ureteral blood supply. The ureter is not divided until the kidney and renal vessels have been completely dissected to prevent rotation of the kidney and torsion of the renal vessels. The kidney is freed laterally and flipped medially to allow exposure and dissection of the posterior surfaces of the renal vessels. The division of the renal vessels is rehearsed with the surgical team to ensure that all instruments are present and working and that the order of their use is familiar to all. Exposure of the renal vessels is greatly facilitated by retraction of the kidney with the intraperitoneal hand. **F,** The artery is ligated with three long titanium clips or with a vascular load (2.0- to 2.5-mm staples) of the endoscopic stapler. Either the Endo GIA or Endo TA stapling devices are used (U.S. Surgical, Norwalk, CT). The Endo TA stapling device only places three rows of staples and allows inspection of the staple line before division of the vessel with the endoscopic scissors. The lack of distal staples will gain 3 to 4 mm in vessel length. Roticulating staplers are preferred. **G,** The vein is stapled and divided as described for the artery. The kidney is immediately delivered from the periumbilical incision, placed on slush, and flushed with ice-cold preservation solution. The renal fossa, staple lines, and clips on vessels are inspected for bleeding, the colon is returned to its normal position, and the wounds are closed.

graft survivals for kidneys from the very young are due to small anatomic parts and the risk of technical problems. There are, however, reports of successful kidney transplants from small deceased donors that were transplanted either as single units or en bloc with donor aorta and inferior vena cava (Hudnall et al, 1989; Bretan et al, 1997). The transplantation of both kidneys from a deceased donor with abnormal renal function or abnormal biopsy findings has also been used with success as an option to expand the donor pool, but the long-term function of such kidneys is inferior (Light, 1999; Wolters et al, 2005). Table 40–6 shows biopsy guidelines that some have found useful for the selection of transplantable kidneys from ECDs.

**The initial goals of resuscitation of the brain-dead deceased donor are systolic blood pressure of 90 mm Hg or mean arterial pressure of 60 mm Hg and urinary output exceeding 0.5 mL/kg/hr.** Monitoring of central venous pressure, capillary wedge pressure, or pulmonary artery pressure is helpful for managing fluid administration (Soifer and Gelb,

**Table 40–6. Biopsy Grading System for Expanded Criteria Deceased Donor Kidney Allografts**

| | Biopsy Grading System | | | |
|---|---|---|---|---|
| **Finding** | **None** | **1%–20%** | **21%–50%** | **>50%** |
| Glomerulosclerosis | 0 | 1 | 2 | 3 |
| Interstitial fibrosis | 0 | 1 | 2 | 3 |
| Tubular atrophy | 0 | 1 | 2 | 3 |
| Vascular narrowing | 0 | 1 | 2 | 3 |

| Biopsy Score Recommendations | |
|---|---|
| **Score** | **Recommendation** |
| 0-3 | Use as single allograft |
| 4-6 | Transplant both into one recipient |
| 7-12 | Do not use |

Modified from Light JA: A 25-year history of kidney transplantation at the Washington Hospital Center. In Cecka JM, Terasaki PI (eds): Clinical Transplants 1998. Los Angeles, UCLA Tissue Typing Laboratory, 1999, p 165.

1989; Boyd et al, 1991). Serum electrolyte levels are checked every 2 to 4 hours. If the resuscitation goals cannot be met by fluid challenge and the central venous pressure is greater than 15 cm $H_2O$, dopamine or dobutamine at less than 10 µg/kg/min can be infused without causing renal vasospasm.

If bradycardia does not respond to atropine, dopamine, or low-dose epinephrine, a temporary pacemaker can be inserted. If intravascular volume expansion and vasopressors are unsuccessful in promoting a diuresis, furosemide, 1 mg/kg, with or without mannitol, 0.5 to 1 g/kg, can be infused. If diabetes insipidus causes an unmanageable diuresis, aqueous vasopressin can be infused to reduce urinary output. Because hypothermia can cause cardiac irritability and coagulopathy, the head can be wrapped, intravenous fluids can be warmed, and the body can be placed on a warming blanket. Tissue typing and crossmatching can be performed on a peripheral blood sample or groin lymph nodes before organ retrieval. The deceased donor is maintained in the operating room by the anesthesiology team to ensure ventilation and circulatory support and to administer drugs such as diuretics, heparin, and α-adrenergic blocking agents.

Most renal donors are now multiple organ donors, and the classic abdominal midline and cruciate incisions have been largely abandoned in favor of the total midline approach with median sternotomy, even when kidneys alone are retrieved. **The principles of deceased donor organ retrieval are adequate exposure, control of the vessels above and below the organs to be removed, initiation of preservation in situ, the removal of the organs, separation of the organs, completion of preservation, removal of histocompatibility specimens, removal of iliac vessels for vascular reconstruction of pancreas and liver grafts, and organ packaging.** The technical aspects of an en bloc method are illustrated in Figure 40–4 (Nakazato et al, 1992; Barry, 1996). Some retrieval teams prefer to do much more dissection in situ before organ removal. When that occurs, the kidneys are the last transplantable organs to be removed. To avoid renal warming in this situation, it is important to maintain surface cooling of the kidneys by surrounding them with ice slush during liver and pancreas recovery.

## KIDNEY PRESERVATION
### Cellular Injury

Warm ischemic injury is due to failure of oxidative phosphorylation and cell death due to adenosine triphosphate (ATP) depletion (Belzer and Southard, 1988). ATP is required for the cellular sodium-potassium pump to maintain a high intracellular concentration of potassium and a low internal concentration of sodium. **When the sodium-potassium pump is impaired, sodium chloride and water passively diffuse into the cells, resulting in cellular swelling and the "no-reflow" phenomenon after renal revascularization.** Cellular potassium and magnesium are lost, calcium is gained, anaerobic glycolysis and acidosis occur, and lysosomal enzymes are activated. This results in cell death. During reperfusion, hypoxanthine, a product of ATP degradation, is oxidized to xanthine with the formation of free radical scavengers that cause further cell damage.

## Principles of Simple Cold Storage of Kidneys

**Cellular energy requirements are significantly reduced by hypothermia.** This is done by surface cooling, hypothermic pulsatile perfusion, or flushing with an ice-cold solution followed by cold storage. Making the flush solution slightly hyperosmolar with impermeant solutes such as mannitol, lactobionate, raffinose, or hydroxyethyl starch helps prevent endothelial cell swelling and the "no-reflow" phenomenon. When the sodium-potassium pump is impaired, there is passive transfer of ions across the cell membrane; and if the electrolyte composition of the flush solution is nearly the same as that inside the cell, electrolyte balance will be maintained. $ATP\text{-}MgCl_2$ infusions have been evaluated as an energy source. Calcium channel blockers, xanthine oxidase inhibitors, free-radical scavengers, vasoprotective agents, and lysosome stabilizers such as methylprednisolone have all been used to reduce ischemic injury (Marshall et al, 2001).

## Clinical Kidney Transplant Preservation

The basic methods of kidney preservation are pulsatile machine perfusion with a protein-based solution (Belzer et al, 1967) and hypothermic flushing followed by simple cold storage (Collins et al, 1969). After demonstration that the two methods provided equivalent results with ideally harvested dog kidneys after 48 hours of preservation (Halasz and Collins, 1976), simple cold storage became more widely used for human kidney preservation. Machine perfusion has provided reliable human kidney preservation for up to 72 hours (Feduska et al, 1978), and it may be the preferred method of preserving kidneys from non–heart-beating deceased donors. There are reports of successfully extending the preservation time for 48 to 95 hours with cold storage alone or in combination with machine perfusion (Haberal et al, 1984). A review of 33,278 first deceased donor kidney transplants demonstrated no significant differences in graft survivals up to 5 years for kidneys that were preserved by pulsatile machine perfusion or simple cold storage, but the rate of delayed graft function was significantly lower for the pumped kidneys (Cecka, 2002).

The commonly used UW solution (Belzer and Southard, 1988) minimizes cellular swelling with the impermeant solutes lactobionate, raffinose, and hydroxyethyl starch. Phosphate is used for its hydrogen ion buffering qualities, adenosine is for ATP synthesis during reperfusion, glutathione is a free-radical scavenger, allopurinol inhibits xanthine oxidase and the generation of free radicals, and magnesium and dexamethasone are membrane-stabilizing agents. A major advantage of this preservation solution has been its utility as a universal preservation solution for all intra-abdominal organs. A prospectively randomized study of 695 deceased kidney grafts preserved with either UW solution or Euro-Collins solution showed that the UW solution resulted in a significantly more rapid reduction in the postoperative serum creatinine level, a significantly lower postoperative dialysis rate, and a 6% higher 1-year graft survival compared with kidneys preserved by Euro-Collins solution (Ploeg et al, 1992).

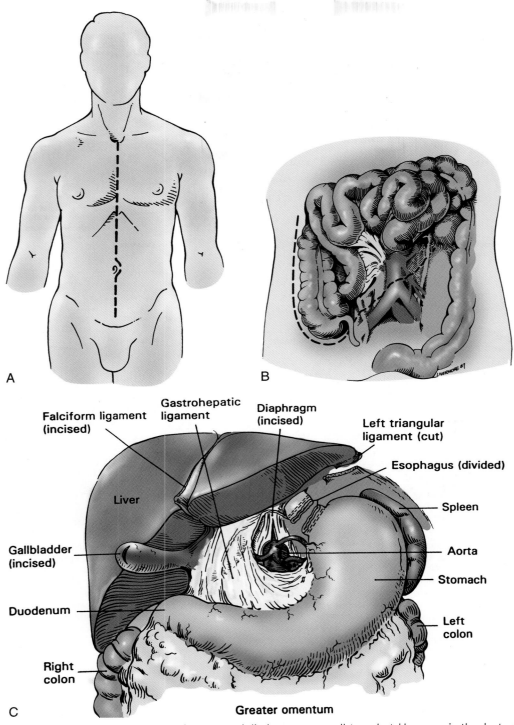

**Figure 40–4.** **A,** A total midline incision with splitting of sternum and diaphragm exposes all transplantable organs in the chest and abdomen. It also provides excellent exposure when retrieving only abdominal organs. **B,** The retroperitoneum is exposed as for a retroperitoneal lymphadenectomy. **C,** For multiple abdominal organ retrieval, the aorta is controlled above the celiac axis. The inferior vena cava (IVC) is controlled above the liver *(not shown)*.

*Continued*

An analysis of the Collaborative Transplant Study database for first deceased kidney transplants performed over a 10-year period revealed that kidney graft survival rates were significantly better for kidneys preserved with UW solution compared with Euro-Collins solution (Opelz and Wujciak, 1996).

The detrimental effects of the events surrounding deceased kidney retrieval and the detrimental effects of preservation injury are shown by the 12% better 5-year graft survival for 5897 living biologically unrelated donor kidney transplants compared with 34,208 primary deceased kidney transplants (Cecka, 2004).

**Expansion of the deceased kidney donor pool by the use of non–heart-beating donors has resulted in renewed interest in pulsatile machine perfusion because it allows**

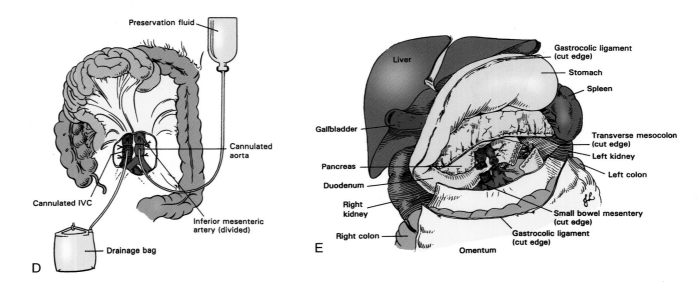

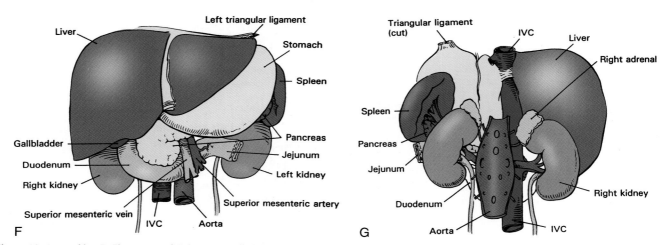

**Figure 40–4, cont'd.** **D,** The aorta and IVC are controlled below the renal vessels, heparin is administered to the donor, and the great vessels are cannulated. The proximal aorta is occluded, the IVC is vented into the chest or through the distal IVC cannula, and in-situ flushing with an ice-cold preservation solution is performed through the aortic cannula. **E,** The gastrocolic ligament is divided, the small bowel mesentery is divided along with the superior mesenteric artery and vein, and the small bowel is divided at the ligament of Treitz. **F,** The esophagus is divided, and, with further dissection, the en bloc specimen consisting of the liver, stomach, spleen, pancreas, both kidneys, aorta, and IVC is removed. **G,** The specimen is placed "face down" in a pan of slush and is separated, first, by splitting the aorta posteriorly between lumbar arteries to identify all renal arteries; second, by transecting the aorta between the superior mesenteric artery and the renal arteries; third, by splitting the anterior aortic wall between the renal arteries; fourth, by transecting the IVC just above the entrance of the renal veins; and fifth, by dividing the left renal vein where it enters the IVC. (**A** and **B** from Barry JM: Cadaver donor nephrectomy. In Novick AC, Streem SB, Pontes JL [eds]: Stewart's Operative Urology. Baltimore, Williams & Wilkins, 1989, pp 294-300; **C** to **G** from Barry JM: Donor nephrectomy. In Marshall FF [ed]: Textbook of Operative Urology. Philadelphia, WB Saunders, 1996, pp 235-247.)

**viability testing with perfusion characteristics** (Light, 1999; Matsuno et al, 2000), and glutathione-S transferase determinations (Gok et al, 2004), and it has been clearly demonstrated in the laboratory to be superior to simple cold storage for kidneys subjected to significant warm ischemia time (Halasz and Collins, 1976).

## RECIPIENT SELECTION FOR DECEASED KIDNEY TRANSPLANTS

**A point system has evolved in the United States for the selection of deceased kidney transplant recipients** (Bryan et al, 2003). Initial screening consists of ABO blood group identity

determination and negative microcytotoxicity lymphocyte crossmatches between donor and recipient. Patients whose serum reacts to a high proportion of lymphocytes on a random or selected panel have high panel reactive antibody levels, and they receive additional points because the probability of obtaining a crossmatch-negative kidney for them is decreased compared with minimally sensitized transplant candidates. The time on the waiting list, histocompatibility between the donor and the recipient, prior vital organ donation, and age younger than 18 years result in additional points. A score is developed for each of the potential recipients, and the candidates are placed in rank order by that score. The patient with the highest score is ranked first for that specific kidney. The kidney graft is then offered in turn to each of the potential recipients by the final rank. If there is no suitable recipient on a local list, the kidney graft is offered to those on a regional list and, if necessary, the national list. There is mandatory distribution of a kidney when there are zero HLA-A, HLA-B, and HLA-DR antigens mismatched between a deceased kidney donor and an ABO blood group–compatible, not identical, recipient on the national waiting list.

Candidates for ECD kidney engraftment must agree to receive one of these kidneys before being placed on the waiting list. These kidney transplants are usually recommended for patients older than the age of 60 years, diabetic patients older than the age of 40 years, and patients who have significant dialysis access problems or who are unable to tolerate dialysis.

## PREOPERATIVE ASSESSMENT

**Just before kidney transplantation, the history, physical examination, and diagnostic studies of the recipient focus on a search for interval medical problems such as symptomatic cardiac disease, active infection, and the need for additional crossmatch testing because of recent blood transfusions or an out-of-date serum sample.** Immunosuppression and infection prophylaxis protocols are assigned, a preliminary determination about the need for an intensive care unit bed is made, a final decision is made to perform the transplant operation, and the team queues up for the operating room. The quality of early renal function is directly correlated with cold ischemia time, and deceased donor kidney transplantation is done on an urgent basis.

## PREPARATION OF KIDNEY GRAFT

A kidney graft removed from a living renal donor by an open technique requires little preparation by the kidney transplant recipient team because most of the preparation has been done in situ by the donor team. Because of the presence of significant amounts of perirenal fat, stapled vessels, and retraction of the renal vein into the renal hilum, significantly more bench work is required for kidneys removed laparoscopically. If not done by the LDN team, prompt identification of the renal

artery and vein, removal of the staple lines, and rapid flushing of the kidney with ice-cold preservation solution is the initial priority, followed by the final dissection. Some programs have adopted a three-row rather than a six-row stapler for the renal vein, followed by distal transection of the vein. This avoids the need to resect the venous staple line at the back table before arterial flushing and reduces venous blood in the kidney. The disadvantage is somewhat more difficult visualization laparoscopically after transecting the renal vein because the distal end is open, permitting venous blood to obscure the operative field.

**For a deceased donor kidney, the short right renal vein can be extended with a variety of techniques that use the inferior vena cava or donor external iliac vein** (Fig. 40–5). Before the use of donor inferior vena cava to provide extension of the right renal vein in deceased donor kidney transplants, the left kidney was preferred because of its longer renal vein. Techniques for the management of multiple renal arteries from deceased and living donors are shown in Figure 40–6.

## RECIPIENT OPERATION

The usual responsibilities of the anesthesia and the surgical teams are depicted in Table 40–7.

A prophylactic antibiotic is administered just before surgery and continued postoperatively until the results of intraopera-

| Table 40–7. Usual Responsibilities of Anesthesia and Surgical Teams during Renal Transplantation | |
|---|---|
| *Anesthesiology* | *Surgery* |
| Anesthetic induction | Patient position |
| Central venous access | Bladder catheterization |
| Administration of antibiotics | Preliminary skin preparation |
| Administration of immunosuppressants | Surgical exposure of operative site |
| Administration of heparin | Renal revascularization |
| Assurance of conditions for diuresis | Urinary tract reconstruction |
| | Wound closure |

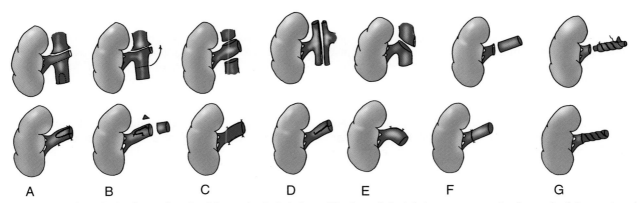

**Figure 40–5.** **A** to **G**, Methods of extending the right renal vein include modifications of the inferior vena cava and a free graft of donor external iliac vein. The first two methods are valuable when the cephalad portion of the right renal vein has been compromised by the separation of the liver graft from the kidney grafts. (**A** and **B** from Barry JM, Lemmers MJ: Patch and flap techniques to repair right renal vein defects caused by cadaver liver retrieval for transplantation. J Urol 1995;153:1803; **C** from Barry JM, Fuchs EF: Right renal vein extension in deceased kidney transplantation. Arch Surg 1978;113:300; **D** and **F** from Barry JM, Hefty TR, Sasaki T: Clam-shell technique for right renal vein extension in cadaver kidney transplantation. J Urol 1988;140:1479; **E** from Corry RJ, Kelley SE: Technic for lengthening the right renal vein of cadaver donor kidneys. Am J Surg 1978;135:867.)

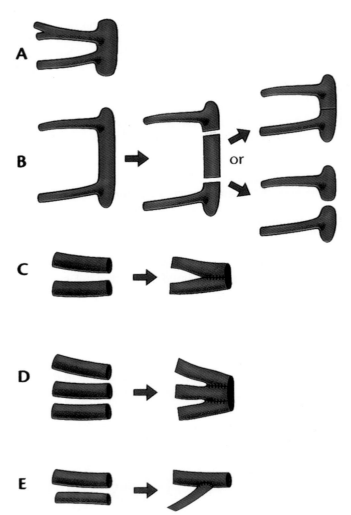

**Figure 40–6.** Preparation of the kidney transplant with multiple renal arteries. **A** and **B,** Use of aortic patches when the kidney is from a deceased donor. **C** and **D,** Pair of pants or three-legged pair of pants is used when an aortic patch is not available, such as when the kidney is from a living donor. **E,** Anastomosis of segmental renal artery to main renal artery. The segmental renal artery can also be anastomosed to the inferior epigastric artery using an end-to-end technique. (**A** to **E** from Barry JM: Technical aspects of renal transplantation. In Schrier RW [ed]: Atlas of Diseases of the Kidney. Philadelphia, Current Medicine, 1998, p 14.4.)

tive cultures are known. Immunosuppression is started just before or during surgery in the deceased kidney graft recipient and, in some programs, in the week before transplantation in the living donor kidney transplant recipient.

After the induction of anesthesia and the placement of a triple-lumen central venous catheter, the genitalia and skin are prepared, and a Foley catheter is placed in the bladder or bladder substitute. **It is helpful to have the catheter attached to a three-way drainage system that allows intraoperative filling and draining of the bladder, especially in a small recipient or in an individual who has a small, defunctionalized bladder.** The bladder or bladder substitute is rinsed with a broad-spectrum antibiotic solution, such as neomycin-polymyxin B, and gravity filled. The catheter tubing is clamped until it is time to do the ureteroneocystostomy. A

self-retaining ring retractor attached to the operating table that has been flexed and rotated toward the surgeon allows the operation to be performed by a surgeon and one assistant (Fig. 40–7). To prevent spinal injury, patients with significant back disease, such as ankylosing spondylitis, should be placed in a comfortable, padded position before anesthetic induction and table flexion should be avoided. Antibiotic irrigation is used liberally during the procedure. Central venous pressure is maintained between 5 and 15 cm $H_2O$ with intravenous fluids. If fluid administration alone cannot maintain the mean arterial pressure at greater than 60 mm Hg and the systolic blood pressure greater than 90 mm Hg, respectively, a dopamine or dobutamine infusion is started.

**In adults and children who weigh more than 20 kg, a first kidney graft is usually placed extraperitoneally in the contralateral iliac fossa by way of a rectus-preserving Gibson incision.** This allows the renal pelvis and ureter to be the most medial structures in case subsequent urinary tract surgery is necessary on the kidney graft. Common exceptions to this principle are the obese recipient in whom it is easier to place a kidney graft in the right iliac fossa because of the more superficial iliac veins and the simultaneous pancreas and kidney transplant recipient in whom it is common to place the left kidney with its longer renal vein in the left iliac fossa. **If there is some doubt about whether there will be enough room in the left pelvis of a small patient for a large kidney, placement of the kidney on the right side will allow access to a wider choice of arteries and veins for vascular reconstruction.** In small children, this is accomplished by extension of the Gibson incision to the right costal margin or by a midline abdominal incision. In men, the spermatic cord is preserved and retracted medially. In women, the round ligament is divided between ligatures. The recipient's target blood vessels are dissected. When the renal vein is short, it is helpful to completely mobilize the external and common iliac veins by dividing the gluteal and internal iliac veins between ligatures or large clips. These branches can be retracted anteriorly with a loop of heavy silk. Lymphatic vessels are divided between ligatures to prevent the development of postoperative lymphocele. **The surgeon must be careful not to mistake the genitofemoral nerve, which sometimes crosses the external iliac artery, for a lymphatic vessel.**

Before temporary vascular occlusion, heparin, 30 units/kg, is commonly given intravenously to the recipient. During the vascular anastomosis, an infusion of mannitol is begun to act as a free-radical scavenger and as an osmotic diuretic. Infusion of an electrolyte solution provides intraoperative volume expansion. The addition of an albumin infusion has been found to be helpful in promoting early renal function in the deceased donor kidney transplant (Dawidson et al, 1994). It is a common practice to keep the kidney transplant cool by wrapping it in a sponge containing crushed saline ice, by dripping an ice-cold electrolyte solution on it, or by placing it in a plastic bag or glove filled with slush. The renal artery is usually anastomosed to the end of the internal iliac artery or to the side of the external iliac artery (Fig. 40–8). Other possible locations for the arterial anastomosis are dictated by the clinical situation, and they include the common iliac artery, the aorta, the splenic artery, and the native renal artery. Moderate arteriosclerosis of the internal iliac artery can be managed by endarterectomy. In the event of significant

**Figure 40-7.** Patient position for kidney transplantation into right iliac fossa. Table flexion opens the iliac fossa and retropubic space, just as for radical cystectomy or open prostatectomy. Rotation of the table toward the surgeon, who stands on the patient's left side, assists in performance of the lateral aspects of the vascular anastomoses. (From Montie JE: Technique of radical cystectomy in the male. In Marshall FF [ed]: Textbook of Operative Urology. Philadelphia, WB Saunders, 1996, p 399.)

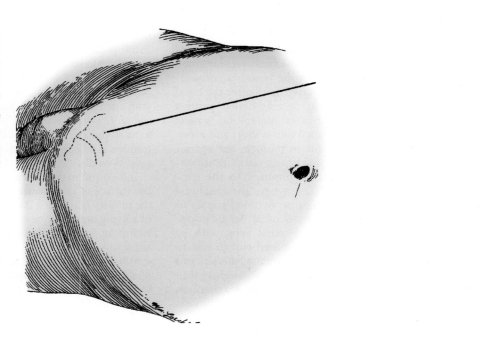

**Figure 40-8.** **A,** The renal vein is anastomosed to the external iliac vein, usually medial to the external iliac artery. When the recipient has a tortuous iliac artery, the venous anastomosis is best performed lateral to the bowed external iliac artery. **B,** In the absence of significant recipient arteriosclerosis, the renal artery is commonly anastomosed to the internal iliac artery with 5-0 or 6-0 monofilament, nonabsorbable sutures. Many prefer to perform the renal artery anastomosis before the venous anastomosis. If significant internal iliac arteriosclerosis is present or the contralateral renal artery has been used in a previous renal transplant in a man, the external or common iliac arteries become the target vessels for renal artery anastomosis. **C,** The completed venous and arterial anastomoses. (**A** to **C** from Salvatierra O Jr: Renal transplantation. In Glenn JF [ed]: Urologic Surgery, 4th ed. Philadelphia, JB Lippincott, 1991, pp 243-251.)

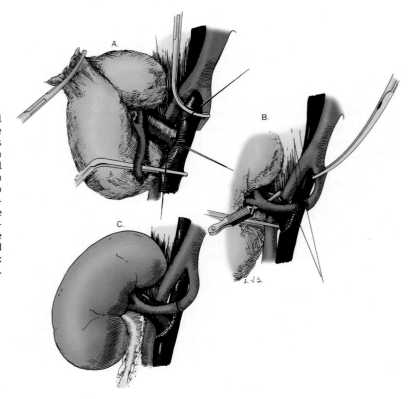

arteriosclerosis of that vessel, the renal artery is anastomosed end to side to the external iliac artery or to the common iliac artery. **A vascular punch is useful for creating a round hole in a rigid or arteriosclerotic vessel and in the common iliac artery or aorta of a child to prevent renal artery coaptation and thrombosis if hypotension occurs.**

When the pelvic vessels are unsuitable for renal revascularization, orthotopic renal transplantation with anastomosis of the renal artery to the splenic artery or native renal artery and venous reconstruction with the renal vein or inferior vena cava can be done (Gil-Vernet et al, 1989).

**It is usually preferable to do the renal artery anastomosis first because it is the more critical of the two vascular anastomoses,** the kidney is not tethered by the venous anastomosis, and venous occlusion can be delayed until after the renal artery anastomosis. This results in decreased iliac venous occlusion time and reduces the risk of iliofemoral venous thrombosis. In cases in which the renal vein is short and exposure is limited, it may be preferable to perform the venous anastomosis first. A man undergoing repeat renal transplantation with the prior transplant anastomosed to the contralateral internal iliac artery should not have the ipsilateral internal iliac artery used. This is to preserve blood supply to the corpora cavernosa and reduce the risk of iatrogenic impotence (Gittes and Waters, 1979). The renal vein, with or without an extension, is usually anastomosed end to side to the external iliac vein or to the junction of the external and common iliac veins. When transplanting an adult kidney into the right retroperitoneum of a small child, the renal vein often has to be shortened to prevent redundancy with anastomosis to the inferior vena cava.

Furosemide is commonly infused just before release of the vascular clamps. After renal revascularization, injection of verapamil, a calcium channel blocker, into the renal arterial circulation of the deceased donor kidney graft has been shown to protect the kidney from reperfusion injury (Dawidson et al, 1994).

Urinary tract reconstruction is usually by antireflux ureteroneocystostomy, of which there are several techniques (Politano and Leadbetter, 1958; MacKinnon et al, 1968; Konnak et al, 1975; Texter et al, 1976; Barry, 1983). **Most surgeons prefer an extravesical rather than the transvesical approach for ureteroneocystostomy because it is faster, a separate cystotomy is not required, and less ureteral length is necessary, thus ensuring a distal ureteral blood supply** (Figs. 40–9 and 40–10). Figure 40–9C demonstrates a rapid technique that can be used with or without a stent when the patient has a very small bladder or the procedure must be quickly completed. **If a prior augmentation cystoplasty had been done, the transplant surgeon will need to know the blood supply of the patch so as not to interfere with it at the time of transplantation.** Indications for ureteroureterostomy and pyeloureterostomy are short or ischemic allograft ureters, very limited bladder capacity, or the surgeon's preference. Double-pigtail ureteral stents are used when there is concern about the ureteroneocystostomy technique, or when ureteroureterostomy or pyeloureterostomy has been performed. The routine use of a ureteral stent for all cases has been shown to reduce the incidence of ureteral complications (Pleass et al, 1995; Mangus and Haag, 2004). Long-term results of renal transplantation into the valve bladder and other abnormali-

ties of the lower urinary tract have been very satisfactory (Luke et al, 2003; Mendizabel et al, 2005).

When a patient with an intestinal conduit undergoes renal transplantation (Surange et al, 2003), the kidney graft should be placed in such a way that it does not interfere with the flat surface at the stoma site and contribute to a poor fit of the urinary appliance and subsequent urinary leakage. The technique of ureteral implantation into an intestinal pouch is the same as that for ureteroneocystostomy. The pouch is irrigated free of mucus with an antibiotic solution, and the best site for the ureteral implantation is chosen with the pouch filled. Intraoperative identification of the conduit and subsequent ureteral anastomosis can be facilitated by cannulation of the stoma with a 14-French Foley catheter and inflating the balloon with 3 to 4 mL of sterile water or staining the conduit with methylene blue. To avoid a kink in the allograft ureter, the kidney transplant can be placed upside down in the iliac fossa so that the ureter is pointing cephalad. The ureteral anastomosis is usually protected with a stent that is left in place for several weeks.

It is common practice to send swab culture specimens from the surface of the deceased donor kidney transplant and from the urinary bladder. It is unnecessary to do so from the surface of a living donor kidney unless there has been a break in sterile technique in the retrieval, perfusion, or transportation of the kidney.

When both kidneys from a deceased donor with marginal renal function are transplanted into the same recipient, one kidney can be transplanted into each iliac fossa by way of a vertical midline incision or by way of separate Gibson's incisions, or both kidneys can be placed in the right retroperitoneum, one on top of the other (Masson and Hefty, 1998). This technique can also be used for simultaneous kidney and pancreas transplantation (Fridell et al, 2004). The first transplant can be anastomosed to the inferior vena cava and common iliac artery, and the second can be anastomosed to the external iliac vein and external or internal iliac artery.

The uncomplicated renal transplantation can be closed by a variety of running or interrupted suture techniques without drains unless anticoagulation is planned. If the rectus-retracting approach has been used, it is not necessary to place any sutures in the rectus muscle; one simply closes the anterior rectus sheath after the external oblique, internal oblique, and transversus abdominis muscles and their fascial layers have been closed in the cephalad aspect of the wound. **A closed suction drain is recommended in the subcutaneous tissue of an obese patient.** A running absorbable subcuticular suture eliminates the need for subsequent suture or clip removal.

## POSTOPERATIVE CARE
### Fluid and Electrolyte Management

Postoperative fluid and electrolyte management are simple for patients with initial kidney graft function. Intravenous fluid of 0.45% saline in 5% dextrose is given to replace estimated insensible losses, and 0.45% saline in 0% dextrose is given at a rate equal to the previous hour's urinary output. When the urinary output is high, this regimen reduces the probability of a glucose-driven diuresis. **An optional method of fluid**

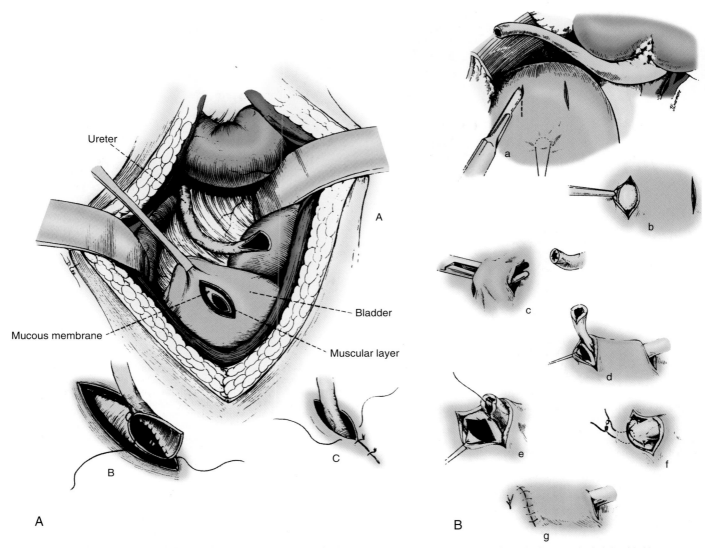

**Figure 40–9.** Three examples of extravesical ureteroneocystostomy. **A,** An anterolateral seromuscular incision is made down to the bulging bladder mucosa. The bladder is drained, the mucosa incised, and the ureter anastomosed to the bladder *(as shown)* with fine absorbable sutures. A distal anchoring stitch to hold the ureter to the bladder is used to prevent proximal migration in the tunnel *(not shown)*. The seromuscular layer is then loosely closed over the ureter. **B,** Steps *a* through *c* are completed with the bladder full of an antibiotic solution. The anesthesiologist unclamps the catheter before mucosal incision, and steps *d* through *g* are completed with fine absorbable sutures.                                    *Continued*

management in the recipient of a living donor kidney transplant is a fixed rate protocol of 125 to 200 mL/hr of 0.45% normal saline in 5% dextrose with an occasional fluid bolus if hypotension ensues (Hatch et al, 1985). Serum electrolyte levels are monitored every 4 to 8 hours, and potassium is added to the intravenous solution when the serum potassium level declines to the middle of the normal range. When delayed graft function occurs, the previously described intravenous fluid is administered at a rate to maintain the central venous pressure at 10 to 15 cm $H_2O$ for 2 to 3 hours, and furosemide is administered intravenously in an effort to induce a diuresis. The oliguric patient may require urgent treatment of hyperkalemia with administration of intravenous calcium chloride, intravenous sodium bicarbonate, insulin, and glucose, or dialysis.

If a diuresis has ensued and the next day's serum creatinine level is significantly reduced, a baseline radioisotope renogram is unnecessary. An ultrasonogram is indicated for delayed graft function, ipsilateral leg swelling, ipsilateral abdominal swelling, or a decreasing hematocrit. When oligoanuria occurs after renal transplantation, radioisotope renograms are commonly performed biweekly until the serum creatinine level begins to decrease without dialysis. If the radioisotope renogram deteriorates, a diagnostic renal biopsy is commonly done.

## Management of Tubes and Drains

A urine culture is obtained just before catheter removal, and the patient is given a single dose of a broad-spectrum

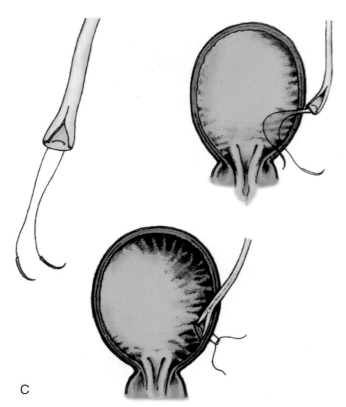

C

**Figure 40–9, cont'd. C,** Double-needle mattress suture is placed through the spatulated ureter, the ends of the suture and ureter are introduced into the bladder lumen, and the suture is tied outside the bladder wall. If the seromuscular incision is too large, it is closed over the ureter with interrupted fine absorbable sutures. (**A** from Konnak JW, Herwig KR, Finkbeiner A, et al: Extravesical ureteroneocystostomy in 170 renal transplant patients. J Urol 1975;113:299-301; **B** from Barry JM: Unstented extravesical ureteroneocystostomy in kidney transplantation. J Urol 1983;129:918-919; **C** reprinted from Texter JH Jr, Bokinsky G, Whitesell Al, et al: Simplified experimental ureteroneocystostomy. Urology 1976;7:21-23, with permission from Elsevier Science.)

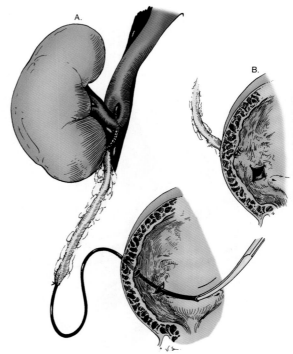

**Figure 40–10.** Transvesical ureteroneocystostomy. **A,** A No. 8 French catheter is passed through the submucosal tunnel and tied to the transplant ureter. **B,** The ureter is drawn through the tunnel, transected, and anastomosed to the bladder with fine absorbable sutures. The distal suture anchors the ureter to the bladder muscularis. Finally, the cystotomy is closed with one or two layers of absorbable sutures. (From Salvatierra O Jr: Renal transplantation. In Glenn JF [ed]: Urologic Surgery, 4th ed. Philadelphia, JB Lippincott, 1991, pp 243-251.)

antibiotic at that time. If the urine culture is subsequently positive, culture-specific therapy is given for 10 to 14 days. The timing of catheter removal is variable, but most catheters are removed within a week. A cystogram is optional. The closed suction drains are removed when the output is less than 50 mL/24 hr or in 3 weeks, whichever comes first. **If a ureteral stent was used to protect the urinary tract reconstruction, it is removed as an outpatient procedure 6 to 12 weeks after the operation.** If the surgeon had attached the stent to the indwelling Foley catheter, it will come out as the Foley catheter is withdrawn.

## Anticoagulation

**Most patients undergoing renal transplantation meet the criteria for low-dose anticoagulation to prevent deep venous thrombosis.** Patients with hypercoagulable states such as systemic lupus erythematosus, factor V Leiden mutation, prothrombin gene mutation, the anticardiolipin antibody syndrome, or deficiencies of protein C, protein S, or

antithrombin III usually receive daily warfarin therapy after the discontinuance of heparin therapy.

## RENAL ALLOGRAFT REJECTION
### Histocompatibility

**The histocompatibility systems of greatest importance in renal transplantation are the ABO blood group and the major histocompatibility complex (MHC)** (Denton et al, 1999; Halloran, 2004). The donor and recipient must be ABO compatible because A and B substances are present on endothelial cells, and most individuals have antibodies to the red blood cell antigens they lack. A common exception is the transplantation of ABO blood group A₂ kidneys into blood group O and B recipients, who have low anti-A2 antibody levels (Alkhunaizi et al, 1999). A rare exception is the transplantation across major ABO incompatibilities by recipient preparation with plasmapheresis to remove anti-A or anti-B antibodies, off-label use of the anti-CD 20 antibody rituximab with or without splenectomy to reduce antibody production, and intense induction immunosuppression (Takahashi et al, 2004; Warren et al, 2004).

The MHC antigens are glycoproteins on the cell membrane. They are encoded by MHC genes on the short arm of chromosome 6. Autosomal class I antigens are known as the HLA-A, HLA-B, and HLA-C antigens, and they are present on

Table 40-8. Influence of Histocompatibility on Standard Criteria Deceased Donor Kidney Transplant Survivals

| HLA Antigens Mismatched | No. | Half-Life (Yr)* |
|---|---|---|
| 0 | 4,182 | 15 |
| 1-3 | 9,391 | 12 |
| 4-6 | 14,186 | 10 |

HLA, human leukocyte antigen.

*Half-life is projected for those kidney transplants surviving the first year.

Data from Cecka JM: The OPTN/UNOS renal transplant registry 2003. In Cecka JM, Terasaki PI (eds): Clinical Transplants 2003. Los Angeles, UCLA Immunogenetics Center, 2004, p 5.

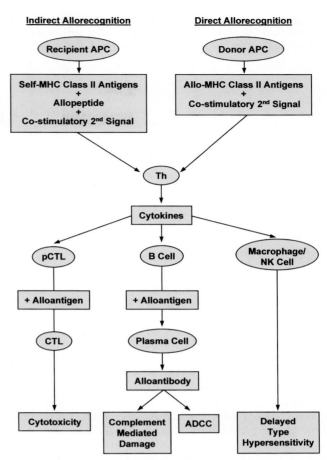

**Figure 40–11.** Cellular interactions in renal transplant rejection. CD4+ helper T cells (Th) are activated by antigen-presenting cells (APCs) that express incompatible major histocompatibility complex (MHC) class II antigens and provide a co-stimulatory second signal. The Th cells produce lymphokines that promote proliferation of B cells, maturation of CD8+ cytotoxic T lymphocytes (CTLs), activation of macrophages and natural killer (NK) cells, and induction of MHC class II antigens on renal cells. ADCC, antibody-dependent cell-mediated cytotoxicity; pCTL, precursor cytotoxic T cell.

nearly all nucleated cells. They are detected by tissue typing T lymphocytes, usually with a DNA polymerase chain reaction amplification technique. HLA-DR, HLA-DQ, and HLA-DP antigens are class II antigens present on B lymphocytes, activated T lymphocytes, monocytes, macrophages, dendritic cells, and some endothelial cells. HLA-DR antigens are detected by tissue typing B lymphocytes. Testing for HLA-DQ and HLA-DP antigens is not routinely done. Recipient circulating cytotoxic antibodies against the MHC antigens of a specific donor are detected by pretransplantation crossmatching techniques, and a positive complement-dependent T-cell lymphocytotoxicity crossmatch is considered to be a contraindication to renal transplantation when the serum used is recently obtained from the transplantation candidate. Protocols have been developed to use kidney transplants when the recipient has a positive crossmatch to the donor, and the crossmatch is rendered negative by plasmapheresis and immunoglobulin administration to permit an otherwise prohibited transplant to take place (Jordan et al, 2004).

Because of inheritance patterns of the HLA antigens, each potential kidney graft recipient is a "half-match," or haploidentical, with his or her parents and children and has a 0.25 probability of HLA identity, a 0.50 probability of haploidentity, and a 0.25 probability of a total HLA mismatch with a sibling. The influence of histocompatibility on deceased kidney transplant survival rates is demonstrated in Table 40–8. Within the past 5 years, the influence of histocompatibility matching on graft survival has decreased in the presence of more effective and less toxic immunosuppressive regimens (Halloran, 2004).

Incompatibility with MHC antigens on donor tissue stimulates the immune response (Fig. 40–11). Class II antigens on donor dendritic cells can directly stimulate recipient CD4+ helper T cells and initiate the rejection process. These MHC antigens are also processed by recipient macrophages, which present these class II alloantigens to the CD4+ helper T cells. **A second, or co-stimulatory, signal must be provided by cognate ligands on the antigen-presenting cell to fully activate CD4+ helper T cells.**

These two signals cause the CD4+ helper T cells to secrete cytokines, most importantly, the T-cell growth factor interleukin-2 (IL-2), and to express new cell surface IL-2 receptors. The cascade of events within the CD4+ helper T cell, after receiving the alloantigenic signal through the T-cell receptor and the co-stimulatory signal, is calcineurin activation; dephosphorylation of the nuclear factor of activated T cells,

enabling it to enter the nucleus and bind to the IL-2 gene promoter; and the production of IL-2.

**IL-2, the third signal, stimulates the IL-2 receptor, and this induces lymphocytes to proliferate.** IL-2 is necessary for the maturation of CD8+ cytotoxic T-cell precursors into cytotoxic T cells. IL-2 also stimulates antigen-activated helper T cells to release other lymphokines, such as IL-3, IL-4, IL-5, IL-6, and interferon-γ. IL-3 is a growth factor for bone marrow stem cells. IL-4, IL-5, and IL-6 enable alloantigen-activated B cells to mature into plasma cells, which produce cytotoxic antibodies against the MHC molecules of the graft. Interferon-γ activates the cytodestructive capabilities of macrophages, augments natural killer cell activity, and induces the expression of MHC class II antigens on kidney graft cells.

## Classification of Rejection

Hyperacute rejection occurs immediately after renal revascularization. It is an irreversible process mediated by preformed circulating cytotoxic antibodies that develop after pregnancy,

**Table 40–9. Mechanisms of Action of Immunosuppressants**

| Immunosuppressant | Mechanism of Action | Interferes with ... |
|---|---|---|
| Glucocorticoids | Reduce transcription of cytokine genes | Intracellular signaling |
| Azathioprine | Inhibits purine synthesis | Lymphocyte proliferation |
| Mycophenolate mofetil | Inhibits purine synthesis | Lymphocyte proliferation |
| Sirolimus | Inhibits cell cycle progression | Lymphocyte proliferation |
| Tacrolimus | Inhibits calcineurin and interleukin-2 production | Intracellular signaling |
| Cyclosporine | Inhibits calcineurin and interleukin-2 production | Intracellular signaling |
| Monomurab CD3 | Depletes T lymphocytes | Antigen recognition |
| Equine antithymocyte globulin | Depletes T lymphocytes | Antigen recognition |
| Rabbit antithymocyte globulin | Depletes T lymphocytes | Antigen recognition |
| Alemtuzumab (off label) | Depletes T and B lymphocytes | Antigen recognition and antibody production |
| Rituximab (off label) | Depletes B lymphocytes | Antibody production |
| Basiliximab | Blocks interleukin-2 receptor | Intercellular signaling |
| Daclizumab | Blocks interleukin-2 receptor | Intercellular signaling |

blood transfusions, or an earlier failed transplantation. It is very rare when the microlymphocytotoxicity crossmatch between recipient serum and donor lymphocytes is negative.

Accelerated rejection is mediated by humoral and cellular components of the immune response. It occurs within days to weeks and often does not respond to antirejection therapy.

Acute rejection can occur any time after transplantation. **The symptoms of acute kidney transplant rejection are those of "the flu," accompanied by pain over an enlarged kidney graft, hypertension, decreased urinary output, fluid retention, increased serum creatinine levels, and radioisotope renography indicating decreased renal blood flow, glomerular filtration, and tubular function.** Acute pyelonephritis must be ruled out by urinalysis and, subsequently, negative urine culture. Needle biopsy of the kidney graft is the standard to confirm the diagnosis of acute rejection. The typical histologic findings of acute renal allograft rejection are mononuclear cellular infiltration, tubulitis, and vasculitis (Gaber et al, 1998). The Banff classification is now accepted as the standard schema for diagnosing rejection (Racusen et al, 2004).

Chronic rejection is characterized by a gradual decline in renal function associated with interstitial fibrosis, vascular changes, and minimal mononuclear cell infiltration. A positive B-cell crossmatch or a positive flow crossmatch against donor B or T cells is considered by some to be predictive of chronic rejection and poorer long-term graft survivals (Ghasemian et al, 1997; Kimball et al, 1998).

## Immunosuppression

**Immunosuppressive drug regimens commonly include a corticosteroid in combination with other drugs such as cyclosporine or tacrolimus (calcineurin inhibitors), azathioprine or mycophenolate mofetil (purine antagonists), and sometimes antilymphocyte antibody preparations.** Triple maintenance immunosuppression with prednisone; cyclosporine or tacrolimus; and azathioprine or mycophenolate mofetil is common. Sirolimus inhibits cell cycle progression, and it is used in combination with corticosteroids or with cyclosporine or tacrolimus in combination with corticosteroids (Groth et al, 1999). The mechanisms and sites of action of clinically useful immunosuppressant medications are listed in Table 40–9 and illustrated in Figure 40–12. An

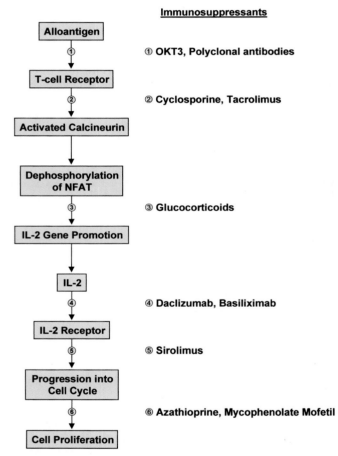

**Figure 40–12.** Sites of action of commonly used immunosuppressants. IL-2, interleukin-2; NFAT, nuclear factor of activated T cells.

example of an immunosuppression algorithm is presented in Figure 40–13. Antilymphocyte antibodies such as muromonab CD3, rabbit antithymocyte globulin, equine antithymocyte globulin, antibodies to the CD25 component of the IL-2 receptor such as daclizumab and basiliximab, or the off-label lymphocyte depleting antibody to CD52, alemtuzumab, are used by some as part of induction immunosuppressive regimens to allow the kidney graft to recover from

**Figure 40–13.** Example of kidney transplant immunosuppression protocol. This algorithm is based on donor and recipient histocompatibility, immunologic risk factors, and immunosuppressant mechanism of action. All receive corticosteroids. Assignment of immunologic risk points: 2 points each for more than 50% panel reactive antibody, positive flow crossmatch; 1 point each for prior transplant, six HLA antigens mismatched, delayed graft function, African American ethnicity, lupus nephropathy; subtract 1 point for age older than 60 years. HLA, human leukocyte antigen; Id, identical; Anti-IL-2R, interleukin-2 receptor antibody; Thymo, rabbit antilymphocyte antibody; MMF, mycophenolate mofetil; Inhib; inhibitor.

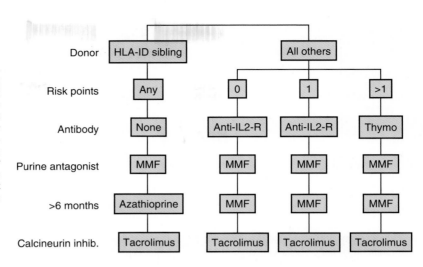

preservation injury before the administration of the nephrotoxic calcineurin inhibitors cyclosporine or tacrolimus (Halloran, 2004).

Corticosteroid therapy is usually started at high doses and then rapidly tapered during the first few weeks after engraftment. Cyclosporine and tacrolimus have similar mechanisms of action, effectiveness, and cost, but slightly different side effect profiles, and they are not used together. Both cyclosporine and tacrolimus are metabolized mainly by the cytochrome P-450 enzyme system. Substances that inhibit that system result in increased blood or plasma levels of these drugs (Table 40–10). Diltiazem and ketoconazole have been used to reduce cyclosporine dosing and cost while maintaining blood levels and the immunosuppressive effect (Patton et al, 1994). Drugs known to induce that enzyme system usually result in increased metabolism of cyclosporine and tacrolimus and decreased whole-blood or plasma levels and immunosuppressive effects. A determination of cyclosporine or tacrolimus blood levels is helpful when toxicity or insufficient immunosuppression is suspected. Drug interactions with sirolimus are very similar to those with the calcineurin inhibitors. Higher and more frequent doses of cyclosporine and tacrolimus are usually necessary in children. Azathioprine and mycophenolate mofetil have similar mechanisms of action, but mycophenolate mofetil is more effective, more toxic, and more expensive (Matthew, 1998). Table 40–11 lists the common organ system targets for toxicity of the drugs used for maintenance immunosuppression. Some programs taper patients off one or more of the maintenance immunosuppressants after many months of stable graft function (Shapiro et al, 2003). The goals of such protocols are to decrease and possibly eliminate maintenance immunosuppression to reduce the long-term complications of malignancy, bone loss, infection, and post-transplant diabetes mellitus and to reduce the costs of transplantation. Tolerance, the achievement of long-term graft acceptance without immunosuppression, has long been a goal of transplantation.

**Conventional treatment for acute renal allograft rejection is high-dose pulses of corticosteroids.** Treatment of corticosteroid-resistant rejection is with antilymphocyte antibody preparations such as muromonab CD3, equine antithymocyte globulin, and rabbit antithymocyte globulin. In some cases, recalcitrant rejection and graft salvage can be achieved by conversion of one baseline immunosuppressive regimen to another, even in the presence of corticosteroid-resistant rejection (Jordan et al, 1997).

Commonly used regimens to prevent infections and peptic ulcer disease are listed in Table 40–12. CMV infection is a significant problem after renal transplantation, and CMV-seronegative recipients have better outcomes than CMV-seropositive recipients, provided the kidney donor is also CMV-seronegative (Cecka, 2000). Recipients of CMV-seropositive deceased donor kidneys had lower 3-year survival rates, whether or not the recipient was CMV seropositive before kidney transplantation. Prophylaxis against CMV infection is possible with ganciclovir, valganciclovir, or valacyclovir (Preiksaitis et al, 2005).

Future immunomodulation strategies in transplantation include blockade of T-cell co-stimulation, blockade of T-cell adhesion molecules, blockade of T-cell accessory molecules, peptide-mediated immunosuppression, gene therapy, and induction of tolerance (Starzl et al, 2003).

**Table 40–10. Potential Drug Interactions with Cyclosporine and Tacrolimus**

| Drugs That Affect Plasma or Whole Blood Concentrations | | Drugs with Nephrotoxic Synergy |
|---|---|---|
| *Decrease* | *Increase* | |
| Rifampin | Diltiazem | Gentamicin |
| Rifabutin | Verapamil | Tobramycin |
| Isoniazid | Nicardipine | Vancomycin |
| Phenobarbital | Erythromycin | Azapropazone |
| Phenytoin | Clarithromycin | Amphotericin B |
| Carbamazepine | Ketoconazole | Cisplatin |
| | Fluconazole | Melphalan |
| | Itraconazole | Cimetidine |
| | Clotrimazole | Ranitidine |
| | Bromocriptine | Diclofenac |
| | Danazol | |
| | Cimetidine | |
| | Methylprednisolone | |
| | Metoclopramide | |

**Table 40–11. Common Organ System Targets for Toxicities of Immunosuppressant Therapy**

| | Prednisone | Cyclosporine | Tacrolimus | Sirolimus | Azathioprine | Mycophenolate |
|---|---|---|---|---|---|---|
| Central nervous system | + | + | + | 0 | 0 | 0 |
| Gastrointestinal system | + | + | + | 0 | + | + |
| Kidney | 0 | + | + | 0 | 0 | 0 |
| Hematopoietic | 0 | 0 | 0 | + | + | + |
| Skin | + | + | 0 | 0 | 0 | 0 |
| Endocrine | + | + | + | + | 0 | 0 |
| Dyslipidemia | + | + | 0 | + | 0 | 0 |
| Wound healing | + | 0 | 0 | + | 0 | 0 |

**Table 40–12. Postoperative Infection and Peptic Ulcer Prophylaxis**

| Problem | Commonly Used Drug Prophylaxis | Alternate(s) |
|---|---|---|
| Urinary tract infection | Trimethoprim-sulfamethoxazole × 3 months | Nitrofurantoin |
| *Pneumocystis* pneumonia | Trimethoprim-sulfamethoxazole × 3 months | Pentamidine inhalant |
| Oral candidiasis | Clotrimazole lozenges × 1-3 months | Nystatin troches |
| Vaginal candidiasis | Clotrimazole vaginal inserts × 1-3 months | Nystatin inserts |
| Herpes simplex virus | Acyclovir × 3 months | Gancyclovir |
| Primary CMV disease | Gancyclovir ± CMV immune globulin × 4 months | Valacyclovir, acyclovir |
| Recurrent CMV disease | Gancyclovir × 3 months or during antibody therapy | Valacyclovir, acyclovir |
| Peptic ulcer disease | H₂ receptor antagonist + antacid if symptomatic | |

CMV, cytomegalovirus.

## PROBLEMS
## Early Graft Dysfunction

**Early graft dysfunction can be due to infection, renal allograft rejection, urinary or vascular obstruction, cyclosporine or tacrolimus nephrotoxicity, hyperglycemia, or dehydration.** The cause can usually be sorted out by following the suggestions in Tables 40–13 and 40–14. Fever is common with infection and/or rejection. Physical examination for sinusitis, dental abscess, pneumonia, cholecystitis, appendicitis, diverticulitis, and kidney graft tenderness can be quickly performed. An ultrasound examination that includes a Doppler flow study can demonstrate renal allograft enlargement, the presence or absence of hydronephrosis, and blood flow in and out of the kidney graft. In addition, it can assess the gallbladder and native kidneys for stones and obstruction. Tremor can be a clue to calcineurin inhibitor toxicity, which can be confirmed by determining the blood level of the calcineurin inhibitor. The pseudorejection of hyperglycemia can be quickly diagnosed with a bedside blood glucose determination. Dehydration can also be quickly diagnosed at the bedside and treated intravenously with a 5- to 10-mL/kg bolus of fluid.

## Vascular Complications

Immediate vascular complications include kinking of the kidney graft's artery or vein, suture line stenosis, or thrombosis. Thrombosis of the kidney graft may occur because of hyperacute rejection or thrombophilia. Renal artery stenosis after renal transplantation is usually diagnosed because of hypertension that is progressively difficult to manage, with or without impaired renal function. Color Doppler sonography has a high sensitivity and specificity for detecting transplant renal artery stenosis (Radermacher et al, 2000). The causes are atheroma, faulty suture technique, clamp trauma, and immunologic mechanisms (Lacombe, 1988). The finding of a bruit over the kidney graft is unreliable because it is a common sign after renal transplantation with or without hypertension; however, the detection of a new bruit may be significant. **Surgical intervention for transplant renal artery stenosis is difficult, with a significant risk of technical failure, and percutaneous transluminal angioplasty, with or without endoluminal stent placement, has become the initial treatment of choice** (Nicita et al, 1998).

Renal allograft rupture is rare and requires immediate operation. It is usually due to acute rejection or renal vein thrombosis. If it is due to the former, rejection crisis treatment and operative repair with bolstered mattress sutures, administration of topical thrombotic agents, and the use of synthetic glue and polyglactin mesh wrap have resulted in graft salvage (Chopin et al, 1989). If it is due to renal vein thrombosis, graft salvage with thrombectomy and repair of graft rupture is rare, and allograft nephrectomy is usually necessary (Richardson et al, 1990).

## Allograft Nephrectomy

**The indications for allograft nephrectomy are to remove a symptomatic irreversibly rejected kidney transplant and, in the case of a chronically rejected asymptomatic graft, to withdraw immunosuppression and to prevent the development of anti-HLA antibodies that could delay or prevent a subsequent transplantation.**

The usual approach is through the original incision. Within the first month after transplantation, allograft nephrectomy is a straightforward procedure, and it is usually possible to

**Table 40–13. Sorting Out Early Graft Dysfunction**

| Cause | Physical Finding | Initial Diagnostics Based on Suspicion |
|---|---|---|
| Infection | Fever, chills, normal or ↓ BP, ± pulmonary findings, ± native or kidney transplant tenderness | Chest radiograph, urinalysis, smears and cultures of sputum, urine, wound drainage, and blood; ultrasonogram of abdomen and kidney graft |
| Rejection | ± Fever, normal or ↑ BP, normal or ↑ CVP, kidney transplant tenderness | Ultrasound of kidney graft, allograft biopsy |
| Obstruction | Vital signs normal unless infected, ± kidney transplant tenderness | Irrigate bladder catheter, ultrasound and Doppler flow study of kidney graft |
| Calcineurin inhibitor toxicity | Afebrile, normal or ↑ BP, normal CVP, ± tremor | Calcineurin inhibitor blood level |
| Hyperglycemia | Afebrile, ↓ BP, ↓ CVP | Blood sugar |
| Dehydration | Afebrile, ↓ BP, ↓ CVP | IV fluid bolus |

BP, blood pressure; CVP, central venous pressure; IV, intravenous.

**Table 40–14. Differentiation of Calcineurin Inhibitor Toxicity from Acute Rejection**

| Characteristic | Tacrolimus or Cyclosporine Toxicity | Acute Rejection |
|---|---|---|
| Fever | No | Yes |
| Urinary output | Usually maintained | Decreased |
| Graft tenderness | No | Yes |
| Graft size | Stable | Increased |
| Serum creatinine level rise | Slow | Rapid |
| Cyclosporine/tacrolimus blood level | High | Normal or low |
| Graft biopsy | May be normal | Cellular infiltration, vasculitis, tubulitis |

remove all of the transplanted tissue. After 4 to 6 weeks, a dense fibrous reaction surrounds the kidney transplant and the procedure can be a formidable one. It is usually accomplished with the subcapsular technique and knowledge of the vascular reconstruction that was done at the time of transplantation. The surgeon must be prepared to occlude the vascular pedicle with a large vascular clamp, transect the vascular pedicle distal to the clamp, and either separately ligate the renal veins and arteries or oversew the stumps of the vessels with 4-0 or 5-0 vascular suture. The renal capsule and the intravesical ureteral stump are left behind. The wound is liberally irrigated with an antibiotic solution, a suction drain is commonly placed, and the wound is closed as described under "Recipient Operation."

Perioperative antibiotic therapy is discontinued, changed, or continued on the basis of intraoperative culture results, and immunosuppression is discontinued within a few weeks. Cyclosporine or tacrolimus is withdrawn immediately; azathioprine, mycophenolate mofetil, or sirolimus is continued for 4 to 6 weeks because of residual allograft tissue, especially in the case of a subcapsular nephrectomy; and prednisone is gradually tapered and withdrawn with the following formula: 1 week of corticosteroid taper for every month of immunosuppression for a maximum of 6 weeks.

## Hematuria

Hematuria immediately after transplantation is usually due to catheter trauma or urinary tract reconstruction. If it cannot

be controlled with catheter irrigation, endoscopy with clot evacuation and fulguration of the bleeding site or sites in the bladder is necessary. If those treatments fail, surgical exploration is indicated.

Late hematuria can be due to medical renal disease in the kidney graft, infection, calculus, or malignancy. If hematuria persists after treatment of a documented urinary tract infection, a standard hematuria workup with microscopy for red blood cell casts or dysmorphic red blood cells should be done, followed, if necessary, by imaging of the native kidneys and kidney transplant, cystoscopy, a bladder wash for cytologic examination, and pertinent urothelial biopsies.

## Fluid Collections

**Most fluid collections after renal transplantation are incidental findings on baseline ultrasound examinations and require no treatment** (Pollak et al, 1988). An algorithm for the evaluation and management of perigraft fluid collections is shown in Figure 40–14. When fluid collections are large or associated with dilatation of the collecting system, pain, fever, or an unexplained decline in renal function, then an ultrasonically guided aspiration can be diagnostic. If the fluid is purulent, microscopic examination of the fluid for pus cells and organisms is performed, and antibiotic treatment is initiated. In the event of infection, cyclosporine or tacrolimus therapy is usually continued; azathioprine, mycophenolate mofetil, or sirolimus therapy is discontinued; and prednisone is reduced to less than 15 mg/day. Although percutaneously placed tube drainage can be effective, open surgical drainage is often necessary for infected fluid collections. Lymph, urine, and blood can be differentiated from each other by creatinine and hematocrit determinations. Lymph has a creatinine concentration that is the same as that of serum, urine has a creatinine concentration higher than that of serum and approaching that of bladder urine, and blood has a high hematocrit level when compared with the other two fluids.

If the symptoms or the urinary tract obstruction are relieved by aspiration and there is no recurrence of the fluid, no further treatment is necessary. If blood reaccumulates, exploration and control of bleeding are usually necessary.

If an uninfected lymphocele recurs, it is usually treated by unroofing it into the peritoneal cavity by either open or laparoscopic technique (Schweitzer et al, 1972; Gill et al, 1995). **Lymphoceles that are lateral to the kidney are**

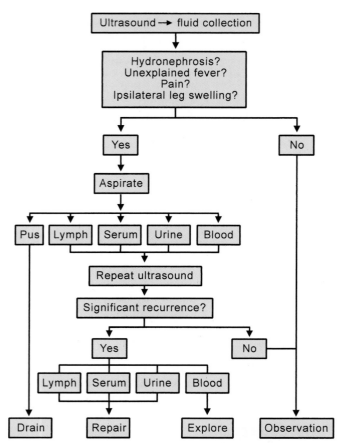

**Figure 40–14.** Algorithm for evaluation and treatment of perigraft fluid collection. (Modified from Barry JM: Renal transplantation. In Krane RJ, Siroky MB, Fitzpatrick JM [eds]: Clinical Urology. Philadelphia, JB Lippincott, 1994, p 325.)

**difficult to access laparoscopically** (Gruessner et al, 1995). Success has been reported with percutaneous sclerosis (Rivera et al, 1996). If the lymphocele is infected, open drainage is often necessary.

Urinary extravasation often requires open surgical repair. A retrograde or CT cystogram will document leakage at the cystotomy or ureteroneocystostomy site. If a retrograde cystogram does not show extravasation, contrast CT may suggest, and percutaneous antegrade pyelography will confirm, a site of extravasation from the ureter or renal pelvis. Excretory urography may also be used but is often impractical in this setting because of inadequate renal function. Some urinary leaks at the ureteroneocystostomy site may be managed simply by bladder catheter drainage, with or without percutaneous nephrostomy, by percutaneous or retrograde passage of a double-J ureteral stent, or by the performance of another ureteroneocystostomy. If open repair is necessary, retrograde pyelography and the passage of a ureteral catheter into the native ureter at the time of repair will facilitate the identification of that structure if it is needed for ureteroureterostomy or ureteropyelostomy. Urinary tract repair is usually protected with a stent for 6 weeks and sometimes a small nephrostomy tube or an omental flap, or both. A suction drain is placed, and antibiotic therapy based on culture and sensitivity results is administered.

## Obstruction and Stones

Figure 40–15 is an algorithm for evaluating hydronephrosis in the transplanted kidney. Ureteral obstruction in the immediate postoperative period is due to technical error, edema, a blood clot, unsuspected donor calculus, or perigraft fluid collection. Although endourologic techniques can be successful, a technical error is usually repaired with a stented ureteroneocystostomy. Edema usually resolves within a few days, and ureteral blood clots lyse with naturally produced urokinase.

The management of fluid collections was discussed previously.

Late causes of urinary tract obstruction are periureteral fibrosis, calculi, tumor, fungus ball, lymphocele, chronic ischemia of the distal ureter with stricture, and BK-related polyomavirus nephropathy. Ureteroneocystostomy meatal stenosis can be managed by endoscopic ureteral meatotomy, by percutaneous ureteral dilatation followed by stent placement (Hobart et al, 2000), or by open surgical repair. **There are reports of long-term success of the endourologic treatment of transplant ureteral stenosis** (Streem et al, 1988; Benoit et al, 1993). Failures are usually apparent within 1 year of treatment, and short, anastomotic strictures are the lesions most successfully treated with these techniques. If the stricture is distal and allograft ureteral length is sufficient, a repeat ureteroneocystostomy will do. For recurrent or long strictures, ureteropyelostomy and ureteroureterostomy as described earlier are reasonable options. Vesicopyelostomy, vesicocalycostomy, and interposition of a small bowel segment between the renal pelvis and the bladder (Orton and Middleton, 1982; Ehrlich et al, 1983; Del Pizzo et al, 1998) have all been used as surgical treatments for an obstructed allograft ureter.

Causes of urinary tract calculi after renal transplantation are considered to be persistent hyperparathyroidism, recurrent urinary tract infections, a foreign body such as a suture or staple, obstruction, a habitual decreased fluid intake, and distal renal tubular acidosis (Hefty, 1991). **Because the renal transplant is denervated, the patient will not experience typical renal colic, and the diagnosis is suspected when renal function suddenly deteriorates or transplant pyelonephritis occurs.** Upper tract calculi are managed by the same techniques as calculi in the normal urinary tract; however, negotiation of the transplanted ureter may be difficult or impossible because of tortuosity, thus favoring percutaneous techniques. Extracorporeal shock wave lithotripsy has been used successfully with clever positioning of the patient in the shock wave path (Wheatley et al, 1991). Small bladder calculi are managed by transurethral extraction and irrigation with or without lithotripsy. If a cystolithotomy is selected as the procedure for a medium to large hard stone, the surgeon must take care not to damage the ureteroneocystostomy.

## Urinary Tract Infection

Urinary tract infections after renal transplantation are present in up to 40% of patients and have been associated with increased mortality after transplantation (Chuang et al, 2005). In addition to immunosuppression and an indwelling bladder catheter, the following risk factors are often present: advanced recipient age, use of deceased donor kidney, female gender, diabetes mellitus, and preexisting urinary tract abnormalities.

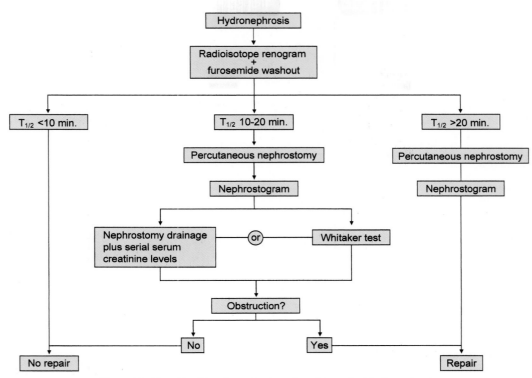

**Figure 40–15.** Algorithm for evaluation of renal transplant hydronephrosis.

During the first 3 months after renal transplantation, prophylactic broad-spectrum antibiotics such as trimethoprim-sulfamethoxazole are usually prescribed. This drug combination also prevents pulmonary *Pneumocystis carinii* infection. Trimethoprim interferes with the tubular secretion of creatinine, and this can cause an increase in the serum creatinine levels. The urinary tract infections that occur months after transplantation are usually benign and respond readily to conventional antimicrobial therapy, guided by urine culture and sensitivity. **Patients with pyelonephritis should be screened with ultrasonography for obstruction or stone.** Graft dysfunction accompanied by fever can be due to either acute pyelonephritis or acute rejection, and it is important to differentiate between the two because increased immunosuppression during an episode of acute pyelonephritis can result in significant sepsis.

*Candida* cystitis often responds to foreign body removal and bladder irrigations with amphotericin B with or without oral fluconazole (Wise, 2002). Cyclosporine and tacrolimus doses usually have to be reduced when fluconazole is given because fluconazole interferes with the metabolism of both those immunosuppressants. Tissue-invasive infections often require intravenous administration of fluconazole or amphotericin B.

Hemorrhagic cystitis can be due to adenovirus (Yagasawa et al, 1995). The disease is usually self-limited and resolves within 1 or 2 weeks. Treatment is by forced hydration and diuresis.

BK polyomavirus is an important, recently recognized uropathogen that can be present in 10% to 45% of recipients and cause significant nephropathy in 6% of infected recipients (Trofe et al, 2004). It can be transmitted from the donor or be reactivated in the recipient by immunosuppression. Recognition and treatment can be challenging because the nephropathy often mimics a rejection crisis, and antirejection therapy can exacerbate the disease. It can also present as ureteral obstruction due to fibrosis. Polymerase chain reaction of both blood and urine can identify the infection. Renal biopsy is often inconclusive. Treatment consists of reduction of immunosuppression, antiviral therapy such as with cidofovir, which has significant nephrotoxicity, and leflunomide (Williams et al, 2005).

## Vesicoureteral Reflux

Although there is some controversy about the need for antireflux ureteroneocystostomy in kidney transplantation, common urologic thinking is that reflux of infected bladder urine or high-pressure reflux is damaging to a kidney. **The indications for antireflux surgery of the kidney transplant ureter are the same as those for nontransplanted patients** (Reinberg et al, 1990). If the reflux is due to high-pressure voiding, relief of the bladder outlet obstruction or augmentation cystoplasty with intermittent catheterization must be considered. Ureteral advancement techniques, ureteroureterostomy to a nonrefluxing native ureter, and submucosal injection techniques are all possible therapies.

## Erectile Dysfunction

Erectile dysfunction after renal transplantation is common (Malavaud et al, 2000) and can be due to any one or a

**Table 40-15. Potential Causes of Erectile Dysfunction after Renal Transplantation**

| Anatomic Location | Examples | Mechanisms |
|---|---|---|
| Central | | |
| Antihypertensives | Clonidine | $\alpha_2$ Agonist |
| | Methyldopa | $\alpha_2$ Agonist, ↑ prolactin |
| | Propranolol | $\beta$ Antagonist |
| Peptides/amino acids | Prednisone | ↓ ACTH |
| ↓ Testosterone | Cimetidine | ↑ Prolactin |
| | Cyclosporine | ↑ Prolactin |
| | Sirolimus | Testis atrophy |
| Anxiety | Stress | ↑ Norepinephrine |
| Autonomic/peripheral nerves | Diabetes mellitus | Axon injury |
| | Uremia | Axon injury |
| Cavernosal blood supply | | |
| Internal iliac arterial tree | Renal artery anastomosis | ↓ Penis blood flow |
| Accelerated arteriosclerosis | Prednisone, cyclosporine, propranolol, diabetes mellitus | ↑ Cholesterol |
| Antihypertensives | Any | ↓ Penis blood pressure and blood flow |
| Diuretics | Any | ↓ Blood volume and penis blood flow |
| Cavernosal smooth muscle | Diabetes mellitus, ↑ cholesterol | Impair nitric oxide–mediated relaxation |
| | Cyclosporine, tacrolimus | ↑ Thromboxane $A_2$ |
| Tunica albuginea of penis | Propranolol | Peyronie's disease |

Modified from Barry JM: The evaluation and treatment of erectile dysfunction following organ transplantation. Semin Urol 1994b;12:147.

combination of the factors outlined in Table 40–15. **Factors unique to the transplant recipient are side effects from immunosuppression and a reduction of cavernosal blood supply by the renal arterial anastomosis.** Sirolimus-treated men have been shown to have lower serum testosterone levels, higher follicle-stimulating hormone and luteinizing hormone concentrations, and no difference in serum prolactin levels when compared with non–sirolimus-treated control subjects (Fritsche et al, 2004).

Treatment options for transplant recipients with erectile dysfunction are presented in Table 40–16. A diagnosis and treatment algorithm for erectile dysfunction after renal transplantation is presented in Figure 40–16 and is similar to those for the immunocompetent patient. Sildenafil has been shown to improve glomerular filtration rates in kidney transplant recipients (Rostaing et al, 2000) and not to alter blood levels of cyclosporine or tacrolimus (Cofan et al, 2002). Intracorporeal injections of vasoactive drugs and implantation of penile prostheses have successfully treated this problem (Lasaponara et al, 2004), but the transplant recipient must be warned of the increased risk of infection when either of these invasive treatment options is used.

**If a penile prosthesis is chosen as the most appropriate therapy, the following criteria are helpful: stable graft function without a rejection crisis for at least 6 months, low doses of maintenance immunosuppressants, a low probability of device malfunction, no intra-abdominal components, minimal tissue dissection, no skin or urinary tract infections, prophylactic antibiotic therapy (parenteral, intraurethral, and wound irrigation), and postoperative oral antibiotics for 2 weeks.** When a stress corticosteroid protocol is used, 25 mg of prednisone (or its equivalent) is given with the preoperative medications and 12 and 24 hours later. Maintenance corticosteroid therapy is resumed on the second postoperative day. The oral doses of cyclosporine or tacrolimus and of azathioprine, mycophenolate mofetil, or rapamycin are not altered. The intravenous doses of

**Table 40-16. Treatment Options for Transplant Recipients with Erectile Dysfunction**

| Treatment | Examples |
|---|---|
| Psychotherapy/counseling | Alternate sexual techniques |
| | Stop alcohol use |
| | Stop tobacco use |
| Medication changes | Treat hypertension with calcium antagonists, angiotensin-converting enzyme inhibitors, or $\alpha_1$ blockers |
| | Change cimetidine to ranitidine, famotidine, or nizatidine |
| | Glucocorticoid withdrawal, if possible |
| Medication additions, if indicated by workup | Testosterone replacement |
| | Thyroid replacement |
| | Bromocriptine |
| | Type 5 phosphodiesterase inhibitors |
| Vacuum erection devices | |
| Intracavernous injections | Prostaglandin $E_1$ |
| Vascular procedures | Angiodilation |
| | Revascularization |
| Penile prostheses | Malleable |
| | Mechanically jointed |
| | Inflatable without prevesical reservoir |

Modified from Barry JM: The evaluation and treatment of erectile dysfunction following organ transplantation. Semin Urol 1994;12:147 and Barry JM: Male sexuality in renal transplant recipients. Transplant Immunol Lett 2000;16:7.

cyclosporine and tacrolimus are one third the oral doses, and they are infused over 24 hours. The intravenous doses of azathioprine and mycophenolate mofetil are the same as the oral doses.

## Pregnancy and Childbearing

After successful kidney transplantation, levels of follicle-stimulating hormone, luteinizing hormone, and testosterone

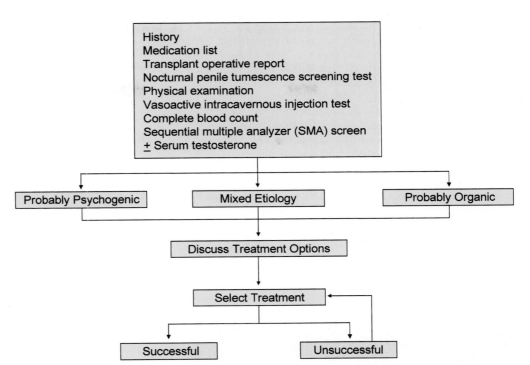

History
Medication list
Transplant operative report
Nocturnal penile tumescence screening test
Physical examination
Vasoactive intracavernous injection test
Complete blood count
Sequential multiple analyzer (SMA) screen
± Serum testosterone

Probably Psychogenic    Mixed Etiology    Probably Organic

Discuss Treatment Options

Select Treatment

Successful    Unsuccessful

**Figure 40–16.** Algorithm for evaluation of men with erectile dysfunction after renal transplantation. Notice that it differs little from treatment-based algorithms for men who have not undergone renal transplantation. (Modified from Barry JM: Male sexuality in renal transplant recipients. Transplant Immunol Lett 2000;16:7.)

usually become normal, and spermatogenesis improves (Akbari et al, 2003; Kheradmand and Javadneia, 2003). **Among male recipients who have fathered children, there has been no increase in congenital abnormalities in the offspring;** however, it is recommended that impregnation be delayed for at least 1 year after transplantation (Armenti et al, 1998).

Successful renal transplantation usually restores fertility in premenopausal women. In a report based on thousands of pregnancies in renal transplant recipients, Davison and Milne (1997) reported the following: 94% of the conceptions that continued beyond the first trimester ended successfully; 50% of the deliveries were preterm; 30% of the women developed hypertension, preeclampsia, or both; intrauterine growth retardation occurred in about 20%; and rejection crises occurred in 10%. **There were no frequent or predominant abnormalities in the children, the transplanted kidney rarely caused dystocia, and the transplanted kidney was not injured during vaginal delivery.** Pregnancy safety information for immunosuppressive drugs is listed in Table 40–17 (Armenti et al, 2003). Guidelines for successful pregnancy are good general health for 2 years after transplantation, minimal proteinuria, no hypertension, no rejection, no urinary tract obstruction, nearly normal renal function, and low doses of maintenance immunosuppressants.

## Pulmonary Infection

Pneumonia in the immunosuppressed kidney transplant recipient is usually due to common bacterial pathogens, however, *Legionella, Nocardia,* mycobacteria, viruses, parasites *(Pneumocystis),* and fungi can all be etiologic agents.

| Table 40–17. **Pregnancy Safety and Immunosuppressants** | |
| --- | --- |
| | *Pregnancy Category* |
| Glucocorticoids | C |
| Azathioprine | D |
| Mycophenolate mofetil | C |
| Sirolimus | C |
| Cyclosporine | C |
| Tacrolimus | C |
| Monomurab CD3 | C |
| Antithymocyte globulin | C |
| Rituximab | C |
| Alemtuzumab | C |
| Daclizumab | C |
| Basiliximab | B |

B, no fetal risk in animals, no controlled studies; C, fetal risk cannot be ruled out; D, evidence of fetal risk.
Data from Armenti VG, Radomski JS, Moritz M, et al: Report from the National Transplantation Pregnancy Registry (NTPR): Outcomes of pregnancy after transplantation. In Cecka JM, Terasaki PI (eds): Clinical Transplants 2002. Los Angeles, UCLA Immunogenetics Center, 2003, p 128; and Physicians Desk Reference, 59th ed. Montvale, NJ, Thomson PDR, 2005.

## Cancer

**Kidney transplant recipients are more likely to develop cancer than age-matched subjects in the general population and patients wait-listed for deceased donor renal transplantation.** Among 35,765 first-time recipients of deceased or living donor renal transplants, the rates for most malignancies were higher after kidney transplantation when compared with the general population and with 46,106 patients wait-listed for kidney transplantation. This was especially true for Kaposi's sarcoma, non-Hodgkins lymphomas, nonmelanoma skin cancers, and kidney cancer (Kasiske et al, 2004).

Although bacille Calmette-Guérin (BCG), a live, attenuated bacterium, has been used successfully to treat superficial bladder cancer in kidney transplant recipients, it should be used with caution, if at all, in immunocompromised transplant recipients because of the risk of systemic infection and the likelihood of diminished therapeutic response. Absorbed thiotepa may have an additive myelosuppressive effect if the patient is also taking azathioprine, mycophenolate mofetil, or sirolimus.

Enterocystoplasty has become recognized as a risk factor for carcinoma in the reconstructed bladder, and it is reasonable to begin bladder cancer surveillance 5 years after the augmentation procedure (Nahas et al, 1999).

## KEY POINTS: RENAL TRANSPLANTATION

- The incidence of end-stage renal disease (ESRD) is greater than any urologic malignancy except prostate cancer.

- More patients die annually of ESRD than of any urologic malignancy.

- The first long-term success with human kidney transplantation occurred in 1954.

- Medicare co-insurance has been one of the most significant advances for the treatment of patients with ESRD.

- Preliminary evaluation of ESRD patients for renal transplantation is important to prevent wastage of kidney grafts because of transplantation into unsuitable recipients.

- Protocols are evolving to deal with the issues of ABO incompatibility and positive crossmatches between donors and recipients.

- Laparoscopic-assisted donor nephrectomy has reduced disincentives for living renal donors.

- Urologists must be aware of the urologic problems that may prevent or impair renal transplant technical success.

- Urologists must be aware of the potential genitourinary problems of transplant recipients.

## Medical Vascular Complications

Nonsurgical hypertension after renal transplantation is common. Causes of this include medications (corticosteroids, cyclosporine, and tacrolimus), intrinsic renal disease, and rejection.

In spite of aggressive preoperative assessment and treatment, myocardial infarction and stroke continue to be leading causes of death in these patients. Prednisone and cyclosporine increase cardiovascular risk because of the hyperlipidemia associated with these drugs, and post-transplant hyperlipidemia should be treated aggressively with dietary changes and, if necessary, anti-lipid medications.

## New Diabetes Mellitus

New diabetes occurs in a significant percentage of kidney transplant recipients (Kasiske et al, 2003). **This is due to the diabetogenic effects of corticosteroids and calcineurin inhibitors.** The incidence of insulin-dependent post-transplant diabetes mellitus is significantly higher in patients treated with tacrolimus than in those treated with cyclosporine.

## SUMMARY

Renal transplantation is the best therapy for most patients with ESRD. Morbidity and mortality have been significantly reduced by attention to pretransplantation evaluations, donor surgery, kidney preservation, recipient selection, recipient surgery, histocompatibility, immunosuppression, and the successful management of complications. **Organ shortage continues to be a significant problem.**

### SUGGESTED READINGS

Belzer FO, Southard JH: Principles of solid-organ preservation by cold storage. Transplantation 1988;45:673.

Halloran PF: Immunosuppressive drugs for kidney transplantation. N Engl J Med 2004;351:2715.

Hobart MG, Streem SB, Gill IS: Renal transplant complications: Minimally invasive management. Urol Clin North Am 2000;27:787.

Irish A: Hypercoagulability in renal transplant recipients: Identifying patients at risk of renal allograft thrombosis and evaluating strategies for prevention. Am J Cardiovasc Drugs 2004;4:139.

Jacobs S, Cho E, Foster C, et al: Laparoscopic live donor nephrectomy: The University of Maryland 6-year experience. J Urol 2004;171:47.

Kasiske BL, Cangro CB, Hariharan S, et al: The evaluation of renal transplant candidates: Clinical practice guidelines. Am J Transplant 2001;2(Suppl 1):5.

Meier-Kriesche HU, Ojo AO, Port FK, et al: Survival improvement among patients with end-stage renal disease: Trends over time for transplant recipients and wait-listed patients. J Am Soc Nephrol 2001;12:1293.

Murray JE, Merrill JP, Harrison JH: Renal homotransplantations in identical twins. Surg Forum 1955;6:432.

Nakazato PZ, Concepcion W, Bry W, et al: Total abdominal evisceration: An en-bloc technique for abdominal organ harvesting. Surgery 1992;111:37.

Warren DS, Zachary AA, Sonnenday CJ, et al: Successful renal transplantation across simultaneous ABO and positive crossmatch barriers. Am J Transplant 2004;4:561.

# 41 Etiology, Pathogenesis, and Management of Renal Failure

DAVID A. GOLDFARB, MD • JOSEPH V. NALLY, JR., MD •
MARTIN J. SCHREIBER, JR., MD

ACUTE RENAL FAILURE

ACUTE TUBULAR NECROSIS

CLINICAL APPROACH TO THE DIFFERENTIAL
DIAGNOSIS OF ACUTE RENAL FAILURE

MANAGEMENT OF ACUTE RENAL FAILURE

CHRONIC RENAL FAILURE

Disorders of renal function are ubiquitous in the contemporary practice of medicine. These can be broadly grouped into two major categories: acute renal failure and chronic renal failure. Urologists are likely to encounter renal function issues and their aberrations on a daily basis. This chapter is designed to give a contemporary insight into the nature of renal failure and its treatment.

## ACUTE RENAL FAILURE
### Definition

Acute renal failure (ARF) is a common problem in the contemporary practice of medicine and urology in the hospitalized patient. Prospective studies have demonstrated that 2% to 5% of all patients admitted to a general medical/surgical hospital unit will develop ARF (Nolan and Anderson, 1998). In selected patients in the intensive care unit (ICU) after cardiovascular or abdominal vascular surgery, the incidence may exceed 20%. Epidemiologic studies indicate that the development of ARF is associated with significant increases in morbidity (which prolongs hospitalization and increases costs) and mortality (Dimick et al, 2003). The high occurrence and substantial morbidity and mortality of ARF demand a logical approach to its early recognition and prevention, as well as prompt diagnosis and management of its complications.

ARF is defined as a rapid reduction in renal function characterized by progressive azotemia (best measured clinically by serum creatinine [SCr]), which may or may not be accompanied by oliguria. This abrupt decline in renal function occurs over the course of hours to days and results in the failure to excrete nitrogenous wastes from the plasma or to maintain normal volume and electrolyte homeostasis. The ARF can be diagnosed with certainty when the patient's prior renal function is known and the reduction in renal function is documented.

The cardinal feature of ARF is a decline in glomerular filtration rate (GFR). While ideally determined by inulin or radioisotopic clearance techniques, it is usually identified in routine clinical practice by a rise in serum blood urea nitrogen (BUN) or creatinine. **It is important to understand the limitations of these common clinical chemistries for them to be properly interpreted. The correlation between BUN, creatinine, and GFR assumes they are delivered into the serum at a constant rate. Therefore, conditions such as hypercatabolic state and massive trauma that may be seen in surgical patients can affect renal function assessment. BUN may be disproportionately elevated in states of marked volume contraction, in hypercatabolic states, and with marked increases in protein loads seen with gastrointestinal bleeding or total parenteral nutrition. Serum creatinine is produced at a constant rate by muscle and more accurately reflects GFR. When renal function deteriorates, tubular secretion represents an increasing proportion of creatinine excretion. Therefore, creatinine clearance may overestimate GFR as renal function slowly declines when measured in the "steady state."** Both the creatinine clearance and the Cockcroft-Gault calculation may be useful tools to estimate GFR because they take into account the patient's body size, age, and SCr value. For example, the Cockcroft-Gault formula states that creatinine clearance = $(140 - \text{age}) \times \text{weight} \times (0.85$ female$)$ divided by $72 \times$ plasma creatinine (Cockcroft and Gault, 1976). Both methodologies have their disadvantages because the urinary creatinine clearance method is cumbersome and the Cockcroft-Gault method may have a margin of error up to about 30% compared with GFR measured by formal $^{125}$I iothalamate techniques. Recently the Modification of Diet in Renal Disease (MDRD) calculations have been used as a way to estimate GFR (Levey et al, 1999). However, none of these techniques is suitable for estimating GFR in the ARF patient because such a "steady state" does not exist (Hoste et al, 2005). Use of "real time" estimates of GFR using infused radioisotopic plasma disappearance techniques in the ICU patient with ARF has been advocated by some but has not achieved wide clinical acceptance. In clinical practice, the experienced nephrologist infers from a rapidly rising SCr value that the patient's true GFR is approaching zero.

# Epidemiology and Classification of ARF

Clinically, it is very useful to separate the causes of ARF into three major categories: prerenal, intrinsic renal, and postrenal. Distinguishing among the three basic categories of ARF is a challenging clinical exercise. Assigning a patient to one of the three categories usually requires a combination of clinical and laboratory evaluations and may require invasive monitoring of central hemodynamics or imaging studies of the genitourinary tract. **The importance of differentiating the major causes of ARF must be stressed, because the initial evaluation and management are tailored to the particular cause.** Because the greatest proportion of hospital-acquired ARF is secondary to acute tubular necrosis (ATN), in this chapter we place special emphasis on the diagnosis, pathophysiology, and management of ATN. For example, a report from Madrid evaluated 748 cases of ARF at 13 tertiary care hospital centers (Liano and Pascual, 1996). The causes of ARF were ATN, 45%; prerenal, 21%; acute or chronic renal failure, 13%; urinary tract obstruction, 10%; glomerulonephritis/vasculitis, 4%; acute interstitial nephritis (AIN), 2%; and atheroembolic renal disease, 1%. Earlier reports had documented that ARF occurs more commonly in the surgical/trauma ICU, medical ICU, and postoperative units.

### Prerenal Azotemia

**Prerenal azotemia is caused by transient renal hypoperfusion that may induce a fall in GFR and produce urinary sodium avidity. The hallmark of prerenal azotemia is its reversibility with treatment of the underlying cause and the lack of structural damage to the kidney. The "gold standard" is the response to appropriate fluid repletion: return of renal function to the previous baseline within 24 to 72 hours is usually considered to represent prerenal disease.**

Under normal circumstances, the kidney can maintain normal renal blood flow (RBF) and GFR down to perfusion pressures of approximately 60 mm Hg. The phenomenon of autoregulation requires a complex interaction of physiologic factors to maintain RBF and GFR. In some hospitalized patients with disordered autoregulation, a reduction in RBF and GFR may occur with modest or even no discernable fall in systemic blood pressure. In the setting of decreased renal perfusion, angiotensin II and vasodilatory prostaglandins play an important role in maintaining glomerular hydrostatic pressure and GFR. The three major determinants of GFR are renal plasma flow, glomerular hydrostatic pressure, and glomerular permeability. **Angiotensin II has selectively greater vasocon-**

| Table 41–1. **Prerenal Causes of Acute Renal Failure** |
| --- |
| *Volume Depletion* |
| Surgical: hemorrhage, shock |
| Gastrointestinal losses: vomiting, diarrhea, fistulas |
| Renal: overdiuresis, salt-wasting disorders |
| *Cardiac Causes: Primary Decrease in Cardiac Output* |
| Acute disorders: myocardial infarction, arrhythmias, malignant hypertension, tamponade, endocarditis |
| Chronic disorders: valvular diseases, chronic cardiomyopathy (ischemic heart disease, hypertensive heart disease) |
| *Redistribution of Extracellular Fluid* |
| Hypoalbuminemic states: nephrotic syndrome, advanced liver disease, malnutrition |
| Physical causes: peritonitis, burns, crush injury |
| Peripheral vasodilatation: sepsis, antihypertensive agents |
| Renal artery stenosis (bilateral) |

strictor effects on the efferent than afferent arteriole, whereas vasodilatory prostaglandins can cause afferent arteriolar vasodilation. Drugs that selectively block angiotensin II synthesis, such as angiotensin-converting enzyme (ACE) inhibitors or angiotensin II receptor binders (angiotensin II receptor blockers), or that inhibit vasodilatory prostaglandin synthesis may cause ARF. This is prone to occur in clinical settings in which GFR is already compromised** (Toto et al, 1991; Whelton, 1999).

Prerenal azotemia may be encountered in both the volume-depleted and volume-overloaded patient (Table 41–1). True volume depletion may result from renal or extrarenal losses that result in systemic hypotension and renal hypoperfusion. In the volume-overloaded patient, with edematous states such as cirrhosis and congestive heart failure, prerenal azotemia may occur because the kidney perceives that the vascular tree is underfilled (i.e., "ineffective arterial blood volume"). This results in renal hypoperfusion. Prerenal azotemia may also occur owing to high-grade bilateral renal artery stenosis or in states of renal hypoperfusion due to redistribution of extracellular fluid with peripheral vasodilation as seen with sepsis. As noted earlier, ACE inhibitors/angiotensin II receptor blockers and nonsteroidal anti-inflammatory drugs (NSAIDs) may alter the vasoconstrictor effects of angiotensin II and the vasodilatory effects of prostaglandins to produce prerenal azotemia. This is especially the case in elderly patients with impaired GFR, subtle volume depletion, or occult renal artery stenosis.

**The pathophysiology of prerenal azotemia relates to the reduction in RBF. Renal hypoperfusion stimulates both the sympathetic nervous system and renin-angiotensin system to cause renal vasoconstriction and sodium avidity. Furthermore, hypotension is a powerful stimulus to the release of antidiuretic hormone, which mediates water reabsorption. Hence, urine production is characterized by low volume, decreased concentration of urinary sodium, increased urinary excretion of creatinine, and a high urine osmolality. Microscopy of the urinary sediment is usually bland. In essence, "prerenal azotemia is a good kidney looking at a bad world."**

Therapy for prerenal azotemia is directed at optimizing volume status with isotonic fluids. In patients with the edematous disorders who have prerenal azotemia, special efforts are directed at treating the underlying disease states (i.e., heart failure, cirrhosis) and optimizing systemic hemodynamics and renal perfusion.

The hepatorenal syndrome (HRS) represents a unique, severe form of prerenal azotemia. HRS refers to the development of ARF in the patient with advanced hepatic disease, often due to cirrhosis but also seen with metastatic tumor or alcoholic hepatitis. The reduction in renal perfusion appears to relate to relative splanchnic vasodilatation, which may be mediated via nitric oxide, the endothelium-derived relaxing factor (Martin et al, 1998; Gines and Arroyo, 1999). HRS is characterized by oliguria, a benign urinalysis, urinary sodium avidity, and a progressive rise in SCr (Cardenas, 2005). HRS is a prerenal disease, because the kidneys are normal histologically and have been successfully used in renal transplantation (Koppel et al, 1969). The diagnosis is one of exclusion, after ATN, acute glomerulonephritis, vasculitis, or correctable forms of reduced renal perfusion have been excluded. Thus, the diagnosis of HRS requires a lack of improvement in renal function after discontinuation of potential nephrotoxins and a trial of fluid repletion. The best hope for reversal of HRS is improvement in hepatic function or successful liver transplantation (Gonwa et al, 1991; Cardenas, 2005); however, not all cases of HRS will resolve with this approach (Pham et al, 2005). Results of medical interventions have been disappointing. Therapy with ACE inhibitors has been complicated by systemic hypotension and reductions in GFR (Gentilini et al, 1993). The antidiuretic hormone analog ornipressin, which should decrease splanchnic dilatation, may also induce renal ischemia (Guevara et al, 1998; Gulberg et al, 1999). Treatment with a prostaglandin analog, misoprostol, has yielded conflicting results, but preliminary evidence with *N*-acetylcysteine suggested improvement in splanchnic dilatation and nitric oxide production in a small series of HRS patients (Holt et al, 1999). Similarly, combination therapy with midodrine (a selective $\alpha_1$-adrenergic agonist) and octreotide (a somatostatin analog) has yielded preliminary information that it may be safe and effective as compared with renal-dose dopamine in a small series of HRS patients (Angeli et al, 1999). Overall, the impact of medical therapy for HRS has been minimal and the outlook for HRS without orthotopic liver transplantation appears bleak. The role of hemodialysis support appears to be limited to those HRS patients awaiting liver transplantation or resolution of their primary hepatic disease, because survival is generally limited by the severity of liver failure. Hemodialysis is often difficult in HRS because of hemodynamic instability.

### Postrenal Azotemia

**Obstruction of the urinary tract may cause ARF. To be the cause of ARF, urinary tract obstruction must involve the outflow tract of both kidneys, unless preexisting renal dysfunction is present, in which case the obstruction may involve only a single kidney.** Patients with acute urinary tract obstruction may present with hematuria, flank or abdominal pain, or signs of uremia. A high index of suspicion for urinary tract obstruction should exist for patients with prior abdominal or pelvic surgery, neoplasia, or radiation therapy. Although oligoanuria suggests complete obstruction, partial obstruction may exist in the presence of adequate urinary output. Oligoanuria is a powerful diagnostic clue that suggests a differential diagnosis of urinary tract obstruction, severe

ATN with cortical necrosis, or bilateral vascular occlusion. Lesions that may cause obstruction can be either intrinsic or extrinsic to the genitourinary tract. If urinary tract obstruction is a diagnostic consideration, the renal ultrasound is sensitive and specific (90% to 95%) in confirming the diagnosis of hydronephrosis. This test may be operator dependent, so the experience of the radiologist is crucial. False-negative tests may be seen with periureteral metastatic disease or retroperitoneal fibrosis (Somerville et al, 1992). Renal radionuclide studies or retrograde pyelography may be helpful in this circumstance. If urinary tract obstruction is a diagnostic consideration, renal ultrasound should be performed, because obstruction represents a potentially reversible cause of ARF.

While urologists are familiar with the various primary pathologies responsible for obstruction, iatrogenic causes should additionally be considered. Any drainage device such as a urethral catheter or ureteral stent should be assessed for patency. Hemorrhage or lymphocele are uncommon sequelae of retroperitoneal surgery but can result in ARF by causing extrinsic compression. **Urinary extravasation or fistula formation is a complication of urinary tract reconstruction. This can cause a rise in the BUN and SCr levels owing to reabsorption, but actual kidney function is preserved.** Diagnosis of urinary extravasation requires analysis of fluid from the area near the reconstructed site. The drain creatinine is compared with the SCr. Ratios of 10:1 are virtually diagnostic for extravasation, but smaller ratios may be observed when the urine has been diluted by other serous fluids. Other ways to confirm urinary extravasation are by intravenous administration of a vital dye excreted by the kidneys (e.g., indigo carmine or methylene blue) or radiographic demonstration of a fistula (isotope renography, retrograde pyelogram, cystogram, computed tomography [CT]). This type of ARF resolves with drainage of the urinoma and definitive treatment of the urinary fistula. The reader is referred to other chapters in this text for more in-depth review of obstructive uropathy.

## Intrinsic Renal Disease

The major causes of ARF due to intrinsic renal disease include acute glomerulonephritis (AGN), AIN, and ATN. Because ATN is the most common cause of ARF in the hospitalized patient, special emphasis will be given here to ATN.

### Acute Glomerulonephritis

**The presence of proteinuria, hematuria, and red blood cell casts is pathognomonic of glomerulonephritis. The importance of the urinalysis in the evaluation of patients with ARF cannot be overemphasized, and the physician must develop skill and expertise in interpreting the microscopic findings.** Such skills are critical in the recognition of AGN as the cause of ARF because the diagnosis of AGN has a tremendous impact on disease management.

The combination of AGN (based on urinalysis findings) and a rapid loss of kidney function defines the clinical syndrome of rapidly progressive glomerulonephritis (RPGN). Discussion of the differential diagnosis and management of RPGN is beyond the scope of this chapter (Little and Pusey, 2004). A simplified differential diagnosis of RPGN is summarized in Table 41–2. It is crucial, however, to appreciate the

**Table 41-2.  Differential Diagnosis of Rapidly Progressive Glomerulonephritis**

*Multisystem Diseases*

Systemic lupus erythematosus
Goodpasture's disease
Henoch-Schönlein purpura
Necrotizing vasculitis (including Wegener's granulomatosis)
Cryoglobulinemia (hepatitis B or C related)
Neoplasia (colon, lung)
Relapsing polychondritis
Behçet's disease

*Superimposed on Primary Glomerular Disease*

Membranoproliferative glomerulonephritis (type I, II)
Membranous glomerulonephritis
IgA nephropathy

*Infectious Diseases*

Post-streptococcal glomerulonephritis
Infectious endocarditis
Visceral sepsis
Hepatitis B or hepatitis C infection

*Drugs and Toxic Agents*

Allopurinol
D-Penicillamine
Hydralazine
Rifampin

*Idiopathic*

Type I: antiglomerular basement membrane antibody disease
Type II: immune complex–mediated disease
Type III: pauci-immune (antineutrophil cytoplasmic autoantibody positive)

**Table 41-3.  Drugs That Cause Acute Interstitial Nephritis**

Nonsteroidal anti-inflammatory agents (particularly fenoprofen)
Penicillins and cephalosporins
Rifampin
Sulfonamides (furosemide, bumetanide, thiazide-type diuretics and trimethoprim-sulfamethoxazole)
Cimetidine
Allopurinol
Ciprofloxacin and perhaps other quinolones
5-Aminosalicylates

impact that urinary microscopic findings of AGN have on the aggressive evaluation and management of patients with this type of ARF. This usually includes a renal biopsy as well as detailed serologic evaluation for the presence of systemic vasculitis, collagen vascular disease, and an infectious process. RPGN comprises a group of glomerulonephritides that progress to renal failure in a matter of days to months in the presence of extensive extracapillary proliferation (i.e., crescent formation in a large percent of glomeruli). Patients with RPGN have been divided into three patterns defined by their immunologic pathogenesis: type I, anti–glomerular basement membrane (anti-GBM) disease (e.g., Goodpasture's syndrome); type II, immune complex deposition disease (e.g., systemic lupus erythematosus, post-streptococcal glomerulonephritis); and type III, pauci-immune (e.g., antineutrophil cytoplasmic autoantibody (ANCA)–positive disease, such as Wegener's granulomatosis). Patients are categorized based on the results of the immunofluorescence of the renal biopsies and results of serologic testing for anti-GBM titer, ANCA, lupus serologies, and so on. Specific therapies (including parenteral corticosteroids, cyclophosphamide or other cytotoxic agents, and possibly plasma exchange) tailored to the disease entity diagnosed may be lifesaving. Hence, early recognition of RPGN based on urinalysis findings is critical.

## Acute Interstitial Nephritis

**The diagnosis of ARF secondary to AIN may be suggested by the urinalysis findings of sterile pyuria, white blood cell casts, and eosinophiluria (using Hansel's stain)** (Michel and

Kelly, 1998). **AIN is most often induced by drug therapy, although sarcoidosis and streptococcal, viral, or *Legionella* infections may also be responsible. The list of offending drugs associated with ATN is extensive, but the most common causes of AIN include those identified in Table 41–3.** The major histologic changes are interstitial edema and marked interstitial infiltrate of T lymphocytes and monocytes (Laberke and Bohle, 1980). Eosinophilic plasma cells and polymorphonuclear cells may also be detected. Granuloma formation, once thought particular to the renal disease of sarcoidosis, can occur in any form of AIN.

The clinical presentation, although variable, usually involves an abnormal urine sediment (described earlier), fever, and a rising SCr value associated with the administration of the offending drug (Nolan et al, 1986). Rash is seen in about 25% of cases. Eosinophilia and eosinophiluria are present in more than 75% of cases, with the exception of AIN due to NSAIDs, in which fever, rash, and eosinophilia are typically absent. Proteinuria with most drugs is usually modest, with less than 0.5 to 1 g/day. Proteinuria in the nephrotic range has been frequently seen with AIN of NSAIDs (especially fenoprofen) and in selected cases with ampicillin, rifampin, ranitidine, and interferon. It is speculated that increased glomerular capillary permeability is related to cytokine release of the infiltrating T cells (Neilson, 1989).

The development of AIN is not dose dependent, and recurrence can occur with second exposures to the same or related drug. The onset of AIN may occur from 3 to 5 days (especially second exposures) to several weeks after drug therapy.

The diagnosis is usually suspected in the ARF patient with characteristic urinary sediment abnormalities and a history of an offending drug therapy. Although the clinical picture may be highly suggestive of AIN, the diagnosis is confirmed only by renal biopsy. Most clinicians will observe the response to withdrawing the offending agent (Kida et al, 1984). No further evaluation or therapy is required if renal function begins to improve in several days. Lack of response, severe ARF, or uncertainty of diagnosis may be indications for definitive diagnosis with renal biopsy. The role of gallium scanning in AIN remains to be clearly defined, because it is often positive with AIN and negative with ATN, but false-positive and false-negative results may occur.

Initial therapy consists of discontinuing the offending drug with the expectation that renal function will begin to improve in 3 to 7 days (Baker and Pusey, 2004). There are no controlled trials evaluating the efficacy of immunosuppressive therapy in the small number of patients reported with biopsy-proven AIN who did not respond to expectant management. There is

## Table 41–4. Causes of Exogenous Toxic Acute Renal Failure

*Antibiotics*

Aminoglycosides
Cephalosporins
Sulfonamide, co-trimoxazole
Tetracyclines
Amphotericin B
Polymyxin, colistin
Bacitracin
Pentamidine
Vancomycin
Acyclovir
Foscarnet

*Anesthetic Agents*

Methoxyflurane
Enflurane

*Contrast Media*

Diatrizoate
Iothalamate
Bunamiodyl
Iopanoic acid

*Antiulcer Regimens*

Cimetidine
Excess of milk-alkali

*Diuretics*

Mercurials
Ticrynafen

*Chemotherapeutic and Immunosuppressive Agents*

Cisplatin
Carboplatin
Ifosfamide
Methotrexate
Nitrosourea
Plicamycin
Cyclosporine
Tacrolimus
D-Penicillamine
Recombinant interleukin-2
Interferon

*Analgesics*

Nonsteroidal anti-inflammatory drugs

*HIV Protease Inhibitors*

Indinavir
Ritonavir

*Organic Solvents*

Glycols (ethylene glycol, diethylene glycol)
Halogenated hydrocarbons ($CCl_4$, tetrachloroethylene and
   trichloroethylene)
Aromatic hydrocarbons (Toluene)
Aliphatic-aromatic hydrocarbons
5-Azacytidine (petrolatum [Vaseline], kerosene, turpentine,
   paraphenylene diamine)

*Heavy Metals and Poisons*

Insecticides (chlordane)
Herbicides (paraquat, diquat)
Rodenticide (elemental phosphorus)
Mushroom
Snake bites*
Stings*
Bacterial toxins*

*Chemicals**

Aniline
Hexol
Cresol
Chlorates
Potassium bromate

*Recreational Drugs†*

Heroin
Amphetamine

*Miscellaneous*

Dextrans
EDTA
Radiation
Silicone
ε-Aminocaproic acid*
Angiotensin-converting enzyme inhibitors

*Direct toxicity or indirect systemic effects (shock, intravascular hemolysis, or coagulation).
†Slow onset of renal failure unless associated with rhabdomyolysis.
From Nally JV: Acute renal failure. In Stoller JK, Ahmed M, Longworth DL (eds): The Cleveland Clinic Intensive Review of Internal Medicine, 2nd ed. Philadelphia, Lippincott Williams & Wilkins, 2000, p 568.

some experimental and suggestive clinical evidence that corticosteroid and/or cytotoxic therapy may be beneficial to hasten recovery of renal function and reduce interstitial fibrosis.

## ACUTE TUBULAR NECROSIS
### Incidence and Etiology

Overall, ARF may affect 2% to 5% of patients in a tertiary care hospital, and the incidence of ARF in the surgical or medical ICU may exceed 20% to 30%. The majority of all hospital-acquired ARF is secondary to ATN (Myers and Moran, 1986; Uchino et al, 2005). Renal hypoperfusion and renal ischemia are the most common causes of ATN, although nephrotoxic insults from various agents are being recognized with increasing frequency. A detailed listing of both exogenous and endogenous nephrotoxic compounds is presented in Tables 41–4 and 41–5.

## Table 41–5. Acute Renal Failure Related to Endogenous Nephrotoxic Products

*Pigment Nephropathy*

Myoglobin
Hemoglobin*
Methemoglobin*

*Intrarenal Crystal Deposition*

Uric acid
Calcium
Oxalate

*Tumor-Specific Syndromes*

Tumor lysis syndrome
Plasma cell dyscrasias (e.g., myeloma kidney)

*Questionable direct nephrotoxic effect.
From Nally JV: Acute renal failure. In Stoller JK, Ahmed M, Longworth DL (eds): The Cleveland Clinic Intensive Review of Internal Medicine, 2nd ed. Philadelphia, Lippincott Williams & Wilkins, 2000, p 567.

Pigment nephropathy may be suspected in the appropriate clinical situation (post-traumatic or atraumatic after intoxications) where there is discrepancy between the finding of hematuria by dipstick and the absence of red blood cells on urinary microscopy. In urology, two clinical circumstances have been identified in association with rhabdomyolysis. This includes protracted extended lithotomy positioning (as seen in urethral stricture cases) (Anema et al, 2000) and after laparoscopic donor nephrectomy (Kuang et al, 2002; Troppmann and Perez, 2003). The combination of renal hypoperfusion and the nephrotoxic insult of myoglobin or hemoglobin within the proximal tubule can result in ATN. Early recognition of this disorder is crucial, because a forced alkaline diuresis is indicated to minimize nephrotoxicity. Similarly, the tumor lysis syndrome may be suspected in the appropriate clinical setting, when marked hyperuricemia/hyperuricosuria and crystalluria are recognized. A forced alkaline diuresis may limit nephrotoxicity and is usually recommended prophylactically before an aggressive chemotherapy regimen.

The list of potential exogenous nephrotoxic agents is exhaustive (see Table 41–4). Simply stated, a patient who develops ATN while receiving medications should have each medication reviewed for the possibility of nephrotoxicity. The most commonly seen nephrotoxins in the hospitalized patient include radiographic contrast material, antibiotics (especially aminoglycosides and amphotericin B), chemotherapeutic agents, NSAIDs, and ACE inhibitors.

More recently, the potential nephrotoxicity of newer agents, such as acyclovir, protease inhibitors, recombinant interleukin 2 (IL-2), interferon, and selected chemotherapeutic agents, is being appreciated.

In the contemporary practice of hospital-based medicine, recognition of ARF in two special patient populations deserves comment. Patients with human immunodeficiency virus (HIV) infection may develop ARF due to the same causes as uninfected patients, but protease inhibitors have been associated with the development of ARF. Ritonavir and indinavir (as well as acyclovir, foscarnet, and sulfadiazine) have been associated with reversible ARF thought secondary to crystalluria and intrarenal obstruction (Olyaei et al, 2000). In addition, patients treated with indinavir may present with renal colic because indinavir renal stones can be associated with urinary tract obstruction (Kohan et al, 1999).

ARF may be quite common after bone marrow transplantation in some centers. Several nephrologic syndromes may be encountered at various times after bone marrow transplantation. In the perioperative period, ATN due to tumor lysis syndrome, bone marrow infusion, sepsis, or antibiotics (especially aminoglycoside and amphotericin B) is likely (Herget-Rosenthal et al, 2000). At days 10 to 16, ARF is commonly attributed to hepatic veno-occlusive disease resulting from radiation- or chemotherapy-related endothelial cell injury. Clinically, the presentation of this entity mimics HRS. After 4 to 12 months, ARF may be due to hemolytic-uremic syndrome, possibly related to cyclosporine or radiation therapy. Therapies with plasma exchange have been disappointing.

## Natural History

The oliguric phase usually begins less than 24 hours after the inciting incident and may last for 1 to 3 weeks. Urine volume averages 150 to 300 mL/day. The oliguric phase may be prolonged in the elderly. During this phase, the clinician must be alert for the expected complications, with special emphasis on metabolic consequences, gastrointestinal bleeding, and infection.

The diuretic phase is characterized by a progressive increase in urine volume, a harbinger of renal recovery. However, the SCr may continue to rise for another 24 to 48 hours before it reaches a plateau and falls. Severe polyuria during this phase is seen less frequently now. Careful management during this phase is crucial, because up to 25% of deaths with ARF may occur in this phase, usually related to fluid and electrolyte abnormalities, as well as infection. Finally, the recovery phase ensues. Renal function returns to near baseline, but abnormalities of urinary concentration and dilution may persist for weeks or months.

## Pathophysiology

Knowledge of the basic processes involved in the development of ATN is a prerequisite to understanding contemporary therapies directed at limiting renal damage and promoting more rapid renal recovery (Fig. 41–1). In hospital practice, ischemic ATN is the most commonly encountered form of the disease; therefore, the following discussion will focus on ischemic renal injury.

A variety of biochemical changes occur during ischemia and reperfusion that are responsible for the cell dysfunction observed in ATN (Myers et al, 1984; Myers and Moran, 1986). The sentinel biochemical event in renal ischemia is the depletion of adenosine triphosphate (ATP), which is the major energy currency for cellular work. ATP is metabolized to adenosine monophosphate (AMP). During prolonged oxygen deprivation, AMP is further metabolized to the nucleosides adenosine, inosine, and hypoxanthine. These compounds diffuse from the cell, resulting in the loss of the substrate reservoir for ATP synthesis after reperfusion (Brady et al, 1996). Furthermore, hypoxanthine becomes an important substrate in the development of oxygen free radicals during the reperfusion period. Provision of exogenous adenine and inosine decreases cellular injury in experimental renal ischemia (Siegel et al, 1980).

ATP depletion results in impaired function of the plasma membrane and intracellular ATPases that are vital to normal cell function. As a consequence of impairment of the $Na^+/K^+$-ATPase, cytosolic concentrations of $Na^+$ and $K^+$ are altered and cell swelling results (Alejandro et al, 1995). Dysfunction of the plasma membrane $Na^+/Ca^{2+}$ ATPase and intracellular $Ca^{2+}$ ATPase leads to high intracellular levels of $Ca^{2+}$. The increase in intracellular $Ca^{2+}$ has been associated with multiple aspects of renal cell injury, including disruption of the cytoskeleton, activation of $Ca^{2+}$-dependent phospholipases, acceleration of the conversion of xanthine dehydrogenase to xanthine oxidase (potentiating reperfusion injury), and uncoupling oxidative phosphorylation (Brady et al, 1996). The activation of phospholipases results in damage to the lipid bilayer, which is critical to the normal function of the plasma membrane and intracellular organelles such as mitochondria. Phospholipase activation leads to an accumulation of free fatty acids and of lysophospholipids,

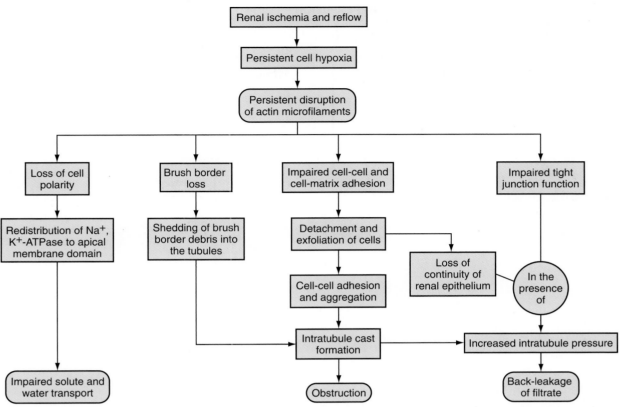

**Figure 41-1.** Pathophysiology of ischemic acute renal failure. The profound reduction in glomerular filtration rate associated with renal ischemia is due to a combination of intrarenal hemodynamic alterations and tubular epithelial injury leading to tubular obstruction and back-leakage of glomerular ultra-filtrate filtrate. (From Brady HR, Brenner BM, Lieberthal W: Acute renal failure. In Brenner BM [ed]: Brenner & Rector's The Kidney. Philadelphia, WB Saunders, 1996, pp 1200-1252.)

which are detrimental to vital cellular function, although the mechanism of such action is not clear.

**Oxidative stress during reperfusion after ischemia is associated with cellular damage** (Fig. 41–2). Recall that ATP is metabolized to hypoxanthine. High levels of intracellular $Ca^{2+}$ activate a calmodulin-dependent protease that converts xanthine dehydrogenase to xanthine oxidase (Brady et al, 1996). The conversion of hypoxanthine to xanthine during reperfusion is the major source of superoxide. This is ultimately metabolized to $OH^-$, which causes cell damage. Finally, the protease calpain is activated and contributes to ischemic renal injury (Edelstein et al, 1997). Calpain regulates membrane channels, kinase activation, and interactions between cytoskeletal proteins.

As the name suggests, ischemic ATN is characterized by renal tubular cell injury. This may be sublethal or lethal. Because obvious necrosis is not a cardinal histopathologic finding in ATN (Racusen et al, 1991), sublethal injury is important. **During normal function of the kidney, the medulla operates at the brink of hypoxia due to the countercurrent diffusion of oxygen from the descending to ascending vasa recta. During prolonged ischemia, medullary hypoxia intensifies and due to the high metabolic requirement of the nephron structures located in the outer** medulla, they are most sensitive to injury. The S3 portion of the proximal tubule sustains the most severe injury (Witzgall et al, 1994). **Other structures that sustain injury in this region include the medullary thick ascending limb (mTAL), which is metabolically active and rich in the energy requiring Na+/K+-ATPase.**

**Sublethal injury to tubular cells leads to aberrations in the cytoskeletal organization of the tubule cells** (Molitoris, 1991) (Fig. 41–3). This is manifest as a loss in the cell polarity. The brush border disappears, and there is redistribution of the basolateral Na+/K+-ATPase and integrins (Lieberthal, 1997). As a result, the normal unidirectional transport of salt and water across tubular cells is disrupted and the ability of the renal epithelium to act as a barrier to the free movement of solute and water is lost. The loss of the tight junctions permits backleak of glomerular filtrate, which has been one of the well-established pathophysiologic features of ATN (see Fig. 41–1). In addition to the loss of tight junctions, there is a loss in cell-matrix adhesion (Gailit and Clark, 1993). The redistribution of the integrins disrupts the normal cell adherence to the tubular basement membrane. As a result, abnormal cell-cell adherence develops and contributes to tubular obstruction. The validation of this concept is provided by research demonstrating that an excess of a matrix protein

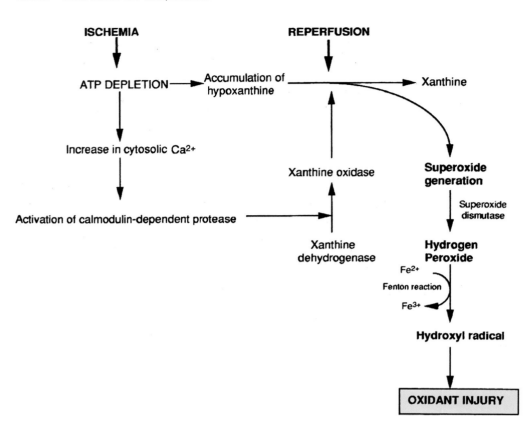

**Figure 41–2.** The pathophysiology of reperfusion injury. The generation of reactive oxygen species. See text for details. (From Brady HR, Brenner BM, Lieberthal W: Acute renal failure. In Brenner BM [ed]: Brenner & Rector's The Kidney. Philadelphia, WB Saunders, 1996, pp 1200-1252.)

sequence (RGD peptides), which is a critical ligand for the β1 integrin, can ameliorate the reduction in GFR in experimental ATN (Noiri et al, 1994). Conceptually this works because the integrin receptors are saturated by the supplemented matrix protein sequence ligand, making them unavailable for abnormal cell-cell adhesion. This can reduce tubular obstruction and backleak of glomerular filtrate.

After sublethal injury, the kidney has a remarkable capacity for repair of normal structure and function. The study of renal recovery from ATN is a relatively new concept with great potential for clinical application. Increased mitotic activity and epithelial regeneration are notable features of ATN (Thadhani et al, 1996). Certain aspects of renal recovery duplicate events in renal development (Witzgall et al, 1994). A number of growth factors play a role in recovery. Epidermal growth factor, insulin-like growth factor-1, and hepatocyte growth factor have been demonstrated to limit renal injury and accelerate renal recovery in experimental ischemic ATN (Thadhani et al, 1996).

**RBF is reduced by 50% or more in ischemic ATN, and the perfusion defect is most marked in the outer medulla. The two predominant reasons for this include vasoconstriction and congestion of the medullary vasculature by leukocytes, red blood cells, and platelets.** Ischemic renal injury is marked by intrarenal vasoconstriction as a result of endothelial cell injury. Vasoconstriction results from the imbalance between endothelin (ET) and endothelial-derived nitric oxide (EDNO) (Lieberthal, 1997). Endothelin receptor blockers have been shown to ameliorate ischemic renal damage and improve renal function (Lieberthal, 1997). The endothelial injury sustained in ATN also leads to decreased production of EDNO by constitutive nitric oxide synthase. The decreased EDNO leads directly to vasoconstriction but also permits increased ET production (Lieberthal, 1998).

The persistent hemodynamic abnormalities in ATN are also maintained by congestion of the medullary vasculature. **Current evidence suggests that ischemic injury results in the release of inflammatory mediators that activate adhesion molecules on leukocytes and upregulates their receptors on the endothelium.** Antibodies directed at leukocyte adhesion molecules or their endothelial ligands (i.e., ICAM-1) ameliorate ischemic renal injury (Kelly et al, 1996; Dragun and Haller, 1999). **Neutrophils play an important part in the injury cascade. In models where the effects of neutrophils are eliminated by delivering antibodies to certain chemokines, injury is ameliorated** (Miura et al, 2001). **Interestingly, the tubular epithelium plays an active role in this inflammatory response by generating chemokines that potentiate recruitment of inflammatory cells** (Bonventre and Zuk, 2004). These include monocyte chemoattractant protein-1 (MCP-1), interleukin 8 (IL-8), regulated-upon activation, normal T cells expressed and secreted (RANTES), and epithelial neutrophil-activating protein 78 (ENA-78). In addition to the role of neutrophils there is evolving evidence that lymphocytes are important in the ischemia/reperfusion injury paradigm. Knockout mice lacking CD4+/CD8+ cell adhesion receptors on T lymphocytes are protected from ischemic injury (Rabb et al, 2000). Also, co-stimulatory blockade can ameliorate ischemic injury (Takada et al, 1997). Newer agents are being developed to deal with the early inflammatory events in renal ischemia that may bear practical application, particularly in the setting of renal transplantation.

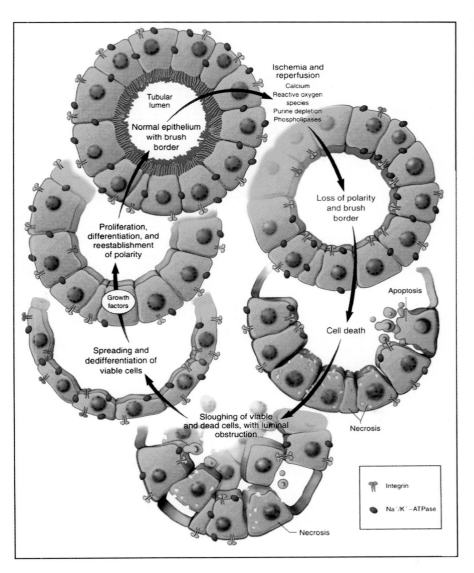

**Figure 41-3.** Tubular-cell injury and repair in ischemic acute renal failure. After ischemia and reperfusion, morphologic changes occur in the proximal tubules. This includes loss of the brush border, loss of cell polarity, and redistribution of integrins and Na$^+$/K$^+$-ATPase to the apical surface. There is sloughing of viable and nonviable cells into the tubular lumen, resulting in the formation of casts and luminal obstruction. The damaged kidney can restore its structure and function. Spreading and dedifferentiation of viable cells occurs during recovery, which duplicates aspects of normal renal development. A variety of growth factors contribute to the restoration of normal renal architecture. (From Thadhani R, Pascual M, Bonventre JV: Acute renal failure. N Engl J Med 1996;334:1448-1460.)

# CLINICAL APPROACH TO THE DIFFERENTIAL DIAGNOSIS OF ACUTE RENAL FAILURE

**Distinguishing between prerenal, intrinsic renal, and postrenal causes of ARF may prove to be a challenging clinical exercise** (Fig. 41–4). **A thorough history and physical examination to assess volume status, cardiovascular hemodynamics, potential nephrotoxic insults, and evidence of systemic disease should be undertaken in ARF patients. All interventions and drug therapies surrounding an ARF event should be outlined against the timeline of changes in renal function. Therefore, it is critical to know the level of pre-existing renal function.** One should identify the presence of risk factors known to be associated with ARF, such as advanced age; comorbid conditions (heart failure, liver failure, renal insufficiency, diabetes); radiocontrast agent exposure; therapy with aminoglycoside antibiotics, NSAIDs, or ACE inhibitors; and atheroembolism. In perioperative ARF, critical

intraoperative issues to identify include the nature and magnitude of the procedure (open vs. endoscopic), blood loss, hemodynamic stability, integrity of the urinary tract, and intraoperative drug treatment.

**On examination, the vital signs and hemodynamic parameters should be critically assessed.** Hypotension, particularly orthostatic hypotension, suggests volume depletion and prerenal ARF. Hypertension with advanced renal insufficiency can be an indicator of volume overload, suggesting the need for diuretics or dialysis. A patient's weight is helpful information, and its daily measurement is important in the diagnosis and management of ARF. An acute decrease in weight over days may indicate volume depletion and prerenal ARF. In contrast, increasing weight in association with a rising creatinine level occurs in ATN with volume overload. After major urologic procedures (e.g., cystectomy, nephrectomy, transplantation), measurement of the central venous pressure or pulmonary artery wedge pressure is the most accurate method to assess volume status. Other clinical parameters that correlate with volume status include neck vein

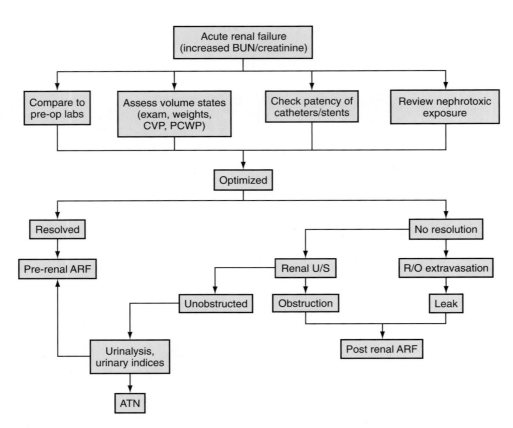

**Figure 41-4.** Algorithm for the differential diagnosis of acute renal failure. See text for details. BUN, blood urea nitrogen; CVP, central venous pressure; PCWP, pulmonary capillary wedge pressure; ARF, acute renal failure; U/S, ultrasound; R/O, rule out. ATN, acute tubular necrosis. (Modified from Goldfarb DA, O'Hara JF: Etiology, pathogenesis, and management of perioperative acute renal failure. AUA Update Series 2001;XX:lesson 4.)

distention, lung rales, and peripheral edema (pretibial or presacral).

The urine output may be a clue to the diagnosis of ARF. The presence of marked oligoanuria suggests urinary tract obstruction, renovascular occlusion, or cortical necrosis. In contrast, nonoliguric ARF is being recognized with increased frequency, and careful monitoring of SCr levels in patients at risk is of paramount importance.

**Examination of the urinalysis results is fundamental to the evaluation of the patient with ARF. The simple urinalysis may distinguish the cause of ARF among the various possibilities. Table 41-6 highlights the various urinary abnormalities associated with the clinical diagnoses.** For example, proteinuria, hematuria, and red blood cell casts are pathognomonic of glomerulonephritis. The classic sediment of ATN includes pigmented (muddy brown) granular casts and renal tubular epithelial cells, which may be seen in nearly 80% of cases of oliguric ARF.

**Determination of urinary chemistry may be helpful in determining the cause of the ARF. The urine sodium and creatinine levels and osmolality should be measured. The fractional excretion of sodium or the renal failure index should be calculated** (Fig. 41-5). Note that a low fractional excretion of sodium (or renal failure index) may be associated with either prerenal azotemia or AGN (Table 41-7). These entities can be separated clinically by examination of the urinalysis results. Conditions associated with prerenal azotemia have bland urinalysis results, whereas proteinuria, red blood cells, and red blood cell casts are seen with AGN. Other causes of ARF associated with a low fractional excretion of sodium

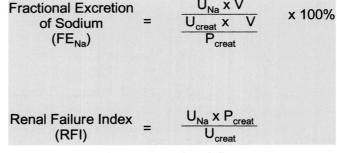

$$FE_{Na} = \frac{\dfrac{U_{Na} \times V}{U_{creat} \times V}}{P_{creat}} \times 100\%$$

$$RFI = \frac{U_{Na} \times P_{creat}}{U_{creat}}$$

**Figure 41-5.** Urinary indices.

| Table 41-6. | **Urine Sediment in Acute Renal Failure** |
|---|---|
| *Sediment Findings* | *Diagnosis* |
| Normal | Prerenal/obstruction |
| Red blood cell casts, red blood cells | Acute glomerulonephritis/vasculitis |
| Eosinophils | Acute interstitial nephritis |
| Pigmented granular casts | Acute tubular necrosis |

include hepatorenal syndrome and selected types of ATN, such as that due to intravenous contrast material, rhabdomyolysis, sepsis, and multisystem organ failure. Both ATN and obstruction may have an increased fractional excretion of sodium or renal failure index. Here, again, the urinalysis is crucial in sorting out the differential diagnosis. ATN has a

Table 41–7. **Patterns of Urinary Indices in Acute Renal Failure**

| | *Prerenal/Acute Glomerulonephritis* | *Acute Tubular Necrosis/ Obstruction* |
|---|---|---|
| Urinary [Na⁺] mEq/L | <20 | >40 |
| Urine: plasma creatinine | >30 | <20 |
| Renal failure index | <1 | >1 |
| FENa | <1 | >1 |
| Urinary osmolality | >500 | <400 |

classic sediment with pigmented coarsely granular casts, but the urinalysis results seen in obstruction are often bland with and without microhematuria.

The urine output may be a clue to the diagnosis of ARF. The presence of marked oligoanuria suggests urinary tract obstruction, renovascular occlusion, or cortical necrosis. In contrast, nonoliguric ARF is being recognized with increased frequency, and careful monitoring of SCr in patients at risk is of paramount importance.

## Imaging

A variety of imaging modalities have clinical utility in the evaluation of ARF. The most widely used is renal ultrasonography. This noninvasive and readily available study is fairly sensitive for the identification of hydronephrosis as discussed earlier in the section on postrenal acute renal failure. Duplex ultrasonography of the renal artery is useful for the identification of renal artery stenosis or thrombosis (Carman et al, 2001). The absence of a Doppler signal from the artery is a noninvasive sign to confirm renal artery thrombosis.

Another common imaging study in ARF is the abdominal plain radiograph to identify the presence or location of renal calculi or both. Additionally, the abdominal plain radiograph is particularly helpful to discern the proper position of the stents and drains. **The radionuclide renal scan is a useful imaging study in selected clinical circumstances. $^{99m}$Tc-labeled mercaptoacetyltriglycine (MAG3) is a more useful imaging agent in renal insufficiency than $^{99m}$Tc-labeled diethylenetriaminepentaacetic acid (DTPA) and is able to evaluate both renal flow and function** (Taylor, 1999). **The renal scan is a simple way to evaluate for renal flow in situations in which renal artery thrombosis is a serious consideration, such as after partial nephrectomy or renal transplantation.** It is especially useful when there is renal insufficiency that prohibits the use of iodinated contrast media (Jafri et al, 1988). Urinary extravasation can also be assessed by isotope renography.

Radiocontrast studies (intravenous pyelography [IVP], CT, angiography) are of limited value during ARF because of their ability to worsen renal insufficiency. Angiography is used to confirm renal artery thrombosis, stenosis, or dissection. Studies such as an IVP yield poor-quality images in azotemic patients, owing to the inability to adequately excrete contrast agent. Notwithstanding, radiocontrast studies are frequently performed just proximal to surgery and may contribute in this manner to perioperative ARF.

Table 41–8. **Complications of Acute Renal Failure**

*Fluid Overload*
- Hypertension
- Edema
- Acute pulmonary edema

*Electrolyte Disturbances*
- Hyponatremia
- Hyperkalemia
- Hypermagnesemia
- Hyperphosphatemia
- Hypocalcemia
- Hypercalcemia (post rhabdomyolysis)
- Hyperuricemia
- Metabolic acidosis

*Uremic Signs and Symptoms*
- Gastrointestinal
  - Nausea
  - Vomiting
  - Upper gastrointestinal bleeding
- Neurologic
  - Mental status changes
  - Encephalopathy
  - Coma
  - Seizures
  - Peripheral neuropathy
- Cardiac
  - Pericarditis
  - Uremic cardiomyopathy
- Pulmonary
  - Pleuritis
  - Uremic cardiomyopathy
- Hematologic
  - Bleeding
  - Anemia
- Immunologic
  - Impaired granulocyte function
  - Impaired lymphocyte function

# MANAGEMENT OF ACUTE RENAL FAILURE

**Management of ARF is based on its cause** (Alkhunaizi and Schrier, 1996; DuBose et al, 1997). **When ARF is identified as prerenal, correction of the precipitating factors and restoration of renal perfusion usually lead to its resolution. Nephrotoxic drugs should be eliminated when clinically appropriate. Maintaining normal volume status is essential. In the postoperative setting, this implies judicious replacement of crystalloid, colloid, and blood with close monitoring of the central venous pressure. The management of postrenal ARF will depend on its etiology. Any obstruction needs appropriate drainage, and urinary extravasation needs to be controlled.**

**The management of ATN focuses on the prevention of complications and providing an environment that is conducive to renal recovery** (Table 41–8). Early consultation with a nephrologist improves the outcome of patients with ARF. Mehta and colleagues (2002a) showed that nephrology consultation was delayed in 28% of ICU patients with ARF. Delay in consultation was associated with higher mortality, longer ICU length of stay, and increased number of systems failing at the time of consultation. During the initial evaluation, it is imperative to search for reversible causes, such as volume depletion, obstruction, and vascular occlusion. During the initial stages, a trial of parenteral hydration with isotonic fluids may correct ARF secondary to prerenal causes. Thereafter, fluid status should be monitored vigilantly to maintain euvolemia. In a patient with oliguria, special attention must be given to avoiding excessive hydration and volume overload that might precipitate the need for dialysis. Consideration may be given to using pharmacologic intervention to convert the patient from an oliguric to a nonoliguric state. In general, increases in urinary volume make it easier to address problems of volume overload, hyperkalemia, and metabolic acidosis. Increases in urine volume may also provide room for supplemental total parenteral nutrition in the critically ill patient. Historically, the morbidity, need for dialysis, and mortality was considered lower in the de novo nonoliguric form of ATN, but recent data challenge this notion (Liangos et al, 2005).

## Pharmacologic Intervention

Pharmacologic intervention to convert oliguric ATN to nonoliguric ATN is a salutary goal for the reasons noted earlier. Experimental studies on the use of diuretics, dopamine, atrial natriuretic peptide (ANP), and calcium channel blockers that attempt to convert oliguria to nonoliguric ARF have been performed. The applicability of these experimental studies to patients with ARF remains unproved. **Uncontrolled studies suggest that patients who respond to mannitol, furosemide, or dopamine with an increased urine output have better outcomes than nonresponders** (Cosentino, 1995). The responders may simply have had less severe disease from the outset. Although de novo nonoliguric ARF has been associated with a lower mortality rate, there is little evidence that conversion from an oliguric to nonoliguric state decreased the mortality rate. **For the patients with established ATN, therapy with loop diuretics may increase urine output but has little effect on the severity or duration of the ARF** (Cosentino et al, 1994). Results of clinical trials involving diuretics, dopamine, ANP, and calcium channel blockers for established ATN are reviewed here.

**Both loop diuretics and mannitol administration have been proved to minimize the degree of renal injury if given at the time of the ischemic insult** (Hanley and Davidson, 1981; Schrier et al, 1984; Cosentino, 1995). **Both diuretics are capable of inducing a diuresis to wash out obstructive debris and casts. Loop diuretics (e.g., ethacrynic acid, furosemide, and bumetanide) exert their pharmacologic effect in the loop of Henle, causing a large solute diuresis. Additionally, they decrease active NaCl transport in the thick ascending limb of Henle and thereby limit energy requirements in the metabolically active segment, which often bears significant ischemic insult.** There are several theoretical reasons why loop diuretics may be of benefit in ARF. Loop diuretics may protect cells of the ascending limb of Henle from hypoxic damage, increase tubular flow to prevent intratubular obstruction, inhibit tubuloglomerular feedback to maintain a favorable GFR, and increase RBF by decreasing renal vascular resistance. The available clinical data do not support an improved outcome in patients who respond to loop diuretics (Shilliday and Allison, 1994). A prospective, randomized placebo-controlled study examining the effect of loop diuretics on renal recovery, dialysis, and death in patients with ARF

found no effect (Shilliday et al, 1997). Observational data suggested that diuretic use in critically ill patients with ARF is associated with an increased mortality rate using multivariate analysis and propensity scores (Mehta et al, 2002b). A more recent prospective, multicenter, epidemiologic study found that the use of loop diuretics was not associated with higher mortality (Uchino et al, 2004). Therefore, it is reasonable to give a trial of a loop diuretic in escalating doses, and if the patient does not respond, the drug should not be readministered because large doses of loop diuretics may be ototoxic and the large infusion volume may cause pulmonary edema.

**Mannitol, an osmotic diuretic, theoretically ameliorates ARF by flushing intratubular casts, increasing RBF, increasing urine flow, reducing hypoxic cell swelling, protecting mitochondrial function, and scavenging free radicals. Mannitol use continues to be promoted prophylactically in certain high-risk patient groups because of the demonstrated benefit in animal models of ARF** (Burke et al, 1983; Shilliday and Allison, 1994). **Mannitol has shown some benefit in the clinical setting of ARF** (Novick, 1983; Weimar et al, 1983), **particularly when administered prophylactically or within a short time after an ischemic or nephrotoxic insult.** The best clinical example of this is its administration before renal artery clamping during partial nephrectomy. However, studies in humans failed to demonstrate the effectiveness of mannitol in prevention or treatment of ischemic or toxic ARF (Shilliday and Allison, 1994; Lee et al, 2004) .

Dopamine has selective renal vasodilator properties that cause natriuresis and increased urine output. Low-dose "renal-dose" dopamine (0.4 to 2.0 µg/kg/min) activates dopamine-1 receptors, which induce renal vasodilation and increased RBF. **Objective review of controlled studies demonstrates that these benefits remain speculative** (Denton et al, 1996; Lassnigg et al, 2000). **Bellomo and colleagues (2000) reported on 328 critically ill patients with ARF who were randomly assigned to continuous infusion of placebo or low-dose dopamine (2 µg/kg/min). Peak SCr concentration, requirement for dialysis, length of hospital stay, and mortality rate did not differ between the two groups. Also, prophylactic use of low-dose dopamine in patients undergoing coronary artery bypass surgery has not been shown to be effective in preventing the development of renal impairment in these patients** (Woo et al, 2002). Use of dopamine has also been associated with serious cardiac, vascular, and metabolic complications in the critically ill and, therefore, should be used with caution (Power et al, 1999). Other than dopamine, the literature provides little guidance on the effects of other vasoactive agents on the kidney and, thus, there is a need for large randomized, controlled studies to clarify this issue (Lee et al, 2004).

**Fenoldopam is a selective dopamine-1 receptor agonist (DA-1) that causes DA-1 receptor–mediated vasodilation and does not stimulate DA-2 or α- or β-adrenergic receptors** (Lee et al, 2004). **Fenoldopam reduces renal vascular resistance and increases RBF and fractional excretion of sodium and free water clearance in studies in normal volunteers and hypertensive patients** (Mathur et al, 1999). A few studies in animal models (Singer and Epstein, 1998; Halpenny et al, 2001b) are consistent with the notion that DA-1 agonists may be useful in preventing or treating ARF. Some clinical studies have shown encouraging results with the use of DA-1 agonists in the treatment (Tumlin et al, 2002) and prevention (Kini et al, 2002a, 2002b) of contrast agent–induced nephropathy and perioperatively in cardiovascular surgery (Halpenny et al, 2001a). A recent multicenter trial, however, did not find any protective benefit of the selective DA-1 agonist fenoldopam mesylate in the prevention of contrast agent–induced renal dysfunction in an at-risk population (Stone et al, 2003). One study showed that when fenoldopam was used prophylactically in patients undergoing aortic surgery its use was associated with improvement in renal function and reductions in dialysis requirements, length of hospital stay, and mortality (Gilbert et al, 2001). Again, because these studies were small, defining fenoldopam's role in clinical situations is difficult without a large-scale randomized controlled trial.

**In some animal studies the effects of ischemic ARF could be reversed with the use of an intrarenal arterial infusion of ANP** (Nakamoto et al, 1987; Shaw et al, 1987), **but other experimental studies have been contradictory. The proposed mechanism by which this occurs is the vasodilatory action of ANP.** In experimental models of established ATN, the combination of ANP with dopamine to prevent systemic hypotension resulted in a rise in GFR induced by arteriolar vasodilatation. The treated animals also exhibited less tubular necrosis and fewer casts, suggesting tubular recovery was promoted. **The efficacy of ANP in established ATN in humans has been evaluated in two trials** (Rahman et al, 1994). **First was a small randomized trial suggesting a benefit of ANP therapy. More recently, a prospective, multicenter, randomized study with ANP in patients with ATN (oliguric and nonoliguric) has been reported. Overall, there was no established benefit on morbidity and mortality with ANP. However, in a subset of patients with oliguric ATN, clinical improvement was seen with ANP infusion.** Further studies in such a select population did not demonstrate benefit (Lewis et al, 2000). ANP is still considered an investigational drug, and its role in the management of patients with ATN remains uncertain.

Experimental studies suggest the possibility of accelerating the rate of tubular regeneration in ATN by administration of growth factors such as insulin-like growth factor-1 (IGF-1) (Miller et al, 1992) and epidermal growth factor (EGF) (Hammerman, 1999). The recovery process involves both tubular cell regeneration and differentiation into mature functioning cells. The applicability of these observations to human disease remains to be determined. A report of a randomized trial of ARF patients of less than 7 days' duration found no benefit in patients treated with IGF-1 (Hirschberg et al, 1999). In a large randomized, double-blind, placebo-controlled trial in ICUs in 20 teaching hospitals involving 72 patients, it was shown that IGF-1 does not accelerate the recovery of renal function in ARF patients with substantial comorbidities (Hirschberg et al, 1999). Similarly, there is no role for thyroxine in modifying the course and outcome in ARF; in fact, it could have a negative effect on outcome through prolonged suppression of thyroid-stimulating hormone (Acker et al, 2000). **Therefore, based on current evidence, there is no role for the use of growth factors to treat ARF.**

Calcium channel blockers inhibit voltage-gated calcium entry into cells and are reported to reverse vascular constriction, increase GFR, and improve renal plasma flow (Epstein, 1993). A few limited animal studies in experimental ARF generally support a protective benefit of calcium channel blockers. **The clinical benefit of calcium channel blockers most**

widely studied has been the effect on graft function in renal transplant recipients (Alkhunaizi and Schrier, 1996).

**In summary, review of the data regarding pharmacologic intervention for established ATN supports a trial of isotonic fluid repletion. Judicious use of intravenous loop diuretics may increase urine output, but the ability of these agents to have an impact on improved patient survival in ARF is still unproven. Similarly, the clinical data on "renal-dose" dopamine are scant and do not support its widespread use in established ATN. If a trial of dopamine is considered, it should be limited to a 24- to 48-hour infusion. Additional studies on the use of ANP, ANP with dopamine, calcium channel blockers, and growth factors are warranted to examine their impact on the course of ischemic or nephrotoxic ATN.**

## Conservative Management

Once the clinical diagnosis of ATN is made, conservative medical management is in order (Table 41–9). **This would include attempts to minimize further renal parenchymal injury, ensure provision of nutrition, maintain the metabolic balance, and promote recovery of renal function.**

**Optimizing the patient's volume status is imperative, particularly in patients with oliguric ARF** (DiBona, 1994). If such patients are administered large volumes of intravenous fluid or allowed free access to oral fluids, they are at risk for developing fluid overload. In the oliguric patient, fluids should be restricted to total output plus insensible losses. If required, pharmacologic intervention with loop diuretics may promote increases in urinary volume.

**Providing adequate nutrition is important for the recovery of the critically ill patient with ARF. Preexisting or hospital-acquired malnutrition is an important factor contributing to high mortality seen in patients with ARF** (Druml, 1998a; Star, 1998). ARF not only affects water, electrolyte, and acid-base metabolism but also induces specific alterations in protein and amino acid, carbohydrate, and lipid metabolism (Druml, 1992). The metabolic alterations in ARF

---

**Table 41–9. Conservative Medical Management of Acute Tubular Necrosis**

*Fluid Balance*

Carefully monitor intake/output and weights.
Restrict fluids.

*Electrolytes and Acid-Base Balance*

Prevent and treat hyperkalemia.
Avoid hyponatremia.
Keep serum bicarbonate > 15 mEq/L.
Minimize hyperphosphatemia.
Treat hypocalcemia only if symptomatic or if intravenous bicarbonate is required.

*Uremia and Nutrition*

Administer protein (1.0-1.8 g/kg/day) and maintain caloric intake; consider forms of nutritional support.
Keep carbohydrate intake at least 100 g/day to minimize ketosis and endogenous protein catabolism.

*Drugs*

Review all medications.
Stop magnesium-containing medications.
Adjust dosage for renal failure; readjust with improvement of glomerular filtration rate.

patients are determined not only by acute loss of renal function but also by the underlying disease process (i.e., sepsis, trauma, or multiple-organ failure) and by the type and intensity of renal replacement therapy (RRT) (Druml, 1992, 2005).

The hallmark of metabolic alterations in ARF is activation of protein catabolism with excessive release of amino acids from skeletal muscle and sustained negative nitrogen balance (Druml, 1998b; Price et al, 1998). Hepatic extraction of amino acids from the circulation, gluconeogenesis, and ureagenesis are all increased. Several additional catabolic factors (secretion of catabolic hormones, hyperparathyroidism, suppression and decreased sensitivities to growth factors, and release of inflammatory mediators) are operative in ARF. All of these factors mediate protein breakdown (Cianciaruso et al, 1991).

Frequently, ARF is associated with hyperglycemia caused by insulin resistance (Klouche and Beraud, 1998). When plasma insulin concentration is elevated, maximal insulin-stimulating glucose uptake by skeletal muscle is decreased by 50%. ARF is also associated with accelerated hepatic gluconeogenesis, mainly from conversion of amino acids released during protein catabolism, which cannot be suppressed by exogenous glucose infusions (Druml, 1992).

The triglyceride content of plasma lipoprotein is increased in ARF, whereas total cholesterol and high-density lipoprotein (HDL) cholesterol are decreased (Schneeweiss et al, 1990). The major cause of lipid abnormalities in ARF is impairment of lipolysis. RRTs themselves may have significant metabolic and nutritional consequences.

Appropriate nutritional therapy in patients with ARF may be beneficial in promoting recovery. Caloric intake should be maintained and carbohydrate intake should be at least 100 g/day to minimize ketosis and endogenous protein catabolism. A moderate protein intake of about 1.0 to 1.8 g/kg/day may be required to maintain positive nitrogen balance. Higher protein intakes of up to 2.5 g/kg/day have been needed to improve nitrogen balance in critically ill ARF patients on continuous dialysis, although no survival advantage was noted. Hence, it should be stressed that a low-protein intake (<0.5 g/kg/day) may be unnecessary and protein intake should not be severely restricted in ARF to limit the need for dialysis. In terms of types of amino acids utilized, diet or solutions including both essential and nonessential amino acids in standard proportions is recommended. Dietary phosphorus, potassium, and sodium chloride may be restricted. In the critically ill patient, nutritional support via total parenteral nutrition or enteral feedings should be considered. Prior studies demonstrate that provision of adequate nutrition to the ARF population may improve survival (Chertow et al, 2000). Patients with ARF are candidates to develop significant electrolyte abnormalities such as hyperkalemia, metabolic acidosis, hyperphosphatemia, and hypocalcemia. These problems may be minimized by the prophylactic institution of a low-potassium diet accompanied by fluid restriction and oral phosphate binders.

Hyperkalemia is the most common and most dangerous electrolyte abnormality in the ARF setting. If the serum potassium level exceeds 6.0 mEq/L, an electrocardiogram should be performed with subsequent therapy based on the findings. With hyperkalemia, the earliest changes demonstrate peaked T waves with subsequent broadening of the PR interval and eventual QRS broadening, which may mature into a sine wave form. The stages of therapy for acute hyperkalemia with electrocardiographic changes include (1) stabilizing the electrical membrane of the cardiac conduction system, (2) shifting potassium back intracellularly, and (3) eventual elimination of potassium from the body. Stabilizing the membrane of the cardiac conduction system may be accomplished with intravenous calcium salts, which have an immediate effect and a rather short duration of action. Shifting potassium into cells may be accomplished by a combination of intravenous glucose and insulin or intravenous sodium bicarbonate. Elimination of potassium from the body in a patient with ARF may be accomplished via the gastrointestinal tract with a cationic binding resin (Kayexalate). If severe hyperkalemia exists, dialysis may be required.

## Dialytic Interventions

Despite adequate medical therapy, dialysis may be required for patients with severe ARF. The indications for the initiation of dialysis include volume overload, severe hyperkalemia, severe metabolic acidosis, pericarditis, selected poisonings, and uremic symptomatology.

The initiation of dialysis for patients with ARF is usually precipitated by one or more of the specific indications. Despite earlier recommendations that patient morbidity and mortality might be improved by early, more intensive dialysis to keep the BUN less than 80 to 100 mg/dL, recent studies fail to document significant benefits. Therefore, patients with ARF should begin dialysis on detection of severe fluid or electrolyte abnormalities or uremic symptomatology, rather than specific BUN or SCr thresholds. A theoretical concern exists that the dialysis treatment itself may have a detrimental impact on the course of ARF from ATN. Three potential mechanisms have been postulated: a fall in urine volume, dialysis-induced hypotension, and complement activation resulting from the blood-dialysis membrane interaction. Removal of excess volume and urea may both contribute to the fall in urine volume. Whether this reduction has an impact on clinical recovery of ATN is speculative. Hypotension is a common complication of hemodialysis in patients with ARF. Because autoregulation is impaired in ATN, such patients may be particularly sensitive to renal hypoperfusion, perhaps due to vascular injury of the endothelium and its vasodilatory products, such as prostacyclin and nitric oxide. As a result, recurrent ischemic injury is more likely to occur and possibly delay the restoration of renal function. Complement activation during the blood-dialyzer interaction is a third possible mechanism for dialysis-induced renal injury. Animal models suggest that blood interaction with cuprophane membranes (but not more biocompatible membranes) can lead to neutrophilic infiltration into the kidney and prolong the course of ARF.

### Dialysis Prescription and Modality

The contribution of the type of RRTs to clinical outcomes in ARF remains unresolved. Several factors operative during RRT for ARF may impact clinical outcome. These include dialysis modality, dialyzer membrane characteristics, and dosing strategies. Hemodialysis (HD) is the standard dialytic modality for hemodynamically stable patients with ARF. To perform acute hemodialysis, access to the circulation is required and usually involves placement of a venous catheter in the jugular, subclavian, or femoral vein. Blood is transported by a blood pump to the dialyzer, where it comes into close proximity with the dialysate solution across a semipermeable membrane. Contact of the blood with dialysate allows the removal of solutes by the process of diffusion, driven by a concentration gradient from blood to dialysate. Fluid may also be removed by the process of ultrafiltration driven by a pressure gradient across the dialyzer. HD treatments may be stressful hemodynamically and possibly complicated by hypotension, hypoxia, bleeding related to anticoagulant administered (usually heparin), and dialysis disequilibrium, with its manifestations ranging from cramps and headaches to seizures and coma.

In the hemodynamically unstable patient, slow fluid and solute removal can be achieved with continuous renal replacement therapy (CRRT). In addition to being better tolerated hemodynamically, CRRT is also as efficient at removing solutes over the course of 24 to 48 hours as conventional hemodialysis. Although the clearance rates of some small solutes such as urea are slower, the rates are closer at 24 hours and more urea is removed over 48 hours with CRRT than with a single, intermittent run of standard hemodialysis.

Peritoneal dialysis (PD) permits the removal of solutes and fluid by using the peritoneal membrane as the dialyzer. This process does not require access to the circulation and is generally less stressful hemodynamically than standard HD. For this procedure, dialysate is instilled into the peritoneal space via a catheter, which is percutaneously placed. Fluid is allowed to dwell for a period of time and is then removed, taking with it uremic solutes by diffusion, as well as accomplishing ultrafiltration of fluid from an osmotic pressure gradient induced by high concentrations of glucose in the dialysate. For a noncatabolic patient, the less efficient PD allows the nephrologist to maintain fluid and electrolyte homeostasis while preventing uremic symptomatology.

Nephrologists caring for ARF patients must select a continuous or intermittent method of dialysis. **An analysis of nine published studies comparing CRRT to intermittent HD in patients with ARF showed no significant difference in clinical outcomes between the two groups** (Tonelli et al, 2002). **A more recent meta-analysis of 13 clinical trials, totaling 1400 patients, also observed no mortality difference between CRRT and intermittent HD. However, after adjusting for severity of illness and study quality, mortality seemed to be lower in the CRRT group** (Kellum et al, 2002). Similarly, a recent well-designed study of 80 critically ill patients with ARF found no difference in survival or renal recovery between continuous venovenous hemodialysis (CVVHD) and intermittent HD groups (Augustine et al, 2004).

Dialysis membranes may be classified as cellulose-derived or non–cellulose-derived membranes. The non–cellulose-derived membranes are synthetic polymers and are generally more biocompatible but more expensive. **A meta-analysis of clinical trials comparing biocompatible versus nonbiocompatible membranes found no difference in mortality between groups** (Jaber et al, 2002). **Given the profound morbidity of patients with ARF, if a survival advantage attributable to biocompatible membranes exists, it is at best small.**

Similarly, high-flux membranes have not demonstrated a survival benefit, recovery of renal function, or duration of dialysis (Ponikvar et al, 2001).

**The dose of dialysis may be important in outcome.** Several studies have attempted to link urea removal to clinical outcomes in patients with ARF. Earlier reports suggested that critically ill patients with ARF may benefit with adequate dialysis dosage. More recently, a trial of 172 patients with ARF who were randomized to either daily or alternate-day dialysis using biocompatible high-flux dialyzers was reported (Schiffl, 2002). Overall mortality was significantly improved in the daily dialysis group, which had a higher weekly dose of delivered dialysis. This is the first study to demonstrate that the amount of dialysis is an independent determinant of mortality in critically ill patients with ARF.

## Prognosis of ATN

The prognosis of ATN is dependent on the underlying primary disease that resulted in the ARF, as well as any complications that arise (e.g., infection, cardiovascular, gastrointestinal bleeding, or CNS). The mortality rate for patients with ATN is nearly 50% (Biesenbach et al, 1992). This pessimistic outlook has changed very little in the past 4 decades, despite the advent of effective dialysis (Lewers et al, 1970; Liano et al, 1993; Liano and Pascual 1996; Uchino et al, 2005). Mortality rates remain high today despite effective control of uremia, since we are caring for an older, sicker population with severe concomitant illnesses. Mortality rates have been quantified as high as 75% recently in several series in the ICU population. Higher mortality rates are seen in elderly patients and in patients with respiratory failure, multiple-organ failure, preexisting chronic diseases, and systemic hypotension (Obialo et al, 1999). In a prospective multicenter study of mortality with critically ill patients with ATN, the factors predictive of early mortality were male gender, oliguria, mechanical ventilation, acute myocardial infarction, cerebrovascular accident/seizure, and chronic immunosuppression (Parker et al, 1998). Leading causes of death include bronchopulmonary infections, sepsis, cardiovascular disease, and bleeding disorders. Of patients who survive ATN, nearly half will have a complete recovery of renal function and a majority of the remainder have an incomplete recovery (Fig. 41–6) (Spurney et al, 1991). Only about 5% of all ARF patients require chronic maintenance dialysis. In short, with ARF "you either die or you get better."

A separate question is whether the development of ARF itself directly contributes to mortality. The answer appears to be a resounding "Yes!" In a prospective study of 183 patients who developed ARF after exposure to an intravenous contrast agent, the in-hospital mortality rate was substantially higher in the ARF group (34% vs. 7%) than a matched control group (Levy et al, 1996). This effect persisted after the adjustment of other comorbid diseases (relative risk = 5.5). The development of ARF is also known to increase morbidity of patients, to prolong hospitalizations, and to increase hospital costs.

## Prevention of ATN

**Because the management of ATN is primarily one of conservative care and support, special attention should be**

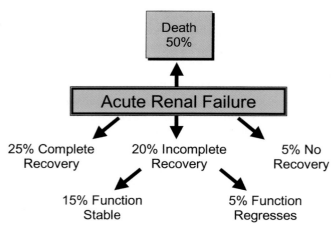

**Figure 41–6.** Prognosis of acute tubular necrosis.

focused on the prevention of ARF. Patients at high risk (i.e., patients with preexisting azotemia, the elderly, volume-depleted individuals, diabetics) warrant careful clinical consideration of the relative risks and benefits of diagnostic or therapeutic interventions that have a potential for nephrotoxicity. This is especially true for patients at risk undergoing cardiac catheterization or other diagnostic studies requiring intravenous contrast material. Several recent studies deserve comment.

A study by Solomon and coworkers (1994) confirmed that intravenous hydration with saline was critical in diminishing the nephrotoxic effects of coronary arteriography for patients with preexisting azotemia. The addition of either a loop diuretic or mannitol did not improve outcome. Rudnick and associates (1995) published a prospective, randomized trial of nearly 1200 well-hydrated patients undergoing cardiac catheterization to examine the effects of the newer nonionic contrast material. Patients were stratified for the presence or absence of azotemia (SCr $\geq$ 1.5 mg/dL) or diabetes mellitus. In patients without azotemia (with or without diabetes mellitus), the incidence of contrast agent–induced renal dysfunction was low (i.e., <1% to 2%) with either the ionic or nonionic contrast material. In contrast, those with preexisting azotemia had a 50% reduction in contrast agent–associated renal dysfunction with the nonionic material. These data suggest that in azotemic patients who require cardiac angiography, a protocol of intravenous hydration and use of a nonionic contrast material appear warranted.

In addition to these maneuvers in high-risk patients, pretreatment with N-acetylcysteine (600 mg orally twice daily for 48 hours) has been shown to reduce the incidence of radiocontrast agent–induced nephropathy (Tepel et al, 2000). A meta-analysis of randomized clinical trials using N-acetylcysteine in patients with reduced renal function clearly showed risk reduction for acute radiocontrast injury (Alonso et al, 2004). In contradistinction, a separately conducted meta-analysis of randomized controlled trials using N-acetylcysteine for the prevention of radiocontrast agent–induced nephropathy did not warrant a strong recommendation for its clinical use (Kshirsagar et al, 2004).

**Recent trials compared the benefits of two hydration protocols in reducing radiocontrast agent–induced nephropa-**thy. **A trial involving 1620 patients undergoing coronary angioplasty demonstrated a benefit of isotonic hydration as superior to half-isotonic hydration in prevention of nephropathy** (Mueller et al, 2002). **A smaller, single-center prospective randomized trial showed the benefit of intravenous hydration with sodium bicarbonate over sodium chloride given 1 hour before contrast agent exposure in the prophylaxis of contrast agent–induced renal dysfunction** (Merten et al, 2004). **The latter protocol has the advantage of timing because it was initiated 1 hour before the anticipated contrast study, rather than requiring 48 hours of pretreatment with N-acetylcysteine.** A recent multicenter trial did not find any protective benefit of the selective DA-1 agonist fenoldopam mesylate in the prevention of contrast agent–induced renal dysfunction in an at-risk population (Stone et al, 2003). Similarly, a meta-analysis did not find any compelling benefit for the use of theophylline, an adenosine antagonist, in the prevention of contrast agent–induced nephropathy (Bagshaw and Ghali, 2005). In the aggregate, the

## KEY POINTS: ACUTE RENAL FAILURE

- Creatinine as an assessment of renal function needs to be interpreted in the context of clinical events that are occurring in the patient.

- Acute renal failure is categorized based on pathophysiology as prerenal, postrenal, or intrinsic renal. The etiology and the pathogenesis determine management.

- Prerenal azotemia is transient renal hypoperfusion and responds well to isotonic fluid replacement.

- In considering postrenal causes of ARF, do not forget fistula as an iatrogenic cause.

- The inflammatory response is important in the pathogenesis of ATN and may become a future target for therapeutic intervention.

- Conservative management predominates for ATN. This entails dialysis support as needed with prevention of complications.

- Review of the data regarding pharmacologic intervention for established ATN supports a trial of isotonic fluid repletion. Judicious use of intravenous loop diuretics may increase urine output, but the ability of these agents to have an impact on improved patient survival in ARF is still not proven. Similarly, the clinical data on "renal-dose" dopamine are scant and do not support its widespread use in established ATN.

- Recommendations for the azotemic patients who require radiocontrast procedures warrant a protocol of intravenous hydration and the use of nonionic contrast material in the lowest dose possible. Treatment with N-acetylcysteine for 48 hours before the procedure and/or special hydration with prestudy sodium bicarbonate are deserving of further study.

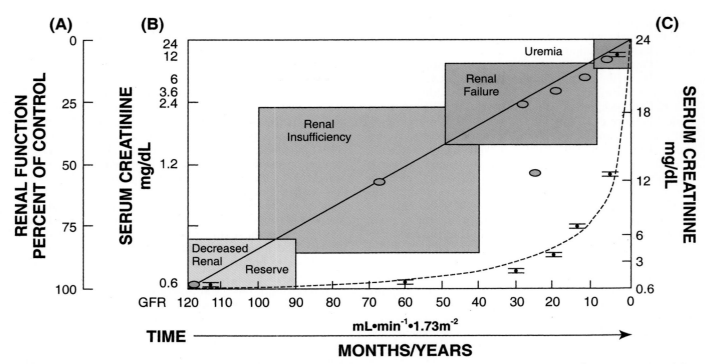

**Figure 41–7.** The course of progressive renal disease. The course of a patient who began with normal renal function corresponding to a serum creatinine concentration of 0.6 mg/dL and glomerular filtration rate (GFR) of 120 mL/min/1.73 m² is shown. *Y-axes:* The geometric serum creatinine ordinate at the left (B) applies to the solid line of identity *(open circles)* and the *rectangles* depict the various stages of progressive renal disease. The serum creatinine ordinate at the right side of the figure (C) should be used with the *dashed curve (ax-heads)* only. The ordinate at the extreme left (A), which describes the percentage of renal function remaining, applies generally. *Line of identity:* This line shows a decrease in function from 100% to 9% of normal corresponding to the diminution in GFR from 120 to 0 mL/min/1.73 m². The matching creatinine scale (A) is geometric. *Dashed curve:* Because GFR equals the daily creatinine excretion/serum creatinine concentration and because the creatinine excretion is equal to daily production, which is constant, this equation is of the form $y = k/x$, which defines a hyperbola. This relationship remains valid over the course of chronic renal disease unless the creatinine production changes. The curve emphasizes that large changes in GFR may produce small and clinically imperceptible changes in serum creatinine concentration when overall renal function is near normal. Conversely, trivial changes in GFR produce large changes in serum creatinine concentration when the GFR is low. The rate of progression throughout the delineated stages depends on the nature of the underlying renal disease, host factors, treatment, and compliance with the medical regimen. (From Kimmel PL: Management of the patient with chronic renal disease. In Greenberg A [ed]: Primer on Kidney Disease, 2nd ed. San Diego, CA, Academic Press, 1998, p 434.)

aforementioned recommendations for the azotemic patients who require radiocontrast procedures warrant a protocol of intravenous hydration and the use of nonionic contrast material in the lowest dose possible. Treatment with *N*-acetylcysteine for 48 hours before the procedure and/or special hydration with prestudy sodium bicarbonate are deserving of further study.

## CHRONIC RENAL FAILURE

Approximately 20 million individuals in the United States have chronic kidney disease (CKD). The diagnosis of CKD implies a persistent abnormality in GFR with a wide spectrum of causes. The Workgroup of the U.S. National Kidney Foundation, Kidney Disease Outcomes Quality Initiative (K/DOQI) Advisory Board recommended that "chronic kidney disease" should be defined as sustained kidney damage greater than 3 months resulting in a GFR of less than 60 mL/min/1.73 m² (National Kidney Foundation, 2002). After an initial kidney insult, if the acute injury does not completely resolve, a continuing attrition of functional nephrons occurs over time. Figure 41–7 depicts the renal failure continuum consisting of several stages of functional deterioration associ-

ated with specific clinical and biochemical abnormalities. Small changes in the SCr measurement correlate with significant alterations in the GFR when renal function is greater than 60 mL/min. This concept is illustrated by the SCr ordinate on the left side of Figure 41–7 matched to the GFR line of identity crossing through the four different phases of progressive renal disease. However, the relationship between the SCr level and the GFR changes as the renal function deteriorates to less than 60 mL/min. As noted on the right side of Figure 41–7, changes in the GFR (dashed, curved line) are represented by significantly larger increases in SCr level depicted on the right ordinate. This is especially true in CKD as the GFR decreases to levels below 30 mL/min. Although an initial insult may decrease an individual's renal reserve, biochemical abnormalities are uncommon before the "renal insufficiency" stage. Once severe "renal failure" occurs, clinical symptoms become more common.

**The degree of adaptation taking place at each stage determines the extent of clinical and biochemical abnormalities.** When kidney function is minimally impaired ($\leq 60\%$), physiologic adaptation is complete. As the GFR falls usually below 20% of normal, progressive anorexia with nausea, salt retention, acidosis, insomnia, anemia, muscle fatigue, and worsening blood pressure control may occur. Structurally, after the GFR in humans falls below 50% of normal, a relentless progressive loss of function ensues even when the initial disease becomes inactive (Mitch et al, 1976). There is significant interest in those clinical and public health initiatives that can potentially identify and prevent progressive kidney failure. The National Kidney Foundation developed and published clinical practice guidelines for CKD in 2002 to more consistently diagnose and treat CKD and its comorbidities (National Kidney Foundation, 2002; Patel et al, 2002; Eknoyan, 2003).

While the clinical course of progressive renal disease as illustrated in Figure 41–7 moves through several different phases, which include decreased renal reserve, renal insufficiency, renal failure, and frank uremia, the K/DOQI guidelines have developed a more uniform classification of the stages of CKD. These guidelines will have an impact on education between patients and providers, enhance the public's understanding of the different levels of kidney disease, and promote dissemination of specific research results for each stage. Because the GFR has been accepted as the best overall measure of kidney function, the new staging schema (Table 41–10) is divided according to GFR levels. This classification represents a series of evidence-based clinical practice guidelines that describe specific recommendations for optimal CKD patient care (Patel et al, 2002).

## Renal Mass Reduction and Chronic Kidney Disease

**Recent evidence supports the view that deficits in nephron number predispose to progressive renal disease and hypertension** (Chertow et al, 1996). Nephron number averages approximately 600,000 per kidney in the normal kidney with standard deviation of more than 200,000 (Nyengaard et al, 1992). Conceptually, partial ablation of renal mass through renal insult or surgical partial nephrectomy initiates a cycle of progressive glomerular injury in the remnant kidney. In this setting, the injury is associated with hyperfiltration, glomerular hypertrophy, and systemic hypertension (Brenner and Mackenzie, 1997). In human studies, Novick and associates (1991) demonstrated that with a greater than 50% reduction in total renal mass, the extent of proteinuria correlated directly with the duration of follow-up and inversely with the amount of renal tissue remaining. This discovery suggests that ongoing

renal injury occurs when a specific "set point" reduction in nephron number occurs. In certain population groups birth weight may be a risk factor for progressive renal failure if associated with intrauterine growth retardation. Low birth weight can lead to a 20% decrease in overall nephron number (Lopes and Port, 1995; Hughson et al, 2003; Keller et al, 2003). Glomerular size in African Americans is larger than in whites, possibly reflecting smaller nephron number (Pesce, 1998) and perhaps attributable to lower birth weight (Garrett et al, 1994). Theoretically, the increased risk for African Americans to develop "nephrosclerosis" could be linked to this low birth weight risk concept. Even allograft nephron number (donor kidney size compared with recipient body size) may be relevant in the development of chronic rejection and failure in the human transplantation setting (Brenner and Mackenzie, 1997). When the body mass of the donor is small, the functional demands on the allograft will be strained and may contribute to ongoing injury over time, leading to allograft failure.

**Interestingly, the age at loss of renal mass influences the kidney's response in humans.** In patients undergoing unilateral nephrectomy for Wilms' tumors, renal growth was most marked in those individuals who had surgery at a younger age (Di Tullio et al, 1996). This finding can be applied to the contrasting observations comparing outcomes in congenital solitary kidney versus surgical unilateral nephrectomy. The volume of glomeruli in a congenital solitary kidney is five to six times that observed in a normal kidney (Bhathena et al, 1985). This increase in volume with decreased nephron number could explain the higher risk for ongoing parenchymal injury compared with surgical nephrectomy cases. These reports support the concept that the true response to decreased renal mass in humans varies according to age at time of reduction, underlying conditions (causative agent, etiology), and the actual degree of reduction.

## Mechanisms of Progression

**Apoptosis (programmed cell death) triggered by ischemia, toxins, or endogenous mediators of damage can be the initial insult that causes renal damage.** Apoptotic cell death is an active process under molecular control of regulatory proteins and is characterized by both morphologic and functional changes. These changes usually occur as a response to the cell

**Table 41–10. Clinical Action Plan for Chronic Kidney Disease by Glomerular Filtration Rate Levels**

| Stage | Description | GFR (mL/min/1.73 m²) | Action |
|---|---|---|---|
| | At increased risk | ≥90 (with CKD risk factors) | Screening, CKD risk reduction |
| 1 | Kidney damage with normal or increased GFR | ≥90 | Diagnosis and treatment, treatment of comorbid conditions, slowing progression, cardiovascular risk reduction |
| 2 | Kidney damage with mild decrease in GFR | 60 to 89 | Estimating progression |
| 3 | Moderate decrease in GFR | 30 to 59 | Evaluating and treating complications |
| 4 | Severe decrease in GFR | 15 to 29 | Evaluating and treating complications |
| 5 | Kidney failure | <15 (or dialysis) | Replacement (if uremia present) |

*Shaded area* identifies patients who have chronic kidney disease; nonshaded area designates individuals who are at increased risk for developing CKD. CKD is defined as either kidney damage or GFR < 60 mL/min/1.73 m² for ≥ 3 months. Kidney damage is defined as pathologic abnormalities or markers of damage, including abnormalities in blood or urine tests or imaging studies.
From National Kidney Foundation: Clinical practice guidelines for chronic kidney disease: Evaluation, classification and stratification. Am J Kidney Dis 2002;39:S19.

and microenvironment in which the presence of certain "lethal factors" (e.g., tumor necrosis factor, Fas-ligand) or the absence of "survivor factors" (e.g., EGF, IGF-1, IGF-2, basic fibroblast growth factor [bFGF]) promote apoptosis. Lethal factors can either activate specific cell death receptors or damage the cells in the absence of receptor activation (Ortiz, 2000). Although growth factors regulate hypertrophy and cell proliferation, they may also mediate apoptosis as a healing response. Understanding the role and regulation of apoptosis in renal disease will be a central theme in designing future therapeutic agents.

**A reduction in nephron mass follows cell death. Figure 41–8 illustrates the mosaic of events that occur with progressive nephron mass loss linking sympathetic nervous system activation, renal structural remodeling, altered gene expression/regulation, and several additional regulatory mechanisms for progression. Renal protective interventions are designed to counter those events that adversely affect the cortex and interstitium of the kidney. Both hemodynamic and nonhemodynamic factors are involved in the sustained renal injury after an initial insult. The hemodynamic events causing an increase in single nephron glomerular filtration rate (SNGFR) include increased glomerular plasma flow rates and capillary hydrostatic pressures in the remaining glomeruli.** Elevated glomerular hydrostatic pressure is a major factor in renal injury after renal mass reduction (Meyer and Rennke, 1988). However, hyperfiltration alone in response

to decreased nephron mass is not sufficient to induce pathologic glomerulosclerosis and interstitial fibrosis. Neurogenic factors and hypertension also play a significant role in ongoing renal injury. Increases in angiotensin II and nitric oxide (NO) activate the sympathetic nervous system (SNS), which plays a dominant role in the pathogenesis of hypertension in CKD (Myers et al, 1975). The rise in central SNS activity is generated by increased local expression of nitric oxide synthase (NOS)-mRNA and NO production coupled to an upregulation of NO production by interleukin-1 (IL-1) in the brain (Campese, 2000).

**Nonhemodynamic mechanisms for renal injury involve a number of complex interactions for remodeling: these include structural changes (injury modeling), multiple growth factors, and cytokines.** Abnormal glomerular growth is associated with, and may be a marker for, the activation of these specific mechanisms leading to sclerosis during the remodeling phase after renal injury (Fogo, 2000). Injury remodeling, involving both glomerular hyperplasia (increase in cell number) and glomerular hypertrophy (increase in cell size), can occur within 2 days of a significant decrease in overall renal mass (5/6 nephrectomy). Glomerular growth can occur because of increases in any of the cellular components. Structural changes in the glomeruli during remodeling include increased extracellular matrix (ECM) production, glomerular hypertrophy, glomerular proliferation (increase in cell number: epithelial, endothelial, mesangial cells), and

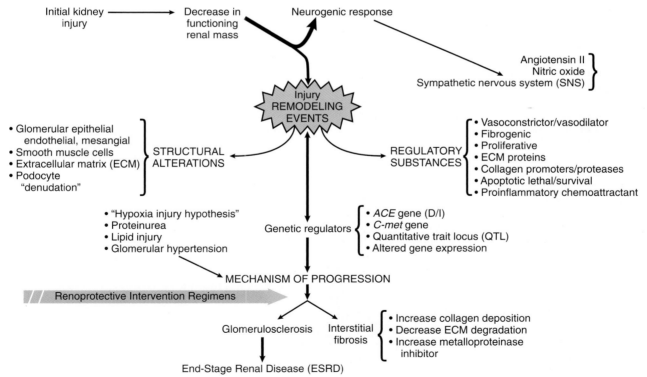

**Figure 41–8.** Kidney injury mosaic for progressive renal failure. *Fibrogenic factors:* Transforming growth factor-β (TGF-β), hepatocyte growth factor (HGF), matrix metalloproteinases (MMP-2 and MMP-9), nuclear factor-κB (NF-κB). *Vasoconstrictors:* Basic fibroblastic growth factor (bFGF), TGF-β, angiotensin II. *Vasodilators:* Prostaglandin E$_1$ (PGE$_1$), nitric oxide (NO). *Proliferative factors:* Vascular endothelial growth factors (VEGF), epidermal growth factor (EGF), growth factor (GF). *ECM expanders:* Platelet-derived growth factor (PDGF), TGF-β. *Glomerular cell proliferation:* Angiotensin II, bFGF, PDGF, and EGF. *Collagen promoting:* PDGF, TGF-β, MMP-2. *Chemoattractant:* Macrophage colony-stimulating factor (MCSF), chemoattractant protein-1. *Apoptotic lethal factors:* Fas-ligand. *Apoptotic survival factors:* Epithelial growth factor, bFGF, PDGF, insulin-like growth factor-1, insulin-like growth factor-2.

glomerular basement membrane (GBM) modification (Harris et al, 1992).

Foam cells are frequently located in segments of the glomerulus undergoing sclerosis and in the interstitium of diseased kidneys. Oxidized low-density lipoprotein (LDL) stimulates inflammation and fibrogenic cytokine production and can cause an increase in cell apoptosis, and the production of endothelin and thromboxane. It also causes an increase in the release of renin from juxtaglomerular cells, thus enhancing vasoconstriction (Keane, 2000).

Many diseases have been associated with an imbalance of ECM synthesis and degradation. The glomerular mesangial cell responds to varied growth factors by proliferation and increased ECM production. An increase in collagen deposition and a decrease in the degradation of ECM components lead to interstitial fibrosis. The degree of tubular interstitial fibrosis has been closely correlated with the reduction in GFR in many different animal and human studies. Angiotensin II upregulates transforming growth factor-$\beta$1 (TGF-$\beta$1), which is a potent fibrogenic factor playing a key role in the pathogenesis of interstitial fibrosis. The major physiologic regulators of ECM degradation in the glomerulus are matrix metalloproteinases (MMPs) (Lenz, 2000). MMPs are distinct, matrix-degrading enzymes such as stromelysins, gelatinases, elastases, and interstitial collagenases. Changes in MMP expression or activity can alter ECM turnover, which, in turn, may lead to glomerular scarring and a decline in renal function. MMPs may also indirectly affect regulation of certain growth factors, which play a role in ECM turnover. Conceptually, progressive glomerular sclerosis may result from this shift in ECM turnover (attributable to MMP imbalance) toward increased matrix accumulation, a decreased filtration area, and progressive renal failure.

**A wide range of conditions or substances can promote intrarenal growth and glomerular sclerosis in experimental models.** These include a loss of renal mass, high-protein or high-salt diet, growth hormone, IGF-1, androgens, corticosteroids, angiotensin, aldosterone, and endothelin. Aldosterone may promote fibrosis by several mechanisms, including plasminogen activator inhibitor-1 expression with consequent alterations of vascular fibrinolysis through stimulation of TGF-$\beta$1 and reactive oxygen species. Whereas significant evidence has accumulated to implicate angiotensin II in mediating renal disease, recent evidence suggests aldosterone is also an important factor in causing progressive renal disease through both hemodynamic and direct cellular actions. Circulating aldosterone may mediate vascular fibrosis by a direct interaction with high-affinity, low-capacity corticoid receptors located in the cytosol of vascular fibroblasts (Epstein, 2001).

Angiotensin II upregulates the expression of multiple growth factors and cytokines. A number of cell-specific growth responses (glomerular cells, endothelial cells, glomerular visceral epithelial cells, mesangial cells) regulate glomerular growth. Endothelial cells inhibit smooth muscle cell migration and proliferation and produce vascular endothelial growth factors, nitric oxide, endothelin, and platelet-derived growth factor (PDGF) (Fogo, 1999). Vascular endothelial growth factors stimulate angiogenesis, whereas endothelin promotes hypertrophy and increased mesangial cell matrix.

In addition to regulatory substances, additional hypotheses have been developed to explain progression of different renal diseases. Fine and associates (1998) proposed a "chronic hypoxia hypothesis," suggesting that chronic oxygen deprivation to the tubular interstitial compartment can result in scarring. Within glomeruli, blood flow and oxygen delivery into the interstitial capillary network are reduced, resulting in lowered oxygen tension in the remaining vasodilated glomeruli with a high-flow tubular capillary system (hyperfiltration). Postglomerular capillaries exposed to the elevated pressure and increased flow develop endothelial swelling and functional changes that infringe on distal blood flow and oxygen delivery, resulting in ischemia over time.

## Genetic Factors

Family members of patients with kidney disease are disproportionately affected with progressive renal failure. The familial clustering of nephropathy has been reported in diabetes, hypertension, systemic lupus erythematosus, and HIV-associated nephropathy. Interestingly, **an individual's family history of end-stage renal disease (ESRD) is a better predictor of the future risk for renal failure than is blood pressure or blood glucose** (Freedman et al, 1997; Satko and Freedman, 2004). A study sponsored by the National Kidney Foundation of Singapore, which screened over 210,000 adults with renal disease, demonstrated a significant relationship between a family history and proteinuria with the potential for future renal failure (Ramirez et al, 2002).

Our understanding of those mechanisms involved in progression to sclerosis has expanded since the early 1990s. It is now clear that genetic traits may contribute to the structural and functional adaptations to a reduction in renal mass. In diabetes, genetic signaling in response to a metabolic injury may explain why only approximately 40% of those with type 1 diabetes develop diabetic nephropathy. In the Appropriate Blood Pressure Control and Diabetic (ABCD) study, the ACE DD genotype was the strongest predictor for the presence of nephropathy (14.2% of DD homozygotes have nephropathy versus 7.8% of non-DD homozygotes) (Jeffers et al, 1997). The Génétique de la Néphropathie Diabétique study demonstrated a significant association between the D-allele frequency and progressive nephropathy in type 2 diabetics (Marre et al, 1997). Even in nondiabetic glomerular injury (IgA nephropathy) there was a greater reduction in GFR and worse biopsy in patients carrying the D allele. Not only does the DD genotype impart increased risk of progression, but this genotype is also associated with an earlier need for dialysis.

The National Institute of Diabetic, Digestive, and Kidney Disease (NIDDK) is currently recruiting diabetic siblings for a family-based linkage analysis of diabetic nephropathy. It is hoped that a large, collaborative genetic analysis will identify the genes underlying diabetic nephropathy and determine if the loci identified in prior smaller studies can be duplicated (Satko and Freedman, 2004, 2005). The National Kidney Foundation sponsored the Kidney Early Evaluation Program (KEEP) and the Southeastern Kidney Council/ESRD Network. These programs are currently screening high-risk American populations assessing the link between family history and kidney disease (Brown et al, 2003).

Studies in human renal disease have begun to map the loci of key growth factors. Zidek and colleagues (1998) uncovered a quantitative trait locus on chromosome 2 of a mouse model that is linked to genetic modulation of kidney compensatory growth. This quantitative trait locus is located close to the gene for ACE, growth hormone, and neurogrowth factor receptor (Schena et al, 1999), all of which influence renal growth. **Furthermore, altered gene expression in certain pathophysiologic settings that induce upregulation or inhibition of various growth factors may regulate the degree of response to an initial renal injury.** This may lead to hypertrophy, proliferation, or an increase in ECM. These growth factors include platelet-derived growth factor (PDGF), TGF-$\beta$, TGF-$\alpha$, IGF-1, EGF, IL-1 and IL-6, tumor necrosis factor-$\alpha$ (TNF-$\alpha$), angiotensin II, and endothelin. Angiotensin II, PDGF, and TGF-$\beta$ play key roles in sclerosis and fibrosis. IGF-1, fibroblast growth factor (FGF), PDGF, and EGF may be altered in diabetes mellitus, leading to progressive renal injury and kidney failure in this patient cohort.

Therefore, a more thorough understanding of susceptibility genes, regulatory genes for kidney disease progression, and treatment response genes may significantly improve our approach to CKD in the future.

## Etiology of CKD

The causes of progressive CKD parallel the most common causes of ESRD. Table 41–11 lists the incident causes of ESRD of varied causes by diagnosis from the year 2004 (U.S. Renal Data System, 2004). **Diabetes mellitus and hypertension account for the largest percentage of cases (76.2%) followed by glomerular diseases (8.9%). In patients younger than age 40 years, CKD is most commonly caused by focal segmental glomerulosclerosis (FSGS), systemic lupus erythematosus (SLE), and then congenital abnormalities of the urinary tract or membranous glomerulonephritis.** Membranoproliferative glomerulonephritis (MPGN), scleroderma, and autosomal dominant polycystic kidney disease (ADPKD) account for the majority of cases of CKD developing in patients between the ages of 40 and 55 years. In the cohort of patients

older than 55 years, atheroembolic disease, paraproteinemia (multiple myeloma, amyloid), nephrosclerosis, and analgesic nephropathy are the main causes of CKD. Table 41–12 (National Kidney Foundation, 2002) illustrates the prevalence of individuals with multiple different diseases who are at increased risk for CKD. The number of individuals older than the age of 70 developing CKD is growing exponentially.

**The primary parenchymal renal diseases that have the greatest propensity to progress are FSGS, RPGN, chronic glomerulonephritis, and MPGN.** The development of CKD in patients with minimal change disease is rare in children and adults with a corticosteroid-responsive clinical course. Patients at highest risk are those who do not respond to corticosteroid therapy or who become late nonresponders. The course of untreated FSGS is usually progressive to ESRD. Both children and adults usually develop ESRD 5 to 20 years from presentation. Malignant FSGS on biopsy exhibits a more rapid

**Table 41–11. Incidence of Reported End-Stage Renal Disease by Detailed Primary Renal Diagnosis, 1998-2002**

| *Diagnosis* | % |
|---|---|
| Diabetes mellitus | 49.3* |
| Hypertensive/large vessel disease | 26.9 |
| Glomerulonephritis | 8.9 |
| Secondary glomerulonephritis/vasculitis | 2.2 |
| Interstitial nephritis/pyelonephritis | 4.2 |
| Cause uncertain | 3.9 |
| Miscellaneous† | 4.1 |
| Cystic hereditary/congenital disease | 3.2 |
| Neoplasms/tumor | 2.0 |
| Missing | 1.5 |

*Type 1 juvenile, 4.7%; type 2 adult onset or unspecified, 44.6%.
†Sickle cell disease; AIDS nephropathy; traumatic, surgical loss of kidney; hepatorenal syndrome; tubular necrosis without recovery, postpartum renal failure.
From U.S. Renal Data System: USRDS Annual Data Report: Atlas of End-Stage Renal Disease in the United States. Bethesda, MD, National Institutes of Health, National Institute of Diabetes, Digestive and Kidney Diseases, 2004.

**Table 41–12. Prevalence of Individuals at Increased Risk for Chronic Kidney Disease**

| Risk Factor | Prevalence | |
|---|---|---|
| | *Estimated %* | *Estimated No.* |
| Diabetes mellitus | Diagnosed: 5.1% of adults age ≥ 20 Undiagnosed: 2.7% of adults age ≥ 20 | 10.2 million |
| Hypertension | 24.0% of adults age ≥ 18 | 43.1 million |
| Systemic lupus erythematosus | ~0.05% definite or suspected | ~239,000 |
| Functioning kidney graft | ~0.03% | 88,311 as of 12/31/1998 |
| African American | 12.3% | 34.7 million |
| Hispanic or Latino (of any race) | 12.5% | 35.3 million |
| American Indian and Alaska Native | 0.9 | 2.5 million |
| Age 60 to 70 | 7.3% | 20.3 million |
| Age ≥ 70 | 92.0% | 25.5 million |
| Acute kidney failure | ~0.14% | ~363,000 nonfederal hospital stays in 1997 |
| Daily use of nonsteroidal anti-inflammatory drug | ~5.2% with rheumatoid arthritis or osteoarthritis (assumed daily use)- ~30% yearly use | ~13 million assumed daily use ~75 million yearly use |

From National Kidney Foundation: Clinical practice guidelines for chronic kidney disease: Evaluation, classification and stratification. Am J Kidney Dis 2002;39:S74.

course to ESRD in 2 to 3 years. Those features associated with a more accelerated course are proteinuria greater than 10 to 15 g/day, SCr greater than 1.5 mg/dL at presentation, significant interstitial fibrosis, and glomerular sclerosis on biopsy.

Although MPGN type 1 is a slowly progressive disease, type 2 is more aggressive with a higher percentage of sclerotic glomeruli, crescent number, and greater degree of interstitial fibrosis. These features portend a poor outcome. Progressive renal insufficiency can occur in 20% to 25% of patients, with MPGN progressing to ESRD over 20 years. At presentation, it is difficult to predict the renal outcome in most membranous patients compared with those with MPGN.

Forty percent of individuals with IgA nephropathy progress to ESRD after approximately 20 years of clinical disease. Markers of poor outcomes are persistent hypertension, proteinuria greater than 2 g/24 hr, initial abnormal SCr value at time of biopsy, and severe sclerotic changes and interstitial fibrosis on biopsy.

A number of systemic diseases involve the kidney and can lead to progressive renal insufficiency (Table 41–13). **Progressive deterioration in renal function can occur in systemic vasculitis due to Goodpasture's syndrome, Wegener's granulomatosis, Henoch-Schönlein purpura, and cryoglobulinemia with or without hepatitis C.** Serologic tests (cryoglobulins, ANCA analysis, immune complex markers, antibodies to hepatitis B or C, antistreptolysin O, and hemolytic complement levels CH50 and C3) and biopsy of the temporal artery or kidney are useful in classifying the clinical presentation into the correct vasculitis category. A significant glomerular insult on biopsy coupled with a poor response to therapy signifies patients at risk for developing worsening renal dysfunction and eventual ESRD.

Forty-nine percent of all new patients entered into the Medicare ESRD program from 1998 to 2002 were classified with diabetic nephropathy. Once proteinuria develops and renal function declines, 50% of patients will reach ESRD between 7 to 10 years after the onset of proteinuria in type 1 diabetes. In most patients with type 2 diabetes the time of onset is unknown, thus complicating the ability to predict the course of renal failure. Moreover, a significant percent have concomitant risk factors (smoking, hypertension, hyperlipidemia) along with the proteinuria (>3 g) and nephrosclerosis, which may accelerate the time to ESRD.

Monoclonal immunoglobulins or light chains in both the serum and urine are observed in dysproteinemic states of light-chain nephropathy, amyloid, and cryoglobulinemia. Patients usually present with undiagnosed increases in SCr level and proteinuria and are usually older than 40 years. Treatment of light-chain deposition disease (LCDD) is suboptimal, with a significant percentage of patients progressing to ESRD if their presenting SCr values were greater than 4 mg/dL.

Malignancies of the gastrointestinal tract, breast, renal cell, prostate, skin, and so on can mediate an immune complex nephropathy potentially leading to CKD. Urologic, gynecologic, and lymphoproliferative malignancies can also result in renal injury and progressive chronic renal insufficiency. Non-Hodgkin's lymphoma is associated with membranous glomerulonephritis, and retroperitoneal tumors can cause ureteral obstruction and parenchymal infiltration or both.

**Certain hereditary diseases (sickle cell nephropathy; ADPKD; medullary cystic and acquired cystic diseases; aplastic, dysplastic or hypoplastic kidneys) can also lead to CKD.** ADPKD is the most common hereditary renal disorder leading to ESRD. Gene linkage may be helpful in identifying the ADPKD gene loci on the short arm of chromosome 16. This test can be carried out in utero in children and in adults before cyst development. Only about 50% of ADPKD patients progress to renal failure. Risk factors for progression include male gender, African origin, early age at presentation, *ADPKD1* gene, hypertension, and gross hematuria. Diverticular disease, cardiac valvular disease, and intracranial aneurysms are more common in ADPKD patients than in the general population and need to be considered in their care.

Medullary cystic disease sometimes can be confused with the benign condition of medullary sponge kidney. Medullary cystic disease presents in childhood with tubular cystic lesions at the cortical medullary junction and can be most accurately detected by kidney biopsy. The kidneys are usually small and the disease progresses to ESRD at a variable rate.

Tubular interstitial disease accounts for 3.8% of patients with CKD. Clinical manifestations depend on the degree of involvement, the tubular sites involved, and the level of compensation that the uninvolved areas provide. The diagnosis of

---

**Table 41–13. Causes of Progressive Chronic Kidney Disease**

*Tubulointerstitial*

Hematopoietic: sickle cell disease, lymphoproliferative, dysproteinemia, neoplastic
Urologic: ureteral obstructions, reflux, prune-belly syndrome, prostatic hypertrophy
Vascular: radiation, hypertension, atheroemboli
Metabolic: cystinosis, oxalosis, uric acid nephropathy, hypercalcemia
Immunologic: renal allograft rejection, Sjögren's syndrome
Toxic: analgesic, nonsteroidal anti-inflammatory drugs, chemotherapy
Immunosuppression: tacrolimus, cyclosporine
Heavy metals: lead, lithium

*Hereditary*

Sickle cell disease
Cystic disease: autosomal dominant polycystic kidney disease, medullary cystic disease
Alport's syndrome
Karyomegalic interstitial nephritis

*Primary Renal Disease*

Glomerular: idiopathic glomerulonephritis
Minimal change disease
Focal segmental glomerulosclerosis
Membranous glomerulonephritis
IgA nephropathy

*Systemic Diseases*

Diabetes mellitus
Infection-related glomerulonephritis
Systemic lupus erythematosus, Henoch-Schönlein purpura, systemic sclerosis
Dysproteinemias/amyloid
Thrombotic microangiopathies
Vasculitis: crescentic glomerulonephritis, acute diffuse glomerulonephritis, antineutrophil cytoplasmic antibody glomerulonephritis (microscopic polyangiitis), Wegener's granulomatosis, Churg-Strauss syndrome, Goodpasture's syndrome, granular cell arteritis

chronic interstitial nephritis depends on the urinalysis and clinical history. The urine findings are variable and white blood cells may be present. Obtaining an accurate medication history is essential, considering the broad range of causes. Three to 20 percent of patients treated with lithium over time develop CKD (Boton et al, 1987). Chronic lead nephropathy may demonstrate a protracted course that is gradually irreversible, as evidenced by small contracted kidneys. Lead nephropathy can be associated with renal adenocarcinoma. Another form of chronic interstitial nephritis that progresses to ESRD is analgesic nephropathy. The course in analgesic nephropathy is variable, depending on the number of pills consumed.

Obstructive uropathy involving the ureter, bladder, or urethra can lead to progressive renal insufficiency. Undetected ureteropelvic junction obstruction and posterior urethral valves are the most common types of congenital causes for progressive renal failure. Newer spiral CT methods may prove helpful in identification of the obstructing lesion. The percentage of ESRD population attributable to reflux nephropathy and nonreflux nephropathy has increased since the early 1990s (Craig et al, 2000). The rate of deterioration has been significantly associated with age, with a downward trend in incidence as age decreases. Women with reflux nephropathy demonstrate an increased risk of accelerated progression during pregnancy if the SCr value is ≥2.49 mg/dL. The risk for permanent renal failure increases with the duration of obstruction. Regaining renal function after obstruction is dependent on both the degree and duration of obstruction (<2 weeks) and preservation of specific tubular acidifying abilities. Vesicoureteral reflux may result in CKD from renal scarring. Vesicoureteral reflux may be either unilateral or bilateral, and progression to renal failure is related to the severity of reflux. Renal biopsy can be diagnostic as well as prognostic in obstructive neuropathy when relief of obstruction is not followed by restoration of renal function to baseline.

Over time, untreated urolithiasis can result in CKD. Gupta and colleagues (1994) reviewed the natural history of 33 urinary stone patients with a presenting SCr value greater than 2.0 mg/dL before surgical intervention and after placement of ureteral stent or percutaneous nephrostomy tube. The mean decrease in SCr with treatment was 1.2 mg/dL. There was no statistical difference in the rate of decrease between patients with pretreatment SCr levels of 2 to 2.9 mg/dL versus those with levels greater than 3 mg/dL.

Renal artery stenosis can result in progressive azotemia (Olin, 2002). "Flash" pulmonary edema with oliguria and azotemia may suggest the presence of bilateral renal artery stenosis, warranting further evaluation. Usually, when the SCr is greater than 3 mg/dL there is an underlying parenchymal abnormality contributing to kidney failure, in addition to the renal artery stenosis. Dejani and colleagues (2000) have reported that only 25% of elderly patients with CKD (SCr greater than 2 mg/dL) and proximal renal artery stenosis improved with renal revascularization. Renal artery stenting can improve the GFR of treated kidney, although the overall GFR may not change, perhaps reflecting the differential function of the contralateral kidney counterbalanced by the beneficial effect of the treated kidney (Grubb, 2000; Dharnidharka et al, 2002; Leertouwer et al, 2002).

Accurately monitoring the rate of decline in residual renal function (RRF) is important to determine whether the observed change in RRF is consistent with the natural history of the underlying disease or the result of an acute insult. If the RRF decline is inconsistent, an evaluation to uncover an alternate cause is warranted. Patients with CKD are at risk for ARF from a broad range of causes. Nephrotoxic agents, infection, volume depletion, hypotension, progressive renal artery stenosis, hypercalcemia, and hyperuricemia may all lead to worsening of underlying stable CKD, as shown in Table 41–14.

## Table 41–14. Factors Associated with Acute Deteriorations in Chronic Kidney Disease

*Nephrotoxic*

Contrast agents
Pharmacologic agents
Aminoglycoside antibiotics
Nonsteroidal anti-inflammatory drugs
Cyclooxygenase-2 inhibitors
Chemotherapeutic agents
Anti-rejection agents (cyclosporine, tacrolimus)
Anesthetic agents

*Autoregulatory Dysfunction*

Angiotensin-converting enzyme inhibitors
Angiotensin receptor blocker

*Anatomic/Structural*

Autosomal dominant polycystic kidney disease and angiotensin-converting enzyme inhibitors
Obstruction
Progressive renal artery stenosis
Renal vein thrombosis
Nephrolithiasis

*Hemodynamic/Perfusion Disorders*

Congestive heart failure
Perioperative hypotension
Volume depletion
Gastrointestinal: bleeding, diarrhea, vomiting
Excessive diuresis
Sepsis with vasodilation

*Parenchymal Injury*

Acute myocardial infarction
Valvular dysfunction
Superimposed "new" glomerulonephritis

*Interstitial*

Hypercalcemia
Hyperuricosuria
Atheroemboli

*Drug-Induced*

Penicillin analogs
Cephalosporins
Sulfonamides
Rifampin
Diuretics
Thiazide
Furosemide

*Miscellaneous*

Phenytoin
Allopurinol
Cimetidine

## Clinical Assessment of CKD (Function, Proteinuria, Radiology, and Biopsy)

In practice, once the GFR decreases to less than 60 mL/min/1.73 m$^2$ for 3 months or more, patients are classified as having CKD. The adjusted relative risk from a population survey adjusted for age, proteinuria, hematuria, and hypertension found that changes in GFR occurred at a cutoff SCr clearance value of 1.2 mg/dL (105 μm/L for women) and 1.4 mg/dL (125 μm/L for men) (Couchoud et al, 1999). However, in extrapolating SCr values to the actual GFR, the relationship may not be linear (see Fig. 41–7).

Other measurements that complement the SCr value may give a better index to the underlying, predicted GFR. Creatinine clearance, creatinine clearance plus urea clearance divided by 2, GFR measurements (inulin iothalamate), and cystatin C all provide information on the level of renal dysfunction. Although the iothalamate GFR is the "gold standard" for measuring renal function, a dedicated staff and laboratory are mandatory to implement this test. The Cockcroft-Gault formula [creatinine clearance = (140 − age) × weight × (0.85 if female) divided by 72 × plasma creatinine] is widely used throughout the world to estimate RRF (Cockcroft and Gault, 1976). Cystatin C, a 13-kD nonglycosylated basic protein produced by all tissues, may have an advantage in detecting minor alterations in GFR, whereas SCr may be more accurate at lower levels of GFR (Grubb, 2000; Dharnidharka et al, 2002; Stevens and Levey, 2005).

Most forms of CKD gradually and inevitably progress to ESRD over a 2- to 10-year time course, depending on the underlying renal lesion responsible for the CKD, combined with patient-specific factors. The K/DOQI staging and the approach to treatment of CKD depend on the assessment of GFR (function assessment), level of proteinuria, and clinical comorbidities. **The National Institutes of Health (NIH) Consensus Conference of 1993 recommended that patients with CKD be referred to a nephrologist when the SCr value has increased to 1.5 mg/dL in females and 2.0 mg/dL in males** (National Institutes of Health, 1994).

### Function Assessment

Although the SCr level is widely used as an index of RRF, the measured value is affected by factors other than the GFR. At any given GFR the SCr concentration is significantly higher in men than in women and in blacks than in whites. Total creatinine clearance (TCrCl) usually exceeds the GFR because of tubular secretion, whereas the urea clearance is usually lower than the GFR because of tubular reabsorption. The mean of the creatinine and the urea clearance is a more accurate estimate of the GFR than either is separately. Factors associated with creatinine excretion (age, gender, ethnicity, tubular creatinine secretion and inhibition) may affect the accuracy of standard SCr measurements. **The MDRD study equation to predict the GFR incorporates SCr concentration, demographic characteristics (age, gender, ethnicity), and other serum factors (urea, serum albumin). It is more accurate than other more widely used predictive equations or parameters (SCr level, 1/SCr, TCrCl + Urea clearance/2, Cockcroft-Gault formula).** The MDRD equation for demographic and serum variables is:

$$GFR = 170 \times [P_{Cr}]^{-0.999} \times [age]^{-0.176} \times [0.762 \text{ if patient is female}] \times [1.180 \text{ if patient is black}] \times [SUN]^{-0.170} \times [Alb]^{-0.318}$$

Although the MDRD equation is better than other standard measures for GFR, it is inaccurate for patients not in a steady state for creatinine balance or those with a medical condition interfering with creatinine excretion or creatinine assay or both (diabetic ketoacidosis, or therapy with certain cephalosporins) (Levey et al, 1999).

Individuals with nephrosclerosis appear to progress at individual rates until their GFR decreases to less than 40 mL/min. Most glomerular diseases that result in eventual ESRD progress slowly over 5 to 10 years. Patients presenting with RPGN, accelerated FSGS, Goodpasture's syndrome, or Wegener's granulomatosis can reach ESRD over a period of several months. In the MDRD study of 249 patients with a wide variety of nondiabetic renal disease, the GFR declined in 85% of patients whose initial GFR ranged from 13 to 55 mL/min (Hunsicker et al, 1997). The average rate of decline in nondiabetic renal disease was 4 mL/min/yr in patients whose disease progressed.

Considering the current K/DOQI staging of renal function linked to level of GFR, a number of medical centers and commercial laboratories are using estimated GFR (eGFR) from SCr as a primary method of reporting kidney function because of inadequacies in SCr alone. The MDRD study equation is used most commonly to estimate GFR. The estimation of GFR from the MDRD study equation is not appropriate for patients who have rapidly changing kidney function, are at the extremes of age and body size, exhibit malnutrition or obesity, are paraplegic or quadriplegic, consume a vegetarian diet, or have diseases that have an impact on the skeletal muscle status. Moreover, in sick, hospitalized patients with moderately advanced renal failure, the Cockcroft-Gault, MDRD equations, and eGFR perform poorly when estimating GFR in this patient population and are not reliable measurements of RRF (Poggio et al, 2005). In instances when the eGFR may not be accurate, a 24-hour urine collection for creatinine plus urea clearance divided by 2 is recommended.

### Proteinuria

Increased excretion of albumin is a sensitive marker for CKD attributable to diabetes mellitus, glomerular disease, interstitial disease, and hypertension. The American Diabetes Association and the National Kidney Foundation have recommended screening assessment using proteinuria measurement to detect CKD (Levey et al, 1998; American Diabetes Association, 2001). In adults albuminuria can be identified by the use of albumin dipstick, urinary albumin concentration (UAC), albumin/creatinine ratio (ACR) measured in a spot morning urine sample, or urinary albumin excretion greater than or equal to 30 mg over 24 hours (Gansevoort et al, 2005). Traditionally the cutoff value indicating a urinary albumin excretion greater than 30 mg/24 hr has been 3 mg/L (Keane and Eknoyan, 1999). The standard urine protein dipstick is insensitive for low concentrations of albumin (<10 mg/dL) and for some immunoglobulin light chains. Dehydration, hematuria, exercise, infection, and extremely alkaline urine (pH > 8) can cause false-positive dipstick readings.

## Radiographic Assessment

The radiographic assessment of CKD patients should take into account the impact of contrast on RRF. Imaging techniques in CKD are usually utilized for investigation of new ARF or for investigation of potential problems in nonrenal sites (e.g., cardiac catheterization, peripheral vascular concerns, abdominal investigations). Contrast material can induce worsening of underlying renal disease to the point of requiring RRT. **All patients with abnormal SCr greater than 2 mg/dL should be considered for alternative diagnostic testing and prophylactic preventive strategies to avoid worsening renal function.** Specific measures may help lower the risk for ARF in patients with CKD undergoing radiographic assessment. These include volume expansion, hydration with intravenous administration of normal saline solution (sodium chloride 0.9%), one-half strength saline solution (sodium chloride 0.45%), sodium bicarbonate solution, infusion of mannitol, administration of atrial natriuretic peptide, loop diuretics, calcium antagonists, theophylline, dopamine, *N*-acetylcysteine, low-osmolar contrast, iso-osmolar contrast media, use of gadolinium-based contrast medium, $CO_2$ angiography, hemodialysis shortly after contrast agent administration, and avoidance of short intervals between contrast studies (Thomsen, 2003; Liss et al, 2005). (See previous discussion in the section on prevention of ATN for recommendations.)

A number of reports have emphasized the value of normal saline solution hydration in patients with CKD and diabetes mellitus to generate a urine flow rate of 100 to 150 mL/hr, thus decreasing the risk for contrast agent–induced nephropathy (Solomon et al, 1994). Merely hydrating patients without ensuring effective urine flow is less valuable. There is no additional benefit to mannitol in the diabetic patient undergoing radiocontrast procedures; however, sodium bicarbonate solution infusion along with *N*-acetylcysteine may be of help. The antioxidant *N*-acetylcysteine (600 mg orally twice a day on the day before and on the day of administration of the contrast agent) along with hydration using a 0.45% saline solution intravenously may decrease the risk of ARF from radiographic contrast agents in this patient group (Tepel et al, 2000; Efrati et al, 2003).

## Urinalysis and Kidney Biopsy

The urine sediment examination is helpful in detection of CKD and the identification of the type of kidney disease. All patients with CKD should undergo a urinary sediment examination. Cells can originate from the kidney or from other sites within the urinary tract. The presence of a red blood cell cast strongly suggests glomerulonephritis especially if the red blood cells are dysmorphic. Urinary eosinophils are usually associated with allergic tubular interstitial nephritis. If the urinalysis is negative, despite the patient's having apparent CKD, a second specimen should be examined at another time. The urine sediment should be examined because urinary dipsticks cannot detect tubular epithelial cells (that are casts in the urine), crystals, fungus, or parasites.

A renal biopsy is not usually performed to evaluate asymptomatic hematuria but is warranted if the GFR is less than 60 mL/min/1.73 m$^2$ and the urinalysis is abnormal. The approach to performing kidney biopsy whether closed (CT-guided, ultrasound-guided) or open (standard or laparoscopic) depends on the overall clinical status, body habitus, patient's clotting parameters, and cumulative experience of the physician. The structural severity of glomerular injury and the immunopathologic category of disease are helpful in predicting renal outcome.

## Renal Protective Strategies

Regardless of the nature of the initial insult, once a critical number of nephrons is destroyed, a steady decline in GFR occurs as the progressive loss in viable nephrons occurs. Strategies for delaying the relentless loss in nephron mass (Brenner, 2003) are inconsistently employed across a population with CKD. **And yet, it is becoming increasingly clear that well-designed renal assessment and management programs are feasible and can be systematically applied to large numbers of CKD patients to decrease the rate of progression.**

A report of the International Society of Nephrology 2004 Consensus Workshop on Prevention of Progression of Renal Disease (Li et al, 2005) identified a number of therapeutic measures to prevent the progression of CKD, including lifestyle modifications, blood pressure control, glycemic control, reduction of proteinuria, protein restriction, lipid control, avoidance of nephrotoxic agents, early referral to a nephrologist, correction of anemia, optimization of calcium-phosphorus product, correction of acidosis, and maintenance of fluid balance.

Various pharmacologic trials comparing different medications have shown that patients with better blood pressure control have significantly slower rates of deteriorating kidney function. Yet all agents have not been shown to slow progression based on blood pressure effect alone. Clinical trials have suggested that reducing mean arterial pressure to 82 mm Hg (125/75 mm Hg) provides more optimal renal function stability in patients with diabetes and proteinuria (>1.5 g/day), compared with more conventional mean arterial pressure targets of 107 mm Hg (140/90 mm Hg).

Conceptually, angiotensin II is critical in causing progressive renal disease by both hemodynamic and nonhemodynamic mechanisms. Blockade of the renin-angiotensin system contributes to preservation of renal function by decreasing glomerular pressure and proteinuria. Because proteinuria plays a sentinel role in renal scarring, a reduction in proteinuria correlates with slowing of disease progression (Fine et al, 2000). A recent meta-analysis of randomized clinical trials confirmed the predictive value of proteinuria and the renal protective effect of proteinuria reduction by ACE inhibitor therapy in large patient series (Chiurchiu et al, 2005). Clinical research findings support the view that preservation of renal function through angiotensin blockade can be achieved in patients with either diabetes mellitus or nondiabetic nephropathy (Kshirsagar et al, 2000b). Reductions in proteinuria are greater with ACE inhibitors than with any other antihypertensive agent at the same level of blood pressure control. Multiple ACE inhibitors have been evaluated in CKD. In the Microalbuminuria Cardiovascular and Renal Outcomes—Heart Outcome Prevention Evaluation (MICRO-HOPE) a subset of 35,077 patients with diabetes mellitus and microalbuminuria were treated with ramipril (Heart Outcomes

Prevention Evaluation Study Investigators, 2000). Ramipril reduced the progression from microalbuminuria to overt nephropathy by 24% (*P* = .027). In the ACE Inhibitor in Progression of Renal Insufficiency (AIPRI) study, only part of the risk reduction in the ACE inhibitor group could be explained by the antihypertensive or antiproteinuric effect (Maschio et al, 1996). The AIPRI group performed a meta-analysis of 11 randomized clinical trials consisting of 17,060 patients with nondiabetic renal disease. This study concluded that antihypertensive regimens containing ACE inhibitors are more effective in slowing progression than regimens without ACE inhibitors. This same finding was observed in the Ramipril Efficacy in Nephropathy (REIN) study (GISEN Group, 1997).

Jafar and associates (1999) proposed that ACE inhibitors act by mechanisms in addition to their blood pressure lowering and antiproteinuric effects. ACE inhibitors also prevent the slow decline in $PO_2$ within the kidney. Considering the "hypoxia injury hypothesis," a potentially important renoprotective mechanism of ACE inhibition could stem from this improvement in interstitial capillary $PO_2$ levels, therefore decreasing the risk of renal sclerosis.

Angiotensin receptor blockers (ARBs) inhibit the type I angiotensin II receptor. Two large prospective, randomized trials have demonstrated that ARBs delay the progression of CKD in type 2 diabetic patients with overt nephropathy (Lewis et al, 2001; Parving et al, 2001). The Irbesartan Diabetic Nephropathy Trial (IDNT) examined the effect of ARBs (irbesartan) versus conventional therapy or the calcium channel blocker amlodipine in 1715 patients with type 2 diabetes. The doubling of SCr was 29% (*P* = .009) and 39% (*P* < .001) less than the risk in placebo and amlodipine-treated groups, respectively. Moreover, the Microalbuminuria Reduction with Valsartan (MARVEL) trial (Parving et al, 2001) supported the view that ARBs can potentially retard the progression of CKD in patients with type 2 diabetes.

**Combining ACE inhibitors and ARBs has led to further reductions in CKD progression, along with blood pressure, proteinuria, and microalbuminuria** (Campbell et al, 2003; Segura et al, 2003). Some CKD patients on ACE inhibitors may experience an acute decrease in RRF with low renal perfusion states due to dehydration, congestive heart failure, and hypotension. Individuals with bilateral renal artery stenosis and ADPKD patients with cyst size larger than 10 cm may also experience a decrease in RRF while on ACE inhibitor therapy. A rise in SCr of more than 1 mg/dL after beginning ACE inhibitor therapy should prompt a clinical evaluation to explain the change in baseline function.

An intricate relationship exists between hemodynamic factors that regulate vascular tone and metabolic factors that govern circulating lipids. It is now apparent that the 3-hydroxy-3-methylglutaryl coenzyme A (HMG-CoA) reductase inhibitors reduce production of molecules involved in fibrogenesis, reduce mesangial and smooth muscle cell proliferation, and decrease production of integrin adhesion molecules (Keane, 2000). Also, HMG-CoA reductase inhibition modulates small G-protein isoprenylation (involved in early gene product C-*fos* and C-*jun* transcription factors) and changes in cell-cycle regulatory proteins. These are involved in intracellular cholesterol metabolism and cell damage at the membrane level. **In view of these findings,**

**HMG-CoA reductase drugs should be part of the CKD treatment regimen.**

For over 25 years it has been known that protein restriction can ameliorate many symptoms of renal insufficiency and prevent its progression. However, without regular dietary consultation, patients on a low-protein diet may experience a decrease in protein intake and deterioration of several nutritional parameters. A number of different diets have been used to help slow the progression of CKD. These dietary formulations include low-protein (0.6 g protein/kg ideal body weight) diets, very low-protein diet (0.3 g protein/kg/day predominantly vegetable protein) supplemented with essential amino acids, or very low-protein diet supplemented with both essential amino acids and nitrogen-free analogs of amino acids (ketoacids). **The overall dietary requirement in CKD is approximately 0.6 g of protein/kg/day.** A recent in-depth analysis of the MDRD study results did note that each 0.2 g/kg/day reduction in protein intake was associated with a 29% slower rate of loss of GFR and a 51% prolongation in the time to dialysis for nondiabetic patients (Mitch, 2000). Two additional studies have demonstrated the beneficial effect of dietary protein restriction on retarding the progression of CKD in both diabetic and nondiabetic patients (Pedrini et al, 1996; Kasiske et al, 1998).

Table 41–15 summarizes a comprehensive strategy to achieve renal protection in patients with CKD (Jafar et al, 1999; Zandi-Nejad and Brenner, 2005). The comprehensive strategy illustrates specific interventions, treatment approaches, monitoring, and target benchmarks of treatment. Future therapies may mobilize progenitor cells for natural "renal repair" similar to those initiatives involving the heart and peripheral arterial disease (Kale et al, 2003; Zandi-Nejad and Brenner, 2005). The progenitor cells from the bone marrow may integrate after ischemic injury with potential for a functional improvement in the insulted organ remodeling. Progenitor cells may amplify biochemical signaling cascades (i.e., vascular and endothelial growth factor, IGF-1, stromal cell–derived factor [SDF]) involved in rescue. Optimal organ targeting will require an ability to amplify the progenitor cell impact. Newer pharmacologic strategies of manipulating resident progenitor cells to treat ischemic renal disease, regenerate glomeruli or tubules, or address transplant vascular disease may offer hope for improved renal reserve in the future (Masuya et al, 2003; Regele and Bohmig, 2003). Preventing renal injury in at-risk settings may also be a direction of treatment for the future. Experimental data in an ischemia-reperfusion rat kidney model have shown that a single systemic dose of erythropoietin before ischemia or just before perfusion prevents injury (Sharples et al, 2004). These findings may have major implications in the prophylaxis against ischemic injury of tubules in humans.

## Preoperative Evaluation of CKD/ESRD

**In CKD patients scheduled for an elective surgical procedure, a thorough preoperative assessment to define risk is warranted. Preoperative risk falls into three categories: patient-specific, procedure-specific, and anesthesia-specific risks** (Bronson, 2000). CKD patients should be closely evaluated because they may have multiple comorbidities that would affect outcome. The risk of a specific procedure is propor-

**Table 41–15. Comprehensive Renoprotection Strategy**

| Focus Area | Goal | Treatment |
|---|---|---|
| Blood pressure control | <130/80 if proteinuria < 1 g/day<br><125/75 if proteinuria > 1 g/day | Angiotensin-converting enzyme inhibitor<br>Angiotensin receptor blocker<br>Salt restriction<br>Diuresis |
| Reduction in proteinuria | <0.5 g/day | Angiotensin-converting enzyme inhibitor<br>Angiotensin receptor blocker<br>? Aldosterone blockade |
| Glycemic control | $HbA_{1c}$ < 7% | Oral hypoglycemic agents<br>Diet<br>Insulin |
| Dietary protein restriction | 0.6 to 0.8 g/kg/d* | Dietary consult |
| Lipid lowering | Low-density lipoprotein level ≥ 70 mg/dL[†] | Statin[††]<br>Triglyceride-lowering agent |
| Anemia management | Hemoglobin > 12 g/dL | Erythropoietin<br>Iron |
| Lifestyle modifications | Ideal body weight*<br>Smoking cessation<br>Exercise three times per week<br>Depression modification | Weight loss program (dietary counseling, surgery)<br>Antidepressants |
| Calcium × phosphorus product | <4.5 mmol/L<br><55 mg/dL<br>Phosphorus < 5.5 mg/dL (1.78 mmol)<br>Intact parathyroid hormone level of 70 to 110 pg/mL<br>  (CKD stage 4)<br>30-70 pg/mL (CKD stage 3)<br>25(OH)vitamin D > 30 ng/mL | Vitamin D supplementation<br>Use of dietary phosphorus restriction<br>Phosphate binders |

*Avoid malnutrition.
[†]Consider measuring nontraditional risk factors: homocysteine, lipoprotein A, C-reactive protein, fibrinogen.
[‡]Treat hyperhomocysteinemia with folic acid.

tional to the physiologic stress associated with the procedure. The American Society of Anesthesiologists' physical status scale defines five classes, each with a specific 7-day mortality from 0.07% (no organic or psychiatric disease) to 33.58% (moribund with little chance of survival). However, this scale does not consider procedure-related risks. There is no set risk profile specific for CKD. In general, procedures associated with a higher level of risk include major joint replacement, craniotomy, cardiac procedures, large bowel procedure, and exploratory laparotomies. The anesthesia-specific risk takes into account the effects of anesthetic agents and physiologic responses to a host of possible operative events such as hypotension, hypertension, blood loss, tachycardia, hypoxia, myocardial depression, and the acute worsening of renal function. In the CKD/ESRD population the major predictors of cardiac events are the presence of active ischemia, poor left ventricular function, and baseline ventricular arrhythmia.

Formal cardiac testing may be warranted preoperatively for patients with established ischemia, ventricular arrhythmias, and abnormal left ventricular ejection fraction. While it is preferable to obtain an exercise imaging study rather than pharmacologic imaging study, a significant percentage of CKD/ESRD patients will not achieve maximal predicted heart rate secondary to limited exercise capacity and medications. Pharmacologic testing with dobutamine stress echocardiography may be the best screening test for coronary disease in CKD (Marwick et al, 1998). A negative study had a low frequency of events over the short term (Chertow et al, 1997).

Hypertension also plays a role in determining operative risk. A blood pressure value of 180/110 mm Hg or more is associated with a greater risk for preoperative ischemic events. When possible, surgery should be delayed to bring blood pressure down to an acceptable level in patients with hypertension and CKD.

CKD patients with chronic obstructive pulmonary disease, active asthma, or a current infection are at high risk for pulmonary complications. Upper abdominal and thoracic surgery carry the greatest risk of compromising pulmonary function. If the forced expiratory volume vital capacity in 1 second ($FEV_1$) is greater than 2 L, the risk of a complication is low. An $FEV_1$ less than 1 L is associated with a significantly greater risk. Discontinuing smoking at least 3 months before surgery can significantly decrease the risk of pulmonary complications.

CKD patients with diabetes mellitus should achieve optimal control (<200 mg/dL) before surgery. The risk for infectious complications increases with blood glucose level greater than 300 mg/dL. CKD patients with diabetes on oral hypoglycemic agents should be carefully monitored because hypoglycemia with sepsis and/or malnutrition can markedly increase morbidity and mortality.

Elective surgery should be avoided in CKD/ESRD patients in a malnourished state. Serum albumin levels less than 3.5 g/dL, prealbumin levels less than 30 mg/dL, protein-nitrogen appearance or protein catabolic rate less than 0.8 g/kg/day, and subjective global nutritional assessment score of less than 5 signify malnutrition. Nutritional (protein/calorie) supplements should be used preoperatively to improve the baseline nutritional status. In the setting of anorexia, all offending drugs should be eliminated and consideration given for using pharmacologic appetite-stimulating agents (megestrol acetate).

**Drug dosing in CKD/ESRD should be closely monitored to avoid both reversible and irreversible toxicities.** Avoiding drugs that have the potential to accelerate loss of RRF is of paramount importance. The risk of adverse events may be linked to the patient's degree of residual renal dysfunction. Uremic toxins may modulate cytokine P450 enzyme activity, decrease glomerular filtration of drugs, and alter tubular secretion. High-risk therapies in the setting of CKD/ESRD include ACE inhibitors, radiographic contrast media, volume depletion, NSAIDs, cyclooxygenase-2 inhibitors, and aminoglycosides.

## Conservative Management: Prevention of Uremic Complications

**A comprehensive approach to achieving optimal renal care begins with the early detection of renal failure followed by the initiation of interventions that delay progression, prevent uremic complications, modify comorbidities, and, when necessary, prepare patients for RRT to optimize patient survival. The components of an optimal disease management program are depicted in Figure 41–9** (Pereira, 2000).

Decreased GFR is associated with complications in most organ systems. The most important complications include high blood pressure, anemia, malnutrition, bone disease, neuropathy, and alterations in quality of life. As the patient moves from stage 2 to higher stages, he or she is more likely to develop additional comorbidities. The level of scrutiny and

search for comorbidities increases as the stage of kidney disease advances. A number of factors increase cardiovascular risk. These include diabetes mellitus, hypertension, dyslipidemia, smoking, physical activity, psychological factors, anemia, arterial stiffness, vascular/valvular calcifications, and calcium and metabolic bone disease status.

The seventh report of the Joint National Committee on Prevention, Detection, Evaluation, and Treatment of High Blood Pressure (JNC VII) has defined hypertension in adults and the general population as systolic blood pressure of 140 to 159 mm Hg and diastolic blood pressure of 90 to 99 mm Hg. Normal blood pressure is defined as less than 120/80 mm Hg. A new category, "Prehypertension," is defined as 120 to 139 mm Hg systolic and 80 to 89 mm Hg diastolic (Chobanian et al, 2003). In patients with CKD, particularly those with proteinuria greater than 1 g in 24 hours, the target blood pressure goal (125/75 mm Hg) provides maximal protection against progression of renal disease (Klahr et al, 1994). Aggressive blood pressure control should also be a goal for patients on dialysis (K/DOQI stage 5), as outlined in Figure 41–10.

Data have shown that mild renal failure (SCr ≥ 1.4 but < 2.4 mg/dL) in high-risk patients had a 40% increase in the risk of cardiovascular death, myocardial infarction, or stroke compared with those patients with lower SCr levels (Mann et al, 2001). Because a large percentage of patients with CKD die of cardiovascular events before reaching dialysis (>60%), attention to risk factors is critical to extend survival. For optimal control of blood pressure a combination regimen that includes a diuretic, ACE inhibitor, or ARB is essential not only to achieving blood pressure control but also to retard the rate of progression of CKD. If the SCr is elevated (GFR less than 30 mL/min), a loop diuretic should be substituted for a standard thiazide.

Traditional atherosclerotic risk factors are frequently present in CKD. Low HDL level, elevated homocysteine level,

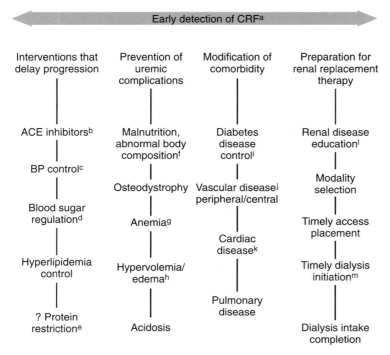

Early detection of CRF[a]

| Interventions that delay progression | Prevention of uremic complications | Modification of comorbidity | Preparation for renal replacement therapy |
|---|---|---|---|
| ACE inhibitors[b] | Malnutrition, abnormal body composition[f] | Diabetes disease control[i] | Renal disease education[l] |
| BP control[c] | | | Modality selection |
| Blood sugar regulation[d] | Osteodystrophy | Vascular disease[j] peripheral/central | |
| | Anemia[g] | | Timely access placement |
| Hyperlipidemia control | Hypervolemia/edema[h] | Cardiac disease[k] | Timely dialysis initiation[m] |
| ? Protein restriction[e] | Acidosis | Pulmonary disease | Dialysis intake completion |

**Figure 41–9.** Optimization of kidney disease care. *a.* Screening high-risk patients; serum creatinine >1.2 mg/dL. *b.* May require higher doses of angiotensin-converting enzyme inhibitors (or ATI-receptor blockers) to achieve target blood pressure. *c.* Control blood pressure: target level: mean arterial pressure less than or equal to 92 mm Hg. *d.* Blood sugar target of HbA$_{1c}$ less than 7%, glucose before meals of 80 to 120 mg/dL, glucose at bedtime of 100 to 140 mg/dL. *e.* Protein restriction, 0.67 g/kg/day with dietary consultation and objective measurements to avoid malnutrition. *f.* Parameters should include serum albumin plus subjective global assessment, anthropometrics or measurements of lean body mass (fat-free mass). *g.* Pre–end-stage renal disease target hematocrit greater than or equal to 30%, end-stage renal disease target hematocrit 30% to 36%. *h.* Effective volume equilibration is essential to avoid congestive heart failure, cellulitis/limb loss; increased admissions may require early initiation of dialysis. *i.* Avoid neuropathy, foot abnormalities, blindness. *j.* Peripheral vascular disease increases the risk for coronary artery disease; evaluate peripheral vascular flow. *k.* Echocardiography to assess left ventricular hypertrophy; dobutamine stress echocardiogram for addressing ischemia; screening in high-risk individuals. *l.* Refer for education when creatinine clearance is less than 25 mL/min; referral to nephrology for screening evaluation. *m.* Initiate dialysis when $K_t/V_{Urea}$ is less than 2.0 with signs of malnutrition. (Adapted from Pereira BJ: Optimization of pre-ESRD care: The key to improved dialysis outcomes. Kidney Int 2000;57:351-365.)

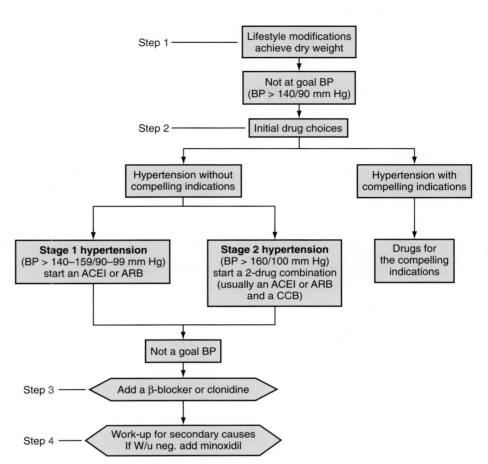

**Figure 41–10.** Algorithm for blood pressure management in chronic kidney disease. BP, blood pressure; ACEI, angiotensin-converting enzyme inhibitor; ARB, angiotensin receptor blocker; CCB, calcium channel blocker. (From National Kidney Foundation: Clinical practice guidelines for chronic kidney disease: Evaluation, classification and stratification. Am J Kidney Dis 2002;39[2].)

elevated LDL level, and elevated lipoprotein A level all define patients at high risk for cardiovascular events warranting lipid-lowering therapy and close cardiovascular screening (i.e., stress echocardiography, cardiac echocardiography). The Executive Summary of the Third Report of the National Cholesterol Education Program (NCEP) (2001) suggested that based on results from the Heart Protection study and the PROVE-IT study that additional benefit may be achieved by reducing LDL cholesterol levels to substantially below 100 mg/L especially in high-risk patients. Not only should medications be used by patients before stage 5 of CKD, but they also should be maintained once the patient starts dialysis or undergoes a kidney transplant. A meta-analysis comparing the efficacy of various antilipidemic therapies for PD, HD, and transplant recipients demonstrated the effectiveness of HMG-CoA reductase inhibitors (Massy and Kasiske, 1996). Both statin and fibric acid derivatives have proven effective, although individual differences mandate periodic monitoring of fasting lipid levels and liver function tests.

Cigarette smoking is universally recognized as an independent risk factor for cardiovascular disease and should be discouraged with this disease. There is a significant association between current smoking and cardiovascular outcomes that further emphasizes the importance of smoking cessation.

Both vascular calcification and valvular calcifications have been found to be more common in CKD patients and impact on survival (Blacher et al, 1999; London et al, 2004). While there are no randomized trials that have evaluated whether treatment of calcium-phosphorus abnormalities or reduction

in the use of calcium-based phosphate binders reduces the risk of cardiovascular disease outcomes, the recommendation from K/DOQI clinical practice guidelines for bone metabolism and disease in CKD is that non–calcium-based binders be used if there is evidence of severe vascular calcification (National Kidney Foundation, 2003). The stage of CKD in which bone disease begins to develop has not been well documented nor has a consensus been reached regarding the optimal screening methods for identifying early abnormalities of calcium-phosphorus metabolism and bone disease in CKD patients. Below a GFR of approximately 60 mL/min/1.73 m$^2$ there is a higher prevalence of abnormalities of bone metabolism.

Being overweight and obese are associated with increasing risks for a variety of cardiovascular complications and with higher all-cause mortality. Weight reduction is an important lifestyle modification for overweight patients. Although protein-energy malnutrition and wasting are common among CKD patients, no single nutritional marker is helpful in defining malnutrition. Changes in lean body mass over time in CKD may signal not only worsening uremia but also an increased risk for cardiovascular disease. Specific methods for evaluating raising nutritional status include multifrequency bioimpedance (BIA), dual x-ray absorptiometry (DEXA), subjective global assessment (SGA), and hand-grip strength (HGS).

All patients with CKD should follow the American Diabetes Association's guidelines for blood glucose control. Recommendations have been based on evidence from the Diabetes

Control and Complications Trial (DCCT) (National Kidney Foundation, 1993; U.K. Prospective Diabetes Study Group, 1998). The target for diabetes control should be a hemoglobin $A_{1C}$ level of less than 7%, a preprandial glucose level of 80 to 100 mg/dL, and a bedtime glucose level of 100 to 140 mg/dL.

Observational studies have shown an association between anemia and adverse cardiovascular outcomes in CKD patients. It is unclear whether treatment of anemia prevents cardiovascular events in CKD patients. Recombinant human erythropoietin (rHu-EPO) is most likely to benefit the CKD patient who is symptomatic with a hematocrit value less than 30%. The treatment goal should be to achieve hemoglobin of ~12 g/dL. Hypertension can be more difficult to control as the hemoglobin is increased with erythropoietin therapy. Hypertension worsens in approximately 23.5% of patients treated with rHU-EPO (Eschbach et al, 1987).

Cardiovascular disease begins early in the course of CKD. Among patients with creatinine clearance of less than 25 to 30 mL/min, left ventricular hypertrophy is present in 38% to 45% of patients compared with a prevalence rate of 16% to 31% among patients with higher levels of RRF.

Noninvasive testing of patients with kidney failure for cardiovascular disease is helpful especially in high-risk patients. The diagnostic accuracy of perfusion imaging is lower than in patients not in renal failure. Dobutamine echocardiography has been reported to have a sensitivity of 96% and specificity of 86% and is the preferred screening instrument for coronary artery disease in CKD/ESRD patients.

Aggressively addressing comorbidities in CKD that may shorten survival is critical to extending life years for these patients.

## Initiation of Renal Replacement Therapy

**The K/DOQI guidelines recommend that dialysis be initiated when weekly renal $K_rT/V_{Urea}$ ($K_rT$ = kidney excretion over a 24-hour time period; $V_{Urea}$ = urea distribution volume) decreases to less than 2, unless all three of the following criteria are met: (1) stable or increased edema-free body weight, (2) a random protein equivalent of total nitrogen appearance greater than 0.8 kg/day, and (3) an absence of clinical symptoms and signs attributable to uremia.** The patient should begin some form of RRT if the $K_rT/V_{Urea}$ value is less than 2 and greater than 6% involuntary reduction in edema-free weight exists, or if the patient is at less than 9% of standard body weight for National Health and Nutrition Examination III, or there is a reduction of serum albumin level by more than 0.3 g/dL. Despite these recommendations, a significant percentage of patients have RRF less than 10 mL/min/1.73 m² at the start of dialysis. Obrador and colleagues (1999) examined data on 90,897 patients who began dialysis in the United States from April 1995 to September 1997. The mean ± standard deviation SCr level at initiation was 8.5 ± 3.8 mg/dL. The mean predicted GFR was 7.1 ± 3.1 mL/min/1.73 m². Historically, mortality among late referrals is consistently higher than among those with more timely initiated RRT patterns. Holland and Lam (2000) identified independent predictors of delayed referral among a retrospective cohort of 362

predialysis patients, including age ≥50 years, female gender, and congestive heart failure.

The rationale for timely initiation of RRT is based on several different, independent lines of evidence. As renal function declines, spontaneous dietary protein restriction occurs. Declining renal function is associated with abnormal protein metabolism, malnutrition, and poor clinical outcomes. A lower serum albumin level correlates with an increased mortality risk for both HD and PD patients (Port, 1994).

## End-Stage Renal Disease Demographics and Treatment Options

There is a steady growth of ESRD patients (stage 5) on RRT throughout the world. The incidence in the United States is 330 new cases per million of population. The ESRD program in the United States comprises 431,284 patients: 308,910 on dialysis and 122,374 with a functioning transplant. In the United States the number of transplants continues to grow, with 16,004 performed in 2004 (9,357 from deceased donors and 6,647 from living donors). Transplants from living donors in the United States now constitute 41% of all transplants performed. Schena and associates (1999) demonstrated that differences in the distribution of patients receiving RRT throughout the world are influenced by the level of gross domestic product. Diabetes is the primary cause of ESRD in 44% of patients initiated on ESRD therapy. The number of new patients beginning dialysis has increased 139% since 1988 (U.S. Renal Data System, 2004). The most common diseases responsible for ESRD vary depending on the country of origin, as noted from worldwide registries depicted in Table 41–16.

Critically important to all ESRD patients worldwide is a thorough understanding by the physician of dialysis practices that yield improved outcomes. The Dialysis Outcomes and Practice Patterns (DOPPS) study is a prospective, longitudinal study of hemodialysis practices from seven countries with large populations of dialysis patients (France, Germany, Italy, Japan, Spain, United Kingdom, and the United States) (Young, 2000). Linking the DOPPS scope of work with the K/DOQI goals will help to develop continuous quality improvement

**Table 41–16. Causes of End-Stage Renal Disease in Worldwide Renal Registries**

|  | USRDS* | CORR | ANZDATA | JSDT |
|---|---|---|---|---|
| *Incidence* | | | | |
| Diabetes | 49.3 | 28.2 | 18.6 | 33.8 |
| Hypertension | 26.9 | 9.9 | 9.7 | 6.5 |
| Glomerulonephritis | 8.9 | 16.1 | 34.5 | 38.2 |
| *Point Prevalence* | | | | |
| Diabetes | 35.7 | 23.0 | 29.6 | 21.7 |
| Hypertension | 23.7 | 9.3 | 12.2 | 3.9 |
| Glomerulonephritis | 15.6 | 20.3 | 22.0 | 53.5 |

USRDS, United States Renal Data System; CORR, Canadian Organ Replacement Registry; ANZDATA, Australian-New Zealand Dialysis and Transplant Registry; JSDT, Japanese Society of Dialysis Therapy.
*USRDS 2004 Annual Report
Adapted from Schena FP: Kidney Int 2000;57(Suppl 74):S39-S43.

programs and provide direct feedback to participating dialysis centers worldwide (Port and Eknoyan, 2004). The DOPPS has collected information that will have an impact on those issues that relate to anemia management, modifiable hemodialysis practices to optimize outcome, vascular access, mortality and hospitalization, nutritional indicators, depression assessment, prescription utilization, acidosis, and vitamin prescriptions.

The mortality rate of RRT patients is strongly influenced by the percentage of enrolled diabetic patients, the dialysis dose, the type of hemodialytic membrane, erythropoietin therapy, and the nutritional status. Adjusted mortality rates of prevalent dialysis patients in the United States continue to fall for those with less than 5 years on therapy. But since 1994, mortality increased in patients on dialysis for greater than or equal to 5 years. Rates for patients on the modality 5 years or more have increased 14% since their lowest point in 1994 to a 2002 level of 286 deaths per 1000-patient-years. This observation may signal a need for more attention to comorbidities that develop in patients over time on dialysis (lipid disorders, worsening diabetes, vascular disease, cardiovascular disease, and infectious complications).

Poor long-term survival of ESRD patients is illustrated by comparing the expected remaining lifetime on dialysis or transplant with the general U.S. population (Table 41–17). The expected remaining lifetime for white dialysis patients was only one-fourth to one-sixth that of the general population, with differences being highest among women age 40 to 65 years. By modality, the expected lifetimes for transplant patients are double those of dialysis patients among black males and more than three times as high for white males age 20 and older. Expected remaining lifetimes in transplant patients are still, however, only 52% to 69% of those of the general population. Compared with males, females have poorer outcomes in terms of more frequent hospitalizations, frequency of anemia, vascular access problems, malnutrition, poorer quality of life, and access to transplantation (Sehgal, 2000).

Multiple different RRTs are available for treatment of ESRD patients. The most commonly utilized RRTs are HD, PD, and renal transplantation. Other treatment options include hemodiafiltration (combination of intermittent hemofiltration with simultaneous HD) and nocturnal home HD (slow flow HD for extended period overnight). **Outcome comparison suggests that renal transplantation is still the best overall treatment for ESRD patients, despite advances in dialytic options.** The time on dialysis may have an impact on the success of replacement therapy. Patients on HD for more than 10 years have a poorer outcome when transplanted compared with individuals receiving transplants with less time on dialysis. This finding is probably related to fixed vascular defects that occur in patients on chronic dialysis therapy. Reports confirm that longer waiting time on dialysis negatively impacts on post-transplant graft and patient survival (Meier-Kriesche et al, 2000). This effect was independent of age, race, donor characteristics, and original disease. Therefore, patients who reach ESRD should undergo preemptive transplantation or transplantation as soon as possible, once on dialysis.

In comparing outcomes between different RRTs for nondiabetic patients, it is essential to consider the type of statistical model used to evaluate mortality (Cox proportional hazards regression versus Poisson regression), the type of analysis employed (intent to treat versus as treated), and the type of study patient (prevalent vs. incident) (Vonesh et al, 2000). Vonesh and associates (2004) reported that specific results are closely linked to stratification by age and modality. Appropriate patient selection is critical to optimizing the life-years per patient with ESRD. PD has an early survival advantage compared with HD, whereas patients older than 45 with diabetes may have a survival advantage (in months) if started on HD.

**Not all patients will benefit from RRT.** Recommendations for withholding or withdrawing dialysis from suboptimal adult ESRD patients were recently published. These were based on feedback from the U.S. Renal Physicians Association (RPA) and American Society of Nephrology (ASN) in conjunction with broad representation from ESRD patients, family, and non-nephrologists (Galla, 2000).

Currently in the United States 92% of dialysis patients are treated with HD and 8% with PD. Between 1998 and 2002 the prevalent HD and transplant population grew 3.2% and 4.3%, respectively, whereas the PD population decreased almost 3.5% per year. **The renal disease continuum** (see Fig. 41–11) **demonstrates the critical junctures in renal disease care extending from the early diagnosis to management of the patient on dialysis. Processes of care for each stage should be developed from evidence-based recommendations and linked to auditing tools that can provide organizations and health care teams ongoing feedback for optimizing results. The concept of RRT assignment in an integrated fashion is a key to prolonging ESRD survival. An integrated approach combining HD, PD, and renal transplant over the life of an ESRD patient may provide the best approach to optimizing survival. An integrated care approach whereby patients are started on PD and transferred in a timely fashion to HD, when PD- or patient-related problems occur, demonstrates an increase in survival compared with those remaining on HD for their entire life span** (Van Biesen et al, 2000). Table 41–18 indicates transition points that may stimulate transfer from one modality to another. RRF is preserved longer on PD than on HD. Blood pressure is better controlled and ventricular arrhythmias are observed less often on PD than on HD. Weight gain and inadequate dialysis after 3 years are more common on PD than with HD. Although vascular access problems and hemodynamic instability are the most common reasons for transfer to PD from HD, other reasons include infection (peritonitis, catheter, tunnel infections), inadequate dialysis, and catheter malfunction. K/DOQI has established specific guideline recommendations for both HD and PD. Quality guidelines are established for HD adequacy, PD adequacy, vascular access, anemia management, bone metabolism, and nutrition.

In 1997, the NKF's DOQI clinical guidelines on HD and PD were published. For HD, DOQI recommended a single pool $K_rT/V_{Urea}$ of 1.3, urea reduction ratio (URR) more than 70%, allowing for errors or compliance problems in delivering the recommended dose of at least 1.2. Barriers to adequate HD include underprescription, inadequate vascular access, dialysis membrane, clotting, shortened treatment times, and "no show." The projected 2005 DOQI guidelines for PD will require a weekly $K_rT/V_{Urea}$ of more than 1.7. Typically, patients with high- to high-average transport characteristics are ideal

**Table 41–17. Expected Remaining Lifetimes (Years) of the General U.S. Population, and of Prevalent Dialysis and Transplant Patients, by Race and Gender from the 2004 USRDS Annual Data Report**

*General U.S. Population, 2001*

| | All Races | | | White | | | Black | | |
|---|---|---|---|---|---|---|---|---|---|
| Age | All | M | F | All | M | F | All | M | F |
| 0 | 77.2 | 74.4 | 79.8 | 77.7 | 75.0 | 80.2 | 72.2 | 68.6 | 75.5 |
| 1 | 76.7 | 74.0 | 79.3 | 77.1 | 74.5 | 79.6 | 72.2 | 68.6 | 75.4 |
| 5 | 72.8 | 70.1 | 75.4 | 73.2 | 70.6 | 75.7 | 68.3 | 64.8 | 71.5 |
| 10 | 67.9 | 65.2 | 70.4 | 68.3 | 65.6 | 70.8 | 63.4 | 59.8 | 66.6 |
| 15 | 62.9 | 60.2 | 65.5 | 63.3 | 60.7 | 65.8 | 58.5 | 54.9 | 61.7 |
| 20 | 58.1 | 55.5 | 60.6 | 58.5 | 56.0 | 60.9 | 53.7 | 50.3 | 56.8 |
| 25 | 53.4 | 50.9 | 55.7 | 53.8 | 51.3 | 56.1 | 49.1 | 45.8 | 52.0 |
| 30 | 48.6 | 46.2 | 50.9 | 49.0 | 46.6 | 51.2 | 44.5 | 41.4 | 47.2 |
| 35 | 43.9 | 41.5 | 46.0 | 44.2 | 41.9 | 46.3 | 39.9 | 36.9 | 42.5 |
| 40 | 39.2 | 37.0 | 41.3 | 39.5 | 37.3 | 41.6 | 35.5 | 32.5 | 38.0 |
| 45 | 34.7 | 32.5 | 36.6 | 34.9 | 32.8 | 36.9 | 31.2 | 28.4 | 33.6 |
| 50 | 30.3 | 28.2 | 32.1 | 30.5 | 28.4 | 32.3 | 27.1 | 24.4 | 29.3 |
| 55 | 26.0 | 24.0 | 27.7 | 26.1 | 24.2 | 27.8 | 23.3 | 20.8 | 25.3 |
| 60 | 21.9 | 20.1 | 23.4 | 22.0 | 20.2 | 23.5 | 19.7 | 17.5 | 21.5 |
| 65 | 18.1 | 16.4 | 19.4 | 18.2 | 16.5 | 19.5 | 16.4 | 14.4 | 17.9 |
| 70 | 14.6 | 13.1 | 15.7 | 14.6 | 13.2 | 15.7 | 13.5 | 11.7 | 14.7 |
| 75 | 11.5 | 10.2 | 12.4 | 11.5 | 10.2 | 12.3 | 10.8 | 9.3 | 11.7 |
| 80 | 8.8 | 7.7 | 9.4 | 8.7 | 7.7 | 9.3 | 8.6 | 7.3 | 9.2 |
| 85 | 6.5 | 5.7 | 6.9 | 6.4 | 5.6 | 6.7 | 6.7 | 5.7 | 7.0 |
| 90 | 4.8 | 4.2 | 5.0 | 4.6 | 4.1 | 4.8 | 5.1 | 4.5 | 5.3 |
| 95 | 3.6 | 3.2 | 3.7 | 3.4 | 3.0 | 3.4 | 3.9 | 3.6 | 4.0 |
| 100 | 2.7 | 2.5 | 2.8 | 2.4 | 2.3 | 2.5 | 3.0 | 2.9 | 3.0 |

*ESRD: Dialysis 2002*

| | All Races | | | White | | | Black | | | Native American | | | Asian | | |
|---|---|---|---|---|---|---|---|---|---|---|---|---|---|---|---|
| Age | All | M | F | All | M | F | All | M | F | All | M | F | All | M | F |
| 0-14 | 20.1 | 21.2 | 18.9 | 20.1 | 21.0 | 19.1 | 19.0 | 20.5 | 17.5 | 22.9 | 23.4 | 22.5 | 32.2 | 32.8 | 31.5 |
| 15-19 | 17.2 | 18.1 | 16.1 | 16.6 | 17.4 | 15.8 | 17.1 | 18.5 | 15.8 | 18.4 | 18.9 | 17.9 | 25.0 | 25.5 | 24.5 |
| 20-24 | 14.6 | 15.5 | 13.6 | 14.0 | 14.6 | 13.2 | 14.8 | 16.1 | 13.4 | 15.3 | 15.9 | 14.9 | 21.8 | 22.2 | 21.3 |
| 25-29 | 12.5 | 13.2 | 11.7 | 11.8 | 12.3 | 11.1 | 13.0 | 14.0 | 11.9 | 12.8 | 13.1 | 12.6 | 18.9 | 19.2 | 18.5 |
| 30-34 | 10.8 | 11.3 | 10.2 | 9.9 | 10.2 | 9.5 | 11.5 | 12.3 | 10.6 | 11.1 | 11.0 | 11.1 | 16.2 | 16.4 | 16.0 |
| 35-39 | 9.3 | 9.6 | 8.8 | 8.4 | 8.6 | 8.2 | 10.0 | 10.6 | 9.2 | 9.4 | 9.3 | 9.5 | 13.7 | 13.8 | 13.6 |
| 40-44 | 8.0 | 8.3 | 7.6 | 7.2 | 7.4 | 7.0 | 8.7 | 9.3 | 8.1 | 8.0 | 7.9 | 8.0 | 11.5 | 11.4 | 11.5 |
| 45-49 | 6.9 | 7.1 | 6.6 | 6.3 | 6.5 | 6.0 | 7.5 | 7.8 | 7.1 | 6.8 | 6.9 | 6.8 | 9.5 | 9.5 | 9.6 |
| 50-54 | 5.9 | 6.0 | 5.8 | 5.4 | 5.5 | 5.3 | 6.5 | 6.8 | 6.2 | 6.1 | 6.0 | 6.2 | 8.0 | 7.9 | 8.0 |
| 55-59 | 5.0 | 5.1 | 5.0 | 4.6 | 4.6 | 4.5 | 5.6 | 5.7 | 5.5 | 5.4 | 5.3 | 5.4 | 6.6 | 6.5 | 6.7 |
| 60-64 | 4.3 | 4.3 | 4.3 | 3.9 | 4.0 | 3.9 | 4.9 | 4.9 | 4.8 | 4.6 | 4.5 | 4.7 | 5.6 | 5.6 | 5.6 |
| 65-69 | 3.6 | 3.6 | 3.6 | 3.3 | 3.3 | 3.3 | 4.1 | 4.2 | 4.0 | 3.9 | 3.8 | 4.0 | 4.8 | 4.8 | 4.9 |
| 70-74 | 3.1 | 3.0 | 3.1 | 2.9 | 2.8 | 2.9 | 3.4 | 3.5 | 3.4 | 3.3 | 3.1 | 3.5 | 4.0 | 3.9 | 4.1 |
| 75-79 | 2.6 | 2.6 | 2.6 | 2.5 | 2.5 | 2.5 | 2.9 | 2.9 | 2.8 | 2.8 | 2.6 | 2.9 | 3.4 | 3.4 | 3.4 |
| 80-84 | 2.2 | 2.2 | 2.2 | 2.1 | 2.1 | 2.1 | 2.4 | 2.5 | 2.4 | 2.4 | 2.3 | 2.4 | 2.8 | 2.7 | 2.9 |
| 85+ | 1.8 | 1.7 | 1.8 | 1.7 | 1.7 | 1.7 | 1.9 | 1.9 | 2.0 | 1.9 | 1.8 | 1.9 | 2.2 | 2.2 | 2.2 |

*Transplant, 2002*

| | All Races | | | White | | | Black | | | Native American | | | Asian | | |
|---|---|---|---|---|---|---|---|---|---|---|---|---|---|---|---|
| Age | All | M | F | All | M | F | All | M | F | All | M | F | All | M | F |
| 0-14 | 49.5 | 49.7 | 49.2 | 50.3 | 50.6 | 50.0 | 45.4 | 45.7 | 44.8 | 38.8 | 39.4 | 38.0 | 57.1 | 56.2 | 58.6 |
| 15-19 | 39.3 | 39.3 | 39.6 | 39.8 | 39.8 | 40.0 | 36.5 | 36.5 | 36.5 | 33.7 | 34.1 | 33.4 | 46.5 | 45.5 | 48.1 |
| 20-24 | 35.6 | 35.5 | 35.9 | 36.0 | 35.9 | 36.3 | 33.0 | 33.0 | 33.2 | 31.2 | 31.5 | 30.9 | 42.7 | 41.6 | 44.3 |
| 25-29 | 31.9 | 31.7 | 32.3 | 32.2 | 32.1 | 32.6 | 29.7 | 29.5 | 29.9 | 28.6 | 29.0 | 28.4 | 38.8 | 37.6 | 40.5 |
| 30-34 | 28.4 | 28.1 | 28.9 | 28.6 | 28.4 | 29.2 | 26.4 | 26.2 | 26.8 | 26.2 | 26.3 | 26.2 | 34.9 | 33.7 | 36.8 |
| 35-39 | 25.0 | 24.6 | 25.7 | 25.2 | 24.9 | 25.9 | 23.2 | 22.8 | 23.8 | 23.7 | 23.5 | 24.2 | 31.1 | 29.8 | 33.1 |
| 40-44 | 21.8 | 21.3 | 22.8 | 22.1 | 21.6 | 23.0 | 20.1 | 19.6 | 20.7 | 21.4 | 20.9 | 22.1 | 27.4 | 26.0 | 29.5 |
| 45-49 | 19.0 | 18.4 | 20.0 | 19.2 | 18.7 | 20.3 | 17.3 | 16.8 | 18.0 | 19.1 | 18.6 | 19.9 | 23.8 | 22.5 | 25.9 |
| 50-54 | 16.4 | 15.8 | 17.5 | 16.7 | 16.1 | 17.8 | 14.7 | 14.3 | 15.5 | 17.0 | 16.5 | 17.7 | 20.6 | 19.4 | 22.6 |
| 55-59 | 14.0 | 13.4 | 15.1 | 14.2 | 13.6 | 15.4 | 12.4 | 11.9 | 13.2 | 15.2 | 14.7 | 16.0 | 17.6 | 16.4 | 19.6 |
| 60-64 | 11.8 | 11.2 | 12.9 | 12.0 | 11.4 | 13.1 | 10.5 | 9.9 | 11.3 | 13.8 | 13.2 | 14.7 | 14.9 | 13.8 | 16.9 |
| 65-69 | 9.9 | 9.3 | 11.1 | 10.0 | 9.4 | 11.2 | 8.8 | 8.2 | 9.8 | 12.6 | 11.8 | 13.8 | 12.8 | 11.7 | 14.7 |
| 70-74 | 8.3 | 7.7 | 9.6 | 8.3 | 7.7 | 9.6 | 7.4 | 6.7 | 8.6 | 11.3 | 10.5 | 12.5 | 10.9 | 9.9 | 12.9 |
| 75-79 | 7.3 | 6.8 | 8.5 | 7.3 | 6.8 | 8.5 | 6.7 | 5.9 | 7.9 | 10.8 | 10.0 | 12.2 | 9.8 | 9.0 | 11.6 |

Courtesy of the U.S. Renal Data System: USRDS 2004 Annual Data Report: Atlas of End-Stage Renal Disease in the United States. Bethesda, MD, National Institutes of Health, National Institute of Diabetes, Digestive and Kidney Disease, 2004.

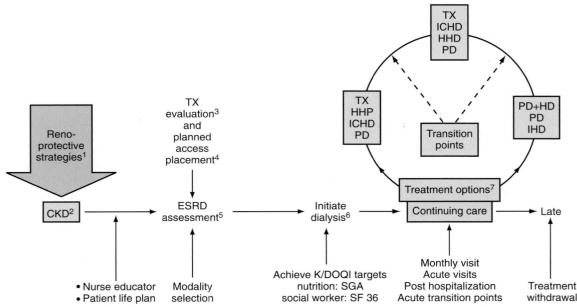

**Figure 41–11.** Kidney disease continuum. (1) Population screening (serum creatinine >1.2 mg/dL), delay progression (stage 1: 60 to 90 mL/min/ 1.73 m²). (2) Preserve residual renal function, educate, assess comorbidities (stage 3, 4: 30 to 59 mL/min/1.73 m²). (3) Preemptive transplant. (4) Peritoneal dialysis/hemodialysis modalities. (5) Evaluate complication/risk; residual renal function 15 to 29 mL/min/1.73 m²: prepare for renal replacement therapy. (6) Initiate dialysis. $K_tT/V_{Urea}$ (residual renal function) less than 2, avoid uremic complications, define physician problem-based care (stage 5: <15 mL/min/1.73 m²). (7) Integrate different therapies over time dependent on critical junctures to extend survival years and control comorbidities: malnutrition, uncontrolled blood pressure, inadequate solute/water removal, access failure, residual renal function preservation.

| Table 41–18. | **Transition Points for Modality Transfers** |
| --- | --- |

*Peritoneal Dialysis Transfer to Hemodialysis:*

Recurrent infection
Catheter malfunction
Ultrafiltration failure
Adequacy (solute) failure
Psychological burnout
Activities of daily living failure
Hospitalization/surgery
Uncontrolled diabetes
Bond composition morbidity delta
Hypotension

*Hemodialysis Transfer to Peritoneal Dialysis*

Recurrent congestive heart failure
Access failure (steal, recurrent [3], lower extremity, option)
Hypercoagulability
Malnutrition
Intradialysis hypotension
Nursing home care

candidates for automated PD, which uses an automated cycling device to perform dialysis exchanges at night. Low- to low-average transport characteristic patients seem to do best on the standard manual exchanges performed during the day. Several options are available to help PD patients meet adequacy targets combining standard manual exchanges with automated cycling devices.

## Hospitalization Risk in CKD/ESRD

**CKD patients are 10 times more likely to be hospitalized; and, on average, hospitalization lasts 1 day longer compared with non–renal failure patients** (Thamer et al, 1996). Hospital admissions for ESRD patients in the United States have remained relatively stable since 1993, and the number of hospital days has fallen 12% for HD patients, 16% for transplant, and 19% for PD patients. ESRD patients secondary to diabetes are admitted most frequently—2.3 times per year in 2002. Inpatient hospital care accounts for 41% of the total ESRD costs (Bruns et al, 1998). The total hospital discharges by general diagnostic related charges from 1996 to 1998 for ESRD patients in the United States showed that the four most common causes for admission were circulatory (36.4%), renal system (15.6%), respiratory system (7.4%), and infection (5.7%). Patients undergoing RRT are often hospitalized with general medical problems most often stemming from comorbid conditions. The length of stay for HD patients differed by the medical service to which they were admitted. Overall costs for hospitalization tended to be less on the nephrology service than on internal medicine service (6.3 days vs. 8.1 days) (Kshirsagar et al, 2000a). Total cost per admission was $2,848 more for an HD admission to internal medicine service versus nephrology service and, yet, the risk of readmission was not significantly higher.

Rocco and coworkers (1996) identified specific risk factors for hospital utilization in chronic dialysis patients from a cohort of 1572 patients in Network VI (states of North Carolina, South Carolina, and Georgia). **By using multiple regression analysis, the strongest predictors of the number of hospitalizations per year of patient risk included low serum albumin, decreased activity level, diabetes mellitus as a primary cause of ESRD, peripheral vascular disease, white race, increasing age, and congestive heart failure.** Both nutritional status (serum albumin, creatinine, transferrin, prealbumin, and lean body mass [bioelectrical impedance]) and inflammatory response (i.e., C-reactive protein) are independent predictors of hospitalization in chronic HD patients (Ikizler et al, 1999).

**Sarnak and Jaber (2000) demonstrated that mortality rates secondary to sepsis are one to several hundredfold higher in dialysis patients (HD and PD) compared with the general population.** Renal transplant recipients have sepsis-associated mortality rates approximately 20-fold higher than the general population but 15-fold lower than dialysis patients. Infection is the second leading cause of death in patients with ESRD. Sepsis accounts for more than 75% of the infection deaths. Acquired immune deficiencies with uremia, advanced age, and a broad array of comorbid conditions contribute to the observed infection risk and admission rate for kidney disease patients.

Acute worsening of renal function may occur in hospitalized CKD patients. The proposed criteria for initiation of RRT in this setting are listed in Table 41–19 (Bellomo and Ronco, 1998). For ESRD patients undergoing high-risk surgery,

sequential daily dialysis for 3 days preoperatively should be entertained to optimize fluid and ensure stable serum potassium and solute levels.

In patients requiring RRT, aggressive volume and solute control are essential to achieving optimal postoperative recovery. Outpatient dialysis schedules may not meet the needs of in-hospital patients. Some individuals may require more intensive therapy either daily or continuously if hemodynamically unstable. A number of different therapies can be utilized to treat critically ill patients requiring RRT (Table 41–20). Ideally, the BUN-to-albumin ratio should decrease to less than 17 through aggressive dialysis. Patients with serum albumin levels less than 3 g/dL with correspondingly low prealbumin values less than 25 g/dL should undergo enteral feedings or aggressive oral supplementation. Total parenteral nutrition may be used if the gastrointestinal tract is nonfunctional. Aggressive ultrafiltration either alone or in conjunction with regular HD should be implemented to control edema and decrease the risk for intubation or reintubation, congestive heart failure, and related infectious complications.

Pulmonary diffusion capacity and pulmonary capillary blood volume are compromised in diabetic CKD patients preoperatively. Low $FIO_2$ and high central venous pressures are indicators of pulmonary compromise. The alveolar oxygen gradient and respiratory index are more abnormal postoperatively in diabetics versus nondiabetics at similar volume levels. Therefore, smaller elevations in pulmonary capillary wedge pressure carry more significant pulmonary morbidity in diabetics versus nondiabetics, warranting close attention to volume status. CKD patients have a poorly responsive ventilator control system, which impedes timely ventilator weaning (Seki et al, 1993). Therefore re-intubation has a significantly higher morbidity and mortality in CKD and should be avoided. Other preventive strategies involve vaccinations (Pneumovax, influenza, hepatitis), hypertension control, identification of high-risk patients for congestive heart failure, early treatment of upper respiratory tract infection/

---

**Table 41–19. Proposed Criteria for Initiation of Renal Replacement Therapy**

Oliguria (urine output < 200 mL/12 hr)
Anuria or extreme oliguria (urine output < 50 mL/12 hr)
Hyperkalemia ([K⁺] > 6.5 mmol/L)
Severe acidemia (pH < 7.1)
Azotemia ([urea] > 30 mmol/L)
Clinically significant organ (especially lung) edema
Uremic encephalopathy
Uremic pericarditis
Uremic neuropathy/myopathy
Severe dysnatremia ([Na] > 160 or < 115 mmol/L)
Drug overdose with dialyzable toxin

From Bellomo R, Ronco C: Indications and criteria for initiating renal replacement therapy in the intensive care unit. Kidney Int Suppl 1998;66: S106-S109.

---

**Table 41–20. Defining Therapies for Acute Renal Failure in Patients with Chronic Kidney Disease**

| Therapy | Definition | Indication | Modality Option |
|---|---|---|---|
| Hemodialysis (HD) | Convective-based process across semipermeable membrane | Solute/$H_2O$ removal<br>Hyperkalemia | IHD, DHD, CAVHD, CVVHD |
| Hemofiltration | Convective-based solute removal with plasma water filtered across highly permeable membrane | Volume control, acid-base disorders, azotemia, congestive heart failure, multiple organ failure | IHD, CVVH, CAVH |
| Hemodiafiltration | Convective and diffusive process across semipermeable membrane, increased small and large molecule removal | Acidosis, possible multiple organ failure, ARDS, dialysis instability | IHDF, CAVHDF, CVVHDF |
| Ultrafiltration (UF) | Plasma water removal, 2 to 5 L/24 hr | Fluid removal, congestive heart failure, total body anasarca, intubation or re-intubation risk | SCUF, CVVUF, IUF |
| Sustained low efficiency dialysis | Slow, convective-based process across semipermeable membrane | IHD treatment failure due to hypotension or inadequate clearance | SLED |
| Peritoneal dialysis (PD) | Diffusive and convective transport across peritoneal membrane | Azotemia, volume control, hypotension, without access to continuous hemodialysis treatments | CAPD, CCPD (APD) |

ARDS, acute respiratory distress syndrome; IHD, intermittent HD; DHD, daily HD; CAVH, continuous arteriovenous hemofiltration; CVVHD, continuous venovenous HD; IHDF, intermittent hemodiafiltration; CAVHDF, continuous arteriovenous diafiltration; CVVHDF, continuous venovenous hemodiafiltration, SCUF, slow continuous ultrafiltration; CVVUF, continuous venovenous ultrafiltration; IUF, intermittent ultrafiltration; SLED, sustained low efficiency dialysis; CAPD, continuous ambulatory peritoneal dialysis; CCPD, continuous cyclic peritoneal dialysis; APD, automated peritoneal dialysis.

bronchitis, and optimization of functional status (vision assessment, exercise, cognitive stability). Identifying patients with risk characteristics that lead to hospitalization and designing a management plan to modify risk are essential and deserving of further study.

## KEY POINTS: CHRONIC RENAL FAILURE

■ The National Kidney Foundation developed and published clinical practice guidelines for CKD in 2002 to more consistently diagnose and treat CKD and its comorbidities.

■ At a set point (usually >50% reduction in GFR), a relentless progressive loss of renal function ensues even when the initial insult becomes inactive: the hyperfiltration hypothesis.

■ Progression of renal insufficiency involves hemodynamic and nonhemodynamic mechanisms.

■ ACE inhibitors are the most effective agents in slowing the progression of renal disease by both hemodynamic and nonhemodynamic mechanisms.

■ The most common causes of CKD are diabetes and hypertension.

■ Comorbidities associated with CKD need treatment to optimize survival and diminish morbidity. This includes managing hypertension, blood lipids, smoking cessation, target weight, anemia, and glycemic control.

■ Major surgical interventions mandate thorough medical evaluation, particularly cardiovascular health. The best cardiac noninvasive screening assessment is a dobutamine echocardiogram.

## SUGGESTED READINGS

Bellomo R, Chapman M, Finfer S, et al: Low-dose dopamine in patients with early renal dysfunction: A placebo-controlled randomised trial. Australian and New Zealand Intensive Care Society (ANZICS) Clinical Trials Group. Lancet 2000;356:2139-2143.

Bonventre JV, Zuk A: Ischemic acute renal failure: An inflammatory disease? Kidney Int 2004;66:480-485.

Brenner BM, Mackenzie HS: Nephron mass as a risk factor for progression of renal disease. Kidney Int Suppl 1997;63:S124-S127.

Bronson D: Preoperative evaluation and management before major non-cardiac surgery. In Stoller J, Ahmad M, Longworth D (eds): Intensive Review of Internal Medicine, 2nd ed. Philadelphia, Lippincott, Williams & Wilkins, 2000, pp 74-81.

Chiurchiu C, Remuzzi G, Ruggenenti P: Angiotensin-converting enzyme inhibition and renal protection in nondiabetic patients: The data of the meta-analyses. J Am Soc Nephrol 2005;16(Suppl 1):S58-S63.

Fogo AB: Glomerular hypertension, abnormal glomerular growth, and progression of renal diseases. Kidney Int Suppl 2000;75:S15-S21.

Goldfarb DA, O'Hara J: Etiology, pathogenesis, and management of pre-operative acute renal failure. AUA Update Series 2001;20(Lesson 4):26-31.

Levey AS, Bosch JP, Lewis JB, et al: A more accurate method to estimate glomerular filtration rate from serum creatinine: A new prediction equation. Modification of Diet in Renal Disease Study Group [see comments]. Ann Intern Med 1999;130:461-470.

National Kidney Foundation: K/DOQI clinical practice guidelines for chronic kidney disease: Evaluation, classification, and stratification. Am J Kidney Dis 2002;39:S1-S266.

Shilliday IR, Quinn KJ, Allison ME: Loop diuretics in the management of acute renal failure: A prospective, double-blind, placebo-controlled, randomized study. Nephrol Dial Transplant 1997;12:2592-2596.

Solomon R, Werner C, Mann D, et al: Effects of saline, mannitol, and furosemide to prevent acute decreases in renal function induced by radio-contrast agents [see comments]. N Engl J Med 1994;331:1416-1420.

Tepel M, van der Giet M, Schwarzfeld C, et al: Prevention of radiographic-contrast-agent-induced reductions in renal function by acetylcysteine [see comments]. N Engl J Med 2000;343:180-184.

Thadhani R, Pascual M, Bonventre JV: Acute renal failure [see comments]. N Engl J Med 1996;334:1448-1460.

U.S. Renal Data System: USRDS Annual Data Report: Atlas of End-Stage Renal Disease in the United States. Bethesda, MD, National Institutes of Health, National Institute of Diabetes, Digestive and Kidney Diseases, 2004.

# SECTION XI

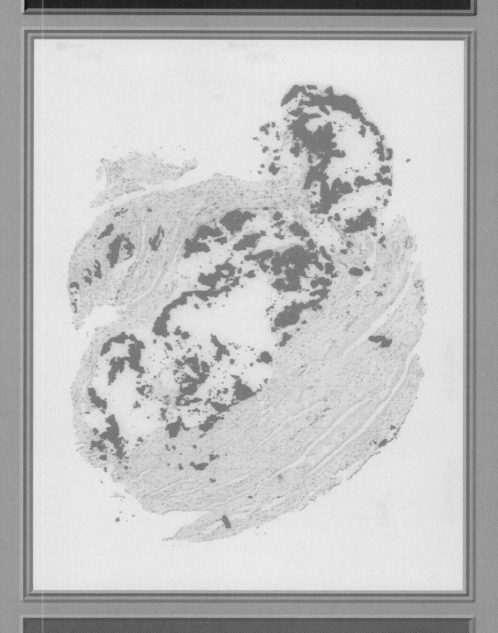

# URINARY LITHIASIS
# AND
# ENDOUROLOGY

# 42 Urinary Lithiasis: Etiology, Epidemiology, and Pathogenesis

MARGARET S. PEARLE, MD, PhD • YAIR LOTAN, MD

EPIDEMIOLOGY OF RENAL CALCULI

PHYSICOCHEMISTRY

MINERAL METABOLISM

PATHOGENESIS OF UPPER URINARY TRACT CALCULI

Although stone disease is one of the most common afflictions of modern society, it has been described since antiquity. With Westernization of global culture, however, the site of stone formation has migrated from the lower to the upper urinary tract and the disease once limited to men is increasingly gender blind. Revolutionary advances in the minimally invasive and noninvasive management of stone disease over the past 2 decades have greatly facilitated the ease with which stones are removed. However, surgical treatments, although they remove the offending stone, do little to alter the course of the disease. Indeed the overall estimated annual expenditure for individuals with claims corresponding to a diagnosis of nephrolithiasis was nearly $2.1 billion in 2000, reflecting a 50% increase since 1994 (Pearle et al, 2005). Given the frequency with which stones recur, the development of a medical prophylactic program to prevent stone recurrences is desirable. To this end, a thorough understanding of the etiology, epidemiology, and pathogenesis of urinary tract stone disease is necessary.

## EPIDEMIOLOGY OF RENAL CALCULI

The lifetime prevalence of kidney stone disease is estimated at 1% to 15%, with the probability of having a stone varying according to age, gender, race, and geographic location. **In the United States, the prevalence of stone disease has been estimated at 10% to 15%** (Norlin et al, 1976; Sierakowski et al, 1978; Johnson et al, 1979). Using data derived from the United States National Health and Nutrition Examination Survey dataset (NHANES II and III), Stamatelou and colleagues (2003) established a 5.2% prevalence of kidney stone disease from 1988 to 1994, which represents a 37% increase from 1976 to 1980 for which a 3.8% prevalence rate was determined. The finding of an increase in the prevalence of stone disease has been observed by others (Norlin et al, 1976; Yoshida and Okada, 1990; Serio et al, 1999; Trinchieri et al, 2000).

## Gender

**Stone disease typically affects adult men more commonly than adult women. By a variety of indicators, including inpatient admissions, outpatient office visits, and emergency department visits, men are affected two to three times more frequently than women** (Hiatt et al, 1982; Soucie et al, 1994; Pearle et al, 2005). However, there is some evidence that the difference in incidence between men and women is narrowing. Using the National Inpatient Sample dataset representing hospital discharges, Scales and colleagues found that while overall population-adjusted discharges for a diagnosis of renal or ureteral calculus increased by only 1.6% from 1997 to 2002, discharges for women increased by 17%, whereas discharges for men decreased by 8.1% (Scales et al, 2005). This trend reflects a change in the ratio of male-to-female discharges from 1.7 in 1997 to 1.3 in 2002. Indeed, in 2002, hospital discharges were the same for men and women in this dataset. Whether trends in hospital discharges accurately reflect trends in the overall prevalence of the disease, however, is not clear. Stamatelou and associates (2003) also noted a slight decrease in the male-to-female ratio of stone disease, from 1.75 (between 1976 and 1980) to 1.54 (between 1988 and 1994) using the NHANES dataset.

## Race/Ethnicity

Racial/ethnic differences in the incidence of stone disease have been observed. **Among U.S. men, Soucie and colleagues (1994) found the highest prevalence of stone disease in whites, followed by Hispanics, Asians, and African Americans, who had prevalences of 70%, 63%, and 44% of whites, respectively.** Among U.S. women, the prevalence was highest among whites but lowest among Asian women (about half that of whites). Others found an even higher differential (threefold to fourfold) between whites and African Americans (Sarmina et al, 1987). Interestingly, despite differences in prevalence of stone disease according to ethnicity, Maloney and colleagues (2005) observed a remarkably similar incidence of metabolic abnormalities between white and nonwhite stone formers from the same geographic region, although the distribution of abnormalities differed, suggesting that dietary and other environmental factors may outweigh the contribution of ethnicity in determining stone risk.

**The gender distribution of stone disease varies according to race. Sarmina and colleagues (1987) noted a male-to-female ratio among whites of 2.3 and among African Americans of 0.65.** Michaels and coworkers (1994) also noted a reversal of the male predisposition to stone disease in Hispanics and African Americans, reporting a male-to-female ratio of 1.8 among Asians, 1.6 among whites, 0.7 among Hispanics, and 0.5 among African Americans, among a group of patients undergoing extracorporal shock wave lithotripsy. Soucie and associates (1994) observed a similar trend in the male-to-female ratio of the lifetime incidence of stone disease of 3.4 among Asians, 2.6 among whites, 2.1 among Hispanics, and 1.8 among African Americans, although the actual ratios differed in the two studies. Dall'era and colleagues (2005) reviewed emergency department records to identify patients presenting with symptomatic renal or ureteral calculi and found a male-to-female ratio of 1.17 among Hispanic patients compared with 2.05 for white patients.

## Age

**Stone occurrence is relatively uncommon before age 20 but peaks in incidence in the fourth to sixth decades of life** (Marshall et al, 1975; Johnson et al, 1979; Hiatt et al, 1982). It has been observed that women show a bimodal distribution of stone disease, demonstrating a second peak in incidence in the sixth decade of life, corresponding to the onset of menopause (Marshall et al, 1975; Johnson et al, 1979). This finding, and the lower incidence of stone disease in women compared with men, has been attributed to the protective effect of estrogen against stone formation in premenopausal women, owing to enhanced renal calcium absorption and reduced bone resorption (McKane et al, 1995; Nordin et al, 1999). Indeed, Heller and colleagues (2002) identified lower urinary saturation of calcium oxalate and brushite in women compared with men. Moreover, urinary calcium was lower in women than in men until age 50, after which it reached equivalence in the two groups. Estrogen-treated postmenopausal women had lower urinary calcium and saturation of calcium oxalate than untreated women.

Alternatively, Fan and associates (1999) found that androgens increased and estrogens decreased urinary and serum oxalate in an experimental rat model, perhaps accounting for the reduced risk of stone formation in women. However, Van Aswegen and coworkers (1989) found lower levels of urinary testosterone in stone formers compared with non–stone-forming control subjects, further confusing the issue.

## Geography

The geographic distribution of stone disease tends to roughly follow environmental risk factors; **a higher prevalence of stone disease is found in hot, arid, or dry climates such as the mountains, desert, or tropical areas.** However, genetic factors and dietary influences may outweigh the effects of

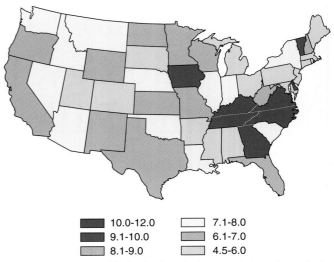

| | |
|---|---|
| ■ 10.0-12.0 | □ 7.1-8.0 |
| ■ 9.1-10.0 | ▨ 6.1-7.0 |
| ▨ 8.1-9.0 | ▨ 4.5-6.0 |

**Figure 42–1.** Geographic distribution of urinary tract stone disease in the U.S. veteran population from 1983 to 1986. Data are expressed as urinary tract stone patients per 1000 hospital discharges. (From Mandel NS, Mandel GS: Urinary tract stone disease in the United States veteran population: II. Geographical analysis of variations in composition. J Urol 1989;142:1516.)

geography. Finlayson (1974) reviewed several worldwide geographic surveys and found that areas of high stone prevalence included the United States, British Isles, Scandinavian and Mediterranean countries, northern India and Pakistan, northern Australia, Central Europe, portions of the Malay peninsula, and China. Within the United States, **Mandel and Mandel (1989a, 1989b) identified the highest rates of hospital discharge for patients with calcium oxalate stones in the Southeast and for uric acid stones in the East, among the veteran patient population. Soucie and associates (1994) found increasing age-adjusted prevalence rates in both men and women going from north to south and west to east, with the highest prevalence observed in the Southeast** (Fig. 42–1). After controlling for other risk factors, the authors determined that ambient temperature and sunlight were independently associated with stone prevalence (Soucie et al, 1996).

## Climate

Seasonal variation in stone disease is likely related to temperature by way of fluid losses through perspiration and perhaps by sunlight-induced increases in vitamin D. Prince and Scardino (1960) noted the highest incidence of stone disease in the summer months, July through September, with the peak occurring within 1 to 2 months of maximal mean temperatures (Prince et al, 1956). Likewise, Bateson (1973) reported a peak incidence of stone disease between December and March in Australia, corresponding to the summer season.

The study of military personnel translocated to desert locations has provided a unique opportunity to study the effect of climate on a defined population. Pierce and Bloom (1945) reported that American soldiers in an undisclosed desert location had an increase in symptomatic episodes of renal colic during the summer season. Another study of military personnel who developed symptomatic stones after arrival in Kuwait and Iraq disclosed a mean time interval to stone formation of

93 days (Evans et al, 2005). Finally, Parry and Lister (1975) measured urinary calcium and magnesium levels in soldiers before and 10 days after transfer to the Persian Gulf and noted increased urinary calcium levels from baseline in those soldiers transferred during the summer months but not among those transferred during the "cold season," which was attributed to sunlight-induced increased production of 1,25-dihydroxyvitamin $D_3$ (1,25[OH]$_2D_3$). Thus it is likely that climate and geography influence the prevalence of stone disease indirectly, through effects on temperature and possibly sunlight.

## Occupation

Heat exposure and dehydration constitute occupational risk factors for stone disease as well. Cooks and engineering room personnel, both of whom are exposed to high temperatures, were found to have the highest rates of stone formation among personnel of the Royal Navy (Blacklock, 1969). Likewise, Atan and colleagues (2005) found a significantly higher incidence of stones among steel workers exposed to high temperatures (8%) compared with those working in normal temperatures (0.9%). Metabolic evaluation of these two groups of workers showed a higher incidence of low urine volume and hypocitraturia among the workers in the hot area. Borghi and colleagues (1993) also noted differences in the incidence of stone disease and urinary stone risk factors among workers at a glass plant who were or were not chronically exposed to high temperatures causing massive perspiration. Those exposed to high temperatures exhibited lower urine volumes and pH, higher uric acid levels, and higher urine specific gravity, leading to higher urinary saturation of uric acid. Accordingly, those workers who formed stones had a remarkably high incidence of uric acid stones (38%).

Individuals with sedentary occupations, such as those in managerial or professional positions, have been found to carry an increased risk of stone formation for unclear reasons (Blacklock, 1969). This finding is consistent with the work of Robertson and associates (1980b), who reported an increased risk of stone disease in affluent individuals, countries, and societies, which may be reflective of a more indulgent diet and lifestyle.

## Body Mass Index and Weight

The association of body size and incidence of stone disease has been investigated. In two large prospective cohort studies of men and women, **the prevalence and incident risk of stone disease were directly correlated with weight and body mass index in both sexes, although the magnitude of the association was greater in women than men** (Curhan et al, 1998; Taylor et al, 2005). Although these investigators identified a reduced risk of incident stone formation with high intake of fluid (men and women) and low protein intake (men) (Curhan et al, 1993, 1997), they found that obesity and weight gain were independent risk factors for incident stone formation and could not be accounted for by diet alone (Taylor et al, 2005). Recent evidence linking obesity and insulin resistance with low urine pH and uric acid stones (Maalouf et al, 2004a, 2004b) as well as an association between hyperinsulinemia and hypercalciuria (Kerstetter et al, 1991;

Shimamoto et al, 1995; Nowicki et al, 1998) could account for an increased risk of uric acid and/or calcium stones in obese patients.

## Water

The beneficial effect of a high fluid intake on stone prevention has long been recognized. In two large observational studies, fluid intake was found to be inversely related to the risk of incident kidney stone formation (Curhan et al, 1993, 1997). Furthermore, in a prospective, randomized trial assessing the effect of fluid intake on stone recurrence among first-time idiopathic calcium stone formers, urine volume was significantly higher in the group assigned to a high fluid intake compared with the control group receiving no recommendations, and, accordingly, stone recurrence rates were significantly lower (12% vs. 27%, respectively) (Borghi et al, 1996).

Geographic differences in the incidence of stone disease have been ascribed in some cases to differences in the mineral and electrolyte content of water in different areas. Although several investigators reported a lower incidence of stone disease in geographic regions with a "hard" water supply compared with a "soft" water supply, where water "hardness" is determined by content of calcium carbonate (Churchill et al, 1978; Sierakowski et al, 1979), others found no difference. Schwartz and coworkers (2002) found no association between water hardness and incidence of stone episodes, although they did observe a correlation between water hardness and urinary magnesium, calcium, and citrate levels.

---

### KEY POINTS: EPIDEMIOLOGY

- Upper urinary tract stones occur more commonly in men than women by a ratio of 2 to 3:1.

- Whites have the highest incidence of upper tract stones compared with Asians, Hispanics, and African Americans.

- Prevalence of stone disease shows geographic variability, with the highest prevalence of stone disease in the Southeast.

- The risk of stone disease correlates with weight and body mass index.

---

## PHYSICOCHEMISTRY

The physical process of stone formation is a complex cascade of events that occurs as the glomerular filtrate traverses the nephron. It begins with urine that becomes supersaturated with respect to stone-forming salts, such that dissolved ions or molecules precipitate out of solution and form crystals or nuclei. Once formed, crystals may flow out with the urine or become retained in the kidney at anchoring sites that promote growth and aggregation, ultimately leading to stone formation. The discussion that follows describes the process of stone formation from a physicochemical standpoint.

# State of Saturation

A solution containing ions or molecules of a sparingly soluble salt is described by the *concentration product,* which is a mathematical expression of the product of the concentrations of the pure chemical components (ions or molecules) of the salt. For example, the concentration product (CP) expression for sodium chloride is $CP = [Na^+][Cl^-]$. A pure aqueous solution of a salt is considered *saturated* when it reaches the point at which no further added salt crystals will dissolve. The concentration product at the point of saturation is called the *thermodynamic solubility product,* $K_{sp}$, which is the point at which the dissolved and crystalline components are in equilibrium for a specific set of conditions. At this point, addition of further crystals to the saturated solution will cause the crystals to precipitate unless the conditions of the solution, such as pH or temperature, are changed.

**In urine, despite concentration products of stone-forming salt components, such as calcium oxalate, that exceed the solubility product, crystallization does not necessarily occur because of the presence of inhibitors and other molecules** that allow higher concentrations of calcium oxalate to be held in solution before precipitation or crystallization occurs. In this state of saturation, urine is considered to be *metastable* with respect to the salt. As concentrations of the salt increase further, the point at which it can no longer be held in solution is reached and crystals form. The concentration product at this point is called the *formation product,* $K_f$.

The solubility product and the formation product differentiate the three major states of saturation in urine: undersaturated, metastable, and unstable (Fig. 42–2). Below the solubility product, crystals will not form under any circumstances and dissolution of crystals is theoretically possible. At concentrations above the formation product, the solution is unstable and crystals will form. In the metastable range, between the solubility product and the formation product and in which the concentration products of most common stone components reside, spontaneous nucleation or precipitation does not occur despite urine that is supersaturated. It is in this area that modulation of factors controlling stone formation can take place and therapeutic intervention is directed.

In the metastable range of concentration products, although crystal growth can occur on existing crystals, de novo formation of crystals cannot occur in the length of time it normally takes for the filtered urine to reach the bladder. However, crystal formation can occur in this range under certain circumstances. First, in parts of the nephron local concentration products may exceed the formation product for long enough time periods to allow nucleation to occur. Second, local areas of obstruction or stasis in the upper

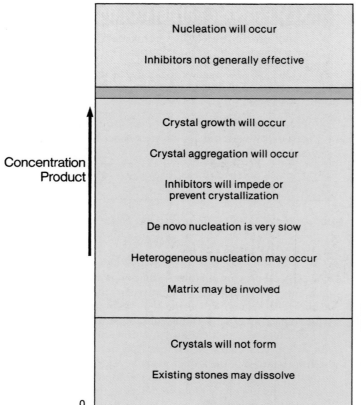

**Phenomena**

Nucleation will occur

Inhibitors not generally effective

Formation Product

Crystal growth will occur

Crystal aggregation will occur

Inhibitors will impede or prevent crystallization

De novo nucleation is very slow

Heterogeneous nucleation may occur

Matrix may be involved

Solubility Product

Crystals will not form

Existing stones may dissolve

Concentration Product

0

**Figure 42–2.** States of saturation. Listed are solid-solution phenomena that are likely to occur at a given range of concentration products. Three general situations are considered: (1) concentrations less than the solubility product (undersaturation), (2) concentrations that are metastable with respect to de novo precipitation (between the solubility product and the formation product), and (3) concentrations that are greater than the formation product (unstable). (From Meyer JL: Physicochemistry of stone formation. In Resnick MI, Pak CYC [eds]: Urolithiasis: A Medical and Surgical Reference. Philadelphia, WB Saunders, 1990, pp 11-34.)

urinary tract may prolong urinary transit time and allow crystal formation to occur in the metastable urine. Finally, microscopic impurities or other constituents in the urine can facilitate the nucleation process by adsorption of the crystal components in a geometric way that resembles the native crystal. The energy required for this "heterogeneous nucleation" process is much less than that required for "homogeneous nucleation."

To estimate the state of saturation for any given crystal system, such as calcium oxalate or calcium phosphate, Pak and Chu (1973) developed a mathematical formula, the *activity product ratio*, that takes into account urine pH and the ionic activities of all major ion species directly involved in the stone-forming process or those that affect the overall ionic strength of the urine. Finlayson subsequently developed a computer program to measure the state of saturation, EQUIL 2, which is commonly used today (Werness et al, 1985). The *relative saturation ratio* or *concentration product ratio* is defined as the ratio of the concentration product of the urine to the solubility product of the specified stone-forming salt. A reduction in the numerator will lead to undersaturation of the urine with respect to the stone-forming salt and consequently reduce the likelihood of precipitation. This can be accomplished by reducing the urinary concentrations of the stone components (e.g., calcium or oxalate), by reducing the filtered load, or by increasing urinary reabsorption. In addition, complexation with substances such as citrate, reduce available free ionic calcium and decrease the relative saturation ratio. On the other hand, manipulation of factors such as pH can significantly impact the concentration of ions such as phosphate, the generation of which is highly pH dependent. Manipulation of pH has little effect on oxalate concentration, however, because oxalic acid is a strong acid (pK = 4) and pH changes within the physiologic range will have little effect on oxalate concentration.

Historically, urinary oxalate has been considered a more important contributor to calcium oxalate stone formation than urinary calcium (Nordin et al, 1972; Robertson and Peacock, 1980). This assumption is based on the findings of Nordin and colleagues (1972), who noted that a rise in urinary calcium concentration had less of an effect than a rise in oxalate concentration in increasing urinary saturation of calcium oxalate. They further showed that at high urinary calcium concentrations the saturation of calcium oxalate reached a plateau that did not exceed the theoretic formation product of calcium oxalate, whereas high oxalate concentrations did, thereby increasing the risk of calcium oxalate crystal formation. Pak and colleagues (2004), however, challenged the notion that urinary oxalate exerts a greater pathogenetic role than calcium in calcium oxalate stone formation. They demonstrated that the choice of stability constant used for calculating relative saturation ratio determines the relative effects of urinary calcium and oxalate concentration. Using the commonly accepted stability constant of $2.746 \times 10^3$ (used in the EQUIL 2 program), the effect of urinary calcium and oxalate proved to be equivalent. Thus, they concluded that **urinary calcium and oxalate are both important and equal contributors to calcium oxalate stone formation.** As such, reduction in both calcium and oxalate will be effective in reducing the relative saturation ratio, and intervention to prevent stone formation can be directed at either.

# Nucleation and Crystal Growth, Aggregation, and Retention

In normal human urine, the concentration of calcium oxalate is four times higher than its solubility in water. Urinary factors favoring stone formation, including low volume and citrate and increased calcium, oxalate, phosphate and uric acid, all increase calcium oxalate supersaturation. Once the concentration product of calcium oxalate exceeds the solubility product, crystallization can potentially occur. However, in the presence of urinary inhibitors and other substances, calcium oxalate precipitation occurs only when supersaturation exceeds the solubility by 7 to 11 times.

Homogeneous nucleation is the process by which nuclei form in pure solution. Nuclei are the earliest crystal structure that will not dissolve. Small nuclei are unstable; below a critical size threshold, dissolution of the crystal is favored over crystal growth. If the driving force (supersaturation level) and the stability of the nuclei are adequate and the lag time to nucleation is sufficiently short compared with the transit time of urine through the nephron, the nuclei will persist. Inhibitors, like citrate, destabilize nuclei, whereas promoters stabilize nuclei by providing a surface with a binding site that accommodates the crystal structure of the nucleus. In urine, crystal nuclei usually form through heterogeneous nucleation by adsorption onto existing surfaces of epithelial cells (Umekawa et al, 2001), cell debris (Fasano et al, 2001), or other crystals (Kok, 1997).

Within the time frame of transit of urine through the nephron, estimated at 5 to 7 minutes, crystals cannot grow to reach a size sufficient to occlude the tubular lumen. However, if enough nuclei form and grow, aggregation of the crystals will form larger particles within minutes that can occlude the tubular lumen. Inhibitors can prevent the process of crystal growth or aggregation. Magnesium and citrate inhibit crystal aggregation. Nephrocalcin, an acidic glycoprotein made in the kidney, inhibits calcium oxalate nucleation, growth, and aggregation (Nakagawa et al, 1987; Asplin et al, 1991). Tamm-Horsfall mucoprotein, the most abundant protein in urine, inhibits aggregation (Hess et al, 1991), and uropontin inhibits crystal growth (Shiraga et al, 1992). Bikunin, the light chain of inter-alpha inhibitor, has been shown to be an efficient inhibitor of crystal nucleation and aggregation.

Opposing views regarding the formation and growth of crystal particles have led to controversy over the concept of free crystal particle growth versus fixed particle growth. Although it was initially concluded that free particle stone formation was impossible within the normal transit time through the nephron (Finlayson et al, 1978b), later recalculation using current nephron dimensions, supersaturation, and crystal growth rates determined that crystalline particles can be formed that are large enough to be retained during normal transit time through the kidney (Kok and Khan, 1994).

Fixed particle growth theory presupposes an anchoring site to which crystals bind, thereby prolonging the time the crystals are exposed to supersaturated urine and facilitating crystal growth and aggregation. A number of mechanisms have been proposed to account for crystal fixation. One favored theory proposes that oxalate-induced injury to renal tubular epithelial cells promotes adherence of calcium oxalate crystals (Miller et al, 2000). In animal models of stone formation in which administration of high oxalate loads leads to calcium oxalate crystal formation, elevated urinary levels of enzyme markers of cell injury, including N-acetyl-β-glucosidase and alkaline phosphatase, imply damage to renal tubular epithelial cells (Khan et al, 1992; Thamilselvan and Khan, 1998). Although the exact mechanism of oxalate-induced cell injury is not known, several studies have suggested that it is mediated by free radical formation (Thamilselvan and Khan, 1998; Thamilselvan et al, 1999). Not only are high concentrations of oxalate toxic to renal tubular cells, but calcium oxalate crystals themselves have also been shown to promote damage to cells (Khan et al, 1993, 1999; Thamilselvan and Khan, 1998; Thamilselvan et al, 1999). Despite these findings in animal models and in-vitro systems, **evidence for oxalate-induced tubular damage in humans has been lacking.** Indeed, Holmes and Assimos (2004) observed no increase in markers of oxidative stress or renal cell injury in normal individuals after ingestion of a large oxalate load, although the response in stone formers has not yet been determined.

How oxalate-induced renal tubular cell damage potentially promotes crystal retention is not known. Randall (1937) first observed areas of damage associated with subepithelial plaques on the renal papillae. Later, structural analyses in hyperoxaluric rats demonstrated crystals attached to the injured epithelium lining the collecting ducts (Khan, 1991). In-vitro studies confirmed increased binding of calcium oxalate crystals to injured renal epithelial cells in culture (Verkoelen et al, 1998). Whether the renal tubular cells or the interstitium constitutes the primary site of stone formation is unclear. Evidence of endocytosis of calcium oxalate crystals into renal tubular cells has been demonstrated in patients with disorders of oxalate metabolism (Saxon et al, 1974; Mandell et al, 1980; Lieske et al, 1992). Intracellular incorporation of these crystals could potentially lead to cell death and deposition of crystals in the interstitium, or transport of the crystals from the luminal to the basement membrane side could promote cell damage and subsequent erosion through to the papillary surface. Knoll and colleagues (2004) demonstrated in cell culture that oxalate-induced damage was more pronounced in renal nontubular compared with tubular cell lines and, further, that renal epithelial cells were more vulnerable to the toxic effects of oxalate on their basolateral side compared with their apical (luminal) side, implicating the interstitium as a possible site of primary stone formation.

In light of these recent findings, a number of investigators have revisited the role of Randall's plaques in the pathogenesis of stone formation. Low and Stoller (1997) mapped the papillae of patients undergoing endoscopic stone removal, as well as control subjects undergoing endoscopy for unrelated reasons, and found that papillary plaques occurred in 74% of stone formers compared with only 43% of control subjects. Stoller and colleagues (2004) hypothesized that the inciting event in the pathogenesis of stones may be vascular injury to the vasa recta near the renal papilla. Repair of damaged vessel walls could involve an atherosclerotic-like reaction that results in calcification of the endothelial wall, followed by erosion into the papillary interstitium and then into the collecting ducts, where it could serve as a nidus for stone formation.

Evan and coworkers presented an alternative view of the pathogenesis of stone formation based on extensive analysis of papillary plaques derived from biopsies obtained during percutaneous nephrolithotomy in idiopathic calcium oxalate stone formers. **They localized the origin of the plaque to the basement membrane of the thin limbs of the loops of Henle and demonstrated that the plaque subsequently extends through the medullary interstitium to a subepithelial location** (Fig. 42–3) (Evan et al, 2003). **Once these plaques, which are invariably composed of calcium apatite, erode through the urothelium, they constitute a stable, anchored surface on which calcium oxalate crystals can nucleate and grow as attached stones.** They further noted that among idiopathic calcium oxalate stone formers, the volume of papillary surface covered by plaque correlated negatively with urine volume and positively with hypercalciuria (Kuo et al, 2003a, 2003b) and the number of stones formed (Kim et al, 2005a), providing further corroborating clinical evidence for the sequence of events they proposed.

In contrast, **patients with enteric hyperoxaluria due to intestinal bypass for obesity demonstrated no plaque but did show apatite crystal deposits plugging the terminal collecting duct lumen and associated epithelial cell damage with inflammation and fibrosis of the interstitium** (Fig. 42–4) (Evan et al, 2003). Patients who form brushite stones were found to have intermediate pathology between the calcium oxalate stone formers and the intestinal bypass patients, demonstrating interstitial apatite plaque and apatite plugging of the terminal collecting ducts, along with associated collecting duct injury and interstitial fibrosis (Fig. 42–5) (Evan et al, 2005). The pathogenesis of brushite stones was postulated to occur by way of crystallization of apatite in the collecting duct, followed by collecting duct injury and cell death leading to enlarged collecting ducts, interstitial inflammation as a result of the injured cells, and, finally, progressive involvement of adjacent renal tissue.

The finding of distinct morphologic subtypes characterizing particular patient phenotypes is consistent with their divergent underlying pathophysiologic abnormalities and supports the role of both urine chemistry/state of saturation as well as local factors in the pathogenesis of stone formation.

## Inhibitors and Promoters of Crystal Formation

At the concentrations that most stone-forming salt components are present in urine, including calcium, oxalate, and phosphate, urine is supersaturated, thereby favoring crystal formation. However, **the presence of molecules that raise the supersaturation needed to initiate crystal nucleation or reduce the rate of crystal growth or aggregation prevents stone formation from occurring on a routine basis.** Although inhibitors have been identified for calcium oxalate and calcium phosphate, no specific inhibitors are known that affect uric acid crystallization.

Whole urine, when added to a solution of calcium phosphate, raises the supersaturation level required to initiate calcium phosphate crystallization (formation product) (Fleisch et al, 1962). Inorganic pyrophosphate was found to be responsible for 25% to 50% of the inhibitory activity of whole urine against calcium phosphate crystallization. By using different methodology, however, citrate, magnesium, and pyrophosphate together were noted to account for

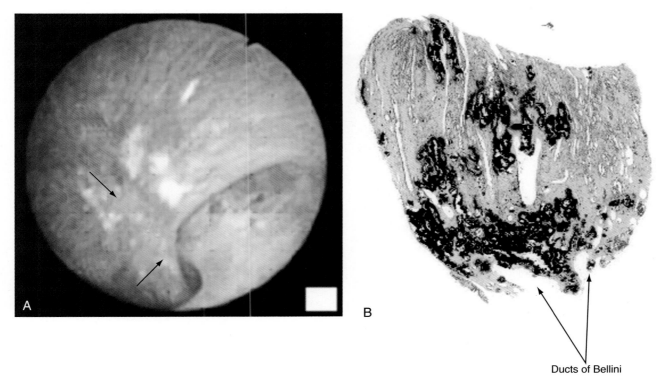

Ducts of Bellini

**Figure 42–3.** Endoscopic (**A**) and histologic (**B**) images of Randall's plaques in calcium oxalate patients. In **A**, sites of Randall's plaques *(arrows)* appear as irregular white areas beneath the urothelium. In **B**, a low-magnification light-microscopic image of a papillary biopsy specimen is shown. Sites of calcium deposits were stained black by the Yasue metal substitution method for calcium histochemistry. (From Evan AP, Lingeman JE, Coe FL, et al: Randall's plaque of patients with nephrolithiasis begins in basement membranes of thin loops of Henle. J Clin Invest 2003;111:607-616.)

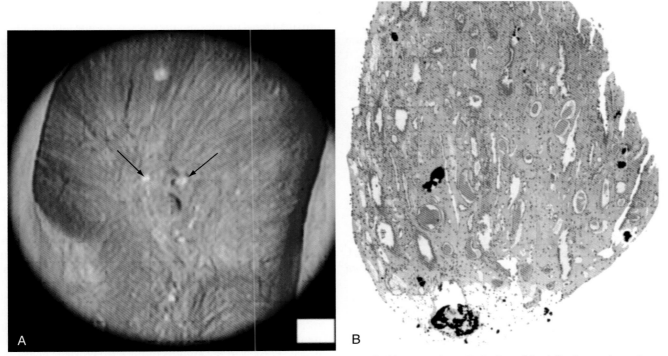

**Figure 42–4.** Endoscopic (**A**) and histologic (**B**) images of Randall's plaques in intestinal bypass patients. In **A**, sites of Randall's plaques *(arrows)* appear as irregular white areas beneath the urothelium. In **B**, a low-magnification light-microscopic image of a papillary biopsy specimen is shown. Sites of calcium deposits were stained black by the Yasue metal substitution method for calcium histochemistry. (From Evan AP, Lingeman JE, Coe FL, et al: Randall's plaque of patients with nephrolithiasis begins in basement membranes of thin loops of Henle. J Clin Invest 2003;111:607-616.)

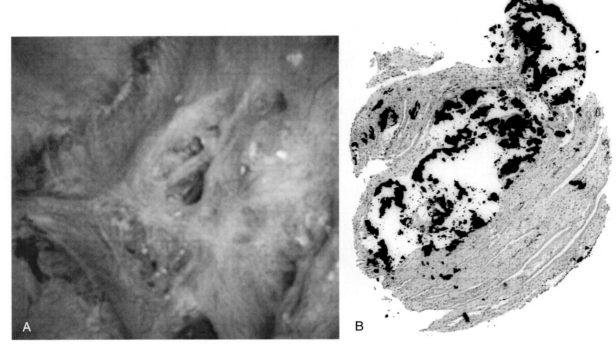

**Figure 42–5.** Endoscopic (**A**) and histologic (**B**) images of Randall's plaques in brushite patients. In **A**, sites of Randall's plaque appear as irregular white areas of crystalline deposit beneath the urothelium. In addition, a yellowish crystalline deposit is apparent at the opening of the ducts of Bellini. In **B**, a low-magnification light-microscopic image of a papillary biopsy specimen is shown. Sites of calcium deposits were stained black by the Yasue metal substitution method for calcium histochemistry. A large amount of Yasue-positive material is seen in the ducts of Bellini. (From Evan AP, et al: Kidney Int 2005;67:576-591.)

approximately 20% of the inhibitory activity of whole urine, with citrate comprising the most important factor of the three (Bisaz et al, 1978).

**Citrate acts as an inhibitor of calcium oxalate and calcium phosphate stone formation** by a variety of actions. First, it complexes with calcium, reducing the availability of ionic calcium to interact with oxalate or phosphate (Meyer et al, 1975; Pak et al, 1982). Second, it directly inhibits the spontaneous precipitation of calcium oxalate (Nicar et al, 1987) and prevents the agglomeration of calcium oxalate crystals (Kok et al, 1986). Although it has limited inhibitory effect on calcium oxalate crystal growth, it has more potent activity in reducing calcium phosphate growth (Meyer et al, 1975). Lastly, citrate prevents heterogeneous nucleation of calcium oxalate by monosodium urate (Pak and Peterson, 1986).

The inhibitory activity of magnesium is derived from its complexation with oxalate, which reduces ionic oxalate concentration and calcium oxalate supersaturation (Meyer et al, 1975). In addition, magnesium reduces the rate of calcium oxalate crystal growth in vitro (Desmars et al, 1973).

Polyanions, including glycosaminoglycans, acid mucopolysaccharides, and RNA have been shown to inhibit crystal nucleation and growth. Among the glycosaminoglycans, heparin sulfate interacts most strongly with calcium oxalate monohydrate crystals (Yamaguchi et al, 1993).

**Two urinary glycoproteins, nephrocalcin and Tamm-Horsfall glycoprotein, are potent inhibitors of calcium oxalate monohydrate crystal aggregation** (Nakagawa et al,

1987). Nephrocalcin is an acidic glycoprotein containing predominantly acidic amino acids that is synthesized in the proximal renal tubules and the thick ascending limb. In simple solution, nephrocalcin strongly inhibits the growth of calcium oxalate monohydrate crystals (Nakagawa et al, 1987). Nephrocalcin has been identified in four isoforms; non–stone formers excrete greater quantities of two isoforms associated with the most inhibitory activity, whereas stone formers excrete urine enriched for the two isoforms lacking inhibitory activity (Nakagawa, 1997). The isoforms with inhibitory activity were found to contain γ-carboxyglutamic acid residues that were lacking in the isoforms isolated from stone formers.

Tamm-Horsfall protein is expressed by renal epithelial cells in the thick ascending limb and the distal convoluted tubule as a membrane-anchored protein that is released into the urine after cleavage of the anchoring site by phospholipases or proteases. **Tamm-Horsfall is the most abundant protein found in the urine and a potent inhibitor of calcium oxalate monohydrate crystal aggregation, but not growth.** The role of Tamm-Horsfall as an inhibitor, promoter, or bystander is controversial and may depend on the state of the molecule itself, which can self-aggregate under certain conditions. A recent study using a Tamm-Horsfall (THP) knockout mouse model demonstrated spontaneous formation of calcium oxalate crystals in the kidneys of mice fed ethylene glycol and vitamin D, suggesting a protective role of Tamm-Horsfall protein against crystallization of calcium salts (Mo et al, 2004).

Osteopontin, or uropontin, is an acidic phosphorylated glycoprotein expressed in bone matrix and renal epithelial cells of the ascending limb of the loop of Henle and the distal tubule. **Osteopontin has been shown to inhibit nucleation, growth, and aggregation of calcium oxalate crystals as well as to reduce binding of crystals to renal epithelial cells in vitro** (Asplin et al, 1998; Wesson et al, 1998). In an osteopontin knockout mouse model, intratubular calcium oxalate crystals can be induced in mice exposed to high levels of oxalate by ethylene glycol feeding (Wesson et al, 2003). Interestingly, in a THP knockout mouse model, mice fed ethylene glycol and vitamin D exhibited a dramatic increase in osteopontin levels over baseline but still formed calcium oxalate crystals (Mo et al, 2004). The authors concluded that osteopontin may constitute an inducible inhibitor of calcium oxalate crystallization that works in conjunction with constitutively expressed Tamm-Horsfall protein to prevent crystallization.

Lastly, inter-α-trypsin is a glycoprotein synthesized in the liver that is composed of three polypeptides (two heavy chains and one light chain), of which bikunin comprises the light chain. Bikunin is a strong inhibitor of calcium oxalate crystallization, aggregation, and growth in vitro (Hochstrasser et al, 1984; Atmani et al, 1999), and its expression has been shown to be upregulated in a rat model when exposed to oxalate.

## Matrix

Renal calculi consist of both crystalline and noncrystalline components. The noncrystalline component is termed *matrix*, which typically accounts for about 2.5% of the weight of the stone (Boyce and Garvey, 1956). In some cases, matrix comprises the majority of the stone (up to 65%), usually in association with chronic urinary tract infection (Boyce and Garvey, 1956; Allen and Spence, 1966). The exact composition of matrix is difficult to ascertain because only 25% of it is soluble (Ryall, 1993); however, chemical analysis reveals a heterogeneous mixture consisting of 65% protein, 9% non-amino sugars, 5% glucosamine, 10% bound water, and 12% organic ash (Boyce, 1968). Among the proteins incorporated into the matrix substance are Tamm-Horsfall protein, nephrocalcin, a γ-carboxyglutamic acid–rich protein, renal lithostathine, albumin, glycosaminoglycans, free carbohydrates, and a mucoprotein called matrix substance A (Hess et al, 1996). Boyce and associates (1962) found that substance A is immunologically unique and present in the matrix component of all stone formers. Moore and Gowland (1975) determined that substance A is composed of three or four distinct antigens unique to stones that were detected in the urine of 85% of stone formers but in no normal individuals. The exact role of matrix in stone formation, whether as a promoter, an inhibitor, or a passive bystander has yet to be elucidated.

## MINERAL METABOLISM
## Calcium

Thirty to 40 percent of dietary calcium is absorbed from the intestine, with most being absorbed in the small intestine and only approximately 10% absorbed in the colon (Bronner et al,

1999). By a process of intestinal adaptation, absorption of calcium varies with calcium intake. At times of low calcium intake, fractional calcium absorption is enhanced; during high calcium intake, fractional calcium absorption is reduced. With a calcium-rich diet, a nonsaturable, paracellular pathway for calcium absorption predominates. A saturable, vitamin D–dependent transcellular pathway constitutes the major pathway for intestinal calcium absorption when calcium intake is limited; this pathway is downregulated by a diet replete in calcium (Buckley et al, 1980; Bronner et al, 1986). Because of the saturable component of calcium transport, a larger portion of calcium is absorbed when it is divided into several doses taken hours apart compared with a large single dose (Phang et al, 1968). A small amount of calcium is secreted into the lumen of the intestine, thereby reducing net calcium absorption, such that, overall, 100 to 300 mg of a total average calcium intake of 600 to 1200 mg daily will be absorbed.

Calcium is absorbed in the ionic state, and incomplete calcium absorption is due in part to formation of soluble calcium complexes in the intestinal lumen. **As such, substances that complex calcium such as phosphate, citrate, oxalate, sulfate, and fatty acids reduce the availability of ionic calcium for absorption** (Allen, 1982). Calcium readily complexes with phosphate in the intestinal lumen, but because calcium phosphate formation is dependent on pH (pK = 6.1), high luminal pH favors calcium phosphate complexation, thereby reducing calcium availability. On the other hand, calcium oxalate complex formation displays less pH dependence and complex formation is less reversible. Consequently, an oxalate-rich diet reduces calcium absorption. Transcellular calcium absorption is mediated by $1,25(OH)_2D_3$ (calcitriol), which is reported to enhance calcium permeability at the brush border of the intestinal epithelial cells (Fontaine et al, 1981).

**The active form of vitamin D, $1,25(OH)_2D_3$, is the most potent stimulator of intestinal calcium absorption.** After conversion of 7-dehydrocholesterol in the skin to previtamin $D_3$ promoted by sunlight, previtamin $D_3$ is hydroxylated in the liver to 25-hydroxyvitamin $D_3$, which is further hydroxylated in the proximal renal tubule to $1,25(OH)_2D_3$. The conversion of 25-hydroxyvitamin $D_3$ to $1,25(OH)_2D_3$ is stimulated by parathyroid hormone (PTH) and by hypophosphatemia. **A decrease in serum calcium increases secretion of PTH, which in turn directly stimulates the enzyme 1α-hydroxylase, which is located in the mitochondria of the proximal renal tubule.** After transport via the bloodstream to the intestine, $1,25(OH)_2D_3$, binds to the vitamin D receptor in the brush border membrane epithelial cells to enhance calcium absorption.

Calcitriol also acts on the bone and kidney in addition to its action in increasing calcium absorption from the intestine. In the bone, $1,25(OH)_2D_3$, along with PTH, promotes the recruitment and differentiation of osteoclasts that subsequently mobilize calcium from the bone. Consequently, the filtered load of calcium and phosphate increases. However, PTH increases renal calcium reabsorption and enhances phosphate excretion, leading to a net increase in serum calcium, which ultimately suppresses further PTH secretion and synthesis of $1,25(OH)_2D_3$.

PTH is critical in maintaining normal concentration of calcium in the extracellular fluid. PTH is an 84 amino acid protein that is the cleavage product of the precursor protein preproPTH. **Only mature PTH is secreted from the parathyroid gland, and the most potent stimulus for its secretion is a decrease in serum calcium** (Sherwood et al, 1968). PTH stimulates mobilization of calcium from bone through the action of osteoclasts, further raising serum calcium and phosphorus. The action of PTH is mediated through changes in cyclic adenosine monophosphate (AMP) and phospholipase C (Dunlay et al, 1990; Muff et al, 1992). **At the kidney, PTH enhances renal calcium reabsorption and reduces renal tubular reabsorption of phosphate.** It also stimulates synthesis of $1,25(OH)_2D_3$, which leads to enhanced intestinal calcium and phosphate absorption. PTH has no direct effect on intestinal calcium absorption.

## Phosphorus

Like calcium, inorganic phosphate absorption is dependent on both saturable, transcellular and nonsaturable, paracellular transport. At low phosphorus concentrations (1 to 3 mmol/L), saturable, absorptive transport occurs. At higher phosphorus levels, absorption increases without saturation (Walton et al, 1979). Approximately 60% of the phosphate in the diet is absorbed by the intestine. Active absorption of phosphate from the intestine involves a $1,25(OH)_2D_3$-regulated, sodium-dependent transport process (Danisi et al, 1980; Lee et al, 1986). Phosphate absorption is highly pH dependent; low luminal pH reduces phosphate transport, whereas high luminal pH enhances phosphate transport.

Approximately 65% of absorbed phosphate is excreted by the kidney and the remainder by the intestine. In normal healthy adults, 80% to 90% of the filtered load of phosphate is reabsorbed by the renal tubules and 10% to 20% is excreted in the urine. **Regulation of renal phosphate handling is primarily by way of PTH, which inhibits renal tubular reabsorption of filtered phosphate.**

## Magnesium

Magnesium is absorbed from the intestine by passive diffusion or active transport, although passive diffusion accounts for most of the net magnesium absorption. Magnesium is absorbed in both the large and small intestine, with the majority absorbed from the distal small intestine. Hormonal regulation of magnesium is primarily through vitamin D.

## Oxalate

Oxalate metabolism differs markedly from calcium metabolism. Whereas 30% to 40% of ingested calcium is absorbed from the intestine, only 6% to 14% of ingested oxalate is absorbed (Holmes et al, 1995; Hesse et al, 1999). Oxalate absorption occurs throughout the intestinal tract, with about half occurring in the small intestine and half in the colon (Holmes et al, 1995). Although oxalate absorption is difficult to measure directly, it has been estimated by urinary oxalate excretion. A recent study suggested that hyperoxaluric stone formers absorb more oxalate in response to an oral oxalate load than stone formers with normal oxalate excretion (Krishnamurthy et al, 2003). Likewise, in patients with small bowel disease or intestinal resection and an intact colon, oxalate absorption is markedly increased (Barilla et al, 1978a). Historically, the contribution of dietary oxalate to urinary oxalate was presumed to be no greater than 20%. However, Holmes and colleagues (2001) demonstrated that the relationship between ingested oxalate and urinary oxalate is curvilinear, owing to higher absorption of oxalate at low intake compared with high intake.

**A number of factors can influence oxalate absorption, including the presence of oxalate-binding cations such as calcium or magnesium and oxalate-degrading bacteria.** Co-ingestion of calcium and oxalate-containing foods leads to formation of a calcium oxalate complex, which limits the availability of free oxalate ion for absorption (Liebman and Chai, 1997; Hess et al, 1998). Oxalate-degrading bacteria, notably *Oxalobacter formigenes*, utilize oxalate as an energy source and consequently reduce intestinal oxalate absorption. Recent studies have demonstrated that stone formers have reduced levels or absent colonization with *Oxalobacter* compared with non–stone-forming control subjects, and those individuals lacking the bacteria have higher urinary oxalate levels (Sidhu et al, 1999; Mikami et al, 2003; Troxel et al, 2003). The contribution of *Oxalobacter* to the overall risk of stone formation is not fully understood at this time.

Absorbed oxalate is nearly completely excreted in the urine (Hodgkinson et al, 1974; Prenan et al, 1982). However, up to 80% of urinary oxalate is derived from endogenous production in the liver (40% from ascorbic acid, 40% from glycine) and 20% or more is derived from dietary sources. It is estimated that greater than 98% of oxalate is filterable, but oxalate reabsorption is negligible. However, there is evidence from a number of animal models of a secretory pathway for oxalate that likely resides in the proximal renal tubules (Cattell et al, 1962; Williams et al, 1971; Knight et al, 1981; Tremaine et al, 1985).

## KEY POINTS: MINERAL METABOLISM

- Calcium absorption occurs primarily in the small intestine at a rate that is dependent on calcium intake.

- 1,25-Dihydroxyvitamin $D_3$ is the most potent stimulator of intestinal calcium absorption.

- PTH stimulates $1\alpha$-hydroxylase in the proximal tubule of the kidney to convert 25-dihydroxyvitamin $D_3$ to $1,25(OH)_2D_3$.

- PTH enhances proximal tubular reabsorption of calcium and reduces renal phosphate excretion.

- Intestinal oxalate absorption is influenced by luminal calcium, magnesium, and oxalate-degrading bacteria.

# PATHOGENESIS OF UPPER URINARY TRACT CALCULI

## Classification of Nephrolithiasis

The most common component of urinary calculi is calcium, which is a major constituent in nearly 75% of stones. Calcium oxalate makes up about 60% of all stones; mixed calcium oxalate and hydroxyapatite, 20%; and brushite stones, 2%. Both uric acid and struvite (magnesium ammonium phosphate) stones occur approximately 10% of the time, whereas cystine stones are rare (1%) (Table 42–1) (Wilson, 1989). Stones associated with medications and their by-products such as triamterene, adenosine, silica, indinavir, and ephedrine are very uncommon and usually preventable.

Most classification systems for nephrolithiasis differentiate stones on the basis of the underlying metabolic or environ-

mental abnormalities with which they are associated (Table 42–2). A number of pathophysiologic derangements contribute to calcium stone formation either alone or in combination, including hypercalciuria (Zerwekh et al, 1988), hypocitraturia (Pak and Fuller, 1986; Pak, 1987; Coe et al, 1992; Bushinsky, 1998), hyperuricosuria, and hyperoxaluria. Uric acid, cystine, and struvite stones form in relatively unique settings: uric acid stones form only in an acid urine (Halabe et al, 1994; Asplin, 1996), cystine stones are the result of impaired renal reabsorption of cystine (Marshall et al, 1976; Stephens, 1989; Joly et al, 1999; Nakagawa et al, 2000), and infection stones occur in an alkaline urine produced by urease-producing bacteria (Marshall et al, 1976). For some stones, such as cystine, knowledge of the chemical composition of the stone may provide sufficient information to initi-

### Table 42–1. Stone Composition and Relative Occurrence

| Stone Composition | Occurrence (%) |
|---|---|
| *Calcium-Containing Stones* | |
| Calcium oxalate | 60 |
| Hydroxyapatite | 20 |
| Brushite | 2 |
| *Non–Calcium-Containing Stones* | |
| Uric acid | 7 |
| Struvite | 7 |
| Cystine | 1-3 |
| Triamterene | <1 |
| Silica | <1 |
| 2,8-Dihyroxyadenine | <1 |

From Pearle MS, Pak YC: Renal calculi: A practical approach to medical evaluation and management. In Andreucci VE, Fine LG (eds): International Yearbook of Nephrology. New York, Oxford University Press, 1996, pp 69-80, Table 7-1, p 69.

### Table 42–2. Diagnostic Classification of Nephrolithiasis

| Condition | Metabolic/Environmental Defect | Prevalence (%) |
|---|---|---|
| Absorptive hypercalciuria | | 20-40 |
| Type I | Increased gastrointestinal calcium absorption | |
| Type II | Increased gastrointestinal calcium absorption | |
| Renal phosphate leak | Impaired renal phosphorus absorption | |
| Renal hypercalciuria | Impaired renal calcium reabsorption | 5-8 |
| Resorptive hypercalciuria | Primary hyperparathyroidism | 3-5 |
| Hyperuricosuric calcium nephrolithiasis | Dietary purine excess, uric acid overproduction | 10-40 |
| Hypocitraturic calcium nephrolithiasis | | 10-50 |
| Isolated | Idiopathic | |
| Chronic diarrheal syndrome | Gastrointestinal alkali loss | |
| Distal renal tubular acidosis | Impaired renal acid excretion | |
| Thiazide-induced | Hypokalemia | |
| Hyperoxaluric calcium nephrolithiasis | | 2-15 |
| Primary hyperoxaluria | Oxalate overproduction | |
| Dietary hyperoxaluria | Increased dietary oxalate | |
| Enteric hyperoxaluria | Increased intestinal oxalate absorption | |
| Hypomagnesiuric calcium nephrolithiasis | Decreased intestinal magnesium absorption | 5-10 |
| Gouty diathesis | Low urinary pH | 15-30 |
| Cystinuria | Impaired renal cystine reabsorption | <1 |
| Infection stones | Infection with urease-producing bacteria | 1-5 |
| Low urine volume | Inadequate fluid intake | 10-50 |
| Miscellaneous or no abnormality | NA | <3 |

From Pearle MS, Pak CY: Renal calculi: A practical approach to medical evaluation and management. In Andreucci VE, Fine LG (eds): International Yearbook of Nephrology. New York, Oxford University Press, 1996, pp 69-80, Table 7-2, p 70.

ate appropriate therapy. However, due to the multiple causes associated with calcium-based stones, an understanding of the underlying metabolic disorders and environmental factors that predispose to stone formation is required to implement a rational treatment plan (Wall et al, 1988; Wall and Tiselius, 1990). Recent investigation into the molecular and genetic causes of stone formation may ultimately translate into newer treatment strategies (Frick et al, 2003; Langman, 2004).

## Calcium Stones

### Hypercalciuria

Hypercalciuria is the most common abnormality identified in calcium stone formers (Pak et al, 1982; Coe et al, 1992; Bushinsky, 1998). However, the role of hypercalciuria in stone formation is controversial, owing to the overlap in urine calcium levels between stone formers and non–stone formers (Robertson and Morgan, 1972; Coe et al, 1992). There are several lines of evidence that support a pathogenetic role for hypercalciuria in stone formation. First, hypercalciuria is common in stone-forming patients, occurring in 35% to 65% of patients (Coe and Kavalach, 1974; Menon, 1986). Indeed, treatment strategies aimed at reducing urinary calcium levels are associated with a reduction in stone recurrence rates (Yendt and Cohanim, 1978), and medical therapy often fails in patients with persistent hypercalciuria (Strauss et al, 1982). Studies on genetic hypercalciuric stone-forming rats have suggested that hypercalciuria and subsequent calcium phosphate supersaturation play a critical role in stone formation (Bushinsky et al, 2000). Lastly, recent investigations of Randall's plaques as potential precursors to calcium stone formation have shown that plaques occur more commonly in stone formers and their number is directly correlated with urine calcium levels and number of stone episodes (Kuo et al, 2003a; Kim et al, 2005b).

High urinary calcium concentrations lead to increased urinary saturation of calcium salts (Pak et al, 1976b) and reduced urinary inhibitory activity by way of complexation with negatively charged inhibitors such as citrate and chondroitin sulfate (Zerwekh et al, 1988). The normal kidney filters approximately 270 mmol of calcium daily and reabsorbs all but 4 mmol (Bushinsky, 1998). However, a variety of conditions lead to elevated urinary calcium levels and increased urinary saturation of calcium salts. Criteria defining hypercalciuria are variable, but **the strictest definition classifies hypercalciuria as greater than 200 mg of urinary calcium/day after adherence to a 400-mg calcium, 100-mg sodium diet for 1 week** (Menon, 1986). **Parks and Coe** (1986) **defined hypercalciuria as excretion of calcium of greater than 4 mg/kg/day or greater than 7 mmol/day (men) or 6 mmol/day (women).**

Historically, the term *idiopathic hypercalciuria* was applied to stone formers for whom classification of their metabolic abnormality was difficult. Calcium transport is regulated at three sites: intestine, bone, and kidney. Dysregulation at any of these sites can lead to hypercalciuria. Furthermore, calcium transport pathways may be interrelated; studies in genetic hypercalciuric rats have demonstrated that hypercalciuria may involve the dysregulation of multiple calcium transport systems (Frick et al, 2003). In 1974, Pak and colleagues divided hypercalciuria into three distinct subtypes based on unique pathophysiologic abnormalities: absorptive hypercalciuria due to increased intestinal absorption of calcium, renal hypercalciuria due to primary renal leak of calcium, and resorptive hypercalciuria due to increased bone demineralization (Pak et al, 1974).

Although this classification system is still widely utilized due to its utility in simplifying the understanding and treatment of specific metabolic derangements, many have argued that hypercalciuria is associated with multiple, interrelated disturbances that cannot be readily separated into a specific organ system (Coe et al, 1992). Furthermore, studies into the molecular mechanisms of stone formation have identified gene mutations that can affect several organ systems, culminating in hypercalciuria (Frick et al, 2003; Langman, 2004). Improved understanding of the molecular and genetic causes of stone disease may well change the categorization and management of stones in the future.

**Absorptive Hypercalciuria.** Absorptive hypercalciuria (AH) is defined by increased urinary calcium excretion (>0.2 mg/mg creatinine) after an oral calcium load. Although fasting urinary calcium is usually normal in AH (<0.11 mg/dL glomerular filtration), severe forms of AH may occasionally be associated with fasting hypercalciuria as well. The underlying pathophysiologic abnormality in AH is increased intestinal absorption of calcium, which occurs in approximately 55% of stone formers (Menon, 1986). AH is classified as type I when urinary calcium remains high despite a low calcium diet (400 mg dietary calcium daily) and type II when urinary calcium normalizes with a restricted calcium intake. **The added systemic load of calcium due to intestinal calcium hyperabsorption results in a transient increase in serum calcium, which suppresses serum PTH and results in increased renal filtration of calcium, ultimately leading to hypercalciuria. Because the increase in intestinal absorption of calcium is matched by enhanced renal calcium excretion, serum calcium level remains normal.**

**The cause of increased intestinal absorption of calcium has been variously ascribed to vitamin D–independent and dependent processes, as well as to upregulation of the vitamin D receptor** (Breslau et al, 1992). However, no proposed mechanism completely accounts for all the findings associated with absorptive hypercalciuria, and there is no clear evidence that upregulation of intestinal calcium absorption is the primary cause. However, hypersensitivity to vitamin D has been shown to increase intestinal calcium absorption (Bushinsky and Monk, 1998). Moreover, several studies have linked hypercalciuria with the vitamin D receptor (VDR) gene. Jackman and coworkers (1999) identified a polymorphism in the VDR gene in 19 patients with a family history of nephrolithiasis and hypercalciuria, thereby establishing a potential link. Likewise, Scott and colleagues (1999) identified linkage between a microsatellite marker and the VDR locus on chromosome 12q12-14 in a cohort of 47 French Canadian pedigrees with idiopathic hypercalciuria and calcium nephrolithiasis.

Other studies, however, failed to confirm the association of VDR abnormalities with hypercalciuria (Zerwekh et al, 1995, 1998). Indeed, other genetic loci have been identified in association with AH. Reed and colleagues (1999, 2002) mapped the locus for an inherited form of AH to chromosome

1q23.3-q24 and found a putative gene (subsequently shown by others to be homologous with the rat soluble adenylate cyclase gene) in this region in 12 unrelated white AH patients.

Another proposed etiology of AH is renal phosphate wasting leading to a subsequent increase in active vitamin D. Patients with hereditary hypophosphatemic rickets with hypercalciuria (HHRH) manifest this abnormality (Tieder et al, 1987). These patients manifest decreased renal reabsorption of phosphate and a subsequent increase in vitamin D levels, leading to enhanced absorption of calcium in the intestine. The mutations associated with HHRH are thought to be inherited in an autosomal recessive pattern. Renal phosphate leak, however, is a rare cause of nephrolithiasis, affecting only at best 2% to 4% of patients (Levy et al, 1995).

**Renal Hypercalciuria.** The kidney filters approximately 270 mmol of calcium and must reabsorb more than 98% of it to maintain calcium homeostasis (Bushinsky, 1998). Approximately 70% of calcium reabsorption occurs in the proximal tubule, with paracellular pathways predominating (Frick et al, 2003). In renal hypercalciuria, impaired renal tubular reabsorption of calcium results in elevated urinary calcium levels leading to secondary hyperparathyroidism (Coe et al, 1973). Serum calcium level remains normal because the renal loss of calcium is compensated by enhanced intestinal absorption of calcium and bone resorption as a result of increased secretion of PTH and enhanced synthesis of $1,25(OH)_2D_3$. **High fasting urinary calcium levels (>0.11 mg/dL glomerular filtration) with a normal serum calcium value are characteristic of renal hypercalciuria.** The elevated fasting urinary calcium and serum PTH levels differentiate renal from absorptive hypercalciuria.

Several lines of evidence support the existence of primary renal calcium leak. First, a subset of patients with fasting hypercalciuria and elevated PTH levels show no improvement in urinary calcium levels with ingestion of sodium cellulose phosphate (which binds intraluminal cations, including calcium) despite reduced intestinal calcium absorption (Pak and Galosy, 1979). Second, patients with renal hypercalciuria and secondary elevation in serum PTH have an exaggerated response to hydrochlorothiazide (HCTZ), implying a renal tubular defect in solute reabsorption (Sakhaee et al, 1985). In addition, calcium excretion was higher at baseline and the calciuric response to an oral glucose load (100 g) was significantly higher 3 hours after glucose ingestion in patients with renal hypercalciuria compared with AH patients and normal subjects (Barilla et al, 1978b).

The actual cause of renal calcium leak is not known, although various theories have been proposed involving renal injury, structural abnormalities, and functional defects (Sutton et al, 1980; Yendt et al, 1981). Excessive dietary sodium intake may lead to changes similar to those seen in patients with renal hypercalciuria (Breslau et al, 1982). However, Pak found that restricting sodium alone does not correct biochemical changes seen in patients with renal hypercalciuria (Pak, 1990).

Another theory implicates urine prostaglandins in the pathogenesis of renal hypercalciuria. Patients with hyperprostaglandin E syndrome/antenatal Bartter's syndrome typically exhibit renal salt wasting, hypercalciuria, nephrocalcinosis, and secondary hyperaldosteronism (Nusing et al, 2001). Administration of the cyclooxygenase-2 specific inhibitor nimesulide to patients with hyperprostaglandin E syndrome/antenatal Bartter's syndrome was shown to block renal prostaglandin $E_2$ synthesis, thereby relieving the hyperprostaglandinuria and secondary hyperaldosteronism and correcting the hypercalciuria (Nusing et al, 2001). Other studies have also supported the association of prostaglandin elevation with hypercalciuria and shown correction of hypercalciuria with prostaglandin inhibitors (Buck et al, 1981; Houser et al, 1984; Hasanoglu et al, 1997). Baggio and associates (2000) noted that patients with nephrolithiasis had significantly higher levels of plasma phospholipid arachidonic acid content, prostaglandin $E_2$, vitamin D, and urinary calcium compared with controls. Institution of a 30-day fish oil diet resulted in a reduction in plasma phospholipid arachidonic acid levels, and, with the exception of serum 25-dihydroxyvitamin $D_3$ levels, baseline blood and urinary parameters normalized, as did intestinal calcium absorption. Calo and colleagues (1990) also found that HCTZ, which is typically used to treat renal hypercalciuria, promoted a significant decrease in urinary prostaglandin $E_2$ levels.

New insights into the abnormalities associated with renal hypercalciuria have come from studies of several genetic disorders. Dent's disease (X-linked recessive nephrolithiasis), characterized by hypercalciuria, proteinuria, nephrolithiasis, and nephrocalcinosis, and X-linked hypophosphatemic rickets/osteomalacia (XLR) are both linked to defects in the CLC-5 chloride channel (Pook et al, 1993; Fisher et al, 1994; Lloyd et al, 1996; Igarashi et al, 1998). The gene for CLC-5 is associated with nine known voltage-gated, transmembrane-spanning chloride channels found in renal tubule and bone cells that are associated with diverse cellular functions, such as transepithelial transport, intravesicular acidification, volume regulation, and transmembrane potential homeostasis (Gunther et al, 1998; Langman, 2004). Although the exact mechanism by which loss of CLC-5 chloride channels results in hypercalciuria is not understood, it may involve abnormal regulation of vitamin D and PTH (Frick et al, 2003; Langman, 2004). DNA screening analysis for common hot spots in the CLCN5 gene is currently available commercially and may play a role in future genetic counseling if associated with one of the X-linked recessive disorders (Langman, 2004).

Bartter's syndrome is characterized by hypokalemic, hypochloremic metabolic alkalosis that arises from defects in one of three genes involving the thick ascending limb of the kidney: the $Na^+$-$K^+$-$2Cl^-$ gene NKCC2, the $K^+$ channel gene ROMK, or the chloride channel gene CLCNKB. Each of these mutations is associated with hypercalciuria and nephrolithiasis.

**Resorptive Hypercalciuria.** Resorptive hypercalciuria is an infrequent abnormality most commonly associated with primary hyperparathyroidism. Primary hyperparathyroidism is the cause of nephrolithiasis in about 5% of cases (Broadus, 1989). Excessive PTH secretion from a parathyroid adenoma leads to excessive bone resorption and increased renal synthesis of $1,25(OH)_2D_3$, which in turn enhances intestinal absorption of calcium; the net effect is elevated serum and urine calcium levels and reduced serum phosphorus levels. Although most patients with primary hyperparathyroidism demonstrate hypercalcemia and hypercalciuria, a normal serum calcium level in the presence of an inappropriately high serum PTH value may be seen in some cases, making the diagnosis more difficult. Administration of a thiazide diuretic will enhance renal calcium reabsorption and exacerbate the hypercalcemia, thereby facilitating the diagnosis ("thiazide challenge") (Coffey et al, 1977). When diagnosing primary hyperparathyroidism, other causes of hypercalcemia should be excluded.

Primary hyperparathyroidism is associated with nephrolithiasis in less than 5% of affected individuals (Heath et al, 1980; Parks et al, 1980). However, the diagnosis should be suspected in patients with nephrolithiasis and serum calcium levels greater than 10.1 mg/dL (Broadus et al, 1980; Menon, 1986). Serum calcium levels can vary by up to 5%, and patients with mild hyperparathyroidism may exhibit relatively small increases of serum calcium (Yendt and Gagne, 1968). As such, repeated measurements of serum calcium may be necessary to make the diagnosis. Measurement of serum ionized calcium may help in equivocal cases, because it may be elevated in the setting of normal serum calcium (Yendt and Gagne, 1968). Urinary cyclic AMP levels have been used to diagnose primary hyperparathyroidism, because PTH promotes release of cyclic AMP from the kidney, leading to increased urinary cyclic AMP levels (Broadus et al, 1980). However, this test has been largely abandoned in favor of direct measurement of serum PTH. PTH also increases excretion of bicarbonate and phosphorus from the proximal renal tubule, resulting in phosphaturia and mild hyperchloremic acidosis. Aro and colleagues (1977) noted that a serum chloride:phosphate ratio greater than 33, along with a phosphate level below 2.5 mg/dL, should raise suspicion of hyperparathyroidism.

*Sarcoid and Granulomatous Disease.* Additional, rare causes of resorptive hypercalciuria include hypercalcemia of malignancy, sarcoidosis, thyrotoxicosis, and vitamin D toxicity. Many granulomatous diseases including tuberculosis, sarcoidosis, histoplasmosis, leprosy, and silicosis have been reported to produce hypercalcemia. Among these, sarcoidosis is most commonly associated with urolithiasis. **The sarcoid granuloma produces $1,25(OH)_2D_3$, causing increased intestinal absorption of calcium, hypercalcemia, and hypercalciuria** (Hendrix, 1966; Bell et al, 1979). Pulmonary alveolar cells and lymph node homogenates in patients with sarcoidosis are capable of synthesizing vitamin D, a function usually limited to the kidney. Most patients with sarcoidosis have a suppressed level of PTH secondary to hypercalcemia (Cushard et al, 1972). Sarcoidosis can also be differentiated from other diagnoses by the rapid resolution of hypercalcemia with initiation of corticosteroid therapy (Breslau et al, 1982).

*Malignancy-Associated Hypercalcemia.* **Whereas primary hyperparathyroidism is the most common cause of hypercalcemia in an outpatient setting, malignancy is the main cause of hypercalcemia in hospitalized patients** (Rizzoli and Bonjour, 1992). An assay for intact PTH can help distinguish patients with hyperparathyroidism from those with other causes of hypercalcemia (Table 42–3) (Burtis et al, 1990). Tumors in patients with humoral hypercalcemia produce a PTH-related protein (PTHrP) (Burtis et al, 1990). Lung and breast cancers account for about 60% of malignancy-associated hypercalcemia, whereas renal cell (10% to 15%), head and neck (10%), and hematologic cancers such as lymphoma and myeloma (10%) account for the rest. While direct mechanical destruction of bone constitutes one cause of hypercalcemia, many tumors secrete humoral factors, including PTHrP, transforming growth factor-α, and cytokines such as interleukin-1 and tumor necrosis factor, which activate osteoclasts and result in bone lysis and hypercalcemia (Burtis et al, 1990; Mundy, 1990; Edelson et al, 1995).

*Glucocorticoid-Induced Hypercalcemia.* Glucocorticoids can significantly alter calcium metabolism through their actions on bone, intestine, and parathyroid glands. Their most potent effect is related to calcium metabolism in bones, where

### Table 42–3. Hypercalcemic States

| Condition | Parathyroid Hormone | Phosphorus | Urine Calcium | Glomerular Filtration Rate | Other |
|---|---|---|---|---|---|
| Thiazide | N | N | L | N | Low $K^+$ |
| Malignant tumors | NLH | L/N | H | N/L | Osteolytic or sclerotic bone lesions |
| Vitamin D excess | L | N/H | H | N/L | |
| Sarcoidosis | L | N | H | N/L | High $1,25(OH)_2D_3$ |
| Coccidioidomycosis | L | N | H | N/L | High $1,25(OH)_2D_3$ |
| Silicosis | L | N | H | N/L | High $1,25(OH)_2D_3$ |
| Plasma cell granuloma | N | N | — | L | High $1,25(OH)_2D_3$ |
| Leprosy | N | N | H | L | High $1,25(OH)_2D_3$ |
| Hypothyroidism | N | N | H | N | High $1,25(OH)_2D_3$ |
| Primary increase in $1,25(OH)_2D_3$ | L | N | H | N | High $1,25(OH)_2D_3$ |
| Pheochromocytoma | L/N | N | H | N | High $1,25(OH)_2D_3$ |
| Hyperthyroidism | N | N | L/N | N | High calcitonin has been reported |
| Tuberculosis | L | H | H | L | |
| Addison's disease | N | N | L/N | N | |
| Familial hypocalciuric hypercalcemia | H | N | N | N | |
| Lithium | N | — | — | — | Asymptomatic |
| Theophylline | L | N | H | N | |
| Paget's disease | L | N | H | N | |
| Immobilization | L | L/N | — | — | |
| Acquired immunodeficiency syndrome | | | | | Usually only hypercalciuric Low $1,25(OH)_2D_3$ |

H, high; L, low; N, normal; $1,25(OH)_2D_3$, 1,25-dihydroxyvitamin $D_3$.
From Coe FL, Park JH (eds): Nephrolithiasis: Pathogenesis and Treatment. Chicago, Year Book Medical Publishers, 1988, p 85.

glucocorticoids promote bone resorption and reduce bone formation, ultimately leading to osteopenia with chronic use (Manelli and Giustina, 2000). Additionally, they stimulate release of PTH (Fucik et al, 1975). On the other hand, glucocorticoids inhibit intestinal absorption of calcium, which accounts for their effectiveness in preventing hypercalciuria induced by sarcoidosis (Manelli and Giustina, 2000). The net effect probably favors promotion of stone formation because nephrolithiasis is common in patients with Cushing's syndrome (Faggiano et al, 2003). In one study, stones were found in 50% of patients with active Cushing's syndrome, 27% of cured patients, and 6.5% of controls. Compared with controls, patients with active disease had a significantly higher prevalence of hypercalciuria, hypocitraturia, and hyperuricosuria, but these patients were also at greater risk of obesity and diabetes, which have been linked to stone formation (Faggiano et al, 2003).

## Hyperoxaluria

Hyperoxaluria, defined as urinary oxalate greater than 40 mg/day, leads to increased urinary saturation of calcium oxalate and subsequent promotion of calcium oxalate stones. Additionally, oxalate has been implicated in crystal growth and retention by means of renal tubular cell injury mediated by lipid peroxidation and the generation of oxygen free radicals (Ravichandran and Selvam, 1990). Membrane injury facilitates the fixation of calcium oxalate crystals and subsequent crystal growth. Antioxidant therapy has been shown to prevent calcium oxalate precipitation in the rat kidney and to

reduce oxalate excretion in stone patients (Selvam, 2002). Similarly, calcium oxalate crystal deposition on urothelium in vitro was prevented by free radical scavengers such as phytic acid and mannitol, purportedly by protecting the membrane from free radical–mediated damage (Thamilselvan and Selvam, 1997; Selvam, 2002). Recent human studies, however, failed to demonstrate increases in markers of oxidative stress or renal injury in normal subjects ingesting large doses of oxalate (up to 8 mmol), thus calling into question the importance of oxalate-induced cell membrane damage in calcium oxalate stone formation (Holmes and Assimos, 2004).

**Causes of hyperoxaluria include disorders in biosynthetic pathways (primary hyperoxaluria); intestinal malabsorptive states associated with inflammatory bowel disease, celiac sprue, or intestinal resection (enteric hyperoxaluria); and excessive dietary intake or high substrate levels (vitamin C) (dietary hyperoxaluria).**

**Primary Hyperoxaluria.** Primary hyperoxaluria is the result of a rare autosomal recessive disorder in glyoxylate metabolism by which the normal conversion of glyoxylate to glycine is prevented, leading to preferential oxidative conversion of glyoxylate to oxalate, an end product of metabolism (Fig. 42–6). Consequently, markedly high levels of urinary oxalate ensue (>100 mg/day), leading to increased saturation of calcium oxalate, aggressive stone formation, and marked nephrocalcinosis. The primary enzyme catalyzing glyoxylate conversion to glycine is alanine glyoxylate aminotransferase (AGT), which is synthesized in the liver. Mutations in this gene result in primary hyperoxaluria type 1. Elucidation of the

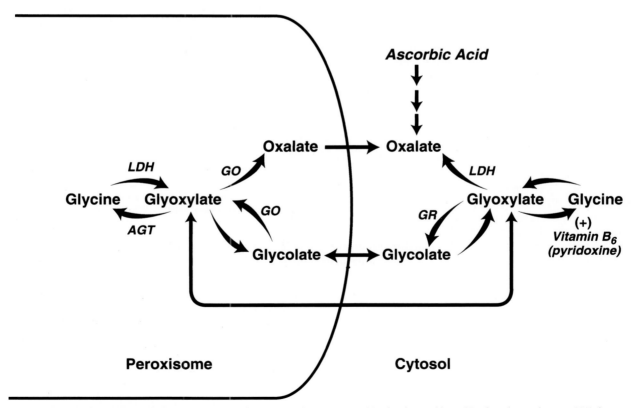

**Figure 42–6.** Pathway of oxalate metabolism. AGT, alanine:glyoxylate aminotransferase; GO, glycolate oxidase; GR, glyoxylate reductase; LDH, lactate dehydrogenase. (From Ruml LA, Pearle MS, Pak CYC: Medical therapy—calcium oxalate-nephrolithiasis. Urol Clin North Am 1997;24:117-133.)

crystal structure of AGT to 2.5A° has improved our understanding of mutations of this protein (Zhang et al, 2003). The most common mutation of the AGT gene *(AGXT)* results in a substitution of glycine by arginine at position 170, which results in failure of the enzyme to dimerize, thereby causing the enzyme to inappropriately target the liver mitochondria rather than the liver peroxisomes (Danpure et al, 2003). In-vitro experiments have shown that by varying the temperature in the presence of glycerol, the enzyme can be induced to dimerize correctly, thus becoming completely functional (Lumb et al, 2003). Other mutations result in accelerated AGT proteolysis, intraperoxisomal aggregation, and loss of catalytic activity (Langman, 2004). Improved understanding of these mutations may allow for rational treatment strategies using small molecule chaperones or ribozyme-based therapeutics (Langman, 2004). Primary hyperoxaluria type 2 is associated with a mutation in glyoxylate reductase *(GRHPR* gene) in the liver, resulting in hyperoxaluric nephrolithiasis, but with a less aggressive course with regard to renal failure (Johnson et al, 2002).

If untreated, primary hyperoxaluria inevitably leads to end-stage renal failure, which occurs by age 15 in 50% of affected patients and is associated with an overall death rate of approximately 30% (Cochat et al, 1999). Because the liver is the only organ responsible for the detoxification of glyoxylate, combined liver-kidney transplant is accepted treatment for most patients with severe primary hyperoxaluria. Patient survival after transplantation approximates 80% at 5 years and 70% at 10 years. Furthermore, the renal function of survivors reportedly remains stable over time (Cochat et al, 1999; Hoppe and Langman, 2003).

**Enteric Hyperoxaluria.** The most common cause of acquired hyperoxaluria is enteric hyperoxaluria. This abnormality is associated with chronic diarrheal states, by which **fat malabsorption results in saponification of fatty acids with divalent cations such as calcium and magnesium, thereby reducing calcium oxalate complexation and increasing the pool of available oxalate for reabsorption** (Earnest et al, 1975). The poorly absorbed fatty acids and bile salts may increase colonic permeability to oxalate, further enhancing intestinal oxalate absorption (Dobbins et al, 1976). There is a strong relationship between fecal fat and urinary oxalate excretion, which has been demonstrated in patients with steatorrhea (Fig. 42–7) (Andersson, 1974; Dobbins et al, 1977; McDonald et al, 1977; Stauffer, 1977; Modigliani et al, 1978). Dehydration, hypokalemia, hypomagnesuria, hypocitraturia, and low urine pH also increase the risk of calcium oxalate stone formation in patients with chronic diarrheal syndrome. Malabsorption of any cause can lead to increased intestinal absorption of oxalate. As such, small bowel resection (Smith et al, 1972), intrinsic disease, and jejunoileal bypass (Cryer et al, 1975) have all been associated with hyperoxaluria.

**Dietary Hyperoxaluria.** Overindulgence in oxalate-rich foods such as nuts, chocolate, brewed tea, spinach, broccoli, strawberries, and rhubarb can result in hyperoxaluria in otherwise normal patients. Increased animal protein can also increase urinary levels of calcium and oxalate (Robertson et al, 1979). In addition, severe calcium restriction may result in reduced intestinal binding of oxalate and increased intestinal oxalate absorption. Ascorbic acid supplementation has

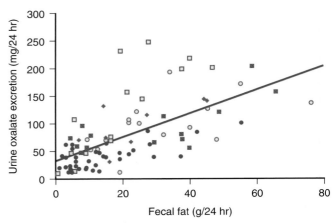

**Figure 42–7.** The relationship between fecal fat and urinary oxalate excretion in patients with steatorrhea. Diet oxalate was 300-500 mg/day in all but one study in which it was 55-90 mg/day; diet calcium 500-900 mg/day in all studies when reported. Normal urine citrate was less than 50 mg/day in all studies, except one in which it was <34 mg/day. Oxalate = 2.1 × fecal fat + 30.7 ($r^2$ = 0.4, n = 96, P < .001). (From Worcester EM: Stones due to bowel disease. In Coe F, Favus M, Pak C, et al [eds]: Kidney Stones: Medical and Surgical Management. New York, Lippincott-Raven, 1996, pp 883-903.)

been shown to increase urinary oxalate levels by in vivo conversion to oxalate (Traxer et al, 2003), although increased clinical rates of stone formation have not been unequivocally linked to ascorbic acid use (Curhan et al, 1996, 1999).

Recent studies have also implicated *Oxalobacter formigenes,* an oxalate-degrading intestinal bacterium, as a potential modulator of intestinal oxalate levels and decreased oxalate absorption in some stone formers (Duncan et al, 2002). Several studies have linked the absence of *Oxalobacter formigenes* with increased stone formation (Sidhu et al, 2001; Mikami et al, 2003) and increased oxalate excretion in stone formers (Troxel et al, 2003).

**Idiopathic Hyperoxaluria.** Several studies have suggested that mild hyperoxaluria is as important a factor as hypercalciuria in the pathogenesis of idiopathic calcium oxalate stones (Menon, 1986; Robertson et al, 1993). In some populations such as those inhabiting the Arabian Peninsula, the prevalence of calcium-containing stones is considerably higher than in the West despite the almost complete absence of hypercalciuria (Robertson and Hughes, 1993). Hyperoxaluria is implicated as the predominant risk factor in this population.

Abnormalities in the metabolism and transport of oxalate may contribute to calcium oxalate nephrolithiasis. Baggio and associates (1986) detected a higher rate of oxalate flux across the red blood cell membrane at steady state in 114 patients with a history of calcium oxalate kidney stones compared with control subjects. Treatment with oral HCTZ (50 mg/day), amiloride (5 mg/ day), or both restored normal or nearly normal red blood cell oxalate exchange in all of the patients who initially demonstrated increased rates. Up to 50% of the time, however, the abnormality in red blood cell oxalate transport is not associated with hyperoxaluria. Furthermore, Motola and colleagues found high rates of oxalate flux in non–calcium oxalate stone formers as well, thus leading some to question the importance of this mechanism in calcium oxalate stone formation (Motola et al, 1992).

## Hyperuricosuria

Hyperuricosuria is defined by urinary uric acid exceeding 600 mg/day. Up to 10% of calcium stone formers have high urinary uric acid levels as the only abnormality (Menon, 1986). Hyperuricosuria increases urinary levels of monosodium urate, which in turn promotes calcium oxalate stone formation. At pH less than 5.5, the undissociated form of uric acid predominates, leading to uric acid and/or calcium oxalate stone formation. **At pH greater than 5.5, sodium urate formation promotes calcium oxalate stone formation through heterologous nucleation** (Grover et al, 1994). Uric acid may reduce the effectiveness of naturally occurring inhibitors of crystallization (Robertson et al, 1976); **uric acid crystals can bind urinary glycosaminoglycans such as heparin that inhibit crystallization of calcium oxalate** (Finlayson et al, 1978a; Grover et al, 1994). Several studies have shown that patients with hyperuricosuria and calcium stones have higher rates of stone formation and more severe symptoms than those stone formers with normouricosuria (Coe and Kavalach, 1974; Favus et al, 1980; Fellstrom et al, 1982).

The most common cause of hyperuricosuria is increased dietary purine intake. However, acquired and hereditary diseases may also be accompanied by hyperuricosuria, including gout, myeloproliferative and lymphoproliferative disorders, multiple myeloma, secondary polycythemia, pernicious anemia, hemolytic disorders, hemoglobinopathies and thalassemia, complete or partial hypoxanthine-guanine phosphoribosyltransferase deficiency, superactivity of phosphoribosylpyrophosphate synthetase, and hereditary renal hypouricemia (Halabe and Sperling, 1994). The recent identification of a urate transporter in the proximal tubule, the anion exchanger URAT1, may provide new insight into the causes of hyperuricosuria (Enomoto et al, 2002; Ichida et al, 2004). Mutations in the gene coding for URAT1, *SLC22A12*, have been shown to cause hyperuricosuric hypouricemia, or renal uric acid leak (Enomoto et al, 2002; Ichida et al, 2004; Iwai et al, 2004).

Another potential gene abnormality, characterized by an increased prevalence of uric acid stones, has been identified in a small, isolated founder population in Sardinia. A susceptibility locus was identified on chromosome 10q21-q22 that codes for a protein with unknown function but that has a strong association with uric acid stones (Ombra et al, 2001; Gianfrancesco et al, 2003).

## Hypocitraturia

**Hypocitraturia is an important and correctable abnormality associated with nephrolithiasis that exists as an isolated abnormality in up to 10% of calcium stone formers and is associated with other abnormalities in 20% to 60%** (Menon and Mahle, 1983; Pak and Fuller, 1986; Pak, 1994; Pak et al, 1985; Levy et al, 1995). Citrate is an important inhibitor that can reduce calcium stone formation by several mechanisms. First, citrate reduces urinary saturation of calcium salts by complexing with calcium (Pak et al, 1982). Second, citrate directly prevents spontaneous nucleation of calcium oxalate (Sakhaee et al, 1987). Third, citrate inhibits agglomeration and sedimentation of calcium oxalate crystals (Kok et al, 1986;

Tiselius et al, 1993a, 1993b) as well as the growth of calcium oxalate and calcium phosphate crystals (Meyer and Smith, 1975). Finally, normal urinary citrate levels can enhance the inhibitory effect of Tamm-Horsfall glycoprotein (Hess et al, 1993).

Hypocitraturia is defined as a urinary citrate level less than 320 mg/day (Pak, 1987) or less than 0.6 mmol (men) or 1.03 mmol (women) daily (Menon and Mahle, 1983). **Acid-base state is the primary determinant of urinary citrate excretion. Metabolic acidosis reduces urinary citrate levels secondary to enhanced renal tubular reabsorption and decreased synthesis of citrate in peritubular cells** (Jenkins et al, 1985). A study comparing normal subjects and stone formers noted comparable mean serum citrate levels and filtered citrate loads in the two groups; however, 24-hour urinary citrate and fasting citrate:creatinine ratio were significantly reduced and mean tubular reabsorption of citrate was significantly increased in the stone formers compared with control subjects (Minisola et al, 1989).

Indirect evidence for a primarily renal etiology of hypocitraturia comes from a study comparing intestinal absorption of citrate in idiopathic hypocitraturic stone formers and normal subjects (Fegan et al, 1992). Oral ingestion of citrate was followed by rapid and efficient absorption in both groups, with 96% to 98% absorbed within 3 hours. As such, hypocitraturia is unlikely to arise from impaired gastrointestinal absorption of citrate in stone formers without overt bowel disease.

Low urinary citrate results from a variety of pathologic states associated with acidosis. Distal renal tubular acidosis (RTA) is characterized by high urine pH (>6.8), high serum chloride, and low serum bicarbonate and potassium (Preminger et al, 1985). The inability to acidify urine in response to an oral acid (ammonium chloride) load confirms the diagnosis of RTA. Chronic diarrheal states cause intestinal alkali loss in the stool with subsequent systemic acidosis and hypocitraturia (Rudman et al, 1980). Excessive animal protein can provide an acid load, reducing citrate levels (Breslau et al, 1988). Indeed, a recent metabolic study evaluating the effect of a high protein, low carbohydrate diet demonstrated a significant reduction in urinary citrate and pH, likely as a result of low citrus and high animal protein intake (Reddy et al, 2002). Diuretics such as thiazides induce hypokalemia and intracellular acidosis (Nicar et al, 1984). Enalapril can cause hypocitraturia independently of systemic acidosis or hypokalemia perhaps due to intracellular acidosis (Melnick et al, 1998). Finally, strenuous exercise may induce lactic acidosis (Sakhaee et al, 1987). However, hypocitraturia may also represent an isolated abnormality unrelated to an acidotic state.

Citrate levels in the urine increase in alkalotic states, as well as with elevated levels of PTH, estrogen, growth hormone, and vitamin D.

### Low Urine pH

At low urine pH (<5.5), the undissociated form of uric acid predominates, leading to uric acid and/or calcium stone formation. Calcium oxalate stones form as a result of heterologous nucleation with uric acid crystals (Coe and Kavalach, 1974; Pak et al, 1976a). Any disorder leading to low urine pH may predispose to stone formation. Chronic metabolic acidosis can lead to low urine pH, hypercalciuria, and hypocitraturia. Acidosis increases bone resorption and produces renal calcium leak (Lemann, 1999; Lemann et al, 2003). "Gouty diathesis" refers to a stone-forming propensity characterized by low urine pH of unknown etiology with or without associated gouty arthritis (Levy et al, 1995).

## Renal Tubular Acidosis

**RTA is a clinical syndrome characterized by metabolic acidosis resulting from defects in renal tubular hydrogen ion secretion and urinary acidification.** There are three types of RTA: 1, 2, and 4. Type 1 (distal) RTA is of particular significance to urologists not only because it is the most common form of RTA but also because it is the form of RTA most frequently associated with stone formation, which occurs in up to 70% of affected individuals (Van den Berg et al, 1983; Caruana et al, 1988). Indeed, symptoms associated with nephrolithiasis lead to the initial diagnosis of RTA in upward of 50% of cases (Van den Berg et al, 1983).

Acid-base balance is maintained by the kidney through several mechanisms involving both the proximal and distal nephron. Because bicarbonate is freely filtered at the glomerulus, the **kidney must reabsorb or regenerate nearly all of the filtered bicarbonate each day** (approximately 4500 mmol) to maintain its buffering capacity (Pohlman et al, 1984). **Furthermore, the kidney must excrete excess acid,** which accumulates from the breakdown of carbohydrates, fats, and proteins and as a result of bicarbonate loss in the stool (Kinkead et al, 1995). A defect in either bicarbonate reabsorption or acid excretion will lead to metabolic acidosis.

Filtered bicarbonate ($HCO_3^-$) is almost completely reabsorbed in the proximal renal tubule through an indirect mechanism (Laing et al, 2005). As sodium ($Na^+$) is pumped out of the proximal tubule cell by the $Na^+/K^+$-ATPase exchanger located in the basolateral membrane, intracellular sodium decreases, driving the $Na^+/H^+$ exchanger in the apical membrane. Carbonic anhydrase in the tubular cells generates $H^+$ and $HCO_3^-$, thereby providing $H^+$ ions that are secreted into the tubular lumen. $HCO_3^-$ is then transferred via a basolateral $Na^+/HCO_3^-$ co-transporter (Unwin et al, 2002). **The proximal nephron is a high-capacity, low-gradient transport system that allows reabsorption of filtered $HCO_3^-$ without causing net $H^+$ secretion or significant changes in urinary pH** (Rocher and Tannen, 1986; Kinkead et al, 1995).

In the distal nephron, 10% to 20% of the filtered bicarbonate is reabsorbed in a similar manner as in the proximal nephron. Net elimination of $H^+$ occurs through several mechanisms. **Hydrogen binds with urinary buffers such as phosphate and ammonia, allowing net elimination of hydrogen in the form of $NH_4^+$. Net $H^+$ excretion occurs through active secretion from $\alpha$-intercalated cells.** These cells secrete $H^+$ using an $H^+$ ATPase and an $H^+/K^+$ ATPase exchanger (Laing et al, 2005). The intercalated cells also have a $Cl^-/HCO_3^-$ anion exchanger that transports $HCO_3^-$ into the blood and is homologous to the red cell anion exchanger known as "band 3" (eAE1) (Alper, 1991; Shayakul et al, 2004a, 2004b). **These active pumps generate a 1000:1 hydrogen ion gradient between the cell and the tubular lumen, allowing reduction of urine pH to as low as 4.5** (Kinkead et al, 1995). Another contributing factor is the lack of luminal carbonic anhydrase

that prevents the rapid dissociation of carbonic acid catalyzed by the enzyme.

**RTA occurs as a result of impairment of net excretion of acid into the urine (type 1) or of reabsorption of bicarbonate (type 2)** (Kinkead et al, 1995). Distinction between these abnormalities provides the means for classification of RTA into proximal or distal, although both share the characteristic findings of hyperchloremic metabolic acidosis associated with inappropriately high urinary pH.

**Type 1 (Distal) RTA.** Type 1 RTA comprises a syndrome of **abnormal collecting duct function characterized by inability to acidify the urine in the presence of systemic acidosis.** The classic findings include hypokalemic, hyperchloremic, non–anion gap metabolic acidosis along with nephrolithiasis, nephrocalcinosis, and elevated urine pH (>6.0) (Pohlman et al, 1984). Patients with incomplete RTA have normal serum electrolytes but demonstrate defective renal acid excretion manifest as failure to lower urine pH below 5.5 after an acid load (Osther et al, 1989).

Patients with distal RTA commonly present as adults with symptoms of nephrolithiasis (Caruana et al, 1988). However, children comprise a third of affected individuals, and they often present with vomiting or diarrhea, failure to thrive, or growth retardation. The most common type of stone associated with distal RTA is calcium phosphate as a result of **hypercalciuria, hypocitraturia, and increased urinary pH** (Fig. 42–8) (Van den Berg et al, 1983; Pohlman et al, 1984). The metabolic acidosis promotes bone demineralization, which leads to secondary hyperparathyroidism and hypercalciuria. **Profound hypocitraturia, perhaps the most important factor in stone formation, is due to impaired citrate excretion as a result of metabolic acidosis,** but may also be related to abnormal renal tubular citrate transport or migration of citrate into the mitochondria due to intracellular acidosis (Kinkead et al, 1995; Osther et al, 1989).

Type 1 RTA is a heterogeneous disorder that may be hereditary, idiopathic, or acquired. Most cases of distal RTA are sporadic, but both autosomal dominant (AD) and autosomal recessive (AR) genetic defects have been identified. Most mutations associated with distal RTA occur in either the $Cl^-/HCO_3^-$ anion exchanger (*SLC4A1* gene) or the $H^+$ ATPase (gene *ATP6V0A4*) (Laing et al, 2005). RTA is endemic in Southeast Asia, where it has been associated with sudden unexplained nocturnal death, hypokalemic periodic paralysis, and renal stones (Nimmannit et al, 1991, 1996). RTA in this population was found to be associated with *SLC4A1* AR mutations (Sritippayawan et al, 2004).

**The molecular defects associated with distal RTA include abnormalities in the $H^+$ ATPase that are responsible for excretion of excess acid into the distal tubule** (Karet et al, 1999). Early childhood features of autosomal recessive distal RTA include severe metabolic acidosis with inappropriately alkaline urine, poor growth, rickets, and renal calcification. Secondary distal RTA in sporadic cases is commonly associated with autoimmune diseases, such as Sjögren's syndrome and systemic lupus erythematosus, and it occurs more frequently in women than men (Buckalew, 1989). Secondary RTA is also associated with obstructive uropathy, pyelonephritis, acute tubular necrosis, hyperparathyroidism, and idiopathic hypercalciuria.

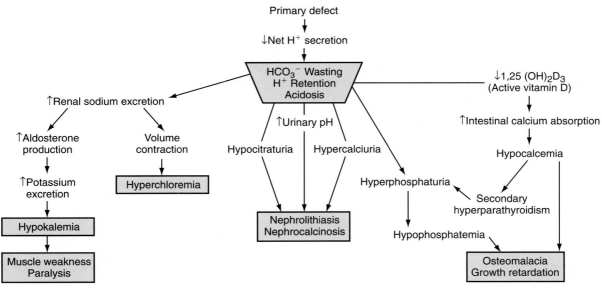

**Figure 42–8.** Pathophysiologic mechanisms for clinical features seen in type 1 (distal) renal tubular acidosis. Primary defects in renal acid excretion lead directly and through hormonally mediated pathways to metabolic abnormalities that produce the clinical syndromes seen in renal tubular acidosis. (From Kinkead TM, Menon M: Renal tubular acidosis. AUA Update 1995;14:54.)

**Type 2 (Proximal) RTA.** Proximal RTA is characterized by a defect in $HCO_3^-$ reabsorption associated with initial high urine pH that normalizes as plasma $HCO_3^-$ decreases and the amount of filtered $HCO_3^-$ falls (Laing et al, 2005). Initially, when serum $HCO_3^-$ levels are normal, more than 15% of filtered $HCO_3^-$ is lost. This syndrome is usually associated with generalized defects in proximal tubule function similar to Fanconi's syndrome, with loss of glycogen, protein, uric acid, and phosphate (Rocher and Tannen, 1986). **Nephrolithiasis is uncommon in this disorder owing to relatively normal urinary citrate excretion** (Laing et al, 2005). The clinical manifestations of proximal RTA include growth retardation and hypokalemia in children due to metabolic acidosis. Metabolic bone disease is seen more frequently with proximal RTA due to associated abnormalities in vitamin D metabolism and hypophosphatemia (Kinkead et al, 1995).

Most cases of proximal RTA are sporadic, but inherited diseases associated with proximal RTA have been described. In humans and terrestrial vertebrates, the kidneys control systemic pH in part by absorbing filtered $HCO_3^-$ in the proximal tubule via an electrogenic $Na^+/HCO_3^-$ co-transporter (NBCe1/SLC4A4). Homozygous point mutations in NBCe1 cause proximal renal tubular acidosis (pRTA), glaucoma, and cataracts (Igarashi et al, 1999). Other mutations in this gene have been identified that cause voltage- and $Na^+$-dependent transport reabnormalities, thereby causing both insufficient $HCO_3^-$ reabsorption by the kidney (proximal RTA) and inappropriate anterior chamber fluid transport (glaucoma) (Dinour et al, 2004).

Carbonic anhydrase II catalyzes the hydration/dehydration of $CO_2$ and $H_2CO_3$ and is expressed in the renal proximal tubule, loop of Henle, and intercalating cells of the collecting duct as well as in brain glial cells and bone osteoclasts (Laing et al, 2005). Deficiency of carbonic anhydrase II (carbonate hydrolyase, EC 4.2.1.1) is the primary defect in the syndrome of osteopetrosis, proximal renal tubular acidosis, and cerebral calcification. Fortunately, this is a rare abnormality (Sly et al, 1985; Roth et al, 1992).

**Type 4 (Distal) RTA. Type 4 RTA is associated with chronic renal damage, usually seen in patients with interstitial renal disease and diabetic nephropathy.** Reduction in glomerular filtration results in hyperkalemic, hyperchloremic metabolic acidosis due to loss of $HCO_3^-$ in the urine and decreased excretion of ammonium (Pohlman et al, 1984). Aldosterone resistance is commonly associated with type 4 RTA (Davidman et al, 1988). Because aldosterone contributes to stimulation of distal acidification and $H^+/K^+$ exchange, aldosterone resistance results in decreased ammonia generation and further exacerbates hyperkalemia (Davidman et al, 1988). Patients with type 4 RTA can still generate acidic urine in response to an acid challenge.

Renal stone formation is uncommon in patients with type 4 RTA. A study comparing patients with type 4 RTA and matched subjects with a similar degree of renal impairment found that patients with type 4 RTA had significantly lower urinary pH and decreased urinary calcium excretion compared with controls (Uribarri et al, 1994). **The protection against renal stone formation in these patients may be attributed to reduced renal excretion of stone-forming substances, such as calcium and uric acid, owing to impaired renal function.**

### Hypomagnesuria

Hypomagnesuria is a rare cause of nephrolithiasis, affecting less than 1% of stone formers as an isolated abnormality, although it can be found in conjunction with other abnormalities in 6% to 11% of cases (Levy et al, 1995; Schwartz et al, 2001). Magnesium complexes with oxalate and calcium salts, and therefore such low magnesium levels result in reduced inhibitory activity. Low urinary magnesium is also associated with decreased urinary citrate levels, which may further contribute to stone formation (Preminger et al, 1989; Schwartz et al, 2001). Whether low magnesium is the cause or an effect of low citrate is not clear. Low magnesium levels occur with poor dietary intake (Pfab et al, 1985) or as a result of reduced intestinal absorption associated with intestinal abnormalities producing chronic diarrheal syndrome (Rudman et al, 1980).

Although a number of studies in rats have implicated hypomagnesuria as a factor in stone formation (Rushton and Spector, 1982), others (Faragalla et al, 1963; Borden et al, 1969; Rattan et al, 1993) have questioned the impact of magnesium (Su et al, 1991). Clinical studies regarding the role of magnesium are contradictory. Schwartz and colleagues (2001) found that hypomagnesiuric patients had higher stone recurrence rates than patients with normal urinary magnesium. However, other studies found no difference in magnesium excretion between stone patients and controls (Johansson et al, 1980; Esen et al, 1991). Of note, the lack of difference in mean magnesium levels may be a result of the small fraction of stone formers with low urinary magnesium levels.

Although magnesium has been shown to increase urinary pH, citrate, and magnesium and therefore to decrease urinary saturation of calcium oxalate in vitro (Khan et al, 1993) and in vivo (Curhan et al, 2001), two randomized trials comparing magnesium oxide with placebo or no treatment in stone formers have failed to demonstrate clinical benefit (Wilson et al, 1984; Ettinger et al, 1988).

## Uric Acid Stones

All mammals, except humans and Dalmatians, synthesize the enzyme uricase, which catalyzes the conversion of uric acid to allantoin, the end product of purine metabolism (Yu, 1981; Bannasch et al, 2004). Consequently, humans accumulate significantly higher levels of uric acid in their blood and urine (Watts, 1976; Yu, 1981). Because allantoin is 10 to 100 times more soluble in urine than uric acid, humans are prone to uric acid stone formation.

Uric acid is a weak acid with a pKa of 5.35 at 37°C. At that pH, half of the uric acid is present as the urate salt and half as free uric acid. Because sodium urate is approximately 20 times more soluble than the free acid, the relative proportion present as free uric acid strongly determines the risk of stone formation. **Urine pH is a critical factor in determining uric acid solubility;** at pH 5, even modest amounts of uric acid exceed uric acid solubility, whereas at pH 6.5, concentrations of uric acid exceeding 1200 mg/L remain soluble (Fig. 42–9) (Asplin, 1996). Because daily uric acid excretion averages 500 to 600 mg/L, urine may reach supersaturation at pH less than 6. Consequently, low urine pH increases concentrations of sparingly soluble undissociated uric acid, which leads to direct precipitation of uric acid. Of note, uric acid and sodium urate can also serve as a nidus for calcium oxalate stones through heterologous nucleation, and, thus, low urine pH is a risk factor for both uric acid and calcium oxalate stones (Coe and Kavalach, 1974; Levy et al, 1995).

The process of uric acid stone formation once uric acid crystals precipitate has not been fully elucidated. Although some investigators have suggested that uric acid crystal adhesion to kidney epithelial cells (Koka et al, 2000) and inhibitors such as glycosaminoglycans (Ombra et al, 2003) may play a role in uric acid stone formation, the involvement or importance of these factors in uric acid stone formation is unclear (Pak et al, 1976a).

**The three main determinants of uric acid stone formation are low pH, low urine volume, and hyperuricosuria** (Fig. 42–10). **The most important pathogenetic factor is low urine pH, because most patients with uric acid stones have normal uric acid excretion but invariably demonstrate persistent low urine pH** (Pak et al, 1985, 2003a). Uric acid stones can develop as a result of congenital, acquired, or idiopathic causes. Congenital disorders associated with uric acid stones involve renal tubular urate transport or uric acid metabolism. Acquired causes of uric acid stones, such as chronic diarrhea, volume depletion, myeloproliferative disorders, high animal protein intake, and uricosuric drugs, may affect any of the three factors determining uric acid stone formation. Patients with "gouty diathesis" or idiopathic low urine pH typically demonstrate decreased fractional excretion of urate and do not have gout (Maalouf et al, 2004a). Patients with gouty diathesis differ from those with hyperuricosuric calcium nephrolithiasis in that the former generally have normal urinary uric acid levels and acidic urine, whereas the latter have hyperuricosuria and normal urine pH. Patients with hyperuricosuria frequently have high urinary sodium and calcium levels leading to increased urinary saturation of sodium urate and calcium oxalate, placing them at risk for calcium oxalate stones (Sorensen and Chandhoke, 2002). Most patients with uric acid stones, however, have normal urinary uric acid levels and low urinary pH (Pak et al, 2003a).

### Pathogenesis of Low Urine pH

Although the pathogenesis of low urine pH in idiopathic uric acid stone formers is not known with certainty and may be multifactorial, several potential mechanisms have been proposed. Sakhaee and colleagues (2002) first observed that normouricosuric individuals with pure uric acid stones were more likely to have diabetes mellitus or to demonstrate glucose intolerance than normal individuals or those with mixed uric acid/calcium oxalate or pure calcium oxalate stones. Furthermore, when a group of normouricosuric uric acid stone formers were placed on a controlled metabolic diet, their urinary pH was lower than that of either normal volunteers or other stone formers (mixed uric acid/calcium oxalate or calcium oxalate). Further investigation revealed that the uric acid stone formers excreted less acid into the urine as ammonium and proportionately more titratable acid and less citrate in order to maintain normal overall acid-base balance. This apparent impairment in ammonium excretion in uric acid stone formers has been putatively linked to an insulin-resistant state.

Supporting this hypothesis, Pak and colleagues (2003b) noted a higher prevalence of uric acid stones and low urinary pH among patients with non–insulin-dependent diabetes (34%) than among nondiabetic stone formers. Furthermore, uric acid stone formers have been found to share many of the characteristic features of the metabolic syndrome (a condition defined by insulin resistance), including hypertriglyceridemia, hyperglycemia, obesity, and hypertension (Sakhaee et al, 2002;

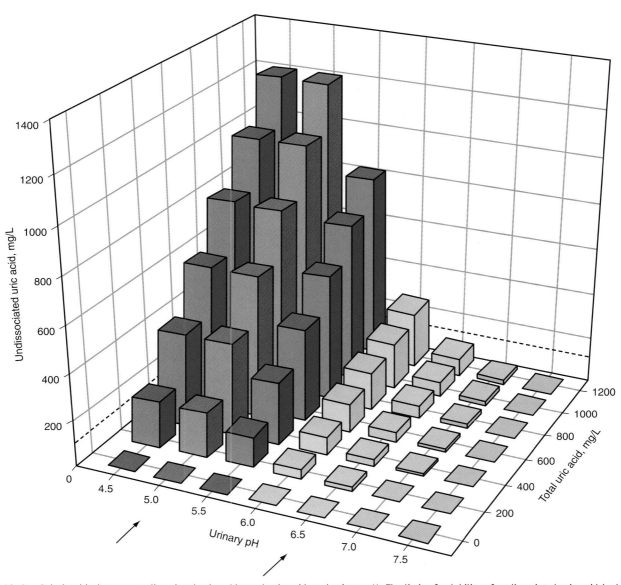

**Figure 42–9.** Relationship between undissociated uric acid, total uric acid, and urinary pH. The limit of solubility of undissociated uric acid is depicted by the *dotted line* (approximately 100 mg/L). Two hypothetical urine pH values are considered *(arrows)*. At low pH (e.g., 5.0), even a modest amount of total urinary uric acid will exceed its solubility. At high pH (e.g., 6.5), even massive hyperuricosuria is well tolerated. (From Maalouf NM, Cameron MA, Moe OW, Sakhaee K: Novel insights into the pathogenesis of uric acid nephrolithiasis. Curr Opin Nephrol Hypertens 2004a;13:181-189.)

**Figure 42–10.** Pathophysiology and etiology of uric acid nephrolithiasis. The three major pathophysiologic mechanisms that contribute to uric acid nephrolithiasis are low urine volume, low urinary pH, and hyperuricosuria. Each of these mechanisms can result from diverse etiologies. The most important pathogenetic factor is low urinary pH. (From Maalouf NM, Cameron MA, Moe OW, Sakhaee K: Novel insights into the pathogenesis of uric acid nephrolithiasis. Curr Opin Nephrol Hypertens 2004a;13:181-189.)

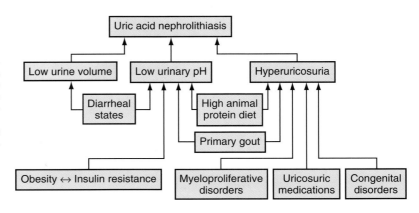

Pak et al, 2003b). In an elegant series of experiments, Abate and colleagues (2004) performed hyperinsulinemic euglycemic clamps to measure insulin sensitivity in a diverse group of non–stone-forming normal volunteers and a group of uric acid stone formers and determined that among normal subjects, low urine pH correlated with low rates of glucose disposal (indicating insulin resistance). Uric acid stone formers displayed the most severe levels of insulin resistance. This association of insulin resistance and low urinary pH was further corroborated by the finding of a strong inverse association of body weight (known to be associated with peripheral insulin resistance) and urinary pH, even after adjusting for urinary sulfate (a marker of animal protein intake) (Maalouf et al, 2004b).

The mechanism by which insulin resistance leads to low urine pH is not known. However, insulin has been shown to promote renal ammoniagenesis from the substrate glutamine (Chobanian et al, 1987; Nissim et al, 1995) and also to stimulate the Na$^+$/H$^+$ exchanger in the proximal tubule, which is responsible for either the direct transport or trapping of ammonium in the urine (Klisic et al, 2002). Impaired ammonium production or excretion as a result of insulin resistance could leave hydrogen ions unbuffered in the urine, thereby leading to reduction in urine pH (Fig. 42–11). Alternatively, free fatty acids, which are present in increased amounts in the blood in states of insulin resistance, could compete with α-ketoglutarate, the end product of glutamine metabolism, for entry into the Krebs cycle, thereby reducing ammonia production that normally results from glutamine deamination (Maalouf et al, 2004a).

Another potential mechanism for uric acid stone formation is loss of diurnal variation in urinary pH. In most individuals there is diurnal variation in both serum and urine pH, with alkalinization of the urine noted in the morning and after meals (Niv and Fraser, 2002). After consumption of a meal, secretion of gastric acid into the stomach lumen leads to com-

pensatory base excretion by the parietal cells into the serum, resulting in transient alkalinization of the blood and urine, the so-called alkaline tide. Support for this hypothesis comes from the findings that vagotomy prevents postprandial alkalinization of the urine (Gibaldi et al, 1975) and administration of antacids is associated with an increase in urine pH (Ahmad, 1986). Bilobrov and colleagues (1990) compared normal individuals and stone formers and found wide variations in urinary pH in normal individuals but persistently low urine pH among stone formers. Murayama and coworkers (1993, 2001) also found consistently low urinary pH (<6) in uric acid stone formers evaluated on both controlled metabolic and random diets and found absence of the postprandial and morning alkaline tides. In contrast, calcium oxalate stone formers maintained diurnal variation in urinary pH. Transient alkalinization of the urine may be sufficient to protect normal individuals from uric acid stone formation. The underlying cause of the absence of a urinary alkaline tide in uric acid stone formers is unknown but may be due to a renal defect rather than a gastric one (Maalouf et al, 2004a).

Dietary content also plays a role in determining urine acidity. Breslau and colleagues evaluated 15 normal subjects in a three-way randomized, crossover study involving three, 12-day phases of study in which subjects were maintained on a controlled metabolic diet containing vegetable protein, vegetable and egg protein, or animal protein, with increasing sulfate content, respectively, in the three diets (Breslau et al, 1988). As the fixed acid content of the diets increased, urinary calcium excretion increased from 103 mg/day on the vegetarian diet to 150 mg/day on the animal protein diet ($P < .02$). Moreover, the animal protein–rich diet was associated with the highest excretion of undissociated uric acid and lowest excretion of citrate due to the reduction in urinary pH. Urinary crystallization studies revealed that the animal protein diet, when matched for electrolyte composition and quantity of protein with the vegetarian diet, conferred an

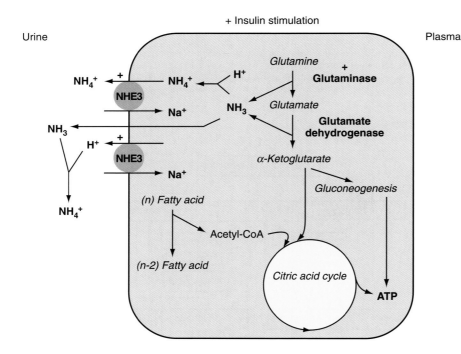

**Figure 42-11.** Potential effects of the insulin-resistant state on the generation and secretion of ammonium in the proximal tubule. The deamination of glutamine and glutamate provide ammonia. Insulin stimulates glutamine metabolism as well as the sodium/hydrogen exchanger NHE3. NHE3 mediates ammonium transport by either directly carrying the ammonium ion or providing the luminal hydrogen ion to trap ammonia. The end-product of glutamine metabolism is α-ketoglutarate, which can enter the Krebs cycle or gluconeogenesis to generate adenosine triphosphate (ATP). Alternatively, the metabolism of free fatty acids may generate acetyl-coenzymeA (CoA), which may compete with α-ketoglutarate to enter the Krebs cycle, thus providing energy to the cell but diminishing ammonia production. (n)-Fatty acid and (n-2)-Fatty acid represent fatty acids made of a skeleton of n and n-2 carbon atoms, respectively. (From Maalouf NM, Cameron MA, Moe OW, Sakhaee K: Novel insights into the pathogenesis of uric acid nephrolithiasis. Curr Opin Nephrol Hypertens 2004a;13:181-189.)

increased risk of uric acid stones, but, because of opposing factors, not of calcium oxalate or calcium phosphate stones.

## Hyperuricosuria

Hyperuricosuria is defined as urinary uric acid less than 600 mg/day (Menon, 1986). Hyperuricosuria predisposes to calcium oxalate or uric acid stone formation by causing supersaturation of the urine with respect to monosodium urate. Patients with gout and urinary uric acid levels less than 600 mg/day had significantly fewer stones than those with uric acid levels greater than 1000 mg/day (Hall et al, 1967; Yu and Gutman, 1967). The causes of hyperuricosuria have been discussed previously but include dietary factors as well as acquired and hereditary diseases and defects in the urate transporter.

## Low Urinary Volume

All conditions that contribute to low urinary volume increase the risk of uric acid supersaturation. Borghi and colleagues (1993) noted high uric acid relative supersaturation in workers exposed to hot temperatures compared with those working in normal temperatures. Likewise, high rates of uric acid stone formation have been found in populations living in warmer climates such as Israel (Shekarriz and Stoller, 2002).

# Cystine Stones

Cystinuria is an autosomal recessive disorder characterized by a defect in intestinal and renal tubular transport of dibasic amino acids, resulting in excessive urinary excretion of cystine (Ng and Streem, 1999, 2001). Although the defect results in high urinary concentrations of lysine, ornithine, and arginine as well, the poor solubility of cystine leads to stone formation. Cystine stones are rare, occurring in the United States and Europe with an incidence of only 1 in 1,000 to 1 in 17,000 (Cabello-Tomas et al, 1999; Knoll et al, 2005). In children, cystinuria is the cause of up to 10% of all stones (Faerber, 2001; Erbagci et al, 2003; Knoll et al, 2005).

Under normal conditions amino acids are freely filtered by the glomerulus and almost completely reabsorbed in the proximal tubules. In cystinuria, the defect in transport of cystine results in high urinary levels. There are several factors that determine the solubility of cystine, including cystine concentration, pH, ionic strength, and urinary macromolecules. The main contributor to cystine crystallization is supersaturation because there is no specific inhibitor of cystine crystallization in the urine (Pak and Fuller, 1983). Because of the poor solubility of cystine in urine, precipitation of cystine and subsequent stone formation occur at physiologic urine conditions (Joly et al, 1999). The solubility of cystine is highly pH dependent, with solubilities of 300 mg/L, 400 mg/L, and 1000 mg/L at pH levels of 5, 7, and 9, respectively (Dent et al, 1955). Ionic strength also influences solubility, and as much as 70 mg of additional cystine can be dissolved in each liter of solution as ionic strength increases from 0.005 to 0.3 (Pak and Fuller, 1983). Macromolecules such as colloid also increase cystine solubility, although the mechanism is unclear (Pak and Fuller, 1983). Therefore, cystine is more soluble in urine than in synthetic solution (Fig. 42–12).

Other factors may contribute to stone formation in cystinuric patients as well. Sakhaee and colleagues evaluated 27

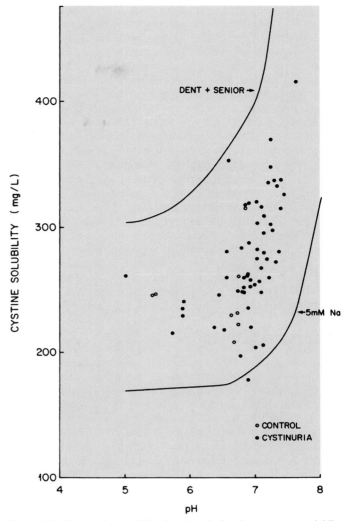

**Figure 42–12.** Cystine solubility in urine. Each point represents solubility of cystine determined in a separate urine sample by incubation with an excess of solid cystine. The solubility curve of Dent and Senior and that obtained in a 5-mM sodium cacodylate solution are plotted for comparison. (From Pak CY, Fuller CJ: Assessment of cystine solubility in urine and of heterogeneous nucleation. J Urol 1983;129:1066-1070.)

patients with documented cystine nephrolithiasis and identified hypercalciuria in 19%, hyperuricosuria in 22%, and hypocitraturia in 44% of patients, which could contribute to formation of not only cystine stones but also to stones composed of a combination of cystine and calcium oxalate (Sakhaee et al, 1989).

The genetics of cystinuria have been studied extensively. To date, two genes involved in the disease have been identified, *SLC3A1* and *SLC7A9*, which have been found to be associated with defects in heteromeric amino acid transporters (HATs). Historically, three types of cystinuria have been recognized in humans: type I, type II, and type III (Rosenberg et al, 1966). However, this classification correlates poorly with molecular findings, and therefore it has recently been revised by International Cystinuria Consortium (ICC) to take into account the chromosomal localization of the mutation: type A (chromosome 2), type B (chromosome 19), and type AB (both chromosomes) (Dello Strologo et al, 2002). Homozygotes with the condition exhibit urinary cystine levels as high as 2000 µmol/g of creatinine. Review by the ICC revealed that the average age at first stone diagnosis was 12.2 years, with mean number of stone episodes of 0.42 and 0.21 per year occurring in men and women, respectively (Dello Strologo et al, 2002). Although mean urinary cystine levels are significantly higher in heterozygotes with type B abnormalities (475 µmol/g creatinine) compared with those with type A abnormalities (70 µmol/g creatinine), there is no difference in stone formation between the two groups, and, in fact, stone formation is uncommon (Dello Strologo et al, 2002).

Little information is available on the relative distribution of the types of cystinuria in specific populations. In 97 well-characterized families in the database of the ICC cohort of patients, which hail primarily from Italy, Spain, and Israel, 38%, 47%, and 14% transmitted type I, non–type I, and mixed cystinuria, respectively (Dello Strologo et al, 2002). In another study of 85 family members of 24 cystine stone formers, 24 additional family members were found to excrete excessive amounts of cystine, although only 5 of them (21%) had produced cystine calculi (Trinchieri et al, 2004).

## Infection Stones

Infection stones (Bichler et al, 2002) are composed primarily of magnesium ammonium phosphate hexahydrate ($MgNH_4PO_4 \cdot 6H_2O$) but may in addition contain calcium phosphate in the form of carbonate apatite ($Ca_{10}[PO_4]_6 \cdot CO_3$). A Swedish geologist discovered magnesium ammonium phosphate in guano and named it "struvite" after his mentor, naturalist H. C. G. von Struve (Griffith and Osborne, 1987). Brown first theorized that bacteria split urea, thereby setting up the condition for stone formation, and indeed he later isolated *Proteus vulgaris* from a stone (Brown, 1901). In 1925, Hager and Magath (1925) postulated that a bacterial enzyme hydrolyzed urea, and Sumner (1926) isolated urease from *Canavalia ensiformis*. It is now well established that struvite stones (magnesium ammonium phosphate) occur only in association with urinary infection by urea-splitting bacteria (Griffith and Musher, 1973).

### Pathogenesis

**The process of urealysis provides an alkaline urinary environment and sufficient concentrations of carbonate and ammonia to induce the formation of infection stones.** Because urease is not present in sterile human urine, **infection with urease-producing bacteria is a prerequisite for the formation of infection stones.** A cascade of chemical reactions generates the conditions conducive to the formation of infection stones. Urinary urea, a constituent of normal urine, is first hydrolyzed to ammonia and carbon dioxide in the presence of bacterial urease:

$$(NH_2)_2CO + H_2O \rightarrow 2NH_3 + CO_2$$

The alkaline urine that results from this reaction (pH 7.2 to 8.0) favors the formation of ammonium:

$$NH_3 + H_2O \rightarrow NH_4^+ + OH^-  \quad pK = 9.0$$

Under physiologic conditions, the alkaline urine would prevent further generation of further ammonium. However,

in the presence of urease, ammonia continues to be produced despite alkaline urine, further increasing urinary pH. The alkaline environment also promotes the hydration of carbon dioxide to carbonic acid, which then dissociates into $HCO_3^-$ and $H^+$. Further dissociation of $HCO_3^-$ yields carbonate and two hydrogen ions:

$$CO_2 + H_2O \rightarrow H_2CO_3  \quad pK = 4.5$$
$$H_2CO_3 \rightarrow H^+ + HCO_3^-  \quad pK = 6.3$$
$$HCO_3^- \rightarrow H^+ + CO_3^{2-}  \quad pK = 10.2$$

The dissociation of hydrogen phosphate under alkaline conditions provides phosphate, thereby completing the generating of constituent ions for infection stone formation:

$$H_2PO_4^- \rightarrow H^+ + HPO_4^{2-}  \quad pK = 7.2$$
$$HPO_4^{2-} \rightarrow H^+ + PO_4^{3-}  \quad pK = 12.4$$

This chemical cascade, along with physiologic concentrations of magnesium, provides the constituents necessary for precipitation of struvite. In addition, the concentrations of calcium, phosphate, and carbonate allow precipitation of carbonate apatite and hydroxyapatite, thereby comprising the components of infection stones (Fig. 42–13).

Although infection stones are a direct result of persistent or recurrent infection with urease-producing bacteria, they may also be associated with or exacerbated by urinary obstruction or stasis (Bichler et al, 2002). As such, growth of infection stones can progress at a very rapid rate (Hinman, 1979).

### Bacteriology

Although the family Enterobacteriaceae comprise the majority of urease-producing pathogens, a variety of gram-positive

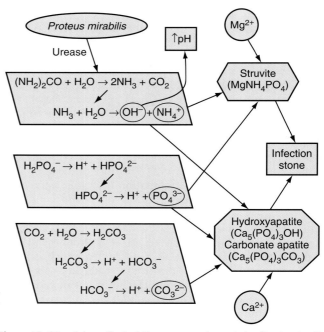

**Figure 42–13.** Schematic depicting concurrent events leading to struvite stone formation. (From Johnson DB, Pearle MS: Struvite stones. In Stoller ML, Meng MV [eds]: Urinary Stone Disease: The Practical Guide to Medical and Surgical Management. Totowa, NJ, Humana Press, in press.)

## Table 42-4. Organisms That May Produce Urease

| Organisms | Usually (>90% of Isolates) | Occasionally (5%-30% of Isolates) |
|---|---|---|
| Gram negative | Proteus rettgeri<br>Proteus vulgaris<br>Proteus mirabilis<br>Proteus morganii<br>Providencia stuartii<br>Haemophilus influenzae<br>Bordetella pertussis<br>Bacteroides corrodens<br>Yersinia enterocolitica<br>Brucella species | Klebsiella pneumoniae<br>Klebsiella oxytoca<br>Serratia marcescens<br>Haemophilus parainfluenzae<br>Bordetella bronchiseptica<br>Aeromonas hydrophila<br>Pseudomonas aeruginosa<br>Pasteurella species |
| Gram positive | Flavobacterium species<br>Staphylococcus aureus<br>Micrococcus<br>Corynebacterium ulcerans<br>Corynebacterium renale<br>Corynebacterium ovis<br>Corynebacterium hofmannii | Staphylococcus epidermidis<br>Bacillus species<br>Corynebacterium murium<br>Corynebacterium equi<br>Peptococcus asaccharolyticus<br>Clostridium tetani<br>Mycobacterium rhodochrous group |
| Mycoplasma | T-strain Mycoplasma<br>Ureaplasma urealyticum | |
| Yeasts | Cryptococcus<br>Rhodotorula<br>Sporobolomyces<br>Candida humicola<br>Trichosporon cutaneum | |

From Gleeson MJ, Griffith DP: Infection stones. In Resnick MI, Pak CYC (eds): Urolithiasis: A Medical and Surgical Reference. Philadelphia, WB Saunders, 1990, p 115.

and gram-negative bacteria and some yeasts and *Mycoplasma* species have the capacity to synthesize urease (Table 42–4). **The most common urease-producing pathogens are *Proteus*, *Klebsiella*, *Pseudomonas*, and *Staphylococcus* species** (Griffith and Osborne, 1987), **with *Proteus mirabilis* the most common organism associated with infection stones** (Silverman and Stamey, 1983). Although *Escherichia coli* is a common cause of urinary tract infections, rare species of *E. coli* produce urease (Bichler et al, 2002). Bacterial urease can be detected by the Urea-Rapid Test, a urea-indole medium from Bio-Merieux, Inc. (Durham, NC) (Bichler et al, 2002).

Bacteria may be involved in stone formation by damaging the mucosal layer of the urinary tract, resulting in both increased bacterial colonization and crystal adherence (Parsons et al, 1984; Grenabo et al, 1988). It has been proposed that ammonium, generated as a result of urealysis, may alter the glycosaminoglycan layer present on the surface of the transitional cell layer and significantly increase bacterial adherence to normal bladder mucosa, further exacerbating infection risk (Parsons et al, 1984). In addition, a study in rats found that injury to the bladder mucosa increased crystal adherence to the bladder wall, a process that was potentiated by the presence of common bacteria such as *Proteus, E. coli, Enterococcus,* and *Ureaplasma urealyticum* (Grenabo et al, 1988). Another potential mechanism for increased stone formation in the presence of bacteria is the finding that particular bacteria, such as *E. coli* and *Proteus,* may alter the activity of urokinase and sialidase, whereas organisms not typically associated with infection stones do not (du Toit et al, 1992). This altered enzymatic activity may explain the frequent association of *E.*

*coli* with stone formation despite lacking urease activity (Holmgren et al, 1989).

## Epidemiology

Infection stones comprise 5% to 15% of all stones (Levy et al, 1995). However, struvite/carbonate apatite was the most common stone composition among a population of African American stone formers in Ohio, accounting for a third of stones in males and nearly half the females in this population (Sarmina et al, 1987). **Because infection stones occur most commonly in those prone to frequent urinary tract infections, struvite stones occur more often in women than men by a ratio of 2:1** (Resnick, 1981). Other populations at risk of recurrent infection include the elderly (Kohri et al, 1991), premature infants or infants born with congenital urinary tract malformation, diabetics, and those with urinary stasis as a result of urinary tract obstruction, urinary diversion, or neurologic disorders. Spinal cord–injured patients are at particular risk for both infection and metabolic stones owing to neurogenic urinary tract dysfunction and hypercalciuria related to immobility. Patients with a functionally complete cord transection are at highest risk of developing a staghorn calculus (DeVivo et al, 1984).

## Miscellaneous Stones

### Xanthine and Dihydroxyadenine Stones

Xanthine stones are comprised of a rare stone type that is often confused with uric acid stones because both are radiolucent. They form as a result of an inherited disorder in the catabolic enzyme xanthine dehydrogenase (XDH) or xanthine oxidase, which catalyzes the conversion of xanthine to uric acid. Because xanthine is poorly soluble in urine, the high levels of xanthine that accumulate in XDH deficiency lead to xanthine stones (Seegmiller, 1968; de Vries et al, 1977; Cameron et al, 1993).

Allopurinol, which inhibits XDH and consequently is used to treat hyperuricemia and hyperuricosuria, can, at very high levels, predispose to xanthine stones. This side effect is distinctly uncommon, because the drug causes only partial inhibition of the enzyme and rarely reduces serum uric acid to levels lower than 3 mg/dL. Patients with Lesch-Nyhan syndrome who suffer from an inherited deficiency of the purine salvage enzyme hypoxanthine-guanine phosphoribosyltransferase (HPRT) are occasionally treated with high enough doses of allopurinol to place them at risk for xanthine stones (Cameron et al, 1993).

Children with inherited deficiencies of adenine phosphoribosyltransferase (APRT) can also present in infancy with renal complications and stones (Cameron et al, 1993). Children with APRT deficiency may be difficult to distinguish from those with HPRT deficiency because the insoluble product excreted, 2,8-dihydroxyadenine (2,8-DHA), is chemically similar to uric acid. Like xanthine stones, 2,8-DHA stones are extremely insoluble at any pH, but stone formation can be averted by the administration of allopurinol.

### Ammonium Acid Urate Stones

Ammonium acid urate stones represent less than 1% of all stones (Herring, 1962; Klohn et al, 1986). In developing countries, however, endemic ammonium acid urate urolithiasis is still observed because they comprise bladder calculi in children (Minon Cifuentes and Pourmand, 1983; Vanwaeyenbergh et al, 1995). **Conditions associated with ammonium acid urate crystallization include laxative abuse, recurrent urinary tract infection, recurrent uric acid stone formation, and inflammatory bowel disease** (Borden and Dean, 1979; Klohn et al, 1986; Dick et al, 1990; Pichette et al, 1997; Soble et al, 1999). Soble and associates (1999) reviewed their experience with 44 patients identified as having stones composed of ammonium acid urate, although the ammonium acid urate contribution varied from 2% to 60%. Among these patients, 25% had a history of inflammatory bowel disease, 14% had a history of significant laxative abuse, 41% were morbidly obese, 36% had history of recurrent urinary tract infections, and 21% had a history of recurrent uric acid stones. The subgroup of patients with inflammatory bowel disease and ileostomy as the sole clinical risk factor had the highest mean ammonium acid urate content (39%), and ammonium acid urate constituted the predominant stone type in 7 of 8 such patients.

Patients with ileostomy after colectomy have markedly reduced urinary volume, pH, and sodium and are not prone to hyperoxaluria like other individuals with bowel disease because the colon is the main site of dietary oxalate absorption (Kennedy et al, 1982). As such, these patients are prone to ammonium acid urate and uric acid stones rather than calcium oxalate stones. **The underlying pathophysiologic mechanism of ammonium acid urate stone formation due to laxative abuse has been postulated to be the result of dehydration due to gastrointestinal fluid loss causing intracellular acidosis and enhanced ammonia excretion. Because urinary sodium is very low with laxative use, urate complexes with abundant ammonia, thereby leading to urinary supersaturation of ammonium acid urate.**

Bowyer and colleagues (1979) demonstrated that ammonium acid urate precipitation is favored at pH 6.2 to 6.3. The association of recurrent uric acid stones with ammonium acid urate stones is likely related to the shared risk factors of low urine volume and pH. Soble and colleagues (1999) identified 9 patients with stones of mixed composition, containing both uric acid and ammonium acid urate (mean ammonium acid urate content 27%), although 8 of the 9 patients had uric acid as the predominant constituent (range: 40% to 95%). They theorized that transient fluctuations in urinary acidity and ammonium and sodium levels may shift the balance between uric acid and sodium- or ammonium-bound urate excretion.

Among the ammonium acid urate stone producers in Sobel and colleagues' study, obesity (body mass index greater than 30) was the most prevalent characteristic in 41% of patients, after excluding patients with inflammatory bowel disease and ileostomy (none of whom was obese). Indeed, a statistically significant correlation was found between body mass index and ammonium acid urate content. This is consistent with recent evidence suggesting a correlation between stone risk and obesity (Powell et al, 2000) and between obesity and low urine pH (Maalouf et al, 2004b).

## Matrix Stones

The association between urinary proteins and stone formation has long been recognized. Early experiments demonstrated that protein suspensions could promote calcium stone formation (Kimura et al, 1976). Both osteopontin and calprotectin have been shown to play a role in forming the matrix structure of urinary calcium stones (Tawada et al, 1999; Kleinman et al, 2004). However, stones composed predominantly of matrix are rare; these "stones" are typically radiolucent and may be mistaken for tumor or uric acid stones depending on the imaging study obtained (Bani-Hani et al, 2005). The literature regarding matrix stones is sparse, consisting mostly of anecdotal case reports (Boyce and King, 1963; Allen and Spence, 1966; Bani-Hani et al, 2005). The matrix component of calcium-based stones comprises only 2.5% of the dry weight of the stone, whereas pure matrix stones may contain upward of 65% protein (Allen and Spence, 1966). Boyce and Garvey (1956) determined that the composition of matrix stones was approximately two thirds mucoprotein and one third mucopolysaccharide by weight. Furthermore, they found that the matrix substance in crystalline calculi is closely related to the matrix substance found in matrix calculi. However, it is unclear why some matrix calculi fail to fully calcify. While some have theorized that reduced urinary calcium levels may account for the preferential formation of matrix stones (Boyce and King, 1959; Allen and Spence, 1966), a recent metabolic evaluation of 5 patients with matrix stones revealed normal urinary calcium excretion (Bani-Hani et al, 2005). In renal failure patients undergoing dialysis, proteinuria may contribute to an increased risk of matrix stone formation. In these patients, matrix stones have been shown to include both microfibrillar protein (Bommer et al, 1979) and $\beta_2$-microglobulin (Linke et al, 1986).

## Medication-Related Stones

Drug-induced stones form either directly due to precipitation and crystallization of a drug or its metabolite or indirectly by altering the urinary environment, making it favorable for metabolic stone formation (Daudon, 1999). Drugs such as loop diuretics (furosemide, bumetanide), acetazolamide, topiramate, and zonisamide contribute to calcium stone formation (Matlaga et al, 2003). Ephedrine (Powell et al, 1998; Assimos et al, 1999), triamterene (Ettinger et al, 1980; Carr et al, 1990), guaifenesin (Assimos et al, 1999), silicate (Farrer and Rajfer, 1984), indinavir (Bruce et al, 1997; Gentle et al, 1997), and ciprofloxacin (Matlaga et al, 2003) have all been associated with stones composed of the drug itself in patients who consumed excessive amounts.

### Medications That Directly Promote Stone Formation

*Indinavir Stones.* Indinavir sulfate is a protease inhibitor that has been shown to be effective in increasing CD4+ cell counts and decreasing HIV-RNA titers in patients infected with human immunodeficiency virus (HIV) or who have the acquired immunodeficiency syndrome (Wu and Stoller, 2000). However, indinavir poses a risk for indinavir stone formation in treated patients, leading to an estimated incidence of 4% to 13% (Wu and Stoller, 2000). Indinavir is rapidly absorbed from the intestine, achieving peak plasma concentrations in less than 1 hour. The drug is metabolized in the liver and eliminated primarily in the stool, but about half of the ingested dose of indinavir is excreted essentially unchanged in the urine (Sutherland et al, 1997). In pure form, indinavir is relatively insoluble in aqueous solution, although the solubility is pH dependent. With a pKa of 5.5, indinavir has a solubility of 0.300 mg/mL at pH 5, 0.035 mg/mL at pH 6.0, and 0.020 mg/mL at pH 7.0 (Daudon et al, 1997; Hermieu et al, 1999). Although indinavir solubility increases significantly at pH levels below 5.5, the standard dose of indinavir in an individual with an average urine volume and pH would produce a urinary concentration of indinavir near the limit of solubility 3 hours after ingestion (Daudon et al, 1997). As such, **individuals taking indinavir on a regular basis are at high risk of producing indinavir stones due to the high urinary excretion and poor solubility of the drug at physiologic urinary pH.** Initiation of indinavir in 54 asymptomatic indinavir-naive HIV-positive individuals led to indinavir crystalluria in 67% of subjects (Gagnon et al, 2000). After the first 2 weeks, indinavir crystalluria remained constant at a frequency of approximately 25% of urine sediments examined at each test point.

*Triamterene Stones.* Triamterene is a potassium-sparing diuretic commonly used for the treatment of hypertension. It is a very uncommon stone composition, accounting for only 0.4% of 50,000 calculi in one report, with only one third of the stones composed largely or entirely of triamterene (Ettinger et al, 1980). An evaluation of triamterene stone formers revealed no significant differences between patients and matched control subjects with respect to total recovery of the drug, hourly excretion patterns, and urinary concentrations of triamterene and its sulfate metabolite (Ettinger, 1985). Approximately half of all subjects tested demonstrated urine concentrations of the sulfate metabolite that exceeded the observed solubility limit. One investigation determined that triamterene is more likely to become incorporated into existing stones or stone nidi than to promote stone formation independently (Werness et al, 1982). This may account for the rarity of this stone in non–stone formers as well as the finding that hospitalization rate for urinary stones did not differ between patients prescribed triameterene and HCTZ (Jick et al, 1982).

*Guaifenesin and Ephedrine.* Consumption of large quantities of guaifenesin and ephedrine can lead to stones composed of their metabolites (Powell et al, 1998; Assimos et al, 1999). Most of the patients reported to have these stones are found to have consumed large quantities of over-the-counter preparations of cold medicine for the stimulatory properties of the ephedrine component, and a history of drug abuse is not uncommon (Assimos et al, 1999). Herbal ecstasy and Ma Huang are also popular ephedrine-containing preparations that are abused for stimulatory properties (Mack, 1997). Unfortunately, chronic ephedrine use leads to tachyphylaxis and prompts the use of increasing doses to achieve a comparable effect. Serious toxicity may result from ephedrine abuse, including death, cardiomyopathy, stroke, hypertension, and seizures.

*Silicate Stones.* Silica is a common element seen in vegetables, whole grains, seafood, and even drinking water that is easily excreted in the urine (Matlaga et al, 2003). Silicate stones are extremely rare and have been associated with consumption of large amounts of silicate-containing antacids, such as magnesium trisilicate (Daudon, 1999; Haddad and Kouyoumdjian, 1986).

**Medications That Indirectly Promote Stone Formation.** Other medications indirectly promote stone formation by increasing urinary stone risk factors. Corticosteroids, vitamin D, and phosphate-binding antacids can induce hypercalciuria. Thiazides cause intracellular acidosis and subsequent hypocitraturia (Nicar et al, 1984). Loop diuretics such as furosemide and bumetanide inhibit sodium and calcium resorption in the thick ascending loop of Henle, which in addition to a diuretic effect results in hypercalciuria (Matlaga et al, 2003). Renal calculi have been identified in up to 64% of low-birth-weight infants receiving furosemide therapy, and stones are consistently composed of calcium oxalate (Hufnagle et al, 1982; Shukla et al, 2001). Carbonic anhydrase inhibitors such as acetazolamide block resorption of sodium bicarbonate in the proximal tubule, leading to urinary alkalinization (Parfitt, 1969). Chronic use results in a hyperchloremic metabolic acidosis with subsequent hypocitraturia and increased risk for calcium phosphate stones (Matlaga et al, 2003). Topiramate is a widely used antiepileptic agent that inhibits certain isoenzymes of carbonic anhydrase with subsequent stone-potentiating effects (Matlaga et al, 2003). Zonisamide is a sulfonamide agent that also exerts an antiepileptic effect and has a weak carbonic anhydrase activity (Peters and Sorkin, 1993). Laxatives can lead to persistent diarrhea and increase the risk of ammonium acid urate stones. Patients abusing laxatives excrete large amounts of ammonia in the urine to eliminate excess acid, resulting in low urine pH. In the setting of low urine volume due to dehydration, the urine of these patients can be highly supersaturated with respect to ammonium urate (Matlaga et al, 2003). Lastly, cytotoxic agents promote a high cell turnover, resulting in urinary excretion of large amounts of uric acid.

## Anatomic Predisposition to Stones

Patients with anatomic anomalies associated with urinary obstruction and/or stasis have been noted to have a high incidence of associated stones. It has long been debated whether the predisposition to stone disease is a result of urinary stasis and delayed transit time through the nephron, leading to higher likelihood of crystal formation and retention, or if these patients form stones as a result of the same or unique metabolic abnormalities associated with stone formation.

### Ureteropelvic Junction Obstruction

The incidence of renal calculi in patients with ureteropelvic junction (UPJ) obstruction is nearly 20% (David and Lavengood, 1975; Lowe and Marshall, 1984; Clark and Malek, 1987). However, **Husmann and colleagues** (1995) **provided several lines of evidence to suggest that patients with UPJ obstruction and concurrent renal calculi carry the same metabolic risks as other stone formers in the general population.** First, among 111 adult patients with UPJ obstruction and stones for whom long-term follow-up was available, 62% developed recurrent stones after treatment of the UPJ obstruction and 43% of the recurrences occurred in the contralateral kidney. These findings suggest that a metabolic predisposition persisted despite correction of the obstruction. Second, 76% of 42 patients with noninfectious stones who underwent a metabolic evaluation demonstrated an underlying metabolic abnormality that could account for the stones, a rate comparable to that of other stone formers (Pak, 1982; Yagisawa et al, 1999). Finally, the type and distribution of metabolic abnormalities identified in these patients were similar to that of the general stone-forming population: hypercalciuria in 46% of patients, hyperuricosuria in 11%, hypocitraturia in 13%, primary hyperparathyroidism in 13%, and RTA in 3% (Pak et al, 1980). Treatment of patients with identifiable abnormalities significantly reduced their rate of recurrence, from 55% in patients managed conservatively to 17% in treated patients.

Matin and Streem also performed metabolic evaluations before definitive repair in 47 patients with UPJ obstruction with or without associated stones (Matin and Streem, 2000). An identifiable abnormality was found in 67% of the stone patients compared with only 33% of the control group; urinary calcium and the incidence of hypercalciuria and hyperuricosuria were significantly higher in the patients with stones compared with the controls, further underscoring the contribution of pathophysiologic background to stone-forming risk in patients with anatomic abnormalities.

Similar findings in two series of children with UPJ obstruction and concurrent renal calculi further support a metabolic contribution to stone formation in the presence of renal obstruction. Tekin and associates (2001) prospectively compared children with UPJ obstruction with and without stones to a control group of calcium stone formers without UPJ obstruction. Both groups of stone formers, those with and without UPJ obstruction, exhibited significantly higher urinary levels of citrate and lower levels of oxalate compared with the non–stone-forming children with UPJ obstruction. Husmann and coworkers (1996) reported a 70-fold increased risk of stone formation in the pediatric population with UPJ obstruction compared with normal children. Among 22 children who underwent treatment of their stones and UPJ obstruction, 68% of patients with nonstruvite stones developed a recurrence after surgical treatment and a metabolic abnormality was identified in 68%. Among the 7 patients with nonstruvite renal calculi who did not experience a recurrence, only 29% had an identifiable metabolic abnormality. As such, correction of the UPJ obstruction did not prevent recurrent stones in most patients, further emphasizing the role of underlying metabolic abnormalities in the etiology of renal calculi in patients with UPJ obstruction.

## Horseshoe Kidneys

Horseshoe kidneys occur with a prevalence of 0.25% but have an associated rate of renal calculi of 20% (Janetschek et al, 1988; Cussenot et al, 1992). Because of the high insertion of the ureter into the renal pelvis, there is a relative impairment of renal drainage, predisposing to UPJ obstruction. As such, the risk of stone formation has been attributed to urinary stasis rather than to metabolic derangements. Raj and colleagues (2004) reviewed 37 patients with horseshoe kidneys and stones and identified at least one metabolic abnormality in all 11 patients in whom 24-hour urine collections were available. Compared with a group of stone formers with normal renal anatomy, the patients with horseshoe kidneys exhibited a similar distribution of metabolic derangements, with the exception that hypocitraturia was overrepresented (55% in the patients with horseshoe kidneys vs. 31% in controls). It seems clear that **although urinary stasis likely contributes to a propensity toward stone for-**

**mation in patients with horseshoe kidneys, an underlying metabolic abnormality is required for stone formation to occur.**

## Caliceal Diverticula

Caliceal diverticula are associated with stones in up to 40% of patients (Middleton and Pfister, 1974). Like stones in horseshoe kidneys, it is unclear whether the stones are caused by local anatomic obstruction and urinary stasis or are due to underlying metabolic factors. Two groups of investigators addressed the issue. Hsu and Streem (1998) identified metabolic abnormalities, including hypercalciuria, hyperoxaluria and hyperuricosuria, in 50% of 14 patients with stone-bearing caliceal diverticula. Notably, 64% of patients reported a history of synchronous or metachronous stones at a site distinct from the diverticulum, supporting the idea of an underlying metabolic risk as a contributing cause of the stones. In contrast, Liatsikos and coworkers (2000) compared 49 patients with caliceal diverticula and stones with 44 stone formers without diverticula and found a low rate of metabolic abnormalities in both groups (25% in patients with diverticula and 23% in the control patients). Of note, however, the metabolic evaluation in this study involved measurement of only urinary volume, creatinine, calcium, phosphorus, oxalate, and uric acid. As it has been shown that low urinary pH and hypocitraturia are identified in approximately 10% and 28% of recurrent stone formers, respectively (Levy et al, 1995), the number of metabolic abnormalities reported in this series is likely underrepresented.

## Medullary Sponge Kidney

Medullary sponge kidney (MSK) is a disorder characterized by ectasia of the renal collecting ducts. Nephrocalcinosis and renal calculi are frequent complications of MSK (Lavan et al, 1971; Parks et al, 1982; Sage et al, 1982; Ginalski et al, 1990), but the exact risk factors for stone formation are not clearly understood. Although recurrent infection and urinary stasis within the ectatic tubules pose a risk for stone formation (Ginalski et al, 1990), renal tubular defects, including hypercalciuria, impaired renal concentrating ability, and defective urinary acidification after an ammonium chloride load have been detected in some MSK patients (Granberg et al, 1971), further potentiating the risk of stone formation. Deck (1965) reported three cases of MSK associated with RTA, which led him to suggest that the acidification defect may constitute the primary event leading to MSK. Osther and colleagues (1988) performed ammonium chloride load tests in 13 patients with MSK and found renal acidification defects in 9 patients: 8 with distal RTA and 1 with proximal RTA. Likewise, Higashihara and associates (1984) reported renal acidification defects in 80% of patients (36% with distal RTA) and impaired concentrating ability in 90% of 11 MSK patients.

Despite these findings, three studies performed specifically on MSK patients with nephrolithiasis revealed no case of associated RTA (O'Neill et al, 1981; Parks et al, 1982; Yagisawa et al, 2001). O'Neill and associates (1981) identified hypercalciuria as the most common metabolic abnormality in 17 patients with MSK and nephrolithiasis, occurring in 88% of patients and attributed to absorptive hypercalciuria in most cases (59%). The spectrum of abnormalities in these patients was judged to be comparable to that of the general stone-forming population. Other investigators identified hypercalciuria less frequently, in only 9% to 44% of MSK patients with nephrolithiasis. In some cases, the cause of the hypercalciuria was attributed to renal calcium leak by which renal calcium reabsorption was presumed to be impaired by damaged renal tubules (Yendt, 1981; Parks et al, 1982; Yagisawa et al, 2001). Yagisawa identified hypocitraturia as the most common metabolic abnormality, occurring in 77% of 22 MSK patients (Yagisawa et al, 2001). Kinoshita (1990) likewise reported hypocitraturia in 58% of MSK patients. **Thus, it appears that although renal tubular defects may be associated with MSK, RTA has not been firmly established as a major cause of stone formation in patients with MSK, and hypercalciuria and hypocitraturia are likely the primary risk factors.**

## Stones in Pregnancy

Symptomatic stones during pregnancy occur at a rate of 1 in 250 (Lewis et al, 2003) to 1 in 3000 (Butler et al, 2000) pregnant women. Like stones in nonpregnant women, they occur more commonly in white than African American women (Lewis et al, 2003). The majority of symptomatic stones occur in the second and third trimester of pregnancy, heralded by symptoms of flank pain or hematuria (Stothers and Lee, 1992; Butler et al, 2000; Biyani et al, 2002; Lewis et al, 2003). The diagnosis can be difficult in this patient population; up to 28% of women are misdiagnosed with appendicitis, diverticulitis, or placental abruption (Stothers and Lee, 1992).

Although most stones pass spontaneously and complications are rare, one report identified an increased risk of premature rupture of the membranes in association with stone passage (Lewis et al, 2003). Although ultrasound constitutes the first-line imaging modality when renal colic is suspected, ultrasound has been reported to miss up to 40% of stones, and a limited, or one-shot intravenous urogram, was found to be more reliable (Butler et al, 2000).

A number of physiologic changes occur during pregnancy. Physiologic hydronephrosis occurs in up to 90% of pregnant women and persists up to 4 to 6 weeks post partum (Swanson et al, 1995). Although hydronephrosis may be in part due to the effects of progesterone, compression of the ureters by the gravid uterus is at least a contributory, if not the primary, factor (Gorton and Whitfield, 1997; McAleer and Loughlin, 2004). Dilation is typically greater on the right ureter as a result of the engorged uterine vein and derotation of the enlarged uterus (Biyani et al, 2002). The physiologic dilatation may promote crystallization due to urinary stasis (Swanson et al, 1995), and the increased renal pelvic pressure has been suggested to increase the likelihood of stone movement and symptoms.

Important physiologic changes in the kidney occur during pregnancy that modulate urinary stone risk factors. Renal blood flow increases, leading to a 30% to 50% rise in glomerular filtration rate, which subsequently increases the filtered loads of calcium, sodium, and uric acid. (McAleer et al, 2004). Hypercalciuria is further enhanced by placental production of $1,25(OH)_2D_3$, which increases intestinal calcium absorption and secondarily suppresses PTH (Gertner et al, 1986; Biyani et al, 2002). Hyperuricosuria has also been reported as a result of increased filtered load of uric acid (Swanson et al, 1995).

Despite increases in a number of stone-inducing analytes, pregnant women have been shown to excrete increased amount of inhibitors such as citrate, magnesium, and glycoproteins (Maikranz et al, 1987; Smith et al, 2001). As such, the overall stone risk of stone formation has been reported to be similar in gravid and nongravid women, and stone composition is similar between the two groups (Coe et al, 1978; Drago et al, 1982).

## KEY POINTS: PATHOGENESIS

- Absorptive hypercalciuria is characterized by normal serum calcium, normal or suppressed PTH, normal fasting urinary calcium, and elevated urinary calcium.

- Renal hypercalciuria is due to impaired renal calcium reabsorption, which stimulates PTH secretion and leads to fasting hypercalciuria.

- Resorptive hypercalciuria is primarily due to primary hyperparathyroidism but may be seen with granulomatous diseases that elaborate $1,25(OH)_2D_3$.

- The most important determinant of uric acid stone formation is low urinary pH.

- Low urine pH seen in uric acid stone formers is likely due to impaired ammoniagenesis as a result of insulin resistance.

- In distal renal tubular acidosis, a defective $H^+$ ATPase accounts for excretion of excess acid into the distal tubule.

- Formation of infection stones requires alkaline urine that can be achieved only with infection with urease-producing bacteria.

## SUGGESTED READINGS

Biyani CS, Joyce AD: Urolithiasis in pregnancy: I. Pathophysiology, fetal considerations and diagnosis. BJU Int 2002;89:811-818; quiz i-ii.

Borghi L, Meschi T, Amato F, et al: Urinary volume, water and recurrences in idiopathic calcium nephrolithiasis: A 5-year randomized prospective study. J Urol 1996;155:839-843.

Evan AP, Lingeman JE, Coe FL, et al: Randall's plaque of patients with nephrolithiasis begins in basement membranes of thin loops of Henle. J Clin Invest 2003;111:607-616.

Griffith DP, Osborne CA: Infection (urease) stones. Miner Electrolyte Metab 1987;13:278-285.

Holmes RP, Assimos DG: The impact of dietary oxalate on kidney stone formation. Urol Res 2004;32:311-316.

Kok DJ, Khan SR: Calcium oxalate nephrolithiasis, a free or fixed particle disease. Kidney Int 1994;46:847-854.

Laing CM, Toye AM, Capasso G, Unwin RJ: Renal tubular acidosis: Developments in our understanding of the molecular basis. Int J Biochem Cell Biol 2005;37:1151-1161.

Maalouf NM, Cameron MA, Moe OW, Sakhaee K: Novel insights into the pathogenesis of uric acid nephrolithiasis. Curr Opin Nephrol Hypertens 2004;13:181-189.

Pak CY: Citrate and renal calculi: An update. Miner Electrolyte Metab 1994;20:371-377.

Pak CY, Adams-Huet B, Poindexter JR, et al: Rapid communication: Relative effect of urinary calcium and oxalate on saturation of calcium oxalate. Kidney Int 2004;66:2032-2037.

Pearle MS, Calhoun EA, Curhan GC: Urologic diseases in America project: Urolithiasis. J Urol 2005;173:848-857.

Stamatelou KK, Francis ME, Jones CA, et al: Time trends in reported prevalence of kidney stones in the United States: 1976-1994. Kidney Int 2003;63:1817-1823.

Thamilselvan S, Khan SR: Oxalate and calcium oxalate crystals are injurious to renal epithelial cells: Results of in vivo and in vitro studies. J Nephrol 1998;11(Suppl 1):66-69.

Trinchieri A, Coppi F, Montanari E, et al: Increase in the prevalence of symptomatic upper urinary tract stones during the last ten years. Eur Urol 2000;37:23-25.

Troxel SA, Sidhu H, Kaul P, Low RK: Intestinal *Oxalobacter formigenes* colonization in calcium oxalate stone formers and its relation to urinary oxalate. J Endourol 2003;17:173-176.

# 43 | Evaluation and Medical Management of Urinary Lithiasis

PAUL K. PIETROW, MD • GLENN M. PREMINGER, MD

DIAGNOSTIC EVALUATION OF NEPHROLITHIASIS

CLASSIFICATION OF NEPHROLITHIASIS AND DIAGNOSTIC CRITERIA

USE OF STONE ANALYSIS TO DETERMINE METABOLIC ABNORMALITIES

THE ECONOMICS OF METABOLIC EVALUATION

CONSERVATIVE MEDICAL MANAGEMENT

SELECTIVE MEDICAL THERAPY FOR NEPHROLITHIASIS

MISCELLANEOUS SCENARIOS

SUMMARY

## DIAGNOSTIC EVALUATION OF NEPHROLITHIASIS

There is no doubt that a symptomatic urinary calculus can cause considerable discomfort to the patient. Although many stones pass spontaneously, the methods used to treat calculi may also cause significant morbidity. In addition to physical consequences, patients may suffer financial pain because of the expense of emergency department visits, office visits, surgical procedures, or time lost from work. It follows, then, that most patients are interested in learning how to prevent a recurrence of such an episode. **Through even a rudimentary understanding of the physiologic causes of urinary calculus formation, physicians may offer a straightforward approach to elucidation of the metabolic basis of nephrolithiasis for any given patient. This evaluation should be simple to** perform; **it must be economically viable, and it should provide information that can be applied toward a selective, rational therapy for stone disease** (Pak et al, 1980a).

Any evaluation should be able to identify associated metabolic disorders responsible for recurrent stone disease. These metabolic problems include distal renal tubular acidosis, primary hyperparathyroidism, enteric hyperoxaluria, cystinuria, and gouty diathesis. In many of these relatively uncommon conditions, it is generally agreed that selective medical therapy is indicated not only to prevent further stone formation but also to correct the underlying physiologic disturbance that may lead to nonrenal complications (Pak et al, 2002a, 2003a).

## Selection of Patients for Metabolic Evaluation

**Debate continues regarding which patients merit the performance of a metabolic evaluation. First-time stone formers have often been estimated to have a 50% risk of recurrence within the subsequent 10 years** (Uribarri et al, 1989). In two separate studies, Ljunghall and colleagues attempted to measure the incidence of a stone recurrence in a northern European population. A retrospective review estimated the chance of recurrence as nearly 50% at 5 years, whereas a prospective evaluation noted a lower overall rate of 53% within 8 years (Ljunghall and Danielson, 1984; Ljunghall, 1987). Males had a higher incidence of calculi overall as well as a higher recurrence rate. Patients had a higher risk for recurrent stones in the years immediately after the first episode. It is not completely apparent whether these were preexisting stones that passed later or represented the formation of new calculi. **In fact, recent evidence suggests that the incidence of stone disease may be increasing, along with a higher percentage of female stone formers** (Scales et al, 2005).

Conversely, Ahlstrand noted that only 26% of patients observed for 10 years had a recurrence, significantly below previously quoted rates (Ahlstrand and Tiselius, 1990). With

1393

this in mind, it may not be financially sound to perform a complete diagnostic panel for every patient since it is unclear what percentage will not be bothered by recurrent episodes. Perhaps new stone formers should simply be given empirical fluid and dietary recommendations and asked to return if they suffer a recurrence. Indeed, a study of single stone formers prescribed a conservative program of high fluid intake and avoidance of dietary excess revealed a low incidence of recurrent stone disease (Hosking et al, 1983). Calling this finding the "stone clinic effect," Hosking and colleagues noted metabolic inactivity in nearly 60% of all patients observed for more than 5 years.

The debate continues, however, as Pak has found that single stone formers have just as high an incidence of metabolic abnormalities as recurrent stone formers do (Pak, 1982). In addition, these derangements are just as severe, leading the author to conclude that single stone formers should undergo the same evaluation as recurrent stone formers do. Similar findings were reported in a series of 182 patients; half of the patients had hypercalciuria or hyperuricosuria, whereas approximately 20% had a systemic disorder that predisposed the patients to the formation of calculi (Strauss et al, 1982). The remainder, 29.1%, had no metabolic disorder. Surprisingly, the incidence of hypercalciuria was actually lower in the patients with multiple stones, although not dramatically so. Patients with single stones tended to be older when they passed their stones and required a greater rate of intervention for treatment of the calculus. The recurrence for both groups of patients was similar (around 10% at 3 years). Since the authors did not note substantial differences between solitary and recurrent stone disease, they recommended that first-time stone formers be evaluated like patients with recurrent stone disease.

However, this approach has been partially refuted by Yagisawa and coworkers (1998), who noted that men with recurrent calculi had a higher rate of metabolic derangements than did first-time stone formers. Whereas women had a trend toward the same pattern, this achieved statistical significance only with regard to decreased levels of urinary citrate (hypocitraturia) (Yagisawa et al, 1998). A more complete discussion of the economic aspects surrounding the decision to perform a metabolic evaluation is found later in this chapter.

**Importantly, the formation of a first stone may be the harbinger of a more severe underlying systemic disorder, such as renal tubular acidosis, bone disease, or hypercalcemia due to hyperparathyroidism. In such patients, metabolic evaluation is justified solely to make the correct diagnosis to prevent extrarenal complications.** With the development of reliable parathyroid hormone assays, it is unacceptable to wait for bone loss before embarking on curative therapy. Whereas the clinical significance of normocalcemic hyperparathyroidism has been questioned and it is frequently simply observed, current practice favors the treatment of those with symptoms that can be attributed to the disorder (such as nephrolithiasis and osteoporosis) (Bilezikian and Silverberg, 2004).

The decision to thoroughly investigate a first-time stone former should ideally be shared by the physician and the patient. Some first-time stone formers will readily accept and follow conservative therapy; others may elect to undergo a thorough evaluation. It is reasonable to determine the extent of evaluation according to the estimation of potential or risk for recurrent stone formation (Smith, 1984). **Patients at higher risk for repeated episodes are those with a family history of stones and those with intestinal disease (particularly when it is causing chronic diarrheal states), pathologic skeletal fractures, osteoporosis, urinary tract infection, or gout.** In these patients, an extensive evaluation is recommended. Any patients with stones composed of cystine, uric acid, or struvite should undergo a complete metabolic workup.

**All children should be required to undergo a complete investigation because they have been found to have a significant risk of underlying metabolic disturbances** (Polito et al, 2000; Tekin et al, 2001; Pietrow et al, 2002; Coward et al, 2003; Bartosh, 2004). In addition, these young patients have more at stake; early, repeated episodes of urinary obstruction with a threat of urinary tract infection could put their developing kidneys at significant risk. To complicate matters, there is a lack of consensus regarding the safety of surgical intervention in these patients (Lottmann et al, 1995, 2000; Gough and Baillie, 2000; Brinkmann et al, 2001; Villanyi et al, 2001). It is no surprise that the performance of an open anatrophic pyelolithotomy can have a deleterious effect on a child's future renal function, causing a decline of 6% to 16% on nuclear scintigraphy (Gough and Baillie, 2000). It is additionally disconcerting that 20 years after its introduction, authors do not agree on the risks associated with exposure of developing renal parenchyma to shockwave energy.

African Americans have been observed to have a significantly lower incidence of nephrolithiasis than their white counterparts. Indeed, in a study by Sarmina and colleagues (1987), white patients had urinary calculi three to four times as often as black subjects did. However, the male-to-female prevalence is not as drastic as it is for white subjects (1 to 1.55 compared with 2.3 to 1, respectively). This finding is taken one step further in a study by Michaels and colleagues (1994), in which the women made up approximately 60% of the African American patients, thereby reversing the expected gender ratio. However, Sarmina found a higher incidence of infection calculi in the African American population in his study, and these stone types were excluded from analysis in the study by Michaels. Following the assumption that a lower incidence of calculi might imply a significant risk of a metabolic or anatomic abnormality in those patients who still manage to make calculi, it seems reasonable to advocate the performance of a metabolic evaluation for all patients of African American descent. This suggestion is supported by a study that assessed the underlying metabolic abnormalities of nonwhite stone formers. **African Americans, Asians, and Hispanics have a surprisingly similar incidence of underlying metabolic disturbances compared with white stone formers. These results suggest that dietary and environmental factors may be as important as ethnicity in the etiology of stone disease** (Beukes et al, 1987; Maloney et al, 2005).

Regardless of whether a particular, individual patient requires a full metabolic evaluation, it is prudent to perform at least a screening evaluation to assess for underlying systemic syndromes that may cause recurrent calculi and extrarenal complications. This assessment should also screen for those patients at an increased risk for stone recurrence as outlined in the preceding paragraphs (Table 43–1).

**Table 43–1. Indications for a Metabolic Stone Evaluation**

Recurrent stone formers
Strong family history of stones
Intestinal disease (particularly chronic diarrhea)
Pathologic skeletal fractures
Osteoporosis
History of urinary tract infection with calculi
Personal history of gout
Infirm health (unable to tolerate repeated stone episodes)
Solitary kidney
Anatomic abnormalities
Renal insufficiency
Stones composed of cystine, uric acid, or struvite

**Table 43–2. Abbreviated Evaluation of Single Stone Formers**

History
  Underlying predisposing conditions (as in Table 43–1)
  Medications (calcium, vitamin C, vitamin D, acetazolamide, steroids)
  Dietary excesses; inadequate fluid intake or excessive fluid loss
Multichannel blood screen
  Basic metabolic panel (sodium, potassium, chloride, carbon dioxide, blood urea nitrogen, creatinine)
  Calcium
  Intact parathyroid hormone
  Uric acid
Urine
  Urinalysis
    pH > 7.5: infection lithiasis
    pH < 5.5: uric acid lithiasis
    Sediment for crystalluria
  Urine culture
    Urea-splitting organisms: suggestive of infection lithiasis
  Qualitative cystine
Radiography
  Radiopaque stones: calcium oxalate, calcium phosphate, magnesium ammonium phosphate (struvite), cystine
  Radiolucent stones: uric acid, xanthine, triamterene
Intravenous pyelography: radiolucent stones, anatomic abnormalities
Stone analysis

## KEY POINTS: SELECTION OF PATIENTS FOR METABOLIC EVALUATION

■ The incidence of nephrolithiasis is increasing.

■ The historic male predominance of stone formers is disappearing.

■ Racial protection may be overcome by dietary indiscretions.

■ Children are generally evaluated because of concerns about renal damage and long-term sequelae of stone recurrence.

## Abbreviated Protocol for Low-Risk Single Stone Formers

**In single stone formers without increased risk, the following abbreviated protocol may be applied** (Table 43–2). A thorough medical history should be obtained for any underlying conditions that may have contributed to the stone disease. Because of the association between bowel disease and calcium oxalate nephrolithiasis (enteric hyperoxaluria), a careful history of bowel habits and bowel disease should be sought (Smith et al, 1972; Bohles et al, 1988; Lindsjo et al, 1989; McConnell et al, 2002; Worcester, 2002; Parks et al, 2003b). This includes questions about chronic diarrhea that could be caused by inflammatory bowel disease (Crohn's disease, ulcerative colitis) or irritable bowel syndrome. A history of gout should be sought as this finding may predispose the patient to hyperuricosuria or gouty diathesis with either uric acid calculi or calcium oxalate stone formation (Grover and Ryall, 1994; Khatchadourian et al, 1995; Kramer and Curhan, 2002). As described by Pak and colleagues, patients with a history of diabetes mellitus may be at an increased risk for development of a gouty diathesis, with altered ammonium management, acidic urine, and a predisposition for a mixture of calcium oxalate and uric acid stones (Pak et al, 2003c).

**In addition, information should be gleaned about the patient's dietary habits, including fluid consumption and excessive intake of certain foods as well as all medications taken. A social history may provide obvious clues about the hydration status of these patients.** Do they have access to fluids on a regular basis or are they sequestered in an environment that does not allow easy access to fluids (such as along an assembly line or in the operating suite)? Do they perform daily tasks that would increase the insensible loss of fluids (manual labor, prolonged outdoor exposure)? Some have suggested that a sedentary lifestyle may actually increase the risk of stone formation above that of those who perform manual labor. Even a brief family history will reveal a potential genetic predisposition to urinary calculi if there is a history of close relatives affected by nephrolithiasis. Age at onset of the patient or of affected relatives may give clues about genetic disorders, such as autosomal recessive cystinuria.

**A multichannel blood screen can be helpful in identifying certain systemic problems.** These include primary hyperparathyroidism (high serum calcium and low serum phosphorus levels), renal phosphate leak (hypophosphatemia), uric acid lithiasis (hyperuricemia), and distal renal tubular acidosis (hypokalemia, decreased carbon dioxide).

Voided urine specimens should be obtained for comprehensive urinalysis and culture. The urinalysis should include pH determination (preferably with an electrode). A pH above 7.0 is suggestive of infection lithiasis or of renal tubular acidosis; a pH below 5.5 suggests uric acid lithiasis secondary to gouty diathesis.

**The urine sediment should be examined for crystalluria since particular crystal types may give a clue as to the composition of stones the patient is forming** (Fig. 43–1). Tetrahedral "envelopes" are seen in calcium oxalate lithiasis; rectangular "coffin-lid" crystals are often seen in patients with struvite calculi. Hexagonal crystals confirm cystinuria; uric acid crystals may be seen as amorphous fibers or as irregular plates. The microscopic appearances of common calculi are summarized in Table 43–3.

**Figure 43–1.** Scanning electron micrographs of various urinary crystals. **A,** Apatite. **B,** Struvite. **C,** Calcium oxalate dihydrate. **D,** Calcium oxalate monohydrate. **E,** Cystine. **F,** Ammonium acid urate. **G,** Brushite. (Courtesy of Dr. S. R. Khan, University of Florida, Gainesville.)

**Urine cultures are performed if there is a suspicion of infection-related calculi or if there are signs or symptoms of a urinary tract infection.** A culture that is positive for urea-splitting organisms such as *Proteus, Pseudomonas,* and *Klebsiella* would help explain the formation of a struvite calculus. A positive culture will also warrant therapy with appropriate

antibiotics before the initiation of any surgical procedure to remove the stone. The surgical management of a calculus during an active infection will place the patient at great risk for bacteremia or sepsis. **Unfortunately, many infected calculi will harbor bacteria even after treatment with broad-spectrum antibiotics.** Indeed, Rocha and Santos (1969)

**Table 43–3. Microscopic Appearance of Common Urinary Calculi**

| Chemical Type | Appearance |
| --- | --- |
| Calcium oxalate monohydrate | Hourglass |
| Calcium oxalate dihydrate | Envelope, tetrahedral |
| Calcium phosphate–apatite | Amorphous |
| Brushite | Needle shaped |
| Magnesium ammonium phosphate (struvite) | Rectangular, coffin-lid |
| Cystine | Hexagonal |
| Uric acid | Amorphous shards, plates |

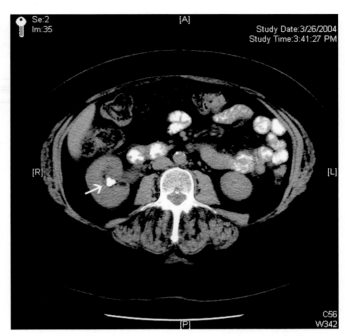

**Figure 43–2.** CT image of a urinary calculus. All stones (with the exception of some medication calculi) appear as dense, white objects within the urinary collecting system.

demonstrated that bacteria can still be cultured from the interior of a calculus despite its being soaked in iodine and alcohol for 6 hours. Furthermore, McAleer and associates (2003) have shown that infection calculi contain large quantities of endotoxin after disintegration. In a comparison of infected and noninfected calculi, infected stones contained 36 times more endotoxin. Half of the infected calculi grew bacteria on culture that were different from those of the preoperative urine specimens. The same investigators have described how endotoxin can cause a vascular collapse as it induces physiologic changes consistent with septic shock (McAleer et al, 2002).

**Abdominal radiographs should be obtained to document the existence of any residual stones within the urinary tract.** The radiopacity of any existing stones may suggest the type of stones that are present. Whereas magnesium ammonium phosphate and cystine stones are often radiopaque, they are not as dense as calcium oxalate or calcium phosphate stones. A plain abdominal film is also useful in identifying nephrocalcinosis (suggestive of renal tubular acidosis) and staghorn calculi (likely due to infection lithiasis). An intravenous pyelogram may be obtained to confirm the presence of radiolucent stones and also to identify any anatomic abnormalities that may predispose the patient to stone formation. The radiographic evaluation of a patient during a metabolic workup for stone disease will differ from an approach taken during an episode of acute renal colic. In these instances, patients are frequently examined with multislice, non–contrast-enhanced computed tomography (CT), which is able to quickly image the entire collecting system in a rapid sequence (Fig. 43–2) (Smith et al, 1995; Sommer et al, 1995; Katz et al, 1996; Fielding et al, 1997).

**Available stones should be analyzed to determine their crystalline composition.** The presence of uric acid or cystine suggests gouty diathesis or cystinuria, respectively. The finding of struvite, carbonate apatite, and magnesium ammonium phosphate suggests infection lithiasis. A predominance of a hydroxyapatite component suggests renal tubular acidosis or primary hyperparathyroidism and warrants an assessment of basic electrolytes. Stones composed of pure calcium oxalate or mixed calcium oxalate and hydroxyapatite are less useful diagnostically since they may occur in several entities, including absorptive and renal hypercalciuria, hyperuricosuric calcium nephrolithiasis, enteric hyperoxaluria, hypocitraturic calcium nephrolithiasis, and low urine volume (Kourambas et al, 2001; Pak et al, 2004).

## KEY POINTS: ABBREVIATED PROTOCOL FOR LOW-RISK SINGLE STONE FORMERS

■ A complete history should be obtained from all stone formers.

■ Patients should be screened for medical diseases that predispose to calculi.

■ Serum metabolic panel and urinalysis are performed.

■ Urine microscopy for crystals may provide clues to diagnosis.

■ Stone analysis can remove the need for further evaluation.

■ Basic radiography (plain films) screens for remaining calculi.

## Extensive Diagnostic Evaluation

A more extensive evaluation, directed at the identification of underlying physiologic derangements, should be performed in patients with recurrent nephrolithiasis as well as in stone formers at increased risk for further stone formation.

**Pak initially described an extensive outpatient (ambulatory) evaluation in 1980 and subsequently made minor revisions to help simplify the process** (Pak et al, 1980a; Levy et al, 1995). The basic strategy involves two outpatient visits, and most of the required laboratory analyses can be performed in a routine clinical laboratory; only a few of the specialized techniques are performed in a more sophisticated laboratory. **The entire schedule of visits and tests is outlined in Table 43–4.**

Before and throughout the period of evaluation, the patient is instructed to discontinue any medication that is known to interfere with the metabolism of calcium, uric acid, or oxalate. These medications include vitamin D, calcium supplements, antacids, diuretics, acetazolamide, and vitamin C. Any current medication for stone treatment (thiazides, phosphate, allopurinol, or magnesium) should be discontinued as well to better understand the patient's baseline physiology (and pathophysiology). Three 24-hour urine samples are collected. The first two 24-hour specimens are obtained with the patient on a random diet, which is reflective of the usual dietary intake. It is important to stress to the patients that they are not to "perform" during the urine collections. An attempt on the patient's part to suddenly eat well or to increase fluid consumption for the sake of the test will only mask the underlying cause of the stone disease.

**Most patients will require detailed instructions on the proper collection of a complete 24-hour urine specimen.** The patient should choose a day when all voids can be completely captured and when the specimen will represent a "typical" day. The first morning void is discarded, since this represents urine from the previous night and may not have had a predictable starting point. From that point on, all urine must be collected in the appropriate laboratory-provided container. The canister may need to be kept on ice or preservatives should have been added according to the requirements of the specific laboratory. When the patient awakens the next morning, the first morning void is collected with the rest of the specimen, thereby completing a full 24 hours. Total urinary creatinine should be measured to provide an internal check. Males will be expected to have produced approximately 15 to 20 mg of creatinine for every kilogram of body weight during the 24-hour period. Females generally have less muscle mass and therefore will typically produce 10 to 15 mg of creatinine for every kilogram of body weight in 24 hours. Significant aberrations in total creatinine excretion from these estimated values imply incomplete collection, overcollection, greater than expected muscle mass, or less than expected muscle mass.

A third 24-hour sample may be collected after 1 week with the patient on a calcium-, sodium-, and oxalate-restricted diet. This dietary restriction is imposed to standardize the diagnostic tests, to better assess the cause of hypercalciuria, and to prepare for the "fast and calcium load" test, which is performed on the second visit. Blood samples are obtained on both visits as outlined in Table 43–4.

## Fast and Calcium Load Test

**A fast and calcium load study is performed on the morning of the second visit** (Pak et al, 1975). The purpose of this exercise is to help delineate various causes of hypercalciuria. As explained in Chapter 42 in greater detail, some patients are too efficient at absorbing calcium from the alimentary canal (absorptive hypercalciuria, types 1 and 2), whereas others suffer from a constant loss of calcium from the renal tubules (renal calcium leak). A third subset of patients has an overabundance of circulating parathyroid hormone, usually from a single parathyroid adenoma, with a constant loss of calcium and phosphate (resorptive hypercalciuria or primary hyperthyroidism).

To differentiate between these three hypercalciuric subtypes, it is essential that the patients have adhered to the restricted diet for at least 7 days before this testing to eliminate the effects of absorbed calcium on fasting calcium excretion. To ensure adequate hydration, distilled water (300 mL) is taken 12 hours and 9 hours before the calcium loading. Other than water ingestion at these times, the patients are to be fasting. Two hours before the scheduled calcium loading, patients empty the bladder completely, discard this urine, and drink an additional 600 mL of distilled water. All urine produced during the next 2 hours is collected as a pooled sample before an oral calcium load is taken (fasting urine). After the 2-hour fasting urine collection has been completed, a 1-g oral calcium load is administered by 250 mL of a liquid synthetic diet (Calcitest) as a carrier solution. This synthetic "meal" is prepared by adding 500 mL of water to a can of Calcitest. Since 250 mL of the synthetic meal contains only 100 mg of calcium, 39 mL of Neocalglucon (900 mg of calcium) must be added to bring the total calcium up to 1 g. The final mixture should be taken slowly during a 5- to 10-minute period.

For the next 4 hours, urine is again collected as a pooled sample (post-load urine). Both fasting and post-load samples are then assayed for calcium and creatinine. Fasting urinary calcium excretion is expressed as milligrams per deciliter of glomerular filtrate since it is reflective of renal function. To obtain this unit of measurement, the urinary calcium concentration (in milligrams per milligram of creatinine) is multiplied by the serum creatinine concentration (in milligrams per deciliter). Normal fasting urinary calcium excretion is less

| Table 43–4. | **Outline of Extensive Ambulatory Protocol** | | | | | | | | | | | |
|---|---|---|---|---|---|---|---|---|---|---|---|---|
| | **Blood** | | | | | **Urine** | | | | | | |
| | Complete Blood Count | SMA | PTH | Calcium | Uric Acid | Creatinine | Sodium | pH | Total Volume | Oxalate | Citrate | Qualitative Cystine |
| Visit 1* | | X | X | X | X | X | X | X | X | X | X | X |
| Visit 2† | | X | X | X | X | X | X | X | X | X | X | X |
| Fast | | | | | X | | X | | | X | | |
| Load | | | | | X | | X | | X | | | |

*History and physical examination, diet history, radiologic evaluation, two 24-hour urine specimens on random diet, and dietary instruction for restricted diet.
†A 24-hour urine specimen on restricted diet (400 mg calcium and 100 mEq sodium/day), fast and load test.
Modified from Pak CY, Britton F, Peterson R, et al: Ambulatory evaluation of nephrolithiasis. Classification, clinical presentation and diagnostic criteria. Am J Med 1980;69:19-30.

than 0.11 mg per deciliter of glomerular filtrate. The post-load urinary calcium excretion is best expressed as milligrams per milligram of creatinine as it is a function of a fixed oral calcium load. The normal value for this measurement is less than 0.2 mg calcium per milligram of creatinine.

**Most clinicians have moved away from the performance of a comprehensive metabolic evaluation that entails a calcium loading test. As explained later, the treatment of both absorptive hypercalciuria and renal leak hypercalciuria is now similar.** With little therapeutic distinction, there is no longer as much of an incentive to discriminate between either type of hypercalciuria. **However, differentiation between absorptive and renal hypercalciuria is essential if one plans to prescribe a calcium-binding resin to a patient with absorptive hypercalciuria** (see "Selective Medical Therapy for Nephrolithiasis" later in this chapter).

## KEY POINTS: EXTENSIVE DIAGNOSTIC EVALUATION

- A complete metabolic evaluation may be obtained on an outpatient basis.

- Calcium fast and load tests can discriminate between the various forms of hypercalciuria.

- Routine performance of calcium fast and load tests is not required to complete a metabolic evaluation.

## Simplified Metabolic Evaluation

The extensive ambulatory protocol affords the physician a high diagnostic yield and is reliable. Unfortunately, many practicing physicians have found this protocol to be time-consuming and difficult to perform because of the inability to find a reliable local laboratory or perceived complexities of the evaluation protocol. Indeed, the full evaluation does entail several office visits and requires strict adherence to fluid protocols during the calcium fast and load tests.

**Several authors have suggested a more simplified approach that uses the same standard principles and procedures as the full outpatient evaluation.** These simplified protocols typically do not include the calcium fast and loading tests and can often be performed in one office visit. Rivers and colleagues (2000) have recommended the collection of two separate 24-hour urine specimens. One is collected while the patient is on a restricted diet; the other allows a random (typical) diet. Such manipulation is well tolerated by the patient and may allow identification of the various types of hypercalciuria with reasonable certainty.

Pak has also recognized the cumbersome nature of a full evaluation and has made similar recommendations (Pak, 1997). On the basis of the findings of a single 24-hour urine collection, patients are evaluated and treated without all steps of fasting and loading calcium challenges. Separation into complicated and uncomplicated calcium stone disease is made on the basis of the presence or absence of normocalcemia, normouricemia, or calcium stones and the absence of urinary tract infection, bowel disease, or marked hyperoxaluria.

Uncomplicated calcium stone disease, represented by the majority of patients, is further separated into a hypercalciuric group and a normocalciuric group. Medical therapy is then based on this distinction.

Lifshitz and colleagues (1999) have also advocated a less complex approach. All patients undergo a basic metabolic screening in search of systemic disorders that could pose a long-term health risk. They suggest that all patients should be advised about conservative nonspecific preventive measures. High-risk patients should have a more extensive metabolic evaluation based on two 24-hour urine samples.

**The cornerstone of these simplified protocols has been the development of a urine preservation method that allows collection of urine without refrigeration.** The patient is then able to submit an aliquot to a central laboratory for the analysis of various stone-forming substances (Nicar et al, 1987). The urine constituents most commonly assayed include calcium, oxalate, citrate, total volume, sodium, magnesium, potassium, pH, uric acid, and sulfate. Whereas most of these parameters are self-evident, sulfate is added to the list to assess the volume of protein loading from animal meat. From such determinations, the urine saturation with respect to stone-forming salts can be calculated.

At present, there are two private companies that offer laboratory services focused on simplified, accurate 24-hour urine assessment for stone-forming risk factors—Mission Pharmacal (San Antonio, Texas) and LithoLink (Chicago, Illinois). Both provide collection containers with chemical preservatives (obviating iced storage and transport), and both laboratories extrapolate 24-hour cumulative data from the submission of a small aliquot of the entire collection. After the values of all urine constituents and saturations have been determined, the physician receives a computerized printout that provides a numeric display of the test results (Fig. 43–3). A graphic display of this information may also be generated, highlighting the increased or reduced risk for each environmental, metabolic, or physicochemical factor (Fig. 43–4). These results should aid the physician in formulating a metabolic and physiologic diagnosis. However, it is usually not possible to make a definitive diagnosis of a particular metabolic derangement without further testing. For example, it is desirable to confirm hypocitraturia or hyperuricosuria by repeated measurements. In addition, whereas this graphic analysis will demonstrate hypercalciuria, routine 24-hour urine analysis is not able to differentiate between the different forms of hypercalciuria.

There is controversy about the necessity of collecting two separate 24-hour urine specimens. As noted earlier, Rivers has advocated the collection of two samples on different diets (random and restricted) (Rivers et al, 2000). Assuming that the patient complies, these data may be able to discern between type 2 absorptive hypercalciuria and renal leak (hypercalciuria disappears on the restricted diet in type 2 absorptive hypercalciuria). Researchers from Dallas have suggested that only one single 24-hour collection is required (Pak et al, 2001). Their study retrospectively reviewed and compared the results of two 24-hour urine samples that were collected on random diets. They noted no significant difference in the excretion of urinary calcium, oxalate, uric acid, citrate, pH, total volume, sodium, potassium, sulfate, or phosphorus. They concluded that the reproducibility of urinary stone risk

**Litholink Laboratory Reporting System™**

# Patient Results Report

| PATIENT | DATE OF BIRTH | PHYSICIAN |
|---|---|---|
| **Sample, Patient** | **06/03/1951** | **Sample, Physician** |

## Stone Risk Factors / Cystine Screening: Negative (12/03/04)

Values larger, bolder and more towards red indicate increasing risk for kidney stone formation.

| DATE | SAMPLE ID | Vol 24 | SS CaOx | Ca 24 | Ox 24 | Cit 24 | SS CaP | pH | SS UA | UA 24 |
|---|---|---|---|---|---|---|---|---|---|---|
| 12/04/04 | 089979 | 2.35 | **12.3** | **375** | **52** | 401 | .95 | 6.04 | 0.6 | 0.85 |
| 12/03/04 | 089978 | 2.17 | **17.9** | **423** | **61** | 471 | 0.9 | 5.72 | 1.6 | 1.01 |

| ABBR. | ANALYTE | NORMAL RANGE | TREATMENT RECOMMENDATION |
|---|---|---|---|
| **Vol 24** | Urine Volume | 1/d: 0.5 - 4 L | *Raise vol at least 2L* |
| **SS CaOx** | Supersaturation CaOx | 6-10 | *Raise urine vol and cit, lower ox and ca.* |
| **Ca 24** | Urine Calcium | men <250, women <200 | *IH, consider Hydrochlorothiazide 25 mg bid or chlorthalidone 25 mg qam, urine Na <100.* |
| **Ox 24** | Urine Oxalate | 20-40 | *usually dietary; if enteric, consider cholestyramine, oral calcium 1-2 gm with meals; if >80, may be primary hperoxauria.* |
| **Cit 24** | Urine Citrate | men >450, women >550 | *consider K citrate 25 bid; if from RTA (urine pH > 6.5) also use K citrate* |
| **SS CaP** | Supersaturation CaP | 0.5-2 | *Urine usually pH > 6.5, IH common.* |
| **pH** | 24 Hour Urine pH | 5.8-6.2 | *<5.8 consider K or Na citrate 25-30 mEq BID; 6.5, RTA if citrate is low; >8, urea splitting infection.* |
| **SS UA** | Supersaturation Uric Acid | 0-1 | *urine pH <6, creates UA stones. Treated with alkali* |
| **UA 24** | Urine Uric Acid | g/day: men <0.800, women <0.750 | *dietary; if stones are severe and low protein diet fails try allopurinol 200 mg/d* |

\*\*Cystine Screening: positive result may be seen in patients with homozygous cystinuria and cystine stone disease, some individuals heterozygous for cystinuria without cystine stone disease, or in patients taking medications such as captopril or penicillamine.

**Figure 43–3.** Commercial 24-hour urine results are available and simplify the collection and reporting process. (Courtesy of LithoLink Corporation, Chicago.)

factors was adequate in repeated samples, enough so that therapy would not have been altered.

**Conversely, Parks and colleagues from Chicago have noted significant disparities between two separate collections** (Parks et al, 2002). More than 1000 patients were examined from both private practice and academic settings. They noted that within nearly 70% of the comparisons, there were large enough differences such that the standard deviation would contain clinically relevant disparities. The authors therefore concluded that relying on one specimen alone could easily lead to misdiagnosis and, consequently, mismanagement.

**The "normal limits" cited on commercially available urine analysis packages may not be the same as those normal values that have been quoted previously. Therefore, one should pay close attention to those patients who may fall in the "gray zone" when a commercially available urine analysis package is used.**

## KEY POINTS: SIMPLIFIED METABOLIC EVALUATION

- A simplified metabolic evaluation has been established.
- Commercial laboratories may facilitate the collection of 24-hour urine studies.
- There is no consensus regarding the need for one versus two 24-hour urine collections during an initial evaluation (although the authors prefer two collections).

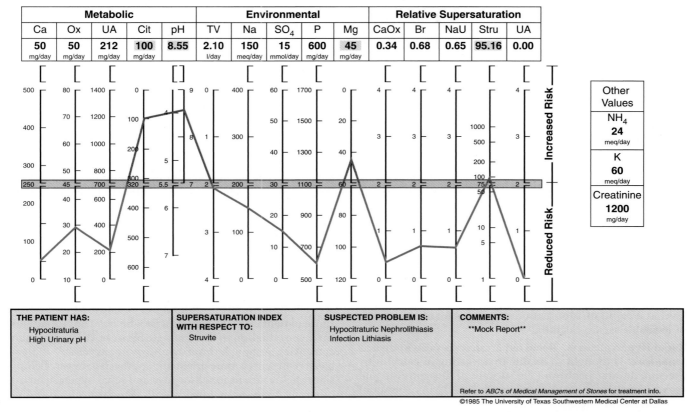

| PATIENT INFORMATION | | LAB INFORMATION |
|---|---|---|
| SSN 111-11-1111 | **StoneRisk** | No. 81324 |
| Patient Name | **Diagnostic Profile** | Control Number 11A22456 |
| Physician Name | | Date Sample Collected 01/01/2005 |
| Laboratory Mission Pharmacal Reference | | Date Sample Received 01/03/2005 |

| Metabolic | | | | | Environmental | | | | | Relative Supersaturation | | | | |
|---|---|---|---|---|---|---|---|---|---|---|---|---|---|---|
| Ca | Ox | UA | Cit | pH | TV | Na | SO$_4$ | P | Mg | CaOx | Br | NaU | Stru | UA |
| **50** | **50** | **212** | **100** | **8.55** | **2.10** | **150** | **15** | **600** | **45** | **0.34** | **0.68** | **0.65** | **95.16** | **0.00** |
| mg/day | mg/day | mg/day | mg/day | | l/day | meq/day | mmol/day | mg/day | mg/day | | | | | |

Other Values

NH$_4$ **24** meq/day

K **60** meq/day

Creatinine **1200** mg/day

Increased Risk — Reduced Risk

| THE PATIENT HAS: | SUPERSATURATION INDEX WITH RESPECT TO: | SUSPECTED PROBLEM IS: | COMMENTS: |
|---|---|---|---|
| Hypocitraturia High Urinary pH | Struvite | Hypocitraturic Nephrolithiasis Infection Lithiasis | **Mock Report** |

Refer to *ABC's of Medical Management of Stones* for treatment info.

©1985 The University of Texas Southwestern Medical Center at Dallas

**Figure 43–4.** The 24-hour urine results may be presented graphically to assist with interpretation and planning. (Courtesy of Mission Pharmacal, Inc., San Antonio, Texas.)

# CLASSIFICATION OF NEPHROLITHIASIS AND DIAGNOSTIC CRITERIA

**With use of an ambulatory protocol, the etiology of nephrolithiasis can be classified into 12 separate categories reflecting specific physiologic derangements.** The details regarding the physiology and pathophysiology of these distinct entities are included in Chapter 42. These categories are listed in Table 43–5 along with the relative frequency of their occurrence as noted by Pak and colleagues at a dedicated stone clinic in an academic medical center (Levy et al, 1995). An argument can be made that these relative incidences may not be representative of the general population for two reasons. First, referral to an academic center may imply a more serious version of stone disease and may therefore represent a selection bias. Second, recognizing that there are at least some regional variations of stone incidence (Harvey et al, 1990), this particular population of patients may be distinctly different from those populations in different regions of the United States and other regions of the world.

# Calcium-Based Calculi

## Hypercalciuria (>200 mg/day)

The classification of nephrolithiasis recognizes three broad categories of hypercalciuria.

**Absorptive Hypercalciuria.** Absorptive hypercalciuria involves an increase in the amount of calcium that is absorbed by the intestinal tract. In absorptive hypercalciuria type 1, this increased absorption will occur regardless of the amount of calcium in the patient's diet. Therefore, these subjects will demonstrate an increased urinary excretion of calcium on both the fasting and the loading specimens. In contrast, patients with absorptive hypercalciuria type 2 will have a normal amount of urinary calcium excretion during calcium restriction but will show elevations during their regular diet. Patients with both subtypes of absorptive hypercalciuria will have normal serum calcium concentration and a normal level of circulating intact parathyroid hormone (iPTH). In fact, **these patients often demonstrate a low iPTH**

**Table 43–5. Classification of Nephrolithiasis**

| | Percentage | |
|---|---|---|
| | Sole Occurrence | Combined Occurrence |
| Absorptive hypercalciuria | 20 | 40 |
|   Type 1 | | |
|   Type 2 | | |
| Renal hypercalciuria | 5 | 8 |
| Primary hyperparathyroidism | 3 | 8 |
| Unclassified calcium nephrolithiasis | 15 | 25 |
| Hyperoxaluric calcium nephrolithiasis | 2 | 15 |
|   Enteric hyperoxaluria | | |
|   Primary hyperoxaluria | | |
|   Dietary hyperoxaluria | | |
| Hypocitraturic calcium nephrolithiasis | 10 | 50 |
|   Distal renal tubular acidosis | | |
|   Chronic diarrheal syndrome | | |
|   Thiazide induced | | |
|   Idiopathic | | |
| Hypomagnesiuric calcium nephrolithiasis | 5 | 10 |
| Gouty diathesis | 15 | 30 |
| Cystinuria | <1 | |
| Infection stones | 1 | 5 |
| Low urine volume | 10 | 50 |
| No disturbance and miscellaneous | ≤3 | |
| | 100 | |

Modified from Levy FL, Adams-Huet B, Pak CY: Ambulatory evaluation of nephrolithiasis: An update of a 1980 protocol. Am J Med 1995;98:50-59.

**Table 43–6. Differential Diagnosis of Hypercalciuria**

| | Absorptive | Renal | Resorptive |
|---|---|---|---|
| Serum calcium | Normal | Normal | Elevated |
| Parathyroid function | Suppressed | Stimulated (secondarily) | Stimulated (primarily) |
| Fasting urinary calcium | Normal | Elevated | Elevated |
| Intestinal calcium absorption | Elevated (primarily) | Elevated (secondarily) | Elevated (secondarily) |

level as a result of suppression from a constant abundance of available serum calcium.

**Renal Hypercalciuria.** Renal hypercalciuria (also known as renal leak) is thought to be due to a wasting of calcium by the functioning nephron. The details of this process and various hypotheses are outlined in Chapter 42. As a result of constant loss of calcium from the distal tubules, these patients will demonstrate hypercalciuria during all phases of fasting, loading, or restriction of dietary calcium. **Most patients with renal hypercalciuria will have a normal serum calcium concentration but may exhibit a mild elevation of iPTH as the regulatory systems attempt to "keep up" with the constant loss of calcium.**

**Resorptive Hypercalciuria (Primary Hyperparathyroidism).** Patients with this disorder suffer from an overproduction of parathyroid hormone from either one dominant adenoma or diffuse hyperplasia of all four glands. The hallmark of this disorder is the persistence of increased urinary calcium during all parts of the dietary calcium manipulations. In addition, these patients frequently demonstrate hypercalcemia and elevations of parathyroid hormone. The measurement of only the intact portion of the hormone (iPTH) has avoided confusion from the measurement of fragments of the same molecule (Kao et al, 1982; Nussbaum et al, 1987) and has greatly enhanced the ability to make this diagnosis.

Unfortunately, some patients may have normocalcemic hyperparathyroidism. These patients may be difficult to distinguish from those with renal leak hypercalciuria, during which serum calcium concentration will be normal but a mild elevation of the iPTH can occur, causing a secondary hyper-

parathyroidism. In these instances, the patients can be treated with a 2-week course of a thiazide diuretic, such as chlorthalidone (25 mg daily). If the patient actually suffers from renal leak, the calcium loss should be suppressed and the iPTH level should return to normal (Aroldi et al, 1979; Barilla and Pak, 1979; Zechner et al, 1981). Those with true primary hyperparathyroidism will continue to circulate elevated levels of iPTH and may become mildly hypercalcemic, although this feature has been debated in the literature (Klimiuk et al, 1981; Farquhar et al, 1990; Strong et al, 1991).

**Idiopathic Hypercalciuria.** Idiopathic hypercalciuria can be found both in normal people and among stone formers (Coe et al, 1979). These patients may demonstrate elevated amounts of urine calcium in all phases of the dietary calcium manipulation but will not demonstrate serum abnormalities. **On a cautionary note, this term does not always enjoy a strict definition and is sometimes substituted to describe those patients with hypercalciuria who have not undergone further evaluation to discriminate between the various subcategories.** Although this diagnosis is not as "clean" as possible, it represents a more pragmatic approach to hypercalciuria, since the treatment for absorptive and renal hypercalciuria is often the same (as outlined later in this chapter). Table 43–6 summarizes the laboratory parameters that help delineate the various types of hypercalciuria.

## KEY POINTS: HYPERCALCIURIA

- Hypercalciuria can be divided into three causes: excessive gastrointestinal absorption, renal tubular leak, hyperparathyroidism.

- Idiopathic hypercalciuria refers to unknown etiology or unevaluated etiology.

### Hyperuricosuric Calcium Nephrolithiasis

**Patients with hyperuricosuria may be prone to the formation of calcium oxalate calculi through a process called heterogeneous nucleation** (also referred to as epitaxy) (Coe and Kavalach, 1974; Pak and Arnold, 1975; Coe, 1980). The details of this process are outlined in Chapter 42. These patients give a history of calcium oxalate nephrolithiasis and may have a history of hyperuricemia with symptomatic gout. On metabolic evaluation, they will demonstrate hyperuricosuria (>800 mg/day).

## Hyperoxaluria (>40 mg/day)

**Enteric Hyperoxaluria. This entity is often one of the most striking findings during a metabolic evaluation because it involves multiple anomalies, all a result of chronic diarrhea with its attendant dehydration and bicarbonate losses** (Worcester, 2002). The main hallmark is, of course, hyperoxaluria with values that can be quite high (i.e., >50 mg/day). As a result of intestinal fluid loss, patients will often exhibit low urine volumes. The bicarbonate loss (and the consumption of citrate as an acid-base buffer) can also cause a low urine pH and hypocitraturia (Rudman et al, 1980). Urine calcium excretion is often low because of the saponification of oral calcium with poorly absorbed fats in the intestinal tract.

**Primary Hyperoxaluria. This disorder is caused by an inborn error of metabolism.** The more common variant, type 1, is due to a defect of the enzyme alanine-glyoxylate transaminase through an autosomal recessive inheritance. Type 2 is a less common variant thought secondary to a defect in D-glycerate dehydrogenase and glyoxylate reductase. Both of these types usually present during childhood with early stone formation, tissue deposition of oxalate (oxalosis), and renal failure due to nephrocalcinosis. Death often occurs before the age of 20 years in untreated patients (Williams and Smith, 1968; Leumann and Hoppe, 1999). Metabolic evaluation reveals high urine oxalate excretion as well as high serum levels of this molecule.

**Mild Metabolic Hyperoxaluria (Dietary).** The importance of dietary oxalate and the possibility of an inheritable sensitivity to oral oxalate loads are debated and have already been discussed in the preceding chapter. Just as interesting is the possibility that a deficiency of a bacterium found within intestinal flora (*Oxalobacter formigenes*) could be a factor in the formation of calcium oxalate calculi (Allison et al, 1986; Sidhu et al, 1999; Troxel et al, 2003). Regardless of the underlying etiology, some patients without primary hyperoxaluria or without a history of bowel disorders will demonstrate an elevation of oxalate in the 24-hour urine collection. A review of the patient's dietary habits may reveal a predisposition for those foods that are particularly high in oxalate. **Whereas this molecule is ubiquitous and cannot be avoided, certain foods can deliver substantial amounts of oxalate in one serving.** An abbreviated list of foods that are particularly high in oxalate is contained in Table 43–7 (Assimos and Holmes, 2000; Holmes and Assimo, 2004).

## Hypocitraturic Calcium Nephrolithiasis (<550 mg, female; <450 mg, male)

**There is some controversy about the definition of normal urinary citrate excretion. Women tend to have higher urinary citrate measurements than men do, particularly before menopause** (Pak, 1990). Menon and Mahle (1983) define hypocitraturia as citrate excretion of less than 110 mg for men and 200 mg for women. Despite noting gender differences, Pak (1990) defined normal urinary citrate as more than 320 mg for both genders. In some of the earlier studies from Dallas, hypocitraturia was found in up to 50% of all patients evaluated, frequently in association with other abnormalities (Nicar et al, 1983). Parks and Coe (1986) have also noted the importance of urinary citrate for the prevention of calcareous stones and have set the limits of normal at higher

| Table 43–7. **High-Oxalate Foods** |
|---|
| Tea (black) |
| Cocoa |
| Spinach |
| Mustard greens |
| Pokeweed |
| Swiss chard |
| Beets |
| Rhubarb |
| Okra |
| Berries (some) |
| Chocolate |
| Nuts |
| Wheat germ |
| Soy crackers |
| Pepper |

values (men, >450 mg daily; women, >550 mg daily). Nevertheless, hypocitraturia is considered one of the more common metabolic diagnoses, probably second only to hypercalciuria. There are four causes of hypocitraturia:

**Distal Renal Tubular Acidosis (Type 1). Patients may have either an acquired or an inheritable version of renal tubular acidosis, with the incomplete version representing a less serious clinical pattern. Regardless of the actual cause, the laboratory hallmark of this disease is a low urine citrate concentration (hypocitraturia) with an inappropriately high urine pH.** Often, the measured 24-hour urine citrate will be quite diminished with values below 100 mg/day. The urine pH will be elevated to 6.5 or above. Hypokalemia is often evident on the serum studies, as is hyperchloremia. A non–anion gap acidosis may be present as well with carbon dioxide values in the mid teens (Preminger et al, 1985). First-void urine specimens can be evaluated to assess the urine pH and to screen for a renal tubular acidosis. Patients with renal tubular acidosis will be unable to acidify the urine overnight and should have a urine pH no lower than 5.5.

Distal renal tubular acidosis may present as an isolated entity or may be the secondary manifestation of a variety of systemic and renal disorders. More than two thirds of patients with distal renal tubular acidosis are adults, but children will occasionally be identified with this disorder. Infants generally present with vomiting or diarrhea, failure to thrive, and growth retardation. Children often present with metabolic bone disease and renal stones; adults frequently present with symptoms attributable to nephrolithiasis and nephrocalcinosis.

**Up to 70% of adults with distal renal tubular acidosis have kidney stones** (Caruana and Buckalew, 1988). Those patients with onset at an early age or with severe forms of the disorder may develop nephrocalcinosis and eventual renal insufficiency (Fig. 43–5). Renal tubular acidosis is more common in women, accounting for nearly 80% of all cases. Secondary renal tubular acidosis can be induced by many common urologic disorders that may also be sought after a diagnosis of acquired renal tubular acidosis. These include obstructive uropathy, pyelonephritis, acute tubular necrosis, renal transplantation, analgesic nephropathy, sarcoidosis, idiopathic

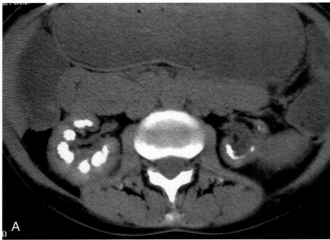

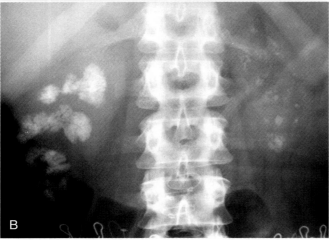

**Figure 43–5.** CT image (**A**) and plain film (**B**) of a patient with renal tubular acidosis and renal failure. Both kidneys demonstrate severe calcification of the medullary pyramids consistent with nephrocalcinosis. Notice the atrophic left kidney on the CT image.

| Table 43–8. Causes of Acquired Renal Tubular Acidosis |
|---|
| Obstructive uropathy |
| Recurrent pyelonephritis |
| Acute tubular necrosis |
| Renal transplantation |
| Analgesic nephropathy |
| Sarcoidosis |
| Idiopathic hypercalciuria |
| Primary hyperparathyroidism |

hypercalciuria, and primary hyperparathyroidism (Buckalew, 1989) (Table 43–8).

Some patients will have an incomplete variant of the disease with less marked hypocitraturia and a more normal urine pH. Incomplete variants can be diagnosed with an ammonium chloride loading challenge. In this evaluation, the fasting patient is given 0.1 g of ammonium chloride per kilogram of body weight in crushed granules mixed with a soft drink. Subsequently, hourly measurements of urine pH and bihourly measurements of serum pH or bicarbonate are taken during 4 to 6 hours (Pohlman et al, 1984). If the serum pH falls below 7.32 or the bicarbonate level falls below 16 mmol/L but urine pH remains at or above 5.5, the diagnosis of incomplete distal renal tubular acidosis is confirmed. If at any time the urine pH falls below 5.5, the diagnosis of incomplete distal renal tubular acidosis is excluded (Preminger et al, 1985, 1987, 1988).

**Chronic Diarrheal States.** The laboratory findings in a patient with a chronic diarrheal disorder are similar to those in patients described with enteric hyperoxaluria. However, these patients do not tend to suffer from the bowel inflammation and subsequent heightened permeability to oxalate. Therefore, urinary oxalate may be mildly elevated, but usually not to the extent found in those patients with bowel resection or inflammatory disorders. These patients are likely to demonstrate moderate decreases in urinary citrate excretion with associated low urine volumes (Fegan et al, 1992; Caudarella et al, 1993; Worcester, 2002; Parks et al, 2003b).

**Thiazide-Induced Hypocitraturia. One of the side effects of thiazide therapy is hypocitraturia.** This defect is presumably secondary to the hypokalemia and resultant intracellular acidosis that may develop after prolonged therapy with thiazides (Pak et al, 1985a). Such patients will demonstrate the effects of this medication. That is, they often have mild to moderate hypocitraturia and mild to moderate hypokalemia. Since thiazides are still widely used as a diuretic and for the management of hypertension, some patients may present with a stone episode after prolonged therapy with this medication. Patients with stone disease who are treated with thiazides for the control of hypercalciuria should be screened for these metabolic disturbances (Pak et al, 1985b).

**Idiopathic Hypocitraturia.** Patients with idiopathic hypocitraturia include all those with 24-hour urine citrate measurements less than 550 mg (males) or 450 mg (females) in the absence of any of the noted disease states. It is important to consider unrecognized incomplete renal tubular acidosis as a potential diagnosis, since this disorder carries with it a significant risk of long-term morbidity. In addition, a careful history should be taken to screen for bowel dysfunction.

## KEY POINTS: HYPOCITRATURIA

- The definition of hypocitraturia may vary greatly.
- Severe hypocitraturia should immediately suggest renal tubular acidosis.
- Hypocitraturia frequently accompanies other diagnostic categories.

### Hypomagnesiuric Calcium Nephrolithiasis (<80 mg)

**Hypomagnesiuric calcium nephrolithiasis is characterized by low urinary magnesium concentration, hypocitraturia, and low urine volume. It is frequently associated with chronic thiazide therapy** (Ljunghall et al, 1981; Preminger et al, 1989). More commonly, inflammatory bowel disorders, particularly those that cause malabsorption, have been implicated in this process (Preminger et al, 1989). Excessive dependence on laxatives may also induce a pattern similar to a chronic diarrheal state (Dick et al, 1990; Soble et al, 1999). The importance of this disorder has been questioned, however, with the suggestion that the stone-risk association of hypomagnesiuria may actually be due to its effect on urinary citrate (Schwartz et al, 2001).

## Uric Acid–Based Calculi

### Gouty Diathesis

The pathophysiologic mechanism of uric acid nephrolithiasis is explained in detail in Chapter 42, but it does deserve some mention to better understand its diagnosis. Since there are no known inhibitors of uric acid crystallization, undissociated uric acid will precipitate when the urine becomes supersaturated. The sigmoidal solubility curve will predict that at a pH of 6.5, more than 90% of all uric acid is ionized and therefore soluble; 50% of uric acid will be soluble at a pH of approximately 5.5 (pKa) (Gutman and Yu, 1968). By definition, patients with gouty diathesis have a urine pH below 5.5.

It follows, then, that patients with gouty diathesis and uric acid calculi will tend to have lower urine pH than in normal subjects (Gutman and Yu, 1968). The 24-hour measurements of this molecule will often be more than 800 mg. Up to 20% of patients with gout will develop uric acid calculi, prompting examination of serum for hyperuricemia. Oftentimes, 24-hour urine collections can underestimate the total amount of uric acid if the specimen pH drops lower than 5.5. In this scenario, the uric acid forms precipitates and settles to the bottom of the collection container.

**It should not be difficult to distinguish between those patients with hyperuricosuric calcium nephrolithiasis, who form calcium oxalate stones, and those with gouty diathesis, who can form either uric acid or calcium oxalate calculi. Patients with hyperuricosuric calcium nephrolithiasis present with normal urine pH and hyperuricosuria, accompanied sometimes by hypercalciuria. In contrast, those with gouty diathesis have a low fractional excretion of urate (that contributes to hyperuricemia) and low urine pH (that leads to increased amount of undissociated uric acid)** (Khatchadourian et al, 1995; Pak et al, 2003c). The varying biochemical and physicochemical presentations of the two conditions can be ascribed to overindulgence with purine-rich foods in those with hyperuricosuric calcium nephrolithiasis and underlying primary gout in those with gouty diathesis (Pak et al, 2002b).

A dietary history should be obtained from all patients with uric acid calculi because they may have a tendency to purine gluttony (high intake of animal protein, specifically red meat). An astute clinician will at least give a brief consideration to the possibility of a neoplastic or myeloproliferative disorder. Patients with diabetes mellitus may also form uric acid calculi as a result of disorders in ammonium handling with subsequent low urine pH (Pak et al, 2003c).

Uric acid calculi can be notoriously radiolucent. Tomography may overcome this difficulty (Fig. 43–6), as can the

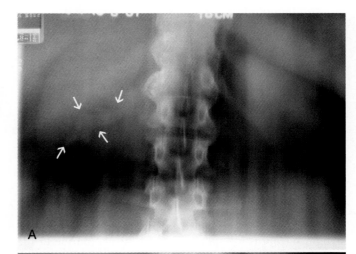

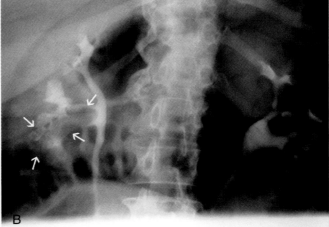

**Figure 43–6.** **A,** Plain film tomographic appearance of a lower pole partial staghorn uric acid calculus. **B,** The addition of intravenous contrast material demonstrates the stone as a filling defect during the excretory portion of the intravenous pyelogram.

acquisition of a non–contrast-enhanced renal CT. These stones frequently have an orange appearance, especially when they are viewed endoscopically. Uric acid stone formers can have a propensity to produce large volumes of very small calculi that may cause obstruction as they pass down the ureter.

### KEY POINTS: URIC ACID–BASED CALCULI

- Hyperuricosuria may be associated with pure uric acid calculi or calcium oxalate calculi.

- Patients with gout may be predisposed to uric acid stones.

- Dietary indiscretion (purine gluttony) should always be suspected.

# Cystinuria

**Cystinuria is caused by an autosomal recessive error of transepithelial transport involving the intestine and the kidneys** (Thier et al, 1965; Pak and Fuller, 1983). In this disease, patients are unable to reabsorb the dibasic amino acids cystine, ornithine, lysine, and arginine. The resultant **accumulation of cystine causes crystallization when concentrations rise above the saturation point (approximately 250 mg cystine per liter of urine)** (Pak and Fuller, 1983).

Patients with this disorder may present at a young age and may have affected first-degree relatives. The stones are often yellow and waxy in appearance and are relatively faint on plain radiography. Staghorn calculi or multiple, filled calyces are common (Fig. 43–7).

Historically, a diagnosis of cystinuria was made with a sodium nitroprusside spot test, which turned purple in the presence of cystine (Smith, 1977). Although this test is a helpful screening adjunct, quantitative measurements of cystine can be difficult to perform owing to interference from other sulfhydryl-containing compounds (such as medications used to treat this disorder) or significant variances with minor changes in urine pH or creatinine content (Pak and Fuller, 1983). Coe and colleagues have developed a more reliable method of cystine supersaturation measurement that may greatly aid in the diagnosis and especially the management of cystinuria (Nakagawa et al, 2000; Coe et al, 2001).

Cystinurics may also demonstrate additional metabolic anomalies on 24-hour urine studies (Sakhaee et al, 1989). In controlled dietary assessment of 27 patients with cystinuria, hypercalciuria was noted in 18.5% of patients, hyperuricosuria in 22.2%. Hypocitraturia was identified in 44.4% and was associated with defective renal acidification in 80% of the patients in whom it was tested. The authors noted that hypercalciuria, hyperuricosuria, and hypocitraturia frequently accompany cystinuria and speculated that these conditions might be renal in origin rather than a result of dietary or environmental aberrations. They further concluded that these unrelated anomalies may contribute to the formation of calcium and uric acid stones, which sometimes complicate cystine nephrolithiasis.

## KEY POINTS: CYSTINURIA

- Cystinuria is manifested when concentrations exceed 250 mg/L.
- Cystinuria may be accompanied by other metabolic abnormalities.

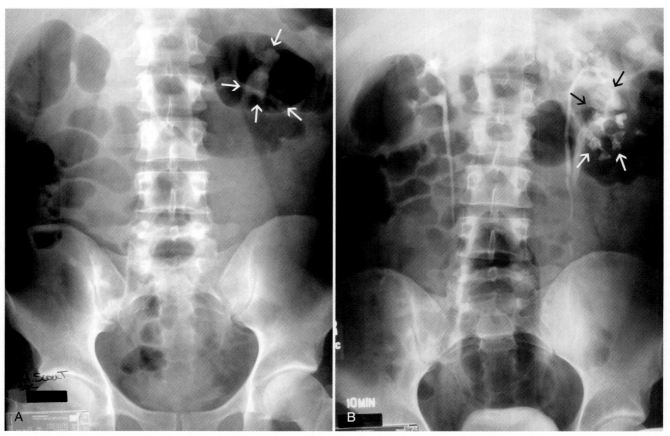

**Figure 43–7.** Cystine calculi are radiopaque on plain film but are less dense than other calcium-based calculi. Notice the stone within the lower pole of this duplicated system (**A**). Similar to uric acid stones, the cystine calculus is more clearly distinguished during the excretory phase of the intravenous pyelogram (**B**).

# Infection Calculi (Struvite)

Struvite calculi form in the presence of alkaline urine (pH above 7.2) and in an environment rich in ammonia (Nemoy and Stamey, 1971). **The ammonia is thought to be produced through the splitting of urea by colonization with bacteria that produce urease.** The details of this process are presented in Chapter 42. Many bacterial organisms are able to produce this enzyme (Table 43–9), the most notorious of which is *Proteus mirabilis*. Although *Escherichia coli* is not able to spilt urea, it may be associated with struvite calculi in up to 13% of infections (perhaps through a metachronous infection).

Patients with these calculi may present with the symptoms of acute pyelonephritis, including fevers, chills, flank pain, dysuria, frequency, urgency, and malodorous, cloudy urine. Some patients may exhibit more chronic symptoms of malaise, fatigue, loss of appetite, and generalized weakness. Rarely, infections and obstruction have lasted long enough to produce a xanthogranulomatous pyelonephritis. Xanthogranulomatous pyelonephritis may cause the failure of an entire kidney or may affect just a portion. Spontaneous fistulas may develop to external surfaces or to peritoneal contents (Fig. 43–8).

**Women are more often affected with struvite calculi than are men, probably because of an increased susceptibility to urinary tract colonization.** A history of a foreign body (e.g., forgotten stent, suture material, staple) or of a neurogenic bladder may be noted. Struvite calculi can be quite large and often fill multiple calyces or even the entire collecting system (Fig. 43–9). **This stone type accounts for the majority of all staghorn calculi.** Urine cultures will often reveal a bacterial

### Table 43–9.  Organisms That May Produce Urease

| Organisms | Usually (>90% of Isolates) | Occasionally (5%–30% of Isolates) |
|---|---|---|
| Gram positive | Proteus rettgeri<br>Proteus vulgaris<br>Proteus mirabilis<br>Proteus morganii<br>Providencia stuartii<br>Haemophilus influenzae<br>Bordetella pertussis<br>Bacteroides corrodens<br>Yersinia enterocolitica<br>Brucella spp. | Klebsiella pneumoniae<br>Klebsiella oxytoca<br>Serratia marcescens<br>Haemophilus para-<br>  influenzae<br>Bordetella bronchiseptica<br>Aeromonas hydrophila<br>Pseudomonas aeruginosa<br>Pasteurella spp. |
| Gram positive | Flavobacterium spp.<br>Staphylococcus aureus<br>Micrococcus<br>Corynebacterium<br>  ulcerans<br>Corynebacterium<br>  renale<br>Corynebacterium<br>  ovis<br>Corynebacterium<br>  hofmannii | Staphylococcus epidermidis<br>Bacillus spp.<br>Corynebacterium<br>  murium<br>Corynebacterium<br>  equi<br>Peptococcus asaccharolyticus<br>Clostridium tetani<br>Mycobacterium rhodochrous<br>  group |
| Mycoplasma | T-strain Mycoplasma<br>Ureaplasma urealyticum | |
| Yeasts | Cryptococcus<br>Rhodotorula<br>Sporobolomyces<br>Candida humicola<br>Trichosporon cutaneum | |

From Gleeson MJ, Griffith DP: Infection stones. In Resnick MI, Pak CYC, eds: Urolithiasis: A Medical and Surgical Reference. Philadelphia, WB Saunders, 1990:115.

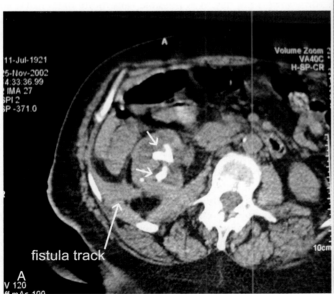

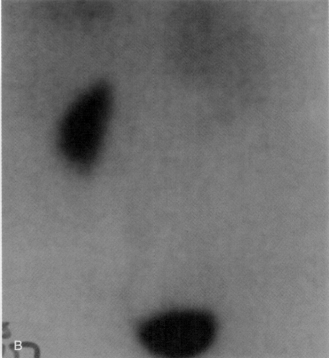

**Figure 43–8.**  **A,** CT image of a staghorn calculus within the right kidney (*short arrows*). The *long arrow* points to a fistula that spontaneously eroded through Petit's triangle. This patient denied a history of recurrent urinary tract infections. **B,** Nuclear renogram of the same patient in **A.** Note the complete lack of function of the affected kidney. This organ was removed laparoscopically.

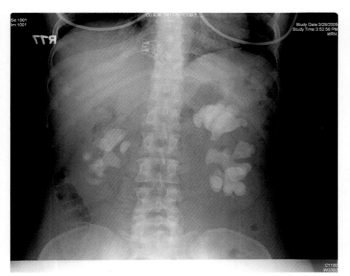

**Figure 43–9.** Plain film of a patient with bilateral staghorn calculi composed entirely of struvite. This patient had a history of recurrent urinary tract infections dating back 15 years.

pathogen, although a sterile urine culture does not preclude the sequestration of bacteria within the calculus itself.

**There is debate about the incidence of associated metabolic anomalies in patients with struvite calculi.** Resnick has advocated the performance of a metabolic evaluation for all patients with infection calculi because of a high incidence of positive findings. Conversely, Lingeman has studied 22 patients with infection calculi and noted that patients with pure struvite calculi were significantly less likely to have metabolic anomalies on 24-hour urine evaluation than were those patients with mixed compositions of struvite and calcium oxalate (Resnick, 1981; Lingeman et al, 1995).

---

### KEY POINTS: INFECTION CALCULI (STRUVITE)

■ Women produce more infection calculi than men do.

■ The urine pH is usually above 6.5 to 7.0.

■ Urea-splitting organisms are frequent.

■ Infection calculi are the most likely to produce staghorn stones.

---

## Low Urine Volumes (<2000 mL)

**Some patients will exhibit few abnormalities on a complete evaluation other than low urine volumes.** From a simplistic view, a low volume of urine output will concentrate the molecular components of crystal formation and raise the supersaturation risk. Intuitively, a patient with a relative state of dehydration will trend toward acidic urine, lowering the urine pH toward the pKa of uric acid (5.5) and potentially consuming titratable buffers such as citrate.

---

### Table 43–10. Potential Causes of Erroneous 24-Hour Urine Collection

Error in collection technique (e.g., improper use of preservatives, ice)
Failure to collect a full 24 hours' worth of urine
Changes in the patient's diet for the sake of the study
Intermittent indiscretions in diet
Failure of specimen to accurately represent "typical" day
Bacterial contamination

---

Many patients with low urine volumes work in professions that induce high insensible losses of fluid (manual labor, outdoor exposure) (Sakhaee et al, 1987; Borghi et al, 1990, 1993a). Many work in environs that do not allow easy access to fluids and work breaks (assembly line, surgeons). A focused social history should elucidate these factors and allow proper identification and subsequent counseling.

## No Disturbances

**Pak has estimated that 3% of all patients undergoing a full metabolic evaluation will demonstrate no abnormalities** (Pak et al, 1980a). **Whereas, on the surface, these patients may present less of a diagnostic challenge, there is always a concern that the collections are not representative of the patient's true metabolic state** (Table 43–10). This could be secondary to an error in collection technique, failure to collect a full 24 hours' worth of urine, changes in the patient's diet for the sake of the study, or intermittent indiscretions in diet. Furthermore, a 24-hour urine collection represents a pooled sample. Heavy oxalate loading at one particular meal or bolus replacement of fluids at the end of a workday may produce average values that look normal but actually hide periods of extreme urine parameters that promote stone formation. Finally, most patients will collect the requested 24-hour specimens on days when they are home and able to stay close to the collection container. For most, this occurs on a weekend or nonworking day. It is possible (and quite likely) that collections on these days do not represent the patient's typical metabolic milieu that exists during the rest of the week (Rodgers et al, 1994, 1995; Norman, 1996; Hess et al, 1997).

The diagnostic criteria for the 12 principal classifications described in this section are summarized in Table 43–11.

## USE OF STONE ANALYSIS TO DETERMINE METABOLIC ABNORMALITIES

Questions have arisen about the necessity of both chemical stone analysis and metabolic evaluation for patients with nephrolithiasis. **Although stone composition analysis is not always feasible or desirable, there is helpful information from such an investigation that can aid with preventive therapy.** Unfortunately, chemical and mineralogic names of common calculi are sometimes used interchangeably, causing significant confusion for the clinician. A list of these names is therefore provided in Table 43–12.

Parks demonstrated that urine supersaturation values do in fact coincide with the stones that patients actually produce (Parks et al, 1997). Although this may seem intuitive, it is

**Table 43–11. Diagnostic Criteria**

| | Serum | | | Urine | | | | | | | |
|---|---|---|---|---|---|---|---|---|---|---|---|
| | Ca | P | PTH | Ca Fasting | Ca Load | Ca Restricted | UA | Ox | Cit | pH | Mg |
| Absorptive hypercalciuria type 1 | N | N | N | N | ↑ | ↑ | N | N | N | N | N |
| Absorptive hypercalciuria type 2 | N | N | N | N | ↑ | N | N | N | N | N | N |
| Renal hypercalciuria | N | N | ↑ | ↑ | ↑ | ↑ | N | N | N | N | N |
| Primary hyperparathyroidism | ↑ | ↓ | ↑ | ↑ | ↑ | ↑ | N | N | N | N | N |
| Unclassified hypercalciuria | N | N/↓ | N | ↑ | ↑ | ↑ | N | N | N | N | N |
| Hyperuricosuria | N | N | N | N | N | N | ↑ | N | N | N | N |
| Enteric hyperoxaluria | N/↓ | N/↓ | N/↓ | ↓ | ↓ | ↓ | ↓ | ↑ | ↓ | N | N |
| Hypocitraturia | N | N | N | N | N | N | N | N | ↓ | N | N |
| Renal tubular acidosis | N | N | N/↑ | ↑ | N | N/↑ | N | N | ↓ | N/↑ | N |
| Hypomagnesiuria | N | N | N | N | N | N | N/↓ | N | N | N | ↓ |
| Gouty diathesis | N | N | N | N | N | N | N/↑ | N | N/↓ | ↓ | N |
| Infection lithiasis | N | N | N | N | N | N | N | N | ↓ | ↑ | N |

Fasting samples represent 2-hour collections obtained in the morning after an overnight fast. Calcium load samples are obtained during a 4-hour period subsequent to oral ingestion of 1 g calcium.
PTH, immunoreactive parathyroid hormone; ↑ high; ↓ low; N, normal; UA, uric acid; Ox, oxalate; Cit, citrate; Mg, magnesium.

**Table 43–12. Mineralogic Names of Renal Calculi**

| | |
|---|---|
| Calcium oxalate monohydrate | Whewellite |
| Calcium oxalate dihydrate | Weddellite |
| Calcium hydrogen phosphate dihydrate | Brushite |
| Tricalcium phosphate | Whitlockite |
| Carbonite-apatite | Carbonite-apatite |
| Magnesium ammonium phosphate | Struvite |
| Cystine | None |
| Uric acid | None |

important to know that medications used to target specific pathophysiologic processes will produce the necessary desired effects. Indeed, in their study, treatments that reduced stone rates also reduced the supersaturation values for the historical stone composition for that patient. If the development of calculi is due to prolonged supersaturation of various crystals (e.g., calcium oxalate, urate), then it is further reassuring that "snapshot," pooled urine supersaturation measurements accurately track stone admixtures and are a reliable index of long-term, "average" renal and urine supersaturations.

Other investigators have found that knowledge of the stone composition can be a helpful adjunct to a metabolic evaluation. **Since most stones are a mixture of more than one component, the relative ratios or predominance of any particular molecule may have predictive value.** In an analysis of almost 1400 patients who had both stone analysis and a complete metabolic evaluation, Pak noted that calcium apatite and mixed calcium oxalate–calcium apatite stones were associated with the diagnoses of renal tubular acidosis and primary hyperparathyroidism (odds ratio ≥ 2) but not with chronic diarrheal syndromes (Pak et al, 2003b). As the phosphate content of the stone increased from calcium oxalate to mixed calcium oxalate–calcium apatite and finally to calcium apatite, the percentage of patients with renal tubular acidosis increased from 5% to 39%, and the percentage of those with primary hyperparathyroidism increased from 2% to 10%. Not surprisingly, pure and mixed uric acid stones were strongly associated with a gouty diathesis; brushite stones were associated with renal tubular acidosis. As expected, there was a

strong association between infection stones and infection and between cystine stones and cystinuria.

These findings were further supported by Kourambas and colleagues (2001). In a consecutive series of 100 patients, they correlated the findings of stone composition with metabolic results. Like Pak, they noted a significant risk of renal tubular acidosis in those producing predominantly calcium phosphate calculi. They suggested that the finding of a noncalcareous stone could simplify an evaluation by focusing the ensuing evaluation on the most obvious cause. Pure uric acid calculi are found in gouty diathesis and may not therefore require further testing. Likewise, pure cystine calculi do not require further testing.

Finally, Lingeman and associates (1995) noted that the finding of pure struvite or calcium apatite in a staghorn calculus predicted a low likelihood of finding other metabolic abnormalities during a workup. In their series, only 2 of 14 patients with pure infection stones had additional abnormalities compared with 7 of 7 patients with mixed chemical compositions. They therefore suggest that those patients with pure infection stones will not benefit from additional evaluation.

## KEY POINTS: STONE ANALYSIS

- Stone analysis may obviate the need for a complete metabolic evaluation.

- Stone composition can direct metabolic investigation.

## THE ECONOMICS OF METABOLIC EVALUATION

**There is no doubt that the costs associated with the treatment of nephrolithiasis are substantial.** In 1984, Shuster and Scheaffer estimated that the average stone episode cost approximately $2000, exclusive of recurrences. At the time, this was based on a predominance of open surgical approaches with an average hospital stay lasting 4 to 5 days. The average annual cost of recurrence for a current stone case was conservatively estimated to be in the $300 to $400 range. On the basis of these *conservative* projections, they estimated that the entire national population of white men in the age range of 18 to 60 years yielded an annual cost due to kidney stones approaching $315,000,000.

By 1993, the estimated costs continued to climb, despite advances in technology and decreases in inpatient care. Indeed, Clark and associates (1995) performed a review of prevalence data for urolithiasis and the relative frequency of surgical treatments from Civilian Health and Medical Program of the Uniformed Services claims data. They found that the total charges for evaluation, hospitalization, and treatment were estimated to be $1.23 billion per year. Professional charges for those who were hospitalized were estimated to be $183 million. Outpatient evaluation of urolithiasis was expected to cost $278 million. Indirect costs for lost wages were estimated to be $139 million. This totaled a staggering annual cost of $1.83 billion in the United States alone.

As we begin the 21st century, one can only assume that costs have not decreased but rather have continued their meteoric climb. **Recent evidence that obesity confers an increased risk of nephrolithiasis is sobering, considering the epidemic of obesity that is enveloping the United States** (Curhan et al, 1998a; Ekeruo et al, 2004; Morrill and Chinn, 2004; Rigby et al, 2004; Strumpf, 2004; Taylor et al, 2005).

With these figures in mind, prudence dictates that medical prevention could help curb runaway costs and prevent long-term sequelae of recurrent nephrolithiasis. As an example, Madore has found an association between nephrolithiasis and the eventual development of hypertension (Madore et al, 1998a, 1998b). This ubiquitous condition has its own attendant costs and risk of end-organ damage, such as cardiovascular disease and renal failure. As these subsequent disorders have their own costs and risks, any reasonable chance to break the chain of events should be sought.

The emergence and instant appeal of shockwave lithotripsy and improved endoscopy in the mid-1980s prompted some authors to remind the urologic community that medical assessment was still a viable option (Resnick and Pak, 1987; Preminger, 1994). **However, office visits, serum studies, and 24-hour urine studies have their own costs. Is there a break-even point at which the costs of a metabolic evaluation, pharmacologic prophylaxis, and continued office visits are less than the expense of surgical management?** This question has been the topic of several studies.

Chandhoke (2002) compared the cost of medical prophylaxis with the cost of clinical management of recurrent stone episodes. In addition, he determined the stone recurrence rate without prophylaxis (stone frequency) at which these two treatment approaches became cost equivalent. This review conducted a cost survey in 10 countries to compare costs of medical prophylaxis and management of recurrent acute stone episodes. Costs of an acute stone episode included an emergency department visit, associated radiographic imaging to confirm diagnosis of a symptomatic stone, and outpatient treatment of upper urinary tract stones that did not pass spontaneously. Costs of medical management included an initial limited metabolic evaluation, drug therapy, follow-up office visit every 6 months that included a 24-hour urinalysis, and

radiographic imaging of the kidneys, ureters, and bladder once a year. Not surprisingly, the costs of medical prophylaxis and management of an acute stone episode varied significantly from country to country. The stone frequency at which costs of these management options became equivalent ranged from 0.3 to 4 stone episodes a year. **This study concluded that medical management of a first stone episode is not cost-effective and that individual decisions should be determined by local costs.**

Researchers at the University of Texas, Southwestern Medical Center have formulated a decision tree model to evaluate the cost-effectiveness and stone recurrence rates of common management strategies in stone formers (Lotan et al, 2004). They evaluated six common medical strategies, namely, dietary measures alone (conservative), empirical drug treatment (empirical), and directed drug therapy based on simple or comprehensive metabolic evaluation. The model made reasonable assumptions about costs for evaluation, medications, emergency treatment, and surgery for stone recurrence. A review of the literature guided estimations of stone recurrence and risk reduction from various medical therapies. They found that first-time stone formers were best treated with a conservative approach since it was the least costly and yielded a stone formation rate of 0.07 stone per patient yearly. For recurrent stone formers, conservative treatment was less costly than drug treatments, but it was associated with a higher stone recurrence rate (0.3 stone per patient yearly). Directed medical therapies were more costly than conservative treatment ($885 to $1187 versus $258 yearly), but they provided the obvious advantage of decreasing recurrence rates by 60% to 86%.

The authors went on to compare the expense of the simple medical evaluation and associated management as described earlier in this chapter and noted it to be more costly than empirical treatment but also more effective. Importantly, a complete evaluation with attendant treatment offered no advantage in cost or efficacy over empirical treatment or modified simple metabolic evaluation and management. The Dallas authors recommended that first-time stone formers be treated with conservative therapy because it is both cost-effective and efficacious. In contrast, however, **recurrent stone formers should be treated medically after a simplified evaluation because of the high recurrence rate of stone formation.**

---

## KEY POINTS: ECONOMICS OF METABOLIC EVALUATION

- A metabolic evaluation may not be economically sound if it is applied to all patients with stone disease.

- Most first-time stone formers may not benefit economically from a metabolic evaluation unless initial screening puts them in a high-risk category.

- Recurrent stone formers are best treated with a metabolic evaluation and directed medical therapy.

# CONSERVATIVE MEDICAL MANAGEMENT

Certain conservative recommendations should be made for all patients regardless of the underlying cause of the stone disease. Unfortunately, it can be difficult to reach consensus regarding specific details from the available literature.

## Fluid Recommendations

### Volume

**One mainstay of conservative management is the forced increase in fluid intake to achieve a daily urine output of 2 liters** (Borghi et al, 1999). Increased urine output may have two effects. First, the mechanical diuresis that ensues may prevent urine stagnation and the formation of symptomatic calculi. More likely is that the dilute urine alters the supersaturation of stone components. Indeed, Pak and colleagues measured in vitro and in vivo effects of urine dilution and discovered that both significantly reduced the urinary activity product ratio (state of saturation) of calcium phosphate, calcium oxalate, and monosodium urate (Pak et al, 1980b). Moreover, the formation product ratio, that is, the minimum supersaturation needed to elicit spontaneous nucleation of calcium oxalate, significantly increased.

Researchers at the University of Chicago have demonstrated that failure to increase urine output is one of three strong predictors of relapse for those patients observed in a dedicated stone clinic (Strauss et al, 1982a). The previously described stone clinic effect has primarily been attributed to increases in fluid intake and attendant increases in urine output (Hosking et al, 1983).

However, although the concept of increased fluid intake is simple, it can be difficult to achieve compliance of patients. Anecdotally, most physicians with an interest in kidney stone disease have seen that many patients are unable to maintain increased urine output over the long term. This general impression has been borne out in an analysis of urine output changes from a large series of 2877 patients (Parks et al, 2003a). In this amalgam of university and private practice patients, the average increase in urine volume was only 0.3 liter per day. In addition, intermittent compliance may not be effective, as small, early stones may develop during periods of intense dehydration. At least one author has suggested that if a patient is able to voluntarily force fluid intake long enough to dilute renal concentrating abilities, thirst mechanisms will take over and help maintain a high fluid intake and high urine output (Burns and Finlayson, 1981). Unfortunately, the more recent data from Parks and colleagues has not proved this finding to be reliable.

### Water Hardness

If water intake is so important, is there a difference in water hardness that might ameliorate or augment its benefit? This concept has been the topic of conflicting articles within the general urologic and epidemiologic literature. In one interesting study, patients with a known history of calcium nephrolithiasis were divided according to postal zip codes; 24-hour urine measurements were compared, as was the history of stone episodes (Schwartz et al, 2002). Although the 24-hour urine calcium, magnesium, and citrate levels increased directly with drinking water hardness, no significant change was found in urinary oxalate, uric acid, pH, or volume. Most important, the number of total lifetime stone episodes was similar between patients residing in areas with soft public water and hard public water. Patients consuming the softest water decile formed 3.4 lifetime stones, and those who consumed the hardest water developed 3.0 lifetime stones. **The authors noted that although water hardness can alter urinary parameters, this ultimately appears to have little effect on clinical outcome.**

These findings are further supported by earlier work from Shuster and associates (1982). They examined 2295 patients from two regions: the Carolinas, which had soft water and high stone incidence; and the Rockies, which had hard water and low stone incidence. Home tap water samples of patients hospitalized for urinary stones were compared with those of controls. After adjustment for environmental factors, no significant difference between the two groups was obtained in tap water calcium, magnesium, and sodium concentrations. An incidental but potentially important finding was that those consuming water from a private well had an estimated relative risk of stone formation of 1.5 compared with those using public water. **They ultimately concluded that water hardness should be a minor concern with respect to stone formation.**

Unfortunately, this issue has not been completely put to rest; there is still evidence that hard water may confer some excess risk of stone formation. In a well-controlled study involving fixed diets and a crossover design, 18 subjects with a history of calcium nephrolithiasis drank hard water, soft water, or tap water (Bellizzi et al, 1999). The urinary levels of calcium demonstrated a significant 50% increase in the absence of changes of oxalate excretion. Whereas these changes are of concern, stone events were not used as a primary outcome.

### Carbonated Beverages

**A number of studies suggest that carbonated water offers increased protection against recurrent stone formation compared with still water** (Rodgers, 1997, 1998; Bren et al, 1998; Caudarella et al, 1998; Coen et al, 2001). These studies focused primarily on carbonated water, which has been demonstrated to increase urinary citrate levels.

Other types of carbonated beverages have also been examined. One study has demonstrated that increased intake of soda can confer an increased risk of subsequent stone recurrence (Shuster et al, 1992). The study sample consisted of 1009 male subjects, who reported consuming at least 160 mL/day of soft drinks. Half of the subjects were randomized to refrain from consuming soft drinks; the remaining subjects served as controls. The intervention group had an observed 6.4% advantage in actuarial 3-year freedom from recurrence over the control group. One important secondary finding was that those who reported that their most consumed drink was acidified by phosphoric acid but not citric acid had a 15% higher 3-year recurrence-free rate than the controls. Meanwhile, those who consumed drinks acidified by citric acid had no increase in stone episodes compared with controls.

Additional epidemiologic studies have demonstrated the effects of particular fluids on the risk of stone recurrence (Curhan et al, 1996a, 1998b). For both men and women, there was a decrease in the risk of nephrolithiasis for those who consumed increased volumes of water, caffeinated or decaffeinated coffee, tea, beer, and wine. Conversely, daily servings of apple or grapefruit juice increased the risk of stone events. **Despite the epidemiologic evidence, the supersaturation risks associated with grapefruit juice have largely been discredited by subsequent evaluations** (Goldfarb and Asplin, 2001; Trinchieri et al, 2002; Honow et al, 2003).

In contrast to these epidemiologic findings, recent evidence suggests that caffeine intake may increase the risk of stone recurrence in calcium stone formers by increasing the excretion of calcium. Caffeine increased urinary calcium/creatinine, magnesium/creatinine, citrate/creatinine, and sodium/creatinine but not oxalate/creatinine in stone formers and controls. Furthermore, supersaturation calculations increased, despite the noted increases in the inhibitors citrate and magnesium (Massey and Sutton, 2004).

### Increased Citrus Juices

**Lemonade and orange juice have long been used as an adjunct to water to provide increased urine volume as well as increased urinary citrate excretion.** In a study of 12 hypocitraturic patients, lemonade made from reconstituted lemon juice provided enough citrate to correct the hypocitraturia in seven subjects (Seltzer et al, 1996). Urinary calcium excretion decreased an average of 39 mg daily, whereas oxalate excretion was unchanged. The lemonade mixture was well tolerated; only two patients complained of mild indigestion that did not require cessation of therapy. Wabner and Pak (1993) have similarly evaluated the effects of orange juice on the urinary parameters of normal subjects and found that compared with potassium citrate, orange juice delivered an equivalent alkali load and caused a similar increase in urine pH (6.48 versus 6.75 from 5.71) and urinary citrate (952 versus 944 from 571 mg/day). Therefore, orange juice, like potassium citrate, decreased urinary undissociated uric acid levels and increased the inhibitor activity (formation product) of brushite (calcium phosphate). However, orange juice increased urinary oxalate and did not alter calcium excretion, whereas potassium citrate decreased urinary calcium without altering urinary oxalate. They concluded that orange juice could be beneficial in the control of calcareous and uric acid nephrolithiasis.

**Overall, most evidence suggests that it is not the type of fluid ingested that is important for stone prevention but the absolute amount of fluid taken in per day. We therefore encourage all of our stone formers to drink at least 3000 mL/day to maintain a urine output of more than 2500 mL/24 hours.**

## Dietary Recommendations

**Although metabolic abnormalities probably contribute to the majority of risk factors for recurrent nephrolithiasis, increasing evidence suggests that dietary changes are having an important impact on renal stone disease.** Indeed, studies have documented an increasing incidence of nephrolithiasis along with a greater propensity of female stone disease; a more complete discussion of these trends can be found in Chapter 42 (Pak et al, 1997; Ramello et al, 2000; Trinchieri et al, 2000; Coward et al, 2003; Hesse et al, 2003; Stamatelou et al, 2003; Amato et al, 2004). Therefore, alterations in diet and physical

---

### KEY POINTS: FLUID RECOMMENDATIONS

- Patients should be strongly encouraged to consume enough fluids to produce 2 liters of urine per day.

- Water hardness is unlikely to play a significant role in recurrence risk.

- Carbonated water may confer some protective benefit.

- Soda flavored with phosphoric acid may increase stone risk, whereas soda with citric acid may decrease risk.

- Citrus juices (particularly lemon juice) may be a useful adjunct to stone prevention.

---

activity may significantly reduce the incidence of recurrent nephrolithiasis.

### Protein Restriction

**Epidemiologic studies from a number of countries have shown that the incidence of renal stones is higher in populations in which there is an increased animal protein intake.** For example, in the northern and western regions of India, animal protein intake is approximately 100% greater than in the southern and eastern regions, and the rate of kidney stones is four times greater. In the United Kingdom, the frequency of upper tract stone disease correlates with the per capita expenditure on foodstuffs (Robertson et al, 1979, 1982). This effect may be partly because protein intake is higher in affluent people, and stone formation, for some reason, seems to be higher in the economically advantaged. When populations are matched for economic status, the intake of protein and other dietary constituents does not differ in patients with recurrent stones and controls. Even in subjects thus matched, however, patients with stone disease secrete greater quantities of calcium in the urine than do controls for a given intake of protein (Wasserstein et al, 1987). Thus, patients with stone disease may be more sensitive to dietary protein loading than are normal subjects.

**Protein intake increases urinary calcium, oxalate, and uric acid excretion and the mathematically calculated probability of stone formation even in normal subjects.** Indeed, according to Burns and Finlayson (1981), ingestion of protein is second only to ingestion of vitamin D in enhancing intestinal absorption of calcium. Early investigations of purine loading in controlled clinical laboratory settings confirmed the risk of hypercalciuria and hyperuricosuria with a diet high in animal protein (Pak et al, 1978; Fellstrom et al, 1983; Breslau et al, 1988). Patients with stone disease also exhibit inappropriate hypercalciuria in response to carbohydrate, sodium, and oxalate intake. In one acute study, dietary protein restriction resulted in a decrease in calcium, phosphate, and oxalate (Liatsikos and Barbalias, 1999). In another study in hypercalciuric patients, protein restriction resulted in decreased urinary uric acid and increased urinary citrate as well (Giannini et al, 1999).

Borghi and colleagues (2002) have provided further support to the importance of dietary protein in stone formation. In a prospective fashion, patients were randomized to either a low-protein, low-salt, moderate-calcium diet or a low-calcium diet. Although it is difficult to separate the potential effects of the three facets of the first diet, there was a convincing 50% reduction in stone events compared with those patients on the low-calcium diet.

Not all investigators have noticed the relationship between intake of meat and hypercalciuria. Brockis and colleagues (1982) demonstrated that mean urinary excretion patterns of calcium and oxalate were similar in matched groups of Seventh Day Adventists (vegetarians) and Mormons (nonvegetarians). A large study at the University of Pennsylvania found that patients with recurrent nephrolithiasis consumed a diet similar in composition to that of case controls (Goldfarb, 1994). Most studies, however, suggest that an increased intake of meat may exacerbate calcium oxalate stone disease.

## Sodium Restriction

**Sodium restriction has been widely recommended as an important element of dietary prevention of recurrent nephrolithiasis** (Massey and Whiting, 1995). Indeed, the evidence implicating excess sodium ingestion as a cause of calcium stone disease comes from several authors in different countries. Ito and colleagues from Japan have noticed that calcium stone formers had increased levels of sodium ingestion compared with the daily recommended allowances for the Japanese nation (Ito et al, 1993). They also found that stone formers consumed larger amounts of animal protein. They did not comment on whether the increased sodium ingestion was caused by the protein excess or whether it acted as an independent risk factor.

Researchers in Dallas, Texas, have confirmed the effects of salt loading in a controlled crossover study involving normal volunteers. In their study, 14 normal subjects participated in two phases of study of 10 days' duration each—a low-sodium phase (basal metabolic diet containing 50 mmol sodium per day) and a high-sodium phase (basal diet plus 250 mmol sodium chloride per day). The high sodium intake significantly increased urinary sodium (34 to 267 mmol/day), calcium (2.73 to 3.93 mmol/day), and pH (5.79 to 6.15) and significantly decreased urinary citrate (3.14 to 2.52 mmol/day). They noted that a high sodium intake not only increased calcium excretion but also increased urine pH and decreased citrate excretion. **The net effect of a high sodium diet was an increased propensity for the crystallization of calcium salts in urine** (Sakhaee et al, 1993).

The investigation by Borghi involving dietary manipulation additionally included a low-salt diet, limited to 50 mmol of sodium chloride per day (Borghi et al, 2002). **In combination with animal protein restriction and moderate calcium ingestion, a reduced sodium diet will decrease stone episodes by approximately 50%.** Further work from Italy has demonstrated that calcium stone formers who ingest large quantities of daily salt are more likely to suffer from decreased bone mineral density (Martini et al, 2000). In this study of 85 patients, all female patients were premenopausal, underscoring the risks of further osteopenia that they might suffer later in life. After adjustment for calcium and protein intakes, age, weight, body mass index, urinary calcium excretion, urinary citrate and uric acid excretion, and duration of stone disease, multiple-regression analysis showed that a high sodium chloride intake (≥16 g/day) was the single variable that was predictive of risk of low bone density in calcium stone–forming patients (odds ratio = 3.8).

---

### KEY POINTS: DIETARY RECOMMENDATIONS

- Randomized studies have confirmed the advantage of a diet with moderate animal protein (meat) intake.

- Randomized trials have demonstrated a benefit of dietary sodium restriction in both normal volunteers and stone formers.

---

## Obesity

Obesity has been associated with impaired carbohydrate tolerance and an inappropriate calcium response to glucose ingestion. Thus, the hypercalciuria seen in meat eaters may be a function of increased body weight (Menon and Krishnan, 1983). Trinchieri and colleagues found that daily urinary oxalate excretion was related to body mass index in a group of stone formers (Trinchieri et al, 1998b). The association between body size and risk of stone formation was studied formally by the Curhan group (Curhan et al, 1998a). In two large cohorts, the Health Professionals Follow-Up Study and the Nurses' Health Study, the prevalence of stone disease history and the incidence of new stone formation were directly associated with weight and body mass index. The magnitude of the association was greater in women than in men.

These same cohorts of patients have been continually observed, and the group from Boston has provided an update on the role of obesity and nephrolithiasis. **They demonstrated that increased body mass index, larger waist size, and weight gain correlated with an increased risk of stone episodes. This increased stone risk was still more pronounced for women than for men** (Taylor et al, 2005).

In a review of a large national database, Powell and colleagues (2000) examined the serum and 24-hour urine parameters from nearly 6000 patients with a history of nephrolithiasis. Within this cohort, obese patients had increased urinary excretion of sodium, calcium, magnesium, citrate, sulfate, phosphate, oxalate, uric acid, and cystine. Furthermore, obesity was associated with increased urine volumes and urine osmolality compared with the nonobese patients. Interestingly, these metabolic changes were associated with an increased rate of stone episodes only for obese women, rather than for obese men.

Clinicians at Duke University have specifically evaluated the metabolic disturbances of obese patients, defined as a body mass index greater than 30 (Ekeruo et al, 2004). They determined that the most common presenting metabolic abnormalities among obese patients included gouty diathesis (54%), hypocitraturia (54%), and hyperuricosuria (43%), which presented at levels that were significantly higher than those found in nonobese stone formers. Chemical stone analysis showed a predominance of uric acid calculi, implicating excessively acid urine in these subjects. Directed medical therapy and dietary recommendations were able to dramatically reduce stone episodes for these patients.

**Studies suggest that the increased incidence of uric acid stone formation in obese stone formers may be secondary to the production of more acidic urine than in "normal-sized" patients.** Combined data from the two largest stone centers in the United States found that urine pH appears to be directly correlated with body size (Maalouf et al, 2004). As body mass increases, the urine pH will decrease. This finding does not appear to be associated with diet but is probably a result of the increased incidence of type 2 diabetes in obese patients. As diabetics have impaired ammonium excretion, these patients have been shown to have an increased incidence of uric acid stone formation (Pak et al, 2003c; Abate et al, 2004).

If obesity is a risk for stone disease, what is the impact of weight-reducing diets on stone formation? Current dietary fads include low-carbohydrate, high-protein, high-fat diets (Atkins diet, South Beach diet, Sugar Busters diet). Experimental evidence suggests that such diets may predispose a patient to increased stone risk (Reddy et al, 2002). In a study of the Atkins diet, 10 healthy subjects engaged in a low-carbohydrate, high-protein diet for 6 weeks under the care of a clinical dietitian. After 6 weeks, urine pH decreased from 6.09 to 5.67, net acid excretion increased by 51 mEq/day, and urine citrate levels decreased from 763 mg/day to 449 mg/day. In addition, urine saturation of undissociated uric acid increased more than twofold; urinary calcium levels increased from 160 mg/day to 248 mg/day, causing an estimated calcium balance decrease of 90 mg/day. **Therefore, the consumption of a low-carbohydrate diet delivers a marked acid load to the kidney, increases the risk for stone formation, and may increase the risk for bone loss.** To date, there have been no well-performed investigations of the long-term clinical effects of this type of diet with respect to actual stone formation. Yet, evidence suggests that alkali therapy may significantly combat acidosis and the potential for stone formation in patients on a low-carbohydrate, high-protein diet.

### KEY POINTS: OBESITY

- Obesity is an independent risk factor for nephrolithiasis, particularly for women.
- Obese patients have a higher propensity for uric acid calculi.
- High-protein, low-carbohydrate diets may increase the risk of stone formation.

## Role of Dietary Calcium

**The preponderance of evidence now supports the maintenance of a moderate calcium intake in the face of calcareous nephrolithiasis** (Curhan et al, 1993; Curhan, 1997; Takei et al, 1998; Trinchieri et al, 1998a; Martini and Wood, 2000; Lewandowski et al, 2001; Borghi et al, 2002; Heller et al, 2003; Taylor et al, 2004). **Older recommendations to significantly restrict calcium intake probably led to an increase in available intestinal oxalate. As a result, this limitation in dietary**

**calcium may subsequently increase oxalate absorption, thereby raising the supersaturation of calcium oxalate.** As noted earlier, a prospective, randomized study has shown that patients on a moderate-calcium diet, combined with salt restriction and moderation of animal protein, had half as many stone episodes as those who attempted to follow a calcium-restricted diet (Borghi et al, 2002). Review of a large cohort of middle-aged nurses revealed that there was a decreased incidence of nephrolithiasis in those subjects who had increased levels of dietary calcium (Curhan, 1997; Curhan et al, 1997). Interestingly, this protection did not remain for those who received increased calcium intake from supplements instead of from dietary sources (i.e., dairy products).

There is further evidence to suggest that calcium supplementation can be safe if attention is paid to preparation and especially to timing. In a review of postmenopausal women, authors have demonstrated that initiation of calcium supplementation does not have deleterious effects on urinary calcium, oxalate, or citrate levels. Furthermore, calcium supplement with a meal or combined calcium supplement and estrogen therapy was not associated with a significant increased risk of calcium oxalate stone formation in the majority of postmenopausal osteoporotic patients (Domrongkitchaiporn et al, 2002b). Additional work from the same group has determined that the timing of calcium supplementation may have positive or negative effects (Domrongkitchaiporn et al, 2004). In a study of healthy male recruits, the authors compared the urinary effects of calcium carbonate supplementation taken with meals versus at bedtime. In both instances, urinary calcium excretion increased equal amounts. However, for those taking the calcium supplement with meals, this increase was offset by an equally significant decrease in urinary oxalate. As a result, there was no increase in urine supersaturation of calcium oxalate when calcium supplementation was taken with meals, a protection that did not remain for the nighttime bolus ingestion.

**Evidence also suggests that the type of calcium supplementation may have an impact on the potential of stone formation.** Two long-term studies from researchers in Dallas document that supplementation with calcium citrate does not have a significant impact on stone formation. Calcium citrate is an over-the-counter calcium preparation that provides 950 mg of calcium citrate and 200 mg of elemental calcium in each tablet. Like other available calcium supplements, calcium citrate will significantly increase urinary calcium excretion; yet, this preparation offers the benefit of also increasing urinary citrate excretion. The concomitant increase in citraturia potentially offsets the lithogenic potential of calcium supplement–induced hypercalciuria and therefore provides a more "stone-friendly" calcium supplement (Sakhaee et al, 2004).

A clinical trial was completed that further studied the effects of long-term calcium citrate supplementation in premenopausal women. This study demonstrated that the urine saturation of calcium oxalate and calcium phosphate (brushite) did not significantly change during calcium citrate therapy. It appears that the lack of calcium supplement–induced hypercalciuria was secondary to the downregulation of intestinal calcium absorption due to prolonged calcium supplementation and the inhibitory effects of citrate included in the calcium citrate preparation. The results of this long-term calcium citrate trial suggest that calcium supplementation with calcium citrate does not increase the propensity for crystallization of calcium salts within the urine. This protective effect is most likely due to an attenuated increase in urinary calcium excretion (from a decrease in fractional intestinal calcium absorption), a decrease in urinary phosphorus, and an increased citraturic response (Sakhaee et al, 1994).

### KEY POINTS: OXALATE AVOIDANCE

■ Avoidance of excess dietary oxalate loading is reasonable and intuitive.

■ Vitamin C in large doses may increase the risk of stone recurrence. Doses should probably be limited to 2 g/day.

### KEY POINTS: ROLE OF DIETARY CALCIUM

■ Dietary calcium avoidance actually increases stone recurrence risk.

■ Calcium supplementation is likely to be safest when it is taken with meals.

■ Calcium citrate appears to be a more stone-friendly calcium supplement because of the additional inhibitor action of citrate.

## Oxalate Avoidance

**Since less than 10% to 15% of urinary oxalate is usually derived from dietary sources, it is unclear how helpful it is to promote the strict avoidance of oral oxalate loading.** This is compounded by the fact that oxalate is ubiquitous and found in most vegetable matter. However, it does seem intuitive to avoid large portions of foodstuffs that are rich in oxalate, such as spinach, beets, chocolate, nuts, and tea. Although general advice on a restricted oxalate intake might be given to patients with recurrent nephrolithiasis, a low-oxalate diet would be most useful in patients with enteric hyperoxaluria or those with underlying bowel abnormalities (Holmes and Assimos, 2004). A more extensive list of high-oxalate foods may be found in Table 43–7.

There have been repeated concerns raised regarding the risk of vitamin C (ascorbic acid) ingestion and the possibility of its conversion to oxalate with subsequent urinary excretion. Unfortunately, conflicting evidence has been presented by multiple authors (Weaver, 1983; Trinchieri et al, 1991, 1998b; Urivetzky et al, 1992; Curhan et al, 1996b, 1999; Baxmann et al, 2003; Traxer et al, 2003). In fact, conflicting conclusions have even been reported from the same group of authors, underscoring the need for close scrutiny of presented data. Some of the confusion stems from differences in study endpoints. Whereas the ingestion of large amounts of vitamin C may demonstrate increases in 24-hour oxalate excretion and therefore calcium oxalate supersaturation, this does not guarantee an eventual increase in the formation of symptomatic calculi.

**In the end, it seems reasonable to avoid heavy dosing of vitamin C. Limiting one's intake to a maximum daily dose of less than 2 g is an easy recommendation to follow** (Traxer et al, 2003).

## Conservative Management Summary

It is anticipated that with these conservative measures alone, a significant number of patients may be able to normalize their urinary risk factors for stone formation. Thus, only these conservative measures may be necessary to keep their stone disease under control. After 3 to 4 months of conservative management, patients should be re-evaluated by either standard laboratory assays or a less comprehensive automated urinalysis package. If the patient's metabolic or environmental abnormalities have been corrected, the conservative therapy can be continued and the patient observed every 6 to 12 months with repeated 24-hour urine testing. It is believed that follow-up is essential not only to monitor the efficiency of treatment but also to encourage the patient's compliance. If, however, a metabolic defect persists, a more selective medical therapy may be instituted. For example, if significant hyperuricosuria (urinary uric acid greater than 800 mg/day) persists even after dietary restriction of meat products, medical therapy with allopurinol may be instituted.

## SELECTIVE MEDICAL THERAPY FOR NEPHROLITHIASIS

Improved elucidation of the pathophysiologic mechanisms of nephrolithiasis and the formulation of diagnostic criteria for its different causes have made feasible the adoption of selective treatment programs (Pak et al, 1981; Preminger and Pak, 1985). Such programs should reverse the underlying physicochemical and physiologic derangements, inhibit new stone formation, overcome nonrenal complications of the disease process, and be free of serious side effects. The rationale for the selection of certain treatments is the assumption that the particular physicochemical and physiologic aberrations identified with the given disorder are etiologically important in the formation of renal stones (as previously discussed) and that the correction of these disturbances would prevent stone formation. Moreover, **it is assumed that such a selective treatment program is more effective and safe than "random" therapy. Despite a lack of conclusive experimental verification, these hypotheses appear reasonable and logical.** Common medications used to treat urinary stone disease and their expected actions are summarized in Table 43–13. Medication dosages are noted in Table 43–14, and side effects are outlined in Table 43–15. A simplified treatment algorithm outlining basic evaluation and management is illustrated in Figure 43–10.

**Table 43–13. Physicochemical and Physiologic Effects of Pharmacologic Therapy**

| | Sodium Cellulose Phosphate | Orthophosphate | Thiazide | Allopurinol | Potassium Citrate |
|---|---|---|---|---|---|
| Urinary calcium | Marked decrease | Mild decrease | Moderate decrease | No change | Mild decrease or no change |
| Urinary phosphorus | Mild increase | Marked increase | Mild increase or no change | No change | No change |
| Urinary uric acid | No change | No change | Mild increase or no change | Marked decrease | No change |
| Urinary oxalate | Mild increase | Mild increase | Mild increase or no change | No change or mild decrease | No change |
| Urinary citrate | No change | Mild increase | Mild decrease | No change | Marked increase |
| Calcium oxalate saturation | Mild decrease or no change | Mild decrease | Mild decrease | No change | Moderate decrease |
| Brushite saturation | Moderate decrease | Mild increase | Mild decrease | No change | No change |

**Table 43–14. Dosages of Common Medications Used to Prevent Urinary Calculi**

| | |
|---|---|
| Thiazide diuretics | |
|   Hydrochlorothiazide | 25 mg PO bid |
|   Chlorthalidone | 25-50 mg PO daily |
|   Indapamide | 2.5 mg PO daily |
| Sodium cellulose phosphate | 10-15 g/day divided with meals |
| Orthophosphate | 0.5 g PO tid |
| Potassium citrate | 20 mEq PO bid-tid |
| Allopurinol | 300 mg PO daily |
| Magnesium gluconate | 0.5-1.0 g tid |
| Pyridoxine (B$_6$) | 100 mg PO daily |
| D-Penicillamine | 250 mg PO daily (titrated to effect) |
| α-Mercaptopropionylglycine | 100 mg PO bid (titrated to effect) |
| Captopril | 25 mg PO bid-tid |
| Acetohydroxamic acid | 250 mg PO bid-tid |

**Table 43–15. Potential Side Effects of Medications Used to Prevent Urinary Lithiasis**

| Medication | Side Effect |
|---|---|
| Thiazide diuretics: hydrochlorothiazide, chlorthalidone, indapamide | Potassium wasting, muscle cramps, hyperuricosuria, intracellular acidosis, hypocitraturia |
| Sodium cellulose phosphate | Gastrointestinal distress, hypomagnesemia, hyperoxaluria, parathyroid hormone stimulation |
| Orthophosphate | Similar to sodium cellulose phosphate, soft tissue calcification |
| Potassium citrate | Gastrointestinal upset, hyperkalemia |
| Allopurinol | Rash, myalgia |
| Magnesium gluconate | Diarrhea |
| Pyridoxine (B$_6$) | Diarrhea |
| D-Penicillamine | Nephrotic syndrome, dermatitis, pancytopenia |
| α-Mercaptopropionylglycine | Rash, asthenia, rheumatologic complaints, gastrointestinal distress, mental status changes |
| Captopril | Rash, cough, hypotension |
| Acetohydroxamic acid | Thromboembolic phenomena, tremor, headache, palpitations, edema, gastrointestinal distress, loss of taste, rash, alopecia, anemia, abdominal pain |

## Efficacy Outside of an Academic Center

One potential criticism of the "selective" metabolic management of nephrolithiasis is that the collection of multiple urine and serum studies can be too time-consuming to be feasible outside of an academic medical center with its dedicated research staff. **Whereas a commitment to follow-up can be tedious, it should be no worse for patients with kidney stones than it is for those observed for cancer or voiding dysfunction.**

Indeed, Lingeman and colleagues (1998) compared the results of patient management from seven private practices with that achieved by a dedicated university clinic. Of note, the specialized stone management software and laboratory resources of the university clinic supported the private centers. They found that supersaturation values were effectively reduced in the network and stone clinic and that the reduction was proportional to the initial supersaturation value and increase in urine volume. The stone clinic achieved a greater supersaturation reduction, higher fraction of patient follow-up, and greater increase in urine volume, but the treatment effects in the network were nevertheless substantial and significant.

This finding is supported by another study demonstrating the efficacy of medical prophylaxis administered in a private practice setting (Mardis et al, 2004). Compared with conservative measures of dietary recommendations and fluid management, active pharmacologic treatment achieved a significantly greater reduction in stone episodes. These findings prompted the authors to conclude that medications validated in trials and guided by metabolic evaluation lower stone recurrence when they are used in a private practice setting as they do in clinical trials from academic medical centers.

## Absorptive Hypercalciuria

### Sodium Cellulose Phosphate

**There is currently no treatment program that is capable of correcting the basic abnormality of absorptive hypercalciuria type 1,** although several drugs are available that have been shown to restore normal calcium excretion. When sodium cellulose phosphate is given orally, this nonabsorbable ion exchange resin binds calcium and inhibits calcium absorption (Pak et al, 1974). However, this inhibition is caused by limitation of the amount of intraluminal calcium available for

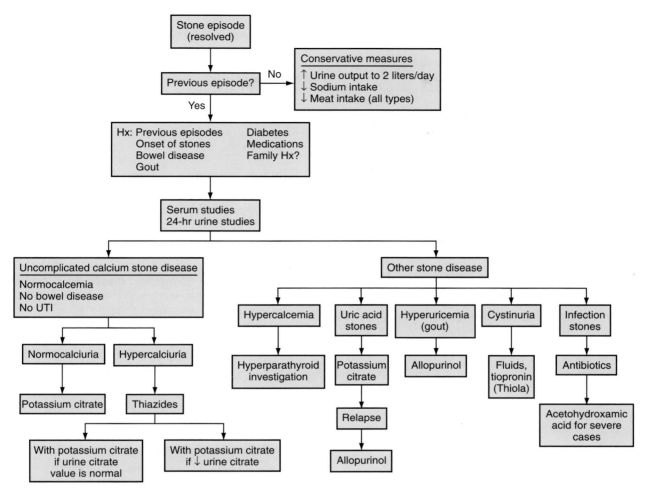

**Figure 43–10.**  Simplified treatment algorithm for the evaluation and medical management of urinary lithiasis. (Modified from C. Y. Pak.)

absorption, not by correction of the basic disturbance in calcium transport. Nevertheless, in one series, sodium cellulose phosphate decreased intestinal calcium absorption by 85% in patients with absorptive hypercalciuria and recurrent nephrolithiasis (Blacklock and Macleod, 1974). Acute treatment with cellulose phosphate can decrease urinary calcium excretion by 50% to 70% (Hayashi et al, 1975).

This mode of action accounts for the three potential complications of sodium cellulose phosphate therapy. First, sodium cellulose phosphate may cause a negative calcium balance and parathyroid stimulation when it is used in patients with normal intestinal calcium absorption or with renal or resorptive hypercalciuria. Second, the treatment may cause magnesium depletion by binding magnesium as well. Third, sodium cellulose phosphate may produce secondary hyperoxaluria by binding divalent cations in the intestinal tract, reducing divalent cation–oxalate complexation, and making more oxalate available for absorption (Hayashi et al, 1975). These complications may be overcome by using the drug only in documented cases of absorptive hypercalciuria type 1, applying oral magnesium supplementation (1.0 to 1.5 g magnesium gluconate twice per day, separately from sodium cellulose phosphate), and imposing a moderate

dietary restriction of oxalate (Pak, 1981). When these precautions are followed, sodium cellulose phosphate at a dosage of 10 to 15 g/day (given with meals) has been shown to reduce urinary calcium and the saturation of calcium salts (calcium phosphate as well as calcium oxalate). In this same study, stone events were reduced by 78%.

The clinical efficacy of this medication has been questioned, however, as Backman and colleagues (1980) have demonstrated that patients with calcareous nephrolithiasis tolerated sodium cellulose phosphate poorly with a high rate of gastrointestinal distress. In addition, they noted a 47% recurrence rate at 2 years. Hautmann and coworkers (1978) had previously demonstrated better efficacy for this medication but also noted significant oxaluria, with 8 of 27 patients having to stop the medication for this reason alone.

**Unfortunately, despite early enthusiasm, the use of sodium cellulose phosphate has largely fallen out of favor because of excessive gastrointestinal side effects and costs. The use of sodium cellulose phosphate may still make sense for patients with intractable stone disease due to profound absorptive hypercalciuria type 1 (urinary calcium excretion above 500 mg/day), but only after all other treatment options have been exhausted.**

## Thiazides

Thiazide diuretics are not considered a selective therapy for absorptive hypercalciuria since they do not decrease intestinal calcium absorption in this condition (Pak, 1979). However, this class of medications has been widely used to treat absorptive hypercalciuria because of its hypocalciuric action and the high cost and inconvenience of alternative therapy (sodium cellulose phosphate). The use of thiazides was first described by Yendt and colleagues (1966) for the treatment of undifferentiated hypercalciuria.

**Thiazides directly stimulate calcium resorption in the distal nephron while promoting excretion of sodium.** Long-term thiazide therapy results in volume depletion, extracellular volume contraction, and proximal tubular resorption of sodium and calcium. Thiazides may increase urinary excretion of magnesium and zinc, but these responses are not consistent. Potassium losses from thiazide therapy can cause hypocitraturia due to hypokalemia with intracellular acidosis.

**Studies indicate that thiazide may have a limited long-term effectiveness in absorptive hypercalciuria type 1** (Zerwekh and Pak, 1980; Preminger and Pak, 1987). Despite an initial reduction in urinary excretion, the intestinal calcium absorption remains persistently elevated. These studies suggest that the retained calcium may be accreted in bone at least during the first few years of therapy. Bone density, determined in the distal third of the radius by photon absorptiometry, increases significantly during thiazide treatment in absorptive hypercalciuria, with an annual increment of 1.34%. With continued treatment, however, the rise in bone density stabilizes and the hypocalciuric effect of thiazide becomes attenuated. These results suggest that thiazide treatment may cause a low turnover state of bone that interferes with a continued calcium accretion in the skeleton. The "rejected" calcium would then be excreted in urine. In contrast, bone density is not significantly altered in renal hypercalciuria, in which thiazide has been shown to cause a decline in intestinal calcium absorption commensurate with a reduction in urinary calcium.

Further work on this topic has been reported (Pak et al, 2003a). In this study, 28 patients with absorptive hypercalciuria type 1 were managed with thiazide (20) or indapamide (8) and potassium citrate for 1 to 11 years while they were maintained on a diet low in calcium oxalate. Serum and urine chemistry studies and bone mineral density were obtained at baseline and at the end of treatment. During treatment, urinary calcium significantly decreased but urinary oxalate did not change. Urine pH and citrate significantly increased, and urine saturation of calcium oxalate significantly decreased by 46%. Stone formation rate decreased significantly from 2.94 to 0.05 per year. Notably, L2-4 bone mineral density increased significantly by 5.7% compared with normal peak value and by 7.1% compared with normal age- and gender-matched values. The authors concluded that **dietary restriction of calcium and oxalate, combined with thiazide and potassium citrate, satisfactorily controlled hypercalciuria but prevented complications commonly associated with sodium cellulose phosphate therapy.**

Although side effects are generally mild, they occur in about 30% to 35% of patients treated with thiazide. Side effects are usually seen on initiation of treatment but disappear with continued treatment. Lassitude and sleepiness are the most common symptoms and can occur in the absence of hypokalemia. **Potassium supplementation should always be considered, particularly in patients with evident potassium deficiency, patients receiving digitalis therapy, and those individuals who develop hypocitraturia.** On occasion, thiazides unmask or induce primary hyperparathyroidism. They may also cause impaired carbohydrate tolerance and hyperuricemia. A more distressing complication is decreased libido or sexual dysfunction seen in a small percentage of patients.

## Guidelines for the Use of Sodium Cellulose Phosphate or Thiazides in Absorptive Hypercalciuria

Neither sodium cellulose phosphate nor thiazides correct the basic, underlying physiologic defect in absorptive hypercalciuria. Some guidelines are offered until more selective therapy can be developed.

**Sodium cellulose phosphate should be used only in patients with severe absorptive hypercalciuria type 1 who are resistant to or intolerant of thiazide therapy.** In patients with absorptive hypercalciuria type 1 who may be at risk for bone disease (growing children, postmenopausal women), thiazide is the first choice and should be combined with potassium citrate and dietary restrictions. If thiazide loses its hypocalciuric action (after long-term treatment), a drug holiday may be instituted and then thiazide therapy may be resumed. The authors recommend that potassium citrate and dietary alterations continue during this time.

### Other Hypocalciuric Agents

**Other agents may be used in place of hydrochlorothiazide for the treatment of hypercalciuria.** These medications include chlorthalidone (25 to 50 mg/day) and indapamide (2.5 mg/day). Indapamide is technically not a thiazide but does share a successful hypocalciuric effect with the other agents. Trichlormethiazide has also been employed at a dose of 4 mg/day, yet this medication is no longer available in the United States. All three agents have been shown to be equally efficacious yet may improve compliance of patients with more convenient once-a-day dosing (Jaeger et al, 1986; Lemieux, 1986; Coe et al, 1988; Ettinger et al, 1988; Ohkawa et al, 1992; Borghi et al, 1993b; Martins et al, 1996).

Amiloride in combination with thiazide (Moduretic) may be more effective than thiazide alone in reducing calcium excretion (Maschio et al, 1981; Leppla et al, 1983). However, this medication does not augment citrate excretion. Since amiloride is a potassium-sparing agent, potassium replacement is not necessary and could, in fact, be problematic. **It is not advisable to provide potassium citrate to patients receiving a potassium-sparing diuretic.** Whereas the potassium-sparing effects of amiloride may be beneficial, the use of triamterene, another potassium-sparing agent, should be undertaken with caution because of reports of triamterene stone formation (Watson et al, 1981; Werness et al, 1982; Ettinger, 1985; Sorgel et al, 1985).

### Absorptive Hypercalciuria Type 2

In absorptive hypercalciuria type 2, no specific drug treatment may be necessary since the physiologic defect is not as severe as in absorptive hypercalciuria type 1. In addition, many patients show disdain for drinking fluids and therefore excrete concentrated urine. A low calcium intake (400 to 600 mg/day) and high fluid intake (sufficient to achieve a minimum urine output of more than 2 liters/day) would seem ideally indicated, since normocalciuria could be restored by dietary calcium restriction alone, and increased urine volume has been shown to reduce urine saturation of calcium oxalate.

## Orthophosphate

**Orthophosphate (neutral or alkaline salt of sodium or potassium, 0.5 g phosphorus three to four times/day) has been shown to inhibit 1,25-dihydroxyvitamin D synthesis** (Van Den Berg et al, 1980; Insogna et al, 1989). **However, there is as yet no convincing evidence from randomized trials that this treatment restores normal intestinal calcium absorption.** Orthophosphate reduces urinary calcium probably by directly impairing the renal tubular reabsorption of calcium and by binding calcium in the intestinal tract. Urinary phosphorus is markedly increased during therapy, a finding that reflects the absorbability of soluble phosphate. Physicochemically, orthophosphate reduces the urine saturation of calcium oxalate but increases that of brushite. Moreover, the urinary inhibitor activity is increased, probably owing to the stimulated renal excretion of pyrophosphate and citrate. Although contrary reports have appeared, this treatment program has been reported to cause soft tissue calcification and parathyroid stimulation (Dudley and Blackburn, 1970). It may be particularly indicated in absorptive hypercalciuria type 3. Orthophosphate is contraindicated in nephrolithiasis complicated by urinary tract infection because of the increased phosphorus load.

A formulation of low-release, neutral potassium phosphate has been developed to obviate the aforementioned problems with currently available orthophosphate preparations. This potassium phosphate preparation (UroPhos-K) is embedded in a wax matrix to provide slow release of the orthophosphate. This restricted release limits the amount of gastrointestinal upset found with most current orthophosphate preparations. In addition, UroPhos-K contains phosphate salts of potassium and does not contain sodium. Therefore, this preparation does not provide a sodium load that could offset the hypocalciuric action of the orthophosphate. Finally, this medication is designed to yield a pH of 7.0 compared with 7.3 for some available orthophosphate preparations. Therefore, it is less likely that the crystallization of calcium phosphate may occur in the urine (Breslau et al, 1995).

A randomized prospective double-blind trial was performed in 21 patients with documented stone formation and absorptive hypercalciuria type 1. Patients received either UroPhos-K or placebo in a double-blinded fashion. No significant gastrointestinal side effects were noted with the slow-release potassium phosphate preparation, nor was there a significant increase in fasting serum potassium or phosphorus concentration. However, the UroPhos-K treatment did significantly reduce urinary calcium from 288 mg/day to 171 mg/day without altering oxalate excretion. Moreover, the urine saturation of calcium oxalate was significantly reduced without altering brushite saturation. Also noted was a significant increase of inhibitor activity secondary to increased urinary citrate and pyrophosphate, thereby inhibiting the

potential crystallization of calcium oxalate in the urine (Breslau et al, 1998; Heller et al, 1998). This medication is not yet approved for use in the United States.

## Dietary Bran

Rice bran also binds intestinal calcium and increases urinary pyrophosphate (Ebisuno et al, 1991). In an uncontrolled long-term study, rice bran reduced stone recurrences. In another study, 73 patients with recurrent urinary stone formation were treated with 40 g of unprocessed bran daily. Hydrochlorothiazide was added during the summer months. During a 2-year follow-up, three fourths of the patients were free of stones. The combination of thiazide and bran was superior to bran alone in preventing stone formation (Ala-Opas et al, 1987).

---

### KEY POINTS: ABSORPTIVE HYPERCALCIURIA

- Sodium cellulose phosphate effectively decreases the absorption of intestinal calcium but has largely been abandoned because of gastrointestinal intolerance and side effects.

- Thiazides do not treat the underlying cause of absorptive hypercalciuria but do manage its symptoms.

- Orthophosphates may have a role in the treatment of absorptive hypercalciuria when other methods are ineffective.

---

## Renal Hypercalciuria

**Thiazide is ideally indicated for the treatment of renal hypercalciuria. This diuretic has been shown to correct the renal leak of calcium by augmenting calcium reabsorption in the distal tubule and by causing extracellular volume depletion and stimulating proximal tubular reabsorption of calcium.** The ensuing correction of secondary hyperparathyroidism restores normal serum 1,25-dihydroxyvitamin D concentration and intestinal calcium absorption. Thiazide has been shown to provide a sustained correction of hypercalciuria commensurate with a restoration of normal serum 1,25-dihydroxyvitamin D concentration and intestinal calcium absorption for up to 10 years of therapy (Preminger and Pak, 1987).

Physicochemically, the urinary environment becomes less saturated with respect to calcium oxalate and brushite during thiazide treatment, largely because of the reduced calcium excretion. Moreover, urinary inhibitor activity, as reflected in the limit of metastability, is increased by an unknown mechanism. These effects are shared by hydrochlorothiazide (25 mg twice/day), chlorthalidone (25 to 50 mg/day), and indapamide (2.5 mg/day). **Potassium citrate supplementation (40 to 60 mEq/day) is advised, since this medication has been shown to be effective in averting hypokalemia and in increasing urinary citrate when it is administered to patients with calcium nephrolithiasis taking thiazide** (Nicar et al, 1984; Pak et al, 1985b).

A more complete discussion of the mechanism of action, efficacy, and side effects of thiazides for the treatment of hypercalciuria is presented in the preceding section. Furthermore, Table 43–16 provides a summary of the results of randomized trials involving the use of thiazides for the treatment of hypercalciuria. Of note, a meta-analysis of medical therapies for calculus prevention demonstrated that only thiazides have shown strong evidence for efficacy in randomized trials (Pearle et al, 1999).

---

### KEY POINT: RENAL HYPERCALCIURIA

- Thiazides are first-line therapy for renal leak hypercalciuria.

---

## Primary Hyperparathyroidism

**Parathyroidectomy is the optimum treatment of nephrolithiasis in patients with primary hyperparathyroidism** (Parks et al, 1980; Fraker, 2000). This therapy may include the resection of a dominant adenoma or removal of all four hyperplastic glands. After removal of abnormal parathyroid tissue, urinary calcium is expected to return to a normal level, commensurate with a decline in serum calcium concentration and intestinal calcium absorption. However, these findings are not always dependable; some patients may suffer from changes in tubular and glomerular functions as a result of long-standing hypercalcemia or hypercalciuria (Farias et al, 1996).

There is no established medical therapy for the nephrolithiasis of primary hyperparathyroidism. Although orthophosphates have been recommended for the disease of mild to moderate severity, their safety or efficacy has not yet been proved. These medications should be used only when parathyroid surgery cannot be undertaken. Estrogen has been reported to be useful in reducing serum and urine concentration of calcium in postmenopausal women with primary hyperparathyroidism (Herbai and Ljunghall, 1983; Marcus et al, 1984; Coe et al, 1986; Selby and Peacock, 1986; Boucher et al, 1989; Diamond et al, 1996; Orr-Walker et al, 2000).

---

### KEY POINT: PRIMARY HYPERPARATHYROIDISM

- Hyperparathyroidism complicated by stone disease is best treated with surgical excision of the adenoma.

---

## Hyperuricosuric Calcium Oxalate Nephrolithiasis

There are two pharmacologic approaches to the management of hyperuricosuric calcium oxalate nephrolithiasis. The first approach involves decreasing the production of uric acid. For this management, allopurinol (300 mg/day) may be used to interfere with the ability of xanthine oxidase to convert xanthine to uric acid (Coe, 1978). The resultant decrease in serum uric acid will ultimately lead to a decrease in urinary uric acid as well. **The use of allopurinol in hyperuricosuria associated with dietary purine overindulgence may also be reasonable if patients are unable or unwilling to comply with dietary purine restriction.** Physicochemical changes ensuing from restoration of a normal urinary uric acid level include an increase in the urinary limit of metastability of calcium oxalate (Pak et al, 1978). Thus, the spontaneous nucleation of calcium oxalate is retarded by treatment, probably by inhibition of monosodium urate–induced stimulation of calcium oxalate crystallization (Pak et al, 1979; Coe et al, 1980). Because of the potential exaggeration of monosodium urate–induced calcium oxalate crystallization, a moderate sodium restriction (150 mEq/day) is also advisable.

There are few convincing randomized trials demonstrating the efficacy of allopurinol for the treatment of hyperuricosuria. However, one study by Ettinger and colleagues (1986) does stand out. In this double-blind, prospective, randomized trial, allopurinol was given to 60 patients with hyperuricosuria, normocalciuria, and recurrent calcium oxalate stones. A 6-month "grace period" was established, during which time any new calculus that was passed was not considered to represent failure of therapy. With a follow-up of up to 39 months, new stone events (stone growth or recurrence) occurred in 58% of the patients receiving placebo and in 31% of the patients receiving allopurinol. The placebo group had 63.4% fewer calculi, whereas the allopurinol group had 81.2% fewer calculi. The mean rate of calculus events was 0.26 per patient per year in the placebo group and 0.12 in the allopurinol group. The allopurinol group had a significantly longer time before the recurrence of stones.

**Alternatively, management of hyperuricosuria may be approached by altering the urinary milieu such that uric acid remains in a dissolved state** (Pak and Peterson, 1986). Central to this approach would be the obvious advantage of copious amounts of dilute urine to maintain uric acid at a low concentration. Attempts to maintain the urine at a pH above the pKa may also be successful by promoting dissolution of this molecule (Pak et al, 1986b). This effect is usually achieved by the use of an alkalinizing agent such as potassium citrate (at a dose of 30 to 60 mEq/day in divided doses). In the study by Pak, the treatment produced a sustained rise in urine pH by 0.55 to 0.85 to the high-normal range. Urinary citrate levels rose by 249 to 402 mg/day. Commensurate with these changes, urine saturation of calcium oxalate (relative saturation ratio) and the amount of undissociated uric acid declined significantly. Stone formation declined from 1.55 per patient-year to 0.38 per patient-year during a mean treatment period of 2.35 years. Stones ceased to form in 16 of 19 patients during treatment.

There is some evidence that changes in urine pH alone are inadequate for the management of hyperuricosuria (Pak et al, 2002b). If this is the case, the efficacy of citrate for the management of hyperuricosuric calcium nephrolithiasis may stem from the inhibitory activity of citrate with respect to calcium and oxalate crystallization.

Potassium citrate may be particularly useful in patients with mild to moderate hyperuricosuria (<800 mg/day), especially in whom hypocitraturia is also present.

## Table 43–16.  Randomized Trials of Diuretic Therapy for the Prevention of Calcium Oxalate Stones

| Year | Author | Diagnosis | Agent | No. of Patients | No. of Controls | Efficacy | Follow-up | Comments |
|------|--------|-----------|-------|-----------------|-----------------|----------|-----------|----------|
| 1981 | Brocks et al | Recurrent calcium stones | Bendroflumethiazide, 2.5 mg tid | 29 | 33 | 83% remission in controls, 85% in treated: not significant | 1.6 years | Not all patients were hypercalciuric<br>Only 16% of expected stones formed in controls, 24% in treated |
| 1982 | Scholz et al | Recurrent calcium stones | Hydrochlorothiazide, 25 mg bid | 25 | 26 | 77% remission in controls, 76% in treated: not significant | 1 year | Fasting urinary calcium increased before treatment, decreased with thiazides, but not in controls<br>Urine output increased in both groups, indicating that hydration was sufficient |
| 1984 | Laerun and Larsen | Recurrent stone formers | Hydrochlorothiazide, 25 mg bid | 25 | 25 | 45% remission in controls, 75% in treated: significant difference<br>Controls formed 21 stones, treated formed 230 stones: not significant | 3 years | General practice study<br>75% of patients did not have hypercalciuria<br>Differences seen only after 18 months |
| 1988 | Ettinger et al | Recurrent calcium stones | Chlorthalidone, 25 or 50 mg/day | 42 | 31 | 55% remission in controls, 86% in treated: significant | 3 years | Only 15% of patients had hypercalciuria<br>Compliance to diet not encouraged or assessed; to drugs, assessed<br>Urine output not measured<br>16% dropout rate in controls, 35%–40% dropout rate with chlorthalidone |
| 1984 | Wilson et al | Recurrent calcium stones | Hydrochlorothiazide, 100 mg/day | 21 | 23 | 65% remission in controls, 70% in treated: not significant<br>0.32 stone per year in controls; 0.15 stone per year in treated: significant | <3 years | Not all patients hypercalciuric<br>Other treatments—phosphates, magnesium, allopurinol—were ineffective |
| 1992 | Okhawa et al | Idiopathic hypercalciuria | Trichlormethiazide, 4 mg/day | 82 | 93 | 86% remission in controls, 92% in treated: not significant<br>Stone formation rate significantly lowered in treated patients | 3 years | Multi-institutional study<br>All patients had hypercalciuria<br>Many were single stone formers |
| 1993 | Borghi et al | Idiopathic hypercalciuria | Indapamide, 2.5 mg/day, or indapamide plus allopurinol, 300 mg/day | 25 | 25 | 65% remission in controls, 95% in treated: significant | | Urinary output did not rise in either group; thus, hydration may not have been effective |
| | Total | | | 249 | 256 | 73% remission in controls, 85% in treated patients | | Beneficial effects with treatment seen only in trials with follow-up of ≥2 years |

---

**KEY POINTS: HYPERURICOSURIC CALCIUM OXALATE NEPHROLITHIASIS**

- Patients with hyperuricosuria should be instructed to decrease dietary purine intake.

- Allopurinol can decrease uric acid production and may be ideal for those patients with a history of gout.

- Potassium citrate can effectively alter the urinary milieu in patients with hyperuricosuria by decreasing the supersaturation of uric acid and calcium oxalate.

## Enteric Hyperoxaluria

**The management of patients with enteric hyperoxaluria usually involves directed therapy that addresses several abnormalities or abnormal physiology.** Oral administration of large amounts of calcium (0.25 to 1.0 g, four times/day) or magnesium has been recommended for the control of calcium nephrolithiasis of ileal disease (Worcester, 2002). Although urinary oxalate may decrease (probably from binding of oxalate by divalent cations), the concurrent rise in urinary calcium may obviate the beneficial effect of this therapy, at least in some patients (Barilla et al, 1978). Lindsjo and colleagues (1989) described an interesting organic marine hydrocolloid that had been charged with calcium (Ox-Absorb) for the purposes of oxalate binding in patients with enteric hyperoxaluria. In their clinical studies of 19 patients with intestinal disorders and stone formation, urinary oxalate excretion was significantly lower during treatment with the organic marine colloid than off treatment. Most patients experienced improvement of bowel function, and those with severe stone formation showed decreases in incidence.

Cholestyramine has also been suggested for the management of calculi in this disorder (Stauffer, 1977). This medication may be useful by binding bile salts in the bowel lumen, thereby decreasing the irritation of the colonic mucosa and the subsequent hyperabsorption of oxalate (Caspary et al, 1977). The replacement of dietary fat with medium-chain triglycerides may be helpful in those patients who also have malabsorption.

Patients may exhibit hypomagnesiuria due to impaired intestinal absorption of magnesium. Since magnesium has been shown to complex oxalate, hypomagnesiuria may increase the urine saturation of calcium oxalate (Caudarella et al, 1993). Whereas oral magnesium supplements may correct hypomagnesiuria, they may also provoke further diarrhea. Magnesium gluconate (0.5 to 1.0 g, three times/day) appears to be better tolerated than magnesium oxide or hydroxide. **Treatment with potassium citrate (60 to 120 mEq/day) may correct the hypokalemia and metabolic acidosis in patients with enteric hyperoxaluria and, in some individuals, increase urinary citrate toward normal.** Consideration should be given to providing the liquid form of potassium citrate in patients with rapid gastrointestinal transit times; the liquid form of this medication may be better absorbed than the slow-release, wax matrix pills.

A high fluid intake is recommended to ensure adequate urine volume. Since excessive fluid loss may be present, an antidiarrheal agent may be necessary before sufficient urine output can be achieved. Calcium citrate may theoretically have a role in management of enteric hyperoxaluria. This treatment may lower urinary oxalate by binding oxalate in the intestinal tract. Calcium citrate may also raise the urine concentration of citrate and pH by providing an alkali load (Harvey et al, 1985). Finally, calcium citrate may correct the malabsorption of calcium and adverse effects on skeleton by providing an efficiently absorbed formulation of calcium.

---

**KEY POINTS: ENTERIC HYPEROXALURIA**

- Fluid intake should be strongly encouraged to correct the relative state of dehydration.

- Dietary calcium may help bind intestinal oxalate and decrease its absorption.

- Slow-release formulations of citrate should be avoided.

---

## Hypocitraturic Calcium Oxalate Nephrolithiasis

In patients with hypocitraturic calcium oxalate nephrolithiasis, potassium citrate treatment is capable of restoring the normal urinary citrate level, lowering the urine saturation, and inhibiting the crystallization of calcium salts. Since hypocitraturia is found in a number of different conditions, each is addressed individually.

### Distal Renal Tubular Acidosis

**Potassium citrate therapy is able to correct the metabolic acidosis and hypokalemia found in patients with distal renal tubular acidosis** (Preminger et al, 1985). In addition, this medication is capable of restoring normal urinary citrate levels, although large doses (up to 120 mEq/day) may be required in severe acidotic states. With correction of the acidosis, urinary calcium should decline into the normal range. Since urine pH is generally high to begin with in patients with renal tubular acidosis, the overall rise in urine pH is small.

Potassium citrate therapy typically produces a sustained decline in the urine saturation of calcium oxalate (from reduction in urinary calcium and in citrate complexation of calcium). The urine saturation of calcium phosphate does not increase since the rise in phosphate dissociation is relatively small and is adequately compensated by a decline in ionic calcium concentration. In addition, the inhibitory activity against the crystallization of calcium oxalate and calcium phosphate is augmented by the direct action of citrate.

Investigators from Thailand have suggested that the target dose of potassium citrate for children with distal renal tubular acidosis should be 3 to 4 mEq/kg/day in divided doses (Domrongkitchaiporn et al, 2002c; Tapaneya-Olarn et al, 2002).

### Chronic Diarrheal States

The full management of enteric stone disease is discussed earlier in this chapter. Part of the entire management should involve the use of citrate to correct the acidosis that accompanies the chronic bicarbonate losses with diarrhea. The amount of potassium citrate depends on the severity of hypocitraturia in these patients; dosages range from 60 to 120 mEq in three or four divided doses.

**It is recommended that a liquid preparation of potassium citrate be used rather than the slow-release tablet preparation since the slow-release medication may be poorly absorbed as a result of rapid intestinal transit time.** In addition, frequent dose schedules (three or four times a day) for the liquid preparation are necessary because this form of the medication has a relatively short duration of biologic action.

### Thiazide-Induced Hypocitraturia

Noted previously, thiazide therapy may cause hypocitraturia due to thiazide-induced hypokalemia with resultant intracellular acidosis (Nicar et al, 1984). Therefore, it should be a common practice to administer potassium supplementation, preferably in the form of potassium citrate, to patients receiving thiazides for treatment of hypercalciuria. Potassium citrate has been shown to be as effective as potassium chloride in correction of thiazide-induced hypokalemia. Moreover, the addition of potassium citrate not only prevents a fall in urinary citrate during thiazide therapy but may raise citrate excretion (Pak et al, 1985b).

### Idiopathic Hypocitraturic Calcium Oxalate Nephrolithiasis

This entity includes hypocitraturia occurring alone as well as in conjunction with other abnormalities (e.g., hypercalciuria or hyperuricosuria). Stones formed in this condition are predominantly composed of calcium oxalate. Potassium citrate therapy may produce a sustained increase in urinary citrate and a decline in the urine saturation of calcium oxalate (Pak and Fuller, 1986). Two agents have been used for the treatment of hypocitraturia: sodium-potassium citrate, commonly used in Europe; and potassium citrate, in liquid form or as a wax matrix tablet, used in the United States. The usual therapeutic dose is 30 to 60 mEq/day given in divided doses or as a single evening dose (Berg et al, 1992). Sodium citrate does not lower urinary calcium excretion, perhaps as a result of the increased sodium load associated with this therapy (Sakhaee et al, 1983; Preminger et al, 1988).

In general, citrate is well tolerated, although the potential for gastric upset is real. The current formulation of potassium citrate embedded within a wax matrix may help alleviate the risk of gastric irritation. Patients are strongly encouraged to take this medication with meals to act as a further buffer.

---

### KEY POINTS: HYPOCITRATURIC CALCIUM OXALATE NEPHROLITHIASIS

- Citrates are generally well tolerated with only a small risk of gastrointestinal upset.

- Citrates are first-line therapy for renal tubular acidosis, thiazide-induced hypocitraturia, and idiopathic hypocitraturia.

---

## Hypomagnesiuric Calcium Nephrolithiasis

Hypomagnesiuric calcium nephrolithiasis is characterized by low urinary magnesium level, hypocitraturia, and low urine volume. Therefore, **management should include restoration of urinary magnesium levels with either magnesium oxide or magnesium hydroxide as well as correction of the hypocitraturia with potassium citrate.** The administration of magnesium salts was first advocated on the grounds that it reduced urinary excretion of oxalate. Some magnesium salts increase urinary magnesium excretion and thus produce a more favorable magnesium-to-calcium ratio in the urine, a condition that offers relative protection against stone formation. Magnesium decreases renal tubular citrate resorption through the chelation of citrate and thus increases urinary citrate excretion. Melnick and coworkers (1971) found that stone recurrence dropped from 6 stones per year to 0.073 stone per year in a group of 149 recurrent calcium oxalate stone formers treated with magnesium oxide. Prien and Gershoff (1974) reported that about 70% of patients administered 300 mg of magnesium oxide and 100 mg of pyridoxine demonstrated complete cessation of stone formation. Johansson and associates (1980) treated 56 patients with 400 to 500 mg of magnesium hydroxide; 80% of the treated patients were free of stones, in comparison to 50% who did not receive magnesium supplementation. The rate of stone formation dropped from 0.8 stone per year to 0.03 stone per year in the treated patients and from 0.5 stone per year to 0.22 stone per year in the control subjects. At least one randomized trial showed no difference in recurrence rates between treated and untreated patients (Ettinger et al, 1988).

Several magnesium salts have been used for the treatment of stone disease. Magnesium oxide and magnesium hydroxide are poorly absorbed and produce only a slight decrease in urinary oxalate and a modest increase in urinary magnesium (Barilla et al, 1978; Johansson et al, 1980). Urinary calcium levels are increased during magnesium oxide supplementation (Melnick et al, 1971; Fetner et al, 1978; Tiselius et al, 1980), and thus urine saturation of calcium oxalate is not significantly lowered with magnesium oxide. Lindberg and colleagues (1990) found that either magnesium citrate or magnesium oxide induced only modest beneficial changes in urinary biochemistry when administered on an empty stomach. When the magnesium salts were provided with meals, however, they caused more prominent changes in urinary biochemistry and lowered the relative saturation of urine with calcium oxalate or brushite.

**Gastrointestinal intolerance is the major side effect of magnesium therapy. At this time, magnesium supplementation is not widely used.** Magnesium supplementation may be used with sodium cellulose phosphate in the treatment of patients with absorptive hypercalciuria type 1 and with potassium citrate in patients with chronic diarrheal syndromes.

A new magnesium preparation (potassium-magnesium citrate) that provides both magnesium and citrate in the same tablet has been developed but is not yet approved for use. This formulation of potassium-magnesium citrate has been shown to provide as much bioavailable potassium as other preparations (Koenig et al, 1991). In addition, magnesium excretion was significantly increased, as was the excretion of urinary citrate. The ability to deliver potassium has been further studied as it relates to thiazide-induced hypokalemia. This medication was demonstrated to provide just as much bioavailable potassium as other, standard agents (Wuermser et al, 2000).

Finally, Ettinger (1997) has reported on a randomized, double-blind trial of potassium-magnesium citrate versus placebo. In the study, new calculi formed in 63.6% of subjects receiving placebo and in 12.9% of subjects receiving potassium-magnesium citrate. Compared with placebo, the relative risk of treatment failure for potassium-magnesium citrate was 0.16. The authors concluded that potassium-magnesium citrate effectively prevents recurrent calcium oxalate stones and could be depended on to provide up to 85% protection for 3 years.

## KEY POINTS: HYPOMAGNESIURIC CALCIUM NEPHROLITHIASIS

- Magnesium supplementation can provide benefits in stone reduction.

- The use of magnesium has been limited by the risk of diarrhea.

- Potassium-magnesium may restore urinary magnesium and citrate levels with minimal gastrointestinal side effects.

## Gouty Diathesis

**The major goal in the management of gouty diathesis is to increase the urine pH above 5.5, preferably between 6.5 and 7.0** (Khatchadourian et al, 1995). In the past, urine alkalinization has been accomplished with either sodium bicarbonate or various combinations of sodium and potassium alkali therapy. Whereas sodium alkali may enhance dissociation of uric acid and inhibit uric acid stone formation by raising urine pH, this medication may be complicated by the development of calcium-containing stones (calcium phosphate or calcium oxalate). Potassium citrate is advantageous because it not only is a good alkalinizing agent but appears to be devoid of the complication of calcium stones. Potassium citrate should be given at a dose sufficient to maintain urine pH at approximately 6.5 (30 to 60 mEq/day in two or three divided doses). **Attempts at alkalinization of the urine to a pH higher than 7.0 should be avoided. At a higher pH, there is a danger of increasing the risk of calcium phosphate stone formation.** If the urinary uric acid excretion is elevated or hyperuricemia exists, allopurinol (300 mg/day) should be added.

## Cystinuria

**The object of treatment of cystinuria is to reduce the urine concentration of cystine to below its solubility limit (200 to 300 mg/L)** (Pak and Fuller, 1983). The initial treatment program includes a high fluid intake to attempt to produce 2.5 to 3 liters of urine per day. This amount of urine output will dramatically raise the denominator of the concentration fraction and help reduce the supersaturation of urine with respect

to cystine. Others have recommended the oral administration of soluble alkali (potassium citrate) at a dose sufficient to raise the urine pH to 6.5 to 7.0 (Chow and Streem, 1998; Joly et al, 1999). This treatment strategy attempts to increase the solubility of the filtered cystine to prevent crystal formation. Whereas alkali therapy may help, it is important to remember that the pKa of cystine is 8.3, which causes two problems. First, it is difficult to achieve a urine pH this high, making excessive alkalinization an unrealistic target. Second, raising the urine pH to these levels will put the patient at risk for the formation of calcium phosphate calculi.

**There is good evidence that excess dietary sodium can lead to increases in cystine excretion** (Norman and Manette, 1990; Lindell et al, 1995; Rodriguez et al, 1995; Fjellstedt et al, 2001). Indeed, these authors have demonstrated that the restriction of dietary sodium should be an integral aspect of the global management of cystinuric patients. Fjellstedt has even shown that the use of sodium citrate rather than potassium citrate may diminish the efficacy of other medical interventions, such as the sulfhydryl-containing compound α-mercaptopropionylglycine.

When this conservative program is ineffective, **the next line of therapy involves the use of agents that increase cystine solubility in urine through formation of a more soluble mixed disulfide bond (i.e., cystine to drug, rather than cystine to cystine). These agents include D-penicillamine (Cuprimine), α-mercaptopropionylglycine (Thiola, tiopronin), and captopril.**

The first agent studied was D-penicillamine. Interestingly, little has been written specifically about this agent and its use in the treatment of cystinuria since the 1960s and 1970s (Crawhall and Thompson, 1965; McDonald and Henneman, 1965; Lotz et al, 1966; Combe et al, 1993). Although moderately effective, D-penicillamine quickly became associated with frequent side effects including nephrotic syndrome, dermatitis, and pancytopenia. Typical doses start at 250 mg/day and are titrated to effect.

**The next medication to be introduced for the treatment of cystinuria was** α-mercaptopropionylglycine (Remien et al, 1975; Hautmann et al, 1977; Johansen et al, 1980). This agent also contains a sulfhydryl group that forms a disulfide bond with cystine. Although this agent has been shown to be slightly less effective at capturing cystine molecules in vivo (Harbar et al, 1986), α-mercaptopropionylglycine is better tolerated than D-penicillamine and therefore enjoys clinical superiority (Pak et al, 1986a). However, side effects are still possible. Indeed, Pak demonstrated that overall, side effects to α-mercaptopropionylglycine were relatively common and occurred in 64.7% without a history of D-penicillamine treatment, compared with 83.7% who suffered toxic effects of D-penicillamine. Moreover, serious adverse reactions requiring cessation of therapy were less common with α-mercaptopropionylglycine. Among the patients who took both drugs, 30.6% had to stop taking α-mercaptopropionylglycine, whereas 69.4% could not tolerate D-penicillamine. Common side effects include asthenia, gastrointestinal distress, rash, joint aches, and mental status changes. Dosages start at 100 mg, taken orally two times per day, and are titrated to achieve urine concentrations of cystine less than 250 mg per liter of urine. Pak has reported total daily doses as high as 1200 mg (Pak et al, 1986a).

As described earlier in this chapter, Coe and colleagues (2001) have presented an assessment of cystine prophylaxis based on the supersaturation of cystine in the presence of thiol-based medications. In essence, this assay measures how much "room" there is in the patient's urine for more cystine. Demonstration that the urine is not yet fully saturated implies a lower risk for spontaneous stone formation.

Finally, the angiotensin-converting enzyme inhibitor captopril has been used to treat cystinuria because of its available sulfhydryl group. Although this agent enjoyed early enthusiasm (Sloand and Izzo, 1987; Streem and Hall, 1989; Cohen et al, 1995), its popularity seems to have waned (Michelakakis et al, 1993). Side effects are less severe than with the other agents and include fatigue, hypotension, and chronic cough. **Yet, there have been no long-term clinical trials demonstrating the effectiveness of captopril in preventing recurrent cystine stone formation.**

**The medical management of cystinuria can be challenging. Whereas the array of medication choices is not particularly complicated, it is often difficult to achieve the patient's compliance** (Barbey et al, 2000). Indeed, because of the genetic nature of the disease process, these patients frequently begin their stone formation at a young age, thereby exposing their kidneys to the risk of chronic stone passage and potential parenchymal loss (Lindell et al, 1997) (Fig. 43–11). Assimos and colleagues (2002) have examined the clinical status of 40 cystinuric patients observed at two medical centers and compared their "kidney health" with that of 3964 calcium oxalate stone formers enrolled in a database. The mean serum creatinine concentration for stone-forming cystinuric patients was significantly higher than that of the calcium oxalate cohort. Male gender, increasing number of open surgical stone-removing procedures, and nephrectomy were significant variables associated with an increased serum creatinine concentration. An alarming number of cystinuric patients had undergone nephrectomy for any reason (14%) versus the patients in the calcium oxalate cohort (3%).

Unfortunately, despite the obvious consequences of poor medical compliance, a study suggests that few patients are able to achieve and to maintain targeted goals of medical intervention (Pietrow et al, 2003). Of the 26 patients observed at a dedicated stone center, only 15% achieved and maintained therapeutic success, as defined by urine cystine concentration less than 300 mg/L. An additional 42% achieved therapeutic success but subsequently had failure at an average of 16 months (range, 6 to 27). Of these patients, two thirds were able to regain therapeutic success at an average of 9.4 months (range, 4 to 20); 19% never achieved therapeutic success, whereas an additional 23% failed to present to follow-up appointments or to provide subsequent 24-hour urine studies despite their having been referred to a tertiary care center. The patients' self-assessment of medical compliance was uniformly high regardless of physicians' perceptions or treatment results.

### KEY POINTS: CYSTINURIA

- The medical compliance of patients with cystinuria can be poor.

- Treatment consists of aggressive fluid intake, urine alkalinization, salt avoidance, and use of a cystine-binding agent.

- α-Mercaptopropionylglycine (Thiola) is the most frequently used cystine-binding agent.

## Infection Lithiasis

The preferred management of struvite calculi involves aggressive surgical approaches. **The American Urological Association Guidelines Committee has released updated guidelines that strongly recommend endoscopy-based therapy (i.e., percutaneous nephrolithotomy) as the first-line therapy for management of complex renal staghorn calculi** (Preminger et al, 2005). **This report noted that complete elimination of all infected stone material is essential for the prevention of recurrent struvite stone formation.** A complete discussion of surgical therapy for large calculi is beyond the scope of this chapter and can be found in Chapter 44.

**The medical management of infection calculi centers on the prevention of recurrence rather than medical dissolution.** As such, **long-standing effective control of infection with urea-splitting organisms should be achieved if at all possible with improved bladder health, adequate urine drainage, and suppressive antibiotics** (Hess, 1990; Bichler et al, 2002). Unfortunately, such control is difficult to obtain in the face of residual calculi since stones often harbor organisms and endotoxin within their interstices (Rocha and Santos, 1969; McAleer et al, 2002, 2003). Antibiotics should be tailored to the predominant organism found on culture and sensitivity screening (Hugosson et al, 1990). Notably, culture results do not always correlate well between a patient's urine and a resuspension of stone material (Fowler, 1984).

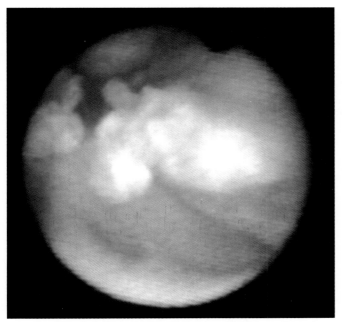

**Figure 43–11.** Endoscopic view of a renal papilla that has been partially replaced by a cystine calculus.

Therefore, strong clinical suspicion is always indicated, and all patients undergoing removal of presumed struvite calculi should be covered with broad-spectrum antibiotics that account for local resistance patterns. Although cultures may become negative during treatment, recurrence of colonization is likely if residual fragments remain within the collecting system.

After surgical stone removal, residual fragments may be dissolved with hemiacidrin irrigation (Renacidin) under careful observation. Historically, use of this agent was associated with significant toxicity and even death. Closer scrutiny revealed that many if not most of these cases involved the use of irrigation in infected urine or sepsis. Therefore, this agent should be employed only after urinary tract infection or colonization has been brought under control. The renal pelvis is first irrigated with sterile saline solution at a rate of 120 mL/hr for 24 to 48 hours, beginning on the fourth or fifth postoperative day. The height of irrigation is adjusted to the lowest level necessary to maintain the flow rate at 120 mL/hr. If there is leakage around a surgical drain or through the incision, irrigation is stopped until additional healing occurs. The patient is observed carefully for development of fever or any flank discomfort and for elevation of serum creatinine, magnesium, or phosphate levels (Dretler and Pfister, 1984). Occurrence of any of these conditions requires immediate cessation of irrigation.

If, after 48 hours, the patient's condition remains satisfactory and there is no infection, no leakage, and no fever or flank discomfort, irrigation is begun with an appropriate solution. Flow rate is continued at 120 mL/hr through the irrigation tube or catheter. Most authors (Jacobs and Gittes, 1976; Nemoy and Stamey, 1976; Palmer et al, 1987) instruct their patients to stop the irrigation themselves if there is evidence of flank pain at any time.

The progress of irrigation is followed by radiographic tomography of the calculi at intervals. Irrigation is continued for 24 to 48 hours after the last radiographically visible fragments have disappeared. In some instances, the rate of irrigation may be reduced to prevent irritation of the kidney or bladder, or sterile saline solutions may be alternated with irrigating solutions. Chemolysis with various agents is no longer routinely used for the management of struvite calculi.

**Acetohydroxamic acid, a urease inhibitor, may reduce the urine saturation of struvite and therefore retard stone formation** (Griffith et al, 1978). **When given at a dose of 250 mg three times per day, acetohydroxamic acid has been shown to prevent recurrence of new stones and to inhibit the growth of stones in patients with chronic urea-splitting infections.** At least two studies have demonstrated significant efficacy in randomized, placebo-controlled trials (Williams et al, 1984; Griffith et al, 1991). In these investigations, patients were treated with acetohydroxamic acid as well as with antibiotics. Recurrence rates and subsequent stone growth were significantly less for patients treated with drug therapy compared with placebo. In addition, in a limited number of patients, this agent has caused dissolution of existing struvite calculi (Rodman et al, 1983). **However, a significant percentage of patients receiving chronic acetohydroxamic acid therapy have experienced minor side effects, and 15% developed deep venous thrombosis.** Indeed, Rodman and colleagues (1987) have demonstrated that patients receiving acetohydroxamic acid enter into a state of low-grade intravascular

coagulation, requiring careful follow-up for signs of thrombosis.

Several authors have reported high rates of medication cessation due to intolerable side effects. In the randomized studies noted, 22% to 68% of treated patients had to stop therapy and withdraw from the investigation. Reported side effects have been varied and include thromboembolic phenomena, tremor, headache, palpitations, edema, gastrointestinal distress, loss of taste, rash, alopecia, anemia, and abdominal pain. Because of these concerns, this agent is frequently reserved for those patients deemed too ill for surgical management. Other acidifying agents have been reported by Wall and Tiselius (1990) but do not appear to have been widely used. These include ammonium chloride, methenamine hippurate, and ascorbic acid.

> ## KEY POINTS: INFECTION LITHIASIS
>
> ■ Struvite calculi are best managed with surgical removal rather than by chemical dissolution.
>
> ■ Recurrent infections (and therefore recurrent calculi) may be avoided with antibiotic prophylaxis.
>
> ■ Acetohydroxamic acid (Lithostat) can effectively inhibit urease, but its widespread use is precluded by significant side effects.

## Ammonium Acid Urate Stones

**Ammonium acid urate calculi are infrequently seen in industrialized nations and are often associated with laxative abuse** (Dick et al, 1990; Kato et al, 2004). The largest described series has been reported by Soble and colleagues (1999) from the Cleveland Clinic. In their series, 23 women and 21 men ranging in age from 20 to 81 years (mean, 48.7 years) were treated for stones partly composed of ammonium acid urate. Stone composition ranged from 2% to 60% ammonium acid urate (mean, 24.1%) of the total stone mass. No patient had a pure ammonium acid urate stone, although 11 (25%) had stones with ammonium acid urate as the predominant crystal. The authors identified one or more potential risk factors for ammonium acid urate for most patients. Of the patients, 25% had a history of inflammatory bowel disease, with 22.7% having undergone ileostomy diversion; 13.6% admitted to a history of significant laxative use or abuse, 40.9% were morbidly obese, 36.4% had a history of recurrent urinary tract infections, and 20.5% had a history of recurrent uric acid stones. On the basis of these findings, the authors suggested that laxative abuse should not be assumed for all patients with ammonium acid urate calculi; rather, a metabolic evaluation or full history should be sought for each patient.

Medical treatment of these calculi is determined by the underlying cause of the stone. Those with laxative abuse are strongly encouraged to develop a healthier bowel regimen. Those with chronic infections are treated much like those with struvite calculi. Bowel disease is treated, if possible, and standard recommendations of fluid intake, oral calcium, alkalinization, and oxalate reduction are made. Those with a history of uric acid calculi are also treated in a similar manner with

**Table 43–17. Medications Associated with Renal Calculus Formation**

*Calculi formed from drug*
Indinavir
Ephedrine
Triamterene
Magnesium trisilicate antacids (silicates)
Sulfamethoxazole-trimethoprim

*Calculi provoked by drug*
Carbonic anhydrase inhibitors
Topiramate
Furosemide
Vitamin C (excess)
Vitamin D (excess)
Laxatives

---

increased fluid intake, protein and salt restriction, and possibly use of citrates or allopurinol.

## Miscellaneous and Drug-Induced Stones

**Some stones are formed from supersaturation of medications themselves or may be due to the effects of a particular agent. Several medications have been associated with stone disease and are listed in Table 43–17.**

Calculi formed from antiretroviral medications used to treat human immunodeficiency virus infection have been described, particularly with indinavir (Crixivan) (Bach and Godofsky, 1997; Hug et al, 1999; Sundaram and Saltzman, 1999; Saltel et al, 2000). These calculi can be quite soft and often dissipate rapidly during endoscopy or shockwave lithotripsy. **Difficulties may arise during diagnosis as indinavir stones may not be visible on plain film radiography and may even be undetectable on stone protocol CT** (Gentle et al, 1997; Sundaram and Saltzman, 1999). Treatment entails aggressive hydration and endoscopy for those stones that do not pass spontaneously. The radiolucency of the calculi often precludes successful treatment with shockwave lithotripsy. In the short term, patients may be temporarily taken off of indinavir until an aggressive fluid habit can be established. Some patients require cessation of this antiretroviral and the initiation of a different agent.

As described earlier, triamterene, a potassium-sparing antihypertensive agent, may crystallize in the urinary tract, requiring cessation of this medication (Werness et al, 1982; Sorgel et al, 1985). For this reason, triamterene is not recommended as an adjunct to thiazides during the treatment of hypercalciuric states.

**Carbonic anhydrase inhibitors may be associated with the formation of calcium-based calculi, particularly calcium phosphate** (Kondo et al, 1968; Parfitt, 1969). In this scenario, the use of the medication creates a chronic intracellular acidosis. This in turn creates a urinary milieu reminiscent of a distal tubular acidosis with hyperchloremic acidosis, high urine pH, extremely low urinary citrate, and hypercalciuria. Treatment may be accomplished with potassium citrate replacement or, more logically, cessation of the medication.

Topiramate is a relatively new antiepileptic medication with significant promise for the treatment of refractory epilepsy. Unfortunately, it may mimic the effect of a carbonic anhydrase inhibitor and lead to the formation of urinary calculi (Kossoff et al, 2002; Kuo et al, 2002; Lamb et al, 2004). The incidence of such an effect has been reported to be approximately 5% (Kossoff et al, 2002).

Finally, **multiple authors have described calculi that have formed in patients taking supplements containing ephedrine** (Blau, 1998; Powell et al, 1998; Assimos et al, 1999; Hoffman et al, 2003; Bennett et al, 2004; Smith et al, 2004; Whelan and Schwartz, 2004). These calculi are likely to be radiolucent but have been reported to be "visible" on non–contrast-enhanced CT. Ephedrine stones have been treated with a variety of methods, including shockwave lithotripsy, endoscopy, and even alkalinization therapy. Because this supplement has a risk of abuse, it may be difficult to effectively interfere with the formation of future stone events.

## MISCELLANEOUS SCENARIOS
## Medical Management of Bladder Calculi

**In the United States, bladder calculi usually occur in men older than 50 years and are associated with bladder outlet obstruction.** The diagnosis of a bladder stone should result in a complete urologic evaluation for factors that cause urine stasis, such as urethral stricture, benign prostatic hyperplasia, bladder diverticulum, and neurogenic bladder.

In contrast to renal stones, **bladder stones are usually composed of uric acid (in noninfected urine) or struvite (in infected urine).** Reports from the United States revealed uric acid stones in nearly 50% of patients with bladder stones (Douenias et al, 1991). Such patients often have bladder outlet obstruction, causing them to decrease fluid intake with the resultant production of concentrated, acidic urine. The occurrence of calcium oxalate or cystine stones in the bladder suggests the presence of calculi in the kidney with subsequent ureteral passage and entrapment in the bladder.

**Bladder calculi are usually solitary but may develop in large numbers in the presence of urine stasis** (Sarica et al, 1994). **The typical symptoms of a vesical stone are intermittent, painful voiding and terminal hematuria.** Discomfort may be dull, aching, or sharp suprapubic pain, which is aggravated by exercise and sudden movement. Severe pain usually occurs near the end of micturition, as the stone becomes impacted at the bladder neck. Relief may be afforded by assuming a recumbent position. The pain may be referred to the tip of the penis, the scrotum, or the perineum and on occasion to the back or the hip. **Besides pain, there may be an interruption of the urinary stream from impaction of the stone at the bladder neck or urethra.**

Bladder calculi are frequently missed on plain film because of a high component of uric acid and overlying prostatic tissue. Such stones form negative shadows in the cystogram phase of intravenous urography. Ultrasonography is useful for detecting radiolucent calculi. Cystoscopic examination is the surest method for detecting vesical calculi.

**Most bladder calculi can be removed by endoscopic techniques.** Various lithotripters have been used, including ultrasonic handpieces, lasers, pneumatic devices, and electrohydraulic probes (Ikari et al, 1993; Razvi et al, 1996). Transurethral and percutaneous approaches have been described with good success. Stone dissolution is feasible with the use of Suby G or M solution. This method is protracted and now rarely employed. **Suby's solutions or Renacidin may prove beneficial in irrigating indwelling suprapubic or urethral catheters to decrease and to prevent encrustation and occlusion** (Kennedy et al, 1992; Getliffe et al, 2000). Twice-daily or thrice-daily irrigation with 0.25% or 0.5% acetic acid solution also serves as beneficial prophylaxis against recurrent struvite calculi when catheters must be left indwelling for long periods. Uric acid calculi may be dissolved by irrigation with alkaline solutions.

**The mainstay of therapy for the prevention of recurrent bladder calculi involves relief of the bladder outlet obstruction.** This treatment may include the performance of a transurethral resection of the prostate or an open prostatectomy, if the gland is large.

## Medical Management of Pediatric Calculi

Children may develop urinary calculi from several underlying causes as outlined in Chapter 42. Evaluation and management depend on the causative process.

### Neonatal Nephrolithiasis

**Neonates with furosemide-induced nephrolithiasis present with hematuria, worsening renal function, and calcific densities on ultrasonography or plain film radiography. Nephrocalcinosis is often present on imaging studies.** This same process has been seen in other infants with severe low birth weight or prematurity and no history of loop diuretic use.

Management of neonatal nephrolithiasis entails the obvious optimization of the infant's overall health. **Cessation of furosemide diuresis is considered helpful and standard therapy. There has been previous suggestion that treatment with thiazide diuretics may actually promote the resolution of this process and reverse the likely parenchymal injury** (Noe et al, 1984). **This observation has not been supported by other investigators, however.** Pope and colleagues (1996) noted a 50% resolution rate of the nephrocalcinosis after cessation of loop diuretics, but this was unrelated to any other factor, including the use of thiazides. Instead, a low calcium/creatinine ratio at the time of diagnosis was the best predictor of resolution. Further research by Knoll and Alon (2000) with an animal model of the disease did not demonstrate a therapeutic effect of the use of thiazides on furosemide-induced nephrocalcinosis.

At the very least, this evidence suggests that **neonates treated with loop diuretics should be screened for the development of nephrocalcinosis. Whereas switching to a thiazide diuretic may not actively cause the dissolution of calculi, it at least removes the causative agent and allows the kidney an opportunity to heal and clear the calcium deposits.**

### Children and Adolescents

As children reach physical maturity at a younger age, it is not surprising that the incidence of urinary calculi in adolescence appears to be increasing. Within the United States, this finding is probably further related to the increasing prevalence of obesity within this same age group. **Nevertheless, the appearance of urinary calculi during childhood should raise the distinct possibility of an inherited genetic disorder, such as cystinuria, distal renal tubular acidosis, or primary hyperoxaluria.**

**The evaluation of pediatric nephrolithiasis has been hampered in the past by a lack of consensus regarding normal laboratory values during 24-hour urine collections in children.** Clinicians have therefore relied on calculated ratios to correct for the wide variation in weight within this diverse population of patients. The most important of these has been the urinary calcium/creatinine ratio. A calculated urinary calcium/creatinine ratio above 0.2 has been considered abnormal and frequently prompts intervention.

**Several investigators have explored the use of urine supersaturation calculations to assess for stone risk factors in children** (Battino et al, 2002; Lande et al, 2005). These calculations may detect abnormalities otherwise overlooked by "traditional" cumulative measurements. At least one of these authors, however, noted that the importance of supersaturation wanes considerably in the face of low urine volumes (Lande et al, 2005).

**The medical management of nephrolithiasis and the prevention of subsequent recurrences in children do not differ dramatically from the approaches undertaken for adults. All patients (and their parents) are counseled to improve fluid intake. Dietary recommendations are similar to those made for adults.** Dietary calcium is not to be avoided in this age group. Rather, calcium should be sought through the ingestion of dairy and other natural sources rather than with the use of supplements. Such sources will also bind dietary oxalate during meals and may decrease calcium oxalate supersaturation in the urine.

Children with cystinuria or hyperoxaluria are managed as outlined in the previous section within this chapter. The exception to this is a general reticence to begin sulfur-binding agents in cystinuric children without first maximizing fluid intake and the use of citrates to alkalinize the urine.

Children with documented hypocitraturia or distal renal tubular acidosis are usually treated with citrates at a dose of 4 mEq/kg/day (Domrongkitchaiporn et al, 2002a). Hypercalciuria may respond to increased fluid intake and decreased sodium (salt) ingestion, much like in the adult population. Thiazides may be employed for recalcitrant hypercalciuria. The long-term efficacy and safety of thiazides in the pediatric population have not been well studied and established.

## Medical Management of Calculi During Pregnancy

The management of calculi during pregnancy is currently undergoing a transformation. These changes, however, are developing mainly within the realm of surgical intervention, not medical therapy. As noted in Chapter 42, **pregnant women create a unique urinary environment that is prone** to stone formation. Whereas the amount of urinary calcium rises notably (Gertner et al, 1986), **this effect is offset by an accompanying increase in urinary citrate. As a result, it is widely assumed that there is no net increase or decrease in the risk of calculi formation during pregnancy** (Coe et al, 1978; Maikranz et al, 1987). **Because of these temporary physiologic changes, a metabolic evaluation is not generally undertaken to determine the cause of the stone disease until after the woman has delivered and returned to her baseline state of health.**

The acute evaluation of a pregnant woman with suspected renal colic begins with a thorough history and physical examination. A urinalysis specimen is obtained and examined for signs of active urinary tract infection. Patients may also present with vague abdominal pain, unexplained fevers, recurrent urinary tract infections, persistent bacteriuria, or microscopic hematuria. A previous history of nephrolithiasis should also be sought as the increased dilation of the ureters during pregnancy may increase the risk that a preformed stone will break loose and attempt to pass.

**Radiation exposure to the fetus should be avidly avoided. Therefore, ultrasonography has become the first-line imaging study to search for calculi during pregnancy.** Although this modality provides adequate images of the kidneys, it can be difficult to fully discern the ureters and their contents. In addition, hydronephrosis of pregnancy may be confused with hydronephrosis from an obstructing calculus. **Limited intravenous pyelography may be performed that consists of one scout image followed by one plate taken approximately 30 minutes after the injection of contrast material. Each plain film exposes the fetus to 0.1 to 0.2 rad, well below the threshold of 1.2 rad, when the risk begins to increase.** Radiation exposure should be particularly avoided in the first trimester during the time of organogenesis and the greatest fetal risk.

**Approximately 66% to 85% of pregnant women with ureteric colic spontaneously pass the calculi when they are treated conservatively with hydration, analgesics, and, if infected, antibiotics** (Jones et al, 1979; Stothers and Lee, 1992). The goal of therapy for the remaining patients is to do the least required to keep the kidney functioning, the patient free from symptoms, and the urine uninfected. **Stents should be placed cystoscopically with minimal radiographic or sonographic monitoring** (Loughlin and Bailey, 1986; Jarrard et al, 1993). Some studies have demonstrated increased encrustation of stents, requiring frequent changes. In some instances, the stents migrated down the ureter because of the physiologic dilation (Stothers and Lee, 1992). Stents are often exchanged every 4 to 6 weeks to avoid excessive encrustation and the risk of obstruction.

Since many expectant mothers take calcium supplementation, a more stone-friendly form of this mineral has been developed (Citracal Prenatal Rx). In this formulation, calcium is bound to citrate, which delivers extra stone inhibitor into the urine, thereby offsetting the effects of worsening absorptive hypercalciuria. Iron and folate are also added to complete the elements commonly found in prenatal multivitamin supplements. Although there are no randomized data to support the use of this supplement, its use does make intuitive sense for patients at risk for recurrent calculi during pregnancy.

A full discussion of the surgical management of calculi during pregnancy is beyond the scope of this chapter. **There is growing evidence, though, that ureteroscopy, with holmium laser lithotripsy performed later during pregnancy, is safe and free of increased risk** (Lifshitz and Lingeman, 2002; Watterson et al, 2002). Indeed, the definitive nature of one uncomplicated ureteroscopy probably represents less risk than the anesthesia associated with multiple stent changes plus the infectious risk of an indwelling foreign body.

## KEY POINTS: MEDICAL MANAGEMENT OF CALCULI

- Bladder calculi are best managed with endoscopic techniques. Subsequent recurrence is prevented by relief of the bladder outlet obstruction.
- Neonatal nephrocalcinosis is frequently caused by loop diuretics. Cessation of this medication is essential.
- Neonatal nephrocalcinosis may be reversed by the use of thiazides.
- The majority of ureteral calculi during pregnancy pass spontaneously.
- There is a growing trend toward endoscopic relief of symptomatic calculi during pregnancy.

## SUMMARY

**Selective medical therapy for nephrolithiasis is highly effective in preventing new stone formation. A remission rate of more than 80% and overall reduction in individual stone formation rate of more than 90% can be obtained in patients with nephrolithiasis.** In patients with mild to moderate severity of stone disease, virtually total control of stone disease can be achieved with a remission rate of more than 95%.

Selective pharmacologic therapy for nephrolithiasis also encompasses the advantages of overcoming nonrenal complications as well as averting certain side effects that may be caused by nonselective medical therapy. Despite these advantages, it is clear that selective medical therapy cannot provide total control of stone disease. **A satisfactory response requires continued, dedicated compliance of patients with the recommended program and a commitment by the physician to provide long-term follow-up and care.**

## SUGGESTED READINGS

Borghi L, Meschi T, Schianchi T, et al: Urine volume: Stone risk factor and preventive measure. Nephron 1999;81(suppl 1):31-37.

Borghi L, Schianchi T, Meschi T, et al: Comparison of two diets for the prevention of recurrent stones in idiopathic hypercalciuria. N Engl J Med 2002;346:77-84.

Curhan GC, Willett WC, Rimm EB, Stampfer MJ: A prospective study of dietary calcium and other nutrients and the risk of symptomatic kidney stones. N Engl J Med 1993;328:833-838.

Levy FL, Adams-Huet B, Pak CY: Ambulatory evaluation of nephrolithiasis: An update of a 1980 protocol. Am J Med 1995;98:50-59.

Lingeman JE, Siegel YI, Steele B: Metabolic evaluation of infected renal lithiasis: Clinical relevance. J Endourol 1995;9:51-54.

Pak CY: Southwestern Internal Medicine Conference: Medical management of nephrolithiasis—a new, simplified approach for general practice. Am J Med Sci 1997;313:215-219.

Pearle MS, Roehrborn CG, Pak CY: Meta-analysis of randomized trials for medical prevention of calcium oxalate nephrolithiasis. J Endourol 1999; 13:679-685.

Preminger GM, Pak CY: The practical evaluation and selective medical management of nephrolithiasis. Semin Urol 1985;3:170-184.

Preminger GM, Pak CY: Eventual attenuation of hypocalciuric response to hydrochlorothiazide in absorptive hypercalciuria. J Urol 1987;137:1104-1109.

Preminger GM, Sakhaee K, Skurla C, Pak CY: Prevention of recurrent calcium stone formation with potassium citrate therapy in patients with distal renal tubular acidosis. J Urol 1985;134:20-23.

# 44 Surgical Management of Upper Urinary Tract Calculi

JAMES E. LINGEMAN, MD • BRIAN R. MATLAGA, MD, MPH • ANDREW P. EVAN, PhD

---

HISTORICAL OVERVIEW

RENAL CALCULI

URETERAL CALCULI

URINARY CALCULI DURING PREGNANCY

STONE REMOVAL: SURGICAL TECHNIQUES AND TECHNOLOGY

## HISTORICAL OVERVIEW
### Kidney Calculi

Although calculi in the kidney were rare before the Industrial Revolution (Shah et al, 2002), the existence of nephrolithiasis was known to Hippocrates, who described the symptoms of renal colic: "An acute pain is felt in the kidney, the loins, the flank and the testis of the affected side; the patient passes urine frequently; gradually the urine is suppressed. With the urine, sand is passed." It is not certain that Hippocrates performed surgery on patients with renal calculi, but he did describe the following operations: the drainage of tuberculous and nontuberculous pyelonephritic abscesses, the incision of swelling in the loin due to renal tumefaction resulting from stone, and the drainage of kidneys presenting with acute congestion caused by pyelonephritis (Wershub, 1970). In the centuries that followed Hippocrates, there was little scientific progress in the surgical therapy for patients with renal calculi. The alleged first account of a surgical attempt to remove a stone from a patient's kidney is the case of the French archer of Bagnolet. Little is known of the authenticity of this tale of a condemned man afflicted with a renal calculus who agreed to allow surgery on the affected kidney on the condition that if he survived, he would be freed. According to the anecdote, the man survived the open surgical stone removal and was freed in 1474

(Herman, 1973). Unfortunately, neither the hospital nor the surgeons involved maintained any first-hand record of this event, so the veracity of this claim is uncertain. The first verifiable account of renal stone surgery was in 1550, when Cardan of Milan opened a lumbar abscess on a young girl and removed 18 calculi (Desnos, 1972). For the following two centuries, most surgeons were in agreement that the only indication for open renal surgery was the infected calculous kidney, distended by the accumulation of purulent matter, or those kidneys in which the calculus could be palpated in the organ itself.

In 1734, Lafite incised a swelling in a patient's loin and drained considerable purulence. Twenty-two days later, the pus reaccumulated; he probed the incision and found a stone in the region of the kidney. Lafite widened the prior incision and removed two calculi, and the patient recovered well. Four years later, Lafite again removed stones from a man who had undergone drainage of a lumbar swelling 11 years before and who had a persistent urinary fistula. Lafite concluded that it was possible to remove the stones at the time of the first surgical intervention rather than subject the patient to multiple procedures (Ballenger et al, 1933). In 1872, William Ingalls of the Boston City Hospital removed a large calculus from the right kidney of a 31-year-old woman with a persistent pyelocutaneous fistula (Spirnak and Resnick, 1983). Ingalls incised the sinus track of the fistula and extracted the stone with forceps, thus performing the first recorded nephrolithotomy in America. In 1880, Henry Morris of England was the first to remove a stone from an otherwise healthy kidney by nephrolithotomy, extracting a 31-g mulberry calculus from the kidney of a young woman (Dudley, 1973).

As the surgical techniques of nephrolithotomy evolved, renal parenchymal incisions were made in a variety of different ways in an effort to reduce hemorrhagic morbidity. Heineke, in 1879, first described a pyelotomy incision for the extraction of calculi. The operation rapidly found favor and was employed by many surgeons, although it was not possible to extend the incision to permit extraction of large renal calculi without damaging the retropelvic renal artery (Wershub, 1970). Josef Hyrtl in 1882 and Max Brödel in 1902 described a relatively avascular plane near the midline (5 mm posterior) of the convex border of the kidney through which the collecting system of the kidney could be entered. In Europe, credit for the plane was given to Hyrtl; but in England and the United States, it was called Brödel's bloodless line or Brödel's white line (Schultheiss et al, 2000). Although the existence of this avascular plane was an important discovery, surgeons continued to find that bleeding during nephrolithotomy was a considerable problem. Zuckerkandl described an inferior pyelonephrolithotomy, in which a pyelotomy incision was extended into the lower pole of the kidney. Partner recommended a V-shaped incision with two limbs radiating toward the poles of the kidney. Other attempts were made to control the persistent problem of bleeding, including compression of the hilar vessels and various methods of suturing. In 1887, Czerny was the first to approximate the cut edges of the incised kidney with suture to control hemorrhage and to prevent fistula formation. In the same year, Felix Guyon reported that nephrectomy, although efficacious in curing patients suffering from calculous pyonephrosis, was more dangerous than nephrolithotomy because lithiasis was often bilateral (Wershub, 1970). In 1889, Kümmell was the first surgeon to perform a partial nephrectomy for calculous pyonephrosis (Redman, 1983). Lower in 1913 revived interest in pyelolithotomy when he suggested that this technique may be a safer and easier method of removing renal calculi than nephrolithotomy. Although several small series of cases indicated that there might be a higher incidence of stone recurrence after pyelolithotomy, other studies showed that recurrence was no more common than it was after nephrolithotomy (Murphy, 1972). These findings, in conjunction with rapid advancements in the field of radiography, brought about a decided preference for pyelolithotomy (Gil-Vernet and Culla, 1981). In 1943, Dees and Fox reported the first use of coagulum to remove small stones and stone fragments from the renal pelvis and calyces (Marshall, 1983). Fibrinogen and thrombin were used to make a coagulum that was injected into the renal pelvis and produced a flexible cast of the pelvis and calyces. The use of this technique was limited initially owing to the scarcity of materials and the risk of blood-borne disease transmission. However, interest in coagulum pyelolithotomy was renewed when cryoprecipitate was found to be a safe and readily available source of concentrated fibrinogen (Fischer et al, 1980).

An important advance in the open surgical approach to the kidney was the intrasinusally extended pyelolithotomy, pioneered by Gil-Vernet in 1965. Because of its wide applicability and minimal morbidity, this approach to the renal collecting system became the procedure of choice for the majority of renal pelvic calculi. Patients harboring large or complex calculi could be effectively treated with extended pyelolithotomy combined with multiple radial nephrotomies (Wickham et al, 1974). In 1968, **Smith and Boyce described anatrophic nephrolithotomy, a procedure that derived its name from the technique of incising the renal parenchyma along the avascular plane between the anterior and posterior vascular distributions. Because an incision in this plane does not interrupt the blood supply to the renal parenchyma, it does not result in atrophy, hence the term** *anatrophic.* This procedure permits a relatively bloodless operation that encompasses stone removal, reconstruction of the calyceal system, and closure of the renal capsule with preservation of renal function. **Although stone-free rates of these modern surgical techniques were excellent, morbidity was significant, and the search for new techniques and technologies continued.**

## Ureteral Calculi

Ambroise Paré is credited with the first account of ureteral calculi in 1564, as he described "the cruel pain [that] tormented the patient in that place where the stone lodged." Paré also stated that death was the consequence of having calculi impacted in both ureters (Murphy, 1972). However, Morris reported in 1898 that "operations on the ureter are an advance of the last few years, but not many have been recorded up to the present time" (Ballenger et al, 1933). Thomas Emmet of New York published an account in 1879 of three female patients with stones impacted at the distal aspect of the ureter. In one patient, he opened the bladder and removed the stone with forceps; in a second patient, he removed a stone by cutting down on it through the vaginal wall. These procedures were the first recordings of a surgeon making a definite diagnosis of ureteral calculus and deliberately and successfully performing a ureterolithotomy. In the years that followed, numerous approaches were used, including intraperitoneal, perineal, sacral, transrectal, and transvaginal. In 1910, **Gibson of New York described an incision parallel to and just above Poupart's ligament, wholly extraperitoneal, by which the lower ureter, even down to its entrance into the bladder, could be readily exposed.** This safe and comparatively easy approach to the ureter placed open ureterolithotomy on sound footing.

## The Rise of Endourology

Before the development of endoscopy, attempts to blindly extract calculi were not uncommon. In 1889, Gustav Kolisher performed the first successful stone manipulation, reporting that he "located the stone with a metal-tipped catheter several inches above the ureteric orifice and through it injected 30 cc of sterile oil," displacing the stone (Murphy, 1972).

The development of minimally invasive surgical techniques for the treatment of patients suffering from urinary lithiasis has been greatly dependent on technologic advances in the fields of **fiberoptics, radiographic imaging, and lithotripsy (shockwave, ultrasonic, electrohydraulic, and laser).** These advancements have accelerated the evolution of modern techniques of calculus removal, including **ureteroscopy, percutaneous nephrolithotomy (PNL), and extracorporeal shockwave lithotripsy (SWL). In 1979, Arthur Smith defined the term** *endourology* **as closed controlled manipulation within the genitourinary tract** (Smith et al, 1979).

### Ureteroscopy

The practice of ureteroscopy began by happenstance when, in 1912, Hugh Hampton Young introduced a pediatric cystoscope into the massively dilated ureter of a child with posterior urethral valves (Young and McKay, 1929). Aided by the child's secondary ureteral dilation, Young was able to advance the cystoscope to the level of the renal pelvis, thus becoming the first urologist to view the intrarenal collecting system endoscopically. Unfortunately, the following three decades held few significant advances in ureteroscopic technology until knowledge of fiberoptics could be put to clinical use. By 1957, Curtiss and Hirschowitz combined a large number of glass fibers into a coherent bundle and fused the fibers at their ends to allow them to move individually along their length, thus creating the first flexible endoscope (Hirschowitz et al, 1957). In 1964, Marshall reported the first urologic use of this new type of flexible endoscope when he passed the scope through an open ureterotomy to the level of the renal pelvis, thereby performing the first flexible ureteroscopy. Subsequently, two of his associates, McGovern and Walzak, performed the first transurethral flexible ureteroscopy when they passed the same 9 French flexible endoscope to inspect a ureteral calculus. Since then, developments in optics and mechanics have greatly improved the design of flexible ureteroscopes.

Currently available ureteroscopes range from 54 to 70 cm in length and have a tapered shaft diameter that increases proximally. As the tip of the ureteroscope is inserted into the ureter and passed retrograde, the ureter is slowly dilated. Initial ureteroscopes had neither a working nor an irrigating channel. Most modern ureteroscopes have a single working channel, and some have a second irrigation channel that serves to distend the ureter and maintain visualization.

Early flexible ureteroscopes were passive, and the subsequent incorporation of active tip deflection has greatly increased their utility. Active deflection refers to deflection of the tip of the endoscope, which is controlled by the surgeon through a lever mechanism on the handle of the endoscope. Flexible ureteroscopes have been introduced with two segments of active deflection, with the active primary site of deflection providing 170 to 180 degrees of up and down movement; the secondary active deflection, located several centimeters proximal to the primary deflection, is a 130-degree one-way downward deflection. This design greatly facilitates entry into the lower pole infundibulum. Other manufacturers have designed flexible ureteroscopes with 270 degrees of deflection, which also facilitates entry into the lower pole infundibulum.

Interestingly, the first reports of rigid ureteroscopy trailed those of flexible ureteroscopy by almost one decade. In 1977, Goodman reported on three cases in which a pediatric cystoscope was used to treat patients with ureteral maladies. These initial rigid ureteroscopes employed a rod-lens system that was large (10 to 13 French) and inflexible, although it provided an optimal image. Most rigid ureteroscopes have replaced this rod-lens system of image transmission with fiberoptics, which allows significant reduction in the size of the endoscope. In addition, the flexibility of the fiberoptic bundles allows the shaft of the endoscope to become somewhat bendable along its vertical axis, hence the term *semirigid ureteroscope*.

Parallel to improvements in rigid and flexible ureteroscopes were advances in intracorporeal lithotripters, including ultrasonic, electrohydraulic, pneumatic, and laser probes, allowing efficient stone fragmentation through the miniaturized modern ureteroscopic equipment. Many new stone retrieval devices, designed to pass through the working channel of a ureteroscope, have been introduced with the capability for manipulation and deflection.

## Percutaneous Stone Removal

The first description of percutaneous stone removal was that of Rupel and Brown (1941) of Indianapolis, who removed a stone through a previously established surgical nephrostomy track. It was not until 1955, however, that Goodwin described the first placement of a percutaneous nephrostomy tube to drain a grossly hydronephrotic kidney (Goodwin et al, 1955). Goodwin did not have the benefit of radiographic guidance, and so the drainage tube was placed without imaging. In 1976, Fernstrom and Johannson first reported the establishment of percutaneous access with the specific intention of removing a renal stone. Subsequent advances in endoscopes, imaging equipment, and intracorporeal lithotripters allowed urologists and radiologists to refine these percutaneous techniques through the late 1970s and early 1980s into well-established methods for removal of upper urinary tract calculi.

## Extracorporeal Shockwave Lithotripsy

The phenomenon that sound waves can be focused has been known since antiquity. The ancient Greeks, as taught by Dionysius, used this knowledge to construct vaults that allowed them to overhear the conversations of their imprisoned enemies. In the 18th and 19th centuries, cabinets constructed with echo or sound mirrors were capable of transmitting the ticking of a pocket watch over a distance exceeding 60 feet.

High-energy shockwaves have been recognized for many years. Examples of high-energy shockwaves include the potentially window-shattering sonic boom created when aircraft pass beyond the speed of sound and the blast effect associated with explosions. Engineers at Dornier Medical Systems in what was then West Germany, during research on the effects of shockwaves on military hardware, demonstrated that shockwaves are reflectable and therefore focusable. The possibility of application of mechanical shockwaves to human tissue was discovered when, by chance, a test engineer touched a target body at the very moment of impact of a high-velocity projectile. The engineer felt a sensation similar to an electric shock, although the contact point at the skin showed no damage at all (Hepp, 1984). This observation and its potential military applications led Dornier to pursue a method of generating a reproducible shockwave.

Beginning in 1969 and funded by the German Ministry of Defense, Dornier began a study of the effects of shockwaves on tissue. Specifically, the study was to determine if the shockwaves generated by a projectile striking the wall of a military tank would damage the lungs of a crew member leaning against the same wall. During the study, Dornier engineers developed techniques to reproducibly generate shockwaves. In the course of this effort, the engineers discovered that shockwaves generated in water could pass through living tissue (except for the lung) without discernible damage to the tissue but that brittle materials in the path of the shockwaves were fragmented.

At some point, a possible medical application of shockwaves became apparent: if shockwaves could safely pass through tissue but fragment brittle materials, perhaps they could be used to break up kidney stones. Dornier engineers found that lower energy shockwaves, which would be appropriate for medical applications, could be generated in a predictable and reproducible manner by an underwater electrical spark discharge.

In 1972, on the basis of preliminary studies performed by Dornier Medical Systems, an agreement was reached with Egbert Schmiedt, director of the urologic clinic at the University of Munich, to proceed with further investigation of the therapeutic potential of this technology (Chaussy and Fuchs, 1986). This research was supported by the West German Federal Ministry of Research and Technology, and the development of the Dornier lithotripter progressed through several prototypes, ultimately culminating in February 1980 with the first treatment of a human by SWL. The production and distribution of the Dornier HM3 lithotripter began in late 1983, and SWL was approved by the U.S. Food and Drug Administration in 1984. Since Dornier's pioneering work, numerous other companies have demonstrated that shockwaves capable of stone fragmentation may be generated by electromagnetic induction, microexplosions, focused lasers, and piezoelectric crystals. To date, more than 3000 lithotripters of all types have been placed worldwide, and more than 1 million patients are treated annually with SWL.

## RENAL CALCULI

**The primary goal of surgical stone management is to achieve maximal stone clearance with minimal morbidity to the patient.** The introduction of SWL as well as continuing advancements in the field of endourology has allowed most patients with renal stones to be treated in a minimally invasive fashion. However, as the armamentarium of treatment modalities available to the urologist has increased, new controversies regarding the indications for these therapies have developed. Currently, urologists face the challenge of selecting the optimal treatment modality on the basis of the patient's and the stone's characteristics. Four minimally invasive treatment modalities are available for the treatment of patients with kidney stones and are detailed in this chapter: SWL, PNL, ureteroscopy, and laparoscopic stone surgery. SWL has also been used in combination with PNL ("sandwich technique") as well as with ureterorenoscopic lithotripsy. Recent advancements in endoscopic technology and surgical technique have dramatically reduced the need for open surgical procedures to treat patients with renal and ureteral calculi.

**Most (about 80% to 85%) patients harboring "simple" renal calculi can be treated satisfactorily with SWL** (Chaussy and Schmiedt, 1984; Krings et al, 1992; Wickham, 1993). To better define those patients with upper urinary tract calculi who are less likely to have a successful outcome after treatment with SWL, Grasso and colleagues (1995a) reviewed a series of 121 patients whose initial SWL treatment session failed. **Several factors were found to be associated with poor stone clearance rates: large renal calculi (mean, 22.2 mm), stones within dependent or obstructed portions of the collecting system, stone composition (mostly calcium oxalate monohydrate and brushite), obesity or a body habitus that inhibits imaging, and unsatisfactory targeting of the stone.** For patients with these clinical characteristics, the authors suggest the consideration of alternative treatment modalities. The urologist, then, when treating a patient with a renal calculus, must ask himself or herself, **Is the patient an appro**priate candidate for SWL or should other treatment modalities be used?

One must consider stone-related factors (size, number, location, composition), renal anatomy, and clinical factors of the patient (Table 44–1) as well as the morbidity inherent in each treatment modality and the availability of the requisite equipment before selecting the optimal therapy. Although treatment decisions are ultimately the result of an integrated analysis of a multiplicity of factors, for the sake of simplicity, these factors and considerations in management of kidney calculi are reviewed separately.

## Preoperative Evaluation

The evaluation of patients with urolithiasis in the current era of minimally invasive therapies has not changed substantially from that of the previous era of open stone surgery. Although standard imaging of urinary tract calculi has previously used plain abdominal radiography and intravenous urography, recent evidence suggests that unenhanced helical computed tomography (CT) has gained widespread acceptance (Heidenreich et al, 2002). Nephrotomography, radionuclide studies, and retrograde contrast-enhanced studies are occasionally necessary to obtain more detailed anatomic and functional information.

Bacteriologic evaluation of the urine is mandatory for all patients. The composition of any previous stone material passed or removed from the patient is extremely important. If previous stones have contained significant amounts of calcium oxalate monohydrate (whewellite) or brushite, fragmentation with SWL may be expected to be more difficult. If a stone of such composition is of a large size, the patient may achieve a better outcome with a percutaneous or ureteroscopic procedure rather than with SWL. Cystinuria may be revealed by previous stone analysis or by the characteristic cystine crystals on urinalysis. Any patient whose stone or stones have radiographic features suggestive of cystine (low radiodensity, ground-glass appearance, smooth edges, bilateral stones) should be screened for cystinuria before treatment because these stones are often not well fragmented by SWL. Many stones may harbor bacteria even though bacteriuria is only intermittently present. This is particularly true in the patient who has received antibiotics in the past. Mariappan and associates (2005) have also reported that **the best predictor of post-PNL urosepsis is stone culture or renal pelvic urine culture results, rather than bladder urine culture results. The fragmentation of stones, despite sterile urine, may**

| Table 44–1. | Factors Affecting Management of Renal Stones | |
|---|---|---|
| **Stone Factors** | **Renal Anatomic Factors** | **Clinical (Patient) Factors** |
| Size | Obstruction or stasis | Infection |
| Number | Hydronephrosis | Obesity |
| Composition | Ureteropelvic junction obstruction | Body habitus deformity |
| | Calyceal diverticulum | Coagulopathy |
| | Horseshoe kidney | Juvenile |
| | Renal ectopia or fusion | Elderly |
| | Lower pole | Hypertension |
| | | Renal failure |

release preformed bacterial endotoxins and viable bacteria that place the patient at risk for septic complications (Scherz and Parsons, 1987; McAleer et al, 2002, 2003; Paterson et al, 2003). Therefore, patients who have radiographic or clinical features suggestive of struvite or in whom infection is suspected should receive a minimum of 2 weeks of broad-spectrum antibiotics before surgery to reduce the risk of sepsis. Parenteral antibiotics should be administered preoperatively in any patient in whom urinary infection is suspected.

## Natural History

### Calyceal Stones

Before the introduction of minimally invasive therapies, urologists were often reluctant to remove incidentally found, asymptomatic, or minimally symptomatic calyceal stones because of the high morbidity associated with open surgery. Although the traditional indications for intervention, including pain, infection, and obstruction, have not changed, the introduction of minimally invasive procedures has allowed patients with mild or no symptoms to consider these less morbid treatments. However, the decision for intervention should be based on a thorough understanding of the natural history of calyceal stones.

Hubner and Porpaczy (1990) reviewed the natural history of calyceal stones in 63 patients during an average of 7.4 years. They reported that of 80 stones, 6% were dissolved with alkali therapy, 16% passed spontaneously, 40% required surgical intervention, and 38% remained in situ. During the observation period, 45% of the stones increased in size, 68% of the patients experienced symptoms of infection, and 51% of the patients experienced pain. Thus, **most calyceal stones, in the absence of intervention, are likely to increase in size, causing symptoms of pain or infection.** Furthermore, as time progressed and stone size increased, the likelihood of spontaneous stone passage decreased. Glowacki and associates (1992) reviewed **the natural history of 107 patients with asymptomatic calyceal stones and found that the cumulative 5-year probability of a symptomatic event was 48.5%; half of these events required active intervention.** A linear association was identified between the development of a symptomatic event and the number of previous stones as well as the number of asymptomatic stones at presentation. Burgher and associates (2004) reported a series of 300 patients initially presenting with asymptomatic renal calculi who were observed for a mean of 3.26 years. **Seventy-seven percent of patients experienced progression of calculi, with 26% requiring surgical intervention.** Those **patients who initially presented with calculi larger than 4 mm were more likely to fail observation** than were patients with smaller solitary calculi. Keeley and colleagues (2001) reported the results of a randomized prospective trial of SWL versus observation for 200 patients with small asymptomatic calyceal calculi. Although the authors found little difference in the number of patients in each group requiring additional treatment, the **interventions in the observation group were more invasive. Patients in the SWL group required no invasive treatment** on follow-up and could be adequately managed with analgesia or antibiotics. In 1988, a National Institutes of Health Consensus Conference addressed the issue of small, asymptomatic calyceal stones and

stated that the use of SWL for small (<5 mm), incidentally discovered, asymptomatic kidney calculi was controversial and that more data were required (Consensus conference. Prevention and treatment of kidney stones, 1988). Furthermore, although SWL, with its low morbidity, might be considered a good option for the prophylactic treatment of patients with small, asymptomatic calyceal stones, the targeting of stones smaller than 5 mm may be difficult because of focusing problems with either a fluoroscopic or an ultrasound-guided lithotripter (Motola and Smith, 1990). Collins and Keeley (2002) reported that they did not detect a benefit after treatment in a randomized controlled trial of prophylactic SWL for patients with asymptomatic calyceal stones. **The necessity of treating patients with small (<5 mm), nonobstructive, asymptomatic stones in a prophylactic fashion remains undetermined.** However, **patients must be advised about the need for regular follow-up; a significant proportion of these calculi will eventually become symptomatic and require intervention.** Treatment decisions in these situations should be based on the individual patient's risk factors and the patient's preference. In several groups of patients, including pediatric patients, patients with a solitary kidney, patients in high-risk professions (e.g., pilots), and women considering pregnancy, treatment of asymptomatic calyceal stones may be indicated.

Historically, simple calyceal stones documented to be immobile and not causing obstruction have been thought to be unlikely causes of flank pain. However, it has been reported that **the pain induced by nonobstructive calyceal stones is characterized by a dull, deep ache, different from the classic pain of renal colic** (Coury et al, 1988). Several groups have reported that patients experience excellent pain relief after the removal of small calyceal stones by SWL, PNL, or ureteroscopy (Andersson and Sylven, 1983; Brannen et al, 1986; Fernandez and Carson, 1989; Brandt et al, 1993; Andreassen et al, 1997). Therefore, **a patient who is thought to be symptomatic from a calyceal stone should be treated.**

### Staghorn Calculi

Staghorn calculi are those stones that fill the major part of the renal collecting system. Typically, they occupy the renal pelvis and branch into most of the calyces, mimicking the horns of a deer or stag (Fig. 44–1). Most staghorn stones are composed of struvite (Segura et al, 1994). Until the early 1970s, some physicians believed that patients harboring staghorn calculi should not be treated (Segura, 1997). However, a better understanding of the natural history of staghorn stones has evolved.

Blandy and Singh (1976) compared untreated staghorn stones in 60 patients with operative removal of staghorn stones in 125 patients. **The 10-year mortality was 28% for patients with untreated staghorn stones versus 7% for patients treated by surgical intervention.** Koga and associates (1991) reported on 167 patients with staghorn stones, of whom 61 were treated conservatively and followed up for an average of 7.8 years. Chronic renal failure occurred in 36% of the patients treated conservatively, and this cohort also experienced higher morbidity and mortality. Teichman and coworkers (1995) reviewed the records of 177 consecutive patients with staghorn calculi for a mean follow-up of 7.7 years. In those patients managed surgically, they noted 28% and 17% overall rates of renal deterioration and mortality,

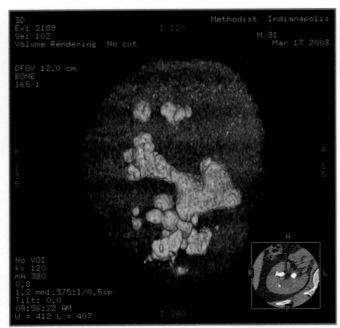

**Figure 44–1.** Three-dimensional computed tomographic reconstruction of a staghorn calculus.

respectively. Renal deterioration was more frequently associated with a solitary kidney (77% versus 21%), previous stones (39% versus 14%), stone burden (partial staghorn 13% versus complete staghorn 34%), urinary diversion (58% versus 18%), and neurogenic bladder (47% versus 28%). Of note, stone recurrence was a significant predictor of the patient's becoming dialysis dependent. No patient with complete stone clearance died of kidney-related causes, compared with 3% of those without clearance of fragments and 67% of those who refused treatment.

Thus, **untreated struvite staghorn calculi eventually destroy the kidney and pose a significant risk to the patient's life.** The American Urological Association (AUA) Nephrolithiasis Clinical Guidelines, released in 2005, recommended that in otherwise healthy individuals, **newly diagnosed struvite staghorn calculi should be treated surgically** (Preminger et al, 2005). Moreover, **struvite stones must be removed completely to minimize the risk of continued urea-splitting bacteriuria.**

## Stone Factors

Stone factors to be considered in the treatment of patients with kidney calculi include **stone burden (size and number), stone composition, and stone location.** Because a significant issue in renal stone location is the treatment of a lower pole stone and the influence of renal anatomy on the treatment results of such calculi, further discussion of this topic is included in the section on renal anatomic factors.

### Treatment Decisions by Stone Burden

**Stone burden (size and number) is perhaps the single most important factor in determining the appropriate treatment modality for a patient with renal calculi** (Motola and Smith,

1990). However, cutoff points for stone size that would categorize those who should be treated by SWL and those who should undergo other treatment modalities have yet to be definitively determined. For now, kidney calculi are conveniently divided into nonstaghorn and staghorn stones, and most controversy is in the area of nonstaghorn stones.

**Nonstaghorn Calculi.** In examining the efficacy of SWL in treatment of patients with renal calculi, passage of stone debris rather than fragmentation of the stone is the primary limiting factor (Renner et al, 1999). There is general agreement that **stone free is the most rigorous definition of successful outcome of any stone removal procedure, and complete stone clearance should be the preferred goal** (Psihramis et al, 1992). However, because SWL outcome is dependent on spontaneous stone clearance, treatment results are often reported in terms of "success rates," which may be defined as patients who are either stone free or who have asymptomatic, small, residual fragments. Various cutoff points between 2 and 5 mm are used in the literature to define the size of these fragments, making study comparisons difficult. A prospective analysis of 121 SWL treatment failures concluded that for almost half of the cases, treatment failure was due to a failure to clear stone fragments (Grasso et al, 1995a). The mean stone size before SWL therapy was 22.2 mm. Steinstrasse, a significant morbid complication, occurred in 8% of those patients who had a mean stone size of 33.7 mm. **Failure to clear stone fragments resulted in a higher re-treatment rate as well as a higher number of ancillary procedures.** Clayman and associates (1989) suggested that in comparing the results of SWL and PNL or in comparing different lithotripters, the parameters of stone-free rate, re-treatment rate, and number of auxiliary procedures should be combined into an effectiveness quotient that may better express treatment results and allow one to compare different treatment modalities:

$$\frac{\% \text{ stone free}}{100\% + \% \text{ re-treatment} + \% \text{ auxiliary procedures}} \times 100$$

For example, Netto and associates (1991), in a study comparing PNL and SWL for patients with lower pole calculi, reported overall stone-free rates of 93.6% and 79.2% for PNL and SWL, respectively; these values were not significantly different. However, the effectiveness quotients of 93.7% and 55.9% for PNL and SWL did differ significantly as this incorporated the 41% re-treatment rate for the SWL group.

**The negative effect of an increasing stone burden (size and number) on the results of SWL has been reported by many groups using a variety of lithotripters** (Drach et al, 1986; Lingeman et al, 1986a; Politis and Griffith, 1987; el-Damanhoury et al, 1991). A now-axiomatic principle of SWL is that **as stone burden increases, the stone-free rate declines and the need for ancillary procedures and re-treatment rises.** Furthermore, larger stone burdens are associated with a higher rate of residual stones, a point of particular concern in the treatment of patients with struvite calculi (Segura, 1989). The presence of multiple stones also adversely affects the results of SWL treatment (Drach et al, 1986; Cass, 1995).

Figure 44–2 illustrates the effect of the size of solitary renal stones on the results of SWL. PNL, although more invasive and often associated with higher morbidity, achieves better

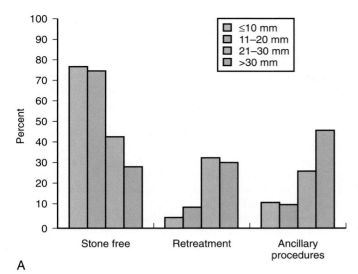

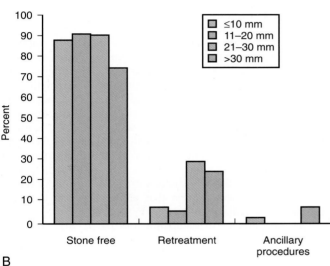

**Figure 44–2.** **A,** Solitary nonstaghorn calculi treated by SWL, stratified by size. **B,** Solitary nonstaghorn calculi treated by PNL, stratified by size.

stone-free rates than does SWL and is not affected by stone size (Lingeman et al, 1987b). Ureteroscopy, another treatment alternative for patients with renal calculi, is also negatively affected by increasing stone burden but possibly to a lesser degree than is SWL because stone fragments are often removed or vaporized. Fabrizio and colleagues (1998) evaluated the characteristics of residual calculi after ureteroscopy in a group of 100 patients and found that increased stone burden led to a higher percentage of patients with residual fragments. For patients with stones smaller than 10 mm, only 20% were found to have residual fragments, whereas more than 50% of patients with stones larger than 16 mm harbored residual fragments. Thus, as stone burden increases, PNL becomes more efficient than either SWL or ureteroscopy.

**Treatment algorithms for patients with nonstaghorn calculi are commonly organized by stone size.** The mean overall stone-free rates of SWL for the treatment of patients with solitary stones stratified by size are 79.9% (range, 63% to 90%), 64.1% (range, 50% to 82.7%), and 53.7% (range,

33.3% to 81.4%) for stones 10 mm or less, 11 to 20 mm, and larger than 20 mm, respectively (Clayman et al, 1989; Psihramis et al, 1992; Lingeman et al, 1994; Cass, 1995; Logarakis et al, 2000).

Approximately **50% to 60% of all solitary renal calculi are less than 10 mm in diameter** (Cass, 1995; Renner and Rassweiler, 1999; Logarakis et al, 2000). **Treatment results of SWL for this substantial group of patients are generally satisfactory** and independent of stone location or composition. Although better results can be achieved with PNL or ureteroscopy for patients with stones smaller than 10 mm, these procedures are more invasive, are associated with greater morbidity, and may be reserved for special circumstances (e.g., anatomic malformation causing obstruction, SWL failure).

**Patients with calculi between 10 and 20 mm are often treated with SWL as first-line management.** However, stone composition and location also affect the results of SWL for patients with calculi in this size range and should be carefully considered. For example, SWL results for patients with 10- to 20-mm stones in the lower pole are inferior (55%) to SWL results for patients with stones in the upper and middle pole calyces (71.8% and 76.5%, respectively) (Saw and Lingeman, 1999). Havel and associates (1998) compared stone-free rates for patients with a solitary lower pole stone managed with either SWL or PNL. For patients with stones smaller than 10 mm, both therapeutic modalities were equally effective. However, **for patients with 10- to 20-mm lower pole stones, significantly better clearance rates were achieved with PNL rather than with SWL** (73% versus 57%). Stone composition is also a factor to consider in treatment of patients with stones larger than 10 mm. Cystine calculi respond poorly to SWL treatment, particularly stones larger than 15 to 20 mm (Hockley et al, 1989; Kachel et al, 1991). Likewise, brushite calculi have demonstrated an in vitro and in vivo resistance to fragmentation that is surpassed only by cystine calculi (Dretler, 1988; Klee et al, 1991). Patients with renal stones of 10 to 20 mm and factors predicting poor treatment outcomes with SWL should be advised about alternative therapeutic modalities. Both PNL and ureteroscopy are less affected by stone location and composition, and good results may be attained with these modalities for patients with 10- to 20-mm renal stones (Lingeman et al, 1994; Grasso and Ficazzola, 1999).

Lingeman and associates (1987b) showed that the frequency of multiple treatments increased from 10% to 33% when SWL was used to treat patients with stones of 1 to 2 cm and 2 to 3 cm, respectively. In addition, the stone-free rate was only 34% compared with a 90% stone-free rate for those patients treated by PNL. Psihramis and colleagues (1992) described 94 patients with renal stones larger than 2 cm treated by SWL, with only 31 patients (33%) becoming stone free. Interestingly, patients with multiple stones had a similar stone-free rate of 32%. These high re-treatment rates and increased need for auxiliary procedures were the basis for the National Institutes of Health Consensus Conference recommendation that patients with stones larger than 2 cm be initially treated with PNL followed, if necessary, by SWL (Consensus conference. Prevention and treatment of kidney stones, 1988). However, because the stone-free rates for patients with renal stones of 2- to 3-cm range treated by SWL can have a wide variability (33% to 65%), SWL in combination with ureteral stent placement may still be considered an option, provided the patient is advised about the higher retreatment rate and the lower likelihood of achieving a stone-free state in comparison with PNL (Renner and Rassweiler, 1999).

Grasso and associates (1998) described 51 patients with 66 large (≥2 cm) upper urinary tract (45 renal, 21 ureteral) stones treated by ureteroscopy. One third of patients with renal stones required a second-look endoscopy; and in three patients with renal calculi, conversion to PNL was necessary. The overall success rate, defined as pulverization of the stone to dust or fragments smaller than 2 mm, after the second ureteroscopy procedure was 91%, which is comparable to PNL results. However, the 6-month follow-up data, which were available for 25 patients, demonstrated that only 60% of patients were stone free, whereas 24% had small lower pole debris and 16% had new stone growth.

Murray and coworkers (1995) reported on 65 treatments for renal calculi larger than 3 cm with SWL monotherapy. The overall success rate for SWL was only 27% at 3 months. The best stone-free rate (60%) was obtained for stones smaller than 500 mm² that were located primarily within the renal pelvis. The stone-free rate for stones with surface areas larger than 1000 mm² was a dismal 8%. Notably, steinstrasse occurred in 23% of patients. Likewise, Lingeman and colleagues (1987b) reported on 13 nonstaghorn stones larger than 3 cm treated with SWL monotherapy. Seventy-seven percent of the patients required further treatment, whereas only 29% were rendered stone free.

**In summary, for patients harboring nonstaghorn stones smaller than 10 mm, SWL is usually the primary approach. For patients with stones between 10 and 20 mm, SWL can still be considered a first-line treatment unless factors of stone composition, location, or renal anatomy suggest that a more optimal outcome may be achieved with a more invasive treatment modality (PNL or ureteroscopy). Patients with stones larger than 20 mm should primarily be treated by PNL unless specific indications for ureteroscopy are present (e.g., bleeding diathesis, obesity).**

**Staghorn Calculi.** Patients suffering from staghorn calculi remain a challenging problem for the practicing urologist. **Most staghorn stones are composed of struvite,** and factors that predispose to urinary tract infection and retained urine increase the likelihood of struvite stone formation (Gettman and Segura, 1999). However, other crystals, including cystine, calcium oxalate monohydrate, and uric acid, can assume a staghorn configuration (Segura, 1997).

The conservative treatment of patients with staghorn calculi exposes the patient to an increased risk of renal loss as well as a mortality rate of up to 30% (Blandy and Singh, 1976; Rous and Turner, 1977; Koga et al, 1991). Therefore, the ideal management of patients with staghorn calculi is composed of three stages. First, complete surgical removal of the entire stone burden is essential. **If all of the infected stone debris is not evacuated, urea-splitting bacteriuria may persist, which can ultimately lead to eventual stone regrowth.** The urologist should select the procedure or combination of procedures most likely to render the patient free of stone material while minimizing the risk of morbidity and mortality. Second, any metabolic abnormalities must be identified and appropriately

treated. It has been reported that metabolic abnormalities are not uncommon in patients with infected stones (Segura et al, 1981). However, others have found that stone recurrence after complete elimination of calculi is uncommon (Silverman and Stamey, 1983). Different definitions of the term *infection stone,* and in particular the inclusion of mixed struvite and calcium oxalate stones in studies, probably explain these contradictory reports. In a group of patients with infection stones, those with pure struvite stones were significantly less likely to have metabolic abnormalities than were patients who had stones composed of a mixture of struvite and calcium oxalate (Lingeman, 1995; Lingeman et al, 1995c). Finally, anatomic abnormalities that may contribute to stasis within the urinary tract should be addressed.

***Classification of Staghorn Calculi.*** Reported stone-free rates for patients with staghorn calculi treated by SWL or PNL (with or without SWL) range from 31% to 85% and from 23% to 86%, respectively (Lam et al, 1992a). These wide variations may be due to the difficulty in accurately assessing stone burden in patients with staghorn calculi. The traditional definition of staghorn calculus is a renal pelvic stone with extension into at least two calyceal groups. Historically, staghorn calculi were classified as partial or complete. Partial staghorn calculi were defined as renal pelvic calculi extending into two calyceal groups, and complete staghorn stones were defined as renal pelvic calculi extending into all major calyceal groups, filling at least 80% of the collecting system. At the time this definition was popularized, there was only one treatment option for patients with these calculi: open surgery. With the introduction of newer and less invasive treatment modalities such as SWL that are highly sensitive to stone burden, there is a greater need to classify staghorn calculi according to reproducible, quantitative criteria that allow clinicians to better evaluate treatment outcomes.

The morphologic classification into partial and complete staghorn calculi is inadequate, as demonstrated by Lam and colleagues (1992b), who reported considerable overlap in stone burdens of calculi grouped as partial or complete staghorn stones. When stone burden was assessed by stone surface area as measured on a kidney, ureter, bladder (KUB) radiographic image, for stones between 501 and 1500 mm², an overlap between partial and complete staghorn calculi occurred in 66% and 56.1% of cases, respectively. To remedy this limitation, several groups have proposed new classification schemes to better define staghorn calculi (Rocco et al, 1984; Griffith and Valiquette, 1987; Ackermann et al, 1989; Di Silverio et al, 1990). However, the cumbersome and subjective nature of these classification approaches has resulted in limited clinical use.

Currently, the most accurate method to estimate the volume of a staghorn calculus is CT imaging with three-dimensional reconstruction. This technique permits highly accurate determination of stone volume as well as the three linear dimensions of renal calculi (Olcott and Sommer, 1999). In addition, Hubert and associates (1997) reported that three-dimensional reconstructions of staghorn calculi assisted in the preoperative determination of the optimal routes for percutaneous access. This technique correlates well with the actual volume of the stone, as measured by water displacement (Lam et al, 1992b). However, three-dimensional CT reconstructions are costly, time-consuming, and not widely available, thus limiting the utility of this technology. Nadler and associates (2004) have reported use of coronal reconstructions of axial CT images to calculate the craniocaudal length of stones, which can facilitate stone volume calculations.

***Surgical Management of Staghorn Calculi.*** Overall, the stone-free rate after open surgery for patients with struvite stones is about 85%, with a 30% stone recurrence rate during 6 years (Griffith et al, 1978). In a comparison of the results of a combination treatment regimen of PNL and SWL with previously reported results of anatrophic nephrolithotomy, Lingeman and associates (1987b) demonstrated that the stone-free rates (191 of 224, or 85% of all staghorn cases treated with combination therapy) were similar. However, convalescence and hospital stay for the PNL cohort were shorter and blood loss was less. Similarly, Snyder and Smith (1986) compared PNL and anatrophic nephrolithotomy for patients with staghorn calculi and found that although patients undergoing PNL had a higher retained stone fragment rate (13% versus 0%, respectively), shorter procedure times, less need for blood transfusions and narcotics, and more rapid return to work ultimately favored PNL over the open surgical procedure.

Increasing experience with PNL (with or without SWL) has further improved treatment outcomes for patients with staghorn calculi. Lam and coworkers (1992c) compared 252 patients treated from 1984 to 1987 with 91 patients treated from 1988 to 1990. In the first group, renal access was performed by a radiologist; in the second group, access was established exclusively by the urologist. The authors noted a significant decrease in the proportion of cases managed by combination therapy (PNL plus SWL) in the second group (35%) compared with the first group (65%). Although the overall stone-free rates (83.3% and 86.8%) were not significantly different between the two groups, the second group had a greater proportion of staghorn stones and also had a greater use of multiple tracks. Of note, the pulmonary complication rate was greater in the second group (8.8% versus 2.8%), reflecting increased use of upper pole access.

**When PNL was compared with SWL monotherapy in the treatment of patients with staghorn stones, the overall stone-free rate for PNL with or without SWL was 84.2% compared with 51.2% for SWL monotherapy** (Lam et al, 1992a). Approximately **one third (30.5%) of patients in the SWL group required auxiliary procedures compared with 3.4% in the PNL group.** The success rate of PNL as initial therapy was independent of stone composition and superior to SWL for all types of stone material. SWL monotherapy was successful (stone-free rate, 92%) in only a small group of patients, those with 500 mm$^2$ or smaller stone burden in nondilated collecting systems. However, this subgroup represented only 3% of the staghorn stone cohort. In a prospective randomized study, Meretyk and associates (1997) compared 27 patients treated by SWL with 23 patients treated by PNL (with or without SWL). Stone-free rates were 74% and 22% in the PNL and SWL groups, respectively. They reported a significantly higher complication rate and number of ancillary procedures in the SWL group compared with the PNL group. The authors concluded that PNL followed by SWL, if needed, is superior to SWL monotherapy in the treatment of patients with staghorn stones. The use of SWL monotherapy in treating struvite stones may be particularly problematic because

residual, "insignificant" fragments can prevent the sterilization of urine, increasing the risk of stone regrowth.

The use of multiple endourologic techniques for the treatment of patients with staghorn stones is referred to as combination therapy. The most frequently used regimen was described by Streem and colleagues (1997) as sandwich therapy, which consisted of primary percutaneous stone debulking followed by SWL of any inaccessible, residual infundibulocalyceal stone extensions or fragments. After SWL, a secondary percutaneous procedure was performed. These various stages are usually separated by 1 or 2 days. Stone-free rates for combined therapy are similar to those obtained by PNL alone or by open surgery (Lam et al, 1992c). **The management of patients with staghorn stones by a combined approach must be viewed as primarily percutaneous in nature, with SWL being used only as an adjunct to minimize the number of access tracks required.** Improved PNL techniques, incorporating the increasing use of flexible nephroscopy and providing complete or nearly complete clearance of stone material at the time of the primary procedure, may have decreased or eliminated the need for additional SWL treatment (Lam et al, 1992c; Beaghler et al, 1999).

The 2005 AUA Nephrolithiasis Committee has published recommendations for the management of patients with staghorn calculi based on a meta-analysis of outcome data from published, peer-reviewed articles. According to the committee, all treatment options (SWL, PNL, combined PNL and SWL, open surgery) must be discussed with the patient (Preminger et al, 2005). As a guideline, however, **PNL, followed by either SWL or repeated PNL, should be used for most patients with struvite staghorn calculi, with PNL being the initial element of the combination therapy.** SWL and open surgery should not be used for most of these patients as a first-line treatment. PNL and SWL are equally effective in treating patients with small-volume staghorn stones when the renal anatomy is normal or nearly normal. Open surgery may be an option in unusual situations in which a staghorn stone is not expected to be removed by a reasonable number of PNL or SWL procedures. Nephrectomy is an option for the patient with a poorly functioning kidney harboring a staghorn stone. Although there are limited data for the treatment of pediatric patients with staghorn calculi, PNL is a safe and effective therapy. Pediatric patients often experience better stone-free rates than do adults with treatment by SWL. The stone-free rate with SWL monotherapy, reported by studies including only pediatric patients, is 78%; an average of 2.9 procedures are performed, and complications are infrequent. However, the developing kidney may be more susceptible to the bioeffects of SWL (Lifshitz et al, 1998).

## Treatment Decisions by Stone Composition

Dretler (1988) first introduced the concept of stone fragility. The readiness with which a stone is fragmented by SWL is variable among stones of different composition. Furthermore, even stones of the same composition may fragment differently (Bhatta et al, 1989; Sakamoto et al, 1991; Wang et al, 1993; Wu et al, 1993; Pittomvils et al, 1994). The efficacy of intracorporeal lithotripters, as well, is dependent on stone composition. Teichman and colleagues (1998b) reported that the holmium laser in vitro was the most effective lithotrite for fragmenting struvite stones and the least effective lithotrite for calcium oxalate monohydrate stones. These results are consistent with the known thermal threshold for each stone composition. Saw and Lingeman (1999) reported that adjusted for size, cystine and brushite calculi are the most resistant to SWL, followed by calcium oxalate monohydrate; following, in descending order of resistance to fragmentation, are struvite, calcium oxalate dihydrate, and uric acid stones (Pittomvils et al, 1994; Saw and Lingeman, 1999). Stone composition affects not just resistance to fragmentation but also the type of fragments produced. Cystine and calcium oxalate monohydrate, in addition to being difficult to fragment, tend to produce relatively large pieces that may be difficult to clear from the collecting system (Pittomvils et al, 1994; Rutchik and Resnick, 1998). In general, **patients with such stones (i.e., brushite, cystine, calcium oxalate monohydrate) should be treated by SWL only when the stone burden is small** (i.e., <1.5 cm). Those patients with larger stones should preferentially be treated with PNL or ureteroscopy.

Patients suffering from cystinuria present a unique challenge to the urologist. Assimos and associates (2002) reported that **cystinuric patients have higher serum creatinine levels compared with a cohort of calcium oxalate stone formers**. Importantly, they also reported that **cystinuric patients are at greater risk for renal loss than are calcium oxalate stone formers** and that open stone surgery for these patients is associated with higher serum creatinine concentration and potential renal loss. Furthermore, patients with cystinuria have been reported to be poorly compliant with medical therapy, increasing the likelihood of recurrent stone events (Pietrow et al, 2003). Chow and Streem (1998) analyzed 31 cystinuric patients who underwent selected intervention for 61 stone events and reported that the probability of stone recurrence at 1 and 5 years was 27% and 73%, respectively. Achieving stone-free status prolonged the time to stone recurrence compared with patients left with residual fragments, a finding confirmed by Knoll and associates (1988). The high likelihood of repeated procedures underlines the need to select not just the least invasive treatment modality but also the most effective treatment modality. Treatment efficacy is of particular importance, as Barbey and associates (2000) reported that decreased renal function was more pronounced in cystinuric patients subjected to more stone removal procedures.

**When stone removal is required, therefore, a minimally invasive approach is preferred.** SWL, when it is used unselectively to treat patients with cystine stones, yields poor results. Hockley and colleagues (1989) described 43 cystinuric patients treated by SWL and PNL. Stone-free rates with use of SWL for calculi 20 mm or smaller and for calculi larger than 20 mm were 70.5% and 41%, respectively, whereas the stone-free rates for those who underwent PNL were 100% and 92%, respectively. Kachel and associates (1991) reviewed 18 patients with cystine stones and suggested a treatment algorithm based on their experience and the reported experience of others. They recommended SWL monotherapy for cystine renal calculi 15 mm or smaller and PNL for stones larger than 15 mm in diameter. Chow and Streem (1998) reported selective treatment, adjusted for stone size, in 31 cystinuric patients with an overall stone-free rate of 86.9%. Rudnick and colleagues (1999) reported success with retrograde ureterorenoscopic fragmentation in patients with 1.5- to 3.0-cm renal

calculi. This approach is especially appealing as it has an inherently low morbidity.

**Brushite** calculi have a resistance to fragmentation that is surpassed only by that of cystine calculi (Dretler, 1988). Klee and associates (1991) described 30 patients with a total of 46 brushite stones. The overall success rate for patients treated by SWL monotherapy was 65% (success defined as fragments smaller than 4 mm), with a mean of 1.5 SWL sessions required per stone. However, only 11% of patients became stone free. PNL and ureteroscopy achieved 100% success rates and stone-free rates of 100% and 66%, respectively. Of 20 kidneys with residual fragments smaller than 4 mm, 12 had rapid regrowth to significant size within 3 to 12 months. Parks and associates (2004) found that SWL use was more frequent among brushite stone formers than among a similar cohort of calcium oxalate stone formers. Therefore, **when brushite calculi are suspected or confirmed, a surgical treatment algorithm similar to that for cystine stones should be applied.**

Although resistance to SWL is generally common for very hard stones, it also characterizes the rare and very soft **matrix** calculi that are composed of as much as 65% organic matter (compared with 2% to 3% organic matter in most noninfected urinary calculi). Matrix stones are radiolucent and are often associated with urea-splitting bacteriuria. SWL is not an effective treatment modality for patients with these stones. These situations are usually best treated with PNL (O'Connor et al, 1990). SWL is usually ineffective because of the stone's gelatinous nature, and ureteroscopy may be compromised by the large volume of stone material present (Bani-Hani et al, 2005).

Another soft radiolucent stone is composed of **indinavir,** a protease inhibitor commonly used in the treatment of human immunodeficiency virus infection (Daudon et al, 1997). A significant number of patients who receive this drug develop symptoms or signs of indinavir nephrolithiasis (Saltel et al, 2000; Nadler et al, 2003). Reiter and coworkers (1999) reported an incidence of symptomatic stone episodes in 12.4% of 105 patients treated with indinavir. The mean time from the initiation of indinavir therapy until the acute stone episode was 21.5 weeks. Twelve of 16 stones were passed spontaneously. Kohan and colleagues (1999) described 13 symptomatic patients with indinavir stones; conservative therapy was successful in 11 patients, and 2 patients were treated by stent placement. Pure indinavir stones are not detectable with standard radiography or CT. However, some patients form indinavir stones that contain a calcium component, which may be radiographically visible (Sundaram and Saltzman, 1999). Hydration and analgesic therapy are recommended for the initial treatment of patients with indinavir stones. Indinavir therapy may need to be temporarily or permanently discontinued, in which case another protease inhibitor may be substituted. Invasive intervention may be necessary for patients with prolonged renal obstruction, signs of sepsis, or unremitting symptoms.

The ability to predict stone composition and, consequently, the number of shockwaves required for complete stone fragmentation would be of great benefit in selecting appropriate treatment of patients with stone disease. If a stone is of a type not amenable to treatment by SWL, other modes of treatment can be pursued. However, except for cystinuric patients and patients who have had previous stone analysis, accurate prediction of stone composition based on imaging and the patient's history is difficult. The ability of plain radiography to differentiate subtypes of calcium oxalate stones and possible relationships to stone fragility was first suggested by Dretler (Dretler, 1988; Dretler and Polykoff, 1996). Using x-ray patterns to predict stone fragility, Wang and colleagues (1993) found that smooth-edged stones with a homogeneous structure required significantly more shockwaves to be completely fragmented, compared with round, radially reticulated stones with spiculated edges or stones with an irregular margin and structure. In a retrospective study of 485 patients, Bon and colleagues (1996) found that smooth, uniform, bulging stones that appeared more dense than bone (with use of either the 12th rib or a transverse process as a reference point) responded poorly to SWL; the stone-free rates for patients with smooth, radiographically dense stones versus those harboring stones with irregular outlines were 34% and 79%, respectively. However, in a prospective study, the overall accuracy of predicting stone composition from plain radiographs was reported to be only 39% and therefore inadequate for clinical use (Ramakumar et al, 1999).

Non–contrast-enhanced helical CT, an increasingly popular method of evaluating patients with suspected renal colic, may be used to identify stone composition. Several in vitro investigations of this technology have been reported. Mostafavi and associates (1998b) performed an in vitro study that used the attenuation levels acquired by CT imaging to accurately predict the chemical composition of pure urinary calculi. Similarly, Saw and associates (2000) found that CT at 1-mm collimation (120 kV) was able to differentiate in vitro between stone groups (each containing at least 60% of one stone constituent) on the basis of absolute attenuation values. The authors noted that both stone size and beam collimation affected the attenuation measurements. Joseph and associates (2002) reported an in vivo study of 30 patients with renal calculi who underwent SWL treatment. They reported that the success rate was significantly lower for those calculi with attenuation values greater than 1000 Hounsfield units than for those calculi with attenuation values less than 1000 Hounsfield units.

Although CT attenuation values can distinguish some stone types in vivo, such as uric acid from calcium stones, the use of attenuation values alone results in considerable overlap; the range of values for calcium oxalate monohydrate and struvite stones does not allow these types to be confidently distinguished. Furthermore, it is not certain that the ease with which

a stone is fragmented by SWL can be predicted by knowing only the major mineral composition of the stone. For example, cystine stones, which are considered difficult to break, have been shown in certain cases to break easily (Bhatta et al, 1989). Williams and associates (2003), too, reported that **the variability in stone fragility to shockwaves is large, even within groups defined by mineral composition.** It is likely that **this variability in fragility could be due to variation in stone composition or structure,** including variable amounts of secondary mineral in the stone, variation in the spatial arrangement of the secondary mineral within the stone, and variation in the layer structures of the primary and secondary minerals within a stone. Williams and associates (2002) also reported that displaying the data acquired by helical CT with use of bone windows can reveal remarkable internal structural detail of kidney calculi (Fig. 44–3). It is clear that CT provides a wealth of information about stone characteristics. However, additional work is needed to determine the utility of this powerful imaging tool in determining the susceptibility of a given stone to SWL.

## Renal Anatomic Factors

There are certain anatomic factors, either congenital or acquired, that can hinder stone clearance after SWL. Congenital anomalies manifest not uncommonly in the upper urinary tract, and almost all that affect the drainage of the kidney are associated with increased incidence of calculous disease. Renal anatomic anomalies associated with an increased risk of stone formation include ureteropelvic junction obstruction, horseshoe kidney, and other ectopic or fusion anomalies as well as calyceal diverticula (Jones et al, 1991; Husmann et al, 1996; Cohen and Preminger, 1997). The dependent position of lower pole calyces may also affect stone clearance after SWL. In addition, stone-free rates after SWL for patients with hydronephrosis or obstruction are poor (Drach et al, 1986; Winfield et al, 1988). A retrospective study identified a significant association of hydronephrosis with the failure to clear residual fragments (Shigeta et al, 1999). Any patient with obstruction distal to the targeted stone should not undergo SWL treatment. If both obstruction and infection are present, SWL may result in life-threatening urosepsis (Meretyk et al, 1992a). Furthermore, the patient is unlikely to clear stone fragments unless the concomitant obstruction is alleviated.

**Figure 44–3.** Photographic and helical CT images show structural variability in stones of the same type. Note that although all stones depicted are calcium oxalate in type, some have a mottled structure and others have a lamellar structure.

## Ureteropelvic Junction Obstruction

Ureteropelvic junction obstruction in adults is commonly associated with urinary calculi. Furthermore, a stone at the ureteropelvic junction can exacerbate the degree of preexisting obstruction and further compromise the renal unit (Rutchik and Resnick, 1998). The role of anatomic obstruction and associated urinary stasis in stone formation is not clearly established. Husmann and colleagues (1995) reviewed the records of 111 patients with simultaneous ureteropelvic junction obstruction and renal calculi. They found that 71% of patients with nonstruvite stones had significant metabolic abnormalities. Furthermore, more than 60% of recurrent calculi in the nonstruvite group occurred in the patient's contralateral kidney. Likewise, 68% of 22 pediatric patients treated for ureteropelvic junction obstruction associated with renal calculus had recurrent stones at a median follow-up of 9 years (Husmann et al, 1996). Thus, **in addition to anatomic obstruction, underlying metabolic abnormalities are commonly present in patients with ureteropelvic junction obstruction.**

Although patients with stones and concomitant ureteropelvic junction obstruction have traditionally been treated by open pyeloplasty and stone extraction, PNL with concomitant endopyelotomy can achieve good results with less morbidity. Endopyelotomy, defined as incision of the ureteropelvic junction obstruction intraluminally, has an overall success rate between 63% and 88% (Ramsay et al, 1984; Van Cangh et al, 1989, 1994; Motola et al, 1993; Kletscher et al, 1995; Nadler et al, 1996; Preminger et al, 1997; Albani et al, 2004; Knudsen et al, 2004). Percutaneous endopyelotomy can easily be combined with PNL, which permits efficient stone removal as well as careful endoscopic inspection of the ureteropelvic junction. Success rates for combined PNL and endopyelotomy have been reported to range from 64% to 85% (Cassis et al, 1991; Meretyk et al, 1992b; Motola et al, 1993). Although retrograde endopyelotomy can also be performed, the antegrade approach is preferable when renal calculi are present. Ramakumar and colleagues (2002) have reported that laparoscopic pyeloplasty with concomitant pyelolithotomy is a feasible technique for this population of patients as well. However, Ball and associates (2004) have observed that **laparoscopic pyeloplasty with concomitant pyelolithotomy is most efficacious when it is applied to patients with limited stone burdens.**

## Calyceal Diverticula

Calyceal diverticula are congenitally derived, nonsecretory, urothelium-lined eventrations of the renal collecting system that are filled with urine. A narrow neck communicating with the collecting system is typically present, which permits the diverticulum to fill passively with urine. Calyceal diverticula are uncommon, having been reported as incidental findings in 0.2% to 0.6% of individuals undergoing renal imaging (Middleton and Pfister, 1974; Timmons et al, 1975; Wulfsohn, 1980; Michel et al, 1985). Stones have been reported to form in 9.5% to 50% of these cavities and can cause pain and hematuria or harbor bacteria (Yow and Bunts, 1955; Williams et al, 1969; Middleton and Pfister, 1974). The role of metabolic factors versus urinary stasis in the pathogenesis of stone formation in calyceal diverticula is controversial. Burns and coworkers (1984) suggested that particle retention time, espe-

cially in the setting of a diverticulum, could be the cause of stone formation. However, several studies examining metabolic data have drawn conflicting conclusions. Although Hsu and Streem (1998) have reported metabolic abnormalities in 50% of 14 patients with calyceal diverticular calculi, Liatsikos and associates (2000) found a low incidence of metabolic abnormalities in 49 patients with calyceal diverticular stones.

Historically, patients with calyceal diverticula were treated by open surgical nephrotomy with closure of the infundibulum, marsupialization and fulguration of the diverticular cavity, or partial nephrectomy. However, with the development of minimally invasive surgical therapies, including PNL, ureteroscopy, SWL, and laparoscopic surgery, open surgical treatments are uncommon. The use of SWL for the treatment of patients with diverticular calculi is controversial. Most investigators agree that **to prevent stone recurrence, eradication of the diverticulum should accompany stone removal,** a goal that is not achieved with SWL (Cohen and Preminger, 1997). Furthermore, **the stone-free rate for patients with calculi within calyceal diverticula who are treated by SWL averages only 21%** (range, 4% to 58%) (Renner and Rassweiler, 1999). However, an average of 60% (range, 36% to 86%) of patients will become symptom free after SWL. The follow-up in series showing the highest symptom-free rates is relatively short (3 to 6 months); on extended follow-up, Jones and associates (1991) demonstrated that some of the patients initially rendered symptom free will subsequently become symptomatic and require re-treatment. The highest success rate with SWL was reported by Streem and Yost (1992), who treated a series of 19 patients harboring calyceal diverticular calculi smaller than 1.5 cm and a functionally patent diverticular neck. An initial stone-free rate of 58% and a symptom-free rate of 86% were achieved, probably a result of careful selection of patients; all of the diverticula filled with contrast material on preoperative intravenous pyelography, and the ostia were well visualized. In addition, the aggregate stone size was smaller than 1.5 cm. However, recurrent stone growth was demonstrated in one patient during the follow-up period, and six of nine patients with infection presumed to be secondary to the diverticulum developed recurrent infections.

**The percutaneous approach for the management of subjects with diverticular stones provides the patient with the best chance of becoming stone and symptom free, 88% and 91%, respectively** (Hulbert et al, 1986; Hedelin et al, 1988; Kriegmair et al, 1990; Ellis et al, 1991; Jones et al, 1991; Lang, 1991; Hendrikx et al, 1992; Bellman et al, 1993; Shalhav et al, 1998; Donnellan et al, 1999; Al-Basam et al, 2000; Monga et al, 2000; Auge et al, 2002b). Furthermore, there is an excellent chance of ablating the diverticular cavity by this approach. **A direct percutaneous approach to the calyceal diverticulum is preferable because it allows use of a rigid nephroscope for stone extraction, dilation and incision of the diverticular neck, and fulguration of the diverticular epithelium.** Kim and associates (2005a) reported a novel, single-stage procedure that does not require ureteral catheter placement or entrance into the renal collecting system. Percutaneous access is directed onto the diverticular cavity harboring stone, two movable core J wires are coiled in the diverticular cavity, and the track is balloon dilated. Once the stone material is removed, the cavity is fulgurated.

**Retrograde ureteroscopic management is a reasonable option for certain patients with diverticula in the upper and**

middle portions of the kidney when the stone burden is less than 2 cm and the diverticular neck is short and accessible (Grasso et al, 1995c). Ureteroscopy also offers the ability to use a laser fiber or electrocautery probe to fulgurate the diverticular epithelium (Cohen and Preminger, 1997). Fuchs and David (1989) reported a stone-free rate of 73% and a symptom-free rate of 86%. Batter and Dretler (1997) attempted this approach in 26 patients. They were able to access the diverticular cavity in only 18, and 15 were rendered stone free. All of the 18 patients in whom the diverticulum could be entered were symptom free at a mean follow-up of 39 months. Auge and associates (2002b) reported a symptom-free rate of 35% and stone-free rate of 19% for this technique. For those patients harboring larger diverticular stones, a combined ureteroscopic and antegrade approach was reported to improve the outcome of PNL (Grasso et al, 1995c).

Laparoscopic management of patients with symptomatic calyceal diverticula has been described in several small series and case reports (Gluckman et al, 1993; Ruckle and Segura, 1994; Harewood et al, 1996; Hoznek et al, 1998; Curran et al, 1999). Miller and associates (2002) reported a series of five patients with symptomatic, stone-bearing calyceal diverticula who underwent retroperitoneoscopic surgical therapy. The authors concluded that the optimal candidates for this approach are those with a symptomatic calyceal diverticulum with thin overlying renal parenchyma, those with a large stone burden, and those with an anterior lesion inaccessible to or unsuccessfully managed by other approaches. However, the laparoscopic approach is more invasive than PNL and therefore is usually limited to diverticula in anterior calyces, which are otherwise difficult to access with a percutaneous approach.

### Horseshoe Kidney and Renal Ectopia

Horseshoe kidney is the most common congenital renal anomaly, and patients with this condition are often affected by urolithiasis (Evans and Resnick, 1981). A horseshoe kidney is considered the result of a median fusion of metanephric tissue during early gestation. Subsequent entrapment of the fused lower pole isthmus by the inferior mesenteric artery results in an incomplete cephalad migration and an associated malrotation of the kidney (Hohenfellner et al, 1992). In many cases, the ureteropelvic junction is anomalous because of a high ureteral insertion into an elongated renal pelvis. This can cause impaired urine drainage, a likely reason that up to two thirds of such patients are found on evaluation to have hydronephrosis, infection, or urolithiasis (Lampel et al, 1996). Although SWL can be used to treat patients with calyceal stones in a horseshoe kidney, the anomalous orientation of the calyces makes localization of the calculi more difficult, especially for stones in the anteromedial calyces. Placement of the patient in a prone position may facilitate localization of the stone (Jenkins and Gillenwater, 1988). Alternatively, a "blast path" technique, which uses the observation that sufficient acoustic pressure for stone fragmentation exists beyond F2 along the axis of the shockwave in many lithotripters, may be employed (Locke et al, 1990). Reported results of SWL treatment of patients with horseshoe kidney stones are variable; stone-free rates between 28% and 78% have been reported (Esuvaranathan et al, 1991; Vandeursen and Baert, 1992; Theiss et al, 1993; Kirkali et al, 1996; Lampel et al, 1996; Kupeli

et al, 1999). Much of the wide range of results can be explained by variability in stone size and location among the different studies. Theiss and colleagues (1993) stratified stones by location and found, as expected, that the clearance rate for lower calyceal stones was inferior to that of middle and upper calyceal stones (a stone-free rate of 53.8% versus 100%). Kirkali and associates (1996) studied a series of 18 patients with calculi larger than 10 mm and found a stone-free rate of 28%. Patients with renal calculi in horseshoe kidneys treated by SWL required a higher number of shockwaves per treatment and also experienced a higher re-treatment rate (30% versus 10%) than did patients with similar stones in orthotopic renal units (Chaussy and Schmiedt, 1984; Drach et al, 1986; Lingeman et al, 1986a). Lampel and associates (1996) reported a recurrence rate of 86% for patients harboring persistent fragments after SWL compared with a 14% recurrence rate for patients who were stone free. Despite the negative implications of these studies, **SWL can achieve satisfactory results in the properly selected patient with a stone burden smaller than 1.5 cm and nonobstructed urine drainage.**

For patients with larger calculi or for those who demonstrate evidence of poor urine drainage, PNL should be the primary approach. **The results of PNL for patients with calculi in a horseshoe kidney are generally superior to those achieved with SWL, with an average stone-free rate of 84%** (range, 75% to 100%) (Esuvaranathan et al, 1991; Jones et al, 1991; Al-Otaibi and Hosking, 1999; Raj et al, 2003; Shokeir et al, 2004). The **optimal point of entry for these kidneys is through a posterior calyx, which is typically more medial than in the normal kidney** because of the altered renal axis and rotation associated with the midline fusion. Except in the isthmus of the horseshoe kidney, where the vascular supply can be variable, **vessels tend to enter the kidney anteriorly. An upper pole collecting system puncture is often appealing as the entire kidney is usually subcostal.** In most cases, the lower pole calyces are anterior and inaccessible percutaneously. During PNL, the flexible nephroscope often aids in accessing stones within anteromedial calyces, which may be difficult to reach with a rigid nephroscope.

An ectopic kidney can be found in a pelvic, iliac, abdominal, thoracic, or crossed position. The most common site of ectopia is the pelvis, and the incidence of pelvic kidney is estimated to be 1 in 2200 to 1 in 3000 patients. See Chapter 113, "Anomalies of the Upper Urinary Tract." Although the ectopic location of the kidney can cause positioning problems during SWL treatment, calculi in these kidneys should be approached initially with SWL, if it is feasible (Harmon et al, 1996; Zafar and Lingeman, 1996). If the bony pelvis shields the targeted stone from the shockwave of the lithotripter, a prone position may be necessary. Kupeli and associates (1999) reported in a series of seven patients with calculi in pelvic kidneys that although successful fragmentation was achieved for most patients at the time of treatment, the stone-free rate at 3 months was only 54%.

For those situations in which SWL therapy is either unsuccessful or not possible, alternative modalities should be used. Laparoscopy-assisted percutaneous transperitoneal nephrolithotomy has been described (Fig. 44–4) (Eshghi et al, 1985; Figge, 1988; Lee and Smith, 1992; Toth et al, 1993). Holman and Toth (1998) described 15 patients treated by laparoscopy-assisted PNL with good results and no major

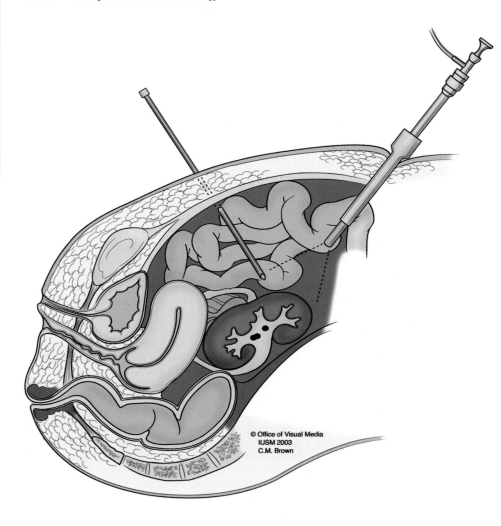

**Figure 44–4.** Laparoscopy-assisted PNL technique, in which the bowel is reflected off of the ectopic kidney before radiographically and laparoscopically guided percutaneous access.

© Office of Visual Media
IUSM 2003
C.M. Brown

complications. Alternatively, laparoscopic retroperitoneal pyelolithotomy in a pelvic kidney has been reported (Harmon et al, 1996). Flexible ureteroscopy is also an attractive alternative for this unusual problem if the stone burden is not large. Weizer and associates (2005) reported a series of eight patients with renal calculi in either a horseshoe kidney or an ectopic kidney who were treated successfully with ureteroscopy. Alternatively, CT guidance can permit percutaneous access into the ectopic renal collecting system without injury to adjacent organs (Matlaga et al, 2003b).

## Lower Pole Calculi

Although SWL is the preferred method for treatment of most patients with symptomatic upper tract calculi, there is considerable controversy concerning the management of patients with lower pole calculi (Tolley and Downey, 1999). The limitations of SWL for treatment of patients with lower pole renal calculi were first noted in a meta-analytic study by Lingeman and associates (1994). These investigators reported that the stone-free results achieved with PNL were superior to those of SWL: **the overall stone-free rate for SWL applied to lower pole calculi was 60% compared with 90% for PNL.** Stratified according to stone size, patients with stones smaller than 10 mm had stone-free rates of 74% when they were treated by SWL compared with 100% by PNL. Among patients with

stones of 10 to 20 mm, stone-free rates were 56% for the SWL group compared with 89% for the PNL group. A regression analysis demonstrated that increasing stone burden was associated with progressively less successful stone-free outcomes for patients treated with SWL, whereas for PNL-treated patients, stone-free rates were not different across categories of stone size. This study has prompted a number of groups to assess the impact of lower calyceal anatomy; studies reported stone-free rates for calculi 10 mm or smaller, 11 to 20 mm, and 20 mm or larger of 67.8%, 54.6%, and 28.8%, respectively (Havel et al, 1998; Kupeli et al, 1998; May and Chandhoke, 1998; Talic and El Faqih, 1998; Keeley et al, 1999b). Importantly, since the mid-1980s, a significant change in renal stone distribution has been noted, with an increase in the percentage of SWL treatments for patients with renal calculi being performed for lower calyceal stones (2% in 1984 to 48% in 1991) (Lingeman et al, 1994). This change in stone distribution may be explained by the tendency of small, radiographically undetectable fragments to gravitate to more dependent calyces after SWL therapy and to act as a nidus for new stone growth (Carr et al, 1996).

The reasons for poor clearance of fragments from the lower pole after SWL are unclear. Intuitively, the gravity-dependent position of the lower pole calyx may impede the passage of stone fragments (Elbahnasy et al, 1998). However, several investigators have proposed that in addition to the gravity-dependent positioning of the lower pole calyces, anatomic features may play an important role in the evacuation of stone fragments from this location. Anatomic factors were first suggested by Sampaio and Aragao (1992, 1994), who described the anatomy of the lower pole by use of polyester resin endocasts of the intrarenal collecting system obtained from adult cadavers. They examined 146 three-dimensional casts from 73 cadavers and noted that in many cases, the spatial anatomy of the lower pole region had peculiar features that were thought to be potentially important factors for the clearance of stone fragments. In 83 of 146 casts (56.8%), the inferior pole was drained by multiple infundibula. The authors hypothesized that an inferior pole with multiple infundibula might have poor drainage and consequently less possibility of eliminating stone fragments than would an inferior pole drained by a single infundibulum receiving fused calyces. In addition, the authors found that 39.7% of the kidneys had calyceal infundibular diameters of less than 4 mm. Again, the authors hypothesized that such a small diameter may hinder passage of stone fragments. The authors also examined the angle formed between the lower infundibulum and the renal pelvis, believing that an angle greater than 90 degrees should facilitate drainage of fragments from the lower pole. In 26% of the casts, the authors noted that this angle was less than 90 degrees and hypothesized that this could perhaps hinder stone clearance. In a prospective study, Sampaio and associates (1997) found that 39 of 52 patients (72%) became stone free when the lower pole infundibulopelvic angle was greater than 90 degrees, whereas only 5 of 22 patients (23%) were stone free when the angle was less than 90 degrees.

A number of other investigators have analyzed the impact of lower pole anatomy on SWL stone clearance (Table 44–2). Sabnis and colleagues (1997) reported that patients with favorable lower calyceal anatomy, as defined by Sampaio, had a post-SWL clearance rate of 70% or more, whereas those with unfavorable factors had a clearance rate of less than 20%. Elbahnasy and associates (1998) assessed the infundibulopelvic angle, infundibular length, and infundibular width in a retrospective study of 34 patients with solitary lower calyceal calculi treated with SWL. These anatomic features were measured by preoperative intravenous pyelography. Overall, the mean infundibulopelvic angle was significantly greater, 45 degrees versus 51 degrees, in SWL stone-free patients compared with those with residual stones after SWL. Furthermore, all patients with an infundibulopelvic angle greater than 90 degrees were stone free. The authors also found that there was a direct, statistically significant relationship between infundibular width and stone-free rate after SWL; only 33% of patients with an infundibular width of 5 mm or less became stone free after SWL compared with a 60% stone-free rate for patients with an infundibular width greater than 5 mm. Furthermore, there was a statistically significant inverse relationship between infundibular length and stone-free status after SWL; the infundibular length was 32 mm in stone-free cases versus 38 mm in cases with residual stone. They concluded that successful SWL is highly sensitive to lower pole anatomy. The combination of an infundibulopelvic angle of 90 degrees or greater, an infundibular length of less than 3 cm, and an infundibular width of more than 5 mm was associated with a successful outcome for lower pole calculi of 15 mm or less. The combination of an infundibulopelvic angle of less than 90 degrees, an infundibular length of more than 3 cm, and an infundibular width of 5 mm or less was associated with treatment failure. Keeley and associates (1999b) reported that collecting system anatomy affected the results in 116 patients with lower pole calculi measuring 11 to 20 mm treated with SWL. The overall stone-free rate was 52%. However, an obtuse infundibulopelvic angle was the only factor to attain significance in predicting stone-free status. Combining the three unfavorable factors (acute angle, distorted calyx, and narrow infundibulum), the stone-free rate was 9%; whereas with three favorable factors, the stone-free rate was 71%.

Others have not found collecting system anatomy to be predictive of lower pole stone clearance with SWL. Madbouly and colleagues (2001) employed the same methods to measure the three aforementioned anatomic parameters in 108 patients undergoing SWL treatment of lower pole stones. The mean infundibular length, the mean infundibular width, and the mean lower pole infundibulopelvic angle were not significant outcome predictors. However, the authors did find that patients with renal scarring had the least chance of becoming stone free.

Sorenson and Chandhoke (2002) reported a series of 190 patients with lower pole calculi who underwent SWL therapy. The patients were all evaluated with intravenous pyelography preoperatively, and these studies were used to measure the infundibular length, infundibular width, and infundibu-

| Table 44–2. | **Factors Affecting Clearance of Lower Pole Calculi** | | | | |
|---|---|---|---|---|---|
| | **Significance of Infundibular** | | | | |
| *Citation* | *Angle* | *Width* | *Length* | *Height* | *Complex Calyx* |
| Sampaio et al, 1997 | Yes | — | — | — | — |
| Sabnis et al, 1997 | Yes | Yes | — | — | — |
| Elbahnasy et al, 1998a | Yes | Yes | Yes | — | — |
| Elbahnasy et al, 1998b | No | Yes | Yes | — | — |
| Lojanapiwat et al, 1999 | Yes | — | — | — | — |
| Keeley et al, 1999b | Yes | No | No | Yes | No |
| Gupta et al, 2000[†] | Yes | Yes | No | — | No |
| Tuckey et al, 2000 | — | Yes | — | Yes* | — |
| Madbouly et al, 2001 | No | No | No | — | — |
| Albala et al (Lower Pole I), 2001 | No | No | No | — | — |
| Sumino et al, 2002 | No | Yes | No | Yes | — |

*Used calyceal pelvic height.
[†]Infundibulopelvic and infundibular to vertical ureteral angles.

lopelvic angle. Calyceal anatomy was not predictive of success, even when the stones were stratified by size. There was no difference in stone-free outcome when patients were grouped by favorable anatomy (infundibular angle greater than 70 degrees, infundibular length less than 30 mm, and infundibular width more than 5 mm) versus unfavorable anatomy (infundibular angle less than 70 degrees, infundibular length more than 30 mm, infundibular width less than 5 mm). Albala and associates (2001), of the Lower Pole I study group, reported on 38 cases in a randomized trial comparing SWL with PNL for the treatment of patients with lower pole calculi. In all of the SWL cases, infundibular length, infundibular width, and infundibulopelvic angle were calculated and recorded. In this study, there was no significant difference in mean lower pole infundibular width, lower pole infundibular length, and lower pole infundibulopelvic angle among patients undergoing SWL who had residual calculi and those rendered stone free.

**One of the confounding issues in examining lower pole outcomes is the reproducibility of lower pole anatomic measurements.** Pace and colleagues (2000) reported that there is wide variability in lower calyceal infundibular width between different intravenous pyelography phases. The authors found that the width was greatest on the compression film and smallest on the postvoid film, which prompted them to suggest the use of standardized timing when infundibular width is measured from an intravenous pyelogram. Likewise, Keeley and associates (1999b) suggested that because peristalsis changes the diameter of the infundibulum, measurement of this variable from a single x-ray film is imprecise. Although some of the disparity regarding the lower pole anatomic influences on stone-free status may be due to the techniques in which the parameters were measured, other sources of variability may be due to the type of lithotripter employed. In addition, stone composition, an important variable, is often neglected in these studies. However, it is likely that an obtuse versus an acute lower pole infundibulopelvic angle is important in fragment clearance after SWL. The most appropriate method for measuring lower pole infundibulopelvic angle and its relevant cutoff values as well as the significance of other lower pole anatomic features as predictive factors of stone clearance are yet to be determined.

Despite the lower stone-free rates achieved with SWL therapy, a number of clinicians advocate this modality for the treatment of patients with lower pole calculi. Elbahnasy and associates (1998b) compared the outcomes of patients with lower pole calculi treated by either SWL or PNL. The authors found that the stone-free rate with SWL was significantly lower compared with PNL (56% versus 85%). However, the clinical stone recurrence rates of the two groups at 20 months were similar (10% versus 11%). Cass (1996a) reviewed the results of 968 lower pole calculi treated by SWL and compared these results with four published series of PNL therapy for lower pole calculi. The author concluded that although the stone-free rate achieved with PNL is greater than that achieved with SWL, lower complication rates, lower repeated treatment and secondary procedure rates, shorter hospital stays, and similar recurrent stone rates make SWL more clinically effective as a primary therapy for patients with lower pole calculi less than 2 cm in diameter. Obek and associates (2001) reported a series of 455 patients with isolated lower pole

calculi treated with SWL. After a single SWL treatment, the stone-free rate for patients with isolated lower pole calculi was 63%. However, the stone-free rate dropped to 49% for patients with calculi larger than 2 cm, leading the authors to recommend SWL for primary treatment of patients with lower calyceal stones smaller than 2 cm. Chen and Streem (1996) reported a series of 206 patients with isolated lower pole calculi in 220 renal units who were treated with SWL. The stone-free rate at 1 month of follow-up was 48%, with another 6.3% of patients becoming stone-free during extended follow-up. Of those patients with residual stones, 9% required secondary intervention.

The poor stone clearance rates for patients with lower pole calculi treated by SWL have prompted investigators to examine techniques to facilitate fragment passage. McCullough (1989) anecdotally reported that postural drainage may assist in the elimination of retained fragments from dependent calyces. Brownlee and associates (1990) subsequently treated patients with residual lower pole fragments with controlled inversion therapy, using intravenous hydration, inversion, and percussion. D'A Honey and associates (2000) reported a pilot study to determine whether mechanical percussion with inversion therapy and furosemide-induced diuresis can move stone fragments out of the lower pole of the kidney. At a mean time of 63 days after SWL, this group reported an 83% stone passage rate. In a subsequent study, Pace and associates (2001) compared the effectiveness of mechanical percussion, inversion, and furosemide-induced diuresis with observation for elimination of lower calyceal fragments after SWL. They reported that 40% of patients with residual lower pole fragments treated with this regimen became stone free compared with 3% in the observation group; the observation group was then treated with this regimen as part of a crossover design, and 43% were rendered stone free. Other authors have reported lower pole irrigation techniques as adjuncts to SWL. Nicely and associates (1992) performed retrograde irrigation of the lower pole with a cobra angiographic catheter during SWL and found that the irrigation group had a 71% stone-free rate at 1 month of follow-up compared with 33% in the control group. Graham and Nelson (1994) placed a small percutaneous nephrostomy tube into the lower pole collecting system before SWL and performed a continuous saline irrigation of the collecting system. All patients became stone free with this therapy. None of these techniques, however, has gained widespread acceptance.

As previously described retrospective studies have indicated, **the results of SWL of lower pole calculi are inferior to those of PNL and depend on stone size.** Albala and associates (2001) have performed a multicenter, randomized, prospective study (Lower Pole I) that compared the treatment outcomes for patients with lower pole calculi after either PNL or SWL. The stone-free rate at 3 months after treatment, as measured by nephrotomograms, was 95% for those undergoing PNL and 37% for those undergoing SWL. Of note, **stone clearance from the lower pole after SWL was especially poor as stone size increased above 10 mm.** For patients with stones smaller than 10 mm, 20 of 20 (100%) patients treated with PNL were stone free, whereas 12 of 19 (63%) treated with SWL were stone free. For those patients with calculi of 11 to 20 mm, 26 of 28 (93%) treated with PNL were stone free, whereas 6 of 26 (23%) treated with SWL were stone free. Finally, for patients with calculi of 21 to 30 mm, 6 of 7 (86%) treated with PNL were stone free, whereas 1 of 7 (14%) treated with SWL was stone free. The main advantage of SWL was the lower associated morbidity.

A number of significant advances in endourologic technology have facilitated the treatment of lower pole calculi through a retrograde endoscopic technique. Grasso and Ficazzola (1999) reviewed a series of 79 patients with 90 lower pole calculi treated through a retrograde approach by small-diameter, actively deflectable, flexible ureteroscopes and holmium laser intracorporeal lithotripsy. In this series, the overall stone-free rate was 76%. Stratified by stone size, the stone-free rates were 82%, 71%, and 65% for patients with stones 1 to 10 mm, 11 to 20 mm, and more than 20 mm, respectively. A long lower pole infundibulum and infundibular stenosis were associated with treatment failures. Hollenbeck and associates (2001) reviewed 61 patients who underwent 68 ureteroscopic procedures for the treatment of lower pole calculi. Laser lithotripsy was performed in situ, without displacement of the stone from the lower pole. After a single procedure, 62% were stone free, and after a second procedure, 69% were stone free. Stratified by size, 71% of patients with stones smaller than 10 mm and 75% of patients with calculi of 10 to 20 mm were stone free.

Recognizing the technologic advances in ureteroscopy, the **Lower Pole Stone Study Group compared ureteroscopy and PNL for patients with 10- to 25-mm lower pole stones and found a significant difference in stone clearance, with only 31% of the ureteroscopy cohort stone free at 3 months versus 76% of the PNL cohort.** The definition of stone free was strict, based on CT imaging. If the definition is broadened to include fragments smaller than 4 mm, the stone-free rate improved to 80% for the ureteroscopy cohort and to 100% for the PNL cohort (Kuo et al, 2003). Thus, **ureteroscopy for patients with a large renal stone burden is probably inferior to PNL and should be used only for those patients who are poor candidates for PNL.** The Lower Pole Stone Study Group also performed a prospective, randomized study of SWL and ureteroscopy for lower pole stones smaller than 10 mm and reported that there was no significant difference in stone-free rates between the two techniques (Pearle et al, 2005).

Placement of an instrument through a flexible ureteroscope impedes scope deflection, which may make it difficult or impossible to perform laser lithotripsy of lower pole calculi. Nitinol baskets and flexible grasping devices have less of a negative effect on deflection than laser fibers do and can be used to displace the targeted stone to the mid or upper portions of the collecting system, facilitating laser lithotripsy (Auge et al, 2001). Kourambas and associates (2000a) reviewed a series of 34 patients with 36 lower pole calculi treated through a retrograde approach. Twenty-six stones were fragmented in situ in the lower pole, whereas 10 calculi were moved to a more favorable position in the collecting system. The stone-free rate of patients who were treated with stone displacement before fragmentation was 90% compared with a stone-free rate of 83% for those patients who underwent in situ fragmentation. Schuster and associates (2002) similarly reported a 77% stone-free rate for patients with lower pole calculi smaller than 1 cm treated in situ versus an 89% stone-free rate for those treated with displacement first. For patients with calculi larger than 1 cm, 100% of those undergoing displacement first were

treated successfully compared with 29% of those treated in situ.

**The optimal approach for management of patients with lower pole stones is still evolving. SWL is a reasonable consideration for individuals with lower pole stones of 1 cm or less in aggregate size. There is a reasonable chance of achieving a stone-free state with minimal attendant morbidity with this technique. Patients with lower pole stones of 2 cm or more are still best served with PNL as this offers them the best chance of being rendered stone free with one procedure. Much of the controversy regarding treatment of lower pole stones is limited to stones of 10 to 20 mm in diameter. PNL, ureteroscopy, and SWL are all acceptable options. Stone composition and lower pole anatomy should be considered in recommending a treatment modality for these patients. Patients with an acute lower pole infundibulopelvic angle (with or without other unfavorable anatomic features), patients whose SWL treatment has failed, and patients known to have stones resistant to SWL should be treated with PNL or ureteroscopy.** In the future, it may be possible to predict which patients among this group will have good results with the different treatment modalities.

## Clinical Factors

The treatment of urinary tract calculi must be viewed in the context of the patient as a whole. Any coexisting clinical factors that may affect the safety and the efficacy of the selected treatment must be considered.

### Urinary Tract Infection

Urinary tract infection, in the presence of renal calculi, can be difficult to eradicate unless the offending stones are completely removed. For these patients, then, PNL or ureteroscopy, both of which permit the complete removal of stone fragments, may be preferable to SWL. The reported incidence of sepsis after SWL is less than 1%, although a staghorn calculus increases this rate substantially to 2.7% to 56% (Lam et al, 1992a; Meretyk et al, 1997). The risk of sepsis increases if the urine culture demonstrates bacterial growth before SWL (Zink, 1988). Furthermore, the risk of sepsis is also greater in the presence of obstruction (Meretyk et al, 1992a). Therefore, **SWL should be performed only if the urine is sterile and there is no distal obstruction.** In general, prophylactic antibiotics are not required before SWL but should be considered in high-risk patients (Kattan et al, 1993; Bierkens et al, 1997).

### Morbid Obesity

Morbid obesity, which may be defined as more than 100 pounds overweight, greater than 200% of ideal body weight, or a body mass index (a value obtained by weight in kilograms divided by height in meters$^2$) greater than 40, poses a number of physiologic and technical challenges to the successful treatment of kidney stones (Giblin et al, 1995; Freedman et al, 2002). The respiratory and cardiovascular morbidities inherent in a morbidly obese state can significantly increase the perioperative risk associated with even a minimally invasive procedure. Morbid obesity may make SWL impractical or technically impossible because of weight limitations on the lithotripter table or gantry, inability to target the stone radiographically, or skin to stone distance that exceeds the maximum allowable focal distance of the lithotripter. When the increased distance from the skin surface to the stone renders positioning of the stone at the focus of the shockwave impossible, a blast path technique that relies on high pressures produced at a point located coaxially beyond F2 may be required (Whelan et al, 1988; Locke et al, 1990). Although the successful treatment of obese patients with SWL has been reported, with an overall stone-free rate of 68% at 3 months, high-energy settings of the lithotripter were required (Thomas and Cass, 1993). Should the urologist treating a morbidly obese patient have a choice among different SWL machines, the machine with the greatest focal length and highest peak pressure should be selected (Hofmann and Stoller, 1992).

Despite these potential maneuvers, the morbidly obese may still achieve a suboptimal outcome after SWL. Ackermann and associates (1994) reported a multivariate analysis that found body mass index to be a significant negative predictor of a stone-free outcome after SWL. Portis and associates (2003) have reported similar findings. In many cases, PNL is the only effective treatment option for the morbidly obese patient with a complex renal calculus. The judicious use of an extralong working sheath, along with extralong rigid nephroscopes, flexible nephroscopes, and longer instruments, can overcome the increased distance between skin surface and stone in these patients. Pearle and associates (1998) described 57 obese patients (body mass index greater than 30) who underwent PNL. The overall stone-free rate (88.3%) and the complication and transfusion rates (12.8% and 5%, respectively) were comparable to the results of PNL in an unselected population of patients. Koo and associates (2004) similarly reported that **the outcome of PNL is independent of the patient's body mass index.**

Significant alterations in technique are not required when a ureteroscopic approach is selected for the morbidly obese patient with a renal calculus. **For morbidly obese patients who do not harbor an excessively large stone burden, the ureteroscopic approach may be preferable** (Fabrizio et al, 1998; Nguyen and Belis, 1998).

### Spinal Deformity or Limb Contractures

Patients with spinal deformity or limb contractures may also be difficult to position within the lithotripter. Alternative treatment modalities, including PNL and ureteroscopy with flexible instruments, may be preferable in these patients. Owing to the unusual anatomy that is often present, **a preoperative CT scan can help in planning percutaneous access.** In certain cases, CT guidance may be necessary to safely obtain percutaneous access into the renal collecting system (Matlaga et al, 2003b).

### Uncorrected Coagulopathy

Although **SWL or PNL treatment of patients with uncorrected coagulopathy can result in life-threatening hemorrhage,** such patients can be safely treated once the bleeding diathesis has been corrected (Streem and Yost, 1990). However, **if the patient's coagulopathy is the result of a pharmacologic therapy that cannot be safely discontinued, ureteroscopy with holmium:yttrium-aluminum-garnet (holmium:YAG) laser lithotripsy is the preferable approach.** Grasso and Chalik (1998) have reported that this is a safe and effective technique for patients with uncorrected coagu-

lopathies. Watterson and associates (2002b) conducted a multicenter retrospective analysis and also reported that upper tract calculi in patients with uncorrected bleeding diathesis can be safely managed by a ureteroscopic approach.

### Other Groups

The management of renal calculi in children is discussed in Chapter 131. However, when children as well as the elderly, the hypertensive, and those with impaired renal function are treated with SWL, enhancement of the adverse effects of the shockwaves may occur. Care should be taken to limit the number and energy of shockwaves applied in such circumstances (Janetschek et al, 1997; Evan et al, 1998; Lifshitz et al, 1998).

## Assessment and Fate of Residual Fragments

In the era of open stone surgery, residual fragments of any size suggested a failed procedure. However, the increasing popularity of SWL as the treatment of choice for most patients with upper tract urinary calculi has changed the definition of a successful outcome, introducing the concept of **clinically insignificant residual fragments** (Newman et al, 1988). Newer definitions of treatment success were required after the observation that **although many patients had successful stone fragmentation, not all patients completely and spontaneously passed all of the stone fragments.** Furthermore, the clearance of stone fragments produced by shockwaves is not immediate; as many as 85% of patients have radiologic evidence of residual fragments in the kidney several days after SWL (Drach et al, 1986). Although most fragments will pass spontaneously during the first 3 months after SWL, continued clearance of fragments can occur for more than 24 months after treatment (Chaussy and Schmiedt, 1984; Graff et al, 1988; Kohrmann et al, 1993). Therefore, since the introduction of SWL, treatment outcomes for patients with renal calculi have been reported by two different terms: stone-free rate and success rate. The stone-free rate is self-explanatory, but the success rate includes patients who are stone free as well as those with clinically insignificant residual fragments. These different methods of reporting treatment results, the lack of consensus regarding the definition of clinically insignificant residual fragments, and the various modalities used for assessing postprocedural stone-free status (KUB radiography, nephrotomography, ultrasonography, CT) make the comparison of endourologic stone removal procedures with SWL difficult.

Clinically insignificant residual fragments were initially defined as residual fragments 4 mm or smaller in diameter associated with sterile urine in an otherwise asymptomatic patient (Newman et al, 1988). However, **small residual stones often become clinically symptomatic** (Streem et al, 1996; Zanetti et al, 1997; Candau et al, 2000). Streem and colleagues (1996) reported on a prospective, long-term follow-up study of 160 patients after SWL who had small, residual, asymptomatic, calcium oxalate or calcium phosphate stones (4 mm or smaller). At a mean follow-up of 23 months, 43% of patients had suffered a significant symptomatic episode or required intervention. Likewise, Zanetti and associates (1997) followed up 129 patients with residual stones smaller than 4 mm after SWL and noted that 22% became symptomatic or required intervention.

**Residual fragments not only may become symptomatic but also can act as a nidus for new stone growth.** Complete stone removal will decrease the risk of stone recurrence and regrowth (Singh et al, 1975; Patterson et al, 1987; Newman et al, 1988). Stone recurrence rates of 6% to 15% have been reported for patients who were rendered stone free after SWL compared with rates of 17% to 80% when residual fragments were present (Graff et al, 1988; Newman et al, 1988; Nijman et al, 1989; Beck and Riehle, 1991; Fuchs et al, 1991; Zanetti et al, 1991; Nakamoto et al, 1993). In a long-term prospective study, residual fragments (<4 mm) after SWL were found to pass spontaneously in 24% of patients, whereas increased, decreased, and stable amounts of residual fragments were noted in 18%, 16%, and 42% of patients, respectively (Streem et al, 1996). Similarly, a retrospective study of 83 patients with residual fragments (<4 mm) after SWL found complete stone clearance or a decreased, stable, or increased amount of residual stone at a mean follow-up of 40 months in 33%, 1%, 29%, and 37% of the patients, respectively (Candau et al, 2000). Furthermore, the size of the residual fragment (2 mm or smaller versus 2 to 4 mm) influences the risk of its becoming symptomatic (Candau et al, 2000).

Many investigators have noted that **after SWL, residual fragments are commonly localized to lower pole calyces, no matter where the stone was treated in the kidney** (Drach et al, 1986; Graff et al, 1988; Liedle et al, 1988; Zanetti et al, 1991; Kohrmann et al, 1993). As well, the incidence of stone recurrence is higher in the lower pole calyces (Zanetti et al, 1991; Kohrmann et al, 1993). Carr and associates (1996) compared SWL with PNL and at 1-year follow-up reported a significantly greater rate of new stone formation in the SWL group. They also demonstrated a greater likelihood of stone recurrence in lower and middle calyces. A plausible explanation for these results is that fine debris, undetectable by KUB radiography, persists after SWL and, because of gravity, tends to settle in the most dependent calyces, serving as a nidus for new stone formation.

In patients with infection-related calculi, the consequence of residual fragments is particularly harmful. Residual fragments may harbor the offending bacteria and thus perpetuate postoperative bacteriuria and persistent infection. Furthermore, stone regrowth has been reported in up to 75% of such patients after SWL, compared with 10% of patients who experienced complete stone removal (Beck and Riehle, 1991; Zanetti et al, 1991).

For patients with metabolic stone disease (such as those with cystinuria), complete stone removal does not prevent stone recurrence, but it does prolong treatment intervals (Chow and Streem, 1998). Thus, residual stones, including small stones, may not have an immediate clinical relevance but are likely to affect the patient's well-being in the long term. In these situations, it is important to select a treatment approach that is most likely to render the patient stone free.

The sensitivity of the method used to detect residual stones after a stone removal procedure has important effects on the incidence and size of residual fragments. In early studies investigating stone clearance after SWL, plain radiography was commonly used to determine stone-free status. A plain radiograph can detect an opaque stone fragment as small as 2 mm (Thornbury and Parker, 1982). However, Denstedt and

coworkers (1991) reported that in 29 patients with large renal calculi treated with a combination of PNL and SWL, plain radiography and renal tomography, overestimated stone-free rates by 35% and 17%, respectively, compared with flexible nephroscopy, leading the authors to conclude that plain radiography is inadequate to accurately determine stone-free status after SWL. Several groups have reported that nephrotomography is superior to plain radiography in evaluating stone-free status; additional residual stone fragments are detected in 12% to 47% of patients (Hjollund Madsen, 1972; Schwartz et al, 1984; Goldwasser et al, 1989). Sonography is inferior to plain radiography and is particularly inadequate in detecting ureteral stones, with a sensitivity of only 19% (Yilmaz et al, 1998; Older and Jenkins, 2000). Although ultrasonography should not be used as a single modality for detecting residual stones, it is effective in diagnosing hydronephrosis and should be considered following all ureteroscopic procedures, as silent obstruction has been reported to occur in certain, albeit rare, instances (Weizer et al, 2002). A prospective study comparing the relative efficacy of abdominal radiography and renal ultrasonography with excretory urography for the evaluation of asymptomatic patients 1 month after SWL treatment demonstrated that the combination of ultrasonography and abdominal radiography was as good as or better than intravenous urography in identifying residual stone fragments and renal abnormalities, including hydronephrosis (Coughlin et al, 1989). The authors suggested that **routine radiologic evaluation of asymptomatic patients after SWL could be limited to abdominal radiography and ultrasonography.**

Although plain films of the abdomen and nephrotomograms were at one time commonly used to identify retained fragments after PNL, antegrade nephrostograms and second-look nephroscopy have now became commonplace (Waldmann et al, 1999). Although flexible nephroscopy may be considered the "gold standard" for assessment of residual stones after PNL, its routine use has been challenged by studies showing the high sensitivity of CT in detecting residual stones after PNL. Pearle and coworkers (1999) noted that CT had 100% sensitivity for detecting residual stones after PNL in 36 patients evaluated with both CT and flexible nephroscopy. Selective use of flexible nephroscopy based on positive CT findings would have avoided an unnecessary procedure in 20% of patients. In a retrospective study of 121 patients who underwent CT after PNL (including 59% stone-free patients and 16% patients with fragments of 1 to 3 mm), Waldmann and associates (1999) reported that routine nephroscopy would not have been required in 75% of cases. Given its wide availability and high sensitivity, non–contrast-enhanced CT is likely to become the primary method for evaluation of patients after PNL.

## Adjunctive Medical Treatment

Any patient who requires surgical stone removal should be offered a metabolic evaluation and stone analysis. **Appropriate medical therapy can decrease the risk of stone recurrence and stone regrowth** (Lifshitz et al, 1999a).

In a retrospective study, Fine and associates (1995) examined the effect of medical management on residual fragments and recurrent stone formation after SWL; they reported that selective medical therapy decreased the stone formation rate compared with the control group by 91% versus 35%, respectively, if the patient was stone free and by 81% versus 17%, respectively, in the presence of residual fragments. Likewise, Lee and colleagues (1999) conducted a retrospective study of patients with upper urinary tract calculi observed for 24 to 60 months and found a significant decrease in the stone recurrence rate in patients who received medical prophylaxis compared with those who were managed expectantly (7.8% versus 46.2%, respectively). In a prospective study, Cicerello and coworkers (1994) found that for patients with either calcium oxalate or struvite stones, alkaline citrate therapy improved stone clearance at 6 and 12 months and also decreased stone regrowth after SWL. The use of long-term (for more than 3 months) antibiotics was reported to decrease the risk of stone recurrence from 90% to 15% after open surgery for struvite stones, suggesting that a prolonged course of antibiotic treatment may also be beneficial after PNL, SWL, and ureteroscopy (Husmann et al, 1995).

Mardis and associates (2004) emphasized the importance of the administration of validated medical therapies, guided by metabolic evaluation, in reducing stone recurrence rates after treatment. Medical therapy in patients with hypercalciuria confers a secondary advantage, as Pak and associates (2003) have reported that appropriate treatment can increase bone density in these patients. However, any postprocedural medical management should not supercede the choice of a treatment approach that gives the patient the best chance to achieve a stone-free status with minimal morbidity.

### KEY POINTS: RENAL CALCULI

- The majority of patients with renal calculi have a normal kidney and a small stone burden, and can be managed best with SWL. Patients with lower pole calculi larger than 10 mm will experience significantly better stone-free rates after PNL than after SWL.

- The procedure of choice for patients with staghorn calculi is PNL. When they are left untreated, staghorn calculi are associated with the loss of renal function and increased mortality.

- Patients harboring stones that are resistant to fragmentation (cystine, brushite, calcium oxalate monohydrate) should undergo SWL only when the stone burden is small.

- The percutaneous approach to patients with calculi in calyceal diverticula provides the best chance for a stone- and symptom-free outcome.

- The outcome of PNL is independent of the patient's body mass index, and therefore PNL is a good treatment option for the morbidly obese with a large stone burden. For the morbidly obese with a small stone burden, ureteroscopy is the optimal approach.

## URETERAL CALCULI

The goal of the surgical treatment of patients suffering from ureteral calculi is to achieve complete stone clearance with minimal attendant morbidity. Improvements in surgical tech-

nology, such as SWL, rigid and flexible ureteroscopes, the holmium:YAG laser, and basket devices, have greatly augmented the urologist's ability to efficiently treat such patients, regardless of the size or location of the ureteral calculus. Although the treatment options available to the urologist are greater now than they have ever been, most patients with ureteral calculi do not require intervention. Ureteral calculi 4 mm or smaller will usually pass spontaneously, although in some cases with discomfort and expense to the patient. Ureteral calculi of any size may be associated with renal obstruction, and care must be taken to prevent irreversible damage to the kidney, whether the patient selects expectant or active treatment.

Perhaps the greatest dilemma facing the urologist today is "to blast or not to blast" (i.e., to choose between the two most frequently used modalities in ureteral stone treatment—SWL and ureteroscopy). PNL is a less commonly used treatment option and is usually reserved for a limited group of patients with large, proximal ureteral stones. Open ureterolithotomy is rarely indicated, although it may be an option as a salvage procedure. Laparoscopic ureterolithotomy has been described both as a salvage procedure in lieu of an open ureterolithotomy and as a first-line therapy (Turk et al, 1998; Keeley et al, 1999a; Gaur et al, 2002). The ultimate role of this procedure in the urologic armamentarium is yet to be determined, although it is effective for a select group of patients.

The factors that the urologist must consider when recommending treatment to patients with ureteral calculi may be grouped into three broad categories: stone-related factors (location, size, composition, duration, and degree of obstruction), clinical factors (the patient's tolerance of symptomatic events, the patient's expectation, associated infection, single kidney, abnormal ureteral anatomy, and clinical factors previously mentioned in the treatment of renal calculi), and technical factors (equipment available for treatment, costs) (Table 44–3). These factors may be thought of as treatment modifiers; the presence or absence of one or more of these factors may shift the balance toward a certain treatment modality.

## Natural History

The indications for intervention in the management of patients with ureteral calculi have clearly been affected by the increased efficiency and lower morbidity of minimally invasive treatment modalities. Although the traditional indications for intervention (intolerable or intractable symptoms, infection, obstruction, and a stone that is unlikely to pass spontaneously) have not changed, the array of technologies currently available allows almost any symptomatic patient to be considered a candidate for stone removal. Lingeman and

**Table 44–3. Factors Affecting Management of Ureteral Stones**

| Stone Factors | Clinical Factors | Technical Factors |
|---|---|---|
| Location | Symptom severity | Available equipment |
| Size | Patient's expectations | Cost |
| Composition | Associated infection | |
| Degree of obstruction | Solitary kidney | |
| | Abnormal ureteral anatomy | |

associates (1986b) reported that when a patient requires hospitalization, it is less costly to remove the patient's stone with either SWL or ureteroscopy than to attempt to control the patient's symptoms with pharmacotherapy only. However, many patients will pass the stone spontaneously. A thorough knowledge, then, of the natural history of ureteral stones permits a well-informed judgment of when conservative measures (e.g., observation), rather than intervention, are indicated. Furthermore, such data help the patient consider the spectrum of options and decide whether to try to endure further symptoms or to elect immediate stone removal.

In the absence of external ureteral compression or internal narrowing, **the width of the stone is the most significant measurement affecting the likelihood of stone passage** (Ueno et al, 1977). However, the measurement of stone size from a plain radiograph can be misleading. Otnes and Sandnes (1978) reported that stone size was overestimated in 59% of cases, was underestimated in 15%, and correlated accurately with the actual size in only 26%. Ueno and colleagues (1977) reported that in a series of 520 patients with ureteral stones, **those with stones smaller than 4 mm, 4 to 6 mm, and larger than 6 mm experienced rates of spontaneous passage of 80%, 59%, and 21%, respectively.** Morse and Resnick (1991) showed that **the rate of spontaneous passage is highly dependent on stone location; passage rates from the proximal, middle, and distal ureter were 22%, 46%, and 71%, respectively.** Hubner and associates (1993) also reported that the likelihood of spontaneous stone passage was directly related to stone size and location at the time of presentation. The rate of spontaneous passage for stones smaller than 4 mm was 38% compared with 1.2% for those larger than 6 mm, irrespective of their position in the ureter at the time of presentation. Calculi discovered in the distal third of the ureter had a spontaneous passage rate of 45%, compared with 22% for the middle third and 12% for the proximal third. Two thirds of all stones that passed did so within 4 weeks after the onset of symptoms. Segura and associates (1997) reported in the AUA guidelines on the management of patients with ureteral calculi that for stones smaller than 5 mm, the spontaneous passage rate in the distal ureter and proximal ureter ranged from 71% to 98% and from 29% to 98%, respectively, whereas stones larger than 5 mm had a lower spontaneous passage rate, ranging from 10% to 53% and 25% to 53% for proximal and distal ureteral calculi, respectively. These rates have been affirmed by a more recent review of CT imaging of ureteral calculi (Coll et al, 2002). Therefore, **for patients with stones of 5 mm or less, conservative management should be considered,** whereas the chance of spontaneous passage for larger stones diminishes considerably, and intervention should be more readily contemplated.

Miller and Kane (1999) analyzed 75 patients with ureteral calculi and found that the interval to stone passage was highly variable and dependent on stone size, location, and side: for 95% of stones to pass, 31 days were required for stones 2 mm or less, and about 40 days were required for stones 2 to 6 mm. Furthermore, only 4.8% of patients with stones smaller than 2 mm required intervention compared with 50% of patients with stones 4 to 6 mm. Cummings and coworkers (2000) trained an artificial neural network to predict outcome in patients with ureteral stones with 76% accuracy. The duration of symptoms before initial presentation was the most influ-

ential factor, followed by degree of hydronephrosis. The importance of symptom duration was reported by several other authors, who concluded that if significant progress has not occurred after 1 month of observation, intervention is usually required (Ibrahim et al, 1991; Hubner et al, 1993; Singal and Denstedt, 1997).

Several groups have investigated the role of pharmacologic therapy to facilitate spontaneous stone passage. Borghi and associates (1994) reported a randomized, double-blind, placebo-controlled study that compared the effectiveness of nifedipine plus methylprednisolone with the effectiveness of the steroid alone in hastening stone passage. The authors found that the combination treatment of calcium channel blocker and steroid increased the rate of spontaneous stone passage over the steroid alone. Porpiglia and associates (2000) and Cooper and associates (2000) investigated the efficacy of a calcium channel blocker and steroid combination in the management of patients with distal ureteral stones, comparing this treatment regimen with a control arm that did not receive any medical therapy beyond analgesia. Both of these studies found that the medical treatment arms had a significantly reduced stone expulsion time and a significantly increased stone expulsion rate. Dellabella and colleagues (2003), in a study performed to investigate the efficacy of tamsulosin in facilitating ureteral stone passage, randomized 60 patients to receive either tamsulosin or florogluucine-trimetossibenzene, a spasmolytic. Both groups received deflazacort, a steroid. The authors found that tamsulosin therapy was associated with an increased stone expulsion rate and a decreased time to stone expulsion. Porpiglia and associates (2004), in a similar study, compared tamsulosin with nifedipine and found that tamsulosin treatment was associated with a reduced time to stone expulsion; as in the preceding studies, both groups of patients were also treated with steroids.

## Factors Affecting Treatment Decisions

### Stone Factors

**Location.** The location at which the passage of a ureteral stone is arrested is an important factor in assessing the likelihood of spontaneous passage as well as in determining the optimal treatment options and their relative successes. The statistical **probability of spontaneous ureteral stone passage is directly related to the distance of the ureter to be traversed and inversely related to stone size.**

Ureteral stones usually become impacted at three distinct sites where the caliber of the ureter narrows: the ureteropelvic junction, the iliac vessels, and the ureterovesical junction. Historically, the ureter was divided into thirds: the proximal ureter, from the ureteropelvic junction to the upper edge of the sacrum; the middle ureter, from the superior to the inferior margin of the sacroiliac joint; and the distal ureter, from the inferior margin of the sacrum to the ureterovesical junction. This three-part division was based on the different open surgical approaches to stones in the ureter. However, with the development of minimally invasive techniques, open surgery is rarely indicated, and the ureter is more often now divided into two segments, proximal and distal; the point of division is the narrow part of the ureter where it crosses the iliac vessels, reflecting a technical impediment for rigid ureteroscopy (Segura et al, 1997). Anatomic location has an important effect on what treatment modality has a higher stone-free rate. In the 1980s, proximal ureteral stones were commonly treated with SWL, whereas distal ureteral stones were treated with ureteroscopy (Sosa et al, 1987). Since that time, the treatment paradigms for ureteral stones have evolved; they are defined further in the sections on proximal and distal ureteral stones.

**Stone Burden.** The stone burden, in terms of both size and number, may affect what form of therapy will be the most efficient and confer the highest stone-free rate. The majority of ureteral stones pass spontaneously, especially stones less than 5 mm in diameter, and thus can be treated with expectant management (Kinder et al, 1987; Segura et al, 1997). Stones larger than 8 mm, however, are unlikely to pass spontaneously in a timely fashion without causing significant symptoms and possible renal damage from obstruction (Ueno et al, 1977). Experience with various treatment modalities has demonstrated differences in efficacy when they are applied to large ureteral stones. In the meta-analysis performed by the AUA, SWL for the in situ treatment of large (>1 cm) ureteral stones achieved a stone-free rate of 76%, independent of initial stone location (Segura et al, 1997). However, if the same stones are manipulated into the renal pelvis before SWL treatment, the stone-free rate increases to 82% (Drach et al, 1986). Some investigators have reported that patients with stones larger than 50 mm$^2$ treated by SWL have a higher likelihood of requiring more than one SWL treatment session (Bierkens et al, 1998; Mattelaer et al, 1994).

For patients with proximal ureteral calculi, ureteroscopy will produce a stone-free rate of 90% to 97%, and this modality is less affected by stone size than is SWL (Erhard et al, 1996; Grasso et al, 1998). Therefore, ureteroscopy may be more efficient for patients with larger stones in the ureter. SWL efficiency also decreases with very small stones because they are more difficult to locate radiographically. Fortunately, such small stones usually pass spontaneously or are easily retrieved with the ureteroscope.

**Composition.** Stone composition, if it is known, is useful information to help discern which treatment strategy may be favored (e.g., SWL for fragile calcium oxalate dihydrate stones or ureteroscopy and intracorporeal lithotripsy for cystine or brushite stones that are relatively resistant to SWL). In general, most ureteral stones are resistant to medical therapy. However, in the moderately symptomatic or asymptomatic patient with an incomplete obstruction caused by a uric acid stone, urine pH manipulation may be attempted as part of a conservative treatment approach. Urine pH manipulation should also be considered for the patient who does not desire or cannot medically tolerate anesthesia for SWL or ureteroscopy and who is thought to harbor a uric acid stone.

**Duration of Presence.** The management of patients with ureteral stones may be affected by the duration of a stone's presence or the patient's symptoms. The length of time a stone has been in the ureter is significant because of the potential for irreversible loss of renal function. However, even with complete ureteral obstruction, irreversible loss of renal function does not occur before 2 weeks, although it can progress to total renal unit loss at up to 6 weeks (Vaughan and Gillenwater, 1971).

Andren-Sandberg (1983) reported that in 358 patients with ureteral stones, nuclear renography detected impaired renal function in 27% of patients who were asymptomatic. Furthermore, 7% of these patients had persistent renal impairment up to 17 months after stone passage. Holm-Nielsen and associates (1981) reported that of 134 patients with unilateral ureteral stones, one third of the patients with obstruction lasting more than 4 weeks suffered irreversible renal damage. Similarly, Kelleher and associates (1991) found that sequential renal scintigraphy performed on 76 patients with obstructive ureteral calculi demonstrated an 18% incidence of reduced renal function (defined as a decrease in relative function greater than 7%). Two of the 14 patients had persistent loss of renal function after treatment. These two patients had undergone previous unsuccessful attempts at stone removal, emphasizing the importance of achieving stone-free status at the time of the initial procedure. Irving and associates (2000) studied 54 patients with ureteral calculi and reported that 28% of patients had silent loss of renal function at presentation. Interestingly, small calculi were as likely to be associated with diminished renal function as were larger stones, and patients who underwent early intervention (before 7 days) for diminished renal function had a better outcome than did patients with delayed intervention. **Because the patient's symptoms and stone size do not predict loss of renal function, and because there is no clear time threshold for irreversible damage, intervention should be considered in any patient with ureteral obstruction unless the ability to closely monitor renal function is available.**

## Clinical Factors

**Pain.** Pain (renal or ureteral colic) is the primary presenting symptom of most patients with ureteral obstruction and is the source of considerable morbidity. The pain of ureteral colic is mediated by prostaglandins released by the ureter in response to obstruction. Prostaglandins act to increase ureteral peristalsis to aid in stone passage and also to sensitize nociceptors to stimuli such as bradykinins that induce pain and visceral responses (nausea, vomiting) (Selmy et al, 1994). For these reasons, prostaglandin inhibitors such as indomethacin and ketorolac are particularly effective in relieving the pain and nausea of ureteral obstruction (Cordell, 1996). However, **prostaglandins must be used with caution or avoided altogether in patients with compromised renal function; infusion of ketorolac in an acute unilateral ureteral obstruction model decreased ipsilateral renal blood flow by 35%** (Perlmutter et al, 1993).

Management of ureteral obstruction on the basis of symptoms should be tailored to the amount of time the symptoms have persisted. Patients presenting with early symptoms of renal colic may be managed expectantly for stone passage as long as their symptoms are controllable with oral medical therapy. Patients with symptoms of longer duration may be more appropriately managed by relieving the ureteral obstruction through either the placement of a ureteral stent or definitive stone treatment. Patients with ureteral stones causing severe symptoms refractory to conservative and medical therapy require prompt treatment.

**Infection.** Infection associated with ureteral stones, or obstructed pyelonephritis, is a not uncommon and potentially life-threatening urologic emergency. Such patients are typically febrile and may present with signs of septic shock, such as hypotension. Urgent drainage of the obstructed portion of the urinary tract by either ureteral catheter or percutaneous nephrostomy is essential. A urine culture specimen from the obstructed segment will aid in directing antibiotic therapy. Definitive stone therapy should be delayed until urine cultures are negative and the patient has recovered completely.

**Patient's Expectations.** The patient's expectations must be considered in recommending different treatment modalities. For ureteral stones with low probability of spontaneous passage, the patient must be informed of the available treatments, including the relative benefits and risks associated with each. Although ureteroscopy is more invasive than SWL, the patient may achieve immediate or nearly immediate stone-free status with a single procedure. Although SWL is less invasive, a patient may be reluctant to select this modality because it entails an often lengthy follow-up until fragment clearance as well as the risk of unplanned additional invasive procedures and re-treatments (Wolf et al, 1995; Peschel et al, 1999). Conversely, patients may select SWL as a consequence of apprehension of the anesthesia associated with ureteroscopy or the possibility of a temporary ureteral stent.

**Solitary Kidney.** Patients with ureteral stones in either surgically or functionally solitary kidneys require a modification of standard treatment algorithms. **A ureteral stone obstructing a solitary kidney demands prompt attention,** usually with internal drainage and definitive stone treatment (SWL or ureteroscopy).

**Aberrant Anatomy.** Ureteral stones in patients with abnormal anatomy (ureteral ectopia, ureteroceles, megaureters) may have impaired egress because of obstructive or functional factors (Kajikawa et al, 1985; Diamond et al, 1994; Dretler, 1995). These patients may not respond to therapies such as SWL with the same level of success as do those with normal ureteral anatomy. The anatomic abnormality may need to be corrected or circumvented to permit successful treatment of ureteral stones. For example, patients with recurrent stones that become lodged and obstruct the ureter in a ureterocele should have the ureterocele treated (by either endoscopic incision or open excision with reimplantation) simultaneously with ureteral stone removal.

## Technical Factors

The treatment of patients with ureteral calculi depends on multiple surgical technologies, and the availability of certain equipment will affect the possible options for treatment. Few operating environments will have all possible lithotripters, ureteroscopes, lithotrites, or stone retrieval devices immediately available. In addition, the surgeon's preference and technical expertise will also affect the technique chosen. The majority of urologists and patients with stone disease in the United States do not have direct access to a fixed lithotripter on an unlimited basis. Therefore, treatment decisions may need to be modified according to lithotripter availability. Patients with symptomatic ureteral stones and no immediate lithotripter access have several options: they may be clinically observed with pain and emetic control; they can undergo placement of an internal ureteral stent to relieve the symptoms of renal colic (but then may suffer stent-related morbidities);

or they may have primary ureteroscopic removal of the stone, provided the requisite endoscopic equipment is available.

Because of recent pressures to decrease resource use, there is increasing emphasis in the modern medical environment on the reduction of cost. Economic pressures have promoted the movement toward less invasive, more cost-effective therapy for patients with ureteral stones. Grasso and colleagues (1995b) analyzed the cost of ureteroscopy and SWL for 112 patients with ureteral calculi. When they compared outpatient ureteroscopic lithotripsy with SWL monotherapy, treatment costs were similar. However, the addition of re-treatments and auxiliary procedures after SWL more than doubled the costs and weighed heavily against this modality's cost-effectiveness. Wolf and associates (1995) used a literature-based probability decision tree to determine the more effective and cost-efficient therapy for patients with distal ureteral calculi and found that although initial SWL was only slightly more expensive than ureteroscopy, the cost differential increased when additional complications and re-treatments were calculated. Kapoor and associates (1992) compared the treatment costs of 20 patients treated by SWL and 32 patients treated by ureteroscopy, with success rates of 75% and 97%, respectively, recorded. They reported that ureteroscopy was 60% less costly than SWL.

In contradistinction to these studies, Bierkens and associates (1998) reported that ureteroscopy was more expensive than SWL for the treatment of patients with middle and distal ureteral stones. However, the average hospital stay for patients who underwent ureteroscopy was more than 3 days, whereas SWL was performed as an outpatient procedure. When ureteroscopy was performed on an outpatient basis, the cost of SWL was greater than that of ureteroscopy. Lotan and associates (2002) performed a decision tree model to identify the most cost-effective treatment option for patients with ureteral calculi. On the basis of a comprehensive literature review to determine the average success rate of observation, SWL, and ureteroscopy, they found that **ureteroscopy is the most cost-effective treatment strategy for ureteral stones at all locations, after observation fails.**

## Proximal Ureteral Stones

The surgical treatment options for patients with proximal ureteral stones include SWL with or without stone manipulation, ureteroscopy, PNL, and, rarely, open or laparoscopic stone surgery. The AUA Ureteral Stones Clinical Guidelines Panel performed a meta-analysis of all articles on ureteral calculi published during a 30-year period from 1966 to 1996 (Segura et al, 1997). The results were analyzed for SWL in situ, SWL after "pushback," SWL after stent insertion, PNL, ureteroscopy, and open surgical stone removal. The stone-free rates of SWL and ureteroscopy were 84% and 56%, respectively, for stones smaller than 1 cm and 72% and 44%, respectively, for stones larger than 1 cm. The risks of significant complications after SWL and ureteroscopy were 4% and 11%, respectively. Although open stone surgery had a median stone-free rate of 97%, it was associated with longer hospitalization and greater postoperative morbidity and therefore was not recommended as a first-line intervention. As a guideline, because of its greater efficacy and lower morbidity, the panel suggested that SWL, either in situ or after pushback, should be the primary approach for stones smaller than 1 cm in the proximal ureter. For stones larger than 1 cm in diameter, SWL, PNL, and ureteroscopy are all acceptable choices. Initial experience with SWL suggested that placement of a ureteral stent before treatment facilitated stone fragmentation and passage (Liong et al, 1989). However, the AUA meta-analysis demonstrated no improvement in stone fragmentation for these patients, so this practice was discouraged. Placement of a ureteral stent may be appropriate for other indications, such as in the management of pain, for the relief of obstruction, and in the treatment of difficult-to-visualize stones. Stent placement is mandatory in patients who have a solitary obstructed kidney.

Since the publication of the AUA guidelines, significant improvements have been made in ureteroscopic technology. In 2001, the European Association of Urology published "Guidelines on Urolithiasis," in which they performed an analysis of the relevant literature for the 3 years after the AUA publication (Tiselius et al, 2001). They detected a significant improvement in stone-free rates; **semirigid and flexible ureteroscopes provided a 90% to 100% stone-free rate for distal ureteral calculi and a 74% stone-free rate for proximal ureteral calculi.** These results are considerably better than those reported by the AUA panel. In addition, 95% of patients could be successfully treated with only one endoscopic procedure, and the best results were reported with holmium:YAG laser lithotripsy in the proximal ureter.

Currently available flexible ureteroscopes are easily accommodated by even unstented ureteral orifices and allow immediate access to ureteral calculi. As well, the introduction of increasingly efficient lithotrites, such as the holmium:YAG laser, facilitates the endoscopic treatment of ureteral calculi of any size, composition, and location. Several investigators have demonstrated excellent outcomes for patients with proximal as well as distal ureteral calculi. Mean stone-free rates of 95%, with a less than 1% incidence of complications such as stricture or perforation, have been reported for patients with proximal as well as distal calculi treated ureteroscopically. Park and associates (1998) analyzed the outcomes of patients with proximal or distal ureteral calculi treated by either SWL or ureteroscopy and found that the efficacy of SWL worsened significantly for stones larger than 1 cm (83.6% versus 42.1%), whereas the stone-free rate for ureteroscopic treatment was unaffected by size (88.9% versus 86.6%).

An impacted stone may be defined as a stone that cannot be bypassed by a wire or catheter or a stone that remains at the same site in the ureter for more than 2 months (Morgentaler et al, 1990; Roberts et al, 1998). **Impacted stones are often more resistant to fragmentation by SWL** (Green and Lytton, 1985; Farsi et al, 1994). Both Mueller and associates (1986) and Park and colleagues (1998) have performed in vitro studies demonstrating that the confinement of a model stone is associated with substantial reduction in fragmentation, which may be due to the lack of a liquid interface surrounding the stone, thus reducing cavitation activity. Mugiya and colleagues (2000) reported a series of 104 patients with impacted ureteral stones, including 83 in the proximal ureter, of which 100 (96.2%) were completely fragmented by a single endoscopic procedure. At 1 month, the stone-free rate was 100%, and there were no significant complications.

Although these reports suggest that ureteroscopy may be the optimal approach to the impacted ureteral stone, some

urologists still favor SWL as the initial approach for stones smaller than 1 cm in the proximal ureter. However, flexible ureteroscopy may be the treatment of choice for patients whose SWL treatment failed, for patients with cystinuria, for patients with distal obstruction, for patients with impacted stones, for obese patients, for patients with bleeding diathesis, and when SWL is not readily available (Tawfiek and Bagley, 1999). If a ureteral stent is required for SWL, a pushback technique of manipulating the stone into the intrarenal collecting system may provide a greater likelihood of complete stone fragmentation (Mueller et al, 1986; Riehle and Naslund, 1987; Liong et al, 1989; Bolton et al, 1991). Gross and coworkers (1998) compared 105 patients who underwent pre-SWL ureteral stone manipulation with 93 patients undergoing SWL of ureteral stones in situ and found that the practice of stone manipulation was successful in 91.4% of patients; the mean number of SWL treatments was 1.4 in the pushback group and 2.1 in the in situ group. Other prospective studies have failed to demonstrate an improved stone-free rate with pushback technique versus in situ SWL, although stones treated in situ did require significantly more shockwaves, administered at higher voltages, than did those treated with pre-SWL manipulation (Rassweiler et al, 1986; Hendrikx et al, 1990; Danuser et al, 1993). When stone manipulation is planned under regional or general anesthesia or when a ureteral stent is to be placed before SWL, consideration should be given to immediate flexible ureteroscopy as it is more definitive and associated with a higher success rate (Grasso, 1999). For patients with proximal ureteral stones larger than 1 cm, a better outcome may be achieved with flexible ureteroscopic lithotripsy as the primary approach.

Alternatively, PNL is a reasonable option for select patients with proximal ureteral calculi. A dilated proximal ureter facilitates access to these stones with large-caliber instruments that can fragment and remove stone burden efficiently (Srivastava et al, 1992). Stone-free rates of 86% have been reported (Segura et al, 1997). Although PNL permits rapid stone removal, it does require general anesthesia and can be associated with longer convalescence and higher complication rates. Therefore, **PNL is usually reserved for the patient with complex, proximal ureteral stones.** Particularly good candidates for this approach include those with impacted calculi that are refractory to other modes of stone removal, those with dilated renal collecting systems, those with large stone burdens, and those with distal ureteral strictures (Preminger, 1992).

## Distal Ureteral Stones

The optimal therapy for patients requiring removal of distal ureteral calculi is controversial. SWL and ureteroscopy are both effective treatments associated with high success rates and limited morbidity. A 1997 meta-analysis performed by the AUA Ureteral Stones Clinical Guidelines Panel established that both ureteroscopy and SWL are acceptable treatment options for patients with distal ureteral stones. This recommendation was based on the stone-free results, morbidity, and re-treatment rates for each respective therapy. However, this report used data that were derived from older lithotripsy and endoscopic technology; in addition, costs and patients' satisfaction or preferences were not addressed. Although blind basket extraction (without fluoroscopy and a safety wire) had an overall success rate of 73%, the panel's expert opinion was that "guided stone manipulation (concomitant use of fluoroscopy and safety guide wire) or ureteroscopic basketing would be safer and more efficacious treatment options." Therefore, the panel recommended that blind basketing of ureteral stones not be encouraged as a treatment option. In addition, the panel also recommended (as a standard) that open stone surgery not be used as a primary approach for distal ureteral stones.

Both recommended treatment options, SWL and ureteroscopy, have valid advantages and disadvantages. The primary goal in treating patients with ureteral calculi is a stone-free state, and the AUA guidelines panel's meta-analytic study reported that 85% of 9422 patients subjected to SWL were rendered stone free compared with 89% of 3978 patients undergoing ureteroscopy. There have been two randomized prospective studies comparing ureteroscopy and SWL for treatment of patients with distal ureteral stones subsequent to the guidelines document. Peschel and associates (1999) randomized 80 patients and found that those undergoing ureteroscopy achieved stone-free status more rapidly, regardless of initial stone size, than did those treated by SWL. All of the patients undergoing ureteroscopy were rendered stone free, whereas 10% of the SWL cohort required subsequent ureteroscopy to achieve a stone-free status. Pearle and associates (2001) randomized 64 patients and reported that 100% of individuals who completed radiographic follow-up subsequent to either SWL or ureteroscopy became stone free. One possible reason for the difference in this outcome compared with the prior study is that an unmodified Dornier HM3 lithotripter, which is known to fragment stones more efficiently, was used in Pearle's study rather than the Dornier MFL5000 used in Peschel's study.

There is no validated instrument available to assess the satisfaction of patients for either of these procedures, although this is an important concern. Peschel and associates (1999) measured patients' satisfaction after ureteroscopy or SWL. They found that for patients with stones smaller than 5 mm, all patients undergoing ureteroscopy reported complete satisfaction, compared with 75% of those undergoing SWL. For those with stones larger than 5 mm, all patients undergoing ureteroscopy were satisfied, compared with 95% of those undergoing SWL. Pearle and associates (2001) also measured patients' satisfaction and found no significant difference between SWL (96%) and ureteroscopy (89%). Neither of these studies used a validated questionnaire, and the divergent conclusions of these two analyses emphasize the need for the development of such a device.

**Supporters of SWL claim that it is effective and noninvasive, is associated with less morbidity, requires less anesthesia than ureteroscopy, and seldom requires ureteral stents. Critics argue that the success rates are not as high as those of ureteroscopy, equipment availability may be limited, visualization of the stone is often difficult, attainment of a stone-free state requires a longer time and follow-up, retreatment rates are higher, and costs are higher. Supporters of ureteroscopy claim that it is highly successful and minimally invasive, is associated with minimal morbidity, can be used with larger and multiple stones, and has high immediate stone-free rates. Critics argue that it requires specialized**

**training, requires more anesthesia, and more often requires ureteral stent placement. Continued studies are warranted to better define the roles of each in the management of patients with distal ureteral calculi because both are highly effective.**

## Laparoscopic Ureterolithotomy

Laparoscopy should be considered whenever one contemplates the open surgical removal of a ureteral calculus. Although the indications for this surgery are not common, there are certain patients for whom this may be an acceptable approach, such as those with concomitant upper tract abnormalities (e.g., ureteral stricture, ureteropelvic junction obstruction) requiring surgical repair.

Both transperitoneal and retroperitoneal approaches have been described for laparoscopic ureterolithotomy (Wuernschimmel and Lipsky, 1993; Gaur et al, 1994). Keeley and associates (1999a) reported on a series of 14 patients undergoing transperitoneal laparoscopic ureterolithotomy, which represented 1.1% of the 1240 patients with stone disease treated in a 5-year period. The authors considered stones that could not be accessed ureteroscopically or did not fragment with other treatment modalities as well as large (>1.5 cm) proximal ureteral stones as indications for the procedure. Three patients with associated ureteral strictures underwent laparoscopic incision of the stricture at the time of ureterotomy; two of these patients subsequently required further dilation but ultimately had a successful result. Turk and colleagues (1998) described 26 patients who underwent laparoscopic ureterolithotomy for stones ranging from 20 to 45 mm. A transperitoneal approach was performed in 21 patients, and a retroperitoneal approach was performed in 5 patients. In two cases, the calculus could not be located, necessitating conversion to open surgery. No intraoperative complications were encountered, and patients were discharged between 2 and 5 days after surgery. Gaur and associates (2002) reported long-term follow-up of a series of 101 patients undergoing laparoscopic ureterolithotomy, performed through a retroperitoneal approach in all but one patient. The procedure was successful in 93 patients. The duration of urine leakage was 5.5 days in those patients whose ureter was neither stented nor sutured

---

### KEY POINTS: URETERAL CALCULI

■ Conservative management for a patient with a ureteral stone smaller than 5 mm is appropriate as there is a high likelihood of stone passage. Ureteral stones larger than 5 mm are unlikely to pass spontaneously.

■ Obstructed pyelonephritis due to a ureteral calculus is a not uncommon and potentially life-threatening emergency that is best treated by urgent decompression of the urinary tract.

■ Both SWL and ureteroscopy are highly effective for patients with ureteral calculi.

■ Medical expulsive therapies with agents such as tamsulosin may promote spontaneous stone passage.

after ureterolithotomy and 3.2 days for those patients whose ureter was both stented and sutured. Although the authors suggest that laparoscopic ureterolithotomy may be used as a primary procedure, it is more likely that this operation will be reserved for those patients who require a salvage procedure after failed ureteroscopy or SWL or who have another indication for a laparoscopic procedure.

## URINARY CALCULI DURING PREGNANCY

Urolithiasis is an infrequent complication of pregnancy. However, pain from renal colic is the most common nonobstetric reason for hospital admission during pregnancy (Rodriguez and Klein, 1988). Furthermore, the occurrence of urinary calculi during pregnancy presents danger not only to the mother but also to the fetus as renal colic, infection, and obstruction are all associated with premature labor (Maikranz et al, 1987; Hendricks et al, 1991). The reported incidence of symptomatic urinary calculi during pregnancy ranges from 1 in 200 to 1 in 2500 pregnancies; the wide variation in reported incidence may be due to the small numbers of patients in these studies (Gorton and Whitfield, 1997). However, **the incidence of symptomatic urinary calculi has been calculated to be the same for pregnant women as for nonpregnant women of childbearing age** (Coe et al, 1978; Hendricks et al, 1991). Multiparous women have been reported to be affected more often than primiparous women, in some cases by a ratio of about 3:1 (Horowitz and Schmidt, 1985; Rodriguez and Klein, 1988). However, when it is adjusted for age, the incidence for multiparous women is no greater than that for primiparous women (Swanson et al, 1995). Calculi present with equal frequency on the left and right sides, although ureteral calculi occur almost twice as frequently as renal calculi (Stothers and Lee, 1992; Parulkar et al, 1998). The majority of patients with symptomatic calculi present during the second or third trimesters but rarely during the first trimester (Denstedt and Razvi, 1992; Stothers and Lee, 1992; Swanson et al, 1995).

Pregnancy induces significant physiologic alterations, some of which affect the urinary system. The most remarkable anatomic change is the dilation of the renal calyces, pelvis, and ureters, which is usually evident by the first 6 to 10 weeks of gestation. Pregnancy-induced hydronephrosis is the most common cause of dilation of the urinary tract in pregnancy and may cause flank discomfort or even mimic renal colic. **Upper tract dilation is seen in up to 90% of pregnant women by the third trimester** and may persist for as long as 12 weeks post partum (Boridy et al, 1996). The **right ureter tends to be more dilated than the left,** and the dilation rarely is observed distal to the pelvic brim (Schulman and Herlinger, 1975). Rarely, spontaneous rupture of the kidney may occur, and if it does, it more commonly happens on the right side (MacNeily et al, 1991; Loughlin, 1994). Both **humoral as well as mechanical factors have been implicated in the etiology of hydronephrosis in pregnant women.** Circulating progesterone, a humoral factor that is increased in pregnancy, causes relaxation of ureteral smooth muscle, reducing ureteral peristalsis. Paller and Ferris (1996) have reported that dilation of the urinary collecting system can be reproduced in an animal model by the administration of estrogen and progesterone.

However, recent evidence suggests that mechanical factors, in particular the gravid uterus directly compressing the ureters, are likely to be primary in the pathogenesis of this condition; women with an altered upper urinary tract in whom the ureter does not cross the pelvic brim, such as those with ileal conduit or renal ectopia, do not experience hydronephrosis during pregnancy (Rasmussen and Nielsen, 1988; Dafnis and Sabatini, 1992; Swanson et al, 1995). Although the exact etiology of hydronephrosis of pregnancy is not yet well defined, most would agree that both mechanical and humoral factors play a role in the pathogenesis of this condition.

Other important physiologic changes in pregnancy include an increase in renal plasma flow, which induces a 30% to 50% increase in glomerular filtration rate. As a result of this physiologic alteration, **the normal ranges of serum creatinine and blood urea nitrogen are approximately 25% lower for the pregnant patient.** Importantly then, a serum creatinine value that is in the normal range for the nonpregnant population may actually represent a decrease in renal function for the pregnant patient (Paller and Ferris, 1996). **The increase in renal plasma flow and glomerular filtration rate also increases the filtered loads of sodium, calcium, and uric acid, causing a state of hypercalciuria and hyperuricosuria** (Boyle et al, 1966; Howarth et al, 1977; Gertner et al, 1986). Hypercalciuria is further exacerbated by the suppression of parathyroid hormone and the increase in circulating 1,25-dihydroxycholecalciferol produced by the placenta, which increases intestinal absorption of calcium. However, **these potentially lithogenic physiologic changes are offset by an increase in the excretion of urinary inhibitors, such as citrate and magnesium, as well as an increase in urine output** (Biyani and Joyce, 2002). It has been postulated that metabolic alterations in the urine may contribute to the accelerated encrustation of ureteral stents during pregnancy (Denstedt and Razvi, 1992; Loughlin, 1994).

Although renal colic is the most common nonobstetric cause of abdominal pain in hospitalized pregnant women, the diagnosis of urolithiasis in the pregnant patient can be challenging; many of the usual presenting signs and symptoms may be masked by the patient's gravid status. As gestation progresses, the perception and localization of pain may be altered. Stothers and Lee (1992) reported that 28% of pregnant patients ultimately diagnosed with an obstructing stone were initially, and incorrectly, diagnosed with appendicitis, diverticulitis, or placental abruption. For most patients, though, **the most common presenting symptom is flank pain, usually accompanied by either macroscopic or microscopic hematuria** and, in some cases, urinary tract infection (Stothers and Lee, 1992). Hematuria can occasionally occur in the normal course of pregnancy; however, hematuria without discomfort is unusual in a patient with stone disease (Swanson et al, 1995). It is particularly important to obtain a urine specimen for culture from these patients because pyuria may commonly be seen in the urinalysis of a pregnant patient, which diminishes the sensitivity of this test in detecting urinary tract infection (Hendricks et al, 1991; Houshiar and Ercole, 1996; Parulkar et al, 1998). A diagnosis of urinary calculi should be considered in evaluation of a pregnant patient who suffers from persistent urinary tract infection or infection with a urea-splitting organism. Other symptoms that may indicate urolithiasis include irritative voiding symptoms, chills, nausea, and vomiting. However, these symptoms may also occur with other intra-abdominal conditions, so the urologist must maintain a high index of suspicion when examining these patients.

An important factor in the radiographic evaluation of pregnant patients suffering from stone disease is the risk of ionizing radiation exposure to the fetus. The principal effects of irradiation on the fetus include teratogenesis, carcinogenesis, and mutagenesis. However, the risk associated with radiation depends critically on the gestational age and the amount of radiation delivered (Biyani and Joyce, 2002). **During the first trimester, the period of early organogenesis and rapid cell division, the embryo is sensitive to the effects of radiation** (Swartz and Reichling, 1978). Although the fetus has diminished sensitivity to the teratogenic effects of radiation in the second and third trimesters, such exposure may increase the risk for development of childhood malignant neoplasia (Harvey et al, 1985).

As the radiation dose below which no deleterious effects on the fetus may occur has not been defined with certainty, it may be presumed that exposure to any level of radiation will carry some degree of risk. For this reason, **ultrasonography has become the standard initial study in evaluation of the pregnant patient thought to be experiencing renal colic.** Unfortunately, it can be difficult to adequately visualize the ureter with ultrasound examination as well as to distinguish dilation of the ureter that may be associated with a normal pregnancy from ureteral obstruction due to calculus. Stothers and Lee (1992) reported that renal ultrasonography for the detection of calculi had a sensitivity of 34% and a specificity of 86%. Butler and associates (2000) similarly reported that ultrasonography diagnosed 60% of 35 women who were later proven to have nephrolithiasis. Several techniques have been recommended to improve the diagnostic capability of this technology. Color Doppler imaging allows the sonographer to differentiate the iliac artery and vein from the dilated ureter. MacNeily and associates (1991) reported that the use of this technique can distinguish a dilated infrailiac ureter, which was strongly correlated with ureteral obstruction. Color Doppler imaging can also demonstrate jets of urine expelled from the ureter into the bladder. Deyoe and associates (1995) reported that if there are no ureteral jets on the suspected side of obstruction, ureteral obstruction can be diagnosed with a sensitivity of 100% and a specificity of 91%. However, Burke and Washowich (1998) reported that there is variation in ureteral jet symmetry in later pregnancy and recommended the use of this technique with caution. Renal vascular resistance increases in the presence of acute obstruction, and duplex ultrasonography allows the quantification of this alteration by calculating the kidney's resistive index (Ulrich et al, 1995). Shokeir and Abdulmaaboud (1999) prospectively evaluated 117 nonpregnant patients with ultrasonography; they reported that resistive index measurements had 77% sensitivity and 83% specificity in diagnosis of ureteral calculi and that change in resistive index had 88% sensitivity and 98% specificity. Horrigan and associates (1996) reported that **renal resistive index remains unchanged from the nonpregnant state throughout the course of pregnancy and also is unaffected by the physiologic hydronephrosis of pregnancy, which suggests that this imaging modality may be useful in detecting acute obstruction in this population.** Shokeir and

associates (2000) evaluated pregnant women in a manner similar to their initial study and found that resistive index had a sensitivity of 45% and a specificity of 91% in detecting an obstructing ureteral calculus; change in resistive index had a sensitivity of 95% and a specificity of 100%. If an obstructing calculus cannot be visualized by conventional renal sonography, **transvaginal ultrasonography can provide imaging of the distal ureter.** In a series of 13 women, 6 of whom were pregnant, Laing and associates (1994) identified distal ureteral stones in all 13 patients with transvaginal ultrasonography and in only 2 by transabdominal ultrasonography.

If the clinician determines that ultrasound evaluation is inadequate, other imaging studies may be considered. **If intravenous pyelography is required, a limited study is recommended.** Stothers and Lee (1992) were able to visualize calculi in 16 of 17 pregnant patients with a three-film study, obtaining a scout, a 30-second, and a 20-minute film. Nuclear renography is a technique that can provide a functional assessment of pregnant patients with suspected ureteral obstruction while exposing them to a limited amount of radiation. However, the radioisotope is excreted in the urine, and the bladder reservoir can provide a significant source of radiation exposure to the fetus, necessitating high fluid intake and frequent voiding for these patients (Biyani and Joyce, 2002). This radiographic technique unfortunately does not provide good anatomic detail or visualization of calculi. Magnetic resonance imaging (MRI) does not rely on ionizing radiation or contrast medium, making it a potentially attractive tool to evaluate pregnant patients. Because MRI does not visualize calcium, stones are seen as filling defects overlying the high signal intensity of urine. The visualization of smaller stones with this technique is difficult (Hattery and King, 1995; Roy et al, 1995). Spencer and associates (2004) reported on the use of MRI to evaluate pregnant women with hydronephrosis and flank pain. The authors reported that this technique enabled the accurate distinguishing of physiologic hydronephrosis of pregnancy from hydronephrosis due to an obstructing ureteral calculus. **CT imaging should be avoided during pregnancy because the radiation dose is particularly high.**

Approximately **50% to 80% of pregnant patients with symptomatic calculi will pass their stones spontaneously when treated conservatively with hydration and analgesia** (Denstedt and Razvi, 1992; Stothers and Lee, 1992; Gorton and Whitfield, 1997; Parulkar et al, 1998). Intervention is required in approximately one third of patients, usually for pain uncontrolled by analgesia or signs of persistent obstruction and infection. Once intervention is elected, some advocate temporary measures, such as ureteral stent placement or percutaneous nephrostomy, with definitive management deferred until after delivery. One rationale for this paradigm is that ureteral stents can be placed with local anesthesia under sonographic or minimal radiographic monitoring (Jarrard et al, 1993; Loughlin, 1994; Swanson et al, 1995). However, accelerated encrustation and stent occlusion that may be encountered during pregnancy can necessitate frequent stent replacement, and the optimal indwelling time for a ureteral stent in a pregnant patient is not known and is likely to be highly variable; Kavoussi and associates (1992) have recommended that stents be changed at least every 6 to 8 weeks. Because patients subjected to ureteral stent placement in early pregnancy will probably require multiple stent exchanges,

Denstedt and Razvi (1992) have suggested limiting ureteral stent placements to the later stages of pregnancy (after 22 weeks) and placing a nephrostomy tube in early pregnancy. However, obstruction of the nephrostomy tube may occur as well, requiring frequent tube irrigation and changes (Kavoussi et al, 1992).

**Improvements in ureteroscopic technology and intracorporeal lithotripters have made it possible to access and to treat any stone in the upper urinary tract successfully, even in the pregnant patient.** Since Rittenberg and Bagley (1988) first described the safe and successful use of flexible ureteroscopy in pregnant patients, several groups have published their experiences with larger series of patients. Scarpa and associates (1996) reported a series of 15 pregnant patients who underwent rigid ureteroscopy for renal colic. In all cases, ureteroscopy was performed successfully, and there were no pregnancy-related complications. Lifshitz and Lingeman (2002) reported a series of pregnant patients with renal colic who underwent ureteroscopy, including one who underwent a bilateral procedure. No complications related to the surgery or the pregnancy occurred. Similarly, Watterson and associates (2002a) conducted a retrospective analysis of eight patients who underwent ureteroscopy with holmium:YAG laser lithotripsy. No obstetric or urologic complications occurred, and the overall success rate of the procedures was 91%. With the currently available rigid and flexible ureteroscopes, these procedures can be performed with minimal anesthesia. Although ureteral dilatation is usually unnecessary, in the event it is required, tactile sensation from sequential ureteral dilators, rather than radiographic imaging, can be used to guide the process. Although the use of a rigid ureteroscope in the latter stages of gestation is possible, the flexible ureteroscope is easier to manipulate in a tortuous ureter and reduces the risk of perforation. Most calculi can be extracted intact with a basket or grasper device. If lithotripsy is required, both the holmium:YAG laser and the pneumatic lithotrite devices are safe. Ultrasonic lithotripters should be avoided as the high-pitched audible sound may induce hearing injury in the fetus, although investigation in this area is ongoing and definitive data are not available (Ulvik et al, 1995; Karlsen et al, 2001). In all cases of ureteroscopic exploration of the pregnant patient, **it is important to minimize radiation exposure to the patient by use of a below-the-patient x-ray source and placement of a lead apron under the patient's pelvis and lower abdomen.**

Other treatment modalities that are effective in the nonpregnant patient are not appropriate for this population. Although there have been reports of the inadvertent treatment of pregnant patients with SWL, with no adverse sequelae to the fetus, pregnancy remains a contraindication to this treatment modality (Chaussy and Fuchs, 1989; Frankenschmidt and Sommerkamp, 1998). PNL should be deferred until after birth because this procedure often requires prolonged anesthesia and radiation exposure.

## STONE REMOVAL: SURGICAL TECHNIQUES AND TECHNOLOGY
### Intracorporeal Lithotripters

Ureteroscopy and PNL occupy an essential place in the treatment of urinary calculi as increasing technologic advance-

---

### KEY POINTS: URINARY CALCULI DURING PREGNANCY

- Ultrasonography is the standard initial imaging study in evaluation of a pregnant patient.

- Improvements in ureteroscopy technology now permit ureteroscopic access to and treatment of stones at any location in the collecting system of the pregnant patient.

- It is important to minimize ionizing radiation exposure to the pregnant patient during ureteroscopy by use of a below-table x-ray source and to shield the fetus with a lead apron placed below the patient.

---

ments allow easier access to stones in all parts of the kidney and ureter. In particular, improvements in ureteroscopic equipment emphasize the need for appropriate and effective miniaturized intracorporeal lithotripsy devices. Smaller ureteral stones can be extracted intact with endoscopic baskets or grasping devices after ureteral dilation, if necessary. However, larger ureteral stones require lithotripsy to permit the safe extraction of calculus fragments. The fragmentation of renal stones during PNL requires an approach different from that applied to ureteral intracorporeal lithotripsy. Although small and flexible endoscopic lithotrites are essential for the occasional difficult-to-approach kidney stone, renal stones can be visualized with a rigid nephroscope in most cases. In these situations, with a large kidney stone burden, the efficiency of the lithotrite is the most important requirement, and size and flexibility are of secondary importance. The urologist who treats patients suffering from urolithiasis, then, requires an armamentarium of intracorporeal lithotripsy devices, each maximizing a different quality (e.g., size, flexibility, efficiency).

Four techniques are available for intracorporeal lithotripsy: electrohydraulic lithotripsy (EHL), laser lithotripsy, ultrasonic lithotripsy, and ballistic lithotripsy. These techniques can be divided into those lithotrites that are flexible (laser lithotripsy and EHL) and those that are rigid (ultrasonic and ballistic lithotripsy). Herein, the mechanisms, advantages, disadvantages, and surgical techniques of the various flexible and rigid intracorporeal lithotripters are reviewed.

### Flexible Lithotripters

**Electrohydraulic Lithotripsy.** EHL was invented in 1955 by Yutkin, an engineer at the University of Kiev, and was the first technique developed for intracorporeal lithotripsy (Grocela and Dretler, 1997). The first reported use of EHL outside the Eastern bloc was in 1960, when a modified version of Yutkin's invention, the Urat-1, was used to fragment bladder calculi (Rouvalis, 1970). EHL was first applied to renal calculi during an open surgical lithotomy in 1975 (Raney and Handler, 1975). In 1985, Lytton reported the first experience treating patients with ureteral stones with a rigid ureteroscope and a 5 French EHL probe; no immediate or long-term complications were encountered (Green and Lytton, 1985). The use of smaller EHL probes through a flexible ureteroscope was first reported in 1988 (Begun et al, 1988).

**The EHL probe is essentially an underwater spark plug** composed of two concentric electrodes of different voltage polarities, separated by insulation. When a current sufficient to overcome the insulative gap is applied, a spark is produced. The spark discharge causes the explosive formation of a plasma channel and vaporization of the water surrounding the electrode. The rapidly expanding plasma causes a hydraulic shockwave followed by formation of a cavitation bubble (Fig. 44–5). Depending on the proximity of the probe to the stone surface, the collapse of the cavitation bubble may be symmetrical (at a distance of about 1 mm from the stone), resulting in a strong secondary shockwave, or asymmetrical (at a distance equivalent to a maximum bubble radius of about 3 mm), leading to the formation of high-speed microjets (Vorreuther et al, 1995; Zhong et al, 1997). **Unlike in SWL, the shockwave is not focused, so the stone must be placed where the shockwave is generated.** The first EHL probes developed were of larger diameters (9 French), which, because of their size, had a narrow margin of safety. Later improvements in technology allowed the development of smaller probes, from 1.6 to 5 French, that were safer and had the ability to be passed through small-diameter, flexible ureteroscopes without occluding the irrigation or working channel. There is little difference in fragmentation ability among the different-sized probes, but the larger probes tended to be more durable (Segura, 1999). Subsequent improvements in the EHL generator allowed the surgeon more control over energy discharge, pulse, and duration. Although it was originally hypothesized to function optimally in a $^1/_6$ to $^1/_7$ normal saline solution, Denstedt and Clayman (1990) demonstrated that EHL works equally well in a normal saline solution, eliminating the hazard of irrigating the upper urinary tract with a hypotonic solution.

***Advantages and Disadvantages.*** **The major disadvantage of EHL is its propensity to damage the ureteral mucosa and its association with ureteral perforation.** Raney (1978) reported that with a 9 French probe, 90% of ureteral stones could be successfully fragmented, but there was a 40% incidence of ureteral extravasation. Ureteral perforation remained

an issue of concern with EHL in the ureter despite advancements in technology and technique. Hofbauer and coworkers (1995), in a prospective study of 72 patients, reported a perforation rate of 17.6% with EHL versus 2.6% with pneumatic lithotripsy. However, others have reported a lower rate of perforation, with a mean incidence of 8.5% recorded. Vorreuther and associates (1995) suggested that the mechanism of damage is the expansion of the cavitation bubble, and thus injury may occur even when the probe is not in direct contact with the mucosa. The diameter of the cavitation bubble depends on the energy used and can expand to more than 1.5 cm when energies greater than 1300 mJ are employed. Therefore, **the risk of perforation is greater with higher energies, such as in treatment of a hard stone.** Even with smaller probes and lower energy settings, perforation may occur if repeated pulses are applied close to the mucosa. Santa-Cruz and colleagues (1998), in a comparative in vitro study, reported that the holmium laser and EHL were associated with a higher risk of perforation compared with the coumarin pulsed-dye laser and pneumatic lithotripter. When the authors placed a 3 French probe 0.5 mm from the ureteral wall, perforation was induced with an average of 24 pulses. The **risk of perforation may be higher for impacted stones** associated with significant mucosal edema or if vision is impaired by the minor hemorrhage that commonly occurs during EHL (Hofbauer et al, 1995).

As with most lithotrites, **retrograde propulsion of calculi and fragments can occur during EHL and is more pronounced than with holmium:YAG lithotripsy** (Teichman et al, 1997). In a series of 43 patients treated for proximal ureteral calculi, 14% required subsequent SWL for stones that migrated into the kidney (Yang and Hong, 1996). Placement of a basket or other retention device above the stone may prevent stone retropulsion. However, care should be taken not to activate the EHL device directly on the basket wires or the guide wire. Another disadvantage of EHL compared with holmium:YAG lithotripsy is the larger number and size of fragments produced, especially for stones larger than 15 mm. The repeated passage of the ureteroscope to extract the multiple stone fragments produced during EHL may exacerbate mucosal irritation (Teichman et al, 1997).

**EHL will successfully fragment 90% of stones.** However, treatment failures may be due to a variety of stone compositions. Stone surface characteristics may also play a role in fragmentation efficiency; rough calculi have been reported to fragment more readily than smooth calculi (Basar et al, 1997). Although EHL successfully fragments most ureteral stones, the average 3-month stone-free rate is only 84% because some of the fragments created during lithotripsy and not removed may be retained in the ureter (Table 44–4). Stone-free rates decrease with ureteral stones larger than 15 mm and are significantly lower than those reported for holmium:YAG lithotripsy (67% versus 100%) (Teichman et al, 1997).

The advantages of EHL include probe flexibility, especially the smaller probes such as the 1.9 French, which allows intracorporeal lithotripsy throughout the entire upper urinary tract through rigid or flexible ureteroscopes. Only the holmium:YAG laser, configured with the 200-μm fiber, offers comparable size and flexibility advantages (Elashry et al, 1996). The 1.6 French EHL probe may be even more flexible than the 200-μm laser fiber (Poon et al, 1997).

**Figure 44–5.** Photograph of liquid microjet produced by an asymmetrically collapsing cavitation bubble. (Courtesy of Dr. Larry Crum.)

**Table 44-4. Electrohydraulic Lithotripsy for Ureteral Stones: Outcomes and Complications**

| Author | Patients | Probe Size (French) | Perforation (%) | Successful Fragmentation (%) | Stone Free (%) |
|---|---|---|---|---|---|
| Hofbauer et al, 1995 | 34 | 2.4 | 17.6 | 85.3 | 89.5 |
| Basar et al, 1997 | 198 | 3, 4.5 | 39 | 90.3 | 57.5 |
| Elashry et al, 1996 | 45 | 1.9 | 0 | 98 | 92 |
| Young et al, 1996 | 43 | 3 | 9 | 84 | N/A |
| See et al, 1997 | 89 | N/A | 4.5 | 91.5 | N/A |
| Teichman et al, 1997 | 23 | 1.9 | 13 | N/A | 87 |
| Kupeli et al, 1998 | 33 | 5 | 12.1 | N/A | 90.9 |
| **Weighted average** | **465** | | **8.5** | **90** | **84** |

EHL is also the least costly intracorporeal device, requiring the purchase of a comparatively inexpensive generator and probes. An average of 1 to 1.3 probes are used per case, except in instances of harder stones (e.g., calcium oxalate monohydrate stones), when two or more EHL probes may be needed (Elashry et al, 1996; Huang et al, 1998).

*Technique.* For intraureteral lithotripsy, the smaller 1.6 and 1.9 French probes should be used. **The EHL fiber tip should be positioned approximately 2 to 5 mm distal to the end of the ureteroscope** to protect the lens system from being damaged when the probe is discharged. Before the EHL generator is activated, the stone must be clearly visible. **The probe is placed about 1 mm from the stone surface,** a distance allowing maximum shockwave emission (Zhong et al, 1997). Initially, low voltage (50 to 60 V) and short intermittent or single pulses are used to enhance safety. The generator output is increased as needed to fragment the stone. However, it is recommended that the treating physician limit the maximum output used in treating ureteral stones to minimize the risk of perforation. The goal of the treatment is to create fragments that can be removed with grasping forceps or a basket device or fragments that are likely to pass spontaneously. Attempts to reduce the stone to fragments smaller than 2 mm are not recommended because damage to the urothelium may occur (Denstedt and Clayman, 1990). After 50 to 60 seconds of firing, the insulation at the tip of the probe may peel away, and at this point, a new probe should be used (Segura, 1999).

**Laser Lithotripsy.** Laser is an acronym for light amplification by stimulated emission of radiation, which is a concise description of how a laser works. Laser energy is produced when an atom is stimulated by an external energy source, which creates a population of electrons in an excited state. These excited or higher energy electrons can release their excess energy in the form of photons or light energy. Laser light differs from natural light in that it is coherent (all photons are in phase with one another), collimated (photons travel parallel to each other), and monochromatic (all photons have the same wavelength (Floratos and de la Rosette, 1999). These unique features of laser light allow considerable energy to be transmitted in a highly concentrated manner. Lasers are named after the laser medium generating a specific wavelength. The laser was developed in 1960, and the first medium used was the ruby. In 1968, Mulvaney and Beck reported that although the ruby laser could effectively fragment urinary calculi, the ruby laser generated excessive heat and was not appropriate for clinical use. This continuous-wave laser simply heats the stone until vaporization occurs, which requires the laser to generate heat greater than the melting point of the stone.

A solution for this problem came with the development of pulsed lasers. The application of pulsed energy results in high power density at the stone's surface but little heat dissipation. As the pulse duration decreases, the power density increases proportionally. When it is applied to the stone surface, the pulsed laser causes release of electrons and formation of a "plasma" bubble (Floratos and de la Rosette, 1999). The expansion followed by the subsequent collapse of the plasma bubble generates a shockwave that is responsible for the stone fragmentation effect of most pulsed lasers (except the holmium laser, which is reviewed separately), a mechanism defined as photoacoustic (Watson and Wickham, 1986). The first widely available laser lithotrite was the pulsed-dye laser, which employed a coumarin green dye as the liquid laser medium. When the coumarin dye was excited with a flash lamp, pulses of green light 1 μs in duration with a wavelength of 504 nm were emitted and delivered through optical quartz fibers. **The coumarin wavelength was chosen because it is absorbed by all stone materials except cystine but not by surrounding tissues,** thus maximizing its margin of safety (Grocela and Dretler, 1997). Ureteral perforation induced by the pulsed-dye coumarin laser was noted only after multiple high-energy pulses were applied directly to the ureteral wall (Santa-Cruz et al, 1998). The coumarin pulsed-dye laser represented a major advancement in intracorporeal lithotripsy. The 200-μm fiber allowed the use of small-diameter semirigid and flexible ureteroscopes, although only a limited amount of energy (60 mJ) could be delivered through the small-diameter fiber. Calculi throughout the urinary system were fragmented, with success rates of 80% to 95% reported (Floratos and de la Rosette, 1999). However, the degree of stone fragmentation with the coumarin laser was related to stone composition; calcium oxalate monohydrate stones were reported to be more difficult to treat and often yielded larger, sharp-edged fragments (Coptcoat et al, 1988a; Grasso and Chalik, 1998). Furthermore, cystine calculi do not absorb the 504-nm laser light and cannot be fragmented with the coumarin pulsed-dye laser. Other limitations of the coumarin pulsed-dye laser include the initial high cost of the device and the cost of toxic disposables (coumarin dye). In addition, the coumarin laser requires about 20 minutes before it is ready to function, and the required eye protection (amber glass) makes visualization of the stone and laser fiber difficult (Segura, 1999).

Technologic advancements eventually led to the development of the holmium:YAG laser. The holmium laser is a solid-state laser system that operates at a wavelength of 2140 nm in the pulsed mode. Pulse duration of the holmium laser ranges from 250 to 350 μs and is substantially longer than the pulse duration in pulsed-dye lasers. The holmium laser is highly absorbed by water, and as tissues are composed mainly of water, the majority of the holmium laser energy is absorbed superficially, which results in superficial cutting or ablation. **The zone of thermal injury associated with laser ablation ranges from 0.5 to 1.0 mm** (Wollin and Denstedt, 1998). The mechanism of stone fragmentation of the holmium:YAG laser is different from that of the pulsed-dye lasers. **The long holmium:YAG pulse duration produces an elongated cavitation bubble that generates only a weak shockwave,** in contradistinction to the strong shockwave produced by short-pulse lasers. Vassar and associates (1999) demonstrated that during holmium lithotripsy, stone fragmentation began before bubble collapse and shockwave production. Furthermore, no stone fragmentation occurred when the fiber was discharged at an incident angle of 90 degrees. Lithotripsy was more efficient for dry stones in air, indicating that the holmium laser requires direct absorption of laser energy. These data as well as the presence of thermal products after holmium irradiation, such as glowing hot stone fragments, indicate that **holmium laser lithotripsy occurs primarily through a photothermal mechanism that causes stone vaporization** (Dushinski and Lingeman, 1998; Wollin and Denstedt, 1998; Vassar et al, 1999).

*Advantages and Disadvantages.* The holmium:YAG laser can transmit its energy through a flexible fiber, which facilitates intracorporeal lithotripsy throughout the entire collecting system. However, compared with EHL, the holmium:YAG laser is safer and more efficient. Whereas EHL may cause injury to the ureter even when the probe is activated several millimeters away from the ureteral wall, the holmium laser may be safely activated at a distance of 0.5 to 1 mm from the ureteral wall (Santa-Cruz et al, 1998). **The ability of the holmium laser to fragment all stones regardless of composition is a clear advantage** over the coumarin pulsed-dye laser. Successful fragmentation of ureteral stones of all compositions has been reported in 91% to 100% of cases, with a mean stone-free rate of 95%. Failures are due mostly to stone migration. Mean perforation and stricture rates are 1.1% and 1.2%, respectively (Table 44–5). During PNL, the holmium laser is most helpful in clearing smaller stones (<2 cm) when the use of flexible instruments is required for access to stones in a calyx remote from the nephrostomy track (Wollin and Denstedt, 1998). The **holmium laser is one of the safest, most**

effective, and most versatile intracorporeal lithotripters. Further advantages of the holmium laser include its production of significantly smaller fragments compared with other lithotrites. Holmium laser lithotripsy results in small stone debris, which is easily irrigated, reducing the need for extraction of the fragments with basket or grasping devices (Teichman et al, 1998a). **The holmium laser produces a weak shockwave, which reduces the likelihood of retropulsion of the stone** or stone fragments compared with EHL or pneumatic lithotrites (Teichman et al, 1998a; Vassar et al, 1999; Sofer and Denstedt, 2000). However, the 365-μm and 550-μm laser fibers will cause significantly more retropulsion than the 200-μm fiber (White et al, 1998). The holmium laser has several distinct operating advantages compared with the coumarin pulsed-dye laser. The required eye protection for the holmium laser does not compromise the ureteroscopic view of the stone or the fiber (Segura, 1999). In fact, the holmium laser properties are such that with use of energy levels applied for stone disease (i.e., less than 15 watts), the operator's cornea would be damaged only if it were positioned at a distance of 10 cm or less from the fiber (Scarpa et al, 1999). The holmium laser machine is more compact than the coumarin laser, requires minimal maintenance, and is ready for use 1 minute after it is turned on.

The major disadvantage of the holmium laser is the initial high cost of the device and the cost of the laser fibers. Elashry and coworkers (1996) noted an advantage of EHL over holmium laser lithotripsy in capital and service contract cost and lithotripter cost per case. However, **the holmium laser has multiple soft tissue applications and can be used to treat patients with benign prostatic hyperplasia, strictures, and urothelial tumors.** In addition, the laser fibers are reusable, so that the effective cost of the holmium laser device and reusable fibers may be lower than that of EHL (Teichman et al, 1998a).

A potential side effect of holmium laser lithotripsy is the production of cyanide when uric acid stones are treated, which has been reported in vitro. However, a **review of clinical experience suggests no significant cyanide toxicity from holmium laser lithotripsy** (Teichman et al, 1998c).

*Technique.* The technique of holmium laser lithotripsy is relatively straightforward and involves placement of the fiber on the stone surface before the laser is activated (Table 44–6). Clear vision is essential at all times to avoid mucosal perforation. After initiation of holmium laser lithotripsy, a short pause is often required because of the "snowstorm effect" created by the scattering of minute stone fragments, which can be cleared by endoscopic irrigation (Scarpa et al, 1999).

| Table 44–5. | **Holmium:YAG Laser Ureteroscopic Lithotripsy of Ureteral Calculi** | | | | |
|---|---|---|---|---|---|
| **Author** | **Patients** | **Perforation (%)** | **Stricture (%)** | **Successful Fragmentation (%)** | **Stone Free (%)** |
| Shroff et al, 1996 | 100 | 3 | 3 | 100 | 87 |
| Gould, 1998 | 127 | 0 | 0 | N/A | 97 |
| Devarajan et al, 1998 | 265 | 4 | 3 | 100 | 93 |
| Yip et al, 1998 | 69 | 0 | 1.4 | 91 | N/A |
| Biyani et al, 1998 | 48 | 2 | N/A | 100 | 98 |
| Grasso and Chalik, 1998 | 109 | 0 | 0 | 100 | 100 |
| Scarpa et al, 1999 | 150 | 0 | 0 | 92.6 | 92.6 |
| Sofer and Denstedt, 2000 | 598 | 0.1 | 1.1 | 97 | 97 |
| **Weighted average** | **1466** | **1.1** | **1.2** | **97.3** | **95.3** |

| Table 44–6. Holmium Laser Lithotripsy Points of Technique |
| --- |
| *Do* |
| Keep the fiber tip in view at all times. |
| Start at low settings and increase only as necessary. |
| Work from the inside of the stone outward. |
| Keep the fiber tip at least 2 mm from the urothelium. |
| *Don't* |
| Do not have one person controlling the fiber and another the foot pedal. |
| Do not discharge the laser fiber inside the working channel or on guide wires and baskets. |
| Do not pass the fiber tip through the back wall of stones. |
| Do not get impatient—holmium:YAG laser lithotripsy is not necessarily fast. |

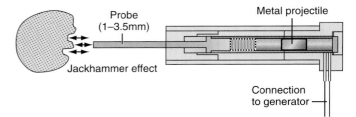

**Figure 44–6.** Schematic illustration of the LithoClast (Electromedical Systems, Kaufering, Germany) handpiece mechanism. An oscillating pellet provides ballistic energy to the probe, resulting in a jackhammer-like effect on calculi. (Courtesy of Dr. John Denstedt.)

Caution must be exercised in operating the holmium laser near a guide wire or a basket as **the holmium laser is capable of cutting through metal** (Freiha et al, 1997). Furthermore, the laser fiber should extend at least 2 mm beyond the tip of the endoscope to avoid destroying the lens system or the working channel of the endoscope. Baskets used to stabilize calculi during laser lithotripsy should be the preformed type and not the type manufactured by bending of the wire, so if they are inadvertently transected by the holmium laser, they will retain the basket shape and will not cause a sharp barbed effect (Grasso and Chalik, 1998).

Holmium laser fibers are available in 200-, 365-, 550-, and 1000-μm diameters as well as end- or side-firing fibers. However, only the 200- and 365-μm-diameter fibers are used for flexible intracorporeal lithotripsy. Teichman and colleagues (1998b) reported that the 550-μm side-firing fiber is more effective than the end-firing fiber during PNL, suggesting that the more nearly normal (perpendicular) laser-to-calculus incident angle provided by the side-firing fiber enhances lithotripsy. However, in treatment of ureteral stones, the end-firing fiber may produce a better angle of attack. **Lithotripsy with the holmium laser depends on the pulse energy output and the diameter of the optical delivery fiber, suggesting that lithotripsy efficiency correlates with energy density** (Vassar et al, 1998). Energy density increases with decreasing fiber diameter, although Calvano and associates (1999) demonstrated, in vitro, that peak lithotripsy occurred with 365- and 550-μm fibers, whereas the 200-μm fiber can act as a fine drill, which is less effective. Compared with some of the soft tissue applications of the holmium laser, the power used for stone fragmentation is considerably lower. In general, pulse energies of 0.6 to 1.2 J and pulse rates of 5 to 15 Hz are used (Wollin and Denstedt, 1998; Spore et al, 1999). Because high-pulse energy narrows the safety margin and may increase stone retropulsion as well as fiber damage, **it is recommended that treatment be commenced with low-pulse energy (e.g., 0.6 J) with a pulse rate of 6 Hz and that pulse frequency be increased (in preference to increasing pulse energy) as needed to speed fragmentation** (Spore et al, 1999). To maximize lithotripsy efficiency, the treating physician should move the laser fiber over the stone surface in a "painting" fashion, vaporizing the stone rather than fragmenting it, and avoid drilling into the stone, fracturing the fiber tip, or drilling past the stone, damaging the urothelium (Segura, 1999). The laser

fiber should be kept at least 1 mm from the urothelium, and lithotripsy should proceed until the stone fragments are small enough to be passed spontaneously or can be safely retrieved with a basket or grasping device.

### Rigid Lithotripters

**Ballistic Lithotripsy.** Ballistic lithotripsy relies on energy generated by the movement of a projectile (Fig. 44–6). The initial movement of the projectile can be induced by a variety of stimuli, but once the projectile is in contact with another object, the ballistic energy is transferred to the object. Flexible objects preserve the momentum of the energy, but inflexible objects, such as a stone, fragment on impact (a "jackhammer" effect).

The Swiss LithoClast, introduced in the early 1990s, was the first ballistic lithotrite. The metal projectile in the handpiece of the LithoClast is propelled by measured bursts of compressed air against the head of a metal probe at a frequency of 12 cycles per second. The probe tip is placed against the stone, and the LithoClast is activated by a foot pedal (Denstedt et al, 1992). In the mid-1990s, the electrokinetic lithotripter was introduced (Menezes et al, 2000). The electrokinetic lithotripter consists of a rheostat and a handset containing an electric coil that generates an electromagnetic field, which then vibrates the probe at 15 to 30 cycles per second. Whereas the LithoClast is connected to the hospital central air supply or to a compressed air tank, the electrokinetic lithotripter requires electrical power. In both instruments, the discharged probe is brought back into its former position by a rubber bushing around the base of the probe (Vorreuther et al, 1998). Studies comparing the LithoClast and the electrokinetic lithotripter, using the same stone fragmentation mechanism, showed no significant difference in stone fragmentation, proximal stone migration, and safety margin. However, the handpiece of the electrokinetic lithotripter is heavier than that of the LithoClast (Vorreuther et al, 1998; Menezes et al, 2000). Probes for the ballistic lithotrites range from 0.8 to 2.5 mm.

Two potential improvements to the ballistic lithotripter have been introduced. A suction device connecting to the LithoClast probe allows evacuation of stone particles, and a flexible nickel-titanium (nitinol) probe allows use of the LithoClast through a flexible ureteroscope (Tawfiek et al, 1997; Delvecchio et al, 2000).

***Advantages and Disadvantages.*** **The ballistic lithotrites provide an effective means for stone fragmentation in the entire urinary tract, with a wide margin of safety.** Successful

**Table 44–7. Ureteroscopic Ballistic Lithotripsy**

| Author | Patients | Stone Migration (%) | Ureteral Perforation (%) | Successful Fragmentation with Ballistic Device Only (%) |
|--------|----------|---------------------|--------------------------|----------------------------------------------------------|
| Hofbauer et al, 1995 | 38 | 14.7 | 2.6 | 89.5 |
| Oktay et al, 1996 | 92 | 2.1 | 0 | 95 |
| Murthy et al, 1997 | 122 | 1.6 | 0 | 93.4 |
| Leidi et al, 1997 | 49 | 9.3 | 0 | 90.7 |
| Knispel et al, 1998 | 143 | 12.5 | 3.5 | 73.7 |
| Kok et al, 1998 | 74 | 2.7 | 0 | 89.7 |
| Keeley et al, 1999 | 121 | 12 | 1.6 | 96.5 |
| Menezes et al, 2000 | 46 | 17.3 | 0 | 87.0 |
| Delvecchio et al, 2000 | 21 | 4.7 | 0 | 100 |
| Aghamir et al, 2003 | 340 | 5.5 | 0.3 | 88.7 |
| **Weighted average** | **1046** | **7.3** | **0.8** | **89.0** |

fragmentation of ureteral stones of all compositions has been reported in 73% to 100% of cases (Table 44–7), a success rate similar to that of EHL. The lower success rate of 73.7% reported by Knispel and associates (1998) suggests reduced efficiency of the LithoClast when it is applied through the deflected working channel (30 degrees) of the 6.9 French semirigid ureteroscope. As well, a significant decrease in the maximum tip displacement and velocity of the LithoClast 0.89-mm flexible probe occurs when it is used through a flexible ureteroscope deflected more than 24 degrees (Zhu et al, 2000). Grocela and Dretler (1997) also reported that for the current ballistic devices, **bowing of the probe during lithotripsy results in significant power loss.** Ballistic devices may be especially advantageous when large or hard stones are encountered during PNL or endoscopic lithotripsy of bladder calculi. In contrast to ureteral stones, **kidney stones are easily "pinned down" against the urothelium during ballistic lithotripsy, allowing a rapid and more efficient fragmentation method than ultrasonic lithotripsy.** Once the bulk of the calculus is fragmented, lithotripsy can be completed with the ultrasonic lithotripter, which can also aspirate minute stone fragments (Denstedt, 1993; Teh et al, 1998; Yavascaoglu et al, 1999). Compared with EHL, ultrasonic lithotripsy, and laser lithotripsy, ballistic devices have a significantly lower risk of ureteral perforation (Piergiovanni et al, 1994). In an animal model, despite 6 minutes of activation in direct contact with the ureteral wall, a ballistic lithotripter was unable to cause perforation (Santa-Cruz et al, 1998). The average risk of ureteral perforation during ureteroscopic ballistic lithotripsy is less than 1%. Furthermore, because no heat is produced during lithotripsy, the risk of thermal injury to the urothelium is eliminated.

One of the advantages of ballistic lithotrites is their relatively low cost and low maintenance. Although the devices are more expensive than EHL, there are no disposable costs and the probes have an extremely long life span (Hofbauer et al, 1995).

Disadvantages of ballistic devices include the rigid nature of the technology, which requires ureteroscopes or nephroscopes with straight working channels. In addition, **ballistic lithotripsy is associated with a relatively high rate of stone retropulsion,** reported in 2% to 17% of ureteral stone treatments. Often, failure to fragment a stone is related to an inability to trap a ureteral stone in a capacious ureter (Denstedt et al, 1992). The migration rate depends on the initial stone location; there is a higher chance of stone migration for proximal ureteral stones compared with distal ureteral stones (Knispel et al, 1998). Limited data are available on the beneficial effects of suction devices, such as the LithoVac, in limiting stone migration. Delvecchio and colleagues (2000) reported the use of the 0.8-mm pneumatic lithotripsy probe placed through a 4.8 French hollow LithoVac suction probe in 21 patients with ureteral stones. Overall stone-free rate at 3 months was 95%, and the suction device reportedly facilitated lithotripsy by preventing stone migration and maintaining a clear endoscopic view.

Teichman and associates (1998a) reported that fragments larger than 4 mm are produced by all types of endoscopic lithotrites, with the exception of the holmium:YAG laser. Fragmenting a stone into pieces smaller than 4 mm with a ballistic lithotripter can be challenging, especially a hard stone in a dilated ureter. Fragments larger than 4 mm are associated with a higher rate of repeated ureteroscopy and therefore should be removed with baskets or stone graspers during the initial procedure (Keeley et al, 1999c).

*Technique.* Like other lithotrites, the ballistic lithotripter should be activated only when there is a clear view of the stone and the probe position can be identified. Fixation of the stone is rarely difficult in the kidney or the bladder but may be a problem in the ureter. Fixation of ureteral stones with a basket or proximal placement of a ureteral occlusion balloon is sometimes necessary. The goal of ballistic lithotripsy in the ureter is to generate fragments that are small enough to permit spontaneous passage (<2 mm). However, more often, larger fragments have to be removed with a basket or grasping device. The relatively atraumatic nature of ballistic lithotripsy may allow the avoidance of stent placement after ureteroscopy. Tan and colleagues (1998) reported the use of stent in only 9 of 68 patients undergoing ballistic lithotripsy. In this series, difficult ureteral access and severe edema and trauma at the site of stone impaction were indications for stent placement.

**Ultrasonic Lithotripsy.** Mulvaney first reported the use of ultrasound vibrations to break renal calculi in 1953. Since then, ultrasonic lithotripsy has become a commonly used modality for the treatment of renal calculi during PNL as well as for the fragmentation of bladder and ureteral stones. The ultrasound probe works by applying electrical energy to excite a piezoceramic plate in the ultrasound transducer (Fig. 44–7). The plate resonates at a specific frequency and generates

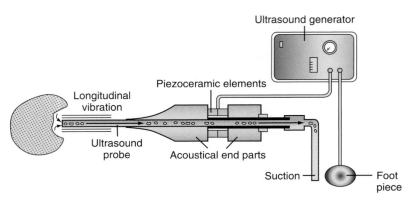

**Figure 44–7.** Ultrasound lithotripsy generator and hand-piece.

ultrasonic waves at a frequency of approximately 23,000 to 25,000 Hz. At operating frequencies, there is no audible sound, although 98 dB of ultrasonic inaudible noise levels have been measured (Segura and LeRoy, 1984).

Ultrasound energy is transformed into longitudinal and transverse vibrations of the hollow steel probe, which then transmits the energy to the calculus. The probe tip causes the stone to resonate at high frequency and to break; but when the probe is placed on compliant tissue, such as urothelium, damage is minimal because the tissue does not resonate with the vibrational energy (Grocela and Dretler, 1997). Although some heat may develop at the end of the probe during lithotripsy, with an irrigation rate of 30 mL per minute, the temperature increase at the tip of the probe can be reduced to a maximum of 1.4° C (Marberger, 1983). Because irrigation may be limited during ureteroscopy, **ultrasonic lithotripsy is more efficient during PNL owing to the greater flow of irrigant through the larger diameter ultrasonic probes that can be used.** The ultrasonic lithotripter system is connected to suction so that debris from the stone is removed continuously with the irrigating fluid during lithotripsy. In addition, the flow of fluid through the hollow probe serves to cool the instrument. Heating of the ultrasound transducer should alert the surgeon to possible occlusion in the probe lumen, an occurrence more commonly encountered with small-diameter probes that are used in the ureter. Although many manufacturers provide an integrated power and suction foot switch for the ultrasonic unit, wall suction with intermittent clamping of the suction tubing by an assistant is a simple and inexpensive alternative. In general, suction is applied only when the ultrasonic lithotripter is activated, and suction pressures in the range of 60 to 80 cm $H_2O$ are sufficient to maintain adequate flow of irrigant during lithotripsy. Higher suction pressures tend to draw air bubbles into the system, impeding vision. Ultrasonic probes are available at sizes ranging from 2.5 to 12 French. The 2.5 French probe is solid and contains no hollow center for suction. Therefore, when it is used in the ureter, heat dissipation is slow. Bending the probe results in energy loss at the convexity of the bend, with the energy being transformed to heat (Marberger, 1983).

Stones vary in their susceptibility to destruction with ultrasound. Although the chemical composition of the stone influences the time required for complete disintegration (cystine, calcium oxalate monohydrate, and uric acid being the most resistant to fragmentation), the size, density, and surface structure of the calculus appear to be more important. Smaller stones are more rapidly destroyed, as are rough stones.

Smooth-surfaced large stones may be more difficult to fragment (Marberger, 1983; Segura and LeRoy, 1984).

Auge and associates (2002a) have reported on a new combination intracorporeal lithotripter that incorporates ballistic lithotripsy and ultrasonic lithotripsy modalities (LithoClast Ultra). In their in vitro study of this device, it was found to more efficiently fragment and clear phantom stones compared with a standard ultrasonic or ballistic device. These findings were confirmed in a subsequent in vitro study by Kuo and associates (2004).

***Advantages and Disadvantages.*** The major advantage of ultrasonic lithotripsy is the efficient combination of stone fragmentation and simultaneous fragment removal. Fragments smaller than 2 mm are aspirated through the hollow lithotrite along with the irrigation fluid. Larger fragments may be removed with forceps or baskets. The efficiency of this technique coupled with the minimal risk of serious tissue damage has made this technology popular. Ultrasonic lithotripsy is often the first modality used for stone fragmentation during PNL.

However, the rigid nature of ultrasonic probes and their small diameter limit the appeal of this technology in treatment of ureteral stones. A ureteroscope with a straight working channel is required. Furthermore, a relatively large 5 French working channel is needed to accommodate the 4.5 French hollow probe. However, success rates between 69% and 100% have been reported (Denstedt, 1996; Gur et al, 2004). The technology may be particularly useful for patients with large ureteral stones as well as for those suffering from steinstrasse because removal of stone debris is facilitated. Excellent results have also been reported for distal ureteral stones easily accessible to the rigid ureteroscope (Grocela and Dretler, 1997; Segura, 1999). Chaussy and colleagues (1987) reported a 96.6% complete fragmentation rate in 118 patients with a 2.5 French solid probe that can be used with smaller ureteroscopes, and Fuchs (1988) has reported similar results. However, in a later report, Murthy and associates (1997) compared a group of 25 patients treated by a rigid ureteroscope and the 3 French ultrasonic solid probe with a group of 122 patients treated by the LithoClast ballistic device, and the overall success rate was significantly higher for the LithoClast group than for the ultrasonic group (97.3% versus 84%, respectively).

***Technique.*** When ultrasonic lithotripsy is applied during PNL, the stone should first be trapped between the probe and the urothelium. The application of gentle pressure to the stone enhances fragmentation, but the temptation to push too hard should be avoided as calculi can easily be pushed through the urothelium. The risk of perforation increases with smaller or more ruggedly surfaced stones as the force applied to the stone is transferred to a smaller surface area of the urothelium. The risk of perforation is particularly high in the thin-walled renal pelvis or ureter rather than in a calyx that is backed by renal parenchyma.

When ureteral stones are treated, the ureter may need to be dilated to allow passage of the offset rigid ureteroscope. The ultrasonic probe is passed through the working channel and placed directly on the stone. If necessary, the stone can be engaged in a stone basket to prevent proximal migration. As with other intracorporeal lithotripsy devices, the goal of treatment is either to fragment the stone completely or to generate fragments that are small enough to be extracted or passed spontaneously.

## Conclusion

The current technology of intracorporeal lithotripsy provides the urologist with several effective options, depending on the type of endoscope used (rigid or flexible) and the location and accessibility of the stone. **The holmium laser has become the mainstay of ureterorenoscopic lithotripsy by virtue of its ability to fragment all stones. As well, the use of small-diameter fibers allows access to all areas of the ureter and intrarenal collecting system. However, for patients with complex, large-volume calculi undergoing PNL, the ultrasonic or pneumatic lithotripters will permit more efficient fragmentation of the stone.** When selecting a lithotripter for purchase, the institution must take into account the number and nature of stone-related procedures performed to maximize the utility and cost-effectiveness of the device.

## Extracorporeal Shockwave Lithotripsy

### Methods and Physical Principles of SWL

In extracorporeal SWL, shockwaves are generated by a source external to the patient's body and are then propagated into the body and focused on a kidney stone. **The uniqueness of this device is in its exploitation of shockwave focusing. Relatively weak, nonintrusive waves are generated externally and transmitted through the body. The shockwaves build to sufficient strength only at the target, where they generate enough force to fragment a stone.**

When energy is deposited rapidly into a fluid, a shockwave invariably results. **Shockwaves are surfaces that divide material ahead, not yet affected by the disturbance, from that behind, which has been compressed as a consequence of energy input at the source** (Sturtevant, 1996). These waves move faster than the speed of sound, and the stronger the initial shock, the faster the shockwave moves. Their behavior is characteristic of the propagation of nonlinear waves. Although the shockwaves in lithotripters generate large pressures, they are relatively weak in that they induce only slight compression and deformation of a material.

**Generator Type.** There are three primary types of shockwave generators: electrohydraulic (spark gap), electromagnetic, and piezoelectric.

*Electrohydraulic (Spark Gap) Generator.* In the electrohydraulic shockwave lithotripter (Table 44–8), **a spherically**

**expanding shockwave is generated by an underwater spark discharge** (Cleveland et al, 2000). High voltage is applied to two opposing electrodes positioned about 1 mm apart. The high-voltage spark discharge causes the explosive vaporization of water at the electrode tip. **For the spherically expanding shockwave to be focused onto a calculus, the electrode is placed at one focus (termed F1) of an ellipsoid, and the target (the kidney stone) is placed at the other focus (termed F2).** Figure 44–8 shows a hemiellipsoid reflector and a spark gap typical of those used in the older electrohydraulic machines. This arrangement allows the projection of the majority of the original shockwave energy from the electrode tip to the stone, provided the electrode tip is precisely at F1. The body of the electrode varies in orientation among machines in that it is positioned within the ellipsoid to provide an easy means of replacement as it deteriorates.

**The clear advantage of this generator is its effectiveness in breaking kidney stones** (Lingeman, 1997). **Disadvantages are the substantial pressure fluctuations from shock to shock and a relatively short electrode life.** New longer life electrodes (like the NewTrode by HMT) have been developed to overcome these drawbacks. Another issue to consider is that as the electrode deteriorates, it wears down, and a 1-mm displacement of the electrode tip off of F1 can shift F2 up to 1 cm off of the initial target.

*Electromagnetic Generator.* Whereas the electrohydraulic lithotripter produces focused shockwaves by bouncing spherically expanding shocks off of an ellipsoid reflector, **the electromagnetic (see Table 44–8) generators produce either plane or cylindrical shockwaves.** The plane waves are focused by an acoustic lens (Fig. 44–9); the cylindrical waves are

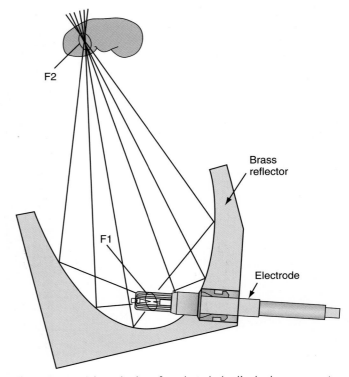

**Figure 44–8.** Schematic view of an electrohydraulic shockwave generator. An electrode is used to generate a shockwave.

**Table 44-8. Mechanical Aspects**

| Company | Machine | Method of Focusing Shockwave | Aperture (cm) | Focal Distance (cm) | Peak Pressure at Focal Point (PVDF) | Focal Zone (W × L, mm) | Electrode Life Span (shockwaves) | Shockwave Coupling |
|---|---|---|---|---|---|---|---|---|
| *Electrohydraulic lithotripters* | | | | | | | | |
| Dornier Medical Systems | HM3* | Ellipsoid reflector | 15.6 | | 220-360 | 15 × 90 | | Water bath |
| | | | 17.2 | 13 | 320-390 | | | Water cushion |
| Medispec Ltd. | Econolith | Ellipsoid reflector | 17.6§ | 13.5 | 760 | 10 × 40 | 2000 | Water cushion |
| Medispec Ltd. | E-2000 | Ellipsoid reflector | 17.6 | 13.5, 15.0 | 760 | 13 × 60 | 3000 | Water cushion |
| Medispec Ltd. | E-3000 | Ellipsoid reflector | 17.6 | 13.5, 15.5 | 910 | 13 × 60 | 3000 | Water cushion |
| HealthTronics | LithoTron | Ellipsoid reflector | 20 | 15 | 530 | 13 × 60 | 8000 | Water cushion |
| HealthTronics | LithoTron Ultra | Ellipsoid reflector | 20 | 15 | 530 | 8 × 38 | 8000 | Water cushion |
| HMT-USA | LithoDiamond | Ellipsoid reflector | 20 | 15 | 580 | 8 × 38 | 20,000 | Coupling water cushion |
| | | | | | | 11 × 96 | | |
| Comair Professor H. Wiksell AB | Lithocut C-3000S† | Ellipsoid reflector | 23 | 15 | 820 | 5 × 16 | approx. 5 sessions | Water cushion |
| Comair Professor H. Wiksell AB | Lithocut C-3000A† | Ellipsoid reflector | 23 | 15 | 200-820 | 3.5 × 12 | approx. 5 sessions | Water cushion |
| Direx Systems Corp. | Tripter X-1 Compact | Ellipsoid reflector | 18.1 | 13.5 | 240-440 | 13 × 48 | 3000 | Water cushion |
| Direx Systems Corp. | Duet | Dual ellipsoid reflectors | 18.1 | 14.2 | 240-480 | 13 × 48 | 3000-12,000 | Dual water cushion |
| Direx Systems Corp. | Nova Ultima† | Rotating ellipsoid reflector | 18.1 | 13.5 | 240-440 | 13 × 48 | 3000-12,000 | Water cushion |
| Medstone International | STS | Ellipsoid reflector | 15 | 15 | 481 | 12 × 90 | 3600 | Water cushion |
| Medstone International | STS-TC | Ellipsoid reflector | 15 | 15 | 481 | 12 × 90 | 3600 | Water cushion |
| ELMED Lithotripsy Systems | Multimed Classic† | Ellipsoid reflector | 17.6 | 13.5 | N/A | 7.5 × 22 | 4500 | Water cushion |
| ELMED Lithotripsy Systems | Complit† | Isocentric movable ellipsoid reflector | 17.6 | 13.5 | N/A | 7.5 × 22 | 4500 | Water cushion |
| EDAP Technomed | Sonolith Praktis | Ellipsoid reflector | 21.9 | 13 | 106 | 25 × 3.6 | 27,000 at 100% | Water cushion |
| EDAP Technomed | Sonolith Vision | Ellipsoid reflector | 21.9 | 13 | 106 | 25 × 3.6 | 27,000 at 20 kV | Water cushion |
| FMD, LLC | Twinheads TH101 | Ellipsoid reflector | 14.7 | 12.7 | 1100 | 15.4 × 15.6 | 3000 | 2 water cushions |
| FMD, LLC | Twinheads TH103 | Ellipsoid reflector | 14.7 | 12.7 | 1100 | 15.4 × 15.6 | 3000 | 2 water cushions |

*Electromagnetic lithotripters*

| Manufacturer | Lithotripter | Focusing | | | | | | Coupling |
|---|---|---|---|---|---|---|---|---|
| Siemens Medical Systems | Lithostar Multiline | Acoustic lens | 17 | 12 | 800 | 5 × 80 | 1 million | Water cushion |
| Siemens Medical Systems | Lithostar Modularis | Acoustic lens | 12.5 | 14 | 570 | 12 × 130 to 13 × 146 | 1.5 million | Water cushion |
| Siemens Medical Systems | Lithostar Modularis Vario† (with Cplus) | Acoustic lens | 12.5 | 14 | 570 | 12 × 130 to 13 × 146 | 1.5 million | Water cushion |
| Siemens Medical Systems | Lithostar Modularis (with Cplus†) Siemens U-11 (Pulso)† New machine presented at AUA, 2005 | Acoustic lens | | 16 | | | | |
| Karl Storz Lithotripsy | Modulith SL20‡ | Parabolic reflector | 30 | 16.5 | 189-1056 | 4.6 × 34 to 2.8 × 37 | 6 million | Water cushion |
| Karl Storz Lithotripsy | Modulith SLX-MX | Parabolic reflector | 30 | 16.5 | 189-1056 | 4.6 × 34 to 2.8 × 37 | 8 million | Water cushion |
| Karl Storz Lithotripsy | Modulith SLX-T | Parabolic reflector | 30 | 16.5 | 189-1056 | 4.6 × 34 to 2.8 × 37 | 8 million | Water cushion |
| Karl Storz Lithotripsy | Modulith SLX-F2 | Parabolic reflector | 30 | 16.5 | 90-160 | 2.0 × 22 to 3.5 × 50 | N/A | Water cushion |
| Dornier MedTech | Compact Delta | Acoustic lens | 14 | 15 | 315-550 | 4.7 × 57 | 1 million | Water cushion |
| Dornier MedTech | Compact Sigma | Acoustic lens | 14 | 15 | 315-550 | 4.7 × 57 | 1 million | Water cushion |
| Dornier MedTech | DoLi S, 140 | Acoustic lens | 14 | 15 | 160-550 | 4.7 × 57 | 1 million | Water cushion |
| Dornier MedTech | DoLi S, 220 | Acoustic lens | 22 | 15 | 288-991 | 2.5 × 41 | 1 million | Water cushion |
| Dornier MedTech | DoLi S, 220-XP‡ | Acoustic lens | 22 | 15 | 200-900 | 3.4 × 46 | 1 million | Water cushion |
| Dornier MedTech | DoLi S, 220-XXP‡ | Acoustic lens | 22 | 15 | 490-900 | 4.1 × 60.5 | 1 million | Water cushion |
| Dornier MedTech | DoLi S II, 140 | Acoustic lens | 14 | 15 | 160-550 | 4.7 × 57 | 1 million | Water cushion |
| Dornier MedTech | DoLi S II, 220 | Acoustic lens | 22 | 15 | 288-991 | 2.5 × 41 | 1 million | Water cushion |
| Dornier MedTech | DoLi S II, 220-XP‡ | Acoustic lens | 22 | 15 | 200-900 | 3.4 × 46 | 1 million | Water cushion |
| Dornier MedTech | DoLi S II, 220-XXP‡ | Acoustic lens | 22 | 15 | 490-900 | 4.1 × 60.5 | 1 million | Water cushion |

*Piezoelectric lithotripters*

| Manufacturer | Lithotripter | Focusing | | | | | | Coupling |
|---|---|---|---|---|---|---|---|---|
| Wolf | P3000† | Concave dish | 26 | 15 | 1320 | 3 × 16 | >5 million | Water cushion |

*No longer manufactured.
†Not approved by the Food and Drug Administration.
‡Not sold in the United States.
§Not interchangeable with Econolith 2000 ellipsoids.

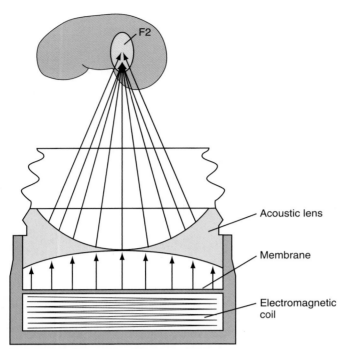

**Figure 44–9.** Schematic view of an electromagnetic shockwave generator that uses an acoustic lens to focus the shockwave. An electromagnetic coil is used to generate the shockwave.

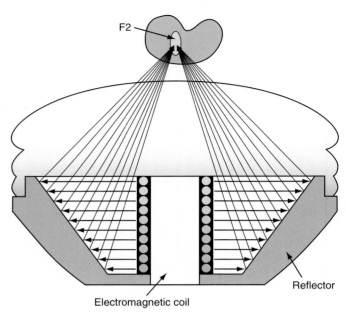

**Figure 44–10.** Schematic view of an electromagnetic shockwave generator that uses a parabolic reflector to focus the shockwave. An electromagnetic coil is used to generate the shockwave.

reflected by a parabolic reflector (Fig. 44–10) and transformed into a spherical wave. The basic design of an electromagnetic generator is simple. Figure 44–9 shows a system that uses a water-filled shock tube containing two conducting cylindrical plates separated by a thin insulating sheet. When an electrical current is sent through one or both of the conductors, a strong magnetic field is produced between the conductors, moving the plate against the water and thereby generating a pressure wave. The electromagnetic force that is generated, termed magnetic pressure, causes a corresponding pressure (shockwave) in the water. The shock front produced is a plane wave that is of the same diameter as the current-carrying plates. **The energy in the shockwave is concentrated onto the target by focusing it with an acoustic lens.** The electromagnetic system that uses a cylindrical source (see Fig. 44–10) also has a coil (cylindrical in shape) surrounded by a cylindrical membrane that is pushed away from the coil by the induction of a magnetic field between the two components. In both systems, the pressure pulse has only one focal point (F2) that is positioned on the target.

**Electromagnetic generators are more controllable and reproducible than electrohydraulic generators because they do not incorporate a variable in their design such as the underwater spark discharge. Other advantages include the introduction of energy into the patient's body over a large skin area, which may cause less pain. In addition, a small focal point can be achieved with high-energy densities, which may increase its effectiveness in breaking stones.** This generator will deliver several hundred thousand shockwaves before servicing, thereby eliminating the need for frequent electrode replacement, which is required with most electrohydraulic machines. **A disadvantage of this design may be that the small focal region of high energy results in an increased**

**rate of subcapsular hematoma formation.** The rate of subcapsular hematoma formation for the Storz Modulith has been suggested to be 3.1 to 3.7% (Dhar et al, 2004). Piper and associates (2001) suggested that perinephric hematomas may occur in up to 12% of patients treated with a DoLi S. In contrast, perinephric hematomas were reported to occur in approximately 0.6% of patients undergoing SWL with the unmodified Dornier HM3 (Chaussy and Schmiedt, 1984; Knapp et al, 1987).

***Piezoelectric Generator.*** **The piezoelectric lithotripter** (see Table 44–8) **also produces plane shockwaves with directly converging shock fronts.** These generators are made of a mosaic of small, polarized, polycrystalline, ceramic elements (barium titanate), each of which can be induced to rapidly expand by the application of a high-voltage pulse (Fig. 44–11). Owing to the limited power of a single piezoelectric element, 300 to 3000 crystals are necessary for the generation of a sufficiently large shock pressure. The piezoelectric elements are usually placed on the inside of a spherical dish to permit convergence of the shock front. The focus of the system is at the geometric center of the spherical dish.

**The advantages of this generator include the focusing accuracy, a long service life, and the possibility of an anesthetic-free treatment because of the relatively low energy density at the skin entry point of the shockwave.** For this reason, piezoelectric lithotripters in general tend to produce less discomfort than do lithotripters with other energy sources. **A major disadvantage of this system is the insufficient power it delivers, which hampers its ability to effectively break renal stones.** The piezoelectric energy sources produce some of the highest peak pressures of any lithotripter, but the actual energy delivered to the stone per shockwave pulse is several orders of magnitude lower than that delivered by an electrohydraulic machine because of the extremely tiny volume of F2.

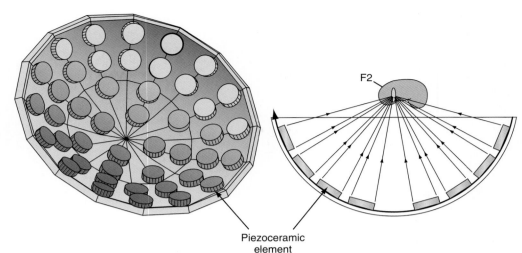

**Figure 44–11.** Schematic view of a piezoelectric shockwave generator. Numerous polarized polycrystalline ceramic elements are positioned on the inside of a spherical dish.

*Other Generators.* Microexplosive generators have also been produced but have not gained widespread acceptance. The explosion of tiny lead azide pellets within a parabolic reflector generates the device's shockwave (Kuwahara et al, 1987). Despite the effectiveness of this type of generator in producing shockwaves, this technology has not met with commercial success because of concerns about the storage and handling of the volatile lead azide pellets. Still other methods of shockwave generation use a laser beam or a multistage light gas gun, but these too have not been well received commercially.

**Imaging Systems.** There are **three basic designs** used by lithotripter manufacturers for stone localization (Table 44–9). They are **ultrasonography alone, fluoroscopy alone, and the combination of ultrasonography and fluoroscopy.**

*Fluoroscopy Alone.* The original Dornier HM3 lithotripter used two x-ray converters arranged at oblique angles to the patient and 90 degrees from each other to localize the stone effectively at F2. To reduce the cost of lithotripters, an adjustable C-arm has been subsequently introduced on many devices. There is presently a remarkable similarity in the fluoroscopic systems used among manufacturers. This appears to be primarily the result of a common theme in the industry to develop multifunctional tables around these machines. The fluoroscopic system typically consists of a high-quality digitized x-ray imaging system mounted on a rotatable C-arm with isocentrically integrated shockwave source. Because the shockwave head can be rotated out of the field of the fluoroscopic system, the table can be used for routine urologic fluoroscopic applications.

The primary advantages of fluoroscopy still include its familiarity to most urologists, the ability to visualize radiopaque calculi throughout the urinary tract, the ability to use iodinated contrast agents to aid in stone localization, and the ability to display anatomic detail. The disadvantages include the exposure of the staff and patient to ionizing radiation, the high maintenance demands of the equipment, and the inability to visualize radiolucent calculi without the use of radiographic contrast agents.

*Ultrasonography Alone.* Ultrasonic localization was initially designed to aid multifunctional lithotripters for treatment of both urinary and biliary stones. It is presently used in several low-cost machines because it is inexpensive to manufacture and to maintain compared with fluoroscopic systems. Another major advantage of this technology is in the treatment of children and infants when one is concerned about the dose of ionizing radiation. In addition, ultrasonography can localize slightly opaque or nonopaque calculi.

Despite its advantages, there are a number of significant disadvantages of ultrasound imaging. Sonographic localization of a kidney stone requires a highly trained operator. To complicate the issue of stone detection is the fact that it is almost impossible to view a kidney stone in areas such as the middle third of the ureter or when there is an indwelling ureteral catheter. Once a stone is fragmented, it is difficult to identify each individual stone piece. Unfortunately, these disadvantages tend to overshadow the advantages of ultrasound imaging.

*Combination of Ultrasonography and Fluoroscopy.* As the demand for interdisciplinary lithotripters has increased, the lithotripsy industry has responded, in some cases combining ultrasonography and fluoroscopy for stone localization. Table 44–9 lists a number of the variations that exist for these two imaging systems. There are clearly advantages to these setups, but each system has a drawback that limits one of the functions of the system.

**Anesthesia.** The approach to anesthesia for lithotripsy has changed considerably since clinical SWL began in 1980. At that time, regional or general anesthesia was used in all instances because the unmodified HM3 device (15.6-cm ellipsoid; 80 nF generator) produced a powerful shockwave and treatment at recommended energy levels caused intolerable pain. Subsequently, urologists and lithotripter manufacturers recognized that the HM3 is considerably more powerful at the recommended energy setting than is necessary for the fragmentation of most renal calculi, an observation that spawned interest in less powerful lithotripters with lessened anesthesia requirements (Marberger et al, 1988; Wilbert et al, 1987). Several researchers have noted that the original HM3 lithotripter without modification produces excellent clinical results when it is used at lower energy settings (Pettersson et al, 1989; Tiselius, 1991; Tolley et al, 1991). In addition, such

**Table 44–9.  Imaging and Financial Aspects**

| Company | Machine | ECG Gating | Endourology Capability | Stone Localization | Portability | Purchase Price | Service Contract | Upgrade Possibility | Upgrade Cost |
|---|---|---|---|---|---|---|---|---|---|
| *Electrohydraulic lithotripters* | | | | | | | | | |
| Dornier Medical Systems | HM3* | Yes | No | X-ray | Semi-trailer | $25,000 used (disassembly and reinstallation: add $55,000) | $45,000 | Digital x-ray | $60,000 |
| Medispec Ltd | Econolith | Optional | Yes | X-ray, portable C-arm, optional US | Yes | $350,000 | $15,000–$21,000 | ECG monitor, endo., C-arm upgrades, computer console | N/A |
| Medispec Ltd | E-2000 | Optional | Yes | X-ray, portable C-arm, optional US | Yes | $380,000 | $15,000–$26,000 | ECG monitor, endo., C-arm upgrades | N/A |
| Medispec Ltd | E-3000 | Optional | Yes | X-ray, portable C-arm, optional US | Yes | $399,000 | $15,000–$26,000 | ECG monitor, 4- or 5-axis endourology table, console, C-arm upgrades | N/A |
| HealthTronics | LithoTron | Optional | Yes | X-ray, portable C-arm, optional US | Yes | $350,000–$400,000 | $48,000 | No | N/A |
| HealthTronics | LithoTron Ultra | Optional | Yes | X-ray, optional US | No | $700,000 | $65,000 | N/A | N/A |
| HMT-USA | LithoDiamond | Optional | Yes | X-ray, optional US | Yes | $400,000 | N/A | N/A | N/A |
| Comair Professor H. Wiksell AB | Lithocut C-3000S† | Yes/no | Yes | X-ray, optional US | Yes | $250,000 | Subunit exchange system | N/A | N/A |
| Comair Professor H. Wiksell AB | Lithocut C-3000A† | Yes/no | Yes | X-ray, optional US | Yes | $200,000 | Subunit exchange system | N/A | N/A |
| Direx Systems Corp. | Tripter X-1 Compact | Yes | Yes | X-ray, portable C-arm | Yes | $395,000 | $28,000–$35,000 | Triple generator, non-ECG gating | N/A |
| Direx Systems Corp. | Duet | Yes | Yes | X-ray, portable C-arm, optional US | Yes | $435,000 | $35,000 | US | N/A |
| Direx Systems Corp. | Nova Ultima† | Yes | Yes | X-ray, portable C-arm, optional US | Yes | N/A | N/A | Triple generator | N/A |
| Medstone International | STS | Yes | Yes | Digital x-ray, US | No | $500,000 | $25,000–$80,000 | Yes | Variable |
| Medstone International | STS-TC | Yes | Yes | Digital x-ray, US | Yes | $433,350 | $20,000–$55,000 | Yes | $49,500–$54,000 |
| ELMED Lithotripsy Systems | Multimed Classic† | Yes | Yes | X-ray, US | Yes | $55,000–$135,000 | $25,000 | Computer-controlled US localization | $15,000 |
| ELMED Lithotripsy Systems | Complit† | Yes | Yes | X-ray, US | Yes | $65,000–$145,000 | $25,000 | Computer-controlled US localization | $15,000 |
| EDAP Technomed | Sonolith Praktis | Optional | Yes | X-ray and US | Yes | $400,000 | $35,000 | Yes | N/A |
| EDAP Technomed | Sonolith Vision | Optional | Yes | X-ray and US | Yes | $500,000 | $50,000 | Yes | N/A |
| FMD, LLC | Twinheads TH101 | Yes | Yes | Fluoroscopy, integrated U-arm | Semiportable | $540,000 | $50,000 | US, laser printer, DICOM 3 | $9,800–$56,000 |
| FMD, LLC | Twinheads TH103 | Yes | Yes | Works with stand-alone C-arm | Semiportable | $495,000 | $40,000 | US, laser printer, DICOM 3 | $9,800–$56,000 |
| *Electromagnetic lithotripters* | | | | | | | | | |
| Siemens Medical Systems | Lithostar Multiline | Yes | Yes | X-ray, in-line US | No | $650,000 | N/A | N/A | N/A |
| Siemens Medical Systems | Lithostar Modularis (with Cplus) | Yes | Yes | X-ray, coaxial US | Yes | $495,000 | N/A | N/A | N/A |

| | | | | | | | | | |
|---|---|---|---|---|---|---|---|---|---|
| Siemens Medical Systems | Lithostar Modularis Vario (with Cplus) | Yes | Yes | X-ray, coaxial US | Yes | $455,000 | N/A | N/A | NA |
| Siemens Medical Systems | Siemens U-11 (Pulso)† New machine presented at AUA, 2005 | | Yes | | | | | | |
| Karl Storz Lithotripsy | Modulith SL20 | No | Yes | In-line x-ray and US | No | $295,000 used (disassembly and reinstallation: add $20,000) | $69,000 | No | N/A |
| Karl Storz Lithotripsy | Modulith SLX-MX | No | Yes | In-line x-ray and US | No | $695,000 | $80,000 | No | N/A |
| Karl Storz Lithotripsy | Modulith SLX-T | No | Yes | In-line x-ray and US | Yes | $525,000 | $62,500 | No | N/A |
| Karl Storz Lithotripsy | Modulith SLX-F2 | No | Yes | In-line x-ray and US | N/A | N/A | N/A | N/A | N/A |
| Dornier MedTech | Compact Delta | Optional | Yes | X-ray, US optional, isocentric fluoroscopy | Yes | $430,000 | $52,000 | US, laser printer, DICOM 3 | $50,000 / $10,000 / $25,000 |
| Dornier MedTech | Compact Sigma | Optional | Yes | X-ray, US optional, mobile C-arm | Yes | $440,000 | $52,000 | US, laser printer, DICOM 3 | $50,000 / $10,000 / $7,000 |
| Dornier MedTech | DoLi S, 140 | Optional | Yes | X-ray, US optional, isocentric fluoroscopy | No | $695,000 | $73,500 | US, laser printer, DICOM 3 | $50,000 / $10,000 / $25,000 |
| Dornier MedTech | DoLi S, 220 | Optional | Yes | X-ray, US optional, isocentric fluoroscopy | No | $695,000 | $73,500 | US, laser printer, DICOM 3 | $50,000 / $10,000 / $25,000 |
| Dornier MedTech | DoLi S, 220-XP‡ | Optional | Yes | X-ray, US optional, isocentric fluoroscopy | No | N/A | N/A | US, laser printer, DICOM 3 | N/A |
| Dornier MedTech | DoLi S, 220-XXP‡ | Optional | Yes | X-ray, US optional, isocentric fluoroscopy | No | N/A | N/A | N/A | N/A |
| Dornier MedTech | DoLi S II, 140 | Optional | Yes | X-ray, US optional, isocentric fluoroscopy | No | $695,000 | $73,500 | US DICOM 3 included | $50,000 |
| Dornier MedTech | DoLi S II, 220 | Optional | Yes | X-ray, US optional, isocentric fluoroscopy | No | $695,000 | $73,500 | US DICOM 3 included | $50,000 |
| Dornier MedTech | DoLi S II, 220-XP‡ | Optional | Yes | X-ray, US optional, isocentric fluoroscopy | No | N/A | N/A | US DICOM 3 included | N/A |
| Dornier MedTech | DoLi S II, 220-XXP‡ | Optional | Yes | X-ray, US optional, isocentric fluoroscopy | No | N/A (disassembly and reinstallation: add $53,000) | N/A | US DICOM 3 included | N/A |
| *Piezoelectric lithotripters* | | | | | | | | | |
| Wolf | P3000† | No | Yes | Coaxial x-ray and US | Yes | N/A | N/A | Yes | N/A |

ECG, electrocardiographic; US, ultrasonography.
*No longer manufactured.
†Not approved by the Food and Drug Administration.
‡Not sold in the United States.

settings create a smaller lesion at F2 in experimental animals (Connors et al, 2000).

**The discomfort experienced during SWL is related directly to the energy density of the shockwave as it passes through the skin as well as the size of the focal point.** The last decade has produced many new and useful anesthetic techniques adaptable to SWL that were not available at the time SWL was introduced:

- Short-acting parenteral sedative-narcotics: alfentanil, midazolam, propofol
- Topical agents: EMLA cream

Short-acting agents, such as the narcotic alfentanil and the sedative-hypnotics midazolam and propofol, have been used in various combinations to allow most SWL treatments with any lithotripter (including the unmodified Dornier HM3) to be accomplished comfortably for the patient without the need for general or regional anesthesia, if the patient so desires. For this reason, anesthesia considerations have not been included in the technical data on lithotripters in Tables 44-8 and 44-9. Monk and associates (1991) compared two sedative-analgesic techniques (midazolam-alfentanil versus fentanyl-propofol) and found that both techniques provided adequate anesthesia for SWL with use of an unmodified Dornier HM3. Anesthesia and recovery times were significantly shorter than those recorded for epidural anesthesia techniques. These findings have been confirmed by others (Nelson et al, 2001; Burmeister et al, 2002; Ozcan et al, 2002).

Another approach to minimize anesthesia requirements during SWL has been the use of topical agents. EMLA cream, a eutectic mixture of lidocaine and prilocaine, has been shown significantly to reduce anesthesia requirements during SWL (Pettersson et al, 1989; Tiselius, 1989; Basar et al, 2003). A topical agent, EMLA cream should be applied at least 45 minutes before SWL. The combination of topical agents and short-acting intravenous agents is likely to minimize the amount of these agents required and to shorten recovery times (Monk et al, 1991).

Not all patients are well served by treatment with a low-energy SWL technique, and therefore a variety of factors need to be considered in choosing the preferred approach for SWL. Calculi composed of cystine, calcium oxalate monohydrate, or brushite are known to be resistant to fragmentation; if their presence is anticipated, delivery of higher levels of shockwave energy with attendant increased anesthesia requirements should be expected (Dretler, 1988; Klee et al, 1991). Thin patients have more pain during SWL because the converging shockwave is more concentrated at the point of skin penetration. Children and extremely anxious individuals may be served best by general anesthesia. If a lengthy treatment session is anticipated (i.e., bilateral SWL or treatment of ureteral and renal stones), the larger amount of topical and intravenous agents required lessens their appeal.

One important observation regarding the issue of general anesthesia versus intravenous sedation was reported by Sorensen and colleagues (2002). In a comparison of patients treated with the DoLi 50 lithotripter, those patients who received general anesthesia experienced a significantly greater stone-free rate than did those patients who underwent intravenous sedation. One possible explanation for this finding is the more controlled respiratory excursion that is conferred by the general anesthetic.

## Lithotripter Comparisons

Information about currently available extracorporeal shockwave lithotripters marketed by several manufacturers is presented in Tables 44-8 and 44-9. Lithotripters that were not commercially viable and are no longer produced have not been included (i.e., Diasonics Therasonic LTS, Northgate SD3, and Yachioda microexplosion lithotripter). Furthermore, although there are a large number of Chinese lithotripters, no reliable technical or clinical information is available and so these devices were not included.

Although there was a surge in publications in the urologic literature in the mid-1980s addressing lithotripsy, few if any appropriately designed comparative trials of lithotripters have been published. In addition, **there are no validated standards within the lithotripsy industry regarding a method of quantification of the power and efficiency of lithotripters, a problem further compounded by a lack of knowledge of the number of shockwaves that can be safely administered to a kidney during any single SWL session with any lithotripter.** Although there is a general consensus that re-treatment rates are an appropriate indicator of lithotripter effectiveness, the lack of clinical agreement about the appropriate outcome of lithotripsy (i.e., stone free versus residual fragments of various size) further hampers comparisons of lithotripters (Tolley et al, 1991).

Only a small part of the literature published to date on the outcomes of SWL presents data that are stratified sufficiently to permit a meaningful comparative analysis, but there is a significant amount of reasonably well stratified data regarding two early lithotripters, the unmodified Dornier HM3 and the Siemens Lithostar (Lingeman et al, 1989b; Tolley et al, 1991). The HM3 and Lithostar were compared by integration of stone-free rates stratified by size into a regression model (Fig. 44-12). The stone-free rate achieved with the unmodified HM3 lithotripter was significantly better than that with the less powerful Lithostar. To date, despite the proliferation of lithotripters and the variety of solutions devised for stone targeting and shockwave delivery, no other lithotripter system has convincingly equaled or surpassed the results produced by the unmodified Dornier HM3 device. That the most effective

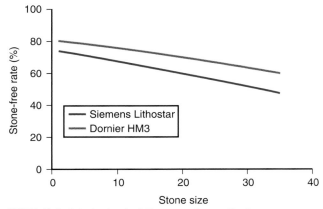

NOTE: Calculated using logistic regression methods.

**Figure 44–12.** Comparison of stone-free rates stratified by stone size for the Dornier HM3 and the Siemens Lithostar.

## Table 44–10.  Shockwave Lithotripsy Outcomes

| Citation | Device | No. of Patients | Mean Stone Size | Stone Free (%) |
|----------|--------|-----------------|-----------------|----------------|
| Albala et al, 2005 | Medstone STS-T | 326 | 8.2 mm | 53 |
| Jain et al, 2004 | LithoTron | 298 | 8 mm | 66 |
| Johnson et al, 2003 | DoLi S | 176 | 9.7 mm | 73 |
| Portis et al, 2003 | HM3 | 38 | 9.6 mm | 79 |
| | LithoTron | 38 | 9.9 mm | 58 |
| Sorensen et al, 2002 | DoLi U50 | 42 with IV sedation | <10 mm (8.1) | 55 |
| | | 89 with general anesthesia | <10 mm (7.3) | 88 |
| | | 18 with IV sedation | 11-20 mm (15.0) | 56 |
| | | 37 with general anesthesia | 11-20 mm (14.4) | 84 |
| Matin et al, 2001 | MFL 5000 | 356 | 103 mm$^2$ | 77 |
| | Modulith SLX | 173 | 71 mm$^2$ | 67 |
| Fallon et al, 2000 | MFL 5000 | 105 | 70% < 10 mm | 47 |

Weighted average stone-free outcome: 66.7%

lithotripter was invented first is a remarkable achievement for Dornier. In general, the less powerful lithotripters with smaller focal points result in lower stone-free rates or higher re-treatment rates (Table 44–10).

Several comparative trials of lithotripters have been reported, most of which involve studies of second-generation machines (the modified HM3 is considered a second-generation device). Tan and associates (1991) from Singapore reported a small nonrandomized series comparing an unmodified Dornier HM3 with an EDAP LT.01 and Sonolith 2000 (an earlier version of the Sonolith 3000) in which they found 3-month stone-free rates of 66%, 67%, and 58%, respectively, with re-treatment rates of 4%, 42%, and 26%, respectively. **This is the only direct (albeit nonrandomized) trial reported in the literature noting equivalent stone-free rates between the unmodified Dornier HM3 and second-generation lithotripters.** In the only other study comparing first- and second-generation lithotripters, Sofras and associates (1991) found that the unmodified Dornier HM3 achieved significantly higher stone-free rates overall than did the EDAP LT.01. However, for small renal calculi (<1 cm), the machines achieved equivalent stone-free rates. The re-treatment rates and running costs were higher for the EDAP LT.01. No other comparative trials have been reported that included an unmodified HM3 device.

Rassweiler and colleagues (1989) compared a modified (low-pressure generator and small F2) Dornier HM3 and Wolf Piezolith 2200 (predecessor of the Piezolith 2300). Stone-free rates were not reported, but stone fragmentation rates were equivalent. Re-treatment was necessary in 12% of the modified Dornier HM3 patients and 54% of the Wolf Piezolith cases. In addition, this was one of the first reports to note problems with sonographic stone localization of ureteral calculi; 5% of ureteral stones failed to be localized with ultrasound. Siebold and associates (1988) also compared a modified Dornier HM3 with another Dornier device, the MPL 9000, once again noting problems with ultrasound for stone localization and assessment of stone fragmentation. Fragmentation rates were lower for the MPL 9000 than for the modified HM3 (73% versus 95% successful disintegration). In addition, 18% of patients initially starting therapy with the MPL 9000 eventually crossed over to complete their lithotripsy therapy in the modified HM3 device, whereas only

3% of patients being treated with the modified HM3 crossed over to the MPL 9000. The Dornier HM4 lithotripter with a low-pressure generator was compared with the Dornier MPL 9000 in a study by Tailly (1990). Tailly noted that the MPL 9000 appeared to be a more efficient machine, with a slightly lower re-treatment rate than the modified Dornier HM4 (1.11 versus 1.17), but he also noted problems with sonographic stone localization for both ureteral stones and obese patients. The MPL 9000 device was initially produced only with ultrasound imaging (as it was intended primarily for biliary applications) but subsequently became available with an integrated x-ray system.

Bierkens and associates (1992) examined five second-generation lithotripters (Siemens Lithostar, Dornier HM4, Wolf Piezolith 2300, Direx Tripter X-1, and Breakstone) in a multicenter trial involving more than 1800 patients. The overall stone-free rate was only 45% with a re-treatment rate of 20%. There were no significant differences in the stone-free rates among the various machines (Siemens Lithostar, 49%; Dornier HM4, 53%; Wolf Piezolith 2300, 45%; Direx Tripter X-1, 50%; Breakstone, 60%). Re-treatment rates were higher with the Wolf Piezolith 2300 than with the other lithotripters. A prospective randomized trial comparing the modified Dornier HM3 with the Dornier MFL 5000 was reported by Chan and colleagues (1995). Although more patients with larger stones were treated with the HM3, overall stone-free results were equivalent for the two machines. Of further interest, they noted that the stone-free rate achieved in the lower pole for the modified HM3 was significantly better than that achieved by the MFL 5000 (80% versus 56%; $P = .05$). Chan's group also noted that treatment times were significantly shorter with the unmodified HM3 device and concluded that the MFL 5000 lithotripter offered no significant clinical advantage over the modified HM3 in terms of lithotripsy efficacy, although the multifunctional table did provide more versatility for stone treatment (i.e., ureteral stones). Since these two lithotripters use the same ellipsoid and shockwave generator, this study supports the observation of others that a water bath is the ideal mechanism for transmitting shockwave energy into the body (Rassweiler et al, 1992).

**It is now recognized that SWL inflicts a trauma similar to a renal contusion, which occasionally can result in adverse clinical sequelae.** Potential concerns about the long-term effects of lithotripsy with the unmodified Dornier HM3 device may have been one motivating factor in the trend within the lithotripsy industry toward, at first, lower power but eventually higher power lithotripters with smaller focal points, with the goal that the efficacy of lithotripsy could be maintained while producing fewer deleterious effects on renal tissue (Fig. 44–13). Unfortunately, **the newer lithotripters are less efficacious than the original Dornier device, and no published information is available to suggest that newer lithotripters produce fewer adverse effects for equivalent degrees of efficacy.** Fortunately, although further study is necessary to fully characterize the bioeffects of SWL, early concerns about a markedly adverse long-term effect of lithotripsy to all patients receiving this form of treatment have not materialized, thereby eliminating any reason to move away from the concept of a powerful lithotripter with a large F2 such as the unmodified Dornier HM3 (Williams et al, 1988; Lingeman et al, 1990). The amount of lithotripsy that can be safely tolerated by a kidney during a single session of SWL remains to be determined for any of the currently available lithotripters. This is an unfortunate circumstance and one that should be addressed by the development of appropriate animal models allowing the proper dose of lithotripsy to be established for each device (Evan et al, 1991, 1998). **On the positive side, research in lithotripsy has provided a much better understanding of the mechanisms of shockwave action in SWL and has made progress in defining the characteristics of renal injury and the consequences of shockwave trauma. This research has also been an important stimulus to the effort to improve lithotripters and has suggested new strategies that may improve outcomes of patients.**

## Mechanisms of Stone Comminution

**Present knowledge in the field of SWL suggests that comminution of a renal stone in a lithotripter field is the consequence of failure of the stone material due to the mechanical stresses produced either directly by the incident shockwave or indirectly by the collapse of cavitation bubbles.** These events could be occurring simultaneously or separately at the surface of the stone or within the interior of the stone (Fig. 44–14). Several potential mechanisms for SWL stone breakage have been described: spall fracture, squeezing, shear stress, superfocusing, acoustic cavitation, and dynamic fatigue.

Before each of these mechanisms is discussed, consideration of the typical shockwave profile is required. A typical pressure pulse generated by an electrohydraulic shockwave lithotripter is shown in Figure 44–15. It involves **an initial short and steep compressive front with pressures of about 40 MPa that is followed by a longer, lower amplitude negative (tensile) pressure of 10 MPa, with the entire pulse lasting for a duration of 4 μs.** Note that the ratio of the positive to negative peak pressures is approximately 5. Pressure measurements near the focal region of a Dornier unmodified HM3 indicate a 6-dB beam, of a width of approximately 15 mm. Since kidney stones are also generally of this dimension, the wave front incident on the stone can be considered a plane wave (Muller, 1990; Cleveland et al, 2000).

**The first mechanism by which a stone might break is through spall fracture.** Once the shockwave enters the stone, it will be reflected at sites of impedance mismatch. One such location is at the distal surface of the stone at the stone-fluid

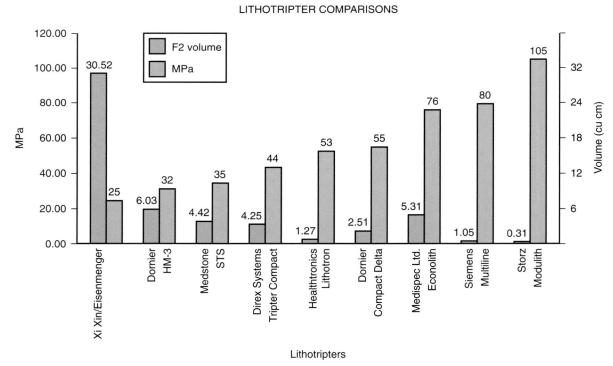

**Figure 44–13.** Comparison of the peak amplitude and size of the focal volume of nine different lithotripters. The general trend (from left to right) is a decrease in the device focal volume and an increase in the peak positive pressure. At the far left is the Xi Xin/Eisenmenger lithotripter, a new design that goes against the trend with a diminished peak amplitude and enlarged focal area.

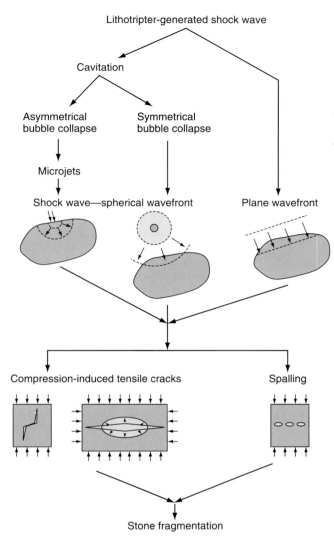

Figure 44–14. Summary of how the various mechanical forces generated by a lithotripsy shockwave might cause a kidney stone to fracture. (Reproduced with permission of Dr. Bradley Sturtevant.)

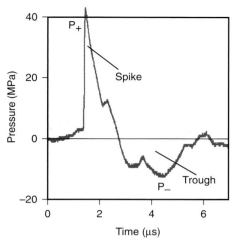

Figure 44–15. A typical pressure pulse at the lithotripter focus (F2) as measured by a PVDF membrane hydrophone. First, there is a steep positive pressure front of about 40 MPa, which is followed by a negative pressure of 10 MPa, with the entire pulse lasting for a duration of 4 μs. (From Coleman AJ, Saunders JE, Preston RC, et al: Pressure waveforms generated by a Dornier extracorporeal shockwave lithotriptor. Ultrasound Med Biol 1987;13:651-657.)

(urine) interface (although there could be other internal sites, such as cavities in the stone and interfaces of crystalline and matrix materials). As the shockwave is reflected, it is inverted in phase to a tensile (negative) wave. If the tensile wave exceeds the tensile strength of the stone, there is an induction of nucleation and growth of microcracks that eventually coalesce, resulting in stone fragmentation, which is termed spallation. The failure plane is located perpendicular to the applied tensile stress. This mechanism is thought to be of considerable importance in that kidney stones, like most brittle materials, will be much more likely to fail under tension rather than compression (Johrde and Cocks, 1985). Lokhandwalla and Sturtevant (2000) have suggested that the trailing negative pressure of the lithotripter pulse also exerts tensile stresses of an order of magnitude similar to that of the spall mechanism. Contributing factors to the effectiveness of spallation in generating stone breakage appear to be the size and the shape of the stone as well as its physical properties (i.e., fracture toughness, acoustic speed, density, and void dimensions). More spherically shaped stones may focus the tensile

wave after reflection and thus further increase the tensile stress. Stones with larger diameters may allow sufficient tensile stress to be generated so that the tensile strength of the stone can more easily be exceeded. If these factors are important, then smaller, irregularly shaped stones may not fracture by spallation.

Eisenmenger (1998) has suggested that **the second mechanism for stone breakage, termed squeezing-splitting or circumferential compression, occurs because of the difference in sound speed between the stone and the surrounding fluid.** The shockwave inside the stone advances faster through the stone than the shockwave propagating in the fluid outside of the stone. The shockwave that propagates in the fluid outside of the stone thus produces a circumferential force on the stone, resulting in a tensile stress in the stone that is at its maximum at the proximal and distal ends of the stone. The resulting squeezing force could split the stone either in a plane parallel to the shockwave propagation direction or, depending on the elastic properties of the stone, possibly in a plane parallel to the shockwave front. It has been theorized that squeezing should be enhanced when the entire stone falls within the diameter of the focal zone. Thus, current third-generation lithotripters that have very small focal zones will not make use of this mechanism, as the stone size is typically greater than the focal zone, whereas the original Dornier HM3 machine would.

**The third mechanism is shear stress.** Shear stress will be generated by shear waves (also termed transverse waves) that develop as the shockwave passes into the stone. The shear waves propagate through the stone and will result in regions of high shear stress inside the stone. In contrast to compression waves, which move the molecules in the direction of propagation, a shear wave results in translation of molecules transverse to the direction of propagation, and therefore the molecules are not compressed but are shifted sideways by the wave. Many materials are weak in shear, particularly if they consist of layers, as the bonding strength of the matrix between layers often has a low ultimate shear stress. Calcium oxalate stones commonly possess alternating layers of mineral and matrix, and the shear stress induced by the transverse wave could cause such stones to fail. Theoretical work by Sapozhnikov and colleagues (2003) suggests that the shear wave mechanism will lead to a tensile strain in cylindrical stones that is 5 to 10 times larger than that induced by spall. They also suggest that cracks will be initiated in the center of the stone and grow in a direction perpendicular to the axis of the stone.

**The fourth mechanism for stone breakage, superfocusing, is the amplification of stresses inside the stone due to the geometry of that stone.** The shockwave that is reflected at the distal surface of the stone can be focused either by refraction or by diffraction from the corners of the stone. Several groups have demonstrated that these reflected waves can be focused to regions of high stress in the interior of the stone and that this can lead to failure (Gracewski et al, 1993; Xi and Zhong, 2001). The regions of high stress (both tensile and shear) are dependent on the geometry of the stone as well as its elastic properties.

**The fifth potential mechanism for SWL stone breakage is cavitation** (Coleman et al, 1987; Crum, 1988; Vakil and Everbach, 1993; Zhong and Chuong, 1993; Zhong et al, 1993). Cavitation is defined as the formation and subsequent dynamic behavior of bubbles. The lithotripter-generated pressure field has been found to induce cavitation in both in vitro and in vivo studies. The negative pressure in the trailing part of the pulse causes bubbles to grow at nucleation sites. A nucleation site is an inhomogeneity in the fluid, which leads to preferential formation of free gas under stress. During the negative pressure wave, the pressure inside the bubble falls below the vapor pressure of the fluid, and the bubble fills with vapor and grows rapidly in size (almost three orders of magnitude). As these bubbles grow, they oscillate in size for about 200 µs and then collapse violently, giving rise to high pressures and temperatures. In the absence of any boundaries, a cavitation bubble remains spherical during collapse, releasing energy primarily by sound radiation, the majority of which is in the form of a shockwave (see Fig. 44–14). This shockwave generates a positive and negative wave and therefore can induce all of the fragmentation mechanisms described in the preceding. However, in the presence of a boundary, a liquid jet, also termed a cavitation microjet, forms inside the bubble during the collapse (see Fig. 44–5) (Crum, 1979, 1988). This jet can accelerate to extremely large speeds because it converts most of its kinetic energy from the collapse of the cavity interface to the jet itself. The typical bubble radii found in SWL vary from 1 µm to 1 mm, and bubble jet velocities range from 22 m/s to 800 m/s. In actual jet-impact cases, the duration of the pressure pulse is only a few microseconds, and in most instances, the peak pressure lasts for only about 1 µs. If the liquid jet is near the surface of a stone, it creates a locally compressive stress field in the stone, which propagates spherically into the stone interior.

Numerous investigators have exposed either aluminum foil or brass plates to the focused shockwave generated by a Dornier HM3 and observed significant microjet damage (pitting) on the surfaces of these metals. If this event occurs at the surface of a kidney stone, erosion of this surface would be expected; Averkiou and Crum (1996) reported this event

for SWL-treated plaster of Paris target stones. To determine if cavitation is the primary mechanism of stone fragmentation, investigators have developed in vitro systems that would eliminate or dampen cavitational events. Such systems have included a viscous medium that possesses a much lower number of nucleation sites and a chamber that allows one to increase the ambient pressure that surrounds the growing cavitation bubbles (Delius, 1997; Stonehill et al, 1998; Vakil et al, 1991). These in vitro systems have shown reduced stone damage along with a reduction in cavitation activity. Work by Bailey and associates (1998, 1999), in which the positive and negative waves were inverted with a pressure release reflector, also showed a reduction in stone comminution. All of these studies suggest that cavitation plays a significant role in damaging brittle objects.

**The final mechanism of stone fragmentation to be considered defines stone breakage in terms of a dynamic fracture process, in which the damage induced by SWL accumulates during the course of the treatment, leading to the eventual destruction of the stone.** Essential to this process is nucleation, growth, and coalescence of flaws within the stone caused by a tensile or shear stress (Fig. 44–16; see also Fig. 44–14). As renal calculi are not homogeneous but rather have either a lamellar crystalline structure bonded by an organic matrix material or an agglomeration of crystalline and noncrystalline material, there are numerous sites of preexisting flaws (microcracks). All of the fracture mechanisms described have the potential to generate progressive damage to the interior of the stone. By use of the cohesive-zone model, a mathematical approach of predicting the qualitative features of transient microcrack damage accumulation, Lokhandwalla and Sturtevant (2000) were able to calculate the number of shockwaves required for a spall-like failure to occur in a

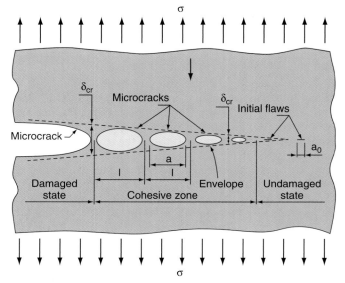

**Figure 44–16.** Coalescence of microcracks with a main crack. The undamaged stone has some initial flaws or microcracks of known length. These flaws occur in renal calculi either at a lamellar crystalline structure bonded by an organic matrix material or at an agglomerate of crystalline and noncrystalline material. When stressed, these microcracks grow until they coalesce with the main crack, and because this event is repeated throughout the stone, it eventually fragments. (Reproduced with permission of Dr. Bradley Sturtevant.)

typical calcium oxalate monohydrate calculus. The values they determined had a range of two orders of magnitude (30 to 3000 shocks), which is well within the clinical dose presently used to treat patients. These investigators further suggested that mechanisms other than spall are also likely to inflict damage to stones, and spall may be a factor only in a small portion of the stone.

## Bioeffects: Clinical Studies

**Acute Extrarenal Damage. SWL induces acute injury in a variety of extrarenal tissues** (Evan et al, 1991, 1998). Patients receiving more than 200 shocks show gross hematuria, which generally resolves within 12 hours (Chaussy and Schmiedt, 1984; Kaude et al, 1985). Hematuria occurs regardless of the type of lithotripter employed. Evan and associates (1989) have noted that the SWL-induced lesion extends from the kidney capsule to the tip of the medulla, which suggests that **hematuria is the result of direct injury to the renal parenchyma.** Patients treated with an unmodified HM3 device at 18- to 24-kV settings commonly complain of pain localized to the posterior body wall (flank) near the site of shockwave entry (Lingeman et al, 1986a). The unmodified HM3 has been associated with significant trauma to such organs as the liver and skeletal muscle as detected by elevated levels of bilirubin, lactate dehydrogenase, serum aspartate transaminase, and creatine phosphokinase within 24 hours of treatment (Lingeman et al, 1986a; Ruiz Marcellan and Ibarz Servio, 1986; Parr et al, 1988). These parameters begin to fall within 3 to 7 days of SWL treatment and are normal at 3 months. Most of these deleterious effects were associated with the use of an unmodified HM3 lithotripter. However, this does not mean that the unmodified HM3 device is more likely to induce injury; rather, current clinical studies of second- and third-generation machines may have inadequately reported such complications.

Changes such as gastric and duodenal erosion have been identified and are thought to represent a common extrarenal complication of SWL therapy (Al Karawi et al, 1987). The lung parenchyma can suffer injury if it is exposed directly to shockwaves (Chaussy and Fuchs, 1986). Several cases of clinically typical acute pancreatitis, associated with a marked rise in serum amylase and lipase levels, have been observed, and even in the absence of the symptoms of overt pancreatitis, increased amylase levels have been detected (Drach et al, 1986; Lingeman et al, 1986a). Hematochezia immediately after SWL secondary to mucosal damage of the colon has also been documented (Cass, 1988). Myocardial infarctions, cerebral vascular accidents, and brachial plexus palsy have been noted after SWL. In addition, early clinical studies noted that shockwaves could induce cardiac arrhythmia, an observation that led to electrocardiographic synchronization with R-wave triggering on the Dornier HM3 device (Chaussy and Schmiedt, 1984). However, later clinical studies with non-water bath lithotripters have concluded that ungating is safe. As a consequence, many clinicians began to treat at faster rates, up to 2 Hertz, which was not possible with the gated devices. Paterson and associates first questioned the effect an accelerated treatment rate may have on stone breakage in a series of porcine studies that demonstrated inferior stone fragmentation at higher treatment rates (Paterson et al, 2002). These data were confirmed in prospective randomized studies per-

formed by Madbouly and associates and Pace and associates (Madbouly et al, 2005; Pace et al, 2005). However, **recent evidence has demonstrated that increasing the rate of SWL delivery reduces the efficiency of stone breakage** (Paterson et al, 2002; Madbouly et al, 2005; Pace et al, 2005).

**Acute Renal Injury: Structural and Functional Changes.** SWL is now known to induce acute structural changes in the treated kidney in the majority if not all of SWL patients. Morphologic studies using both MRI and quantitative radionuclide renography have suggested that 63% to 85% of all SWL patients treated with an unmodified HM3 lithotripter exhibit one or more forms of renal injury within 24 hours of treatment (Kaude et al, 1985; Knapp et al, 1987; Wilson et al, 1989). These values are much larger than those reported by Chaussy and Schmiedt (1984), who described the sonographic detection of clinical hematomas in 0.6% of cases. These changes are not specific to any particular lithotripter, and numerous reports have documented identical renal bioeffects induced by second- and third-generation lithotripters (Thuroff et al, 1988; Ueda et al, 1993; Kohrmann et al, 1995; Piper et al, 2001).

**The two most common renal side effects seen immediately after SWL are hemorrhage and edema within or around the kidney.** Frequently, the kidney is enlarged and there is a loss of corticomedullary demarcation, suggesting acute intrarenal edema; although clinically significant fluid collections were initially determined to occur in less than 1% of SWL treatments, this incidence rises when CT or MRI is used for screening (Chaussy and Schmiedt 1984; Kaude et al, 1985; Rubin et al, 1987; Knapp et al, 1988; Mobley et al, 1993; Krishnamurthi and Streem, 1995). In addition, the newer generation lithotripters that have small focal areas and extremely high peak positive pressures are reported to produce higher clinically significant hematoma rates (3% to 12%), a trend that is worrisome (Thuroff et al, 1988; Ueda et al, 1993; Kohrmann et al, 1995; Piper et al, 2001). Dhar and associates (2004) reported clinical results with a Storz Modulith that demonstrated the probability for development of a subcapsular hematoma increased 2.2 times for every 10-year increase in the patient's age. The appearance of these changes can range in severity from a mild contusion localized within the renal parenchyma to a large hematoma (Fig. 44–17) associated with severe bleeding, possibly necessitating blood transfusion or rarely even arteriographic embolization. Such hemorrhage may produce a state of acute renal failure, and death may result if the condition is not identified in a timely fashion (Stoller et al, 1989). Rubin and associates (1987), with CT imaging, found an increase in the number of septal strands and a thickening of Gerota's fascia after SWL, suggesting focal regions of edema. In general, perirenal fluid disappears within a few days, whereas subcapsular fluid or blood may take 6 weeks to 6 months (or more) to resolve (Knapp et al, 1988).

Rigatti and associates (1989) performed a histopathologic study documenting acute changes in the kidney and surrounding tissues of SWL-treated patients. Renal biopsy specimens obtained within 1 week of SWL treatment revealed marked tubular, vascular, and interstitial changes that were localized to the plane of the pressure wave. Most renal corpuscles in this zone were disrupted, and the rest of the nephron showed mild degenerative changes with an

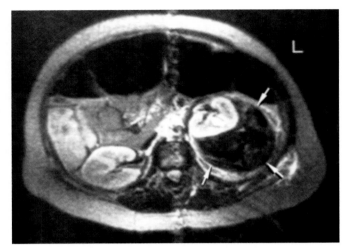

**Figure 44–17.** MRI scan taken 24 hours after SWL with 1200 shocks at 22 kV (by an unmodified Dornier HM3 lithotripter) shows a large subcapsular hematoma *(arrows)* in the treated (left) kidney.

accumulation of hemosiderin granules and cast material. Alterations in the microvasculature included dilation of veins, with evidence of endothelial damage and thrombus formation. Seitz and colleagues (1991) studied the kidneys from four patients treated with a piezoelectric lithotripter and detected sites of intraparenchymal hemorrhage at the corticomedullary junction that increased in severity with increasing numbers of shocks (4000 to 20,000). They commented that the gross and histologic appearances of these four SWL-treated kidneys mirrored exactly the results of animal studies published by others. Another approach used to determine the type and degree of injury induced by SWL in the human kidney has been to treat a human cadaver kidney with SWL (Brewer et al, 1988; Roessler et al, 1993). These studies clearly show that **a clinical dose always induced injury to the nephrons and small to medium-sized blood vessels within F2.** As the number of shockwaves was increased, so too was the amount of damage detected. In addition, Roessler and colleagues (1996) determined the size of a lesion induced by an electromagnetic versus an electrohydraulic lithotripter. They found a much larger lesion with the electrohydraulic machines; however, the electromagnetic machine produced complete cellular destruction at F2, an observation that may explain the higher rate of subcapsular hemorrhage for electromagnetic lithotripters. The ex vivo nature of this model has numerous disadvantages that limit the applicability of these studies to an in vivo setting.

There have been numerous observations documenting injury to the nephron, as defined by the elevation of several tubular enzymes in the urine immediately after SWL (Assimos et al, 1989a; Ruiz Marcellan and Ibarz Servio, 1986). Krongrad and colleagues (1991) noted in five men with unilateral urolithiasis that urine levels of $N$-acetyl-$\beta$-$D$-glucosaminidase, $\gamma$-glutamyltransferase, and $\beta_2$-microglobulin in diseased kidneys were elevated compared with the contralateral normal kidneys; however, there was not a statistically significant increase during the initial 24 hours after SWL. They suggested that the elevation was a result of a tubular defect in association with stone disease and not in response to SWL treatment. Nonetheless, the majority of observations suggest that all

portions of the kidney and surrounding tissues are vulnerable to shockwaves, and the microvasculature may be the most susceptible.

Acute alterations in renal function have not been well described in SWL patients as few studies have attempted to follow parameters of renal function after SWL. Kaude and associates (1985) found an immediate decrease in effective plasma flow, measured by renal scans, in 30% of kidneys treated with SWL. Others have also noted a delay in excretion of contrast material in unobstructed kidneys undergoing SWL (Grantham et al, 1986). The decrease in renal function has been linked to the number of shocks administered. These studies are supported by observations that there is an apparent transient reduction of intrarenal blood flow at F2 as well as in the untreated kidney (Bomanji et al, 1987; Eterovic et al, 1999; Kataoka et al, 1993; Mostafavi et al, 1998a). These changes can be blocked with pretreatment pharmacologic manipulations (Strohmaier et al, 1994; Chan et al, 2000). Thomas and associates (1988) have reported that a treatment regimen of approximately 1500 shocks is safe, and others have demonstrated that the administration of greater numbers of shocks will induce a fall in renal plasma flow (Graff et al, 1988). Orestano and associates (1989) noted that fewer than 2500 shocks produced changes in renal function that totally regressed by 30 days after SWL. Their observations showed that more than 2500 shocks induced more extensive changes in renal function (reduction in creatinine clearance, prolonged $^{131}$I-Hippuran transit time) in the treated kidney as well as in the contralateral kidney. In a study of solitary kidneys, Karlsen and Berg (1991) reported a significant reduction in glomerular filtration rate 3 months after SWL.

A group of investigators from the University of Innsbruck has conducted a prospective study in which they measured resistive index in a group of patients receiving a clinical dose of shockwaves sufficient to comminute a stone (mean, 2725 shockwaves; 16 to 28 kV, Dornier MFL 5000 lithotripter) (Janetschek et al, 1997). The results were stratified by age of the patients, and the only patients who were excluded from the study were those who had documented vascular disease. Resistive indices were elevated immediately after SWL in the treated kidney (but not in the contralateral kidney) of patients older than 60 years. Seventy-five percent of the patients in this age group exhibited a pathologically high resistive index, and at 26 months, 15 of the 20 patients in this group still demonstrated a statistically elevated value. Aoki and colleagues (1999) also found a larger increase in resistive index in elderly patients. In 45% (9 of 20) of these patients, resistive indices continued to increase, and these patients also developed new-onset hypertension. No changes were found in the plasma renin activity at any time point. The authors concluded that there is a strong positive correlation between elevated resistive index and blood pressure, that this is indicative of underlying renovascular disease, and that age is a risk factor for long-term complications in SWL.

All of the studies cited in this section indicate that **renal function is adversely affected, acutely, in some patients and that the primary change appears to be a vasoconstrictive response resulting in a fall in renal blood flow and glomerular filtration rate.** There are reports that SWL can result in a significant improvement in renal function in some patients (Chaussy and Schmiedt, 1984). However, many such patients

**Table 44–11. Acute Renal Side Effects: Risk Factors for Shockwave Lithotripsy**

Age
Obesity
Coagulopathies
Thrombocytopenia
Diabetes mellitus
Coronary heart disease
Preexisting hypertension

show evidence of ureteral obstruction before treatment, thereby biasing such findings.

Risk factors may predispose SWL patients to increased acute renal injury. Knapp and associates (1988) found **patients with existing hypertension to be at increased risk for the development of perinephric hematomas as a consequence of SWL** (Table 44–11). In particular, those patients having unsatisfactory control of their hypertension at the time of SWL had the highest incidence of hematoma formation. Dhar and colleagues (2004) reported that the probability for development of a subcapsular hematoma after SWL with a Storz Modulith increased 2.2 times for every 10-year increase in the patient's age. Additional risk factors included increased thromboplastin time and the use of aspirin (even when it was discontinued up to 2 weeks before treatment). When the voltage applied and the number of shockwaves administered were evaluated as potential risk factors, no correlation with hematoma formation was found. Newman and Saltzman (1989) have also confirmed these observations, noting that patients with coagulopathies and thrombocytopenia were at greater risk for development of a subcapsular hematoma. Additional risk factors for hemorrhage were diabetes mellitus, coronary artery disease, and obesity, all of which suggest a link to a vascular disorder (see Table 44–11). In relation to risk factors, an interesting observation is that some patients with preexisting hypertension require increased doses of their blood pressure medication after SWL therapy (Kaude et al, 1985). Age is a factor on both ends of the spectrum in that children and the elderly both appear to be at increased risk for structural and functional changes (Janetschek et al, 1997; Lifshitz et al, 1998).

In addition to the risk factors described, another set of risk factors are linked to the parameters of treatment. These factors include discharge voltage, number of total shockwaves administered, rate of shockwave delivery, and type of lithotripsy. Most of these data have been collected in animals and are reviewed later.

**Chronic Renal Injury: Structural and Functional Changes.** Although there still remains a paucity of information on the subject, **four potential chronic renal changes that follow SWL are emerging. They are an accelerated rise in systemic blood pressure, a decrease in renal function, an increase in the rate of stone recurrence, and the induction of brushite stone disease. All four effects appear to be linked to the observation that the acute injury does progress to scar formation at F2.** Lechevallier and associates (1993) performed pre- and post-SWL (30 days) single-photon emission computed tomography studies in 12 patients treated with a piezoelectric lithotripter. All SWL-treated kidneys showed some loss of renal function; 4 of the 12 kidneys showed a loss of local tracer uptake of more than 4%. In addition, seven scars were detected in the region of F2. Umekawa and associates (1994) examined the kidney of a patient in acute renal failure that occurred 90 days after SWL treatment and found evidence of anti–glomerular basement membrane antibody production in glomeruli at F2.

The possibility that SWL might be associated with significant changes in systemic blood pressure was first suggested by Peterson and Finlayson (1986) and has been investigated by others (Table 44–12). Lingeman and coworkers (1987a) reported that 8.2% of 243 patients who were normotensive at the time of SWL developed blood pressure changes requiring antihypertensive medication. Mean follow-up in this group of patients was 1.5 years, giving an annualized incidence of hypertension of 5.5%. Similar data have been reported by Williams and Thomas (1989). Following these reports suggesting that hypertension could be a long-term complication of SWL, a large study involving almost 1000 patients was undertaken at the Methodist Hospital of Indiana (Lingeman et al, 1990). This study found a small but statistically significant change in diastolic blood pressure associated with SWL therapy. The observed effect of SWL on diastolic pressure change persisted even after controlling statistically for other

**Table 44–12. Blood Pressure Changes in Shockwave Lithotripsy–Treated Patients**

| Reference | Length of Study (months) | Range | Mean | Change in Incidence of Hypertension | Change in Diastolic Blood Pressure |
|---|---|---|---|---|---|
| Liedl et al, 1988 | 40 | Not recorded | 1043 | No change | Not recorded |
| Williams et al, 1988 | 21 | 800-2000 | 1400 | Increased | Increased |
| Puppo et al, 1989 | 12 | 1100-1900 | 1380 | No change | No change |
| Montgomery et al, 1989 | 29 | 110-3300 | 1429 | Increased | No change |
| Lingeman et al, 1990 | | Not recorded | 1289 | No change | Increased |
| Yokoyama et al, 1992 | 19 | 1500-3000 | Not recorded | Not recorded | Increased |
| Janetschek et al, 1997 | 26 | 2600-3000 | 2735 | Increased (60- to 80-year-old age group) | Increased (60- to 80-year-old age group) |
| Jewett et al, 1998 | 24 | Not recorded | 4411 | No change | No change |
| Strohmaier et al, 2000 | 24 | | | Increased | Increased |
| Elves et al, 2000 | 26.4 | Not recorded | 5281 | No change* | No change* |
| Krambeck et al, in press | 228 | 500-4500 | 1125 | Increased | Not recorded |

*Shockwave lithotripsy–treated patients compared with control group not undergoing therapy.

variables that might be associated with variation in blood pressure, such as age, sex, pretreatment baseline blood pressure, and number of treatment sessions. Strohmaier and colleagues (2000) studied 252 patients with stone disease during a 24-month period to determine if treatment modality influenced their blood pressure after stone removal. The different treatment protocols for stone removal included SWL, ureteroscopy, PNL, and spontaneous passage of renal and ureteral stones. All patients regardless of stone location or treatment type showed a rise in blood pressure. Eterovic and colleagues (2005) obtained blood pressure measurements and renal vascular resistance before and 3 months after stone removal in 30 patients treated by SWL and in another 30 patients treated by Gil-Vernet intrasinus pyelolithotomy. They noted a drop in blood pressure and renal vascular resistance from baseline in the pyelolithotomy-treated patients but no change in the SWL-treated patients, suggesting that SWL results reflect a balance between the relief of obstruction and an SWL-induced lesion. Janetschek and colleagues (1997) showed that by stratifying their results by age of the patient, there was a long-term change in both blood pressure and resistive index. What is not known at this time is the future health risk for these patients or who is at risk. Because the long-term effects of hypertension, if it is occurring, include an increased risk of stroke, myocardial infarction, and renal failure, any therapy that might increase the incidence of hypertension should be rigorously examined.

The possibility that SWL treatment might be associated with a long-term reduction in renal function has been suggested by several investigators. Williams and associates (1988) found a **significant decrease in the percentage of effective renal plasma flow 17 to 21 months after SWL for patients with two kidneys.** Orestano and colleagues (1989) noted that patients receiving more than 2500 shocks had a reduction in creatinine clearance and a prolongation of $^{131}$I-Hippuran transit time 30 days after SWL in the treated kidney; in some cases, similar findings were noted in the contralateral kidney. Lingeman and associates have reported that patients with a solitary kidney demonstrated elevated serum creatinine levels 5 years after SWL (Brito et al, 1990). These observations stand in contrast to the early reports by Chaussy and Fuchs (1986), which suggested a significant increase in renal function 3 months to 1 year after SWL. In addition, a longer follow-up study of patients treated in Munich has failed to confirm this increase in renal function (Liedle et al, 1988).

An additional concern is that **stone recurrence rates may be higher after SWL because of residual stone debris** (Pearle et al, 1999). A study by Carr and associates (1996) documented new stone formation in 298 consecutive patients who initially were determined to be stone free after SWL and compared those findings with those of 62 patients treated by PNL. Their data showed a significant increase in the rate of new stone formation within 1 year of SWL treatment compared with PNL. The authors suggested that fine sand debris generated from SWL treatment remained in the kidney and gravity acted to position it as a nidus in the calyceal system.

There has been reported to be a significant increase in the number of calcium phosphate stone formers during the last three decades (Mandel et al, 2003; Parks et al, 2004). An intriguing finding in Parks' work was that when all kidney stone formers were analyzed for the number of SWL proce-

dures, the **calcium phosphate stone formers had received a significantly higher number of procedures than did the idiopathic calcium oxalate stone formers when rates were adjusted for number of stones and duration of stone disease.** Furthermore, the brushite stone formers had received a significantly greater number of SWL treatments than had the apatite stone formers. The histopathologic examination of the brushite stone formers revealed advanced levels of tissue changes in the renal cortex and papilla that included interstitial fibrosis, tubular atrophy, glomerular obsolescence, and deposition of large amounts of biologic hydroxyapatite in the lumens of inner medullary collection ducts (Evan et al, 2005). Although these data do not establish a cause and effect relationship, clearly there is an association between brushite stone disease and high levels of SWL treatment sessions. As apatite stone disease is likely to be related to higher urine pH levels in these patients, animal studies that showed the initial site of SWL injury to be localized to the microvessels and collecting duct of the renal papilla may explain the loss of control over normal urinary fluid pH.

## Bioeffects: Experimental Animal Studies

**Acute Renal Injury: Structural and Functional Changes.** After the introduction of SWL, there was an early misperception that shockwaves did not produce injury and passed harmlessly through the body (Chaussy and Fuchs, 1986). Subsequent studies have demonstrated that SWL does, indeed, affect organ structure and function (Table 44–13).

On macroscopic examination, the acute changes noted in dog and pig kidneys treated with a clinical dose of shockwaves are strikingly similar to those described for SWL patients. This lesion is predictable in size, focal in location, and unique in the types of injuries (primarily vascular insult) induced. These changes include hematuria, contusion-like lesions, subcapsular hematomas, hemorrhage, and kidney enlargement. Although hemorrhage has been found in three general locations, perirenal, subcapsular, and intraparenchymal (Figs. 44–18 and 44-19), it is always at or near F2. The perirenal fat is a common site of extensive hemorrhage. Subcapsular hemorrhage is found to spread diffusely along the length of the capsule or to form discrete hematomas. Sites of intra-

**Table 44–13. Renal Side Effects of Shockwave Lithotripsy in Experimental Animal Models (Canine and Porcine)**

*Acute histologic changes*

Venous thrombi
Cellular disruption and necrosis
Mild tubular necrosis (ischemic changes)
Intraparenchymal hemorrhage
Tubular dilation and cast formation
Damage and rupture of veins and small arteries
Rupture of glomerular and peritubular capillaries

*Chronic histologic changes*

Nephron loss
Dilated veins
Streaky fibrosis
Diffuse interstitial fibrosis
Calcium and hemosiderin deposits
Hyalinized and acellular scars from cortex to medulla

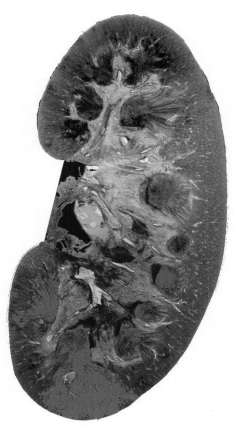

**Figure 44–18.** Macroscopic photomicrograph of a coronal section through the kidney of a juvenile pig (about 6 weeks old) treated with 2000 shocks at 24 kV by an unmodified Dornier HM3 lithotripter and examined 4 hours after treatment. The region of intraparenchymal hemorrhage has been colored red by an automated computer color recognition program. Note that the lesion involves multiple papillae and in some regions extends through the cortex to the renal capsule, where a subcapsular hematoma may develop.

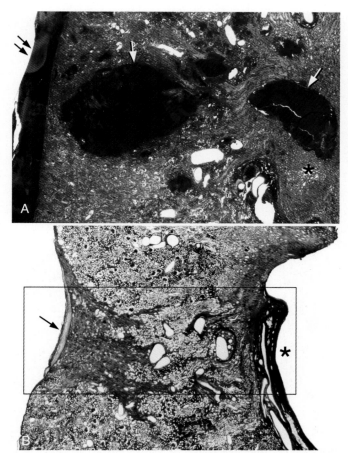

**Figure 44–19.** Light micrographs of an acute SWL-induced lesion at F2 (**A**) and subsequent chronic changes at a similar site 3 months after SWL treatment (**B**). Each pig kidney was treated with 2000 shockwaves at 24 kV by an unmodified Dornier HM3 lithotripter. The acute lesion is characterized by numerous sites of hemorrhage *(arrows)* that extend from individual renal papilla *(asterisk)* to the outer cortex of the kidney. Note a subcapsular hematoma in **B** is similar in location to that seen in **A** but is shown at 3 months after SWL. A rectangle outlines the site of F2. Within that region, there is complete loss of the renal papilla (the asterisk indicates where it should be), and only scar tissue is found in the adjacent cortical tissue *(arrow)*.

parenchymal hemorrhage are generally wedge shaped, being most severe at the corticomedullary junction and extending from the papillary tip to the capsule (see Fig. 44–19). Hematomas localized within the renal parenchyma or subcapsular zone may be up to 0.5 cm in diameter and may number up to 10 per kidney (Delius et al, 1988a, 1988b; Jaeger et al, 1988; Newman et al, 1987). The hemorrhagic lesion can occupy approximately 2% of the functional mass in an adult pig kidney that has been treated by an unmodified HM3 device with 2000 shocks at 24 kV (Willis et al, 1999). The larger hematomas appear to compress the adjacent tissue, interstitial edema is common, and the diffuse nature of this change would appear to account for enlargement of the kidney.

**Regions of hemorrhage are always near the site of F2, and these regions are typically characterized by the rupture of small vessels such as thin-walled veins, small arteries, and glomerular and peritubular capillaries** (Fig. 44–20; see also Figs. 44–18 and 44–19) (Evan et al, 1991; Willis et al, 1999). Furthermore, these findings correlate with the vasoconstriction measured in both the treated and untreated kidneys. Venous thrombi are frequently associated with interlobular and arcuate veins at the sites of hemorrhage. Evidence of extensive endothelial damage in these veins is noted by a loss

of endothelial cells, the immediate attachment of numerous polymorphonuclear cells and activated platelets to the luminal surface of these vessels, and the appearance of vasculitis; damage to both the nephron and the vasculature is always seen first in the renal papilla and then in the cortex (Connors et al, 2000; Shao et al, 2003) (Fig. 44–21). Nephrons near areas of marked hemorrhage show evidence of direct damage from the shockwave and secondary changes that appear to be related to ischemia. These alterations consist of vacuolar changes in individual cells, tubular dilation, cast formation (hyaline-like, red blood cells), and mild tubular necrosis. These observations demonstrate that both the microvasculature and nephron are susceptible to shockwave damage; however, the primary injury appears to be a vascular insult.

Of great interest are those experimental animal studies that have determined factors of SWL administration that appear to influence the degree of renal trauma induced by shockwaves (Table 44–14). Several groups have noted that as shock

### Table 44–14. Factors That Influence Degree of Renal Trauma in Animals

*Aggravating factors*

Increasing the number of shocks delivered
Administering a large number of shocks over a short period of time
Selecting a high voltage or high power setting
Treating a juvenile kidney or a kidney with impaired function

*Mitigating factors*

Pretreating with 100 to 500 shocks at low energy level

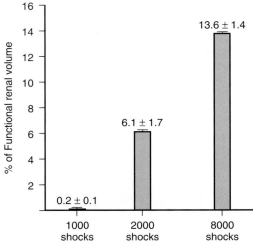

**EFFECT OF SHOCK NUMBER ON SWL LESION SIZE**
(six-week-old pigs, 24kV)

**Figure 44–22.** Effect of shock number (1000, 2000, and 8000 at 24 kV) on lesion size (percentage of functional renal volume) of 6-week-old pigs. Data are expressed as mean ± SEM, and all groups are statistically different from each other ($P < .05$).

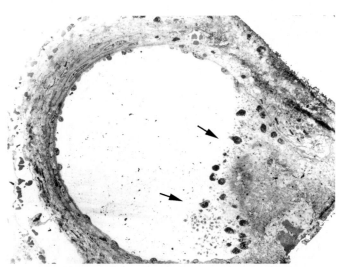

**Figure 44–20.** Low-magnification transmission electron micrograph demonstrating injury to a medium-sized artery located within F2 of a pig treated with 2000 shockwaves at 24 kV. The shockwave-induced injury to the right side of this vessel resulted in a rupture site that permitted extravasation of blood into the nearby interstitium. The site of injury in the vessel wall is plugged with a clot *(arrows)*.

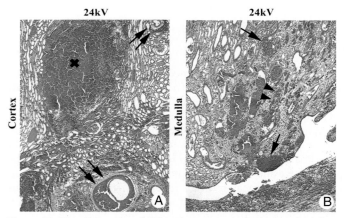

**Figure 44–21.** This series of light microscope panels depicts the injury seen in the cortex and medulla from an animal treated with 2000 shockwaves at 24 kV by an unmodified Dornier HM3 lithotripter. **A** and **B** illustrate extensive injury in both cortex and medulla. Within the cortex, disruption of arterial walls with hemorrhage *(double arrows)* is noted near sites of intraparenchymal bleeding *(x)*. The first site of injury appears to occur in the renal medulla, where damage is noted to small vessels, which causes intraparenchymal hemorrhage *(arrows)* adjacent to damaged collecting ducts *(arrowheads)*.

number is increased (1000 to 8000 shocks), a greater number of hematomas are formed and lesion size increases, although not as a direct correlation with shock number (Delius et al, 1988b; Willis et al, 1999). An increased number of shockwaves also was associated with larger hematomas, probably related to the fact that larger arteries are injured at high shock numbers. It appears that 1000 shockwaves represents the threshold for tissue injury with the unmodified HM3 in that lesions begin to appear at this shock number and then grow rapidly in size as the shock number is increased (Fig. 44–22) (Willis et al, 2005). Delius and associates (1988b, 1990) have also reported that more massive hemorrhage and tubular damage are induced by increasing the rate (1 shock/second to 100 shocks/second) at which the shocks are administered and by administering the shockwaves in pairs. Kidney size has been shown to be a risk factor for increased intraparenchymal hemorrhage; lesion size has been reported to be 7% in a juvenile pig and 2% in an adult pig (Willis et al, 1996; Evan et al, 1998). In addition, Evan and associates (1999) noted that the degree of injury induced by a clinical dose of SWL is potentiated by a preexisting condition such as acute pyelonephritis. Under such conditions, a 2000-shock dose acts like an 8000-shock dose. Although the degree of renal injury has been linked to the type of shockwave generator used, these data are difficult to compare as the parameters for shockwave delivery are so variable among instruments (Morris et al, 1989).

An obvious void in the experimental SWL literature has been studies that examine changes in renal function after shockwave administration. Jaeger and Constantinides (1989) reported a significant decrease in creatinine clearance and an elevation of glucose excretion 1 hour after SWL in dogs treated with 3000 shocks (1500 shocks per pole of kidney). Both values returned to normal by 24 hours after SWL. They also noted an increase in serum aspartate transaminase and alanine transaminase levels at 1 hour after SWL. Karlsen and associates (1990) detected an increase in urine osmolality and urine flow while renal plasma flow was reduced by approximately one third at 2 hours after SWL in dogs treated with 1500 shocks at 18 kV. However, these authors found no change in glomerular filtration rate or urinary electrolyte excretion. A series of experiments by Willis and associates (1996) have expanded these observations to include bilateral kidney function in the pig. These studies show that the application of 2000 shocks at 24 kV with an unmodified Dornier HM3 lithotripter to one kidney consistently reduces renal blood flow and glomerular filtration rate in that kidney. At 1 hour after SWL, the fall in renal blood flow was 27% in the young adult animals and 50% in the juvenile pigs. By 4 hours after SWL, renal blood flow returned to baseline in the young adult pigs but was still significantly reduced in the juvenile pigs. Glomerular filtration rate followed a similar course but was reduced to a lesser extent than renal blood flow measurements. In addition, these studies found a significant reduction in renal blood flow in the untreated kidney at the 1-hour post-SWL time point. These investigators also measured tubular function by use of *p*-aminohippurate extraction and found a significant reduction in the treated kidney but no fall in the untreated kidney. Again, the greatest reduction occurred in the juvenile pig compared with the young adults. These results show that the major change in renal function is vasoconstriction, and small kidney size does appear to be a risk factor for increased side effects. If the shock number is reduced to 1000 shockwaves, no detectable changes can be found acutely in renal hemodynamics. To demonstrate that the reduction in renal blood flow was focal, images of the blood flow in treated kidneys were obtained with positron emission tomographic scanning. Figure 44–23 compares blood flow in a treated and an untreated kidney by use of radiolabeled copper 62 microspheres, demonstrating **a loss of blood flow at the site of F2.** Willis and associates (2005) have found that high shock numbers (8000 shocks) do not generate a greater decrease in renal blood flow at 1 hour after SWL, but they do induce a sustained reduction at the 24 hour post-treatment mark. Connors and colleagues (2000) evaluated the effect of energy level on both renal blood flow and lesion size and found that lesion size increased as the energy level was increased from 12 to 24 kV. However, the maximal vasoconstrictive response was already induced at the 12 kV level and remained there regardless of the energy level used. These studies demonstrate the sensitivity of the renal vasculature to SWL. What is not known is whether electromagnetic lithotripters also induce renal vasoconstriction at a clinical dose.

It was known early in the era of lithotripsy that shockwaves induce a vasoconstrictive event in blood vessels. In a series of studies by Brendel and associates in 1987, video microscopy demonstrated that when shockwaves were directed at a simple microvascular bed, acute spasms of arterioles and hemorrhage of venules occurred. Vasoconstriction reached its maximum after 20 to 30 seconds and lasted between 4 and 10 minutes. Dilation followed the constriction event. In addition to the sites of microhemorrhage in the small veins were areas of macromolecule leakage and platelet aggregation. These authors also suggested that vasoconstriction is most pronounced in the region of peak pressure generated by the shockwave.

Willis (2006) reported **a practical way to protect the treated kidney from the predicted lesion induced by a clini-**

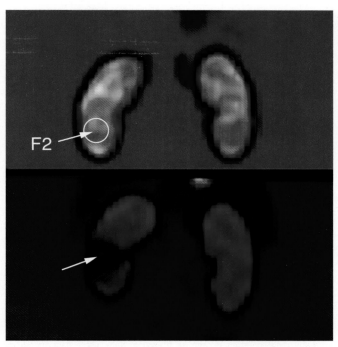

**Figure 44–23.** SWL-treated and control kidneys, imaged by positron emission tomographic scanning before and immediately after treatment with 3500 shockwaves to the lower pole, at level six, with a DoLi 50 device. The site of F2 (lower pole) on the shocked kidney shows a 50% reduction of renal blood flow *(arrow)*.

**cal dose of shockwaves. Before the administration of a clinical dose of 2000 shocks at 24 kV with an unmodified HM3 lithotripter, a pretreatment dose of 100 to 500 shockwaves at 12 kV is administered, followed by the full clinical dose to the same site. Under these conditions, the normal lesion of approximately 6% is reduced to approximately 0.3%, a highly significant change** (Fig. 44–24). One hypothesis of a possible mechanism of this outcome is that the pre-dose of shockwaves induces a significant vasoconstrictive event that prevents an incoming stress from shearing the vessel wall or perhaps prevents or reduces the number of cavitation events. A reduction in cavitation potentially protects the parenchyma from cavitation-induced injury. A clinical trial is needed to test this result in patients.

Vascular injury may potentiate ischemic damage to the renal parenchyma (Delvecchio et al, 2003). Both Cohen and associates (1998) and Brown and associates (2000) performed studies to confirm that the clinical dose of shockwaves induces lipid peroxidation and free radical formation in the treated kidney. The concern for ischemic changes is for both the treated and the untreated kidney, as SWL induces a vasoconstrictive response in both kidneys (Willis et al, 1999). Further evidence of the bilateral effects of SWL was provided by Delvecchio and associates (2003), who reported a dose-related increase in conjugated diene levels from the pole of the treated kidney and to a lesser degree from the untreated kidney.

Chronic changes in renal structure after shockwave treatment have received minimal investigation. At 2 weeks after SWL, Jaeger and Constantinides (1989) noted calcium deposits, streaky fibrosis, and encapsulation of sites of acute hemorrhage. Newman and coworkers (1987) identified permanent morphologic changes in the dog kidney 30 days after

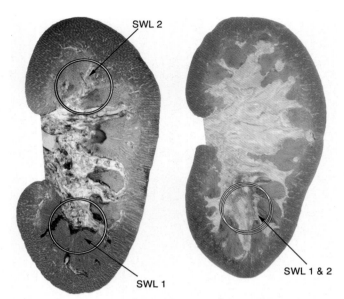

**Figure 44–24.** On the left is a coronal section of a kidney from an animal treated with 2000 shocks at 24 kV first to the lower pole (SWL 1) and then an additional 2000 shocks at 24 kV to the upper pole (SWL 2) of the same kidney. The typical lesion (colored in red) is seen at the lower pole; however, a greatly reduced lesion is seen on the upper pole. These data suggested that a pretreatment protocol might reduce the lesion induced by a clinical dose of shockwaves. The panel on the right shows lesion size in an animal first treated at the lower pole with 500 shocks at 12 kV (SWL 1) and then treated again at the lower pole with 2000 shocks at 24 kV (SWL 2). A greatly reduced lesion is also noted for this protocol.

| Table 44–15. **Reversible and Irreversible Injury** |
|---|
| *Reversible changes* |
| Mild tubular necrosis |
| Casts and red blood cells in tubular lumen |
| Vacuolar changes of tubular lumen |
| Mild interstitial edema and hemorrhage |
| *Irreversible changes resulting in loss of renal tissue* |
| Disruption of nephrons |
| Extensive interstitial edema |
| Large hematomas of cortex and medulla |
| Rupture and occlusion of veins and arteries |
| Fracture of glomerular and peritubular capillaries |

SWL treatment. These alterations consisted of diffuse interstitial fibrosis, focal areas of calcification, nephron loss, dilated veins, and hyalinized and acellular scars from the cortex to the medulla. Morris and colleagues (1991) found a direct correlation between the number of shockwaves and the size of the resulting scar; as the number of shocks was increased from 1000 to 2000, the size of the scar increased from 1.4% to 12.8%. In addition, Banner and associates (1991) have noted mesangioproliferative glomerulopathy in pigs treated with either the HM3 or the EDAP lithotripter. With time, deposits of complement C3 and traces of immunoglobulin G were found to increase in amount in the mesangium. Interestingly, these changes were noted to occur in both the treated and the untreated kidney to about the same degree, suggesting the induction of a systemic factor or bilateral injury induced by SWL. Delius and associates (1990) have reported that most of these renal alterations were reversible in several weeks except for some of the large hematomas. These observations suggest that the **acute changes induced in the kidney can be classified as either reversible or irreversible** (Table 44–15); **however, a clinical dose of SWL always induces irreversible injury that ultimately forms a region of scar.**

**Chronic Renal Injury: Structural and Functional Changes.** Only a few studies have attempted to determine the chronic changes in renal function induced by SWL. Neal and associates (1991) treated infant and adult rhesus monkeys with 1500 shocks at 15 kV or 2000 shocks at 18 kV to each kidney. A highly significant decrease in effective renal plasma flow was noted in the infant group 6 months after treatment when those values were indexed to body surface area. In another study, immature rabbits receiving 1000 to 2000 shocks

developed a significant rise in mean arterial blood pressure at 4 and 8 weeks after SWL compared with controls (Feagins et al, 1991). Pretreatment of these animals with either allopurinol or mannitol prevented the development of hypertension. Both of these studies strongly suggest that **there can be long-term functional consequences to a clinical dose of SWL, and the young or immature kidney is at great risk for such complications.**

### Mechanism for Tissue Injury

The mechanism for the traumatic effects of SWL is not known, although Delius and colleagues (1988b) have speculated that the violent collapse of cavitation bubbles generated by the shockwaves is primarily responsible for the cellular changes. This concept is based on data showing that cavitation bubbles are present during shockwave application and that lithotripter shockwaves can cavitate water and blood in vitro (Coleman et al, 1987). Crum (1988) documented that SWL does produce acoustic cavitation, possibly as the result of the high intensity of the shockwave amplitude, and noted that the cavitation microjets are sufficiently forceful to pit or deform metal test foils. Zhong and coworkers (2001) suggested that it is expansion of the bubbles in a vessel that will lead to rupture of the wall of that blood vessel, testing this in an in vitro setting.

No group had been able to positively detect and validate acoustic cavitation within the kidney during SWL treatment until Bailey and associates (2005) created a passive cavitation detection system using two confocal spherical bowl PZT transducers. This device was used for coincidence detection of cavitation bubble emissions within a $2 \times 2 \times 2$-mm sampling volume centered on F2 of a Dornier HM3 lithotripter. An ultrasound scan head targeted at this spot was used to image echogenicity in and around the sample volume. Signal (passive cavitation detection, hyperechoic spots) was intense in the urinary space during SWL treatment, and a signal was also seen in the renal cortex after only 1000 shocks. At that time, a small fluid space was noted at the site of the parenchymal signal. These data suggest that **once blood vessels have been ruptured and blood has collected in pools, there is a greater potential for cavitation to occur. The pooling of blood provides a large fluid-filled space for cavitation bubbles to grow and collapse.** In this model, the accuracy of tissue targeting was confirmed by inducing a lesion with high-intensity focused ultrasound. Further evidence that cavitation plays a role in tissue injury comes from a study by Evan and associates (2002) in which the degree of tissue injury was compared between a standard rigid reflector and a pressure release reflector. The pressure release reflector generates a shockwave where the negative tail precedes the positive peak, resulting in a suppression of cavitation activity. No injury was detected in the kidneys treated with the pressure release reflector; the standard rigid reflector induced the expected lesion.

## KEY POINTS: SHOCK WAVE LITHOTRIPSY

- Most patients with uncomplicated kidney stones can be successfully treated with SWL.

- Shock waves break stones via multiple different mechanisms, including both compressive and tensile forces.

- SWL is associated with both anatomic and functional injuries to the kidney.

- The harmful effects of SWL can be minimized by pre-treating with low energy shock waves and treating at the lowest power setting that fractures the stone.

- Stone breakage can be promoted by treating at slower rates, such as 1 Hz (60 shocks per minute).

## Percutaneous Nephrolithotomy

Fernstrom and Johansson first reported the technique of establishing a percutaneous track specifically to remove a stone in 1976. Subsequent reports have established PNL as a routinely used technique to treat patients with large or otherwise complex calculi (Alken et al, 1981; Wickham and Kellett, 1981; Segura et al, 1982; Clayman et al, 1984). Advances in surgical technique and technology have allowed the urologist to remove calculi percutaneously with increasing efficiency. As the percutaneous approach to stone removal is superior to the open approach in terms of morbidity, convalescence, and cost, PNL has replaced open surgical removal of large or complex calculi at most institutions (Brannen et al, 1985). Herein the specific aspects of percutaneous techniques as they relate to stone removal are delineated.

### Preparation of the Patient

The initial evaluation of the patient who is being considered for PNL should be a complete history and physical examination. A complete medical history will **identify those patients with an absolute contraindication to PNL, such as uncorrected coagulopathy, as well as those with an active, untreated urinary tract infection.** The placement of a percutaneous nephrostomy drain, without manipulation of the calculus, may be an appropriate therapy if the stone is associated with obstruction of the renal unit and sepsis. If it is medically feasible, **aspirin and other antiplatelet medications should be discontinued 7 days before the date of surgery** (Mak and Amoroso, 2003).

Preoperative laboratory evaluation of patients scheduled for PNL should include a complete blood count as well as serum electrolyte determinations and renal function tests. Martin and colleagues (2000) have reported that it is unnecessary to obtain screening coagulation studies before PNL for

an otherwise healthy patient. **Urine culture is mandatory for all patients who undergo PNL;** perioperative antibiotics can be appropriately tailored to culture-specific organisms. Typing and screening of the patient's blood should be performed, although preoperative crossmatching is usually not necessary.

Historically, it has been viewed as mandatory to evaluate the patient's collecting system by either intravenous urography or retrograde pyelography. Recently, as more patients are initially evaluated with helical CT imaging, it is no longer mandatory to have these studies at the preoperative evaluation. **In most cases, the decision to perform PNL may be based on the stone burden displayed on the CT images.** A KUB radiographic image should be obtained immediately before the procedure to verify stone location. Retrograde pyelography can be performed at the time of the surgical procedure, acquiring information about calyceal anatomy that may aid in selecting the targeted puncture site. However, for certain patients, such as **those with calyceal diverticula, for whom the surgical approach is affected by the diverticulum's relationship to the collecting system, intravenous or retrograde pyelography may be required at the time of initial evaluation.** Retrorenal colon has been reported to be present in less than 1% of all patients, but its incidence may be higher in those who have undergone jejunoileal bypass, those in a nursing home, or those with spinal cord injury (Sherman et al, 1985). These patients may benefit from initial CT imaging. Patients with ectopic kidneys, both congenital and iatrogenic (e.g., due to renal allograft, autotransplantation), as well as patients with dysmorphic body habitus due to congenital malformations such as spinal dysraphism may also benefit from cross-sectional imaging before PNL; intra-abdominal structures, such as the bowel, may be located in the targeted track. Radionuclide scanning may be necessary in select patients, particularly those harboring staghorn calculi, to evaluate differential renal function (Schnapp and Smith, 1995).

**Antibiotics. Urinary calculi may harbor bacteria even though bacteriuria is only intermittently present.** This is particularly true in the patient who has been taking antibiotics in the past. For those patients who do have preoperative bacteriuria, stone cultures produced bacteria in 77% of cases in a series reported by Larsen and associates (1986). The most frequently identified organisms were *Proteus mirabilis*, *Escherichia coli*, *Klebsiella* species, *Pseudomonas* species, *Enterococcus* species, and *Enterobacter* species. Sterile urine does not preclude postoperative bacteriuria, however, as Charton and colleagues (1986) reported a 35% incidence of bacteriuria after PNL among patients with sterile preoperative urine culture specimens in whom prophylactic antibiotic therapy was not used. Mariappan and associates (2005) have also reported that the best correlate with post-PNL sepsis is stone culture or renal pelvic urine culture, not bladder urine culture. **The fragmentation of stones, despite sterile urine, may release preformed bacterial endotoxins and viable bacteria that place the patient at risk for septic complications** (Scherz and Parsons, 1987; McAleer et al, 2002, 2003; Paterson et al, 2003). Therefore, patients who have radiographic or clinical features suggestive of struvite or in whom infection is suspected should receive 2 weeks of broad-spectrum antibiotics before surgery to reduce the risk of sepsis. Antibiotic treatment may also reduce bleeding secondary to inflammation and friability of renal parenchyma. Approximately one third of patients with an indwelling ureteral stent will, despite sterile urine on a preoperative analysis, be colonized with bacteria; *Enterococcus* and *Staphylococcus epidermidis* are the most frequent offending organisms (Reid et al, 1992; Lifshitz et al, 1999b). For patients with indwelling stents, then, antibiotic prophylaxis, particularly for gram-positive organisms, may be beneficial before instrumentation.

**Patients without a history of urinary infection should receive prophylactic antibiotics before endourologic interventions; all urologic endoscopic procedures are regarded as clean-contaminated,** even if infection is not evident. Inglis and Tolley (1988), in a randomized prospective study, demonstrated that antibiotic prophylaxis before PNL reduced the incidence of postoperative urinary tract infection in those patients found with sterile urine on preoperative culture. **Cephalosporins are the most appropriate antibiotic for prophylaxis before surgical procedures in noninfected patients as the most common secondarily infecting organism is *S. epidermidis.*** High-risk patients can be treated with intravenous ampicillin and gentamicin. The use of gentamicin has become simplified since the introduction of a single daily dosing schedule (Santucci and Krieger, 2000).

**Anesthesia.** PNL can be performed after the administration of general, epidural, or local anesthesia. Local anesthesia, usually in combination with intravenous sedatives and analgesics, has been reported in a number of centers (Clayman et al, 1983; Hulbert et al, 1986; Preminger et al, 1986; Ohlsen and Kinn, 1993). Local anesthesia may be an option when general anesthesia is contraindicated. A local anesthetic, such as lidocaine, can be delivered into the access track by use of an 8.3 French anesthetic injection catheter with multiple side holes or with a dual-lumen ureteral access catheter (Dalela et al, 2004). Regional anesthesia (e.g., epidural, spinal) can be used for percutaneous procedures, but several problems may be associated with these regional anesthetic techniques. First, a relatively high block is necessary to eliminate all renal pain. Second, distention of the renal pelvis during PNL may cause a vasovagal reaction that is not always prevented by regional anesthesia (Grasso and Taylor, 1997). General anesthesia is usually preferred when a more lengthy procedure is planned because it is the best means of protecting the airway when patients are in a prone position. **In cases in which upper pole puncture is contemplated, general anesthesia should be used as it permits control of respiratory movements** which is essential to minimize the risk of pulmonary complications.

**Opacification of the Collecting System.** The collecting system can be visualized in several ways in preparation for PNL. When it is performed as a single-stage procedure, PNL is initiated by the cystoscopic placement of a ureteral catheter. If the stone burden is large or when the proximal ureter is dilated, the use of a 7 French occlusion balloon catheter should be considered to prevent the migration of fragments into the ureter (Fig. 44–25). **A ureteral catheter serves several purposes: to opacify and to distend the collecting system, to provide an optimal target for percutaneous puncture, to minimize passage of stone fragments into the ureter during lithotripsy, to allow retrograde irrigation, and to instill contrast material during the procedure** (Beckmann and Roth, 1985; Littleton et al, 1986). Iodinated contrast material is the most widely used means of opacifying the collecting system in

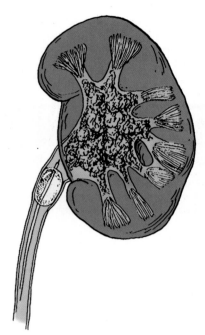

**Figure 44–25.** Occlusion balloon catheter at the ureteropelvic junction in preparation for PNL.

a retrograde fashion. However, as contrast material is more dense than urine, the contrast agent may layer in the more dependent, anterior calyces, making the delineation of the posterior calyces difficult. If this occurs, carbon dioxide or room air (<20 mL) can be used to outline the posterior calyces, although the resolution will not be as great as with iodinated contrast material (Lee et al, 1986; Young, 1986). However, **air embolism after air pyelography has been reported, so care must be exercised in performing this technique** (Miller et al, 1984; Cadeddu et al, 1997).

**Percutaneous access is best achieved as a single-stage procedure, performed in the operating room by the urologist** or, if necessary, a radiologist, by use of biplanar C-arm fluoroscopic imaging, followed immediately by track dilation and stone removal. However, in many institutions, antegrade access is created as a separate procedure by an interventional radiologist in the radiology suite (two-stage PNL). When it is done in this manner, opacification of the collecting system can be achieved with retrograde pyelography as described. Alternatively, intravenous injection of contrast material or percutaneous antegrade pyelography can be performed with a 22-gauge Chiba needle. The risk of clinically significant hemorrhage or renal damage with such a thin needle is negligible (Dunnick et al, 1985; Zagoria and Dyer, 1999). The renal collecting system is located fluoroscopically after intravenous injection of contrast material or by sonographic imaging. Alternatively, a "blind" puncture can be performed just lateral (1 to 1.5 cm) to the vertebral transverse process at the L1-2 level. In the average-sized adult patient, the renal collecting system is usually within 7 to 10 cm of the skin, and the minimal distance to the renal capsule is about 4 cm. Continuous aspiration is applied to the needle as it is slowly withdrawn, until urine appears. Entrance into the collecting system with this method can usually be achieved with three or fewer passes (Castaneda-Zuniga et al, 1986; Robert et al,

1999). Once the renal collecting system has been entered, dilute contrast material is injected to opacify the collecting system. The Chiba needle can also be used in a one-step procedure when retrograde opacification is difficult or impossible.

For solitary calculi in difficult-to-access locations or in a calyceal diverticulum, it is often best to avoid contrast material injection into the collecting system and to direct the puncture at the stone itself (Ohlsen and Kinn, 1993; Kim et al, 2005a).

**Positioning of the Patient.** PNL is performed with the patient in a prone position, and the stone-containing side is elevated on a foam pad to approximately 30 degrees (Fig. 44–26). This position aids in ventilation of the patient and tends to bring the posterior calyces into a vertical position that is helpful during PNL puncture. The posterior calyces are usually oriented toward the avascular area between the anterior and posterior arterial divisions of the kidney (Brödel's bloodless line of incision), the ideal point of entry. A puncture through a posterior calyx usually traverses this line, avoiding the major branches of the renal artery (Dyer et al, 1997). Pressure points are identified and padded, and careful attention is focused on the positioning of the patient's arms. The arm on the side of the stone is flexed at the elbow and placed on an arm board, and the contralateral arm is placed at the patient's side. Intravenous extension tubing is connected to the ureteral catheter or the occlusion balloon port to allow inflation or deflation of the balloon or the instillation of contrast material or irrigation.

## Choosing Renal Access for Percutaneous Nephrolithotomy

PNL is usually performed through antegrade percutaneous access. Alternatively, percutaneous access can be achieved in a

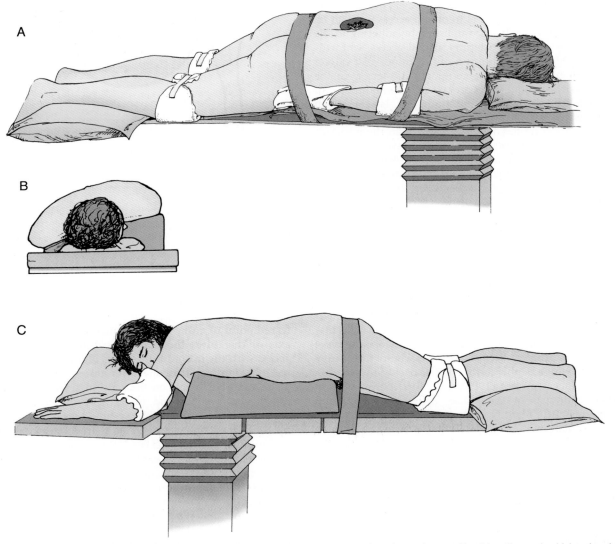

**Figure 44–26.** Position of the patient for PNL. **A,** Side to be treated is elevated approximately 30 degrees. The "down" arm should be placed at the patient's side. **B,** All pressure points are carefully padded. **C,** The "up" arm should be placed in an abducted position. The patient is placed far enough down the table so that the center post of the table does not impede movement of the C-arm.

retrograde fashion. The retrograde technique was first described as an attempt to simplify access for urologists, particularly in treating nondilated collecting systems (Hunter et al, 1983; Lawson et al, 1983; Kidd and Conlin, 2003). Regardless of the access technique, the selection of the calyx to enter as well as the point of puncture is critical for a successful outcome. The surgeon must select the optimal approach for stone removal, recognizing the restraints conferred by renal anatomy.

**Anatomic Considerations.** Familiarity with basic renal anatomy is essential for access to be obtained safely. The main renal artery typically divides into an anterior and a posterior division. The avascular field between the anterior and posterior divisions, known as Brödel's bloodless line, is the ideal point of renal entry. Because of the orientation of the kidney in the body, entry through a posterior calyx usually traverses this line (Dyer et al, 1997). **A posterior calyx is a preferred site of entry; it is usually easier to negotiate a wire out of the calyx and into the ureter when the site of puncture is a posterior rather than an anterior calyx.** However, in certain situations, it may be more optimal to obtain access through an anterior calyx; this may be accomplished by adhering to the same principles as for a posterior calyceal access. Unfortunately, it is only at the midportion of the kidney that calyces are arranged into two rows, anterior and posterior. In the polar regions, the major calyces are typically compound, with great variability in calyceal orientation (Fig. 44–27). When they are viewed on intravenous pyelography, the anterior calyces are usually more laterally situated than the posterior calyces; however, some variability exists (Kaye and Reinke, 1984). Therefore, determination of calyceal orientation and choice of the most favorable calyx for puncture are best done when the patient is in the prone position with use of biplanar C-arm fluoroscopy. Regardless of the exact calyceal orientation, the ideal subcostal percutaneous access track begins inside the posterior axillary line and traverses the renal parenchyma at the posterolateral aspect of the kidney (Fig. 44–28). Biplanar fluoroscopy also permits close attention to the point of entry into the collecting system, avoiding through-and-through puncture. **The collecting system should be accessed along the direction of the infundibulum to avoid blood vessels adjacent to the infundibulum.** Inadvertent puncture beyond the anterior aspect of the collecting system risks vascular injury of the large anterior segmental vessels; this is a problem because these vessels are not readily tamponaded with a nephrostomy tube or occlusion balloon.

Sampaio and associates (1992) studied 62 polyester resin corrosion endocasts of the kidney collecting system and intrarenal vessels to identify the preferred anatomic point of puncture into a calyx. Before performance of the endocast, a retrograde pyelogram was obtained on each kidney, and the superior, middle, and lower poles of each kidney were punctured under fluoroscopic guidance. Puncture through the infundibulum of the upper, middle, and lower poles was associated with vascular injury in 67.6%, 38.4%, and 68.2% of the kidneys, respectively. Puncture through the upper pole infundibulum was the most dangerous because the posterior segmental artery crosses the posterior surface of the infundibulum in 57% of cases (Sampaio and Aragao, 1990). Puncture through the fornix proved to be much safer and was

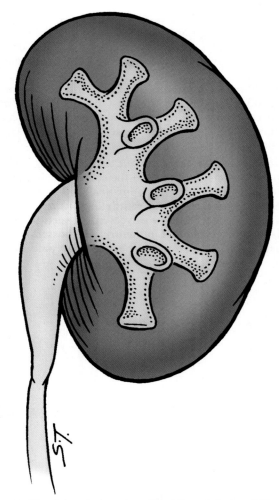

**Figure 44–27.** Calyceal orientation of the kidney. Only the middle calyces are arranged in two rows (anterior and posterior). Polar calyceal orientation is variable.

associated with less than 8% venous injury and no arterial lesions. Direct puncture into the renal pelvis injured large retropelvic vessels in one third of cases. Therefore, **the preferred point of entry into the collecting system is along the axis of the calyx, through the papilla. Alignment of the access with the infundibulum also allows the most efficient use of a rigid nephroscope and reduces the need for one to place excessive torque on the rigid instruments,** which may cause renal trauma and bleeding. Infundibular puncture should be avoided, if possible, as should direct puncture of the renal pelvis with its elevated risk of vascular injury, potential prolonged urine leak, and easy tube dislodgment.

The retroperitoneal location of the kidney and its relation to diaphragm and pleura, liver, spleen, and right and left colon as well as the skin entrance site are important extrarenal anatomic details the urologist must keep in mind in planning a PNL puncture. When it is possible, **the kidney should be approached from below the 12th rib to reduce the risk of pleural complications.** The site of entry on the skin is usually just inferior and several centimeters medial to the tip of the 12th rib (Clayman et al, 1984). A puncture too close to the rib

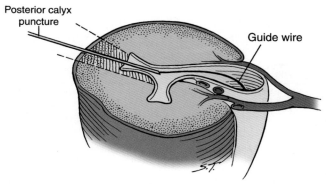

**Figure 44–28.** The ideal subcostal percutaneous access traverses the renal parenchyma at the posterolateral aspect of the kidney through the relatively avascular Brödel's zone, entering a posterior calyx. This approach minimizes the chance of vascular injury and allows a relatively direct path into the renal pelvis.

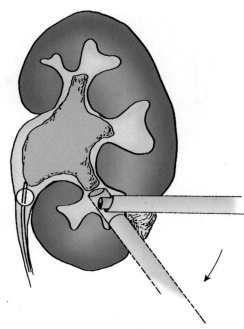

**Figure 44–29.** Access that is not aligned with the infundibulum requires torque to be placed on the nephroscope to achieve optimal visibility, which may traumatize renal parenchyma and cause bleeding. Aligning the access with the infundibulum allows the most efficient and least traumatic use of the rigid nephroscope.

may injure the intercostal vessels and nerve, exacerbating postoperative pain. A more medially sited track (i.e., paraspinal) is uncomfortable to the patient and may traverse the renal parenchyma too medially, increasing the risk of bleeding (Lang, 1987). A puncture placed too laterally (lateral to the posterior axillary line) may injure the colon, as the position of the retroperitoneal colon is usually anterior or anterolateral to the lateral renal border (Lang, 1987; Lee et al, 1987a). Patients with displacement of the colon posterior to the kidney are at increased risk of colon perforation, and a retrorenal colon is most likely to be situated near the inferior pole of the kidney. Hopper and coworkers (1987a, 1987b), in a study of 500 CT scans of the abdomen, reported that **the overall frequency of retrorenal colon in the supine patient is 1.9%.** When 90 patients were studied in the prone position, a retrorenal colon was found in 10% (Hopper et al, 1987a). Posterior colonic displacement is more likely in thin female patients with very little retroperitoneal fat and in elderly patients as well as in those who have been subjected to jejunoileal bypass. Other factors increasing the risk of colon injury include anterior calyceal puncture, previous extensive renal surgery, horseshoe kidney, and kyphoscoliosis; retrorenal colon is more commonly found on the left (LeRoy et al, 1985; Dyer et al, 1997; Wolf, 1998).

The liver and spleen may also be at risk for injury during percutaneous access. However, in the absence of splenomegaly or hepatomegaly, injury to these organs is extremely rare for those patients treated with a puncture below the 12th rib. The risk may be somewhat greater with upper pole punctures, especially if the puncture is incorrectly performed, such as during the inspiratory phase of respiration rather than the expiratory phase, or if the puncture is placed above the 11th rib (Hopper and Yakes, 1990; Robert et al, 1999). In an upper pole access, the skin puncture site should be as far medial as possible, adjacent to the lateral border of the paraspinal muscles, to reduce the risk of damage to the liver or spleen. **The main risk of a supracostal puncture, though, is injury to the lung and pleura;** the upper poles of both kidneys rest immediately anterior to the posterior portion of the 11th and 12th ribs or, occasionally, as high as the 10th rib (Fuchs and Forsyth, 1990). **The risk of pleural injury is much greater**

during the inspiratory phase of respiration, so a supracostal puncture should be performed only during full expiration. A supracostal puncture is associated with pulmonary morbidity in approximately 16% of cases (Young et al, 1985; Picus et al, 1986; Fuchs and Forsyth, 1990; Narasimham et al, 1991; Golijanin et al, 1998; Stening and Bourne, 1998; Munver et al, 2001). Most complications are minor pleural effusions that can be managed conservatively, although there are certain patients who will require an intervention to drain an accumulation of fluid or air. Supracostal puncture has also been associated with increased postoperative pain (Fuchs and Forsyth, 1990). To reduce the morbidity of a supracostal access, the puncture site should be placed in the middle of the intercostal space, just lateral to the paraspinal muscles. If it is at all possible, puncture above the 11th rib should be avoided.

**Puncture Site Selection.** Stone location and stone burden should be the primary considerations in selection of the optimal access for stone removal. The lower pole approach has been associated with fewer complications, making lower pole renal access preferable, unless an upper pole access is specifically indicated. The guiding principle should be that **the goal of all approaches is the removal of the greatest stone burden with a rigid nephroscope.** A rigid nephroscope that is aligned with the infundibular access allows optimal visualization of the stone and easier access into the renal pelvis (Fig. 44–29). The risk of renal trauma is reduced, as there should be little need to place significant torque on the rigid instruments. For patients with a solitary calyceal stone, the preferred approach is usually directly into the calyx containing the stone (Hulbert et al, 1986). However, stones in anterior calyces may be difficult to access in this manner; a direct puncture into the calyx

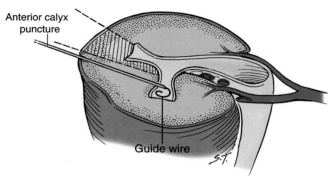

**Figure 44-30.** In puncture of an anterior calyx, it may be difficult to pass a wire or an instrument through the infundibulum owing to the acute angle created between the line of puncture and the infundibulum. Anterior calyx puncture may also be associated with an increased risk of vascular injury.

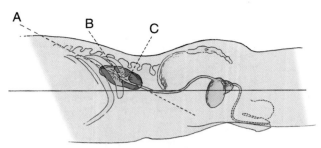

**Figure 44-31.** Angle of entry. Lateral view of abdomen demonstrates the renal axis (**A**). PNL through the upper pole (**B**) provides a less acute angle of entry into the collecting system than does lower pole access (**C**).

is often at an acute angle with the collecting system, making access into the renal pelvis difficult not only with a rigid instrument but also with a flexible endoscope (Glanz et al, 1986). Therefore, for smaller stones in an anterior calyx, an indirect approach through a posterior calyx followed by flexible nephroscopy may be preferred (Fig. 44-30). However, for those patients with large stones, a direct approach may be required to maximize the efficiency of the procedure (Coleman, 1986). Nonstaghorn stones usually can be accessed from a posterior lower or mid-kidney calyx (Coleman, 1986; Lee et al, 1986).

**A supracostal puncture is usually necessary when the predominant distribution of stone material is in the upper calyces, when there is an associated ureteropelvic junction stricture requiring endopyelotomy, in cases of multiple lower pole infundibula and calyces containing stone material or an associated ureteral stone, in staghorn calculi with substantial upper pole stone burden, and in horseshoe kidneys** (Lam et al, 1992c). A supracostal puncture may also be used when stone removal is incomplete through a lower pole access (Munver et al, 2001). The major advantage of a supracostal puncture is that the line of puncture aligns the access track most closely with the renal axis (Fig. 44-31 and Table 44-16).

Upper pole renal access can be performed through an infracostal, intercostal, or supracostal puncture (Fig. 44-32). For a solitary stone in an upper pole calyx or an upper pole calyceal diverticulum, a subcostal puncture directed toward the upper

pole may be used. However, directing a rigid nephroscope from the upper pole into the renal pelvis after such a puncture may be impossible or unduly traumatic. On occasion, the upper pole can be reached through a laterally situated track between the tips of the 11th and 12th ribs. Although by strict definition this is an intercostal access track, the risk for pleural injury is significantly lower than when a vertical supracostal puncture is selected (LeRoy et al, 1985). Karlin and Smith (1989) described a technique of renal displacement that may be used to avoid a supracostal puncture. An Amplatz sheath passed through a central or lower pole calyx is used to displace the kidney caudally, and a second puncture is performed toward the upper pole. The authors reported that failures have occurred in patients with kidneys that are immobile due to previous operations.

**Multiple accesses should be considered when any calyx contains a stone larger than 2 cm and is unreachable through the primary access with a rigid instrument or when stones are smaller than 2 cm but cannot be reached with a flexible instrument through the primary access.** In general, additional accesses may be undertaken during the primary PNL, unless the procedure has been unduly prolonged or bleeding is deemed excessive. In such instances, further intervention may be best delayed until the time of secondary PNL. The frequency of multiple accesses varies widely. Newmark and colleagues reported that in a group of 229 patients (246 renal units) with staghorn stones, 13.4% of the kidneys required access with track dilation in addition to the primary track (Lingeman et al, 1995). Furthermore, 7.3% of kidneys required an additional puncture without track dilation to

| Table 44-16. **Percutaneous Nephrolithotomy Through Supracostal Access** | | | | | |
|---|---|---|---|---|---|
| *Author* | *Overall PNL Patients (n)* | *No. of Supracostal Punctures (%)* | *Overall Pleural Complications (%)* | *Pleural Complications Treated (%)* | *Stone-Free Rate (%)* |
| Young et al, 1985 | 140 | 24 (17) | 37 | 4.2 | N/A |
| Picus et al, 1986 | 154 | 50 (32) | 32 | 8 | 90 |
| Fuchs and Forsyth, 1990 | 344 | 106 (31) | N/A | 4.7 | N/A |
| Narasimham et al, 1991 | 231 | 56 (24) | 9 | 3.5 | 95 |
| Lam et al, 1992b | 91 | 25 (27) | 28 | 2.2 | N/A |
| Golijanin et al, 1998 | 320 | 104 (36) | 8.7 | 4.3 | 87 |
| Stening and Bourne, 1998 | N/A | 21 | None | None | 75 |
| Munver et al, 2001 | 300 | 98 (33) | 2.6 | 2.3 | 98 |
| **Weighted average** | **1580** | **484 (30)** | **14.8** | **4.1** | **92.2** |

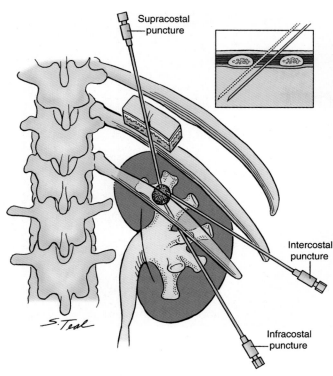

**Figure 44–32.** Upper pole access can be achieved with a supracostal, intercostal, or infracostal approach. A supracostal approach most closely aligns the puncture with the renal axis, whereas an infracostal puncture allows access to the upper pole only. Supracostal puncture should be initiated closer to the upper rib to allow proper passage of the needle through the intercostal space (inset). A midline puncture (inset, dotted line) risks hitting the lower rib.

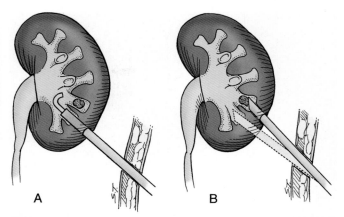

**Figure 44–33.** When a stone in an adjoining calyx cannot be reached with a flexible nephroscope (**A**), the Amplatz sheath is withdrawn to just beyond the renal capsule, and a second puncture with use of the same skin incision (Y puncture) is directed into the neighboring calyx (**B**).

assist in identification of a stone-containing calyx during flexible nephroscopy. Matlaga and associates (2004) reported on a series of 133 patients with large-volume calculi, of whom 16.5% required multiple access tracks. In comparison, multiple accesses were used by Lee and associates (1987b) in 73% and by Merhej and coworkers (1998) in 78% of patients treated for staghorn stones. These differences may reflect different preferences in the use of flexible nephroscopy during PNL for staghorn stones. Multiple accesses are usually best created as separate punctures. However, when calculi are located in parallel or adjacent calyces, a Y puncture, in which the secondary puncture angles off the existing nephrostomy track, can be considered (Lange et al, 1984; Hulbert et al, 1986). Once the first calyx has been completely cleared, the Amplatz sheath is retracted outside of the renal capsule and angled toward the second calyx. The second puncture is made through the Amplatz sheath (Fig. 44–33).

**Access and Track Dilation.** Once the point of puncture and the preferred calyx have been selected, the C-arm unit is angled in the direction opposite the line of puncture (i.e., to the head for a lower pole puncture or to the feet for an upper pole puncture) to minimize x-ray exposure of the surgeon's hands. **After the targeted calyx is identified with fluoroscopy, an 18-gauge needle is directed into it by the triangulation method. Mediolateral adjustments of the needle (showing the point of entrance to the calyx) are made with the C-arm directed parallel to the needle** (Fig. 44–34). **Cephalad or caudad adjustments of the needle (showing the depth of penetration) are made with the C-arm rotated obliquely as much as is feasible relative to the needle axis** (Fig. 44–35). It is critical to maintain the needle orientation in one plane while adjustments in the other plane are made. If the surgeon rests his or her forearm on the patient's torso, the line of puncture is stabilized and drift is minimized, facilitating precise puncture. After the direction of puncture is correctly aligned in both planes, the needle is advanced, with the C-arm rotated obliquely to the sagittal plane of the needle so that the depth of puncture can be monitored. Before the renal capsule is entered, final adjustments are made. Manipulation of the needle after renal parenchyma is entered is a problem because movements of the needle invariably displace the kidney and thus affect the position of the target calyx as well.

Proper location of the needle is verified by aspiration of urine. On occasion, the needle must be withdrawn gradually while constant suction is applied until urine appears in the suction tubing. **After the needle is satisfactorily positioned in the collecting system, a hydrophilic guide wire is passed. A hydrophilic wire is preferred for entering the collecting system as it is the most flexible and maneuverable wire currently available.** Ideally, the guide wire is advanced into the ureter, a most secure position. **When a lower pole puncture is performed, an angiographic catheter (i.e., Cobra) is often helpful in directing the guide wire through the ureteropelvic junction.** When an upper pole puncture is used, manipulation of the guide wire into the ureter is usually straightforward. If the guide wire cannot be manipulated down the ureter, the wire should be coiled as much as possible in a calyx or the renal pelvis. Care should be taken to avoid excessive force in this situation because perforations of the calyx and renal pelvis are distressingly easy to create. **Once the guide wire is positioned in the ureter, it is exchanged for a stiffer, Teflon-coated working wire such as an Amplatz super-stiff wire. An 8-10 French coaxial dilating system is then used to place a second safety wire. Renal track dilation should not proceed without a safety wire in place.** Several methods of track dilation are available, including metal telescoping dilators, semirigid Amplatz dilators, and balloon dilators (Alken

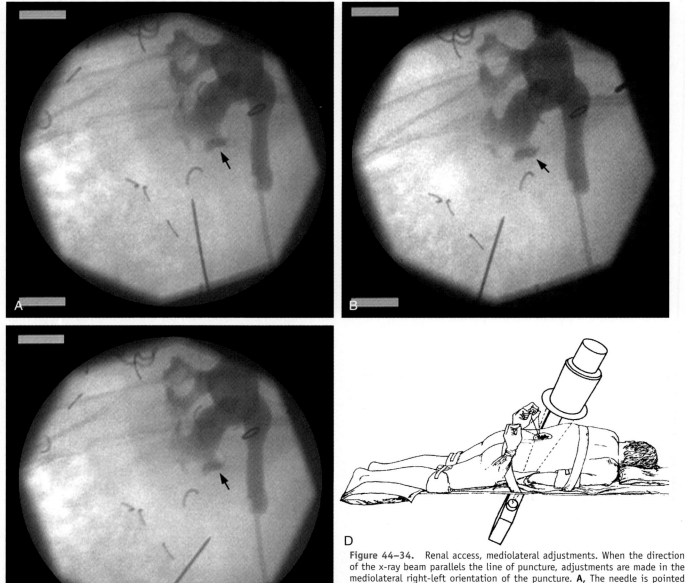

**Figure 44–34.** Renal access, mediolateral adjustments. When the direction of the x-ray beam parallels the line of puncture, adjustments are made in the mediolateral right-left orientation of the puncture. **A,** The needle is pointed too laterally. **B,** The needle is properly aligned with the lower pole calyx. **C,** The needle is pointed too medially. Notice the C-arm is angled away from the line of puncture to protect the surgeon's hands. **D,** With the C-arm parallel to the saglttal plane of the needle, mediolateral adjustments to the needle are made.

et al, 1981; Clayman et al, 1983; Kerlan et al, 1984). **Balloon dilators, although more costly, are often quicker and safer than the other dilators.** Davidoff and Bellman (1997) reported that use of balloon dilators was associated with significantly less bleeding as well as a reduced rate of transfusion compared with Amplatz dilation. In select cases, such as those patients with extensive perirenal fibrosis after open renal surgery, balloon dilation may not be possible, and Amplatz or metal dilators may be necessary. Excessive force, especially with use of Amplatz or metal dilators, can lead to perforation of the renal pelvis, causing significant hemorrhage and urine extravasation. In the presence of flank scarring, a 4.5-mm

fascial incising needle that can be placed over the working wire will often facilitate subsequent balloon dilation.

After track dilation, the operating nephroscope is inserted through an **open, low-pressure system** with an Amplatz working sheath or through a **closed, high-pressure system** with the nephroscope serving as its own sheath. The advantages of the closed system are that the nephrostomy track is smaller (depending on the nephroscope used), hydrodistention of the collecting system occurs (which facilitates intrarenal inspection), and bleeding may be reduced (Segura, 1998). However, **a closed system is a low-flow, high-pressure (16 to 33 cm H$_2$O) system that can lead to significant fluid**

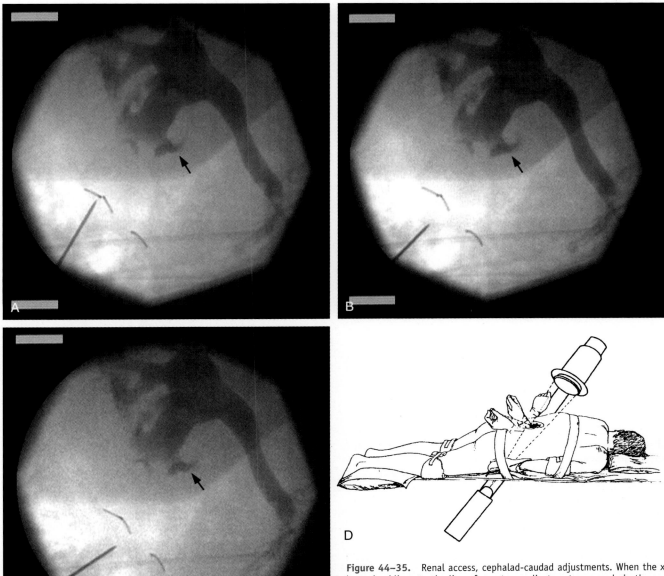

**Figure 44–35.** Renal access, cephalad-caudad adjustments. When the x-ray beam is oblique to the line of puncture, adjustments are made in the cephalad-caudad (up-down) orientation of the line of puncture. **A,** The needle is pointed too cephalad. **B,** The needle is properly aligned with the lower pole calyx. **C,** The needle is pointed too caudad. **D,** After the C-arm is rotated approximately 90 degrees, adjustments in the cephalocaudad direction of the puncture can be made.

**absorption.** When an Amplatz working sheath is used, pressures remain below 16 cm $H_2O$ at all times and usually below 7 cm $H_2O$ (Saltzman et al, 1987). Absorption of irrigant into the circulation and the risk of a large-volume extravasation event are higher when a closed system is used. For these reasons, use of an Amplatz sheath during PNL is always preferred. Furthermore, the use of a working sheath allows easy insertion and removal of the nephroscope and permits a simple exchange from rigid to flexible nephroscopy. In addition, the internal diameter of the Amplatz sheath is larger than that of the operating nephroscope, allowing the grasping and basketing of larger stone fragments. When the Amplatz working sheath is advanced over the dilating system into the

calyx of puncture, care must be taken not to overadvance the dilator and sheath. This is a common and potentially serious error in obtaining access for PNL and may result in significant trauma to the renal collecting system or extensive hemorrhage (Fig. 44–36).

*"Mini-Perc" and Nondilated Punctures.* The "mini-perc" technique was first developed for use in children. An 11 to 15 French peel-away vascular access sheath was used, instead of the more commonly used 24 to 30 French Amplatz sheaths. PNL was performed with pediatric instruments (Helal et al, 1997; Jackman et al, 1998). The mini-perc technique was adapted to adult patients with stones smaller than 2 cm by use of a 13 French ureteroscopy sheath for percutaneous access,

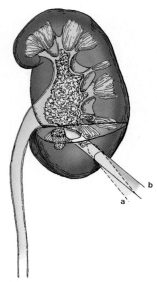

**Figure 44–36.** Placement of dilator–working sheath for staghorn calculus. Care should be taken to avoid overadvancement of dilators. The correct position, *a*, is just short of the renal collecting system. Overadvancement, *b*, slides past the stone-containing calyx and traumatizes adjacent renal parenchyma.

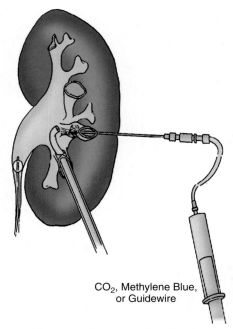

CO$_2$, Methylene Blue, or Guidewire

**Figure 44–37.** Adjuvant needle puncture (nondilated puncture) to aid in identification of difficult-to-locate calyx. Methylene blue, carbon dioxide, or a guide wire is instilled to mark entry into the desired calyx.

6.9 French rigid or 7.2 French flexible ureteroscopes, and a 7.7 French rigid offset pediatric cystoscope. Lithotripsy was achieved with a holmium:YAG laser and a 4.5 French ultrasonic probe. The authors reported a stone-free rate of 89% with minimal morbidity. Monga and Oglevie (2000) used an 18 French balloon dilation catheter, a 20 French nephrostomy sheath, and a 9.8 French rigid or 15.5 French flexible endoscope and reported similar results in a series of 16 patients with an average stone size of 2.8 cm. **The miniperc technique requires longer operative time and fragmentation of relatively small, otherwise extractable stones.** The advantages of this technique over standard PNL remain to be established.

Several clinical situations may require a nondilated puncture during the course of PNL. For example, when an eccentric calyx is encountered that is difficult to locate through an established access, a needle puncture into the desired calyx without track dilation can be helpful. Methylene blue or carbon dioxide can be injected through the needle, and the colored stream or gas bubbles may be used to guide a flexible nephroscope into the appropriate calyx (Fig. 44–37). If the stone-containing calyx still cannot be identified after this maneuver, a glide wire may be passed through the calyx into the renal pelvis and grasped with the nephroscope. If a narrow infundibulum precludes advancement of the nephroscope, a flexible ureteroscope may be required; alternatively, the infundibulum may be dilated with a balloon. The flexible nephroscope can also be backloaded onto the guide wire and passed into the desired calyx with a push-pull technique (Lingeman, 1995). A nondilated puncture may also be used for the insertion of a small-diameter nephrostomy tube into a lower pole calyx when the initial access was placed through an upper pole calyx. Kim and associates (2005b) reported use of this technique for patients undergoing PNL through an upper pole access, when the patients were judged to have

minimal or no residual stones at the conclusion of the procedure. Puncture of the lower pole was directed onto a flexible nephroscope that was inserted through the upper pole access and placed into the desired lower pole calyx. In cases in which secondary PNL was required, the procedure could be accomplished successfully by a flexible ureteroscope inserted through the nondilated lower pole access. When indicated, the insertion of a lower pole nephrostomy tube in patients undergoing PNL through upper pole access provided the benefits of a supracostal puncture with less discomfort of the patient postoperatively. This technique allows the surgeon to take advantage of the benefits of a supracostal access while minimizing postoperative discomfort.

**Stone Removal.** After the track has been appropriately dilated and the Amplatz sheath positioned, the urologist can proceed with stone removal by endoscopic techniques. In the early days of PNL, several authors reported the successful extraction of renal calculi with Randall's forceps (modified to allow passage over a guide wire) or stone baskets under only fluoroscopic, not visual, guidance (Castaneda-Zuniga et al, 1982; Pollack and Banner, 1984). However, fluoroscopically guided stone removal is no longer recommended because it is not as safe or as efficient as the removal of calculi under direct vision.

**Physiologic solutions should be used for irrigation during PNL to minimize the risk of dilutional hyponatremia in the event of large-volume extravasation** (Carson, 1986). The height of the irrigant should be maintained at 80 cm or less above the patient to minimize intrapelvic pressure and to prevent fluid absorption through pyelovenous backflow (Miller and Whitfield, 1985). The use of an Amplatz working sheath also prevents elevated intrapelvic pressures. Rigid nephroscopy is performed initially, and stones up to 1 cm in diameter can be grasped with rigid graspers or stone baskets and extracted intact through the 30 French Amplatz sheath. Stones larger than 1 cm require fragmentation before extraction. Several intracorporeal lithotripsy techniques are available.

Rigid nephroscopy is the preferred method for stone removal; however, only the simplest intrarenal collecting systems can be completely inspected with a rigid nephroscope through a single access. Therefore, **flexible nephroscopy should be used during every PNL to survey the entire intrarenal collecting system for residual stone fragments.** Pressurization of irrigation fluid (to 300 mm Hg) during flexible nephroscopy is necessary to adequately distend the collecting system and to improve visualization (the use of an Amplatz sheath is mandatory when pressurized irrigation is used). The entire collecting system should be examined systematically, including the proximal ureter. Injection of contrast material through the flexible nephroscope is helpful in maintaining orientation and verifying that each calyx has been inspected. Small stone fragments can be removed with a stone basket passed through the flexible instrument, and larger stones can be fragmented with laser or EHL. Alternatively, fragments may be flushed or manipulated into the renal pelvis with a combination of high-pressure irrigant and a floppy-tipped J wire, where they may be retrieved more easily with rigid instruments. The goal of PNL is complete or nearly complete clearance of stone material at the time of the primary procedure, which greatly simplifies secondary procedures, if necessary. Furosemide is administered intravenously when the nephrostomy tube is placed at the conclusion of PNL to promote and to maintain diuresis.

**Postoperative Considerations: Nephrostomy Tubes.** After completion of PNL, percutaneous drainage through a nephrostomy tube is usually advocated. The nephrostomy tube serves several purposes: to tamponade bleeding emanating from the nephrostomy track, to allow the renal puncture to heal, to allow proper drainage of urine, and to allow access to the collecting system if a secondary PNL is required (Winfield et al, 1986). Various nephrostomy tubes are available that may be divided into several categories: catheters without self-retention features (such as red rubber Robinson-type catheters), self-retaining catheters (pigtail, Cope loop, Malecot, and balloon catheters), nephrostomy-stent combinations (reentry catheters), and circle nephrostomy tubes (U-loop catheters) (Fig. 44–38) (Babayan, 1993; Lee, 1995).

The size and type of catheter used are largely dependent on the extent of stone manipulation and urothelial trauma during PNL, the extent of hemorrhage during and after the procedure, the patient's body habitus, and the surgeon's preferences. Self-retaining catheters have an obvious advantage over catheters without self-retention properties as they are less likely to migrate or to be dislodged. Smaller, softer, self-retaining tubes (such as 10 French Cope loop catheters) cause less discomfort to the patient than do stiffer, larger diameter tubes (Kim et al, 2005b). In addition, the smaller nephrostomy track closes more readily after tube removal. However, in the presence of significant bleeding, smaller tubes may be more likely to occlude and may be insufficient to tamponade the nephrostomy track. The reentry catheter consists of a Malecot catheter with a ureteral catheter attached to the tip of the Malecot, which extends across the ureteropelvic junction into the midureter. The benefit of the reentry catheter is that access to the collecting system is maintained even when the nephrostomy tube is partially dislodged. Therefore, its use is preferable in patients prone to tube dislodgment, such as the morbidly obese. If tube dislodgment is a concern, a ureteral catheter or an angiographic catheter may also be placed through the access track in addition to the nephrostomy tube, allowing easy access to the ureter, if necessary. Finally, a circle (or loop) nephrostomy tube is a useful option after PNL with multiple accesses. After tube placement, a nephrostogram is usually obtained 24 to 48 hours after PNL. If all the stones have been removed and there is free flow of contrast material down the ureter without extravasation, the nephrostomy tube can be removed or clamped and then removed.

Bellman and associates (1997) have suggested that to minimize PNL morbidity, no nephrostomy tube may be placed after PNL in select patients. The concept of "tubeless" PNL is not new. In 1984, Wickham and coworkers omitted percutaneous drainage in selected patients, with good outcomes reported. However, Winfield and associates (1986) reported significant morbidity in two patients in whom nephrostomy tube drainage was not used after PNL, concluding that a nephrostomy tube is essential to ensure an uncomplicated postoperative course; in these two cases, no alternative form of upper tract drainage was used. Bellman and associates (1997) described 50 patients who had early removal of the nephrostomy tube after PNL. The first 30 patients had a nephrostomy tube removed within 2 to 3 hours after surgery, and the remaining 20 patients had the nephrostomy tube removed in the operating room. All patients had a double-J stent placed during PNL, and a Foley catheter was left in place for 24 hours. Patients with significant residual stone burden, procedures longer than 2 hours, multiple accesses, perforation of the collecting system, or significant bleeding were excluded. The authors reported no significant complications in this cohort, and hospitalization, analgesia requirements, and time to return to normal activity were significantly reduced in the group with double-J stent drainage compared with a control group in whom nephrostomy tubes were placed. However, no data were presented regarding postoperative assessment of residual calculi possibly necessitating secondary PNL.

Goh and Wolf (1999) reported on 10 of 26 renal units treated with an internal stent or externalized ureteral catheter placed for 1 or 2 days after PNL. Exclusion criteria included stone burden larger than 3 cm, more than one access, obstructive renal anatomy, need for a second-look procedure, and significant bleeding or perforation during the procedure. The authors reported a reduction in hospital stay in the tubeless group with morbidity comparable to that of patients with standard nephrostomy tube drainage. However, 4-mm residual fragments were noted in two patients. Delnay and Wake (1998) described 33 patients in whom an internal stent was placed in lieu of a nephrostomy tube after PNL with use of similar exclusion criteria. Average hospital stay was 1.5 days, and no significant complications occurred, but several patients harbored residual calculi that necessitated additional procedures (SWL) after PNL. Limb and Bellman (2002)

SECTION XI

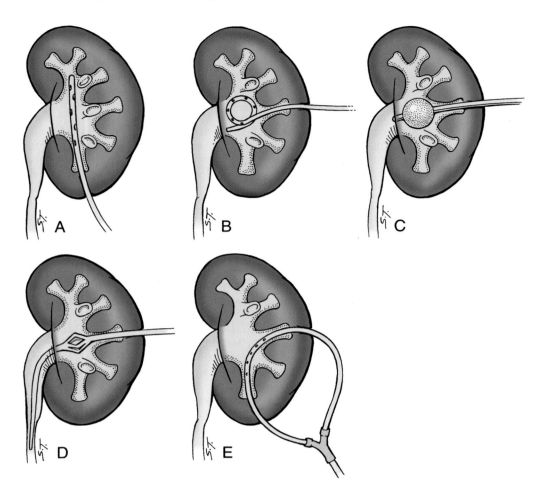

**Figure 44–38.** Various nephrostomy tubes. Without self-retention: a red rubber catheter (**A**). Self-retaining catheters: Cope loop (**B**), Foley catheter (**C**), nephrostomy-stent combination or reentry catheter (**D**). Multiaccess drainage: a circle (U-loop) tube (**E**).

described 112 patients undergoing tubeless PNL; strict criteria were used to select these patients, who had a mean stone burden of 3.30 cm$^2$. The authors reported a 93% stone-free rate and a mean length of hospitalization of 1.56 days; 7% required subsequent SWL ancillary treatments. Feng and associates (2001) performed a randomized controlled study comparing standard PNL, mini-PNL, and tubeless PNL. They found no advantage for the mini-PNL over the standard PNL and also found that the tubeless cohort experienced the least morbidity. Desai and associates (2004) also performed a prospective randomized study of patients undergoing PNL with conventional large-bore nephrostomy drainage, small-bore nephrostomy drainage, or no nephrostomy drainage. The authors reported that tubeless PNL was associated with the least pain. However, they did not comment on the need for ancillary procedures or the stone-free status of the patients.

Tubeless PNL (with internal drainage) remains controversial but may be considered for select, relatively straightforward cases for which the urologist is certain that no secondary procedures will be required. An important caveat is that all tubeless procedures have been reported to include the placement of an internalized ureteral stent, which requires a second procedure to accomplish stent removal.

## Percutaneous Nephrolithotomy in Special Situations

### Calyceal Diverticula

Calyceal diverticula are nonsecretory, transitional cell epithelium–lined cystic cavities within the renal parenchyma. A narrow communication with the pelvicalyceal system almost always exists. The incidence of calyceal diverticula diagnosed on routine intravenous pyelography ranges from 0.21% to 0.45% (Hulbert et al, 1986). Calculi have been reported in 9.5% to 50% of calyceal diverticula (Jones et al, 1991). Percutaneous access into stone-bearing diverticula poses several unique problems. Direct puncture is often difficult because of the small size of the cavity and the frequent occurrence of calyceal diverticula in the upper pole of the kidney. After successful puncture is achieved, negotiation of a guide wire into the renal pelvis is often not possible. A similar situation can occur when a stone fills a calyx so completely that a guide wire cannot be passed through the infundibulum into the renal pelvis or in the rare case of infundibular stenosis. To overcome these difficulties, a special access technique is required.

Contrast media can be instilled through a ureteral catheter to localize the diverticulum. However, if the stones are visible on fluoroscopy, it is often preferred to puncture directly onto the stone (Ohlsen and Kinn, 1993). **Direct puncture into the diverticulum allows use of rigid instruments that provide superior visualization compared with flexible instruments that are used in an indirect approach.** Optimal visualization is essential in trying to identify the communication between the diverticulum and the renal collecting system. Direct access is also beneficial because fulguration of the urothelium can easily be achieved by a resectoscope equipped with a roller-ball electrode. Jones and colleagues (1991) reported that direct percutaneous access into the diverticulum could be established in all but 2 of 24 patients. Likewise, Shalhav and associates (1998) reported that in a group of 30 patients with calyceal diverticula, direct access was performed in 28 patients. When direct puncture fails, a neighboring calyx can be punctured and the diverticulum entered indirectly by perforating the wall of the diverticulum or by entering in a retrograde fashion, through the diverticular neck (Hedelin et al, 1988). However, the results with an indirect approach are inferior (Jarrett and Smith, 1986).

Kim and associates (2005a) have described a single-stage technique for the treatment of patients with calculi residing in a calyceal diverticulum (Fig. 44–39). Once the diverticulum is punctured, a 0.035-inch movable core J wire is coiled within the diverticulum. It is important to ensure that not only the floppy tip of the wire but also the solid core is coiled within the diverticulum, so that sufficient stabilization is provided for proper placement of coaxial dilators. A second 0.035-inch movable core J wire serving as a safety wire is then passed through the 10 French sheath of the coaxial dilator. With two guide wires coiled within the diverticular lumen, balloon dilation of the track can be performed safely. Care should be taken to avoid perforation of the back wall of the diverticulum. Once the balloon dilator is inflated, the working sheath is passed over the balloon as close as possible to the diverticulum without advancing the balloon. In small diverticula, this results in the placement of the sheath outside the diverticu-lum. An 11 French alligator forceps is passed through the rigid nephroscope and used to follow the wire and gently spread renal parenchyma to allow entry into the calyceal diverticu-lum under direct vision. Stone material is extracted with grasping forceps or ultrasonic lithotripsy. Careful inspection of the urothelium with the rigid nephroscope is performed in an effort to identify a flattened renal papilla, which suggests an obstructed calyx rather than a diverticulum. The neck of the diverticulum is often difficult to identify as it can be diminutive. Methylene blue injected through the ureteral catheter can facilitate visualization of the ostium. Once a guide wire is passed into the renal pelvis, the neck of the diver-ticulum can be balloon dilated or incised.

Because calyceal diverticula are lined by a nonsecretory endothelium, most authors advocate fulguration at the time of PNL as this will ablate 76% to 100% of diverticula (Ellis et al, 1991; Jones et al, 1991; Shalhav et al, 1998; Monga, 2000). Alternatively, Hulbert and coworkers (1986) reported treating 10 patients with calyceal diverticula and suggested that trauma to the wall of the diverticulum caused by the dilation process is sufficient to ablate the diverticular lumen. In this series, a nephrostomy tube was left in place for 2 weeks. However, Donnellan and colleagues (1999) reported that treatment of 20 patients with calyceal diverticula by dilation or incision of the diverticular neck without fulguration resulted in complete ablation of the diverticulum in only 30% of patients, leading the authors to conclude that fulguration should be performed routinely to ensure diverticular ablation. Typically, after abla-tion of the diverticulum, a nephrostomy tube is placed for 48 to 72 hours.

### Horseshoe Kidney

Horseshoe kidney is the most common congenital renal anomaly, with an estimated incidence of 1 in 400 and a male-to-female ratio of 2:1 (Jones et al, 1991). The unique location and orientation of the horseshoe kidney are due to the incom-plete cephalad migration and malrotation of the kidney, a

**Figure 44–39.** Access into small diverticula. **A,** Balloon dilator is advanced as far as possible without perforating the back wall of the diverticulum. The working sheath is placed just outside the diverticu-lum. **B,** Alligator forceps spread the parenchyma and allow advancement of the nephroscope under vision into the diverticulum. The working sheath is then advanced over the nephro-scope and into the diverticulum (**C**).

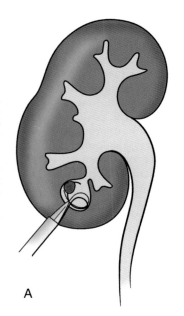
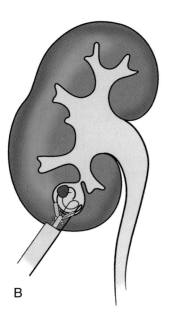
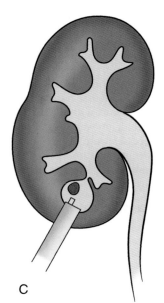

A                    B                    C

consequence of the entrapment of the isthmus under the inferior mesenteric artery (Hohenfellner et al, 1992). The ureteropelvic junction is commonly deformed owing to the high insertion of the ureter into a typically elongated renal pelvis. The course of the proximal ureter is similarly aberrant; it drapes ventrally over the renal symphysis, where it may be compressed by vessels supplying the lower pole and isthmus. Ureteral obstruction that may result from these anomalies can give rise to hydronephrosis, urinary stasis, sepsis, and calculi formation in up to 70% of patients (Jones et al, 1991; Lampel et al, 1996).

In considering PNL in a horseshoe kidney, the characteristic lower and centrally oriented position of the kidney, the orientation of the collecting system, and the abnormal blood supply should be taken into account. Janetschek and Kunzel (1988) performed postmortem examinations of six horseshoe kidneys, in situ, and found normal renal arteries in all specimens. However, accessory arteries entering the renal hilum, aberrant polar and isthmus arteries originating from the aorta, and hypogastric and common iliac arteries were noted as well; all blood vessels, except a select few supplying the isthmus, entered the kidney from its ventromedial aspect. Therefore, **a puncture of the dorsal or dorsolateral aspect of the kidney will be well away from major renal vessels.**

Skoog and associates (1985) have reported an association between horseshoe kidney and retrorenal colon. A preoperative CT scan can be of assistance, then, in determining the presence of a retrorenal colon as well as in defining the stone-bearing calyces. **The lower pole calyces lie within a coronal plane, angled medially, and are seldom suitable for direct puncture** (Al-Otaibi and Hosking, 1999). However, the **upper pole calyces are more posterior and lateral and are often subcostal, providing a convenient and relatively safe route for PNL access.** The standard site for PNL (inside the posterior axillary line just caudad to the 12th rib) is punctured, but the angle of the puncture is caudad rather than cephalad. Because most of the calyces of horseshoe kidneys point either dorsomedially or dorsolaterally, they are more favorably positioned for puncture than are normal renal units (Janetschek and Kunzel, 1988). Because of the malrotation of the kidney, the renal pelvis may be more anteriorly located, and the length of the nephrostomy track may exceed the length of the rigid nephroscope, necessitating the use of flexible nephroscopy or multiple accesses. Flexible nephroscopy may also be required to gain access to the lower medial calyces, where stones are often found (Jones et al, 1991; Al-Otaibi and Hosking, 1999).

Raj and associates (2003) reported a multicenter analysis of 24 patients with calculi in a horseshoe kidney who underwent PNL. The overall stone-free rate was greater than 90%, most accesses were upper pole, and flexible nephroscopy was performed in almost all patients. The authors noted that the rigid nephroscope was rarely sufficient to remove the whole stone burden.

## Transplantation and Pelvic Kidneys

Urolithiasis is uncommon in patients who have undergone renal transplantation, with a reported incidence of 0.5% to 3% (Harper et al, 1994; Shoskes et al, 1995; Del Pizzo and Sklar, 1999). Factors that may predispose transplant recipients to form calculi include metabolic abnormalities, foreign bodies (nonabsorbable suture material, forgotten stents), recurrent infection, and papillary necrosis. On occasion, calculi may have been present in the donor kidney (Pardalidis et al, 1994). Typical renal colic does not occur because the transplantation kidney and ureter are denervated; the presentation may instead resemble acute rejection or acute tubular necrosis (Harper et al, 1994; Rhee et al, 1999). Benoit and colleagues (1996) reported that in a series of 1500 transplantation patients, 12 (0.8%) were diagnosed with urinary calculi. Three patients presented with obstructive anuria, one patient presented with abdominal pain, and eight patients were asymptomatic and diagnosed by ultrasonography.

Renal allografts present a unique anatomic situation for PNL. The most common surgical anatomy is for the donor left kidney to be placed extraperitoneally into the recipient's right iliac fossa; alternatively, the right kidney is transplanted in the left iliac fossa. In either case, the renal pelvis is located medially, requiring that the kidney be rotated 180 degrees on its axis. Thus, the posterior calyces point anteriorly, and consequently an anterior approach to the kidney is similar to a posterior approach to native kidneys. In the usual percutaneous approach to a transplanted kidney, the patient is placed in the lithotomy position, which allows simultaneous cystoscopic access to the bladder. A ureteral catheter is inserted for instillation of contrast material. Access is most safely established (i.e., avoiding intraperitoneal contents) into the lower pole with the skin puncture as caudal as possible. Percutaneous access to transplanted kidneys is actually facilitated by their superficial location. However, scar formation around the graft may make the initial needle puncture and track dilation more difficult (Rhee et al, 1999). Once access is established, PNL can be performed by standard methods (Pardalidis et al, 1994). Del Pizzo and Sklar (1999) have reported the use of a mini-perc technique in 14 transplantation patients in whom access was established with the aid of intraoperative ultrasonography with a 16 French suprapubic peel-away introducer and sheath. No data are available to show an advantage of the mini-perc technique compared with the larger diameter working sheaths. Although delayed closure of the access track after catheter removal in immunosuppressed transplantation patients is a concern, most authors report that dilated tracks closed normally (Caldwell and Burns, 1988; Gedroyc et al, 1989; Del Pizzo and Sklar, 1999).

Patients with ectopic pelvic kidneys necessitate a different and more complicated approach for PNL as a result of their unique anatomy. The incidence of pelvic kidney has been estimated to range from 1 in 2200 to 1 in 3000 in autopsy series (Zafar and Lingeman, 1996). The pelvic kidney is retroperitoneal, posterior to the peritoneum and anterior to the sacrum. Interposing bowel loops between the kidney and the anterior abdominal wall prevent a direct puncture through the anterior abdominal wall. Eshghi and colleagues (1985) first described a laparoscopically assisted PNL technique for pelvic kidneys. Holman and Toth (1998) reported a series of 15 patients treated with laparoscopically assisted percutaneous transperitoneal nephrolithotomy. With patients in the Trendelenburg position under laparoscopic control, the bowel was mobilized until the kidney became visible, allowing percutaneous access. All stones were removed successfully with minimal morbidity. Zafar and Lingeman (1996) described a modification of the laparoscopic technique in which intracorporeal suturing of the nephrotomy site and ureteral stent placement allowed elimination of a transperitoneal nephrostomy tube. Alternatively, Matlaga and associates (2003b) reported the utility of obtaining percutaneous access with CT guidance for select patients harboring calculi in ectopic renal units.

## Morbid Obesity

Patients suffering from morbid obesity, defined as more than 100 pounds overweight, greater than 200% of ideal body weight, or a body mass index (a value obtained by weight in kilograms divided by height in meters$^2$) greater than 40, present technical as well as anesthetic challenges (Freedman et al, 2002). Often, one or more comorbid factors complicate management of these patients. Pearle and coworkers (1998) described a group of 57 patients undergoing PNL. Of the patients, 59.6% were classified by the anesthesiologist as American Society of Anesthesiologists class II and 40.4% as class III. General anesthesia may be a special concern for patients in the prone position because of restricted respiratory capacity that may require higher ventilation pressures intraoperatively. Some studies suggest an increased postoperative morbidity in morbidly obese patients, mostly because of the higher incidence of wound infection and thromboembolic events.

However, when Carson and colleagues (1988) compared 44 obese patients with 226 nonobese patients undergoing PNL, they found **no significant difference in postoperative morbidity.** Pearle and associates (1998), too, reported **no significant difference in complication and transfusion rates as well as in length of hospitalization** between obese and nonobese patients. Koo and colleagues (2004) similarly reported that **the outcome of PNL is independent of the patient's body mass index.**

There are a number of challenges in performing a radiographic evaluation of a morbidly obese patient suffering from renal or ureteral calculi. Attenuation of the ultrasound beam can make identification of the kidney difficult. Weight limitations of CT gantries (usually in the range of 300 pounds) as well as the wide girth of these patients may restrict the use of CT (Hofmann and Stoller, 1992). However, imaging is essential not only to evaluate the stone burden and location but also to determine the distance from skin to stone.

PNL in morbidly obese patients presents several unique challenges. Positioning the patient can be difficult, and in particular for large patients, two surgical tables may need to be secured together (Hofmann and Stoller, 1992). Kerbl and colleagues (1994) reported use of the flank position in two very obese patients to facilitate ventilation. However, the lateral decubitus position resulted in greater renal mobility and a longer nephrostomy track. Furthermore, Hoffman and Stoller (1992) described a morbidly obese patient who developed acute rhabdomyolysis secondary to crush injuries from placement in the lateral approach. The major difficulty in performing PNL in the morbidly obese patient is the long distance from the skin to the collecting system, which may exceed the length of the working sheath or the length of the rigid nephroscope. **Extralong Amplatz working sheaths (20 cm or more) and extralong rigid nephroscopes are now available that can overcome this challenge.** Alternatively, the Amplatz sheath can be secured by a suture, allowing easy retrieval even when it migrates under the skin (Nguyen and

Belis, 1998). On occasion, when the long Amplatz sheath is not sufficient to reach the kidney, an incision can be made through the subcutaneous tissue to the muscles of the flank, and the PNL track is created from the level of the muscle sheath (Curtis et al, 1997). Giblin and colleagues (1995) described the successful use of extralong Amplatz sheaths (18 to 24 cm) and a 30 French gynecologic laparoscope (with a working length of 27 cm) in five patients in whom the skin-to-stone distance precluded the use of standard percutaneous access sheaths and nephroscopes. Another possibility is to dilate the track and place a nephrostomy tube for 1 week to let the track mature. Flexible nephroscopy can then be performed through the mature track. In some cases, maturation of the track allows the kidney to fall back posteriorly closer to the skin, allowing the use of standard nephroscopic instrumentation (Hofmann and Stoller, 1992). Liberal use of flexible nephroscopy in obese patients improves the stone-free rate and decreases the need for additional access (Pearle et al, 1998).

After stone removal, consideration should be given to the type of nephrostomy tube used. **Tube displacement tends to occur more often in morbidly obese patients,** so balloon-type catheters or reentry Malecot catheters may be preferable (Carson et al, 1988). Alternatively, if a Cope loop catheter is used, placement of a ureteral catheter should be considered to ensure that access to the kidney is not lost should the nephrostomy tube become displaced.

## Bilateral Simultaneous Percutaneous Nephrolithotomy

Patients with large, bilateral stone burdens present a formidable challenge to the urologist; rendering these patients stone free can require separate staged procedures and multiple anesthetics. In 1987, Colon-Perez and associates (1987) first reported simultaneous bilateral PNL in a series of three patients. Since that time, the procedure has evolved, and several dictums have been established. It is recommended that either the side that is more symptomatic or the side that is more difficult be treated first. Patients may be positioned prone or with the treated side elevated.

Dushinski and Lingeman (1997) reported their experience with 48 patients with a mean stone surface area of 929 mm (approximately half of the stones were staghorn stones). Mean operative time was 269 minutes, and mean hospital stay was 5.6 days. Of these patients, 96.6% were rendered stone free. Complications were infrequent, and intrathecal morphine injections at the end of the case decreased the need for postoperative narcotics, possibly shortening the length of hospitalization. Nadler and coworkers (1998) compared a group of four patients undergoing simultaneous bilateral PNL under general anesthesia plus subarachnoid spinal anesthesia with a group of four patients undergoing staged bilateral PNL without subarachnoid spinal anesthesia. A marked advantage in hospital stay (4.8 days versus 11 days) and postoperative narcotics requirements was demonstrated for the simultaneous bilateral PNL group, leading the authors to conclude that simultaneous bilateral PNL provides the patient with a less morbid, more rapid method of stone resolution than does staged PNL or a sandwich technique (PNL followed by SWL followed by PNL). Silverstein and associates (2004) also reported that stone-free rates, blood loss per operation, and transfusion rates for simultaneous and staged bilateral PNL were similar. Furthermore, the reduced total operative time, hospital stay, and total blood loss along with the requirement for only one anesthesia session makes simultaneous bilateral PNL an attractive option for select patients. The authors recommend, though, that the decision should be made to pursue the second side only if no significant bleeding is encountered on the first side, the first side did not take an undue amount of time, the patient is clinically stable, and the anesthesia team is agreeable. Holman and associates (2002) confirmed these findings in a larger series, reporting that simultaneous bilateral PNL was not associated with greater hazards than was unilateral PNL.

## Complications

Even for the most experienced urologist, major complications can still occur in 1.1% to 7% of patients undergoing PNL, and minor complications may be encountered in 11% to 25% of patients. **Hemorrhage is the most significant complication of PNL, with transfusion rates reported to be from less than 1% to 10%.** Bleeding from an arteriovenous fistula or pseudoaneurysm that requires angiographic embolization occurs in less than 0.5% of patients. Other potential complications include sepsis in 0.3% to 2.5% (postoperative temperature below 38.5°C is found in almost one fourth of patients), adjacent organ injury (bowel, spleen) in less than 0.5%, failed access in less than 5%, and perforation of renal pelvis and ureter in less than 2%. The need for open surgery is rare and mostly reported as part of early experience in various studies. The mortality rate of PNL is between 0.046% and 0.8% (Lang, 1987; Lee et al, 1987a; Henriksson et al, 1989; Jones et al, 1991; Lam et al, 1992c; Segura et al, 1994; Dyer et al, 1997; Matlaga et al, 2004). When supracostal puncture is performed, the risk of pneumothorax or pleural effusion requiring drainage is 4% to 12% (Young et al, 1985; Picus et al, 1986; Fuchs and Forsyth, 1990; Narasimham et al, 1991; Golijanin et al, 1998; Munver et al, 2001) (see Table 44–16). Finally, failure of equipment is an often-ignored but significant potential complication.

During initial experiences with PNL, concern was expressed about the extent of renal damage caused by the creation and dilation of the transparenchymal nephrostomy track. However, several studies have shown that although some scarring occurs along the percutaneous track, there is little or no significant effect on renal function (Eshghi et al, 1989).

As the kidney is an extremely vascular organ, some degree of bleeding occurs during every PNL. Significant bleeding usually requires cessation of the procedure because of impaired visualization. In most cases, the source of hemorrhage is venous, and placement of a nephrostomy tube is usually sufficient to control the bleeding. If bleeding persists despite the placement of a nephrostomy tube, clamping the tube for a time may facilitate the tamponade of any bleeding points (Carson, 1986). If these measures do not control the hemorrhage, a Kaye nephrostomy tamponade balloon catheter should be placed. The Kaye nephrostomy tube incorporates a low-pressure 12-mm balloon that may be left inflated for prolonged periods to tamponade bleeding from the nephrostomy track (Kaye and Clayman, 1986). If bleeding persists despite placement of a Kaye catheter, immediate angiography should be performed to identify a possible arteriovenous fistula or false aneurysm. Angiography is both

diagnostic and therapeutic, as arteriovenous fistulas and false aneurysms are best managed by embolization. In the rare event that bleeding cannot be controlled with angiography, partial nephrectomy may be required.

PNL can lead to some absorption of irrigation fluid; therefore, the use of physiologic irrigating solutions is mandatory. The amount of absorbed fluid depends mostly on the irrigant pressure and the length of the procedure. Larger amounts of fluid absorption may occur with extravasation of fluid due to collecting system perforation. Extravasation usually occurs into the retroperitoneal tissue and may be noted by medial displacement of the kidney during fluoroscopy. Minor perforations are common during PNL; premature termination of the procedure is usually not necessary if a low-pressure system (i.e., Amplatz sheath) is being used. However, with more significant perforations, termination of the procedure and nephrostomy drainage are advisable (Irby et al, 1999). Intraperitoneal extravasation is a less common but potentially more serious complication than retroperitoneal extravasation. As the patient is prone, abdominal distention may be difficult to recognize, although the anesthesiologist will usually note a gradual rise in the patient's diastolic blood pressure with consequent narrowing of the pulse pressure and increase in central venous pressure; in advanced cases, ventilation may become difficult because of increased abdominal pressure (Carson, 1986). Early recognition of major extravasation is crucial. Some authors have suggested that irrigant input and output should be monitored during PNL, and if a discrepancy of more than 500 mL is encountered, cessation of the procedure should be considered (Lee et al, 1986; Segura, 1993). This is often not possible and should not be considered mandatory. Intraperitoneal extravasation may be treated by vigorous diuresis; alternatively, peritoneal drainage has been reported (Carson and Nesbitt, 1985).

When a supracostal puncture is performed, extravasation of irrigant into the pleural cavity may occur. The use of a working sheath tends to minimize extravasation into this space because intrarenal pressure remains low. The chest should be examined at the end of PNL procedures in which a supracostal puncture is used. Fluoroscopy with use of the C-arm is usually sufficient to examine for pneumothorax or hydrothorax (Ogan et al, 2003). If the surgeon has a high index of suspicion for a thoracic complication, a chest radiograph may be obtained postoperatively. If a greater than 10% pneumothorax or hydrothorax occurs, aspiration is generally sufficient because lung injury is extremely rare. Should the pneumothorax recur, a chest tube should be placed. Ogan and Pearle (2002) have described placement of a chest tube under fluoroscopic guidance at the time of the PNL.

Colonic injury is an unusual complication and is often diagnosed on postoperative nephrostogram, although passage of gas or feculent material through the nephrostomy track, intraoperative diarrhea, and hematochezia or peritonitis are all signs of a possible colonic perforation. Typically, the injury is retroperitoneal; thus, signs and symptoms of peritonitis are infrequent. If the perforation is extraperitoneal, management may be expectant, with placement of a ureteral catheter or double-J stent to decompress the collecting system and withdrawal of the nephrostomy tube from an intrarenal position to an intracolonic position to serve as a colostomy tube (Gerspach et al, 1997). The colostomy tube is left in place for a minimum of 7 days and is removed after a nephrostogram or a retrograde pyelogram shows no communication between the colon and the kidney (LeRoy et al, 1985; Wolf, 1998).

## Ureteroscopic Management of Ureteral Stones

Basic ureteroscopic techniques and intracorporeal lithotripsy techniques have been reviewed elsewhere. Herein, issues of anesthesia and specific points of technique and complications of ureteral stone management are reviewed.

The increasing miniaturization of and improvements in the technology of ureteroscopy have greatly altered the anesthetic considerations associated with this procedure. Ureteroscopy was initially performed exclusively under general or regional anesthesia as a consequence of the large-caliber ureteroscopes that were available. However, as ureteroscopes have become more diminutive, intravenous sedation, or sedoanalgesia, has provided another practical anesthetic option for patients harboring ureteral stones. The short duration of modern sedoanalgesic agents allows rapid relief of pain, efficient titration of analgesia, and rapid recovery after the procedure. Ureteroscopy can be safely and efficiently performed under local or intravenous sedation, with success rates equivalent to those of patients undergoing general regional anesthesia (Rittenberg and Bagley, 1988; Abdel-Razzak and Bagley, 1992, 1993; Grasso and Bagley, 1998; Cybulski et al, 2004). As most ureteral orifices will accommodate a 6 to 7 French device, immediate access to ureteral calculi with a 7 French flexible ureteroscope is possible. Furthermore, the small-diameter fibers of the holmium:YAG laser allow the immediate treatment of ureteral calculi.

The ability to fragment and remove calculi with a ureteroscope has dramatically advanced the urologist's ability to render patients stone free with one procedure. Early stone-free results with flexible ureteroscopy did not greatly exceed those of in situ SWL, both being approximately 80% (Drach et al, 1986; Bagley, 1990; Frang et al, 1992; Mogensen and Andersen, 1994). However, as smaller ureteroscopes were introduced and the holmium:YAG laser became available, success rates increased (Grasso et al, 1998). Although it is a more invasive technique than SWL, ureteroscopy with small, rigid or flexible endoscopes is the most efficient technique for treatment and removal of ureteral stones. Patients desiring a single procedure with maximal efficacy should consider primary ureteroscopy.

When the ureteral orifice is too narrow to accommodate a ureteroscope, dilation may be accomplished with serial dilators, balloons, or even the ureteroscope itself. The anatomy of male patients may not allow a rigid ureteroscope to be easily passed above the iliac vessels, but a flexible ureteroscope can usually be advanced over a guide wire. The entire ureter can be more easily accessed with a rigid ureteroscope in female patients. Once the stone is visualized, fragmentation with the lithotrite of choice is performed. Complete fragmentation to a size less than that of the safety wire (0.035 inch) should allow passage of all fragments without sequelae. Alternatively, fragmentation to a size sufficient for extraction by a stone retrieval device achieves a stone-free state for the patient at the end of the procedure.

Ureteral access sheaths have been developed to facilitate difficult ureteroscopic access. Kourambas and associates (2001) reported a randomized controlled study comparing patients who underwent ureteroscopy with a 12 to 14 French ureteral access sheath and those who underwent ureteroscopy with no access sheath. They found that use of the access sheath decreased operating time and costs and simplified ureteral reentry. Others have reported that intrapelvic pressures remain low when an access sheath is employed, a potentially significant finding when patients with infection-related calculi are treated (Rehman et al, 2003).

If significant ureteral edema or manipulation occurs, a post-ureteroscopy stent should be placed to prevent colic and obstruction. If the clinical situation does not allow primary ureteroscopy (sepsis, inability to advance the ureteroscope, ureteral injury, equipment failure), a ureteral stent is placed and the problem corrected. Secondary or post-stent ureteroscopy has the advantage of working through a dilated ureter, often allowing the use of larger rigid ureteroscopes.

### Steinstrasse

Steinstrasse, literally "street of stones," describes the accumulation of stone fragments in the ureter, obstructing the collecting system, after SWL. This complication has been reported in 2% to 10% of SWL cases and directly correlates with increasing stone burden (Coptcoat et al, 1987; Weinerth et al, 1989; Sulaiman et al, 1999; Madbouly et al, 2002). Large stone burden, staghorn calculi, bilateral SWL, and preexisting ureteral obstruction are all known to be risk factors for steinstrasse (Weinerth et al, 1989). Steinstrasse may occur in as many as 41% of patients undergoing SWL monotherapy for staghorn calculi, although with the increasing use of PNL in the treatment of patients with large stones, the incidence of steinstrasse has lessened (Coptcoat et al, 1987; Wirth et al, 1992).

The spectrum of presentation of patients suffering from steinstrasse is variable. Some patients may be entirely asymptomatic; others will present with the typical symptoms of renal colic, urinary tract infection, and renal insufficiency, with a time to presentation ranging from hours to months after SWL. More than 70% of steinstrasse occurs in the distal ureter (Coptcoat et al, 1987; Fedullo et al, 1988; Al-Awadi et al, 1999b; Sulaiman et al, 1999).

The placement of a ureteral stent before SWL therapy may decrease although not eliminate the risk of steinstrasse. However, the benefit of ureteral stent placement is probably limited to those patients with large stone burdens or solitary kidneys (Coptcoat et al, 1987; Riehle and Naslund, 1987; Libby et al, 1988; Sulaiman et al, 1999). Sulaiman and associates (1999) reviewed 1087 patients who underwent treatment for renal calculi with a piezoelectric lithotripter and found the incidence of steinstrasse to be 6.3%. The authors routinely placed a ureteral stent in all patients with a stone burden of more than 20 mm. However, regardless of ureteral stent placement, steinstrasse occurred in 4%, 14%, and 30% of patients with stones of 10 to 19 mm, 20 to 29 mm, and more than 30 mm, respectively. No patient with a stone smaller than 10 mm developed steinstrasse. Libby and associates (1988) reviewed 283 patients harboring a stone burden larger than 2.5 cm; they found a significant reduction in complications, most commonly ureteral obstruction, from 26% to 7%, and a significant reduction in ancillary procedures, from 15% to 6%, favoring ureteral stent placement before SWL. Al-Awadi and associates (1999b) reported a prospective, randomized study comparing 400 patients harboring calculi of 1.5 to 3.5 cm mean diameter who underwent SWL treatment; 200 patients underwent ureteral stent placement before treatment, and the other 200 did not. The authors found that the placement of a ureteral stent significantly reduced the incidence of steinstrasse. However, regardless of the placement of a ureteral stent, steinstrasse occurred more commonly as stone burden increased.

It may be particularly beneficial for patients with stones larger than 20 mm to undergo ureteral stent placement before SWL treatment. Sulaiman and colleagues (1999) reported that steinstrasse developed in 15% of patients with a ureteral stent versus 38% of patients without a ureteral stent. The authors also reported a reduced rate of hospitalization after SWL for those patients who underwent ureteral stent placement than for those who did not have a ureteral stent placed (5% versus 23%).

However, other authors have reported that there is no benefit to placement of a ureteral stent before SWL. Pryor and Jenkins (1990), in a prospective randomized comparison of 25 patients who underwent pre-SWL ureteral stent placement and 25 patients who did not, found no benefit to routine ureteral stent placement in the prevention of steinstrasse; the stone burden in this study was 7 to 25 mm. Interestingly, Kirkali and associates (1993) reported that in a series of 351 patients with stones larger than 30 mm who were treated by SWL, there was no significant difference in the need for auxiliary treatment for steinstrasse between the group of 85 patients who had undergone stent placement and the 266 patients who did not. However, there was a significant increase in the rate of steinstrasse; 24% of patients in the non-stent group experienced this complication compared with 15% in the stent group.

As there are a wide variety of manifestations of the symptoms of steinstrasse, the management of these patients depends on their clinical presentation. Patients with steinstrasse who are asymptomatic can often be observed initially; spontaneous stone clearance occurs in 60% to 80% of cases (Fedullo et al, 1988; Preminger et al, 1989; Kim et al, 1991). Fedullo and associates (1988) reported that steinstrasse occurred in 20% of the first 1000 patients they treated with the HM3 lithotripter, 65% of which resolved spontaneously. Preminger and colleagues (1989) reported a 1.7% incidence of steinstrasse in 302 patients treated by an HM3 lithotripter, with all cases resolving at 6 weeks after treatment. Kirkali and associates (1993) also reported that steinstrasse spontaneously resolved in 50 of 64 cases (82%). Sayed and associates (2001) similarly reported that in a series of 52 patients who developed steinstrasse after SWL, conservative management was successful in 25 patients. However, patients with bilateral obstruction, obstruction of a solitary kidney, severe refractory pain, or infected hydronephrosis should be managed with prompt urinary tract decompression by internal ureteral stenting, nephrostomy tube drainage, or ureteroscopic management. Large leading fragments unlikely to pass spontaneously and failure of expectant management are additional indications for intervention (Coptcoat et al, 1987; Weinerth et al, 1989).

When intervention is required, a minimally invasive approach is often successful. Coptcoat and associates (1988b) reported that percutaneous nephrostomy alone permitted passage of all stone fragments in 75% of cases. Dretler (1994) also recommended placement of a percutaneous nephrostomy tube for patients with pain or sepsis, reserving endoscopic intervention for afebrile patients with large leading fragments or after at least 4 weeks of observation. However, Weinerth and colleagues (1989) found that seven of nine patients initially treated with percutaneous nephrostomy eventually required ureteroscopic basket extraction or lithotripsy. The use of prophylactic antibiotics in expectantly managed cases is recommended, as are frequent radiologic and ultrasound examinations. Failure of steinstrasse to resolve within 3 to 4 weeks may necessitate intervention (Coptcoat et al, 1987).

In those cases that do require intervention, ureteroscopy is often used; basket extraction of larger fragments or additional lithotripsy is easily accomplished and has a success rate approaching 100% (Coptcoat et al, 1988a; Weinerth et al, 1989). Coptcoat and associates (1988a) employed ureteroscopic pulsed-dye laser lithotripsy, after initial renal decompression by percutaneous nephrostomy, in five patients with large leading fragments, reporting successful outcomes in all cases. However, primary ureteroscopic intervention without initial decompression was difficult, and successful outcomes were reported in only 60% of cases. Weinerth and colleagues (1989) reported a 3% incidence (19 of 650 cases) of large steinstrasse (a third or more of the ureteral length), which was not always prevented by the placement of ureteral stents or percutaneous nephrostomy tubes. In 37% of cases, the steinstrasse spontaneously cleared, and ureteroscopic ultrasonic lithotripsy was successful in all 10 cases. Sulaiman and colleagues (1999) reported that ureteroscopic laser lithotripsy or basket extraction was used in 31% of non-stented and 45% of stented patients with steinstrasse, with success in 96% of cases.

Caution is warranted in undertaking the retrograde endoscopic treatment of a patient with steinstrasse; the complication rate of ureteroscopy may be increased over that of percutaneous nephrostomy or SWL. Al-Awadi and associates (1999b) reported that steinstrasse resolved in 50% of cases (19 of 38); but during three of seven attempted ureteroscopies, ureteral perforations occurred that necessitated open surgery.

SWL of the lead fragment of steinstrasse has a high reported success rate and has been associated with few complications. Kim and colleagues (1991), using a piezoelectric lithotripter, noted a 6% incidence of steinstrasse in a series of 958 SWL cases; 64% resolved spontaneously, and 90% of the refractory cases were treated successfully with additional SWL. The authors reported some difficulty in the retrograde placement of a ureteral catheter in those patients who suffered steinstrasse as well as a higher incidence of spontaneous passage of distal, rather than proximal, ureteral steinstrasse (82% versus 33%). Sulaiman and colleagues (1999) reported success with SWL in persistent steinstrasse for seven of nine patients who had undergone ureteral stent placement before SWL and three of three patients who did not undergo ureteral stent placement.

PNL, with or without concomitant ureteroscopy, can also be used to treat patients suffering from steinstrasse. Coptcoat and associates (1988b) reported 100% success in three cases of proximal ureteral steinstrasse. PNL is particularly appealing if significant stone burden remains in the kidney, as is commonly the case. Open ureterolithotomy has been reported by multiple authors as a salvage procedure for steinstrasse but is rarely required in the modern endoscopic era (Kim et al, 1991; Al-Awadi et al, 1999b; Sulaiman et al, 1999).

In summary, steinstrasse is a well-known complication of SWL, with most cases resolving spontaneously. When intervention is required, percutaneous nephrostomy alone has a success rate of more than 70%. Ureteroscopic intervention is definitive and predictable with an immediate success rate approaching 100%. Additional SWL may be successful, but the results are less predictable than with ureteroscopy. PNL may be used as a salvage procedure, with open ureterolithotomy reserved for failure or for complications of less invasive modalities.

## Complications of Ureteral Stone Management

As modern ureteroscopes have become smaller and less traumatic, as safer intracorporeal lithotripters have become widely available, and as a better understanding of the technical principles of ureteroscopy has been developed, the number of complications arising from the management of ureteral stones has been steadily decreasing. Grasso and Bagley (1998) reviewed their experience with 492 patients undergoing 584 ureteroscopic procedures and reported an overall complication rate of less than 1%, with no ureteral perforations, avulsions, septic episodes, or deaths.

Fortunately, most of the complications caused by ureteral stones and their management respond favorably to simple drainage of urine with ureteral catheters or stents.

**Perforation.** Perforation of the ureter is decreasing in frequency, in part because of the widespread availability of smaller flexible endoscopes, lithotrites with more precise energy delivery, and increasing experience with ureteroscopy. However, ureteral perforation does occasionally still occur, and it is a significant risk factor for the development of a ureteral stricture. The incidence of ureteral perforation varies among the different intracorporeal lithotrites; the highest incidence of ureteral perforation occurs with EHL (see Table 44–4). The treatment of patients who suffer ureteral perforation consists of immediate termination of the procedure, placement of a ureteral stent for 2 to 4 weeks, and careful radiographic follow-up.

**Stricture.** Ureteral strictures occur secondary to ureteral trauma or alternatively from stone impaction, iatrogenic injury (perforation, lithotrite or stone retrieval device use), or retained stone fragments in the ureteral wall. Duration of stone impaction and ureteral perforation were found to be significant risk factors for ureteral stricture formation by Roberts and coworkers (1998), who reported a 24% stricture rate for stones that had been impacted an average of 11 months. Concomitant iatrogenic ureteral perforation occurred in four of five patients who developed ureteral stricture. If significant trauma does occur, placement of a ureteral stent for an extended period (4 to 6 weeks) may prevent the development of a ureteral stricture. If a ureteral stricture occurs, incision (with cold knife, cautery, or laser) and ureteral stent placement may be successful; balloon dilation with subsequent placement of a ureteral stent is another treatment option (Singal and Denstedt, 1997). Open repair with either excision or

bypass of the strictured segment may be necessary if endoscopic measures fail (Matlaga et al, 2003a).

**Submucosal Stone.** Submucosal stones, defined as calculi iatrogenically displaced into the wall of the ureter, are a problematic complication. Removal of such stones is difficult, ureteral perforation with urinoma can occur, and intense fibrosis may result. If submucosal stones are encountered, laser excision followed by ureteral stent placement is recommended. If laser excision fails, open resection of the affected segment of ureter may be necessary.

**Lost Stone.** The lost stone, or a stone that has been manipulated to a position outside the ureter, is usually harmless and requires no further treatment. The process (i.e., perforation) that placed the stone outside the ureter may induce stricture formation or other complications. If the stone is associated with infection, a retroperitoneal abscess can result.

**Avulsion.** Ureteral avulsion is the most severe ureteral complication. It usually occurs when aggressive stone removal maneuvers result in entrapment of a portion of the ureter with the stone during basket extraction or when excessively large stones are withdrawn through narrow areas of the ureter. To reduce the risk of avulsion, some urologists advocate the use of grasping devices instead of baskets for stone retrieval. If ureteral avulsion does occur, open repair of the avulsed ureter is usually required, although if the continuity of the ureter can be re-established by a guide wire already in place, a trial of ureteral stent drainage for several months to allow the ureter to heal may be attempted. However, ureteral stricture is a common outcome. Conversely, if no safety wire is in place or if the ureteral injury is severe, immediate open reconstruction of the ureter is required. All surgical options for replacing ureteral loss, including ureteral reimplantation and psoas hitch of the bladder, ileal ureter, and autotransplantation, must be entertained (Matlaga et al, 2003a).

# Ureteroscopic Management of Intrarenal Calculi

Huffman and associates (1983) first described the removal of large ureteral and renal pelvic calculi with a rigid rod-lens ureteroscope and an ultrasonic lithotripter. However, rigid ureteroscopy is limited to stones in certain renal locations, such as the renal pelvis and upper pole calyces. As advancements in fiberoptic technology have facilitated the development of practical flexible ureteroscopes, the therapeutic potential of flexible ureteroscopes has also been improved by several design changes, including a working channel to allow irrigation and passage of flexible instruments and active tip deflection combined with passive deflection to allow access to the entire collecting system. Concomitant improvements in flexible intracorporeal lithotripters have allowed the use of flexible ureteroscopes for the treatment of upper urinary tract calculi with a high degree of success.

Fuchs and Fuchs (1990) reported the first large series (208 patients) of renal calculi treated by ureteroscopy, using a flexible deflectable ureteroscope after a 1- to 2-week period of ureteral stent placement. Indications for ureteroscopy included patients whose SWL treatment failed (single stone smaller than 1 cm or up to five stones smaller than 5 mm), patients with radiolucent stones (smaller than 1.5 cm), patients with concomitant ureteral and renal stones, patients with renal stones associated with intrarenal stenosis, patients with nephrocalcinosis or urinary diversion, patients with a need for complete stone removal (e.g., pilots), and patients with bleeding disorders. The overall stone-free rate was 87%, and the only complications reported were two cases of sepsis. The subsequent introduction of flexible, actively deflectable ureteroscopes (7.5 French) has permitted more procedures to be performed without routine ureteral dilation. In a series of 598 patients with ureteral and renal stones treated by holmium laser lithotripsy, ureteral dilation was necessary in only 185 (31%) (Sofer and Denstedt, 2000). Numerous baskets and graspers now allow full deflection of flexible ureteroscopes, facilitating treatment of often difficult-to-access lower pole stones (Honey, 1998; Lukasewycz et al, 2004).

As improvements in technique and technology have led to increased numbers of patients treated with ureteroscopy, a review of the literature (Table 44–17) shows that the mean overall success (defined as successful fragmentation with complete stone clearance or presence of "insignificant" residual fragments) of ureteroscopy for the treatment of patients with renal stones (mostly smaller than 3 cm) in a single session is 86%. Higher success rates can be achieved after a second-look procedure. About half the stones treated were located in the lower pole, and a mean success rate of greater than 80% was reported. Complication rates are low (between 0% and 4%); fever and urinary tract infection are the most common complications.

Fabrizio and associates (1998) evaluated the characteristics of residual calculi after ureteroscopy in a group of 100 patients treated for renal stones. As expected, increased stone burden correlated with a higher percentage of patients with residual fragments. Residual fragments were present in only 20% of patients with stones 10 mm or smaller, whereas patients with stones larger than 16 mm were left with residual fragments in

more than 50% of cases. In addition, as the number of stones increased, the percentage of patients with residual fragments increased. When success rates of ureteroscopy were stratified by intrarenal location and size, the results for lower pole calculi compared with middle and upper pole calculi were 84%, 93%, and 100%, respectively. A multicenter study evaluated the results of ureteroscopy in 51 patients with 66 large (2 to 6 cm) upper urinary tract stones. Many of the patients failed prior SWL or failed or refused prior PNL. Of 51 patients, 48 were treated solely in a retrograde ureteroscopic manner; 3 were converted to PNL as a result of failure to access the lower pole or because infectious material was encountered on initial endoscopy. One third of the patients with large renal calculi underwent a second-look procedure, and the initial and subsequent success rates after a second treatment session were 76% and 91%, respectively. No intraoperative complications were noted, and the postoperative complication rate was 3% (Grasso et al, 1998).

Treatment of staghorn stones with ureteroscopy has been described, but it is not a widely used technique. In 1990, Aso and colleagues described 34 patients with complete and partial staghorn stones treated with flexible ureteroscopic lithotripsy with a success rate of 88%. In 1994, Dretler proposed ureterorenoscopic fragmentation followed by SWL as an alternative technique for select patients harboring large-volume renal stones (>500 mm$^2$). In this small series, seven of eight patients became stone free after an average of 2.6 procedures. Female patients with moderate-volume, fragile-looking (i.e., struvite) stones as well as patients with bleeding disorders or a solitary kidney were proposed as possible candidates for the combined ureteroscopic and SWL technique. Mugiya and associates (1998) described 27 patients with partial and complete staghorn stones treated by ureteroscopic lithotripsy followed by SWL, reporting stone-free rates of 61% and 80% for complete and partial staghorn stones, respectively; however, 3 to 26 SWL sessions (mean, 8.4) were required per patient.

| Table 44–17. | Ureteroscopic Treatment of Renal Stones | | | | | | | |
|---|---|---|---|---|---|---|---|---|
| Authors | Patients | Ureteral Stones | Renal Stones | Lower Pole Stones (%) | Stone Size (Mean:Range) | Intracorporeal Lithotripter | Overall Success (%) | Lower Pole Success (%) |
| Elashry et al, 1996 | 45 | 32 | 57 | 37 (65) | Mean:8.5mm <25 mm:58 | 1.9 French EHL | 98 (residual < 2 mm) 91 | 94 |
| Gould, 1998 | 86 | — | 86 | 30 (35) | 25-30 mm:22 >30 mm:6 | Holmium laser | 86 0 | |
| Grasso and Chalik, 1998 | 210 | 137 | 112 | 48 (43) | Mean:15.4 mm 1-10 mm:75 | Holmium laser | 97 | 73 |
| Fabrizio et al, 1998 | 199 | 56 | 199 | 63 (63) | 11-15 mm:14 15-20 mm:5 >20 mm:6 5-10 mm:40 | Holmium laser EHL | 77 | N/A |
| Menezes et al, 2000 | 37 | 15 | 40 | 14 (35) | 11-15 mm:14 16-20 mm:1 | EHL | 75 (residual < 5 mm) | 80 |
| Tawfiek and Bagley, 1999 | 155 | 82 | 73 | 23(31) | Mean:6-8 mm 1-10 mm:47 | Holmium laser EHL | 87.6 (residual < 3 mm) | 87 |
| Grasso and Ficazzola, 1999 | 79 | — | 90 | 90 (100) | 11-20 mm:21 >20 mm:22 | Holmium laser | 84 (residual < 2 mm) | 82 |
| Kourambas et al, 2000 | 36 | 0 | 0 | 36 (100) | <15 mm:32 >15 mm:4 | Holmium laser | 85 | 85 |
| El-Anany et al, 2001 | 30 | 0 | 40 | 11 (27) | >2 cm:30 | Holmium laser | 23 (76) | 60 |
| Sofer and Denstedt, 2000 | 598 | 542 | 56 | N/A | Mean:13.3 mm | Holmium laser EHL | 84 (residual < 2 mm) | N/A |

EHL, electrohydraulic lithotripsy.

Gould (1998) reported a success rate of only 33% in the treatment of patients with partial staghorn calculi by retrograde flexible ureterorenoscopic holmium laser lithotripsy. Therefore, except in unusual circumstances, ureteroscopic treatment of staghorn stones is inefficient and is generally not an appropriate alternative to PNL.

## Technique

Proximal ureteral and intrarenal calculi can be accessed with actively deflectable, flexible ureteroscopes. Although, historically, a ureteral stent was left indwelling before ureterorenoscopy, this maneuver is currently necessary only when difficulty is encountered introducing the flexible ureteroscope into the ureter. If necessary, the stent is left for 2 to 4 weeks before the procedure (Erhard et al, 1996). The use of small-diameter ureteroscopes minimizes the necessity of ureteral dilation for stone access and may decrease associated morbidity. In a series of 155 ureteroscopic treatments for upper tract calculi, ureteral dilation was performed in only 8.3% of patients (Tawfiek and Bagley, 1999). In cases of multiple stones or large stone burden requiring multiple passages of a basket, a ureteral access sheath may facilitate stone removal (Elashry et al, 1996). A comparative study of ureteroscopic lithotripsy with or without access sheath showed that operative time was significantly reduced by use of the access sheath, despite a greater mean stone burden in the access sheath group (Kourambas et al, 2001).

When a retrograde ureteroscopic approach is used to treat patients with intrarenal calculi, two wires are placed initially. The flexible ureteroscope is passed over one working wire in a monorail fashion. Saline is used for irrigation. When an implement is present within the working channel, simple gravity irrigation is inadequate, and pressurized irrigation is required. The holmium:YAG laser lithotripter is used in almost all cases, and the laser energy required usually does not exceed 1 J and 15 Hz (Gould, 1998; Sofer and Denstedt, 2000). Stones in lower pole calyces can be treated in situ or moved, with flexible 2.5 French graspers or a basket, into a position that allows better visualization. A head-down position with the ipsilateral flank elevated may help with stone and fragment visualization because fragments tend to migrate superiorly and are thus more easily localized during treatment (Grasso and Chalik, 1998). When access into the lower pole is difficult, prone positioning of the patient with the head down 20 degrees has been shown to provide the broadest angle of entry to the lower pole infundibulum (Bercowsky et al, 1999). The goal of holmium laser lithotripsy is to reduce the stone to fine

dust and to small fragments 2 mm or less in diameter. If the stone is large, the collecting system may often become lined with fine dust and debris, which can obscure residual stones. Furthermore, poor visualization may lead to perforation. In such cases, retrograde catheters can be placed to allow irrigation of the collecting system postoperatively and planning of a staged procedure (Grasso, 1999). Alternatively, the irrigant in the intrarenal collecting system may be aspirated through the ureteroscope, which may also provide a clearer field in which to work.

Fragmentation of stones in situ in the lower pole can be challenging. One technique to aid in the application of the laser fiber to a lower pole stone is to first coil an open-ended 0.035-inch guide wire into the calyx of interest, then pass the flexible ureteroscope over the wire into the calyx. The laser fiber is then passed through the open-ended wire onto the stone for fragmentation (Perez and Pahira, 1995). Alternatively, the ureteroscope can be passively directed into the calyx with the laser fiber already extended, obviating the need to advance the fiber through the ureteroscope when it is maximally deflected. Finally, if the infundibulum is accommodating, the easiest way to treat the stone is to engage it in a nitinol basket and displace it to the renal pelvis or an upper pole calyx. Disassembly of the basket device with removal of the sheath, to create a "bare naked basket," will also enhance the deflectability of the ureteroscope (Landman et al, 2002).

## Open Stone Surgery

Historically, most patients with symptomatic upper urinary tract calculi underwent open surgical lithotomy. Those patients with a small to moderate stone burden typically underwent pyelolithotomy, radial nephrolithotomy, or ureterolithotomy. For those patients harboring staghorn calculi, more extensive procedures were required, including anatrophic nephrolithotomy, extended pyelolithotomy combined with radial lithotomies, and bench surgery with autotransplantation. However, the introduction of SWL and the development of endourologic techniques for stone removal have dramatically diminished the role of open stone surgery, especially for stone removal procedures, and open surgery is now one of the least common treatments of patients harboring upper urinary tract calculi. Matlaga and Assimos (2002) reported that of 986 surgical procedures for stone removal performed at their institution between 1998 and 2001, 0.7% were open surgical procedures. Others have reported similar findings (Table 44–18), with an incidence of open stone

| Table 44–18. Open Stone Surgery in the Modern Era | | | | |
|---|---|---|---|---|
| | *Assimos et al, 1989* | *Kare et al, 1995* | *Paik et al, 1998* | *Matlaga and Assimos, 2002* |
| Number of open stone surgery cases (% of total stone removal procedures) | 37 (4.1) | 25 (3.13) | 42 (5.4) | 7 (0.7) |
| Stone-free rate (%) | 100 | 71 | 93 | 100 |
| *Indications (%)* | | | | |
| Complex stone burden | 3 (8.1) | 3 (12) | 23 (55) | 0 |
| Endoscopic treatment failure | 18 (49) | 51 (20) | 12 (29) | 1 (14) |
| Anatomic abnormality or concomitant open surgery | 13 (35) | 8 (32) | 11 (46) | 6 (86) |
| Body habitus | 5 (14) | 5 (19) | 4 (10) | 0 |
| Other | 2 (5) | 6 (24) | 4 (10) | 0 |

surgery ranging from 0.3% to 5.4% (Assimos et al, 1989b; Segura, 1990; Kane et al, 1995; Paik et al, 1998).

## Renal Calculi

Minimally invasive techniques have clear advantages over open surgical techniques for patients harboring small to moderate burdens in otherwise normal kidneys. In 1985, Brannen and associates retrospectively compared PNL and open surgery for the treatment of patients with renal and proximal ureteral stones. Although the overall stone-free rate was similar, those patients treated by PNL experienced a shorter hospital stay, a lower narcotic requirement, and a shorter recovery period. Preminger and associates (1985) compared 88 patients undergoing PNL with 41 patients undergoing open stone surgery and found that PNL was associated with lower postoperative morbidity, more rapid convalescence, greater satisfaction of the patient, and reduced hospital costs for stones smaller than 2.5 cm. Brown and associates (1986) have also demonstrated that PNL is more cost-effective than open stone surgery because of its reduced morbidity.

A more controversial issue has been the treatment of patients harboring staghorn calculi, a condition that carries a significant risk of mortality if it is untreated. Boyce and Elkins (1974) established anatrophic nephrolithotomy as a standard treatment of patients with staghorn stones in the United States. Overall, the reported stone-free rate after open surgery for struvite calculi is about 85%, with a 30% stone recurrence rate during 6 years (Griffith, 1978). In comparing results for a combination of PNL and SWL with reported results of anatrophic nephrolithotomy, Kahnoski and associates (1986) reported stone-free rates (85%) similar to those for the open surgical procedures, although convalescence and hospital stay for PNL were shorter and blood loss was less.

Snyder and Smith (1986) compared PNL with anatrophic nephrolithotomy for patients with staghorn calculi. They reported that although the retained stone fragment rate was higher for PNL than for anatrophic nephrolithotomy (13% versus 0%), shorter procedure times, reduced need for blood transfusions and narcotics, and far more rapid return to work were achieved with PNL.

A meta-analysis undertaken by the AUA documented stone-free rates of 81.6% for open stone surgery, 80.8% for combined PNL and SWL, 73.3% for PNL, and only 50% for SWL monotherapy (Segura et al, 1994; Preminger et al, 2005). The more invasive the procedure, the greater the stone-free rate; however, morbidity was higher as well. Although SWL carried the lowest morbidity, a greater number of unplanned post-treatment interventions were necessary. The AUA concluded that for most patients, neither SWL monotherapy nor open stone surgery should be the first-line treatment of staghorn stones. As a guideline, PNL, followed by SWL or repeated PNL procedures as warranted, should be used for most patients with struvite staghorn calculi.

There are no strict guidelines that define which patient should undergo an open surgical procedure for stone removal. Some indications, such as a stone burden too large for PNL, clearly rely on the surgeon's judgment and experience and the availability of equipment. Also, those patients harboring calculi that may require multiple PNL or SWL treatments may be good candidates for an open procedure. Although a single open surgical procedure may seem to be the optimal procedure in the short term, the inevitable scar tissue that develops will compromise any future stone removal procedures. A small group of patients who are refractory to PNL, SWL, and ureteroscopy may require an open surgical procedure as a salvage technique.

Nephrectomy remains an option for patients with nonfunctioning kidneys or stone disease with a normal contralateral kidney. Partial nephrectomy is also an option for a stone in a localized area of irrevocably poor function. In addition, patients with an associated anatomic abnormality requiring open operative intervention, such as ureteropelvic obstruction and infundibular stenosis, may be candidates for an open surgical approach. Some patients requiring open surgery unrelated to their urologic problem may also benefit from a simultaneously performed open procedure.

## Ureteral Calculi

Although ureterolithotomy has been a time-honored technique for many decades, it is seldom performed in the modern, endourologic era. A meta-analysis undertaken by Segura and associates (1997) for the AUA demonstrated median stone-free rates of 87% and 90% for stones in the distal ureter treated by open surgical removal and ureteroscopy, respectively. In the proximal ureter, the stone-free rate for ureterolithotomy was 97% compared with 83% and 72% for SWL and ureteroscopy, respectively. Although the results of open surgery in the proximal ureter were somewhat better than those of minimally invasive techniques, the greater morbidity and longer hospitalization associated with open surgery favored a primary endourologic solution for ureteral stones. Further miniaturization of ureteroscopes, combined with the now widespread availability of the holmium:YAG laser, has increased the success rate for a ureteroscopic approach to proximal ureteral calculi. Grasso and Bagley (1998) have reported a large series of patients undergoing ureteroscopy for proximal ureteral calculi, finding a 97% stone-free rate. Open surgery for patients with ureteral stones is now indicated only as a salvage procedure, when a planned abdominal operation coincides with a symptomatic ureteral stone episode, or when another ureteral abnormality requires open surgical repair.

# Laparoscopic Stone Removal

The advent of laparoscopic stone removal procedures has provided the urologist with another means to circumvent open stone surgery. Every type of "lithotomy" procedure has been reported by use of a laparoscopic approach (Raboy et al, 1992; Winfield et al, 1993; Ruckle and Segura, 1994; Van Cangh et al, 1995; Harmon et al, 1996; Deger et al, 2004). However, a laparoscopic approach to stone removal should be considered only if the results with SWL or endoscopic approaches are expected to be poor.

There are certain cases in which a laparoscopic lithotomy may be considered a reasonable therapy. Situations that may benefit from a laparoscopic approach include the following: pyeloplasty with pyelolithotomy; patients harboring stones in poorly functioning polar areas or with nonfunctioning kidneys; pelvic kidneys containing a large stone volume, in which laparoscopic techniques can be used to reflect overlying bowel, allowing pyelolithotomy or percutaneous stone removal; and ureterolithotomy for the extremely rare endoscopic failure.

## KEY POINTS: STONE REMOVAL: SURGICAL TECHNIQUES AND TECHNOLOGY

■ The holmium:YAG laser is one of the safest, most versatile, and most effective intracorporeal lithotripters and has become the standard lithotrite for the ureteroscopic approach.

■ For patients undergoing PNL, a rigid lithotripter such as a ballistic or ultrasonic device will provide for more efficient stone removal than will a flexible lithotripter.

■ For PNL, the preferred point of entry into the collecting system is along the axis of the calyx, through the papilla.

■ The goal in selecting access for PNL is to remove the greatest stone burden with the rigid nephroscope thereby maximizing the efficiency of the procedure.

## SUGGESTED READINGS

Albala DM, Assimos DG, Clayman RV, et al: Lower pole I: A prospective randomized trial of extracorporeal shockwave lithotripsy and percutaneous nephrostolithotomy for lower pole nephrolithiasis—initial results. J Urol 2001;166:2072-2080.

Assimos DG, Leslie SW, Ng C, et al: The impact of cystinuria on renal function. J Urol 2002;168:27-30.

Evan AP, Willis LR, Connors B, et al: Shockwave lithotripsy–induced renal injury. Am J Kidney Dis 1991;17:445-450.

Evan AP, Willis LR, Lingeman JE, et al: Renal trauma and the risk of long-term complications in shockwave lithotripsy. Nephron 1998;78:1-8.

Grasso M, Ficazzola M: Retrograde ureteropyeloscopy for lower pole caliceal calculi. J Urol 1999;162:1904-1908.

Grasso M, Loisides P, Beaghler M, et al: The case for primary endoscopic management of upper urinary tract calculi: I. A critical review of 121 extracorporeal shockwave lithotripsy failures. Urology 1995;45:363-371.

Janetschek G, Frauscher F, Knapp R, et al: New onset hypertension after extracorporeal shockwave lithotripsy: Age related incidence and prediction by intrarenal resistive index. J Urol 1997;158:346-351.

Kim SC, Tinmouth WW, Kuo RL, et al: Using and choosing a nephrostomy tube after percutaneous nephrolithotomy for large or complex stone disease: A treatment strategy. J Endourol 2005;19:348-352.

Kourambas J, Byrne RR, Preminger GM: Does a ureteral access sheath facilitate ureteroscopy? J Urol 2001;165:789-793.

Lifshitz DA, Lingeman JE: Ureteroscopy as a first-line intervention for ureteral calculi in pregnancy. J Endourol 2002;16:19-22.

Lingeman JE, Woods JR, Toth PD: Blood pressure changes following extracorporeal shockwave lithotripsy and other forms of treatment for nephrolithiasis. JAMA 1990;263:1789-1794.

Lingeman JE, Siegel YI, Steele B, et al: Management of lower pole nephrolithiasis: A critical analysis. J Urol 1994;151:663-667.

Mariappan P, Smith G, Bariol SV, et al: Stone and pelvic urine culture and sensitivity are better than bladder urine as predictors of urosepsis following percutaneous nephrolithotomy: A prospective clinical study. J Urol 2005;173:1610-1614.

Matlaga BR, Assimos DG: Changing indications of open stone surgery. Urology 2002;59:490-493; discussion 493-494.

Monga M, Smith R, Ferral H, et al: Percutaneous ablation of caliceal diverticulum: Long-term followup. J Urol 2000;163:28-32.

Pace KT, Ghiculete D, Harju M, et al: Shockwave lithotripsy at 60 or 120 shocks per minute: A randomized, double-blind trial. J Urol 2005;174:595-599.

Pearle MS, Nakada SY, Womack JS, et al: Outcomes of contemporary percutaneous nephrostolithotomy in morbidly obese patients. J Urol 1998;160(pt 1):669-673.

Pearle MS, Nadler R, Bercowsky E, et al: Prospective randomized trial comparing shockwave lithotripsy and ureteroscopy for management of distal ureteral calculi. J Urol 2001;166:1255-1260.

Pearle MS, Lingeman JE, Leveillee R, et al: Prospective, randomized trial comparing shockwave lithotripsy and ureteroscopy for lower pole caliceal calculi 1 cm or less. J Urol 2005;173:2005-2009.

Peschel R, Janetschek G, Bartsch G: Extracorporeal shockwave lithotripsy versus ureteroscopy for distal ureteral calculi: A prospective randomized study. J Urol 1999;162:1909-1912.

Portis AJ, Yan Y, Pattaras JG, et al: Matched pair analysis of shockwave lithotripsy effectiveness for comparison of lithotriptors. J Urol 2003;169:58-62.

Preminger GM, Assimos DG, Lingeman JE, et al: Chapter 1: AUA guideline on management of staghorn calculi: Diagnosis and treatment recommendations. J Urol 2005;173:1991-2000.

Sampaio FJ, Aragao AH: Anatomical relationship between the intrarenal arteries and the kidney collecting system. J Urol 1990;143:679-681.

Segura JW, Preminger GM, Assimos DG, et al: Ureteral Stones Clinical Guidelines Panel summary report on the management of ureteral calculi. The American Urological Association. J Urol 1997;158:1915-1921.

Streem SB, Yost A, Mascha E: Clinical implications of clinically insignificant stone fragments after extracorporeal shockwave lithotripsy. J Urol 1996;155:1186-1190.

Tiselius HG, Ackermann D, Alken P, et al: Guidelines on urolithiasis. Eur Urol 2001;40:362-371.

Watterson JD, Girvan AR, Cook AJ, et al: Safety and efficacy of holmium:YAG laser lithotripsy in patients with bleeding diatheses. J Urol 2002;168:442-445.

Willis LR, Evan AP, Connors BA, et al: Shockwave lithotripsy: Dose-related effects on renal structure, hemodynamics, and tubular function. J Endourol 2005;19:90-101.

# Ureteroscopy and Retrograde Ureteral Access

BEN H. CHEW, MD, MSc, FRCSC •
JOHN D. DENSTEDT, MD, FRCSC

INDICATIONS FOR URETEROSCOPY AND RETROGRADE ACCESS

EQUIPMENT NECESSARY FOR URETEROSCOPY AND RETROGRADE ACCESS

STEP-BY-STEP URETEROSCOPY IN THE TREATMENT OF URETERONEPHROLITHIASIS

IS ROUTINE STENTING NECESSARY FOLLOWING URETEROSCOPY?

URETERAL STENTS AND BIOMATERIALS

POSTOPERATIVE CARE

RESULTS OF URETEROSCOPY FOR TREATMENT OF URETERAL STONES

URETEROSCOPY IN SPECIAL CASES

RETROGRADE URETEROSCOPIC TREATMENT OF URETERAL STRICTURES

URETEROSCOPIC MANAGEMENT OF UPPER TRACT TRANSITIONAL CELL CARCINOMA

COMPLICATIONS OF URETEROSCOPY

CONCLUSIONS

## INDICATIONS FOR URETEROSCOPY AND RETROGRADE ACCESS

Ureteroscopy has become a standard urologic technique and is used in a wide variety of situations for diagnosis and treatment. The diagnostic and therapeutic indications for ureteroscopy are summarized in Table 45–1. The main use for the technique of supravesical endoscopy is in the treatment of urolithiasis. The advent of smaller semirigid and flexible fiberoptic endoscopes has allowed routine retrograde access to the proximal ureter and kidney, and when combined with the holmium:yttrium-aluminum-garnet (YAG) laser, provides a safe and highly effective retrograde method of intracorporeal lithotripsy. The current generation of flexible, actively deflectable fiberoptic endoscopes makes virtually every part of the kidney, including the lower pole, accessible for the treatment of calculi.

Ureteroscopy is also used in the diagnosis and treatment of upper tract transitional cell carcinoma, ureteral strictures, and ureteropelvic junction obstruction. The investigation of undiagnosed hematuria or filling defects seen on intravenous or retrograde pyelography may also include ureteroscopy.

## EQUIPMENT NECESSARY FOR URETEROSCOPY AND RETROGRADE ACCESS
### Endoscopes

The first ureteroscopy was performed in 1912 by Hugh Hampton Young in a patient with posterior urethral valves when a rigid cystoscope was advanced into the dilated ureter (Young and McKay, 1929). In the 1960s a rudimentary ureteroscope was placed into a ureter through a ureterolithotomy during open surgery (Marshall, 1964). Initially, all ureteroscopes were rigid in design and consisted of a rod-lens system with outer diameters ranging from 12 to 13.5 Fr. These endoscopes required routine dilation of the ureter in order to gain access as well as an indwelling stent postoperatively. By the mid-1980s, improvements in design and engineering had resulted in miniaturization of ureteroscopes and a corresponding decrease in trauma associated with the procedure. Rigid endoscopes were reduced to 8.5 Fr in diameter and contained a working channel (Huffman, 1989a; Huffman, 1989b). It was not until 1989 that the next generation of "semirigid" ureteroscopes was developed and contained fiberoptics rather than a rod-lens system (Dretler and Cho, 1989), and in 1993 the current generation of smaller endoscopes was available for use (Abdel-Razzak and Bagley, 1993; Bagley et al, 2004).

Ureteroscopes are produced as semirigid (a rigid instrument able to accommodate a small amount of bend) or flexible instruments. Semirigid ureteroscopes typically have a tapered distal tip (e.g., 6.75 to 9.0 Fr) that dilates to a larger diameter shaft closer to the eyepiece (e.g., 8.4 to 10.1 Fr). The advantages of the semirigid ureteroscope include a large working channel, faster irrigation flow, and a larger field of view because of the larger number of fiberoptic bundles compared with the corresponding flexible instruments. Semirigid ureteroscopes are typically used for treatment of ureteral pathology below the iliac vessels but may be utilized above the iliac vessels especially in female patients. Caution must be used as the semirigid instrument can accommodate some bend but may sustain damage or even fracture when the metal fatigues. This is particularly hazardous in patients with large psoas muscles and longer urethras (i.e., males), in whom it is often difficult to use the semirigid ureteroscope above the iliac vessels.

**Flexible, actively deflectable ureteroscopes range from 6.75 to 9 Fr in diameter at the tip and offer the distinct advantage of being able to reach the entire urinary system including the lower pole of the kidney.** Table 45–2 lists some of the currently available flexible ureteroscopes. Typical endoscopes offer 120 to 170 degrees of deflection in one direction and 170 to 270 degrees in the other (Ferraro et al, 1999; Chiu et al, 2004; Johnson and Grasso, 2004); however, the degree of deflection may be altered with instruments (such as laser fibers) in the working channel that increase the stiffness and resistance to deflection of the endoscope (Poon et al, 1997; Landman et al, 2002a ; Parkin et al, 2002). The extra flexibility of such instruments comes with the disadvantages of inferior image quality compared with semirigid ureteroscopes and frequent repairs for a variety of problems including damaged fiberoptic bundles, perforation of the working channel by accessory instruments, or malfunctioning deflection mechanisms (Afane et al, 2000; Pietrow et al, 2002; Landman et al,

2003a). Active dual-deflection ureteroscopes are now available and offer two deflection points in the shaft of the instrument to facilitate access to all calyces, particularly the lower pole (Fig. 45–1) (Grasso and Bagley, 1998; Ankem et al, 2004; Shvarts et al, 2004). In addition to increased repair costs, the capital costs of flexible ureteroscopes are greater than those of semirigid instruments (Elashry et al, 1997; Ferraro et al, 1999; Afane et al, 2000; Chiu et al, 2004). **The flexible ureteroscope is used almost exclusively in cases with ureteral stones and pathology above the iliac vessels at the authors' institution.** Attempting to work in the most distal portion of the ureter with a flexible ureteroscope can be difficult because of a lack of "purchase" by the instrument.

## Ancillary Equipment

A variety of ancillary equipment is required for the effective and safe performance of ureteroscopy as outlined in Table 45–3 and Figure 45–2. Fluoroscopy by way of a C-arm or fixed urology-specific endoscopy table is necessary for retrograde pyelography, ureteral stenting, and localizing equipment and instruments within the urinary tract intraoperatively. Operating room personnel must take the proper protective precautions including wearing lead aprons, thyroid protectors, and lead glasses. Radioprotective shields are also available to protect anesthesia staff. A video tower consisting of a monitor, fiberoptic light source, camera source, and optional documentation components should be placed near the head of the table facing the surgeon.

A variety of instruments and hardware should be at the urologist's disposal, but not all equipment is opened before surgery because it is unknown exactly which accessories may be needed or which difficulties may be encountered during endoscopic cases. Waste of disposable devices and single-use accessories should be minimized during ureteroscopy; therefore, it is recommended that these items be opened on an as-needed basis.

### Guide Wires

Guide wires can vary in their tips, shaft rigidity, material, and shaft diameter. Polytetrafluorethylene (PTFE)-coated guide wires with a stainless steel core and a floppy tip are commonly used utilitarian guide wires. Various guide wires and their different characteristics are outlined in Table 45–3 and Figure 45–3. Hydrophilic-tipped guide wires require sterile water or

---

| Table 45–1.  **Indications for Ureteroscopy** |
|---|

*Therapeutic Indications*

Urolithiasis
Endoureterotomy for ureteral stricture
Retrograde endopyelotomy for ureteropelvic junction obstruction
Biopsy/ablation of upper tract transitional cell carcinoma (TCC)
Retrieval of migrated ureteral stent

*Diagnostic Indications*

Evaluation of positive cytology with normal cystoscopy
Monitoring of previous upper tract TCC
Evaluation of filling defects on intravenous pyelography/retrograde pyelography
Undiagnosed gross hematuria

---

| Table 45–2.  **Characteristics of Available Flexible Ureteroscopes** | | | | | | | |
|---|---|---|---|---|---|---|---|
| | *ACMI DUR 8 Elite* | *ACMI DUR 8* | *Storz 11274AA* | *Storz Flex-X (11278A)* | *Wolf 7325.172 7.5 F* | *Wolf 7330.072 9.0 F* | *Olympus URF-P3* |
| Tip size (Fr) | 6.75 | 6.75 | 7.5 | 7.5 | 7.5 | 9.0 | 6.9 |
| Shaft size (Fr) | 8.7-10.1 | 8.7-10.1 | 8.6 | 8.4 | 8.0-9.0 | 9.0 | 8.4 |
| Working channel (Fr) | 3.6 | 3.6 | 3.6 | 3.6 | 3.6 | 4.0 | 3.6 |
| Working length (cm) | 64 | 65 | 70 | 67.5 | 70 | 60 | 70 |
| Field of view (°) | 80 | 80 | | 90 | 95 | 60 | 90 |
| Active tip deflection | 180/170 −130 down with dual deflection | 180/170 | 170/120 | 270/270 (dual deflection) | 160/130 | 160/130 | 180/180 |
| Active deflection | Primary and secondary | Primary | Primary | Primary and secondary | Primary | Primary | Primary |

Data from User et al., 2004; Monga et al., 2004; Shvarts et al., 2004; Parkin et al., 2002.

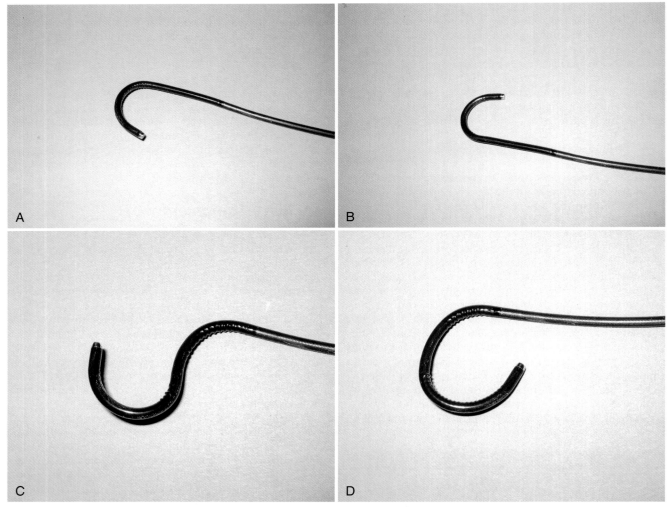

**Figure 45–1.** An active dual deflection flexible ureteroscope. **A** and **B** display typical primary up and down deflection. **C** and **D** display the active secondary deflection to facilitate access into lower pole calyces.

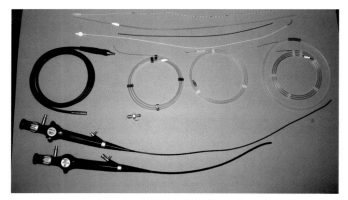

**Figure 45–2.** Equipment necessary for retrograde endoscopic ureteral access. From top to bottom, left to right: 5 Fr open-ended ureteral catheter (yellow), 8/10 Fr coaxial dilator (blue), metal-tipped stent pusher (red), 5 Fr angled vascular catheter (light blue), endoscope fiberoptic light cable, polytetrafluoroethylene (PTFE)-coated guide wire, hydrophilic-tipped guide wire, extra stiff PTFE-coated guide wire, combination hydrophilic-tipped wire and PTFE body, cysto tap, flexible ureteroscope, flexible cystoscope.

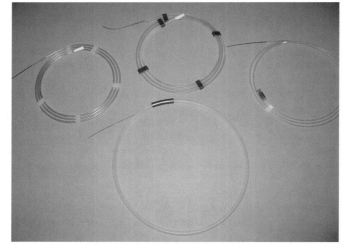

**Figure 45–3.** An assortment of guide wires. From left to right: Combination hydrophilic-tipped wire with polytetrafluoroethylene (PTFE) shaft (Sensor wire, Microvasive, Boston Scientific), PTFE-coated Bentson wire (Cook Urological), hydrophilic wire (Terumo), and below the stiff Amplatz wire (Cook Urological).

**Table 45–3. Equipment Necessary for Ureteroscopy and Retrograde Access**

| Equipment | Factors to Consider |
|---|---|
| Fluoroscopy | |
| Operating room table | Documentation devices including digital capture devices for still photographs and motion pictures |
| Video tower with monitor | |
| Endoscopes | |
|   Cystoscopes (rigid/flexible) | Flexible cystoscopes offer various angles and are more comfortable for the patient |
|   Ureteroscope (semirigid) | Typically for stones below the iliac vessels<br>**Advantages:** more durable, larger working channel for larger instruments (e.g., laser fibers, baskets), better visibility related to increased irrigating ability<br>**Disadvantages:** may be more traumatic to the urethra/ureter, limited access within the ureter |
|   Ureteroscope (flexible) | Typically used for stones above the iliac vessels and in the kidney<br>Can reach every part of the urinary tract (including lower pole of the kidney)<br>Some models have "double deflection" allowing easier access to all calyces<br>**Disadvantages:** flexible fiberoptics require frequent repairs, which are costly; smaller working channels have lower flow rates; the image is not as sharp as with semirigid endoscopes because of the smaller fiberoptic bundles |
| Ureteral catheters | |
|   5 Fr open ended, straight or angled | These catheters can be used to provide backing to help maneuver guide wires<br>Angled vascular catheters are useful in manipulating guide wires past obstructions and tight areas |
| Guide wires | |
|   Polytetrafluoroethylene (PTFE) coated | PTFE is the commonest wire and is a good utilitarian wire. The floppy tip prevents urothelial damage |
|   Hydrophilic | Hydrophilic wires absorb water and have a very decreased coefficient of friction, making them very slippery to help maneuver past obstructions |
|   Extra stiff | The extra stiff wire is more resistant to kinking than regular PTFE guide wires and is a good backing for coaxial or balloon dilation and insertion of ureteral access sheaths |
|   Combination wires | Combination wires combine a hydrophilic tip with a more robust and easier to manipulate PTFE body |
|   Double floppy tip | Double floppy tips may be used to backload flexible ureteroscopes in an attempt to prevent damage to the working channel of the ureteroscope |
|   Exchange wire | An exchange wire is longer than a typical guide wire to facilitate certain procedures |
| Dilators | |
|   8/10 coaxial dilators | These are used in serial fashion using progressively larger dilators<br>A good dilator to dilate the ureter and orifice to accommodate semirigid and flexible ureteroscopes<br>Is also helpful for inserting ureteral stents under fluoroscopic guidance<br>Is also used to introduce the second guide wire for flexible ureteroscopy |
|   Balloon dilator | Potentially less traumatic than coaxial dilation and very efficient for dilating tight ureteral orifices, ureters, and ureteral strictures in one step |
| Irrigation devices | |
|   Hand pressure irrigation (large syringes or self-refilling pistol grip syringes) | |
|   Pressure bag | |
|   Foot pump | |
| Laser fiber (holmium:YAG) | These come in a variety of sizes ranging from 200 to 1000 μm. |
| Laser fiber sealing device for the endoscope | Typically, fibers ranging from 200 to μm or 400 μm are utilized in ureteroscopic lithotripsy |
| Working channel graspers/baskets | These are typically made of a nickel-titanium (nitinol) combination that provides a strong metal that is thin and flexible but also retains its original shape (memory) when deployed |
|   Stone baskets | |
|   Stone graspers | |
|   Specialty baskets that have a working channel in the middle to allow a laser fiber to break up a stone being held in the basket or special coils that prevent ureteral stones from migrating proximally during lithotripsy | |
| Ureteral access sheath | These come in a variety of sizes ranging from 9 to 18 Fr and a variety of lengths. The shorter lengths are generally used in women and the longer sheaths in men |
| Biopsy forceps | These are small enough to fit in the channel of the ureteroscope to biopsy any ureteral or renal pelvic masses |
| Intracorporeal lithotriptors | |
|   Holmium:YAG laser | Ho:YAG lasers can fragment all stone compositions and have a high margin of safety. |
|   Electrohydraulic lithotriptor | |
|   Pneumatic ballistic lithotriptor | |
|   Ultrasonic lithotriptor | |
| Self-retaining ureteral stents (double pigtails) | These come in a variety of sizes and a diameter of 5 to 7 Fr is standard. |

YAG, yttrium-aluminum-garnet.

saline flushes through the holding jacket before use. The hydrophilic material absorbs water and becomes slippery to facilitate manipulation past tight obstructions. The main disadvantage of the hydrophilic wire is also its slipperiness, which allows it to slide easily out of the ureter. Stenting over a hydrophilic wire is difficult, and a ureteral catheter (Fig. 45–4) may be used to exchange to a PTFE-coated guide wire before ureteral stenting. A hybrid wire combines a hydrophilic tip to facilitate maneuverability with a PTFE-coated nitinol shaft for stiffness and grip. Ureteral stents can be easily placed over hybrid guide wires.

Guide wires are also used to facilitate the insertion of endoscopes. Advancing a flexible ureteroscope over a rigid guide wire can damage the working channel, necessitating costly repairs (Vanlangendonck and Landman, 2004). Double floppy tipped guide wires may be less traumatic to the working channel and reduce the possibility of endoscope damage (Monga et al, 2001). Semirigid ureteroscopes are typically advanced adjacent to guide wires.

### Ureteral Dilation

**Ureteral catheters** (see Fig. 45–4) **and dilators** (Fig. 45–5) **are important for retrograde access** and include 5 Fr open-ended catheters both for the instillation of contrast material and to provide a buttress for guide wire manipulation past tight junctions or obstructing stones.

Ureteral dilation, if required, is typically performed at the narrowest point, the ureteral orifice, in order to facilitate passage of the ureteroscope. Occasionally, the ureter more proximal to the orifice requires dilation. Sets of progressively larger **polyethylene coaxial dilators** are available for dilation of the ureter but may produce a shearing force and ureteral trauma (Ford et al, 1984; Gaylis et al, 2000). **Balloon dilators** (see Fig. 45–5) provide radial dilation with less trauma and come in 5 to 7 Fr catheter shaft diameters with balloons ranging from 4 to 10 mm in diameter that can exert up to 220 psi (15 atm) (Huffman and Bagley, 1988; Garvin and

Clayman, 1991). After the balloon is positioned fluoroscopically with the area requiring dilation between the two radiopaque markers, an assistant uses a locking screw syringe or other inflating device to instill contrast material into the balloon while the surgeon steadies the dilating catheter to prevent inadvertent movement during dilation. Care must be taken to avoid overinflation of the balloon, which may burst, resulting in ureteral damage (Huffman and Bagley, 1988).

**Ureteral dilation is not necessary in every ureteroscopic case and should be performed only if passage of the ureteroscope is met with difficulty** (Rodrigues et al, 1990; Stoller et al, 1992). **The earlier generation of ureteroscopes required routine dilation, but with newer, smaller endoscopes and miniaturized intracorporeal lithotripsy devices, ureteral dilation is seldom necessary (<14% of cases), particularly when the endoscopes used are 9 Fr or smaller in diameter** (Rodrigues et al, 1990; Stoller et al, 1992; Elashry et al, 1997; Harmon et al, 1997).

### Irrigation

Adequate irrigation flow is necessary to maintain visibility. Ureteroscopes have either two separate channels (one working channel for an instrument such as a laser fiber and the second for irrigation) or one common channel for both irrigation and working instruments. Irrigation can be provided by gravity, a pressure bag, or a variety of hand or foot pumps. Manual hand irrigation has been shown to produce pressures greater than 100 mm Hg in the kidney (Auge et al, 2004). Theoretically, this may lead to bacteremia and sepsis in an infected system because of pyelovenous and pyelolymphatic backflow. Distention of the renal pelvis during ureterorenoscopy may also interfere with maneuverability of the ureteroscope inside the kidney if the pelvis is so capacious that it cannot provide a "backboard" for secondary deflection of the ureteroscope. Furthermore, higher pressures may result in increased fluid absorption by the patient. One study measured fluid absorp-

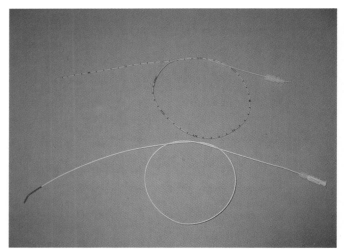

**Figure 45–4.** **Top,** 5 Fr open-ended ureteral catheter. Utilized for injecting contrast medium, performing retrograde pyelograms, and manipulating or exchanging guide wires. **Bottom,** A 5 Fr angled vascular catheter used to manipulate guide wires past obstructions.

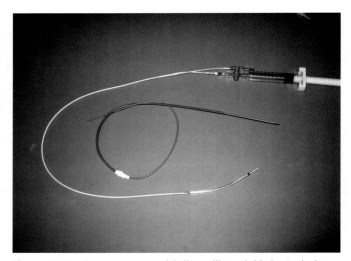

**Figure 45–5.** A one-step ureteral balloon dilator (white) attached to a locking screw syringe (white). A 8/10 Fr coaxial dilator used for ureteral dilation and insertion of a secondary guide wire (blue). Serial ureteral coaxial dilators are not shown in this picture.

tion of approximately 135 mL per hour by the patient during ureteroscopy (Cybulski et al, 2004a). Care should be taken to apply the correct level of pressure irrigation necessary for visualization and to avoid fluid overload and fluid extravasation. Ureteral access sheaths may be used to decrease renal pressure from irrigation during ureteroscopy (Landman et al, 2002b; Auge et al, 2004).

## Ureteral Access Sheath

This accessory was originally developed in the 1970s to facilitate insertion of the flexible ureteroscope (Takayasu and Aso, 1974) and has been shown to decrease renal pressures during ureteroscopy (Landman et al, 2002b; Auge et al, 2004). A variety of companies produce **ureteral access sheaths** (UASs), which come in sizes ranging from 9 to 18 Fr and are inserted with a tapered dilating obturator over a guide wire. UASs can provide ureteral dilation because of the tapered tip, and there has been one report of less postoperative pain following ureteroscopy utilizing a UAS for dilation compared with balloon dilation (Kourambas et al, 2001). As an open conduit into the kidney, the UAS allows irrigation to flow in through the endoscope and back out of the kidney, thus preventing high renal pressures (Kourambas et al, 2001; Landman et al, 2002b; Rehman et al, 2003; Auge et al, 2004). **Shorter operating room times and greater cost savings have been demonstrated when UASs are utilized in conjunction with ureteroscopy** (Kourambas et al, 2001; Monga et al, 2001). The shortened surgical times are thought to be due to the ease of repeated insertion of the flexible ureteroscope and thus facilitation of basketing to remove stone fragments from the kidney, which would otherwise require intracorporeal lithotripsy into small enough fragments to pass spontaneously. **Part of the overall decrease in costs was due to a decreased incidence of ureteroscope damage.** As the ureteroscope is not in direct contact with a potentially tight ureter undergoing axial forces during insertion, the endoscope appears to sustain less damage over time and can be used in more cases before servicing is required (Pietrow et al, 2002). Previous concerns that UASs may cause ureteral ischemia and necrosis resulting in a ureteral stricture have been unfounded, as the stricture incidence has been demonstrated to be the same as that with ureteroscopy alone (~1.4%) (Delvecchio et al, 2003; Vanlangendonck and Landman, 2004).

Although use of UASs has been reported to decrease operating times and cost, there has been only a single study to date regarding stone-free rates (L'Esperance et al, 2004). In 181 patients, the overall stone-free rate was higher in patients who underwent ureteroscopy utilizing a UAS compared with control subjects who underwent ureteroscopy without a UAS (L'Esperance et al, 2004).

Flexible ureteroscopy is better facilitated by UASs than semirigid ureteroscopy. De Sio and colleagues (2004) managed distal ureteral stones with semirigid ureteroscopy and used UASs but found that in 5 of 12 (42%) of the patients, the procedure could not be completed until the sheath was removed. There were no differences in operating time or stone-free rates. Thus, UASs do not appear to be useful in semirigid ureteroscopic management of distal ureteral stones.

The use of UASs has been extended to simultaneous ureteroscopic access during percutaneous nephrolithotomy

(Landman et al, 2003b) and extracorporeal shockwave lithotripsy (SWL) for large stone burdens in patients surgically unfit for percutaneous nephrolithotomy (Okeke et al, 2004).

**In summary, use of UASs during flexible ureteroscopy shortens operating times, reduces renal pelvic pressures, and can limit endoscope damage.**

## Intracorporeal Lithotriptors

**A variety of devices for intracorporeal lithotripsy are reviewed in detail in Chapter 46. The holmium:YAG laser is the current "gold standard" because of its effectiveness in fragmenting any stone composition and its excellent safety profile.** Before the advent of the holmium:YAG laser, other methods of intracorporeal lithotripsy included ultrasonic lithotripsy, which was first described in 1973 using a hollow rigid probe (Goodfriend, 1973). Ultrasound was not used with flexible ureteroscopy until a flexible solid wire probe later became available. Briefly, electrical energy is delivered to piezoceramic elements in the handpiece, which generates sound waves at frequencies of 23,000 to 25,000 Hz. Vibrations of the hollow probe are then transmitted to the stone, resulting in fragmentation. The hollow center allows simultaneous suction to evacuate stone fragments. A disadvantage, however, is that ultrasonic lithotripsy probes are rather large and require a semirigid ureteroscope. More flexible ureteral probes available for use in flexible ureteroscopy are solid and do not contain a suctioning device, making them less efficient than their rigid counterparts. Because of the lack of simultaneous suction, the solid-wire probes failed to gain widespread popularity. Ultrasonic lithotripsy in combination with ureteroscopy is now rarely used because of the drawbacks of the larger rigid probes (Gur et al, 2004).

**Ballistic lithotripsy involves energy generated from an electrokinetic source** (Keeley et al, 1999) **or more commonly a pneumatic energy source** (Leidi et al, 1997; Yinghao et al, 2000; Aghamir et al, 2003). Ballistic lithotripsy utilizes compressed air or electrokinetic energy to propel a missile or ballistic body against the probe that strikes the stone, producing a "jackhammer" effect. Advantages of ballistic lithotripsy include relatively inexpensive equipment with reusable components and a high margin of safety because very little heat is generated at the probe tip. Disadvantages include the inability to remove fragments simultaneously, stone retropulsion, and the lack of efficacy of flexible probes for use in flexible ureteroscopy. In an effort to improve simultaneous fragment removal, ballistic lithotripsy was combined with a suction device (Delvecchio et al, 2000). The overall stone-free rate was 95% at 3 months, and the authors found the addition of suction to aid in fragment removal and prevent fragment migration. However, the combined ballistic lithotripsy–suction device can be used only with rigid probes and, therefore, can be utilized only with rigid ureteroscopy.

**Electrohydraulic lithotripsy** (EHL) utilizes electrical energy that overcomes the insulative gap of an electrode to produce a spark and an ensuing cavitation bubble (Yang and Hong, 1996). Symmetrical collapse of the cavitation bubble results in a secondary shockwave or high-speed microjets if the bubble collapses asymmetrically. Both the secondary shockwave and microjets are responsible for stone fragmentation (Willscher et al, 1988; Denstedt and Clayman, 1990). An advantage of EHL is its low capital cost compared with laser units. EHL probes are a disposable component and, depending on stone hardness, more than one probe may be required to achieve complete stone fragmentation. The probes are more flexible than laser fibers and do not affect the deflection of flexible ureteroscopes to the same extent as quartz laser fibers. The two most important disadvantages of EHL are that some stones are resistant to fragmentation and that high peak pressures are generated at a distance from the probe tip, producing a narrow margin of safety (Vorreuther, 1993). High peak pressures can result in ureteral perforation. Two studies reported extravasation rates of 18% to 40% using EHL as an intracorporeal lithotriptor for ureteral stones (Raney, 1978; Hofbauer et al, 1995).

The first laser employed to fragment a stone was the **long-pulsed ruby laser,** which in 1968 was utilized in vitro. The ruby laser was never used clinically because of the large amount of energy delivered to surrounding tissues, resulting in damage (Mulvaney and Beck, 1968). **The carbon dioxide ($CO_2$) and neodymium:yttrium-aluminum-garnet (Nd:YAG)** lasers subsequently became available for general clinical use; however, the $CO_2$ laser lacked fibers for endoscopic use and the Nd:YAG converted much of the energy to heat, causing thermal tissue damage. It was not until 1988 that the Nd:YAG was altered to enable the first clinically applicable laser lithotriptor (Hofmann and Hartung, 1988). The Nd:YAG laser was combined with Q-switching and a specially designed coupling tip to produce short-pulse laser beams that generated high peak pressures with reduced heat. This modification improved the safety of the laser even when directly discharged on urothelium in an animal model (Hofmann and Hartung, 1988). The drawbacks of the Nd:YAG laser are the inability to fragment calcium oxalate monohydrate and brushite stones, the relatively large-diameter fiber, and the fragile delivery system (Zheng and Denstedt, 2000). Three additional laser lithotripsy platforms for clinical use have since been developed: the pulsed-dye, alexandrite, and holmium:YAG lasers.

One of the most important developments in the endoscopic approach to urolithiasis has been the **holmium:YAG laser** for intracorporeal lithotripsy. The holmium:YAG laser is now recognized to be the gold standard for ureteroscopic intracorporeal lithotripsy. The active medium is the rare earth element holmium combined with a YAG crystal. This pulsed solid-state laser system operates at 2100 nm, which is in the near infrared portion of the electromagnetic spectrum and, therefore, invisible to the human eye. The holmium:YAG laser was successfully used in ophthalmology, otolaryngology, and orthopedics before it was introduced to urology in 1993 (Webb et al, 1993). As the 2100 nm wavelength can be transmitted through flexible silica quartz fibers, the holmium laser is especially suited for endoscopic procedures using both flexible and rigid endoscopes.

The method of stone fragmentation using the holmium:YAG laser differs from the photoacoustic method utilized by other lasers. **Energy from the holmium:YAG laser produces a photothermal effect resulting in vaporization of the stone** (Dushinski and Lingeman, 1998; Wollin and Denstedt, 1998). **The 2100 nm holmium:YAG laser energy is strongly absorbed by water and travels no farther than 0.5 to 1.0 mm in a liquid medium, providing a substantial margin of safety in preventing ureteral damage** (Grasso and Chalik, 1998; Wollin and Denstedt, 1998). Furthermore, when the laser fiber is oriented in the same direction as the ureter during ureteroscopy, there is a high laser incident angle with the mucosa, causing low mucosal damage after accidental exposure (Vassar et al, 1999). In addition, because of the paucity of holmium:YAG shockwaves, there is little risk of shockwave-induced collateral injury (Vassar et al, 1999). In vitro studies have demonstrated that the holmium:YAG laser cuts and incises soft tissue with precision and fragments all types of calculi, which is a distinct advantage over the other lasers used in urology (Wollin and Denstedt, 1998). **Stone-free rates using this method of intracorporeal lithotripsy are in excess of 90% in several series** (Grasso, 1996; Hosking and Bard, 1996; Devarajan et al, 1998; Yip et al, 1998; Sofer et al, 2002). Fibers are available in sizes 200, 365, 400, 550, and 1000 μm. Typically, 200 to 400 μm fibers are utilized during ureteroscopy.

## STEP-BY-STEP URETEROSCOPY IN THE TREATMENT OF URETERONEPHROLITHIASIS
### Preparation of the Patient

A variety of techniques and nuances exist in performing successful ureteroscopy, and the method presented here reflects the technique employed by the authors. The basic principles of the procedure remain the same even for the most experienced endoscopist.

**Preparation of the patient includes informed consent and explanation of the potential complications and the possibility of insertion of an indwelling ureteral stent.** Other preoperative considerations include the type of anesthesia, preoperative antibiotics, and imaging. Typically, **general anesthesia** is used, but **neuroleptic anesthesia** is also feasible (Abdel-Razzak and Bagley, 1993; Hosking and Bard, 1996; Elashry et al, 1997; Miroglu and Saporta, 1997; Hosking et al, 2003; Cybulski et al, 2004b). The majority of ureteroscopic cases can be treated as an outpatient day surgical procedure.

### Antibiotic Prophylaxis

The rate of urinary tract infection (UTI) following ureteroscopy varies between 4% and 25% of cases even when prophylactic antibiotics are administered (Rao et al, 1991; Hendrikx et al, 1999; Puppo et al, 1999; Christiano et al, 2000; Grabe, 2001; Grabe, 2004). **European guidelines advocate a single dose of preoperative antibiotic prophylaxis** (Naber et al, 2001); **however, a randomized study by Knopf and colleagues revealed no difference in the rate of clinical UTI between patients randomly assigned to antibiotic prophylaxis and those without antibiotic prophylaxis** (Knopf et al, 2003). This study demonstrated a higher rate of postoperative bacteriuria in those who did not receive antibiotic prophylaxis (12.5%) than in those who did receive prophylaxis (1.8%); however, there were no clinically active UTIs in either group, suggesting that postoperative asymptomatic bacteriuria does not necessarily lead to a clinical UTI (Christiano et al, 2000; Knopf et al, 2003).

In a review of the literature reported by Grabe, it is recommended that intravenous antibiotic prophylaxis be given to patients undergoing ureteroscopy for the treatment of a proximal or impacted stone (Grabe, 2004). **Grabe further recommends that antibiotic prophylaxis is not necessary in the ureteroscopic treatment of more distal stones in uncomplicated cases but should be utilized in patients at risk (e.g., significant comorbidities, diabetes). Patients with a preoperative stent, catheter, or nephrostomy tube should be treated with prophylactic antibiotics** (Grabe, 2004). Christiano and associates (2000) determined that a single preoperative oral dose of ciprofloxacin provided protection equivalent to that of a single intravenous dose of cefazolin at reduced cost.

**Patients with heart valves and murmurs at risk for bacterial endocarditis require antibiotic prophylaxis** (Amin, 1992). The American Urological Association (AUA) and American Academy of Orthopaedic Surgeons (2003) published a joint advisory statement regarding antibiotic prophylaxis stating that **all patients who have undergone prosthetic joint replacement within the past 2 years are at increased risk for bacteremia and should be administered prophylactic antibiotics. Immunocompromised patients with inflammatory arthropathies, those with drug- or radiation-induced immunosuppression, and patients with comorbidities (malnourishment, hemophilia, human immunodeficiency virus, diabetes, or malignancy) should also undergo antibiotic prophylaxis.**

## Video Monitoring and Camera

Video monitoring of ureteroscopy provides several advantages. The camera is ergonomically beneficial, particularly when using the semirigid ureteroscope and for teaching trainees and coordinating operating room personnel. Documentation devices such as digital capture devices can take still photographs as well as digital motion film through the endoscope. Digital capture allows endoscopic images to be filed into a patient's electronic chart or electronic radiology file for later reference.

## Positioning of the Patient

Ureteroscopy has been described with patients in the supine, prone, and flank positions (Clayman et al, 1987; Bercowsky et al, 1999; Herrell and Buchanan, 2002). Flank positioning requires the exclusive use of flexible instruments and has the advantage of placing the renal pelvis in the most dependent position to facilitate stone clearance and access to fragments during intracorporeal lithotripsy (Herrell and Buchanan, 2002). **The authors' preference is to position the patient in the dorsal lithotomy position** with the ipsilateral leg somewhat straighter and lower than the contralateral leg to allow the surgeon more room to operate rigid instruments in line with the affected ureter. The lower, straighter ipsilateral leg is also believed to align the affected ureter in order to facilitate ureteroscopy. **When operating in the proximal ureter or kidney, slight Trendelenburg positioning may help the stone or any fragments to be displaced into an upper calyx, which is typically in line with the ureter and is easier to reach than the lower pole.**

## Cystoscopy

Flexible or rigid cystoscopes can be used for initial guide wire placement into the ureter; the technique depends on the urologist's training and available equipment. At the authors' institution, flexible cystoscopy is the preferred modality. Although rigid cystoscopes are more durable, they may cause more urethral trauma and discomfort, particularly in males. Rigid ureteroscopes produce clearer images because of the glass rod-lens system. Various angles that are not attainable with a rigid instrument may, however, be achieved with a flexible cystoscope. For instance, in males with a prominent prostate and large median lobe, it may be difficult to visualize and cannulate the ureteral orifice with a rigid cystoscope, whereas the flexible counterpart has increased maneuverability to perform this task. **Cystoscopy** is carried out in order to insert a 0.035- or 0.038-inch PTFE-coated floppy-tip guide wire into the ureter up to the renal pelvis until it is coiled in the kidney. If difficulty occurs in visualizing the ureteral orifice, certain steps may be taken: (1) identify the contralateral orifice and look across the intertrigonal ridge, (2) empty the bladder if it is full, (3) fill the bladder if it is empty, and (4) switch from the flexible to rigid cystoscope or vice versa. A colored dye may also be given intravenously (e.g., indigo carmine), but this may be time consuming while waiting for renal filtration.

## Safety Guide Wire

Fluoroscopy is used to confirm the position of the guide wire as it is advanced. For ureteral stones, the wire should be advanced past the stone before beginning intracorporeal lithotripsy. In this manner, **the wire acts as a safety wire, and should ureteral perforation or excessive bleeding occur such that vision is obscured and the procedure can no longer be safely performed, access to the kidney is preserved and a ureteral stent may be left indwelling. A general principle of ureteroscopy is always to have a safety guide wire present intraoperatively.** If the wire cannot traverse past an obstructing stone, the wire is left at the level of the obstruction, the cystoscope is removed, and the following steps may be attempted:

1. Insert a 5 Fr ureteral catheter over the guide wire to buttress the guide wire and provide backing to propel the guide wire past the stone. If this is unsuccessful . . .
2. Exchange the PTFE guide wire for an angled hydrophilic wire or combination wire with an angled hydrophilic tip and attempt to maneuver past the stone (Leveillee and Bird, 2000; Hofmann et al, 1995). If this is unsuccessful . . .
3. Exchange the 5 Fr ureteral catheter for an angled ureteral catheter or vascular catheter (see Fig. 45–4) in combination with the angled hydrophilic wire to manipulate past the obstructing stone (Schwalb and Eshghi, 1994).

If there is any question about where the guide wire has traversed, a 5 Fr ureteral catheter can be exchanged over the guide wire and a retrograde pyelogram obtained to outline the collecting system. Ureteral edema, inflammation, and thinning of the mucosa may occur with an obstructing stone, resulting in ureteral perforation during wire manipulation indicated by extravasation of contrast material on the retrograde pyelogram. If the wire cannot be manipulated into the collecting system and confirmed with contrast, antegrade percutaneous nephrostomy tube drainage is indicated to relieve obstruction and prevent urinary extravasation.

## Ureteroscope Insertion

When a safety guide wire is in place, the cystoscope is backed out and a straight urethral catheter is inserted and removed to drain the bladder. The next step depends on whether rigid or flexible ureteroscopy is planned. During **rigid ureteroscopy**, the endoscope is generally inserted alongside the guide wire under direct vision (Abdel-Razzak and Bagley, 1993). Care must be taken to observe the presence of the wire at all times to avoid creation of a false passage. The ureteroscope is advanced only when the instrument slides freely and there is a clear field of view. When performing **flexible ureteroscopy**, a second "working" wire must be inserted in order to backload the endoscope, allowing the wire to act as a guide for the instrument to be advanced into the ureter or kidney under fluoroscopic guidance (Afane et al, 2000). Placement of a second wire can be achieved by insertion of a dual-lumen catheter (6/10 Fr) or an 8/10 Fr coaxial dilator inserted over the initial guide wire. Adequate tension should be placed on the guide wire by the assistant as the ureteroscope is advanced. The ureteral orifice is a location where advancement of the endoscope may be hindered because the working channel is typically eccentrically located in ureteroscopes. Simply rotating the ureteroscope during advancement often overcomes this obstacle. Failing this, the ureter should be gently dilated using an 8/10 Fr coaxial or similar dilator and insertion attempted again (Table 45–4). This degree of dilation is typically sufficient to insert the current generation of small flexible ureteroscopes. A UAS can also dilate the ureter, improve irrigation and visibility, and facilitate repeated ureteroscope insertions as noted previously (Aslan et al, 1998).

---

**Table 45–4. Algorithm for Troubleshooting Advancement of the Flexible Ureteroscope**

1. **Rotate the ureteroscope at the ureteral orifice while attempting to advance.** Rotation of the eccentrically placed working channel where the guide wire exits often allows passage of the flexible ureteroscope into the ureter. If this fails, . . .
2. **Dilate ureteral orifice using an 8/10 Fr coaxial dilator over a guide wire.** Reattempt ureteroscope insertion. If this fails, . . .
3. **One-step dilation with a balloon dilator or serial dilation using coaxial dilators.** One-step dilators may be less traumatic. Deflation of the balloon is necessary before removing the balloon. If the balloon cannot be advanced, use an extra-stiff guide wire, which is likely to buckle. If it cannot be advanced over the stiff wire, load an 8/10 Fr coaxial dilator and remove the 8 Fr dilator leaving the 10 Fr sheath. Pass the balloon dilator over the wire through the 10 Fr sheath, which gives it backing to advance through the tight part of the ureter. If this fails, . . .
4. Place a **ureteral access sheath** that has a dilating obturator that, once removed, provides a conduit for insertion of the ureteroscope. If this fails, . . .
5. The last resort is to **leave a self-retaining ureteral stent and defer the definitive procedure.** The stent passively dilates the ureter after 7 to 10 days and ureteroscopy can be attempted again at that time.

---

**If the ureteroscope still cannot be advanced, the last step is to leave a ureteral stent, defer the definitive procedure, and return after 7 to 10 days when the stent has passively dilated the ureter.**

Upon successful advancement of the endoscope, fluoroscopy is used to guide the flexible ureteroscope to the area of interest, which is then visualized directly. Instillation of contrast material through the ureteroscope and concurrent fluoroscopy are used to provide intrarenal orientation, and the endoscope is manipulated into each calyx and visually evaluated. All calyces should be systematically inspected to ensure a complete examination.

## IS ROUTINE STENTING NECESSARY FOLLOWING URETEROSCOPY?

Placement of a ureteral catheter or internal ureteral stent has been the standard of care following ureteroscopy. The main advantage of a postoperative ureteral stent is to prevent renal colic from obstruction related to stone fragments or ureteral edema from balloon dilation. Furthermore, passive ureteral dilation by the stent is thought to facilitate passage of stone fragments when the stent is removed. Stenting the ureter is also thought to prevent ureteral stricture formation and to facilitate ureteral healing. Disadvantages of ureteral stents include morbidity associated with infection, dysuria, flank pain, hematuria, or stent migration (Stoller et al, 1992; Joshi et al, 2002; Joshi et al, 2003).

Randomized controlled clinical trials have demonstrated that not all patients require routine stenting after ureteroscopy. Of 93 patients who were not stented following ureteroscopy, 40 had no postoperative discomfort, and of the 53 patients with discomfort, 45 complained of only mild discomfort that was easily resolved by oral analgesics (Hosking et al, 1999). Although this was a case series and there were no controls, this was the first report to demonstrate that ureteroscopy patients did not routinely require a ureteral stent (Hosking et al, 1999). **Patients prospectively randomly assigned to ureteral stents following ureteroscopy have increased pain compared with nonstented patients, yet the incidence of emergency room visits, urosepsis, and hospitalization and stone-free rates did not differ between the two groups** (Borboroglu et al, 2001; Denstedt et al, 2001). Similarly, nonstented patients did not have more complications than patients in whom a stent was left indwelling. Several randomized controlled trials have shown similar results (Cheung et al, 2001a; Hollenbeck et al, 2001; Netto et al, 2001; Byrne et al, 2002; Cheung et al, 2003; Srivastava et al, 2003; Damiano et al, 2004). **At our institution, if the stone burden is small, the ureter has not been balloon dilated, and the holmium:YAG laser has been used without ureteral trauma, a ureteral stent is not routinely placed** (Denstedt et al, 2001). Other authors have demonstrated that a stent is not necessary even with balloon or coaxial ureteral dilation (Hosking et al, 1999; Borboroglu et al, 2001; Hollenbeck et al, 2001; Byrne et al, 2002). **Ureteral stenting after ureteroscopy is not routinely necessary and should be determined on a case-by-case basis** (Knudsen et al, 2004). Indications for insertion of a ureteral stent following ureteroscopy and lithotripsy are outlined in Table 45–5.

| Table 45–5. Indications for Ureteral Stent Placement following Ureteroscopy |
|---|
| Ureteral perforation intraoperatively |
| Ureteral dilation greater than 10 Fr (either coaxial or balloon dilator) |
| Significant ureteral edema due to stone (e.g., impacted stone) |
| Failure to advance the ureteroscope due to a narrow ureter or ureteral orifice and in preparation for a subsequent ureteroscopy after 7 days |
| Infected urinary system with an obstructing system |
| Large stone burden with many fragments remaining to pass |
| Solitary kidney |

## URETERAL STENTS AND BIOMATERIALS

All stents may cause morbidity such as flank pain, dysuria, hematuria, infection, migration, and encrustation. **The ideal stent material should be biocompatible and radiopaque, relieve intraluminal and extraluminal obstruction, resist encrustation and infection, cause little discomfort to the patient, and be widely available at a reasonable cost. To date, no stent material meets all of these criteria.**

**Polyethylene** was the first synthetic polymer used to produce stents, but it has been abandoned because of its fragility and tendency to fracture (Mitty et al, 1987; Mardis and Kroeger, 1988; Roemer, 2000). Various materials have been utilized to manufacture stents including silicone and polyurethane. **Silicone** stents are the most biocompatible of materials used, but they lack rigidity because of their flexibility and elasticity and are difficult to manipulate within the urinary tract. The low tensile strength of silicone makes it easy to compress the stent extrinsically. The development of biomaterials has evolved to produce **polyurethane, the commonest polymer used in today's stents.** As a single polymer, polyurethane is very rigid and causes discomfort in patients and ureteral ulceration and erosion in animal ureters (Marx et al, 1988). Blended polymers of polyurethane have a reduced tendency to cause mucosal damage. Newer materials and combination polymers are softer, more comfortable, and easier to maneuver within the urinary tract (Beiko et al, 2004; Chew and Denstedt, 2004). Examples include various proprietary blends such as Percuflex (Boston Scientific Corporation, Natick, MA), Silitek (Surgitek, Medical Engineering Corporation, Racine, WI), C-Flex (Consolidated Polymer Technologies, Clearwater, FL), Tecoflex (Thermedics, Wilmington, MA), and ethylene vinyl acetate (from the polyolefin family, of which polyethylene is a member).

**Infection and encrustation, in particular, limit long-term use of stents to the extent that patients who require long-term indwelling stents must undergo stent changes every 3 to 4 months. Infection and encrustation arise from the formation of biofilm on the surface of the stent, which occurs within hours after insertion** (Tieszer et al, 1998; Wollin et al, 1998). After a conditioning film coats the surface of any foreign object in the urinary system, glycoproteins, exopolymer, and matrix form a biofilm in which bacteria may become embedded (Choong and Whitfield, 2000). Embedded bacteria in biofilms are difficult to eradicate as antibiotics poorly penetrate the biofilm, the bacteria upregulate genes to produce resistance, or the bacteria enter a low-energy hiber-

nation state that is immune to antibiotics that rely on high cellular metabolism for their bactericidal activity. Improvements in biomaterials and surface coatings have attempted to reduce biofilm formation and, thus, subsequent infection and encrustation (Roemer, 2000; Beiko et al, 2004; Chew and Denstedt, 2004). Coatings such as hydrophilic polymers (Gorman et al, 1998), heparin (Riedl et al, 2002), pentosan polysulfate (Zupkas et al, 2000), or oxalate-degrading enzymes (Watterson et al, 2003) have been used in an attempt to reduce stent encrustation.

**Stent design has varied in newer stents, including biodegradable, spiral, tail, and dual durometer stents. Biodegradable stents** are composed of a polymer containing poly-L-lactic and glycolic acids that is designed to disintegrate after 48 hours in the urinary tract after it has provided kidney drainage following ureteroscopy (Lingeman et al, 2003b). Although it successfully provided drainage for 48 hours in 78% of patients (68 of 81), its widespread use was prevented by such complications as early disintegration (<48 hours) and retained fragments (>3 months) requiring SWL and ureteroscopic removal (Lingeman et al, 2003a). **Spiral stents** were designed with a helical ridge that spiral from proximal to distal and were believed to facilitate stone fragment expulsion after lithotripsy (Stoller et al, 2000). A clinical prospective study found no difference in stone clearance rates following extracorporeal SWL in patients with spiral stents compared with control stents (Gerber et al, 2004). **Tail stents** have a regular 7 Fr hollow lumen proximal pigtail within the kidney and a tapered 3 Fr lumenless tail that starts in the distal ureter and extends into the bladder but does not coil (Dunn et al, 2000). In one clinical trial, the tail stent was reported to produce less irritative stent symptoms than control stents (Liatsikos et al, 2002). **Dual durometer stents** are composed of materials with different stiffness in the bladder pigtail compared with the kidney pigtail. The proximal pigtail is more rigid to prevent stent migration, whereas the bladder portion is softer and hypothesized to produce less irritative symptoms. To date, there are no clinical trials evaluating symptoms associated with dual durometer stents.

Encrustation and bacterial colonization related to stents and catheters are problematic and potentially lead to morbidity such as infection, sepsis, or renal failure. Between 44% and 69% of indwelling stents have bacteria adherent to their surface (Reid et al, 1992; Wollin et al, 1998; Paick et al, 2003; Kehinde et al, 2004). Oral antibiotics administered at the time of stent insertion have been found to be adsorbed to the stent surface biofilm (Reid et al, 2001). This provides evidence for the short-term administration of oral antibiotics following ureteral stent insertion. The utility of long-term antibiotic use in patients with indwelling stents has not been proved, and such patients should be treated only if symptomatic (Kehinde et al, 2004).

Loading the antimicrobial triclosan, a common antimicrobial constituent of many commercial products such as soaps and toothpaste, directly into the ureteral stent to elute over time has resulted in clearance of bacteria in an animal model of UTI (Chew et al, 2004). This type of drug-eluting stent may reduce biofilm formation and, hence, infection and encrustation. The next generation of stents will see drugs delivered directly out of the stent to decrease stent-related irritation, infection, and encrustation.

## Technique of Ureteral Stent Placement

A variety of techniques have been described for stent placement. The general principles include fluoroscopic observation and passage over a guide wire. The first step is to cystoscopically insert a guide wire up to the kidney. A retrograde pyelogram to outline the collecting system may be obtained by exchanging the wire for a 5 Fr ureteral catheter. The stent can be inserted directly over the wire through the cystoscope as it is visualized directly and a stent pusher is used to deploy the stent. Alternatively, the cystoscope can be removed and the stent can be inserted using fluoroscopy and a stent pusher with a radiopaque tip. Care must be taken not to advance the distal end of the stent too far proximally into the ureter. A stenting method using a UAS and fluoroscopy has been described (Wu et al, 2001).

## POSTOPERATIVE CARE

Ureteroscopy is typically performed as an outpatient day surgery procedure. If a stent is left indwelling, it is typically removed 3 to 10 days after the procedure. Postoperative radiographs are obtained within 1 to 2 weeks to determine the success of the procedure. **Small stone fragments (<4 mm) normally pass after the stent has been removed because of the passive ureteral dilation that occurs from stenting** (Deliveliotis et al, 1996a, 1996b). Patients are asked to strain their urine and collect any fragments for stone analysis if samples were not obtained during surgery.

The requirement for routine imaging to rule out obstruction after ureteroscopy is controversial. Postoperative imaging has been recommended in a routine fashion to determine whether there are any residual calculi (Biester and Gillenwater, 1986; Harmon et al, 1997; Roberts et al, 1998). Silent obstruction may occur secondarily from ureteral edema, trauma, or stricture and result in renal failure if it remains undetected (Biester and Gillenwater, 1986; Harmon et al, 1997; Roberts et al, 1998). Weizer and colleagues (2002) reviewed a series of 241 patients of whom 30 had obstruction postoperatively and 7 of these 30 had silent obstruction. They recommended that all patients undergo postoperative imaging as 28% of obstructed patients had silent obstruction and did not have any identifiable risk factors for ureteral stricture at the time of surgery. Others believe that routine imaging is not necessary if there is no history of preexisting ureteral stricture, ureteral perforation, or significant stone impaction at the time of surgery (Karod et al, 1999; Bugg et al, 2002; Beiko et al, 2003). Asymptomatic patients had normal postoperative imaging, and urinary obstruction was present only in patients who experienced flank pain or had identifiable risk factors at surgery such as preexisting evidence of ureteral stricture or significant ureteral trauma intraoperatively.

Postoperative imaging of asymptomatic patients to rule out urinary obstruction and ureteral stricture remains a point of controversy.

## RESULTS OF URETEROSCOPY FOR TREATMENT OF URETERAL STONES

**The 1997 AUA panel guidelines recommended ureteroscopy or shockwave lithotripsy as acceptable treatment for stones in the distal ureter that are unlikely to pass spontaneously or cause significant symptoms requiring multiple hospital visits** (Segura et al, 1997). Stone-free rates in the distal ureter exceed 95% after ureteroscopy (Peschel et al, 1999; Strohmaier et al, 1999; Sofer et al, 2002) and 75% to 97% after SWL (Eden et al, 1998; Park et al, 1998; Peschel et al, 1999; Turk and Jenkins, 1999; Pearle et al, 2001). Ureteroscopy may produce consistently higher stone-free rates but is more invasive than SWL. Furthermore, SWL is likely to require more than one session, ancillary treatments, and is not as widely available as ureteroscopy in some healthcare settings. For distal ureteral stones larger than 1 cm, ureteroscopy and intracorporeal lithotripsy decrease the need for ancillary treatment and typically render the patient stone free following one treatment compared with SWL. **Studies comparing SWL with ureteroscopy for distal stones demonstrate that patients treated with ureteroscopy not only had higher stone-free rates but also required less operating room time, less fluoroscopy time, and less time to achieve a stone-free status** (Hendrikx et al, 1999; Peschel et al, 1999; Chang et al, 2001; Hautmann et al, 2004). **Both ureteroscopy and SWL are viable options in the treatment of distal ureteral stones, and the decision on which treatment to employ should be based on patients' preferences and the availability of each modality** (Segura et al, 1997).

**AUA panel guidelines recommend SWL as first-line therapy for proximal ureteral stones smaller than 1 cm. Ureteroscopy and percutaneous nephrolithotomy are acceptable choices for failed SWL.** SWL produces stone-free rates ranging from 65% to 75% for proximal ureteral stones (Schmidt et al, 1995; Kim et al, 1996; Osti et al, 1997; Park et al, 1998). Ureteroscopy and holmium:YAG laser lithotripsy produce excellent stone-free rates (>92%) in the treatment of proximal ureteral stones smaller than 1 cm (Psihramis, 1992; Erhard et al, 1996; Lam et al, 2002; Wu et al, 2004).

**For proximal ureteral stones larger than 1 cm, SWL, percutaneous nephrolithotomy, and ureteroscopy are all equally viable options according to AUA panel guidelines** (Segura et al, 1997). Patients with stones larger than 1 cm in the proximal ureter treated by ureteroscopy have excellent stone-free rates ranging from 92% to 97% (Lam et al, 2002; Sofer et al, 2002; Wu et al, 2004) compared with 65% to 75% in those treated with SWL (Schmidt et al, 1995; Kim et al, 1996; Osti et al, 1997; Park et al, 1998). Table 45–6 outlines the stone- and patient-related considerations for when ureteroscopy is preferable to SWL in the treatment of ureteral stones.

Ureteroscopy for intrarenal stones is very effective and produces stone-free rates ranging from 84% to 92% (Andersen et al, 1993; Grasso and Chalik, 1998; Grasso et al, 1998; Tawfiek and Bagley, 1999; Sofer et al, 2002; Chow et al, 2003). Intrarenal stones smaller than 2 cm may be successfully treated ureteroscopically while larger stones (>2 cm) are better managed with a percutaneous approach. One study with a small number of patients with stones larger than 2 cm reported a success rate (fragments < 2 mm) of 76% using ureteroscopy in patients who were medically unfit to undergo a percutaneous procedure (Grasso et al, 1998). Stones located in the lower pole usually have lower rates of clearance compared to other intrarenal locations and the optimal management of stones in this location is controversial. Success rates

**Table 45-6. Indications for Ureteroscopy Rather than Shockwave Lithotripsy in Stone Ureteral Disease**

Salvage for failed shockwave lithotripsy (SWL)
Known hard stone (calcium oxalate monohydrate, cystine, brushite)
Morbidly obese (>300 lb or above the focusing limit of the lithotriptor)
Uncorrectable bleeding diathesis (or in a patient in whom it is unsafe to discontinue anticoagulation)
Multiple proximal ureteral stones
Stones >1 cm (decreased rate of success with SWL when stone is >1 cm)
Radiolucent stones
Patient's preference
Social reasons (i.e., for patients who must be completely stone free, such as pilots, bus drivers)

of 85% have been reported for lower pole stones treated ureteroscopically (Grasso and Chalik, 1998). A randomized, prospective trial of SWL versus ureteroscopy in the treatment of lower pole stones revealed no statistically significant difference between stone-free rates at 3 months (35% vs 50%, respectively) (Pearle et al, 2005). Using a flexible ureteroscope and nitinol basket or graspers to re-position lower pole stones smaller than 1 cm to an upper calyx before employing intracorporeal lithotripsy improved the stone-free rate from 77% to 89% (Schuster et al, 2002). Ureteroscopy for intrarenal stones smaller than 2 cm provides good success rates.

## Salvage Ureteroscopy after Failed Extracorporeal Shockwave Lithotripsy

Ureteroscopy is typically recommended as a salvage ancillary procedure for ureteral stones after failed SWL (Boline and Belis, 1993; Singal et al, 1998). Pace and coworkers (2000) determined that after one SWL treatment, the stone-free rate is 68%, and with the addition of a second treatment, a small incremental improvement up to 76% is achieved. Subsequent SWL treatments increase the cumulative stone-free rate to 77% and 78% for the third and fourth treatments, respectively. Results of this study strongly suggest that after one failed SWL treatment, salvage ureteroscopy provides the best chance for a stone-free status (Singal et al, 1998; Pace et al, 2000).

## URETEROSCOPY IN SPECIAL CASES
## Urolithiasis in Pregnancy

Urolithiasis in pregnancy is relatively uncommon with an incidence rate of approximately 1 in 1000 pregnancies (Stothers and Lee, 1992). It must be differentiated from hydronephrosis of pregnancy, which can occur in 90% of pregnant women by the third trimester (Puskar et al, 2001). **More than 84% of pregnant women with renal colic pass their stone spontaneously, making conservative therapy the first-line treatment** (Rodriguez and Klein, 1988; Hendricks et al, 1991; Stothers and Lee, 1992). Initial management should include intravenous hydration, analgesics, antiemetics, and antibiotics where appropriate. Urinary sepsis, obstruction, or azotemia in conjunction with urolithiasis requires urgent urinary decompression. Conservative management itself is not entirely benign and can result in premature labor or pyelonephritis (Parulkar et al, 1998). Given the high rate of spontaneous stone passage, a trial of conservative management is advocated. The urologist can always proceed to more invasive therapies if symptoms or obstruction persists. If urinary drainage is required for sepsis or persistent obstruction, nephrostomy tube or ureteral stent drainage may be used to provide upper tract drainage until after the time of delivery with postpartum treatment of the stone (Denstedt and Razvi, 1992; Evans and Wollin, 2001; McAleer and Loughlin, 2004).

Pregnant women have been shown to have an increased incidence of hypercalciuria compared with their nongravid counterparts, yet stone formation rates and stone composition types are no different (Swanson et al, 1995). The increase in urinary calcium is caused by an increased filtered load and intestinal hyperabsorption from elevated serum vitamin D levels during gestation. An increase in urinary excretion of inhibitors such as citrate, magnesium, and glycoproteins occurs during pregnancy to offset the lithogenic tendency of hypercalciuria.

The diagnosis of urolithiasis typically requires diagnostic tests utilizing radiation. Exposure to potentially teratogenic ionizing radiation must be reduced or eliminated in pregnant patients. Ultrasonography is a safe initial radiologic study of choice for evaluating urolithiasis during pregnancy. A limited intravenous pyelogram may be obtained safely with proper shielding and produces only 200 millirads, well below the 1-rad threshold that has been linked to teratogenic effects (Gianopoulos, 1995). The fetus is thought to be most susceptible during organogenesis (4 to 10 weeks of gestation) to radiation-induced malformation (Houston, 1977). After this time frame, much higher radiation doses are required to induce anomalies. If fluoroscopy is required, pulsed fluoroscopy minimizes radiation to the fetus. With radiation, there is a small but tangible risk of future malignancy in the child. There is an epidemiologic link between diagnostic irradiation and solid malignancy and leukemia (Stewart and Kneale, 1973; Harvey et al, 1985).

In the management of pregnant patients with urolithiasis, anesthesia may be necessary for procedures to provide urinary drainage or to treat the stone definitively. Special consideration must be given as many anesthetic agents are highly lipid soluble and cross the placenta. During the first trimester, an estimated risk of 0.5% of morphogenic anomaly may be associated with volatile gas anesthetic agents (Pedersen and Finster, 1979); therefore, nonemergent surgery should be delayed until the second trimester, when organogenesis is complete. Furthermore, there is an increased risk of spontaneous abortion during the first and second trimesters in women who have undergone general anesthesia for various procedures (Duncan et al, 1986).

Not all of the potential modalities normally used to treat urolithiasis are available in the treatment of pregnant patients. Extracorporeal SWL is absolutely contraindicated in pregnant patients as animal studies have demonstrated deleterious effects of shockwaves on developing fetal tissue (Chaussy and Fuchs, 1989). With the myriad of other available treatment options, SWL should be deferred until the postpartum period. Ureteroscopic manipulation of stones during pregnancy is possible, but not all methods of intracorporeal lithotripsy are compatible with pregnancy. The peak pressures generated by EHL are transmitted some distance from the probe, may harm the fetus, and should be avoided in pregnancy (Vorreuther, 1993). Ultrasonic lithotripsy is theorized to produce fetal hearing damage and should likewise be avoided during pregnancy (Ulvik et al, 1995). **The intracorporeal modality of choice in the pregnant patient is the holmium:YAG laser because of its excellent safety profile** (Carringer et al, 1996; Gross, 1996; Scarpa et al, 1996; Scarpa et al, 1997; Irving et al, 1998; Shokeir and Mutabagani, 1998; Evans and Wollin, 2001; Lifshitz and Lingeman, 2002; Watterson et al, 2002a). Other methods such as pulsed dye laser and pneumatic lithotripsy have been utilized, but the latter is available only in conjunction with semirigid ureteroscopy because of the rigid nature of the pneumatic probe. Reported stone-free rates with the holmium:YAG laser are greater than 90% with no episodes of preterm labor. Regional anesthesia can be used in the first and second trimesters with general anesthesia in the third trimester without increasing the risk of spontaneous abortion or developmental anomaly. **If conservative therapy fails, ureteroscopy may be performed safely and effectively in pregnant patients with urolithiasis** (Lifshitz and Lingeman, 2002; Watterson et al, 2002a).

## Ureteroscopy in Children

Urolithiasis in children may be managed with the same modalities utilized in the adult, namely percutaneous nephrolithotomy, ureteroscopy, and SWL. SWL provides stone-free rates ranging from 60% to 100%, depending on the size and location of the stone (Demirkesen et al, 1999; Delakas et al, 2001; Gofrit et al, 2001; Tan et al, 2004).

Advances in technology including the miniaturization of ureteroscopes have made ureteroscopy with intracorporeal lithotripsy in children feasible in cases in which SWL would have been considered first-line treatment. Ureteroscopy has produced excellent stone-free rates in excess of 92%, similar to those achieved in adults (Schuster et al, 2002; Al-Busaidy et al, 2004). The smaller endoscopes allow access to the majority of ureters without ureteral dilation. **All three modalities of intracorporeal lithotripsy (holmium:YAG laser, pneumatic lithotripsy, EHL) and basket extraction have been used successfully and safely with both flexible and semirigid ureteroscopy** (Shroff and Watson, 1995; al Busaidy et al, 1997; Wollin et al, 1999; Bassiri et al, 2002; Schuster et al, 2002; Al-Busaidy et al, 2004; Satar et al, 2004; Tan et al, 2005). The holmium:YAG laser is the intracorporeal lithotriptor of choice because of its effectiveness against all stone compositions and high margin of safety. The rate of complications remains similar to those reported in adults; for example, ureteral perforation occurs in 1.4% of pediatric cases (Schuster et al, 2002).

Ureteroscopy for the treatment of renal and ureteral calculi has become more feasible, safe, and efficient in the pediatric population and rivals SWL as a first-line treatment in many clinical scenarios. At our institution, ureteroscopy is emerging as the preferred first-line therapy for many of our pediatric patients with urinary tract stones, especially those with stones in the distal ureter.

## Ureteroscopy in the Morbidly Obese Patient

Obesity is a major health care issue in the developed world and is a factor contributing to the increasing incidence of stone disease (Meschi et al, 2004; Straub and Hautmann, 2005). Obese patients present a particular challenge and are often not amenable to extracorporeal SWL because of focal length limitations and positioning difficulty on SWL machines. Nguyen and Belis (1998) reported on ureteroscopy in 52 patients with an average weight of 288 pounds (205 to 385 pounds) with a stone-free rate of 78% after one procedure and 97% after a second procedure with no significant complications. Dash and colleagues (2002) demonstrated that the stone-free and complication rates are equal in morbidly obese patients and nonobese patients. Special attention should be given to anesthetic concerns, particularly regarding airway management, ventilation, and obesity-related diseases. Equipment such as the surgical bed and stirrups must be able to sustain the weight of morbidly obese patients. **The ureteroscopic techniques and principles used in nonobese patients are the same as those for obese patients, in whom they are only marginally more difficult. Ureteroscopy and intracorporeal lithotripsy offer the obese population a minimally invasive treatment with results that rival stone-free rates in nonobese patients.**

## Patients with Bleeding Diatheses

Endourologic management of upper tract urinary calculi in patients with a bleeding diathesis can present a therapeutic challenge. Uncorrected coagulopathy remains an absolute contraindication to SWL and percutaneous nephrolithotomy. Traditionally, the management of bleeding diathesis includes preoperative normalization of hemostatic parameters to minimize the risk of bleeding. However, perioperative discontinuation and reinitiation of anticoagulation increase health care costs and hospitalization and can be associated with increased bleeding and thromboembolic complications. Furthermore, the administration of clotting factors and platelet concentrates can be complicated by transfusion reactions and the transmission of bloodborne disease. With the improved ureteroscopic instrumentation, complete access to the upper urinary tract can be achieved in a relatively atraumatic manner without the need for ureteral dilation. Furthermore, the holmium:YAG laser has been shown to be an extremely safe modality for intracorporeal lithotripsy. A series of 29 patients with urolithiasis and an average international normalized ratio of 2.3 were treated by ureteroscopy and holmium:YAG laser lithotripsy (Watterson et al, 2002b). The stone-free rate was 93%, and 27 of 30 surgeries were performed as same-day outpatient procedures. Only one patient who was treated using EHL suffered from retroperitoneal bleeding postoperatively and required a blood transfusion. None of the patients treated with the holmium:YAG laser had any bleeding complications because of its excellent margin of safety.

**Points to consider during ureteroscopy of patients with bleeding diatheses include avoiding EHL (because of the high peak pressures that may be transmitted beyond the ureter, resulting in significant bleeding), using only the**

holmium:YAG laser, avoiding high-pressure irrigation, minimizing ureteral dilation (8/10 Fr coaxial dilation is typically sufficient), and routinely stenting all patients (Kuo et al, 1998; Watterson et al, 2002b). With these points in mind, ureteroscopy may be safely performed in fully anticoagulated patients on an outpatient surgery basis, providing significant health cost savings.

## Ureteroscopic Treatment of Calyceal Diverticula

Calyceal diverticula are thought to be ureteral buds that failed to degenerate and are incidentally found in up to 0.45% of intravenous pyelograms (Canales and Monga, 2003). Flank pain and associated stones are the presenting features in the majority of patients. Prior to the availability of endourologic procedures, standard treatment was open surgery. Percutaneous, retrograde ureteroscopic and laparoscopic approaches all present less invasive alternatives to open surgery for the treatment of calyceal diverticula. SWL is an unattractive option for management of stones within calyceal diverticula as fragments are unlikely to evacuate through the narrow infundibulum, leaving persistent stones and symptoms (Psihramis and Dretler, 1987).

The technique for retrograde treatment of calyceal diverticula begins with flexible ureteroscopy to inspect the entire renal pelvis for the narrow infundibulum connecting to the calyceal diverticulum. Using fluoroscopy and contrast material infused through the endoscope, a "road map" is established to identify the infundibulum of the diverticulum. Once it is located, a guide wire is traversed through the narrow opening and a balloon dilator or holmium:YAG laser is used to incise and enlarge the infundibulum, after which a stent is left indwelling. In up to 30% of patients, however, the opening cannot be found ureteroscopically and these patients require a percutaneous or laparoscopic approach (Batter and Dretler, 1997; Auge et al, 2002; Canales and Monga, 2003). **Percutaneous neoinfundibulotomy and nephrolithotomy remain the standard for treatment of calyceal diverticula. Ureteroscopy is less attractive for lower pole diverticula and is more likely to be successful in upper pole anterior calyces in patients with a small stone burden** (Canales and Monga, 2003).

## Urolithiasis in Anomalous Kidneys

Anomalous kidneys include abnormalities in fusion, ascent, and form during development of the kidney. Horseshoe and pelvic kidneys are most common. The stone-free rate for treatment of intrarenal calculi in pelvic kidneys treated with SWL is 54% (Kupeli et al, 1999), compared with 75% to 87% in patients treated with ureteroscopy (Rigatti et al, 1991; Weizer et al, 2005). Holmium:YAG laser, nitinol baskets, and graspers are effectively utilized in the ureteroscopic treatment of urolithiasis in pelvic and horseshoe kidneys to provide an effective first-line therapy (Weizer et al, 2005). Larger stones and those failing ureteroscopy require treatment by percutaneous nephrolithotomy (Shokeir et al, 2004). UASs can facilitate ureteroscope insertion and repeated removal of small stone fragments with nitinol baskets in horseshoe kidneys

(Andreoni et al, 2000). In summary, percutaneous nephrolithotomy is performed in anomalous kidneys with large stone burdens, and ureteroscopy may be successfully employed for smaller stone burdens in anomalous kidneys.

## RETROGRADE URETEROSCOPIC TREATMENT OF URETERAL STRICTURES

Ureteral strictures result from ureteral injury during surgery. Strictures occur with a reported rate of 0.5% to 11% of all surgeries involving upper tract manipulation in urology, gynecology, and general surgery (Selzman and Spirnak, 1996). Other causes include urinary reconstruction, radiation, malignancy, spontaneous stone passage, and chronic inflammatory disorders (e.g., tuberculosis and schistosomiasis). Davis and colleagues (1948) were the first to describe reepithelialization of ureteral defects, a principle of the modern endourologic endoureterotomy procedure. The standard treatment of strictures has been open repair, but advances in endourologic techniques and instrumentation as well as in interventional radiology have led to minimally invasive approaches to ureteral stricture resulting in decreased morbidity, operative time, hospitalization, and cost.

Various endourologic techniques in the treatment of ureteral strictures have been described including holmium:YAG laser incision (Gerber et al, 1999; Giddens and Grasso, 2000; Kristo et al, 2003), cold-knife incision (Poulakis et al, 2003), electrocautery, and hot-wire balloon dilation (Wolf et al, 1997; Erdogru et al, 2005). Simple balloon dilatation is effective in patients with nonischemic strictures that are short in length but ineffective in longer strictures caused by ischemia (Netto Junior et al, 1990; Osther et al, 1998; Richter et al, 2000; Byun et al, 2003). Ischemic strictures, in general, respond poorly to endourologic procedures compared with open reconstruction (Byun et al, 2003). The length of stricture is one of the most important factors in predicting success of endourologic treatment. Success rates for strictures shorter than 1.5 to 2 cm are significantly better than for longer strictures treated by ureteroscopic endoureterotomy (Meretyk et al, 1992; Razdan et al, 2005). In addition to the postoperative ureteral stent that is left indwelling, urine flow through the area of incision appears to be necessary for successful endourologic treatment of strictures. Renal units contributing less than 25% of the total renal function were more likely to fail ureteroscopic endoureterotomy than highly functioning kidneys (Wolf et al, 1997).

The widespread use of bowel segments in urinary reconstruction has resulted in a subset of strictures that present a particular challenge to urologists. The reported incidence of ureterointestinal stricture is 4% to 8% in patients who undergo ureteral ileal conduit procedures (Sullivan et al, 1980; Weijerman et al, 1998) with a higher rate of stenosis in those with nonrefluxing continent urinary diversions (13%) (Studer et al, 1996) or ureterosigmoidostomy (22%) (Allen, 1993). The management of ureterointestinal strictures in patients who have undergone urinary diversion typically required open surgical reimplantation. Open surgery has been relegated from its role as primary therapy to salvage therapy for failed endourologic management of ureterointestinal strictures. Endoscopic ureteral incision utilizing the holmium:YAG laser provides a precise incision with good hemostatic qualities and is the modality of choice (Singal et al, 1997; Watterson et al, 2002c; Razdan et al, 2005).

Currently, the endourologic techniques for managing ureteral stricture do not have the same success rates as open surgery. However, these approaches are preferred for initial treatment because of decreased associated morbidity, operative time, hospitalization, and cost. If required, subsequent open revision does not seem to be compromised by initial endourologic procedures.

## Retrograde Ureteroscopic Treatment of Ureteropelvic Junction Obstruction

In addition to open or laparoscopic pyeloplasty, minimally invasive techniques such as antegrade and retrograde endopyelotomy are accepted forms of treatment for ureteropelvic junction (UPJ) obstruction (Nakada and Johnson, 2000). Retrograde endopyelotomy may be performed with balloon dilation (Osther et al, 1998; Albani et al, 2004), hot-wire balloon dilation (Sofras et al, 2004), laser incision (Biyani et al, 2000; Hibi et al, 2002; Matin et al, 2003; Bagley, 2004), or a combination of laser and balloon dilation (Van Cangh et al, 2001; Ng and Streem, 2004). A combined antegrade approach with percutaneous introduction of a guide wire followed by retrograde ureteroscopy and laser endoureterotomy has also been described (Lopatkin et al, 2000). Following endopyelotomy, a ureteral stent is left indwelling in an attempt to provide a larger lumen when the UPJ heals.

**Reported success rates for retrograde endopyelotomy range from approximately 65%** (Lopatkin et al, 2000; Matin et al, 2003; Albani et al, 2004) **to 87%** (Conlin and Bagley, 1998; Tawfiek et al, 1998; Biyani et al, 2000; Gerber and Kim, 2000; Giddens and Grasso, 2000; Hibi et al, 2002). In these series, various methods of retrograde ureteroscopic endopyelotomy as mentioned previously were utilized. Balloon dilation alone has a low success rate and should be used only in conjunction with another modality (Osther et al, 1998).

**In summary, retrograde endopyelotomy provides a 65% to 87% chance of success in the treatment of UPJ obstruction, and patients need to be followed up with imaging for at least 3 years for recurrence of symptoms or obstruction** (Albani et al, 2004).

## URETEROSCOPIC MANAGEMENT OF UPPER TRACT TRANSITIONAL CELL CARCINOMA

Upper tract transitional cell carcinoma (TCC) constitutes approximately 5% of urothelial tumors, and the standard treatment has been radical extirpative surgery of the kidney, ureter, and cuff of bladder (Anderstrom et al, 1989; Munoz and Ellison, 2000). Radical nephroureterectomy is an extensive procedure with significant potential morbidity and mortality, particularly in the older age group in which TCC is more prevalent. In patients with significant comorbidities, conservative minimally invasive renal-sparing techniques have been applied with the thought that these patients would succumb to their comorbidities before the TCC could

recur and progress. Surprisingly, many of these patients not only outlived their comorbidities but also were successfully treated for their upper tract TCC (Brown and Roumani, 1974; Elliott et al, 1996; Engelmyer and Belis, 1996; Martinez-Pineiro et al, 1996; Fuchs, 1997; Keeley et al, 1997a; Stoller et al, 1997).

Filling defects seen on intravenous or retrograde pyelography, positive cytology with normal cystoscopic findings, and lesions seen during ureteroscopy should lead to the suspicion of ureteral or renal pelvis TCC (Figs. 45–6 to 45–8) (Chen and Bagley, 2001). **Ureteroscopy is particularly indicated in the patient who has positive cytology in combination with a normal bladder on cystoscopy** (Chen et al, 2000; Dooley and Pietrow, 2004). Biopsy of any urothelial lesions can be performed through the ureteroscope using a basket for papillary tumors or cup biopsy forceps for sessile tumors (Keeley et al, 1997b; Shiraishi et al, 2003). The accuracy of visually grading TCC ureteral tumors by ureteroscopy was reported as 70%, suggesting that biopsies are necessary for the proper diagnosis and treatment of this disease (El-Hakim et al, 2004). Metastatic evaluation should be performed, and in combination with the pathology results of the biopsy, discussions with the patient should determine the appropriate treatment options.

Small or low-grade TCCs have been successfully treated retrogradely with ureteroscopy and a variety of energy sources

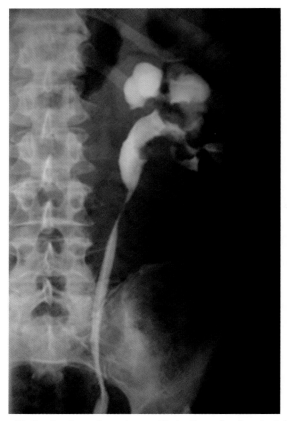

**Figure 45–6.** A retrograde pyelogram illustrating a "moth-eaten" filling defect in the left renal pelvis. The pathology demonstrated transitional cell carcinoma. (Photograph courtesy of Dr. Justin Amann.)

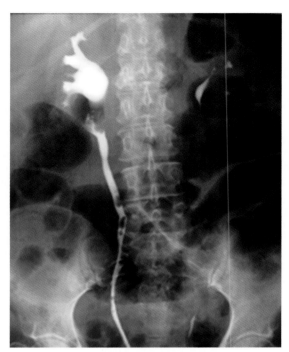

**Figure 45–7.** A proximal ureteral filling defect on retrograde pyelogram. Note that the radiolucencies in the ureter at the iliac level represent injected air bubbles. (Photograph courtesy of Dr. Stephen E. Pautler.)

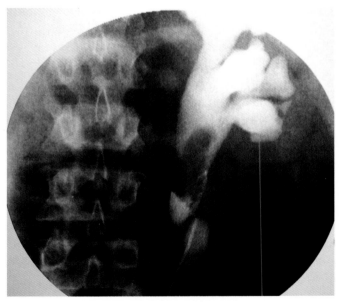

**Figure 45–8.** A large filling defect seen on retrograde pyelogram. The final diagnosis was fibroepithelial polyp. (Photograph courtesy of Dr. Justin Amann.)

including the holmium:YAG laser (Johnson and Grasso, 2005), electrocautery (Grasso et al, 1999; Elliott et al, 2001), and the Nd:YAG laser (Kaufman and Carson, 1993; Bagley, 1998; Lee et al, 2002).

The best success rates in terms of cure are in patients with low-grade, small tumor burdens (Martinez-Pineiro et al, 1996; Elliott et al, 2001; Deligne et al, 2002; Lee et al, 2002). It is rec-

| Table 45–7. | **Complications of Ureteroscopy** |
|---|---|

*Intraoperative*

Failure to access (ureter, kidney, or stone)
Failure to fragment the stone
Stone migration into the ureteral wall
Mucosal trauma
Ureteral perforation
Ureteral avulsion

*Early Postoperative*

Gross hematuria
Renal colic (small residual stone fragments, blood clot, or ureteral edema)
Large residual stone fragments (that require ancillary procedures)
Pyelonephritis
Urinoma
Ureteral stent symptoms

*Late Postoperative*

Ureteral stricture
"Forgotten" encrusted ureteral stent

ommended that healthy patients with a normal contralateral kidney with high-grade TCC undergo radical nephroureterectomy by an open or laparoscopic approach; however, it has been shown that even healthy patients with a normal contralateral kidney and low-grade disease may undergo conservative therapy provided that they are compliant with regular ureteroscopic follow-up with a urologist who is vigilant and is ready to perform a nephroureterectomy in the event of recurrence or progression (Hendin et al, 1999; Chen and Bagley, 2000; Elliott et al, 2001; Liatsikos et al, 2001; Yamada et al, 2003). In carefully selected patients who are compliant with strict follow-up, the death rate from progression and recurrence has been very low, approaching 0%.

In patients appropriately chosen for conservative management, the next decision is whether to perform percutaneous resection or retrograde ureteroscopy. In larger tumors of the renal pelvis and proximal ureter, the percutaneous approach is favored. Smaller tumors located in the kidney and ureter are accessible by the flexible ureteroscope and may be ablated with the holmium:YAG laser, Nd:YAG laser, or electrocautery. When performing retrograde ureteroscopy, ureteral tumors may be managed with the semirigid ureteroscope and a 365 or 400 μm laser fiber with initial settings of 0.8 J and a pulse rate of 15 Hz. A safety guide wire should be in place and coiled within the renal pelvis for ureteral stent insertion at completion of the case. The holmium:YAG laser should be "defocused" by not placing it directly on the tumor. When held 2 to 3 mm away from the tumor, it has a coagulative and ablative effect on tumor tissue. The tumor should be resected at the stalk if possible. When the tumor has been resected, a ureteral stent should be left in place to reduce the possibility of extravasation and ureteral stricture. If there is a suspicion of residual tumor, a second ureteroscopy in 1 to 2 weeks with further ablation should be carried out.

**Postoperative bacillus Calmette-Guérin (BCG) immunotherapy is difficult to deliver to the upper tracts and has been instilled by percutaneous nephrostomy tubes or intravesically with a ureteral stent in place to allow the medication to reflux to the diseased area. Although the benefits of BCG have been demonstrated in TCC of the bladder, its**

role has not been proved in upper tract TCC and remains controversial (Chen and Bagley, 2000; Elliott et al, 2001; Lam and Gupta, 2004).

Ureteroscopic management in select cases of upper tract TCC can provide good results. Patients treated with this modality must undergo routine diagnostic ureteroscopy (e.g., every 3 to 6 months) in addition to urine cytology and renal imaging studies to rule out recurrence (Martinez-Pineiro et al, 1996; Lam and Gupta, 2004).

## COMPLICATIONS OF URETEROSCOPY
### Ureteral Stricture

Complications during ureteroscopy (Table 45–7) have decreased over the past 20 years because of improvements in ureteroscopes, ancillary devices, intracorporeal lithotriptors, and surgical skills. In 1986, Carter and coauthors reported that 8% of patients suffered ureteral perforation or stricture and 3% of patients required a ureteral reimplantation. More recent experience has demonstrated that the perforation rate has decreased to between 0% and 4.7% (Harmon et al, 1997; Daneshmand et al, 2003; Boorjian et al, 2004). Risk factors for ureteral perforation included longer operating room times, stones located in the kidney, use of EHL, and surgeon inexperience.

Decreasing the rate of ureteral perforation has significantly decreased the rate of ureteral stricture formation. The reported ureteral stricture rate of approximately 3.5% increases to 5.9% if a ureteral perforation occurs (Stoller et al, 1992; Harmon et al, 1997; Netto Junior et al, 1997; Grasso and Ficazzola, 1999; Tawfiek and Bagley, 1999; Schuster et al, 2001; Chow et al, 2003). Both smaller endoscopes and use of the holmium:YAG laser have contributed to this improvement. Other general tips to prevent ureteral trauma include (1) advancing the semirigid ureteroscope under direct vision only when the lumen is in view and a safety guide wire is in place, (2) using the holmium:YAG laser as the primary modality for intracorporeal lithotripsy, and (3) performing less basket extraction of stones or performing the extraction through a UAS.

### Ureteral Avulsion

Ureteral avulsion is an uncommon but serious complication of ureteroscopy. **Avulsion typically occurs during basket extraction of a stone fragment that is too large and becomes caught in ureteral mucosa, telescoping and avulsing the ureter as the stone is extracted.** Open surgery is necessary and ureteroureterostomy or ureteroneocystotomy is performed if only a short segment of the ureter is avulsed (Bernhard and Reddy, 1996; Alapont et al, 2003). If complete avulsion of the ureter occurs, the treatment options become ileal interposition, autotransplantation, and nephrectomy (Puppo et al, 1999; Gupta et al, 2005). To avoid ureteral avulsion, stones must be broken into fragments small enough to pass spontaneously or be extracted by a basket inserted through the ureteroscope. **To reduce catastrophic complications, a safety guide wire should be present, and when basket extraction is used, the basket and stone should be positioned slightly away from the tip of the ureteroscope so that the lumen can** be visualized during extraction. Excluding basket extraction altogether reduces the chances of ureteral avulsion.

## Urosepsis

In patients who present with an infected collecting system and an obstructing stone, urinary decompression in combination with antibiotics is the initial treatment. Manipulation of the stone in the presence of infection is likely to result in bacteremia and possible urosepsis. Insertion of a percutaneous nephrostomy tube or ureteral stent has been demonstrated to drain the kidney equally well (Fabrizio et al, 2000; Shekarriz et al, 2001; Lutter et al, 2002). When the infection has been adequately treated, definitive management of the stone can proceed. Challenges arise when dealing with infection and stones in patients who cannot completely clear their infection until they are free of their stone but cannot be treated for their stone until their urine is clear. In these cases, a few days of preoperative oral antibiotics followed by intravenous antibiotic prophylaxis at the time of surgery decreases the rate of septicemia.

Postoperative bacteremia and sepsis should be treated with culture-sensitive intravenous antibiotics followed by oral antibiotics when the patient has defervesced. Imaging should be carried out, and if obstruction is present, upper tract drainage in addition to antibiotics is necessary.

## Ureteroscope Damage

All components of the ureteroscope including the working channel, deflection tip, cables, and the entire length of the fiberoptic bundles are susceptible to damage by several mechanisms. Gentle care and handling should be used at all times, particularly at the end of the procedure, when equipment tends to accumulate on the operating room table, potentially crushing delicate endoscopes. The ureteroscope should be kept as "straight" as possible during manipulation and handling, as bending tends to break the delicate fiberoptic bundles. Ureteroscopes should be stored carefully in suitable containers. Reports have demonstrated that the current generation of ureteroscopes require maintenance or repairs ranging from every 6 to 15 uses (Pearle et al, 1998; Mokhmalji et al, 2001) to 10 to 34 uses (Afane et al, 2000).

The working channel can be damaged by sharp objects such as a beveled laser fiber, which should be inserted gently and with the endoscope, particularly the deflecting tip, as straight as possible. **Channel perforation by manipulation of laser fibers is a common cause of endoscope damage** (Pietrow et al, 2002; User et al, 2004). Laser fibers are prone to breakage, particularly during maximal deflection as when accessing the lower pole calyces (User et al, 2004). Laser fiber fracture while in the ureteroscope can have devastating effects on the instrument, including perforation of the entire sealed channel. Communication between surgeon and operating room staff needs to be clear, and placing the laser on standby when the laser fiber is within the endoscope prevents accidental triggering of the laser and ureteroscope damage (Nazif et al, 2004).

Use of a UAS has been shown to decrease the number of repairs to flexible ureteroscopes by relieving the endoscope of the axial forces and the requirement for backloading of a guide wire normally used to "railroad" the endoscope into the kidney (McDougall et al, 2001). The type of cleaning method (Steris versus Cidex) does not affect the durability of ureteroscopes; however, human handling has been documented to be responsible for many instances of endoscope damage outside the operating room (Pietrow et al, 2002).

## CONCLUSIONS

Almost any patent ureteral lumen, no matter how narrow, can be cannulated and reached if the correct wires and equipment are available. Ureteroscopy is a mainstay in the treatment of urologic stone disease, and despite the introduction of extracorporeal SWL in the 1980s, ureteroscopy has remained a prominent therapy for stones. It provides an effective method of lithotripsy with stone-free rates in excess of 90% and can also be used for the diagnosis and treatment of upper tract transitional cell cancer, ureteral stricture, and ureteropelvic junction obstruction.

## Acknowledgments

The authors wish to acknowledge and thank Linda Nott, Peter Cadieux, Dr. Anthony Bella, Dr. Chris Neville, Dr. Tony Chen, Dr. Justin Amann, Dr. Hassan Razvi, and Dr. Stephen Pautler.

### SUGGESTED READINGS

Bagley DH: Ureteroscopic surgery: Changing times and perspectives. Urol Clin North Am 2004;31:1-4, vii.

Grasso M, Fraiman M, Levine M: Ureteropyeloscopic diagnosis and treatment of upper urinary tract urothelial malignancies. Urology 1999;54:240-246.

Sofer M, Watterson JD, Wollin TA, et al: Holmium:YAG laser lithotripsy for upper urinary tract calculi in 598 patients. J Urol 2002;167:31-34.

Sprunger JK, Herrell SD III: Techniques of ureteroscopy. Urol Clin North Am 2004;31:61-69.

## KEY POINTS: URETEROSCOPY AND RETROGRADE URETERAL ACCESS

- Retrograde ureteral access is achievable in nearly every case provided the proper equipment, including endoscopes, guide wires, and catheters is available.

- Flexible ureteroscopes are used to gain access to the entire renal system, particularly above the iliac vessels. Semirigid ureteroscopes are typically used in the distal ureter below the iliac vessels but can be advanced up to the middle and proximal ureter, especially in female patients, with the advantages of a larger working channel and better optics.

- The holmium:YAG laser is a safe and effective method of intracorporeal lithotripsy as its energy travels only 0.5 mm in a liquid medium. This modality has been proved safe and effective in children, obese patients, pregnant patients, and patients with bleeding diatheses.

- Ureteral dilation is not routinely necessary for ureteroscopy.

- Placement of a ureteral stent is not routinely necessary following uncomplicated ureteroscopy.

# 46 Percutaneous Management of the Upper Urinary Tract

MANTU GUPTA, MD • MICHAEL C. OST, MD •
JAY B. SHAH, MD • ELSPETH M. McDOUGALL, MD •
ARTHUR D. SMITH, MD

INDICATIONS FOR PERCUTANEOUS NEPHROSTOMY

PERTINENT RENAL ANATOMY

IMAGING MODALITIES FOR PERCUTANEOUS ACCESS

RETROGRADE AND RETROGRADE-ASSISTED PERCUTANEOUS RENAL ACCESS

TECHNICAL ASPECTS OF PERCUTANEOUS ENTRY

DILATION OF THE NEPHROSTOMY TRACT

COMPLICATIONS OF PERCUTANEOUS RENAL SURGERY

PERCUTANEOUS PROCEDURES OF THE UPPER URINARY TRACT

NEPHROSTOMY DRAINAGE

FUTURE DIRECTIONS

Since 1955, when Willard Goodwin and colleagues first described the use of a needle to decompress a hydronephrotic kidney, the discipline of endourology has grown to encompass a vast array of percutaneous procedures involving the kidneys and upper urinary tracts. When percutaneous nephrostomy was first performed in the late 1970s, the primary indications were limited to diversion of urine and treatment of stone disease in poor surgical candidates. By the early 1980s percutaneous nephrolithotomy had gained widespread popularity for treatment of all renal stones. With the advent of extracorporeal shockwave lithotripsy (ESWL) in the mid 1980s, the indications for percutaneous stone extraction were narrowed. However, **as the limitations of ESWL were recognized, percutaneous surgery once again rose in popularity with a redefined role in stone management.** In addition, continued experience with percutaneous access has led to an extraordinary expansion in the indications for establishment of a nephrostomy tract.

## INDICATIONS FOR PERCUTANEOUS NEPHROSTOMY

Percutaneous nephrostomy is the cornerstone of every percutaneous procedure of the upper urinary tract. As a minimally invasive conduit to the pelvicalyceal system, the percutaneous approach provides a convenient route for the diagnosis of upper tract pathology. The majority of diseases affecting the upper urinary tract fall into one of four categories—(1) stone disease, (2) obstruction, (3) malignant or benign tumors, and (4) infection—and percutaneous procedures have been used to manage each of these entities.

Whereas ESWL remains appropriate for patients with uncomplicated renal stones and normal renal anatomy, percutaneous stone extraction is the preferred treatment for patients with large, obstructing renal stones (e.g., staghorn calculi) or stones with composition resistant to fragmentation with extracorporeal lithotripsy. In addition, for patients with concomitant renal stones and distal narrowing (e.g., infundibular stenoses and coexisting calyceal stones, stones in calyceal diverticula, or renal stones with ureteropelvic junction [UPJ] narrowing), the percutaneous route allows a convenient approach to address both problems simultaneously. For patients with UPJ obstruction (even in the absence of stones), percutaneous endopyelotomy provides an effective alternative to laparoscopic or open pyeloplasty with acceptable success rates (Bernardo and Smith, 1999).

Although nephroureterectomy was previously considered the standard of care for all upper tract transitional cell carcinoma, in recent decades it has been shown that percutaneous resection of the tumor and instillation of chemotherapeutic agents into the upper tract can provide acceptable outcomes for select patients (Goel et al, 2003; Palou et al, 2004). For these patients, the nephrostomy tract serves as both a conduit for tumor resection as well as a channel for antegrade chemotherapy instillation if necessary (See, 2000).

**In some cases, percutaneous nephrostomy may be preferable to retrograde ureteral stenting for patients presenting with ureteral obstruction and signs of impending sepsis** (Ng et al, 2002). The percutaneous route can also be used to manage less common entities affecting the kidneys. Renal cysts, fungal bezoars, and fibroepithelial polyps have all been safely treated via a percutaneous nephrostomy.

Although patient preference is not considered an absolute indication, **patients generally favor the decreased morbidity of a percutaneous renal procedure to that of open surgery.** The less invasive nature of percutaneous surgery affords patients both a quicker recovery and a more desirable cosmetic result. It also translates into shorter lengths of stay and lower overall costs for the hospital. It was initially believed that percutaneous renal surgery would have limited efficacy in obese patients. However, it has since been shown that with slight modifications in technique and instrumentation, obese patients have similar outcomes to control subjects after percutaneous nephrolithotomy (Hofmann and Stoller, 1992; Giblin et al, 1995; Curtis et al, 1997; Pearle et al, 1998).

Despite the numerous indications for the establishment of a percutaneous nephrostomy tract, many urologists have only limited experience obtaining access to the pelvicalyceal system and are dependent on the assistance of an interventional radiologist. **In the age of minimally invasive surgery, urologists who are able to master the technique of percutaneous renal access have a distinct advantage in remaining at the forefront of the rapidly evolving field of endourology.** The current chapter can serve to help motivated urologists achieve competence with percutaneous access. After reviewing the relevant anatomy of the kidneys and surrounding structures and presenting the various imaging modalities available for percutaneous access, the technical aspects of establishing a percutaneous nephrostomy tract are reviewed. In the second half of the chapter, various procedures of the upper urinary tract that can be performed via a nephrostomy tract are reviewed. Percutaneous management of stone disease, UPJ obstruction, and upper tract transitional cell carcinoma are covered elsewhere in this textbook and are not discussed at length in this chapter.

## PERTINENT RENAL ANATOMY

An intimate understanding of the anatomic relationships of the kidneys and surrounding structures is crucial for successful and safe percutaneous entry into the renal collecting system. The unique anatomic considerations of the right and left kidneys as well as variability in intrarenal anatomy can make the attainment of percutaneous access frustrating for the inexperienced surgeon.

### Perirenal Anatomy

The kidneys are retroperitoneal structures located in the paravertebral gutters between the levels of the 12th thoracic vertebra and the 2nd or 3rd lumbar vertebrae (Fig. 46–1). The superior poles are located more medially than the inferior poles, and both kidneys are angled 30 degrees posterior to the frontal plane of the body. The longitudinal axis of each kidney parallels the oblique course of the adjacent psoas major muscle. The right kidney lies 2 to 3 cm lower than the left kidney owing to the large size of the right lobe of the liver.

The anteromedial aspect of the superior pole of each kidney is covered by the corresponding adrenal gland (Fig. 46–2A). The right kidney is related to the liver superiorly, the descending portion of the duodenum medially, and the right colic flexure anteriorly. The left kidney is bounded anteriorly by the stomach and spleen at the superior pole and the descending

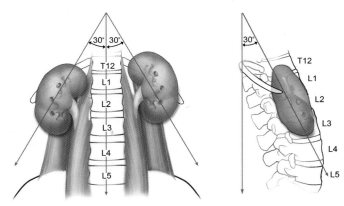

**Figure 46–1.** Location of kidneys in the retroperitoneum.

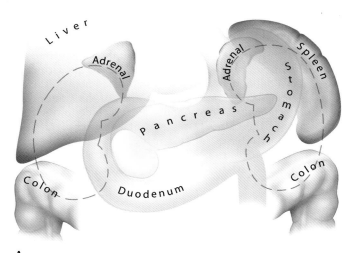

A

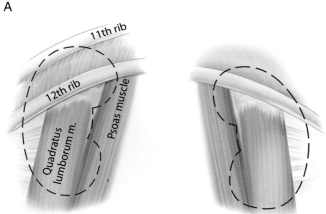

B

**Figure 46–2.** Anterior (**A**) and posterior (**B**) relations of kidneys to adjacent organs.

colon at the inferior pole. The tail of the pancreas lies immediately anterior to the left renal hilum. During attempted percutaneous puncture of the kidneys, any of these adjacent organs are at risk for inadvertent injury. The colon is particularly susceptible to injury because up to 16% of patients may demonstrate a retrorenal colon during percutaneous puncture

(Hopper et al, 1987; Boon et al, 2001). Thin female patients are especially prone to this phenomenon.

Posteriorly, the kidneys are supported by several muscle layers (see Fig. 46–2B). The inferior two thirds of each kidney is intimately related to the quadratus lumborum and psoas major muscles. The superior pole of each kidney is in direct contact with the diaphragm, which separates it from the pleural cavity and 12th rib. Movement of the diaphragm with breathing causes the kidney to move downward in inspiration and upward in expiration. In addition, when the patient is anesthetized the abdominal wall musculature relaxes and more extensive excursions of the kidney are seen. When the patient is in the prone position with bolsters under the chest and upper abdomen, the kidneys may be displaced further cephalad.

## Intrarenal Anatomy

### Renal Vasculature

The main renal artery divides into two branches: the anterior and the posterior renal arteries (Fig. 46–3). The anterior division further subdivides into four anterior segmental arteries, which supply the anterior and polar areas of the kidney. The posterior segmental artery supplies the remainder of the posterior area of the kidney. The segmental arteries divide into the interlobar arteries after crossing the renal sinus and become the arcuate arteries at the corticomedullary junction. The interlobular arteries branch from the arcuate arteries at right angles and run to the periphery giving rise to the afferent arterioles of the glomeruli. **Brödel's line delineates an avascular plane between the anterior and posterior segmental blood supplies.**

The intrarenal veins do not have a segmental structure. Unlike the arteries, there is free circulation throughout the renal venous system. Multiple anastomotic arcades between the veins prevent parenchymal congestion and ischemia from venous injury.

### Collecting System Anatomy

The anatomic landmarks dividing the renal parenchyma from the collecting system are the renal papilla. Calyces in direct apposition to the renal papilla are defined as minor calyces and vary in number from 5 to 14 (mean: 8). A minor calyx may be single (draining only one papilla) or compound (draining two or three papillae). Minor calyces may drain directly into an infundibulum or join to form major calyces, which then drain into an infundibulum (Fig. 46–4). The infundibula are the principal divisions of the pelvicalyceal system, draining directly into the renal pelvis.

There are usually three renal calyceal groups: the superior, midzone, and inferior major calyces. Barcellos Sampaio and Mandarim-de-Lacerda (1988) analyzed 140 three-dimensional polyester resin corrosion endocasts of human kidneys and contributed significantly to our understanding of the intricate anatomy of the pelvicalyceal system. They observed that the superior and inferior major calyces usually consist of compound calyces that project toward the polar regions at various angles (Fig. 46–5). The midzone calyces, on the other hand, are generally arranged in paired sets of anterior and posterior calyces. These paired calyces have been observed to display one of two configurations (Fig. 46–6). In the Brödel type configuration, the anterior calyx is short and medially directed (forming a 70-degree angle to the frontal plane of the kidney), whereas the posterior calyx is longer and more laterally directed (positioned only 20 degrees from the frontal plane of the kidney). The second configuration is the Hodson type in which the posterior calyx is shorter and more medially directed and the anterior calyx is longer and closer to the lateral edge of the kidney. It has been shown that 69% of right kidneys exhibit the Brödel configuration and 79% of left kidneys exhibit the Hodson configuration (Kaye and Reinke, 1984).

In studying the pelvicalyceal endocasts, Barcellos Sampaio (1988) noted significant variability in the drainage patterns of the three calyceal groups. The midzone calyceal group was variably found to have drainage dependent on one of the polar calyceal groups (62%) or to drain directly into the renal pelvis independent of either polar group (38%). In 18% of the endocasts studied, the kidney midzone was drained simultaneously by crossed calyces, one draining into the superior calyceal group and the other draining into the inferior calyceal group. In addition, a perpendicular minor calyx draining directly into the renal pelvis was noted in 11% of the endocasts. **The only**

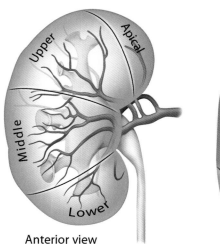

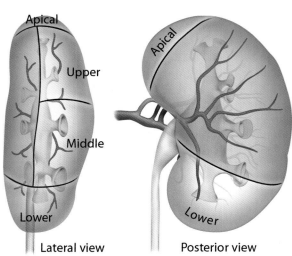

**Figure 46–3.** Arterial supply to the kidney. The kidney is supplied by the anterior and posterior segmental branches of the main renal artery. The anterior segmental artery supplies both the anterior half of the kidney and the polar regions. The posterior segmental artery supplies only the posterior aspect of the kidney *(represented by the shaded region)*. An avascular plane, known as Brödel's line, separates the anterior and posterior circulations.

Anterior view | Lateral view | Posterior view

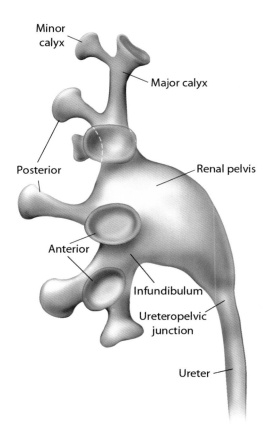

Figure 46–4. Basic pelvicalyceal anatomy.

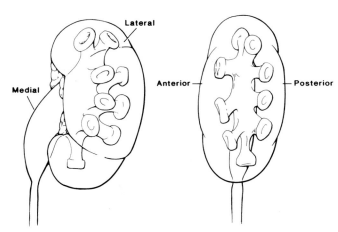

**Figure 46–5.** Calyceal orientations of the kidney. Polar regions have minor calyces that are oriented toward their respective poles, and the middle calyces have anterior and posterior orientations. (From Smith AD [ed]: Controversies in Endourology. Philadelphia, WB Saunders, 1995.)

consistently noted findings were that the superior calyceal group was drained by only one midline infundibulum in 99% of the endocasts and that the midzone was drained by paired calyces arranged in two rows (anterior and posterior) in 96% of cases.

## Clinical Relevance of Intrarenal Anatomy

A thorough understanding of intrarenal anatomy can greatly facilitate percutaneous entry into the renal collecting system and minimize complications. Appreciation of the anterior and posterior segmental blood supply of the kidney can allow the urologist to utilize Brödel's line during percutaneous puncture. A needle traversing the renal parenchyma posterolaterally through this avascular plane avoids damage to any major blood vessels (see Fig. 46–1). In more than 50% of kidneys, the posterior segmental artery (retropelvic artery) is located in the middle or upper half of the posterior renal surface, and it may be damaged with an excessively medial needle puncture of an upper calyx. **The posterior segmental artery is the most commonly injured vessel in endourologic procedures.**

Knowledge of the Hodson and Brödel configurations of calyceal anatomy is crucial for precise preoperative localization of a stone or other lesion on intravenous pyelogram. Awareness of the great variability in calyceal drainage patterns can aid greatly during intraoperative decision-making for appropriate puncture sites. The results of the Sampaio endocast studies imply that it is easier to access a polar region drained by a single infundibulum than a polar region drained by paired calyces. Furthermore, the anatomic relationships of

the intrarenal vessels to the kidney collecting system predict a high rate of vascular injury for attempted puncture directly into any infundibulum. **This suggests that percutaneous entry directly into the fornix of a calyx is the safest route** (Sampaio, 1996).

Preview of any renal access involves examination of the desired calyx. The calyx is inspected for three factors: relation to the 12th rib, extent of hydronephrosis, and presence of malrotation. Whether the desired calyx resides above or below the 12th rib has critical significance for the technique chosen for renal access and the possibility of thoracic complications. The degree of hydronephrosis influences the difficulty of renal access. Although dilated calyces are technically less demanding to puncture, improper technique may still result in failure. Finally, the unusual case of the malrotated or ectopic kidney may necessitate minor adjustments in the access technique.

## KEY POINTS: PERTINENT RENAL ANATOMY

- The anterior and posterior segmental blood supply of the kidney is divided by Brödel's line, an avascular plane that may be used to guide safe percutaneous puncture.

- Excessively medial needle punctures risk damage to the posterior segmental artery, the most frequently injured vessel during endourologic procedures.

- Despite the significant variability in pelvicalyceal drainage patterns, the superior pole is generally drained by a single midline infundibulum and the midzone is drained by paired calyces arranged in two rows (anterior and posterior).

- Needle puncture directly into the fornix of a calyx is the safest route of percutaneous entry into the renal collecting system.

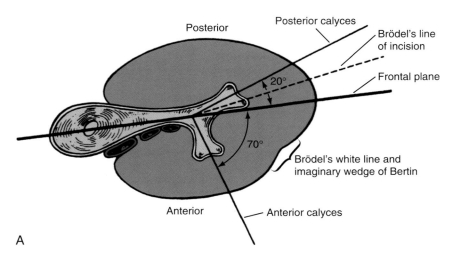

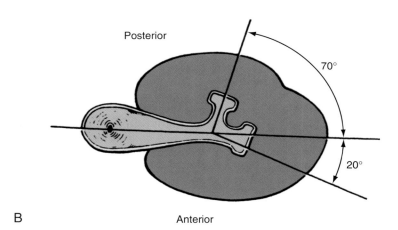

**Figure 46–6.** Calyceal orientations in the Brödel and Hodson configurations. In the Brödel-type kidney (**A**), the longer posterior calyx is positioned 20 degrees from the frontal plane of the kidney and the shorter anterior calyx forms a 70-degree angle with the frontal plane. In the Hodson-type kidney (**B**), the shorter posterior calyx is positioned 70 degrees from the frontal plane of the kidney and the larger anterior calyx forms a 20-degree angle with the frontal plane. (From Smith AD [ed]: Controversies in Endourology. Philadelphia, WB Saunders, 1995.)

# IMAGING MODALITIES FOR PERCUTANEOUS ACCESS
## Ultrasonography

Percutaneous ultrasound-guided nephrostomy is perhaps the simplest and most direct technique to access and drain a hydronephrotic collecting system. It is most often utilized to place a temporary urinary diversion in the instances of an obstructing stone or pyonephrosis and has also been used successfully to relieve obstruction secondary to malignant compression. Although the technique has been especially popular among interventional radiologists, it has gained popularity among endourologists who are comfortable with ultrasonography. Allergies to topical or injectable local anesthetic and coagulopathy are the only relative contraindications to ultrasound-guided renal access. The ultrasonographic approach has the advantages of minimizing radiation exposure and allowing imaging of intervening structures between skin and kidney.

When the kidney is evaluated with ultrasound, its various compartments have different sonographic appearances that can be seen quickly and accurately in three-dimensional orientation. The renal capsule is clearly visible. The renal

cortex produces low-level homogeneous echoes, and the medulla presents as a relatively sonolucent structure. Most importantly, **hydronephrosis can easily be identified as a hypoechoic cavity surrounded by a central echo complex** (Kumari-Subaiya and Phillips, 1995).

The principles of a successful ultrasound-guided puncture do not differ from those of the fluoroscopic approach. However, sonographic identification of the needle may be technically demanding. There are a variety of transducers with lumens designed to accommodate the needle to help guide the puncture more easily (Fig. 46–7). Because the tip of the needle is difficult to visualize, successful puncture of the collecting system is ultimately confirmed by the return of urine through the needle. Porcine experiments on ultrasound-guided nephrostomy with the aid of a magnetic field–based navigation device have addressed this limitation, allowing for accurate puncture needle placement in plane or out of plane from any direction, independent of transducer position (Krombach et al, 2001).

Large retrospective studies have shown ultrasound-guided percutaneous nephrostomy insertion to be highly successful (88% to 99%) with a low complication rate (4% to 8%) (Farrell and Hicks, 1997; Wah et al, 2004). In instances of malignant ureteral obstruction with hydroureteronephrosis,

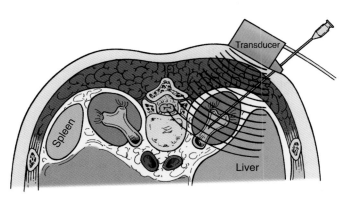

**Figure 46–7.** The needle is advanced using ultrasound guidance.

**Table 46–1. Radiation Safety for Urologists**

Put fluoroscopy beam under table.
Use lead apron and thyroid shields.
Use minimal fluoroscopic time: "Think before or after fluoroscopy, not during."
Collimate.
Wear radiation detection devices.
Wear lead-impregnated glasses.
Use lead gloves?

diversion by percutaneous puncture utilizing *both* ultrasonic and fluoroscopic imaging modalities has been shown to be successful 99% of the time (Pappas et al, 2000). Ultrasound-fluoroscopic guided access can be more precise than the fluoroscopic guided access alone, making the procedure less invasive and more precise for surgical planning (Montanari et al, 1999).

The main indication for the ultrasound-guided approach is percutaneous drainage of an obstructed and hydronephrotic kidney. However, application of the ultrasound-guided approach for antegrade collecting system access before percutaneous nephrolithotomy has also proved to be safe and efficacious in the pediatric population (Desai et al, 1999) and in the instances of both transplanted kidneys (Francesca et al, 2002) and pelvic renal ectopia (Desai and Jasani, 2000). Although bowel may be visualized ultrasonically, **one should remain wary of the risk of viscus injury during ultrasound-guided access to an ectopic pelvic kidney.** In light of this, preventive measures with Trendelenburg positioning and tilting the table away from the pelvic kidney of interest will reduce the risk of bowel injury. Digital subtraction angiography–assisted ultrasound has also been described as an alternative modality to help reduce the risk of enteric and vascular injury when accessing a pelvic kidney (Touloupidis et al, 2003).

The ultrasonic depiction of the dilated calyces is easily obtained. However, when the pelvicalyceal system is not dilated, localization and puncture of the specific calyx may require special expertise. Use of a diuretic to transiently dilate collapsed calyces has been reported to facilitate ultrasound-guided puncture without complications (Gupta et al, 1998). **Ultrasound-guided nephrostomy puncture is also preferred for patients in whom retrograde ureteral catheterization is unsuccessful and in pregnant women in whom there is a need for decompression of an obstructed kidney** (von der Recke et al, 1994; Gupta et al, 1997; Gupta et al, 1998; Khoo et al, 2004). **A distinct disadvantage of using ultrasound is the inability to clearly visualize and manipulate a guide wire once it is placed through the percutaneous access site.**

## Fluoroscopy

The technical aspects of using fluoroscopy for percutaneous access are discussed later in this chapter. In this section, we focus on the issue of radiation safety. Presently, endourologic procedures most often rely on fluoroscopy. Although the risk is relatively small, the patient, surgeon, and participating staff will be exposed to some level of ionizing radiation. The endourologist, in particular, must undertake protective measures because he or she will likely be exposed to radiation on a regular and cumulative basis (Table 46–1). Likewise, certain patients such as children with nephrolithiasis secondary to cystinuria may be subjected to repeated fluoroscopy-based procedures. In this regard, radiation dose is an extremely important issue in the young child, who is significantly more radiosensitive and more likely to manifest radiation-induced changes over his or her lifetime (Seibert, 2004). In fact, radiation exposure has been linked to malignancies, including leukemia and thyroid cancer.

**The main principle for protection from radiation energy is ALARA: as low as reasonably achievable. The maximum yearly whole-body exposure recommended by the National Council on Radiation Protection is 5000 mrem, or 5 rem** (Giblin et al, 1996). Dosages exceeding the standard limits likely carry with them only a small short-term health risk. Nevertheless, particularly over the course of a professional lifetime, the hazards of radiation exposure may be substantial (Castaneda, 1996; Brateman, 1999). Experimental data suggest that a mixture of dietary antioxidants and glutathione-elevating agents may protect tissues from radiation's mutagenic effects (Prasad et al, 2004). The use of such antioxidant preparations may soon extend the concept of ALARA from dose to biologic damage.

Time, distance, and shielding are critical factors that determine radiation exposure. **Limiting fluoroscopy time during endourologic procedures is of paramount importance, because the radiation dose to the operating room personnel is a function of exposure time.** Modern fluoroscopic equipment features, including under-table fluoroscopic sources, timer alarms, collimation of the x-ray beam, and last-image-hold/memory capability help the urologist limit the fluoroscopy time. **Grid-controlled fluoroscopic technique may also reduce overall radiation dose by decreasing the selected film frame rate.** Use of this technique, as opposed to continuous fluoroscopy, has led to substantial dose reduction for the patient and fluoroscopy operator without sacrificing image quality or diagnostic confidence (Boland et al, 2000).

**The major source of radiation to the endourologist is scatter from the patient's body.** Radiation is emitted from a source in all directions, and its intensity decreases proportionally as the square of the distance from the source. **Because scattered radiation follows the inverse square law, operators near the radiation beam can make significant reductions in**

exposure by increasing their distance from the patient (Ramakumar and Jarrett, 2000). For example, if one stands 3 feet from the fluoroscopy table during imaging, there is one ninth the radiation exposure, or an approximate 89% dose reduction. At a distance of 12 feet, however, the dose will approximate natural background levels, not registering on radiation monitoring devices (dosimeters).

During fluoroscopy, the kilovoltage and milliamperage are adjusted automatically and the operator can control only the duration of the exposure. Exposure doses may be reduced significantly by minimizing the total "active" fluoroscopic time for a procedure through cautious use of the exposure switch to ensure that irradiation occurs only when there is a need for active viewing of the image. **The use of a last-image-hold feature is of great importance in reducing the overall irradiation time.** With this feature, anatomic details can be scrutinized without a competing concern about additional radiation dose. Thus, all fluoroscopes used for percutaneous surgery should have a last-image-hold feature so the urologist does not need to "think with a foot on the pedal."

The irradiated site of the patient affects the scatter rate to the endourologist. When the field is closer to the midline of the patient, less radiation is scattered to the operator because it is attenuated through a greater thickness of overlying tissue. When the field is more lateral, the radiation is less attenuated by the patient and thus there is more radiation scatter. Furthermore, obese patients require more primary radiation than do thinner patients to allow the formation of an adequate image, creating a potential for more scatter. Protective surgical drapes composed primarily of bismuth, specialized urologic radiation shields, and special radioprotective gloves can be used to substantially reduce scattered radiation dose (King et al, 2002; Yang et al, 2002).

Collimation narrows the beam and limits the imaging area to the exact position of interest, thus reducing the scattered radiation to and from the patient. Keeping the image receiver as close to the patient as possible minimizes the distance between the focal spot and the image receptor, keeps the fluoroscopic beam intensity as low as possible, decreases image blur, and serves as a scatter barrier between the patient and the operator. In addition, **the direction of the beam significantly influences the amount of scattered radiation reaching the operator.** When the tube is above the operating table, there is a combination of leakage and scattered radiation. However, when the image intensifier is placed superiorly, radiation leakage is minimized, as the emission tube is shielded by an additional layer of material. The scattered radiation to the operator is also reduced (Fig. 46–8).

Shielding involves the use of flexible protective clothing such as aprons, skirts, thyroid shields, eyeglasses, and gloves. The basic protection for every urologist during percutaneous surgery is a lead apron, thyroid shield, and eyeglasses. The use of protective glasses is prudent, even though there is debate about their absolute necessity. Nevertheless, approximately 1100 mrem/hr may be deviated toward the urologist's upper extremities as a result of radiation scatter, which certainly suggests that the use of eye protection may be beneficial (Bowsher et al, 1992; Brateman, 1999). The standard flexible material for protective clothing is lead-impregnated rubber. The goal is to provide a barrier between the radiation source and the operator so that radiation is attenuated by the shield. Lead aprons

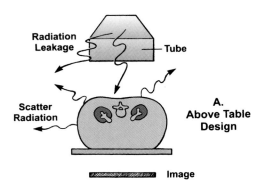

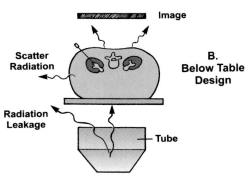

**Figure 46–8.** Emission tube placed over (**A**) and under (**B**) the operating table. In the first case, there is a combination of leakage and scattered radiation to the urologist. In the second case, the leakage is greatly reduced.

are heavy and can become uncomfortable when the operator is wearing them for a protracted period of time. The amount of lead required for efficacy has been established as 0.5 mm, and it has been estimated that the weight of aprons with this much lead ranges from 2.5 to 7 kg. Today, however, some aprons are made of composites of lead with elements of lower atomic numbers so that the weight can be reduced but the efficacy maintained (Castaneda, 1996; Giblin et al, 1996; Brateman, 1999).

Finally, **all personnel exposed to radiation should wear dosimeters** positioned where the operator receives the maximal radiation. It has been estimated that the radiation exposure to the underlying body is as little as 1% of the measured value. In modern radiation protection practices, active personal dosimeters are absolutely essential operational tools for satisfying the ALARA principle (Bolognese-Milsztajn et al, 2004).

## Computed Tomography and Magnetic Resonance Imaging

Although some investigators have advocated the use of CT-guided percutaneous access (Barbaric et al, 1997), cross-sectional imaging is only needed to facilitate safe percutaneous access in special circumstances. A CT- or MRI-guided approach is a time-consuming and expensive method that is not practical for most patients and needs to be considered only if the aforementioned techniques are not feasible or do not provide good results or if sophisticated preoperative planning is necessary.

Preoperative evaluation with the aid of either CT or MRI may aid in minimizing the risk of pulmonary, visceral, splenic, or hepatic injury if a percutaneous puncture of the upper pole of the kidney above the 11th rib is necessary (Robert et al, 1999). **Patients with a retrorenal colon or a severely distorted body habitus due to spinal dysraphism predictably require cross-sectional imaging to facilitate safe access before percutaneous nephrostolithotomy** (Matlaga et al, 2003). In addition, the CT-guided approach may be useful in obtaining renal access in patients with ileal conduits, renal uric acid stones, or nephrolithiasis in the presence of angiomyolipomas at risk for bleeding (Eiley et al, 1999). Three-dimensional CT has been described as a valuable tool for obtaining percutaneous access in the morbidly obese with malrotated kidneys and large staghorn calculi (Buchholz, 2000). Newer technology involving real-time CT fluoroscopy under laser guidance has also allowed for efficient and safe percutaneous nephrostomy placement when difficult access to the pelvicalyceal system has been encountered (LeMaitre et al, 2000). This newer imaging modality can maximize operator hand distances away from the gantry (>25 cm) and reduce the radiation dose to the operator's hand to 0.4 mrad/s (4 μGy/s) (de Mey et al, 2000). In the instance of nephrostomy dislodgement or malpositioning, CT may be used to successfully reposition drainage tubes into the collecting system (Jones and McGahan, 1999). There are no specific indications for MRI-guided percutaneous nephrostomy, although the technique has been shown to be feasible and accurate in nondilated

collecting systems (Hagspiel et al, 1998; Nolte-Ernsting et al, 1999; Merkle et al, 1999).

## Percutaneous Access without Imaging—"Blind Access"

Attempting percutaneous access without the aid of imaging is reserved for the rare instances when retrograde or intravenous opacification is precluded, the pelvicalyceal system cannot be opacified, or imaging machinery such as a fluoroscopic unit or sonography is inaccessible. Poor renal function in the presence of ureteral obstruction, for example, may represent such a situation, especially if emergent collecting system decompression is required (i.e., urosepsis from pyonephrosis). Percutaneous access without imaging relies on anatomic landmarks and the assumption that anatomy is not aberrant.

The lumbar notch, bounded superiorly by the latissimus dorsi muscle and the 12th rib, medially by the sacrospinalis and the quadratus lumborum muscles, and laterally by the transversus abdominis and the external oblique muscles, has been shown to be a useful anatomic window for successful blind percutaneous calyceal access (Chien and Bellman, 2002). An 18-gauge access needle can be inserted into the notch at a 30-degree angle directed cephalad under the 12th rib to a depth of 3 to 4 cm (Fig. 46–9). Alternatively, the renal pelvis may be accessed at a point 1.0 to 1.5 cm lateral to the L1 vertebral body. A 22-gauge "skinny" needle may be used to perform a blind perpendicular puncture lateral to the psoas and just below the level of the 12th rib. Often, initial blind access through the lumbar notch or perpendicular to the psoas may be suboptimal. Once urine can be aspirated from the

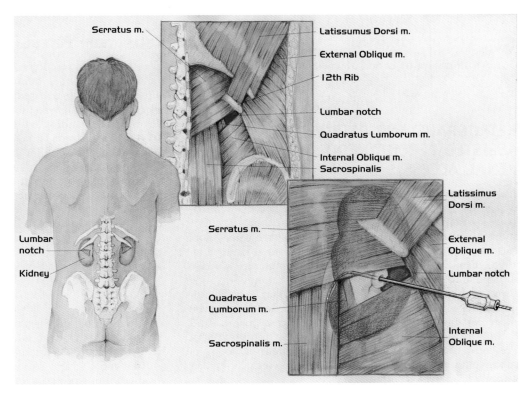

**Figure 46–9.** The lumbar notch is a useful anatomic landmark for blind percutaneous access to the renal collecting system. It is bounded superiorly by the latissimus dorsi muscle and the 12th rib, medially by the sacrospinalis and quadratus lumborum muscles, laterally by the transverses abdominis and external oblique muscles, and inferiorly by the internal oblique muscle.

Serratus m.
Latissumus Dorsi m.
External Oblique m.
12th Rib
Lumbar notch
Quadratus Lumborum m.
Internal Oblique m.
Sacrospinalis
Lumbar notch
Kidney
Serratus m.
Quadratus Lumborum m.
Sacrospinalis m.
Latissimus Dorsi m.
External Oblique m.
Lumbar notch
Internal Oblique m.

initial access needle, contrast material can be instilled to outline the upper collecting system and direct an appropriate calyceal puncture. If a smaller access needle is used there is less of a chance of causing an arteriovenous fistula should any vessels be traversed. If doubt exists as to whether the collecting system has been entered with the puncture needle (e.g., no return of urine), attempts to opacify the system should not be undertaken because extravasated contrast media can distort anatomic landmarks.

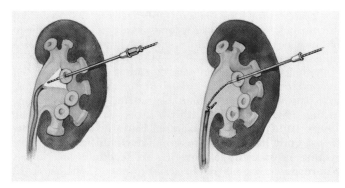

**Figure 46–10.** Retrograde ureteroscopic visualization of the desired calyx of entry can be used to facilitate percutaneous access.

---

## KEY POINTS: IMAGING MODALITIES FOR PERCUTANEOUS ACCESS

■ Percutaneous access to the upper urinary tract is most commonly performed with fluoroscopic guidance. Ultrasonography is preferred for patients in whom retrograde ureteral catheterization is unsuccessful and in pregnant women in whom there is a need for decompression of an obstructed kidney.

■ The main principle for protection from radiation energy during fluoroscopy and CT fluoroscopy is ALARA: as low as reasonably achievable. The maximum yearly whole-body exposure as recommended by the National Council on Radiation Protection is 5000 mrem, or 5 rem. Urologists performing radiation-based procedures should wear dosimeters, which should be positioned where the operator receives the maximal radiation.

■ Urologists are mostly exposed to scattered radiation, which follows the inverse square law; operators near the radiation beam can make significant reductions in exposure by increasing their distance from the patient and assuring that the radiation source is positioned under the patient.

■ Blind access is reserved primarily for emergent situations and relies on known anatomic landmarks.

---

## RETROGRADE AND RETROGRADE-ASSISTED PERCUTANEOUS RENAL ACCESS

Although uncommon, some urologists may chose to obtain upper tract access by a pure retrograde method or by retrograde-assisted techniques. Retrograde nephrostomy has been shown to be a safe procedure that can be mastered with a short learning curve and minimal radiation exposure (Wong et al, 1995). Conditions that make standard percutaneous access difficult may be overcome by utilizing a retrograde route. **Cases of morbid obesity, tightly branched staghorn calculi, and a hypermobile, malrotated, or ptotic kidney may be more amenable to retrograde-based access** (Gupta and Smith, 1996; Hosking, 1996; Kidd and Conlin, 2003). Presently, ureteroscopically assisted percutaneous access is more commonly utilized than older fluoroscopically guided retrograde access techniques.

## Ureteroscopically Assisted Percutaneous Access

With the patient in a prone split-leg position, wire access to the collecting system is obtained by flexible cystoscopy. Under direct vision a flexible ureteroscope with either single or dual deflection is advanced to select the exact calyx of interest. A fluoroscopically guided percutaneous puncture is performed using the distal end of the ureteroscope as a landmark. The tip of the puncture needle is in correct position when confirmed endoscopically (Fig. 46–10). An antegrade guide wire can then be advanced through a ureteroscopically positioned snare or basket and withdrawn through the urethra. With this through-and-through guide wire access, standard percutaneous access, tract dilation, and percutaneous procedures of choice can be performed expeditiously (Grasso et al, 1995; Kidd and Conlin, 2003).

## Retrograde Percutaneous Access

A retrograde transcutaneous nephrostomy is performed transurethrally under fluoroscopic guidance. **A sharp wire is passed through a ureteral catheter and directed out the selected calyx.** The selection of the appropriate calyx can be technically demanding and time consuming.

Presently, retrograde percutaneous access to the kidney can be obtained using the Lawson Retrograde Nephrostomy Wire Puncture Set (Cook Urological; Spencer, IN). This technique is primarily utilized in centers not familiar with the more direct and controlled approach of antegrade percutaneous access. Increasing expertise with antegrade access ureteroscopic assistance has decreased the indications for retrograde nephrostomy. Nevertheless, this technique has proved to be successful for the management of complex nephrolithiasis (Mokulis and Peretsman, 1997).

## Technique

Retrograde urography is performed, and a floppy-tip, 0.038-inch guide wire is advanced into the collecting system. A 7.5-Fr Torcon deflectable catheter is passed over the guide wire, and the guide wire is removed (Fig. 46–11). The catheter is advanced into a posterior calyx under fluoroscopic control to

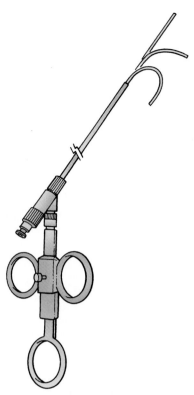

**Figure 46–11.** A 7.5-Fr Torcon deflectable catheter used for retrograde fluoroscopic access.

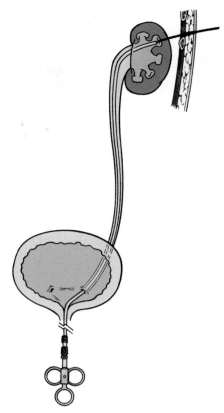

**Figure 46–12.** Retrograde fluoroscopic nephrostomy access. A puncture wire is advanced through the Torcon catheter into the calyx and through the abdominal wall to the skin.

ascertain accurate placement. **A posterior calyx is always chosen to avoid injuring adjacent structures (i.e., liver, spleen, bowel, and lung).** On fluoroscopy, the catheter should be aiming away from the spine. The Torcon catheter can be actively deflected from 0 to 140 degrees and locked into any desired position.

A sheathed puncture wire (3-Fr sheath, 0.017-inch wire) is advanced through the Torcon catheter and into the calyx and is secured with its Luer-Lok fitting. The wire is pushed through the kidney and subcutaneous tissues under fluoroscopic control (Fig. 46–12). If the needle finds any obstacles on its way to the skin (e.g., rib) it should be withdrawn and readvanced until it finds the correct path. A small skin incision may be needed to grasp the wire and advance it out, gaining through-and-through access.

**If organ injury is suspected, CT can confirm the course of the needle. It is crucial not to dilate the tract unless the urologist is certain that the tract is posterior and inferior enough to avoid organ injury.**

The tract is sequentially dilated to 10 Fr with the aid of fascial dilators passed over the puncture wire. The Torcon catheter is advanced out through the tract, and the wire is exchanged for a 0.038-inch Lunderquist-Ring torque wire. The torque wire is clamped near the urethra and has a dual function of a safety and a working wire, thus obviating the need for a second wire (Gupta and Smith, 1996; Hosking, 1996).

## KEY POINTS: RETROGRADE AND RETROGRADE-ASSISTED PERCUTANEOUS RENAL ACCESS

■ Retrograde nephrostomy is safe, has a short learning curve, and involves minimal radiation exposure to the urologist.

■ Ureteroscopically assisted percutaneous access is more commonly employed than older fluoroscopically guided retrograde access techniques.

■ During retrograde percutaneous access, it is crucial not to dilate the tract unless the urologist is certain that the tract is sufficiently posterior and inferior to avoid injury to adjacent organs.

## TECHNICAL ASPECTS OF PERCUTANEOUS ENTRY

Percutaneous entry is the initial and most important part of percutaneous renal surgery. Improper site selection can lead to difficulty performing the procedure at best and devastating complications at worst. This is also the portion of the procedure most often feared and often relegated to interventional radiology colleagues. Anatomic considerations were discussed earlier. In this section we describe technical aspects of entry and complications.

## Preoperative Preparation

**Urine sterility is mandatory for all elective procedures.** This should be achieved by urine culture followed by sensitivity-specific antibiotics for 5 to 7 days before the procedure. Documented follow-up sterile urine is preferable but may not always be feasible (e.g., indwelling nephrostomy or urethral catheter, struvite stone). Consideration should be given for 1 to 2 days or more of preoperative intravenous antibiotics in select patients with a history of urosepsis, struvite calculi, or indwelling tubes. In patients with indwelling tubes, urine should be obtained directly from the catheter lumen, not from the drainage bag. **Percutaneous entry in the setting of untreated urinary tract infection risks sepsis and death.** In emergency situations where drainage is necessary but sterility is not immediately achievable or is unknown, broad-spectrum intravenous antibiotics should be administered and minimal manipulation should be performed. Even in patients with documented urine sterility, preoperative intravenous antibiotic prophylaxis is desirable.

Intravenous analgesia and sedation combined with local anesthetic injection may be sufficient for patients undergoing drainage procedures. Patients having more extensive percutaneous renal surgery require spinal blockade or general anesthesia. Because patients will most likely be in the prone position, airway access is poor and endotracheal intubation is necessary if general anesthesia is being administered. In patients receiving spinal blockade, a higher level than usually utilized for lower urinary tract procedures is desirable, but not to the detriment of pulmonary function.

## Patient Positioning

**Correct patient positioning is mandatory to facilitate the procedure and prevent respiratory problems, neurologic damage (e.g., brachial plexus injury), compression injury (including compartment syndrome and rhabdomyolysis), and adjacent organ injury.** After induction of anesthesia the patient is repositioned in low dorsal lithotomy (if cystoscopy is to be performed), flank (for ultrasound-guided nephrostomy placement), or prone position with or without spreader bars. If retrograde access is being used to opacify the collecting system or distend it with saline, cystoscopy can be performed with the patient in lithotomy or prone position with spreader bars for placement of a urethral catheter. Bladder drainage should be provided by means of an indwelling urethral catheter.

Options for ureteral catheterization include a 5- or 6-Fr open-ended catheter, an occlusion balloon catheter, a dual-lumen catheter, or a ureteral access sheath. Each has its advantages and disadvantages. Simple open-ended catheters are generally nonobstructive, thereby preventing high intrarenal pressure. In addition, they generally are least likely to cause ureteral injury. They may not prevent stone fragments from migrating down the ureter during the procedure, however. A dual-lumen catheter has the advantage of allowing simultaneous retrograde injection of more than one medium (e.g., contrast medium and/or indigo carmine), allowing simulta-

neous guide wire access and contrast agent or saline injection, providing drainage via one lumen and injection through the other to prevent high pressure, and preventing stone fragment migration. It does dilate the ureter, however, and may result in ureteral edema or injury requiring stent placement. An occlusion balloon prevents fragment migration but can cause ureteral injury and high intrarenal pressure. A ureteral access sheath facilitates fragment passage and prevents high pressure while allowing for injection via the inner dilator but significantly dilates the ureter (thereby mandating stent placement), can cause ureteral injury, does not provide adequate remaining urethral lumen for bladder drainage, and requires a makeshift drainage apparatus at its distal end.

For more extensive percutaneous procedures prone positioning is preferable (Fig. 46–13). Specifically designed mirrored head rests with foam inserts are now available to allow the anesthesiologist to access the oral and nasal cavities,

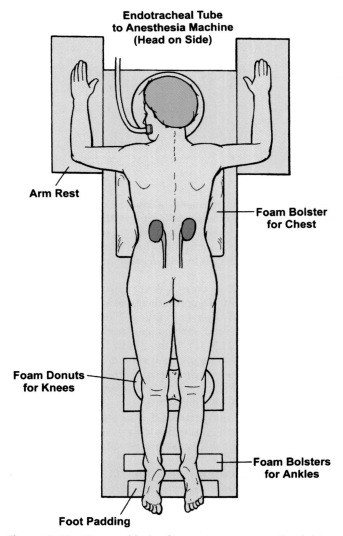

**Figure 46–13.** Prone positioning for percutaneous access. Two bolsters are placed on each side of the chest to facilitate ventilation; additional bolsters are placed under the knees and ankles. The head is carefully supported by an additional bolster.

prevent ocular compression, and visualize the airway during the procedure. Bolsters are placed under the patient from the shoulder to the iliac crest on each side to facilitate ventilation. Care should be taken in female patients to place the breasts medial to the longitudinal bolsters to prevent compression injury. The patient's arms are brought up at right angles to the body with the elbows bent to remove the arms from the path of the fluoroscopic beam and to allow the anesthesiologist to access the arms. The thighs, knees, legs, ankles, and feet are also padded, supported, and secured. Cleansing alcohol can be applied after a povidone-iodine skin preparation to enhance adhesion of the surgical drapes. A specially designed sterile endourology drape with a plastic side pouch for the collection of irrigation fluid is generally used.

For patients who cannot tolerate the prone position, the supine oblique position (with the kidney of interest elevated off the table) can be used. This position results in a more lateral renal puncture site and may theoretically increase the risk of injury to major renal vessels or adjacent organs. However, multiple investigators have reported success and complication rates with percutaneous nephrolithotomy in the supine position comparable to the prone approach (Urìa et al, 1998; Shoma et al, 2002, Ng et al, 2004). For ultrasound-guided access the supine position avoids rib-generated artifacts often seen with patients in the prone position. For CT-guided access, precise delineation of the relations of the kidney to surrounding structures allows for safe percutaneous entry even in the supine position.

## Site Selection

It is very important to select the percutaneous nephrostomy tract that is most suited for a particular procedure. The preferred approach is by way of a posterior calyx because major vascular structures surrounding the renal pelvis are avoided and the transparenchymal route stabilizes the nephrostomy catheter in an appropriate position. However, puncture of anterior calyces may be required for some stones or a calyceal diverticulum but is used only if access from posterior calyces is not possible. In addition, access from an anterior calyx to the renal pelvis is technically demanding because it requires directing the wire backward. Direct puncture of the renal pelvis should be avoided because it carries a significant risk of injury to the posterior branch of the renal artery. In general, the risk of injuring larger branches of the renal artery increases with progressively more medial punctures. In addition, the tract created from such a medial puncture provides no stability for the nephrostomy tube because it lacks parenchymal support (Niles and Smith, 1996).

Injection of contrast material through the ureteral catheter may assist opacification of the collecting system. Alternatively, a small amount of air may be injected to provide an air pyelogram. The advantage of air is that it is lighter than urine or contrast material and therefore identifies the posterior calyces first, with the patient in the prone position. The typical appearance of air in a posterior calyx filled with contrast agent has been described as "Mickey Mouse ears." With a single stone in the renal pelvis or when the anatomy is unclear, the use of contrast material is recommended to precisely delineate the intrarenal anatomy. However, in the case of multiple radiopaque calyceal or complete staghorn calculi, an air pyelogram outlines the collecting system satisfactorily and will not interfere with the evaluation of residual stones or fragments due to retained or extravasated contrast material. **In general, anterior calyces are more laterally located and posterior calyces are more medially located (mnemonic LAMP: Lateral-Anterior, Medial-Posterior).**

**Subcostal Approach.** With the C-arm in the vertical position, the collecting system is inspected and the appropriate calyx is identified. The ideal site provides the shortest tract to the calyx from below the 12th rib (Fig. 46–14). Examination with the C-arm at 90 degrees defines the medial vertical plane for entry into the calyx. The C-arm is then rotated approximately 30 degrees toward the surgeon. This places the axis of the C-arm in the same central posterior plane of the kidney, providing a direct end-on view of the posterior calyces. After the calyx has been identified, the overlying skin site is marked with a curved hemostat (Kessaris and Smith, 1995; LeRoy, 1996; Niles and Smith, 1996).

An 18-gauge translumbar angiography needle is advanced in the plane of the fluoroscope beam with the C-arm in the 30-degree position. The diamond tip prevents deflection by sharply cutting through muscle and fascia while causing minimal shearing (Fig. 46–15). In general, the shorter the needle (11 to 15 cm) the easier it is to control. Longer needles are necessary for obese patients or when triangulation is utilized (see later), because this latter technique may require a longer tract or more flexibility to "bend around" a rib. **The appropriate direction for needle advancement is determined by obtaining a "bull's-eye sign" on the fluoroscopic screen.** This effect can be observed only when the needle hub is superimposed on the needle shaft and is evident when the plane of the needle is the same as that of the x-ray beam. If the axis of the needle advancement is not parallel to the axis of the C-arm beam, a segment of the needle shaft is visible (Fig. 46–16).

After determination of the appropriate plane, the needle is advanced in 1- to 2-cm increments using a hemostat to minimize radiation exposure to the surgeon. The needle should

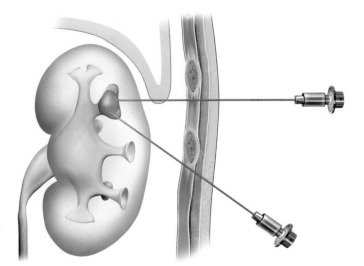

**Figure 46–14.** The ideal site for percutaneous puncture is one that provides the shortest tract to the calyx from below the 12th rib. In this particular case, although an intercostal approach would provide the shortest tract, it would also greatly increase the risk of injury to the pleura or lung.

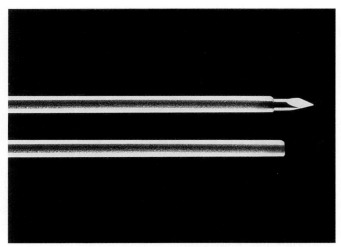

**Figure 46–15.** An 18-gauge translumbar angiography diamond-tipped needle. Notice that the tip protrudes approximately 1 mm from the distal end of the trocar.

approximate the avascular line of Brödel, because this provides the safest access to the posterior calyceal system. A transparenchymal route avoids the hilar vessels and seals the nephrostomy tract from urine leakage. **The depth of needle penetration is monitored by rotating the C-arm back to the vertical position.** With the C-arm in the vertical position, the approximation of the tip of the needle to the predetermined calyx can be seen and guided fluoroscopically. For example, the needle is too deep if it appears to be past the calyx on the fluoroscopic screen. Periodically, it is important to evaluate the correct direction of needle advancement by rotating the C-arm 30 degrees toward the surgeon and observing for the bull's-eye effect. Both the appropriate axis and the needle depth are prerequisites for a successful percutaneous access. The needle has reached its intended target when its tip is in the desired calyx on both planes of fluoroscopy.

When the needle appears to be in a calyx, the stylet is removed and the correct needle position is verified by aspira-

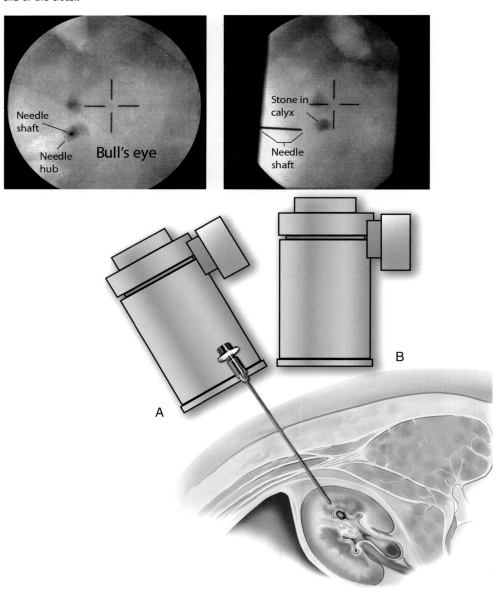

**Figure 46–16.** The use of two-plane fluoroscopy to achieve accurate needle entry. With the C-arm rotated 30 degrees from the vertical position (**A**), the "bull's eye" sign confirms passage of the needle at the proper angle. The depth of needle penetration can be checked by intermittently rotating the C-arm to the vertical position (**B**).

tion of urine or air, or both. A 0.038-inch floppy-tip J-shaped guide wire is inserted into the needle and either advanced across the UPJ or coiled within the renal pelvis. With the needle left in place, a 1-cm skin incision is made. The needle is then removed and the tract is dilated over the wire.

**Intercostal Approach.** **The risk of hydrothorax and hemothorax is increased when percutaneous access to the calyces is performed above the 12th rib.** Several endourologic techniques to access the superior calyces while minimizing complications have been described (Lang and Glorioso, 1986; Irby et al, 1999). The direct intercostal approach, triangulation, indirect access by way of lower calyces, and retrograde percutaneous nephrostomy have all been described.

**Direct percutaneous access to an upper pole calyx can be difficult by a subcostal approach, and the endourologist needs to be familiar with the intercostal approach.** Many urologists favor this approach for gaining access to the upper pole and suggest that it provides direct and optimal access to most staghorn calculi, even though it carries a slight and acceptable increase in morbidity (Fuchs and Forsyth, 1990; Golijanin et al, 1998). Contemporary series, in contrast to older literature, indicate that with caution intercostal puncture may be safe and effective. In particular, care should always be taken to ensure that the access sheath always remains in the collecting system.

Karlin and Smith (1989) described a technique for minimizing the potential morbidity of the intercostal approach by displacing the kidney caudally. This is achieved by placing an Amplatz sheath through a central or lower pole calyx and rotating the back of the dilator cranially, which causes caudal displacement of the kidney that can be viewed fluoroscopically. A second distinct puncture or a Y-tract is created into the upper pole. This method was successful in 21 of 25 cases

without complications (Fig. 46–17). Also, an occlusion balloon catheter can be used to apply gentle caudal traction and displace the kidney downward and below the costal margin during the initial access approach. Alternatively, the needle can be advanced gradually only when the kidney is at its lowest excursion point, either incrementally during consecutive end-inspirations or while the patient is made to perform a Valsalva maneuver by the anesthesiologist.

Another frequently used technique for access to a superior calyx is triangulation. The C-arm is placed over the patient in the vertical position. A retrograde pyelogram is obtained, and the skin over the desired calyx is marked with a hemostat while the C-arm is maintained in the vertical position. This plane defines the medial extent of needle penetration for access to the desired calyx. The C-arm is then rotated 30 degrees toward the surgeon for an end-on view of the posterior group of calyces. With the C-arm at 30 degrees, the skin site over the calyx is marked lateral to the first site. The surgeon uses this point on the skin surface to move in a vertical line inferiorly until a site 1 to 2 cm below the 12th rib is reached. This third site is marked and serves as the site of needle entry. From this point, the needle is advanced to the junction of the vertical plane and the 30-degree plane. Access is achieved at the junction of all three axes, hence the term *triangulation* (Niles and Smith, 1996) (Fig. 46–18).

In the latter approach, the bull's-eye sign does not exist; and thus the axis for needle advancement is based on the surgeon's appreciation of the principles of two-plane fluoroscopic viewing, especially regarding the needle tip and calyceal position. It is also very important to be familiar with the perception of the angle of advancement of the needle as it relates to the depth of penetration along the medially defined plane described previously. This approach is technically more demanding and requires more experience with percutaneous

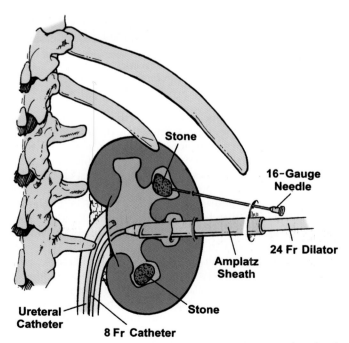

**Figure 46–17.** Caudal mobilization of the kidney using an Amplatz sheath in a middle calyx presents a lower position for superior calyceal puncture.

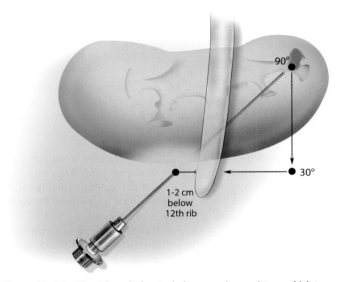

**Figure 46–18.** The triangulation technique can be used to avoid intercostal needle puncture. The vertical (90-degree) plane defines the medial extent of needle penetration, and the 30-degree plane provides an end-on view of the posterior calyces. In the triangulation technique, the needle is advanced from a point 1 to 2 cm below the 12th rib to the junction of the vertical and 30-degree planes.

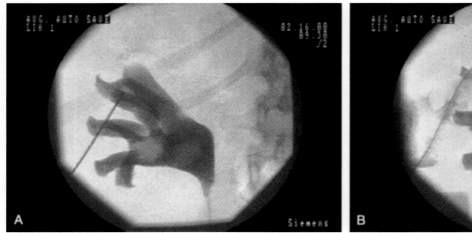
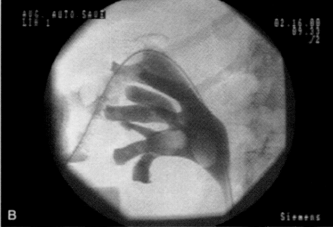

**Figure 46–19.**  **A,** Subcostal point of entry with the tip of the needle puncturing the superior pole calyx. **B,** After aspiration of urine confirms the correct position, the guide wire is advanced into the ureter.

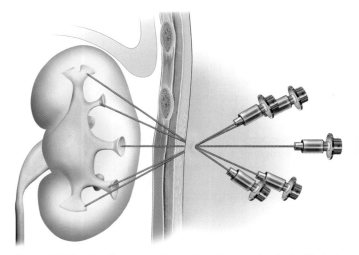

**Figure 46–20.**  The Y-tract technique allows the use of a single skin incision to gain access to multiple calyces.

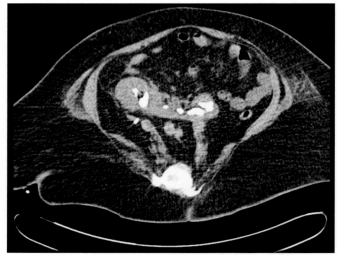

**Figure 46–21.**  Horseshoe kidneys tend to be more anteriorly and inferiorly located than orthotopic kidneys. In morbidly obese patients such as this one, extra-long dilators and nephroscopes are required.

punctures (Figs. 46-19 and 46-20). This procedure can place some torque on the renal parenchyma and should only be used when the normal renal excursion allows the superior calyces to be close to the level of the 12th rib.

**Special Circumstances.** Percutaneous access to anomalous kidneys for endourologic procedures requires excellent radiographic imaging for guidance. CT or MRI is imperative to properly define anatomy and guide puncture. In some instances laparoscopic guidance may be needed.

Malrotated kidneys and horseshoe kidneys are relatively easy to access percutaneously (Janetschek and Kunzel, 1988; Jones et al, 1991; Al-Otaibi and Hosking, 1999; Shokeir et al, 2004). In these kidneys, the majority of the calyces are facing posteriorly while the renal pelvis is anterior. In general, the more medial the calyx, the more likely it is to be posterior. Because of the possible aberrant vasculature, however, preoperative CT is extremely helpful in deciding which calyx is best to access in terms of safety and efficacy (being able to reach

the pathologic site). One advantage of horseshoe kidneys is that their embryologic ascent is limited by the inferior mesenteric artery, resulting in an inferior location compared with orthotopic kidneys. This results in a low incidence of pulmonary complications because the tract is almost always subcostal. The tract may be long, however, because these kidneys are more anterior; and in obese patients extra-long dilators and nephroscopes may be necessary (Fig. 46–21). Also, these kidneys tend to have supernumerary calyces, making maneuvering from one calyx to another difficult.

Access is more difficult with pelvic kidneys and cross-fused ectopic kidneys. The very anterior location of these kidneys with surrounding bowel often precludes safe access (Eshghi et al, 1985). Laparoscopic displacement of bowel with subsequent combined laparoscopic and fluoroscopically guided puncture has been used successfully (Troxel et al, 2002; Dos Santos et al, 2004; Aron et al, 2005). Cross-fused ectopic kidneys associated with UPJ obstruction may be able to be accessed through the anterior abdominal wall providing there are no intervening bowel segments. This can be ensured with a combination of a preoperative CT scan and intraoperative ultrasound and/or cross-table lateral fluoroscopy to guide the puncture.

## Guide Wires and Catheters

In general, the wire preferred by most surgeons for initial access is the J-wire. This wire has the benefit of being non-perforating, because its distal end is in the shape of a soft J. It has a tendency to coil in the calyx of access or in the renal pelvis and can be maneuvered in the collecting system with low risk of injury. J-wires come in various lengths, coatings, and stiffness, each having distinct advantages and disadvantages, which are beyond the scope of this chapter to discuss. Hydrophilic coated wires are also commonly used for initial access, because they are very slippery and are most likely to find their way through a tight infundibulum, past an impacted stone, or through the UPJ. The major advantages of these wires are their ability to find their way through obstructions, to coil generously in the collecting system or bladder, and to have innate resistance to kinking. Their four disadvantages are their extreme slipperiness when wet, which can result in inadvertent loss of access; their blunt tip, which can cause perforation of the collecting system; their high coefficient of friction when dry, which can cause difficulty passing catheters over them; and their lack of memory, which can result in recoil if not physically held in position. A third wire commonly used for access as well as for manipulating down the UPJ is the coaxial wire. This wire has an inner movable core, allowing the end of the wire to be flexible or stiff, depending on the desire of the surgeon and the particular situation. Once access is obtained to the collecting system with the distal end of the wire being flexible, the shaft of the wire leading into the collecting system can be stiffened, allowing for easier dilation and preventing kinking and loss of access.

Catheters are necessary once guide wire access has been obtained to the collecting system. The tract initially should be serially expanded to 10 to 12 Fr. This can be achieved using short fascial dilators. These are tapered, Teflon-coated, and malleable but stiff enough to go over a guide wire and dilate through fascia, muscle, and renal capsule. If a guide wire gets kinked during passage of a dilator, the kinked portion can be pulled into the dilator and the dilator is then advanced with back tension on the wire. Once the dilating catheter is in the collecting system, the wire can be exchanged for a stiffer wire or an attempt can be made to maneuver a new wire down the UPJ. Other catheters, such as a coudé-tipped catheter, Kumpe catheter, or a Cobra catheter, can be used to manipulate the guide wire into desired locations. These catheters have tapered ends that are curved to varying degrees, allowing access around corners or tortuosities.

In patients who have had previous renal surgery or have scarring from infections, the fascia may be too fibrotic to dilate with a Teflon-coated catheter or a balloon. In these situations a fascial incising needle may be helpful. This device is a butterfly-shaped needle that goes over a guide wire. The wings have cutting surfaces that can slice through the scar, allowing subsequent catheter placement.

## DILATION OF THE NEPHROSTOMY TRACT

Needle entry into the desired location of the pelvicalyceal system represents the first step of a successful percutaneous intervention. The tract also must be secured and dilated to allow for the passage of nephroscopic equipment or drainage catheters. In the early experience with percutaneous techniques, dilation of existing nephrostomy tracts was carried out gradually using sequentially larger telescopic dilators over a period of 8 days. Castañeda-Zúñiga (1982) first described acute dilation of the nephrostomy tract in a single session with no untoward effects. **Since then, multiple techniques have been developed that allow for safe, rapid nephrostomy tract dilation so that percutaneous access and intrarenal surgery now can be routinely performed during the same setting.**

## Guide Wire Introduction

The main principle of acute tract dilation is that it must *always* be performed over a guide wire. After needle entry into the collecting system is confirmed by return of urine after removal of the stylet, the Seldinger technique is used to advance a guide wire through the needle into the collecting system. The wire should be stiff enough to support the subsequent dilation. Passage of the wire down the ureter into the bladder should be attempted to minimize the risk of wire dislodgement during fascial dilation. In situations in which this is not possible (e.g., impacted ureteral stone, narrow UPJ), the wire should be positioned in a calyx that is distant from the initial nephrostomy tract to prevent dislodgement during dilation. In patients with complete staghorn calculi, the guide wire may coil within the punctured calyx because it cannot pass into the renal pelvis. In this case, dilation must be performed very gently because the guide wire can be easily displaced.

In addition to the initial working guide wire, a second safety guide wire may also be used. The safety wire is inserted immediately adjacent to the working wire and serves to protect access to the nephrostomy tract in case the working wire becomes kinked or displaced. Insertion of the safety guide wire requires the use of a double-lumen catheter or a coaxial system to accommodate two wires. This coaxial system consists of an inner dilator tapered to the size of the guide wire and an outer sheath. After the inner dilator is removed, the external sheath allows the safe insertion of the second guide wire, ensuring its correct positioning within the ureteral lumen. Various safety guide wire introducers are available (Press and Smith, 1995).

## Types of Dilators

A variety of techniques exist for acute dilation of the nephrostomy tract. **The most commonly used systems include progressive fascial dilators, malleable dilators, metal coaxial dilators, and high-pressure balloon dilators.** The decision of which type of dilation system is used varies among urologists on the basis of personal preference and experience. Multiple investigators have found no differences in renal parenchymal damage among the various dilation methods (Clayman et al, 1987; Stoller et al, 1994). It should be noted, however, that when comparing balloon dilators and malleable dilators several groups of investigators observed lower renal hemorrhage rates and lower transfusion rates in patients undergoing balloon dilation (Davidoff and Bellman, 1997; Safak et al, 2003).

**Fascial Dilators.** The fascial dilator system consists of progressively larger polytetrafluoroethylene (Teflon) tubes designed to slide over a 0.038-inch guide wire. They range in size from 8 to 36 Fr and are inserted in a rotating, screw-type fashion with the entire dilation procedure performed under fluoroscopic control. The main advantage of this system is that it is safe. Once the 8-Fr catheter is in place, subsequent dilation is unlikely to kink the guide wire. The stability conferred by the firm polytef composition also makes fascial dilators ideal for dilation of fibrous tracts such as may be seen in patients with a history of retroperitoneal surgery, percutaneous surgery, or inflammatory processes of the kidney (Press and Smith, 1995). The main drawback of this system is its dependence on the integrity of the guide wire (LeRoy, 1996). In addition, despite their purported safety, caution must be exercised when introducing fascial dilators because their tips can perforate the renal pelvis medially, causing excessive blood loss or extravasation of irrigating fluid into the retroperitoneum.

**Malleable Dilators.** Malleable dilators were developed in 1982 by Kurt Amplatz to improve upon some of the weaknesses of the older fascial dilators and are now widely referred to as Amplatz dilators (Rusnak et al, 1982). A tapered 8-Fr angiographic catheter is initially inserted down the ureter over the working guide wire, and progressively larger polyurethane catheters are serially passed over the catheter/guide wire combination. The additional stability conferred by the tapered

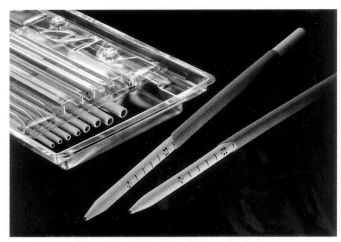

**Figure 46–22.** Amplatz dilator and sheath set.

8-Fr catheter facilitates the entire dilation process by preventing the guide wire from kinking and by allowing the larger dilating catheters to slide more easily. These dilating catheters range in diameter from 12 to 30 Fr in increments of 2 Fr (Fig. 46–22).

The nephrostomy tract either can be dilated in a stepwise fashion with the full set of dilators or some sizes can be skipped. The dilators must be advanced over the working guide wire until they enter the calyceal lumen. However, further insertion may damage the integrity of the pelvicalyceal system and should be avoided. Thus, to avoid collecting system tears, the distal end of the dilators should not be advanced across the UPJ. When nephrostomy tract dilation is performed to treat large renal stones, the dilators should be advanced only to the peripheral edge of the stone. Calyceal or infundibular lacerations have been reported when large dilators were forced past stones that were impacted in the pelvicalyceal system (LeRoy, 1996).

Once the tract is adequately dilated, an outer sheath is passed in coaxial fashion over the polyurethane dilators. The external sheath secures access to the kidney and allows the repeated introduction and withdrawal of endourologic equipment. The sheaths range in size from 28 to 34 Fr, and the outer diameter exceeds the inner diameter by 4 Fr; thus, the 34-Fr sheath is designed to slide over the 30-Fr dilator. The sheaths are impregnated with polytef to reduce the coefficient of friction and to minimize buckling.

Complications that may occur with the malleable dilators include perforation of the pelvicalyceal system, hemorrhage, extravasation, and trauma to the renal capsule. Dilation of the nephrostomy tract must always be performed under fluoroscopic observation. If excessive force is used during the insertion of the dilators, the renal pelvis may be perforated despite the presence of the 8-Fr catheter. When the medial segment of the renal pelvis is perforated, there is the possibility of extravasation of irrigation fluid into the retroperitoneum. Trauma to the renal capsule with resultant perirenal hematoma can be caused by irregularities on the leading edge of the Amplatz dilator. The disposable dilator sets ensure a smooth leading edge on the sheath each time (Press and Smith, 1995).

**Metal Coaxial Dilators.** Metal coaxial dilators are made of stainless steel and are mounted together in a telescopic fashion, mimicking a collapsible radio antenna. Progressively larger dilators are added until the tract is dilated to the desired size (Alken, 1985). The metal telescopic dilators consist of an 8-Fr hollow guide rod that slides over a guide wire and a set of six metal tubes ranging in diameter from 9 to 24 Fr. Each dilator adapts exactly to the lumen of the next dilator. A bulge at the end of the rod represents the endpoint for the progression of the dilators, ensuring that they cannot be advanced farther. After all dilators have been advanced, their tips are in the same horizontal plane, close to the tip of the guide rod.

The metal coaxial dilation system is rigid and theoretically is excellent for patients with previous surgery and associated perirenal fibrous tissue. However, several notable drawbacks have limited its use. The main disadvantage is that it is difficult to control the pressure exerted during dilation. The central core of the apparatus must be held firmly while the outer dilator is advanced to avoid untoward events such as perforation of the renal pelvis and the resultant risks of extravasation and hemorrhage (Seeman and Alken, 1995).

**Balloon Dilation Catheters.** For the fascial, malleable, and metal coaxial dilation systems, the major risk of injury stems from the uncontrolled repetitive passage of progressively larger dilators. In an attempt to minimize the morbidity of nephrostomy tract dilation, balloon dilation catheters capable of achieving tract dilation in a single step were developed (Fig. 46–23). Before inserting the balloon catheter, a 30-Fr polytef working sheath is backloaded behind the uninflated balloon. The catheter is then inserted over the guide wire until the inflatable segment traverses the nephrostomy tract. The tip of the balloon, indicated by the radiographic marker, is advanced just inside the calyx. Passing the balloon tip beyond the calyx or stone may result in infundibular tears or urothelial injury from the impaction of the stone. Once appropriately positioned, the balloon is inflated to acutely dilate the tract. Pressures of 15 to 20 atm can easily be reached with the balloon catheter. In patients with no previous renal surgery, pressures of 4 to 5 atm are usually enough to dilate a nephrostomy tract. In those who have had surgery, higher pressures are required to achieve the final dilatation. As the balloon is inflated, a characteristic "waist" appears in areas of high resistance, such as the renal capsule or a previous operative scar (Fig. 46–24).

With persistent inflation, the balloon expands fully and the waist disappears, allowing the backloaded sheath to be advanced into the collecting system in a rotating fashion. This sheath is advanced into the tract to the end of the balloon, not the end of the catheter. The balloon is then deflated and retrieved from the tract. The working sheath provides the access for further endourologic manipulations.

**The purpose of balloon dilation is to achieve tract formation in a single step, avoiding the need for serial dilation.** Among the major advantages of the balloon dilation system is its ease of use. Also, unlike serial dilators, which repetitively generate angular shearing forces, the balloons generate lateral compressive forces and are therefore less traumatic. Theoretically, balloon dilation should generate less hemorrhage, but this has yet to be definitively proved. Among the drawbacks of the balloon dilation system are the relative inability to dilate dense fascial tissue or scar tissue and the greater expense compared with other dilation systems.

**Novel Dilation Methods.** Several groups have reported on alternative techniques of nephrostomy tract dilation to avoid the morbidity associated with repetitive insertion and withdrawal of malleable dilators. In contrast to the traditional method, which employs sequential insertion of dilators of increasing size, a "one-shot" method consisting of a single dilation of the tract with a 25- or 30-Fr Amplatz dilator has been described (Travis et al, 1991; Frattini et al, 2001). Similar to the "one-shot" method, single-step dilation using an expanding malleable sheath preloaded on a laparoscopic trocar has also been described (Goharderakhshan et al, 2001). Preliminary results using these novel methods suggest that they may be feasible and perhaps less time consuming than some of the traditional methods of tract dilation (Frattini et al, 2001; Goharderakhshan et al, 2001).

The indication for percutaneous access and the size of the endoscopic instruments that will be used dictate the final extent of tract dilation. With the access tract dilated, either endourologic equipment or a nephrostomy tube is

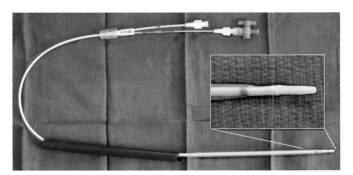

**Figure 46–23.** Balloon dilation catheter and preloaded sheath. As shown in the *inset,* the balloon cuff does not extend to the distal tip of the catheter. This must be kept in mind during advancement of the balloon dilation catheter into the collecting system.

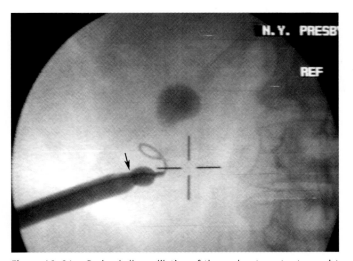

**Figure 46–24.** During balloon dilation of the nephrostomy tract, a waist can be seen at areas of high resistance such as the renal capsule and previous operative scar. In this instance, the waist *(arrow)* corresponds to dilation of the renal capsule.

introduced. When simple renal drainage is needed, a 10-Fr nephrostomy tube may be sufficient and there is no need for greater tract dilation. The final diameter of the tract should exceed the tube or instrument size by 2 to 4 Fr, to allow adequate flow of fluid around the instrument. When percutaneous access is needed for the management of stone disease, the tract is usually dilated to 30 Fr to accommodate a rigid nephroscope. Various authors have investigated the use of a "mini-perc" technique in which the tract is dilated between 13 and 20 Fr. The early literature suggests that a smaller volume of renal parenchyma is dilated, leading to a corresponding decrease in blood loss and postoperative pain (Jackman et al, 1998; Monga and Oglevie, 2000). **However, the only randomized study in the literature comparing the mini-perc and standard techniques showed no advantage with the mini-perc technique,** suggesting instead that poorer visualization and more difficult instrument handling may even place the mini-perc technique at a slight disadvantage (Feng et al, 2001).

---

### KEY POINTS: DILATION OF THE NEPHROSTOMY TRACT

- Modern nephrostomy tract dilation techniques allow for establishment of a nephrostomy tract and performance of complex intrarenal surgery at the same setting.

- Progressive dilators such as fascial dilators, malleable dilators, and metal coaxial dilators achieve tract formation by the generation of repetitive angular shearing forces.

- Balloon dilators achieve tract formation using lateral compressive forces and are theoretically less traumatic.

- Both standard and "mini-perc" techniques have been used successfully for tract dilation, but no clear advantage has yet been demonstrated for either technique.

---

## COMPLICATIONS OF PERCUTANEOUS RENAL SURGERY

Although percutaneous procedures of the kidney are associated with less morbidity than open surgery, the potential for significant complications still exists (Farrell and Hicks, 1997). Prompt recognition and management of complications are critical. Equally important are prevention and minimization of these complications.

### Hemorrhage

Blood loss is a common occurrence during percutaneous procedures of the kidney. **In particular, excessively medial punctures, multiple punctures, and punctures into kidneys with abnormal anatomy are associated with an increased risk of bleeding** (Sampaio, 1996; Martin et al, 1999). In addition,

patients on anticoagulant or antiplatelet medications are more likely to experience bleeding. In the majority of cases, the amount of blood lost during percutaneous procedures is not significant enough to require transfusion and conservative management is generally sufficient. Occasionally, blood transfusion may be warranted depending on baseline hematocrit, presence of comorbidities, and amount of blood lost. Rarely, angiographic embolization of the injured vessel is necessary. In a series of 2200 patients who underwent percutaneous renal surgery, only 17 patients (0.8%) had uncontrollable bleeding requiring angiography and embolization (Kessaris et al, 1995). The most common sources of refractory bleeding in this series were arteriovenous fistulas (41%) and pseudoaneurysms (35%). For patients with bleeding refractory to angiographic embolization, open surgical exploration is warranted.

Acute bleeding associated with percutaneous renal surgery may be secondary to injury to renal parenchymal vasculature or to branches of the renal vein or artery adjacent to the pelvicalyceal system. Parenchymal bleeding is usually seen at the site of nephrostomy tract dilation. Advancement of the distal segment of the working sheath into the collecting system provides effective parenchymal tamponade, allowing the procedure to continue. After completion of surgery, a large-bore nephrostomy tube (26 or 28 Fr) is usually sufficient to quell oozing from the tract. **When tract bleeding is refractory to this or is brisk, a nephrostomy tamponading balloon catheter (Kaye catheter) may be invaluable and should be readily available in the surgical suite.** This is essentially a large nephrostomy tube surrounded by a balloon that can be inflated with varying pressure, thereby providing effective tamponade from the pelvicalyceal system to the skin. This can be maintained for 2 to 4 days if necessary. Urine drainage is provided through the inner lumen of the catheter (Kaye and Clayman, 1986; Kerbl et al, 1994). This high-pressure Kaye tamponade balloon catheter should be removed under fluoroscopic control with guide wire access down the ureter. This allows immediate reinsertion if bleeding recurs. Several studies have demonstrated that dilation of the tract using balloon dilating catheters as opposed to metal Alken telescopic dilators or the Teflon-coated Amplatz dilators results in less blood loss. They may also cause less renal damage. The reason is that the balloon dilates radially and minimizes the shearing forces associated with other methods.

Renal venous lacerations are not uncommon and may also be managed conservatively. The insertion of a large (26 or 28 Fr) nephrostomy tube aids in controlling venous bleeding. The tube can be clamped, allowing the pelvicalyceal system to fill with clot and creating enough pressure to tamponade venous bleeding. This maneuver may not be sufficient if bleeding is brisk or from a large branch of the renal vein. Gupta and coworkers (1997) presented a technique utilizing a selectively positioned and inflated Councill balloon catheter that was successful in controlling hemorrhage without affecting renal function in five patients with renal vein injury during percutaneous renal surgery. The technique involves first a nephrostogram at the end of the procedure to delineate the exact site of egress of contrast medium into a vein (Fig. 46–25A). Usually a blush will be seen entering the branch vein and then subsequently the main renal vein and even the inferior vena cava. The most common sites of injury are an

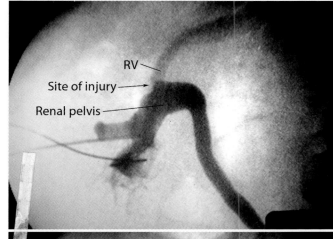

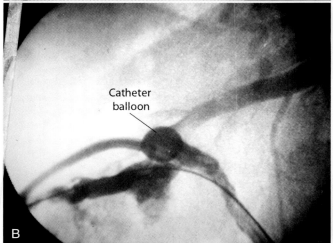

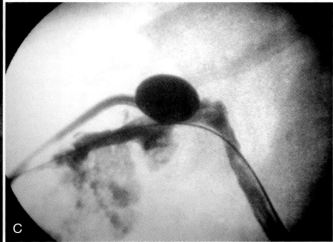

**Figure 46–25.** **A** to **C,** The renal vein (RV) may be inadvertently injured during any percutaneous procedure of the upper urinary tract. With opacification of the collecting system, contrast medium can be seen entering the renal vein.

infundibulum between the renal pelvis and a calyx or the wall of a calyx and the renal pelvis after endoscopic resection of malignant tumor. A guide wire is passed through the infundibulum if it is not already present, and a Councill catheter (18 to 26 Fr) is placed over the guide wire. Before the catheter is passed, an extra side hole should be created proximal to the balloon (Fig. 46–26). This can be achieved by placing a curved mosquito clamp through an existing side hole and passing it through the lumen of the catheter proximally until its tip is felt to be beyond the area of the balloon. The clamp should be curved away from the balloon lumen, which is on the same side of the catheter as the balloon inflation port. A sharp tenotomy scissors or scalpel can then be used to cut over the tip of the clamp as the tip is pressing into the wall of the catheter. A tiny window is thus created that can then be enlarged by grasping a cut edge and trimming further. This proximal side hole serves to allow drainage of the calyx or calyces that are about to be obstructed by the balloon of the Councill catheter. If this is not done, the patient may have tremendous flank pain due to the obstructed calyx or calyces and/or may have copious extravasation of urine into the retroperitoneum or through the skin adjacent to the catheter. Next the balloon is positioned such that it is straddling the infundibulum or the site of egress in the calyx or renal pelvis

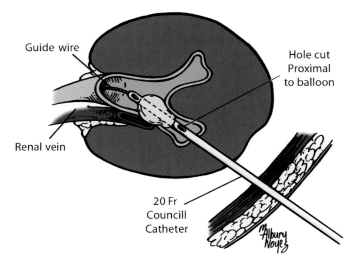

**Figure 46–26.** When using a Councill catheter to effect tamponade of an injured renal vein, an extra side hole should be created proximal to the catheter balloon. This allows for drainage of any calyces obstructed by the balloon.

(see Fig. 46–25B). The balloon is inflated with dilute contrast solution in slow increments until contrast agent instilled through the catheter no longer demonstrates extravasation into a vein (see Fig. 46–25C). The catheter should not be removed for at least 48 hours. The decision of whether the balloon is ready to be deflated should be made in the fluoroscopy suite. A nephrostogram should rule out continued venous egress as the balloon is partially deflated. Delakas and colleagues (1994) reported their experience with two cases of renal vein laceration large enough to allow entry of a 24-Fr rigid nephroscope. In both cases, inflation of a Councill catheter balloon adjacent to the injured venous segment successfully controlled the bleeding.

Arterial bleeding is relatively rare during percutaneous renal surgery but may be encountered intraoperatively or in the early or late postoperative period. Intraoperatively, it may present as pulsatile efflux of bright red blood through the puncture needle or working sheath and may not respond to conservative measures. If it occurs during dilation of the tract, the vessel is usually a tiny arteriole and tamponade may be successful. Endoscopic fulguration of parenchymal bleeding is rarely successful and is more likely to exacerbate than ameliorate the situation. If the injury is more central (i.e., near the collecting system), endoscopic fulguration may succeed for tiny vessels. Most of the time, however, bleeding is brisk enough to prevent continuation of surgery and angiographic evaluation is necessary and should not be delayed. As a temporizing method, the Kaye tamponade balloon catheter may be maximally inflated to limit blood loss in preparation for definitive management. Many patients require blood transfusion and subsequent superselective embolization under angiographic control (Beaujeux et al, 1995; Martin et al, 2000). **If the exact site of bleeding can be identified, angiographic embolization is virtually universally successful in controlling hemorrhage.** Open surgical exploration in these situations rarely succeeds and most often results in nephrectomy.

**Delayed bleeding after percutaneous procedures is almost always secondary to pseudoaneurysms or arteriovenous fistulas** (Fig. 46–27). The former occur from partial vessel laceration during initial access or dilation with subsequent weakening of the vessel wall and eventually intermittent rupture into the collecting system, resulting in spasmodic bleeding that is intermittently severely brisk and then spontaneously resolves only to recur hours or days later. The key to successful management is renal angiography during active bleeding (with the aid of an arterial vasodilator such as papaverine if necessary). Arteriovenous fistulas usually result from injury to proximate artery and veins, allowing blood to flow from the high pressure artery to the low pressure vein without tamponade from surrounding tissues (Fig. 46–28). The bleeding can be immediate or delayed but is more likely to be continuous compared with pseudoaneurysms. The treatment of choice again is highly selective angiographic embolization (Fig. 46–29). In rare situations in which embolization is relatively contraindicated due to preexisting moderate to severe renal insufficiency, the Gupta Councill catheter technique described earlier has proven successful.

The reported incidence of serious arterial injuries ranges from 0.9% to 3% after percutaneous procedures. Patterson and coworkers (1985) reported success in all seven of their angiographic embolizations. Martin and associates (2000)

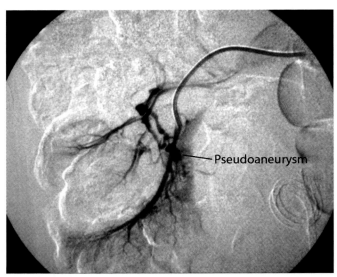

**Figure 46–27.** Angiography demonstrates a pseudoaneurysm in the lower pole of the right kidney. This patient presented with persistent severe hematuria after a percutaneous renal procedure. His pseudoaneurysm most likely developed after a percutaneous endopyelotomy performed 2 years earlier.

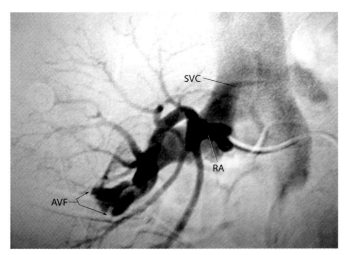

**Figure 46–28.** Injection of contrast medium into the renal artery (RA) promptly results in a blush in the superior vena cava (SVC), suggesting the presence of an arteriovenous fistula (AVF).

reported a 1% incidence of severe bleeding after percutaneous nephrolithotomy requiring superselective embolization. The need for a blood transfusion is dictated by a variety of factors, including operative technique, the patient's general condition, and the initial stone burden. The incidence of transfusion after percutaneous procedures differs among series. Segura and associates (1985) reported a need for transfusion in only 3% of their patients, whereas Stoller and colleagues (1994) had a 23% transfusion rate. In the literature, the reported transfusion rate among patients with large, complex stones is approximately 11%. An aggressive approach is associated with increased blood loss and a higher transfusion rate. **For technically demanding cases such as those involving multiple angular punctures for complex staghorn calculi, transfusion**

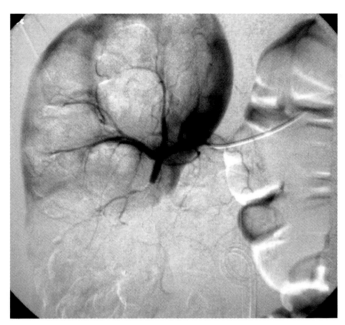

**Figure 46–29.** Embolization of the pseudoaneurysm pictured in Figure 46–27 resulted in complete absence of filling of the lower pole of the kidney as well as prompt resolution of hematuria.

**rates may approach 50%.** Martin and coworkers (1999) reported their results with the treatment of staghorn calculi and showed that transfusion rates increased from 20% when one or two punctures were required to 42% when more than two punctures were deemed necessary.

## Injury to the Renal Pelvis

Perforation of the renal pelvis is usually diagnosed intraoperatively. The most frequent causes of perforation are aggressive passage of serial dilators and percutaneous lithotripsy-induced damage. Perforation during dilation of the nephrostomy tract can result from transgression of the medial pelvic wall during initial passage of a guide wire or needle. Dilation over the inappropriately positioned guide wire then results in a relatively large tear. Perforation by the guide wire can also occur during passage of serial dilators, especially if the initial tract is tortuous, access is too medial, the dilating catheter is too large and requires excessive force to pass, or a kink is created in the guide wire. Kinks usually occur when the dilator cannot pass smoothly over the guide wire because of angulation or unusual resistance from fibrosis. Angulation tends to occur at the renal capsule, because the kidney moves up and down but the body wall stays stationary, at the junction between a calyx and renal pelvis (infundibulum), and at the medial pelvic wall where the guide wire curves down toward the UPJ or a lower pole calyx or up toward an upper pole calyx (especially in lower pole punctures). The incidence of kinking and angulation is higher for lower pole punctures. In the case of a kink, the force of dilation is misdirected to the kinked portion, resulting in the entire kinked portion of the guide wire being forced outside the collecting system. Balloon dilation over a guide wire that has traversed through the

collecting system or through a tight infundibulum can also result in renal pelvis perforation.

Lithotripsy using mechanical devices such as rigid ultrasound probes or pneumatic probes can also result in renal pelvis perforation. This is especially likely if the force of lithotripsy is being directed directly against the medial pelvic wall. Recent infection or inflammation can make the renal pelvis more friable and susceptible to perforation. Careful attention to technique may prevent perforation. First, undue pressure of the probe against the stone should not be used. In cases of very durable stones that do not fragment without mechanical pressure of the probe, gentle continuous pressure is preferable to intermittent "banging" of the probe against the stone. Moving the probe to multiple positions on the stone (so-called painting the stone) can aid in fragmentation. Also helpful is to relocate the stone to another location away from the medial wall (e.g., toward the upper pole, lower pole, or UPJ) before lithotripsy is employed. Rotating the stone such that a softer portion of the stone is tackled first may be effective. The use of stronger suction so that less mechanical pressure is required may also help.

If perforation is recognized, the rate of irrigation should be slowed, the fluid should be switched to normal saline, and judgment should be used as to whether the procedure can continue. In the case of a relatively short procedure (e.g., solitary relatively small stone at the UPJ that is clearly visible and does not require lithotripsy) the procedure can sometimes be expeditiously completed by placing the access sheath past the perforation to minimize extravasation. **In the vast majority of such situations, however, the procedure should be discontinued and ureteral stent placement and nephrostomy tube drainage should be accomplished and are usually sufficient** (Pardalidis and Smith, 1995; Dyer et al, 1997). An antegrade nephrostogram confirming resolution of extravasation of contrast material dictates when a secondary percutaneous procedure can occur or when removal of the nephrostomy tube or ureteral stent is possible.

## Fluid Absorption

Patients with venous injury or collecting system perforation should be monitored for volume overload. Continued high-pressure irrigation in the presence of venous injury or perforation can lead to intravascular absorption of large volumes of fluid. Irrigation should always be performed with normal saline to minimize the risk of dilutional hyponatremia (Gallucci et al, 1998). In cases in which electrocautery is being used, glycine should be used in place of saline to prevent the hemolysis associated with use of nonisotonic solutions such as sterile water. A "TUR" syndrome can occur similar to that described for transurethral prostate resection. The treatment of this is identical to that described for prostate surgery and its discussion is beyond the scope of this chapter.

## Injury to the Pleural Cavity

Pulmonary complications may be encountered during formation of a percutaneous nephrostomy tract. **The risk of injury to the lungs or pleura increases with more superior punctures: subcostal approaches have the lowest risk and intercostal approaches between the 10th and 11th ribs have the**

**highest risk.** In addition, needle advancements during end inspiration increase the risk of intrathoracic complications. Hopper and Yakes (1990) reported their experience with intercostal punctures and suggested that the incidence of lung injury during full expiration was 29% on the right side and 14% on the left side. Other investigators have reported pneumothorax rates from 0% to 4% and pleural effusion rates from 0% to 8% with intercostal punctures (Picus et al, 1986; Forsyth and Fuchs, 1987; Stening and Bourne, 1998). Pardalidis and Smith (1995) suggested that in the case of nephrostomy access between the 11th and 12th ribs, approximately 10% of patients present with fluid accumulation within the pleural space. Intraoperative fluoroscopy of the chest should be used in every case of intercostal access to evaluate for fluid. Of particular use is visualization of the normally sharp costophrenic angle. If a small effusion is recognized, it may be tapped with relative ease with the patient still under anesthesia. If the effusion is larger or contains bloody fluid, a thoracostomy tube can be easily placed with the patient still prone and under anesthesia. Even in cases when intraoperative fluoroscopy is negative, some patients do present later with pneumothorax or pleural effusion (Ogan et al, 2003). The vast majority of these cases will be detected by a postoperative chest radiograph in the recovery room. **Therefore, a postoperative chest radiograph is deemed necessary to rule out hydrothorax or pneumothorax in all patients undergoing intercostal punctures.** If the clinical findings suggest either of these complications, placement of a chest tube is mandatory. Immediate aspiration is performed, and the tube is removed within 24 hours. If the hemothorax is extensive, a large chest tube is advisable.

## Bowel Perforation

Colonic perforation is a rare complication of the percutaneous procedures, being reported in less than 1% of cases (Neustein et al, 1986; Morse et al, 1988; Gerspach et al, 1997). After studying the anatomic relation of the colon to the kidneys, Hadar and Gadoth (1984) reported finding a retrorenal colon in 0.6% of the evaluated cases. A retrorenal colon is more common in thin female patients. Patients with horseshoe kidneys and other irregularities of renal anatomy (e.g., renal fusion, ectopia) and those with previous jejunoileal surgery present a higher incidence of colonic perforation during percutaneous procedures. In addition, patients in whom the nephrostomy puncture is performed too laterally have an increased risk of colon injury. CT should be considered if colon enlargement is suspected, the patient is very thin, or the patient has had prior renal surgery or retroperitoneal surgery. Because usually most patients have a preoperative CT, it should be available and used to guide the puncture. The diagnosis of colonic perforation should be considered in the presence of intraoperative hematochezia, peritonitis or sepsis, or drainage of gas or feces from the nephrostomy tube. Colonic perforation may have a silent onset and eventually present only during the postoperative nephrostography, when contrast medium is seen entering the colon.

If the perforation is extraperitoneal, it can be treated conservatively. A double-pigtail ureteral stent is positioned to ensure adequate urinary drainage, and the nephrostomy tube is withdrawn to lie within the lumen of the colon. **Separation** of the gastrointestinal and urinary systems is achieved and healing is facilitated, thus avoiding fistula formation. Broad-spectrum antibiotics are administered, and radiographic studies are performed through the colostomy tube 7 to 10 days after the initial manipulation. If there is no communication between the gastrointestinal and urinary tracts, the tube is removed. Surgical correction is considered only in cases of intraperitoneal perforation of the colon or in the presence of peritonitis or sepsis.

The duodenum is positioned anteromedial to the right kidney and can be injured during right-sided percutaneous procedures if a needle or an instrument is advanced too deeply. In addition, the duodenum can be perforated if the back, stiff part of a guide wire is erroneously used for dilatation of the nephrostomy tract. This complication is less common than colonic perforation (Culkin et al, 1985). Diagnosis is based on the formation of a nephroduodenal fistula, which is seen when the postoperative nephrostography is performed.

Duodenal perforation can usually be treated conservatively with the placement of a nephrostomy tube and of a nasogastric tube to divert gastric secretions. In addition, parenteral hyperalimentation is advised. Appropriate radiographic evaluation is performed 2 weeks after the initial procedure to determine resolution of the fistula.

## Injury to the Spleen and Liver

Injury of the spleen is an uncommon finding, especially when the dimensions of the organ are within the normal range. Hopper and Yakes (1990) evaluated the anatomic relations of the kidney, spleen, and ribs and showed that when a supracostal approach was used, the incidence of splenic laceration was very low. In cases of splenomegaly, the incidence of injury is higher and CT-guided nephrostomy puncture is advised to avoid perforation of the spleen. If the spleen is perforated or lacerated, there is usually significant bleeding and a surgical exploration is necessary, often leading to splenectomy.

Injuries to the liver are less common than injuries to the spleen. In cases of hepatomegaly, an increased risk arises. CT-guided nephrostomy is advised in these cases to ensure a correct and uneventful percutaneous puncture. Treatment of liver injuries is usually conservative, and open surgical exploration is rarely needed.

## Sepsis

It is advised that all patients undergoing percutaneous procedures have urine cultures preoperatively with the administration of an appropriate antibiotic to sterilize the urine. Despite this precaution, sepsis has been reported in 0.25% to 1.5% of patients undergoing percutaneous stone removal (Segura et al, 1985; Rao et al, 1991). In these cases, infected urine has been systemically absorbed. Segura and colleagues (1985) suggested that 600 mL of infected extravasated fluid is enough to overcome the patient's defense mechanisms and cause sepsis. When staghorn calculi are treated, the antibiotic administered should be effective against the patient's specific pathogen as well as the usual urease-producing organisms associated with stones.

## KEY POINTS: COMPLICATIONS OF PERCUTANEOUS RENAL SURGERY

■ The risk of blood loss during percutaneous renal surgery is increased by excessively medial punctures, multiple punctures, and punctures into kidneys with abnormal anatomy.

■ A tamponading balloon catheter (Kaye catheter) should be readily available in the surgical suite in case brisk bleeding or bleeding refractory to a large-bore nephrostomy catheter is encountered.

■ Delayed bleeding after percutaneous procedures usually indicates the presence of a pseudoaneurysm or an arteriovenous fistula.

■ If the renal pelvis is perforated during percutaneous surgery, maximal decompression with a ureteral stent and a nephrostomy tube should be accomplished and the procedure should be discontinued.

■ Because the risk of injury to the lungs or pleura increases with more superior punctures, a postoperative chest radiograph should be obtained for all patients in whom an intercostal puncture is performed.

■ In the case of colonic perforation during percutaneous renal surgery, the gastrointestinal and urinary systems should be separated to avoid fistula formation. A double-pigtail stent should be placed in the ureter and a nephrostomy tube should be placed in the colon.

## PERCUTANEOUS PROCEDURES OF THE UPPER URINARY TRACT

Successful entry into the collecting system and dilation of the nephrostomy tract represent the common initial pathway of all percutaneous procedures of the upper urinary tract. Once secure access into the collecting system has been achieved, numerous therapeutic options are available to the urologist. From this vantage point, the urologist may choose to address disease processes as varied as kidney stones, UPJ obstruction, malignant or benign tumors, infections of the collecting system, and symptomatic renal cysts among many others. We review here the treatment of various disease processes of the upper urinary tract. Percutaneous management of stone disease, UPJ obstruction, and upper tract transitional cell carcinoma is covered elsewhere in this textbook.

### Drainage Procedures

The most common indication for percutaneous drainage of the collecting system is obstruction that cannot be decompressed by internal retrograde means. This may be in the form of either intrinsic or extrinsic obstruction affecting the ureter, UPJ, or an infundibulum. Obstruction may be intraluminal (e.g., stone or tumor), in the ureteral wall (e.g., scarring from

prior instrumentation), or extrinsic. Extrinsic obstruction is often the result of malignant compression (e.g., metastatic colon cancer, cervical cancer) or an inflammatory and fibrotic process (e.g., retroperitoneal fibrosis, prior pelvic radiation). The indications for nephrostomy tube placement include preservation of renal function, relief of pain, and emergency drainage of infected urine in the setting of obstruction.

**In the instance of obstructing ureterolithiasis, either a percutaneous nephrostomy or a ureteral stent may serve to decompress the upper tract. The efficacy of one modality over the other remains controversial.** One randomized prospective trial has demonstrated the superiority of percutaneous nephrostomy to ureteral stenting in the decompression of hydronephrosis caused by obstructing stones, especially in patients who are febrile (Mokhmalji et al, 2001). Yet, in a different randomized prospective trial, including patients presenting with obstructing ureteral calculi and clinical signs of infection (temperature >38°C [100.4°F] and/or a white blood cell count >17,000/mm$^3$), there was no advantage to percutaneous nephrostomy over retrograde stenting in terms of recovery (Pearle et al, 1998). Some studies indicate that in the instance of an obstructing stone, ureteral stenting causes more irritative urinary symptoms and local discomfort than nephrostomy tube drainage (Joshi et al, 2001). The decision of which mode of drainage to use can therefore be largely based on the clinical scenario, patient's preference, and urologist's discretion.

Similarly, the optimal method of drainage in the situation of extrinsic ureteral obstruction is controversial. In one retrospective study involving 148 patients with malignant ureteral obstruction, the difference in overall stent-related or catheter-related complications between the internal ureteral stent and percutaneous nephrostomy groups was not statistically significant (Ku et al, 2004b). However, primary stenting has demonstrated early failure rates in 51% to 58% of this patient population, ultimately necessitating percutaneous drainage (Feng et al, 1999; Shekarriz et al, 1999). In light of this, percutaneous nephrostomy drainage has been recommended as the management option of choice in instances of extrinsic obstruction by cervical cancer, bladder cancer, and other advanced abdominal malignancies (Ekici et al, 2001; Park et al, 2002; Little et al, 2003). For patients in whom life-long nephrostomy drainage is necessary, a novel technique involving subcutaneous tunneling of a nephrostomy tube with insertion of the distal end of the tube into the bladder has been reported with encouraging early results (Paterson and Forrester, 1997; Jabbour et al, 2001). **Alternatively, in the instance of malignant compression, placing two ureteral stents into one collecting system (double ureteral stenting) may be beneficial** (Fromer et al, 2002).

### Uninfected Obstruction

**Technique.** The goal in these patients is simply to place a small percutaneous drainage tube to decompress the system with minimal manipulation. A dilated system contributes to the high success rate of this procedure. Often, because of the obstruction, the collecting system cannot be visualized by the intravenous administration of contrast material. Ultrasound guidance may be of assistance or one may use anatomic landmarks as described in the section "Percutaneous Access without Imaging." Passage of a 22-gauge Chiba needle opposite the second lumbar process usually results in puncture of the dilated renal pelvis. With the stylet in place, the needle is advanced in increments. Every 1 to 2 cm, the stylet is removed and a syringe is placed on the end of the Chiba needle. The syringe is used to aspirate while the needle is held in place. If no urine can be aspirated, the stylet is replaced and the needle is advanced farther. It is important to prevent advancement of the needle without the stylet in place because this can clog the needle and prevent aspiration of urine even after the collecting system is entered. With alternating advancement and aspiration of the needle the collecting system is gradually approached. The aspiration of urine into the syringe signals entry of the needle tip into the collecting system. The collecting system can then be opacified by injecting contrast medium to guide a larger needle from a more appropriate posterolateral location.

The safest, most expeditious entry is by way of a posterior lower pole calyx. A 10-Fr Cope loop-type catheter is positioned in the renal pelvis and secured to the flank. When placing a nephrostomy tube, consideration should be given to the site of the lesion and to the eventual treatment modality to be used. For example, if an antegrade endopyelotomy is planned, attempts should be made to place the nephrostomy tube in an upper or middle posterior calyx to provide straight-line access to the obstructed UPJ.

**Results.** Successful percutaneous access to the obstructed collecting system is routinely achieved in 99% of adult patients (Pappas et al, 2000; Sim et al, 2002). Failure is most often associated with a collecting system that has become decompressed because of a ruptured fornix. In these rare instances, retrograde access may be necessary and is recommended. Interestingly, in a pediatric cohort with unilateral UPJ obstruction in a poorly functioning kidney (split renal function < 10%), placement of a nephrostomy tube improved renal function in 12 (71%) of 17 children. In these 12 patients, mean split renal function increased to 29% on the affected side (Gupta et al, 2001).

## Pyonephrosis and Emphysematous Pyelonephritis

**Natural History and Presentation.** Pyonephrosis or pyocalyx most often results secondary to an obstructing calculus in a patient with infected urine. Patients present with acute septicemia or a chronic condition with minimal symptoms. **In the acute case, emergency drainage of the obstructed collecting system is mandatory because any delay in establishing drainage can be fatal.** In the instance of acute pyonephrosis, percutaneous nephrostomy drainage is associated with minimal morbidity, facilitates definitive treatment, and provides therapeutic benefit (Ng et al, 2002). It is important that bacterial cultures are taken from the nephrostomy at the time of placement to define causative organisms and appropriate antibiotic sensitivities.

In the instance of chronic pyonephrosis the patient's symptoms may be so minimal that the diagnosis is not initially entertained. Indeed, the patient may be afebrile and complain of only a slight amount of flank discomfort. These patients may have only a mild leukocytosis. The urine culture is often

sterile. In some patients, nonvisualization of the stone-bearing calyx (e.g., "missing" or "phantom" calyx) on the intravenous urogram is the first sign of a pyocalyx (Brennan and Pollack, 1979; Meretyk et al, 1992). For any patient undergoing ESWL, intravenous urograms must be carefully reviewed to identify the presence of a phantom calyx. If a pyocalyx is inadvertently missed, the result of ESWL can be immediate urosepsis and septicemia, necessitating emergency hospital admission with subsequent percutaneous drainage of the pyocalyx and delayed percutaneous stone removal (Albala et al, 1991; Meretyk et al, 1992).

Immediate nephrectomy has been considered the standard treatment for the rare instance of emphysematous pyelonephritis (Shokeir et al, 1997). Evidence exists, however, that a minimally invasive approach consisting of CT-guided percutaneous drainage and intravenous antibiotics may be an acceptable alternative for treatment of this life-threatening condition (Chen et al, 1997; Lim et al, 2000; Mallet et al, 2002; Narlawar et al, 2004). Percutaneous drainage as opposed to immediate nephrectomy may be considered a first-line therapy more readily in those patients with emphysematous pyelonephritis who are too unstable to tolerate an operation or cannot afford additional nephron loss (e.g., renal transplant allograft) (Cheng et al, 2001). Alternatively, percutaneous drainage may complement nephrectomy if the need exists; and, therefore, treatment may be staged (Mydlo et al, 2003).

**Technique.** Treatment of pyonephrosis, pyocalyx, or emphysematous pyelonephritis can be most rapidly done with percutaneous antegrade drainage of the affected calyx or renal pelvis. Initially, a 22-gauge Chiba needle is passed into the obstructed system under CT or ultrasound guidance. On return of purulent material, a slight amount of contrast material is introduced to opacify the affected area of obstruction; the amount of contrast material instilled should be less than the amount of purulent material removed to preclude any pyelovenous or pyelosinus backflow and resultant septicemia. Injection of contrast agent should be avoided in the instances of emphysematous pyelonephritis or existing sepsis. Aspirated material is sent for bacterial and fungal cultures. To avoid an incidental pleurotomy, the recommended approach for the nephrostomy catheter is by way of the subcostal puncture, especially if the affected calyx is in the upper pole. As such, when trying to drain an upper pole calyx, the needle may need to be steeply angled caudally to ensure entry into the calyx below the 12th rib.

Next, a 10- or 12-Fr locking loop-type catheter is placed using a trocar or guide wire technique as previously described. As mentioned previously, no attempt is made at this time to obtain an antegrade nephrostogram because injection of contrast material into a pressurized, infected system may result in iatrogenic septicemia.

Attempts at retrograde drainage of a pyonephrotic kidney by way of a ureteral catheter are not recommended. This approach requires significant anesthesia, is more invasive, and provides less effective drainage (e.g., smaller catheter) than a percutaneous antegrade approach. In addition, maneuvering the catheter beyond the obstructed lesion may be difficult and could result in potential ureteral perforation. Also, in the situation of a pyocalyx, the placement of a retrograde catheter into the affected obstructed calyx may not be possible, especially if the calyx is in the lower pole.

**Results.** Among patients with pyonephrosis or pyocalyx, adherence to the aforementioned principles can give excellent results. The importance of a subcostal approach, however, cannot be overemphasized. Indeed, in one series in which two patients were managed with intercostal (e.g., 11th intercostal space) puncture, pulmonary complications resulted. In one patient, a massive pleural effusion developed, requiring prolonged chest tube drainage. A second patient developed empyema and needed open drainage.

## Renal Cysts

**Presentation and Natural History.** With increasing use of abdominal ultrasonography and CT over the past 3 decades, it has become apparent that simple renal cysts are a common finding in the general population. They are more often seen in men and in the elderly. By 40 years of age 27% of adults have radiographically detectable cysts; by 80 years of age, this number increases to 61% (Carrim and Murchison, 2003). In the modern era, the majority of renal cysts are discovered incidentally during abdominal imaging for nonurologic indications.

Renal cysts may grow in both number and size over time, but the majority remain clinically insignificant and do not require treatment (Terada et al, 2002). Very few patients experience symptomatic progression. Studies exploring the association between simple renal cysts and symptoms such as flank pain, hematuria, erythrocytosis, and hypertension have shown mixed results (Caglioti et al, 1993; Terada et al, 2004). It should be noted, however, that among patients with autosomal dominant polycystic kidney disease, a greater constellation of cyst-related complications may be seen: back and abdominal pain (47%), urinary tract infection (41%), urolithiasis (34%), hypertension (69%), palpable mass (15%), macroscopic hematuria (31%), and renal failure (47%) (Delaney et al, 1985; Milutinovic et al, 1990).

Most patients presenting to a urologist for treatment of renal cysts do so for relief of symptoms caused by the large size of the cysts. In the majority of these patients, the cysts have grown large enough to cause obstruction of the renal collecting system and/or compression of adjacent organs.

Percutaneous options for treatment of renal cysts include aspiration and sclerotherapy or endoscopic resection. In the past, percutaneous aspiration of cyst fluid followed by injection of sclerosing agents was considered first-line therapy for all renal cysts. Early reports suggested acceptable outcomes with this technique (Wahlqvist and Grumstedt, 1966; Ozgur et al, 1988). However, long-term data supporting the durability of sclerotherapy are not available. In addition, with reports of an increasing number of significant complications, including UPJ obstruction, cyst abscess formation, fever, pain, and recurrences, the role of cyst puncture has been limited (Perugia and Hubner, 1991; Paananen et al, 2001). **For those patients who fail sclerotherapy, have cysts in communication with the collecting system, or have cysts deemed too large to be adequately treated with aspiration and sclerotherapy, percutaneous resection should be considered.**

**Technique.** For both aspiration/sclerotherapy and percutaneous resection, access must first be gained directly into the cyst to be treated. Before percutaneous puncture, retrograde opacification of the collecting system using a mixture of diluted contrast material and indigo carmine can aid in directing needle entry into the cyst. Aspiration of blue fluid suggests inadvertent entry into the collecting system instead of the cyst and requires the needle to be passed again. Once access is obtained, the contents of the cyst are drained and sent for laboratory evaluation (culture, cytology, protein, lactate dehydrogenase, creatinine). A thin, clear yellow fluid is suggestive of a benign cyst, whereas sanguineous fluid may be associated with a traumatic puncture or a neoplasm. Contrast material is injected into the cyst to be certain it does not communicate with the collecting system. In addition, a slight amount of air may be injected into the cyst, thereby providing additional contrast for determining if there is any nodularity along the cyst wall; a benign cyst should have a completely smooth wall.

To proceed with sclerotherapy, after the cyst is drained, 95% ethanol (equal to 25% of the cyst volume) is instilled into the cyst. It has been shown that the epithelial lining cells are fixed by the ethanol within 3 minutes of exposure (Ozgur et al, 1988). In practice, the ethanol is left indwelling for 10 to 20 minutes to ensure complete fixation. Alternative cyst-sclerosing agents that have been reported include bismuth phosphate, tetracycline, povidone-iodine, and polidocanol among many others (Holmberg and Hietala, 1989; Peyromaure et al, 2002; Brunken et al, 2002).

After direct access into the cyst has been gained, the nephrostomy tract is dilated over a guide wire and a 30-Fr sheath is placed into the cyst if percutaneous resection is to be carried out. After the cyst is internally inspected with a 26-Fr rigid nephroscope, a standard 26-Fr resectoscope is inserted. The entire cyst wall is fulgurated using a rollerball electrode. Glycine is used for irrigation throughout the procedure. After the fulguration, a portion of cyst wall can be excised with grasping forceps to marsupialize the cyst into the retroperitoneum. Alternatively, the cyst can be marsupialized directly into the collecting system, either to the renal pelvis or a calyx by viewing the indigo carmine in the collecting system through the nearly transparent cyst wall (Fig. 46–30) (Kang et al, 2001). Marsupialization of the cyst cavity into the collecting system does not necessarily reduce the risk of recurrence and some urologists do not consider it an imperative step of the procedure. In all patients, a percutaneous drain is left inside the cyst cavity overnight and the patient is discharged after its removal.

As an alternative to the direct method of percutaneous resection, the cyst may be approached indirectly from the collecting system. With the indirect method, a calyx adjacent to the cyst is accessed and the cyst is approached from within the collecting system. Similar to the direct method, the cyst is marsupialized into the collecting system and the portions of the cyst wall that do not border the collecting system are fulgurated to promote obliteration of the cystic cavity.

**Results.** Aspiration without sclerosis is known to be of little therapeutic value (Raskin et al, 1975). With aspiration alone, only 10% to 20% of the cysts disappear or have a 50% or more reduction in volume over the ensuing follow-up (Wahlquist

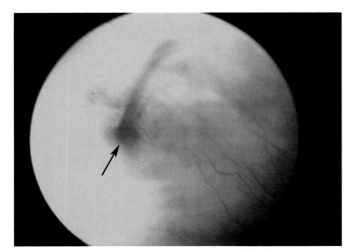

**Figure 46–30.** Indigo blue dye seen entering a renal cyst *(arrow)* through small communication channel.

and Grumstedt, 1966; Holmberg and Hietala, 1989). Sclerotherapy results in a satisfactory outcome in 75% to 100% of patients with small cysts (Bean, 1981; Zachrisson, 1982; Ozgur et al, 1988; Holmberg and Hiatala, 1989). Some investigators have found multiple sessions of percutaneous sclerotherapy for simple renal cysts to be more effective in reducing the recurrence of simple renal cysts than single-session percutaneous sclerotherapy (Hanna and Dahniya, 1996; Chung et al, 2000). Chung and colleagues (2000) noted 95% complete regression of simple cysts with two sclerotherapy sessions compared with only 19% complete regression with single-session percutaneous sclerotherapy. Long-term data supporting the durability of sclerotherapy to 5 years or beyond, however, are not available. Also, some physicians have not been able to duplicate the initial sanguine reports previously cited. Perugia and associates (1991) noted that with a 20% volume of the cyst replaced with 98% ethanol, none of five patients had a satisfactory result (defined as >50% decrease in the size of the renal cyst).

Reports of an endoscopic approach to simple renal cysts have appeared sporadically in the literature (Eikenberg, 1985; Hulbert et al, 1988b; Wong and Griffith, 1994). Hubner and colleagues (1990) reported one of the largest experiences and noted an early success rate of 93%; however, when follow-up was extended to 46 months in 10 patients, 50% of the treated cysts were again either detectable or close to their preoperative size (Plas and Hubner, 1993). In a modern series of 9 patients followed for a mean of 21 months after percutaneous cyst resection, Kang and colleagues (2001) reported complete resolution of pain in 8 patients (89%) and complete obliteration of the cyst in 7 patients (78%).

**Alternative Treatment Options.** Other methods that may be considered in the management of renal cysts include open and laparoscopic cyst decortication. These modalities are often reserved for patients who fail percutaneous resection or who are deemed poor candidates for the percutaneous approach. In particular, patients with multiple cysts or cysts difficult to approach percutaneously (e.g., anteriorly located cysts) may

be treated most effectively with the laparoscopic approach (Hemal, 2001; Lam and Gupta, 2002).

## Calyceal Diverticula

**Presentation and Natural History.** Calyceal diverticula are congenital cystic extensions of the renal collecting system into the normal renal parenchyma that communicate with the main collecting system via a narrow channel. They are lined with nonsecretory transitional cell epithelium and are thought to arise from minor calyceal fornices. Unlike a hydrocalyx, which may be acquired later in life, calyceal diverticula are believed to be congenital lesions. They are relatively rare entities, diagnosed in less than 0.5 % of all intravenous urograms. One third to one half of patients with calyceal diverticula present with pain, infection, hematuria, or calculi (Timmons et al, 1975).

Calyceal diverticula do not produce urine because their epithelial lining is nonsecretory. They do, however, fill with urine flowing retrograde from the collecting system. Hence, they may sometimes only be seen on delayed images of an intravenous urogram or by relatively high-pressure retrograde pyelography.

For patients with incidentally discovered calyceal diverticula no treatment is necessary. However, for patients presenting with pain, recurrent urinary tract infection, hematuria, symptomatic calculi, or progressive renal damage, treatment should be undertaken. The surgical approach to these lesions involves either excision or marsupialization of the diverticulum with occlusion of the neck of the diverticulum by suture or electrocautery. If the diverticulum is large, a partial nephrectomy may be necessary (Abeshouse and Abeshouse, 1963). Since the early 1990s, the treatment of calyceal diverticula has shifted increasingly toward minimally invasive methods (Clayman et al, 1984; Hulbert et al, 1988a). Minimally invasive treatment has included ESWL (of stones in a diverticulum), ureteroscopy (dilation or incision of the neck with or without fulguration of the lining), and percutaneous methods (fulguration of the lining, dilation or incision of the neck, or both).

**Technique.** After retrograde placement of an occlusion balloon ureteral catheter, the collecting system is opacified until the calyceal diverticulum is well outlined. Then, using an 18-gauge nephrostomy needle a fluoroscopically guided puncture is made directly into the calyceal diverticulum itself. A hydrophilic coated guide wire may be successful with perseverance in slipping through the neck of the diverticulum, but more often than not the neck is not blindly accessible and the wire must be coiled in the diverticular cavity. If the diverticulum is large enough to accommodate a second wire, a safety wire is also placed before the nephrostomy tract is dilated. For dilation, a 10-mm balloon catheter may be preferable. Dilating the tract with sheath dilators is more difficult and may result in an anterior false passage of the diverticulum. A 30-Fr Amplatz sheath is placed into the diverticulum, after which the rigid nephroscope is introduced. Any calculus present is treated by either intact removal or ultrasonic nephrolithotripsy (Clayman et al, 1984).

Next, saline with indigo carmine stain, or room air, is gently instilled through the retrograde ureteral occlusion balloon catheter while the surgeon examines the interior of the calyceal diverticulum with the rigid or flexible nephroscope. Blue fluid or air bubbles should be seen traversing the neck of the diverticulum. If this is not the case, the Amplatz sheath may be too deep into the diverticulum. The sheath should be carefully withdrawn 1 to 2 cm under endoscopic control while the assistant continues to instill air (10-mL bolus) or fluid gently into the retrograde ureteral catheter. Once the neck of the diverticulum is visualized, a guide wire can be passed across the neck of the diverticulum and coiled in the renal pelvis. If a metal guide wire is used, after its passage across the diverticular neck, a 5-Fr angiographic catheter is passed over the guide wire to insulate it. In the case of an anterior calyceal diverticulum, the neck will likely never be seen, in which case cannulation will not be possible and the interior of the diverticulum should be thoroughly fulgurated.

At this point, the rollerball or barrel electrode mounted on a standard 24- or 26-Fr resectoscope is introduced into the diverticular cavity. The entire surface of the diverticulum is then electrocoagulated except for the immediate area surrounding the neck of the diverticulum (Fig. 46–31) (Hulbert et al, 1987).

Next, the neck of the diverticulum is treated. This can be done most simply by balloon dilation of the neck of the diverticulum with a 4-cm-long ureteral dilating balloon. Some urologists prefer to cut the neck of the diverticulum under direct vision with either a cold knife (e.g., direct vision urethrotome), electrosurgical probe (2- or 3-Fr Greenwald electrode) or holmium:yttrium-aluminum-garnet (YAG) laser. Again, if electrosurgery is to be used, any metal guide wire in the surgical field must be covered with a 5-Fr angiographic catheter so that no electric current is transmitted to the guide wire. Several shallow incisions (2 to 4 mm) are made in the

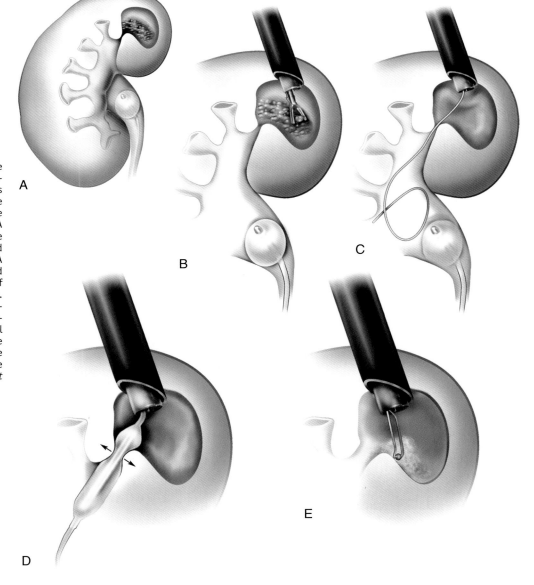

**Figure 46–31. A,** Superior pole calyceal diverticulum containing multiple small stones. **B,** A percutaneous tract is established directly into the diverticulum and the stones are extracted with grasping forceps. **C,** A guide wire is negotiated through the narrow neck of the diverticulum and into the main collecting system. **D,** A balloon dilation catheter is advanced over the wire until the balloon cuff sits in the neck of the diverticulum. Inflation of the balloon in this position allows for dilation of the diverticular neck. **E,** A rollerball or barrel electrode is used to fulgurate the diverticular cavity. Last, a large-bore nephrostomy tube traversing the diverticular neck is placed *(not shown).*

neck of the diverticulum in a radial fashion (12, 3, 6, and 9 o'clock). A solitary deep cut into the diverticular neck should be avoided because this may result in significant hemorrhage (Clayman et al, 1984).

After the neck of the diverticulum is opened, a large-bore (22 Fr) nephrostomy tube is placed such that its shaft traverses the diverticulum and the tip of the catheter lies in the renal pelvis. The nephrostomy tube can be removed as early as 3 days after the procedure (Hulbert et al, 1986). Indeed, prolonged drainage of the kidney and stenting of the diverticular neck do not appear to improve results (Hulbert et al, 1988a; Jones et al, 1991).

A faster, and perhaps simpler, alternative is not to identify the diverticular neck. Instead, the entire surface of the diverticulum, including the area of the unidentified diverticular neck, is thoroughly cauterized using the roller electrode. A 22-Fr drainage catheter is placed only to tamponade the percutaneous tract; the tip of the catheter thus resides in the calyceal diverticulum. The "calycostomy" tube is removed on the following morning, provided that there is no drainage.

In addition to the direct antegrade percutaneous approach to calyceal diverticula, an *indirect* percutaneous approach has also been reported (Hulbert et al, 1986). For this approach, access to the collecting system is obtained at a site removed from the calyceal diverticulum and the diverticulum is approached from within the collecting system. This method is not preferred by many endourologists and is fraught with difficulty and poor results. First, a usually nonhydronephrotic collecting system must be punctured. Next, the surgeon must locate the diminutive communication between the calyceal diverticulum and the collecting system. After this step, the neck must be opened and the diverticulum entered. Incising the neck of the diverticulum, however, often results in bleeding, which obscures visibility and impairs subsequent treatment of the diverticular wall. In addition, removal of any stones within the diverticulum is complicated by the steep angle of entry into the diverticulum as well as by any bleeding caused by dilating or incising the neck of the diverticulum. Ureteroscopic and ESWL techniques for dealing with the stone-laden calyceal diverticulum are discussed elsewhere in this textbook.

**Results.** Multiple authors have reported fairly high success rates with the direct antegrade percutaneous approach for treating calyceal diverticula (Eshghi et al, 1987; Hulbert et al, 1988a; Janetschek, 1988; Ellis et al, 1991; Jones et al, 1991; Lang, 1991; Schneider et al, 1991; Hendrikx et al, 1992; Bellman et al, 1993; Van Cangh et al, 1994; Grasso et al, 1995; Soble et al, 1995). **Combining the results of these individual studies, of 134 patients with a calyceal diverticulum and a stone, the percutaneous approach resulted in removal of the stone in 86% and obliteration of the diverticulum in 80% of the patients.** Recent studies confirm these findings with stone-free rates of 78% to 95% and diverticular obliteration rates around 80% (Donnellan and Harewood, 1999; Auge et al, 2002). The indirect percutaneous method has poor results. Hulbert and colleagues (1986) noted that in their three patients approached with indirect punctures, the diverticula were still present in all three on follow-up radiographic studies 4 to 14 months later.

**Alternative Treatments.** Nonpercutaneous minimally invasive modalities for treatment of calyceal diverticula include ureteroscopy, ESWL, or a combination of ureteroscopy and ESWL. With ureteroscopy, Mikkelsen and coworkers (1989) successfully treated only two of six calyceal diverticula. In one of the successful cases, two ureteroscopic procedures were required because of postoperative bleeding from the diverticulum. In their series of 17 patients treated ureteroscopically for calyceal diverticula, Auge and colleagues (2002) reported a stone-free rate of only 19%.

Similarly, with ESWL as front-line therapy, Psihramis and Dretler (1987) noted that 70% of patients became asymptomatic after treatment. At the time of follow-up, however, 80% still had stone fragments within the diverticula. In all patients studied, the diverticula remained intact. Indeed, even under the most favorable circumstances, the stone-free rate after ESWL is only 40% (Streem and Yost, 1992; Van Cangh et al, 1994) and can be as poor as 6% (Jones et al, 1991). In none of the ESWL patients did the calyceal diverticulum disappear.

Fuchs and David (1989) have combined ESWL with ureteroscopy for dilation of the calyceal neck and stone extraction in 15 patients with stone-containing calyceal diverticula. Their overall stone-free rate of 73% is an improvement over ESWL monotherapy; however, although less morbid, it is not as effective as an antegrade percutaneous approach. Likewise, treatment of the diverticulum was limited to balloon dilatation of the neck of the diverticulum; in only 47% of the cases was obliteration or a decrease in size of the diverticulum noted. With this technique, only diverticula in the upper and middle portion of the kidney can be effectively accessed.

More recently, several investigators have reported on laparoscopic treatment of calyceal diverticula. Hoznek and coworkers (1998) employed an extraperitoneal laparoscopic approach in three women with symptomatic calyceal diverticula and successfully obtained watertight obliteration of the diverticular cavity using gelatin resorcinol formaldehyde glue. Similarly, Miller and associates (2002) successfully used the laparoscopic approach to treat five patients with anterior calyceal diverticula.

**Complications.** The narrow ostium of many calyceal diverticula often precludes passage of a guide wire into the main renal collecting system. Hence, the guide wire is advanced only into the diverticulum. This small amount of wire provides little mechanical advantage and can easily become kinked or dislodged during tract dilation. The repetitive insertion and removal of serial dilators in this situation can lead to the creation of a false passage. Even if a balloon dilation catheter is used, caution must be exercised during tract dilation if the guide wire cannot be negotiated through the diverticular neck.

In addition to the increased risks of nephrostomy tract dilation, the potential complications of significant hemorrhage, retroperitoneal extravasation, pneumothorax, hemothorax, and adjacent organ injury should be kept in mind.

## Infundibular Stenosis

**Presentation and Natural History.** Infundibular stenosis is a rare clinical entity that may be caused by extrinsic compression or intrinsic narrowing of a renal infundibulum. Extrinsic causes include retroperitoneal malignancy and retroperitoneal fibrosis. Intrinsic conditions affecting the wall of the infundibulum include neoplasm, tuberculosis, and chronic scarring induced by multiple renal calculi, long-standing calculi, prior renal surgery, and so on. Rarely, infundibular obstruction may be caused by an upper pole crossing a segmental artery, in which case the condition is known as Fraley's syndrome (Fraley, 1966; Eshghi et al, 1987). In some situations, infundibular stenosis may be complete, resulting in a condition described as an excluded calyx (Elashry et al, 1996).

Similar to patients with calyceal diverticula, patients with infundibular stenosis may present with flank pain, hematuria, recurrent urinary tract infection, or, less commonly, progressive renal damage. They also commonly present with a radiologic finding of a dilated calyx (hydrocalyx). Hydrocalyces and calyceal diverticula often can be difficult to distinguish only from clinical and radiologic information. In these instances, nephroscopy can be useful because the presence (hydrocalyx) or absence (calyceal diverticulum) of a renal papilla is diagnostic. Treatment of patients with infundibular stenosis is indicated to relieve obstruction and to restore adequate drainage of urine into the main collecting system. If one suspects the presence of an obstructing crossing segmental renal artery, an arteriogram should be obtained before any endourologic therapeutic maneuvers because this condition mandates an open surgical repair (Eshghi et al, 1987).

**Technique.** The percutaneous antegrade technique for infundibular stenosis is initially similar to the approach for treating a calyceal diverticulum (Fig. 46–32). Retrograde opacification of the collecting system with a ureteral occlusion balloon catheter is used to facilitate direct percutaneous puncture onto the hydrocalyx. If the calyx is not visualized, as in the case of an excluded calyx, ultrasound or CT guidance may be necessary for puncture. After insertion of a working wire (and safety wire if possible) the nephrostomy tract is dilated and an Amplatz sheath is advanced directly into the calyx. The stenotic infundibulum is visualized and cannulated with a wire if possible. If the mouth of the infundibulum cannot be located, air or dilute indigo carmine may be injected via the retrograde catheter to facilitate detection of the opening. In the situation of an excluded calyx, a wire may be advanced up the retrograde catheter (under fluoroscopic guidance) and directed up to the point of obstruction. Manipulation of the wire from below while the operator observes with the nephroscope may permit successful cutdown through the stenosed segment.

Once a wire has been negotiated into the main collecting system, the narrowed segment may be addressed in one of several ways. It may be dilated with a balloon dilation catheter, incised with a direct vision urethrotome, cauterized with a 2- or 3-Fr electrosurgical probe, or radially incised with a holmium:YAG laser. If electrocautery is to be used, the metal guide wire must either be insulated with a 5-Fr angiographic catheter or exchanged for a nonconductive plastic wire. According to anatomic studies by Sampaio (1996), the incision should be made along the less vascular superior and inferior aspects of the middle calyceal infundibulum or the medial and lateral aspects of the upper calyceal infundibulum. Usually, a 2-mm incision is made on the superior and the inferior aspect of the infundibulum. A single deep cut is to be

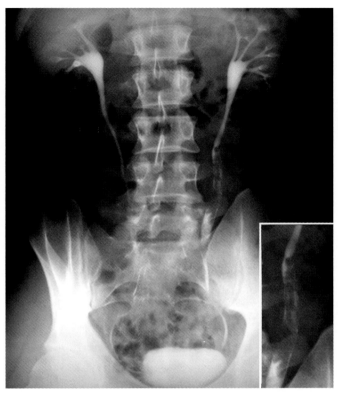

**Figure 46–32.** Intravenous pyelogram shows a radiolucent filling defect of the left ureter in a healthy young woman who presented with left flank pain. The patient underwent percutaneous resection of the mass, and pathologic examination revealed fibrovascular stroma covered by nonpapillary transitional cell epithelium consistent with the diagnosis of fibroepithelial polyp.

avoided because this may result in marked bleeding. Before making an incision, the area to be incised should be carefully inspected for the presence of any arterial pulsations. After the incision is completed, the patency of the infundibulum can be further gauged by passing a 7-mm dilating balloon catheter across the incised infundibulum. The balloon should inflate to 21 Fr at low pressure (less than 1 atm).

For postoperative drainage a nephrostomy tube of any size can be left through the infundibulum to drain the renal pelvis with or without a separate double-pigtail stent and Foley catheter. Alternatively, a large caliber (e.g., 8 Fr) double-pigtail stent can be placed to drain the hydrocalyx across its infundibulum and a separate nephrostomy tube placed into the hydrocalyx. No studies have ever demonstrated that eventual patency of the infundibulum is dependent on the type, size, or duration of drainage used.

Another therapeutic approach to infundibular stenosis is an indirect percutaneous approach. Puncturing the collecting system through an unaffected calyx and trying to approach the stenotic infundibulum in a retrograde fashion with a nephroscope is tedious and may be less efficacious than a direct antegrade approach. As with calyceal diverticula, this approach should be avoided.

**Results.** Reported series of percutaneously treated infundibular stenoses are few. Commonly, reports on calyceal diverticula are mixed with cases of hydrocalyx, such that the "true" success rates may appear overly sanguine (Eshghi et al, 1987; Janetschek, 1988). Lang (1991) reported a 60% success rate in six patients with an isolated hydrocalyx using simple balloon dilation of the infundibular stenosis and a 4-week period of stenting. With regard to actual incision of the infundibulum, Schneider and coworkers reported a 67% success rate in nine patients with infundibular stenosis with a mean follow-up of 15 months (Schneider et al, 1991). More recently, Hwang and Park (1994) recorded an 80% success rate in 10 patients with tuberculous infundibular strictures who had undergone a cold knife incision. **It appears that in contrast to calyceal diverticula, in which a successful outcome is obtainable in nearly 90%, infundibular stenosis is a more difficult entity to treat via the endourologic approach, with only a 60% to 80% success rate.**

## Fungal Bezoars

Fungal bezoars are rare infectious concretions of the kidney that may be seen in patients with funguria. They have been reported in patients with fulminant fungal pyelonephritis as well as in patients with asymptomatic fungal colonization of the urine. The clinical presentation can vary greatly ranging from urinary obstruction to gross hematuria to sepsis. *Candida* species are most commonly associated with fungal bezoars, but *Aspergillus* infections have also been reported (Irby et al, 1990). Risk factors for the development of fungal bezoars include diabetes mellitus, neurogenic bladder, chronic antibiotic use, and the presence of indwelling urinary catheters (Schonebeck and Ansehn, 1972; Dembner and Pfister, 1977). Elderly, transplant, and human immunodeficiency virus–infected patients as well as premature infants may also be at risk depending on their level of immunocompromise (Wise, 2001; Ku et al, 2004a).

Fungal bezoars may be treated with medical and surgical therapies. In the preoperative or seriously ill patient, a course of amphotericin B or flucytosine is initiated. Once adequate serum levels are obtained, topical irrigation of the affected collecting system with amphotericin B (50 mg/L at 25 to 50 ml/hr) can be given through either two retrograde ureteral catheters (one for inflow; one for outflow) or an antegrade nephrostomy tube (Harbach et al, 1970; Wise, 1990). After antibiotic coverage has resulted in sterile urine cultures, the bezoar can be removed percutaneously or by open surgery (Karlin et al, 1987).

**Technique.** Percutaneous removal of a fungal bezoar requires meticulous attention to detail. Initially, the renal pelvis is irrigated with amphotericin B via a retrograde catheter to decrease the hypothetical possibility of retroperitoneal seeding of fungus. A subcostal lower pole approach is used to access the collecting system, and the nephrostomy tract is dilated with a 10-mm balloon dilation catheter. An intercostal approach should be avoided because inadvertent entry into the pleural cavity may result in fungal empyema.

Manipulation of the renal parenchyma and the potential for retroperitoneal extravasation are minimized by the use of a balloon dilation catheter and a 30-Fr Amplatz sheath.

On visual inspection bezoars have a gray-white or yellow-gray appearance. The consistency is similar to that of a blood clot. If smaller than 1 cm, the bezoar may be extracted intact from the collecting system; however, for larger concretions, the suction on the ultrasonic lithotriptor probe is useful for bezoar evacuation. The flexible nephroscope is helpful to access every calyx to ensure that all fungal concretions have been cleared from the collecting system. At the end of the procedure, a large catheter is secured as a nephrostomy tube and the retrograde ureteral catheter can be left in place. If antegrade nephrostogram on postoperative day 1 reveals no extravasation and no remaining concretions, irrigation with amphotericin B (50 mg/L at 50 mL/hr) can be performed by way of the ureteral catheter for 48 to 72 hours (Wise et al, 1982).

**Results.** In general, reports of fungal bezoars are rare. Schonebeck and Ansehn (1972) noted only 29 cases of upper tract fungal concretions in the literature. The presence of an upper tract fungal bezoar in association with an unrelieved ureteral obstruction has a mortality rate in the 80% range. Given the infrequent occurrence of this problem, it is not surprising that there is a paucity of experience with regard to the percutaneous management and removal of fungal concretions (Dembner and Pfister, 1977; Abramowitz et al, 1986; Karlin et al, 1987; Banner et al, 1988; Doemeny et al, 1988; Keane et al, 1993). Since the early 1990s, fewer than 50 cases of percutaneous therapy for renal fungal bezoars have been reported (Irby et al, 1990; Babut et al, 1995; Karpman et al, 2003; Campbell et al, 2004; Ku et al, 2004a). In this limited group of patients, successful endourologic treatment has occurred in approximately 80% with minimal attendant morbidity and mortality.

## Fibroepithelial Polyps

Fibroepithelial polyps of the renal pelvis and ureter are rare benign mesodermal tumors. Grossly, most fibroepithelial polyps are long slender projections with a smooth surface presenting as a single or multiple fronds arising from a common base. Histologically, these polyps are composed of a cone of fibrovascular stroma emerging from the submucosa and covered by a layer of nonpapillary transitional cell epithelium (Bolton et al, 1994). These lesions are typically found in young patients, with the most common presenting complaints being hematuria and flank pain. In children, fibroepithelial polyps have been described as an uncommon cause of UPJ obstruction (Macksood et al, 1985). A fibroepithelial polyp should be suspected when an intravenous urogram or a retrograde pyelogram reveals a radiolucent filling defect of the upper urinary tract with persistently negative urine cytology (see Fig. 46–32). The treatment of these benign polyps is dictated by the degree of obstruction, involvement of the urinary tract, and intraoperative impression of carcinoma. In the past, open exploration and resection was the mainstay of therapy. Recently, percutaneous resection also has been shown to be an effective treatment option (Lam et al, 2003).

**Technique.** With the assistance of retrograde opacification, a percutaneous access tract into an upper or middle pole posterior calyx is created and secured. Nephroscopy is used to identify the stalk of the fibroepithelial polyp, and a resectoscope with a thin wire loop is used to excise the stalk completely from the renal pelvis. Biopsy forceps are then used to extract the mass in piecemeal fashion until it is removed in its entirety.

For polyps located in the ureter, a 12/14-Fr ureteral access sheath is placed down the ureter after the percutaneous tract is established. A flexible 7-Fr ureteroscope is used to identify the stalk of the polyp, and a holmium:YAG laser is used to resect the base of the stalk from the ureteral wall. A large ureteroscopic basket is used to remove the specimen in its entirety.

At the end of the procedure, both a ureteral stent and a nephrostomy tube are placed. The nephrostomy tube is removed before discharge from the hospital. An intravenous urogram may be performed 3 months after fibroepithelial polyp resection to confirm disappearance of the filling defect.

**Results.** Fibroepithelial polyps are rarely encountered in clinical practice. Fewer than 200 cases have been documented in published reports. Experience with percutaneous resection of fibroepithelial polyps remains predictably limited. One patient with a large polyp (>20 cm) in the renal pelvis and two patients with smaller ureteral polyps were all successfully managed with percutaneous resection (Lam et al, 2003). With a mean follow-up period of 19.6 months, all three patients remained free of recurrence and none developed ureteral strictures.

## Ureteroenteric Anastomotic Strictures

In patients who have undergone urinary diversion or bladder substitution with bowel segments, strictures at the ureteroenteric anastomotic site occur not uncommonly. Early strictures are typically due to ureteral ischemia, and late strictures may be due to fibrosis or progression of malignant disease. Retrograde endoscopic management often proves impossible, owing to acute angulation at the ureteral insertion sites. Although frequently employed, open surgical repair can be complicated by dense scarring and adhesions as well as by comorbid conditions in these generally elderly patients.

Percutaneous approaches to ureteroenteric anastomotic strictures have been described (Gupta and Smith, 1996). After establishment of a nephrostomy tract, strictures may be treated by balloon dilation or endoscopic incisional ureterotomy followed by stent placement across the anastomosis. Results of balloon dilation of ureteroenteric strictures vary widely in the literature (Martin et al, 1982; Banner and Pollack, 1984; Shapiro et al, 1988). One series of 14 patients who underwent endoscopic incisional ureterotomy for ureteroenteric strictures reported a 57% success rate with over 2 years of follow-up (Meretyk et al, 1991).

## Other Therapeutic Uses

The urologic conditions discussed earlier represent only a minority of the disease processes of the upper urinary tract that may be managed percutaneously. Currently, the most common indications for establishment of a nephrostomy tract are management of large burden stone disease, treatment of UPJ obstruction, and decompression of an acutely obstructed urinary system. Treatment of upper tract transitional cell carcinoma via the percutaneous route is also becoming increasingly more common.

As experience with percutaneous access to the renal collecting system has increased, this approach has been broadened for the treatment of other intra-abdominal pathology. Interventional radiologists are frequently called on to drain retroperitoneal fluid collections such as perinephric abscesses, urinomas, and lymphoceles with percutaneously placed catheters.

The percutaneous approach to the kidney has also been used for diagnostic purposes. Radiologists and nephrologists routinely perform percutaneous renal biopsies for patients with medicorenal disease. For patients in whom UPJ obstruction is suspected and radionuclide renal imaging is equivocal, the Whitaker test represents another option for diagnosing UPJ obstruction (Whitaker, 1979). Although rarely performed, it remains an accurate method for quantifying hydrostatic pressure differences between the renal pelvis and the bladder.

---

### KEY POINTS: PERCUTANEOUS PROCEDURES OF THE UPPER URINARY TRACT

- In the instance of urosepsis secondary to collecting system obstruction, drainage by a percutaneous nephrostomy tube or a ureteral stent is mandatory because any delay in establishing drainage can be fatal.

---

## NEPHROSTOMY DRAINAGE
### Nephrostomy Drainage and Addressing the Access Tract

External drainage of the pelvicalyceal system after percutaneous procedures of the upper urinary tract (i.e., percutaneous nephrolithotomy) has been routine practice among endourologists. Evidence that once suggested there was not a definitive role for external drainage after some percutaneous procedures (Wickham et al, 1984; Bellman et al, 1997; Delaney and Wake, 1998; Goh and Wolf, 1999) has translated into the modality of "tubeless percutaneous renal surgery" in select patients at some institutions (Limb and Bellman, 2002). In addition, use of hemostatic sealants at the renal parenchymal defect after tubeless percutaneous procedures (i.e., nephrolithotomy) has shown some benefit in limiting postoperative urine extravasation and aiding in hemostasis (Mikhail et al, 2003; Lee et al, 2004; Noller et al, 2004). Nevertheless, **postoperative drainage with a nephrostomy tube after percutaneous renal surgery remains a safe and standard practice.** The decision on which type of external drainage device, if any, to use postoperatively largely depends on the extent of postprocedure bleeding and whether a repeat intervention through the nephrostomy tract will be undertaken in a relative short period of time.

**The main function of a postprocedure nephrostomy tube is to divert and drain urine from the structures acutely expanded and inflamed during dilatation and instrumenta-**

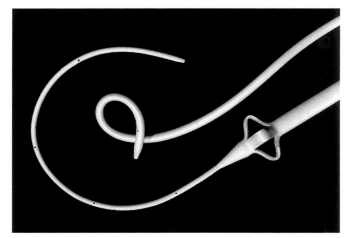

Figure 46–33. Pigtail nephrostomy catheter.

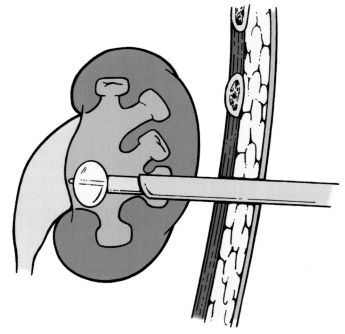

Figure 46–34. Councill catheter.

tion of the renal parenchyma and urothelium. Postprocedure edema will obstruct antegrade urinary flow. Furthermore, a sizeable nephrostomy tube will rapidly drain bloody urine before obstructing clot forms and serve to tamponade postoperative bleeding. The minimal diameter of the nephrostomy tube required for satisfactory percutaneous urinary drainage is considered to be 8 or 10 Fr. The untoward event of tube dislodgment has greatly been reduced by the use of self-locking pigtail nephrostomy catheters, which are available in sizes up to 14 Fr (Fig. 46–33). Many investigators favor the use of larger catheters for urinary drainage after acute tract dilatation to 24 to 30 Fr. Among the most widely used tubes are the Councill-type catheters with a retention balloon close to their tips. These tubes can be inserted by sliding them over a guide wire. If a working sheath is being used during the endoscopic procedure, a large nephrostomy drainage tube can be inserted through it before its removal. The sheath will then have to be excised with scissors (Fig. 46–34). One disadvantage of these catheters is that the balloon can occlude certain calyces and can subsequently cause pain.

## Malecot Tubes

Other commonly used nephrostomy drainage tubes are those with Malecot tips. The mushroom-style tip design of these catheters allows for unimpeded nephrostomy drainage without the concern of obstructing a calyx. A very popular variation of these catheters is available with a distal 18-cm extension that is 5 to 8 Fr. This re-entry Malecot catheter is inserted over a guide wire and is provided with an internal stiffener. When the stiffener is introduced, the wings collapse and the tube is easily placed. When the tube is in position, it provides external urinary drainage with the Malecot tip in the renal pelvis while its 8-Fr tip lies within the distal end of the ureteral lumen. These catheters have the advantage of maintaining ureteral access if needed and also provide stenting at the UPJ if needed. A disadvantage of these catheters, however, is that their retention mechanism is not very secure (Fig. 46–35).

## Pigtail Catheters

The standard pigtail external drainage catheter is an angiographic-type polyethylene tube, usually ranging in size from 5 to 14 Fr, with the distal end tapered (see Fig. 46–33). Pigtail catheters are typically used for simple percutaneous drainage. Urinary drainage is ensured by multiple side holes in the pigtail portion. Pigtail catheters are available in polyethylene, polyurethane, silicone, C-Flex, and Percuflex. **Percuflex offers the best ratio of internal to external diameter, excellent tensile strength and coil retention, a relatively low coefficient of friction, and good biocompatibility.** C-Flex is not as strong as Percuflex but has good coil retention strength, durability, and biocompatibility. Polyurethane has a high tensile strength and strong coil retentive properties but suboptimal biocompatibility. Silicone and hydrogel-coated catheters seem to be more biocompatible (Mardis et al, 1993; Cormio et al, 1995).

**The pigtail design of the distal segment reduces the risk of accidental dislocation.** The small diameter of these catheters facilitates their insertion and provides satisfactory drainage, obviating use of a larger tube. Even though they are equipped with the pigtail form, they do not have a self-retaining mechanism. Thus, one of the greatest drawbacks of these catheters is the ease with which they can move out of their original position, hindering drainage.

**The Cope loop catheter was designed to overcome this problem of the standard pigtail catheters** (Fig. 46–36). The Cope catheter has a nylon suture connecting the most distal side hole to the end of the catheter. When traction is exerted on this suture, a loop is formed by a locking mechanism triggered when the suture is tied to the external end of the catheter just below the hub and covered with a rubber sleeve. The catheter is secured to the skin either by a plastic retention disk

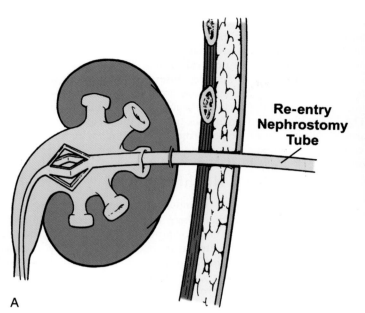

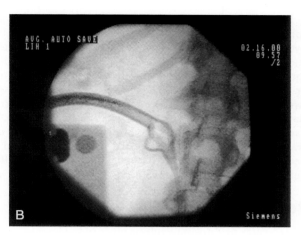

**Figure 46–35.** **A** and **B,** Malecot catheter.

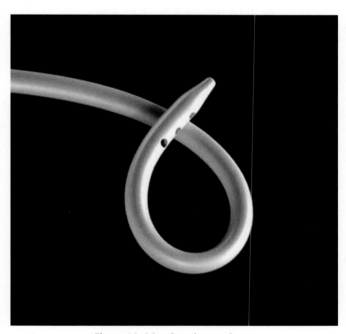

**Figure 46–36.** Cope loop catheter.

or a nylon suture. A simple gravity drainage bag is connected to the system (Lee, 1995).

**The self-locking capability, softness, and high coefficient of friction of C-Flex material are the main advantages of the Cope loop catheter** (Banner and Pollack, 1985). Its insertion can be simplified with the use of a flexible cannula stiffener that slides over a 0.038-inch guide wire, following gentle curves along the tract.

Even the Cope loop catheter presents certain drawbacks. The main problem is that if a **tight loop forms and the end hole becomes encrusted, the catheter becomes very difficult to remove. In addition, if the catheter is mistakenly cut, string may be left within the collecting system acting as a nidus for infection and stone formation.** Furthermore, the passage of the guide wire for catheter exchange can be very demanding. This catheter is suitable mainly for patients with a large renal pelvis. The loop formation requires the insertion of approximately 3 cm of pigtail catheter into the renal pelvis. Thus, the insertion of the catheter into a nondilated system could become particularly difficult. The tension of the nylon string of the locking mechanism in a patient with a small pelvis can cause serious tears by an action mimicking that of a cheese cutter. For this same reason, it is absolutely necessary to fully release the string before removing this catheter to avoid a serious renal parenchymal laceration.

Even though smaller catheters may be appealing, they have limitations in function and drainage capabilities. **The retention mechanism of the Malecot and the pigtail catheters often proves to be inefficient. In obese and hypermobile patients, these tubes are often pulled out.** The tubes also may not serve their purpose in patients with significant intrarenal bleeding, fragmented calculi, or mucus production. Furthermore, if there is a need to use the nephrostomy tract for repeated percutaneous procedures, a larger tube may allow such intervention, under local anesthesia and without the need for further tract dilatation.

## Balloon Retention Catheters: Councill and Foley

Because of the problems of tube dislodgement, many urologists favor the use of a larger, self-retaining nephrostomy drainage catheter. One of the design specifications of all nephrostomy catheters is an end hole for passing a guide wire through the catheter tip. The presence of this wire is essential for initial placement, subsequent replacement, and repeat access to the kidney.

Most Councill and Foley catheters are constructed of latex rubber with a variety of coatings. Silicone, polytef, and hydrophilic coatings are available for these latex catheters (Carson, 1995) (see Fig. 46–34). Self-retaining balloon catheters have balloon capacities of 5 mL and range from 12 Fr to 32 Fr. Drainage through the Foley catheters is through two side holes located in offset positions on the distal portion. **Balloons should always be inflated with water or saline. The use of contrast material should be avoided, because the contrast materials have a higher viscosity than water and can occlude the balloon inflation port, jeopardizing balloon deflation for catheter removal.**

## Re-entry Tubes

The re-entry nephrostomy tube is made of C-Flex and is structured as a 24-Fr Malecot catheter in association with an 18-cm extension from the distal end of the Malecot tip. This extension has a diameter of 8 Fr, and its distal tip has drainage holes. The Malecot configuration secures the catheter within the renal pelvis. When a hollow introducer is inserted, the Malecot wings are flattened, enabling catheter insertion. **The advantages of the re-entry tube are the ability to access the renal pelvis and ureter, a wider lumen for drainage, softer material (and thus more comfort for the patient), and the safety of removing the tube.**

The percutaneous tract is dilated to a minimum of 26 Fr, and the guide wire is advanced down the ureter toward the bladder. The re-entry tube, with an introducer in place and the wings collapsed, is advanced over the guide wire under fluoroscopic control. We favor the use of a guide wire, thus avoiding kinking of the wire or buckling of the tube in the pelvicalyceal system. **The final position of the nephrostomy tube is ascertained fluoroscopically to be certain the Malecot wings are within the renal pelvis, the distal tip of the catheter is at the UPJ, and its tail is down the ureter** (see Fig. 46–35).

One of the great advantages of this tube is that, as its names indicates, **it enables easy access to the pelvicalyceal system and ureter when re-entry is needed.** The introducer is inserted under fluoroscopic control and locked into the Luer-Lok exterior end of the tube. This connection must be made cautiously because the distal end of the introducer may exit the Malecot wings. If this occurs, the tube should be slowly and partly withdrawn, causing the collapse of the Malecot wings against the renal parenchyma. With this technique, the introducer can be aligned with the tube, and then a guide wire can be advanced down the ureter. After wire placement, the tube can safely be removed (Badlani, 1995).

When debris is present, the guide wire often cannot be advanced through the tip of the re-entry tube. The tube should be retracted until the tip of the Malecot catheter is seen to protrude outside the nephrostomy tract. Access to the ureter is maintained by the 18-cm tail of the tube. A guide wire can then be forwarded directly through the tip.

In addition, when the nephrostomy tube is removed (48 to 72 hours after the initial percutaneous procedure), the re-entry tube enables the **safe monitoring of any potential bleeding from the tract.** This can be achieved by removing the Malecot wings from the nephrostomy tract. The tract should then be observed before removing the tail. In case of bleeding, a wire can easily be passed down the 8-Fr segment of the re-entry tube.

**The main disadvantage of the re-entry tube is the tip location within the ureteral lumen.** The distal segment is one length (18 cm), and, depending on the patient's dimensions, it can be located anywhere from the site of the common iliac vessels to the ureterovesical junction. Caution must be exercised when advancing the tip down the ureter, a maneuver that should always be performed over a guide wire to avoid complications such as perforation.

## Circle Loop Nephrostomy

The circle tube or U-loop nephrostomy was introduced in 1954, and since then there has been a great evolution in ureteral stents and nephrostomy catheters. However, the circle tube remains an alternative because it is easily changed, rarely encourages infection or stone formation, causes little intrarenal trauma, and can be used for irrigation. **It remains a suitable alternative for patients who require long-term upper tract diversion, necessitating fewer tube changes than the single nephrostomy catheters** (Oshinsky and Smith, 1995).

Initially, percutaneous access is achieved through a lower pole calyx, the tract is dilated to 12 Fr, and a Malecot-type catheter is positioned. With the aid of fluoroscopy, a second site is selected for the next percutaneous access. The new site must not be in proximity to the previous one: otherwise, the circle tube may kink in the renal pelvis. After the correct position has been identified, an 18-gauge needle is inserted into the predetermined calyx and a guide wire is advanced through the needle into the renal pelvis.

A flexible nephroscope or a rigid ureteroscope is then inserted through the lower pole tract, sliding along the guide wire, and the guide wire in the upper tract is grasped. After through-and-through communication has been established between the two tracts, an 8-Fr coaxial dilator is advanced over the guide wire and the circle tube is advanced over this catheter. The circle tube must have radiopaque markings in the region of the drainage holes to assist with positioning under fluoroscopic guidance such that the drainage holes are within the pelvicalyceal system.

When the insertion is concluded, the circle tube is clamped and nephrostography is performed to confirm its accurate position. The ends of the tube are then assembled to a Y-connector and connected to a drainage bag (Fig. 46–37).

## Large Bore versus Small Bore

Nephrostomy tubes are available in sizes ranging from 5 to 32 Fr. Larger tubes usually provide better drainage at the expense of greater patient discomfort and urinary leak. In one prospective study, for example, there was a statistically significant difference in the analgesic need and the duration of urinary leak, favoring use of a 9-Fr pigtail catheter over a 28-Fr nephrostomy tube after percutaneous nephrolithotomy (Maheshwari et al, 2000). In an additional percutaneous nephrolithotomy (PCNL) study, use of smaller drainage catheters after PCNL (10-Fr pigtail vs. 22-Fr Councill) was associated with lower pain scores during the immediate postoperative period. However, no statistical benefit, with regard

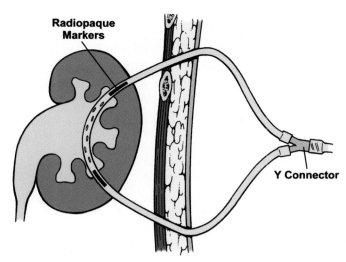

**Figure 46–37.** Circle loop nephrostomy.

to comfort, was demonstrated regardless of tube size after 6 hours (Pietrow et al, 2003). Similarly, 7-Fr tail stents have been better tolerated after PCNL compared with 24-Fr re-entry Malecot nephrostomy tubes (Liatsikos et al, 2002). Desai and colleagues (2004) compared postoperative outcomes among tubeless, conventional large-bore (20 Fr) and small-bore nephrostomy (9 Fr) drainage after PCNL in a randomized prospective fashion. Postoperative analgesic requirements, urinary extravasation, duration of hematuria, duration of urinary leak, decrease in hematocrit, and hospital stay were compared among the three groups. Tubeless PCNL was associated with the least postoperative pain, urinary leakage, and hospital stay. Important to note was that there was no difference in duration of hematuria or decrease in hematocrit whether a nephrostomy tube was used or not, regardless of size. In contrast, a prospective randomized study comparing use of either a 24-Fr re-entry tube, an 8-Fr pigtail catheter, or a ureteral stent (with removal of an 18-Fr Councill catheter on postoperative day 1) after PCNL, there was no overwhelming advantage of any one drainage system over the other (Marcovich et al, 2004).

With regard to prolonged urinary drainage from a nephrostomy tract after PCNL without evidence of obstruction, oral desmopressin has been shown to be an alternative modality to decrease urinary leak (Cimentepe et al, 2004).

## Tubeless Nephrostomy and Use of Sealants and Hemostatic Agents

Just over 20 years ago, Wickham and associates (1984) introduced the concept of a one-stage tubeless nephrolithotomy with a reported high success rate. What was once conceptual and novel in practice has now become routine at some institutions in select cases. Tubeless percutaneous renal surgery has also been shown to be safe and effective in the morbidly obese requiring PCNL or endopyelotomy (Yang and Bellman, 2004) and in instances of bilateral percutaneous nephrolithotomy (Weld and Wake, 2000).

Approaching the realm of tubeless renal surgery, Lojanapiwat and colleagues (2001) demonstrated a reduction in

patient discomfort in patients who underwent an uncomplicated tubeless PCNL with an externalized 6-Fr ureteral stent for 48 hours. However, Feng and associates (2001) performed a prospective randomized trial to assess the efficacy and morbidity of standard PCNL (34-Fr sheath), "mini-PCNL" (26-Fr sheath), and tubeless PCNL (double J ureteral stent used for drainage). Compared with those who underwent standard and "mini" PCNL, the tubeless PCNL population required less morphine and had a decreased length of hospitalization. In addition, the tubeless technique was associated with the least morbidity and greatest cost efficiency.

Limb and Bellman (2002) also assessed the outcomes and safety of tubeless percutaneous renal surgery in select patients who underwent PCNL (n = 86; mean stone burden = 3.30 cm²) and antegrade endopyelotomy (n = 26). When internal ureteral stents were placed without external drainage tubes in this cohort, there was a reduction in hospital stay and analgesic requirements with an earlier return to normal activities. These findings have recently been reproduced in similar, albeit smaller, studies (Aghamir et al, 2004; Karami and Gholamrezaie, 2004; Patel and Abubacker, 2004). To overcome the possible bothersome bladder symptoms and need for cystoscopic removal of a standard ureteral stent, use of a 7-Fr/3-Fr tail stent with the string exiting the urethral meatus has been described as a modification to the standard tubeless nephrostomy technique (Yew and Bellman, 2003). In addition to the obvious clinical benefit of tubeless percutaneous renal surgery, it is important to note the economic advantage when utilizing the tubeless technique (Bellman et al, 1997; Candela et al, 1997; Feng et al, 2001).

Mikhail and coworkers (2003) retrospectively compared outcomes after the use of fibrin glue (Tissel Vapor Heated Fibrin Sealant, Baxter Healthcare) in the nephrostomy tract after tubeless PCNL. Differences in the hematocrit drop between the experimental and control groups were not statistically different. **Although the use of fibrin glue was demonstrated to be safe in this study, a definitive clinical benefit was not demonstrated.** In contrast, a noncomparative study by Noller and colleagues (2004) assessed the ability of fibrin sealant (2 mL of HEMASEEL APR—Hemacure Corp., Sarasota, FL) to facilitate tubeless PCNL in 10 renal units with an average stone burden of 3.37 cm². The goal was to prevent urinary extravasation and promote early hospital discharge without the inconvenience of urinary leak from the access site after antegrade placement of a ureteral stent. All patients in this study were discharged on postoperative day 1 without evidence of soaked dressings or extravasation on postoperative CT. Similarly, in a small pilot study (n = 2), injection of a gelatin matrix hemostatic sealant (FloSeal, Baxter Medical, Fremont, CA) into the nephrostomy tract after tubeless PCNL demonstrated value in providing immediate and effective hemostasis (Lee et al, 2004). **It is clear that injection of hemostatic agents into nephrostomy tracts after tubeless PCNL is safe and feasible. However, additional clinical studies are needed to prove a definitive clinical benefit after percutaneous renal surgery.**

## Cauterization of the Access Tract

Placement of a large-bore nephrostomy tube at the conclusion of an extensive percutaneous procedure such as a PCNL has been the traditional method to control and tamponade post-operative hemorrhage. In an effort to reduce bleeding after a percutaneous procedure, the efficacy and safety of access tract cauterization has been investigated. Jou and colleagues (2004a, 2004b), for example, described the use of an 8-Fr, 20-inch elongated electrode probe through the working channel of a nephroscope to cauterize obvious points of bleeding in a large cohort of patients after tubeless PCNL. In these studies, use of electrocautery proved to be safe and effective in decreasing the transfusion rate without increasing patient morbidity. In contrast, Aron and associates (2004) showed no statistical difference between change in hemoglobin after tubeless PCNL with or without the use of diathermy coagulation. Interestingly, however, the length of hospitalization and postoperative analgesic requirements were significantly less in the fulguration group. If one wishes to cauterize identifiable bleeding points after percutaneous renal surgery a holmium:YAG laser or a flexible Bugbee cautery may alternatively be used. **It is difficult to fulgurate bleeding of renal parenchymal origin; in doing so, bleeding may be aggravated rather than quelled.**

## Conclusions

If used, the *ideal* nephrostomy tube should have excellent bio-compatibility and strength, be well tolerated by the patient, resist obstruction or dislodging, and be simple to insert and replace (Paul et al, 2003). Regardless of these parameters, there is really no panacea for drainage after percutaneous surgeries (Marcovich et al, 2004). **The choice as to which drainage modality used is largely dependent on the clinical scenario (i.e., complicated vs. uncomplicated, degree of bleeding, likelihood of obstructing edema), the endourologist's preference, the likelihood of repeat interventions, and patient tolerability** (Table 46–2). Foregoing placement of nephrostomy drainage after a percutaneous procedure (tubeless nephrostomy) is safe and feasible in select patients (i.e., minimal bleeding and no need for repeat nephroscopy). Future studies on tubeless percutaneous procedures with the use of hemostatic agents and sealants, with or without the use of cautery, will determine the exact role of these compounds in percutaneous renal surgery.

---

### KEY POINTS: NEPHROSTOMY DRAINAGE

- Postoperative drainage with a nephrostomy tube after percutaneous renal surgery remains a safe and standard practice. Choice of tube placement is largely dependent on the clinical scenario.

- The advantages of using a Malecot re-entry tube are the ability to access the renal pelvis and ureter, a wider lumen for drainage, softer material (and thus more comfort for the patient), and the safety of removing the tube.

- Tubeless nephrostomy is an option in select patients when there is no significant postprocedure bleeding, perforation, or extravasation; the renal unit is not obstructed; and repeat nephroscopy will not be required.

- If an obvious site of bleeding is noted in the nephrostomy tract, cautery may be used to promote hemostasis; fibrin sealant may then be used to seal the tract or a large-bore nephrostomy tube can be placed.

---

## FUTURE DIRECTIONS

The future for percutaneous renal surgery is bright. Continued technologic advancements in endourologic training (Hammond et al, 2004), imaging (Krombach et al, 2001), ureteroscopic design (Ankem et al, 2004; Bratslavsky et al, 2004; Monga and Beeman, 2004), bio-impedance–based access needles (Hernandez et al, 2001), and robotic systems (Eichel et al, 2004) will ultimately refine assisted percutaneous access techniques to pinpoint accuracy. Ongoing evolution and progression in endourologic science will translate into more efficacious percutaneous renal surgeries for the disease processes affecting the upper urinary tracts.

## Innovations in Imaging

Although significant advances have been made in CT and MRI to perfect three-dimensional tissue imaging, the future role that these expensive and cumbersome imaging modalities will play in access for standard percutaneous renal surgery access is questionable. CT and MRI, however, will continue to facilitate safer percutaneous access in special circumstances (i.e., retrorenal colon, spinal dysraphism) in which other imaging modalities cannot ensure secure access. Newer technology involving **real-time CT fluoroscopy under laser guidance** has also allowed for efficient and safe percutaneous nephrostomy placement when difficult access to the pelvicalyceal system has been encountered while minimizing radiation exposure (LeMaitre et al, 2000). This advanced imaging modality can maximize operator hand distances away from the gantry (>25 cm) and reduce the radiation dose to the operator's hand to 0.4 mrad/s (4 μGy/s) (de Mey et al, 2000).

Successful puncture of the collecting system, however, is ultimately confirmed by the return of urine through the needle. Porcine experiments on **ultrasound-guided nephros-**

---

### Table 46-2. Choosing Appropriate Nephrostomy Tube Drainage

| Clinical Indication | Suggested Nephrostomy Tube and Tract Management |
| --- | --- |
| Acute obstruction, simple temporary drainage | Pigtail, Cope loop catheter |
| Uncomplicated percutaneous renal surgery | Tubeless ± cautery or hemostatic sealants, Malecot catheter, Balloon catheter |
| Complicated percutaneous renal surgery | Councill tip Catheter, Kaye tamponade catheter |
| Minor mucosal damage or post-endopyelotomy care | Malecot re-entry tube, Smith endopyelotomy stent (14 Fr/7 Fr) |
| Long-term drainage, administration of topical chemotherapy, pyelopyelostomy | Circle loop nephrostomy tube |

## Innovations in Access: PAKY, Smart Needle, and Ureteroscopically Assisted Access (UAA)

Attempts have been made to apply robotics to nephrostomy puncture, with the intent to make access easier and more precise. The Urobotics Laboratory at Johns Hopkins University (Caddedu et al, 1997, 1998) has developed and assessed a fluoroscopic-based mechanical robot arm with an active remote center of motion translational device for percutaneous access to the kidney (PAKY-RCM). The device is mounted to the operating table and works in conjunction with a fluoroscopic unit to monitor the path and depth of needle insertion. Important to note is that the PAKY-RCM system does not require computer-based image processing for image correction and calibration (Kim and Schulman, 2004).

In pilot studies the PAKY-RCM arm has provided a steady needle holder and an effective method for obtaining percutaneous renal access. Early findings suggested that the PAKY might be the mechanical platform necessary for the development of a complete robotic system for ensuring percutaneous renal access. Since then robotic **PAKY has proved to be a safe and efficacious method of obtaining access before percutaneous nephrolithotomy** (Su et al, 2002); the number of attempts, blood loss, and time to access are comparable to those of standard manual percutaneous access techniques. Use of the PAKY-RCM system has also proved to be safe and effective in international telementoring, promoting collaborative efforts to teach percutaneous access techniques among urologists at remote locations (Micali et al, 2000; Bauer et al, 2001; Netto et al, 2003). Perhaps in the future, robotic technology will continue to be a driving force in the progress of percutaneous renal surgery.

Standard percutaneous access to the upper urinary tract without a robotic system relies on a sound foundation of renal anatomy coupled with the aid of imaging modalities. Even so, multiple attempts to enter a desired calyx may often have to be undertaken to ensure proper placement. Furthermore, until urine is aspirated or flows from the needle sheath, appropriate access cannot be confirmed. In light of this, **an impedance-based percutaneous Smart Needle system has been developed to provide an objective means to confirm proper collecting system access** (Hernandez et al, 2001). The impedance system is built into an 18-gauge percutaneous access needle system in which the inner stylet is electrically insulated from the outer sheath. In ex-vivo porcine kidneys, a characteristic drop in resistivity can be demonstrated when the needle transitions from the renal parenchyma into a saline-infused collecting system. An impedance-based percutaneous access system may prove to be useful to endourolo-

tomy with the aid of a magnetic field-based navigation device have addressed this limitation, allowing for accurate puncture needle placement in plane or out of plane from any direction, independently of the position of the transducer (Krombach et al, 2001). Perhaps in the future, this technology may play an increased role in effective real-time imaging for obtaining standard percutaneous access.

gists performing percutaneous renal surgery, easily differentiating between renal parenchyma, blood, and urine.

Advances in flexible dual active deflection ureteroscope design (e.g., ACMI DUR-8 Elite, Storz Flex-X) have facilitated retrograde access to any calyx of interest (Ankem et al, 2004). As discussed in the section on retrograde access techniques, ureteroscopic-assisted access is a technique that may be utilized in instances of morbid obesity, tightly branched staghorn calculi, and a hypermobile, malrotated, or ptotic kidney. The present status of ureteroscopic design allows for better retrograde assisted access technique. Further innovations in ureteroscope technology and durability will continue to perfect ureteroscopically assisted access as an option for retrograde access.

## Innovations in Drainage

As discussed in the section on nephrostomy drainage, the concept of tubeless nephrostomy in select cases (i.e., uncomplicated without urothelial damage or significant bleeding) has proved to be a well-tolerated and economically beneficial modality at the conclusion of some percutaneous renal surgeries. Any future innovations in nephrostomy tube drainage will adhere to the principles of excellent biocompatibility and strength and resistance to obstruction or dislodgement, will be well tolerated, and be simple to insert and replace. It is clear that injection of hemostatic agents into nephrostomy tracts after tubeless PCNL is safe and feasible. However, additional clinical studies will clarify the role of such agents in the paradigm of percutaneous renal surgery.

### SUGGESTED READINGS

Chen M, Huang C, Chou Y: Percutaneous drainage in the treatment of emphysematous pyelonephritis: 10-year experience. J Urol 1997;157:1569-1573.

Chien GW, Bellman GC: Blind percutaneous renal access. J Endourol 2002;16:93-96.

Fuchs EF, Forsyth MJ: Supracostal approach for percutaneous ultrasonic lithotripsy. Urol Clin North Am 1990;17:99-102.

Giblin JG, Rubenstein J, Taylor A, et al: Radiation risk to the urologist during endourologic procedures, and a new shield that reduces exposure. Urology 1996;48:624-627.

Gupta M, Bellman GC, Smith AD: Massive hemorrhage from renal vein injury during percutaneous renal surgery: Endourological management. J Urol 1997;157:795-797.

Kessaris DN, Smith AD: Fluoroscopic access in prone position with C arm. In Smith AD (ed): Controversies in Endourology. Philadelphia, WB Saunders, 1995, pp 10-17.

Kidd CR, Conlin MJ: Ureteroscopically assisted percutaneous renal access. Urology 2003;61:1244-1245.

Ku JH, Lee SW, Jeon HG, et al: Percutaneous nephrostomy versus indwelling ureteral stents in the management of extrinsic ureteral obstruction in advanced malignancies: Are there differences? Urology 2004;64:895-899.

Niles BS, Smith AD: Techniques of antegrade nephrostomy. Atlas Urol Clin North Am 1996;4:1.

Pardalidis N, Smith AD: Complications of stone treatment. In Smith AD (ed): Controversies in Endourology. Philadelphia, WB Saunders, 1995, pp 179-185.

Patel U, Hussain FF: Percutaneous nephrostomy of nondilated renal collecting systems with fluoroscopic guidance: Technique and results. Radiology 2004;233:226-233.

Paul EM, Marcovich R, Lee BR, et al: Choosing the ideal nephrostomy tube. BJU Int 2003;92:672-677.

Sampaio FJB: Surgical anatomy of the kidney. In Smith AD (ed): Smith's Textbook of Endourology. St. Louis, Quality Medical, 1996, pp 153-184.

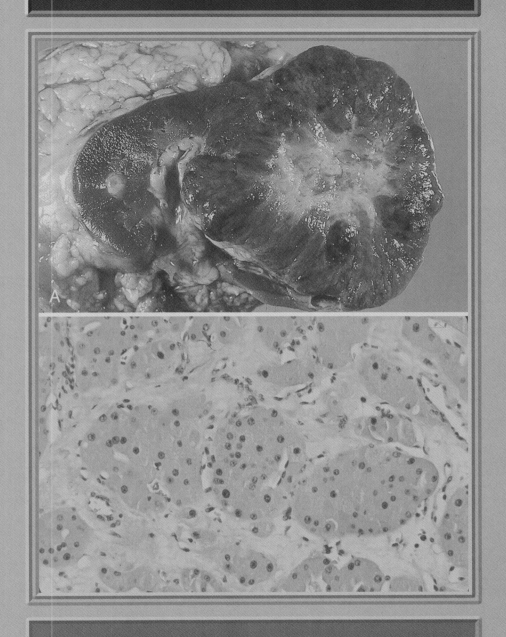

# NEOPLASMS OF
# THE UPPER
# URINARY TRACT

# 47 Renal Tumors

STEVEN C. CAMPBELL, MD, PhD •
ANDREW C. NOVICK, MD • RONALD M. BUKOWSKI, MD

**HISTORICAL CONSIDERATIONS**

**CLASSIFICATION**

**RADIOGRAPHIC EVALUATION OF RENAL MASSES**

**BENIGN RENAL TUMORS**

**RENAL CELL CARCINOMA**

**TREATMENT OF LOCALIZED RENAL CELL CARCINOMA**

**TREATMENT OF LOCALLY ADVANCED RENAL CELL CARCINOMA**

**TREATMENT OF METASTATIC RENAL CELL CARCINOMA**

**OTHER MALIGNANT RENAL TUMORS**

## HISTORICAL CONSIDERATIONS

The introduction of nephrectomy and other subsequent surgical interventions for renal diseases provided the clinical information and histopathologic insight that form the basis of current concepts of renal tumors. Harris (1882) reported on 100 surgical extirpations of the kidney, a sufficient number to permit analysis of clinical, surgical, and pathologic features of renal disorders that require surgery. The first documented nephrectomy was apparently accomplished in 1861 by Wolcott, who operated with the mistaken assumption that the tumor mass was a hepatoma. In 1867, Spiegelberg removed a kidney incidentally in the course of excising an echinococcus cyst. The first planned nephrectomy was performed by Simon in 1869 for persistent ureteral fistula, and this patient survived with cure of the fistula. One year later (1870), the first planned nephrectomy in the United States was successfully accomplished by Gilmore in Mobile, Alabama, for treatment of atrophic pyelonephritis and persistent urinary tract infection (Glenn, 1980).

With surgical intervention, tissue became available to pathologists for histologic interpretation. Unfortunately, such interpretation was not always accurate, and there were often serious professional differences of opinion. According to Carson (1928), the first accurate gross description of kidney tumors dates to 1826, with Konig's observations. In 1855, Robin examined solid tumors apparently arising in the kidney and concluded that renal carcinoma arose from renal tubular epithelium. This interpretation was confirmed by Waldeyer in 1867. Unfortunately, theoretical and practical considerations of renal tumors were confused by Grawitz (1883), who contended that such apparent renal tumors arose from adrenal rests within the kidney. He introduced the terminology *struma lipomatodes aberrata renis* as descriptive nomenclature for the tumors of clear cells that he believed were derived from the adrenal glands. He based his conclusions not only on the fatty content of the tumors, analogous to that seen in the adrenal glands, but also on the location of the tumors beneath the renal capsule, the approximation to the adrenal glands, the lack of similarity of the cells to uriniferous tubules, and the demonstration of amyloid similar to that seen with adrenal degeneration.

This histogenetic concept was adopted by subsequent investigators, and pathologists of the era readily embraced the idea that renal tumors truly arose from the adrenal glands. In 1894, Lubarch endorsed the idea of a suprarenal origin of renal tumors, and the term *hypernephroid tumors,* indicating origin above the kidneys, was advocated by Birch-Hirschfeld (Birch-Hirschfeld and Doederlein, 1894). This semantic and conceptual mistake led to the introduction of the term *hypernephroma,* which predominates in the literature describing parenchymal tumors of primary renal origin.

Weichselbaum and Greenish (1883) described renal adenomas containing both papillary and alveolar cell types. Some clarification of the histopathology of renal tumors is derived from the work of Albarran and Imbert (1903), and the four-volume contribution of Wolff (1883), written between 1883 and 1928, adds further historical significance to the understanding of renal tumors today (Glenn, 1980).

**The modern era has brought an appreciation that renal cell carcinoma includes a number of distinct subtypes derived from the various parts of the nephron, each with a unique genetic basis and tumor biology** (Linehan et al, 2003). **Other major advances in the past several decades have included the introduction of radical nephrectomy followed by a trend toward nephron-sparing surgery and, more recently, a variety of minimally invasive approaches** (Robson, 1963; Uzzo and Novick, 2001; Abreu and Gill, 2003; Herr, 2005). **One common theme that has persisted is that renal cell carcinoma remains primarily a surgical disease— it is still considered the paradigm of the chemorefractory tumor,** and although immune-based therapies have shown promise, overall response rates remain low (Negrier et al, 2002; Milowsky and Nanus, 2003). Recent efforts have focused on multimodal strategies in addition to a variety of novel therapeutic approaches (Flanigan et al, 2004). Unfortunately, the incidence of renal cell carcinoma is gradually increasing, and despite a trend toward earlier detection, mortality rates remain high.

# CLASSIFICATION

The most comprehensive classification of renal tumors is that offered by Deming and Harvard (1970) in a previous edition of this text. They established 11 categories of renal tumors, with multiple subdivisions embracing virtually every known new growth that may involve the kidney, including various renal cystic disorders as well as perirenal retroperitoneal tumors that may involve the kidney secondarily. This classification is reproduced here (Table 47–1) because it provides the most succinct presentation of renal tumors yet retains accuracy and inclusiveness.

An effort must be made, however, to provide a classification that is both complete and uncomplicated, embracing all the lesions that predispose an individual to a renal mass or new growth. Such a simplified classification was proposed by Glenn (1980) (Table 47–2). Benign tumors include those of the renal capsule (such as fibroma), renal parenchymatous adenomas, vascular tumors, various cystic lesions and dysplasias, heteroplastic and mesenchymal tumors, and even various hydronephroses. Tumors of the renal pelvis, not a primary consideration here, include benign papillomas as well as transitional, squamous, and adenocarcinomatous malignant neoplasms. Pararenal tumors are those that involve the kidney by extension and invasion, and they may be either benign or malignant. Embryonic tumors include predominantly nephroblastoma (Wilms' tumor) and the embryonic or mesotheliomatous carcinomas and sarcomas of childhood.

## Table 47–1. Classification of Renal Tumors

| | |
|---|---|
| *Tumors of the Renal Capsule* | *Neurogenic Tumors* |
| Fibroma | Neuroblastoma |
| Leiomyoma | Sympathicoblastoma |
| Lipoma | Schwannoma |
| Mixed | |
| | *Heteroplastic Tissue Tumors* |
| *Tumors of the Mature Renal Parenchyma* | Adipose |
| Adenoma | Smooth muscle |
| Adenocarcinoma | Adrenal rests |
|   Hypernephroma | Endometriosis |
|   Renal cell carcinoma | Cartilage |
|   Alveolar carcinoma | Bone |
| | *Mesenchymal Derivatives* |
| *Tumors of the Immature Renal Parenchyma* | Connective tissue |
| Nephroblastoma (Wilms' tumor) |   Fibroma |
| Embryonic carcinoma |   Fibrosarcoma |
| Sarcoma | Osteogenic sarcoma |
| | Adipose tissue |
| *Epithelial Tumors of the Renal Pelvis* |   Lipoma |
| Transitional cell papilloma |   Liposarcoma |
| Transitional cell carcinoma | Fibrosarcoma |
| Squamous cell carcinoma | Muscle tissue |
| Adenocarcinoma |   Leiomyoma |
| |   Leiomyosarcoma |
| *Cysts* | |
| Solitary | *Pararenal or Perirenal Solid Tumors* |
| Unilateral multiple | Lipoma |
| Calyceal | Sarcoma |
| Pyogenic | Liposarcoma |
| Calcified | Fibrosarcoma |
| Tubular ectasia | Lymphangiosarcoma |
| Tuberous sclerosis | Cancer |
| Cystadenoma | Teratoma |
| Papillary cystadenoma | Lymphoblastoma |
| Dermoid | Neuroblastoma |
| Pararenal or perirenal cysts | Hodgkin's disease |
|   Hydrocele renalis | |
|   Lymphatic | *Secondary Tumors* |
|   Wolffian | Cancer |
| Malignant | Sarcoma |
| | Blastoma |
| *Vascular Tumors* | Granuloma |
| Hemangioma | Thymoma |
| Hamartoma | Testicular |
| Lymphangioma | Renal |

| Table 47-2. | Simplified Classification of Renal Tumors |
|---|---|

*Benign Tumors*

Renal capsule
Renal parenchyma
Vascular tumors
Cystic lesions, dysplasia, hydronephrosis
Heteroplastic, mesenchymal tumors
True oncocytoma

*Tumors of Renal Pelvis*

Benign papilloma
Transitional and squamous cell carcinomas, adenocarcinomas

*Pararenal Tumors*

Benign
Malignant

*Embryonic Tumors*

Nephroblastoma (Wilms' tumor)
Embryonic, mesotheliomatous tumors
Sarcomas

*Nephrocarcinoma*

Renal cell carcinoma, adenocarcinoma, "hypernephroma"
Papillary cystadenocarcinoma

*Other Malignant Tumors*

Primary: mesenchymal, hemangiopericytoma, myeloma
Secondary: metastatic lesions

**Table 47-3. Renal Masses Classified by Pathologic Features**

| Malignant | Benign | Inflammatory |
|---|---|---|
| Renal cell carcinoma | Simple cyst | Abscess |
| Conventional | Angiomyolipoma | Focal pyelonephritis |
| Chromophilic | Oncocytoma | Xanthogranulomatous |
| Chromophobic | Renal adenoma | pyelonephritis |
| Collecting duct | Metanephric adenoma | Infected renal cyst |
| Urothelium based | Cystic nephroma | Tuberculosis |
| Transitional cell | Mixed epithelial- | Rheumatic granuloma |
| carcinoma | stromal tumor | |
| Squamous cell | Reninoma (JG cell | |
| carcinoma | tumor) | |
| Adenocarcinoma | Leiomyoma | |
| Sarcoma | Fibroma | |
| Leiomyosarcoma | Hemangioma | |
| Liposarcoma | Vascular | |
| Angiosarcoma | Renal artery | |
| Hemangiopericytoma | aneurysm | |
| Malignant fibrous | Arteriovenous | |
| histiocytoma | malformation | |
| Synovial sarcoma | Pseudotumor | |
| Osteogenic sarcoma | | |
| Clear cell sarcoma | | |
| Rhabdomyosarcoma | | |
| Wilms' tumor | | |
| Primitive | | |
| neuroectodermal | | |
| tumor | | |
| Carcinoid | | |
| Lymphoma | | |
| Leukemia | | |
| Metastases | | |
| Invasion by adjacent | | |
| neoplasm | | |

Wilms' tumor, the common renal malignant neoplasm of childhood, is addressed elsewhere in this book, as are neuroblastoma, renal cystic disorders, and primary retroperitoneal tumors. Nephrocarcinoma is the generic category that includes adult renal parenchymatous malignant neoplasms, primarily the classic hypernephroma and papillary adenocarcinoma. The category of other malignant tumors comprises relatively rare mesenchymal malignant neoplasms, such as the various sarcomas, hemangiopericytomas, infiltrative malignant neoplasms such as myeloma, and secondary or metastatic malignant neoplasms manifesting within the renal substance. Oncocytoma has been added to Glenn's original classification in the category of benign tumors.

**Another approach has been taken by Barbaric (1994) in which renal masses are classified on the basis of pathologic features (malignant, benign, or inflammatory) (Table 47-3) or radiographic appearance (simple cysts, complex cysts, fatty tumors, and others) (Table 47-4).** We have updated this classification scheme on the basis of current knowledge about the distinct subtypes of renal cell carcinoma and recent advances in our understanding of the various benign and malignant tumors of the kidney. This classification is practical and should assist in the differential diagnosis of renal masses.

## RADIOGRAPHIC EVALUATION OF RENAL MASSES

Several radiographic modalities are currently available for detection and evaluation of renal masses, each with relative strengths and weaknesses (Davidson et al, 1997; Zagoria, 2000; Israel and Bosniak, 2003a). A systematic method is necessary to ensure complete evaluation of suspected renal masses, given

the large differential diagnosis and considerable overlap between benign and malignant renal lesions (Fig. 47-1; see Table 47-4).

Intravenous pyelography remains a commonly used test for the evaluation of hematuria; in the past, it was often the first test that indicated a renal mass in many patients. However, the lack of sensitivity and specificity of intravenous pyelography for the detection of parenchyma tumors is well documented. In particular, intravenous pyelography may miss small anterior or posterior lesions that do not distort the collecting system or the contour of the kidney. **When a renal mass is identified on intravenous pyelography, features suggestive of malignancy include calcification within the mass, increased tissue density, irregularity of the margin, and distortion of the collecting system** (Zagoria, 2000).

**When a renal mass is identified by intravenous pyelography, unless the mass has features suggestive of malignancy, ultrasonography should be the next study performed because it is noninvasive, accurate, and relatively inexpensive** (Davidson et al, 1997). Ultrasonography is reliable for differentiation of solid tissue from fluid and can establish the diagnosis of a simple renal cyst. **Strict sonographic criteria for simple cysts have been defined and include a smooth cyst wall, a round or oval shape without internal echoes, and through-transmission with strong acoustic shadows posteriorly.** If these criteria are met, observation is sufficient in an asymptomatic patient.

**Table 47-4. Renal Masses Classified by Radiographic Appearance**

| Simple Cystic | Complex Cystic | Fatty Tumors | All Others |
|---|---|---|---|
| Cyst | Cystic nephroma | Angiomyolipoma | Renal cell carcinoma |
| Multiple cysts | Cystic renal cell | Lipoma | Sarcomas |
| Peripelvic cysts | carcinoma | Liposarcoma | Lymphoma, leukemia |
| Calyceal | Hemorrhagic cyst | | Metastases |
| diverticulum | Infected cyst | | Lobar nephronia |
| Hydronephrosis | Renal abscess | | Abscess |
| | Septated cyst | | Tuberculosis |
| | Hydrocalyx | | Xanthogranulomatous |
| | Cystic Wilms' tumor | | pyelonephritis |
| | Mixed epithelial-stromal tumor | | Urothelium-based tumors |
| | Vascular | | Transitional cell carcinoma |
| | Renal artery aneurysm | | Squamous cell carcinoma |
| | Arteriovenous malformation | | Adenocarcinoma |
| | Tuberculosis | | Wilms' tumor |
| | | | Oncocytoma |
| | | | Renal adenoma |
| | | | Metanephric adenoma |
| | | | Reninoma (JG cell tumor) |
| | | | Leiomyoma |
| | | | Fibroma |
| | | | Hemangioma |
| | | | Carcinoid |
| | | | Primitive neuroectodermal tumor |

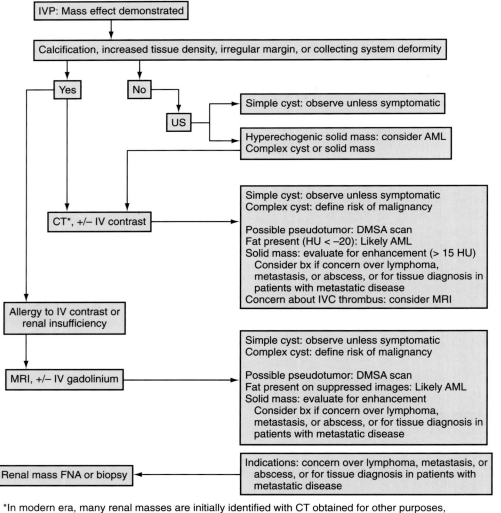

**Figure 47-1.** Algorithm for radiographic evaluation of renal masses. IVP, intravenous pyelography; US, ultrasonography; AML, angiomyolipoma; CT, computed tomography; DMSA, dimercaptosuccinic acid; MRI, magnetic resonance imaging; FNA, fine-needle aspiration.

*In modern era, many renal masses are initially identified with CT obtained for other purposes, and in this setting a dedicated CT of the kidneys should be considered.

In evaluating complicated renal cysts, important sonographic features include thickness and contour of the cyst wall, number and thickness of any septa, presence of any calcifications, density of the renal cyst fluid, and presence of solid components. Sonography is helpful in suggesting the fat content of an angiomyolipoma (AML) by its characteristic increased echogenicity (Nelson and Sanda, 2002). **A renal mass that is not clearly a simple cyst by strict ultrasound criteria should be evaluated further with computed tomography (CT) scanning.** Percutaneous needle puncture of cysts with aspiration of cystic fluid for cytology and biochemical studies and further injection of the cyst cavity with contrast medium for radiographic evaluation were often performed in the past. However, these assessments are frequently nondiagnostic and have thus largely been abandoned.

**A dedicated (thin-slice) renal CT scan remains the single most important radiographic test for delineating the nature of a renal mass.** CT scanning, with and without the administration of contrast material, is necessary to take full advantage of the contrast enhancement characteristics of highly vascular renal parenchymal tumors (Davidson et al, 1997; Zagoria, 2000). **In general, any renal mass that enhances with intravenous administration of contrast material on CT scanning by more than 15 Hounsfield units (HU) should be considered a renal cell carcinoma (RCC) until proved otherwise** (Fig. 47–2) (Hartman et al, 2004). **Solid masses that also have substantial areas of negative CT attenuation numbers (below −20 HU) indicative of fat are diagnostic of AMLs** (Nelson and Sanda, 2002). In approximately 10% of solid renal masses, CT findings are indeterminate, and additional testing or surgical exploration is needed to establish a definitive diagnosis. On occasion, CT scanning demonstrates an enhancing renal segment that is isodense with the remainder of the kidney, suggestive of a renal pseudotumor. Renal pseudotumors may be due to a hypertrophied column of Bertin, renal dysmorphism, or an unusually shaped kidney. In this situation, the diagnosis of a pseudotumor can be confirmed by isotope renography with technetium-labeled dimercaptosuccinic acid or glucoheptonate (Fig. 47–3). These isotope studies demonstrate an area of increased density if the mass is a pseudotumor and an area of decreased density if the mass is a cyst or solid tumor (Israel and Bosniak, 2003b).

Magnetic resonance imaging (MRI) was initially employed only infrequently for evaluation of renal masses because routine sequences were not specific or sensitive enough to characterize these lesions. However, with the introduction of gadolinium-enhanced MRI, its use has increased significantly (Pretorius et al, 2000). **A basic consideration in the evaluation of a renal mass is that for such a mass to be considered malignant, it must enhance with the intravenous administration of contrast material. Such enhancement can now be determined equally well by magnetic resonance angiography with intravenous gadolinium-labeled diethylenetriaminepentaacetic acid.** On T1-weighted scans before and after administration of gadolinium, enhancement (vascularity) of the mass is detected (Fig. 47–4). This technique is most helpful in patients for whom iodinated contrast medium is contraindicated because of significant renal insufficiency or severe allergy.

Renal arteriography has a limited role in the diagnostic evaluation of renal masses. In equivocal cases, the presence or

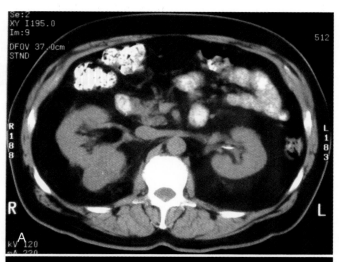

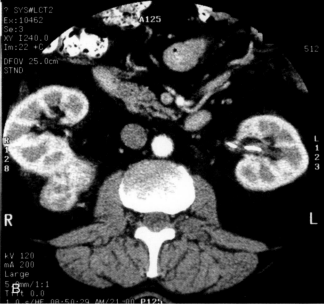

**Figure 47–2.** **A,** CT scan without administration of contrast material shows solid, right posterior renal mass. **B,** After administration of the contrast agent, CT scan shows that the mass enhances more than 20 Hounsfield units and is thus highly suggestive of renal cell carcinoma. This mass was excised and confirmed to be a clear cell renal cell carcinoma. (Courtesy of Dr. Terrence Demos, Maywood, Illinois.)

absence of neovascularity may help establish the diagnosis of RCC. However, approximately 20% to 25% of RCCs are angiographically indistinct, even though most of these tumors are not truly avascular and demonstrate contrast enhancement by 10 to 25 HU on CT scanning.

**Fine-needle aspiration or biopsy has traditionally been of limited value in the evaluation of renal masses.** Although there have been relatively few reports of spread of tumor by needle puncture of an RCC, this is an invasive study that occasionally causes perirenal bleeding. The major problems with this technique are the high incidence of false-negative biopsy findings in patients with renal malignant neoplasms and the difficulty differentiating renal oncocytoma from the common eosinophilic variants of RCC with limited pathologic material

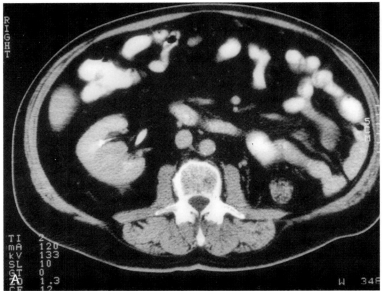

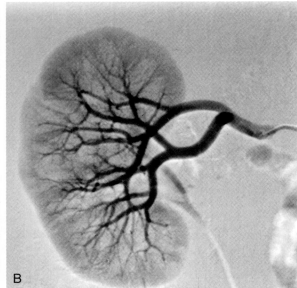

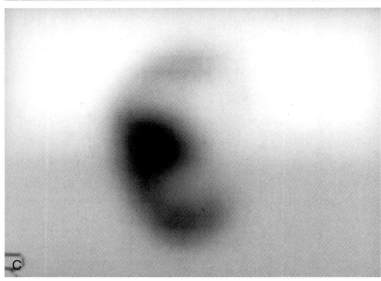

**Figure 47–3. A,** CT scan with administration of contrast material shows isodense hilar mass in solitary right kidney. **B,** Right renal arteriography shows no neovascularity. **C,** Glucoheptonate isotope renal scan shows increased density of mass indicative of hypertrophied column of Bertin.

(Herts and Baker, 1995; Schatz and Lieber, 2003). **The primary indications for needle aspiration or biopsy of a renal mass are when a renal abscess or infected cyst is suspected and when RCC must be differentiated from metastatic malignant disease or renal lymphoma** (Herts and Remer, 2000). More recently, fine-needle aspiration or biopsy has been reevaluated; several series suggested an improved sensitivity and specificity, particularly when it is combined with molecular analysis (Truong et al, 1999; Wood et al, 1999; Lechevallier et al, 2000; Richter et al, 2000; Hara et al, 2001; Liu and Fanning, 2001; Caoili et al, 2002; Rybicki et al, 2003). In one such study, fine-needle aspiration was combined with molecular analysis for *MN/CA9* gene expression that is characteristic of conventional RCC, yielding promising results (Li et al, 2004).

The differentiation between a benign renal cyst and a cystic RCC remains one of the more common and difficult problems in renal imaging (Balci et al, 1999; Harada et al, 2002; Kausik

et al, 2002). When a complicated renal cyst is identified, determination of its benign or malignant nature is based on evaluation of the wall of the lesion; its thickness and contour; the number, contour, and thickness of any septa; the amount, character, and location of any calcifications; the density of fluid in the lesion; and the margination of the lesion and the presence of solid components. **Bosniak has developed a useful classification scheme that divides renal cystic lesions into four categories that are distinct from one another in terms of the likelihood of malignancy** (Bosniak, 1997). Category I lesions are uncomplicated, simple, benign cysts of the kidney that are straightforward to diagnose on ultrasonography, CT scan, or MRI scan. These are by far the most common renal cystic lesions, and in the absence of associated symptoms, no treatment is necessary.

**Category II lesions are minimally complicated cysts** that are benign but have some radiologic findings that cause concern (Fig. 47–5). These lesions include septated cysts, cysts

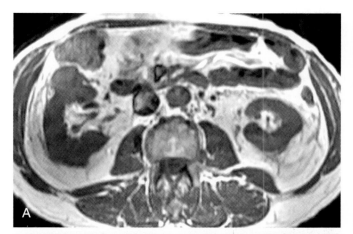

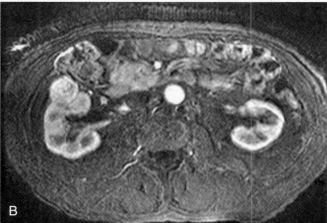

**Figure 47–4.** **A,** Magnetic resonance scan of kidneys without administration of gadolinium suggests anterior right renal mass. **B,** After intravenous administration of gadolinium-labeled diethylenetriaminepentaacetic acid, MRI shows enhancement of this mass indicative of malignancy. (Courtesy of Dr. Terrence Demos, Maywood, Illinois.)

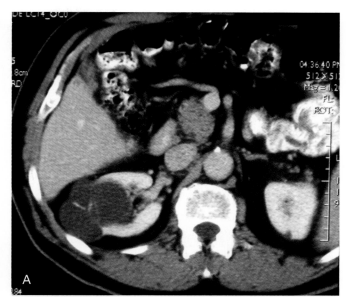

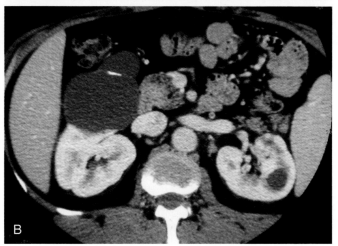

**Figure 47–5.** Bosniak's class II renal cysts. **A,** CT scan shows right renal cyst with thin internal septation. **B,** CT scan in another patient shows relatively thin, curvilinear calcification in the septa of the wall of right renal cyst. (Courtesy of Dr. Terrence Demos, Maywood, Illinois.)

with minimal calcium in the wall or septum, infected cysts, and hyperdense (high-density) cysts (Bosniak, 1997). Hyperdense cysts are benign lesions that contain old, degenerated, or clotted blood; therefore, the CT attenuation of their contents is increased (>20 HU). Classic hyperdense renal cysts are small (<3 cm), round, and sharply marginated and do not enhance after the administration of contrast material (Fig. 47–6). **The risk of malignancy for category II renal cysts is 0% to 5%, and these lesions should be observed with periodic renal imaging** (Kausik, 2002; Israel and Bosniak, 2003b).

**Category III lesions are more complicated renal cysts that are indeterminate and cannot be confidently distinguished from malignant neoplasms** (Kausik, 2002). **The radiographic features include an irregular margin, thickened septa, and thick irregular calcification** (Fig. 47–7). In the absence of a mitigating factor such as renal trauma or infection, surgical exploration is usually indicated in young patients of good operative risk. About 50% of these lesions are malignant; the remainder prove to be benign multiloculated, hemorrhagic, or densely calcified cysts (see Table 47–4). Fine-needle aspiration of complex cysts is rarely performed because of concern about sampling error and tumor cell spillage.

However, one report suggested that analysis of cyst fluid for expression of matrix metalloproteins might differentiate benign lesions from malignant, which express elevated levels of matrix metalloproteinases 2 and 9 (Harada et al, 2002).

**Category IV lesions have large cystic components; irregular, shaggy margins; and, most important, some solid enhancing portions that provide a definitive diagnosis of malignancy** (Fig. 47–8) (Bosniak, 1997; Israel and Bosniak, 2003c). Category IV lesions are invariably cystic RCCs that, if localized, require surgical treatment.

For radiographically detected solid renal masses, the differential diagnosis is extensive and includes conditions such as RCC, renal adenoma, oncocytoma, AML, transitional cell carcinoma, metastatic tumor, abscess, infarct, vascular malformation, and renal pseudotumor (see Table 47–4). The diagnosis of most of these lesions can be established on the basis of the clinical presentation and the characteristic

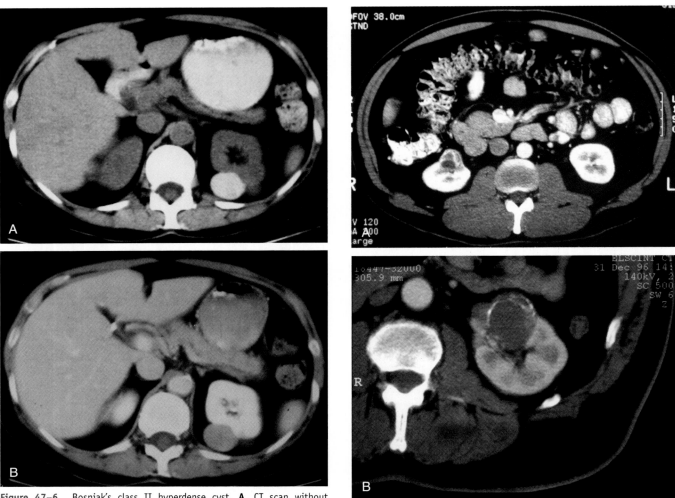

**Figure 47–6.** Bosniak's class II hyperdense cyst. **A,** CT scan without administration of contrast material shows small, smooth-walled, high-density left renal cyst. **B,** CT scan after administration of contrast material shows no enhancement of the cyst. This is an extreme example of a hyper-dense cyst. (Courtesy of Dr. Terrence Demos, Maywood, Illinois.)

**Figure 47–7.** Bosniak's class III cysts. **A,** CT scan shows complex right renal cyst with thick and irregular septa and inhomogeneous character. **B,** CT scan shows somewhat thick-walled, complex left renal cyst also exhibiting irregular calcification and moderate heterogeneity. (Courtesy of Dr. Terrence Demos, Maywood, Illinois.)

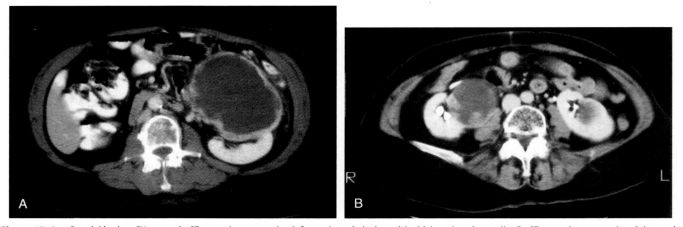

**Figure 47–8.** Bosniak's class IV cysts. **A,** CT scan shows complex left renal cystic lesion with thick, enhancing walls. **B,** CT scan shows complex right cystic lesion with enhancing nodular areas and inhomogeneity. Both lesions proved to be renal cell carcinoma. (Courtesy of Dr. Terrence Demos, Maywood, Illinois.)

radiographic features, occasionally combined with endourologic studies or needle biopsy of the mass. **However, it is not possible to reliably distinguish RCC, adenoma, and oncocytoma with current diagnostic techniques. Approximately 10% to 20% of small, solid, CT-enhancing renal masses with features suggestive of RCC prove to be benign after surgical excision** (Silver et al, 1997). Although oncocytoma is a benign tumor, associated RCC in the same or the opposite kidney has been found in as many as 30% of patients (Licht, 1995).

## KEY POINTS: COMPLEX RENAL CYSTS

| Bosniak Classification | Radiographic Features | Risk of Malignancy | Management |
|---|---|---|---|
| I | Water density | None | Only if symptomatic |
|  | Homogeneous |  | Surveillance not necessary |
|  | No septa |  |  |
|  | No calcification |  |  |
|  | No enhancement |  |  |
| II | Thin septa | 0%-5% | Periodic surveillance |
|  | Thin, curvilinear calcification |  |  |
|  | No enhancement |  |  |
|  | Hyperdense lesion with no enhancement | 0%-5% | Periodic surveillance |
| III | Thick or irregular septa | 50% | Surgical excision |
|  | Thick or irregular calcification |  |  |
|  | Mild to moderate heterogeneity |  |  |
|  | No enhancement |  |  |
| IV | Thick walls or nodular areas | 75%-90% | Surgical excision |
|  | Marked heterogeneity |  |  |
|  | Enhancement |  |  |

## BENIGN RENAL TUMORS

Benign renal tumors may arise from cortical tissue (e.g., adenoma, oncocytoma) or from the various mesenchymal derivatives within the parenchyma or capsule of the kidney. Differentiation from malignant renal masses by radiographic or clinical means can be challenging if not impossible in some instances, and some benign renal masses can also achieve clinical significance by growth to large size that leads to flank pain or, more acutely, by hemorrhage. **Women are more likely to have benign histologic types, and in one series, young women (<45 years) with renal masses suggestive of RCC were found to have benign pathologic processes in 36% of cases** (Eggener et al, 2004).

## Benign Renal Cyst

**Simple cysts, the most common benign renal lesions, represent more than 70% of all asymptomatic renal masses.**

**Benign renal cysts are more common in men than in women (2:1 ratio) and can be solitary or multiple** (Terada et al, 2002). **Prevalence increases with age, and renal cysts can be found in more than 50% of patients older than 50 years** (Kissane, 1976). Longitudinal study of more than 1700 individuals demonstrated a mean growth rate of 2.8 mm per year, and these lesions tended to grow more rapidly in younger individuals (Terada et al, 2002).

Renal cysts are readily identified and characterized radiographically, as previously described. They may, however, grow to large size and become symptomatic, and various minimally invasive techniques for drainage or sclerosis have been described. One common outpatient protocol uses percutaneous drainage and sclerosis with 95% alcohol, resulting in successful ablation of the cyst cavity in more than 90% of cases (Hanna and Dahniya, 1996). One relative contraindication to percutaneous management is peripelvic location adjacent to the renal vessels; in this circumstance, laparoscopic approaches may be safer (Hemal, 2001; Roberts et al, 2001). However, all patients should be advised that multiple treatment sessions may be required to achieve complete ablation and that chronic pain may persist.

## Renal Cortical Adenoma

**Small, evidently benign, solid renal cortical lesions have been found at autopsy with an incidence of 7% to 23% and have been designated renal adenomas** (Licht, 1995; Renshaw, 2002; Minor et al, 2003). The majority of such lesions are solitary; 25% are multicentric (Corwin, 1940). Incidence increases with the patient's age, and renal adenomas have also been found to be more common in patients with von Hippel–Lindau disease and acquired renal cystic disease associated with end-stage renal failure (Grantham and Levine, 1985; Solomon and Schwartz, 1988). The male-to-female ratio is 3:1, slightly higher than that for RCC, and an association with tobacco use has also been reported (Bennington et al, 1968; Xipell, 1971). The overwhelming majority of renal adenomas remain asymptomatic, and most are undetectable radiographically because of size less than 1 cm. A large ultrasound screening effort designed to detect renal tumors in more than 40,000 asymptomatic adults yielded an incidence of adenoma of significantly less than 1% (Tosaka et al, 1990).

**The histologic appearance of a typical renal adenoma is a small, well-circumscribed lesion characterized by uniform basophilic or eosinophilic cells with monotonous nuclear and cellular characteristics, often arranged in a tubulopapillary or purely papillary growth pattern** (Fig. 47–9). Many lesions classified as renal adenoma exhibit trisomy of chromosomes 7 and 17 and thus share cytogenetic features with papillary RCC (Minor et al, 2003). Although most pathologists would be comfortable making this diagnosis in an autopsy setting, a pathologic diagnosis of renal adenoma is rendered much less often after surgical excision or biopsy because most pathologists believe that there are no reliable histopathologic, ultrastructural, or immunohistochemical criteria to distinguish benign from malignant renal epithelium–derived neoplasms (Cooper and Waisman, 1973; Bennington, 1987; Licht, 1995). Tumor size has historically been evoked in an effort to make this important but difficult differentiation. In his original autopsy series, Bell found 1 of

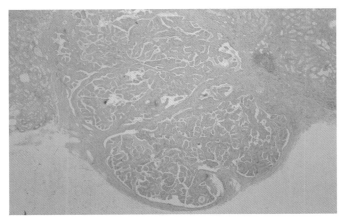

**Figure 47–9.** Small renal cortical adenoma demonstrating typical papillary architecture.

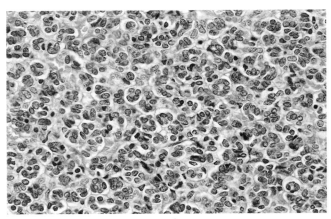

**Figure 47–10.** Classic metanephric adenoma with small, intensely basophilic cells arranged in an acinar pattern.

38 renal cortical tumors smaller than 3 cm in diameter to be associated with metastases, in contrast to 70 of 106 tumors larger than 3 cm (Bell, 1938). A subsequent update revealed that 3 of 62 tumors smaller than 3 cm had metastasized, reflecting the unpredictable behavior of RCC (Bell, 1950). **Nevertheless, the "3-cm rule" remained pervasive in the urologic literature for many years, despite the documented 5% incidence of metastasis and Bell's precaution that he could not make a definitive distinction between adenoma and carcinoma on the basis of histologic analysis.** Many pathologists continue to use tumor size for the classification of renal adenoma. Thoenes and colleagues (1986), in their provocative reassessment of the histologic classification of renal tumors, defined renal adenoma as tumors with nuclear grade 1 and diameter of more than 1 cm. Most authors agree that larger tumors or those with clear cell histology or any degree of cytologic atypia should not be classified as renal cortical adenoma.

**The diagnosis of renal adenoma remains controversial; many believe that all solid renal epithelium–derived masses are potentially malignant and should be treated as such** (Renshaw, 2002; Minor et al, 2003). **Renal exploration and wedge resection or other ablative therapies should be strongly considered for all such clinically evident lesions, with appropriate consideration of the patient's age, comorbidities, and other relevant factors.**

## Metanephric Adenoma

In 1995, Davis and colleagues reported 50 cases of an unusual and novel renal mass lesion with distinctive histologic features and a benign clinical course despite occasional symptomatic presentation and large tumor size (Davis et al, 1995a). In this series, mean tumor size was 5.5 cm (range, 0.3 to 15 cm), and 22 patients presented with flank pain, gross hematuria, or a palpable mass. Six additional patients presented with polycythemia, and hypercalcemia has also been reported in association with this tumor type, which was designated *metanephric adenoma* (Davis et al, 1995a; Mahoney et al, 1997; Kuroda et al, 2003b). The male-to-female ratio in the series of Davis and colleagues was 2:1, but a female predominance has been reported in other series (Jones et al, 1995). Incidental

presentation is most common, and peak incidence is in the fifth decade of life (Renshaw, 2002).

On microscopic examination, these tumors consist of very small, often highly basophilic epithelial cells that form small acini and occasionally tubular or papillary structures within a predominantly acellular stroma (Fig. 47–10). Davis and colleagues (1995a) argued that metanephric adenoma might be histologically related to epithelial Wilms' tumor because they believed that it exhibited histologic similarities to the metanephric, hamartomatous elements of nephroblastomatosis. Along these lines, it is interesting to note that many of these tumors exhibit evidence of regression in the form of scarring or calcification. In addition, Muir and colleagues (2001) have shown positive staining for the Wilms' tumor protein WT-1 and an immunohistochemical staining profile that suggests a histogenetic relationship to Wilms' tumor. An alternative theory for the origin of metanephric adenoma was proposed by Brown and associates (1997), who found gain of chromosomes 7 and 17 by fluorescent in situ hybridization in 8 of 11 of these tumors. These findings suggest a clonal neoplastic disorder potentially related to papillary RCC, but others have argued that this series may have been contaminated by inclusion of some cases of papillary RCC, which can be difficult to differentiate from metanephric adenoma (Brown et al, 1997; Renshaw, 2002; Brunelli et al, 2003a). Pesti and colleagues (2001) have described a putative tumor suppressor gene for metanephric adenoma at chromosome 2p13.

**Only one case of metastasis has been described in association with classic metanephric adenoma, into a regional lymph node, and death related to this entity has not been reported** (Renshaw, 2002). **However, Picken and colleagues (2001) have described malignant stromal elements associated with a metanephric neoplasm of the kidney in a 21-year-old woman who died of progressive cancer, and they have proposed that there may be a spectrum of metanephric tumors that includes rare, aggressive variants. Given these concerns about the true natural history of metanephric adenomas, its rarity, and the lack of clinical, radiographic, or cytologic means to establish a definite diagnosis, metanephric adenoma remains primarily a pathologic diagnosis. Most if not all patients require surgical excision because of concern about malignancy.**

# Oncocytoma

The diagnosis of renal oncocytoma first gained acceptance as a distinct clinicopathologic entity after a report of 13 cases by Klein and Valensi in 1976. Since then, several reports have further characterized this essentially benign renal histiotype, which represents 3% to 7% of all solid renal masses (Lieber et al, 1987; Davis et al, 1991; Licht et al, 1993; Lieber, 1993; Amin et al, 1997b; Perez-Ordonez et al, 1997; Dechet et al, 1999; Chao et al, 2002a; Kuroda et al, 2003d). In gross appearance, these tumors are light brown or tan, homogeneous, and well circumscribed, but like most renal tumors, they are not truly encapsulated (Fig. 47–11). A central scar is commonly found, but prominent necrosis or hypervascularity is lacking. On microscopic examination, uniform round or polygonal eosinophilic cells predominate, most commonly arranged in a nested or organoid growth pattern (Farrow, 1997; Renshaw, 2002).

**Ultrastructurally, oncocytomas are packed with numerous large mitochondria, which contributes to their distinctive staining characteristics** (Farrow, 1997). Although most oncocytomas are cytologically low grade, prominent nucleoli are not uncommon, and conspicuous pleomorphism or cellular atypia has been reported in 12% to 30% of cases. Such findings are generally accepted within the diagnosis of renal

oncocytoma if all other diagnostic criteria are met (Amin et al, 1997b; Perez-Ordonez et al, 1997). Other atypical features include hemorrhage, which is found in 20% to 30% of cases, and extension into the perinephric fat, which has been reported in 11% to 20% of cases (Amin et al, 1997b; Perez-Ordonez et al, 1997). In light of this information, it is interesting to note that Rainwater and colleagues (1986) found that 50% of their oncocytomas were nondiploid and that more than 20% were frankly aneuploid. The acceptance of tumors with such atypical features as oncocytomas has not been complete, and despite the almost uniformly benign course for these lesions, some pathologists prefer to reserve the diagnosis of oncocytoma for tumors exhibiting only low-grade characteristics.

Common cytogenetic findings for oncocytomas include loss of the first and Y chromosomes, loss of heterozygosity on chromosome 14q, and rearrangements at 11q13 (Crotty et al, 1992; Schwerdtle et al, 1997; Chao et al, 2002a; Polascik et al, 2002; Lindgren et al, 2004). In contrast, abnormalities of chromosomes 3, 7, and 17 are rarely found in association with oncocytomas (Minor et al, 2003). The genetic alterations observed with renal oncocytomas are thus characteristic and distinct from those described for the various subtypes of RCC. Oncocytoma and chromophobe cell carcinoma are both derived from the distal tubules, and histologic similarities do exist, particularly for the eosinophilic variant of chromophobic carcinoma (Weiss et al, 1995; Renshaw, 2002). A transitional histiotype has been described in the Birt-Hogg-Dubé syndrome, in which renal oncocytomas, chromophobe RCC, and distinctive cutaneous lesions commonly develop (Minor et al, 2003). These transitional neoplasms exhibit features of both oncocytoma and chromophobe RCC, and some authors have hypothesized that there may be a spectrum of tumors spanning both of these histiotypes (Chao et al, 2002a; Linehan et al, 2003; Minor et al, 2003; Pavlovich et al, 2005). Nevertheless, the distinctive cytogenetics and immunohistochemical staining profiles suggest an individuality of these tumor types (Leroy et al, 2000; Chu and Weiss, 2001; Chao et al, 2002a).

**Unfortunately, most renal oncocytomas cannot be differentiated from malignant RCC by clinical or radiographic means** (Chao et al, 2002a). Mean age at presentation and male-to-female predominance are similar for oncocytoma and RCC, and although oncocytomas are more likely to be asymptomatic (58% to 83%), most RCCs are now also diagnosed incidentally (Lieber et al, 1987; Davis et al, 1991; Licht et al, 1993; Lieber, 1993; Amin et al, 1997b; Perez-Ordonez et al, 1997; Dechet et al, 1999). Mean tumor size for oncocytomas has ranged from 4 to 6 cm in most series—again, similar to RCC. The central stellate scar observed on CT scan and the spoke-wheel pattern of feeding arteries observed on angiography can suggest the diagnosis of oncocytoma, but extended experience has proved these findings to be unreliable and of poor predictive value (Levine and Huntrakoon, 1983; Davidson et al, 1993; Licht et al, 1993; Licht, 1995). The nuclear agent technetium sestamibi is evidently retained in mitochondria, and Gormley and colleagues (1996) reported increased uptake in oncocytomas compared with RCC, AML, and renal cysts. The biologic rationale for nuclear scanning is therefore strong, but these results have not been confirmed, and their clinical utility has not been defined. Characteristic

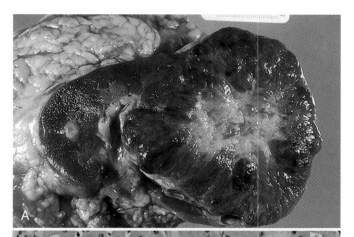

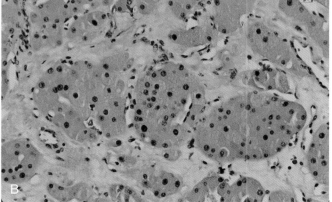

**Figure 47–11.** **A,** Bivalved renal oncocytoma demonstrating central scar. **B,** Oncocytoma with large eosinophilic cells arranged in distinct nests.

findings for oncocytoma on MRI include well-defined capsule, central stellate scar, and distinctive intensities on T1 and T2 images, all of which can suggest the diagnosis but cannot be considered definitive (Harmon et al, 1996). **Renal fine-needle aspiration or biopsy is compromised by difficulty distinguishing oncocytoma from the granular forms of conventional RCC or the eosinophilic variants of chromophobe or chromophilic RCC** (Weiss et al, 1995). Another factor limiting the utility of fine-needle aspiration or biopsy is the well-documented coexistence of RCC and oncocytoma in the same lesion or at other locations in the same kidney, which has been reported in 7% to 32% of cases (Davis et al, 1991; Licht et al, 1993; Licht, 1995).

**Given these uncertainties about a preoperative diagnosis, most authors have emphasized the need to treat these tumors aggressively with thermal ablation, partial nephrectomy, or radical nephrectomy, depending on the clinical circumstances** (Licht, 1995). A nephron-sparing approach is clearly desirable if oncocytoma is suspected and if tumor size and location are amenable, given the propensity of these tumors for multicentricity, bilaterality, and metachronous recurrence, all of which have been reported in 4% to 13% of cases (Lieber et al, 1987; Davis et al, 1991; Licht et al, 1993; Lieber, 1993; Amin et al, 1997b; Perez-Ordonez et al, 1997; Dechet et al, 1999; Tickoo et al, 1999; Minor et al, 2003). A thermal ablative approach unfortunately condemns the patient to long-term surveillance, given uncertainty about the diagnosis of oncocytoma, even if a biopsy was performed before ablation. Nephron-sparing approaches are also preferred in patients with familial renal oncocytomatosis, which was identified by Weirich and colleagues (1998) at the National Cancer Institute. They described five families with this syndrome, which exhibits an increased propensity for bilaterality, multicentricity, and early age at onset. The molecular genetics responsible for the development of this syndrome have not been defined.

## Angiomyolipoma

**AML is a benign clonal neoplasm consisting of varying amounts of mature adipose tissue, smooth muscle, and thick-walled vessels** (Tamboli et al, 2000; Nelson and Sanda, 2002; Bissler and Kingswood, 2004). This tumor type, which is found in 0.3% of all autopsies and in 0.13% of the population screened by ultrasonography, was originally identified by Fischer in 1911 and was designated AML by Morgan in 1951 (Eble, 1998). AML is most likely derived from the perivascular epithelioid cells, and its growth may be hormone dependent, as suggested by its female predominance and rarity before puberty. **Approximately 20% to 30% of AMLs are found in patients with tuberous sclerosis syndrome (TS), an autosomal dominant disorder characterized by mental retardation, epilepsy, and adenoma sebaceum, a distinctive skin lesion** (Eble, 1998; Neumann et al, 1998; Tamboli et al, 2000; Minor et al, 2003; Lendvay and Marshall, 2003). Penetrance for each of these traits is far from complete, and approximately 50% of patients with TS develop AMLs. Among this group, mean age at presentation is 30 years, and a female-to-male predominance of 2:1 has been observed (Lendvay and Marshall, 2003). In contrast, of the 70% to 80% of patients with AML who do not have TS, a more pronounced female

predominance is found, and most patients present later in life, during the fifth or sixth decade (Eble, 1998; Neumann et al, 1998). AML in TS is more likely to be bilateral and multicentric, and a tendency toward accelerated growth rates and symptomatic presentation has been reported (Neumann et al, 1998; Lendvay and Marshall, 2003).

Previously, most AMLs were diagnosed only after symptomatic presentation, and much of the data correlating tumor size and symptoms were derived from this era. **Massive retroperitoneal hemorrhage from AML, also known as Wunderlich's syndrome,** has been found in up to 10% of patients and represents the most significant and feared complication (Oesterling et al, 1986; Eble, 1998). Common signs or symptoms include flank pain, hematuria, palpable mass, and hypovolemic shock, which can be fatal if it is not identified and promptly treated (Oesterling et al, 1986; Steiner et al, 1993; Eble, 1998). Pregnancy appears to increase the risk of hemorrhage from AML, a factor that can influence clinical decision-making (Eble, 1998). More subtle presentations of AML include anemia and hypertension, and more than 50% of AMLs are now found incidentally because of the more prevalent use of abdominal imaging for the evaluation of a wide variety of nonspecific complaints (Lemaitre et al, 1997).

A number of distinctive radiographic findings associated with AML allow a definitive diagnosis in the majority of cases (Fig. 47–12). CT scan has been the most useful and reliable modality for this purpose (Lemaitre et al, 1997). **The presence of even a small amount of fat within a renal lesion on CT scan (confirmed by a value of −20 HU or lower) virtually excludes the diagnosis of RCC and is considered diagnostic of AML** (Jinkazi et al, 1997; Lemaitre et al, 1997; Bosniak et al, 1998). All five reported cases of RCC containing fat density have also been calcified, and even these extremely rare exceptions can thus be identified because calcification has never been reported within an AML (Henderson et al, 1997; Lemaitre et al, 1997; Roy et al, 1998). In 14% of AMLs, fat cannot be identified with CT, presumably related to a reduced proportion of mature adipose tissue, and a definite diagnosis cannot be made (Lemaitre et al, 1997; Kim et al, 2004; Milner et al, 2005). Patients with tumors with indeterminate features or calcifications should be managed proactively because the likely diagnosis in most such cases is RCC. The typical but not diagnostic finding of AML on ultrasonography is a well-circumscribed, highly echogenic lesion, often associated with shadowing (Siegel et al, 1996; Lemaitre et al, 1997). The finding of shadowing should suggest an AML rather than a small, echogenic RCC, which rarely shadows (Siegel et al, 1996). Aneurysmal dilation is found in 50% of AMLs when they are visualized by angiography and can also suggest the diagnosis (Lemaitre et al, 1997). Finally, fat-suppressed images on MRI may be helpful in difficult cases or when CT is contraindicated for other reasons.

Although a benign status is well accepted for AML, extrarenal occurrences have been reported in the hilar lymph nodes, retroperitoneum, and liver, and direct extension into the venous system has been reported in 21 cases (Eble, 1998; Turker Koksal et al, 2000; Gogus et al, 2001; Nelson and Sanda, 2002; Bissler and Kingswood, 2004). A uniformly benign clinical course in such cases has argued in favor of multicentric origin rather than metastasis. Many AMLs exhibit regions of

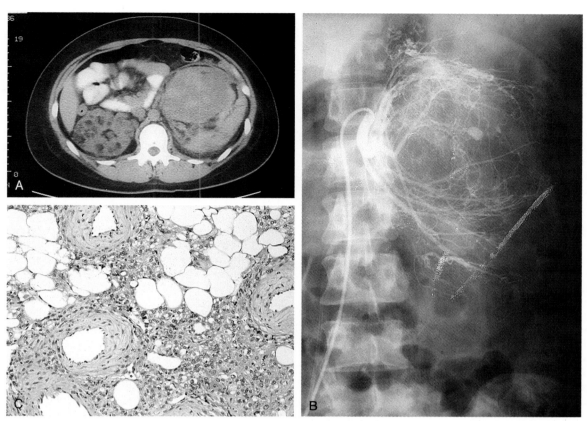

**Figure 47–12.** **A,** CT scan demonstrates large bilateral renal angiomyolipomas in a patient with tuberous sclerosis. **B,** Renal angiogram shows increased vascularity and aneurysmal dilation characteristic of angiomyolipoma. **C,** Typical microscopic appearance of angiomyolipoma with admixture of mature adipose tissue, smooth muscle, and thick-walled blood vessels.

cellular atypia, and the pathologic differential diagnosis can include a number of subtypes of sarcoma, including fibrosarcoma, leiomyosarcoma, and liposarcoma, depending on the relative amounts of adipose, vascular, or smooth muscle tissue present (Wang et al, 2002). **Positive immunoreactivity for HMB-45, a monoclonal antibody raised against a melanoma-associated antigen, is characteristic for AML and can be used to differentiate AML from sarcoma in such cases** (Eble, 1998). Nevertheless, one should be aware that there have been two reports of high-grade and eventually lethal leiomyosarcoma arising within an AML, and Christiano and colleagues (1999) have described a highly pleomorphic AML that was associated with the development of multiple pulmonary nodules, the majority of which stained positive for HMB-45 (Ferry et al, 1991). They believed that this case represented a malignant transformation of AML, which—if it does occur—must be exceedingly rare. More recently, a malignant epithelioid variant of AML has been described that can metastasize (Cibas et al, 2001; Nelson and Sanda, 2002; Saito et al, 2002; Yamamoto et al, 2002; Bissler and Kingswood, 2004). Such malignant variants of AML are extremely rare; the overwhelming majority pursue a benign course.

**The management of AML must take into account the natural history and, in particular, the risk of hemorrhage. In general, most symptomatic AMLs have been relatively large, and most studies in the literature have focused on a**

**4-cm cut point** (Nelson and Sanda, 2002). On the basis of an extensive literature review, Oesterling and coworkers (1986) reported that 82% of patients with AMLs larger than 4 cm in diameter were symptomatic, with 9% in hemorrhagic shock at the time of presentation; in contrast, patients with smaller tumors were symptomatic 23% of the time. Echoing these findings, Dickinson and colleagues (1998) reported that all 18 patients with AMLs smaller than 4 cm in their series were asymptomatic, whereas 7 of 13 with AMLs of 4 to 8 cm and 5 of 6 with tumors larger than 8 cm required intervention, primarily related to pain or bleeding. These observations have been confirmed and extended by a number of investigators (Blute et al, 1988; Steiner et al, 1993; Lemaitre et al, 1995; De Luca et al, 1999). Steiner and colleagues (1993) reported that patients with AMLs larger than 4 cm were symptomatic 52% of the time, with 30% requiring surgical intervention, whereas patients with smaller tumors never required surgery and were asymptomatic 76% of the time. Although it was primarily retrospective, limited follow-up with a mean of 4 years was available for 24 patients with 28 AMLs in this series. Interval growth was documented in 6 of 13 tumors with diameter of more than 4 cm and in 4 of 15 tumors smaller than 4 cm. A slower growth rate and a low risk of hemorrhage for smaller tumors was also supported by Kennelly and colleagues (1994), who observed 17 AMLs with tumor size of less than 4 cm for a mean of 3.8 years. They reported that only one such tumor demonstrated interval growth, and even it remained asymptomatic for 18 years; no patients in this series required intervention. Similarly, De Luca and colleagues (1999) studied 32 incidentally discovered AMLs smaller than 5 cm in diameter and found that 92% remained asymptomatic and unchanged in size. **Multicentric AMLs and those in patients with TS represent a special group that has demonstrated increased growth rates of approximately 20% per year, in contrast with a mean growth rate of 5% per year for solitary AMLs** (Steiner et al, 1993; Nelson and Sanda, 2002; Harabayashi et al, 2004).

Although a large prospective study providing long-term outcomes of AMLs of various sizes has not yet been reported, the information reviewed here allows one to propose guidelines for management. **In general, asymptomatic, smaller AMLs, which by convention have been those with tumor diameter of less than 4 cm, can be observed expectantly, with repeated evaluation and imaging at 6- to 12-month intervals to define the growth rate and clinical significance. Intervention should be considered for larger tumors, particularly if the patient is symptomatic, taking into account the patient's age, comorbidities, and other related factors. Women of childbearing age and patients with limited access to surveillance or to emergency care should also consider a proactive approach** (Nelson and Sanda, 2002). **A nephron-sparing approach, by either selective embolization or partial nephrectomy, is clearly preferred in patients with small AMLs requiring intervention because of symptoms, in patients with TS or multicentric AML, and in patients for whom preservation of renal function is at issue.** The feasibility and efficacy of partial nephrectomy in patients with AML are established, with preservation of renal function achieved even in patients with large lesions and a solitary kidney (Fazeli-Matin and Novick, 1998). Selective embolization is now often chosen as the preferred modality, and data of 76 patients in six series have documented long-term success in most cases (Nelson and Sanda, 2002; Harabayashi et al, 2004). However, 17% of patients experienced recurrence of symptoms or hemorrhage, and most of these required repeated embolization (Hamlin et al, 1997; Han et al, 1997; Nelson and Sanda, 2002). The overall complication rate with embolization in these series was 10% and included abscess formation or sterile liquefaction of the tumor requiring percutaneous drainage or surgical intervention. These data highlight the need for extended follow-up after selective embolization (Nelson and Sanda, 2002).

**Most patients with acute or potentially life-threatening hemorrhage require total nephrectomy if it is explored; and if a patient has TS, bilateral disease, preexisting renal insufficiency, or other medical or urologic disease that could affect renal function in the future, selective embolization should be considered. In such circumstances, selective embolization can temporize and in many cases prove definitive.**

## Cystic Nephroma

**Cystic nephroma is a characteristic renal lesion with a bimodal age distribution and a benign clinical course** (Tamboli et al, 2000; Minor et al, 2003; Truong et al, 2003). **A wide variety of synonyms have been used in the past, most notably multiloculated cystic nephroma, but the more simple terminology is now preferred.** In gross appearance, these lesions are well circumscribed and encapsulated and consist of multiple, noncommunicating, fluid-filled spaces partitioned by septa. On microscopic examination, the cysts are lined by cuboidal epithelial cells arranged in a hobnailed pattern, and the intervening stroma is characteristic for its pronounced cellularity (Fig. 47–13). The age distribution is bimodal, occurring primarily in the first 2 to 3 years of life and again primarily in the fourth and fifth decades (Madewell et al, 1983; Upadhyay and Neely, 1989; Castillo et al, 1991; Kajani et al, 1993; Murphy et al, 1994). **A male predominance is observed in children, and a female predominance is observed in adults. Children tend to present with an asymptomatic abdominal mass detected on routine physical examination, whereas symptomatic presentation with abdominal pain, hematuria, urinary tract infection, or hypertension is more common in adults** (Madewell et al, 1983; Castillo et al, 1991; Minor et al, 2003). Familial cases are rare, and most cystic nephromas are unilateral and unifocal.

Most cystic nephromas are centrally located, and distinctive radiographic findings have been described but are not universally present and cannot be considered diagnostic (Minor et al, 2003). **All cystic nephromas are, by definition, multilocular, and almost all qualify as a complex renal cyst suspicious for malignancy, specifically class III-IV in Bosniak's classification scheme** (Madewell et al, 1983). Curvilinear calcification and herniation into the renal pelvis occur in 10% to 20% of cases and can suggest the diagnosis of cystic nephroma, but this must be proved pathologically (Gettman and Segura, 1999). Most lesions are avascular or hypovascular on angiography, but hypervascular variants have been reported, and enhancement within the septa on CT or MRI is not uncommon (Madewell et al, 1983). **At present, there is no reliable clinical or radiographic means to differentiate cystic nephroma from cystic RCC in adults or from cystic Wilms' tumor in children.**

**Most cystic nephromas in adults have traditionally been managed with radical nephrectomy because of the concern for malignancy.** Now many such lesions are being managed with partial nephrectomy, and this is certainly a reasonable option when tumor size and location are amenable and when the diagnosis of cystic nephroma is suspected on the basis of clinical and radiologic characteristics. Most children continue to be managed by radical nephrectomy related to concern for cystic Wilms' tumor, which is much more common in this population (Vujanic et al, 2000). Although this condition is generally considered a benign neoplasm, sarcomatous stromal elements have been reported in some adult patients with cystic nephroma, and foci of nephroblastoma, including blastemal, epithelial, or mesenchymal elements alone or in combination, have been reported in children with this diagnosis (Tamboli et al, 2000). Careful microscopic inspection for such potentially malignant features is indicated because metastases from the sarcomatous stromal elements were reported in three adults in the Armed Forces Institute of Pathology series (Madewell et al, 1983). However, classification of such tumors as cystic nephromas is controversial; many pathologists prefer to exclude lesions with such ominous features.

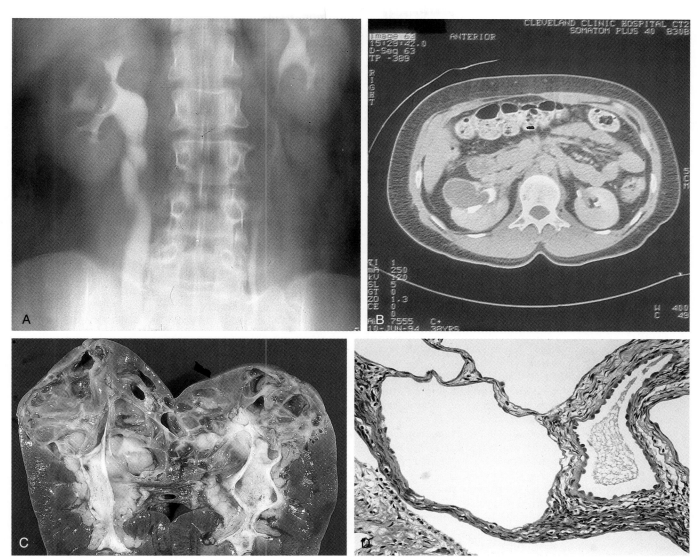

**Figure 47–13.** **A,** Intravenous urogram demonstrates indentation of the midportion of the right renal pelvis, suggesting a mass effect. **B,** CT scan reveals a multiloculated cystic mass herniating into the collecting system. **C,** Nephrectomy specimen harboring a multiloculated mass that protrudes into the collecting system. **D,** Cystic nephroma illustrating diagnostic findings: multiple cysts lined by hobnail-shaped epithelial cells and intervening stroma notable for increased cellularity.

## Mixed Epithelial Stromal Tumor of the Kidney

Mixed epithelial stromal tumor of the kidney (MESTK) has only recently been described, and its essential characteristics are still being defined (Adsay et al, 2000; Beiko et al, 2001; Pierson et al, 2001; Minor et al, 2003). As the name implies, these tumors are composed of a mixture of epithelial and stromal elements that form solid and cystic growth patterns. The epithelial elements tend to be scattered among the stromal cells, occasionally organized into large cysts lined by eosinophilic cells, often with a hobnail appearance. The stromal component can range from scarlike fibrous tissue to interlacing fascicles suggestive of leiomyoma, and these cells tend to stain strongly for desmin and smooth muscle actin (Adsay et al, 2000). **A gross cystic appearance is common, and a complex cystic pattern is predominant radiographi-**

cally, typically classifying as Bosniak III-IV lesion (Adsay et al, 2000). It was originally thought that most tumors previously classified as adult mesoblastic nephroma were actually MESTK, but molecular analysis refutes this (Pierson et al, 2001). **The current theory is that MESTK may be related to cystic nephroma and that there may be a spectrum of lesions that lies between these two entities.**

MESTK occurs primarily in perimenopausal women, a large proportion of whom are receiving estrogen therapy; in Adsay's series, the only man with MESTK had a long history of androgen deprivation therapy for prostate cancer (Adsay et al, 2000). **In addition, most MESTKs stain positively for estrogen and progesterone receptors, further suggesting that the hormonal milieu may play an important role in the pathogenesis of this tumor type.** Mean age at presentation in Adsay's series was 56 years; six patients presented symptomatically and six were incidentally discovered (Adsay et al,

2000). A preoperative diagnosis of MESTK should be considered in perimenopausal women receiving hormone therapy, and a nephron-sparing approach is preferred if this diagnosis is suspected. In Adsay's series, all patients were managed with radical nephrectomy and have remained cancer free at mean follow-up of 49 months (Adsay et al, 2000). A benign clinical course is also supported by other reports in the literature, but further data are required to define the natural history and malignant potential of MESTK.

## Leiomyoma

**Renal leiomyoma, a slow-growing, benign neoplasm, can arise from the capsule or peripelvic tissues and, less often, from the renal vein** (Uchida et al, 1980; Wells et al, 1981; Steiner et al, 1989; O'Brien et al, 1992; Mohammed et al, 1999; Tamboli et al, 2000). These lesions are found at autopsy with a frequency of 4.2% to 5.2%, but only a minority are discovered clinically (Minor et al, 2003). In the past, most of these tumors presented symptomatically with pain, hematuria, or gastrointestinal complaints, and many were large and palpable on routine abdominal examination. Of the 30 renal leiomyomas reported as of 1989 and reviewed by Steiner and colleagues (1989), the average size was 12.3 cm, and the largest tumor was 57 cm in diameter.

Now, renal leiomyomas are diagnosed with increased frequency; most are small and asymptomatic, representing a significant change in clinical presentation. Radiographic appearance can be highly variable, ranging from purely cystic to complex cystic or purely solid (Steiner et al, 1989). Some renal leiomyomas enhance with contrast material, and in most cases, differentiation from RCC is not possible by clinical or radiographic means (Steiner et al, 1989; Inoue et al, 2000; Rao et al, 2001). **A clearly capsular origin may suggest the diagnosis but cannot be considered diagnostic.** On microscopic examination, leiomyomas are spindle cell tumors with rare mitoses and no pleomorphism. Increased mitotic rate or significant pleomorphism should suggest a diagnosis of leiomyosarcoma, the malignant counterpart. Large lesions have traditionally been managed with radical nephrectomy, but nephron-sparing approaches should be considered for peripherally located lesions, particularly if they are small and apparently derived from the capsule.

## Other Benign Tumors

**Other benign renal tumors, all of which are rare, are derived primarily from the various mesenchymal derivatives present within the kidney and its environs. These include virtually all conceivable histiotypes, such as fibromas, lipomas, lymphangiomas, and hemangiomas** (Tamboli et al, 2000; Minor et al, 2003). Small medullary fibromas (1 to 7 mm in diameter) are commonly found at autopsy, usually escaping radiologic detection. Ten clinically evident cases have been reported, most presenting with hematuria or filling defect on urography or retrograde pyelography (Ohkawa et al, 1993). Renal lipoma can grow to a large size, typically presents with pain or hematuria, and must be differentiated from liposarcoma (Robertson and Hand, 1941; Safak et al, 1989; Mydlo et al, 1991). Renal lipomas can easily be confused with AMLs on the basis of clinical and radiographic evaluation, but most are confined to the renal capsule, and microscopic features and staining for HMB-45 should allow differentiation of these entities. Average age at presentation of the 20 patients described with lymphangioma cavernosum of the kidney was 34 years, and as with most of these lesions, a female predominance was reported (Joost et al, 1977; Nakai et al, 1999; Honma et al, 2002). Solitary fibrous tumor has also been described in the kidney, with two case reports (Wang et al, 2001; Magro et al, 2002). All these lesions are best managed with wide surgical excision, given the possible presence of sarcomatous elements. In most cases, this has required radical nephrectomy, although partial nephrectomy is a reasonable option, depending on the clinical circumstances.

**Another rare but fascinating benign renal tumor is the renin-secreting juxtaglomerular tumor, or reninoma** (Martin et al, 2001; Rubenstein et al, 2002). First described by Robertson and colleagues (1967), this tumor is actually a specialized form of a hemangiopericytoma, specifically derived from the juxtaglomerular cell. Strong immunostaining for factor VIII and factor VIII–related antigens is characteristic and confirms derivation from endothelial cell lineage (Sanfillipo et al, 1982). Most are small (<3 cm), solitary, and hypovascular and are well visualized by ultrasonography or CT scan as a solid parenchymal mass (Dunnick et al, 1983; Tanabe et al, 2001). **Clinical presentation is dominated by hypersecretion of renin and includes hypertension and hypokalemia and associated symptoms such as polydipsia, polyuria, myalgia, and headaches** (Dunnick et al, 1983). Most patients are in the third or fourth decade of life; predominantly females are affected. Almost all patients may be cured with surgical excision, which typically leads to normalization of blood pressure and resolution of other related symptoms (Dunnick et al, 1983; Schoenfeld et al, 1991). The first case of a juxtaglomerular cell tumor demonstrating metastatic behavior was recently reported (Duan et al, 2004). The 70 previously reported cases of this tumor type all exhibited benign clinical course, suggesting that this is an uncommon occurrence. The diagnosis of juxtaglomerular tumor should be considered in any patient with pronounced hyperreninemia and hypertension in whom renal artery disease has been rigorously excluded.

## RENAL CELL CARCINOMA
## Incidence

RCC, which accounts for 2% to 3% of all adult malignant neoplasms, is the most lethal of the urologic cancers. Traditionally, more than 40% of patients with RCC have died of their cancer, in contrast with the 20% mortality rates associated with prostate and bladder carcinomas (Landis et al, 1999; Pantuck et al, 2001b). Approximately 31,000 new diagnoses of RCC are made each year in the United States, and 11,900 patients die of disease (Landis et al, 1999; Pantuck et al, 2001b). Overall, 8.9 new cases are diagnosed per 100,000 population per year, with a male-to-female predominance of 3:2 (Landis et al, 1999). This is primarily a disease of the elderly patient, with typical presentation in the sixth and seventh decades of life (Pantuck et al, 2001b). Incidence rates are 10% to 20% higher in African Americans for unknown reasons (Chow et al, 1999). The majority of cases of RCC are believed

## KEY POINTS: BENIGN RENAL TUMORS

| Tumor Type | Distinctive Features |
|---|---|
| Benign renal cyst | Typically asymptomatic |
| | Water density and homogeneous |
| Renal cortical adenoma | Commonly found at autopsy |
| | Difficult to differentiate from RCC—controversial |
| | More commonly found with papillary RCC and in end-stage renal failure |
| | Working definition: small (<1 cm), well circumscribed, low grade, and papillary |
| Metanephric adenoma | Incidental presentation, peak incidence is fifth decade |
| | May be related to Wilms' tumor or papillary RCC |
| | Cannot be differentiated from RCC by clinical or radiographic means |
| Oncocytoma | Typically tan and homogeneous in gross appearance |
| | Eosinophilic with nested or organoid appearance |
| | Multiple mitochondria on electron microscopy |
| | Common loss of chromosomes 1 and Y; alterations of 14q and 11q13 |
| | Seen along with chromophobe RCC in Birt-Hogg-Dubé syndrome |
| | Cannot be differentiated from RCC by clinical or radiographic means |
| Angiomyolipoma | Sporadic or associated with tuberous sclerosis syndrome |
| | Fat density found with CT; hyperechoic on ultrasonography |
| | Stains positive for HMB-45 |
| | Typically intervene if symptomatic or large (>4 cm) |
| | Options for management: selective embolization, partial nephrectomy |
| Cystic nephroma | Middle-aged women or young males |
| | Radiographically presents as Bosniak III-IV cyst |
| | Herniation into collecting system can be clinical clue |
| | Difficult to differentiate from cystic malignancy |
| | Partial nephrectomy if diagnosis suspected |
| MESTK | Perimenopausal women, typically with history of hormonal manipulation |
| | Often stains for estrogen or progesterone receptors |
| Leiomyoma | Often arises from the capsule |
| Reninoma | Derived from juxtaglomerular cells |
| | Secretes renin; associated with hypertension and hypokalemia |

the 1980s, and this was observed in all ethnic and both sex groups. They reported that the incidence of advanced tumors per unit population has also increased and that although the proportion of advanced tumors has decreased, the mortality rate per unit population has been negatively affected (Chow et al, 1999; Hock et al, 2002). This suggests that a deleterious change in tumor biology may have occurred during the past several decades, perhaps related to environmental factors such as diet, tobacco use, and exposure to other carcinogens. The mortality rates from RCC would presumably be even higher if not for the trend toward incidental detection (Chow et al, 1999; Pantuck et al, 2001b; Hock et al, 2002; Parsons et al, 2002).

RCC in childhood is uncommon, representing only 2.3% to 6.6% of all renal tumors in children (Castellanos et al, 1974; Chan et al, 1983; Freedman et al, 1996; Asanuma et al, 1999; Broecker, 2000). Mean age at presentation in children is 8 to 9 years, and the incidence is similar in boys and in girls. Although Wilms' tumor is much more common in younger children, RCC is as common as Wilms' tumor during the second decade of life. RCC in children and young adults is more likely to exhibit papillary histology and a predilection for locally advanced, high-grade disease, and unfavorable histologic subtypes have also been reported (Freedman et al, 1996; Renshaw et al, 1999; Sanchez-Ortiz et al, 2004b). TFE3 protein overexpression, which correlates with the presence of *ASPL-TFE3* and *PRCC-TFE3* gene translocation events involving the X and first chromosomes, is relatively common in children and young adults with RCC and is unique to this population (Heimann et al, 2001). The clinical significance of TFE3 protein overexpression is not well defined, although preliminary data suggest that these tumors may show differential sensitivity to certain chemotherapeutic agents (Argani et al, 2002; Heimann et al, 2001; Perot et al, 2003; Bruder et al, 2004). Most studies suggest that stage for stage, children and young adults with RCC may respond better to surgical therapy, and a number of long-term survivors have been reported after radical nephrectomy and lymphadenectomy for lymph node–positive disease (Freedman et al, 1996; Asanuma et al, 1999; Abou El Fettouh et al, 2002; Geller et al, 2004; Sanchez-Ortiz et al, 2004b). An aggressive surgical approach with formal lymphadenectomy has thus been recommended at the time of radical nephrectomy when RCC is suspected in children or young adults (Freedman et al, 1996; Asanuma et al, 1999; Geller et al, 2004).

## Etiology

RCCs were traditionally thought to arise primarily from the proximal convoluted tubules, and this is probably true for most clear cell and papillary variants. However, more recent data suggest that the other histologic subtypes of RCC, such as chromophobe and collecting duct RCC, are derived from the more distal components of the nephron (Störkel, 1996; Oyasu, 1998; Pantuck et al, 2001a).

**The only generally accepted environmental risk factor for RCC is tobacco exposure, although the relative associated risks have been modest, ranging from 1.4 to 2.5 compared with controls.** All forms of tobacco use have been implicated, and risk increases with cumulative dose or pack-years (Kantor, 1977; La Vecchia et al, 1990; McLaughlin et al, 1995;

to be sporadic; the National Cancer Institute estimates that only 4% are familial.

**The incidence of RCC has increased since the 1970s by an average of 3% per year for whites and 4% per year for African Americans,** largely related to the more prevalent use of ultrasonography and CT scan for the evaluation of a variety of abdominal or gastrointestinal complaints (Chow et al, 1999). This trend has correlated with an increased proportion of incidentally discovered and localized tumors and with improved 5-year survival rates for patients with this stage of disease (Konnak and Grossman, 1985; Thompson and Peek, 1988; Kessler et al, 1994; Pantuck et al, 2001b; Parsons et al, 2001). However, other factors must also be at play because Chow and colleagues (1999) have documented a steadily increasing mortality rate from RCC per unit population since

McLaughlin and Lipworth, 2000; Moyad, 2001; Dhote et al, 2004; Lindblad, 2004). Relative risk is directly related to duration of smoking and begins to fall after cessation, further supporting a cause-and-effect relationship (La Vecchia et al, 1990; McLaughlin et al, 1995; Parker et al, 2003b). A particularly high risk for RCC has been reported in smokers who also chew tobacco (Goodman et al, 1986). The relative risk associated with tobacco use in women has approached normality in some of the more highly powered case-control studies, suggesting that smoking may not be as important a risk factor for RCC in women (McLaughlin et al, 1995).

**Although a number of potential etiologic factors have been identified in animal models, including viruses, lead compounds, and more than 100 chemicals such as aromatic hydrocarbons, no specific agent has been definitively established as causative in human RCC** (Bennington and Beckwith, 1947; Kantor, 1977). The potential role of trichloroethylene exposure has been actively investigated; some studies showed relative risks ranging from twofold to sixfold, but others have argued that inherent biases may account for these results (Vamvakas et al, 2000; Mandel, 2001; Moyad, 2001; Bruning et al, 2003). However, Brauch and colleagues (1999) have reported an increased incidence and unique pattern of von Hippel–Lindau gene (*VHL*) mutations in this population, which would argue in favor of a causative role for this compound. Slightly increased relative risks for RCC have been reported for workers in the metal, chemical, rubber, and printing industries and those exposed to asbestos or cadmium, but the data are not particularly convincing (Kolonel, 1976; Pesch et al, 2000; Hu et al, 2002; Dhote et al, 2004; Lindblad, 2004; Moyad, 2001). One report described a 13.1-fold increased risk of RCC for workers in factories that synthesize vitamins A and E, but this has not yet been validated (Richard et al, 2004).

Case-control studies have shown that RCC is more common among individuals with long-standing obesity, low socioeconomic status, and urban background, although the causative factors have not been defined (Kantor, 1977; Goodman et al, 1986; Muscat et al, 1995; Yuan et al, 1998). The typical modern Western diet (high in fat and protein and low in fruits and vegetables), increased intake of dairy products, and increased consumption of coffee or tea have been associated with RCC, but the relative risks have been modest, and conflicting data are available in most instances (Yu et al, 1986; Lindblad et al, 1997; Moyad, 2001; Handa and Kreiger, 2002; Dhote et al, 2004; Lindblad, 2004). A family history of RCC may also be a factor; one study showed a relative risk of 2.9 for individuals with a first- or second-degree relative with RCC (Gago-Dominguez et al, 2001).

Other potential iatrogenic causes include Thorotrast (which was used as a contrast agent in the past), radiation therapy, and antihypertensive medications; but again, the relative risks are low (Wenz, 1967; Romanenko et al, 2000). Vogelzang and colleagues (1998) reported four cases of RCC developing in a previously irradiated field, and a slightly increased incidence of RCC has been reported in men who received retroperitoneal irradiation for the treatment of testicular cancer. Survivors of childhood Wilms' tumor also appear to be at increased risk for RCC, possibly related to prior radiation therapy or chemotherapy (Cherullo et al, 2001). A 1.4- to 2-fold increased risk of RCC has been reported

in patients with hypertension, and diuretics, particularly thiazides, and other antihypertensive medications have been implicated (Mellemgaard et al, 1992; Hiatt et al, 1994; McLaughlin et al, 1995; Yuan et al, 1998; Shapiro et al, 1999; Chow et al, 2000; Schmieder et al, 2000; Grossman et al, 2001; Mimi and Ross, 2001; Moyad, 2001; Gago-Dominguez et al, 2002; Dhote et al, 2004; Lindblad, 2004). However, in some studies, the relative risk associated with diuretic use has evaporated when multivariate analysis has been applied, suggesting that the real risk factor is hypertension (Shapiro et al, 1999). An increased incidence of RCC is also observed in patients with end-stage renal failure and certain familial syndromes such as TS, as discussed later (Ishikawa et al, 1990; Bjornsson et al, 1996; Neumann et al, 1998).

## Familial Renal Cell Carcinoma and Molecular Genetics

Since the early 1990s, significant advances have been made in our understanding of the molecular genetics of RCC. Novel familial syndromes of RCC have been identified, and the tumor suppressor genes and oncogenes contributing to the development of both sporadic and familial forms of this malignant disease have been characterized (Table 47–5) (Linehan et al, 1995; Zbar et al, 1995; Schmidt et al, 1997; Weirich et al, 1998; Choyke et al, 2003; Linehan et al, 2003; Pavlovich et al, 2003; Zimmer and Iliopoulos, 2003; Pavlovich and Schmidt, 2004). The impact of this new information should not be underestimated because it has changed our perceptions about RCC. **We now, more than ever, recognize the distinct nature of the various histologic subtypes of RCC, and advances in molecular genetics have contributed to a major revision in the histologic classification of this malignant neoplasm** (Oyasu, 1998; Linehan et al, 2003). In certain cases, a direct and beneficial impact on management of patients has also been achieved, and potential therapeutic targets have been identified (Linehan, 2002).

Knudson and Strong recognized that familial forms of cancer might hold the key to the identification of important

**Table 47–5. Familial Renal Cell Carcinoma Syndromes**

| Syndrome | Genetic Element | Major Clinical Manifestations |
|---|---|---|
| von Hippel–Lindau | *VHL* gene (chromosome 3p25-26) | Clear cell RCC Hemangioblastomas of the central nervous system Retinal angiomas Pheochromocytoma |
| Hereditary papillary RCC | c-*met* proto-oncogene (chromosome 7q34) | Type 1 papillary RCC |
| Familial leiomyomatosis and RCC | Fumarate hydratase (chromosome 1q42-43) | Type 2 papillary RCC Cutaneous leiomyomas Uterine leiomyomas |
| Birt-Hogg-Dubé | *BHD1* gene (chromosome 17p11.2) | Chromophobe RCC Oncocytoma Transitional tumors* Cutaneous fibrofolliculomas Lung cysts Pneumothorax |

*Features of both chromophobe RCC and oncocytoma.
Linehan, 2002; Choyke et al, 2003; Linehan et al, 2003; Maranchie and Linehan, 2003; Pavlovich et al, 2003; Pavlovich and Schmidt, 2004.

regulatory elements known as tumor suppressor genes (Knudson, 1971; Knudson and Strong, 1972). Their observations about the childhood tumor retinoblastoma, in which familial cases tend to be multifocal and early onset (whereas sporadic tumors tend to be unifocal and late onset), led them to propose a two-hit theory of carcinogenesis. They hypothesized that a gene product that could suppress tumor development must be involved and that both alleles of this "tumor suppressor gene" must be mutated or inactivated for tumorigenesis to occur. Furthermore, Knudson postulated that patients with the familial form of the cancer would be born with one mutant allele and that all cells in that organ or tissue would be at risk, accounting for the early onset and multifocal nature of the disease. In contrast, sporadic tumors would develop only if a mutation occurred in both alleles within the same cell, and because each event would be expected to occur with low frequency, most tumors would develop late in life and in a unifocal manner (Knudson, 1971; Knudson and Strong, 1972). Knudson's hypothesis has proved true for retinoblastoma and a number of other tumor types, including RCC (Choyke et al, 2003; Linehan et al, 2003; Pavlovich et al, 2003; Zimmer and Iliopoulos, 2003; Pavlovich and Schmidt, 2004). Identification of familial cases of RCC is particularly important because it allows linkage analysis between affected family members.

## von Hippel–Lindau Disease, *VHL* Gene, and Genetics of Clear Cell Renal Cell Carcinoma

**The familial form of the common clear cell variant of RCC is von Hippel–Lindau disease.** This is a relatively rare autosomal dominant disorder that occurs with a frequency of 1 per 36,000 population. **Major manifestations include the development of RCC, pheochromocytoma, retinal angiomas, and hemangioblastomas of the brain stem, cerebellum, or spinal cord** (Table 47–6) (Horton et al, 1976; Go et al, 1984; Green, 1986; Jennings et al, 1988; Lamiell et al, 1989; Maher et al, 1990; Neumann and Zbar, 1997). All these tumor types are highly vascular and can lead to substantial morbidity, much of which can be avoided with prompt recognition and careful, skilled management. In particular, central nervous system lesions can lead to paralysis or death and the retinal lesions to blindness if they are not identified and managed in an expedient manner. Other common or important manifestations of

von Hippel–Lindau disease include renal and pancreatic cysts, inner ear tumors, and papillary cystadenomas of the epididymis (Neumann and Zbar, 1997). An increased incidence of neuroendocrine tumors of the pancreas has also been reported in von Hippel–Lindau disease (Zbar et al, 1999). Penetrance for all of these traits is far from complete, and some, such as pheochromocytomas, tend to be clustered in certain families but do not occur in others (Neumann and Zbar, 1997). **RCC develops in about 50% of patients with von Hippel–Lindau disease and is distinctive for its early age at onset, often in the third, fourth, or fifth decade of life, and for its bilateral and multifocal involvement** (Horton et al, 1976; Go et al, 1984; Green, 1986; Jennings et al, 1988; Lamiell et al, 1989; Maher et al, 1990; Neumann and Zbar, 1997). With improved management of the central nervous system manifestations of the disease, RCC has now become the most common cause of mortality in patients with von Hippel–Lindau disease (Maher et al, 1990; Neumann and Zbar, 1997). Screening for von Hippel–Lindau disease and important considerations for the management of RCC in von Hippel–Lindau disease are reviewed later in this chapter.

Early clues to the genetic elements involved in the development of RCC came from cytogenetics. These studies demonstrated a common loss of chromosome 3 in kidney cancer, particularly the clear cell variants, and led to intensive efforts to find a tumor suppressor gene in this region (Zbar et al, 1987; Seizinger et al, 1988; Hosoe et al, 1990; Lerman et al, 1991). Reports by Kovacs and colleagues (1989) and Cohen and associates (1979) of translocations involving chromosome 3 further implicated this chromosome as an important regulatory element. Southern blot testing and analysis for restriction fragment length polymorphisms with a wide variety of genetic markers subsequently demonstrated loss of heterozygosity in distinct regions on the short arm of chromosome 3 (reviewed by Jennings et al, 1995). **Sophisticated molecular genetic linkage studies in patients with von Hippel–Lindau disease eventually led to the identification of the *VHL* tumor suppressor gene** (Latif et al, 1993). **This gene, which is located at chromosome 3p25-26, has now been completely sequenced, and its role as a tumor suppressor gene for both the sporadic and the familial forms of clear cell RCC has been confirmed** (Gnarra et al, 1994; Linehan et al, 1995; Zbar, 1995). The *VHL* gene consists of three exons, and it encodes a protein of 213 amino acids. A large number of common mutations or "hot spots" in the gene have been identified, and a direct correlation between genotype and phenotype has been established in some cases (Gnarra et al, 1994; Linehan et al, 1995; Zbar, 1995; Brauch et al, 2000; Pavlovich and Schmidt, 2004). For instance, missense mutations (type 2 mutations) that result in a full-length but nonfunctional protein are commonly found in families with von Hippel–Lindau disease that develop pheochromocytomas, whereas deletions leading to a truncated protein (type 1 mutations) are typically found in families that do not develop pheochromocytomas (Crossey et al, 1994; Linehan et al, 1995; Maher and Kaelin, 1997; Neumann and Zbar, 1997; Walther et al, 1999b; Hes et al, 2000; Friedrich, 2001; Pavlovich and Schmidt, 2004). The identification of this tumor suppressor gene represented a major advance in the field and required close collaboration between clinical urologic-oncologists and molecular geneticists. The important historical steps in solving this challenging puzzle

### Table 47–6. Manifestations of the von Hippel–Lindau Syndrome

| Organ System | Lesion | Incidence (%) |
|---|---|---|
| Eye | Benign retinal angiomas | 49-59 |
| Central nervous system | Benign hemangioblastomas | 42-72 |
| Kidney | Clear cell RCC | 24-70 |
| | Renal cysts | 22-59 |
| Adrenal gland | Pheochromocytoma | 18 |
| Pancreas | Islet cell tumors | 12 |
| | Malignant islet cell tumor | 2 |
| | Pancreatic cysts | 21-72 |
| Epididymis | Cystadenoma | 10-26 |
| Ear | Endolymphatic sac tumor | 10 |

Horton et al, 1976; Green, 1986; Lamiell et al, 1989; Maher et al, 1990; Neumann and Zbar, 1997; Friedrich, 1999; Choyke et al, 2003; Linehan et al, 2003; Maranchie and Linehan, 2003; Pavlovich et al, 2003.

were reviewed by Linehan and colleagues (1995) and Zbar (1995), who spearheaded this important effort.

**As with most tumor suppressor genes, both alleles of the *VHL* gene must be mutated or inactivated for development of the disease; the observed inheritance patterns have conformed to Knudson's hypotheses.** As expected, almost all patients with von Hippel–Lindau disease were found to have germline mutations of one allele of the *VHL* tumor suppressor gene, and autosomal dominant inheritance from the affected parent was confirmed (Gnarra et al, 1994; Linehan et al, 1995, 2003). The second allele is commonly lost by gene or chromosome deletion (Zbar, 1995). Also, as predicted, most sporadic clear cell RCCs were found to harbor mutations or other genetic mechanisms that inactivated both alleles of the *VHL* gene (Zbar, 1995; Linehan et al, 2003). However, they differ in that both mutations must be acquired after birth, accounting for the late onset and the unifocal nature of the sporadic form of the disease. Knudson's hypothesis about tumor suppressor genes and their role in familial and sporadic tumors thus holds true for RCC.

Subsequent work has focused on the function of the VHL protein and its potential mechanisms of action. The VHL protein is known to bind to elongins B and C and CUL-2 to form an E3 ubiquitin ligase complex and may thereby influence the degradation of important regulatory proteins (Gorospe et al, 1999; Lisztwan et al, 1999; Zbar et al, 1999; Wiesener et al, 2001; George and Kaelin, 2003; Linehan et al, 2003; Pavlovich and Schmidt, 2004). **A critically important function of the VHL protein complex is to target the hypoxia-inducible factor 1 (HIF-1) for ubiquitin-mediated degradation, keeping the levels of HIF-1 low under normal conditions. HIF-1 is an intracellular protein that plays an important role in regulating cellular responses to hypoxia, starvation, and other stresses. Inactivation or mutation of the *VHL* gene leads to dysregulated expression of HIF-1** (Maxwell et al, 1999; Yu et al, 2001), and this protein begins to accumulate in the cell. **This in turn leads to a several-fold upregulation of the expression of vascular endothelial growth factor (VEGF), the primary proangiogenic growth factor in RCC, contributing to the pronounced neovascularity associated with clear cell RCC** (Gnarra et al, 1996; Iliopoulos et al, 1996; Gunningham et al, 2001; Igarashi et al, 2002; Linehan et al, 2003). HIF-1 also upregulates the expression of tumor growth factor-α, platelet-derived growth factor (PDGF), glucose transporter (Glut 1), erythropoietin, and carbonic anhydrase 9 (CA-9), a tumor-associated antigen with specificity for clear cell RCC (Fig. 47–14) (Zbar et al, 1999; Wykoff et al, 2000; Turner et al, 2002; Wiesener et al, 2002; Linehan et al, 2003; Grabmaier et al, 2004). In addition, the VHL protein appears to influence the cell cycle, cellular differentiation, and intracellular processing of important matrix molecules such as fibronectin; all these functions may contribute to the pathogenesis and distinctive character of this disease (Lieubeau-Teillet et al, 1998; Kamada et al, 2001; Bindra et al, 2002; Hergovich et al, 2003; Linehan et al, 2003; Na et al, 2003; Pavlovich and Schmidt, 2004).

Other genetic elements potentially involved in the development of sporadic clear cell RCC include the *p53* tumor suppressor gene, the PTEN/Akt pathway, and additional loci on the short arm of chromosome 3. Sophisticated and thorough molecular analysis, including complete gene sequencing and assessment for inactivation by hypermethylation of the promoter, has failed to reveal *VHL* gene abnormalities in a small proportion of sporadic clear cell RCCs, and the search for additional regulatory elements has continued (Clifford et al, 1998b; Hamano et al, 2002). Loss of heterozygosity has also been observed at 3p12-p14 and 3p21.2-p21.3 and is particularly common in tumors with wild-type VHL status (Shridhar et al, 1997; van den Berg and Buys, 1997; Clifford et al, 1998a; Lott et al, 1998; Velickovic et al, 2001; Bodmer et al, 2002). The functional importance of these loci is suggested by experiments showing that the transfer of fragments of chromosome

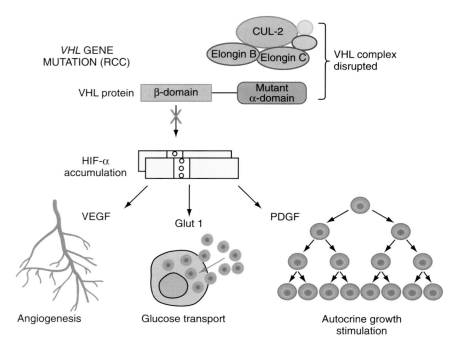

**Figure 47–14.** Biologic functions of the VHL protein. The wild-type VHL protein targets HIF-α for degradation. Mutation of the *VHL* gene allows HIF-α to accumulate, leading to increased expression of VEGF, Glut 1, and PDGF. This in turn has important implications with respect to tumor angiogenesis, metabolic activity, and autocrine stimulation. (From Linehan WM, Walther MM, Zbar B: The genetic basis of cancer of the kidney. J Urol 2003;170:2163-2172.)

3 containing only these genetic elements can suppress tumorigenesis in RCC cell lines (van den Berg and Buys, 1997; Lovell et al, 1999; Bodmer et al, 2002). A candidate tumor suppressor gene at 3p12 has been described and may contribute to a *VHL*-independent pathway to RCC (Lovell et al, 1999). Increased immunostaining for p53 has been reported in 6% to 40% of RCCs, with some studies suggesting a correlation with tumor grade and stage (Reiter et al, 1993; Uhlman et al, 1994; Haitel et al, 1999). Gurova and colleagues (2004) have shown inactivation of the p53 pathway in RCC cell lines in the absence of mutations in the gene itself, and a dominant mechanism was demonstrated suggesting suppression by an inhibitor of *p53* transactivation. However, the data regarding *p53* in RCC have been controversial, and no clear consensus is available at this time.

Oncogenes, such as c-*myc*, c-*erbB-1*, c-*Ha-ras*, c-*fos*, and *raf-1*, have also been studied in RCC, but the available data suggest limited involvement (Slamon et al, 1984). Finally, studies suggest that mutations in the PTEN/Akt pathway may play a role in the progression of clear cell RCC, with mutations commonly found in patients with advanced disease (Brenner et al, 2002; Velickovic et al, 2002; Horiguchi et al, 2003; Shin et al, 2003; Hara et al, 2004). Downregulation of DNA mismatch repair genes may contribute to genetic instability in RCC and allow accumulation of multiple genetic defects (Deguchi et al, 2003).

### Familial Papillary Renal Cell Carcinoma and Genetics of Papillary Renal Cell Carcinoma

**Several studies have documented distinct cytogenetic findings in non–clear cell histiotypes of RCC; chromosome 3 and *VHL* gene abnormalities are uncommon in these variants** (Störkel et al, 1997; Oyasu, 1998). These observations suggested a distinct genetic basis for non–clear cell RCC. Papillary RCC, the second most common histologic subtype of RCC, is characterized by trisomy for chromosomes 7 and 17 as well as by abnormalities on chromosomes 1, 12, 16, 20, and Y (Störkel et al, 1997; Oyasu, 1998; Pavlovich et al, 2003). In 1995, Zbar and colleagues at the National Cancer Institute reported a **second familial form of RCC, the hereditary papillary RCC (HPRCC).** This followed a number of isolated case reports that suggested clustering of papillary RCCs within certain families (Zbar et al, 1994). In Zbar's series, there were 10 families with 41 affected members (29 men and 12 women). Median age at diagnosis was 45 years, and most patients developed multifocal and bilateral papillary RCC (Zbar et al, 1995). Type 1 papillary RCC is typically found in this syndrome rather than type 2, which is commonly seen in the familial leiomyomatosis and RCC syndrome. Unlike in von Hippel–Lindau disease, there have been only occasional reports of associated tumors in other organ systems (Czene and Hemminki, 2003). Mean survival in affected individuals was only 52 years in Zbar's series, although the number of patients dying of RCC was not defined, and it is not known whether a more aggressive course is characteristic (Zbar et al, 1995).

**Studies of families with HPRCC demonstrate an autosomal dominant mode of transmission** and provide insight into the molecular genetics of papillary RCC (Zbar et al, 1995; Linehan et al, 2003). Schmidt and colleagues (1997) reported the identification and characterization of a gene that appears

to be responsible for the development of type 1 papillary RCC. Again, molecular linkage analysis in affected families played a key role in the discovery of this gene, which was localized to chromosome 7q31-34. However, in this case, activation of a proto-oncogene is the inciting event, rather than inactivation of a tumor suppressor gene. **Missense mutations of the *met* proto-oncogene at 7q31 were found to segregate with the disease, implicating it as the relevant genetic locus** (Schmidt et al, 1997; Pavlovich et al, 2003). The protein product of this gene is the receptor tyrosine kinase for the hepatocyte growth factor (also known as scatter factor), which plays an important role in the regulation of the proliferation and differentiation of epithelial and endothelial cells in a wide variety of organs, including the kidney. **Most of the mutations in HPRCC have been found in the tyrosine kinase domain of *met* and apparently lead to constitutive activation** (Schmidt et al, 1997; Pavlovich et al, 2003). The mutated met protein can transform NIH 3T3 murine fibroblasts and has proved to be tumorigenic in immunodeficient murine models. Trisomy for chromosome 7, which is commonly found in HPRCC and sporadic papillary RCC, develops primarily through duplication of the chromosome harboring the mutant allele of the *met* proto-oncogene and effectively increases the dosage of the activated receptor (Zhuang et al, 1998). It is thought that this nonrandom event also contributes to the development of the tumor diathesis (Zhuang et al, 1998). Early onset and multifocality in HPRCC are due to inheritance of the mutated *met* gene, which places all the cells in the kidney at risk from birth, but the incomplete penetrance and variable clinical courses associated with this syndrome have not been explained and suggest that additional genetic loci or epigenetic phenomena may modulate the phenotype (Choyke et al, 2003; Linehan et al, 2003; Pavlovich et al, 2003; Pavlovich and Schmidt, 2004). Schmidt and colleagues (2004) have described three more families with HPRCC and have shown age-dependent penetrance and a variable clinical course according to the site of mutation and family involved. Whereas tumors in HPRCC tend to be less aggressive, Schmidt and colleagues (2004) have emphasized that some can metastasize and lead to mortality.

### Hereditary Leiomyomatosis and Renal Cell Carcinoma

**In 2001, Launonen and colleagues described a new familial renal cancer syndrome in which patients commonly develop cutaneous and uterine leiomyomas and type 2 papillary RCC** (Choyke et al, 2003; Pavlovich and Schmidt, 2004). **Renal tumors in this syndrome are unusual for familial RCC in that they are often solitary and unilateral, and they are more likely to be aggressive than are other forms of familial RCC** (Linehan et al, 2003; Maranchie and Linehan, 2003; Pavlovich and Schmidt, 2004). Collecting duct RCC, another highly malignant variant of RCC, has also been observed in this syndrome, which was named **hereditary leiomyomatosis and renal cell cancer (HLRCC) syndrome** (Linehan et al, 2003). The HLRCC locus was mapped to a region on 1q42-44, and this was later shown to be the site of the fumarate hydratase gene (Tomlinson et al, 2002; Linehan et al, 2003; Toro et al, 2003; Pavlovich and Schmidt, 2004). Fumarate hydratase is an essential enzyme in the Krebs cycle of oxidative metabolism. Again, autosomal dominant inheritance was observed, and this appears to be a tumor suppressor gene rather than an oncogene (Linehan et al, 2003; Pavlovich and Schmidt, 2004). The mechanistic link between a metabolic enzyme located in the mitochondria and tumorigenesis is still an enigma and is now an active area of investigation (Pollard et al, 2003; Pavlovich and Schmidt, 2004). Penetrance for RCC is lower than for the cutaneous and uterine manifestations, with only a minority (20%) of patients developing RCC (Choyke et al, 2003). In contrast, almost all individuals with this syndrome will develop cutaneous leiomyomas and uterine fibroids (female patients), usually manifesting at the age of 20 to 35 years. A high proportion of women have had a hysterectomy for fibroids before formal diagnosis of this syndrome. Prompt surgical management of the renal tumors is recommended in this syndrome, given their tendency toward invasive and aggressive behavior (Linehan et al, 2003; Grubb et al, 2005b).

### Birt-Hogg-Dubé Syndrome

**Birt-Hogg-Dubé syndrome, in which patients develop cutaneous fibrofolliculomas, lung cysts, spontaneous pneumothoraces, and a variety of renal tumors primarily derived from the distal nephron, is named after three Canadian physicians who first described the cutaneous lesions in 1977** (Toro et al, 1999; Linehan et al, 2003; Pavlovich et al, 2003, 2005; Pavlovich and Schmidt, 2004). **The renal tumors typically include chromophobe RCC, oncocytomas, and hybrid or transitional tumors that exhibit features of both of these entities.** However, other forms of RCC, even a substantial proportion of clear cell RCC, have been observed in this syndrome (Pavlovich et al, 2002). Overall penetrance for renal tumors is about 20% to 30%, but when they occur, they are often bilateral and multifocal (Choyke et al, 2003; Pavlovich et al, 2002; Linehan et al, 2003; Pavlovich and Schmidt, 2004). The *BHD1* gene responsible for this syndrome has been mapped to chromosome 17p11.2 and is now fully sequenced (Khoo et al, 2001). Germline mutations in this gene have been found in 89% of kindreds. As with all of the familial RCC syndromes, an autosomal dominant pattern of inheritance is observed (Choyke et al, 2003; Maranchie and Linehan, 2003; Pavlovich et al, 2005).

## Tumor Biology and Clinical Implications

### Immunobiology and Immune Tolerance

**Several lines of evidence demonstrate that RCC is immunogenic, and this knowledge has stimulated intensive efforts to harness the immune system to improve outcomes for patients with advanced disease. RCC has been shown to express a variety of tumor-associated antigens, including PRAME, RAGE-1, MUC-1, gp47, and CA-9, which contribute to its immunogenicity** (Liao et al, 1997; McKiernan et al, 1997; Neumann E et al, 1998; Mulders et al, 2003; Uzzo et al, 2003). Tumor-infiltrating immune cells can be readily isolated from RCC, including natural killer cells, cytotoxic T cells with specificity for autologous tumor cells, and helper T cells and dendritic cells, which express interleukin (IL)-1 and IL-2 and function as antigen-presenting cells (Finke et al, 1992; Gaudin et al, 1995; Elsasser-Beile et al, 1999; Schwaab et al, 1999). **Of the tumor-associated antigens for RCC, CA-9 (also known as MN-9) has demonstrated the most specificity** (Liao et al,

1997; McKiernan et al, 1997). **This antigen, which is recognized by the G250 monoclonal antibody, is expressed in 70% to 90% of RCCs, primarily of clear cell histology.** In normal tissues, the expression of CA-9 is restricted to the gastric mucosa, large bile ducts, and pancreas, and its expression in normal renal epithelial cells is suppressed by wild-type VHL protein (McKiernan et al, 1997; Ivanov et al, 1998; Vissers et al, 1999). Peptides derived from CA-9 can activate cytotoxic T cells, suggesting functional relevance of CA-9 in the generation of the immune response (Vissers et al, 1999). Radioactively labeled G250 has shown promise for the detection of RCC metastases by radionuclide scanning (Brouwers et al, 2003), and conjugates between G250 and various toxins have proved effective in the renal carcinoma cell line (RenCa) animal model of RCC (Steffens et al, 1999). CA-9 is also being investigated for reverse transcriptase–polymerase chain reaction detection of circulating RCC cells in the peripheral blood (McKiernan et al, 1999), and a CA-9 based vaccine protocol has been developed (Hernandez et al, 2002). All these potential applications of MN-9 are, at present, promising but experimental.

**Clinical observations such as spontaneous tumor regression, prolonged disease stabilization, and durable responses to immunotherapy also support the immunogenicity of RCC.** Spontaneous regression is seen in all types of cancer, but more than 50% of reported cases have been associated with neuroblastoma, RCC, melanoma, lymphoma, or leukemia (Papac, 1998; Elhilali et al, 2000). As of 1986, there were more than 80 reported cases of spontaneous regression of RCC in the literature, and 22 were histologically proved (Kavoussi et al, 1986). The estimated incidence of spontaneous regression of RCC has ranged from 0.3% to as high as 7%, although most experienced clinicians believe that the lower figure is more accurate (Oliver et al, 1989; Vogelzang et al, 1992). Most responses have been noted in patients with pulmonary metastases and have occurred after cytoreductive nephrectomy, but regression of primary RCC has also been reported in the absence of any form of treatment (Vogelzang et al, 1992). Remission can be durable, and this phenomenon, although rare, is thought to be real (Young, 1998). It has been assumed to be due to immune surveillance, although other possibilities cannot be excluded (Papac, 1998). Response of RCC to immunomodulators, such as protocols employing IL-2, interferon alfa, and tumor-infiltrating lymphocytes, can be durable and also argues in favor of an important role for the immune system in the tumor biology of RCC (Rosenberg et al, 1998; Motzer and Russo, 2000).

**Unfortunately, response rates of immunotherapy for RCC have been disappointing, typically ranging from 15% to 20% despite a variety of creative treatment strategies, suggesting immune tolerance** (Motzer and Russo, 2000; Ng et al, 2002). A number of observations support impaired immune surveillance in RCC, and a variety of mechanisms affecting virtually all levels of regulation of the immune system have been proposed. These mechanisms include deficient recruitment and activation of dendritic cells (Troy et al, 1998); reduced expression of major histocompatibility complex (MHC) antigens by tumor cells (Seliger et al, 1996); deficient processing of MHC antigens by lymphocytes (Kallfelz et al, 1999); impaired proliferation, locomotion, and cytotoxicity of tumor-infiltrating lymphocytes (Alexander et al, 1993); enhanced expression of various immunosuppressive cytokines, such as IL-10 (Lahn et al, 1999); reduced expression of caspases required for immune-mediated apoptosis of RCC cells (Kolenko et al, 1999); and increased expression of the Fas receptor (CD95) by tumor-infiltrating lymphocytes (Cardi et al, 1998; Wu et al, 2000). Interaction between the Fas ligand, which is expressed by most RCCs, and its receptor results in apoptosis and depletion of the tumor-infiltrating lymphocytes (Uzzo et al, 1999b).

Data suggest that defects in signal transduction in lymphocytes may also play an important role in the immunotolerance of RCC (Ng et al, 2002). Uzzo and colleagues have shown that nuclear factor κB (NF-κB), a transcription factor that regulates lymphocyte activity and viability, is integrally involved in these signaling pathways (Bukowski et al, 1998; Uzzo et al, 1999a, 1999b). They report impaired activation of NF-κB in tumor-infiltrating lymphocytes and dendritic cells of 60% of RCCs, which predisposes the lymphocytes to induction of apoptosis and contributes to immune dysfunction (Finke et al, 2001; Thornton et al, 2004). Defects in IL-2 receptor signaling and aberrant regulation of IκBα, which sequesters NF-κB in an inactive form in the cytoplasm, contribute to this process (Kolenko et al, 1997; Ling et al, 1998; Uzzo et al, 1999). VEGF, which is produced by the tumor cells at high levels, also promotes immunotolerance by blocking activation of NF-κB in hematopoietic progenitor cells and thereby inhibiting the maturation of dendritic cells (Gabrilovich et al, 1998; Oyama et al, 1998). This defect may be particularly important because dendritic cells are the most efficient antigen-presenting cells in the immune system. Improved understanding of the mechanisms contributing to immunotolerance in RCC should suggest novel and rational strategies for improving outcomes for patients with advanced disease.

## Multidrug Resistance

**Expression of multidrug resistance (MDR) proteins, such as MDR-1 (also known as P-glycoprotein), also contributes to the refractory nature of advanced RCC. P-glycoprotein is a 170-kD transmembrane protein expressed by 80% to 90% of RCCs that acts as an energy-dependent efflux pump for a wide variety of large hydrophobic compounds, including several cytotoxic drugs** (Fojo et al, 1987; Kakehi et al, 1988; Mickisch, 1994). The vinca alkaloids paclitaxel, actinomycin D, and mitomycin C are processed by P-glycoprotein, thereby lowering their effective intracellular concentrations (Mickisch, 1994; Chapman and Goldstein, 1995). P-glycoprotein is expressed by proximal tubule cells in the normal kidney and tends to be downregulated in high-grade tumors and metastases, suggesting that other resistance mechanisms must also be operative (Tobe et al, 1995; Gamelin et al, 1999). Resistance of RCC to cisplatin-based therapy and to other agents that are not recognized or handled by P-glycoprotein also suggests redundancy in resistance mechanisms. The MDR-related protein, another transmembrane efflux protein, glutathione detoxification mechanisms, and altered topoisomerase activity have all been reported in RCC and may contribute to this redundancy (Mickisch, 1994; Chapman and Goldstein, 1995; Ramp et al, 2000).

A variety of drugs that can reverse the MDR-1 phenotype have been described and tested, both in vitro and in clinical trials. These agents include calcium channel blockers, calmodulin antagonists, steroids, cyclosporine, tamoxifen,

toremifene, amiodarone, and quinidine (Mickisch, 1994; Chapman and Goldstein, 1995; Braybrooke et al, 2000). The primary mode of action is to bind P-glycoprotein competitively and prevent it from interacting with cytotoxic agents. A transgenic murine model with increased expression of P-glycoprotein is available and has facilitated studies in this field, allowing identification of synergistic or additive combinations of drugs (Mickisch et al, 1991). Thus far, however, clinical trials of such strategies have not significantly enhanced the response rates for cytotoxic therapies for RCC, and further research is required to define more efficacious approaches (Mickisch, 1994; Motzer and Russo, 2000).

## Angiogenesis

**RCC has long been recognized as one of the most vascular of cancers as reflected by the distinctive neovascular pattern exhibited on renal angiography** (Fig. 47–15). Dependence on angiogenesis is also suggested by a number of studies assessing the effect of antiangiogenic agents in experimental models, such as the RenCa or xenograft models of RCC in mice. In these studies, the growth and metastasis of RCC have been blocked by endostatin, IL-12, ZD1839, PTK787/ZK 222584, and TNP-40 (fumagillin analog), all well-established antiangiogenic compounds (Fujioka et al, 1996; Tan et al, 1996; Dhanabal et al, 1999; Drevs et al, 2000). In contrast, microvessel density studies in RCC have often been inconclusive, perhaps reflecting the fact that the kidney is a highly vascular organ at baseline, making detection of increased microvessel density within tumors more difficult (Yoshino et al, 1995; Delahunt et al, 1997; Gelb et al, 1997; Nativ et al, 1998). **The primary angiogenesis inducer in clear cell RCC appears to be VEGF, which is suppressed by the wild-type VHL protein under normal conditions and is dramatically upregulated during tumor development**

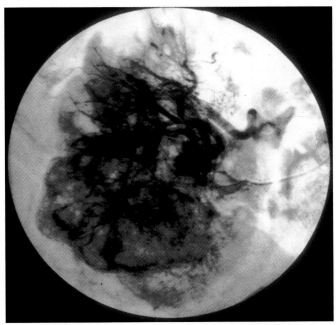

**Figure 47–15.** Neovascularity associated with renal cell carcinoma. Right renal angiogram shows right renal mass exhibiting markedly increased neovascularity consistent with renal cell carcinoma.

(Gnarra et al, 1996; Iliopoulos et al, 1996; Tomisawa et al, 1999). Functional relevance of VEGF is demonstrated by studies showing increased levels of VEGF transcript in most hypervascular tumors, whereas the less common hypovascular counterparts exhibit reduced expression of VEGF (Takahashi et al, 1994). Increased levels of VEGF have also been found in the serum and urine of patients with RCC, and a correlation with stage and grade has been reported (Tsuchiya et al, 1998; Chang et al, 2001; Horstmann et al, 2005). Elevated serum levels of basic fibroblast growth factor have also been reported in RCC, and other putative angiogenesis inducers for this malignant neoplasm include placental growth factor, tumor growth factor-β1, angiogenin, angiopoietins, IL-8, and hepatocyte growth factor, all of which have been detected at increased levels in patients with RCC compared with normal controls (Campbell, 1997; Slaton et al, 2001; Currie et al, 2002; Yagasaki et al, 2003).

**Given the angiogenesis dependence of RCC and the lack of generally effective forms of systemic therapies, it is not surprising that RCC has been targeted for antiangiogenic approaches.** Thus far, TNP-470 and roquinimex (Linomide), an oral antibiotic with antiangiogenic activity, have demonstrated only limited activity in patients with advanced RCC (de Wit et al, 1997; Pawinski et al, 1997; Stadler et al, 1998). Thalidomide has been investigated extensively for patients with RCC because of its antiangiogenic effects but has likewise shown only rare responses. In addition, toxicity with thalidomide can be substantial, including thrombotic events and neurologic morbidity (Daliani et al, 2002; Escudier et al, 2002b; Nathan et al, 2002; Fanelli et al, 2003; Matthews and McCoy, 2003). The most promising results have been reported for bevacizumab, a humanized anti-VEGF antibody, which was associated with a significant delay in time to progression for patients with metastatic RCC compared with placebo (Yang et al, 2003a). Partial responses were uncommon and there were no complete responses, consistent with a tumoristatic rather than a tumoricidal mechanism of action. A number of other agents that target the VEGF pathway are now being tested in clinical trials, including SU5416, SU11248, and PTK787/ZK 222584, and various combinations of these drugs and interferon alfa are also under study (Lara et al, 2003; Pantuck et al, 2003b).

Antiangiogenic agents offer a number of potential advantages because they are not genotoxic and target stable endothelial cells rather than genetically unstable tumor cells. They are thus unlikely to induce secondary cancers or tumor resistance. In addition, many antiangiogenic agents have proved to be synergistic with one another and with cytotoxic therapies, and their side effects are limited and should not overlap those of conventional forms of therapy (Campbell, 1997). Antiangiogenic agents have been tested primarily as monotherapy in patients with refractory disease, and it is likely that more potent combinations of agents or multimodal approaches will be required to optimize results.

## Growth Factors, Signal Transduction, and Regulation of the Cell Cycle

**Proliferative index, as defined by PCNA or Ki-67 staining, has correlated with pathologic parameters and clinical outcomes in RCC, suggesting that regulation of the cell cycle plays an important role in the tumor biology of RCC** (de Riese et al, 1993; Delahunt et al, 1995; Tannapfel et al, 1996).

Increased expression of tumor growth factor-α and its receptor tyrosine kinase, the epidermal growth factor receptor (EGFR), have been reported in RCC and may contribute to tumorigenesis by promoting cell proliferation or transformation through an autocrine mechanism (Gomella et al, 1989; Mydlo et al, 1989; Sargent et al, 1989; Lager et al, 1994; Moch et al, 1997; Ramp et al, 1997). The functional relevance of EGFR in the development of RCC is also suggested by studies testing the efficacy of the C225 monoclonal antibody, which binds and neutralizes EGFR. In murine xenograft models of RCC, C225 can block tumor growth and metastasis (Prewett et al, 1998; Brouwers et al, 2004). Increased expression of the proto-oncogene *erbB-2,* which is homologous to EGFR, has also been reported in RCC, and a correlation between EGFR and erbB-2 staining and tumor grade and stage has been observed in some studies (Stumm et al, 1996). Agents that target the EGFR, such as erlotinib (Tarceva), gefitinib (Iressa, ZD1839), and C225, are now being tested in clinical trials for RCC (Tian and Dawson, 2001; Drucker et al, 2003; Mendelsohn and Baselga, 2003; Motzer et al, 2003; Dancey, 2004).

**Aberrant activation of signal transduction pathways in RCC may also contribute to altered cell cycle kinetics and represent excellent targets for therapeutic intervention.** Constitutive activity of the Ras, Raf-1, MEK, and other mitogen-activated protein (MAP) kinases, which mediate the effects of growth factor–EGFR interactions, have been reported in RCC, potentially increasing the proliferative index (Oka et al, 1995). **Small molecule inhibitors of these and other pathways are currently being studied in patients with advanced RCC, and this "targeted molecular approach" has generated much interest and excitement.** Many of these agents, such as BAY43-9006 (sorafenib), are multifunctional inhibitors of various tyrosine receptor kinases and may block several pathways important for tumor growth and metastasis. BAY43-9006 blocks receptors for VEGF and PDGF, and in a study of 63 evaluable patients with advanced RCC, oral treatment with this agent for a 12-week course yielded 25 responders (39.7%) and 18 patients with stable disease (Ratain et al, 2005; Sridhar et al, 2005). A subsequent phase III study with this agent reported improved progression-free survival for patients with advanced RCC. In this study, mean progression-free survival for controls was 12 weeks versus 24 weeks for actively treated patients (Escudier et al, 2005). Other signal transduction pathways involving the mTOR protein also appear to be important in the tumor biology of RCC and are being targeted for molecular therapeutics, in this case rapamycin and related compounds such as CCI-779 (Atkins et al, 2004).

Other important growth regulatory elements in RCC include the insulin-like growth factor axis (Takahashi et al, 2005), telomerase, and Bcl-2. Insulin-like growth factor receptor expression has been documented in RCC, and Parker and colleagues (2003a) have correlated this factor with survival. Increased telomerase activity, which has been found in 56% to 93% of RCCs, may also affect the cell cycle by maintaining telomere length (Mehle et al, 1996; Yoshida et al, 1998; Orlando et al, 2001). Progressive telomere loss occurs each time a normal cell divides and eventually leads to growth inhibition and cellular senescence. Increased expression of Bcl-2, which protects against programmed cell death, has also been reported in RCC and may contribute to tumor viability and treatment failure (Huang et al, 1999; Gobe et al, 2002).

The hepatocyte growth factor and its receptor, the *met* proto-oncogene, may also contribute to the pathogenesis of RCC (Sweeney et al, 2002a). The role of activating mutations of the *met* proto-oncogene in the etiology of both sporadic and familial forms of papillary RCC has already been discussed, but data suggest that upregulated expression of the ligand may occur in most of the histologic subtypes of RCC (Natali et al, 1996; Pisters et al, 1997; Schmidt et al, 1997; Clifford et al, 1998a; Horie et al, 1999). Hepatocyte growth factor (also known as scatter factor) is expressed by proximal tubular cells in the normal kidney, where it is involved in the branching tubulogenesis of the developing kidney and regeneration after renal injury. In vitro, hepatocyte growth factor has mitogenic, motogenic, and morphogenic effects on renal epithelial cells (Clifford et al, 1998a). Expression of hepatocyte growth factor and its receptor has been found in the majority of RCCs, including most histiotypes, and correlation with tumor volume was reported in one study (Horie et al, 1999). Increased serum levels of hepatocyte growth factor have also been reported in most patients with RCC, independent of histologic subtype (Petri et al, 1997). Taken together, these data suggest that hepatocyte growth factor and its receptor may play an important role in the tumor biology of RCC, although constitutive activation of the receptor, which may be the most potent mechanism, appears to be limited to papillary RCC.

## Proteases, Adhesion, and the Extracellular Matrix

Interactions among cancer cells, adjacent cells, and the surrounding matrix can strongly influence their pathogenic potential. Altered intracellular processing and secretion of fibronectin and other matrix proteins is found in RCC, representing one consequence of *VHL* gene mutation (Lieubeau-Teillet et al, 1998; Ohh et al, 1998). This fundamental defect most likely has important effects on tumor biology, given the important role of the matrix in regulating cellular differentiation and tumor invasiveness and metastasis. Increased expression of proteases, such as plasmin and the matrix metalloproteinases, has correlated with reduced survival in RCC and may also contribute to the aggressive behavior of RCC (Walther et al, 1997a; Kugler et al, 1998). **Downregulation of E-cadherin and cadherin-6, which mediate adhesion between cancer cells, is well documented in RCC and has correlated with poor outcomes in most studies** (Morton et al, 1995; Paul et al, 2004). Aberrant regulation of α-catenins, the cytoplasmic proteins that bind cadherins and mediate their effects on the cytoskeleton, has also been observed in RCC, and a correlation with compromised survival has been reported (Shimazui et al, 1996; Paul et al, 1997).

Other studies have defined the adhesion molecules that facilitate interactions between tumor cells and endothelial cells in RCC. Steinbach and colleagues (1996) have shown that sialyl-Lewis^x/endothelial leukocyte adhesion molecule 1 and VLA-4/vascular cell adhesion molecule 1 interactions regulate this process, which presumably influences the ability of tumor cells to move into or out of the vascular system during the metastatic cascade.

## Pathology

**Most RCCs are round to ovoid and circumscribed by a pseudocapsule of compressed parenchyma and fibrous** tissue rather than a true histologic capsule. Unlike upper tract transitional cell carcinomas, most RCCs are not grossly infiltrative, with the notable exception of collecting duct RCC and some sarcomatoid variants (Farrow, 1997). Tumor size has ranged from 5 to 8 cm in most series but can vary from a few millimeters to large enough to fill the entire abdomen. Tumors smaller than 3 cm were previously classified as benign adenomas, but some small tumors have been associated with metastases, and most pathologists agree that with the exception of oncocytoma, there are no reliable histologic or ultrastructural criteria to differentiate benign from malignant renal epithelial tumors (Farrow, 1997). When they are bivalved, RCCs consist of yellow, tan, or brown tumor interspersed with fibrotic, necrotic, or hemorrhagic areas; few are uniform in gross appearance. Cystic degeneration is found in 10% to 25% of RCCs and appears to be associated with a better prognosis compared with purely solid RCC (Corica et al, 1999; Koga et al, 2000; Onishi et al, 2001; Nassir et al, 2002; Imura et al, 2004). Calcification can be stippled or plaquelike and is found in 10% to 20% of RCCs.

**Nuclear features can be highly variable, and a number of grading systems have been based on such features as nuclear size and shape and the presence or absence of prominent nucleoli. Fuhrman's system has been most generally adopted and is now recognized as an important independent prognostic factor for RCC** (Table 47–7) (Fuhrman et al, 1982; Pantuck et al, 2001a).

Aggressive local behavior is not uncommon with RCC and can be expressed in a variety of ways. **Frank invasion and perforation of the collecting system or renal capsule are found in approximately 20% of cases, although displacement of these structures is a more common finding.** Further spread to involve adjacent organs or the abdominal wall is often precluded by Gerota's fascia, although some high-grade RCCs are able to overcome this natural barrier. One unique feature of RCC is its predilection for involvement of the venous system, which is found in 10% of RCCs, more often than in any other tumor type (Skinner et al, 1972; Schefft et al, 1978). This is most commonly manifested in the form of a contiguous tumor thrombus that can extend into the inferior vena cava as high as the right atrium. Many such tumor thrombi are highly vascularized by arterial blood flow (Novick et al, 1990).

**Most sporadic RCCs are unilateral and unifocal. Bilateral involvement can be synchronous or asynchronous and is found in 2% to 4% of sporadic RCCs, although it is considerably more common in patients with von Hippel–Lindau disease or other familial forms of RCC** (Farrow, 1997; Linehan et al, 2003). Multicentricity, which is found in 10% to 20% of cases, is more common in association with papil-

**Table 47–7. Fuhrman's Classification System for Nuclear Grade in Renal Cell Carcinoma**

| Grade | Nuclear Size | Nuclear Outline | Nucleoli |
|-------|-------------|-----------------|----------|
| 1 | 10 mm | Round, uniform | Absent or inconspicuous |
| 2 | 15 mm | Irregular | Small (visible at 400× magnification) |
| 3 | 20 mm | Irregular | Prominent |
| 4 | ≥20 mm | Bizarre, often multilobed | Prominent, heavy chromatin clumps present |

lary histology and familial RCC (Mukamel et al, 1988; Cheng et al, 1991; Whang et al, 1995; Campbell et al, 1997; Richstone et al, 2004). Satellite lesions are often small and difficult to identify by preoperative imaging, intraoperative ultrasonography, or visual inspection; they appear to be the main factor contributing to local recurrence after partial nephrectomy (Campbell et al, 1996a; Richstone et al, 2004). Microsatellite analysis suggests a clonal origin for most multifocal RCC within the same kidney (Junker et al, 2002), but tumor in the contralateral kidney is likely to be an independent growth if it is synchronous or a metastasis if it is asynchronous (Kito et al, 2002).

**All RCCs are, by definition, adenocarcinomas, derived from renal tubular epithelial cells** (Zambrano et al, 1999; Pantuck et al, 2001a; Renshaw, 2002). **Most RCCs share ultrastructural features, such as surface microvilli and complex intracellular junctions, with normal proximal tubular cells, and they are believed to be derived from this region of the nephron** (reviewed in Farrow, 1997). Similarly, immunohistochemistry for lectins and other cell surface antigens has supported derivation from the proximal convoluted tubule (Kim and Kim, 2002). **However, more recent data suggest that this information applies primarily to the more common conventional and chromophilic variants of RCC** (Table 47–8), **whereas most other histologic subtypes of RCC appear to be derived from the more distal elements of the nephron** (Störkel et al, 1997; Zambrano et al, 1999; Pantuck et al, 2001a; Renshaw, 2002; Linehan et al, 2003; Pavlovich and Schmidt, 2004). Almost all RCCs express keratins 8 and 18, and 50% express vimentin, which is more commonly found in associ-

ation with sarcomatoid differentiation (DeLong et al, 1993; Farrow, 1997).

**Since the early 1990s, the histologic classification of RCC has undergone a major revision** (Zambrano et al, 1999; Renshaw, 2002; Linehan et al, 2003). **Traditionally, RCC was divided into four histologic subtypes: clear cell, granular cell, tubulopapillary, and sarcomatoid. On the basis of advances in the molecular genetics of RCC and a more discerning interpretation of histologic and ultrastructural features, a new classification scheme was proposed by Kovacs** (1993). This new classification system was reviewed by Weiss and colleagues (1995) and was approved by an international consensus workshop of clinicians and researchers in the field (see Table 47–8) (Störkel et al, 1997; Zambrano et al, 1999; Pantuck et al, 2001a; Renshaw, 2002; Linehan et al, 2003; Pavlovich and Schmidt, 2004). Major changes included the addition of a new histologic subtype, the chromophobe cell carcinoma; the reclassification of granular cell tumors into other categories; and the recognition that sarcomatoid lesions represent poorly differentiated elements derived from other histologic subtypes rather than a distinct tumor type (Weiss et al, 1995; Störkel et al, 1997; Oyasu, 1998; Zambrano et al, 1999; Renshaw, 2002; Linehan et al, 2003; Pavlovich and Schmidt, 2004). With respect to the last point, current practice is to identify the primary histologic subtype and comment on the presence and extent of sarcomatoid differentiation rather than to separate these tumors into a distinct category, although the prognostic implications have not changed (Mian et al, 2002; Cheville et al, 2004). Depending on well-defined histologic and ultrastructural criteria, granular cell tumors are

**Table 47–8. Histologic Classification of Renal Cell Carcinoma[1]**

| Histology | Subtype | Genetic Factors | Characteristics |
|---|---|---|---|
| Conventional (70%–80%) | Clear cell<br>Granular<br>Mixed | Deletions of chromosome 3p<br>Mutations of *VHL* gene<br>Loss of chromosomes 8p, 9p, and 14q<br>Gain of chromosome 5q | Hypervascular<br>Aggressive behavior more common<br>May respond to immunotherapy<br>Familial form is von Hippel–Lindau syndrome<br>From proximal tubule |
| Chromophilic[2] (10%–15%) | Type 1<br>Type 2 | Trisomy of chromosomes 7 and 17<br>Abnormalities of *met* proto-oncogene<br>Loss of chromosomes 14 and Y<br>Gain of chromosomes 12, 16, and 20 | Typically hypovascular<br>Multicentricity common<br>Prognosis variable<br>Type 2: worse prognosis<br>Type 1 seen in HPRCC[3]<br>Type 2 seen in HLRCC[4]<br>Common in acquired renal cystic disease<br>From proximal tubule |
| Chromophobic (3%–5%) | Type 1—classic<br>Type 2—eosinophilic | Loss of chromosomes 1, 2, 6, 10, 13, 17, and 21 | Prognosis better than conventional<br>Aggressive variants exist<br>Seen in Birt-Hogg-Dubé syndrome<br>From intercalated cells of collecting duct |
| Collecting duct (1%) | Medullary cell is one variant | Loss of chromosomes 1, 6, 8, 11, 18, 21, and Y<br>Gain of chromosomes 7, 12, 17, and 20 | Centrally located<br>Infiltrative<br>Poor prognosis<br>May respond to chemotherapy<br>From collecting duct |
| Unclassified (1%) | | Poorly defined | Poor prognosis<br>Origin not defined |

[1]Sarcomatoid variants of all of these subtypes have been described and are associated with compromised prognosis.
[2]Also known as papillary RCC.
[3]Hereditary papillary RCC.
[4]Hereditary leiomyomatosis and RCC.
Störkel et al, 1997; Zambrano et al, 1999; Pantuck et al, 2001; Renshaw, 2002; Linehan et al, 2003; Pavlovich and Schmidt, 2004.

now reclassified as papillary RCC, collecting duct RCC, or eosinophilic variants of chromophobic RCC, or they are combined with clear cell RCC into a broader category that has been designated common or conventional RCC (Weiss et al, 1995; Kovacs et al, 1997; Störkel et al, 1997; Oyasu, 1998; Zambrano et al, 1999; Renshaw, 2002). Another important development has been the identification of the medullary cell variant of RCC that is common in young African Americans with sickle cell trait (Davis et al, 1995b; Störkel et al, 1997).

All of these recent developments indicate that RCC is not a single malignant neoplasm but rather comprises several different tumor subtypes, each with a distinct genetic basis and unique clinical features (see Table 47–8). Sophisticated gene expression profiling and proteomic analyses support the individuality of each of these tumor subtypes and hold great promise for differentiating these subtypes in the future (Takahashi et al, 2003, 2004; Amy-Bazille et al, 2004; Furge et al, 2004; Sugimura et al, 2004; Yang et al, 2004). This is clearly a field in evolution, with changes stimulated by basic science advances and astute clinical observation.

**Conventional RCC accounts for approximately 70% to 80% of all RCCs, representing the garden variety of RCC** (Störkel et al, 1997). **These tumors are typically yellow when they are bivalved and are highly vascular,** containing a network of delicate vascular sinusoids interspersed between sheets or acini of tumor cells (Fig. 47–16). **On microscopic examination, common or conventional RCC can include clear cell, granular cell, or mixed types.** Clear cells are typically round or polygonal with abundant cytoplasm containing glycogen, cholesterol, cholesterol esters, and phospholipids, all of which are readily extracted by the solvents used in routine histologic preparations, contributing to the clear appearance of the tumor cells (Farrow, 1997). However, granular cells, which have eosinophilic cytoplasm and abundant mitochondria, can predominate. Two percent to 5% of conventional RCCs also demonstrate sarcomatoid features, and conventional RCC is more likely to exhibit venous tumor extension than is any other subtype of RCC (Rabbani et al, 2004). **In general, patients with conventional RCC have a worse prognosis compared with chromophilic or chromophobic RCC, even after stratification for stage and grade** (Cheville et al, 2003; Beck et al, 2004). **However, most responders in immunotherapy protocols have had conventional RCC, and these protocols are now being reserved primarily for this population** (Childs et al, 2000; Drachenberg and Childs, 2003). **Chromosome 3 alterations and *VHL* mutations are common in conventional RCC, and mutation or inactivation of this gene has been found in a majority of sporadic cases** (Clifford et al, 1998b; Zambrano et al, 1999; Renshaw, 2002; Linehan et al, 2003). The familial form of clear cell RCC, the von Hippel–Lindau syndrome, has already been reviewed.

**Chromophilic RCC, which has also been designated papillary RCC in other classification schemes, is the second**

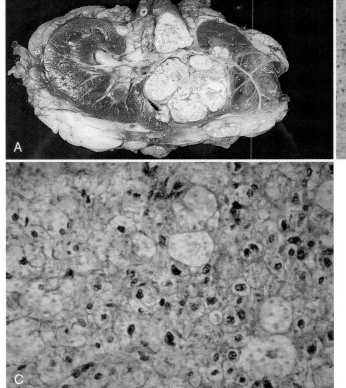

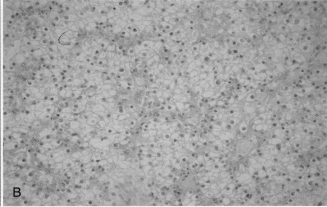

**Figure 47–16.** **A,** Conventional renal cell carcinoma with medial extension into the renal vein within the hilum. **B,** Classic clear cell variant of conventional renal cell carcinoma. **C,** High-grade, conventional renal cell carcinoma with both clear and granular cell features.

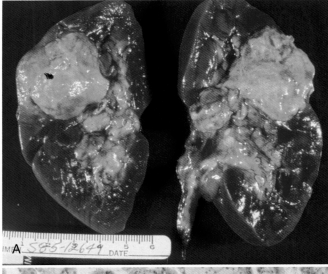

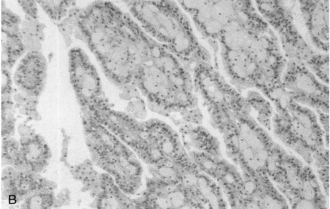

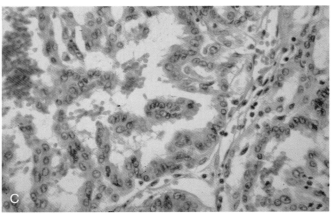

**Figure 47–17. A,** Papillary (chromophilic) renal cell carcinoma extending into the collecting system. **B** and **C,** Low- and high-power views of papillary renal cell carcinoma illustrating prototypic histologic findings.

**most common histologic subtype** (Störkel et al, 1997). It represents 10% to 15% of all RCCs, although it is more commonly found in certain populations, such as patients with end-stage renal failure and acquired renal cystic disease (Ishikawa and Kovacs, 1993; Störkel et al, 1997). On microscopic examination, most tumors in this category consist of basophilic or eosinophilic cells arranged in papillary or tubular configuration; previously, more than 50% or more than 75% of the tumor had to exhibit such architectural features to qualify as a papillary RCC (Fig. 47–17). More recently, solid variants of chromophilic RCC have been described by characteristic cytogenetics and immunostaining profiles (Renshaw et al, 1997). In the future, it is likely that distinct cytogenetic and molecular features will take precedence over histologic findings in the classification of this and other subtypes of RCC (Renshaw et al, 1997; Störkel et al, 1997; Oyasu, 1998). Delahunt and colleagues (2001) have described two subtypes of chromophilic RCC: type 1, consisting of basophilic cells with scant cytoplasm; and the potentially more aggressive type 2 variant, with eosinophilic cells and abundant granular cytoplasm (Amsellem-Ouazana et al, 2002; Leroy et al, 2002; Renshaw, 2002; Choyke et al, 2003; Gunawan et al, 2003).

**Small papillary tumors are commonly found at autopsy, are often well encapsulated and low grade, and appear to have low malignant potential** (Farrow, 1997; Renshaw, 2002). These lesions, which possess many of the same genetic alterations found in larger papillary RCCs, have been classified as renal adenomas. Indeed, many pathologists believe that if renal adenoma does exist as a distinct entity, small, well-differentiated papillary tumors are the most likely candidates (Farrow, 1997; Renshaw, 2002).

**The cytogenetic abnormalities associated with chromophilic RCC are characteristic and include trisomy of chromosomes 7 and 17 and loss of the Y chromosome.** Other common findings include gain of chromosomes 12, 16, and 20 and loss of heterozygosity on chromosome 14 (Oyasu, 1998; Brunelli et al, 2003b; Kuroda et al, 2003a; Pavlovich and Schmidt, 2004). *VHL* mutations are rare in chromophilic RCC, confirming distinct genetic pathways to tumorigenesis (Kenck et al, 1996; Zambrano et al, 1999; Linehan et al, 2003). Chromophilic RCC is more likely to be hypovascular, perhaps owing to the lack of *VHL* mutations that regulate VEGF, the primary proangiogenic molecule in RCC (Blath et al, 1976; Herts et al, 2002; Kim JK et al, 2002). As discussed earlier, activating mutations of the *met* proto-oncogene located on chromosome 7, which encodes the receptor for hepatocyte growth factor, appear to be common and pathogenic in chromophilic RCC (Schmidt et al, 1997; Pavlovich and Schmidt, 2004). Indeed, this genetic defect is now being targeted for novel treatment approaches with use of small molecule inhibitors (Schmidt et al, 1997; Linehan et al, 2003). **Another unique feature of chromophilic RCC is its tendency toward multicentricity, which approaches 40% in many series** (Renshaw and Corless, 1995; Amin et al, 1997a; Campbell et al, 1997; Baltaci et al, 2000; Chow et al, 2001).

The prognosis associated with chromophilic RCC remains controversial. Many older studies suggested a tendency toward low-grade disease, and one literature review found that 80% of papillary RCCs were confined to the kidney, which has obvious prognostic implications (Blath et al, 1976; Mancilla-Jimenez et al, 1976; Boczko et al, 1979; Mydlo and Bard, 1987; Farrow, 1997; Chow et al, 2001). On the other hand, more recent studies contain an increased proportion of high-grade and advanced tumors, often leading to the patient's demise (Lager et al, 1995; Amin et al, 1997a; Renshaw, 2002). Evolving definitions of this entity and corresponding differences in interpretation and classification may contribute to the lack of consensus about this issue. **At present, many authors believe that grade for grade and stage for stage, a significant difference in outcome for patients with chromophilic RCC versus conventional RCC may be difficult to demonstrate** (Renshaw et al, 1997; Renshaw, 2002).

**Chromophobe cell carcinoma,** first described by Thoenes and colleagues in 1985, is a distinctive histologic subtype of RCC that appears to be derived from the cortical portion of the collecting duct (Störkel et al, 1997). It represents 3% to 5% of all RCCs (Oyasu, 1998). The tumor cells typically exhibit a relatively transparent cytoplasm with a fine reticular pattern that has been described as a "plant cell" appearance. The chromophobic nature of this classic variant is responsible for the name of this histologic subtype (Fig. 47–18) (Nagashima, 2000; Kuroda et al, 2003a). However, eosinophilic variants of chromophobic RCC have also been described and constitute about 30% of cases (Thoenes et al, 1988; Störkel et al, 1997; Latham et al, 1999; Kuroda et al, 2003a). In either case, **a perinuclear halo is typically found, and electron microscopic findings consist of numerous 150- to 300-nm microvesicles, which are the single most distinctive and defining feature of chromophobe cell carcinoma** (Nagashima, 2000; Krishnan and Truong, 2002). **These microvesicles characteristically stain positive for Hale's colloidal iron, indicating the presence of a mucopolysaccharide unique to RCC** (Thoenes et al, 1988). Most chromophobic RCCs also stain positive for various cytokeratins, but most are negative for vimentin (Cochand-Priollet et al, 1997). Genetic analysis has revealed loss of heterozygosity at chromosomes 1, 2, 6, 10, 13, 17, and 21, and flow cytometric analysis has demonstrated hypodiploid DNA content in most cases (Schwerdtle et al, 1996; Bugert et al, 1997; Iqbal et al, 2000; Polascik et al, 2002). Some studies have reported an increased incidence of *p53* mutations in this histologic subtype, and upregulated expression of the c-*kit* oncogene has also been reported (Contractor et al, 1997; Yamazaki et al, 2003; Pan et al, 2004; Petit et al, 2004). The latter finding may have clinical relevance because it suggests that such tumors may respond to imatinib mesylate (Gleevec) (Voelzke et al, 2002). Again, chromosome 3 abnormalities and *VHL* mutations are uncommon (Schwerdtle et al, 1996). Chromophobic RCC is commonly seen in the Birt-Hogg-Dubé syndrome, but most cases are sporadic (Pavlovich et al, 2002).

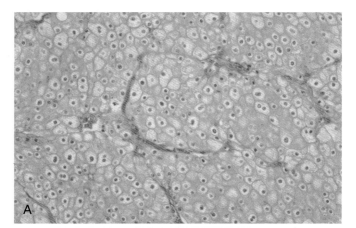

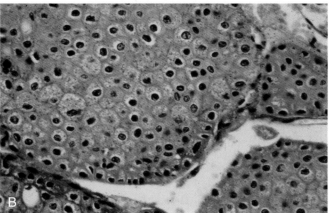

**Figure 47–18.** **A** and **B,** Chromophobic renal cell carcinoma with admixture of classic (chromophobic) and eosinophilic cells. Characteristic features include distinct cytoplasmic borders and perinuclear halos. The classic variant is notable for its "plant cell" appearance. Both variants stain positive for Hale's colloidal iron (**B**) and demonstrate multiple microvesicles on analysis by electron microscopy.

The clinical behavior of chromophobic RCC has not yet been adequately defined, although must studies suggest a better prognosis than for conventional RCC (Polascik et al, 2002; Peyromaure et al, 2003). Most early reports suggested a tendency to remain localized despite growth to large size as well as a predominance of low-grade disease (Thoenes et al, 1988). Crotty and colleagues (1995) reported that 86% of their 50 cases of chromophobic RCC were Robson stage I, and 94% remained cancer free with mean follow-up of 6 years. Similarly, in the series from Memorial Sloan-Kettering Cancer Center, 48 of 49 chromophobic RCCs were confined to Gerota's fascia, and 45 patients (92%) remained cancer free with mean follow-up of 52 months (Campbell et al, 1996b). Peyromaure and colleagues (2003) also reported good outcomes for patients with chromophobic RCC, with no recurrences in a series of 61 patients. In contrast, Renshaw and colleagues (1996) reported a more adverse prognosis associated with chromophobic RCC. In their series, high-grade disease was common, and 7 of 25 patients eventually developed metastatic disease. In addition, sarcomatoid differentiation has been reported in association with chromophobe cell carcinoma, and such tumors are almost invariably aggressive (Campbell et al, 1996b; Kuroda et al, 2003a).

Collecting duct, or Bellini's duct, carcinoma is a relatively rare subtype of RCC, accounting for less than 1% of all RCCs (Kennedy et al, 1990; Rumpelt et al, 1991; Carter et al, 1992; Störkel et al, 1997; Srigley and Eble, 1998; Swartz et al, 2002). Many reported cases have occurred in younger patients, often in the third, fourth, or fifth decade of life (Carter et al, 1992). Affinity for the *Ulex europaeus* lectin and expression of high-molecular-weight keratins (34βE12) support a collecting duct origin (Rumpelt et al, 1991; Oyasu, 1998; Polascik et al, 2002). Collecting duct carcinomas are derived from the medulla, but many are infiltrative, and extension into the cortex is common (Pickhardt et al, 2001). On microscopic examination, these tumors consist of an admixture of dilated tubules and papillary structures typically lined by a single layer of cuboidal cells, often creating a cobblestone appearance. Deletions on chromosome 1q and monosomy of chromosomes 6, 8, 11, 18, 21, and Y have been reported, but the number of tumors analyzed thus far has been limited (Fuzesi et al, 1992; Steiner et al, 1996; Polascik et al, 2002). Most reported cases have been high grade and advanced stage and have not responded to conventional therapies (Carter et al, 1992; Chao et al, 2002b; Polascik et al, 2002; Mejean et al, 2003; Tokuda et al, 2004). Most patients are symptomatic at presentation (Tokuda et al, 2004). Immunohistochemical and molecular analyses suggest that collecting duct RCC may resemble transitional cell carcinoma, and some patients with advanced collecting duct RCC have responded to cisplatin- or gemcitabine-based chemotherapy (Milowsky et al, 2002; Peyromaure et al, 2003).

**Renal medullary carcinoma is a relatively new subtype of RCC that occurs almost exclusively in association with the sickle cell trait. It is typically diagnosed in young African Americans, often in the third decade of life** (Davis et al, 1995b; Polascik et al, 2002; Swartz et al, 2002). Renal medullary carcinoma is thought to arise from the calyceal epithelium near the renal papillae but is often highly infiltrative (Davidson et al, 1995; Davis et al, 1995b). Many cases are both locally advanced and metastatic at the time of diagnosis. Most patients do not respond to therapy and succumb to their disease in a few to several months (Davis et al, 1995b; Herring et al, 1997; Figenshau et al, 1998; Polascik et al, 2002). Mean survival in Davis and coworkers' series (1995b), which consisted of 34 patients, was only 15 weeks. **This tumor shares**

many histologic features with collecting duct carcinoma, and some consider it a subtype of collecting duct carcinoma or at least a closely related tumor (Störkel et al, 1997; Polascik et al, 2002; Swartz et al, 2002). The site of origin (renal papillae) and association with sickle cell trait suggest that a relatively hypoxic environment may contribute to tumorigenesis.

**Sarcomatoid variants of almost all the histologic subtypes of RCC have been described, and this entity has now been reclassified because it is no longer considered a distinct histologic subtype of RCC** (Weiss et al, 1995; Störkel et al, 1997; Oyasu, 1998; Delahunt, 1999; de Peralta-Venturina et al, 2001; Kuroda et al, 2003e; Cheville et al, 2004). Thorough search for epithelium-derived malignant components is almost always fruitful; it is rare to find a truly pure sarcomatoid renal mass (Delahunt, 1999). Most authors now believe that sarcomatoid lesions represent poorly differentiated regions of other histologic subtypes of RCC rather than independently derived tumors (DeLong et al, 1993; Oyasu, 1998; Delahunt, 1999). Sarcomatoid differentiation is found in 1% to 5% of RCCs, most commonly in association with conventional or chromophobic RCC (Oyasu, 1998; Cheville et al, 2004). It is characterized by spindle cell histology, positive staining for vimentin, infiltrative growth pattern, aggressive local and metastatic behavior, and poor prognosis (Fig. 47–19) (Ro et al, 1987; DeLong et al, 1993; Cangiano et al, 1999). Invasion of adjacent organs is common, and median survival has been less than 1 year in most series (Ro et al, 1987; Cangiano et al, 1999; Escudier et al, 2002a; Mian et al, 2002; Nanus et al, 2004). Multimodal approaches should be considered if performance status allows because Cangiano and colleagues (1999) reported improved response rates in patients receiving IL-2–based immunotherapy and surgery compared with patients receiving surgery alone. Other reports suggest occasional responses to chemotherapy (Bangalore et al, 2001). Some sarcomatoid tumors may express the *c-kit* proto-oncogene, suggesting that they may respond to imatinib mesylate, but clinical experience with this is limited (Voelzke et al, 2002; Castillo et al, 2004).

Unclassified RCC represents a small minority of cases (<3%) of presumed RCC with features that remain indeterminate even after careful analysis (Zisman et al, 2002a). Most

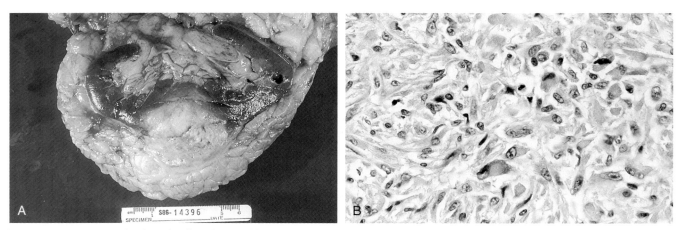

**Figure 47–19.** **A,** Conventional renal cell carcinoma with sarcomatoid differentiation demonstrating infiltrative growth pattern. **B,** High-grade renal cell carcinoma with sarcomatoid differentiation and rhabdoid cells.

are poorly differentiated and are associated with a highly aggressive biologic behavior and a particularly poor prognosis (Zisman et al, 2002a).

## Clinical Presentation

**Because of the sequestered location of the kidney within the retroperitoneum, many renal masses remain asymptomatic and nonpalpable until they are advanced. With the more pervasive use of noninvasive imaging for the evaluation of a variety of nonspecific symptom complexes, more than 50% of RCCs are now detected incidentally** (Pantuck et al, 2000). Several studies have shown that such tumors are more likely to be confined to the kidney, and a positive impact on survival of patients has been reported, although the potential contributions of lead and length time biases have not been defined (Konnak and Grossman, 1985; Thompson and Peek, 1988; Kessler et al, 1994; Tsui et al, 2000b; Parsons et al, 2001; Lee et al, 2002; Leslie et al, 2003). **Symptoms associated with RCC can be due to local tumor growth, hemorrhage, paraneoplastic syndromes, or metastatic disease.** Flank pain is usually due to hemorrhage and clot obstruction, although it can also occur with locally advanced or invasive disease. **The classic triad of flank pain, gross hematuria, and palpable abdominal mass is now rarely found** (Jayson and Sanders, 1998). This is fortunate because this constellation of findings almost always denotes advanced disease, and some refer to it as the "too late triad." Before the advent of ultrasonography and CT scanning, most patients with RCC presented with one or more of these signs or symptoms, and many were incurable. Other indicators of advanced disease include constitutional symptoms, such as weight loss, fever, and night sweats; physical examination findings such as palpable cervical lymphadenopathy, nonreducing varicocele, and bilateral lower extremity edema suggest venous involvement. A minority of patients present with symptoms directly related to metastatic disease, such as bone pain or persistent cough. A less common but important presentation of RCC is that of spontaneous perirenal hemorrhage, although the underlying mass is often obscured by the blood. Zhang and colleagues (2002) have shown that more than 50% of patients with perirenal hematoma of unclear etiology have an occult renal tumor, most often AML or RCC. Repeated CT a few months later will often provide a definitive diagnosis.

**Paraneoplastic syndromes are found in 20% of patients with RCC,** and few tumors are associated with the diversity of such syndromes (Table 47–9). **In fact, RCC was previously referred to as the internist's tumor because of the predominance of systemic rather than local manifestations** (Sufrin et al, 1989; Gold et al, 1996; Moein and Dehghani, 2000; De Luca et al, 2002; Kamra et al, 2002). Now, a more appropriate name would be the radiologist's tumor, given the frequency of incidental detection (Parsons et al, 2001). Nevertheless, it is still important to evaluate for paraneoplastic phenomena because they can be a source of major morbidity and can affect clinical decision-making. Under normal circumstances, the kidney produces 1,25-dihydroxycholecalciferol, renin, erythropoietin, and various prostaglandins, all of which are tightly regulated to maintain homeostasis. RCC may produce these substances in pathologic amounts, and it may also elaborate a variety of other physiologically important factors, such as parathyroid hormone–like peptides, lupus-type anticoagulant, human chorionic gonadotropin, insulin, and various cytokines and inflammatory mediators (Sufrin et al, 1989; Gold et al, 1996; Ather et al, 2002). These substances are believed to be responsible for the development of constitutional symptoms such as weight loss, fever, and anemia.

**Hypercalcemia has been reported in up to 13% of patients with RCC and can be due to either paraneoplastic phenomena or osteolytic metastatic involvement of the bone** (Sufrin et al, 1989; Gold et al, 1996; Magera et al, 2004). The production of parathyroid hormone–like peptides is the most common paraneoplastic etiology, although tumor-derived 1,25-dihydroxycholecalciferol and prostaglandins may contribute in a minority of cases (Goldberg et al, 1964; Mangin et al, 1988; Sufrin et al, 1989; Gold et al, 1996; Walther et al, 1997b; Magera et al, 2004; Massfelder et al, 2004). Recent data suggest that the expression of parathyroid hormone–like peptides is suppressed by the wild-type VHL protein, and these peptides may act as potent growth factors for RCC (Massfelder et al, 2004). This may account in part for the observation that patients with RCC who present with hypercalcemia have a compromised prognosis, with a relative risk of death from cancer progression of 1.78 compared with patients with normal serum calcium levels (Magera et al, 2004). **The signs and symptoms of hypercalcemia are often nonspecific and include nausea, anorexia, fatigue, and decreased deep tendon reflexes. Medical management predominates and includes vigorous hydration followed by diuresis with furosemide and the selective use of bisphosphonates, corticosteroids, or calcitonin** (reviewed in Gold et al, 1996; Coleman, 2004). Bisphosphonate therapy is now established as standard of care for patients with hypercalcemia of malignancy, as long as renal function is adequate. Zoledronic acid, 4 mg intravenously every 4 weeks, appears to be particularly effective in patients with RCC but must be withheld in the presence of renal insufficiency (Lipton et al, 2003, 2004; Coleman et al, 2004). Indomethacin has also proved useful in a minority of cases (Gold et al, 1996; Walther et al, 1997b). More definite management would include nephrectomy or cytoreductive nephrectomy, depending on the clinical circumstances, and systemic immunotherapy to reduce the burden of disease (Goldberg et al, 1980). Hypercalcemia related to extensive osteolytic metastases is much more difficult to palliate because it is unresponsive to cytoreductive nephrectomy, but many such patients may respond to bisphosphonate therapy (Lipton et al, 2003, 2004; Coleman et al, 2004). Some patients with hypercalcemia related to osteolytic

| Table 47–9. Incidence of Systemic Syndromes Associated with Renal Cell Carcinoma | |
|---|---|
| **Syndrome** | **Percentage** |
| Elevated erythrocyte sedimentation rate | 55.6 |
| Hypertension | 37.5 |
| Anemia | 36.3 |
| Cachexia, weight loss | 34.5 |
| Pyrexia | 17.2 |
| Abnormal liver function | 14.4 |
| Hypercalcemia | 4.9 |
| Polycythemia | 3.5 |
| Neuromyopathy | 3.2 |
| Amyloidosis | 2.0 |

metastases may benefit from focused radiation therapy if limited sites of involvement can be identified (Gold et al, 1996).

**Hypertension and polycythemia are other important paraneoplastic syndromes commonly found in patients with RCC** (Moein and Dehghani, 2000). Hypertension associated with RCC can be secondary to increased production of renin directly by the tumor; compression or encasement of the renal artery or its branches, effectively leading to renal artery stenosis; or arteriovenous fistula within the tumor (Robertson et al, 1967; Sufrin et al, 1989). Less common causes include polycythemia, hypercalcemia, ureteral obstruction, and increased intracranial pressure associated with cerebral metastases (Sufrin et al, 1989). Polycythemia associated with RCC can be due to increased production of erythropoietin, either directly by the tumor or by the adjacent parenchyma in response to hypoxia induced by tumor growth (Gross et al, 1994).

**One of the more fascinating paraneoplastic syndromes associated with RCC is nonmetastatic hepatic dysfunction, or Stauffer's syndrome, which has been reported in 3% to 20% of cases** (Stauffer, 1961; Rosenblum, 1987). Almost all patients with Stauffer's syndrome have elevated serum alkaline phosphatase, 67% have elevated prothrombin time or hypoalbuminemia, and 20% to 30% have elevated serum bilirubin or transaminases (Sufrin et al, 1989). Other common findings include thrombocytopenia and neutropenia, and typical symptoms include fever and weight loss, which is not surprising given that many patients are found to harbor discrete regions of hepatic necrosis (Sufrin et al, 1989; Gold et al, 1996). Hepatic metastases must be excluded. Biopsy, when it is indicated, often demonstrates nonspecific hepatitis associated with a prominent lymphocytic infiltrate (Hanash, 1982). Elevated serum levels of IL-6 have been found in patients with Stauffer's syndrome, and it is believed that this and other cytokines may play a pathogenic role (Blay et al, 1997). Hepatic function normalizes after nephrectomy in 60% to 70% of cases. Persistence or recurrence of hepatic dysfunction is almost always indicative of the presence of viable tumor and thus represents a poor prognostic finding (reviewed in Sufrin, 1989).

A variety of other less common paraneoplastic syndromes associated with RCC have been reviewed by Sufrin and colleagues (1989), including Cushing's syndrome, hyperglycemia, galactorrhea, neuromyopathy, and clotting disorders (Ather et al, 2002; Kamra et al, 2002).

**In general, treatment of paraneoplastic syndromes associated with RCC has required nephrectomy or systemic immunotherapy, and except for hypercalcemia, medical therapies have not proved helpful.**

## Screening and Clinical Associations

**A number of factors make screening for RCC appealing** (Cohn and Campbell, 2000). **Most important, RCC remains primarily a surgical disease requiring early diagnosis to optimize the opportunity for cure.** Unfortunately, our ability to salvage patients with advanced disease remains limited. Consistent with these observations, several studies have demonstrated an apparent advantage to early or incidental diagnosis of RCC (Konnak and Grossman, 1985; Thompson and Peek, 1988; Kessler et al, 1994; Cohn and Campbell, 2000;

Tsui et al, 2000b; Parsons et al, 2001; Lee et al, 2002; Leslie et al, 2003).

**The primary factor that limits the widespread implementation of screening for RCC is the relatively low incidence of RCC in the general population** (8.9 cases per 100,000 population/year) (Landis et al, 1999; Cohn and Campbell, 2000). A screening test needs to be almost 100% specific to avoid an unacceptably high false-positive rate, which would lead to unnecessary, expensive, and potentially harmful diagnostic or therapeutic procedures. In addition, even if the test were 100% sensitive and specific, the yield from screening would be so low that it would not be considered cost-effective (Cohn and Campbell, 2000). Even when one considers populations with established risk factors for RCC, such as male sex, increased age, and heavy tobacco use, generalized screening would be difficult to justify because the increase in relative risk associated with each of these factors is at best twofold to threefold (Paganini-Hill et al, 1988; Cohn and Campbell, 2000). Another confounding factor is the prevalence of clinically insignificant tumors such as renal adenomas, which are found at autopsy in 10% to 20% of individuals, and other benign or slow-growing tumors (Xipell, 1971; Bosniak et al, 1995; Cohn and Campbell, 2000; Pantuck et al, 2000; Parsons et al, 2001). There is clearly a risk that such clinically insignificant lesions could be detected, leading to unnecessary evaluation and treatment (Pantuck et al, 2000; Parsons et al, 2001). All these factors recommend against generalized screening efforts for the detection of RCC.

Review of the literature describing the use of dipstick analysis for hematuria and ultrasonography or CT scanning for screening for RCC supports these conclusions (Cohn and Campbell, 2000). Urinalysis is simple and inexpensive, but the yield of RCC in several screening studies has been exceedingly low (Mohr et al, 1986; Thompson, 1987; Mariani et al, 1989; Murakami et al, 1990). In part, this may be due to the fact that small RCCs are often not associated with hematuria (gross or microscopic) because this is a parenchymal rather than a urothelium-based malignant neoplasm (Tosaka et al, 1990). The incidence of RCC in ultrasound or CT screening studies has ranged from 23 to 300 per 100,000 population, and an apparent advantage of screening has been debated because an increased proportion of organ-confined tumors has been found in screened populations compared with historical controls (Sohma et al, 1989; Tosaka et al, 1990; Spouge et al, 1996; Tsuboi et al, 2000; Filipas et al, 2003; Fenton and Weiss, 2004). However, although the yield of RCC has been higher than expected, it is still relatively low, and it is unlikely that such efforts would be considered cost-effective (Cohn and Campbell, 2000). Overall, the yield of RCC in such studies is more than an order lower than the yield from prostate-specific antigen–based screening for prostate cancer, and many of the same controversies about lead and length time biases that have plagued the debate about screening for prostate cancer also apply to RCC (Cohn and Campbell, 2000; Pantuck et al, 2000; Parsons et al, 2001; Fenton and Weiss, 2004). Because of these considerations, it is difficult to justify generalized screening efforts for RCC given the currently available technology.

Several investigators are now reporting novel molecular assays to detect RCC-related biomarkers in the urine or serum that may substantially alter our perspective about screening for RCC. These assays can detect microsatellite alterations in the DNA, *VHL* gene mutations or hypermethylation of the

*VHL* gene, expression of RCC-specific proteins such as CA-9, or upregulation of angiogenic factors such as VEGF (Eisenberger et al, 1999; de la Taille et al, 2000; Chang et al, 2001; Ashida et al, 2003; Battagli et al, 2003; Chen and Getzenberg, 2004; Uzzo et al, 2004). Proteomic profiling of the urine to detect RCC-specific markers also holds much promise for the future (Rogers et al, 2003).

**For now, however, the focus for screening for RCC must be on well-defined target populations, such as patients with end-stage renal failure and acquired renal cystic disease, TS, and familial RCC** (Table 47–10). Eighty percent of patients with end-stage renal failure eventually develop acquired renal cystic disease, and 1% to 2% of this subgroup develops RCC (Ishikawa et al, 1980, 1990; Matson and Cohen, 1990; Levine et al, 1991; Cheuk et al, 2002; Brown, 2004). **Overall, the relative risk of RCC in patients with end-stage renal failure has been estimated to be 5- to 20-fold higher than that in the general population** (Ishikawa et al, 1990; Matson and Cohen, 1990; Ishikawa, 1991, 2004; Levine et al, 1991; Levine, 1992; Cowie, 2002; Denton et al, 2002; Brown, 2004). Fifteen percent of patients with RCC in the setting of end-stage renal failure have metastases at the time of presentation, and many such patients die of malignant progression (Levine et al, 1991; Brown, 2004; Ishikawa, 2004). Given these considerations, screening for RCC is recommended in this population, which is substantial, representing almost 300,000 patients in the United States alone. There are, however, a number of problems associated with screening this population of patients. These include concerns about short life expectancy, increased incidence of adenomas (20% to 40% versus 10% to 20% in the general population), complexity of imaging given the altered architecture associated with acquired renal cystic disease, and inevitable cost-related issues (Mindell, 1989; Levine et al, 1991, 1997; Sarasin et al, 1995; Cowie, 2002). **A reasonable compromise is to target end-stage renal failure**

---

### Table 47–10. Screening for Renal Cell Carcinoma: Target Populations

*Patients with end-stage renal failure*

Screen only patients with long life expectancy and no major comorbidities

Periodic ultrasound examination or CT scan beginning during third year on dialysis

*Patients with known von Hippel–Lindau syndrome*

Obtain biannual abdominal CT or ultrasound study beginning at the age of 15 to 20 years

Periodic clinical and radiographic screening for nonrenal manifestations

*Relatives of patients with von Hippel–Lindau syndrome*

Obtain genetic analysis
   If positive, follow screening recommendations for patients with known von Hippel–Lindau syndrome
   If negative, less stringent follow-up is required

*Relatives of patients with other familial forms of RCC*

Obtain periodic ultrasound or CT study and consider genetic analysis

*Patients with tuberous sclerosis*

Periodic screening with ultrasound examination or CT scan

*Patients with autosomal-dominant polycystic kidney disease*

Routine screening not justified

---

**patients without other major comorbidities, to delay screening until the third year on dialysis, and to take into account the sex and type of renal replacement therapy, although data about the last factors are admittedly controversial** (Brown, 2004). Ishizuka and colleagues (2000) have demonstrated elevated serum levels of VEGF in dialysis patients with RCC, suggesting a potential role for biomarkers for screening this population in the future. Interestingly, recent data suggest that renal transplant recipients remain at high risk for RCC in the native kidneys, and Neuzillet and colleagues (2004) have recommended continued periodic radiologic screening even after transplantation.

**An increased incidence of RCC has also been debated in TS, an autosomal dominant disorder in which patients can develop adenoma sebaceum (a distinctive skin lesion), epilepsy, mental retardation, and renal cysts and AMLs** (Shapiro et al, 1984; Bernstein et al, 1986; Washecka and Hanna, 1991; Aoyama et al, 1996; Bjornsson et al, 1996; Robertson et al, 1996; Sampson, 1996; Tello et al, 1998; Choyke et al, 2003; Lendvay and Marshall, 2003; Narayanan, 2003). Many cases of RCC in this syndrome have been characterized by early onset and multifocality, suggesting a genetic predisposition (Washecka and Hanna, 1991; Lendvay and Marshall, 2003). In addition, the Eker rat, which is mutant for the rodent homologue of the *TSC2* gene responsible for the development of TS in humans, develops RCC at high frequency, as do *Tsc2*-deficient knockout mice (Yeung et al, 1994; Kobayashi et al, 1997, 1999; Hino et al, 1999; Lendvay and Marshall, 2003; McDorman and Wolf, 2002). Furthermore, an increased incidence of *TSC2* mutations has been found in human RCC (Duffy et al, 2002; Lendvay and Marshall, 2003), and Liu and colleagues (2003) have shown that loss of this tumor suppressor gene leads to upregulated expression of VEGF through an mTOR and HIF-2α–mediated mechanism, analogous to the role of the VHL protein. **Such biologic and clinical observations argue in favor of an increased predisposition for RCC in this syndrome, which is consistent with most, although admittedly not all, relevant demographic data** (Shapiro et al, 1984; Bernstein et al, 1986; Washecka and Hanna, 1991; Aoyama et al, 1996; Bjornsson et al, 1996; Robertson et al, 1996; Sampson, 1996; Tello et al, 1998; Lendvay and Marshall, 2003; Martignoni et al, 2003). **A reasonable conclusion is that periodic renal imaging should be pursued in patients with TS; such a policy will also facilitate follow-up for the development and progression of AML.**

Screening for RCC in autosomal dominant polycystic kidney disease (ADPKD) was previously recommended, but several factors have prompted a reassessment of this policy. More recent studies suggest no significantly increased risk of RCC in ADPKD, and imaging is extremely difficult in this population related to the altered intrarenal architecture (Torres et al, 1985; Gregoire et al, 1987; Keith et al, 1994; Sessa et al, 1997; Soderdahl et al, 1997; Cohn and Campbell, 2000; Gupta et al, 2000; Mosetti et al, 2003). The increased incidence of adenomas in ADPKD would also militate against a potential benefit of screening (Torres et al, 1985; Gregoire et al, 1987). **Taken together, these considerations suggest that screening for RCC in patients with ADPKD should not be pursued.**

Special consideration should also be given to von Hippel–Lindau disease in any discussion of the value of

**screening for RCC.** This syndrome should be considered in any patient with early-onset or multifocal RCC or RCC in combination with any of the following: a history of visual or neurologic symptoms; a family history of blindness, central nervous system tumors, or renal cancer; or coexistent pancreatic cysts, epididymal lesions, or inner ear tumors (Neumann and Zbar, 1997; Choyke et al, 2003; Linehan et al, 2003; Pavlovich and Schmidt, 2004). Patients suspected of having von Hippel–Lindau disease, or the appropriate relatives of those with documented disease, should strongly consider genetic evaluation. The entire *VHL* gene has now been sequenced and detailed, and sophisticated molecular analysis is readily available and offers a number of important advantages (Zbar et al, 1999; Linehan et al, 2003). Patients with germline mutations can be identified and offered clinical and radiographic screening that can identify the major manifestations of von Hippel–Lindau disease at a presymptomatic phase, allowing potential amelioration of the considerable morbidity associated with this syndrome (Glenn et al, 1992; Maranchie and Linehan, 2003). Investigators at the National Institutes of Health have recommended that such patients be evaluated with (1) annual physical examination and ophthalmologic evaluation beginning in infancy; (2) estimation of urinary catecholamines at the age of 2 years and every 1 to 2 years thereafter; (3) MRI of the central nervous system biannually beginning at the age of 11 years; (4) ultrasound examination of the abdomen and pelvis annually beginning at the age of 11 years, followed by CT scanning every 6 months if cysts or tumors develop; and (5) periodic auditory examinations (Choyke et al, 1995; Friedrich, 1999; Maranchie and Linehan, 2003). Individuals who are found to be wild type for both alleles of *VHL* also benefit because they can be spared much of the expense and anxiety associated with such intensive surveillance protocols.

Molecular screening is also available for patients suspected of having hereditary papillary RCC and other familial forms of RCC and should be discussed with appropriate family members (Schmidt et al, 1997; Linehan et al, 2003). Again, individuals at risk, as defined by the presence of mutations of the *met* proto-oncogene or other relevant genetic alterations, and those with suggestive clinical or family histories should be evaluated with abdominal ultrasonography or CT scanning at periodic intervals. Further testing may be indicated according to the syndrome involved.

## Staging and Diagnosis

**Until the 1990s, the most commonly used staging system for RCC was Robson's modification of the system of Flocks and Kadesky, and this schema is still embedded in the mindset of most urologists** (Fig. 47–20) (Robson, 1963; Robson et al, 1969). In retrospect, the limitations of this classification scheme are readily evident. The primary problem can be found in stage III, where tumors with lymphatic metastases, a very poor prognostic finding, were combined with those with venous involvement, many of which can be treated and potentially cured with an aggressive surgical approach (Gettman and Blute, 2002; Leibovich et al, 2003b). Further imprecision resulted from the fact that the extent of nodal and venous involvement was not delineated in this system. The net effect was that the prognostic significance of the various stages was

STAGING OF RENAL CELL CARCINOMA

**Stage I**

Tumor within capsule

**Stage II**

Tumor invasion of perinephric fat (confined to Gerota's fascia)

**Stage III**

Tumor involvement of regional lymph nodes and/or renal vein and cava

**Stage IV**

Adjacent organs or distant metastases

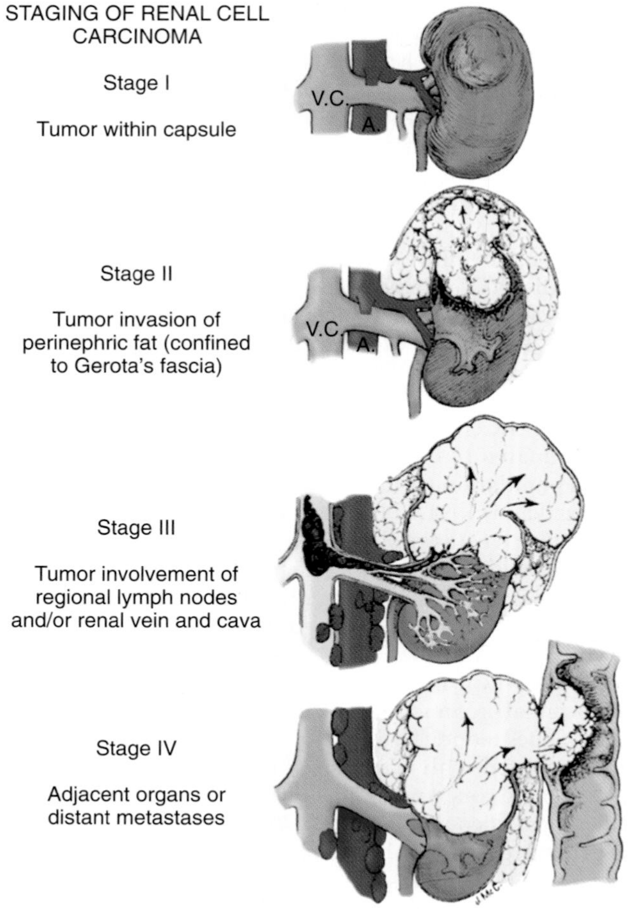

**Figure 47–20.** Staging of renal cell carcinoma as proposed by Holland, in accordance with classification systems developed by Robson, Murphy, and Flocks and Kadesky. (From Holland JM: Cancer of the kidney: Natural history and staging. Cancer 1973;32:1030. Copyright © 1973 American Cancer Society.)

blunted, with some studies reporting equivalent survival for patients with stage II and stage III tumors (Skinner et al, 1971).

**The tumor, nodes, and metastasis (TNM) system proposed by the International Union Against Cancer represented a major improvement because it separated tumors with venous involvement from those with lymphatic invasion, quantified each, and defined the anatomic extent of disease more explicitly** (Beahrs et al, 1988; Leibovich et al, 2003b). Another advantage of the TNM system is that it has facilitated comparison of clinical and pathologic data from various centers across the globe (Leung and Ghavamian, 2002; Leibovich et al, 2003b).

**In 2002, the American Joint Committee on Cancer proposed a revision of the TNM system that is now the recommended staging system for RCC** (Tables 47–11 and 47–12). This staging classification has undergone several modifications in the past two decades in an effort to more accurately reflect tumor biology and prognosis and to guide clinical management. It is important to be cognizant of these changes in comparing studies from different eras. In 1997, the previous division of stages T1 and T2 at tumor size of 2.5 cm was

### Table 47–11. International TNM Staging System for Renal Cell Carcinoma

*T: Primary tumor*

TX: Primary tumor cannot be assessed
T0: No evidence of primary tumor
T1a: Tumor ≤ 4.0 cm and confined to the kidney
T1b: Tumor > 4.0 cm and ≤ 7.0 cm and confined to the kidney
T2: Tumor > 7.0 cm and confined to the kidney
T3a: Tumor invades adrenal gland or perinephric fat but not beyond Gerota's fascia
T3b: Tumor extents into the renal vein (or its segmental branches) or vena cava below diaphragm
T3c: Tumor extends into the vena cava above the diaphragm or invades the wall of the vena cava
T4: Tumor invades beyond Gerota's fascia

*N: Regional lymph nodes*

NX: Regional lymph nodes cannot be assessed
N0: No regional lymph nodes metastasis
N1: Metastasis in a single regional lymph node
N2: Metastases in more than one regional lymph node

*M: Distant metastases*

MX: Distant metastasis cannot be assessed
M0: No distant metastasis
M1: Distant metastasis present

*Stage grouping*

| | | | |
|---|---|---|---|
| Stage I | T1 | N0 | M0 |
| Stage II | T2 | N0 | M0 |
| Stage III | T1 or T2 | N1 | M0 |
| | T3 | N0 or N1 | M0 |
| Stage IV | T4 | any N | M0 |
| | any T | N2 | M0 |
| | any T | any N | M1 |

Modified from the AJCC Cancer Staging Manual, 6th ed. New York, Springer-Verlag, 2002.

### Table 47–12. Comparison of Robson and TNM Staging Systems for Renal Cell Carcinoma

| Tumor Status | Robson Stage | TNM Stage (2002) |
|---|---|---|
| Tumor ≤ 4.0 cm, confined to kidney | I | T1a |
| Tumor > 4.0 cm and ≤ 7.0 cm and confined to kidney | I | T1b |
| Tumor > 7.0 cm and confined to kidney | I | T2 |
| Extension to adrenal gland or perinephric fat | II | T3a |
| Renal vein or vena caval involvement below diaphragm | IIIa | T3b |
| Vena caval involvement above the diaphragm | IIIa | T3c |
| Single lymph node involved | IIIb | N1 |
| More than one lymph node involved | IIIb | N2 |
| Combination of venous and nodal involvement | IIIc | T3b or c, N1 or N2 |
| Local extension beyond Gerota's fascia | IVa | T4 |
| Distant metastasis | IVb | M1 |

abandoned because several studies showed no prognostic significance at this level. Analysis of the Surveillance, Epidemiology, and End Results (SEER) program database demonstrated survival differences associated with 5-, 7.5-, and 10-cm cut points, and the 7-cm cut point between stages T1 and T2 was adopted because it reflected the mean tumor size in the database (Guinan et al, 1995a; Gettman et al, 2001a). Other significant changes included a reclassification of venous tumor thrombi and a simplification of the classification of extent of nodal involvement (Guinan et al, 1997). These changes were substantiated by Gettmann and colleagues (2001a), who showed that this schema provided improved prognostication. Another important change clarified the status of tumors that invade the perinephric fat medially, near the renal sinus. These tumors were often classified as stage pT2 in the past. Consensus is that these tumors should now be classified as T3a because there is no biologic rationale for excluding them from this category, and studies suggest that such tumors actually may be at increased risk for metastasis related to enhanced access to the venous system (Bonsib et al, 2000; Uzzo et al, 2002). Regarding venous involvement, macroscopic invasion of the caval wall is now classified as stage T3c since this has been found to be a poor prognostic indicator (Hatcher et al, 1991).

In the 2002 version, stage T1 was subdivided; T1a represents tumor size of 4 cm or less and T1b represents tumor size between 4 and 7 cm, reflecting data in the literature demonstrating excellent outcomes for patients with small (4 cm or less), unilateral, confined tumors managed by either partial or radical nephrectomy (Butler et al, 1994; Lerner et al, 1996; Hafez et al, 1999; Igarashi et al, 2001). This change was validated in a large review of 1593 patients with nonmetastatic clear cell RCC treated with radical nephrectomy at the Mayo Clinic (Frank et al, 2004b). Subclassification of T2 tumors into T2a (7 to 10 cm) and T2b (>10.0 cm) has also been proposed by Frank and colleagues (2005b), who presented data showing a substantial prognostic difference between these two subgroups of patients. Nevertheless, the cut point for classification of organ-confined RCC remains controversial; some authors argue that a single cut point of 4.5 to 5.5 cm would provide optimal prognostication while having the advantage of simplicity (Zisman et al, 2001a; Sagalowsky, 2002; Elmore et al, 2003; Ficarra et al, 2004).

Other proposed changes in the staging system for RCC have focused on patients with stages T3a-c, specifically related to adrenal gland involvement, tumor thrombus, and invasion of the perinephric fat. Several reports now document a poor prognosis associated with adrenal metastasis from RCC, and one proposal is to reclassify tumors with direct extension into the adrenal gland as T4 and others as M1, reflecting a likely hematogenous route of spread (Sagalowsky et al, 1994; Sandock et al, 1997; Paul et al, 2001a; von Knobloch et al, 2004; Lam et al, 2005; Siemer et al, 2005; Thompson et al, 2005). Leibovich and colleagues (2005) have proposed reclassification of patients with T3 RCC into four categories: (1) tumor thrombus limited to renal vein but no invasion of the perinephric fat; (2) invasion of the perinephric fat but no tumor thrombus; (3) tumor thrombus limited to the renal vein and invasion of the perinephric fat *or* caval thrombus below the diaphragm; and (4) caval thrombus below the diaphragm and invasion of the perinephric fat *or* caval thrombus above the diaphragm. Their series of 675 patients with pT3 RCC demonstrated substantially improved prognostication with this combined classification system, which also makes intuitive sense with respect to the tumor biology of the disease (deKernion, 2005). Five-year cancer-specific survival rates in these four groups were 64%, 55%, 42%, and 26%, respectively.

**The clinical staging of renal malignant disease begins with a thorough history, physical examination, and judicious use of laboratory tests. Symptomatic presentation, significant weight loss (>10% of body weight), bone pain, and poor performance status all suggest advanced disease, as do physical examination findings of a palpable mass or lymphadenopathy.** A nonreducing varicocele and lower extremity edema suggest venous involvement. Abnormal liver function test results, elevated serum alkaline phosphatase or sedimentation rate, and significant anemia point to the probability of advanced disease (Gelb, 1997; Srigley et al, 1997).

**The radiographic staging of RCC can be accomplished with a high-quality abdominal CT scan and a routine chest radiograph in most cases,** with selective use of MRI and other studies as indicated (reviewed in Bechtold and Zagoria, 1997; Choyke et al, 2001). MRI can be reserved primarily for patients with locally advanced malignant disease, possible venous involvement, renal insufficiency, or allergy to intravenous contrast material (Choyke, 1997; Pretorius et al, 2000; Choyke et al, 2001). CT findings suggestive of extension into the perinephric fat include perinephric stranding (Fig. 47–21), which is a nonspecific finding, and a distinct soft tissue density within the perinephric space, which is an uncommon finding (Bechtold and Zagoria, 1997). Overall, the accuracy of CT or MRI for detection of involvement of the perinephric fat is low, reflecting the fact that extracapsular spread often occurs microscopically (Pretorius et al, 2000; Choyke et al, 2001; Leung and Ghavamian, 2002; Kamel et al, 2004). Most of these cases are managed with radical nephrectomy, so the clinical relevance of this imprecision in staging is blunted. Ipsilateral adrenal involvement can be assessed with reasonable accuracy through a combination of preoperative CT and intraoperative inspection. **Patients with an enlarged adrenal gland on CT,**

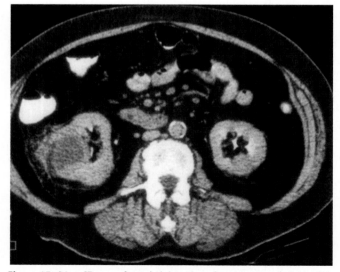

**Figure 47–21.** CT scan after administration of contrast agent shows right renal tumor with perinephric stranding suggesting invasion of the perinephric fat.

**upper pole tumor location, extensive malignant replacement of the kidney, or palpably abnormal adrenal gland are at risk for ipsilateral adrenal involvement and should be managed accordingly** (Sagalowsky et al, 1994; Sandock et al, 1997; Tsui et al, 2000a; Sawai et al, 2002; Kobayashi et al, 2003). **Enlarged hilar or retroperitoneal lymph nodes 2 cm or more in diameter on CT almost always harbor malignant change, but this should be confirmed by percutaneous aspiration or surgical exploration. Many smaller nodes prove to be inflammatory rather than neoplastic and should not preclude surgical therapy** (Studer et al, 1990; Choyke et al, 2001; Israel and Bosniak, 2003b). MRI can add specificity to the evaluation of retroperitoneal nodes by distinguishing vascular structures from lymphatic ones (Bechtold and Zagoria, 1997). MRI is the premier study for evaluation of invasion of tumor into adjacent structures and for surgical planning in these challenging cases (Bechtold and Zagoria, 1997; Choyke, 1997; Pretorius et al, 2000; Choyke et al, 2001). Obliteration of the fat plane between the tumor and the adjacent organs (such as the liver) can be a misleading finding on CT and should prompt further imaging with MRI.

**The sensitivities of CT for detection of renal venous tumor thrombus and inferior vena caval involvement are 78% and 96%, respectively** (Bechtold and Zagoria, 1997). CT findings suggestive of venous involvement include venous enlargement, abrupt change in the caliber of the vein, and intraluminal areas of decreased density or filling defects. The diagnosis is strengthened by the demonstration of collateral vessels. Most false negatives occur in patients with right-sided tumors in whom the short length of the vein and the mass effect from the tumor combine to make detection of the tumor thrombus difficult (Bechtold and Zagoria, 1997). Fortunately, such cases are readily identified and dealt with intraoperatively. **MRI is well established as the premier study for the evaluation and staging of inferior vena caval tumor thrombus, although recent data suggest that multiplanar CT may be equivalent** (Goldfarb et al, 1990; Kallman et al, 1992; Bechtold and Zagoria, 1997; Choyke, 1997; Oto et al, 1998; Sun et al, 1999; Pretorius et al, 2000; Choyke et al, 1987; Sohaib et al, 2002; Israel and Bosniak, 2003a; Ergen et al, 2004; Hallscheidt et al, 2004). MRI provides reliable information about both the cephalad and caudad extent of the thrombus and can often distinguish bland from tumor thrombus. In addition, MRI is noninvasive and does not place the patient at risk for contrast nephropathy (Pretorius et al, 2000; Choyke et al, 2001). **Venacavography is now best reserved for patients with equivocal MRI findings and for patients who cannot tolerate MRI or have other contraindications to MRI.** Transesophageal echocardiography also appears to be accurate for establishing the cephalad extent of the tumor thrombus, but it is invasive and provides no distinct advantages over MRI in the preoperative setting (Glazer and Novick, 1997). Doppler ultrasonography is operator dependent and does not provide the anatomic resolution available with MRI (Habboub et al, 1997).

**Metastatic evaluation in all cases should include a routine chest radiograph, careful and systematic review of the abdominal and pelvic CT findings, and liver function tests** (Choyke et al, 1987). Most investigators agree that a bone scan can be reserved for patients with elevated serum alkaline phosphatase or bone pain and that a chest CT scan can be reserved for patients with pulmonary symptoms or an abnormal chest radiograph (Lim and Carter, 1993; Seaman et al, 1996; Choyke et al, 2001). However, patients with locally advanced disease, enlarged retroperitoneal lymph nodes, or significant comorbid disease may mandate more thorough imaging to rule out metastatic disease and to aid in treatment planning (Choyke et al, 2001). As always, evaluation and management must be individualized on the basis of the clinical circumstances. Shvarts and colleagues (2004) have shown that performance status is a powerful predictor of bone metastasis. In their analysis, patients with good performance status (Eastern Cooperative Oncology Group performance status score of 0), no evidence of extraosseous metastases, and no bone pain were extremely low risk and did not benefit from bone scanning. They recommended a bone scan for all other patients, and the incidence of bone metastasis in this group was above 15%.

Positron emission tomography has also been investigated for patients with high risk or metastatic RCC, with most studies showing good specificity but suboptimal sensitivity. At present, its best role is for patients with equivocal findings on conventional imaging. In this setting, an abnormal positron emission tomographic scan indicates metastatic disease and could strongly influence further evaluation and management (Hoh et al, 1998; Ramdave et al, 2001; Nimeh et al, 2002; Jadvar et al, 2003; Kang et al, 2004). Immunoscintigraphy with radiolabeled monoclonal antibodies to CA-9 is also being explored in this population, analogous to the ProstaScint scan for prostate cancer (Brouwers et al, 2002).

**The indications for percutaneous renal biopsy or aspiration in the evaluation of renal masses have traditionally been limited, primarily related to concerns about sampling error, difficulty interpreting limited tissue given the inherent similarities between the eosinophilic variants of RCC and oncocytoma, and recognition of the improved diagnostic accuracy of cross-sectional imaging such as CT or MRI** (Herts and Baker, 1995; Schatz and Lieber, 2003). Eighty-three percent to 90% of solid renal masses thought to be suspicious for RCC based on careful radiographic evaluation prove to be RCC on final pathologic analysis (Silver et al, 1997). Fine-needle aspiration biopsy (FNAB) cannot significantly improve on this degree of diagnostic certainty and is unlikely to influence clinical management in the majority of cases (Dechet et al, 2003). **The sensitivities and specificities of FNAB for the diagnosis of RCC are well documented and range from 80% to 95%** (Herts and Baker, 1995; Dechet et al, 2003; Neuzillet et al, 2004). Five percent to 15% of RCCs are thus misdiagnosed by FNAB, and given the high likelihood of malignancy, most investigators are appropriately unwilling to proceed with this invasive procedure. Notable exceptions include patients suspected of having metastatic disease, renal abscess, or lymphoma, all of which are primarily managed medically (Herts and Baker, 1995; Herts and Remer, 2000). Patients with flank pain, febrile urinary tract infection, and renal mass may be considered for percutaneous biopsy or aspiration to establish a diagnosis of renal abscess rather than malignant disease; a drainage tube can be placed concomitantly if it is clinically indicated. Lymphoma should be suspected in patients with massive retroperitoneal lymphadenopathy, especially in the setting of distant lymphadenopathy or splenomegaly, and a percutaneous biopsy is often diagnostic, precluding the need

for major surgery. Metastasis to the kidney is usually multifocal and is particularly common in patients with lung, breast, and gastrointestinal cancers and malignant melanoma (Choyke et al, 1987; Pollack et al, 1987). However, FNAB should be strongly considered in any patient with a history of primary nonrenal malignant disease, unless clinical circumstances, such as a prolonged interval between diagnoses and unifocal renal involvement with a well-vascularized mass, point toward RCC rather than metastatic disease. Another indication for FNAB is a need to establish a pathologic diagnosis of RCC in patients presenting with disseminated metastases or unresectable primary tumors or in patients with extensive comorbid disease or other contraindications to surgery. In this setting, FNAB can confirm the diagnosis, guide management, and potentially obviate the need for surgery.

More recently, FNAB has been reassessed, and several groups have shown enthusiasm for this approach. Some studies suggest improved sensitivity and specificity, particularly when FNAB is combined with molecular analysis for CA-9 expression or other markers for RCC (Truong et al, 2001; Wood et al, 1999; Lechevallier et al, 2000; Richter et al, 2000; Hara et al, 2001; Liu and Fanning, 2001; Caoili et al, 2002; Rybicki et al, 2003; Li et al, 2004). Molecular analysis could also assess HMB-45 expression to evaluate for atypical AML, and genetic analysis for oncocytoma may also be available in the near future. In addition, FNAB could influence clinical management of small renal masses if markers of clinical aggressiveness could be established and reliably evaluated on limited pathologic material (Neuzillet et al, 2004).

**The potential complications of FNAB include bleeding, infection, arteriovenous fistula, needle track seeding, and pneumothorax** (reviewed in Herts and Baker, 1995). In general, the incidence of complications has been reduced significantly since the introduction of smaller gauge needles. Tumor location, operator expertise, and number of biopsy attempts can also influence complication rates. Perinephric bleeding can be detected by CT scan in 90% of cases, but clinically significant hemorrhage resulting in gross hematuria is much less common (5% to 7%) and is almost always self-limited (Hopper and Yakes, 1990; Vassiliades and Bernardino, 1991). Blood transfusion is only rarely required. Persistent bleeding may indicate an arteriovenous fistula or a laceration of a major branch artery or vein and may require angiography and embolization. All other complications of FNAB are uncommon, with clinically significant morbidity occurring in less than 5% of cases. Only five cases of needle track seeding have been reported with RCC. Overall, the estimated incidence of needle track seeding with urologic malignant neoplasms is less than 0.01%; most occur with poorly differentiated transitional cell carcinoma (Herts and Baker, 1995).

## Prognostic Factors

**Important prognostic factors for RCC include specific clinical signs or symptoms, tumor-related factors, and various laboratory findings** (Kontak and Campbell, 2003). **Overall, tumor-related factors such as pathologic stage, tumor size, nuclear grade, and histologic subtype have the greatest utility on an independent basis. However, an integrative approach, combining a variety of factors that have proved to**

**Table 47-13. Robson Tumor Stage and 5-Year Survival for Renal Cell Carcinoma**

| Author | Total No. | Number of Patients (% 5-year Survivors) | | | |
|---|---|---|---|---|---|
| | | I | II | III | IV |
| Robson et al (1969) | 88 | 32 (66) | 14 (64) | 24 (42) | 9 (11) |
| Skinner et al (1971) | 309 | 91 (65) | 17 (47) | 100 (51) | 77 (8) |
| McNichols et al (1981) | 506 | 177 (67) | 57 (51) | 209 (34) | 56 (14) |
| Selli et al (1983) | 115 | (93) | (63) | (80) | (13) |
| Golimbu et al (1986) | 326 | 52 (88) | 39 (67) | 73 (40) | 88 (2) |
| Hermanek and Schrott (1990) | 872 | 278 (92) | 165 (77) | 296 (47) | 133 (12) |
| Dinney et al (1992) | 312 | (73) | (68) | (51) | (20) |
| Guinan et al (1995) | 2473 | 1048 (75) | 473 (63) | 511 (38) | 411 (11) |

Modified from Thrasher JB, Paulson DF: Prognostic factors in renal cancer. Urol Clin North Am 1993;20:247-262.

**have independent value on multivariate analysis, appears to be most powerful** (Kattan et al, 2001; Zisman et al, 2001b; Kontak and Campbell, 2003; Patard et al, 2004a).

Clinical findings suggestive of a compromised prognosis include symptomatic presentation, weight loss of more than 10% of body weight, and poor performance status (Gelb, 1997; Srigley et al, 1997; Zisman et al, 2001b; Kim et al, 2003; Kontak and Campbell, 2003; Schips et al, 2003). Anemia, thrombocytosis, hypercalcemia, albuminuria, elevated serum alkaline phosphatase or erythrocyte sedimentation rate, and other paraneoplastic signs or symptoms have also correlated with poor outcomes for patients with RCC (Gelb, 1997; Srigley et al, 1997; Symbas et al, 2000; O'Keefe et al, 2002; Kim et al, 2003; Kontak and Campbell, 2003; Vaglio et al, 2003). Several molecular markers are now showing prognostic significance and may provide important insight into the tumor biology (Bui et al, 2001; Han et al, 2003; Kontak and Campbell, 2003). The most promising of these factors appears to be CA-9, which is regulated by the *VHL* gene and is overexpressed in many conventional RCCs (Bui et al, 2003, 2004). High CA-9 expression has correlated with improved survival in this population, suggesting that tumors with *VHL*-independent pathogenesis may have increased aggressiveness, and Yao and colleagues (2002) have presented data to support this (Mukouyama et al, 2004). Decreased proliferative index as assessed by Ki-67 has also correlated with improved survival in clear cell RCC (Bui et al, 2004). Other factors that may prove to be useful include apoptotic indices; the status of various genetic elements, such as *p53* (Shvarts et al, 2005); and evaluation of the expression and function of various growth factors and their receptors, proteins that regulate apoptosis (Miyake et al, 2002), and important adhesion molecules and proteases (see section on tumor biology) (Bui et al, 2001; Zhou and Rubin, 2001; Uchida et al, 2002; Cho et al, 2003; Kontak and Campbell, 2003; Shimazui et al, 2004). Assays for the levels of proangiogenic factors such as VEGF or basic fibroblast growth factor in the serum or urine may also improve prognostication (Gelb, 1997; Srigley et al, 1997; Jacobsen et al, 2000; Zhou and Rubin, 2001; Mizutani et al, 2003). Gene array and proteomic technology are likely to identify additional prognostic factors in the near future (Kim et al, 2004b).

**Pathologic stage has proved to be the single most important prognostic factor for RCC** (Thrasher and Paulson, 1993; Delahunt, 1998; Kontak and Campbell, 2003). Various studies have shown a strong correlation between Robson's pathologic

**Table 47-14. TNM Stage and 5-Year Survival for Renal Cell Carcinoma**

| Findings | Robson Stage | TNM (2002) | 5-Year Survival (%) |
|---|---|---|---|
| Organ confined (overall) | I | T1-2 N0 M0 | 70-90 |
| (≤4.0 cm) | I | T1a N0 M0 | 90-100 |
| (>4.0 cm, ≤7.0 cm) | I | T1b N0 M0 | 80-90 |
| (>7.0 cm) | I | T2 N0 M0 | 70-80 |
| Invasion of perinephric fat | II | T3a N0 M0 | 60-80 |
| Adrenal involvement | II | T3a N0 M0 | 0-40 |
| Venous involvement | IIIA | T3b-c N0 M0 | 40-60 |
| Locally advanced | IVA | T4 N0 M0 | 0-20 |
| Lymphatic involvement | IIIB | any T, N+ M0 | 0-20 |
| Systemic metastases | IVB | any T, any N, M1 | 0-10 |

Butler et al, 1994; Sagalowsky et al, 1994; Targonski et al, 1994; Guinan et al, 1995; Lerner et al, 1996; Sandock et al, 1997; Hafez et al, 1999; Motzer et al, 1999; Igarashi et al, 2001; Paul et al, 2001; Vasselli et al, 2001; Pantuck et al, 2002; Kontak and Campbell, 2003; von Knobloch et al, 2004; Patard et al, 2004; Phillips and Taneja, 2004; Leibovich et al, 2005; Siemer et al, 2005; Thompson et al, 2005.

stage and 5-year survival rates for RCC, as shown in Table 47-13. Similar but more discerning results have been reported for tumors staged with the TNM classification system (Table 47-14), confirming that the extent of locoregional or systemic disease at diagnosis is the primary determinant of outcome for this disease (Bassil et al, 1985; Hermanek and Schrott, 1990; Kontak and Campbell, 2003). These studies demonstrate 5-year survival rates of 70% to 90% for organ-confined disease and document a 15% to 20% reduction in survival associated with invasion of the perinephric fat (Kontak and Campbell, 2003; Leibovich et al, 2005). Renal sinus involvement should definitely be classified as T3a, and studies suggest that these patients may be at higher risk for metastasis related to increased access to the venous system (Bonsib et al, 2000; Uzzo et al, 2002). Several reports have shown that most patients with ipsilateral adrenal involvement, which is found in 1% to 2% of cases, eventually succumb to systemic disease progression, suggesting a hematogenous route of dissemination or a highly invasive phenotype (Sagalowsky et al, 1994; Sandock et al, 1997; Paul et al, 2001a; von Knobloch et al, 2004; Siemer et al, 2005; Thompson et al, 2005). Some authors have proposed that such tumors be reclassified as T4 if there is direct invasion of the adrenal gland, or M1 otherwise, to reflect this poor prognosis (Guinan et al, 1997; Thompson et al, 2005).

Venous involvement was once thought to be a poor prognostic finding for RCC, but several reports demonstrate that many patients with tumor thrombi can be salvaged with an aggressive surgical approach. These studies document 45% to 69% 5-year survival rates for patients with venous tumor thrombi as long as the tumor is otherwise confined to the kidney (Table 47–15). At one extreme, Golimbu and associates (1986) reported 84% 5-year survival in the best of circumstances—tumor thrombus limited to the main renal vein and tumor otherwise confined to the kidney. Patients with venous tumor thrombi and concomitant lymph node or systemic metastases have markedly decreased survival, and those with tumor extending into the perinephric fat have intermediate survival (see Table 47–15) (Montie et al, 1991; Glazer and Novick, 1996; Gettman et al, 1999; Naitoh et al, 1999; Sweeney et al, 2002b; Bissada et al, 2003; Kim et al, 2004a; Moinzadeh and Libertino, 2004; Leibovich et al, 2005). The importance of tumor invasion into the perinephric fat and its negative impact on prognosis for patients with tumor thrombi are highlighted in the series by Leibovich and colleagues (2005).

The prognostic significance of the cephalad extent of tumor thrombus has been controversial, and it is difficult to compare various series because of differences in selection of patients and related covariables (Leibovich et al, 2005). In a series by Sosa and coworkers (1984), the incidence of advanced locoregional or systemic disease increased with the cephalad extent of the tumor thrombus, accounting for the reduced survival associated with tumor thrombus extending into or above the level of the hepatic veins. However, other data suggest that the cephalad extent of tumor thrombus is not of prognostic significance as long as the tumor is otherwise confined. Libertino and colleagues (1987) reported no difference in survival of patients with supradiaphragmatic versus infradiaphragmatic tumor thrombi, and Glazer and Novick (1996) reported an excellent 5-year survival of 56% in 18 patients with tumor thrombus extending into the right atrium, demonstrating that many patients with tumor thrombi even at this extreme can be salvaged. Again, the caveat is that the tumor is otherwise confined, and this is less likely with level 3-4 inferior vena cava thrombi (Sosa et al, 1984; Kim et al, 2004a; Moinzadeh and Libertino, 2004). Direct invasion of the wall of the vein appears to be a more important prognostic factor than cepha-

lad extent of tumor thrombus and should be noted during tumor staging. Hatcher and colleagues (1991) reported 69% 5-year survival when the wall of the vein was clean, which was reduced to 25% when direct invasion of the caval wall was observed.

**The major drop in prognosis comes in patients whose tumor extends beyond Gerota's fascia to involve contiguous organs, which is rarely associated with 5-year survival, and in patients with lymph node or systemic metastases** (Thrasher and Paulson, 1993; Thompson et al, 2005). **Lymph node involvement has long been recognized as a dire prognostic sign because it is associated with 5- and 10-year survival rates of 5% to 30% and 0% to 5%, respectively** (Bassil et al, 1985; Phillips and Taneja, 2004). Some have argued that an extensive lymph node dissection can improve survival in this setting, particularly for patients with early or microscopic involvement of the nodes. At one extreme, Giuliani and associates (1990) reported 52% 5-year survival for 25 patients with node-positive disease managed with radical nephrectomy and extensive lymph node dissection, which is certainly better than historical controls. Other studies suggest improved survival in patients with pathologic stage N0 disease managed with extensive lymph node dissection, and proponents of this procedure have argued that a small but finite proportion of patients with microscopically occult positive nodes may benefit from a more proactive surgical approach (Golimbu et al, 1986; Herrlinger et al, 1991; Phillips and Taneja, 2004). However, randomized data to prove the therapeutic value of an extensive lymph node dissection for RCC are not available, and these results could also be explained by more accurate staging. Identification of tumors with early nodal involvement, which is facilitated by an extensive lymph node dissection, allows them to be classified as stage N+ rather than stage N0, which would improve outcomes for both groups. The stage N0 group is improved by the removal of a small proportion of patients who actually have positive nodes, and the N+ group is improved by the addition of a subgroup with early nodal involvement (Phillips and Taneja, 2004). Although it is likely that the controversy about the therapeutic value of lymphadenectomy for RCC will persist, most authors agree that a limited dissection should be considered in most patients primarily for staging and prognostic purposes.

**Systemic metastases portend a particularly poor prognosis for RCC, with 1-year survival of less than 50%, 5-year survival of 5% to 30%, and 10-year survival of 0% to 5%** (Motzer et al, 1999; Motzer and Russo, 2000; Negrier et al, 2002; Sella et al, 2003). The statistics for patients presenting with synchronous metastases are even worse, with most patients dying of disease progression within a year. For patients with asynchronous metastases, the metastasis-free interval has proved to be a useful prognosticator because it reflects the tempo of disease progression (Maldazys and deKernion, 1986; Negrier et al, 2002). Other important prognostic factors for patients with systemic metastases include performance status, number and sites of metastases, anemia, hypercalcemia, elevated alkaline phosphatase or lactate dehydrogenase levels, and sarcomatoid histology (Maldazys and deKernion, 1986; Motzer and Russo, 2000; Negrier et al, 2002; Leibovich et al, 2003b; Motzer et al, 2004). Visceral metastases have been associated with a particularly poor prognosis, in contrast to pulmonary-only disease, which accounts for most

**Table 47–15. Survival for Patients with Renal Cell Carcinoma and Inferior Vena Cava Tumor Thrombus: Effect of Associated Metastases***

| Author | N | M0 | N+ | M1 |
|---|---|---|---|---|
| Novick et al (1990) | 43 | 64% | | 11% |
| Thrasher and Paulson (1993) | 44 | 69% | | 0% |
| Swierzewski et al (1994) | 100 | 64% | | 20% |
| Staehler and Brkovic (2000) | 79 | 39%[†] | | |
| Quek et al (2001) | 99 | 59% | 33% | 0% |
| Zisman et al (2003) | 100 | 72% | | |
| Blute et al (2004) | 191 | 59% | 17% | 15% |

*Data represent 5-year survival except in the series by Novick et al, which reported 3-year survival percentages.
[†]Predominance of level III and level IV inferior vena cava thrombi (29 of 59 with M0 disease, 49%) probably accounts for lower survival in this series.

of the complete remissions observed in immunotherapy trials (Negrier et al, 2002). Bulky retroperitoneal lymphadenopathy is now also established as a strong negative prognostic factor in patients with metastatic RCC (Vasselli et al, 2001; Pantuck et al, 2003a, 2003b). Prior nephrectomy has correlated with improved survival in this population of patients, although it has been difficult to determine whether this is due to selection bias rather than a direct effect achieved by surgical debulking (Motzer et al, 1999; Negrier et al, 2002). Recent randomized data suggest that cytoreductive nephrectomy may provide a modest survival benefit, although the mechanism for this is still under debate (Flanigan et al, 2001).

**Another significant prognostic factor for RCC is tumor size,** particularly at the ends of the spectrum (Kontak and Campbell, 2003). Giuliani and colleagues (1990) reported 5-year survival rates of 84% for patients with tumor diameter less than 5 cm, 50% for tumors between 5 and 10 cm, and 0% for tumors more than 10 cm in diameter. To a large extent, this is due to a strong correlation between tumor size and pathologic tumor stage, but Guinan and coworkers (1995b) have also shown that tumor size can function as an independent prognostic factor. In their review of the SEER database of 2473 patients with RCC, tumor size was found to provide prognostic information for patients with Robson stages II, III, and IV disease. Organ-confined tumors tended to do well regardless of tumor size, but Frank and colleagues (2003a) have shown that larger tumors are more likely to exhibit clear cell histology and high nuclear grade, and both of these factors correlate with a compromised prognosis. A review of 1771 patients with organ-confined RCC showed 10-year cancer-specific survival rates of 90% to 95%, 80% to 85%, and 75% for patients with pT1a, pT1b, and pT2 tumor, respectively (Patard et al, 2004a). Other studies have also shown a particularly favorable prognosis for the unilateral pT1a tumors that are now being discovered with increased frequency. In series from the Cleveland Clinic and the Mayo Clinic, such tumors were associated with greater than 95% 5-year survival rates, whether they were managed with nephron-sparing surgery or radical nephrectomy (Butler et al, 1994; Lerner et al, 1996; Cheville et al, 2001).

**Other important prognostic factors for RCC include nuclear grade and histologic subtype.** Several grading systems for RCC have been proposed on the basis of nuclear size and morphology and presence or absence of nucleoli. Unfortunately, interobserver variability is common in the assignment of nuclear grade because it is primarily a subjective exercise; there is no ideal classification system that can overcome this subjectivity. Nevertheless, almost all the proposed grading systems have provided prognostic information for RCC, and nuclear grade has proved in many cases to be an independent prognostic factor when it is subjected to multivariate analysis (Goldstein, 1997; Ficarra et al, 2001; Kattan et al, 2001; Zisman et al, 2001b; Lohse et al, 2002; True, 2002; Kontak and Campbell, 2003; Patard et al, 2004; Lang et al, 2005). In North America, Fuhrman's classification system has been most generally adopted. In Fuhrman's original report, the 5-year survival rates for grades 1 to 4 were 64%, 34%, 31%, and 10%, respectively, and nuclear grade proved to be the most significant prognostic factor for stage I tumors in this series (Fuhrman et al, 1982). Similarly, Bretheau and colleagues (1995) evaluated 190 patients with RCC and reported

a correlation between Fuhrman's nuclear grade and tumor stage, synchronous metastases, lymph node involvement, venous tumor thrombi, tumor size, and invasion of the perinephric fat. In this series, the 5-year survival rates for grades 1 to 4 were 76%, 72%, 51%, and 35%, respectively, with significant differences observed between tumors of grades 1/2 and those of grades 3/4. In most series, prognostic significance has been found primarily at the ends of the spectrum (i.e., grades 1 and 4), and given the difficulties of distinguishing the intermediate grades, a consensus conference on tumor grading for RCC recommended changing to a three-tiered system (Medeiros et al, 1997; Lang et al, 2005).

**Histologic subtype can also carry prognostic significance, although, again, primarily at the ends of the spectrum.** The presence of sarcomatoid differentiation or collecting duct or medullary cell histologic subtype denotes a poor prognosis (Carter et al, 1992; Davis et al, 1995b; Chao et al, 2002b; Escudier et al, 2002a; Mian et al, 2002; Polascik et al, 2002; Mejean et al, 2003; Nanus et al, 2004; Tokuda et al, 2004). Several studies now suggest that conventional RCC may have a better prognosis on average compared with chromophilic or chromophobic RCC, although there are clearly poorly differentiated tumors in each of these subcategories that can be lethal (Moch et al, 2000; Amin et al, 2002; Lau et al, 2002; Cheville et al, 2003; Krejci et al, 2003; Beck et al, 2004).

Estimates of DNA ploidy and assessment of nuclear morphometry have also correlated with outcomes for patients with RCC, but the main utility of ploidy appears to be in patients with organ-confined disease, and the role of nuclear morphometry has not yet been defined (di Silverio et al, 2000; Abou-Rebyeh et al, 2001). Focusing on patients with Robson stage I tumors, Grignon and colleagues (1989) reported 10-year cancer-related mortality rates of 37% in patients with nondiploid tumors versus 8% in patients with diploid tumors. Similar studies have confirmed these findings, and Rainwater and associates (1987) reported that ploidy analysis can also separate patients with low-grade RCC into distinct prognostic groups. Carducci and colleagues (1999) showed that nuclear morphometry improved the prognostication of stage and grade in a multivariate model, confirming previous studies in the literature (Monge et al, 1999).

**Several investigators have now combined various prognostic factors, and this has greatly improved our predictive capacity** (Cindolo et al, 2005). For instance, Kattan and colleagues (2001) have combined manner of presentation (incidental, or local versus systemic symptoms), tumor histology, tumor size, and pathologic stage to develop a nomogram (Fig. 47–22) that predicts cancer-free survival after nephrectomy. Tumor grade was not included in this analysis because its role for nonconventional RCC has not been clearly defined. A subsequent analysis from this same group focused only on patients with conventional RCC and incorporated tumor grade, assessment of tumor necrosis, and vascular invasion to further improve prognostication (Sorbellini et al, 2005). A similar model for conventional RCC has also been proposed by Frank and colleagues (2002), in this case incorporating 1997 TNM stage, tumor size, nuclear grade, and presence of tumor necrosis to predict recurrence and survival after radical nephrectomy (Sengupta et al, 2005).

Pantuck and colleagues (2001a) have also performed an integrated analysis of prognostic factors for RCC, although

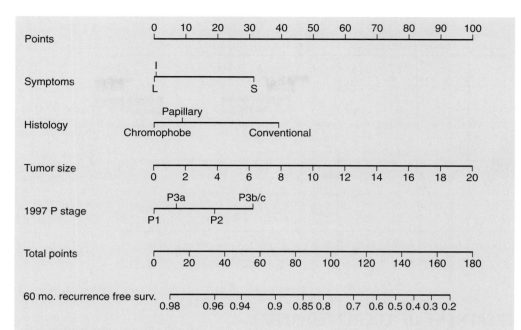

**Figure 47–22.** Nomogram for estimating the probability of 5-year recurrence-free survival after radical nephrectomy for renal cell carcinoma. (From Kattan MW, Reuter V, Motzer RJ, et al: A postoperative prognostic nomogram for renal cell carcinoma. J Urol 2001;166:63-67.)

**Instructions for physician:** Locate the patient's symptoms (I=incidental, L=local, S=systemic) on the Symptoms axis. Draw a line straight upwards to the Points axis to determine how many points towards recurrence the patient receives for his symptoms. Repeat this process for the other axes, each time drawing straight upward to the Points axis. Sum the points achieved for each predictor and locate this sum on the Total points axis. Draw a line straight down to find the patient's probability of remaining recurrence free for 5 years assuming he or she does not die of another cause first.

**Instruction to patient:** "Mr. X, if we had 100 men or women exactly like you, we would expect between <predicted percentage from nomogram – 10%> and <predicted percentage + 10%> to remain free of their disease at 5 years following surgery, though recurrence after 5 years is still possible."

their analysis included patients with all stages of the disease (Fig. 47–23). **A sophisticated multivariate analysis revealed three independent prognostic factors that were most robust for predicting outcomes, namely, TNM stage, performance status, and tumor grade** (Zisman et al, 2001b). Prediction of survival of patients has proved to be powerful, and this approach has now been validated in an independent analysis of 4202 patients from eight academic centers (Patard et al, 2004c). Subsequent reports segregated patients with N0 M0 tumors from those with N+ or M1 tumors and provided separate analyses for each subgroup, and this should be even more useful for the practicing clinician (Zisman et al, 2002c). Molecular factors such as staining for CA-9 and p53 and assessment of proliferation status with Ki-67 are now also being incorporated into algorithms to predict outcomes for patients with RCC (Kim et al, 2005).

For patients with clinically localized disease, Patard and colleagues (2004a) have shown that mode of presentation (incidental versus symptomatic) can be combined with tumor size to better stratify patients after primary surgical management. They have proposed a novel staging system for organ-confined RCC:

T1a: ≤4.0 cm and incidental
T1b: ≤4.0 cm and symptomatic or >4.0 cm and incidental

T2a: >4 to ≤7 cm and symptomatic
T2b: >7 cm and symptomatic

Cancer-specific mortality rates at 5 years of follow-up were 1.9%, 4.1%, 13.8%, and 23.7%, respectively, showing that this simple modification could potentially improve prognostication for this population of patients (Patard et al, 2004a). Improved prognostication such as this will help guide counseling and management of patients and is likely to stimulate a reassessment of the current staging protocols for RCC.

## KEY POINTS: PROGNOSTIC FACTORS FOR RCC

| Tumor Related | Patient Related | Laboratory |
|---|---|---|
| Stage | Performance status | Anemia |
| Grade | Symptomatic | Thrombocytosis |
| Size | presentation | Hypercalcemia |
| Histologic subtype | Constitutional | Elevated erythrocyte |
| Sarcomatoid | symptoms | sedimentation rate |
| histology | Paraneoplastic | Elevated alkaline |
| Tumor necrosis | syndromes | phosphatase level |
| Sites of metastasis | Metastasis-free | CA-9 expression |
| Burden of metastasis | interval | |

| UISS | TNM stage | ECOG PS | Grade | 2 yr (%) | 5 yr (%) |
|------|-----------|---------|-------|----------|----------|
| I | I | 0 | 1, 2 | 96 | 94 |
| II | I | 0 | 3, 4 | 89 | 67 |
| | II | any | any | | |
| | III | 0 | any | | |
| | III | 1+ | 1 | | |
| III | III | 1+ | 2–4 | 66 | 39 |
| | IV | 0 | 1, 2 | | |
| IV | IV | 0 | 3, 4 | 42 | 23 |
| | | 1+ | 1–3 | | |
| V | IV | 1+ | 4 | 9 | 0 |

**Figure 47–23.** UCLA Integrated Staging System for patients with renal cell carcinoma. This classification system incorporates stage, grade, and performance status and provides estimates of 2-year and 5-year survival rates. (From Pantuck AJ, Zisman A, Belldegrun A: Biology of renal cell carcinoma: Changing concepts in classification and staging. Semin Urol Oncol 2001;19:72-79.)

# TREATMENT OF LOCALIZED RENAL CELL CARCINOMA
## Radical Nephrectomy

Notwithstanding advances in our understanding of the genetics and biology of RCC, **surgery remains the mainstay for curative treatment of this disease. The objective of surgical therapy is to excise all tumor with an adequate surgical margin.** Simple nephrectomy was practiced for many decades but has been supplanted by radical nephrectomy, which is the treatment of choice for many patients with localized RCC.

Robson and colleagues (1969) established radical nephrectomy as the "gold standard" curative operation for localized RCC with their report of 66% and 64% overall survival for stages I and II tumors, respectively. These results demonstrated improved survival rates compared with those of patients treated by pericapsular nephrectomy. More recent reports indicate 5-year survival rates of 73% to 92% after radical nephrectomy for Robson stage I (pT1-pT2) RCC (see Table 47–13). Radical nephrectomy remains the established form of treatment for patients with localized unilateral RCC and a normal contralateral kidney (Fig. 47–24) (Lam et al, 2004b).

**The prototypical concept of radical nephrectomy encompasses the basic principles of early ligation of the renal artery and vein, removal of the kidney outside Gerota's fascia, excision of the ipsilateral adrenal gland, and performance of a complete regional lymphadenectomy from the crus of the diaphragm to the aortic bifurcation. Controversy has arisen concerning the need for some of these practices in all patients** (Lam et al, 2004b). Performance of a perifascial nephrectomy is of undoubted importance in preventing postoperative local tumor recurrence because approximately 25% of localized RCCs manifest perinephric fat involvement. Preliminary renal arterial ligation remains an accepted practice; however, in large tumors with abundant collateral vascular supply, it is not always possible to achieve complete preliminary control of the arterial circulation. It has been well demonstrated that removal of the ipsilateral adrenal gland is not routinely necessary in the absence of radiographic adrenal enlargement unless the malignant lesion extensively involves the kidney, is locally advanced, or is located in the upper portion of the kidney immediately adjacent to the adrenal gland (Sagalowsky et al, 1994; Leibovitch et al, 1995; Kletscher et al, 1996; Kozak et al, 1996; Sandock et al, 1997; Tsui et al, 2000a; Paul et al, 2001a; Lam et al, 2004a; Siemer et al, 2004).

The need for a complete regional lymphadenectomy in all patients undergoing radical nephrectomy remains controversial (Blom et al, 1999; Schafhauser et al, 1999; Terrone et al, 2003; Blute et al, 2004a; Phillips and Taneja, 2004). Regional lymph node extension is an important prognostic factor usually associated with poor survival (Pantuck et al, 2003b). However, several characteristics of RCC argue against a therapeutic role for lymphadenectomy. First, the tumor metastasizes through the bloodstream and the lymphatic system with equal frequency. Consequently, most patients with positive lymph nodes eventually develop bloodborne metastases despite undergoing lymphadenectomy, and many patients with RCC will develop disseminated metastases without ever having lymphatic involvement. In addition, the lymphatic drainage of the kidney is variable, and even an extensive retroperitoneal dissection cannot reasonably be expected to remove all possible sites of metastasis. These considerations militate against a therapeutic benefit for routine lymphadenectomy for most patients with localized RCC, and most believe that only a relatively small percentage of patients are likely to benefit (<2% to 3%), namely, the subset of patients with micrometastatic disease (Golimbu et al, 1986; Giuliani et al, 1990; Herrlinger et al, 1991). In all likelihood, the involved lymph nodes in these patients would be removed by a conventional radical nephrectomy, which incorporates the renal hilar and immediately adjacent paracaval or paraaortic lymph nodes. At the other end of the spectrum, patients with advanced disease undergoing cytoreductive nephrectomy should have all grossly enlarged lymph nodes removed if possible. Pantuck and colleagues (2003c) have shown that this subgroup of patients has a better outcome than do those in whom lymphadenectomy is not performed.

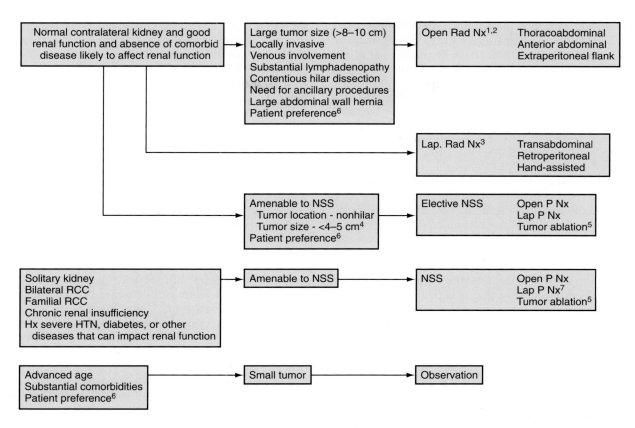

**Figure 47–24.** Algorithm for management of localized renal cell carcinoma (RCC).

1. Rad Nx = radical nephrectomy, NSS = nephron sparing surgery, P Nx = partial nephrectomy, lap = laparoscopic
2. Surgical approach dependent on tumor size, location, body habitus, etc.
3. Surgical approach dependent on tumor size, location, and surgeon experience and expertise
4. Prognostic data about outcomes after partial nephrectomy support good results for pathologic tumor size of 4.0 cm or less, but corresponding radiographic sizes are 10–20% higher due to blood flow in vivo.
5. Long-term efficacy not established, but less invasive and a good option for elderly patients and/or those with substantial comorbid disease. Percutaneous approach can be considered when pancreas, bowel, or ureter not adjacent to mass.
6. Patient preference takes precedence assuming balanced counseling about various options and their potential advantages and disadvantages.
7. Assumes adequate expertise

Although performance of a complete regional lymphadenectomy allows more accurate staging of the extent of RCC, the therapeutic value of this information is limited because there is no established form of systemic treatment for patients with advanced disease. **At present, the need for routine performance of a complete lymphadenectomy in all cases is not well defined, and there remains a divergence of clinical practice among urologists with respect to this aspect of radical nephrectomy** (Blom et al, 1999; Blute et al, 2004a; Daneshmand et al, 2004; Phillips and Taneja, 2004). Blute and colleagues (2004a) have reported risk factors for lymphatic involvement with RCC including high tumor grade, sarcomatoid component, histologic tumor necrosis, tumor size larger than 10 cm, and tumor stage pT3 or pT4. The incidence of lymph node involvement in their series was 10% if two or more of these factors were present and only 0.6% if fewer than two were present. Most of these factors can be assessed preoperatively or with intraoperative frozen-section analysis, and this analysis could be used to guide decision-making with respect to lymphadenectomy. With this approach, only the hilar and regional lymph nodes would be removed for low-risk patients.

Open surgical techniques for radical nephrectomy are described in detail in Chapter 50. **The surgical approach for radical nephrectomy is determined by the size and location of the tumor as well as by the body habitus of the patient.** The operation is usually performed through a transperitoneal incision to allow abdominal exploration for metastatic disease and early access to the renal vessels with minimal manipulation of the tumor. The authors prefer an extended subcostal or a bilateral subcostal incision for most patients undergoing radical nephrectomy. The thoracoabdominal approach is employed when radical nephrectomy is performed in patients with large tumors involving the upper portion of the kidney. On occasion, an extraperitoneal flank incision is appropriate in elderly patients or patients of poor surgical risk, but exposure can be limiting, particularly in patients with large tumors or those with contentious hilar anatomy.

**Laparoscopic radical nephrectomy has emerged as a less morbid alternative to open surgery in the management of low- to moderate-volume (8 to 10 cm or smaller), localized RCCs with no local invasion, renal vein involvement, or lymphadenopathy** (see Fig. 47–24). Laparoscopic radical nephrectomy is associated with diminished postoperative discomfort and shortened recovery, and costs compare favorably with the open approach (Meraney and Gill, 2002). Available outcome data suggest that cancer-specific survival after laparoscopic radical nephrectomy is comparable to that after open radical nephrectomy (Cadeddu et al, 1998; Dunn et al, 2000; Meraney et al, 2000; Chan et al, 2001; Gill et al, 2001; Portis et al, 2002; Saika et al, 2003; Wille et al, 2004; Permpongkosol et al, 2005; Yoshino et al, 2005). In a multi-institutional report of 157 patients undergoing laparoscopic radical nephrectomy for clinical stage I (T1-2) RCC, the 5-year actuarial disease-free rate for all patients was 91% (Cadeddu et al, 1998). Only five patients developed retroperitoneal or metastatic tumor recurrence, and there were no port site recurrences. Current laparoscopic techniques allow replication of the important tenets of radical nephrectomy, and outcome data reflect this at several centers (Cadeddu et al, 1998; Dunn et al, 2000; Meraney et al, 2000; Chan et al, 2001; Gill et al, 2001; Portis et al, 2002; Saika et al, 2003; Wille et al, 2004). A variety of approaches including transperitoneal, retroperitoneal, and hand assisted have been popularized and are described elsewhere in this text (Cadeddu et al, 1998; Gill et al, 2000b; Nelson and Wolf, 2002; Desai et al, 2005). Studies suggest that elderly and morbidly obese patients, those with a history of previous abdominal surgery, and those with large tumor size may also be considered for laparoscopic renal surgery, although selection of patients must be careful, and surgical expertise and experience should also be taken into account (Fazeli-Matin et al, 1999; Parsons et al, 2002; Matin et al, 2003; Cobb et al, 2004; Fugita et al, 2004; Steinberg et al, 2004). The potential applications for laparoscopic approaches to the surgical management of RCC are evolving rapidly (Desai et al, 2003a, 2003b; Meraney et al, 2003; Steinberg et al, 2003; Abreu et al, 2004; Fenn and Gill, 2004; Finelli et al, 2004a, 2004b, 2005; Johnston et al, 2005).

Previously, there was no consensus regarding an appropriate follow-up regimen for patients who had undergone radical nephrectomy for localized RCC. **Several studies on outcomes after radical nephrectomy for localized RCC have now demonstrated that the risk for postoperative recurrent malignant disease is stage dependent** (Sandock et al, 1995; Levy et al, 1998; Eggener et al, 2001; Janzen et al, 2003; Stephenson et al, 2004a; Theodorescu et al, 2004). For instance, in a study from M. D. Anderson Cancer Center (Levy et al, 1998), 68 of 286 patients (23.8%) developed metastatic RCC after radical nephrectomy, and the incidence of this event, according to the initial pathologic tumor stage, was as follows: 7.1% for T1 N0 M0, 26.5% for T2 N0 M0, and 39.4%

for T3 N0 M0. The risk for development of recurrent malignant disease was greatest during the first 3 postoperative years. Stephenson and colleagues (2004a) also reported substantially increased risk of recurrence in patients with stage pT3a and pT3b compared with pT1 and pT2, and recurrences were diagnosed earlier in the former, with a median of 12 versus 26 months.

**These data indicate that surveillance for recurrent malignant disease after radical nephrectomy for RCC can be tailored according to the initial pathologic tumor stage.** The recommended surveillance scheme is depicted in Table 47–16. All patients should be evaluated with a medical history, physical examination, and selected blood studies on a yearly or twice-yearly basis. For patients with stage T1 N0 M0 tumors, routine postoperative radiographic imaging is not necessary because of the low risk for recurrent malignant disease. For patients with stage T2 N0 M0 tumors, a chest radiograph every year and an abdominal CT scan every 2 years are recommended. Patients with stage T3 N0 M0 tumors have a higher risk for development of recurrent malignant disease, particularly during the first 3 years after radical nephrectomy, and may benefit from more frequent laboratory and radiographic follow-up as outlined in Table 47–16. Postoperative bone scans, bone plain films, and head CT scans are necessary only in the presence of related symptoms. This surveillance scheme is cost-effective and enables early detection of most cases of recurrent RCC after radical nephrectomy for localized disease. Other important prognostic factors for RCC, such as tumor size, grade, and histologic subtype, can also influence the risk and pattern of recurrence and are now integrated into predictive algorithms that will be useful for more individualized surveillance in the near future (Kattan et al, 2001; Pantuck et al, 2001a; Zisman et al, 2002c; Frank et al, 2003b, 2004b, 2005b; Sorbellini et al, 2005).

## Nephron-Sparing Surgery

Nephron-sparing surgery for the treatment of a renal tumor was first described by Czerny in 1890 (reviewed in Herr, 2005). However, high morbidity limited its application. In 1950, Vermooten suggested that peripheral encapsulated renal neoplasms could be excised locally while leaving a margin of normal parenchyma around the tumor. **Interest in nephron-sparing surgery for RCC has been stimulated by advances in renal imaging, experience with renal vascular surgery for other conditions, improved methods of preventing ischemic renal damage, growing numbers of incidentally discovered low-stage RCCs, and good long-term survival in patients undergoing this form of treatment** (Uzzo and Novick, 2001). Nephron-sparing surgery entails complete local resection of a renal tumor while leaving the largest possible amount of normal functioning parenchyma in the involved kidney.

**Table 47–16. Postoperative Surveillance after Radical Nephrectomy for Localized Renal Cell Carcinoma**

| Pathologic Tumor Stage | History, Examination, and Blood Tests | Chest Radiograph | Abdominal CT Scan |
|---|---|---|---|
| T1 N0 M0 | Yearly | — | — |
| T2 N0 M0 | Yearly | Yearly | Every 2 years |
| T3a-c N0 M0 | Every 6 months for 3 years, then yearly | Every 6 months for 3 years, then yearly | At 1 year, then every 2 years |

Accepted indications for nephron-sparing surgery include situations in which radical nephrectomy would render the patient anephric or at high risk for ultimate need of dialysis (see Fig. 47–24) (Licht et al, 1994; Ghavamian and Zincke, 2001; Uzzo and Novick, 2001). This encompasses patients with bilateral RCC or RCC involving a solitary functioning kidney. The solitary functioning kidney may be the result of unilateral renal agenesis, prior removal of the contralateral kidney, or irreversible impairment of contralateral renal function by a benign disorder. Another accepted indication for nephron-sparing surgery is represented by patients with unilateral carcinoma and a functioning opposite kidney affected by a condition that might threaten its future function, such as renal artery stenosis (Campbell et al, 1993; Hafez et al, 2000), hydronephrosis, chronic pyelonephritis, ureteral reflux, calculus disease, or systemic diseases such as diabetes and nephrosclerosis (Gilbert et al, 2003; Uzzo and Novick, 2001).

In patients with bilateral synchronous RCC, the authors' philosophy has been to attempt to preserve as much functioning renal tissue as possible. This entails performing bilateral nephron-sparing operations when feasible, usually as staged procedures if the tumors are relatively large. When a locally extensive tumor on one side precludes nephron-sparing surgery, a radical nephrectomy is performed on the more involved side along with a contralateral partial nephrectomy. Margin width appears to be immaterial as long as the final margins are negative, and this is particularly relevant when the tumor is located within the hilum and preservation of renal function is at a premium (Castilla et al, 2002; Sutherland et al, 2002). Patients with RCC involving a functionally or anatomically solitary kidney must be advised about the potential need of temporary or permanent dialysis postoperatively, which, according to our experience, occurs in 8% and 4% of cases, respectively (Campbell et al, 1994). Similarly, Ghavamian and colleagues (2002) reported a 12.7% incidence

of acute renal failure when operating on a solitary kidney, with 15.9% developing proteinuria and 12.7% experiencing chronic renal insufficiency on a long-term basis. A functioning renal remnant of at least 20% of one normal kidney is necessary to avoid end-stage renal failure.

**Evaluation of patients with RCC for nephron-sparing surgery should include preoperative testing to rule out locally extensive or metastatic disease and additional specific renal imaging to delineate the relationship of the tumor to the intrarenal vascular supply and collecting system.** For centrally located tumors, this information has traditionally been obtained with a combination of studies including CT scanning, renal arteriography, and occasionally renal venography. Three-dimensional volume-rendered CT (or MRI) is now established as a noninvasive imaging modality that can accurately depict the renal parenchymal and vascular anatomy in a format familiar to urologic surgeons (Coll et al, 1999; Uzzo et al, 2000b; Berman et al, 2001; VanderBrink et al, 2004). This study integrates essential information from arteriography, venography, excretory urography, and conventional two-dimensional CT scanning into a single imaging modality and obviates the need for more invasive renal imaging (Derweesh et al, 2004).

The surgical techniques for performing nephron-sparing surgery in patients with RCC are reviewed in Chapter 50. **The technical success rate of nephron-sparing surgery for RCC is excellent, and many studies have reported extended cancer-specific survival rates of 78% to 100% in such patients** (Campbell et al, 1994; Uzzo and Novick, 2001) (Table 47–17). These survival rates are comparable to those obtained after radical nephrectomy, particularly for low-stage RCC. The major disadvantage of nephron-sparing surgery is the risk of postoperative local recurrence in the kidney that was operated on, which has occurred in up to 10% of patients. These local recurrences are most likely a manifestation of undetected

| Table 47–17. Results of Nephron-Sparing Surgery for Renal Cell Carcinoma* |||||
|---|---|---|---|---|
| *Series* | *No. of Patients* | *Disease-Specific Survival (%)* | *Local Recurrence (%)* | *Mean Follow-up (months)* |
| Jacobs et al (1980) | 51 | 84 | 10 | 60 |
| Marberger et al (1981) | 72 | 78 | 8 | N/A |
| Marshall and Walsh (1984) | 10 | 90 | 10 | 24.5 |
| Bazeed et al (1986) | 51 | 96 | 4 | 35.8 |
| Carini et al (1988) | 35 | 89 | 3 | 45.8 |
| Gohji et al (1990) | 21 | 100 | 0 | N/A |
| Morgan and Zincke (1990) | 104 | 89 | 6 | 60 |
| Selli et al (1991) | 56 | 90 | 4 | 46.2 |
| Provet et al (1991) | 44 | 88 | 2 | 36 |
| Steinbach et al (1992) | 121 | 90 | 4.1 | 47 |
| Moll et al (1993) | 142 | 98 | 1.4 | 34.8 |
| Thrasher et al (1994) | 21 | 100 | 0 | 40 |
| Lerner et al (1996) | 185 | 89 | 5.9 | 44 |
| D'Armiento et al (1997) | 19 | 95 | 0 | 70 |
| Indudhara et al (1997) | 35 | 100 | 0 | 37 |
| van Poppel et al (1998) | 76 | 96 | 0 | 75 |
| Hafez et al (1999) | 485 | 92 | 3.2 | 47 |
| Barbalias et al (1999) | 41 | 97.5 | 7.3 | 59 |
| Belldegrun et al (1999) | 146 | 93 | 2.7 | 74 |
| Lee et al (2000) | 79 | 95 | 0 | 40 |
| Krejci et al* (2003) | 344 | 94.4 | 1.7 | 54 |
| Patard et al (2004) | 379 | 97 | 1.3 | 62.5 |
| Total | 2517 | 78-100 | 0-10 | 24-75 |

*Data for conventional RCC only.

microscopic multifocal RCC in the renal remnant—most are found distant from the previous tumor bed. The risk of local recurrence after radical nephrectomy has not been well studied, but it is presumably very low.

The largest reported study of partial nephrectomy is from the Cleveland Clinic and reviewed the results of nephron-sparing surgery for the treatment of localized, sporadic RCC in 485 patients (Hafez et al, 1999). The mean postoperative follow-up was 4 years, and overall and cancer-specific 5-year survival rates for patients in this series were 81% and 92%, respectively. Recurrent RCC developed postoperatively in 44 patients (9%), including 16 (3.2%) with local recurrence in the remnant kidney and 28 (5.8%) with metastatic disease. In another study from the Cleveland Clinic, longer term results of nephron-sparing surgery were reviewed in 107 patients with localized sporadic RCC treated before 1988, almost exclusively for imperative indications (Fergany et al, 2000). All patients were observed for a minimum of 10 years or until death. Cancer-specific survival was 88.2% at 5 years and 73% at 10 years. Long-term renal function was preserved in 100 patients (93%). Ten-year follow-up was also provided by Herr (1999), who reported that 97% of patients remained cancer free after partial nephrectomy in the setting of a normal contralateral kidney, a more select population of patients. These data confirm that **nephron-sparing surgery provides effective long-term therapy for patients with localized RCC and can preserve renal function when necessary** (Saad et al, 2005).

**A more recent trend has been to perform partial nephrectomy by minimally invasive approaches, a considerable challenge given concerns about hemostasis and margin status without direct visualization and tactile input. Nevertheless, several series have now reported encouraging results, mostly with relatively small, polar or peripherally located tumors** (Gill et al, 2002, 2003; Hsu et al, 2002; Guillonneau et al, 2003; Simon et al, 2003; Allaf et al, 2004; Finelli et al, 2004; Kane et al, 2004; Mabjeesh et al, 2004). Gill and colleagues (2002, 2003) have now essentially duplicated the open surgical technique, including occlusion of the renal vasculature, application of saline ice slush, and intracorporeal suturing to close the collecting system and repair the capsular defect (Desai et al, 2003a). Other methods to achieve renal hypothermia are also being explored, including antegrade perfusion of the renal artery or retrograde perfusion of the collecting system with cold solutions (Landman et al, 2002; Janetschek et al, 2004). Interestingly, recent data suggest that the kidney may tolerate longer periods of warm ischemia than previously appreciated, but this will require further study (Bhayani et al, 2004; Laven et al, 2004; Shekarriz et al, 2004). Hemostasis remains the primary concern, and a variety of approaches have been explored to accomplish this, including

the use of hemostatic dissecting devices and tissue sealants (Gettman et al, 2001b; Yoshimura et al, 2001; Richter et al, 2003; Hasan et al, 2004a, 2004b; Herrell et al, 2004; Urena et al, 2004; Finley et al, 2005). Efficacy data including margin status and recurrence rates appear promising but must be considered preliminary, and further data will be required to substantiate these approaches (Kaouk et al, 2004; Porpiglia et al, 2005). Major complications are hemorrhagic, occasionally requiring delayed nephrectomy or embolization, but they have been reduced substantially with more extended experience and routine use of tissue sealants during reconstruction of the kidney (Ramani et al, 2005). Even centrally located tumors are now being managed laparoscopically (Gill et al, 2003; Frank et al, 2005c), and this field is rapidly progressing. Please refer to the chapter on laparoscopic renal surgery in this text for further details about these surgical developments.

Clinical guidelines for long-term surveillance after nephron-sparing surgery for sporadic localized RCC have been developed (Eggener et al, 2001; Janzen et al, 2003; Theodorescu et al, 2004), primarily based on a detailed analysis of tumor recurrence patterns in 327 patients treated at the Cleveland Clinic (Hafez et al, 1997). In this series, recurrent RCC developed after nephron-sparing surgery in 38 patients (11.6%), including 13 patients (4%) who developed local recurrence and 25 patients (7.6%) who developed metastatic disease (Hafez et al, 1997). The incidence of postoperative local recurrence and metastatic disease varied according to the initial pathologic tumor stage as follows: 0% and 4.4% for T1 N0 M0 tumors, 2% and 5.3% for T2 N0 M0 tumors, 8.2% and 11.5% for T3a N0 M0 tumors, and 10.6% and 14.9% for T3b N0 M0 tumors. The peak postoperative intervals for development of local recurrence were 6 to 24 months (in T3 tumors) and more than 48 months (in T2 tumors). T1 tumor stage in this series represented tumor size of less than 2.5 cm, based on the previous TNM classification system.

**These data indicate that surveillance for recurrent malignant disease after nephron-sparing surgery for sporadic RCC can be tailored according to the initial pathologic tumor stage and tumor size.** The recommended surveillance scheme is depicted in Table 47–18. All patients should be evaluated with a medical history, physical examination, and selected blood studies on a yearly or twice-yearly basis. The blood studies should include serum calcium, alkaline phosphatase, liver function, blood urea nitrogen, serum creatinine, and electrolyte studies.

The need for postoperative radiographic surveillance studies after nephron-sparing surgery varies according to the initial pathologic tumor stage. Patients who undergo nephron-sparing surgery for small (<2.5 cm) T1 N0 M0 tumors do not require radiographic imaging postoperatively in view of the low risk for recurrent malignant disease. A

| Table 47–18. | Postoperative Surveillance after Partial Nephrectomy for Localized Renal Cell Carcinoma | | |
|---|---|---|---|
| *Pathologic Tumor Stage* | *History, Examination, and Blood Tests* | *Chest Radiograph* | *Abdominal CT Scan* |
| T1 N0 M0* | Yearly | — | — |
| T2 N0 M0* | Yearly | Yearly | Every 2 years |
| T3 N0 M0 | Every 6 months for 3 years, then yearly | Every 6 months for 3 years, then yearly | Every 6 months for 3 years, then every 2 years |

*Based on 1997 AJCC classification system, with T1 ≤ 2.5 cm and T2 > 2.5 cm.

yearly chest radiograph is recommended after nephron-sparing surgery for other patients with confined RCC (stage T1 and larger than 2.5 cm or stage T2 N0 M0 tumors) because the lung is the most common site of postoperative metastasis. Abdominal or retroperitoneal tumor recurrence is uncommon in this group, particularly early after nephron-sparing surgery, and these patients require only occasional follow-up abdominal CT scanning; the authors recommend that this be done every 2 years. Patients with stage T3 N0 M0 tumors have a higher risk for development of local recurrence and metastatic disease, particularly during the first 2 years after partial nephrectomy, and may benefit from more frequent follow-up with chest radiography and abdominal CT scanning initially; the authors recommend that these be done every 6 months during the first 3 years, after which a chest radiograph is obtained yearly and an abdominal CT scan is done every 2 years.

**Patients who undergo nephron-sparing surgery for RCC may be left with a relatively small amount of renal tissue and are at risk for development of long-term renal functional impairment from hyperfiltration renal injury** (Modlin and Novick, 2001; Abdi et al, 2003). In a study of 14 patients observed for up to 17 years after partial nephrectomy in a solitary kidney, patients with more than 50% reduction in overall renal mass were found to be at increased risk for development of proteinuria, focal segmental glomerulosclerosis, and progressive renal failure (Novick et al, 1990). The development of proteinuria correlated directly with the length of follow-up and inversely with the amount of remaining renal tissue. Renal biopsy revealed focal segmental glomerulosclerosis in several patients with severe proteinuria (Fig. 47–25). These findings mirror those observed in experimental animal models of partial renal ablation (Brenner, 1983). Because proteinuria is the initial manifestation of this phenomenon, a 24-hour urinary protein measurement should be obtained yearly in patients with a solitary remnant kidney to screen for hyperfiltration nephropathy.

**Efforts to prevent or to ameliorate the damaging effects of renal hyperfiltration have primarily focused on dietary and pharmacologic intervention** (Modlin and Novick, 2001). Animal studies have suggested that dietary restriction of protein and angiotensin-converting enzyme inhibitor (ACEI) agents may mitigate this type of glomerulopathy (Meyer et al, 1985). Preliminary clinical data appear to support this concept. Novick and Schreiber (1995) studied five patients who had developed proteinuria with stable renal function after partial nephrectomy in a solitary kidney. Four of these patients had documented focal segmental glomerulosclerosis on renal biopsy. All five patients had normal renal morphologic features at the time of surgery. Treatment with ACEI therapy and a low-protein diet decreased the level of proteinuria in four patients. Data from other studies have also suggested that ACEI therapy can significantly diminish proteinuria in patients with established renal disease (Goldfarb, 1995). This information suggests that ACEI therapy and a low-protein diet may improve the long-term renal functional outcome for patients with a remnant kidney after partial nephrectomy. The optimal time for initiating the regimen is not clear, and it may be best to implement this therapy as early as possible to obviate the maladaptive

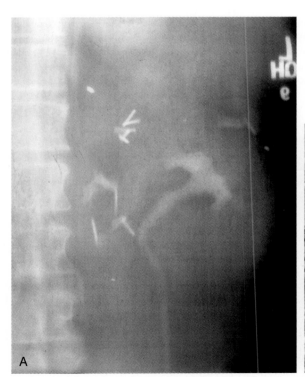
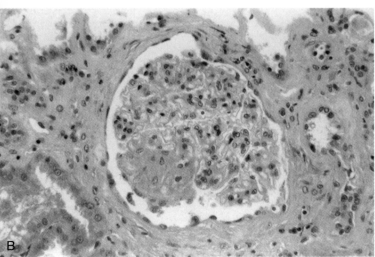

**Figure 47–25.** **A,** Ten years after partial nephrectomy for large tumor in solitary left kidney, intravenous pyelogram shows function of small remnant kidney. The patient had developed nephrotic syndrome at this time. **B,** Renal biopsy specimen shows focal segmental glomerulosclerosis indicative of hyperfiltration nephropathy.

responses that can lead to progressive sclerosis and renal failure in this setting.

There is experimental evidence that nonhemodynamic processes may also contribute to progression of sclerosis in the remnant kidney (Goldfarb, 1995). This raises other therapeutic possibilities, such as thromboxane inhibitors, anticoagulants, lipid-lowering agents, and other pharmacologic agents. Future clinical trials, it is hoped, will clarify the potential value of these treatment approaches.

### Nephron-Sparing Surgery with a Normal Opposite Kidney

Although radical nephrectomy remains the standard treatment of localized renal carcinoma in patients with an anatomically and functionally normal opposite kidney, a growing number of authors have reported excellent results with nephron-sparing surgery in this "elective" setting (see Fig. 47–24) (Campbell and Novick, 1995). Table 47–19 details the outcome of nephron-sparing surgery in 909 patients with unilateral localized RCC and a normal opposite kidney. Extended cancer-specific survival ranges from 90% to 100%, and there have been only 20 cases of postoperative local tumor recurrence (2%). Significantly, the mean tumor size in most of these reports was less than 4 cm. Clearly, selection of patients on the basis of small tumor size was a significant factor accounting for the favorable outcome after nephron-sparing surgery in these studies.

Previous studies have defined optimal candidates for elective partial nephrectomy. In a study from the Cleveland Clinic, the outcome of nephron-sparing surgery was reviewed in 216 patients with sporadic RCC, mostly for imperative indications (Licht et al, 1994). The findings confirmed that extended cancer-free survival after partial nephrectomy was significantly improved in patients with small (<4 cm) tumors compared with patients with larger tumors. Other factors associated with significantly improved survival were unilateral renal involvement, low pathologic tumor stage, and presence of a solitary tumor. There were no postoperative tumor recurrences, and the cancer-specific 5-year survival rate was 100% in patients with small, unilateral, stage T1-2 RCCs.

These data suggest that **nephron-sparing surgery may be an acceptable therapeutic approach in patients who have a single, small (<4 cm) RCC and a normal contralateral kidney.** This hypothesis was tested in two subsequent studies (Butler et al, 1994; Lerner et al, 1996), in which the outcome after radical nephrectomy versus nephron-sparing surgery was compared in patients with a single, small, localized, unilateral, sporadic RCC. Butler noted cancer-specific 5-year survival rates for patients in the radical and nephron-sparing surgical groups of 97% and 100%, respectively. Similarly, Lerner reported cancer-specific survival rates for patients in the radical and nephron-sparing surgical groups of 96% and 92%, respectively. The data from these two studies affirm that radical nephrectomy and nephron-sparing surgery provide equally effective curative treatment of patients with a single, small, unilateral, localized RCC.

A related issue is whether the location of the tumor in the involved kidney is a significant factor affecting treatment outcome in patients with a single, small, unilateral, localized, sporadic RCC. This issue was addressed in another study wherein tumor characteristics and cancer-free survival were compared in patients with centrally versus peripherally located RCCs that fulfilled these criteria (Hafez et al, 1999). The study comprised 145 patients treated with either radical nephrectomy or nephron-sparing surgery, and the mean postoperative follow-up was 4.3 years. Pathologic tumor stage was T1-2 in 94% and 82% of central versus peripheral RCCs, respectively. Postoperatively, in comparing patients with central versus peripheral RCCs, there was no difference in 5-year cancer-specific survival (100% versus 97%), tumor recurrence (5.7% versus 4.5%), or renal function (mean serum creatinine concentration, 1.43 mg/dL in both groups). These parameters were also equivalent in patients treated with nephron-sparing surgery versus radical nephrectomy, both overall and within the central versus peripheral RCC subgroups. The results of this study indicate that **there are no**

**Table 47–19. Results of Elective Nephron-Sparing Surgery for Unilateral Renal Cell Carcinoma with a Normal Opposite Kidney**

| Series | No. of Patients | Disease-Specific Survival (%) | Local Recurrence (%) | Mean Tumor Size (cm) |
|---|---|---|---|---|
| Bazeed et al (1986) | 23 | 100 | 0 | 3.3 |
| Carini et al (1988) | 10 | 90 | 0 | 3.5 |
| Morgan and Zincke (1990) | 20 | 100 | 0 | 3.1 |
| Selli et al (1991) | 20 | 90 | 0 | <3.5 |
| Provet et al (1991) | 19 | 100 | 0 | 2.6 |
| Steinbach et al (1992) | 72 | 94.4 | 2.7 (2 cases) | N/A |
| Moll et al (1993) | 98 | 100 | 1 (1 case) | 4 |
| Thrasher et al (1994) | 6 | — | 0 | 4.3 |
| Lerner et al (1996) | 54 | 92 | 5.6 (3 cases) | <4 |
| D'Armiento et al (1997) | 19 | 96 | 0 | 3.34 |
| van Poppel et al (1998) | 51 | 98 | 0 | 3 |
| Herr (1999) | 70 | 97.5 | 1.5 (2 cases) | 3 |
| Hafez et al (1999) | 45 | 100 | 0 | <4 |
| Barbalias et al (1999) | 41 | 97.5 | 7.3 (3 cases) | 3.5 |
| Belldegrun et al (1999) | 63 | 100 | 3.2 (2 cases) | <4 |
| Filipas et al (2000) | 180 | 98 | 1.6 (3 cases) | 3.3 |
| Delakas et al (2002) | 118 | 97.3 | 3.9 (4 cases) | 3.4 |
| Total | 909 | 90-100 | 0-7.3 | 2-4.3 cm |

significant biologic differences between centrally and peripherally located small, solitary, unilateral RCCs. Moreover, nephron-sparing surgery and radical nephrectomy appear to be equally effective treatments regardless of tumor location in these patients.

The primary advantages of elective partial nephrectomy are preservation of renal function and the very real possibility that the lesion of interest might be benign, particularly if it is small (<4.0 cm) (Johannes et al, 2005). Silver and colleagues (1997) found that 17% of all renal masses excised with radical nephrectomy at Memorial Sloan-Kettering Cancer Center were benign, and in the series from Young and colleagues (2002), 28% of renal masses smaller than 3.5 cm were benign compared with only 8% for larger tumors. A direct relationship between tumor size and risk of malignancy and high-risk features has also been reported by Frank and colleagues (2003a). In addition, matched comparisons demonstrate a small but statistically significant increased incidence of renal insufficiency after radical nephrectomy compared with nephron-sparing surgery, even when controlling for preoperative risk factors such as diabetes, hypertension, preoperative serum creatinine level, age, and other relevant comorbidities (Lau et al, 2000; Matin et al, 2002; McKiernan et al, 2002b). This decline in renal function is often not evident for several years but can lead to dialysis dependency in a small minority of patients (Weber et al, 2000). Factors that predict renal insufficiency after radical nephrectomy include elevated preoperative serum creatinine level, hypertension, and proteinuria (Ito et al, 2004), and a nomogram to predict renal insufficiency after radical nephrectomy has been reported (Sorbellini et al, 2005).

Analysis of costs and potential morbidity of partial nephrectomy versus radical nephrectomy, particularly by minimally invasive approaches, should also be taken into account in evaluating patients with a renal mass and a normal contralateral kidney (Campbell and Novick, 1995). Recent analyses suggest that the costs of these two procedures are similar when they are performed at a tertiary care center, and morbidity profiles are also comparable given careful selection of patients and honest and realistic assessment of the individual surgeon's experience and expertise (Uzzo et al, 1999c; McKiernan et al, 2002a; Shekarriz et al, 2002; Stephenson et al, 2004b). Interestingly, reports suggest that quality of life and psychological adaptation may be better after elective partial nephrectomy compared with radical nephrectomy (Clark et al, 2001; Poulakis et al, 2003). Minimally invasive approaches to elective partial nephrectomy and improved perioperative care could further tip the balance in favor of a nephron-sparing approach for some patients (Gill et al, 2002, 2003b; DiBlasio et al, 2004a, 2004b).

Given these considerations, some centers are now expanding their indications for elective partial nephrectomy to include select patients with larger tumors (4 to 7 cm). Leibovich and colleagues (2004) reported similar outcomes after elective partial nephrectomy and radical nephrectomy in this population of patients after adjusting for important pathologic features such as stage, grade, and histologic subtype, and other series support these findings (DiBlasio et al, 2004b; Lam et al, 2004a; Patard J, et al, 2004b). However, selection of patients is likely to play an important role in these series, and definitive data to support a strong consideration for elective partial nephrectomy in the general population of patients with clinical stage T1b tumor is clearly lacking at this time.

## Nephron-Sparing Surgery in von Hippel–Lindau Disease

RCC in von Hippel–Lindau disease differs from its sporadic counterpart in that the diagnosis is made at a young age, and there are usually multiple bilateral renal tumors (Maher and Kaelin, 1997; Uzzo and Novick, 1999; Zbar et al, 1999). Although these are generally low-stage tumors, they are capable of progression with metastasis and represent a frequent cause of death in patients with von Hippel–Lindau disease. RCC in these patients is characterized histopathologically by both solid tumors and renal cysts that contain either frank carcinoma or a lining of hyperplastic clear cells representing incipient carcinoma (Fig. 47–26) (Christenson et al, 1982; Walther et al, 1995). **Therefore, adequate surgical**

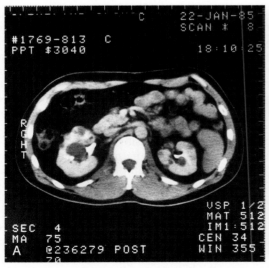
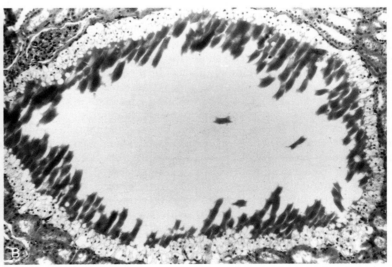

**Figure 47–26.** **A,** CT scan after administration of contrast agent shows bilateral solid and cystic renal masses in patient with von Hippel–Lindau disease. **B,** Histopathologic section of one of the renal cysts shows lining of clear cells representing incipient carcinoma.

treatment of localized RCC in von Hippel–Lindau disease requires excision of all solid and cystic renal lesions. Choyke and colleagues (2001) have shown that intraoperative ultrasonography may be a valuable adjunct for this population of patients. In their series, this study identified additional tumors in 25% of patients with hereditary renal cancer undergoing renal exploration.

The surgical options in patients with bilateral RCC and von Hippel–Lindau disease are bilateral nephrectomy and renal replacement therapy or partial nephrectomy to avoid end-stage renal failure (Herring et al, 2001; Roupret et al, 2003; Drachenberg et al, 2004). The general philosophy has been to pursue nephron-sparing surgery if possible, given the multifocal nature of the disease, even for centrally located tumors (Drachenberg et al, 2004). Although early results of partial nephrectomy were promising, subsequent studies suggested a high incidence of postoperative tumor recurrence in the remaining portion of the kidney (Novick and Streem, 1992). It is likely that most of these local recurrences were a manifestation of residual microscopic RCC that was not removed at the time of the original partial nephrectomy (Walther et al, 1995).

One multicenter study delineated the long-term outcomes after surgical treatment of localized RCC in 65 patients with von Hippel–Lindau disease managed at eight medical centers in the United States (Steinbach et al, 1995). RCC was present bilaterally and unilaterally in 54 and 11 patients, respectively. Radical nephrectomy and partial nephrectomy were performed in 16 and 49 patients, respectively. The mean postoperative follow-up interval was 68 months. The 5-year and 10-year cancer-specific survival rates for all patients were 95% and 77%, respectively. The corresponding rates for patients treated with partial nephrectomy were 100% and 81%, respectively. In the latter group, 25 patients (51%) developed postoperative local recurrence; however, only two of these patients had concomitant metastatic disease. Survival free of local recurrence was 71% at 5 years but only 15% at 10 years. Similarly, Roupret and colleagues (2003) **reported a 27.4% incidence of local recurrence at mean follow-up of 55.9 months after partial nephrectomy for patients with von Hippel–Lindau disease, confirming that these patients are at much higher risk for local recurrence than are patients with sporadic RCC.**

**Duffey and colleagues (2004) at the National Cancer Institute have defined a 3-cm threshold for intervention in patients with von Hippel–Lindau disease.** In their series, a total of 108 patients with von Hippel–Lindau disease and solid renal tumors smaller than 3 cm were observed a mean of 58 months, and none developed metastatic disease. In contrast, metastases developed in 20 of 73 patients (27.4%) with tumor larger than 3 cm, and the frequency of metastases increased with increasing tumor size. A 3-cm cut point has thus been proposed to reduce the number of surgical interventions, to optimize renal function, and to minimize the risk of metastatic disease. The authors have emphasized that this recommendation also applies to patients with the hereditary papillary RCC and Birt-Hogg-Dubé syndromes (Walther et al, 1999a; Herring et al, 2001; Duffey et al, 2004; Grubb et al, 2005a).

Taken together, these studies suggest that **partial nephrectomy can provide effective initial treatment of patients with** RCC and von Hippel–Lindau disease but should be withheld until tumor size reaches or eclipses 3.0 cm. After nephron-sparing surgery, patients with von Hippel–Lindau disease must be observed closely because most will eventually develop locally recurrent RCC with the concomitant need for repeated renal surgery (Campbell and Novick, 1995). In this setting, repeated partial nephrectomy can be challenging because of postoperative fibrosis, and some centers are moving toward thermal ablative modalities to reclaim local control (Shingleton and Sewell, 2002; Hwang et al, 2004; Mabjeesh et al, 2004). When removal of all renal tissue is necessary to achieve control of malignant disease, renal transplantation can provide satisfactory replacement therapy for end-stage renal disease and appears to be safe despite the tumor diathesis (Goldfarb et al, 1997).

## Thermal Ablative Therapies

**Thermal ablative therapies, including renal cryosurgery and radiofrequency ablation, have emerged as alternative nephron-sparing treatments of localized RCC** (Marshall, 1999; Murphy and Gill, 2001; Lowry and Nakada, 2003; Hinshaw and Lee, 2004; Mabjeesh et al, 2004). **Both can be administered percutaneously or through laparoscopic exposure and thus offer the potential for reduced morbidity and more rapid recovery** (Johnson et al, 2004). **However, long-term efficacy is not established,** and preliminary data suggest that the local recurrence rate may be somewhat higher than that reported for traditional surgical approaches. Another concern has been the lack of accurate histologic and pathologic staging associated with these modalities, since the treated lesion is left in situ. **The ideal candidates for thermal ablative procedures may be patients with advanced age or significant comorbidities who prefer a proactive approach but are not considered good candidates for conventional surgery, patients with local recurrence after previous nephron-sparing surgery, and patients with hereditary renal cancer who present with multifocal lesions for which multiple partial nephrectomies might be cumbersome if not impossible.** In the last circumstance, a combination of conventional partial nephrectomy for select lesions complemented by thermal ablative approaches for the remainder may represent the optimal treatment plan. The patient's preference must also be considered, and some patients not fitting these criteria may also select thermal ablation, a decision that can be supported as long as balanced counseling about the current status of these modalities has been provided (see Fig. 47–24). Finally, tumor size can also be an important factor in selection of patients because the current technology does not allow reliable treatment of lesions larger than 3.5 cm in diameter.

Experience with renal cryosurgery predates that of radiofrequency ablation and has been much more extensive. The kidney may be an anatomically favored organ for cryosurgery, particularly compared with the prostate, another target organ for cryoablation. Unlike the prostate, which is in intimate, fixed contact with the rectum and the sphincteric mechanism, the kidney can be laparoscopically mobilized, thereby minimizing the risk of injury to adjacent vital structures. Furthermore, although the prostate often harbors multifocal carcinoma, the kidney usually presents with unifocal malignancy. Because the renal tumor can be readily visualized with ultrasonography, the ice ball can be confirmed to completely and circumferentially obliterate the tumor margins, including a surrounding margin of healthy tissue, with increased precision and confidence. An extensive body of experimental work is now available to guide and support clinical cryoablation (Hinshaw and Lee, 2004).

**Established prerequisites for successful cryosurgery include rapid freezing, gradual thawing, and a repetition of the freeze-thaw cycle. The mechanism underlying tissue cryodestruction is thought to involve immediate cellular damage and delayed microcirculatory failure** (Gill and Novick, 1999). Ice formation occurs initially in the extracellular space, causing the extracellular fluid to become hyperosmotic. To equilibrate chemical osmolality, water permeates from the intracellular compartment into the extracellular compartment. Osmolality of the intracellular fluid is thus increased, leading to intracellular solute concentration and dehydration, which cause desiccation trauma—the first step of chemical cellular injury. Continued rapid supercooling leads to the second step of cellular damage—intracellular ice formation. Intracellular ice irreversibly disrupts cell organelles and the cell membrane, a lethal event. Delayed microcirculatory failure occurs during the slow thaw phase of the freeze-thaw cycle, leading to circulation arrest and cellular anoxia. Progressive failure of the microcirculation occurs along a cascade of events: vasoconstriction, endothelial cell destruction causing vessel walls to become porous, interstitial edema, platelet aggregation, microthrombi, and, ultimately, vascular congestion and obliteration. Cells that survive the initial cryogenic assault are destroyed by this secondary insult of ischemia. Repetition of the rapid freeze–slow thaw cycle potentiates the damage. The cryoablation area is thus rendered ischemic, leading ultimately to a circumcised necrosis (Hinshaw and Lee, 2004).

Further work has defined treatment parameters required to bring this treatment into the clinical sphere. Chosy and colleagues (1996) demonstrated that complete necrosis of in vivo porcine renal parenchyma could be consistently achieved only at temperatures of −19.4°C or lower; necrosis was incomplete and suboptimal at temperatures above this threshold. Campbell and coworkers (1998) confirmed that the target lethal temperature of −20°C was achieved at a distance of 3.1 mm inside the leading edge of the ice ball as visualized by real-time ultrasonography. Thus, to ensure complete cell kill, the ice ball must extend well beyond the visible margins of the targeted tumor. In practice, we routinely extend the ice ball approximately 1 cm beyond the edge of the tumor, as determined by both laparoscopic and real-time ultrasonographic imaging (Gill et al, 1998). The availability of sophisticated and reliable ultrasonography and the introduction of finer cryoprobes that allow more accurate and less traumatic probe placement have contributed to the current resurgence of interest in visceral cryosurgery (Onik et al, 1993; Pantuck et al, 2002b).

**Clinical experience and follow-up of patients after renal cryoablative therapy remain somewhat limited, as summarized in Table 47–20.** Diagnosis of local recurrence after thermal ablative treatments can be challenging because evolving fibrosis within the tumor bed can be difficult to differentiate from residual cancer. **In general, enhancement within the tumor bed on extended follow-up has been considered diagnostic of local recurrence, and the clinical experience thus far has supported this.** However, only one study has included routine post-therapy biopsies to provide histologic confirmation (Gill et al, 2000a). Reported rates of local recurrence in some of these series may be underestimates because 10% to 25% of small renal masses may be benign rather than RCC (Silver et al, 1997; Young et al, 2002). In addition, patients may have a recurrence at other sites in the kidney, and this should also be considered local recurrence although the mechanism is different (novel tumor occurrence due to multifocality rather than treatment failure). Hasan and colleagues (2004a) reported two such ipsilateral occurrences when their patients were observed for a minimum of 48 months, so the true incidence of local recurrence in the treated kidney in this series was 10%, not 5%, and somewhat higher than would be expected for conventional partial nephrectomy for an analogous population of patients with small renal tumors. Indeed, in this setting, recurrence in the tumor bed after conventional

**Table 47–20.** **Local Recurrence after Thermal Ablative Therapies for Renal Cell Carcinoma**

| Author | N | Exposure | LR* | Mean Tumor Size (cm) | Mean Follow-up (months) |
|---|---|---|---|---|---|
| *Cryoablation* | | | | | |
| Cestari et al (2004) | 37 | Laparoscopic | 1 (3.4%) | 2.6 | N/A |
| Hasan et al (2004a) | 40 | Laparoscopic | 2 (5%)[†] | 2.4 | 48+ |
| Shingleton and Sewell (2004) | 90 | Image guided | 7 (7.8%) | 3.0 | 30 |
| Lee et al (2003) | 20 | Laparoscopic | 0 (0%) | 2.6 | 14 |
| Nadler et al (2003) | 15[‡] | Laparoscopic | 1 (10%) | 2.2 | 15 |
| Rukstalis et al (2001) | 29[§] | Open | 1 (5.9%) | 2.0 | 16 |
| *Radiofrequency Ablation* | | | | | |
| Hwang et al (2004) | 24 | Image guided | 1 (4.2%) | 2.2 | 13 |
| Matsumoto et al (2004) | 28 | Laparoscopic | 1 (3.6%) | 3.6 | 13 |
| Zagoria et al (2004) | 24 | Image guided | 0 (0%) | 3.5 | 7 |
| Farrell et al (2003) | 35 | Image guided | 0 (0%) | 1.7 | 9 |
| Gervais et al (2003) | 34 | Image guided | 6 (17.6%) | 3.2 | 13 |
| Mayo-Smith et al (2003) | 32 | Image guided | 0 (0%) | 2.6 | 9 |
| Su et al (2003) | 29 | Image guided | 0 (0%) | 2.2 | 9 |

*LR, local recurrence (treatment failure).
[†]Two patients also had recurrence at other sites in the kidney.
[‡]10 of 15 had RCC on intraoperative biopsy before treatment.
[§]17 of 29 had biopsy-proved RCC.

partial nephrectomy is uncommon; most local recurrences are distant from the original tumor site. This limited experience suggests that local control after cryoablative therapy approaches but may not reach that attained by conventional surgical excision.

**The experience with radiofrequency ablation, also summarized in Table 47–20, is even more limited—this technology is clearly at an earlier state of development than cryoablation** (Corwin et al, 2001; Murphy and Gill, 2001; Rendon et al, 2001; Zelkovic and Resnick, 2003; Mabjeesh et al, 2004). Mechanistically, heat above 45°C leads to irreversible cellular damage, and temperatures higher than 55°C to 60°C result in immediate cell death. Application of high-frequency electrical current by radiofrequency ablation induces excitation of ions, frictional forces, and heat, which in turn causes denaturation of intracellular proteins and melting of cellular membranes, a lethal sequence of events. These effects are observed at tissue temperatures above 41°C but increase directly with increasing temperature and duration of treatment (Mabjeesh et al, 2004). Temperatures in excess of 100°C are typically obtained at the tips of the probes, and thermosensors near the tips are used to monitor progress during active treatment. Temperature dissipates at points more distant from the probe tip, and multiple probes are typically required to achieve adequate heating of the region of interest (Murphy and Gill, 2001). One disadvantage of radiofrequency ablation is that the treatment effect is more difficult to monitor in real time—there is no true "ice ball" equivalent (Zelkovic and Resnick, 2003). Rather, treatment is typically based on empirical results from previous probe alignments, and this allows a fairly predictable target zone of up to 4.0 cm to be treated in most cases. Successfully treated tumors demonstrate no enhancement during extended follow-up, similar to cryoablation (Matsumoto et al, 2004b; Svatek et al, 2005).

Early experience suggested that tumor kill might not be as reliable after radiofrequency ablation compared with cryoablation (Matlaga et al, 2002; Michaels et al, 2002; Rendon et al, 2002), but subsequent reports look more promising, probably reflecting improvements in the technology and increased operative experience (see Table 47–20). Most contemporary series report low rates of local recurrence, although some patients have required repeated treatments to achieve local control, an infrequent event with cryoablation and conventional treatments of localized RCC (Anderson et al, 2005; Coleman et al, 2005; Schenk et al, 2005). Complications are

uncommon but have included acute renal failure, stricture of the ureteropelvic junction, necrotizing pancreatitis, and lumbar radiculopathy, so careful and judicious selection of patients is essential (Ogan et al, 2002; Coskun et al, 2003; Elias et al, 2004; Schenk et al, 2005; Weizer et al, 2005). Direct comparison with cryoablation is inevitable but perhaps unfair because radiofrequency ablation is earlier in its development, and recent advances suggest great promise (Anderson et al, 2005; Coleman et al, 2005; Schenk et al, 2005).

Other exciting new technologies, such as high-intensity focused ultrasound and frameless, image-guided radiosurgical treatments (CyberKnife), are also under development and may allow extracorporeal treatment of small renal tumors in the future (Kohrmann et al, 2002; Ponsky et al, 2003; Wu et al, 2003).

## Observation

There was once relatively little information about the growth rate of RCC because when a renal tumor was detected, it was usually removed. The incidental discovery of many small RCCs in asymptomatic elderly patients or those of poor surgical risk has provided the opportunity to observe the growth rate of these tumors in patients who are unable or unwilling to undergo surgery (Table 47–21) (Derweesh and Novick, 2003). Bosniak and associates (1996) reported the largest such series that included 72 small (<3.5 cm) renal tumors in 68 patients who were observed with serial imaging studies for intervals ranging from 2 to 10 years (mean, 3.3 years). On CT scan, these were well-marginated, homogeneous, solid, enhancing tumors consistent with RCC. During the period of observation, these tumors grew at slow and variable rates of up to 1.1 cm per year, with a median growth rate of 0.36 cm per year. In 32 patients whose tumors grew larger than 3 cm, surgical excision was performed; all the excised tumors proved to be stage I RCCs, and the majority were grade 1 tumors. Significantly, none of the patients developed metastasis during the period of observation.

Subsequent series have confirmed that many small renal masses will grow relatively slowly (see Table 47–21), and there have been only two patients with metastasis in these series, suggesting that this may be a reasonable management strategy in carefully selected patients who are not candidates for conventional surgery or thermal ablative approaches (Chawla et al, 2005). However, a critical review of these data is required to recognize the limitations of this database. First, this is a

| Table 47–21. | **Observation of Renal Masses** | | | | |
|---|---|---|---|---|---|
| **Author** | **N** | **Mean Tumor Size (cm)** | **Mean Follow-up (months)** | **Growth Rate (cm/yr)** | **No. with Metastasis** |
| Bosniak et al (1996) | 72 | 1.8 | 40 | 0.36* | 0 (0%) |
| Frank et al (2001) | 30 | 1.7 | 30 | 0.01[†] | 0 (0%) |
| Chawla et al (2004) | 25 | 2.8 | 38 | 0.14[†] | 0 (0%) |
| Kassouf et al (2004) | 24 | 3.3 | 29 | 0.49[†] | 0 (0%) |
| Kato et al (2004) | 18 | 2.0 | 23 | 0.42[†] | 0 (0%) |
| Sowery and Siemens (2004) | 22 | 4.1 | 21 | 0.86[†] | 1 (4.5%) |
| Volpe et al (2004) | 32 | 2.7 | 28 | 0.10[†] | 0 (0%) |
| Siu et al (2005) | 45 | 2.1 | 29 | 0.26[†] | 1 (2%) |

*Median growth rate.
[†]Mean growth rate.

highly select population; most series included only relatively small, well-marginated, and homogeneous renal masses, a substantial proportion (approximately 20%) of which may have been benign (Frank et al, 2003b). Second, in some cases, the growth rate was calculated backward by obtaining old films for which the lesion of interest was either previously missed or dismissed, introducing a clear selection bias (Bosniak et al, 1996). Finally, in most of these series, there is a subpopulation of patients with rapidly growing tumors that appear to have more aggressive characteristics. For instance, in the series from Volpe and colleagues (2004), 25% of the masses doubled in volume in 12 months and 22% reached a diameter of 4 cm, triggering surgical intervention.

**Nevertheless, these studies suggest that patients with small, solid, enhancing, well-marginated, homogeneous renal lesions, who are elderly or poor surgical risks, can safely be managed with observation and serial renal imaging at 6-month or 1-year intervals** (Chawla et al, 2005; Viterbo et al, 2005). **This approach is not appropriate for patients with larger (>3 cm), poorly marginated, or nonhomogeneous solid renal lesions. Observation is also not advisable in younger, otherwise healthy patients with small, solid tumors that have radiographic characteristics consistent with RCC.** Even if these lesions are smaller than 3 cm, the current database (see Table 47–21) indicates that most will grow and eventually reach a size at which metastasis becomes more likely. Therefore, in this setting, it is more appropriate to undertake surgical excision of the tumor (or thermal ablation) when it is small, clearly localized, and potentially amenable to nephron-sparing approaches.

## TREATMENT OF LOCALLY ADVANCED RENAL CELL CARCINOMA
### Inferior Vena Caval Involvement

One of the unique features of RCC is its frequent pattern of growth intraluminally into the renal venous circulation, also known as venous tumor thrombus. In extreme cases, this growth may extend into the inferior vena cava (IVC) with cephalad migration as far as the right atrium. The absence of metastases in many patients with vena caval extension is an intriguing aspect of this cancer's behavior (Gettman and Blute, 2002). Approximately 45% to 70% of patients with RCC and IVC thrombus can be cured with an aggressive surgical approach including radical nephrectomy and IVC thrombectomy (see Table 47–15). In general, patients with tumor that is otherwise confined to the kidney and free-floating thrombi have the best prognosis; those with tumor extending into the perinephric fat, lymph node involvement, or direct invasion of the wall of the IVC are at much higher risk for recurrence (Hatcher et al, 1991; Montie et al, 1991; Glazer and Novick, 1996; Gettman et al, 1999; Naitoh et al, 1999; Sweeney et al, 2002b; Bissada et al, 2003; Kim et al, 2004a; Moinzadeh and Libertino, 2004; Leibovich et al, 2005).

**Overall, involvement of the IVC with RCC occurs in 4% to 10% of patients. Venous tumor thrombus should be suspected in patients with a renal tumor who also have lower extremity edema, isolated right-sided varicocele or one that does not collapse with recumbency, dilated superficial abdominal veins, proteinuria, pulmonary embolism, right**

**atrial mass, or nonfunction of the involved kidney. Staging of the level of IVC thrombus is as follows: I, adjacent to the ostium of renal vein; II, extending up to the lower aspect of the liver; III, involving the intrahepatic portion of the IVC but below the diaphragm; and IV, extending above the diaphragm.** The prognostic significance of the cephalad extent of the IVC thrombus has been controversial. Most studies suggest that the incidence of locoregional or systemic progression is higher in patients with level III-IV IVC thrombus, and this probably accounts for the reduced survival reported in this subgroup in some series (Sosa et al, 1984; Quek et al, 2001; Zisman et al, 2003; Kim et al, 2004a; Leibovich et al, 2005). However, other reports confirm that many patients with level IV IVC thrombi can be cured of disease with surgical resection, as long as the tumor is otherwise confined (Libertino et al, 1987; Glazer and Novick, 1996; Sweeney et al, 2002b).

Accurate information about the presence and complete extent of IVC involvement is essential for surgical planning. Routine CT scanning and abdominal ultrasonography usually detect gross renal vein and inferior vena caval involvement but are less reliable in delineating the cephalad extent of a thrombus (Goldfarb et al, 1990). Transesophageal echocardiography and transabdominal color flow Doppler ultrasonography are occasionally employed in this setting (Glazer and Novick, 1997). Contrast inferior venacavography remains an accurate diagnostic study for assessment of IVC involvement (Fig. 47–27). However, this is an invasive technique that entails

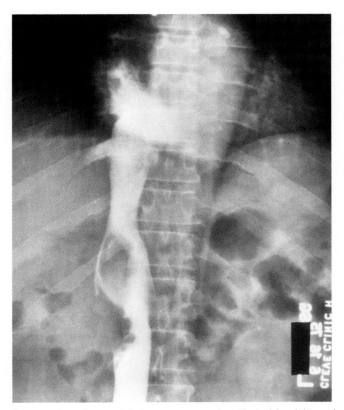

**Figure 47–27.** Contrast inferior venacavogram in patient with a right renal tumor shows involvement of the subdiaphragmatic vena cava.

administration of contrast material, and a single antegrade study may be insufficient in patients with complete caval occlusion (Fig. 47–28). In such cases, a second retrograde injection of the vena cava may be needed to define the distal limits of the thrombus.

**MRI is a noninvasive and accurate modality for demonstrating both the presence and the cephalad extent of vena caval involvement and has become the preferred diagnostic study at most centers** (Fig. 47–29) (Goldfarb et al, 1990; Kallman et al, 1992; Choyke, 1997). Venous thrombus detection, characterization, and extent are best evaluated by MRI on gradient-recalled echo sequences. Individual gradient-recalled echo sequences can be reconstructed by maximum-intensity projection algorithms to create magnetic resonance venograms. Gadolinium chelates can be given to patients with known thrombus to differentiate between tumor thrombus and bland thrombus. Most tumor thrombi will demonstrate enhancement after gadolinium administration, whereas this finding is absent in bland thrombi. A limitation of current vena caval imaging modalities is the inability to differentiate extrinsic vena caval compression from actual invasion of the vena caval wall, which is generally associated with a poor prognosis; unfortunately, the determination is most often established at the time of surgical exploration.

**Renal arteriography remains a useful preoperative study in patients with RCC involving the inferior vena cava because in 35% to 40% of cases, distinct vascularization of a tumor thrombus is observed** (Fig. 47–30). When this finding is present, preoperative embolization of the kidney often causes shrinkage of the thrombus, which can facilitate

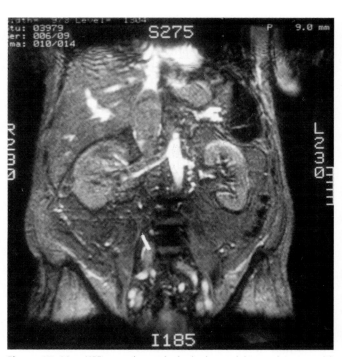

**Figure 47–29.** MRI scan (coronal view) shows right renal tumor with thrombus extending to intrahepatic vena cava.

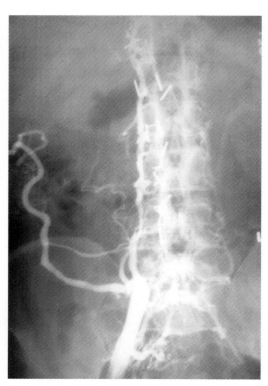

**Figure 47–28.** Transfemoral venogram shows complete occlusion of the inferior vena cava in patient with renal tumor.

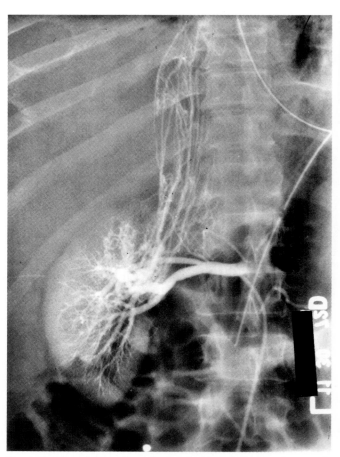

**Figure 47–30.** Right renal arteriogram shows arterialization of a supradiaphragmatic vena caval thrombus.

its intraoperative removal. In patients with extensive supradiaphragmatic vena caval thrombi, when adjunctive cardiopulmonary bypass with deep hypothermic circulatory arrest is considered, coronary angiography is also performed preoperatively (Novick et al, 1990). If significant obstructing coronary lesions are found, these can be repaired simultaneously during cardiopulmonary bypass.

**Contrast inferior venacavography is reserved for patients in whom MRI findings are equivocal or for whom MRI is contraindicated,** as in patients with claustrophobia, cardiac pacemakers, certain intracerebral vascular clips, cochlear implants, or intraocular foreign bodies. Another option in this group of patients is multiplanar CT, and recent data suggest that this study may approach the accuracy of MRI in the identification and characterization of IVC thrombi (Pretorius et al, 2000; Sohaib et al, 2002; Ergen et al, 2004; Hallscheidt et al, 2004).

Although involvement of the IVC with RCC renders the task of complete surgical excision more complicated, operative removal offers the only realistic hope for cure for most patients (Quek et al, 2001; Blute et al, 2004b). After mobilization of the kidney and ligation and transection of the arterial blood supply, vascular control of the involved portion of the IVC is then obtained. In general, level I thrombi are isolated by a Satinsky clamp and are thus readily removed. Level II thrombi require sequential clamping of the caudal IVC, contralateral renal vein, and cephalad IVC along with mobilization of the relevant segment of the IVC and occlusion of lumbar veins. The renal ostium is then opened and the thrombus is removed, all in a bloodless field. On occasion, a tumor thrombus may locally invade the wall of the vena cava. Aggressive resection of the vena caval wall and attainment of negative surgical margins in these patients appear to provide a survival benefit (Hatcher et al, 1991). IVC grafting or reconstitution is required in some instances, but patients with a completely occluded IVC do not require this because of collateral blood flow (Sarkar et al, 1998). Bland thrombus may be left in situ, although the cephalad IVC level should be occluded or clipped in this instance to prevent pulmonary embolism.

Vascular control for level III and level IV IVC thrombi requires more extensive dissection or cardiopulmonary bypass and hypothermic circulatory arrest. For level III thrombi, mobilization of the liver and exposure of the intrahepatic IVC will often allow the thrombus to be mobilized proximal to the hepatic veins, and dissection can then proceed as for a level II thrombus (Gallucci et al, 2004). If this is not possible, the IVC can be clamped above the liver and a Pringle maneuver can be performed, whereby the portal triad is temporarily occluded (Burt, 1991; Ciancio and Soloway, 2001, 2002; Vaidya et al, 2003; Jibiki et al, 2004). Venovenous bypass is commonly used in these cases but may not be required if adequate collateral flow is present (Ciancio et al, 2002). Level IV IVC thrombi have traditionally been managed with cardiopulmonary bypass and hypothermic circulatory arrest, and this is still the preferred approach in complex cases. However, many centers are now trying to avoid hypothermic circulatory arrest and the associated hypocoagulable state that ensues after coming off the pump and the increased risk of cerebrovascular accident and myocardial infarction that accompanies this procedure (Shinghal, 2003; Tasca et al, 2003). In this case, the thrombus is mobilized below the atrium, allowing sequential vascular control to be achieved without opening the heart. Further detail about these procedures can be found in Chapter 50.

Mortality rates associated with radical nephrectomy and IVC thrombectomy have ranged as high as 5% to 10% for upper level thrombi, depending on the patient's comorbidities and tumor characteristics, and the risk of morbidity can also be substantial in this setting (Staehler and Brkovic, 2000; Blute et al, 2004b). Hence, selection of patients is of paramount importance (Gettman et al, 2003), and this procedure has for the most part been reserved for patients with good performance status in whom preoperative studies show no substantial lymphadenopathy or systemic metastasis. However, there may be a palliative role for surgery in some patients with metastasis who experience severe disability from intractable edema, ascites, cardiac dysfunction, or associated local symptoms such as abdominal pain and hematuria (Slaton et al, 1997). In addition, cytoreductive nephrectomy and IVC thrombectomy can also be considered in some patients with metastatic disease, particularly those with level I-II or readily managed level III thrombi (Zisman et al, 2002b, 2003).

## Locally Invasive Renal Cell Carcinoma

The sequestered location and propensity for aggressive behavior of RCC result in occasional patients presenting with large primary tumors that invade adjacent structures. **Such patients usually present with pain, generally from invasion of the posterior abdominal wall, nerve roots, or paraspinous muscles.** Liver extension is uncommon, and intrahepatic metastases occur more often than local extension. The capsules of large tumors may indent and compress adjacent liver parenchyma but seldom actually grow by direct extension into the liver. Duodenal and pancreatic invasion is uncommon and a poor prognostic sign. The propensity for RCC to parasitize vessels may account for extension into the colon and its mesentery. **In evaluation of patients with large, invasive upper quadrant abdominal masses, a broad differential diagnosis should be considered, including adrenocorticoid carcinoma, infiltrative transitional cell carcinoma, sarcoma, and lymphoma in addition to locally invasive RCC.**

**Because surgical therapy is the only effective management for RCC, extended operations with en bloc resection of adjacent organs are sometimes indicated. Complete excision of the tumor, including resection of the involved bowel, spleen, or abdominal wall muscles, is the aim of therapy.** En bloc partial hepatectomy is rarely curative but may occasionally be worthwhile. Important perioperative concerns for patients with locally advanced RCC include a full bowel preparation and consideration for preoperative embolization of the renal arterial blood supply, which can substantially facilitate the dissection.

Partial excision of the large primary tumor, or debulking, is rarely indicated. In one study, only 12% of patients who underwent incomplete excision of locally extensive tumor were alive at 1 year (deKernion et al, 1978). Most reports suggest that less than 5% of patients with extension into adjacent viscera (stage pT4) survive 5 years after surgery. The randomized studies evaluating the role of cytoreductive nephrectomy (Flanigan et al, 2004) did not include a substantial number of patients with this subcategory of disease, and their conclusions should not be extrapolated to this population of patients. Resection of locally advanced disease can be a major undertaking, and its primary indication should be curative or palliative intent.

The role of radiation therapy in the treatment of locally extensive RCC is controversial. Several early studies suggested that preoperative radiotherapy could improve survival (Richie, 1966; Cox et al, 1970). A subsequent study by van der Werf–Messing (1973), however, compared results for preoperative therapy with those for no preoperative therapy and found no survival difference at 5 years. Routine postoperative radiotherapy has not been shown to influence overall survival and can be hazardous because of proximity of small bowel, which is highly radiosensitive. When tumor is known to have been left behind in the renal fossa or adjacent structures, postoperative radiotherapy may occasionally retard regrowth of tumor mass (Kao et al, 1994). This approach is rarely used today and has largely been replaced by the use of systemic immunotherapy.

## Local Recurrence after Radical Nephrectomy or Nephron-Sparing Surgery

**Local recurrence of RCC after radical nephrectomy is an uncommon event, occurring in approximately 2% to 4% of cases** (Uson, 1982; Sandock et al, 1995; Levy et al, 1998; Ljungberg et al, 1999; Itano et al, 2000; Schrodter et al, 2002; Dimarco et al, 2004; Stephenson et al, 2004a). **Risk factors include increasing T stage and locally advanced or node-positive disease** (Esrig et al, 1992; Sandock et al, 1995; Levy et al, 1998). In contrast, local recurrence after radical nephrectomy is rare in patients with low-stage pT1-2 N0 M0 RCC. **Only about 40% of local recurrences are isolated; the majority of patients with local recurrence also have systemic disease, and a thorough metastatic evaluation should be pursued** (Uson, 1982; Phillips and Messing, 1993; Sandock et al, 1995; Itano et al, 2000; Schrodter et al, 2002). Isolated local recurrence of RCC after radical nephrectomy should be considered for surgical resection, which can provide long-term cancer-free status for about 30% to 40% of patients with this dilemma (Esrig et al, 1992; Tanguay et al, 1996a; Itano et al, 2000; Schrodter et al, 2002; Wiesner et al, 2002; Gogus et al, 2003). However, this is often a formidable task because the natural tissue barriers are no longer present and invasion of contiguous organs is not uncommon. En bloc resection of adjacent organs is often required, and the risk of morbidity can be substantial (Esrig et al, 1992; Tanguay et al, 1996a; Itano et al, 2000; Wiesner et al, 2002; Gogus et al, 2003). Radiation therapy may be of value for palliation of symptomatic local recurrence in patients who are not operative candidates.

**Local recurrence in the remnant kidney after nephron-sparing surgery for RCC has been reported in 1.4% to 10% of patients, and the main risk factor is advanced T stage** (see Table 47–17). Most of these local recurrences are distant from the tumor bed and are thus probably a result of unrecognized tumor multicentricity or de novo occurrence rather than true treatment failure (Campbell and Novick, 1994). Patients with isolated local recurrence after partial nephrectomy can be considered for repeated partial nephrectomy, completion nephrectomy, or thermal ablative therapies. The last option is now being used more frequently in this setting because of concern about fibrosis within the renal fossa, but conventional partial nephrectomy can and should be performed when preservation of renal function is important and the anatomy or tumor characteristics are not favorable for ablative modalities (Gittes and Blute, 1982; Moll et al, 1993; Campbell and Novick, 1994; Frank et al, 2005a).

Local recurrence after thermal ablative modalities often represents treatment failure; many local recurrences develop within the previous tumor bed (see Table 47–20). The true incidence of local recurrence in this population is not well defined because most series do not include longitudinal follow-up. Diagnosis of local recurrence in this setting is established by the demonstration of persistent enhancement within the tumor bed or at any other site within the ipsilateral kidney. Again, management is primarily surgical and most often will entail repeated thermal ablation or completion nephrectomy.

## Adjuvant Therapy for Renal Cell Carcinoma

**Although RCC can be cured surgically, recurrence develops in a significant proportion of patients.** Rabinovitch and coworkers (1994) reviewed patterns of disease relapse in 172 patients after nephrectomy, and their experience is typical—**distant metastases developed in 26% and local recurrence in only 5%.** In view of these findings, a strong rationale for systemic postoperative adjuvant therapy exists in high-risk patients.

**Studies have attempted to identify patients who are appropriate candidates for adjuvant therapy trials.** Zisman and colleagues (2001b) investigated 661 patients who underwent nephrectomy, and **five patient groups were segregated on the basis of clinical and pathologic parameters with 5-year survival rates of 94%, 67%, 39%, 23%, and 0%, respectively.** This system was validated by an international cohort of 4202 patients (Patard et al, 2004c) with localized RCC. This group has reported a variety of molecular markers, such as CA-9, Ki-67, and EpCAM (Bui et al, 2004), that may also be useful biomarkers to predict outcomes. Approaches integrating clinical factors and molecular markers to define risk of recurrence will be employed to select patients for adjuvant trials in the future.

**Clinical endpoints used in adjuvant trials include progression-free survival, time to progression, and overall survival.** The determination of time to progression or progression-free survival requires either placebo-controlled and blinded designs or independent review of radiographic and clinical data. **The majority of adjuvant trials performed in patients with RCC have been underpowered to detect small differences in survival; endpoints of time to progression or progression-free survival have been difficult to assess in view of the study designs.**

**Several different therapeutic modalities and systemic agents have been used in an adjuvant setting** for patients with RCC, including hormonal manipulation, radiotherapy, vaccines, and cytokines. Most of these trials have been randomized and have incorporated a control arm of observation only. A series of clinical trials using postoperative medroxyprogesterone acetate (Pizzocaro et al, 1987) or perioperative radiotherapy (van der Werf–Messing, 1973; Kjaer et al, 1987) were all negative, **with no survival advantage demonstrated.**

**A variety of autologous tumor vaccine–based approaches have been used to immunize RCC patients in the postoperative setting, most with negative results and one with controversial results** (Table 47–22). Galligioni and associates (1996) conducted a prospective controlled trial in which patients were treated with three intradermal injections of $10^7$ autologous irradiated tumor cells mixed with $10^7$ bacille Calmette-Guérin (first two injections) or observed. A total of 120 patients were randomized, and at a median follow-up of 61 months, no difference in progression-free survival or overall survival was seen. Jocham and colleagues (2004) reported a prospective trial in which a group of 553 patients were apparently randomized to observation or intradermal treatment with an autologous vaccine. The final report included 202 patients on observation and 177 on active treatment, and this cohort of 379 patients was referred to as the intent-to-treat group by the investigators. At 5 years, the progression-free survival rates were significantly improved for the vaccine-treated group ($P = .0204$). However, this trial was not blinded, did not include a placebo control, and did not undergo external review of data; therefore, a confirmatory study is required. In addition, this study may not have included a true intent-to-treat analysis, and this has raised concern about potential bias.

Finally, Wood and colleagues (2004) have now conducted the largest adjuvant clinical trial testing an autologous tumor vaccine for RCC, in this case targeting patients with clear cell histology and incorporating autologous heat shock protein HSPPC-96 (Oncophage). HSPPC-96 binds peptide fragments and can act as a chaperone for antigen presentation. More than 2000 patients have been evaluated; 809 were eligible. This group was randomized to observation alone or therapy with intradermal HSPPC-96 (25 mg weekly × 4, then 1 every 4 weeks until vaccine supply was exhausted). A placebo arm was not incorporated, but independent review of the radiologic studies is planned. The review committee will independently determine time to progression. Accrual to this trial is complete, but results remain preliminary. **Despite this series of studies, it remains unclear whether adjuvant administration of a tumor vaccine influences the natural history of RCC.** Clearly, the nature of the vaccine, the population treated, and the trial design are major issues in these studies.

**In view of their antitumor effects in patients with demonstrable metastatic disease, IL-2 and interferon alfa have also been studied in postoperative adjuvant trials.** Four randomized studies have been performed, three with interferon alfa and one with IL-2 (Table 47–23). No improvement in disease-free or overall survival for treated patients has been found. The studies investigating interferon used various doses, preparations (L-interferon, interferon alfa-2a, interferon alfa-2b), and duration of therapy (6 to 12 months). The results demonstrate no protective effect of postoperative adjuvant interferon; however, only one trial (Messing et al, 2003) evaluated survival as the primary endpoint. In addition, these studies included patients with all histologic subtypes of RCC, which may not be optimal in view of the limited effects of systemic interferon alfa in non–clear cell histologic types (Motzer et al, 2002). Finally, lack of external review or a blinded design does not permit conclusions about time to progression. Given the modest survival benefit reported with interferon alfa in patients with metastatic RCC, further adjuvant trials with interferon alfa may be of interest.

IL-2 has also been evaluated in a postoperative adjuvant trial without success. Clark and colleagues (2003) randomized patients to observation alone or to high-dose IL-2 (600,000 units/kg every 8 hours on days 1 to 5 and 15 to 19). A total of 69 patients were registered, 25 with resected M1 disease and 38 with locally advanced but resectable disease. An interim analysis prompted closure of the trial with adjuvant IL-2 having demonstrated no clinically meaningful benefit for the population as a whole or in either subgroup.

**In summary, the majority of postoperative adjuvant trials in patients with resected renal cancer have been negative, and the standard of care remains observation. In the future, trials using targeted oral agents such as sorafenib or SU11248 are planned for the population of patients with surgically resectable RCC who are at high risk for recurrence.**

## TREATMENT OF METASTATIC RENAL CELL CARCINOMA

### Nephrectomy

Approximately one third of patients with RCC have metastatic disease at the time of initial diagnosis (synchronous metastatic disease), and 40% to 50% will develop distant metastases after initial diagnosis (Bukowski, 1997). **The value**

---

**Table 47–22.** **Randomized Adjuvant Trials with Autologous Tumor Cell Preparations: Renal Cell Carcinoma**

| Author | Patients Eligible | Treatment Groups | No. of Patients | 5-yr PFS | 5-yr OS |
|--------|-------------------|------------------|-----------------|----------|---------|
| Galligioni et al (1996) | T1 N0-1 M0 | Evaluated | 184 | — | — |
| | | Control | 60 | 72% | 78% |
| | | Vaccine + BCG | 60 | 63% | 69% |
| Jocham et al (2004) | T2-3b N0-3 M0 | Evaluated | 553 | Not stated | Not stated |
| | | Control | 202 | 67.8% | Not stated |
| | | Vaccine | 177 | 77.4% | Not stated |
| Wood et al (2004) | T2 N0 M0 (grade 3, 4) | Evaluated | 2024 | — | Not stated |
| | T3a-c N0-1 M0 | Control | 409 | Too early | Too early |
| | T4 N1-2 M0 | HSPPC-96 | 409 | Too early | Too early |

PFS, progression-free survival; OS, overall survival; BCG, bacille Calmette-Guérin.

**Table 47–23. Randomized Trials of Adjuvant Cytokine Therapy: Renal Cell Carcinoma**

| Author | Patients Eligible | Treatment Type | No. of Patients | 3-yr PFS | 3-yr OS | 5-yr PFS | 5-yr OS |
|---|---|---|---|---|---|---|---|
| Porzsolt (1992) | T3-4 N0/+ M0 | Interferon alfa-2a 9 million IU 3 times per week for 12 months | 133 | 60%* | 80% | Not stated | Not stated |
| | | Control | 137 | 60% | 80% | Not stated | Not stated |
| Pizzocaro et al (2001) | T3a N0 M0 T3b N0 M0 T2/3 N1-3 M0 | Interferon alfa-2b 6 million IU 3 times per week for 6 months | 123 | 64% | 83% | 67% | 66% |
| | | Control | 124 | 75% | 80% | 57% | 66% |
| Messing et al (2003) | T1-2 N1-3 M0 T3a-c N0-3 M0 T4a N0-3 M0 | Interferon alfa-NL 3 million IU/m$^2$ day 1 5 million IU/m$^2$ day 2 20 million IU/m$^2$ days 3-5 12 cycles every 3 weeks | 140 | 44% | 62% | 37% | 51% |
| | | Control | 143 | 48% | 70% | 41% | 62% |
| Clark et al (2003) | T3a-c N1-2 M0 any T, any N, M1R | IL-2 (SC) 600,000 units/kg every 8 hours on days 1-5 and 15-19 | 33 | 32% | 80% | Too early | Too early |
| | | Control | 36 | 45% | 86% | Too early | Too early |

*Time to treatment failure at 30 months.
PFS, progression-free survival; OS, overall survival.

**Table 47–24. Interferon alfa Monotherapy or Interferon alfa with Cytoreductive Nephrectomy: Metastatic Renal Cell Carcinoma**

| | Flanigan (2001) | | Mickisch (2001) | |
|---|---|---|---|---|
| | Interferon alfa* | Interferon alfa–Nephrectomy | Interferon alfa | Interferon alfa–Nephrectomy |
| Patients accrued | 121 | 120 | 43 | 42 |
| Efficacy | | | | |
| Complete response | 0 | 0 | 1 (20%) | 5 (12%) |
| Partial response | 3/83 (3.6%) | 3/92 (3.3%) | 4/43 (10%) | 3/42 (7%) |
| Overall response | 3.6% | 3.3% | 12% | 19% |
| Progression-free survival (months) | Not available | Not available | 3.0† | 5.0 |
| Median survival (months) | 8.1‡ | 11.1‡ | 7.0§ | 17.0§ |
| 1-year survival | 38.6% | 49% | 35% | 63% |

*Recombinant human interferon alfa-2b.
†$P = .04$.
‡$P = .012$.
§$P = .03$.

of nephrectomy has been examined retrospectively in patients with synchronous metastases. Prospective controlled trials have also examined the value of nephrectomy (Flanigan et al, 2001; Mickisch et al, 2001). Initially, the rationale for nephrectomy included palliation for severe bleeding, pain, and paraneoplastic symptoms. In addition, there have been occasional patients who demonstrate regression of metastases after nephrectomy; the frequency of this finding has been estimated as 1% to 2% (Walther et al, 1997c). These responses have been predominantly in pulmonary nodules, with a median duration of approximately 6 months. Several retrospective studies suggested that prior nephrectomy was a good prognostic factor for patients with metastatic RCC, but concerns about selection bias predominated. About 10% to 30% of patients undergoing cytoreductive nephrectomy were unable to receive systemic therapy because of postoperative medical complications or rapid cancer progression.

Two prospective trials have been reported in which untreated patients with synchronous metastatic disease were randomized to either nephrectomy followed by systemic interferon alfa or interferon alfa monotherapy alone (Table 47–24). The results demonstrate that cytoreductive nephrectomy followed by systemic treatment should be considered in patients with synchronous metastatic disease. Careful selection of patients remains of paramount importance. Eligibility for these trials included the histologic confirmation of RCC before study entry, a primary tumor considered surgically resectable, and an Eastern Cooperative Oncology Group performance status score of 0 to 1. Interferon alfa-2b (Intron A) was administered subcutaneously at a dose of $5 \times 10^6$ IU/m$^2$ three times weekly. In the study reported by Flanigan and colleagues (2001), the dose was gradually escalated from $1.25 \times 10^6$ IU/m$^2$ during 3 days, and interferon alfa was initiated in almost all patients within 4 weeks of nephrectomy. In a meta-analysis of both trials (Flanigan et al, 2004), the median survival in the nephrectomy-interferon group was found to be 13.6 months (95% CI, 9.7 to 17.4) versus 7.8 months (95% CI, 5.9 to 9.7) for patients receiving interferon alfa alone (HR, 0.69; 95% CI, 0.55 to 0.87; $P = .002$). The greatest survival advantages were observed in patients with good performance status (17.4 versus 11.7 months median survival) and those with pulmonary-only metastasis (14.3 versus 10.3 months median survival), but this survival benefit of 30% to 50% persisted in other subgroups as well. Surgical morbidity and mortality were minimal, with a 1% operative and perioperative mortality noted in the Southwest Oncology Group trial. **These data therefore support the concept of cytoreductive nephrectomy before systemic therapy with a cytokine such as interferon.**

Two retrospective series (Walther et al, 1997c; Pantuck et al, 2002a) have examined institutional experience with cytoreductive nephrectomy followed by IL-2–based therapy. In the series from Walther and associates (1997c), 195 patients underwent cytoreductive nephrectomy but 31% did not subsequently receive systemic treatment because of postsurgical complications (9%) or rapidly progressive disease (22%). Pantuck and colleagues (2002a) reviewed 89 patients treated at the University of California, Los Angeles with nephrectomy followed by IL-2–based treatment. The median survival of this group was 16.7 months, somewhat better than that reported in the Southwest Oncology Group and European Organisation for Research and Treatment of Cancer trials with interferon-based systemic therapy. However, in view of potential selection bias in these trials, related in part to the high-dose IL-2 regimen used, comparisons to the data from the nephrectomy–interferon alfa trials is not possible. Nevertheless, the Walther and Pantuck reports do demonstrate that nephrectomy followed by high-dose IL-2 is possible.

Selection of patients for nephrectomy followed by cytokine therapy in the setting of advanced disease must be careful—this is not a pathway that should be used indiscriminately. **Individuals with advanced symptoms (performance status ≥ 2), metastases in critical areas (central nervous system,** spinal cord compression), major organ dysfunction, and significant comorbid illnesses are not candidates for such approaches.** Figure 47–31 highlights the indications for cytoreductive nephrectomy and other treatment options for the management of patients with advanced RCC. **The role of this approach in patients with non–clear cell carcinoma is not well defined.**

## Hormonal Therapy

**The use of hormonal therapy for patients with metastatic RCC has minimal value.** It was originally thought that progestational agents would be useful since they inhibit the growth of diethylstilbestrol-induced renal tumors in Syrian hamsters. Unfortunately, the collective experience with medroxyprogesterone acetate, androgens, and antiestrogens has shown that such preclinical models of renal cancer do not correlate with human RCC. Although the initial clinical trials using progestins for patients with advanced RCC looked promising, studies using modern objective response criteria have demonstrated only limited activity.

Two multicenter randomized trials (Medical Research Council Renal Cancer Collaborators, 1999; Negrier et al, 2005) tested oral medroxyprogesterone acetate as initial therapy for patients with metastatic RCC. In these reports, 174 and 123 patients received medroxyprogesterone acetate, 300 mg/day and 200 mg/day, respectively. Response rates to medroxyprogesterone acetate were uniformly low (2.0% and 2.5%, respectively), and overall median survival of the patients varied from 6.0 months (Medical Research Council Renal Cancer Collaborators, 1999) to more than 15.0 months (Negrier et al, 2005). The difference in survival probably reflects patient entry criteria used in the two studies rather

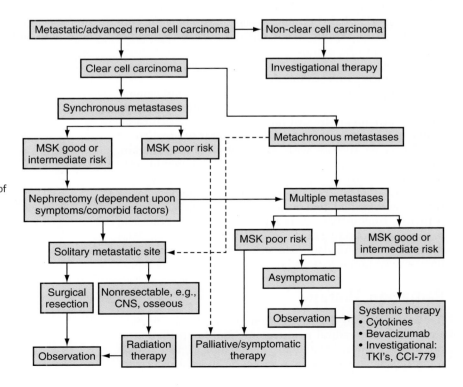

**Figure 47–31.** Algorithm for management of advanced RCC. MSK, Memorial Sloan Kettering.

than a true difference in biologic responsiveness. **Therefore, whereas progestational agents may be useful for symptom palliation, they do not appear to have any significant value in the treatment of patients with metastatic RCC.**

## Chemotherapy

**Multiple clinical trials performed during the 1980s established RCC as a prototype of a chemotherapy-resistant tumor.** Yagoda and associates (1995) reviewed a total of 4542 patients treated with a variety of chemotherapeutic agents in a series of clinical trials (1983-1993) and found an overall response rate of 6.0% (95% CI, 5.3% to 6.8%). This series was updated by Ruiz and colleagues (2000), who reviewed an additional 2327 patients treated with chemotherapy between 1993 and 1998. The overall response rate in this review was 18.5%, but protocols incorporated immunotherapy in combination with chemotherapy, and this probably accounts for the marginal increase in activity. In the past, it has been suggested that the fluoropyrimidines or vinblastine might have antitumor activity in patients with metastatic RCC. However, when vinblastine was tested in a randomized prospective setting, the response rate was 2.5% in 81 patients receiving chemotherapy alone, and overall survival was inferior to the combination of vinblastine and interferon alfa (Pyrhonen et al, 1999). **Virtually every other cytotoxic agent has been tested for this disease, either alone or in combination with other chemotherapeutic approaches, almost uniformly with discouraging results.**

One factor contributing to this phenomenon is the expression of the MDR-associated glycoprotein on the surface of RCC cells (Fojo et al, 1987). *MDR1,* which encodes a 170-kD membrane glycoprotein (P-glycoprotein), can act as an efflux pump, reducing intracellular concentrations of agents such as vinblastine. In view of this, compounds inhibiting P-glycoprotein, such as toremifene, verapamil, nifedipine, and cyclosporine, have been investigated in combination with vinblastine (Braybrooke, 2000). To date, these approaches have not improved response rates to vinblastine. It is likely that additional mechanisms also contribute to chemoresistance in patients with advanced RCC.

**Currently available data of chemotherapy do not demonstrate reproducible antitumor activity or improvement in survival of patients treated for metastatic clear cell carcinoma. In patients with metastatic non–clear cell malignant neoplasms or tumors with sarcomatoid differentiation, various agents including doxorubicin and gemcitabine may have clinical activity.** Nanus and colleagues (2004) reported a response rate of 39% (two complete responses) in 18 patients with sarcomatoid or rapidly progressing RCC treated with this combination. Anecdotal reports of responses in patients with collecting duct cancers (Peyromaure et al, 2003) to agents such as cisplatin and gemcitabine suggest that this type of renal tumor may also be sensitive to chemotherapy.

## Radiation Therapy

**Radiation therapy has been used primarily as adjuvant treatment after radical nephrectomy and for palliation of metastatic lesions.** Most studies have failed to demonstrate improvement in survival or a reduction in local recurrence rates after postoperative radiation therapy. **At present, the main role of radiation therapy for patients with metastatic RCC is for the palliation of symptomatic osseous metastases** (Halperin and Harisiadis, 1983; Cutuli et al, 1990). Radiation therapy has also been combined with surgery for the treatment of vertebral body metastases with spinal cord compression, allowing substantially reduced blood loss (Sundaresan et al, 1986). Standard radiation therapy may also be employed for palliation of brain metastases (Halperin and Harisiadis, 1983; Maor et al, 1988; Cutuli et al, 1990). Stereotactic radiosurgery has shown promise for the treatment of select patients with brain metastases, thereby avoiding the risks associated with craniotomy (Coffey et al, 1991).

## Cytokines and Immunologic Therapy

**The therapeutic potential of cytokines and immunotherapy has been investigated for the last 30 years in patients with metastatic RCC and has shown real but limited efficacy. The demonstration of T-cell infiltrates** (Finke et al, 1988), **the development of T-cell lines (CD8[+]) with specificity for autologous tumor** (Finke et al, 1994), **and the finding of tumor-associated antigens on renal tumors that are MHC restricted** (Tatsumi et al, 2002) **provide laboratory evidence for a specific antitumor immune response.** Coincident with these observations, a series of clinical trials demonstrated the antitumor activity of cytokines such as interferon alfa and IL-2 in patients with advanced disease.

Interferon alfa is one member of a pleiotropic group of proteins with antiviral, immunomodulatory, and antiproliferative activities (Vestal et al, 2001) related to modulation of gene expression in selected cell populations. IL-2 is a T-cell growth factor that was first described by Morgan and colleagues (1976) and is produced when T lymphocytes are activated (Alatrash et al, 2001). Its biologic effects are mediated by binding to the IL-2 receptor, with subsequent clonal expansion of cytotoxic T cells. **Since the 1980s, these two cytokines have been tested alone or in combination as therapy for metastatic RCC.** In a review of phase II and randomized phase III trials (Bukowski, 1997), the aggregate response rates for these cytokines were characterized (Fig. 47–32). With single-

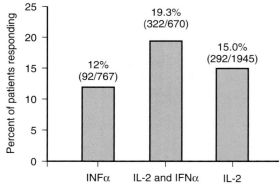

**Figure 47–32.** Overall response rates (complete and partial responses) in a review of therapy with various cytokines including interferon alfa (INF-α), interleukin-2 (IL-2), and the combination of interleukin-2 and interferon alfa. Patients included in prospective phase II and phase III trials receiving various doses and schedules of the cytokines are included.

agent interferon alfa or IL-2, the overall response rates were approximately 13% to 15%. With combination therapy, this increased to more than 20%.

**The responses seen with interferon alfa monotherapy are generally partial, with a complete response rate of only 1.8%.** Prospective phase III trials have examined the activity of interferon alfa in untreated patients compared with other agents with or without interferon alfa. Representative studies summarized in Table 47–25 demonstrate that interferon alfa monotherapy has a modest effect compared with medroxyprogesterone acetate or vinblastine. Increases in objective response rates, overall survival, and progression-free survival (Medical Research Council Renal Cancer Collaborators, 1999; Pyrhonen et al, 1999) were found. Addition of agents such as vinblastine and *cis*-retinoic acid to interferon alfa does not appear to improve results.

**A series of meta-analyses have been performed to examine results of interferon alfa monotherapy in patients with metastatic RCC.** Coppin and colleagues (2005) found four randomized controlled trials containing 644 patients that critically examined survival in patients receiving interferon alfa compared with a control population of patients treated with inactive or ineffective therapies. **The improvement in median survival (interferon alfa–treated patients) was 3.8 months (11.4 versus 7.6 months; hazard ratio, 0.74), with an overall response rate of 12.5% versus 1.5% in control patients.** In one such study, Motzer and colleagues (2001) examined their results with interferon alfa therapy in 463 patients receiving first-line therapy. The overall median survival was 13.0 months, and median progression-free survival was 4.7 months. The individuals most likely to benefit had good to intermediate risk status (Motzer et al, 2001), clear cell histology (Motzer et al, 2002), and lung or soft tissue predominant disease (Bukowski, 1997).

IL-2 has been the other primary immunotherapeutic agent used to treat patients with metastatic RCC (Bukowski, 1997). As shown in Figure 47–32, the overall response rate in 1714 patients treated with single-agent IL-2 is 15.0%. **IL-2 can be administered in a variety of ways, including bolus intravenous infusion, continuous intravenous infusion, and subcutaneous injection. These schedules use different dose levels and were developed in an effort to maintain efficacy while decreasing side effects, in particular the "vascular leak**

syndrome" that is associated with high-dose therapy. This syndrome can include hypotension, oliguria, and organ failure if it is not treated aggressively with fluid resuscitation and careful hemodynamic monitoring.**

**In the United States, IL-2 is registered and approved for treatment of metastatic RCC on the basis of data from a high-dose bolus intravenous infusion protocol in which patients were given cytokine every 8 hours for 5 days (15 doses). This regimen may be more efficacious in terms of complete durable responses (≥5%), but it is associated with significant morbidity and requires hospitalization.**

Several randomized trials and a retrospective analysis have investigated the optimal dose and schedule for IL-2 administration. Negrier and colleagues (2005) have reported preliminary results from a phase III trial comparing subcutaneous IL-2, interferon alfa, the combination of IL-2 and interferon alfa, and medroxyprogesterone in patients with an intermediate-prognosis RCC. A total of 492 patients were randomized, and no differences in overall survival between the treatment arms were detected (median overall survival, 15.0 months). Atzpodien and colleagues (2004) reported a randomized trial comparing various outpatient combinations of interferon alfa and IL-2 (Table 47–25). When the arms containing IL-2 and interferon alfa were compared with interferon alfa and vinblastine, median survival was significantly increased. Indirectly, this report suggests that adding IL-2 to interferon alfa and 5-fluorouracil may have an impact on survival.

Baaten and colleagues (2004) reviewed published results with IL-2 to assess the effects of the administration schedule (Fig. 47–33); 4946 patients receiving either intravenous bolus (1108 patients), subcutaneous (2394 patients), or continuous intravenous (1444 patients) IL-2–based therapy were described. Complete responses were seen less frequently in patients receiving continuous intravenous IL-2, and durable complete responses (≥36 months) were most frequent in patients receiving high-dose bolus IL-2. The heterogeneity of the patients treated, the variability in the regimens, and the absence of survival data make any conclusions tentative.

Table 47–26 summarizes a series of prospective phase III trials in which IL-2 monotherapy was included as a treatment arm. In one trial comparing IL-2 and interferon alfa (Negrier et al, 1998), essentially no differences were observed. In two reports (Yang et al, 2003b; McDermott el, 2005) comparing

**Table 47–25.  Phase III Trials with Single-Agent Interferon alfa in Metastatic Renal Cell Carcinoma**

| Author | No. of Patients | OS | 3-yr OS | 3-yr PFS | Median OS (months) | Median PFS (months) |
|---|---|---|---|---|---|---|
| Motzer et al, 2000 | | | | | | |
| Interferon alfa | 145 | 6% | 18% | 6% | 15.0 | 5.0 |
| Interferon alfa + CRA | 139 | 13% | 25% | 10% | 5.0 | 5.0 |
| Medical Research Council, 1999 | | | | | | |
| Interferon alfa | 174 | 14% | 43% (1 yr) | Not stated | 8.5 | 4.0 |
| MPA | 176 | 2% | 31% (1 yr) | Not stated | 6.0 | 3.0 |
| Pyrhonen et al, 1999 | | | | | | |
| Interferon alfa + vinblastine | 79 | 16% | 12% | 6% | 16.9 | 3.3 |
| Vinblastine | 81 | 2.5% | 7% | 3% | 9.4 | 2.3 |
| Atzpodien et al, 2004 | | | | | | |
| Interferon alfa + vinblastine | 63 | 20% | 21.4% | 8.4% | 16.0 | 5.0 |
| Interferon alfa + IL-2 + 5-FU | 132 | 31% | 37.2% | 15.6% | 25.0 | 6.0 |
| Interferon alfa + IL-2 + 5-FU + CRA | 146 | 26% | 41% | 17.7% | 27.0 | 7.0 |

OS, overall survival; PFS, progression-free survival; CRA, cis-retinoic acid; MPA, medroxyprogesterone acetate; 5-FU, 5-fluorouracil.

high-dose bolus IL-2 with lower doses of IL-2 or the combination of IL-2 and interferon alfa, the overall and complete response rates with high-dose IL-2 were increased, but no significant increase in survival or progression-free survival was seen.

High-dose IL-2 has been the schedule and dose recommended by a variety of investigators (Yang et al, 2003b; McDermott et al, 2005) on the basis of the frequency of complete durable responses. These are generally seen in 6% (Yang et al, 2003b) to 8% (McDermott et al, 2005) of selected patients. **However, in view of the significant toxicity associated with this approach, rigorous selection of patients is required, and these individuals may not represent the average patient with metastatic RCC, potentially biasing**

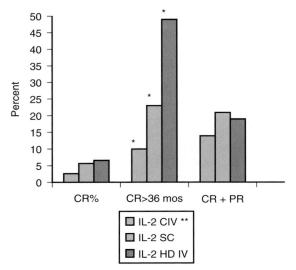

\* CIV 3/30, SC 8/35, HD IVB 36/74 - patients included in assessment of CR duration
\*\* Total number of patients evaluated: CIV - 1444, SC - 2394, HD IV - 1108

**Figure 47–33.** Complete and partial response rates in 4946 patients treated with interleukin-2 administered in a variety of ways and at various dose levels (Baaten et al, 2004). The data suggest that durable complete responses are more frequent in patients treated with intravenous bolus IL-2 at higher doses. CIV, continuous intravenous infusion; SC, subcutaneous; HD IV, high-dose intravenous.

**these results in a favorable manner. The absence of a demonstrable survival or progression-free survival improvement with this approach remains problematic.**

In view of the single-agent data with IL-2 and interferon alfa and the preclinical data demonstrating potential synergy (Chikkala et al, 1990), these two cytokines have been combined. Data summarized in Figure 47–33 and Table 47–26 suggest that the combination has a higher response rate than monotherapy does, but no differences in overall survival have been reported (Negrier et al, 1998). The toxicity of regimens including IL-2 is increased; and in the absence of a survival benefit, careful selection of patients for a cytokine regimen such as IL-2 and interferon alfa is required.

Reports that address the issue of prognostic factors for response to cytokine therapy are useful for selection of patients (Motzer et al, 2001; Mekhail et al, 2005). More than 700 patients were included in these studies; the results are outlined in Table 47–27. **These studies demonstrate that prognosis in patients with metastatic RCC can be defined by a series of clinical criteria including performance status, metastasis-free interval, and several laboratory findings (hemoglobin, lactate dehydrogenase, and corrected calcium concentrations). Patients can then be divided into groups of favorable, intermediate, and poor risk differentiated by median survival as outlined in Table 47–27.** The initial analysis by Motzer and colleagues (2001) was then validated on an independent data set (Mekhail, 2005). This method provides a clinically defined set of criteria that can be used to select patients for various treatment approaches with cytokines. Patients in the poor-risk group (20% to 25%) have a short median survival, are unlikely to tolerate or to benefit from aggressive therapy, and may experience significant toxicity. The other two groups have median survivals of 14.0 and more than 26.0 months (intermediate and favorable risk, respectively) and are appropriate candidates for IL-2, interferon alfa, or investigational trials.

**The overall approach to patients with metastatic RCC is outlined in Figure 47–31 and highlights the use of prognostic criteria for selecting initial treatment.** In addition, information such as this can be used for clinical trial design to determine sample size and eligibility of patients. **Patients are also segregated on the basis of histology (clear cell versus non–clear cell) and the type of metastatic disease (synchronous versus metachronous). For patients receiving systemic**

| Table 47–26. | Phase III Clinical Trials with Single-Agent IL-2 in Metastatic Renal Cancer | | | | | | |
|---|---|---|---|---|---|---|---|
| *Author* | *No. of Patients* | *CR* | *OS* | *3-yr OS* | *3-yr PFS* | *Median OS (months)* | *Median PFS (months)* |
| Negrier et al, 1998 | | | | | | | |
|   IL-2 (CIV) | 138 | NS | 6.8% | 32% | 8% | 12.0 | 3.0 |
|   Interferon alfa | 147 | NS | 7.5% | 25% | 8% | 13.0 | 3.0 |
|   IL-2 (CIV) + interferon alfa | 140 | NS | 18% | 31% | 8% | 17.0 | 4.0 |
| Yang et al, 2003 | | | | | | | |
|   IL-2 (HD IVB) | 96 | 6% | 21% | 31% | NS | 18.0 | NS |
|   IL-2 (LD IVB) | 92 | 1% | 11% | 21% | NS | 18.0 | NS |
|   IL-2 (SC) | 93 | 2% | 10% | 25% | NS | 18.0 | NS |
| McDermott et al, 2005 | | | | | | | |
|   IL-2 (HD IVB) | 95 | 8% | 23.2% | 32% | 10.5% | 17.0 | 4.0 |
|   IL-2 (SC) + interferon alfa | 91 | 3% | 9.9% | 21% | 3.3% | 13.0 | 4.0 |

CR, complete response; OS, overall survival; PFS, progression-free survival; CIV, continuous intravenous infusion; HD, high dose; LD, low dose; IVB, intravenous bolus; SC, subcutaneous; NS, not stated.

**Table 47-27. Prognostic Factors in Patients with Metastatic Renal Cancer**

| Author | No. of Patients | Median OS (months) | Favorable Risk* | | Intermediate Risk† | | Poor Risk‡ | |
|---|---|---|---|---|---|---|---|---|
| | | | No. of Patients | Median OS (months) | No. of Patients | Median OS (months) | No. of Patients | Median OS (months) |
| Motzer et al, 2002 | 437 | 13.1 | 80 | 30.0 | 269 | 14.0 | 88 | 5.0 |
| Mekhail et al, 2005 | 308 | 14.8 | 114 | 26.0 | 108 | 14.0 | 86 | 7.3 |

Risk grouping:
  *Favorable—no poor prognostic factors.
  †Intermediate ≤ 2 poor prognostic factors.
  ‡Poor ≥ 3 poor prognostic factors.
Prognostic factors: Karnofsky performance status below 80%; time from diagnosis of metastatic disease less than 12 months; hemoglobin level below the lower limit of normal; lactate dehydrogenase level more than 1.5 times the upper limit of normal; corrected calcium concentration above 10.0 mg/dL.

therapy, the current standards include IL-2, interferon alfa, and investigational therapy.

## Cytokine Combinations

**IL-2 and interferon alfa have been combined, and currently available data suggest an increase in response rate but no improvement in overall survival.** The randomized trial reported by Negrier and colleagues (1998) did find an increase in 1-year event-free survival (20%) associated with IL-2 and interferon alfa therapy (15%, IL-2; 12%, interferon alfa; $P = .01$), but the toxicity of the regimen was thought to preclude its general use.

IL-2 and interferon alfa have also been combined with other agents, including other cytokines (granulocyte-monocyte colony-stimulating factor, interferon gamma, IL-12), chemotherapeutic agents (5-fluorouracil, vinblastine, capecitabine, gemcitabine), and miscellaneous agents (cis-retinoic acid, thalidomide). Studies in which interferon alfa monotherapy or the combination of IL-2 and interferon has been compared with the same regimens plus vinblastine (Pyrhonen et al, 1999), 5-fluorouracil (Negrier et al, 2000), or cis-retinoic acid (Motzer et al, 2000; Fossa et al, 2004) have also been conducted but have not demonstrated improved outcomes compared with the standard cytokine protocols.

## Adoptive Immunotherapy

In view of the T-cell response to RCC (Finke et al, 1994), a series of clinical studies investigating the role of adoptive transfer of autologous lymphocytes for treatment of metastatic RCC have been performed. These trials used various immune cell populations obtained from peripheral blood, including lymphokine-activated killer cells (Rosenberg et al, 1993), T lymphocytes (Graham et al, 1993), lymph node cells (Chang et al, 1997), and tumor-infiltrating T cells (Bukowski et al, 1991), which were then expanded ex vivo through exposure to IL-2. **Randomized trials comparing IL-2 monotherapy with IL-2 plus adoptive transfer cells have not demonstrated significant differences compared with cytokine therapy alone** (Figlin et al, 1999). **At present, use of adoptive immunotherapy remains investigational. It is unclear whether the addition of any ex vivo–expanded cell population enhances the clinical results with IL-2 monotherapy.**

## Vaccines

Active specific immunotherapy refers to treatment of patients with biologic preparations designed to directly (antibodies) or indirectly (vaccines) enhance an immune response. In view of the active immune response in patients with RCC, a variety of vaccines have been employed as therapy for advanced disease. These can be administered with adjuvants, such as bacille Calmette-Guérin or incomplete Freund's adjuvant. **Vaccine preparations that have been employed in patients with RCC include autologous tumor cells** (Galligioni et al, 1996; Jocham et al, 2004), **autologous tumor cells fused with allogeneic dendritic cells** (Avigan, 2004), **autologous dendritic cells** (Gitlitz et al, 2003; Arroyo et al, 2004), **and heat shock protein** (Hoos and Levey, 2003). Of particular interest is the use of dendritic cells, which function as potent antigen-presenting cells for antigen in the context of MHC molecules, thereby stimulating T lymphocytes. These cells are found in a low frequency in peripheral blood (Banchereau and Palucka, 2005) and can be expanded ex vivo with growth factors such as IL-4, granulocyte-monocyte colony-stimulating factor, and tumor necrosis factor. The optimal preparation for clinical immunization remains unclear. Dendritic cells can be loaded with autologous tumor lysates, tumor antigens, or peptide sequences of defined tumor-associated antigens and administered intradermally, intravenously, or by lymphatic infusion. **Currently, use of tumor vaccines in patients with advanced renal cancer remains investigational.**

## Targeted Agents

**The VHL gene has been cloned, functions of the protein have been elucidated, and a high frequency of mutations or epigenetic silencing of this gene in sporadic clear cell carcinoma has been recognized. These findings led to a series of studies identifying the VEGF and PDGF pathways as molecular targets in this tumor** (Kaelin, 2004). These growth factors bind to receptor tyrosine kinases that regulate cell proliferation and survival and can promote tumor-associated angiogenesis and growth. Inhibition of the VEGF and PDGF signaling pathways may therefore inhibit angiogenesis and tumor progression (Fig. 47–34). A series of agents inhibiting VEGF or tyrosine kinase receptors such as VEGFR types 1 to 3 and PDGFR are now under investigation and appear to have

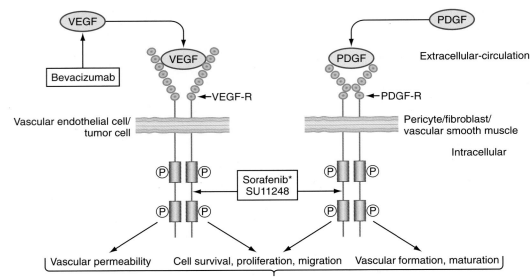

* Sorafenib also inhibits Raf kinase

**Figure 47–34.** Illustration of the effects of various targeted agents (bevacizumab, sorafenib, SU011248) on endothelial and tumor cells. Bevacizumab binds and sequesters VEGF, and sorafenib and SU011248 inhibit the receptors for VEGF and PDGF.

antitumor effects in renal cancer patients. Table 47–28 outlines the preliminary results of several phase II and phase III trials in which these drugs have been investigated.

**Bevacizumab is an IgG1 monoclonal antibody recognizing and binding all VEGF isoforms** (Ferrara et al, 2003). **This agent inhibits signaling through the VEGF pathway by sequestering the circulating ligand.** Yang and colleagues (2003a) conducted a phase II randomized, placebo-controlled trial in patients with cytokine-refractory clear cell carcinoma. Two dose levels of bevacizumab (3.0 mg/kg and 10 mg/kg) were compared with a placebo; **116 patients were randomized, but the trial was stopped early when an interim analysis demonstrated that patients receiving 10.0 mg/kg had significant prolongation of time to progression (4.8 months) compared with the placebo group (2.5 months).** Partial responses (4 of 37, 10%) were seen in patients receiving 10.0 mg/kg bevacizumab every 2 weeks, in contrast to no partial responses in the other two arms. No overall survival advantage was seen, but the crossover design or the relatively small sample size studied may have precluded this. **A report** (Spigel et al, 2005) **tested the combination of erlotinib (150 mg/day) and bevacizumab (10 mg/kg intravenously every 2 weeks) in an effort to improve on these results.** Erlotinib is an orally administered tyrosine kinase inhibitor that blocks signaling through the EGFR. **Preclinical studies have suggested that dual inhibition of both the VEGF and EGF pathways can have additive antitumor effects for renal cancer** (Rini et al, 2005). Sixty-three patients with metastatic clear cell carcinoma of the kidney were treated. **An overall response rate of 26% and a progression-free survival of 11.0 months were found.** Therefore, at both the clinical and preclinical levels, co-administration of these two agents may enhance results. A phase II randomized trial with this combination is in progress. Finally, the activity of bevacizumab in untreated patients with metastatic clear cell carcinoma is under investi-

**Table 47–28. Targeted Therapy for Cytokine-Refractory Renal Cell Carcinoma: Summary of Clinical Trials**

| Agent/Trial | No. of Patients | ORR | TTP/PFS (months) |
|---|---|---|---|
| SU11248 (Motzer et al, 2004, 2005) | | | |
|   Trial 1 | 63 | 40% | 8.7 |
|   Trial 2 | 106 | 39% | Too early |
| AG-013736 (Rini et al, 2005) | 52 | 40% | Too early |
| Sorafenib (Escudier et al, 2005) | | | |
|   Sorafenib | 384 | 2% | 6.0 |
|   Placebo | 385 | 0 | 3.0 |
| Bevacizumab (Yang et al, 2003) | | | |
|   Bevacizumab (10 mg/kg) | 39 | 10% | 4.8 |
|   Bevacizumab (3.0 mg/kg) | 37 | 0 | 3.0 |
|   Placebo | 40 | 0 | 2.5 |
| Bevacizumab + erlotinib (Spigel et al, 2005) | 63 | 26% | 11.0 |

ORR, overall response rate; TTP, time to progression; PFS, progression-free survival.

gation in two prospectively randomized, phase III trials comparing the combination of interferon alfa and bevacizumab with interferon alfa monotherapy (Rini et al, 2005).

A series of oral agents that inhibit various tyrosine kinase receptors have also been studied in patients with cytokine-refractory clear cell carcinoma. **Three of these agents are outlined in Table 47–28, including SU11248** (Motzer et al, 2004, 2005), **AG-013736** (Rini et al, 2005), **and sorafenib** (Escudier et al, 2005). **These agents inhibit multiple tyrosine kinases, including VEGFR-2, PDGFR, c-Kit, and Flt3, and sorafenib also inhibits Raf kinase. SU11248** (Motzer et al, 2004, 2005) **and AG-013736** (Rini et al, 2005) **have been studied in a series of phase II trials, and the preliminary results demonstrate partial response rates of 38% to 40%, with**

**progression-free survival and median survival rates that are still preliminary.** A phase III randomized trial comparing SU11248 with interferon alfa in untreated patients with metastatic clear cell carcinoma is currently in progress.

**Sorafenib is an oral tyrosine kinase inhibitor that has an excellent toxicity profile and encouraging antitumor activity in patients with RCC** (Escudier et al, 2005). A phase III trial was recently completed in which 905 cytokine-refractory patients with clear cell RCC were randomized to either sorafenib (400 mg twice daily) or a placebo. **An interim analysis in 763 individuals demonstrated a significant ($P = .000001$) prolongation of progression-free survival in patients receiving sorafenib compared with placebo (6.0 months versus 3.0 months).** The overall regression rate in patients receiving sorafenib was 2%; however, more than 70% of patients demonstrated a regression in tumor size, albeit not adequate to be scored as a partial or complete response. The study was terminated after this initial analysis in view of the large differences noted, and all patients were crossed over to active drug. Survival data in this trial remain preliminary, but again, these are encouraging results.

These results (see Table 47–28) clearly demonstrate that agents targeting the VEGF pathway can have significant antitumor effects in patients with advanced clear cell carcinoma. The studies that have been completed and those in progress will define the role of these and other targeted agents in patients with RCC. **The preliminary results suggest that targeted molecular therapeutics will have a role in the treatment paradigm for metastatic RCC in the near future.**

## Multimodal Therapy

Combined modality approaches integrating surgery and systemic therapy have been applied successfully in genitourinary oncology, the best example being testicular cancer. In patients with either synchronous or metachronous metastatic RCC, multidisciplinary therapeutic approaches have been applied and are illustrated in Figure 47–35. **For patients presenting with synchronous metastatic disease, nephrectomy is often performed before initiation of systemic therapy, as reviewed before** (Flanigan et al, 2001; Mickisch et al, 2001). Two prospective randomized trials have demonstrated that median

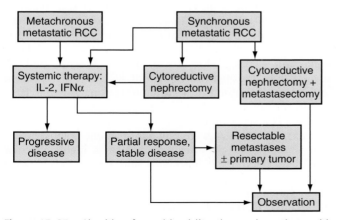

**Figure 47–35.** Algorithm for multimodality therapy in patients with metastatic renal cell carcinoma (RCC).

overall survival can be significantly improved in patients undergoing surgery followed by interferon alfa compared with treatment with interferon alfa alone. Immunosuppression induced by the primary tumor may contribute to this phenomenon. **In patients with advanced RCC, multiple T-cell abnormalities have been described. These include alterations in signal transduction pathways, abnormal activity of DNA-binding proteins, poor proliferative responses** (Bukowski et al, 1998; Uzzo et al, 1999a), **and increase in T-lymphocyte apoptosis** (Uzzo et al, 1999b). In vitro studies in which normal T lymphocytes are incubated with renal cancer supernatants can reproduce some of these deficiencies (Uzzo et al, 2000a). **When the primary tumor is resected, the factors responsible for this acquired immune dysfunction may be eliminated or removed, with subsequent normalization of T-cell function including cytokine production and tumor cell lysis.** An alternative hypothesis to explain the beneficial effects of cytoreductive surgery is that the primary tumor may express proangiogenic factors or other tumor-promoting growth factors, and removal of this source may allow a less aggressive course at other sites.

**Other combined approaches in which surgery and immunotherapy have been used include initial immunotherapy followed by adjuvant nephrectomy in responding individuals, and immunotherapy with or without nephrectomy followed by resection of residual or recurrent metastatic lesions. The optimal timing of adjuvant nephrectomy in the setting of multimodality treatment remains unclear.** Most investigators have advocated nephrectomy before cytokine or adoptive immune therapy, but a potential drawback of this approach is that many patients may undergo surgery without subsequently receiving immunotherapy. Postoperative mortality rates of 0% to 17% have been reported after nephrectomy in patients with metastatic renal cancer (reviewed in Flanigan, 2004). Some patients who undergo nephrectomy are unable to receive cytokine therapy because of rapid tumor progression or postoperative complications. In a series from the National Cancer Institute, 37 of 93 patients (40%) who underwent nephrectomy did not receive subsequent immunotherapy (Walther et al, 1993). In a study from the Cleveland Clinic, 8 of 37 RCC patients (22%) were unable to receive immunotherapy after nephrectomy for one of these reasons (Rackley et al, 1994).

For this problem to be avoided, the alternative of delayed nephrectomy has been proposed. This involves initial systemic treatment with delayed nephrectomy only in patients who demonstrate regression or stability of their metastatic lesions (Fleischmann and Kim, 1991). Rackley and associates (1994) found that patients treated with initial immunotherapy had slightly higher objective response rates and longer median survival times compared with patients undergoing primary nephrectomy and subsequent immunotherapy. Similarly, Tanguay and associates (1996b) compared initial and adjuvant surgery in patients with pulmonary metastases and observed higher survival rates in patients who received initial immunotherapy. A less common situation in which this approach has been applied involves the patient with metastatic renal cancer and a solitary, functioning kidney. In this setting, immunotherapy is administered first; and in patients whose metastatic lesions regress, a partial nephrectomy can be performed (Krishnamurthi et al, 1996).

The presence of a large primary tumor may decrease the effects of therapy, and response to systemic therapy is uncommon in this setting. Thus, the optimal timing of nephrectomy is still controversial in many patients. Delayed nephrectomy allows selection of patients who have biologically more responsive tumors, theoretically reserving the more aggressive pathway for this subgroup that may be more likely to benefit. A prospective, controlled comparison of appropriate systemic therapy combined with initial or delayed nephrectomy is needed to clarify the optimal timing of nephrectomy.

An aggressive surgical approach to RCC often offers the best chance for a long-term cure. In an effort to consolidate therapy, metastasectomy either before or after administration of systemic therapy should be considered in select patients with solitary or limited metastases. The prognostic factors associated with prolonged survival after resection of metastatic RCC lesions have been investigated and should be carefully evaluated during clinical decision-making—an individualized approach to each patient is of paramount importance.

Several reports provide useful information about selection of patients in this challenging population. Friedel and colleagues (1999) reviewed 77 patients who underwent resection of pulmonary metastases from RCC and reported a long disease-free interval (>48 months) with resected solitary metastases. In this study, solitary versus multiple metastases were also associated with prolonged survival. Piltz and associates (2002) reviewed 105 patients who underwent resection of pulmonary metastases. The median survival of the entire group was 43 months; 40% of these patients were alive at 5 years. In this study, a multivariate analysis identified complete surgical resection, metastases less than 4.0 cm in diameter, and tumor-free regional lymph nodes as independent prognostic factors. These studies involved patients with pulmonary metastases who had not received preoperative cytokine therapy. The literature suggests that pulmonary metastases may have a more favorable prognosis than metastases at other sites, both for response to systemic therapy and for surgical consolidation. This should also be taken into account during the decision-making process.

In addition to this approach, so-called salvage metastasectomy can be employed in patients with residual or recurrent metastatic RCC after an incomplete response to therapy. Kim and Louie (1992) described 11 patients with a partial response to IL-2–based therapy after a cytoreductive nephrectomy who then underwent surgical excision of residual metastases. At median follow-up of 21 months, all patients were alive and disease free, an encouraging finding for this disease. Similarly, Sella and colleagues (1993) described 17 patients who underwent excision of residual metastatic lesions after a partial response to interferon-based therapy. Eleven patients were alive and disease free at a median follow-up of 12 months. In a report from the Cleveland Clinic (Krishnamurthi et al, 1998), 14 patients underwent initial immunotherapy followed by surgical resection of the primary tumor and metastatic lesions. After immunotherapy, nine patients manifested an objective response; five patients had stable disease. All patients were then rendered disease free by surgery. Cancer-specific survival at 3 years was 81.5%.

Finally, Kavolius and associates (1998) reviewed a group of 278 patients who underwent "curative" metastasectomy. The 5-year overall survival was 44% compared with 14% for 67 patients who had noncurative surgery. A multivariate analysis indicated that a solitary metastatic site, curative surgical resection, prolonged disease-free interval (>12 months), and metachronous metastatic disease were associated with prolonged survival. These results are echoed by a study from the Cleveland Clinic (Murthy et al, 2005) that reviewed 417 patients with pulmonary metastases. Ninety-two individuals underwent metastasectomy, and 20 (22%) of these had received preoperative immunotherapy. Multivariate analysis identified incomplete resection as the strongest predictor of decreased survival (8% versus 45% 5-year survival for patients with complete resection). Of interest, preoperative cytokine therapy was not a factor associated with improved survival.

Taken together, these reports suggest that salvage surgery for removal of residual metastatic lesions may extend survival for some patients with metastatic RCC. Selection of patients clearly plays a role, and randomized clinical trials are required to validate this approach and to clarify the optimal timing of surgery relative to systemic therapy. In view of the low response rates associated with cytokine therapy, it seems unlikely this will occur. Finally, the multimodality approaches discussed have been applied primarily to patients with clear cell tumors; their application to patients with non–clear cell tumors is unknown.

## OTHER MALIGNANT RENAL TUMORS
### Sarcomas of the Kidney

Sarcomas represent 1% to 2% of all malignant renal tumors in adults, with a peak incidence in the fifth decade of life (Srinivas et al, 1984; Russo, 1991; Spellman et al, 1995; Frank et al, 2000). Renal sarcoma is less common but more lethal than sarcoma of any other genitourinary site, including the prostate, bladder, and paratesticular region (Russo, 1991; Russo et al, 1992). Differentiation of renal sarcoma from sarcomatoid RCC is often difficult on the basis of clinical presentation, radiographic findings, and, in some cases, pathologic analysis. Identification of any features of the various subtypes of RCC excludes the diagnosis of primary renal sarcoma. The common signs and symptoms associated with renal sarcoma in adults include palpable mass, abdominal or flank pain, and hematuria, similar to those seen with large, rapidly growing RCCs (Economou et al, 1987). Abdominal CT scan typically demonstrates a large soft tissue mass involving or derived from the kidney, a finding that is again similar to that associated with many sarcomatoid RCCs (Farrow et al, 1968; Shirkhoda and Lewis, 1987; Russo, 1991). Specific findings suggestive of sarcoma rather than of RCC include apparent origin from the capsule or perisinuous region, growth to large size in the absence of lymphadenopathy, presence of fat or bone suggestive of liposarcoma or osteosarcoma, and hypovascular pattern on angiography, although one notable exception is the hemangiopericytoma, which is highly vascular (Smullens et al, 1982; Shirkhoda and Lewis, 1987). Renal sarcoma should be suspected in any of these circumstances or in any patient with a very large or rapidly growing renal mass.

Sarcomas of the kidney, like sarcomas of any other site, share in common a distinct tumor biology that has important implications with respect to management (reviewed in

Russo, 1991). **These tumors are derived from mesenchymal components and are thus free of many of the natural barriers to dissemination that confine other tumor types. They are typically surrounded by a pseudocapsule that is readily identifiable but that cannot be relied on for surgical dissection because it is often infiltrated with cancer cells,** which can extend for some distance into the surrounding tissues. In many cases, this cannot be recognized macroscopically, although it is often manifested in the form of local recurrences, which are common after surgical extirpation, even when a wide excision has been performed. **High-grade sarcomas often metastasize, with the lungs being a primary site of spread, and prognosis is poor; many patients die of disease progression in a matter of months. Low-grade sarcomas tend to pursue a more indolent course,** although local recurrences often require repeated resection to prolong survival and minimize morbidity.

In general, the most important prognostic factors for sarcomas are margin status and tumor grade. The initial resection is the key event because, for many patients, this is their best chance for a long-term cure. For renal sarcomas, this often mandates radical nephrectomy along with en bloc excision of adjacent organs (Srinivas et al, 1984). MRI can be useful for preoperative planning by defining tissue planes and proximity to vital structures. This is primarily a surgical disease, and wide excision is the goal with intraoperative monitoring of margin status. Chemotherapeutic agents that have demonstrated activity against metastatic sarcomas include doxycycline and ifosfamide, but even in the best of circumstances, response rates are disappointing (Antman et al, 1993). A renal primary sarcoma is far from the best of circumstances, given the poor prognosis associated with this site of origin. The combination of radiation therapy and chemotherapy, which has proved effective in an adjuvant setting for the management of sarcomas of the extremity, has not provided much benefit for renal or retroperitoneal sarcomas (Russo, 1991). At present, the role of such adjuvant approaches for the management of renal sarcomas is not well defined, although a multimodal approach is often pursued if performance status allows, given the poor prognosis.

The largest single-institution series of renal sarcomas include only 15 to 26 cases and represent a composite experience extending for a period of several years (Farrow et al, 1968; Srinivas et al, 1984; Shirkhoda and Lewis, 1987). In all such series, leiomyosarcoma has been the most common histologic subtype, and in many series, liposarcoma has been the second most common. In contrast, for retroperitoneal sarcomas, the order is reversed, with liposarcoma being the most common histologic subtype (Karakousis et al, 1995). All such series report a poor prognosis; the experience of Srinivas and colleagues (1984) at Memorial Sloan-Kettering Cancer Center is representative. In this series of 16 patients with renal sarcomas, 15 underwent nephrectomy, often with en bloc excision of adjacent organs; 5 received adjuvant radiation therapy and chemotherapy without apparent benefit; and 13 died within 6 months after surgery. Vogelzang and associates (1993) reported a more encouraging experience with 21 patients with primary renal sarcomas; they had 6 long-term survivors after surgery alone. A predominance of low-grade disease may account for these favorable outcomes. However, even in this series, the majority of patients died of progressive disease within a few to several months after diagnosis. Saitoh and colleagues (1982) defined the common sites of metastases of renal sarcomas: lung first and foremost, but also lymph nodes and liver.

**Leiomyosarcoma is the most common histologic subtype of renal sarcoma, accounting for 50% to 60% of such tumors** (Fig. 47–36). The cell of origin is the smooth muscle cell of the capsule or other perinephric structures (Moudouni et al, 2001; Deyrup et al, 2004). Niceta and associates (1974) identified 66 cases of renal leiomyosarcoma in the literature and reported a female predominance; most patients presented in the fourth through sixth decades of life. Renal leiomyosarcoma, like many renal sarcomas, tends to displace rather than to invade the parenchyma, and it is characterized by rapid growth rate, frequent metastasis, and high local and systemic recurrence rates (Pollack et al, 1987; Deyrup et al, 2004). In the cases reviewed by Niceta, most patients were treated primarily with radical nephrectomy and died within 2 years. In the Mayo Clinic series, 14 of 15 patients with renal leiomyosarcoma died of disease progression within 4 months to 5.5 years after surgery (Farrow et al, 1968).

Other than leiomyosarcoma, a wide variety of histologic subtypes have been described because almost every con-

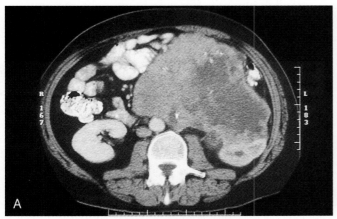 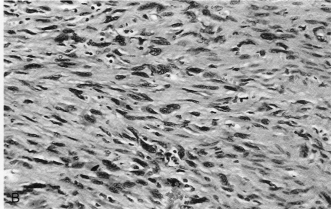

**Figure 47–36.** **A,** CT scan demonstrates a large leiomyosarcoma of the left kidney. **B,** Microscopic features of leiomyosarcoma include spindle cells, blunt-ended nuclei, and eosinophilic cytoplasm. (Courtesy of Dr. Michael McGuire, Evanston, Illinois.)

ceivable type of sarcoma has been found in the kidney. Liposarcoma is readily distinguished from RCC because of the presence of adipose tissue, but it is often confused with AMLs or with large, benign renal lipomas (Frank et al, 2000). Renal liposarcoma typically develops in the fifth and sixth decades of life and often grows to extremely large size (Economou et al, 1987). Response to radiation therapy and cisplatin-based chemotherapy in an adjuvant setting has been reported by Belldegrun and deKernion (1987) and should be considered in patients with high-grade disease or positive margins. Osteogenic sarcoma is a rare but distinctive form of renal sarcoma that contains calcium and is often rock hard (Micolonghi et al, 1984; Leventis et al, 1997). Extensive calcification in a large, hypovascular tumor should suggest the diagnosis. The appearance on plain films can mimic a staghorn calculus, but the readily evident mass effect should suggest xanthogranulomatous disease or, more rarely, osteogenic sarcoma. Again, prognosis is poor; most patients die of disease progression within a few years after diagnosis. Less common histologic subtypes include rhabdomyosarcoma, fibrosarcoma, carcinosarcoma, malignant fibrous histiocytoma, synovial sarcoma, angiosarcoma, and malignant hemangiopericytoma (Raghavaiah et al, 1979; Weiss et al, 1984; Mordkin et al, 1997; Tsuda et al, 1997; Cerilli et al, 1998; Merchant et al, 1998; Chhieng et al, 1999; Koyama et al, 2001; Bella et al, 2002; Chen et al, 2003). Malignant hemangiopericytomas are notable for their extensive vascularity. Preoperative catheter embolization has been described and can simplify surgical excision (Smullens et al, 1982).

## Renal Lymphoma and Leukemia

**Renal involvement with hematologic malignant neoplasms, which include the various lymphomas and leukemias, is common—found at autopsy in approximately 34% of patients dying of progressive lymphoma or leukemia. However, these processes are uncommonly seen in clinical practice** because they are often silent and generally occur only as a late manifestation of systemic disease (Richmond et al, 1962; Pollack et al, 1987; McVary, 1991). The role of the urologist in the evaluation of renal lymphoma or leukemia is critically important and can include differentiation from other renal malignant neoplasms, timely provision of a pathologic diagnosis, and preservation of renal parenchyma and function (reviewed in McVary, 1991). Renal involvement is more common with non-Hodgkin's lymphoma than with Hodgkin's disease, and as with most other forms of extranodal non-Hodgkin's lymphoma, histologically diffuse forms predominate over nodular forms (Richmond et al, 1962; Pollack et al, 1987; Yasunaga et al, 1997; O'Riordan et al, 2001). Primary renal lymphoma is rare, with only a few well-documented case reports in the literature (Kandel et al, 1987; Pollack et al, 1987; Arranz-Arija et al, 1994; Dimopoulos et al, 1996; Yasunaga et al, 1997; Tuzel et al, 2003). This is not surprising given the relative paucity of lymphoid tissue in the normal renal parenchyma. Hematogenous dissemination of lymphoma to the kidney is most common and is thought to occur in 90% of cases; direct extension from retroperitoneal lymph nodes accounts for the remainder. Hartman and colleagues (1982) have correlated pathologic and radiographic patterns and have shown that the most common pattern of

renal involvement consists of multiple small renal nodules that tend to develop between the individual nephrons. Eventually, these nodules become confluent, forming radiographically detectable masses. At the extreme, they can replace the entire parenchyma of the kidney, leading to renal failure.

**The CT scan is the radiographic modality of choice for the diagnosis of renal lymphoma and for monitoring response to therapy** (Jafri et al, 1982; Pollack et al, 1987; Sheeran and Sussman, 1998; Urban and Fishman, 2000). The common radiographic patterns associated with renal lymphoma have been defined by Heiken and associates (1991) and confirmed by a number of other investigators (Table 47–29). Renal lymphoma can present as multiple distinct renal masses; as a solitary renal mass, which can be difficult to differentiate from RCC; as diffuse renal infiltration; or as direct invasion of the kidney from enlarged retroperitoneal nodes (Cohan et al, 1990; Heiken et al, 1991; Eisenberg et al, 1994; Sheeran and Sussman, 1998). A hypovascular pattern on angiography is typical for renal lymphoma (Pollack et al, 1987). **Renal lymphoma should be suspected in patients with massive retroperitoneal lymphadenopathy, splenomegaly, or lymphadenopathy in other regions of the body or atypical regions within the retroperitoneum** (Jafri et al, 1982; Dimopoulos et al, 1996). Along these lines, the main landing zones for RCC should be kept in mind—the interaortocaval region for right RCC and para-aortic region for left RCC—and lymphadenopathy centered outside of these areas should raise suspicion for lymphoma. Any patient with a prior history of lymphoma and a renal mass should also be evaluated for renal recurrence rather than for RCC. In general, lymphomas are more common in patients with iatrogenic immune suppression, acquired immunodeficiency syndrome (AIDS), autoimmune diseases, or graft-versus-host disease and in patients with a history of radiation therapy (McVary, 1991). These clinical associations may also increase the index of suspicion about a diagnosis of systemic lymphoma.

Renal involvement related to leukemia is more common in children, paralleling the demographics of the disease, and is more commonly due to lymphocytic leukemia than the myelogenous forms (Araki, 1982; Pollack et al, 1987). Leukemia typically involves the kidney in a diffusely infiltrative pattern and most often represents a late manifestation of systemic disease. However, as for renal lymphoma, a variety of other radiographic patterns have been observed, as reviewed by Pollack and colleagues (1987).

**Table 47–29. Radiographic Findings Associated with Lymphoma**

| Computed Tomography | Incidence (%) |
| --- | --- |
| Multiple renal masses | 45 |
| Solitary renal mass | 15 |
| Renal invasion from enlarged retroperitoneal lymph nodes | 25 |
| Diffuse renal involvement | 10 |
| Predominantly perinephric involvement | 5 |

Data from Pollack HM, Banner MP, Amendola MA: Other malignant neoplasms of the renal parenchyma. Semin Roentgenol 1987;22:260-274; and Heiken JP, Gold RP, Schnur MJ: Computed tomography of renal lymphoma with ultrasound correlation. J Comput Assist Tomogr 1991;1:245-250.

If lymphoma or leukemic renal involvement is suspected, consideration should be given to percutaneous biopsy to obtain a pathologic diagnosis, and if exploratory surgery is necessary, intraoperative biopsy and frozen-section analysis should take priority. If lymphoma or leukemia is confirmed, the kidney should be spared, and complete staging of the neoplasm should be performed to preclude the need for a secondary procedure (McVary, 1991). Truong and colleagues (2001) have demonstrated the utility of fine-needle aspiration in the diagnosis of renal lymphoma, although additional tissue may be required in many cases to classify the lymphoma accurately and to guide further therapy. Extirpative surgery should be avoided if renal lymphoma and leukemia are suspected because the treatment of these processes is generally systemic chemotherapy with or without radiation therapy. The classic chemotherapy regimen for non-Hodgkin's lymphoma is the CHOP protocol, which includes cyclophosphamide, doxorubicin, vincristine, and prednisolone (Colevas et al, 2000). Nephrectomy is seldom indicated except in patients with severe symptoms, such as uncontrollable hemorrhage. The other notable exception is the extremely rare patient with primary renal lymphoma in whom a combination of nephrectomy and systemic chemotherapy may represent optimal therapy (Okuno et al, 1995).

Both renal lymphoma and leukemia are commonly silent but can be associated with hematuria, flank pain, or progressive renal failure. Fever, weight loss, and fatigue, the so-called B symptoms of lymphoma, are much more common (Yasunaga et al, 1997). Renal failure can be due to extensive replacement of the functioning parenchyma or bilateral ureteral obstruction associated with enlarged retroperitoneal lymph nodes (more common with lymphoma) (reviewed in McVary, 1991). In reality, renal failure in such patients is more often related to medical causes, such as hypercalcemia or urate nephropathy, that can develop during systemic treatment of advanced disease. The diagnosis of renal failure related to parenchymal replacement by lymphoma or leukemia requires exclusion of other related causes of renal failure and demonstration of improvement in renal function after administration of systemic chemotherapy or radiation therapy (Choi et al, 1997; O'Riordan et al, 2001).

## Metastatic Tumors

Metastatic tumors are the most common malignant neoplasms in the kidney, outnumbering primary renal tumors by a wide margin. Autopsy studies have shown that 12% of patients dying of cancer have renal metastases, making the kidney one of the most common sites for metastatic dissemination (Pollack et al, 1987). The high blood flow and profuse vascularity of the kidney make it a fertile soil for the deposition and growth of cancer cells. Almost all renal metastases develop through a hematogenous route of spread; only a small minority are caused by direct invasion of tumors derived from adjacent organs such as the pancreas, colon, and adrenal gland. The most common sources of renal metastases include lung, breast, and gastrointestinal cancers; malignant melanoma; and the hematologic malignant neoplasms, which are reviewed in the preceding section (Klinger, 1951; Choyke et al, 1987; Pollack et al, 1987; Sanchez-Ortiz et al, 2004b). Of the solid malignant neoplasms, lung cancer is most commonly

associated with renal metastases. Olsson and colleagues (1971) found that 20% of patients dying of lung cancer had renal metastases, 60% of which were bilateral. Klinger (1951) reviewed 5000 autopsies and found 17 cases of renal metastases from lung cancer, 11 from gastric cancer, 9 from breast cancer, 7 from pancreatic cancer, 4 from esophageal cancer, 6 from other gastrointestinal primary cancers, and 1 from malignant melanoma. In a series of 27 renal metastases reviewed by Choyke and associates (1987), 7 patients had primary lung cancer, 7 had gastrointestinal malignant neoplasms, 4 had malignant melanoma, 2 had breast cancer, and 2 had endometrial carcinoma. Most renal metastases are multifocal, and almost all are associated with widespread nonrenal metastases (Choyke et al, 1987; Pollack et al, 1987). Choyke and associates (1987) reported that renal metastases from lung, breast, and colon carcinomas are notable because they are occasionally large and solitary, making them difficult to differentiate from RCC.

The typical pattern of renal metastases consists of multiple small nodules that are often clinically silent, although they can lead to hematuria or flank pain in exceptional circumstances (Walther et al, 1979; Pollack et al, 1987). CT scan is the primary diagnostic modality for renal metastases and typically demonstrates isodense masses that enhance only moderately (5 to 30 HU) after administration of intravenous contrast material (Pollack et al, 1987; Ferrozzi et al, 1997). Arteriography usually shows a hypovascular pattern (Pollack et al, 1987).

Renal metastases should be suspected in any patient with multiple renal lesions and widespread systemic metastases or a history of nonrenal primary cancer. If there is any uncertainty about the diagnosis, a CT- or ultrasound-guided percutaneous renal biopsy usually provides pathologic confirmation (Sanchez-Ortiz, 2004a). Most patients with renal metastases are managed with systemic therapy or placed on a palliative care pathway, depending on the clinical circumstances. Nephrectomy is almost never required except in extenuating circumstances, such as uncontrollable renal hemorrhage. Patients with a solitary, strongly enhancing renal lesion and a history of organ-confined, nonrenal malignant disease are more likely to have RCC, particularly if the interval between the two diagnoses is substantial. However, even in this circumstance, a renal biopsy should be considered because it may preclude the need for surgical intervention.

## Other Malignant Tumors of the Kidney

Other malignant tumors of the kidney include renal carcinoid, adult Wilms' tumor, primitive neuroectodermal tumor (PNET), and small cell carcinoma. All are relatively uncommon, but each has a distinct tumor biology.

Carcinoid tumors arise from neuroendocrine cells, which are not normally present in the kidney, and this is a rare renal malignant neoplasm with fewer than 40 cases reported in the English literature (Kawajiri et al, 2004). Primitive stem cells within the kidney or retained neural crest tissue may give rise to these tumors (Krishnan et al, 1997; Begin et al, 1998). A correlation with horseshoe kidneys has been reported, with previous studies showing an increased relative risk of 82-fold compared with normal kidneys (Begin et al, 1998). Carcinoid tumors stain positive for markers of neuroendocrine tissue such as neuron-specific enolase and chromogranin (Kulke and Mayer, 1999). **Measurement of urinary or plasma serotonin or its metabolites can be diagnostic** (Kulke and Mayer, 1999). **Most patients are asymptomatic; a minority will present with the carcinoid syndrome—episodic flushing, wheezing, and diarrhea** (Jensen and Doherty, 2001). CT findings are nonspecific, and most renal carcinoids are small and nonaggressive. Surgical excision is the mainstay of treatment (Kawajiri et al, 2004). Nephron-sparing surgery is preferred if the diagnosis is suspected preoperatively. Prognosis is good, particularly when it is associated with a horseshoe kidney (Krishnan et al, 1997; Begin et al, 1998). Patients with renal carcinoid should be considered for evaluation with colonoscopy and esophagogastroscopy to assess for multifocal disease.

Wilms' tumor is the most common abdominal malignant neoplasm in children, but 3% of Wilms' tumors are seen in adults. Of these, 20% are found between the ages of 15 and 20 years, and the remaining 80% are distributed between the third and seventh decades of life (Winter et al, 1996). Adult and pediatric Wilms' tumors are histologically similar with a distinctive triphasic pattern consisting of varying amounts of blastema, epithelium, and stroma (Orditura et al, 1997). **Pathologic staging is the same as for pediatric Wilms' tumor, and most authors recommend treating adult patients with the same therapeutic protocols that have been tested and proven in children** (Firoozi and Kogan, 2003). Adult Wilms' tumor typically presents as a heterogeneous intrarenal mass on CT with a relatively hypovascular pattern, but differentiation from RCC can be difficult if not impossible in many cases (Winter et al, 1996; Orditura et al, 1997; Reinhard et al, 2004). Clinical presentation of adult Wilms' tumor is also similar to that of RCC, and this tends to be an unsuspected pathologic diagnosis in most cases. Multimodal therapy should be considered as in the treatment protocols for pediatric Wilms' tumor (Bozeman et al, 1995; Green, 1997; Neville and Ritchey, 2000; Terenziani et al, 2004). Prognosis is worse for adults with Wilms' tumor than for children with this malignant neoplasm because adults are more likely to present with advanced disease and a sudden drop in performance status (Winter et al, 1996; Akmansu et al, 1998).

PNET is related to the Ewing's sarcoma family of tumors that are more common in the pediatric population, typically manifesting in the bone or soft tissues of the extremities, trunk, and head and neck and only rarely in the viscera or kidneys (Jimenez et al, 2002; Maly et al, 2004). However, any age may be affected, and several cases of PNET have been reported in the kidneys of adults (Rodriquez-Galindo et al, 1997; Karnes et al, 2000; Doerfler et al, 2001; Parham et al, 2001; Thomas et al, 2002; Pomara et al, 2004). These tumors are derived from primitive neural crest cells, and positive staining for CD99 in addition to vimentin, cytokeratin, and neuron-specific enolase strongly supports the diagnosis (Gonlusen et al, 2001; Parham et al, 2001; Ginsberg et al, 2002; Maly et al, 2004). On microscopic examination, renal PNET typically shows small round cells that may form characteristic Homer Wright rosettes (Marley et al, 1997; Pomara et al, 2004). A characteristic t(11;22)(q24;q12) translocation is highly specific for PNET and can help differentiate it from neuroblastoma or adult Wilms' tumor (Marley et al, 1997; Quezado et al, 1997; Parham et al, 2001; Jimenez et al, 2002).

Clinical symptoms are nonspecific, and CT often demonstrates a heterogeneous ill-defined mass with areas of necrosis (Doerfler et al, 2001). Again, minimal enhancement with contrast medium is typical, but differentiation from RCC is often difficult. Renal PNET appears to behave more aggressively than similar tumors at other sites and may represent a distinct clinical entity (Rodriquez-Galindo et al, 1997; Parham et al, 2001; Jimenez et al, 2002; Pomara et al, 2004). A strong propensity for local recurrence and early metastasis to lymph nodes, lung, liver, and bone has been described (Quezado et al, 1997; Rodriquez-Galindo, 1997; Gonlusen et al, 2001). **Multimodal treatment protocols combining tumor debulking, chemotherapy, and radiotherapy are often employed, but prognosis is poor with overall 5-year disease-free survival of 45% to 55%** (Casella et al, 2001).

**Approximately 30 cases of small cell carcinoma of the kidney have been reported for which another primary site could not be identified** (Mackey et al, 1998; Gonzalez-Lois et al, 2001; Akkaya et al, 2003; Majhail et al, 2003). **On pathologic examination, small cell carcinoma has features of neuroendocrine and epithelial neoplasms and must be differentiated from Wilms' tumor, PNET, lymphoma, and metastasis from pulmonary small cell carcinoma** (Gonzalez-Lois et al, 2001; Akkaya et al, 2003). **Positive staining for neuron-specific enolase, chromogranin, and synaptophysin is characteristic** (Akkaya et al, 2003). Preoperative differentiation from RCC is difficult, although a relatively hypovascular pattern may be an indication. Many small cell carcinomas of the kidney are locally advanced or metastatic at presentation, and flank pain or hematuria is common (Majhail et al, 2003). Multimodal therapy with nephrectomy or tumor debulking combined with platinum-based chemotherapy regimens is advocated for extrapulmonary small cell carcinoma in general and may also be useful for the renal manifestation of this malignant neoplasm (Majhail et al, 2003). Long-term survivors are described, but rare and new treatment regimens are needed.

## SUGGESTED READINGS

Argani P, Antonescu CR, Couturier J, et al: PRCC-TFE3 renal carcinomas. Morphologic, immunohistochemical, ultrastructural, and molecular analysis of an entity associated with the t(X;1)(p11.2;q21). Am J Surg Pathol 2002;26:1553-1566.

Atkins MB, Hidalgo M, Stadler WM, et al: Randomized phase II study of multiple dose levels of CCI-779, a novel mammalian target of rapamycin kinase inhibitor, in patients with advanced refractory renal cell carcinoma. J Clin Oncol 2004;22:909-918.

Bell ET: Renal Disease. Philadelphia, Lea & Febiger, 1950.

Blute ML, Leibovich BC, Lohse CM, et al: The Mayo Clinic experience with surgical management complications and outcome for patients with renal cell carcinoma and venous tumour thrombus. BJU Int 2004;94:33-41.

Bosniak MA: The use of the Bosniak classification system for renal cysts and cystic tumors. J Urol 1997;157:1852.

Bukowski RM: Natural history and therapy of metastatic renal cell carcinoma: The role of interleukin-2. Cancer 1997;80:1198-1220.

Cangiano T, Liao J, Naitoh J, et al: Sarcomatoid renal cell carcinoma: Biologic behavior, prognosis and response to combined surgical resection and immunotherapy. J Clin Oncol 1999;17:523-528.

Childs R, Chernoff A, Cotentin N, et al: Regression of metastatic renal-cell carcinoma after nonmyeloablative allogeneic peripheral-blood stem-cell transplantation. N Engl J Med 2000;343:750-758.

Chow WH, Devesa SS, Warren JL, Fraumeni JF Jr: Rising incidence of renal cell cancer in the United States. JAMA 1999;281:1628-1631.

Choyke PL, White EM, Zeman RK, et al: Renal metastases: Clinicopathologic and radiologic correlation. Radiology 1987;162:359-363.

Cohn EB, Campbell SC: Screening for renal cell carcinoma. In Bukowski RM, Novick AC (eds): Renal cell carcinoma: Molecular biology, immunology, and clinical management. Totowa, NJ, Humana Press, 2000.

Coppin C, Porzsolt F, Awa A, et al: Immunotherapy for advanced renal cell cancer. Cochrane Database Syst Rev 2005;CD001425.

Crotty TB, Farrow GM, Lieber MM: Chromophobe cell renal carcinoma: Clinicopathological features of 50 cases. J Urol 1995;154:964-967.

Davis CJ, Barton JH, Sesterhenn IA, Mostofi FK: Metanephric adenoma: Clinicopathological study of fifty patients. Am J Surg Pathol 1995;19:1101-1114.

Davis CJ, Mostofi FK, Sesterhenn IA: Renal medullary carcinoma: The seventh sickle cell nephropathy. Am J Surg Pathol 1995;19:1-11.

Eggener S, Reiher FK, Campbell SC: Surveillance for renal cell carcinoma after surgical management. Am Urol 2001;20:202-207.

Esrig D, Ahlering TE, Lieskovsky G, et al: Experience with fossa recurrence of renal cell carcinoma. J Urol 1992;147:1491-1494.

Fergany AF, Hafez KS, Novick AC: Long-term results of nephron sparing surgery for localized renal cell carcinoma: 10-year follow-up. J Urol 2000;163:442.

Flanigan RC, Salmon SE, Blumenstein BA, et al: Nephrectomy followed by interferon alfa-2b compared with interferon alfa-2b alone for metastatic renal cell cancer. N Engl J Med 2001;345:1655-1659.

Flanigan RC, Mickisch G, Sylvester R, et al: Cytoreductive nephrectomy in patients with metastatic renal cancer: A combined analysis. J Urol 2004;171:1071-1076.

Frank I, Blute ML, Cheville JC, et al: An outcome prediction model for patients with clear cell renal cell carcinoma treated with radical nephrectomy based on tumor stage, size, grade and necrosis: The SSIGN score. J Urol 2002;168:2395-2400.

Furge KA, Lucas KA, Takahashi M, et al: Robust classification of renal cell carcinoma based on gene expression data and predicted cytogenetic profiles. Cancer Res 2004;64:4117-4121.

Gill IS, Schweizer D, Hobart MG, et al: Retroperitoneal laparoscopic radical nephrectomy: The Cleveland Clinic experience. J Urol 2000;163:1665-1670.

Gill IS, Matin SF, Desai MM, et al: Comparative analysis of laparoscopic versus open partial nephrectomy for renal tumors in 200 patients. J Urol 2003;170:64-68.

Gold PJ, Fefer A, Thompson JA: Paraneoplastic manifestations of renal cell carcinoma. Semin Urol Oncol 1996;14:216-222.

Guinan PD, Vogelzang NJ, Fremgen AM, et al: Renal cell carcinoma: Tumor size, stage and survival. J Urol 1995;153:901-903.

Hafez KS, Novick AC, Campbell SC: Patterns of tumor recurrence and guidelines for follow-up after nephron sparing surgery for sporadic renal cell carcinoma. J Urol 1997;157:2067.

Hafez KS, Novick AC, Butler BP: Management of small solitary unilateral renal cell carcinomas: Impact of central versus peripheral tumor location. J Urol 1998;159:1156.

Hafez KS, Fergany AF, Novick AC: Nephron sparing surgery for localized renal call carcinoma: Impact of tumor size on patient survival, tumor recurrence and TNM staging. J Urol 1999;162:1930.

Herr HW: Partial nephrectomy for unilateral renal carcinoma and a normal contralateral kidney: 10-year follow-up. J Urol 1999;161:33-35.

Herts BR, Baker ME: The current role of percutaneous biopsy in the evaluation of renal masses. Semin Urol Oncol 1995;13:254-261.

Herts BR, Remer EM: The role of percutaneous biopsy in the evaluation of renal and adrenal mass. AUA Update Series 2000;19:282-287.

Jocham D, Richter A, Hoffmann L, et al: Adjuvant autologous renal tumor cell vaccine and risk of tumour progression in patients with renal-cell carcinoma after radical nephrectomy: Phase III randomized controlled trial. Lancet 2004;363:594-599.

Kausik S, Segura J, King BF: Classification and management of simple and complex renal cysts. AUA Update Series 2002;21:82-87.

Lam JS, Shvarts O, Pantuck AJ: Changing concepts in the surgical management of renal call carcinoma. Eur Urol 2004;45:692-705.

Latif F, Tory K, Gnarra J, et al: Identification of the von Hippel–Lindau disease tumor suppressor gene. Science 1993;260:1317-1320.

Leibovich BC, Pantuck AJ, Bui MHT, et al: Current staging of renal cell carcinoma. Urol Clin North Am 2003;30:481-497.

Lendvay TS, Marshall FF: The tuberous sclerosis complex and its highly variable manifestations. J Urol 2003;169:1635-1642.

Licht MR, Novick AC, Goormastic M: Nephron sparing surgery in incidental versus suspected renal cell carcinoma. J Urol 1994;152:39-42.

Linehan WM, Walther MM, Zbar B: The genetic basis of cancer of the kidney. J Urol 2003;170:2163-2172.

Mabjeesh NJ, Avidor Y, Haim M: Emerging nephron sparing treatments for kidney tumors: A continuum of modalities from energy ablation to laparoscopic partial nephrectomy. J Urol 2004;171:553-560.

McKiernan JM, Simmons R, Katz J, et al: Natural history of chronic renal insufficiency after partial and radical nephrectomy. Urology 2002;59:816-820.

Messing EM, Manola J, Wilding G, et al: Phase III study of interferon alfa-NL as adjuvant treatment for resectable renal cell carcinoma: An Eastern Cooperative Oncology/Intergroup trial. J Clin Oncol 2003;21:1214-1222.

Minor LD, Picken MM, Campbell SC, et al: Benign renal tumors. AUA Update 2003;22:170-175.

Motzer RJ, Mazumdar M, Bacik J, et al: Survival and prognostic stratification of 670 patients with advanced renal cell carcinoma. J Clin Oncol 1999;17:2530-2540.

Motzer RJ, Bacik J, Murphy BA, et al: Interferon-alfa as a comparative treatment for clinical trials of new therapies against advanced renal cell carcinoma. J Clin Oncol 2001;20:289-296.

Motzer RJ, Bacik J, Mariani T, et al: Treatment outcome and survival associated with metastatic renal cell carcinoma of non–clear-cell histology. J Clin Oncol 2002;20:2376-2381.

Nelson CP, Sanda MG: Contemporary diagnosis and management of renal angiomyolipoma. J Urol 2002;168:1315-1325.

Neumann HP, Zbar B: Renal cysts, renal cancer, and von Hippel–Lindau disease. Kidney Int 1997;51:16-26.

Patard JJ, Kim HL, Lam JS, et al: Use of the University of California Los Angeles integrated staging system to predict survival in renal call carcinoma: An international multicenter study. J Clin Oncol 2004;22:3316-3322.

Pavlovich CP, McClellan MW, Eyler RA, et al: Renal tumors in the Birt-Hogg-Dubé syndrome. Am J Surg Pathol 2002;26:1542-1552.

Phillips CK, Taneja SS: The role of lymphadenectomy in the surgical management of renal cell carcinoma. Urol Oncol 2004;22:214-224.

Robson CJ, Churchill BM, Anderson W: The results of radical nephrectomy for renal cell carcinoma. J Urol 1969;101:297.

Schatz SM, Lieber MM: Update on oncocytoma. Curr Urol Rep 2003;4:30-35.

Schmidt L, Duh FM, Kishida T, et al: Germline and somatic mutations in the tyrosine kinase domain of the MET proto-oncogene in papillary renal carcinomas. Nat Genet 1997;16:68-73.

Schmidt LS, Nickerson ML, Angeloni D, et al: Early onset hereditary papillary renal carcinoma: Germline missense mutations in the tyrosine kinase domain of the met proto-oncogene. J Urol 2004;172:1256-1261.

Sorbellini M, Kattan MW, Snyder ME, et al: A postoperative prognostic nomogram predicting recurrence for patients with conventional clear cell renal cell carcinoma. J Urol 2005;173:48-51.

Srigley JR, Eble JN: Collecting duct carcinoma of kidney. Semin Diagn Pathol 1998;5:54-67.

Steinberg AP, Finelli A, Desai MM, et al: Laparoscopic radical nephrectomy for large (greater than 7 cm, T2) renal tumors. J Urol 2004;172:2172-2176.

Toro JR, Nickerson ML, Wei MH, et al: Mutations in the fumarate hydratase gene cause hereditary leiomyomatosis and renal cell cancer in families in North America. Am J Hum Genet 2003;73:95-106.

Tsui KH, Shvarts O, Barbaric Z, et al: Is adrenalectomy a necessary component of radical nephrectomy? UCLA experience with 511 radical nephrectomies. J Urol 2000;163:437-441.

Uzzo RG, Coll D, Novick AC: The role of three dimensional computed tomography in renal imaging. Am Urol Assoc 2000;(updated series)19:298-303.

Yagoda A, Abi-Rached B, Petrylak D: Chemotherapy for advanced renal cell carcinoma: 1983-1993. Semin Oncol 1995;22:42-60.

Yang JC, Haworth L, Sherry RM, et al: A randomized trial of bevacizumab, an anti-vascular endothelial growth factor antibody, for metastatic renal cancer. N Engl J Med 2003a;349:427-434.

Yang JC, Sherry RM, Steinberg SM, et al: Randomized study of high-dose and low-dose interleukin-2 in patients with metastatic renal cancer. J Clin Oncol 2003b;21:3127-3132.

Zbar B, Tory K, Merino M, et al: Hereditary papillary renal cell carcinoma. J Urol 1994;151:561-566.

# 48 Urothelial Tumors of the Upper Urinary Tract

ROBERT C. FLANIGAN, MD

**BASIC AND CLINICAL BIOLOGY**

**EPIDEMIOLOGY**

**NATURAL HISTORY**

**PATHOLOGY**

**PROGNOSTIC FACTORS**

**DIAGNOSIS**

**STAGING**

**TREATMENT**

## BASIC AND CLINICAL BIOLOGY

Upper urinary tract tumors can be defined as any neoplastic growth that affects the lining of the urinary tract from the calyces to the distal ureter. These tumors display behaviors that are similar to those of tumors arising in bladder, but they also have many characteristics that separate them from those tumors. For example, unlike bladder urothelial cancers, upper tract cancers are relatively less common and are associated with several familial syndromes. They are more difficult to visualize directly and to reach with topical therapies, and given the anatomic difference between the upper and lower urinary tracts in terms of muscle thickness and other factors, they may have different prognoses.

## EPIDEMIOLOGY
### Incidence and Mortality Rates

Upper urinary tract urothelial tumors involving the renal pelvis or ureter are relatively uncommon, accounting for about 5% to 7% of all renal tumors and about 5% of all urothelial tumors (Fraley, 1978; Melamed and Reuter, 1993; Jemal et al, 2004). Because renal pelvic tumors are generally not reported separately, worldwide statistics vary substantially between nations and are not accurate. However, the highest incidence appears to occur in Balkan countries, where urothelial cancers represent 40% of all renal cancers.

The peak incidence of upper tract tumors is 10 per 100,000 per year, occurring in the age range of 75 to 79 years. Fortunately, synchronous bilateral urothelial upper urinary tract tumors are very rare (Holmang and Johansson, 2004). In one series from Sweden, the percentage of upper tract tumors that were bilateral was 1.6%, preceded in 80% of cases by a bladder cancer diagnosis. There may be a decreasing incidence of bilaterality secondary to the prohibition of phenacetin-containing analgesics in the 1960s. An evaluation of data from 1973 to 1996 with use of the Surveillance, Epidemiology, and End Results (SEER) database showed 9072 cases, 5379 of the renal pelvis and 3678 of the ureter.

In comparison of age-adjusted annual incidence rates, an increase in ureteral neoplasms from 0.69 to 0.73 per 100,000 person-years was found, but no change in the incidence of renal pelvic tumors was apparent. In addition, the rate of in situ neoplasm increased from 7.2% to 23.1%. Upper tract urothelial tumors are rarely diagnosed at autopsy but rather present clinically during the patient's lifetime (Ressequie et al, 1978). It also appears that the true incidence of upper tract tumors is increasing as the population ages. Patients with upper tract cancer are generally older than patients with bladder tumors (Melamed and Reuter, 1993). Upper tract tumors rarely present before the age of 40 years, and the mean age at presentation is 65 years (Anderstrom et al, 1989). **SEER data also demonstrate a 5-year overall survival rate that is significantly different as related to tumor stage (95.1% in situ, 88.9% localized, 62.6% regional, and 16.5% distant)** (Munoz and Ellison, 2000). **In conclusion, there appears to be a slight increase in the U.S. national incidence of ureteral cancers during the last two decades. Fortunately, this has been associated with a slight improvement in the overall and disease-specific survival of patients with upper tract malignant neoplasms.**

## Variations by Sex and Race

Men are about twice as likely to develop upper tract tumors as are women (Greenlee et al, 2000). In addition, whites are about twice as likely as African Americans to develop upper tract tumors (Greenlee et al, 2000). On the other hand, SEER data suggest that disease-specific annual mortality is greater in black men than in white men (7.4% versus 4.9%) and greater in women than in men (6.1% versus 4.4%) (Munoz and Ellison, 2000). As is the case with bladder cancer, women who develop upper tract cancer are 25% more likely than men to die of the cancer (Greenlee et al, 2000). Accurate data regarding racial differences in mortality are not available.

## Upper Tract Tumors after Known Bladder Cancer

On the basis of SEER data from the period 1973 to 1996, upper tract cancers developed in 657 of 91,245 cases of bladder cancer with adequate follow-up (4.1 years median) (Rabbani et al, 2001). The relative risk for upper tract tumors for white men and women was 64.2% and 75.4% at or before 2 years, 44.3% and 40.5% at 2 to 5 years, 50.8% and 42.1% at 5 to 10 years, and 43.2 and 22.2% at more than 10 years. These authors concluded that the incidence of upper tract cancers is stable on long-term follow-up and that upper tract surveillance must remain rigorous for an extended period. **The incidence of upper tract recurrence has been shown to be higher in patients with carcinoma in situ than in patients with superficial transitional cell carcinoma and in patients treated with cystectomy for carcinoma in situ rather than for invasive cancer** (Solsona et al, 1997). On pathologic evaluation, recurrence is most likely to be superficial (Ta, T1, Tis) and to occur in the distal ureter only (47%). However, this finding has not been reported in all series. For example, in patients with Ta, T1, and Tis bladder cancers treated with bacille Calmette-Guérin (BCG), Herr and colleagues (1996) reported a 21% upper tract recurrence rate after a median interval of 7.3 years; the majority were invasive, and 38.8% of patients with recurrence died of their upper tract disease.

## Etiology and Risk Factors

**Balkan Nephropathy.** Balkan nephropathy is characterized by a degenerative interstitial nephropathy occurring in Balkan countries. Afflicted families display a much higher incidence of upper tract transitional cell cancer, in some areas 100 to 200 times greater than in nonaffected individuals (Petkovic, 1975). Curiously, bladder cancer incidence is not affected. Tumors are generally low grade and are more frequently multiple and bilateral than are upper tract transitional cell carcinomas due to other causes (Radovanovic et al, 1985). Balkan nephropathy is familial but not obviously inherited, suggesting an environmental etiology that has yet to be identified. Interestingly, family members who leave home early in life may not be affected (Radovanovic et al, 1985).

**Smoking.** Cigarette smoking appears to be the most important of the modifiable risk factors for upper tract cancer, producing an incidence three times as that seen in nonsmokers. It appears that this risk is dose related, with a rate as high as 7.2 times normal for long-term (>45 years) smokers (McLaughlin et al, 1992). Former smokers also have a twofold increased risk compared with age-matched persons with no smoking history. This risk declines only partially after smoking ceases. In addition, the risk from smoking seems to more often lead to ureteral rather than to renal pelvic tumors.

**Coffee Consumption.** A relative risk of 1.8 times normal has been described in individuals who consumed more than seven cups of coffee per day (Ross et al, 1989). However, after controlling for cigarette smoking, this risk decreased to 1.3.

**Analgesics.** Analgesic abuse is a well-documented risk factor associated with the development of upper tract cancers (Morrison, 1984; McCredie et al, 1986). In one study, 22% of patients with renal pelvic tumors and 11% of patients with ureteral tumors reported a history of analgesic abuse with a latency period of approximately 2 years (Steffens and Nagel, 1988). Renal papillary necrosis and phenacetin consumption also appear to be independent but synergistic risk factors. Each alone resulted in relative risk factors of 6.9 and 3.6, respectively, but together increased risk 20 times (McCredie et al, 1986). Although phenacetin is the most well described causative agent in analgesic nephropathy, most patients have reported taking combination preparations that included caffeine, codeine, acetaminophen, and aspirin or other salicylates (De Broe and Elseviers, 1998). Histologic findings associated with analgesic abuse include thickening of the basement membrane (pathognomonic) and papillary scarring. Thickening of the basement membrane has been demonstrated in 15% of patients with upper tract tumors and should alert the physician to the presence of this etiologic agent and the subsequent risk of contralateral involvement (Palvio et al, 1987). The degree of papillary scarring also appears to be closely related to tumor grade although not with the development of squamous metaplasia or squamous cancer (Stewart et al, 1999).

**Occupation.** A significantly increased risk for upper tract tumors has been reported for persons employed in chemical, petroleum, and plastic industries (relative risk of 4); patients with exposure to coal or coke (relative risk of 4); and patients with exposure to asphalt or tar (relative risk of 5.5) (Jensen et al, 1988). Aniline dyes, β-naphthylamine, and benzidine have been implicated as causative agents, and tumors can occur at long intervals (up to 15 years or more) after exposure.

**Chronic Inflammation, Infection, or Exposure to Chemotherapies.** The development of squamous cell cancer (and less commonly adenocarcinoma) has been shown to be related to chronic bacterial infection associated with urinary stones and obstruction (Godec and Murrah, 1985; Spires et al, 1993). In addition, exposure to cyclophosphamide, an alkylating agent, also appears to confer an increased risk (Brenner and Schellhammer, 1987).

**Heredity.** Several familial syndromes have been associated with the development of upper tract transitional cell cancer (Frischer et al, 1985; Orphali et al, 1986; Lynch et al, 1990). Lynch syndrome II, for example, is characterized by the early development of colonic tumors (without polyposis) and extracolonic neoplasms, including upper tract urothelial tumors. Unlike with nonhereditary cancers, these patients are typically younger (mean, 55 years) and are more likely to be female (Lynch et al, 1990).

## NATURAL HISTORY
## Molecular Biology (Chromosome Abnormalities)

The molecular and genetic basis of upper tract transitional cell cancers appears to be similar to that of transitional cell cancers of the bladder. These events have been better described in bladder cancers and are reported in detail in Chapter 77.

Briefly, the genetic events leading to the development of upper tract tumors seem to be associated with the presence of tumor suppressor genes, including *p53* (on chromosome 17p), the retinoblastoma gene (*RB*) on chromosome 13q, and several gene foci on chromosome 9 (including the genes for p18 and p16 proteins located at 9p21 and 9p32-33). It is generally thought that chromosome 9 abnormalities occur early in the development of these cancers but are not typically associated with high grade and dysplastic changes, whereas *p53* is more often associated with increased grade and dysplasia. It would also seem, however, that by the time the tumor has been able to invade into the lamina propria, both genetic events are likely to have occurred (Spruck et al, 1994).

## Location and Distribution of Tumors

**Ureteral tumors occur more commonly in the lower than in the upper ureter. Overall, about 70% of ureteral tumors occur in the distal ureter, 25% in the midureter, and 5% in the proximal ureter** (Anderstrom et al, 1989; Messing and Catalona, 1998). This phenomenon may be a reflection of downstream implantation. One area of consensus is that removal of the entire ureter is mandatory when upper urinary tract cancers are removed by nephroureterectomy. Bilateral involvement (either synchronous or metachronous) occurs in 1.6% to 6% of sporadic upper tract transitional cell cancers (Babaian et al, 1980; Murphy et al, 1981; Kang et al, 2003).

**Patients with upper tract tumors are at risk for development of bladder cancer, with an estimated incidence that varies in multiple reports from 15% to 75% within 5 years of the development of the upper tract cancer** (Kakizoe et al, 1980; Huben et al, 1988; Anderstrom et al, 1989; Hisataki et al, 2000; Miyake et al, 2000; Kang et al, 2003). **This high incidence of metachronous bladder involvement suggests that routine bladder surveillance should be performed.** Why are upper tract cancers followed by bladder cancers more often than bladder cancers are followed by upper tract cancers? Theories include downstream seeding, longer exposure time to carcinogens in the bladder, and greater number of urothelial cells in the bladder that are subject to random carcinogenic events. Studies have suggested that in high-grade cancers (with associated *p53* gene mutations), which also tend to be more rapidly recurrent, specific gene mutations noted in upper tract cancers are also demonstrated in subsequent bladder cancers (Harris and Neal, 1992; Lunec et al, 1992; Habuchi et al, 1993). In contrast, microsatellite studies in low-grade upper tract cancers, which tend to recur less rapidly in the bladder, have suggested genetic discordance between these upper tract tumors and subsequent bladder cancers in 46% of cases (Takahashi et al, 2000).

Upper tract cancers have traditionally been reported to develop in 2% to 4% of patients with bladder cancer, with a mean interval to recurrence of 17 to 170 months (Oldbring et al, 1989; Solsona et al, 1997; Rabbani et al, 2001). **Risk factors that have been reported to predict a higher likelihood of the development of upper tract cancers after bladder cancer treatment include stage, grade, multiplicity of tumors in the bladder, presence of ureteral reflux, presence of recurrent carcinoma in situ in the bladder after BCG treatment, multifocal carcinoma in situ in the bladder at the time of cystectomy, and presence of bladder cancers arising close to** a ureteral orifice (Hudson and Herr, 1995; Herr et al, 1992; Zincke et al, 1994). Two long-term follow-up series have reported that upper tract recurrence after bladder cancer diagnosis may be much higher than previously thought, occurring in approximately 25% of cases. This phenomenon may be the result of selection of patients, with more high-grade and dysplastic tumors reported in these series (Solsona et al, 1997; Herr et al, 1996).

Delayed recurrence is more common in the ureter than in the renal pelvis and appears to occur earlier (at 40 versus 67 months). In patients treated with BCG for carcinoma in situ of the bladder, upper tract cancer is even more common (about 30% of cases) and appears to occur distally (in the distal, juxtavesical, and intramural portions of the ureter), especially in those patients subjected to cystectomy who are BCG refractory. Therefore, in cases of high-risk bladder cancer (high-grade T1 disease or carcinoma in situ), upper tract imaging should probably be performed annually as part of routine follow-up (Herr et al, 1996).

**Upper tract urothelial cancers are often associated with a poor prognosis. Up to 19% of patients with upper tract transitional cell carcinoma have been reported to present initially with metastatic disease** (Akaza et al, 1970). **Several studies have suggested that renal pelvic tumors have a better overall prognosis and 5-year disease-specific and recurrence-free survival than do ureteral tumors** (Park et al, 2004). **However, overall prognosis of upper tract tumors seems to be principally related to tumor stage and to a lesser degree to tumor grade.** In one series, 5-year survival was 100% for Ta and Tis, 91.7% for T1, 72.6% for T2, and 40.5% for T3 tumors. Multivariate analysis in this series showed that tumor stage ($P = .0001$) and age of the patient ($P = .042$) were the only statistically significant predictors of survival (Hall et al, 1998).

## Progression to Muscle Invasion and Metastases

The thin muscle layer of the renal pelvis and ureter probably allows earlier penetration of invasive upper tract tumors through the thinned muscle layer than is seen in bladder cancers (Cummings, 1980; Richie, 1988). In a recent report, 164 patients with upper tract tumors were compared with 2197 patients with bladder cancer. High-grade and deeply invasive transitional cell carcinoma occurred in 28.2% of bladder cancers compared with 39.5% of upper tract tumors (Stewart et al, 2005). The renal parenchyma itself may be a barrier to the spread of stage T3 cancers, whereas periureteral tumor extension is a risk factor for early tumor dissemination (Batata and Grabstald, 1976; Guinan et al, 1992). This anatomic phenomenon may be at least part of the explanation as to why renal pelvic tumors appear to have a better prognosis than ureteral tumors. In one large series of 611 patients treated at 97 hospitals, the 5-year survival rates of patients with stage T3 tumors of the renal pelvis and ureter were 54% and 24%, respectively (Guinan et al, 1992).

## Patterns of Spread

Transitional cell carcinomas of the upper urinary tract may spread in several different ways, including direct invasion into the renal parenchyma or surrounding structures, lymphatic or vascular invasion, and epithelial spread by seeding or direct extension. It is clear that high-grade tumors demonstrate a greater propensity to invade and that renal parenchymal invasion is the most significant predictor of the development of metastases (95%), followed by vascular invasion (83%) and lymphatic invasion (77%) (Davis et al, 1987).

**Epithelial.** To describe the clonal nature of urothelial tumors of the bladder and upper tract, two theories of the nature of this phenomenon have been proposed. The monoclonality theory describes the multiple tumors as the descendants of a single genetically transformed cell that populates the urothelium. In contrast, the field theory assumes a diffuse "cancerization" that is the result of exposure to a carcinogen and results in the independent development of nonrelated tumors at different sites. Although the majority of the evidence supports the monoclonality theory, most of this evidence has resulted from the study of advanced invasive cancers. It seems that a small but significant proportion of multifocal cancers are in fact derived from different clones (Hafner et al, 2002).

Epithelial spreading may occur in both antegrade (most common) and retrograde manners. Antegrade seeding is thought to be the most likely explanation for the high incidence of recurrence in patients in whom a ureteral stump is left in situ after nephrectomy and incomplete ureterectomy (Johnson and Babaian, 1979).

**Lymphatic.** Lymphatic spread from the upper urinary tract extends to the para-aortic, paracaval, and ipsilateral common iliac and pelvic lymph nodes (Batata and Grabstald, 1976). This extension, of course, depends on the location of the primary tumor and is directly related to the depth of invasion of the primary tumor. Whether lymphadenectomy should be performed routinely and the extent of lymphadenectomy remain controversial (Nakazono and Muraki, 1993; Komatsu et al, 1997). In a series of nephroureterectomy and lymph node dissection, Secin and associates (2005) reported positive lymph nodes in 20% of cases (mean number of lymph nodes sampled, 7.3; range, 1 to 17). Death from disease was 25% for patients with N0 tumors compared with 66.7% in the N1-2 group ($P < .001$). In this series, the presence of suspicious lymph nodes on preoperative imaging studies was the only preoperative predictor of lymph node metastasis on multivariate analysis ($P = .02$).

**Hematogenous.** The most common sites of hematogenous metastases from upper tract tumors are the liver, lung, and bone (Batata et al, 1975). Although it is very rare, direct extension into the renal veins and vena cava may occur in renal pelvic tumors (Jitsukawa et al, 1985; Geiger et al, 1986).

## PATHOLOGY

The majority of upper tract tumors are urothelial cancers. Of these, the majority are transitional cell in origin; squamous cell cancers and adenocarcinomas represent a small minority (Bennington et al, 1975; Vincente et al, 1995; Flanigan and Kim, 2004).

## Normal Upper Tract Urothelium

**The urothelial lining of the upper urinary tract closely approximates that of the bladder except for the markedly reduced thickness of the muscle layer and the abutting of the urothelium to the renal parenchyma proximally.** The epithelial layer is continuous from the level of the calyces to the distal ureter. It has been postulated that the urothelial layer may even "extend" into the collecting ducts, raising the possibility that collecting duct renal cancers may be closely related to urothelial cancers and perhaps better treated by agents used for urothelial cancers (Orsola et al, 2005). This observation needs further confirmation.

**Renal Pelvis and Calyces** (Fig. 48–1). The walls of the calyces and the pelvis contain fibrous connective tissue and two layers of smooth muscle and are lined on their inner surfaces by transitional epithelium (Dixon and Gosling, 1982) (Fig. 48–2). Thin muscle layers originate in the minor calyces and form a spiral, helical arrangement (Fig. 48–3).

**Ureter.** The ureter demonstrates two continuous thin muscle layers with a loosely spiraled internal layer and a more tightly spiraled external layer. In the lower third of the ureter, a third outer longitudinal layer is present. All three layers merge with the three layers (inner longitudinal, middle circular, and outer longitudinal) of the bladder wall, which run longitudinally, transversely, and obliquely. Beneath the outer muscle coat is the serosa, made up of loose connective tissue and containing

**Figure 48–1.** Low-magnification view of a section through the kidney. The renal medulla ends in the pointed renal papilla. Urine empties into the Y-shaped space made up of the renal calyces (the arms of the Y) and the pelvis (the base of the Y).

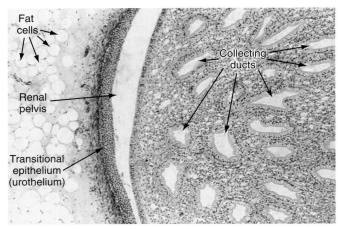

**Figure 48–2.** This image shows several large collecting ducts near the end of a medullary pyramid (i.e., close to their opening into the pelvis). The transitional epithelium of the renal pelvis is continuous with that of the ureters and bladder.

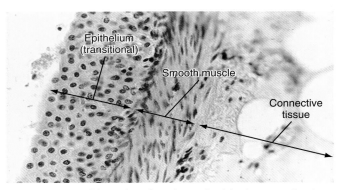

**Figure 48–3.** In this specimen from the renal pelvis, the connective tissue immediately beneath the epithelium is inconspicuous, obscured by a layer of smooth muscle (note elongated nuclei). Beneath the smooth muscle is loose connective tissue, including conspicuous adipocytes.

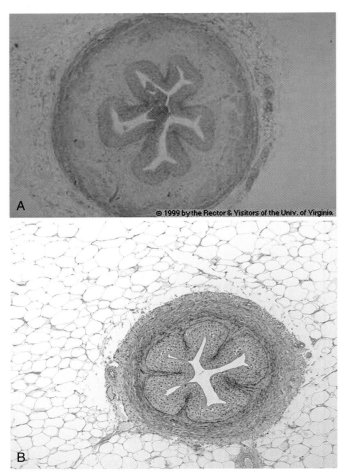

**Figure 48–4.** Cross section of ureter. The ureter has an irregular lumen, which is lined by transitional epithelium. Under the epithelium is a connective tissue layer and, beneath that, three layers of smooth muscle: inner longitudinal, middle circular, and outer longitudinal.

blood vessels and lymphatics (Hanna et al, 1976; Notley, 1978) (Figs. 48–4 and 48–5).

## Abnormal Urothelium

**Metaplasia and Dysplasia. Several studies have suggested that upper tract urothelial cancers progress through histologic changes from hyperplasia to dysplasia to frank carcinoma in situ in a significant proportion of patients** (Heney et al, 1981; McCarron et al, 1982). Carcinoma in situ may be patchy and may extend proximally to the collecting ducts of the kidney (Mahadevia et al, 1983). More severe urothelial dysplastic changes are associated with a greater risk for tumor recurrence in the distal ureter and bladder and a reduced prognosis.

**Benign Lesions: Inverted Papillomas and von Brunn's Nests.** Inverted papillomas, although generally considered benign lesions, have been shown to often be associated with either synchronous or metachronous upper tract urothelial tumors (Renfer et al, 1988; Stower et al, 1990; Chan et al, 1996; Cheville et al, 2000). One series demonstrated an 18% incidence of malignancy associated with inverted papilloma of the

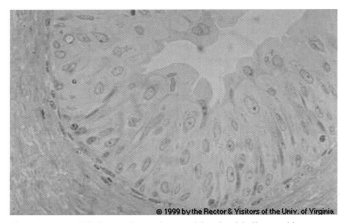

**Figure 48–5.** This image shows the transitional epithelium and loose connective tissue that compose the mucosa of the urinary tract. A transitional epithelium superficially resembles a nonkeratinized stratified squamous epithelium; but note that the epithelial cells nearest to the apical (outer) surface are not flattened but cuboidal. Transitional epithelium is a stratified epithelium characterized by the fact that the most apical cells are the roundest and largest in diameter. It is designed to be able to increase its surface area as the lumen is dilated by urine.

ureter (Grainger et al, 1990). Other studies have suggested that there are two types of urinary inverted papilloma. The lesions of type 1 behave in a benign fashion, whereas those of type 2 may have a malignant potential. Since there is currently no way to distinguish between these two types, it has been advised that follow-up for all cases of inverted papilloma be continued for at least 2 years after initial diagnosis (Asano et al, 2003). Similarly, these findings suggest close surveillance of the upper tracts for malignancy is warranted when inverted papilloma is diagnosed.

**Transitional Cell Carcinoma.** Transitional cell carcinoma makes up more than 90% of upper tract tumors, may present as papillary or sessile lesions, and may be unifocal or multifocal. On histologic examination, these lesions are similar to transitional cell cancers of the bladder, but the relative thinness of the muscle layer of the renal pelvis and ureter makes invasion through the muscle coat an earlier event. Carcinoma in situ, as in the bladder, can be particularly difficult to identify and can vary in appearance from a whitish plaque to epithelial hyperplasia or a velvety red patch due to increased submucosal vascularity (Melamed and Reuter, 1993). Progression to muscle invasion or invasion into the renal parenchyma or adventitial tissues may occur and is more likely, given the relative thinness of the muscle coat of the upper tracts.

**Nontransitional Cell Tumors.** Nontransitional cell tumors of the upper tracts represent a wide spectrum of lesions, from benign to highly malignant. The most common of these are squamous cell cancers and adenocarcinomas.

*Squamous Cell Cancers.* Squamous cell cancers make up 0.7% to 7% of upper tract cancers (Babaian and Johnson, 1980; Blacker et al, 1985). Squamous cancers are frequently associated with a condition of chronic inflammation or infection or with analgesic abuse (Stewart et al, 1999). These tumors occur six times more frequently in the renal pelvis than in the ureter and are generally moderately to poorly differentiated and more likely to be invasive at the time of presentation.

*Adenocarcinoma.* Adenocarcinomas account for less than 1% of all renal pelvic tumors and are typically associated with long-term obstruction, inflammation, or urinary calculi (Stein et al, 1988; Spires et al, 1993). These tumors typically present at advanced stage and display a poor prognosis.

**Other Miscellaneous Tumors.** Fibroepithelial polyps (benign) (Musselman and Kay, 1986; Blank et al, 1987) and neurofibromas (benign) (Varela-Duran, 1987) are uncommon lesions that are typically treated by simple excision.

Multiple types of sarcomas have also been reported to involve the upper urinary tracts, including leiomyosarcomas (Madgar et al, 1988), plasmacytomas (Igel et al, 1991), and angiosarcomas (Coup, 1988). Because of the rare nature of these tumors, they are typically treated by excision with adjuvant therapy that is based on the experience with tumors of similar histology occurring elsewhere in the body.

## PROGNOSTIC FACTORS
### Stage

**Stage is currently the most important predictor of survival in patients with upper tract urothelial tumors.** The most commonly used staging system is the TNM system (see later section on staging). Upper tract cancers can spread by direct invasion, mucosal seeding, and hematologic and lymphatic routes. Prognosis decreases as stage increases; the most significant decrease in survival is observed in T3 tumors that have penetrated into the perirenal or periureteral fat (Grabstald et al, 1971).

### Grade

The traditional grading system used for bladder cancer is also applicable to upper tract tumors. Broder's original system, modified by Ash, grades tumors from grade 1 to grade 4; grade 1 tumors are primarily papillomas, and grade 4 tumors are highly anaplastic and poorly differentiated tumors (Melamed and Reuter, 1993). The World Health Organization's system, proposed by Mostofi, eliminates papillomas and grades tumors from grade 1 to grade 3. Recently, tumor grading has been divided into low grade and high grade (Epstein, 1998). Papillomas and papillary urothelial neoplasms of low malignant potential are also described. **Certainly, tumors of high grade are more likely to invade into the underlying connective tissue, muscle, and surrounding tissues. Tumors of high grade are also more likely to be associated with concomitant carcinoma in situ.**

### Location

There remains disagreement as to whether the location of an upper tract tumor affects prognosis. Several studies have suggested that renal pelvic tumors have a better prognosis than ureteral cancers (Park et al, 2004). In contrast, others have argued that when renal pelvic and ureteral tumors are matched for stage, there is no significant difference in prognosis (Hall et al, 1998).

### Associated Carcinoma In Situ

**As in bladder cancer, carcinoma in situ of the upper tract is associated with a poor prognosis and a likelihood of future development of invasive urothelial cancers.** Carcinoma in situ of the distal ureter is most common in patients with bladder carcinoma in situ treated with BCG (30% likelihood).

### Molecular Markers

**p53.** The p53 nuclear protein staining of cytology specimens obtained ureteroscopically appears to correlate well with the presence of upper tract transitional cell carcinoma. In one study, of 36 p53-positive specimens, 28 had simultaneous evidence of upper tract transitional cell carcinoma; 80% of the remaining patients who were evaluated serially also had confirmed transitional cell carcinoma. All 14 p53-negative studies occurred in patients with no sign of concurrent malignant disease on ureteroscopy (Keeley et al, 1997c).

**Lymphovascular Invasion.** **Lymphovascular invasion has been suggested to be an independent prognostic factor for disease-specific survival in upper tract transitional cell carcinoma.** In a Japanese study, 173 consecutive patients undergoing surgical treatment of upper tract transitional cell carcinoma had lymphovascular invasion determined (Kikuchi et al, 2005). Lymphovascular invasion was found in 30% of cases and was more frequent in advanced pathologic stage. Overall 5- and 10-year survival rates were 84.9% and 80.4%, respectively, in the absence of lymphovascular invasion compared with 40.2% and 21.1% with lymphovascular invasion. Further prospective, large-scale studies are needed to confirm this observation.

**Loss of Heterozygosity.** Loss of heterozygosity at 9p21 has been observed in bladder cancer and now in upper tract transitional cell carcinoma by microsatellite instability analysis. It has been shown that transitional cell carcinoma can occur in patients with hereditary nonpolyposis colorectal cancer syndrome. Patients with this syndrome show genomic lesions in DNA mismatch repair genes (Amira et al, 2003). Furthermore, an inverted growth pattern of cancer has also been associated with microsatellite instability, with a sensitivity and specificity of 0.82 in one study. This finding suggests that microsatellite instability may serve as a marker for inverted growth in upper tract cancers (Hartmann et al, 2003).

**Ploidy–Flow Cytometry.** Tumor ploidy has been shown to correlate with survival in upper tract tumors. In one study, tumor aneuploidy was associated with poor 5- and 10-year survival rates of 25% and 0%, respectively (Blute et al, 1988).

**Other Markers.** Telomerase activity has been shown to be present in most (>95%) upper tract urothelial cancers. It can be detected in exfoliated urinary specimens in a high percentage of patients and thus may prove to be a potentially useful marker (in addition to conventional cytology) to identify upper tract cancers (Wu et al, 2000).

Urinary levels of NMP22, a nuclear matrix protein–based marker, have been found to be elevated in patients with upper tract cancer (Carpinito et al, 1996). Although the sensitivity of this test for determining the presence of low-grade tumors is probably higher than that of cytology, the specificity is low.

Rapid urine tests for urothelial malignant neoplasms have been studied extensively for the purpose of identifying lower urinary tract tumors. Less is known about their value in upper tract cancers. In one series, an analysis of fibrinogen-fibrin degradation products (AuraTek FDP) was compared with the bladder tumor antigen (BTA) test and urine cytology. In this study, the accuracy of the FDP test was 83% compared with 62% for BTA and 59% for cytology (Siemens et al, 2003).

p27, a cyclin-dependent kinase inhibitor, has also been shown to predict the prognosis of upper tract tumors. In one study, low levels of p27 staining were indicative of a worse disease-specific survival (Kamai et al, 2000).

# DIAGNOSIS
## Symptoms and Signs

**The most common presenting symptom of upper tract urothelial tumors is hematuria, either gross or microscopic.** This occurs in 56% to 98% of patients (Murphy et al, 1981; Guinan et al, 1992; Raabe et al, 1992). Flank pain is the second most common symptom, occurring in 30% of tumors. This pain is typically dull and believed to be secondary to a gradual onset of obstruction and hydronephrotic distention. In some cases, pain can be acute and mimic renal colic, typically ascribed to the passage of clots that acutely obstruct the collecting system. About 15% of patients are asymptomatic at presentation and are diagnosed when an incidental lesion is found on radiologic evaluation. Patients may also present with symptoms of advanced disease, including flank or abdominal mass, weight loss, anorexia, and bone pain. Nearly all upper tract tumors are diagnosed during the patient's life, and therefore upper tract urothelial cancer represents a rare autopsy finding (Ressequie et al, 1978).

## Radiologic Evaluation

**Although intravenous pyelography has been the traditional means for diagnosis of upper tract lesions, computed tomographic (CT) urography is increasingly performed today.** CT scanning is easier to perform and less labor intensive. It also has a higher degree of accuracy in determining the presence of renal parenchymal lesions. On the other hand, small urinary filling defects (<5 mm) may be missed between the "cuts" of the traditional CT scan. More recently, CT urography has been performed to obtain a three-dimensional image of the upper tracts. This technique appears to be equal to intravenous pyelography in imaging the ureters and renal pelvis (McTavish et al, 2002). With CT urography, the sensitivity for detecting upper tract malignant disease has been reported to approach 100%, with a specificity of 60% and a negative predictive value of 100% (Caoili et al, 2002). CT urography does, however, expose the patient to higher doses of radiation.

**Radiolucent filling defects, obstruction or incomplete filling of a part of the upper tract, and nonvisualization of the collecting system are the typical findings suggestive of an upper tract tumor.** Filling defects, which account for 50% to 75% of cases, typically require the intravenous administration of contrast material to be identified (Fein and McClennan, 1986; Murphy et al, 1981). The differential diagnosis of these defects includes blood clot, stones, overlying bowel gas, external compression, sloughed papilla, and fungus ball. Stones can be ruled out most easily by confirmation of calcification by renal ultrasonography or CT scanning. Transitional cell cancers have an average density of 46 Hounsfield units (HU) and a range of 10 to 70 HU (Lantz and Hattery, 1984). This is in contrast to an average of 100 HU seen in radiolucent uric acid stones (range, 80 to 250 HU). Thus, CT scanning can be useful in distinguishing between these two common causes of radiolucent filling defect on excretory urography or retrograde ureterography.

Radiolucent, noncalcified lesions may require additional evaluation by retrograde urography or ureteroscopy, with or without biopsy and cytology. Overall, retrograde urography has an accuracy of 75% in diagnosis of an upper tract malignant neoplasm (Murphy et al, 1981). An incompletely filled or obstructed renal infundibulum or calyx, occurring in 10% to 30% of cases, again typically requires retrograde urography or ureteroscopy to confirm the diagnosis. Obstruction of the urinary tract is a poor prognostic sign for tumor invasion (Babaian and Johnson, 1980).

**Evaluation of the contralateral kidney is important not only because of possible bilaterality of the disease but also because it allows a determination of the functionality of the contralateral kidney.** This is an extremely important part of the management process. At times, a split-function renal scan may be helpful in determining the contribution of both the "diseased" and the presumed "normal" kidney to the patient's overall renal function.

Some have suggested that ultrasonography has sensitivity equal to that of urography in evaluating patients with painless gross hematuria for upper tract malignant disease (Yip et al, 1999; Data et al, 2002). For staging purposes, CT or magnetic resonance scanning is most useful in determining the extent of invasion, an associated mass lesion outside the collecting system, and the presence of lymph node or distant metastases (Milestone et al, 1990). CT is also more sensitive than conventional radiography in determining minimally radiopaque substances, making it useful in identifying urine excreted by poorly functioning areas of kidney (as in obstructed areas) (Kenney and Stanley, 1987). The greatest downside of CT or magnetic resonance scanning is in the detection of small lesions that may be lost in volume averaging. In one series, CT scanning predicted TNM stage in 60% of patients; it understaged 16% and overstaged 24% (Scolieri et al, 2000).

## Cystoscopy

Because upper tract tumors are often associated with bladder cancers, cystoscopy is mandatory in the evaluation to exclude coexistent bladder lesions.

## Ureteroscopic Evaluation and Biopsy

The technical advances achieved in the realm of endoscopic equipment have made the flexible and rigid ureteroscope a key part of the evaluation (and treatment) of upper tract tumors. **Diagnostic accuracy can be improved from approximately 75% with excretory or retrograde urography alone to approximately 85% to 90% when it is combined with ureteroscopy** (Streem et al, 1986; Blute et al, 1989). Although pyelovenous and pyelolymphatic migration has been reported with ureteroscopy, this phenomenon appears to be uncommon and should not preclude its use (Lim et al, 1993).

**As with bladder tumors, 55% to 75% of ureteral tumors are low grade and low stage** (Cummings, 1980; Richie, 1988; Williams, 1991). **Also, like bladder cancers, approximately 85% of renal pelvic tumors are papillary and the remainder sessile.** Invasion of the lamina propria or muscle (stage T1 or T2) occurs in 50% of papillary and in more than 80% of sessile tumors. Overall, therefore, 50% to 60% of renal pelvic tumors are invasive into either the lamina propria or muscle. In ureteral tumors, invasion is also more common than in bladder tumors (Anderstrom et al, 1989; Williams, 1991).

In addition to visualization of the tumor, ureteroscopy allows more accurate biopsy of suspected areas, with either biopsy forceps or brushing (Fig. 48–6). Good histologic correlation (78% to 92%) between the ureteroscopic biopsy specimen and the final pathologic specimen has been established (Keeley et al, 1997b; Guarnizo et al, 2000). It appears that fresh samples obtained ureteroscopically provide the best chance of predicting eventual pathologic findings. In one study, a cell block from biopsies was prepared when a visible tumor was present, and grades of ureteroscopic biopsy specimens were compared with grades and stages of surgical specimens in 42 cases. Of 30 low- or moderate-grade specimens, 29 (90%) proved to be low- or moderate-grade transitional cell carcinoma; 11 of 12 high-grade specimens (92%) proved to be high-grade transitional cell carcinoma, and 8 (67%) were invasive (T2 or T3) (Keeley et al, 1997b). In contrast, the urologist's impression of the tumor grade based on ureteroscopic appearance is likely to be correct in only 70% of cases, suggesting that biopsy is also needed to further define this important aspect of staging (El-Hakim et al, 2004).

**Because of the small size of ureteroscopic biopsy specimens, a precise correlation with eventual tumor *stage* is difficult. Therefore, in predicting the tumor stage, a combination of the radiographic studies, the visualized appearance of the tumor, and the tumor grade provides the surgeon with the best estimation of eventual tumor stage.** Although, as stated before, grading of the tumors may be fairly accurate, staging is much more problematic. Of 40 urothelial tumors staged in one series (40% in the renal pelvis, 20% in the proximal ureter, and 40% in the distal ureter), ureteroscopic grade matched surgical grade in 78% of cases and was less than surgical grade in the remaining 22%. Lamina propria was present in 68% of biopsy specimens (62% of cup biopsies and 100% of loop biopsies), but tumors thought to be Ta were upstaged to T1 to T3 in 45% of cases at the time of complete resection of the lesion (Guarnizo et al, 2000). Therefore, accurate tumor grading on ureteroscopic biopsy is critical in estimating tumor stage. In one series, a biopsy specimen showing grade 3 tumor accurately predicted tumor stage in more than 90% of cases (Skolarikos et al, 2003).

Is ureteroscopy (with or without biopsy) necessary in all cases of suspected upper tract tumors? No. In fact, ureteroscopy should probably be reserved for situations in which the diagnosis remains in question after conventional radiographic studies and for those patients in whom the treatment plan may be modified on the basis of the ureteroscopic findings, for example, endoscopic resection. Although there is no evidence that ureteroscopy diminishes the prognosis of a patient destined to proceed to nephroureterectomy, and although the risks of tumor seeding, extravasations, and dissemination are low in experienced hands, these risks are real and should preclude ureteroscopy when it is unnecessary (Hendin et al, 1999).

## Antegrade Endoscopy

In some cases of upper tract tumors, percutaneous access to the renal pelvis may be required for diagnosis or treatment. In such cases, antegrade urography and uroscopy may be useful for tumor resection, biopsy, or simple visualization. Larger caliber scopes that can be passed into the renal pelvis in this manner may be particularly helpful in resecting or debulking larger volumes of tumor in this area (Streem et al, 1986; Blute et al, 1989). One must remember, however, that tumor cell implantation in the retroperitoneum and along the nephrostomy tube track has been reported after these procedures (Tomera et al, 1982; Huang et al, 1995).

## Role of Cytology and Other Tumor Markers

Urine cytology is a specific tool that is useful in the diagnosis of upper tract carcinomas. On the other hand, the sensitivity

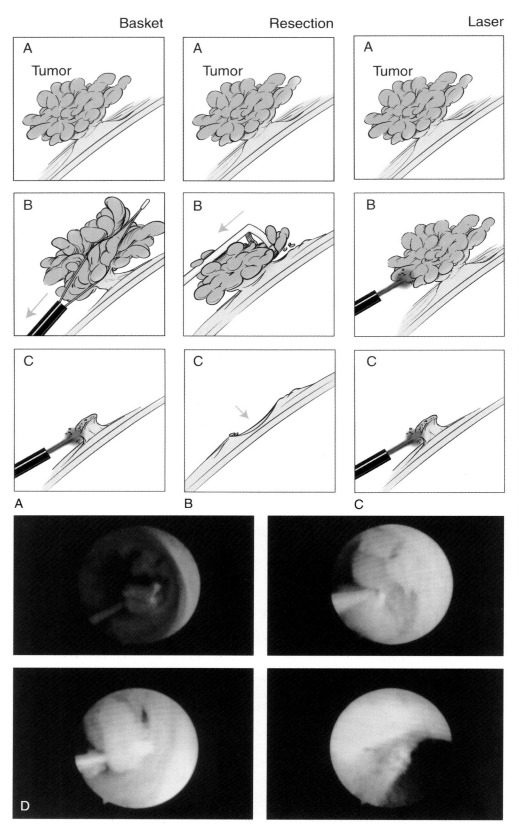

**Figure 48–6.** Techniques for ureteroscopic treatment of ureteral and renal tumors. **A,** The tumor is identified and removed piecemeal by grasping forceps to its base. **B,** Alternatively, a flat wire basket can be deployed alongside the tumor. The tumor is engaged and removed, with care taken not to avulse the adjacent ureter. With either of these techniques, the base is treated with electrocautery or a laser energy source. **C,** The tumor is identified and removed by a ureteroscopic resectoscope. The technique differs from the technique for bladder tumors in that only intraluminal tumor is resected. No attempt is made to resect deeply, as with a bladder tumor. The scope is not arching deep into the tissue. **D,** The tumor is sampled for diagnostic purposes. The bulk of the tumor is then ablated with electrosurgical or laser energy. Laser energy is generally preferred because it has more reliable delivery of energy and depth of penetration. The two most commonly used energy sources are holmium:yttrium-aluminum-garnet and neodymium:yttrium-aluminum-garnet.

of cytology remains an issue. In general, the sensitivity of voided urine (or bladder wash) cytology is directly related to tumor grade. Overall accuracy estimates of the sensitivity of cytology have ranged from about 20% for grade 1 tumors to 45% and 75% for grade 2 and grade 3 tumors, respectively (Murphy and Soloway, 1982; Konety and Getzenberg, 2001).

Even if a voided cytology specimen is abnormal in a patient with an upper tract filling defect, one must be cautious in determining the site of origin of the malignant cells. Ureteral catheterization for collection of urine or washings may provide more accurate cytologic results. However, even in this setting, a substantial false-negative or false-positive result (22% to 35%) can be expected (Zincke et al, 1976). It would appear that saline washing provides a better cell yield and improves cytologic results secondary to the release by hydroscopic forces of loosely adherent cells from the urothelium. Still better accuracy can be achieved by brush biopsy through a retrograde catheter or ureteroscope. Sensitivity in the 90% range with specificity approaching 90% may be possible with these techniques (Blute et al, 1989; Streem et al, 1986). Brush biopsies have, however, also been reported to result in severe complications, including massive hemorrhage and perforation of the urinary tract with extravasation (Blute et al, 1981).

It appears that the exposure of urothelial cells to ionic, high-osmolar contrast agents as in retrograde pyelography may worsen cytologic abnormalities. Thus, it is probably prudent to obtain cytologic specimens before the use of these agents (Terris, 2004).

## STAGING
## TNM Staging System

The TNM staging system is the most commonly used system.

| Primary tumor (T) | |
|---|---|
| TX | Primary tumor cannot be assessed |
| T0 | No evidence of primary tumor |
| Ta | Papillary noninvasive carcinoma |
| Tis | Carcinoma in situ |
| T1 | Tumor invades subepithelial connective tissue |
| T2 | Tumor invades the muscularis |
| T3 | Tumor invades periureteral fat |
| | [for renal pelvis only] Tumor invades beyond muscularis into perinephric fat or the renal parenchyma |
| T4 | Tumor invades adjacent organ, or through the kidney into the perinephric fat |
| Lymph nodes (N) | |
| NX | Regional lymph nodes cannot be assessed |
| N0 | No regional lymph node metastases |
| N1 | Metastasis to a single lymph node, 2 cm or less in greatest dimension |
| N2 | Metastasis in a single lymph node, more than 2 cm but not more than 5 cm in greatest dimension; or multiple lymph nodes, none more than 5 cm in greatest dimension |
| N3 | Metastasis in a lymph node, more than 5 cm in greatest dimension |
| Distant metastasis (M) | |
| MX | Distant metastasis cannot be assessed |
| M0 | No distant metastasis |
| M1 | Distant metastasis |

The American Joint Committee on Cancer (AJCC) staging system and the TNM system compare as follows:

| AJCC | TNM |
|---|---|
| Stage 0 | T0 |
| Stage I | Ta, Tis, T1, N0, M0 |
| Stage II | T2, N0, M0 |
| Stage III | T3, N0, M0 |
| Stage IV | T4 or any T, N+, M+ |

## TREATMENT
## Role and Limitations of Various Therapies

### Endoscopic Resection or Fulguration (Retrograde and Antegrade)

Technical advances have made it possible to reach all parts of the urinary tract with instruments capable of visualizing lesions, obtaining specimens for histologic evaluation, and delivering treatment modalities. Tumors of the distal ureter can be typically managed well with use of a rigid ureteroscope. Tumors of the upper urinary tract can be reached by retrograde and antegrade approaches. In the retrograde approach, flexible ureteroscopy is most often used. In general, retrograde approaches are characterized as being less invasive than antegrade approaches but are limited to some degree by the size of instrument that can be introduced through the ureter. In contrast, antegrade approaches are characterized as being more invasive (requiring placement of a percutaneous nephrostomy tube) but also able to deliver larger instruments. The basic principles for the endoscopic treatment of urothelial cancers of the upper urinary tract are similar to those for treatment of bladder cancers. Endoscopic treatment of patients with upper tract transitional cell carcinoma is generally recommended in those patients with a solitary kidney, bilateral disease, renal dysfunction, or significant intercurrent illness that precludes a major abdominal procedure. **Endoscopic management may also be appropriate in selected patients with small, low-grade lesions in the presence of a normal contralateral kidney** (Gerber and Steinberg, 1999). **However, most series suggest that recurrence is likely even with frequent reinspection and that progression to invasive disease occurs in a significant number of patients, depending on the stage and grade of the initial tumor.**

The lesion is first sampled and then the underlying tissue is ablated by electrocautery or laser energy. Endoscopic resection is generally best suited for the treatment of low-grade, low-stage lesions, for which results with this approach are excellent. In high-grade lesions, even if they are noninvasive, the procedure is limited by the field effect or by the dysplasia or carcinoma in situ commonly associated with these lesions. In the case of invasive lesions (T1 or T2), the adequacy of determination of the depth of tumor invasion is problematic as deep biopsy of the renal pelvis or ureter can be associated with massive bleeding or penetration of the urinary tract. Retrospective reviews of patients who have undergone ureteroscopic biopsy followed by nephroureterectomy have demonstrated an accuracy of 89% to 94% in determining the diagnosis and 78% to 92% in determining grade. The depth of invasion is best estimated by the tumor grade; about 85% of grade 1 and grade 2 tumors are Ta or T1, whereas 67% of

**Table 48-1. Results of Endoscopic Ablation of Upper Tract Tumors**

| Author | No. of Patients | Complication Rate (%) | Recurrence Site | Subsequent Nephroureterectomy (%) | Follow-up (months) |
|---|---|---|---|---|---|
| Englemeyer and Belis (1996) | 10 | 20 | 2 P, 5 U | — | 24-66 |
| Elliott et al (1996) | 37 | 22 | 8 P, 9 U, 19 B | 16 | 3-132 |
| Martinez-Pineiro et al (1996) | 28 | 43 | 2 P, 6 U | 11 | 2-119 |
| Keeley et al (1997) | 41 | 5 | 3 P, 5 U, 15 B | 20 | 3-116 |
| Chen et al (2000) | 23 | 9 | 5 P, 8 U, 7 B | 17 | 8-103 |
| Blute et al (1989) | 13 U | 0 | 2 U, 4 B | 0 | 6-50 |
|  | 6 RP | 0 | 1 P | 0 | 12-48 |
| Schilling et al (1986) | 10 | 0 | 1 B | 0 | 3-31 |
| Matsuoka (2003) | 30 | 3.3 | 1 P, 6 U, 5 B | 0 | 17-48 |
| Iborra et al (2003) | 54 | 14.2 | 23 UT, 4 B | 5.5 | 36-210 |
| Daneshmand et al (2003) | 30 | 16.7 | all but 3 recurred | 10 | 4-106 |

B, bladder; P, renal pelvis; RP, retroperitoneal; U, ureter; UT, upper tract.

grade 4 tumors demonstrate invasion (stage T2 or T3) (Chasko et al, 1981; Heney et al, 1981). Thus, patients with high-grade and high-stage lesions are probably best treated by formal resection, by either open or laparoscopic methods. On the other hand, patients who are at high risk for open or laparoscopic surgeries because of underlying comorbidities or patients with tumor in a solitary kidney or with impaired renal function, when resection of the kidney may result in renal insufficiency and dialysis, may be treated with some success with repeated endoscopic tumor ablation or topical immunotherapy or chemotherapy.

**Results.** Multiple studies have demonstrated the safety and efficacy of ureteroscopic treatment of upper urinary tract tumors (Elliott et al, 1996; Martinez-Pineiro et al, 1996; Keeley et al, 1997a; Chen and Bagley, 2000) (Table 48-1). **In one literature review of 205 patients, overall recurrence rates for ureteral and renal pelvic tumors were 33% and 31%, respectively** (Tawfiek and Bagley, 1997). **The risk of bladder recurrence in this review was 43%. The most important predictors of tumor recurrence are tumor grade and stage.** The recurrence rate for grade 1 tumors is about 25%, whereas it is about 45% for grade 2 tumors (Keeley et al, 1997b). It seems clear that frequent reinspections of the upper tract are necessary, probably every 3 months until "tumor free" and every 6 months thereafter (Chen et al, 2000). It also seems clear that this approach is best suited for low-grade, low-stage lesions, for which the risk of progression to invasion is lowest (Chen et al, 2000). Serious complications due to ureteroscopy are uncommon, including primarily ureteral perforation and ureteral stricture. These complications have become less common because of smaller endoscopes, improved sources of energy administration, and improved surgical techniques. Ureteral perforation can be effectively treated with ureteral stenting in most cases.

A percutaneous approach to upper tract lesions is typically indicated by tumor volume, location, or increased grade when complete resection of the lesions is the goal. The technical approach to the tumor depends on its location within the collecting system. High-grade and high-stage upper tract tumors are aggressive and associated with a high likelihood of progression and even death. In one series comparing percutaneous and open management of upper tract transitional cell carcinoma observed for 13 years, 26 of 110 patients

(24%) died of metastases, and 60% of these were noted to have grade 3 disease initially (mean cancer survival period was 15.2 months after the initial procedure in this group). Although results with open management were better for patients with grade 3 tumors in this series with long-term follow-up, disease-specific survival rates for grade 2 tumors were similar for open (53.8 months) and percutaneous (53.3 months) approaches. Therefore, in high-grade cancers, nephroureterectomy is warranted if the patient is a surgical candidate (Lee et al, 1999) (Fig. 48-7).

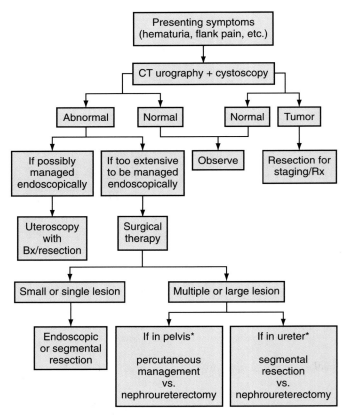

*High grade lesions are often invasive and associated with CIS, making NU more appropriate

**Figure 48-7.** Algorithm for the management of upper tract tumors.

## Segmental Resection (Nephron-Sparing Surgery) of Renal Pelvic Tumors

Although it is today largely supplanted by endoscopic approaches, open nephron-sparing surgery may be indicated in the rare patient with a large, localized tumor in a solitary kidney and synchronous bilateral tumors. Furthermore, in approaching a tumor located in the renal pelvis, a laparoscopic approach to partial nephrectomy *may* be less indicated than an open approach because of the significant likelihood for tumor spillage and subsequent implantation. In the open approach to a renal pelvic tumor, after standard flank incision and dissection of the kidney and renal pelvis are accomplished, pyelotomy and resection of the tumor are undertaken, and its base (if it is abutting the renal parenchyma) is cauterized with electrocautery, laser, or argon bean coagulator. Once resection is complete, the pyelotomy is closed. A temporary ureteral stent or percutaneous tube diversion is not always used but may be indicated in particularly aggressive resections of large-volume tumors. In larger tumors that invade the renal parenchyma, standard partial nephrectomy may be used, as is typical in cases of renal cell cancer, and it may be accomplished with open or laparoscopic techniques.

**Results.** The overall risk of tumor recurrence in the ipsilateral renal pelvis after segmental resection varies widely from 7% to 70% (Zincke and Neves, 1984; Ziegelbaum et al, 1987; Messing and Catalona, 1998). This risk is high correlated with the grade of tumor removed and ranges from 10% for grade 1 tumors to 30% for grade 2 and 60% for grade 3. This risk of recurrence is primarily determined by the inherent multifocal atypia and field change seen with increased tumor grade (Heney et al, 1981; Nocks et al, 1982; Mahadevia et al, 1983; McCarron et al, 1983). Estimation of overall and cancer-specific survival for these highly selected patients with significant comorbidities is difficult. In one series, patients with grade 1 tumors displayed a 75% 5-year survival; those with grade 2 tumors displayed a 46% 2-year survival (Murphy et al, 1980). It therefore seems that high-grade, muscle-invasive, organ-confined tumors may be best treated by nephroureterectomy even if this means that dialysis will be necessary (Gittes, 1980; McCarron et al, 1983). On the other hand, dialysis is not without morbidity and mortality in the elderly, making thorough discussion of treatment options critical to the patient's decision process (Table 48–2).

## Segmental (Partial) Ureterectomy

**Segmental ureterectomy with ureteroureterotomy or bladder reimplantation is indicated for noninvasive, grade 1 or grade 2 tumors of the proximal or middle ureter that are too large for endoscopic management and for grade 3 or invasive tumors when nephron sparing must be done to preserve renal function.**

**Results.** As with other approaches for removal of upper tract lesions, the outcome associated with segmental ureterectomy depends largely on tumor stage and grade. High-grade tumors are often associated with dysplasia or carcinoma in situ, and when possible, the proximal ureter should be inspected or even sampled to confirm or to disprove the presence of these conditions. When the upper ureter cannot be visualized preoperatively secondary to ureteral obstruction or the surgeon's preference not to pass the tumor with a scope, intraoperative flexible ureteroscopy may be easily performed to exclude proximal lesions. The outcomes for ureteral tumors are shown in Table 48–3. Reported 5-year survival is generally excellent for grade 1 and grade 2 Ta tumors. One series reported no tumor-related deaths and only one recurrence in 21 patients with low-grade, low-stage tumors treated with segmental ureterectomy who were observed for a median of 83 months (Anderstrom et al, 1989). In contrast, reported 5-year survival is approximately 65% for stage T1 tumors and approximately 50% for stage T2 tumors (McCarron et al, 1983). In the same series, 5-year survival for Ta tumors was similar for patients treated by open ureteral resection and endoscopic management. The risk of ipsilateral recurrence after segmental resection is 44% to 50% (Mazeman, 1976; Babaian et al, 1980; Williams, 1991). Lifelong periodic investigation is warranted because of this risk (Herr et al, 1996).

## Nephroureterectomy

**Radical nephroureterectomy with resection of a bladder cuff remains the "gold standard" for the treatment of upper tract tumors, especially those that are large, high grade, and invasive, and for large, multifocal or rapidly recurring, medium-grade, noninvasive tumors of the renal pelvis or proximal ureter** (Batata and Grabstald, 1976; Babaian et al, 1980; Cummings, 1980; Murphy et al, 1981; Nocks et al, 1982; McCarron et al, 1983; Richie, 1988; Williams, 1991; Messing and Catalona, 1998). This approach is based on the biologic behavior

**Table 48–2. Results of Segmental Resection and Reimplantation**

| Author | No. of Patients | Local Recurrence (%) | Follow-up (months) |
|---|---|---|---|
| Johnson and Babaian (1979) | 6 | 16.6 | 44 |
| Zungri et al (1990) | 35 | 8.5 | 86 |
| Maier et al (1990) | 17 | 17.6 | 41.4 |
| Wallace et al (1981) | 7 | 14.3 | 93.6 |
| Anderstrom et al (1989) | 21 | 4.7 | 83 |

**Table 48–3. Segmental Ureteral Resection for Localized Upper Tract Tumors**

| Author | No. of Patients | Ureteral Recurrence (%) | Follow-up (months) |
|---|---|---|---|
| Zungri et al (1990) | 35 | 8.5 | 86 |
| Anderstrom et al (1989) | 21 | 4.7 | 83 |
| Maier et al (1990) | 17 | 17.6 | 41 |
| Wallace et al (1981) | 7 | 14.3 | 94 |
| Johnson and Babaian (1979) | 6 | 16.6 | 44 |

of these tumors that is characterized by multifocality, a high incidence of ipsilateral recurrence after partial resection, and a low (<5%) incidence of contralateral disease. Nephroureterectomy can be done totally by open technique, totally laparoscopically, and by a combination of laparoscopic and open techniques (usually laparoscopic nephrectomy and ureterectomy except for the distal or intramural portion, which is done by an open approach).

Traditionally, ipsilateral adrenalectomy has been included in the procedure and is still probably useful in cases of advanced disease because the adrenal is a not-infrequent site of metastases in this disease. However, there appears to be little evidence for an advantage derived from removal of the adrenal gland unless the tumor is superior, appears to involve the gland by direct extension on preoperative radiographic evaluation, or is palpably abnormal intraoperatively.

**The entire ureter, including the intramural portion and ureteral orifice, should be removed. The risk of tumor recurrence in a remaining ureteral stump is 33% to 75%** (Bloom et al, 1970; Babaian et al, 1980; Kakizoe et al, 1980; McCarron et al, 1983). The entire specimen, including the kidney and ureter, may be removed en bloc or after division of the ureter at a site not involved with cancer. In this case, one must be aware of the possibility of tumor spillage and take appropriate steps to minimize its impact.

Regional lymphadenectomy is generally included in open nephroureterectomy. Although there are few data that confirm its value in terms of survival, extrapolation from bladder tumor data suggests that if lymph node metastases are confirmed, adjuvant chemotherapy is potentially useful. The limits of lymphadenectomy are also not as well defined as in bladder cancer; but for renal pelvic tumors, it probably should include the ipsilateral hilar lymph nodes and proceed medially to the adjacent para-aortic and paracaval lymph nodes. A series of 168 patients showed that 39 (23%) had lymph node metastases, including, on the right side, 30% in renal pelvic tumors, 14% in upper ureteral tumors, 20% in middle ureteral tumors, and 27% in lower ureteral tumors, and on the left side, 19%, 9%, 33%, and 18%, respectively (Kondo et al, 2005). This series also suggested that for right-sided tumors, interaortocaval nodes should be removed. What factors predict the presence of lymph node metastases? In another report of 120 patients with upper tract cancers, only suspicious lymph nodes on preoperative imaging studies significantly predicted lymph node metastases (44% of these patients had pathologically proven lymph node metastases) (Secin et al, 2005).

**Laparoscopic nephroureterectomy can be performed by pure laparoscopic technique or a hand-assisted technique with an incision in the lower abdomen.** With the hand-assisted approach, the lower incision is positioned to facilitate removal of the entire specimen en bloc and the bladder cuff. The indications for any of the laparoscopic approaches are identical to those for the open approach. In addition, either laparoscopic approach may be complemented by removal of the distal ureter and bladder cuff by an open, endoscopic, or pure laparoscopic approach. Long-term data are currently not available, but recent data suggest that this technique can be done safely. Local recurrence and port site seeding continue to be of some concern. At least three cases of port site recurrence have been reported; but in two of these cases, principles of surgical oncology were not employed. A report described long-term cancer control in 89 patients treated laparoscopically with a variety of techniques for distal ureterectomy, open in 36 cases and endoscopic stapling in 53 cases (Hattori et al, 2005). These data were compared with results seen by the authors with open nephroureterectomy. In this series, patients' survival and metastasis-free rates were 79% and 75% for the open group, 80% and 80% for the combined laparoscopic and open group, and 78% and 72% for the pure laparoscopic group, respectively. In this nonrandomized series, the authors reported no significant difference in the groups (Sagalowsky and Jarrett, 2002) (Table 48–4).

**Results.** Numerous series have demonstrated that the outcome after nephroureterectomy strongly correlates with tumor stage and grade (see Table 48–4). Nearly all series suggest that nephroureterectomy provides an improved 5-year survival rate compared with simple nephrectomy or endoscopic management, particularly in patients with high-grade or locally advanced (stage T3 or T4, N1 or N2) disease (Batata et al, 1975; Johansson and Wahlquist, 1979; Murphy et al, 1980; McCarron et al, 1983; Zungri et al, 1990). For example, one series reported a survival advantage at 5 years of 84% with radical nephroureterectomy versus 51% with simple nephrectomy, and 74% versus 37%, respectively, for patients with high-stage tumors (Johansson and Wahlquist, 1979). Unfortunately, the retrospective, uncontrolled nature of all of these reports limits the conclusions that may be drawn from them. In summary, however, radical nephroureterectomy is warranted in patients with high-grade invasive disease that is organ confined (T1-2, N0) or locally advanced (T3-4, N0 or N+). Tumor-specific survival rates are high in patients with

| Author | Laparoscopic Approach | No. of Cases | Type of Ureteral Resection | Pathologic Features | Follow-up (months) | Local Recurrence (%) |
|--------|----------------------|--------------|---------------------------|---------------------|---------------------|----------------------|
| Chung et al (1996) | RP | 14 | Open cuff | NA | 12 | 15 (bladder) |
| McNeill et al (2000) | TP | 25 | Open cuff | T1-3, grade 1-3 | 35 | 16 |
| Shalhav et al (2000) | TP | 25 | Stapled | Ta-3, grade 1-4 | 39 | 28 (bladder) 12 (local) |
| Yoshino et al (2003) | RP | 23 | Stapled | Ta-4, grade 1-3 | 19 | 17 (bladder) |
| Landman et al (2002) | TP | 11 | Cysto unroof | Ta-1, grade 1-4 | 27 | 30 (bladder) |

**Table 48–4. Laparoscopic Nephroureterectomy with Open Versus Endoscopic Management of the Distal Ureter**

RP, retroperitoneal; TP, transperitoneal.

organ-confined disease and are guarded to poor in patients with locally advanced disease.

**The precise role of adjuvant chemotherapy in the setting of locally advanced disease has not been defined, given the relatively low number of patients at risk and the absence of clinical trials.** Despite this lack of definitive information, most patients with disease invasion outside the muscle layer or positive lymph node metastases are currently considered for adjuvant chemotherapy with drug regimens developed to treat urothelial cancers of the bladder.

**The usefulness of regional lymphadenectomy in this disease has not been firmly established. Although it is recommended by many investigators, little therapeutic value has been established, and nearly every patient with positive nodal metastases has developed early systemic metastases** (Cummings, 1980; Heney et al, 1981; McCarron et al, 1983; Richie, 1988; Williams, 1991; Messing and Catalona, 1998). However, regional lymphadenectomy adds little to the time or morbidity of the procedure and may have some therapeutic value. In one series, a 5-year survival of 23% was noted when patients with T3 or T4, N1 or N2 disease had all disease resected (Batata and Grabstald, 1976).

### Use of Topical Immunotherapy and Chemotherapy

**Topical immunotherapy or chemotherapy can be used successfully to reduce recurrence and definitely treat upper tract urothelial transitional cell cancers. Installation can be accomplished in several ways, including infusion through a percutaneous tube (the author's preference), retrograde reflux from the bladder with a double-J indwelling stent in place or after iatrogenic creation of ureteral reflux, and instillation through a retrograde catheter.** In addition, repeated ureteral catheterization for instillation of agents has also been reported. Low pressure in the upper urinary tract and care to minimize infection are critical to help prevent systemic absorption of the agent and sepsis. In all cases, continued topical exposure of the urothelium over time and with low intrapelvic pressure are the goals. Several agents have successfully been employed, including BCG (Smith et al, 1987; Studer, et al, 1989; Eastham and Huffman, 1993; Sharpe et al, 1993; Jarrett et al, 1995), mitomycin C (Eastham and Huffman 1993; Weston et al, 1993; Martinez-Pineiro et al, 1996; Keeley et al, 1997a), doxorubicin (See, 2000), and thiotepa (Elliott et al, 1996; Patel et al, 1996). Most investigators have reported satisfactory results with these drugs, but no series has been large enough to show statistically improved survival or decreased recurrence rate. The most common complication reported is sepsis; however, granulomatous involvement of the kidney and systemic signs of BCG infection have also been reported (Bellman et al, 1994).

The agent most commonly employed for treatment or adjuvant therapy is BCG (Table 48–5). Complete resection or destruction of existing tumors has been employed in most cases, but in some, the agent has been used in the presence of incompletely resected lesions.

### Chemotherapy for Advanced Disease

Upper tract transitional cell cancers, like bladder cancers, are relatively chemosensitive, with reasonable response rates reported. Because of the relative low frequency of these tumors, however, few clinical trials have been performed, and much of what is the basis for our treatments comes from the experience with bladder cancer trials. Because single-agent chemotherapy with cisplatin, methotrexate, cyclophosphamide, or gemcitabine has yielded response rates only in the 25% to 35% range, combination therapies have commonly employed MVAC (methotrexate, vinblastine, doxorubicin, cisplatin) or combinations of gemcitabine and taxanes.

**Table 48–5. Percutaneous BCG Instillation**

| Author | No. of Patients | No. of Renal Units | Recurrence (%) | DOD (%) | Mean Follow-up (months) |
|---|---|---|---|---|---|
| Thalmann et al (2002) | 37 | 41 | 49 | 38 | 42 |
| Clark et al (1999) | 17 | 18 | 35 | 35 | 20.5 |
| Jarrett et al (1995) | 30 | — | 33 | — | 55 |

DOD, dead of disease.

### KEY POINTS: DIAGNOSIS AND TREATMENT OF UPPER TRACT TUMORS

■ CT urography with the administration of contrast material provides more information than does excretory urography.

■ Urine cytology for upper tract tumors, although highly sensitive, is of low specificity.

■ A combination of radiologic studies, tumor grade, and tumor visualization is most useful in identifying invasive upper tract cancers.

■ Nephroureterectomy, by whatever technique, is the gold standard therapy for upper tract cancers, especially for larger, high-grade, and invasive lesions.

■ Endoscopic management is most indicated when nephron sparing is an issue and for low-grade, low-stage lesions.

### SUGGESTED READINGS

Dixon JS, Gosling JA: The musculature of the human renal calyces, pelvis, and ureter. J Anat 1982;135:129.

Gerber GS, Steinberg GD: Endoscopic treatment of renal pelvic and ureteral transitional cell carcinoma. Tech Urol 1999;5:77.

Hartmann A, Dietmaier W, Hofstadter F, et al: Urothelial carcinoma of the upper urinary tract: Inverted growth pattern is predictive of microsatellite instability. Pathology 2003;34:222.

Herr HW, Wartinger DD, Oettgen HF: Bacillus Calmette-Guérin therapy for superficial bladder cancer: A 10-year follow-up. J Urol 1992;147:1020.

Huben RP, Mounzer AM, Murphy GP: Tumor grade and stage as prognostic variables in upper tract urothelial tumors. Cancer 1988;62:2016.

Jarrett TW, Sweetser PM, Weiss GH, Smith AD: Percutaneous management of transitional cell carcinoma of the renal collecting system: 9-year experience. J Urol 1995;154:1629.

Keeley FX, Bibbo M, McCue PA, Bagley DH: Use of p53 in the diagnosis of upper tract transitional cell carcinoma. Urology 1997;49:181.

Konety BR, Getzenberg RH: Urine based markers of urologic malignancy. J Urol 2001;165:600.

McCarron JP Jr, Mills C, Vaughn ED Jr: Tumors of the renal pelvis and ureter: Current concepts and management. Semin Urol 1983;1:75.

McTavish JD, Jinzaki M, Zou KH, et al: Multi–detector row CT urography: Comparison of strategies for depicting the normal urinary collecting system. Radiology 2002;225:783.

Messing EM, Catalona W: Urothelial tumors of the urinary tract. In Walsh PC, Retik AD, Vaughan ED, et al, eds: Campbell's Urology, 7th ed. Philadelphia, WB Saunders, 1998:2327.

Munoz JJ, Ellison LM: Upper tract neoplasms: Incidence and survival during the last 2 decades. J Urol 2000;164:1523.

Park S, Hong B, Kim CS, Ahn H: The impact of tumor localization on prognosis of transitional cell carcinoma of the upper urinary tract. J Urol 2004;171:621.

Solsona E, Iborra I, Rirus JV, et al: Upper urinary tract involvement in patients with bladder carcinoma in situ (CIS): Its impact on management. Urology 1997;49:347.

Tawfiek ER, Bagley D: Upper-tract transitional cell carcinoma. Urology 1997;50:321.

# 49 | Management of Urothelial Tumors of the Renal Pelvis and Ureter

ARTHUR I. SAGALOWSKY, MD • THOMAS W. JARRETT, MD

OPEN NEPHRON-SPARING SURGERY FOR RENAL PELVIS TUMORS: PYELOTOMY AND TUMOR ABLATION AND PARTIAL NEPHRECTOMY

OPEN RADICAL NEPHROURETERECTOMY

LAPAROSCOPIC RADICAL NEPHROURETERECTOMY

OPEN SEGMENTAL URETERECTOMY

ENDOSCOPIC TREATMENT

ISOLATED UPPER TRACT CYTOLOGIC ABNORMALITY OR URINARY MARKER

ADJUVANT THERAPY

FOLLOW-UP

TREATMENT OF METASTATIC DISEASE

least ablative treatment necessary for safe control of the tumor is preferred. Most upper tract urothelial tumors are not large or bulky. Thus, laparoscopic surgery is ideal, at least for the renal portion of radical nephroureterectomy when the tumor warrants removal of the entire renal unit (see later). A variety of approaches with various combinations of laparoscopic and open techniques are employed for distal ureterectomy. Low-grade noninvasive upper tract tumors are managed initially by ablative renal-sparing surgery. Retrograde ureteroscopy and ureteropyeloscopy are preferred when tumor size, number, and access allow complete tumor ablation. Percutaneous antegrade tumor ablation is chosen when the anatomy and the tumor do not allow complete ablation through a retrograde approach.

## KEY POINT: UPPER TRACT UROTHELIAL TUMORS

■ The frequency of urothelial tumors of the upper tract is increasing.

The treatment of upper tract urothelial tumors has undergone significant changes. **The relatively low frequency of these lesions and the lack of prospective randomized trials do not permit absolute conclusions about treatment impact on outcomes.** In the past, treatment recommendations were based, at least in part, on practical limitations in follow-up and detection of local disease recurrence. Technologic improvements in imaging and, most important, direct endoscopic visualization of all levels of the urinary tract allow earlier and more accurate initial diagnosis and treatment and improved follow-up. Treatment may be based primarily on the risk the tumor poses and on the efficacy of a specific treatment rather than on other considerations. The specific indications and techniques for each form of treatment (open versus laparoscopic radical nephroureterectomy; open versus retrograde endoscopic versus percutaneous renal-sparing tumor ablation) are addressed later in this chapter. However, the following introductory considerations apply. The least invasive and

**The frequency of urothelial tumors of the upper tract is increasing,** even though the tumors represent only a small percentage of all urothelial neoplasms (McCarron et al, 1982; Richie, 1988; Williams, 1991; Herr, 1998; Messing and Catalona, 1998; Munoz and Ellison, 2000). The incidence of ureteral and renal pelvis tumors in the United States from 1985 to 1994 was 0.73 and 1.0 each per 100,000 person-years, respectively, based on the National Cancer Institute Surveillance, Epidemiology, and End Results (SEER) database (Munoz and Ellison, 2000). The 5-year disease-specific survival was 75% overall and 95%, 88.9%, 62.5%, and 16.5% for in situ, localized, regional, and distant disease, respectively. Several factors account for this increase. Survival of patients with the more prevalent transitional cell carcinoma of the bladder is improved owing to more effective diagnosis and treatment. This produces a length-time bias of longer time at risk for development of upper tract tumors.

The etiology, natural history, pathology, detection, and staging of urothelial tumors are presented in Chapter 75. Only the features that differentiate upper tract tumors from bladder tumors and that are pertinent to treatment are revisited here. The common symptoms of localized disease (hematuria, dysuria) and of advanced upper tract tumors (weight loss, fatigue, anemia, bone pain) are similar in type and frequency to those of bladder cancer. However, flank pain due to obstruction by tumor or clot is more prevalent in upper tract tumors, having been reported in 10% to 40% of cases (Babaian and Johnson, 1980; McCarron et al, 1983; Richie, 1988; Williams, 1991; Melamed and Reuter, 1993). Flank pain in patients with upper tract tumors does not correlate with either locally advanced tumor stage or worse prognosis, as is the case with bladder cancer.

A filling defect is the most common finding on imaging studies. The impact of hydronephrosis and nonvisualization for renal pelvis tumors versus ureteral tumors as indicators of a higher stage is uncertain. Nonvisualization is reported in 20% of renal pelvis tumors, only 33% of which are invasive (McCarron et al, 1983). Nonvisualization is reported in 37% to 45% of ureteral tumors and carried a 60% risk of invasion in one series (McCarron et al, 1983). In other reports, there is no correlation of nonvisualization and stage (Batata and Grabstald, 1976; Anderstrom et al, 1989). Hydronephrosis with or without an associated filling defect is linked with invasion in 80% of ureteral tumors (McCarron et al, 1983).

The histologic characteristics and biology of upper tract tumors still affect treatment decisions, technologic improvements notwithstanding. The entity of benign papilloma, which responds favorably regardless of the extent of treatment, is well described in older series of upper tract tumors (Bloom et al, 1970; Batata and Grabstald, 1976). The existence of similar low-grade papillomas of low-grade malignant potential in the bladder remains controversial (Cheng et al, 1999; Cheng and Bostwick, 2000; Oyasu, 2000). It is unclear whether the differences between upper tract papillomas and bladder papillomas are biologic or semantic. **Approximately 85% of renal pelvis tumors are papillary;** the remainder are sessile. This distribution is similar to that of bladder tumors. However, the stage of upper tract tumors is T1 or T2 in approximately 50% of papillary and 80% of sessile lesions, respectively (Cummings, 1980; Richie, 1988; Williams, 1991). Thus, 50% to 60% of renal pelvis tumors are invasive, in contrast to most bladder tumors, which are noninvasive; 55% to 75% of ureteral tumors are low grade and low stage, but invasion is still more common than among bladder tumors (Anderstrom et al, 1989; Williams, 1991). Patients with upper tract tumors present most often in the sixth or seventh decade of life and thus are generally older than patients with bladder tumors (Melamed and Reuter, 1993).

Tumors of the renal pelvis are slightly more common than ureteral tumors (Batata and Grabstald, 1976; Richie, 1988; Maulard-Durdux et al, 1996). Ureteral tumors occur in the distal, middle, and proximal segments in 70%, 25%, and 5% of cases, respectively (Babaian and Johnson, 1980; Anderstrom et al, 1989; Williams, 1991; Messing and Catalona, 1998). **After conservative treatment, ipsilateral upper tract tumor recurrence is common in a proximal to distal direction and is seen in 33% to 55% of cases** (Mazeman, 1976; Johnson and Babaian, 1979; Babaian and Johnson, 1980; Cummings, 1980; McCarron et al, 1983). Recurrence proximal to the original lesion is rare.

**This high rate of ipsilateral recurrence is due in part to a multifocal field change,** which is even more pronounced than in bladder cancer. Areas of atypia, dysplasia, or carcinoma in situ are reported in 60% to 95% of specimens after nephroureterectomy for renal pelvis tumor (Johansson et al, 1976; Kakizoe et al, 1980; Heney et al, 1981; Nocks et al, 1982; McCarron et al, 1983; Melamed and Reuter, 1993). Molecular techniques demonstrate that downward seeding of tumor accounts for some recurrences (Harris and Neal, 1992). Tumor multifocality does not lessen survival of patients independent of stage (Messing and Catalona, 1998).

**The occurrence of bladder tumors after upper tract tumors, and vice versa, is another expression of the field change, multifocal risk that affects initial treatment decisions.** Carcinoma in situ is present in the distal ureter at the time of cystectomy in 7% to 25% of cases (Melamed and Reuter, 1993; Solsona et al, 1997; Herr, 1998); 15% to 50% of all cases of upper tract tumor occur in patients with a history of bladder tumor (Batata and Grabstald, 1976; Babaian and Johnson, 1980). The incidence of upper tract tumor after bladder tumor is 2% to 4% with a mean time to occurrence of 70 months (Shinka et al, 1988; Oldbring et al, 1989; Melamed and Reuter, 1993; Herr et al, 1996). Upper tract tumors are reported in 3% to 9% of patients after cystectomy for bladder cancer in older series (Zincke and Neves, 1984; Mufti et al, 1988).

Particular insight into the contemporary risk for upper tract tumor after treatment of bladder cancer is provided in several large series (Solsona et al, 1997; Herr, 1998; Rabbani et al, 2001; Mullerad et al, 2004; Sved et al, 2004). Herr found that among 307 patients with bladder tumor followed up for a median of 12 years, there was an overall incidence of upper tract tumors of 23%. The cumulative risks for upper tract tumors were 10%, 26%, and 34% at follow-ups of 5 years, 5 to 10 years, and 15 years, respectively. Upper tract tumors occurred in 26% of another subgroup of 87 patients with bladder tumor followed up for more than 15 years. Delayed upper tract tumors were more common in the ureter than in the renal pelvis and appeared at a median follow-up of 56 months. Median time to delayed ureteral versus renal pelvis tumors was 40 months versus 67 months, respectively. Ureteral tumors occurred in 29% of 66 patients who were successfully treated with intravesical bacille Calmette-Guérin (BCG) for carcinoma in situ. In a subset of 105 patients who underwent cystectomy for BCG-refractory carcinoma in situ, ureteral carcinoma in situ was present in the distal, juxtavesical, and intramural portions of the ureter in 35%, 68%, and 81% of cases, respectively. In a retrospective study from the same center, treatment outcome in patients with upper tract tumor was worse in patients with a prior history of bladder cancer (superficial or invasive) independent of upper tumor stage (Mullerad et al, 2004). Similarly, Sved and colleagues (2004) reported upper tract tumors in 2% of patients (5 of 235) observed for a mean of 42 months after radical cystectomy for bladder cancer. Upper tract tumor was diagnosed at a mean follow-up of 39.6 months, because of hematuria in four cases and on routine intravenous urography in the remaining case. Presence of tumor in the prostatic urethra of the cystectomy specimen was the only initial tumor feature that was associated with a higher risk of subsequent upper tract tumor. This may be a predictor of a higher risk of multifocal tumor in such cases. Outcome was poor with disease-related mortality in four of the cases. In contrast, in a review of 91,245 patients with bladder cancer from the SEER database for 1973 to 1996, upper tract tumor occurred in 657 patients (0.7%) at a median follow-up of 4.1 years (Rabbani et al, 2001). These patients had lower tumor stage and improved disease-specific survival than did patients with primary upper tract tumors.

Solsona and colleagues (1997) reported that carcinoma in situ was present in the distal ureter in 25% of 138 cystectomies performed for bladder carcinoma in situ, compared with only 2.3% and 2.9% among 786 and 179 cases of stage Ta to T1 versus stage T2 disease, respectively. This may indicate that bladder carcinoma in situ carries a higher risk of multifocal disease than do other forms of bladder tumor.

The incidence of bladder tumor after treatment of upper tract tumor is 20% to 75% (Batata and Grabstald, 1976; Kakizoe et al, 1980; Nocks et al, 1982; Huben et al, 1988; Anderstrom et al, 1989; Williams, 1991; Melamed and Reuter, 1993; Kang et al, 2003; Matsui et al, 2005). Bladder tumor after upper tract tumor occurs earlier than the reverse, at a median of 21 months versus 86 months afterward, respectively. Both bladder tumor and contralateral upper tract tumor after initial unilateral upper tract tumor are examples of the multifocal nature of urothelial tumor. In one study, subsequent bladder tumors appeared earlier than did contralateral upper tract tumors (Kang et al, 2003). Renal insufficiency was associated with a higher risk of contralateral upper tract tumor.

The occurrence of bladder tumor after treatment of upper tract tumor may be due to a field effect, distal tumor seeding, or both. Association of a higher bladder tumor incidence after upper tract tumor multiplicity supports a role of distal seeding (Matsui et al, 2005). However, reports of distinct tumor clones by microsatellite analysis support a field effect (Takahashi et al, 2001). The paradoxical finding that the risk of subsequent bladder tumor is inversely related to upper tract tumor size and stage may reflect a higher and earlier risk of death from the primary tumor in these cases.

**Two particular forms of upper tract urothelial tumor, those seen in Balkan nephropathy and those seen in association with analgesic abuse, have an even higher tendency to multiple and bilateral recurrences than do sporadic tumors** (Markovic, 1972; Petkovic, 1975; Mahoney et al, 1977; Johansson and Wahlquist, 1979; Melamed and Reuter, 1993; Stewart et al, 1999). The typically low-grade nature of the tumors and the frequent renal insufficiency seen in Balkan nephropathy underscore the importance of conservative treatment when possible. The degree of scarring of renal papillae seen in phenacetin abuse correlates in a dose-dependent manner with the risk of high tumor grade and progression. Calcification of renal papillae after analgesic abuse is associated with development of squamous carcinoma of the renal pelvis (Stewart et al, 1999).

**The staging of upper tract tumors parallels the staging of bladder tumors** as presented in Chapter 75. There is a strong

### Table 49-1. Correlation of Tumor Stage and Grade for Upper Tract Urothelial Tumors

| Location and Stage | High Grade (%) |
|---|---|
| Pelvis | |
| Low | 5 |
| High | 91 |
| Ureter | |
| Low | 26 |
| High | 64 |

Data from McCarron JP Jr, Mills C, Vaughn ED Jr: Tumors of the renal pelvis and ureter: Current concepts and management. Semin Urol 1983;1:75-81.

### Table 49-2. Literature Review of Survival of Patients with Upper Tract Urothelial Tumors

| Tumor | 5-Year Survival (%) |
|---|---|
| Grade | |
| 1-2 | 40-87 |
| 3-4 | 0-33 |
| T stage | |
| a, 1, cis | 60-90 |
| 2 | 43-75 |
| 3 | 16-33 |
| 4 | 0-5 |
| N+ | 0-4 |
| M+ | 0 |

correlation of grade and stage for upper tract tumors (Table 49-1). **The single most important determinant of outcome is tumor stage** (Table 49-2) (Bloom et al, 1970; Grabstald et al, 1971; Batata et al, 1975; Wagle et al, 1975; Babaian and Johnson, 1980; Cummings, 1980; McCarron et al, 1983; Huben et al, 1988; Anderstrom et al, 1989; Guinan et al, 1992b; Terrell et al, 1995; Messing and Catalona, 1998). The evolving understanding of molecular predictors of behavior for upper tract urothelial cancer parallels that for bladder cancer. In a recent publication, decreased p63 immunoreactivity and p53 overexpression in upper tract tumors were significantly associated with advanced tumor stage and poor prognosis (Zigeuner et al, 2004). However, these findings were not independent of stage and grade in multivariate analysis.

## KEY POINTS: STAGING OF UPPER TRACT TUMORS

- Staging of upper tract tumors parallels that of bladder cancer.

- Stage is the most important determinant of outcome.

The primary tumor characteristics that suggest invasion, the high incidence of ipsilateral multifocal abnormality, and the risk of recurrence distal to the primary lesion are all offered in support of radical excision of large, proximal, and likely invasive tumors of the upper tract. Conversely, the same risks of multiple recurrence and the fact that tumor stage is the main determinant of outcome support conservative nephron-sparing surgery in many cases.

Upper tract tumors spread in the same ways as bladder tumors do, through lymphatic and hematogenous routes and by direct extension into contiguous structures. Thus, **the common metastatic sites are the lungs, liver, bones, and regional lymph nodes.** Preoperative evaluation for the extent of disease includes chest radiography, abdominal computed tomography, liver function tests, and occasional bone scan. The thin muscle layer of the renal pelvis and ureter may allow earlier penetration of invasive upper tract tumors than is seen in bladder neoplasms (Cummings, 1980; Richie, 1988). However, this is not a valid reason for radical versus conservative treatment if a lesion is either noninvasive or invasive and organ confined (stage T2) (Gittes, 1980). The renal parenchyma may be a barrier, slowing distant spread of stage T3 renal pelvis tumors. In contrast, periureteral tumor extension carries a high risk of early tumor dissemination along the periureteral vascular and lymphatic supply. Improved survival of patients with stage T3 renal pelvis tumors versus ureteral tumors has been reported by several investigators (Batata and Grabstald, 1976; Guinan et al, 1992a; Park et al, 2004). Guinan and colleagues confirmed this observation among 611 patients treated at 97 hospitals and in a collection of 250 cases reported in the literature (Guinan et al, 1992a). The 5-year survival rates for patients with stage T3 tumors of the renal pelvis and ureter were 54% and 24%, respectively. In a multivariate analysis, patients with ureteral tumors had a higher local and distant failure rate than did those with renal pelvis tumors of the same stage and grade (Park et al, 2004). Renal pelvis and upper ureteral tumors spread initially to para-aortic and paracaval nodes, whereas distal ureteral tumors spread to pelvic nodes (Batata et al, 1975; Heney et al, 1981; Nocks et al, 1982; McCarron et al, 1983; Mahadevia et al, 1983; Jitsukawa et al, 1985; Geiger et al, 1986).

## OPEN NEPHRON-SPARING SURGERY FOR RENAL PELVIS TUMORS: PYELOTOMY AND TUMOR ABLATION AND PARTIAL NEPHRECTOMY
### Indications

**Open conservative surgery may be applied in selected cases when nephron sparing for preservation of renal function is required** (Gittes, 1966, 1980; Petkovic, 1972a, 1972b; Mazeman, 1976; Johnson and Babaian, 1979; Babaian and Johnson, 1980; Cummings, 1980; Wallace et al, 1981; Tomera et al, 1982; McCarron et al, 1983; Zincke and Neves, 1984; Bazeed et al, 1986; Ziegelbaum et al, 1987; Messing and Catalona, 1998). Tumor in a solitary kidney, synchronous bilateral tumors, and predisposition to form multiple recurrences, as in endemic Balkan nephropathy, are all reasons to consider nephron sparing (Fig. 49–1). Pyeloscopy as an initial diagnostic component to open conservative surgery has been supplanted by retrograde or percutaneous antegrade renal endoscopy (Huffman et al, 1985). Direct endoscopic visualization of the lesion and biopsy with cup forceps or brush establish a definitive diagnosis and tumor grade (Gill et al, 1973). The brush biopsy has renewed value because tissue obtained by small cup biopsy forceps used through narrow-caliber flexible endoscopes is limited. Preoperative determi-

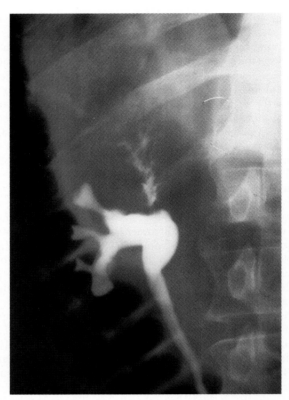

**Figure 49–1.** Patient with an invasive tumor of the upper calyx of a solitary kidney. The patient elected an upper pole partial nephrectomy.

nation of the stage of renal pelvis tumors remains difficult. Large size, broad base, and nonpapillary pattern favor tumor invasiveness. These improvements in initial diagnosis and assessment of tumor stage and grade allow more specific treatment, including conservative surgery when it is indicated.

The documented risk of wound implantation by tumor is low after open conservative surgery if simple precautions are followed to minimize spillage (Gittes, 1980; Tomera et al, 1982; McCarron et al, 1983). Modern percutaneous antegrade renal surgery allows resection of virtually any lesion formerly treated by open pyeloscopy, and the risk of tumor spillage is even lower (see following discussion).

### Technique

Preoperative arteriography is not routinely obtained. However, it may be helpful before partial nephrectomy of rare hypervascular renal pelvis tumors. The affected segmental renal artery may be embolized or more easily identified at the time of surgery on the basis of the arteriogram.

The patient is placed in either a full flank or a torque position, as shown in Chapter 50. The full flank position provides optimal exposure to the renal pelvis for pyelotomy and excision of a large noninvasive tumor. The torque position allows both anterior and posterior exposure to the renal pedicle for partial nephrectomy. An extrapleural, extraperitoneal flank, or thoracoabdominal incision is made. Removal of a portion of the 11th or 12th rib provides maximal exposure to the kidney and aids in mobilization of the upper pole and in gaining access to the renal vessels. Removal of a rib is especially helpful in obese patients or in those with a high kidney. An incision off the tip of the 12th rib suffices in thin patients with a low kidney and is accompanied by less potential wound discomfort or morbidity. After the incision is completed, Gerota's fascia is opened posteriorly, and the entire kidney is mobilized. The renal vessels and the ureter are each isolated with a vessel loop.

The wound is packed with dry sponges to isolate the kidney before any intrarenal incisions are made. For pyelotomy and tumor excision, the renal pelvis and the major calyceal infundibula are exposed by dissecting the hilar and renal sinus fat as for an extended pyelolithotomy. A gentle curvilinear incision is made in the renal pelvis, and the tumor is excised; the base is cauterized with electrocautery, laser, or argon beam coagulator. Finally, the pelvis is closed with 4-0 chromic catgut or other absorbable suture.

The techniques of partial nephrectomy for renal pelvis tumors are essentially the same as those described in Chapter 50, with the added proviso of taking care to minimize the risk of tumor spillage. The involved segment of the intrarenal collecting system is clamped before removal of the tumor-bearing portion of the kidney is begun. The collecting system of the renal remnant is closed with absorbable 4-0 suture. Identified individual bleeding points are oversewn with 4-0 vascular Prolene or polydioxanone suture. Additional hemostasis is provided by use of electrocautery and the argon beam coagulator on the raw parenchymal surface. The edges of the renal defect and the adjoining renal capsule are approximated over Surgicel bolsters with 2-0 chromic catgut suture.

A suction drain is placed in the renal bed in all cases. A temporary urinary diversion stent is not used routinely unless difficulty is encountered in closing the collecting system.

## Results

The reported overall risk of tumor recurrence in the ipsilateral renal pelvis after initial pyelotomy or partial nephrectomy varies from 7% to 60% (Mazeman, 1976; Murphy et al, 1980, 1981; Wallace et al, 1981; McCarron et al, 1983; Zincke and Neves, 1984; Ziegelbaum et al, 1987; Messing and Catalona, 1998). The risk of recurrence after conservative surgery increases with tumor stage from less than 10% for grade 1 to 28% to 60% for grades 2 and 3. The moderate to high risk of recurrence primarily reflects the inherent multifocal atypia and field change of the renal pelvis (Heney et al, 1981; Nocks et al, 1982; Mahadevia et al, 1983; McCarron et al, 1983). The possibility of incomplete initial treatment of the primary tumor cannot be totally excluded.

Estimates of overall and cancer-specific survival after conservative surgery of renal pelvis tumors are hampered by the lack of prospective, controlled, randomized trials and the small numbers of affected patients. The inherent bias introduced by selection of patients for conservative treatment based on medical comorbidities is another variable. Murphy reported 5-year survival of 75% and 2-year survival of 46% after conservative surgery in patients with grade 1 and grade 2 renal pelvis tumors, respectively (Murphy et al, 1980). McCarron and associates reported rates of cures, cancer-related deaths, and deaths due to unrelated causes of 33% each in nine patients who underwent conservative surgery

(McCarron et al, 1983). **Radical nephroureterectomy and dialysis still offer the best chance of cure and survival in patients with a large, invasive, high-grade, organ-confined renal pelvis tumor (T2, N0, M0) in a solitary kidney** (Gittes, 1980; McCarron et al, 1983).

## OPEN RADICAL NEPHROURETERECTOMY
### Indications

**Radical nephroureterectomy with excision of a bladder cuff is recommended for large, high-grade, invasive tumors of the renal pelvis and proximal ureter** (Batata and Grabstald, 1976; Skinner, 1978; Babaian and Johnson, 1980; Cummings, 1980; Murphy et al, 1981; Nocks et al, 1982; McCarron et al, 1983; Richie, 1988; Williams, 1991; Messing and Catalona, 1998). Radical surgery also retains a role in treatment of medium-grade, noninvasive tumors of the renal pelvis and upper ureter when they are large, multifocal, or rapidly recurring despite maximal efforts at conservative surgery.

> ### KEY POINT: INDICATIONS FOR RADICAL NEPHROURETERECTOMY
>
> ■ The treatment of large, invasive tumors of the renal pelvis and proximal ureter is radical nephroureterectomy with removal of a bladder cuff.

## Technique
### Choice of Incision

Radical nephroureterectomy may be performed through a variety of approaches. The choice of incision is largely one of the surgeon's preference and is based on the surgeon's experience, the patient's body habitus and medical comorbidities, and the size of the kidney. The operation may be performed through one incision with the patient placed in a flank torque position as shown in Chapter 50 and as described in the section on open nephron-sparing surgery (Fig. 49–2). In male patients, the genitalia are included in the surgical field so that the bladder catheter may be accessed during the procedure. An extrapleural, extraperitoneal, thoracoabdominal incision is begun over the 11th or 12th rib or off the tip of the 12th rib as described earlier. In contrast to the incision for partial nephrectomy, for which adequate exposure to the kidney is the primary concern, the lower ureter and the bladder must also be exposed for nephroureterectomy. Thus, the middle and anterior portions of the skin incision angle down toward the pelvis rather than in a subcostal direction (see Fig. 49–2). The peritoneum may be opened at any time to increase exposure as necessary. The thoracoabdominal approach offers the best exposure to the kidney but may cause a greater degree of postoperative atelectasis than the anterior subcostal approach. This may be an important consideration in patients with chronic lung disease.

The operation may also be performed through a single long midline incision and intraperitoneal exposure. However, exposure to the kidney is limited from this approach, particularly for left-sided tumors.

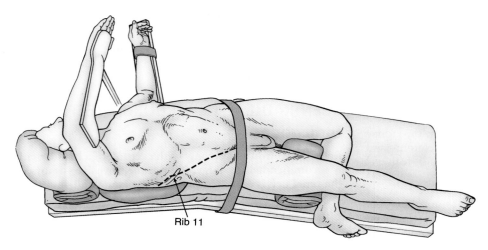

**Figure 49-2.** Patient in torque flank position for radical nephroureterectomy through a single thoracoabdominal incision. The shoulder girdle is rotated into a full flank position. The pelvic girdle is rolled back nearly to a supine position. All potential pressure points are carefully padded.

Rib 11

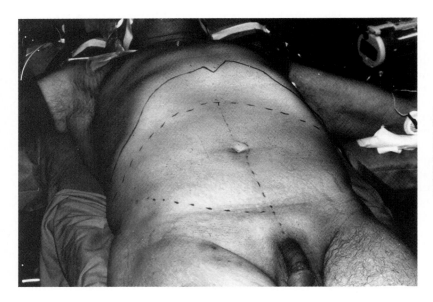

**Figure 49-3.** Radical nephroureterectomy may be performed through a long midline incision or through a subcostal plus Gibson, lower midline, or Pfannenstiel incision. The patient is supine, and the table is mildly flexed. Placement of a small roll under the edge of the rib cage is helpful. (From Sagalowsky AI: Renal transplantation and autotransplantation. In Marshall F, ed: The Textbook of Operative Urology. Philadelphia, WB Saunders, 1996:320-330.)

Alternatively, the patient may be positioned supine with a small roll placed behind the rib cage on the affected side. The nephroureterectomy is performed through an upper anterior subcostal incision and a lower quadrant Gibson incision as for renal transplantation. A lower midline or Pfannenstiel incision may be substituted (Fig. 49–3). A lower midline incision avoids dividing muscles, is fast, and provides direct exposure to the prevesical space. However, a Gibson incision provides easier exposure to the distal ureter. Nephrectomy may be difficult from an anterior subcostal approach in obese patients.

## Radical Nephrectomy

The entire kidney, along with all the perinephric fat and Gerota's fascia, is fully mobilized (Figs. 49–4 and 49–5). The renal vessels are dissected and individually secured and divided in a standard manner. The authors prefer at least one 0 silk tie and 4-0 vascular Prolene suture ligature on an RB needle for each renal artery and renal vein. Combinations of ties plus large hemoclips may be substituted for the suture ligature. The adrenal is a not-infrequent site of metastasis for urothelial tumor. Traditionally, the ipsilateral adrenal gland has been included with the specimen. However, as in the case of renal cell carcinoma, **adrenalectomy adds little to the cure for upper tract tumors.** One may omit adrenalectomy if the gland appears normal on preoperative imaging studies and is grossly normal at the time of surgery and if the disease seems localized within the renal pelvis. However, adrenalectomy is prudent for maximal control if locally advanced disease is discovered.

## Distal Ureterectomy

Complete distal ureterectomy with a bladder cuff is necessary with nephroureterectomy and represents a distinct portion of the case, whether an open or laparoscopic approach to the kidney is used. General principles include intact complete ureteral excision with controlled occlusion of the ureteral orifice. **The entire distal ureter, including the intramural portion and the ureteral orifice, is removed.** Failure to completely remove the entire distal ureter and ureteral orifice is associated with a high rate of tumor recurrence. The ureter may be kept in continuity with the kidney to obviate the risk of tumor spillage from the lumen. However, the attached

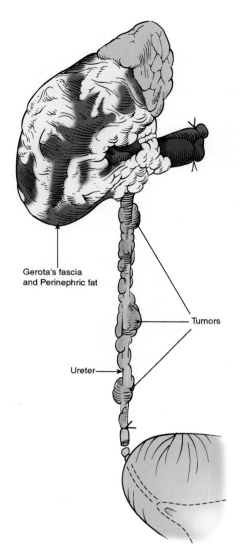

Gerota's fascia
and Perinephric fat

Tumors

Ureter

**Figure 49–4.** Radical nephroureterectomy specimen including the kidney, Gerota's fascia, and perinephric fat, with or without the ipsilateral adrenal gland. Note that the ureter is divided distally in the pelvis between ties for a separate distal ureterectomy.

kidney is cumbersome, and this technique is not necessary as long as the distal ureter is divided between ties or clips at a location that is free of gross abnormality. Following are the options available for management of the distal ureter, whether an open or laparoscopic approach is used. If a laparoscopic approach is chosen, the incision can be placed to facilitate both intact specimen extraction and dissection of the distal ureter. One should keep in mind that transitional cell carcinoma is a tumor that has the potential to seed nonurothelial surfaces, and maintenance of a "closed system" is important, especially with high-grade tumors.

**Traditional Open Distal Ureterectomy.** This can be done through Gibson, low midline, and Pfannenstiel incisions, depending on the patient's anatomy and the extent of proximal ureteral dissection required. Transvesical, extravesical, and combined approaches have been described. The transvesical approach is the most reliable approach for ensuring

complete ureteral excision. An anterior cystotomy may be made and intravesical and extravesical dissection performed as for ureteral neocystostomy (Fig. 49–6); 1 cm of bladder mucosa is included circumferentially around the ureteral orifice. The defect in the bladder wall at the ureteral hiatus is closed in two layers from within the bladder with interrupted 2-0 or 3-0 absorbable suture on the muscle and 4-0 suture on the mucosa. The anterior cystotomy is closed carefully in two layers with running 3-0 absorbable suture. The urethral catheter is maintained for 5 to 7 days; a suprapubic catheter is not routinely used. A flat suction drain is left in the perivesical space.

Complete distal ureterectomy may be performed entirely by extravesical (Fig. 49–7) dissection of the distal ureter and the intramural portion within the bladder wall all the way to the ureteral orifice. The need for a cystotomy is avoided with this approach. The ureter is tented up, and the bladder mucosa is divided between clamps. The defect in the bladder wall is closed in layers as described previously. Care must be taken to ensure a complete dissection of the intramural portion of the ureter and to avoid contralateral injury from excessive traction.

**Transurethral Resection of the Ureteral Orifice.** This approach, also referred to as the pluck technique, should be reserved for proximal, low-grade tumors (Abercrombie et al, 1988; Palou et al, 2000). The patient is placed in the lithotomy position, and the ureteral orifice and intramural ureter are aggressively resected to the extravesical space (Fig. 49–8). The patient is then positioned for the nephrectomy portion of the procedure, in which dissection must extend down to the perivesical space. The advantage is avoidance of a second incision in performing an open nephroureterectomy. The advantages are less apparent with laparoscopic nephrectomy, in which an incision is necessary for specimen extraction, and this can be used for dissection of the distal ureter. In addition, there is exposure of nonurothelial surfaces, which may predispose to local recurrence, especially with more dysplastic tumor (Jones and Moisey, 1993; Arango et al, 1997).

**Intussusception (Stripping) Technique.** Several variations of this procedure have been described (McDonald, 1953; Clayman et al, 1983; Roth et al, 1996; Angulo et al, 1998). Basically, a ureteral catheter is placed in the ipsilateral ureter at the beginning of the procedure. The nephrectomy portion of the procedure is carried out, and the ureter is dissected as far distally as possible. The ureter is then ligated and transected with the ureteral catheter secured to the proximal end of the distal ureter (Fig. 49–9). After nephrectomy, the patient is moved to the lithotomy position; the ureter is intussuscepted by traction into the bladder, and a resectoscope is used to excise the bladder cuff and free the ureter from the bladder. Concerns with this technique are presented by Giovansili and associates (2004), who described a failure rate of 18.7% in which there may have been disruption of the ureter and the need for an additional surgical incision.

**Transvesical Laparoscopic Ligation and Detachment Technique.** This technique most closely mimics the open technique. Before the nephrectomy portion of the procedure, the patient is placed in the low lithotomy position, a ureteral catheter is placed, and two suprapubic 3-mm trocars

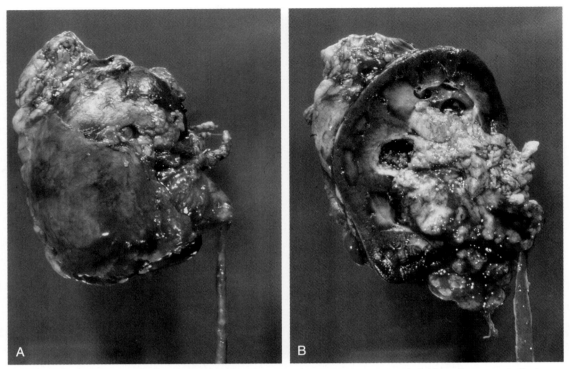

**Figure 49–5.** **A,** Intact nephroureterectomy specimen for a large renal pelvis tumor. **B,** Bivalved specimen reveals the tumor.

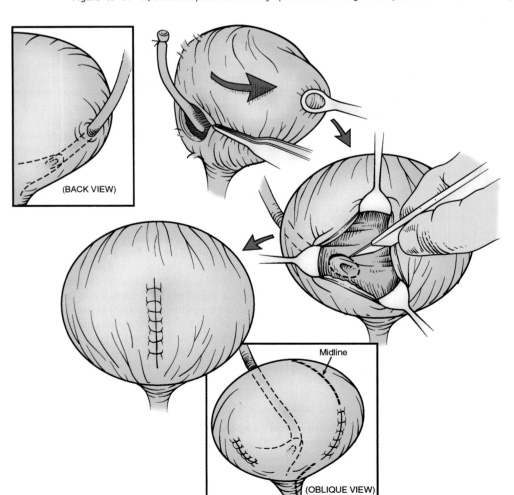

**Figure 49–6.** Complete distal ureterectomy with bladder cuff is performed by combined extravesical and transvesical dissection.

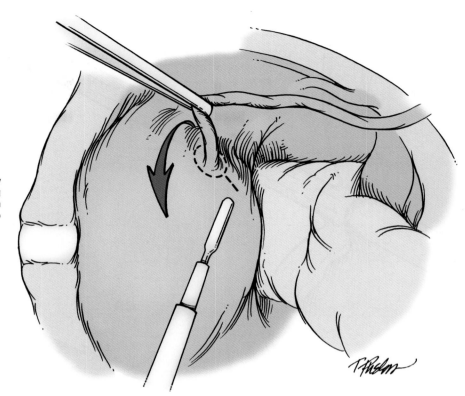

**Figure 49–7.** Complete distal ureterectomy by extravesical approach. Traction is placed, everting the orifice outside the bladder. Care must be taken to ensure complete removal and to avoid injury to the contralateral ureteral orifice.

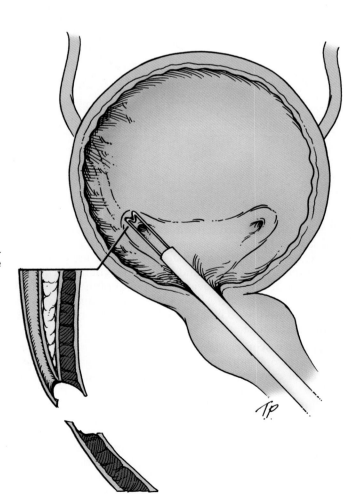

**Figure 49–8.** The entire orifice and intramural ureter are resected transurethrally until the extravesical fat is seen. This portion is usually done at the beginning but can be done at the end of the procedure.

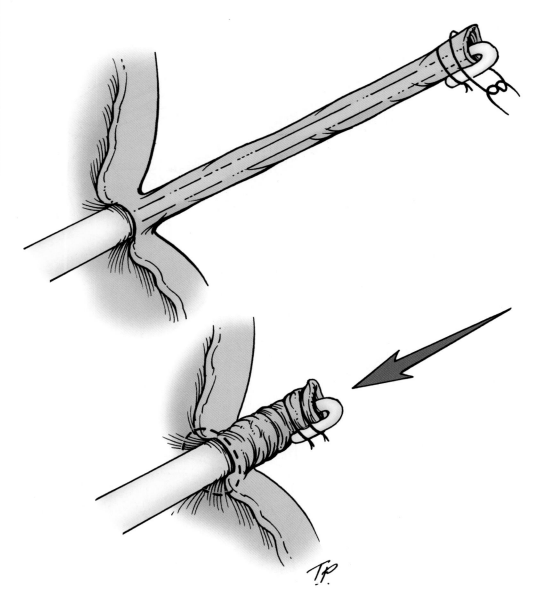

**Figure 49–9.** With the intussusception technique, a ureteral catheter is placed at the beginning of the case. After nephrectomy, the ureter is divided, and the catheter is secured to the distal portion of the ureter. The patient is moved to the lithotomy position, and the ureter is intussuscepted into the bladder with retrograde traction. A resectoscope is used to excise the attached orifice.

(Fig. 49–10) are placed transvesically. The ureter is tented up, and a loop ligature is placed around the catheter and the orifice, creating a "closed" system. A Collins knife circumscribes the ureteral orifice, and further dissection is facilitated by the grasper, which provides traction until the extravesical space is reached. There has been excellent clinical success reported with this technique (Gill et al, 1999), but it can be technically difficult.

**Total Laparoscopic.** Flexible cystoscopy is performed before the laparoscopic portion of the case, and a Bugbee electrode is used to cauterize the orifice and intramural ureter completely. Cauterization of the intramural portion of the ureter is important for identification of the distal limits of the dissection during the laparoscopic portion of the procedure. A 20 or 22 French Foley catheter is placed before proceeding to the laparoscopic portion. The nephrectomy and ureteral dissection are carried down to the detrusor muscle. Antegrade traction is placed on the ureter, everting the orifice out of the

bladder, and an endovascular stapling device is placed as distally as possible (Fig. 49–11). A flexible cystoscope can be placed at this time if there is any question of the adequacy of the specimen or concern of disturbance of the contralateral ureteral orifice. The endovascular stapling device is then deployed, laying two rows of staples on the bladder and specimen sides. This allows a closed system after division of the ureter.

## Lymphadenectomy

**Regional lymphadenectomy is included with radical nephroureterectomy.** For renal pelvis and proximal or middle ureteral tumors, the ipsilateral renal hilar nodes and the adjacent para-aortic or paracaval nodes are resected. This dissection adds little time or morbidity to the surgery. On occasion, lymphadenectomy is more hazardous in patients with severe atherosclerosis of the aorta or grossly positive and fixed nodes. Node dissection is limited or omitted in these cases.

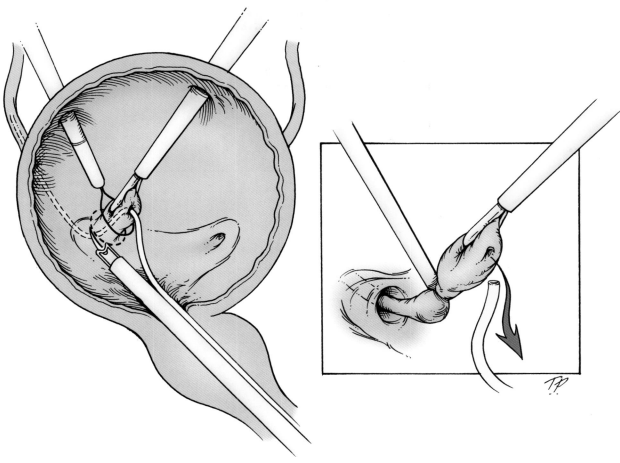

**Figure 49–10.** A ureteral catheter is placed, and two laparoscopic ports are placed transvesically. The ureteral orifice is tented up; a loop is placed around the orifice to occlude the opening and to place traction on the ureter. A Collins knife then facilitates the dissection to the extravesical space.

## KEY POINT: LYMPHADENECTOMY WITH RADICAL NEPHROURETERECTOMY

■ Regional lymphadenectomy is included with radical nephroureterectomy.

## Results

**The outcome strongly correlates with tumor stage and grade** as summarized in Table 49–2, compiled from numerous series. The role of complete distal ureterectomy with excision of a bladder cuff in radical nephroureterectomy for upper tract tumors is well established. The risk of tumor recurrence in a remaining ureteral stump is 30% to 75% (Bloom et al, 1970; Strong et al, 1976; Johansson and Wahlquist, 1979; Babaian and Johnson, 1980; Kakizoe et al, 1980; Mullen and Kovacs, 1980; McCarron et al, 1983). This risk is likely to remain or even to increase as the use of radical nephroureterectomy becomes more selective for patients, mainly those with higher risk tumors. All patients who underwent an extravesical dissection and tenting up of the ureter in

the series by Strong and associates retained a portion of the ureter and the ureteral orifice; this demonstrates that the transvesical dissection of the ureter must be thorough to avoid such an error. Complete ureterectomy with a bowel cuff should accompany nephroureterectomy of a renal unit draining into a urinary diversion. Mufti and coworkers (1988) reported a tumor recurrence rate of 37.5% when the ureteroenteric anastomosis was not removed.

**The need or benefit of radical nephroureterectomy versus simple nephrectomy or conservative nephron-sparing surgery is less well defined.** Radical nephroureterectomy is recommended as providing optimal chance for survival in numerous series (Batata et al, 1975; Johansson and Wahlquist, 1979; Murphy et al, 1980; McCarron et al, 1983; Zungri et al, 1990). Batata and colleagues reported that radical nephroureterectomy provided a 5-year survival rate of 23% among patients with locally advanced disease (stage T3 to T4, N1 to N2). Johansson and Wahlquist reported survival advantage at 5 years for radical versus simple nephrectomy of 84% versus 51%, respectively, and of 74% versus 37%, respectively, for patients with high-stage tumors only. McCarron and associates reported that the subgroup of patients with large, high-grade, but organ-confined disease obtained the most benefit from radical versus conservative surgery. The death rate due

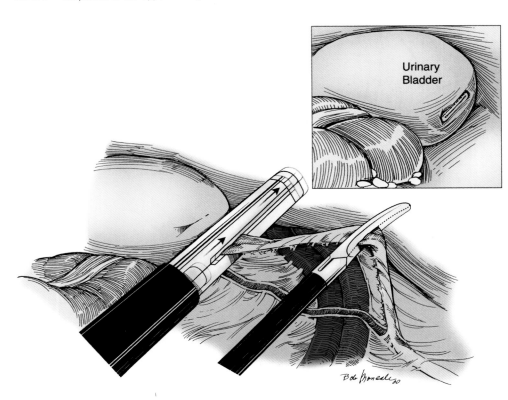

**Figure 49–11.** The ureter is dissected extravesically to the ureteral orifice. Lateral traction is placed on the ureter, everting the orifice, and the endovascular stapling device is placed at the distal margin, providing simultaneous ligation and division of the distal ureter at the level of the bladder. A cystoscope can be placed to ensure that the entire ureter is removed.

to tumor was 29% versus 89% for the radical and conservative surgery groups, respectively. In the series reported by Murphy, radical surgery conferred a survival advantage over conservative surgery at 5 years of 88% versus 75% for grade 1 tumors and of 90% versus 46% for grade 2 tumors. The retrospective, uncontrolled nature of all these series limits the conclusions that may be drawn. In summary, radical nephroureterectomy is warranted for patients with high-grade invasive disease that is organ confined (stage T1 to T2, N0) or is only locally advanced (stage T3 to T4, N0 to N2, M0). Tumor-free survival rates are high after radical nephroureterectomy for organ-confined disease and are guarded to poor for locally advanced disease. Treatment decisions in patients with compromised renal function must balance the potential beneficial effect of radical surgery on control of the tumor versus the morbidity, mortality, and quality of life risks associated with dialysis.

Regional lymphadenectomy is a recommended accompaniment of radical nephroureterectomy for upper tract tumors in multiple reports (Grabstald et al, 1971; Batata et al, 1975; Batata and Grabstald, 1976; Skinner, 1978; Johansson and Wahlquist, 1979; Babaian and Johnson, 1980; Cummings, 1980; Heney et al, 1981; McCarron et al, 1983; Richie, 1988; Williams, 1991; Messing and Catalona, 1998). However, the authors in nearly every one of these series find little therapeutic value from lymphadenectomy, and almost every patient with node-positive disease develops early distant metastases. **The rationale for continuing regional lymphadenectomy is that it adds little time or morbidity to the surgery, is important for prognosis, and may occasionally have therapeutic value.** In the series by Batata and Grabstald, 5-year survival

was seen in 23% of patients with completely resected stage T3 to T4, N1 to N2 disease. Earlier diagnosis in contemporary experience may identify more patients with limited nodal metastases who might benefit from radical surgery. Patients with proven nodal disease are obvious candidates for more careful follow-up and for trials exploring the role of adjuvant therapy.

## LAPAROSCOPIC RADICAL NEPHROURETERECTOMY

The indications for laparoscopic nephroureterectomy are the same as those for open nephroureterectomy. Laparoscopic nephroureterectomy can be performed by transperitoneal, retroperitoneal, and hand-assisted approaches. All show a significant decrease in morbidity compared with an open surgical approach for appropriately selected patients. All laparoscopic techniques involve two distinct portions of the procedure, nephrectomy and excision of the distal ureter with intact specimen extraction for accurate staging. Management of the distal ureter is described previously in the chapter. One should bear in mind several factors with laparoscopic nephroureterectomy, including the risk of tumor seeding from both the ureter and the bladder. For these reasons, removal of an intact specimen is desirable. The incision should be strategically placed for both extraction of the specimen and dissection of the distal ureter. Since an incision is necessary regardless of the approach chosen, some techniques for avoidance of a second incision for the distal ureter described previously have less utility.

# Technique

## Transperitoneal Laparoscopic Nephroureterectomy

**Laparoscopic Removal of Kidney Down to Midureter.** The patient is placed supine with the ipsilateral hip and shoulder rotated approximately 20 degrees (Fig. 49–12). The patient is secured to the table and can be easily moved from the flank position (nephrectomy portion) to the modified supine position (open portion) by rotating the operative table. The ipsilateral flank and urethra are prepared and draped, and a Foley catheter is placed before insufflation of the abdomen.

*Port Insertion and Configuration.* The abdomen is insufflated, and three or four trocars are placed as outlined in Figure 49–13, with the first usually being the lateral trocar. Subsequent trocars are placed under direct vision. With this configuration, the camera is kept at the umbilicus for the entire procedure. The upper midline and lateral trocars are used by the surgeon for the dissection of the kidney and the proximal half of the ureter. The lower midline and lateral trocars are used for the dissection of the distal ureter. A 3-mm

trocar just below the xiphoid can be helpful in retracting the spleen and liver for left- and right-sided lesions, respectively. The exception is with obese patients, when shifting of the trocars may be necessary to provide optimal visualization (Fig. 49–14).

*Mobilization of the Colon.* The table is rotated so the patient is in the flank position. The peritoneum is incised along the white line of Toldt from the level of the iliac vessels to the hepatic flexure on the right and to the splenic flexure on the left. The colon is moved medially by releasing the renocolic ligaments while leaving the lateral attachments of Gerota's fascia in place to prevent the kidney from "flopping" medially.

**Proximal Ureteronephrectomy.** The proximal ureter is identified, just medial to the lower pole of the kidney, and dissected toward the renal pelvis. If an invasive ureteral lesion is suspected, the dissection should include a wide margin of tissue. The renal hilum is identified, and its vessels are carefully exposed with a combination of blunt and sharp dissection. The artery is ligated and divided by use of a gastrointestinal stapling device with a vascular load or

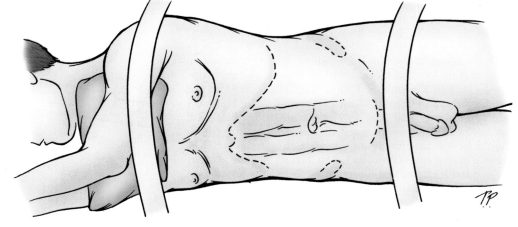

**Figure 49–12.** The patient is positioned on the table in a modified lateral decubitus position with the ipsilateral flank rotated up 15 degrees. The patient is secured to the table at the chest, waist, and lower extremity. This setup allows the patient to be moved to the full flank or supine position with simple rotation of the operating table. (From Jarrett TW: Laparoscopic nephroureterectomy. In Bishoff JT, Kavoussi LR, eds: Atlas of Laparoscopic Retroperitoneal Surgery. Philadelphia, WB Saunders, 2000:105.)

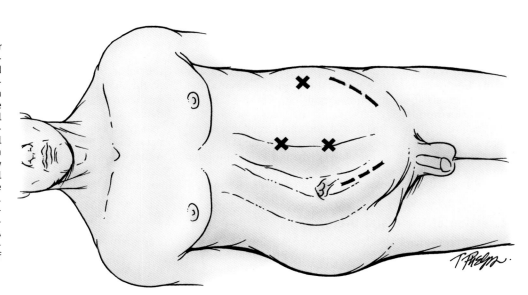

**Figure 49–13.** Port configuration for laparoscopic-assisted nephroureterectomy. Three ports are generally used for the kidney and upper ureteral dissection. A fourth midline port between the umbilicus and symphysis can be placed, if needed, for further ureteral dissection. The incision is then strategically placed to allow the distal ureteral dissection and specimen removal. The choice of incision largely depends on patient factors and level of dissection reached during the laparoscopic portion of the procedure. A low abdominal (midline or Pfannenstiel) incision is favored if the dissection is below the iliac vessels. A Gibson-type incision will give exposure of the more proximal ureter, if necessary.

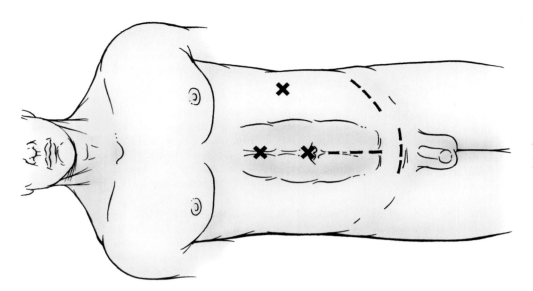

**Figure 49–14.** For obese patients, the trocars are shifted laterally to accommodate the increased distance from the kidney.

multiple clips. The renal vein is then divided in a similar fashion (Fig. 49–15). With vascular control ensured, the kidney is dissected free, either inside or outside Gerota's fascia, depending on the tumor location and stage. For upper pole lesions thought to invade the parenchyma, the ipsilateral adrenal should be removed.

The ureteral dissection is continued distally, keeping in mind that the ureteral blood supply is generally anteromedially located in the proximal third, medially located in the middle third, and laterally located in the distal third. Dissection of the lower half may require placement of the fourth trocar. In the area of primary disease, surrounding tissue should be left to provide an adequate tumor margin. The ureteral dissection is continued as far as is technically feasible. If the distal limits of the dissection are below the level of the iliac vessels, the remainder of the procedure can easily be completed through a lower abdominal incision. The specimen is placed in the pelvis, and the renal bed is inspected meticulously for bleeding. At this time, the 10-mm port sites are closed before proceeding to the open portion of the case.

### Open Distal Ureterectomy with Excision of Bladder Cuff

The patient is now moved to the supine position, which can usually be done without repreparation, and a low midline Pfannenstiel or Gibson incision is made (see Fig. 49–13). The choice of incision largely depends on the area of disease, the body habitus of the patient, and the most caudal level of ureteral dissection attained during the laparoscopic portion. The Gibson incision is preferable when the distal ureter cannot be freed laparoscopically to the level of the iliac vessels. The open distal ureterectomy is described in the section on open techniques.

### Dissection of the Distal Ureter

If one is to consider a total laparoscopic procedure or to minimize the open distal portion, the ureteral dissection needs to continue to the level of the bladder. The patient is placed in the Trendelenburg position to move the bowel contents out of

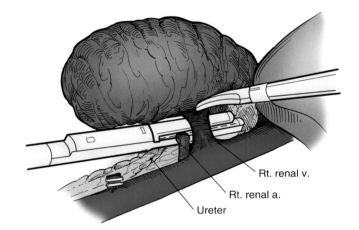

**Figure 49–15.** The vessels of the renal hilum are carefully dissected, and the endovascular stapling device, with a vascular load, is used to simultaneously ligate and divide the vessels in a controlled environment. (From Jarrett TW: Laparoscopic nephroureterectomy. In Bishoff JT, Kavoussi LR, eds: Atlas of Laparoscopic Retroperitoneal Surgery. Philadelphia, WB Saunders, 2000:112.)

the pelvis. The peritoneal incision is extended from the level of the iliac vessels into the pelvis lateral to the bladder and medial to the medial umbilical ligament (Fig. 49–16). The vas deferens in male patients and the round ligament in female patients is clipped and divided. The ureter can now be traced between the bladder and the medial umbilical ligament down to its origin at the bladder. The bladder cuff may be dissected extravesically, freeing the ureter from the surrounding detrusor muscle.

### Results

The first laparoscopic nephroureterectomy was performed in 1991 by Clayman and associates. Since that time, the technical aspects and safety of laparoscopic procedures have been well established. There are multiple published series of

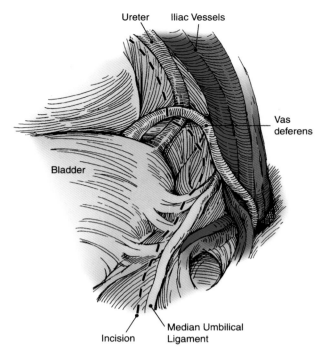

**Figure 49–16.** The peritoneal incision is continued below the iliac vessels medial to the median umbilical ligament and lateral to the bladder. The vas deferens is divided between clips in the male patient. In the female patient, the round ligament is divided, giving full exposure of the distal ureter to the bladder.

laparoscopic nephroureterectomy (Chung et al, 1996; Keeley and Tolley, 1998; Salomon et al, 1999; Shalhav et al, 2000; Jarrett et al, 2001; Stifleman et al, 2001; Bariol et al, 2004; Hsueh et al, 2004; Matin and Gill, 2005; Wolf et al, 2005). Each varies with regard to approach (transperitoneal versus retroperitoneal), management of the distal ureter by open removal, transurethral resection, and total laparoscopic management. As with other laparoscopic renal procedures, there is no clear-cut benefit of any one approach with regard to morbidity, cosmesis, or return to activity. All, however, show a benefit with regard to morbidity compared with open surgery.

The efficacy of laparoscopic nephroureterectomy is being established for cancer control. With intermediate follow-up, cancer-related outcomes appear comparable to those of the open counterpart. El Fettouh and colleagues (2002), in a multi-institutional study with 116 patients, showed the local and bladder recurrence rates to be 2% and 24%, respectively. The rate of distant metastasis was 9%, and positive margins were seen in 4.5% of cases. This compares favorably with open nephroureterectomy, although longer evaluation is necessary.

Local recurrence and port site seeding are major concerns. There have been five reported instances of port site seeding involving transitional cell carcinoma of the upper urinary tract. Two of these cases were discovered after simple nephrectomy for presumed benign disease in which the principles of surgical oncology were inadvertently not followed (Ahmed et al, 1998; Otani et al, 1999). Three instances were for intended nephroureterectomy for high-grade disease (Ong et al, 2003; Matsui et al, 2004; Barrett, verbal communication, September 1998). Although the potential for seeding exists, it does not

appear any higher than that for the open surgical counterpart as long as good surgical principles are followed.

## OPEN SEGMENTAL URETERECTOMY

### Ureteroureterostomy

#### Indications

**Segmental ureterectomy and ureteroureterostomy are indicated for noninvasive grade 1 and grade 2 tumors of the proximal ureter or midureter that are too large for complete endoscopic ablation and for grade 3 or invasive tumors when nephron sparing for preservation of renal function is a goal.**

#### Technique

The patient is placed in a modified flank position for lesions of the proximal ureter or in a supine position with a roll under the ipsilateral lumbar space for midureteral tumors. An angular extraperitoneal incision from the tip of the 12th rib toward the pelvis provides good exposure to the midureter. The ureter is identified, mobilized, and secured with vessel loops proximally and distally. The approximate location of the lesion is known from preoperative imaging and ureteroscopy. The tumor is palpated, and the ureter is ligated 1 to 2 cm proximal and distal to the tumor (Fig. 49–17A). The involved ureteral segment is excised and sent for frozen-section analysis to confirm the diagnosis, grade, and stage and to verify that both ends of the ureter are tumor free. A regional lymphadenectomy is performed. The ureter is repaired by mobilizing both ends to allow a tension-free anastomosis. A defect of up to 4 cm is amenable to ureteroureterostomy in most cases. The entire kidney may be mobilized downward to provide additional length to the proximal ureter when necessary. The periureteral blood supply is preserved as the ureter is mobilized. The ureteral ends are spatulated and anastomosed with interrupted absorbable 4-0 sutures (Fig. 49–17B and C). A ureteral stent is placed as the anastomosis is in progress, and a closed-suction drain is placed in the retroperitoneal space, near to but not touching the repair (Fig. 49–17D).

## Distal Ureterectomy and Direct Neocystostomy or Ureteroneocystostomy with a Bladder Psoas Muscle Hitch or a Boari Flap

### Indications

**Complete distal ureterectomy is recommended for tumors in the distal ureter that cannot be removed completely by endoscopic means** (Bloom et al, 1970; Johnson and Babaian, 1979; Babaian and Johnson, 1980; Johnson et al, 1988; Pagano, 1984; Anderstrom et al, 1989; Williams, 1991; Messing and Catalona, 1998). Larger, high-grade, organ-confined, invasive lesions constitute the majority of these tumors.

### Technique

The patient is placed in the supine position. It is desirable to include the genitalia in the surgical field so that a bladder catheter may be placed and accessible during the procedure.

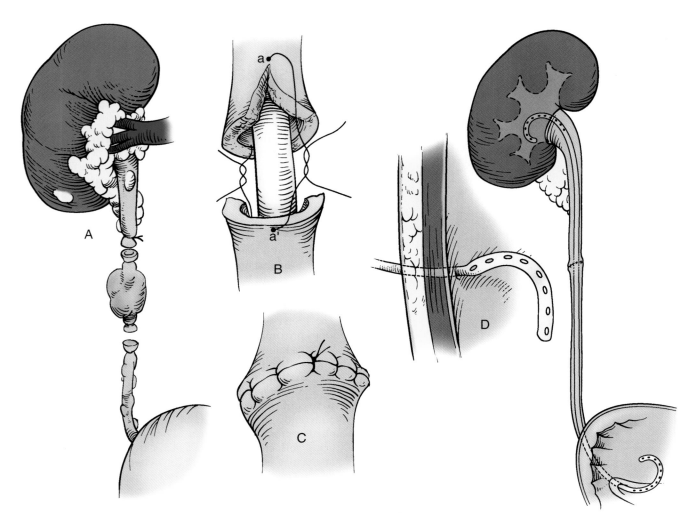

**Figure 49–17.** **A,** Segmental ureterectomy between ties for a large, invasive tumor of the midureter. **B** and **C,** Ureteroureterostomy of spatulated ends of the ureter. The repair is performed over an internal stent. **D,** Completed repair with closed-suction drain in retroperitoneal space.

A Gibson, Pfannenstiel, or lower midline incision provides good exposure to the distal ureter and bladder for the ureteral excision and the repair. The distal ureterectomy is performed as described in the section on radical nephroureterectomy. Extra care is warranted to avoid spillage of known tumor in the distal ureteral segment.

The choice of a nonrefluxing or refluxing anastomosis is controversial (Pagano, 1984). The nonrefluxing anastomosis may limit infections as well as seeding of the upper tract with tumors from the bladder. The refluxing anastomosis may facilitate follow-up surveillance of the upper tract with imaging studies and ureteroscopy.

Direct ureteroneocystostomy may be possible if only a short segment of the juxtavesical and intramural ureter is removed. Additional techniques are required when the entire distal ureter is removed. The first choice is a bladder psoas muscle hitch. The superior vesical attachments on the opposite side of the bladder are freed. An anterior cystotomy is made, and the bladder is mobilized upward over the iliac vessels to the psoas muscle at the level of the iliac crest (Fig. 49–18A and B). The bladder is secured to the psoas muscle and tendon with a

row of interrupted 2-0 chromic sutures. Entrapment of the genitofemoral nerve is avoided. The ureteral end is spatulated and brought through an opening in the uppermost portion of the bladder. Angulation must be avoided at the ureteral hiatus. A nonrefluxing anastomosis is performed by placing the ureter in a mucosal trough or tunnel if there is sufficient ureteral length (Fig. 49–18C). The anastomosis is completed with interrupted 4-0 chromic sutures. A ureteral stent, a urethral catheter, and a closed-suction drain in the perivesical space are placed in all cases (Fig. 49–18D). The anterior cystotomy is closed in two layers with 3-0 absorbable suture. Insertion of a suprapubic catheter is optional.

The bladder psoas muscle hitch provides considerable length if the bladder is of normal size and compliance. However, if an even greater gap must be bridged, a Boari flap from the anterior bladder wall combined with a psoas muscle hitch will reach the proximal ureter (Figs. 49–19 and 49–20). If the need for a Boari flap is anticipated, the incisions for the flap should be marked before making the cystotomy and psoas hitch. The spatulated end of the ureter is anastomosed to the cephalad end of the bladder flap as described previously. The

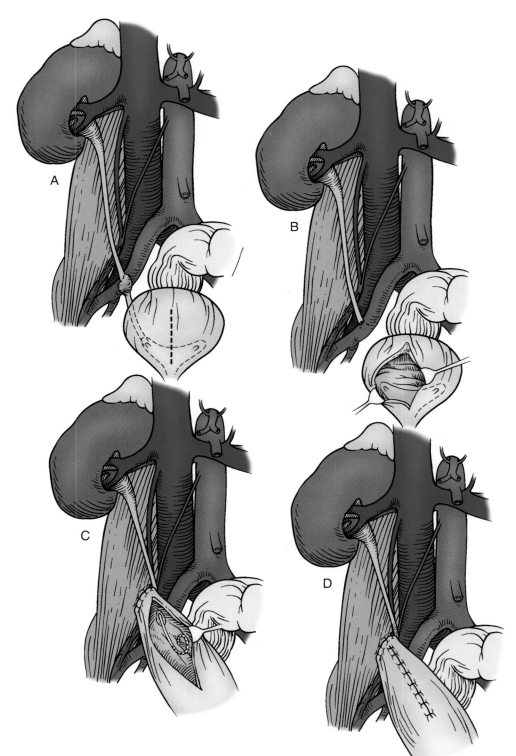

**Figure 49–18.** **A** and **B,** Distal ureterectomy for invasive tumor of the distal ureter. **C,** The bladder is advanced and secured to the psoas muscle. The ureter is anastomosed to the posterior upper aspect of the bladder hitch. **D,** The anterior cystotomy is closed. A closed-suction drain, ureteral stent, and bladder catheter are placed (not shown).

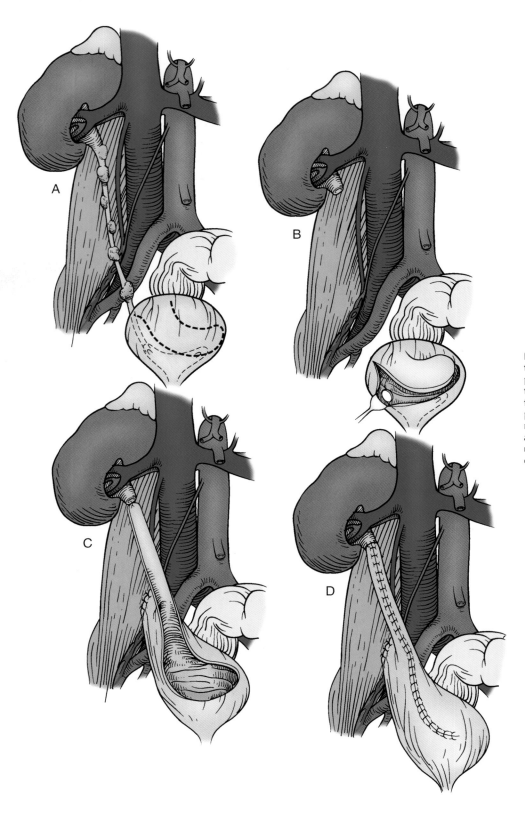

**Figure 49–19.** **A,** Subtotal ureterectomy required for nephron sparing in a patient with multiple diffuse ureteral tumors. **B,** A spiral flap is fashioned from the anterior bladder wall. **C,** The psoas hitch plus Boari flap reaches the remaining proximal ureter. **D,** Completed anastomosis and bladder closure. The ureteral stent, bladder catheter, and closed-suction drain are not shown.

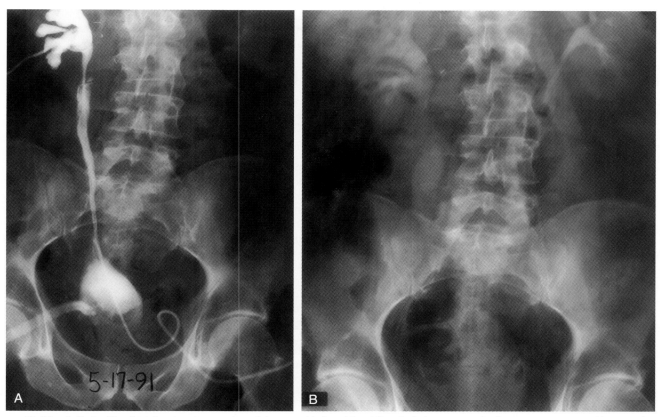

**Figure 49–20.**   Patient with subtotal ureterectomy and repair by psoas hitch and Boari flap. **A,** Early postoperative intravenous urogram with external stent in place. **B,** Intravenous urogram 10-minute film 2 years postoperatively shows good renal function and drainage across ureteral repair.

bladder tube is folded and closed in two layers with running 3-0 absorbable suture.

## Subtotal Ureterectomy

### Indications

Some tumors may require removal of long segments of the ureter by virtue of multifocality and number. However, the tumor grade and stage may not warrant nephroureterectomy. In addition, nephron sparing may be necessary because of compromised function of the contralateral kidney.

### Technique

Complete ileal ureteral substitution may be performed as described in Chapter 80. The proximal ileal segment is anastomosed to the renal pelvis, and the distal ileum is connected to the bladder. Ileal interposition may be performed to repair a long midureteral defect when neither ureteroureterostomy nor bladder mobilization is feasible. A suitable length of ileum to bridge the gap is selected. The ileum is narrowed over a 14 French catheter held along the mesenteric edge of the bowel to approximate the diameter of the ureter. Discarding excess bowel from the antimesenteric edge decreases problems with mucus plugging, preserves intestinal blood supply, and allows more efficient peristalsis of urine across the ileal segment. The vermiform appendix has also been used for segmental ureteral substitution (Goldwasser et al, 1994). A preoperative bowel

preparation is indicated when possible use of intestine is anticipated.

Finally, total ureterectomy, renal autotransplantation to the iliac fossa, and pyelocystostomy are options when the entire ureter is involved with multiple tumors (Pettersson et al, 1984). However, modern endoscopic techniques provide less invasive means of tumor control with lower morbidity in most cases.

## Results

In the past, some authors recommended radical nephroureterectomy for all patients with upper tract urothelial tumors (Skinner, 1978). Others suggested segmental ureterectomy only for patients with low-grade, noninvasive tumors of the distal ureter (Babaian and Johnson, 1980). The cumulative results from the series in Table 49–2 for patients with upper tract tumors of the renal pelvis or ureter reveal that **outcome strongly correlates with tumor stage and grade. Moreover, the results are similar for radical or nephron-sparing surgery.** The outcomes for only ureteral tumors are shown for three series in Table 49–3. Again, overall survival strongly correlates with stage and grade regardless of the extent of surgical treatment. Overall 5-year survival is excellent for patients with grade 1 and grade 2 noninvasive ureteral tumors. Five-year survival remains approximately 50% for patients with stage T2 disease but falls dramatically for stage T3. McCarron and associates (1983) reported 5-year survival

**Table 49–3. 5-Year Survival (%) for Patients with Ureteral Tumors**

| Tumor | Bloom et al, 1970 (n = 102) | Batata and Grabstald, 1976 (n = 77) | McCarron et al, 1983 |
|---|---|---|---|
| Grade | | | |
| 1-2 | 56-83 | 50-80 | 60-87 |
| 3-4 | 16 | 0-20 | 15 |
| T stage | | | |
| a, 1, cis | 62 | 60-90 | 64-81 |
| 2 | 50 | 43 | 46 |
| 3 | 33 | 16 | 22 |
| 4 | — | — | — |
| N+ | 0 | 0 | 4 |
| M+ | 0 | 0 | — |

of 64% for patients with stage Ta tumors treated by either segmental ureterectomy or endoscopic tumor ablation. In the same series, 5-year tumor-free survival was 66% and 50% for stage T1 and T2 tumors, respectively, treated with segmental or distal ureterectomy. Anderstrom and colleagues (1989) reported no tumor-related deaths and only one recurrence among 21 patients treated with segmental ureterectomy for low-grade, noninvasive ureteral tumors who were followed up for a median of 83 months.

Booth and associates (1980) reported 5-year survival of 72% versus 31% among 144 patients with ureteral tumors having either superficial or deep ureteral muscle invasion, respectively. This observation has not been duplicated in other series. The concept is of doubtful validity owing to the thin nature of the ureteral wall.

One of the few reports of 5-year cancer-specific survival by stage for patients with ureteral tumors comes from Grabstald and coworkers (1971). Disease-specific survival was 64% and 100% for stage Ta to T1 and stage T2 disease, respectively. All deaths were due to unrelated causes. In contrast, for patients with stage T3 disease, cancer-specific survival was only 7%, and the death rate due to tumor was 87%.

**The risk of ipsilateral recurrence after conservative treatment of ureteral tumors is 33% to 55%** (Mazeman, 1976; Johnson and Babaian, 1979; Babaian and Johnson, 1980; McCarron et al, 1983; Williams, 1991). Most recurrences are distal to the original lesion, but proximal recurrences are also seen (Strong et al, 1976). The risk for recurrence and the need for follow-up are lifelong (Herr, 1998). Grossman (1978) reported a stage T2 local recurrence in a patient 16 years after segmental ureterectomy and ureteroureterostomy for a grade 1, stage Ta, midureteral tumor. The authors have seen a recurrence of a grade 2, stage Ta tumor in the distal ureter 18 years after segmental ureterectomy of a grade 1, stage Ta tumor of the proximal ureter (Sagalowsky, unpublished data, 1999).

The following are general recommendations for treatment of ureteral tumors in patients with good contralateral renal function. **Segmental ureterectomy is offered for grade 1 to grade 2, stage Ta to stage T1 tumors of the proximal ureter or midureter that are not amenable to complete ablation by endoscopic means because of size or multiplicity. Segmental excision also is offered for grade 1 to grade 2, stage T2 tumors of the proximal ureter or midureter. Distal ureterectomy and neocystostomy are offered for low-grade, low-**stage tumors that are not controlled by endoscopic means. Ureteral excision may also be suitable for some high-grade, locally invasive tumors of the distal ureter.**

## ENDOSCOPIC TREATMENT
### Basic Attributes

Hugh Hampton Young described the first endoscopic evaluation of the upper urinary tract in 1912. Subsequent advances in technology allow us to reach all parts of the urinary tract with minimal morbidity through antegrade and retrograde approaches. Diagnosis and treatment of upper tract transitional cell carcinoma have become possible with these improvements because tumor biopsy and ablation by various energy sources are possible even through the smallest instruments. In addition, miniaturization has made follow-up surveillance of the upper tract more practical with the use of smaller ureteroscopes, which usually do not require previous stenting, or with active dilation of the distal ureter.

Tumors of the upper urinary tract can be approached in a retrograde or antegrade fashion. The approach chosen depends largely on the tumor location and size. In general, a retrograde ureteroscopic approach is used for low-volume ureteral and renal tumors. An antegrade percutaneous approach is preferred for larger tumors of the upper ureter or kidney and for those that cannot be adequately manipulated in a retrograde approach because of location (e.g., lower pole calyx) or previous urinary diversion. In cases with multifocal involvement, combined antegrade and retrograde approaches can be considered (Figs. 49–21 and 49–22).

The basic principles for treatment of transitional cell carcinoma of the upper urinary tract are similar to those for the bladder counterpart (Fig. 49–23). The tumor is sampled and ablated by electrocautery or laser energy sources. A staged procedure should be considered for high-volume disease or disease that is thought to represent high pathologic grade or stage. In such cases, when subsequent nephroureterectomy most likely will be necessary for cure, only biopsy and partial ablation are performed to minimize the risks of perforation or major complications. Endoscopic management is completed only after the pathologic examination shows that the patient is an acceptable candidate for continued minimally invasive endoscopic management. If the pathologic process is unresectable, high grade, or invasive, the patient should proceed immediately to nephroureterectomy, provided he or she is medically fit. Patients who undergo renal-sparing therapy must be committed to a lifetime of follow-up with radiographs and endoscopy.

## Ureteroscopy and Ureteropyeloscopy

The ureteroscopic approach to tumors was first described by Goodman in 1984 and is generally favored for ureteral and smaller renal tumors. With the advent of small-diameter rigid and flexible ureteroscopes, tumor location is less of a limiting factor than it used to be. **The advantage of a ureteroscopic approach is lower morbidity than that of the percutaneous and open surgical counterparts, with the maintenance of a closed system. With a closed system, nonurothelial surfaces are not exposed to the possibility of tumor seeding.**

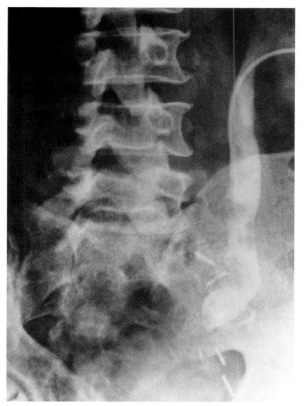

**Figure 49–21.** Retrograde pyelogram of a patient with a solitary kidney and multifocal low-grade tumors, which required both antegrade and retrograde approaches.

The major disadvantages of a retrograde approach are related to the smaller instruments required. Smaller endoscopes have a smaller field of view and working channel. This limits the size of tumor that can be approached in a retrograde fashion. In addition, some portions of the upper urinary tract, such as the lower pole calyces, cannot be reliably reached with working instruments. Smaller instruments limit the ability to remove large tumors and to obtain deep specimens for reliable staging. Retrograde ureteroscopy is difficult in patients with prior urinary diversion.

## KEY POINT: URETEROSCOPY

■ Ureteroscopy offers lower morbidity and a closed-system approach to the tumor.

### Technique and Instrumentation

A wide variety of ureteroscopic instruments are available, each with its own distinct advantages and disadvantages. In general, rigid ureteroscopes are used primarily for the distal ureter and midureter. Access to the upper ureter and kidney with rigid endoscopy is unreliable, especially in the male patient. Larger, rigid ureteroscopes provide better visualization because of their larger field of view and better irrigation. Smaller rigid ureteroscopes (8 French) generally do not require active dilation of the ureteral orifice (Fig. 49–24A).

Newer generation, flexible ureteropyeloscopes are available in sizes smaller than 8 French to allow simple and reliable passage to most portions of the urinary tract (Abdel-Razzak

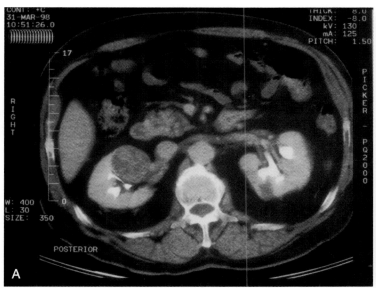

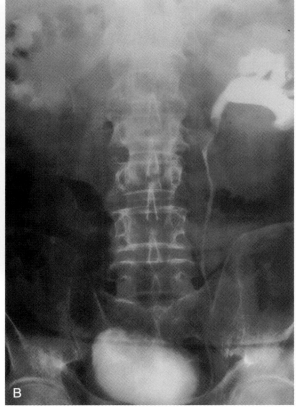

**Figure 49–22.** Patient with synchronous bilateral tumors. **A,** Right renal cell carcinoma that required radical nephrectomy. **B,** Left proximal ureteral tumor that required combined ureteroscopic and antegrade percutaneous ablation.

and Bagley, 1993; Grasso and Bagley, 1994). These are generally preferred in the upper ureter and kidney, where the rigid ureteroscope cannot be reliably passed. **Flexible ureteroscopes, however, have technical limitations, such as a small working channel, that limit irrigant flow and the diameter of working instruments. Further limitations of flexible ureteroscopy include reduced access to certain areas of the kidney, such as the lower pole, where the infundibulopelvic**

**angle may limit passage of the scope, and prior urinary diversion** (Fig. 49–24B).

### Steps

**Endoscopic Evaluation and Collection of Urine Cytology Specimen.** Cystoscopy is performed and the bladder inspected for concomitant bladder disease. The ureteral orifice is identified and inspected for lateralizing hematuria. A small-diameter ureteroscope is passed directly (6.9 or 7.5 French) into the ureteral orifice, and the distal ureter is inspected for any trauma from a previously placed guide wire or dilation. A guide wire is then placed through the ureteroscope and up the ureter to the level of the renal pelvis under fluoroscopic guidance. The flexible ureteroscope is used to visualize the remaining urothelium. **When a lesion or suspicious area is seen, a normal saline washing of the area is performed before biopsy or intervention** (Bian et al, 1995). If the ureter does not accept the smaller ureteroscope, active dilation of the ureter is necessary.

**Special circumstances include prior urinary diversion and tumor confined to the intramural ureter.** With cases of prior urinary diversion, identification of the ureteroenteric anastomosis is difficult and may require antegrade percutaneous passage of a guide wire down the ureter before endoscopy. The wire can be retrieved from the diversion, and the ureteroscope can be passed in a retrograde fashion. The nephrostomy track does not need to be fully dilated in this setting. A second type of case is tumor in the intramural ureter. When a tumor protrudes from the ureteral orifice, complete ureteroscopic ablation of the tumor or aggressive

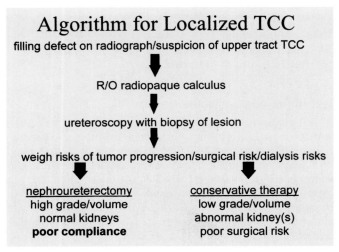

**Figure 49–23.** Algorithm for endoscopic approach to upper tract transitional cell carcinoma (TCC).

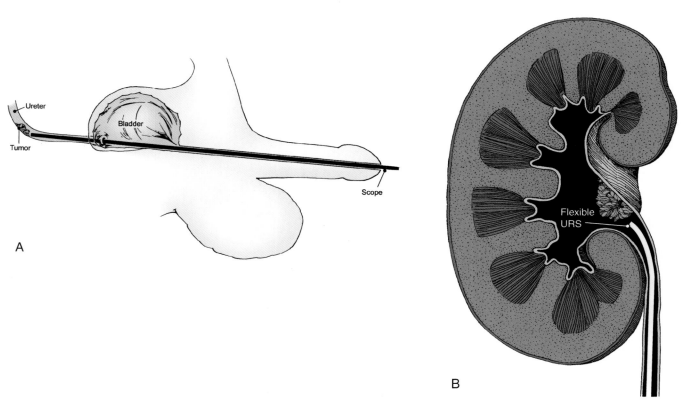

**Figure 49–24.** **A,** Rigid ureteroscopic approach. **B,** Flexible ureteroscopic approach. URS, ureteroscope.

transurethral resection of the entire most distal ureter can be done with acceptable results (Palou et al, 2000).

**Biopsy and Definitive Treatment.** Three general approaches can be used for tumor ablation: bulk excision with ablation of the base, resection of the tumor to its base, and diagnostic biopsy followed by ablation with electrocautery or laser energy sources. Regardless of technique used, special attention to biopsy specimens is necessary. Specimens are frequently minute and should be placed in fixative at once and specially labeled for either histologic or cytologic evaluation (Tawfiek et al, 1997).

*Ureteroscopic Techniques.* The tumor is debulked by use of either grasping forceps or a flat wire basket engaged adjacent to the tumor (Fig. 49–25*A*). Next, the tumor base is treated with either electrocautery or laser energy sources. This technique is especially useful for low-grade papillary tumor on a narrow stalk. The specimen is sent for pathologic evaluation.

A ureteroscopic resectoscope is used to remove the tumor (Fig. 49–25*B*). Only the intraluminal tumor is resected, and no attempt is made to resect deep (beyond the lamina propria). Extra care is necessary in the midureter and upper ureter, where the wall is thin and prone to perforation. Ureteral resectoscopes are approximately 12 French and require more extensive dilation of the ureteral orifice. With larger volume disease of the distal ureter, Jarrett and associates (1995a) described extensive dilation of the ureter followed by resection with a long standard resectoscope. **The tumor is adequately sampled with forceps and sent to the pathology laboratory for diagnostic evaluation. The tumor bulk is then ablated to its base with laser or electrosurgical energy** (Fig. 49–25*C* and *D*). Multiple biopsy specimens are often required when small, flexible, 3 French biopsy forceps are used. Electrocautery delivered through a small Bugbee electrode (2 or 3 French) can be used to fulgurate tumors. However, the variable depth of penetration can make its use in the ureter dangerous, and circumferential fulguration should be avoided because of the high risk of stricture formation. More recently, laser energy with either neodymium:yttrium-aluminum-garnet (Nd:YAG) (Smith et al, 1984; Schmeller and Hofstetter, 1989; Carson, 1991) or holmium:YAG (Bagley and Erhard, 1995; Razvi et al, 1995) sources has been popular. Each has characteristic advantages (Fig. 49–26) and can be delivered through small, flexible fibers (200 or 365 μm) that fit through small, flexible ureteroscopes without significant alteration of irrigant flow or scope deflection.

## KEY POINT: BIOPSY AND ABLATION

- The lesion is sampled first for histopathologic staging, if possible; then it is ablated.

The holmium:YAG laser is well suited for use in the ureter. The tissue penetration is less than 0.5 mm, which allows tumor ablation with excellent hemostasis and minimal risk of full-thickness injury to the ureter. Its shallow penetration may, however, make its use cumbersome with larger tumors, especially in the renal pelvis. Settings most commonly used for holmium:YAG are energy of 0.6 to 1 joule with frequency of 10 hertz. The neodymium:YAG laser has a tissue penetration

of up to 5 to 6 mm, depending on laser settings and duration of treatment. In contrast to the holmium:YAG laser, which ablates tumor, the Nd:YAG laser works by coagulative necrosis with subsequent sloughing of the necrotic tumor. The safety margin is significantly lower and can limit its use in the ureter, where the ureteral wall is thin. Settings most commonly used for the Nd:YAG laser are 15 watts for 2 seconds for ablation of tumor and 5 to 10 watts for 2 seconds for coagulation.

A ureteral stent is placed for a variable duration to aid with the healing process. Large tumors usually require multiple treatment sessions during several months.

### Results

Multiple series have shown the safety and efficacy of ureteroscopic treatment of upper tract transitional cell carcinoma (Elliott et al, 1996; Martinez-Pineiro et al, 1996; Keeley et al, 1997a, 1997b). In a literature review of 205 patients (Tawfiek and Bagley, 1997), the overall recurrence rates for ureteral and renal pelvic lesions were 33% and 31.2%, respectively, and the risk of bladder recurrence was 43%. In the two largest series (Keeley et al, 1997a), there was a single cancer death directly attributed to recurrent upper tract disease. As with any transitional cell carcinoma, the most important prognostic indicator for tumor recurrence was grade. Keeley and associates (1997b) showed a recurrence rate of 26% for grade 1 tumors and 44% for grade 2 tumors, which roughly correlated with previously established recurrence rates for open conservative surgery. More recently, Daneshmand and colleagues (2003) showed the long-term feasibility of ureteroscopic management but a large number of recurrences (3.4 recurrences per patient). This is important in considering patients with a normal contralateral kidney. They must be counseled in the need for lifetime follow-up and possible treatment of ipsilateral recurrence.

Complications were uncommon and usually related to the patient's comorbidities. Complications specific to ureteroscopic therapy included ureteral perforation, which can be managed with indwelling ureteral stent, and ureteral stricture. Stricture formation rate ranged from 5% to 13% (Elliott et al, 1996; Martinez-Pineiro et al, 1996; Keeley et al, 1997a). The complication rates have dropped in more contemporary series, most likely related to smaller endoscopes, improved laser energy sources, and refinements in endoscopic techniques.

Two major concerns of the ureteroscopic approach are the accuracy of ureteroscopic biopsies and the limitations of biopsies, especially with regard to staging (Huffman, 1988). Retrospective reviews of patients who underwent ureteroscopic biopsy followed by nephroureterectomy found the accuracy of ureteroscopic diagnosis to be 89% to 94% and the pathologic grading to match the open surgical technique in 78% to 92% (Keeley et al, 1997a; Guarnizo et al, 2000). From prior studies, we know that there is an excellent correlation between grade of lesion and stage (Chasko et al, 1981; Heney et al, 1981). This holds true for the ureteroscopic approach (Keeley et al, 1997b) because 87% of patients with grade 1 or grade 2 tumors had noninvasive disease (stage Ta or T1), whereas 67% of patients with grade 3 tumors had invasive disease (stage T2 or T3). This information supports the notion that tumor grade is the most important prognostic factor, and although stage cannot be directly assessed, noninvasive disease can be expected in most cases of low-grade tumor.

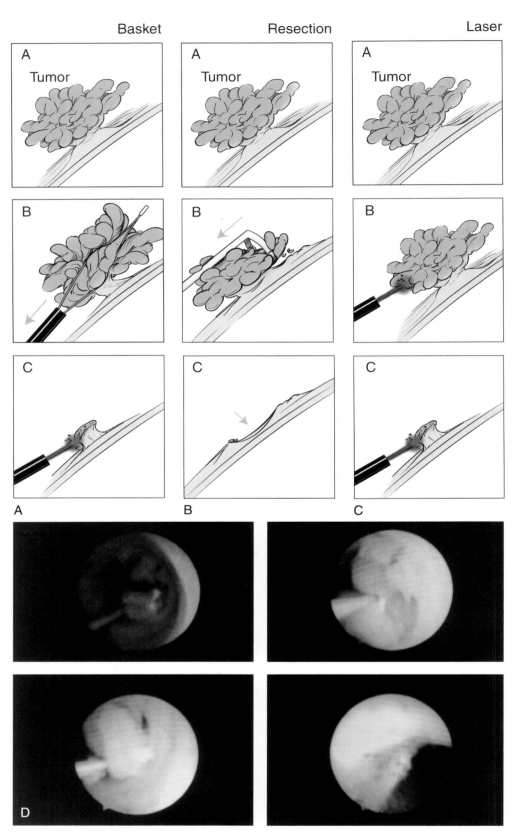

**Figure 49–25.** Techniques for ureteroscopic treatment of ureteral and renal tumors. **A,** The tumor is identified and removed piecemeal by grasping forceps to its base. **B,** Alternatively, a flat wire basket can be deployed alongside the tumor. The tumor is engaged and removed, with care taken not to avulse the adjacent ureter. With either of these techniques, the base is treated with electrocautery or a laser energy source. **C,** The tumor is identified and removed by a ureteroscopic resectoscope. The technique differs from the technique for bladder tumors in that only intraluminal tumor is resected. No attempt is made to resect deep, as with a bladder tumor. The scope is not arching deep into the tissue. **D,** The tumor is sampled for diagnostic purposes. The bulk of the tumor is then ablated with electrosurgical or laser energy. Laser energy is generally preferred because it has more reliable delivery of energy and depth of penetration. The two most commonly used energy sources are holmium:yttrium-aluminum-garnet and neodymium:yttrium-aluminum-garnet.

Ho:YAG

Minimal penetration (<05 mm)

Efficient ablation of tumor

Precise cutting

Settings  0.6-1.2 joules/8-10 Hz

Nd:YAG

Deep penetration (5-6mm)

Excellent hemostasis

Tumor ablation by coagulative necrosis

Settings – 20-30 watts

**Figure 49-26.** Characteristics of holmium:YAG and neodymium:YAG laser energy sources. YAG, yttrium-aluminum-garnet.

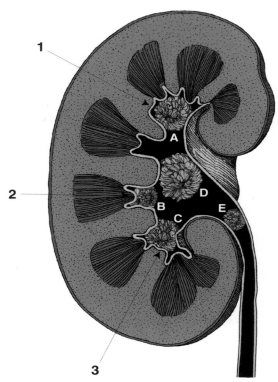

**Figure 49-27.** Nephrostomy track puncture site. Position of the nephrostomy is imperative for successful percutaneous resection of transitional cell carcinoma of the renal collecting system and upper ureter and requires careful preoperative evaluation of radiographs for tumor location. Tumors in peripheral calyces (A to C) are best approached by direct puncture as far distally in the calyx as possible. Tumors in the renal pelvis (D) and upper ureter (E) are best approached by puncture to an upper (1) or middle (2) calyx, which allows the scope to be maneuvered in the renal pelvis and down the ureter. Tumors in the lower calyx are approached by lower calyx puncture (3).

A final concern is whether ureteroscopy promotes progression or spread of disease to other urothelial surfaces or metastatic sites. There have been reports of increased tumor appearance in refluxing ureters of patients with bladder tumors (de Torres Mateos et al, 1987) and in the ipsilateral urinary tract and bladder of patients after ureteroscopic treatment. However, Kulp and Bagley (1994) reported on 13 patients who underwent multiple ureteroscopic treatments followed by nephroureterectomy; they found no unusual propagation of transitional cell carcinoma in the specimens. Concerns that ureteroscopy may promote metastatic spread were raised by Lim and associates (1993), who found tumor cells in renal lymphatics after ureteroscopy. However, Hendin and colleagues (1999) reported no increased risk of metastatic disease in a group of patients who underwent ureteroscopy before nephroureterectomy compared with a group undergoing nephroureterectomy alone.

## Percutaneous Approach

The percutaneous approach was first described by Tomera and coworkers in 1982 and is generally favored for larger tumors located proximally in the renal pelvis or proximal ureter. **The main advantage of the percutaneous approach is the ability to use larger instruments that can remove a large volume of tumor** in any portion of the renal collecting system. Because deeper biopsy specimens are obtained, tumor staging as well as grading is usually possible. In addition, a percutaneous approach may avoid the limitations of flexible ureteroscopy, especially in complicated calyceal systems or areas difficult to access, such as the lower pole calyx or the upper urinary tract of patients with urinary diversion. With a percutaneous approach, the established nephrostomy track can be maintained for immediate postoperative nephroscopy and administration of topical adjuvant therapy.

The main disadvantages are the increased morbidity compared with ureteroscopy and the potential for tumor seeding outside the urinary tract. Establishment of the nephrostomy track has inherent risks, and the procedure usually requires inpatient admission. Distinct risks related to a percutaneous approach are loss of urothelial integrity and exposure of nonurothelial surfaces to tumor cells. This open system provides the possibility of tumor implantation in the nephrostomy track.

### Technique and Instrumentation

**Establishment of the Nephrostomy Track.** Cystoscopy is performed, and an open-ended ureteral catheter is positioned in the pelvis. Contrast material is injected to define the calyceal anatomy, and a percutaneous nephrostomy track is established through the desired calyx (Fig. 49-27). Tumors in peripheral calyces are best approached with direct puncture distal to the tumor (Fig. 49-28). Disease in the renal pelvis and upper ureter is best approached through an upper or middle pole access to allow scope maneuvering through the collecting system and down the ureteropelvic junction. The track is dilated by either sequential (Amplatz) or balloon dilation to accommodate a 30 French sheath. Correct positioning of the nephrostomy track is crucial to the success of the procedure

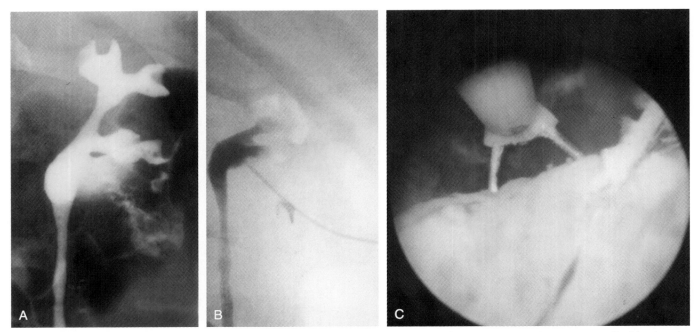

**Figure 49–28.** **A,** Retrograde pyelogram of a man with transitional cell carcinoma of the lower calyx in a solitary kidney. **B,** Access distal in the calyx allows a clear view of the tumor. **C,** Subsequent resection.

and should be done by the urologist or by the radiologist after direct consultation with the operating surgeon.

A nephroscope is inserted, and the ureteral catheter is grasped, brought out the track, and exchanged for a stiff guide wire, thus providing both antegrade and retrograde control. Complete nephroscopy is performed with rigid and flexible endoscopes when necessary. Any suspicion of upper ureteral involvement warrants antegrade ureteroscopy.

**Biopsy and Definitive Therapy. After identification, the tumors are removed by one of the following four techniques** (Fig. 49–29). In the first technique, which uses a cold-cup biopsy forceps through a standard nephroscope, the bulk of the tumor is grasped by forceps and removed in piecemeal fashion until the base is reached (Fig. 49–29A). A separate biopsy of the base is performed for staging purposes, and the base is cauterized with a Bugbee electrode and cautery. Low-grade papillary lesions on a thin stalk are easily treated in this manner with minimal bleeding.

Alternatively, a cutting loop from a standard resectoscope is used to remove the tumor to its base (Fig. 49–29B). Once again, the base should be resected and sent separately for staging purposes. This approach is more effective for larger, broad-based tumors for which simple debulking to a stalk is not possible.

For the third technique, which uses flexible or rigid endoscopes, the tumor is sampled and treated with holmium:YAG or Nd:YAG laser at 25 to 30 watts (Fig. 49–29C and D). Tissue may also be obtained with a small snare used for gastrointestinal polyps.

Regardless of approach, a nephrostomy tube is left in place. This access can be used for second-look follow-up nephroscopy to ensure complete tumor removal (Fig. 49–30). Nephroureterectomy is indicated if the pathologic examination shows high-grade or invasive disease.

## Second-Look Nephroscopy

Follow-up nephroscopy is performed 4 to 14 days later to allow adequate healing. The tumor resection site is identified, and any residual tumor is removed. If no tumor is identified, the base should be sampled and treated by cautery or the Nd:YAG laser (15 to 20 watts and 3-second exposures). The nephrostomy tube can be removed several days later if all tumors have been removed. If the patient is being considered for adjuvant topical therapy, a small, 8 French nephrostomy tube is left to provide access for instillations. Some authors advocate third-look nephroscopy before final nephrostomy tube removal (Jarrett et al, 1995b).

## Results

Because of the rarity of the disease, there are only several retrospective series with adequate numbers and follow-up from which to draw reasonable conclusions (Jarrett et al, 1995b; Patel et al, 1996; Clark et al, 1999; Goel et al, 2003; Palou et al, 2004). In a literature review of 84 patients, Okada and colleagues (1997) found an overall recurrence rate of 27%. Tumor grade strongly predicted outcomes; Jarrett and associates showed the recurrence rate for grades 1, 2, and 3 lesions to be 18%, 33%, and 50%, respectively. The only cancer-related mortalities in this series were in patients with high-grade disease. Lee and colleagues (1999) reviewed their 13-year experience with percutaneous management, comparing 50 patients who underwent percutaneous management with 60 patients who underwent nephroureterectomy, and found no significant difference in overall survival. As expected, patients with low-grade disease did well regardless of modality, and patients with high-grade disease did poorly regardless of treatment option.

Most would agree from the literature that percutaneous management is acceptable in patients with low-grade (grade

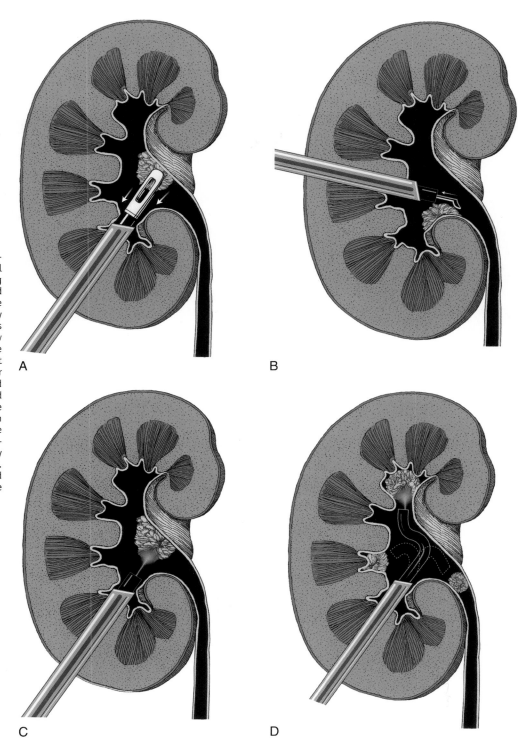

**Figure 49–29.** Techniques for percutaneous removal of transitional cell carcinoma of the renal collecting system. **A,** The tumor is identified and debulked by forceps to its base. The base is sampled and sent separately for evaluation. This technique works well for papillary tumors on a narrow stalk. Broad-based tumors may cause excessive bleeding and are best approached with resection or laser therapy. **B,** With use of a standard resectoscope, the tumor is identified and resected to its base. Special care should be taken to avoid resection into major renal vasculature. The tumor is identified, sampled for diagnostic purposes, and treated by holmium or neodymium laser sources. This can be done through a standard nephroscope (**C**) or with a flexible cystoscope (**D**).

A

B

C

D

1) disease regardless of the status of the contralateral kidney, provided the patient is committed to lifelong endoscopic follow-up. Patients with grade 3 disease do poorly regardless of modality chosen but should probably undergo nephro-ureterectomy to maximize cancer therapy (provided they are medically fit). The largest area of controversy surrounds the

use of percutaneous management for patients with grade 2 disease and a normal contralateral kidney. Jabbour and associates (2000) retrospectively evaluated 24 patients and found a disease-specific survival of 95% overall and 100% and 80% for stage Ta and stage T1 lesions, respectively. This study shows an acceptable result with conservative treatment of noninva-

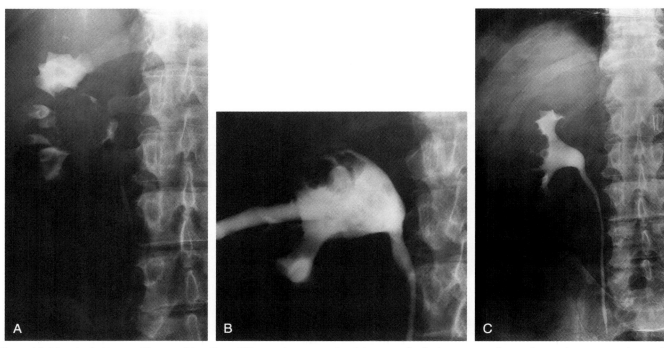

**Figure 49–30. A,** A 65-year-old man with solitary kidney and 5-cm renal pelvis tumor. **B,** Nephrostogram after patient underwent staged resection. **C,** Three-month follow-up retrograde pyelogram after completed resection. The patient showed grade 1 transitional cell carcinoma without invasion to submucosa.

sive grade 2 disease. With more invasive lesions, the potential for disease progression and metastatic disease is significant, and nephroureterectomy should be considered.

Complications from percutaneous management of tumors are similar to those for benign renal processes and include bleeding, perforation of the collecting system, and secondary ureteropelvic junction obstruction. Complications increase in number and severity with higher tumor grade (Jarrett et al, 1995b). This finding is probably due to the more extensive pathologic process and treatments necessary to eradicate the tumor. Unlike ureteroscopic resection, the percutaneous method can stage tumors, and as expected, stage increases with tumor grade.

A major concern of the percutaneous approach is the potential seeding of nonurothelial surfaces with tumor cells. Although there have been multiple reported cases of nephrostomy track infiltration with high-grade tumors (Tomera et al, 1982; Slywotzky and Maya, 1994; Huang et al, 1995; Oefelein and MacLennan, 2003; Treuthardt et al, 2004), there were no reported occurrences in the three largest series (Jarrett et al, 1995b; Patel et al, 1996; Clark et al, 1999). Track seeding is a possibility but appears to be an uncommon event.

## ISOLATED UPPER TRACT CYTOLOGIC ABNORMALITY OR URINARY MARKER

On occasion, one is faced with a patient who has an isolated abnormal cytologic finding or other urinary marker from the upper urinary tract. **By definition, the patient should have normal intravenous urography and retrograde pyelography,** **normal cystoscopy, and normal biopsy findings from the bladder and urethra.** Radical nephroureterectomy was performed in the past for a unilateral cytologic abnormality of the upper tract to eliminate presumed carcinoma in situ. This practice is not recommended (Gittes, 1980; McCarron et al, 1983; Williams, 1991; Messing and Catalona, 1998). Upper tract cytology suffers from the same limitations in specificity as does bladder cytology. Further, properly collected upper tract samples are of limited volume and cell count compared with bladder washings. Any source of inflammation, such as urinary infection or calculus, may produce a false-positive result. A subsequent cytologic abnormality from the contralateral side during follow-up is not rare in cases of true positives from early carcinoma in situ (Murphy et al, 1974; Khan et al, 1979). A variety of urinary markers are being studied to aid in detection of urothelial tumor recurrence. At this time, both urine fluorescence in situ hybridization and urine nuclear matrix protein show particular promise.

**Ureteropyeloscopy is indicated in such cases because the yield for direct visualization of small lesions is superior to that of retrograde pyelography.** An attempt to perform biopsy and confirm the diagnosis is indicated before treatment is considered. A consistently abnormal finding on upper tract cytology may signify carcinoma in situ. Current treatment options are limited. Instillation of topical immunotherapy or chemotherapy may be performed through ureteral catheters or a small percutaneous nephrostomy. However, the contact time of the agent with the urothelium is minimal. Reports of efficacy are uncontrolled and anecdotal.

Frequent-interval reevaluation with urinalysis, bladder cytology, cystoscopy every 3 months, and retrograde pyelography or ureteropyeloscopy every 6 months is indicated for 1 to 2 years. However, one must avoid overtreatment and excessive evaluation and instrumentation of a patient who may have had a single false-positive result.

## ADJUVANT THERAPY
## After Organ-Sparing Therapy

Any procedure short of nephroureterectomy has a higher local recurrence due to the established risk of ipsilateral recurrence. Several approaches are available to minimize these risks. They fall into two basic categories: instillation of immunotherapeutic or chemotherapeutic agents and brachytherapy of the nephrostomy track.

### Instillation Therapy

Instillation therapy can be accomplished in several ways. Accepted techniques include antegrade instillation through a nephrostomy tube (Fig. 49–31) and retrograde instillation directly into a ureteral catheter or by reflux in a patient with an indwelling ureteral stent or iatrogenically created vesicoureteral reflux. Patel and Fuchs (1998) described a convenient technique of outpatient instillation through a ureteral catheter placed suprapubically. Regardless of the technique chosen, administration to the upper urinary tract should be done under low pressure and in the absence of active infection to minimize the risk of bacterial sepsis or systemic absorption of the agent.

**Results. The same agents used to treat urothelial carcinoma of the bladder are used to treat tumors of the upper tracts. Many studies have described small, retrospective, uncontrolled series of patients undergoing therapy with thiotepa** (Elliott et al, 1996; Patel et al, 1996), **mitomycin** (Eastham and Huffman, 1993; Weston et al, 1993; Martinez-Pineiro et al, 1996; Keeley et al, 1997a), **and BCG** (Smith et al, 1987; Studer et al, 1989; Eastham and Huffman, 1993; Sharpe et al, 1993;

Jarrett et al, 1995b; Hayashida, 2004). Although the cumulative experience appears encouraging, no individual study has shown statistical improvement with relation to survival and recurrence rates. Possible reasons for this include (1) insufficient numbers to show clinical significance because of the relative rarity of the disease; (2) tumors of the upper urinary tract, which have a tumor biology different from that of their bladder counterparts; and (3) inadequate delivery system that, unlike in the bladder, does not allow uniform delivery of the agent with adequate dwell time to enable a clinical response. Further, in the report by Hayashida and colleagues (2004) with intrarenal perfusion of BCG, despite initial return of cytology results to normal, 50% of patients (5 of 10) developed disease recurrence after a mean follow-up of 50.9 months, and all of these suffered cancer-specific mortality. There is no doubt that more studies are required to settle this issue. The attempt to decrease multiple recurrences in the upper tract is reasonable in well-selected patients.

The most common complication of instillation therapy is bacterial sepsis. To minimize this problem, patients must be evaluated for active infection before each treatment, and only a low-pressure delivery system should be used. Agent-specific complications of the various therapies include ramification of systemic absorption of the agent. Bellman and colleagues (1994) described upper urinary tract complications of percutaneous BCG instillation. Granulomatous involvement of the kidney in the absence of systemic signs of BCG infection was most commonly seen. Mukamel and associates (1991) saw an inordinate decrease in renal function for patients receiving BCG who had vesicoureteral reflux.

### Brachytherapy

Brachytherapy to the nephrostomy track through iridium wire or delivery system was described by Patel and coworkers (1996) and Nurse and colleagues (1989). There were no instances of track recurrences in this series, although the authors acknowledged the rarity of the event. The only major complication attributed to the brachytherapy was cutaneous fistula formation requiring nephroureterectomy.

## After Complete Excision
### Radiation Therapy

The rationale for focal radiation therapy is to decrease the risk of local relapse after radical surgery for locally advanced non–organ-confined disease (stage T3 to T4, N+). Most series concluding that postoperative irradiation is beneficial are small or even anecdotal, uncontrolled, and retrospective (Holtz, 1962; Brady et al, 1968; Leiber and Lupu, 1978). In one series with 41 patients, postoperative radiation therapy decreased local recurrence but had no effect on distant relapse or survival (Brookland and Richter, 1985). Maulard-Durdux and associates (1996) retrospectively reviewed 26 patients who received 46 Gy to the wound bed after radical surgery for upper tract tumors. Tumors were grade 2 in 40% and grade 3 in 60% of cases. Tumor stage was T2, T3, and N+ in 42%, 58%, and 35% of cases, respectively. Five-year survival is shown in Table 49–4. Overall 5-year survival was 49%, with 30% remaining disease free. All patients with local relapse also had distant relapse, leading the authors to conclude that adjuvant radiation therapy is not beneficial.

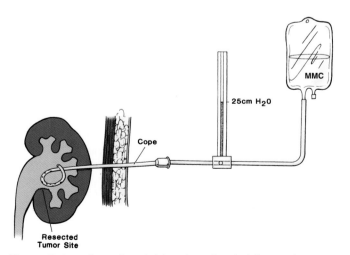

**Figure 49–31.** Setup for administration of topical immunotherapy or chemotherapy to the upper urinary tract through a previously placed nephrostomy tube. Therapy is instilled by gravity with a mechanism that prevents excessive intrarenal pressures. High pressures have been linked to complications of systemic absorption and bacterial sepsis.

**Table 49-4.  5-Year Survival after Postoperative Adjuvant Radiation Therapy for Upper Tract Urothelial Tumors**

| Tumor | 5-Year Survival (%) |
| --- | --- |
| Grade | |
| 2 | 90 |
| 3 | 0  P < .01 |
| T stage | |
| 2 | 60 |
| 3 | 19 |
| N0 | 49  P = .04 |
| N+ | 15 |

Data from Maulard-Durdux C, Dufour B, Hennequin C, et al: Postoperative radiation therapy in 29 patients with invasive transitional cell carcinoma of the upper urinary tract: No impact on survival? J Urol 1996;155: 115-117.

The largest experience addressing this issue is that reported by Hall and associates (1998). A retrospective review of 252 patients with upper tract tumors who were followed up for a median of 64 months was performed. Radical nephroureterectomy was performed in 77% of cases. Initial tumor stage was T3 in 19% and T4 in 10% of cases; 50% and 52%, respectively, of patients with stage T3 and stage T4 tumors received 40 Gy to the wound bed postoperatively. Disease-specific and overall 5-year survival was 41% and 28%, respectively, for patients with stage T3 disease. Actuarial 5-year disease-specific survival for stage T3 with or without adjuvant radiation therapy was 45% and 40%, respectively. Median survival was 6 months for stage T4 disease. There were no long-term survivors in this group. Local relapse occurred in only 9% of the entire series and was seen only in patients with stage T3 and stage T4 disease. Among the patients who received adjuvant radiation, isolated local relapse without distant metastases occurred in only 10% and 4% of stage T3 and stage T4 cases, respectively. Thus, **radical nephroureterectomy alone provides a high rate of local control. Adjuvant radiation for high-stage disease does not decrease local relapse or protect against a high rate of distant failure.**

### Systemic Chemotherapy

**The major limitation to long-term survival for patients with locally advanced upper tract tumors is distant relapse with metastatic disease. Both induction (neoadjuvant) and adjuvant systemic therapy with agents used for proven metastatic disease (see following discussion) are reasonable. However, there are no controlled trials that establish the efficacy of either induction or adjuvant chemotherapy in this setting.** The small number of cases treated with adjuvant chemotherapy are anecdotal and preclude definitive conclusions of efficacy.

### KEY POINT: METASTATIC DISEASE

■ Distant relapse with metastatic disease is the main limitation in survival of patients, not local recurrence.

## FOLLOW-UP

## Issues in Assessing for Recurrence

The propensity of upper tract tumors for multifocal recurrence and metastatic spread with more dysplastic lesions makes follow-up complicated. Postoperative evaluation must routinely include evaluation of the bladder, the ipsilateral (if organ-sparing therapy was chosen) and contralateral urinary tracts, and the extraurinary sites for local and metastatic spread. A follow-up regimen is thus dependent on the time from surgery, the approach chosen (organ sparing versus radical), and the potential for metastatic spread. General recommendations for time intervals are listed in Figure 49–32.

## General Procedures

All patients should be assessed at 3-month intervals the first year after they are rendered tumor free by endoscopic or open surgical approaches (Keeley et al, 1997a). This schedule is largely based on work with bladder transitional cell carcinoma that shows that most tumor recurrences after bladder resection develop in the first year (Varkarakis et al, 1974; Loening et al, 1980). The upper urinary tract is more difficult to monitor, and delayed recognition of upper tract tumor recurrence may lead to disease progression and poor results (Mazeman, 1976). Evaluation should include history, physical examination, urinalysis, and office cystoscopy because of the high risk of bladder recurrences in patients treated both conservatively and with nephroureterectomy (Mazeman, 1976). If the patient requires endoscopic evaluation of the upper urinary tract, cystoscopy can be done in conjunction with that procedure.

**Urine cytology may be helpful in assessing for upper tract recurrence, especially for high-grade tumors** (Murphy et al, 1981). The utility, however, is decreased with less dysplastic tumors (Grace et al, 1967; Sarnacki et al, 1971; Zincke et al, 1976). The same tumor markers under study for bladder transitional cell carcinoma are promising for upper urinary tract transitional cell carcinoma (Brown, 2000). One marker that may be preferentially more involved in upper tract transitional cell carcinoma than in bladder transitional cell carcinoma is the DNA mismatch repair gene *hMSH2* (Leach et al, 2000).

## Specific Procedures

Bilateral disease, either synchronous or metachronous, is seen in 1% to 4% of patients (Petkovic, 1975; Babaian and Johnson, 1980; Murphy et al, 1981), and thus imaging of the contralateral kidney is required on a regular basis. Yearly intravenous urography is usually sufficient. However, retrograde pyelography may be necessary if the patient is not a candidate for injection of contrast medium or if intravenous urography is not diagnostic. Computed tomography or sonography is helpful in distinguishing stones from soft tissue densities. Further evaluation of filling defects on imaging studies usually requires ureteroscopic evaluation.

If an organ-sparing approach is chosen, the ipsilateral urinary tract must be assessed as well as the remainder of the urinary tract. The frequency and duration of the follow-up assessments depend largely on the grade and stage of the o   **Physical examination, urine cytology (only for high grade lesions) and cystoscopy**

    o   every 3 months – first year

    o   every 6 months thereafter – years 2 –3

    o   yearly – thereafter

o   **Contralateral Imaging (IVU or retrograde pyelography) – yearly**

o   **Ipsilateral Endoscopy (patients undergoing organ-sparing therapy) –**

    o   every 6 months – first several years

    o   yearly – thereafter

o   **Metastatic Evaluation – necessary in all patients with significant risk of disease progression (i.e., high grade or invasive disease)**

    o   Physical examination, chest x-ray, comprehensive metabolic panel with liver enzymes

        ■   Every 3 months – first year

        ■   Every 6 months – years 2 through 3

        ■   Yearly – years 4 and 5

        ■   After 5 years – evaluation of urothelium only

    o   Computed tomography or MRI of abdomen and pelvis –

        ■   Every 6 months – years 1 and 2

        ■   Yearly – years 3 – 5

    o   Bone scan – only for elevated alkaline phosphatase or symptoms of bone pain

**Figure 49–32.** Follow-up begins after open surgery or when the patient is rendered tumor free by endoscopic management. The commencement of follow-up may be altered according to the potential for disease progression.

lesion, but they are usually every 6 months for several years and annually thereafter. Radiographic evaluation of the upper tracts alone is not adequate because Keeley and colleagues (1997a) showed that 75% of early tumor recurrences were visible endoscopically and not radiographically. With tumors approached in a percutaneous fashion, immediate follow-up nephroscopy can be performed through the established nephrostomy track.

In the past, the burden of repeated endoscopic evaluation of the upper urinary tracts was a major deterrent to conservative therapy. The use of smaller, 7.5 French flexible ureteroscopes has greatly eased the burden of follow-up because ureteroscopes can be reliably passed up the ureter without the need for dilation of the ureteral orifice or prior stenting. Others have advocated resection of the ureteral orifice to facilitate subsequent surveillance ureteroscopy in the office setting (Kerbl and Clayman, 1993). Even though technology has somewhat facilitated follow-up, both physician and patient must be committed to nephron-sparing treatment.

## Metastatic Restaging

Metastatic restaging is required in all patients at significant risk for disease progression to local or distant sites. This group

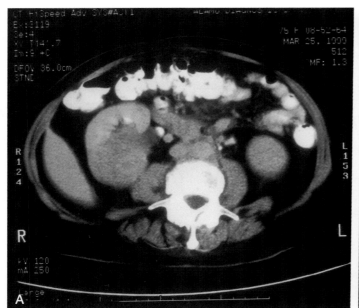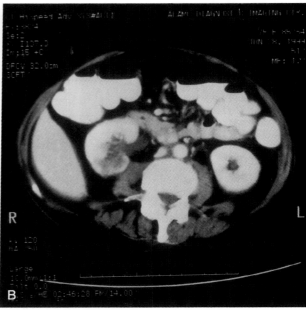

**Figure 49–33.** Patient with a large, biopsy-proven transitional cell carcinoma of the kidney as well as lung and axillary metastases. **A,** Initial appearance of the renal tumor. **B,** Marked shrinkage of the tumor after four courses of paclitaxel and gemcitabine. The lung and axillary metastases disappeared, and nephroureterectomy was performed. During the next year, the patient developed a brain metastasis. (Courtesy of Dr. Randall Singleton.)

includes those with high-grade or high-stage disease. Metastatic restaging is generally not necessary for low-grade disease when the risks of invasive and subsequent metastatic disease are negligible. Included in metastatic restaging is imaging of the ipsilateral renal bed for recurrence with cross-sectional imaging. Follow-up restaging includes chest radiograph, liver function tests, cross-sectional body imaging, and selective use of bone scan based on an understanding of natural disease history and metastatic pathways (Korman et al, 1996).

## TREATMENT OF METASTATIC DISEASE

Outcomes are poor in patients with metastatic urothelial tumors of the upper urinary tract. **The systemic chemotherapy regimens offered for treatment are the same as those used for transitional cell carcinoma of the bladder.** These regimens are discussed in Chapter 77. Only limited data on response rates of advanced upper tract tumors to chemotherapy are available because of the rarity of these lesions. Prospective randomized trials comparing chemotherapeutic regimens for upper tract tumors are not feasible for this reason. Patients with advanced upper tract tumors are excluded from most trials on treatment of advanced bladder cancer. Therefore, one must extrapolate likely chemotherapy response rates for upper tract disease from observations in bladder cancer trials.

The MVAC (methotrexate, vinblastine, doxorubicin, cisplatin) regimen continues to have the highest response rate (Sternberg et al, 1989). However, complete responses are rare, and the duration of response is limited, with overall survival of approximately 12 to 24 months. Toxicity is high and dose

limited in some patients. For all these reasons, there is considerable ongoing investigation with newer agents, including paclitaxel, ifosfamide, carboplatin, and gemcitabine, used in various combinations and sequences (Roth et al, 1994; Bajorin et al, 1998; Redman et al, 1998; Vaughn et al, 1998; Kaufman et al, 2000; Lorusso et al, 2000). Many of these show initial overall response rates similar to the response rate to MVAC and lower toxicity. Occasional major responses are seen (Fig. 49–33). However, thus far, complete responses are rare, and neither durability of response nor survival is better than that seen with MVAC. In summary, upper tract urothelial cancer, like bladder cancer, is chemosensitive. It is to be hoped that additional improvements in treatment efficacy and safety are forthcoming, with further experience with new chemotherapeutic regimens. Alternative strategies, such as biologic response modifiers and gene therapy, also should be explored.

## KEY POINTS: CHEMOTHERAPY

- The chemotherapy for advanced upper tract transitional cell carcinoma is the same as for bladder cancer.

- Controlled trials limited to upper tract tumors are not practical because of the low prevalence of disease.

# SUGGESTED READINGS

Batata MA, Grabstald H: Upper urinary tract urothelial tumors. Urol Clin North Am 1976;3:79-86.

Daneshmand S, Quek ML, Huffman JL: Endoscopic management of upper urinary tract transitional cell carcinoma: Long-term experience. Cancer 2003;98:55-60.

El Fettouh HA, Rassweiler JJ, Schulze M, et al: Laparoscopic radical nephroureterectomy: Results of an international multicenter study. Eur Urol 2002;42:447-452.

Elliott DS, Blute ML, Patterson DE, et al: Long-term follow-up of endoscopically treated upper urinary tract transitional cell carcinoma. Urology 1996;47:819-825.

Hall MC, Womack S, Roehrborn CG, et al: Advanced transitional cell carcinoma of the upper urinary tract: Patterns of failure, survival and impact of postoperative adjuvant radiotherapy. J Urol 1998;160:703-706.

Hall MC, Womack S, Sagalowsky AI, et al: Prognostic factors, recurrence, and survival in transitional cell carcinoma of the upper urinary tract: A 30-year experience in 252 patients. Urology 1998;52:594-601.

Hayashida Y, Nomata K, Noguchi M, et al: Long-term effects of bacille Calmette-Guérin perfusion therapy for treatment of transitional cell carcinoma in situ of upper urinary tract. Urology 2004;63:1084-1088.

Herr HW: Long-term results of BCG therapy: Concern about upper tract tumors. Semin Urol Oncol 1998;16:13-16.

Jarrett TW, Sweetser PM, Weiss GH, Smith AD: Percutaneous management of transitional cell carcinoma of the renal collecting system: 9-year experience. J Urol 1995;154:1629-1635.

Jarrett T, Abbou CC, Tolley DA, et al: Laparoscopic radical nephroureterectomy: Results of an international multicenter study. Eur Urol 2002;42:447-452.

Kang CH, Yu TJ, Hsieh HH, et al: The development of bladder tumors and contralateral upper urinary tract tumors after primary transitional cell carcinoma of the upper urinary tract. Cancer 2003;98:1620-1626.

Matin SF, Gill IS: Recurrence and survival following laparoscopic radical nephroureterectomy with various forms of bladder cuff control. J Urol 2005;173:395-400.

Mullerad M, Russo P, Golijanin D, et al: Bladder cancer as a prognostic factor for upper tract transitional cell carcinoma. J Urol 2004;172:2177-2181.

Munoz JJ, Ellison LM: Upper tract urothelial neoplasms: Incidence and survival the last 2 decades. J Urol 2000;164:1523-1525.

Park S, Hong B, Kim CS, Ahn H: The impact of tumor location on prognosis of transitional cell carcinoma of the upper urinary tract. J Urol 2004;171:621-625.

Sternberg DW, Yagoda A, Scher HI, et al: Methotrexate, vinblastine, doxorubicin, and cisplatin for advanced transitional cell carcinoma of the urothelium: Efficacy and patterns of response and relapse. Cancer 1989;64: 2448-2458.

Tawfiek ER, Bagley D: Upper-tract transitional cell carcinoma. Urology 1997;50:321-329.

Zincke H, Neves RJ: Feasibility of conservative surgery for transitional cell cancer of the upper urinary tract. Urol Clin North Am 1984;11:717-724.

# 50 Open Surgery of the Kidney

ANDREW C. NOVICK, MD

**HISTORICAL ASPECTS**

**SURGICAL ANATOMY**

**PREOPERATIVE PREPARATION**

**INTRAOPERATIVE RENAL ISCHEMIA**

**SURGICAL APPROACHES TO THE KIDNEY**

**SIMPLE NEPHRECTOMY**

**RADICAL NEPHRECTOMY**

**PARTIAL NEPHRECTOMY FOR MALIGNANT DISEASE**

**PARTIAL NEPHRECTOMY FOR BENIGN DISEASE**

**RENAL ARTERIAL RECONSTRUCTION**

**INDICATIONS FOR TREATMENT**

**PREOPERATIVE CONSIDERATIONS**

**AORTORENAL BYPASS**

**ALTERNATIVE BYPASS TECHNIQUES**

**POSTOPERATIVE CARE**

**CLINICAL RESULTS**

**COMPLICATIONS**

**MISCELLANEOUS RENAL OPERATIONS**

## HISTORICAL ASPECTS

The first nephrectomies were probably performed serendipitously. Early reports of removal of large ovarian tumors indicate that the surgeon was occasionally surprised to find the kidney included in the surgical specimen. Definitive renal surgery was first performed in 1869 by Gustav Simon, who carried out a planned nephrectomy for treatment of a ureterovaginal fistula. The operation was preceded by extensive experimental investigation of uninephrectomy in dogs to demonstrate that they could survive normally with only one kidney. This application of an experimental model to a clinical problem was the forerunner of the method by which many current surgical procedures were developed.

In 1881, Morris was the first to perform nephrolithotomy in an otherwise healthy kidney, and he later defined the terms *nephrolithiasis, nephrolithotomy, nephrectomy,* and *nephrotomy*. The first partial nephrectomy was performed in 1884 by Wells for removal of a perirenal fibrolipoma. In 1887, Czerny was the first to use partial nephrectomy for excision of a renal neoplasm. Kuster performed the first successful pyeloplasty (a dismembered procedure) in 1891 on the solitary kidney of a 13-year-old boy. In 1892, Fenger applied the Heineke-Mikulicz principle for pyloric stenosis to ureteropelvic junction obstruction. In 1903, Zondek emphasized the importance of thorough knowledge of renal arterial circulation in performing partial nephrectomy.

There was great controversy among early surgeons regarding the relative merits of retroperitoneal versus transperitoneal exposure of the kidney. Kocher and Langham performed an anterior transperitoneal nephrectomy through a midline incision as early as 1878. A transverse abdominal incision was employed in 1913 by Berg, who also mobilized the colon laterally to expose the great vessels and thus secure the renal pedicle with greater safety. Berg was able to remove vena caval tumor thrombi through a cavotomy after control of the veins by vascular clamps. Rehn actually reimplanted the contralateral renal vein after resecting the inferior vena cava (IVC) in 1922. However, the high incidence of peritonitis and other abdominal complications led most urologists to adopt a retroperitoneal flank approach to the kidney during the first half of the 20th century. During the late 1950s, the development of safe abdominal and vascular surgical techniques led to a revival of the anterior approach in patients undergoing renal surgery (Culp and Winterringer, 1955; Poutasse, 1961).

## SURGICAL ANATOMY

The kidneys are paired vital organs located on either side of the vertebral column in the lumbar fossa of the retroperitoneal space. Each kidney is surrounded by a layer of perinephric fat, which is in turn covered by a distinct fascial layer termed Gerota's fascia. Posteriorly, both kidneys lie on the psoas major and quadratus lumborum muscles. They are also in relationship with the medial and lateral lumbocostal arches and the tendon of the transverse abdominal muscle. Posteriorly and superiorly, the upper pole of each kidney is in contact with the diaphragm (Fig. 50–1).

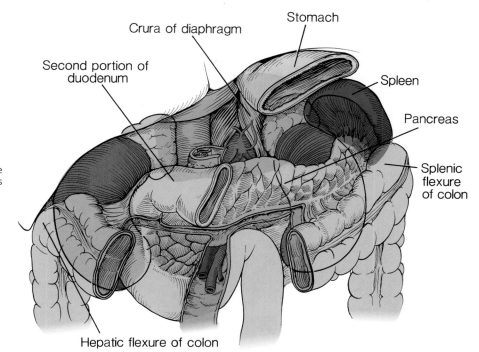

Figure 50–1. The anatomic relationship of the kidneys to surrounding structures. The liver is retracted superiorly.

A small segment of the anterior medial surface of the right kidney is in contact with the right adrenal gland. However, the major anterior relationships of the right kidney are with the liver, which overlies the upper two thirds of the anterior surface, and the hepatic flexure of the colon, which overlies the lower third. The second portion of the duodenum covers the right renal hilum.

A small segment of the anterior medial surface of the left kidney is also covered by the left adrenal gland. The major anterior relationships of the left kidney are with the spleen, the body of the pancreas, the stomach, and the splenic flexure of the colon.

**The kidney has four constant vascular segments, which are termed apical, anterior, posterior, and basilar**. The anterior segment is the largest and extends beyond the midplane of the kidney onto the posterior surface. A true avascular line exists at the junction of the anterior and posterior segments on the posterior surface of the kidney.

Each vascular segment of the kidney is supplied by one or more major arterial branches (Fig. 50–2). Although the origin of the branches supplying these segments may vary, the anatomic position of the segments is constant. All segmental arteries are end arteries with no collateral circulation; therefore, in performing renal surgery, failure to preserve one of these branches leads to devitalization of functioning renal tissue. Most individuals have a single main artery to each kidney originating from the lateral aspect of the aorta just below the superior mesenteric artery (SMA). Multiple renal arteries occur unilaterally and bilaterally in 23% and 10% of the population, respectively.

The normal renal venous anatomy is depicted in Figure 50–3. The left and right renal veins both terminate in the lateral aspect of the IVC. The left renal vein is longer and has a thicker muscle layer than the right renal vein. These are the gonadal vein inferiorly, the left adrenal vein superiorly, and

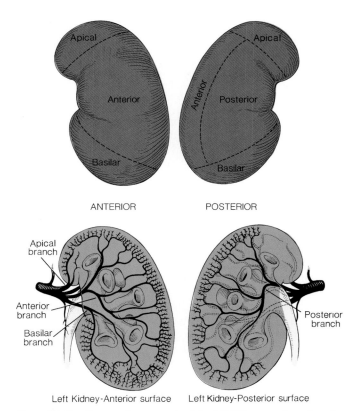

Figure 50–2. The vascular segments of the left kidney, as shown in anterior and posterior projections, and the corresponding segmental arterial supply to each segment.

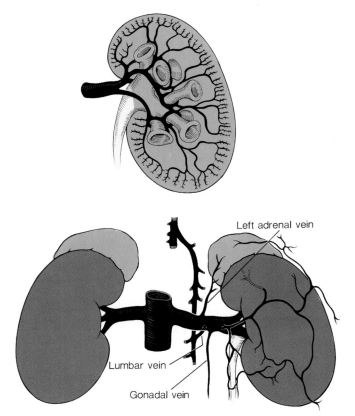

**Figure 50–3.** The normal renal venous anatomy, including branches of the left renal vein *(bottom)*. The intrarenal venous drainage parallels the segmental arterial supply and is depicted for the left kidney *(top)*.

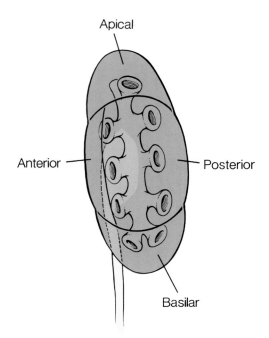

**Figure 50–4.** The intrarenal collecting system in relation to major vascular segments of the kidney.

one or two large lumbar veins posteriorly. There are no significant branches draining into the right renal vein. Multiple renal veins are less common than multiple renal arteries.

The renal venous drainage system differs significantly from the arterial blood supply in that the intrarenal venous branches intercommunicate freely among the various renal segments. Ligation of a branch of the renal vein, therefore, does not result in segmental infarction of the kidney because collateral venous blood supply provides adequate drainage. This is important clinically because it enables one to obtain surgical access to structures in the renal hilum by ligation and division of small adjacent or overlying venous branches.

With regard to the intrarenal collecting system, there are 8 to 10 major calyces that open into the renal pelvis (Fig. 50–4). The apical segment has one major calyx that lies in the mid-frontal plane and receives two minor calyces, which are lateral and medial. The basilar segment has a single major calyx in the median plane and receives two minor calyces, which are anterior and posterior. There are three major calyces in the anterior segment that enter the renal pelvis at a 20-degree angle to the midfrontal plane and three major calyces in the posterior segment that enter the renal pelvis at a 75-degree angle to the midfrontal plane.

## PREOPERATIVE PREPARATION

A thorough preoperative evaluation is important in patients undergoing renal surgery because of the special positions in

which the patient may have to be placed intraoperatively and the systemic disturbances that may occur secondary to renal infections and impairment of renal function.

Cardiorespiratory function is evaluated by eliciting any history of heart disease, chest pain, smoking, or respiratory distress on exertion. An electrocardiogram, chest radiograph, and complete blood count should be obtained for all patients. The flank position with lateral flexion of the spine is known to cause embarrassment of ventilatory capacity, and the venous return may be significantly diminished in this position, resulting in hypotension. Therefore, alternatives to the flank approach should be used whenever possible in patients with a decreased pulmonary reserve. Preoperative pulmonary function studies and blood gas analysis are mandatory in patients thought to have impaired respiratory function. In the event of impairment, use of an anterior surgical approach with the patient in the supine position is preferred.

Regardless of the surgical incision used, respiration may be seriously impaired postoperatively as a result of transection of upper abdominal or flank muscles and, occasionally, removal of a rib. Also, the upper poles of the kidneys encroach on the undersurface of the diaphragm, and the removal of a large upper pole renal mass may interfere temporarily with its function. Preoperative breathing exercises, alleviation of bronchospasm, cessation of smoking, and evaluation of cardiopulmonary function are helpful in improving respiratory function and in preventing postoperative cardiorespiratory problems.

Bleeding tendencies are assessed by examination of platelet function and coagulation factors. Patients should be questioned about excess alcohol intake and ingestion of drugs, such as aspirin, that can influence blood clotting.

A thorough anatomic examination of the urinary tract should be made in all patients undergoing renal surgery.

Available studies include intravenous pyelography, cystoscopy, retrograde pyelography, ureteroscopy, cystourethrography, computed axial tomography, ultrasonography, magnetic resonance imaging, renal arteriography, and renal venography. Three-dimensional volume-rendered computed tomography (CT) is an accurate imaging modality for surgical planning before reconstructive renal surgery (Coll et al, 1999). These tests and their usefulness in evaluating patients for specific renal operations are reviewed in other chapters of this text.

Overall, renal function is evaluated by estimation of the serum creatinine level and either endogenous creatinine clearance or iothalamate glomerular filtration rate. Differential renal function can be assessed noninvasively by computed isotope renography with hippuric acid I 131 or technetium 99. Hippuric acid I 131 is cleared by both glomeruli and tubules and is most useful for measuring unilateral renal dysfunction when overall renal function is normal. Technetium chelated with diethylenetriaminepentaacetic acid is filtered only by the glomeruli and is thus more helpful in assessing differential renal perfusion. Both of these isotopes are excreted in the urine, and in the presence of obstruction, parenchymal concentration is obscured by the high concentration of isotope in the accumulated urine.

Patients with either upper or lower urinary tract infection should receive organism-specific antibiotic therapy preoperatively. With suspected or proven upper tract infection, at least 48 hours of antibiotic therapy is indicated before renal surgery. Severe bacteremia can occur during operation on an infected kidney, with significant resulting morbidity and potential mortality.

Percutaneous embolization of the kidney is occasionally helpful before radical nephrectomy is performed for large renal malignant neoplasms. The major value of this adjunct procedure is for patients with an arterialized vena caval tumor thrombus or a medial extension of tumor that interferes with early ligation of the renal artery. Subsequent transient flank pain is common and often requires analgesic medication for control.

Patients are often concerned about how the removal of a kidney will affect their renal function. After nephrectomy for unilateral renal disease, the opposite kidney undergoes compensatory hypertrophy, and the glomerular filtration rate is ultimately maintained at 75% of the normal value (Aperia et al, 1977; Robitaille et al, 1985). Several long-term studies have shown no increase in hypertension or proteinuria, stable overall renal function, and normal life expectancy after unilateral nephrectomy with a normal contralateral kidney (Kretschmer, 1943; Goldstein, 1956; Anderson et al, 1968). This information should be shared with patients to alleviate their anxiety before surgery.

## INTRAOPERATIVE RENAL ISCHEMIA

Temporary occlusion of the renal artery is necessary for a variety of operations, such as partial nephrectomy, renal vascular reconstruction, anatrophic nephrolithotomy, and repair of traumatic renal injury. In such cases, temporary arterial occlusion not only diminishes intraoperative renal bleeding but also improves access to intrarenal structures by causing the kidney to contract and by reducing renal tissue turgor. Performance of these operations requires an understanding of

renal responses to warm ischemia and available methods of protecting the kidney when the period of arterial occlusion exceeds that which may be safely tolerated.

## Mechanisms of Renal Ischemic Injury

In recent years, there have been significant insights into the pathophysiologic process of renal ischemia. In animal models as well as in humans, postischemic reductions in glomerular filtration rate have been attributed to persistent vasoconstriction, due in part to activation of tubuloglomerular feedback as a result of enhanced delivery of solute to the macula densa. Increased solute delivery to the distal nephron is caused by impaired tight junction integrity resulting in decreased sodium reabsorption due to loss of cell polarity in the proximal tubule with mislocalization of the $Na^+,K^+$-ATPase (Kwon et al, 1998).

Endothelial injury results in cell swelling and enhanced expression of cell adhesion molecules. This, together with leukocyte activation, leads to enhanced leukocyte–endothelial cell interactions, which can promote injury and swelling of the endothelial cell, physically impede blood flow, contribute to the production of local factors promoting vasoconstriction, and add to effects of vasoconstriction on local blood flow and tubule cell metabolism (Thadhani et al, 1996).

Endothelial injury also leads to changes in the response to vasoactive substances. Arterioles from postischemic kidneys have increased basal tone and reactivity to vasoconstrictive agents and decreased vasodilatory responses compared with arterioles from normal kidneys. Alterations in local levels of vasoconstrictors (angiotensin II, thromboxane $A_2$, leukotrienes, adenosine, endothelin-1) have been implicated in abnormal vascular tone. Vascular responses may be attributed to enhanced responses to angiotensin II through activation of endothelin B or prostaglandin $H_2$–thromboxane $A_2$ receptors. Systemic endothelin-1 levels increase with ischemia, and administration of antiendothelin antibodies or endothelin receptor antagonists has been reported to protect against ischemia-reperfusion injury (Newaz and Oyekan, 2001). Nitric oxide is vasodilatory and decreases endothelin expression and activity in the vascular endothelium, effects that should be protective against ischemic renal injury. With endothelial injury, endothelial nitric oxide synthase is inhibited (Kourembanas et al, 1993). Nevertheless, despite extensive data suggesting that enhanced vasoconstriction is a fundamental contributor to the pathophysiologic process of ischemic acute renal failure, vasodilators have not been found to be clinically useful in prevention or treatment of acute renal failure associated with tubular necrosis in humans.

An important feature of the pathophysiologic mechanism of ischemic injury is related to reductions in medullary blood flow with reduction in oxygen delivery to the tubular structures in this region of the kidney and resultant cellular injury due to imbalance between oxygen delivery and demand. Endothelial activation and injury together with increased leukocyte–endothelial cell interactions and activation of coagulation pathways may have a greater effect on outer medullary ischemia than arteriolar vasoconstriction, as there can be markedly impaired oxygen delivery to the outer medulla despite adequate renal blood flow (Thadhani et al, 1996).

Endothelial cell injury leading to upregulation of adhesion molecules and cell swelling and loss of the patency of the endothelial barrier potentiates interactions with leukocytes and platelets and leads to small vessel–mechanical obstruction. Locally derived cytokines, chemokines, eicosanoids, and reactive oxygen species recruit and activate leukocytes. Activated leukocytes generate reactive oxygen species and eicosanoids, which further the inflammatory response and enhance vascular tone, stimulating further injury.

Infiltration of neutrophils and mononuclear cells is important in reperfusion injury. Tissue injury is ameliorated by prevention of neutrophil accumulation (Suwa et al, 2001). Macrophages and T lymphocytes predominate over neutrophils in the later recovery phase of postischemic injury. Blockade of T-cell CD28-B7 costimulation protects against ischemic injury in rats (Takada et al, 1997). Chemokines are upregulated by inflammatory cytokines such as interleukin-1 and tumor necrosis factor-α. Infusion of a tumor necrosis factor-α–binding protein decreases neutrophil infiltration and is renoprotective. Activation of coagulation pathways also contributes to postischemic injury. An oral inhibitor of platelet-activating factor is protective against ischemic injury in animal models. Attenuation of complement C5 protects against late inflammation and resulting renal dysfunction (Bonventre and Weinberg, 2003).

## Renal Tolerance to Warm Ischemia

The extent of renal damage after normothermic arterial occlusion depends on the duration of the ischemic insult. Canine studies have shown that warm ischemic intervals of up to 30 minutes can be sustained with eventual full recovery of renal function (Ward, 1975). **For periods of warm ischemia beyond 30 minutes, there is generally significant, immediate functional loss, and late recovery of renal function is either incomplete or absent. On histologic evaluation, renal ischemia is most damaging to the proximal tubular cells,** which may show varying degrees of necrosis and regeneration, whereas the glomeruli and blood vessels are generally spared.

Human tolerance to warm renal ischemia closely parallels that seen in experimental canine observations, and in general, 30 minutes is the maximum tolerable period of arterial occlusion before permanent damage is sustained. In some clinical situations, this admonition may not apply, and a longer period of ischemia may be safely tolerated. It is acknowledged that the solitary kidney is more resistant to ischemic damage than the paired kidney, although precise limits have not been defined (Askari et al, 1982). Another situation that may enhance renal tolerance to temporary arterial occlusion is the presence of an extensive collateral vascular supply. This is generally observed only in patients with renal arterial occlusive disease (Schefft et al, 1980).

**Another determinant of renal ischemic damage is the method employed to achieve vascular control of the kidney. Animal studies have shown that functional impairment is least when the renal artery alone is continuously occluded.** Continuous occlusion of the renal artery and vein for an equivalent time interval is more damaging because it prevents retrograde perfusion of the kidney through the renal vein and may also produce venous congestion of the kidney (Neely and Turner, 1959; Leary et al, 1963; Schirmer et al, 1966).

Intermittent clamping of the renal artery with short periods of recirculation is also more damaging than continuous arterial occlusion, possibly because of the release and trapping of damaging vasoconstrictor agents within the kidney (Neely and Turner, 1959; Schirmer et al, 1966; Wilson et al, 1971; McLoughlin et al, 1978). Animal studies have further demonstrated that the use of manual renal compression to control intraoperative hemorrhage is more deleterious than simple arterial occlusion (Neely and Turner, 1959).

## Prevention of Ischemic Renal Damage

Several general adjunctive measures should be employed in all patients undergoing operations that involve a period of temporary renal arterial occlusion. These include generous preoperative and intraoperative hydration, prevention of hypotension during the period of anesthesia, avoidance of unnecessary manipulation or traction on the renal artery, and intraoperative administration of mannitol. These measures help limit postischemic renal injury by ensuring optimal perfusion with an absence of cortical vasospasm at the time of arterial occlusion, which allows uniform restoration of blood flow throughout the kidney when the renal artery is unclamped. Mannitol is most effective when it is given 5 to 15 minutes before arterial occlusion (Collins et al, 1980), and it is beneficial because it increases renal plasma flow, decreases intrarenal vascular resistance, minimizes intracellular edema, and promotes an osmotic diuresis when renal circulation is restored (Nosowsky and Kaufman, 1963). Systemic or regional heparinization before renal arterial occlusion is not necessary, unless there is existing small vessel or parenchymal renal disease.

**When the anticipated period of intraoperative renal ischemia is longer than 30 minutes, additional specific protective measures are indicated to prevent permanent damage to the kidney.** Local hypothermia is the most effective and commonly employed method for protecting the kidney from ischemic damage. Lowering renal temperature reduces energy-dependent metabolic activity of the cortical cells, with a resultant decrease in both the consumption of oxygen and the breakdown of adenosine triphosphate (Harvey, 1959; Levy, 1959). The optimum temperature for hypothermic in situ renal preservation is 15°C, based on canine experiments conducted by Ward (1975). In clinical renal surgery, it is difficult to achieve uniform cooling to this level because of the temperature of adjacent tissues and the need to have a portion of the kidney exposed to perform the operation. For practical reasons, a temperature of 20°C to 25°C is easier to maintain and represents a compromise that renders renal surgery technically feasible while still allowing a renal preservative effect. Both animal and human studies have shown that this level of hypothermia provides complete renal protection from arterial occlusion of up to 3 hours (Wickham et al, 1967; Luttrop et al, 1976; Petersen et al, 1977; Wagenknecht et al, 1977; Marberger et al, 1978; Stubbs et al, 1978; Kyriakidis et al, 1979).

In situ renal hypothermia can be achieved with external surface cooling or perfusion of the kidney with a cold solution instilled into the renal artery. These two methods are equally effective; however, the latter is an invasive technique that requires direct entry into the renal artery (Leary et al,

1963; Farcon et al, 1974; Kyriakidis et al, 1979; Abele et al, 1981). Surface cooling of the kidney is a simpler and more widely used method that has been accomplished by a variety of techniques, such as surrounding the kidney with a cold solution (Mitchell, 1959) or applying an external cooling device to the kidney (Cockett, 1961). These methods require complete renal mobilization to achieve effective surface cooling.

**Most urologists prefer ice-slush cooling for surface renal hypothermia because of its relative ease and simplicity.** The mobilized kidney is surrounded with a rubber sheet on which sterile ice slush is placed to completely immerse the kidney. An important caveat with this method is to keep the entire kidney covered with ice for 10 to 15 minutes immediately after the renal artery is occluded and before the renal operation is commenced. This amount of time is needed to obtain core renal cooling to a temperature (approximately 20°C) that optimizes in situ renal preservation. During performance of the renal operation, invariably, large portions of the kidney are no longer covered with ice slush, and in the absence of adequate prior core renal cooling, rapid rewarming and ischemic renal injury can occur. This technique is effective for in situ renal preservation. Stubbs and associates (1978) described 30 patients with a solitary kidney in whom anatrophic nephrolithotomy was performed with ice-slush surface hypothermia; despite a mean renal artery clamp time of longer than 2 hours and as long as 4 hours in some cases, renal function was completely preserved in all patients.

Another approach to in situ renal preservation that does not involve hypothermia is pretreatment with one or more pharmacologic agents to prevent postischemic renal failure (Novick, 1983).

**Whereas agents such as renal-dose dopamine and inosine, captopril, and adenosine triphosphate–magnesium chloride have been proposed to minimize ischemic renal damage, reports have failed to show a consistent renoprotective effect in the setting of transient renal ischemia during solitary partial nephrectomy or in single-kidney animal models.** A prospective controlled study from the Cleveland Clinic showed no beneficial effect of perioperative dopamine on renal function after partial nephrectomy in a solitary kidney (O'Hara et al, 2002).

## SURGICAL APPROACHES TO THE KIDNEY

Exposure of the kidney during surgery must be adequate to perform the operation and to deal with any possible complications. This is particularly important in renal surgery because the kidney is deeply placed in the upper retroperitoneum with access limited by the lower ribs, liver, and spleen. Injuries to large renal vessels may be difficult to control or to repair through small incisions, particularly in the presence of a large tumor or inflamed perinephric tissues. Poor exposure renders the operation unnecessarily difficult and also leads to excessive retraction, with bruising of the muscles and possible injury to the intercostal nerves, which can increase postoperative pain.

**Factors to consider in selecting an appropriate incision for renal surgery include operation to be performed,** underlying renal disease, previous operations, concurrent extrarenal disease that requires another operation to be done simultaneously, need for bilateral renal operations, and body habitus. Physical abnormalities in the patient, such as kyphoscoliosis or severe pulmonary disease, may also dictate that certain approaches, such as the standard flank incision, not be used.

The kidney may be approached by four principal routes: an extraperitoneal flank approach, a dorsal lumbotomy, an abdominal incision, and a thoracoabdominal incision. The indications, relative advantages, and technical performance of each approach are reviewed separately.

## Flank Approach

This approach provides good access to the renal parenchyma and collecting system (Woodruff, 1955). It is an extraperitoneal approach and involves minimal disturbance to other viscera. Contamination of the peritoneal cavity is avoided, and drainage of the perirenal space is readily established. This approach is particularly useful in the obese patient because most of the panniculus falls forward, making this incision relatively straightforward even in the very large person. **The principal disadvantage of the flank incision is that exposure in the area of the renal pedicle is not as good as with anterior transperitoneal approaches. In addition, the flank incision may prove unsuitable for the patient with scoliosis or cardiorespiratory problems.**

The most commonly used flank approach to the kidney is through the bed of the 11th or 12th rib (Hess, 1939; Hughes, 1949; Bodner and Briskin, 1950). The choice of rib depends on the position of the kidney and on whether the upper or lower pole is the site of disease. With a flank incision, the midportion of the wound and the site of maximal exposure are in the midaxillary line. Access in the posterior part, at the neck of the rib, is limited by the sacrospinal muscle. The appropriate level of the incision is therefore best determined by drawing a horizontal line on the urogram from the hilum of the kidney to the most lateral rib that it intersects (Fig. 50–5).

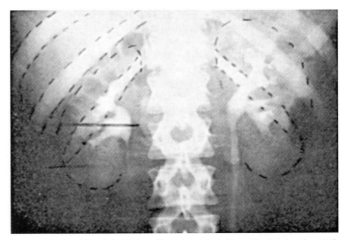

**Figure 50–5.** The right kidney is traversed at its midpoint by the 12th rib. The ideal incision is chosen by drawing a horizontal line from the hilum to the lateral rib cage.

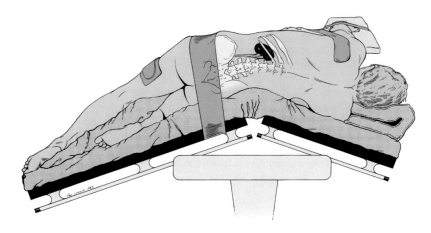

**Figure 50–6.** Position of the patient for the flank approach. Note the axillary pad. The kidney rest may be elevated if further lateral extension is needed.

When access to the upper renal pole is required, the rib above is selected.

The patient is placed in the lateral position after being anesthetized and having an endotracheal tube inserted. The back should be placed fairly close to the edge of the operating table to ensure unimpeded access by the surgeon, and the patient should be positioned so that the tip of the 12th rib is over the kidney rest. The bottom leg is flexed to 90 degrees with the top leg straight to maintain stability. A pillow is placed between the knees, and a sponge pad is placed under the axilla to prevent compression of the axillary vessels and nerves. The patient is secured in this position with a wide adhesive tape passed over the greater trochanter and attached to the moveable portion of the table (Fig. 50–6). The extended upper arm can be supported on a padded Mayo stand, which is adjusted to the appropriate height to maintain the arm in a horizontal position with the shoulder rotated slightly forward.

Flexion of the table and elevation of the kidney rest should be performed slowly and may be delayed until the surgeon is ready to make the skin incision to minimize the time spent in this position. The flexion increases the space between the costal margin and the iliac crest and puts the flank muscles and skin on tension. Care must be taken with patients who have stiff spines to ensure that their extremities remain in contact with the table because their range of lateral flexion is limited. This position may not be well tolerated by elderly patients or by those with impaired cardiopulmonary function because it results in decreased venous return due to compression of the IVC and the dependent position of the legs. It also limits aeration of the lung on the dependent side. It is important to determine the blood pressure after the patient has been turned on the side and again after the table has been flexed and the kidney rest elevated. The rest may have to be lowered and the table unflexed if hypotension is observed. **Table flexion with elevation of the kidney rest may also cause ischemic damage to a previously operated on contralateral kidney** (Matin and Novick, 2001).

The flank incision is made directly over the appropriate rib, beginning at the lateral border of the sacrospinal muscle (Fig. 50–7). A left-sided 12th rib incision is demonstrated in Figures 50–7 to 50-12. After the external oblique and latissimus dorsi muscles and the slips of the underlying serratus inferior posterior muscles are divided (Fig. 50–8), the periosteum over the

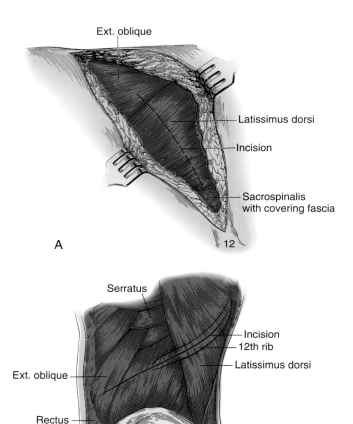

**Figure 50–7.** **A,** Left flank incision. The anterior edge of the latissimus dorsi muscle overlies the posterior edge of the external oblique muscle. **B,** The relationship of the 12th rib to the overlying muscles.

rib is incised with a scalpel or by diathermy. The flat periosteal elevator is used to reflect the periosteum off the rib (Fig. 50–9). Mobilization of the periosteum is completed by separating it from the inner aspect of the rib with use of a Doyen periosteal elevator (Fig. 50–10). The proximal end of the rib is then transected as far back as possible with the guillotine

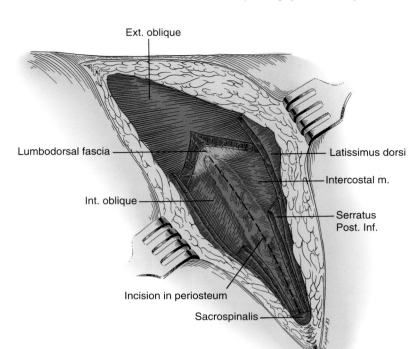

**Figure 50–8.** The muscles in the posterior part of the wound have been divided to expose the rib for incision of the periosteum.

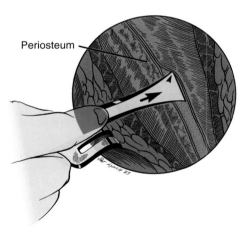

**Figure 50–9.** The periosteum is reflected off the upper surface of the rib. Note that the periosteal elevator is moved distally or downward on the upper edge of the rib against the direction of the intercostal muscle fibers.

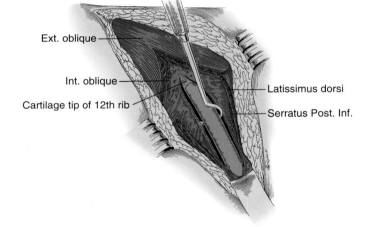

**Figure 50–10.** The periosteum is dissected off the rib, with use of a Doyen periosteal elevator, before resection of the rib.

rib resector. The retracted muscle mass is allowed to fall back over the sharp cut edge, protecting the operator from injury. The rib is grasped with a Kocher clamp and is separated by sharp dissection from the muscles attached anteriorly to complete its removal.

When the 11th rib is resected, attention must be directed at the pleural reflection, which crosses its lower border at the junction of the anterior and middle thirds and occupies the posterior part of the wound as it lies on the lower fibers of the diaphragm. The pleura may be reflected upward by sharply dividing the fascial attachments to the diaphragm. Alternatively, the lower fibers of the diaphragm can be detached from their insertion into the posterior inner aspect

of the 12th rib. This allows the lower diaphragm and pleura to be retracted upward, out of the wound.

An incision is now made through the periosteal bed of the rib to expose Gerota's fascia (Fig. 50–11). The incision is completed anteriorly by incising the lumbar fascia and inserting two fingers into the perinephric space to push the underlying peritoneum forward. The lateral peritoneal reflection is peeled off the undersurface of the anterior abdominal wall and the transversalis fascia by sweeping it forward with the fingers. The external and internal oblique muscles are divided by incising them sharply or with electrocautery while they are tented

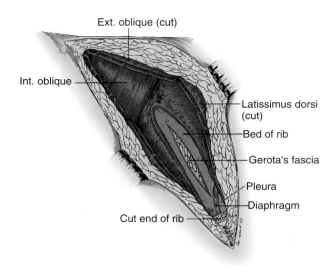

**Figure 50–11.** The rib has been resected, exposing the diaphragm and pleura in the posterior part of the wound. The slips of the diaphragm inserting into the rib have been divided, allowing the pleura to be displaced upward. An incision is made through the periosteal bed of the wound to expose Gerota's fascia.

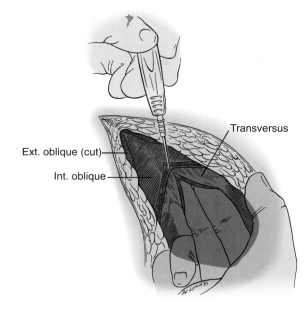

**Figure 50–12.** Two fingers are inserted into the incision in the posterior part of the transverse muscle to sweep the peritoneal reflection forward and divide the anterior abdominal muscles.

up over the two fingers inserted below the transverse muscle (Fig. 50–12). A little upward pressure controls bleeding from the severed vessels, allowing them to be clamped or cauterized by the assistant. This should expose the intercostal neurovascular bundle as it courses forward and downward between the internal oblique and transverse muscles. The transverse fibers of the transverse muscle may be split by blunt dissection below the nerve, allowing it to fall away with the upper margin of the incision.

A Finochietto retractor is used to maintain the exposure. The blades of the retractor are placed over moistened gauze sponges to avoid breaking a rib. The perinephric space is entered by incising Gerota's fascia posteriorly to avoid injury to the peritoneum. Care should be taken to avoid injury to the iliohypogastric and ilioinguinal nerves as they emerge from behind the lateral border of the psoas muscle and pass down over the anterior surface of the quadratus lumborum in the renal fossa.

The incision is closed by careful approximation of the corresponding muscle and fascial layers. To facilitate this, the kidney rest is lowered, and the table is returned to the horizontal position. Care must be taken to avoid inclusion of any intercostal nerves or branches during closure of the transverse muscle. Injection of 0.5% bupivacaine into the fascial sheath around the intercostal nerves as they emerge from the intervertebral foramina is helpful in diminishing postoperative pain and involuntary splinting of the lower chest. Drains are usually brought out posteriorly through a separate stab incision below the wound.

On occasion, a subcostal flank incision is indicated for surgery on the lower renal pole or upper ureter, insertion of a nephrostomy tube, or drainage of a perinephric abscess. It has the disadvantage of being low in relation to the usual position of the kidney, which makes access to the pedicle and renal pelvis more difficult. Exposure may be hampered by the iliac crest and subcostal nerve. The subcostal incision does not have

these disadvantages in children, in whom it provides good access to the kidney because the lower ribs are soft and easily displaced upward.

The subcostal incision is begun at the lateral border of the sacrospinal muscle where it crosses the inferior edge of the 12th rib and is carried forward about a fingerbreadth below the lower border of the last rib onto the anterior abdominal wall. The medial end of the incision is curved slightly downward as it passes the midaxillary line to avoid the subcostal nerve and may be extended as far as the lateral border of the rectus abdominis muscle. The extent of the incision is modified, depending on the location of the kidney and the nature of the disease.

With a subcostal incision, the latissimus dorsi muscle is divided in the posterior part of the wound to expose the posterior edge of the external oblique muscle (Fig. 50–13). The serratus inferior posterior muscles, arising from the lumbar fascia and inserting into the lower four ribs, are divided in the posterior portion of the wound. The external oblique muscle is divided anteriorly. The fused layers of the lumbodorsal fascia are now exposed, giving origin to the internal oblique and transverse muscles. After the internal oblique muscle is divided, the transverse muscle is separated bluntly either above or below the subcostal nerve, depending on the course of the nerve in relation to the incision (Fig. 50–14). Every effort should be made to avoid injury to the intercostal nerves; this may cause persistent postoperative pain or bulging in the flank due to paresis of the denervated muscle. The lumbar fascia and the lateral border of the sacrospinal muscle may need to be incised to improve exposure in the posterior part of the wound. Division of the costotransverse ligament as it passes up to the neck of the 12th rib allows the rib to be retracted upward to further improve the exposure. The closure is as described for a flank incision.

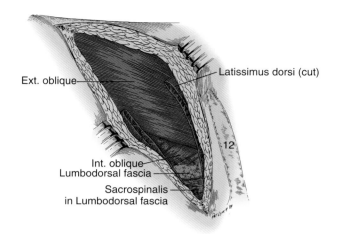

**Figure 50–13.** Left subcostal incision. The latissimus dorsi muscle has been divided to expose the lumbodorsal fascia and the posterior aspects of the abdominal muscles.

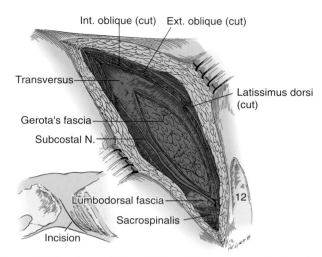

**Figure 50–14.** The lumbodorsal fascia and transverse muscles have been divided to expose Gerota's fascia. The subcostal nerve and vessels pierce the lumbodorsal fascia posteriorly and course forward on the transverse muscle.

## Dorsal Lumbotomy

The dorsal lumbotomy incision is a potentially useful approach for removal of a small kidney, for bilateral nephrectomy in patients with end-stage renal disease, or for open renal biopsy. It has also been used in the past for pyeloplasty, for pyelolithotomy, and for upper ureterolithotomy (Novick, 1980). This approach offers several advantages in performing these operations (Gardiner et al, 1979). Unlike with the standard flank incision, no muscles are transected, and access to the kidney is obtained by simply incising the posterior fascial layers. This approach is more rapid, provides strong wound closure with less postoperative pain, and obviates anterolateral bulging of the abdomen that commonly results from flank incisions. With detachment of the costovertebral ligament, the 12th rib can be retracted widely laterally, rendering resection of the rib unnecessary.

The dorsal lumbotomy approach is also advantageous in patients with prior abdominal or flank operations on the kidney because it permits dissection of fresh tissue planes. **The major disadvantage of dorsal lumbotomy is its limited access to the kidney and renal vessels, which can pose a problem if there are intraoperative complications such as migration of a calculus or injury to major renal vessels with bleeding.**

When bilateral nephrectomy is done, the patient is placed in the prone position with the table flexed to increase the distance between the 12th rib and the iliac crest. In this position, the patient is supported over the sternum and pubis so that there is free excursion of the anterior abdominal wall to prevent embarrassment of respiration and venous return. For unilateral renal operations, the patient may be placed in the lateral position with the table flexed to extend the lumbar region. In this position, a sandbag is placed between the abdomen and the table for support and to help push the kidney posteriorly.

A vertical lumbar incision is made along the lateral margin of the sacrospinal muscle. The incision begins at the upper margin of the 12th rib superiorly and follows a gentle lateral curve to the iliac crest inferiorly (Fig. 50–15A). The incision is carried through the lumbodorsal fascia just lateral to the sacrospinal and quadratus lumborum muscles, which are then retracted medially to approach the renal fossa (Fig. 50–15B). The transverse fascia is incised to expose the kidney contained within Gerota's fascia (Fig. 50–15C). Exposure of the kidney is thus obtained without transection of any muscle fibers. If additional superior exposure is needed, the costovertebral ligamentous attachment of the 12th rib is divided to allow lateral and superior retraction of the rib (Fig. 50–15D and E). The kidney can be mobilized and delivered down into the incision, provided the lower third of the kidney is below the 12th rib on preoperative radiographs. However, for high-lying or enlarged kidneys, the dorsal lumbotomy approach is cumbersome, and either a flank or an anterior incision provides better exposure. To close the incision, the retracted muscles are allowed to return to their original position, and the lumbodorsal fascia is reapproximated.

## Abdominal Incisions

**The principal advantage of the abdominal approach is that exposure in the area of the renal pedicle is excellent. The principal disadvantage is the somewhat longer period of postoperative ileus and the possible long-term complication of intra-abdominal adhesions leading to bowel obstruction.** The choice between a vertical and a transverse type of abdominal incision is determined by the patient's anatomy and disease entity. A vertical incision is easier and quicker to perform and repair because it involves division of only the linea alba or the anterior and posterior layers of the rectus sheath rather than several muscle layers. The vertical incision may be used in patients with a narrow subcostal angle and is preferred in patients with renal injury because it allows better access for inspection of the remainder of the abdominal contents for associated injuries. A transverse incision is preferable for patients with a wide subcostal angle and for exploration or removal of renal mass lesions (Chute et al, 1967). This incision provides better access to the lateral and superior portion

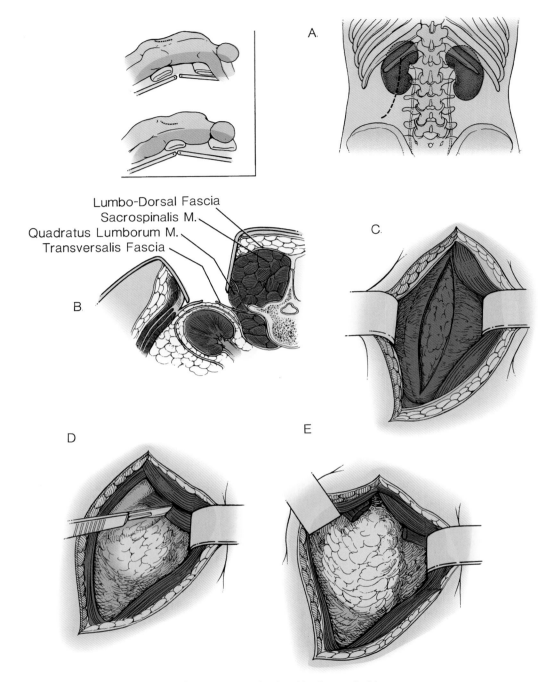

Lumbo-Dorsal Fascia
Sacrospinalis M.
Quadratus Lumborum M.
Transversalis Fascia

**Figure 50–15.** The dorsal lumbotomy incision.

of the kidney. A unilateral subcostal incision can be extended across the midline as a chevron incision to provide excellent exposure of both kidneys along with the aorta and the IVC.

When an anterior subcostal incision is employed, the patient is in the supine position with a rolled sheet beneath the upper lumbar spine. The incision begins approximately 1 to 2 fingerbreadths below the costal margin in the anterior axillary line and then extends with a gentle curve across the midline, ending at the midportion of the opposite rectus muscle. The incision is carried through the subcutaneous tissues to the anterior fascia, which is divided in the direction of the incision. In the lateral aspect of the incision, a portion

of the latissimus dorsi muscle is divided. The external oblique muscle is divided, exposing the fibers of the internal oblique muscle (Fig. 50–16A). The rectus, internal oblique, and transverse abdominal muscles are divided along with the posterior rectus sheath (Fig. 50–16B and C). The peritoneal cavity is entered in the midline, and the ligamentum teres is divided (Fig. 50–16D).

The bilateral subcostal incision is performed as described for the unilateral incision, except that both sides are involved (Fig. 50–17). It extends from one anterior axillary line to the opposite anterior axillary line, with a gentle upward curve as it crosses the midline. This incision provides better exposure

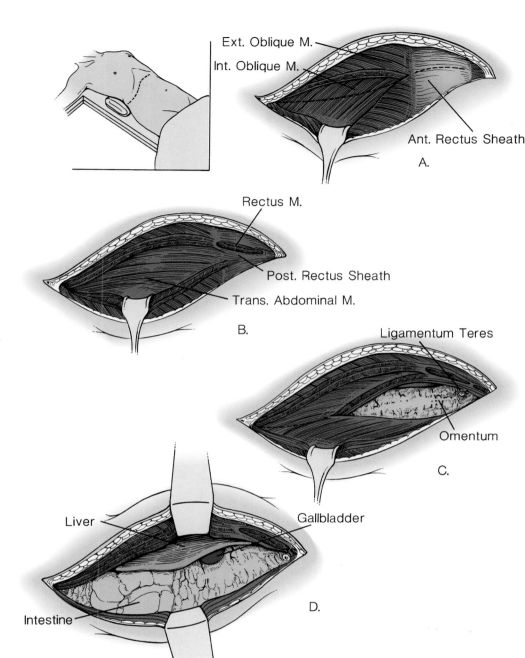

**Figure 50–16.** Unilateral anterior subcostal transperitoneal incision.

of both kidneys than does a midline incision, particularly in obese patients with a wide subcostal angle. The disadvantage is that it involves extensive transection of the abdominal wall musculature.

An extraperitoneal anterior subcostal approach may be useful to perform open renal biopsy or nephrectomy, particularly when there has been a previous intra-abdominal procedure or when there is a possibility that the patient may require peritoneal dialysis postoperatively (Lyon, 1958). The peritoneal cavity is not entered, thereby minimizing postoperative ileus and the chance of intra-abdominal complications. Reflection of the peritoneum off the anterior abdominal

wall may at times be difficult, and access to the renal pedicle may be less satisfactory than with a transperitoneal incision.

The patient is placed in a semioblique position with a rolled sheet beneath the side on which the incision is to be made. The muscle layers are divided as they are for a unilateral subcostal incision, except that the peritoneal cavity is not entered. The peritoneum is mobilized intact from the undersurface of the lateral musculature and rectus sheath and is then retracted medially to expose the retroperitoneal space (Fig. 50–18).

When a midline upper abdominal incision is employed, the patient is placed supine on the operating table with a rolled sheet beneath the upper lumbar spine. The incision extends

SECTION XII

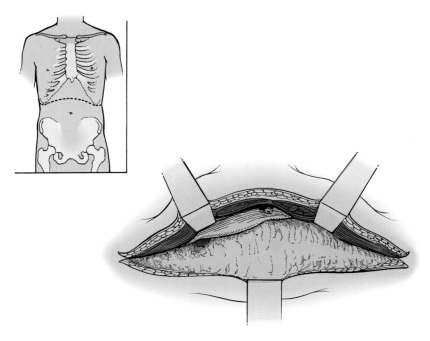

**Figure 50–17.** Bilateral anterior subcostal transperitoneal incision.

from the xiphoid to the umbilicus and can be extended around the umbilicus on either side if necessary. The incision is carried down through the subcutaneous tissues to the linea alba, which is the midline fusion of the tendinous fibers of the anterior rectus sheath. The linea alba is divided to expose the extraperitoneal fat and peritoneum, which is then entered (Fig. 50–19).

A paramedian incision is another type of vertical abdominal incision that may be preferred because the separate closure of the two layers of the rectus sheath makes the wound more secure. The incision is made about 3 cm lateral to the midline to provide an adequate margin of rectus sheath medially (Fig. 50–20). The anterior sheath is divided and reflected medially off the underlying muscle by sharp division of the tendinous intersections. The free medial edge of the muscle is retracted laterally to allow the posterior rectus sheath and peritoneum to be incised (Fig. 50–21). An extraperitoneal approach to the kidney can also be made through a paramedian incision by carefully reflecting the peritoneum off the posterior rectus sheath after it has been divided (Tessler et al, 1975).

## Thoracoabdominal Incision

**The thoracoabdominal approach is desirable for performing radical nephrectomy in patients with large tumors involving the upper portion of the kidney** (Clarke et al, 1958; Khoury, 1966; Middleton and Presto, 1973; Chute et al, 1949). It is particularly advantageous on the right side, where the liver and its venous drainage into the upper vena cava can limit exposure and impair vascular control as the tumor mass is being removed. There is less need for a thoracoabdominal incision on the left side because the spleen and pancreas can usually be readily elevated away from the tumor mass. The thoracoabdominal incision optimizes exposure of the suprarenal area. Nevertheless, because it involves additional operative time and greater potential pulmonary morbidity, I reserve this approach for patients in whom additional

exposure over that provided by an anterior subcostal incision is considered important to achieve complete and safe tumor removal.

The patient is placed in a semioblique position with a rolled sheet placed longitudinally beneath the flank. The lower leg is flexed and the upper one is extended with a pillow beneath the legs. The pelvis assumes a more horizontal position, tilted only about 10 to 15 degrees, which allows free access to the anterior abdominal wall. The incision is begun in the eighth or ninth intercostal space near the angle of the rib and carried across the costal margin to the midpoint of the opposite rectus muscle just above the umbilicus. The incision is carried down to the fascia, which is divided in the direction of the incision (Fig. 50–22A). The latissimus dorsi, external oblique, rectus, and intercostal muscles are also divided in the direction of the incision. The costal cartilage between the tips of the adjacent ribs is divided (Fig. 50–22B). The pleura in the posterior portion of the incision is opened to obtain complete exposure of the diaphragm (Fig. 50–22C).

The diaphragmatic incision is begun at the periphery about 2 cm inside its attachment to the chest wall; the incision is then carried around circumferentially to the posterior aspect of the diaphragm (Fig. 50–22D). In doing this, there must be at least 2 or 3 cm of diaphragm left attached to the rib cage to allow later reconstruction. By dividing the diaphragm in a circumferential manner from anterior to posterior, damage to the phrenic nerve is avoided. This also develops a diaphragmatic flap that can be pushed into the chest to provide complete exposure of the liver, which is then simply retracted upward (Fig. 50–22E). If further mobilization of the liver is needed, the right triangular ligament and coronary ligament can be incised to mobilize the entire right lobe of the liver upward. This provides excellent additional exposure of the suprarenal vena cava. Medial to the ribs, the internal oblique and transverse abdominal muscles are divided and the peritoneal cavity is entered. The colon and duodenum are mobilized medially, and the liver is

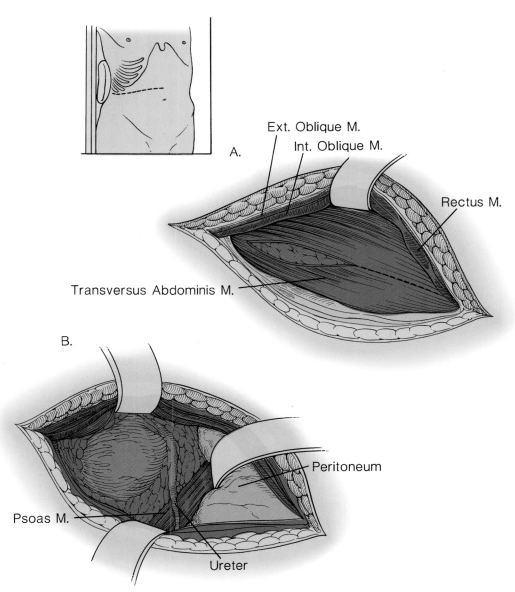

**A.**

Ext. Oblique M.

Int. Oblique M.

Rectus M.

Transversus Abdominis M.

**B.**

Peritoneum

Psoas M.

Ureter

**Figure 50–18.** Extraperitoneal anterior subcostal incision.

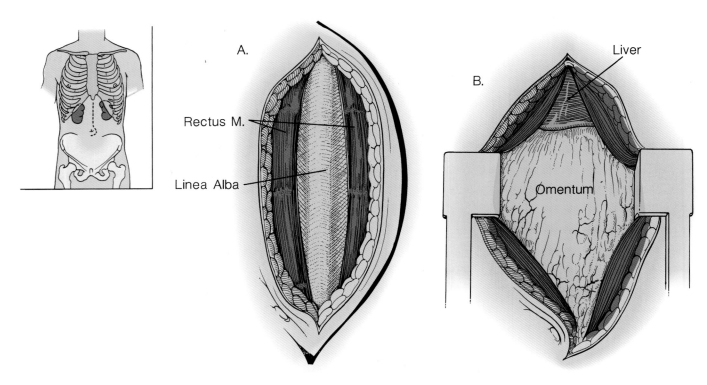

A.

Rectus M.

Linea Alba

B.

Liver

Omentum

**Figure 50–19.** Midline upper abdominal incision.

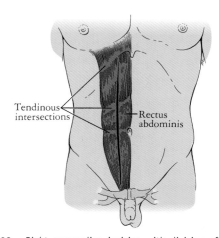

Tendinous intersections

Rectus abdominis

**Figure 50–20.** Right paramedian incision with division of the anterior rectus sheath.

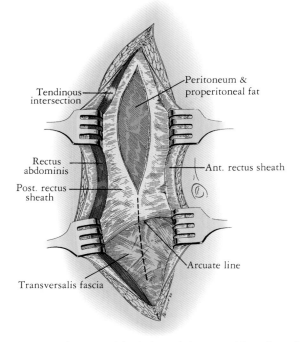

Tendinous intersection

Peritoneum & properitoneal fat

Rectus abdominis

Ant. rectus sheath

Post. rectus sheath

Arcuate line

Transversalis fascia

**Figure 50–21.** The rectus abdominal muscle is retracted laterally, and the posterior rectus sheath and transverse fascia are then incised to expose the properitoneal space.

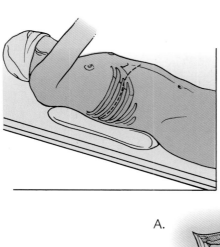

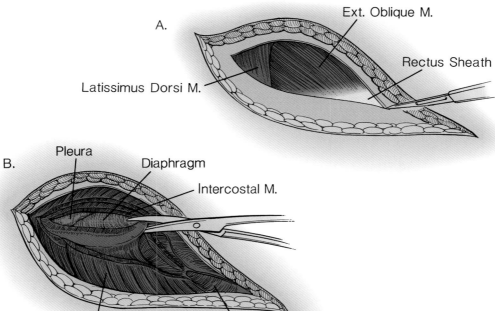

A.

Ext. Oblique M.

Rectus Sheath

Latissimus Dorsi M.

B.

Pleura    Diaphragm

Intercostal M.

External Oblique M.

Abdominis Rectus M.

**Figure 50–22.**   Right thoracoabdominal incision.   *Continued*

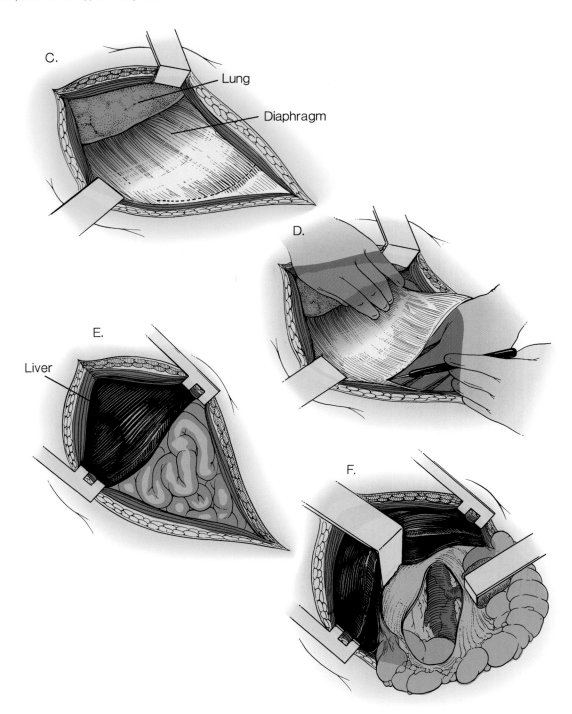

**Figure 50–22, cont'd.**

retracted upward to expose the kidney and great vessels (Fig. 50–22F).

At the completion of the procedure, the abdominal viscera are replaced in their anatomic position. The diaphragm is repaired with interrupted 2-0 silk mattress sutures with the knots tied on the undersurface. The chest wall is reapproximated by passing 0-0 polyglycolic sutures around the ribs above and below. The sutures should be passed on a tapered needle to avoid cutting any vessels, with care taken to avoid the neurovascular bundle. Before the pleura is closed, a 20 French chest tube is placed in the pleural cavity and brought out through a stab wound below the incision in the posterior axillary line. The transected muscle and fascial layers are reapproximated separately. The chest tube is connected to an underwater drain; it is usually removed 24 to 48 hours postoperatively, provided there is no persistent leakage of air and a chest radiograph shows satisfactory lung expansion.

## SIMPLE NEPHRECTOMY
### Indications

Simple nephrectomy is indicated in patients with an irreversibly damaged kidney due to symptomatic chronic infection, obstruction, calculus disease, or severe traumatic injury. It is occasionally appropriate to remove a functioning kidney involved with one of these conditions when the patient's age or general condition is too poor to permit a reconstructive operation and provided the opposite kidney is normal. Nephrectomy may also be indicated to treat renovascular hypertension due to noncorrectable renal artery disease or severe unilateral parenchymal damage from nephrosclerosis, pyelonephritis, reflux, or congenital dysplasia.

Simple nephrectomy can be performed through a variety of incisions. **An extraperitoneal flank approach is usually preferable when the kidney is chronically infected, when the patient is obese, or when multiple prior abdominal operations have been performed.** A subcapsular approach is indicated when severe perirenal inflammation or adhesions obscure anatomic relationships between the kidney and the surrounding structures. A transperitoneal approach is preferable in patients who cannot tolerate the flank position, in patients with end-stage renal disease undergoing bilateral nephrectomy for polycystic kidney disease, and in cases of traumatic renal injury in which early access to the pedicle is necessary. The transperitoneal approach is also useful when multiple operations have been performed previously through the flank with resulting dense adhesions around the kidney. Bilateral nephrectomy in patients with small end-stage kidneys can be done through a bilateral simultaneous posterior approach (Novick, 1980).

### Flank Approach

Once the perinephric space is entered, access to the kidney is obtained by incising Gerota's fascia on the lateral aspect of the kidney to avoid injury to the overlying peritoneum (Fig. 50–23A). The plane of cleavage between the perinephric fat and the renal capsule is usually developed easily. The kidney is mobilized by blunt dissection, and on the left side, the

pancreas and duodenum are carefully reflected medially along with the peritoneum. The ureter is identified during mobilization of the lower renal pole. It is preferable to divide the ureter after ligation of the pedicle to avoid congestion of the kidney. The kidney is pulled downward, and the upper pole is dissected free. There is normally a separate compartment in Gerota's fascia for the adrenal gland, which enables it to be readily separated from the upper pole.

The kidney is pulled laterally to identify the renal artery and vein, which are separated from surrounding fatty and lymphatic tissues by blunt dissection (Fig. 50–23B). Whenever possible, it is preferable to secure the vessels individually away from the hilum, and the artery should always be ligated first. The renal vein is usually visualized easily and is mobilized by ligating and dividing the gonadal, adrenal, and lumbar branches. The vein can then be retracted to expose the artery, which lies posteriorly. Alternatively, the renal vein can be approached posteriorly by mobilizing the kidney and retracting it up into the wound. The renal artery and vein are individually secured with 2-0 silk ligatures and then divided (Fig. 50–23C). The ureter is clamped and divided, and the distal end is ligated with 2-0 chromic catgut to complete the nephrectomy (Fig. 50–23D).

### Subcapsular Technique

Subcapsular nephrectomy is indicated when severe perirenal inflammation precludes satisfactory dissection between the kidney and the surrounding structures (Kimbrough and Morse, 1953; Kittredge and Fridge, 1958). After the retroperitoneal space has been entered, the renal capsule is identified, and a longitudinal incision is made over the lateral surface of the kidney (Fig. 50–24A). Once the capsule has been entered, a plane is developed between the renal parenchyma and the capsule over the entire surface of the kidney down to the level of the hilum (Fig. 50–24B and C). The renal parenchyma is retracted laterally to expose the major renal vessels as they enter the hilum. Vascular branches are ligated and transected as far laterally as possible to allow satisfactory proximal control of each branch (Fig. 50–24D). The upper ureter is then ligated and divided to complete the nephrectomy.

### Transperitoneal Approach

In transperitoneal simple nephrectomy, a subcostal incision is made, and the peritoneal cavity is entered. On the left side, the colon, pancreas, and spleen are reflected upward and medially to expose the left renal vein. A self-retaining ring retractor is useful to maintain exposure of the surgical field (Fig. 50–25A).

The renal vein and artery are mobilized, ligated, and transected (Fig. 50–25B). The artery is occluded first to avoid excessive blood loss into the kidney. The kidney is then mobilized laterally, superiorly, and inferiorly by sharp and blunt dissection. It is best to initiate the dissection laterally to obtain maximum mobilization before approaching the posterior renal hilum, where friable lumbar veins may be present (Fig. 50–25C). In cases of severe perirenal fibrosis, it may be necessary to remove some of the posterior psoas fascia together

SECTION XII

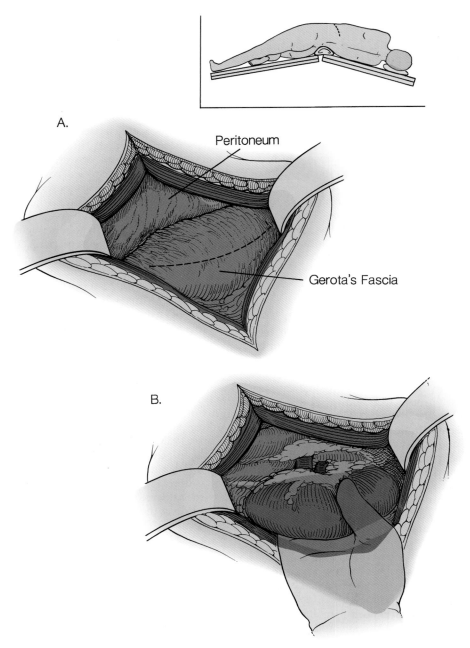

A.

Peritoneum

Gerota's Fascia

B.

**Figure 50–23.** Technique of simple left nephrectomy through an extraperitoneal flank incision. *Continued*

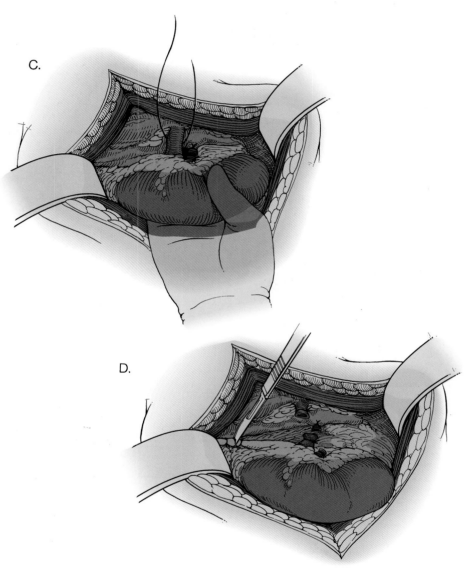

**Figure 50–23, cont'd.**

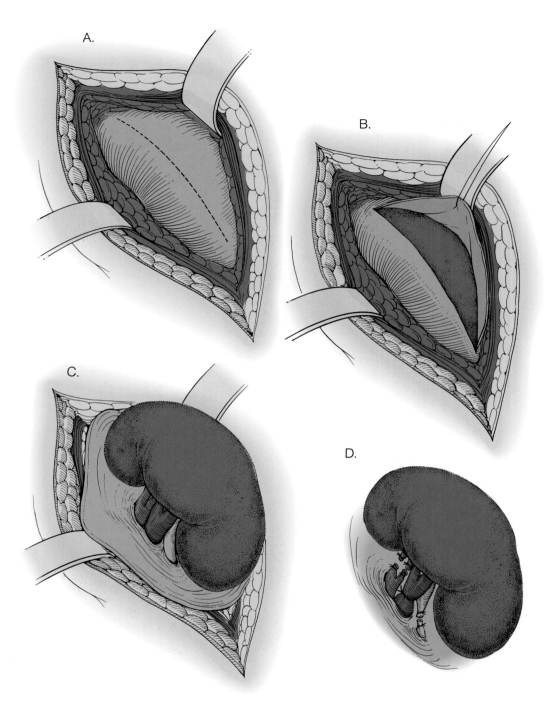

**Figure 50–24.** Technique of subcapsular nephrectomy.

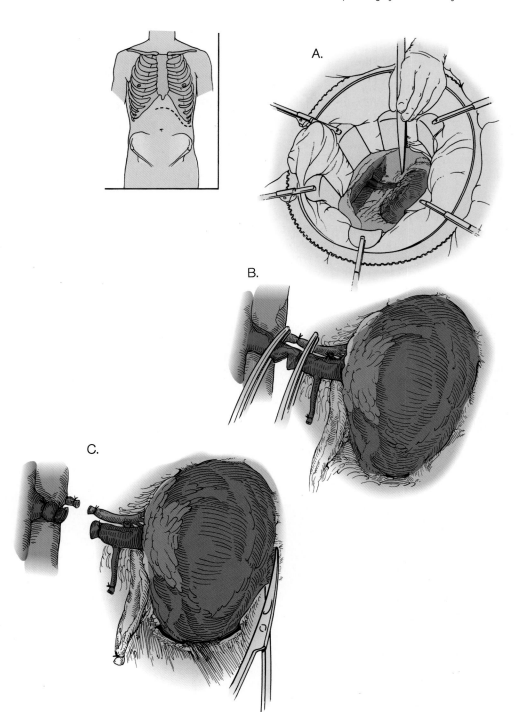

**Figure 50–25.** Technique of transperitoneal simple nephrectomy through an anterior subcostal incision.

with the kidney. After complete renal mobilization, the ureter is ligated and divided to complete the nephrectomy.

## RADICAL NEPHRECTOMY
### Indications and Evaluation

**Radical nephrectomy is the treatment of choice for patients with localized renal cell carcinoma (RCC)** (Robson et al, 1969; Skinner et al, 1971). The preoperative evaluation of patients with RCC has changed considerably during the past 2 decades owing to the advent of new imaging modalities such as ultrasonography, CT scanning, and magnetic resonance imaging. In many patients, a complete preliminary evaluation can be performed with these noninvasive modalities. Renal arteriography is no longer routinely necessary before radical nephrectomy. All patients should undergo a metastatic evaluation including a chest radiograph, an abdominal CT scan, and occasionally a bone scan; the last is necessary only in patients with bone pain or elevated serum alkaline phosphatase. Radical nephrectomy is occasionally done in patients with metastatic disease to palliate severe associated local symptoms or to allow entry into a biologic response modifier treatment protocol or concomitant with resection of a solitary metastatic lesion.

Involvement of the IVC with RCC occurs in 4% to 10% of cases and renders the task of complete surgical excision more complicated (Schefft et al, 1978). However, operative removal offers the only hope for cure, and when there are no metastases, an aggressive approach is justified. Five-year survival rates of 40% to 68% have been reported after complete surgical excision (Libertino et al, 1987; Neves and Zincke, 1987; Skinner et al, 1989; Novick et al, 1990). The best results have been achieved when the tumor does not involve the perinephric fat and regional lymph nodes (Cherrie et al, 1982). The cephalad extent of vena caval involvement is not prognostically important, and even with intra-atrial tumor thrombi, extended cancer-free survival is possible after surgical treatment when there is no nodal or distant metastasis (Glazer and Novick, 1996). In planning the appropriate operative approach for tumor removal, it is essential for preoperative radiographic studies to define accurately the distal limits of a vena caval tumor thrombus.

RCC involving the IVC should be suspected in patients who have lower extremity edema, varicocele, dilated superficial abdominal veins, proteinuria, pulmonary embolism, right atrial mass, or nonfunction of the involved kidney. Magnetic resonance imaging is the preferred diagnostic study for demonstrating both the presence and the distal extent of IVC involvement (Pritchett et al, 1987; Goldfarb et al, 1990). Transesophageal echocardiography (Fig. 50–26) (Treiger et al, 1991;

Glazer and Novick, 1997) and transabdominal color Doppler ultrasonography (McGahan et al, 1993) have also proved to be useful diagnostic studies in this regard. Inferior venacavography is reserved for patients in whom a magnetic resonance imaging or ultrasound study is either nondiagnostic or contraindicated. Renal arteriography may be helpful in patients with RCC involving the IVC when distinct arterialization of a tumor thrombus is observed. When this finding is present, preoperative embolization of the kidney often causes shrinkage of the thrombus, which facilitates its intraoperative removal. When adjunctive cardiopulmonary bypass with deep hypothermic circulatory arrest is considered, coronary angiography is also performed preoperatively (Belis et al, 1989; Novick et al, 1990). If significant obstructing coronary lesions are found, these can be repaired simultaneously during cardiopulmonary bypass.

## Standard Technique

Radical nephrectomy encompasses the basic principles of early ligation of the renal artery and vein, removal of the kidney outside Gerota's fascia, removal of the ipsilateral adrenal gland, and performance of a complete regional lymphadenectomy from the crus of the diaphragm to the aortic bifurcation (Robson et al, 1969). **Perhaps the most important aspect of radical nephrectomy is removal of the kidney outside Gerota's fascia because capsular invasion with perinephric fat involvement occurs in 25% of patients. It has been shown that removal of the ipsilateral adrenal gland is not routinely necessary unless the malignant neoplasm either extensively involves the kidney or is located in the upper portion of the kidney** (Sagalowsky et al, 1994). Although lymphadenectomy allows more accurate pathologic staging, its therapeutic value remains controversial. Nevertheless, there may be a subset of patients with micrometastatic lymph node involvement who can benefit from lymphadenectomy (Giuliani et al, 1990). The need for routine performance of a complete lymphadenectomy in all cases is unresolved, and there remains a divergence of clinical practice among urologists with respect to this aspect of radical nephrectomy.

The surgical approach for radical nephrectomy is determined by the size and location of the tumor as well as by the habitus of the patient. The operation is usually performed through a transperitoneal incision to allow abdominal exploration for metastatic disease and early access to the renal vessels with minimal manipulation of the tumor. **I prefer an extended subcostal or bilateral subcostal incision for most patients. A thoracoabdominal incision is used for patients with large upper pole tumors** (Fig. 50–27). I occasionally employ an extraperitoneal flank incision to perform radical nephrectomy in elderly or poor-risk patients with a small tumor.

In radical nephrectomy through a subcostal transperitoneal incision, a thorough exploration for metastatic disease is performed after the abdominal cavity is opened. On the left side, the colon is reflected medially to expose the great vessels. This is facilitated by division of the splenocolic ligaments, which also helps avoid excessive traction on and injury to the spleen.

On the right side, the colon and duodenum are reflected medially to expose the vena cava and aorta (Fig. 50–28).

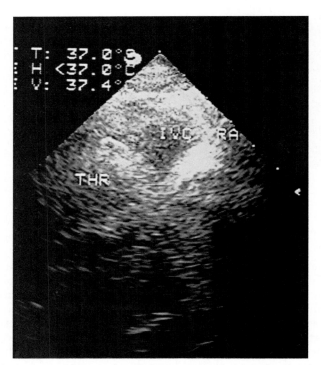

**Figure 50–26.** Transesophageal ultrasonography demonstrating thrombus (THR) in the intrahepatic inferior vena cava (IVC) proximal to the right atrium (RA).

The operation is initiated with dissection of the renal pedicle. On the right side, the renal vein is short, and care must be taken not to injure the vena cava. The right renal artery may be mobilized either lateral to the vena cava or, with a large medial tumor, between the vena cava and the aorta (Fig. 50–29).

On the left side, the renal vein is quite long as it passes over the aorta. The vein is mobilized completely by ligating and dividing gonadal, adrenal, and lumbar tributaries. The vein can then be retracted to posteriorly expose the artery, which is then mobilized toward the aorta (Fig. 50–30). The renal artery is ligated with 2-0 silk ligatures and divided, and the renal vein is then similarly managed (Fig. 50–31).

The kidney is mobilized outside Gerota's fascia with blunt and sharp dissection as needed. The remaining vascular attachments are secured with nonabsorbable sutures or metal clips. The ureter is then ligated and divided to complete the removal of the kidney and adrenal gland (Fig. 50–32).

**The classic radical nephrectomy procedure includes the performance of a complete regional lymphadenectomy. The lymph nodes can be removed either en bloc with the kidney and adrenal gland or separately after the nephrectomy.** Lymph node dissection is begun at the crura of the diaphragm just below the origin of the SMA. There is a readily definable periadventitial plane close to the aorta that can be entered so that the dissection may be carried along the aorta and onto the origin of the major vessels to remove all periaortic lymphatic tissue. Care must be taken to avoid injury to the origins of the celiac artery and SMA superiorly as they arise from the anterior surface of the aorta. The dissection of the periaortic and pericaval lymph nodes is then carried downward en bloc to the origin of the inferior mesenteric artery. The sympathetic ganglia and nerves are removed together with the lymphatic tissue. The cisterna chyli is identified medial to the right crus, and entering lymphatic vessels are secured to prevent the development of chylous ascites.

**A thoracoabdominal incision is preferable in performing radical nephrectomy for a large upper pole tumor.** This

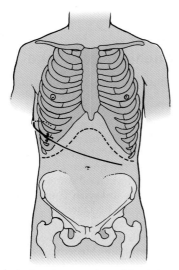

**Figure 50–27.** Radical nephrectomy is performed through either a bilateral subcostal or a thoracoabdominal incision.

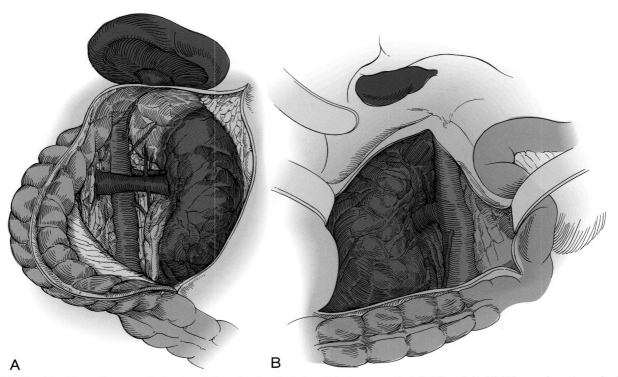

A                    B

**Figure 50–28.** After the peritoneal cavity is entered, the colon is reflected medially to expose the left (**A**) or right (**B**) kidney and great vessels. (Reproduced with permission from Novick AC, Streem SB, Pontes E, eds: Stewart's Operative Urology, 2nd ed. Baltimore, Williams & Wilkins, 1989.)

approach is demonstrated in Figures 50-33 to 50-35 for a right-sided tumor. Once the liver has been retracted upward into the chest, the hepatic flexure of the colon and the duodenum are reflected medially to expose the anterior surface of the kidney and great vessels (Fig. 50–33). The renal artery is

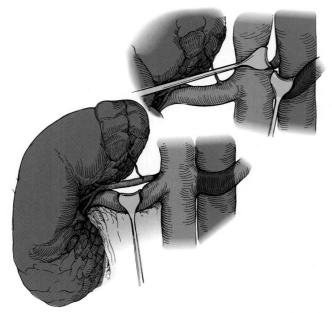

**Figure 50–29.** The right renal artery may be mobilized either lateral to the vena cava or between the vena cava and the aorta. (Reproduced with permission from Novick AC, Streem SB, Pontes E, eds: Stewart's Operative Urology, 2nd ed. Baltimore, Williams & Wilkins, 1989.)

secured with 2-0 silk ligatures and divided, and the renal vein is then similarly managed (Fig. 50–34). The ureter and right gonadal vein are ligated and divided, and the kidney is mobilized outside Gerota's fascia. Downward and lateral traction of the kidney exposes the superior vascular attachments of the tumor and adrenal gland. Exposure of these vessels is also facilitated by medial retraction of the IVC (Fig. 50–35). Care is taken to preserve small hepatic venous branches entering the vena cava at the superior margin of the tumor mass. The tumor mass is then gently separated from the undersurface of the liver to complete the resection.

## Management of Retroperitoneal Hemorrhage

During performance of radical nephrectomy, intraoperative hemorrhage can occur from the IVC or its tributaries. The urologist should be familiar with methods of preventing or controlling this problem. In most cases, vena caval hemorrhage is caused by the laceration or avulsion of large yet fragile veins entering the vena cava at predictable locations.

**Lumbar veins enter the posterolateral aspect of the vena cava at each vertebral level, and undue traction on the cava can result in their avulsion with troublesome bleeding.** To prevent this, care should be taken to retract the vena cava gently with curved vein retractors during its dissection; if additional mobilization is necessary, these veins should be dissected free from surrounding structures, ligated, and divided. In ligating venous tributaries entering the vena cava, 3-0 to 4-0 suture material should be used, and the ligatures should not be tied too tightly because this can cause shearing through the

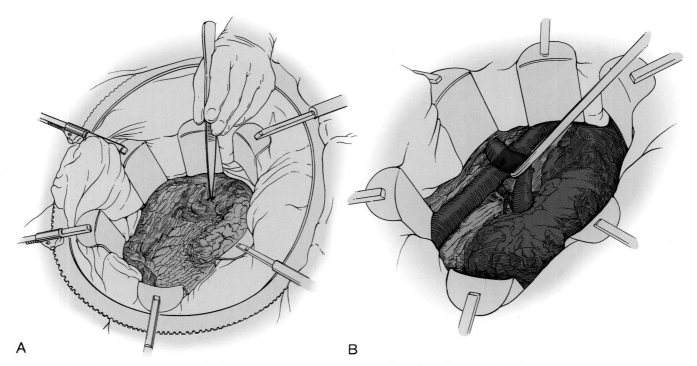

**A**                    **B**

**Figure 50–30.** **A,** Self-retaining ring retractor is inserted to maintain exposure. **B,** Left renal vein is mobilized by ligation of its major branches to expose the artery posteriorly. (Reproduced with permission from Novick AC, Streem SB, Pontes E, eds: Stewart's Operative Urology, 2nd ed. Baltimore, Williams & Wilkins, 1989.)

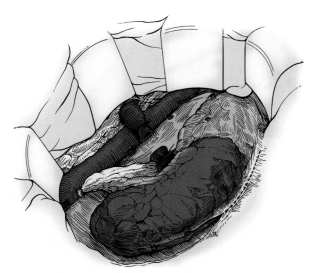

**Figure 50–31.** After the pedicle is secured and the ureter divided, the kidney is mobilized outside Gerota's fascia. (Reproduced with permission from Novick AC, Streem SB, Pontes E, eds: Stewart's Operative Urology, 2nd ed. Baltimore, Williams & Wilkins, 1989.)

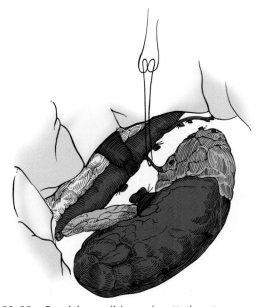

**Figure 50–32.** Remaining medial vascular attachments are secured and divided to complete the nephrectomy. (Reproduced with permission from Novick AC, Streem SB, Pontes E, eds: Stewart's Operative Urology, 2nd ed. Baltimore, Williams & Wilkins, 1989.)

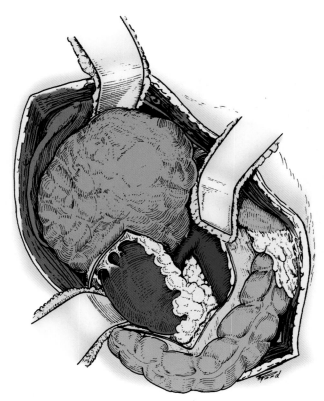

**Figure 50–33.** Exposure of large right upper pole tumor through a thoracoabdominal incision. (Reproduced with permission from Novick AC, Streem SB, Pontes E, eds: Stewart's Operative Urology, 2nd ed. Baltimore, Williams & Wilkins, 1989.)

fragile venous wall with further hemorrhage. After the ligature has been applied, it should not be pulled too tightly before the ends of the ligature are cut, again for fear of avulsing the entrance of the vein into the vena cava.

**A second predictable bleeding site is the entry of the right gonadal vein into the anterolateral surface of the vena cava.** This is an extremely thin-walled vein, and excessive traction or mobilization of the cava at this level can lead to its avulsion, with resulting hemorrhage.

**A third predictable site of bleeding lies at the level of the renal veins, where large lumbar veins often course posteriorly from the left renal vein just lateral to the aorta or from**

**the posterior aspect of the vena cava close to the entry of the right renal vein.** Injudicious mobilization of the renal veins, without consideration of these fragile and often large-caliber veins, can result in severe hemorrhage that may be difficult to control.

**A fourth predictable site of bleeding is at the level of the right adrenal vein that enters the IVC.** This vein is large and friable, frequently lies higher than the surgeon expects, and must be carefully dissected free from surrounding structures to avoid avulsion from the vena cava.

Finally, excessive vena caval hemorrhage can be prevented by careful dissection in proper tissue planes along the vena cava. This may be difficult when tumor involves the vena cava, but a plane can usually be established along the vena caval wall that, if followed, allows safe and relatively bloodless exposure. One should follow the general principle of isolating a relatively normal area of vena cava and working upward or downward from that level to expose the diseased portion.

If inadvertent vena caval laceration or avulsion of entering veins occurs, control of hemorrhage can be accomplished by a variety of techniques. Direct pressure on the site of bleeding gives immediate control until additional exposure can be gained, the field properly illuminated, and additional suckers or retractors brought in if necessary. If the laceration involves the anterior or lateral caval wall and is of considerable length, it can readily be controlled by applying a series of Allis clamps over the edges of the laceration in serial fashion. The edges of the laceration are then oversewn with running 5-0 vascular suture material (Fig. 50–36).

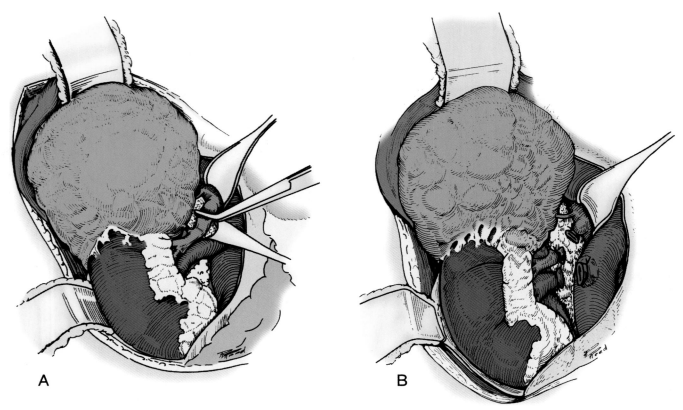

**Figure 50–34.** The renal artery and vein are secured and divided. (Reproduced with permission from Novick AC, Streem SB, Pontes E, eds: Stewart's Operative Urology, 2nd ed. Baltimore, Williams & Wilkins, 1989.)

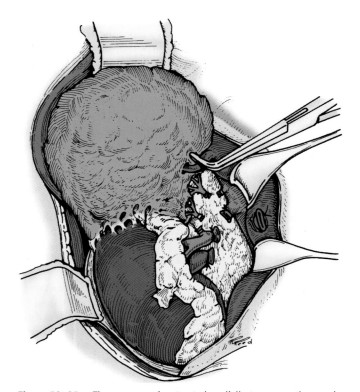

**Figure 50–35.** The vena cava is retracted medially to expose the remaining superior vascular attachments, which are secured and divided. (Reproduced with permission from Novick AC, Streem SB, Pontes E, eds: Stewart's Operative Urology, 2nd ed. Baltimore, Williams & Wilkins, 1989.)

If avulsion of an entering lumbar vein is the cause of bleeding, the vena cava should be rolled medially, with digital compression above and below the site of bleeding, until the posterolateral entry of the avulsed vein is exposed. This is then grasped with one or two Allis clamps, which can be used as tractors to bring the avulsion into better view for oversewing with vascular suture material. Persistent bleeding can occur from the proximal end of an avulsed lumbar vein, which may retract into the psoas muscle and be difficult to secure. This can be controlled in some cases by grasping the end of the vein with a hemostat and then twisting the hemostat to bring the end of the vein into better view for suture ligation (Fig. 50–37). If this is not possible, bleeding can be controlled by inserting a figure-of-eight 2-0 silk suture through the muscle overlying the vein.

Bleeding from large lumbar veins entering the posterior aspect of the left renal vein or the posterior wall of the vena cava near the entry of the right renal vein can be particularly troublesome (Fig. 50–38). Further mobilization of the vena cava and renal veins is often needed while compression is maintained on the bleeding site. It may be necessary to apply a Satinsky side clamp across the entry of the renal vein, as well as a distal bulldog clamp beyond the bleeding point in the renal vein, to control the hemorrhage and allow closure of the venous defect. Mobilization and gentle rotation of the vena cava or the renal veins may also be necessary to gain optimal exposure. In this situation, as well, distal entry of the lumbar vein into the posterior musculature can cause troublesome bleeding and must be controlled as described previously.

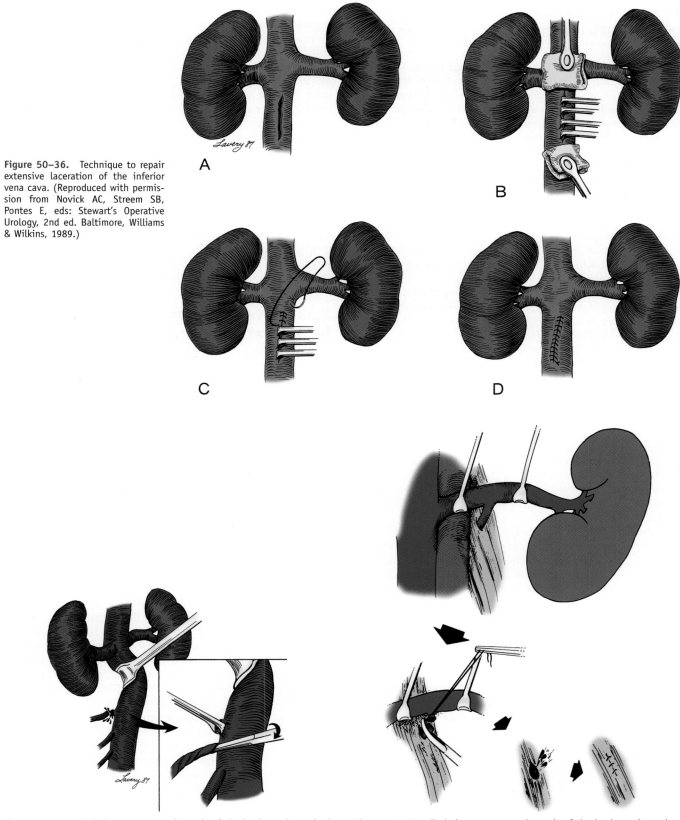

**Figure 50–36.** Technique to repair extensive laceration of the inferior vena cava. (Reproduced with permission from Novick AC, Streem SB, Pontes E, eds: Stewart's Operative Urology, 2nd ed. Baltimore, Williams & Wilkins, 1989.)

A

B

C

D

**Figure 50–37.** Technique to secure the ends of the lumbar vein avulsed from the inferior vena cava. (Reproduced with permission from Novick AC, Streem SB, Pontes E, eds: Stewart's Operative Urology, 2nd ed. Baltimore, Williams & Wilkins, 1989.)

**Figure 50–38.** Technique to secure the ends of the lumbar vein avulsed from the left renal vein. (Reproduced with permission from Novick AC, Streem SB, Pontes E, eds: Stewart's Operative Urology, 2nd ed. Baltimore, Williams & Wilkins, 1989.)

## Radical Nephrectomy with Infrahepatic Vena Caval Involvement

There are four levels of vena caval involvement in RCC that are characterized according to the distal extent of the tumor thrombus (Fig. 50–39). **A bilateral subcostal transperitoneal incision usually provides excellent exposure for performance of radical nephrectomy and removal of a perirenal or infrahepatic IVC thrombus. For extremely large tumors involving the upper pole of the kidney, a thoracoabdominal incision may alternatively be used.** After the abdomen is entered, the colon is reflected medially, and a self-retaining ring retractor is inserted to maintain exposure of the retroperitoneum (Fig. 50–40A). The renal artery and the ureter are ligated and divided, and the entire kidney is mobilized outside Gerota's fascia, leaving the kidney attached by only the renal vein (Fig. 50–40B and C). During the initial dissection, care is taken to avoid unnecessary manipulation of the renal vein and vena cava.

The vena cava is then completely dissected from surrounding structures above and below the renal vein, and the opposite renal vein is also mobilized. It is essential to obtain exposure and control of the suprarenal vena cava above the level of the tumor thrombus. If necessary, perforating veins to the caudate lobe of the liver are secured and divided to allow separation of the caudate lobe from the vena cava. This maneuver can allow an additional 2 to 3 cm of vena cava to be exposed superiorly. **Mobilization of the liver off of the IVC can further enhance exposure of the intra-abdominal vena cava** (Ciancio et al, 2002). The infrarenal vena cava is then occluded below the thrombus with a Satinsky venous clamp, and the opposite renal vein is gently secured with a small bulldog vascular clamp. Finally, in preparation for tumor thrombectomy, a curved Satinsky clamp is placed around the suprarenal vena cava above the level of the thrombus (Fig. 50–40D).

The anterior surface of the renal vein is then incised over the tumor thrombus, and the incision is continued posteriorly with scissors, passing just beneath the thrombus (Fig. 50–40E). In most cases, there is no attachment of the thrombus to the wall of the vena cava. After the renal vein has been circumscribed, gentle downward traction is exerted on the kidney to extract the tumor thrombus from the vena cava (Fig. 50–40F). After the gross specimen is removed, the suprarenal vena caval clamp may be released temporarily as the anesthetist applies positive pulmonary pressure; this maneuver can ensure that any small remaining fragments of thrombus are flushed free from the vena cava. When the tumor thrombectomy is completed, the cavotomy incision is repaired with a continuous 5-0 vascular suture (Fig. 50–40G).

In occasional cases, there is direct caval invasion of the tumor at the level of the entrance of the renal vein and for varying distances. This requires resection of a portion of the vena caval wall. Narrowing of the caval lumen by up to 50% does not adversely affect maintenance of caval patency. If further narrowing appears likely, caval reconstruction can be performed with a free graft of pericardium or polytetrafluoroethylene (Sarkar et al, 1998).

In some patients, more extensive direct growth of tumor into the wall of the vena cava is found at surgery. The prognosis for these patients is generally poor, particularly when hepatic venous tributaries are also involved, and the decision to proceed with radical surgical excision must be carefully considered. Several important principles must be kept in mind when en bloc vena caval resection is undertaken. Resection of the infrarenal portion of the vena cava can usually be done safely because an extensive collateral venous supply has developed in most cases. With right-sided kidney tumors, resection of the suprarenal vena cava is also possible, provided the left renal vein is ligated distal to the gonadal and adrenal tributaries, which then provide collateral venous drainage from the left kidney. With left-sided kidney tumors, the suprarenal vena cava cannot be resected safely owing to the paucity of collateral venous drainage from the right kidney. In such cases, right renal venous drainage can be maintained by preserving a tumor-free strip of vena cava, augmented, if necessary, with a pericardial patch; alternatively, the right kidney can be autotransplanted to the pelvis, or an interposition graft of saphenous vein may be placed from the right renal vein to the splenic, inferior mesenteric, or portal vein (Fig. 50–41).

## Radical Nephrectomy with Intrahepatic or Suprahepatic Vena Caval Involvement

In patients with RCC and an intrahepatic or suprahepatic IVC thrombus, the difficulty of surgical excision is significantly increased. In such cases, the operative technique must be modified because it is not possible to obtain subdiaphragmatic control of the vena cava above the tumor thrombus. Several different surgical maneuvers have been used to provide adequate exposure, to prevent severe bleeding, and to achieve complete tumor removal in this setting (Cummings et al, 1979; Novick, 1980; Foster et al, 1988; Skinner et al, 1989; Burt, 1991; Ciancio et al, 2002).

One technique for obtaining vascular control involves temporary occlusion of the suprahepatic intrapericardial portion of the IVC. To reduce hepatic venous congestion and troublesome backbleeding, the porta hepatis and SMA are also temporarily occluded (Skinner et al, 1989). A disadvantage of this approach is that occlusion of these vessels can be safely tolerated for only 20 minutes. This approach is also not applicable in cases of tumor extension into the right atrium. **At the Cleveland Clinic, the preferred approach is to employ cardiopulmonary bypass with deep hypothermic circulatory arrest for most patients with complex supradiaphragmatic tumor thrombi and for all patients with right atrial tumor thrombi** (Marshall and Reitz, 1986). A favorable experience with this approach was reported in 43 patients (Novick et al, 1990), and a subsequent study showed excellent long-term cancer-free survival after its use in patients with right atrial thrombi (Glazer and Novick, 1996). The relevant technical aspects are described subsequently.

A bilateral subcostal incision is used for the abdominal portion of the operation. After resectability is confirmed, a median sternotomy is made (Fig. 50–42). Intraoperative monitoring is accomplished with an arterial line, a multiple-lumen central venous pressure catheter, and a pulmonary artery catheter. Nasopharyngeal and bladder temperatures are monitored. Anesthesia is induced with fentanyl, sufentanil, or

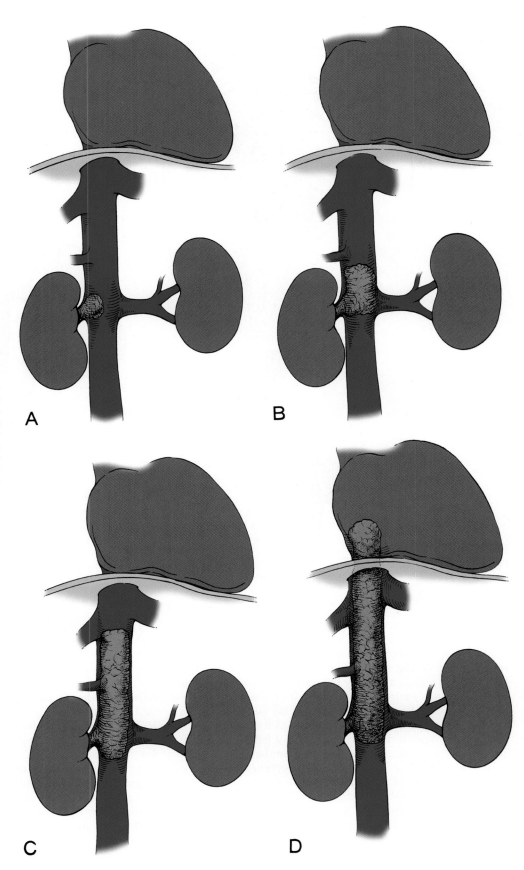

**Figure 50–39.** Classification of inferior vena caval tumor thrombus from renal cell carcinoma, according to the distal extent of the thrombus, as perirenal (**A**), infrahepatic (**B**), intrahepatic (**C**), and suprahepatic (**D**). (Reproduced with permission from Novick AC, Streem SB, Pontes E, eds: Stewart's Operative Urology, 2nd ed. Baltimore, Williams & Wilkins, 1989.)

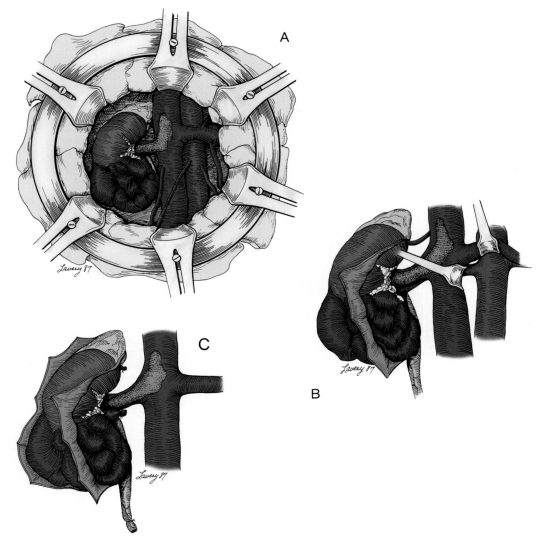

**Figure 50–40.** Technique of radical nephrectomy and vena caval tumor thrombectomy with infrahepatic tumor thrombus. (Reproduced with permission from Novick AC, Streem SB, Pontes E, eds: Stewart's Operative Urology, 2nd ed. Baltimore, Williams & Wilkins, 1989.) *Continued*

thiopental and is maintained with a narcotic inhalation agent (Welch et al, 1989).

The kidney is completely mobilized outside Gerota's fascia with division of the renal artery and ureter, such that the kidney is left attached by only the renal vein. The infrarenal vena cava and contralateral renal vein are also exposed. Extensive dissection and mobilization of the suprarenal vena cava are not necessary with this approach. Adequate exposure is somewhat more difficult to achieve for a left renal tumor. Simultaneous exposure of the vena cava on the right and the tumor on the left is not readily accomplished simply by reflecting the left colon medially. I have dealt with this by transposing the mobilized left kidney anteriorly through a window in the mesentery of the left colon while leaving the renal vein attached. This maneuver yields excellent exposure of the abdominal vena cava with the attached left renal vein and kidney. Precise retroperitoneal hemostasis is essential before proceeding with cardiopulmonary bypass because of the risk of bleeding associated with systemic heparinization.

The heart and great vessels are exposed through the median sternotomy. The patient is heparinized, ascending aortic and right atrial venous cannulas are placed, and cardiopulmonary bypass is initiated (Fig. 50–43). When the heart fibrillates, the aorta is clamped, and crystalloid cardioplegic solution is infused. Under circulatory arrest, deep hypothermia is initiated by reducing arterial inflow blood temperature as low as 10°C. The head and abdomen are packed in ice during the cooling process. After approximately 15 to 30 minutes, a core temperature of 18°C to 20°C is achieved.

At this point, flow through the perfusion machine is stopped, and 95% of the blood volume is drained into the pump with no flow to any organ.

The tumor thrombus can now be removed in an essentially bloodless operative field. An incision is made in the IVC at the entrance of the involved renal vein, and the ostium is circumscribed. When the tumor extends into the right atrium, the atrium is opened at the same time (Fig. 50–44A). If possible, the tumor thrombus is removed intact with the kidney.

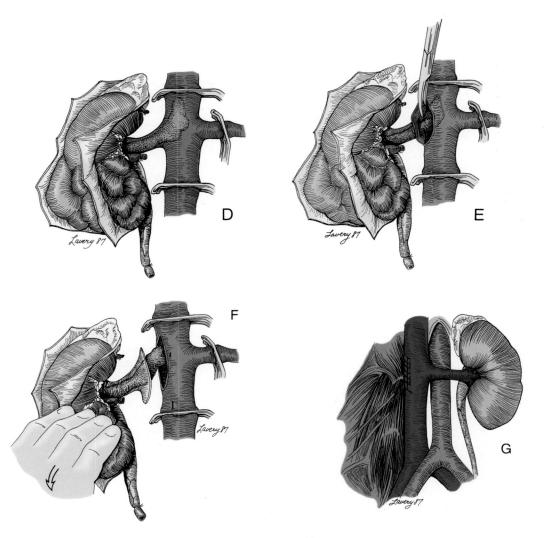

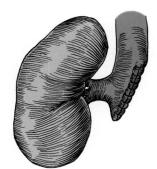

**Figure 50–40, cont'd.**

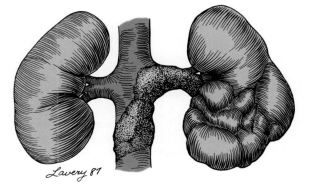

**Figure 50–41.** With vena cava resection, right renal venous drainage can be maintained by preserving a tumor-free strip of vena cava. (Reproduced with permission from Novick AC, Streem SB, Pontes E, eds: Stewart's Operative Urology, 2nd ed. Baltimore, Williams & Wilkins, 1989.)

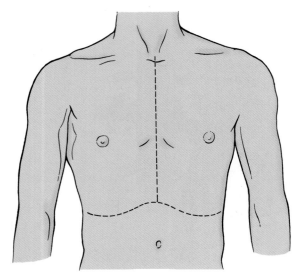

**Figure 50–42.** Surgical incision for radical nephrectomy with removal of suprahepatic vena caval tumor thrombus. (Reproduced with permission from Novick AC, Streem SB, Pontes E, eds: Stewart's Operative Urology, 2nd ed. Baltimore, Williams & Wilkins, 1989.)

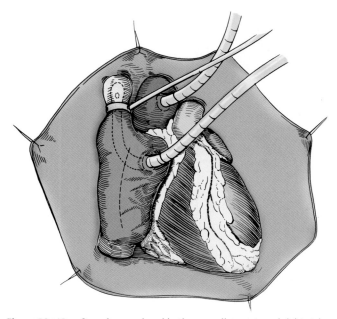

**Figure 50–43.** Cannulas are placed in the ascending aorta and right atrium in preparation for cardiopulmonary bypass. The planned incision into the right atrium is shown. (Reproduced with permission from Novick AC, Streem SB, Pontes E, eds: Stewart's Operative Urology, 2nd ed. Baltimore, Williams & Wilkins, 1989.)

Frequently, this step is not possible because of the friability of the thrombus and its adherence to the vena caval wall. In such cases, piecemeal removal of the thrombus from above and below is necessary. **Under deep hypothermic circulatory arrest, the entire interior lumen of the vena cava can be directly inspected to ensure that all fragments of thrombus are completely removed.** Hypothermic circulatory arrest can be safely maintained for at least 40 minutes without incurring a cerebral ischemic event (Svensson et al, 1993). In difficult cases, this interval can be extended either by maintenance of

"trickle" blood flow at a rate of 5 to 10 mL/kg per minute (Mault et al, 1993) or by adjunctive retrograde cerebral perfusion (Pagano et al, 1995).

After complete removal of all tumor thrombus, the vena cava is closed with a continuous 5-0 vascular suture and the right atrium is closed (Fig. 50–44B). As soon as the vena cava and right atrium have been repaired, rewarming of the patient is initiated. If coronary artery bypass grafting is necessary, it is done during the rewarming period. Rewarming takes 20 to 45 minutes and is continued until a core temperature of approximately 37°C is obtained. Cardiopulmonary bypass is then terminated. Decannulation takes place, and protamine sulfate is administered to reverse the effects of the heparin. Platelets, fresh frozen plasma, desmopressin acetate, or a combination may be provided when coagulopathy is suspected. Aprotinin has also proved effective in reversing the coagulopathy associated with cardiopulmonary bypass (Bidstrup et al, 1989) but may induce thrombotic complications. Mediastinal chest tubes are placed, but the abdomen is not routinely drained.

**In patients with nonadherent supradiaphragmatic vena caval tumor thrombi that do not extend into the right atrium, venovenous bypass in the form of a caval-atrial shunt is a useful technique** (Foster et al, 1988; Burt, 1991). In this approach, the intrapericardial vena cava, infrarenal vena cava, and opposite renal vein are temporarily occluded. Cannulas are then inserted into the right atrium and infrarenal vena cava. These cannulas are connected to a primed pump to maintain adequate flow from the vena cava to the right side of the heart (Fig. 50–45). This avoids the obligatory hypotension associated with temporary occlusion alone of the intrapericardial and infrarenal vena cava. After venovenous bypass is initiated, the abdominal vena cava is opened and the thrombus is removed. If bleeding from the hepatic veins is troublesome during extraction of the thrombus, the porta hepatis may also be occluded (Pringle's maneuver). After the thrombus is removed, repair of the vena cava is performed as previously described. This technique is simpler than cardiopulmonary bypass with hypothermic circulatory arrest but may entail more operative bleeding.

## Complications

**After radical nephrectomy, postoperative complications occur in approximately 20% of patients, and the operative mortality rate is approximately 2%** (Swanson and Borges, 1983). Systemic complications may occur as after any surgical procedure. These include myocardial infarction, cerebrovascular accident, congestive heart failure, pulmonary embolism, atelectasis, pneumonia, and thrombophlebitis. The incidence of these problems can be reduced by adequate preoperative preparation, avoidance of intraoperative hypotension, appropriate blood and fluid replacement, postoperative breathing exercises, early mobilization, and elastic support of the legs both during and after surgery.

**An intraoperative gastrointestinal injury should always be checked for during the procedure, and lacerations should be repaired and drained.** Tears of the liver may be repaired with mattress sutures. Splenic injuries usually require splenectomy, although small lacerations may be managed by application of Avitene or Oxycel. Injuries to the tail of the pancreas,

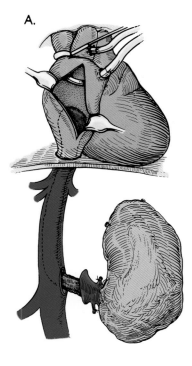

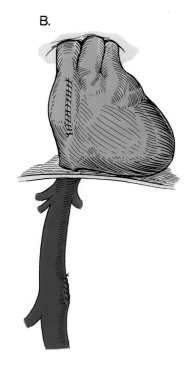

**Figure 50–44. A,** The ostium of the renal vein is circumferentially incised and the right atrium is opened. **B,** After removal of the tumor thrombus, the atriotomy and vena cavotomy incisions are closed.

which may occur with left radical nephrectomy, are best managed by partial amputation.

**A particularly distressing postoperative complication is the development of a pancreatic fistula due to unrecognized intraoperative injury to the pancreas.** This is usually manifested in the immediate postoperative period with signs and symptoms of acute pancreatitis and drainage of alkaline fluid from the incision. A CT scan of the abdomen demonstrates fluid collection in the retroperitoneum. Fluid draining from the incision should be analyzed for pH and the presence of amylase. Treatment involves percutaneous or surgical drainage of the fluid collection to avoid the development of a pancreatic pseudocyst or abscess (Zinner et al, 1974; Spirnak et al, 1984). Most fistulas close spontaneously with the establishment of adequate drainage. Because the healing of a pancreatic fistula is usually a slow process, the patient is also supported with hyperalimentation. Surgical closure by excision of the fistulous track and construction of an anastomosis between the pancreas and a Roux-en-Y limb of the jejunum is only occasionally necessary in patients with prolonged drainage.

Other gastrointestinal problems that may occur include a generalized ileus or a functional obstruction caused by a localized ileus of the colon overlying the surgical renal fossa. Oral feedings should not be given until adequate bowel sounds are present and the patient has passed flatus. Nasogastric suction is used in more severe cases. When a prolonged period of ileus is anticipated, or if the patient is in a poor nutritional state, parenteral hyperalimentation should be instituted.

Secondary hemorrhage may occur after radical nephrectomy and is manifested by pain, signs of shock, abdominal or flank swelling, and drainage of blood through the incision or a drain site. Bleeding may be from the kidney or renal pedicle but is occasionally from an unrecognized injury to a neighboring structure such as the spleen, the liver, or a mesenteric vessel. Patients should be given blood and fluid replacement as needed. In most cases, it is best to reopen the wound, evacuate the hematoma, and secure the bleeding point. In the event of diffuse bleeding from a clotting disorder, it may be necessary to temporarily pack the wound with gauze, which can then be gradually removed after 24 to 48 hours.

**Pneumothorax may occur during thoracoabdominal or flank incisions. Pleural injuries are usually recognized immediately and repaired with a running 3-0 or 4-0 chromic suture.** Before complete closure of the incision, a red rubber catheter is inserted into the pleural cavity and a purse-string suture is tied around the catheter. The anesthesiologist is then asked to hyperinflate the lungs. With hyperinflation and suction on the catheter, air and fluid in the hemithorax are forced out through the red rubber catheter, which is then removed, and the purse-string suture is secured. An alternative method is to place the distal end of the catheter in a basin of water. As the anesthesiologist hyperinflates the lung, air and fluid are forced out of the pleural cavity through the red rubber catheter and into the basin of water. When the pleura is entered, a chest radiograph should be obtained in the recovery room to ensure adequate re-expansion of the lung. Pneumothorax greater than 10%, tension pneumothorax, or

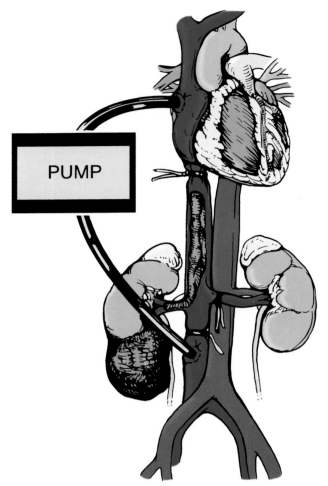

PUMP

**Figure 50–45.** Technique of venovenous bypass for removal of supradiaphragmatic vena caval tumor thrombus.

pneumothorax that is causing respiratory distress requires insertion of a chest tube.

Postoperative atelectasis is common in patients undergoing radical nephrectomy and is probably secondary to the positioning of the patient during the procedure. This is a common cause of fever postoperatively and may be effectively treated with pulmonary physiotherapy, including deep breathing, coughing, and incentive spirometry.

Infection is a common complication encountered in the postoperative period. Superficial wound infections are best managed by removal of skin sutures or staples to allow drainage. Deeper infections must be treated by the establishment of adequate drainage and the administration of appropriate antibiotics when there are systemic manifestations of the infection. If the drainage is persistent and profuse, the possibility of a retained foreign body or a fistulous communication with the intestine should be considered. Accumulations of lymph or serous fluid in the renal fossa or pleura are best managed expectantly, unless they are causing respiratory embarrassment. Such accumulations may become infected or may be complicated by bleeding if they are treated by needle aspiration.

**Temporary renal insufficiency may develop postoperatively after ligation of the left renal vein in conjunction with**

right radical nephrectomy and extension of a vena caval tumor thrombus (Clark, 1961; Pathak, 1971). Renal failure in this setting is probably secondary to venous obstruction and usually resolves as drainage improves with the development of venous collaterals, although temporary hemodialysis may occasionally be needed. It is always preferable, if possible, to preserve left renal venous drainage into the vena cava to diminish the risk of this complication. As previously mentioned, ligation of the right renal vein leads to permanent and complete renal failure.

When a flank incision is used to perform nephrectomy, an incisional hernia or bulge may occur postoperatively. The intracostal nerve lies immediately below the corresponding rib between the internal oblique and the transverse abdominal muscles. At surgery, an effort should be made to spare this nerve by dissecting both proximally and distally, enabling careful padding and retraction of the nerve out of the operative field, because transection may lead to muscle denervation. Postoperatively, muscle denervation with flank bulging must be differentiated from a flank incisional hernia, which is rare. With the hernia, a fascial defect is usually palpable.

## PARTIAL NEPHRECTOMY FOR MALIGNANT DISEASE

Interest in partial nephrectomy, or nephron-sparing surgery, for RCC has been stimulated by advances in renal imaging, improved surgical techniques, increasing numbers of incidentally discovered low-stage RCCs, and good long-term survival in patients undergoing this form of treatment. Partial nephrectomy entails complete local resection of a renal tumor while leaving the largest possible amount of normal functioning parenchyma in the involved kidney.

**Accepted indications for partial nephrectomy include situations in which radical nephrectomy would render the patient anephric with subsequent immediate need for dialysis. This encompasses patients with bilateral RCC or RCC involving a solitary functioning kidney.** The patient may have a solitary functioning kidney because of unilateral renal agenesis, prior removal of the contralateral kidney, or irreversible impairment of contralateral renal function from a benign disorder. Another indication for partial nephrectomy is represented by patients with unilateral RCC and a functioning opposite kidney affected by a condition that might threaten its future function, such as calculus disease, chronic pyelonephritis, renal artery stenosis, ureteral reflux, or systemic diseases such as diabetes and nephrosclerosis (Licht and Novick, 1994).

Studies have clarified the role of partial nephrectomy in patients with localized unilateral RCC and a normal contralateral kidney. These data indicate that **radical nephrectomy and partial nephrectomy provide equally effective curative treatment for patients who present with a single, small (<4 cm), and clearly localized RCC** (Butler et al, 1995; Lerner et al, 1996; Uzzo and Novick, 2001). The long-term renal functional advantage of partial nephrectomy with a normal opposite kidney requires further study. Partial nephrectomy is also occasionally indicated in the management of patients with renal pelvic transitional cell carcinoma or Wilms' tumor when preservation of functioning renal parenchyma is a clinically relevant consideration (Zincke and Neves, 1984; Ziegelbaum et al, 1987).

**The technical success rate with partial nephrectomy for RCC is excellent, and several large studies have reported 5-year cancer-specific survival rates of 87% to 90% in such patients** (Morgan and Zincke, 1990; Steinbach et al, 1992; Licht and Novick, 1994). These survival rates are comparable to those obtained after radical nephrectomy, particularly for low-stage RCC. The major disadvantage of partial nephrectomy for RCC is the risk of postoperative local tumor recurrence in the kidney that was operated on, which has been observed in 4% to 6% of patients (Morgan and Zincke, 1990; Steinbach et al, 1992; Licht and Novick, 1994). These local recurrences are most likely a manifestation of undetected microscopic multifocal RCC in the renal remnant. The risk of local tumor recurrence after radical nephrectomy has not been studied, but it is presumably very low.

A study from the Cleveland Clinic reviewed the results of partial nephrectomy for treatment of localized sporadic RCC in 485 patients. The mean postoperative follow-up was 4 years (Hafez et al, 1999). The overall and cancer-specific 5-year patient survival rates in the series were 81% and 92%, respectively. Recurrent RCC developed postoperatively in 44 patients (9%), including 16 (3.2%) with local recurrence in the remnant kidney and 28 (5.8%) with metastatic disease.

In a subsequent study, Fergany and colleagues (2000) reviewed the results of partial nephrectomy in 107 patients with localized sporadic RCC treated before 1988 and observed a minimum of 10 years at the Cleveland Clinic. Tumors were symptomatic in 73 patients (68%), and indications for surgery were imperative in 96 (90%). All patients were observed for at least 10 years or until death. Cancer-specific survival was 88.2% at 5 years and 73% at 10 years, and 26% of the patients died of metastatic disease. Long-term preservation of renal function was achieved in 93% of patients.

In a more recent study from the Cleveland Clinic, Fergany reviewed the long-term results of open partial nephrectomy in 400 patients with RCC in a solitary kidney. Postoperatively, 97% of patients maintained satisfactory renal function without the need for dialysis. Cancer-specific survival was 89% at 5 years and 82% at 10 years (Fergany et al, 2005). These results attest to the long-term biologic and functional efficacy of partial nephrectomy for localized RCC.

**Evaluation of patients with RCC for partial nephrectomy should include preoperative testing to rule out locally extensive or metastatic disease.** Previously, preoperative renal arteriography was routinely performed to delineate the intrarenal vasculature so that the tumor could be excised with minimal blood loss and damage to adjacent normal parenchyma. Selective renal venography was performed in patients with large or centrally located tumors to evaluate for intrarenal venous thrombosis secondary to malignant disease, which, if present, implies a more advanced local tumor stage and also increases the technical complexity of tumor excision. These invasive studies have been replaced by three-dimensional volume-rendered CT, which can accurately and less invasively depict the renal parenchymal and vascular anatomy in a format familiar to urologic surgeons (Coll et al, 1999). The data integrate essential information from arteriography, venography, excretory urography, and conventional two-dimensional CT into a single imaging modality and obviate the need for more

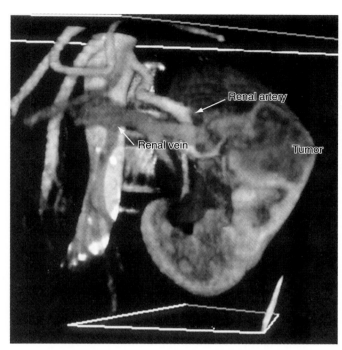

**Figure 50–46.** Three-dimensional CT scan shows tumor in upper part of left kidney with renal arterial and venous supply.

invasive imaging (Fig. 50–46). **Three-dimensional CT scanning is additionally advantageous by accurately demonstrating involvement of the collecting system with a localized renal tumor** (Derweesh et al, 2005).

In patients with bilateral large synchronous RCCs, I usually approach the kidney most amenable to a partial nephrectomy first. Then, approximately 1 month after a technically successful result has been documented, I perform a second partial nephrectomy or a radical nephrectomy on the opposite kidney. Staging surgery in this fashion obviates the need for temporary dialysis if ischemic renal failure occurs after nephron-sparing excision of RCC. In patients with bilateral, small, synchronous RCCs, bilateral simultaneous partial nephrectomies are performed.

**It is usually possible to perform partial nephrectomy for a malignant neoplasm in situ by using an operative approach that optimizes exposure of the kidney and by combining meticulous surgical technique with an understanding of the renal vascular anatomy** in relation to the tumor. Preoperative hydration and mannitol administration are important adjuncts to ensure optimal renal perfusion at operation. I employ an extraperitoneal flank incision through the bed of the 11th or 12th rib for almost all these operations; I occasionally use a thoracoabdominal incision for very large tumors involving the upper portion of the kidney. These incisions allow the surgeon to operate on the mobilized kidney almost at skin level and provide excellent exposure of the peripheral renal vessels (Fig. 50–47). With an anterior subcostal transperitoneal incision, the kidney is invariably located in the depth of the wound, and the surgical exposure is simply not as good. Extracorporeal surgery is rarely necessary in these patients today.

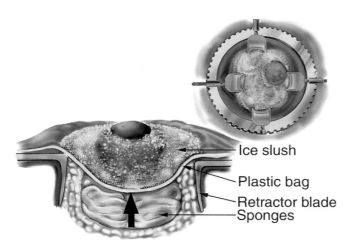

Ice slush

Plastic bag

Retractor blade

Sponges

**Figure 50–47.** Elevation of the mobilized kidney to skin level is demonstrated by placement of sponges under the plastic bag containing the kidney and ice slush.

**A report highlighted the potential for renal dysfunction associated with staged bilateral renal exploration through the flank. Specifically, when the second renal operation is performed, flexion with elevation of the kidney rest may cause ischemic damage to the previously operated on contralateral kidney, which has become fixed in place by postoperative scarring. In such cases, the second flank operation should be performed without elevation of the kidney rest.** Alternatively, an anterior surgical approach may be elected for the second operation (Matin and Novick, 2001).

When in situ partial nephrectomy is performed for malignant disease, the kidney is mobilized within Gerota's fascia while the perirenal fat around the tumor is left intact. For small, peripheral renal tumors, it is not necessary to control the renal artery. In most other cases, however, partial nephrectomy is most effectively performed after temporary renal arterial occlusion. This measure not only limits intraoperative bleeding but also, by reducing renal tissue turgor, improves access to intrarenal structures. When possible, it is helpful to leave the renal vein patent throughout the operation. This measure decreases intraoperative renal ischemia and, by allowing venous backbleeding, facilitates hemostasis by enabling identification of small, transected renal veins. In patients with centrally located tumors, it is necessary to occlude the renal vein temporarily to minimize intraoperative bleeding from transected major venous branches.

When the renal circulation is temporarily interrupted, in situ renal hypothermia is used to protect against postischemic renal injury. Surface cooling of the kidney with ice slush allows up to 3 hours of safe ischemia without permanent renal injury. An important caveat with this method is to keep the entire kidney covered with ice slush for 10 to 15 minutes immediately after the renal artery is occluded and before the partial nephrectomy is commenced (see Fig. 50–47). This amount of time is needed to obtain core renal cooling to a temperature (approximately 20°C) that optimizes in situ renal preservation. During excision of the tumor, invariably, large portions of the kidney are no longer covered with ice slush, and in the absence of adequate prior renal cooling, rapid rewarming and ischemic renal injury can occur. Cooling by perfusion of the

kidney with a cold solution instilled through the renal artery is not recommended because of the theoretical risk of tumor dissemination. **Mannitol is given intravenously 5 to 10 minutes before temporary renal arterial occlusion. Systemic or regional anticoagulation to prevent intrarenal vascular thrombosis is not necessary.** A prospective controlled study from the Cleveland Clinic demonstrated that perioperative dopamine does not help preserve renal function in partial nephrectomy operations (O'Hara et al, 2002).

**A variety of surgical techniques are available for performing partial nephrectomy in patients with malignant disease** (Novick, 1998). These include simple enucleation, polar segmental nephrectomy, wedge resection, transverse resection, and extracorporeal partial nephrectomy with renal autotransplantation. All these techniques require adherence to basic principles of early vascular control, avoidance of ischemic renal damage, complete tumor excision with free margins, precise closure of the collecting system, careful hemostasis, and closure or coverage of the renal defect with adjacent fat, fascia, peritoneum, or Oxycel. Whichever technique is employed, the tumor is removed with a small surrounding margin of grossly normal renal parenchyma. **Data have shown that as long as a histologic tumor-free margin of resection is present, the width of the resection margin is of no biologic or prognostic significance** (Castilla et al, 2002). Intraoperative ultrasonography is helpful in achieving accurate tumor localization, particularly for intrarenal lesions that are not visible or palpable from the external surface of the kidney (Assimos et al, 1991; Campbell et al, 1996) (Fig. 50–48).

**In performing a transverse resection of the upper part of the kidney, care must be taken to avoid injury to the posterior segmental renal arterial branch, which may also occasionally supply the basilar renal segment** (Fig. 50–49). Preoperative vascular imaging with three-dimensional CT scanning is integral to the identification and preservation of the posterior segmental artery at surgery to avoid devascularization of a major portion of the healthy remnant kidney. Midrenal resections may also be particularly complicated because the arterial supply comprises branches of anterior and posterior renal artery divisions, and the calyces often enter the same infundibula as those draining the upper and lower poles.

Whatever nephron-sparing technique is used, the parenchyma around the tumor is divided with a combination of sharp and blunt dissection. In many cases, the tumor extends deeply into the kidney, and the collecting system is entered. Often, renal arterial and venous branches supplying the tumor can be identified as the parenchyma is being incised, and these should be directly suture ligated at that time while they are most visible (Fig. 50–50). Similarly, in many cases, direct entry into the collecting system may be avoided by isolation and ligation of major infundibula draining the tumor-bearing renal segment as the incision into the parenchyma is developed (see Fig. 50–50).

After excision of the tumor, the remaining transected blood vessels on the renal surface are secured with figure-of-eight 4-0 chromic sutures. Bleeding at this point is usually minimal, and the operative field can be kept satisfactorily clear by gentle suction during placement of hemostatic sutures. Residual collecting system defects are similarly closed with interrupted or continuous 4-0 chromic sutures. At this point, with the renal artery still clamped but with the renal vein open, the anesthe-

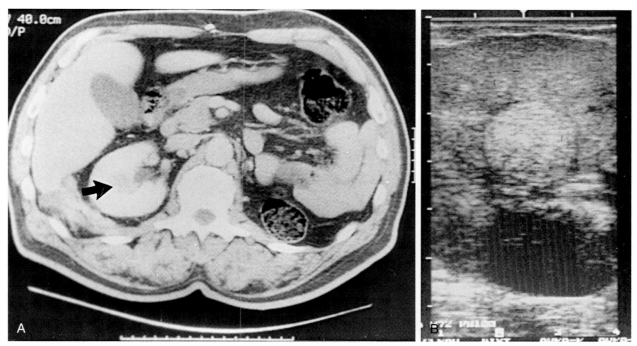

**Figure 50–48.** **A,** CT scan shows small tumor within the center of a solitary kidney. **B,** Intraoperative ultrasonography demonstrates localization of this intrarenal tumor.

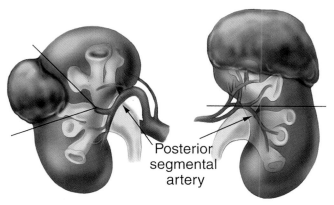

**Figure 50–49.** Injury to the posterior segmental renal arterial branch must be avoided during upper or midrenal resections.

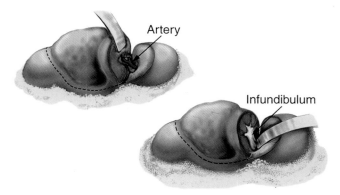

**Figure 50–50.** As the parenchyma around the tumor is incised, major vessels supplying the tumor are identified and secured. Similarly, infundibula draining the tumor-bearing portion of the kidney are also identified and secured.

siologist is asked to hyperinflate the lungs and thereby raise the central and renal venous pressures. This forces blood out through residual, unsecured, transected veins on the renal surface and thereby facilitates their detection (Fig. 50–51). Once identified, these veins are secured with interrupted figure-of-eight 4-0 chromic sutures. The argon beam coagulator is a useful adjunct for achieving hemostasis on the transected peripheral renal surface.

**In most cases, after the renal vasculature and the collecting system are secured, the kidney is closed on itself by approximating the transected cortical margins with simple interrupted 3-0 chromic sutures after placement of a small piece of Oxycel at the base of the defect.** This is an important additional hemostatic measure. When it is done, the suture line must be free of tension and the blood vessels supplying

the kidney must be free of significant angulation or kinking. After the renal defect is closed, the renal artery is unclamped, and circulation to the kidney is restored. When the remnant kidney resides within a large retroperitoneal fossa, the kidney is fixed to the posterior musculature with interrupted 3-0 chromic sutures to prevent postoperative movement or rotation of the kidney, which may compromise the blood supply (Fig. 50–52). A retroperitoneal drain is always left in place for at least 7 days, and an intraoperative ureteral stent is placed only when major reconstruction of the intrarenal collecting system has been performed.

**In patients with RCC or transitional cell carcinoma, partial nephrectomy is contraindicated in the presence of**

Lung hyperinflation

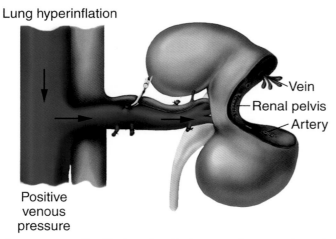

**Figure 50–51.** Identification of residual unsecured transected vessels (particularly veins) on the renal surface is facilitated by increasing the renal venous pressure through hyperinflation of the lungs.

Nephropexy of Remnant Kidney

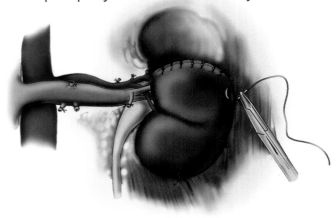

**Figure 50–52.** Nephropexy of the remnant kidney to the retroperitoneum is achieved with several interrupted sutures.

**lymph node metastasis because the prognosis for these patients is poor.** Biopsy of enlarged or suspicious-looking lymph nodes should be done before the renal resection is initiated. When partial nephrectomy is performed, after excision of all gross tumor, absence of malignant change in the remaining portion of the kidney should be verified intraoperatively by frozen-section examinations of biopsy specimens obtained at random from the renal margin of excision. Such biopsies do not usually demonstrate residual tumor, but if they do, additional renal tissue must be excised.

## Segmental Polar Nephrectomy

In patients with a malignant neoplasm confined to the upper or lower pole of the kidney, partial nephrectomy can be performed by isolation and ligation of the segmental apical or basilar arterial branch while unrepaired perfusion is allowed to the remainder of the kidney from the main renal artery. This procedure is illustrated in Figure 50–53 for a tumor confined to the apical vascular segment. The apical artery is dissected away from the adjacent structures, ligated, and divided. A corresponding venous branch is often present, and it is similarly ligated and divided. An ischemic line of demarcation then generally appears on the surface of the kidney and outlines the segment to be excised. If this area is not obvious, a few milliliters of methylene blue can be directly injected distally into the ligated apical artery to better outline the limits of the involved renal segment. An incision is then made in the renal cortex at the line of demarcation, which should be several millimeters away from the visible edge of the cancer. The parenchyma is divided by sharp and blunt dissection, and the polar segment is removed. In cases of malignant disease, it is not possible to preserve a strip of capsule beyond the parenchymal line of resection for use in closing the renal defect. When the collecting system and vasculature have been repaired, the edges of the kidney are reapproximated as an additional hemostatic measure with simple, interrupted 3-0 chromic sutures inserted through the capsule and a small amount of parenchyma. Before these sutures are tied, perire-

nal fat or Oxycel can be inserted into the defect for inclusion in the renal closure.

## Wedge Resection

Wedge resection is an appropriate technique for removal of peripheral tumors on the surface of the kidney, particularly ones that are larger or not confined to either renal pole. Because these lesions often encompass more than one renal segment and because this technique is generally associated with heavier bleeding, it is best to perform wedge resection with temporary renal arterial occlusion and surface hypothermia.

In a wedge resection, the tumor is removed with a several-millimeter surrounding margin of grossly normal renal parenchyma (Fig. 50–54). The parenchyma is divided by a combination of sharp and blunt dissection. Often, prominent intrarenal vessels are identified as the parenchyma is being incised. These may be directly suture ligated at the time, while they are most visible. After excision of the tumor, the collecting system and vasculature are then repaired as needed. The renal defect can then be closed in one of two ways (see Fig. 50–54). The kidney may be closed on itself by approximating the transected cortical margins with simple interrupted 3-0 chromic sutures after placement of a small piece of Oxycel at the base of the defect. If this is done, there must be no tension on the suture line and no significant angulation or kinking of blood vessels supplying the kidney. Alternatively, a portion of perirenal fat may simply be inserted into the base of the renal defect as a hemostatic measure and sutured to the parenchymal margins with interrupted 4-0 chromic sutures. After closure or coverage of the renal defect, the renal artery is unclamped, and circulation to the kidney is restored.

## Major Transverse Resection

A transverse resection is done to remove large tumors that extensively involve the upper or lower portion of the kidney.

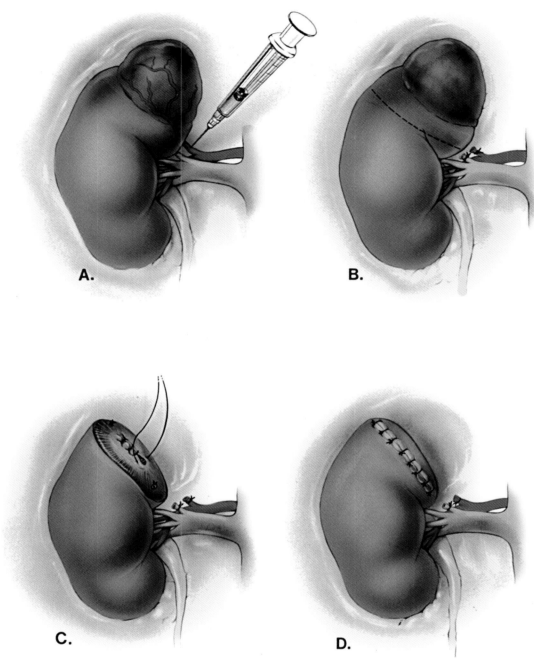

**Figure 50–53.** Technique of segmental (apical) polar nephrectomy with preliminary ligation of apical arterial and venous branches. (From Novick AC: Partial nephrectomy for renal cell carcinoma. Urol Clin North Am 1987;14:419.)

This technique is performed with surface hypothermia after temporary occlusion of the renal artery. Major branches of the renal artery and vein supplying the tumor-bearing portion of the kidney are identified in the renal hilum, ligated, and divided (Fig. 50–55A). If possible, this should be done before the renal artery is temporarily occluded to minimize the overall period of renal ischemia.

After the renal artery is occluded, the parenchyma is divided by blunt and sharp dissection, leaving a several-millimeter margin of grossly normal tissue around the tumor (Fig. 50–55B). Transected blood vessels on the renal surface are secured as previously described, and the hilum is inspected carefully for remaining unligated segmental vessels. If possible, the renal defect is sutured together with one of the techniques previously described (Fig. 50–55C). If this suture cannot be placed without tension or without distorting the renal vessels, a piece of peritoneum or perirenal fat is sutured in place to cover the defect.

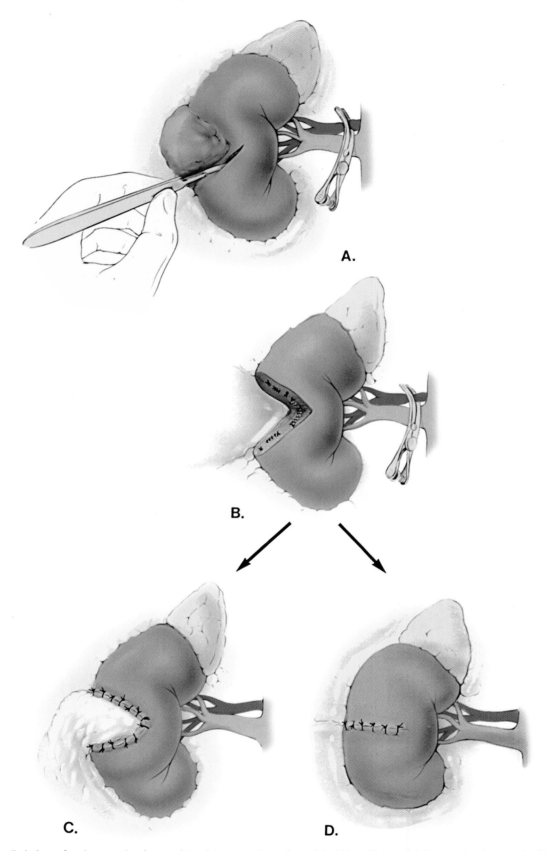

**Figure 50–54.** Technique of wedge resection for a peripheral tumor on the surface of the kidney. The renal defect may be closed on itself or covered with perirenal fat. (From Novick AC: Partial nephrectomy for renal cell carcinoma. Urol Clin North Am 1987;14:419.)

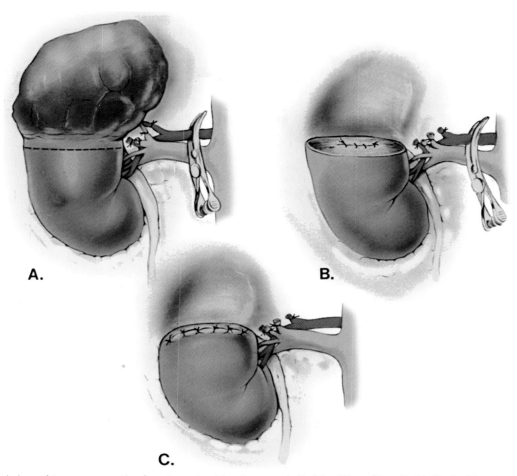

**Figure 50–55.** Technique of transverse resection for a tumor involving the upper half of the kidney. (From Novick AC: Partial nephrectomy for renal cell carcinoma. Urol Clin North Am 1987;14:419.)

## Partial Nephrectomy for Central Tumors

**For patients with central tumors, complete delineation of the renal arterial and venous supply is mandatory for surgical planning. As stated, this information can now be obtained with three-dimensional CT scanning, and invasive vascular imaging studies are no longer necessary** (Coll et al, 1999). In patients with central tumors, partial nephrectomy is most effectively performed after temporary occlusion of the renal artery and vein. Renal vein occlusion is important to minimize intraoperative bleeding from transected major venous branches. The renal artery and vein are occluded separately with individual atraumatic vascular clamps.

During the preliminary dissection, the kidney is mobilized within Gerota's fascia while the perirenal fat around the tumor is left intact. There may be relatively little perirenal fat to preserve with central tumors that extend into the renal hilum. The tumor is mobilized and isolated as much as possible by dissecting away adjacent segmental renal vessels that provide critical blood supply to the **non–tumor-bearing part of the kidney that is to be preserved.**

**The differences between the renal arterial and venous circulations must be borne in mind and may be used to advantage in these operations.** Because all segmental arteries are end-arteries with no collateral circulation, all branches supplying tumor-free parenchyma must be preserved to avoid devitalization of functioning renal tissue. However, the renal venous drainage system is different, in that intrarenal venous branches intercommunicate freely among the various renal segments. Therefore, ligation of a branch of the renal vein does not result in segmental infarction of the kidney because collateral venous blood supply provides adequate drainage. This is important clinically because it enables one to obtain safe surgical access to central tumors in the renal hilum by ligation and division of small adjacent or overlying venous branches. This allows the main renal vein to be completely mobilized and freely retracted in either direction to expose a central tumor with no vascular compromise of uninvolved parenchyma (Fig. 50–56). At this stage, small, segmental arterial branches that directly supply the tumor can also be secured and divided. If the portion of kidney or tumor supplied by a segmental artery is not readily apparent, temporary occlusion of the branch with a miniature vascular clamp can resolve this by enabling direct visualization of the ischemic supplied renal tissue. In dissecting on the posterior renal surface, particular care must be taken to avoid injury to the posterior segmental renal arterial branch, which has a variable

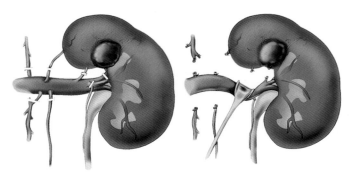

**Figure 50–56.** Mobilization of the left renal vein to obtain better exposure of a tumor in the renal hilum by ligation and division of small renal venous branches.

location and may also occasionally supply the basilar renal segment; if this is the case, failure to identify and preserve this branch can lead to devascularization of a major portion of the healthy remnant kidney.

The object of the preliminary dissection is to isolate the tumor and to secure as much of its direct blood supply as possible before clamping the main renal artery and vein, so that overall warm renal ischemia time can be minimized. Intraoperative ultrasonography is also performed before temporary renal vascular occlusion for the same reason. The primary value of this adjunctive imaging modality is for localization of intrarenal tumors that are not visible or palpable from the external surface of the kidney. A prospective study demonstrated that intraoperative ultrasonography is of limited value for detecting occult multicentric tumors in the kidney (Campbell et al, 1996).

After temporary occlusion of the renal artery and vein, the mobilized and isolated tumor is resected by incision of the attachment to the renal parenchyma. Small renal arterial and venous branches supplying the tumor can often be identified as the parenchyma is being incised, and these should be directly suture ligated at that time while they are most visible. Whereas a surrounding margin of normal parenchyma should be removed with the tumor, a wide margin of normal renal tissue is often not available for hilar tumors that may, in part, impinge directly on the central collecting system. It is sufficient to remove these tumors with all adjacent renal sinus fat and with a 3- to 4-mm margin of surrounding normal parenchyma where this is available.

In most cases, after the renal vessels and the collecting system are secured, the kidney is closed on itself by approximating the transected cortical margins with interrupted sutures as an additional hemostatic measure. When this is done, the parenchymal suture line must be free of tension and the blood vessels supplying the kidney must be free of significant angulation or kinking. After closure of the renal defect, the renal artery is unclamped, and circulation to the kidney is restored.

## Simple Enucleation

Some RCCs are surrounded by a distinct pseudocapsule of fibrous tissue (Vermooten, 1950). The technique of simple enucleation implies circumferential incision of the renal parenchyma around the tumors simply and rapidly at any

location, often with no vascular occlusion and with maximal preservation of normal parenchyma.

Initial reports indicated satisfactory short-term clinical results after enucleation, with good survival of patients and low rate of local tumor recurrence (Graham and Glenn, 1979; Jaeger et al, 1985). However, **most studies suggested a higher risk of leaving residual malignant cells in the kidney when enucleation is performed** (Rosenthal et al, 1984; Marshall et al, 1986; Blackley et al, 1988). These reports included several carefully done histopathologic studies that demonstrated frequent microscopic tumor penetration of the pseudocapsule surrounding the neoplasm. These data indicated that it is not always possible to be assured of complete tumor encapsulation before surgery. Local recurrence of tumor in the treated kidney is a grave complication of partial nephrectomy for RCC, and every attempt should be made to prevent it. Therefore, it is my view that a surrounding margin of normal parenchyma should be removed with the tumor whenever possible. This provides an added margin of safety against the development of local tumor recurrence and, in most cases, does not appreciably increase the technical difficulty of the operation. The technique of enucleation is currently employed only in occasional patients with von Hippel–Lindau disease and multiple low-stage encapsulated tumors involving both kidneys (Spencer et al, 1988).

## Extracorporeal Partial Nephrectomy and Autotransplantation

Extracorporeal partial nephrectomy for RCC with autotransplantation of the renal remnant was initially described by several surgeons (Calne, 1973; Gittes and McCullough, 1975) as an approach to facilitate successful excision of large complex tumors involving the renal hilum. Reconstruction of kidneys with RCC as well as with renal artery disease may be facilitated by this approach (Campbell et al, 1993). The practical and theoretical advantages of an extracorporeal approach include optimum exposure, bloodless surgical field, ability to perform a more precise operation with maximum conservation of renal parenchyma, and greater protection of the kidney from prolonged ischemia. Disadvantages of extracorporeal surgery include longer operative time with the need for vascular and ureteral anastomoses and increased risk of temporary and permanent renal failure (Campbell et al, 1994); the latter presumably reflects a more severe intraoperative ischemic insult to the kidney. **Whereas some urologic surgeons have found that almost all patients undergoing partial nephrectomy for RCC can be managed satisfactorily in situ** (Novick et al, 1989), others have continued to recommend an extracorporeal approach for selected patients (Morgan and Zincke, 1990).

Extracorporeal partial nephrectomy and renal autotransplantation are generally performed through a single midline incision. The kidney is mobilized and removed outside Gerota's fascia with ligation and division of the renal artery and vein as the last steps in the operation (Fig. 50–57A). Immediately after the renal vessels are divided, the removed kidney is flushed with 500 mL of a chilled intracellular electrolyte solution and submerged in a basin of ice-slush saline solution to maintain hypothermia. Under these conditions, if warm renal ischemia has been minimal, the kidney can safely

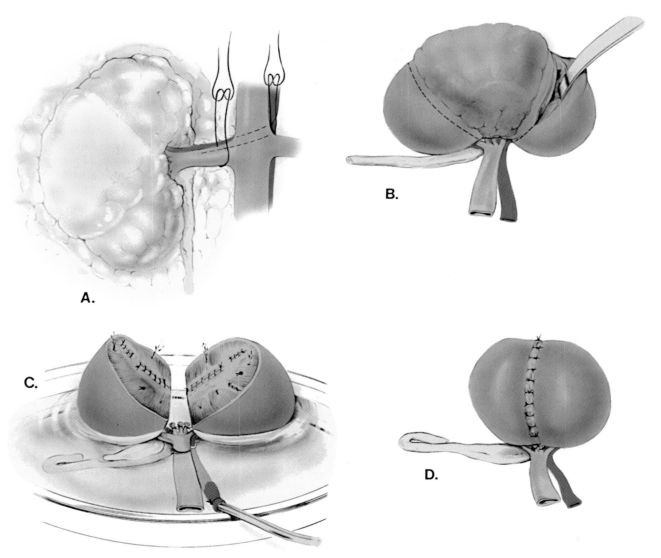

**Figure 50–57.** Technique of extracorporeal partial nephrectomy for a large central tumor. **A,** The kidney is removed outside Gerota's fascia. **B,** The tumor is excised extracorporeally while the vascular branches to uninvolved parenchyma are preserved. **C,** Pulsatile perfusion or reflushing is used to identify transected blood vessels. **D,** The kidney is closed on itself. (From Novick AC: Partial nephrectomy for renal cell carcinoma. Urol Clin North Am 1987;14:419.)

be preserved outside the body for as much time as needed to perform extracorporeal partial nephrectomy.

**If possible, it is best to leave the ureter attached in such cases to preserve its distal collateral vascular supply, particularly with large hilar or lower renal tumors in which complex excision may unavoidably compromise the blood supply to the pelvis, ureter, or both.** When this procedure is done, the extracorporeal operation is performed on the abdominal wall. If the ureter is left attached, it must be occluded temporarily to prevent retrograde blood flow to the kidney when it is outside the body. Often, unless the patient is thin, working on the abdominal wall with the ureter attached is cumbersome because of the tethering and restricted movement of the kidney. If these are observed, the ureter should be divided and the kidney placed on a separate workbench. This practice provides better exposure for the extracorporeal operation, and as this is being done, a second surgical team can simultaneously prepare the iliac fossa for

autotransplantation. If concern exists about the adequacy of ureteral blood supply, the risk of postoperative urinary extravasation can be diminished by restoration of urinary continuity through direct anastomosis of the renal pelvis to the retained distal ureter.

Extracorporeal partial nephrectomy is performed with the flushed kidney preserved under surface hypothermia (Fig. 50–57B). After the tumor has been completely resected, the renal remnant may be reflushed or placed on the pulsatile perfusion unit to facilitate identification and suture ligation of remaining potential bleeding points (Fig. 50–57C). The kidney can alternatively be perfused through the renal artery and vein to ensure both arterial and venous hemostasis. Because the flushing solution and perfusate lack clotting ability, there may continue to be some parenchymal oozing, which can safely be ignored. If possible, the defect made by the partial nephrectomy is closed by suturing the kidney on itself to further ensure a watertight repair (Fig. 50–57D).

Autotransplantation into the iliac fossa is done by the same vascular technique as for renal allotransplantation. Urinary continuity may be restored with ureteroneocystostomy or pyeloureterostomy, leaving an internal ureteral stent in place. After autotransplantation, a Penrose drain is positioned extraperitoneally in the iliac fossa away from the vascular anastomotic sites.

## Complications

**Complications of partial nephrectomy include hemorrhage, urinary fistula formation, ureteral obstruction, renal insufficiency, and infection.** Significant intraoperative bleeding can occur in patients who are undergoing partial nephrectomy. The need for early control and ready access to the renal artery is emphasized. Postoperative hemorrhage may be self-limited, if it is confined to the retroperitoneum, or it may be associated with gross hematuria. The initial management of postoperative hemorrhage is expectant, with bed rest, serial hemoglobin and hematocrit determinations, frequent monitoring of vital signs, and blood transfusions as needed. Angiography may be helpful in some patients to localize actively bleeding segmental renal arteries, which may be controlled by angioinfarction. Severe intractable hemorrhage may necessitate re-exploration with early control of the renal vessels and ligation of the active bleeding points.

**Postoperative urinary flank drainage after a partial nephrectomy is common and usually resolves as the collecting system closes with healing.** Persistent drainage suggests the development of a urinary cutaneous fistula. This diagnosis can be confirmed by determination of the creatinine level of the drainage fluid and by intravenous injection of indigo carmine with subsequent appearance of the dye in the drainage fluid. The majority of urinary fistulas resolve spontaneously if there is no obstruction of urinary drainage from the involved renal unit. If the perirenal space is not adequately drained, a urinoma or abscess may develop. An intravenous pyelogram or a retrograde pyelogram should be obtained to rule out obstruction of the involved urinary collecting system. In the event of hydronephrosis or persistent urinary leakage, an internal ureteral stent is placed. If this is not possible, a percutaneous nephrostomy may be inserted. Most urinary fistulas resolve spontaneously with proper conservative management, although it may take several weeks in some cases. A second operation to close the urinary fistula is rarely necessary.

**Ureteral obstruction can occur after partial nephrectomy because of postoperative bleeding into the collecting system with resulting clot obstruction of the ureter and pelvis.** This obstruction can lead to temporary extravasation of urine from the renal suture line. In most cases, expectant management is appropriate, and the obstruction resolves spontaneously with lysis of the clots. When urinary leakage is excessive, or in the presence of intercurrent urinary infection, placement of an internal ureteral stent can help maintain antegrade ureteral drainage.

Varying degrees of **renal insufficiency** often occur postoperatively when partial nephrectomy is performed in a patient with a solitary kidney. This insufficiency is a consequence of both intraoperative renal ischemia and removal of some normal parenchyma along with the diseased portion of the kidney. Such renal insufficiency is usually mild and resolves spontaneously with proper fluid and electrolyte management. Also, in most cases, the remaining parenchyma undergoes compensatory hypertrophy that serves to further improve renal function. Severe renal insufficiency may require temporary or permanent hemodialysis, and the patient should be aware of this possibility preoperatively.

Postoperative infections are usually self-limited if the operative site is well drained and in the absence of existing untreated urinary infection at the time of surgery. Unusual complications of partial nephrectomy include transient postoperative hypertension and aneurysm or arteriovenous fistula in the remaining portion of the parenchyma (Snodgrass and Robinson, 1964; Rezvani et al, 1973).

A study detailed the incidence and clinical outcome of technical or kidney-related complications occurring after 259 partial nephrectomies for renal tumors at the Cleveland Clinic (Campbell et al, 1994). In the overall series, local or kidney-related complications occurred after 78 operations (30.1%). The incidence of complications was significantly less for operations performed after 1988 and significantly less for incidentally detected versus suspected tumors. The most common complications were urinary fistula formation and acute renal failure. A urinary fistula occurred after 45 of 259 operations (17%). Significant predisposing factors for a urinary fistula included central tumor location, tumor smaller than 4 cm, need for major reconstruction of the collecting system, and ex vivo surgery. Only one urinary fistula required open operative repair; the remainder resolved either spontaneously (n = 30) or with endoscopic management (n = 14).

Acute renal failure occurred after 30 of 115 operations (26%) performed on a solitary kidney. Significant predisposing factors for acute renal failure were tumor larger than 7 cm, parenchymal excision of more than 50%, ischemia time longer than 60 minutes, and ex vivo surgery. **Acute renal failure resolved completely in 25 patients, of whom 9 (8%) required temporary dialysis; 5 patients (4%) required permanent dialysis.**

Overall, only eight complications (3.1%) required repeated open surgery for treatment, whereas all other complications resolved with nonintervention or endourologic management. Surgical complications contributed to an adverse clinical outcome in only seven patients (2.9%). These data indicate that partial nephrectomy can be performed safely with preservation of renal function in most patients with renal tumors.

**With increasing experience, the morbidity of open partial nephrectomy continues to diminish. A study from the Cleveland Clinic detailed the outcome of open partial nephrectomy in 100 consecutive patients** (Gill et al, 2003). **A postoperative renal or urologic complication occurred in only two patients (one urine leak, one ureteral obstruction), and both of these resolved with appropriate management.**

## Postoperative Follow-up

Patients who undergo nephron-sparing surgery for RCC are advised to return for initial follow-up 4 to 6 weeks postoperatively. At that time, a serum creatinine measurement and intravenous pyelogram are obtained to document renal function and anatomy; in patients with impaired overall renal function, a renal ultrasound study is obtained instead of an intravenous pyelogram.

A study from the Cleveland Clinic analyzed tumor recurrence patterns after partial nephrectomy in 327 patients with sporadic localized RCC (Hafez et al, 1997). The purpose of this study was to develop appropriate guidelines for long-term surveillance after nephron-sparing surgery for RCC. RCC occurred postoperatively in 38 patients (11.6%), including 13 patients (4.0%) who developed local tumor recurrence and 25 patients (7.6%) who developed metastatic disease. The incidence of postoperative local tumor recurrence and metastatic disease, respectively, according to initial pathologic tumor stage was as follows: 0% and 4.4% for stage T1 RCC, 2% and 5.3% for stage T2 RCC, 8.2% and 11.5% for stage T3a RCC, and 10.6% and 14.9% for stage T3b RCC. The peak postoperative intervals for development of local tumor recurrence were 6 to 24 months (in patients with stage T3 RCC) and more than 48 months (in patients with stage T2 RCC).

These data indicate that surveillance for recurrent malignant disease after nephron-sparing surgery for RCC can be tailored according to the initial pathologic tumor stage. All patients should be evaluated with medical history, physical examination, and selected blood studies on a yearly basis. The blood studies should include serum calcium, alkaline phosphatase, blood urea nitrogen, serum creatinine, and electrolyte determinations and liver function tests.

The need for postoperative radiographic surveillance studies varies according to the initial pathologic tumor (pT) stage. Patients who undergo nephron-sparing surgery for pT1 RCC do not require radiographic imaging postoperatively in view of the very low risk for recurrent malignant disease. A yearly chest radiograph is recommended after nephron-sparing surgery for pT2 or pT3 RCC because the lung is the most common site of postoperative metastasis in both groups. Abdominal or retroperitoneal tumor recurrence is uncommon in patients assigned to stage pT2, particularly early after nephron-sparing surgery, and these patients require only occasional follow-up abdominal CT scanning; I recommend that this be done every 2 years for this category. Patients with pT3 RCC have a higher risk for local tumor recurrence, particularly during the first 2 years after nephron-sparing surgery, and they may benefit from more frequent follow-up abdominal CT scanning initially; I recommend that this be done every 6 months for 3 years and every 2 years thereafter. If a local recurrence is found without metastatic disease, either a second partial nephrectomy or a total nephrectomy may be performed (Novick and Straffon, 1987).

Patients with less than one kidney are at higher risk for development of proteinuria, glomerular damage, and impaired renal function as a result of glomerular hyperfiltration (Solomon et al, 1985; Foster et al, 1991). In one study, long-term renal function was evaluated in 14 patients with a solitary kidney who underwent partial nephrectomy for localized malignant disease (Novick et al, 1991). Preoperatively, there was no clinical or histopathologic evidence of primary renal disease. Postoperative renal function remained stable in 12 patients, whereas 2 patients developed end-stage renal failure. A total of nine patients had proteinuria: low grade (<750 mg/day) in four patients and moderate to severe (930 to 6740 mg/day) in five patients. A statistically significant association was found between more proteinuria and a reduced

amount of remaining renal tissue as well as a longer follow-up interval. A renal biopsy was done in four patients with moderate to severe proteinuria that, in each case, showed focal segmental or global glomerulosclerosis.

**These data suggest that patients with more than 50% reduction in overall renal mass are at the greatest risk for proteinuria, glomerulopathy, and progressive renal failure. Structural or functional renal damage in such cases is usually antedated by the appearance of proteinuria. Therefore, the follow-up of patients after partial nephrectomy in a solitary kidney should include a 24-hour urinary protein determination in addition to the usual renal function and tumor surveillance studies. Patients who have proteinuria (>150 mg/day) may be treated with a low-protein diet and a converting enzyme inhibitor agent, which appear to be beneficial in preventing glomerulopathy caused by reduced renal mass** (Meyer et al, 1985; Novick and Schreiber, 1995).

## PARTIAL NEPHRECTOMY FOR BENIGN DISEASE

Partial nephrectomy is also indicated in selected patients with localized benign disease of the kidney (Leach and Lieber, 1980). The indications include hydronephrosis with parenchymal atrophy or atrophic pyelonephritis in a duplicated renal segment; calyceal diverticulum complicated by infection, stones, or both; calculus disease with obstruction of the lower pole calyx or segmental parenchyma disease with impaired drainage (Papathanassiadis and Swinney, 1966; Bates et al, 1981); renovascular hypertension due to segmental parenchymal damage or noncorrectable branch renal artery disease (Aoi et al, 1981; Parrott et al, 1984); traumatic renal injury with irreversible damage to a portion of the kidney (Gibson et al, 1982); and removal of a benign renal tumor, such as an angiomyolipoma or oncocytoma (Maatman et al, 1984).

The preoperative considerations are similar to those in patients undergoing partial nephrectomy for malignant disease. In most cases, a vascular imaging study should be performed to delineate the main and segmental renal arterial supplies. The same measures should be taken to minimize intraoperative renal damage from ischemia. The preferred surgical approach is usually through an extraperitoneal flank incision, except in cases of renal trauma, which are best approached anteriorly. The surgical techniques are similar to those described for malignant renal disease.

In performing an apical or basilar partial nephrectomy for benign disease, the segmental apical or basilar arterial branch is secured and the parenchyma is divided at the ischemic line of demarcation, without the need for temporary renal arterial occlusion. More complex transverse or wedge renal resections are best performed with temporary renal arterial occlusion and ice-slush surface hypothermia. When the technique of transverse renal resection is employed for a benign disorder, the renal capsule is excised and reflected off the diseased parenchyma for subsequent use in covering the renal defect (Fig. 50–58). The technical aspects of partial nephrectomy for benign disease are otherwise the same as those described for malignant disease, with adherence to the same basic principles of appropriate vascular control, avoidance of ischemic renal

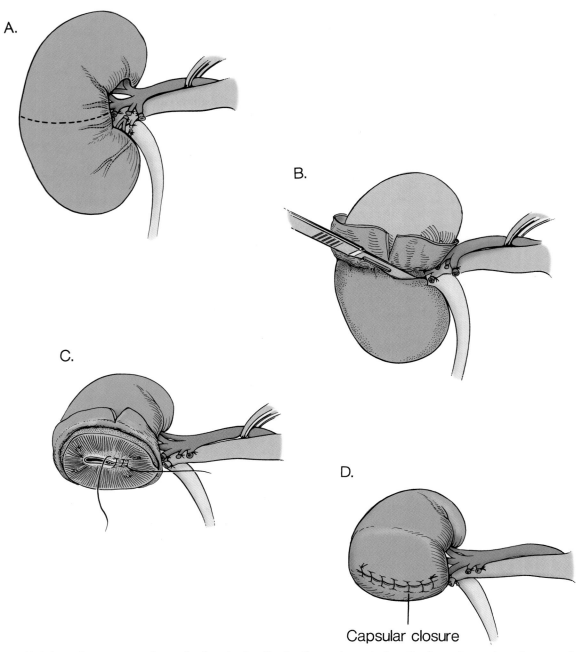

A.

B.

C.

D.

Capsular closure

**Figure 50–58.** Technique of transverse renal resection for a benign disorder. The renal capsule from the diseased parenchyma is preserved and used to cover the transected renal surface.

damage, precise closure of the collecting system, careful hemostasis, and closure or coverage of the renal defect.

## Heminephrectomy in Duplicated Collecting Systems

Because the indications for partial nephrectomy in this setting are usually hydronephrosis and parenchymal atrophy of one of the two segments, the demarcation of the tissue to be removed is usually evident. The atrophic parenchyma lining the dilated system can be further delineated by blue pyelo-tubular backflow if the ureter is ligated and the affected collecting system is distended by blue dye under pressure. In such cases, there is also often a dual arterial supply with distinct segmental branches to the upper and lower halves of the kidney. Segmental arterial and venous branches to the diseased portion of the kidney are ligated and divided. After a strip of renal capsule is preserved, the parenchyma is divided at the observed line of demarcation. There is usually minimal bleeding from the renal surface, and temporary occlusion of the arterial supply to the nondiseased segment is often unnecessary. There should be no entry into the collecting system over the transected renal surface, which is then closed or covered as described previously.

## RENAL ARTERIAL RECONSTRUCTION

**Two main categories of renal artery disease, atherosclerosis and fibrous dysplasia, account for approximately 80% and 20% of all such lesions,** respectively. Other unusual causes of renal artery disease include arterial aneurysm, arteriovenous fistula, neurofibromatosis, extrinsic obstruction of the renal artery, middle aortic syndrome, and renal artery thrombosis or embolism. Intervention may be indicated in these disorders to treat associated hypertension, to preserve renal function, or to prevent rupture of an arterial aneurysm.

**The role of surgical therapy in the management of these patients has changed for several reasons** (Novick and McElroy, 1985). These include the advent of percutaneous transluminal angioplasty (PTA) and stenting as alternative effective forms of treatment for certain patients, the development of new and more effective techniques for surgical revascularization, and an enhanced appreciation of advanced atherosclerotic renal artery disease as a correctable cause of renal failure. Surgical revascularization remains the definitive treatment of choice for patients with branch renal artery disease, with an ostial atherosclerotic lesion, with an arterial aneurysm, or in whom endovascular therapy has been unsuccessful. Surgical revascularization continues to provide excellent long-term results in properly selected patients with renal artery disease (Novick et al, 1987; Steinbach et al, 1997).

A variety of factors must be assessed in determining whether surgical treatment is appropriate for a given patient. These include the causal relationship of renal vascular disease to hypertension, the adequacy of blood pressure control with medical therapy, the natural history of untreated renal vascular disease with attention to the risk for renal function impairment, the medical condition of the patient, and the known results of surgical therapy and other interventions such as PTA or renal artery stents.

**Advances in surgical renovascular reconstruction have limited the role of total or partial nephrectomy in the management of patients with renal artery disease.** These operations are occasionally indicated in patients with renal infarction, severe arteriolar nephrosclerosis, severe renal atrophy, and noncorrectable renovascular lesions. Nephrectomy may also be indicated in elderly, poor–surgical risk patients with a normal contralateral kidney or after a failed revascularization procedure.

## INDICATIONS FOR TREATMENT
### Renovascular Hypertension

**The coexistence of hypertension and renal artery disease does not always imply a causal relationship between the two. Renal artery disease is far more common than renovascular hypertension.** Classically, renovascular hypertension is a retrospective diagnosis rendered when hypertension resolves after intervention to correct a renal artery lesion. The term now commonly refers to renin-mediated hypertension as a result of renal artery disease. Clinical clues to suggest renovascular hypertension include age younger than 30 years or older than 50 years, abrupt onset and short duration of hypertension, presence of extrarenal vascular disease, end-organ damage such as left ventricular hypertrophy or high-grade hypertensive retinopathy, systolic-diastolic abdominal bruit, and deterioration of renal function in response to an angiotensin-converting enzyme inhibitor. In patients who have a moderate clinical suggestion of renovascular hypertension, a number of noninvasive tests have been developed that identify patients with renovascular hypertension and help predict the outcome of intervention treatment.

**For patients with renovascular hypertension due to fibrous dysplasia, candidacy for surgical intervention is guided by the specific pathologic process, as determined by angiographic findings, and its associated natural history** (Stewart et al, 1970). Medical management of medial fibroplasia is the initial approach because loss of renal function from progressive obstruction is uncommon, and intervention is reserved for those patients with difficult-to-control hypertension. Renal artery disease due to intimal or perimedial fibroplasia is often associated with progressive obstruction, which can result in ischemic renal atrophy. Therefore, early intervention is recommended to improve blood pressure control and to preserve renal function.

The known results of PTA are important in assessing the need for surgery in patients with fibrous dysplasia. **Technical and clinical success rates with PTA for fibrous disease of the main renal artery are 90% to 95% and are no different from results obtainable with surgery** (Novick, 1994a, 1994b). Still, up to 30% of patients may present with branch disease or aneurysm that is not amenable to PTA. Surgery is then reserved for patients with peripheral, complex branch disease or for those whose PTA has failed.

**Renal artery aneurysms may require repair if they result in significant hypertension or for prevention of rupture when they are larger than 2 cm and noncalcified** (Novick, 1982). This is a particular concern in women of reproductive age because of the predisposition for rupture during pregnancy.

For patients with atherosclerosis and renovascular hypertension, the indications for intervention are more restrictive because of the frequent presence of concomitant extrarenal vascular disease. More vigorous attempts at medical management for this group are warranted. Surgical revascularization is reserved for those patients whose hypertension cannot be satisfactorily controlled with medication or whose renal function becomes threatened by advanced vascular disease. **Whereas PTA is associated with a successful blood pressure result for nonostial atherosclerosis, the long-term success rate with ostial lesions is poor because of a higher incidence of restenosis** (Novick, 1994a, 1994b). The results with endovascular stenting for ostial lesions are better than those with PTA; however, surgical revascularization remains the definitive long-term therapy for these patients (Steinbach et al, 1997).

### Ischemic Nephropathy

Epidemiologic studies suggest that atherosclerotic renovascular disease is common in patients with generalized atherosclerosis obliterans regardless of the presence of renovascular hypertension. **The development of chronic renal insufficiency from atherosclerotic renal artery disease, known as ischemic nephropathy, has become an important clinical issue that is separate and distinct from the problem of renovascular hypertension.** Knowledge of the natural history of atherosclerotic renal artery disease permits identification of patients at risk for ischemic nephropathy (Schreiber et al, 1984).

**Those at highest risk are patients with high-grade stenosis (>75%) involving the entire renal mass (bilateral disease or disease in a solitary kidney). Intervention in these patients is for the purpose of preservation of renal function.** Many of these patients are older, with diffuse extrarenal vascular disease and ostial renal artery disease. Clinical clues suggesting ischemic nephropathy include azotemia (unexplained or associated with angiotensin-converting enzyme inhibitor treatment), diminished renal size, and vascular disease in other sites (cerebrovascular disease, coronary artery disease, or peripheral vascular disease).

In considering a patient for revascularization, a determination of the potential for renal salvage must be made (Novick, 1996a, 1996b). All testing in this regard is aimed at identifying severe underlying renal parenchymal disease, in which case restoration of renal blood flow would not result in recovery of renal function. Successful revascularization usually results when the affected kidney is larger than 9 cm and demonstrates some evidence of function (usually assessed by isotopic renal scan). Total occlusion of the renal artery is not a contraindication for repair because the viability of the kidney can be maintained by collateral circulation, which is demonstrable by angiography. **Patients with mild to moderate renal dysfunction are acceptable surgical candidates; however, surgical revascularization is generally not worthwhile for patients with advanced azotemia (serum creatinine concentration of more than 4 mg/dL) because of significant underlying renal parenchymal disease. An exception to this rule is the small number of patients with significant renal functional impairment and bilateral total renal artery occlusion when one or both kidneys remain viable on the basis of collateral circulation.** Such kidneys otherwise meet criteria for revascularization (i.e., adequate size and with minimal parenchymal disease). Although such a presentation is uncommon, these patients can have favorable outcomes with surgical revascularization. Finally, in equivocal cases, a renal biopsy is performed at the time of revascularization. Preservation of the majority of glomeruli is the most important element of a favorable biopsy finding. Excessive glomerular hyalinization precludes performance of surgical revascularization. Tubular atrophy, interstitial fibrosis, and arteriolar sclerosis are less important and do not preclude consideration for revascularization.

## PREOPERATIVE CONSIDERATIONS

**Patients with atherosclerotic renal artery disease who are considered for surgical revascularization should undergo screening and correction of significant associated extrarenal vascular disease, such as coronary and carotid disease.** With aggressive treatment of coexisting extrarenal vascular disease before surgical renal revascularization, perioperative morbidity and mortality can be minimized.

**Before surgery, all patients require catheter arteriography** with iodinated contrast material for accurate anatomic information to be obtained. In selected cases, carbon dioxide angiography can be used, which eliminates the risk for contrast-related nephrotoxicity. In addition to anteroposterior views of the renal artery and aorta, I routinely obtain a lateral aortogram to assess the celiac artery and a view of the lower thoracic aorta. These additional views are obtained in anticipation of the use of extra-anatomic bypass procedures.

Many patients have bilateral disease, especially those with ischemic nephropathy. Because the morbidity of bilateral procedures is greater and disease is frequently asymmetrical, I usually perform unilateral renal revascularization. In cases of renovascular hypertension, the more extensively diseased artery is repaired, and for ischemic nephropathy, the larger kidney is repaired.

**All patients undergoing surgical renal revascularization are well hydrated before surgery.** Because renovascular hypertension is associated with secondary hyperaldosteronism, potassium supplementation and monitoring of serum potassium levels are needed to guard against hypokalemia. To further ensure optimal renal perfusion and an active diuresis intraoperatively, 12.5 g of mannitol is given intravenously before the operation is commenced; equivalent doses of mannitol are subsequently given before revascularization, immediately after revascularization, and again in the recovery room.

## AORTORENAL BYPASS

Although a variety of surgical revascularization techniques are available for treatment of patients with renal artery disease, **aortorenal bypass with a free graft of autogenous saphenous vein or hypogastric artery remains the preferred method in patients with a nondiseased abdominal aorta** (Straffon and Siegel, 1975; Novick et al, 1977a, 1977b; Stoney and Olofsson, 1988). Although an arterial autograft is theoretically advantageous, use of the hypogastric artery as a bypass graft is limited by its short length and frequent involvement with atherosclerosis. Therefore, the autogenous saphenous vein is most often employed, and excellent clinical results continue to be achieved with this type of bypass graft. The gonadal vein should never be used as a renal artery bypass graft. This vein is extremely friable and may either rupture postoperatively or undergo severe dilation. Currently, aortorenal bypass with a synthetic material is indicated only when an autogenous vascular graft is not available, and polytetrafluoroethylene has become the synthetic graft of choice in such cases (Khauli et al, 1984; Cormier et al, 1990).

For an aortorenal bypass on the right side, the kidney is exposed by reflection of the ascending colon medially and Kocher's maneuver on the duodenum (Fig. 50–59). The liver and gallbladder are retracted upward, with care taken to protect the hepatic ligament with its vessels and common bile duct. Exposure of the right renal artery, right renal vein, IVC, and aorta is thereby obtained. The Buckwalter self-retaining ring retractor is inserted to maintain exposure. Gerota's fascia is opened laterally to expose the surface of the kidney so that its color and consistency may be observed.

The aorta is exposed from the level of the left renal vein to the inferior mesenteric artery; overlying lymphatic vessels and lumbar segmental branches are ligated as necessary to gain

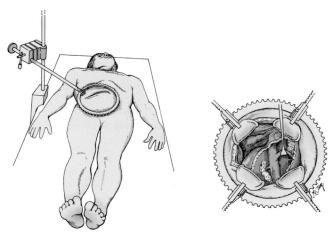

**Figure 50–59.** Transperitoneal exposure of the right kidney and renal vessels for aortorenal bypass.

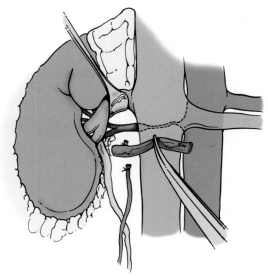

**Figure 50–60.** The bypass graft is measured for alignment with the aorta and distal renal artery.

exposure. The proximal aspect of the right renal artery is exposed by mobilizing and retracting the vena cava laterally and the left renal vein superiorly, carrying the dissection along the anterolateral aspect of the aortic wall until the renal artery origin is encountered.

The distal two thirds of the main right renal artery are exposed by retracting the mobilized vena cava medially and the right renal vein superiorly. To accomplish this, it is often necessary to secure and divide one or more lumbar veins entering the posterior aspect of the vena cava. There are generally no significant tributaries of the right renal vein. After exposure of the right renal artery, it is then mobilized from its attached and surrounding lymphatics and nerves. Small vessels and lymphatics are secured by light electrocautery or fine suture ligatures.

The bypass graft is placed along the lateral aortic wall to determine the best position for placement of the graft (Fig. 50–60). At this point, the ring retractor blades are relaxed to allow the aorta to return to its normal position and to prevent distortion of an otherwise well-placed graft after the final retraction is released.

On the right side, it is important to bring the graft off the anterolateral aspect of the aortic wall to avoid kinking of the proximal anastomosis as the graft passes in front of the vena cava. If the aortotomy is made too far anteriorly or posteriorly, the graft may kink, with subsequent development of stenosis or thrombosis. On the left side, the graft may be placed directly off the lateral aspect of the aorta.

An end-to-side anastomosis of the bypass graft to the aorta is done first to minimize the time of renal ischemia (Fig. 50–61). A DeBakey clamp is placed to occlude the aorta, with care taken to avoid compression of the mesenteric and contralateral renal arteries. In most cases, the lateral aortic wall is only partially occluded, thereby preserving distal aortic flow and obviating the need for systemic heparinization. In some patients with a small abdominal aorta (e.g., children, young women), better exposure is obtained by placing the DeBakey clamp completely across the aorta; this maneuver totally interrupts aortic blood flow, and in this event, systemic heparinization is initiated before aortic clamping.

An oval aortotomy is made on the anterolateral wall of the aorta. If significant atherosclerosis of the perirenal aorta is present, a local endarterectomy is performed to remove atheromatous plaque from the region of the anastomosis.

The bypass graft is spatulated for a short distance, and if length permits, the apex of the spatulation is generally placed at the caudal end of the aortotomy so that the graft can follow a gentle curve as it emerges from the aorta. If the aortotomy is located a significant distance below the distal renal artery or if the graft is short, as on the side, the apex is reversed cephalad to avoid kinking of the aortorenal bypass graft. Two corner sutures of 6-0 silk are inserted 180 degrees apart to begin the anastomosis.

The anastomosis is performed with interrupted 6-0 arterial sutures, and the anterior wall of the anastomosis is completed first. The aorta is rotated anteriorly to expose the posterior wall of the anastomosis, which is similarly completed with interrupted 6-0 arterial sutures. The graft is occluded beyond its origin with a bulldog clamp, and the aortic clamp is gently released. An arterial leakage is corrected at this time with additional sutures as needed. The bulldog clamp is intermittently released to ensure good blood flow and to flush the graft free of any atherosclerotic fragments. The graft distal to the clamp is then irrigated with heparin solution.

The main renal artery is then mobilized in its entirety, if this has not already been done. The renal artery is ligated proximally, a bulldog clamp is placed distally, and the diseased arterial segment is excised and sent for pathologic examination (Fig. 50–62). Before the distal anastomosis is performed, 10 mL of diluted heparin solution is instilled into the distal renal artery.

The bypass graft is brought anterior to the vena cava to lie in proximity to the distal renal artery. The graft is trimmed as necessary to allow a tension-free end-to-end anastomosis with no redundancy in the length of the graft. The graft and distal renal artery are spatulated to create a wider anastomosis, which minimizes the possibility of subsequent stenosis. The

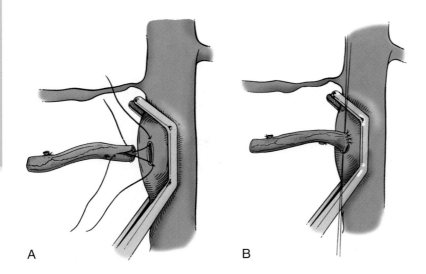

**Figure 50–61.** **A** and **B,** End-to-side anastomosis of the graft to the aorta is performed.

A

B

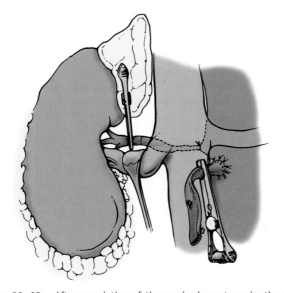

**Figure 50–62.** After completion of the proximal anastomosis, the distal renal artery is temporarily occluded before its division.

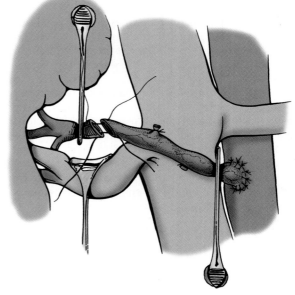

**Figure 50–63.** Performance of end-to-end anastomosis between the graft and the distal renal artery.

anastomosis is performed with 6-0 arterial sutures. Stay sutures, 180 degrees apart, are placed in the cephalic and caudal margins of the anastomosis. An end-to-end anastomosis of the graft to the renal artery is preferred to an end-to-side technique because it provides better flow rates, is easier to perform, and allows removal of the diseased renal arterial segment for pathologic study. The anastomosis is performed with interrupted 6-0 arterial sutures (Fig. 50–63).

The proximal and distal bulldog clamps are released, and circulation to the kidney is restored. Adequate renal perfusion is verified by palpating the pulse in the distal renal artery and by visually inspecting the renal surface. Arterial anastomotic leakage, if present, is controlled with Oxycel cotton or additional 6-0 interrupted arterial sutures (Fig. 50–64).

**Surgical revascularization is more complicated when the disease extends into the branches of the renal artery or when vascular reconstruction is required for a kidney supplied by multiple renal arteries. When disease-free distal arterial**

**branches occur outside the renal hilum, aortorenal bypass operation can usually be done in situ.** The size of the involved vessels is not a significant factor; with use of microvascular instruments and optical magnification, vessels as small as 1.5 mm in diameter can be repaired in situ. There are several variations of the standard aortorenal bypass technique that may be used to repair branch renal artery disease. Because the bypass graft must be sufficiently long to reach the renal artery branches, an autogenous saphenous vein graft is the graft of choice in these cases.

In patients with disease involving two or more renal artery branches, I have found that aortorenal bypass with a branched vascular graft offers the most useful and versatile technique for in situ vascular reconstruction (Fig. 50–65) (Streem and Novick, 1982). These end-to-side anastomoses are done with interrupted 7-0 arterial sutures and lead to construction of a

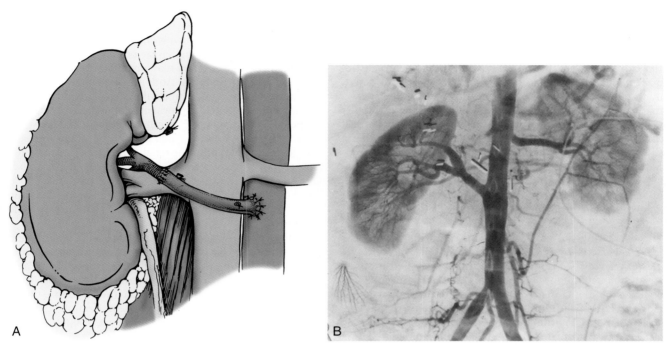

**Figure 50–64.** **A,** Completed right aortorenal bypass operation. **B,** Postoperative abdominal aortogram after successful right aortorenal bypass.

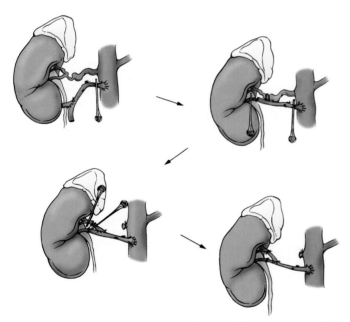

**Figure 50–65.** Technique of aortorenal bypass with a branched graft of autogenous saphenous vein.

multibranched graft that can be used to replace several diseased renal artery branches. After insertion of the proximal graft into the aorta, direct end-to-end anastomosis of each graft branch to a renal artery branch is done. During performance of each individual branch anastomosis, the remainder of the kidney continues to be perfused, and overall renal ischemia is thus limited to the time required for completion

of a single end-to-end anastomosis (approximately 15 to 20 minutes), which is an important advantage.

Renal artery aneurysms have a variable presentation, and vascular involvement may be focal or diffuse (Poutasse, 1976; Novick, 1982). **Saccular aneurysms are the most commonly encountered type of renal artery aneurysm and are often located at the initial bifurcation or trifurcation of the main renal artery.** When the aneurysm is outside the renal hilum, in situ excision may be done. If the renal artery wall at the base of the aneurysm is intact, aneurysmectomy by either primary closure or patch angioplasty with a segment of saphenous vein can be performed (Fig. 50–66). If the entire circumference of the renal artery wall is diseased, aortorenal bypass with a branched autogenous vascular graft is done as described earlier (Ortenberg et al, 1983).

## ALTERNATIVE BYPASS TECHNIQUES

**In older patients with renal artery disease, involvement of the abdominal aorta with severe atherosclerosis, aneurysmal disease, or dense fibrosis from a prior operation may render an aortorenal bypass or endarterectomy technically difficult and potentially hazardous to perform.** Simultaneous aortic replacement and renal revascularization have been associated with operative mortality rates of 5% to 30% (Brewster et al, 1976; Shahian et al, 1980; Dean et al, 1984; Tarazi et al, 1987) compared with rates of 2% to 6% (Novick et al, 1987; Libertino et al, 1992) for renal revascularization without aortic replacement. Dean and associates (1984) analyzed various risk factors to identify patients at greatest risk from a combined aortic and renal operation. The most significant risk factors were myocardial infarction, existing myocardial ischemia or ventricular hypertrophy, serum creatinine level higher than 3 mg/dL, diffuse peripheral vascular disease, and revascularization of both renal arteries at the time of aortic replacement. Although operative mortality was 0% if none of these risk factors were present, it increased to 63% if three or more were present. Therefore, simultaneous aortic replacement and renal revascularization should be considered only in patients with a significant aortic aneurysm or symptomatic aortoiliac occlusive disease. In the absence of a definite indication for aortic replacement, alternative bypass techniques are preferable because they can safely and effectively restore renal arterial blood flow while avoiding the need for a more hazardous operation. These alternative bypass operations include hepatorenal bypass, splenorenal bypass, iliorenal bypass, thoracic aortorenal bypass, and mesenterorenal bypass. The relative indications, surgical technique, and efficacy of these approaches are reviewed here.

In considering the patient's eligibility for alternative visceral–renal arterial bypass operations, the absence of occlusive disease involving the donor artery must be verified by preliminary arteriography. **Candidates for hepatorenal or splenorenal bypass must be evaluated with both anteroposterior and lateral abdominal aortography to ensure that the celiac artery and its branches are unobstructed. Pelvic arteriography is a requisite study in patients considered for an iliorenal bypass. If thoracic aortorenal revascularization is contemplated, lower thoracic aortography must be obtained.**

**Surgical revascularization has been performed more often to preserve renal function in patients with ischemic nephropathy from atherosclerotic renal artery disease.** Such patients are generally older, with ostial renal artery lesions and diffuse atherosclerosis involving other major abdominal vessels. Significant atherosclerotic occlusive disease involving the celiac and iliac arteries may preclude use of these vessels for renal revascularization. Abdominal aortographic findings were reviewed in 254 patients with atherosclerotic renal artery disease to document the prevalence of associated abdominal aortic and visceral arterial atherosclerosis (Fergany et al, 1995). All patients were evaluated with both anteroposterior and lateral aortography. The renal, celiac, superior mesenteric, and common iliac arteries were evaluated for the presence and severity of stenosis. The incidence of moderate (50% to 75%) or severe (>75%) visceral artery stenosis was determined in patients with varying degrees of renal artery stenosis (Table 50–1).

In the overall group of 254 patients with atherosclerotic renal artery stenosis, the incidence of significant celiac and iliac artery stenosis was 54% and 50%, respectively. Patients with severe renal artery stenosis bilaterally or in a solitary kidney are of greatest interest because they compose the most common candidate group for revascularization to preserve renal function. In this group, the incidence of significant celiac and iliac artery stenosis was 59% and 58%, respectively. Patients with severe unilateral renal artery stenosis also occasionally require revascularization for treatment of poorly controlled hypertension. In this group, the incidence of significant celiac and iliac stenosis was 52% and 30%, respectively (Fig. 50–67). A majority (75% to 81%) of patients in both of these groups had significant abdominal aortic atherosclerosis, which would preclude abdominal aortorenal revascularization. These findings underscore the prevalence of celiac and iliac arterial occlusive disease in these patients; if it is present, it obviates use of these vessels for renal revascularization. The only other published study relevant to this issue is from Valentine and colleagues (1991), who noted celiac artery stenosis in 17 of 50 patients (34%) with more than 50% renal artery stenosis and in 10 of 20 patients (50%) with more than 75% renal artery stenosis.

## Splenorenal Bypass

**Splenorenal bypass is the preferred vascular reconstructive technique for patients with a troublesome aorta who require left renal revascularization** (Khauli et al, 1985; Brewster and Darling, 1979). Transposition of the splenic artery by retroduodenal passage for right renal revascularization has been unsatisfactory and is not recommended. A requisite for performing splenorenal bypass is the demonstration on preoperative aortography, with both anteroposterior and lateral views,

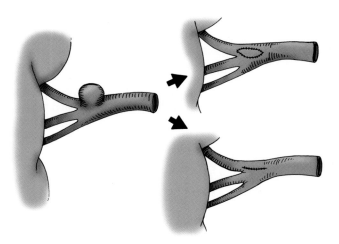

**Figure 50–66.** Technique of renal artery aneurysmectomy with primary closure *(bottom)* or patch angioplasty *(top)*.

**Table 50-1. Incidence of Significant Aortic Disease and Visceral Artery Stenosis in Patients with Renal Artery Stenosis**

| Renal Artery Status | Aortic Disease (%) | Celiac Stenosis (%) | SMA Stenosis (%) | Iliac Stenosis (%) |
| --- | --- | --- | --- | --- |
| Unilateral mild or moderate stenosis (N = 45) | 89 | 53 | 31 | 48 |
| Unilateral severe stenosis (N = 44) | 75 | 52 | 20 | 30 |
| Bilateral mild or moderate stenosis (N = 36) | 72 | 39 | 25 | 47 |
| Severe stenosis bilaterally or in a solitary kidney (N = 129) | 81 | 59 | 29 | 58 |

SMA, superior mesenteric artery.

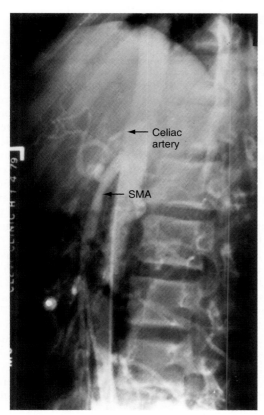

**Figure 50–67.** Lateral abdominal aortography shows significant stenosis at the origin of the celiac artery. SMA, superior mesenteric artery.

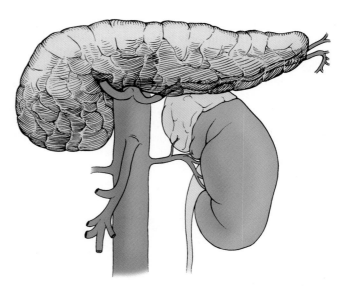

**Figure 50–68.** The normal anatomic relationships of the celiac, splenic, and left renal arteries.

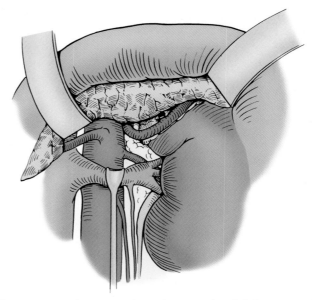

**Figure 50–69.** The pancreas is gently retracted cephalad to expose the splenic artery. The left renal vein is retracted inferiorly to expose the left renal artery.

of widely patent celiac and splenic arteries. The splenic artery must also be carefully examined intraoperatively for intramural atheromatous disease, which may be minimally occlusive and therefore not apparent on angiography but significant nonetheless. This problem, which is more commonly observed in women than in men, also militates against use of the splenic artery for renal revascularization.

The normal anatomic relationships of the splenic and renal vessels are shown in Figure 50–68. For splenorenal bypass, an extended left subcostal transperitoneal incision is made, and the left colon and duodenum are reflected medially. The plane between Gerota's fascia and the pancreas is developed by blunt dissection, and the pancreas and spleen are gently retracted cephalad. The left renal vein is mobilized and retracted inferiorly to expose the main left renal artery. The pancreas is gently retracted upward to permit access to the splenic vessels (Fig. 50–69). The splenic artery may be palpated posterior and superior to the splenic vein, and that portion lying closest to the distal aspect of the renal artery is chosen for mobilization. Small pancreatic arterial branches are divided and secured with fine silk sutures. The splenic artery may be tortuous and should be mobilized proximally as close to the celiac artery as possible, where the vessel wall is thicker and the luminal diameter larger.

After mobilization, the splenic artery is occluded proximally with a bulldog clamp, ligated distally with a 2-0 silk suture, and transected. It is not necessary to remove the spleen, which

receives adequate collateral supply from the short gastric and gastric epiploic vessels to maintain its viability. After transection, the splenic artery is often observed to be in spasm with a considerably reduced luminal size. After irrigation of the lumen with diluted heparin solution, the spasm can be relieved by gentle dilation of the splenic artery with graduated sounds. In general, there is no significant disparity in the caliber of the splenic and renal arteries, and a direct end-to-end anastomosis is performed (Fig. 50–70). I prefer this type of anastomosis because it provides better flow, is easier to perform, and allows removal of the diseased arterial segment for pathologic study (Fig. 50–71). An alternative method for splenorenal bypass involves end-to-side anastomosis of the

SECTION XII

splenic artery to the distal disease-free renal artery. I have employed this technique only in the unusual event of significant disparity in the caliber of the splenic and renal arteries.

**The advantages of the splenorenal bypass technique are that the operation is done well away from the aorta, that only a single vascular anastomosis is necessary, and that revascularization is accomplished with an autogenous vascular graft.** In properly selected patients, splenorenal bypass is an excellent method for vascular reconstruction of the left kidney.

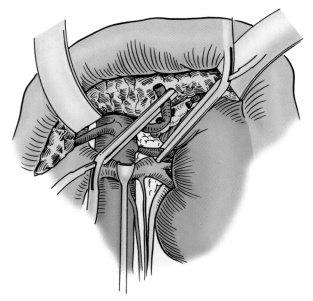

**Figure 50–70.** The splenic artery has been transected and is temporarily occluded proximally. The left renal artery is being prepared for anastomosis to the splenic artery.

## Hepatorenal Bypass

**Hepatorenal bypass is the preferred vascular reconstructive technique for patients with a troublesome aorta who require right renal revascularization. The hepatic circulation is ideally suited for a visceral–right renal arterial bypass operation. The liver receives 28% of the cardiac output in resting adults and is unique in having dual circulation from the portal vein and the hepatic artery, which contribute 80% and 20% of hepatic blood flow, respectively. Hepatic oxygenation is equally derived from these two circulations. It has been well demonstrated that hepatic artery flow can be safely interrupted.** When this occurs, hepatic function and morphologic appearance are maintained by increased extraction of oxygen from portal venous blood and by rapid development of an extensive collateral arterial flow to the liver (Novick et al, 1979).

The hepatic artery arises from the celiac axis and runs anterior to the portal vein and to the left of the common bile duct. The first major branch is the gastroduodenal artery, and thereafter the hepatic artery divides into its right and left branches. In considering a hepatorenal bypass operation, one of the more clinically significant anatomic variations is origin of the right hepatic artery from the SMA, which occurs in about 12% of patients. The left hepatic artery arises from the gastric artery in approximately 11.5% of patients.

In patients considered for a hepatorenal bypass operation, preoperative aortography with lateral views must demonstrate patent celiac and hepatic arteries. In my experience, the hepatic artery is rarely involved with atherosclerosis—certainly less often than the splenic artery. Hepatorenal bypass should also be undertaken only when preoperative biochemical screening reveals normal liver function. The most common method of performing hepatorenal bypass is with an interposition saphenous vein graft anastomosed end-to-side to the common hepatic artery, just beyond the gastroduodenal origin, and then end-to-end to the right renal artery

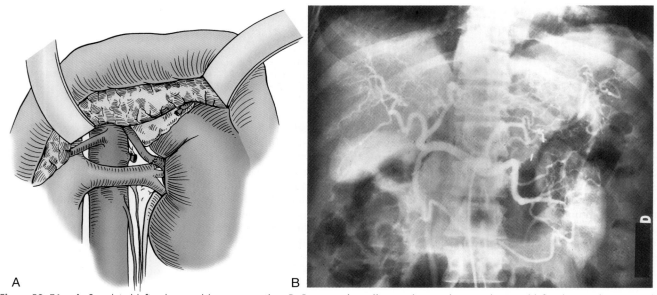

A                                                      B

**Figure 50–71.**  **A,** Completed left splenorenal bypass operation.  **B,** Postoperative celiac arteriogram shows unobstructed left splenorenal anastomosis.

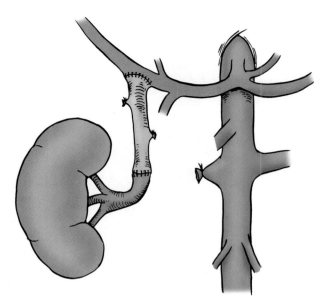

**Figure 50–72.** The most common method of performing hepatorenal bypass, with an interposition saphenous vein graft anastomosed end-to-side to the common hepatic artery and end-to-end to the right renal artery.

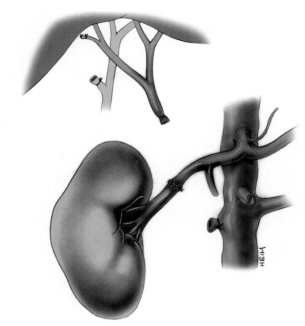

**Figure 50–73.** Performance of hepatorenal bypass by direct end-to-end anastomosis of the common hepatic artery to the right renal artery.

(Fig. 50–72). This technique preserves distal hepatic arterial flow and thereby reduces the risk of ischemic liver damage.

In some patients, the common hepatic artery cannot be employed in this manner for hepatorenal revascularization, either because it is smaller than the renal artery or because of an anatomic variation in which the right and left hepatic arterial branches have separate origins. In these situations, the available major hepatic arteries are generally of insufficient caliber to maintain adequate blood flow to both the liver and the right kidney. It is then preferable to perform end-to-end anastomosis of the common, right, or left hepatic arteries to the right renal artery (Fig. 50–73) (Novick and McElroy, 1985). In some patients, a direct tension-free anastomosis of these vessels can be done; otherwise, an interposition saphenous vein graft is needed. Despite the resulting total or segmental hepatic dearterialization in these patients, postoperative liver function studies have remained normal. However, **the gallbladder is more susceptible to ischemic damage and may undergo necrosis when its blood supply from the right hepatic artery is interrupted.**

Strategies are available to avoid the complication of gallbladder ischemia in patients undergoing end-to-end hepatorenal revascularization. First, when separate right and left hepatic arteries are present, the left hepatic artery should be used preferentially for anastomosis with the renal artery. Second, if it is necessary to use the common or right hepatic arteries in this manner, an adjunctive cholecystectomy should be performed. A third option is to perform end-to-end anastomosis of the gastroduodenal and renal arteries, with an interposition saphenous vein graft if necessary (Fig. 50–74). However, the origin and course of the gastroduodenal artery must be such that proximal kinking does not occur when this vessel is rotated toward the right kidney. It is also somewhat more difficult to mobilize an adequate length of this artery, and care must be taken to avoid damage to the duodenum or

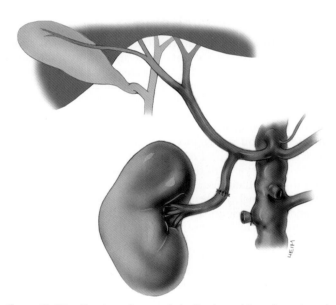

**Figure 50–74.** Hepatorenal revascularization by end-to-end anastomosis of the gastroduodenal and right renal arteries.

pancreas. This technique is not as widely applicable as other methods of hepatorenal revascularization, but it does offer the advantage of preserving hepatic arterial flow.

The results of hepatorenal bypass for right renal arterial occlusive disease have been excellent (Fig. 50–75) and indicate that this is a safe and effective operative approach in properly selected patients with a diseased abdominal aorta (Chibaro et al, 1984).

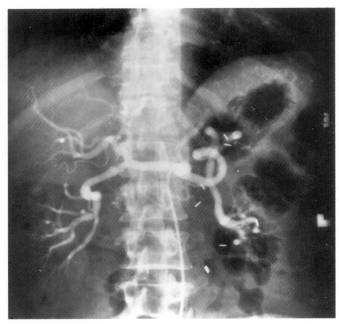

**Figure 50–75.** Postoperative selective celiac arteriogram after successful right hepatorenal and left splenorenal bypass operations.

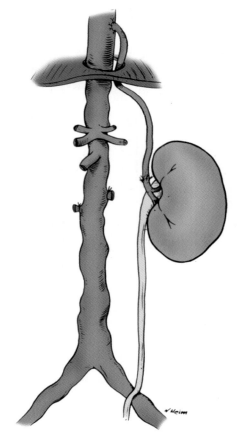

**Figure 50–76.** Technique of left thoracic aortorenal revascularization.

## Thoracic Aortorenal Bypass

**Use of the thoracic aorta for renal revascularization is a surgical alternative for patients with significant abdominal aortic atherosclerosis, celiac artery stenosis, and no primary indication for replacement of the abdominal aorta. The subdiaphragmatic supraceliac and descending thoracic aorta are often relatively free of disease in such patients and can be used to achieve renal vascular reconstruction with an interposition saphenous vein graft** (Fry and Fry, 1989; Novick, 1994a, 1994b). Preoperative angiographic evaluation should include views of the supraceliac aorta and the thoracic aorta to verify their disease-free status.

For left renal revascularization, I have employed the descending thoracic aorta as a donor site because I believe that it is more readily accessible than the subdiaphragmatic supraceliac aorta (Fig. 50–76). A left thoracoabdominal incision is made below the eighth rib and extended medially across the midline. This incision provides excellent simultaneous exposure of the thoracic aorta and renal artery with no need for extensive abdominal visceral mobilization. The left colon is reflected medially to expose the kidney and renal artery. The descending thoracic aorta is exposed above the diaphragm and partially occluded laterally with a DeBakey clamp. A small aortotomy is made, a reversed saphenous vein graft is anastomosed end-to-side to the aorta, and the aortic clamp is then removed. During performance of the proximal anastomosis, distal aortic flow is preserved and systemic heparinization is therefore not employed. A 2-cm incision is then made in the diaphragm just lateral to the aorta to enlarge the hiatus. The saphenous vein graft is passed alongside the aorta, through the diaphragmatic hiatus, posterior to the pancreas, and into the left retroperitoneum. End-to-end anastomosis of the vein graft and distal left renal artery is performed

to complete the operation (Fig. 50–77). On the right side, the subdiaphragmatic supraceliac or lower thoracic aorta is equally accessible through an anterior bilateral subcostal incision. The technique of thoracic aortorenal bypass is otherwise analogous to that described on the left side.

I reported my initial results with thoracic aortorenal bypass in 23 patients with hypertension, abdominal aortic atherosclerosis, and celiac artery stenosis; in 21 patients, renal artery stenosis was present bilaterally or in a solitary kidney (Novick, 1994a, 1994b). There was one operative death due to myocardial infarction. Postoperatively, among the remaining 22 patients, hypertension was cured or improved in 19 (86%), and renal function was stable or improved in 21 (95%).

Thoracic aortorenal revascularization is an attractive approach for several reasons. The thoracic aorta provides an excellent inflow source, and the proximal end-to-side vein graft anastomosis yields an antegrade acute angle that is hemodynamically advantageous. Because the thoracic aorta is only partially occluded during performance of the proximal anastomosis, distal aortic flow is preserved and systemic heparinization is unnecessary. The potential morbidity of aortic cross-clamping, which includes the risk of spinal cord ischemia, is avoided. The period of renal ischemia is also minimal and is limited to the time required for completion of the distal anastomosis, which is 15 to 20 minutes. Revascularization of the kidney is achieved with an autogenous vascular graft, which is the optimal material for renal

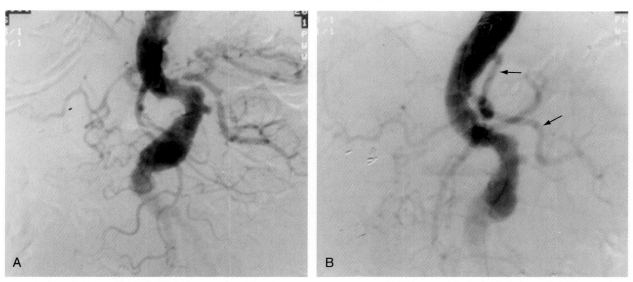

**Figure 50–77.** **A,** Preoperative abdominal aortogram shows solitary left kidney with high-grade stenosis. **B,** Postoperative aortogram shows patent thoracic aortorenal saphenous vein bypass graft.

artery replacement. Finally, use of the invariably healthy thoracic aorta minimizes the risk of peripheral embolization.

## Iliorenal Bypass

**Iliorenal bypass is an occasionally useful technique for revascularization in patients with severe aortic atherosclerosis, provided there is satisfactory flow through the diseased aorta and absence of significant iliac disease** (Novick and Banowsky, 1979). My approach is to consider this operation only when a splenorenal, hepatorenal, or thoracic aortorenal bypass cannot be done. This preference is based on the fact that aortic atherosclerosis may continue to progress in these patients, and if so, this process is most likely to involve the intrarenal aorta. Such a development might then compromise flow to a revascularized kidney whose blood supply is derived exclusively from one of the iliac arteries. The suprarenal aorta and supraceliac aorta are more often spared from progressive atherosclerosis—hence, my preference for bypass procedures originating from these locations.

In general, iliorenal bypass is performed with use of the ipsilateral iliac artery because this simplifies exposure of the operative field (Fig. 50–78). This is a relatively minor consideration, and use of the contralateral common iliac artery is also satisfactory, particularly if it is less diseased than the ipsilateral counterpart. Iliorenal bypass is performed through a midline transperitoneal incision after harvesting of a long saphenous vein graft. The colon is reflected medially to obtain simultaneous exposure of the ipsilateral common iliac and renal arteries. The common iliac artery is occluded proximally and distally with bulldog clamps. An oval arteriotomy is made on the anterolateral aspect of the common iliac artery. The distal clamp is temporarily released to enable 20 mL of diluted heparin solution to be instilled into the distal iliac and femoral arteries. Systemic heparinization is not routinely employed.

The proximal end of the saphenous vein graft is spatulated, and the apex of the spatulation is placed at the cephalic end

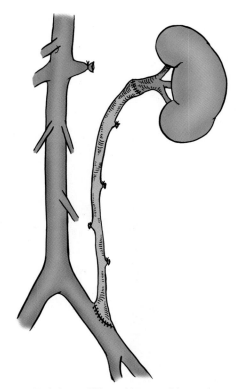

**Figure 50–78.** Technique of iliorenal bypass with a saphenous vein graft.

of the arteriotomy. Stay sutures are placed in both cephalic and caudal margins of the anastomosis, which is then completed with interrupted 6-0 arterial sutures. A bulldog clamp is placed across the proximal portion of the vein graft, and the iliac clamps are removed, restoring circulation to the lower extremity. The saphenous vein graft follows a direct cephalad course toward the ipsilateral renal artery between the aorta medially and the ureter laterally. An end-to-end anastomosis of the saphenous vein graft to the distal disease-free renal artery is then performed with interrupted 6-0 arterial sutures. The graft is positioned to allow a tension-free distal anastomosis while avoiding angulation or kinking of the renal artery.

## Mesenterorenal Bypass

**In unusual cases, aortography reveals an enlarged SMA that may then be employed for visceral arterial bypass to either kidney** (Fig. 50–79). I have employed the superior mesenterorenal bypass technique in occasional patients with a troublesome aorta in whom a bypass to the kidney from the celiac or iliac arteries was not possible (Khauli et al, 1985a, 1985b). The finding of an enlarged and widely patent SMA is most often observed in patients with total occlusion of the infrarenal aorta. In such cases, the SMA has a wider caliber than normal because it is supplying collateral vessels to areas ordinarily vascularized from the infrarenal aorta (i.e., large bowel, pelvis, and lower extremities). Use of such an enlarged SMA for performance of a mesenterorenal bypass has been well tolerated, with no compromise of intestinal blood flow. I have not used this approach in patients with normal-sized SMA and cannot comment on its efficacy in this setting.

For mesenterorenal bypass, the abdomen is entered through a midline incision. During revascularization of the left kidney, the descending colon and splenic flexure are reflected medially, and a plane of dissection is developed between the pancreas and Gerota's fascia. Exposure of the suprarenal aorta is obtained by gentle retraction of the pancreas and the first portion of jejunum cephalad; the mesocolon is reflected medially. If necessary, additional exposure may be obtained by mobilization and evisceration of the right colon and small bowel, as is done commonly for retroperitoneal lymphadenectomy. The SMA can be palpated readily at its origin from the aorta approximately 1 to 2 cm above the level of the renal arteries. The vessel lies against the neck of the pancreas as it courses between the neck and the uncinate process. The artery then crosses the third part of the duodenum to enter the large bowel mesentery, where it lies posterior and to the left of the superior mesenteric vein. The SMA is mobilized for a distance of 2 to 3 cm beyond its origin, where it is most accessible and without branches. The left renal artery then is exposed and isolated similarly. A reversed segment of saphenous vein is anastomosed end-to-side to the lateral aspect of the SMA with interrupted 6-0 vascular sutures. After completion of this anastomosis, which generally takes 15 to 20 minutes, blood flow through the SMA is restored immediately, and the saphenous vein graft is occluded temporarily. End-to-end anastomosis of the vein graft to the left renal artery is then done with interrupted 6-0 vascular sutures.

During revascularization of the right kidney, the ascending colon and duodenum are reflected medially to gain exposure of the aorta and right renal artery. The ascending colon and small bowel are then rotated back to their normal position,

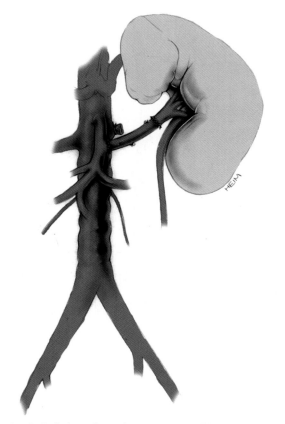

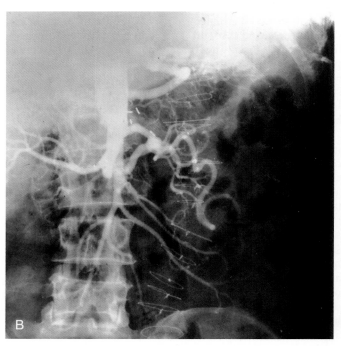

**Figure 50–79. A,** Technique of superior mesenterorenal bypass to the left kidney with a saphenous vein graft. **B,** Aortogram in a patient who underwent left mesenterorenal saphenous vein bypass shows excellent flow to the left kidney.

and the SMA is palpated where it crosses the third portion of the duodenum. The SMA is mobilized and isolated in this location for a distance of 3 to 4 cm. A saphenous vein graft is sutured end-to-side to this portion of the SMA, and the graft is then passed through a tunnel in the root of the small bowel mesentery, after a gentle curve as it crosses the third portion of the duodenum to enter the right retroperitoneum. End-to-end anastomosis of the graft to the right renal artery is performed to complete the operation.

## Extracorporeal Microvascular Branch Renal Artery Reconstruction

**Vascular disease involving the branches of the renal artery is most often caused by one of the fibrous dysplasias, namely, intimal, medial, or perimedial fibroplasia. Other causes of branch disease include arterial aneurysm, arteriovenous malformation, Takayasu's arteritis, neurofibromatosis, trauma, and, rarely, atherosclerosis.** In such cases, the task of renovascular reconstruction is considerably more complicated because it necessitates multiple vascular anastomoses to renal artery branches that may be difficult to expose and are small in caliber. For these reasons, many patients in this category were formerly considered inoperable or candidates for total or partial nephrectomy. However, technical advances have improved this outlook, and successful vascular reconstruction is now possible in most patients. This evolution has primarily been due to the incorporation of microvascular and extracorporeal techniques into the armamentarium of the renovascular surgeon.

**Branch renal artery lesions can often be repaired in situ with an aortorenal bypass when distal branches free of disease are present outside the renal hilum** (Novick, 1980). Extracorporeal branch arterial repair and autotransplantation are indicated primarily when preoperative arteriography, with oblique views, demonstrates intrarenal extension of renovascular disease (Salvatierra et al, 1978; Novick, 1981a, 1981b; Dubernard et al, 1985; Dean et al, 1986). The advantages of an extracorporeal surgical approach include optimum exposure and illumination, bloodless surgical field, greater protection of the kidney from ischemia, and more facile employment of microvascular techniques and optical magnification. Removal and flushing of the kidney also cause it to contract in size, thereby enabling more peripheral dissection in the renal sinus for mobilization of distal arterial branches. Finally, the completed branch anastomosis can be tested for patency and integrity before autotransplantation.

**In evaluating patients for extracorporeal revascularization and autotransplantation, preoperative renal and pelvic arteriography should be performed to define renal arterial anatomy, to ensure disease-free iliac vessels, and to assess the hypogastric artery and its branches for use as a reconstructive graft.** Assuming the presence of a viable functioning kidney, the only absolute contraindication to this approach is such severe aortoiliac vascular disease as to preclude renal autotransplantation. It is also best to avoid autotransplantation of kidneys involved by severe renal parenchymal or small vessel disease. Such kidneys generally flush poorly after their removal, often leading to irreversible ischemic damage and nonfunction.

Extracorporeal revascularization and autotransplantation are generally performed through an anterior subcostal transperitoneal incision combined with a separate, lower quadrant, transverse semilunar incision. For nonobese patients, a single midline incision extending from the xiphoid process to the symphysis pubis may be used. The same intraoperative measures are taken as in live donor nephrectomy for allotransplantation to ensure minimal renal ischemia and immediate function after revascularization. These measures include prevention of hypotension during anesthesia, administration of mannitol, minimal surgical manipulation of the kidney, and rapid flushing and cooling of the kidney after its removal. Systemic heparinization before nephrectomy is unnecessary.

Immediately after its removal, the kidney is flushed intra-arterially with 500 mL of a chilled intracellular electrolyte solution and then submerged in a basin of ice-slush saline to maintain hypothermia (Fig. 50–80). The extracorporeal operation is completed under ice-slush surface hypothermia, and if there has been minimal warm renal ischemia, the kidney can be safely preserved in this manner for many more hours than are needed to perform even the most complex renal repair. In performing extracorporeal revascularization, I have found it cumbersome to work on the abdominal wall with the ureter attached. It is preferable to divide the ureter and place the kidney on a separate workbench. This provides better exposure for the extracorporeal operation and allows a second surgical team to prepare the iliac fossa simultaneously. This approach is also justified by the low incidence of complications after ureteroneocystostomy in renal allotransplantation.

Extracorporeal branch arterial reconstruction is performed with microvascular instruments, 7-0 to 9-0 suture material, and optical magnification with loupes (3.5× or 6×) or an operating microscope. The basic instruments required for microvascular surgery include a microneedle holder, microscissors, fine jeweler's forceps, small vessel dilators, microvascular clamps, and a 10-mL syringe with a 27-gauge blunt needle for irrigation.

After removal and flushing of the kidney, and with maintenance of surface hypothermia, the renal artery branches are mobilized distally in the renal sinus beyond the area of

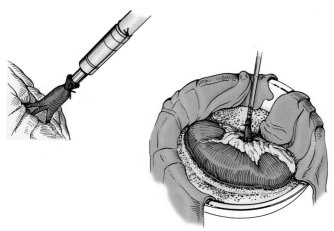

**Figure 50–80.** The removed kidney is flushed intra-arterially with a cold electrolyte solution and is placed in a basin of ice slush to maintain hypothermia.

vascular disease (Fig. 50–81). During this dissection, care is taken not to interfere with ureteral or renal pelvic blood supply. When the diseased renal artery branches are completely exposed, an appropriate technique for vascular reconstruction is selected.

The optimal method for extracorporeal branch renal artery repair involves the use of a branched autogenous vascular graft (Novick, 1981a, 1981b). This technique permits separate end-to-end microvascular anastomosis of each graft branch to a distal renal artery branch (Fig. 50–82). A hypogastric arterial

autograft is the preferred material for vascular reconstruction because this vessel may be obtained intact with several of its branches (Fig. 50–83).

On occasion, the hypogastric artery is not suitable for use as a reconstructive graft because of atherosclerotic degeneration. When this occurs, a long segment of saphenous vein can be harvested, and by sequential end-to-side microvascular anastomoses, a branched graft can be fashioned from this vessel. This branched graft is then used in a similar manner to achieve reconstruction of the diseased renal artery branches (Fig. 50–84).

Branched grafts of the hypogastric artery and saphenous vein may occasionally prove too large in caliber for

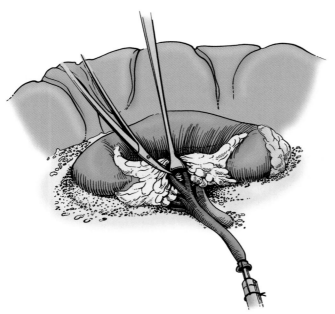

**Figure 50–81.** Under surface hypothermia, the diseased renal artery branches are mobilized in the renal sinus.

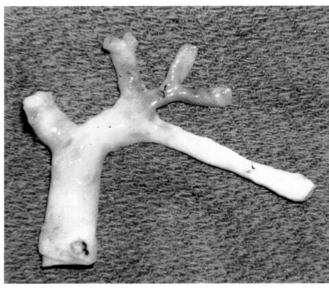

**Figure 50–83.** Operative photograph of the hypogastric artery removed intact with its branches.

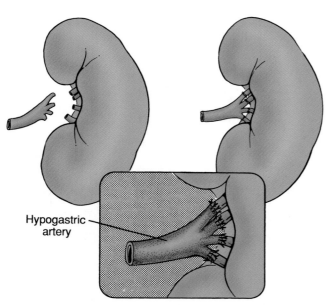

**Figure 50–82.** Extracorporeal repair with a branched hypogastric arterial autograft.

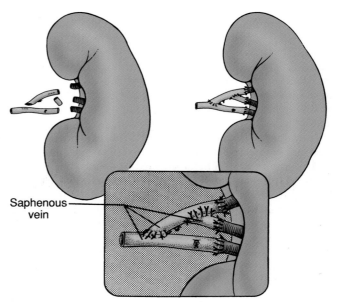

**Figure 50–84.** Extracorporeal repair with a branched saphenous vein graft.

anastomosis to small secondary or tertiary renal arterial branches. In these cases, the inferior epigastric artery provides an excellent alternative free graft for extracorporeal microvascular repair (Novick, 1981a, 1981b). This artery measures 1.5 to 2 mm in diameter, is rarely diseased, and coapts nicely in caliber and thickness to small renal artery branches (Fig. 50–85). The inferior epigastric artery may also be employed as a branched graft, either individually or in conjunction with a segment of saphenous vein (Fig. 50–86).

Although use of a branched autogenous vascular graft provides a simple, versatile, and effective method for branch renal

arterial reconstruction, other techniques are occasionally preferable, depending on the extent of vascular disease. In some patients with localized segmental intrarenal branch lesions, there may be other arterial branches that either are uninvolved or have more proximally located vascular disease. Such branches with longer disease-free distal segments may be anastomosed end-to-side, either into a larger arterial branch or into the reconstructive vascular graft (Fig. 50–87).

On occasion, two distal arterial branches of similar diameter and free of disease are found adjacent to one another. When this occurs, the two adjacent branches can be conjoined and then anastomosed end-to-end to a single limb of the branched graft (Fig. 50–88).

Renal artery aneurysms have a variable presentation, and the method of extracorporeal repair is determined by whether

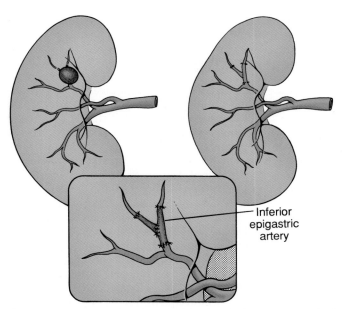

**Figure 50–85.** Extracorporeal repair with a branched autogenous graft of the inferior epigastric artery.

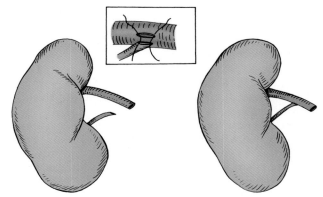

**Figure 50–87.** End-to-side reimplantation of a small renal artery branch into a larger one.

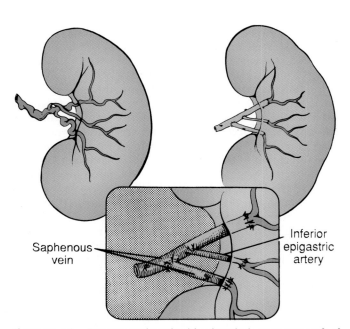

**Figure 50–86.** Extracorporeal repair with a branched autogenous graft of the saphenous vein and inferior epigastric artery.

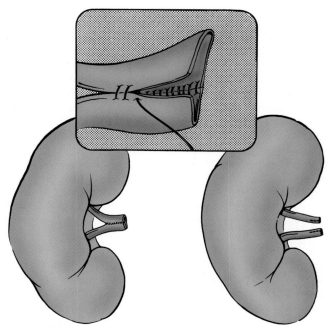

**Figure 50–88.** Side-to-side (conjoined) anastomosis of equal-caliber renal artery branches.

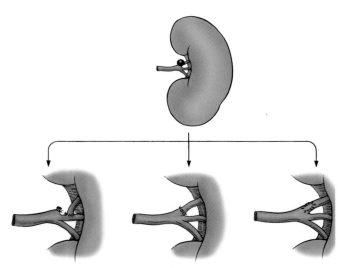

**Figure 50–89.** Technique for renal artery aneurysmectomy with patch angioplasty *(right)*, resection and reanastomosis *(middle)*, or end-to-side reimplantation *(left)*.

renovascular involvement is focal or diffuse. If the renal artery wall at the base of an aneurysm is intact, aneurysmectomy with patch angioplasty can be performed.

Aneurysms with short focal involvement of renal artery branches may also be simply resected with end-to-side branch reanastomosis or end-to-side reimplantation into an adjacent branch. In other cases, with more extensive vascular disease, aneurysmectomy and revascularization with a branched autogenous graft are indicated (Fig. 50–89).

These extracorporeal vascular techniques are performed with interrupted sutures, except for the conjoined anastomosis, for which a continuous suture is used. In revascularizing multiple arterial branches, one must anticipate the position that the various branches will assume in relation to one another on completion of the repair. Individual branch anastomoses are then done with careful attention to avoid subsequent malrotation, angulation, or tension. In all cases, extracorporeal repair leads to formation of a single main renal artery so that autotransplantation may be performed with one arterial anastomosis and no increase in revascularization time. When extracorporeal revascularization has been completed, the kidney is either reflushed or placed on the hypothermic pulsatile perfusion unit to verify patency and integrity of the repaired branches. Renal autotransplantation into the iliac fossa is then performed, with anastomosis of the renal vessels to the iliac vessels and restoration of urinary continuity by ureteroneocystostomy.

## POSTOPERATIVE CARE

Patients undergoing surgical renal revascularization may experience wide fluctuations in blood pressure in the early postoperative period; either hypotensive or hypertensive episodes may predispose to graft thrombosis or bleeding from vascular anastomotic sites, respectively. Therefore, these patients are placed in the intensive care unit for monitoring of central venous pressure, urine output, pulse rate, and serum levels of hemoglobin and creatinine. During this period, dias-

tolic blood pressure is maintained at approximately 90 mm Hg to ensure satisfactory renal perfusion. If hypertensive episodes occur, they are managed with intravenous infusion of sodium nitroprusside. Within the first 24 hours postoperatively, a technetium 99m renal scan is obtained to verify perfusion of the revascularized kidney. If clear evidence of perfusion is not present, arteriography should be done immediately to examine the repaired renal artery.

If the patient's condition is stable, the nasogastric tube, central venous line, arterial line, and urethral catheter are removed 48 hours postoperatively, and intensive care monitoring is discontinued. Most patients are discharged from the hospital 1 week postoperatively. Subsequent follow-up is performed by periodic evaluation of blood pressure and serum creatinine level and technetium 99m renal scanning.

## CLINICAL RESULTS

Experiences with alternative bypass techniques for renal revascularization at the Cleveland Clinic from January 1980 to December 1992 were analyzed (Fergany et al, 1995). A total of 175 revascularization operations were performed in 171 patients. In all patients, alternative bypass techniques were employed because of severe abdominal aortic atherosclerosis or previous aortic surgery. The revascularization operations comprised hepatorenal bypass (n = 59), splenorenal bypass (n = 54), iliorenal bypass (n = 37), thoracic aortorenal bypass (n = 23), renal autotransplantation (n = 1), and superior mesenterorenal bypass (n = 1). Surgical renal revascularization was indicated for treatment of poorly controlled hypertension in 13 patients and ischemic nephropathy in 158 patients; all patients in the latter group had severe renal artery stenosis bilaterally or in a solitary kidney.

There were five patient deaths within the first postoperative month for an overall operative mortality rate of 2.9%. Postoperative thrombosis of the repaired renal artery occurred after 7 of 175 revascularization operations (4%). In the 13 patients with severe hypertension, the mean preoperative blood pressure was 176/101 mm Hg, and the mean postoperative blood pressure was 142/78 mm Hg. The mean preoperative and postoperative serum creatinine levels in this group were 1.2 mg/dL and 1 mg/dL, respectively.

**In patients with ischemic nephropathy, postoperative renal function was improved in 41%, stable in 44%, and deteriorated in 15%. The best results were obtained in patients with a preoperative serum creatinine level of less than 2 mg/dL; 90% experienced postoperative improvement or stabilization of renal function.** Although preservation of renal function was the predominant indication for intervention in the ischemic nephropathy group, all these patients also had hypertension that was controlled with medical therapy. Postoperatively, hypertension was cured in 14%, improved in 63%, and unchanged in 23%. The results of this study affirmed the efficacy of alternative bypass techniques for renal revascularization when the prerequisite conditions for their use were present.

From 1976 to 1991, extracorporeal microvascular reconstruction and autotransplantation were performed in 66 patients with complex branch renal artery disease at the Cleveland Clinic (Novick, 1996a, 1996b). This series included 50 female patients and 16 male patients ranging in age from 4 to

62 years. Renovascular disease was caused by fibrous dysplasia in 42 patients, arterial aneurysm in 13 patients, atherosclerosis in 7 patients, primary dissection in 2 patients, arteriovenous fistula in 1 patient, and arteritis in 1 patient. Eighteen patients presented with branch disease in a solitary kidney, 27 patients had bilateral renovascular disease, and 21 patients had unilateral branch disease with a normal contralateral kidney. Renal revascularization was indicated for treatment of renovascular hypertension in 58 patients, for prevention of rupture of an arterial aneurysm in 7 patients, and for treatment of an asymptomatic arteriovenous fistula in 1 patient.

In the 66 patients who underwent extracorporeal branch reconstruction and autotransplantation (including one bilateral autotransplantation), a total of 187 diseased renal artery branches were repaired (mean, 2.8 branches per operation). The period of cold renal ischemia needed for extracorporeal microvascular repair to be performed ranged from 1 to 3.5 hours. All patients were studied postoperatively with isotope renography and, in many cases, with arteriography as well. Postoperative follow-up in these cases ranged from 1 to 15 years. In 64 patients, branch arterial reconstruction was technically successful, whereas 2 patients suffered postoperative occlusion of the repaired renal artery. Fortunately, in both of these patients, a normal contralateral kidney was present. Currently, all 66 patients are normotensive, including 11 patients who continue to require low-dose antihypertensive medication. The current level of renal function is stable or improved in all patients. These results attest to the efficacy of extracorporeal microvascular reconstruction in enabling revascularization with preservation of renal parenchyma to be achieved in patients with complex branch arterial lesions.

## COMPLICATIONS
### Operative Mortality

**Most patients with nonatherosclerotic lesions, such as fibrous dysplasia or aneurysm, are young and otherwise healthy. Therefore, the risk of operative death in this group is minimal.** However, several studies during the 1970s indicated significant operative mortality rates of 6% to 10% in patients with atherosclerotic renal artery disease. These patients compose an older group and often have associated coronary, cerebrovascular, or peripheral vascular disease. In the National Cooperative Study, coronary artery disease was the leading cause of operative mortality after surgical treatment for atherosclerotic renal artery disease (Franklin et al, 1975). Other significant risk factors included magnitude of the operation performed and presence of extracranial cerebrovascular disease.

**Several policies have been adopted to reduce operative mortality after surgical revascularization in patients with atherosclerotic renal artery disease. These include preliminary screening and correction of existing coronary or cerebrovascular occlusive disease, avoidance of bilateral simultaneous renal operations, and reliance on methods of revascularization that avoid operation on a severely diseased aorta.** The impact of these policies at the Cleveland Clinic was evaluated in a review of surgical revascularization for renal artery disease in 361 patients from 1975 to 1984

(Novick et al, 1987). The cause of renal artery disease was atherosclerosis in 241 patients and fibrous dysplasia or an arterial aneurysm in 120 patients. The operative mortality rate was 21% and 0% in the former and latter groups, respectively. These data indicate that when appropriate measures are taken, the risk of operative mortality after renal revascularization is small even in older patients with generalized atherosclerosis.

### Hypertension

Patients undergoing renal revascularization often experience hypertension postoperatively, even with technically satisfactory vascular repair. This hypertension may be due to hypervolemia, vasoconstriction from total body hypothermia, poorly controlled incisional pain, or renal ischemia sustained intraoperatively. Such blood pressure elevation may be severe immediately after surgery and, if not properly controlled, can promote hemorrhage from fresh vascular anastomoses. Therefore, these patients are initially placed in an intensive care unit for monitoring of the central venous pressure, blood pressure, urine output, pulse rate, and serum levels of hemoglobin and creatinine. During this time, diastolic blood pressure is maintained at 90 to 100 mm Hg to ensure satisfactory renal perfusion. I prefer to manage postoperative hypertension with continuous intravenous infusion of sodium nitroprusside for the first 24 to 36 hours. At this time, if hypertension persists, maintenance therapy with oral agents is initiated, and the nitroprusside infusion is gradually discontinued.

Approximately 50% of patients who are ultimately cured of hypertension by renal revascularization experience blood pressure elevation for a time postoperatively. In fact, it is not uncommon for such hypertension to persist for several weeks after surgery before gradually resolving. Of course, when this occurs, patency of the reconstructed renal artery must be confirmed with isotope renography or angiography.

### Hemorrhage

Early hemorrhage after renal revascularization is generally a consequence of poor surgical technique. Bleeding from a vascular anastomotic site can occur if it is under tension, if one or both of the anastomosed vessels are diseased, or if the vascular sutures have not been placed sufficiently close together. Eversion of intima through the anastomosis may also predispose to hemorrhage and should be avoided.

Early hemorrhage may also be due to poor surgical hemostasis. This complication is most likely to occur because of unsecured collateral vessels in the renal hilum; because of damage to the left adrenal gland, which is often closely apposed to the left renal artery; or because of inadequately secured lumbar arteries that have been divided during aortic mobilization. When a saphenous vein bypass graft has been used, bleeding can occur from avulsion of a ligature applied to one of the branches of the vein graft; this can be avoided by suture ligation of all such branches.

Factors that predispose to early postoperative hemorrhage include incomplete reversal of systemic heparinization, episode of hypertension, or unrecognized coagulopathy. Mild bleeding that ceases spontaneously in an asymptomatic patient does not require reoperation. Such small hematomas generally undergo complete reabsorption without sequelae, although extrinsic cicatricial stenosis of the repaired renal artery may occasionally result. With severe or uncontrolled bleeding, immediate reoperation is indicated to evacuate the accumulated blood and secure hemostasis.

In unusual cases, late hemorrhage can occur weeks, months, or even years after renal revascularization. This may be due to infection involving the vascular suture line (Nerstrom and Engell, 1972; Szilagy et al, 1971), rupture of a noninfected false aneurysm at the anastomotic site into the retroperitoneum or gastrointestinal tract (Moore and Hall, 1970), or erosion of a prosthetic bypass graft into the duodenum (Cerny et al, 1972). All present as sudden catastrophic hemorrhage that requires immediate operation. Prosthetic graft erosion can be avoided at the original operation by interposition of peritoneum or omentum between such grafts and the duodenum or by placement of the graft retrocaval on the right side. It is also appropriate to state that prosthetic renal artery bypass grafts should be used only when an autogenous vascular graft is not available.

## Renal Artery Thrombosis

**Thrombosis of the repaired renal artery is an uncommon complication that occurs in less than 5% of patients undergoing revascularization, generally within the first few days of surgery.** Postoperative hypotension, a hypercoagulable state, and hypovolemia are factors that predispose to this problem. Significant intrarenal arteriolar nephrosclerosis causes poor runoff, which can also lead to arterial thrombosis. Nevertheless, arterial thrombosis is usually due to poor technical performance of revascularization, and in this regard, several points deserve emphasis.

All the vessels used for anastomosis should be free of disease that may cause subsequent occlusion. Complete excision of all renal artery disease is necessary. On occasion, a local aortic endarterectomy is performed when an aortorenal bypass is done. All vascular anastomoses must be done precisely to avoid intraluminal intrusion of adventitia and trauma to the intima. Intimal trauma may result from improperly applied surgical forceps or vascular clamps and is known to promote intraluminal platelet aggregation, fibrin deposition, and development of a thrombus. When an endarterectomy is done, the resulting traumatized arterial surface can also predispose to thrombus formation.

If an intimal flap is present in the distal renal artery at revascularization, it must be tacked down with interrupted sutures to avoid intramural dissection and occlusion after restoration of blood flow. End-to-end anastomosis of vessels that are more than 50% disparate in diameter should also be avoided. This invariably leads to bunching of the smaller vessel and unfavorable hemodynamics that can lead eventually to thrombus formation and vascular occlusion.

When a renal artery bypass procedure is performed, the bypass graft must be properly placed to avoid angulation, kinking, or malrotation with the renal artery. Figures 50–90 and 50–91 illustrate the most common errors in the positioning of an aortorenal bypass graft that can lead to thrombosis or stenosis. These same considerations apply to all renal revascularization operations, especially extracorporeal branch repairs. In these repairs, multiple renal arterial branch

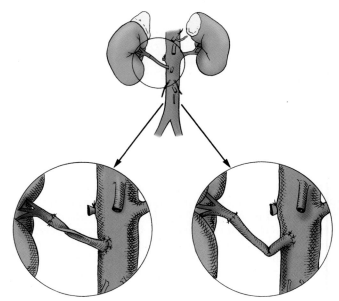

**Figure 50–90.** Improper placement of an aortorenal bypass graft with longitudinal torsion *(left)* or angulation *(right)* that can lead to postoperative thrombosis or stenosis.

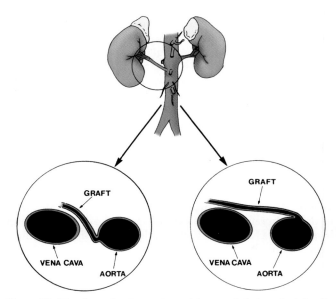

**Figure 50–91.** In performing aortorenal bypass, it is important for the graft to be brought off the anterolateral aspect of the aorta. If the graft originates too far posteriorly *(left)* or anteriorly *(right)*, it can predispose to postoperative thrombosis or stenosis at the origin of the graft.

anastomoses are commonly done, and it is important to anticipate the position that the various branches will assume in relation to one another on completion of the repair and after autotransplantation.

Embolization of an atheroma from a traumatized aorta into the kidney and external compression of the repaired artery by retroperitoneal fluid collection are additional causes of postoperative thrombosis. Finally, although thrombosis is typically an early event, occlusion of an aortorenal bypass graft can occur months or years later from progressive aortic atherosclerosis at the origin of the graft.

The diagnosis of renal artery thrombosis must be established almost immediately for salvage of the kidney to be possible. In some cases, subtotally occlusive thrombus and extensive collateral renal arterial supply allow additional time for successful intervention to be undertaken. The most helpful clinical clues to postoperative thrombosis are persistent or sudden hypertension and elevated serum creatinine level. However, both of these findings may initially be present with a patent vascular repair. Therefore, a radiographic renal imaging study should be routinely done within the first 24 hours of surgery; in this regard, I have found isotope renography with technetium to be an excellent noninvasive method. Because I always perform direct end-to-end anastomosis of the bypass graft to the distal renal artery, renal uptake of isotope ensures patency of the vascular repair. This study is less reliable if an end-to-side anastomosis of the bypass graft to the distal renal artery has been done. If isotope renographic findings are equivocal or clinical suspicion for arterial thrombosis remains high, angiography should be done immediately.

The traditional treatment of postoperative renal arterial thrombosis has been emergency surgical re-exploration with thrombectomy or graft revision if the kidney is found to be viable. More commonly, the kidney is no longer viable, and a nephrectomy is done. Percutaneous low-dose intra-arterial infusion of streptokinase may be undertaken as an alternative to surgery (Berni et al, 1983; Cronan and Dorfman, 1983; Dardik et al, 1984). Although successful clot lysis has been reported with this technique, there also appears to be an increased risk of bleeding from hypofibrinogenemia. Percutaneous transcatheter thrombectomy has also been described as treatment of acute renal artery thrombosis or embolism; however, this technique cannot be safely done in the presence of a fresh vascular anastomosis (Millan et al, 1978). Systemic anticoagulation with heparin is not effective as primary therapy for postoperative arterial thrombosis but is a useful adjunctive measure after surgical thrombectomy or intra-arterial streptokinase infusion.

## Renal Artery Stenosis

**The incidence of stenosis of a surgically reconstructed renal artery is less than 10% with current techniques, and this complication typically occurs weeks, months, or even years after revascularization.** Many of the causes are similar to those outlined for postoperative thrombosis, such as faulty suture technique, intimal trauma, incomplete excision of primary vascular disease, wide disparity in vessel size, dissection of a distal intimal flap constructed at surgery, and torsion, angulation, or kinking of the vessels. When an end-to-end vascular anastomosis is performed, the likelihood of subsequent stenosis can be minimized by spatulating the ends of the two vessels to fashion a suture line that is wider than the normal circumference of the renal artery. Tension on the vascular suture line can also cause narrowing in this area and should be avoided. Finally, during procurement of a saphenous vein graft, care should be taken not to overdistend the vein or injudiciously dissect periadventitial tissue, both of which may cause devascularization of the graft that leads to subsequent stenosis.

Other causes of late postoperative renal artery stenosis include diffuse subendothelial fibroplastic proliferation in saphenous vein grafts, neointimal proliferation at the suture line of synthetic grafts, recurrent primary vascular disease, and obstruction from a valve in a segment of saphenous vein (Dean et al, 1974). With the last cause, grafts should always be reversed so that blood flow is directed toward the cephalic end, which allows venous valves to assume a neutral position. However, even when this is done, such valves may undergo fibrotic contracture to produce a weblike stenosis of the vein graft. This occurrence, although rare, suggests that a valveless segment of vein should be used, if possible.

**All patients undergoing renal revascularization should be followed up at yearly intervals with blood pressure measurements, determination of renal function, and isotope renography with technetium.** Postoperative renal artery stenosis that is more than 70% occlusive is invariably accompanied by an elevation in blood pressure and, not uncommonly, evidence of deteriorating renal function. When either of these conditions is present, or if there is isotope renographic evidence of diminished renal perfusion, angiography should be done. Recurrent arterial stenosis is most often located at a vascular suture line but may present anywhere along the course of the reconstruction renal arterial supply. The therapeutic options are surgical reoperation and PTA-stenting. Because secondary revascularization in such cases is difficult and may lead to nephrectomy, PTA-stenting is a reasonable initial approach to therapy if it is technically feasible.

## Renal Artery Aneurysm

Long-term angiographic studies of patients who underwent aortorenal saphenous vein bypass revealed graft dilation in 25% to 52% of patients and frank aneurysm formation in 5% to 8% of patients (Stanley et al, 1973; Dean et al, 1974). These findings have been observed more often in children than in adults. The clinical significance of these abnormal-appearing vein grafts remains uncertain because most of these patients continue to be normotensive with excellent renal function. In some cases, graft dilation has been associated with a distal anastomotic stenosis, suggesting this as a possible inciting factor (Fig. 50–92). However, in other cases, similar dilation has been found with no evidence of stenosis (Fig. 50–93). This problem has only rarely been encountered with autogenous arterial grafts. It may be possible to prevent saphenous vein graft dilation by more careful procurement and storage of the graft in chilled heparinized lactated Ringer irrigation or autologous blood to prevent transmural ischemia. When severe aneurysmal dilation is present, or if graft expansion is associated with recurrent hypertension, reoperation and attempted secondary revascularization are indicated.

Postoperative aneurysm formation has also been associated with use of the spermatic or ovarian veins for renal artery bypass surgery. These veins are extremely friable, cannot withstand the stress of arterial pressure, and undergo severe dilation or frank rupture. Therefore, their use as bypass grafts in arterial reconstruction is absolutely contraindicated.

After renal revascularization, a false aneurysm may develop at a vascular anastomotic site months or years later. Mycotic false aneurysms are caused by deep wound infection involving the vascular suture line (Nerstrom and Engell, 1972). Contrary to a widely held impression, there is no increased risk of infection with vascular silk sutures when they are used for

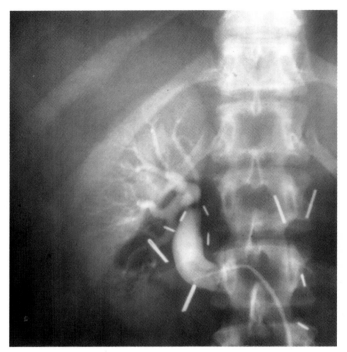

**Figure 50–92.** Right renal arteriogram after aortorenal saphenous vein bypass demonstrates dilation of the graft with distal anastomotic stenosis.

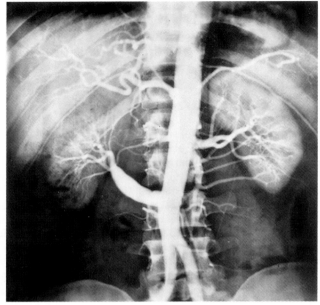

**Figure 50–93.** Abdominal aortogram after right aortorenal saphenous vein bypass demonstrates aneurysmal dilation of the bypass graft with no evidence of stenosis.

anastomosis of autogenous vessels. Noninfected false aneurysms have most often been associated with synthetic bypass grafts because anastomoses of native vessels with these grafts never acquire significant strength other than that determined by the suture line (Moore and Hall, 1970). For this reason, synthetic graft anastomoses should always be done with a nonresorbable suture, such as polypropylene, rather than with silk, which loses its tensile strength over time. Infected or uninfected false anastomotic aneurysms can rupture spontaneously and should be repaired as soon as the diagnosis is established.

## Aortic Complications

During an aortorenal bypass operation, clamping and unclamping of the abdominal aorta is performed. When the aorta is involved with atherosclerosis, this maneuver can cause dislodgment of plaque, resulting in aortic thrombosis or distal embolization. This occurrence can be minimized by selecting the healthiest portion of the abdominal aorta for use in such operations. Intraoperative systemic heparinization also helps prevent this problem. Ultimately, the most effective prevention is to avoid operation on the extensively diseased aorta by use of alternative techniques, such as hepatorenal or splenorenal bypass.

Whenever aortic surgery is undertaken, the peripheral pulses and lower extremities should always be examined before and immediately after revascularization. If there is evidence of compromised peripheral circulation postoperatively, emergency transbrachial abdominal aortography should be done. Immediate surgical thromboembolectomy is indicated to relieve aortic or major peripheral vascular occlusion. Minor

discoloration of the toes from cholesterol microemboli can be observed easily when good peripheral pulses are present. This problem generally resolves spontaneously, and digital amputation is rarely necessary.

Clamping and unclamping of the aorta may also produce an intraluminal aortic dissection, especially if a local endarterectomy has been done. This can be prevented by suturing down distal flaps of intima within the aorta when the lumen is exposed. This type of aortic dissection can cause peripheral ischemia or may be entirely asymptomatic, in which case simple observation is sufficient.

## Visceral Complications

Visceral–renal arterial bypass operations are indicated in patients with severe aortic disease and may be associated with specific complications. When splenorenal bypass is done, splenic viability is maintained by collateral vascular supply from the short gastric and gastroepiploic arteries. Nevertheless, a retractor-induced splenic laceration may be sustained during mobilization of the splenic artery, which necessitates performance of an incidental splenectomy. In an initial series of splenorenal bypasses, this complication occurred in 5 of 32 cases (16%) (Novick et al, 1977a, 1977b). During mobilization of the splenic artery, the splenic vein, which is thin walled and directly adjacent to the artery, may be inadvertently damaged. Lacerations of the splenic vein are repaired with interrupted 5-0 vascular sutures. Injury to the pancreas, with resulting pancreatitis or pseudocyst formation, is a potential complication of splenorenal bypass that I have not yet encountered.

In hepatorenal bypass, the common hepatic artery and its major branches can be mobilized readily without damage to the portal vein or common bile duct. Hepatorenal bypass is usually done by end-to-side anastomosis of a saphenous vein graft to the common hepatic artery, which allows preservation of distal hepatic arterial flow (Chibaro et al, 1984). However, in some cases, a direct end-to-end anastomosis of the hepatic and right renal arteries is done, which produces complete hepatic dearterialization (Novick and McElroy, 1985). This is well tolerated by the liver because of the increased extraction of oxygen from portal venous blood and the fairly rapid development of collateral hepatic arterial flow. Thus, although transient abnormalities in liver function parameters may occur, permanent hepatic damage has not yet been observed. However, the gallbladder is more susceptible to ischemic damage and may undergo postoperative necrosis when its blood supply from the right hepatic artery is interrupted. This problem can be avoided by an adjunctive cholecystectomy in patients whose blood flow through the common hepatic artery is totally diverted to the kidney.

A bypass from the SMA to the kidney is occasionally an option in patients with severe aortic atherosclerosis (Khauli et al, 1985a, 1985b). Because the SMA is the only source of blood supply to a large portion of the bowel, this operation may produce postoperative intestinal ischemia. Such ischemia can be avoided by limiting this approach to patients with infrarenal aortic occlusion, in whom a significantly enlarged SMA is invariably present.

## Acute Renal Failure

**Acute renal failure induced by ischemia is a potential complication of surgical revascularization that, fortunately, can be prevented in most cases.** Because all revascularization operations require temporary occlusion of the renal artery, it is important to understand renal responses to warm ischemia. If the period of arterial occlusion exceeds that which may be safely tolerated, specific renal preservation measures are indicated.

**In general, 30 minutes is the maximum period of arterial occlusion that the kidney can withstand before permanent damage is sustained** (Novick, 1983). In some clinical situations, this time may not apply, and a longer period of ischemia may be safely tolerated. It is acknowledged that the solitary kidney is more resistant to ischemic damage than the paired kidney, although precise limits have not been defined. I reviewed the outcome of renal revascularization in 43 patients with a solitary kidney in whom warm ischemic intervals ranged from 14 to 59 minutes and in whom no specific renal protective measures were employed. In this series, there were no cases of acute renal failure postoperatively, which indicated in many of these patients the ability of the solitary kidney to safely withstand periods of warm ischemia longer than 30 minutes (Askari et al, 1982). Another situation that may enhance renal tolerance to temporary arterial occlusion is the presence of an extensive collateral vascular supply, which is often observed in patients with renal arterial occlusive disease.

When postoperative acute renal failure occurs, it is generally manifested by a fall in urine output and a rise in serum creatinine level. Alternatively, nonoliguric renal insufficiency may be observed. The cornerstone of therapy for such acute renal failure is judicious fluid management to ensure normal extracellular volume and sodium content. In older patients, central venous pressure is not reliable for monitoring fluid replacement, and pulmonary artery wedge pressure provides a more accurate measurement of left ventricular filling pressure. This information allows precise control of the volume and rate of fluid infusion so that maximum cardiac output can be achieved without inducing left ventricular decompensation. The role of diuretic and vasoactive drug therapy for improving renal perfusion after ischemic injury is controversial. Furosemide administration appears to be of value because it is known to increase renal blood flow by stimulating the release of intrarenal alprostadil, a potent dilator of the afferent renal arterioles (Patak et al, 1975).

## MISCELLANEOUS RENAL OPERATIONS
## Open Renal Biopsy

Open renal biopsy may be necessary to establish a tissue diagnosis in patients with renal disease, to assess the severity of such disease, or to evaluate the potential for salvable renal function in patients with a known correctable disorder who are candidates for a reconstructive operation. Open biopsy is usually preferred to the percutaneous technique in patients with a solitary kidney, coagulopathy, atypical anatomy, or other factors that may increase the risk of a closed biopsy. An open biopsy also provides more tissue for study and minimizes the potential for complications such as arteriovenous fistula, perirenal hematoma, and gross hematuria.

An open renal biopsy may be performed through an extraperitoneal flank or posterior incision. General anesthesia is preferable; however, in a thin, cooperative patient, local anesthesia may be employed. Biopsy of the right kidney is usually done because of its more caudal location.

After the surgical incision is made, Gerota's fascia is opened and the lower pole of the kidney is exposed. An elliptical incision is made in the renal capsule, which is usually 1 to 2 cm long and 0.5 to 1 cm wide (Fig. 50–94A). The incision is deepened on either side with a scalpel and beveled so that the final wedge depth includes an adequate segment of cortical tissue, usually 5 to 8 mm deep. Fine Metzenbaum scissors are used to complete the transection of cortex at the bottom of the wedge, and the tissue is gently lifted out with the slightly spread scissor blades rather than a forceps, which might crush the specimen (Fig. 50–94B). Suction is avoided during this final maneuver to prevent loss of tissue into the suction tip. This technique of elliptical wedge biopsy is preferred to open needle biopsy because bleeding is more readily controlled and more renal tissue is obtained. The renal incision is closed with absorbable 2-0 or 3-0 sutures placed across the defect and gently tied over Oxycel (Fig. 50–94C).

## Surgery for Simple Renal Cysts

Simple renal cysts usually present as mass lesions and are often detected during renal imaging studies performed for unrelated reasons. A small number of patients require exploration to distinguish between a cyst and an atypical tumor mass. Large renal cysts causing obstruction may also occasionally require open surgical drainage with unroofing (Stanisic et al, 1977).

The preferred surgical approach for drainage of a renal cyst is through an extraperitoneal posterior, flank, or anterior

SECTION XII

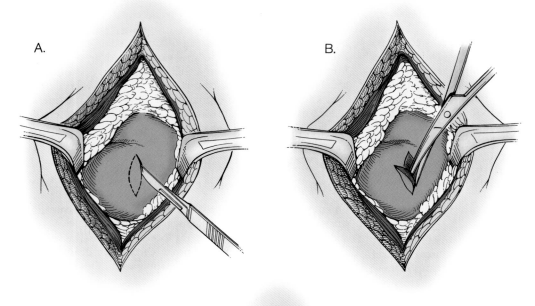

A.

B.

**Figure 50–94.** Technique of open renal biopsy.

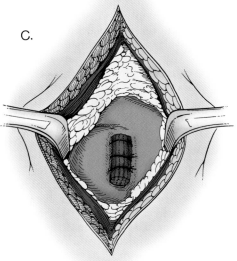

C.

incision, according to the number and location of lesions. Gerota's fascia is opened, and the cystic lesion is exposed by dissection of perirenal fat from the cyst and adjacent parenchyma (Fig. 50–95*A*). The surrounding area is packed off, and cyst fluid is aspirated for diagnostic study. The cyst wall is then entered sharply and resected near its junction with normal parenchyma (Fig. 50–95*B*). The base of the cyst cavity is inspected, and biopsy of any suspicious areas is performed with immediate frozen-section examination. After unroofing, the perimeter of the cyst wall is oversewn with an absorbable 3-0 or 4-0 continuous suture to achieve hemostasis (Fig. 50–95*C*). Alternatively, the edge of the cyst wall may be cauterized and persistent bleeders controlled with interrupted figure-of-eight absorbable sutures. Drainage is not required unless the cyst is infected.

## Open Nephrostomy Insertion

Nephrostomy tube drainage is usually achieved by the percutaneous approach, but an open operation is occasionally necessary because of difficult anatomy or a minimally dilated upper urinary tract. Open nephrostomy insertion may also be performed intraoperatively during reconstructive procedures such as pyeloplasty and ureterocalicostomy.

Primary nephrostomy insertion is usually performed through an extraperitoneal flank incision. After the kidney is mobilized, the renal pelvis is exposed and opened. A Willscher nephrostomy tube, as illustrated in Figure 50–96, is particularly simple to place because of a built-in malleable stylet within a smoothly tapered sheath (Noble, 1989). The stylet of the catheter is passed through the pyelotomy and then used to

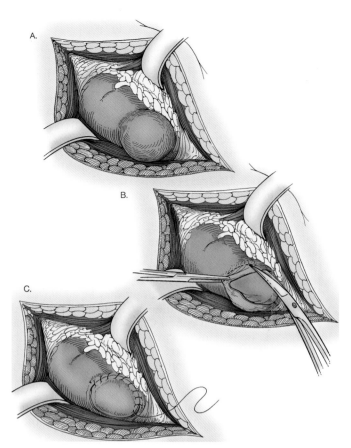

**Figure 50–95.** Technique of excision of renal cyst.

puncture the cortex from within a calyx (Fig. 50–96A). It is important to ensure that the nephrostomy is made near the convex border of the kidney and not in the anterior or posterior surface; this allows better positioning of the tube and minimizes the risk of injury to large intrarenal vessels. Usually, a 22 or 24 French catheter is used. The Willscher tube has a flared portion with wide openings followed by a long tip, which may be used as a splint through the ureteropelvic junction if necessary. The catheter is pulled through the cortex until the flared portion lies in good position within the collecting system, usually in the pelvic calyx or a dependent calyx (Fig. 50–96B). The nephrostomy tube is secured to the renal capsule with a 3-0 absorbable purse-string suture. The pyelotomy is closed with 3-0 or 4-0 absorbable suture. The stylet of the nephrostomy tube is passed through the flank muscles, subcutaneous tissue, and skin, with care taken to ensure proper alignment of the tube as it passes from the kidney to the exterior. Heavy 2-0 skin sutures are inserted to secure the tube near the flank wall exit point to prevent inadvertent dislodgment. A Penrose drain is placed near the pyelotomy site and brought out through a separate stab wound in the flank.

Ongoing care of a nephrostomy tube is important to prevent infection and to ensure unobstructed drainage. Periodic urine culture specimens are obtained, and significant intercurrent urinary infection is appropriately treated. If the tube is dislodged within 7 to 10 days of its insertion, it may not be possible to replace it through the track, and a second-

ary procedure may be necessary. Even with the best of care, encrustations form around the tube and require periodic tube replacement at 6- to 8-week intervals. This is usually readily performed under fluoroscopic guidance once a chronic track has been established.

## Surgery for Polycystic Kidney Disease

Bilateral nephrectomy may be necessary in selected patients with end-stage renal failure from polycystic kidney disease who are candidates for renal transplantation. Indications for bilateral nephrectomy in this setting include a history of significant bleeding or renal infection and massively enlarged kidneys that may interfere with placement of an allograft in the pelvis. This operation is best performed through an anterior bilateral subcostal or midline transperitoneal incision.

Unilateral nephrectomy is occasionally required before end-stage renal failure develops or when the polycystic kidney is a site of complications such as infection, severe pain due to bleeding or obstruction, or development of a tumor. Cyst puncture and unroofing of cysts may be helpful when they obstruct the collecting system or cause flank pain (Lue et al, 1966). **Multiple cyst punctures and unroofing of cysts (Rovsing's operation) do not appear to improve renal function or to prevent further deterioration** (Milam et al, 1963). However, this approach can provide long-term pain relief in symptomatic patients (Elzinga et al, 1993).

## Isthmusectomy for Horseshoe Kidney

Horseshoe kidney occurs in about 1 in 700 individuals and is frequently associated with other urologic anomalies. The isthmus that joins the kidneys usually lies anterior to the great vessels. Ureteral obstruction with hydronephrosis, stone formation, or infection is the most common problem with this condition and may require surgical treatment (Culp and Winterringer, 1955). In patients with ureteral or ureteropelvic junction obstruction, division of the isthmus alone is insufficient, and appropriate correction of the obstruction is required; in such cases, isthmusectomy may be a useful adjunctive measure to allow repositioning of the kidney and maintenance of an unobstructed upper urinary tract. Abdominal pain in the absence of any demonstrable renal symptoms is rarely due to polar fusion and is not an indication for isthmusectomy.

When surgery is performed on a horseshoe kidney, an anterior subcostal extraperitoneal approach is preferred. This provides good access to the isthmus as well as to the pelvis and ureter, which are rotated anteriorly. Horseshoe kidneys are generally supplied by multiple renal vessels that, in some cases, can enter the isthmus directly. The isthmus may be fibrous but often consists of parenchyma tissue. Isthmusectomy is performed by mobilizing the isthmus from the great vessels, being careful to avoid injury to any anomalous vessels, and placing mattress sutures of 0-0 chromic catgut through the parenchyma about 1 cm on either side of the line of section to control bleeding. The divided ends can be further oversewn with sutures passed through the capsule of the cut edges. Two or three sutures through the divided isthmus and into the fascia overlying the muscles of the posterior abdominal wall are used to fix the lower pole, which is rotated outward to

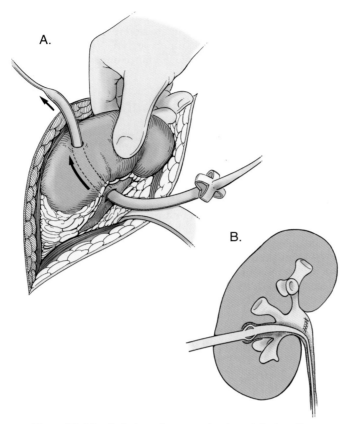

**Figure 50–96.** Technique of open nephrostomy tube insertion.

allow room for the ureter to lie on the posterior abdominal wall.

## Local Excision of Renal Pelvic Tumor

**In patients with localized transitional cell carcinoma of the renal pelvis, nephroureterectomy with a bladder cuff is the treatment of choice. A nephron-sparing operation may be indicated in selected patients with low-grade, noninvasive malignant disease present bilaterally or in a solitary kidney to avoid the need for dialytic renal replacement therapy.** A variety of conservative surgical approaches are available in such cases, including open pyelotomy with tumor excision and fulguration, partial nephrectomy (Fig. 50–97), and endourologic techniques with or without adjunctive topical chemotherapy (Zincke and Neves, 1984; Huffman et al, 1985; Streem and Pontes, 1986; Smith et al, 1987; Ziegelbaum et al, 1987; Vasavada et al, 1995). The last two approaches are reviewed elsewhere.

Open pyelotomy and tumor excision may be employed in patients with noninvasive transitional cell carcinoma confined to a portion of the renal pelvis. On occasion, small lesions involving an infundibulum may be accessible by this approach. This operation is performed through an extraperitoneal flank incision after mobilization of the entire kidney within Gerota's fascia.

The upper ureter and renal pelvis are mobilized along the posterior renal aspect. Renal pelvic dissection is carried into the renal sinus, which often also exposes one or more infundibula. Small vein or Gil-Vernet retractors are used to maintain this operative exposure (Fig. 50–98A). The renal

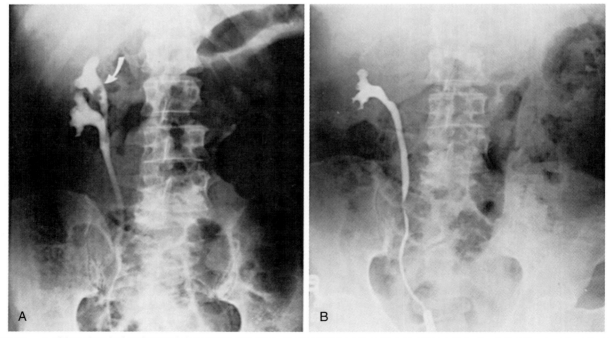

**Figure 50–97. A,** This patient had undergone left nephroureterectomy for transitional cell carcinoma of the left renal pelvis. Intravenous pyelography suggests a lesion in the upper infundibulum of the remaining right kidney *(arrow).* This is confirmed at the time of retrograde pyelography. **B,** Upper pole partial nephrectomy is performed, leaving the pelvis and lower infundibulocalyceal system intact, as demonstrated on this postoperative retrograde pyelogram. (Reproduced with permission from Novick AC, Streem SB, Pontes E, eds: Stewart's Operative Urology, 2nd ed. Baltimore, Williams & Wilkins, 1989.)

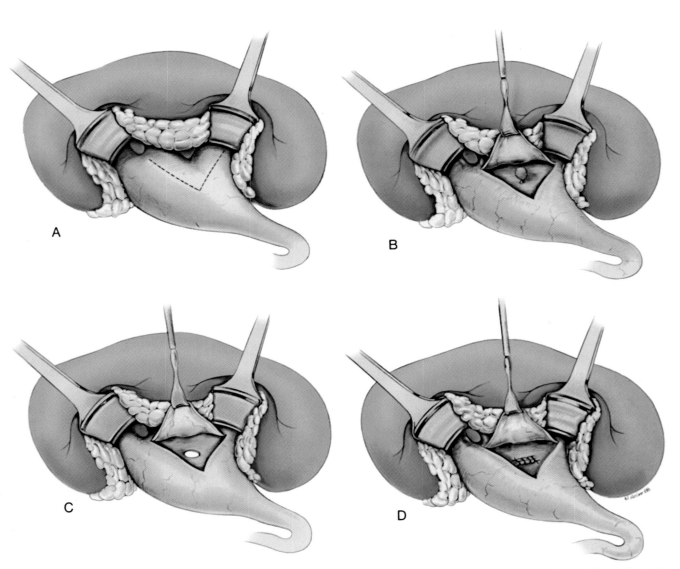

**Figure 50–98.** Technique of open pyelotomy and tumor excision for transitional cell carcinoma of the renal pelvis. (Reproduced with permission from Novick AC, Streem SB, Pontes E, eds: Stewart's Operative Urology, 2nd ed. Baltimore, Williams & Wilkins, 1989.)

pelvic incision is made to expose the tumor-bearing portion of the renal pelvis (Fig. 50–98*B*). This incision may be extended into an infundibulum if necessary. It is preferable to excise a full-thickness segment of the renal pelvis encompassing the tumor (Fig. 50–98*C*). Frozen sections are prepared to ensure that the resected margins are free of disease. An alternative approach is to sharply excise the tumor at its base while preserving the integrity of the renal pelvic wall and then to fulgurate the base and surrounding area extensively. After excision of all gross tumor, operative pyeloscopy is used to examine the intrarenal collecting system for any remaining lesions. The site of renal pelvic tumor excision is repaired with 4-0 chromic suture (Fig. 50–98*D*), and the pyelotomy incision is then similarly closed. A Penrose drain is placed near the pyelotomy and brought out through a separate stab wound in the flank.

## SUGGESTED READINGS

Castilla E, Liou L, Abrahams N, et al: Prognostic importance of resection margin width after nephron-sparing surgery for renal cell carcinoma. Urology 2002;60:993.

Coll DM, Uzzo RG, Herts BR, et al: 3-dimensional volume rendered computerized tomography for preoperative evaluation and intraoperative treatment of patients undergoing nephron-sparing surgery. J Urol 1999;161:1097.

Fergany A, Kolletis P, Novick AC: The contemporary role of extra-anatomic surgical renal revascularization in patients with atherosclerotic renal artery disease. J Urol 1995;153:1798.

Fergany AF, Hafez KS, Novick AC: Long-term results of nephron-sparing surgery for localized renal cell carcinoma: 10-year follow-up. J Urol 2000;163:442.

Gill IS, Matin SF, Desai M, et al: Comparative analysis of laparoscopic versus open partial nephrectomy for renal tumors in 200 patients. J Urol 2003;170:64.

Hafez KS, Novick AC, Campbell SD: Patterns of tumor recurrence and guidelines for follow-up after nephron-sparing surgery for sporadic renal cell carcinoma. J Urol 1997;157:2067.

Hafez KS, Fergany AF, Novick AC: Nephron-sparing surgery for localized renal cell carcinoma: Impact of tumor size on patient survival, tumor recurrence, and TNM staging. J Urol 1999;162:1930.

Libertino JA, Bosco PJ, Ying CY, et al: Renal revascularization to preserve and restore renal function. J Urol 1992;147:1485.

Marshall FF, Powell KD: Lymphadenectomy for renal cell carcinoma: Anatomical and therapeutic considerations. J Urol 1982;128:677.

Novick AC: Anatomic approaches in nephron-sparing surgery for renal cell carcinoma. Atlas Urol Clin North Am 1998;6:39.

Novick AC, Ziegelbaum M, Vidt DG, et al: Trends in surgical revascularization for renal artery disease: Ten year's experience. JAMA 1987;257:498.

Novick AC, Kaye M, Cosgrove D, et al: Experience with cardiopulmonary bypass and deep hypothermic circulatory arrest in the management of retroperitoneal tumors with large vena caval thrombi. Ann Surg 1990;212:472.

Novick AC, Gephardt G, Guz B, et al: Long-term follow-up after partial removal of a solitary kidney. N Engl J Med 1991;325:1058.

Steinbach F, Novick AC, Campbell S, Dykstra D: Long-term survival after surgical revascularization for atherosclerotic renal artery disease. J Urol 1997;158:38.

Uzzo R, Novick AC: Nephron-sparing surgery for renal tumors: Indications, techniques and outcomes. J Urol 2001;166:6.

## KEY POINTS: SURGERY OF THE KIDNEY

- During reconstructive renal surgery, when renal vascular occlusion is employed for a period of more than 30 minutes, adjunctive surface renal hypothermia is needed to prevent permanent ischemic renal damage.

- Radical nephrectomy with removal of a perirenal or infrahepatic IVC thrombus is best performed through a bilateral subcostal transperitoneal incision.

- Radical nephrectomy with removal of an atrial thrombus is best performed with adjunctive cardiopulmonary bypass and deep hypothermic circulatory arrest.

- Techniques for partial nephrectomy require adherence to basic principles of early vascular control, avoidance of ischemic renal damage, complete tumor excision with free margins, precise closure of the collecting system, careful hemostasis, and closure or coverage of the renal defect.

- The two primary kidney-threatening complications of partial nephrectomy are hemorrhage and ischemic renal failure.

- Patients with atherosclerotic renal artery disease who are considered for surgical revascularization should undergo screening and correction of significant associated extrarenal vascular disease, such as coronary and carotid disease.

- In older patients with renal artery disease, involvement of the abdominal aorta with severe atherosclerosis or aneurysmal disease may render an aortorenal bypass technically difficult and hazardous to perform. In such cases, alternative extra-anatomic bypass techniques, such as hepatorenal or splenorenal bypass, are preferable.

- Extracorporeal revascularization and autotransplantation are indicated for intrarenal branch arterial lesions due to fibrous dysplasia or aneurysmal disease.

# 51 Laparoscopic Surgery of the Kidney

JAY T. BISHOFF, MD • LOUIS R. KAVOUSSI, MD

HISTORICAL OVERVIEW

PATIENT EVALUATION AND PREPARATION

SURGICAL APPROACHES

SIMPLE NEPHRECTOMY

RENAL BIOPSY

RENAL CYSTIC DISEASE

NEPHROPEXY

PYELOLITHOTOMY AND URETEROLITHOTOMY

CALYCEAL DIVERTICULECTOMY

LAPAROSCOPY FOR RENAL MALIGNANCY

TRANSPERITONEAL RADICAL NEPHRECTOMY

RETROPERITONEAL RADICAL NEPHRECTOMY

HAND-ASSISTED RADICAL NEPHRECTOMY

NEPHRON-SPARING SURGERY

LAPAROSCOPIC ABLATIVE TECHNIQUES

COMPLICATIONS OF LAPAROSCOPIC RENAL SURGERY

SUMMARY

## HISTORICAL OVERVIEW

The current practice of laparoscopic renal surgery evolved slowly over a period of almost 200 years. In 1804, Bozzini developed the first reproducible device to illuminate dark cavities previously unseen in the living body. Seventy years later, Nitze and Leiter laid the foundation for the modern urologic endoscope. In parallel, surgeons began toying with the idea of filling the abdominal cavity with air to create a diagnostic space. These technologies fused in 1901 when Jacobius used room air to fill the abdomen of 15 patients and then inserted a laparoscope to assist with the diagnosis of ascites. Progress from a simple diagnostic modality to therapeutic intervention finally occurred in 1983, when Semm removed an appendix laparoscopically (Clayman, 2004).

Only recently has laparoscopy become a practical and acceptable alternative to treat complex urologic surgical diseases. William Schuessler conceived the first urologic laparoscopic procedure: the pelvic lymphadenectomy for patients with prostate cancer (Griffith et al, 1990). Shortly thereafter, in 1990, Clayman and coworkers at Washington University developed a solution to laparoscopic solid organ removal by performing the first laparoscopic nephrectomy. During an operation that lasted more than 7 hours, an elderly patient with a 3-cm solid renal mass underwent laparoscopic radical nephrectomy through five trocar sites. Inside the abdomen, the kidney was placed in an impermeable bag and morcellated into small pieces. The entire radical nephrectomy specimen was extracted through a 12-mm incision (Clayman et al, 1991). This work has paved the way for a variety of both extraperitoneal and reconstructive renal surgical procedures.

**The proven benefits of laparoscopic surgery, compared with open surgery, are now recognized in the treatment of renal disease and include decreased requirements for pain medication, shorter hospital stay, improved cosmetic result, and a more rapid return to full activity.**

## PATIENT EVALUATION AND PREPARATION

Patient preparation for laparoscopic kidney surgery is similar to that for comparable open surgical procedures. **Informed consent should include a discussion of possible complications, including injury to the diaphragm, vascular structures, nerves, bowel, spleen, and pancreas. In addition, the patient should be informed that conversion to open surgery may be necessary to safely complete the planned procedure.**

For the surgeon to assess for operative contraindications, the preoperative evaluation should include a careful history and detailed physical examination. **Laparoscopic renal surgery requires controlled ventilation and, therefore, is restricted in patients who are not candidates for a general** anesthetic (Monk and Weldon, 1992). Prior abdominal surgery may alter the choice between transperitoneal or retroperitoneal approaches, patient positioning, and the placement site of trocars but is not a contraindication to laparoscopic surgery (Chen et al, 1998; Cadeddu et al, 1999). Severe cardiac or pulmonary disease may place the patient at risk for complications due to the pneumoperitoneum, which can compromise ventilation and limit venous return (Arthure, 1970; Hodgson et al, 1970; Nunn, 1987; Lew et al, 1992). Patients with chronic obstructive pulmonary disease may not be able to compensate for hypercarbia induced by the pneumoperitoneum and may require lower insufflation pressures, use of an alternative insufflant insufflator such as helium, or conversion to open surgery (Monk and Weldon, 1992; Wolf, 1996).

**Obesity is not a contraindication to laparoscopic transperitoneal, retroperitoneal, or hand-assisted kidney procedures. However, fatty tissue can make identification of anatomic structures challenging. Moreover, the increased distance to the operative field may require alterations in traditional trocar site selection** (Mendoza et al, 1996; Doublet and Belair, 2000; Jacobs et al, 2000). The weight of the pannus may raise the intra-abdominal pressure and limit the working space. Obese patients are at increased risk for complications from open or laparoscopic surgery (Fazeli-Matin et al, 1999) and may have a greater chance of conversion to open surgery. Of note, postoperative pulmonary and wound complications are often lower in obese patients undergoing laparoscopic surgery compared with the open approach (Fugita et al, 2004; Hedican et al, 2004; Kapoor et al, 2004). Rhabdomyolysis is a rare complication of prolonged laparoscopic renal surgery in the obese population as well as extremely muscular individuals (Troppmann et al, 2003).

Laparoscopy during pregnancy should be approached with care and has been reported in cases of adrenal pheochromocytoma and Cushing's syndrome. There are also published cases of laparoscopic radical nephrectomy for renal cell carcinoma diagnosed during pregnancy. No complications were reported in any of these cases, and all pregnancies were carried to term (O'Conner et al, 2004; Sainsbury et al, 2004).

Anticoagulated patients are managed in cooperation with their primary physician. One should have results of blood studies available for patients with bleeding disorders. Platelets and fresh frozen plasma can be given if needed before the procedure. Patients with thrombocytopenia receive platelets 30 minutes before the incision, to increase their platelet count to greater than 50,000/mL. Additional platelet transfusion should not be necessary in the absence of symptomatic bleeding. Uremic patients with prolonged bleeding time may benefit from infusion of desmopressin acetate (0.3 to 0.4 µg/kg) 1 hour before the procedure to improve platelet function.

The patient's medical history dictates the laboratory and imaging studies to be obtained. An electrocardiogram and a chest radiograph may be obtained before surgery. Pulmonary function studies are performed only in those patients with known respiratory disease or those at risk based on the history and physical examination. It is recommended that patients have their blood typed and screened. For complex reconstructive procedures, one may consider crossmatching blood. Bowel preparation varies according to the procedure, likelihood of bowel adhesions, and the physician's preference. For left-sided transperitoneal procedures, we prefer to evacuate the colon the evening before surgery with enemas or laxatives.

Preoperative abdominal axial imaging with computed tomography (CT) or magnetic resonance imaging (MRI) is helpful in defining renal pathology as well as individual anatomy. Areas of perinephric stranding discovered on CT may indicate significant inflammation and adhesions, increasing the chance for conversion to an open procedure (Fig. 51–1). In addition, the contrast medium–enhanced scans provide data on the appearance and function of the contralateral kidney. Differential function can be determined with a diethylenetriaminepentaacetic acid renal scan if needed. Angiography, embolization, or placement of a ureteral stent may be helpful in select patients but is not routine.

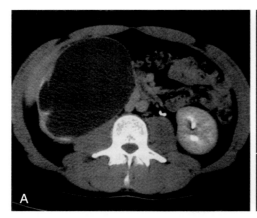 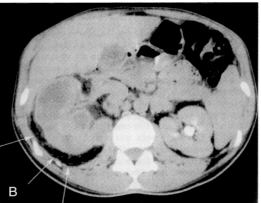

**Figure 51–1.** Preoperative abdominal CT scans from two different patients before simple nephrectomy for nonfunctioning kidneys. **A,** Minimal perinephric stranding is seen, and an uncomplicated laparoscopic nephrectomy was performed. **B,** *Arrows* show significant perinephric stranding. These represent dense adhesions that required conversion to open surgery to complete the nephrectomy. (From Bishoff JT, Kavoussi LR [eds]: Atlas of Laparoscopic Retroperitoneal Surgery. Philadelphia, WB Saunders, 2000).

# SURGICAL APPROACHES

**There are three basic laparoscopic approaches for laparoscopic nephrectomy: transperitoneal, retroperitoneal, and hand-assisted.**

## Transperitoneal Approach

The transperitoneal approach is the traditional method used to perform laparoscopic surgery. It results in small incisions and gives latitude in the location of trocar placement. It also affords an optimal working space and facilitates orientation from readily identifiable anatomic landmarks. Nambirajan and colleagues (2004) performed a prospective randomized study between the transperitoneal and retroperitoneal approaches. They showed no significant operative differences between the two approaches but did report that resumption of oral intake was significantly faster in the transperitoneal group.

## Retroperitoneal Approach

The retroperitoneal approach mimics traditional open surgery in that the kidney is approached without entry into the peritoneal cavity. A potential space must be developed to allow adequate visualization of the surgical field. Even though urologists have conventionally approached the kidney through the retroperitoneum, the laparoscopic approach can appear unfamiliar owing to overlying adipose tissue and the limited working space. For the novice, this can cause difficulty with orientation, visualization, instrument manipulation, and organ entrapment.

There are patients in whom retroperitoneal access is preferred over the transperitoneal approach. Patients with a history of multiple abdominal surgical procedures or peritonitis may benefit from this approach. Initial retroperitoneal access can be achieved with subsequent opening of the peritoneum as indicated (Cadeddu et al, 1999). Also, patients with abnormalities on the posterior surface of the kidney (exophytic cyst or mass) may be better served through retroperitoneal access. Consequently, the laparoscopic surgeon should be familiar with both transperitoneal and retroperitoneal approaches.

## Hand-Assisted Approach

To facilitate learning of laparoscopic techniques and to increase the availability of less invasive procedures, hand-assisted endoscopic techniques have been introduced. The first hand-assisted laparoscopic nephrectomy (HALN) was reported by Nakada and coworkers in 1997. The hand-assisted devices offer a bridge between laparoscopic and open surgery and may help surgeons without advanced laparoscopic training gain the necessary experience. At the time of this writing, there were three devices available to maintain the pneumoperitoneum during HALN: the Gelport (Applied Medical, Rancho Santa Margarita, CA), the LapDisc (Ethicon Endosurgery, Cincinnati, OH), and the Omniport (Advanced Surgical Concepts, Ireland; distributed in the US by Weck Closure, Raleigh, NC) (Table 51–1) (Rane et al, 2003; Patel and Stifelman, 2004; Wolf et al, 2005). Hand-assisted laparoscopic surgery has the advantage of restoring tactile feedback and use of the hand to assist with dissection, retraction, extraction, and rapid control of bleeding if needed. An incision large enough to allow the surgeon or assistant to insert a hand must be created, and this site can be utilized for organ extraction. Hand-assisted dissection may be helpful in those patients whose pathologic condition makes laparoscopy more difficult, such as infectious processes or prior renal surgery. Multiple series have documented the utility of the hand-assisted technique for most kidney procedures (Keeley et al, 1997; Wolf et al, 1998; Nakada et al, 1997, 1999).

# SIMPLE NEPHRECTOMY

## Indications and Contraindications

**Laparoscopic simple nephrectomy is indicated in the treatment of most benign renal diseases, including renovascular hypertension, symptomatic acquired renal cystic disease**

---

**Table 51–1. Characteristics of Commercially Available Devices for Hand-Assisted Laparoscopy**

| Characteristic | Gelport | Lap Disc | Omniport |
|---|---|---|---|
| Manufacturer | Applied Medical, Rancho Santa Margarita, CA | Ethicon Endo-Surgery, Cincinnati, OH | Advanced Surgical Concepts, Ireland, Distributed in US by Weck Closure, Raleigh, NC |
| Device diameter | 13 cm | 12 cm | 12 cm |
| No. of different sizes | 2 | 2 | 1 |
| No. of components | 3 pieces: flexible skirt, rigid base, gel cap | One piece | 2 pieces: cuff with retention rings, insufflation device |
| Advantages | Gel cap maintains pneumoperitoneum with or without instruments and allows instrument to be placed directly though cap device. | Small and simple to work. An iris configuration allows opening to be large enough for hand or tightly placed around a trocar. | Able to maintain pneumoperitoneum even when incision is too long. |
| Disadvantages | Gas leak if incision is too long | Gas leak if incision is too long | Loss of pneumoperitoneum when hand is removed |
| Cost per device | $575 | $490 | $415 |

Data from Wolf JS: Tips and tricks for hand-assisted surgery. AUA Update Series 2005;24:2; Rane A, Dasgupta P: Prospective experience with a second-generation hand-assisted laparoscopic device and comparison with first-generation devices. J Endourol 2003;17:895-897; and Rupa P, Stifelman MD: Hand-assisted laparoscopic devices: The second generation. J Endourol 2004;18:649-653.

in dialysis patients, nephrosclerosis, symptomatic patients with autosomal dominant polycystic kidney disease (ADPKD), chronic pain of renal origin refractory to conservative measures, chronic pyelonephritis, reflux or obstructive nephropathy, and multicystic dysplastic kidney (Fricke et al, 1998).

Prior abdominal surgery may result in the formation of intra-abdominal adhesions and potentially increase injury to bowel during insufflation, trocar placement, or dissection. The initial entry site in these patients should be away from scars and prior surgical fields. Open trocar placement or a retroperitoneal approach may be necessary to minimize access injuries (Hassan, 1971). **Patients with large, dilated loops of bowel from either functional or obstructive ileus should be approached cautiously because the dilated intestinal segments can limit the working space and may be injured during access, dissection, and trocar site closure** (Borten, 1986). Other contraindications include an uncorrected coagulopathy, untreated infection, and hypovolemic shock (Capelouto and Kavoussi, 1993). Although not a contraindication, xanthogranulomatous pyelonephritis and renal tuberculosis (Gupta et al, 1997; Bercowsky et al, 1999) can be associated with dense adhesions and lead to conversion to open surgery. Of note, Lee and associates (2002) reported successful retroperitoneal laparoscopic simple nephrectomy in 30 of 31 patients with nonfunctioning kidneys secondary to tuberculosis.

## Patient Positioning

For transperitoneal laparoscopic nephrectomy, the patient is initially positioned supine for intravenous access, the induction of general anesthesia, endotracheal intubation, bladder catheterization, and orogastric tube placement. The patient is then positioned in a modified lateral decubitus position. Approximately 30 degrees of rotation of the chest and abdomen is used. The table can be flexed as needed, an axillary roll is placed, and padding is used to support the buttocks and flank. **The patient is taped in position with multiple strips of wide cloth tape so that the patient's arms, legs, and abdomen remain securely in place while the table is rolled toward the surgeon to assist with gravity retraction of the bowel** (Fig. 51–2).

The equipment in the operating room is configured to maximize the use of operating room space and to allow all members of the surgical team to view the procedure (Fig. 51–3). During the skin preparation and towel placement, the entire flank and abdomen are included in case conversion to an open procedure is required.

## Insufflation and Trocar Placement

Once a pneumoperitoneum is established, a 12-mm port is placed lateral to the rectus muscle at the level of the umbilicus. This can be accomplished blindly or with the aid of a visual obturator to allow entry into the abdomen under direct vision. Once the port is in place, the abdomen is then inspected for any injury from Veress needle placement. Also, one should inspect for adhesions in areas where the secondary ports will be placed. Remaining trocars are inserted under direct vision.

The use of local anesthesia to prevent postoperative trocar site pain may be helpful. Khaira and Wolf (2004) performed a double-blind, randomized placebo-controlled trial showing that the infiltration of trocar and hand-assisted sites with 0.5% bupivacaine before incision or port placement decreased postoperative narcotic requirements at all time points compared with placebo injection.

Three to five trocars are utilized to complete the dissection. **A 12-mm trocar is placed lateral to the rectus at the level of the umbilicus; this trocar is used for instrumentation and the passage of staplers to secure and divide hilar vessels. A 10- or 12-mm trocar is placed at the umbilicus for the camera, and a 5-mm port is inserted in the midline between the umbilicus and the xiphoid process.** In obese patients, all trocar sites are moved laterally (Fig. 51–4). A lower midline additional trocar may be needed for retraction or to complete the hilar dissection or assist with organ entrapment (Fig. 51–5). A subxiphoid 3- to 5-mm retractor may be needed to retract the liver for right-sided procedures.

## Procedure

### Reflection of the Colon

For a left nephrectomy, the white line of Toldt is incised from the level of the iliac vessels inferiorly, extending above the spleen superiorly. The lienocolic ligament should be incised to allow the spleen to fall medially along with the pancreas and

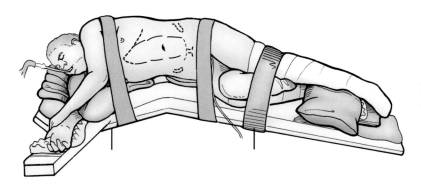

**Figure 51–2.** The patient is placed in a modified flank position, with the umbilicus over the break in the operating table. This position allows the arms to be placed on the table in a "praying mantis" position or crossed over the chest with two pillows placed between them.

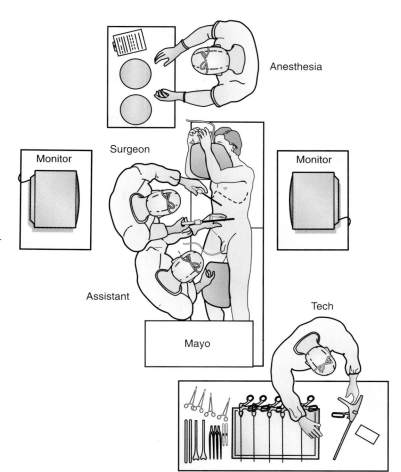

**Figure 51–3.** The operating room is configured for left nephrectomy. Two monitors allow the assistant to follow the procedure.

the colon (Fig. 51–6). Care must be taken to avoid injuring the diaphragm with this maneuver. Also, the surgeon must be cognizant of the stomach as superior attachments are incised. During a right-sided nephrectomy the hepatic flexure of the colon is usually below the lower pole of the kidney. As such, the peritoneal incision begins at the hepatic flexure and is carried cephalad, above the hepatic flexure, including the right triangular and right anterior coronary ligaments. On both sides, medial traction on the colon reveals colorenal attachments that must be divided to complete mobilization (Fig. 51–7).

### Dissection of the Ureter

Once the colon has been freed, the psoas muscle and psoas tendon should be identified. When the psoas muscle is followed medially, the gonadal vessels are usually first encountered. These should be swept laterally and the ureter is usually located just deep to these vessels. The ureter is usually more medial than anticipated. Peristalsis of the ureter can help differentiate from the gonadal vein. **Once identified, the ureter alone on the right side or both the ureter and gonadal vessels together on the left side are elevated and followed proximally to the lower pole and hilum of the kidney. The ureter is not divided at this time because it can be used to help elevate the kidney** (Fig. 51–8).

### Identification of the Renal Hilum

Safe dissection of the renal hilum requires two conditions: (1) medial retraction of the colon and bowel by gravity or an additional retractor and (2) lateral retraction of the kidney by lifting it out of the renal fossa. **Lateral retraction of the kidney, with a grasper placed under the lower pole, will place the vessels on tension, allowing for visualization and control of bleeding vessels should a small accessory vessel be avulsed. This is accomplished by gently placing the lateral grasper under the ureter and lower pole of the kidney until the grasper abuts against the abdominal sidewall. It is important to be sure that the grasper is not into the renal parenchyma.** With the ureter and lower pole of the kidney elevated, layer-by-layer anterior dissection is performed with the irrigator aspirator until the renal vein is uncovered. Gonadal, lumbar, and accessory venous branches can then be clipped and divided as encountered (Fig. 51–9).

### Securing the Renal Blood Vessels

By clearing off anterior Gerota's fascia and inferior lymphatics, one can identify the renal artery. If the irrigator-aspirator tip is not precise enough for meticulous dissection, a hook electrode can be used to dissect the lymphatic vessels free of the vein and artery. It has been our experience that smokers,

*Text continued on p. 1768.*

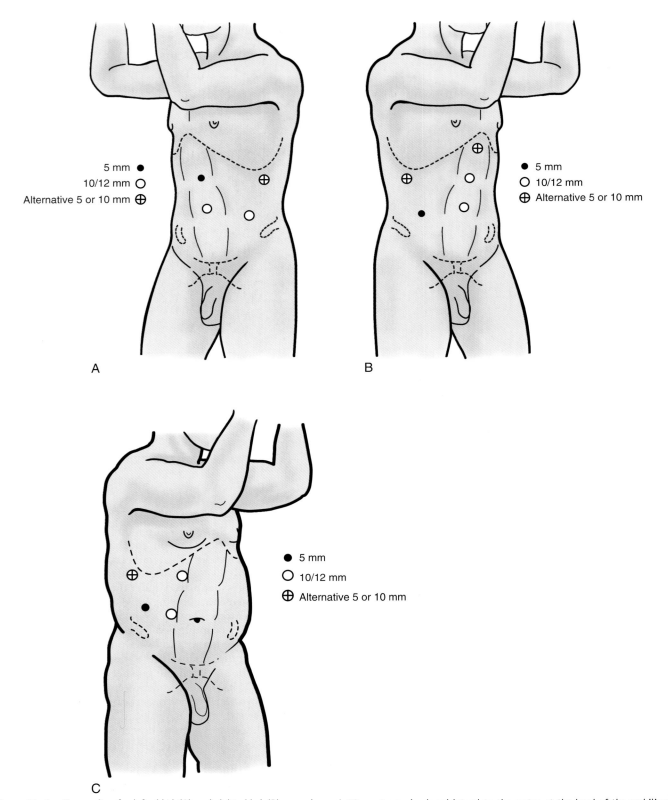

**Figure 51–4.** Trocar sites for left-sided (**A**) and right-sided (**B**) procedures. A 12-mm trocar is placed lateral to the rectus at the level of the umbilicus, a second 10-mm trocar is placed at the umbilicus, and a 5-mm trocar is inserted in the midline between the umbilicus and the xiphoid process. **C,** In obese patients, all trocars are shifted laterally.

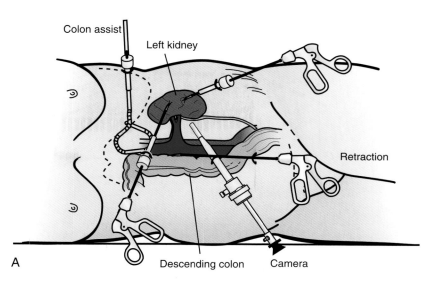

A

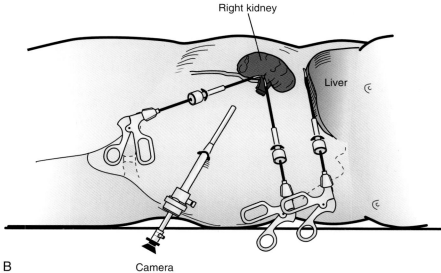

B

**Figure 51–5. A,** Additional retraction during left-sided procedures can be accomplished with the use of a blunt instrument passed through a 5- or 10-mm trocar placed above the symphysis pubis or a 5-mm instrument and retractor passed through a subcostal incision. **B,** In right-sided procedures, the liver and bowel can be retracted through a 3- or 5-mm trocar placed in the midline. **C,** In right-sided procedures the liver and bowel can be retracted through a 5-mm trocar with a 5-mm instrument.

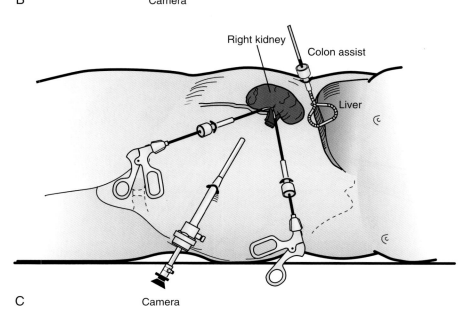

C

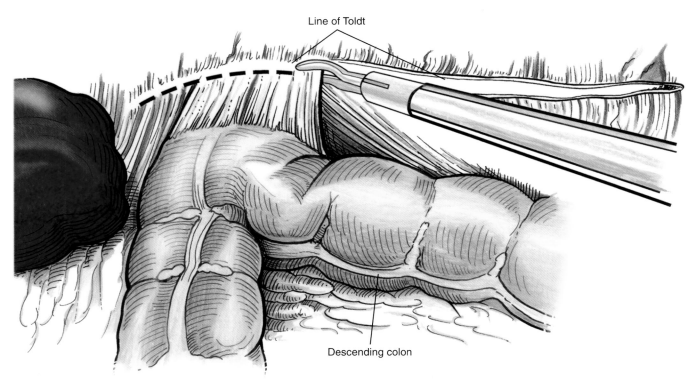

Line of Toldt

Descending colon

**Figure 51–6.** Incision of the white line of Toldt with endoshears, bipolar cautery, or ultrasonic energy allows reflection of the colon.

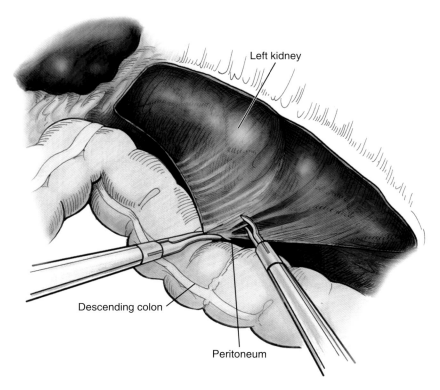

Left kidney

Descending colon

Peritoneum

**Figure 51–7.** Medial traction on the colon helps identify additional colorenal attachments and assists in differentiating the undersurface of the large bowel mesentery.

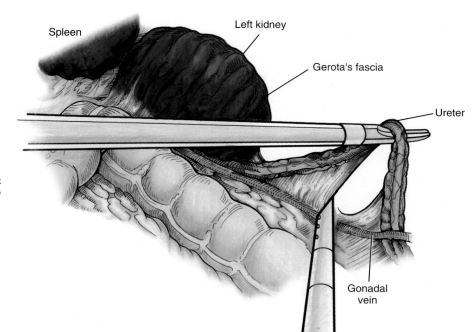

**Figure 51–8.** A curved dissector, in the left hand, is placed beneath the ureter and used to provide anterolateral elevation.

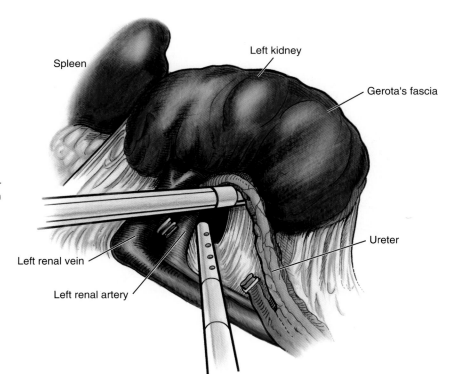

**Figure 51–9.** The lower pole of the kidney and ureter are firmly retracted anterolaterally, placing the hilum on stretch.

particularly users of marijuana, will have lymphatics that are more tenacious and dense than nonsmokers. **Clips or staples can be used on the artery** (Fig. 51–10). The artery is divided first, followed by the vein. We prefer to use an endovascular gastrointestinal anastomosis (GIA) stapler on both the artery and vein, because three rows of staples will be

left on the vessel stump and are unlikely to be dislodged during subsequent dissection. Occasionally, oozing may be seen from the stump when using a GIA stapler. In these cases, a reinforcing clip may be helpful. On the left side, to preserve the adrenal gland, the GIA stapler is fired distally to the take-off of the adrenal vein.

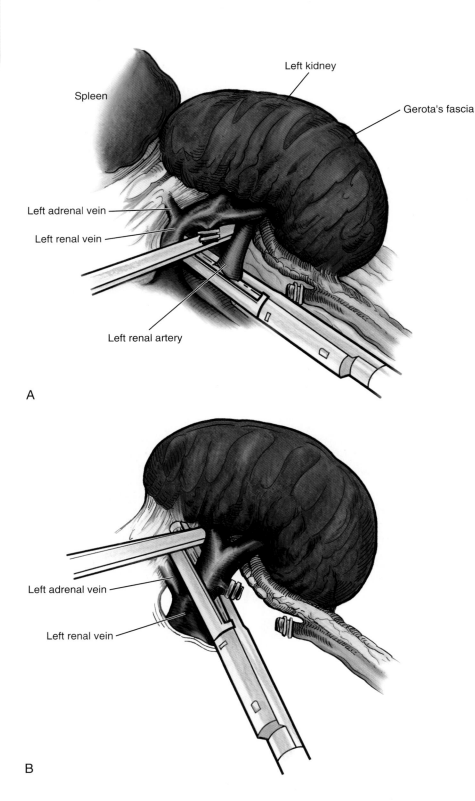

A

B

**Figure 51–10. A,** First, the renal artery is stapled using an endovascular gastrointestinal anastomosis (GIA) stapler. **B,** The renal vein is secured lateral to the adrenal vein with the GIA stapler. If clips are used on the gonadal or adrenal vessels, the surgeon must be careful to exclude them from the jaws of the stapler.

## Isolation of the Upper Pole

Once all the hilar vessels have been divided, the dissection continues posteriorly and superiorly to the upper pole. The adrenal gland is preserved in cases of simple nephrectomy by first applying the GIA stapler distal to the takeoff of the adrenal vein. Gerota's fat is then peeled off circumferentially above the upper pole of the kidney (Fig. 51–11). At this point during the dissection, it may be necessary to clip and transect the ureter. This allows the kidney to be rotated anteriorly above the liver (right) or spleen (left) to facilitate incision of the uppermost attachments under direct vision.

In cases of extreme fibrosis, a subcapsular nephrectomy can be performed once the artery and vein have been controlled (Moore et al, 1998). Long, blunt instruments such as the closed stapler or the 10-mm LigaSure Atlas (Valleylab, Tyco Healthcare Group, Boulder, CO) are particularly well suited for reaching and freeing the upper pole and adrenal attachments.

## Organ Entrapment

The kidney can be removed intact through an enlarged incision or after morcellation. When morcellation is performed, the specimen should be placed into a sturdy entrapment sac such as the LapSac (Cook Urological, Spencer, IN) (Urban et al, 1993). This minimizes the risk of rupture during mechanical morcellation of the tissue (Walther et al, 1999; Landman et al, 2000). By using ring forceps and a Kocher clamp the kidney and collecting system can be morcellated and removed in small pieces. Alternatively, the kidney can be removed intact through an incision after placement into a sac. The kidney can be worked out of an extended trocar site or Pfannenstiel incision. For trocar sites greater than 5 mm, it is helpful to place the closure sutures before removing the kidney. Once the sutures are placed, trocars can be reinserted for kidney entrapment and removal.

## Postoperative Management

The orogastric tube is removed at the conclusion of the procedure. The patient can begin a diet as tolerated. The Foley catheter should be removed once the patient is comfortably ambulating. The patient is discharged when tolerating a regular diet. Unrestricted activity can usually be resumed according to the patient's comfort. If a specimen has been removed through an incision, lifting is limited to 6 weeks.

## Results

The postoperative results of the laparoscopic nephrectomy are comparable to that of open surgery with much less pain and shorter convalescence. **Postoperative pain requirements are approximately four times less than with traditional open incisions. Hospital stays have been decreased by 50%, and the time to full convalescence has been reported to be markedly less than with open removal.** In early series, the mean operative times were greater than 300 minutes. However, with advances in techniques, experience, and equipment, current operative times have decreased dramatically (Kerbl et al, 1994a, 1994b; Nicol et al, 1994; Perez et al, 1994; Parra et al, 1995; Baba et al, 1996; Rassweiler et al, 1998a, 1998b; Permpongkosol et al, 2005).

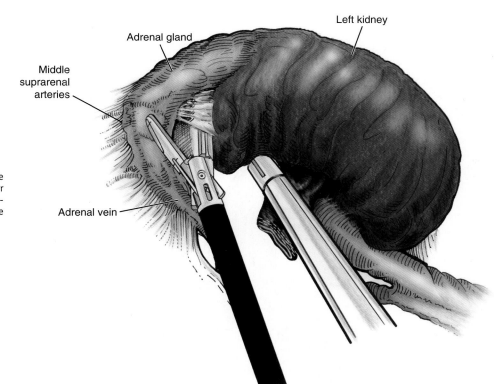

**Figure 51–11.** The adrenal gland can be preserved during simple nephrectomy or radical nephrectomy as indicated by dissecting it from the superior pole of the kidney.

# RENAL BIOPSY

Renal biopsy can play an important role in the assessment of proteinuria or unexplained medical disease of the kidney. Histologic information is often pivotal in making treatment decisions and prognosis (Morel-Maroger, 1982; Gault and Muehrcke, 1983; Manoligod and Pirani, 1985). **Ultrasound-guided percutaneous needle biopsy, under local anesthesia, is the current standard for obtaining renal tissue. Unfortunately, there is a 5% rate of significant hemorrhagic complications, and as many as 5% to 20% of cases yield inadequate tissue for accurate diagnosis** (Wickre and Golper, 1982). In morbidly obese patients it can be difficult or impossible to identify the kidney using ultrasound, prohibiting biopsy. When percutaneous or transjugular biopsy fails or is considered to have risk, patients may benefit from surgical renal biopsy. This allows hemostasis to be achieved under direct vision and provides the pathologist with adequate tissue to make a diagnosis. Laparoscopic renal biopsy offers the advantages of open biopsy with the decreased morbidity of a two-port outpatient procedure and can be performed in the morbidly obese.

## Indications

**Renal biopsy under direct vision is indicated in three primary categories of patients: failed percutaneous needle or transjugular biopsy, anatomic variations, and a risk of bleeding complication. Factors that may make a patient unsuitable for percutaneous biopsy include morbid obesity, multiple bilateral cysts, a body habitus that makes localization impossible, and a solitary functioning kidney.** Renal imaging with CT or ultrasonography is performed to determine any abnormality, such as renal cysts or solitary kidney, that may alter the choice of kidney for biopsy.

## Patient Positioning

The patient is placed in the full flank position with the umbilicus over the table break. The table is fully flexed to help increase the distance between the ribs and the iliac crest. Grounding pads for electrocautery and the argon beam coagulator are placed on the exposed upper thigh.

## Procedure

### Retroperitoneal Access

A 10-mm transverse incision is made in the skin midway between the iliac crest and the tip of the 12th rib in the posterior axillary line. A 0-degree lens and visual obturator (Visiport, AutoSuture, Norwalk CT; or Optiview, Ethicon Endosurgery, Cincinnati, OH) are placed in the incision. Holding the trocar with the laparoscope in the visual obturator perpendicular to the skin and aiming approximately 10 degrees anteriorly, the surgeon enters the retroperitoneum under direct vision. Characteristic retroperitoneal fat helps identify the correct space. **Straying too far anteriorly can result in peritoneal entry or colon injury, whereas veering posteriorly can cause bleeding in the quadratus or psoas muscles.**

Once entry is made into the retroperitoneum, the visual obturator is removed, leaving behind the 10-mm trocar. Carbon dioxide insufflation is begun at a pressure of 20 mm Hg. Blunt dissection, using only the laparoscope, is initially used to create a retroperitoneal working space. Anteriorly, the peritoneum is swept medially, exposing the underside of the transversalis fascia (Fig. 51–12). Once anterior dissection has mobilized the peritoneum medially, a 5-mm port is placed in the anterior axillary line at the same level as the first port (Fig. 51–13).

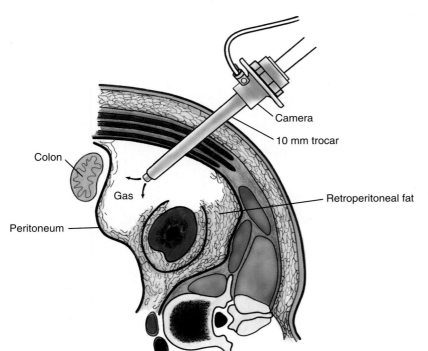

Colon

Gas

Peritoneum

Camera

10 mm trocar

Retroperitoneal fat

**Figure 51–12.** Standing behind the patient, the surgeon places the visual obturator in the posterior axillary line. The 0-degree laparoscope is used to bluntly push the peritoneum medially, creating a working space large enough to allow placement of the second trocar.

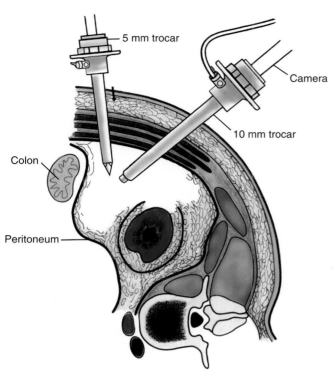

**Figure 51–13.** A 5-mm trocar is placed under direct vision. The working instruments are passed through this port. The camera can be used to assist with dissection and is frequently cleaned to maintain adequate visualization.

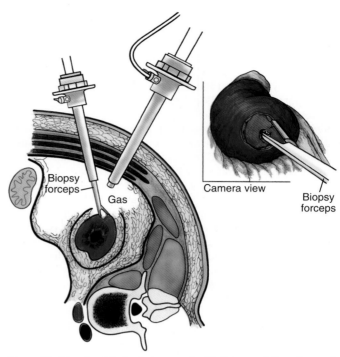

**Figure 51–14.** Gerota's fascia is opened with the use of the scissors. A 5-mm two-tooth laparoscopic biopsy forceps is used to take two to three samples from the lower pole of the kidney.

### Kidney Exposure and Biopsy

The lower pole of the kidney is located, and Gerota's fascia is opened using blunt and sharp dissection. **In anatomically challenging patients such as those who are morbidly obese, preoperative transcutaneous or intraoperative ultrasonography may be valuable in localizing the kidney** (Chen et al, 1997). Once Gerota's fascia is incised, the perirenal fat is swept aside to expose the lower pole. A 5-mm biopsy forceps is used to take several cortical samples (Fig. 51–14). Only a small amount of tissue is needed to obtain adequate sampling of the glomeruli for diagnosis. To prevent errors in tissue processing, the fresh renal biopsy specimen may be placed in formalin but transferred fresh, directly to a nephrologist or pathologist for immediate frozen section confirmation and then processing.

### Hemostasis and Closure

**Hemostasis is obtained with the argon beam coagulator. During activation of the argon beam, it is important to open an insufflation port, because the flow of argon gas can markedly increase the intra-abdominal pressure.** Once adequate hemostasis is achieved, the insufflation pressure is lowered to 5 mm Hg for at least 5 minutes and the entire retroperitoneum is inspected for hemostasis. Persistent bleeding from the biopsy site is treated with repeated argon beam coagulation. Once hemostasis has been confirmed under low pressure, oxidized cellulose is packed into the biopsy site and direct pressure is applied. The skin incisions are irrigated, inspected for hemostasis, and closed with a 4-0 absorbable subcuticular suture.

## Postoperative Considerations

The length of hospital stay depends on the patient's health status. Specific attention is given to control of blood pressure. **Care must be taken in patients requiring postoperative resumption of anticoagulation. Usually, patients can resume oral warfarin or subcutaneous injection anticoagulation therapy 24 to 48 hours after surgery. Patients who require intravenous heparin must be observed very closely to ensure that they do not become supratherapeutic and bleed from the biopsy site.** Most nonhospitalized patients can be discharged the same day as the biopsy.

## Results

A report of 32 consecutive patients who underwent laparoscopic renal biopsy showed 100% success in obtaining adequate tissue for histopathologic diagnosis (Gimenez et al, 1998). The mean blood loss was 26 mL, the operative time was 1.5 hours, and the hospital stay was 1.7 days. Sixteen patients (50%) were treated as outpatients. Complications included one inadvertent biopsy of the spleen without consequence and one 300-mL hematoma that resolved without a need for intervention. The overall complication rate was 6% (2 of 32) and included a patient who was a Jehovah's Witness and on high-dose corticosteroid therapy who developed a perforated gastric ulcer and died 7 days after surgery.

A multi-institutional study over a period of 9 years and 74 patients undergoing laparoscopic renal biopsy showed that adequate tissue was retrieved from 96% of patients. The mean operating room time was 123 minutes (range: 9 to 261 minutes) and the mean estimated blood loss was 67 mL (range: 5 to 2000 mL) (Shetye et al, 2003).

In another series of 17 patients, a balloon was inserted into the retroperitoneum to create the working space (Gaur et al, 1994). Adequate renal tissue for diagnosis was obtained in each case. The mean operative time was 35 minutes, excluding anesthesia time, with a range of 20 to 45 minutes. Fifteen patients were discharged within 24 hours, and 2 patients remained hospitalized for 4 days. Complications were seen in 11% of the patients (2 of 17), including severe bleeding requiring conversion to an open procedure and 1 patient with marked gross hematuria. **Hemorrhage is the most common major complication associated with laparoscopic renal biopsy. Slow resumption of anticoagulation is important to prevent bleeding from the biopsy site. The cause of a persistent decline in hematocrit or symptoms of hypovolemia should be evaluated by CT.**

## RENAL CYSTIC DISEASE

**Renal cysts are present in over one third of patients older than 50 years, and few require surgical intervention** (Hoenig et al, 1997; Wolf, 1998). Patients with pain, infection, or obstruction may need cyst excision. Moreover, with the advent of CT and ultrasonography, the detection of indeterminate renal masses and complex renal cysts has become a frequent occurrence. Classification schemes have been devised based on CT criteria to help surgeons determine whether further diagnostic or therapeutic maneuvers are necessary (Table 51–2) (Bosniak, 1986). Unfortunately, imaging studies are not always diagnostic, and surgical removal may be needed to exclude the possibility of malignancy.

Approximately 600,000 individuals suffer from autosomal dominant polycystic kidney disease (ADPKD). The clinical course of ADPKD is usually dominated by symptoms of abdominal fullness or pain and may require surgical treatment for symptomatic relief. End-stage ADPKD may occasionally require bilateral or unilateral nephrectomy for the treatment of cyst complications, bleeding, infection, or pain.

## Indications

**Needle aspiration with or without sclerosis of symptomatic solitary renal cysts is often the first line of therapy and diagnosis. Resolution of symptoms after drainage and then recurrent symptoms with reaccumulation of cyst fluid**

**increases the likelihood that laparoscopic cyst decortication will be successful in eliminating the patient's pain** (Rane, 2004). **However, cyst aspiration and sclerosis is not always effective and can pose a risk of fibrosis when peripelvic cysts are treated in this manner** (Wehle and Grabstald, 1986; Hulbert et al, 1988; McDougall, 1998; Santiago et al, 1998). Symptomatic parapelvic renal cysts are usually treated with laparoscopic decortication (Doumas et al, 2004). Renal cysts may also obstruct the collecting system, compress renal parenchyma, or spontaneously hemorrhage, inducing pain and hematuria. In addition, they may become infected and cause obstructive uropathy or hypertension. Complex cysts can be explored laparoscopically and sampled, and definitive treatment can be initiated if renal cell carcinoma is confirmed on frozen section histopathologic examination.

In patients with ADPKD, laparoscopic renal cyst marsupialization, decortication, or unroofing large numbers of cysts has been successful in providing pain relief in up to 83% of patients (Bennett et al, 1987; Rubenstein et al, 1993; Teichman and Hulbert, 1995; Brown et al, 1996; Elashry et al, 1996; Lifson et al, 1998). Some patients with renal cysts may experience pain. Those patients in whom standard medical therapies have failed to treat pain may be candidates for laparoscopic cyst decortication. In addition to pain, patients with hypertension, hematuria, or infections may also benefit from treatment. Bilateral synchronous laparoscopic nephrectomy and hand-assisted nephrectomy have also been reported in ADPKD patients with end-stage renal disease and symptoms from enlarged or infected kidneys (Dunn et al, 2000; Kaouk et al, 2000; Bendavid et al, 2004; Luke and Spodek, 2004).

Surgical approaches for complex renal cysts include exploration with biopsy, enucleation, partial nephrectomy, or radical nephrectomy. Radiographic evaluation utilizing the Bosniak classification can help select those patients who should undergo laparoscopic exploration (Bosniak, 1986) (see Table 51–2). Bosniak class 3 and class 4 cysts have an increased chance of malignancy and may benefit from excision (Cloix et al, 1996; Santiago et al, 1998).

Caution should be used in patients with intraparenchymal cysts. Although intraoperative ultrasonography is helpful for locating deep parenchymal renal cysts, removal of the cysts may be challenging and there is a risk of injuring the collecting system or causing significant bleeding (Polascik and Marshall, 1997). Laparoscopic or percutaneous cryoablation may be helpful in these cases.

## Patient Preparation

All patients undergoing laparoscopic cyst biopsy should be informed that if malignancy is detected, more extensive resec-

| Table 51–2. | **Renal Cyst Classification Based on Bosniak Criteria** | | | | |
|---|---|---|---|---|---|
| **Type** | **Wall** | **Septations** | **Calcification** | **Precontrast Density** | **Enhancement** |
| I | Thin | None | None | 0–20 | None |
| II | Thin | None or few | Minimal | 0–20 | None |
| III | Increased thickness | Multiple | Moderate | 0–20 | None |
| IV | Thick | Many | Coarse | >20 | Present |

From Bosniak M: The current radiological approach to renal cyst. Radiology 1986;158:1-10.

tion may be performed, including simple enucleation, partial nephrectomy, or radical nephrectomy. If a lesion is clearly peripheral and does not involve the collecting system, a ureteral stent or catheter is not necessary. **If there is any question that a cyst may be in proximity to the collecting system, cystoscopy and placement of an open-ended ureteral catheter can be performed at the time of surgery and used to instill contrast material or methylene blue intraoperatively to evaluate the integrity of the collecting system after cyst excision.**

## Patient Positioning

Patient positioning depends on the type of approach (extraperitoneal vs. transperitoneal). If cystoscopy and ureteral catheter placement are required, the patient is first placed in the supine position for flexible cystoscopy or in the dorsal lithotomy position if rigid cystoscopy is used. For patients with cysts located in the anterior portion of the kidney, a transperitoneal approach is preferred. The patient is placed in a 45-degree modified flank position. Posterior lesions may be easier to approach through the retroperitoneum, where the patient is placed in the full flank position.

## Procedure

### Transperitoneal Approach

Trocar placement and renal exposure are as previously described. For right-sided dissections, caution should be exercised when dissecting the medial attachments, because the duodenum lies in close proximity. For middle pole or medial

lesions, it is often necessary to mobilize the duodenum with a Kocher maneuver (Fig. 51–15). This should be done with a combination of sharp and gentle blunt dissection. The use of cautery in this area should be avoided, because an injury to the duodenum can lead to significant morbidity or death. The cyst usually appears as a well-defined blue dome protruding from the surface of the kidney. If there is difficulty in identifying the location of the cyst, intraoperative ultrasonography can be performed. After visual inspection, the cyst is decompressed using a laparoscopic cyst aspiration needle. If suspect, the fluid can be sent for cytopathologic analysis; however, in our experience, this is of limited utility. At this point, the cyst wall is excised at its junction with the parenchyma and sent for pathologic interpretation (Fig. 51–16). If the cyst wall is too large to be easily removed through the 12-mm trocar, it should be placed in a laparoscopic retrieval sac and removed directly through the abdominal wall trocar site. **The edge of the cyst wall where normal parenchyma is encountered should be inspected and biopsies performed using the 5-mm laparoscopic biopsy forceps. If there is no evidence of malignancy, the parenchymal surface of the cyst wall can be fulgurated with electrocautery or the argon beam coagulator. Biopsy or cauterization of the center of the cyst can cause entry into the collecting system.** Surgical cellulose (Surgicel, Johnson & Johnson, Arlington, TX) can be packed into the cyst base. If malignancy is noted, the patient should have a partial or radical nephrectomy, as indicated.

A drain is usually not required; however, if the collecting system has been violated, it should be closed and a drain placed. This is accomplished by passing a hemostat through a small stab incision in a posterior axillary line under direct

**Figure 51–15.** On the right side, the colon is reflected and a Kocher maneuver may be performed to completely expose the kidney and the renal hilum.

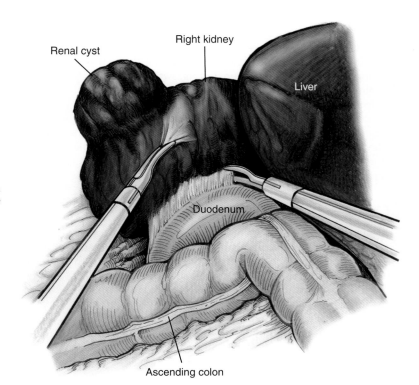

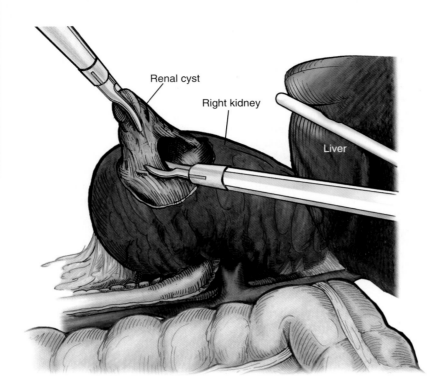

**Figure 51–16.** The cyst fluid is aspirated with a laparoscopic aspiration needle and sent for cytologic study. After decompression of the cyst, the wall can easily be grasped and manipulated. The cyst is elevated with a grasper and scissors or ultrasonic shears to circumferentially excise the cyst wall. The edge of the cyst is carefully inspected, and biopsies are performed using the 5-mm laparoscopic biopsy forceps as needed.

vision. A round suction drain is placed through a 10-mm trocar site and placed on one of the jaws of the hemostat (Fig. 51–17). The holes of the drain are placed in a dependent position.

### Retroperitoneal Approach

The retroperitoneal approach is used for posterior or lower pole lesions. With the patient in a full flank position, a 10-mm trocar is placed in the posterior axillary line, halfway between the iliac crest and the 12th rib. Once the trocar is in place, a pneumoretroperitoneum is established and the anterior abdominal wall is identified with gentle dissection of the retroperitoneal fat. The peritoneum is swept medially by "hugging" the anterior abdominal wall. The second 5-mm port is placed under direct vision in the anterior axillary line as described. A third 5-mm port can be placed superior to the second port below the rib cage. By using the perinephric fat to elevate the kidney, the surgeon readily sees the lower pole and posterior surfaces. The remainder of the procedure is as described for the transperitoneal approach.

### Results

The laparoscopic approach to symptomatic renal cystic disease has been found to be effective in decompression and pain control (Hulbert, 1992; Morgan and Rader, 1992; Munch et al, 1992; Roberts et al, 2001). Iannelli and colleagues (2003) showed that, at a mean follow-up of 60 months, 80% to 90% of patients with symptomatic renal cysts will have complete resolution of pain after laparoscopic cyst decortication. In another series of nine patients with solitary symptomatic renal cysts, 100% remained pain free at an average follow-up of 26 months (range: 3 to 63 months) (Lifson et al, 1998). Similar pain-free rates were reported by Rubenstein and associates

(1993) in 10 patients. However, in their series, 20% of the patients (2 of 10) were found to have malignancy on cyst wall biopsy, despite a negative cytologic appearance on cyst aspiration, and subsequently underwent radical nephrectomy. Santiago and associates (1998) also found unsuspected renal cell carcinoma in 4 of 35 patients with renal cysts undergoing laparoscopic exploration and cyst decortication. These series underscore the need to treat cystic tissue as though it contained renal cancer cells, by removal of specimens in closed systems (i.e., spoon grasper or entrapment sac).

## Autosomal Dominant Polycystic Kidney Disease

In cases of symptomatic ADPKD and adequate renal function, multiple cysts must be marsupialized by aspirating the cyst fluid and unroofing the cyst wall with electrocautery or ultrasonic energy. It is often necessary to unroof 100 or more cysts to adequately relieve pain (Bennett et al, 1987; Elzinga et al, 1992; Elashry et al, 1996). Because of marked distortion of the anatomy, care should be taken to avoid entering the collecting system (Cherullo et al, 1999). Laparoscopic intraoperative ultrasonography can be particularly helpful in evaluating and ablating perihilar cysts, which may be in close proximity to renal vessels.

Patients with symptomatic ADPKD and renal failure are approached as described under "Simple Nephrectomy." Multiple cysts are aspirated to decrease the size of the kidney, allowing access to the renal vessels for ligation and for ease of entrapment for removal or morcellation. Occasionally, the size, even after aspiration of many cysts, is too great to be manipulated into a retrieval device and requires removal through a low midline incision. Because these kidneys are

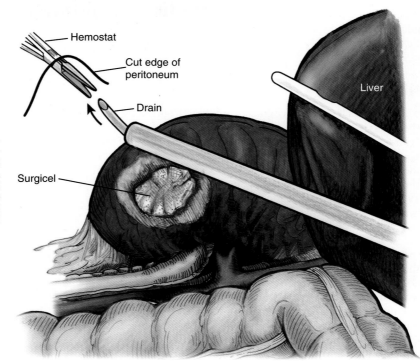

**Figure 51–17.** If the collecting system has been entered, it is closed and a drain placed. To insert the drain, a hemostat is passed through a small stab incision in the side and advanced into the abdominal cavity under direct vision. A 7-mm drain is placed through a trocar site and advanced toward the open hemostat using the trocar to direct the drain. The colon is brought back over the kidney and attached to the sidewall to "reperitonealize" the kidney and drain.

often too large to fit into an entrapment sac they may be removed by enlarging a midline incision or directly through a hand-assisted port, if used for the dissection (Jenkins et al, 2002).

## Postoperative Management

Postoperative management is as with nephrectomy; however, if there is any concern regarding an injury to the collecting system, a double-pigtail stent can be left in place for up to 4 weeks. In the postoperative period, a urinoma should be in the differential diagnosis with any patient who develops a fever (>38.5°C [101.3°F]), persistent ileus, abdominal pain, nausea or vomiting, or an elevated white blood cell count with a left shift. Retroperitoneal hematomas can also occur, and the majority of these patients can be treated conservatively with observation and other supportive measures (including transfusion). Rarely, arteriography may be required to identify and treat a source of active bleeding.

## Results

The experience with laparoscopic cyst decortication in cases of symptomatic ADPKD is increasing, and results demonstrate decreased pain and occasionally improvement in hypertension. Lee and coworkers (2003) reported unroofing an average of 220 cysts in 29 patients and found that 81% of patients had greater than 50% improvement in pain up to a mean of 3 years after cyst decortication. Furthermore, no patient showed a significant decrease in renal function and several patients had decreased blood pressure after the procedure. Their results were similar to those from historical open series (Elzinga et al, 1993). Other published series report pain-free rates ranging from 75% to 100% at 6 to 40 months of

follow-up (Barry and Lowe, 1992; Chehval et al, 1995; Segura et al, 1995; Teichman et al, 1995; Brown et al, 1996; Elashry et al, 1996; Kaouk et al, 2000; Dunn et al, 2001). Laparoscopic decortication for symptomatic ADPKD is technically feasible and less morbid than open surgery.

Laparoscopic nephrectomy is occasionally indicated in symptomatic ADPKD patients with end-stage renal disease. Several series demonstrate the feasibility of laparoscopic removal with lower morbidity when compared with open removal. However, laparoscopic nephrectomy in the ADPKD patient can be challenging owing to the large size of the kidney causing difficulty in the dissection of the renal hilum. Bendavid and associates (2004) reported their series of 22 laparoscopic nephrectomies in 19 patients with ADPKD. The mean size was 22 cm, and the mean operative time was 255 minutes. They experienced an 8% intraoperative and a 32% postoperative complication rate. Conversion to open surgery was required in 18%. Gill and colleagues (2001) compared a series of 10 bilateral synchronous laparoscopic nephrectomies performed for symptomatic ADPKD to 10 open procedures performed for the same indication. None of the laparoscopic procedures required conversion to open surgery. There was no difference in operating time, specimen weight, or blood loss between the two groups. However, there was a significant difference in the length of the hospital stay (2.4 vs. 8.1 days, $P = .001$) and narcotic use (30 vs. 177 mg, $P = .001$), favoring the laparoscopic approach. Two patients in the laparoscopic group had a retroperitoneal hematoma that did not require surgical intervention.

Because an incision is often needed to remove the large ADPKD specimens, a hand-assisted dissection may be helpful in exposure and manipulation of the kidney specimen. Several series support the use of hand-assisted surgery for bilateral ADPKD nephrectomy. The hand port is placed in the midline to allow access to both kidneys through one device, and additional trocars are placed as described for hand-assisted nephrectomy in this chapter (Rehman et al, 2001; Jenkins et al, 2002).

## NEPHROPEXY

Nephroptosis has been recognized and treated surgically since the 1800s, when nephropexy was described in Berlin by Hahn (Harrison, 1969). In one of the first urology texts, Hugh Hampton Young defined *nephroptosis* as the inferior displacement of the kidney by more than 5 cm, when the patient moves from a supine to an erect position (Young and Davis, 1926). William Mayo diagnosed "floating kidneys" in 20% of random patients, and William Osler (1892) had recorded over 700 cases of nephroptosis. The ptotic kidney has also been blamed for abnormalities and symptoms in other organs, including stomach, bowel, and pancreas. It has been estimated that over 170 innovative procedures have been described to adhere the kidney to the retroperitoneum to prevent descent while standing (Kelly, 1910; Deming, 1930; Moss, 1997).

Unfortunately, in the past nephroptosis was frequently cited as the cause of a variety of symptoms, many unrelated to the kidney, and surgical repair was greatly overutilized. Because repair did not afford patients relief of symptoms, this diagnosis was questioned to the point of extinction. Time has borne out that there are patients in whom positional changes can result in obstruction of the collecting system or blood flow to the kidney. These patients may benefit from laparoscopic surgical repair.

## Indications

Nephroptosis is characterized by a significant downward displacement (>5 cm) of the kidney as the patient moves from the supine to the erect position, causing pain in the abdomen or flank. The most severe manifestation causes *Dietl's crisis,* which is heralded by severe colicky flank pain, nausea, chills, tachycardia, oliguria, and transient hematuria or proteinuria (Irwin, 1948). The exact cause of pain is not known but is likely to be from transient renal ischemia or urinary tract obstruction (Moss, 1997). Patients who are symptomatic are generally young, thin females, who complain of pain in the erect position as the primary symptom. Several different means of evaluating the ptotic kidney are available. **The diagnosis can be made using color Doppler imaging in the supine and upright positions where diminished blood flow to the ptotic kidney in the upright position would be detected. Also, erect and supine intravenous urograms or renal scans documenting obstruction are good diagnostic studies for nephroptosis. Descent of the symptomatic kidney by two vertebral bodies and obstruction or diminished flow to the symptomatic side should be documented before surgical repair.**

## Procedure

In the transperitoneal approach, a three-port midline configuration is used (see Fig. 51–4). The kidney is fully mobilized by freeing the lower, lateral, posterior attachments (Fig. 51–18). Once cleared, the fascia overlying the quadratus lumborum and psoas muscle is easily exposed. Beginning at the upper pole, three interrupted sutures are placed laparoscopically between the lateral edge of the capsule of the kidney and the fascia overlying the quadratus lumborum or psoas muscle (Fig. 51–19). The subhepatic parietal peritoneum may also be sutured to the anterior portion of the renal capsule to provide additional support for the kidney. Sutures with a pre-placed LapraTY clip (Ethicon Endosurgery, Cincinnati, OH) can facilitate this procedure. The suture with a LapraTy clip is used for the initial pass though the quadratus lumborum or psoas muscle and then a second LapraTy is used to secure the suture on the kidney.

A retroperitoneal approach can also be used with success and may be useful in patients with prior abdominal surgery (Chueh et al, 2002; Ichikawa et al, 2003; Matsui et al, 2004). Symptomatic evaluation, along with erect and supine radiographic studies, is performed 12 weeks after surgery to evaluate the efficacy of the repair.

## Results

In a series of 26 symptomatic patients with renal ptosis evaluated with Doppler ultrasound and isotope renal scans in the supine and upright positions, Strohmeyer and colleagues (2004) showed improved blood flow and decreased symptoms in 20 of 26 patients and marked improvement in symptoms in the remaining 6 patients treated laparoscopically.

McDougall and associates (2000) reported a series of laparoscopic nephropexy done in 14 women with right flank pain and documented nephroptosis. At a mean follow-up of 3.3 years, patients reported an average of 80% improvement in pain (range: 56% to 100% improvement).

Fornara and coworkers (1997) reported their results from 23 patients (22 women and 1 man) who underwent laparoscopic nephropexy. The mean operative time was 60 minutes, and there were no complications or conversions to an open procedure. Split renal function while erect improved from 38% preoperatively to 47% postoperatively ($P = .03$). At a mean follow-up of 13 months (range: 2 to 37 months), pain intensity had improved in 21 patients. The laparoscopic group was retrospectively compared with a series of 12 patients treated with open nephropexy. Follow-up in the open group at a mean 7.6 years showed 4 patients free of pain, 5 with occasional pain, and 3 without any resolution of symptoms.

## PYELOLITHOTOMY AND URETEROLITHOTOMY

The treatment of renal and ureteral stones has gone through dramatic changes with the advent of extracorporeal shock wave lithotripsy (ESWL), percutaneous nephrolithotomy, and ureteroscopic laser lithotripsy. These new techniques have almost eliminated the need for pyelolithotomy to remove renal stones; however, there are some patients who benefit from laparoscopic pyelolithotomy. **Individuals to be considered for this approach include those who have failed ESWL or percutaneous or ureteroscopic procedures, patients with unusual anatomy such as the pelvic kidney, and patients with stones resistant to fragmentation, such as those of cystine composition. In addition, patients with**

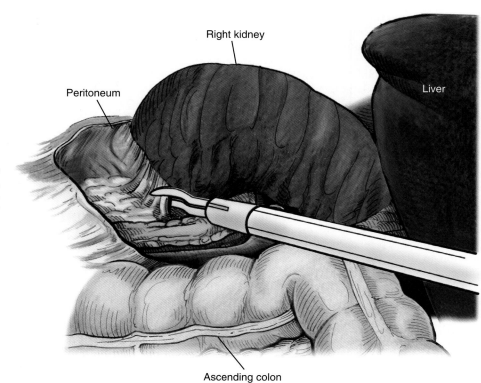

**Figure 51–18.** The kidney is stripped of overlying Gerota's fascia down to the surface of the renal capsule. All remaining attachments are divided, allowing full mobility for repositioning.

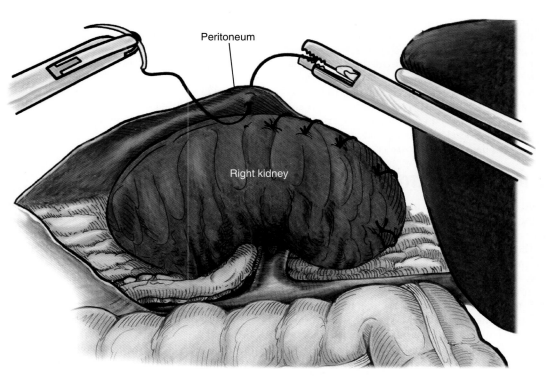

**Figure 51–19.** Once the kidney is free of lateral and posterior attachments, multiple 2-0 sutures are placed into the capsule and the lateral edge of the fascia overlying the abdominal wall.

ureteropelvic junction obstruction and renal stones undergoing laparoscopic reconstruction can have stones removed during the same procedure using a flexible cystoscope (Ball et al, 2004; Whelan et al, 2004). Successful laparoscopic transperitoneal pyelolithotomy has been reported in ectopic kidneys with stones as large as 4 cm (Chang and Dretler, 1996; Harmon et al, 1996; Hoenig et al, 1997). Laparoscopic anatrophic nephrolithotomy has also been described in several small series with low morbidity and preservation of kidney function (Gaur et al, 2002; Deger et al, 2004).

When stones develop in pelvic or ectopic kidneys, treatment may be challenging. ESWL is acceptable for initial treatment but may not be successful because of the stones' composition or position or the anatomy of the renal collecting system. Percutaneous techniques risk damage to anomalous vasculature with subsequent bleeding. To avoid damage to vessels in ectopic kidneys, several authors have used laparoscopic visualization to direct percutaneous access (Eshghi et al, 1985; Toth et al, 1993; Troxel et al, 2002).

In 1994, Gaur and colleagues reported successfully removing five of eight stones utilizing retroperitoneal laparoscopic pyelolithotomy. In two patients, the kidney was not accessed because of failure in retroperitoneal dilatation techniques. Once access to the kidney was obtained, the stones were successfully removed in five of six cases. In one case, attempts to palpate the stone in the renal pelvis before pyelotomy dislodged the stone into an upper pole calyx requiring open conversion for removal. Others have also described the retroperitoneal approach to kidney stones (Goel and Hemal, 2003).

Ureteral stones can also be approached laparoscopically. In a series of 31 patients with ureteral stones, Hemal and associates (2003) performed ureteral lithotomy with intracorporeal suturing of the ureterotomy with a mean operating room time of 67 minutes and a mean hospital stay of 2.4 days. Gaur and colleagues (2002a, 2002b) performed laparoscopic ureterolithotomy in 93 patients with only eight failed attempts, which were due to difficulty in locating the stone. The mean operating room time was 80 minutes. In many patients the ureter was not closed and subsequent urine leak ensued. When the ureter was closed, urine leak was seen for 3 days, compared with 6 days when the ureter was not closed.

## CALYCEAL DIVERTICULECTOMY

The management of calyceal diverticula with stones has always been challenging. The classic management was by open surgery. Partial nephrectomy and open marsupialization with fulguration of the diverticulum and even total nephrectomy have been used in the past (Devine et al, 1969; Williams et al, 1969; Middleton and Pfister, 1974; Timmons et al, 1975; Wulfsohn, 1980; Donnellan et al, 1999). Advances in less invasive equipment and techniques have changed the treatment of these difficult cases. **The ideal means of treating symptomatic calyceal diverticula includes removal of the stones and widening of the infundibulum to prevent urine stasis or ablation of the diverticula cavity.** Percutaneous treatment is most often used for treatment in symptomatic cases (Donnellan et al, 1999). ESWL and ureteroscopy have also been applied, but anatomic factors can result in a lower rate of achieving stone clearance (Jones et al, 1991; Pang et al, 1992;

Stream et al, 1992). Recurrence of symptoms and stones can occur if the diverticulum has not been ablated.

## Indications

**Large peripheral diverticula, those located medially near the renal hilum and those in an anterior location, may be treated using laparoscopic techniques.** A laparoscopic approach allows evacuation of the stone fragments, careful inspection, and fulguration of the cavity using argon beam or standard monopolar coagulation. Additionally, perirenal fat or biological agents can be inserted into the cavity to decrease the chance for recurrence.

## Procedure

As with the treatment of renal cysts, the location of the diverticulum dictates a transabdominal or retroperitoneal approach. Gerota's fascia is opened and perirenal fat is cleared from the surface of the kidney. **The exact location of the diverticulum in the kidney can be difficult to find. Once Gerota's fat has been removed from the kidney, the diverticulum can usually be identified by the presence of dense adhesions from the surface of the kidney to surrounding fat and a "dimpling" on the surface of the kidney.** Intraoperative fluoroscopy or ultrasonography may be necessary to confirm the correct location of the diverticulum and stones before attempting entry into the renal parenchyma. Once located, the thin parenchyma over the cavity is cauterized and opened. Spoon graspers are useful for removing stones intact. Milk of calcium stones and many small stone fragments can be encountered, despite the appearance of a solitary dense stone on conventional radiographs. Argon beam coagulation or monopolar cautery is used to fulgurate the lining of the cavity to prevent recurrence. Methylene blue can be given intravenously, and careful inspection allows detection of blue urine in the cavity, indicating communication with the collecting system. The collecting system can be closed using laparoscopic suturing techniques and perirenal fat inserted into the cavity. Stenting and drainage are performed as indicated.

## Results

Several authors have reported successful laparoscopic treatment of calyceal diverticula. This approach is associated with high stone-free rates and allows definitive management of the diverticulum to decrease the incidence of recurrence (Gluckman et al, 1993; Ruckle and Segura, 1994; Harewood et al, 1996; Wolf, 2000; Miller et al, 2002; Canales and Monga, 2003).

## LAPAROSCOPY FOR RENAL MALIGNANCY

The initial use of laparoscopy in the treatment of renal malignancies initially generated controversy based on fear of inadequate cancer control. Early laparoscopic experiences in the surgical and gynecologic literature raised concerns regarding the risk of port site seeding, inadequate surgical margins, and inaccurate staging due to morcellation. Five- and 10-year follow-up studies established the role of laparoscopy in safely treating urologic cancers. Experience has borne out that laparoscopic removal of urologic cancers provides equivalent cancer control when compared with traditional open approaches.

## Trocar or Port Site Recurrence

Port site recurrence after laparoscopic procedures in cancer patients has been described in the general surgery, gynecology, and urology literature. In a broad survey of over 1050 European general surgery programs, port site recurrence occurred in 17% of laparoscopic cholecystectomies for incidental gallbladder carcinoma and in 4.6% of cases of colorectal cancer (Paolucci et al, 1999). Studies have demonstrated that tumor cells may be deposited at the port site during laparoscopy either directly from contaminated instruments or indirectly by way of insufflation gas (Neuhaus et al, 1998; Schaeff et al, 1998; Whelan and Lee, 1999).

In the urologic literature, there have been rare reports of laparoscopic port site seeding of transitional cell carcinoma, adrenal, prostate, and renal cell carcinomas. Bangma and coworkers (1995) reported on the first patient with port site seeding from prostate cancer after laparoscopic pelvic lymph node dissection (LPLND). In contrast, Cadeddu and associates (1996) found no cases of port site seeding after 372 cases of LPLND. A review of a subset of 40 patients with positive pelvic lymph nodes for prostate cancer (at the time of LPLND) revealed no instance of port site seeding up to 3 years after surgery. Furthermore, there was no acceleration in the natural history of the disease after laparoscopic pelvic lymph node procedures (Kavoussi et al, 1993) (Table 51–3).

In the laparoscopic staging and treatment of transitional cell carcinoma, there have been seven reports of port site seeding (Stolla et al, 1994; Anderson and Steven, 1995; Ahmed et al, 1998; Elbahnasy et al, 1998; Altieri et al, 1998; Otani et al, 1999; Ong et al, 2003). In three instances, port site recurrence developed after laparoscopic staging with a biopsy or LPLND of a primary bladder tumor and in one case laparoscopic staging and biopsy of the kidney. In one of three cases related to nephrectomy, seeding developed in a patient with a tuberculous atrophic kidney containing unsuspected transitional cell carcinoma.

To date, there have been four reports of port site seeding after laparoscopic radical nephrectomy for renal cell carcinoma. In a series of 94 laparoscopic radical nephrectomies with specimen morcellation, one patient with T3 N0 M0 (Fuhrman grade IV/IV) disease suffered a solitary recurrence at one trocar site, 25 months after radical nephrectomy (Fentie et al, 2000). In the second case, a patient with a T1 N0 M0 renal cell carcinoma (Furhman grade II) underwent transperitoneal radical laparoscopic nephrectomy with morcellation of the specimen. Five months later, the patient developed disseminated metastatic renal cell carcinoma, carcinomatosis, and recurrence at all the trocar sites (Castilho et al, 2001). Port site recurrence has been reported in one radical HALN. A patient with a 10-cm T2 N0 M0, Fuhrman grade III, renal cell carcinoma was without initial tumor violation and negative surgical margins but had the specimen delivered intact through the hand port without entrapment. Specific delivery through the hand port orifice or wound (with wound protector) was not detailed. At 9 months after nephrectomy,

however, a 6 × 5-cm hand port site mass was seen. The patient was treated with wide local excision and immunotherapy (Chen et al, 2003) (Fig. 51–20). Finally, at 39 weeks after left retroperitoneoscopic radical nephrectomy, Iwamura and colleagues (2004) reported the most recent abdominal wall recurrence in a patient with a primary T3a, Fuhrman grade II, clear cell renal cell carcinoma. Importantly, tissue entrapment was not used in this case.

The exact incidence of laparoscopic port site seeding with recurrence after laparoscopic radical nephrectomy is not known. However, wound metastases after open radical nephrectomy for renal cell carcinoma are reported in approximately 0.4% (2 of 518) of cases (Uson, 1982). In open colon surgery for known cancer there is a 1.5% wound recurrence rate reported in the literature (Reilly et al, 1996). In a retrospective multicenter study, with a mean follow-up of 19.2 months (range: 1 to 72 months; 51 with greater than 2 years' follow-up), Cadeddu and coworkers (1998) reported no port site recurrence from laparoscopic nephrectomy for renal cell carcinoma in 157 cases. Comparison of long-term open versus laparoscopic nephrectomy by Portis and others (2002) demonstrates no significant differences in local or distant metastatic recurrence rates, with no wound or port site recurrence.

**Several steps should be taken to prevent port site seeding and tumor spillage. First, the basic principles of cancer surgery should be followed. Direct handling of the tissue must be minimized and all attempts made to prevent violation of the tumor. An en-bloc dissection to obtain an adequate surgical margin should be performed. All potentially cancerous tissue should be entrapped in an impermeable sack before extracting though a trocar site or hand-assisted incision. The field should be draped before morcellation or extraction** (Urban et al, 1993) (Table 51–4).

Morcellation of specimens for extraction has raised concerns about accurate pathologic staging. CT has been proved

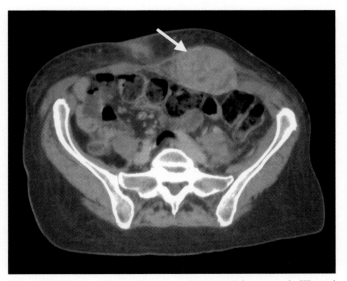

**Figure 51–20.** A patient with a 10-cm T2 N0 M0 Fuhrman grade III renal cell carcinoma was treated using hand-assisted laparoscopic nephrectomy with intact specimen removal through the hand port. Nine months after surgery he presented with 6 × 5-cm mass that was found to be renal cell carcinoma. (Courtesy of Y. T. Chen.)

**Table 51–3. Trocar or Port Site Recurrence (PSR) after Laparoscopic Surgery**

| Author | Pathology (Primary TNM Stage, Grade) | Primary Laparoscopic Approach | Recurrence Identification/ Month Post-Op | Management |
|---|---|---|---|---|
| Iwamura et al, 2004 | Renal cell carcinoma | Retroperitoneoscopic, extracted intact without entrapment sac or wound protector | CT mass in left flank at 39 mos | Refused further treatment |
| Chen et al, 2003 | Renal cell carcinoma T2N0M0, Fuhrman III/IV | Hand-assisted, transperitoneal | Clinically palpable with CT confirmation at 9 months | Operative excision, biopsy, and immunotherapy referral |
| Castilho et al, 2001 | Renal cell carcinoma (morcellated specimen, stage not reported, Fuhrman IV/IV) | Transperitoneal | Abdominal masses identified on CT | Interferon-alfa immunotherapy. Patient died 8 months post nephrectomy. |
| Fentie et al, 2000 | Renal cell carcinoma (T3N0M0, Fuhrman IV/IV) | Transperitoneal | Port site discomfort with solid mass CT confirmation at 25 months | Surgical excision, every 3-month clinical and radiographic (CXR, CT) follow-up. No evidence of disease at 35 months post nephrectomy. |
| Ong et al, 2003 | Ureteral transitional cell carcinoma (T1NxMx, "high grade") | Extraperitoneal | Clinically palpable with CT confirmation at 12 months | Operative excision with negative pathologic margins and 18-month follow-up |
| Otani et al 1999 | Transitional cell carcinoma (TNM not reported, "high grade"). TCC invasive into renal parenchyma with one positive hilar lymph node | Extraperitoneal. | Painful mass at trocar site, with CT confirmation at 3 months | Ultrasound biopsy for confirmation. No other management reported. |
| Ahmed et al, 1998 | Transitional cell carcinoma (stage not reported, "high grade"). TCC invasion with small vascular focus of invasion | "Laparoscopic" nephrectomy | Painful umbilical port site 8 months post nephrectomy | Open positive biopsy with CT follow-up demonstrating residual local recurrence at renal fossa, along psoas muscle, and hepatic metastases. Patient referred for chemotherapy. No follow-up was reported. |
| Andersen et al, 1995 | Transitional cell carcinoma T4bNxM0, grade 2 | Transperitoneal laparoscopic staging and biopsy | Palpable nodule "shortly after" biopsy | Open exploration with positive biopsy. Tumor involvement of urachus, anterior abdominal wall, and preaortic lymph nodes |
| Altieri et al, 1998 | Transitional cell carcinoma (T2NxM0, grade 2 (at time of LPLND; T3N0M0, grade 3 after open cystectomy and ureterosigmoidoscopy) | Transperitoneal | Right lower extremity edema 3 months post cystectomy, with positive CT for right pelvic lymphadenopathy and 3 cm right superior port site mass | Open biopsy positive for TCC. Patient refused chemotherapy and died 3 months later. |
| Bangma et al, 1995 | LPLND for CaP (T3N1M0, grade 2) | Transperitoneal | Clinically palpable at 6 months | Aspiration cytologic confirmation with no other diagnostic or therapeutic maneuvers. Patient died 8 months post lymphadenectomy. |
| Stolla et al, 1994 | LPLND for transitional cell carcinoma (T3N1M0, grade 2) | Transperitoneal | Clinically palpable subcutaneous masses at multiple port sites, with CT confirmation | Observation secondary to previous post-LPLND failure of M-VAC chemotherapy and external-beam irradiation. Hepatic mass identified on CT. Patient died 1 month after PSR recognition. |
| Matsui et al, 2004 | Squamous cell carcinoma of the renal pelvis (T3N0M0) | Retroperitoneoscopic nephroureterectomy | Clinically palpable with CT confirmation at 6 months | Surgical excision with mesh repair of aponeurotic defect. Disease free at 6-month follow-up from excision. |
| Rassweiler et al, 2003 | Metastatic small cell carcinoma to adrenal. (TNM not reported) Nonseminomatous germ cell tumor to the retroperitoneum. (TNM not reported) | Not reported | CT (adrenal lesion)/month not reported | Not reported. Each patient died within 6 months after identification of PSR. |
| Chen et al, J Urol 2002 | Metastatic small cell carcinoma to adrenal (stage IIb small cell carcinoma of lung) | Transperitoneal | Clinically palpable with CT confirmation at 5 months | Palliative external-beam irradiation; patient died 10 10 months post-adrenalectomy. |

CT, computed tomography; LPLND, laparoscopic lymph node dissection; CXR, chest radiograph; CaP, carcinoma of the prostate.

to be an effective tool for planning surgery and predicting pathologic findings. The overall accuracy of CT in staging renal cell carcinoma ranges from 72% to 90% (Johnson et al, 1987; London et al, 1989; Parks and Kelley, 1994; Zagoria et al, 1995). Roberts and colleagues (2005) retrospectively reviewed the records of 296 patients treated for renal cell carcinoma with nephrectomy between 1990 and 1999 who had CT or MRI preoperatively. Pathologic results were then compared with preoperative imaging for staging comparison. Of the patients with clinical T1 tumors, 67% had pathologic T1 tumors and 31% had pathologic T3a tumors. Mean tumor size for the pT1 group was 3.9 cm, and it was 3.8 cm for the pT3a patients. Kaplan-Meier analysis showed the 5-year recurrence-free survival to be the same for the pT1 (91%) and pT3a (98%) groups.

In a review of 172 renal tumors treated with open radical nephrectomy, Shalhav and coworkers (1998) correlated the preoperative CT-based clinical stage with the final pathologic tumor stage. They found 1 tumor (0.6%) to be understaged and 7 tumors (4%) overstaged by preoperative CT. They concluded that clinical CT staging of low-stage renal tumors is reliable and tends to overstage rather than understage renal tumors. Currently, if a patient with clinically localized renal cell carcinoma is found to have microscopically advanced disease, there is no effective adjunct therapy. Thus, morcellation does not alter subsequent follow-up, treatment, or survival in pT1 and pT3a patients. The long-term follow-up in laparoscopic series in which kidneys are morcellated compared with open radical nephrectomy shows equivalent cancer-free survival (Barrett et al, 1998; Ono et al, 2000; Chan et al, 2001). When pathologic staging is required, the specimen may be removed intact through a low midline or Pfannenstiel incision. Landman and coworkers (2000) reported on the ability of pathologists to read renal specimens before and after morcellation. They found that morcellation of kidneys after radical nephrectomy did not change the determination of histopathology, grade, or local invasion compared with findings in nonmorcellated specimens.

## TRANSPERITONEAL RADICAL NEPHRECTOMY

Radical nephrectomy for patients with clinically localized renal cell carcinoma provides the best opportunity for cure. However, the pain, morbidity, and cosmetic changes associated with an open flank incision can be significant. The laparoscopic approach to renal cell carcinoma has evolved into a safe and effective minimally invasive alternative to open surgery. The disease-free and cancer-specific survival rates for laparoscopic radical nephrectomy are comparable with those of open surgery (Permpongkosol et al, 2005) (Table 51–5).

## Indications and Contraindications

Laparoscopic radical nephrectomy is indicated in patients with T1 to T3a renal tumors. In addition, laparoscopic radical nephrectomy has been applied to patients with advanced stages of renal cell carcinoma and those with large tumors (Walther et al, 1999; Pautler et al, 2002). Some patients with tumor thrombus extending into the renal vein can also be treated with laparoscopic radical nephrectomy (Desai et al, 2003). Patients with a prior history of ipsilateral renal surgery, perinephric inflammation, or extensive intra-abdominal surgery are still candidates for laparoscopic surgery, based on the experience of the surgeon and an informed patient who understands that it may be necessary to convert to open surgery. Although tumors with a small vein thrombus have been treated laparoscopically, with current limits in technology renal tumors with thrombus extending to the level of the liver represent a challenge to the laparoscopic approach.

## Preoperative Evaluation

The preoperative evaluation of the patient with a suspected renal malignancy is the same whether an open or a laparoscopic approach is planned. A complete metastatic evaluation is necessary and includes an abdominal CT and chest radiograph or chest CT. A bone scan is obtained in patients with elevated serum calcium or alkaline phosphatase levels and in those with symptomatic bone pain. If there is a question of renal vein tumor thrombus, then an appropriate study (MRI, venography, sonography, or three-dimensional CT) to preoperatively evaluate the vein is required. Contralateral renal function is assessed before radical nephrectomy by measuring serum creatinine levels and evaluating the kidney appearance on contrast medium–enhanced CT. In equivocal cases, a functional renal scan and 24-hour urinary creatinine clearance studies can be obtained. The presence of renal insufficiency should prompt the surgeon to consider partial nephrectomy.

## Positioning and Trocar Placement

Patient positioning and trocar placement are similar to those described for the simple nephrectomy (see Fig. 51–4). Three ports are generally sufficient to complete the procedure, although a fourth trocar may be necessary for organ entrapment or liver or bowel retraction during nephrectomy.

## Procedure

### Reflection of the Colon

The colon is reflected to provide adequate visualization of the anterior surface of Gerota's fascia. On the right, the duodenum is mobilized medially, using the Kocher maneuver, until the vena cava is clearly visualized.

---

**Table 51–4. Prevention of Port Site Seeding during Laparoscopy for Malignancy**

- Avoid resection and excision of tissue in presence of carcinomatosis.
- Isolate ascitic fluid to be sent for cytology from all wounds.
- Minimize direct tumor handling to prevent iatrogenic tumor violation.
- Ensure wide en-bloc dissection of tumor and surrounding tissues.
- Place all tissues within an impermeable laparoscopic sac before morcellation or tissue extraction.
- Re-drape port sites at time of tissue removal.
- Remove all possible contaminated instrumentation from the newly towel-draped operative field.
- Change the surgeons' and technicians' gloves before formal peritoneal closure.

## Table 51–5. Results of Laparoscopic Radical Nephrectomy

| Author | Approach | Indication | OR Time | LOH | EBL | Conversion | Complications | Morcellation | Intact | Follow-up | Local Recurrence | Metastatic Disease |
|---|---|---|---|---|---|---|---|---|---|---|---|---|
| McDougall et al, 1996 | Transperitoneal N = 17 | T1-T2 | 414 min | 4 days | 105 mL | 6% | 18% | 29% | 71% | 14 mo | 0 | 0 |
| Cadeddu et al, 1998 | Transperitoneal N = 139 | T1, T2 | NA | NA | NA | 4% | 10% | 90% | 10% | 19 mo | 1% | 3% |
| | Retroperitoneal N = 18 | | | | | | | | | | | |
| Abbou et al, 1999 | Retroperitoneal N = 29 | T1 | 145 min | 5 days | 100 mL | 0 | 8% | 0 | 100% | | 3% | 0 |
| Ono et al, 1999 | Transperitoneal N = 34 | T1, T2 | 300 min | 11 days | 225 mL | 2% | | | | 60 mo | 0 | 3% |
| | Retroperitoneal N = 15 | | | | | | | | | | | |
| Barrett and Fentie, 1999 | Transperitoneal N = 94 | T1-T4 | 173 min | 4.6 days | | 10% | 9% | 89% | 11% | 36 mo | 4% | 2% |
| Gill et al, 2000 | Retroperitoneal N = 53 | T1, T2 | 180 min | 2 days | 128 mL | 4% | 17% | 0 | 100% | 13 mo | 0 | 4% |
| Jeschke et al, 2000 | Transperitoneal N = 51 | T1, T2 | 125 min | 7 days | | 0 | 4% | 0 | 100% | 8 mo | 0 | 0 |
| Janetschek et al, 2000 | Transperitoneal N = 100 | T1, T2 | 137 min | 7 days | 168 mL | 0 | 10% | 0 | 100% | 14 mo | 0 | 0 |
| Dunn et al, 2000 | Transperitoneal N = 55 | T1, T2, T3 | 330 min | 3.4 days | 172 mL | 1% | 3%* | 65% | 35% | 25 mo | 0 | 8% |
| | Retroperitoneal N = 6 | | | | | | | | | | | |
| Chan et al, 2001 | Transperitoneal N = 67 | T1, T2 | 256 min | 3.8 | 289 mL | 1% | 15% | 60% | 40% | 21 mo | 0 | 3% |

*Major complications.
LOH, length of hospitalization; EBL, estimated blood loss.

## Dissection of the Ureter

The midureter is located in the retroperitoneal fat medial to the psoas muscle. During proximal mobilization, the gonadal vein is usually first encountered and may be elevated with the ureter. The ureter is located just posterior to the gonadal vein, anterior to the psoas muscle. The psoas tendon is a reliable landmark when searching for the gonadal and ureter (Fig. 51–21). Once located, the ureter is elevated, revealing the psoas muscle and traced proximally to identify the renal hilum.

## Mobilization of the Lower Pole

As opposed to a simple nephrectomy, the radical nephrectomy preserves Gerota's fascia so that the renal parenchyma and mass are not visualized during this operation. Once the ureter is mobilized up to the ureteropelvic junction, forceps are inserted beneath Gerota's fascia and lower pole along the psoas fascia. The specimen is lifted superolaterally; and with the use of the suction-irrigator and electrosurgical scissors, the inferior and posterior sidewall attachments are divided. The inferior cone of Gerota's fascia lateral to the ureter is also divided. To facilitate this dissection and assist with lateral specimen retraction during the hilar dissection, the fourth port may be necessary, as outlined earlier. Dissection of the renal hilum requires (1) the kidney to be displaced laterally to render the renal vessels taut and (2) the bowel must be retracted medially by gravity or with assistance from a laparoscopic retractor to fully expose the renal hilum.

## Securing the Renal Blood Vessels

During right-sided radical nephrectomies, retraction of the liver to improve visualization of the renal hilum and upper pole is usually necessary and can be accomplished by passing a 3- or 5-mm instrument through a fourth trocar placed below the ribs in the anterior axillary line. Visualization of the renal vein is accomplished by using the tip of the irrigator-aspirator to dissect individual layers of lymphatics and tissue from the lower pole of the kidney to the renal hilum. The renal artery and vein are usually individually dissected and divided. The surgeon places the renal hilum on gentle tension by lifting the lower pole laterally. With the use of the electrosurgical scissors and the suction-irrigator, the hilum is identified by moving cephalad along the medial aspect of the ureter and renal pelvis. From an anterior approach, the renal vein is first identified.

Once the renal vein is dissected, the renal artery can readily be identified and transected with the GIA stapler (Fig. 51–22). On the left side the gonadal, lumbar, and adrenal branches of the renal vein are identified and divided using either bipolar cautery, ultrasonic energy, or clips. The renal vein is ligated and transected with a GIA stapler. **If nylon or metal clips to secure renal branches are used, the surgeon must ensure that these clips are not included in the jaws of the stapler. The clips will prevent anticipated activation of the staples and result in bleeding.** Alternating clips can be used to secure the artery and vein. When using clips, three should be placed proximally to minimize the risk of dislodgement. Extended lymphadenectomy can be readily performed once the vessels are identified and dissected circumferentially. On occasion (i.e., large tumors, bleeding) one may need to transect the renal vein before occluding the artery.

## Dissection of the Upper Pole

The decision whether to remove the ipsilateral adrenal with the specimen determines the superior margin of dissection. If

**Figure 51–21.** The ureter alone or the ureter and gonadal vein together are elevated with a grasper and mobilized cephalad. As the cephalad dissection approaches the renal hilum, the gonadal vein crosses anterior to the ureter. On the right side the angle of insertion from the gonadal to the vena cava can be a source of significant bleeding if torn during elevation.

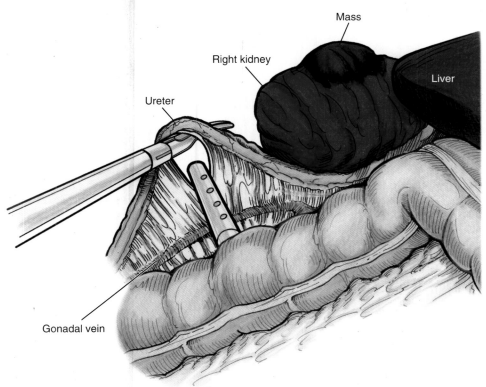

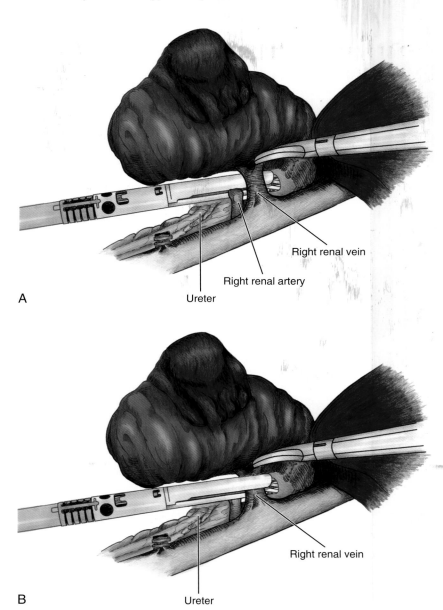

Right renal vein

Right renal artery

A

Ureter

Right renal vein

B

Ureter

**Figure 51–22.** **A,** After mobilization of the lower pole and posterior attachments, the renal hilum is exposed. The vein is displaced to expose the artery, and a plane is dissected to allow the introduction of the vascular GIA stapler. **B,** The renal vein is also divided with an endovascular vascular stapler after the artery or arteries have been secured. After passing the tips of the stapler around the renal vein, the vein is positioned in the middle of the jaws of the stapler.

the adrenal gland is not removed, upper and lateral attachments to Gerota's fascia are incised. Care must be taken to avoid injury to the diaphragm at this point. If the adrenal gland is to be removed on the right side with the specimen, control and division of the adrenal vein is imperative. Dissection cephalad along the vena cava identifies the adrenal vein. Once it is divided, the superior, medial, and posterior attachments of the adrenal are mobilized (Fig. 51–23). For left-sided tumors, the GIA is placed proximal to the adrenal vein if the adrenal gland is to be taken with the specimen. If the gland is to be left, the GIA is positioned distal to the adrenal vein.

## Specimen Entrapment and Extraction

Intra-abdominal entrapment of the excised specimen is performed to facilitate removal. If it is to be removed intact through an incision, a 15-mm deployable sac is recommended. It consists of a plastic bag attached to a self-opening, flexible metal ring. The primary advantage of a self-opening

bag is that the specimen can be easily manipulated into the opening of the bag with a single grasper.

The retrieval device is 15 mm and thus needs to be placed through one of the 10-mm trocar sites after the trocar has been removed (Fig. 51–24). Once the specimen is placed into the sac, the opening is withdrawn through the trocar site. Using electrocautery, the trocar site is enlarged to allow extraction of the specimen, and the specimen and sac are protected by the surgeon's finger positioned through the trocar site alongside the specimen (Fig. 51–25). Alternatively, the kidney can be removed through a Pfannenstiel incision.

If the specimen is to be morcellated, a LapSac (Cook Urological, Inc., Spencer, IN) fabricated from a double layer of plastic and nondistensible nylon should be used. This sac has been shown to be impermeable to bacteria and tumor cells even after its use for morcellation (Urban et al, 1993). The LapSac is prepared by passing a moistened hydrophilic wire alternating through every third hole in the sac. The sac is then

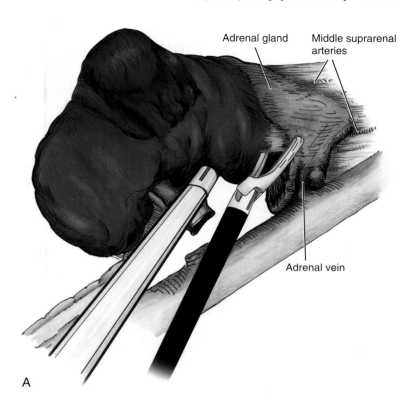

Adrenal gland

Middle suprarenal arteries

Adrenal vein

**A**

**Figure 51–23.** **A,** Adrenal-sparing right radical nephrectomy. Bipolar or ultrasonic energy devices are used to release all adreno-colic attachments. Inferior retraction of the specimen facilitates exposure of this surgical plane. **B,** Inclusion of the adrenal gland with right radical nephrectomy can be readily accomplished using ultrasonic or bipolar shears to control the multiple arterial branches to the adrenal gland.

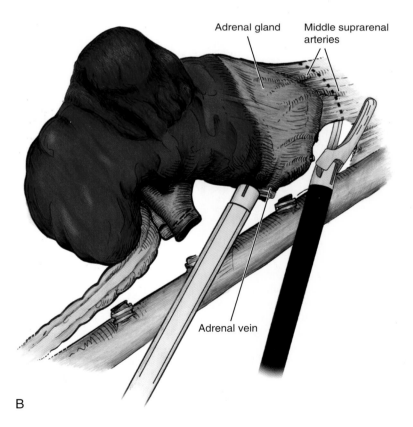

Adrenal gland

Middle suprarenal arteries

Adrenal vein

**B**

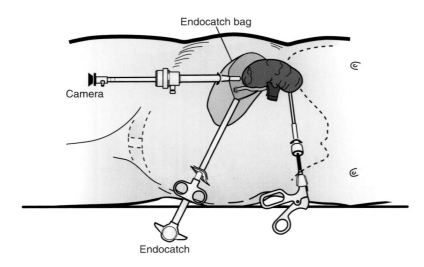

**Figure 51–24.** Placement of a specimen into an opened Endocatch device placed through an umbilical trocar site. Note that the camera is positioned in the lateral port and the specimen is maneuvered through the upper midline trocar. (From Bishoff JT, Kavoussi LR [eds]: Atlas of Laparoscopic Retroperitoneal Surgery. Philadelphia, WB Saunders, 2000.)

**Figure 51–25.** For removal of the intact specimen, a 4- to 6-cm incision is made including one of the trocar sites. The surgeon's finger protects the specimen and underlying structures from injury.

rolled from the bottom of the sac toward the top and the roll placed though a 12-mm trocar site with the free ends of the wire protruding from the trocar site. The trocar is then replaced alongside the wires. The sac is unrolled, and the wire will help to hold the mouth of the sac in an open position (Wakabayashi et al, 2003). Once introduced, it is held open with several graspers and the specimen is placed in the entrapment sac (Fig. 51–26). The wire is then withdrawn and the drawstring is grasped, tightened, and withdrawn into the 10-mm umbilical port. The neck of the sac is pulled tightly against the abdomen. Enlarging the trocar site by 1 cm will allow small amounts of tissue to protrude through the mouth of the sac. The morcellation process is performed by grasping only tissue protruding from the mouth of the sac with alternating bites from a ring forceps to break up the parenchyma

and a Kocher clamp to pull apart the tenacious collecting system. Deep passes into the sac should be avoided because bowel resting near the edge of the sac can be inadvertently grasped and pulled into the sac and injured. All of the morcellated tissue is carefully collected and sent for histopathologic evaluation. The pneumoperitoneum should be preserved throughout the morcellation process so that the intraabdominal portion of the sac can be monitored laparoscopically for possible perforation. Surgical towels are placed around the sac, and the entire surgical field is covered to prevent port site contamination with any spillage of the morcellated specimen (Fig. 51–27).

In a series comparing patient outcomes of 33 morcellated specimens and 23 intact kidneys, the patents had no difference in surgical time, postoperative pain, or hospital stay. The only

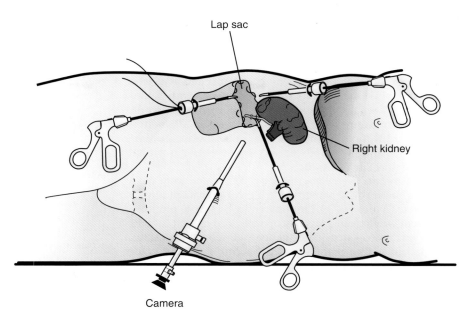

**Figure 51–26.** In cases in which the kidney is morcellated, the LapSac (Cook Urological, Inc., Spencer, IN) entrapment sac is introduced through the lateral 10-mm trocar site after passing a hydrophilic wire through the opening of the LapSac. After the entrapment sac is released within the abdomen, the 10-mm port is replaced and the sac is unfurled. The wire will facilitate opening the bag and placement of the specimen. A lateral 5- or 3-mm port may be necessary to assist with holding placement of the specimen inside the LapSac. Once the specimen is within the LapSac, the wire is removed, the bag cinched closed, and the opening withdrawn through the 10-mm trocar site.

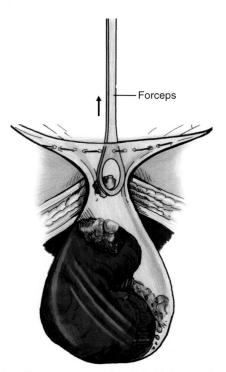

**Figure 51–27.** The entrapment sac is pulled tightly up against the abdominal wall with two hands pushing part of the specimen to appear through the opening of the LapSac. After the site is carefully draped, manual morcellation with ring forceps or a Kelly clamp can be used, and the entrapment sac is removed once the remaining specimen fragments are small enough to be extracted through the trocar site. Only the tissue visible from the opening is grasped. Blind passes into the bag may injure surrounding bowel segments.

**Table 51–6. Laparoscopic Radical Nephrectomy for Renal Cell Carcinoma: Long-Term Cancer-Specific Survival in 248 Patients**

| Pathologic Stage | No. of Patients | 5 Year | 10 Year |
|---|---|---|---|
| T1a N0 M0 | 169 | 94% | 88% |
| T1b N0 M0 | 69 | 90% | NA |
| T2 N0 M0 | 10 | 100% | NA |

From Ono Y, Hattori R, Gotoh M, et al: Laparoscopic radical nephrectomy for renal cell carcinoma: The standard of care already? Curr Opin Urol 2005;15:75-78.

significant difference was the length of incision, which was a mean 1.2 cm in the morcellation group and 7 cm in the intact removal group (Hernandez et al, 2003).

## Results

Five- and 10-year cancer survival data demonstrate that laparoscopic radical nephrectomy is equivalent to open radical nephrectomy in the treatment of renal cancer. Consequently, laparoscopic radical nephrectomy has become a standard of care for most renal malignancies. Ono and associates (2005) reported their results from 312 patients with histopathologically proved renal cell carcinoma. They found 5- and 10-year cancer-specific survival equal to that seen in open series (Table 51–6). Others have reported similar long-term survival using the laparoscopic approach. Portis and colleagues (2002) reported results from three different centers that started performing laparoscopic nephrectomy in the early 1990s. This report compared the surgical outcomes of laparoscopic and open nephrectomy for renal cancer with a median follow-up of 54 months (range: 0 to 94 months) for the laparoscopic group and 69 months (range: 8 to 114 months) in the open group. Kaplan-Meier analysis showed 5-year recurrence-free survival of 92% for laparoscopy and 91% for open nephrectomy ($P = .583$). The 5-year cancer-specific survival was found to be 98% for laparoscopy and 92% for open surgery ($P = .124$).

In one of the largest published series, Saika and associates (2003) presented their results from 195 patients with pathologic stage T1 renal cell carcinoma treated with laparoscopic radical nephrectomy. At a median follow-up of 40 months (range: 2 to 121 months) they found a 5-year disease-free survival of 91% and overall 5-year survival of 94%. No patient developed port site recurrence.

Similar results were described by Fentie and colleagues (2000) in a series of 57 patients with T1 to T4 renal cell tumors followed for a mean of 33.4 months (range: 14 to 70 months). All patients were treated laparoscopically, and in each case the kidney was morcellated. Three patients developed metastasis. One patient with a pathologic T3 N0 M0, Fuhrman grade III/IV tumor developed a recurrence in the renal fossa and chest metastasis 14 months after surgery. A second patient with a pathologic T2 N0 M0, Fuhrman grade II/IV tumor developed metastasis to the bone 20 months after radical nephrectomy. Finally, a patient with a pathologic T3 N0 M0 Fuhrman grade IV/IV tumor developed a solitary port site recurrence more than 2 years after nephrectomy (Barrett and Fentie, 1999).

Permpongkosol and associates (2005) reported their experience comparing 67 laparoscopic nephrectomies with 54 patients undergoing open removal. All patients were clinical stage cT1 to cT2 N0 M0. There were no differences in patient age, tumor size, and estimated blood loss differences between the two procedures. The patients in the laparoscopic group, however, did consistently have a shorter period of hospitalization. The mean operating time was 193 minutes in the open group, which was faster than in the laparoscopic group (256 minutes). A significant operating time difference between the first 34 and last 33 laparoscopic radical nephrectomies existed, reinforcing the notion of the learning curve. **The calculated disease-free survival rates for laparoscopic and open radical nephrectomy were 95% and 89%, respectively, at 10 years, and the actuarial survival rates for laparoscopic and open radical nephrectomy were 86% and 75%, respectively, at 10 years.** These differences were not statistically significant, and no laparoscopic trocar site implantation was identified. One operative conversion (1.5%) was required in the laparoscopic group. Complications occurred in 10 patients (15%) in the laparoscopic group and 8 (15%) in the open group. Six laparoscopic patients required blood transfusions (8%), compared with 11 in the open group.

Gill and associates (2000) compared a series of 53 laparoscopic radical nephrectomies to 34 open radical nephrectomies. There were no differences in body mass index, age, American Society of Anesthesiologists status, tumor size, specimen weight, or surgical time between the two groups. In the 53 laparoscopic radical nephrectomies for tumors with a mean size of 4.6 cm (range: 2 to 12 cm), the mean specimen weight was 484 g. All specimens were removed intact. Minor complications occurred in eight patients (17%,) and major complications requiring conversion to open surgery occurred in two patients (4%). The laparoscopic approach was found to have less blood loss ($P = .001$), a shorter hospital stay ($P = .001$), lower analgesic requirements ($P = .001$), and shorter

convalescence ($P = .005$) compared with open radical nephrectomy. Complications were seen in 13% of the laparoscopic patients and in 24% of the open surgical candidates. Similar results have been reported by other investigators comparing open and laparoscopic radical nephrectomy (Kerbl et al, 1994; McDougall et al, 1996; Clayman et al, 1997).

# RETROPERITONEAL RADICAL NEPHRECTOMY

Access to the kidney through the retroperitoneum requires creation of a working space from a potential space. Clayman and associates (1991) were the first to perform a complete retroperitoneal nephrectomy. Gaur (1992) described a simple technique using readily available and inexpensive equipment to create a balloon for access to the retroperitoneum. The utility of this approach has been shown in many different series for all laparoscopic kidney procedures as well as ureteral and adrenal surgery.

## Indications and Contraindications

The indications for laparoscopic retroperitoneal nephrectomy (LRPN) are the same as those for open, laparoscopic, and hand-assisted nephrectomy. In addition, patients with extensive transperitoneal surgery may still maintain well-preserved tissue planes in the retroperitoneum, allowing the surgeon to avoid abdominal adhesions. Additional potential advantages include more direct access to the renal vessels for early control.

Relative contraindications include previous retroperitoneal surgery, large tumors with possible adjacent organ involvement, and infectious disease processes. Because the retroperitoneal space is a potential space that must be created, prior renal surgery may make it difficult to approach using LRPN. Dense adhesions may result from recurrent infections, tuberculosis, xanthogranulomatous pyelonephritis, prior episodes of pyelonephritis, and extracorporeal shock wave lithotripsy. Typically, uncomplicated percutaneous stone procedures do not create extensive scar tissue preventing access to the kidney using LRPN. Evaluation with preoperative CT may reveal adhesions that may be difficult to approach with LRPN. Disadvantages include disorientation due to unfamiliar landmarks being obscured by adipose tissue. The small working space can make trocar placement, instrument movement, and organ manipulation difficult.

## Positioning and Trocar Placement

The patient is placed in the full lateral position, similar to open nephrectomy, with the hips flexed and the kidney rest elevated. A 15-mm incision is made off the tip of the 12th rib, which will serve as the middle trocar and is usually used for the camera port (Fig. 51–28). The index finger is inserted through the incision and used for blunt dissection to create a hole from the skin through the muscle into the retroperitoneal space. If the finger is in the correct position, the surgeon should feel the smooth surface of psoas muscle and the lower pole of the kidney covered by Gerota's fascia (Fig. 51–29).

The potential working space can be created with a balloon made from the two fingers of a size 8 or 9 glove secured with silk suture over a red rubber catheter (Fig. 51–30). Commercial balloons are available and offer the advantage of dilation under direct vision. The empty balloon catheter is inserted into the space and directed under the kidney. It is then filled to 600- to 800-mL capacity with normal saline and removed. Usually an instrument trocar is placed posterior to the initial trocar site by directing the nonbladed trocar onto the tip of an inserted finger. A Blunt Tip Trocar (U.S. Surgical, Norwalk, CT) is used to seal the trocar site and because of its low profile, it will not obstruct the view or working space (Fig. 51–31). The retroperitoneum is insufflated to 15 to 20 mm Hg. The posterior trocar allows use of a dissector or aspirator to push the peritoneum medially allowing adequate space for placement of the anterior secondary trocars. These include a 12-mm trocar to allow placement of an endovascular stapler and a fourth trocar for retraction and elevation of the kidney.

## Procedure

The first step in the LRPN is to identify the psoas muscle and psoas tendon. From the psoas tendon, medial dissection will reveal the ureter, which is then elevated and followed to the lower pole of the kidney. Because the instruments are being placed perpendicular to the ureter during dissection, the surgeon must be aware of the close proximity of the ureter to the aorta on the left and the vena cava on the right. Elevation of the lower pole of the kidney places the renal vessels on stretch, assisting with dissection. Visualization of the ureter and psoas helps with orientation, which can be especially valuable on the right side where the vena cava is close to the renal hilum.

By dissecting medially, the renal artery is identified. The pulsating artery is dissected with a right-angled dissector and divided with an endovascular stapler or with clips according to the surgeon's preference. On the left side the lumbar vein may be encountered first or intimately involved with the renal artery and can be unwittingly injured during dissection of the artery. Once the artery is divided, the vein is usually readily apparent and, once circumferentially dissected, can be divided with an endovascular stapler. **However when the vein is identified, the surgeon should recheck the orientation of the camera and the relationship of the vein to the ureter and psoas to ensure that the identified structure is the renal vein and not the vena cava. Care must be taken because there are reports of dividing the vena cava during LRPN with the**

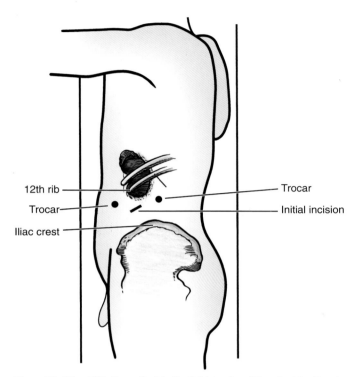

**Figure 51–28.** With the patient in the full lateral position, the hips flexed, and the kidney rest elevated, a 15-mm incision is made 2 cm below the tip of the 12th rib, between the rib and the anterior superior iliac spine.

**Figure 51–29.** The index finger is inserted through the incision and used for blunt dissection to create a hole from the skin through the muscle into the retroperitoneal space. If the finger is in the correct position, the surgeon should feel the smooth surface of psoas muscle and the lower pole of the kidney covered by Gerota's fascia.

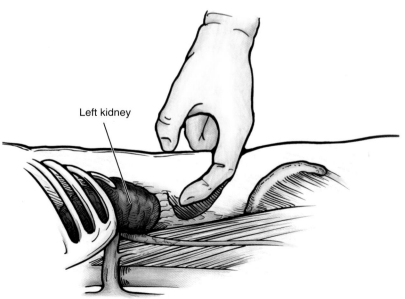

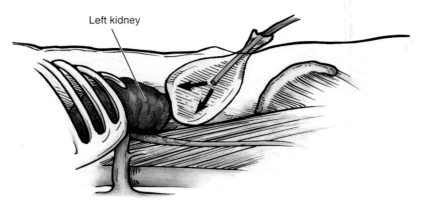

Left kidney

**Figure 51–30.** To quickly create the working space, we insert an inexpensive Gaur balloon created from the two fingers of a size 8 or 9 glove, secured with silk suture over a simple red rubber catheter. The balloon is then filled with 600 to 800 mL of saline.

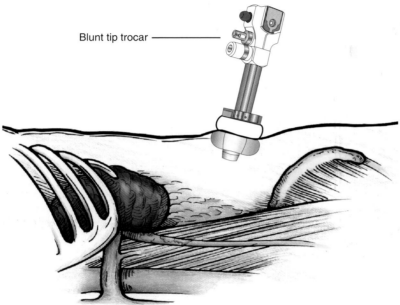

Blunt tip trocar

**Figure 51–31.** A Blunt Tip Trocar (U.S. Surgical, Norwalk, CT) is used to seal the trocar site. Because of its low profile it will not obstruct the view or take up useful space in the retroperitoneum. The balloon/collar configuration eliminates the need for sutures and allows 360-degree rotation.

**endovascular stapler** (see "Complications of Laparoscopic Renal Surgery" later in this chapter).

Next the lower pole attachments are dissected and the gonadal vessel is divided. The posterior attachments along the length of the kidney are freed, and the kidney is then lowered so that the anterior surface can be dissected. Depending on the indication for nephrectomy the adrenal gland is removed with the specimen or left in place. The retroperitoneal approach offers excellent visualization of the adrenal gland.

Entrapment of the specimen is done with an entrapment bag if removed intact or with a LapSac when morcellated. With intact removal the patient should be warned about the possibility of nerve injury and a resulting flank bulge, even with a small flank incision.

## Results

**Compared with a transperitoneal approach, a retroperitoneal approach offers similar outcomes in complication rates, pain medication requirements, length of hospital stay, and time to return to normal activity** (McDougall et al, 1996). Even with an extraperitoneal operation, injury to intra-abdominal organs can occur, and a hernia can be created during balloon dilatation of the extraperitoneal space.

There are two prospective randomized transperitoneal versus retroperitoneal laparoscopic nephrectomy series reported in the literature. Desai and colleagues (2005) published results on 50 patients randomized to transperitoneal and 52 patients to an LRPN for renal tumors averaging 5 cm in size. They found no difference in blood loss, narcotic requirements, hospital stay, or complications. The retroperitoneal approach had a shorter mean operative time of 150 minutes compared with 207 minutes in the transperitoneal series ($P = .001$).

Nambirajan and associates (2004) randomized 40 patients into two equal groups with a mean tumor size of 4.5 cm. They found no difference between the two approaches for laparoscopic kidney removal when comparing number and size of trocars, pathologic stage, operating room time, blood loss, length of hospital stay, or incidence of complications. Operating room times in the retroperitoneal group were slightly longer than in the transperitoneal group but did not reach statistical significance. Interestingly, Nambirajan and associates report that all patients in the transperitoneal group resumed oral intake by postoperative day 1 but only 75% did so in the retroperitoneal group. Although the retroperitoneal group had difficulty scores greater than the transperitoneal group, the difference did not reach statistical significance.

## HAND-ASSISTED RADICAL NEPHRECTOMY

The first HALN was performed in 1997 by Nakada to remove a nonfunctioning, obstructed kidney. Several clinical reports have demonstrated the utility of the hand-assisted technique for radical nephrectomy, simple nephrectomy, autosomal dominant polycystic kidneys, nephroureterectomy, donor nephrectomy, partial nephrectomy, and pyeloplasty.

Pure laparoscopic nephrectomy requires a different set of surgical skills compared with open surgery. The hand-assisted devices have increased the availability of minimally invasive kidney surgery by offering urologists a technique that helps transfer many open surgery skills to the less invasive approach. The hand-assisted approach has the potential to decrease the learning curve of laparoscopic surgery. It can be useful for cases in which the specimen is going to be extracted intact or when a difficult dissection is anticipated. Some surgeons see the hand-assisted device as a bridge to learn pure laparoscopy when starting out learning laparoscopy, when unable to progress the case using laparoscopic techniques, or to assist in learning new complex procedures (Batker et al, 2001).

The popularity of the hand-assisted technique has also launched an ongoing debate between the hand-assisted surgeons and those who prefer pure laparoscopy, centered on the advantages and disadvantages of these two approaches. Proponents of the hand-assisted technique assert the benefits of tactile sensation for dissection of blood vessels and obscured organs, spatial orientation, as well as the use of the hand for dissection, retraction, and suturing. When bilateral procedures are being performed, a midline hand-assisted port can be of value in working on both kidneys and preventing repositioning of the patient. One of the greatest benefits of the hand-assisted technique may be the ability to control bleeding, which would otherwise result in conversion to open surgery or at least permit conversion to open surgery in a more controlled fashion than may be required during laparoscopic surgery. Disadvantages include the fact that even if the kidney is to be extracted intact, the hand-assisted approach requires a larger incision than that of a complete laparoscopic approach. Moreover, one is limited as to the placement of the hand-assisted incision. In some patients it is difficult to maintain an adequate airtight seal with the hand-assisted device (Rane et al, 2003). Once the incision is made it can be difficult to partially close in order to stop gas escaping from the edge of the insertion site. Chronic loss of the pneumoperitoneum can result in difficulty maintaining adequate visualization during the procedure. Some surgeons who use this technique report forearm compression with tingling, numbness, or pain in the forearm and hand (Wolf et al, 2000). Recent studies have shown that these devices exert between 30 to 100 mm Hg pressure on the hand and arm and vary in the ease of hand insertion and removal (Monga et al, 2004).

Currently, there are three devices marketed for hand-assisted surgery (see Table 51–1). The surgeon must be familiar with the particular characteristics of the chosen hand device to maximize its effectiveness and to prevent loss of pneumoperitoneum during the procedure.

## Indications and Contraindications

Indications for HALN are identical to those for laparoscopic nephrectomy. Favorable characteristics for this approach include thin or normal body habitus, left-sided tumors, no prior surgery, and patients with tumors not in the area of the renal hilum. Prior abdominal surgery and obesity are not contraindications to HALN but can make the dissection more difficult. Patients undergoing surgery to remove kidneys destroyed by infectious processes may benefit from the hand-assisted approach to help dissect adhesions. Patients with well-developed abdominal musculature may not allow adequate distention of the abdomen, resulting in a diminished working space and less room for intra-abdominal placement of the surgeon's hand. Relative contraindications include large tumors (>15 cm), history of peritonitis, extensive abdominal surgery, inferior vena cava thrombus, or ipsilateral abdominal wall stoma.

## Positioning and Hand Port and Trocar Placement

The patient is placed in a 30-degree lateral decubitus position. Once in position the patient is secured to the table with 3- or 4-inch cloth tape. All pressure points should be carefully checked and padded to prevent nerve or muscle injury. It is helpful to mark the midline before positioning on the table. Once the patient is prepped and draped the incision is made for hand port placement through the skin and fascia into the abdominal cavity. The success of the operation can be compromised if the initial incision for hand port placement is too large because gas will escape, resulting in a small working space.

After the hand port is placed and the hand inserted, the additional nonbladed trocars can quickly be placed using palpation with the intra-abdominal hand and gently inserting the trocars directly onto the finger inside the abdomen. The hand in the abdomen can also be used to identify and avoid adhesions if present. Alternatively, a trocar can be inserted through the hand-assisted port and the abdomen insufflated (Fig. 51–32). With the camera placed through the hand port, the secondary trocars can be placed under direct vision.

Hand port and trocar placement is different for left and right kidney surgery and between right- and left-handed surgeons. In general, the nondominant hand is inserted into the abdomen for dissection and the dominant hand is used to operate the laparoscopic instruments. Incorrect placement of the hand port may prevent ready access to the hilum and interfere with the instruments or the camera (Figs. 51–33 and 51–34).

## Procedure

### Reflection of the Colon

The colon is reflected after incising the peritoneum along the line of Toldt from the spleen or liver superiorly to the

*Text continued on p. 1796.*

SECTION XII

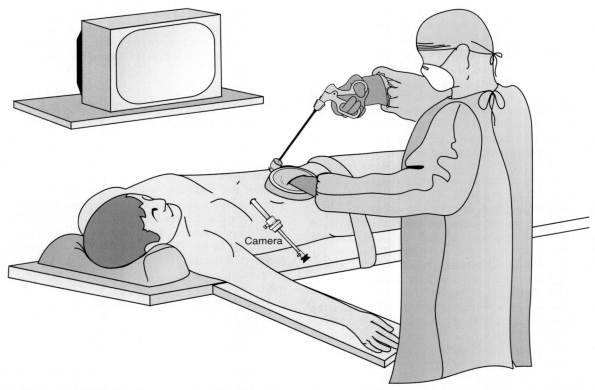

**Figure 51-32.** A right-handed surgeon working on the left kidney will usually insert the left hand through the working port while using instruments for dissection, cautery, and stapling with the dominant right hand.

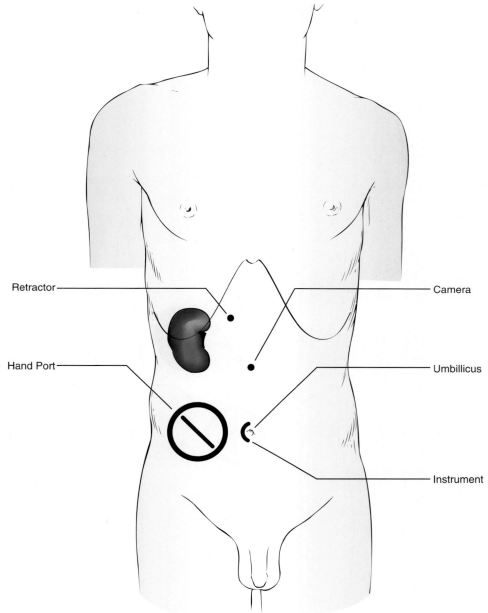

**Figure 51–33. A,** In a right-handed surgeon operating on a right-sided kidney, the hand-assisted device is placed in the right lower quadrant for insertion of the left hand and dissection is performed with instruments in the right hand placed through an umbilical trocar. The camera is placed several centimeters above the umbilicus in the midline. On the right side, retraction of the liver is usually necessary to allow visualization and dissection of the renal hilum. A liver or bowel retractor can be placed through a subcostal trocar to assist with visualization or irrigation/aspiration. *Continued*

A

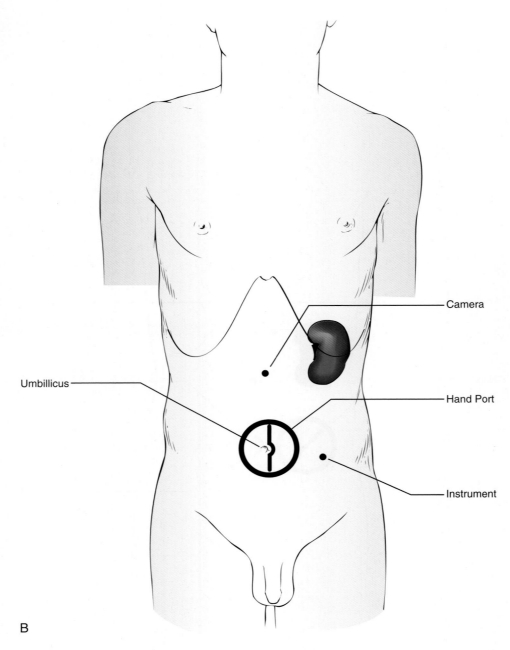

Camera

Umbillicus

Hand Port

Instrument

B

**Figure 51–33, cont'd. B,** For a right-handed surgeon operating on the left kidney the hand-assisted device and left hand are placed though a periumbilical incision and dissection is performed with the right hand using an instrument placed in the subcostal margin just medial to the nipple. The camera is placed several centimeters lateral to the edge of the actual hand-assisted device (not the edge of the incision). Additional assistance can be delivered through the most lateral trocar site.

**Figure 51–34.**  **A,** When operating on the right kidney a left-handed surgeon places the hand-assisted port in the periumbilical location for insertion of the right hand. The working port for the left hand is placed lateral to the rectus muscle, in line with or just inferior to the level of the umbilicus. The camera is placed through a lateral trocar in the anterior axillary line. Additional assistance with retraction of the liver can be accomplished through a subcostal trocar.    *Continued*

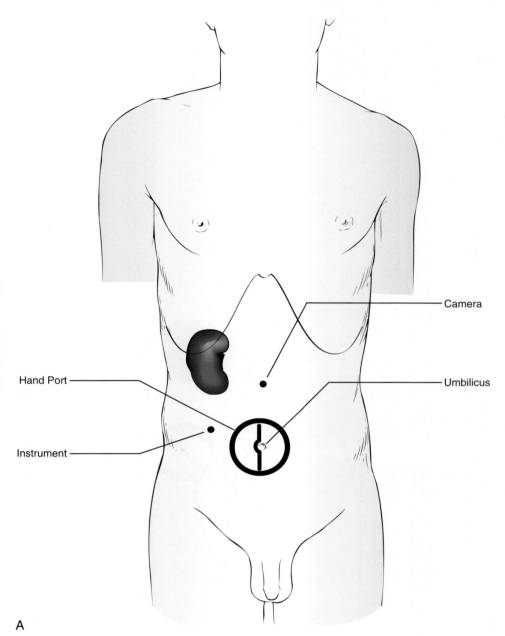

Camera

Hand Port

Umbilicus

Instrument

A

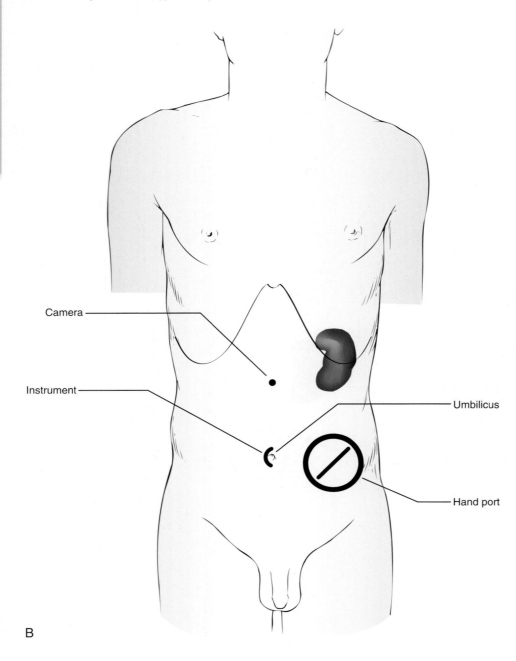

Camera

Instrument

Umbilicus

Hand port

Figure 51–34, cont'd. **B,** For a left-handed surgeon operating on the left kidney the hand-assisted port is placed in the left lower quadrant for insertion of the right hand. The left hand works with the instrument passed through an umbilical trocar, and the camera is placed midway between the umbilicus and the xiphoid process. Additional assistance with retraction or aspiration can be accomplished through a fourth trocar placed at the sub-costal margin.

B

iliac vessels inferiorly. The nondominant hand is used to retract the colon medially, while the dominant hand uses the irrigator-aspirator to bluntly dissect the correct plane and divide tissue as needed to develop the correct plane between the posterior aspect of the large bowel mesentery and underlying structures. Lateral traction of the kidney by the assistant can help identify correct tissue planes (Fig. 51–35). It is important to enter the correct plane between the large bowel mesentery and Gerota's fascia. If the surgeon wanders too far medially, significant bleeding can occur from mesenteric vessels; and if movement is too far laterally, Gerota's fascia will be violated. Lateral countertraction on the kidney from the assistant will help demonstrate the correct plane of dissection. For left-sided nephrectomy the spleen can be retracted with the inserted hand while sidewall attachments of splenorenal

ligaments are divided, allowing the spleen to be retracted medially.

### Dissection of the Ureter

Once the colon is reflected the psoas muscle can be identified and the ureter elevated. The gonadal vessel is usually included with the ureteral packet on the left side. On the right, the gonadal vessel is reflected medially. The ureter is followed to the renal hilum. Once the hand palpates the lower pole, the kidney is displaced laterally with the fingers while the thumb pushes the bowel and mesentery medially. Some surgeons divide the ureter after the lower pole of the kidney is identified, because the hand can be used to elevate the kidney for further dissection. In contrast, during transperitoneal laparoscopic surgery the ureter is left intact until the upper pole and

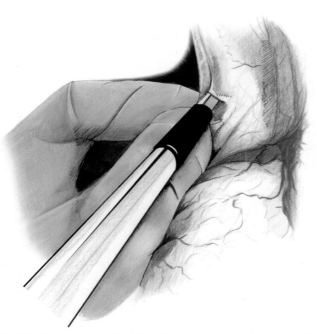

**Figure 51–35.** The nondominant hand is used to retract the colon medially and to dissect tissue planes, while the dominant hand uses endoscopic scissors to divide colon attachments.

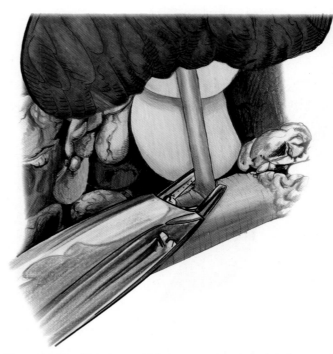

**Figure 51–36.** With the renal hilum on stretch and the bowel retracted medially to expose the vessels, the fingers can be used to palpate the renal artery and guide a stapler or clip applier to secure and divide the artery.

lateral and posterior attachments are divided and the kidney is completely mobilized.

## Dissection: Lateral Attachments and Upper Pole

In the case of hand-assisted laparoscopic radical nephrectomy the surgeon must ensure that Gerota's fascia is not violated but dissected intact from the lateral body sidewall attachments and from the psoas muscle. Retraction and dissection with the hand can allow division of the lateral attachments with harmonic shears or bipolar cautery. If the adrenal gland is to be removed with the specimen, ultrasonic energy or bipolar cautery can be used to divide all medial and superior adrenal attachments, which include the remaining branches from the aorta and inferior phrenic arteries. The hand can be used for retraction and exposure but not usually dissection of the adrenal gland, because this will usually result in bleeding from adrenal vessels or a fragile adrenal gland. If the adrenal gland is to remain in place, then the surgeon's fingers can be used to dissect the plane between the adrenal gland and the kidney. Medial retraction of the kidney can displace the diaphragm and cause perforation of the diaphragm during dissection.

## Securing the Renal Blood Vessels

On the left side, the gonadal branch will lead the surgeon to the renal vein. The gonadal vessel can be divided using bipolar cautery or clips. If clips are used, the surgeon must be careful to note the exact location of the clips to prevent inadvertently placing the clip within the jaws of the endovascular stapler, which will result in a misfire. On the left side, a lumbar vein will usually course posterior to the renal vein and be intimately involved with the renal artery. On the right side, the

surgeon may divide the gonadal vessel as it enters the vena cava to avoid bleeding. On the left side, the adrenal vein should be identified and spared in the case of simple nephrectomy or divided for radical nephrectomy if appropriate. To dissect the renal hilum, the kidney should be retracted laterally and the bowel retracted medially. This maneuver places the artery and vein on stretch and if injured keeps the vessels elevated so that vascular control can be achieved with clips or staplers. Palpation of the hilum can help with identifying the artery, which can be dissected with the tip of the irrigator-aspirator while the vessels are on stretch and the fingers are directing the tip of the irrigator-aspirator. When the lateral and posterior attachments are divided, the kidney can be retracted medially, exposing the posterior view of the renal hilum. Some surgeons will dissect the vessels from a posterior approach, allowing the fingertips to surround the renal hilum and exposing the renal artery first, followed by the renal vein (Fig. 51–36).

Clips, staples, or a tie can be used on the artery. We prefer to use staples on the renal artery because clips can interfere with stapling of the vein and have been displaced during subsequent dissection of the upper pole and posterior attachments during hand-assisted surgery (Maartense et al, 2003). Once the artery is divided, the renal vein is freed circumferentially and divided with an endovascular stapler (Fig. 51–37).

## Aspiration

Placement of the hand-assisted device allows placement of a laparotomy sponge at the start of the case that can be used to assist with retraction and absorption of blood. If the sponge is saturated, the aspirator can be used to remove blood from

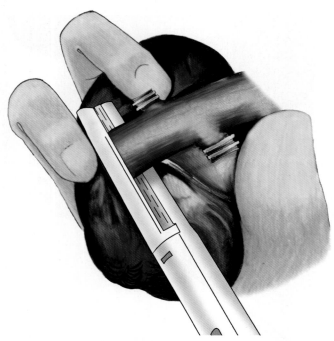

**Figure 51–37.** Once the artery is divided, the renal vein is freed circumferentially and divided with an endovascular stapler.

the compressed sponge or replace it through the hand port. Because the sponge is often out of the surgeon's view, the surgeon must remember to remove the laparotomy sponge at the end of the case.

### Specimen Entrapment and Extraction

The incision for hand placement allows rapid removal of the kidney specimen. Tissue should not be directly pulled across unprotected wound edges. Metastasis of renal cell carcinoma at the site of the hand port has been reported (Chen et al, 2003). An unsuspected renal malignancy may be present even in cases of simple nephrectomy. We recommend that renal specimens be placed in a removal device before being extracted through the hand-assisted site to prevent wound edge contamination.

### Port and Trocar Site Closure

The inserted hand can facilitate closure of trocar sites greater than 10 mm with a suture-passing device. Hand-assisted incision sites can be a location for hernia formation and complications. **Several authors have reported problems with wound complications and a 4% hernia incidence, with all hernias presenting at least 3 months after HALN** (Okeke et al, 2002; Wolf, 2005).

### Cost Comparison

With increased use of the hand-assisted devices the manufacturers have reduced the cost of the devices to make them more cost-effective. Baldwin and associates (2003) found the overall cost of laparoscopic nephrectomy to be 21% lower than both HALN and open radical nephrectomy. However, Velidedeoglu and coworkers (2002) showed decreased cost with HALN owing to shorter operative times and decreased hospital stay compared with open surgery.

## Results

The efficacy, operative times, complication rates, narcotic requirements, length of hospital stay, and convalescence outcomes for simple HALN are comparable to the laparoscopic technique. Nelson and Wolf (2002) compared 22 HALNs to 16 laparoscopic radical nephrectomy procedures and found HALN to be shorter (205 vs. 270 minutes), but the HALN patients had more abdominal pain and more wound complications.

A large number of radical HALN series are reported in the literature, but the vast majority give only a comparison of the overall short-term morbidity and operative outcomes between laparoscopy, HALN, and open surgery. In the treatment of renal cell carcinoma, the laparoscopic radical nephrectomy had a 6-year head start on HALN and, as a result, long-term cancer survival data for radical HALN are not yet available. Several series with short-term follow-up data demonstrate promising results. Stifelman and coworkers (2003) have published a multi-institutional series of 95 radical HALNs in which a comparison was made between patients according to tumor size. Thirty-two patients had tumors greater than 7 cm, and 63 patients had tumors less than 7 cm. At a mean follow-up of 12 months the investigators found no difference between the two groups, comparing positive margins, local recurrence, or metastasis. Patel and Leveillee (2003) reported on a series of 60 radical HALNs for T1 or T2 renal tumors with a mean follow-up of 11 months and showed no recurrence or trocar site seeding.

Several authors have demonstrated the use of hand-assisted surgery in the management of renal cell carcinoma with tumor thrombus extension into the renal vein or vena cava. Sundaram and associates (2002) used hand-assisted laparoscopy in a patient with T3b renal cancer with inferior vena cava thrombus. Using the hand-assisted device they controlled the inferior vena cava with vessel loops, and an endoscopic Satinsky clamp was placed to open the vena cava and remove the tumor thrombus; the defect was then closed with 4-0 vascular polypropylene suture. A similar procedure was reported by Troxel and colleagues (2002) for a level 1 renal vein tumor thrombus.

## Summary

Laparoscopic radical nephrectomy has become a standard of care for most renal tumors. This approach has proved itself to be less morbid than open surgery, with contemporary operative times comparable to open operative times. Follow-up data have now established laparoscopic radical nephrectomy as an effective means of treating renal cell carcinoma comparable to open radical nephrectomy. This can be accomplished via a hand-assisted or radical laparoscopic approach. Hand-assisted laparoscopy offers benefit when the renal specimen is going to be removed intact, in treating large tumors, and in learning laparoscopic surgery.

Laparoscopic surgery on the kidney through a retroperitoneal approach has similar outcomes compared with the transperitoneal laparoscopic approach. Although there are distinct advantages to both procedures, a laparoscopic surgeon should be familiar with both approaches to maximize safety and efficiency of laparoscopic renal surgery for a given surgical condition and the particular patient's prior history.

## NEPHRON-SPARING SURGERY

Nephron-sparing surgery (NSS) was initially reserved for patients at high risk for developing renal failure after kidney surgery to treat renal cancer. **Several series have shown open partial nephrectomy to be equivalent to open radical nephrectomy in terms of long-term cancer-free survival with unilateral renal involvement, unifocal disease, and a tumor size less than 4 cm.** Fergnany and coworkers (2000) reported a 10-year cancer-specific survival of 100% in this subset of patients. Lee and associates (2000) reported a series of 79 patients treated with open partial nephrectomy for tumors less than 4 cm compared with 183 patients with the same stage of renal cancers treated with open radical nephrectomy. They found no local recurrence and no significant difference between the two groups in disease-specific, disease-free, or overall survival. **In a matched comparison of 1566 open radical nephrectomies and 164 nephron-sparing procedures, Lau and colleagues (2000) reported no overall or cause-specific survival advantage at 5, 10, and 15 years for the radical nephrectomy group. Additionally, they found comparable early complications and similar rates of local recurrence and distant metastasis. The only difference discovered was an increased risk of developing renal insufficiency after open radical nephrectomy** ($P = .002$).

The widespread use of modern imaging techniques has resulted in a 32% decrease in the mean tumor size since the early 1990s. The result is a staged migration, with lower stages being discovered at the time of initial diagnosis (Lee et al, 2000). Thus, many individuals are advocating the use of NSS in patients with small renal tumors.

An extension of laparoscopy in the treatment of small renal lesions has been laparoscopic nephron-sparing surgery (LNSS), which mimics the fundamentals of open surgery. Tissue is removed under direct vision, with the margin status assessed intraoperatively. Direct vision and laparoscopic ultrasonography permit the laparoscopist to identify multifocal tumors, determine an adequate surgical margin, and maintain orientation with respect to the collecting system and renal hilum. If necessary, the collecting system can be resected with the surgical specimen to obtain adequate margins and then repaired. Endoscopic retrieval pouches allow safe removal of the tumor specimen.

## Indications and Contraindications

Paramount to the application of LNSS is patient selection. Peripheral, well-circumscribed lesions, with enhancement on preoperative imaging that are less than 4 cm (the latter criterion being seen in up to 40% of all renal tumors) can usually be approached laparoscopically. Intrarenal, endophytic, and centrally located tumors are amenable to larger resections with adequate collecting system closure and hemostasis. Studies evaluating the utility of LNSS include patients with solitary renal units, bilateral tumors, significant renal insufficiency, recurrent or metastatic disease, compromised function of the contralateral kidney, previous renal surgery, obesity, and comorbid disease. Unique patient populations with a predis-

position to renal tumors, such as von Hippel–Lindau disease, tuberous sclerosis, and hereditary papillary renal cell carcinoma are optimal candidates for LNSS and ablative techniques. Superior polar lesions with adrenal invasion may be amenable to en-bloc resection (Ramani et al, 2003).

## Preoperative Preparation

All patients anticipating LNSS should complete a metastatic evaluation before the procedure. Patients should be prescribed a bowel preparation the day before surgery. Broad-spectrum intravenous antibiotics are administered in the preoperative holding area. Blood is typed and screened. Crossmatching of blood is done, and 2 units of typed, screened, and crossmatched blood is usually reserved for each patient.

## Patient Positioning and Operating Room Configuration

After induction of general anesthesia and placement of calf sequential compression devices, the umbilicus is positioned over the operative table break and the patient is placed in a modified lateral decubitus position. The ipsilateral chest and shoulder are placed 30- to 45-degrees off the table using the same position as transperitoneal laparoscopic nephrectomy. Throughout the case, rotating the operative table toward the surgeon facilitates the medial displacement of the colon within the pneumoperitoneum (Schulam et al, 2002). A laparotomy set, including vascular clamps, is open on the instrument table for immediate access if needed.

In select cases, an open-ended 5-Fr catheter is passed cystoscopically up the ipsilateral ureter. This is connected to a syringe of methylene blue solution. Injecting fluid once the collecting system is transected can aid in closure.

## Trocar Placement

Veress needle insufflation is performed as previously described. Trocar placement is similar to laparoscopic nephrectomy (see Figs. 51–4 and 51–28).

## Procedure

Renal mobilization ensures inspection of the entire capsular surface for possible satellite metastasis. Complete hilar control allows excellent visualization, to ensure negative margins at the posterior aspect of the dissection. Arterial and venous clamping can be achieved with laparoscopic bulldog devices or a Satinsky clamp (Klein Medical, San Antonio, TX). Clamping of the renal vessels (with or without intrarenal or extrarenal cooling) mimics open techniques, facilitates tumor resection, and is associated with less blood loss and shorter operative times (Guillonneau et al, 2003). Intraoperative laparoscopic ultrasound (IOLUS) augments the visual inspection, helping the surgeon gain further understanding of the intrarenal margins of a primary tumor and assessment for possible satellite lesions.

Circumscription and lesion excision is completed with scissors, ultrasonic shears, or an endoscopic scalpel. The scalpel can be fashioned from a No. 15 scalpel blade affixed with Steri-

Strips to a blunt laparoscopic dissector and visually directed through a 5-mm trocar (Fig. 51–38).

Incisional hemostatic devices (i.e., TissueLink, TissueLink Medical, Inc., Dover, NH) may allow the resection of some renal lesions without the need for hilar control (Yoshihiko et al, 1998; Sundaram et al, 2003; Urena et al, 2004) (Fig. 51–39). Surgeons must recognize that with these devices severe bleeding can suddenly occur as the dissection progresses into the kidney with deeper lesions. Consequently, the hilum should be ready for hilar occlusion if bleeding occurs.

Collecting system defects can be visualized and closed with absorbable suture material using intracorporeal suture techniques. Intentional calyceal entry (to obviate positive surgical margins) is effectively repaired in a watertight manner by intracorporeal and extracorporeal laparoscopic suture maneuvers (Desai et al, 2003) (Fig. 51–40). Arterial branches may be clipped or oversewn.

Argon beam coagulation for hemostasis of the parenchymal bed is useful, taking great care to ensure its deployment is directed only at the cut renal parenchymal surface. Some authors also use a fibrin sealant product applied to the parenchymal bed (Ramakumar et al, 2002; User and Nadler, 2003).

A preplaced oxidized cellulose bolster can be used for larger defects to compress the parenchyma and aid in closure. Interrupted, horizontal mattress sutures (0-Polyglactin) on a CTX or SH needle are used for capsular closure. Continued intracorporeal suture techniques are employed, and complete renal defect closure is ensured before removal of the laparoscopic bulldog clamps. Drain placement is at the discretion of the surgeon.

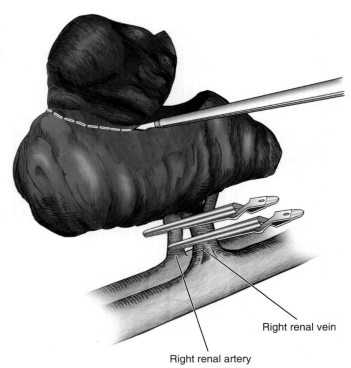

Right renal vein

Right renal artery

**Figure 51–38.** After the renal artery and vein are identified, laparoscopic bulldog clips are placed on the artery and vein. An endoscopic scalpel is used to rapidly and precisely excise the renal mass with a large rim of normal parenchyma. The excised mass is placed in an entrapment sac and left in the abdomen during kidney reconstruction.

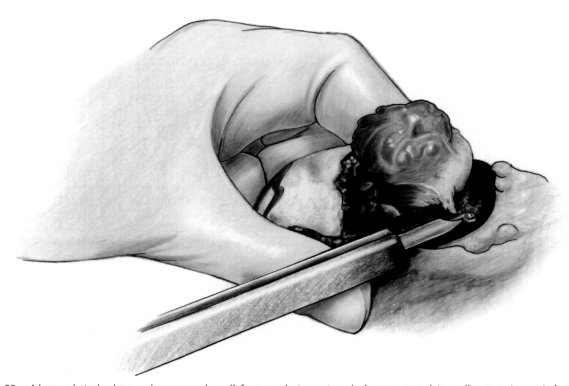

**Figure 51–39.** Advances in technology, such as monopolar radiofrequency instruments and microwave coagulators, allow some tumors to be excised without the need for renal ischemia.

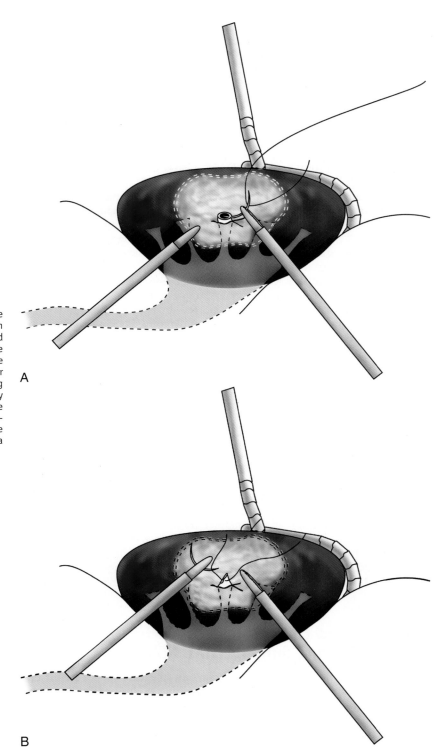

**Figure 51–40.** **A,** When deep resection is required, the collecting system will often be transected. With occlusion of the renal vessels these defects can easily be identified and closed using absorbable sutures. The cut edge of the collecting system is identified with the tip of the needle and elevated. **B,** An interrupted figure-of-eight suture or running suture is used to completely close the collecting system. The integrity of the repair can be determined by intravenous indigo carmine administration or retrograde instillation if a ureteral catheter was placed at the beginning of the case. Care must be taken not to destroy the suture if argon beam coagulation of the parenchyma surface will be performed.

A

B

**Oxidized cellulose** (Surgicel, Ethicon, Inc., Cincinnati, OH) **is often placed in the defect created after removal of the renal mass. In the early postoperative period this may appear as a gas-containing abscess, owing to air in the gauze spaces, when no real infection is present.** This appearance on CT has been reported as long as 30 days after surgery (Farina Perez et al, 2004).

## Renal Cooling and Special Considerations

Renal hypothermia has long been a part of open partial nephrectomy. To date, two primary laparoscopic renal cooling techniques have been reported: intrarenal and extrarenal. Several authors have described unique means of placing ice on the kidney after occlusion of the renal hilum. Gill and colleagues (2003) reported the initial novel technique of laparoscopic extrarenal cooling using an Endocatch II (U.S. Surgical, Norwalk, CT) bag with drawstring cinched around a clamped hilum. Ice slush was then introduced through an opened isolated inferior portion of the bag through a 12-mm port site with thermocouple-measured nadir renal parenchymal temperature of 5°C. Temperatures less than 20°C during in situ renal preservation have been reported for open partial nephrectomy (Novick, 2002). Wakabayashi and associates (2004) used a cylindrical tube to deliver ice slush directly to the kidney surface, resulting in a temperature of 18.4°C.

Landman and colleagues (2003) have reported intrarenal cooling through the infusion of ice-cold saline through ureteral catheters with cortical and medullary temperatures of 21°C and 27°C, respectively. However, the renal cooling in a recent porcine model with this type of catheter scheme demonstrated mean temperatures of only 26.1°C, which exceeds the temperatures for adequate renal preservation hypothermia, so the exact utility remains in question.

Janetschek and coworkers (2004) reported an aggressive renal hypothermia program in 15 patients undergoing LNSS. Continuous perfusion of the kidney was performed with Ringer's lactate solution at 4°C instilled directly through a needle placed in the clamped renal artery. Their mean ischemic time was 40 minutes (range: 27 to 101 minutes) with no report of decreased renal function.

## Retroperitoneal Approach

There are several contemporary adult laparoscopic retroperitoneal partial nephrectomy reports (Gill et al, 1994; Hoznek et al, 1999). To date, the posterior approach appears to grant access to the renal pedicle in the pediatric population, but peritoneal tears in the younger peritoneum appear common.

Most masses approached in this manner are small and exophytic (Tanaka et al, 2000). The limited working space creates a challenge for adequate visualization and for suturing. Murota and colleagues (2002) have used the microwave coagulator to achieve hemostasis in the retroperitoneum for NSS surgery.

## Hand-Assisted Laparoscopic Nephron-Sparing Surgery (HAL NSS)

In HAL partial nephrectomy the hand plays an integral part with both placement and removal of the bulldog occlusion clamp or compression of the renal parenchyma for hemostasis during the dissection. In a series of 15 HAL NSS procedures Pruthi and associates (2004) used the inserted hand to compress the kidney during resection of the mass followed by application of argon beam coagulation and then Tisseel (Baxter, Inc, Deerfield, IL) to the fresh resection edge while hand compression was maintained. They reported excellent hemostasis without the need for additional hemostatic measures and without delayed bleeding or formation of a urinoma.

Brown and colleagues (2004) published their results in 30 patients undergoing NSS with HAL and hand compression without vascular occlusion and reported delayed bleeding and urine leakage. Argon beam coagulation and fibrin glue were used for hemostasis. In the postoperative period, 6 patients required transfusion of red blood cells and 6 patients had urinary extravasation with 1 patient requiring a ureteral stent. Patients with centrally located tumors were more likely to have postoperative complications than those with peripheral or polar lesions.

Stifelman and coworkers (2001) have published their results from 11 HAL NSS procedures for tumors with a mean size of 2 cm. No patient required hilar occlusion; however, one patient was converted to a full open procedure to successfully complete the surgery. The mean estimated blood loss was 320 mL. No patient has shown a recurrence of renal cell carcinoma.

## In-Situ Ablation and Resection

The use of in-situ laparoscopic applications of ablative technologies (i.e., radiofrequency [RF] ablation and microwave tissue coagulation) before lesion extirpation is advocated by some to facilitate hemostasis (Gettman et al, 2001; Itoh et al, 2002). Jacomides and coworkers (2003) have employed laparoscopic RF ablation followed by tissue excision in a small series of five renal tumors with excellent results and low incidence of bleeding during LNSS. We reported our initial series of 10 patients treated in a similar fashion in tumors with a mean size of 2.1 cm (range: 1.0 to 3.2 cm) and found it to be of assistance in facilitating LNSS for both exophytic and endophytic lesions, while avoiding renal ischemia.

Microwave tissue coagulation (MTC) is being used with increasing frequency as a means for hemostatic extirpation of renal tissue during laparoscopic partial nephrectomy without renal ischemia. The MTC probe is placed sequentially around the area to be removed in a circumferential manner, and the tumor is then excised. Even when the collecting system is involved in the resection, the MTC techniques appear to be effective. Several recent reports on MTC have demonstrated positive margins, delayed bleeding, or formation of a urinoma (Maito et al, 1998; Furuya et al, 2003; Hiroya et al, 2003; Iinuma et al, 2004; Terai et al, 2004).

## Results

Multiple series have shown the feasibility and low morbidity of LNSS in the treatment of renal cell carcinoma (Table 51–7). The effect of warm ischemia on renal function is a major concern after LNSS. Bhayani and coworkers (2004) evaluated serum creatinine values in 188 LNSS patients divided into three groups: group I, no warm ischemia (N = 42); group II, warm ischemia less than 30 minutes (N = 49); and group III, warm ischemia greater than 30 minutes (N = 28). At a mean follow-up of 28 months there were no differences in serum creatinine values between the three groups and no progression to renal insufficiency after LNSS. Shekarriz and associates (2004) prospectively evaluated patients with renal tumors treated with LNSS with renal scans performed 1 month before surgery and 3 months after LNSS in 17 patients with mean warm ischemic time of 23 minutes (range: 10 to 40 minutes). They found no significant difference in glomerular filtration rate before or after surgery and no association with clamp time and changes in renal function. Kane and colleagues (2004) found similar results in 27 patients who also had

**Table 51–7. Laparoscopic Partial Nephrectomy Series**

| Author | No. Patients | Mean Tumor Size (cm) | TP/RP* | Ischemic Time (min) | Renal Cooling | OR Time (Mean) (min) | Mean EBL (mL) | Hospital Stay (days) | Mean Follow-up | Pathology/ Margin Status | Complications |
|---|---|---|---|---|---|---|---|---|---|---|---|
| Ramani et al, 2005 | 200 | 2.9 cm | 122 TP 76 RP | 29 (range: 15-58) | NA | 200 (range: 45-360) | 247 (range: 25-1500) | NA | NA | NA | Two cases converted to open surgery. Intraoperative hemorrhage 4%, delayed hemorrhage after discharge 4%, urine leakage 5%, 4 patients required reoperation. |
| Baughman et al, 2005 | 47 | 2.1 | 41 TP/6 RP | 20.5 (range: 20-55 ) | Select cases/ intrarenal | 193 (range: 50-300) | 188 (range: 50-800) | 2.4 | 22 mo | 35 RCC: 12 benign/all margins negative, mean margin distance = 4.18 mm (range: 0.5-7 mm) | 3 Urinomas; 3 trocar site infections; 1 each: pneumothorax, pulmonary edema, open conversion; no recurrence to date. |
| Allaf et al, 2004 | 48 | 2.4 | TP | NA | NA | NA | NA | NA | 38 (range: 32-81 mo) | 48 RCC: 1 positive margin/2 recurrences | NA |
| Janetschek et al, 2004 | 15 | 2.7 | 14 TP 1 RP | 40 (range: 27-101) | Yes | 185 (range: 135-220) | 160 (range: 30-650) | NA | NA | RCC: 13 AML, 2 positive margins | Reoperation for hemorrhage in 1 patient |
| Bermudez et al, 2003 | 19 | 25.8 | TP | 28.5 | Yes Intrarenal | 125 (range: 60-210) | 290 (range: 25-1200) | 5 (range: 2-10) | 3 mo | 11 RCC: 3 oncocytomas, 5 AML/mean margin 3 cm, all margins negative | Two transfusions, 4 renal insufficiency Three-month follow-up, no recurrences |
| Simon et al, 2003 | 19 | 2.1 | TP | No clamps used | No | 130 (range: 60-120) | 120 (range: 200-400) | 2.4 | 8 mo | 14 RCC: 1 AML, 3 oncocytoma, 3 benign | Tumor fragmentation, postoperative dyspnea, bleeding, pneumonia |
| Rassweiler, et al, 2000 | 53 | 2.4 | 15 TP 38 RP | NA | NA | 191 (range: 90-320) | 725 (range: 20-1500) | 5.4 | 24 mo | 37 RCC: 15 benign, 3 oncocytoma, 1 lymphoma | Argon beam coagulator-induced pneumothorax, 4 conversion to open, 1 reoperation for bleeding and 14 urinomas. |

EBL, estimated blood loss; TP, transperitoneal; RP, retroperitoneal; AML, angiomyolipoma; RCC, renal cell carcinoma; NA, data not available from publication.

postoperative renal scans after LNSS with mean warm ischemic time of 43 minutes (range: 25 to 65 minutes). They found no change in serum creatinine values after surgery and no change in differential renal function postoperatively.

Data suggest that LNSS for small solid renal masses can be performed safely utilizing innovative modalities to achieve hemostasis. This technique closely approximates the surgical goals of open NSS.

Allaf and associates (2004) have reported on their series of 48 patients treated with LNSS for T1 renal tumors less than 4 cm in size. The mean tumor size was 2.4 cm (range: 1.0 to 4 cm). This study had follow-up at a mean of 38 months (range: 22 to 84 months) with two recurrences. In a patient with von Hippel–Lindau disease a new tumor was seen at the edge of the initial LNSS site 18 months after surgery and the second was in a patient who demonstrated a new tumor remote from the original surgical site 46 months after his first procedure.

## Complications

Complications associated with LNSS are uncommon (Table 51–8). Kim and coworkers (2003) found no difference in the incidence of complications in 35 patients undergoing laparoscopic radical nephrectomy and 79 patients undergoing LNSS. Gill and associates (2003) described their complications in a series of 100 open NSS procedures compared with 100 LNSS procedures. The laparoscopic approach was found to have a longer warm ischemic time: 28 minutes versus 18 minutes ($P < .001$). In the laparoscopic group, intraoperative complications occurred in 5% of patients, compared with 0% in the open group. Positive margins were seen in 3% of the laparoscopic group and 0% of the open series. There was no difference in postoperative complications between the two groups. Transfusion needs are reported in many series, with hemorrhage necessitating open nephrectomy in one (Gill et al, 2002). Tension pneumothorax secondary to use of argon beam coagulation during pediatric laparoscopic partial nephrectomy is also noted in the literature (Shanberg et al, 2002). With experience, these complications are approaching the rates seen with open surgery.

A review of complications after LNSS in 200 patients was reported by Ramani and colleagues (2005). The mean tumor size was 3 cm (range: 1 to 10 cm), and the mean ischemic time was 29 minutes (range: 15 to 58 minutes). Only two patients required conversion to open surgery. Bleeding was one of the most common complications reported. The mean blood loss was 250 mL (range: 25 to 1500 mL). Intraoperative hemorrhage was seen in 4% of cases and postoperative bleeding in 6%, including 8 patients who had hemorrhage after discharge

### Table 51–8. Reported Complications of Laparoscopic Partial Nephrectomy

Urinoma
Completion nephrectomy
Trocar site infection
Pneumothorax/tension pneumothorax
Pulmonary edema
Tumor fragmentation
Transfusion
Pneumonia
Renal insufficiency

to home. Intraoperative bleeding occurred due to bulldog or vascular clamp malposition or malfunction. Urine extravasation from the kidney resection site was seen in 5% of patients and was treated with stent placement or percutaneous drainage. Fifteen patients had solitary kidneys, and 4 of these patients needed hemodialysis in the postoperative period. Finally, 4 patients required reoperation to treat a complication.

## Summary

In its current form, LNSS mimics the gold standard techniques for open partial nephrectomy and current results are encouraging. Capsular inspection, tumor extirpation, and margin status also meet the standards set by open NSS. Intraoperative identification and repair of collecting system defects and hemorrhagic foci ensure early postoperative success.

## LAPAROSCOPIC ABLATIVE TECHNIQUES

With an increasing incidence of renal cell carcinoma and stage migration to lower stage at the time of diagnosis, there is continued ongoing pursuit of minimally invasive treatments for renal cancer. Several new methods are being investigated to treat small renal lesions in situ. These techniques have the potential to minimize blood loss, dissection, and complications when compared with extirpative approaches. Moreover, these modalities have the potential to be used in an image-guided percutaneous manner on an outpatient basis, eliminating the need for surgical intervention. Cryotherapy, RF ablation, high-intensity focused ultrasonography, microwave therapy, and high-intensity radiation have all been investigated as tools to ablate renal tumors. The future and ultimate goal of ablative technologies in the treatment of renal carcinoma rests on our ability to develop techniques that ensure complete tumor destruction and are delivered percutaneously, as an outpatient procedure. Not all tumors are accessible percutaneously and may require direct visualization and manipulation through the laparoscopic approach. Cryoablation and RF ablation have received the most attention for clinical applications.

## Cryoablation

The indications are similar for all of the ablative technologies and include hereditary renal cell, solitary renal unit, tumors located adjacent to bowel or vital organs, bilateral renal tumors, patients with renal insufficiency, patients with significant comorbid disease, and at the informed patient's request. This technique may be best suited for the treatment of exophytic lesions 3.0 cm or less. Small renal lesions in close proximity to the renal hilum can be difficult to remove using open or laparoscopic extirpative techniques and may be treated with laparoscopic delivery of cryosurgical ablation.

The laparoscopic delivery of renal cryotherapy calls on standard transperitoneal or retroperitoneal techniques to gain access to the kidney. The only variable is the location of the mass. Those tumors located in the posterior aspect of the kidney may be easily visualized and treated through the retroperitoneal approach and those more anteriorly located through a transabdominal technique. Laparoscopic delivery of cryoablation permits visualization of probe placement, and with the use of intraoperative laparoscopic ultrasonography the progression of the ice ball can be monitored.

Once the kidney is mobilized, Gerota's fascia is opened and the tumor is localized. The perirenal fat overlying the tumor should be dissected off of the lesion, placed in a retrieval bag, and extracted for evaluation of histopathology. Complete mobilization of the kidney will allow the use of intraoperative ultrasound to monitor the size and location of the cryolesion as well as to identify multifocal lesions. Once the lesion has been visualized, an 18-gauge biopsy needle is inserted into the mass and biopsy samples are taken. If frozen section analysis will not change the planned procedure, the samples are sent for permanent pathologic section evaluation.

Initially, researchers used a single freeze-thaw cycle to destroy tumor cells. However, most current clinical series have utilized double freeze-thaw cycles in an attempt at greater tumor destruction (Gill and Novick, 1999; Gill et al, 2000; Johnson et al, 2001). Although there is concern that vascular flow to the kidney may affect the freezing of tissue, renal artery occlusion does not significantly alter the freezing process and provided no practical advantage in an animal model (Campbell et al, 1998).

Because of the destructive nature of the ice ball and the inability to rapidly arrest its progression, the developing edge must be constantly monitored during freezing. Furthermore, direct vision is not a sufficient predictor of tissue destruction, with incomplete ablation noted in 11% of samples taken within the visible margins of the ice ball (Chosy et al, 1998). Real-time ultrasound is the most common monitoring modality for use during laparoscopic application. The evolving renal ice ball is visualized as a hyperechoic, crescentic advancing edge with posterior acoustic shadowing. On the other hand, renal tumors are mildly hyperechoic or of mixed echogenicity and the renal sinus fat is hyperechoic. The ultrasound probe is placed opposite the tumor, allowing precise placement of the cryoprobe up to the deep margin of the tumor. Zegel and colleagues (1998) found that intraoperative ultrasonography accurately delineated tumor size, cryoprobe placement, and depth of freezing. An echogenic interface was generated by the marked differences at the junction of the normal renal parenchyma and frozen tissue.

**Potential complications of cryosurgery include urinary fistula formation, post-treatment hemorrhage, and injury to adjacent structures including the collecting system, bowel, and liver** (Campbell et al, 1998). Bishoff and coworkers (1999) in a porcine model noted severe adhesions between cryoablated kidney and overlying bowel in non-retroperitonealized kidneys. There was no evidence of bowel injury or fistulas. Gill and Novick (1999) reported the complication of small bowel obstruction when the cryoprobe inadvertently contacted a loop of small bowel during porcine laparoscopic renal cryoablation. Campbell and associates (1998) described an obstructive stricture at the ureteropelvic junction.

## Results

Cryotherapy has been one of the most studied ablative techniques, with multiple investigators having demonstrated the ability of temperatures of −20°C to induce tissue necrosis (Chosy et al, 1996; Campbell et al, 1998; Bishoff et al, 1999; Gill and Novick, 1999). In cryoablation, target tissue destruc-

tion is achieved through rapid freezing with liquid nitrogen or argon to a central, core temperature of approximately −195°C. Rapid freezing causes crystal formation in the microvasculature, extracellular spaces, and within the cells, eventually resulting in uncoupling of oxidative phosphorylation and rupturing of plasma cell membranes with subsequent solute shifts. Progressive failure of the microvasculature results in endothelial cell damage, edema, and platelet aggregation, with thrombosis and vascular occlusion. Thirteen weeks after ablation, fibrous collagen bundles replace the region of coagulation necrosis.

**Chosy and associates** (1996) **demonstrated that a renal tissue temperature less than −20°C was necessary to create tissue necrosis.** Uchida and colleagues (1995) evaluated renal cancer cell lines in culture by phase microscopy 24 hours after subjecting them to 60 minutes of −5°C, −10°C, −20°C, and −30°C. Approximately 95% of renal cancer cells survived after cooling for 60 minutes at temperature about −10°C but only 15% survived at a temperature of −20°C. Schmidlin and colleagues (2001) also found the threshold temperature for complete tissue ablation to be −16.1°C.

Despite the low temperatures achieved at the center of the probe during renal cryoablation, there is rapid warming of surrounding tissue toward the periphery of the ice ball. The margin of cell death beyond the probe is an important consideration in deciding the depth of probe deployment. Campbell and coworkers (1998) demonstrated that a temperature less than −20°C was achieved 3.1 mm behind the leading edge of the ice ball. These types of reports have encouraged surgeons to extend the ice ball to a minimum of 1 cm beyond the edge of the target lesion.

Sharp and associates (2003) demonstrated considerable variability in the actual tissue temperature created in the kidney during cryoablation. A single cryoprobe of 3 or 5 mm, with a central core temperature of −143°C (range: −133°C to −153°C), was used to take measurements at predetermined points moving away from the center of the probe. At only 8 mm from the center of the probe significant variability was found in tissue temperatures, ranging from −60° to −16°C. At a distance of 15 mm from the center of the probe tissue temperatures ranged from −50° to +13.5°C. These data may explain incomplete ablations reported, despite the ice ball extending beyond the margin of the lesion.

Microscopic examination of the ablation site immediately after the procedure demonstrates extensive hemorrhage into the glomerular and tubular urinary spaces. One week after cryosurgery, the lesion reflects four distinct histologic zones from the center: (1) complete necrosis, (2) inflammatory infiltrate, (3) hemorrhage, and (4) fibrosis and regeneration. By 13 weeks, these zones are replaced by fibrous connective tissue with occasional necrotic cellular debris (Bishoff et al, 1999).

Both CT and MRI have been used to assess patients after cryoablation. Gill and Novick (1999) used MRI for follow-up and noted that the primary criterion for successful cryoablation is nonenhancement of lesions after gadolinium administration. All cryolesions are isointense to the adjacent normal parenchyma on T1-weighted images and hypointense on T2-weighted images. On day 1, half the cases may have a hyperintense peripheral rim at the border of the cryolesion and normal kidney. On day 30, the cryolesions demonstrate an increase in signal intensity on both T1- and T2-weighted images but no enhancement. MRI also demonstrates sequential contraction of the cryolesion (Gill et al, 2000). The disadvantage of radiologic follow-up, however, is that most cryolesions do not resolve completely (Rodriguez et al, 2000; Chan et al, 2001).

Rukstalis and coworkers (2001) performed open renal cryoablation on 29 patients with a median preoperative lesion size of 2.2 cm. Serious adverse events occurred in 5 patients, with only one event directly related to the procedure. One patient experienced a biopsy-proved local recurrence, and 91.3% of patients (median follow-up 16 months) demonstrated a complete radiographic response with only a residual scar or small, nonenhancing cyst.

Cestari and associates (2004) reported on 29 patients with renal cell carcinoma who underwent laparoscopic cryoablation for lesions averaging 2.6 cm (range: 1.0 to 6.0 cm). Close follow-up with MRI at day 1 and then at 1, 3, 6, 12, and 24 months and biopsy of the cryo site was done at 6 months. They found a progressive decrease in size of the renal lesion over time as determined by sequential MRI evaluation, with a mean size of 3.7 cm at 1 month and a mean size of 0.7 cm at 24 months. At a mean overall follow-up of 20.5 months they reported 2 of 29 patients with documented recurrence or inadequate treatment.

Gill and associates (2000) reported their results from a series of 32 patients with a pathologically proved renal cell carcinoma (mean tumor size of 2.3 cm) treated with laparoscopic cryoablation who had a minimum follow-up of 3 years. Two patients had positive biopsy for renal cell carcinoma at 6 months, and 3 patients developed new renal cell carcinoma lesions in the cryoablated kidney. Cancer-free survival was 98%.

## Radiofrequency Interstitial Tissue Ablation

RF ablation has been utilized in a number of different clinical applications, including ablation of cardiac dysrhythmias and treatment of lesions arising from the liver, nervous system, and bone (Zlotta et al, 1997; McGovern et al, 1999; Nakada, 1999; Crowley et al, 2001). Urologists have used this technology to treat benign prostatic hypertrophy through a transurethral approach. RF energy can be introduced percutaneously, laparoscopically, or through an open approach under ultrasonographic, fluoroscopic, CT, or MRI guidance. The RF energy returns to the RF generator by way of a grounding pad that completes the electric circuit. The probe carries an alternating current of high-frequency radiowaves that causes the local ions to vibrate, and the resistance in the tissue creates heat to the point of desiccation (thermal coagulation). Microscopic examination reveals intense stromal and epithelial edema with marked hypereosinophilia and pyknosis immediately after RF treatment (Zlotta et al, 1997). This is replaced in a matter of days to weeks by coagulative necrosis with concentric zones of inflammatory infiltrate, hemorrhage, and fibrosis (Crowley et al, 2001).

Precise control of the size of the lesion can be achieved by temperature-based or impedance-based monitoring. Temperature-based systems depend on thermocouples imbedded within the tips of the electrodes. Sufficient amounts of RF

energy (10 to 90 W) are applied to raise the tissue temperature to the minimal 60°C required to induce coagulative necrosis (Crowley et al, 2001). However, the observation that temperatures recorded at the limit of ablation have been found to be 20°C to 30°C cooler than temperatures recorded at the thermocouples makes sufficient tissue desiccation uncertain. For this reason, some authors favor an impedance-based system, which applies RF energy through the electric circuit until the tissue becomes sufficiently desiccated to become an insulator. In this manner, the flow of RF energy back to the return pad is blocked. A gradual decrease in tissue impedance suggests that the thermal lesion is continuing to evolve; a rise in impedance (to approximately 200 Ω) suggests that the tissue is desiccated and that further thermal lesion growth is unlikely (Lewin et al, 1998).

Although ultrasonography, fluoroscopy, CT, and MRI have all been used for positioning of the patient and for percutaneous placement of the RF probe, none of these modalities has proved reliable for the intraoperative monitoring of the RF lesion. On ultrasound imaging, there is no immediate change in the echotexture in the area of RF ablation, and color and power Doppler ultrasonography are of no added benefit because of variable and inconsistent findings (Crowley et al, 2001). Moreover, RF treatment can sometimes disturb ultrasound imaging (Zlotta et al, 1997).

Walther and coworkers (2000) explored 14 tumors less than 5 cm in 4 patients with multiple renal lesions and performed RF ablation just before surgical excision. A complete immediate treatment effect was noted in 10 of 11 patients; in the final case, only 35% of the tumor was ablated. Excluding any technical inconsistencies, as with the early results of cryoablation, this early treatment failure needs to be put into the context of long-term, prospective clinical trials.

The definition of success after RF ablation is similar to that for cryoablation in that lack of enhancement on radiographic imaging is currently considered to be successful ablation. Matsumoto and associates (2004) describe contrast medium–enhanced images in a series of 64 patients treated with either percutaneous (34), laparoscopic (28), or open RF ablation. At a median follow-up of 14 months, 62 lesions demonstrated no enhancement on CT. Endophytic tumors developed a low-density, nonenhancing, wedge-shaped defect with fat infiltration between the ablated tissue and normal kidney. Exophytic tumors maintained their shape but had no enhancement on CT. Two patients had pathologic confirmation of recurrence after RF ablation.

## Complications

In a multi-institutional review of 139 cryoablation procedures and 133 RF procedures Johnson and associates (2004) reported an 11% complication rate with 1.8% major and 9% minor complications. In this series, 181 procedures were performed percutaneously and 90 performed laparoscopically. Significant complications included hemorrhage, ileus, ureteropelvic junction obstruction, urinoma, conversion to open surgery, and death (from aspiration pneumonia). In the laparoscopic subgroup, complications were seen in 9% of patients; 4% were directly related to the laparoscopic approach, 4% were attributed to the ablation procedure, and there was one iatrogenic case of pneumonia. The most common complication in the series was pain or paresthesia at the ablation probe insertion site (Johnson et al, 2004).

# COMPLICATIONS OF LAPAROSCOPIC RENAL SURGERY

Complications are an unavoidable consequence of surgical practice. Even when the surgery is in the most experienced hands, factors related to the patient, operating room environment, and chaotic forces can lead to an untoward event. Thus, efforts at prevention and the patients' understanding should be maximized. Moreover, if complications occur, the consequences can often be minimized through early recognition and appropriate intervention.

Life-threatening vascular injuries usually occur during dissection of the renal hilum. The acute angle of insertion of the right gonadal vein into the inferior vena cava is a potential site of injury and bleeding during elevation of the gonadal and ureter. Injury to arteries, veins, branches, and accessory vessels can result in bleeding that may require conversion to open surgery. **There are also reports of complete transection of the vena cava during retroperitoneoscopic nephrectomy** (McAllister et al, 2004). As such, one must be certain of anatomic relationships before firing a stapling device. A multi-institutional review of endovascular stapler complications showed a malfunction rate of 1.7% (10 of 565 cases), with 8 cases involving the renal vein and 2 cases involving the renal artery. Blood loss resulting from the malfunction was between 200 and 1200 mL. Conversion to open surgery for hemostasis was required in 20% of the malfunction cases. The etiology of stapler failure was due directly to the instrument in 3 cases and to preventable causes in 7 cases. Preventable causes included stapling over clips or incomplete transection due to incorrect placement (Chan et al, 2000).

Recently, reports of patient concern over body image alteration after renal surgery have appeared in the literature. These studies show that flank incisions, as traditionally made for open surgery and some hand-assisted cases, result in significantly larger postoperative, surface area and volume changes on the operated side compared with the noninvolved flank. Furthermore, patients reported dissatisfaction with the body changes occurring in up to 60% of flank incisions (Chatterjee et al, 2004; Kobayashi et al, 2004). These types of body image changes have not been reported from laparoscopic or transperitoneal (midline or subcostal) surgical approaches.

Complications can arise during each step of the laparoscopic nephrectomy. Access-related problems such as solid organ injury, bowel injury, abdominal wall hematomas, and epigastric vessel injuries have been reported. **Bleeding complications can be minimized by carefully inspecting the abdomen at the conclusion of surgery. Examination after lowering the intra-abdominal pressure can reveal bleeding veins tamponaded by the pneumoperitoneum. One also needs to carefully inspect the area of surgical dissection and the trocar sites for adequate hemostasis. Common areas of postoperative intra-abdominal bleeding include the adrenal gland, renal hilum, mesentery, gonadal vessels, and ureteral stump.**

Coagulation of the surface of the kidney with the argon beam coagulator will increase the intra-abdominal pressure to dangerously elevated levels if the gas is not allowed to escape or be actively evacuated during coagulation. There is one case report of a tension pneumothorax caused by the argon beam coagulator during laparoscopic partial nephrectomy (Shanberg et al, 2002).

Patients undergoing laparoscopic renal surgery can experience intravascular volume overload, because the laparoscopic approach is associated with far less insensible fluid loss compared with the open procedures. There is also a vascular-mediated oliguria that should not be aggressively treated because diuresis is seen after release of the pneumoperitoneum. Volume overload in patients with diminished cardiac reserve can result in congestive heart failure manifested by oliguria. Poor urine output or hemodynamic instability in the postoperative period should initiate an evaluation to rule out bleeding; if the workup is negative, diuresis can be induced if clinically indicated.

Additionally reported common complications include incision hernia after intact specimen removal, transient thigh numbness, prolonged ileus, pulmonary embolus, pneumonia, brachial nerve injury, and unrecognized bowel injury (Copcoat et al, 1992; Kavoussi et al, 1993; Kerbl et al 1993a, 1993b, 1994; Rassweiler et al, 1993, 1996, 1998; Nicol et al, 1994; Perez et al, 1994; Parra et al, 1995; Keeley and Tolley, 1998; Rozenberg et al, 1999).

Unrecognized bowel injury is a potential complication of any transabdominal or retroperitoneal surgical procedure. **One of the most devastating complications occurring as a result of laparoscopic surgery is unrecognized bowel injury. Because only 10% of the laparoscopic instrument is in the visual field, these injuries can occur out of the surgeon's field of view. The combined incidence of bowel injury in the literature is 1.3 in 1000 cases.** Most injuries (69%) are not recognized at the time of surgery. Small bowel segments account for 58% of injuries, followed by colon (32%) and stomach (7%). Fifty percent of bowel injuries are caused by electrocautery, and 32% occur during Veress needle or trocar insertion. The presentation of bowel injuries in the laparoscopic group differs from that described with open postoperative injury with peritonitis. Patients with unrecognized bowel injury after laparoscopy typically present with persistent and increased trocar site pain at the site closest to the bowel injury. Later, signs and symptoms include nausea, diarrhea, anorexia, low-grade fever, persistent bowel sounds, and a low or normal white blood cell count. The patient's condition can rapidly deteriorate to hemodynamic instability and death if the injury is not quickly recognized and treated (Bishoff et al, 1999). CT is the initial diagnostic modality of choice (Cadeddu et al, 1997), and open exploration is usually required to evacuate bowel spillage and perform the necessary repair (Fig. 51–41).

Insufflation-related complications include subcutaneous emphysema and gas embolism. The laparoscopic surgeon should be aware that the subcutaneous space communicates with the anterior mediastinum. Consequently, leaking trocar sites or incorrectly positioned trocars can allow gas to travel under the skin into the mediastinum, resulting in a pneumomediastinum or pneumothorax (Bruyere et al, 2001; Siu et al, 2003).

Diaphragm injury is uncommon and is usually immediately recognized as peak airway pressures suddenly increase and ventilation of the patient becomes difficult. Immediate

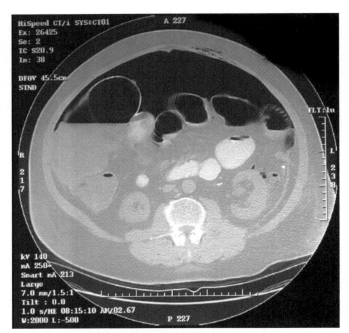

**Figure 51–41.** CT scan taken 9 days after partial nephrectomy when the patient presented to the clinic for routine follow-up complaining of distention and worsening abdominal pain for the past 3 days, low-grade fever, leukopenia, and pain out of proportion at a single trocar site. CT shows dilated loops of large bowel and significant amounts of free air. Exploration revealed a small perforation in the cecum.

treatment is needed to prevent a tension pneumothorax. This complication usually occurs during dissection of the upper pole of the kidney. It can be successfully treated laparoscopically with placement of a percutaneous meter to relieve the pneumothorax (Del Pizzo et al, 2003).

Complication rates have been reported in several large multi-institutional reviews of laparoscopic simple nephrectomy. In a series of 185 patients, Gill and coworkers (1995) reported an overall complication rate of 12% for benign disease, with 5% of patients requiring conversion to open surgery. In their series, the incidence of complications decreased markedly with increasing experience. **In fact, 70% of the complications occurred during the first 20 cases at each institution. A learning curve of approximately 20 laparoscopic nephrectomy cases is also supported by other reports** (Keeley and Tolley, 1998; Rassweiler et al 1998; Fahlenkamp et al, 1999). Rassweiler and colleagues (1998) published the results of a series of 482 laparoscopic nephrectomies (444 procedures for benign disease) performed by 20 surgeons at 14 different European medical centers. They reported a 6% overall complication rate, with 10% of the cases converted to open surgery. **The majority of patients converted to open surgery had infectious causes of renal abnormality as the leading indication for kidney removal.** Bleeding was the most common cause of open conversion, followed by the surgeon's inability to visualize the renal hilum for dissection. Hemal and associates (1999) presented a series of 126 laparoscopic nephrectomies performed for benign disease. In their series, 12% (15 of 126) of the patients required conversion to an open surgical procedure. The

overall incidence of major and minor complications was 17% (22 of 126).

In 1998, Cadeddu and colleagues reported a minor and major complication rate of 9.6% in a series of 157 laparoscopic radical nephrectomies.

**In several different contemporary series, comparing open, hand-assisted, and laparoscopic nephrectomy for malignancy the complication rates were 10%, 17%, and 12%, respectively** ($P = .133$) (Chan et al, 2001; Shuford et al, 2004).

Varkarakis and associates (2004) compared complication rates between 28 patients younger than 75 years of age and 33 patients older than 75 years of age and found no difference in surgical or longer-term morbidity between these two groups. In patients at high risk for perioperative complications determined by the American Society of Anesthesiologists score greater than or equal to 3, no significant differences were noted in complication rates between HALN and open radical nephrectomy (Baldwin et al, 2003).

Rare or unusual complications include nerve injury, chronic pain syndrome, and orchialgia. Several authors have reported cases of chronic pain syndrome or nerve injury after laparoscopic radical nephrectomy presenting as constant burning discomfort in the ipsilateral flank requiring narcotics and pain clinic consultation for chronic management (Wolf et al, 2000; Oefelein and Bayazit, 2003). In a series of 381 laparoscopic donor nephrectomies, Kim and colleagues (2003) reported ipsilateral orchialgia in 10% of patients. Onset of pain occurred at a mean of 5 days after surgery (range: 6 to 52 months), and at 6 months 50% had complete spontaneous resolution.

## SUMMARY

The laparoscopic approach to renal disease has emerged as a standard treatment of renal pathology. In a wide variety of

---

### KEY POINTS: LAPAROSCOPIC SURGERY OF THE KIDNEY

- Laparoscopic radical and partial nephrectomies provide equivalent cancer control compared with open techniques.

- When ablating renal lesions, temperatures less than 20°C are necessary for cell death. Moreover, the leading edge of the ice ball should be 1 cm beyond the tumor.

- Unrecognized laparoscopic bowel injuries usually present as indolent signs compared with injuries sustained after open surgery.

- Patients with a laparoscopic bowel injury are usually afebrile with a normal to low serum white blood cell count, focal abdominal discomfort, and mild ileus.

- Vascular injuries are the most common cause of conversion to open surgery with laparoscopic renal surgery. This is more commonly seen in patients undergoing nephrectomies for chronic inflammatory processes.

applications, patients benefit from decreased morbidity without sacrificing therapeutic outcomes. Results are similar to those obtained with open surgery. Early results with ablative techniques hold promise for eventual nonoperative management of many renal lesions.

## SUGGESTED READINGS

Fadden P, Nakada S: Hand-assisted laparoscopic renal surgery. Urol Clin North Am 2001;28:167-176.

Gaur DD: Laparoscopic operative retroperitoneoscopy: Use of a new device. J Urol 1992;148:1137-1139.

Gill IS: Renal cryotherapy: Pro. Urology 2005;65:415-418.

Gill IS, Rassweiler JJ: Retroperitoneoscopic renal surgery: Our approach. Urology 1999;54:734-738.

Johnson DB, Solomon SB, Su LM, et al: Defining the complications of cryoablation and radiofrequency ablation of small renal tumors: A multi-institutional review. J Urol 2004;172:874-877.

Nambirajan T, Jeschke S, Al-Zahrani H, et al: Prospective, randomized controlled study: Transperitoneal laparoscopic versus retroperitoneoscopic radical nephrectomy. Urology 2004;64:919-924.

Russo P: Renal cryoablation: Study with care—proceed with caution. Urology 2005;65:419-421.

Shichman S, Wagner J: Minimally invasive hand-assisted nephrectomy for the treatment of renal cancer. In Moore R, Bishoff J (eds): Minimally Invasive Uro-oncologic Surgery. Taylor & Francis, Oxfordshire, UK, 2005, pp 191-201.

Terranova SA, Siddiqui KM, Preminger GM, Albala DM: Hand-assisted laparoscopic renal surgery: Hand-port incision complications. J Endourol 2004;18:775-779.

Wolf J: Tips and tricks for hand-assisted laparoscopy. AUA Update Series 2005;24:lesson 2.

# 52 Ablative Therapy of Renal Tumors

MICHAEL MARBERGER, MD, FRCSEd • JULIAN MAUERMANN, MD

RATIONALE FOR ENERGY ABLATIVE THERAPY

DEFINING SUCCESSFUL ABLATION

CRYOABLATION

RADIOFREQUENCY ABLATION

MICROWAVE ABLATION

INTERSTITIAL LASER COAGULATION

HIGH-INTENSITY FOCUSED ULTRASOUND

RADIOSURGERY

CONCLUSION

## RATIONALE FOR ENERGY ABLATIVE THERAPY

Modern imaging techniques have resulted in a dramatic change in the clinical landscape of renal tumors, with a significant migration to smaller and lower stage lesions in asymptomatic patients (Chow et al, 1999; Pantuck et al, 2001). Incidentally detected renal cell carcinoma (RCC) has a more favorable prognosis (Hsu et al, 2004), and there is an inverse correlation between tumor size and the odds of having clear cell versus papillary and high-grade versus low-grade RCC (Duchene et al, 2003; Frank et al, 2003). Even with most advanced cross-sectional imaging techniques it remains difficult to differentiate between RCC and some solid benign tumors, especially oncocytoma (Herts, 2003; Walter et al, 2003). Twenty percent to 22% of tumors 4 cm or less in diameter and up to 46% of tumors smaller than 1 cm prove to be benign at histologic examination (Duchene et al, 2003; Frank et al, 2003).

Not surprisingly, the majority of small renal masses grow slowly, with growth rates in diameter of 0.22 to 0.54 cm per year (Volpe et al, 2004; Wehle et al, 2004) having been observed in patients managed by surveillance only. A small number, however, progress rapidly, and at present there is no way these can be identified by imaging. Magnetic resonance imaging (MRI) or computed tomography (CT)–guided fine needle aspiration biopsy correctly defines most benign lesions, but it is usually insufficient for subclassification or grading of RCC (Tuncali et al, 2004). Core biopsies taken with larger caliber needles permit this more reliably but carry an inherent, albeit low, risk of tumor cell seeding and hemorrhage (Wolf, 1998). Even advocates of surveillance strategies consider higher nuclear grade RCC unsuited for a "watchful waiting" approach (Renshaw, 2004). Given the fact that up to 38% of incidentally discovered RCCs smaller than 3 cm in diameter have extracapsular extension (>T3) and up to 28% are Fuhrman grade greater than 3 (Hsu et al, 2004), surgical removal remains the standard therapy.

Nephron-sparing partial nephrectomy has been shown to be as effective as radical nephrectomy in achieving cure for tumors less than 4 cm in diameter (Herr, 1999; Fergany et al, 2000; Lau et al, 2000) regardless of whether they are in a peripheral or central location (Hafez et al, 1998). To reduce access trauma, laparoscopic partial nephrectomy is rapidly gaining acceptance (Janetschek et al, 2000; Gill et al, 2002; Janetschek, et al, 2004). Nevertheless, the learning curve in mastering laparoscopic partial nephrectomy remains substantial, with a reported median surgical time of 3 hours and a median warm renal ischemia time of 27.8 minutes in one of the largest series (Gill et al, 2003). Given the low tendency of the majority of small renal tumors to progress and the fact that the largest increase in their incidence occurred in the seventh to ninth decade age groups (Chow et al, 1999) with inherently high comorbidity, less invasive treatment options appear very attractive.

Less invasive treatment can be achieved by targeted destruction of the tumor with energy-based ablation techniques. These techniques were initially employed to provide an ischemic plane at nephron-sparing partial nephrectomy to reduce bleeding, but destruction of the entire tumor with or without subsequent removal is now the objective. Small renal tumors are good targets as they often have a spherical shape, are unifocal, and are surrounded by homogeneous renal parenchyma and perirenal fat. The entire surface of the kidney is fairly simple to reach either laparoscopically or percutaneously, and real-time monitoring of tissue destruction can be attempted by intraoperative thermometry, ultrasonography, CT, or MRI. Conversely, high renal perfusion poses real challenges for this approach. Needle puncture of the renal capsule immediately results in bleeding along the tract, with the risk of seeding tumor cells and losing ablative energy. Even more significant are the proximity to large intrarenal vessels, which may drain ablative energy by conduction in a manner that is difficult to control. Attempts at needle chemoablation have proved disappointing in the kidney for this reason, as the chemoablative agent tends to spread in an irregular and unpredictable manner (Rehman et al, 2003). Only ablative techniques that destroy renal tissue in a homogeneous, safe, and rapid manner can adequately destroy renal tumors. At present, this appears possible only by freezing, heating, or radiosurgery.

## DEFINING SUCCESSFUL ABLATION

To gain clinical acceptance, the techniques have to achieve oncologically complete destruction of the tumor with less morbidity than with standard surgical procedures. Moreover, these must be of technical complexity that allows widespread adoption. Definitive proof of their efficacy requires long-term data on disease-free survival. Given the slow growth rate of most of the lesions, intermediate evaluation has to be based on experimental data showing dose-dependent tissue destruction in the target area, on intraoperative monitoring of the lesion with subsequent histologic evaluation, and on clinical data on complications and intermediate follow-up.

Complete loss of contrast enhancement on follow-up CT or MRI scans has been considered a sign of complete tissue destruction (Matsumoto et al, 2004). Of note, viable residual tumor has been demonstrated in nonenhancing lesions (Rendon et al, 2002) after radiofrequency (RF) ablation. The lesion should also show progressive shrinking after therapy as proof of remission, although this may take months and is less pronounced after RF ablation (Lee et al, 2003; Lowry and Nakada, 2003; Nakada et al, 2004). The role of biopsies remains controversial. A preoperative needle biopsy establishes the diagnosis and is important for assessing outcome results, but frozen sections of intraoperative needle biopsy specimens are fairly inaccurate and unreliable for clinical decision-making (Dechet et al, 1999, Zagoria et al, 2004). Likewise, perioperative biopsies may be misleading as to the viability of residual structures, and negative results in masses less than 3 cm in diameter should always be viewed with caution (Lechevallier et al, 2000; Raj et al, 2003; Rybicki et al, 2003). Whatever ablative technique is used, patients need close post-procedural follow-up with serial CT or MRI scans performed by a dedicated radiologist every 3 months for 12 to 18 months followed by long-term surveillance either until complete regression or, if a lesion becomes stable, annually to ensure no potential recurrence from a margin (Lowry and Nakada, 2003; Nakada et al, 2004). Failure of the lesion to shrink within 6 months after therapy or any growth mandates renal biopsy regardless of contrast enhancement. In addition, 3.7% of renal cell cancers less than 3 cm in diameter have multifocal satellite lesions (Nissenkorn and Bernheim, 1995), a possible reason for recurrent tumors after any form of nephron-sparing therapy (Jang et al, 2005).

## CRYOABLATION
## Mode of Action and Experimental Data

Tissue destruction by freezing and thawing has been utilized for a variety of medical indications for over 150 years, but it was not until vacuum-insulated liquid nitrogen or argon-cooled probes were developed that targeted cryoablation of kidney tumors came within clinical reach (Gage, 1998). Through the Joule-Thomson effect (i.e., rapid cooling of the tip of a probe by highly compressed liquid nitrogen or argon expanding though a restricted orifice to the gaseous state), temperatures of −175° C to −190° C can be pinpointed within soft tissues. Cryoprobes 1.5 to 8 mm in diameter are now available. An ice ball is rapidly generated around this core and can be monitored by real-time intraoperative ultrasonography, CT, or MRI. Tissue necrosis is achieved by direct damage on a cellular level and indirect damage from malperfusion during the thawing phase. The former are complex sequelae of intracellular ice formation with mechanical cell destruction and extracellular ice formation with subsequent dehydration injury and solute effects on cellular lipid and protein biophysics (Hoffmann and Bischof, 2002). Even if primarily sublethal, secondary reperfusion injury ultimately results in cell death. Histologically, the ultimate outcome is coagulation necrosis, followed by fibrosis and scarring (Campbell et al, 1998; Chosy et al, 1998).

Renal cryoablation has been shown to produce predictable and reproducible tissue destruction in animal models (Campbell et al, 1998; Chosy et al, 1998; Collier et al, 2004). Its extent depends on the speed of freezing, the number of freeze-thaw cycles, the size as well as area of contact of the cryoprobe, and, most important, on the lowest temperatures reached and the hold time at subzero temperatures (Smith DJ et al, 1999; Finelli et al, 2003). Complete destruction of normal renal parenchyma occurs at temperatures below −19.4° C (Chosy et al, 1998). Cancer cells may need even lower temperatures for reliable cell death (Larson et al, 2000). In experimental settings, these temperatures were reached only 4 to 6 mm inside the edge of the forming ice ball (Campbell et al, 1998; Chosy et al, 1998). Histologic data on cryotherapy-assisted partial nephrectomy of large RCCs confirm this (Bargman et al, 2003). In clinical practice, the ice ball is therefore in general extended 5 to 10 mm beyond the tumor margin. Thus, for reliable treatment of tumors 2.5 cm in diameter, a cryoprobe of 3.4 mm or greater or multiple thinner probes must be used (Gill et al, 2000; Rukstalis et al, 2001). Not all structures are equally cryosensitive. The renal collecting system has been shown to remain intact in spite of being within the ice ball, provided it is not lacerated mechanically (Sung, 2003).

Comparing lesion size and volumes of confluent necrosis, significantly larger lesions were noted with double-freeze cycles than with a single freeze (Woolley et al, 2002). In contrast to previous assumptions, active thawing with helium gas at 15° C to 20° C/min does not infringe on lesion size but reduces procedural time significantly (Gage, 1998; Gill and Novick, 1999). Occlusion of the renal artery during freezing increases the size of the cryolesion only marginally (Campbell et al, 1998; Collier et al, 2004). In clinical practice, real-time monitoring of the advancing ice ball, with an extension 10 mm beyond the tumor margins, has proved a reliable clinical endpoint (Gill et al, 2000). Thermometry with thermocouples at the tumor margin targeting a margin temperature of $-40°$ C and on-line MRI monitoring have been reported to be comparable (Rukstalis et al, 2001; Shingleton and Sewell, 2001). As the freeze process depends on probe contact, puncture cryoablation is the preferred technique today. It can be achieved by open surgical access, laparoscopically, or percutaneously.

## Open Surgical and Laparoscopic Cryoablation

After isolated case reports on cryoablation using open access (Delworth et al, 1996), a first report on systematic use of this approach to treat 29 tumors averaging 2.2 cm in diameter in 29 patients was published (Rukstalis et al, 2001). Using intraoperative ultrasound monitoring and targeting thermosensor-controlled margin temperatures of $-40°$ C, double-freeze sequences were performed with one to three cryoprobes. With a median follow-up of 16 months, only one patient had a biopsy-confirmed recurrent tumor. Postoperative morbidity was moderate, with five patients needing some intervention after cryoablation to control bleeding from the ablation site. Cryotherapy-assisted nephron-sparing removal of larger renal masses using a single-freeze ice ball along the tumor margin as a guide for excision has also been utilized to reduce the morbidity of open partial nephrectomy (Bargman et al, 2003).

The laparoscopic approach permits similar exposure and visualization of the kidney with less access trauma. Anterior or medially located tumors are approached transperitoneally, and posterior tumors by retroperitoneal access. A deflectable, laparoscopic ultrasound transducer is used for precise insertion of the cryoprobe and for monitoring the advancing ice ball (Gill et al, 2000). After withdrawing the cryoprobe, hemostasis is ascertained by local compression with bioadhesive bolsters or argon beam coagulation, or both. In the first larger

clinical series 32 patients with small peripheral renal tumors were treated. Using a double freeze-thaw cycle, cryoablation time averaged 15.1 minutes and surgical time 2.9 hours. Morbidity was minimal with a mean blood loss of 67 mL, no complication requiring an additional intervention, and an average hospital stay of 1.8 days. Five of 20 patients followed up by sequential MRI had no demonstrable residual lesion after 1 year, and in the other 15 the lesions had decreased in size by an average 66% (Gill et al, 2000). Subsequently, the group presented 3-year follow-up data for the first 56 patients with a mean tumor size of 2.3 cm (range 1 to 4 cm) and biopsy-confirmed renal cancer in 36 patients (Steinberg et al, 2002; Spaliviero et al, 2004). Only two patients had biopsy-confirmed recurrences and subsequently had a radical nephrectomy. Other authors reproduced these results (Table 52–1; Fig. 52–1). Negative biopsies or loss of gadolinium enhancement and shrinkage of the tumor on follow-up MRI or CT or both were achieved in 84 of 91 patients with histologically confirmed renal cell cancer, although some lesions required retreatment. This represents an approximately 8% failure rate, which is higher than that for standard partial nephrectomy, especially given the lack of long-term follow-up. Failure mainly occurs with tumors more than 3 cm in diameter and centrally located tumors (Jang et al, 2005).

## Percutaneous Cryoablation

The first attempts at cryoablation of kidney tumors in humans were performed percutaneously but proved unsatisfactory because of technical limitations (Uchida et al, 1995). The development of ultrathin nonmagnetic cryoprobes and open access interventional MRI systems, which permit simultaneous monitoring of the procedure in sagittal and coronal planes with imaging beyond the ice ball, provided technical breakthroughs (Harada et al, 2001). Shingleton and Sewell (2001) used a 2- or 3-mm cryoprobe, 5-mm margins, and triple

**Table 52–1. Clinical Experience with Cryoablation of Renal Masses under Laparoscopic Control***

| Authors | Techniques | Patients (N) | Median Follow-up (mo) | Biopsy-Proved Renal Cell Carcinoma | Renal Cell Carcinoma Persisting/Recurrent Disease (Patients) |
|---|---|---|---|---|---|
| Lee et al, 2003 | Ultrasound (US) guided Laparoscopic (retroperitoneal) Double-freeze technique | 20 | 14.2 | 11 | 0 |
| Harmon et al, 2003 | US guided Open or laparoscopic Double freeze-thaw cycles | 76 | 17 | n.s. | 3 |
| Spaliviero et al, 2004 (Gill) | Visual + US guided Laparoscopic (transperitoneal or retroperitoneal) Double freeze-thaw cycles | 56 | Minimum 36 | 36 | 2 |
| Cestari et al, 2004 | Visual Laparoscopic (transperitoneal or retroperitoneal) Two freeze-thaw cycles | 37 | 20.5 | 29 | 1 |
| Moon et al, 2004 | US guided Laparoscopic (transperitoneal or retroperitoneal) Two freeze-thaw cycles | 16 | 9.6 | 5 | 0 |
| Jang et al, 2005 | Visual + US guided Laparoscopic (transperitoneal or retroperitoneal) Double freeze–passive thaw cycles | 15 | 15 | 10 | 1 |
| | | 220 | | 91 | 7 |

*Only series with 15 patients or more and only latest publication of series listed. N.S., not stated.

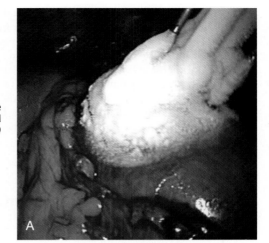

**Figure 52–1.** Biopsy-proved clear cell renal cell cancer 2.5 cm in diameter: intraoperative image during laparoscopic cryoablation with evolving ice ball (**A**), unenhanced and contrast-enhanced computed tomography scans preoperatively (**B** and **C**), after 3 months (**D** and **E**), and after 9 months (**F** and **G**) showing complete loss of enhancement and progressive shrinking of lesion.

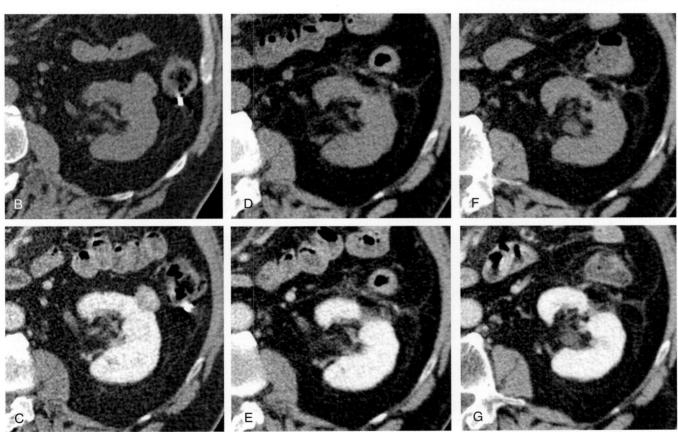

freeze-thaw sequences of −80° C to −70° C. To treat larger tumors, the probe was inserted repeatedly to create overlying ice balls. The procedure was performed with general anesthesia or sedation, with a hospital stay less than 24 hours in 95% of patients treated. They updated their experience in 70 patients, including patients with von Hippel–Lindau disease and RCC in a transplanted kidney (Shingleton, 2003). With an average follow-up of 24 months for 59 patients, 9 (15%) patients required retreatment because of incomplete initial tumor ablation. Only one patient required transfusions secondary to a perinephric hematoma and there were no cancer-related deaths. In spite of the encouraging results, the efficacy of percutaneous cryoablation in achieving complete tumor ablation has not been confirmed histologically in clinical series. Moreover, the need for an open access MRI unit or fluoroscopy capable CT scanner for intraoperative monitoring can limit availability. Percutaneous cryoablation with sonographic guidance has been described (Bassignani et al, 2004), but the poor echogenicity of the cryoprobes, difficult monitoring of the situation anterior to the ice ball, and the mobility of the kidney at puncture render this a potentially suboptimal approach.

In conclusion, experimental data document the potential of cryoablation for treating renal tumors. Promising clinical results are emerging that show that this is a minimally invasive and feasible approach for treating peripheral lesions less than 3 cm in diameter. Morbidity is low and mainly consists of probe site pain and paresthesia and minor hemorrhage, with a higher incidence after percutaneous cryoablation (Johnson et al, 2004). Major complications have been reported in about 2% of patients, mainly from hemorrhage and urinary fistula (Johnson et al, 2004).

# RADIOFREQUENCY ABLATION
## Mode of Action and Experimental Data

Heating above 60° C results in instantaneous and irreversible coagulation necrosis of all biologic tissues, with denaturation of cellular proteins, melting of lipids, and disintegration of cell membranes. Temperatures in this range are reached consistently by delivering alternating electric current with a frequency in the radio segment of the electromagnetic spectrum to the target area through an interstitial needle electrode (Leveen, 1997; Rendon et al, 2001; Rehman et al, 2004). This can be achieved either with bipolar electrodes, where the current flows from an active electrode to a negative electrode built into the delivery needle, or with a monopolar system. With the latter, the patient is grounded with an electrode pad applied to the skin to complete the electric circuit and RF energy is released at the uninsulated monopolar needle tip. RF energy administered to the tissue causes ionic agitation in the cells and, as a result of electrical impedance of the tissue, local heating. The energy then dissipates by conductive heating. Provided the electrical impedance of the tissue remains low, a dynamically expanding sphere of heat-induced tissue damage is created outward from the electrode (Leveen, 1997).

Tissue death depends on the distance from the electrode, RF current intensity, and the duration of its application. If the current is too high or applied too rapidly, desiccation and charring occur, impedance increases sharply, and the heating process comes to a standstill (Djavan et al, 2000). Lesion volume is then smaller than desired and, because of scattered areas of water vaporization, may have an irregular shape. Multiarray electrodes from which up to 10 evenly spaced wire electrodes are deployed into the tissue in an umbrella-like manner at a constant radius from an axial insulated sheath achieve more regular spherical lesions. As tissue impedance adjacent to a particular electrode rises, the current is automatically redistributed to areas of lower impedance, resulting in more homogeneous lesions (Leveen, 1997).

In experimental studies, only multitine RF has been shown to cause complete necrosis consistently. Single-needle RF alone, regardless of whether monopolar or bipolar, always produced lesions with skip areas of viable cells (Rehman et al, 2004). Rapid increase of impedance can be avoided by cooling the electrode with circulating chilled water. The tissues closest to the electrode are not overheated, permitting greater overall energy deposition and subsequently larger lesions (Lorentzen, 1992). Alternatively, hypertonic saline or gel can be perfused into the tissue through a cannulated RF probe. The electrically conductive agent facilitates the delivery of energy from the electrode to surrounding tissue, rendering it a much larger, "virtual" electrode. Impedance remains lower and larger volumes are ablated (Leveillee and Hoey, 2003). Saline diffusion depends on the anatomic structure. In the kidneys of laboratory animals, "wet" RF has consistently been shown to produce larger lesions (Patel et al, 2000; Renshaw, 2004), although, in contrast to cryoablation, not always complete necrosis.

With all thermal ablation techniques the "heat sink" effect of large blood vessels near the target zone may conduct energy away to an extent that complete cell killing is not achieved. In swine kidneys, dry RF ablation usually caused slightly larger and more homogeneous lesions if the renal artery was occluded during ablation, but the difference from lesions obtained in normally perfused kidneys appeared marginal (Corwin et al, 2001; Marcovich et al, 2002) and not worth risking renal infarction peripheral to the thermal lesion (Kariya et al, 2003).

Because of the low intrinsic contrast between normal and ablated tissues and artifacts from gas bubble formation, real-time imaging of the developing thermal lesion with intraoperative ultrasonography, MRI, or CT has proved unreliable (Renshaw, 2004). In general, imaging techniques are used only to place the electrodes (Fig. 52–2), and RF is monitored by measuring temperature or impedance changes, or both, usually with feedback from thermosensors integrated at the end of the RF tines. Provided the treatment protocols recommended by the manufacturer are adhered to, temperature-based and impedance-based RF generators seem equally effective (Gettman et al, 2002a). Temperatures over 70° C throughout the entire target zone are needed for complete ablation. To achieve this consistently, temperatures of 105° C have to be targeted at the tip of each RF tine, and this may even be insufficient with central tumors located in the vicinity of large vessels (Ogan and Cadeddu, 2002a). Infrared thermography with a laparoscopic infrared camera reliably documents renal temperatures above 70° C but only at the surface of the organ (Ogan et al, 2003).

Ultimately, monitoring of the spatial distribution of heating with real-time image-based thermometry is needed. Attempts to achieve this using ultrasonography, MRI thermometry, impedance tomography, or microwave radiometry appear promising but are still experimental (Varghese et al, 2002). Simpler visualization of the expanding RF lesion may be another advantage of wet RF ablation, especially if a temperature-modulated vapor appearing hyperechoic at ultrasonography is used (Johnson et al, 2003).

## Laparoscopic Radiofrequency Ablation

RF ablation has been utilized laparoscopically, both for in situ ablation of tumors and to secure hemostasis at partial nephrectomy. In one series (Jacomides et al, 2003), 11 tumors 1.1 to 3.6 cm in diameter, which were located in positions where partial nephrectomy was considered difficult, were ablated. The RF probe was introduced percutaneously and, under laparoscopic control, the tumor was ablated at 105° C, with impedance less than 75 ohm, and the target zone extended at least 1 cm over the tumor diameter. With a mean follow-up of 9.8 months, no lesion showed enhancement on serial CT studies and five lesions disappeared completely. The authors nevertheless recommend excision after RF ablation

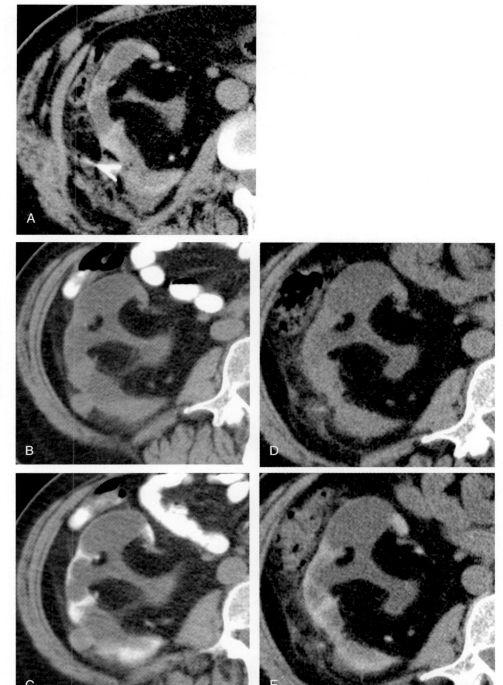

**Figure 52–2.** Percutaneous radiofrequency (RF) ablation of biopsy-proved papillary cancer in a hydronephrotic kidney after multiple stone episodes: monopolar RF probe in tumor (**A**) and unenhanced and contrast-enhanced computed tomography scans before (**B** and **C**) and 6 months (**D** and **E**) after RF ablation showing complete loss of contrast enhancement and fibrotic shrinking of lesion.

where this is technically simple, and they performed it without complication in six patients. One of these patients had a focal positive margin at histologic evaluation. RF has also been employed for circumferential coagulation around the tumor to be used as a plane of resection at laparoscopic partial nephrectomy (Coleman et al, 2003). Histologic evaluation of the specimen was not impaired. Laparoscopic control does, however, not rule out complications from damage to adjacent structures such as the collecting system (Johnson et al, 2003)

or loss of renal function from overzealous tissue ablation (Ogan et al, 2002).

## Percutaneous Radiofrequency Ablation

The thinner diameters of RF probes render a percutaneous approach using CT guidance most attractive. Since a first report in 1997 (Zlotta et al, 1997), a number of phase II studies have been published (Table 52–2). Tumor persistence or

**Table 52–2. Clinical Experience with Percutaneous Radiofrequency Ablation of Renal Masses and Follow-up by Serial Computed Tomography or Magnetic Resonance Imaging Scans and Biopsies\***

| Authors | Techniques | Patients (N) | Median Follow-up (mo) | Biopsy Proven Renal Cell Carcinoma | Renal Cell Carcinoma Persisting/Recurrent Disease (Patients) |
|---|---|---|---|---|---|
| Pavlovich et al, 2002 | Ultrasound (US) and/or computed tomography (CT) guided Percutaneous Temperature controlled 2 or 3 cycles | 21 | 2 | n.st. | 5 |
| Farrell et al, 2003 | US or CT guided Percutaneous Impedance or temperature controlled | 20 | 9 | n.st. | 0 |
| Mayo-Smith et al, 2003 | US or CT guided Percutaneous Temperature and impedance controlled 1 to 6 cycles | 32 | 9 | 18 | 6 |
| Su et al, 2003 (Kavoussi) | CT guided Percutaneous Impedance or temperature controlled | 29 | 9 | 20 | 2 |
| McGovern et al, 2003 | CT guided Percutaneous Impedance or temperature controlled | 62 | 9.9 | 62 | 7[†] |
| Lisson et al, 2003 | CT guided Percutaneous Temperature controlled | 21 | 12.1 | 6 | 3 |
| Hwang et al, 2004 | CT + US guided (laparoscopic—9 patients) US guided (percutaneous—8 patients) Temperature controlled 1 to 4 cycles | 17 | 12.8 | n.st. | 1 |
| Zagoria et al, 2004 | CT guided Percutaneous Impedance controlled 1 to 9 cycles | 22 | 7 | 17 | 3 |
| Matsumoto et al, 2004 (Cadeddu) | CT guided percutaneous (34 tumors) US guided laparoscopic radiofrequency ablation (RFA) (28 tumors) Open RFA (2 tumors) Temperature controlled 2 cycles | 60 | 13.7 | 41 | 2 |
| | | 284 | | 164 | 29 |

\*Only series with 15 patients or more detailed follow-up and only latest publication of series listed.
[†]All tumors >3 cm in diameter. N.St., not stated.

recurrence seems to depend mainly on selection of patients. With small exophytic, peripheral tumors radiographic complete remission was achieved in 50 of 51 (98%) masses treated in one series, whereas this was accomplished in only 16 of 22 (72%) masses located centrally, although of comparable size (McGovern et al, 2003). Morbidity is low and in general limited to minor perinephric hematomas, although bile and urine fistulas, pancreatic pseudocysts, and a ureteric stricture have been reported (Johnson et al, 2004; Zagoria et al, 2004).

These enthusiastic reports are dampened by three studies in which renal tumors were removed after "curative" RF therapy (Matlaga et al, 2002; Michaels et al, 2002; Rendon et al, 2002). At histologic examination the majority of tumors still showed areas of viable-appearing tumor cells. Standard histology may be misleading immediately after RF application, and loss of reduced nicotinamide adenine dinucleotide (NADH) activity has been postulated as a definitive sign of cell death (Ogan and Cadeddu, 2002b). Six of 13 (46%) tumors had residual NADH activity after RF ablation (Matlaga et al, 2002; Michaels et al, 2002). These findings question the therapeutic efficacy of RF ablation with the techniques presently used. Clearly,

tumor cells are destroyed, but the unreliability of cell kill at least in the border region renders the technique problematic. The use of higher energy generators, multiple treatment cycles, wet RF, and better cooling of the electrodes seem to produce more reliable results (Rehman et al, 2004; Zagoria et al, 2004), but further refinement of the RF delivery systems, better selection of patients, standardization of the technique, and, most important, improved intraoperative monitoring are needed.

## MICROWAVE ABLATION

Early experimental studies with microwave thermotherapy and needle-shaped antennas have shown that temperatures around 60° C can be reached and sustained over time in rabbit kidneys, resulting in focal coagulative necrosis (Hradec and Fuchs, 1969; Kigure et al, 1996). Higher temperatures are difficult to achieve in a normally perfused kidney, and hence multiple needle placements and treatments are necessary for ablating larger lesions. A microwave tissue coagulator based on this principle has been developed to facilitate hemostasis at partial resection of parenchymal organs without ischemia. A needle antenna 10 to 40 mm long is inserted into the parenchyma along the planned plane of resection and a cone-shaped area of coagulative necrosis is produced between the needle and a circle electrode at its base. Parenchymal dissection then follows this plane in a bloodless field. Large clinical series document that the technique permits safe partial nephrectomy for small renal tumors without the need to clamp hilar vessels (Naito et al, 1998; Hirao et al, 2002; Hiroya et al, 2003), but the instruments presently available limit this to open access.

## INTERSTITIAL LASER COAGULATION

By inserting bare-tip laser fibers directly into tissue, laser energy can be utilized for focal tissue ablation by a combination of cavitation and thermal processes. Both neodymium:yttrium-aluminum-garnet (Nd:YAG, 1064 nm) lasers and diode lasers (830 to 980 nm) have been utilized experimentally and in selected patients for interstitial application in the kidney (Lofti et al, 1994; De Jode et al, 1999; Williams et al, 2000; Gettman et al, 2002b). Dose-dependent areas of coagulative necrosis were achieved with target temperatures up to 85° C, but small areas staining NADH positive consistently documented viable residual tissue (Gettman et al, 2002b). The use of diffusing laser tips and multiple laser fiber treatments might bring improvements. Moreover, treatment success also crucially depends on precise delivery of the laser fiber to the target zone, with a stabilization system of the probe during energy delivery to compensate for respiratory movement, and on real-time monitoring of the treatment effect.

## HIGH-INTENSITY FOCUSED ULTRASOUND
## Mode of Action and Experimental Data

As an ultrasound wave propagates through biologic tissues, it is progressively absorbed and energy is converted to heat. If the ultrasound beam is brought to a tight focus at a selected depth within the body, the high energy density produced in this region results in temperatures exceeding the threshold level of protein denaturation. As a consequence, coagulative necrosis occurs. The energy drops sharply outside the focal zone so that surrounding tissues remain unchanged. Utilization of these physical principles open a new prospect in minimally invasive therapy—**targeted tissue ablation from an extracorporeal approach**. Size and location of the ablated region depend on the shape of the piezoceramic element and its focusing system, ultrasound frequency, exposure duration, absorption coefficient of the incident tissues, and in situ intensity achieved (Madersbacher et al, 1995). With higher site intensities (>3500 W/cm$^3$) cavitation phenomena occur, which are more difficult to control. In a multitude of experimental studies, high-intensity focused ultrasound (HIFU) of malignant tumors has not been shown to cause tumor cell dissemination or an increased rate of metastases (Gelet and Chapelon, 1995).

Some of the first attempts at extracorporeal HIFU of renal tissue used a system of multiple piezoceramic elements arranged on a concave disk that targeted a common focal area. Devised from piezoelectric lithotriptors, they generated site intensities in excess of 10,000 W/cm$^3$ and hence predominantly cavitation-induced lesions. Although studies on porcine kidneys and limited clinical trials demonstrated renal lesions (Vallancien et al, 1991, 1992), focusing proved to be too unreliable for clinical use.

All systems presently employed for therapeutic HIFU have single transducers, which are focused either by having a concave shape or with acoustic lenses. The former are smaller and have been employed clinically mainly for intracavitary use, such as transrectal HIFU in the prostate (Madersbacher 1995). As the focal lengths are smaller, frequencies in the 3 to 4 MHz range can be used. They produce smaller but better defined lesions. A modified system of this type was developed for laparoscopic use, which in porcine kidneys permitted reproducible partial kidney ablation with no damage to surrounding structures (Paterson et al, 2003). For extracorporeal HIFU ablation, penetration at this frequency is too short, even in small laboratory animals (Adams et al, 1996). In the 1 to 1.5 MHz range penetration increases, and in animal studies significant renal lesions were obtained at this frequency with an extracorporeal approach (Chapelon et al, 1992; Watkin et al, 1997).

## Extracorporeal High-Intensity Focused Ultrasound: Clinical Experience

Using a prototype system based on a 1-MHz piezoelement focused at a depth of 10 cm with a parabolic reflector and with an integrated 3.5-MHz ultrasonic transducer for real-time imaging, Köhrmann and colleagues (2002) were able to achieve radiologic regression of two of three tumors treated in a solitary kidney. Another system with exchangeable transducers of 0.8, 1.2, and 1.6 MHz and focal lengths of 100 to 160 mm has been tested extensively in China (Wu et al, 2002). Site intensities of 5000 to 20,000 W/cm$^3$ are targeted and the bubble formation in the tissue from cavitation effects is used for real-time ultrasound monitoring. To ablate larger volumes, the focal spot is moved continuously over the target zone, that is, "painting" it rather than spacing one individual lesion next to another. In 13 patients with advanced renal cancer, 3 renal tumors treated in this manner were ablated completely and 10 partially without significant complications (Wu, 2003).

In contrast, a report on the use of these two systems for the treatment of 18 kidney tumors that were subsequently removed and examined histologically found incomplete ablation of the tumors in all patients (Marberger et al, 2005). The disappointing results are due mainly to difficult targeting because of the respiratory movements of the kidney, the complexity of acoustic interphases from intervening structures of the abdominal wall and ribs, and the acoustic inhomogeneities within the tumor. These problems could be overcome by individualizing treatment parameters if a reliable method were available for on-line assessment of the treatment effect. As standard thermosensors cannot be used with HIFU because of acoustic interference, at present this is possible only by complex MRI thermometry (Smith NB et al, 1999; Damianou, 2004). In contrast to applications in other organs, HIFU ablation in the kidney must therefore still be categorized as experimental.

## RADIOSURGERY

In contrast to thermal ablation techniques, radiation destroys dividing tumor cells by mitosis-linked death. Because it is temperature independent, loss of efficacy near larger vessels is avoided. High-energy external-beam radiation affects tissues surrounding the target area with wide margins and even with modern planning techniques can therefore not be applied for truly focal tissue ablation in radiosensitive organs. Brachytherapy permits sharply defined ablation but relies on precise placement of radioactive seeds, which is difficult to achieve in highly perfused mobile organs such as the kidney. All these problems are overcome by using stereotactic techniques to apply highly focused radiation. Pioneered in neurosurgery for the treatment of intracranial tumors, two "radiosurgical" methods have so far been evaluated for tissue ablation in the kidney.

In **interstitial photon radiation**, a miniature linear accelerator generates x-ray photons when accelerated electrons collide with a metal target at the tip of a 3.2-mm needle-shaped target tube. The tube is inserted into the target to deliver a spherical field of radiation with an extremely sharp dose fall-off curve with minimal exposure to surrounding tissues. A dose of 15 Gy of local radiation at a radius of 1.3 cm resulted in well-defined lesions of coagulative necrosis averaging 2.5 cm in diameter, regardless of whether they were in a hilar or peripheral location (Chan et al, 2000). Real-time monitoring of the developing lesion is not possible, but serial CT scans showed a loss of enhancement and shrinkage over time similar to that observed with other ablative techniques (Solomon et al, 2001).

A strictly extracorporeal approach using a frameless image-guided radiosurgical device (**cyberknife**) for focal renal ablation appears even more attractive. The system combines a lightweight 6-V linear accelerator mounted on a robotic arm with an image-to-image algorithm for target localization. An adequate conformal radiation dose is delivered by focusing a multitude of radiation beams at the target zone, yet directing the individual beams along different pathways so that the surrounding tissues are not exposed to a harmful dose. With a targeted dose of up to 40 Gy, complete fibrosis of the target zone without any apparent damage to the surrounding structures was achieved in porcine kidneys (Ponsky et al, 2003). With more than 30 units of this type already operating in clinical radiation oncology centers worldwide, further experimental and also first clinical data on the ablation of renal tumors will presumably soon become available.

## CONCLUSION

A variety of energy ablative techniques have been shown to achieve focal destruction of renal tissue in experimental set-tings and, to a more limited extent, of renal tumors clinically. Morbidity appears to be lower than with the standard surgical procedures. The main problem with the approach remains adequate intraoperative monitoring of the developing lesions to administer the energy needed for complete tumor ablation on an individualized basis. At present, cryoablation under laparoscopic control appears to be most consistent in achieving this goal and intermediate clinical data are encouraging. Given the low growth rate of small renal tumors, long-term clinical follow-up data are needed. Patients should be treated within well-controlled studies, with defined treatment parameters and the possibility of precise follow-up. Selection of patients appears crucial. At present, only renal masses smaller than 3 cm in diameter and located peripherally on the convexity of the kidney, in an easily accessible position, can be considered curable. Standard nephron-sparing procedures achieve excellent results in tumors of this size, so that energy ablative techniques appear justified only if a less invasive approach is mandated because the patient has significant comorbidity.

---

### KEY POINTS: ENERGY ABLATION OF RENAL TUMORS

- Small renal tumors can be destroyed by heat or freezing with low morbidity.

- At present, percutaneous or laparoscopic cryoablation and RF ablation are the only techniques with emerging clinical data.

- Reliable results are obtained with peripheral tumors less than 3 cm in diameter.

- Adherence to technical details with defined treatment parameters and precise long-term follow-up with sequential cross-sectional imaging and frequent biopsy are mandatory.

- Long-term results are emerging.

- This is an alternative for patients unsuited for standard therapy.

---

## SUGGESTED READINGS

Gill IS: Minimally invasive nephron-sparing surgery. Urol Clin North Am 2003;30:551-579.

Kennedy JE, Ter Haar GR, Cranston D: High intensity focused ultrasound: Surgery of the future. Br J Radiol 2003;76:590-599.

Rehman J, Landman J, Lee D, et al: Needle-based ablation of renal parenchyma using microwave, cryoablation, impedance and temperature based monopolar and bipolar radiofrequency, and liquid and gel chemoablation: Laboratory studies and review of the literature. J Endourol 2004;18:83-104.

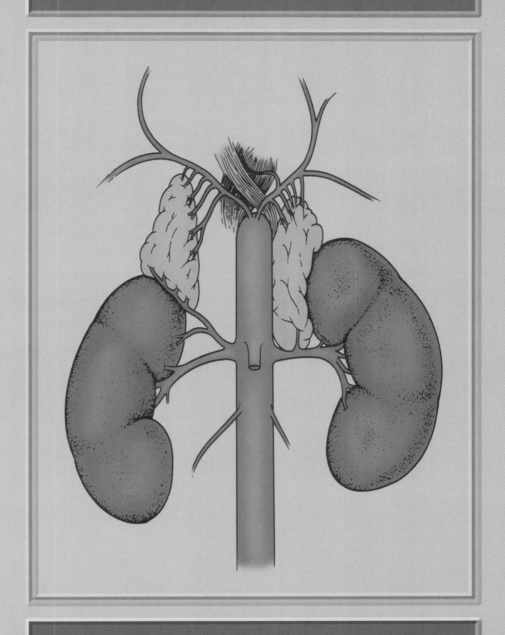

# THE ADRENALS

# 53 Pathophysiology, Evaluation, and Medical Management of Adrenal Disorders

E. DARRACOTT VAUGHAN, JR., MD • JON D. BLUMENFELD, MD

HISTORICAL BACKGROUND

ANATOMY, HISTOLOGY, AND EMBRYOLOGY

ADRENAL PHYSIOLOGY

CUSHING'S SYNDROME

ADRENAL CARCINOMA

ADRENAL ONCOCYTOMA

ADRENAL CYSTS

ADRENAL INSUFFICIENCY

PRIMARY HYPERALDOSTERONISM

PHEOCHROMOCYTOMA

MALIGNANT PHEOCHROMOCYTOMA

## HISTORICAL BACKGROUND

Understanding of the essential physiologic role of the adrenal glands has evolved from the initial description by Eustachius in *Opuscula Anatomica* in 1563 to the elegant biochemical analysis of adrenal secretory products and the precise radiologic imaging studies currently available. Despite earlier recognition of the presence of the adrenals and their division into cortex and medulla (Cuvier and Baron, 1800-1805), it was not until the precise observations of Addison in 1855 that the essential role of these glands was recognized in patients who died with adrenal destruction secondary to tuberculosis. Soon thereafter, Brown-Séquard (1856) performed bilateral adrenalectomies in animals and predicted that the adrenals were essential for life.

Hyperfunction of the adrenal cortex was not documented until 1912, with a definitive report in 1932 of 11 patients with basophilic adenomas of the pituitary that described the now-classic characteristics of Cushing's syndrome (Cushing, 1912, 1932). It was not until the purification of adrenocortical extracts, however, that adrenalectomized animals could be maintained; the adrenal cortex was then documented as the site of critical and essential steroid production (Hartman et al, 1927). Progressive and sequential advances in the understanding of adrenal steroid production have led to the development of precise diagnostic tests to identify patients with Cushing's syndrome (Orth, 1995), adrenocortical forms of hypertension (Biglieri et al, 1995), congenital adrenal hyperplasia (New et al, 2003; Merke and Bornstein, 2005), adrenal carcinoma (Schulick and Brennan, 1999), and other adrenal disorders.

Fränkel first described a medullary adrenal tumor in 1886. London physiologists demonstrated a pressor substance from the adrenal medulla, which they named *adrenaline* (Oliver and Sharpey-Schafer, 1895). Subsequently, Abel (1897) coined the term *epinephrine*, and Kohn (1902) described the chromaffin system. In 1912, the pathologist Pick formulated the descriptive term *pheochromocytoma*, from the Greek *phaios* (dark or dusty) and *chroma* (color), to describe adrenal medullary tumors with their chromaffin reaction.

The development of precise urine and plasma tests led to the accurate identification of patients with adrenal medullary disorders (Rosano et al, 1991; Stein and Black, 1991). Moreover, it is particularly in the identification and localization of pheochromocytomas that imaging techniques have become highly accurate and essential (Heinz-Peer et al, 1999; Sohaib and Reznek, 2000; Teeger et al, 2003).

The diagnosis of the major adrenal disorders is actually simpler now than in the past because of precise diagnostic assays and radiologic tests. The evaluation of a patient for a potential adrenal disorder can be performed efficiently, usually without hospitalization, by a practicing urologist knowledgeable in adrenal disease. Moreover, the surgical approaches are well within the expertise of the urologist and are precisely described (Vaughan, 2004). Finally, laparoscopic adrenalectomy is now the surgical procedure of choice for most adrenal tumors (Gagner et al, 1992).

This chapter reviews the relevant adrenal anatomy, pathology, and physiology that serve as the bases for the clinical, biologic, and radiologic diagnoses of the major adrenal disorders. The adrenal disorders of neuroblastoma and congenital adrenal hyperplasia are reviewed in detail elsewhere in this book and are mentioned only briefly here.

## ANATOMY, HISTOLOGY, AND EMBRYOLOGY

The adrenal glands are paired retroperitoneal organs that lie within perinephric fat at the anterosuperior and medial aspects of the kidneys. They measure up to 5 cm in length by 3 cm in width and are 1 cm thick. In the healthy, nonstressed adult, the glands weigh about 5 g each. **In contrast, the adrenal weight at birth is large (5 to 10 g) because of the fetal adrenal cortex, which may play a major role in fetal embryogenesis and homeostasis** (Pepe and Albrecht, 1990; Anand et al, 1998). The fetal adrenal cortex regresses rapidly during the first 6 weeks of life (Scott, 1990); adrenal tissue remodeling is due to apoptotic cell death at birth after the fetal adrenal serves as a reservoir of progenitor cells that move centrally to populate the definitive zones of the adult adrenal (Jaffe et al, 1998; Wolkersdorfer and Bornstein, 1998). The presence of pituitary adenylate cyclase–activating peptide receptors in developing chromaffin cells in the human fetal adrenal suggests a role for neuropeptides in adrenal development (Breault et al, 1998), but the adrenal is susceptible to hemorrhage at the time of birth, a condition now readily diagnosed by magnetic resonance imaging (Fig. 53–1).

Sectional imaging has provided a better understanding of the precise appearance of the adrenals. Both glands are flat-tened anteriorly with a thick central ridge and thinner medial and lateral rami (Markisz and Kazam, 1989). Cortical infoldings, especially seen on sagittal sections, may be confused with small adenomas, especially in primary aldosteronism, in which the lesions are small.

The right adrenal lies above the kidney posterolateral to the inferior vena cava. The anterior surface is in immediate contact with the inferior-posterior surface of the liver. Thus, from an anterior approach, the anterior surface of the adrenal can be exposed extraperitoneally by gently lifting the liver cephalad, the inferior vena cava being medial. The posterior surface of both adrenals is in contact with the posterior diaphragm (Fig. 53–2). Both adrenals lie more posteriorly as they follow the lumbar curve of the spine, thus falling away from the surgeon for the superior dissection.

The left adrenal is in more intimate contact with the kidney, and the main left renal artery often lies deep to the left adrenal vein as it enters the left renal vein. The gland overlies the upper pole of the kidney, with its anterior surface and medial aspect behind the pancreas and splenic artery (see Fig. 53–2). The anterior surface of the left adrenal can be exposed by remaining retroperitoneal and by gently retracting the spleen cephalad within the peritoneum. Division of the splenorenal ligament facilitates this dissection.

The adrenals have a delicate and rich blood supply estimated to be 6 to 7 mL/g per minute, without a dominant single artery. The inferior phrenic artery is the main blood supply, with additional branches from the aorta and the renal artery (Fig. 53–3) (Pick and Anson, 1940; Anson et al, 1947). In addition, there can be an adrenal arterial supply arising from the gonadal arteries in 60% of fetal adrenal vascular dissections (Bianchi and Ferrari, 1991). The small arteries penetrate the gland in a circumferential stellate fashion, leaving both anterior and posterior surfaces avascular. The venous drainage is usually a common vein on the right, exiting the apex of the gland and **entering the posterior surface of the**

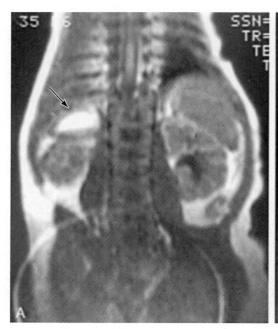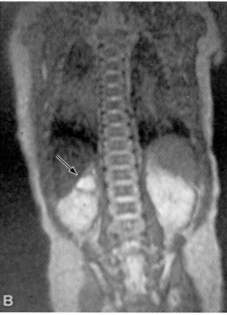

**Figure 53–1.** Adrenal hemorrhage (**A**) bright on magnetic resonance image *(arrow)* and showing later resolution (**B**).

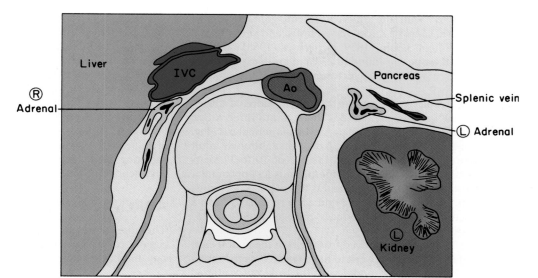

**Figure 53-2.** Line schematic of an anatomic specimen showing position of the adrenal glands in relation to the diaphragm, inferior vena cava (IVC), and kidneys. Ao, aorta. (From Vaughan ED Jr, Carey RM, eds: Adrenal Disorders. New York, Thieme Medical, 1989.)

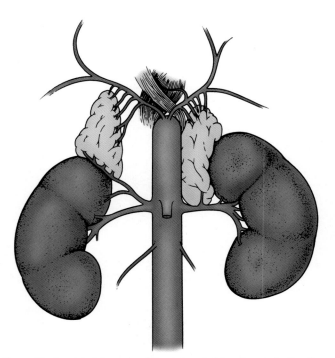

**Figure 53-3.** Arterial supply of the left and right adrenal glands. (From Vaughan ED Jr, Carey RM, eds: Adrenal Disorders. New York, Thieme Medical, 1989.)

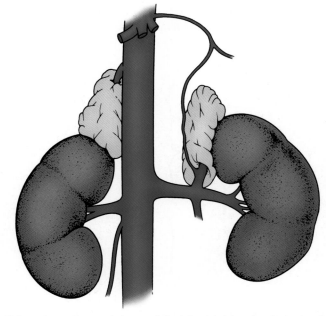

**Figure 53-4.** Venous drainage of the left and right adrenal glands with particular attention to the intercommunicating vein on the left, which is medial and drains into the phrenic system. (From Vaughan ED Jr, Carey RM, eds: Adrenal Disorders. New York, Thieme Medical, 1989.)

**inferior vena cava; this vein is short, fragile, and the most common source of troublesome bleeding during right adrenalectomy** (Fig. 53-4). Uncommonly, the right adrenal vein is joined by a hepatic vein that enters the undersurface of the liver. The left vein empties directly into the left renal vein, about 3 cm from the inferior vena cava and often opposite the gonadal vein (Johnstone, 1957). Not well recognized is the left inferior phrenic vein, which typically communicates with the adrenal vein but then courses medially and can be injured during dissection of the medial edge of the gland.

The adrenal cortex develops from mesoderm, and the medulla develops from neuroectoderm. During the fifth week of development, mesothelial cells located between the root of the mesentery and the developing gonad proliferate and invade the mesenchyme. These cells form the fetal cortex, whereas a second migration of cells forms the definitive cortex; an additional cell type is of mesonephric origin (Crowder, 1957). The intimate relationship with the developing gonad, kidney, and adrenal generally explains the finding of ectopic or aberrant adrenal tissue. Heterotopic adrenal tissue is usually associated with the kidney but is also reported to be associated with the broad ligament, gonadal vessels, spermatic cord, canal of Zuck, uterus, testis, and sites of peritoneal attachment (Culp, 1959; Schechter, 1968). Ectopic adrenocortical tissue was found in 2.7% of groin explorations in male children, with none detected in females (Sullivan et al, 2005).

On microscopic examination, the mature adrenal cortex constitutes 90% of the gland and is divided into three zones: zona glomerulosa, zona fasciculata, and zona reticularis (Fig. 53–5). Zonation is complete by 18 months, although adult configuration is not reached until the age of 10 to 12 years (Moore et al, 1989). The zona glomerulosa is less prominent in humans than in other species and is the site of aldosterone production. The zona fasciculata and zona reticularis form a single functional zone that produces glucocorticoids, androgens, and estrogens.

The adrenal medulla is derived from cells of the neural crest that migrate at the seventh week to form collections that enter the fetal cortex, leaving nodules of neuroblasts scattered throughout the cortex. Neuroblastic cortical nodules regress as the medulla forms, but they can persist and should not be confused with an in situ neuroblastoma. By the 20th week, there is a primitive medulla, but the distinct medulla is not present until atrophy of the fetal cortex.

The medulla is soft and currant jelly–like and can be bluntly dissected free from the cortex for adrenal medullary transplantation (Madrazo et al, 1987). The medulla produces both norepinephrine and epinephrine, with the reaction facilitated in the presence of glucocorticoids. Moreover, there is morphologic evidence for a close interaction of chromaffin cells with cortical cells of the adrenal gland, suggesting a possible paracrine role for neuroregulation of the adrenal cortex (Bornstein et al, 1991). The chromaffin cells are polyhedral, arranged in cords, and richly innervated. Epinephrine-secreting and norepinephrine-secreting cells are distinct (Tannenbaum, 1970).

## ADRENAL PHYSIOLOGY

The adrenal can be thought of functionally as two distinct organs, cortex and medulla. Each has its own unique physiology and hormonally active secretory products.

### Adrenal Cortex

From a common precursor, the zones of the adrenal cortex produce a series of steroid hormones that have an array of actions, including salt retention, metabolic homeostasis, and

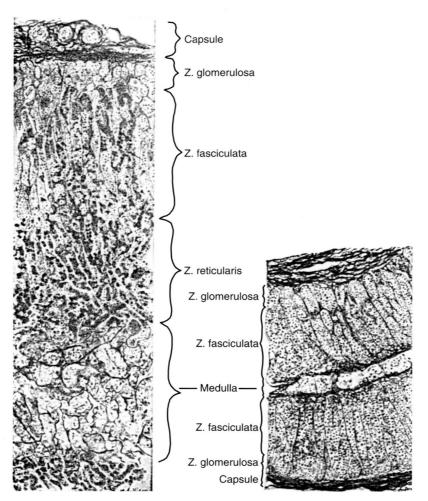

Capsule

Z. glomerulosa

Z. fasciculata

Z. reticularis

Z. glomerulosa

Z. fasciculata

Medulla

Z. fasciculata

Z. glomerulosa

Capsule

**Figure 53–5.** Section of an adrenal of a man *(left)* and of a 6-month-old infant *(right)* (Mallory's azan stain, about ×105). (From Fawcett DW: Bloom and Fawcett: A Textbook of Histology, 11th ed. Philadelphia, WB Saunders, 1986. With permission from Dr. Don W. Fawcett.)

adrenarche development. The basic steroid structure of pregnenolone as derived from cholesterol is shown in Figure 53–6. The zona glomerulosa is the only source of the major mineralocorticoid aldosterone, which regulates sodium resorption in the kidney, gut, and salivary and sweat glands (Carey and Sen, 1986). The other zones produce and secrete cortisol, the major glucocorticoid in humans, and the **principal androgens dehydroepiandrosterone (DHEA), DHEA sulfate (DHEAS), and androstenedione.** The pathways for production of these steroids are shown in Figures 53–7 and 53–8. The rate-limiting step for the formation of all these hormones is the production of pregnenolone (see Fig. 53–6) (Lindzey and Korach, 1997).

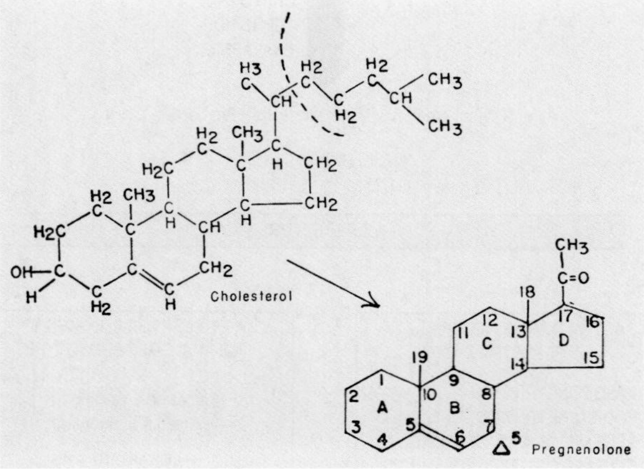

As is discussed in detail elsewhere in this text, it is the deficiency of one of the five enzymes necessary to convert cholesterol to cortisol that leads to the family of diseases termed congenital adrenal hyperplasia (New, 2003); the presenting symptom complexes depend on the specific enzyme deficiency, the lack of necessary pituitary feedback, and the resultant adrenal hyperplasia and proximal precursor excess. The excess of one or numerous steroid products gives the characteristic signs and symptoms of Cushing's syndrome, primary hyperaldosteronism (Conn's syndrome), or adrenal carcinoma.

Now that these pathways have been established clearly, it is possible to perturb the system purposely for diagnostic purposes. Thus, the system can be stimulated with adrenocorticotropic hormone (ACTH), also known as corticotropin, to search for adrenal insufficiency; suppressed with dexamethasone, a synthetic glucocorticoid, to identify different types of Cushing's syndrome; or interrupted with a drug such as metyrapone, which inhibits the enzyme 11β-hydroxylase, thus decreasing circulating cortisol and thereby stimulating the hypothalamic-pituitary axis to increase ACTH (Liu et al, 2003).

### Regulation of Hormone Release

**The regulation of corticosteroid release involves a complex interaction of the hypothalamus, pituitary gland, and adrenal gland.** ACTH is a 39–amino acid polypeptide that exerts a major influence on the adrenal cortex (Hoffman, 1974). ACTH is produced from a large protein (290 amino acids) termed pro-opiomelanocortin. Other peptides derived from pro-opiomelanocortin include β-lipotropin, α-melanocyte–stimulating hormone, β-melanocyte–stimulating hormone, β-endorphin, and methionine enkephalin (Fig.

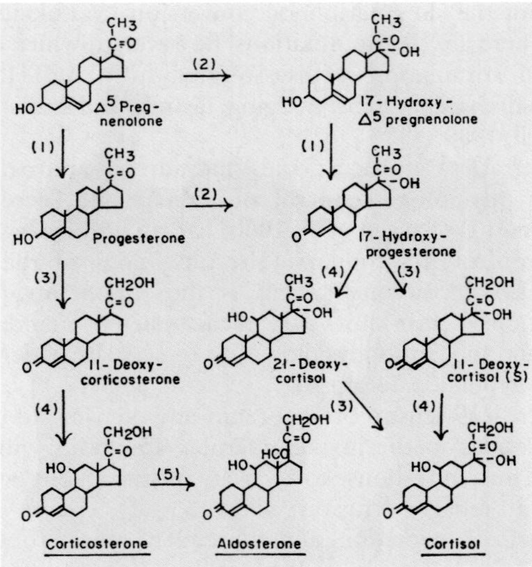

**Figure 53–6.** Conversion of cholesterol to pregnenolone. The cholesterol formula shows the complete steroid structure; the pregnenolone formula shows the conventional representation of the steroid molecule with the rings designated by letter and the carbon atoms numbered.

**Figure 53–7.** Corticosteroid synthesis in the adrenal cortex. Enzyme systems are numbered: 1, β-hydroxysteroid dehydrogenase–β5-oxosteroid isomerase complex; 2, C-17-hydroxylase; 3, C-21-hydroxylase; 4, C-11-hydroxylase; 5, C-18-hydroxylase. The β signifies a double bond, and the attached number shows its position in the nucleus.

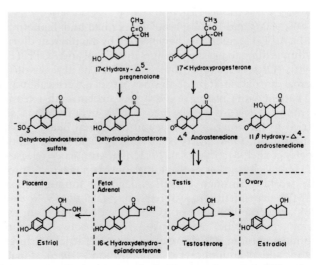

**Figure 53–8.** Sex hormone synthesis. The upper two panels of the scheme show the synthesis of adrenal androgens. The lower panel shows conversion of androstenedione to testosterone (testis, adrenal cortex, and, to a small degree, liver), 16β-hydroxylation of dehydroepiandrosterone by the fetal adrenal and conversion to estrogen in the placenta, and conversion of androgen to estrogen in the ovary. Note that the initial steps in sex hormone synthesis are the same in all these organs.

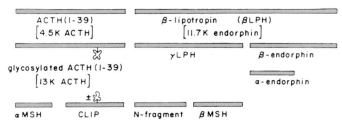

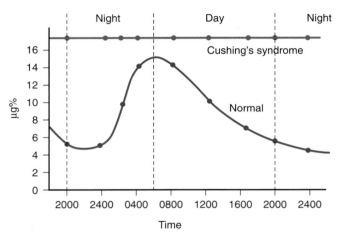

**Figure 53–9.** Structural relationships of peptides with a parental compound of pro-opiomelanocortin. (Modified from Eipper BA, Mains RE: Structure and biosynthesis of pro-adrenocorticotropin/endorphin and related peptides. Endocr Rev 1980;1:2.)

**Figure 53–10.** Circadian rhythm in cortisol secretion of plasma in a normal subject contrasted with absence of rhythm in a patient with Cushing's syndrome. (From Bergland RM, Harrison TS: Pituitary and adrenal. In Schwartz SI, ed: Principles of Surgery, 3rd ed. New York, McGraw-Hill, 1979:1493.)

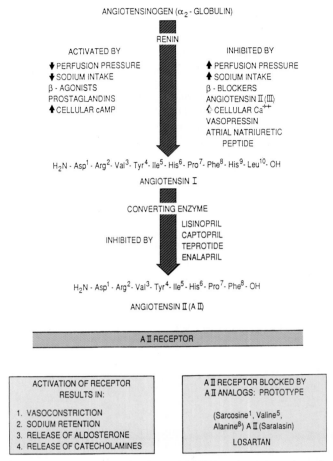

**Figure 53–11.** Factors activating and inhibiting the renin-angiotensin-aldosterone system.

53–9) (Mains and Eipper, 1980; Tepperman and Tepperman, 1987). ACTH secretion is characterized by an inherent diurnal rhythm leading to parallel changes in cortisol and ACTH (Fig. 53–10) (Orth et al, 1967; Kreiger, 1975). The absence of the normal diurnal variation of plasma cortisol is a critical finding in a patient with Cushing's syndrome. Corticotropin-releasing hormone (CRH) is synthesized in the hypothalamus and carried to the anterior pituitary in the portal blood (Taylor and Fishman, 1988). CRH is a 41–amino acid linear peptide (Speiss et al, 1981; Vale et al, 1981) that stimulates release of ACTH as well as other pro-opiomelanocortin products, probably working through a cyclic adenosine monophosphate (cAMP)–dependent process requiring calcium (Vale et al, 1981). Other stimulators of ACTH include vasopressin, oxytocin, epinephrine, angiotensin II, vasoactive intestinal peptide, serotonin, gastrin-releasing peptide, atrial natriuretic factor, and γ-aminobutyric acid (Antoni, 1986). Finally, ACTH secretion is reciprocally related to the circulating cortisol level.

Adrenal androgen production in the reticular and fascicular zones is also under the influence of ACTH, but other mechanisms are involved. DHEA level rises after administration of ACTH; a later elevation of DHEAS level occurs, presumably

because of the slow peripheral conversion (Vaitukaitis et al, 1969). There are clearly situations, however, in which adrenal androgen stimulation is disassociated from ACTH. These include adrenarche, puberty, aging, fasting, and stress (Parker and Odell, 1980).

In contrast to glucocorticoids and adrenal androgens, the **primary physiologic control of aldosterone secretion is angiotensin II** (Laragh et al, 1960; Laragh and Sealey, 1992). ACTH control is secondary. The physiology of the renin-angiotensin-aldosterone system is thoroughly reviewed in Chapters 36. A clear knowledge of the system is mandatory to understand the pathophysiology and to evaluate patients with primary hyperaldosteronism.

The critical sensor of the renin-angiotensin-aldosterone system resides in the juxtaglomerular apparatus within the kidney. Thus, in response to a variety of stimuli but primarily decreased renal perfusion (Fig. 53–11), renin release, angiotensin II formation, and subsequent aldosterone secretion occur, resulting in sodium retention in an attempt to restore renal perfusion (Fig. 53–12). Conversely, if there is sodium retention, renin secretion is suppressed, aldosterone secretion falls, and urinary sodium rises. The inverse relationship found between plasma renin activity or aldosterone and urinary sodium excretion in normal volunteers is shown in Figure 53–13.

**A second, less potent stimulus for aldosterone release is potassium;** thus, there is a second cybernetic system for the control of serum potassium involving the renin-angiotensin-aldosterone system (Laragh and Sealey, 1992). Hypokalemia blunts the adrenal's ability to synthesize aldosterone and can result in the lowering of the plasma aldosterone to a normal range in patients with hypokalemia and hyperaldosteronism (Herf et al, 1979).

## Hormone Actions

All steroid hormones diffuse passively into cells and bind to and activate nuclear steroid receptor proteins. The activated steroid receptor–ligand complexes then bind to specific DNA sequences, termed steroid response elements, which are associated with promoter regions that regulate transcription of genes (Lindzey and Korach, 1997). In the absence of hormone estrogen receptors, androgen receptors and progesterone receptors are primarily localized in the nucleus, whereas glucocorticoid receptors are localized in the cytoplasm.

In addition, glucocorticoids have a non-nuclear pathway that is important in the control of ACTH. The numerous activities of this pathway include inhibition of prostaglandin synthesis, inhibition of calcium flux, inhibition of cAMP protein kinase, and others (Hubbard et al, 1990).

Glucocorticoids are essential for life, even after mineralocorticoid replacement. Glucocorticoids exert their effects on a wide spectrum of cellular metabolism, including accumulation of glycogen in liver and muscle, enhanced gluconeogen-

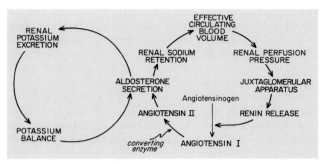

**Figure 53–12.** Control of aldosterone secretion by means of interrelationships between the potassium and renin-angiotensin feedback loops.

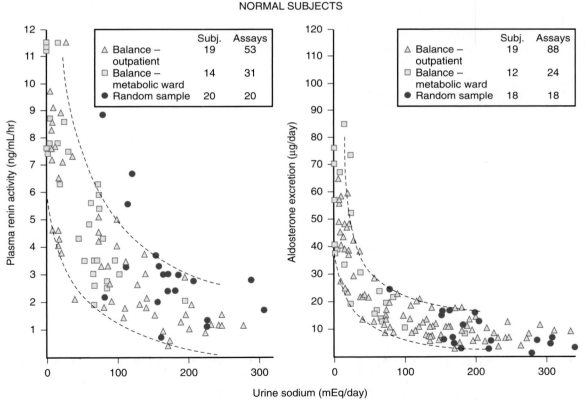

**Figure 53–13.** Relation of renin activity in plasma samples obtained at noon and the corresponding 24-hour urinary excretion of aldosterone to the concurrent daily rate of sodium excretion. For these normal subjects, the data describe a dynamic hyperbolic relationship between each hormone and sodium excretion. The dynamic fluctuations in renin in response to changes in sodium intake help maintain constant blood pressure in the presence of wide changes in sodium balance. The renin and aldosterone responses work together in the kidney to conserve or to eliminate sodium in response to changes in dietary sodium intake. Subjects who were studied while on random diets outside the hospital or on carefully controlled diets in the hospital exhibited similar relationships—a finding that validates the use of this nomogram in the study of outpatients or subjects not on controlled diets. (From Laragh JH, Baer L, Brunner MR, et al: Angiotensin—the renin-aldosterone system in pathogenesis and management of hypertensive vascular diseases. In Laragh JH, ed: Hypertension Manual. New York, Yorke Medical, 1974:313.)

**Table 53–1. Effects and Implications of Glucocorticoids**

| Effects | Clinical Implications |
|---------|----------------------|
| Enhance skeletal and cardiac muscle contraction | Absence results in weakness |
| Cause protein catabolism | Excess results in wastage and weakness |
| Inhibit bone formation | Excess decreases bone mass |
| Inhibit collagen synthesis | Excess causes thin skin and fragile capillaries |
| Increase vascular contractility and decrease permeability | Absence makes it difficult to maintain blood pressure |
| Have anti-inflammatory activity | Exogenous steroid is useful in treating inflammatory diseases |
| Have anti-immune system activity | Exogenous steroids are useful in treating transplantation and various immune diseases |
| Maintain normal glomerular filtration | Absence reduces glomerular filtration |

From Howards SS, Carey RM: The adrenals. In Gillenwater JY, Grayhack JT, Howards SS, Duckett JW, eds: Adult and Pediatric Urology, 2nd ed. Chicago, Year Book, 1991.

esis, impaired peripheral glucose utilization, muscle wasting and myopathy, osteopenia, immune-mediated inflammation, and numerous interactions with other hormones (Table 53–1) (Howards and Carey, 1991; Chrousos, 1995).

Aldosterone accounts for 95% of adrenal mineralocorticoid activity and serves to maintain sodium and potassium balance, as previously stated. The active sites include the kidney, gut, salivary glands, and sweat glands. In all sites, there is the effect of stimulating sodium reabsorption and the increased secretion of potassium and hydrogen through activation of $Na^+,K^+$-ATPase activity or activation of permease in the luminal membrane (Biglieri et al, 1990).

Adrenal androgens are only weakly active, in contrast to testosterone. They appear to be relevant only in pathologic states, such as congenital adrenal hyperplasia, in which there may be excess production.

### Metabolism

The release of these steroids and their metabolism and route of excretion play a critical role in understanding the tests used to diagnose adrenal disorders. In the circulation, 80% of cortisol is bound to corticosterone-binding globulin, 10% to 15% is bound to albumin, and 7% to 10% is free.

Therefore, variations in binding proteins influence the total plasma cortisol value but not the free cortisol, which is metabolically active (Baxter and Tyrrell, 1981). Accurate plasma cortisol assays are now available. Thus, the diurnal variation of plasma cortisol and its response to dexamethasone suppression have evolved as critical tests in the evaluation of patients for possible Cushing's syndrome (Orth, 1995; Liu et al, 2003). Urinary free cortisol is also used as a screening test, although about 3.3% of lean, obese, or chronically ill individuals have elevated values, and values are not well established in children. Difficulties have also been found in establishing upper limits of 17-hydroxysteroid secretion. They are most valuable in evaluation of normal adrenal function,

particularly in looking for adrenal insufficiency or congenital adrenal hyperplasia, in which 17-hydroxysteroid levels are low and 11-hydroxylase levels are high.

The precise control of adrenal androgens is not totally understood, although there is some ACTH control. Peripheral conversion of DHEA to DHEAS contributes to the DHEAS level (Liu et al, 2003). DHEA does show some diurnal variation. DHEA is not produced in significant quantities by other tissues except occasionally in polycystic ovarian disease and gonadal androgen-producing tumors (Osborn and Yannone, 1971; Nelson, 1980). Patients with high DHEA levels also have high 17-ketosteroids, whereas those with virilization caused by elevated testosterone do not. Elevated levels of DHEA, androstenedione, or 17-ketosteroids out of proportion to glucocorticoid production call to mind the diagnosis of adrenal carcinoma (Cohn et al, 1986). Of these tests of adrenal androgen function, the plasma DHEAS value is more commonly used today and is more accurate than the androstenedione value. **Elevated serum concentrations of testosterone and DHEA are the hallmarks of adrenal tumors in women who present with hirsutism** and are used to identify the 5% of women with hirsutism who have a significant adrenal pathologic process (Derksen et al, 1994).

Aldosterone, the major sodium-retaining hormone secreted by the zona glomerulosa, is poorly bound to albumin and plasma protein (Laragh and Sealey, 1992) and has a short half-life of 20 to 30 minutes. Plasma aldosterone can be measured by radioimmunoassay. The plasma value has to be related to the sodium status of the patient and should be measured in conjunction with the plasma renin activity. Equally accurate is urinary aldosterone excretion analyzed in a similar fashion (see Fig. 53–13).

## Adrenal Medulla

The adrenal medulla is composed of large chromaffin cells, which secrete primarily epinephrine but also norepinephrine and dopamine. The fact that the cells stain brown when they are exposed to chromium salts as the result of oxidation of epinephrine and norepinephrine is the origin of the term *chromaffin cell* (Fig. 53–14). The enzyme phenylethanolamine-N-methyltransferase (PNMT), which catalyzes the methylation of norepinephrine to form epinephrine, is almost solely localized to the adrenal medulla (Axelrod, 1962). Thus, if there is excessive production of both norepinephrine and epinephrine, the offending lesion is almost always within the adrenal and not the other sites of chromaffin tissue. Data suggest that high levels of glucocorticoids are necessary to maintain high levels of PNMT and thus epinephrine secretion (Wurtman and Axelrod, 1965). These observations explain the unique location of the adrenal medulla and the central venous drainage system within the adrenal bathing the medullary cells with high levels of glucocorticoids.

Catecholamine synthesis begins with dietary tyrosine and phenylalanine, which are the substrates (Fig. 53–15). Catecholamine synthesis occurs in the adrenal, the central nervous system, and the adrenergic nerve terminals. Activation and suppression of tyrosine hydroxylase activity are the major regulators of catecholamine biosynthesis and may be influenced by the adrenal cortex (Mueller et al, 1970). Norepinephrine is

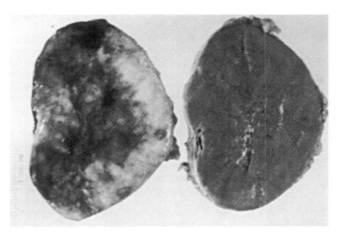

**Figure 53–14.** Pheochromocytoma showing chromaffin reaction 1 *(right)*.

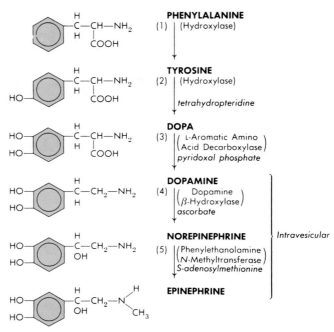

**Figure 53–15.** Enzymatic pathway for dopamine, norepinephrine, and epinephrine synthesis. Enzymes are in parentheses; cofactors are in italics. (Modified from Goodman AG, Goodman LS, Gilman A, eds: The Pharmacologic Basis of Therapeutics, 6th ed. New York, Macmillan, 1980:72.)

the major catecholamine secreted by sympathetic neurons. Studies of healthy humans indicate that plasma dopamine accounts for 13% of the free catechols; epinephrine, 14%; and norepinephrine, 73% (Manger and Gifford, 1990).

Catecholamines are stored in separate vesicles along with adenosine triphosphate, chromogranins, and the enzyme dopamine β-hydroxylase. Stimulation of the preganglionic sympathetic nerves during stress, pain, cold, heat, asphyxia, hypotension, hypoglycemia, and sodium depletion increases catecholamine release (Lewis, 1975). After stimulation, the contents of the vesicles are released by exocytosis (Winkler and Smith, 1975). In addition, catechols may be released without sympathetic stimulation and possibly without exocytosis—a phenomenon postulated in patients with pheochromocytomas.

## Catecholamine Metabolism

Catecholamines are rapidly removed from the circulation with a plasma half-life of less than 20 seconds (Ferrerira and Vane, 1967). The metabolic pathways for catecholamines are shown in Figure 53–16. Neuronal reuptake is of major importance in the removal of norepinephrine from the synaptic gap for re-release and has been termed uptake (Iverson, 1975). Catecholamines are degraded by the action of catechol-*O*-methyltransferase and monoamine oxidase, with either enzyme beginning the degrading process. **The primary metabolite in the urine is vanillylmandelic acid; metanephrine, normetanephrine, and their derivatives contribute to total metabolic products,** which are often measured in evaluation of patients with pheochromocytomas (Bravo and Tagle, 2003).

## Catecholamine Actions

Catecholamines exert varied effects by stimulating specific cellular receptors (adrenoreceptors), which are protein-binding sites (Table 53–2). The diversity of effects of circulating catecholamines on various organs acting at specific receptors accounts for the diversity of symptoms exhibited by patients with pheochromocytomas. Moreover, different tumors can produce different proportions of norepinephrine, epinephrine, or dopamine.

| Table 53–2. **Catecholamine Receptors** |
| --- |
| $\alpha_1$-*Adrenergic* |
| Postsynaptic agonists |
| Vascular smooth muscle—vasoconstriction |
| Prostate—contraction |
| Liver—glycogenesis |
| $\alpha_2$-*Adrenergic* |
| Presynaptic—inhibit norepinephrine release |
| Postsynaptic—agonist |
| Large veins—venoconstrictor |
| Brain—decrease sympathetic outflow |
| Pancreas—inhibit insulin secretion |
| Gut—relaxation |
| Adipocyte—inhibit lipolysis |
| $\beta_1$-*Adrenergic* |
| Heart—inotropic and chromotropic effect |
| Adipocyte—lipolysis |
| Kidney—stimulate renin release |
| $\beta_2$-*Adrenergic* |
| Lung—bronchodilatation |
| Vascular smooth muscle—vasodilatation |
| Liver—gluconeogenesis |
| Uterus—relaxation |
| Gut—relaxation |
| *Dopaminergic* |
| $D_1$: Vascular—vasodilatation |
| $D_2$: Presynaptic—inhibit norepinephrine release |

The actions of epinephrine and norepinephrine are not totally independent and are dose dependent. Hence, the classification of naturally occurring adrenergic hormones as α-adrenergic or β-adrenergic or as blocking agents, such as an $\alpha_1$ antagonist, is useful but does not fully characterize

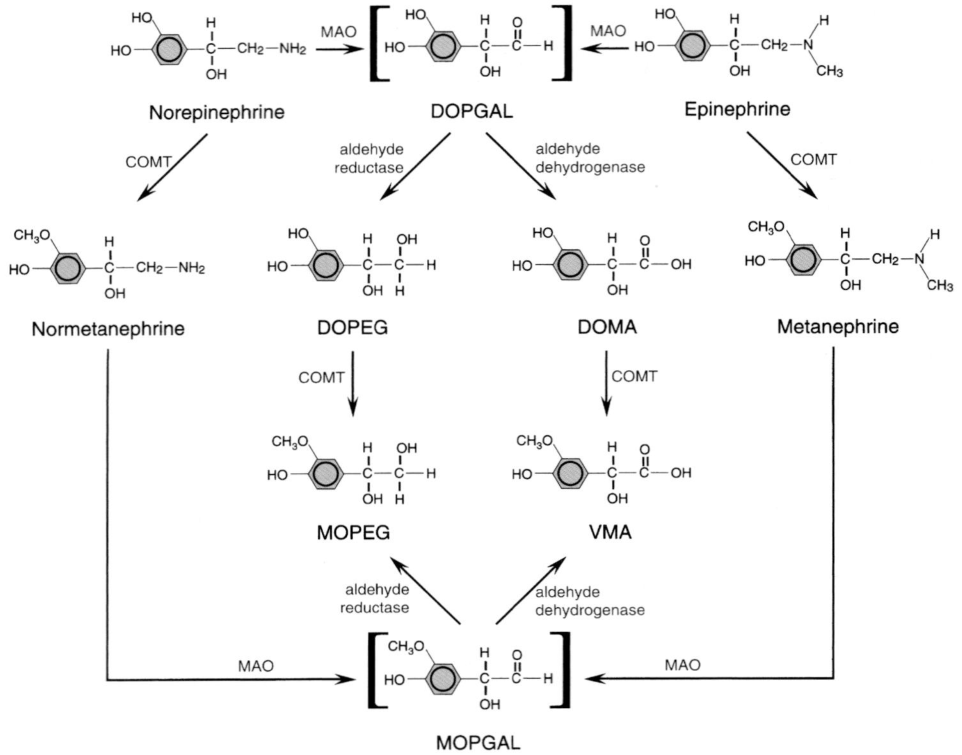

**Figure 53–16.** Steps in the metabolic disposition of catecholamines. Both norepinephrine and epinephrine are first oxidatively deaminated by monoamine oxidase (MAO) to 3,4-dihydroxyphenylglycoaldehyde (DOPGAL) and then either reduced to 3,4-dihydroxyphenylethylene glycol (DOPEG) or oxidized to 3,4-dihydroxymandelic acid (DOMA). Alternatively, they can be initially methylated by catechol-*O*-methyltransferase (COMT) to normetanephrine and metanephrine, respectively. Most of the products of either type of reaction are then metabolized by the other enzyme to form the major excretory products 3-methoxy-4-hydroxyphenylethylene glycol (MOPEG or MHPG) and 3-methoxy-4-hydroxymandelic acid (VMA). Free MOPEG is largely converted to VMA. The glycol and, to some extent, the *O*-methylated amines and the catecholamines may be conjugated to the corresponding sulfates or glucuronides. (From Hardman JG, Limbird LE, Molinoff PB, et al: Neurotransmission: The autonomic and somatic nervous system. In Lefkowitz RJ, Hoffman BB, Taylor P, eds: Goodman and Gilman's The Pharmacological Basis of Therapeutics, 9th ed. New York, McGraw-Hill, 1996:105.)

the activity of the hormone or antagonist in all clinical settings.

# CUSHING'S SYNDROME

Cushing's syndrome describes the symptom complex caused by excess circulating glucocorticoids (Cushing, 1912, 1932; Arnaldi et al, 2003; Findling and Raff, 2005). The term is all-encompassing and includes patients with pituitary hypersecretion of ACTH (corticotropin); **patients with Cushing's disease, who account for 75% to 85% of patients with endogenous Cushing's syndrome;** patients with adrenal adenomas or carcinomas; and patients with ectopic secretion of ACTH or CRH (Carey et al, 1984), or about 20% of those with ACTH-dependent disease (Meador et al, 1962; Scott, 1990) (Tables 53–3 and 53–4).

The entity is rare, occurs most often in young adults, and is more common in females. **An exogenous source of Cushing's syndrome should always be excluded first because therapeutic steroids are the most common cause.** Often, the patient does not even realize he or she is using a steroid-containing preparation, especially creams or lotions (Champion, 1974; Flavin et al, 1983). The manifestations of the disease are legion and are the result of the manifold actions of glucocorticoids (see Table 53–1). There are few diseases in which the clinical appearance of the patient can be as useful in suggesting the diagnosis (Figs. 53–17 and 53–18). Old photographs are helpful in documenting the changes in appearance that have occurred. The more common clinical manifestations of Cushing's syndrome, found in several series of patients, are

**Table 53–3. Relative Prevalence of Various Types of Cushing's Syndrome Among 630 Patients Studied at Different Times***

| Diagnosis | Percentage of Patients |
|---|---|
| Corticotropin-dependent Cushing's syndrome | |
|     Cushing's disease | 68 |
|     Ectopic corticotropin syndrome | 12 |
|     Ectopic corticotropin-releasing hormone syndrome | <1 |
| Corticotropin-dependent Cushing's syndrome | |
|     Adrenal adenoma | 10 |
|     Adrenal carcinoma | 8 |
|     Micronodular hyperplasia | <1 |
|     Macronodular hyperplasia | <1 |
| Pseudo–Cushing's syndrome | |
|     Major depressive disorder | <1 |
|     Alcoholism | <1 |

*Data are based on a study of 146 consecutive patients seen at Vanderbilt University Medical Center before 1993 and on published reports describing a total of 484 patients. Because these and most other published series were reported by major referral centers, the proportion of patients with unusual diagnoses may be exaggerated compared with that of patients with more common diagnoses. The prevalence of pseudo–Cushing's syndrome depends largely on the individual physician's threshold of clinical suspicion. The proportions of children and adolescents with the different causes of Cushing's syndrome may differ slightly from the proportions of adults; for example, ectopic corticotropin syndrome is less common in children.
From Orth DN: Cushing's syndrome. N Engl J Med 1995;332:791.

described in Table 53–5. The clinical findings do not distinguish patients with Cushing's disease from those with adrenal adenomas or carcinomas. Most patients with ectopic ACTH do not present with the typical features (Bagshaw, 1960) but exhibit cachexia due to underlying tumor as well as hypertension, hypokalemic alkalosis, and skin pigmentation (Bagshaw, 1960; Schambelan et al, 1971). The most common characteristics in children are weight gain and growth retardation (Magiakou et al, 1994). Virilization in the female or feminization in the male should raise the question of adrenal carcinoma, although more patients present with traditional manifestations of glucocorticoid excess (Luton et al, 1990; Ng and Libertino, 2003).

The goals of management of Cushing's syndrome have been articulated by investigators who have a long-standing interest in this disease: lowering of daily cortisol secretion to normal, eradication of any tumor threatening health, production of no permanent endocrine deficiency, and avoidance of permanent dependence on medications (Orth and Liddle, 1971; Orth, 1995). Obviously, not all of these goals can be met in all

### Table 53–4. Sources of Ectopic ACTH in 100 Cases

| Tumor | Number |
|---|---|
| Carcinoma of lung | 52 |
| Carcinoma of pancreas (including carcinoid) | 11 |
| Thymoma | 11 |
| Benign bronchial adenoma (including carcinoid) | 5 |
| Pheochromocytoma | 3 |
| Carcinoma of thyroid | 2 |
| Carcinoma of liver | 2 |
| Carcinoma of prostate | 2 |
| Carcinoma of ovary | 2 |
| Undifferentiated carcinoma of mediastinum | 2 |
| Carcinoma of breast | 1 |
| Carcinoma of parotid gland | 1 |
| Carcinoma of esophagus | 1 |
| Paraganglioma | 1 |
| Ganglioma | 1 |
| Primary site uncertain | 3 |

From Scott HW Jr, Orth DN: Hypercortisolism (Cushing's syndrome). In Scott HW, ed: Surgery of the Adrenal Glands. Philadelphia, JB Lippincott, 1990:145.

### Table 53–5. Clinical Manifestations of Cushing's Syndrome

| Manifestation | All (%)* | Disease (%)† | Adenoma or Carcinoma (%)‡ |
|---|---|---|---|
| Obesity | 90 | 91 | 93 |
| Hypertension | 80 | 63 | 93 |
| Diabetes | 80 | 32 | 79 |
| Centripetal obesity | 80 | — | — |
| Weakness | 80 | 25 | 82 |
| Muscle atrophy | 70 | 34 | — |
| Hirsutism | 70 | 59 | 79 |
| Menstrual abnormalities, sexual dysfunction | 70 | 46 | 75 |
| Purple striae | 70 | 46 | 36 |
| Moon facies | 60 | — | — |
| Osteoporosis | 50 | 29 | 54 |
| Early bruising | 50 | 54 | 57 |
| Acne, pigmentation | 50 | 32 | — |
| Mental changes | 50 | 47 | 57 |
| Edema | 50 | 15 | — |
| Headache | 40 | 21 | 46 |
| Poor healing | 40 | — | — |

*Hunt and Tyrrell, 1978.
†Wilson, 1984.
‡Scott, 1973.
From Scott HW Jr: Surgery of the Adrenal Glands. Philadelphia, JB Lippincott, 1990.

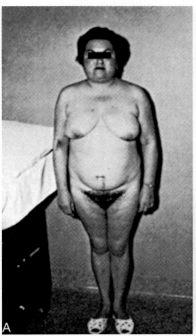
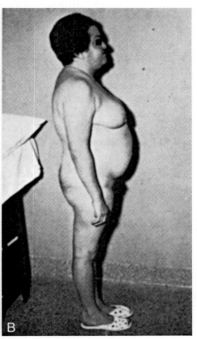

**Figure 53–17. A,** A 34-year-old woman with Cushing's syndrome. The patient shows truncal obesity and mild hirsutism. **B,** Note that cutaneous striae and ecchymoses are absent, in contrast to most cases shown in textbooks.

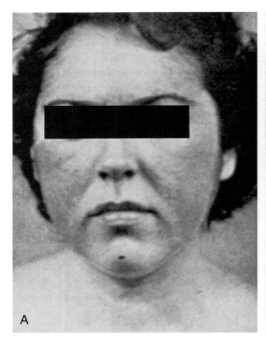 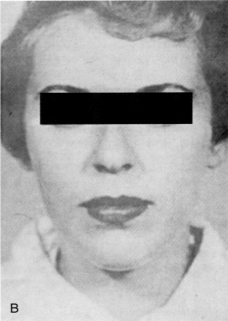

**Figure 53–18.** **A,** A 23-year-old woman 6 months after the development of moon face and other early signs of Cushing's syndrome due to an adrenocortical adenoma on the left side. **B,** Same patient 6 months after surgical removal of the adenoma of the adrenal cortex. (From Harrison JH: Surgery of the adrenals. In Davis L, ed: Christopher's Textbook of Surgery, 8th ed. Philadelphia, WB Saunders, 1964.)

patients; however, they serve as a thoughtful frame of reference. To initiate evaluation, the cause of Cushing's syndrome in a given patient must be established. **Importantly, patients with nonendocrine disorders that mimic the clinical and sometimes biochemical manifestations of Cushing's syndrome must be separated from those patients with true Cushing's syndrome;** these patients have been said to have pseudo–Cushing's syndrome. Abnormally regulated cortical secretion, albeit mild, may exist in as many as 80% of patients with major depression and can occur commonly in patients with chronic alcoholism (Gold et al, 1986; Stewart et al, 1993; Orth, 1995). Finally, although Cushing's syndrome has always been described as rare, about two or three cases per million (Findling and Raff, 2005), it is now recognized that there is an entity termed subclinical Cushing's syndrome. **Remarkably, in early studies of the common "metabolic syndrome," 3% to 5% of patients have been found to have this entity** (Catargi et al, 2003). Moreover, in a study of patients with incidentalomas, 24% had subclinical Cushing's syndrome after careful evaluation, and clinical features of the syndrome improved after adrenalectomy in a selected group of patients (Rossi et al, 2000). Thus, the indications for screening for Cushing's syndrome have expanded (Table 53–6) (Findling and Raff, 2005). In the future, many more patients with this entity may be diagnosed and treated.

## Laboratory Diagnosis

A panoply of tests of glucocorticoid function have evolved that are used to establish the presence of Cushing's syndrome and to distinguish between pituitary and adrenal causes as well as ectopic ACTH secretion (Orth, 1995; Liu et al, 2003; Raff and Findling, 2003) (Fig. 53–19). The clinical diagnosis of Cushing's syndrome is confirmed by the demonstration of cortisol hypersecretion. **The determination of 24-hour excre-**

| Table 53–6. **Who Should Be Screened for Cushing's Syndrome?** |
|---|
| *Signs and Symptoms* |
| Central obesity with |
|     Facial rounding with plethora |
|     Increased supraclavicular and dorsocervical fat |
|     Cutaneous wasting with ecchymoses |
|     Wide violaceous striae (>1 cm) |
|     Proximal myopathy |
|     Increased lanugo hair |
|     Superficial fungal infections |
|     Growth retardation (in children) |
| *Clinical Diagnosis* |
| Metabolic syndrome X |
|     Diabetes mellitus (Hgb $A_{1c}$ > 8%) |
|     Hypertension |
|     Hyperlipidemia |
|     Polycystic ovary syndrome |
| Hypogonadotropic hypogonadism |
|     Oligomenorrhea, amenorrhea, infertility |
|     Decreased libido and impotence |
| Osteoporosis (especially rib fracture) |
|     Patients aged < 65 yr |
| Incidental adrenal mass |

**tion of cortisol in the urine is the most direct and reliable index of cortisol secretion.** A consensus statement on the diagnosis of Cushing's syndrome (Arnaldi et al, 2003) recommended that urinary cortisol be measured in two or preferably three consecutive 24-hour urine specimens collected on an outpatient basis. If cortisol excretion results are normal in three collections, Cushing's syndrome is unlikely. Multiple collections are necessary because of the possibility of errors in collection and because of variations in hour-to-hour or day-to-day cortisol excretion. As for other 24-hour urine

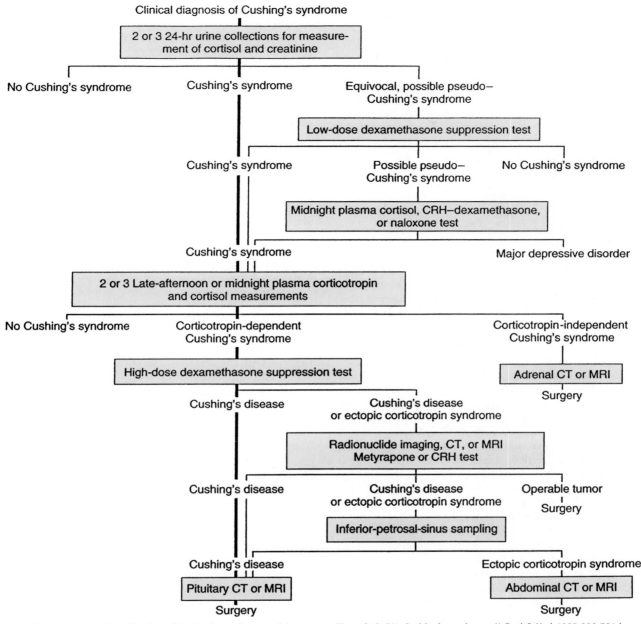

**Figure 53–19.** Identification of Cushing's syndrome and its causes. (From Orth DN: Cushing's syndrome. N Engl J Med 1995;332:791.)

collections, cortisol excretion should be calculated as a function of creatinine excretion.

In the patient with elevated 24-hour urinary cortisol, we advocate determining the presence or absence of the normal circadian rhythm in plasma cortisol by obtaining ambulatory morning and evening plasma cortisol levels to continue the diagnosis. After ACTH release, healthy subjects show a characteristic rise in plasma cortisol in the morning, with a fall to less than 5 ng/dL in the evening (see Fig. 53–10). Patients with Cushing's syndrome lose the diurnal variation (Besser and Edwards, 1972) or show some variations, but at higher basal levels (Glass et al, 1984).

Commonly, the next test used is the dexamethasone suppression test as developed by Liddle (1960). Pituitary ACTH

secretion is regulated with negative feedback inhibition by cortisol. Liddle used the synthetic steroid dexamethasone, 30 times as potent as cortisol, to study the pituitary feedback mechanism in patients with suspected Cushing's syndrome. In normal subjects, 0.5 mg orally every 6 hours for 2 days causes a dramatic fall in 17-hydroxycorticosteroid, urinary free cortisol, or plasma cortisol (<5 ng/dL). A simplification of the test is to administer a single 1-mg oral dose between 11 PM and midnight and to measure the plasma cortisol level between 8 AM and 9 AM (Fig. 53–20) (Paulotos et al, 1965; Sarvin et al, 1968). The test is less reliable, however, than the formal low-dose 2-day test, especially in obese patients. Patients with Cushing's syndrome show resistance to suppression with low-dose dexamethasone. This failure of suppression has been

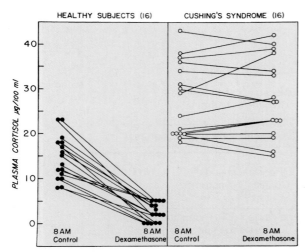

HEALTHY SUBJECTS (16)   CUSHING'S SYNDROME (16)

**Figure 53-20.** The rapid dexamethasone suppression test distinguishes patients with Cushing's syndrome from healthy subjects or other obese subjects. Note the overlap in cortisol levels between the two groups before suppression. The patients with high basal cortisol levels were those with ectopic ACTH production by a nonendocrine tumor as the underlying cause. (From Melby J: Assessment of adrenocortical function. N Engl J Med 1971;285:735.)

found to be characteristic of all patients with Cushing's syndrome studied by Scott and Orth (1990). These low-dose suppression tests are now reserved primarily for patients with equivocal 24-hour urinary cortisol excretion (Orth, 1995) and are especially useful for identifying patients with pseudo–Cushing's syndrome. **A recently described test that is likely to be used more commonly by endocrinologists is the late-night salivary cortisol concentration measurement** (Arnaldi et al, 2003; Findling and Raff, 2005). The test has high sensitivity and specificity and may be combined with the low-dose overnight dexamethasone test.

Alternatively, **the ideal way to determine whether a patient has ACTH-dependent or ACTH-independent hypercortisolism is the concurrent measurement of both plasma ACTH and cortisol** (Raff and Findling, 1989). Despite the fact that the ideal time to measure these hormones is between midnight and 2 AM, when the concentrations are at the lowest, a more practical approach is to measure the test late in the afternoon. Again, Orth (1995) recommends the measurement of the two hormones at least on 2 and preferably 3 separate days. If the plasma cortisol concentration is more than 50 μg/dL and the corticotropin concentration is less than 5 pg/mL, cortical secretion is ACTH independent (the patient has primary adrenal Cushing's syndrome). If the plasma ACTH level is more than 50 pg/mL, the cortical secretion is ACTH dependent (the patient has Cushing's disease or ectopic ACTH or CRH syndrome) (Orth, 1995). In situations in which the two-site immunoradiometric assay test is not available, the high-dose dexamethasone suppression test has always been the standard test to differentiate between pituitary and adrenal Cushing's syndrome. Patients are given high-dose dexamethasone (2 mg every 6 hours for 2 days), and plasma cortisol and urinary free cortisol levels are measured. In patients with pituitary disease, there should be a 50% or greater suppression in cortisol. Patients with adrenal adenomas or carcinomas fail to suppress cortisol secretion. In addition, the tests

usually distinguish Cushing's disease, in which there is only relative resistance to glucocorticoid negative feedback, from ectopic ACTH syndrome, in which there is usually complete resistance. A number of different criteria have been established to try to obtain greater sensitivity in correctly identifying patients with Cushing's disease; but in almost all the different studies, patients with ectopic ACTH as well as those with primary adrenal disease have uniformly failed to suppress cortisol (Avgerinos et al, 1994; Miller and Crapo, 1994).

Additional tests in use to differentiate between pituitary Cushing's disease and ectopic ACTH secretion are metyrapone stimulation tests and petrosal venous sinus catheterization. The metyrapone stimulation test was originally used to determine pituitary insufficiency. Metyrapone blocks conversion of 11-desoxycortisol to cortisol, and as the plasma cortisol concentration falls, the pituitary secretes more ACTH, and there is an increase in urinary 17-hydroxycorticosteroid concentration. Patients with Cushing's disease have a normal or supernormal increase in urinary excretion of 17-hydroxycorticosteroids, in contrast to patients with ectopic ACTH-secreting tumors, who have little or no increase in either value because of the suppression of pituitary ACTH (Avgerinos et al, 1994). **Obviously, the most direct way to demonstrate pituitary hypersecretion of ACTH is to measure its level in the petrosal venous sinus and compare the level with the peripheral level.** Sampling can also be done before and after stimulation with CRH. This is an invasive procedure, however, and significant complications have been reported (Oldfield et al, 1991; Miller et al, 1992). Before petrosal sinus catheterization is indicated, thorough studies should be performed to identify occult ACTH-secreting tumors. Many of these tumors can be identified with standard computed tomography (CT) or magnetic resonance imaging (MRI) and, more recently, unique radionuclide imaging for somatostatin receptors, which are present in small cell lung carcinomas and thymic carcinoid tumors (Phlipponneau et al, 1994).

At this point, despite the availability of numerous stimulatory and inhibitory tests (Liu et al, 2003), the dramatic advances in radiologic localizing tests usually make further biochemical studies unnecessary.

## Radiographic Localization

The development of computer-aided sectional imaging and MRI has revolutionized adrenal imaging. Accordingly, older tests such as intravenous urography with tomography, ultrasonography, and adrenal arteriography and venography are only rarely used today. In general, CT has become the initial imaging procedure.

In patients with Cushing's disease, additional information can be obtained with CT or MRI of the sella turcica in search of a pituitary adenoma (Fig. 53–21) (Mitty and Yeh, 1982). More recently, both unenhanced and gadolinium-enhanced MRI is used; however, only 50% of microadenomas are detected (Klibanski and Zervas, 1991; Hall et al, 1994).

Patients with hyperplasia can show diffuse thickening and elongation of the adrenal rami (Fig. 53–22) or, unfortunately, prominent glands bilaterally that fall within normal range (Teeger et al, 2003). A second variant, found in 10% to 20% of cases, is nodular cortical hyperplasia characterized by

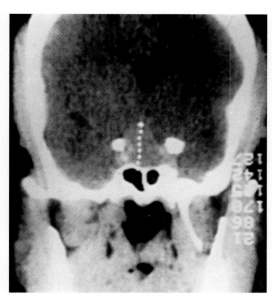

**Figure 53–21.** CT scan of a chromophobe adenoma in the sella turcica of a patient with Cushing's syndrome presenting with hyperpigmentation, headaches, and a visual field defect.

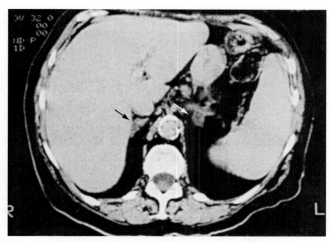

**Figure 53–23.** CT scan showing a patient with macronodular adrenal hyperplasia.

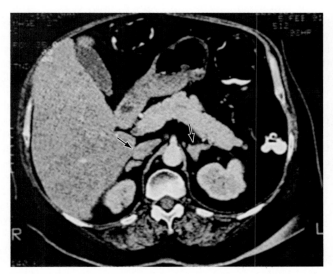

**Figure 53–22.** CT scan showing bilateral adrenal hyperplasia in a patient with Cushing's disease.

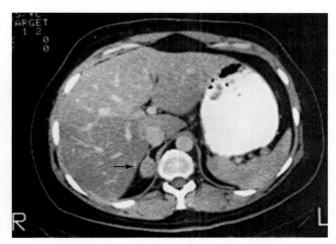

**Figure 53–24.** CT scan of a patient with right adrenal adenoma.

multinodularity of both adrenals (Fig. 53–23). The CT appearance does not distinguish between patients with glucocorticoid excess and patients with idiopathic hyperaldosteronism (pseudo–primary hyperaldosteronism) because of bilateral adrenal hyperplasia. The small size (<2 cm) and multiplicity of the nodules as well as the bilateral distribution are the distinguishing features from Cushing's adenomas. Rarely, patients with macronodular hyperplasia develop autonomous glucocorticoid secretion and may require adrenalectomy.

Adrenal adenomas are usually larger than 2 cm, solitary, and associated with atrophy of the opposite gland. The density is low because of the high concentration of lipid. Sonography and study after the administration of contrast material showing enhancement avoid misdiagnosis of an adrenal cyst

(Fig. 53–24) (Huebener and Treugut, 1984). However, large benign adenomas (5 cm or larger) often show calcification, heterogenicity, and cystic characteristics on CT and have regions of high signal intensity on T2-weighted MRI (Newhouse et al, 1999). Thus, these large adenomas share the radiologic characteristics of adrenal carcinoma.

Adrenal carcinomas are often indistinguishable from adenomas except for the larger size (>6 cm) (Fig. 53–25) (Belldegrun and deKernion, 1989). **Necrosis and calcification are also more common in association with adrenal carcinoma but are not diagnostic.** Clearly, large, irregular adrenal lesions with invasion represent carcinoma; however, metastatic carcinoma to the adrenal has the same appearance.

MRI is not usually necessary in patients with Cushing's syndrome unless adrenal carcinoma is suspected. In that clinical setting, **the signal intensity may be much higher with carcinoma than that in the spleen, accurately differentiating adenomas from carcinomas** (Bilbey et al, 1995). MRI may also provide useful information about adjacent-organ or vascular invasion.

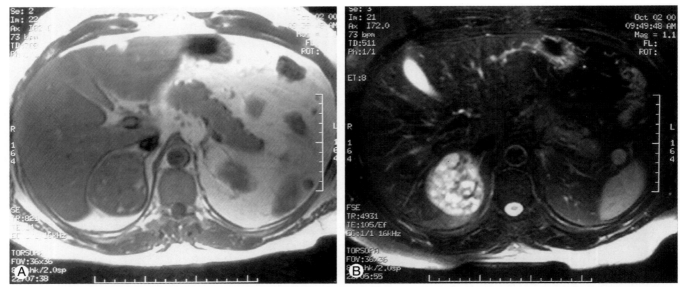

**Figure 53-25.** Large right adrenal carcinoma showing a heterogeneous pattern (**A**) and bright enhancement on a T2-weighted magnetic resonance image (**B**).

Adrenal cortical scanning with iodinated cholesterol agents is no longer routinely used but can be helpful in differentiating functional adrenal tissue from other retroperitoneal lesions (Kazerooni et al, 1990; Nakajo et al, 1993) and in identifying residual cortical tissues. It is not useful for the identification of adrenal carcinoma (Pasieka et al, 1992). Positron emission tomography has recently been used to image adrenal masses. To date, there is evidence that a variety of agents can discriminate between cortical lesions and either metastatic disease or neural tumors but not between benign and malignant cortical tumors (Hoh et al, 1998; Yun et al, 2001; Zettinig et al, 2004).

## Treatment

### Cushing's Disease and Ectopic ACTH Syndrome

In recalling the goals of management of Cushing's syndrome as outlined by Liddle, it is obvious that precise diagnosis is critical. Accordingly, in the patient with ectopic ACTH syndrome, treatment is directed to the primary tumor. Reduction of secretion of functional steroids by use of blocking agents can further ameliorate symptoms. Agents include aminoglutethimide, which blocks the conversion of cholesterol to pregnenolone; metyrapone, which blocks the conversion of 11-desoxycortisol to cortisone and ketoconazole; and an antifungal agent that blocks cytochrome P-450–mediated side chain cleavage and hydroxylation at both early and late steps in steroid biosynthesis (Loose et al, 1983; Farwell et al, 1988; Mortimer et al, 1991). Patients given aminoglutethimide must be observed for adrenocortical insufficiency because aldosterone production is also impaired. Metyrapone does not normally result in salt wasting at the usual dose of 250 to 500 mg three times daily because of increased production of desoxycorticosterone, a potent mineralocorticoid (see Figs. 53–7 and 53–8) (Scott and Orth, 1990). Other agents used with some success are ketoconazole (Sonino et al, 1991) and the cortisol receptor blocker mifepristone (Bertagna et al, 1986).

The synthesis of cortisol in 1950 (Wendler et al, 1950) led to the availability of replacement steroids not only for patients with Addison's disease but also for those with bilateral adrenalectomy for Cushing's disease. Thus, bilateral adrenalectomy through a bilateral posterior approach was used in patients with severe Cushing's disease. In general, patients did well with resolution of the disease (Scott et al, 1977, 1990). **However, 10% to 20% of patients subsequently developed pituitary tumors, usually chromophobe adenomas, perhaps caused by the lack of hypothalamic-pituitary feedback and the high levels of ACTH and related compounds** (Nelson et al, 1958; Cohen et al, 1978). This entity, called Nelson's syndrome, may arise many years after bilateral adrenalectomy. Thus, patients must be followed up with determination of ACTH levels and evaluation of the sella turcica (Fig. 53–26). The development of Nelson's syndrome may be prevented by prophylactic pituitary radiotherapy (Jenkins et al, 1995).

The development of pituitary irradiation subsequently limited the use of bilateral adrenalectomy for Cushing's disease beginning in the 1950s (Orth and Liddle, 1971). Long-term follow-up reveals an 83% remission rate after unsuccessful transsphenoidal surgery, which is the initial treatment of choice (Estrada et al, 1997). Irradiation is useful to treat Nelson's syndrome. Heavy particle proton beam therapy may be more effective but also is more likely to induce panhypopituitarism (Burch, 1985).

In 1971, Hardy reported his experience with transsphenoidal hypophyseal microsurgery for removal of pituitary adenomas with preservation of pituitary function. Subsequently, this technique evolved as the single most effective and safest treatment of Cushing's disease. Cure rates are 85% to 95%, results are immediate, complications are low, and recurrences are rare (Ludecke, 1991; Swearingen et al, 1999). Patients often have transient decreases in cortisol levels and may need replacement therapy and monitoring for some months (Fitzgerald et al, 1982). Transient diabetes insipidus may also occur. In adults, irradiation is reserved for patients

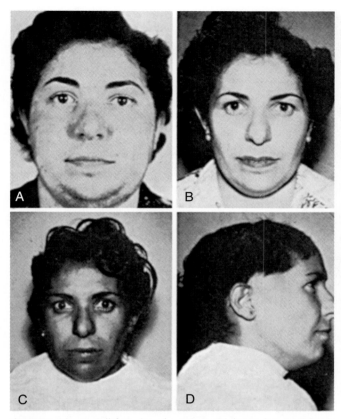

**Figure 53–26.** **A,** Full-face view of a patient with hyperadrenocorticism in 1954, treated by total adrenalectomy at that time. **B,** The same patient 6 months after total adrenalectomy, showing striking improvement. All symptoms and signs of Cushing's syndrome have disappeared. **C,** Deep pigmentation, headache, and failing vision supervened in 1957; emergency craniotomy was necessary after radiation therapy. **D,** Disappearance of pigmentation is shown in the facial view after removal of chromophobe adenoma of pituitary by Dr. Donald Matson. (From Rothenberg RE, ed: Reoperative Surgery. New York, McGraw-Hill, 1969.)

| Table 53–7. **Adrenocortical Carcinoma: Clinical Features (N = 602)** |
| --- |
| 38% Nonfunctional |
| 62% Functional |
| 39.5%  Cushing's syndrome |
| 24%  Cushing's + virilization |
| 20%  Virilization alone* |
| 6%  Feminization |
| 2.5%  Hyperaldosteronism |

*Primarily in children; 3% to 5% in adults.
From Ng L, Libertino JM: Adrenocortical carcinoma: Diagnosis, evaluation and treatment. J Urol 2003;169:5-11.

not cured by transsphenoidal surgery (Estrada et al, 1997). Finally, although it is unusual, there may be spontaneous regression of Cushing's disease (Dickstein et al, 1991).

Medical management is also available for specific hormone-secreting pituitary adenomas. Often, medical management is part of a multimodal, integrated therapeutic approach (Shimon and Melmed, 1998).

### Cushing's Syndrome during Pregnancy

Adrenal tumors (Harrington et al, 1999) including those producing Cushing's syndrome during pregnancy are rare (Mulder et al, 1990; Guilhaume et al, 1992; Kamiya et al, 1998) because of the menstrual irregularities characteristic of the disease. Of cases reported, 59% have been ACTH independent and 33% ACTH dependent. The others were not classified. During normal pregnancy, plasma cortisol-binding protein and plasma protein bound and unbound cortisone levels rise; however, the normal diurnal variation persists (Liu et al, 2003). The urinary free cortisol level also rises slightly. Moreover, there is some resistance to dexamethasone suppression that progresses with each trimester; however, some suppression remains so that the total absence of suppression

to low-dose dexamethasone is compatible with Cushing's syndrome.

Obviously, imaging studies are contraindicated during pregnancy, especially in the first trimester. **We have used MRI to identify an adenoma in a pregnant patient with Cushing's syndrome** (Fig. 53–27).

Both maternal and fetal morbidity are reduced with treatment. Surgical removal of an adenoma can be successfully achieved during pregnancy, as was done in our patient, especially during the second trimester. Alternatively, some patients have been treated with metyrapone or transsphenoidal adenectomy when indicated (Casson et al, 1987).

Fortunately, because of the low transplacental transfer of adrenal corticosteroids, the fetus is not affected in most cases and does not require steroid replacement after birth. However, the prematurity rate is high.

### Adrenal Adenoma

Adrenal adenomas causing Cushing's syndrome are treated by surgical removal, which is discussed in Chapter 54.

## ADRENAL CARCINOMA

Adrenal carcinoma is a rare disease and has a poor overall survival of 16% to 37% despite treatment (Novakovic et al, 2004; Ng and Libertino, 2003). The incidence is estimated as 1 case per 1.7 million, accounting for 0.02% of cancers and 0.2% of all cancer deaths (Nader et al, 1983; Plager, 1984; Brennan, 1987). Most adrenal tumors are sporadic and unilateral, but 2% to 6% are bilateral and associated with Li-Fraumeni syndrome, multiple endocrine neoplasia type I, Beckwith-Wiedemann syndrome, and the Carney complex primarily in children (Novakovic et al, 2004).

The etiology is unknown. Chromosomal heterozygosity on chromosomes 11p, 13q, and 17p may play a role (Fogt et al, 1998; Schulick and Brennan, 2003). In addition, *p53* abnormalities have been reported but may represent a late event (McNicol et al, 1997).

**A practical subclassification for adrenal carcinomas is according to their ability to produce adrenal hormones. The varieties and distribution of the types identified in a review of the literature are shown in Table 53–7.** Most tumors secrete multiple compounds. A review of 62 patients with functional tumors reported that 53% had Cushing's syndrome, 21% only virilization, 10% Cushing's syndrome and virilization, 8% feminization, and 5% hyperaldosteronism (Schulick and Brennan, 2003). In a series by Luton and

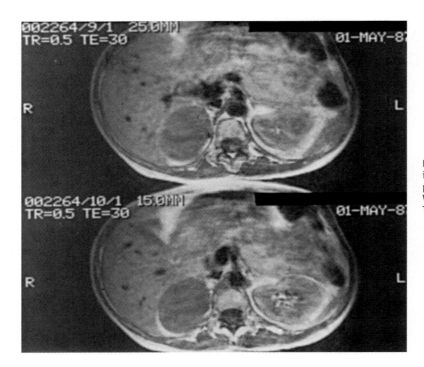

**Figure 53–27.** Magnetic resonance T1- and T2-weighted images of patient who developed Cushing's syndrome during pregnancy, showing the large right adrenal adenoma. (From Vaughan ED Jr, Carey RM, eds: Adrenal Disorders. New York, Thieme Medical, 1989.)

coworkers (1990), 79% of adrenal tumors were functional, a higher percentage than previously reported, probably because of more sensitive assays. In addition, nonfunctional tumors may become functional, or a tumor may subsequently produce multiple hormones (Grunberg, 1982; Arteaga et al, 1984). Moreover, tumors may produce metabolites that are nonfunctional or in such low amounts as not to cause physiologic changes. Thus, although convenient, a classification of tumors by product is somewhat contrived, and debate exists as to whether "nonfunctioning" tumors carry a worse prognosis for the patient than do functioning tumors (Heinbecker et al, 1957; Lewinsky et al, 1974).

## Incidentally Discovered Adrenal Masses

The increased use of abdominal ultrasonography and CT scanning has led to the frequent finding of an unexpected adrenal mass, an "incidentaloma" (Fig. 53–28). Evolving experience with this entity led to a consensus conference on the topic at the National Institute of Health in 2002 (Grumbach et al, 2003). Numerous observations were made. Three fourths of lesions found in patients with cancer are metastatic; in contrast, two thirds of masses in patients without a cancer diagnosis are benign. **Moreover, adrenal cortical carcinoma accounts for 2% of tumors that are smaller than 4 cm, 6% of tumors that are 4.1 to 6.0 cm, and 25% of tumors that are larger than 6.0 cm, confirming earlier studies.** This observation supports the prior observation that **adrenal malignant neoplasms are usually larger than 6 cm.** Belldegrun and coworkers (1986), **reviewing six series, found that 105 of 114 adrenocortical carcinomas were larger than 6 cm** (Heinbecker et al, 1957; Knight et al, 1960; Lewinsky et al, 1974; Sullivan et al, 1978; Bertagna and Orth, 1981).

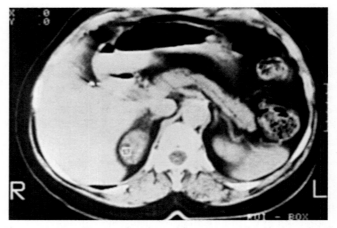

**Figure 53–28.** CT scan of patient with a 5-cm nonfunctioning adrenal mass found incidentally.

Accordingly, solid adrenal lesions of more than 6 cm should be considered malignant until proved otherwise by exploration and adrenalectomy. Follow-up of patients with smaller nodules reveals that 5% to 25% increase in size by at least 1 cm during a varied time, the risk of malignancy is 1 of 1000, and up to 20% develop hormonal hyperfunction, especially if the tumor is larger than 3 cm (Rossi et al, 2000; Grumbach et al, 2003).

The problem arises in the management of incidentally found adrenal lesions smaller than 6 cm. Unsuspected adrenal masses have been detected in 0.6% to 1.3% of upper abdominal CT studies (Copeland, 1983; Abecassis et al, 1985; Ross and Aron, 1990). Moreover, the prevalence of benign, clinically silent adrenal adenomas found on autopsy series ranges from less than 1% in patients younger than 30 years to 7% in patients 70 years or older (Grumbach et al, 2003). In contrast, occult nonfunctioning adrenocortical carcinoma is rarely found on autopsy. Accordingly, attention has turned to the appropriate management of the incidentaloma (Ross and Aron, 1990; Rossi et al, 2000; Grumbach et al, 2003).

One approach is shown in Table 53–8. Several points do not engender controversy. First, there is agreement that all patients with solid adrenal masses should undergo biochemical assessment. If biochemical abnormalities are identified, the lesions should be treated appropriately as described elsewhere in this chapter—usually by removal of the offending lesion. The extent of the biochemical evaluation has been reviewed (Ross and Aron, 1990; Grumbach et al, 2003). A selective approach has been outlined, which markedly limits cost without sacrificing diagnostic accuracy. A limited evaluation is recommended, including urine or plasma metanephrine determinations to rule out pheochromocytoma; a 1-mg dexamethasone suppression test to rule out Cushing's syndrome; and in patients with hypertension, serum potassium concentration and plasma renin-to-aldosterone ratio. The test recommendations have expanded since 1990 following the demonstration of more subclinical hormonal abnormalities. Because of the likelihood that nonfunctioning solid lesions larger than 6 cm are malignant, these lesions should be removed. **CT scanning may underestimate the size of an adrenal lesion, and we suggest that exploration be performed when the lesion is larger than 5 cm on CT or MRI** (Cerfolio et al, 1993). Furthermore, lesions clearly proved to be cystic by CT, MRI, or cyst puncture, which is often not

necessary, can also be observed. Other approaches include removal of smaller (3 cm) lesions in patients younger than 50 years (Staren and Prinz, 1995) and use of 4-cm criteria for removal (Barzon and Boscaro, 2000). Lesions smaller than 4 cm are rarely malignant, and it is thought that these lesions can be observed with repeated CT at 6- to 12-month intervals (Grumbach et al, 2003). However controversy still arises concerning the management strategy of lesions smaller than 4 cm. Glazer and coworkers (1982) suggested that adrenalectomy be considered for solid lesions larger than 3 to 4 cm. Prinz and associates (1982) also suggested a surgical approach, especially in younger patients. Copeland (1983) challenged the 3- to 4-cm criterion and suggested observation for all patients with nonfunctioning lesions smaller than 6 cm. **These authors estimate that more than 4000 adrenalectomies would have to be done on patients with masses 1.5 cm or larger in diameter to remove one carcinoma.** In a review of 311 incidentally found lesions, 22 were proved to be carcinoma, with tumor sizes from 3.2 cm to 20 cm. Importantly, both localized disease and survival were greater than in a group of 51 patients with clinically apparent adrenal carcinoma (Kasperlik-Zaluska et al, 1998).

Thus, the 4- to 6-cm, solid, nonfunctioning adrenal mass incidentally found remains the major area of controversy. Certainly, on statistical grounds, the majority are benign. An occasional mass, however, is malignant and potentially curable, a situation not frequently encountered in patients with adrenal carcinomas. Fine-needle adrenal biopsy guided by ultrasound and CT is now available and is well tolerated by the patient and associated with minimal complications. The nondiagnostic rate is as high as 28%, but of diagnostic aspirates, the ability to identify the current adrenal lesion accurately is greater than 95% (Nguyen and Akin, 1998). In addition, with polymerase chain reaction and microdissection, loss of heterozygosity of several suppressor genes has been suggested to separate adrenal carcinomas from adenomas (Abati et al, 1999).

An additional useful test is MRI; a high signal intensity ratio on T2 images suggests that the lesion is not a benign adenoma (see Fig. 53–25) (Reinig et al, 1986). There is controversy over the ability of signal characteristics to reliably differentiate benign from malignant masses (Lubat and Weinreb, 1990; Bilbey et al, 1995; Teeger et al, 2003). **A number of entities other than adrenal carcinoma, however, can cause high intensity, including neural tumors, metastatic tumors to the adrenal, and hemorrhage into a variety of adrenal lesions** (Lubat and Weinreb, 1990).

## Myelolipoma

In the past, this nonfunctioning benign lesion was incidentally found at autopsy. These lesions are generally smaller than 5 cm, unilateral, asymptomatic, and benign, containing hematopoietic and fatty elements (Del Gaudio and Solidoro, 1986; Del Gaudio et al, 1992; Sanders et al, 1995; Han et al, 1997).

The lesion has been recognized with increasing frequency because it has a characteristic appearance on CT scanning and MRI (Casey et al, 1994) that establishes the diagnosis and excludes the need for extensive metabolic evaluation or surgical exploration. The exception may be large lesions (Fig. 53–29), in which confusion with necrotic adrenal carcinoma

**Table 53–8. Evaluation of Incidentally Found Adrenal Mass**

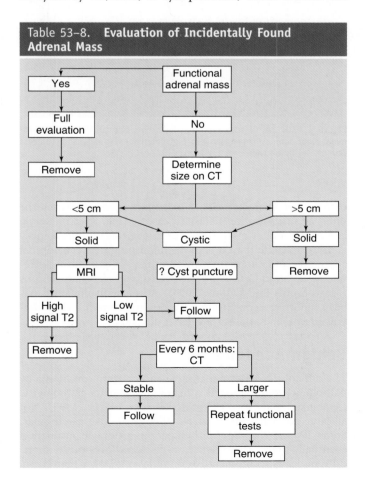

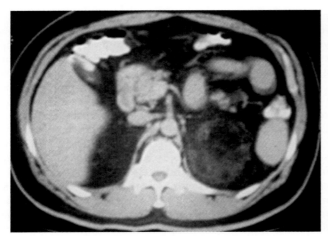

Figure 53–29.   Myelolipoma, left adrenal.

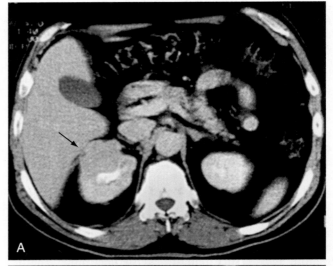

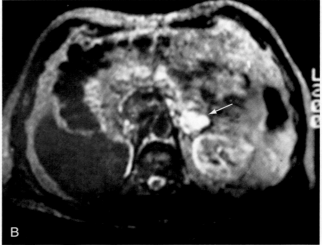

Figure 53–30.   **A,** CT scan showing a left renal cell carcinoma. **B,** Subsequent right adrenal metastasis with high intensity. The pathologic process was proved by excision.

could occur (Wilhelmus et al, 1981). Rarely, pure adrenal lipomas may occur; these should be removed to exclude the possibility of a retroperitoneal liposarcoma (Milatianakis et al, 2002) or an adrenal leiomyosarcoma (Thamboo et al, 2003).

The cause of the lesion is unknown, but it may be part of a group of entities characterized by deposition of myeloid and adipose tissue (Papavasiliou et al, 1990). Patients are predominantly obese, with a male-to-female ratio of 1.75:1. Pain is the most common presenting symptom. The lesions are rarely calcified or hormonally active. Hormone levels should be obtained, however, because coexisting functional cortical adenoma and myelolipoma have been reported (Hisamatsu et al, 2004).

## Adrenal Metastasis

Primary adrenocortical carcinoma is actually less common than metastatic tumor to the adrenal. In a series of 500 autopsy cases, Willis (1952) found adrenal metastasis in 9%. Specifically, the adrenal has been found to be a site of metastasis in more than 50% of patients with melanomas and carcinomas of the breast and lung; in 40% of patients with renal cell carcinomas; and in patients with, in order of frequency, carcinomas of the contralateral adrenal, bladder, colon, esophagus, gallbladder, liver, pancreas, prostate, stomach, and uterus (Bullock and Hirst, 1953).

Now that adrenal imaging with CT and MRI is commonplace, more adrenal lesions are identified earlier in the course of patients with cancer (Thomas et al, 1982). Management is obviously predicated on the underlying malignant neoplasm. The major clinical point is not to confuse a metastatic adrenal lesion with a primary adrenal process. In general, the adrenal lesion is part of the clinical picture of diffuse metastatic disease. Long-term survival after adrenalectomy and aggressive treatment of the primary process, however, has been reported in patients with pulmonary carcinoma and adrenal metastasis (Porte et al, 2001). In addition, it is routine to include the adrenal with a radical nephrectomy in patients with T3-4 renal cell carcinoma, large upper pole lesions, or CT evidence of adrenal invasion (Siemer et al, 2004). Moreover, the finding of an unsuspected adrenal mass should heighten the clinical suspicion of a neoplasm elsewhere. An MRI

pattern not characteristic of a benign adenoma raises the index of suspicion for metastatic disease (Fig. 53–30) (Reinig et al, 1986; Bilbey et al, 1995). In this setting, adrenal biopsy is more accurate than it is in distinguishing between adrenal adenomas and carcinoma. In addition, CT-guided radiofrequency ablation has been described to treat metastatic lesions (Mayo-Smith and Dupuy, 2004). Adrenal insufficiency has been reported secondary to both benign adenomas and bilateral adrenal metastases (Sheeler et al, 1983).

## Benign Adenoma

The difficulty in discriminating adenoma from carcinoma by pathologic examination is a major problem for pathologists (Amberson and Gray, 1989; Medeiros and Weiss, 1992). Not all large adrenal lesions behave biologically like carcinomas. Some lesions that appear benign on histologic evaluation eventually metastasize. Hence, as discussed previously, surgical removal is recommended for all lesions larger than 5 cm.

| Table 53–9. | **Adrenocortical Carcinoma: Weiss Criteria** |
|---|---|

High mitotic rate (>5 per 50 high-power field)
Atypical mitoses
Venous invasion
High nuclear grade (Fuhrman 3-4)
Absence of cells with clear cytoplasm (<25% of cells)
A diffuse growth pattern (more than one third of tumor)
Necrosis
Sinusoidal invasion
Capsular invasion

Three or more are needed for diagnosis of carcinoma.

Weiss, 1984.

In an attempt to better determine the prognosis of these lesions and to predict the metastatic potential, Weiss proposed nine histologic criteria (Table 53–9); if more than three are present, the lesion is considered malignant (Weiss, 1984; Aubert et al, 2002).

**Klein and coworkers** (1985) **reported that flow cytometry accurately demonstrated aneuploid stem lines in four cases classified histologically as carcinoma.** We also found that all but one patient exhibiting subsequent metastatic disease had aneuploid primary tumors (Fig. 53–31) (Amberson et al, 1987).

Others have also shown that adrenal carcinomas can demonstrate either aneuploid or diploid characteristics; however, there is some evidence that there may be longer disease-free survival in patients with hypodiploid or hyperdiploid carcinomas, in contrast to those with aneuploid patterns (Haak et al, 1993a). Abnormalities in DNA content may not be as useful in children with adrenal cortical tumors (Moore et al, 1993). Also, DNA tetraploidy by fluorescence in situ hybridization is common in adrenal cortical adenomas associated with primary aldosteronism (Shono et al, 2002). Determination of mutations of *p53* (Sameshima et al, 1992; Reincke et al, 1994) may be helpful in predicting prognosis. However, in a comprehensive analysis of 67 primary adrenal and 36 metastatic tumors, multimolecular phenotyping showed molecular complexity and heterogeneity to the extent that any therapy based on this type of analysis would have to be patient specific (Stojadinovic et al, 2002). Interestingly, the use of a modification of the Weiss criteria predicted prognosis, whereas cell cycle proteins and multimolecular phenotypic expression did not.

## Functional Tumors

### Cushing's Syndrome

Cushing's syndrome has been discussed in detail, adrenal carcinoma being one of the causes of corticosteroid excess. This form of functional tumor is the most common in its pure form or with associated virilization. In a study comparing clinical and laboratory studies of patients with Cushing's syndrome caused by adenoma and carcinoma, Bertagna and Orth (1981) found that virilization without evidence of cortisol excess was indicative of carcinoma, except in children. Other clinical parameters were not helpful except for hirsutism, which is more common in patients with carcinoma. Thin skin, purple striae, thin hair, and temporal hair loss were more common in patients with adenomas. From a metabolic standpoint, 17-ketosteroid (Forbes and Albright, 1951) and DHEAS levels (Yamaji et al, 1984) are often high in patients with carcinomas, usually in conjunction with elevated glucocorticoid production (Luton et al, 1990). Prognosis is poor.

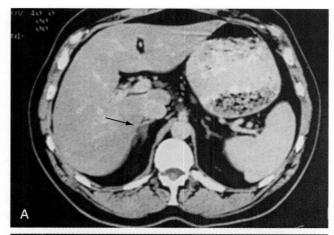

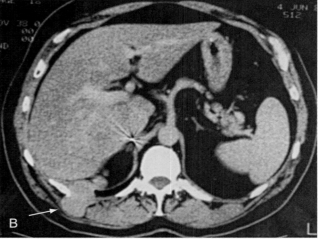

**Figure 53–31.** Patient with a small, right, aldosterone-producing adenoma (**A**), which was malignant and recurred in the adrenal bed and at the site of the flank incision (**B**). The disease caused the death of the patient.

### Testosterone-Secreting Adrenal Cortical Tumors

Virilization is the hallmark of Cushing's syndrome secondary to adrenal carcinoma. Virilization in the absence of elevated urinary 17-ketosteroids, however, is uncommon and should raise the possibility of testosterone-secreting ovarian or adrenal lesions (Imperato-McGinley et al, 1981; Del Gaudio and Del Gaudio, 1993). Of the two sites of origin, adrenal cortical tumors that secrete testosterone are exceedingly rare. Most adrenal tumors have been adenomas, but several have been ganglioneuromas with Leydig cell nodules (Aguirre and Sculley, 1983) or Leydig cell adenoma (Trost et al, 1981). Most tumors have been found in women, although they have been reported in men and children. Testosterone secretion can be autonomous, under gonadotropin control (Werk et al, 1973), or under ACTH control (Trost et al, 1981).

In contrast to the other tumors described in this chapter, these tumors are usually smaller than 6 cm, and they behave in a benign fashion. In a review of 47 documented cases of testosterone-producing neoplasms, however, eight were virilizing carcinomas (Gabrilove et al, 1981; Mattox and Phelan, 1987).

### Estrogen-Secreting Adrenal Cortical Tumors

Most feminizing tumors occur in men 25 to 50 years old, and in contradistinction to testosterone-secreting tumors, they are usually larger, often palpable, and highly malignant (Gabrilove et al, 1965). Characteristically, the patients present with gynecomastia. In addition, they may exhibit testicular atrophy, impotence, or decreased libido. In one of our patients, the clinical presentation was infertility and oligospermia.

These tumors secrete androstenedione, which is converted peripherally to estrogens. Other steroids may also be secreted, and the clinical picture may be mixed, with associated cushingoid features.

Of these tumors, 80% are malignant. Half the patients with this disease expire within 18 months of diagnosis. Three-year survival is less than 20%.

The prime therapy is surgical, usually employing a thoracoabdominal approach with wide excision of the tumor, the adjacent organs if necessary, and the regional lymph nodes. Despite wide resection, the patient's prognosis remains poor, and no effective adjunctive therapy has been developed.

### Aldosterone-Secreting Adrenal Cortical Carcinoma

Primary hyperaldosteronism is almost always due to a small, benign, solitary adenoma; Conn's syndrome; or bilateral adrenal hyperplasia. The syndrome in its pure form, however, may rarely be caused by adrenal carcinoma (Vaughan and Carey, 1989). In fact, in most cases with evidence of mineralocorticoid excess and hypokalemia due to adrenal carcinoma, there are also signs of abnormalities in glucocorticoid or androgen secretion.

On review of the cases, the striking difference between the tumors found in these patients and in those with Conn's syndrome caused by benign adenoma is the size of the tumor. Benign adenomas are rarely larger than 3 cm. In contrast, all but two reported aldosterone-secreting carcinomas were larger than 3 cm (Vaughan and Carey, 1989). Accordingly, the clinical and biochemical syndrome of hyperaldosteronism and the CT evidence of a large adrenal mass strongly suggest carcinoma. Similar to most other patients with tumors as described, these patients do poorly despite initial resection of the tumor. Adjunctive therapy is ineffective.

## Adrenocortical Carcinoma in Children

Adrenocortical carcinoma constitutes only 0.002% of all childhood malignant neoplasms (Young and Miller, 1975) and only 6% of childhood malignant adrenal tumors—the majority being neuroblastomas (Stewart et al, 1974). Despite the finding that survival is better in children—double that in adults—the entity is still highly lethal and refractory to adjunctive therapy, although adequate trials have not been carried out (Kay et al, 1983; Teinturier et al, 1999).

In contrast to tumors in adults, most of these tumors in children are hormonally active, and perhaps earlier detection

is the reason for their better survival. The clinical syndromes include Cushing's syndrome, commonly as a result of carcinoma—not adenoma—in children; virilization in girls; and isosexual precocious puberty in boys. Evaluation follows the same lines as those described for adults, with careful examination for steroid precursors and byproducts. These may be of later use as tumor markers after initial tumor removal. In addition to recurrence, late occurrence of other tumors has also been reported (Andler et al, 1978). Adrenocortical carcinoma is also found in excess in children with Beckwith-Wiedemann syndrome, among children with isolated hemihypertrophy, and in association with Li-Fraumeni syndrome. Tumors have been found to show a high frequency of germline *p53* mutations, as are found in Li-Fraumeni syndrome, suggesting a potential relationship (Wagner et al, 1994; Venara et al, 1998).

## Management of Adrenocortical Carcinoma

Except for testosterone-secreting tumors, adrenocortical carcinomas are highly malignant, with both local and hematogenous spread and a 5-year survival rate of about 35% (Icard et al, 1992; Schulick and Brennan, 1999). In a series by Richie and Gittes (1980), the most common sites of metastasis were lung, liver, and lymph nodes. A large autopsy study of 132 cases showed metastases to lungs (60%), liver (50%), lymph nodes (48%), bone (24%), and pleura and heart (10%) (Didolkar et al, 1981). In addition, these tumors often extend directly into adjacent structures, especially the kidney, and may involve the inferior vena cava (Long et al, 1993) or splenic vein (Stein et al, 1998). Treatment is surgical removal of the primary tumor, with an attempt to remove the entire lesion even if resection of adjacent organs (e.g., kidney, spleen) and of local lymph nodes en bloc is necessary, and any caval thrombus that is present (Ekici and Ciancio, 2004). In one review, patients with complete resection had a higher 5-year survival rate (38% to 62%) than the overall survival in the series reported (16% to 37%) (Schulick and Brennan, 2003). After surgical removal of functioning adrenal tumors, the patient can be followed up with appropriate hormone levels as markers for tumor recurrence.

### Medical Therapy

Despite the current accuracy in anatomic and biochemical definition of adrenal carcinoma, about 40% of patients present with metastatic disease. Unfortunately, many patients with locally resectable disease eventually die of recurrent local or distant disease. The search for effective adjunctive therapy has been frustrating; radiation therapy has not been useful except for palliation (Percarpio and Knowlton, 1976). In addition, conventional chemotherapy, although not widely studied in a systematic fashion, has not been effective, probably because of P-glycoprotein expression (Flynn et al, 1992; Haak et al, 1993b).

The most success has been reported with adrenolytic drugs (1,1-dichloro-2-[*o*-chlorophenyl]-2-[*p*-chlorophenyl]ethane; *o,p*′-DDD) or mitotane (Bergenstal et al, 1960). This DDT derivative was shown by Hutter and Kayhoe (1966) to induce tumor response in 34%; Wooten and King (1993), in a review of 551 cases reported in the literature, showed tumor response in 35%. The major use has been for patients with metastatic disease, and despite the response rates given, survival time has not been prolonged (Hoffman and Mattox, 1972; Luton et al, 1990) unless high serum levels are obtained (Haak et al, 1994; Khorram-Manesh et al, 1998) or it is given postoperatively in an adjuvant fashion (Vassilopoulou-Sellin et al, 1993). Moreover, the usual treatment regimen is to increase the dosage to 8 to 10 g/day until toxicity occurs. Significant toxicity includes gastrointestinal, neurologic, and dermatologic disorders, most of which regress on cessation of therapy.

During management, adrenal insufficiency can occur, and cortisol and aldosterone levels should be monitored. Because of the high fat solubility of the drug, traces of it can be found several months after the drug has been discontinued, warranting continued steroid monitoring during this period.

The overall response to mitotane has been disappointing, even in combination regimens (Bukowski et al, 1993). Suramin, the antiparasitic agent, also has limited efficacy (Arit et al, 1994). The antifungal drug ketoconazole, which has an adrenolytic effect, has also induced regression in metastatic adrenal carcinoma (Contreras et al, 1985), as have cisplatin and etoposide (Berruti et al, 1998; Bonacci et al, 1998).

Thus, drugs such as mitotane, ketoconazole, metyrapone, and aminoglutethimide may help relieve the devastating symptoms of glucocorticoid or mineralocorticoid excess. Little evidence exists, however, showing that survival is extended in most cases.

Transarterial embolization has been reported to achieve partial remission of symptoms in a patient with metastatic disease (Koh et al, 1991).

## ADRENAL ONCOCYTOMA

Oncocytic tumors are rare neoplasms that are histologically composed of epithelial cells with abundant acidophilic granular cytoplasm that can be arranged in alveolar, tubular, or solid patterns (Chang and Harawi, 1992). Oncocytic neoplasms of the adrenal are nonfunctional, usually benign, and often large before being detected (Lin et al, 1998; Baloch and LiVolsi, 1999). Because they cannot be distinguished from adrenal carcinomas, treatment is surgical removal (Kitching et al, 1999). An additional rare benign tumor of the adrenal is an adenomatoid tumor of mesothelial origin (Isotalo et al, 2003).

## ADRENAL CYSTS

These are usually unilateral lesions discovered incidentally during imaging procedures or surgery and at autopsy. Calcifications may be found in approximately 15% of cases and need not imply malignancy. Endothelial or lymphangiomatous cysts account for nearly 45% of these lesions and are usually small, measuring 0.1 to 1.5 cm in diameter. Adrenal pseudocysts that lack an epithelial lining are the next most common variety (39%) and most likely represent encapsulated residua of previous adrenal hemorrhages. Pseudocysts may become massive and may cause symptoms because of the compression of adjacent structures (Fig. 53–32). The acute hemorrhage in the case shown was readily distinguished by MRI. Traumatic rupture of adrenal cysts has also been

reported (Favorito et al, 2004). Parasitic cysts due to echinococcal disease (7%) and true epithelial cysts (9%) account for the remainder of adrenal cysts (Kazam et al, 1989; Sroujieh et al, 1990). **Most cystic adrenal lesions are found incidentally and can be observed; symptomatic cysts can be percutaneously drained or laparoscopically decorticated** (Yoder and Wolf, 2004).

## ADRENAL INSUFFICIENCY

Adrenal insufficiency is rarely encountered in the practice of urology. Because it is potentially fatal if it is not recognized, the salient features of the entity are worthy of review. In addition, delayed adrenal insufficiency can rarely be seen after unilateral adrenalectomy (Kazama et al, 2005).

Addison's disease is rare, the death rate being approximately 0.3 per 100,000; the most common cause in the past was either tuberculosis or adrenal atrophy (Dunlop, 1963; Irvine and Barnes, 1972; Eason et al, 1982). **However, at present in industrialized countries, the most common cause is autoimmune destruction of the adrenal gland** (Lovas and Husebye, 2005). The diagnosis is based on the presence of adrenal autoantibodies, of which 21-hydroxylase is the most important. Addison's disease may be a part of autoimmune polyendocrine syndrome type I and type II, syndromes that may also include primary hypogonadism. Other causes include malignant infiltration (Cedermark et al, 1977), sarcoidosis (Rickards and Barrett, 1954; Irvine and Barnes, 1972), histoplasmosis (Crispel et al, 1956), North American blastomycosis (Fish et al, 1960), South American blastomycosis (Osa et al, 1981), and coccidioidomycosis (Moloney, 1952). The general term *adrenal atrophy* actually refers to a pathologic process of lymphocytic adenitis with fibrosis (Maisey and Stevens, 1969). From a clinical point of view, however, symptoms of adrenal insufficiency usually appear in hospitalized patients in whom a history of the long-term use of exogenous steroids has not been obtained and acute withdrawal from steroids has occurred. Adrenal insufficiency may be an important aspect of the care of a patient with cancer and may be due to replacement of the adrenals with metastases, infiltration with lymphoma, hemorrhagic necrosis in association with anticoagulation or sepsis, and impaired adrenal steroidogenesis in patients receiving aminoglutethimide, ketoconazole, mitotane, or suramin (Ihde et al, 1990).

The symptoms and signs of chronic adrenal insufficiency are nonspecific and may be associated with numerous other diseases (Table 53–10). Similarly, abnormalities determined with routine laboratory tests are also nonspecific. The most common abnormalities are hyponatremia and hyperkalemia, with at least one electrolyte abnormality being found in 99 of 108 patients in one series (Nerup, 1974). The classic triad of hyponatremia, hyperkalemia, and azotemia was present in only 50% to 60% of cases. Hypercalcemia may also be an initial abnormality. Other endocrine disorders, including hyperthyroidism or hypothyroidism (17%), diabetes mellitus (12%), gonadal dysfunction (12%), and hypothyroidism (5%), occur in about 10% to 30% of patients with Addison's disease (May et al, 1989).

The symptoms of acute adrenal insufficiency "crisis," usually caused by withdrawal of exogenous steroids, sepsis, bilateral adrenal hemorrhage, or postadrenalectomy state,

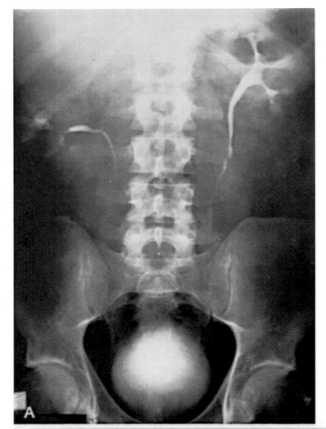

Figure 53–32. **A,** Massive right adrenal cyst. The patient presented with fever, pain, and anemia. **B,** CT scan of cyst. **C,** MRI image of bright hemorrhage into the lumen and cyst proved at exploration.

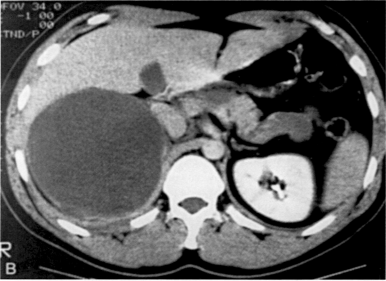

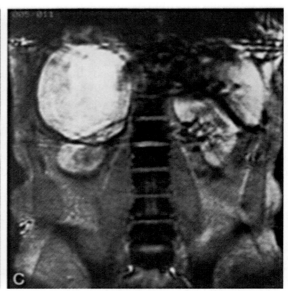

differ somewhat from those of Addison's disease, particularly fever, which occurs in 70% of patients (see Table 53–10) (Liu et al, 1982). Abdominal pain is also often present and may be due to unilateral or bilateral adrenal hemorrhage, which can be diagnosed by CT (Liu et al, 1982) or MRI (Falke et al, 1987). A useful screening test is an 8 AM measure of serum cortisol level (Dullaart et al, 1999).

However, the critical test to confirm Addison's disease is the demonstration of a failure to increase plasma (Perkoff et al,

1954) or urine corticosteroid level into the normal range with ACTH infusions (Renold et al, 1952; Schlaghecke et al, 1992). A provocative test is particularly important because there are numerous reports of patients with primary adrenal insufficiency having normal-based plasma cortisol or urine 17-hydroxycorticoid levels (May et al, 1989). Plasma ACTH levels may be markedly elevated, but such an assay is not always available. The simplest screening test is the rapid ACTH test, whereby plasma cortisol levels are measured before and 60

## Table 53–10. Signs and Symptoms of Chronic Addison's Disease and Acute Adrenal Insufficiency

| Prevalence | | |
| --- | --- | --- |
| **Number** | **%** | **Symptom** |
| *Addison's Disease* | | |
| 435/462 | 94 | Weakness, tiredness, fatigue |
| 393/438 | 90 | Weight loss |
| 303/351 | 86 | Anorexia |
| 178/268 | 66 | Nausea, vomiting |
| 100/164 | 61 | Unspecified gastrointestinal complaints |
| 35/127 | 28 | Abdominal pain |
| 44/246 | 18 | Diarrhea |
| 15/94 | 16 | Muscle pain |
| 24/168 | 14 | Salt craving |
| 24/166 | 14 | Orthostatic hypotension, dizziness, or syncope |
| 4/33 | 12 | Lethargy, disorientation |
| *Acute Adrenal Insufficiency* | | |
| 165/165 | 100 | Severe clinical deterioration |
| 98/140 | 70 | Fever |
| 20/31 | 64 | Nausea, vomiting |
| 21/46 | 46 | Abdominal or flank pain |
| 59/165 | 36 | Hypotension |
| 9/28 | 32 | Abdominal distention |
| 25/101 | 26 | Lethargy, obtundation |
| 55/122 | 45 | Hyponatremia |
| 21/83 | 25 | Hyperkalemia |

From May ME, Vaughan ED Jr, Carey RM: Adrenocortical insufficiency—clinical aspects. In Vaughan ED Jr, Carey RM, eds: Adrenal Disorders. New York, Thieme Medical, 1989.

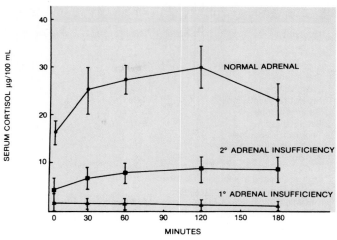

**Figure 53–33.** Serum cortisol response and response to ACTH infusion in normal persons and in patients with primary and secondary adrenal insufficiency. (From Vaughan ED Jr, Carey RM, eds: Adrenal Disorders. New York, Thieme Medical, 1989.)

## Table 53–11. Treatment of Adrenal Crisis

*Emergency Treatment*

Establish 19-gauge IV line. Obtain stat serum electrolytes, glucose, cortisol, and plasma ACTH. Do not wait for results.

Infuse 2-3 L 0.9% saline solution (154 mmol/L) or 5% dextrose (50 g/L) in 0.9% saline solution as quickly as possible. Monitor for fluid overload by observing central or peripheral venous pressure or listening for pulmonary rales. Reduce infusion rate if indicated.

Inject 4 mg dexamethasone sodium phosphate (Decadron) IV at beginning of IV infusion or give 100 mg hydrocortisone sodium succinate (Solu-Cortef) or hydrocortisone sodium phosphate (Hydrocortone Phosphate) IV and 100 mg every 8 hours thereafter.

Provide supportive measures as needed.

Mineralocorticoids are unnecessary; ACTH is useless.

*Subacute Treatment after Stabilization of Patient*

Continue IV infusion of 0.9% saline solution at a lower rate for 24-48 hours as needed.

Search for and treat, if possible, precipitating cause of adrenal crisis.

In patient not known to have Addison's disease, and if not already done, perform short ACTH stimulation test to confirm diagnosis of adrenal insufficiency.

Taper glucocorticoid to maintenance dosage over 1-3 days if precipitating or complicating disease permits.

Begin or resume mineralocorticoid replacement with fludrocortisone (Florinef), 0.1 mg orally daily, when saline infusion is stopped.

From Magiakou MA, Chrousos GP: Corticosteroid therapy, nonendocrine disease, and corticosteroid withdrawal. In Bardin CW, ed: Current Therapy in Endocrinology and Metabolism, 5th ed. St. Louis, CV Mosby, 1994:120.

minutes after 0.25 mg of cosyntropin is given intravenously; cortisol levels should be higher than 18 μg/dL at 60 minutes (Fig. 53–33) (Speckard et al, 1971). Alternatively, 100 μg of human CRH can be used (Schlaghecke et al, 1992). A patient with a relative or an absolute lack of ACTH may respond normally to cosyntropin but not respond properly to surgical stress (Jasani et al, 1968; Kehlet and Binder, 1973). Most of these patients, however, tolerate surgical stress without steroid coverage. If treatment is mandated in a patient with suspected adrenal insufficiency, the ACTH stimulation test can be performed when treatment is with the synthetic steroid dexamethasone (Sheridan and Mattingly, 1975). Other, more definitive but more complex and longer infusion tests also can be used (Liu et al, 2003).

The treatment of acute or chronic adrenal insufficiency is obviously the administration of glucocorticoids. In acute adrenal crisis, stress-level dexamethasone (8 to 12 mg/day) is given, along with replacement saline (Smith and Byrne, 1981) and a simultaneous ACTH stimulation test to confirm the diagnosis (Sheridan and Mattingly, 1975) (Table 53–11).

The treatment of chronic Addison's disease is maintenance therapy—approximately 30 mg of hydrocortisone plus 0.05 to 0.1 μg fluorohydrocortisone per day orally, or a synthetic steroid (Table 53–12).

Replacement therapy after unilateral adrenalectomy is discussed elsewhere. The same guidelines pertain, however, and it is helpful to maintain patients on dexamethasone so that the ACTH test can be used to follow the recovery of the contralateral gland.

## Selective Adrenal Insufficiency

Selective hypoaldosteronism is rare and is usually due to hyporeninemia or functional hypoaldosteronism caused by tubular insensitivity to normal aldosterone levels (Schambelan et al, 1972; Williams et al, 1983). The urologist occasionally observes this phenomenon in an adult or a child who exhibits unexplained hyperkalemia after relief of chronic obstructive uropathy, especially in association with azotemia (Schambelan et al, 1980; Pelleya et al, 1983; Kozeny et al, 1986).

**Table 53–12.** **Comparison of Half-life and Biologic Activity of Various Natural and Synthetic Steroids**

| Compound | Biologic Half-life (hr) | Plasma Half-life (hr) | Equivalent Dose (mg) | Relative Sodium-Retaining Activity |
|---|---|---|---|---|
| Cortisone* | 8–12 | 0.5 | 25 | 0.8 |
| Cortisol (hydrocortisone) | 8–12 | 1.5 | 20 | 1 |
| Prednisone* | 12–36 | 1 | 5 | 0.8 |
| Prednisolone | 12–36 | 2–4 | 5 | 0.8 |
| 6α-Methylprednisolone | 12–36 | 1–3 | 4 | 0.5 |
| Dexamethasone | 36–72 | 2–3 | 0.75 | 0–2 |
| Betamethasone | 36–72 | | 0.60 | 0 |
| Deoxycorticosterone† | | | 0 | 20 |
| 9α-Fluorohydrocortisone | | | 2 | 125–400 |
| Aldosterone | | 0.2 | 0.1 | 400 |

*Requires hepatic metabolism for bioactivity.
†Inactivated on oral administration.
From May ME, Vaughan ED Jr, Carey RM: Adrenocortical insufficiency—clinical aspects. In Vaughan ED Jr, Carey RM, eds: Adrenal Disorders. New York, Thieme Medical, 1989.

Other selective hypoaldosteronism may occur from primary disturbances of the zona glomerulosa, endogenous impairment of angiotensin II production (Findling et al, 1987), or aldosterone receptor deficiency (Armanini et al, 1985). Congenital primary hypoaldosteronism may be sporadic or familial (May et al, 1989).

Selective familial glucocorticoid deficiency has been well described, almost totally in the pediatric literature (May et al, 1989). The clinical presentation is dominated by recurrent hypoglycemia, both fasting and reactive, with subsequent seizures. The children usually have normal findings of electrolytes, which often delays the proper diagnosis.

## PRIMARY HYPERALDOSTERONISM

The term *primary hyperaldosteronism* was originally coined by Conn (1955a, 1955b) to describe the clinical syndrome characterized by hypertension, hypokalemia, hypernatremia, alkalosis, and periodic paralysis caused by an aldosterone-secreting adenoma. As diagnostic tests for quantifying the components of the renin-angiotensin-aldosterone system have become available, the syndrome of primary hyperaldosteronism (PAL) is now identified by hypertension, suppressed plasma renin activity (PRA), and high urine and plasma aldosterone levels. However, there remain several unresolved issues related to the diagnosis and management of this disorder. What is the prevalence of primary aldosteronism, and which diagnostic screening tests should be used? Moreover, the term *primary hyperaldosteronism* encompasses a family of adrenal disorders, including variants that cannot be cured by adrenalectomy (Young, 2003; Mulatero et al, 2005; New et al, 2005). Which diagnostic tests are most likely to identify patients with surgically remediable subtypes? The following section provides evidence to support a diagnostic and therapeutic approach to the patient with primary aldosteronism.

## Pathophysiology

The normal physiology of the renin-angiotensin-aldosterone system including the stimuli for aldosterone release is reviewed in Chapter 36. When aldosterone is secreted in amounts that are inappropriately high for the state of sodium balance, sodium reabsorption is augmented by the distal nephron (O'Neil, 1990; Rossier, 2003; Verrey et al, 2003; Kahle et al, 2005). Extracellular sodium content is increased and is accompanied by water so that isotonicity is maintained as body volume increases. Sodium accumulation is usually gradual and is dependent on its availability and on the magnitude of aldosterone excess. After a gain of about 1.5 kg of extracellular fluid, however, there is diminished renal sodium reabsorption. This phenomenon, which accounts for the absence of edema in this disorder, is referred to as mineralocorticoid escape; it enables the kidney to overcome the sodium-retaining effects of mineralocorticoid excess and consequently maintains sodium balance (Knowlton and Laragh, 1970; Knepper et al, 2003). Aldosterone-induced increases in glomerular filtration rate and fractional excretion of sodium are required for mineralocorticoid escape, and thus it is a manifestation of the pressure-natriuresis phenomenon (Hall et al, 1984). In addition, atrial natriuretic peptide participates in this response (de Bold et al, 2001). More recently, dynamic regulation of sodium transport by the distal nephron has been shown to contribute importantly to this adaptation to high levels of aldosterone (Meneton et al, 2004). For example, increased excretion of sodium during mineralocorticoid escape is associated with a major decrease in the abundance of the thiazide-sensitive $Na^+-Cl^-$ cotransporter in the distal nephrons (Knepper et al, 2003).

As the understanding of adrenal physiology, biochemistry, histopathology, molecular biology, and genetics has advanced, it has become evident that there are distinct subsets of PAL. Reports from several centers indicate that the majority of patients with PAL can have hypertension and metabolic abnormalities ameliorated by unilateral adrenalectomy (Blumenfeld et al, 1994; Stowasser et al, 2003; Young et al, 2004). **Patients who are most likely to respond favorably to surgery are those in whom aldosterone production is highly autonomous from renin-angiotensin** (Mulatero et al, 2005) (see "Diagnostic Tests"). **Among the features that identify autonomy are**

1. **limited effect on aldosterone production by maneuvers that either increase the angiotensin II level (e.g., angiotensin II infusion or postural stimulation) or**

decrease it (e.g., saline infusion, fludrocortisone administration, angiotensin-converting enzyme inhibition);
2. increased levels of aldosterone biosynthetic precursors (e.g., ratio of 18-hydroxycorticosterone to cortisol);
3. elevated levels of "hybrid" steroids (e.g., urinary cortisol C-18–methyloxygenated metabolites [18-hydroxycortisol and 18-oxocortisol]) (Ulick et al, 1992; Blumenfeld et al, 1994); and
4. **lateralization of aldosterone secretion to one adrenal gland** (Blumenfeld et al, 1994; Espiner et al, 2003; Stowasser and Gordon, 2004; Young et al, 2004).

Identification of patients with these diagnostic features has important implications for determining clinical management and for predicting the response to treatment.

The response of PRA to aldosterone-induced sodium retention and blood pressure elevation is the cornerstone of early diagnosis of PAL (Fig. 53–34). Accordingly, the normal renal juxtaglomerular responses to increased blood pressure (the baroreceptor mechanism) and the increased distal delivery of sodium chloride (the macula densa mechanism) result in suppression of PRA (Laragh and Sealey, 1992; Komlosi et al, 2004; Schweda and Kurtz, 2004). Moreover, PRA remains low even in the presence of sodium depletion or acute furosemide administration (Weinberger et al, 1979). This observation is in marked contrast to the elevated PRA seen in patients with secondary aldosteronism, whereby oversecretion of aldosterone is the consequence of excess production of renin and angiotensin II usually caused by renal arterial or parenchymal disease (Laragh and Sealey, 1992) (see Chapters 35 and 36).

Measurements of urine and plasma aldosterone have provided further insight into abnormalities of aldosterone secretion (Laragh and Sealey, 1992; Gordon et al, 2005). Hence, in contrast with healthy subjects, the oversecretion of aldosterone is not suppressed by sodium loading in primary aldosteronism (Weinberger et al, 1979; Mulatero et al, 2005). Conversely, with ambulation, patients with an aldosterone-producing adenoma (APA) do not exhibit the characteristic rise in aldosterone secretion found in normal subjects (Ganguly et al, 1973; Ganguly, 1998). These observations highlight the autonomous secretion that is present in patients with APA and identify differences in the pathophysiology of APA and other subtypes of primary aldosteronism (Fontes et al, 1991; Ganguly, 1998; Espiner et al, 2003).

In a subset of APAs, aldosterone production is stimulated by the renin-angiotensin-aldosterone system, as determined by angiotensin II infusion and postural stimulation (Tunny et al, 1991). In these cases, angiotensin II infusion no longer stimulates aldosterone release shortly after adrenalectomy, suggesting that the adenoma is the sole source of aldosterone. This variant, referred to as angiotensin II responsive (AII-R) APA, has other unique biochemical and histologic features (Tunny et al, 1991). In contrast to the typical APA, which is angiotensin II unresponsive (AII-U APA) and in which there is overproduction of cortisol C-18–oxygenated metabolites (i.e., 18-oxocortisol, 18-hydroxycortisol), AII-R APA is not associated with increased levels of these hybrid steroids. In addition, plasma cortisol levels are suppressible in AII-U APA but not in AII-R APA. These findings indicate that autonomous overproduction of cortisol occurs from some APAs (Imai et al, 1991). These heterogeneous biochemical responses are consistent with the histologic characteristics: AII-U APAs consist predominantly of fasciculata-like cells, whereas AII-R APAs are primarily composed of glomerulosa-like cells. Tunny and coworkers (1991) found a reciprocal relationship between the increment in plasma aldosterone during angiotensin II infusion and the percentage of fasciculata-type cells in the adenoma and concluded that the aldosterone responsiveness to angiotensin II was related to the predominant tumor cell type.

Biglieri and coworkers (Banks et al, 1984; Irony et al, 1990) and others (Blumenfeld et al, 1994; Young et al, 2004) have characterized a subset of patients with autonomous aldosterone production in whom an adrenal adenoma could not be identified. This variant has been referred to as primary adrenal hyperplasia. The adrenal glands in primary adrenal hyperplasia are hyperplastic, frequently with a dominant nodule. As in AII-R APA, aldosterone production in primary adrenal hyperplasia is autonomous (Fontes et al, 1991). Furthermore, correction of the metabolic abnormalities and hypertension in this subset occurs after unilateral adrenalectomy.

Adrenal carcinoma is an extremely rare cause of PAL (Arteaga et al, 1984; Isles et al, 1987). Of 141 patients with adrenal carcinoma presenting to the Mayo Clinic for surgery, 15 patients were identified with aldosterone-secreting adrenal carcinoma (Kendrick et al, 2002). Isolated aldosterone hypersecretion was present in 10 patients, and mixed hormonal secretion was detected in 5. Mean tumor size and weight were 10.8 cm and 453 g, respectively. Surgical resection was curative in 10 patients (67%), although the perioperative mortality was 20% and the disease recurrence rate was 70%, with a median interval of 17 months. Five-year survival was 52%.

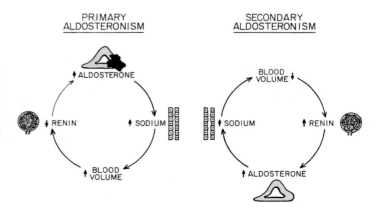

**Figure 53–34.** Hyperaldosteronism may be seen in association with elevated (secondary) or depressed (primary) levels of plasma renin activity. In primary aldosteronism, an adrenal neoplasm or bilateral hyperplasia is the initiating event. Secondary aldosteronism is most commonly seen in edematous disorders (e.g., cirrhosis, renal failure), in which the elevated renin levels are a physiologic adjustment to a contracted blood volume; it is also present in renal artery stenosis, secondary to the stimulus of elevated levels of renin and angiotensin II.

Patients with aldosterone-secreting adrenal carcinoma had an increased risk of perioperative mortality compared with those with an adrenal carcinoma that did not secrete aldosterone (20% versus 5%), although overall survival was longer in aldosterone-secreting adrenal carcinoma (63 months versus 19 months).

The pathogenesis of idiopathic hyperaldosteronism associated with bilateral adrenal hyperplasia remains uncertain. However, a systemic stimulus other than angiotensin II or ACTH seems to be responsible. Less common disorders associated with bilateral adrenal hyperplasia and hyperaldosteronism have been identified and characterized (see preceding, primary adrenal hyperplasia). Glucocorticoid-remediable aldosteronism (GRA), also termed familial hyperaldosteronism type I (FH-I), is an autosomal dominant disorder in which aldosterone biosynthesis is regulated by ACTH rather than by the renin-angiotensin-aldosterone system (Sutherland et al, 1966; Isles et al, 1987; Lifton et al, 1992; McMahon and Dluhy, 2004; Mulatero et al, 2004a). The exaggerated aldosterone responsiveness to ACTH in GRA can be corrected by glucocorticoid treatment (McMahon and Dluhy, 2004; New et al, 2005). Clinical features include a strong family history of hypertension, early-onset hypertension, and increased risk of intracerebral hemorrhage or aortic dissection. The most common, routine laboratory finding is low PRA; however, other biochemical evidence of aldosterone excess may be absent (e.g., hypokalemia) (Rich et al, 1992; Litchfield et al, 1997). A key diagnostic feature is the overproduction of C-18 cortisol-aldosterone structural hybrids, 18-hydroxycortisol and 18-oxocortisol, which are formed when cortisol is accepted by aldosterone synthase as a substrate for methyloxidation (Ulick and Chan, 1989) (Fig. 53–35). Normally, this enzyme is expressed predominantly in the adrenal glomerulosa zone (White, 1994, 2001). On the basis of these biochemical features and the associated hyperplasia of the zona fasciculata, Ulick and associates proposed that the fascicular zone acquires aldosterone synthase activity, thereby abrogating the normal zonation of adrenal function (Ulick and Chan, 1989; Ulick et al, 1992). This hypothesis was supported by the finding that GRA is caused by a chimeric gene duplication that results from unequal crossing over between the highly homologous 11-hydroxylase (*CYP11B1*) and aldosterone synthase (*CYP11B2*) genes, which are located in proximity on chromosome 8 (Lifton et al, 1992; Dluhy and Lifton, 1999). This chimeric gene represents a fusion of the 5′ ACTH-responsive promoter region of the 11-hydroxylase gene and 3′ coding sequences of the aldosterone synthase gene. It results in ectopic expression of aldosterone synthase activity in the cortisol-producing zona fasciculata that is stimulated by ACTH instead of angiotensin II (Fig. 53–36). Furthermore, because of its aberrant expression in the fascicular zone, the enzymatic product of this chimeric gene uses cortisol as a substrate for C-18 oxidation to the cortisol-aldosterone hybrid steroids. Treatment of this syndrome with low doses of exogenous glucocorticoid inhibits ACTH secretion, suppresses aldosterone production (thereby promoting natriuresis), normalizes PRA, and consequently reduces blood pressure and corrects metabolic abnormalities caused by mineralocorticoid excess.

Although GRA is a rare disorder, several previously undiagnosed patients were discovered when elevated urinary levels of 18-hydroxycortisol and 18-oxocortisol were used to screen the relatives of a proband with GRA (Rich et al, 1992). All affected adults were hypertensive before the age of 20 years and had lower PRA than their unaffected family members.

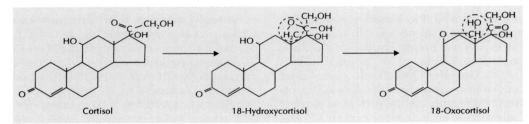

**Figure 53–35.** Biosynthesis of the C-18 methyloxygenation metabolites of cortisol. (From Blumenfeld JD: Hypertension and adrenal disorders. Curr Opin Nephrol Hypertens 1993;2:274.)

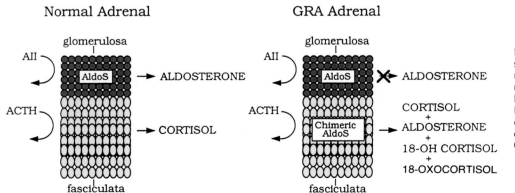

**Figure 53–36.** Adrenal cortex responsiveness to ACTH and angiotensin II in normal subjects and in glucocorticoid-remediable aldosteronism (GRA). (From Lifton RP, Dluhy RG, Powers M, et al: Hereditary hypertension caused by chimeric gene duplications and ectopic expression of aldosterone synthase. Nat Genet 1992;2:66-74.)

Surprisingly, none of those affected were hypokalemic, and their urinary aldosterone excretion overlapped with the unaffected group. An attenuated aldosterone response to potassium in GRA has been described in association with a sharp diurnal decline in aldosterone in this ACTH-regulated syndrome (Litchfield et al, 1997). It has been proposed that these pathophysiologic responses in GRA cause milder clinical and laboratory manifestations of hyperaldosteronism compared with other forms of primary aldosteronism, thereby producing volume expansion with minimal renal potassium wasting (Litchfield et al, 1997).

Diagnostic tests for GRA include direct genetic analysis to identify the chimeric *CYP11B1/CYP11B2* gene; 24-hour urine collection, demonstrating overproduction of cortisol C-18 oxidation metabolites (i.e., 18-hydroxycortisol, 18-oxocortisol); and dexamethasone suppression test (Dluhy and Lifton, 1999). Although C-18 hybrid steroids are also present in APA, the chimeric *CYP11B1/CYP11B2* gene has not been identified in these tumors (Pilon et al, 1999).

Gordon and colleagues have described another familial form of primary aldosteronism termed FH-II, distinct from GRA (FH-I), in which aldosterone production is not suppressed by glucocorticoid treatment (Stowasser et al, 2001; Gordon et al, 2005). The inheritance pattern of FH-II has not been completely determined, and there is no common histologic presentation encompassing family members with AII-R APA, AII-U APA, and bilateral hypersecretion of aldosterone.

Apparent mineralocorticoid excess type 1 is characterized by hypertension, low PRA, low urinary aldosterone excretion rate, and increased urinary excretion of metabolites of cortisol rather than cortisone (ratio of free cortisol to cortisone and of tetrahydrocortisols to tetrahydrocortisone) (Ulick et al, 1979; Quinkler and Stewart, 2003; New et al, 2005). Normally, the mineralocorticoid receptor in vitro binds cortisol and aldosterone with equal affinity, whereas cortisone binding is less avid (Arriza et al, 1987; Quinkler and Stewart, 2003). Although the serum concentration of cortisol is normally 1000-fold greater than that of aldosterone, cortisol is inactivated by conversion to cortisone (which has a relatively low affinity for the mineralocorticoid receptor) by 11β-hydroxysteroid dehydrogenase at mineralocorticoid-responsive tissues. This allows aldosterone, rather than cortisol, to gain access to the mineralocorticoid receptor. **Thus, it is 11β-hydroxysteroid dehydrogenase rather than the mineralocorticoid receptor that confers tissue specificity for aldosterone.** Hypothalamic-pituitary-adrenal axis responsiveness is normal in apparent mineralocorticoid excess, and the serum cortisol concentration is normal and does not aid in the diagnosis.

Treatment options in apparent mineralocorticoid excess include (1) blockade of either the mineralocorticoid receptor (e.g., spironolactone) or the renal apical sodium channel (amiloride) and (2) suppression of endogenous cortisol production with dexamethasone, which has a low affinity for the mineralocorticoid receptor. In patients with Cushing's syndrome, cortisol can become the active mineralocorticoid, especially in the ectopic ACTH syndrome, in which cortisol secretion is extremely high (Ulick et al, 1992; Stewart, 1999). In this disorder, mechanisms of cortisol inactivation are overwhelmed, allowing it to gain access to the mineralocorticoid receptor.

Licorice ingestion can cause hypertension with features that are similar to apparent mineralocorticoid excess (Stewart et al, 1987; Edwards et al, 1988; Farese et al, 1991; Stewart, 1999). **Glycerrhizic acid and its hydrolytic product (glycyrrhetenic acid) are the active ingredients of licorice that inhibit 11β-hydroxysteroid dehydrogenase and thereby allow cortisol to gain access to the mineralocorticoid receptor.** Aldosterone receptor antagonism normalizes blood pressure, prevents upregulation of vascular endothelin-1, and restores nitric oxide–mediated endothelial dysfunction in an animal model of glycyrrhizic acid–induced hypertension (Quaschning et al, 2001).

Liddle's syndrome is an autosomal dominant condition characterized by low-renin hypertension, hypokalemia, renal potassium wasting, and low levels of aldosterone (Liddle and Coppage, 1963). The genetic defects responsible for this syndrome are deletion mutations in the C terminus of the β/γ subunits of the renal epithelial sodium channel (ENaC) (Shimkets et al, 1994; Schild et al, 1995; Warnock, 1998; O'Shaughnessy and Karet, 2004). These gain of function mutations lead to constitutive activation of ENaC, resulting in electrogenic sodium reabsorption and kaliuresis. Amiloride, which blocks the apical sodium channel, is effective treatment. By contrast, mineralocorticoid receptor blockade (e.g., spironolactone) is ineffective because renin, angiotensin II, and aldosterone levels are all suppressed by the sodium-dependent hypertension.

## Epidemiology

PAL has traditionally been considered a rare form of hypertension, affecting 1% to 2% of hypertensive patients, with APA the most prevalent diagnostic subset (Weinberger et al, 1979; Bravo et al, 1983; Blumenfeld et al, 1994). However, results of screening efforts at several large centers, which rely primarily on the ratio of plasma aldosterone to plasma renin activity (see later), suggest that the prevalence of PAL is substantially higher than previously thought. After the aldosterone-to-renin ratio was introduced as a screening strategy, the reported prevalence of PAL increased by 5- to 15-fold at five medical centers, with detection rates of PAL ranging from 3% to 32% of all hypertensive patients (Stowasser et al, 2003; Mulatero et al, 2004b). This screening strategy has also uncovered a higher proportion of PAL patients with milder laboratory abnormalities, accounting for the observation that hypokalemia was found in only 9% to 37% of patients. Moreover, a dramatic change in the prevalence of diagnostic subsets of PAL has been reported. Whereas APA was reported as the cause of PAL in two thirds of patients before screening by the aldosterone-to-renin ratio was introduced (Weinberger et al, 1979; Bravo et al, 1983; Blumenfeld et al, 1994), a marked increase in the proportion of patients with bilateral adrenal hyperplasia has since been reported and the prevalence of patients with APA has decreased to the range of 9% to 50% (Stowasser et al, 2003; Mulatero et al, 2004b; Stowasser and Gordon, 2004; Young et al, 2004). However, use of the aldosterone-to-renin ratio as the cornerstone for PAL screening has been challenged and the validity of this apparent dramatic shift in the epidemiology of PAL questioned (Padfield, 2002; Kaplan, 2004) (see later).

**Table 53–13. Age Distribution of 266 Tumors of the Adrenal Cortex in Hyperaldosteronism with Low Plasma Renin**

| Adrenal Changes (No. of Cases) | Sex | 15-20 | 21-30 | 31-40 | 41-50 | 51-60 | 61-70 | >70 | Total |
|---|---|---|---|---|---|---|---|---|---|
| Adenoma (241) | Female | 6 | 16 | 59 | 67 | 17 | 5 | 1 | 171 |
| | Male | 2 | 7 | 20 | 28 | 9 | 3 | 1 | 70 |
| Carcinomas (25) | Female | — | 2 | 5 | 3 | 5 | 1 | — | 16 |
| | Male | — | 1 | 4 | 1 | 2 | 1 | — | 9 |

From Neville AM, O'Hare MJ: The Human Adrenal Cortex: Pathology and Biology—An Integrated Approach. New York, Springer-Verlag, 1982.

## Clinical Characteristics

The clinical findings in patients with this syndrome are primarily due to the increased total body sodium content and deficit in total body potassium (Ferriss et al, 1978). Symptoms include nocturia and urinary frequency, reflecting the urine concentrating defect induced by the potassium deficit, although patients may not be aware of these symptoms and thus the history may have to be elicited. In patients with more severe hypokalemia and other manifestations, muscle weakness, frontal headaches, polydipsia, paresthesias, visual disturbances, temporary paralysis, cramps, and tetany may occur. If the patient is normokalemic, these characteristic symptoms are usually mild or absent.

An adenoma is more likely to be detected in younger patients and in women. The age and gender distribution of 266 tumors in patients with hyperaldosteronism is shown in Table 53–13. The weights and sites of adrenal adenomas and adrenal carcinomas are shown in Table 53–14.

**Patients with PAL are not edematous because sodium retention in this syndrome is limited by the mineralocorticoid escape phenomenon** (Nakada et al, 1989) (see earlier). Patients with an adenoma, however, usually have more extensive manifestations of mineralocorticoid excess than do those with hyperplasia, including more severe hypertension (Ferriss et al, 1978; Blumenfeld et al, 1994). The physical examination findings are not usually distinguishable from essential hypertension, unless hypokalemia is severe. Malignant hypertension occurs rarely.

Hypertension is present in virtually all patients with primary aldosteronism. Moreover, the prevalence of primary aldosteronism is reportedly higher in patients with more severe hypertension. For example, of 609 hypertensive patients evaluated for PAL at primary care centers in Chile, PAL prevalence was 2% in patients with blood pressure of 140-159/90-99 mm Hg, 8% in those with blood pressure of 160-179/100-109 mm Hg, and 13.2% in those with blood pressure above 180/110 mm Hg (Mosso et al, 2003).

At our center, after withdrawal of antihypertensive medication, patients with an adenoma had significantly higher systolic (184 versus 161 mm Hg) and diastolic (112 versus 105 mm Hg) levels than did those with adrenal hyperplasia (Blumenfeld et al, 1994). Systolic blood pressure was 175 mm Hg or higher in 66% with adenoma, compared with only 15% with hyperplasia. Diastolic pressure was 114 mm Hg or higher in 50% of patients with adenoma, compared with only 19% of those in the hyperplasia group. There was a direct relationship ($r = 0.58$) between the urinary aldosterone excre-

**Table 53–14. Hyperaldosteronism**

| Weights of 151 Adrenal Adenomas | | | Weights of 25 Adrenal Carcinomas | |
|---|---|---|---|---|
| Weight (g) | No. | % | Weight (g) | No. |
| <2 | 51 | 34 | <30 | 1 |
| 2-4 | 36 | 24 | 30-100 | 5 |
| 4-5 | 16 | 11 | 100-200 | 3 |
| 5-10 | 26 | 17 | 200-500 | 4 |
| 10-20 | 11 | 7 | 500-1000 | 6 |
| 20-30 | 3 | 3.5 | 1000-2000 | 5 |
| >30 | 8 | 3.5 | >2000 | 1 |
| Total | 151 | 100 | | 25 |

**Site Distribution of Adrenal Adenomas in 218 Patients**

| Site | Male | Female | Total |
|---|---|---|---|
| Single | | | |
| Right adrenal | 22 | 37 | 59 |
| Left adrenal | 25 | 70 | 95 |
| Bilateral | 2 | 1 | 3 |
| Unknown | 14 | 40 | 54 |
| Subtotal | 63 (91%) | 148 (93%) | 201 (92%) |
| Multiple | | | |
| Right adrenal | 4 | 2 | 6 |
| Left adrenal | 1 | 8 | 9 |
| Bilateral | 1 | 1 | 2 |
| Unknown | — | — | — |
| Subtotal | 6 (9%) | 11 (7%) | 17 (8%) |
| Total | 69 (30%) | 159 (70%) | 218 (100%) |

From Neville AM, O'Hare MJ: The Human Adrenal Cortex: Pathology and Biology—An Integrated Approach. New York, Springer-Verlag, 1982.

tion rate and the mean arterial pressure among the adenoma patients.

In contrast to the escape from sodium retention that occurs in this syndrome, aldosterone-mediated renal secretion of potassium is persistent and causes total body potassium deficit, hypokalemia, nephrogenic diabetes insipidus, and related symptoms (Ferriss et al, 1978). In the Cornell study, serum potassium levels were significantly lower in the patients with adenoma (3.0 versus 3.5 mEq/L) (Blumenfeld et al, 1994). Levels below 2.8 mEq/L occurred in 44% of the adenoma group compared with only 6% of the group with hyperplasia. The profound hypokalemia that occurs in patients with an adenoma contributes to its marked metabolic alkalosis. Conversely, 18% of the hyperplasia group had a serum potassium concentration above 3.5 mEq/L compared with only 6% of those with an adenoma. Several previous studies have also reported normal serum potassium levels in approximately 20% of patients with PAL (Conn et al, 1966; Bravo et al, 1983; Melby, 1984; Takeda et al, 1995; Mosso et al, 2003; Mulatero et al, 2004b; Stowasser and Gordon, 2004), most commonly in patients with adrenal hyperplasia. **Because severe hypokalemia occurs less frequently in patients with restricted dietary sodium intake, the authors do not recommend screening patients for this syndrome unless they are adequately sodium loaded** (see "Diagnostic Tests").

**Cardiovascular Disease.** Although case reports and other studies with relatively few patients illustrate that cardiovascular complications can occur in patients with PAL, there is little information about the prevalence of these complications (Suzuki et al, 1988; Rossi et al, 1996, 1997, 2002, 2003; Porodko et al, 2002; Rossi, 2005). However, a case-control study identified 124 patients with PAL (APA in 52%) from a rigorously screened population of 5500 patients referred for evaluation of hypertension (Milliez et al, 2005). Compared with the control group of 465 patients with essential hypertension in that study, those with PAL were at significantly greater risk of atrial fibrillation (7.3% versus 0.6%), myocardial infarction (4% versus 0.6%), stroke (12.9% versus 3.4%), and left ventricular hypertrophy (by electrocardiography: 32% versus 14%; by echocardiography: 34% versus 24%) during a mean follow-up period of 13.6 months. Blood pressure was reportedly controlled during follow-up by unilateral adrenalectomy or antihypertensive drug treatment. The risk of complications was not preferentially associated with either diagnostic subtype of PAL. The clinical characteristics, blood pressure (mean, ~175/105 mm Hg), and other risk factors were reportedly well matched, with the exception of a slightly greater serum cholesterol level in the essential hypertension group. The cardiovascular complication rates reported in this study were unusually high, and those results will have to be confirmed in subsequent studies. However, treatment with mineralocorticoid receptor blockade (i.e., spironolactone, eplerenone) in patients with severe heart failure, which is commonly associated with secondary hyperaldosteronism, improves survival and decreases the risk of cardiovascular complications (Pitt et al, 1999, 2003). Although there is a temptation to relate the cardiovascular impact of secondary hyperaldosteronism in heart failure with that of primary aldosteronism, this comparison has significant and obvious limitations. Nevertheless, whether the dramatically high prevalence of cardiovascular complications reported by Milliez and coworkers (2005) can be generalized to all patients with primary aldosteronism will require further investigation.

## Diagnostic Tests

The diagnostic tests described here are designed to screen the large hypertensive population for PAL and to identify patients with surgically remediable subtypes of PAL. The absence of a reliable clinical picture of hyperaldosteronism has led to an array of tests suggested to accomplish these goals.

**Unprovoked hypokalemia is the hallmark of hyperaldosteronism, but as already discussed, serum potassium levels between 3.5 and 4.0 mEq/L are relatively common in patients subsequently proved to have PAL.** Moreover, patients with essential hypertension may exhibit hypokalemia, especially during treatment with thiazide and loop diuretics.

Monitoring serum potassium concentration after salt loading increases the likelihood that hypokalemia will be observed, but the entity of normokalemic PAL is well recognized (Weinberger et al, 1979; Blumenfeld et al, 1994; Stowasser et al, 2003).

### Plasma Renin Activity

The first breakthrough followed the ability to determine PRA accurately. In 1964, Conn and associates demonstrated the suppression of PRA in patients with PAL (Conn, 1964). Until that time, a major diagnostic dilemma was distinguishing patients with PAL from those with excessive secretion of aldosterone as the consequence of high levels of renin due to primary renal parenchymal or renovascular diseases (secondary hyperaldosteronism). This problem was solved by the accurate measurement of PRA (Streeten et al, 1990; Laragh and Sealey, 1992).

Two methods are now commonly used to measure plasma renin. The PRA enzyme kinetic assay quantifies the amount of angiotensin I generated during incubation of plasma. PRA is expressed as the hourly rate of angiotensin I generation (as nanograms per milliliter per hour). It reflects the net capacity of the blood to generate angiotensin II because angiotensin-converting enzyme is not normally rate limiting unless it is pharmacologically blocked (Sealey et al, 2005). This is the most sensitive method available for quantifying the low levels of renin activity that are characteristic of PAL.

The direct renin assay is an alternative method that is based on a chemiluminescence assay (expressed as microunits per milliliter). Unlike the PRA measurement by the enzyme kinetic assay, the direct renin method does not measure angiotensin I generation and lacks its sensitivity (Sealey et al, 2005).

Although approximately one third of patients with essential hypertension also exhibit low PRA (Brunner et al, 1972), with an increased prevalence of low-renin essential hypertension among black patients (Alderman et al, 2004), these patients are normokalemic and have normal aldosterone responses to changes in posture, sodium depletion, and saline loading.

### Aldosterone-to-Renin Ratio

An elevated ratio of plasma aldosterone to PRA is another indicator of autonomous aldosterone secretion that is now widely used as a screening test for PAL (Hiramatsu et al, 1981; Young, 2003; Mulatero et al, 2004b; Stowasser and Gordon, 2004). Dunn and Espiner (1976) first reported the use of the aldosterone-to-renin ratio (ARR) as a screening test for PAL, and Hiramatsu and colleagues (1981) showed that an ARR above 40 (aldosterone [ng/dL] to PRA [ng/mL/hr]) successfully identified untreated patients with APA. Since then, investigators from several centers have used ARR cutoff values ranging from 14 to 50 (Blumenfeld et al, 1994; Mosso et al, 2003; Mulatero et al, 2004b; Young et al, 2004) and consequently have identified PAL in significantly higher proportions of patients with previously diagnosed essential hypertension. However, a precise partition value for the ARR has not been established in the diagnosis of PAL. In the Cornell study, a plasma ARR above 50 was more commonly observed in PAL than in essential hypertension, including patients with low-renin essential hypertension (Blumenfeld et al, 1994). However, there was considerable overlap between the hyperplasia and adenoma patients, and the magnitude of ARR was not predictive of surgical cure. Therefore, ARR is not a useful index for differentiating these diagnostic subsets or the potential for surgical cure.

Several factors can have an impact on the measurements of plasma renin and aldosterone and thus influence the interpretation of the ARR. **When the PRA is less than 1 ng/mL/hr, which is a characteristic finding in patients with PAL, the ARR is disproportionately affected by small changes in the renin level** (Auchus, 2003). For example, a patient with essential hypertension with a PRA of 0.6 ng/mL/hr and a serum aldosterone level of 8 ng/dL (ARR = 13) would be misdiagnosed with PAL if the PRA was erroneously reported as 0.2 ng/mL/hr (ARR = 40). The risk of a false-positive screening test result and hence the likelihood of an incorrect diagnosis of PAL is amplified because the accuracy of the PRA measurement is limited at these low levels. The large intrapatient and interpatient variations in plasma aldosterone concentration, PRA, and ARR in patients with APA highlight this problem. In fact, only 37% of PAL patients always have the characteristic profile associated with APA (i.e., plasma aldosterone > 15 ng/dL, PRA < 0.5 ng/mL/hr, ARR > 35) (Tanabe et al, 2003).

To minimize the risk that the ARR will result in an incorrect diagnosis, several additional steps should be employed before proceeding with the ARR as a screening test for primary aldosteronism (Stowasser and Gordon, 2004).

1. The patient should be seated when blood samples are obtained.
2. Hypokalemia should be corrected with oral potassium supplementation because potassium depletion attenuates aldosterone secretion and leads to a false-negative ARR.
3. Plasma (or serum) aldosterone concentration (PAC) above 15 ng/dL: Although there is no clearly defined level, a PAC of less than 15 ng/dL is unlikely to occur in patients with PAL (especially those with APA). However, a false-positive ARR can occur with very low PRA encountered in patients with low-renin essential hypertension (e.g., PRA of 0.1 ng/mL/hr, PAC of 6 ng/dL, ARR of 60) (Mulatero et al, 2005).
4. Antihypertensive medications:
   False-negative ARR: Diuretics (amiloride, spironolactone, thiazide and loop diuretics) stimulate renin secretion and should be discontinued 4 weeks before testing to decrease the chance of a false-negative test result. Dihydropyridine calcium channel blockers can inhibit aldosterone secretion and increase renin and should be discontinued at least 2 weeks before testing.
   False-positive ARR: β-Adrenergic receptor blockers, clonidine, and methyldopa suppress PRA and should be discontinued for at least 2 weeks before testing to reduce the chance of a false-positive test result.
5. Captopril test: Angiotensin-converting enzyme inhibitors and angiotensin receptor blockers stimulate renin secretion and should be discontinued 2 weeks before testing to reduce the likelihood of potentially false-negative ARR, particularly in patients with idiopathic hyperaldosteronism or an angiotensin II–responsive adenoma. However, several investigators have reported that acute administration of a single dose of captopril (25 to 50 mg 1 to 2 hours before measurement of plasma renin and aldosterone levels) enhances the accuracy for diagnosis of patients with primary aldosteronism and have recommended its use for screening (Agharazii et al, 2001; Castro et al, 2002; Racine et al, 2002; Rossi E et al, 2002).
   If antihypertensive medication is required, verapamil and $\alpha_1$-adrenergic receptor blockers do not significantly influence renin or aldosterone secretion and thus are less likely to confound the ARR.
6. If the ARR screening test result is positive (>25 to 50), a salt-loading suppression test is indicated (see later).

**Problems with the ARR as a Screening Test for PAL.** The ARR has gained broad acceptance and is now widely used to screen patients for primary aldosteronism. However, several methodologic inconsistencies have limited the interpretation of the ARR results (Kaplan, 2004). As discussed before, the elevated ARR is predominantly an indicator of low PRA and is especially vulnerable to variability in this assay that can occur from antihypertensive medication use and volume depletion (Padfield, 2002). Several centers that have reported ARR for the diagnosis of PAL do not use sodium suppression protocols (Kaplan, 2004). Moreover, only limited data exist regarding the sensitivity and specificity of ARR. In one study of patients in whom the adrenal status was clearly defined, an ARR of 32 or higher had a specificity of 61% (Hirohara et al, 2001). Some investigators do not require an absolutely elevated plasma aldosterone level for the interpretation of an elevated ARR (Stowasser et al, 2003). Critics of ARR for PAL screening raise other issues, including the risks of potentially unnecessary invasive testing and treatment (e.g., adrenal vein sampling, adrenalectomy; see later). Moreover, bilateral adrenal hyperplasia predominates in patients with PAL that is detected by an elevated ARR. This diagnostic variant is not surgically remediable and requires treatment with antihypertensive medication, preferably a selective mineralocorticoid receptor antagonist (i.e., spironolactone or eplerenone). Hence, critics question the necessity of these elaborate maneuvers when treatment with a mineralocorticoid receptor antagonist is the most likely outcome. The true sensitivity and specificity, cost-efficacy, and safety can best be defined by properly designed clinical studies. Moreover, any safe screening test that can facilitate the stratification of patients with essential hypertension into more clearly defined pathophysiologic subgroups and improve treatment efficacy is desirable.

### Postural Stimulation Test

**Stimulation of renin and aldosterone secretion occurs in normal individuals during upright posture** (Laragh and Sealey, 1992). **In subsets of PAL associated with autonomous aldosterone production (including angiotensin II–unresponsive adenoma and primary adrenal hyperplasia), however, postural stimulation of aldosterone does not occur** (Ganguly et al, 1973; Fontes et al, 1991; Blumenfeld et al, 1994). The postural stimulation test is conducted by drawing plasma cortisol and aldosterone samples at 8:00 AM with the patient supine after an overnight recumbency and again while the patient is upright after 2 to 4 hours of ambulation. In patients with angiotensin II–unresponsive adenoma and primary adrenal hyperplasia who have highly autonomous aldosterone production, plasma aldosterone levels *decrease* during this test, reflecting the diurnal fall in ACTH. **Normally, ACTH is a relatively minor stimulus for aldosterone production, but this effect is accentuated in angiotensin II–unresponsive adenoma and primary adrenal hyperplasia because renin-angiotensin levels are highly suppressed** (Schambelan et al, 1976). A false-negative response, which might occur during a stress-related increase in ACTH, can be detected if plasma cortisol levels rise during upright posture. By contrast, in patients with idiopathic hyperaldosteronism or angiotensin II–responsive adenoma, renin and angiotensin II levels increase slightly during upright posture and aldosterone production increases because of the increased sensitivity of the zona glomerulosa to angiotensin II (Tunny et al, 1991). In GRA, aldosterone production falls during the test because of the ACTH dependency of aldosterone biosynthesis. This response may lead to an inaccurate diagnosis.

### Sodium Loading

Sodium-loading maneuvers are useful for identifying patients with PAL (Weinberger et al, 1979; Arteaga et al, 1985; Stowasser and Gordon, 2004; Mulatero et al, 2005). Accordingly, during volume expansion in normal individuals or in patients with essential hypertension, PRA levels decrease and consequently aldosterone secretion falls. **In patients with PAL, renin secretion is suppressed before salt loading, and therefore additional volume expansion does not decrease aldosterone levels to the same extent as in normal subjects or patients with essential hypertension.** Several salt-loading protocols have been validated for diagnostic screening (Mulatero et al, 2005):

1. Oral sodium loading for 3 to 5 days (≥200 mEq/day; 5 g of sodium per day). This may be accomplished by instructing the patient to eat a high-salt diet or to supplement the diet with sodium chloride tablets (1 g NaCl = 17 mEq Na). On the last day of the high-salt diet, a 24-hour urine specimen is collected to measure sodium, potassium, and aldosterone concentrations. The test result is positive if the aldosterone level is greater than 14 μg with a concomitant sodium content above 200 mEq. Because sodium loading can cause kaliuresis and exacerbate hypokalemia, potassium chloride supplementation is required.
2. Intravenous saline loading. Plasma aldosterone concentration is measured after the infusion of 2 liters 0.9% NaCl during 4 hours. PAL is ruled out if the plasma aldosterone level is less than 5 ng/dL and is confirmed if the level exceeds 10 ng/dL. Although a plasma aldosterone level in the range of 5 to 10 ng/dL after sodium loading is considered equivocal by some investigators, many consider a level above 5 ng/dL diagnostic of PAL (Mulatero et al, 2005).

Although this maneuver is useful for identifying patients with PAL, it does not adequately discriminate patients with an APA from those with nonadenomatous adrenal hyperplasia. By contrast, measurement of morning levels of plasma cortisol, aldosterone, and 18-hydroxycorticosterone after intravenous saline loading (1.25 to 2.0 liters during 90 to 120 minutes) reportedly can distinguish these diagnostic subsets. In APA, the ratio of aldosterone to cortisol is greater than 2.2, or the ratio of 18-hydroxycorticosterone to cortisol is greater than 3; whereas for patients with idiopathic hyperaldosteronism, the ratios are lower (Arteaga et al, 1985). With a normal sodium intake, a supine morning 18-hydroxycorticosterone plasma level above 50 ng/dL is characteristic of PAL, and a level of 100 ng/dL or more is diagnostic of aldosteronoma (Biglieri and Schambelan, 1979; Bravo et al, 1983).

3. Fludrocortisone suppression test. Plasma aldosterone and cortisol levels are measured in an upright position at 10 AM after 4 days of administration of fludrocortisone (0.1 mg every 6 hours) and sodium chloride supplementation (30 mEq thrice daily) with a corresponding 24-hour urine sodium excretion rate of 3 mEq/kg/day. This test is diagnostic of PAL if, on day 4, the plasma aldosterone level exceeds 5 ng/dL, provided the concurrent PRA is less than 1 ng/mL/hr, the serum potassium level is normal, and the plasma cortisol level at 10 AM is no higher than at 7 AM (Stowasser et al, 2003; Mulatero et al, 2005).

### Cortisol Metabolites

C-18–methyloxygenated metabolites of cortisol, 18-hydroxycortisol and 18-oxocortisol, are increased in PAL when it is caused by adenoma but not by nonadenomatous adrenal hyperplasia (Ulick and Chan, 1989; Ulick et al, 1992). This steroid pattern appears to reflect the loss of normal functional zonation of the adrenal gland (see previously). In the Cornell study, two of the adenoma patients with hybrid steroid levels in hyperplasia range also had a negative postural stimulation test response, and their blood pressures were improved but not cured by surgery (Blumenfeld et al, 1994). These findings are in accord with a previous report that patients with adenomas who increase aldosterone production during upright posture or infusion of exogenous angiotensin II have low levels of these hybrid cortisol metabolites (Gordon et al, 1987).

## Lateralizing Tests

### Adrenal Vein Sampling

The diagnostic tests provide the biochemical evidence necessary to confirm the diagnosis of PAL. Although the results of these tests may identify surgically remediable variants (e.g., lack of postural stimulation of aldosterone in patients with an APA), they do not locate the tumor and thus fail to guide surgical treatment. Adrenal CT and MRI lack sufficient sensitivity and specificity to identify adrenal tumors less than 1.5 cm in diameter and thus cannot reliably distinguish APA from bilateral adrenal hyperplasia (Espiner et al, 2003; Young et al, 2004). **Thus, scans can appear normal when a small APA is not identified because of limited spatial resolution or when an APA is not detected because of the concomitant benign unilateral or bilateral adrenal nodularity that occurs normally with aging.**

The ability to measure plasma aldosterone concentration from selectively catheterized adrenal veins has added an important dimension to the localization of APA (Melby, 1984; Blumenfeld et al, 1994; Phillips et al, 2000; Rossi et al, 2001; Espiner et al, 2003; Young et al, 2004). Adrenal veins are catheterized by the percutaneous femoral approach, and blood is obtained from both adrenal veins and from the inferior vena cava below the level of the renal veins. Aldosterone and cortisol levels are measured from both adrenal veins and from the inferior vena cava. **To minimize stress-induced fluctuations in cortisol and aldosterone, continuous infusion of cosyntropin (50 μg/hr) is recommended, beginning 30 minutes before the catheterization and continuing throughout the procedure.** Adrenal vein catheterization is considered to be technically successful if the cortisol level measured from the adrenal vein is significantly higher than that obtained from the inferior vena cava. **The specific adrenal–inferior vena cava ratio cutoff value of 2 or greater for the cortisol concentration identifies a successful adrenal vein cannulation.** Studies have reported ratios ranging from 1.1 to 5 (Phillips et al, 2000; Rossi et al, 2001; Espiner et al, 2003; Young et al, 2004).

Studies have evaluated several criteria for lateralization of aldosterone secretion by adrenal vein sampling in which these levels are normalized for the corresponding adrenal venous cortisol concentrations (Espiner et al, 2003):

1. *Lateralized ratio:* the aldosterone-to-cortisol ratio of the dominant adrenal vein divided by the aldosterone-to-cortisol ratio of the nondominant adrenal vein. **The patient with a lateralized ratio exceeding 5, together with a peripheral venous aldosterone level above 15 ng/dL, reportedly has about 180 times the odds of having an APA compared with the patient having a peripheral venous aldosterone level below 15 ng/dL and a lateralized ratio below 5** (Phillips et al, 2000). Others have reported a lateralized ratio above 4 to have a positive predictive index of 89% (Espiner et al, 2003) and a sensitivity of 96% for the diagnosis of APA (Young et al, 2004). In a large series in which cosyntropin stimulation was not employed during adrenal vein sampling and a low adrenal–inferior vena cava cortisol ratio was used to confirm successful adrenal vein catheterization, a lateralized ratio above 2 reportedly had a sensitivity of 80% for identification of APA (Rossi et al, 2001).

2. *Contralateral ratio:* the aldosterone-to-cortisol ratio of the nondominant adrenal vein divided by the aldosterone-to-cortisol ratio in the matching antecubital vein or inferior vena cava. When this value is less than 1, it indicates suppression of aldosterone secretion by the uninvolved adrenal gland and has been reported to have a high positive predictive value in patients with APA. It has been proposed that a contralateral ratio below 1 is diagnostic of APA and is thus an important consideration when the vein from the affected adrenal gland (i.e., with the adenoma) is not successfully sampled. However, there is considerable disagreement about the importance of this value in separating the diagnosis of APA from bilateral adrenal hyperplasia (Doppman et al, 1992; Espiner et al, 2003; Young et al, 2004).

3. *Ipsilateral ratio:* the aldosterone-to-cortisol ratio in the dominant adrenal vein divided by the aldosterone-to-cortisol ratio in the matching antecubital vein or inferior vena cava. This value does not aid in distinguishing APA from bilateral adrenal hyperplasia (Espiner et al, 2003).

Technical problems that are encountered during adrenal vein sampling include difficulty in catheterization of the short right adrenal vein; trauma, including adrenal hemorrhage that can result in acute adrenal insufficiency; dilution of blood by blood from nonadrenal sources; and episodic changes in aldosterone secretion coincident with changes in cortisol (Weinberger et al, 1979). Most of these problems can be controlled by careful catheter localization, simultaneous plasma cortisol measurements to document appropriate catheter placement, and collection of blood during ACTH administration.

### Radionuclide Scintigraphy

[$^{131}$I]6β-Iodomethyl-19-norcholesterol (NP-59) scintigraphy has the potential to correlate anatomy and function of APA. However, this test is limited by poor tracer uptake by tumors less than 1.5 cm in diameter and by the exposure to and disposal of a radioactive isotope (Young et al, 2004). This test is not routinely used at most centers for the diagnostic evaluation of primary aldosteronism.

The sensitivity and specificity of adrenal imaging techniques may differ substantially among medical centers, depending on the local resources and expertise. Incidental, nonfunctioning adrenal masses are relatively common; they are found in 0.6% of all CT scans of the abdomen, and 2% to 9% of adults have grossly visible adenomas at autopsy. Conversely, a subset of patients with surgically curable PAL have radiographically normal adrenal glands (Radin et al, 1992; Blumenfeld et al, 1994; Young et al, 2004). **Therefore, to minimize confusion during diagnostic evaluation, radiographic imaging procedures should be withheld until after biochemical confirmation of PAL has been accomplished** (Radin et al, 1992).

## Diagnostic Strategy

The results of diagnostic screening of patients with this syndrome are often ambiguous, especially when the serum potassium level is in the normal range. Relatively simple tests that can improve the diagnostic accuracy include the following:

1. 24-hour urinary aldosterone excretion rate above 14 μg or higher and PRA less than 1.0 ng/mL/hr, after sodium loading for at least 3 days (urine sodium content > 250 mEq/day) (Bravo et al, 1983);

2. ratio of plasma aldosterone to renin activity above 50, although a lower ratio is used by others with a concurrent serum aldosterone concentration above 15 ng/dL (Blumenfeld et al, 1994; Stowasser et al, 2003; Young et al, 2004; Mulatero et al, 2005);

3. failure to increase PRA after sodium restriction, furosemide-induced diuresis (Weinberger et al, 1979) and;

4. supine plasma 18-hydroxycorticosterone levels above 50 ng/dL or ratio of plasma 18-hydroxycorticosterone to cortisol greater than 3 after saline infusion (Biglieri and Schambelan, 1979; Bravo et al, 1983; Arteaga et al, 1985).

Measurements of aldosterone should be performed only after potassium supplementation because aldosterone secretion is attenuated by the potassium deficit and thus may obfuscate the diagnosis. The presence of hypokalemia and renal potassium wasting (24-hour urine potassium concentration above 40 mEq), together with the characteristics described before, confirms the diagnosis of primary aldosteronism.

The sensitivity and specificity of each of these diagnostic maneuvers can be adversely influenced by concurrent use of antihypertensive medications. For example, β-adrenoceptor antagonists markedly decrease PRA in essential hypertension and may alter the interpretation of these tests (Buhler et al, 1972; Blumenfeld et al, 1999). Hypokalemia, when it is caused by thiazide diuretics, may be difficult to distinguish from PAL, although the PRA is often elevated during diuretic use in patients with essential hypertension (Laragh and Sealey, 1992). Angiotensin-converting enzyme inhibitors and calcium channel antagonists reportedly reduce aldosterone biosynthesis and improve hypokalemia in some patients with PAL

(Melby, 1984; Nadler et al, 1985) (see later). Therefore, antihypertensive medications should be discontinued for at least 2 weeks before diagnostic evaluation and potassium supplements provided to hypokalemic patients. Spironolactone should be discontinued for at least 1 month before these biochemical assessments because it has a long duration of action.

Figure 53–37 is a diagnostic algorithm that can be useful for directing treatment when biochemical screening tests are indicative of PAL. Hypertensive patients with a low PRA (<0.65 ng/mL/hr) warrant measurement of plasma aldosterone level, particularly if their blood pressure is difficult to control. Those patients with an ARR above 25 to 50 should

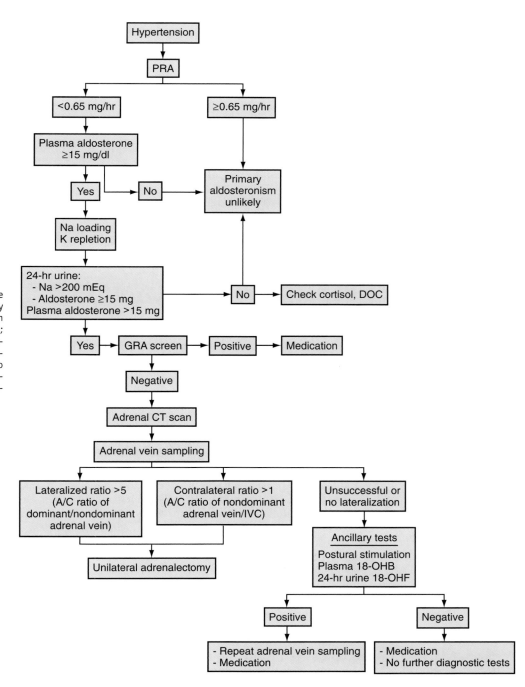

**Figure 53–37.** Algorithm for the diagnosis and treatment of primary aldosteronism. PRA, plasma renin activity; DOC, deoxycorticosterone; GRA, glucocorticoid-remediable aldosteronism; A/C, ratio of the concentration of plasma aldosteronism to cortisol; IVC, inferior vena cava; 18-OHB, 18-hydroxycorticosterone; 18-OHF, 18-hydroxycortisol.

undergo either an oral or intravenous sodium loading protocol followed by a repeated measurement of either plasma or 24-hour urine aldosterone level. Failure to suppress aldosterone by sodium loading is diagnostic of primary aldosteronism. To exclude GRA, screening for the chimeric gene is indicated, particularly if there is a personal history or family history of early-onset hypertension, stroke, or aortic dissection; if results are negative, adrenal vein sampling is warranted. Adrenal imaging, preferably by CT scan, does not reliably exclude or confirm the diagnosis of APA, but it is reasonable at this point because it can assist the interventional radiologist in identifying anatomic landmarks. A positive lateralized ratio or, perhaps less reliably, a positive contralateral ratio is suggestive of a surgically remediable lesion regardless of the radiographic appearance of the adrenal gland. In those patients with nondiagnostic or unsuccessful adrenal vein sampling results, a positive postural stimulation test result and elevated levels of serum 18-hydroxycorticosterone and 24-hour urine 18-hydroxycortisol are strongly suggestive of a surgically remediable diagnostic subtype. In that case, we often treat the patient medically with a mineralocorticoid receptor antagonist (e.g., spironolactone, eplerenone) for 6 to 12 months and then repeat adrenal vein sampling after withdrawal of this medication for 4 to 6 weeks. **Adrenalectomy should be preceded by several weeks of adequate control of hypertension and correction of hypokalemia and other metabolic abnormalities** (see later).

If the patient fails to lateralize aldosterone secretion during adrenal vein sampling, the postural stimulation test result is negative, and levels of 18-hydroxycorticosterone and 18-hydroxycortisol are normal, adrenalectomy is not indicated and the patient should be treated with a mineralocorticoid receptor antagonist. When a discrete adrenal tumor appears to be present in this situation, unilateral adrenalectomy may be considered, particularly in relatively young (<40 years) patients (Young et al, 2004). However, the risk of persistent hypertension in this situation is not well established but is probably relatively high.

## Treatment

### Idiopathic Hyperaldosteronism (Bilateral Adrenal Hyperplasia)

**The cornerstone of medical therapy in PAL caused by idiopathic hyperaldosteronism is a mineralocorticoid receptor antagonist (i.e., spironolactone, eplerenone).** The efficacy of this drug class relates to the reduction in plasma volume in disorders associated with aldosterone excess. Although a favorable blood pressure response to spironolactone has been associated with improved chances of surgical cure, it does not reliably predict outcome (Celen et al, 1996). Side effects of spironolactone include painful gynecomastia, erectile dysfunction, decreased libido, and menstrual irregularities that are caused by nonspecific binding to cellular receptors for progesterone and dihydrotestosterone. In a study of 182 patients with essential hypertension treated with spironolactone, daily doses of 75 to 100 mg/day lowered blood pressure as effectively as 150 to 300 mg/day. Overall, gynecomastia developed in 13% of patients, and its occurrence was dose related—6.9% of patients taking 50 mg/day were symptomatic

compared with 52% of those taking a dose of 150 mg/day or more (de Gasparo et al, 1989).

Eplerenone is a steroid-based competitive and highly selective mineralocorticoid receptor antagonist that was recently approved for use in patients with essential hypertension. This drug has 0.1% of the binding affinity to androgen receptors and less than 1% of the binding affinity to progesterone receptors compared with spironolactone (Young, 2003). Although eplerenone is reported to be effective, with a side effect profile similar to that of placebo in patients with essential hypertension (Young, 2003), there are no reported studies comparing it with spironolactone in patients with primary aldosteronism.

Amiloride can also effectively lower blood pressure and correct hypokalemia in patients with gynecomastia or other side effects associated with spironolactone (Griffing et al, 1982). The dihydropyridine calcium channel antagonists can acutely decrease blood pressure and aldosterone secretion in patients with this syndrome (Melby, 1984; Nadler et al, 1985). Other studies of longer duration, however, have failed to demonstrate these beneficial effects when nifedipine was used as monotherapy (Bravo et al, 1985; Bursztyn et al, 1988). Angiotensin-converting enzyme inhibitors have been reported to successfully treat some patients with hyperplasia in whom aldosterone production is not completely autonomous from angiotensin II stimulation (Melby, 1984). Phentolamine does not acutely reduce blood pressure; therefore, a role for α-adrenergic receptor blockade has not been established (Bravo et al, 1985). Nevertheless, long-term treatment with prazosin is effective in low-renin essential hypertension, suggesting that α-adrenergic receptor antagonists may have an ancillary role in the treatment of PAL (Bolli et al, 1980).

Subsets of patients with PAL who demonstrate autonomous aldosterone production should be managed with excision of the adrenal gland containing the adenoma or, in the case of nonadenomatous adrenal hyperplasia, the gland from which aldosterone secretion is predominant. This rationale is based on the observation that both the metabolic abnormalities and the hypertension are alleviated by unilateral adrenalectomy in most of these patients (Fontes et al, 1991). By contrast, patients with idiopathic hyperaldosteronism usually do not have significant improvement in hypertension after unilateral or bilateral adrenalectomy.

### Aldosterone-Producing Adenoma

Laparoscopic unilateral adrenalectomy is now the standard of care for patients with an APA. Although more than 90% of patients will have their blood pressure controlled postoperatively, antihypertensive medication is required in 40% to 70% (Blumenfeld et al, 1994; Young, 2003). Factors that have been associated with persistent hypertension after unilateral adrenalectomy include age older than 50 years, duration of hypertension, increased serum creatinine concentration, one first-degree relative with hypertension, and preoperative use of more than two antihypertensive medications (Blumenfeld et al, 1994; Young, 2003). In the Cornell study, preoperative renin system activity was also an important predictor of blood pressure outcome (Blumenfeld et al, 1994). Cured patients had significantly lower pretreatment PRA (0.17 versus 0.50 ng/mL/hr) than did those who were not cured. Furthermore, in cured patients, there was also a correlation between the preoperative urinary aldosterone excretion and the relative decrease in diastolic blood pressure after adrenalectomy (r = 0.59). All patients in whom lateralization of aldosterone secretion occurred had hypertension cured or improved by adrenalectomy.

## Summary

Establishing the diagnosis of PAL is important because hypertension and metabolic disturbances are potentially curable by unilateral adrenalectomy. Furthermore, hypertension associated with PAL is often severe and can be difficult to control solely with antihypertensive medication. The diagnosis may be obscured, however, because the complete clinical and biochemical expression of mineralocorticoid hypertension may not be present, particularly in those with adrenal hyperplasia who present with a serum potassium level in the normal range. Support for the diagnosis is provided by low PRA, elevated 24-hour urinary aldosterone level and ratio of plasma aldosterone to renin activity, positive postural stimulation test result, and elevated urinary excretion of hybrid steroids (i.e., 18-hydroxycortisol). Adrenal vein sampling has a central role in the diagnostic evaluation of PAL because lateralization of aldosterone secretion indicates the presence of a curable lesion regardless of the radiographic findings.

## PHEOCHROMOCYTOMA

Pheochromocytoma is an uncommon entity but one that has fascinated both clinicians and investigators, who have worked together to derive effective means for detection, localization, and management (Bravo and Tagle, 2003; Manger and Gifford, 2002; Lenders et al, 2005). **Although it is the causative factor of hypertension in about 0.1% to 0.6% of the hypertensive population, or 1 or 2 per 100,000 adults per year, detection is mandatory, not only for the potential cure of the hypertension but also to avoid the potentially lethal effects of the unrecognized tumor.**

Clinical manifestations of pheochromocytoma are all due to the physiologic effects of the amines produced by the lesion. Epinephrine and norepinephrine are similar in their metabolic action, although epinephrine is more potent. The symptom complex manifested by the patient depends somewhat on the secretory products, both type and amount, including the more unusual products dopa and dopamine as well as a variety of peptides produced from amine precursor uptake and decarboxylation (APUD)–type cells (Pearse and Polak, 1971; Bolande, 1974). The peptides are ACTH, somatostatin, serotonin, enkephalins, calcitonin, vasoactive intestinal peptide, neuropeptide, lipotropin, β-endorphin, and dynorphin (Robertson et al, 1990). Small tumors generally bind catecholamine poorly. Thus, the severity of symptoms, despite the small size of these tumors, results from direct release of most catecholamines directly into the circulation. Large lesions have high catecholamine content but bind them well and metabolize substantial quantities directly within the tumors. Thus, only relatively small amounts of the vasoactive amines mixed with large amounts of inactive metabolites are secreted.

## Signs and Symptoms

Signs and symptoms of patients with pheochromocytoma, all secondary to secretion of the neurohormonal agents epinephrine and norepinephrine, may be extraordinarily variable. In all reported series, hypertension is by far the most consistent sign (Tables 53–15 and 53–16). Of 106 patients described by Van Heerden and colleagues (1982), 84% were hypertensive. As a sign itself, hypertension may have a variety of manifestations. The three common patterns are as follows:

1. Sustained hypertension. Thirty-seven percent of Van Heerden and colleagues' patients manifested sustained hypertension with little fluctuation, much as in patients with essential hypertension. This form is most common in children and in patients with multiple endocrine adenoma (MEA) type II.
2. Paroxysmal hypertension. "Dramatic attacks" of hypertension, usually associated with other signs and symptoms, punctuated the patient's usual asymptomatic, normotensive status. This pattern more readily provokes the suspicion of and workup for the possibility of an underlying pheochromocytoma and was reported to affect 47% of patients. Females are more likely than males to manifest paroxysmal hypertension.
3. Sustained hypertension with superimposed paroxysms. The phenomenon is self-explanatory. Manger and Gifford (1990) reported a 50% incidence of this manifestation. Scott and coworkers (1976, 1990) reported a 66% incidence.

The frequency of attacks among patients is variable, ranging from a few times per year to multiple daily episodes. Their duration may be minutes to hours, usually with rapid onset and slower subsidence. One or more episodes per week occur in 75% of patients. Daily attacks, or more than one attack each day, occur in nearly all other patients. Among patients with pheochromocytoma, half experience symptoms for a duration of less than 15 minutes. In 80% of patients, attacks last less than an hour. With the passage of time after the initial appearance of symptoms, frequency of attacks tends to increase, although severity may or may not change.

Attacks may occur in the absence of recognizable stimuli. A multitude of associated factors, however, have been reported: compression of the tumor elicited by massage; physical exercise, particularly a certain posture or lying in a certain position; and direct trauma. Similar precursors of attacks are wearing tight clothing, straining to defecate or to void, micturition itself, bladder distention, sexual intercourse, laughing, sneezing, coughing, retching, Valsalva's maneuver, and hyperventilation, which cause increased intra-abdominal pressure. Foods that are rich in tyramine (beer, wine, and aged cheese) may elicit attacks. Potentially provocative drugs are tyramine, histamine, epinephrine and norepinephrine, nicotine, glucagon, tetraethylammonium, methacholine, succinylcholine, phenothiazine, ACTH, and β blockers such as propranolol.

Additional signs and symptoms are numerous but not specific. Among these are headaches, sweating, pallor or flushing, palpitations, tachycardia, abdominal or chest pain, and postural hypotension. Also common are weakness, nausea, emesis, and anorexia. Profound psychological changes are frequently observed. The occasional patient in whom the

**Table 53–15.  Symptoms Reported by 76 Patients (Almost All Adults) with Pheochromocytoma Associated with Paroxysmal or Persistent Hypertension**

| Symptoms | Percentage Paroxysmal (37 patients) | Percentage Persistent (39 patients) |
|---|---|---|
| *Symptoms Presumably Due to Excessive Catecholamines or Hypertension* | | |
| Headache (severe) | 92 | 72 |
| Excessive sweating (generalized) | 65 | 69 |
| Palpitations ± tachycardia | 73 | 51 |
| Anxiety or nervousness (± fear of impending death, panic) | 60 | 28 |
| Tremulousness | 51 | 26 |
| Pain in chest, abdomen (usually epigastric), lumbar regions, lower abdomen, or groin | 48 | 28 |
| Nausea ± vomiting | 43 | 26 |
| Weakness, fatigue, prostration | 38 | 15 |
| Weight loss (severe) | 14 | 15 |
| Dyspnea | 11 | 18 |
| Warmth ± heat intolerance | 13 | 15 |
| Visual disturbances | 3 | 21 |
| Dizziness or faintness | 11 | 3 |
| Constipation | 0 | 13 |
| Paresthesia or pain in arms | 11 | 0 |
| Bradycardia (noted by patient) | 8 | 3 |
| Grand mal | 5 | 3 |
| *Manifestations Due to Complications* | | |
| Congestive heart failure ± cardiomyopathy | | |
| Myocardial infarction | | |
| Cerebrovascular accident | | |
| Ischemic enterocolitis ± megacolon | | |
| Azotemia | | |
| Dissecting aneurysm | | |
| Encephalopathy | | |
| Shock | | |
| Hemorrhagic necrosis in a pheochromocytoma | | |
| *Manifestations Due to Coexisting Diseases or Syndromes* | | |
| Cholelithiasis | | |
| Medullary thyroid carcinoma ± effects of secretions of serotonin, calcitonin, prostaglandin, or ACTH-like substance | | |
| Hyperparathyroidism | | |
| Mucocutaneous neuromas with characteristic facies | | |
| Thickened corneal nerves (seen only with slit lamp) | | |
| Marfanoid habitus | | |
| Alimentary tract ganglioneuromatosis | | |
| Neurofibromatosis and its complications | | |
| Cushing's syndrome (rare) | | |
| von Hippel–Lindau disease (rare) | | |
| Virilism, Addison's disease, acromegaly (extremely rare) | | |
| Symptoms caused by encroachment on adjacent structures or by invasion and pressure effects of metastases | | |

From Manger WM, Gifford RW Jr: Pheochromocytoma. In Laragh JH, Brenner BM, eds: Hypertension: Pathophysiology, Diagnosis, and Management. New York, Raven Press, 1990.

**Table 53–16.  Signs Observed in Patients with Pheochromocytoma**

Blood pressure changes
± Hypertension ± wide fluctuations (rarely, paroxysmal hypotension or hypertension alternating with hypotension)
Hypertension induced by physical maneuver such as exercise, postural change, or palpation and massage of flank or mass elsewhere
Orthostatic hypotension ± postural tachycardia
Paradoxical blood pressure response to certain antihypertensive drugs; marked pressor response with induction of anesthesia
Other signs of catecholamine excess
Hyperhidrosis
Tachycardia or reflex bradycardia, forceful heartbeat, arrhythmia
Pallor of face and upper part of body (rarely flushing; mottled cyanosis)
Anxious, frightened, troubled appearance
Hypertensive retinopathy
Dilated pupils (rarely exophthalmos, lacrimation, scleral pallor, or injection; pupils may not react to light)
Leanness or underweight
Tremor (± shaking)
Raynaud's phenomenon or livedo reticularis (occasionally puffy, red, cyanotic hands in children); skin of extremities wet, cold, clammy, or pale; gooseflesh; occasionally cyanotic nail beds
Fever
Mass lesion (rarely palpable)
Tumor in abdomen or neck (pheochromocytoma, chemodectoma, thyroid carcinoma, or thyroid swelling that is rare and only during hypertensive paroxysm)
Signs caused by encroachment on adjacent structures or by invasion and pressure effects of metastases
Manifestations related to complications or to coexisting diseases or syndromes

From Manger WM, Gifford RW Jr: Pheochromocytoma. In Laragh JH, Brenner BM, eds: Hypertension: Pathophysiology, Diagnosis, and Management. New York, Raven Press, 1990.

diagnosis has not been recognized has sometimes been referred for psychiatric evaluation of what were thought to have been functional symptoms.

Some patients are symptomatic for years before diagnosis. Others may present with convulsions, cerebrovascular accidents, and coma. Others have died of massive intracranial bleeding. The appearance of sudden, severe hypertension during the induction of anesthesia or during the course of a surgical procedure may herald underlying pheochromocytoma.

Patients may have pheochromocytomas without manifesting hypertension. **About 10% of pheochromocytomas are found in normotensive patients** (Scott et al, 1976). About 5% of all incidentalomas are pheochromocytomas, and about 25% of all pheochromocytomas are found incidentally (Lenders et al, 2005). On occasion, during a severe paroxysmal attack, blood pressure may be unobtainable. Herein, the patient is not hypotensive. Marked peripheral vasoconstriction occurs; therefore, one cannot measure the blood pressure with a sphygmomanometer. Hypertension may also be modest in nature, less serious than other signs and symptoms. Flushing, pallor, and signs of hypermetabolism closely mimic the classic appearance of thyrotoxicosis, leading to surgery of the thyroid gland before recognition of the underlying cause of the disease process.

Many reports exist of pheochromocytoma diagnosed during pregnancy (Schenker and Chowers, 1971; Fudge et al,

1980). Symptoms commonly mimic those of eclampsia, preeclampsia, and toxemia. Headache, visual disturbances, palpitations, diaphoresis, and hypertension (paroxysmal or sustained) are common. According to Fudge and associates (1980), the diagnosis of pheochromocytoma in association with pregnancy has been made before delivery in only one third of patients. All too often, it is only with the stress of labor and delivery, although more commonly during the postpartum period, that resultant fulminant hypertension or shock leads to the diagnosis of an underlying pheochromocytoma (Hume, 1960). Maternal and infant mortality rates exceed 40%. Despite a history of prior successful pregnancy, in the presence of hypertension, the diagnosis of pheochromocytoma should be considered in the pregnant patient with labile or postural hypertension, congestive heart failure, or arrhythmias. Appropriate diagnostic studies must be carried out.

Pheochromocytoma may be the underlying causative agent in patients afflicted by other disease states with conditions that may result from excess catecholamine secretion. Common manifestations are cerebrovascular accident, encephalopathy, retinopathy, congestive heart failure, cardiomyopathy, dissecting aneurysm, acute respiratory distress syndrome, shock, renal failure, azotemia, ischemic enterocolitis, and megacolon. Conversely, numerous entities mimic some of the symptoms and signs of pheochromocytoma (Table 53–17).

**One specific entity that has gained more recognition is catecholamine-induced cardiomyopathy** (Imperato-McGinley et al, 1987; Vaughan, 1991; Quigg and Om, 1994). Experimentally injected catecholamines can cause foci of myocardial necrosis, with inflammation and fibrosis (Van Vliet et al, 1966; Rosenbaum et al, 1988). These patients may have a reduction in blood pressure because of a global reduction in myocardial pump functions, considered to be due to both a downregulation of β receptors and a decrease in viable myofibrils (Sardesai et al, 1990). Fortunately, the lesion is usually reversible with the combination of α blockade and α-methylparatyrosine (Imperato-McGinley et al, 1987). All patients with pheochromocytoma should have a complete cardiac evaluation with echocardiography and radionuclide scans before corrective surgery.

An appreciable number of pheochromocytomas have been found in association with several disease entities and hereditary syndromes (see Table 53–17). Among these unusual conditions are the association of tumors of the glomus jugulare region with either pheochromocytoma or ectopic paragangliomas (Hamberger et al, 1967; Sato et al, 1974; Blumenfeld et al, 1993; Mena et al, 1993). It is now recognized that both the tumor in the glomus jugulare region and the other adrenal or nonadrenal chromaffin tumors can secrete catecholamines. It is also apparent that these patients can have multiple lesions (Fig. 53–38). Accordingly, the patients have to have sequential procedures with appropriate blockade and determination of catecholamine secretion after each procedure to determine residual activity. Tank and colleagues (1982) estimated that 95% of pheochromocytomas are sporadic in occurrence but that the remaining 5% have a familial pattern; 10% is often reported. Calkins and Howard (1947) published the first report of familial pheochromocytoma. Familial transmission is believed to be through autosomal dominance, with a locus on chromosome 10 (Simpson et al, 1987) found in the subset designated multiple endocrine neoplasia (MEN) type II.

| Table 53–17. **Differential Diagnosis*** |
|---|
| All hypertensives (sustained and paroxysmal) |
| Anxiety, tension states, psychoneurosis, psychosis |
| Hyperthyroidism |
| Paroxysmal tachycardia |
| Hyperdynamic β-adrenergic circulatory state |
| Menopause |
| Vasodilating headache (migraine and cluster headaches) |
| Coronary insufficiency syndrome |
| Acute hypertensive encephalopathy |
| Diabetes mellitus |
| Renal parenchymal or renal arterial disease with hypertension |
| Local arterial insufficiency of the brain |
| *Intracranial lesions* (with or without increased intracranial pressure) |
| *Autonomic hyperreflexia* |
| *Diencephalic seizures and syndrome* |
| Toxemia of pregnancy (or eclampsia with convulsions) |
| Hypertensive crises associated with monoamine oxidase inhibitors |
| *Carcinoid* |
| *Hypoglycemia* |
| Mastocytosis |
| Familial dysautonomia |
| Acrodynia |
| Neuroblastoma; ganglioneuroblastoma; ganglioneuroma |
| Neurofibromatosis (with or without renal arterial disease) |
| *Adrenocortical carcinoma* |
| Acute infectious disease |
| Rare causes of paroxysmal hypertension (*adrenal medullary hyperplasia, acute porphyria, lead poisoning*, tabetic crisis, encephalitis, *clonidine withdrawal*, hypovolemia with inappropriate vasoconstriction, pulmonary artery fibrosarcoma, portal hypersensitivity, dysregulation of hypothalamus, *tetanus, Guillain-Barré syndrome, factitious*) |
| Fortuitous circumstances simulating pheochromocytoma |
| Conditions sometimes associated with pheochromocytoma |
| Coexisting disease or syndromes |
| Cholelithiasis |
| Medullary thyroid carcinoma |
| Hyperparathyroidism |
| Mucosal neuromas |
| Thickened corneal nerves |
| Marfanoid habitus |
| Alimentary tract ganglioneuromatosis |
| Neurofibromatosis |
| Cushing's syndrome |
| von Hippel–Lindau disease |
| Polycythemia |
| Virilism, Addison's disease, acromegaly |
| Complications |
| Cardiovascular disease[†] |
| Cerebrovascular disease |
| Renovascular disease |
| Circulatory shock |
| Renal insufficiency |
| Hemorrhagic necrosis of pheochromocytoma[†] |
| Dissecting aneurysm[†] |
| Ischemic enterocolitis with or without intestinal obstruction[†] |

*Conditions in italics may have increased excretion of catecholamines or metabolites (or both).
[†]Patient may present as having abdominal or cardiovascular catastrophe.
From Manger WM, Gifford RW Jr: Pheochromocytoma. In Laragh JH, Brenner BM, eds: Hypertension: Pathophysiology, Diagnosis, and Management. New York, Raven Press, 1990.

**Familial pheochromocytomas may be divided into different types of genetic abnormalities.** In 1961, Sipple described the combination of pheochromocytoma and medullary carcinoma of the thyroid (MCT) that came to be known as Sipple's syndrome. In subsequent years, as more cases came to light,

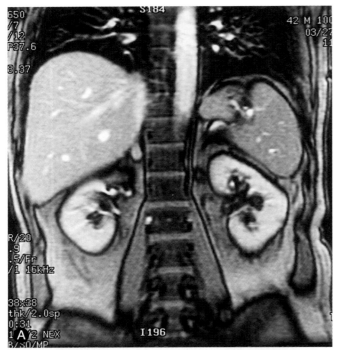

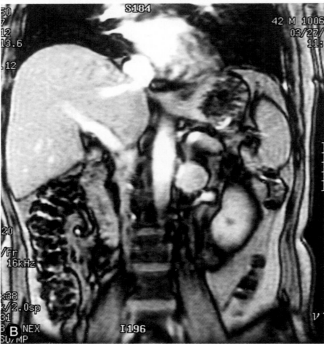

**Figure 53–38.** MRI scan showing bilateral adrenal pheochromocytomas in a patient with bilateral glomus jugulare tumors. The patient was treated with left adrenalectomy and enucleation of the smaller right pheochromocytoma. **A,** Small right pheochromocytoma. **B,** Larger left pheochromocytoma.

new terminology—MEA or MEN—has been popularized, as has a subclassification system: MEA I, MEA II, and MEA III or MEA IIB (Raue et al, 1985; Larsson and Nordenskjold, 1990). Pheochromocytomas occur in MEA II, a triad including pheochromocytoma, MCT, and parathyroid adenomas. The last may be a secondary phenomenon. The parafollicular

cells of MCT elaborate thyrocalcitonin. The resulting decrease in serum calcium concentration leads to parathyroid stimulation with subsequent hyperplasia or development of adenomas. Pheochromocytoma may also be a part of MEN III, which also includes MCT, mucosal neuromas, thickened corneal nerves, alimentary tract ganglioneuromatosis, and frequently a marfanoid habitus (Manger and Gifford, 2002).

Recognition of MEA II and aggressive evaluation of MEA II kindreds are mandatory. Carney and associates (1976) reported 22% mortality from complications of pheochromocytoma in a review of 149 patients with MEA II. MCT has an expected incidence of 50% in MEA II kindreds. The development of DNA technology to identify carriers of the MEN IIA gene (Lips et al, 1994) and the awareness of patients with pheochromocytomas as a component of MEN IIA or von Hippel–Lindau disease have resulted in the recommendation that all patients with pheochromocytoma be screened for these syndromes, as well as family members of patients with these diseases (Lips et al, 1994; Neumann et al, 1995).

Families with von Hippel–Lindau disease and pheochromocytoma are classified as von Hippel–Lindau disease type 2 (Walther et al, 1999). Some of these patients have renal cell carcinoma (type 2A); others do not (type 2B). von Hippel–Lindau disease type 2 is most frequently associated with a missense mutation of the *VHL* gene (Chen et al, 1995). Patients with this entity can be identified at a younger age when the tumors are smaller (Pomares et al, 1998; Walther et al, 1999).

Partial adrenalectomy is indicated because of the high occurrence of bilateral disease (Pavlovich and Walther, 2001; Diner et al, 2005). In addition, in patients with von Hippel–Lindau disease, there may be multiorgan visceral tumors of the adrenal, kidney, and pancreas that can be managed with a single-stage operation (Hwang et al, 2003).

The neuroectodermal dysplasias are a group of related diseases: von Recklinghausen's disease (neurofibromatosis), tuberous sclerosis, Sturge-Weber syndrome, and von Hippel–Lindau disease. All are strongly familial and associated with each other and with pheochromocytoma.

The prevalence of pheochromocytoma in patients with neurofibromatosis is reported as 1% to 2%. Of those patients with pheochromocytoma, 5% have von Recklinghausen's disease. Kalff and associates (1982), having seen 10 patients with pheochromocytoma and neurofibromatosis, reviewed the sample population, selecting patients with both von Recklinghausen's disease and hypertension. They found 17 such patients, 53% of whom had pheochromocytomas.

Pheochromocytoma is distinctly less common than the other neuroectodermal dysplasias (Kalff et al, 1982). The rare association of a somatostatin-rich duodenal carcinoid tumor and pheochromocytoma has also been reported (Wheeler et al, 1986).

The increased incidence of pheochromocytomas in association with neuroectodermal dysplasias and MCT may be explained by the APUD cell system of Pearse. The APUD cells derive from the neural crest of the embryo, sharing common ultrastructural and cytochemical features and elaborating amines by precursor uptake and decarboxylation (Pearse and Polak, 1971; Bolande, 1974). The products of these cells have been previously listed. Immunochemical techniques showing both neuron-specific enolase and chromogranin A in a variety

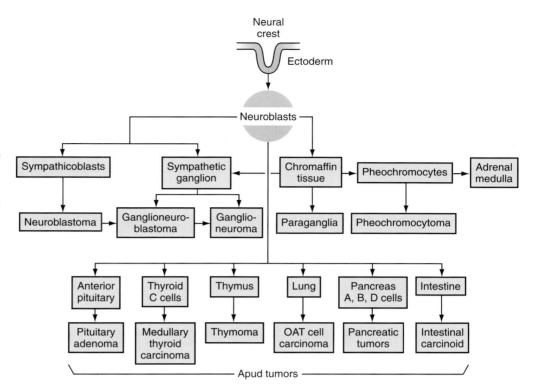

**Figure 53–39.** Ectodermal origin of amine precursor uptake and decarboxylation tumors. (From Manger WM, Gifford RW Jr: Pheochromocytoma: A clinical review. In Laragh JH, Brenner BM, eds: Hypertension: Pathophysiology, Diagnosis, and Management. New York, Raven Press, 1990.)

of polypeptide hormone–producing tissues support the concept of the APUD system (Fig. 53–39) (Lloyd et al, 1984; O'Connor and Deftos, 1986; Hsiao et al, 1991).Considerable information is now available concerning the chromosomal localization and gene in the hereditary forms of pheochromocytoma (Table 53–18), which are useful in screening of families with these syndromes.

## Children

Manifestations of pheochromocytoma in children vary somewhat from those in adults. Headache, nausea or vomiting, weight loss, and visual complaints occur more commonly in children than in adults. Manger and Gifford (1977) reported polydipsia, polyuria, and convulsions—rarely observed in adults—in 25% of children. Puffy, red, and cyanotic appearance of the hands is reported in 11% of children. Of children with pheochromocytomas, 90% have sustained hypertension. Paroxysmal hypertension occurs in less than 10% of children.

**In contrast to adults, children manifest a higher incidence of familial pheochromocytomas (10%) and bilaterality (24%).** Multiple pheochromocytomas have been reported in children with an incidence of 15% to 32%, and extra-adrenal location of pheochromocytomas has been reported in 15% to 31% of the children (Glenn et al, 1968). Glenn and coworkers (1968) believed that on a histologic basis, there was a higher incidence of malignant pheochromocytomas in children. Stackpole and colleagues' review (1963) found a random distribution of age at diagnosis among boys. In girls, the diagnosis was made in 62% during menarche. Because of the tendency toward multiplicity and thus asynchronous recurrence, close follow-up for recurrent symptoms and hypertension is mandatory in children (Ein et al, 1990).

**Table 53–18.   Hereditary Forms of Pheochromocytoma**

| Syndrome | Gene | Chromosome Location |
|---|---|---|
| Multiple endocrine neoplasia type II | *RET* oncogene | 10q11 |
| von Hippel–Lindau disease | *VHL* tumor suppressor gene | 3p25 |
| Neurofibromatosis type 1 | *NF1* | 17q11 |
| Hereditary paraganglioma syndrome | *PGL1* | 11q23 |

From Pacak et al, 2001.

## MALIGNANT PHEOCHROMOCYTOMA

Approximately 10% to 20% of pheochromocytomas are malignant. In the Cleveland Clinic series, 19% of all cases were malignant, which was more common in tumors larger than 5 cm than in smaller tumors (76% versus 24%) and in extra-adrenal tumors (52% versus 9%) (Bravo and Tagle, 2003). A number of markers including Ki-67, p53, telomerase activity, and expression of angiogenesis factors are being studied to differentiate benign from malignant tumors, but none has achieved clinical usefulness (Novakovic et al, 2004; Lenders et al, 2005). In a separate report in 251 patients with MEN IIA, the prevalence of malignancy was 4.4% (Gagel et al, 1988). Treatment is surgical resection with wide excision and resection of involved adjacent organs; debulking is indicated even when it is not curative to diminish symptoms of catecholamine excess and to facilitate medical management. Chemotherapeutic therapy is limited, although partial responses have been reported in about half the patients treated with a neuroblastoma regimen (Averbuch et al, 1988). An

## Laboratory Diagnosis

The clinical diagnosis of pheochromocytoma is based on the subjective evaluation of signs and symptoms. Laboratory confirmation of the clinical diagnosis is mandatory and may be divided into two general categories: biochemical diagnosis and radiologic diagnosis (Fig. 53–40).

**Confirmation of the diagnosis is obtained by demonstrating elevated levels of catecholamines in the blood or urine,** which occur in 95% to 99% of patients with pheochromocytoma. Extremely accurate assays exist (Manger and Gifford, 2002; Bravo and Tagle, 2003; Liu et al, 2003). There are considerable numbers of foods and drugs that can affect urine levels of catecholamines or breakdown products (Table 53–19). Plasma catecholamines are highly responsive to stress, activity, blood loss, and other stimuli.

Because of the severe consequences of the undiagnosed pheochromocytoma, it is recommended that all hypertensive patients be screened. Measurement of urine catecholamines and metanephrines is adequate in most patients.

**Rarely, the concentrations of plasma and urine catecholamines and their metabolites are not elevated, especially if the patient is normotensive at the time of study.** In this clinical setting, if there is a high index of suspicion, studies with [131]I-labeled MIBG scanning (Shapiro et al, 1985), MRI (Newhouse, 1990), or repeated sampling when the patient is hypertensive are indicated. Provocative tests with histamine, glucagon, or phentolamine are rarely used.

In contrast, some patients with essential hypertension and signs or symptoms of pheochromocytoma have slightly elevated plasma catecholamine levels, probably representing a neurogenic component to the hypertension. The clonidine suppression test distinguishes these patients (Bravo et al, 2003). Two to 3 hours after a single 0.3-mg oral dose of clonidine, patients with neurogenic hypertension at rest show a fall in plasma norepinephrine plus epinephrine to a level below 500 pg/mL (Bravo et al, 2003), whereas patients with pheochromocytoma do not.

## Radiologic Tests

As for other adrenal tumors, the development of sectional imaging was a major advancement in the diagnosis and localization of pheochromocytoma (Kazam et al, 1989). For adrenal pheochromocytomas, the CT accuracy for detection is more than 90% (Thomas et al, 1980; Abrams et al, 1982), and CT has rapidly replaced angiography, venography, and ultrasonography for extra-adrenal pheochromocytoma, in which the detection is less (about 75%). CT, however, does not aid in differentiating pheochromocytomas from other adrenal lesions or in predicting malignancy.

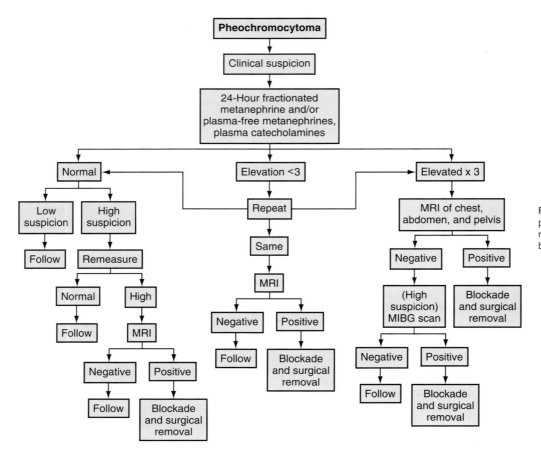

**Figure 53–40.** Identification of pheochromocytoma. MRI, magnetic resonance imaging; MIBG, metaiodobenzylguanidine.

**Table 53–19. Effects of Drugs and Interfering Substances on Concentrations of Urinary Catecholamines and Metabolites***

| Upper Limit of Normal—Adult (mg/24 hr) | Effects | |
| --- | --- | --- |
| | Increases Apparent Value | Decreases Apparent Value |
| Catecholamines<br>  Epinephrine, 0.02<br>  Norepinephrine, 0.08<br>  Total, 0.10<br>  Dopamine, 0.20<br>  Methyldopa | Catecholamines<br>Drugs containing catecholamines<br>Isoprenolol (isoproterenol)[†]<br>Levodopa<br>Labetalol[†]<br>Tetracyclines[†]<br>Erythromycin[†]<br>Chlorpromazine[†]<br>Other fluorescent substances[†]<br>  (e.g., quinine, quinidine, bile in urine)<br>Rapid clonidine withdrawal<br>Ethanol | Fenfluramine (large doses) |
| Metanephrine<br>  Metanephrine, 0.4<br>  Normetanephrine, 0.9<br>  Total 1.3 | Catecholamines<br>Drugs containing catecholamines<br>Monoamine oxidase inhibitors<br>Benzodiazepines<br>Rapid clonidine withdrawal<br>Ethanol | N-Methylglucamine (in Renovist, Renografin)<br>Fenfluramine (large doses) |
| Vanillylmandelic acid, 6.5 | Catecholamines (minimal increase)<br>Drugs containing catecholamines (minimal increase)<br>Levodopa<br>Nalidixic acid[†]<br>Rapid clonidine withdrawal | Clofibrate<br>Disulfiram<br>Ethanol<br>Monoamine oxidase inhibitors<br>Fenfluramine (large doses) |

*As determined by most reliable assays.
[†]Probably spurious interference with fluorescence assays.
From Manger WM, Gifford RW Jr: Pheochromocytoma. In Laragh JH, Brenner BM, eds: Hypertension: Pathophysiology, Diagnosis, and Management. New York, Raven Press, 1990.

We have been impressed with the multiple uses of MRI in patients with pheochromocytoma. The test appears to be as accurate as CT in identifying lesions while having a characteristically bright, "light bulb" image on T2-weighted study (Fig. 53–41) (Reinig et al, 1986). In addition, sagittal and coronal imaging can give excellent anatomic information about the relationship between the tumor and the surrounding vasculature as well as the draining venous channels (Figs. 53–42 and 53–43). We believe that MRI should be the initial scanning procedure in patients with biochemical findings of pheochromocytoma.

An alternative approach that is also useful at times, particularly in the search for residual or multiple pheochromocytoma, is the MIBG scan that images medullary tissue (Shapiro et al, 1985; Campeau et al, 1991). In an experience with 400 cases, the developers of the technique found sensitivity of 78.4% in primary sporadic tumors, 92.4% in malignant lesions, and 94.3% in familial cases, giving an overall sensitivity of 87.4% with 99% specificity. Thus, the test may be more sensitive than CT in patients with extra-adrenal lesions. The isotope may be picked up by other APUD cell–type tumors. In a smaller series involving children, the MIBG scan findings were abnormal in all cases (Deal et al, 1990). The MIBG scan is highly sensitive and is a useful tool, especially if CT and MRI findings are normal or confusing (Fig. 53–44). Sequential venous sampling has been used successfully to identify small extra-adrenal lesions (Newbould et al, 1991). One warning is that the normal adrenal medulla may be visualized in more than 50% to 70% of patients imaged at 24 to 48 hours after injection (Roelants et al, 1998). Positron emission tomographic scanning with a variety of agents remains controversial at this time because of nonspecificity and limited sensitivity (Lenders et al, 2005).

## Preoperative Management

There is unanimity of opinion that surgical extirpation is the only effective treatment of pheochromocytoma. The one accepted exception to this principle is treatment late in pregnancy. The patient should be treated with α-adrenergic blockade by oral administration of phenoxybenzamine until the fetus has reached maturity. At this point, cesarean section with tumor excision should be carried out in one operation, without allowing the patient to undergo the stress of vaginal delivery.

A controversial issue in the management of patients with pheochromocytoma is whether to employ pharmacologic blockade preoperatively, and some with extensive and highly successful experience do not use α-adrenergic blockade (Ulchaker et al, 1999). **We do not believe that this is an issue at present. The evolution of an accurate localization test weakens the argument that α blockade limits the ability to identify the lesion at the time of exploration.**

Moreover, the greater stability of the patient with adequate preoperative preparation greatly facilitates the procedure for both surgeon and anesthesiologist as well as increases the safety to the patient. At our institution, the preoperative medical preparation is of utmost importance to provide an ideal anesthetic and operative environment (Malhotra, 1995). The perioperative course is smoother with adequate preoperative preparation. **Phenoxybenzamine hydrochloride (Dibenzyline), a long-acting α-adrenergic blocker, controls**

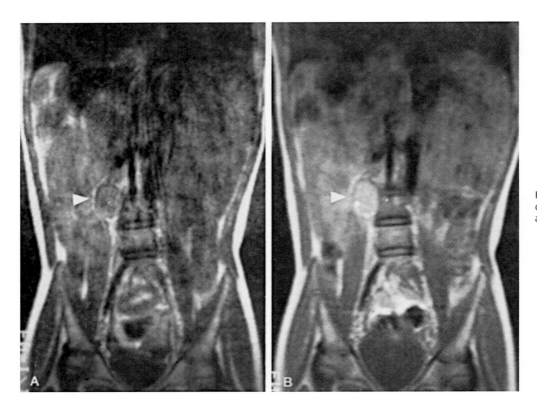

**Figure 53–41.** Extra-adrenal pheochromocytoma showing a T1 image (**A**) and a bright T2 image (**B**).

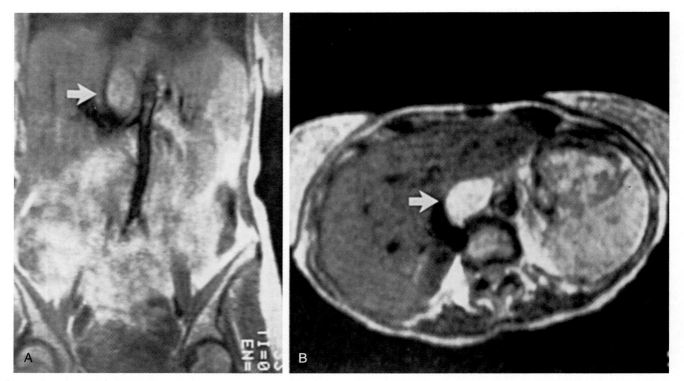

**Figure 53–42.** MRI of pheochromocytoma *(arrows)*. Right adrenal arises from the medial limb, which grew medial to the inferior vena cava above the celiac axis under the caudate lobe of the liver and was missed at first abdominal exploration. Intra-aortocaval location is clearly seen on these films. **A,** Coronal image. **B,** Transverse image.

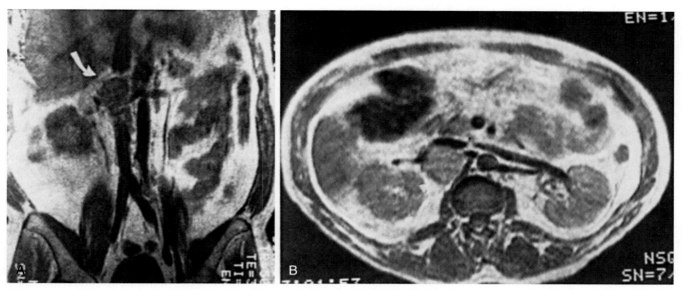

**Figure 53–43.**  MRI of recurrent pheochromocytoma *(arrow)* with an excellent demonstration of an anterior-crossing right renal vein, a feeding lumbar vein, and involvement of a right renal artery. **A,** Coronal image. **B,** Transverse image.

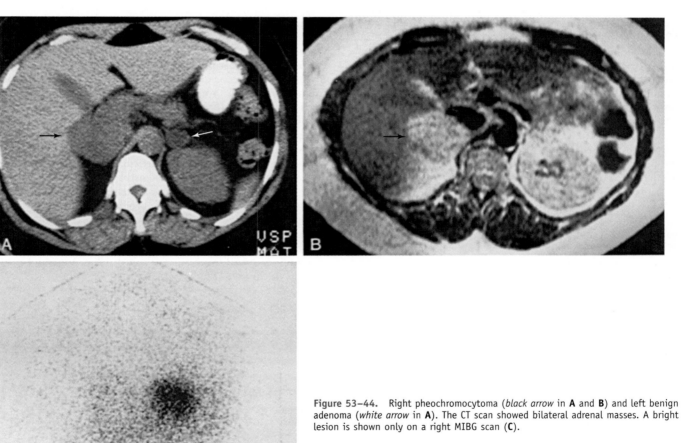

**Figure 53–44.**  Right pheochromocytoma *(black arrow* in **A** and **B**) and left benign adenoma *(white arrow* in **A**). The CT scan showed bilateral adrenal masses. A bright lesion is shown only on a right MIBG scan (**C**).

**blood pressure in patients with pheochromocytoma.** The initial divided dose of 20 to 30 mg is given orally and is increased by 10 to 20 mg/day until the blood pressure has been stabilized and there is mild postural hypotension. Usually, a dose of 40 to 100 mg/day is required.

β-Adrenergic blockers, such as propranolol, have been added to α blockers to prepare patients for anesthesia and surgery. The β blockers protect against arrhythmias and permit reduction in the amount of α-adrenergic blockers necessary to control blood pressure (Ross et al, 1967). The β blockers have also been given when tachyphylaxis to α blockers occurs. However, they must be used carefully. A β-adrenergic blocker should be administered only when α blockade is established; β blockade alone may cause a marked rise in total peripheral vascular resistance, secondary to unopposed α-adrenergic activity. Accordingly, we do not routinely prepare patients with propranolol. A β-adrenergic blocker is provided only when cardiac arrhythmias are prominent. Propranolol is given orally in doses of 20 to 40 mg three or four times daily.

α-Methylparatyrosine (metyrosine, a tyrosine hydroxylase inhibitor) has been recommended in addition to phenoxybenzamine or propranolol during preparation of the patient for anesthesia and surgery (Sjoerdsma et al, 1965; Engelman et al, 1968). Metyrosine decreases the rate of catecholamine synthesis—the conversion of tyrosine to dihydroxyphenylalanine. Adverse effects include crystalluria, sedation, diarrhea, anxiety, psychic disturbance, and extrapyramidal signs. Experience with α-methylparatyrosine is limited, although its combination with α-adrenergic blockade has been recommended (Perry et al, 1990). We therefore do not use it routinely but reserve the drug for patients who have myocardiopathy, multiple catecholamine-secreting paragangliomas, or resistance to α-adrenergic blockers. α-Methylparatyrosine is given in doses of 0.5 to 1 g orally three or four times daily and is usually started before surgery. The dose is determined by repeated catecholamine evaluations.

Prazosin, a specific postsynaptic α1-adrenergic blocker, has gained rapid acceptance as an effective antihypertensive agent. The drug has been evaluated in the medical management of patients with pheochromocytoma either alone (Wallace and Gill, 1978) or in combination with a β blocker. We, however, have experience with four patients who were prepared with prazosin alone for surgical removal of adrenal pheochromocytoma. The control of blood pressure was effective preoperatively but was not adequate during surgical removal of the tumor. Marked blood pressure elevations were present in all four patients. In contrast to phenoxybenzamine, which binds irreversibly to α-adrenergic receptors, prazosin blockade is reversible and may be overwhelmed by the surge in catecholamine secretion during intubation and surgical manipulation. We have since abandoned prazosin in preparing patients for anesthesia and surgery (Nicholson et al, 1983).

In addition to the α-blocking and β-blocking agents, it is important that the state of hydration and blood volume be evaluated because many patients have decreased intravascular volume. Crystalloids may be needed to raise the intravascular volume to accommodate the expanded vascular bed produced by α-blocking agents. To avoid this potential problem, patients receive at least 1 liter of 5% glucose in lactated Ringer's irrigation preoperatively. The α-blocking agent and β-blocking agent (if used) should be continued through the day of surgery.

## Anesthetic Management

Anesthetic management of the patient undergoing surgical removal of a pheochromocytoma is directed toward control of the cardiovascular system (Robertson et al, 1990; Artusio, 1995). Close monitoring is of utmost importance and includes attention to the electrocardiogram, blood pressure (arterial line for continuous arterial pressure reading), urine output, and central venous pressure. A Swan-Ganz catheter may be employed to measure pulmonary capillary wedge pressure if the patient has left ventricular dysfunction.

Patients should arrive in the operating room in a relaxed state, and therefore some form of preanesthesia medication such as a barbiturate (pentobarbital at a dose of 100 to 300 mg) should be given an hour before the patient's arrival to the operating room. **We recommend general anesthesia with a combined approach—induction with an intravenous agent such as thiopental followed by isoflurane as the inhalation agent of choice.** At the time of induction of anesthesia, there may be a marked vasopressor response, and appropriate α-adrenergic and β-adrenergic blocking agents should be available for intravenous use. Acutely, it is recommended that phentolamine (Regitine), a short-acting α blocker, be used to control blood pressure during the induction of anesthesia. Phentolamine can be given in boluses of 1 to 5 mg or by continuous infusion (50 mg of phentolamine per 500 mL of lactated Ringer's irrigation). Alternatively, sodium nitroprusside may be needed to control severe hypertension, and it should be present in a solution of 50 mg in 250 mL of 5% dextrose and water.

Throughout the procedure, particularly during any manipulations of the tumor, hypertensive episodes as well as arrhythmias may occur. The use of general anesthesia allows the anesthesiologist to follow the progress of the surgery, and as the blood supply of the tumor is diminished, fluids can be increased, and the depth of the anesthesia can be decreased. β-Adrenergic blockers, such as esmolol and propranolol, should be reserved for persistent tachycardias or arrhythmias that persist despite α blockade.

A variety of anesthetic agents and drugs should be avoided in patients with pheochromocytoma (Table 53–20). With use

| Table 53–20. Anesthetics and Drugs to Be Avoided in Pheochromocytoma | |
|---|---|
| Inhalation agents | Halothane |
| Intravenous agents | Propofol |
| | Ketamine |
| Tranquilizers | Droperidol |
| Narcotics | Morphine |
| Local anesthetics | Cocaine |
| Muscle relaxants | Tubocurarine |
| | Atracurium |
| | Pancuronium |
| Vasopressors | Ephedrine |
| Adjuvants | Chlorpromazine |
| | Metoclopramide |

From Artusio JF Jr: Anesthesia for pheochromocytoma. In Malhotra V, ed: Anesthesia for Renal and Genitourinary Surgery. New York, McGraw-Hill, 1995. Reproduced by permission of the McGraw-Hill Companies.

## KEY POINTS: ADRENAL DISORDERS

■ An exogenous source of Cushing's syndrome should always be excluded first because therapeutic steroids are the most common cause of the syndrome.

■ Subclinical Cushing's syndrome represents 3% to 5% of the common metabolic syndrome.

■ The determination of 24-hour excretion of cortisol in the urine is the most direct and reliable index of cortisol secretion.

■ Most adrenal carcinomas are larger than 5 cm and show a heterogeneous pattern and high signal intensity on MRI.

■ The critical requirement for potential cure in patients with adrenal carcinoma is complete surgical removal of the primary tumor.

■ Extra-adrenal neural tumors (paragangliomas) are more likely than adrenal pheochromocytoma to be malignant.

■ MRI is the most useful radiologic test to confirm the diagnosis of a pheochromocytoma (bright "light bulb" on T2-weighted imaging). It shows the relationship of the tumor with adjacent structures and identifies multiple lesions.

■ Solid lesions of the adrenal gland that give a high signal intensity on MRI include pheochromocytoma, other neural tumors, metastatic tumors, primary hyperaldosteronism, and adrenal carcinoma.

■ The classic triad for diagnosis of primary hyperaldosteronism is low potassium concentration (after sodium repletion), suppressed plasma renin activity, and high plasma or urine aldosterone level.

■ Metastatic tumors to the adrenal from other primary tumors are more common than primary adrenal tumors.

of this approach and adequate preoperative blockade, at times with both α-adrenergic blocking agents and α-methylparatyrosine, hypotension after removal of the tumor now rarely occurs. If the systolic blood pressure falls below 100 mm Hg, however, norepinephrine (4 to 8 mg per 500 mL normal saline) should be started and blood pressure stabilized above 100 mm Hg. The norepinephrine can usually be withdrawn after further fluid resuscitation.

## SUGGESTED READINGS

Bravo EL, Tagle R: Pheochromocytoma: State-of-the-art and future prospects. Endocr Rev 2003;24:539-553.

Espiner EA, Ross DG, Yandle TG, et al: Predicting surgically remediable primary aldosteronism: Role of adrenal scanning, postural testing, and adrenal vein sampling. J Clin Endocrinol Metab 2003;88:3637-3644.

Findling JW, Raff H: Screening and diagnosis of Cushing's syndrome. Endocrinol Metab Clin North Am 2005;34:385-402.

Hwang JJ, Uchio EM, Pavlovich CT, et al: Surgical management of multiorgan visceral tumors in places with von Hippel–Lindau disease: A single stage approach. J Urol 2003;169:895-898.

Lenders JWM, Eisenhofer G, Mannelli M, et al: Pheochromocytoma. Lancet 2005;366:655-675.

Lovas K, Husebye ES: Addison's disease. Lancet 2005;365:2058-2061.

Lucon AM, Pereira MA, Mendonca BB: Adrenocortical tumors: Results of treatment and study of Weiss's score as a prognostic factor. Rev Hosp Clin Fac Med Sao Paulo 2002;56:251-256.

Merke DP, Bornstein SR: Congenital adrenal hyperplasia. Lancet 2005;265:2125-2136.

Mulatero P, Stowasser M, Loh KC: Increased diagnosis of primary aldosteronism, including surgically correctible forms, in centers from five continents. J Clin Endocrinol Metab 2004;89:1045-1050.

Ng L, Libertino JM: Adrenocortical carcinoma: Diagnosis, evaluation and treatment. J Urol 2003;169:5-11.

Novakovic K, Ersahin C, Picken M, et al: Malignant adrenal tumors. AUA Update Series 2004;23:241-247.

Vaughan ED Jr: Diseases of the adrenal gland. Med Clin North Am 2004;88:443-466.

# 54 Surgery of the Adrenal Glands

GEORGE K. CHOW, MD • MICHAEL L. BLUTE, MD

**HISTORY**

**SURGICAL ANATOMY**

**CLINICAL INDICATIONS AND SELECTION OF PATIENTS**

**PREOPERATIVE MANAGEMENT**

**OPEN ADRENALECTOMY**

**LAPAROSCOPIC ADRENALECTOMY**

**HAND-ASSISTED SURGERY**

**ROBOTIC SURGERY**

**INTRAOPERATIVE ULTRASONOGRAPHY**

**POSTOPERATIVE MANAGEMENT**

**OUTPATIENT AND SHORT-STAY LAPAROSCOPIC ADRENALECTOMY**

**OUTCOMES**

**COMPLICATIONS**

**SPECIAL CONSIDERATIONS**

**NONSURGICAL ALTERNATIVES**

Surgery of the adrenal gland consists of operative procedures to correct endocrine abnormalities or to treat malignant disease. As outlined in Chapter 53, various adrenal disorders can be identified and treated medically. When medical therapy is ineffective or does not exist for a particular adrenal disease, surgery becomes necessary.

Traditional open adrenal surgery has been performed since the late 19th century. Various techniques and anatomic approaches have been described for adrenalectomy, but the essential surgical principles have remained unchanged for a century. The introduction of laparoscopic adrenalectomy has revolutionized adrenal surgery and largely supplanted the open approach. However, we are not yet ready to relegate open adrenal surgery to the history books. There is a diminished but vital role for open adrenal surgery in the management of invasive adrenal carcinoma. Furthermore, all urologic surgeons should be familiar with the open techniques in the event that emergent open surgical conversion is necessary.

The future of adrenal surgery is a study in evolution. New technology, such as robotics and percutaneous ablation, is being developed. These minimally invasive nonsurgical approaches may obviate the skills of the surgeon. Nevertheless, it is important that the urologist be part of the treatment team, either as direct practitioner of the technique or in direct consultation guiding therapy.

## HISTORY

The first adrenalectomy was performed by Thornton in 1889 for a large tumor in a 36-year-old woman (Thornton, 1890). At the time, Thornton was unaware of the adrenal origin of the patient's disease and removed the adrenal en bloc with the kidney. Sargent performed the first planned adrenalectomy in 1914 for a large adrenal adenoma. Charles Mayo performed the first flank adrenalectomy for pheochromocytoma in 1927 (Mayo, 1927). As was often the case in these early forays, Mayo was not aware of the exact nature of the pathologic process with which he was dealing and assumed that he was removing an aberrant retroperitoneal nerve.

In 1936, Young described the posterior approach by a "hockey stick" incision to access both adrenal glands simultaneously (Young, 1936). The thoracoabdominal incision for management of large retroperitoneal masses was first described in 1949 by Chute (Chute et al, 1949). Turner-Warwick developed a supracostal transdiaphragmatic variation of Young's posterior approach in 1965 (Turner-Warwick, 1965).

Gagner performed the first laparoscopic adrenalectomy in 1991 (Gagner et al, 1992). He used a transperitoneal approach to gain access to the adrenal gland. Also in 1992, Gaur developed the first device for balloon dilation of the retroperitoneum (Gaur, 1992). Retroperitoneal access has been developed for both flank (Gasman et al, 1998) and posterior (Baba et al, 1997) approaches.

## SURGICAL ANATOMY

The adrenal glands are situated in the retroperitoneum within Gerota's fascia. The right adrenal gland tends to lie more cephalad than the left adrenal gland. The anatomic borders of the right adrenal gland are the liver anteriorly, the vena cava medially, the right kidney laterally and inferiorly, and the diaphragm along its superior and posterior aspects. The medial aspect of the right adrenal gland will often be retrocaval, and the right adrenal vein will enter the inferior vena cava in a posterolateral position.

The left adrenal gland is bordered by the aorta medially, the stomach and body of the pancreas anteriorly, the kidney inferiorly, the spleen superiorly, and the diaphragm posteriorly. The left adrenal gland is often more elongated than the right adrenal gland and will lie in a more superomedial position to the kidney. This tends to place the gland closer to the left renal hilum, and these structures must be accounted for during dissection. The anatomic relationships of the adrenal glands are summarized in Figure 54–1.

The arterial blood supply to the adrenal gland can be variable but tends to derive from three major sources on each side. Each adrenal gland receives branches from its ipsilateral inferior phrenic artery (superior adrenal arteries), aorta (middle adrenal arteries), and renal artery (inferior adrenal arteries). The venous drainage is typically simple; a single adrenal vein drains into the vena cava directly on the right and into the left renal vein on the left. Accessory veins (5% to 10%) that drain into the right renal vein, right hepatic vein, or inferior phrenic vein can be present (Fig. 54–2).

Lymphatic drainage from the adrenal glands consists of a lateral aortic lymph node chain extending from the diaphragm to the ipsilateral renal artery.

## CLINICAL INDICATIONS AND SELECTION OF PATIENTS
### Clinical Indications

The clinical indications for adrenalectomy are summarized in Table 54–1. The pathophysiology, diagnosis, and treatment of these diseases are detailed in Chapter 53.

### Exclusion Criteria

**Severe coagulopathy and poor cardiopulmonary performance status are absolute contraindications to adrenalectomy by any technique.** As far as laparoscopy is concerned, the

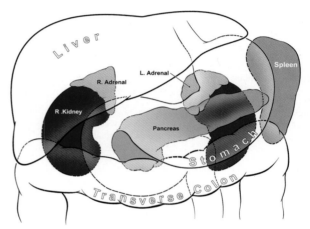

**Figure 54–1.** Regional anatomy of adrenal glands.

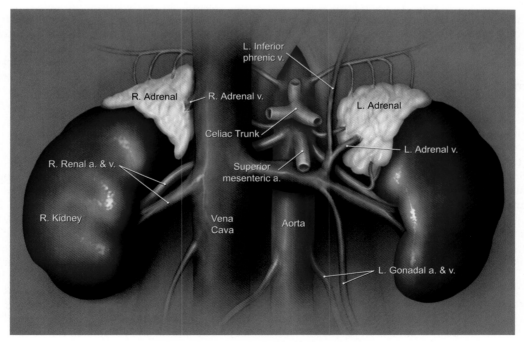

**Figure 54–2.** Vascular supply of adrenal glands.

**Table 54–1. Clinical Indications for Adrenalectomy**

Primary aldosteronism (solitary adenoma versus bilateral adrenal hyperplasia)
Cushing's syndrome
Pheochromocytoma
Adrenal adenoma
Myelolipoma
Adrenal cyst
Metastatic tumor
Adrenocortical carcinoma
Neuroblastoma (pediatric)
Incidentally discovered adrenal mass or "incidentaloma"

**Table 54–2. Surgical Options (Open Adrenalectomy)**

| Disease | Approach |
| --- | --- |
| Primary hyperaldosteronism | Posterior (left or right) |
| | Modified posterior (right) |
| | 11th rib (left > right) |
| | Posterior transthoracic |
| Cushing's adenoma | 11th rib (left or right) |
| | Thoracoabdominal (large) |
| | Posterior (small) |
| Cushing's disease (bilateral hyperplasia) | Bilateral posterior |
| | Bilateral 11th rib (alternating) |
| Adrenal carcinoma | Thoracoabdominal |
| | 11th rib |
| | Transabdominal |
| Bilateral adrenal ablation | Bilateral posterior |
| Pheochromocytoma | Transabdominal chevron |
| | Thoracoabdominal (large, usually right) |
| | 11th rib |
| Neuroblastoma | Transabdominal |
| | 11th rib |

From Vaughn ED: Adrenal surgery. In Marshall F, ed: Operative Urology. Philadelphia, WB Saunders, 1996:222.

shrinking number of contraindications attests to the high level of skill exhibited by pioneering laparoscopic surgeons. These relative contraindications include previous open surgery, tumor size, obesity, and adrenal cortical carcinoma.

### Indications for Open Surgery

The current indications for open adrenalectomy are few but important. First, **adrenal cortical carcinoma with radiographic evidence of extra-adrenal tumor invasion of adjacent organs may benefit from maximal surgical exposure. Similarly, the extension of adrenal vein tumor thrombus into the inferior vena cava necessitates a more invasive approach.** Finally, in developing countries, the resources for laparoscopic surgery may be lacking, and the open approach will be preferred out of necessity. The choice of open surgical approach is dictated by the surgeon's experience and the pathologic process in question. Table 54–2 summarizes the best surgical approach for a given adrenal disease.

### Past Surgical History

Is open surgery indicated when there is a history of previous surgery close to the adrenal gland? The laparoscopic approach can be tailored to deal with past surgical history; a patient with previous transabdominal surgery could have a retroperitoneal

laparoscopic procedure (Caddedu et al, 1999), and a history of previous open flank surgery could be addressed by performing a transperitoneal laparoscopic procedure. Furthermore, Gill and colleagues (2001) have reported their experience with a transthoracic laparoscopic approach that may be ideally suited for this situation. The thoracic cavity is entered thoracoscopically, the diaphragm is divided, and the adrenal gland is approached superiorly.

### Size

Tumor size is a relative contraindication to laparoscopic surgery. In the initial experience of many laparoscopists, a cutoff of 5 or 6 cm was chosen because of the increased risk of treating an adrenal cortical carcinoma. Subsequently, ample empirical evidence has accumulated to suggest that specimen size is not necessarily a contraindication to laparoscopic adrenalectomy. MacGillivray and colleagues (2002) noted no difference in operative time, blood loss, complication rate, and hospital stay between 12 patients with large tumors (mean, 8.2 cm; range, 6 to 12 cm) and 36 patients with small tumors (mean, 2.5 cm; range, 0.4 to 5.6 cm).

In contrast, Hobart and coworkers (2000) noted increased operative time (205 minutes versus 158 minutes; $P = .07$), increased blood loss (400 mL versus 113 mL; $P = .009$), higher complication rate (21.4% versus 8.9%; $P = .21$), and higher open conversion rate (14.3% versus 2.2%; $P = .14$) in comparing 14 large tumors (mean, 8 cm) with 45 small tumors (mean, 2.2 cm). However, Hobart did find that operative time, blood loss, hospital stay, narcotic use, and complication rate were lower with laparoscopic adrenalectomy than with traditional open adrenalectomy for large tumors. Although a higher morbidity could be expected with larger tumors, morbidity was still less than with open surgery.

Conversion to open surgery is most often due to infiltrative adrenal cortical carcinoma. In the largest series, conversion occurred electively after initial laparoscopic exploration and not because of hemorrhage or other emergent causes. MacGillivray concluded that **preoperative computed tomographic scanning can identify those infiltrative tumors that are likely to be invasive carcinoma.**

MacGillivray and Henry recommend an upper size limit of 12 cm for laparoscopic adrenalectomy. However, keep in mind that computed tomographic scanning can underestimate specimen size by as much as 16% (Lau et al, 1999).

### Obesity

With a worldwide epidemic of obesity, it is an increasingly common occurrence to operate on morbidly obese patients. Rather than obesity's being a relative contraindication, laparoscopy may offer a less morbid alternative for adrenalectomy on obese patients. Comparing results between obese patients (body mass index greater than 30) who underwent laparoscopic adrenal or renal surgery and those who underwent open surgery, Fazeli-Matin and associates (1999) noted that patients who underwent laparoscopic surgery had fewer complications (18% versus 47%; $P = .21$), less blood loss (50 mL versus 300 mL; $P = .03$), less narcotic use ($P = .01$), and shorter hospital stay (<24 hours versus 5.5 days; $P = .01$). However, these surgeries were performed by a veteran laparoscopist, and obesity may remain a relative contraindication for less experienced surgeons.

## Adrenal Cortical Carcinoma

Laparoscopic adrenalectomy on adrenal cortical carcinoma can be a daunting task. Adrenal carcinomas tend to be larger (>6 cm). Henry and colleagues (2002) noted that of 150 consecutive laparoscopic adrenalectomies, none of the smaller (<4 cm) tumors (N = 102) was malignant. In contrast, 12.5% of tumors larger than 4 cm (N = 48) were malignant. Using a 6-cm cutoff, Prager and coworkers (2004) noted that 21.2% of tumors larger than 6 cm were malignant versus 1.9% of lesions smaller than 6 cm. Also, the prospect of invasion by infiltrative lesions into surrounding structures can prohibit successful laparoscopic surgery. However, if computed tomography indicates that no local invasion is present and the lesion is not excessively large, laparoscopic adrenalectomy is possible. **Known adrenal vein or vena caval involvement is an absolute contraindication to laparoscopic surgery.** However, in one case report, Kim and associates (2004) described an intraoperatively discovered adrenal vein thrombus with a 7-cm adrenal mass. With use of atraumatic vascular clamps, the renal vein was entered, and the intact tumor thrombus was removed en bloc with the adrenalectomy specimen.

Cancer control is dependent on adherence to the same oncologic principles as in open surgery. Wide local excision with periadrenal fat is necessary for good local control to be obtained. Adrenal cortical carcinoma tends to be an aggressive disease, and locoregional recurrence can develop as often as 60% (Vassilopoulou-Sellin and Schultz, 2001). Most reports of postoperative adrenal cortical carcinoma recurrence have been in case reports. Henry and coworkers (2002) published a summary of 12 cases of carcinoma recurrence in the medical literature. In 25% of the cases, the authors admitted to specimen disruption during the case.

## PREOPERATIVE MANAGEMENT

It is important to correct any electrolyte abnormalities that may result from an endocrinologically active adrenal tumor. Most notably, aldosteronoma can result in hypokalemia that may require potassium repletion and administration of potassium-sparing diuretic. Hypertension should also be treated before surgery.

With pheochromocytoma, α-adrenergic blockade should be started 2 weeks before surgery. Phenoxybenzamine (10 to 40 mg four times daily; maximum, 300 mg/day) is used, starting gradually with a dose of 10 to 20 mg twice per day. Some patients with tachycardia may benefit from concurrent β blockade. Alternatively, an $\alpha_1$-selective blocker such as prazosin or doxazosin can be used. Intraoperatively, high blood pressure can be treated with nitroprusside or a short-acting β blocker like esmolol. Volume repletion is important to prevent the postoperative hypotension secondary to loss of tonic vasoconstriction after removal of a pheochromocytoma.

Patients with Cushing's syndrome require correction of electrolyte abnormalities and hyperglycemia before surgery. These patients may benefit from administration of adrenolytic agents such as mitotane or aminoglutethimide.

Potential errors in preoperative preparation are summarized in Table 54–3.

A mechanical bowel preparation can be helpful for open or laparoscopic transperitoneal surgery. Retroperitoneal surgery

**Table 54–3.** **Errors in Preparation of Patients for Adrenal Surgery**

*Primary aldosteronism*

Potassium repletion
Blood pressure control

*Cushing's syndrome*

Inhibition of glucocorticoid production when there is severe manifestation with metyrapone
Control of diabetes
Preoperative antibiotics
Operative steroid administration

*Incidentalomas*

Anesthetic preparation for pheochromocytoma; 5% have normal diagnostic studies

*Adrenal carcinoma*

Consent for adjacent organ removal
Failure to identify vena cava involvement

*Pheochromocytoma*

Preoperative catecholamine blockade
Volume expansion
Anesthetic consultation

Modified from Vaughn ED: Complications of adrenal surgery. In Taneja SS, Smith RB, Ehrlich RM, eds: Complications of Urologic Surgery: Prevention and Management, 3rd ed. Philadelphia, WB Saunders, 2001:363.

may not require this bowel preparation. All patients should receive appropriate preoperative antibiotics. A nasogastric or orogastric tube can be placed to decompress the bowel, especially helpful for transperitoneal cases. The placement of a urinary catheter to help measure urine output and to decompress the bladder is essential.

## OPEN ADRENALECTOMY

Open adrenalectomy can be performed through either a transperitoneal or retroperitoneal approach. The transperitoneal approaches include midline, subcostal, and thoracoabdominal. The retroperitoneal approaches include flank and posterior lumbodorsal. The advantages of the transperitoneal approaches are better exposure for larger tumors and excellent access to the great vessels and retroperitoneum. The main disadvantages are prolonged ileus and difficult exposure in morbidly obese patients. The retroperitoneal approach results in less ileus and may result in shorter hospital stays. There is a smaller operative field, and access to larger tumors and surrounding involved organs may be difficult. The best surgical approach for a given adrenal disease is indicated in Table 54–2.

### Flank Retroperitoneal Approach

**Right Side.** The patient is placed in flank position with the right side facing up (Fig. 54–3). The bed is placed in maximal flexion, and the kidney rest is deployed to accentuate the space between the costal margin and iliac crest. Palpation is used to identify the course of the 11th rib. The skin and fat overlying the 11th rib are incised, and the fascia and muscle overlying the rib are divided (Fig. 54–4).

Once the anterior surface of the rib is exposed, the anterior periosteum is cauterized and the periosteal elevator is used to scrape it off the anterior rib surface. The edges of the periosteum on the superior and inferior aspects of the rib should now be visible. The periosteal elevator is used to develop a plane between the posterior rib surface and the posterior leaf of the periosteum. The Doyen instrument and surgical cautery are used to strip the periosteum off of the rib from the tip of the rib back toward the paraspinal muscles. With the rib cutter, the 11th rib is excised (Fig. 54–5). A rongeur can be used to remove any sharp remnants on the rib stump. Cautery or bone wax can be used to render the marrow hemostatic.

Next, the neurovascular bundle is identified and freed with sharp and blunt dissection to avoid injury during subsequent dissection and closure (Fig. 54–6). The lumbodorsal fascia is entered sharply with Metzenbaum scissors, and blunt dissection is used to dissect the peritoneum off of the transverse fascia anteriorly. The flank muscles and their accompanying fasciae are divided anteriorly—the external oblique, internal oblique, and transverse abdominal. Next, the posterior muscle diaphragmatic attachments are divided with cautery. The pleura is sharply and bluntly dissected off the superior edge of the 12 rib.

The plane between Gerota's fascia and the peritoneum can be started with the cautery or sharp dissection. Once it is identified, this plane can be maximally developed with blunt dissection. The peritoneum needs to be freed from the superior aspect of Gerota's fascia as well. Once the peritoneum is mobilized, on the right side, the vena cava can be visualized, and with cephalad dissection, the adrenal gland and renal vein can be seen as well. Placement of a self-retaining retractor is essential for maximal exposure to be obtained.

Dissection of the adrenal gland typically begins along the medial border of the gland with the vena cava. The overlying peritoneum is divided, and blunt dissection is used to expose the plane between the medial surface of the adrenal gland and the lateral surface of the vena cava. The adrenal vein is often difficult to identify until this plane is developed. The adrenal vein is dissected out with a right-angled instrument like a Mixter forceps. Surgical ties or clips can be placed to ligate the adrenal vein. In our opinion, surgical ties are more reliable

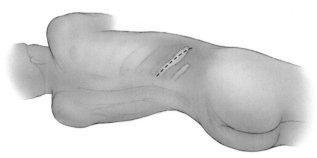

**Figure 54–3.** Surgical incision over 11th rib for flank adrenalectomy. The patient is in flexion with the kidney rest deployed to maximally expose the right retroperitoneum.

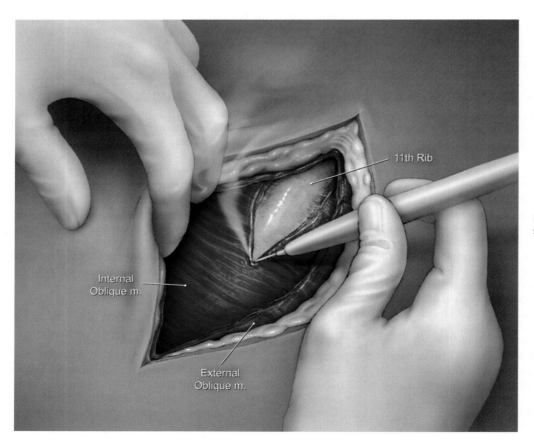

11th Rib

Internal Oblique m.

External Oblique m.

**Figure 54–4.** Flank approach. Incision of muscle overlying 11th rib.

than standard titanium clips. However, locking surgical clips may be substituted for added security. There are numerous arterial branches to the gland that can be ligated and divided individually. Alternatively, many authors attest to the utility of the harmonic scalpel in hemostatically dividing arterial attachments. Once this is done, the psoas muscle is often visible posteriorly. Superior attachments are divided with the aid of surgical cautery or harmonic scalpel. Downward trac-

tion on the kidney assists with this dissection. Inferomedial attachments to the kidney are taken with sharp or cautery hook dissection.

Dissection of the left adrenal gland is similar except that the aorta is visualized, and the adrenal vein originates from the renal vein. Other authors have described supracostal technique with intentional violation of the pleura. This approach may be helpful for larger tumors.

Closure of the incision consists of a two-layer closure with a running No. 1 polydioxanone suture. The deep layer consists of the transverse abdominal muscle and internal oblique muscle and fascia. The outer layer consists of the external oblique muscle and fascia. Skin closure can be completed with surgical staples or absorbable subcuticular suture.

## Lumbodorsal Posterior Approach

The main advantage of this approach is the ability to easily access both adrenal glands for bilateral surgery. The disadvantages include a limited operative field and respiratory limitation. If bleeding is extensive, it can be difficult to control from this position. The posterior approach requires prone positioning of the patient with arms extended cephalad. The procedure has been extensively modified over time—with or without rib resection, transthoracic through the diaphragm, or diaphragm sparing. A rib-resecting, diaphragm-sparing approach is described.

**Right Side.** An incision is made along the course of the right 11th rib (Fig. 54–7). This is taken down to the periosteum, and the rib resection is performed in a manner similar to that described for flank incision. The diaphragm is dissected off the underlying peritoneum and liver. The peritoneum is then dissected off of Gerota's fascia, which is retracted inferiorly. If a bilateral procedure is undertaken, a Finochietto retractor can be used to assist in bilateral exposure (Fig. 54–8). With division of the final hepatic attachments, the adrenal gland

**Figure 54–5.** Flank approach. Excision of 11th rib.

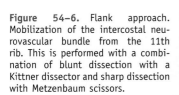

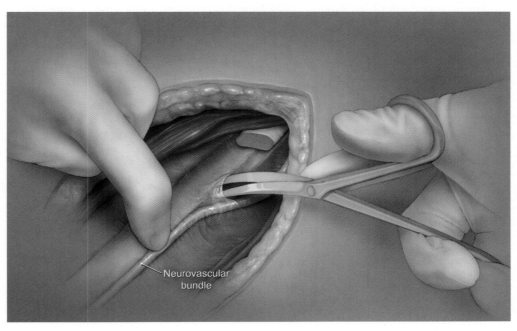

**Figure 54–6.** Flank approach. Mobilization of the intercostal neurovascular bundle from the 11th rib. This is performed with a combination of blunt dissection with a Kittner dissector and sharp dissection with Metzenbaum scissors.

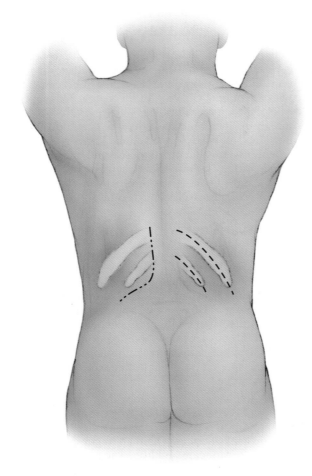

**Figure 54–7.** Posterior approach—possible incisions for lumbodorsal incisions.

becomes visible. The vena cava often becomes visible at this point, and the right adrenal vein is easily identified at its posterolateral origin. After division of arterial branches to the adrenal that course behind the vena cava and anterior to the paraspinal muscles, the adrenal gland can be mobilized posteriorly away from the paraspinal muscles, exposing the anterior vena cava. Given the small operative field, manual retraction of the kidney to assist dissection is not usually possible. Fortunately, division of the vascular attachments is relatively simple, and direct manipulation of the adrenal gland is possible. **The posterior approach should not be used for large tumors or adrenocortical carcinoma.**

## Subcostal Anterior Approach

The anterior approach is useful for larger tumors and can be extended to the contralateral side as a chevron incision for treatment of bilateral lesions (Fig. 54–9). This approach also affords excellent exposure of the great vessels in the event that lymph nodes or venous tumor thrombus needs to be addressed.

**Left Side.** The patient is placed supine on the surgical table. If it is desired, a body roll can be placed under the back at the level of the costal margin to accentuate the costal margin. A skin incision is made approximately two fingerbreadths below the costal margin. This incision is extended medially to the midline or beyond, depending on the degree of exposure needed. The external oblique, internal oblique, and transverse abdominal muscles and their corresponding fasciae are divided laterally, and the rectus muscle and the rectus sheath are divided medially. The peritoneum is entered sharply, and the falciform ligament is divided after it is clamped and ligated with a large-gauge vascular tie (0 or 1 silk). The line of Toldt is incised, and the left colon is mobilized medially. The splenic

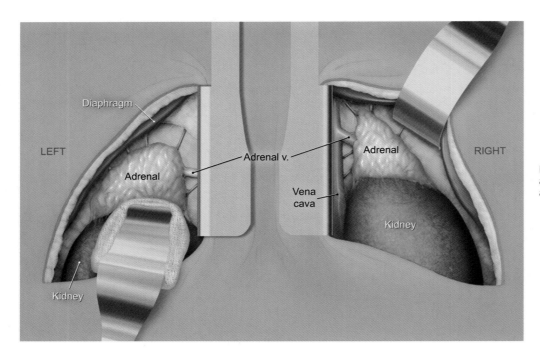

**Figure 54–8.** Bilateral posterior approach—anatomic relations to the adrenal gland as seen from behind.

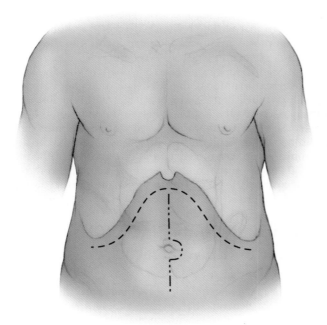

**Figure 54–9.** Anterior approach. The transperitoneal approach may be attempted through a midline incision or subcostal incision. The subcostal incision can be extended into a full chevron for bilateral adrenalectomy or if a large unilateral tumor is encountered.

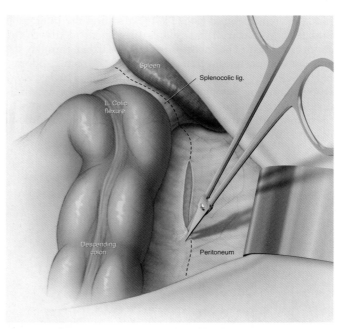

**Figure 54–10.** Anterior approach. Peritoneum lateral to left colon is incised at the line of Toldt and extended cephalad to the splenocolic ligament and inferiorly.

flexure is taken down by dividing the splenocolic ligament (Fig. 54–10). Division of the lienorenal ligament will allow medial mobilization of the spleen. The tail of the pancreas may come into view at this point. In a thin individual, the adrenal may be visible at this point. The left adrenal vein is identified on dissecting out the left renal vein (Fig. 54–11). After ligation and division of the left adrenal vein, medial attachments to the aorta can be taken with the harmonic scalpel or with careful dissection and ligation of small arterial vessels while gentle lateral traction is placed on the gland. The lateral and inferior attachments to the kidney can be taken by blunt and sharp dissection off of the renal capsule. Care must be taken to avoid hitting upper pole renal vascular attachments. After removal of the left adrenal gland, closure of the incision is performed with a running No. 1 polydioxanone suture in two layers; the deep layer consists of the transverse abdominal muscle, transverse fascia, internal oblique muscle and fascia, and posterior rectus sheath, and the superficial layer consists of the external oblique muscle and fascia and the anterior rectus sheath.

For right-sided tumors, the dissection is similar except for the necessity to dissect the duodenum medially by the Kocher maneuver (Fig. 54–12).

## Thoracoabdominal Approach

This approach is a maximally invasive way to ensure superb surgical exposure of the retroperitoneum, adrenal gland, and great vessels. However, this exposure comes at a price: increased incisional pain, prolonged ileus, pulmonary morbidity, and a chest tube. **The thoracoabdominal approach is reserved for large or invasive adrenal carcinomas.**

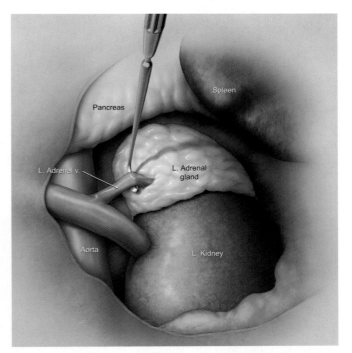

**Figure 54–11.** Anterior approach. The left adrenal vein is dissected out and ligated.

**Right Side.** The patient is placed in an oblique position with the upper torso at a 45-degree angle to the table and the lower body flat on the table. A body roll is used to achieve the 45-degree position, and the right arm is placed in a sling with the arm bent at the elbow (Fig. 54–13). The left arm is secured to an arm board. The incision is made through the eighth or ninth intercostal space (Fig. 54–14), dividing the intercostal muscles and fasciae. The costal cartilage is divided with the surgical cautery. The incision is carried farther through the anterior and posterior rectus sheaths and the rectus abdominal muscle. The pleura is entered, and the lung is packed away with laparotomy sponges (Fig. 54–15). The diaphragm is divided with the cautery. Do not cut directly to the center of the diaphragm as the phrenic nerve can be damaged. Once the diaphragm is divided, a Finochietto self-retaining retractor is placed to expose the surgical area. The rest of the dissection is similar to that of the previously described techniques. The relationship of the thoracoabdominal incision to the adrenal gland is illustrated in Figures 54–16 and 54–17.

Closure of the incision requires closure of the diaphragm and reapproximation of the ribs. The diaphragm is closed with interrupted figure-of-eight stitches with nonabsorbable suture. A chest tube is placed before the anterior thorax is closed. The anterior thorax is closed with several interrupted 0 chromic sutures on blunt-tip liver needles around the superior border of the eighth rib and inferior border of the ninth rib. A 0 Prolene suture on a tapered needle is placed through the cut costal cartilage to bring the costal margin together. The chest tube is placed to a water seal and suction.

# LAPAROSCOPIC ADRENALECTOMY
## Transperitoneal Approach

Transperitoneal laparoscopic adrenalectomy can be performed through either an anterior supine approach or a lateral approach. In general, the anterior supine approach allows bilateral adrenalectomy without having to reposition the patient. The lateral position is advantageous because greater

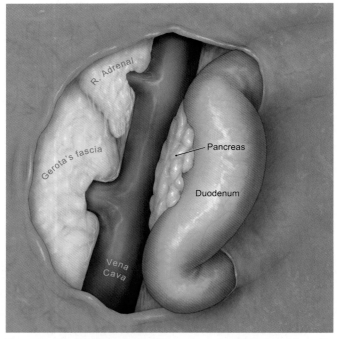

**Figure 54–12.**   Kocher maneuver. The peritoneum is incised, and sharp dissection and blunt dissection are used to mobilize the second stage of the duodenum away from the renal hilum.

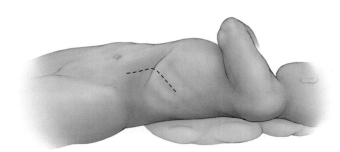

**Figure 54–13.**   Positioning for thoracoabdominal surgery. A body roll elevates the flank on the side of surgery, and the arm and shoulder are rotated away, supported by a sling.

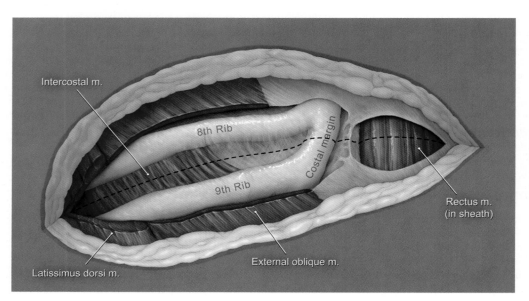

**Figure 54–14.** Thoracoabdominal approach. Incision at the eighth intercostal space. The costal margin, external intercostal muscle and fascia, and anterior rectus sheath are divided.

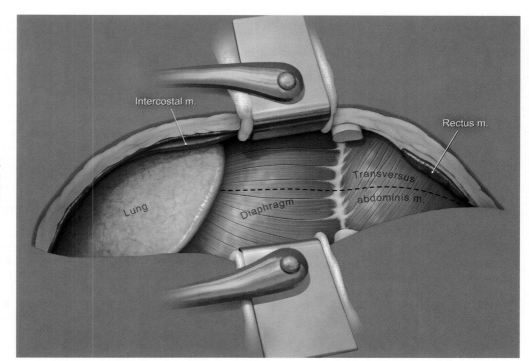

**Figure 54–15.** Thoracoabdominal approach. The Finochietto retractor is placed to expose the anatomy. The lung visible in this view is packed away with laparotomy sponges.

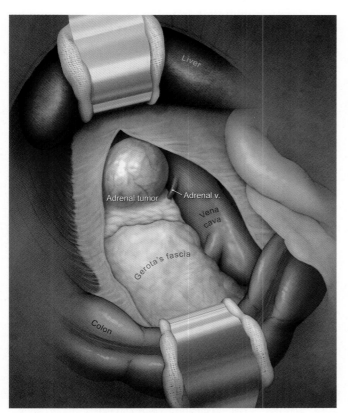

**Figure 54–16.** Thoracoabdominal approach. Exposure of the adrenal.

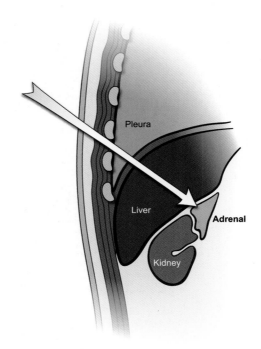

**Figure 54–17.** Demonstration of the route of surgical dissection during thoracoabdominal incision.

workspace is available secondary to gravity-assisted retraction of the bowel. The flank approach is described in detail.

**Left Side.** The patient is positioned in a modified flank position. The patient is angled back about 30 to 45 degrees. After insufflation of the abdomen, four trocars are placed along the left costal margin (Fig. 54–18). The line of Toldt is incised and the left colon medially mobilized (Fig. 54–19). The lienorenal and splenocolic ligaments are divided. The lateral and superior attachments of the spleen can be divided to facilitate medial mobilization of the spleen if necessary. In many cases, the spleen may fall away sufficiently by gravity without having to extend the dissection above the spleen. The renal vein and adrenal vein are dissected free (Fig. 54–20). The left adrenal vein is dissected out, ligated, and divided (Fig. 54–21). Surgical clips are used to control the adrenal vein. It is advisable to leave two clips on the body side of the vein and one on the specimen side. Adrenal arterial supply is divided as the adrenal is dissected free (Fig. 54–22). The harmonic scalpel is effective for performing this dissection. The remaining attachments to the kidney are divided bluntly and with the hook cautery (Fig. 54–23). The specimen is placed in an endoscopic sac and extracted (Fig. 54–24).

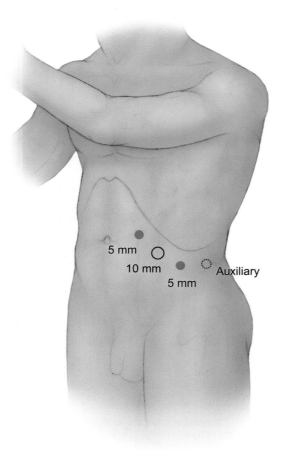

**Figure 54–18.** Four-trocar configuration for left transperitoneal laparoscopic adrenalectomy.

The operative field is examined with the insufflation pressure turned down to 5 mm Hg. If it is hemostatic, the trocar sites are closed with absorbable suture. A drain usually does not need to be placed.

On the right side, the approach is similar. However, the duodenum must be dissected away by the Kocher maneuver. As on the left side, a four-trocar configuration is used (Fig. 54–25). The most medial trocar is used for liver retraction. A 2-mm trocar can be used with a 2-mm locking grasper to fashion a self-retaining retractor of the liver (Fig. 54–26).

## Retroperitoneal Approach

**Left Side.** The patient is placed in flank position with the left side up. The patient is placed in flexion, and the kidney rest is deployed to accentuate the left flank. A 12-mm incision is made near the tip of the 12th rib under the 11th rib. The underlying muscle and fasciae are divided with cautery until the lumbodorsal fascia is visible or palpable. The lumbodorsal fascia is divided with cautery or Metzenbaum scissors, and blunt finger dissection is used to develop a plane between the posterior Gerota's fascia and the psoas fascia. With this plane developed, a retroperitoneal dissection balloon is placed and inflated. Typically, a laparoscope can be placed down the hollow shaft of the dissection balloon to visually confirm the accurate anatomic placement of the balloon between the kidney and psoas. A balloon-tip trocar is placed into the defect and secured in position. After insufflation of the retroperitoneum, a 5- or 10-mm trocar is placed at the angle of the paraspinal muscle and the origin of the 12th rib. A 5- or 10-mm trocar is placed about two fingerbreadths above the iliac crest near the anterior superior iliac spine (Fig. 54–27).

The renal hilum is usually located fairly rapidly in the retroperitoneal approach by direct visualization of arterial pulsations. The left adrenal vein can be isolated from its origin on the left renal vein (Fig. 54–28). The left adrenal vein is dissected out and ligated with surgical clips and divided (Fig. 54–29). The left adrenal gland is then dissected out as described previously; small arterial branches can be clipped or divided hemostatically with a harmonic scalpel. The specimen is placed in a specimen bag and extracted. The trocar sites are closed with absorbable suture after hemostasis is ensured. The right adrenalectomy is performed in similar fashion; anatomic relations of this approach are illustrated in Figure 54–30.

## HAND-ASSISTED SURGERY

The advantage of hand assistance stems from the addition of tactile sensation. This may result in faster dissection and added security in the event of bleeding complications. Also, the learning curve may be shorter with hand assistance. Only case reports exist regarding hand-assisted laparoscopic adrenalectomy. This may be especially advantageous for large adrenal tumors that may require an incision for extraction. Bilateral tumors may also be treated in this fashion.

*Text continued on p. 1884.*

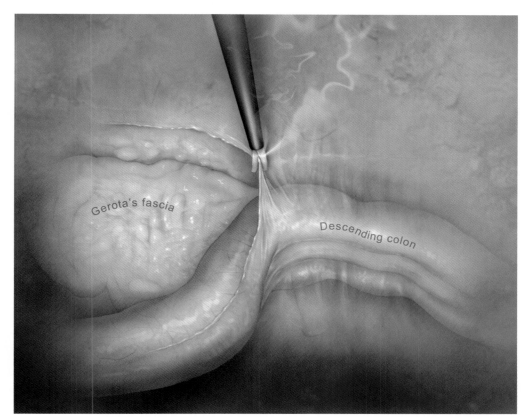

**Figure 54–19.** Transperitoneal laparoscopic adrenalectomy. Incision of the line of Toldt and medial dissection of the left colon with cautery endoscopic scissors.

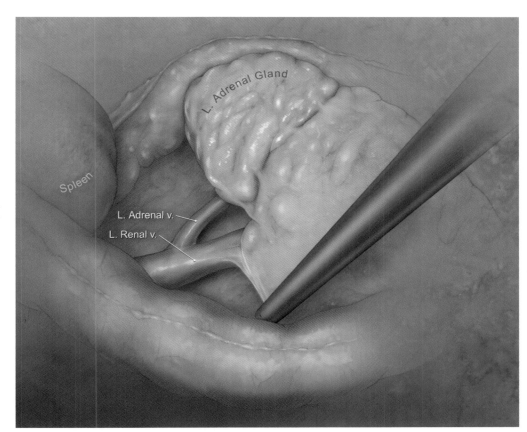

**Figure 54–20.** Transperitoneal laparoscopic adrenalectomy. Exposure and dissection of the renal vein and left adrenal vein.

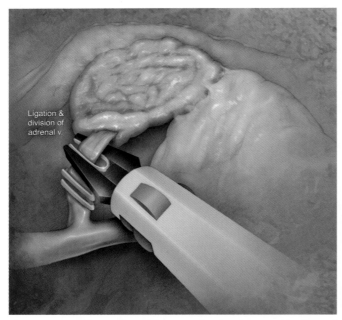

**Figure 54–21.** Transperitoneal laparoscopic adrenalectomy. Ligation and division of left adrenal vein.

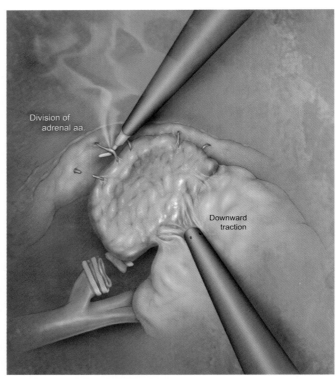

**Figure 54–22.** Transperitoneal laparoscopic adrenalectomy. Division of adrenal arterial supply and superomedial dissection with downward traction on the kidney.

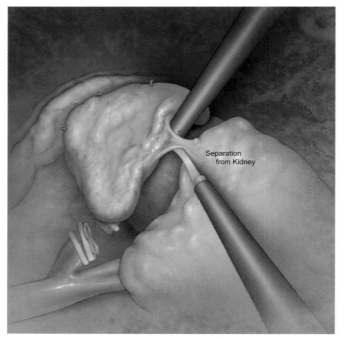

**Figure 54–23.** Transperitoneal laparoscopic adrenalectomy. The adrenal gland is mobilized off the medial aspect of the kidney.

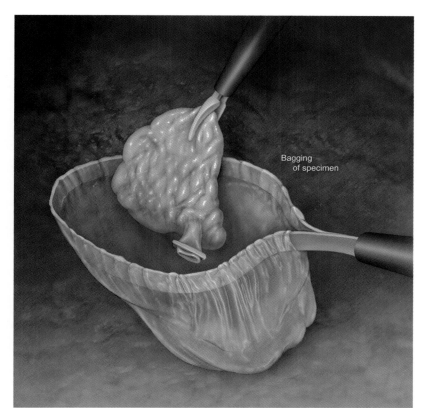

**Figure 54–24.** Transperitoneal laparoscopic adrenalectomy. Placement of specimen in endoscopic extraction sac.

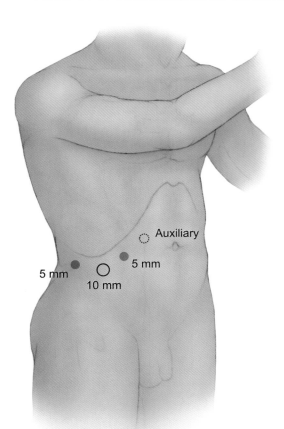

**Figure 54–25.** Four-trocar configuration for right transperitoneal laparoscopic adrenalectomy. Auxiliary site can be used for liver retraction.

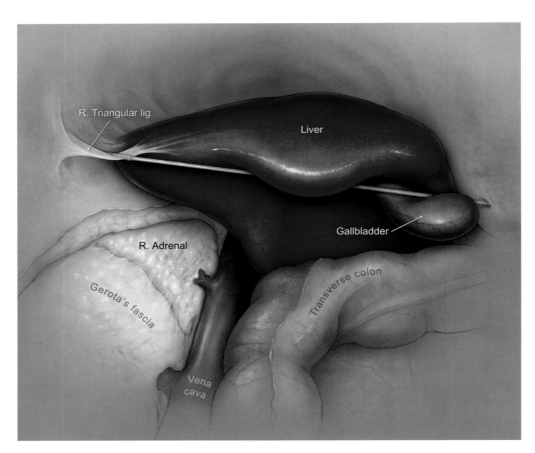

**Figure 54–26.** A 2-mm trocar and locking grasping forceps can be used instead of a larger caliber fan retractor to act as a self-retaining liver retractor. It is important that the trocar be placed just below the xiphoid process to ensure adequate retraction.

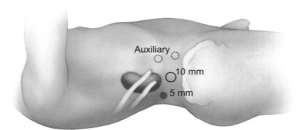

**Figure 54–27.** Trocar placement for retroperitoneal laparoscopy. The dotted circles represent alternative sites for placement of a third port.

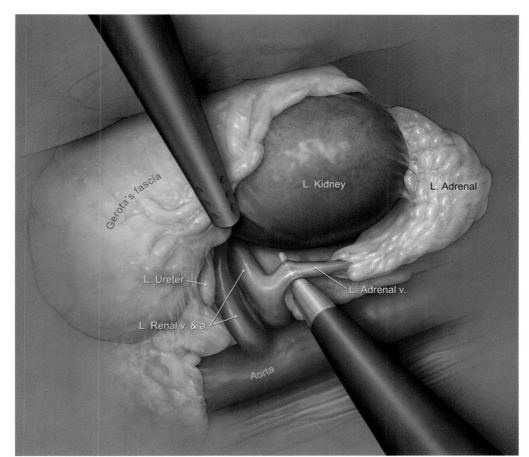

**Figure 54–28.** Retroperitoneal laparoscopic adrenalectomy. Dissection of the left adrenal vein by the retroperitoneal approach.

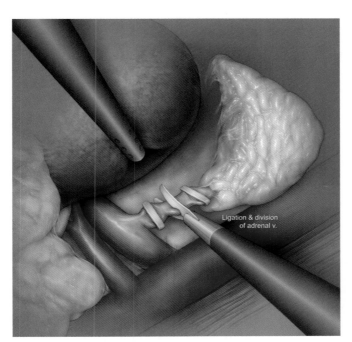

**Figure 54–29.** Retroperitoneal laparoscopic adrenalectomy. Ligation and division of left adrenal vein. The kidney is dissected away from the adrenal gland.

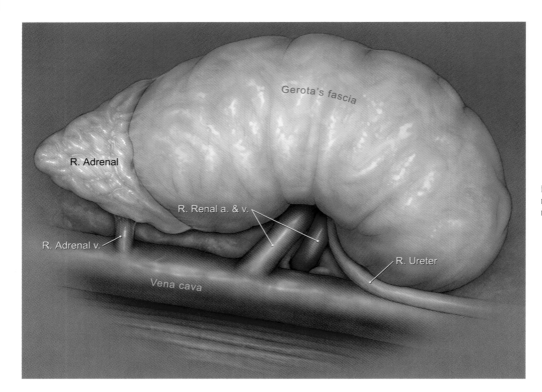

**Figure 54–30.** Anatomic view of right adrenal gland from laparoscopic retroperitoneal approach.

## ROBOTIC SURGERY

Robotic-assisted laparoscopic adrenalectomy has been performed with the da Vinci surgical robotic system.* The robot provides handlike dexterity to laparoscopic surgery. The case reports of a total of five patients were completed successfully without complication, except for one case with a minor capsular tear (Undre et al, 2004).

## INTRAOPERATIVE ULTRASONOGRAPHY

It can be difficult at times to locate the adrenal gland, especially if the patient is obese and there is a lot of intra-abdominal fat. Without tactile feedback, unless the lesion is grossly evident, it can be difficult to localize the adrenal gland during surgery. Ultrasonography of the adrenal gland is extremely difficult as an extracorporeal technique. The ability to directly apply the ultrasound probe to the operative area under laparoscopic guidance facilitates identification of the adrenal gland. Furthermore, **intraoperative ultrasonography can help identify the adrenal vein,** especially on the left side.

Brunt and coworkers (1999) used intraoperative ultrasonography in 28 adrenalectomies and had 100% success in identifying the adrenal gland. Lucas and associates (1999) had similar success with 42 adrenalectomies.

Intraoperative ultrasonography is especially helpful in laparoscopic partial adrenalectomy. It can delineate the tumor within the adrenal gland to facilitate adrenal-sparing surgery. Pautler and colleagues (2002) successfully performed laparoscopic partial adrenalectomy on seven patients with ultra-

---

*Intuitive Surgical, Mountain View, Calif.

sound assistance. There were no complications and no open conversions.

## POSTOPERATIVE MANAGEMENT

Electrolyte values are checked the night of surgery and each morning; this is especially important for patients with Conn's or Cushing's syndrome. The urinary catheter can usually be removed on the first postoperative day when the patient is ambulatory. If a nasogastric tube was placed for open surgery, it can be removed with return of bowel sounds. Diet resumption is usually started on the first postoperative day for laparoscopic surgery and when bowel sounds resume for open surgery.

Blood pressure is carefully evaluated for hypertension or hypotension. Unexplained hypotension, confusion, lethargy, nausea, vomiting, or fever could represent addisonian crisis (adrenal insufficiency). **Adrenal insufficiency is most commonly seen after surgery for Cushing's syndrome as a result of contralateral cortisol suppression.** Stress-dose steroid administration may be necessary. Corticosteroid replacement and mineralocorticoid (fludrocortisone) may be required for the long term. Hospital stay may be prolonged by the necessary adjustment of antihypertensive medications and steroids.

## OUTPATIENT AND SHORT-STAY LAPAROSCOPIC ADRENALECTOMY

In select patients who underwent uneventful surgery, same-day or less than 24-hour hospital discharge has been attempted. Gill and colleagues (2000) were able to discharge 9 of 27 patients who underwent laparoscopic adrenalectomies within 8 hours of surgery. One patient was readmitted for abscess formation. Edwin and coworkers (2001) described 13 patients with aldosteronoma who underwent laparoscopic adrenalectomy. All were discharged within 3 to 6 hours of surgery. None was readmitted. The satisfaction of patients was high for all but one patient who had poorly controlled pain after discharge. Rayan and Hodin (2000) performed 19 laparoscopic adrenalectomies and were able to discharge 47% of patients within 24 hours.

## OUTCOMES

Retrospective studies demonstrate a clear advantage to laparoscopic surgery over open surgery in terms of analgesia, hospital stay, blood loss, and complication rate. The laparoscopic surgeries typically had longer operative times than the open surgery did. There are no randomized prospective studies comparing laparoscopic with open adrenalectomy. In a rare non-randomized prospective study, Prager and colleagues (2004) assigned patients to laparoscopic or open surgery on the basis of a cutoff of 6 cm; lesions smaller than 6 cm were removed laparoscopically. As one would expect, operative times, complication rate, and blood loss were higher in the open surgery group. It is difficult to compare these two groups fairly since the patients assigned to open surgery had larger tumors and a higher incidence of malignant disease (1.9% versus 29.1%) than the laparoscopic cohort did.

Comparison of retroperitoneal with transperitoneal laparoscopy tended to favor the retroperitoneal approach. Bonjer and colleagues (1997) showed an advantage in operative time (75 minutes versus 150 minutes; $P = .005$), blood loss (20 mL versus 150 mL; $P = .01$), postoperative analgesia (6 mg versus 20 mg of morphine sulfate; $P = .003$), and hospital stay (4 versus 6 days; $P = .027$) for retroperitoneal over transperitoneal approach. Suzuki and coworkers (2001) also found less blood loss, shorter convalescence, and faster resumption of oral intake with retroperitoneal surgery than with anterior and lateral transperitoneal procedures. Interestingly, the authors initially attempted to perform a prospective randomized study, but patients expressed strong preference for retroperitoneal surgery.

Is laparoscopic adrenalectomy too costly? In the current era of soaring medical costs, the cost-effectiveness of laparoscopic surgery must be proven to justify its use. Initially, the cost of laparoscopic adrenalectomy was much higher than the cost of open surgery. Thompson and colleagues (1997) noted that hospital charges for laparoscopic adrenalectomy were $1000 higher than for open adrenalectomy. With increased use of disposables and with growing surgical experience, the costs are becoming manageable. Hobart and colleagues (1999) have shown that with 2-mm instrumentation, laparoscopic adrenalectomy resulted in 17.9% less cost than open adrenalectomy. The laparoscopic adrenalectomy had an 18.1% increased intraoperative cost but a 63.4% less postoperative cost. In Spain, Ortega and associates (2002) calculated that laparoscopic adrenalectomy was not more expensive in terms of direct surgical cost (€6306 versus €7581; $P = NS$). However, hospital stay was significantly shorter and cheaper (€742 versus €1191; $P = .004$). Interestingly, the most expensive part of the entire therapeutic process was the preoperative hospitalization for diagnostic workup. In the United States, most diagnostic tests are carried out on an ambulatory outpatient basis, and these costs would be considerably less. Outside of the direct cost of surgery and hospitalization, laparoscopic adrenalectomy is often less expensive than long-term medical therapy for certain adrenal disorders. In Canada, aldosteronoma management with surgery represents a savings of C$31,132 over the lifetime of each patient (Sywak and Pasieka, 2002).

## COMPLICATIONS
### Operative Complications (Table 54–4)

As expected, adrenal surgery, both open and laparoscopic, can involve injury to adjacent organs. Hemorrhage is a potentially catastrophic complication of adrenal surgery. Bleeding can result from injury to the adrenal vein, inferior vena cava, lumbar vein, or renal vein. These injuries are managed initially by application of direct pressure to the injury. Grasping a small injury with an Allis clamp and closing it with suture or by placement of a vascular clamp for a larger vena cava injury may be curative. For laparoscopic cases, the management is more of a problem. In the early days of laparoscopic adrenalectomy, open conversion was the typical consequence of vascular injury. However, with increasing experience with laparoscopic suturing techniques, these injuries are often managed as in the open surgery.

Nonhemorrhagic vascular injuries can occur as well. An upper pole renal artery branch can be divided inadvertently during dissection. If the branch is small and supplies a minimal portion of the kidney, it can be ignored. More substantial injuries may require a revascularization attempt. If the patient has a large tumor, there can be distortion of the regional anatomy, and inadvertent ligation of the superior mesenteric vein is possible. This is a potentially fatal injury, and one must have a high index of suspicion to restore vascular supply to the bowel as soon as possible.

| Table 54–4. **Operative Complications of Adrenal Surgery** |
| --- |
| *Hemorrhage* |
| Inferior vena cava |
| Adrenal vein |
| Lumbar vein |
| Hepatic vein |
| *Vascular* |
| Ligation of renal artery branch |
| Ligation of mesenteric artery |
| Inferior vena cava involvement |
| *Adjacent organ injury* |
| Pneumothorax |
| Pancreas |
| Liver |
| Spleen |
| Stomach |
| Colon |
| Kidney |

From Vaughn ED: Complications of adrenal surgery. In Taneja SS, Smith RB, Ehrlich RM, eds: Complications of Urologic Surgery: Prevention and Management, 3rd ed. Philadelphia, WB Saunders, 2001:366.

The adjacent organs can be injured during dissection of the adrenal gland. The liver can be injured during right adrenalectomy. Liver lacerations can be treated with argon beam coagulation and application of hemostatic agents such as methyl cellulose. More serious injuries may require hemostatic sutures with a blunt-tip liver needle. The spleen can be injured during left adrenalectomy. As with hepatic injury, argon beam coagulation and hemostatic agents can be used to control bleeding. If this is not sufficient, splenorrhaphy can be attempted. If these measures are unsuccessful, splenectomy may be necessary. It is important to remember to give pneumonia vaccination to these patients during postoperative care.

The pancreas can be injured during surgery on either the right or left adrenal gland. If an injury to the tail of the pancreas occurs, distal pancreatectomy may be performed. If the injury is to the pancreatic duct, this may be repaired and surgical drains left. If there is uncertainty of pancreatic injury, leaving closed-suction surgical drains behind is advisable. Postoperative drainage high in triglycerides is indicative of pancreas injury. Management consists of bowel rest with parenteral nutrition. The administration of octreotide can decrease pancreatic secretions while the pancreas heals.

The proximity of the kidney to the adrenal gland can be a problem in cases of large adrenal cortical carcinomas. **It is imperative for all patients undergoing surgery for large adrenal masses to be counseled about the possibility of concurrent en bloc nephrectomy.**

During 11th rib flank adrenalectomy, it is not unusual for pleural injury to be incurred. These injuries can be repaired with a purse-string chromic suture and a red rubber catheter to water seal. Expulsion of air from the pleura followed by cinching of the purse-string usually repairs the defect. Postoperative chest radiography should be routinely performed after flank or thoracoabdominal nephrectomy. If a significant pneumothorax is present, a chest tube should be placed.

With pheochromocytoma, blood pressure fluctuations can be life-threatening. The anesthesiologist typically manages high blood pressure with short-acting $\beta$ blockade, $\alpha$ blockers, or nitroprusside. Arrhythmias are usually treated with $\beta$ blockers. When the adrenal vein is ligated, there can be a sudden drop in blood pressure. It is important to inform the anesthesiologist just before the adrenal vein is ligated to avoid any nasty surprises. Fluid repletion and pressors may be necessary to bring the pressure to normal.

## Postoperative Complications

Table 54–5 summarizes the postoperative complications that can occur. Disease-specific complications must be accounted for to ensure an uneventful postoperative course.

Patients with primary hyperaldosteronism require close monitoring of potassium levels as they can be either hypokalemic or hyperkalemic. Hyperkalemia, secondary to contralateral adrenal zona glomerulosa suppression, should be managed medically with the typical hyperkalemia regimens. Hypokalemia can persist in the immediate period after adrenalectomy, and this should be corrected with potassium

### Table 54–5. Postoperative Complications of Adrenal Surgery

*Primary aldosteronism*

Hypokalemia: secondary to continued potassium loss immediately postoperative
Hyperkalemia: secondary to failure of contralateral adrenal to secrete aldosterone

*Cushing's syndrome*

Inadequate steroid replacement leading to hypocorticoidism
Fracture secondary to osteoporosis
Hyperglycemia
Poor wound healing
Increased risk of infections

*Pheochromocytoma*

Hypotension secondary to $\alpha$-adrenergic blockade after tumor removal

*Generic complications*

Hemorrhage
Inferior vena cava
Adrenal arteries
Pneumothorax
Pancreatitis
Pneumonia
Hiccups

From Vaughn ED: Complications of adrenal surgery. In Taneja SS, Smith RB, Ehrlich RM, eds: Complications of Urologic Surgery: Prevention and Management, 3rd ed. Philadelphia, WB Saunders, 2001:368.

repletion. In patients who had only one adrenal gland to begin with, mineralocorticoid replacement with fludrocortisone is essential.

Patients with Cushing's syndrome will require steroid replacement after surgery until the contralateral gland recovers function. Measurements of plasma cortisol can be useful in determining when steroid replacement can be tapered. Furthermore, these patients have increased risk of fracture secondary to osteoporosis, hyperglycemia, and poor wound healing.

Patients with pheochromocytoma may have hypotension secondary to $\alpha$ blockade. These patients need to be monitored closely until $\alpha$ blockade wears off, often in the intensive care unit. If $\alpha$ blockade was not used preoperatively, as it is done at the Cleveland Clinic, intensive care stay is unnecessary in most cases.

## Laparoscopy Versus Open Adrenalectomy

Brunt (2002) compiled the complication statistics of 50 laparoscopic studies and 48 open studies to evaluate the impact of laparoscopy on adrenalectomy. To limit selection bias, open surgical series with adrenal cortical carcinoma cases were excluded. Laparoscopy resulted in a lower complication rate (10.9% versus 25.2%; $P \leq .0001$) than did open adrenalectomy. Specifically, **pulmonary, wound, and infectious complications were statistically less common with laparoscopic surgery.** There were also fewer injuries to adjacent organs (0.7% versus 2.4%; $P = .05$). Splenic injuries decreased dramatically in incidence (laparoscopic, 0.2%; open, 2.0%). A number of factors account for this decrease, including division of the splenocolic and lienorenal ligaments under magnification and the assistance of gravity in retracting the spleen rather than manual retraction. With retroperitoneal surgery, the spleen would not even be in the surgical field to be injured. A decrease in cardiac complications was observed, but some of the improvement in complication rate was thought to be attributable to improvements in perioperative management of vasoactive tumors. The most common complication of laparoscopic adrenalectomy is bleeding (4.7%). Bleeding is also the most common reason for open conversion of laparoscopic adrenalectomy (30%). Bleeding results from vascular injury to the adrenal vein, injury to the vena cava, direct injury to the adrenal gland, renal capsular tear, or surgical clip dislocation.

## SPECIAL CONSIDERATIONS
## Pediatric

There are relatively few cases of laparoscopic adrenalectomy for pediatric patients. The small body habitus of the patients makes surgery more technically challenging. Neuroblastoma is the most common adrenal tumor in this age group, and this tumor tends to be large and infiltrative, complicating laparoscopic extraction.

Nevertheless, laparoscopic surgery has been successfully performed on pediatric patients. The first case was performed on a small asymptomatic neuroblastoma identified by mass screening of children in Japan (Yamamoto et al, 1996). Comparing open with laparoscopic biopsies and excisions, Iwanaka and colleagues (2001) showed that laparoscopy was associated with shorter hospitalization and rapid resumption of diet. Bilateral laparoscopic adrenalectomy can be performed safely as well (Schier et al, 1998).

In financial terms, laparoscopic adrenalectomy is cost-saving when postoperative stay is accounted for (Stanford et al, 2002). Even though laparoscopic adrenalectomy was more expensive as a procedure ($12,941 versus $4,714; $P < .001$), the overall cost difference between the two procedures was statistically insignificant.

## Pregnancy

The pregnant patient can present with an endocrinologically active adrenal tumor. Pheochromocytoma must be distinguished from preeclampsia or pregnancy-induced hypertension, a more medically accurate term. The main distinguishing factors are the absence of proteinuria in pheochromocytoma and the fact that pregnancy-induced hypertension tends to occur in the third trimester. When pheochromocytoma is diagnosed late in pregnancy, the pregnancy can be taken to term with medical management and the child delivered by cesarean section. If pheochromocytoma is diagnosed in the first or second trimester, the risk of surgery must be weighed against the risk of the pheochromocytoma to the pregnancy.

Laparoscopic adrenalectomy can be successfully performed on a pregnant patient. Several reports exist of successful surgery. Maneuvers to minimize risk include keeping insuf-flation pressure below 15 mm Hg, using open Hasson technique to gain access, and monitoring fetal heart rate and maternal arterial blood gases.

## Partial Adrenalectomy

The main indications for partial adrenalectomy are solitary adrenal gland, bilateral disease, and patients with familial syndromes. Pheochromocytoma has been treated with partial adrenalectomy, especially in patients with von Hippel–Lindau syndrome (Al-Sobhi et al, 2002; Baghai et al, 2002), familial pheochromocytoma, or multiple endocrine neoplasia type IIA (Brauckhoff et al, 2004, Sackett and Bambach, 2003). Aldosteronomas have been removed laparoscopically (Sasagawa et al, 2000; Jeschke et al, 2003).

Partial adrenalectomy is usually performed with an endoscopic stapler. Dividing the adrenal vein does not affect viability of the adrenal gland, so it can be taken with the mass. However, Sasagawa and colleagues (2000) described a technique using the ultrasonic scalpel. Intraoperative ultrasonography can help identify the mass to facilitate surgery (Pautler et al, 2002).

## NONSURGICAL ALTERNATIVES
## Radiofrequency Ablation

Radiofrequency ablation has been used successfully to treat adrenal lesions, primarily adrenal metastases (Rohde et al, 2003) or metastases of adrenal cortical carcinoma (Abraham et al, 2003; Wood et al, 2003) and malignant pheochromocytoma. In the largest series to date, Mayo-Smith and Dupuy (2004) described performing 13 procedures on 12 patients without incident. These procedures can be safely and comfortably employed on an outpatient or overnight-stay basis. However, life-threatening hypertension has been reported in one case of adrenal ablation (Chini et al, 2004). The lesion may have been a pheochromocytoma. Unfortunately, no pathologic examination or preoperative workup for vasoactive adrenal masses was performed. Presumably, **catecholamine release can be caused by thermal injury to the adrenal in the absence of pheochromocytoma.** Onik and colleagues (2003) described their experience with two cases of hypertensive crisis in patients undergoing hepatic radiofrequency ablation. Both cases involved radiofrequency ablation of the posterior right lobe of the liver, close to the right adrenal. In one patient in whom catecholamine levels were measured, the values were 10-fold greater than the upper limit of normal.

## Cryoablation

The clinical experience with cryoablation is fairly limited (Munver and Sosa, 2004). Canine experiments have confirmed that cryotherapy can be delivered to the adrenal gland effectively (Schulsinger et al, 1999). Furthermore, the ability to observe the ice ball under ultrasound examination in a live dynamic fashion allows it to be applied in a controlled, reproducible fashion.

SECTION XIII

## KEY POINTS: SURGERY OF THE ADRENAL GLANDS

■ Laparoscopic adrenalectomy is the current standard of care for adrenal lesions with the exception of invasive adrenocortical carcinoma or adrenocortical carcinoma with caval thrombus.

■ Preoperative computed tomography can help distinguish invasive from noninvasive adrenocortical carcinoma.

■ Percutaneous ablative technologies are an increasingly attractive alternative to surgery for small incidental masses.

■ If you suspect pheochromocytoma, avoid percutaneous ablation because of the risk for catecholamine release.

■ Open adrenal surgery is reserved for lesions not amenable to minimally invasive techniques (i.e., invasive, large carcinomas, or carcinoma with caval involvement).

■ When operating on patients for large invasive adrenocortical carcinoma, be sure to obtain consent for possible en bloc resection of adjacent organs.

## ACKNOWLEDGMENT

Special thanks to Dr. E. Darracott Vaughan for permission to use tables published in previous chapters on adrenal surgery.

## SUGGESTED READINGS

Brunt LM: The positive impact of laparoscopic adrenalectomy on complications of adrenal surgery. Surg Endosc 2002;16:252-257.

Gill IS: The case for laparoscopic adrenalectomy. J Urol 2001;166:429-436.

Hamilton BD: Laparoscopic adrenalectomy: Transperitoneal and retroperitoneal approaches. In Bishoff JT, Kavoussi LR, eds: Atlas of Laparoscopic Retroperitoneal Surgery. Philadelphia, WB Saunders, 2000:191-208.

Jossart GH, Burpee SE, Gagner M: Surgery of the adrenal glands. Endocrinol Metab Clin North Am 2000;29:57-67.

Lal G, Duh QY: Laparoscopic adrenalectomy: Indications and technique. Surg Oncol 2003;12:105-123.

Vaughan ED: Surgical options for open adrenalectomy. World J Urol 1999;17:40-47.

Vaughan ED: Complications of adrenal surgery. In Taneja SS, Smith RB, Ehrlich RM, eds: Complications of Urologic Surgery: Prevention and Management, 3rd ed. Philadelphia, WB Saunders, 2001:362-369.

Welbourn RB: The History of Endocrine Surgery. New York, Praeger, 1990.

Winfield HN, Hamilton BD, Bravo EL: Technique of laparoscopic adrenalectomy. Urol Clin North Am 1997;24:459-465.

# INDEX

Note: Page numbers followed by the letter f refer to figures; those followed by t refer to tables.

## A

ABCDE mnemonic, in renal injury, 1274
Abdomen
  access to, in robotic-assisted laparoscopic radical prostatectomy, 2988-2989
  ecchymosis of, after laparoscopic surgery, 217
  laparoscopic exit from
    complications in, 216
    in robotic-assisted laparoscopic radical prostatectomy, 2996
    port removal in, 197-198
    port site closure in, 198, 198f
    skin closure in, 198
  molluscum contagiosum affecting, 382f
Abdominal aorta. *See* Aorta, abdominal.
Abdominal incisions, in renal surgery, 1695-1698, 1697f-1701f
Abdominal injury, in children, radiographic and endoscopic assessment of, 3930-3932
Abdominal leak point pressure
  definition of, 2005
  in incontinence, 2066, 2066f
  testing for, 2006, 2006f
Abdominal mass
  in bilateral renal ectopia, 3279, 3280f
  in children
    cystic and solid, 3208
    evaluation of, 3199, 3203t
  in neonate, 3195, 3195t
Abdominal pain
  in children
    evaluation of, 3199, 3202t
    features of, 3207, 3207t
    ureteropelvic junction obstruction and, in children, 3363, 3364f
Abdominal pressure, increased, incontinence during, 1975-1976
Abdominal radiography. *See* Radiography.
Abdominal repair, for lateral and combined defects, in vaginal wall prolapse, 2218-2219, 2218t
Abdominal stoma, in intestinal segments, 2551-2553
  complications of, 2553-2554
  flush, 2552
  loop end ileostomy as, 2553, 2553f
  nipple "rosebud," 2552, 2552f
Abdominal ultrasonography. *See* Ultrasonography.
Abdominal wall
  anterior, 38, 40-43
    inguinal canal of, 43, 43f, 44f
    internal surface of, 43, 45f
    muscles of, 40, 41f, 42f
    skin of, 38
    subcutaneous fascia of, 38, 40, 40f, 41f
  defects of
    in bladder exstrophy, 3503
      closure of, 3510, 3511f-3512f, 3513
    in prune-belly syndrome, 3486, 3486f
    reconstruction of, 3493

Abdominal wall *(Continued)*
  posterior, 3-9
    iliacus muscles of, 9, 9f, 9t
    lateral flank muscles of, 8-9, 9t, 10f
    lower rib cage of, 9, 11f
    lumbodorsal fascia of, 3, 8, 8f
    posterior muscles of, 3, 6f-9f, 8-9, 9t
    psoas muscles of, 9, 9f, 9t
Abdominoscrotal hydrocele, 3789
Ablative procedures. *See also specific therapy, e.g., Radiofrequency ablation.*
  for renal tumors, 1810-1818. *See also* Renal tumor(s), ablative therapy for.
  for varicocele, 3796
    outcome of, 3797t
  laparoscopic, 1804-1807
  rationale for, 1810-1811
  success of, 1811
  thermal, for localized renal cell carcinoma, 1616-1618, 1617t
  valvular, in management of posterior urethral valves, 3591, 3592f
ABO blood group(s), in renal transplantation, 1314
  screening of, 1308
ABO blood group antigen(s), influence of, on urinary tract infections, 3237
Abrams-Griffiths nomogram, for outflow obstruction, 1998
Abscess
  perinephric, 276-278, 277f, 278f
    after injury, 1282
    *Candida* causing, 462
    in children, 3246
  periurethral, 302
  prostatic, 325
    *Candida* causing, 460, 462f
  renal, 273-276, 275f
    drainage of, in tuberculosis, 445
    in children, 3246
  seminal vesicle, 1114-1115
  tubo-ovarian, ureteral obstruction due to, 1220
Absence of voiding. *See also* Voiding *entries.*
  in neonate, 3196
Absorbent products, for bladder filling/storage disorders, 2298
Absorptive hypercalciuria, 1374-1375, 1401-1402
  management of, 1416-1419
    drug guidelines in, 1418
Abuse. *See specific type, e.g., Sexual abuse.*
Accessory sex gland(s). *See* Sex accessory gland(s).
ACE. *See* Angiotensin-converting enzyme (ACE) *entries.*
Acellular matrices
  allogeneic, for bladder regeneration, 560
  for tissue engineering, 555-556, 556f
Acetaminophen, for fever, in children, 3206
Acetohydroxamic acid, for infection lithiasis, 1426

*N*-Acetyl-β-D-glucosaminidase, in ureteropelvic junction obstruction, measurement of, 3369
Acetylcholine
  in penile erection, 728, 729
  in ureteral function, 1904
Acetyl-L-carnitine, for Peyronie's disease, 827
*N*-Acetyltransferase, in bladder cancer, 2414
Acid-base balance, 1151-1152
  changes of pH in, 1152
  disorders of, 1152-1154
  in neonate, 3152
  maintenance of pH in, 1151
  with pneumoperitoneum, 200-201, 201-202
Acidemia, 1152
Acidosis, 1152
  metabolic, 1153, 1153t
    after augmentation cystoplasty, 3681-3682
  renal tubular, 1153-1154
  respiratory, 1154
Acne inversa (hidradenitis suppurativa), of male genitalia, 422-423, 422f
Acoustic energy, ultrasound focusing, for prostate cancer, 2945
Acquired immunodeficiency syndrome (AIDS). *See also* Human immunodeficiency virus (HIV) infection.
  definition of, 386
  developed world perspective on, 386-387
  epidemic of
    dynamics of, 387-388, 387t
    global, 387t
  epidemiology of, 386-388
  Fournier's gangrene in, 397
  genitourinary infectious manifestations of, 396-397
  Kaposi's sarcoma in, 398-399, 428, 429f, 962, 963
  non-Hodgkin's lymphoma in, 399
  overt, 391
  prostatic cryptococcosis in, 465, 466f
  renal tuberculosis in, 396
  seborrheic dermatitis in, 415
  squamous genital cancers in, 399
  testicular cancer in, 399-400
  urogenital viral infections in, 394-396, 395f
  voiding dysfunction in, 397, 2036
  worldwide perspective on, 386, 387t
Acrochordons (skin tags), 431, 433
Acrosome reaction, in male infertility, 631
ACTH. *See* Adrenocorticotropic hormone (ACTH) *entries.*
Actin, of smooth muscle, 1891
Action potential, of ureteral smooth muscle, 1892-1895, 1894f, 1895f
Active surveillance, of prostate cancer, 2933-2934
  factors predicting progression in, 2954-2955
  vs. watchful waiting, 2947-2948, 2948t
  with selective definitive therapy, 2951-2955
    outcomes of, 2951-2954, 2953f, 2953t

Activities of daily living, interference with, in benign prostatic hyperplasia, 2742
Activity product ratio, 1367
Acupuncture
    for erectile dysfunction, 770t
    for painful bladder syndrome/interstitial cystitis, 365
    for prostatitis, 324
    for urethral sphincter dysfunction, in children, 3619
    for voiding dysfunction, 2288-2289
    mechanism of action of, 2289
Acute lymphoblastic leukemia. See also Leukemia.
    in children, renal stones associated with, 3224
Acute tubular necrosis
    ATP depletion in, 1330-1331, 1332f
    hemodynamic abnormalities in, 1332
    in acute renal failure, 1329-1332
    incidence and etiology of, 1329-1330, 1329t
    natural history of, 1330
    pathophysiology of, 1330-1332, 1331f-1333f
    prevention of, 1339-1341
    prognosis of, 1339, 1340f
    sublethal injury in, 1331-1332, 1333f
Acyclovir, for herpes simplex virus infection, 374t
    in HIV patients, 394t
Aδ fibers
    of bladder, 2080
    of lower urinary tract, 1938-1939, 1939t
ADAM. See Androgen deficiency in aging male (ADAM) entries.
Addison's disease, 1843
    signs and symptoms of, 1845t
    test for, 1844-1845
    treatment of, 1845, 1846t
Adenitis
    of Skene's glands, 884
    vestibular, 870f, 885
Adenocarcinoma
    associated with urethral diverticula, 2389
    of bladder, 2422
    of prostate, 2875-2880
        Gleason grading of, 2876, 2877f
        location of, 2875
        needle biopsy of, 2878-2879, 2878t
        pathology of, 2875-2880
        radical prostatectomy specimens of, assessment of, 2879-2880
        subtypes of, 2880-2882
        transurethral resection for, 2879
        treatment effect and, 2880
        tumor spread in, 2875
        tumor volume in, 2875
    of seminal vesicles, 1116
    of testis, 929, 932t
    of upper urinary tract, abnormal urothelium in, 1643
Adenofibroma, metanephric, in children, 3899
Adenoma
    adrenal, 1840-1841, 1841f
        in children, 3878
    aldosterone-producing, treatment of, 1856-1857
    metanephric, 1576, 1576f
    nephrogenic
        in children, 3581-3582
        of bladder, 2418
        treatment of, 3883
        within urethral diverticula, 2389
    papillary, of seminal vesicles, 1116
    renal, 1575-1576, 1576f

Adenoma (Continued)
    in acquired renal cystic disease, 3352-3353
    malignant transformation of, 3353
Adenoma sebaceum lesions, in tuberous sclerosis, 3329
Adenomatoid tumor
    of epididymitis, excision of, 1105
    of testicular adnexa, 931-933, 932t
    of testis, 930
Adenosine, in male sexual function, 732
Adenosine monophosphate (AMP), cyclic
    in bladder smooth muscle relaxation, 1954
    in penile smooth muscle relaxation, 732
    in ureteral smooth muscle relaxation, 1900, 1900f
Adenosine triphosphate (ATP)
    action of, on purinergic nerves, 1951-1952
    depletion of, in acute tubular necrosis, 1330-1331, 1332f
Adenosquamous carcinoma, of penis, 990
Adenovirus, in acute hemorrhagic cystitis, 3263
Adenylyl cyclase, in male sexual function, 734
ADH. See Antidiuretic hormone (ADH).
Adhesion(s)
    in renal cell carcinoma, 1591
    of labia minora, 3210, 3841-3842, 3842f
        outpatient lysis of, 3215, 3215f
    penile, after circumcision, 3748
Adhesion molecules. See Cell adhesion molecule(s).
Adjunctive therapy, cryotherapy with, for prostate cancer, 3049
Adjuvant chemotherapy. See Chemotherapy, adjuvant.
Adolescents. See also Children.
    acute scrotum in, 3790-3794. See also Scrotum, acute.
    bladder cancer in, 2409
    female, perineal examination in, 3209, 3209f
    renal calculi in, 1427
    ureteral or vaginal anomalies in, 3203
    urinary tract infections in
        diagnosis of, 3243
        sexual activity associated with, 3240
Adoptive cell therapy
    for melanoma, 499
    for renal cell carcinoma, 499
ADPKD1 gene, 1346
Adrenal adenoma, 1840-1841, 1841f
    in children, 3878
Adrenal artery, 20, 23f, 24
Adrenal carcinoma
    adrenalectomy for, 1870t, 1871. See also Adrenalectomy.
    aldosterone-secreting, 1847-1848
    clinical features of, 1837-1838, 1837t
    functional tumors associated with, 1841-1842
    in children, 1842
    management of, 1842-1843
    metastatic, 1840, 1840f
    Weiss criteria of, 1841t
Adrenal cortex
    development of, 1823-1824
    hormones of
        action of, 1827-1828, 1828t
        metabolism of, 1827f, 1828
        regulation of release of, 1825-1827, 1826f, 1827f
    hyperfunction of, 1821
    physiology of, 1824-1828, 1825f
Adrenal crisis
    symptoms of, 1843-1844
    treatment of, 1845t
Adrenal cysts, 1843, 1844f

Adrenal gland(s), 19-22, 21f-22f, 24
    anatomic relationships of, 20
    anatomy, embryology, and histology of, 1822-1824, 1822f-1824f
    arterial supply to, 20, 23f, 24
    atrophy of, 1843
    blood supply to, 1822-1823, 1823f
    composition of, 20, 23f
    computed tomography of, 132, 133f
    cortex of. See Adrenal cortex.
    disorders of, 1830-1867. See also specific disorder, e.g., Cushing's syndrome.
    dissection of, 21f-22f
    historical background of, 1821-1822
    magnetic resonance imaging of, 135, 137f
    mass in. See also Adrenal tumor(s); specific tumor.
        incidentally found, 1838-1839, 1838f, 1839t
    medulla of. See Adrenal medulla.
    physiology of, 1824-1830
    surgical anatomy of, 1869, 1869f
    ultrasonography of, 122, 124f
    venous drainage of, 23f, 24
Adrenal hemorrhage, in neonates, 3196-3197
Adrenal hyperplasia
    bilateral, treatment of, 1856
    congenital, 3816-3820, 3817f, 3818f
        androgen excess in, 636-637
        emergent evaluation of, 3199
        11β-hydroxylase deficiency in, 3819
        21-hydroxylase steroid deficiency in, 3816-3819, 3817f, 3818f
        in non–salt-losing male, 3818
        male infertility secondary to, 619
        nonclassic form of, 3819
        prenatal diagnosis of, 3819
        salt-losing variant of, 3817
        simple virilizing form of, 3817, 3818f
        treatment of, 3820
            prenatal, 3819-3820
Adrenal insufficiency, 1843-1846
    selective, 1845-1846
    signs and symptoms of, 1843, 1845f
    treatment of, 1845, 1845t
Adrenal medulla
    catecholamines of
        actions of, 1829-1830, 1829t
        metabolism of, 1829, 1830f
    development of, 1824
    physiology of, 1828-1830, 1829t, 1830f
Adrenal surgery, 1868-1888. See also Adrenalectomy.
    anatomy pertinent to, 1869, 1869f
    flank approach to, 1871-1873, 1872f, 1873f
    intraoperative ultrasonography in, 1884
    nonsurgical alternatives to, 1887
    postoperative management in, 1884
    preoperative management in, 1871, 1871t
Adrenal tumor(s)
    adenoma as, 1840-1841, 1841f
    aldosterone-secreting, 1842
    carcinoma as, 1837-1838, 1837t
        in children, 1842
        management of, 1842-1843
    Cushing's syndrome and, 1841
    cysts as, 1843, 1844f
    estrogen-secreting, 1842
    in hyperaldosteronism, age distribution of, 1850t
    incidentally discovered, 1838-1839, 1838f, 1839t
    maternal, virilizing effects of, 3820-3821
    metastatic, 1840, 1840f
    myelolipoma as, 1839-1840, 1840f

Adrenal tumor(s) *(Continued)*
  oncocytoma as, 1843
  pheochromocytoma as. *See*
    Pheochromocytoma.
  testicular, 929-930
  testosterone-secreting, 1841-1842
Adrenal vein, 11f, 14, 23f, 24
  bleeding from, in radical nephrectomy, 1711
Adrenal vein sampling, in primary
    hyperaldosteronism, 1853-1854
Adrenalectomy
  clinical indications for, 1869, 1870t
  complications of
    postoperative, 1886, 1886t
    surgical, 1885-1886, 1885t
  contraindications to, 1869-1870
  for adrenal carcinoma, 1870t, 1871
  for Cushing's syndrome, 1870t, 1871
  for pheochromocytoma, 1870t, 1871
  history of, 1868
  laparoscopic. *See* Laparoscopic adrenalectomy.
  nonsurgical alternatives to, 1887
  obesity and, 1870
  open, 1871-1876
    complications of, 1886-1887
    flank retroperitoneal approach to, 1871-
      1873, 1872f, 1873f
    for specific tumors, 1870t
    indications for, 1870
    lumbodorsal posterior approach to, 1873-
      1874, 1874f
    subcostal anterior approach to, 1874-1875,
      1876f
    thoracoabdominal approach to, 1875-1876,
      1876f, 1877f
  outcomes of, 1885
  partial, 1887
  past surgical history and, 1870
  postoperative management of, 1884
  preoperative management of, 1871
    errors in, 1871t
  prophylactic, for congenital adrenal
    hyperplasia, 3820
  surgical options for, 1870, 1870t
  tumor size and, 1870
Adrenaline, 1821
Adrenergic agonists, effect of, on ureteral
    function, 1905-1906
α-Adrenergic agonists
  causing geriatric incontinence, 2308, 2308t
  for stress incontinence, 2075
  uropharmacology of, 1952
β-Adrenergic agonists
  for urethral sphincter dysfunction, in
    children, 3620
  uropharmacology of, 1952
Adrenergic antagonists, effect of, on ureteral
    function, 1906
α-Adrenergic antagonists
  causing geriatric incontinence, 2308-2309,
    2308t
  for benign prostatic hyperplasia, 2777-2787
    adverse events associated with, 2786
    classification of, 2777-2777, 2778t
    coexisting hypertension and, 2786
    comparison of, 2786-2787
    dose response of, 2778
    effects of
      in elderly, 2786
      on acute urinary retention, 2785-2786
      on bladder outlet obstruction, 2785
    future of, 2787
    literature review of, 2779-2785
    rationale for, 2777

α-Adrenergic antagonists *(Continued)*
    recommended dosage of, 2778t
    study designs for, 2778
  for bladder outlet obstruction, 2318-2319
  for pheochromocytoma, preoperative, 1866,
    1871
  for prostatitis, 321, 325t
  for smooth sphincter dysfunction, 2118-2119
  for urethral sphincter dysfunction, in
    children, 3620
  prophylactic, for postoperative urinary
    retention, 2040-2041
  uropharmacology of, 1952-1953, 1953f
β-Adrenergic antagonists
  erectile dysfunction caused by, 743, 744t
  preoperative, for pheochromocytoma, 1866
  uropharmacology of, 1952
Adrenergic receptors
  α-, 1952
  β-, 1952
α-Adrenoceptor agonists
  combination, 2111
  for stress incontinence, 2109-2111
    nonselective, 2109-2111
    selective, 2111
β-Adrenoceptor agonists
  for overactive bladder/detrusor overactivity,
    2093t, 2103-2104
  for stress incontinence, 2112
Adrenoceptor antagonists, for erectile
    dysfunction, 778-779
α-Adrenoceptor antagonists
  erectile dysfunction caused by, 743, 744t
  for overactive bladder/detrusor overactivity,
    2093t, 2103
β-Adrenoceptor antagonists, for stress
    incontinence, 2111
Adrenocortical tumors, in children, 3878
Adrenocorticotropic hormone (ACTH)
  ectopic, in Cushing's syndrome, 1831t
  production of, 1825-1826
  secretion of, 578, 637
Adrenocorticotropic hormone (ACTH)
    syndrome, Cushing's disease and, 1836-
    1837, 1837f
Adrenoreceptors, action of, on spinal cord,
    1962-1963
Advancement techniques, of hypospadias repair,
    3722, 3723f
Advancement test, in laparoscopic surgery, 180,
    180f
Afferent pathways, in lower urinary tract, 1938-
    1939, 1938f, 1939t
AG-013736, for renal cell carcinoma, 1630, 1630t
Age. *See also* Geriatric patients.
  altered bladder sensation with, 1970
  androgen deficiency and, 850-862. *See also*
    Hypogonadism, late-onset.
  at time of hypospadias repair, 3718
  bladder cancer and, 2409
  bladder contractility and, 1969-1970
  detrusor overactivity and, 1969-1970
  effect of, on ureteral function, 1916-1917,
    1917f
  erectile dysfunction and, 746
  germ cell tumor incidence and, 899-900
  gestational
    fractional excretion of sodium and, 3150
    glomerular filtration rate and, 3151
    maximal renal caliceal diameter according
      to, 1220f
  hormones affected by, 856-857, 856t
    historical perspective on, 850-851
  incontinence and, 2189, 2305-2306, 2306f

Age *(Continued)*
  of hypothalamic-pituitary axis, in males, 580
  onset of hypertension and, 1167
  pediatric urinary tract infections and, 3236
  pelvic organ prolapse and, 2189
  physiologic vs. chronologic, in orthotopic
    urinary diversion, 2616
  postpyelonephritic scarring and, 4338
  prostate cancer diagnosis and, 2856
  prostate cancer screening and
    discontinuation of, 2925-2926
    start of, 2924-2925
  renal calculi and, 1364
  vesicoureteral reflux and, 4324, 4325t
  voiding dysfunction and, 2043
Agenesis
  bladder, antenatal detection of, 3575
  of seminal vesicles, 1113-1114, 1114f
  of vas deferens, 3797-3798
  penile, 3756-3757, 3757f
    in bilateral renal agenesis, 3271
  renal, 3269-3276. *See also* Renal agenesis.
  sacral, 3644-3645, 3645f-3647f, 3647
  vaginal, 3833-3839. *See also* Vaginal agenesis.
Aging Male Survey (AMS), of late-onset
    hypogonadism, 853, 854f
*AGTR2* gene, in vesicoureteral reflux, 4326
AIDS. *See* Acquired immunodeficiency
    syndrome (AIDS).
Albendazole
  for filariasis, 457
  for hydatid disease, 459
Alcock's canal, 71
Alcohol
  consumption of
    benign prostatic hyperplasia and, 2745
    erectile dysfunction caused by, 746
    male infertility and, 645
    patient history of, 88-89
    priapism associated with, 841
    prostate cancer associated with, 2863
  intraspinal injections of, for painful bladder
    syndrome/interstitial cystitis, 366
Aldosterone
  metabolism of, 1828
  secretion of
    in adrenal carcinoma, 1847-1848
    physiologic control of, 1826-1827, 1827f
Aldosterone:cortisol ratio, in primary
    hyperaldosteronism, 1854
Aldosterone-producing adenoma, treatment of,
    1856-1857
Aldosterone:renin ratio, in primary
    hyperaldosteronism, 1851-1852, 1854
Aldosterone-secreting adrenal tumor, 1842
Aldosteronism, glucocorticoid-remediable, 1848-
    1849
  diagnostic tests for, 1849
Alfuzosin
  for benign prostatic hyperplasia, 2784-2785
    dosage of, 2778t, 2785
    efficacy of, 2785t
  for prostatitis, 321, 327t
  uropharmacology of, 2119
  vs. other α-adrenergic blockers, 2787
Alginate, for tissue engineering, 555
Alkalemia, 1152
Alkalosis, 1152
  after augmentation cystoplasty, 3682
    in children, 3682
  metabolic, 1153, 1153t, 1154, 1154t
  renal tubular, 1153-1154
  respiratory, 1154
Allantois, embryology of, 3573

Allergen(s), associated with contact dermatitis, 408, 409f
Allergic dermatitis
  contact, 408-409, 409f
  of male genitalia, 407-410, 407f, 407t, 409f, 410f
Allergy(ies)
  painful bladder syndrome/interstitial cystitis and, 335-336
  patient history of, 89
Alloantigen(s), recognition of, in immune response, 481
Allograft(s). See also Graft(s).
  for slings, 2238
    outcome of, 2248t
  in vaginal prolapse surgery, 2216
Allopurinol
  for calcium oxalate nephrolithiasis, 1420
  for gouty diathesis, 1424
  for prostatitis, 323
Alpha-fetoprotein, in testicular tumors, 906
Alprostadil, for erectile dysfunction
  combination therapy with, 780
  intracavernous injection of, 779-780
  intraurethral, 781
Alprox-TD gel, for erectile dysfunction, 781-782
Alström's syndrome, 3327
Alternative therapies, for erectile dysfunction, 770t
Alveolar rhabdomyosarcoma, 3879
Ambiguous genitalia. See also Hermaphroditism; Pseudohermaphroditism.
  evaluation and management of, 3827-3829, 3828f
Ambulatory urodynamic monitoring, 2008. See also Urodynamic evaluation.
  applications of, 2008-2009
  of incontinent patient, 2009, 2069
  of urethral sphincter dysfunction, in children, 3617-3618, 3617f, 3618f
Amebiasis, 459
Amenorrhea, in 46,XY complete gonadal dysgenesis, 3813
American Association for Surgery of Trauma Organ Injury Severity Scale, for kidney, 1275t, 1282t
American Joint Committee on Cancer (AJCC) staging
  of germ cell tumors, 904, 905t
  of penile cancer, 971-972, 971t
American Society for Therapeutic Radiology and Oncology (ASTRO) definition, of biochemical failure, 3011, 3023, 3071
  adherence to
  in post-radiation therapy prostate cancer, 3011-3012
American Urological Association (AUA) symptom index, 85
Amikacin, for pediatric urinary tract infections, 3248t
Amiloride, with thiazide, for hypercalciuria, 1418
Amine precursor uptake and decarboxylation (APUD) cells, in pheochromocytoma, 1857, 1860-1861, 1861f
Amino acids
  excretion of, in neonate, 3156
  inhibitory, uropharmacology of, 1962
  renal reabsorption of, in proximal convoluted tubules, 1140
γ-Aminobutyric acid. See Gamma-aminobutyric acid.
Aminoglutethimide, for prostate cancer, 3088

Aminoglycosides, for urinary tract infections, 245t, 246t, 247t, 248, 248f, 249f
  in children, 3248t
Aminopenicillins, for urinary tract infections, 245t, 246t, 248
Amitriptyline
  effect of, on ureteral function, 1920
  for painful bladder syndrome/interstitial cystitis, 359-360, 360t
Ammoniagenic coma, conduit urinary diversion causing, 2573
Ammonium acid urate calculi, 1387-1388
  management of, 1426-1427
Amniotic fluid, assessment of, 3178
Amoxicillin
  for urinary tract infections, 245t, 246t, 248
  prophylactic
    for pediatric urinary tract infections, 3250t
    prior to pediatric genitourinary procedures, 3242t
Amoxicillin/clavulanate, for pediatric urinary tract infections, 3248t
AMP. See Adenosine monophosphate (AMP).
Amphotericin B, 468-469
  cost of, 464t
  dosage of, 461t
  for funguria, 299, 300
Ampicillin
  for urinary tract infections, 245t, 246t, 248
    in children, 3248t
  prophylactic, prior to pediatric genitourinary procedures, 3242t
Amplatz dilator and sheath set, 1542, 1542f
Amplatz dilator system, technique of, 166, 167f
Ampulla, of ureteric bud, 3130
Amputation, of penis, 1050-1052, 1051f, 2651
  cancer and, 973-974. See also Penectomy.
  during circumcision, 1045
AMS. See Aging Male Survey (AMS).
AMS Ambicor two-piece inflatable penile prosthesis, 788, 789f, 789t
AMS Ultrex three-piece inflatable penile prosthesis, 788, 789f, 789t
  implantation of, transverse penoscrotal approach to, 790-795, 791f-795f
Amyloid, of seminal vesicles, 1116
Amyloidosis, 1042
Anabolic steroids, abuse of, 611
Anaerobes, in urinary tract, 228
Anal. See also Anus.
Anal cancer, human papillomavirus causing, 380-381
Anal folds, 3141, 3142f
Anal incontinence. See Fecal incontinence.
Anal sphincter, examination of, 2207
Anal triangle, 68
  blood supply to, 69, 70f
Analgesia/analgesics
  abuse of, bladder cancer associated with, 2415
  effect of, on ureteral function, 1919
  for hypospadias repair, 3718
  for painful bladder syndrome/interstitial cystitis, 361-362
  for TRUS-guided prostate biopsy, 2889
  urothelial tumors associated with, 1639
  vanilloid-induced, mechanisms of, 1959
Anaphase, in mitosis, 2712
Anaphylatoxins, C3 and C5 as, 474, 474f
Anaplastic seminoma, 895
Anastomosis
  bladder neck, in radical retropubic prostatectomy, 2971-2972, 2971f, 2972f
  in vasectomy reversal, preparation of vas deferens in, 667-669, 668f, 669f

Anastomosis (Continued)
  in vasoepididymostomy
    end-to-end technique of, 683, 683f-685f
    end-to-side technique of, 683-684, 687f-693f, 690
    intussusception technique of, 690, 692-694, 694f-698f
    two-suture modification in, 693-694, 697f-698f
    methods of, 683-684, 690, 692-694
    side-to-side technique of, 679, 680f
  intestinal. See Intestinal anastomosis.
  microvascular, in penile revascularization, 809-810, 809f, 810f
    mechanical disruption of, 810-811
  small bowel, 2557-2561
    Bricker technique of, 2557, 2557f
    hammock, 2559
    Le Duc technique of, 2559, 2559f
    split-nipple technique of, 2558-2559, 2559f
    tunneled, 2558, 2558f
    Wallace technique of, 2557-2558, 2558f
  tissue, in laparoscopy, 193-194
  ureteral, in Politano-Leadbetter procedure, 4352
  ureteroenteric, stricture formation at, 43-46. See also Ureteroenteric stricture, anastomotic.
  ureterointestinal, 2554-2563. See also Ureterointestinal anastomosis.
  vascular, in renal transplantation, 1310, 1311f, 1312
  vesicourethral
    in radical perineal prostatectomy, 2982-2983, 2982f
    in robotic-assisted laparoscopic radical prostatectomy, 2995-2996, 2997f
Anastomotic strictures, after robotic-assisted laparoscopic radical prostatectomy, 3000-3001
Anderson-Hynes dismembered pyeloplasty, of ureteropelvic junction obstruction, in children, 3373-3374, 3373f, 3374f
Androblastoma, testicular, 927-928
Androgen(s). See also Antiandrogen(s); Dihydrotestosterone; Testosterone.
  action of, 852-853
    abnormal, in male infertility, 638
    role of nuclear matrix in, 2703-2705
  adrenal, 2686t, 2687f, 2688
  and female sexual dysfunction, in postmenopausal women, 880-881
  deficiency of
    definitions of, 850
    historical perspective on, 850-851
    in aging male, 850-862. See also Hypogonadism, late-onset.
  excess of, male infertility and, 636-637
  for infertility, 647
  for micropenis, 3753
  in aging male
    deficiency of, 850-862. See also Hypogonadism, late-onset.
    production of, 851
  in benign prostatic hyperplasia, role of, 2728-2730, 2729f
  in brain, 853
  in male infertility
    abnormal action of, 638
    excess of, 636-637
  in prostate cancer, influence of, 2860-2861, 2863-2864
  in prostate development, 3138-3139

Androgen(s) (*Continued*)
in regulation of prostate growth, at cellular level, 2690-2691, 2691f
in regulation of stromal-epithelial interactions, 2693-2694
in testicular descent, 3766-3767
influencing PSA expression, 2915
maternal administration of, 3820-3821
normal physiology of, 3804, 3805f
replacement therapy with
before hypospadias repair, 3711
for Kallmann's syndrome, 635
for testicular dysfunction, 569
in erectile dysfunction
adequacy of, 772-773
potential adverse effects of, 773
sources of, 3084-3085, 3085t
ablation of, 3085
stimulation with, before hypospadias repair, 3711
supplementation with, before hypospadias repair, 3711
synthesis of, inhibition of, 3088
testicular production of, 2685-2686, 2686t, 2687f
uropharmacology of, 1956
within prostate, metabolism of, 2691-2693, 2692f
Androgen axis blockade. *See also* Androgen deprivation therapy.
mechanisms of, 3085-3088, 3085t, 3087t
response to, 3088-3089
Androgen deficiency in aging male (ADAM), 850
Androgen deficiency in aging male (ADAM) questionnaire, for late-onset hypogonadism, 853, 854t
Androgen deprivation therapy
current forms of, 3083-3084, 3084f
for prostate cancer
combined hormone therapy with, 3092-3095, 3094f, 3095f
complications of, 3089-3091
costs of, 3099
immediate vs. delayed
in localized disease, 3096
in locally advanced or asymptomatic metastatic disease, 3097-3098, 3097f
in lymph node metastatic disease, 3096-3097, 3096f
integration of data in, 3098, 3098f
intermittent, 3099
locally advanced
adjuvant
after radiation therapy, 3064-3065
after radical prostatectomy, 3062-3063, 3063t
intermittent, 3066
neoadjuvant
before radiation therapy, 3063-3064
before radical prostatectomy, 3059-3060, 3059t, 3060t
quality of life after, 3066-3067
timing of, 3065-3066
radiation therapy with, 3091-3092, 3093f, 3093t
radical prostatectomy with, 3091, 3092f, 3092t
response in, 3088-3089
timing of, 3095-3098
therapeutic approaches to, 3085t
Androgen insensitivity syndrome, 638
complete, 3823-3824

Androgen receptor(s)
activation of, 852
mechanism of, 2697, 2698f
CAG repeat lengths of, 852
chaparonin binding by, 2698
defects of, 3823-3825
dimerization of, 2699
DNA-binding domain of, 2698-2699
in benign prostatic hyperplasia, 2729
in initiation and progression of prostate cancer, 2865
in regulation of prostate growth, 2697-2701, 2697f, 2698f
ligand-binding domain of, 2699
nuclear localization of, 2700
post-translational modification of, 2699-2700
selective modulators of, for late-onset hypogonadism, 858
transcriptional activation domains of, 2700-2701, 2700t, 2701f
Androgen receptor co-activators, 2700t
Androgen receptor gene, 2697
Androgen receptor pathway–focused therapy, for prostate cancer, 3099
Androgen receptor protein, structure of, 2697, 2697f
Androgen receptor-dependent chromatin remodeling, in regulation of prostate growth, 2702-2703
Androgen resistance syndrome, partial, 3824-3825
Androgen suppression therapy
for benign prostatic hyperplasia, 2788-2793
classification of agents in, 2788, 2788t
in clinical practice, 2793
interpretation of studies of, 2788
literature review of, 2788-2793
rationale for, 2788
radiation therapy with, for prostate cancer
locally advanced, 3027-3028
node-positive disease, 3028
Androgen-binding proteins
plasma levels of, 2688-2689
Sertoli cell production of, 588-589
AndronGel, for erectile dysfunction, 772
Androstenedione, 2686t, 2687f, 2688
circulation of, 3084-3085, 3085t
Anejaculation, 87
definition of, 715
treatment of, 715-717, 716f
Anemia
androgen deprivation therapy causing, 3091
maternal, bacteriuria and, 291-292
pernicious, voiding dysfunction in, 2012t, 2030
Anesthesia
for circumcision, 3747
for hypospadias repair, 3718
for laparoscopic surgery, complications related to, 210-211
in children, 3917-3918
for open prostatectomy, 2847
for percutaneous nephrolithotomy, 1486
for pheochromocytoma, 1866-1867
drugs to avoid in, 1866t
for radical retropubic prostatectomy, 2959
for renal transplantation, 1309t
for robotic-assisted laparoscopic radical prostatectomy, 2986-2987
for shockwave lithotripsy, 1469, 1472
for tension-free vaginal tape procedures, 2258
for transurethral resection of prostate, 2831
for ureteroscopy, 1501
for vasectomy reversal, 667

Anesthesia (*Continued*)
local
for open testicular biopsy, 655, 655f, 656f
for vasectomy, 1099
for vasectomy reversal, 667
priapism associated with, 840
Anesthetics, topical, for premature ejaculation, 786, 786t
Aneurysm(s). *See also* Pseudoaneurysm(s).
abdominal aortic
as contraindication to laparoscopy, 175
ureteral obstruction due to, 1221, 1222f
berry, in autosomal dominant polycystic kidney disease, 3321
iliac artery
as contraindication to laparoscopy, 175
ureteral obstruction due to, 1222-1223, 1222f
renal artery, 1187, 1188f, 1189, 3296-3297
after renal bypass surgery, 1751-1752, 1752f
dissecting, 1187, 1188f
fusiform, 1187, 1188f
intrarenal, 1187, 1188f
saccular, 1187, 1188f
Angiogenesis
activators of, 542-543
in cancer, 542-545
in hormone-refractory prostate cancer, 3117
in renal cell carcinoma, 1589-1590, 1589f
inhibitors of, 543-545
for neuroblastoma, 3877
steps in, 556-557
Angiography
computed tomographic. *See* Computed tomography (CT) angiography.
contrast, of renovascular hypertension, 1172-1173
magnetic resonance. *See* Magnetic resonance angiography (MRA).
of donor arteries, in penile vascular reconstruction, 803-804, 805f
of genitourinary tuberculosis, 443
of renal angiomyolipoma, 1578, 1579f
of renal injury, in children, 3931
of tumor involvement of inferior vena cava, 1620-1621, 1620f
penile
in priapism, 845
pharmacologic, 760-761, 761f
Angiokeratoma of Fordyce, 430-431, 432f
Angiomyolipoma, renal, 1578-1580, 1579f, 3331
in children, 3899-3900, 3900f
Angioplasty, percutaneous transluminal. *See* Percutaneous transluminal angioplasty (PTA).
Angiosarcoma, of bladder, 2445
Angiotensin, effect of, on ureteral function, 1919
Angiotensin II
adrenal effects of, 1163
effect of, on glomerular circulation, 1163
in initiation of fibrosis, 1204
in renal hemodynamics, 1134
in renin-angiotensin-aldosterone system, 1162-1163
receptors for, 1163-1164
medullary effects of, 1163
tubular effects of, 1163
vascular effects of, 1163
vasoconstrictor effects of, 1326
Angiotensin receptor blockers, renal protection with, 1350
Angiotensin-converting enzyme (ACE)
in kidney development, 3135
in renin-angiotensin-aldosterone system, 1162

Angiotensin-converting enzyme (ACE) gene polymorphisms, implication of, in renal scarring, 3238
Angiotensin-converting enzyme (ACE) inhibitors
    abnormal renal structure and function due to, 3135
    causing geriatric incontinence, 2308t, 2309
    erectile dysfunction caused by, 743, 744t
    for glomerulopathy, after partial nephrectomy, 1613-1614
    renal protection with, 1350
Angiotensinogen, in renin-angiotensin-aldosterone system, 1161
Animal bites, to penis, 2650
    in children, 3945
Animal models, painful bladder syndrome/interstitial cystitis in, 337-338, 338f
Anion(s), transport of, effect of ureteral obstruction on, 1202-1203
Anion gap
    definition of, 1153, 3154
    normal, 1153t
    urinary, 3155
Anogenital cancer, HPV-related, in AIDS patients, 399
Anorchia, bilateral (vanishing testis syndrome), 640
Anorectal malformations
    in bladder exstrophy, 3503
    Wingspread classification of, 3647t
Anorgasmia, 87
Antegrade Continence Enema (ACE) procedure, for fecal continence, in myelomeningocele, 3640
Antegrade continence enemas, in children, 3700-3701, 3700f
Antegrade pyelography. See Pyelography, antegrade.
Anthracyclines, causing congestive heart failure, in children, 3898
Antiandrogen(s)
    androgen blockade with, 3085-3087, 3085t
    erectile dysfunction caused by, 745
    for priapism, 846t
    nonsteroidal, 3086
Antiandrogen withdrawal phenomenon, 3086
Antiangiogenic agents, for renal cell carcinoma, 1590
Antibiotics
    as inhibitors of angiogenesis, 543
    causing interstitial cystitis, 338-339
    effect of, on ureteral function, 1920
    for acute pyelonephritis, 269-270, 270t
    for bacteriuria, in pregnancy, 292-293, 292t
    for cystitis, 256-257, 256t
    for human and animal bite wounds, 2651
    for prostatitis, 318-321
        clinical trial data in, 318-320, 320t
        dosage of, 325t
        pharmacology and pharmacokinetics in, 318
        rationale in, 318
    for renal abscess, 276
    for urinary tract infections
        bacterial resistance to, 244-245
        choice of, 249
        duration of therapy and, 249
        formulary of, 245-249, 245t, 246t-247t
        in children, 3247-3249, 3248t
            dosages of, 3248t
            prophylactic, 3249-3252, 3250t
            selection of, 3249
        mechanism of action of, 245t

Antibiotics (Continued)
    principles of, 243-249, 244t
    prophylactic
        cystoscopy and, 252
        endocarditis risk and, 253-254, 254t
        endoscopic procedures and, 253
        indwelling orthopedic hardware and, 254, 254t
        low-dose, 262-265, 262t
        open and laparoscopic surgery and, 253, 253t
        post-intercourse, 265
        principles of, 250, 250t, 251t
        shockwave lithotripsy and, 252
        transrectal prostate biopsy and, 251-252, 2889
        transurethral procedures and, 252
        ureteroscopy and, 1514-1515
        urethral catheterization and, 250
        urodynamics and, 251
        urologic procedures and, 250-254, 251t
    for urodynamic studies, 1987
        prophylactic, 251
    in bowel preparation
        disadvantages of, 2539
        for urinary tract reconstruction, 2538-2539, 2538t
    intravenous, in hypospadias repair, 3718-3719
    low-dose prophylactic, for recurrent urinary tract infections, 262-265, 262t
        biologic basis in, 262-263
        efficacy of, 264
    perioperative
        for transurethral resection of prostate, 2831
        in vesicovaginal fistula repair, 2332
    post-intercourse prophylactic, for recurrent urinary tract infections, 265
    prophylactic, 225
        for bacteremia, 1515
        for bacterial endocarditis, 1515
        for pediatric urinary tract infections, 3249-3252, 3250t
        for percutaneous nephrolithotomy, 1485-1486
        for ureteroscopy, 253, 1514-1515
        for urodynamic studies, 251
        for vesicoureteral reflux, 4348, 4349t, 4350
    resistance of, to urinary tract infections, 3266-3267
    suppressive, 225
Antibody(ies). See also Immunoglobulin entries.
    antisperm. See Antisperm antibodies.
    monoclonal
        in tumor immunology, 500
        synthesis of, 478
    production of, 478
    structure and binding of, 478, 478f
Antibody assay(s), for HSV infection, 373-374
Anticholinergics
    affecting lower urinary tract function, 3628t
    causing geriatric incontinence, 2308, 2308t
    for painful bladder syndrome/interstitial cystitis, 360t, 361
    uropharmacology of, 1950, 1950t
Anticholinesterase, effect of, on ureteral function, 1905
Antidepressants
    effect of, on ureteral function, 1920
    erectile dysfunction caused by, 745
    for incontinence, in elderly, 2317t
    for overactive bladder/detrusor overactivity, 2093t, 2104-2105
    for painful bladder syndrome/interstitial cystitis, 359-360, 360t

Antidepressants (Continued)
    for premature ejaculation
        on-demand, 786
        serotonergic, 785-786
    for stress incontinence, 2111-2112
    tricyclic
        erectile dysfunction caused by, 744
        for urethral sphincter dysfunction, in children, 3620
        uropharmacology of, 1962
Antidiuretic hormone (ADH)
    actions of, 1137, 1138f
    and renal development, 3159
    in renal hemodynamics, 1134
    release of, factors affecting, 1137-1138, 1137t
Antifungals, 468-469
    cost of, 464t
    dosage of, 461t
    topical
        for seborrheic dermatitis, 415
        for vulvovaginal candidiasis, 385
Antigen(s), 478. See also specific antigen.
    impaired presentation of, mechanism of tumor escape in, 497
    presentation of, in immune response, 480-481, 480f
    tumor-associated, 495-496, 496t
        in cancer vaccines, 499-500
Antigen detection kits, for HSV infection, 374
Antigenic markers, in bladder cancer, 2436
Antigen-presenting cell(s), 477
Antihistamines, for painful bladder syndrome/interstitial cystitis, 360, 360t
Antihypertensive agents, erectile dysfunction caused by, 743, 744t
Antilymphocyte antibodies, in immunosuppressive regimens, 1316-1317
Antimuscarinic agents
    for incontinence, 2071-2072, 2072t
    for overactive bladder/detrusor overactivity, 2093-2099, 2093t
    for urethral sphincter dysfunction, in children, 3620
    quaternary compounds, 2094
    selectivity of, 1951
    tertiary compounds, 2094
    uropharmacology of, 1950, 1950t
Antimuscarinic Clinical Effectiveness Trial (ACET), 2096
Antioxidants, for prostate cancer, chemopreventive, 2870-2871
Antiproliferative factor, in painful bladder syndrome/interstitial cystitis, 347-348, 347t, 348f, 353
Antipsychotics, erectile dysfunction caused by, 744
Antireflux mechanism
    functional anatomy of, 4327-4328, 4327f, 4328t
    incorporation of, in orthotopic urinary diversion, 2630-2633
Antireflux surgery, 4350-4360
    Cohen-Anderson technique of, 4356-4357, 4357f
    complications of
        early, 4360-4361
        long-term, 4361-4362
    cystoscopy in, 4351
    endoscopic, 4362-4366
        follow-up of, 4363-4364
        materials used in, 4364-4365, 4364t
        recurrence of reflux after, 4365-4366
        STING technique of, 4362-4363, 4363f

Antireflux surgery *(Continued)*
 extravesical procedures in, 4357, 4358f, 4359-4360
 Gil-Vernet procedure in, 4366
 Glenn-Anderson technique of, 4356, 4356f
 in children, 3661-3663
  peritoneoscopic, 3926-3927, 3927f
  single ureteral reimplantation as, 3661-3662
  transureteroureterostomy as, 3661-3662, 3661f
  with intestinal segments, 3662
  with psoas hitch, 3662, 3663f
 in exstrophy repair, 3524, 3525f-3526f, 3526
  postoperative care after, 3526
 incision in, 4351
 intravesical procedures in, 4352
 laparoscopic, 4366-4367
 Paquin technique of, 4352, 4356
 patient positioning for, 4351
 Politano-Leadbetter technique of, 4352, 4353f-4355f
 postoperative evaluation in, 4360
 principles of correction in, 4350-4351
Antireflux valves, in ureterointestinal anastomosis, 2561-2562, 2561f, 2562f
Antiretroviral therapy
 and genital secretions, 388
 for HIV infection, 401-403, 402f
Antispasmodics, for painful bladder syndrome/interstitial cystitis, 360t, 361
Antisperm antibodies
 assays for, 624t
 detection of, 624-625
 development of, risk factors for, 623-624
 effect of, on sperm function, 624
 in male infertility, analysis of, 623-625
Antituberculous drugs, for genitourinary tuberculosis, 443-444, 445t
Antrum technique, of gastrocystoplasty, in children, 3678
Anus. *See* Anal; Ano- *entries.*
 imperforate, 3647, 3647t
  associated findings in, 3647-3648
  evaluation of, 3648, 3649f
  in neonate, 3195
  in unilateral renal agenesis, 3275, 3275f
Anxiolytics, erectile dysfunction caused by, 745
Aorta, abdominal, 6f, 9, 13
 aneurysm of
  as contraindication to laparoscopy, 175
  ureteral obstruction due to, 1221, 1222f
 branches of, 9, 11f, 13, 13t
 complications of, after renal bypass surgery, 1752
Aortic syndrome, middle, 1191, 1191f
Aortorenal bypass, 1734-1737, 1735f-1738f
 thoracic, 1742-1743, 1742f, 1743f
*APC* gene, 516
 in colorectal cancer, 516
Aphallia, 3756-3757, 3757f
Aphthous ulcers, of male genitalia, 417-418, 418f
Apical support defects, in vaginal wall prolapse, surgical management of
 abdominal approach to, 2224
 abdominal sacral colpopexy in, 2228, 2229f
 iliococcygeus ligament suspension in, 2227-2228, 2228t
 laparoscopic, 2229-2230, 2230t
 sacrospinous ligament fixation in, 2225-2226, 2226f
 uterosacral ligament suspension in, 2226-2227, 2227f
 vaginal approach to, 2223-2224, 2224f, 2225f

Apnea, sleep, testosterone therapy causing, 859
Apomorphine
 for erectile dysfunction, 782
 in male sexual function, 729
Apoptosis, 488-490, 529-533
 bcl-2 family member-mediated, 530-531, 532
 caspase-mediated, prostate cancer cells and, 2858, 2859f
 cell death and, 531
 cell survival and, 530-531
 death receptor pathway in, 488-489, 489f
 death receptor–dependent receptors in, 530
 death receptor–induced, 529-530, 530f
 global defects in, 532
 in genitourinary malignancies, 531-532
  alternative regulators of, 532-533
 induction of, in transurethral microwave therapy, 2815-2816
 initiation of, caspases in, 531
 ligand-dependent receptors in, 530
 markers of, 2430
 mechanisms of, in cryotherapy, 3035, 3035t
 mitochondrial pathway in, 489-490
 NFκB regulation of, 490
 regulation of, 2730-2731
  in kidney development, 3167, 3167f
  in prostate growth, 2714-2715
 renal damage due to, 1342-1343
 *TP53*-induced, 530, 531f, 532
 tumor-induced, in T cells, 498-499
Appendicovesicostomy, for continent urinary diversion, 3694-3695, 3694f
 results of, 3696-3697
Appendix
 in antegrade continence enemas, for continent urinary diversion, 3700, 3700f
 in ileocecocystoplasty, 3675
Appendix epididymis, 3137, 3792
Appendix testis, 3792
Arcus tendineus fasciae pelvis, 2195, 2196f
Arcus tendineus levator ani, 2195
Areflexia
 definition of, 1981
 of detrusor muscle. *See* Detrusor muscle, areflexia of.
L-Arginine, for painful bladder syndrome/interstitial cystitis, 360t, 361
Argon beam coagulator, in laparoscopy, 192-193
*Aristolochia fangchi* herb, bladder cancer associated with, 2416
Aromatase inhibitors, for benign prostatic hyperplasia, 2797
Arrhythmias
 anesthesia-related, in laparoscopy, 210-211
 pneumoperitoneum and, 200
Arterial embolization, for nonischemic priapism, 848
Arteriography. *See* Angiography.
Arteriovenous fistula
 delayed bleeding due to, following percutaneous procedures, 1546, 1546f
 renal, 1189-1190, 1189f, 3297
  acquired, 1189, 1189f
  congenital, 1189
  idiopathic, 1189
Arteritis, Takayasu's, in children, 1184
Artery(ies). *See also specific artery, e.g.,* Aorta.
 dilation of, penile blood flow and, 758-759, 759f
 kinking of, after renal transplantation, 1318
Artificial sweeteners, bladder cancer associated with, 2415
Artificial urinary bladder. *See also* Bladder.
 for filling/storage disorders, 2297-2298

Artificial urinary sphincter
 evolution of, 2398f
 for bladder filling/storage disorders, 2294
 for bladder neck reconstruction, in children
  results of, 3667-3668
  technique of, 3666-3667, 3667f
 for male incontinence, 2077, 2396-2403
  complications of, 2399-2401
  history and development of, 2396-2397, 2398f
  implantation technique of, 2397, 2399f
  in special circumstances, 2401-2403
  indications for, 2391-2392
  results of, 2397
 for stress incontinence, in females, 2076-2077
 incompetence of
  in children, 2402
  in females, 2401-2402
 mechanical failure of, 2401
ARTs. *See* Assisted reproductive techniques (ARTs).
Ascites
 as complication of post-chemotherapy surgery, 956
 as contraindication to laparoscopy, 175
 chylous, after laparoscopy, 219
 urinary
  in neonate, 3196
  posterior urethral valves causing, 3586t, 3588
ASI stent, 2809
Ask-Upmark kidney, 1191
 clinical features of, 3311
 histopathology of, 3311
 treatment of, 3312
Aspergillosis, 464-465, 465f
*Aspergillus,* 464
Aspiration
 fine-needle. *See* Fine-needle aspiration biopsy.
 in laparoscopy, 196
  of gastric contents, 211
 in radical laparoscopic nephrectomy, hand-assisted, 1797-1798
 of bladder, suprapubic, 238-239
 of renal cysts, 1551, 3347
 of seminal vesicles, in assessment of ejaculatory duct obstruction, 710, 712f
 of sperm
  from epididymis
   microsurgical technique of, 652, 700, 703f-704f
   percutaneous technique of, 652, 700, 702f-703f
  from vas deferens, 700
Aspirin, associated with Reye's syndrome, 3206
Asplenism, risk of priapism with, 840
Assisted reproductive techniques (ARTs), 650-653, 651t
 in vitro fertilization with, 652
 intrauterine insemination with, 651-652
 semen processing in, 651
 sperm retrieval in, 652-653
 success of, 609
Asthenospermia, evaluation of, 622-623, 622f
Ataxia, cerebellar, voiding dysfunction with, 2017
Atelectasis
 after radical nephrectomy, 1720
 as complication of post-chemotherapy surgery, 956
Atheroembolism, ischemic nephropathy due to, 1166

Atherosclerosis
  erectile dysfunction associated with, 741
  renal artery, 1157-1159, 1157t, 1158f. *See also*
      Renovascular hypertension.
    diagnosis of, 1168
    endovascular stenting for, 1184-1187
      complications of, 1186-1187, 1186t
      indications for, 1185
      results of, 1185-1186, 1185t, 1186f
      technique of, 1185
    epidemiologic considerations in, 1167-
        1168, 1167t
    histopathology in, 1176, 1178f
    level of kidney function in, 1175-1176,
        1175f, 1176f
    natural history of, 1158, 1158t
    percutaneous transluminal angioplasty for,
        1180-1184
      complications of, 1181
      mechanisms of, 1181
      technique of, 1180-1181
    screening for, 1168
    severity and extent of disease in, 1174-
        1175, 1174f, 1175f
    surgical revascularization for
      preoperative preparation in, 1177
      results of, 1179-1180, 1179t
      secondary, 1180
      techniques of, 1177-1179
    smoking as risk factor for, 1167
Athlete's foot (tinea pedis), 424
Atopic dermatitis, of male genitalia, 407-408,
    407f
ATP. *See* Adenosine triphosphate (ATP).
Atrasentan, for hormone-refractory prostate
    cancer, 3116
Atresia
  cervical, 3838-3839, 3839f
  vaginal, 3833
Atrial natriuretic peptide
  in acute renal failure, 1337
  in renal development, 3158-3159
  in renal hemodynamics, 1134-1135, 1134f
Atrophic urethritis, in geriatric incontinence,
    2306-2308, 2307t
Atrophic vaginitis, in geriatric incontinence,
    2306-2308, 2307t
Atropine
  effect of, on ureteral function, 1905
  for overactive bladder/detrusor overactivity,
      2093t, 2094
Attachment plaques, ureteral, 1891
AUA-7 Symptom Index, for benign prostatic
    hyperplasia, 2829-2830, 2830t
Audiovisual sexual stimulation, in erectile
    dysfunction, 764
Augmentation cystoplasty. *See* Cystoplasty,
    augmentation.
Autoaugmentation
  bladder, in children, 3688-3690, 3689f
    laparoscopic, 3925
  disadvantage of, 3689-3690
Autocoagulation, postoperative, in renal
    transplant recipient, 1314
Autocrine signals, in prostate, 2690, 2690f
Autoimmunity, in painful bladder
    syndrome/interstitial cystitis, 340-341
Autoinflation, of penile prosthesis, 797
Autologous materials, for endoscopic correction
    of reflux, 4364-4365, 4364f
Automated Endoscopic System for Optimal
    Positioning (AESOP), 173
Autonomic hyperreflexia, voiding dysfunction
    with, 2012t, 2026-2027

Autonomic nervous system
  of corpus cavernosum, in exstrophy patient,
      3504-3505
  of penis, pathways in, 724-725, 725f
  of retroperitoneum, 15, 16f, 17, 17f
  testing of, in erectile dysfunction, 766-767
Autonomic plexus, pelvic, 54-55, 54f, 55f
Autonomous hypothesis, peripheral, of detrusor
    overactivity, 2080-2081, 2081f
Autopsy, prevalence of benign prostatic
    hyperplasia at, 2739, 2739f, 2741f
Autopsy data, in bladder cancer, 2409
Autoregulation, of glomerular filtration rate,
    1132
Autosomal dominant polycystic kidney disease,
    3318, 3320-3326
  bilateral nephrectomy for, 1301
  characteristics of, 3314t
  clinical features of, 3320-3321, 3322f
  emerging therapies for, 3326
  etiology of, 3322-3323
  evaluation of, 3323, 3324f, 3325
  examination of family members for, 3325
  genes responsible for, 3306
  genetic counseling in, 3325
  genetics of, 3320
  histopathology of, 3323
  in chronic renal failure, 1346
  laparoscopic nephrectomy for, 1775-1776
  laparoscopic surgery for, 1774-1775
  manifestations of, variations in, 3306-3307
  renal cell carcinoma in, 3323
    screening for, 1599
  treatment and prognosis of, 3325-3326
  variant form of, 3321, 3322f
  vs. autosomal recessive polycystic kidney
      disease, 3320t
Autosomal dominant simple cyst disease, 3347-
    3348, 3348f
Autosomal recessive polycystic kidney disease,
    3315-3318
  characteristics of, 3314t
  clinical features of, 3316
  evaluation of, 3316-3318, 3317f-3319f
  genetics of, 3315
  histopathology of, 3316
  prenatal diagnosis of, vs. multicystic dysplastic
      kidney, 3183, 3184f
  renal failure in, 3318, 3320
  treatment of, 3318
  vs. autosomal dominant polycystic kidney
      disease, 3320t
Autotransplantation. *See also* Transplantation.
  for upper ureteral injuries, 1287
  for ureteral stricture, 1267
  microvascular, of testes, 3787
  with extracorporeal partial nephrectomy,
      1728-1730, 1730f
Avastin, as inhibitor of angiogenesis, 545
Avoidance strategies, in prevention of bladder
    cancer, 2444
Avulsion injury, ureteral
  management of, 1289
  stone removal causing, 1503
  ureteroscopy causing, 1524
Axial flap(s), 1026, 1027f. *See also* Flap(s).
Axilla, pediculosis of, 384
Azithromycin
  for chancroid, in HIV patients, 397
  for *Chlamydia trachomatis* infection, 378
  for gonorrhea with chlamydial infection,
      379
  for mollicute infections, 384
  for pediatric urinary tract infections, 3248t

Azoospermia
  after vasovasostomy, 678
  causes of, 621-622, 621f, 655
  evaluation of, 621-622, 621f
  genetic abnormalities related to, 717
  history of, 611
  in XYY syndrome, 639
  obstructive, 647-648
    sperm retrieval for, 700
  radiation-induced, 3897
  vasography in, 627
  Y chromosome microdeletions in, 632
Azoospermia factor, 632, 639, 640
Azotemia
  benign prostatic hyperplasia with, 2758
  in renovascular hypertension, 1167
  postrenal, 1327
  prerenal, 1326-1327, 1326t
Aztreonam, for urinary tract infections, 245t,
    246t, 247t, 248

**B**

B cell(s), 476
  activation of, 481-482
  antigen-specific, 481
    clonal expansion in, 485
  memory, 488
Bacille Calmette-Guérin (BCG)
  controversy associated with, 447
  for bladder cancer
    in renal transplant recipients, 1324
    non–muscle-invasive, 2455-2457
      and impact on progression, 2456
      chemotherapy with, 2460
      contraindications to, 2457t
      for carcinoma in situ, 2455
      for tumor prophylaxis, 2456
      interferon with, 2461
      optimum treatment schedule of, 2456-
          2457, 2457t, 2458t
      toxicity of, management of, 2458t
  for painful bladder syndrome/interstitial
      cystitis, 362t, 364
  for urothelial tumors, 1659, 1659t
  granulomatous prostatitis and, 306
  intravesical, for genitourinary tuberculosis,
      447
  postoperative, for transitional cell carcinoma,
      1523
  urologic tumor response to, 522
Back pressure test, of penile prosthesis, 794-795,
    795f
Baclofen
  dosage of, 2121
  for overactive bladder/detrusor overactivity,
      2093t, 2106
  for priapism, 846t
  for prostatitis, clinical trial data on, 322
  uropharmacology of, 2120-2121
Bacteremia. *See also* Sepsis; Septic shock.
  conduit urinary diversion causing,
      2574-2575
  definition of, 287
  prophylactic antibiotics for, 1515
Bacteria. *See also specific bacterium.*
  anaerobic, in urinary tract, 228
  in prostatitis
    anaerobic, 306-307
    gram-negative, 306
    gram-positive, 306
  in urinary sediment, 108, 108f, 109f
  in urinary tract infections
    adherence of, 229-230, 229f, 230f
    in children, 3234

Bacteria *(Continued)*
    periurethral colonization of, 3238
    preputial skin colonization of, 3238-3239
    recurrent, persistence of, 260-261
    virulence of, 229
  resistance of, to antibiotics, 244-245
  urease-producing, 1387, 1387t, 1407, 1407t
  urea-splitting, struvite renal stones caused by, 261
Bacterial adhesins, in urinary tract infections, 229, 229f
Bacterial endocarditis, antibiotic prophylaxis for, 253-254, 254t, 1515
  in pediatric genitourinary procedures, 3242t
Bacterial infections. *See also specific infection.*
  immunity to, 500-501
  in children, fever and, 3206, 3206t
Bacterial pili, in urinary tract infections
  mannose-resistant, 230
  mannose-sensitive, 229-230, 230f
  phase variation of, 230-231, 231f, 232f
Bacteriuria
  after augmentation cystoplasty, 3683-3684
  asymptomatic, 257-258, 258t
  catheter-associated, 296-297
  conduit urinary diversion causing, 2574-2575
  definition of, 223-224
  in geriatric patient, 293-296
    diagnosis of, 294
    epidemiology of, 293, 293t, 294f
    management of, 295-296
    pathogenesis of, 293-294, 295f
    screening for, 294-295
  in pediatric urinary tract infections, factors affecting, 3236-3238, 3236t, 3237f
  in pregnancy, 237, 289-293
    complications of, 291-292
    diagnosis of, 292
    management of, 292-293, 292t
    pathogenesis of, 290
  localizing site of, ureteral catheterization in, 241, 241t
  prevalence of, 226, 226f
  significant, 223
  unresolved
    causes of, 259-260, 259t
    diagnosis and management of, 260
BAD, in apoptosis mediation, 531
Balanitis, 1044
  keratotic, of penis, 960
  of female genitalia, 883
  of male genitalia, 419
    pseudoepitheliomatous, keratotic, and micaceous, 429, 429f
    Zoon's, 431, 432f
Balanitis circinata, of male genitalia, 411, 412f
Balanitis xerotica obliterans. *See* Lichen sclerosus et atrophicus.
Balanoposthitis, of male genitalia, 419, 420f
Balkan nephropathy, urothelial tumors associated with, 1639
Ballistic lithotripsy, 1462-1463, 1462f, 1463t, 1513
Balloon dilatation
  for laparoscopic surgery, 181-182, 182f
  for prostatitis, 324
  of nephrostomy tract, 1543, 1543f
  of ureteral stricture
    antegrade approach to, 1256
    results of, 1256-1257
    retrograde approach to, 1255-1256, 1257f
  transurethral, of ejaculatory duct obstruction, 708

Balloon dilators
  in nephrostomy, 1543, 1543f
  in ureteroscopy, 1511t, 1512, 1512f
Balloon retention catheter, for percutaneous nephrostomy, 1559-1560
Banff classification, of renal allograft rejection, 1316
Barcat balanic groove technique, of hypospadias repair, 3725
Barnes stent, 2806
Baroreceptor mechanism, in renin-angiotensin-aldosterone system, 1162
Barotrauma, with pneumoperitoneum, 205
Bartter syndrome, 1375
  in children, 3229
Basal body temperature, charting of, 612
Basal cell(s), of prostate, 2682-2683
Basal cell carcinoma
  of genitalia, 428, 428f
  of penis, 989
  of prostate, transrectal ultrasonography of, 2887
Base excision repair, of DNA, 527-528
Bashful bladder, voiding dysfunction with, 2039-2040
BAX, in apoptosis mediation, 530-531
B-cell receptor, signaling events transmitted via, 483-484
BCG. *See* Bacille Calmette-Guérin (BCG).
*BCL-2* oncogene, in apoptosis mediation, 530-531, 532
BCL-2 protein
  elevated levels of, in apoptosis, 532
  expression of, in renal cell carcinoma, 1590
*BCR-ABL* oncogene, 514
Beckwith-Wiedemann syndrome, 515t
  Wilms' tumor in, 519
Bed pads, for geriatric incontinence, 2317
Behavior modification
  for incontinence, 2071
  for painful bladder syndrome/interstitial cystitis, 358
  for stress incontinence, 2074
  for urethral sphincter dysfunction, in children, 3618
Behavioral therapy
  for incontinence, 2126-2129, 2126f
    bladder training and timed voiding in, 2127-2128
    decreased caffeine intake in, 2128
    dietary management in, 2129
    fluid management in, 2128-2129
    in elderly, 2314-2316
    lifestyle issues in, 2129
    long-term results of, 2127t
    obesity/weight reduction in, 2129
    pelvic floor education in, 2127
    smoking cessation in, 2128, 2128t
    urge inhibition in, 2129
  for premature ejaculation, 785
  for stress incontinence, 2143
Behçet's disease, of male genitalia, 417-418, 418f
Bellini's duct (collecting duct) renal cell carcinoma, 1592t, 1596
Belt's procedure, 68
Bendroflumethiazide, for calcium oxalate stones, 1421t
Benign bounce phenomenon, post-radiation therapy, prostate cancer and, 3013
Benign multilocular cyst, 3339-3343, 3340f. *See also* Multilocular cyst, benign.
Benign prostatic hyperplasia, 94
  acute urinary retention in, 2758-2759
  alcohol use and, 2745

Benign prostatic hyperplasia *(Continued)*
  anatomic features of, 2734-2735, 2735f
  androgen receptors in, 2729
  androgens in, 2728-2730, 2729f
  autopsy prevalence of, 2739, 2739f, 2741f
  azotemia with, 2758
  bladder calculi with, 2757
  bladder decompression in, 2758
  bladder obstruction in
    effects of α-adrenergic blockers on, 2785
    measures of, 2743
    pathophysiology of, 2737-2738
  body mass index and, 2745
  clinical manifestations of, 2767
  clinical prevalence of, cross-sectional studies of, 2739-2740, 2740f, 2741f
  complications of, 2757-2764
  cytokines in, 2733
  definitions of, 2738-2739
  diagnosis of, 2767-2773
    additional tests in, 2769
    for surgical patients, 2769-2773
  diet and, 2745
  dihydrotestosterone in, 2729
  effect of testosterone therapy on, 859-860
  epidemiology of
    analytic, 2743-2746, 2759-2760, 2760f-2762f
    correlation of parameters in, 2746-2748, 2746f-2748f, 2747t
    descriptive, 2739-2748, 2739f, 2759, 2759t
  estrogens in, 2731
  etiology of, 2727-2734
  familial, 2733-2734, 2733t
  genetic factors in, 2733
  growth factors in, 2731-2732, 2731f
  hematuria in, 2758
    effects of medical therapy on, 2775
  histologic features of, 2735-2736, 2736f
  histologic prevalence of, 2739
  hypertension with, 2745
    α-adrenergic blockers for, 2747
  inflammatory cell infiltrates in, 2733
  initial evaluation of, 2767-2769
  interference with activities of daily living in, 2742
  liver cirrhosis and, 2745
  macroscopic, 2766-2767
  medical history of, 2767
  medical therapy for, 2773-2801
    α-adrenergic blockers in, 2777-2787
      adverse events associated with, 2786
      classification of, 2777-2777, 2778t
      coexisting hypertension and, 2786
      comparison of, 2786-2787
      dose response of, 2778
      effects of
        on acute urinary retention, 2785-2786
        on bladder outlet obstruction, 2785
      future of, 2787
      in elderly, 2786
      literature review of, 2779-2785
      rationale for, 2777
      recommended dosage of, 2778t
      study designs for, 2778
    adverse events in, 2775
    alfuzosin in, 2784-2785, 2785t
    androgen suppression in, 2788-2793
      classification of agents in, 2788, 2788t
      in clinical practice, 2793
      interpretation of studies of, 2788
      literature review of, 2788-2793
      rationale for, 2788

Benign prostatic hyperplasia *(Continued)*
  aromatase inhibitors in, 2797
  candidate selection for, 2776
  cetrorelix in, 2792-2793
  clinical endpoints in, 2773
  combination therapy in, 2793-2797
    Medical Therapy of Prostatic Symptoms
      Study of, 2795-2797
    Veterans Affairs Cooperative Study of,
      2793, 2793t, 2794f, 2795, 2795t,
      2796f
  development of, directed toward
    unrecognized factors, 2801
  doxazosin in, 2780, 2782-2783, 2782t
  dutasteride in, 2792
  effects of
    on bladder emptying, 2774
    on bladder outlet obstruction,
      2773-2774
    on detrusor instability, 2774
    on hematuria, 2775
    on renal insufficiency, 2775
    on symptoms, 2773, 2774f
    on urinary retention, 2774-2775
  eliminating bias in, 2775
  finasteride in, 2788-2792, 2789f, 2790t,
    2791f
  flutamide in, 2792
  future strategies in, 2801
  *Hypoxis rooperi* (South African star grass)
    in, 2800
  impact of, 2776
  phytotherapeutic agents in, 2797-
    2801
    composition of, 2798, 2798t
    mechanism of action of, 2798-2800,
      2798t
    origin of, 2797-2798, 2798t
  prophylactic, 2776
  *Pygeum afrricanum* (African plum) in,
    2799-2800, 2800t
  quantitative outcome measures in,
    2773-2775
  safety and effectiveness of, 2773-2775
  sample size in, 2775
  *Serenoa repens* (saw palmetto berry) in,
    2799, 2799t, 2800t
  tamsulosin in, 2783-2784, 2784t
  terazosin in, 2779-2780, 2779f, 2779t,
    2780t, 2781f
  zantoterone in, 2792
  medications exacerbating, 2746
  microscopic, 2766
  minimally invasive therapy for, 2803-
    2844
    intraprostatic stents in, 2804-2809
      permanent, 2807-2809
      temporary, 2804-2807
    lasers in, 2820-2829. *See also* Laser
      therapy.
    rotoresection of prostate in, 2843
    transurethral ethanol ablation of prostate
      in, 2843
    transurethral incision of prostate in, 2841-
      2842, 2841f, 2842t
    transurethral microwave, 2813-2820. *See
      also* Transurethral microwave therapy
      (TUMT).
    transurethral needle ablation of prostate in,
      2809-2813. *See also* Transurethral
      needle ablation (TUNA), of prostate.
    transurethral resection of prostate in,
      2829-2838. *See also* Transurethral
      resection of prostate (TURP).

Benign prostatic hyperplasia *(Continued)*
    transurethral vaporization of prostate in,
      2838-2841
      water-induced thermotherapy in, 2842
  mortality rate for, 2757
  obesity and, 2745-2746
  pathology of, 2734-2736, 2735f, 2736f
  pathophysiology of, 2734-2738, 2734f
  physical examination for, 2767
  population-based studies of, 2756-2757, 2757f
  postvoid residual urine in, 2770-2771
  pressure-flow studies in, 2771-2772
  prostate size in, 2742-2743, 2742f
  prostate-specific antigen in, 2768
  5α-reductase in, 2729
  religion and, 2743
  serum creatinine in, 2768
  sexual activity and, 2744, 2744f
  sham control arms of device treatment trials
    for
      natural history and disease progression in,
        2753-2754, 2754f, 2755f, 2756t
      sham/placebo effect in, 2753
        relationship between perception of
          improvement and, 2754, 2756
  smoking and, 2745
  smooth muscle, 2736-2737, 2736f
  socioeconomic factors in, 2743
  stromal-epithelial interaction in, 2731
  surgery for, 2761-2763, 2763f, 2764f
    diagnostic tests prior to, 2769-2773
  sympathetic signaling pathways in, 2732-2733
  symptom assessment in, 2768-2769
  symptom severity and frequency of, 2740,
    2741f
  transition zone histology in, 2920
  treatment of
    clinical parameters and outcomes of
      interest in, 2747, 2747f, 2747t
    medical, 2773-2801. *See also* Benign
      prostatic hyperplasia, medical therapy
      for.
    minimally invasive, 2803-2844. *See also*
      Benign prostate hyperplasia,
      minimally invasive therapy for.
    surgical, 2761-2763, 2763f, 2764f
      diagnostic tests prior to, 2769-2773
  untreated
    clinical parameters and outcomes of
      interest in, 2748-2749, 2749t
    natural history of, 2748-2750
      methods of study in, 2749-2750, 2750t
    placebo control groups in, 2752-2753,
      2752t
    watchful waiting in, 2750-2752, 2751f,
      2751t, 2752t, 2776-2777
  upper urinary tract deterioration with, 2758
  urethrocystoscopy in, 2772
  urinalysis in, 2767-2768
  urinary incontinence with, 2758
  urinary retention in
    effects of α-adrenergic blockers on, 2785-
      2786
    effects of medical therapy on, 2774-2775
  urinary tract imaging in, 2772-2773
  urinary tract infection with, 2757-2758
    effects of medical therapy on, 2775
  uroflowmetry in, 2769-2770
  vasectomy and, 2744
Benign Prostatic Hyperplasia Symptom Index,
  2830, 2830t
Benzodiazepines, uropharmacology of, 2120
Berger's disease. *See* IgA nephropathy (Berger's
  disease).

Berry aneurysm, in autosomal dominant
  polycystic kidney disease, 3321
Berry prosthesis, for male incontinence, 2392.
  *See also* Perineal sling, for male
  incontinence.
Bethanechol, to facilitate bladder emptying,
  2114-2115
Bethanechol supersensitivity test, 1995
Bevacizumab
  for metastatic hormone-refractory prostate
    cancer, 3117
  for renal cell carcinoma, 1630, 1630f,
    1630t
Beverages, carbonated, for nephrolithiasis, 1411-
  1412
Bezoar
  *Aspergillus,* 465f
  *Candida*
    imaging of, 463, 463f
    in bladder, 460, 460f
  fungal
    in children, 3265
    percutaneous treatment of, 1556
*BHD1* gene, 1588
Bias, eliminating, in medical therapy for benign
  prostatic hyperplasia, 2775
Bicalutamide
  androgen blockade with, 3085t, 3086
  for priapism, 846t
Bicarbonate, renal reabsorption of
  in cortical collecting tubules, 1145
  in loop of Henle, 1142
  in proximal convoluted tubules, 1139, 1140f
Bicarbonate buffer system, 1152
Bichloroacetic acid, for genital warts, 382
Bicycling, long-distance, erectile dysfunction
  associated with, 769
Bifid pelvis, 3303
Bifid scrotum, 3759
Big bang theory, of postpyelonephritic scarring,
  4338
Bikunin, as calcium oxalate crystal inhibitor,
  1367, 1371
Bilateral electrical stimulation. *See also* Electrical
  stimulation, of bladder.
  of bladder, for storage disorders, 2158
Bilirubin, in urine, 104
Bimanual examination
  of bladder, 91, 91f
    for invasive cancer, 2468
  of kidneys, 90, 90f
Biochemical changes, in sperm, during
  epididymal maturation, 603
Biochemical markers
  in pediatric ureteropelvic junction
    obstruction, 3369-3370
  of ureteropelvic junction obstruction, in
    children, 3369-3370
Biodegradable stents, 1517
  for benign prostatic hyperplasia, 2807
Biofeedback
  for incontinence, 2133, 2133f-2135f
  for prostatitis, 324
  for urethral sphincter dysfunction, in
    children, 3618, 3619f, 3620f
Biofragmentable rings, intestinal anastomosis
  with, 2548
Bioglass injections, for incontinence, 2286
Biologic grafts. *See also* Graft(s).
  in vaginal prolapse surgery, 2216
Biologic therapy(ies), for neuroblastoma,
  noninvasive, 3877
Biological recurrence, of prostate cancer,
  management of, 2943

Biomaterials
  for tissue engineering, 554-556
    design and selection of, 555
    types of, 555-556, 556f
  used in stents, 1517-1518
Bioplastique injections, for incontinence, 2275
Biopsy
  cavernous, of penile smooth muscle, 763
  endometrial, in evaluation of fertility, 612
  fine-needle aspiration. See Fine-needle
    aspiration biopsy.
  for genitourinary tuberculosis, 443
  for prostatitis, 317
  needle, of adenocarcinoma of prostate, 2878-
    2879, 2878t
  of bladder cancer
    non–muscle-invasive, 2452-2453
    site-selected, 2438
  of kidney. See Renal biopsy.
  of penile cancer, 968, 993
  of prostate. See Prostate, biopsy of.
  of retroperitoneal fibrosis, 1216-1217
  of sentinel lymph node, in penile cancer, 979,
    1003-1005, 1004f
  of testis, 633-634, 633f
    complications of, 658
    indications for, 655
    open, 655-657, 656f, 657f
      sperm retrieval through, 701
    percutaneous, 657, 657f
  of urothelial tumors, 1645
Biothesiometry, penile, in erectile dysfunction,
    766
Bipedicled flap. See also Flap(s).
  in penile reconstruction, 1095-1096
Bipolar electrosurgical devices, in laparoscopy,
    192
Bipolar transurethral resection of prostate,
    2838
Birmingham Reflux Study, 3239
Birth
  evaluation of bladder exstrophy at, 3508-3510,
    3508f
  evaluation of cloacal exstrophy at, 3541-3542,
    3541t
Birth weight, low, bilateral renal agenesis and,
    3270
Birt-Hogg-Dubé syndrome, 515t
  inherited susceptibility to cancer in, 518
  renal cell carcinoma associated with, 1584t,
    1588
Bismuth phosphate, sclerotherapy with, for renal
    cysts, 3347
Bisphosphonates, for metastatic prostate cancer,
    3114
Bites, human and animal, to penis, 2651
  in children, 3945
BK polyomavirus infection, after renal
    transplantation, 1321
Blackfoot disease, bladder cancer associated
    with, 2416
Bladder, 57-60
  accommodation of, 1925
    continence and, 2049, 2049f
  activation of, role of urothelium-
    suburothelium in, 2094
  agenesis of, antenatal detection of, 3575
  altered sensation of, aging and, 1970
  anatomic relationships of, 57
  anatomy of, 1923-1924, 1923f, 3605
  anomalies of
    in children, 3573-3582. See also specific
      anomaly.
    classification of, 3574-3582

Bladder (Continued)
    postnatal detection of, 3576-3579, 3576f-
      3578f
    prenatal detection of, 3574-3575, 3575f
  incontinence due to, urodynamic
    observation of, 2053-2054, 2053f,
    2054f
  artificial, for bladder filling/storage disorders,
    2297-2298
  augmentation of. See Bladder augmentation.
  base of, 58
    in females, 65, 66f, 67
  bashful, 2039-2040
  biomechanics of, 1924, 1924f
    function associated with, 1925-1926,
      1926f
  blood supply to, 60, 1932
  bowel-augmented, pediatric urinary tract
    infections and, 3241
  calcifications in, schistosomiasis and, 453,
    453f
  calculi in. See Bladder calculi.
  cancer of. See Bladder cancer.
  candidiasis of, 460, 469f
  capacity of, 57, 1981
    age-based, estimation of, 3657
    calculation of, 3606-3607
    cystometrographic, 1992-1993
    evaluation of, prior urinary tract
      reconstruction, 3659-3660
    in epispadias, 3546
    in exstrophy patient, 3518, 3524
    therapeutic increase in, 2091-2106
  changes of, during pregnancy, 290
  compliance of, 1981
    after augmentation cystoplasty, 3680-3681,
      3681f
    cystometrogram of, 1993, 1993f
    decreased, in valve patients, 3597
    definition of, 1925, 3657
    diminished
      after artificial sphincter placement,
        2401
      during filling and storage, 1977
    evaluation of, prior to urinary tract
      reconstruction, 3659-3660
    low (decreased)
      causes of, 2056, 2056t
      evaluation of, 2240
      incontinence due to, 2054, 2054f
      treatment of, 2071-2074
  computed tomography of, 132-133
  connective tissue support of, 57
  contractility of
    aging and, 1969-1970
    index of, 2000, 2000f
    therapeutic inhibition of, 2091-2106
    therapy to increase, 2114-2117
  contraction of
    muscarinic receptors and, 2091-2093
    normal, in voiding, 1975
  decompression of
    in benign prostatic hyperplasia, 2758
    in utero, indications for, 3187-3188,
      3187f
    postoperative, 2040
  defunctionalized, 2043
  denervation of
    peripheral, 2290-2291
    perivesical, 2290-2291
    potential risks of, 2291
    transvaginal partial, 2290
  detrusor muscle of. See Detrusor muscle.
  development of, 3135-3136, 3573

Bladder (Continued)
  drainage of
    in management of posterior urethral valves,
      3591
    in retropubic suspension surgery, 2175
  duplication of, 3580-3581, 3581f
  dysfunction of, in children, 3657-3659
    elevated filling pressures and, 3658
    etiologic classification of, 3609-3610
    functional classification of, 3610-3611,
      3610f
    incontinence and, 3658-3659
    management of, 3597
  effect of drugs on, 1960-1962
  embryology of, 3122f, 3131-3133
  emptying of, 57, 1976. See also Voiding.
    cystometrographic studies of, 1995
    evaluation of, prior to urinary tract
      reconstruction, 3660
    failure in, 1977-1978
      electrical stimulation for, 2163-2167. See
        also Electrical stimulation, of
        bladder.
    in benign prostatic hyperplasia, effects of
      medical therapy on, 2774
    phases in, 1941-1943, 1944f, 1945f
    reflexes promoting, 2149
    therapy to facilitate, 1980t, 2114-2122,
      2298-2304. See also specific therapy.
    urethral sphincter dysfunction during,
      3612-3613
  endometriosis of, 1220
  epithelial cell receptivity of, in urinary tract
    infections, 233-234, 234f
  examination of, 90-91, 91f
  exstrophy of. See Bladder exstrophy.
  female, 57
  fetal
    absent, 3574-3575
    dilation of, 3574
    nondilated, 3574-3575
    sonographic appearance of, 3178, 3180f,
      3573
    sonographic findings in, 3573
  filling of, 1976
    abnormalities of, 1976-1977
    mechanics in, 1924-1925
    outlet response during, 1974-1975
    rate of, in children, 3627-3628
    response to, 1974
    smooth muscle during, 1929
    storage phase in, 1939-1941, 1940t, 1942f,
      1943f
    therapy to facilitate, 1979t, 2091-2114,
      2288-2298. See also specific therapy.
    ureteral function and, 1909
    urethral sphincter dysfunction during,
      3611-3612
  full valve, 3596-3598
  function of
    active, 3657
    evaluation of, 2239-2240
    in exstrophy patient, 3506
    normal, in children, 3605-3609, 3606f-
      3608f
    parameter changes in, 3606-3607, 3606f
    passive, 3657. See also Bladder, storage
      function of.
    tissue biomechanics and, 1925-1926, 1926f
  fungal bezoar in, 460, 460f
  hemangioma of, in children, 3582
  high-pressure, spinal cord injury with, 237-
    238
  hypoplasia of, antenatal detection of, 3575

Bladder (*Continued*)
  in exstrophy patient. *See also* Bladder
      exstrophy.
    bladder neck repair in
      failed, 3536-3537
      results of, 3533-3534, 3533t
    closure of, 3510, 3511f-3512f, 3513
      combined with epispadias repair,
          3517-3518, 3526, 3527f-3530f,
          3530
        results of, 3531-3533, 3535
        failed, 3535-3536, 3536f
          results of, 3531, 3531t
    defects of, 3505-3507, 3506f, 3507f
    small, unsuitable for closure, management
        of, 3516-3517
  in prune-belly syndrome, 3484, 3484f
  in utero decompression of, indications for,
      3187-3188, 3187t
  infections of, 254-265. *See also* Urinary tract
      infection; *specific infection.*
  inflammation of. *See* Cystitis.
  injury to. *See* Bladder injury.
  innervation of, 60, 3605, 3606f
    afferent pathways in, 1938-1939, 1938f,
        1939t
    interruption of, 2289-2291
    parasympathetic pathways in, 1938
    peripheral, 1937-1939, 1938f
    somatic pathways in, 1938
    sympathetic pathways in, 1938
  internal surface of, 57-58
  lymphatic drainage of, 60
  magnetic resonance imaging of, 135, 137f
  male, dissection of, 58f
  manual compression of, for emptying
      disorders, 2298
  mechanical compression of, for filling/storage
      disorders, 2291-2292
  mucosa of, free graft, for neourethral
      formation in hypospadias repair, 3734,
      3736-3728, 3738f
  muscles. *See* Smooth muscle, bladder.
  myoplasty of, to facilitate emptying, 2299-
      2300
  native, management of, in augmentation
      cystoplasty, 3672-3673, 3673f
  natural defenses of, 235-236
  neck of. *See* Bladder neck.
  neurogenic. *See* Neurogenic bladder.
  outlet obstruction of. *See* Bladder outlet,
      obstruction of.
  overactivity of. *See* Overactive bladder.
  overdistention of, therapeutic, 2288
  pain in. *See also* Painful bladder
      syndrome/interstitial cystitis.
    related to filling, 2084
  paralytic, 1982
  perforation of. *See also* Bladder injury.
    delayed
      after augmentation cystoplasty, 3684-
          3686, 3685f
      etiology of, 3685
      incidence of, 3685-3686
      treatment of, 3686
    resectoscope causing, 2482, 2482f
  reconstruction of, sling procedures associated
      with, 2249
  reflexes of. *See under* Reflex(es).
  regeneration of
    in children, 3690-3691
    matrices for, 559-560
  relationship between brain dysfunctions and,
      in nocturnal enuresis, 3624

Bladder (*Continued*)
  replacement of
    for painful bladder syndrome/interstitial
        cystitis, 367
    tissue engineering in, 561-562, 562f,
        563f
  retrograde flow of urine from. *See*
      Vesicoureteral reflux.
  sensory aspects of, 1976
  sensory input to, therapeutic inhibition of,
      2106-2109
  sphincter of. *See* Urethral sphincter.
    artificial. *See* Artificial urinary sphincter.
  storage function of, 1976
    cystometrographic studies of, 1993, 1993f,
        1995, 1995f
    failure in, 1976-1977
      electrical stimulation for, 2151-2163. *See
          also* Electrical stimulation, of
          bladder.
      functional classification of, 1978-1979,
          1978t, 1979t
      expanded, 1980t
    phases in, 1939-1941, 1940t, 1942f, 1943f
    reflexes promoting, 2149, 2149f
    therapy to facilitate, 1979t, 2091-2114,
        2288-2298. *See also specific therapy.*
  structure of, 57-58, 58f, 59f
  suprapubic aspiration of, in urinary tract
      infection, 238-239
  surgical approaches to, 2483
    laparoscopic, 2506-2532, 2507t. *See also
        specific procedure.*
  surgical compression of, for filling/storage
      disorders, 2293-2294
  tissue engineering of, 558-562, 559f
    artificial replacement by, 561-562, 562f,
        563f
    matrices for, 559-560
    tissue expansion for bladder augmentation
        in, 558-559, 559f
    with cell transplantation, 561, 561f
  transection of, 2290-2291
  trigone of, 59f, 60, 60f
    embryology of, 3132-3133, 3134f
  tuberculosis of, 438, 439f
  tumors of. *See* Bladder cancer.
  ulcers of, schistosomal, 453
  ultrasonography of, 122, 124, 125f
  underactivity of, 1978
  unstable (overactive). *See also* Overactive
      bladder.
    definition of, 2079
  urachal anchoring of, 57
  ureterovesical junction of, 58-59, 60f
  urothelial layer of, 1932-1935, 1933f. *See also*
      Urothelium.
  viscoelastic properties of, 1974
Bladder augmentation
  calculi in, 2666-2667
    management of, 2669-2670, 2671f
  for incontinence, 2074
  for urethral sphincter dysfunction, in
      children, 3620
  laparoscopic technique of, 560
  overactivity in, drug treatment for,
      2108-2109
  tissue expansion for, 558-559, 559f
Bladder autoaugmentation, in children, 3688-
    3690, 3689f
  laparoscopic, 3925
Bladder calculi, 1427, 2663-2670
  after augmentation cystoplasty, 3684
  diagnosis of, 2668

Bladder calculi (*Continued*)
  in augmentations and urinary diversions,
      2666-2667
    management of, 2669-2670, 2671f
  management of, 1428, 2668-2670
    chemolysis in, 2668
    cystolitholapexy in, 2668-2669
    cystolithotomy in, 2669
    endoscopic lithotripsy in, 2669-2670
    shockwave lithotripsy in, 2668
    surgical approach to, 2670, 2671f
  migrant, 2663
  primary idiopathic (endemic), 2663-2664
  secondary, 2664-2666
    foreign body nidus, 2666, 2667f
    related to bladder outlet syndrome, 2664-
        2665, 2664f-2666f
    related to infection or catheterization,
        2665-2666
  symptoms of, 2667-2668
  with benign prostatic hyperplasia, 2757
Bladder cancer, 2407-2446
  adenocarcinoma as, 2422
  age associated with, 2409
  analgesic abuse as, 2415
  apoptosis in, 532
  autopsy data and, 2409
  biology of, 2407
  cystectomy for. *See* Cystectomy.
  diagnosis of, 2430-2432
    flow cytometry in, 2431
    image analysis in, 2432
    microscopic cytology in, 2431
    signs and symptoms in, 2430-2431
    specimen interpretation in, 2432
  early detection of, 2432-2438
    antigenic markers in, 2436
    biases and pitfalls in, 2432-2433
    combination markers studies in, 2436
    CT imaging in, 2437
    cystoscopy in, 2437-2438
    excretory urography in, 2437
    fluorescence cytology tests in, 2436
    microsatellite repeat analyses in, 2435
    nuclear matrix proteins in, 2434-2435
    rationale for, 2432
    reported studies in, 2433-2434
    screening for, 2432-2434
      carcinogen exposure and, 2436-2437
    site-selected biopsies in, 2438
    survivin in, 2435-2436
    telomerase in, 2435
    tumor resection in, 2438
  enterocystoplasty as risk factor for, 1324
  etiology of, 2410-2413
    amplification and overexpression in, 2412-
        2413
    basic biology in, 2410
    *CDKN2A* gene in, 523
    oncogenes in, 2410
    retinoblastoma gene and regulators in,
        2411-2412
    *TP53* gene in, 2411, 2414
    tumor suppressor genes in, 2410-2411
  in renal transplant recipients, 1324, 2416
  in situ carcinoma as, 2418-2419, 2418f
  incidence of, 2407-2408
    regional and national differences in, 2409
  interstitial cystitis and, 335
  invasive, 2468-2476
    bimanual examination of, 2468
    bladder preservation protocols for, 2475-
        2476, 2476t, 2477f
    chemotherapy for

Bladder cancer *(Continued)*
    adjuvant, 2474, 2474t
    hyperthermia and, 2476
    intra-arterial, 2476
    neoadjuvant, 2473, 2473t
    perioperative, 2473
  imaging of, 2469
  molecular markers in, 2478
  presentation of, 2468
  radiation therapy for, 2474, 2476
    preoperative, 2473
  radical cystectomy for, 2469-2473
    adjuncts to, 2473-2474
    complications of, 2472
    efficacy of, 2471, 2471t
    female urethra management after, 2471
    follow-up after, 2472-2473
    indications for, 2469-2470
    lymphadenectomy in, 2472
    male urethra management after, 2470-2471
    technique of, 2470, 2470f, 2470t
    ureteral frozen-section analysis in, 2471
  staging of, laparoscopic, 2469
  standard therapy for, alternatives to, 2474-2476
  transurethral resection for, 2468
    chemotherapy and partial cystectomy with, 2475
    partial cystectomy with, 2474-2475
    restaging, 2468-2469
  metastatic
    chemotherapy for
      newer agents in, 2477-2478
      systemic, 2476-2477
    molecular markers in, 2478
    palliative therapy for, 2478
    salvage cystectomy for, 2478
  mortality rate of, 2408-2409
  natural history of, 2426-2427
  nonepithelial, 2445-2446
    angiosarcoma as, 2445
    hemangioma as, 2445
    leiomyosarcoma as, 2445
    lymphoma as, 2445
    neurofibroma as, 2445
    pheochromocytoma as, 2445
    rhabdomyosarcoma as, 2446
      treatment of, 3880-3883, 3881f, 3882f
  non–muscle-invasive, 2447-2467
    biology of, 2449
    chemotherapy for, 2458-2460
      combination, 2460
      doxorubicin in, 2459
      mitomycin C in, 2459
      novel agents in, 2459-2460
      thiotepa in, 2459
    disease progression in, 2448t
    endoscopic management of, 2450-2454
      fluorescent cystoscopy in, 2454, 2454f, 2455f
      laser therapy in, 2453-2454
      office-based, 2454
      perioperative intravesical therapy in, 2453, 2453t
      role of biopsies in, 2452-2453
      transurethral resection of tumor in, 2451
        complications of, 2451-2452
        repeat of, 2452
    immunotherapy for, 2455-2458
      bacille Calmette-Guérin in, 2455-2457, 2457t, 2458t
      chemotherapy with, 2460

Bladder cancer *(Continued)*
      interferon in, 2457
      investigational agents in, 2457-2458
    pathologic grading of, 2447, 2448f, 2449f
    pathology of, by stage, 2449-2450, 2450t
    refractory disease in, management of, 2460-2462
      alternative options in, 2462
      early cystectomy in, 2461-2462
      salvage intravesical therapy in, 2460-2461
    staging of, 2447-2450, 2448f, 2448t, 2449f, 2450t
      pathologic, 2448-2449
    surveillance of, 2462-2467
      cystoscopic, 2463
      extravesical, 2465-2466, 2466t
      investigational markers in, 2465
      secondary prevention strategies in, 2466-2467
      tumor markers in, 2464-2465, 2464t, 2465f
      urine cytology in, 2463-2464
  nonurothelial, 2444-2445
    carcinosarcoma as, 2444-2445
    metastatic carcinoma as, 2445
    small cell carcinoma as, 2444
  pathology of, 2417-2418
    epithelial hyperplasia and metaplasia in, 2417
    urothelial dysplasia in, 2417-2418, 2418f
  prevalence of, 2408
  prevention of, 2441, 2441t
    avoidance strategies in, 2444
    dietary factors in, 2443-2444
    megavitamins in, 2443
    NSAIDS in, 2444
    polyamine synthesis inhibitors in, 2443
    vitamins in, 2442
  prognostic indicator(s) in, 2427-2430
    cell adhesion molecules as, 2428
    chromosomal abnormalities as, 2429-2430
    clinical and pathologic parameters as, 2427
    extracellular matrix components as, 2428
    genetic abnormalities as, 2429-2430
    growth factors and receptors as, 2428-2429
    laboratory parameters as, 2427
    Lewis blood group antigens as, 2428
    tumor-associated antigens as, 2428
  recurrence of, after cystectomy, 2623-2629
    pelvic, 2628-2629
    urethral, 2623-2628
      in female patient, 2626-2628
      in male patient, 2624-2626
  risk factor(s) for, 2413-2417
    analgesic abuse as, 2415
    *Aristolochia fangchi* herb as, 2416
    artificial sweeteners as, 2415
    blackfoot disease as, 2416
    chronic cystitis as, 2415
    cigarette smoking as, 2413-2415
    coffee and tea drinking as, 2415
    cyclophosphamide as, 2416
    heredity as, 2416-2417
    infectious, 450, 2415-2416
    occupational exposures as, 2413
    pelvic irradiation as, 2416
    renal transplant as, 1324, 2416
  schistosomiasis and, risk of, 450, 2415
  squamous cell carcinoma as
    etiology of, 2421-2422
    histology of, 2422, 2422f
  staging of, 2438-2441
    bone scans in, 2441
    chest radiography in, 2441

Bladder cancer *(Continued)*
    CT imaging in, 2439-2440
    goals of, 2439
    lymphadenectomy in, 2440-2441
    molecular, 2441
    MR imaging in, 2440
    PET imaging in, 2440
    systems of, 2441, 2441t
    ultrasonography in, 2440
  transitional cell carcinoma as, 2419-2421. *See also* Transitional cell carcinoma, of bladder.
  transurethral resection for. *See* Transurethral resection (TUR).
  urachal carcinoma in, 2422-2423
  urethrectomy for. *See* Urethrectomy.
  urothelial carcinoma as, 2418-2423. *See also* Urothelial carcinoma, of bladder.
  urothelial tumors after, 1639, 1654, 1655
    risk of, 1639
  voiding dysfunction with, 2028
Bladder contractility index, 2000, 2000f
Bladder diverticulum(a), 2361-2371, 2362f
  acquired, 2361-2363, 2363f
  classification of, 2361-2363
  conditions associated with, 2365-2367
  congenital, 2361
  endoscopic examination of, 2365, 2366f
  iatrogenic, 2363
  imaging of, 2364-2365, 2364f, 2365f
  in children, 3579-3580, 3579f
  management of, 2367-2371
    algorithm in, 2368f
    endoscopic, 2367
    indications for intervention in, 2367
    observation in, 2367
    surgical, 2369-2371, 2369f-2372f
      complications of, 2371
  presentation of, 2363-2364
  urodynamics of, 2365
  vesicoureteral reflux and, 4343-4344, 4343f
Bladder exstrophy, 4326-4334. *See also* Exstrophy-epispadias complex.
  abdominal wall defects in, 3503
  anatomic considerations in, 4326-4333
  anorectal defects in, 3503
  antenatal detection of, 3575
  duplicate, 3550, 3551f
  embryology of, 3499-3500
  emergent evaluation of, 3199
  entities constituting, 3497, 3498f
  evaluation of, at birth, 3508-3510, 3508f
  genital defects in
    failed repair of, 3537
    female, 3505, 3505f, 3524
    male, 3503-3505, 3504f, 3505f
  initial presentation and management of, 3509t
  long-term adjustment issues in, 3553
  management of. *See also* Bladder exstrophy, reconstruction for.
    at birth, 3508-3510, 3508f
    with small bladder unsuitable for closure, 3516-3517
  obstetric implications of, 3552-3553
  parents of patients with, reassurance and education of, 3509-3510
  pelvic floor defects in, 3502f, 4328-4329
  prenatal diagnosis of, 3507-3508, 3508f
  reconstruction for, 3508-3517, 3509t
    abdominal wall closure in, 3510, 3511f-3512f, 3513
    alternative techniques of, 3537-3538
    at birth, 3508-3510, 3508f
    patient selection for, 3510

Bladder exstrophy (Continued)
    bladder closure in, 3510, 3511f-3512f, 3513
        combined with epispadias repair, 3517-
            3518, 3526, 3527f-3530f, 3530
            results of, 3531-3533, 3535
        results of, 3531, 3531t
    bladder neck repair in
        failed, 3536-3537
        results of, 3533-3534, 3533t
    chordee release in, 3519-3520
    complete primary exstrophy repair in,
        3557-3563
        complete, 3559, 3560f
        in females, 3563-3564, 3563f, 3565f-
            3567f
        initial dissection in, 3557, 3558f, 3559f
        modifications of, 3561, 3563
        penile/urethral dissection in, 3558-3559
        primary closure in, 3559-3561, 3562f,
            3563f
        proximal dissection in, 3559, 3561f
        results of, 3569-3571
    continence and antireflux procedure in,
        3524, 3525f-3526f, 3526
        postoperative care after, 3526
    epispadias repair in, 3518-3519, 3519f
    Erlangen approach to, 3517
        results of, 3534
    failed closure in, 3535-3536, 3536f
    failed genitourinary reconstruction in, 3537
    immobilization techniques in,
        complications of, 3515-3516
    modern staged approaches to, 3510, 3517-
        3530
        outcomes and results of, 3530-3534,
            3531t, 3533t
    modified Cantwell-Ransley repair in, 3520,
        3520f-3523f, 3523-3524
        results of, 3531-3532
    osteotomy in, 3513, 3514f-3516f, 3515
        complications of, 3515-3516
    penile and urethral closure in, 3518-3524
    penile skin closure in, 3520
    postoperative problems with, 3524
    primary closure in
        management after, 3518
        results of, 3531, 3531t
    Seattle approach to, 3517
        results of, 3534-3535
    trigonosigmoidostomy in, 3537-3538
    ureterosigmoidostomy in, 3537
    urethral closure in, 3510, 3511f-3512f, 3513
    urethral reconstruction in, 3520
    urinary diversion in, 3537-3538
        continent, 3538
    Warsaw approach to, 3517
        results of, 3534
    recurrence of, familial risk of, 3497-3499
    sexual function and fertility issues in
        female, 3552
        male, 3550-3552
    skeletal defects in, 3500f, 3501f, 4326-4328
    urinary defects in, 3505-3507, 3506f, 3507f
    with small bladder unsuitable for closure,
        management of, 3516-3517
Bladder injury
    clinical signs and symptoms of, 2656
    diagnosis of, 2655-2657, 2656f, 2657f
    etiology of, 2655
    in children, 3938
        classification of, 3939
        diagnosis of, 3939
        treatment of, 3939
        vs. adult injury, 3938-3939

Bladder injury (Continued)
    in laparoscopy, 214
    management of, 2657-2658, 2657f
    outcome and complications of, 2658
    perforation as. See Bladder, perforation of.
Bladder neck
    anterior, lacerations through, in children vs.
        adults, 3938-3939
    contracture of, radical retropubic
        prostatectomy causing, 2973-2974
    division of, in children, 3672
    dysfunction of
        videourodynamic evaluation of, 2001-2002
        voiding dysfunction with, 2038-2039
    female, 58
    function of, in reproduction, 1924
    in radical retropubic prostatectomy
        division of, 2969-2971, 2970f
        intussusception of, 2971-2972, 2971f, 2972f
        preservation and sparing of, 2974-2975
        reconstruction of, 2971, 2971f
    in robotic-assisted laparoscopic radical
        prostatectomy, transection of, 2992,
        2994f
    incompetence of, after posterior urethral
        injury, Mitrofanoff principle for, 3944
    repair of
        in epispadias, continence after, 3546-3547,
            3546t
        in exstrophy patient
            failed, 3536-3537
            modified Young-Dees-Leadbetter
                procedure in, 3524, 3525f-3526f,
                3526
            results of, 3533-3534, 3533t
    transurethral resection of, 2300
    YV-plasty of, 2300
Bladder neck reconstruction, in children, 3664-
    3672
    artificial urinary sphincter in
        results of, 3667-3668
        technique of, 3666-3667, 3667f
    bladder neck division in, 3672
    bulking agents for, 3665-3666
    fascial sling for, 3665
    Pippi-Salle procedure for
        results of, 3672
        technique of, 3669-3670, 3671f, 3672
    urethral lengthening in, 3668-3669
        results of, 3669
        technique of, 3669, 3670f
    Young-Dees-Leadbetter technique of, 3664-
        3665
Bladder neck suspension
    four-corner, 2219-2221, 2220t, 2221f
    Gittes technique, 2212-2213
    needle, anterior colporrhaphy with, 2220t,
        2221-2222, 2221f
    Raz technique, 2213-2214, 2213f
    six-corner, 2219-2221, 2219f, 2220t
    Stamey needle technique, 2212
Bladder neck urethra, 1030, 1030f
Bladder outlet
    anatomy of, 1923, 1923f
    closure of, for bladder filling/storage
        disorders, 2293-2294
    obstruction of, 1978
        bladder diverticula associated with, 2365-
            2366
        definition of, 2039
        detrusor overactivity due to, 1967-1968,
            1969f
        effects of α-adrenergic blockers on, benign
            prostatic hyperplasia and, 2785

Bladder outlet (Continued)
    fetal, 3574
    geriatric incontinence due to, 2310
        treatment of, 2318-2319
    high flow, 1998
    in benign prostatic hyperplasia
        effects of medical therapy on, 2773-2774
        measures of, 2743
        pathophysiology of, 2737-2738
    plasticity of target organ function and,
        2013-2014
    prenatal diagnosis of, 3181
        fetal interventions for, 3187-3189, 3187t,
            3188f
        vaginal pessaries for, 2137-2138, 2138f,
            2139f
    voiding dysfunction with, 2039
    reconstruction of, for bladder filling/storage
        disorders, 2294
    relationship of, to painful bladder
        syndrome/interstitial cystitis, 333, 333f
    resistance of
        decreased
            at anatomic site obstruction, 2300
            at level of striated sphincter, 2301-2304
            in exstrophy patient, 3518
            therapy for decreasing, 2118-2122
            therapy for increasing, 2109-2113, 2109t,
                2110t
    response of, to filling, 1974-1975
    underactivity of, 1977
Bladder outlet syndrome, bladder calculi related
    to, 2664-2665, 2664f-2666f
Bladder preservation protocols, 2475-2476,
    2476t, 2477f
Bladder pressure. See also Detrusor pressure.
    therapy to increase, 2114-2117
Bladder sensation
    cystometrographic studies of, 1993, 1994t
    measurement of, 2083
Bladder Sensation Scale, 2084, 2084t
Bladder spasm, after hypospadias repair, 3720
Bladder training
    for incontinence, 2127-2128
    for overactive bladder, 2127
Bladder wall
    blood supply to, 1932
    collagen of, 1931
    elastin of, 1932
    stroma of, 1931-1932
    nonfibrillar matrix of, 1932
Blastomycosis, 466-467
Bleeding. See Hemorrhage.
Bleeding diatheses, ureteroscopic management
    of, 1520-1521
Blister(s), in autoimmune cutaneous diseases,
    416-417, 416f, 417f
Blood clots
    patient history of, 83
    retention of, after transurethral resection,
        2482-2483
Blood flow
    in transurethral microwave therapy, 2815
    to bladder, 60
Blood gas determinations, cavernosal, in
    priapism, 845
Blood glucose, in chronic renal failure, control
    of, 1353-1354
Blood group(s), ABO, in renal transplantation,
    1314
    screening of, 1308
Blood group antigen(s)
    influence of, on urinary tract infections,
        3237

Blood group antigen(s) (Continued)
Lewis, as prognostic indicator of bladder cancer, 2428
Blood pressure
changes of, in shockwave lithotripsy–treated patients, 1479-1480, 1479t
effect of terazosin on, in nonhypertensive and hypertensive men, 2780t
high. See Hypertension.
Blood products, preparation of, for laparoscopic surgery, 175
Blood tests, for sexual health problems, in females, 872-873, 872f
Blood urea nitrogen, in acute renal failure, 1325
Blood-epididymis barrier, 598
Blood-testis barrier, 589-591, 590f, 591f
development of, 590
disruption of, vasectomy causing, 1103
importance of, 590-591
Blunt injury, to ureters, 1282
hematuria with, 1275-1276
Boari flap, 2509-2511. See also Flap(s).
for lower ureteral injuries, 1288
for ureteral stricture, 1262, 1264, 1264f
laparoscopic, 1264
results of, 2510, 2510f
technique of, 2510
ureteroneocystostomy with
indications for, 1667
technique of, 1667-1668, 1669f-1671f, 1671
Body composition and strength, effects of testosterone therapy on, 858-859
Body habitus, changes in, androgen deprivation therapy causing, 3090-3091
Body mass index
benign prostatic hyperplasia and, 2745
stone formation associated with
ammonium acid urate, 1388
renal, 1365
Body technique, of gastrocystoplasty, in children, 3678-3679, 3678f
Bone marrow stem cell(s), differentiation of, 475. See also B cell(s); T cell(s).
Bone marrow transplantation
allogeneic, for hematologic malignancies, 500
autologous, chemotherapy with, for nonseminomatous germ cell tumors, 923
Bone metastases, prostate cancer and, palliative therapy for, 3028-3029
Bone mineral density, effects of testosterone therapy on, 859
Bone mineralization, regulation of, 1136-1137, 1136f
Bone scans. See also Scintigraphy.
for bladder cancer, 2441
Bonney test, for stress incontinence, 2206, 2313
Bony pelvis, 38, 39f, 2190-2191, 2191f
abnormalities of, in exstrophy patient, 3500-3501, 3500f
Borrelia burgdorferi, in painful bladder syndrome/interstitial cystitis, 339
Bors-Comarr classification, of voiding dysfunction, 1983-1984, 1983t
Bortezomib, for hormone-refractory prostate cancer, 3116
Bosniak classification, of renal cysts, 1572-1573, 1573f, 1574f, 1575, 1772t
Botryoid sarcomata, of vagina, in neonates, 3194-3195
Botulinum toxin
for detrusor overactivity, 2144
for detrusor-sphincter dyssynergia, 2122
for incontinence, 2072-2073

Botulinum toxin (Continued)
for overactive bladder/detrusor overactivity, 2093t, 2106
for painful bladder syndrome/interstitial cystitis, 364
uropharmacology of, 1959-1960, 2122
Bovine collagen, cross-linked
for bladder neck reconstruction, in children, 3666
for endoscopic correction of reflux, 4364, 4364t
Bowel. See also Intestinal entries; specific part.
Bowel disorders, sacral neuromodulation for, 2158
Bowel emptying regimen, for myelomeningocele, 3640
Bowel entrapment, in laparoscopic surgery, 216
Bowel flora, prophylactic antibiotic effect on, 262-263
Bowel injury
in laparoscopic surgery, 211-213, 212f
laparoscopic renal surgery causing, 1807
Bowel insufflation, complications of, 205
Bowel interposition, for upper ureteral injuries, 1287
Bowel management, for urethral sphincter dysfunction, in children, 3619
Bowel neovagina, creation of, 3836, 3836f, 3837f
Bowel obstruction
after augmentation cystoplasty, 3680
due to intestinal anastomosis, 2549-2550, 2550t, 2551f
Bowel perforation, percutaneous nephrostomy causing, 1548
Bowel preparation
for laparoscopic surgery, 175
for radical cystectomy, 2484
for radical perineal prostatectomy, 2980
for robotic-assisted laparoscopic prostatectomy, 2986
for urinary tract reconstruction, 2536-2539
antibiotic, 2538-2539, 2538t
disadvantages of, 2539
in children, 3660-3661
mechanical, 2537-2538, 2537t
for urodynamic evaluation, 3625-3626
Bowenoid papulosis
of male genitalia, 427, 427f
of penis, 962
Bowen's disease, 426, 964
Bowman's capsule, 31, 32f
Bowman's space, glomerular cysts in, autosomal dominant polycystic kidney disease variant and, 3321, 3322f
Brachial pressure index, penile, 762
Brachytherapy
for penile cancer, 985-986
for prostate cancer, 2941
disease control and quality of life following, 3021-3027
high-dose-rate, 3027
implantation in
deployment of radioactive seeds in, 3022-3023, 3022f, 3023f
outcome of, 3023, 3025t
quality assessment of, 3025
isotopes for, 3024
post-implantation biopsy in, 3023, 3024t
post-treatment PSA assessment in, 3023-3025
potency rates after, 3026-3027
rectal toxicity and, 3026
toxicity of, 3025

Brachytherapy (Continued)
urinary toxicity and, 3026
with external beam irradiation, 3025, 3025t
for urothelial tumors, 1681
rectourethral fistula repair after, 2357
Bradley classification, of voiding dysfunction, 1984-1985
Brain dysfunctions, relationship between bladder and, in nocturnal enuresis, 3624
Brain injury, traumatic, voiding dysfunction after, 2016
Brain stem
dysfunction of, nocturnal enuresis and, 3622, 3624
involved in sexual function, 726t
neurologic lesions at or above, voiding dysfunction with, 2014-2019
stroke in, voiding dysfunction with, 2016
Brain tumor, voiding dysfunction with, 2012t, 2016-2017
Bran, dietary, for nephrolithiasis, 1419
Breast cancer, familial, 516t
Breast feeding, protective effect of, urinary tract infections and, 3239
Bricker technique, of small bowel anastomosis, 2557, 2557f
Brief Male Sexual Function Inventory (BMSFI) questionnaire, 751
Brindley-Finetech system, for sacral root stimulation, 2164, 2164f
results of, 2165
Broad ligament, of uterus, 3145
Brödel's lines, 1528
Broder's classification, of squamous cell carcinoma, of penis, 968-969
Bropirimine, for bladder cancer, non–muscle-invasive, 2458
Brugia malayi, 455. See also Filariasis.
Brugia timori, 455. See also Filariasis.
Brushite calculi, surgical management of, 1440
Bryant's traction, for exstrophy patient, 3515, 3516
Buccal delivery, of testosterone
for erectile dysfunction, 772
for late-onset hypogonadism, 858, 858t
Buckling injuries, to penis, Peyronie's disease due to, 820, 820f
Buck's fascia, 70f, 71, 1031, 1032f
Buck's traction, for exstrophy patient, 3515f
Bud theory, of renal dysplasia, 3309
Buffer systems, 1152
Bulbocavernosus muscle, rhythmic contraction of, 725
Bulbocavernosus reflex, 725, 726t
Bulbomembranous urethra, carcinoma of, 1013-1014, 1014f
Bulbourethral artery, 721, 721f, 1034, 1035f
Bulbourethral glands, 1030
secretions of, 614
Bulbourethral vein, 723f
Bulbous urethra, 1029, 1030f
Bulking agents, for bladder neck reconstruction, in children, 3665-3666
Bulking procedures, periurethral, for bladder filling/storage disorders, 2292
Bullet velocity, calculation of, 1274
Bullous dermatosis, linear IgA, of male genitalia, 416, 416f
Bullous pemphigoid, of male genitalia, 415-416, 416f
Bupivacaine, for hypospadias repair, 3718

Burch colposuspension
  for female incontinence, 2170, 2171f
    results of, 2181, 2253t
    technique of, 2176, 2178, 2178f-2180f
  vs. Marshall-Marchetti-Krantz and
    paravaginal repair procedures, 2187-2188
Burkitt's lymphoma, EBV in, 541
Burn(s)
  genital, 2654
  penile, 1052
Buschke-Löwenstein tumor (verrucous
    carcinoma)
  of male genitalia, 427-428, 428f
  of penis, 963-964
Bypass renal surgery. See Renal surgery, bypass.

C
C3. See Complement component C3.
C5. See Complement component C5.
Cadaver donor(s), for renal transplantation,
    1296. See also under Renal transplantation.
Cadaveric dermis, for slings, outcome of, 2247,
    2249
Cadaveric fascia lata, for slings, 2238
  outcome of, 2247
Cadherin. See E-cadherin.
Café au lait spots, in children, 3207
Caffeine consumption
  decreased, in behavioral therapy for
    incontinence, 2128
  male infertility and, 645
Calcifications
  bladder, in schistosomiasis, 453, 453f
  in chronic renal failure, 1353
  in renal tuberculosis, 438, 438f
Calcified plaque, in Peyronie's disease, 825, 825f,
    826f
Calcineurin, in urinary tract development, 1892
Calcineurin inhibitor toxicity, vs. acute allograft
    rejection, 1319t
Calcitonin gene–related peptide
  in male sexual function, 732
  in testicular descent, 3769
  in ureteral function, 1906
Calcitrol, calcium metabolism and, 1372
Calcium
  dietary, in nephrolithiasis, 1414-1415
  in action potential, 1894-1895
  in excitation-contraction coupling, 1899-1900
  in prostate cancer, epidemiologic studies of,
    2862
  in stone formation, 1367
  in ureteral contractile activity, 1897-1898,
    1898f
  intracellular, activation of, 483
  metabolism of, 1371-1372
  oral, for hyperoxaluria, 1422
  renal reabsorption of
    in distal tubules, 1144
    in loop of Henle, 1142
    in proximal convoluted tubules, 1141, 1141f
  urinary excretion of, in neonate, 3156
Calcium antagonists
  effect of, on ureteral function, 1920
  for overactive bladder/detrusor overactivity,
    2099-2100
Calcium calculi
  classification of, 1401-1405
  composition of, 1373, 1373t
  hypercalciuria in, 1374-1377, 1376t, 1401-
    1402, 1402t
  hyperoxaluria in, 1377-1379, 1377f, 1378f,
    1403, 1403t
  hyperuricosuria in, 1379, 1385, 1402

Calcium calculi (Continued)
  hypocitraturia in, 1379, 1403-1404, 1404f,
    1404t
  hypomagnesuria in, 1381-1382, 1404-1405
  low urine pH in, 1379-1380
  pathogenesis of, 1374-1382
  renal tubular acidosis in, 1380-1381
Calcium channel(s), of bladder smooth muscle,
    1927-1928
Calcium channel blockers
  causing geriatric incontinence, 2308t, 2309
  erectile dysfunction caused by, 743, 744t
  for acute renal failure, 1337
  for incontinence, in elderly, 2317t
  for painful bladder syndrome/interstitial
    cystitis, 360t, 361
  uropharmacology of, 1960-1961
Calcium homeostasis, effect of vitamin D and
    parathyroid hormone on, 1136, 1136f
Calcium hydroxyapatite, injection of, for
    incontinence, 2286
Calcium oxalate crystals
  endocytosis of, 1368
  formation of, inhibitors in, 1367, 1370-1371
Calculus(i)
  anatomic predisposition to, 1389-1391
  bladder. See Bladder calculi.
  calcium-containing. See Calcium calculi.
  cultured, in urinary tract infection, 241
  cystine, 1385-1386, 1385f, 1406, 1406f, 1425f
  formation of, in medullary sponge kidney,
    1390-1391, 3349
  in pregnancy, 1391
    medical management of, 1428-1429
    ureteroscopic management of, 1519-1520
  in seminal vesicles, 1115
    endoscopic removal of, 1125
  infection-based, 1386-1387, 1386f, 1387t
    management of, 1425-1426
      consequences of residual fragments in,
        1449
    struvite, 1407-1408, 1407f, 1408f
  medical management of. See Renal calculi,
    medical management of.
  mineral metabolism and
    calcium in, 1371-1372
    magnesium in, 1372
    oxalate in, 1372
    phosphorus in, 1372
  non-calcium-containing. See also specific type.
    composition of, 1373, 1373t
  physiochemistry of, 1365-1371
    crystal aggregation and retention in, 1368-
      1369, 1369f, 1370f
    crystal formation in, inhibitors and
      promoters of, 1368, 1370-1371
    crystal growth in, 1367-1368
    crystal matrix in, 1371
    crystal nucleation in, 1367
    saturation states in, 1366-1367, 1366f
  preputial, 2672-2673
  renal. See Renal calculi.
  single, low-risk, abbreviated protocol for,
    1395-1397, 1395t, 1396f, 1397f, 1397t
  surgical management of, 1431-1507. See also
    at specific anatomy site.
    historical overview of, 1431-1434
  ureteral. See Ureteral calculi.
  urethral. See Urethral calculi.
  uric acid-based, 1405, 1405f. See also Uric acid
    calculi.
  urinary. See Urinary calculi.
  within urethral diverticulum, 2389-2390,
    2389f

Calicovesicostomy, laparoscopic, for
    ureteropelvic junction obstruction,
    1253
Caloric intake, for acute renal failure, 1338
Calyceal diverticulum(a), 3354. See also Renal
    calyx (calyces), diverticula of.
Camera
  in laparoscopic surgery, 189-190
  video, for ureteroscopy, 1515
Camey II technique, of orthotopic urinary
    diversion, 2634, 2634f
Camper's fascia, 38, 40, 40f
Cancer. See also at anatomic site; specific
    neoplasm.
  adhesion molecules and, 539-540
  advanced, vesicovaginal fistula associated
    with, 2326
  after renal transplantation, 1323-1324
    risk of recurrence of, 1298-1299
  AIDS-associated, 398-400, 428, 429f
  angiogenesis in, 542-545
  apoptosis and, 531-532
    alternative regulators of, 532-533
  cell surface and, 538-540
  cellular signaling and, 535-538
  dysregulation and
    hypermethylation in, 514-515
    mutation in, 513, 513f
    oncogenes in, 513-514
    tumor suppressor genes in, 514
  gene therapy for, 551
  in chronic renal failure, 1346
  increased incidence of, conduit urinary
    diversion and, 2576
  inherited susceptibility to, 515-520, 515t,
    516t
    clues in, 516-517, 516f, 517f
    in Birt-Hogg-Dubé syndrome, 518
    in genitourinary syndromes, 517-519
    in hereditary nonpolyposis colorectal
      cancer, 519
    in hereditary papillary renal cell carcinoma,
      518
    in hereditary prostate cancer, 518
    in von Hippel–Lindau disease, 517-518
    in Wilms' tumor, 519
    polymorphisms and, 519-520, 520f
  late development of, after continent urinary
    diversion, 2581-2582
  membrane-bound receptors and, 538-539
  metastatic. See Metastasis.
  molecular diagnosis of, 547-550
    differential display technology and PCA3
      in, 548-549
    epitomics in, 549
    genetics in, 548
    immunohistochemistry in, 547-548
    microarray technology in, 549
    new modalities in, 550
    proteomics in, 549
  mouse models of, 545-547
  of male genitalia, 423f-427f, 426-430
  priapism associated with, 840
  stem cells and, 533-535
  telomerase and, 533, 534f
  tumor syndromes associated with, 515t
  tumor syndromes not associated with, 516t
Cancer cells, xenografting of, 545
Cancer of Prostate Strategic Urologic Research
    Endeavor (CAPSURE), 157
Cancer Rehabilitation Evaluation System
    (CARES), 150
Cancer Rehabilitation Evaluation System Short
    Form (CARES- SF), 152

Cancer therapy. *See also specific type, e.g.,*
    Chemotherapy.
    spermatogenesis and, 611
    targets for
        death receptors as, 530
        ligands as, 530
Cancer vaccines, 499-500
*Candida*
    in intertrigo, 424, 424f
    in prostatitis, 307
    infection with. *See* Candidiasis.
*Candida albicans*
    in pediatric urinary tract infections, 3265
    in urinary sediment, 106f, 109
    in vaginitis, 385
Candidemia
    in children, 3265
    kidney associated with, 462
    predisposing factors for, 460
Candidiasis, 459-464
    clinical manifestations of, 460, 460f, 462
    cutaneous, 460
    diagnosis of, 462-463
    disseminated, treatment of, 461t, 464
    epidemiology of, 459-460
    in children, 462
    of bladder, 460, 469f
    of female genitalia, 460
    of kidney, 462
        management of, 300
    of male genitalia, 460
    of prostate, 460, 468f
    of ureters, 462
    predisposing factors in, 460
    radiography of, 463, 463f
    systemic, 462
        treatment of, 463-464
    treatment of, 463-464
        antifungals in, 461t, 464t
    vulvovaginal, 385, 460
Candiduria, 460
    treatment of, 463
Cannula site, bleeding at, in laparoscopy, 209,
    209f, 216
Cannulation, tubal, in evaluation of fertility, 612
Cantwell-Ransley repair, modified, of bladder
    exstrophy, 3520, 3520f-3523f, 3523-3524
    results of, 3531-3532
Capacitation, of sperm, 605
Capillary hemangioma, of male genitalia, 433
Capsaicin
    efficacy of, vs. resiniferatoxin, 2107
    for incontinence, 2072
    for painful bladder syndrome/interstitial
        cystitis, 362t, 364
    intravesical therapy with, 2106-2107
    uropharmacology of, 1958
Capsular artery, 63, 63f
Captopril, for cystinuria, 1425
Captopril test, for renovascular hypertension,
    1169
Captopril-enhanced renography, of renovascular
    hypertension, 1170
Caput epididymis, 597, 598. *See also* Epididymis.
Carbohydrate(s), intake of, in acute renal failure,
    1338
Carbon dioxide, for pneumoperitoneum, in
    laparoscopic surgery, 199
Carbon dioxide embolus, pediatric laparoscopy
    and, 3917
Carbon dioxide lasers
    for penile cancer, 973, 993
    in lithotripsy, 1514
Carbon monoxide, in renal hemodynamics, 1135

Carbonated beverages, for nephrolithiasis, 1411-
    1412
Carboplatin, for hormone-refractory prostate
    cancer, 3105t
Carcinoembryonic antigen (CEA), T cell
    recognition of, 496
Carcinogen(s), in bladder cancer, 2413, 2414
    screening for exposure to, 2436-2437
Carcinogenesis
    mutation and, 513, 513f
    prostate, genes implicated in, 2861
Carcinoid(s)
    of kidney, 1635-1636
    of seminal vesicles, 1116
    of testis, 930
Carcinoma. *See specific type, e.g.,* Transitional
    cell carcinoma.
Carcinoma in situ
    of bladder, 2418-2419, 2418f
        BCG therapy for, 2455
    of testes, 896-897, 899t
        cryptorchidism associated with, 3773, 3902
        in adolescents, 3901-3902
        management of, 897, 899, 899t
    of upper urinary tract, 1643, 1655
Carcinosarcoma
    of bladder, 2444-2445
    of prostate, 2881
Cardiac anomalies, in prune-belly syndrome,
    3485t, 3486
Cardiac arrest, in laparoscopy, 211
Cardinal ligaments, 2197, 2198f
Cardiomyopathy, catecholamine-induced,
    pheochromocytoma associated with, 1859
Cardiovascular disease
    erectile dysfunction with, 777-778, 778f
    in primary hyperaldosteronism, 1851
Cardiovascular system, effects of testosterone
    therapy on, 859
Cardiovascular toxicity, of contrast media, 113
Cartilage cells, injections of, for bladder neck
    reconstruction, in children, 3666
Caruncle, urethral, vs. urethral diverticula, 2384-
    2385, 2384f
CASA (computer-assisted semen analysis), 617.
    *See also* Semen analysis.
Casale continent catheterizable stoma, in
    continent vesicostomy, 3698, 3699f
Cascade phenomena, of complement activation,
    474
Case mix, in health care costs, 146-147
Caspases, in regulation of apoptosis, 531, 1205
Caspofungin, 469
    cost of, 464t
    dosage of, 461t
Cast(s), in urinary sediment, 107, 107f, 108f
Castration, for prostate cancer
    medical, 3083, 3087-3088, 3087t
    surgical, 3082-3083, 3085, 3085t
Catecholamine(s)
    action of, 1829-1830, 1829t
    metabolism of, 1829, 1830f
    synthesis of, 1828-1829, 1829f
    urinary, effects of drugs on, 1863t
Catecholamine receptors, action of, 1829t
Catheter(s). *See also specific catheter, e.g.,* Foley
    catheter.
    bacteriuria associated with, 296-297
    condom, for geriatric incontinence, 2317-2318
    dilating
        in percutaneous nephrostomy, 1541, 1558-
            1560, 1558f, 1559f
        postoperative removal of, in renal
            transplant recipient, 1313-1314

Catheter(s) *(Continued)*
    in urodynamic studies, 1988-1989
    indwelling, urinary tract infection associated
        with, 238
    intraurethral, stenting with, 2806
    removal of, after orthotopic urinary diversion,
        2633
    single/dual, in postoperative vesicovaginal
        fistula drainage, 2333
    ureteral
        commonly used, 170f
        for ureteroscopy, 1511t, 1512, 1512f
    urethral. *See* Urethral catheter.
Catheterization
    bladder calculi related to, 2665-2666
    clean intermittent
        for bladder filling/storage disorders, 2294-
            2295
        for cloacal disorders, 3865-3866, 3866f
        for urethral sphincter dysfunction, in
            children, 3620
        in renal transplant recipients, 1300
    continuous, for bladder filling/storage
        disorders, 2295-2297
    ureteral, in localizing site of bacteriuria, 241,
        241t
    urethral. *See* Urethral catheterization.
Catheterizing pouches, continent, for continent
    urinary diversion, 2586-2591
    care of, 2588-2589
    methodology of, 2587-2588
    patient's questions regarding, 2588
    surgical principles in, 2586-2587, 2587f
Cation(s), transport of, effect of ureteral
    obstruction on, 1202-1203
Cauda equina syndrome, 2031
Caudal embryology, 3830-3832, 3831f
Caudal regression syndrome, 3832
Cautery wire balloon endopyelotomy, for
    ureteropelvic junction obstruction
    complications of, 1238-1239
    indications for and contraindications to, 1237,
        1237f
    postoperative care following, 1237
    results of, 1237-1238
    technique of, 1237, 1238f
Cautery wire balloon incision
    in endopyelotomy, 1237
    in ureteral stricture repair, 1257-1258
Caveolae, ureteral, 1891
Caveolin, 540
Cavernosal fibrosis, penile prosthesis for, 798-
    800, 799f, 800f
Cavernosography, pharmacologic, 762, 762f
Cavernosometry, pharmacologic, 761-762
Cavernous artery, 721, 721f, 1035, 1035f
    occlusive pressure of, evaluation of, 760,
        761f
    pharmacologic arteriography of, 760-761, 761f
Cavernous (subcutaneous) hemangioma, of
    male genitalia, 3760
Cavernous nerve, 724, 725f
    stimulation of, 724-725
Cavernous vein, 723f, 1034, 1034f
Cavitation mechanism, of stone fragmentation,
    1476
CD (cluster of differentiation) markers, 475-477,
    476t
CD4+ T cell(s)
    activation and expansion of, 485, 485f
    dendritic cell activation of, 485f
    in HIV infection, 389, 391, 392
    in painful bladder syndrome/interstitial
        cystitis, 341

CD4+ T cell(s) (Continued)
in tumor immunology, 495
stimulation of, 1315
CD8+ T cell(s)
activation and expansion of, 485, 485f
dendritic cell activation of, 485f
in cytolysis of target cells in, 487-488, 487f
in painful bladder syndrome/interstitial cystitis, 341
in tumor immunology, 495
CDKN1A gene, in prostate cancer, 524
CDKN1C gene, in Beckwith-Wiedemann syndrome, 519
CDKN2A gene, in bladder cancer, 523
CEA (carcinoembryonic antigen), T cell recognition of, 496
Cecocystoplasty, in children, 3675
Cecoureterocele, 3383, 3384f
definition of, 3383
Cecum, anatomy of, 2534
Cefepime, for pediatric urinary tract infections, 3248t
Cefixime, for gonorrhea, 379
Cefotaxime, for pediatric urinary tract infections, 3248t
Ceftazidime, for pediatric urinary tract infections, 3248t
Ceftibuten, for pediatric urinary tract infections, 3248t
Ceftriaxone
for gonorrhea, 379
for pediatric urinary tract infection, 3248t
Cefuroxime, for pediatric urinary tract infections, 3248t
Celiac disease, cutaneous manifestation of (dermatitis herpetiformis), 416
Celiac plexus, 15, 17, 17f
Cell(s). See also named cell, e.g., Leydig cell(s).
aging, senescence, and immortality of, in regulation of prostate growth, 2713-2714
in prostate, 2680-2683, 2680t
in urinary sediment, 105-107, 105f-107f
Cell adhesion molecule(s), 539-540, 2694-2696
caveolin as, 540, 2695
E-cadherin as, 540
expression of
in endothelial cells, 493
unregulated, 492-493, 493t
in bladder cancer, 2428
in lymphocyte trafficking, 492-494, 493f, 493t
in prostate cancer, 2695-2696
integrins as, 539-540, 2695
Cell adhesion molecule-1, platelet/endothelial, 493-494
Cell cycle, 520-526
control of, in prostate growth, 2711-2712
$G_1S$ checkpoint in, 521-524
cip/cik function and, 523-524
cyclin-dependent kinase complexes and, 523-524
INK4 function and, 523
retinoblastoma protein and, 524
TP53 in urologic malignancies and, 522-523
TP53 regulator of, 521-522, 522f
$G_2M$ checkpoint in, 525, 525f
regulation of, in renal cell carcinoma, 1590-1591
S phase of, 524-525
steps in, 520-521, 521f
therapeutic implications of, 525-526
Cell death, 531
in regulation of prostate growth, 2714-2715
programmed. See Apoptosis.

Cell death (Continued)
tubular, cellular and molecular mechanisms in, 1205, 1206f
Cell injury, mechanisms of, in cryotherapy, 3034-3035, 3035t
Cell populations
antibodies in, 478, 478f
antigen-presenting cells in, 477
granulocytes in, 477
homing of, 475
immunoresponsive, 475-478, 476f
lymphocytes in, 476-477. See also B cell(s); Natural killer cell(s); T cell(s).
macrophages in, 477
monocytes in, 477
vascular endothelial cells in, 477
Cell signal transduction
B cell receptor pathway in, 483-484
intracellular calcium and protein kinase C in, activation of, 483
Jak/STAT pathway in, 484
Ras pathway in, 483
T cell receptor pathway in, 482-483, 482f
Cell surface, cancer and, 538-540
adhesion molecules in, 539-540
receptors in, 538-539
Cell surface activation
B cells in, 481-482
major histocompatibility complex in, 479, 479f
of immune response, 478-482
presentation of antigen in, 480-481, 480f
recognition of alloantigens in, 481
T-cell receptor in, 479-480
Cell transplantation, in tissue engineering
bladder replacement and, 561-562, 563f, 571f
ex situ bladder tissue formation and, 561
in situ bladder tissue formation and, 561, 561f
principles of, 554, 554f
Cellular injury, of kidney for transplantation, 1306
Cellular signaling, 535-538
epidermal growth factor in, 536
G protein–coupled ligand in, 537-538
insulin-like growth factor in, 537
NKX3-1 in, 536
PTEN in, 535-536
transforming growth factor-β in, 536-537
Cellulitis
in HIV patients, 397
in radiation-induced penile injury, 1052
of male genitalia, 419, 420f
Central nervous system, renin-angiotensin-aldosterone in, 1163
Central pathways, in micturition reflex modulation, 1946-1947
Central tendon, of perineum, 68
Central venous pressure, unreliable reading of, pneumoperitoneum with, 200
Centrally acting drugs, for erectile dysfunction, 782-783
Cephalad renal ectopia, 3281
Cephalexin
for pediatric urinary tract infections, 3248t
prophylactic, 3250t, 3251
low-dose prophylactic, for recurrent urinary tract infections, 262t, 264
Cephalosporins, for urinary tract infections, 245t, 246t, 247t, 248
in children, 3248t
Ceramide, in regulation of apoptosis, 533
Cerebellar ataxia, voiding dysfunction with, 2017

Cerebral palsy
diagnosis of, 3648
etiology of, 3648
findings in, 3648-3651, 3650f
urodynamic, 3650t
lower urinary tract function in, 3650t
management of, 3651
perinatal risk factors in, 3650t
voiding dysfunction in, 2012t, 2017
Cerebrovascular accident. See also Stroke.
brain stem, voiding dysfunction after, 2014-2016
Cernilton, for prostatitis, clinical trial data on, 323
Cervical atresia, 3838-3839, 3839f
Cervical cancer, human papillomavirus causing, 380-381
Cervical mucus, sperm interaction with, 630-631
Cervical myelopathy, voiding dysfunction in, 2028-2029
Cervix
duplication of, unilaterally imperforate vagina with, 3839, 3839f, 3840f
strawberry, trichomoniasis and, 380
Cesarean section, vesicouterine fistula following, 2345
Cetrorelix, for benign prostatic hyperplasia, 2792-2793
dosage of, 2788t
C-fiber(s)
of bladder, 2080
of lower urinary tract, 1939
C-fiber spinal reflex
capsaicin-sensitive, after spinal cord injury, 1966
of lower urinary tract, 1938-1939, 1939t
pharmacotherapy of, 1958
CFTR gene, 611, 621
genetic abnormalities associated with, 717
genetic testing for, 632
vasal anomalies and, 3797
Chancre, syphilitic, penile, 376f, 420f
Chancroid, 420f
diagnosis of, 374-375, 375f
in HIV patients, 395-396
treatment of, 375
Chaparonin, binding of, by androgen receptors, 2698
Charge(s), in health care costs, 145
CHARGE association, vesicoureteral reflux in, 4344
Chemical(s), prostatitis caused by, 309
Chemical vasectomy, 1101. See also Vasectomy.
Chemokine(s)
and tissue recruitment of leukocytes, 494-495
production of, 494
representative, 494t
Chemokine receptors, representative, 494t
Chemolysis, for bladder calculi, 2668
Chemoprevention, of prostate cancer, 2867-2871
antioxidants in, 2870-2871
clinical trial design for, 2867-2868, 2868t
COX-2 inhibitors in, 2871
finasteride in, 2869-2870, 2870t
green tea in, 2871
lycopene in, 2871
models of secondary prevention in, 2868t
other 5α-reductase inhibitors in, 2870
Prostate Cancer Prevention Trial in, 2868-2870, 2869f, 2870t
selective estrogen receptor modulators in, 2871
selenium in, 2870
vitamin E with, 2871

Chemoprevention, of prostate cancer
    (Continued)
  soy in, 2871
  target populations for, 2868t
  vitamin E in, 2870-2871
Chemoprophylaxis, postexposure, for HIV
    infection, 401
Chemotherapeutic agents. See also specific agent.
  as inhibitors of angiogenesis, 543
  erectile dysfunction caused by, 746
Chemotherapy
  adjuvant
    for invasive bladder cancer, 2474, 2474t
    for nonseminomatous germ cell tumors,
        stage IIB, 919, 949
    for renal cell carcinoma, locally advanced,
        1622-1623, 1623t, 1624t
    for urothelial tumors, 1682
  combination
    for bladder cancer, non–muscle-invasive,
        2460
    for penile cancer, 987-988, 988t
    for yolk sac tumors, 3904
  exposure to, urothelial tumors associated
      with, 1639
  for bladder cancer
    invasive
      adjuvant, 2474, 2474t
      hyperthermia and, 2476
      intra-arterial, 2476
      neoadjuvant, 2473, 2473t
      perioperative, 2473
      transurethral resection and partial
          cystectomy with, 2475
    metastatic
      newer agents in, 2477-2478
      systemic, 2476-2477
    non–muscle-invasive, 2458-2460
      bacille Calmette-Guérin with, 2460
      combination, 2460
      doxorubicin in, 2459
      mitomycin C in, 2459
      novel agents in, 2459-2460
      thiotepa in, 2459
  for metastatic renal cell carcinoma, 1626
  for neuroblastoma, 3877
  for nonseminomatous germ cell tumors
    stage I and stage IIA, 918, 918t, 948
    stage IIB, 919-920, 920t
    stage IIC and stage III, 920-921
      residual mass after, 922-923
  for paratesticular and testicular tumors, 933-
      934
  for penile cancer, 987-989, 988t
  for prostate cancer
    hormone therapy with, before radical
        prostatectomy, 3061, 3061t
    hormone-refractory, 3105-3112
      clinical trials of
        docetaxel in, 3108-3110, 3109f, 3110f,
            3110t
        multidrug regimens in, 3106, 3107t,
            3108
        single agents in, 3106, 3106t
        Southwest Oncology Group study in,
            3110, 3110f, 3111f
        survival comparisons in, 3108t
      efficacy of, 3105-3106, 3105t
    radiation therapy with, 3065
  for seminomas
    stage I, 910-911
    stage IIC and stage III, 912, 913t
      residual mass after, 912-913
  for urethral cancer, in males, 1014-1015

Chemotherapy (Continued)
  for urothelial tumors, 1659
  male infertility due to, 643-644
  neoadjuvant, for locally advanced cancer,
      before radical prostatectomy, 3060-3061,
      3061t
  preoperative, for Wilms' tumor, vs. immediate
      nephrectomy, 3895-3897, 3896f
  salvage, for nonseminomatous germ cell
      tumors, stage IIC and stage III, 923-924
  side effect(s) of, second malignancy as, 923-
      924, 3898
  single-agent, for penile cancer, 987
  toxicity of, 923-924
  with hormone therapy, for locally advanced
      cancer, before radical prostatectomy,
      3061, 3061t
Cherney incision, 2483
Chest, bell-shaped, in bilateral renal agenesis,
    3271
Children. See also Infants; Neonates.
  abdominal masses in
    cystic and solid, 3208
    evaluation of, 3199, 3203t
  abdominal pain in, evaluation of, 3199,
      3202t
  abscess in, perinephric and renal, 3246
  acute scrotum in, 3790-3794. See also
      Scrotum, acute.
  adrenal carcinoma in, 1842
  artificial sphincter in, incompetence of, 2402
  augmentation cystoplasty in, 3672-3691. See
      also Cystoplasty, augmentation, in
      children.
  bacterial infections in, fever and, 3206, 3206t
  Bartter syndrome in, 3229
  bladder anomalies in, 3573-3582. See also
      specific anomaly.
    classification of, 3574-3582
    postnatal detection of, 3576
    prenatal detection of, 3574-3575, 3575f
  bladder diverticula in, 3579-3580, 3579f
  bladder duplication in, 3580-3581, 3581f
  bladder function in, normal, 3605-3609,
      3606f-3608f
  bladder hemangioma in, 3582
  café au lait spots in, 3207
  candidiasis in, 462
  cystinuria in, 3223
  cystitis in, 3234-3236, 3235f
    eosinophilic, 3582
    inflammatory hemorrhagic, 3263
    interstitial, 3263-3264
  daytime and nighttime enuresis in, 3204
  developmental milestones in, 3210, 3211t
  dysfunctional elimination syndrome in, 3611,
      3613
  dysfunctional voiding in, 2038
  emergent evaluations of, 3198-3200, 3199t,
      3200t-3201t, 3202t, 3203, 3203t
  Fanconi syndrome in, 3228, 3228t
  focal segmental glomerulosclerosis in, 3225-
      3226
  genitourinary injury in, 3929-3945. See also
      specific anatomic site; specific injury.
    assessment and treatment of, 3930-3932
    grading of, 3931t
    imaging of, indications for, 3930
    vs. adult injury, 3929-3930
  Gitelman's syndrome in, 3229
  glomerular filtration rate in, 3153
  hematuria in
    epidemiology of, 3217-3219
    gross, 3212

Children (Continued)
  microscopic, 3212
  physical examination of, 3219
  screening for, 3218
  treatment algorithm for, 3220f
  hemolytic-uremic syndrome in, 3227-3228
  Henoch-Schönlein purpura in, 3226-3227
  hydrocele in, 3203
  hypercalciuria in, 3222-3223
  hyperoxaluria in, 3223
  hyperuricosuria in, 3223
  IgA nephropathy in, 3226-3227
  incontinence in, injectable therapies for, 2273
    intraurethral technique of, 2280
  inguinal hernia in, 3203
  laparoscopic adrenalectomy in, 1887
  lupus nephritis in, 3227
  macroglossia in, 3208
  megaureter in. See Megaureter(s).
  membranous nephropathy in, 3226
  nephritic syndromes in, 3226-3228
  nephrogenic adenoma in, 3581-3582
  nephrogenic diabetes insipidus in, 3229
  nephrotic syndrome in, 3225
    congenital, 3226
  nocturnal enuresis in, 3621-3624, 3621f-3623f
  pheochromocytoma in, 1861
  posterior urethral valves in. See Urethral
      valves, posterior.
  postinfectious glomerulonephritis in, 3226
  proteinuria in, 3219-3221
    evaluation of, 3220, 3221f
    investigation of, 3220-3221
    quantitation of urinary protein in, 3219
  pyelonephritis in, 3234-3236, 3235f
    radiologic findings in, 3245-3246
    sequelae of, 3256-3258, 3257f, 3259f
    signs and symptoms of, 3245
    xanthogranulomatous, 3258-3259
  renal artery stenosis in, 1184
  renal calculi in, 1427, 3221-3224
    diagnostic approach to, 3224, 3224f, 3225t
    identifiable causes of, 3222t
  renal cell carcinoma in, 1583
  renal disease in, 3217-3231
    cystic, 3313-3357, 3314t. See also Autosomal
        dominant polycystic kidney disease;
        Autosomal recessive polycystic kidney
        disease; Glomerulocystic kidney
        disease; Multicystic dysplastic kidney.
    end-stage, 1296, 3229-3230
      renal transplantation for, 1296
    hypodysplastic, 3310t, 3312-3313, 3312f
    hypoplastic, 3310-3312, 3310t, 3311f
    parenchymal, 3225-3228
    tubular disorders and, 3228-3229
  renal function in, evaluation of, 3153-3156,
      3155f, 3157f
  renal insufficiency in, chronic, 3229-3230
  renal tubular acidosis in, 3154-3155, 3155f,
      3228-3229
  retractile testes in, 3208
  routine evaluations of, 3199t, 3203-3204
  school-aged
    posterior urethral valve presentation in,
        3588. See also Urethral valves,
        posterior.
    urinary values for, 3225t
  semi-urgent evaluations of, 3199t, 3203
  sexual abuse of, evaluation of, 3199, 3203,
      3210
  spinal injury in, 3651-3653, 3651f
  supernumerary nipples in, 3207
  Takayasu's arteritis in, 1184

Children (Continued)
undescended testes in. See Cryptorchidism.
ureteropelvic junction obstruction in, 3359-
3382. See also Ureteropelvic junction
obstruction, in children.
ureteroscopy in, 1520
ureters in, length and diameter of, 4328t
urethral duplication in, 3601, 3602f, 3603
urethral polyps in, 3601, 3601f
urethral prolapse in, 3210
urethral stricture in, 3600, 3601f
urethral valve anomalies in. See Urethral
valves, posterior.
urgent evaluations of, 3199t, 3203
urinary tract infection in, 3232-3268. See also
Urinary tract infection, in children.
urinary tract reconstruction in, 3656-3702.
See also Urinary tract reconstruction, in
children; specific procedure.
urologic office visit for, 3204-3215
hematuria in, 3212
history in, 3205
laboratory examination in, 3211-3212
outpatient procedures in, 3214-3215
physical examination in, 3205-3210, 3206t,
3207t, 3208f, 3209f, 3211f, 3211t
radiologic examination in, 3212-3214,
3214f
surgical procedures performed in, 3215,
3215f
voiding history in, 3205
vaginal bleeding in, 3209
tumors and, 3210
vaginal discharge in, 3209
vesicoureteral reflux in, 4323-4367. See also
Vesicoureteral reflux.
voiding dysfunction in
neuropathic, 3625-3653
central nervous system insults and, 3648-
3653
neurospinal dysraphisms and, 3628-3648
urodynamic evaluation of, 3625-3628
non-neuropathic. See also Urethral
sphincter, dysfunction of.
classification of, 3609-3611, 3610f
epidemiology of, 3609
evaluation of, 3614-3618
management of, 3618-3620
prevalence of, 3609
sacral neuromodulation for, 2157-2158
urinary tract infections and, 3262
Children's Oncology Group Staging System, for
testicular germ cell tumors, 3903t
Chills, patient history of, 88
Chlamydia, in urinary tract infections, 229
Chlamydia pneumoniae, in painful bladder
syndrome/interstitial cystitis, 339
Chlamydia trachomatis
in lymphogranuloma venereum, 377
in proctitis, 371
in prostatitis, 306-307
infection with
diagnosis of, 378
testing for, 627
treatment of, 378-379
prevalence of, 372
Chloramphenicol, for Pasteurella multocida
infection, 2651
Chloride, renal reabsorption of
in cortical collecting tubules, 1144-1145
in distal tubules, 1144
in loop of Henle, 1142
Chloroquine derivatives, for painful bladder
syndrome/interstitial cystitis, 360t, 361

Chlorothiazide, for renal tubular acidosis, in
infant and child, 3155
Chlorthalidone
for absorptive hypercalcemia, 1418
for renal hypercalciuria, 1419, 1421t
Cholesterol, in prostatic secretions, 2718
Cholesterol embolism, of renal artery, 1166
Cholinergic agonists, role of, in ureteral
function, 1904
Cholinergic receptors
in pontine micturition center, 1965
muscarinic, 1949-1951, 1949f, 1950t
drug selectivity for, 1951
Cholinesterase inhibitors, causing geriatric
incontinence, 2308t, 2309
Chondrocyte injections
autologous, for incontinence, 2286
for vesicoureteral reflux, 568, 568f
Chondrocytes, for endoscopic correction of
reflux, 4364t, 4365
Chondroitin sulfate, for painful bladder
syndrome/interstitial cystitis, 362t, 364
Chordee, 1087. See also Penile curvature.
correction of, 1048-1049, 1048f, 1049f
etiology of, 3707-3708
release of, in exstrophy patient, 3519-3520
without hypospadias, 1088-1089, 3756, 3756f
Choriocarcinoma
of bladder, 2445
testicular, 895
incidence, pathology, and presentation of,
898t
Chromaffin cells, 1828, 1829f
Chromatin
abnormal, risk factors for, 626
integrity testing of, in male infertility, 626-627
organization and regulation of, in prostate
growth, 2712-2713
Chromophilic renal cell carcinoma, 1592t, 1593-
1594, 1594f
cytogenetic abnormalities associated with,
1594-1595
Chromophobic renal cell carcinoma, 1592t,
1595, 1595f
Chromosomal abnormalities
in bladder cancer, 2429-2430
in locally advanced prostate cancer, 3055t
in neuroblastoma, 3870
in urothelial tumors, 1639-1640
in Wilms' tumor, 3887-3888, 3892
Chromosomal rearrangement, in proto-
oncogene conversion to oncogene, 514
Chromosomal resistance, of bacteria, to
antibiotics, 244
Chromosomal sex, 3799-3801, 3800f-3802f
Chromosomal syndromes, associated with
genitourinary anomalies, 3201t
Chromosomal translocations, male infertility
and, 640
Chromosome 8p, loss of heterozygosity on, in
prostate cancer, 536
Chromosome 9 deletions, in bladder cancer,
2412, 2429
Chromosome 10q, loss of heterozygosity on, in
prostate cancer, 535
Chromosome 13q deletions, in bladder cancer,
2412, 2429
Chromosome 17p deletions, in bladder cancer,
2429
Chronic obstructive pulmonary disease,
incontinence and, 2190
Chronic pelvic pain syndrome
clinical presentation of, 311-312
cytokine levels in, 317-318

Chronic pelvic pain syndrome (Continued)
diagnostic algorithm for, 318, 318f
evaluation of, 318, 319t
sacral neuromodulation for, 2157
symptom assessment in, 312, 313f
therapeutic algorithm for, 326f
zinc levels in, 318
Chylous ascites, after laparoscopy, 219
Chyluria, 96-97
in filariasis, 457
Cigarette smoking. See Smoking.
Ciliary dyskinesia, primary, 611, 623
Cimetidine, for painful bladder
syndrome/interstitial cystitis, 360, 360t
Cip/cik, G$_1$S checkpoint and, 523-524
Ciprofloxacin
for chancroid, 375
in HIV patients, 395-396
for gonorrhea, 379
for pediatric urinary tract infections, 3248t
for prostatitis, 320t, 321, 327t
Circadian rhythm, in cortisol secretion, 1826,
1826f
Circle loop nephrostomy, 1560, 1561f
Circular stapling device, ileocolonic stapled
intestinal anastomosis with, 2543-2544,
2543f
Circulation, to pelvis, 46, 50f, 51-52, 51f
Circumcaval ureter. See Ureter(s), circumcaval
(retrocaval).
Circumcision, 1045-1046, 1046f, 3747-3750
and limited excision, for penile cancer, 973
anesthesia for, 3747
complications of, 1045, 3748-3750, 3750f
contraindications to, 3747-3748, 3749f
controversies surrounding, 1045
decreased risk of urinary tract infection with,
3232, 3239
female, 3839-3840, 3841f
Gomco clamp for, 1045
HIV and STDs and, 388
in adults, 1046
in pediatric office, 3215
incision in, for corpus cavernosum laceration,
2650, 2650f
meatal stenosis following, 1044-1045, 1045f
neonatal
advantages and benefits of, 3747
prophylactic effect of, on penile cancer, 965,
966
urethral injury after, 3941
Circumferential compression mechanism, of
stone fragmentation, 1475
Circumflex artery, 72, 72f, 721f, 1034, 1035f
Circumflex vein, 72, 72f, 722f, 723f, 1031,
1034f
Cisapride, to facilitate bladder emptying, 2116
Cisplatin
for seminomas, stage IIC and stage III, 912
gemcitabine with, for bladder cancer,
metastatic, 2477
toxicity of, 924
Cisterna chyli, 14
Citrate, as inhibitor of stone formation, 1370
Citric acid, in prostatic secretions, 2716
Citrus juices, increased intake of, for
nephrolithiasis, 1412
C-kit, in cell migration and proliferation, 1896
Clamp(s)
Gomco, 1045
vas deferens fixation, ring-tipped, 1099f
CLCN5 gene, DNA screening for, 1375
Clean intermittent catheterization. See
Catheterization, clean intermittent.

Clear cell carcinoma, genetics of, 1584t, 1585-1587, 1585t, 1586f

Clear cell sarcoma, of kidney, in children, 3898

Clenbuterol, for overactive bladder/detrusor overactivity, 2104

Clindamycin, for bacterial vaginosis, 384

Clinical preservation, of kidney, for transplantation, 1306-1308

Clinical Symptom Scales, in painful bladder syndrome/interstitial cystitis, 354-355, 354t, 355t, 357t

Clipping devices, in laparoscopy, 194f, 195

Clitoris
  atrophy of, 871f
  bifid, in exstrophy patient, 3505, 3505f, 3524
  development of, 3142f, 3143
  dorsal vein of, 51
  glans of, absent, 869f
  hypertrophy of, 3855f
    high vaginal confluence with, management of, 3858-3859, 3859f-3861f
    low vaginal confluence with, management of, 3856-3858, 3858f
    management of, 3858-3859, 3859f-3861f
  nerves of, stimulation of, 2159
  phimosis of, 866, 868f, 869f
  physical examination of, 866, 867f
  sexual pain disorders involving, 883
  suspensory ligament of, 67

Clitoromegaly, in 46,XY complete gonadal dysgenesis, 3813, 3813f

Clitoroplasty, for intersex conditions
  results of, 3863-3864
  simultaneous vaginoplasty and labioplasty with, 3854
  technique of, 3854-3855

Cloaca
  anatomy of, spectrum of, 3853, 3853f
  embryology of, 3831

Cloacal anomaly(ies)
  evaluation of, 3848
  history and physical examination of, 3848-3849, 3850f
  radiographic and endoscopic evaluation of, 3852-3853, 3852f, 3853f
  surgical resection of, 3865-3869
    definitive repair of, 3866-3868
    gastrointestinal decompression in, 3865
    genitourinary decompression in, 3865-3866, 3866f
    initial timing, management, and principles of, 3865
    obstructive urinary pathology repair in, 3866
    operative technique in, 3866-3868, 3867f
    results of, 3868-3869, 3868t

Cloacal exstrophy, 3538-3544
  anatomic considerations in, 3538-3541
  antenatal detection of, 3575
  at birth, evaluation and management of, 3541-3542, 3541t. See also Cloacal exstrophy, reconstruction for.
  cardiopulmonary abnormalities with, 3540
  coding grid for, 3541f
  embryology of, 3499-3500, 3499f
  emergent evaluation of, 3199
  gastrointestinal abnormalities with, 3540
  genitourinary abnormalities with, 3540
  neurospinal abnormalities with, 3538-3539, 3539f
  prenatal diagnosis of, 3540-3541

Cloacal exstrophy (Continued)
  reconstruction for, 3541-3544
    complete primary exstrophy repair in, 3564, 3567-3569, 3567f-3570f
      results of, 3571
    continence after, 3543-3544
    gender assignment in, 3542, 3542f
    immediate, 3542
    long-term issues in, 3544
    modern staged functional, 3541t
    urinary reconstruction in
      modern staged, 3542-3543
      osteotomy in, 3543, 3543f
      single-staged, 3543
  skeletal abnormalities with, 3539-3540

Cloacal fold, development of, 3141, 3141f, 3142f

Clomiphene citrate, for male infertility, 646

Clomipramine, for premature ejaculation, 785, 786, 786t

Clonal anergy, in lymphocyte tolerance, 491

Clonidine suppression test, for pheochromocytoma, 1862

Clorpactin WCS-90, for painful bladder syndrome/interstitial cystitis, 362-363, 362t

Clots, blood. See Blood clots.

Cluster of differentiation (CD) markers, 475-477, 476t. See also CD entries.

Clusterin, in regulation of apoptosis, 532

CMV. See Cytomegalovirus (CMV).

Coagulation
  interstitial laser ablative, of renal tumors, 1817
  of semen, 2725

Coagulopathy, uncorrected, affecting renal calculi surgery, 1448

Coaptite, for endoscopic correction of reflux, 4365

Cobra catheter, 1541

Cocaine, effect of, on ureteral function, 1906

Coccidioidomycosis, 467

Coccygeus muscle, 44, 46f, 2191, 2191f, 2192

Cockcroft-Gault formula, for creatinine clearance, 1133, 1325

Coffee consumption
  bladder cancer associated with, 2415
  urothelial tumors associated with, 1639

Cognitive dysfunction, androgen deprivation therapy causing, 3090

Cohen cross-trigonal technique, of antireflux surgery, 4356-4357, 4357f

Colchicine, for Peyronie's disease, 827

Cold storage, of kidney for transplantation, 1306

Colic artery(ies), 2535, 2535f

Collagen
  cross-linked bovine, for endoscopic correction of reflux, 4364, 4364t
  for tissue engineering, 555, 556f
  of bladder wall, 1931

Collagenase, for Peyronie's disease, 828

Collecting devices, external, for bladder filling/storage disorders, 2298

Collecting duct (Bellini's duct) renal cell carcinoma, 1592t, 1596

Collecting system, renal. See Renal collecting system.

Colles' fascia, 40, 40f, 68, 1031, 1032f, 1036, 1037f

Colon. See also Bowel entries.
  anatomy of, 19, 20f, 2534-2535, 2535f
  injury to, percutaneous nephrolithotomy causing, 1500-1501
  malposition of, in renal ectopia, 3281
  reflection of, in laparoscopic nephrectomy, 1762-1763, 1766f
    hand-assisted, 1791, 1796, 1797f
    transperitoneal approach to, 1781

Colon (Continued)
  selection of, for urinary diversion, 2536
  sigmoid
    harvesting of, for neovagina, 3836, 3836f, 3837f
    in cystoplasty, 3677, 3677f

Colon conduit, in conduit urinary diversion
  complications of, 2568-2569, 2568t
    long-term, 2614t
  preparation for, 2564
  procedure in, 2567-2568, 2568f, 2569f

Colon pouch, right
  for continent urinary diversion, 2607-2609, 2608f
    with intussuscepted terminal ileum, 2596
  for orthotopic urinary diversion, 2642

Colonization, of bacteria, in pediatric urinary tract infections, 3238-3239

Color, of urine, 96, 96t

Colorectal cancer, hereditary nonpolyposis, 515t
  genetic mutations in, 517
  inherited susceptibility to cancer in, 519

Colorectal surgery, ureteral injury caused by, 1283

Colostomy, for cloacal anomalies, 3865

Colpoclesis, for apical vaginal prolapse repair, 2230

Colpopexy, sacral, in apical vaginal prolapse repair, 2228, 2229f
  laparoscopic, 2229-2230, 2230t
  vs. sacrospinous ligament fixation, 2229

Colporrhaphy
  anterior
    for central defect, 2217-2218, 2217f
    with needle bladder neck suspension, 2220t, 2221-2222, 2221f
    with sling procedures, 2220t, 2222
  posterior, and perineorrhaphy, 2230-2232, 2231f

Colposuspension
  Burch, 2170, 2171f
    results of, 2181, 2253t
    technique of, 2176, 2178, 2178f-2180f
  laparoscopic, 2170
  open retropubic, 2170
  vs. tension-free vaginal tape procedure, 2188

Columns of Bertin, 25

Coma, ammoniagenic, conduit urinary diversion causing, 2573

Combination therapy, for benign prostatic hyperplasia, 2793-2797
  Medical Therapy of Prostatic Symptoms Study of, 2795-2797
  Veterans Affairs Cooperative Study of, 2793, 2793t, 2794f, 2795, 2795t, 2796f

Combined Intracavernous Injection and Stimulation (CIS) test, in erectile dysfunction, 757-758

Communicating hydrocele, 3788-3789

Complement component C3, 474, 474f
  in seminal plasma, 2724

Complement component C5, 474, 474f

Complement system
  activation of, 474
  classical and alternate pathways of, 474, 474f

Complete primary exstrophy repair, 3554-3571
  background of, 3554-3555
  disassembly technique of, 3555-3557
    anatomic considerations in, 3555-3556, 3556f, 3557f
    complications of, 3571
  for bladder exstrophy
    complete, 3559, 3560f

Complete primary exstrophy repair *(Continued)*
  in females, 3563-3564, 3563f, 3565f-3567f
    initial dissection in, 3557, 3558f, 3559f
    modifications of, 3561, 3563
    penile/urethral dissection in, 3558-3559
    primary closure in, 3559-3561, 3562f, 3563f
    proximal dissection in, 3559, 3561f
    results of, 3569-3571
    surgical technique in, 3557-3563
  for cloacal exstrophy, 3564, 3567-3569, 3567f-3570f
    results of, 3571
  operative considerations in, 3556
  postoperative care in, 3557, 3558f
  preoperative care in, 3556
  results of, 3569-3571
Compliance issues, in renal transplant recipients, 1299
Compression
  for bladder emptying disorders, manual, 2298
  for bladder filling/storage disorders
    mechanical, 2291-2292
    surgical, 2293-2294
Computed tomography (CT), 127-135
  contrast media in, 127, 129
  in nephrostomy procedures, 1532-1533
  non–contrast-enhanced helical, of renal calculi, 1441, 1441f
  of acquired renal cystic disease, 3353, 3354f
  of acute pyelonephritis, 269
  of adrenal mass, 1838, 1838f
  of adrenals, 132, 133f
  of autosomal dominant polycystic kidney disease, 3323, 3324f
  of autosomal recessive polycystic kidney disease, 3317, 3318f
  of bladder, 132-133
  of bladder cancer, 2437, 2439-2440
    invasive, 2469
  of bladder diverticula, 2364, 2364f
  of bladder injury, 2656-2657, 2657f
  of Cushing's syndrome, 1834-1835, 1835f
  of emphysematous pyelonephritis, 273, 273f, 274f
  of genitourinary tuberculosis, 442, 443f
  of germ cell tumors, 905
  of kidney, 129, 131f, 132, 132f
  of myelolipoma, 1839-1840, 1840f
  of normal genitourinary anatomy, 128f-129f
  of pediatric urologic patient, 3214
  of pelvic lipomatosis, 1218, 1219f
  of penile cancer, 970
  of perinephric abscess, 277-278, 277f, 278f
  of prostate, 133
  of prostate cancer, localized vs. metastatic, 3071-3072
  of renal abscess, 275, 275f
  of renal angiomyolipoma, 1578, 1579f
  of renal cell carcinoma, 1602, 1602f
  of renal cysts, 3344-3345, 3345f, 3346, 3346f
  of renal injury, 1277, 1277f
    in children, 3930-3931
  of renal pelvis laceration, 1283f
  of renal tumors, 1571, 1571f, 1572f
  of retroperitoneal fibrosis, 1216, 1216f, 1271, 1271f
  of seminal vesicles, 133, 1112, 1112f
  of staghorn calculus, 1407f
  of tuberous sclerosis, 3329f, 3331f
  of ureteral injury, 1285-1286
  of ureteral obstruction, 1211

Computed tomography (CT) *(Continued)*
  of ureteropelvic junction obstruction, 1229, 1230f
  of ureterovaginal fistula, 2343, 2344f
  of urinary calculi, 129, 130f, 1397, 1397f
  of urinary tract infections, 243
    in children, 3256
  of urothelial tumors, 1645
  of vesicoenteric fistula, 2352
  of vesicouterine fistula, 2346, 2346f
  of vesicovaginal fistula, 2329, 2329f
  of Wilms' tumor, 3891, 3891f, 3892
  of xanthogranulomatous pyelonephritis, 282, 283f
  prior to laparoscopic surgery, 176
Computed tomography (CT) angiography, 134-135, 135f
  of renovascular hypertension, 1172
Computed tomography (CT) urography, 133-134, 134f
  of urothelial tumors, 1644
Computer-assisted semen analysis (CASA), 617. *See also* Semen analysis.
Computerized planning, for cryotherapy, 3039
Concentric electrode, 1989
Concurrent validity, of HRQOL instruments, 154-155, 154t
Condom catheters, for geriatric incontinence, 2317-2318
Conduction velocity, in ureters, 1897
Conduit conversion, to continent reservoir, in continent urinary diversion, 2607
Condylomata acuminata, 420f
  diagnosis of, 380-381, 380f, 381f
  of penis, 961-962
    giant, 963-964
  treatment of, 381-382, 962
Condylomata lata, 376
Cones, vaginal, for incontinence, 2133, 2133f
Conformal radiation therapy, for prostate cancer, 3014-3017, 3015t, 3016t
  tumor control after, 3017-3018, 3018f
Congenital adrenal hyperplasia. *See* Adrenal hyperplasia, congenital.
Congenital lesions, in seminal vesicles, 1113-1114, 1114f, 1115f
Congenital megacystitis, antenatal detection of, 3574, 3575f
Congenital mesoblastic nephroma, 3898-3899
Congenital nephrosis
  Finnish type, 3328-3329
    characteristics of, 3314t
  with diffuse mesangial sclerosis, 3328-3329
    characteristics of, 3314t
Congenital urethral fistula, 3757-3758
Congestive heart failure, anthracycline-induced, in children, 3898
Connective tissue support(s)
  of bladder, 57
  of pelvic floor, 2194-2198
    anterior, 2195, 2196f, 2197f
    middle, 2195, 2197, 2198f
    posterior, 2197-2198, 2198f
Consent, informed
  for laparoscopic surgery, 175
  for robotic-assisted laparoscopic radical prostatectomy, 2986
Conservative therapy, for painful bladder syndrome/interstitial cystitis, 358-359
Conservative treatment, of locally advanced prostate cancer, 3057t
Constipation
  in children, urinary tract infections and, 3262
  incontinence and, 2190

Constipation *(Continued)*
  pelvic organ prolapse and, 2190
  sacral neuromodulation for, 2158
Construct validity, of HRQOL instruments, 154t, 155
Contact dermatitis, of male genitalia, 408-409, 409f
Contact laser, for benign prostatic hyperplasia, 2822-2823
  clinical results of, 2826
Content validity, of HRQOL instruments, 154, 154t
Continence
  fecal
    after cloacal surgery, 3868-3869, 3868t
    after radical perineal prostatectomy, 2983-2984
  in orthotopic urinary diversion
    mechanisms of, 2618-2619
    preservation of, 2619-2623
      surgical technique of, 2621-2623
        in females, 2623
        in males, 2622-2623
  urinary
    after bladder neck reconstruction, 3533t
      with complete epispadias, 3546, 3546t
    after cloacal exstrophy repair, 3543-3544
    after cloacal surgery, 3868, 3868t
    after complete primary exstrophy repair, 3570
    after functional bladder closure, 3531t
    after radical perineal prostatectomy, 2984
    after radical prostatectomy, 2938
    bladder accommodation and, 2049, 2049f
    definition of, 3536
    evaluation of, after robotic-assisted laparoscopic radical prostatectomy, 2999, 2999t
    exstrophy reconstruction and, 3524, 3525f-3526f, 3526
    myelodysplasia and, management of, 3636-3639, 3638f
Continence enemas, antegrade, in children, 3700-3701, 3700f
Continence mechanisms, development of, 3135-3136
Continence products, 2070-2071
Continent intestinal pouches, renal transplants into, 1300
Continent reservoir, conduit conversion to, in continent urinary diversion, 2607
Continent urinary diversion, in exstrophy patient, 3538
Continent vesicostomy, for urinary diversion, in children, 3697-3698, 3699f
Continuous incontinence, 86, 2047. *See also* Incontinence.
Contracted bladder syndrome, schistosomal, 452
Contractile activity, of ureteral smooth muscle, 1897-1902, 1898f. *See also* Ureter(s), peristalsis of.
  excitation-contraction coupling in, 1899-1900
  proteins in, 1898-1899, 1898f, 1899f
  second messengers in, 1900-1902, 1900f-1902f
Contractile proteins, in ureteral smooth muscle, 1898-1899, 1898f, 1899f
Contractile tissue, of epididymis, 597-598
Contractions, after augmentation cystoplasty, 3680-3681, 3681f
Contracture, bladder neck, radical retropubic prostatectomy causing, 2973-2974
Contrast media
  in computed tomography, 127, 129
  in urinary tract radiography, 111, 113

Contusion, ureteral, management of, 1286, 1286f
Conus medullaris, 2031
Conventional fill urodynamic studies, of urethral sphincter dysfunction, in children, 3617
Cooper's ligament, 38
Cordonnier and Nesbit technique, of ureterocolonic anastomosis, 2557
Core biopsy, extended, TRUS-guided, of prostate, 2890, 2890f, 2890t
Corporotomy incision, in penile prosthesis placement, 790-791, 791f
Corpus amylacea, prostatic secretions causing, 306
Corpus cavernosum
  anatomy of, 69, 69f, 70f, 1028, 1029f
    functional, 720-721
  atrophy of, after complete primary exstrophy repair, 3571
  autonomic innervation of, in exstrophy patient, 3504-3505
  decompression of, in priapism, 845
  electromyography of, in erectile dysfunction, 767
  endothelium of, erectile dysfunction and, 742
  in penile erection, hemodynamics of, 723-724, 723f, 724f
  laceration of, 2650, 2650f
  smooth muscle of, reconstruction of, 564-565, 564f
  venous drainage of, 722-723, 722f
Corpus epididymis, 598. *See also* Epididymis.
Corpus spongiosum
  anatomy of, 69f, 70f, 71, 1028, 1029f
    functional, 721
  in hypospadias repair, 3716, 3718
  in penile erection, hemodynamics of, 724
  venous drainage of, 722-723, 722f
Corrective gene therapy, for prostate cancer, 3030
Cortical microcystic disease, 3329
Corticosteroids
  for cutaneous diseases, of external genitalia, 406-407, 407f
  for immunologically mediated infertility, 649
  for lichen planus, 412-413
  for painful bladder syndrome/interstitial cystitis, 360t, 361
  for retroperitoneal fibrosis, 1217
  immunosuppression with, in renal transplant recipients, 1317
  release of, regulation of, 1825-1826, 1826f
  synthesis of, 1825, 1825f
  topical, for atopic dermatitis, 408
Corticotropin-releasing hormone (CRH), synthesis of, 1826
Cortisol metabolites, in primary hyperaldosteronism, 1853
*Corynebacterium*
  in prostatitis, 306
  in trichomycosis, 423, 423f
*Corynebacterium minutissimum*, in erythrasma, 424
Cosmesis, hypospadias repair and, 3742
Cost(s), of health care, 144-147
Cost-benefit analysis, of health care, 145
Cost-effective analysis, of health care, 145
Coudé catheters, 162, 162f
Coudé-tipped catheter, 1541
Councill catheter, 164, 164f
  in percutaneous nephrostomy, 1545, 1545f, 1558f, 1559-1560
Cowden's disease, 516t
Cowper's glands. *See* Bulbourethral glands.

COX inhibitors. *See* Cyclooxygenase (COX) inhibitors.
Crab louse, 383-384, 425, 425f
C-reactive protein, elevated, in urinary tract infection, 3245
Creatinine
  plasma levels of
    in benign prostatic hyperplasia, 2768
    in glomerular filtration rate, 1133, 1133f
  urinary excretion of, 3219
Creatinine clearance
  Cockcroft-Gault formula for, 1133, 1325
  estimation of glomerular filtration rate by, 3230t
  in children, estimation of, 1134
  in estimation of glomerular filtration rate, 1132-1133
Credé maneuver, 2298, 3630, 3636, 3637f
Cremasteric reflex, absence of, 3790
CRH (corticotropin-releasing hormone), synthesis of, 1826
Criterion validity, of HRQOL instruments, 154, 154t
Crohn's disease, rectourethral fistula due to, 2354, 2354f
Cromakalim, effect of, on ureteral function, 1920
Cross-linked bovine collagen
  for bladder neck reconstruction, in children, 3666
  for endoscopic correction of reflux, 4364, 4364t
Crural vein, 1034, 1034f
Cryogenic systems, third generation, 3038
Cryopreservation, of sperm, at time of vasovasostomy, 678
Cryoprobe(s)
  evolution of, 3034, 3035f
  isotherm curves for, 3042f
  placement of, 3041, 3043f
Cryotherapy
  computerized planning in, 3039
  contraindications to, 3040
  cryogeneration systems in, 3038
  cytotoxic and antineoplastic effects of, 3035t
  equipment for, technical improvements in, 3037-3039, 3037f, 3038f
  for adrenal lesions, 1887
  for genital warts, 381
  for localized renal cell carcinoma, 1616-1618, 1617t
  for prostate cancer, 2944, 3032-3052
    adjunctive therapy with, 3049
    biochemical disease-free survival after, 3045, 3046t, 3047, 3047t
    combination therapy with, 3040, 3040f
    complications of, 3049-3050, 3049t
    costs of, 3051
    cryoprobe placement in, 3041, 3042f, 3043f
    evolution of, 3033t
    focal, 3044-3045
    future directions of, 3051-3052
    generations of, 3032-3034, 3033t, 3038
    local recurrence after, 3048-3049
    monitoring of freezing process in, 3041, 3044
    nerve-sparing, 3044, 3044f
    patient follow-up after, 3045
    patient preparation and, 3040-3041
    patient selection for, 3039-3040
    positive biopsy rate after, 3045, 3047
    postoperative care after, 3045
    primary, 3039
    quality of life after, 3050-3051

Cryotherapy (*Continued*)
    repetition of, 3048
    salvage, 3039-3040
    surgical technique of, 3040-3045
    thermocouple and urethral warmer placement in, 3041, 3043f
    transrectal ultrasound evaluation in, 3041
    vs. other minimally invasive options, 3045-3047
    vs. salvage radical prostatectomy, 3047-3048
  for renal tumors, 1811-1814
  history of, 3032-3034, 3033t, 3034f, 3035f
  laparoscopic, 1804-1805, 1812, 1812t, 1813f
    complications of, 1806-1807
    results of, 1805-1806
  mechanisms of cell injury and death by, 3034-3035, 3035t
  mode of action of, 1811-1812
  open surgical, 1812
  percutaneous, 1813-1814
  primary, 3039
    outcomes after, 3045-3047, 3046t
    rectourethral fistula repair after, 2357
  salvage, 3039-3040
    outcomes after, 3047-3048, 3047t
  templates and stands for, 3038, 3038f
  thermocouples for, 3038
  tissue destruction during, factors affecting, 3036-3037, 3036t
  tissue response to, 3035-3036, 3036f
  transrectal ultrasound systems in, 3037-3038, 3037f
  urethral warming device for, 3038-3039
  warming probes for, 3038
Cryptococcosis, 465-466, 466f
*Cryptococcus neoformas*, 465
Cryptorchidism, 3763-3787
  associated with hypospadias, 3709
  bilateral, 610
  carcinoma in situ associated with, 3773, 3902
  classification of, 3764-3765
  consequences of, 3771-3773
  definition of, 3763
  epidemiology of, 3764
  evaluation of, 3204, 3208
  germ cell tumors associated with, 900-901
  hernia due to, 3773
  histopathology of, 3712-3713
  incidence of, 3763-3764
  infertility due to, 640-641, 3771-3772
  maldescent in, 3766-3770
    calcitonin gene–related peptide in, 3769
    endocrine factors in, 3766-3768
    epididymis related to, 3769-3770
    genitofemoral nerve in, 3769
    gubernaculum in, 3768-3769
    intra-abdominal pressure and, 3770
    theories of, 3766
  management of, 3775-3787
    hormonal therapy in, 3775-3776
    laparoscopic, 3781-3787
      assessment in, 3782-3784, 3783f
      diagnostic, 3782
      technique of, 3782
      vs. surgical exploration, 3784-3785
    laparoscopic orchidopexy in, 3785-3786
      Fowler-Stephens, 3786
    microvascular autotransplantation in, 3787
    orchidopexy in
      complications of, 3787
      for high undescended testes, 3779, 3781
      Fowler-Stephens, 3781
        laparoscopic, 3786
      laparoscopic, 3785-3786

Cryptorchidism (Continued)
  reoperative, 3787
    standard, 3776-3777, 3776f-3780f, 3779
    surgical, 3776-3779
    vs. laparoscopic exploration,
      3784-3785
  tenets of, 3775
  neoplasia due to, 3772-3773
  nonpalpable testis in, 3764
  palpable testis in, 3764
  testicular torsion due to, 3773
  unilateral, 610
  work-up for, 3774-3775, 3774t
Crystals. See also specific crystal.
  in urinary sediment, 107-108, 108f
  urinary
    aggregation and retention in, 1368-1369,
      1369f, 1370f
    formation of, inhibitors and promoters of,
      1368, 1370-1371
    growth of, 1367-1368
    matrix in, 1371
    microscopic appearance of, 1395, 1396f,
      1397t
    nucleation in, 1367
    saturation states in, 1366-1367, 1366f
CT. See Computed tomography (CT).
Cucurbita pepo, for benign prostatic hyperplasia,
  2800
Culp-DeWeerd spiral flap technique, of
  pyeloplasty, 1245, 1246f
Cultural issues, associated with health-related
  quality of life, 155-156
Currarino triad
  associated with familial sacral agenesis,
    3644
  cause of, 3647
Cushing's disease, ectopic ACTH syndrome and,
  1836-1837
Cushing's syndrome, 1830-1837
  adrenal tumors and, 1841
  adrenalectomy for, 1870t, 1871. See also
    Adrenalectomy.
    complications of, 1886, 1886t
  clinical manifestations of, 1830-1831, 1831f,
    1831t, 1832f
  diagnosis of, 1832-1834, 1833f, 1834f
  during pregnancy, 1837, 1838f
  ectopic ACTH in, 1831t
  in children, 3878
  male infertility associated with, 638
  radiographic localization of, 1834-1836,
    1835f, 1836f
  screening for, 1832, 1832t
  treatment of, 1836-1837, 1837f
  types of, 1830t
Cutaneous. See also Skin entries.
Cutaneous fistula, of urinary tract, 2359
Cutaneous hemangioma, of male genitalia,
  3760
Cutaneous horn, of penis, 960
Cutaneous T-cell lymphoma, 430, 431f
Cutaneous vesicostomy
  for prune-belly syndrome, 3490
  in management of posterior urethral valves,
    3591-3592, 3593f-3594f
Cyberknife, 1818
Cyclic adenosine monophosphate (cAMP)
  in bladder smooth muscle relaxation, 1954
  in penile smooth muscle relaxation, 732
  in ureteral smooth muscle relaxation, 1900,
    1900f
Cyclic AMP-signaling pathway, in male sexual
  function, 732-734

Cyclic GMP-signaling pathway, in male sexual
  function, 734-735
Cyclic guanosine monophosphate (cGMP)
  in penile smooth muscle relaxation, 732
  in smooth muscle relaxation, 1954
  in ureteral smooth muscle contraction, 1901
Cyclin(s), in cell cycle, 2712-2713
Cyclin D, expression of, at G$_1$S checkpoint, 523
Cyclin-dependent kinase, 2713
Cyclin-dependent kinase complex, G$_1$S
  checkpoint and, 523-524
Cyclooxygenase (COX) inhibitors
  effect of, on ureteral function, 1919-1920
  for overactive bladder/detrusor overactivity,
    2093t, 2105
  for prostate cancer, chemopreventive, 2871
  for prostatitis, clinical trial data on, 322
  for renal colic, 1213
  in prevention of bladder cancer, 2444
  in prostate cancer, etiology of, 2865
Cyclophosphamide
  for glomerulonephritis, 1300
  for hormone-refractory prostate cancer, 3106t
  for paratesticular and testicular tumors, 933
  use of, bladder cancer associated with, 2416
Cyclosporine
  as immunosuppressant, 1316, 1316f, 1316t
  drug interactions with, 1317, 1317t
  for painful bladder syndrome/interstitial
    cystitis, 360t, 361
Cylinder, penile prosthetic
  erosion of, 797
  inflation and deflation of, 793, 794f
  insertion of, 792, 792f, 793f
  oversized, 797
  selection of, 791-792, 792f
CYP17 deficiency, 3767
CYP19 gene, in virilization of female fetus, 3821
CYP21 gene, in congenital adrenal hyperplasia,
  3816-3817
Cyproterone acetate
  androgen blockade with, 3085-3086, 3085t
  for hot flashes, 3090
Cyst(s)
  adrenal, 1843, 1844f
  epidermoid
    of male genitalia, 433, 434f
    testicular, 929
      in children, 3901, 3903
  epididymal cyst, 3798
  Gartner's duct, 3843, 3843f
  hydatid, 458-459, 459f
  introital, 3842-3843, 3842f, 3843f
  median raphe, 431, 3760
  multilocular. See Multilocular cyst.
  ovarian, ureteral obstruction due to, 1221
  paraurethral, 3842-3843, 3842f
  penile, 3750
  prostatic, transrectal ultrasonography of,
    2886, 2886f
  pyelogenic, 3354
  renal. See Renal cyst(s).
  renal sinus, 3356, 3356f, 3357f
    definition of, 3354, 3356
    parapelvic location of, 3354, 3355f
  seminal vesicle, 1115-1116, 1115f
    imaging of, 1112, 1112f
    laparoscopic surgery for, 2507-2509, 2509f
      in children, 3927
    medical-radiologic treatment of, 1125
  urachal, 3577f, 3578-3579
  urethral, parameatal, 3758
  vaginal wall, vs. urethral diverticula, 2383-
    2384, 2385f

Cystadenoma
  of seminal vesicles, 1116
  of testicular adnexa, 933
Cystatin C, plasma levels of, in glomerular
  filtration rate, 1133
Cystectomy
  bladder cancer recurrence after, 2623-2629
    pelvic, 2628-2629
    urethral, 2623-2628
      in female patient, 2626-2628
      in male patient, 2624-2626
  continence preservation with, 2619-2623
    surgical technique of, 2621-2623
      in females, 2623
      in males, 2622-2623
  for continent urinary diversion, 2580-2581,
    2581f
  for refractory disease, in non–muscle-invasive
    bladder cancer, 2461-2462
  laparoscopic approach to, 2544, 2545f, 2546f
  partial, 2503-2505
    complications of, 2505
    follow-up for, 2505
    for invasive bladder cancer, with
      transurethral resection, 2474-2475
      chemotherapy and, 2475
    indications for, 2503
    laparoscopic, 2515-2516, 2516f
    postoperative management of, 2505
    preoperative considerations in, 2503
    surgical technique of, 2503-2505, 2504f
  radical, 2483-2489
    for invasive bladder cancer, 2469-2473
      adjuncts to, 2473-2474
      complications of, 2472
      efficacy of, 2471, 2471t
      female urethra management after, 2471
      follow-up after, 2472-2473
      indications for, 2469-2470
      lymphadenectomy in, 2472
      male urethra management after, 2470-
        2471
      technique of, 2470, 2470f, 2470t
      ureteral frozen-section analysis in, 2471
    in females, 2493-2501
      anterior exenteration with urethrectomy
        and, 2496-2498, 2497f-2499f
      completion of, 2499
      complications of, 2501
      indications for, 2494
      pelvic dissection in, 2495-2496, 2496f,
        2497f
      pelvic lymphadenectomy with, 2495,
        2495f, 2496f
      postoperative management of, 2499
      preoperative evaluation for, 2494
      surgical technique of, 2494-2495, 2494f
      urethra-sparing, vagina-sparing approach
        to, 2498-2499, 2499f
    in males
      complications of, 2488-2489
      indications for, 2483
      nerve-sparing approach to, 2487-2488,
        2488f, 2489f
      pelvic dissection in, 2485, 2486f-2488f,
        2487
      pelvic lymphadenectomy with, 2484-
        2485, 2485f, 2486f
      postoperative management for, 2488
      preoperative evaluation and management
        for, 2483-2484
      surgical technique of, 2484, 2484f
    laparoscopic, 2516-2523. See also
      Laparoscopic radical cystectomy.

Cystectomy (*Continued*)
  and urinary diversion, 2523-2527. *See also* Urinary diversion, laparoscopic-assisted.
  retained male urethra after, 1015-1018
    considerations in, 1015
    total urethrectomy for
      after cutaneous division, 1015, 1016f-1017f
      after orthotopic division, 1018
  salvage, for metastatic bladder cancer, 2478
  simple, 2501-2503
    complications of, 2503
    indications for, 2501
    postoperative management of, 2502-2503
    surgical technique of, 2501-2502, 2501f, 2502f
  supratrigonal, for painful bladder syndrome/interstitial cystitis, 366-367
  urethral recurrence after, in females, 1021-1022
Cysteinyl leukotriene D4 receptor antagonist, for painful bladder syndrome/interstitial cystitis, 360t, 361
Cystic fibrosis, male infertility in, 611
Cystic fibrosis transmembrane conductance regulator (*CFTR*) gene. *See CFTR* gene.
Cystic nephroma, 1580, 1581f
  multiloculated, 3339-3343, 3340f. *See also* Multilocular cyst.
  in children, 3899
Cystine calculi, 1385-1386, 1385f, 1406, 1406f, 1425f
Cystinuria, 107, 1406, 1406f
  genetics of, 1385-1386
  in children, 3223
  treatment of, 1424
Cystitis
  after renal transplantation, 1321
  chronic, bladder cancer associated with, 2415
  clinical presentation of, 255, 255f
  complicated, 258-259
    host factors in, 258t
    treatment of, 259, 259t
  definition of, 224
  diagnosis of, 255-256
  differential diagnosis of, 256
  in children, 3234-3236, 3235f
    eosinophilic, 3582
    inflammatory hemorrhagic, 3263
    interstitial, 3263-3264
  interstitial. *See also* Painful bladder syndrome/interstitial cystitis.
    antibiotics causing, 338-339
    bladder cancer associated with, 335
    feline, 337-338
    gynecologic problems mimicking, 351
    ICDB Study Eligibility Criteria for, 332, 333t
    in children, 3263-3264
    NIDDK diagnostic criteria for, 332, 332t
    prostatitis and, 309-310
    sacral neuromodulation for, 2156-2157
  management of
    antibiotics in, 256-257, 256t
    cost of therapy in, 257
    duration of therapy in, 257
    follow-up in, 257
  signs and symptoms of, 238
  uncomplicated, 254-258
Cystitis glandularis, in pelvic lipomatosis, 1217

Cystocele. *See also* Vagina, prolapse of.
  leak point pressure measurement in, 2007, 2240-2241, 2242f
  sling procedures for, 2236-2237
Cystography, in vesicoureteral reflux, 4332-4333, 4334f
Cystolithalopexy, for bladder calculi, 2668-2669
Cystolithotomy, for bladder calculi, 2669
Cystolysis, 2290-2291
Cystometrography. *See also* Cystometry.
  bladder capacity in, 1992-1993
  bladder compliance in, 1993, 1993f
  bladder emptying in, 1995
  bladder sensation in, 1993, 1994t
  bladder storage in, 1993, 1993f, 1995, 1995f
  in benign prostatic hyperplasia, 2772
  phases of, 1992
    fill rate of, 1991-1992
  pitfalls in, 1995
  pressure measurement in, 1991
  special testing in, 1995
  studies in, 1991-1995
Cystometry. *See also* Cystometrography.
  for painful bladder syndrome/interstitial cystitis, 352-353, 352f, 353f
  potassium chloride in, 354
  types of, 1992
Cystometry Sensation Scale, 2084t
Cystometry transducers, 1988
Cystoplasty
  augmentation. *See also* Bladder augmentation.
    artificial sphincter placement with, 2402
    for bladder filling/storage disorders, 2291
    for genitourinary tuberculosis, 446
    for incontinence, 2073-2074
    for painful bladder syndrome/interstitial cystitis, 367
    in children, 3672-3691
      alkalosis after, 3682
      alternative(s) to, 3687-3691
        autoaugmentation as, 3688-3690, 3689f
        bladder regeneration as, 3690-3691
        seromuscular enteroplasty as, 3690, 3691f
        ureteroplasty as, 3687-3688, 3688f
      bladder calculi after, 3684
      bladder compliance after, 3680-3681, 3681f
      cecocystoplasty in, 3675
      decreasing necessity for, 3691
      delayed growth after, 3682
      delayed spontaneous bladder perforation after, 3684-3686, 3685f
      gastrocystoplasty in
        antrum technique of, 3678
        body technique of, 3678-3679, 3678f
      gastrointestinal effects of, 3680
      hematuria-dysuria syndrome after, 3682-3683
      ileocecocystoplasty in
        appendix in, 3675
        ileocecal valve in, 3675, 3677
        technique of, 3675, 3675f, 3676f, 3677
      ileocystoplasty in, 3673-3675, 3674f
      intestinal segment choice for, 3686-3687
      intestinal segment management in, 3673
      intestinal segment mucus production after, 3683
      metabolic complications of, 3681-3682
      native bladder management in, 3672-3673, 3673f
      postoperative management of, 3679
      pregnancy following, 3686

Cystoplasty (*Continued*)
      results and complications of, 3679-3687
      sigmoid cystoplasty in, 3677, 3677f
      tumor formation after, 3684
      urinary tract infection after, 3683-3684
    laparoscopic approach to, 2544, 2545f, 2546f
  reduction, 2299
    for prune-belly syndrome, 3491
  sigmoid, in children, 3677, 3677f
  substitution, for painful bladder syndrome/interstitial cystitis, 367
Cystosarcoma phyllodes, of seminal vesicles, 1116
Cystoscopic incision, of ureterocele, 3407-3408, 3407f, 3408f
Cystoscopy
  antibiotic prophylaxis for, 252
  flexible, 166, 167, 168f, 1515
  in benign prostatic hyperplasia, 2769
  in bladder cancer, 2437-2438
    non–muscle-invasive, 2454, 2454f, 2455f
    surveillance, 2463
  in genitourinary tuberculosis, 443
  in pelvic lipomatosis, 1218-1219
  in pelvic organ prolapse, 2209-2210
  in urothelial tumors, 1645
  in vesicoureteral reflux, 4351
  in vesicouterine fistula, 2345, 2345f, 2346f
  in vesicovaginal fistula, 2327-2328, 2328f
  preoperative, for urinary tract reconstruction, in children, 3661
  rigid, 167, 167f, 1515
Cystostomy
  Stamey percutaneous, 164, 165f
  suprapubic, for urethral injury, 2659
Cystourethrectomy, for painful bladder syndrome/interstitial cystitis, 367
Cystourethrography, 116
  of detrusor-sphincter dyssynergia, 2022f, 2023f
  static, 116, 117f
  voiding, 116, 118, 119f, 120f
    of anterior urethral valves, 3600f, 3601f
    of bladder diverticula, 2362f, 2364
      in children, 3579f, 3580
    of bladder duplication, 3581f
    of congenital megacystis, 3574, 3575f
    of ectopic kidney, 3279, 3280f
    of ectopic ureter, 3392, 3392f
    of patent urachus, in children, 3577, 3578f
    of pediatric urologic patient, 3213
    of posterior urethral valves, 3589-3590, 3591f
    of prune-belly syndrome, 3484, 3484f
    of urethral diverticula, 2379-2380, 2380f, 2381f
    of urethrovaginal fistula, 2348, 2348f
    of urinary tract infections, 243
      pediatric, 3254-3255, 3255f
    of vesicovaginal fistula, 2328-2329, 2328f, 2329f
    preoperative, of hypospadias, 3711
Cystourethroscopy, 166-169
  equipment for, 167-168, 167f-169f
  indications for, 166-167
  of urethral diverticula, 2378-2379, 2379f
  patient preparation for, 167
  technique of, 168-169
  video-cystoscopy unit for, 168, 169f
Cytogenetic abnormalities, in chromophilic renal cell carcinoma, 1594-1595

Cytokine(s). *See also specific cytokine.*
during peptide/MCH class II priming, 486-487, 486f
for metastatic renal cell carcinoma, 1626-1628, 1626f, 1627t, 1628t
combination of, 1629
in benign prostatic hyperplasia, 2733
in chronic pelvic pain syndrome, 317-318
in tumor regression, 499
in Wilms' tumor, 3893
production of, 493
representative, 486t
type 1, 486, 487
type 2, 487
Cytology
of bladder cancer, 2431
fluorescence, 2436
non–muscle-invasive, 2463-2464
of urothelial tumors, 1645, 1647
Cytolytic gene therapy, for prostate cancer, 3030
Cytomatrix, of prostate, 2683f, 2684
Cytomegalovirus (CMV)
postoperative infection with, prophylaxis for, 1317, 1318t
serologic testing for, prior to renal transplantation, 1298
Cytometry, flow. *See* Flow cytometry.
Cytotoxicity, of cryotherapy, 3035t

**D**

Dactinomycin, for paratesticular and testicular tumors, 933
Dantrolene
dosage of, 2121
uropharmacology of, 2121-2122
Darifenacin
for incontinence, in elderly, 2316, 2317t
for overactive bladder/detrusor overactivity, 2093t, 2097-2098
Dartos fascia, 40f, 69f, 73, 1031, 1032f
Dartos (subcutaneous) flap. *See also* Flap(s).
in hypospadias repair, 3716, 3716f
Dartos pouch, formation of, in orchidopexy, 3779, 3779f
Data collection, on health-related quality of life, 156
Davis intubated ureterotomy, for ureteropelvic junction obstruction, in children, 3370, 3370f
*DAX1* gene, 3147
in sex determination, 3802f, 3803
*DAZ* gene, in spermatogenesis, 596
*DD3^pca3* gene, in prostate cancer, 2909
Death domain, in apoptosis, 488
Fas-associated, 489
Death receptor(s)
apoptosis and, 529-530, 530f
as cancer therapy targets, 530
Death receptor pathway, in apoptosis, 488-489, 489f
Débridement, in Fournier's gangrene, 301-302
Decision-making, shared, in erectile dysfunction therapy, 756, 756t
Deep venous thrombosis
after laparoscopic surgery, 218
after robotic-assisted laparoscopic radical prostatectomy, 3001
Deferential artery, of vas deferens, 606
Degloving injury, of penis, 1052, 1053f
in Peyronie's disease surgery, 831, 832f
Dehiscence, fascial, after complete primary exstrophy repair, 3571

Dehydration
in early graft dysfunction, 1318
risk of stone formation with, 1365
Dehydroepiandrosterone
affected by aging, 856, 856t
assessment of, in females, 872, 872f
for erectile dysfunction, 772
for sexual dysfunction
in perimenopausal and postmenopausal women, 880
in premenopausal women, 876
metabolism of, 1828
DeLancey's theory, of stress incontinence, 2051-2052, 2051f, 2052f
Delirium, in geriatric incontinence, 2306, 2307t
Delivery disorders, of sperm
ductal obstruction in, 647-648
ejaculatory problems in, 648-649
Dementia, voiding dysfunction in, 2016
Dendritic cell(s)
activation of, tumor necrosis factor-α in, 484
activation of CD4/CD8 T cells by, 485, 485f
Denervation procedures, for incontinence, 2073
Denis-Brown pouch, 3765
Denonvillier's fascia, 40f, 45, 65
Dental sepsis, treatment of, prior to renal transplantation, 1298
Dent's disease, 1375
Denys-Drash syndrome, 3812
mixed gonadal dysgenesis in, 3812
Wilms' tumor in, 519
Deoxyribonucleic acid. *See* DNA *entries.*
Depression, in sexual dysfunction, 770
Dermal graft inlays, in Peyronie's disease surgery, 831, 833
Dermatitis, of male genitalia
atopic (eczematous), 407-408, 407f
contact, 408-409, 409f
factitial, 419
seborrheic, 414-415
Dermatitis herpetiformis, of male genitalia, 416
Dermatofibroma, of male genitalia, 433
Dermatophyte infection, of male genitalia, 424-425, 425f
Dermatosis, linear IgA bullous, of male genitalia, 416, 416f
Descendin, in testicular descent, 3768
Desensitization, vanilloid-induced, 1959
Desmopressin, for nocturnal enuresis, 2113-2114
Detrusor hyperactivity with impaired contractility (DHIC), in elderly, 2310
Detrusor instability. *See* Overactive bladder.
Detrusor leak point pressure
definition of, 2005
in incontinence, 2067, 2067f
measurement of, technique in, 2005-2006, 2005f
Detrusor muscle. *See also* Bladder.
activity of
during bladder filling/storage stage, 3610
during voiding phase, 3611
areflexia of
in herpesvirus infection, 2033
in HIV patients, 2036
in intervertebral disk disease, 2031
in Lyme disease, 2035
in multiple sclerosis, 2020
in reflex sympathetic dystrophy, 2037
in stroke patient, 2014-2015
in syringomyelia, 2036
urodynamic classification of, 1981-1982, 1981t

Detrusor muscle (Continued)
cellular mechanics of, 1927-1931, 1929f-1931f
contraction of
muscarinic receptor-induced, 1949, 1949f
sequence in, 1928t
dysfunction of, pressure-flow micturition studies of, 1996-1997, 1996f
hyperreflexia of
definition of, 2079, 3610
in valve patients, 3597
urodynamic classification of, 1981, 1981t
layers of, 57-58
mast cells in, in interstitial cystitis, 342
overactivity of. *See also* Overactive bladder.
afferent mechanism in, 2080
aging and, 1969-1970
causes of, 2055t
cystometrogram of, 1993, 1995f
evaluation of, 2239-2240
hypotheses of, 2080-2081, 2081f
idiopathic, 2054-2055, 2086-2088
in multiple sclerosis, 2020
incontinence due to, 2053-2054, 2053f
in elderly, 2309-2310
treatment of, 2071-2074, 2314-2318, 2317t
index of, 2088, 2088f
inflammation in, 1968-1969, 1969f
mechanisms of, 1966-1970
neurogenic, 1981, 2055, 2055t, 2086-2088
mechanisms underlying, 1970
spinal cord injury and, 1966-1967, 1967f
phasic, 2087, 2087f
definition of, 2086
terminal, 2087-2088, 2088f
definition of, 2086
treatment of. *See* Overactive bladder, management of.
urodynamic confirmation of, 2085-2088
tone of, 1930
underactivity of
incontinence due to
in elderly, 2310
treatment of, 2319-2320, 2319t, 2320t
International Continence Society classification of, 1981
Detrusor pressure
at filling
elevated, bladder dysfunction and, 3658
oxybutynin to lower, 3633
at voiding, 3607, 3607f
maximal, 1996-1997, 1996f
measurement of, 2004-2005, 2004f
Detrusor-sphincter dyssynergia, 1981
detrusor overactivity with, 2055
in autonomic hyperreflexia, 2026
in neurospinal dysraphisms, 2030, 3631
recommendations for, 3632-3634, 3634f
in stroke patient, 2015
in suprasacral spinal cord injury, 2022, 2022f, 2023f, 2024
in syringomyelia, 2036
kinesiologic studies of, 2002
myelomeningocele and, 3634f
smooth, 1981-1982
striated, 1981
transitory, in infancy, 3609
treatment of, 2118-2119, 2122
voiding dysfunction in, 2037-2038
Detumescence. *See* Penile detumescence.
Developmental milestones, in children, 3210, 3211t

Dexamethasone
  for hormone-refractory prostate cancer, palliative, 3113
  for painful bladder syndrome/interstitial cystitis, 364
  prenatal treatment with, for congenital adrenal hyperplasia, 3819
Dexamethasone suppression test, for Cushing's syndrome, 1833-1834, 1834f
Dextranomer hyaluronic copolymer, for endoscopic correction of reflux, 4364t, 4365
Dextranomer microspheres, injection of, for incontinence, 2286
*DHH* gene, in 46,XY complete gonadal dysgenesis, 3813
DHIC (detrusor hyperactivity with impaired contractility), in elderly, 2310
Diabetes insipidus, nephrogenic, in children, 3229
Diabetes mellitus
  after renal transplantation, 1298, 1324
  erectile dysfunction and, 746-747, 747t
    PDE-5 inhibitors for, 775
  in chronic renal failure, 1358-1359
  urinary tract infections and, 236
  voiding dysfunction in, 2012t, 2033-2035
Diacylglycerol, in ureteral smooth muscle contraction, 1901-1902
Diagnostic algorithms, for male infertility, 619-623, 620t
  absent or low-volume ejaculate and, 619, 620f, 620t, 621
  asthenospermia and, 622-623, 622f
  azoospermia and, 621-622, 621f
  normal seminal parameters and, 623
  oligospermia and, 622
  seminal parameter defects and, 623
  teratospermia and, 623
Diagnostic markers, for painful bladder syndrome/interstitial cystitis, 353-354
Dialysis. *See* Hemodialysis; Peritoneal dialysis.
Dialysis membranes, classification of, 1339
Dialysis Outcomes and practice Patterns (DOPPS) study, 1354-1355
Diapedesis, 493
DIAPERS mnemonic, for incontinence, 2306, 2307t
Diaphragm
  injury to, laparoscopic renal surgery causing, 1807-1808
  pelvic, 2191-2192, 2191f, 2192f
  urogenital, 68-69, 69f, 2192-2194, 2193f
Diaphragmatic hernia, as contraindication to laparoscopy, 175
Diarrhea
  antibiotic bowel preparation causing, 2539
  chronic
    after augmentation cystoplasty, 3680
    hypocitraturic lithiasis and, 1404
    management of, 1422-1423
  hemolytic-uremic syndrome associated with, 3227-3228
Diathesis
  bleeding, ureteroscopic management of, 1520-1521
  gouty, 1405, 1405f
    treatment of, 1424
Diazepam, for prostatitis, clinical trial data on, 322
Dicyclomine, for overactive bladder/detrusor overactivity, 2093t, 2102
Diet
  benign prostatic hyperplasia and, 2745
  prostate cancer and, epidemiologic studies of, 2862

Dietary bran, for nephrolithiasis, 1419
Dietary calcium, in nephrolithiasis, 1414-1415
Dietary factors, in prevention of bladder cancer, 2443-2444
Dietary fat, prostate cancer and, epidemiologic studies of, 2862-2872
Dietary hyperoxaluria, 1378, 1403
Dietary maneuvers, for incontinence, 2129
Dietary restrictions
  for chronic renal failure, 1350
  for nephrolithiasis, 1412-1413
  for painful bladder syndrome/interstitial cystitis, 358-359, 359t
  of protein, after partial nephrectomy, 1613-1614
Diethylcarbamazine, for filariasis, prophylactic, 458
Diethylstilbestrol, in utero exposure to, 611
Dietl's crisis, in nephrotosis, 1776
Differential display technology, in diagnosis of oncology, 548-549
Diffuse mesangial sclerosis, congenital nephrosis with, 3328-3329
  characteristics of, 3314t
Digital rectal examination, 93-94
  for benign prostatic hyperplasia, 2767
  for prostate cancer, 2922-2923
    routine use of, 2913
    tumor staging with, 2929-2930
  of prostate, 313-314
Digital video recorders, in laparoscopic surgery, 190
Digoxin
  erectile dysfunction caused by, 745
  for priapism, 846t
Dihydrotestosterone. *See also* Testosterone.
  circulation of, 3084, 3085t
  conversion of testosterone to, 767
  daily application of, before hypospadias repair, 3711
  fetal secretion of, 3804
  for erectile dysfunction, 772
  for late-onset hypogonadism, 858
  in benign prostatic hyperplasia, 2729
  in epididymis, 603-604
  in prostate, 2678-2679, 2684, 2686t, 2687f
    influence of, 2863-2864
    levels of, 2728-2729, 2729f
  in testicular descent, 3766-3767
Dihydroxyadenine calculi, 1387
Dilatation
  balloon. *See* Balloon dilatation.
  manual, in laparoscopic surgery, 182
  of fetal bladder, 3574
  of nephrolithotomy tract, 1491-1494, 1492f-1494f
  of nephrostomy tract, 1541-1544
    guide wire entry in, 1541-1542
    novel methods in, 1543-1544
    types of dilators in, 1542-1543, 1542f, 1543f
  of ureters, 1511t, 1512, 1512f. *See also* Megaureter(s).
  urethral. *See* Urethral dilatation.
Diltiazem, for incontinence, in elderly, 2317t
Dimercaptosuccinic acid, scanning with, in pediatric renal injury, 3932
Dimethyl sulfoxide
  for overactive bladder/detrusor overactivity, 2106
  for painful bladder syndrome/interstitial cystitis, 362t, 363
Diode laser, in treatment of benign prostatic hyperplasia, 2821
Dip slide test, for urine culture, 240, 240f

Diphallia, 3757
Diphenoxybenzamine, for prostatitis, 321
Dipstick testing
  for hematuria, 98
  for ketones, 104
  in urinalysis, 97
Direct surface plating, for urine culture, 240
Disc kidney, 3284f, 3285-3286
Discomfort, post-biopsy, 2892
Dismembered pyeloplasty, for ureteropelvic junction obstruction, 1242-1243, 1243f, 1244f
  in children, 3370, 3372f, 3373
  laparoscopic, tubularized flap technique of, 1253
Dissecting aneurysm, of renal artery, 1187, 1188f
Dissection, anterior, for continence preservation after orthotopic diversion
  in female patient, 2623
  in male patient, 2622-2623
Distal procedure, in hypospadias repair, 3722-3725
  advancement techniques for, 3722, 3723f
  flap techniques for, 3725, 3726f-3727f
  other techniques for, 3725
  tubularization techniques for, 3722-3723, 3724f, 3725
Distigmine, to facilitate bladder emptying, 2115
Diuresis
  effect of, on ureteral function, 1909
  physiologic postnatal, 3156
  postobstructive
    clinical management of, 1214
    experimental modulation of, 1214
    mechanisms of, 1213-1214
Diuretic scintigraphy, 141f-142f, 142-143
Diuretics. *See also* Thiazides.
  erectile dysfunction caused by, 743, 744t
  for calcium oxalate nephrolithiasis, 1421t
  for hypercalciuria, 1419
  for nocturnal enuresis, 2114
  loop, for acute renal failure, 1336
  renal cell carcinoma associated with, 1584
Diverticulectomy
  bladder
    complications of, 2371
    intravesical and extravesical approach to, 2369, 2371, 2372f
    laparoscopic, 2511-2512, 2511f
    transvesical approach to, 2369, 2369f-2371f
  laparoscopic, 1778
  urethral, in females, 2385-2389
    complications of, 2388, 2388t, 2389f
    excision and reconstruction in, 2385-2386, 2385t
    indications for, 2385, 2386f
    postoperative care in, 2388
    preoperative preparation in, 2386
    symptoms persistence after, 2388-2389
    technique in, 2386-2388, 2387f
Diverticulum(a)
  bladder. *See* Bladder diverticulum(a).
  calyceal, 3354. *See also* Renal calyx (calyces), diverticula of.
  paraureteral, in children, 3579-3580, 3579f
  urachal, 3577f, 3579
  ureteral, 3411-3402, 3413f
  urethral. *See* Urethral diverticulum(a).
  vesicourachal, 3577f, 3579
DNA, 507-510, 508t
  complementary, definition of, 508t
  damaging agents threatening, 526
  hypermethylation of, 514-515
  in gene therapy, 551

DNA (Continued)
  mitochondrial, oocyte-derived, in tissue
      engineering, 571-572, 572f
  mutation of, 513, 513f
  nuclear matrix of, 511
  repair of, 526-529, 526f, 527f
    apoptosis and, 529
    base excision in, 527-528
    double-stranded breaks and, 528-529
    mismatch, 528
    nucleotide excision in, 527
  replication of, 507, 509f
    errors of, 2410
  rudimentary form of, 507, 509f
  sequence of expression of, 508-510, 510f
  sperm
    abnormal, risk factors for, 626
    integrity testing of, 626-627
  synthesis of, in regulation of prostate growth,
      2711-2712
  transcription of, 509, 509f, 510f
    post-transcription modification of, 510
    regulation of, 510
  translation of, 511-512
  tumor
    in neuroblastoma, 3874
    in Wilms' tumor, 3892-3893
    somatic mutations in, 2865-2867
  ubiquitination and, 512
DNA damage, in regulation of prostate growth,
    2714
DNA extract, for bladder cancer, non–muscle-
    invasive, 2458
DNA microarrays, in diagnosis of oncology, 549
DNA screening
  for bladder cancer, 2432
  for CLCN5 gene, 1375
DNA viruses, 507-508
DNA-binding domain, of androgen receptors,
    2698-2699
Docetaxel
  for bladder cancer
    metastatic, 2478
    non–muscle-invasive, 2459
  for hormone-refractory prostate cancer, 3106t
    clinical trials of, 3108-3110, 3109f, 3110f,
      3110t
Donepezil, causing geriatric incontinence, 2309
Donor(s), kidney, 1296. See also under Renal
    transplantation, donor for.
  gene expression profiles of, 503, 504f
Donor artery(ies), angiography of, in penile
    vascular reconstruction, 803-804, 805f
Dopamine
  for acute renal failure, 1336
  in male sexual function, 729
Dopamine agonist, for female sexual
    dysfunction, 881-882
Doppler ultrasonography. See also
    Ultrasonography.
  duplex
    of penile arterial flow, 803, 804f
    of priapism, 845
    of renovascular hypertension, 1170-1171
    of veno-occlusive dysfunction, 760
  of penile blood flow, 758, 758f, 759f
    arterial anatomic variation in, 759-760
    arterial dilation in, 758-759, 759f
    power-mode for, 760
    waveform analysis in, 758, 759f
  of prostate, transrectal color and power, 2892-
    2893, 2893f, 2894f
  of renal transplant candidates, 1299, 1299t
  of scrotal cord torsion, 3791

Doppler ultrasonography (Continued)
  of sexual health problems, in females, 874,
    874f
  power-mode, of penile blood flow, 760
Dorsal artery, 1034-1035, 1035f
  dissection of, in penile revascularization, 806-
    807, 808f
Dorsal lumbotomy incisions, in renal surgery,
    1695, 1696f
Dorsal nerve
  conduction velocity testing of, in erectile
      dysfunction, 766
  of penis, 72, 72f
    stimulation of, 2159
    spinal reflexes in, 726t
Dorsal vein
  division of, in robotic-assisted laparoscopic
      radical prostatectomy, 2993, 2995
  of clitoris, 51
  of penis, 51, 51f, 72, 72f, 1034, 1034f
    mobilization, division, and dissection of, in
      Peyronie's disease surgery, 831, 832f
Dorsal vein complex ligation
  in radical retropubic prostatectomy, 2961-
      2968, 2962f-2968f
    neurovascular bundles in, 2967-2968,
      2967f
      high anterior release of, 2965, 2965f
      identification and preservation of, 2966-
        2967, 2967f
      wide excision of, 2968, 2968f
    standard division in, 2962-2963, 2963f,
      2964f
    urethral division and suture placement in,
      2963-2965, 2964f, 2965f
  in robotic-assisted laparoscopic radical
      prostatectomy, 2991-2992, 2991f, 2992f
Double-stranded breaks, in DNA repair,
    528-529
Douglas (rectouterine) pouch, 56, 56f, 57
Down syndrome, hydronephrosis and, 3184
Doxazosin
  for benign prostatic hyperplasia, 2780, 2782-
      2783
    dosage of, 2778t, 2783
    efficacy of, 2782t
    vs. combination therapy, 2793t, 2795t
  for prostatitis, 321
  uropharmacology of, 2119
  vs. other α-adrenergic blockers, 2787
Doxepin
  for incontinence, in elderly, 2317t
  for overactive bladder/detrusor overactivity,
    2104
Doxorubicin
  for hormone-refractory prostate cancer,
      multidrug regimens with, 3107t
  for non–muscle-invasive bladder cancer,
      2459
    mitomycin C with, 2460
  for painful bladder syndrome/interstitial
      cystitis, 362t, 364
Doxycycline
  for gonorrhea with chlamydial infection,
      379
  for lymphogranuloma venereum, 378
  for mollicute infections, 384
  for syphilis, 377
Drain(s)
  in renal transplant recipient, postoperative
      removal of, 1313-1314
  in retropubic suspension surgery, 2175
  removal of, after orthotopic urinary diversion,
    2633

Drainage
  bladder
    after augmentation cystoplasty, 3679
    in management of posterior urethral valves,
      3591
    in retropubic suspension surgery, 2175
  in percutaneous nephrostomy, 1549, 1557-
    1562. See also Nephrostomy,
    percutaneous, drainage procedures in.
  of obstructed kidney, 1212
  of perinephric abscess, 278
  of prostate abscess, 325
  of renal abscess, 276
    in tuberculosis, 445
  postoperative, after vesicovaginal fistula
    repair, 2333
Dressing techniques, in hypospadias repair, 3720
Drotrecogin alfa, for septic shock, 289
Drug(s). See also Uropharmacology; specific drug
    or drug group.
  abnormal absorption of, conduit urinary
    diversion causing, 2573-2574
  action of, on bladder smooth muscle, 1960-
    1962
  acute interstitial nephritis due to, 1328, 1328t
  development of, 550
  effect of, on ureteral function, 1918-1920
  erectile dysfunction caused by, 742-746
  exacerbating benign prostatic hyperplasia,
    2746
  for urethral sphincter dysfunction, in
    children, 3619-3620
  geriatric incontinence due to, 2307t, 2308-
    2309, 2308t
  HIV resistance to, 389-390, 394
  in patient history, 88
  interactions of, with cyclosporine and
    tacrolimus, 1317, 1317t
  male infertility caused by, 644-645
  priapism caused by, 841, 844
  stone formation caused by, 1388-1389, 1427,
    1427t
  transport of, prostatic secretions and, 2725-
    2726
  urologic side effects of, 89t
Drug eruption, fixed, involving male genitalia,
    414, 414f
Dual durometer stents, 1517
Ductal reflux, intraprostatic, of urine, 308
Ductus deferens. See Vas deferens.
Ductus epididymis. See also Epididymis.
  histology of, 598, 599f
Duloxetine
  for overactive bladder/detrusor overactivity,
    2105
  for stress incontinence, 2075, 2111-2112
  uropharmacology of, 1963-1964
Duodenum, anatomy of, 19, 20f
Duplex ultrasonography. See Doppler
    ultrasonography, duplex.
Duplication
  of bladder, 3580-3581, 3581f
  of cervix, unilaterally imperforate vagina with,
    3839, 3839f, 3840f
  of penis, 3757
  of ureter, 3413-3417. See also Ureter(s),
    duplication of.
  of urethra, 3601, 3602f, 3603
Dupuytren's contracture, Peyronie's disease
    associated with, 818
Dura II semi-rigid penile prosthesis, 788, 789t
Durasphere and Durasphere Exp injections, for
    incontinence, 2274, 2275f
  efficacy of, 2282

Dutasteride
  for benign prostatic hyperplasia, 2792
  for prostate cancer, prophylactic, 2870
Dye test, for incontinence, 2063
Dynamic fracture mechanism, of stone
    fragmentation, 1476-1477, 1476f
Dysfunctional elimination syndrome, of
    childhood, 3611, 3613
Dysgenetic male pseudohermaphroditism
    (partial gonadal dysgenesis), 3812-3813
Dyspareunia, in females, 864
  causes of, 885
Dysplasia, urothelial, 1642
Dysraphism, neurospinal, voiding dysfunction
    in, 2029-2030
Dyssynergia, sphincter. *See also* Detrusor-
    sphincter dyssynergia.
  definition of, 1981
  proximal, 2038
  smooth, 2038
Dystrophy. *See specific type, e.g.*, Reflex
    sympathetic dystrophy.
Dysuria, 84

**E**

EBV. *See* Epstein-Barr virus (EBV).
E-cadherin, 540, 2695
  in prostate cancer, 2866
Ecchymosis, abdominal and scrotal, after
    laparoscopic surgery, 217
Echinococcosis, 458-459, 459f
  renal, 285-286, 286f
Economic considerations
  in androgen deprivation therapy, 3099
  in robotic-assisted laparoscopic radical
    prostatectomy, 3000-3001
Ecthyma gangrenosum, of male genitalia, 424,
    424f
Eczema (atopic dermatitis), 407-408, 407f
Edema
  in infants, 3207
  penile, after penile revascularization, 810
  scrotal
    miscellaneous causes of, 3793
    testicular torsion causing, 3792
Eggplant deformity, of penis, 2649, 2650f
Ehlers-Danlos syndrome, voiding dysfunction
    in, 2042
Ehrlich technique, in management of prune-
    belly syndrome, 3493
Ejaculate
  biochemical properties of, 605-606
  coagulation of, 605
  failure of, 87
  low-volume
    evaluation of, 619, 620f, 620t, 621
    history of, 611
  premature, 87
Ejaculation
  absent, 619, 620f, 621
    history of, 611
  antegrade, preservation of, retroperitoneal
    lymph node dissection and, 940, 941,
    945
  dysfunction of
    in sperm delivery, 648-649
    in spinal cord injury, 619, 649
      management of, 649
  premature, 784-787
    classification of, 784
    definition of, 784
    diagnosis of, components in, 784
    etiology of, 784-785, 784t
    exclusionary factors in, 784

Ejaculation (*Continued*)
    office management of, 786, 787t
    treatment of
      pharmacologic, 785-786, 786t
      psychological/behavioral, 785
  retrograde, 648-649
    after laparoscopic retroperitoneal lymph
      node dissection, 947
    definition of, 715
    management of, 715
    medical therapy for, 648
Ejaculatory duct(s)
  function of, pelvic and retroperitoneal surgery
    affecting, 610-611
  obstruction of, 619, 621
    detection of, 627-628, 628f
    diagnosis of, 707-708, 708f
    surgical management of, 707-714
      complications of, 708
      outcomes of, 708-710, 709t
      seminal vesical aspiration in, 710, 712f
      seminal vesiculography in, 710, 711f
      transrectal ultrasonography in, 707,
        708f
      transurethral balloon dilatation in, 708
      transurethral resection in, 708, 709f
    vasography of, 707-708
      complications of, 714
      technique of, 710-711, 713f, 714, 714f
*ELAC2* gene, in hereditary prostate cancer, 518
Elastin, of bladder wall, 1932
Elderly. *See* Geriatric patient.
Electrical activity
  of bladder smooth muscle, 1927-1928
    propagation of, 1929
  of ureteral smooth muscle, 1892-1897
    propagation of, 1897
Electrical responses, in bladder smooth muscle,
    propagation of, 1929
Electrical stimulation. *See also* Transcutaneous
    electrical nerve stimulation (TENS).
  applications of, for voiding dysfunctions,
    2148t
  for incontinence, 2071, 2135
  for stress incontinence, 2074
  future research in, 2167
  history of, 2147-2148, 2148t
  of bladder
    for emptying disorders, 2163-2167
      direct, 2163-2164
      neurophysiology of, 2148-2150, 2149f-
        2151f
      sacral neuromodulation in, 2166-2167
      to nerve roots, 2164-2165, 2164f
      transurethral, 2165-2166
    for storage disorders, 2151-2163
      bilateral, 2158
      complications of, 2160-2163
      contraindications to, 2152
      criteria for patient selection in, 2151-
        2152
      efficacy and safety of, 2160-2162, 2161f,
        2162f
      neurophysiology of, 2148-2150, 2149f-
        2151f
      sacral neuromodulation in, 2153-2158
        outcome of, 2155
        special populations and, 2155-2158
        technique of, 2153-2155, 2153f-2155f
      sacral rhizotomy in, 2152-2153
      selective nerve stimulation in, 2158-2160
      transurethral, 2152
      troubleshooting algorithm for, 2162-
        2163, 2163f

Electrical stimulation (*Continued*)
  of sacral nerve
    for painful bladder syndrome/interstitial
      cystitis, 365
    responses to, 2148t
Electrocautery, for genital warts, 382
Electrode(s)
  design of, in transurethral vaporization of
    prostate, 2839
  electromyographic, types of, 1989-1990
  in urodynamic studies, 1989-1990
Electroejaculation
  for anejaculation, 715-716, 716f
  for spinal cord-injured men, 649
Electrohydraulic (spark gap) generator, for
    shockwave lithotripsy, 1465, 1465f, 1466t,
    1470t
Electrohydraulic lithotripsy, 1458-1460, 1459f,
    1513-1514
  advantages and disadvantages of, 1459-1460
  technique of, 1460
Electrolyte(s)
  abnormalities of, conduit urinary diversion
    causing, 2570-2573, 2571f, 2571t
  management of
    in neonate, 3156, 3157f
    postoperative, in renal transplant recipient,
      1312-1313
Electromagnetic generator
  for shockwave lithotripsy, 1465, 1467t, 1468,
    1468f
  imaging and financial aspects of, 1470t-1471t
Electromagnetic therapy, for incontinence,
    2136
Electromyography
  corpus cavernosum, in erectile dysfunction,
    767
  equipment for, 1989-1990
  in urodynamic studies, 2002
  of urethral sphincter, 3626-3627, 3628f
  sphincter, 2068
Electronic dip stick flowmeter, 1989
Electronic spread, of current, 1897
Electrosurgical devices, bipolar, in laparoscopy,
    192
Elephantitis
  penile, 457
  scrotal, 456, 456f, 457
    *Onchocerca volvulus* causing, 455
    treatment of, 458
El-Ghorab shunt, for priapism, 847f, 848
Elimination syndrome, dysfunctional, of
    childhood, 3611, 3613
ELISA (enzyme-linked immunosorbent assay)
  for antisperm antibodies, 624t
  for HIV infection, 393
Elsberg syndrome, 2033
Embolization
  arterial, for nonischemic priapism, 848
  of pseudoaneurysm, 1546-1547, 1547f
  percutaneous, in varicocele repair, 662-663
Embolus (embolism)
  carbon dioxide, pediatric laparoscopy and,
    3917
  gas, with pneumoperitoneum, 205
  pulmonary, due to radical retropubic
    prostatectomy, 2973
  renal artery, 1190, 1190t
    cholesterol, 1166
Embryonal carcinoma, testicular, 895
  incidence, pathology, and presentation of,
    897t
Embryonal rhabdomyosarcoma, 3879
Emissary vein(s), 723, 723f

Emphysema
  insufflation-related, laparoscopic renal surgery
    causing, 1807
  subcutaneous, with pneumoperitoneum,
    205-206
Encephalomyelitis, acute disseminated, voiding
  dysfunction in, 2036
Encephalopathy, Wernicke's, voiding dysfunction
  in, 2042
Endemic bladder calculi, 2663-2664
Endocarditis. *See* Bacterial endocarditis.
  in pediatric genitourinary procedures,
    3242t
Endocrine signals, in prostate, 2690, 2690f
Endocrine system
  effect of
    on male infertility, 635-638
    on prostate growth, 2684-2689
  in testicular descent, 3766-3768
Endocrine/paraendocrine mechanisms, in
  renin-angiotensin-aldosterone system,
  1162
Endogenous inhibitors, of angiogenesis, 544
Endometriosis
  definition of, 1220
  painful bladder syndrome/interstitial cystitis
    and, 351
  ureteral obstruction due to, 1220-1221
  within urethral diverticula, 2389
Endometrium, biopsy of, in evaluation of
  fertility, 612
Endopelvic fascia, 2194-2195
  incision of, in radical retropubic
    prostatectomy, 2960-2961, 2961f
Endopyelotomy
  antegrade, for ureteropelvic junction
    obstruction
    complications of, 1236-1237
    in children, 3374-3375, 3375f
    indications for and contraindications to,
      1233, 1233f
    patient preparation in, 1233
    postoperative care following, 1234, 1236
    results of, 1236
    simultaneous nephrolithotomy with, 1234
    technique of, 1233-1234, 1235f, 1236f
  cautery wire balloon, for ureteropelvic
    junction obstruction
    complications of, 1238-1239
    indications for and contraindications to,
      1237, 1237f
    postoperative care following, 1237
    results of, 1237-1238
    technique of, 1237, 1238f
  in children
    access for, 3913
    incision for, 3913
    indications for, 3912-3913
    results of, 3913
  ureteroscopic, for ureteropelvic junction
    obstruction
    complications of, 1241
    indications for and contraindications to,
      1239
    results of, 1241
    success of, 1522
    technique of, 1239, 1240f, 1241
Endoscope(s), pediatric application of, 3908t
Endoscopic lithotripsy, for bladder calculi, 2669-
  2670
Endoscopic resection, of urothelial tumors,
  1647-1648
  percutaneous approach to, 1648
    results of, 1648, 1648t

Endoscopy
  antegrade, of urothelial tumors, 1645
  antibiotic prophylaxis for
    of lower urinary tract, 252
    of upper urinary tract, 253
  in bladder cancer, non–muscle-invasive
    office-based, 2454
    therapeutic, 2450-2454
  in incontinent patient, 2069-2070
  in laparoscopy, 177
  in prostatitis, 316
  in surgical approach, to seminal vesicles, 1125
  in vesicoureteral reflux, 4362-4366
    emerging role of, 4348
    follow-up of, 4363-4364
    materials for, 4364-4365, 4364t
    reflux recurrence after, 4365-4366
    STING technique of, 4362-4363, 4363f
  of bladder diverticula, 2365, 2366f
  of cloacal anomalies, 3852
  of ureterocele, 3406
  of ureteropelvic junction obstruction, in
    children, 3374-3375, 3375f
  of urethral strictures, 2660
  of urogenital sinus anomalies, 3851, 3852f
  of urothelial tumors, 1672-1680
    basic attributes of, 1672, 1673f, 1674f
    biopsy and definitive treatment in, 1675,
      1676f, 1677f
    collection of urine in, 1674-1675
    percutaneous approach to, 1677-1680
      biopsy and definitive treatment in, 1678,
        1679f, 1680f
      establishment of nephrostomy tract in,
        1677-1678, 1677f, 1678f
      results of, 1679-1680
      second-look nephroscopy in, 1679
    results of, 1675, 1677
    steps in, 1674-1675, 1676f, 1677f
    technique and instrumentation in, 1673-
      1674, 1674f
  ureteral injury due to, in children, 3937
Endothelial barrier, traversing, 493-494
Endothelial cell(s)
  adhesion molecule expression on, 493
  T cell interaction with, 493, 493f
  vascular, 477
Endothelial growth factor, in urothelial tumors,
  2425
Endothelin(s), 2711
  effect of, on ureteral function, 1920
  in male sexual function, 728
  in renal hemodynamics, 1134
  uropharmacology of, 1956
Endothelin-1, 537-538, 2711
  in hormone-refractory prostate cancer, 3116
Endothelium, of corpus cavernosum, erectile
  dysfunction and, 742
Endothelium-dependent vasodilation, impaired,
  in erectile dysfunction, 741-742
Endoureterotomy, for ureteral stricture, 1257-
  1259
  antegrade approach to, 1258
  cautery wire balloon incision in, 1257-1258
  combined approaches to, 1259
  retrograde approach to, 1257, 1257f
Endourologic procedures
  for ureteroenteric anastomotic stricture, 1269
  for ureteropelvic junction obstruction, 1232-
    1241
    complications of, 1236-1237, 1238-1239,
      1241
    indications for and contraindications to,
      1232, 1233f, 1237, 1237f, 1239

Endourologic procedures *(Continued)*
    patient preparation in, 1232
    postoperative care following, 1234, 1236,
      1237
    results of, 1236, 1237-1238, 1241
    technique of, 1232-1234, 1235f, 1236f,
      1237, 1238f, 1239, 1240f, 1241
  in children, 3907-3914
  prior to laparoscopy, 176
Endovascular stenting. *See* Stent (stenting).
End-stage renal disease
  acquired renal cystic disease in, 3351
  causes of, 1345
    in worldwide renal registries, 1354t
  drug dosing in, 1352
  family history of, 1344-1345
  hospitalization for, 1357-1359, 1358t
  impotence in, 1301
  in children, 1296, 3229-3230, 3230t
    renal transplantation for, 1296
    urinary tract infection and, 3261
  incidence of, 1295, 1345t
  long-term survival with, 1355, 1356t
  Medicare co-insurance for, 1297
  preoperative evaluation of, 1350-1352
  prevalence of, 1295, 1345t
  renal cell carcinoma in, 3352
  renal transplantation for
    in children, 1296
    results of, 1296, 1296t
  treatment options for, 1295-1296, 1354-1357,
    1356t, 1357f, 1357t
End-to-end ileocolonic sutured anastomosis,
  2542, 2542f
End-to-end stapled anastomosis, ileal-ileal or
  ileocolonic, 2544, 2544f
End-to-side ileocolonic sutured anastomosis,
  2541-2542, 2541f, 2542f
Enemas
  antegrade continence, in children, 3700-3701,
    3700f
  cleansing, for TRUS-guided prostate biopsy,
    2889
Enteric hyperoxaluria, 1378, 1378f, 1403
Enterobiasis, 458
Enterocele(s)
  repair of
    abdominal approach to, 2224
    vaginal approach to, 2223-2224, 2224f, 2225f
  types of, 2200, 2200t, 2201f
*Enterococcus faecalis*, endocarditis due to,
  antibiotic prophylaxis for, 254, 254t
Enterocolitis, pseudomembranous, antibiotic
  bowel preparation causing, 2539
Enterocystoplasty
  as risk factor for bladder cancer, 1324
  laparoscopic, 2512-2515
    in children, 3925
    results of, 2514-2515
    technique of, 2513-2514, 2514f
Enteroenterostomy
  by single-layer sutured anastomosis, 2541,
    2541f
  by two-layer sutured anastomosis, 2540-2541,
    2540f
Enteroplasty, seromuscular, in children, 3690,
  3691f
Enucleation
  in partial nephrectomy, 1728
  of adenoma
    in retropubic prostatectomy, 2848-2849,
      2848f, 2849f
    in suprapubic prostatectomy, 2850, 2850f,
      2851f

Enuresis
  daytime, in children, 3204
  nocturnal. *See* Nocturia.
  patient history of, 86
Environment, role of, in prostate cancer, 2856
Environmental toxins, male infertility due to, 644
Enzyme-linked immunosorbent assay (ELISA)
  for antisperm antibodies, 624t
  for HIV infection, 393
Enzyme-linked receptor(s), 539
Eosinophilia, tropical pulmonary, in filariasis, 457
Eosinophilic cystitis, in children, 3582
Ephedrine
  for retrograde ejaculation, 648
  for stress incontinence, 2109
Ephedrine calculi, 1389
Epidermal growth factor, 2709
  cancer and, 536
  for tubal regeneration, in acute tubular necrosis, 1337
  in benign prostatic hyperplasia, 2731-2732, 2731f
  properties of, 2706t
Epidermal growth factor receptor
  in hormone-refractory prostate cancer, 3115
  in renal cell carcinoma, 1590
Epidermoid cyst
  of male genitalia, 433, 434f
  testicular, 929
    in children, 3901, 3903
Epididymal appendage torsion, in acute scrotum, 3792
Epididymal cyst, 3798
Epididymectomy, 1103
  in genitourinary tuberculosis, 445-446
  surgical technique of, 1103-1104, 1104f
Epididymis, 596-604
  arterial supply to, 74, 598
  aspiration of sperm from
    microsurgical technique of, 652, 700, 703f-704f
    percutaneous technique of, 652, 700, 702f-703f
  blood supply to, 1099t
  contractile tissue of, 597-598
  embryology of, 3124
  epithelial histology of, 598, 599f, 600
  functions of, 600-603
    fluids and secretions affecting, 603
    regulation of, 603-604
  in testicular descent, 3769-3770
  inflammation of. *See* Epididymitis.
  innervation of, 77, 598
  leiomyosarcoma of, 934
  lymphatic drainage of, 598
  obstruction of
    diagnosis of, 680, 682
    tuberculosis-induced, 447
    vasectomy causing, 680
  sperm maturation in, 600-603, 601f
  sperm reserves in, 606
  sperm storage in, 600
  sperm transport in, 600
  structure of, 597, 597f
  surgery of, 1103-1105, 1104f
  tuberculosis of, 438, 440
  vascularization of, 598
Epididymitis
  *Chlamydia trachomatis* in, 378
  chronic, 1107
    congestive, 1108
  classification of, 329, 329t

Epididymitis *(Continued)*
  definition of, 329
  diagnosis of, 329
  in HIV patients, 396
  pathogenesis and etiology of, 328-329
  pediatric urinary tract infection and, 3264-3265
  treatment of, 329
  tuberculous, 440
  tumors of, excision of, 1105
  vs. acute scrotum, 3792-3793
Epididymo-orchitis, 327
  pediatric urinary tract infections and, 3264-3265
Epidural blockade, for painful bladder syndrome/interstitial cystitis, 365
Epidural cord compression, hormone-refractory prostate cancer and, palliative therapy for, 3112-3113, 3113t
Epigastric artery, inferior, 46, 48t, 50f
  harvesting of, in penile revascularization, 807-809, 808f
Epigenetic events, in prostate cancer, 2865
Epinephrine, 1821
  for priapism, 846t
Episiotomy, pelvic floor dysfunction and, 2189
Epispadias, 91, 3544-3550
  female, 3547-3548
    anomalies associated with, 3547
    surgical management of
      objectives in, 3547-3548
      results of, 3548
      techniques of, 3548, 3549f-3550f
  male, 3544-3547, 3545f
    anomalies associated with, 3545
    surgical management of, 3545-3547
      urethroplasty in, 3547
      urinary continence after, 3546-3547, 3546t
  repair of
    combined with exstrophy reconstruction, 3517-3518, 3526, 3527f-3530f, 3530
    results of, 3531-3533, 3535
    in exstrophy patient, 3518-3519, 3519f
Epithelial cell(s)
  in urinary sediment, 106-107, 107f
  of prostate, 2680-2681, 2680t
  permeability of, in painful bladder syndrome/interstitial cystitis, 343-345
  receptivity of, in urinary tract infections, 231-234, 233f, 234f
  stromal cell interactions with, 2693-2694, 2706, 2707f
  in benign prostatic hyperplasia, 2731
  vacuoles within, in adenomatoid tumors, 931
Epithelial growth factor
  in prostate cancer, 2867
  properties of, 2706t
Epithelial growth factor receptor, in prostate cancer, 2867
Epithelial hyperplasia, in bladder cancer, 2417
Epithelial tumor(s)
  of kidney, mixed stromal, 1581-1582
  of testicular adnexa, 931
Epithelium
  of seminiferous tubules, 592
  urothelial tumor spread to, 1641
Epitomics, in diagnosis of oncology, 549
Epitope, of antigen-binding site, 478
Eplerenone, for primary hyperaldosteronism, 1856
Epoöphoron, 3124

Epstein-Barr virus (EBV)
  in Burkitt's lymphoma, 541
  serologic testing for, prior to renal transplantation, 1298
Equipment. *See also* Instrumentation.
  in laparoscopic surgery
    malfunction of, 204
    strategic placement of, 177-178, 177f
  urodynamic, 1988-1990, 1988t
  videourodynamic, 2000-2001, 2001f
*erb* proto-oncogene, 514
*erb-2* oncogene
  in bladder cancer, 2412
  in renal cell carcinoma, 1590
Erectile dysfunction
  after cryotherapy, 3049
  after radical cystectomy, 2488-2489
  after radical prostatectomy, PDE-5 inhibitors for, 775-776
  after radical retropubic prostatectomy, 2974
  after renal transplantation, 1321-1322
    potential causes of, 1322t
    treatment options for, 1322, 1322t, 1323f
  after robotic-assisted laparoscopic radical prostatectomy, 2999-3000
  after urethral injury, 3944
  aging and, 746
  androgen deprivation therapy causing, 3090
  arteriogenic, 740-742
  atherosclerosis affecting, 741
  cardiovascular risk factors in, 777t
  cavernosus (venogenic), 742
  chronic renal failure and, 747-748
  classification of, 738-742, 738f, 739t
  complex, 757-768
    hormonal evaluation of, 767-768
    neurologic evaluation of, 765-767
    penile blood flow studies in
      first-line evaluation of, 757-758
      historical and investigational evaluations of, 762-763
      second-line evaluation of, 758-760, 758f, 759f
      third-line evaluation of, 760-762, 761f, 762f
    psychological evaluation of, 765
    psychophysiologic evaluation of, 763-764, 764f
    vascular evaluation of, 757-763, 757t
  definition of, 715
  diabetes mellitus and, 746-747, 747t
  diagnostic algorithm in, 751f
  drug-induced, 742-746
    antiandrogens in, 745
    antidepressants in, 744, 745
    antihypertensive agents in, 743, 744t
    miscellaneous agents in, 745-746
    psychotropic agents in, 743-745
  endocrinologic, 740
  epidemiology of, 738
  future research on, 783
  hyperlipidemia affecting, 741
  hyperprolactinemia associated with, 637
  hypertension affecting, 741
  impaired vasodilation causing, endothelium-dependent, 741-742
  in Peyronie's disease, 823
  incidence of, 738
  neurogenic, 739-740
  organic, 755, 755t
  pathophysiology of, 738-749
  patient-centered evaluation of, 750-757
    follow-up strategy in, 757
    goal-directed approach in, 750

Erectile dysfunction (Continued)
  ICSM recommendations in, 750-751, 751f, 752f
  laboratory testing in, 756
  medical history in, 752, 755, 755t
  physical examination in, 756
  psychosocial history in, 755-756, 755t
  questionnaires for, 751-752, 753f
  review of findings in, 756
  Sexual Function Scale in, 752, 754f-755f
  shared decision-making and treatment planning in, 756, 756t
  specialist consultation and referral in, 756-757
 perspectives on, 748
 pharmacotherapy for, 773-783
  α-adrenergic antagonists in, 779
  adrenoceptor antagonists in, 778-779
  alprostadil in, 779-780
  apomorphine in, 782
  centrally acting drugs for, 782-783
  intracavernous injection in, 779-781
   adverse effects of, 781
   common agents in, 779t
   contraindications to, 781
   dosage and administration of, 781
   drug combinations in, 780
   patient acceptance and dropout with, 781
  intraurethral, 781
  melanocortin-receptor agonist in, 782-783
  oral preparations in, 773-779
  papaverine in, 779
  phosphodiesterase type-5 inhibitors in, 773-777, 774f, 774t
   cardiovascular safety and, 777-778, 777t, 778f
   combination therapy with, 778
  priapism associated with, 841
  testosterone for, 859
  transdermal, 781-782
  trazodone in, 782
  yohimbine in, 782
 primary, 748
 prosthetic surgery for, 788-801
  approach(es) to, 790, 790f, 790t
   transverse penoscrotal, 790-795, 791f-795f
  complication(s) of, 795-797
   autoinflation as, 797
   infection as, 795-796, 796f
   oversized cylinder or rod as, 797
   perforation and erosion as, 797
   poor glans support as, 797, 798f
   pump, 797
  in cavernosal fibrosis, 798-800, 799f, 800f
  in Peyronie's disease, 798, 798f
  mechanical failure rates in, 800, 800t
  patient-partner satisfaction with, 800-801
  postoperative care after, 795
  preoperative patient-partner counseling and, 788-790
  results of, 800-801, 800t
  types of prosthesis in, 788, 789f, 789t
 psychogenic, 739, 755, 755t
 risk factors for, 738
 structural changes causing, 741
 treatment of
  costs, advantages, and disadvantages of, 756t
  diagnostic algorithm in, 752f
  diagnostic workup in, 751t
  herbal supplements in, 770, 770t
  hormonal therapy in, 771-773, 771t

Erectile dysfunction (Continued)
  lifestyle change in, 769
  medication change in, 769-770
  nonsurgical, 768-783
  pelvic floor exercises in, 770
  pharmacologic therapy in, 773-783. See also Erectile dysfunction, pharmacotherapy for.
  prosthetic surgery for, 788-802. See also Erectile dysfunction, vascular surgery for.
  psychosexual therapy in, 770-771
  shared decision-making in, 756
  vacuum constriction device in, 783
  vascular surgery for, 802-816
 vascular, mechanisms of, 741-742
 vascular surgery for, 802-816
  history and review of, 802-803
  patient counseling for, 803, 803f
  penile arterial reconstruction in, 803-812
   complications of, 810-811
   dorsal artery dissection in, 806-807, 808f
   inferior epigastric artery harvesting in, 807-809, 808f
   microvascular anastomosis in, 809-810, 809f, 810f
   results of, 811-812, 811t
   selection criteria for, 803-805, 803t, 804f, 805f
   technique of, 806-810, 806f, 806t, 807t
  penile venous reconstruction in, 812-816
   complications of, 815-816
   results of, 816, 816t
   selection criteria for, 812, 813f-814f
   technique of, 812, 815, 815f
  recommendations for, 802
 vasoconstriction causing, 741
Erectile Dysfunction Inventory for Treatment Satisfaction (EDITS) questionnaire, 751-752
Erection, penile. See Penile erection.
Erlangen procedure, of bladder exstrophy repair, 3517
 results of, 3534
Erosion
 artificial sphincter placement–induced, of urethra, 2400
 of fascial slings, 2235, 2236f, 2237f, 2246
 tension free vaginal tape–induced
  intravesical, 2262-2263, 2262t
  of urethra, 2260-2262, 2261f
  of vagina, 2259-2260, 2260f
Erysipelas, of male genitalia, 419, 421
Erythema multiforme, of male genitalia, 409-410, 409f
Erythrasma, of male genitalia, 424
Erythroid progenitor cell(s), 1135
Erythromycin
 for chancroid, 375
  in HIV patients, 396
 for Chlamydia trachomatis infection, 378
 for mollicute infections, 384
 neomycin with, in antibiotic bowel preparation, 2538
Erythroplasia of Queyrat, 426-427, 427f, 964. See also Penile cancer.
Erythropoiesis, 1135-1136
 regulation of, 1136
Erythropoietin, renal production of, 1136
Escherichia coli
 epithelial cell receptivity of, 231-234, 233f, 234f
 in acute pyelonephritis, 268
 in prostatitis, 306

Escherichia coli (Continued)
 in renal abscess, 3246
 in urinary tract infections, 228, 229-230, 229f, 230f
  pediatric, 3234
Estradiol
 and female sexual function, 875
 daily production of, in males, 2686t, 2688
Estramustine phosphate, for hormone-refractory prostate cancer, 3105t, 3106, 3108
 multidrug regimens with, 3107t
Estrogen(s)
 assessment of, in females, 872, 872f
 deficiency of
  genital tissue atrophy associated with, 879-880
  menopausal, 879, 879f
 effects of, on prostate, 2679-2680, 2686t, 2687f, 2688
 excess, male infertility and, 637
 fetal secretion of, 3804-3805
 for incontinence, 2107-2108
  in elderly, 2318
 for sexual dysfunction
  in perimenopausal and postmenopausal women, 878-880
  in premenopausal women, 875-876
 for stress incontinence, 2075, 2112-2113
 for vaginal atrophy, 880
 in benign prostatic hyperplasia, 2731
 in prostate growth, 2679-2680
  estrogen-androgen synergism in, 2693
 in testicular descent, 3768
 preoperative, for vaginal surgery, in postmenopausal women, 2215-2216
 prostate cancer and, epidemiologic studies of, 2861
 synergism of, on androgen-induced prostate growth, 2693
 uropharmacology of, 1956
Estrogen receptor modulators, selective, for prostate cancer, chemopreventive, 2871
Estrogen-secreting adrenal tumor, 1842
Ethambutol, for genitourinary tuberculosis, 444, 445t
Ethnicity
 pediatric urinary tract infection and, 3237-3238
 renal stones associated with, 1363-1364
Ethylene vinyl alcohol injections, for incontinence, 2274-2275
 efficacy of, 2282
Ethylsuccinate, for Chlamydia trachomatis infection, 378
Etoposide
 for hormone-refractory prostate cancer, 3105t
 high-dose, for nonseminomatous germ cell tumors, 923
Euchromatin, 2712
Euro-Collins solution, for kidney transplant preservation, 1306-1307
European Organization for Research and Treatment of Cancer Quality of Life Questionnaire (EORTC QLQ-C30), 150-151
Excision, of renal pelvis tumor, local, 1756, 1756f, 1757f, 1758
Excision strategies
 conservative, for penile cancer, 994, 995f, 996
 for hydrocelectomy, 1105, 1105f, 1106f
 for urethral stricture, reanastomosis with, 1062, 1063f, 1064f
 limited, for penile cancer, circumcision and, 973

Excitation, vanilloid-induced, 1959
Excitation-contraction coupling
  in bladder smooth muscle, 1928-1929, 1928t, 1929f
  in ureteral smooth muscle, 1899-1900
Excretory urography. *See* Urography, excretory.
Exenteration, anterior, urethrectomy with, in female radical cystectomy, 2496-2498, 2497f-2499f
Exercise(s)
  incontinence associated with, 2190
  pelvic floor, for erectile dysfunction, 770
Exercise-induced hematuria, 100
Exstrophy
  bladder. *See* Bladder exstrophy.
  cloacal. *See* Cloacal exstrophy.
  in female patient
    obstetric implications of, 3552-3553
    sexual function and fertility issues in, 3552
  in male patient, sexual function and fertility issues in, 3550-3552
  repaired, residual genital defect with, 1047-1049
    chordee as, 1042f, 1048-1049, 1048f
    reconstruction goals in, 1047-1048, 1048f
    urethral construction for, 1049
Exstrophy-epispadias complex, 3497-3500, 4323-4326
  causes of, 4326
  embryology of, 3499-3500, 3499f
  etiologies of, 3498
  historical aspects of, 3497
  incidence of, 3497
  inheritance of, 3497-3499
  omphaloceles in, 3503
  one-stage reconstruction of, 3554-3571
    background in, 3554-3555
    Mitchell technique in. *See* Complete primary exstrophy repair.
  variants of, 3548, 3550, 3551f, 3552f
Extended core biopsy, TRUS-guided, of prostate, 2890, 2890f, 2890t
Extracellular matrix
  components of, in bladder cancer, 2428
  imbalance of, renal disease associated with, 1344
  in renal cell carcinoma, 1591
  prostatic, 2690, 2690f
Extra-chromosomal resistance, of bacteria, to antibiotics, 244-245
Extracorporeal shockwave lithotripsy. *See* Shockwave lithotripsy.
Extragonadal germ cell tumor(s), 924-925
Extramural tunnel, serous-lined, for orthotopic urinary diversion, 2636, 2637f, 2638
Extraperitoneal space, development of, in laparoscopic surgery, 181-189. *See also* Laparoscopic surgery, development of extraperitoneal space in.
Extraperitoneoscopy, 182
  open and closed technique in, 184
Extrarenal calyces, 3301, 3301f
Extrarenal pelvis, 3303
Extrarenal tissues, damage to, shockwave lithotripsy causing, 1477
Extraurethral incontinence, 2047. *See also* Incontinence.
Extravasation, retroperitoneal, percutaneous nephrolithotomy causing, 1500
Extravesical procedures, in antireflux surgery, 4357, 4358f, 4359-4360
*EYA1* gene, in BOR syndrome, 3135
Eyeball urodynamic monitoring, of incontinent patient, 2064, 2064f

Eyelashes, pediculosis of, 384
EZH2 lysine methyltransferase, in prostate cancer, 2867

**F**
Facial appearance, characteristic, in bilateral renal agenesis, 3270-3271, 3271f, 3272
Factitial dermatitis, of male genitalia, 419
Failure to thrive, 3205-3206
  approach to, 3206t
  definition of, 3205
  organic causes of, 3206t
  psychosocial, 3205
Fallopian tubes
  evaluation of, in female fertility, 612
  sparing of, in laparoscopic radical cystectomy, 2521
Famciclovir, for herpes simplex virus infection, 374t
  in HIV patients, 394t
Familial adenomatous polyposis, 516t
Familial aspects, of hypospadias, 3708-3709
Familial benign prostatic hyperplasia, 2733-2734, 2733t
Familial hypoplastic glomerulocystic kidney disease, 3329
  characteristics of, 3314t
Familial papillary renal cell carcinoma, 1584t, 1587
Familial pheochromocytoma, 1860, 1861t
Familial prevalence, of hypospadias, 3708-3709
Familial prostate cancer, 2857-2858, 2857t
  definition of, 2857
Familial renal cell carcinoma
  molecular genetics and, 1584-1585, 1585f
  von Hippel–Lindau disease in, 1584t, 1585-1587, 1585t, 1586f
Family history, 88
Family members, examination of, for autosomal dominant polycystic kidney disease, 3325
Fanconi syndrome, in children, 3228, 3228t
Fas ligand, in cytolysis of target cell, 488
Fas-associated death domain, in apoptosis, 489
Fascia. *See also named fascia.*
  abdominal wall, subcutaneous, 38, 40, 40f, 41f
  endopelvic, 2194-2195
  lumbodorsal, 3, 6f, 7f, 8
  pelvic, 44-46
    components of, 45-46, 48f, 49f
    surgical anatomy of, 2959, 2959f
  perineal, 46, 49f, 73, 73f
  spermatic, 73
Fascia lata, for sling procedures
  autologous, 2247
    indications for, 2236-2237
    outcome of, 2247
  cadaveric, 2238
    outcome of, 2247
    harvesting of, 2237-2238
Fascial dehiscence, after complete primary exstrophy repair, 3571
Fascial dilators, 1542
Fascial sling, for bladder neck reconstruction, in children, 3665
Fasciitis, necrotizing. *See* Fournier's gangrene.
Fasciocutaneous (tissue) flap. *See also* Flap(s).
  in hypospadias repair, 3716-3717
Fas/Fas-L-mediated induction, of apoptosis, 488-489, 489f
Fast and calcium load test, 1398-1399
Fast-twitch muscle fibers, of urethra, 1936-1937
Fat, dietary, prostate cancer and, 2862-2872

Fat injections, autologous, for incontinence, 2275
  efficacy of, 2281
  safety of, 2285
Febrile illness, impaired spermatogenesis due to, 611
Fecal colonization, in pediatric urinary tract infection, 3239
Fecal continence
  after cloacal surgery, 3868-3869
  after radical perineal prostatectomy, 2983-2984
Fecal impaction, in geriatric incontinence, 2307t, 2309
Fecal incontinence
  epidemiology of, 2188
  in exstrophy patient, 3503
  in pelvic organ prolapse, 2204
  myelodysplasia and, management of, 3640
  sacral neuromodulation for, 2158
Feet, soles of, secondary syphilis affecting, 376f
Feline interstitial cystitis, 337-338
Female eunuch syndrome, infertility and, 636
Female-to-male transsexualism, reassignment surgery in, 1096-1097
Femoral artery, 46, 1031, 1033f
Femoral cutaneous nerve
  lateral, 18, 18f
  posterior, 53, 53t
Femoral nerve, 18-19, 18f, 53, 53f, 53t
  palsy of, 53, 53f
    after osteotomy, in exstrophy patient, 3516
Femoral vein, 46, 51
FemSoft urethral insert, 2140, 2140f
Fenoldopam, for acute renal failure, 1336-1337
Fertility
  after hypospadias repair, 3742
  female
    after renal transplantation, 1323
    evaluation of, 611-613
      fallopian tubes in, 612
      ovulation and luteal phase in, 612
      peritoneal cavity in, 612-613
      uterus in, 612
    in exstrophy patient, 3552
  in advanced testicular germ cell tumors, 957
  in low-stage testicular germ cell tumors, 949
  male. *See also* Infertility, male.
    in exstrophy patient, 3550-3552
    sperm maturation and, 602-603
  potential for, in true hermaphrodites, 3816
Fetal tissue, engineering of, 566-567, 567f
Fetus
  bladder anomalies in, prenatal detection of, 3574-3575, 3575f
  bladder in, antenatal sonographic findings of, 3573
  female, differentiation of, 3805, 3807f
  glomerular filtration rate in, 3149-3150
  kidney in
    development of
      anatomic stages in, 3149, 3150f
      functional, 3149-3150
    function of, evaluation of, 3150-3151, 3151f
  male, masculinization of, 3805, 3807f
  plasma renin activity in, 3157
  sex of, determination of, 3573
  sexual differentiation in. *See* Sexual differentiation.
  urologic anomalies in, antenatal diagnosis and management of, 3598, 3598f
  uropathy in. *See also specific pathology, e.g.,* Hydronephrosis, fetal.
    appearance of, 3180-3185, 3181f-3184f

Fetus (*Continued*)
  diagnostic findings in, 3176-3178, 3177f, 3177t, 3179f, 3180f
  incidence of, 3186
  interventions for, 3187-3189, 3187t, 3188f
  management of, 3186-3189
  pathophysiology of, 3185-3186
  postnatal evaluation and management of, 3189-3194, 3190t
  vesicoureteral reflux in, 4324
Fever
  filarial, 456
  in children
    bacterial infections and, 3206, 3206t
    management of, 3206
    urinary tract infection and, 3198, 3203
      management of, 3261
  in early graft dysfunction, 1318, 1319t
  in urinary tract infection, 240-241
  patient history of, 88
Fexofenadine, for Peyronie's disease, 827
Fibrin glue, in laparoscopy, 193
Fibroblast growth factor, 2708-2709
  in activation of angiogenesis, 542
  in benign prostatic hyperplasia, 2731-2732, 2731f
  properties of, 2706t
Fibroepithelial polyps, 431, 433
  in children, 3900
  of upper urinary tract, abnormal urothelium in, 1643
  percutaneous treatment of, 1556-1557
Fibroid. *See* Leiomyoma.
Fibroma
  ovarian, ureteral obstruction due to, 1221
  renal medullary, 1582
Fibromuscular hyperplasia, of renal artery, 1157t, 1161
Fibromyalgia, painful bladder syndrome/interstitial cystitis and, 336
Fibroplasia, of renal artery
  intimal, 1157t, 1159, 1159f, 1160f
  medial, 1157t, 1159-1160, 1160f
  perimedial, 1157t, 1160-1161, 1160f, 1161f
Fibrosis
  associated with intracavernous injection therapy, 781
  cavernosal, penile prosthesis for, 798-800, 799f, 800f
  in urinary tract obstruction
    cellular and molecular changes leading to, 1204
    congenital, 3169-3171, 3170f
    initiation of, angiotensin II in, 1204
  pelvic, as contraindication to laparoscopy, 174-175
  renal, experimental treatment approaches to, 1205-1206
  retroperitoneal. *See* Retroperitoneal fibrosis.
Fibrous dysplasia, percutaneous transluminal angioplasty for, 1181-1182, 1181t, 1182f
Fibular osteocutaneous flap. *See also* Flap(s).
  in penile reconstruction, 1093
Field theory, of epithelial spread, of urothelial tumors, 1641
Filariasis, lymphatic, 455-458
  clinical manifestations of, 456-457
  diagnosis of, 457
  early infection in, 456
  late infection in, 456, 456f
  pathogenesis of, 455-456
  pathology of, 455-456
  prevention of, 458
  treatment of, 457-458

Filiform catheter, 163, 165f
Filmy penile adhesions, after circumcision, 3748
Filtration fraction, in renal blood flow, 1131
Finasteride
  erectile dysfunction caused by, 745
  for benign prostatic hyperplasia, 2788-2792, 2789f, 2791f
    dosage of, 2788t
    efficacy of, 2790t
    vs. combination therapy, 2793, 2795t
  for lowering PSA levels, 2916
  for prostate cancer, prophylactic, 2869-2870, 2870t
  for prostatitis, clinical trial data on, 322-323, 327t
Finasteride Study Group, 741
Fine-needle aspiration biopsy
  of inguinal lymph nodes, in penile cancer, 980
  of prostate, 2891
  of renal cell carcinoma, disease staging with, 1603
  of renal cysts, 1772
  of renal tumors, 1571-1572
  of testicular sperm, 658
  of testis, sperm retrieval through, 701, 703, 705-706, 705f-707f
FISH (fluorescent in situ hybridization), in diagnosis of oncology, 548
Fistula(s)
  arteriovenous
    delayed bleeding due to, following percutaneous procedures, 1546, 1546f
    renal, 1189-1190, 1189f, 3297
  complex, of posterior urethra, reconstructive surgery for, 1086-1087, 1086f
  due to intestinal anastomosis, 2549
  due to ureterointestinal anastomosis, 2556t, 2562
  pancreatic, after radical nephrectomy, 1719
  pyeloenteric, 2353
  pyelovascular, 2357
  rectourethral, after cryotherapy, 3050
  renovascular, 2357
  ureteroenteric, 2353
  ureterovaginal, 2341-2345
    diagnosis of, 2341-2343, 2342f-2344f
    etiology and presentation of, 2341, 2342t
    management of, 2343-2345
  ureterovascular, 2357-2359, 2358t
  urethral, congenital, 3757-3758
  urethrocutaneous, 1042-1043, 1043f
    after hypospadias repair, 3739
  urethrorectal (rectourethral), 2353-2357
    etiology and presentation of, 2354-2355, 2354f, 2355f
    management of, 2355-2357, 2356f
  urethrovaginal, 2347-2351
    diagnosis of, 2348, 2348f, 2349f
    etiology and presentation of, 2347-2348, 2347f, 2348f
    management of, 2348-2351, 2350f
  urinary tract, 2322-2359
    after partial nephrectomy, 1730
    cutaneous, 2359
    general considerations in, 2322-2323
    repair of, 2322-2323, 2323t
    urethrocutaneous, 2359
  uroenteric, 2351-2357
  urogynecologic, 2323-2351
  urovascular, 2357-2359
  vesicoenteric, 2351-2353
    diagnosis of, 2352
    etiology and presentation of, 2351, 2351t
    management of, 2352-2353

Fistula(s) (*Continued*)
  vesicouterine, 2345-2347
    diagnosis of, 2345-2346, 2345f-2346f
    etiology and presentation of, 2345
    management of, 2346-2347
  vesicovaginal, 2323-2340, 2323f. *See also* Vesicovaginal fistula.
Fixed particle growth theory, of crystal formation, 1367-1368
Flank incisions, in renal surgery, 1691-1694, 1691f-1695f
Flank muscles, lateral, 8-9, 9t, 10f
Flank pain
  in urinary tract infection, 240-241
  ureteropelvic junction obstruction and, in children, 3363, 3364f
Flap(s)
  axial, 1026, 1027f
  Boari. *See* Boari flap.
  in correction of Peyronie's disease, H-shaped, 833, 835f, 836, 836f
  in hypospadias repair, 3725, 3726f-3727f
    onlay island, 3725-3726, 3728, 3728f-3729f
    one-stage, 3729, 3731
    split prepuce in-situ technique of, 3725, 3728, 3730f-3731f, 3743
  reoperative, 3740-3741
  subcutaneous (dartos), 3716, 3716f
  tissue (fasciocutaneous), 3716-3717
  transverse preputial island, 3731-3732, 3732f-3733f, 3734
  in penile reconstruction
    bipedicled, 1095-1096
    fibular osteocutaneous, 1093
    forearm, 1092-1093
      disadvantages of, 1093
      modifications of, 1093, 1094f, 1095f
    upper arm, 1094-1095
  in pyeloplasty techniques, 1243-1245, 1245f
  in reconstructive surgery, 1026, 1026f, 1027f, 1028
  in urethral diverticula repair, 2387f, 2388
  in urethral stricture repair, 1067, 1067f-1073f, 1073
  in urethrovaginal fistula repair, 2349, 2351
  in vesicovaginal fistula repair, 2332, 2340
    splitting of, 2333-2335, 2334f, 2335f
  island, 1026, 1027f, 1028
  musculocutaneous, 1026, 1027f
  onlay island, in hypospadias repair, 3725-3726, 3728, 3728f-3729f
    one-stage, 3729, 3731
    split prepuce in-situ technique of, 3725, 3728, 3730f-3731f, 3742
  peninsular, 1026, 1027f
  random, 1026, 1026f
  skin island, 1028
    in urethral stricture repair, 1072f-1074f, 1073-1075
  skin paddle, 1028
  subcutaneous (dartos), in hypospadias repair, 3716, 3716f
  tissue (fasciocutaneous)
    in hypospadias repair, 3716-3717
    in reoperative hypospadias repair, 3740-3741
  transverse preputial island, in hypospadias repair, 3731-3732, 3732f-3733f, 3734
Flavoxate
  for incontinence, in elderly, 2317t
  for overactive bladder/detrusor overactivity, 2093t, 2103
Floating ball electrode, in laparoscopy, 191-192

Flow cytometry
  of bladder cancer, 2431
  of urothelial tumors, 1644
Flowmeters, in urodynamic studies, 1989, 1989t
Fluconazole, 469
  cost of, 464t
  dosage of, 461t
  for funguria, 300
  for pediatric fungal infections, of urinary tract, 3265
  for urinary tract infection, candidal, 463
  for vulvovaginal candidiasis, 385
Flucytosine, 469
  for funguria, 300
Fluid(s)
  absorption of, percutaneous nephrostomy causing
  collection of, after renal transplantation, 1319-1320, 1320f
  for acute renal failure, 1337-1338
  for nephrolithiasis, 1411-1412
  in renal transplant recipient, postoperative management of, 1312-1313
  intake of, renal stones associated with, 1365
  management of, in neonate, 3156, 3157f
  restriction of, in behavioral therapy for incontinence, 2128-2129
  retention of, testosterone therapy causing, 859
Fluorescent in situ hybridization (FISH), in diagnosis of oncology, 548
Fluoroquinolones
  for acute pyelonephritis, 270, 270t
  for cystitis, 256t, 257
  for prostatitis, 320-321, 320t
  for urinary tract infections, 245t, 246t, 247t, 248-249
Fluoroscopy
  in nephrostomy procedures, 1531-1532, 1531f, 1531f
  in shockwave lithotripsy, 1469
  ultrasonography with, 1469, 1470t-1471t
5-Fluorouracil
  for hormone-refractory prostate cancer, 3105t
  for penile cancer, 987
Fluoxetine, for premature ejaculation, 785, 786t
Flush stoma, 2552
Flutamide
  androgen blockade with, 3085t, 3086
  for benign prostatic hyperplasia, 2792
  dosage of, 2788t
  for priapism, 846t
Foam cells, in glomerulus, 1344
Foley catheter, 162, 162f
  for percutaneous nephrostomy, 1559-1560
  in urethral diverticula repair, 2387f, 2388
Foley Y-V plasty technique, for ureteropelvic junction obstruction, 1243-1245, 1245f
  in children, 3370, 3370f
Follicle-stimulating hormone (FSH)
  deficiency of, in male, 636
  for male infertility, 636
  in evaluation of fertility, 612
  in evaluation of infertility, 618-619, 618t
  in male reproductive axis, 577, 578f
  increased levels of, following varicocele repair, 664
  role of, in spermatogenesis, 596
  secretion of, 578
  Sertoli cell stimulation by, 579-580
Folliculitis, of male genitalia, 421, 422f

Foods
  avoidance of, ICA recommendations for, in painful bladder syndrome/interstitial cystitis, 359t
  oxalate-rich, 1378, 1403t
Force-length relations, of ureteral smooth muscle, 1902-1903, 1902f, 1903f
Force-velocity relations, of ureteral smooth muscle, 1903, 1903f
Forearm flap. See also Flap(s).
  in penile reconstruction, 1092-1093
    disadvantages of, 1093
    modifications of, 1093, 1094f, 1095f
Forebrain, involved in sexual function, 726t
Foreign body(ies), bladder calculi related to, 2666, 2667f
Foreskin, neonatal bacterial colonization of, 3238
Fosfomycin, for pediatric urinary tract infections, 3248t
Fossa navicularis, urethral, 1029, 1030f
Four-corner bladder neck suspension, for vaginal wall prolapse, 2219-2221, 2220t, 2221f
Fournier's gangrene, 301-302
  genital skin loss due to, 2654
  in AIDS patients, 397
  of male genitalia, 421, 421f
Fowler syndrome, voiding dysfunction in, 2040
Fowler-Stephens orchidopexy, 3781
  for prune-belly syndrome, 3492-3493
  laparoscopic, 3786
Fowler-Stephens test, 3781
Fractional excretion of sodium
  gestational age and, 3150
  in infant and child, 3154
  in preterm and term neonates, 3151, 3153f
Fracture(s)
  pelvic
    associated with posterior urethral injury, in children, 3940
    urethral disruption related to, 2659
  penile, 2649-2650, 2650f
  straddle, of pubic rami, 2658, 2658f
Frank technique, in creation of neovagina, modification of, 3835
Free graft. See also Graft(s).
  in hypospadias repair, 3716
    neourethral formation and, 3734, 3736-3738, 3738f
    reoperative, 3741
Freeze-thaw cycle, in cryotherapy, 3036-3037
Freezing process, in cryotherapy. See also Cryotherapy.
  monitoring of, 3041, 3044
  tissue response to, 3035-3036, 3035f
Frenulae, sexual pain disorders involving, 883
Frequency, 84
  causes of, 370t
  definition of, 331, 2079
  in elderly, 2311
  measurement of, 2084
  nocturnal, 84
Fructose, in prostatic secretions, 2716
FSH. See Follicle-stimulating hormone (FSH).
Fuhrman's classification, of renal cell carcinoma, 1591, 1591t
Fulguration, of urothelial tumors, 1647-1648
Fumagillin, as inhibitor of angiogenesis, 543
Fungal bezoar(s)
  *Aspergillus,* 465f
  *Candida,* 460, 460f, 463, 463f
  in children, 3265
  percutaneous treatment of, 1556

Fungal infection(s), of genitourinary tract, 459-469. See also specific infection, e.g., Candidiasis.
  pediatric, 3265
Funguria, 299-301
  clinical presentation of, 299
  diagnosis of, 299
  in pediatric urinary tract infections, 3265
  management of, 299-301, 300f
Funiculoepididymitis, 456-457
Furunculosis, of male genitalia, 422, 422f
Fusiform aneurysm, of renal artery, 1187, 1188f
Fusion anomaly(ies). See also specific anomaly.
  of female genitalia
    lateral, 3839, 3839f, 3840f
    vertical, 3832-3839, 3833f-3839f

**G**

G protein, muscarinic receptor-coupling to, 2092
G protein–coupled ligand, cancer and, 537-538
G protein–coupled receptor(s), 539
$G_1S$ checkpoint, in cell cycle, 521-524
  cip/cik function and, 523-524
  cyclin-dependent kinase complexes and, 523-524
  INK4 function and, 523
  retinoblastoma protein and, 524
  *TP53* in urologic malignancies and, 522-523
  TP53 regulator of, 521-522, 522f
$G_2M$ checkpoint, in cell cycle, 525, 525f
Gabapentin, effect of, on detrusor overactivity, 2108
Gallium nitrate, for bladder cancer, metastatic, 2478
Gamma-aminobutyric acid
  in male sexual function, 730
  uropharmacology of, 1962, 1965, 2120-2121
Gamma-glutamyl transpeptidase, in testicular tumors, 907
Ganglioneuroma, 3871, 3871f
Gangliosides, in suppression of tumor immunity, 497
Gangrene
  Fournier's. See Fournier's gangrene.
  necrotizing, genital skin loss due to, 2654, 2655f
Gap junctions
  in penile function, 742
  in ureteral function, 1897
*Gardnerella vaginalis,* in painful bladder syndrome/interstitial cystitis, 339
Gartner's duct, abnormalities of, vs. urethral diverticula, 2383, 2383f
Gartner's duct cyst, 3843, 3843f
Gas embolism
  insufflation-related, laparoscopic renal surgery causing, 1807
  with pneumoperitoneum, 205
Gasless technique, for pneumoperitoneum, 181
Gastric artery, 2533, 2534f
Gastric contents, aspiration of, in laparoscopy, 211
Gastric pouches, for continent urinary diversion, 2604-2606
  postoperative care of, 2606
  procedure in, 2604-2606, 2604f, 2605f
Gastrocystoplasty, in children
  antrum technique of, 3678
  body technique of, 3678-3679, 3678f
Gastroepiploic artery, 2533, 2534f
Gastrointestinal tract. See also specific part.
  anomalies of
    in cloacal exstrophy, 3540
    in prune-belly syndrome, 3485t, 3487

Gastrointestinal tract (*Continued*)
decompression of, for cloacal anomalies, 3865
disorders of
radiation-induced, 3016t
renal pain associated with, 82
effects of augmentation cystoplasty on, 3680
hemorrhage in, as complication of post-
chemotherapy surgery, 956
injury to
laparoscopic, trocar placement causing,
206-207
radical nephrectomy causing, 1718-1719
Gastroparesis, voiding dysfunction in, 2041
Gastrostomy decompression, after intestinal
anastomosis, 2548-2549
Gelatin agglutination test, for antisperm
antibodies, 624t
Gelport device, hand-assist, 186, 186f
Gemcitabine, for bladder cancer
metastatic, 2477
non–muscle-invasive, 2459
Gender
assignment of, 3829
in cloacal exstrophy reconstruction, 3542,
3542f
in true hermaphroditism, 3816
pediatric urinary tract infections and, 3237
reassignment of, micropenis and, 3753
renal stones and, 1363
vesicoureteral reflux and, 4324
Gender identity, 3805, 3808
issues of, in hypospadias, 3742
Gender orientation, 3808
Gene(s). *See also specific gene.*
cancer. *See* Oncogene(s); *specific oncogene.*
hereditary tumor
identification of, 517, 517f
inactivation of, 516
role of, in malignancies, 516-517
hormone response element in, 2703
involved in kidney development, 3134-3135
involved in sexual differentiation, 3802-3803,
3802f
involved in vesicoureteral reflux, 4326
promotor element in, 2702-2703
protein products of, 3306
susceptibility, in prostate cancer, 2858,
2858t
tumor suppressor. *See* Tumor suppressor
gene(s).
Gene amplification, in proto-oncogene
conversion to oncogene, 514
Gene chip, 503
Gene expression
analysis of, in penile cancer, 979
in tumor marker discovery, 2909
of retroviruses, 389
profile of
in transplantation, 503, 504f
in urologic oncology, 503
Gene map, for kallikrein tumor marker, 2897,
2897f
Gene mutations, in hypogonadotropic
hypogonadism, 3767
Gene therapy, 551
for prostate cancer, 3029-3031
corrective, 3030
cytolytic/proapoptotic, 3030
enzyme/prodrug, 3030
General population, prevalence of hypospadias
in, 3708
Genetic counseling, in autosomal dominant
polycystic kidney disease, 3325
Genetic engineering, advances in, 546

Genetic factors
in autosomal dominant polycystic kidney
disease, 3320
in autosomal recessive polycystic kidney
disease, 3315
in benign prostatic hyperplasia, 2733
in bladder cancer, 2429-2430
in chronic renal failure, 1344-1345
in clear cell carcinoma, 1584t, 1585-1587,
1585t, 1586f
in germ cell tumors, 900
in hypospadias, 3709
in juvenile nephronophthisis, 3326, 3326t
in medullary cystic disease, 3326, 3326t
in neuroblastoma, 3870
in papillary renal cell carcinoma, 1584-1585,
1584t, 1587
in pediatric urinary tract infections, 3236-
3237
in pelvic organ prolapse, 2190
in prostate cancer, 2858, 2858t, 2859f
in prune-belly syndrome, 3482
in rhabdomyosarcoma, 3878-3879
in tuberous sclerosis, 3330-3331
in vesicoureteral reflux, 4325-4326
in von Hippel–Lindau disease, 3332-3333
Genetic imprinting, in autosomal dominant
polycystic kidney disease, 3320
Genetic testing, in male infertility work-up, 632-
633
Genital burns, 2654
Genital nerve, dorsal, stimulation of, 2159
Genital ridges, formation of, 3136, 3136f-3138f
Genital secretions, antiretroviral therapy and,
388
Genital squamous cancers, in AIDS patients,
399
Genital tissue, engineering of, 563-566
in females, 565-566
in males, corporal tissues reconstruction for,
564-565, 564f, 565f
Genital tubercle, development of, 3141, 3141f,
3142f
Genital ulcer, 372, 373t
Genital warts, 420f
diagnosis of, 380-381, 380f, 381f
treatment of, 381-382
Genitalia. *See also specific part.*
ambiguous. *See also* Hermaphroditism;
Pseudohermaphroditism.
evaluation and management of, 3827-3829,
3828f
defects of, bladder exstrophy and, failed repair
of, 3537
female
anomalies of. *See also specific anomaly.*
in bladder exstrophy, 3505, 3505f, 3524
in renal ectopia, 3279-3280
in unilateral renal agenesis, 3274, 3274f
lateral fusion, 3839, 3839f, 3840f
nonobstructive, 3840-3846, 3841f-3846f,
3842f-3846f
obstructive, 3832-3840
acquired, 3839-3840, 3841f
vertical fusion, 3832-3839, 3833f-3839f
candidiasis of, 460
development of, 3139-3140, 3140f
molecular mechanism in, 3146f, 3147-
3148
embryology of, 3123f, 3136-3148
external
characterization of, in fetus, 3178
development of, 3140-3141, 3141f-3143f,
3143

Genitalia (*Continued*)
fetal
abnormalities of, prenatal diagnosis of,
3184-3185
external
characterization of, 3178
development of, differentiation in, 3762-
3763
male, 3745-3760
allergic dermatitis of, 407-410, 407f, 407t,
409f, 410f
anomalies of, 3746-3760. *See also specific
anomaly.*
miscellaneous, 3760
penile, 3746-3758
scrotal, 3758-3759, 3758f, 3759f
vascular, 3759-3760
candidiasis of, 460
cutaneous diseases of, 407-435. *See also
specific disease.*
benign, 430-431, 432f
examination of, 405, 406t
malignant, 426-430, 427f-431f
miscellaneous, 431, 433, 434f, 435f
treatment of, 406-407, 407f
defects of, in bladder exstrophy, 3503-3505,
3504f, 3505f
development of, 3136-3137
molecular mechanism in, 3146-3147,
3146f
examination of, 613-614, 613t
external, development of, 3141, 3141f,
3142f
infections of, 419-425, 420f-425f
infestations involving, 425, 425f, 426f
injuries to, 2649-2655
penile, 2649-2652
skin loss in, 2654-2655, 2655f
testicular, 2652-2654, 2653f
noninfectious ulcers of, 417-419, 417t, 418f,
419f
normal, and association with other
abnormalities, 3745-3746, 3746t
papulosquamous disorders of, 410-415,
410t, 411f-414f
secondary syphilis affecting, 376f
vesicobullous disorders of, 415-417, 415t,
416f, 417f
Genitocerebral evoked potential studies, in
erectile dysfunction, 766
Genitofemoral nerve, 18, 18f, 73
in testicular descent, 3769
transection of, cryptorchidism and, 3145
Genitography
of cloacal anomalies, 3852
of urogenital sinus anomalies, 3849, 3851,
3851f
Genitoplasty, feminizing, for congenital adrenal
hyperplasia, 3820
Genitourinary tract
anomalies of
chromosomal syndromes associated with,
3201t
in bladder exstrophy, failed reconstruction
of, 3537
in cloacal exstrophy, 3540
in prune-belly syndrome, 3483-3485,
3483f-3485f
decompression of, for cloacal anomalies,
3865-3866, 3866f
infections of. *See also* Urinary tract infection;
*specific infection.*
fungal, 459-469
HIV-related, 396-397

Genitourinary tract (*Continued*)
  parasitic, 448-459
  pediatric, 3232-3268
  tuberculous, 436-447. *See also* Tuberculosis.
  injury to, in children, 3929-3945. *See also specific anatomic site; specific injury.*
    assessment and treatment of, 3930-3932
    grading of, 3931t
    imaging of, indications for, 3930
    vs. adult injury, 3929-3930
  pediatric urinary tract infections and, 3240-3241. *See also* Urinary tract infection, in children.
  recurrent, 3261-3262
  radiation-induced, 3016t
Gentamicin
  for pediatric urinary tract infections, 3248t
    intravenous, 3249
  prophylactic, prior to pediatric genitourinary procedures, 3242t
Geriatric patient
  bacteriuria in, 293-296, 295f, 1138f
  benign prostatic hyperplasia in, α-adrenergic blockers for, 2786
  detrusor hyperactivity with impaired contractility in, 2310
  frequency in, 2311
  incontinence in, 2306-2309
    cause(s) of
      detrusor overactivity as, 2309-2310
      detrusor underactivity as, 2310
      DIAPERS mnemonic for, 2306, 2307t
      established, 2309-2311
      functional, 2310-2311
      lower urinary tract, 2309-2310
      outlet obstruction as, 2310
      pathologic, 2306-2308, 2307t
      pharmaceutical, 2308-2309, 2308t
    diagnostic categorization of, empirical, 2313-2314
    diagnostic evaluation of, 2059-2070, 2311-2313
    functional, 2310-2311
    history-taking in, 2311-2312, 2312t
    laboratory investigation of, 2313
    physical examination for, 2312-2313
    stress, 2310
    stress testing in, 2313
    transient, causes of, 2059t, 2306-2309, 2307t, 2308t
    treatment of, 2314-2320, 2314f
      adjunctive measures in, 2317-2318
      behavioral therapy in, 2314-2316
      stepwise approach to, 2315t
    urodynamic testing in, 2314
    voiding diary in, 2312, 2312f
  nocturia in, 2311-2312, 2312t
  tension-free vaginal tape procedure in, 2254
Germ cell(s)
  aplasia of, infertility and, 634
  primordial, migration of, 579, 3803, 3803f
  Sertoli cells associated with, 588, 589f, 591-592, 591f
  transformation of, 3803-3804
Germ cell tumor(s), testicular, 893-925. *See also specific type.*
  acquired causes of, 901
  clinical manifestations of, 902-903
  clinical staging of, 903-904, 904t, 905t, 938
  congenital causes of, 900-901
  diagnosis of, delay in
  differential diagnosis of, 903
  epidemiology of, 899-900
  etiology of, 900-901

Germ cell tumor(s), testicular (*Continued*)
  high-stage
    fertility in, 957
    post-chemotherapy pathologic findings in, 951t
    surgery for
      complications of, 955-956
      high-risk post-chemotherapy patients and, 953-954
      histologic findings and controversies in, 950-951
      late-relapse and, 953
      lung resection as, 955
      mediastinal resection as, 955
      neck resection as, 955
      nonseminomatous tumors and, 950-956
      post-chemotherapy RPLND as, 954-955
      predicting necrosis in, 952-953
      preoperative preparation for, 950
      reoperative retroperitoneal, 954-955
      teratomas and, 951-952
      timing of, 950
  histologic classification of, 893-895, 894t
  imaging of, 905
  in children, 3902-3904, 3903t
  incidence of, 899
  intratubular, 896-897, 899, 899t
  low-stage
    fertility in, 949
    treatment options for, 948-949
  natural history of, 901, 938
  nongonadal, 924-925
  nonseminomatous, 895-896. *See also* Nonseminomatous germ cell tumor(s).
  pathogenesis of, 901
  patterns of spread of, 901-902, 939
  scrotal ultrasonography of, 903
  seminomatous, 894-895. *See also* Seminoma(s).
  signs and symptoms of, 903
  treatment of, 936-950. *See also* Orchiectomy; Retroperitoneal lymph node dissection (RPLND).
    anatomic considerations in, 939, 939f
    for nonseminomatous tumors, 913-924, 950-956
      options in, 948-949
    for seminomas, 909-913, 956-957
    organ-preserving surgery in, 908-909
    principles of, 908-924
  tumor markers for, 893, 906-908
Gerota's fascia, 26, 27f, 28
Gestational age
  fractional excretion of sodium and, 3150
  glomerular filtration rate and, 3151
  maximal renal calyceal diameter according to, 1220t
GH (growth hormone), affected by aging, 856t, 857
Gibson incision, in renal transplantation, 1310
Giggle incontinence, in children, 3612
Gil-Vernet procedure, in antireflux surgery, 4366
Ginkgo biloba, for erectile dysfunction, 770t
Ginseng, for erectile dysfunction, 770t
Girlie disease, 1160. *See also* Perimedial fibrodysplasia.
Gishiri cutting, vesicovaginal fistula following, 2325
Gitelman's syndrome, in children, 3229
Gittes bladder neck suspension, for stress incontinence, 2212-2213
Glands of Littre. *See* Periurethral glands.

Glans penis. *See also* Penis.
  anatomy of, functional, 721
  cutaneous lesions of, 960
  in erection, hemodynamics of, 724
  lymphatic drainage of, 1035
  partial removal of, with Mogen clamp, 3748
  poor support of, in penile prosthesis implantation, 797, 798f
  squamous cell carcinoma of, 1012, 1012f
Glansectomy, partial, for squamous cell carcinoma, 1012-1013, 1013f
Glanuloplasty. *See also* Meatoplasty and glanuloplasty (MAGPI) technique.
  in hypospadias repair, 3718
Gleason grading
  of adenocarcinoma of prostate, 2876, 2877f
  of prostate cancer, 2926, 2928t-2929t
Glenn-Anderson technique, of antireflux surgery, 4356, 4356f
Glial cell line–derived neurotrophic factor
  in ureteral development, 1891
  in ureteric bud outgrowth, 3129, 3129f
Global Response Assessment, of painful bladder syndrome/interstitial cystitis, 355, 356t
Globulin, sex hormone–binding, 767
  assessment of, in females, 872
Glomerular circulation, effect of angiotensin II on, 1163
Glomerular filtration rate
  autoregulation of, 1132
  clinical assessment of, 1132-1133
  determinants of, 1131-1132, 1326
  estimation of
    by creatinine clearance, 3230t
    mathematical formulas in, 1133
  factors influencing, 1195
  in acute renal failure, 1325-1326
  in chronic renal failure, 1341-1342, 1342t
  in fetus, 3149-3150
  in infant and child, 3153
  in neonate, 3151-3152, 3152f, 3153f
    regulation of, 3158, 3158f
  oncotic pressure in, 1132
  permeability in, 1132
  plasma markers in, 1133, 1133f
  regulation of, 1132
  renal clearance in, 1132-1133
  renal plasma flow and, 1132
  transglomerular (hydraulic) pressure in, 1131-1132
  tubuloglomerular feedback in, 1132
  urinary tract obstruction and, 1195-1196
Glomerulations, in painful bladder syndrome/interstitial cystitis, 352-353, 352f
Glomerulocystic kidney disease
  familial hypoplastic, 3329
    characteristics of, 3314t
  sporadic, 3350-3351
    characteristics of, 3314t
    conditions associated with, 3350t
Glomerulonephritis
  acute, 1327-1328, 1328t
  focal. *See* IgA nephropathy (Berger's disease).
  membranoproliferative, in chronic renal failure, 1345-1346
  membranous, retroperitoneal fibrosis associated with, 1270-1271
  postinfectious, in children, 3226
  rapidly progressive, differential diagnosis of, 1328t
Glomerulosclerosis
  focal segmental, in children, 3225-3226
  in renal transplant recipient, 1297-1298

Glomerulotubular balance, 1138
Glomerulus(i)
    disorders of, hematuria associated with, 98-99, 99f, 99t
    foam cells of, 1344
    injury to, in children, management of, 3597-3598
    microscopic anatomy of, 31, 32f
Glucocorticoids
    actions of, 1827-1828, 1828t
    excess of, male infertility and, 638
    for cutaneous diseases, of external genitalia, 406
    hypercalcemia associated with, 1376-1377
Glucose
    in urine, 103-104
    metabolism of, 852-853
    renal reabsorption of, in proximal convoluted tubules, 1140, 1141f
    tubular reabsorption of, in neonate, 3156
Glue, fibrin-based, in laparoscopy, 193
Glutamate
    in spinal cord, 1964
    uropharmacology of, 1962-1963
γ-Glutamyl transpeptidase, in testicular tumors, 907
Glutaraldehyde cross-linked bovine collagen (GAX-collagen) injections, for incontinence, 2274
    adverse effects of, 2284t
    efficacy of, 2282-2283
    safety of, 2285
Glutathione S-transferase, in prostate cancer, 2866
Gluteal artery, inferior, 50f, 51
Glycosaminoglycan(s), in painful bladder syndrome/interstitial cystitis, 343-345, 363
Glycosaminoglycan layer, of urothelium, 1932-1933
Glycosides, effect of, on ureteral function, 1920
GMP. See Guanosine monophosphate (GMP).
GnRH. See Gonadotropin-releasing hormone (GnRH).
Gomco clamp, 1045, 3215
Gonad(s). See also Ovary(ies); Testis(es).
    descent of
        in females, 3144f, 3145
        in males, 3143-3145, 3144f
    in sexual differentiation, 3803-3804, 3803f
        disorders in, 3808-3816. See also specific disorder.
    function of, 3804-3805, 3805f
    renin-angiotensin-aldosterone system and, 1163
Gonadal artery, 11f, 13, 13t
Gonadal dysgenesis syndrome(s), 3809-3814
    mixed, 3811-3812
    partial, 3812-3813
    "pure," 3811
    Turner's syndrome as, 3809-3811, 3810f
    46,XY complete, 3813-3814, 3813f, 3814f
Gonadal stromal tumor(s), testicular, 927-928
Gonadal vein, 11f, 13
    excision of, in left-sided laparoscopic RPLND, 946-947
Gonadal vessels, dissection of, in right-sided laparoscopic RPLND, 946
Gonadoblastoma(s), 926t, 928-929
    in children, 3901, 3904-3905
    in complete androgen insensitivity syndrome, risk of, 3824
    in 46,XY complete gonadal dysgenesis, 3814, 3814f

Gonadoblastoma(s) (Continued)
    in mixed gonadal dysgenesis, 3812
    in Turner's syndrome, 3810-3811
Gonadotropin(s). See also specific hormone.
    therapy with, for male infertility, 636, 646
Gonadotropin-releasing hormone (GnRH)
    for cryptorchidism, 3776
    in male reproductive axis, 577, 578f
    in males, 618
    therapy with, for male infertility, 636, 646
Gonadotropin-releasing hormone (GnRH) stimulation test, in males, 619
Gonorrhea, 379
    rates of, 372
Goodwin technique, transcolonic, of ureterointestinal anastomosis, 2556, 2556f
Gouty diathesis, 1405, 1405f
    treatment of, 1424
Gouverneur's syndrome, 2351
Graft(s). See also Allograft(s); Xenograft(s).
    for vesicovaginal fistula repair, 2332, 2340
    free, in hypospadias repair, 3716
        neourethral formation and, 3734, 3736-3738, 3738f
        reoperative, 3741
    full-thickness, 1025
    imbibition of, 1023
    in penile curvature repair, 3714, 3715f
    in penile reconstruction
        saphenous interposition, 1095
        split-thickness, 994, 996, 996f
    in reconstructive surgery, 1023, 1024f-1025f, 1025-1026
    in urethral stricture repair, 1062, 1064-1066f, 1067
    in vaginal prolapse surgery
        biologic, 2216
        synthetic, 2216, 2216t
    in vaginal repair surgery, 2220t, 2222, 2223f
    inosculation of, 1023, 1025
    interposition nerve, in radical retropubic prostatectomy, 2976-2977
    kidney. See Kidney graft.
    mesh, 1025
    saphenous interposition, in penile reconstruction, 1095
    split-thickness, 1025
        in penile reconstruction, 994, 996, 996f
        in reoperative hypospadias repair, 3741
    vascular, placement of, ureteral obstruction due to, 1223
Granular cell myoblastoma, of bladder, 2445
Granulocyte(s), 477
Granulocyte-macrophage colony-stimulating factor, source and activity of, 486t
Granuloma
    after vasovasostomy, 678
    sperm, 1102, 1108
Granulomatous disease, hypercalcemia associated with, 1376
Graspers, laparoscopic, 190, 191f
Gravimetric flowmeter, 1989
Grayhack shunt, for priapism, 848, 848f
Great vessels, anatomy of, 6f, 9, 11f, 13-14, 13t, 14f
    anatomy of. See also specific vessel, e.g., Aorta.
Greater omentum, in vesicovaginal fistula repair, 2339-2340
Green tea
    for prostate cancer, chemopreventive, 2871
    in prevention of bladder cancer, 2443
GRHPR gene, in hyperoxaluria, 1378

Growth
    and development, detrimental effect of conduit urinary diversion on, 2574
    delayed, after augmentation cystoplasty, in children, 3682
    of prostate. See also Prostate, growth of.
        endocrine control of, 2684-2689
        regulation of
            balance of cell replication and death in, 2711-2715
            steroid receptors in, 2696-2705
            steroids and protein growth factors in, 2689-2696
Growth factor(s). See also specific growth factor.
    in benign prostatic hyperplasia, 2731-2732, 2731f
    in bladder cancer, 2428-2429
    in prostate, 2705-2711
    in renal cell carcinoma, 1590
    mechanism of action of, 2706, 2707f
    properties of, 2706t
Growth factor receptors, 2706, 2708-2711
Growth hormone (GH), affected by aging, 856t, 857
Growth pathways, in hormone-refractory prostate cancer, 3115-3116
Guaifenesin calculi, 1389
Guanosine monophosphate (GMP), cyclic
    in penile smooth muscle relaxation, 732
    in smooth muscle relaxation, 1954
    in ureteral smooth muscle contraction, 1901
Guanylyl cyclase, in male sexual function, 735
Guarding reflex, 1975
    in continence, 2049
Gubernaculum
    development of, 3762
    female, 3145
    in testicular descent, 3768-3769
    innervation of, 3145
    male, 3143-3145
Guide wires
    for ureteroscopy, 1509, 1510f, 1511t, 1512, 1512f
    safety, 1515-1516
        cystoscopic placement of, 1515
    in percutaneous nephrostomy, 1541
Guillain-Barré syndrome, voiding dysfunction in, 2035
Gunshot wounds
    to kidney, 1274
    to penis, 1050, 2650-2651
    to ureters, hematuria with, 1284-1285
Gynecomastia, 613
    androgen deprivation therapy causing, 3091
    germ cell tumors associated with, 903
    in Klinefelter's syndrome, 3809
    testosterone therapy causing, 859

**H**

H flap. See also Flap(s).
    in Peyronie's disease surgery, 833, 835f, 836, 836f
HAART (highly active antiretroviral therapy)
    for HIV infection, 401
        immune-based strategies with, 403-404
    for HIVAN, 398
Haemophilis ducreyi, in chancroid, 374
Hailey-Hailey disease, 417, 417f
Hair, in penile strangulation injury, 2652
Hair growth, intraurethral, after hypospadias repair, 3740
Hald-Bradley classification, of voiding dysfunction, 1984, 1984t

Hammock hypothesis, 2195, 2196f
  of stress incontinence, 2051-2052, 2051f, 2052f
Hammock technique, of small bowel anastomosis, 2559
Hand port access, for pneumoperitoneum, 181
Hand-assisted devices, in laparoscopic surgery, 171-173, 186-187, 186f. *See also* Trocar(s).
Hanging drop test, in laparoscopic surgery, 180
Hasson technique
  in extraperitoneoscopy, 184
  in retroperitoneoscopy, 183, 183f, 184f
Hautmann ileal neobladder, for orthotopic urinary diversion, 2635, 2635f
HBV (hepatitis B virus), in hepatocellular carcinoma, 541
hCG. *See* Human chorionic gonadotropin (hCG).
Health care
  access to, 144
  costs of, 144-147
    case mix in, 146-147
    patterns of care and, 146
    terms and methods and, 145
  quality of, 147-149
    challenges in evaluation of, 148-149
    measurement approaches to, 149
    outcomes of care in, 148
    process of care in, 148
    structure of care in, 147-148
Health concerns, sexual, in women, 863-889. *See also* Sexual health concerns, female.
Health maintenance organizations (HMOs), care provided by, 146
Health policy decisions, based on costs, 144-145
Health-related quality of life (HRQOL), 149-156
  comparison groups for, 155
  cultural issues and translations associated with, 155-156
  data collection for, caveats on, 156
  disease-specific, age-adjusted means of, 2746, 2746f
  future implications of, 156-157
  instruments in, 150-152, 151t
    cancer-related, 150-152
    general, 150
    psychometric validation of, 152-155
    reliability assessment of, 152-154, 152t, 153f
    responsiveness of, 155
    selection of, 152
    validity assessment of, 154-155, 154t
Heart and Estrogen/Progestin Replacement Study (HERS), of hormone therapy, 2307
Heart disease, after renal transplantation, 1299
Heart rate, testing variability of, in erectile dysfunction, 766
Heat
  exposure to, risk of stone formation associated with, 1365
  male infertility due to, 644
Heavy lifting, incontinence associated with, 2190
Heineke-Mikulicz technique, in penile curvature repair, 3714
Helium, for pneumoperitoneum, in laparoscopic surgery, 199-200
Hemangioma
  bladder, in children, 3582
  capillary, of male genitalia, 433
  of bladder, 2445
  of male genitalia, 3759-3760
  urethral, 1040-1041
Hematochezia, shockwave lithotripsy causing, 1477

Hematogenous metastasis, of urothelial tumors, 1641
Hematologic dyscrasias, priapism associated with, 840
Hematoma
  after artificial sphincter placement, 2399
  after hydrocelectomy, 1106
  after hypospadias repair, 3739
  after vasectomy, 1102
  after vasoepididymostomy, 699
  after vasovasostomy, 678
Hematospermia, patient history of, 87
Hematuria
  after renal transplantation, 1319
  differential diagnosis of, 98
  essential, 100, 100f
  exercise-induced, 100
  glomerular, 98-100, 99f, 99t
  gross
    in children, 3212
      etiology of, 3218-3219
    in neonate, evaluation of, 3199, 3203
    vs. microscopic hematuria, 83
  in benign prostatic hyperplasia, 2758
    effects of medical therapy on, 2775
  in bladder cancer, 2430-2431
  in children
    epidemiology of, 3217-3219
    gross, 3212
      etiology of, 3218-3219
    microscopic, 3212
    physical examination of, 3219
    screening for, 3218
    treatment algorithm for, 3220f
  in medullary sponge kidney, 3349
  in neonate, 3196
    gross, evaluation of, 3199, 3203
  in urinary tract infection, 239
  in urothelial tumors, 1644
  microscopic
    in children, 3212
    vs. gross hematuria, 83
  nonglomerular, 100, 101f, 102f
  patient history of, 83-84, 97-100
  shockwave lithotripsy causing, 1477
  timing of, 83
  trauma-induced, pediatric vs. adult, 3930
  ureteropelvic junction obstruction and, in children, 3363, 3364f
  with renal injury, 1275
  with ureteral injury, 1275-1276
    incidence of, 1284-1285
Hematuria-dysuria syndrome, after augmentation cystoplasty, 3682-3683
Hemi-Kock procedure, for continent urinary diversion, with augmented valved rectum, 2583-2584
Heminephrectomy, of duplicated collecting system, 1732-1733
Hemizona assay, for infertility, 631
Hemodialysis
  for acute renal failure, 1338-1339, 1358t
  for end-stage renal disease, 1296
  long-term, acquired renal cystic disease associated with, 3351, 3353f
Hemodynamics
  changes of
    in bilateral ureteral obstruction, 1198, 1199f
    in unilateral ureteral obstruction, 1196-1198, 1197f
  in laparoscopic surgery, 202
  of penile erection, 723-724, 723f, 724f

Hemodynamics (*Continued*)
  patient positioning and, 202
  renal. *See* Renal hemodynamics.
Hemolytic-uremic syndrome
  in children, 3227-3228
  in renal transplant recipient, 1298
Hemorrhage
  adrenal, 1822, 1822f
    in neonates, 3196-3197
  adrenal surgery causing, 1885, 1885t
  after artificial sphincter placement, 2399
  after circumcision, 3215
  after hypospadias repair, 3739
  after ileal loop urinary diversion, 2554
  at cannula site, in laparoscopy, 209, 209f, 216
  gastrointestinal, as complication of post-chemotherapy surgery, 956
  in radical perineal prostatectomy, 2983
  intestinal anastomosis causing, 2550
  intracranial, in autosomal dominant polycystic kidney disease, 3321
  partial nephrectomy causing, 1730
  percutaneous nephrolithotomy causing, 1500
  percutaneous nephrostomy causing, 1544-1547, 1545f-1547f
  perineal sling procedure causing, 2395
  post-biopsy, 2892
  post-circumcision, 3748
  post-robotic-assisted laparoscopic radical prostatectomy, 2998-2999
  radical nephrectomy causing, 1719
  radical retropubic prostatectomy causing
    intraoperative, 2972-2973
    postoperative, 2973
  renal, shockwave lithotripsy causing, 1477, 1478f
  renal bypass surgery causing, 1749-1750
  retroperitoneal, during radical nephrectomy, management of, 1710-1712, 1713f
  vaginal tape–induced, 2258, 2259t
Hemostasis
  in hypospadias repair, 3719
  in laparoscopic surgery, 3917
  in renal biopsy, 1771
  in transurethral resection of prostate, management of, 2836
Hemostatic agents
  used in laparoscopy, 193, 193t
  used in percutaneous nephrostomy, 1561
Hemostatic maneuvers
  in retropubic prostatectomy, 2847-2848, 2848f
  in suprapubic prostatectomy, 2850-2851, 2851f
Henderson-Hasselbalch equation, 1152
Henoch-Schönlein purpura, in children, 3226-3227
Heparin, for painful bladder syndrome/interstitial cystitis, 362t, 363
Hepatic cysts, in autosomal dominant polycystic kidney disease, 3321
Hepatitis B virus (HBV), in hepatocellular carcinoma, 541
Hepatocellular carcinoma, HBV in, 541
Hepatocyte growth factor, in renal cell carcinoma, 1591
Hepatorenal bypass, 1740-1741, 1741f, 1742f
Hepatorenal syndrome, 1327
Hepatotoxicity, of rifampin, 443
Hepsin, in prostate cancer, 2909
*HER2/NEU* oncogene, amplification of, in bladder cancer, 2429
HER2/NEU receptors, in diagnosis of oncology, 548

Herbal supplements, for erectile dysfunction, 770, 770t

Hereditary hypophosphatemic rickets, in hypercalciuria, 1375

Hereditary leiomyomatosis and renal cell carcinoma (HLRCC) syndrome, 1584t, 1587-1588

Hereditary nonpolyposis colorectal cancer. See Colorectal cancer, hereditary nonpolyposis.

Hereditary papillary renal cell carcinoma, 515t, 518, 1584t, 1587

Hereditary spastic paraplegia, voiding dysfunction in, 2035

Heredity
   of bladder cancer, 2416-2417
   of urothelial tumors, 1639

Hermaphroditism, true, 3815-3816, 3815f

Hernia(s)
   cryptorchidism and, 3773
   diaphragmatic, as contraindication to laparoscopy, 175
   differential diagnosis of, 3787
   incisional
      after laparoscopy, 217-218
      after radical nephrectomy causing, 1720
      laparoscopic renal surgery causing, 1807
   inguinal
      associated with hypospadias, 3709
      examination for, 92-93, 92f
      in children, 3203
      in exstrophy patient, 3503
   laparoscopic examination of, in children, 3915-3916, 3915f
   parastomal, after ileal loop urinary diversion, 2553-2554
   repair of
      orchialgia after, 1108
      vasal obstruction after, 676-678, 676f-677f
   umbilical, as contraindication to laparoscopy, 175
   ureteral, 3420-3421, 3421f

Hernia uteri inguinale, 3826-3827

Herpes simplex virus (HSV), serologic testing for, prior to renal transplantation, 1298

Herpes simplex virus (HSV) infection
   anogenital, urinary retention associated with, 2033
   genital, 420f
      diagnosis of, 373, 374f, 400f
      treatment of, 374, 374t
   in HIV patients, 394-395, 394t

Herpes zoster virus (HZV), infection with, voiding dysfunction caused by, 2033

Herpesvirus types 1 and 2, in erythema multiforme, 409

Herpesvirus type 8, in Kaposi's sarcoma, 398

Heterochromatin, 2712

Heterozygosity, loss of, in urothelial tumors, 1644

Hidden penis, 3749f, 3751, 3751f

Hidradenitis suppurativa, of male genitalia, 422-423, 422f

High-dose-rate brachytherapy, for prostate cancer, 3027

High-intensity focused ultrasonography
   extracorporeal, 1817-1818
   for prostate cancer, 2945
   mode of action of, 1817

Highly active antiretroviral therapy (HAART)
   for HIV infection, 401
      immune-based strategies with, 403-404
   for HIVAN, 398

Hinman syndrome, 2038, 3612-3613

Hirsutism, in 46,XY complete gonadal dysgenesis, 3813

Histamine, effect of, on ureteral function, 1918

Histamine $H_2$ receptor antagonists, erectile dysfunction caused by, 746

Histocompatibility, in renal transplant rejection, 1314-1315, 1315f, 1315t

Histologic classification, of renal cell carcinoma, 1592-1593, 1592t

Histoplasmosis, 468

HIV. See Human immunodeficiency virus (HIV) entries.

HIV-associated neuropathy (HIVAN), 397-398

hK2 tumor marker, of prostate cancer, 2906-2907

hK3 tumor marker, of prostate cancer, 2897-2906. See also Prostate-specific antigen (PSA).

HLAs (human leukocyte antigens), in allograft rejection, 1314-1315, 1315f, 1315t

HLXB9 gene, in sacral agenesis, 3644

HMB-45 immunoreactivity, in renal angiomyolipoma, 1579

HMOs (health maintenance organizations), care provided by, 146

Holmium laser resection, for benign prostatic hyperplasia, 2823, 2824f
   clinical results of, 2827-2828

Holmium:yttrium-aluminum-garnet (Ho:YAG) laser
   for benign prostatic hyperplasia, 2821
   for bladder cancer, non–muscle-invasive, 2453
   in lithotripsy, 1460-1462, 1461t, 1462t, 1513-1514
   in children, 3908

Homing, of immune cells, 475

Hormonal control, of renal function, during development, 3157-3159, 3158f

Hormonal imprinting, of prostate, 2679-2680

Hormonal manipulation, before hypospadias repair, 3711
   timing of, 3712

Hormone(s). See also specific hormone.
   affected by aging, 856-857, 856t
      historical perspective on, 850-851
   controlling male sexual differentiation, 3761
   effect of, in laparoscopic surgery, 202
   evaluation of
      in erectile dysfunction, 767-768
      in male infertility, 618-619, 618t
   in regulation of renal functional development, 3172
   in regulation of spermatogenesis, 595-596
   in renal physiology, 1133-1138, 1134f, 1134t, 1136f, 1137t, 1138f
   neural, in male sexual function, 729-730
   role of, in painful bladder syndrome/interstitial cystitis, 349
   uropharmacology of, 1956

Hormone response element, in genes, 2703

Hormone therapy. See also specific hormone.
   chemotherapy with, for locally advanced cancer, before radical prostatectomy, 3061, 3061t
   for cryptorchidism, 3775-3776
   for erectile dysfunction, 771-773, 771t
   for metastatic renal cell carcinoma, 1625-1626
   for painful bladder syndrome/interstitial cystitis, 360t, 361
   for prostate cancer, 3082-3099
      adjuvant, 2942
      combined androgen blockade in, 3092-3095, 3094f, 3095f
      economic considerations of, 3099

Hormone therapy (Continued)
   complications of, 3089-3091
   economic considerations in, 3099
   future of, 3099
   historic overview of, 3082-3083
   immediate vs. delayed
      in clinically localized disease, 3096
      in locally advanced or asymptomatic metastatic disease, 3097-3098, 3097f
      in lymph node metastatic disease, 3096-3097, 3096f
      integration of data in, 3098, 3098f
   molecular biology of, 3083-3084, 3084f
   primary, 2943-2944
   response to, 3088-3089
   timing of, 3095-3098
   with radiation therapy, 3091-3092, 3093f, 3093t
   with radical prostatectomy, 3091, 3092f, 3092t
   for prostatitis, 322-323, 325t, 327t
   for sexual health problems
      in perimenopausal women, 878-881, 879f
      in premenopausal women, 875-878
   postmenopausal, incontinence and, 2108
   replacement, testicular, 569, 569f

Horseshoe kidney, 3287-3291
   associated anomalies with, 3289
   blood supply to, 3288, 3289f
   diagnosis of, 3290, 3290f
   embryology of, 3287-3288, 3288f
   features of, 3288
   in Turner's syndrome, 3811
   incidence of, 3287
   isthmusectomy for, 1755-1756
   multicystic dysplastic kidney in, 3336, 3336f
   percutaneous access to, 1540, 1540f
   percutaneous nephrolithotomy into, 1497-1498
   prognosis for, 3290-3291
   renal cell carcinoma in, 3290
   stone formation in, 1390
      surgical management of, 1443
   symptoms of, 3289-3290
   ureteropelvic junction obstruction and, in children, 3362, 3363f
   Wilms' tumor in, 3290-3291

Hospitalization, risk of, for chronic renal failure, 1357-1359, 1358t

Host defense, altered
   in prostatitis, 308
   in urinary tract infections, 236

Hot flashes
   androgen deprivation therapy causing, 3089-3090
   treatment of, 3090

Ho:YAG laser. See Holmium:yttrium-aluminum-garnet (Ho:YAG) laser.

HPV. See Human papillomavirus (HPV).

HRQOL. See Health-related quality of life (HRQOL).

H-shaped incisions, in Peyronie's disease surgery, 833, 833f, 834f

HSP27, in regulation of apoptosis, 532-533

HSV. See Herpes simplex virus (HSV) entries.

Human bites, to penis, 2651

Human chorionic gonadotropin (hCG)
   for cryptorchidism, 3775
   for erectile dysfunction, 772
   in penile development, 3752
   in testicular tumors, 906

Human immunodeficiency virus (HIV)
   detection of, 391-392
   drug-resistant, assays for, 394

Human immunodeficiency virus (HIV)
    (Continued)
    eradication of, prospects for, 392-393
    replication of, 389-390, 390f
    transmission of
        modes of, 386
        multiple cofactors affecting, 387, 387t
    type 1 (HIV-1), 388
    type 2 (HIV-2), 388
    virion of, 388-389, 389f
Human immunodeficiency virus (HIV)
    infection, 371. *See also* Acquired
        immunodeficiency syndrome (AIDS).
    abnormal urinalysis in, 398
    acute renal failure and, 1330
    chronic
        asymptomatic, 391
        virus escape and establishment in, 392
    circumcision status and, 388
    clinical course of, 391
    diagnostic tests and algorithms for, 393
    drug-resistant, assays for, 394
    dynamics of, urologic risk factors in, 387-388,
        387t
    epidemiology of, 386-388
    genitourinary infections with, 396-397
    HIV-negative partner and, intrauterine
        insemination of, 651
    in developing world, 386
    natural history of, 390-391
        early pathogenic events in, 391-392
    neuropathy in, 397-398
    occupational risk of
        associated with specific exposures, 400, 400t
        epidemiology of, 400
        interventions to decrease, 400-401
        postexposure chemoprophylaxis for, 401
    pathogenesis of, 390-393
    primary, 391
        role of lymphoid tissue in, 392
    Reiter's syndrome in, 397
    sexual behaviors associated with, 388
    sexually transmitted infections concurrent
        with, 387-388, 394-396, 394t
    treatment of
        antiretroviral therapy in, 401-403, 402f
        available drugs in, 401, 403, 403t
        evolving strategies in, 403
        HAART in, 401
            immune-based strategies with, 403-404
        monotherapy in, 401
        new investigational drugs in, 403
        prophylactic, 403-404
        side effects of, 403
    urethritis in, 397
    urinary tract infection associated with, 237
    urolithiasis in, 397
    urologic manifestations of, 394-400
        malignant conditions in, 398-400
        nonmalignant conditions in, 394-398, 394t,
            395f
    viral load monitoring in, 393-394
    voiding dysfunction in, 397, 2036
Human leukocyte antigens (HLAs), in allograft
    rejection, 1314-1315, 1315f, 1315t
Human papillomavirus (HPV), 541-542
    cancer associated with
        anogenital, in AIDS patients, 399
        penile, 542, 961-962, 965-966
    causing genital warts, 380-381, 380f, 381f
    in HIV patients, 395, 395f
    prevalence of, 372
Human T-cell lymphoma/leukemia virus, in
    tropical spastic paraparesis, 2035

Hunner's ulcer
    in painful bladder syndrome/interstitial
        cystitis, 352, 353f
    transurethral resection of, 366
H-Y antigen, 3799-3800
Hyaluronic acid
    for painful bladder syndrome/interstitial
        cystitis, 362t, 364
    in bladder cancer, 2465
    injection of, for incontinence, 2286
Hydatid cyst, of seminal vesicles, 1116
Hydatid disease, 458-459, 459f
Hydraulic valves, for continent urinary
    diversion, in children, 3696-3697
Hydrocalycosis, 3298-3299, 3299f
Hydrocele(s), 93, 3788-3789
    abdominoscrotal, 3789
    after laparoscopy, 216-217
    after varicocelectomy, 665
    communicating, 3788-3789
    differential diagnosis of, 3787
    in children, 3203
    in filariasis, 456f, 457
    in infants, 3204
    of spermatic cord, 3789
Hydrocelectomy
    complications of, 1106
    excisional technique of, 1105, 1105f, 1106f
    inguinal approach to, 1105
    plication technique of, 1105-1106, 1106f
    sclerotherapy in, 1106
    scrotal approach to, 1105-1106, 1105f, 1106f
Hydrocephalus, normal pressure, voiding
    dysfunction in, 2017
Hydrochlorothiazide, for renal hypercalciuria,
    1419, 1421t
Hydrocolpos, imperforate hymen with, 3194
Hydrocortisone, for congenital adrenal
    hyperplasia, in children and adolescents,
    3820
Hydrodistention, for painful bladder
    syndrome/interstitial cystitis, 365-366
Hydrogen, renal reabsorption of, in cortical
    collecting tubules, 1145
Hydrogen ion, transport of, ureteral obstruction
    and, 1202
Hydrometrocolpos, 3848
Hydronephrosis, 1195
    after aortic bypass graft surgery, 1223
    after renal transplantation, 1320, 1321f
    Down syndrome and, 3184
    fetal
        bilateral, postnatal evaluation and
            management of, 3190-3191, 3190t
        evaluation of, 3204
        ultrasound appearance of, 3176-3177,
            3177f, 3179f
        unilateral, postnatal evaluation and
            management of, 3191-3193, 3192f
        upper pole, 3182
    in infants, evaluation of, 3198
    in multicystic dysplastic kidney, 3334, 3335f
    in pelvic organ prolapse, prevalence of, 2204
    in pregnancy, 1219-1220
    in urinary tract infections, 276
    intraoperative ureteral manipulation causing,
        1283
    pathophysiology of, 3185-3186
    prenatal diagnosis of, vs. multicystic dysplastic
        kidney, 3183
    schistosomal, 450
    upper pole, with ureterocele, 3398, 3399,
        3399f, 3400f
    with ectopic ureter, 3389, 3390f

Hydronephrosis (Continued)
    with posterior urethral valves
        fetal sonography of, 3590f
        management of, 3596
    with single-system ectopic ureters, 3396,
        3396f
    with ureteral duplication, 3414
Hydroureter, fetal, ultrasound appearance of,
    3177, 3179f
α-Hydroxy acids, polymers of, for tissue
    engineering, 556
Hydroxy-3-methylglutaryl coenzyme A, for
    chronic renal failure, 1350
11β-Hydroxylase deficiency, in congenital
    adrenal hyperplasia, 3819
17α-Hydroxylase deficiency, 3822
21-Hydroxylase steroid deficiency, in congenital
    adrenal hyperplasia, 3816-3819, 3817f,
    3818f
3β-Hydroxysteroid deficiency, 3821-3822
3β-Hydroxysteroid dehydrogenase deficiency
    in congenital adrenal hyperplasia, 3819
    type 2, 3767
17β-Hydroxysteroid dehydrogenase deficiency,
    type 3, 3767
17β-Hydroxysteroid oxidoreductase deficiency,
    3822-3823
5-Hydroxytryptamine receptor sensitivity, in
    premature ejaculation, 785
Hydroxyzine, for painful bladder
    syndrome/interstitial cystitis, 360, 360t
Hylagel Uro injection, for incontinence, 2286
Hymen
    examination of, in adolescents, 3209
    imperforate, 3843-3844, 3844f
        with hydrocolpos, 3194
Hymenal skin tags, 3843, 3843f, 3844f
Hyperaldosteronism, primary, 1846-1857
    adrenal surgery for, 1871t
        postoperative complications of, 1886t
    clinical characteristics of, 1850-1851, 1850t
    diagnostic strategy for, 1854-1856, 1855f
    diagnostic test(s) for, 1851-1853
        aldosterone-to-renin ratio, 1851-1852
        cortisol metabolites, 1853
        lateralizing, 1853-1854
        plasma renin activity, 1851
        postural stimulation, 1852-1853
        sodium loading, 1853
    epidemiology of, 1849-1850
    pathophysiology of, 1846-1849, 1847f, 1848f
    treatment of, 1856-1857
Hypercalcemia
    glucocorticoid-induced, 1376-1377
    in medullary sponge kidney, 3349
    in renal cell carcinoma, 1597-1598, 1597t
    malignancy-associated, 1376, 1376t
    penile cancer associated with, 969
    sarcoid and granulomatous diseases associated
        with, 1376
Hypercalciuria
    absorptive, 1374-1375, 1401-1402
        management of, 1416-1419
            drug guidelines in, 1418
        calcium stone formation associated with,
            1374-1377, 1376t, 1401-1402
    definition of, 1374
    differential diagnosis of, 1402t
    idiopathic, 1374, 1402, 1402t
    in children, 3222-3223, 3222t
        treatment of, 3223
    renal, 1375, 1402
        management of, 1419-1420, 1421t
    resorptive, 1375-1377, 1402

Hypercarbia, laparoscopy and, 210-211, 3917
Hyperchloremia, conduit urinary diversion causing, 2571-2572, 2571t
Hypercholesterolemia, erectile dysfunction associated with, statins for, 769
Hypercontinence, in females undergoing orthotopic reconstruction, 2621
Hypercortisolism, ACTH-dependent vs. ACTH-independent, 1834
Hyperglycemia, in acute renal failure, 1338
Hyperkalemia, 1150-1151, 1151t
    in acute renal failure, 1338
Hyperlipidemia, erectile dysfunction associated with, 741, 768
Hypermethylation, of DNA, 514-515
Hypermobility, in retropubic suspension surgery, contribution of, 2170
Hypernatremia
    clinical approach to, 1149, 1150f
    treatment of, 1149
Hypernephroid tumors, 1567
Hypernephroma, 1567
Hyperoxaluria, 1377-1379, 1403
    definition of, 1377
    dietary, 1378, 1403
    enteric, 1378, 1378f, 1403
        management of, 1422
    idiopathic, 1378-1379
    in children, 3223
    primary, 1377-1378, 1377f, 1403
Hyperparathyroidism, primary, parathyroidectomy for, 1420
Hyperprolactinemia
    erectile dysfunction associated with, 740
    male infertility associated with, 637
Hyperreflexia
    autonomic, voiding dysfunction with, 2012t, 2026-2027
    of detrusor muscle, 1981, 1981t
Hypertension
    after renal bypass surgery, 1749
    after renal injury, 1282
        in children, 3935
    age at onset of, 1167
    anesthesia-related, in laparoscopy, 211
    benign prostatic hyperplasia with, 2745
        α-adrenergic blockers for, 2786
    definition of, 1157
    erectile dysfunction associated with, 741
    family history of, 1167
    in autosomal dominant polycystic kidney disease, 3320-3321
    in chronic renal failure, 1351
    in multicystic dysplastic kidney, 3337, 3339
    in neonate, 3196
    in pheochromocytoma, 1857-1858, 1858t
    in primary hyperaldosteronism, 1850
    in renal cell carcinoma, 1597t, 1598
    in ureteral obstruction, management of, 1211-1212, 1212t
    licorice ingestion causing, 1849
    malignant, 1167
    nonsurgical, after renal transplantation, 1324
    pyelonephritic, pediatric urinary tract infection and, 3259-3260
    renovascular. See Renovascular hypertension.
    vesicoureteral reflux causing, 4340
Hyperthermia
    chemotherapy and, for invasive bladder cancer, 2476
    microwave, for prostatitis, 324

Hyperthyroidism
    erectile dysfunction associated with, 740
    male infertility associated with, 637-638
    voiding dysfunction in, 2041
Hypertrichosis, 3210, 3211f
Hyperuricosuria, 1379, 1385, 1402
    in children, 3223
    management of, 1420
Hypnotics, causing geriatric incontinence, 2308, 2308t
Hypoactive sexual desire disorder, 727, 859
Hypocitraturia, 1379, 1403-1404, 1404f, 1404t
    idiopathic, 1404
    thiazide-induced, 1404
        management of, 1423
Hypoestrogenism, role of, in labial adhesions, 3841
Hypogastric artery. See Iliac artery, internal (hypogastric).
Hypogastric plexus
    inferior, 15, 17, 17f
    superior, 15, 17, 17f
Hypogastric vein. See Iliac vein, internal (hypogastric).
Hypogonadism
    erectile dysfunction in, 740
    hypogonadotropic
        anabolic steroid-induced, 611
        gene mutation in, 3767
        in Kallmann syndrome, 635
        isolated, 635-636
        micropenis in, 3752-3753
    late-onset
        biochemical diagnosis of, 854-856, 855t, 856f
        clinical diagnosis of, 853-854, 853t, 854f, 854t
        clinical manifestations of, 851t
        definition of, 850
        diagnosis of, 853-857
        epidemiology of, 851
        historical perspective on, 850-851
        incidence of, 851
        physiologic principles in, 851-853, 852f
        screening questionnaires for, 853-854, 854f, 854t
        spectrum and severity of, 853t
        treatment of, 857-860
            recommendations and guidelines in, 860-862, 860t
            testosterone in, 857-858, 858t
                adverse effects of, 859-860
                objective effects of, 858-859
    radiation-induced, 3897
Hypokalemia, 1150
    conduit urinary diversion causing, 2571-2573, 2571t
    in primary hyperaldosteronism, 1851
    in renovascular hypertension, 1167
Hypomagnesuria, 1381-1382, 1404-1405
Hyponatremia, 1146-1148
    clinical approach to, 1147, 1148f
    conduit urinary diversion causing, 2571-2572, 2571t
    definition of, 1146
    treatment of, 1147, 1148f, 1149
Hypo-osmotic sperm-swelling test, 631-632
Hypophysectomy, restoration of spermatogenesis after, 595
Hypospadias, 91, 92, 3703-3743. See also Chordee; Penile curvature.
    after complete primary exstrophy repair, 3571
    characteristic defects of, 3706
    chordee without, 1088-1089, 3756, 3756f

Hypospadias (Continued)
    classification of, 3703, 3705f
    cryptorchidism associated with, 3709
    definition of, 3703, 3704f
    developmental considerations in, 3704-3706
    diagnosis of, 3703, 3704f
    embryology of, 3704-3705
    epidemiology of, 3708-3709
    etiology of, 3706-3707, 3707f
    evaluation of, 3204
    genetic associations with, 3709
    inguinal hernia associated with, 3709
    intersex states and, 3709
    long-term follow-up for, 3742
    megameatus intact prepuce (MIP) variant of, 3703, 3704f
    repair of, 3725
    neurovascular anatomy in, 3705-3706
    penile curvature without, etiology of, 3708
    prevalence of, in general population, 3708
    repair of, 714
        anesthesia/analgesia for, 3718
        antibiotics with, 3718-3719
        bladder spasm after, 3720
        complication(s) of, 3738-3740
            balanitis xerotica obliterans as, 3739
            hematoma as, 3739
            hypospadias cripples as, 3740
            infection as, 3739
            intraurethral hair growth as, 3740
            meatal stenosis as, 3739
            recurrent penile curvature as, 3739
            repair breakdown as, 3740
            urethral diverticulum as, 3739
            urethral stricture as, 3739-3740
            urethrocutaneous fistula as, 3739
        current trends in, 3743
        distal procedure in, 3722-3725
            advancement techniques for, 3722, 3723f
            flap techniques for, 3725, 3726f-3727f
            other techniques for, 3725
            tubularization techniques for, 3722-3723, 3724f, 3725
        dressing techniques in, 3720
        failed, management of, 1046-1047, 1047f
        fertility after, 3742
        functional issues after, 3742
        future concepts in, 3743
        general principles in, 3712-3718
        glanuloplasty in, 3718
        hemostasis in, 3719
        historical aspects of, 3712
        hormonal manipulation before, 3711
            timing of, 3712
        indications for, 3710-3711
        intersex evaluation for, 3711
        intraoperative algorithm for, 3720, 3721f, 3722
        laser techniques in, 3719
        meatoplasty in, 3718
        middle procedure in, 3725-3729
            onlay techniques for, 3725-3726, 3728, 3728f-3731f
            tubularization techniques for, 3729
        neourethral intubation in, 3719
        optical magnification in, 3719
        orthoplasty in, 3712-3714, 3713f, 3715f
        patient satisfaction with, 3742
        penile erection after, 3720
        penile shaft skin coverage in, 3718
        perioperative considerations in, 3718-3720
        preoperative considerations in, 3710-3712
        primary procedure in, 3722-3738

Hypospadias *(Continued)*
   distal, 3722-3725. *See also* Hypospadias, repair of, distal procedure in.
   middle, 3725-3729. *See also* Hypospadias, repair of, middle procedure in.
   proximal, 3729-3738. *See also* Hypospadias, repair of, proximal procedure in.
   proximal procedure in, 3729-3738
     one-stage, 3729-3734
      onlay techniques for, 3729-3731
      other, 3734, 3735f
      tubularization techniques for, 3731-3732, 3732f-3733f, 3734
     two-stage, 3734, 3735-3738, 3736f-3737f
      free-graft for neourethral formation in, 3734, 3736-3738, 3738f
   radiologic evaluation for, 3711
   reoperative
     general principles of, 3740
     specific techniques in, 3740-3741
   sexual function after, 3742
   suture technique in, 3719
   timing of (age at), 3718
   urethroplasty in, 3715-3718
     neourethral coverage in, 3716, 3716f, 3717f, 3718
     neourethral formation in, 3715-3716
   uroflow after, 3742
   syndromes associated with, 3709, 3710t
Hypospadias cripples, 3740
Hypospermatogenesis, 634
Hypothalamic-pituitary axis, in males, aging of, 580
Hypothalamic-pituitary-gonadal axis, normal, in testicular descent, 3766
Hypothalamus
   in male reproductive axis, 577-578
   involved in sexual function, 726t
   steroid feedback on, 578-579
Hypothermia
   anesthesia-related, in laparoscopy, 211
   induction of, intraoperative renal ischemia and, 1690-1691
Hypothyroidism, erectile dysfunction associated with, 740
Hypoxia, perinatal, functional response to, 3161
*Hypoxis rooperi* (South African star grass), for benign prostatic hyperplasia, 2800
Hysterectomy
   ureteral injury caused by, 1283
   vesicovaginal fistula following, 2323, 2323f, 2324f, 2326
Hysteresis, 1902
Hysterosalpingography, in evaluation of fertility, 612
HZV (herpes zoster virus), infection with, voiding dysfunction caused by, 2033

**I**

Ice water test, 1995
Idiopathic hypercalciuria, 1374, 1402, 1402t
Idiopathic hyperoxaluria, 1378-1379
Idiopathic hypocitraturia, 1404
Idiotope, of antigen-binding site, 478
Ifosfamide, for nonseminomatous germ cell tumors, 923
IgA nephropathy (Berger's disease)
   after renal transplantation, 1298
   end-stage renal disease and, 1346
   hematuria in, 99-100
   in children, 3226-3227
Ileal bladder substitute, Studer, for orthotopic urinary diversion, 2635, 2636f

Ileal conduit
   in conduit urinary diversion
     complications of, 2566, 2566f, 2566t
      long-term, 2614t
     preparation for, 2564
     procedure in, 2564, 2565f, 2566
   in laparoscopic-assisted urinary diversion, 2523-2524, 2524f-2526f
Ileal neobladder
   for orthotopic urinary diversion
     Hautmann, 2635, 2635f
     T pouch, 2638, 2639f-2640f, 2640
   orthotopic, in laparoscopic-assisted urinary diversion, 2524, 2527f
Ileal neovagina, creation of, 3836-3837, 3837f, 3838f
Ileal pouch, vesical, for orthotopic urinary diversion, 2634
Ileal reservoir (Kock pouch)
   for continent urinary diversion, 2589, 2590f-2591f
   for orthotopic urinary diversion, 2636, 2637f
Ileal union, delayed, after osteotomy, in exstrophy patient, 3516
Ileal ureteral substitution, for ureteral stricture, 1266, 1267f
   laparoscopic, 1266-1267
Ileal valve, intussuscepted, 2561-2562, 2561f
Ileal vesicostomy, 2570
Ileal-ileal stapled anastomosis, end-to-end, 2544, 2544f
Ileocecal conduit, in conduit urinary diversion, 2568
   complications of, 2569
Ileocecal valves
   for continent urinary diversion, in children, 3696
   in ileocecocystoplasty, 3675, 3677
   intussuscepted, 2561, 2561f
   loss of, conduit urinary diversion and, 2575
Ileocecocystoplasty, in children
   appendix in, 3675
   ileocecal valve in, 3675, 3677
   technique of, 3675, 3675f, 3676f, 3677
Ileocolonic anastomosis
   stapled, with circular stapling device, 2543-2544, 2543f
   sutured
     end-to-end, 2542, 2542f
     end-to-side, 2541-2542, 2541f, 2542f
Ileocolonic (Le Bag) pouch, for orthotopic urinary diversion, 2641-2642, 2642f
Ileocystoplasty, in children, 3673-3675, 3674f
Ileostomy, loop end, 2553, 2553f
Ileum
   anatomy of, 2534
   intussuscepted terminal, right colon pouches with, for continent urinary diversion, 2596
   reinforced nipple valves of, for antireflux surgery, in children, 3662
   selection of, for urinary diversion, 2536
Iliac artery
   aneurysm of
     as contraindication to laparoscopy, 175
     ureteral obstruction due to, 1222-1223, 1222f
   external, 46, 48t, 50f
   internal (hypogastric), 46, 48t, 50f, 51
   preureteral, 3420, 3421f
Iliac crest, 38, 39f
Iliac lymph nodes, 52, 52f
Iliac spine, 38, 39f

Iliac vein
   common, 11f, 13, 14f
   external, 52
   internal (hypogastric), 11f, 13, 51, 52
Iliacus muscle, 9, 9f, 9t
Iliococcygeus ligament suspension, in apical vaginal prolapse repair, 2227-2228, 2228t
Iliococcygeus muscle, 44, 46f, 2191, 2191f
Iliohypogastric nerve, 18, 18f, 52, 53t
Ilioinguinal lymphadenectomy, for penile cancer, 982
   radical, 1006-1008, 1006f-1010f, 1011
Ilioinguinal nerve, 18, 18f, 43, 43f, 52, 53t, 73
Iliorenal bypass, 1743-1744, 1743f
Ilium, 38, 39f
Illness(es), patient history of
   present, 81-88
   previous, 88
Imaging, in staging of prostate cancer, 2930
Imaging modalities. *See specific modality.*
Imidazole, 469
Imipramine
   for incontinence, 2072
     in elderly, 2317t
   for overactive bladder/detrusor overactivity, 2093t, 2104
     contraindications to, 2105
   for retrograde ejaculation, 648
   for stress incontinence, 2075, 2111
     in elderly, 2318
Imiprem, for pediatric urinary tract infections, 3248t
Imiquimod cream, for genital warts, 381
Immobilization techniques, in bladder exstrophy repair, 3515, 3515f, 3516f
   complications of, 3515-3516
Immotile cilia syndrome, 611, 623
Immune function, laparoscopic surgery and, 202-203
Immune homeostasis, role of chemokines in, 494-495
Immune modulators, for prostatitis, 322
Immune status, in pediatric urinary tract infection, 3239
Immune system
   adhesion molecules and lymphocyte trafficking in, 492-494, 493f, 493t
   apoptosis in, 488-490, 489f
   cell populations in, 475-478, 476t, 478f
   cell signal transduction in, 482-484, 482f
   cell surface activation of, 479f, 480f
   chemokines and leukocyte recruitment in, 494-495, 494t
   complement and, 474, 474f
   infections affecting, 500-502, 502t
   lymphocyte tolerance in, 490-492
   lymphoid tissue and organs in, 475, 475f
   phagocytosis and, 474
   prostatic, alterations in, 308-309
   T cell activation and effector function in, 484-488, 485f-487f, 486t
   tumor immunology and, 495-500, 496t, 498f
Immune tolerance, in renal cell carcinoma, 1588-1589
Immune-based strategies, with HAART, for HIV infection, 403-404
Immunity
   active, 502
   adaptive, 473
   cell-mediated responses to, 475
   humoral responses to, 475
   initiation of, 478
   innate, 473
     complement in, 474, 474f

Immunity *(Continued)*
  phagocytosis in, 474
  role of, 496
  passive, 502
  primary, 478
  secondary, 478
  T-cell receptor in, 479-480
  to infections, 500-502, 502t
  to uropathogens, 235-236
Immunobead test, for antisperm antibodies, 624t
Immunobiology, of renal cell carcinoma, 1588-1589
Immunoglobulin(s). *See also* Antibody(ies).
  classes of, 478
  in seminal plasma, 2724
Immunoglobulin A, secretion of, 475
Immunohistochemistry, in diagnosis of oncology, 547-548
Immunologic infertility, in males, 649-650
Immunology, molecular, 502-503, 504f
Immunosuppressants
  in renal transplantation, 1316-1317
    infection and peptic ulcer prophylaxis and, 1317, 1318t
    mechanism of action of, 1316t
    potential drug interactions among, 1317, 1317t
    protocol for, 1317, 1317f
    sites of action of, 1316f
    toxicity of, organ targets for, 1317, 1318t
  pregnancy safety and, 1323t
  secretion of, as mechanism of tumor escape, 497-498, 498f
Immunotherapy
  for bladder cancer, non–muscle-invasive, 2455-2458
    bacille Calmette-Guérin in, 2455-2457, 2457t, 2458t
      chemotherapy with, 2460
    interferon in, 2457
    investigational agents in, 2457-2458
  for painful bladder syndrome/interstitial cystitis, 360t, 361
  for prostate cancer, 3030
    hormone-refractory, 3116-3117
  for renal cell carcinoma, 1588-1589
    metastatic, 1629
  for retroperitoneal fibrosis, 1217, 1272
  for tumors, 499-500
  for urothelial tumors, 1651, 1651t
Imperforate anus, 3647, 3647t
  associated findings in, 3647-3648
  evaluation of, 3648, 3649f
  in neonate, 3195
  in unilateral renal agenesis, 3275, 3275f
Imperforate hymen, 3843-3844, 3844f
  with hydrocolpos, 3194
Imperforate vagina, cervix and uterine duplication with, 3839, 3839f, 3840f
Impetigo, in HIV patients, 396-397
Implant, penile. *See* Penile prosthesis.
Implantable microballoons
  for bladder filling/storage disorders, 2292
  for incontinence, 2286-2287
Impotence, 86. *See also* Erectile dysfunction; Penile detumescence; Priapism.
  after urethral distraction injuries, 2661
  arteriogenic, 740-742
  hormonal, 740
  in end-stage renal disease, 1301
  neurogenic, 739-740
  patient history of, 87

Impotence *(Continued)*
  psychogenic, 739
  venogenic, 742
In vitro fertilization. *See also* Assisted reproductive techniques (ARTs).
  with intracytoplasmic sperm injection, 650, 651, 652, 717-718, 718f
Incision(s). *See also specific incision.*
  electrosurgical, 191
  in adrenal surgery
    flank, 1871-1873, 1872f, 1873f
    lumbodorsal, 1873, 1874f
    subcostal, 1874, 1875f
    thoracoabdominal, 1875-1876, 1876f
  in antireflux surgery, 4351
  in radical nephrectomy, thoracoabdominal, 1709-1710, 1711f, 1712f
  in radical retropubic prostatectomy, 2959-2960
    endopelvic fascia, 2960-2961, 2961f
  in renal surgery
    abdominal, 1695-1698, 1697f-1701f
    dorsal lumbotomy, 1695, 1696f
    flank, 1691-1694, 1691f-1695f
    thoracoabdominal, 1698, 1701f-1702f, 1703
  in simple nephrectomy
    flank, 1703, 1703f-1705f
    transperitoneal, 1703, 1707, 1707f
  sites of, in varicocele repair, 659, 660f
Incisional hernia
  after laparoscopy, 217-218
  after radical nephrectomy, 1720
Inconspicuous penis, 3749f, 3751, 3751f
Incontinence, 2046-2077. *See also* Fecal incontinence; Voiding dysfunction.
  after cryotherapy, 3049-3050
  after robotic-assisted laparoscopic radical prostatectomy, 2999, 2999t
  after urethral injury, 3944
  age-related changes and, 2189, 2305-2306, 2306f
  assessment of, initial, 2059
  bladder abnormalities in, 2053-2056, 3658-3659
    conditions causing, 2054-2056, 2055t, 2056f-2058f, 2056t
    urodynamic observation of, 2053-2054, 2053f, 2054f
  causes of, 2049t
    established, 2309-2311
    functional, 2310-2311
    lower urinary tract, 2309-2310
  classification of, 2046-2047
  clinical evaluation of, 2202-2203, 2202t
    self-administered questionnaire in, 2203t
    self-administered short forms in, 2203t
  continuous, 86, 2047
  definition of, 2187
    International Continence Society, 2046, 2082
  detrusor overactivity causing. *See also* Overactive bladder.
    medical treatment of, 2071-2073
    surgical treatment of, 2073-2074
  diagnostic evaluation of, 2059-2070, 2311-2313
    empirical categorization in, 2313-2314
    history in, 2311-2312, 2312t
    laboratory examination in, 2313
    physical examination in, 2312-2313
    stress testing in, 2313
    urodynamic testing in, 2314
    voiding diary in, 2312, 2312f

Incontinence *(Continued)*
  during abdominal pressure increase, 1975-1976
  dye testing for, 2063
  effect of, on quality of life, 2062, 2062t
  endoscopy in, 2069-2070
  epidemiology of, 2047-2049, 2187-2190
  etiology of, 2053-2059
  extraurethral, 2047
  eyeball urodynamics in, 2064, 2064f
  female, 1936, 2047-2048, 2048f
    physical examination for, 2059-2060
    retropubic suspension surgery for, 2168-2185. *See also* Retropubic suspension surgery, for female incontinence.
    sphincter abnormalities and, 2058-2059
  geriatric. *See* Geriatric patient, incontinence in.
  history of, 2059-2060, 2060t
  impact of, 2124-2125, 2125t
    on sexual function, 2204-2205
  in children, 3612
    giggle, 3612
    injection therapy for, 2273
      intraurethral technique of, 2280
    urinary tract infection associated with, 3263
  in schizophrenia, 2041
  in stroke patients, 2014-2015
  in ureterovaginal fistula, 2341
  in urethrovaginal fistula, 2347-2348
  in valve patients, 3597
  incidence of, 2187, 2188, 2188t
  laboratory investigation in, 2313
  leak point pressures in
    abdominal, 2066, 2066f
    detrusor, 2067, 2067f
  low bladder compliance causing, treatment of, 2071-2074
  male, 2048-2049
    physical examination for, 2060
    prosthesis for, history and development of, 2392-2393
    sphincter abnormalities and, 2059
    surgical treatment of, 2391-2403. *See also* Artificial urinary sphincter; Perineal sling.
      contraindications to, 2392
      indications for, 2391-2392
  micturition diary in, 2062
  mixed, 2046, 2084, 2084f, 2202
    management of, 2145
    tension-free vaginal taping for, 2256-2257
  multichannel videourodynamic monitoring of, 2068-2069, 2069f
  myelodysplasia and, management of, 3636-3639, 3638f
  neurologic examination in, 2060
  overflow, 86, 2047
  pad testing for, 2063
  pathophysiology of, 2053-2059
  patient history of, 86
  pelvic examination in, 2060
  physical examination in, 2060-2061, 2312-2313
  postvoid residual volume in, 2060
  pressure-flow relation in, 2068
  prevalence of, 2187, 2188, 2188t
  radical retropubic prostatectomy causing, 2974
  recurrent
    artificial sphincter placement–induced, 2400-2401
    perineal sling procedure causing, 2396

Incontinence (*Continued*)
  risk factors for, 2189-2190, 2199t
  silicone prosthesis for, 553-554
  sphincteric abnormalities in, 2057-2059
    conditions causing, 2057-2059
      in females, 2058-2059
      in males, 2059
    urodynamic observations of, 2057
  stress. *See* Stress incontinence.
  stress testing in, 2313
  transient
    causes of, 2059t
      pathologic, 2306-2308, 2307t
      pharmacologic, 2308-2309, 2308t
    in elderly, 2306-2309
  treatment of, 2070-2077, 2314-2320, 2314f
    adjunctive measures in, 2317-2318
    after orthotopic diversion, 2621
    algorithms in, 2089f, 2090f
    antimuscarinic agents in, 2071-2072, 2072t
    augmentation cystoplasty in, 2073-2074
    behavioral therapy in, 2314-2316
    bladder augmentation in, 2074
    botulinum toxin in, 2072-2073
    capsaicin in, 2072
    condition-specific, 2070t
    conservative (nonsurgical), 2124-2146
      concept of, 2130
      costs of, 2124, 2125t
      data collection in, 2141-2142, 2142t
      description of, 2125-2126
      devices in, 2136-2140. *See also specific
        device.*
      overview of, 2126
      patient goals in, 2140-2141
      practical approach to, 2140-2145
      rationale for, 2125
      rehabilitation as, 2130-2136. *See also*
        Pelvic floor rehabilitation.
      tools of, 2126-2129. *See also* Behavioral
        therapy.
    continence products in, 2070-2071
    denervation procedures in, 2073
    due to detrusor overactivity or low bladder
      compliance, 2071-2074
    due to sphincteric dysfunction, 2074-2077.
      *See also* Stress incontinence, treatment
      of.
    estrogens in, 2107-2108
    imipramine in, 2072
    injectable therapies in, 567-569, 2272-2287.
      *See also* Injection therapy, for
      incontinence.
    intravesical and intradetrusor therapies in,
      2072-2073
    oxybutynin in, 2072
    pharmacologic, 2316-2317, 2317t
    previous and subsequent, perineal sling
      procedure and, 2396
    rehabilitation techniques in, 2071
    resiniferatoxin in, 2072
    sacral nerve neuromodulation for, 2073
    stepwise approach to, 2315t
    surgical, 2073-2074
      retropubic suspension in, 2168-2185. *See
        also* Retropubic suspension surgery,
        for female incontinence.
    therapeutic options in, 2168-2169, 2169t
  unconscious, 2046
  urethral pressure profilometry in, 2067
  urgency. *See* Urgency incontinence.
  urinalysis in, 2060
  urodynamic monitoring in, 2063-2069, 2314
    eyeball, 2064, 2064f

Incontinence (*Continued*)
    multichannel, 2064-2068
      filling/storage phase of, 2065-2067,
        2065f-2067f
      indications for, 2065t
      voiding/emptying phase of, 2068
    uroflowmetry in, 2063
    vaginal examination in, 2060-2061
    videourodynamic evaluation of, 2001
      multichannel, 2068-2069, 2069f
    voiding diary in, 2312, 2312f
    with benign prostatic hyperplasia, 2758
    with ectopic ureter, 3389
Incontinence Grading System, 2280t
Indapamide
  for absorptive hypercalciuria, 1418
  for renal hypercalciuria, 1419, 1421t
Indiana pouch, for continent urinary diversion
    in children, 3696
  postoperative care of, 2602
  procedure in, 2597, 2599f-2600f, 2600-2602,
    2601f
Indinavir calculi, 1388-1389
  surgical management of, 1440
Indomethacin, effect of, on ureteral function,
    1919
Indwelling orthopedic hardware, antibiotic
    prophylaxis for, 254, 254t
Infants. *See also* Children.
  autosomal recessive polycystic kidney disease
    in, 3316. *See also* Autosomal recessive
    polycystic kidney disease.
  bladder function in, normal, 3605-3609,
    3606f-3608f
  edema in, 3207
  glomerular filtration rate in, 3153
  hydrocele in, 3204
  hydronephrosis in, evaluation of, 3198
  intersex condition in, evaluation of, 3208
  myelodysplasia in, surveillance of, 3635t
  newborn. *See* Neonates.
  renal function in, evaluation of, 3153-3156,
    3155f, 3157f
  scrotum in, normal, 3208
  transitory detrusor-sphincter discoordination
    in, 3609
  uncircumcised, urinary tract infections in,
    3747
  urinary tract infection in. *See also* Urinary
    tract infection, in children.
    diagnosis of, 3242, 3243t
    management of, 3246-3247, 3248t
  urine specimen collection from, 96
Infection(s). *See also specific infection.*
  after artificial sphincter placement, 2400
  after hypospadias repair, 3739
  after osteotomy, in exstrophy patient, 3516
  after partial nephrectomy, 1730
  after penile prosthesis implantation, 795-796,
    796f
    salvage procedures for, 796
  after radical nephrectomy, 1720
  after renal transplantation, 1320-1321, 1323
  associated with ureteral calculi, 1452-1453
  bladder calculi related to, 2665-2666
  bladder cancer associated with, 450, 2415-
    2416
  causing painful bladder syndrome/interstitial
    cystitis, 338-340
  detection of, prior to renal transplantation,
    1298
  due to conduit urinary diversion, 2574-2575
  effect of, on ureteral function, 1915
  immunity to, 500-502, 502t

Infection(s) (*Continued*)
  of genitourinary tract
    fungal, 459-469. *See also specific infection.*
    parasitic, 448-459. *See also specific infection.*
  of male genitalia, 419-425, 420f-425f
  of seminal vesicles, 1114-1115
  perineal sling procedure causing, 2395
  post-biopsy, 2892
  postoperative, prophylactic management of,
    1317, 1318t
  preputial, 883
  prostate cancer associated with, 2859-2860,
    2860f
  urinary tract. *See* Urinary tract infection.
  urothelial tumors associated with, 1639
  vaginal tape–induced, 2265-2266
  voiding dysfunction with, 2027-2028
  wound. *See* Wound infections.
Infection-based calculi, 1386-1387
  bacteriology of, 1386-1387, 1387t
  epidemiology of, 1387
  management of, 1425-1426
    consequences of residual fragments in,
      1449
  pathogenesis of, 1386, 1386f
  struvite, 1407-1408, 1407f, 1408f, 1408t
Inferior vena cava, 11f, 13-14, 14f
  bleeding from, in radical nephrectomy, 1711,
    1713f
  double, 3418-3419, 3420f
  embryology of, 3418, 3419f
  transection of, laparoscopic renal surgery
    causing, 1807
  tumor involvement of
    5-year survival for, 1605t
    intrahepatic, radical nephrectomy with,
      1714, 1715f, 1716f
    intrahepatic or suprahepatic, radical
      nephrectomy with, 1714, 1716, 1718,
      1718f-1720f
    treatment of, 1619-1621, 1619f, 1620f
Infertile male syndrome, 3825
Infertility. *See also* Fertility.
  male, 609-653. *See also* Spermatogenesis,
    disorders of.
    abnormal androgen action in, 638
    alcohol-related, 645
    androgen excess in, 636-637
    androgens for, 647
    caffeine-related, 645
    chemotherapy-related, 643-644
    clomiphene citrate for, 646
    cryptorchidism and, 640-641, 3771-3772
    diagnosis of, 635-650
    diagnostic algorithms for, 619-623, 620t
      absent or low-volume ejaculate and, 619,
        620f, 621
      asthenospermia and, 622-623, 622f
      azoospermia and, 621-622, 621f
      normal seminal parameters and, 623
      oligospermia and, 622
      seminal parameter defects and, 623
      teratospermia and, 623
    drug-related, 644-645
    endocrine causes of, 635-638
    environmental toxins-related, 644
    estrogen excess in, 637
    evaluation of
      abdominal ultrasonography in, 630
      acrosome reaction in, 631
      additional testing in, 623-634
      antisperm antibodies in, 623-625,
        624t
      basic laboratory procedures in, 614-619

Infertility *(Continued)*
chromatin/DNA integrity testing in, 626-627
diagnostic algorithms based on, 619-623, 620f-622f, 620t
end-stage testes in, 634
female partner studies in, 611-613
genetic testing in, 632-633
germ cell aplasia in, 634
goals in, 609-610
hemizona assay in, 631
history in, 610-611, 610t
hormone studies in, 618-619, 618t
hypospermatogenesis in, 634
leukocyte staining in, 625
maturation arrest in, 634
normal testes in, 633, 633f
physical examination in, 613-614, 613t
radiologic, 627-630
reactive oxygen species testing in, 632
scrotal ultrasonography in, 629-630
semen analysis in, 614-618. *See also* Semen analysis.
semen cultures in, 625-626
sperm function testing in, 630-632
sperm penetration assay in, 631
sperm viability assay in, 631-632
sperm-cervical mucus interaction in, 630-631
testicular biopsy in, 633-634, 633f
transrectal ultrasonography in, 628-629, 628f
ultrastructural, 627
vasography in, 627-628, 628f
venography in, 629, 629f
glucocorticoid excess in, 638
GnRH therapy for, 646
gonadotropin therapy for, 646
heat-related, 644
idiopathic, 646
immunologically mediated, 649-650
in bilateral anorchia, 640
in chromosomal translocations, 640
in female eunuch syndrome, 636
in isolated FSH deficiency, 636
in isolated hypogonadotropic hypogonadism, 635-636
in Kallmann syndrome, 636
in Klinefelter syndrome, 638-639
in myotonic dystrophy, 643
in Noonan's syndrome, 639
in pituitary disease, 635
in Prader-Willi syndrome, 636
in Sertoli cell–only syndrome, 642-643, 643t
in thyroid disorders, 637-638
in XX male syndrome, 639
in XXY male syndrome, 639
in Y chromosome microdeletions, 639-640
occupational exposures-related, 644
orchitis and, 643
prolactin excess in, 637
radiation-related, 644
smoking-related, 645
sperm delivery disorders in, 647-649
sperm function disorders in, 649-650
surgical treatment of, 654-718
diagnostic procedures in, 655-658
for anatomic, congenital, and organic causes, 714-717
for ejaculatory duct obstruction, 707-714. *See also* Ejaculatory duct, obstruction of.
improved sperm delivery in, 665-700

Infertility *(Continued)*
improved sperm production in, 658-665
in vitro fertilization in, 717-718, 718f
sperm retrieval in, 700-707
epididymal aspiration for, 700, 702f-704f
for obstructive azoospermia, 700
open testicular biopsy for, 701
testis aspiration and needle biopsy for, 701, 703, 705-706, 705f-707f
vasal aspiration for, 700, 701f
varicocele repair in, 658-665, 658t, 659f-664f. *See also* Varicocelectomy.
vasectomy reversal in, 665-679, 667f-678f, 679t. *See also* Vasectomy.
vasoepididymostomy in, 679-700, 680f-698f, 699t. *See also* Vasoepididymostomy.
tamoxifen for, 646
testicular biopsy in
complications of, 658
indications for, 655
open, 655-657, 655f, 656f
percutaneous, 657, 657f
sperm aspiration in, 658
testicular torsion and, 641
testolactone for, 646-647
treatment of
assisted reproductive techniques in, 650-653, 653t. *See also* Assisted reproductive techniques (ARTs).
hormone therapy in, 646-647
miscellaneous, 647
overview of, 634-635
surgical, 654-718. *See also* Infertility, male, surgical treatment of.
varicocele and, 641-642
Infestation(s). *See also* Pediculosis pubis; Scabies.
involving male genitalia, 425, 425f, 426f
Infibulation, 3839-3840, 3841f
Inflammation
after osteotomy, in exstrophy patient, 3516
chronic
immune response to, 501
urothelial tumors associated with, 1639
detrusor overactivity and, 1968-1969, 1969f
in congenital urinary tract obstruction, 3171
painful bladder syndrome/interstitial cystitis associated with, 341
prostate cancer associated with, 2859-2860, 2860f
role of chemokines in, 494
Inflammatory bowel disease, painful bladder syndrome/interstitial cystitis and, 336
Inflammatory hemorrhagic cystitis, in children, 3263
Informed consent
for laparoscopic surgery, 175
for robotic-assisted laparoscopic radical prostatectomy, 2986
Infrapubic penis, 723
Infrared spectrophotometry, 762
Infundibular stenosis, 3302-3303, 3302f
natural history of, 1554-1555
percutaneous treatment of, 1555-1556, 1555f
presentation of, 1554-1555
Infundibulopelvic dysgenesis, 3302-3303, 3302f
Inguinal adenopathy
bulky, nodal metastasis and, 984, 984f
palpable, dissection for, 974, 976

Inguinal canal
anatomy of, 43, 43f, 44f
anomalies of, 3790f
examination of, 92-93, 92f
in children, 3208, 3208f
Inguinal hernia
associated with hypospadias, 3709
in children, 3203
in exstrophy patient, 3503
laparoscopic examination of, in children, 3915-3916, 3915f
Inguinal incision
exploration of communicating hydrocele through, 3789
transverse, in orchidopexy, 3776, 3776f
Inguinal ligation, for varicocele, 3796-3797
Inguinal lymph nodes, 73
anatomy of, 1002-1003, 1003f
in penile cancer
fine-needle aspiration of, 980
sentinel node biopsy of, 979, 1003-1005, 1004f
superficial and modified dissection of, 981
Inguinal lymphadenectomy, for penile cancer, 974-984
bilateral vs. unilateral, 981-982
bulky adenopathy and fixed nodal metastasis and, 984, 984f
complications of, 977t
in high-risk patients, 983f, 984
in low-risk patients, 983-984, 983f
indication for
immediate vs. delayed surgery and, 976
morbidity vs. benefit and, 976-978, 976f, 977f, 977t
palpable adenopathy as, 974, 976
prediction of occult metastases as, 978-979, 979t
prognostic significance of metastatic disease as, 974, 975t, 976t
modified, 1005, 1005f, 1006f
prophylactic, 979-980, 980t
Inguinal region
in penile cancer, radiation therapy to, 986-987
risk-based management of, penile cancer and, 983-974, 983f-984f
Inguinoscrotal incision, for penile arterial and venous reconstruction, 803, 803f
Inherited susceptibility, to cancer, 515-520, 515t, 516t. *See also under* cancer.
Inhibin, in male reproductive axis, 577
β-Inhibin, 2723-2724
Injectable material(s), for incontinence. *See* Injection therapy, for incontinence, injectable material(s) in.
Injection therapy
antireflux, 567-569, 568f
for erectile dysfunction, vasoactive agents in, 779-781, 779t
for incontinence, 567-569, 2272-2287
complications of, 2283-2284, 2284t
efficacy of, 2280-2283, 2280t
after prostatic resection, 2281
after radical prostatectomy, 2281
in females, 2281-2283
in adult females, 2273
in adult males, 2273
in children, 2273
injectable material(s) in, 2273-2275
autologous chondrocytes, 2286
autologous fat, 2275
efficacy of, 2281
safety of, 2285
bioglass, 2286

Injection therapy (Continued)
calcium hydroxyapatite, 2286
dextranomer microspheres, 2286
Durasphere and Durasphere Exp, 2274, 2275f
efficacy of, 2282
ethylene vinyl alcohol, 2274-2275
efficacy of, 2282
future of, 2285-2287
GAX-collagen, 2274
adverse effects of, 2284t
efficacy of, 2282-2283
safety of, 2285
historical chronology of, 2273
hyaluronic acid, 2286
Hylagel Uro, 2286
implantable balloons, 2286-2287
polytetrafluoroethylene, 2273-2274
efficacy of, 2281
safety of, 2284-2285
silicone polymers, 2275
efficacy of, 2281-2282
intraurethral technique of, 2275-2280
in children, 2280
in females, 2277-2280, 2278f, 2279f
in males, 2276-2277, 2276f
patient selection for, 2272-2273
postoperative care following, 2280
safety of, 2284-2285
for late-onset hypogonadism, testosterone in, 857, 858t
for tissue engineering, 567-569, 568f
with bulking agents, for bladder neck reconstruction, in children, 3665-3666
Injury. See Trauma; at anatomic site; specific injury.
INK4, G₁S checkpoint and, 523
Innervation. See Nerve(s); under anatomy.
Innominate bones, 38, 39f
Innovations, in percutaneous nephrostomy, 1563
Insemination, intrauterine. See also Assisted reproductive techniques (ARTs).
natural cycle of, 651
INSL3 gene, in testicular descent, 3145
INSL3 hormone, in testicular descent, 3769
Instillation therapy, for urothelial tumors, 1681, 1681f
Institute of Medicine (IOM) report, on androgen therapy, 860, 860t
Instrumentation. See also Equipment.
for laparoscopic surgery, 189-197. See also Laparoscopic surgery, instrumentation in.
extraperitoneal space development with, 181-189
in children, 3916-3917
for percutaneous nephrolithotomy, in children, 3909-3911, 3910f
for robotic-assisted laparoscopic prostatectomy, 2986t
for transurethral needle ablation of prostate, 2810, 2811f
for ureteroscopy, 1508-1514, 1511t. See also Ureteroscopy, instrumentation for.
in children, 3907, 3908t
for vasectomy reversal, 666-667, 667f
Insufflant system, for pneumoperitoneum, 178-179
choice of, 199-200
Insulin-like growth factor(s)
cancer and, 537
in benign prostatic hyperplasia, 2731, 2731f
Insulin-like growth factor receptor, in renal cell carcinoma, 1590

Insulin-like growth factor-1, 2710-2711
for tubal regeneration, in acute tubular necrosis, 1337
in prostate cancer, epidemiologic studies of, 2861
properties of, 2706t
role of, in compensatory renal growth, 1206-1207
Insulin-like growth factor-2, 2710-2711
properties of, 2706t
Integral theory, of stress incontinence, 2052-2053
Integrins, 539-540, 2695
in activation of leukocytes, 492-493, 493t
Intensity-modulated radiotherapy, for prostate cancer, 3018-3020, 3018f, 3019f
Intercellular communication, in male sexual function, 737
Interferon(s)
as inhibitors of angiogenesis, 544
for non–muscle-invasive bladder cancer, 2457
BCG with, 2461
for Peyronie's disease, 828
Interferon-alpha
for penile cancer, 988-989
for renal cell carcinoma, 1623, 1624t, 1626-1627, 1626f, 1627t
cytoreductive nephrectomy with, 1624-1625, 1624t
interleukin-2 with, 1629
Interferon-gamma
in benign prostatic hyperplasia, 2733
in tumor regression, 499
source and activity of, 486t
Intergroup Rhabdomyosarcoma Study Group
clinical staging of, 3879t
grouping classification of, 3879t
Interlabial mass(es), 3841-3846
hymenal skin tags as, 3843, 3843f, 3844f
imperforate hymen as, 3843-3844, 3844f
introital cysts as, 3842-3843, 3842f, 3843f
labial adhesions as, 3841-3842, 3842f
prolapsed ureterocele as, 3845, 3845f
prolapsed urethra as, 3844-3845, 3845f
urethral polyp as, 3845-3846, 3846f
vaginal rhabdomyosarcoma as, 3846, 3846f
Interleukin(s)
in benign prostatic hyperplasia, 2733
source and activity of, 486t
Interleukin-2
for renal cell carcinoma, 1623, 1624t, 1626f, 1627-1628, 1628t
cytoreductive nephrectomy with, 1625
interferon-alpha with, 1629
in allograft rejection, 1315
in tumor regression, 499
Interleukin-10, in suppression of tumor immunity, 498
Intermesenteric nerve, to testis, 581
Intermittency, urinary, 84
Intermittent therapy, self-start, for recurrent urinary tract infections, 264-265
International Consultation on Sexual Medicine (ICSM) recommendations, for erectile dysfunction, 750-751, 751f, 752f
International Continence Society (ICS)
classification
of incontinence, 2046-2047
of voiding dysfunction, 1980-1981, 1981t
International Continence Society (ICS) criteria, for filling rates during cystometry, 1991
International Continence Society (ICS)
Cystometry Terms, 1994t

International Continence Society (ICS)
definition
of incontinence, 2046, 2082
of overactive bladder, 2079
of painful bladder syndrome, 332
of urgency, 333
International Continence Society (ICS)
provisional nomogram, for outflow obstruction, 1999-2000, 1999f, 2000f
International Continence Society (ICS)
standards, minimal, 1988t
International Index of Erectile Function (IIEF) questionnaire, 751-752, 753f
International Prostate Symptom Score (IPSS), 85-86, 85t, 2768-2769
International Reflux Study in Children, 3239
International Society of Paediatric Oncology, rhabdomyosarcoma clinical trials conducted by, 3894-3895, 3895f
Interpersonal process, in quality of health care, 148
Intersex condition(s)
evaluation of, before hypospadias repair, 3711
hypospadias and, 3709
laparoscopic examination of, in children, 3914-3915, 3914t
surgical reconstruction of, 3853-3864
current operative techniques in, 3855-3862, 3857f
for high vaginal confluence with or without clitoral hypertrophy, 3858-3859, 3859f-3861f
for low vaginal confluence with clitoral hypertrophy, 3856-3858, 3858f
initial management, timing, and principles in, 3853-3855, 3854f-3856f
results of, 3863-3864
urogenital mobilization in, total or partial, 3859-3862, 3861f-3864f
Interstitial cell(s), of bladder, 1929-1930, 1930f
Interstitial cell tumors, testicular, 925-927, 926t. See also Leydig cell tumor(s).
Interstitial cystitis. See also Painful bladder syndrome/interstitial cystitis.
antibiotics causing, 338-339
bladder cancer associated with, 335
feline, 337-338
gynecologic problems mimicking, 351
ICDB Study Eligibility Criteria for, 332, 333t
in children, 3263-3264
NIDDK diagnostic criteria for, 332, 332t
prostatitis and, 309-310
sacral neuromodulation for, 2156-2157
Interstitial Cystitis Association (ICA)
recommendations, of foods to avoid, in painful bladder syndrome/interstitial cystitis, 359t
Interstitial Cystitis Database (ICDB) Study Eligibility Criteria, for interstitial cystitis, 332, 333t
Interstitial laser, for benign prostatic hyperplasia, 2823
clinical results of, 2826-2827
Interstitial nephritis, in acute renal failure, 1328-1329, 1328t
Interstitium, of testis, 581, 581f, 584-585, 585f-587f, 587
Intertrigo, candidal, 424, 424f
Intervertebral disks, disease of, voiding dysfunction with, 2012t, 2031
Intestinal anastomosis, 2539-2551
complication(s) of, 2549-2551, 2550t
bowel obstruction as, 2549-2550, 2550t, 2551f

Intestinal anastomosis (Continued)
    elongation of segment as, 2551, 2551f
    fistulas as, 2549
    hemorrhage as, 2550
    pseudo-obstruction as, 2550-2551
    sepsis as, 2549
    stenosis as, 2550, 2551f
    stricture as, 2551
    laparoscopic, 2542, 2545f-2547f
    postoperative care following, 2548-2549
    principles of, 2539-2540
    stapled, 2542-2544, 2543f, 2544f
        ileocolonic
            end-to-end, 2544, 2544f
            with circular stapling device, 2543-2544,
                2543f
    sutured, 2540-2542, 2540f-2542f
        ileocolonic
            end-to-end, 2542, 2542f
            end-to-side, 2541-2542, 2541f, 2542f
            single-layer, 2541, 2541f
            two-layer, 2540-2541, 2540f
    types of, 2540-2544
    with biofragmenatable rings, 2548
Intestinal antireflux valves, 2561-2562, 2561f
Intestinal conduits, renal transplants into, 1300
Intestinal motility, with pneumoperitoneum,
    201
Intestinal neobladder, overactivity of, drug
    treatment for, 2108-2109
Intestinal neovagina, creation of, 3836-3838,
    3836f-3838f
Intestinal segment(s)
    anastomotic-induced, 2551, 2551f
    neuromechanical aspects of, urinary
        diversion, 2576-2578
    used in antireflux surgery, in children, 3662
    used in augmentation cystoplasty
        choice of, 3686-3687
        management of, 3673
        mucus production with, 3683
    used in urinary diversion, 2533-2578
        abdominal stoma and, 2551-2553
            complications of, 2553-2554
            flush, 2552
            loop end ileostomy as, 2553, 2553f
            nipple "rosebud," 2552, 2552f
        colon as, surgical anatomy of, 2534-2535,
            2535f
        complications of, 2551, 2551f
        preparation of, 2536-2539
            antibiotic, 2538-2539, 2538t
            diarrhea and pseudomembranous
                enterocolitis following, 2539
            mechanical, 2537-2538, 2537t
        renal deterioration after, 2563-2564
        selection of, 2535-2536
        small bowel as, surgical anatomy of, 2534
        stomach as, surgical anatomy of, 2533-
            2534, 2534f
Intestinal stenosis, due to anastomosis, 2550,
    2551f
Intestinal strictures, due to anastomosis, 2551,
    2556t, 2562-2563
Intimal fibroplasia, of renal artery, 1157t, 1159,
    1159f, 1160f
Intracellular mechanisms, in renin-angiotensin-
    aldosterone system, 1162
Intracranial hemorrhage, in autosomal
    dominant polycystic kidney disease, 3321
Intracrine signals, in prostate, 2690, 2690f
Intracytoplasmic injection, of sperm, in vitro
    fertilization with, 650, 651, 652, 717-718,
    718f

Intradetrusor therapy
    for incontinence, 2072-2073
    for painful bladder syndrome/interstitial
        cystitis, 362-364, 362t
Intraprostatic ductal reflux, of urine, 308
Intraprostatic stents, for benign prostatic
    hyperplasia, 2804-2809
    permanent, 2807-2809
        Memotherm, 2809
        UroLume, 2808-2809
    temporary, 2804-2807
        biodegradable, 2807
        polyurethane, 2806-2807, 2807f
        spiral, 2804-2806
Intrarenal aneurysm, of renal artery, 1187, 1188f
Intraspinal alcohol injections, for painful
    bladder syndrome/interstitial cystitis, 366
Intraurethral catheter, stenting with, 2806
Intraurethral hair growth, after hypospadias
    repair, 3740
Intraurethral therapy, for erectile dysfunction,
    781
Intrauterine insemination, 651-652. See also
    Assisted reproductive techniques (ARTs).
    natural cycle of, 651
Intravenous urography. See Urography,
    intravenous.
Intravesical pressure. See Bladder pressure.
Intravesical procedures, in antireflux surgery,
    4352
Intravesical tape erosion, 2262-2263, 2262t
Intravesical therapy
    for incontinence, 2072-2073
    for painful bladder syndrome/interstitial
        cystitis, 362-364, 362t
    of non–muscle-invasive bladder cancer,
        perioperative, 2453, 2453t
Introital cysts, 3842-3843, 3842f, 3843f
Introitus, examination of, pull-down procedure
    in, 3841, 3841f
Intubated ureterotomy
    for ureteral stricture, 1264
    for ureteropelvic junction obstruction, 1245,
        1247, 1247f
Intussusception technique, of anastomosis, in
    vasoepididymostomy, 690, 692-694, 694f-
        698f
    two-suture modification of, 693-694, 697f-
        698f
Inulin, in estimation of glomerular filtration
    rate, 1132
Inverted-Y ureteral duplication, 3417
Investigational agents
    immunotherapeutic, for bladder cancer,
        non–muscle-invasive, 2457-2458
    new, for HIV infection, 403
Investigational markers, of bladder cancer,
    non–muscle-invasive, 2465
Ion channels, in male sexual function, 736-737
Ion transport
    across urothelium, 1934-1935
    metabolic determinants of, 1203-1204
Irrigation
    for ureteroscopy, 1511t, 1512-1513
        in children, 3909
    in laparoscopy, 196
Irritant contact dermatitis, 408
Irritative urinary symptoms, patient history of,
    84
Isaac's syndrome, voiding dysfunction in, 2041-
    2042
Ischemia, renal. See Renal ischemia.
Ischemic nephropathy, renal artery
    reconstruction in, 1733-1734

Ischemic priapism, 841, 843. See also Priapism.
    cavernosal blood gas determinants in, 845
    natural history of, 841
    treatment of, 845-846, 846t, 847f-848f, 848
Ischial tuberosity, 38, 39f
Ischiocavernosus muscle(s), rhythmic
    contraction of, 725
Ischium, 38, 39f
Island flap(s), 1026, 1027f. See also Flap(s).
    skin, 1028
        in urethral stricture repair, 1072f-1074f,
            1073, 1074-1075
Isoniazid, for genitourinary tuberculosis, 443,
    445t
Isoproterenol, effect of, on ureteral function,
    1905
Isotopes, for brachytherapy, 3024
Isthmusectomy, for horseshoe kidney, 1755-1756
Itraconazole, 469
    cost of, 464t
    dosage of, 461t
Ivermectin
    for filariasis, 457
    for onchocerciasis, 458
    for scabies, 383

J

Jak/STAT pathway, in signal transduction, 484
Jarisch-Herxheimer reaction, 377
Jejunal conduit, in conduit urinary diversion,
    2566-2567
    complications of, 2567, 2567t
    preparation for, 2564
Jejunum
    anatomy of, 2534
    significant loss of, conduit urinary diversion
        and, 2575-2576
Jones incision, for orchidopexy, 3779
Joule-Thompson principle, of cryotherapy,
    3033-3034, 3034f
Juvenile nephronophthisis, 3326-3328
    NPH genes in, 3326
Juvenile nephronophthisis/medullary cystic
    disease complex, 3326-3328
    characteristics of, 3314t
    clinical features of, 3326-3327, 3326t
    evaluation of, 3327-3328, 3328f
    genetics of, 3326, 3326t
    histopathology of, 3327, 3327f
    treatment of, 3328
Juxtaglomerular tumor, renin-secreting, 1582

K

Kalicinski plication, for megaureter, 4379,
    4379f
Kallikrein 1, 2719t, 2720
Kallikrein 2, 2719t, 2720
Kallikrein 11, 2720
Kallikrein tumor marker(s), of prostate cancer,
    2897-2907, 2897f
Kallmann syndrome, 611, 635, 636
Kanamycin, in antibiotic bowel preparation,
    2538t
Kaposi's sarcoma
    in AIDS patients, 962, 963
    of male genitalia, 428, 429f
    of penis, 962-963
Kartagener's syndrome, 611, 613, 623
Katayama fever (acute schistosomiasis), 450, 452
Kaufman procedures, for male incontinence,
    2392. See also Perineal sling, for male
    incontinence.
Kaye catheter, 1544
Kegel exercises, 2130

Keratinocytic growth factor, in benign prostatic hyperplasia, 2731-2732, 2731f
Keratosis, seborrheic, of male genitalia, 433, 434f
Keratotic balanitis, of penis, 960
Ketoconazole, 469
  for hormone-refractory prostate cancer, multidrug regimens with, 3107t
  for prostate cancer, 3088
  topical, for seborrheic dermatitis, 415
Ketones, in urine, 104
Ketoprofen, for prostatitis, clinical trial data on, 322
Keyhole-limpet hemocyanin, for bladder cancer, non–muscle-invasive, 2457
Kidney(s), 24-32. *See also* Neph-; Renal *entries.*
  anatomic relationships of, 24f, 25-26, 26f
  anatomy of
    gross, 24-25, 24f
    intrarenal, 1528-1529, 1528f-1530f
    microscopic, 24-25
    perirenal, 1527-1528, 1527f
    surgical, 1527-1529, 1527f-1530f, 1686-1688, 1687f, 1688f
  anomalies of, 1521
    congenital, 3929
    of ascent, 3278-3283
    of collecting system, 3297-3303
    of form and fusion, 3283-3291
    of number, 3269-3278
    of rotation, 3291-3292, 3292f, 3293f
    of vasculature, 3292-3297
    percutaneous nephrostomy and, site selection for, 1540-1541, 1540f
    ultrasonography of, in male infertility work-up, 630
    vesicoureteral reflux and, 4344
  ascent of
    anomalies of, 3278-3283
    normal and abnormal, 3127, 3128f
  Ask-Upmark, 1191, 3311-3312
  biopsy of. *See* Renal biopsy.
  candidiasis of, 462
    management of, 300
  computed tomography of, 129, 131f, 132, 132f
  development of, 3121-3131, 3122f
    anatomic stages in, 3149, 3150f
    apoptosis in, 3167, 3167f
    collecting system in, 3126, 3127f
    early events in, 3121, 3124f
    gene involved in, 3134-3135
    hormonal control in, 3172
    malformation or injury during, functional response to, 3159-3162, 3159t
    mesonephros in, 3121, 3124, 3124f
    metanephros in, 3124-3126, 3125f, 3126f
    molecular mechanism of, 3127-3131, 3128f-3130f
    prenatal renal ascent in, 3127, 3128f
    pronephros in, 3121, 3124f
    urinary tract obstruction in. *See also* Urinary tract obstruction, congenital.
      functional response to, 3160-3161
      pathophysiology of, 3163-3175
  disc, 3284f, 3285-3286
  duplex
    definition of, 3383
    with bifid ureter, 3386
  ectopic. *See* Renal ectopia.
  egress of urine from, 1200
  examination of, 90, 90f
  fetal
    development of
      anatomic stages in, 3149, 3150f
      functional, 3149-3150

Kidney(s) (*Continued*)
  function of, evaluation of, 3150-3151, 3151f
    normal, 3176, 3177f
  for transplantation. *See also* Renal transplantation.
    preservation of
      cellular injury and, 1306
      clinical, 1306-1308
      cold storage in, 1306
  Gerota's fascia of, 26, 27f, 28
  growth of
    regulation of, 3167
    retarded, vesicoureteral reflux causing, 4340
  histopathology of, in renal artery atherosclerosis, 1176, 1178f
  horseshoe. *See* Horseshoe kidney.
  hydatid cysts in, 459, 459f
  hydronephric, growth acceleration in, 3167
  hydronephrotic, regulation of apoptosis in, 3167, 3167f
  in prune-belly syndrome, 3483, 3483f
  increased size of, during pregnancy, 290
  infections of, 265-286. *See also* Urinary tract infection; *specific infection.*
    in AIDS patients, 396
  inflammation of. *See* Pyelonephritis; Urinary tract infection.
  injury to. *See* Renal injury.
  innervation of, 32
  localization of, in diagnosis of urinary tract infection, 240-241, 241t
  L-shaped, 3284f, 3285
  lump, 3284f, 3285
  lymphatic drainage of, 30-31, 31f
  magnetic resonance imaging of, 135, 136f
  medullary sponge. *See* Medullary sponge kidney.
  multicystic dysplastic. *See* Multicystic dysplastic kidney.
  normal opposite, nephron-sparing surgery for renal cell carcinoma with, 1614-1615, 1614f
  obstructed
    drainage of, 1212
    impaired growth of, 3166-3167
  Page's, 1191
  pathophysiology of, 1146-1154
    acid-base disorders in, 1152-1154, 1153t, 1154t
    potassium imbalances in, 1150-1151, 1151t
    sodium imbalances in, 1146-1149, 1148f, 1149t, 1150f
    water imbalances in, 1146, 1147f
  physiology of, 1131-1146
    hormones in, 1133-1138
      antidiuretic, 1137-1138, 1137t, 1138f
      bone mineral regulation and, 1136-1137, 1136f
      erythropoiesis and, 1135-1136
      vasoconstrictors and, 1134-1135, 1134f, 1134t
      vasodilators and, 1134t, 1135
    tubular function in, 1138-1146
      at loop of Henle, 1141-1144, 1142f-1144f
      basic, 1138, 1139f
      cortical collecting, 1144-1145, 1145f, 1146f
      distal, 1144
      medullary collecting, 1145-1146
      proximal convoluted, 1138-1141, 1140f, 1141f

Kidney(s) (*Continued*)
  vascular, 1131-1133, 1133f
    blood flow in, 1131
    glomerular filtration rate in, 1131-1133, 1133f
  pseudotumor of, 3302, 3302f
  reconstruction of, after injury, 1279, 1280f, 1281
  recovery of, after obstruction relief, 1207
  retarded growth of, vesicoureteral reflux causing, 4340
  sigmoid (S-shaped), 3284f, 3285
  solitary, ureteral calculi in patient with, 1453
  structures of, tissue engineering of, 566, 566f
  supernumerary
    associated anomalies with, 3277
    diagnosis of, 3278
    embryology of, 3277
    features of, 3277, 3277f, 3278f
    incidence of, 3276-3277
    symptoms of, 3277-3278
  thoracic
    associated anomalies with, 3282
    diagnosis of, 3282
    embryology of, 3281-3282
    features of, 3282, 3282f
    incidence of, 3281
    prognosis for, 3282-3283
    symptoms of, 3282
  transillumination of, 90
  tuberculosis of, 438, 438f
    in AIDS patients, 396
  ultrasonography of, 122, 122f-124f
  unipapillary, 3301
  unobstructed, compensatory growth of, 1206-1207
  vasculature of, 28-30, 28f-30f, 1528, 1528f, 1687-1688, 1687f, 1688f. *See also* Renal artery(ies); Renal blood flow; Renal plasma flow; Renal vein(s).
    common variants of, 30
    development of, 3131
    injury to, in children, 3935
Kidney graft. *See also* Renal transplantation.
  early dysfunction of, 1318, 1319t
  expanded criteria donor of, 1303, 1305
    candidates for, 1309
    definition of, 1303
  preparation of, 1309, 1309f, 1310f
  preservation of
    cellular injury and, 1306
    clinical, 1306-1308
    cold storage in, 1306
  rejection of, 1314-1317
    classification of, 1315-1316
    histocompatibility in, 1314-1315, 1315f, 1315t
    immunosuppression in, 1316-1317, 1316f, 1317f, 1317t, 1318t
Kinesiologic studies, of voiding dysfunction, 2002-2003, 2003f
Kinins, effect of, on ureteral function, 1919
Klinefelter's syndrome, 3808-3809
  in azoospermic men, 717
  infertility in, 638-639
  mosaic form of, 639
Klippel-Feil syndrome, 3834
  cervical and vaginal atresia with, 3839f
Klippel-Trénaunay-Weber syndrome, 3760
KLK4 tumor marker, of prostate cancer, 2907
KLK11 tumor marker, of prostate cancer, 2907
KLK14 tumor marker, of prostate cancer, 2907
KLK15 tumor marker, of prostate cancer, 2907

Knockout mice, 546
  conditional, 547
Knudson's hypothesis, of hereditary
    malignancies, 516, 516f
Kocher maneuver, in adrenal surgery, 1875,
    1876f
Kock pouch (ileal reservoir)
  for continent urinary diversion, 2589, 2590f-
    2591f
  for orthotopic urinary diversion, 2636, 2637f
Koyanagi repair, of hypospadias, 3734, 3735f
KTP laser. *See* Potassium titanyl phosphate
    (KTP) laser.
Ku protein, in DNA repair, 528
Kumpe catheter, 1541

L
Labia, erosions of, in Stevens-Johnson
    syndrome, 410, 410f
Labia majora, 77
  development of, 3142f, 3143
Labia minora
  adhesions of, 3210, 3841-3842, 3842f
    outpatient lysis of, 3215, 3215f
  atrophy of, 871f
  development of, 3142f, 3143
Labioplasty, for intersex conditions
  simultaneous vaginoplasty and clitoroplasty
    with, 3854
  technique of, 3855, 3856f
Labor, prolonged, vesicovaginal fistula following,
    2324-2325, 2325f
Laboratory test(s)
  for erectile dysfunction, 756
  for male infertility, 614-619
  for penile squamous cell carcinoma, 969
  for priapism, 844-845
  for sexual health problems, in females, 871-
    873
Lacerations. *See at anatomic site.*
Lactate dehydrogenase, in prostate, 2724
Lactic acid dehydrogenase, in testicular tumors,
    906-907
Lacuna magna (sinus of Guérin), 3141
Lamina propria, 1937
Laparoscopes, three-dimensional, 190
Laparoscopic ablation techniques, 1804-1807.
    *See also specific technique.*
Laparoscopic adrenalectomy
  complications of, 1886-1887
  during pregnancy, 1887
  hand-assisted, 1878
  in children, 1887
  outpatient and short-stay, 1884-1885
  postoperative management of, 1884
  retroperitoneal approach to, 1878, 1882f-
    1884f
  robotic, 1884
  transperitoneal approach to, 1876, 1878,
    1878f-1882f
Laparoscopic antireflux surgery, 4366-4367
Laparoscopic bladder autoaugmentation, in
    children, 3925
Laparoscopic calicovesicostomy, for
    ureteropelvic junction obstruction, 1253
Laparoscopic carts, 177
Laparoscopic colposuspension, 2170
Laparoscopic cryotherapy, 1804-1805, 1812,
    1812t, 1813f
  complications of, 1806-1807
  results of, 1805-1806
Laparoscopic dismembered tubularized flap
    pyeloplasty, for ureteropelvic junction
    obstruction, 1253

Laparoscopic diverticulectomy, of bladder, 2511-
    2512, 2511f
Laparoscopic enterocystoplasty, 2512-2515
  in children, 3925
  results of, 2514-2515
  technique of, 2513-2514, 2514f
Laparoscopic intestinal anastomosis, 2542,
    2545f-2547f
Laparoscopic ligation, for varicocele, 3796
Laparoscopic nephrectomy
  donor, hand-assisted, 1303, 1304f-1305f
  for autosomal dominant polycystic kidney
    disease, 1775-1776
  for ectopic ureter, 3395, 3395f
  for malignancy, 1778-1781
    radical, 1609f, 1610
    trocar or port site recurrence after, 1779,
      1779f, 1780t, 1781, 1781t
  in children, 3921
  radical
    hand-assisted, 1791-1799
      indications for and contraindications to,
        1791
      patient positioning and hand port/trocar
        placement in, 1791, 1792f-1796f
      results of, 1798
      technique of, 1791, 1796-1798, 1797f,
        1798f
    retroperitoneal, 1788-1791
      indications for and contraindications to,
        1788
      patient positioning and trocar placement
        in, 1788-1789, 1789f, 1790f
      results of, 1790-1791
      technique of, 1789-1790
    transperitoneal, 1781-1788, 1782t
      dissection of upper pole in, 1783-1784,
        1785f
      dissection of ureter in, 1783, 1783f
      indications for and contraindications to,
        1781
      mobilization of lower pole in, 1783
      organ entrapment in, 1784, 1786-1787,
        1786f, 1787f
      patient positioning and trocar placement
        in, 1781
      preoperative evaluation in, 1781
      reflection of colon in, 1781
      results of, 1787-1788, 1787t
      securing of blood vessels in, 1783, 1784f
  simple, 1761-1769
    dissection of ureter in, 1763, 1767f
    identification of renal hilum in, 1763,
      1767f
    indications for and contraindications to,
      1761-1762
    insufflation and trocar placement in, 1762,
      1764f, 1765f
    isolation of upper pole in, 1769, 1769f
    organ entrapment in, 1769
    patient positioning for, 1762, 1762f, 1763f
    postoperative management of, 1769
    reflection of colon in, 1762-1763, 1766f
    results of, 1769
    securing renal blood vessels in, 1763, 1768,
      1768f
    technique of, 1763-1769
Laparoscopic nephron-sparing surgery. *See*
    Nephron-sparing surgery, laparoscopic.
Laparoscopic nephroureterectomy, 1650, 1650t
  in children, 3921-3922
  radical, 1664-1667
    results of, 1666-1667
    transperitoneal, 1665-1666, 1665f, 1666f

Laparoscopic orchidopexy, 3785-3786
  Fowler-Stephens, 3786
Laparoscopic partial cystectomy, 2515-2516,
    2516f
Laparoscopic pelvic lymph node dissection
  complications of, 3003-3004
  in radical cystectomy, 2521, 2523f
  indications for, 3002
  port site seeding after, 1779
  technique of, 3002-3003, 3002f-3004f
Laparoscopic pyeloplasty, for ureteropelvic
    junction obstruction, 1249-1253, 1251f,
    1252f
  anterior extraperitoneal approach to, 1250
  complications of, 1252, 1252f
  dismembered tubularized flap in, 1253
  in children, 3375-3376, 3376f
    retroperitoneal access for, 3377-3378, 3378f,
      3379f
  indications for and contraindications to,
    1249-1250
  postoperative care following, 1250, 1252
  results of, 1252
  robotic-assisted approach to, 1250
  transperitoneal approach to, 1250, 1251f
    in children, 3378, 3379f
  with concomitant pyelolithotomy, 1253
Laparoscopic radical cystectomy, 2516-2523
  and urinary diversion, 2523-2527. *See also*
    Urinary diversion, laparoscopic-assisted.
  clinical outcome data for, 2527, 2528t, 2529t,
    2530-2532, 2530t, 2531t
    in hand-assisted surgery, 2532
    in robot-assisted surgery, 2531-2532
    intracorporeal vs. extracorporeal,
      comparative characteristics of, 2529t
    oncological outcomes in, 2531t
    operative outcomes in, 2528t
    prostate-sparing and, 2531
  future directions of, 2532
  general considerations in, 2518, 2518f
  historical background in, 2517-2518
  in females, 2520-2521, 2521f-2522f
    uterus/fallopian tube/ovary-sparing, 2521
  in males, 2518, 2519f, 2520, 2520t
    prostate-sparing, 2519f, 2520
      outcome data on, 2531
  indications for and contraindications to, 2518
  laboratory data on, 2518
  pelvic lymph node dissection in, 2521, 2523f
  technique of, 2518-2527
  world experience with, 2517t
Laparoscopic radical prostatectomy, 2935-2936
  robotic-assisted, 2985-3002
    anesthesia for, 2986-2987
    complications of, 3001-3002
    economic considerations in, 3000-3001
    evolution of, 2985-2986
    extraperitoneal approach to, 2996, 2998f
      vs. transperitoneal approach, 2996-2997
    informed consent for, 2986
    operating room personnel, configuration,
      and equipment for, 2986, 2986t, 2987f
    patient positioning for, 2986, 2988f
    patient selection for, 2986
    preoperative preparation for, 2986
    results of, 2997-3000
      functional, 2999-3000, 2999t
      oncologic, 3000
      perioperative, 2998-2999
    surgical technique of, 2987-2997, 2988f
    transperitoneal approach to, 2988-2996
      abdominal access and trocar
        configuration in, 2988-2989, 2989f

Laparoscopic radical prostatectomy (Continued)
    antegrade neurovascular bundle
        preservation in, 2993, 2994f, 2995f
    bladder neck transection in, 2992,
        2994f
    delivery of prostate specimen in, 2996
    developing space of Retzius in, 2991,
        2991f
    dorsal vein complex division in, 2993,
        2995
    dorsal vein complex ligation in, 2991-
        2992, 2991f, 2992f
    exiting abdomen in, 2996
    inspection and entrapment of prostate
        specimen in, 2995
    interfascial dissection of neurovascular
        bundles in, 2992, 2993f
    posterior prostatic dissection in, 2990-
        2991, 2990f, 2991f
    prostatic apical dissection in, 2995
    prostatic pedicle ligation in, 2992-2993,
        2994f
    retrograde neurovascular bundle
        preservation in, 2993
    seminal vesical and vas deferens
        dissection in, 2989-2990, 2989f,
        2990f
    urethral division in, 2995, 2996f
    vesicourethral anastomosis in, 2995-
        2996, 2997f
    vs. extraperitoneal approach to, 2996-
        2997
Laparoscopic renal biopsy, 1770-1772, 1770f,
    1771f
Laparoscopic retroperitoneal lymph node
    dissection, for testicular cancer, 945-948
    bilateral, 947
    complications of, 947
    left-sided, 946-947
    nerve-sparing techniques in, 947
    patient positioning for, 945-946
    patient preparation for, 945
    results and current status of, 947-948
    right-sided, 946
    transperitoneal approach to, 946
Laparoscopic retropubic suspension surgery, for
    female incontinence, 2180, 2182
Laparoscopic sacral colpopexy, for apical vaginal
    prolapse repair, 2229-2230, 2230t
Laparoscopic stone surgery, 1506-1507
Laparoscopic surgery, 171-220
    antibiotic prophylaxis for, 253, 253t
    blood product preparation for, 175
    bowel preparation for, 175
    complication(s) of, 203-219, 203t
        exiting abdomen as, 216
        intraoperative, 211-216
            bowel injury as, 211-213, 212f
            nerve injury as, 215-216
            pancreatic injury as, 215
            splenic injury as, 215
            urinary tract injury as, 214-215
            vascular injury as, 213-214
        minimizing incidence of, 203
        postoperative, 216-218
            deep venous thrombosis as, 218
            hydrocele as, 216-217
            incisional hernia as, 217-218
            late, 218-219
            pain as, 217
            rhabdomyolysis as, 218
            scrotal and abdominal ecchymosis as,
                217
            wound infection as, 218

Laparoscopic surgery (Continued)
    procedural, 203-219
        related to anesthesia, 210-211
        related to pneumoperitoneum, 204-209. See
            also Pneumoperitoneum,
            complication(s) related to.
        secondary trocar placement and, 209-210,
            209f, 210f
    contraindications to, 174-175
    development of extraperitoneal space in
        balloon dilatation in, 181-182, 182f
        extraperitoneoscopy in, 184
        gasless peritoneal laparoscopy in, 182
        instrumentation for, 181-189
        retroperitoneoscopy in, 183, 183f, 184f
        trocar placement in, 185, 185f, 186f, 188f,
            189f
    diagnostic, in children, 3914-3916
        indications for, 3914
        of hernia, 3915-3916, 3915f
        of intersex conditions, 3914-3915, 3914t
        of testis, 3914
    endourologic procedures prior to, 176
    exiting abdomen in
        complications of, 216
        port removal in, 197-198
        port site closure in, 198, 198f
        skin closure in, 198
    extraperitoneal approach to, 173
    for cryptorchidism, 3781-3787
        assessment in, 3782-3784, 3783f
        diagnostic, 3782
        technique of, 3782
        vs. inguinal exploration, 3784-3785
    for ureteral stricture
        Boari flap in, 1264
        ileal ureteral substitution in, 1266-1267
        psoas hitch in, 1261
    for urinary diversion, 2523-2527, 2524f-2526f
    for vesicovaginal fistula, 2512, 2513f
    hand-assist devices in, 171-173, 186-187, 186f
    historical aspects of, 171-174
    in children, 3914-3928
        anesthetic issues in, 3917-3918
        antireflux, 3926-3927
        complications of
            operative, 3919
            related to access, 3918-3919
        for bladder reconstruction, 3924-3926,
            3925f
        indications for, 3916
        instruments for, 3916-3917
        perivesical, 3927
        renal, 3919-3924. See also Renal surgery,
            laparoscopic, in children.
        robotic-assisted, 3927-3928, 3928f
        vaginoplasty as, 3927
    informed consent for, 175
    initial incision in, procedures prior to, 178
    instrumentation in, 189-197
        for aspiration and irrigation, 196
        for grasping and blunt dissection, 190-191,
            191f
        for incising and hemostasis, 191-193
        for morcellation, 195-196
        for retraction, 196-197, 197f
        for specimen entrapment, 195, 196f
        for stapling and clipping, 194-195, 194f
        for suturing and tissue anastomosis, 193-
            194
        for visualization, 189-190
        pediatric, 3916-3917
    of seminal vesicles, 1120, 1122-1125
        patient preparation for, 1120

Laparoscopic surgery (Continued)
    potential complications of, 1124-1125
    retroperitoneal approach to, 1124
    robotic approach to, 1124
    transperitoneal approach to, 1120, 1122-
        1124, 1124f
    operating room setup for, 176, 176t
    patient draping for, 176
    patient positioning for, 176
    patient selection for, 174-175
    physiologic consideration(s) in, 199-203
        acid-base metabolic effects of
            pneumoperitoneum as, 201-202
        cardiovascular effects of
            pneumoperitoneum as, 200, 200t
        choice of insufflant as, 199-200
        choice of pneumoperitoneum pressure as,
            200, 200t
        hemodynamic effects as, 202
        hormonal effects as, 202
        immunologic effects as, 202-203
        metabolic effects as, 202
        renal effects of pneumoperitoneum as,
            201
        respiratory effects of pneumoperitoneum
            as, 200-201
    postoperative management in, 198-199
    preoperative management in, 174-176
    procedures in, 178-198
    radiologic procedures prior to, 176
    retroperitoneal approach to, 173
    robotic-assisted, 173-174
    skin closure in, 198
    standard, 171-173
    strategic placement of team and equipment
        for, 177-178, 177f
    transperitoneal, 171-173
        vs. extraperitoneal pelvic surgery, 220
        vs. retroperitoneoscopy, 219
    transperitoneal access in, 178-181
    troubleshooting in, 203-219, 203t
    ureteral injuries due to, 1283-1284
        in children, 3937
Laparoscopic ureteral reimplantation, 2506-
    2507, 2507f, 2508f
Laparoscopic ureterocalicostomy, for
    ureteropelvic junction obstruction, 1253
Laparoscopic ureterolithotomy, for ureteral
    calculi, 1455
Laparoscopic ureterolysis, for retroperitoneal
    fibrosis, 1273
Laparoscopic ureteroneocystostomy, for ureteral
    stricture, 1261
Laparoscopic ureteronephrectomy, proximal,
    1665-1666, 1666f
Laparoscopic ureteroureterostomy, for ureteral
    stricture, 1261
Laparoscopic varicocelectomy, 659-661, 661f,
    1125-1126
    indications for, 1125
    results of, 1126
    technique of, 1125-1126, 1126f
Lapdisc device, hand-assist, 186-187, 186f
Lapides classification, of voiding dysfunction,
    1982-1983, 1982t
Laplace equation, 1908, 1912, 1924, 1924f
Laser(s). See also specific laser.
    in laparoscopy, 192
    in treatment of benign prostatic hyperplasia,
        2820-2821
Laser lithotripsy, 1460-1462, 1513-1514
    advantages and disadvantages of, 1461,
        1461t
    technique of, 1461-1462, 1462t

Laser therapy
  coagulative, for renal tumors, 1817
  for benign prostatic hyperplasia,
      2820-2829
    methods of delivery in, 2821
    techniques of, 2821-2823
      clinical results of, 2823-2828
    types of lasers used in, 2820-2821
    with contact laser, 2822-2823
      clinical results of, 2826
    with holmium laser resection, 2823,
        2824f
      clinical results of, 2827-2828
    with interstitial laser, 2823
      clinical results of, 2826-2827
    with photoselective KTP laser, 2828
    with side-firing laser, 2822
      clinical results of, 2824-2826
  for bladder cancer, non–muscle-invasive,
      2453-2454
  for cutaneous diseases, of external genitalia,
      407
  for hypospadias, 3719
  for penile cancer, 973, 993-994
  for urethral stricture, 1061-1062
Latex catheters, 161-162, 162f
Latissimus dorsi muscle, 3, 6f, 7f, 8, 9t
Latzko procedure, in vesicovaginal fistula repair,
    2336
Laxative abuse, stone formation associated with,
    1389, 1426
Lazy bladder syndrome, 3612
Le Bag (ileocolonic) pouch, for orthotopic
    urinary diversion, 2641-2642, 2642f
Le Duc technique, of small bowel anastomosis,
    2559, 2559f
Leadbetter and Clarke technique, of
    ureterocolonic anastomosis, 2555-2556,
    2556f
Leak point pressures
  abdominal, 2006, 2006f
    in incontinence, 2066, 2066f
    controversies/pitfalls in, 2006-2007
  detrusor, 2005-2006, 2005f
    in incontinence, 2067, 2067f
  recording of, 2006
    volume at, 2006-2007
  vaginal wall prolapse and, 2007
  Valsalva, measurement of, 2240-2242, 2241f,
    2242f
Leiomyoma
  renal, 1582
  uterine, ureteral obstruction due to, 1221
  vaginal, vs. urethral diverticula, 2382-2383,
    2382f
Leiomyomatosis, hereditary, renal cell carcinoma
    and, 1584t, 1587-1588
Leiomyosarcoma
  of bladder, 2445
  of kidney, 1633, 1633f
  of prostate, 2881
  of testicular adnexa, 934
Length-tension relationships, in bladder smooth
    muscle, 1931
Lentigo simplex, of male genitalia, 433, 434f
Leptin, prostate cancer and, epidemiologic
    studies of, 2861
Lesch-Nyhan syndrome, xanthine stone
    formation associated with, 1387
Leucine aminopeptidase, in prostate, 2724
Leukemia
  acute lymphoblastic, renal stones associated
      with, 3224
  priapism associated with, 840

Leukemia (Continued)
  renal, 1634-1635
  testicular, 930-931
    in children, 3905
Leukocyte(s)
  activation of, integrins in, 492-493, 493t
  in urinary sediment, 106, 106f, 107f
  staining of, in semen, 625
  vs. round cells, 625
Leukocyte esterase activity, in urinalysis, 104-105
Leukocyte esterase test, for pediatric urinary
    tract infection, 3244, 3244t
Leukoplakia
  of penis, 961
  vesical, 2418
Leukotriene D4 receptor antagonist, for painful
    bladder syndrome/interstitial cystitis, 360t,
    361
Leuprolide, for priapism, 846t
Levator ani muscle, 44, 46f, 2191, 2191f
  innervation of, 2192
  palpation of, 2207
Levator plate, 44, 2192
Levofloxacin
  for gonorrhea, 379
  for prostatitis, 320t, 321, 327t
Lewis blood group antigens
  in bladder cancer, 2428
  influence of, on urinary tract infections, 3237
Lewy bodies, in Parkinson's disease, 2018
Leydig cell(s), 3137
  aplasia of, 3821
  as source of androgens, 2685
  fetal, 580
  microencapsulated, for testosterone
      supplementation, 569, 569f
  radioresistance of, 644
  stereogenesis in, 584
    control of, 584-585, 586f
Leydig cell tumor(s), 637, 925-927
  clinical presentation of, 926-927, 926t
  in children, 3904
  prognosis of, 927
  Reinke's crystals in, 3901
  treatment of, 926t, 927
LH (luteinizing hormone), evaluation of, in
    male infertility, 618-619, 618t
LHRH. See Luteinizing hormone–releasing
    hormone (LHRH) entries.
Libido
  in exstrophy patients, 3552
  loss of
    androgen deprivation therapy causing, 3090
    patient history of, 86-87
Lichen nitidus, involving male genitalia, 413
Lichen planus, 884
  involving male genitalia, 412-413, 412f
Lichen sclerosus et atrophicus, 884, 1041-1042,
    1042f
  after hypospadias repair, 3739
  of male genitalia, 413-414, 413f
  of penis, 960
Licorice ingestion, hypertension due to, 1849
Liddle's syndrome, 1849
Lidocaine
  for painful bladder syndrome/interstitial
      cystitis, 362t, 364
  topical, for premature ejaculation, 786, 786t
Life cycle
  of Schistosoma haematobium, 448-449, 448f
  of Wuchereria bancrofti, 455
Life-expectancy, orthotopic urinary diversion
    and, 2616-2617
Lifestyle changes, for erectile dysfunction, 769

Lifestyle interventions, in behavioral therapy for
    incontinence, 2129
Li-Fraumeni syndrome, 516t
Ligament(s). See specific ligament, e.g.,
    Sacrospinous ligament.
Ligand(s)
  as cancer therapy targets, 530
  G protein–coupled, cancer and, 537-538
Ligand-binding domain, of androgen receptors,
    2699
Light sources, in laparoscopic surgery, 190
Limb contractures, affecting renal calculi
    surgery, 1448
Lindane
  for pediculosis pubis, 384
  for scabies, 383
Linear IgA bullous dermatosis, of male genitalia,
    416, 416f
Lipid(s), in prostatic secretions, 2718
Lipid abnormalities, in acute renal failure, 1338
Lipoma, renal, 1582
Lipomatosis, pelvic, ureteral obstruction due to,
    1218-1219, 1218f, 1219f
Lipomeningocele, 3641-3644
  diagnosis of, 3641, 3641t, 3642f
  findings in, 3641, 3643f
  imaging of, 3643-3644, 3644f
  pathogenesis of, 3641, 3643, 3643f
  treatment of, 3644
Liposarcoma, renal, 1634
Lithiasis
  renal. See Renal calculi.
  ureteral. See Ureteral calculi.
  urinary. See Urinary calculi.
Lithotripsy
  ballistic, 1462-1463, 1462f, 1463t
  electrohydraulic, 1458-1460, 1459f
    advantages and disadvantages of, 1459-1460
    technique of, 1460
  endoscopic, for calculi in augmentations and
      urinary diversions, 2669-2670
  laser, 1460-1462
    advantages and disadvantages of, 1461,
        1461t
    technique of, 1461-1462, 1462t
  shockwave. See Shockwave lithotripsy.
  ultrasonic, 1463-1465, 1464f
    advantages and disadvantages of, 1464
    technique of, 1464-1465
Lithotriptors
  comparisons of, 1472-1474, 1472f, 1473t,
      1474f
  flexible, 1458-1462
  intracorporeal, 1458-1465
    for ureteroscopy, 1511t, 1513-1514
  rigid, 1462-1465
Liver cirrhosis, benign prostatic hyperplasia and,
    2745
Liver dysfunction, in renal cell carcinoma, 1597t,
    1598
Liver injury
  adrenal surgery causing, 1885t, 1886
  percutaneous nephrolithotomy causing,
      1489
  percutaneous nephrostomy causing, 1548
Living donor(s), for renal transplantation, 1296.
    See also under Renal transplantation.
Lomefloxacin, for prostatitis, 320t
Loop diuretics. See also Diuretics.
  for acute renal failure, 1336
Loop end ileostomy, 2553, 2553f
Loop of Henle, 31, 33f. See also Nephron(s).
  anatomy of, 1141, 1142f
  function of, 1141-1144, 1143f, 1144f

Loopography, 114, 116, 117f
Loss of libido
  androgen deprivation therapy causing, 3090
  patient history of, 86-87
Louse (lice), crab, 383-384, 425, 425f
Lower extremity(ies), lymphedema of, penile
    cancer and, 976, 976f
Lower motor neuron lesions, voiding
    dysfunction after, classification of, 1983-
    1984, 1983t
Lower urinary tract. See also Urinary tract
    entries.
  calculi in, 2663-2673
    bladder, 2663-2670. See also Bladder.
    prostatic, 2670
    seminal vesicle, 2670
    urethral, 2670-2672. See also Urethral
      calculi.
  dysfunction of
    in pelvic organ prolapse, 2202-2204,
      2203t
    incontinence due to, in elderly, 2309-2310
    neurologic injury causing, 2011-2044. See
      also Voiding dysfunction,
      neurogenic/neuropathic.
    neuropathic, in children, 3625-3653
      central nervous system insults and, 3648-
        3653
      neurospinal dysraphisms and, 3628-3648
      urodynamic evaluation of, 3625-3628
    non-neuropathic, in children, 3604-3624.
      See also Urethral sphincter,
      dysfunction of.
      classification of, 3609-3611, 3610f
      epidemiology of, 3609
      evaluation of, 3614-3618
      management of, 3618-3620
      prevalence of, 3609
  endoscopic procedures in, antibiotic
    prophylaxis for, 252
  evaluation of
    cytologic examination and culture in, 314-
      315, 314f, 315f
    physical examination in, 312-314
  function of
    in cerebral palsy, 3650t
    normal, 1973-1974
    two-phase concept of, 1973-1974. See also
      Micturition cycle.
    mechanisms underlying, 1974-1976
  injury to, posterior urethral valves causing,
    3585-3586, 3586f
  irritative symptoms of, 84
  neural control of, 1937-1948
  obstructive symptoms of, 84-86, 85t
  peripheral nervous system of, 1937-1939,
    1938f
    afferent pathways in, 1938-1939, 1938f,
      1939t
    parasympathetic pathways in, 1938
    somatic pathways in, 1938
    sympathetic pathways in, 1938
  reflex circuitry in, 1939-1943, 1940f, 1940t,
    1941f. See also Micturition reflex.
  urodynamic evaluation of, 1986-2009. See also
    Urodynamic evaluation.
L-shaped kidney, 3284f, 3285
Lumbar artery, 11f, 13, 13t
Lumbar epidural blockade, for painful bladder
    syndrome/interstitial cystitis, 365
Lumbar vein, 11f, 13, 14f
  bleeding from, in radical nephrectomy, 1710-
    1712, 1713f
Lumbodorsal fascia, 3, 8, 8f

Lumbodorsal incisions, in adrenal surgery, 1873,
    1874f
Lumbosacral plexus, 17-18, 17f, 52-53, 53f, 53t
  branches of, 19t
Lumbosacral trunk, 53, 53t
Lumbotomy, posterior, for pediatric
    ureteropelvic junction obstruction, 3374
Lumbotomy incisions, dorsal, in renal surgery,
    1695, 1696f
Lump kidney, 3284f, 3285
Lung(s). See Pulmonary entries.
Lupus nephritis, in children, 3227
Luteal phase, evaluation of, in female fertility,
    612
Luteinizing hormone (LH), evaluation of, in
    male infertility, 618-619, 618t
Luteinizing hormone (LH) receptor
    abnormality, 3821
Luteinizing hormone–releasing hormone
    (LHRH)
  for cryptorchidism, 3775-3776
  in testosterone production, 585, 586f
  inhibition of, 3087-3088
  secretion of, 578
  structure of, 3087t
  therapy with, for male infertility, 636
  urinary and plasma levels of, in female
    fertility, 612
Luteinizing hormone–releasing hormone
    (LHRH) agonists, for prostate cancer, 3087,
    3087t
Luteinizing hormone–releasing hormone
    (LHRH) antagonists, for prostate cancer,
    3087-3087
17,20-Lyase deficiency, 3822
Lycopene, for prostate cancer, chemopreventive,
    2871
Lyme disease, voiding dysfunction in, 2035
Lymph node(s)
  iliac, 52, 52f
    urothelial tumor spread to, 1641
  inguinal. See Inguinal lymph nodes.
  pelvic
    laparoscopic dissection of, 1779, 2521,
      2523f
    urothelial tumor spread to, 1641
  sentinel, biopsy of, in penile cancer, 979,
    1003-1005, 1004f
Lymph node metastasis
  of bladder cancer, 2426
  of penile cancer, prediction of, 978-979, 979t
  of prostate cancer, immediate vs. delayed
    hormone therapy for, 3096-3097, 3096f
Lymphadenectomy
  for bladder cancer, 2440-2441
    invasive, radical cystectomy with, 2472
  in retroperitoneal lymph node dissection,
    943-944, 944f
    left-sided, 947
    right-sided, 946
  inguinal, for penile cancer, 974-984. See also
    Inguinal lymphadenectomy, for penile
    cancer.
  pelvic. See Pelvic lymphadenectomy.
  radical nephroureterectomy with, 1662
Lymphangiography, in penile cancer, 970
Lymphangitis, sclerosing, of male genitalia, 431
Lymphatic mapping, intraoperative, in penile
    cancer, 980-981
Lymphatic vessels
  of bladder, 60
  of kidneys, 30-31, 31f
  of pelvis, 52, 52f
  of penis, 1035

Lymphatic vessels (Continued)
  of perineum, 73
  of retroperitoneum, 14, 15f
  of testes, 14
  of ureters, 37
Lymphedema
  genital, 3756-4175
  in radiation-induced penile injury, 1053
  lower extremity, penile cancer and, 976,
    976f
Lymphocele(s)
  after laparoscopy, 218-219
  after renal transplantation, 1319-1320
Lymphocyte(s), 476-477
  B. See B cell(s).
  circulating, 476
  NK. See Natural killer cell(s).
  T. See T cell(s).
  tolerance of
    central, 490-491
    clonal anergy in, 491
    development of, 490-492
    peripheral, 491-492
    regulatory T cells in, 491-492
  trafficking of, adhesion molecules in, 492-494,
    493f, 493t
Lymphogranuloma venereum, 420f
  diagnosis of, 377-378, 377f, 378f
  treatment of, 378
Lymphoid tissue, 475, 475f
  in HIV infection, 391-392
  role of, 392
Lymphoma
  of bladder, 2445
  of kidney, 1634-1635, 1634t
  of prostate, 2881-2882
    transrectal ultrasonography of, 2887
  of seminal vesicles, imaging of, 1112, 1112f
  of testes, 930, 932t
    in children, 3905
Lymphoreticular malignant neoplasm, of penis,
    990
Lymphovascular invasion, of urothelial tumors,
    1643-1644
Lynch syndrome. See Colorectal cancer,
    hereditary nonpolyposis.

M

Mackie-Stephens bud theory, of renal dysplasia,
    3309
Macrocysts
  in autosomal dominant polycystic kidney
    disease, 3323
  in autosomal recessive polycystic kidney
    disease, 3317
  in multicystic dysplastic kidney, 3336, 3337f
Macroglossia, in children, 3208
Macrophage(s), 477
  in postinfection prostatic fluid, 109, 109f
  lipid-laden, in xanthogranulomatous
    pyelonephritis, 283
Macroplastique injections, for incontinence,
    2275
Macula densa, in renin-angiotensin-aldosterone
    system, 1162
Magnesium
  metabolism of, 1372
  renal reabsorption of
    in distal tubules, 1144
    in loop of Henle, 1142
    in proximal convoluted tubules, 1141
Magnesium gluconate, for hyperoxaluria, 1422
Magnesium hydroxide, for hypomagnesiuric
    calcium nephrolithiasis, 1423-1424

Magnesium oxide, for hypomagnesiuric calcium nephrolithiasis, 1423-1424

Magnetic resonance angiography (MRA), 139-138
of penis, 763
of renovascular hypertension, 1171-1172

Magnetic resonance imaging (MRI), 135-139
in percutaneous procedures, 1532-1533
of adrenal carcinoma, 1835-1836, 1836f
of adrenals, 135, 137f
of autosomal dominant polycystic kidney disease, 3323, 3324f
of autosomal recessive polycystic kidney disease, 3318f
of bladder, 135, 137f
of bladder cancer, 2440
invasive, 2469
of brain
during sexual arousal, 726-727
for female sexual health problems, 874
of ectopic ureter, 3392-3393
of genitourinary tuberculosis, 443
of germ cell tumors, 905
of kidneys, 135, 136f
of lipomeningocele, 3643, 3644f
of myelomeningocele, 3634, 3635f
of neuroblastoma, 3872, 3872f, 3873f
of pelvic organ prolapse, 2210-2211, 2211f
of penile cancer, 970
of pheochromocytoma, 1860f, 1863, 1864f, 1865f
of prostate, 135, 138, 138f, 139f
of prostate cancer
localized vs. metastatic, 3072
locally advanced, 3055, 3055f
of renal cell carcinoma, 1602
of renal cysts, 3345, 3347f
of renal tumors, 1571, 1573f
of retroperitoneal fibrosis, 1216, 1217f
of sacral agenesis, 3645, 3646f
of seminal vesicles, 1112-1113, 1113f
of tumor involvement of inferior vena cava, 1620, 1620f
of ureteropelvic junction obstruction, in children, 3367-3368, 3368f, 3369f
of urethra, 138
of urethral diverticula, 2381-2382, 2381f, 2382f
of urinary tract infections, 243
in children, 3256
of Wilms' tumor, 3891, 3891f, 3895f

Magnetic resonance urography (MRU), 138, 139f
of megaureter, 4374, 4374f
of pediatric patient, 3214, 3214f
of ureteral obstruction, 1211

Magnetic stimulation
for incontinence, 2136
noninvasive, 2160

Mainz ileocecocystoplasty, in children, 3675, 3676f

Mainz pouch, for orthotopic urinary diversion, 2641, 2643f

Mainz pouch I, for continent urinary diversion, 2591, 2593, 2595-2596
postoperative care in, 2595-2596, 2596f-2599f
procedure in, 2593, 2594f, 2595

Mainz pouch II
for continent urinary diversion, with augmented valved rectum, 2584, 2586
in laparoscopic-assisted urinary diversion, 2524, 2527

Major histocompatibility complex (MHC)
in allograft rejection, 1314-1315, 1315f, 1315t
in allorecognition, 481
in immune response, 479, 479f

Malacoplakia
clinical presentation of, 284-285
differential diagnosis of, 285
management of, 285
pathogenesis of, 283-284
pathology of, 284, 284f
radiologic findings in, 285

*Malassezia furfur*, autoimmune response to, seborrheic dermatitis and, 415

Male Sexual Function Scale, 752, 754f-755f

Malecot catheter, 162, 162f

Malecot tubes, for percutaneous nephrostomy, 1558

Malignancy. *See* Cancer; *specific neoplasm.*

Malignant melanoma, of bladder, 2445

Malleable dilators, 1542, 1542f

Malnutrition
due to conduit urinary diversion, 2575
in acute renal failure, 1337-1338
in chronic renal failure, 1353

Malposition, of colon, in renal ectopia, 3281

Malrotation, of kidney, 3291-3292, 3292f, 3293f

Mannitol, for acute renal failure, 1336

Manual compression, for bladder emptying disorders, 2298

MAO (monoamine oxidase) inhibitors, erectile dysfunction caused by, 744

Marsden symptoms scores, 2816, 2819

Marsden-Iversen score, 2819

Marshall test, for stress incontinence, 2206, 2313

Marshall-Marchetti-Krantz procedure
for female incontinence, 2170, 2171f
results of, 2175
technique of, 2174-2175, 2176f
vs. Burch colposuspension and paravaginal repair, 2184-2185

Martius flap. *See also* Flap(s).
in urethrovaginal fistula repair, 2349, 2350f
in vesicovaginal fistula repair, 2338-2339, 2338f

Massachusetts Male Aging Study (MMAS)
of erectile dysfunction, 738, 765
of late-onset hypogonadism, 854

Massage therapy, for prostatitis, 323-324

Mast cells, involvement of, in painful bladder syndrome/interstitial cystitis, 341-343, 342f

Maternal anemia, bacteriuria and, 291-292

Mathieu hypospadias repair, 3725, 3726f-3727f

Matrix (matrices)
extracellular. *See* Extracellular matrix.
for bladder regeneration, 559-560
nonfibrillar, of bladder wall, 1932
nuclear, 511
of urinary stones, 1371

Matrix calculi, 1388

Matrix metalloproteinases
in Peyronie's disease, 821-822
in ureteral obstruction, 1204
in urothelial tumors, 2424-2425

Mayer-Rokitansky-Küster-Hauser syndrome
atypical form of, 3834
genital anomalies associated with, 3833-3834
typical form of, 3834

McIndoe technique, in creation of neovagina, 3835-3836, 3835f

*MCKD1* gene, in medullary cystic disease, 3326

*MCKD2* gene, in medullary cystic disease, 3326

Meares-Stamey four-hour glass test, for prostatitis, 314, 314f

Meatal stenosis
after circumcision, 3215, 3749-3750
after hypospadias repair, 3739

Meatoplasty
for meatal stenosis, after circumcision, 3749-3750
in hypospadias repair, 3718

Meatoplasty and glanuloplasty (MAGPI) technique, of hypospadias repair, 3722, 3723f

Meatotomy, as outpatient procedure, 3215

Mechanical compression, nonsurgical, for bladder filling/storage disorders, 2291-2292

Mechanical failure
of artificial sphincter, 2401
rates of, for penile prosthesis, 800, 800t

Mechanical preparation, of bowel, for urinary tract reconstruction, 2537-2538, 2537t

Mechanical properties, of ureteral smooth muscle, 1902-1903
force-length relations in, 1902-1903, 1902f, 1903f
force-velocity relations in, 1903, 1903f
pressure-length-diameter relations in, 1903

Meconium, passage of, 3210

Medial fibroplasia, of renal artery, 1157t, 1159-1160, 1160f

Mediastinal resection, postchemotherapy, testicular tumors and, 955

Medical history, of erectile dysfunction, 752, 755, 755t

Medical Therapy of Prostatic Symptoms (MTOPS), 2754

Medical Therapy of Prostatic Symptoms (MOPS) study, of combination therapy for benign prostatic hyperplasia, 2795-2797

Medication regimen change, for erectile dysfunction, 769-770

Medullary carcinoma, renal, 1596

Medullary cystic disease, 3326-3328, 3327f, 3328f. *See also* Juvenile nephronophthisis/medullary cystic disease complex.
genetics of, 3326, 3326t
in chronic renal failure, 1346

Medullary fibroma, renal, 1582

Medullary sponge kidney, 3348-3350
asymptomatic, 3349
characteristics of, 3314t
clinical features of, 3349
diagnosis of, 3350
histopathology of, 3349-3350
imaging of, 3349f, 3350
stone formation associated with, 1390-1391, 3349
treatment and prognosis of, 3350

Megacalycosis, 3299-3301, 3300f
definition of, 3299
of renal calyces, 3299-3301, 3300f

Megacystis-megaureter association
postnatal evaluation and management of, 3191
vesicoureteral reflux in, 4344

Megacystitis, congenital, antenatal detection of, 3574, 3575f

Megalourethra, in prune-belly syndrome, 3485, 3485f
surgical repair of, 3491, 3492f

Megameatus intact prepuce (MIP) variant, in hypospadias, 3703, 3704f
repair of, 3725

Megaprepuce, 3749f, 3756

Megathura crenulata, for bladder cancer, non–muscle-invasive, 2458

Megaureter(s), 4367-4381. *See also* Ureter(s).
  adult, 4380-4381
  classification of, 4367, 4368f
  clinical findings in, 4367-4371
  definition of, 4367
  evaluation of, 4372-4374, 4373f, 4374f
  in duplex system, management of, 4380
  in utero diagnosis of, 4368
  magnetic resonance urography of, 3214, 3214f
  management of
    recommendations in, 4374-4375
    surgical options in, 4377, 4377f
    surgical technique(s) in, 4378f-4380f, 4379
      complications of, 4380
      for dilated duplex ureter, 4380
      Kalicinski plication in, 4379, 4380f
      results of, 4380
      Starr plication in, 4379, 4379f
      tapering in, 4379, 4379f
  nonobstructive nonrefluxing
    clinical correlates of, 4375, 4376f, 4377
    primary, 4371-4372, 4372f
      management of, 4375
    secondary, 4372
  obstructive
    primary, 4368-4369, 4369f-4371f
    secondary, 4369-4370
  pathophysiology of, 4368
  refluxing
    obstructive, 4371
      management of, 4375
    primary, 4370-4371
      management of, 4374
    secondary, 4370-4371
      management of, 4375
Megavitamins. *See also* Vitamin *entries.*
  in prevention of bladder cancer, 2443, 2467
Megestrol acetate, for hot flashes, 3090
Meiosis, in spermatogenesis, 593, 593f
Melanocortin(s), in male sexual function, 730
Melanocortin-receptor agonists, for erectile
    dysfunction, 782-783
Melanoma
  adoptive cell therapy for, 499
  of male genitalia, 429
  of penis, 989
Melatonin, affected by aging, 856t, 857
Membrane electrical properties, of bladder
    smooth muscle, 1927-1928
Membranoproliferative glomerulonephritis, in
    chronic renal failure, 1345-1346
Membranous urethra, 63-64, 64f, 1030, 1030f
Memokath stent, 2805
Memory B cell(s). *See also* B cell(s).
  development of, 488
Memory T cell(s). *See also* T cell(s).
  development of, 488
Memotherm permanent stent, for benign
    prostatic hyperplasia, 2809
MEN. *See* Multiple endocrine neoplasia (MEN).
Meningocele
  Arnold-Chiari malformation associated with,
    3630
  closure of, 3629-3630
  definition of, 3629
Menopause
  incontinence associated with, 2189
  pelvic organ prolapse associated with, 2189
Menstrual history, in evaluation of fertility, 612
Mentor Titan three-piece inflatable penile
    prosthesis, 788, 789f, 789t
α-Mercaptopropionylglycine, for cystinuria,
    1424

Meropenem, for pediatric urinary tract
    infections, 3248t
MESA (microsurgical epididymal sperm
    aspiration), 652, 700, 703f-704f
Mesenchymal tumor, of prostate, 2881
  transrectal ultrasonography of, 2887
Mesenchyme, metanephric
  ureteric bud interaction with, 3125, 3125f
  ureteric bud outgrowth toward, 3127, 3129,
    3129f
Mesenteric artery
  inferior, 11f, 13, 13t
  superior, 11f, 13, 13t
Mesenteric blood flow, with
    pneumoperitoneum, 201
Mesenterorenal bypass, 1744-1745, 1744f
Mesoblastic nephroma, congenital, 3898-3899
Mesonephric duct, 3384-3385, 3385f
  persistence of, 3798
Mesonephric tubules, differentiation of, 3124
Mesonephros, 3149, 3150f
Mesothelioma
  of testes, 929
  of testicular adnexa, 932
*MET* oncogene, 513
  in renal cell carcinoma, 1591
Metabolic acidosis, 1153, 1153t
  after augmentation cystoplasty, 3681-3682
Metabolic alkalosis, 1154, 1154t
Metabolic evaluation, in urinary lithiasis
  abbreviated protocol for, 1395-1397, 1395t,
    1396f, 1397f, 1397t
  extensive ambulatory, 1398-1399, 1399t
  fast and calcium load test for, 1398-1399
  patient selection for, 1393-1394, 1395t
  simplified, 1399-1400, 1400f, 1401f
Metabolism, laparoscopic surgery and, 202
Metal coaxial dilators, 1543
Metanephric adenofibroma, in children,
    3899
Metanephric adenoma, 1576, 1576f
Metanephric mesenchyme
  ureteric bud interaction with, 3125, 3125f
  ureteric bud outgrowth toward, 3127, 3129,
    3129f
Metanephros, 3149
  development of, 3124-3126, 3125f, 3126f
Metaphase, in mitosis, 2712
Metaplasia, urothelial, 1642
Metastasectomy, salvage, for renal cell
    carcinoma, 1632
Metastasis
  bone, in prostate cancer, palliative therapy for,
    3028-3029, 3113-3114
  locally advanced or asymptomatic, immediate
    vs. delayed hormone therapy for, 3097-
    3098, 3097f
  lymph node, immediate vs. delayed hormone
    therapy for, 3096-3097, 3096f
  of adrenal cancer, 1840, 1840f
  of bladder cancer, 2426
    chemotherapy for
      newer agents in, 2477-2478
      systemic, 2476-2477
    molecular markers in, 2478
    palliative therapy for, 2478
    salvage cystectomy for, 2478
  of neuroblastoma, 3871-3872
  of penile cancer, 990-991
    nodal
      bulky adenopathy and, 984f, 994
      prediction of, 978-979, 979t
      prognostic significance of, 974, 975t, 976t
  of renal cancer, 1635

Metastasis *(Continued)*
  of renal cell carcinoma, treatment of, 1623-
    1632. *See also* Renal cell carcinoma,
    metastatic, treatment of.
  of testicular cancer, 931
  of urothelial carcinoma, 1640, 2426
  rising PSA levels and
    radiographic tests for, 3071-3072
    risk for development of, 3073, 3075
    vs. local disease, 3073
Methotrexate
  for painful bladder syndrome/interstitial
    cystitis, 360t, 361
  for penile cancer, 987
Methoxamine, for stress incontinence, 2111
7α-Methyl-19-nortestosterone, for late-onset
    hypogonadism, 858
α-Methylacyl-coenzyme A racemase
  in diagnosis of oncology, 548, 549
  in prostate cancer, 2866-2867, 2909
*N*-Methyl-D-aspartate receptors, in painful
    bladder syndrome/interstitial cystitis, 346
α-Methylparatyrosine, preoperative, for
    pheochromocytoma, 1866
Methylprednisolone, for prostatitis, clinical trial
    data on, 322
Metoclopramide, to facilitate bladder emptying,
    2116
Metronidazole
  for bacterial vaginosis, 384
  for trichomoniasis, 380
  neomycin with, in antibiotic bowel
    preparation, 2538t
MHC. *See* Major histocompatibility complex
    (MHC).
Mice, knockout, 546
  conditional, 547
Miconazole, for funguria, 299
Microarray technology, in diagnosis of oncology,
    549
Microballoons, implantable
  for bladder filling/storage disorders, 2292
  for incontinence, 2286-2287
Microbiology, of genitourinary tuberculosis, 440
Microcystic disease, cortical, 3329
Microlithiasis, testicular, in children, 3905
Microorganisms, urinary, in vesicoureteral
    reflux, requirement for, 4337
Micropenis, 748, 3751-3754, 3752f
  androgen therapy for, 3753
  causes of, 3752-3753
  etiology of, 3753t
  gender reassignment and, 3753
  long-term retrospective study of, 3753-3754
Microsatellite repeats
  analyses of, in bladder cancer, 2435
  in polymorphism, 519-520, 520f
Microseminoprotein, 2723-2724
Microsurgical epididymal sperm aspiration
    (MESA), 652, 700, 703f-704f
Microvascular autotransplantation, of testes,
    3787
Microwave ablation, for renal tumors, 1816-1817
Microwave hyperthermia, for prostatitis, 324
Microwave therapy, transurethral. *See*
    Transurethral microwave therapy (TUMT).
Micturition. *See also* Voiding *entries.*
  decreased force of, 84
  incidence of, during sleep states, 3608, 3608f
  initiation of, 2049-2050
  neural control of, 1922, 1923f, 1939-1943,
    1940f, 1940t, 1941f, 3608-3609
  normal, evolution of, 3607-3609, 3608f
  painful, 84

Micturition (Continued)
physiology of, 2049-2053, 2049f
neural pathways in, 2049-2050, 2050f
sphincter mechanism and anatomy in, 2050-2053
in men, 2053
in women, 2050-2053, 2051f, 2052f
pontine control center for, 1946
pressure-flow studies of, 1995-2000. See also Pressure-flow micturition studies.
Micturition cycle
bladder emptying/voiding in, 1941-1943, 1944f, 1945f
bladder filling/urine storage in, 1939-1941, 1940t, 1942f, 1943f
phases of, 1974-1976
process in, 1973
Micturition diary, 2062
Micturition reflex
cholinergic mechanisms in, 1965
dopaminergic mechanisms in, 1965
GABAergic mechanisms in, 1965
glutamatergic mechanisms in, 1962, 1964-1965, 1964f
modulation of, central pathways in, 1946-1947
neonatal, re-emergence of, 1948
promotion or initiation of, 2299
regulation of, pontine control center in, supraspinal mechanisms of, 1964-1966, 1964f
serotonergic pathways in, 1963
spinal pathways in, 1944-1946
drugs affecting, 1962-1964
supraspinal pathways in, 1944-1946
Micturitional urethral pressure profilometry, 2007-2008
Midbrain, involved in sexual function, 726t
Middle procedure, in hypospadias repair, 3725-3729
onlay techniques for, 3725-3726, 3728, 3728f-3731f
tubularization techniques for, 3729
Midodrine, for stress incontinence, 2111
Midurethral sling
tension-free transvaginal taping approach in, 2251-2266. See also Vaginal tape procedure, tension-free.
transobturator approach in, 2266-2271. See also Transobturator sling.
Migrant bladder calculi, 2663
Minimally invasive continent diversion, in continent urinary diversion, 2606-2607
Minimally invasive therapy(ies). See also Laparoscopic entries.
for benign prostatic hyperplasia, 2803-2844
intraprostatic stents in, 2804-2809
permanent, 2807-2809
Memotherm, 2809
UroLume, 2808-2809
temporary, 2804-2807
biodegradable, 2807
polyurethane, 2806-2807, 2807f
spiral, 2804-2806
lasers in, 2820-2831. See also Laser therapy.
rotoresection of prostate in, 2843
transurethral ethanol ablation of prostate in, 2843
transurethral incision of prostate in, 2841-2842, 2842t
clinical efficacy of, 2841
comparative studies of, 2841-2842, 2842t
complications of, 2841
technique of, 2841, 2841f

Minimally invasive therapy(ies) (Continued)
transurethral microwave therapy in, 2813-2820. See also Transurethral microwave therapy (TUMT).
transurethral needle ablation of prostate in, 2809-2813. See also Transurethral needle ablation (TUNA), of prostate.
transurethral resection of prostate in, 2829-2838. See also Transurethral resection of prostate (TURP).
transurethral vaporization of prostate in, 2838-2841
clinical experience with, 2839-2840
comparative studies in, 2840
electrode design in, 2839
mechanism of action of, 2839
vaporization-resection in, 2840
water-induced thermotherapy in, 2842
for prostate cancer, vs. cryotherapy, 3045-3047
for prostatitis, 324-325
for ureteropelvic junction obstruction, in children, 3374-3376
Mini-perc and nondilated punctures, for percutaneous nephrolithotomy, 1493-1494, 1494f
MIS. See Müllerian-inhibiting substance (MIS).
Mismatch repair, of DNA, 528
Mitchell technique, of exstrophy-epispadias complex repair. See Complete primary exstrophy repair.
Mitochondrial pathway, in apoptosis, 489-490
Mitomycin C, for non–muscle-invasive bladder cancer, 2459
doxorubicin with, 2460
perioperative, 2453, 2453t
Mitosis, phases of, 2712
Mitoxantrone
for hormone-refractory prostate cancer, 3106t
multidrug regimens with, 3107t
for locally advanced cancer, before radical prostatectomy, 3061
Mitrofanoff principle
for bladder neck incompetence, after posterior urethral injury, 3944
for continent urinary diversion, 3694
Mixed antiglobulin reaction, for antisperm antibodies, 624t
Mixed epithelial stromal tumor, of kidney, 1581-1582
Mixed gonadal dysgenesis, 3811-3812
Mixed incontinence, 2046, 2084, 2084f, 2202. See also Incontinence.
tension-free vaginal taping for, 2256-2257
Mixed tumors, testicular, 896
incidence, pathology, and presentation of, 898t
MMAS (Massachusetts Male Aging Study)
of erectile dysfunction, 738, 765
of late-onset hypogonadism, 854
MMR protein, in DNA repair, 528
Mobility, restricted, in geriatric incontinence, 2307t, 2309
Modern staged reconstruction, of bladder exstrophy, 3510, 3517-3530
management of primary closure in, 3518
outcomes and results of, 3530-3534, 3531t, 3533t
Modification of diet in renal disease (MDRD) formula, in estimation of glomerular filtration rate, 1133
Mohs micrographic surgery, for penile cancer, 973, 994
Mole(s). See Nevus(i).

Molecular biology
glossary of terms in, 508t
of urothelial tumors, 1639-1640
Molecular diagnosis, in oncology, 547-550
differential display technology and PCA3 in, 548-549
epitomics in, 549
genetics in, 548
immunohistochemistry in, 547-548
microarray technology in, 549
new modalities in, 550
proteomics in, 549
Molecular epidemiology, of prostate cancer, 2860-2862
androgens in, 2860-2861
estrogens in, 2861
insulin-like growth factor-1 in, 2861
lepin in, 2861
vitamin D and calcium in, 2861-2862
Molecular genetics
in diagnosis of oncology, 548
in renal dysgenesis, 3305-3307
of prostate cancer, 2863-2867, 2864f
androgen influence in, 2863-2864
COX enzymes in, 2865
epigenetic changes in, 2865
somatic mutations in, 2865-2867
stem cells in, 2864-2865
Molecular immunology, 502-503, 504f
Molecular markers
of bladder cancer
invasive, 2478
metastatic, 2478
of urothelial tumors, 1643
Molecular mechanism, of penile smooth muscle contraction/relaxation, 731-737, 731f-733f
Molecular staging
of bladder cancer, 2441
of prostate cancer, 2930
Mollicutes, in sexually transmitted disease, 384
Molluscum contagiosum infection, 420f
diagnosis of, 382-383
in HIV patients, 396
treatment of, 382-383
Monfort technique, in management of prune-belly syndrome, 3493, 3494f-3495f, 3496f
Moniliasis. See Candidiasis.
Monoamine oxidase (MAO) inhibitors, erectile dysfunction caused by, 744
Monoclonal antibody(ies)
in tumor immunology, 500
synthesis of, 478
Monoclonality theory, of epithelial spread of urothelial tumors, 1641
Monocyte(s), 477
Monopolar electrode, 1989
Monotherapy, for HIV infection, 401
Montelukast, for painful bladder syndrome/interstitial cystitis, 360t, 361
Morbidity
in open prostatectomy, 2852
in radical perineal prostatectomy, 2983-2984
perioperative, in renal transplant recipient, 1299
Morcellation, in laparoscopy, 195-196
Mortality rates
for benign prostatic hyperplasia, 2757
for bladder cancer, 2408-2409
for Fournier's gangrene, 302
for open prostatectomy, 2852
for prostate cancer, 2854, 2856f
changes in, by country, 2914t
effect of screening on, 2857

Mortality rates *(Continued)*
  positive biopsies and, in low-risk and
    favorable intermediate-risk patients,
    3009, 3009f-3011f
  pretreatment risk groups and, 3007, 3008f
  worldwide, 2855-2856
  for renal bypass surgery, 1749
  for renal replacement therapy, 1355
  for transurethral resection of prostate, 2837-
    2838
  for urothelial tumors, 1638
  prenatal, bacteriuria and, 291
Mosquito hemostat, in vasectomy, 1099, 1100f
Motility
  intestinal, with pneumoperitoneum, 201
  sperm
    defects in, 621-623, 621f, 622f
    maturation and, 601-602, 601f
    reference range for, 618
Motor activity, in conduit urinary diversion,
  2577-2578
Motor unit action potential, neurophysiologic
  studies of, 2003-2004, 2004f
MPB chemotherapy regimen, for penile cancer,
  988t
MRA. *See* Magnetic resonance angiography
  (MRA).
MRI. *See* Magnetic resonance imaging (MRI).
MRU. *See* Magnetic resonance urography
  (MRU).
*MSR1* gene, in hereditary prostate cancer, 518
Mucinous adenocarcinoma, of prostate, 2880
Mucormycosis, 466
Mucus, production of, by intestinal segments
  used in augmentation cystoplasty, 3683
Müllerian aplasia, 3833. *See also* Mayer-
  Rokitansky-Küster-Hauser syndrome.
Müllerian duct, differentiation of, 3805, 3806f,
  3831
Müllerian duct syndrome, persistent, 3826-3827
Müllerian-inhibiting substance (MIS), 3137
  fetal secretion of, 3761-3762
  in gonadal differentiation, 2679
  in sexual differentiation, 3804, 3805, 3806f
  in testicular descent, 3145, 3767-3768
  properties of, 2706t
  Sertoli cell secretion of, 3144-3145
Multichannel urodynamic monitoring, 2004-
  2005, 2004f. *See also* Urodynamic
  evaluation.
  of incontinent patient, 2064-2068
    filling/storage phase in, 2065-2067, 2065f-
      2067f
    indications for, 2065t
    voiding/emptying phase in, 2068
Multichannel videourodynamic monitoring, of
  incontinent patient, 2068-2069, 2069f
Multicystic dysplastic kidney, 3334-3339, 3335f
  bunch of grapes appearance of, 3334, 3335f
  characteristics of, 3314t
  clinical features of, 3335-3336
  etiology of, 3334-3335
  evaluation of, 3337
  genes active in, 3334
  histopathology of, 3336-3337, 3336f
  hydronephrotic form of, 3334, 3335f
  hypertension in, 3337, 3339
  in horseshoe kidney, 3336, 3336f
  in utero diagnosis of, 3336
  involution in, 3336
  prenatal diagnosis of, 3182-3183, 3183f
    differential diagnosis in, 3183, 3184f
    postnatal evaluation and management with,
      3193-3194

Multicystic dysplastic kidney *(Continued)*
  solid cystic form of, 3334, 3335f
  treatment and prognosis of, 3337-3339, 3660t
  vesicoureteral reflux in, 4344
  Wilms' tumors associated with, 3337
Multicystic kidney tumor, benign adenomatous,
  3341
Multidrug regimens, for hormone-refractory
  prostate cancer, clinical trials of, 3106,
  3107t, 3108
Multidrug resistance (MDR) proteins, in renal
  cell carcinoma, 1589, 1626
Multilocular cyst
  benign, 3339-3343, 3340f
    characteristics of, 3314t
    clinical features of, 3340
    evaluation of, 3341, 3343
    histopathology of, 3340-3341, 3342f
    treatment of, 3343
  solitary, in children, 3899
Multimodal therapy, for metastatic renal cell
  carcinoma, 1631-1632, 1631f
Multiple endocrine neoplasia (MEN)
  pheochromocytoma associated with, 1861,
    1862t
  type I, 516t
  type II, 515t
Multiple malformation syndromes, with renal
  cysts, 3329-3339, 3330t. *See also specific
  disorder.*
Multiple punctures, for percutaneous
  nephrolithotomy, 1490-1491, 1491f
Multiple sclerosis
  sacral neuromodulation for, 2156
  voiding dysfunction in, 2012t, 2019-2020
Multiple system atrophy
  voiding dysfunction in, 2012t, 2018-2019
  vs. Parkinson's disease, 2019
Multisystemic disease, syndromes associated
  with, 3200t
Mumps orchitis, infertility due to, 643
Muscarinic receptors
  in bladder contraction, 2091-2093
  location of, 2092
  pharmacologically defined, 2092
  uropharmacology of, 1949-1951, 1949f,
    1950t
  selectivity of, 1951
Muscle(s). *See also named muscle.*
  abdominal wall
    anterior, 40, 41f, 42f
    posterior, 3, 6f-9f, 8, 9t
  pelvic, 43-44, 46f, 47f, 2191-2194, 2191f-2194f
  renal pelvic, urothelial tumor invasion of,
    1640
  smooth. *See* Smooth muscle.
  striated. *See* Striated muscle.
  urethral, 1935-1937
    fiber types of, 1936-1937
Muscle hypertrophy, in ureteral obstruction,
  1911, 1911f
Muscle precursor cells, injectable, for urinary
  incontinence, 568-569
Muscle relaxants
  affecting lower urinary tract function, 3628t
  for prostatitis, 322
Muscular dystrophy, voiding dysfunction in,
  2042-2043
Musculocutaneous flap(s), 1026, 1027f. *See also*
  Flap(s).
Mutagenesis, xenografts and, 545-546
Mutation(s)
  carcinogenesis and, 513, 513f
  of oncogenes, relevance of, 514

Mutation(s) *(Continued)*
  somatic, associated with prostate cancer
    initiation and progression, 2865-2867
Myasthenia gravis, voiding dysfunction in, 2041
*MYC* oncogene, 513
*Mycobacteria,* in urinary tract, 228
*Mycobacterium tuberculosis,* 436, 440. *See also*
  Tuberculosis.
  transmission of, 441
Mycophenolate mofetil, as immunosuppressant,
  1316, 1316f, 1316t
*Mycoplasma genitalium*
  in genital tract, 384
  in urethritis, 625
  testing for, 626
*Mycoplasma hominis*
  in genital tract, 384
  in painful bladder syndrome/interstitial
    cystitis, 339
  in semen cultures, 625-626
Mycosis fungoides, 430, 431f
Myelitis, acute transverse, voiding dysfunction
  in, 2029
Myelodysplasia, 3628-3640
  assessment of, in neonate, 3630-3631
  bowel function and, 3640
  detrusor leak point pressure in, 2005
  familial risk of, 3629t
  neurologic findings in, 3634-3635, 3635f,
    3636f
  pathogenesis of, 3629-3630, 3629f, 3630t
  recommendations for, 3632-3634, 3634f
  sexuality and, 3639-3640
  surveillance of infants with, 3635t
  urinary continence and, management of,
    3636-3639, 3638f
  urodynamic findings in, 3631-3632, 3632f,
    3633f
  vesicoureteral reflux with, management of,
    3635-3636, 3637f
Myelolipoma, adrenal, 1839-1840, 1840f
Myelomeningocele, 3629, 3629f. *See also*
  Myelodysplasia.
  bowel emptying regimen for, 3640
  closure of, 3629-3630
  imaging of, 3634, 3635f
  spinal level of, 3630t
  voiding dysfunction with, 2029-2030
Myelopathy
  cervical, voiding dysfunction in, 2028-2029
  schistosomal, voiding dysfunction in, 2036-
    2037
Myoblastoma, granular cell, of bladder, 2445
Myocardial infarction, after renal
  transplantation, 1324
*MyoD* gene, in rhabdomyosarcoma, 3879
Myofascial trigger point release, for prostatitis,
  323-324
Myogenic failure, in valve patients, 3597
Myogenic hypothesis, of detrusor overactivity,
  2080
Myoid cell(s), peritubular, function of, 588
Myoplasty
  bladder, 2299-2300
  for functional sphincter reconstruction, 2294
Myosin, of smooth muscle, 1891, 1898, 1899f
Myotomy, closure of, in laparoscopic antireflux
  surgery, 4366
Myotonic dystrophy, infertility in, 643

**N**

Nalidixic acid, for pediatric urinary tract
  infections, 3248t
  prophylactic, 3252

Nalmefene, for painful bladder syndrome/interstitial cystitis, 360t, 361

Naloxone, to facilitate bladder emptying, 2117

Narcotic analgesics, effect of, on ureteral function, 1919

Nasogastric decompression, after intestinal anastomosis, 2548-2549

National Health and Social Life Survey (NHSLS), of erectile dysfunction, 738, 765

National Institute of Diabetic and Digestive and Kidney Diseases (NIDDK) diagnostic criteria, for interstitial cystitis, 332, 332t

National Institutes of Health Chronic Prostatitis Symptom Index, 305, 313f

National Institutes of Health classification, of prostatitis, 311, 311t

National Multicystic Kidney Registry, monitoring for, 3340, 3340t

National Wilms' Tumor Study Group, 3893-3894 treatment protocol of, 3894t

Natriuretic peptides, in male sexual function, 734

Natural fill urodynamic studies, of urethral sphincter dysfunction, in children, 3617

Natural killer cell(s), 477 role of, in tumor immunology, 496

Navelbine, for hormone-refractory prostate cancer, 3106t

Nd:YAG laser. See Neodymium:yttrium-aluminum-garnet (Nd:YAG) laser.

Neck resection, postchemotherapy, testicular tumors and, 955

Necrosis. See also at anatomic site. penile, after circumcision, 3748 predicting, in retroperitoneal lymph node dissection, of testicular tumors, 952-953

Necrospermia, 623

Necrotizing fasciitis. See Fournier's gangrene.

Necrotizing gangrene, genital skin loss due to, 2654, 2655f

Needle biopsy in staging of prostate cancer, 2926-2927 of adenocarcinoma of prostate, 2878-2879, 2878t

Needle electrode, 1989 placement of, 2002

Needle suspension procedure anterior colporrhaphy with, 2220t, 2221-2222, 2221f vs. retropubic suspension surgery, for female incontinence, 2184

Neisseria gonorrhoeae, in gonorrhea, 379

Neobladder for orthotopic urinary diversion Hautmann ileal, 2635, 2635f T pouch ileal, 2638, 2639f-2640f, 2640 gastric form of, in urinary tract reconstruction, 2616 intestinal, overactivity of, drug treatment for, 2108-2109 orthotopic for genitourinary tuberculosis, 447 ileal, in laparoscopic-assisted urinary diversion, 2524, 2527f reconstruction of, for painful bladder syndrome/interstitial cystitis, 367

Neocystostomy indications for, 1667 technique of, 1667-1668, 1669f-1671f

Neodymium:yttrium-aluminum-garnet (Nd:YAG) laser for bladder cancer invasive, 2482 non–muscle-invasive, 2453, 2482

Neodymium:yttrium-aluminum-garnet (Nd:YAG) laser (Continued) for penile cancer, 973, 993-994 in lithotripsy, 1514 in treatment of benign prostatic hyperplasia, 2821

Neomycin with erythromycin, in antibiotic bowel preparation, 2538t

Neomycin with metronidazole, in antibiotic bowel preparation, 2538t

Neonates. See also Children; Infants. ambiguous genitalia in, evaluation and management of, 3827-3829, 3828f amino acid excretion in, 3156 bladder exstrophy in, 3555f. See also Bladder exstrophy. complete primary exstrophy repair for, 3557-3563. See also Complete primary exstrophy repair. calcium excretion in, 3156 Chlamydia trachomatis infection in, 378 circumcision in, 3215 advantages and benefits of, 3747 contraindications to, 3747-3748 prophylactic effect of on penile cancer, 965, 966 on urinary tract infections, 3232, 3239. See also Urinary tract infection, in children. fluid and electrolyte management in, 3156, 3157f glomerular filtration rate in, 3151-3152, 3152f, 3153f regulation of, 3158, 3158f hematuria in, gross, 3199, 3203 megaureter in, 4375-4376, 4376f. See also Megaureter(s). myelodysplasia in, assessment of, 3630-3631 oliguric, fractional excretion of sodium in, 3154 posterior urethral valves in, 3588. See also Urethral valves, posterior. prune-belly syndrome in, 3486f, 3488 renal calculi in, 1427 renal function in development of, 3151-3153, 3152f, 3153f impaired, 3159-3162, 3159t serum phosphorus in, 3156 tubular reabsorption of glucose in, 3156 urine specimen collection from, 96 urologic emergencies in, 3194-3196 presenting signs of, 3194t specific diagnoses of, 3196-3197

Neoplasm(s). See Cancer; Tumor entries; at anatomic site; specific neoplasm.

Neotonus device, for incontinence, 2136

Neourethra formation of, 3715-3716 free grafts in, 3734, 3736-3738, 3738f in hypospadias repair coverage of, 3716-3718. See also Urethroplasty. intubation of, 3719

Neourethral intubation, in hypospadias repair, 3719

Neovagina, creation of in children, 3927 intestines used in, 3836-3837, 3836f-3838f advantages and disadvantages of, 3837-3838 optimal timing in, 3838 skin used in, 3835-3836, 3835f

Neovascularity, in renal cell carcinoma, 1589, 1590f

Nephrectomy allograft, indications for, 1318-1319 bilateral, for autosomal dominant polycystic kidney disease, 1301 cytoreductive, for metastatic renal cell carcinoma with interferon-alpha, 1624-1625, 1624t with interleukin-2, 1625 for emphysematous pyelonephritis, 273 for perinephric abscess, 278 for renal injury, indications for, 1282 for renal tuberculosis, 444-445 partial, 445 for upper pole ectopic ureter, 3393-3395, 3394f, 3395f laparoscopic. See Laparoscpic nephrectomy. living donor contraindications to, 1301 laparoscopic, 1303, 1304f-1305f open, 1303 short- and long-term risks of, 1303 partial. See also Nephron-sparing surgery. for benign disease, 1731-1733, 1732f heminephrectomy, as in duplicated collecting system, 1732-1733 for malignancy, 1720-1731, 1721f-1724f central tumors in, 1727-1728, 1728f closure of vasculature and collecting system after, 1722-1723, 1723f complications of, 1730 contraindications to, 1723-1724 exposure and mobilization of kidney in, 1721-1722, 1721f extracorporeal, with autotransplantation, 1728-1730, 1730f indications for, 1720 major transverse resection in, 1724-1725, 1727f patient evaluation in, 1721, 1721f postoperative follow-up in, 1730-1731 segmental polar procedure in, 1724, 1725f simple enucleation in, 1728 success rate of, 1721 wedge resection in, 1724, 1726f for unilateral Wilms' tumor, 3897 in children, 3922-3923, 3923f technique of, 1280f pretransplant, indications for, 1300-1301, 1300t radical, 1707-1720 complication(s) of atelectasis as, 1720 gastrointestinal, 1718-1719 hemorrhage as, 1710-1712, 1713f, 1719 incisional hernia as, 1720 infection as, 1720 pancreatic fistula as, 1719 pneumothorax as, 1719-1720 renal insufficiency as, 1720 for malignancy laparoscopic. See under Laparoscopic nephrectomy. local recurrence after, 1622 localized disease and, 1608-1610, 1609f, 1610t metastatic disease and, 1623-1625, 1624t, 1625f for urothelial tumors, 1658, 1659f, 1660f for Wilms' tumor, 3893 vs. preoperative chemotherapy, 3895-3897, 3896f indications and evaluation for, 1707-1708, 1708f

Nephrectomy (Continued)
retroperitoneal hemorrhage during, management of, 1710-1712, 1713f
technique of, standard, 1708-1710, 1709f-1712f
vena caval involvement in
infrahepatic, 1714, 1715f, 1716f
intrahepatic or suprahepatic, 1714, 1716, 1718, 1718f-1720f
simple
flank approach to, 1703, 1703f-1705f
indications for, 1703
subscapular technique of, 1703, 1706f
transperitoneal approach to, 1703, 1707, 1707f
Nephric ducts, formation of, 3121, 3127
Nephritic syndromes, in children, 3226-3228
Nephritis
bacterial, 265-271
focal or multifocal, 266f, 271, 272f
pediatric, 3245-3246
pathology of, 265, 266f, 267, 267f
granulomatous, 280-286
interstitial, in acute renal failure, 1328-1329, 1328t
lupus, in children, 3227
Nephroblastoma. See Wilms' tumor.
Nephrocalcin, as calcium oxalate crystal inhibitor, 1367, 1370
Nephrogenesis, 3149, 3150f
cell-cell interactions in, 3130-3131, 3130f
Nephrogenic adenoma
in children, 3581-3582
of bladder, 2418
treatment of, 3883
within urethral diverticula, 2389
Nephrogenic rests, in Wilms' tumor, 3889-3890, 3889f
prevalence of, 3889t
Nephrolithiasis. See Renal calculi; Urinary calculi.
Nephrolithotomy
percutaneous, 1485-1496
anesthesia for, 1486
antibiotics for, 1485-1486
bilateral simultaneous, 1499-1500
complications of, 1500-1501
for calyceal diverticular calculi, 1442
for ectopic renal calculi, 1443-1444, 1444f
for horseshoe kidney calculi, 1443
for lower pole calculi, 1446-1447
for nonstaghorn calculi, 1437
for proximal ureteral calculi, 1454
for renal calculi, in morbidly obese patients, 1448
for staghorn calculi, 1439
in children, 3909-3912
access for, 3911
indications for, 3911
instruments for, 3909-3911, 3910f
postprocedure management for, 3912
results of, 3912
stone manipulation using, 3912
in morbidly obese patients, 1499
into calyceal diverticula, 1496-1497, 1497f
into ectopic kidney, 1498-1499
into horseshoe kidney, 1497-1498
into renal allograft, 1498
opacification of collecting system in patient positioning for, 1487, 1487f
patient preparation for, 1485-1487, 1487f
renal access for, 1487-1496
anatomic considerations in, 1488-1489, 1488f, 1489f

Nephrolithotomy (Continued)
in children, 3911
mini-perc and nondilated punctures in, 1493-1494, 1494f
multiple, 1490-1491, 1491f
postoperative considerations in, 1495-1496, 1496f
puncture site selection in, 1489-1491, 1490f-1492f, 1490t
stone removal in, 1494-1495
supracostal puncture in, 1490, 1490f, 1490t, 1491f
track dilation in, 1491-1494, 1492f-1494f
stone removal by, 1494-1495
stone size and, 1437-1438
simultaneous, percutaneous antegrade endopyelotomy with, for ureteropelvic junction obstruction, 1234
Nephroma
cystic, 1580, 1581f
multiloculated, 3339-3343, 3340f. See also Multilocular cyst.
in children, 3899
mesoblastic, congenital, 3898-3899
Nephron(s). See also Renal tubule(s).
development of, 3125-3126, 3125f, 3126f
ion transport in, metabolic determinants of, 1203-1204
reduction of, in chronic renal failure, 1343, 1343f
Nephronia, lobar, pediatric, 3245-3246
Nephron-sparing surgery. See also Nephrectomy, partial.
for renal cell carcinoma
in von Hippel–Lindau disease, 1615-1616, 1615f
local recurrence after, 1622
localized, 1609f, 1610-1616, 1613f
postoperative surveillance after, 1612t
results of, 1611t
with normal opposite kidney, 1614-1615, 1614t
for urothelial tumors, 1649, 1649t
adjuvant therapy after, 1681, 1681f
indications for, 1656, 1656f
results of, 1657
technique of, 1656-1657
laparoscopic, 1799-1804
complications of, 1804, 1804t
hand-assisted, 1802
in situ ablation and resection in, 1802
indications for and contraindications to, 1799
patient position and operating room configuration in, 1799
preoperative preparation for, 1799
renal cooling in, 1801-1802
results of, 1802, 1803t, 1804
retroperitoneal approach to, 1802
technique of, 1799-1801, 1800f, 1801f
trocar placement in, 1799
Nephropathy
Balkan, urothelial tumors associated with, 1639
familial clustering of, 1344
ischemic
atheroembolism and, 1166
clinical features of, 1167-1168, 1167t
pathophysiology of, 1165-1166, 1165f
renal artery reconstruction in, 1733-1734
surgical treatment of
patient selection for, 1174-1177, 1174f-1176f, 1178f
results of, 1179, 1179t

Nephropathy (Continued)
membranous, in children, 3226
obstructive, 1195
causes of, 1196t
characteristics of, 3169-3171, 3170f
congenital, 3163-3175. See also Urinary tract obstruction, congenital.
patterns of, 3165-3166, 3166f
pigment, 1330
radiocontrast agent–induced, 1340
prevention of, 1340-1341
toxic, functional response to, 3161
Nephropexy, laparoscopic, 1776, 1777f
Nephroscope(s)
adult, 3910, 3910f
pediatric, rigid and flexible, 3909-3910
Nephroscopy
for stone removal, 1495
rigid, 1489-1490, 1489f, 1495
second-look, 1678
Nephrosis, congenital
Finnish type, 3328-3329
characteristics of, 3314t
with diffuse mesangial sclerosis, 3328-3329
characteristics of, 3314t
Nephrostography (antegrade urography), 118
Nephrostomy, percutaneous
catheters in, 1541
complication(s) of
bowel perforation as, 1548
fluid absorption as, 1547
hemorrhage as, 1544-1547, 1545f-1547f
liver injury as, 1548
pleural cavity injury as, 1547-1548
renal pelvic injury as, 1547
sepsis as, 1548
splenic injury as, 1548
CT-guided, 1532-1533
drainage procedures in, 1549, 1557-1562
balloon retention catheters for, 1559-1560
choice of appropriate, 1562, 1562t
circle loop, 1560, 1561f
Councill catheters for, 1558f, 1559-1560
Foley catheters for, 1559-1560
for calyceal diverticula, 1552-1554, 1553f
for emphysematous pyelonephritis, 1550-1551
for fibroepithelial polyps, 1556-1557
for fungal bezoars, 1556
for infundibular stenosis, 1554-1556, 1555f
for pyonephrosis, 1550-1551
for ureteroenteric anastomotic strictures, 1557
innovations of, 1563
Malecot tubes for, 1558
of renal cysts, 1551-1552
of uninfected obstruction, 1549-1550
pigtail catheters for, 1558-1559, 1558f, 1559f
re-entry tubes for, 1559f, 1560
fluoroscopic approach to, 1531-1532, 1531f, 1531t
future directions of, 1562-1563
guide wires in, 1541
imaging for, 1530-1534
innovations in, 1562-1563
indications for, 1526-1527
MRI-guided, 1532-1533
patient positioning for, 1536-1537, 1536f
pertinent renal anatomy for, 1527-1529, 1527f-1530f
preoperative preparation for, 1536
retrograde-assisted, 1534-1535, 1534f, 1535f

Nephrostomy, percutaneous *(Continued)*
  sealants and hemostatic agents in, 1561
  site selection for, 1537-1541
    anomalous kidneys and, 1540-1541, 1540f
    intercostal approach in, 1539-1540, 1539f,
      1540f
    subcostal approach in, 1537-1539, 1537f,
      1538f
  stone removal through, 1433
  technical aspects of, 1535-1541
  tract dilation in, 1541-1544
    dilators in, 1542-1544, 1542f, 1543f
    guide wire entry in, 1541-1542
  tubeless, 1561
  ultrasound-guided, 1530-1531, 1531f
Nephrostomy tract
  dilation of, 1541-1544, 1542f, 1543f
  establishment of, 1677-1678, 1677f, 1678f
Nephrostomy tube
  after percutaneous nephrolithotomy, 1495-
    1496, 1496f
  choice of, 1562, 1562t
  insertion of, 1754-1755, 1756
  large bore vs. small bore, 1560-1561
  re-entry, 1559f, 1560
Nephrotic syndrome, in children, 3225
  congenital, 3226
Nephrotosis
  definition of, 1776
  Dietl's crisis in, 1776
Nephrotoxic agents, acute renal failure related
  to, 1329t, 1330
Nephrotoxicity, cisplatin-induced, 924
Nephroureterectomy
  laparoscopic, 1650, 1650t
  in children, 3921-3922
  radical, 1649-1650
    laparoscopic, 1664-1667
      results of, 1666-1667
      transperitoneal, 1665-1666, 1665f,
        1666f
    lymphadenectomy with, 1662
    open, 1657-1664
      choice of incision in, 1657-1658, 1658f
      indications for, 1657
      results of, 1663-1664
      technique of, 1657-1662, 1659f-1664f
    results of, 1650-1651, 1650t
Nernst equation, 1892
Nerve(s). *See also specific nerve.*
  injury to
    in laparoscopic surgery, 215-216
    postchemotherapy surgery causing, 956
  of bladder, 60
  of kidneys, 32
  of pelvis, 52-55, 53f-55f, 53t
  of penis, 581038
  of prostate, 63
  of retroperitoneum, 14-19
    autonomic, 15, 16f, 17, 17f
    somatic, 15f, 17-19, 18f, 19t
  of ureters, 37
Nerve grafting. *See also* Graft(s).
  interposition, in radical retropubic
    prostatectomy, 2976-2977
Nerve roots, electrical stimulation to, for
  bladder emptying disorders, 2164-2165,
  2164f
Nerve-sparing cryotherapy, for prostate cancer,
  3044, 3044f
Nerve-sparing surgery, potency after, 2470t
Nerve-sparing technique(s), in retroperitoneal
  lymph node dissection, 944-945, 945f
  laparoscopic, 947

Nervous system. *See* Autonomic nervous system;
  Central nervous system; Parasympathetic
  system; Somatic nervous system;
  Sympathetic nervous system.
Neural dysregulation, in prostatitis, 309
Neural mechanism, in renin-angiotensin-
  aldosterone system, 1162
Neuroblastoma, 3870-3878
  biologic variables in, 3874-3875
  chemotherapy in, 3877
  chromosomal abnormalities in, 3870
  clinical findings in, 3871, 3872f
  clinical variables in, 3873-3874
  diagnosis of, 3872-3873
  embryology of, 3870-3871
  epidemiology of, 3870-3871
  genetics of, 3870
  imaging of, 3872, 3873f
  in situ, 3870, 3871
  pathology of, 3871, 3871f
  patterns of spread of, 3871-3872
  prenatal diagnosis of, 3185
  screening for, 3872-3873
  spinal cord compression with, treatment of,
    3877-3878
  spontaneous regression of, 3870-3871
  staging of, 3873, 3873t, 3874t
  treatment of, 3875-3878
    chemotherapy in, 3877
    noninvasive biologic therapies in, 3877
    radiation therapy in, 3877
    surgical, 3875-3877
      in high-risk disease, 3876-3877
      in low-risk disease, 3875-3876, 3876f
    with spinal cord compression, 3877-3878
Neuroectodermal tumor, peripheral, of kidney,
  1636
Neuroendocrine cells
  of prostate, 2680t, 2681
  transcriptional activation of, 2702
Neuroendocrine signals, in prostate, 2690,
  2690f
Neurofibroma
  of bladder, 2445
  of male genitalia, 433
Neurofibromatosis
  affecting renal arteries, 1190-1191
  type I, pheochromocytoma associated with,
    1861, 1862t
Neurogenic bladder
  antenatal detection of, 3574
  autonomous, 1982-1983
  dysfunction of, videourodynamic evaluation
    of, 2002
  in children
    neurospinal dysraphisms and, 3628-3648
    urinary tract infections and, 3241
    non-neurogenic (subclinical), 2038, 3612-
      3613
  reflex, 1982
  sacral neuromodulation for, 2155-2156
  uninhibited, 1982
Neurogenic hypothesis, of detrusor overactivity,
  2080
Neurogenic mechanisms, in painful bladder
  syndrome/interstitial cystitis, 345-347,
  346t
Neurogenic priapism, 844. *See also* Priapism.
Neurologic injury, lower urinary tract
  dysfunction due to, 2011-2044. *See also*
  Voiding dysfunction,
  neurogenic/neuropathic.
Neurologic tests, for sexual health problems, in
  females, 875

Neuromodulation
  for painful bladder syndrome/interstitial
    cystitis, 364-365
  for urethral sphincter dysfunction, in
    children, 3619
  sacral. *See* Sacral nerve neuromodulation.
Neuropathy
  HIV-associated, 397-398
  traumatic, sexual pain disorders and, 883
Neuropeptides
  sensory, release of, 1959
  uropharmacology of, 1954-1955
Neurophysiology
  artifacts in, 2004
  of electrical stimulation, for storage and
    emptying disorders, 2148-2150, 2149f-
    2151f
  of motor unit action potentials, 2003-2004,
    2004f
Neurospinal dysraphism. *See also specific
  dysraphism.*
  in children, 3628-3648
  in cloacal exstrophy, 3538-3539, 3539f
  voiding dysfunction in, 2029-2030
Neurostimulation, intraoperative, during
  retroperitoneal lymph node dissection,
  945
Neurotoxicity, cisplatin-induced, 924
Neurotransmitters, in male sexual function, 728-
  730
  central, 729-730
  interaction between nerves and, 729
  peripheral, 728-729
Neurovascular bundles
  in radical cystectomy, preservation of, 2487-
    2488, 2488f, 2489f
  in radical retropubic prostatectomy, 2967-
    2968, 2967f
    high anterior release of, 2965, 2965f
    identification and preservation of, 2966-
      2967, 2967f
    wide excision of, 2968, 2968f
  in robotic-assisted laparoscopic radical
    prostatectomy
    antegrade preservation of, 2993, 2994f,
      2995f
    interfascial dissection of, 2992, 2993f
    retrograde preservation of, 2993
Neutrophils, in injury cascade, 1332
NEVA device, for nocturnal penile tumescence
  testing, 764
Nevus(i), of male genitalia, 433, 434f
NFκB activation, angiotensin II in, 1204
NFκB regulation, of apoptosis, 490
Nicotinic agonists, effect of, in ureteral function,
  1904
Nifedipine
  for autonomic hyperreflexia, 2027
  for incontinence, in elderly, 2317t
  for painful bladder syndrome/interstitial
    cystitis, 360t, 361
Nilutamide, androgen blockade with, 3085t,
  3087
Nimesulide, for prostatitis, clinical trial data on,
  322
Nipple(s), supernumerary, in children, 3207
Nipple "rosebud" stoma, 2552, 2552f
Nipple valves
  for continent urinary diversion, in children,
    3693-3694, 3694f
  in ureterointestinal anastomosis, 2562,
    2562f
  reinforced, of ileum, for antireflux surgery,
    3662

Nitric oxide
and renal development, 3159
in male sexual function, 728-729, 730, 734-735
in obstructive renal fibrosis, 3170
in renal hemodynamics, 1135
in smooth muscle relaxation, 1954
in ureteral smooth muscle contraction, 1901, 1901f
uropharmacology of, 1953-1954, 1957
Nitric oxide donors, for voiding dysfunction, 2119-2120
Nitric oxide synthase, in ureteral smooth muscle contraction, 1901, 1901f
Nitrite tests
for pediatric urinary tract infection, 3244, 3244t
in urinalysis, 104-105
Nitrofurantoin
for cystitis, 256t, 257
for urinary tract infections, 245, 245t, 246t, 247t, 248
in children, 3248t
prophylactic, 3251, 3426
low-dose prophylactic, for recurrent urinary tract infections, 262t, 263-264
Nitrous oxide, for pneumoperitoneum, in laparoscopic surgery, 199
NK cell(s). See Natural killer cell(s).
NK receptors, 1954-1955
NK₁ antagonists, 1954
*NKX3-1* gene, 536
in prostate cancer, 2865-2866
NMP 48 (50.8 kD) protein, in prostate cancer, 2909
NMP22 protein, in urothelial tumors, 1644
N-*myc* oncogene, amplification of, in neuroblastoma, 3874, 3875
Nocturia, 84, 2047
causes of, 2312t
definition of, 2079
in children, 3621-3624
bladder-brain dialogue in, 3624
etiology of, 3621
evaluation of, 3204
role of bladder dysfunction in, 3621-3622, 3623f
sleep arousal disturbance in, 3622, 3624
in elderly, 2311-2312
measurement of, 2084
treatment of, pharmacotherapy in, 2113-2114
Nocturnal penile tumescence, monitoring of, 763-764, 764f
Nodule(s)
painless, in germ cell tumors, 903
postoperative spindle cell, of bladder, 2418
Nonadrenergic noncholinergic mechanism, of bladder emptying, 1975
Nonautologous materials, for endoscopic correction of reflux, 4364-4365, 4364t
Noncompliance, in renal transplant recipients, 1299
Noncutaneous lesions, of penis, benign, 959-960
Nonepithelial tumor(s), of bladder, 2445-2446
angiosarcoma as, 2445
hemangioma as, 2445
leiomyosarcoma as, 2445
lymphoma as, 2445
neurofibroma as, 2445
pheochromocytoma as, 2445
rhabdomyosarcoma as, 2446
Nonfebrile infections, of urinary tract, in children, 3203

Non-Hodgkin's lymphoma, in AIDS patients, 399
Nonhormonal therapy, for sexual health problems, in females, 881-883
Noninfectious ulcers, of male genitalia, 417-419, 417t, 418f, 419f
Nonischemic priapism, 841, 843. See also Priapism.
cavernosal blood gas determinants in, 845
natural history of, 841
treatment of, 848
Non–muscle-invasive bladder cancer, 2447-2467. See also Bladder cancer, non–muscle-invasive.
Non-nociceptive pain, characteristic features of, 346, 346t
Non–nucleoside reverse transcriptase inhibitors, for HIV infection, 401
Nonrenal cystic lesions, prenatal diagnosis of, vs. multicystic dysplastic kidney, 3183
Nonseminomatous germ cell tumor(s), 895-896. See also specific tumor.
high-stage
fertility in, 957
postchemotherapy pathologic findings in, 951t
surgery for
complications of, 955-956
high-risk post-chemotherapy patients and, 953-954
histologic findings and controversies in, 950-951
late-relapse and, 953
lung resection as, 955
mediastinal resection as, 955
neck resection as, 955
post-chemotherapy RPLND as, 954-955
predicting necrosis in, 952-953
preoperative preparation for, 950
reoperative retroperitoneal, 954-955
timing of, 950
histologic classification of, 893, 894t
incidence, pathology, and presentation of, 897t-898t
treatment of, 913-924
algorithm in, 914f
for stage I and stage IIA disease, 913, 915-918
chemotherapy in, 918, 918t, 948
radiation therapy in, 915-916, 916t
retroperitoneal lymph node dissection in, 913, 915, 915f, 916f, 948
surveillance studies after, 916-918, 917t
for stage IIB disease
chemotherapy in, 919-920, 920t
radiation therapy in, 920
retroperitoneal lymph node dissection in, 919, 919t, 949
adjuvant chemotherapy after, 919, 949
for stage IIC and stage III disease
chemotherapy in, 920-921
salvage, 923-924
good-risk vs. poor-risk, 920
post-chemotherapy residual mass after, 922
indications for resection in, 922-923
principles in, 913
vs. seminomas, 956-957
Nonstaghorn calculi, shockwave lithotripsy for, 1436-1437, 1437f
Nonsteroidal anti-inflammatory drugs (NSAIDs)
for prostatitis, 321-322, 325t

Nonsteroidal anti-inflammatory drugs (NSAIDs) (Continued)
for renal colic, 1213
in prevention of bladder cancer, 2444
Nonsurgical therapy, for erectile dysfunction, 768-783
Nontransitional cell carcinoma, of upper urinary tract, abnormal urothelium in, 1643
Nonurothelial tumor(s), of bladder
carcinosarcoma as, 2444-2445
metastatic carcinoma as, 2445
small cell carcinoma as, 2444
Noonan's syndrome, infertility in, 639
Norephedrine, for stress incontinence, 2109-2111
Norepinephrine
in male sexual function, 730
in renal hemodynamics, 1134
in ureteral function, 1905
Norfenefrine, for stress incontinence, 2109
Norfloxacin, for prostatitis, 320t
Northwestern male bulbourethral sling, for incontinence, 2392-2393. See also Perineal sling, for male incontinence.
Norwegian scabies, 383
No-scalpel vasectomy, 1099-1101, 1099f-1101f. See also Vasectomy.
Nosocomial infections, of urinary tract, in children, 3241-3242, 3242t, 3266
Nottingham Health Profile (NHP), 150
*NPH1* gene, in juvenile nephronophthisis, 3326
*NPH2* gene, in juvenile nephronophthisis, 3326
*NPH3* gene, in juvenile nephronophthisis, 3326
*NPHS1* gene
in congenital nephrosis, 3328
in congenital nephrotic syndrome, 3226
NSAIDs. See Nonsteroidal anti-inflammatory drugs (NSAIDs).
Nuclear cloning, in tissue engineering, 570-572, 571f, 572f
Nuclear matrix, 511
of prostate, 2683f, 2684
role of, in androgen action, 2703-2705
Nuclear matrix proteins, in bladder cancer, 2434-2435
Nuclear renography. See Scintigraphy, renographic.
Nuclear scintigraphy. See Scintigraphy.
Nucleation, homogenous, 1367
Nucleic acid amplification test
for *Chlamydia trachomatis* infection, 378
for gonorrhea, 379
Nucleoside reverse transcriptase inhibitors, for HIV infection, 401
Nucleotide, 509f
Nucleotide excision repair, of DNA, 527
Nucleotide polymorphism, single, 519-520, 520f
Numbness, penile, after penile revascularization, 810
Nutritional therapy, for acute renal failure, 1338
Nystatin, for pediatric fungal infections, of urinary tract, 3265

**O**

Obesity
benign prostatic hyperplasia and, 2745-2746
definition of, 1413
erectile dysfunction associated with, 769
incontinence and, 2189
behavioral therapy for, 2129
long-standing, renal cell carcinoma associated with, 1584

Obesity (Continued)
  morbid
    affecting renal calculi surgery, 1447-1448
    as contraindication to laparoscopy, 174
    definition of, 1447, 1499
    percutaneous nephrolithotomy and, 1499
    ureteroscopy and, 1520
  nephrolithiasis and, 1413-1414
  open vs. laparoscopic adrenalectomy and, 1870
  orthotopic urinary diversion and, 2616
  pelvic organ prolapse associated with, 2189
  prostate cancer associated with, 2863
  tension-free vaginal tape procedure and, 2254-2255
Oblique muscle, 8-9, 9t, 10f
  external, 40, 42f
Observation, therapeutic, of renal cell carcinoma, 1618-1619, 1618t
Obstetrical implications, of exstrophy, in female patient, 3552-3553
Obstructive urinary symptoms, in patient history, 84-86, 85t
Obturator artery, 50f, 51
Obturator internus muscle, 43-44, 46f
Obturator lymph nodes, 52, 52f
Obturator nerve, 18f, 19, 53, 53t
Occlusive devices, for bladder filling/storage disorders, 2292
Occupation
  bladder cancer associated with, 2413
  HIV infection associated with
    epidemiology of, 400
    interventions to decrease, 400-401
    postexposure chemoprophylaxis for, 401
    specific exposures and, 400, 400t
  renal stones associated with, 1365
  urothelial tumors associated with, 1639
Occupational exposure(s), infertility due to, 644
Ochoa (urofacial) syndrome, in children, 3613
Office management, of premature ejaculation, 786, 787t
Office surgical procedures, for pediatric urologic patient, 3215, 3215f
Office-based endoscopy, of bladder cancer, non–muscle-invasive, 2454
Ofloxacin
  for Chlamydia trachomatis infection, 378
  for gonorrhea, 379
  for mollicute infections, 384
  for prostatitis, 320t
Oligoasthenoteratospermia
  conditions associated with, 611
  evaluation of, 623
Oligohydramnios
  etiologies of, 3184-3185
  in bilateral renal agenesis, 3271
  in neonate, 3195
  second-trimester, 3181
  timing of onset of, 3186
Oligomeganephronia, 3310, 3311f
Oligospermia
  evaluation of, 622
  in XYY syndrome, 639
  vasography in, 627
  Y chromosome microdeletions in, 632, 717
Oliguria, with pneumoperitoneum, 201
Olmstead County Study, of benign prostatic hyperplasia, 2763
Omniport device, hand-assist, 186, 186f
Omphalocele
  closure of, in cloacal exstrophy, 3542
  in exstrophy-epispadias complex, 3503
Onchocerca volvulus, 455. See also Filariasis.

Onchocerciasis, 458
Oncocytoma
  adrenal, 1843
  renal, 1577-1578, 1577f
  vs. renal cell carcinoma, 1577-1578
Oncogene(s), 513-514. See also specific oncogene.
  definition of, 508t
  in bladder cancer, 2410
  in prostate cancer, 2865, 2866
  mutation of, 514
  tumorigenesis induced by, 546
Oncotic pressure, in glomerular filtration rate, 1132
One-kidney, one-clip constriction, of renal artery, renovascular hypertension in, 1164-1165, 1165t
One-stage proximal procedure, in hypospadias repair, 3729-3734
  onlay techniques for, 3729-3731
  tubularization techniques for, 3731-3732, 3732f-3733f, 3734
Onlay technique(s), of hypospadias repair, 3725-3726, 3728, 3728f-3729f
  split prepuce in-situ technique of, 3725 40, 3728, 3730f-3731f
Open biopsy
  of kidney, 1753, 1754f
  of testis, 655-657, 656f, 657f
Open donor nephrectomy, 1303
Open stone surgery, 1505-1506, 1505t
  for renal calculi, 1506
  for ureteral calculi, 1506
Open-ended vasectomy, 1102. See also Vasectomy.
Operating room setup, for laparoscopic surgery, 176, 176t
Operative team placement, for laparoscopic surgery, 177-178, 177f
Opiate(s), erectile dysfunction caused by, 746
Opiate antagonist, for painful bladder syndrome/interstitial cystitis, 360t, 361
Opioid(s)
  for painful bladder syndrome/interstitial cystitis, 362
  in male sexual function, 730
  uropharmacology of, 1964, 1965
Opioid receptor antagonists, to facilitate bladder emptying, 2117
Opsonin, for phagocytes, 474
Optical magnification, in repair of hypospadias, 3719
Oral cavity, mucocutaneous lesions of, in Behçet's disease, 418, 418f
Oral thrush. See Candidiasis.
Orchialgia
  chronic, 1107-1108
    definition of, 1107
    of undetermined etiology, 1108, 1109f
    post-vasectomy, 1108
  in children, 3207
  patient history of, 83
  post-hernia repair, 1108
Orchidopexy (orchiopexy)
  complications of, 3787
  for high undescended testes, 3779, 3781
  for prune-belly syndrome, 3492-3493
    Fowler-Stephens, 3492-3493
    transabdominal, 3492, 3493f
  Fowler-Stephens, 3781
  laparoscopic, 3786
  in adults, 1106-1107
    for intermittent torsion, 1107
    for retractile testes, 1107

Orchidopexy (orchiopexy) (Continued)
  laparoscopic, 3785-3786
  reoperative, 3787
  standard, 3776-3777, 3776f-3780f, 3779
Orchiectomy
  delayed, for germ cell tumors, 938
  for complete androgen insensitivity, timing of, 3824
  for germ cell tumors, 936-938, 937f
    findings at, 904-905
    prior scrotal violation and, 938
  for prostate cancer, 3082-3083, 3085, 3085t
  partial, for germ cell tumors, 938
  radical
    for germ cell tumors, 936-938, 937f
    for Leydig cell tumors, 926t, 927
    for yolk sac tumors, 3903
Orchitis
  classification of, 327, 327t
  definition of, 327
  diagnosis of, 328
  in HIV patients, 396
  infertility due to, 643
  pathogenesis and etiology of, 327-328
  pediatric urinary tract infections and, 3264-3265
  treatment of, 328
Orciprenaline, effect of, on ureteral function, 1905
Organ entrapment
  in laparoscopic nephrectomy, 1769
    hand-assisted, 1798
    transperitoneal approach to, 1784, 1786-1787, 1786f, 1787f
  in laparoscopic surgery, 195, 196f
Organomegaly, as contraindication to laparoscopy, 175
Organophosphate, for hypercalciuria, 1419
Organ-preserving surgery
  for penile cancer, 972-973
  for testicular tumors, 908-909
Orgasm, absence of, 87
Orgasmic disorder, in females, 864
Orthopedic anomalies, in prune-belly syndrome, 3485t, 3487
Orthopedic hardware, indwelling, antibiotic prophylaxis for, 254, 254t
Orthoplasty, in hypospadias repair, 3712-3714, 3713f, 3715f
  two-stage, 3734, 3736f-3737f
Osmolality, of urine, 97
Osteogenic sarcoma, of kidney, 1634
Osteomalacia, conduit urinary diversion causing, 2574
Osteopontin, as calcium oxalate crystal inhibitor, 1367, 1371
Osteoporosis, androgen deprivation therapy causing, 3089
Osteotomy
  in exstrophy patient, 3513, 3514f-3516f, 3515
    complications of, 3515-3516
    urinary reconstruction and, 3543, 3543f
  with cloacal exstrophy, 3543, 3543f
Ostlin's folds, 3360, 3361f
Ototoxicity, cisplatin-induced, 924
Ouabain, effect of, on ureteral function, 1920
Outpatient procedures, in pediatric urologic patient, 3214-3215
Outpatient surgery, laparoscopic adrenalectomy as, 1884-1885
Outpatient therapy, for urinary tract infections, in children, 3247-3249, 3248t
Ovarian cyst, ureteral obstruction due to, 1221

Ovarian fibroma, ureteral obstruction due to, 1221

Ovarian remnants, ureteral obstruction due to, 1221

Ovarian tumor, maternal, virilizing effects of, 3820-3821

Ovarian vein, thrombophlebitis of, ureteral obstruction due to, 1223

Ovary(ies)
  descent of, 3144f, 3145
  sparing of, in laparoscopic radical cystectomy, 2521
  streak
    in Turner's syndrome, 3810
    in 46,XY complete gonadal dysgenesis, 3813-3814

Overactive bladder, 1978, 2079-2090. *See also* Detrusor muscle, overactivity of.
  afferent mechanisms in, 2080
  after retropubic suspension surgery, 2183
  clinical assessment of, 2082-2084, 2082f, 2084t
  dry, 2081, 2086
  during filling and storage, 1976-1977
  etiology of, 2079-2081, 2081f
  evaluation of, 2239-2240
    questionnaires recommended for, 2062t
  in benign prostatic hyperplasia, effect of medical therapy on, 2774
  in children, 3611
  International Continence Society definition of, 2079
  management of
    algorithms in, 2089f, 2090f
    bladder training in, 2127
    conservative, 2089
    drug, 2089, 2093, 2093t
    multimodality therapy in, 2143, 2144f
  prevalence of, 2081-2082
  refractory, management of, 2143-2145
  risk factors for, 2128, 2128t
  sacral nerve neuromodulation for, mechanism of action of, 2150, 2150f
  urodynamic classification of, 2056, 2056f-2058f
  vs. painful bladder syndrome, 2084-2085, 2085f
  wet, 2081-2082, 2086

Overactive Bladder: Judging Effective Control and Treatment (OBJECT) trial, 2096, 2101

Overactive Bladder: Performance of Extended Release Agents (OPERA) studies, 2096, 2101

Overflow incontinence, 86, 2047. *See also* Incontinence.

Ovulation, evaluation of, in female fertility, 612

Oxalate
  avoidance of, for nephrolithiasis, 1415
  in stone formation, 1367
  metabolism of, 1372

Oxalosis, in renal transplant recipient, 1298

Oxybutynin
  extended-release, 2101
  for incontinence, 2072
    in elderly, 2316, 2317t
  for overactive bladder/detrusor overactivity, 2093t, 2100-2102
  immediate-release, 2101
  rectal administration of, 2102
  to lower detrusor filling pressures, 3633
  transdermal, 2102
  uropharmacology of, 1950, 1950t

Oxygen, modulation of, in male sexual function, 737

Oxygen desaturation, pediatric laparoscopy and, 3917-3918

Oxygen species testing, reactive, of semen, 632

Oxytocin, in male sexual function, 730

**P**

P blood group antigens, influence of, on urinary tract infections, 3237

$P2X_3$ receptors, purinergic, 1951

p27 kinase inhibitor
  in prostate cancer, 2866
  in urothelial tumors, 1644

p53 protein, in urothelial tumors, 1643

Pacemaker activity, of ureteral smooth muscle, 1895-1897, 1896f, 1897f
  latent, 1896-1897

Paclitaxel
  for bladder cancer
    metastatic, 2478
    non-muscle-invasive, 2459
  for hormone-refractory prostate cancer, 3106t

Pad(s), for geriatric incontinence, 2317

Pad test, for incontinence, 2063, 2204

Pagano technique, of ureterocolonic anastomosis, 2557, 2557f

Page's kidney, 1191

Paget's disease
  extramammary, 430, 430f
  of penis, 990
  Peyronie's disease associated with, 818

Pain. *See also at anatomic site.*
  abdominal. *See* Abdominal pain.
  after cryotherapy, 3050
  after laparoscopic surgery, 217
  associated with ureteral calculi, 1452
  complicating sling procedures, 2246
  flank. *See* Flank pain.
  in hormone-refractory prostate cancer, palliative therapy for, 3112-3113, 3113t
  in ureteral obstruction, management of, 1213
  non-nociceptive, characteristic features of, 346, 346t
  patient history of, 82-83
  perception of, in upper urinary tract, 37, 37f
  perineal sling procedure causing, 2396
  post-robotic-assisted laparoscopic radical prostatectomy, 2998
  post-vasectomy, 1102, 1108
  sexual. *See* Dyspareunia; Sexual pain disorders; Vaginismus.

Pain medication, for penile prosthesis placement, 789

Painful bladder syndrome/interstitial cystitis, 330-368. *See also* Cystitis.
  allergies associated with, 335-336
  antiproliferative factor in, 347-348, 347t, 348f, 353
  *Borrelia burgdorferi* in, 339
  *Chlamydia pneumoniae* in, 339
  clinical symptom scales in, 354-355, 354t, 355t, 357t
  definitions of, 331-333
  diagnosis of, 351-354
    algorithm in, 369f
    cystometry in, 352-353, 352f, 353f
    markers in, 353-354
    potassium chloride challenge test in, 354
  diseases associated with, 335-337, 336f
  epidemiology of, 333-337
  etiology of, 337-349, 338f
    animal models in, 337-338, 338f
    autoimmunity in, 340-341
    epithelial permeability barrier in, 343-345

Painful bladder syndrome/interstitial cystitis
    *(Continued)*
    increased sympathetic activity in, 346-347, 346t
    infectious, 338-340
    inflammation in, 341
    mast cell involvement in, 341-343, 342f
    neurogenic mechanisms of, 345-347, 346t
    role of hormones in, 349
    urine abnormalities in, 347
  fibromyalgia associated with, 336
  focal vulvitis associated with, 336-337
  foods to avoid in, ICA recommendations of, 359t
  *Gardnerella vaginalis* in, 339
  Global Response Assessment of, 355, 356t
  glomerulations in, 352-353, 352f
  glycosaminoglycans in, 343-345
  gynecologic problems mimicking, 351
  historical perspective on, 330-331
  Hunner's ulcer in, 352, 353f
  ICS definition of, 332
  inflammatory bowel disease associated with, 336
  *Mycoplasma hominis* in, 339
  *N*-methyl-D-aspartate receptors in, 346
  O'Leary-Sant indices for, 355, 355t
  pathology of, 349-350, 349f, 350t
  pelvic floor dysfunction associated with, 349
  Pelvic Pain and Urgency/Frequency Patient System Scale for, 355, 356t
  population-based studies of, 334-335
  prevalence of, 335
  reflex sympathetic dystrophy in, 346
  relationship of overactive bladder to, 333, 333f
  sexual pain disorder and, 884
  Sjögren's syndrome associated with, 337
  stress in, 348-349
  systemic lupus erythematosus associated with, 336
  T cells in, 341
  treatment of
    acupuncture in, 365
    algorithm in, 369f
    amitriptyline in, 359-360, 360t
    analgesics in, 361-362
    anticholinergics in, 360t, 361
    antihistamines in, 360, 360t
    antispasmodics in, 360t, 361
    L-arginine in, 360t, 361
    assessment of results of, 355-358, 357f
    BCG in, 362t, 364
    behavioral modification therapy in, 358
    botulinum toxin A in, 364
    capsaicin in, 362t, 364
    chloroquine derivatives in, 360t, 361
    chondroitin sulfate in, 362t, 364
    Clorpactin WCS-90 in, 362-363, 362t
    conservative therapy in, 358-359
    corticosteroids in, 360t, 361
    dexamethasone in, 364
    dietary restrictions in, 358-359, 359t
    dimethyl sulfoxide in, 362t, 363
    doxorubicin in, 362t, 364
    glycosaminoglycans in, 363
    heparin in, 362t, 363
    hormones in, 360t, 361
    hyaluronic acid in, 362t, 364
    hydrodistention in, 365-366
    intravesical and intradetrusor therapy in, 362-364, 362t
    lidocaine in, 362t, 364
    lumbar epidural blockade in, 365
    montelukast in, 360t, 361

Painful bladder syndrome/interstitial cystitis
(*Continued*)
    nalmefene in, 360t, 361
    neuromodulation in, 364-365, 2156-2157
    nifedipine in, 360t, 361
    patient education and empowerment in, 358
    pentosan polysulfate in, 360-361, 360t,
      362t, 363-364
    pharmacologic therapy in, 359-362
    placebo effects in, 356-357
    principles of, 368, 369f
    resiniferatoxin in, 362t, 364
    silver nitrate in, 362, 362t
    surgical, 366-368
    tricyclic antidepressants in, 359-360, 360t
    vitamin E in, 360t, 361
  University of Wisconsin Symptom Scale for,
    354-355, 354t
  *Ureaplasma urealyticum* in, 339
  vs. overactive bladder, 2084-2085, 2085f
Palliative therapy
  for hormone-refractory prostate cancer, 3112-
    3114
    bone-targeted approaches to, 3113-3114
    epidural cord compression in, 3112-3113,
      3113t
  for metastatic bladder cancer, 2478
  for prostate cancer, 3028-3029, 3029t
    bone metastases and, 3028-3029
    spinal cord compression and, 3029
Pampiniform plexus, 74, 75f
Pancreas, anatomy of, 19, 20f
Pancreatic fistula, after radical nephrectomy,
  1719
Pancreatic injury
  adrenal surgery causing, 1885t, 1886
  in laparoscopic surgery, 215
Pancreatitis, after post-chemotherapy surgery,
  956
Panendoscopy, in transurethral resection, 2480
Papaverine, for erectile dysfunction
  combination therapy with, 780
  intracavernous injection of, 779
Papillary adenoma, of seminal vesicles, 1116
Papillary renal cell carcinoma, 1594. *See also*
  Renal cell carcinoma.
  familial, 1584t, 1587
  genetics of, 1584-1585, 1584t, 1587
  hereditary, 515t, 518, 1584t, 1587
Papillary urothelial neoplasm of low malignant
  potential (PUNLMP), 2447
Papilloma
  bladder, inverted, 2417-2418, 2418f
    malignant transformation of, 2418
  penile, hirsute, 960
  urothelial, 1642-1643
Papules, penile, pearly, 960
Papulosis, bowenoid
  of male genitalia, 427, 427f
  of penis, 962
Papulosquamous disorders. *See also specific*
  *disorder.*
  of male genitalia, 410-415, 410t, 411f-414f
Paquin technique, of antireflux surgery, 4352,
  4356
Paracrine signals, in prostate, 2690, 2690f
Paradidymis, 3137
Paralytic ileus, prolonged, as complication of
  post-chemotherapy surgery, 956
Parameatal urethral cyst, 3758
Paramesonephric ducts, formation of, 3136,
  3136f-3138f
Paraneoplastic syndromes, in renal cell
  carcinoma, 1597-1598, 1597t

Paraparesis, tropical spastic, voiding dysfunction
  in, 2035-2036
Paraphimosis, 91-92, 1044, 3755. *See also*
  Phimosis.
Paraplegia, hereditary spastic, voiding
  dysfunction in, 2035
Parasites, in urinary sediment, 109, 109f
Parasitic infection(s), of genitourinary tract,
  448-459. *See also specific infection.*
Parastomal hernia, after ileal loop urinary
  diversion, 2553-2554
Parasympathetic blocking agents, effect of, on
  ureteral function, 1905
Parasympathetic nervous system
  of lower urinary tract
    pathways in, 1938
    purinergic mechanisms in, 1951-1952
  role of, in ureteral function, 1904-1905
Parasympathomimetic agents, to facilitate
  bladder emptying, 2114-2116
Paratesticular tumor(s), 932t, 933-934
  leiomyosarcoma as, 934
  management of, 933-934
  rhabdomyosarcoma as, 933
    treatment of, 3883-3884
Parathyroid hormone (PTH)
  calcium metabolism and, 1372
  effect of, on calcium homeostasis, 1136,
    1136f
  in acid-base balance, in neonate, 3153
  regulation of, 1137
  renal effects of, 1137
Parathyroid hormone–related peptide,
  uropharmacology of, 1956
Parathyroidectomy, for primary
  hyperparathyroidism, 1420
Paratope, of antigen-binding site, 478
Paraureteral diverticulum(a), in children, 3579-
  3580, 3579f
Paraurethral cysts, 3842-3843, 3842f
Paraurethral tissue, stress incontinence and,
  1937
Paravaginal repair procedure
  for female incontinence
    results of, 2179-2180
    technique of, 2178-2179, 2179f
  for prolapse, 2218t, 2219
  vs. Burch colposuspension and Marshall-
    Marchetti-Krantz procedures,
    2184-2185
Parenchymal diseases, renal. *See also specific*
  *disease.*
  in children, 3225-3228
Parity
  incontinence and, 2189
  pelvic organ prolapse and, 2189
Parkinsonism, 2017
  vs. Parkinson's disease, 2018
Parkinson's disease
  erectile dysfunction in, 739
  seborrheic dermatitis in, 415
  voiding dysfunction in, 2012t, 2017-2018
  vs. multiple system atrophy, 2019
  vs. parkinsonism, 2018
Paroöphoron, 3124
Paroxetine, for premature ejaculation, 785, 786,
  786t
Partial gonadal dysgenesis (dysgenetic male
  pseudohermaphroditism), 3812-3813
Partner notification, of sexually transmitted
  disease, 372
Patch testing, for allergens, 408, 409f
Patient education and empowerment, in painful
  bladder syndrome/interstitial cystitis, 358

Patient history, 81-109
  alcohol use in, 88-89
  allergies in, 89
  anorgasmia in, 87
  bilirubin in, 104
  bladder examination in, 90-91, 91f
  blood clots in, 83
  chief complaint in, 81-88
  ejaculatory failure in, 87
  enuresis in, 86
  family history in, 88
  fever and chills in, 88
  general observations in, 89-90
  hematospermia in, 87
  hematuria in, 83-84, 97-100
    glomerular, 98-100, 99f, 99t
    nonglomerular, 100, 101f, 102f
  impotence in, 87
  incontinence in, 86
  irritative symptoms in, 84
  leukocyte esterase in, 104-105
  loss of libido in, 86-87
  medications in, 88, 89t
  neurologic examination in, 95, 95f
  nitrite tests in, 104-105
  obstructive symptoms in, 84-86, 85t
  of lower urinary tract symptoms, 84-86
  overview of, 81
  pain in, 82-83
  pelvic examination in, female, 95
  penile examination in, 91-92
  penile pain in, 83
  physical examination in, 89-95
  pneumaturia in, 87
  premature ejaculation in, 87
  present illness in, 81-88
  previous medical illnesses in, 88
  previous surgical procedures in, 88
  prostate examination in, 94
  prostatic pain in, 83
  proteinuria in, 100-103
  rectal examination in, 93-94
  renal examination in, 90, 90f
  renal pain in, 82
  scrotal pain in, 83
  scrotum and content examination in, 92-93,
    92f
  sexual dysfunction in, 86-87
  smoking in, 88-89
  testicular pain in, 83
  ureteral pain in, 82
  urethral discharge in, 87
  urinary glucose in, 103-104
  urinary ketones in, 104
  urinary sediment in, 105-109
    bacteria in, 108, 108f, 109f
    casts in, 107, 107f, 108f
    cells in, 105-107, 105f-107f
    crystals in, 107-108, 108f
    expressed prostatic secretions in, 109, 109f
    parasites in, 109, 109f
    specimen preparation and technique of,
      105
    yeast in, 106f, 109
  urine color in, 96, 96t
  urine dipsticks in, 97
  urine examination in
    chemical, 97-105
    physical, 96-97, 96t
  urine pH in, 97
  urine specimen in
    from females, 96
    from males, 95-96
    from neonates and infants, 96

Patient history (Continued)
  urine turbidity in, 96-97
  urobilinogen in, 104
  vesical pain in, 82-83
Patient-partner counseling, preoperative, in
    penile prosthesis placement, 788-790
Patient-partner satisfaction, with penile
    prosthesis, 800-801
PAX2 gene
  in renal-coloboma syndrome, 3134-3135
  in vesicoureteral reflux, 4326
PBOV1 gene, in prostate cancer, 2909
PCA3, in diagnosis of oncology, 549
Peak systolic velocity
  in penile blood flow, arterial dilation and,
    758-759, 759f
  in renal artery, 1170
Pearly penile papules, 431, 432f
Pedicles
  in radical retropubic prostatectomy, dissection
    and division of, 2968-2969, 2969f
  in robotic-assisted laparoscopic radical
    prostatectomy, ligation of, 2992-2993,
    2994f
Pediculosis pubis, 425, 425f
  diagnosis of, 383-384
  treatment of, 384
PEER retractors, in laparoscopy, 196, 197f
Pelvic artery(ies), 46, 48t, 50f, 51
Pelvic diaphragm, 2191-2192, 2191f, 2192f
Pelvic dissection, in radical cystectomy
  in females, 2495-2496, 2496f, 2497f
  in males, 2485, 2486f-2488f, 2487
Pelvic fibrosis, as contraindication to
    laparoscopy, 174-175
Pelvic floor
  abnormal musculature of, in prostatitis,
    309
  anatomy of, 2190-2198
  defects of, in bladder exstrophy, 3502f, 4328-
    4329
  dysfunction of
    in painful bladder syndrome/interstitial
      cystitis, 349
    sexual pain associated with, 885-886
    vaginal delivery and, 2189
  hyperactivity of, 2002
  massage of, for prostatitis, 323-324
  support structures of
    bony, 2190-2191, 2191f
    connective tissue, 2194-2198
      anterior supports, 2195, 2196f, 2197f
      middle supports, 2195, 2197, 2198f
      posterior supports, 2197-2198, 2198f
    muscular, 2191-2194, 2191f-2194f
Pelvic floor exercises
  for erectile dysfunction, 770
  for geriatric incontinence, 2318
  Kegel, 2130
Pelvic floor muscle training
  definition of, 2130
  for incontinence, 2071, 2130-2132
    effectiveness of, 2131
    vs. other conservative modalities, 2132
  for stress incontinence, 2074, 2142
  implementation of, in clinical practice, 2131-
    2132
  in childbearing women, 2131
  vs. exercises, 2130
Pelvic floor rehabilitation
  for incontinence, 2130-2136
    biofeedback techniques in, 2133, 2133f-
      2135f
    electrical stimulation in, 2135

Pelvic floor rehabilitation (Continued)
    magnetic stimulation in, 2136
    muscle training in, 2130-2132
      implementation of, 2131-2132
      vs. other conservative modalities, 2132
    tools for, 2133, 2134f-2135f
  for urethral sphincter dysfunction, in
    children, 3618, 3619f, 3620f
Pelvic fracture
  associated with posterior urethral injury, in
    children, 3940
  urethral disruption related to, 2659
Pelvic inflammatory disease, tubo-ovarian
    abscess in, 1220
Pelvic kidney, percutaneous access to, 1540-1541
Pelvic lipomatosis, ureteral obstruction due to,
    1218-1219, 1218f, 1219f
Pelvic lymph node dissection. See Pelvic
    lymphadenectomy.
Pelvic lymphadenectomy
  for penile cancer, 982
  in radical retropubic prostatectomy, 2960,
    2960f
  in staging of prostate cancer, 2930-2931
  laparoscopic
    complications of, 3003-3004
    indications for, 3002
    port site seeding after, 1779
    technique of, 3002-3003, 3002f-3004f
    with radical cystectomy, 2521, 2523f
  with radical cystectomy
    in females, 2495, 2495f, 2496f
    in males, 2484-2485, 2485f, 2486f
Pelvic musculature education, in behavioral
    therapy for incontinence, 2127
Pelvic organ prolapse, 2198-2211
  anatomic classification of, 2200, 2200t, 2201f
  clinical classification of, 2207, 2208f, 2209,
    2209f
  clinical evaluation of, 2202-2207, 2202t
  cystoscopy in, 2209-2210
  definition of, 2188-2189
  genetic factors in, 2190
  in anterior compartment, 2200, 2200t
  in middle compartment, 2200, 2200t, 2201f
  in posterior compartment, 2200, 2200t, 2201f
  incidence of, 2189
  magnetic resonance imaging of, 2210-2211,
    2211f
  parity and, 2189
  pathophysiology of, 2198-2199, 2199t
  pelvic examination in, 2205-2207, 2206f
    instrumentation for, 2205
  physical examination in, 2205
  risk factors for, 2189-2190, 2199t
  signs and symptoms of
    bowel, 2204
    local, 2205
    lower urinary tract, 2202-2204, 2203t
    sexual, 2204-2205, 2204t
  sling procedures for, 2249
  stages in, 2207, 2209
  surgical management of
    goals in, 2215t
    vaginal approach to, 2199-2200, 2199f
  tension-free vaginal taping for, 2255-2256
  ultrasonography of, 2210
  urodynamic testing in, 2209, 2210f
  vaginal pessaries for, 2137-2138, 2138f, 2139f,
    2215
  voiding dysfunction in, 2204
Pelvic organ prolapse quantification (POPQ)
    classification system, 2207, 2208f
Pelvic pain, after cryotherapy, 3050

Pelvic Pain and Urgency/Frequency Patient
    System Scale, for painful bladder
    syndrome/interstitial cystitis, 355, 356t
Pelvic pain syndrome, chronic. See Chronic
    pelvic pain syndrome.
Pelvic plexus
  stimulation of, 724-725
  surgical anatomy of, 2957, 2957f
  transvesical infiltration of, 2291
Pelvic radiation therapy, previous, orthotopic
    urinary diversion with, 2629-2630
Pelvic surgery
  erectile dysfunction associated with, 739-740
  extensive, as contraindication to laparoscopy,
    174
  glossary of terms for, 2215t
  incontinence associated with, 2189-2190
  pelvic organ prolapse associated with, 2190
  radical, voiding dysfunction after, 2012t, 2032
  ureteral injury caused by, 1283
Pelvic vein(s), 51-52, 51f
Pelvis
  arterial supply to, 46, 48t, 50f, 51
  benign anomalies of, ureteral obstruction due
    to, 1220-1221
  bifid, 3303
  bladder cancer recurrence in, after cystectomy,
    2628-2629
  bony, 38, 39f, 2190-2191, 2191f
    abnormalities of, in exstrophy patient,
      3500-3501, 3500f
  examination of
    in incontinence, 2060
    in organ prolapse, 2205-2207, 2206f
    landmarks for, 2207, 2208f
  extrarenal, 3303
  fascia of, 44-46
    components in, 45-46, 48f, 49f
  female, 2190-2191, 2191f
    physical examination of, 95
    support in, 67-68
    viscera in, 65, 65f-67f, 67
  innervation of, 52-55, 53f-55f, 53t
  irradiation of, bladder cancer associated with,
    2416
  lymphatics of, 52, 52f
  muscles of, 43-44, 46f, 47f
  soft tissues of, 43-46
  venous supply to, 51-52, 51f
  viscera of, 56-68. See also specific organs.
Pemphigoid, bullous, of male genitalia, 415-416,
    416f
Pemphigus vulgaris, of male genitalia, 415, 416f
Pendulous penis, 723
Penectomy, for penile cancer
  local recurrence after, 998
  partial, 973-974, 996, 997f, 998, 998f
  radical, 998, 1001f, 1002, 1002f
  total, 973-974, 998, 999f-1001f
Penetrating injury
  to kidney, 1274
    hematuria with, 1276
  to penis, 1049-1054
  to ureters, 1282-1283
D-Penicillamine, for cystinuria, 1424
Penicillin(s)
  for pediatric urinary tract infections, 3248t
  Jarisch-Herxheimer reaction to, 377
Penicillin G, for syphilis, 377
  in HIV patients, 395
Penicillin V, for Pasteurella multocida infection,
    2651
Penile adhesions, filmy, after circumcision,
    3748

Penile agenesis, 3756-3757, 3757f
  in bilateral renal agenesis, 3271
Penile artery, 71, 71f, 1033f, 1034, 1035f
  variability of, 71-72, 72f
Penile blood flow, evaluation of
  first-line, 757-758
  historical perspective in, 762
  intracavernous injection and stimulation in,
    757-758
  investigational, 762-763
  second-line, 758-760, 758f, 759f
  third-line, 760-762, 761f, 762f
Penile brachial pressure index, 762
Penile burns, 2654
Penile cancer, 92
  adenosquamous, 990
  basal cell, 989
  brachytherapy for, 985-986
  chemotherapy for, 987-989, 988t
  human papillomavirus and, 542, 961-962,
    965-966
  in uncircumcised males, 3747
  inguinal node involvement in, 1002-1011
    lymphadenectomy for. See also Inguinal
      lymphadenectomy.
      contemporary indications for, 974, 975t,
        976, 976t
      evolving indications for, 976-978, 976f,
        977f, 977t
      impact of histology, stage, grade, and
        vascular invasion in, 978-979, 979t
      prophylactic, 979-980, 980t
      modified procedures for, 980-981
      risk-based management of, 983-984, 983f-
        984f
      traditional procedures for, 981-982
  Kaposi's sarcoma as, 962-963
  lymphoreticular neoplasm as, 990
  metastatic, 990-991
  nonsquamous, 989-991
  Paget's disease in, 990
  radiation therapy for, 984-987
    disadvantages of, 985
    external beam, 984-985
    surgery after, 986, 986t
    to inguinal areas, 986-987
  sarcomas as, 990
    Kaposi's, 962-963
  squamous cell, 964-972
    biopsy of, 968, 993
    diagnosis of, 968-972
      delay in, 968
    differential diagnosis of, 972
    etiology of, 965-966
    histologic features of, 968-969
    in situ, 426-427, 427f, 964
    invasive, 964-965
    laboratory studies of, 969
    natural history of, 967
    physical examination of, 968
    prevention of, 966
    radiologic studies of, 969-970
    signs and symptoms of, 967-968
    staging of, 971-972, 971t, 972f, 972t
  surgical management of
    circumcision and limited excision in, 973
    conservative excision in, 994, 995f, 996
    laser ablation in, 973, 993-994
    Mohs micrographic, 973, 994
    organ preservation in, 972-973
    penectomy in
      partial, 996, 997f, 998, 998f
      radical, 998, 1001f, 1002, 1002f
      total, 973-974, 998, 999f-1001f

Penile cancer (Continued)
  survival associated with
    prognostic indicators in, 975t
    related to nodal metastases, 976t
Penile chancre, syphilitic, 376f, 420f
Penile curvature, 1087-1092. See also Chordee;
    Peyronie's disease.
  acquired, 1091
    without Peyronie's disease, 1091-1092
  assessment of, 3712
    artificial erection in, 1089, 3712, 3713f
    pharmacologic erection in, 3712
  congenital, 1089-1091
    types of, 1087-1088
  dorsal, 3755
  etiology of, 3707-3708
  lateral, 3754-3755
  persistent, options for, 1089
  recurrent, after hypospadias repair, 3739
  surgical treatment of, 1089-1091, 1090f, 3712-
    3714
    artificial erection obtained for, 1090-1091
    corporal rotation in, 3714
    dermal graft in, 3714, 3715f
    Heineke-Mikulicz technique in, 3714
    skin release and transfer in, 3713
    small intestinal submucosa in, 3714
    total penile disassembly in, 3714
    tunica albuginea plication in, 3714
    tunica vaginalis graft in, 3714
  without hypospadias
    etiology of, 3708
    management of, 3712-3714, 3715f
Penile cysts, 3750
Penile detumescence
  neurotransmitters in, 728
  phases of, 723
Penile disassembly technique
  in complete primary exstrophy repair, 3556-
    3557, 3556f-3558f
  complete, 3559, 3560f
    modifications of, 3563
  in penile curvature repair, 3714
Penile elephantitis, 457
Penile erection. See also Erectile dysfunction.
  after hypospadias repair, 3720
  artificial, in evaluation of penile curvature,
    1089
  functional anatomic components in, 719-723,
    719t
  hemodynamics of, 723-724, 723f, 724f
  mechanics of, 723-724
  neuroanatomy of, 724-730, 724f
  neurophysiology of, 724-730
    neurotransmitters in, 728-730
    peripheral pathways in, 724-725, 725f,
      726t
    supraspinal pathways in, 725-728, 726t,
      727t
  nocturnal, 765
  persistent. See Priapism.
  physiology of, 718-737
    historical aspects in, 718-719
    smooth muscle, 730-737. See also Smooth
      muscle, penile.
  psychogenic, 765
  reflexogenic, 739, 765
  return of, after radical prostatectomy, 2938
Penile injury
  amputation as, 1050-1052, 1051f, 2651
  bite as, 2650
  buckling, Peyronie's disease due to, 820, 820f
  degloving, 1052, 1053f
    in Peyronie's disease surgery, 831, 832f

Penile injury (Continued)
  fracture as, 2649-2650, 2650f
  genital burn as, 1052
  gunshot, 1050, 2650-2651
  in children, 3944-3945
  penetrating, 1049-1054
  penile cancer associated with, 966
  priapism associated with, 840-841
  radiation-induced, 1052-1054
  reconstruction after, 1096
  skin loss in, reconstruction for, 2654-2655
  strangulation, 2652
  zipper, 2652
Penile length
  fetal, 3745
  flaccid, 719t
  measurement of, 3752, 3752f
  stretched, 719t
    in normal male, 3746t
Penile necrosis, after circumcision, 3748
Penile pain, patient history of, 83
Penile papules, pearly, 431, 432f, 960
Penile plethysmography, 762
Penile prosthesis, 788-801
  complication(s) of, 795-797
    autoinflation as, 797
    infection as, 795-796, 796f
    oversized cylinder or rod as, 797
    perforation and erosion as, 797
    poor glans support as, 797, 798f
    pump, 797
  concomitant or prior, perineal sling procedure
    and, 2396
  design of, advances in, 796
  engineered, 565, 565f
  for cavernosal fibrosis, 798-800, 799f, 800f
  for erectile dysfunction, after renal
    transplantation, 1322, 1322t
  for Peyronie's disease, 798, 798f, 836-837
  inflatable, 788, 789t
    erection-like state of, 789-790
    historical perspectives on, 788
    mechanical failure rates of, 800, 800t
    three-piece, 788, 789f
    two-piece, 788, 789f
  malleable (semi-rigid), 788, 789t
  patient-partner satisfaction with, 800-801
  placement of, 790, 790f, 790t
    artificial sphincter and, 2402
    back pressure test in, 794-795, 795f
    corporotomy incision in, 790-791, 791f
    cylinder inflation and deflation in, 793,
      794f
    cylinder insertion in, 792, 792f, 793f
    cylinder selection in, 791-792, 792f
    pain medication in, 789
    postoperative care after, 795
    preoperative patient-partner counseling in,
      788-790
    pump insertion in, 792-793, 793f
    results of, 800-801, 800t
    safe reservoir insertion in, 793-794, 794f
    transverse incision in, 790, 791f
    transverse penoscrotal approach to, 790-
      795, 791f-795f
Penile reconstruction
  after injury, 1096, 2654-2655
  in exstrophy patient, 3518-3524
    modified Cantwell-Ransley repair in, 3520,
      3520f-3523f, 3523-3524
    postoperative problems after, 3524
    release of chordee in, 3519-3520
    skin closure in, 3520
    urethral repair in, 3520

Penile reconstruction (Continued)
  total, 1092-1096
    bipedicled flap in, 1095-1096
    fibular osteocutaneous flap in, 1093
    forearm flaps in, 1092-1093
      disadvantages of, 1093
      modifications of, 1093, 1094f, 1095f
    principles of, 1092
    rigidity for intercourse with, 1096
    saphenous interposition graft in, 1095
    upper arm flap, 1094-1095
Penile shaft
  anatomy of, 1028-1031, 1029f-1030f, 1032f-1035f
  coverage of, in hypospadias repair, 3718
  length of, 719t
  rotational defect of, 3754, 3754f
  skin of, 71
Penile sinusoids, loss of compliance of, erectile dysfunction associated with, 742
Penile skin bridges, after circumcision, 3748-3749, 3750f
Penile thermal sensory testing, in erectile dysfunction, 767
Penile torsion, 3754, 3754f
Penile tumescence, nocturnal, monitoring of, 763-764, 764f
Penile tumor(s), 959-991
  benign
    cutaneous, 960
    noncutaneous, 959-960
  Buschke-Löwenstein, 963-964
  malignant. See Penile cancer.
  premalignant
    cutaneous horn as, 960
    keratotic balanitis as, 960
    leukoplakia as, 961
    lichen sclerosus as, 960
    pseudoepitheliomatous micaceous growths as, 960
  viral-related, 961-963
    bowenoid papulosis as, 962
    Kaposi's sarcoma as, 962-963
    malignant transformation of, 961-962
Penile (pendulous) urethra, 1029, 1030f
  carcinoma of, 1012-1013, 1012f, 1013f
Penile vascular surgery
  arterial, 803-812
    complications of, 810-811
    dorsal artery dissection in, 806-807, 808f
    inferior epigastric artery harvesting in, 807-809, 808f
    microvascular anastomosis in, 809-810, 809f, 810f
      disruption following, 810-811
    penile edema following, 810
    penile numbness following, 810
    penile shortening following, 810
    results of, 811-812, 811t
    selection criteria for, 803-805, 803t, 804f, 805f
    technique of, 806-810, 806f, 806t, 807t
  venous, 812-816
    complications of, 815-816
    results of, 816, 816t
    selection criteria for, 812, 813f-814f
    technique of, 812, 815, 815f
Penile vibratory stimulation
  for anejaculation, 715-716, 716f
  for spinal cord–injured men, 649
Penile warts, human papillomavirus causing, 380, 381f

Penis. See also Micropenis.
  anatomy of, 69, 70f-72f, 71-72, 1028-1031, 1029f-1035f
    functional, 719-723, 719t
    of arterial system, 1034-1035, 1035f
    of lymphatics, 1035
    of nerve supply, 1035
    of venous drainage, 1031, 1034, 1034f
  anomalies of, 3746-3758. See also specific anomaly.
  arterial supply to, 721-722, 721f, 1031, 1033f
    anatomy of, 1034-1035, 1035f
  cancer of. See Penile cancer.
  corpus cavernosum of, 69, 69f, 70f. See also Corpus cavernosum.
  corpus spongiosum of, 69f, 70f, 71. See also Corpus spongiosum.
  duplication of, 3757
  edema of, after penile revascularization, 810
  elongation of, 3141, 3142f, 3143
  erectile tissue of, 1028-1029, 1030f. See also Penile erection.
  examination of, 91-92
  flaccid
    length of, 719t
    neurotransmitters in, 728
    smooth muscle contraction in, 723
  hidden, 3749f, 3751, 3751f
  hilum of, 69
  HSV infection of, 374f
  hypersensitivity of, in premature ejaculation, 784-785
  in exstrophy patient, functional and cosmetically pleasing, 3503-3504, 3519
  inconspicuous, 3749f, 3751, 3751f
  infrapubic, 722f, 723
  injury to. See Penile injury.
  innervation of, 724-725, 725f, 726t
    anatomy of, 1035
  lymphatics of, anatomy of, 1035
  molluscum contagiosum affecting, 382f
  neonatal, evaluation of, 3209
  normal, 3745
  numbness of, after penile revascularization, 810
  pendulous, 723
  prosthetic. See Penile prosthesis.
  reconstruction of. See Penile reconstruction.
  scabies affecting, 383f
  shortening of
    after penile revascularization, 810
    in bladder exstrophy, 3501
  strangulation of, 2652
  tissue engineering of, corporal tissues reconstruction in, 564-565, 564f, 565f
  trapped, 3751
    resulting from circumcision, 3750f
  tuberculosis of, 440
  tunica albuginea of, 70f, 72f. See also Tunica albuginea.
  vasculature of, 51, 51f, 71-72, 72f
  venous drainage of, 722-723, 722f, 813f
    anatomy of, 1031, 1034, 1034f
  webbed, 3749f, 3751
Penn pouch, for continent urinary diversion, 2602-2604
  postoperative care of, 2603-2604
  procedure in, 2602-2603, 2603f
Penography, radionuclide, 762-763
Penoscrotal transposition, 3758-3759, 3758f
PENS. See Posterior tibial nerve stimulation (PENS).

Pentosan polysulfate
  for painful bladder syndrome/interstitial cystitis, 360-361, 360t, 362t, 363-364
  for prostatitis, clinical trial data on, 322, 327t
Peptic ulcer, postoperative, prophylactic management of, 1317, 1318t
Peptide(s), excretion of, effect of ureteral obstruction on, 1203
Peptidergic agents, effect of, on ureteral function, 1906
Percussion, of bladder, 90
Percutaneous antegrade endopyelotomy, for ureteropelvic junction obstruction, 1233-1237. See also Endopyelotomy, percutaneous antegrade.
Percutaneous epididymal sperm aspiration (PESA), 652, 700, 702f-703f
Percutaneous nephrolithotomy. See Nephrolithotomy, percutaneous.
Percutaneous nephrostomy. See Nephrostomy, percutaneous.
Percutaneous procedures. See also specific procedure.
  antibiotic prophylaxis for, 253
Percutaneous transluminal angioplasty (PTA)
  complications of, 1181
  for atherosclerotic renal artery stenosis, 1182, 1183f, 1183t, 1184, 1184t
  for fibrous dysplasia, 1181-1182, 1181t, 1182f
  for inflammatory renal artery stenosis, 1184
  for renovascular hypertension, 1180-1184
  in children, 1184
  mechanism of, 1181
  technique of, 1180-1181
  with endovascular stenting, 1185-1186, 1185t
Percutaneous vasectomy, 1101. See also Vasectomy.
Pereyra technique, modified, for stress incontinence, 2212
Perforation. See at anatomic site.
Perfusion studies, of ureteral obstruction, 1913-1914, 1914f
Perimedial fibroplasia, of renal artery, 1157t, 1160-1161, 1160f, 1161f
Perimenopausal women, hormonal therapy for, sexual health problems and, 878-881, 879f
Perineal body, 1036, 1037f, 1039, 2194, 2194f
  defects of, 2200
  examination of, 2207
  fascia of, 46, 49f
Perineal mass, in female neonate, 3194-3195
Perineal membrane, 2193
Perineal pain, in children, 3207
Perineal sling, for male incontinence, 2077, 2393-2396
  complications of, 2395-2396
  implantation technique of, 2393, 2394f
  indications for, 2391-2392
  results of, 2393-2395, 2395t
  special circumstances and, 2396
Perineal space
  deep, 1038f, 1039
  superficial, 1036, 1037f
Perineorrhaphy, posterior colporrhaphy and, 2230-2232, 2231f
Perinephric abscess, 276-278
  after injury, 1282
  Candida causing, 462
  clinical presentation of, 277
  in children, diagnosis of, 3246
  management of, 278
  radiologic findings in, 277-278, 277f, 278f
  vs. acute pyelonephritis, 278

Perineum, 68-77
  anal triangle of, 68
  anatomy of, 1035-1036, 1037f-1039f, 1039
  fascia of, 46, 49f, 73, 73f, 1036, 1037f
  female
    anal triangle of, 68
    urogenital triangle of, 76f, 77
  lymphatic drainage of, 73
  male, urogenital triangle of, 68-69, 70f
  massage of, for prostatitis, 323-324
  muscles of, 68, 1036, 1037f, 1038f, 1039, 2193,
    2193f
Peripheral autonomous hypothesis, of detrusor
    overactivity, 2080-2081, 2081f
Peripheral nervous system, of lower urinary
    tract, 1937-1939, 1938f
  afferent pathways in, 1938-1939, 1938f, 1939t
  parasympathetic pathways in, 1938
  somatic pathways in, 1938
  sympathetic pathways in, 1938
Peripheral neuroectodermal tumor, of kidney,
    1636
Peristalsis, ureteral. See Ureter(s), peristalsis of.
Peritoneal cavity, evaluation of, in female
    fertility, 612-613
Peritoneal dialysis. See also Hemodialysis.
  for acute renal failure, 1339, 1358t
Peritoneal flap. See also Flap(s).
  in vesicovaginal fistula repair, 2339, 2339f
Periurethral abscess, 302
Periurethral bulking procedures, for bladder
    filling/storage disorders, 2292
Periurethral colonization, of bacteria, in
    pediatric urinary tract infections, 3238
Periurethral fascial flap. See also Flap(s).
  in urethral diverticula repair, 2387f, 2388
Periurethral glands, 1030
  secretions of, 614
Periurethral nodules, in benign prostatic
    hyperplasia, 2735-2736, 2736f
Permethrin cream
  for pediculosis pubis, 384
  for scabies, 383
Pernicious anemia, voiding dysfunction in,
    2012t, 2030
Persistent müllerian duct syndrome, 3826-3827
PESA (percutaneous epididymal sperm
    aspiration), 652, 700, 702f-703f
Pessaries, vaginal
  for pelvic organ prolapse, 2137-2138, 2138f,
    2139f
  for stress incontinence, 2137
PET. See Positron emission tomography (PET).
Peyronie's disease, 92, 818-838
  acquired penile curvatures without, 1091-
    1092
  anatomic considerations in, 819-822, 819f-
    822f
  animal models in, 822-823
  buckling penile injuries causing, 820, 820f
  calcified plaque in, 825, 825f, 826f
  carnitine in, 827
  Dupuytren's contracture associated with, 818
  erectile dysfunction in, 823
  etiology of, 819-822
  evaluation of, 825-826, 825f, 826f
  incidence of, 818-819
  matrix metalloproteinases in, 821-822
  natural history of, 823
  Paget's disease associated with, 818
  pathophysiology of, 823-824
  PDE-5 inhibitor therapy and, 819
  plication for, 714-715
  prevalence of, 819

Peyronie's disease (Continued)
  symptoms of, 824-825
  TGF-β accumulation in, 821, 821f, 822f
  treatment of, 826-838
    carnitine in, 827
    colchicine in, 827
    collagenase in, 828
    extracorporeal shockwave therapy in, 828
    fexofenadine in, 827
    interferons in, 828
    medical, 826-828
    penile prosthesis in, 798, 798f, 836-837
    potassium aminobenzoate in, 827
    radiotherapy in, 828
    surgical correction in, 829-831, 831f-836f,
      833, 836
      candidates for, 828-829
      dermal graft inlays in, 831, 833
      dorsal exposure of turnica in, 831, 833f
      H flaps in, 833, 835f, 836, 836f
      H-shaped incisions in, 833, 833f, 834f
      initial incision in, 831, 831f
      mobilization and division of dorsal vein
        in, 831, 832f
      penile degloving in, 831, 832f
    tamoxifen in, 827
    terfenadine in, 827
    vacuum erection device for, 828
    verapamil in, 827-828
    vitamin E in, 827
  urethral instrumentation causing, 818
Pezzer catheter, 162, 162f
PF chemotherapy regimen, for penile cancer,
    988t
Pfannenstiel incision, 2483
  in antireflux surgery, 4351
P-glycoprotein, in renal cell carcinoma, 1589,
    1626
pH
  in acid-base balance
    changes of, 1152
    maintenance of, 1151
  of semen, 617
    reference range for, 618
  of urine. See Urinary pH.
  of vagina, testing for, 871
Phagocytosis, 474
Phallus
  development of
    in females, 3142f, 3143
    in males, 3141, 3142f, 3143
  examination of, genital anomalies and,
    3849
Pharmaceuticals. See Drug(s); specific drug or
    drug group.
Phenoxybenzamine
  dosage of, 2119
  effect of, on ureteral function, 1906
  for pheochromocytoma, preoperative, 1866,
    1871
  for postoperative urinary retention,
    prophylactic, 2040-2041
  for prostatitis, 321
  side effects of, 2119
Phentolamine
  effect of, on ureteral function, 1906
  for erectile dysfunction, 778-779
    combination therapy with, 780
Phenylephrine, for priapism, 845, 846t, 3755
Phenylpropanolamine
  AHCPR guidelines for, 2110
  for stress incontinence, 2109-2111
    complications of, 2110-2111
    in elderly, 2318

Pheochromocytoma, 1857-1867
  adrenalectomy for, 1870t, 1871. See also
    Adrenalectomy.
    intraoperative complications in, 1886
    postoperative complications in, 1886,
      1886t
  anesthetic management of, 1866-1867,
    1866t
  differential diagnosis of, 1859t
  hereditary forms of, 1860, 1861t
  historical background of, 1821
  in children, 1861, 3878
  in von Hippel–Lindau disease, 1861, 1862t,
    3334
  in von Recklinghausen's disease, 1861
  laboratory diagnosis of, 1862, 1862f, 1863t
  malignant, 1861-1862
  MR images of, 1860f, 1863, 1864f, 1865f
  of bladder, 2445
  preoperative management of, 1863, 1866
  radiologic tests for, 1862-1863
  scintigraphy of, 1863, 1865f
  signs and symptoms of, 1857-1861, 1858t
Phimosis, 91, 883, 1044, 3746-3747
  as risk factor for penile cancer, 3747
  circumcision with, 1046, 1046f
  clitoral, 866, 868f, 869f
Phleboliths, radiographic studies of, 111,
    112f
Phosphate, renal reabsorption of, in proximal
    convoluted tubules, 1140-1141, 1141f
Phosphaturia, 96
Phosphodiesterase, in male sexual function, 736,
    736f
Phosphodiesterase type-5 (PDE-5) inhibitors.
    See also specific inhibitor.
  for erectile dysfunction, 773-777, 774f, 774t
    cardiovascular safety and, 777-778, 777t,
      778f
    combination therapy with, 778
    nitrates contraindicated with, 778
  for female sexual dysfunction, 882-883
  for premature ejaculation, 786
  Peyronie's disease and, 819
  synergism of testosterone with, 859
Phosphorus, metabolism of, 1372
Phosphorylcholine, in prostatic secretions,
    2717
Photodynamic therapy
  for cutaneous diseases of external genitalia,
    407
  for refractory disease, in non–muscle-invasive
    bladder cancer, 2462
  for transitional cell carcinoma of bladder,
    2482
Photon radiation, interstitial, 1818
Photoselective potassium titanyl phosphate
    (KTP) laser, in treatment of benign
    prostatic hyperplasia, 2828
Phrenic artery, 20, 23f, 24
Phrenic vein, 11f, 14
Phthirus pubis, 383, 425. See also Crab louse.
Phycomycosis, 466
Physical examination, 89-95
  general observations in, 89-90
  of bladder, 90-91, 91f
  of kidneys, 90, 90f
  of neurologic system, 95, 95f
  of pelvis, female, 94-95
  of penis, 91-92
  of prostate, 94
  of rectum, 93-94
  of scrotum, 92-93, 92f
Physical therapy, for prostatitis, 323-324

Phytotherapeutic agents. *See also specific agent.*
  for benign prostatic hyperplasia, 2797-2801
    composition of, 2798, 2798t
    mechanism of action of, 2798-2800, 2798t
    origin of, 2797-2798, 2798t
  for prostatitis, 323, 325t, 327t
PI3-Kinase/Akt pathway, in hormone-refractory prostate cancer, 3115
Piezoelectric generator, for shockwave lithotripsy, 1467t, 1468, 1469f, 1471t
Pigtail catheter, for percutaneous nephrostomy, 1558-1559, 1558f, 1559f
Pins, osteotomy, in exstrophy patient, 3514f, 3515
Piperacillin, for pediatric urinary tract infections, 3248t
Pippi-Salle procedure, for bladder neck reconstruction, in children
  results of, 3672
  technique of, 3669-3670, 3671f, 3672
Piriformis muscle, 44, 46f
Pituitary
  disorders of, male infertility associated with, 635
  in male reproductive axis, 578, 578f
  steroid feedback on, 578-579
*PKD1* gene, in autosomal dominant polycystic kidney disease, 3306, 3320, 3322
*PKD2* gene, in autosomal dominant polycystic kidney disease, 3306, 3320, 3322
*PKD3* gene, in autosomal dominant polycystic kidney disease, 3306, 3320
Placebo control groups, in untreated benign prostatic hyperplasia, 2752-2753, 2752t
  vs. watchful waiting studies, 2752t
Placental alkaline phosphatase, in testicular tumors, 907
Plant extracts, for benign prostatic hyperplasia, 2797-2801, 2798t. *See also* Phytotherapeutic agents; *specific extract.*
Plaque, calcified, in Peyronie's disease, 825, 825f, 826f
Plasma markers, in glomerular filtration rate, 1133, 1133f
Plasma renin activity
  in fetus, 3157
  in primary hyperaldosteronism, 1851
  in renovascular hypertension, 1169
Plasmacytoma, of bladder, 2445
Plasmin, 544
Plastic constricting device, in penile strangulation injury, 2652
Plasticity, of target organs, voiding dysfunction and, 2013-2014
Platelet-derived growth factor, 2711
  in bladder cancer, 2429
  in renal cell carcinoma, 1629-1630, 1630f, 1630t
  properties of, 2706t
Platelet-derived growth factor receptor, in hormone-refractory prostate cancer, 3115
Platelet/endothelial cell adhesion molecule-1, 493-494
Plethysmography, penile, 762
Pleural injury
  adrenal surgery causing, 1885t, 1886
  percutaneous nephrolithotomy causing, 1489
  percutaneous nephrostomy causing, 1547-1548
Plexus
  nerve. *See specific plexus.*
  pelvic, lateral, 51-52, 51f

Plication technique(s)
  for megaureter, 4379, 4379f
  for Peyronie's disease, 714-715
  of hydrocelectomy, 1105-1106, 1106f
PMB chemotherapy regimen, for penile cancer, 988t
Pneumaturia
  in vesicoenteric fistula, 2351
  patient history of, 87
Pneumomediastinum, with pneumoperitoneum, 206
Pneumonia
  after renal transplantation, 1323
  as complication of post-chemotherapy surgery, 956
Pneumopericardium, with pneumoperitoneum, 206
Pneumoperitoneum
  acid-base effects of, 201-202
  cardiovascular effects of, 200
  closed techniques for, 179-180, 179f, 180f
  complications related to, 204-209
    blind trocar placement and, 206-209, 207t, 208f
    closed access and, 204
    equipment malfunction and, 204
    insufflation and, 205-206
    open access and, 206
  creation of, in laparoscopic varicocele repair, 660
  gas for, 199-200
  gasless technique for, 181
  hand port access for, 181
  insufflant system for, 178-179
    choice of, 199-200
  open techniques for, 180-181, 181f
  pressure for, 200, 200t
  renal effects of, 201
  respiratory effects of, 200-201
  transperitoneal access and, 178-181, 179f-181f
  Veress needle placement for, verification of, 179-180, 179f
  visceral effects of, 201
Pneumothorax
  after radical nephrectomy, 1719-1720
  tension, laparoscopic renal surgery causing, 1808
  with pneumoperitoneum, 206
Pocket site discomfort, in acral nerve neuromodulation, troubleshooting algorithm for, 2162-2163, 2163f
Podocytes, of glomerular capillaries, 31, 32f
Podofilox solution, for genital warts, 381
Podophyllin in tincture of benzoin, for genital warts, 382
Poliomyelitis, voiding dysfunction in, 2030
Politano-Leadbetter technique, of antireflux surgery, 4352, 4353f-4355f
Polyamine(s), in prostatic secretions, 2716-2717
Polyamine synthesis inhibitors, in prevention of bladder cancer, 2443
Polycystic kidney disease. *See also* Autosomal dominant polycystic kidney disease; Autosomal recessive polycystic kidney disease.
  renal surgery for, 1755
Polycythemia
  in renal cell carcinoma, 1597t, 1598
  testosterone therapy causing, 860
Polydimethylsiloxane, for endoscopic correction of reflux, 4364-4365, 4364t
Polyester(s), for tissue engineering, 556
Polyethylene coaxial dilators, for ureteroscopy, 1511t, 1512

Polyethylene glycol-electrolyte lavage solution (GoLYTELY), for mechanical bowel preparation, 2537-2538, 2537t
Polyethylene stents, 1517
Polymer injections, silicone, for incontinence, 2275
  efficacy of, 2281-2282
Polymorphisms
  and susceptibility to cancer, 519-520, 520f
  variants of, prior study of, 520
Polyp(s)
  bladder, in exstrophy patient, 3506, 3506f
  fibroepithelial, 431, 433
    in children, 3900
    of upper urinary tract, abnormal urothelium in, 1643
    percutaneous treatment of, 1556-1557
  urethral, 3845-3846, 3846f
    in children, 3601, 3601f
Polyposis, schistosomal, 450, 450f
Polypropylene monofilament mesh, in tension-free vaginal tape procedure, 2251-2252
Polystyrene sodium sulfonate, for renal tubular acidosis, in infant and child, 3155
Polysynaptic inhibitors, for overactive bladder/detrusor overactivity, 2106
Polytetrafluoroethylene injections
  for bladder neck reconstruction, in children, 3665-3666
  for incontinence, 2273-2274
    efficacy of, 2281
    safety of, 2284-2285
Polytetrafluoroethylene paste, for endoscopic correction of reflux, 4364, 4364t
Polyurethane stents, 1517
  for benign prostatic hyperplasia, 2806-2807
Polyuria, nocturnal, 3621. *See also* Nocturia.
Pontine micturition center, 1946
  supraspinal mechanisms in, 1964-1966, 1964f
Population-based studies, of painful bladder syndrome/interstitial cystitis, 334-335
Port(s)
  in hand-assisted laparoscopic nephrectomy placement of, 1791, 1792f-1796f
  site closure of, 1798
  site seeding of, after laparoscopic surgery, 1779, 1779f, 1780t, 1781, 1781t
Positron emission tomography (PET)
  of bladder cancer, 2440
    invasive, 2469
  of brain, during sexual arousal, 726-728
  of germ cell tumors, 905
  of prostate cancer, localized vs. metastatic, 3072
  of renal cell carcinoma, 1603
Postcoital test, 615
  abnormal, antisperm antibodies in, 624
  normal, 630
  of sperm function, 630-631
Posterior sagittal anorectovaginourethroplasty, for cloacal malformations, 3866-3867, 3867f
Posterior tibial nerve stimulation (PENS), 2159-2160
  for voiding dysfunction, in children, 2157-2158
Postinfectious glomerulonephritis, in children, 3226
Post-intercourse prophylaxis, for recurrent urinary tract infections, 265
Post-massage two-hour glass test, for prostatitis, 314-315, 315f

Postmenopausal women
  hormonal therapy for
    incontinence and, 2108
    sexual health problems and, 878-881, 879f
  recurrent urinary tract infections in, 262
  vaginal surgery in, preoperative estrogens for,
    2215-2216
Postmicturition contraction, 1997
Postmicturition dribble, 84, 2047
  in children, 3613
Postobstructive diuresis
  clinical management of, 1214
  experimental modulation of, 1214
  mechanisms of, 1213-1214
Postoperative spindle cell nodule, of bladder,
  2418
Postural stimulation test, for primary
  hyperaldosteronism, 1852-1853
Post-vasectomy pain syndrome, 1102, 1108
Postvoid residual urine
  definition of, 1997
  in benign prostatic hyperplasia, assessment of,
    2770-2771
  in incontinent patient, assessment of, 2060
Potassium
  in resting membrane potential, 1892-1893,
    1893f
  renal excretion of
    after bilateral ureteral obstruction, 1202
    cortical collecting tubule in, 1145
    loop of Henle in, 1142
    proximal convoluted tubule in, 1139
Potassium aminobenzoate, for Peyronie's
  disease, 827
Potassium channel openers
  effect of, on ureteral function, 1920
  for overactive bladder/detrusor overactivity,
    2100
  uropharmacology of, 1961-1962
Potassium chloride challenge test, for painful
  bladder syndrome/interstitial cystitis, 354
Potassium citrate
  for calcium oxalate nephrolithiasis, 1422, 1423
  for gouty diathesis, 1424
  for hyperoxaluria, 1422
  for hyperuricosuria, 1420
  for renal hypercalciuria, 1419
  for renal tubular acidosis, 1422
Potassium titanyl phosphate (KTP) laser
  for penile cancer, 973, 994
  in treatment of benign prostatic hyperplasia,
    2821
  photoselective, 2828
Potassium-magnesium citrate, for
  hypomagnesiuric calcium nephrolithiasis,
    1423-1424
Potency
  after brachytherapy, 3026-3027
  after radical perineal prostatectomy, 2984
  after radical prostatectomy, 2938
Potter's facies, characteristic, in bilateral renal
  agenesis, 3270-3271, 3271f, 3272
Potter's syndrome, in neonate, 3195
Prader-Willi syndrome, infertility in, 636
Praziquantel, for schistosomiasis, 454
Prazosin
  dosage of, 2119
  preoperative, for pheochromocytoma, 1866
  side effects of, 2119
Precipitancy (urinary)
  definition of, 2311
  in elderly, 2311
Predictive validity, of HRQOL instruments, 154t,
  155

Prednisolone
  for nephrotic syndrome, 3225
  for prostatitis, clinical trial data on, 322
Prednisone
  for nephrotic syndrome, 3225
  for painful bladder syndrome/interstitial
    cystitis, 361
Pregnancy
  after renal transplantation, 1322-1323,
    1323t
  anatomic and physiologic changes during,
    290-291, 290t, 291f
  as contraindication to laparoscopy, 175
  bacteriuria in, 237, 289-293
    complications of, 291-292
    diagnosis of, 292
    management of, 292-293, 292t
    pathogenesis of, 290
  calculi in, 1391
    medical management of, 1428-1429
    ureteroscopic management of, 1519-1520
    urinary, 1455-1458
      evaluation of, 1457
      incidence of, 1456
      spontaneous passage of, 1457
      surgical management of, 1457-1458
  Cushing's syndrome in, 1837, 1838f
  effect of, on ureteral function, 1918
  following augmentation cystoplasty, 3686
  in true hermaphrodites, 3816
  in women with renal insufficiency, 293
  incontinence in, 2189
  laparoscopic adrenalectomy during, 1887
  pelvic organ prolapse and, 2189
  pheochromocytoma in, 1859
  pyelonephritis during, 289, 290
  rates of
    after vasovasostomy, 678-679, 679t
    electroejaculation and, 716
  ureteral obstruction due to, 1219-1220,
    1220t
  urethral diverticula in, 2390
  urinary tract infections in, 237
    effects of, 3241
  vesicoureteral reflux in, 4344-4345
Pregnenolone, production of, 1825, 1825f
Premalignant penile tumor(s), 960-961. See also
  Penile tumor(s).
Pre-massage two-hour glass test, for prostatitis,
  314-315, 315f
Premature ejaculation. See Ejaculation,
  premature.
Prematurity, bacteriuria and, 291
Premenopausal women, hormonal therapy for,
  sexual health problems and, 875-878
Premicturition pressure, 1996
Prenatal mortality, bacteriuria and, 291
Preneoplastic proliferative abnormalities, of
  bladder, 2417
Prentiss maneuver, in orchidopexy techniques,
  3779
Preoperative counseling, in vesicovaginal fistula
  repair, 2333
Preperitoneal laparoscopy, gasless, 182
Prepuce
  atrophy of, 871f
  infections of, 883
  sexual pain disorders involving, 883
Preputial calculi, 2672-2673
Preputial colonization, of bacteria, in pediatric
  urinary tract infection, 3238-3239
Presacral dimple, atypical, 3210
Presacral lymph nodes, 52, 52f
Pressure transmission rate, 2007

Pressure-flow micturition studies, 1995-2000
  ICS nomenclature for, 1994t, 1996-1997,
    1996f
  in benign prostatic hyperplasia, 2771-2772
  in bladder outlet obstruction, 1998
  in incontinence, 2068
  in transurethral needle ablation of prostate,
    2812-2813, 2812t
  in ureteropelvic junction obstruction, in
    children, 3368-3369
  nomogram(s) in, 1998-2000
    Abrams-Griffiths, 1998
    ICS provisional, 1999-2000, 1999f, 2000f
    Schafer, 1998-1999, 1999f
  obstructed, 1997, 1997f
  urethral resistance factors in, 1999
  with detrusor dysfunction, 1996-1997, 1996f
Pressure-length-diameter relations, of ureteral
  smooth muscle, 1903, 1904f
Preureteral vena cava, 3417-3420
  anatomy of, 3417, 3418f
  diagnosis of, 3419
  embryology of, 3417-3419, 3419f, 3420f
  incidence of, 3419
  treatment of, 3419-3420
Priapism, 92, 839-850, 3755
  alcohol-induced, 841
  associated with intracavernous injection
    therapy, 781
  classification of, 843-844
  definition of, 839
  diagnosis of, 844-845, 844f
  drug-induced, 841, 844
  epidemiology of, 839-840
  erectile dysfunction pharmacotherapy
    associated with, 841
  etiology of, 840-841
  hematologic dyscrasias associated with, 840
  idiopathic, 841, 844
  incidence of, 840
  intraoperative, management of, 2836
  ischemic, 841, 843, 3755
    cavernosal blood gas determinants in, 845
    natural history of, 841
    treatment of, 845-846, 846t, 847f-848f, 848
  laboratory tests for, 844-845
  management of, 3755
  natural history of, 841
  neoplastic processes associated with, 840
  neurogenic, 844
  neurologic conditions associated with, 840
  nonischemic, 841, 843, 3755
    cavernosal blood gas determinants in, 845
    natural history of, 841
    treatment of, 848
  painful, in boys, 3203
  pathology of, 841-842
  pathophysiology of, 842-843
  penile injury associated with, 840-841
  physical examination of, 844
  radiologic evaluation of, 845
  refractory, 843-844
  stuttering (intermittent), 3755
  stuttering (recurrent), 843
    natural history of, 841
    treatment of, 848-849
  treatment of, 845-849
    algorithm for, 844f
    medical, 845-846, 846t
    miscellaneous therapies in, 849
    surgical, 846, 847f-848f, 848
  variants of, 843-844
Prilocaine cream, for premature ejaculation, 786,
  786t

Primary ciliary dyskinesia, 611, 623
PRL. *See* Prolactin (PRL).
Proapoptotic gene therapy, for prostate cancer, 3030
Probiotic therapy, prophylactic, for pediatric urinary tract infections, 3252
Processus vaginalis
  ligation of, in orchidopexy, 3777, 3778f
  patent
    in undescended testis, 3773
    laparoscopic examination of, 3915f
  separation and ligation of, in orchiopexy, 3777, 3777f, 3778f
Proctitis, 371
Prodrug gene therapy, for prostate cancer, 3030
Progesterone
  and female sexual function, 875
  for sexual dysfunction
    in perimenopausal and postmenopausal women, 880
    in premenopausal women, 875-876
  for vaginal atrophy, 880
  midluteal phase, in evaluation of fertility, 612
Progestin, maternal administration of, 3820-3821
Programmed cell death. *See* Apoptosis.
Prolactin (PRL)
  effects of, on prostate, 2689
  excess of, in males, 637
  in male sexual function, 730
  secretion of, 578
Prolapse. *See at specific anatomic site.*
Promoter element, in genes, 2702-2703
Pronephros, 3121, 3124f, 3149, 3150f
Propanolamine, for retrograde ejaculation, 648
Propantheline, for overactive bladder/detrusor overactivity, 2093t, 2094-2095
Prophase, in mitosis, 2712
Propiverine, for overactive bladder/detrusor overactivity, 2093t, 2102-2103
Proscar Long Term Efficacy and Safety Study (PLESS), 2753, 2754, 2790, 2791f
Prosta Coil stent, 2805
Prosta Kath stent, 2804-2805
Prostaglandin(s)
  and renal development, 3159
  in male sexual function, 732-734
  in prostatic secretions, 2717-2718
  in ureteral function, 1919-1920
  to facilitate bladder emptying, 2116-2117
  uropharmacology of, 1955
Prostaglandin $E_1$, for erectile dysfunction
  intracavernous injection of, 779-780
  intraurethral, 781
Prostaglandin $E_2$
  in renin secretion, 1162
  inhibition of T cell activity by, 497-498
Prostaglandin $F_{2\alpha}$, in male sexual function, 728
Prostaglandin $I_2$
  in male sexual function, 728
  in renin secretion, 728
Prostanoids, uropharmacology of, 1955
ProstaScint scan, of prostate cancer, localized vs. metastatic, 3072
Prostasoft 2.5 protocol, clinical studies of, 2817
Prostasoft 3.5 protocol, clinical studies of, 2817
Prostate, 61-63
  abscess of
    *Candida* causing, 460, 462f
    drainage of, 325
  anatomic relationships of, 61
  anatomy of
    arterial, 2956-2957, 2956f
    ultrasonographic, 2883, 2884f, 2885

Prostate *(Continued)*
  apex of, 61
    dissection of, in robotic-assisted laparoscopic radical prostatectomy, 2995
  arterial supply to, 63, 63f
  basal cells of, 2682-2683
  benign hyperplasia of. *See* Benign prostatic hyperplasia.
  biopsy of, 2887-2892
    contraindications to, 2889
    extended core, 2890, 2890f, 2890t
    fine-needle aspiration, 2891
    indications for, 2887-2889, 2887t
    patient preparation for, 251-252, 2889
    positive
      after cryotherapy, 3045, 3047
      in intermediate-risk patients, 3007-3009, 3008f
      in low-risk and favorable intermediate-risk patients, 3009, 3009f-3011f
    post-brachytherapy, 3023, 3024t
    post-radiotherapy, 3013-3014, 3013t
    repeat and saturation, 2890-2891, 2891t
    repeated, 2955
    rising PSA levels and, 3072
    risks and complications of, 2892
    sextant, 2890
    systemic results of, 2951
    transperineal, 2891-2892
    transrectal
      antibiotic prophylaxis for, 251-252
      techniques of, 2889-2891
      ultrasound-guided, 2923
        recommendations for, 2925
        techniques of, 2889-2891
    transurethral, 2892
  calculi in, 2670
  cancer of. *See* Prostate cancer.
  candidiasis of, 460, 468f
  cell types in, 2680-2683, 2680t
  central zone of, 63
  computed tomography of, 133
  cystic lesions of, transrectal ultrasonography of, 2886, 2886f
  development of, 3137-3139, 3139f
  dissection of, posterior, in robotic-assisted laparoscopic radical prostatectomy, 2990-2991, 2990f, 2991f
  embryonic development of, 2678-2679
  epithelial cells of, 2680-2681, 2680t
  examination of, 94
  exposure of
    in perineal prostatectomy, 2980-2981, 2980f, 2981f
    in retropubic prostatectomy, 2847, 2847f
      radical, 2960
    in suprapubic prostatectomy, 2850, 2850f
  expressed secretions from, in urinary sediment, 109, 109f
  fibromuscular stroma of, 61, 63, 64f
  glandular elements of, 61
  growth factors in, 2705-2711. *See also* Growth factors.
  growth of
    endocrine control of, 2684-2689
      androgen production in, 2685-2686, 2686t, 2687f
      androgen-binding proteins in, 2688-2689
      estrogens in, 2679-2680, 2686t, 2687f, 2688
      overview of, 2684-2685, 2685f
      prolactin in, 2689

Prostate *(Continued)*
  regulation of
    androgen action in, 2690-2691, 2691f
      nuclear matrix in, 2703-2705
    androgen receptor-dependent chromatin remodeling in, 2702-2703
    androgen receptors in, 2697-2701, 2697f, 2698f
    apoptosis in, 2714-2715
    balance of cell replication and death in, 2711-2715
    by steroids and protein growth factors, 2689-2696
    cell adhesion molecules in, 2694-2696
    cell aging, senescence, and immortality in, 2713-2714
    cell-adhesion molecules in, 2694-2696
    chromatin in, 2712-2713
    DNA damage in, 2714
    DNA synthesis and cell cycle control in, 2711-2712
    estrogens and estrogen-androgen synergism in, 2693
    interactive types of, 2690, 2690f
    5α-reductase and androgen metabolism in, 2691-2693, 2691t, 2692f
    steroid receptors in, 2696-2705
    stromal-epithelial interactions in, 2693-2694
    vitamin A in, 2705
    vitamin D in, 2705
  hormonal imprinting of, 2679-2680
  in exstrophy patient, 3504, 3505f
  in prune-belly syndrome, 3484
  inflammation of. *See* Prostatitis.
  innervation of, 63
  irradiation of, treatment effects of, 2880
  lobes of, 63
  localization of, in diagnosis of urinary tract infection, 242
  lymphatic drainage of, 63
  magnetic resonance imaging of, 135, 138, 138f, 139f
  massage of, for prostatitis, 323
  neuroendocrine cells of, 2680t, 2681
  pain in, patient history of, 83
  peripheral zone of, 63
  periurethral zone of, in benign prostatic hyperplasia, 2734
  postnatal development of, 2679-2680
  resection of. *See also* Prostatectomy.
    efficacy of injectable therapies after, 2281
  secretions of. *See* Prostatic secretions.
  size of, in benign prostatic hyperplasia, 2742-2743, 2742f
  smooth muscle of, adrenergic regulation of, 2737
  sparing of, in laparoscopic radical cystectomy, 2519f, 2520
    clinical outcome data on, 2531
  stem cells of, 2682-2683
  structure of, 61, 62f, 63
  tissue matrix of, 2683-2684, 2683f
  transit-amplifying cells of, 2680t, 2681-2682, 2682f
  transition zone of, 61, 62f, 63
    in benign prostatic hyperplasia, 2734
  transperineal biopsy of, 2891-2892
  transurethral biopsy of, 2892
  transurethral resection of, antibiotic prophylaxis for, 252
  trapped, 2039
  TRUS-guided biopsy of, 2887-2891
    contraindications to, 2889

Prostate (Continued)
  indications for, 2887-2889, 2888t
  patient preparation for, 251-252, 2889
  techniques of, 2889-2891, 2890f, 2890t, 2891t
  tuberculosis of, 440
  ultrasonography of, 124
    transrectal, 2883-2887. See also Transrectal ultrasonography (TRUS).
  venous anatomy of, 2956, 2956f
  zonal anatomy of, 61, 62f, 63
Prostate cancer, 94
  adenocarcinoma as, 2875-2880. See also Adenocarcinoma, of prostate.
  androgen receptor in, 2865
  androgen-refractory, 3084. See also Prostate cancer, hormone-refractory.
  androgens in, influence of, 2860-2861, 2863-2864
  apoptosis in, 532
  biopsy for. See Biopsy, of prostate.
  CDKN1A gene in, 524
  cell adhesion molecules in, 2695-2696
  chemoprevention of, 2867-2871
    antioxidants in, 2870-2871
    clinical trial design for, 2867-2868, 2868t
    COX-2 inhibitors in, 2871
    finasteride in, 2869-2870, 2870t
    green tea in, 2871
    lycopene in, 2871
    models of secondary prevention in, 2868t
    other 5α-reductase inhibitors in, 2870
    Prostate Cancer Prevention Trial in, 2868-2870, 2869f, 2870t
    selective estrogen receptor modulators in, 2871
    selenium in, 2870
      vitamin E with, 2871
    soy in, 2871
    target populations for, 2868t
    vitamin E in, 2870-2871
  classical oncogenes in, 2866
  cyclooxygenase in, 2865
  detection of, 2912-2915
    early, guidelines for, 2923-2925
    future risk of, 2917t, 2918-2919, 2918t
    issues in, 2913
  development of, lifetime risk for, 2948t
  diagnosis of
    age at, 2856
    digital rectal examination in, 2922-2923
    histologic, 2912
    modalities used in, 2915-2923
    prostate-specific antigen test in, 2915-2922. See also Prostate-specific antigen (PSA).
    stage at, 2856, 2856f. See also Prostate cancer, staging of.
    transrectal ultrasound-directed biopsy in, 2923
    recommendations for, 2925
  E-cadherin in, 2866
  effect of testosterone therapy on, 859
  epidemiology of, 2854-2857
    molecular, 2860-2862
  epigenetic changes in, 2865
  epithelial growth factor and epithelial growth factor receptor in, 2867
  etiology and molecular genetics of, 2863-2867
  EZH2 levels in, 2867
  glutathione S-transferase in, 2866
  hereditary, 515t
    susceptibility to cancer in, 518
  histologic form of, 2863

Prostate cancer (Continued)
  hormone-refractory, 3101-3117
    assessment and treatment selection for, 3102-3103, 3102f, 3102t
    clinical considerations in, 3102-3105
    cytotoxic chemotherapy for, 3105-3112
      clinical trials of
        docetaxel in, 3108-3110, 3109f, 3110f, 3110t
        multidrug regimens in, 3106, 3107t, 3108
        single agents in, 3106, 3106t
        Southwest Oncology Group study in, 3110, 3110f, 3111f
        survival comparisons in, 3108t
      efficacy of, 3105-3106, 3105t
      metastatic, 3104-3105, 3104f, 3104t
        survival in, 3102t
      neuroendocrine subtype of, 3110-3112, 3112f
      treatment of, 3112
    nonmetastatic, androgen-independent, castrate disease in, 3103-3104
    novel approach(es) to, 3114-3117
      angiogenesis targets in, 3117
      growth and survival pathways in, 3115-3116
      immunotherapy in, 3116-3117
      rational target overview in, 3114-3115
    palliative therapy for, 3112-3114
      bone-targeted approaches to, 3113-3114
      epidural cord compression in, 3112-3113, 3113t
  incidence of, 2854, 2855f, 2855t
    worldwide, 2855
  indolent, nomogram for predicting, 2951, 2952f
  latent form of, 2863
  localized, radiation therapy for, 3006-3014
    posttreatment prognostic factors in, 3009-3014, 3012t, 3013t
    pretreatment prognostic factors in, 3006-3009, 3007f-3011f
  locally advanced
    chromosome abnormalities associated with, 3055t
    definition of, 3053
    imaging of, 3054-3055, 3054f, 3055f
    incidence of, 3055
    natural history of, 3056-3057, 3057f
    novel markers of, 3055, 3055t
    risk assessment in, 3053-3054
    treatment of
      androgen deprivation in
        intermittent, 3066
        timing of, 3065-3066
      clinical trials in, 3067t, 3068
      conservative, 3057t
      delayed sequelae and, 3067-3068
      quality of life after, 3066-3067
      radiation therapy in, 3063-3065. See also Radiation therapy, for prostate cancer.
      radical prostatectomy in, 3057-3063. See also Prostatectomy, radical, for locally advanced disease.
      trends in, 3055-3056, 3056t
  low-risk of, identification of men with, 2950-2951, 2952f
  lymphoma as, 2881-2882
    transrectal ultrasonography of, 2887
  mesenchymal tumors as, 2881
    transrectal ultrasonography of, 2887
  α-methylacryl-CoA racemase in, 2866-2867

Prostate cancer (Continued)
  mortality rates in, 2854, 2856f
    effect of screening on, 2857
    worldwide, 2855-2856
  NKX3-1 gene in, 2865-2866
  oncogene in, 2865, 2866
  overdiagnosis of, 2934
  p27 in, 2866
  prostate-specific membrane antigen in, 2867
  PTEN gene in, 2866
  racial differences and, 2854-2855
  randomized trials for, 2914-2915
  RB gene in, 524
  rhabdomyosarcoma as, treatment of, 3880-3883, 3881f, 3882f
  risk factor(s) for, 2857-2863
    alcohol consumption as, 2863
    androgens as, 2860-2861, 2863-2864
    calcium as, 2862
    diet as, 2862
    dietary fat as, 2862-2872
    estrogens as, 2861
    familial, 2857-2858, 2857t
    genetic, 2858, 2858t, 2859f
    inflammatory and infectious, 2859-2860, 2860f
    insulin-like growth factor-1 as, 2861
    leptin as, 2861
    obesity as, 2863
    sexual activity as, 2862
    smoking as, 2862
    vasectomy as, 2862
    vitamin D as, 2861-2862
  screening for
    age to begin, 2923-2924
    age to discontinue, 2924-2925
    intervals between, 2924
    simulations and population-based observations of, 2913-2914, 2914t
    specialty group and task force recommendations in, 2913
  staging of, 2925-2931
    clinical system of, 2925-2926, 2927t
      vs. pathologic system, 2925, 2926f
    digital rectal examination in, 2929-2930
    imaging in, 2930
    molecular, 2930
    needle biopsy in, 2926-2927
    pelvic lymphadenectomy in, 2930-2931
    prediction of tumor extent in, 2926-2927, 2928t-2929t
    PSA levels in, 2929
    radioimmunoscintigraphy in, 2930
  stem cells in, 2864-2865
  susceptibility genes in, 2858, 2858t
  telomerase in, 2866
  transitional cell carcinoma as, 2881
  transrectal ultrasonography of, 2886-2887, 2887f
    after treatment, 2887
  treatment of
    active monitoring or watchful waiting in, 2933-2934
    background in, 2932-2933
    brachytherapy in, 2941
    conservative, 2933-2934
    cryotherapy in, 2944, 3032-3052. See also Cryotherapy, for prostate cancer.
    erectile dysfunction after, PDE-5 inhibitors for, 775-776
    expectant management in, 2947-2955
      active surveillance as, 2951-2955. See also Active surveillance, of prostate cancer.

Prostate cancer *(Continued)*
watchful waiting as, 2948-2950. *See also*
Watchful waiting, in prostate cancer.
high-intensity focused ultrasound in, 2945
hormone therapy in, 3082-3099. *See also*
Hormone therapy, for prostate cancer.
adjuvant, 2942
primary, 2943-2944
hormone-refractory. *See under* Prostate
cancer, hormone-refractory.
locally advanced disease and. *See* Prostate
cancer, locally advanced, treatment of.
management of biological recurrence in,
2943
patient evaluation in, 2933
radiation therapy in, 2938-2943, 3006-3031.
*See also* Radiation therapy, for prostate
cancer.
radical prostatectomy in, 2934-2938. *See
also* Prostatectomy, radical.
radiofrequency interstitial tumor ablation
in, 2944-2945
recommendations for, by patient risk
groups, 2945t
rising PSA levels after, 3069-3080. *See also
under* Prostate-specific antigen (PSA).
tumor characterization in, 2933
tumor initiation and progression in, somatic
mutations associated with, 2865-2867
tumor markers of, 2896-2910
epigenetic modifications of, 2908
gene expression in, 2909
genomic alterations and susceptibility of,
2908
kallikreins as, 2897-2907, 2897f. *See also
specific type, e.g.,* Prostate-specific
antigen (PSA).
prostate-specific membrane antigen as,
2907-2908. *See also* Prostate-specific
membrane antigen (PSMA).
proteomics in, 2909
vascular epithelial growth factor in, 2866
Prostate Cancer Prevention Trial (PCPT), 2868-
2870, 2869f
continued debate surrounding, 2869-2870,
2870t
findings in, 2869
Prostate cancer susceptibility genes, 2858, 2858t
Prostate, Lung, Colorectal, and Ovary (PLCO)
cancer trial, 2914-2915
Prostate specimen, in robotic-assisted
laparoscopic radical prostatectomy
delivery of, 2996
inspection and entrapment of, 2995
Prostate stem cell antigen, 2722-2723
Prostatectomy, 2845-2853
open
anesthesia for, 2847
complications of, 2852
indications for, 2846
operating day preparation for, 2847
postoperative management of, 2851-2852
preoperative evaluation for, 2846-2847
surgical technique of, 2847-2851
overview of, 2845-2846
radical
cancer control with, 2934-2938
adjuvant radiation therapy after, 2941-
2942
complications of, 2938
disease control with, 2937-2938
erectile function after, 2938
laparoscopic approach to, 2935-2936
patient selection in, 2936

Prostatectomy *(Continued)*
perineal approach to, 2935
postoperative care after, 2937
salvage, 2936
technique of, 2936-2937
urinary continence after, 2938
vs. radiation therapy, 2942-2943
efficacy of injectable therapies after, 2281
erectile dysfunction after, PDE-5 inhibitors
for, 775-776
erectile function recovery after, facilitation
of, 780-781
for locally advanced disease, 3057-3063
adjuvant androgen deprivation after,
3062-3063, 3063t
adjuvant radiation therapy before, 3061-
3062, 3061t
chemotherapy-hormone therapy before,
3061, 3061t
clinical stage T3 and, 3057-3058, 3058t
neoadjuvant androgen deprivation
before, 3059-3060, 3059t, 3060t
neoadjuvant chemotherapy before, 3060-
3061, 3061t
outcomes of, 3058-3059, 3058f
hormone therapy with, 3091, 3092f, 3092t
laparoscopic and robotic-assisted, 2985-
3002. *See also* Laparoscopic radical
prostatectomy, robotic-assisted.
pathologic findings in, 3056, 3056t
rectourethral fistula following, 2354
rising PSA levels after, 3070-3071
salvage, 2977-2978, 3048-3049
vs. other salvage therapies, 3047-3048
specimens from
assessment of, 2879
prognosis and, 2879-2880
transrectal ultrasonography after, 2887
vs. salvage cryotherapy, 3047-3048
radical perineal, 2979-2984
closure in, 2983
exposure of prostate in, 2980-2981, 2980f,
2981f
morbidity in, 2983-2984
nerve-sparing dissection in, 2981-2982,
2981f, 2982f
pathologic outcomes in, 2983
patient positioning for, 2980, 2980f
patient selection for, 2979-2980
preoperative care in, 2980
vesicourethral anastomosis in, 2982-2983,
2982f
radical retropubic, 2956-2978
anesthesia for, 2959
bladder neck division and seminal vesicle
excision in, 2969-2971, 2970f
bladder neck reconstruction and
anastomosis in, 2971-2972, 2971f,
2972f
complications of
intraoperative, 2972-2973
postoperative, 2973-2974
dorsal vein complex ligation in, 2961-2968,
2962f-2968f
neurovascular bundles in, 2967-2968,
2967f
high anterior release of, 2965, 2965f
identification and preservation of,
2966-2967, 2967f
wide excision of, 2968, 2968f
standard division in, 2962-2963, 2963f,
2964f
urethral division and suture placement
in, 2963-2965, 2964f, 2965f

Prostatectomy *(Continued)*
endopelvic fascia incisions in, 2960-2961,
2961f
erectile dysfunction after, 2974
exposure in, 2960
incisions in, 2959-2960
endopelvic fascia, 2960-2961, 2961f
instruments used in, 2959
pelvic fascia and, 2958f, 2959, 2959f
pelvic lymphadenectomy in, 2960, 2960f
pelvic plexus and, 2957-2958, 2957f
posterior dissection and division of lateral
pedicles in, 2968-2969, 2969f
postoperative management of, 2972
preoperative preparation for, 2959
puboprostatic ligament division in, 2961,
2961f
pudendal artery preservation in, 2961,
2961f
striated urethral sphincter and, 2958, 2958f
surgical anatomy and, 2956-2959
surgical modification(s) to, 2974-2977
bladder neck sparing as, 2974-2975
interposition nerve grafting as, 2976-
2977
seminal vesicle sparing as, 2975-2976
surgical technique of, 2959-2972
venous and arterial anatomy and, 2956-
2957, 2957f
retropubic, 2847-2849
closure in, 2849, 2849f
enucleation of adenoma in, 2848-2849,
2848f, 2849f
exposure of prostate in, 2847, 2847f
hemostatic maneuvers in, 2847-2848, 2848f
incision in, 2847, 2847f
patient positioning for, 2847
radical. *See* Prostatectomy, radical
retropubic.
suprapubic, 2849-2851
closure in, 2851, 2851f
enucleation of adenoma in, 2850, 2850f,
2851f
exposure of prostate in, 2850, 2850f
hemostatic maneuvers in, 2850-2851, 2851f
incision in, 2849-2850, 2850f
patient positioning for, 2849
Prostate-specific antigen (PSA), 2718-2720,
2719t
as tumor marker, 2897-2906, 3069-3070
age-specific levels of, 2900t
clinical use of, 2899-2901, 2899f
density of, 2900, 2900t
factors influencing, 2898-2899
investigational, 2922
molecular derivatives of, 2901-2906, 2901f,
2902t
velocity of, 2900-2901, 2900t
benign, 2905
complexed, 2905-2906
in prostate cancer, 2922
distribution of, by age, 2916t
effect of testosterone therapy on, 859
elevations of, 2915-2916
free, 2901-2902
FDA-approved use of, 2903-2904
in prostate cancer, 2921-2922
isoforms of, 2904-2905, 2904f
in benign prostatic hyperplasia, 2748, 2748f,
2768, 2915
in erectile dysfunction, measurement of, 756
in molecular forms of, 2897, 2897f
in prostate cancer, 2915
after brachytherapy, 3023-3025

Prostate-specific antigen (PSA) *(Continued)*
  approaches to improve, 2919-2922
  changes or variability in, 2921
  clinical use of, 2916-2919, 2916t, 2917f,
      2917t, 2918f, 2918t
  complexed, 2922
  doubling time of, 2953, 2954, 3073, 3075
    concerns about, 3073, 3075
    disease-free survival associated with,
        3075-3076, 3075f
    hormone-refractory disease and, 3103
  factors to consider with, 2915-2916
  free, 2921-2922
  investigational, 2922
  thresholds of, 2919-2920
  volume-based parameters for, 2920
  in prostatic intraepithelial neoplasia, 2874
  in screening for prostate cancer, 2854, 2856,
      2857f
    decline in mortality associated with, 2854
  in staging of prostate cancer, 2929
  lowering, 2916
  molecular forms of, 2897, 2897f
  percent free, 2901-2902
    cutoff thresholds for, 2902t
  response of, to androgen deprivation therapy,
      3089
  rising levels of
    after definitive local therapy, 3069-3080
      disease-specific, 3075-3076, 3075f
      prediction of clinical events associated
          with, 3074t
      prediction of local vs. systemic relapse
          in, 3073
      risk of metastatic disease in, 3073, 3075
      treatment of, 3076-3080
        clinical trial considerations in, 3078-
            3080, 3079f
        local, 3077-3078
        systemic, 3076-3077, 3077t
    after radiation therapy, 3071
    after radical prostatectomy, 3070-3071
    clinical state of, 3070-3071
    definition of, 3070
    in localized and metastatic disease
      biopsy in, 3072
      radiographic determination of, 3071-
          3072
      survival prediction for, 3072-3076, 3074t,
          3075f
    outcome measures for patient with, 3079-
        3080, 3079f
    states-based model for, 3070, 3070f
  test for, 94
Prostate-specific membrane antigen (PSMA),
    2719t, 2721-2722
  as tumor marker, 2907-2908
  in prostate cancer, 2867
Prostate-specific protein 94, 2723-2724
Prostatic acid phosphatase, properties of, 2719t,
    2723
Prostatic hyperplasia, benign. *See* Benign
    prostatic hyperplasia.
Prostatic intraepithelial neoplasia
  high-grade, 2874-2875, 2875f
  low-grade, 2874
  pathology of, 2874-2875
Prostatic pedicle ligation, in robotic-assisted
    laparoscopic radical prostatectomy, 2992-
    2993, 2994f
Prostatic secretions, 2715-2718
  and drug transport, 2725-2726
  cholesterol in, 2718
  citric acid in, 2716

Prostatic secretions *(Continued)*
  fructose in, 2716
  lipids in, 2718
  phosphorylcholine in, 2717
  polyamines in, 2716-2717
  prostaglandins in, 2717-2718
  protein(s) in, 2718-2725, 2719t
    C3 complement, 2724
    immunoglobulins, 2724
    β-inhibin, 2723-2724
    kallikrein 1, 2719t, 2720
    kallikrein 2, 2719t, 2720
    kallikrein 11, 2720
    lactate dehydrogenase, 2724
    leucine aminopeptidase, 2724
    microseminoprotein, 2723-2724
    prostate stem cell antigen, 2722-2723
    prostate-specific antigen, 2718-2720, 2719t
    prostate-specific membrane antigen, 2719t,
        2721-2722
    prostate-specific protein 94, 2723-2724
    prostatic acid phosphatase, 2723
    semenogelins I and II, 2721
    seminal vesicle secretory proteins, 2724-
        2725
    transferrin, 2724
    transglutaminases, 2720-2721
  zinc in, 2718
Prostatic urethra, 61, 62f, 1030, 1030f
  congenital diverticulum in, 1044. *See also*
      Urethral diverticulum(a).
Prostatitis
  acupuncture in, 324
  acute, 94
  altered host defense in, 308
  asymptomatic inflammatory, clinical
      presentation of, 312
  bacterial
    acute
      classification of, 311t
      clinical presentation of, 311
    chronic
      classification of, 311t
      clinical presentation of, 311
      interrelated, pluricausal, multifactorial
          etiology of, 310, 310f
      symptom assessment in, 312, 313f
  biopsy of, 317
  *Candida* in, 307
  chemically-induced, 309
  *Chlamydia* in, 306-307
  classification of
    NIH, 311, 311t
    traditional, 310-311, 311t
  clinical presentation of, 311-312
  condition(s) related to, 326-329
    epididymitis as, 328-329, 329t
    orchitis as, 327-328, 327t
    seminal vesiculitis as, 326-327
  *Corynebacterium* in, 306
  culturing techniques for, 314-315, 314f, 315f
    cytologic considerations in, 315-316, 316f
    microbiologic considerations in, 315
  definition of, 305
  dysfunctional voiding in, 308
  emphysematous, 460
  endoscopy in, 316
  epidemiology of, 304-305
  *Escherichia coli* in, 306
  etiology of, 306-310
  granulomatous, BCG therapy and, 306
  histopathology of, 305-306, 305f
  historical aspects of, 304
  immunologic alterations in, 308-309

Prostatitis *(Continued)*
  in HIV patients, 396
  interstitial cystitis-like causes of, 309-310
  intraprostatic ductal reflux in, 308
  lower urinary tract infection in, evaluation of,
      312-318, 314f-316f
  microbiologic causes of, 306-308
  neural dysregulation in, 309
  nonbacterial. *See also* Chronic pelvic pain
      syndrome.
    classification of, 311t
    clinical presentation of, 311-312
    cytokine levels in, 317-318
    immunologic alterations in, 309
    zinc levels in, 318
  nonculturable organisms in, 307-308
  pelvic floor musculature abnormalities in, 309
  physical examination in, 312-314
  transrectal ultrasonography of, 317
  treatment of, 318-326
    acupuncture in, 324
    α-adrenergic blockers in, 321, 325t
    allopurinol in, 323
    antibiotics in, 318-321, 320t, 325t, 327t
    anti-inflammatory agents in, 321-322, 325t
    balloon dilatation in, 324
    biofeedback in, 324
    hormone therapy in, 322-323, 325t, 327t
    immune modulators in, 322
    microwave hyperthermia in, 324
    minimally invasive therapies in, 324-325
    muscle relaxants in, 322
    myofascial trigger point release in, 323-324
    pelvic floor massage in, 323-324
    perineal massage in, 323-324
    physical therapy in, 323-324
    phytotherapeutic agents in, 323, 325t, 327t
    prostatic massage in, 323
    psychological support in, 324
    pudendal nerve entrapment therapy in, 324
    surgical, 325
    thermotherapy in, 324-325
  *Trichomonas* in, 307
  *Ureaplasma* in, 307
  urodynamics for, 316
Prostatitis Symptom Index, chronic, NIH, 305,
    313f
Prostatodynia, classification of, 311t
Prostatron device, in transurethral microwave
    therapy, 2813, 2814f
Prostatron software 2.0, in transurethral
    microwave therapy, 2816
Prosthesis
  for male incontinence, history and
      development of, 2392-2393
  penile, engineered, 565, 565f
  silicone, for urinary incontinence, 553-554
  urethral stent, 2303-2304
  vaginal support, for stress incontinence, 2137,
      2137f
Protease(s), in renal cell carcinoma, 1591
Protease inhibitors
  for HIV infection, 401, 403, 403t
  of angiogenesis, 544-545
Proteasome inhibitors, for hormone-refractory
    prostate cancer, 3116
Protein(s). *See also named protein.*
  dietary restriction of, after partial
      nephrectomy, 1613-1614
  excretion of, effect of ureteral obstruction on,
      1203
  in prostatic secretions, 2718-2725, 2719t
    C3 complement, 2724
    immunoglobulins, 2724

Protein(s) *(Continued)*
β-inhibin, 2723-2724
kallikrein 1, 2719t, 2720
kallikrein 2, 2719t, 2720
kallikrein 11, 2720
lactate dehydrogenase, 2724
leucine aminopeptidase, 2724
microseminoprotein, 2723-2724
prostate stem cell antigen, 2722-2723
prostate-specific antigen, 2718-2720, 2719t
prostate-specific membrane antigen, 2719t, 2721-2722
prostate-specific protein 94, 2723-2724
prostatic acid phosphatase, 2723
semenogelins I and II, 2721
seminal vesicle secretory proteins, 2724-2725
transferrin, 2724
transglutaminases, 2720-2721
intake of, in acute renal failure, 1338
renal reabsorption of, in proximal convoluted tubules, 1140
restriction of
for nephrolithiasis, 1412-1413
in chronic renal failure, 1350
secretory, of seminal vesicles, 2724-2725
synthesis of, 512
Protein kinase A, in male sexual function, 734
Protein kinase C, activation of, 483
Protein kinase G, in male sexual function, 735
cross-activation of, 736
Protein-polyubiquitin complex, destruction of, 512
Proteinuria
detection of, 101-102
evaluation of, 102-103, 103f
glomerular, 101
in acute interstitial nephritis, 1328
in children, 3219-3221
evaluation of, 3220, 3221f
investigation of, 3220-3221
quantitation of urinary protein in, 3219
in chronic renal failure, 1348
nephrotic-range, definition of, 3225
overflow, 101
pathophysiology of, 101
patient history of, 100-103, 103f
persistent, 102-103
tubular, 101
Proteomics, in diagnosis of oncology, 549
Proton beam therapy, for prostate cancer, 3020-3021, 3020f
Proto-oncogene(s). *See also* Oncogene(s).
conversion of, to oncogene, 514
Proximal procedure, in hypospadias repair, 3729-3738
one-stage, 3729-3734
onlay techniques for, 3729-3731
other, 3734, 3735f
tubularization techniques for, 3731-3732, 3732f-3733f, 3734
two-stage, 3734, 3735-3738, 3736f-3737f
free-graft for neourethral formation in, 3734, 3736-3738, 3738f
Prune-belly syndrome, 3208, 3482-3496
abdominal wall defect in, 3486, 3486f
reconstruction of, 3493
accessory sex organs in, 3484
antenatal detection of, 3574
anterior urethra in, 3484-3485, 3485f
surgical repair of, 3491, 3491f, 3492f
bladder in, 3484, 3484f
cardiac anomalies in, 3485t, 3486
clinical features of, 3483-3487

Prune-belly syndrome *(Continued)*
embryology of, 3482
evaluation of, 3489
extragenitourinary anomalies in, 3485-3487, 3485t
female, 3488-3489
gastrointestinal anomalies in, 3485t, 3487
genetics of, 3482
genitourinary anomalies in, 3483-3485, 3483f-3485f
incidence of, 3482
incomplete, 3488
kidneys in, 3483, 3483f
long-term outlook for, 3493, 3496
management of, 3489-3493
abdominal wall reconstruction in, 3493
anterior urethral reconstruction in, 3491, 3491f, 3492f
controversies of, in category II disease, 3490
cutaneous vesicostomy in, 3490
Ehrlich technique in, 3493
internal urethrotomy in, 3490-3491
Monfort technique in, 3493, 3494f-3496f
orchidopexy in, 3492-3493
Fowler-Stephens, 3492-3493
transabdominal, 3492, 3493f
Randolph technique in, 3493
reduction cystoplasty in, 3491
supravesical urinary diversion in, 3490
surgical, 3490-3493
ureteral reconstruction in, 3491
megalourethra in, 3485, 3485f
surgical repair of, 3491, 3492f
orthopedic anomalies in, 3485t, 3487
prenatal diagnosis of, 3487-3488, 3487f
presentation of, 3487-3489
adult, 3488
neonatal, 3488
prostate in, 3484
pulmonary anomalies in, 3485t, 3486-3487
renal hypodysplasia associated with, 3313
spectrum of disease in, 3488, 3488t
Pruritus
in atopic dermatitis, 408
in scabies, 425
PSA. *See* Prostate-specific antigen (PSA).
Pseudoaneurysm(s). *See also* Aneurysm(s).
delayed bleeding due to, following percutaneous procedures, 1546, 1546f
embolization of, 1546-1547, 1547f
Pseudo-Cushing's syndrome, 1832
Pseudodyssynergia, 2015, 2018
Pseudoephedrine
for retrograde ejaculation, 648
for stress incontinence, 2109
in elderly, 2318
Pseudoepitheliomatous, keratotic, and micaceous balanitis, of male genitalia, 429, 429f
Pseudoepitheliomatous micaceous growth, of penis, 960
Pseudoexstrophy, in adult male, 3550, 3551f
Pseudohermaphroditism, 3816-3827
dysgenetic male, 3812-3813
female, 3816-3821
congenital adrenal hyperplasia in, 3816-3820, 3817f, 3818f
secondary to maternal androgens, progestins, and tumors, 3820-3821
male, 3821-3827
androgen receptor and postreceptor defects in, 3823-3825
17α-hydroxylase deficiency in, 3822
3β-hydroxysteroid deficiency in, 3821-3822

Pseudohermaphroditism *(Continued)*
17β-hydroxysteroid oxidoreductase deficiency in, 3822-3823
Leydig cell aplasia in, 3821
17,20-lyase deficiency in, 3822
persistent müllerian duct syndrome in, 3826-3827
5α-reductase deficiency in, 3825-3826, 3825f, 3826f
StAR deficiency in, 3821
syndrome of complete androgen insensitivity in, 3823-3824
syndrome of partial androgen resistance in, 3824-3825
testosterone biosynthesis disorders in, 3821-3823
Pseudomembranous enterocolitis, antibiotic bowel preparation causing, 2539
Pseudo-obstruction, due to intestinal anastomosis, 2550-2551
Pseudosarcoma, of bladder, 2418
Pseudotumor, of kidney, 3302, 3302f
PSMA. *See* Prostate-specific membrane antigen (PSMA).
Psoas muscle, 9, 9f, 9t
Psoas muscle hitch
for lower ureteral injuries, 1288
for ureteral stricture, 1261, 1262f, 1263f
laparoscopic, 1261
in children, 3662, 3663f
in redo ureteral reimplantation, 4362, 4362f
ureteroneocystostomy with
indications for, 1667
technique of, 1667-1668, 1669f-1671f, 1671
Psoriasis, of male genitalia, 410-411, 411f
Psychological support, for prostatitis, 324
Psychological therapy, for premature ejaculation, 785
Psychometric validation, of HRQOL instruments, 152-154, 152t, 153f
Psychosexual issues, after hypospadias repair, 3742
Psychosexual sexual differentiation, 3805, 3808
Psychosexual therapy, for erectile dysfunction, 770-771
Psychosocial history
of erectile dysfunction, 755-756, 755t
of female sexual health concerns, 865-866
Psychotropic agents, erectile dysfunction caused by, 743-745
Psychotypic sexual differentiation, 3805, 3806f, 3807f
PT-141, for erectile dysfunction, intranasal administration of, 782-783
PTA. *See* Percutaneous transluminal angioplasty (PTA).
*PTEN* gene, 535-536
alterations in, 535
in prostate cancer, 2866
*PTEN/MMAC* tumor suppressor gene, 535
PTH. *See* Parathyroid hormone (PTH).
Puberty
delayed, in 46,XY complete gonadal dysgenesis, 3813
factors affecting, 580
Pubic diastasis, partial recurrence of, after osteotomy, in exstrophy patient, 3516
Pubic rami, straddle fractures of, 2658, 2658f
Pubic tubercle, 38, 39f
Pubis, 38, 39f
Pubococcygeus muscle, 44, 46f, 2191, 2191f, 2192
Puboprostatic ligament, division of, in radical retropubic prostatectomy, 2961, 2961f

Pubovaginal sling, 2234-2249
  fascial
    abdominal approach to, 2243
    autologous
      indications for, 2236-2237
      materials for, 2234, 2237-2238
      outcomes of, 2248t
    indications for, 2234-2237
    patient evaluation for, 2238-2242
      bladder function tests in, 2239-2240
      physical examination in, 2238
      urethral continence function in, 2240
      Valsalva leak point pressure
        measurement in, 2240-2242, 2241f,
        2242f
    preliminary steps in, 2243
    retropubic tunnel development in, 2243
    sling harvest in, 2243
    sling placement and fixation of, 2243-2244
    sling tension in, determination of, 2244
    vaginal approach to, 2243
    wound closure for, 2244
  vs. retropubic suspension surgery, for female
    incontinence, 2184
Pubovisceral muscle, 44, 68
Pudendal artery
  external, 1031, 1033f
  internal, 50f, 51, 721-722, 721f, 722f
  preservation of, in radical retropubic
    prostatectomy, 2961, 2961f
Pudendal lymph nodes, 52, 52f
Pudendal nerve, 69, 70f
  interruption of, 2304
  stimulation of, 2158-2159
Pudendal nerve entrapment therapy, for
  prostatitis, 324
Pudendal vein, internal, 69, 723f
Pull-down maneuver, in examination of
  introitus, 3841, 3841f
Pulmonary anomalies, in prune-belly syndrome,
  3485t, 3486-3487
Pulmonary embolism, due to radical retropubic
  prostatectomy, 2973
Pulmonary eosinophilia, tropical, in filariasis,
  457
Pulmonary hypoplasia
  in bilateral renal agenesis, 3271
  posterior urethral valves causing, 3586t, 3588
Pulmonary infection, after renal transplantation,
  1323
Pulmonary resection, post-chemotherapy,
  testicular tumors and, 955
Pulmonary toxicity, bleomycin-induced, 924
Pump implantation, in penile prosthetic surgery,
  792-793, 793f
  complications of, 797
Puncture sites, for percutaneous
  nephrolithotomy, selection of, 1489-1491,
  1490f-1492f, 1490t
PUNLMP (papillary urothelial neoplasm of low
  malignant potential), 2447
Purinergic nerves
  in lower urinary tract, 1951-1952
  role of, in ureteral function, 1906-1907
PUVA therapy. See Ultraviolet light therapy.
Pyeloenteric fistula, 2353
Pyelogenic cyst, 3354
Pyelography
  antegrade
    of genitourinary tuberculosis, 443
    of ureteral obstruction, 1210
    of ureterovaginal fistula, 2342, 2344f
  intravenous
    of acute renal failure, 1335

Pyelography (Continued)
    of pediatric urologic patient, 3214
    of renal injury, in children, 3931
    of retroperitoneal fibrosis, 1271, 1272f
  retrograde, 118, 121f, 169-170
    indications for, 169-170
    of blind-ending ureteral duplication, 3416,
      3416f
    of genitourinary tuberculosis, 443
    of multiple calyceal diverticula, 3298, 3298f
    of renal injury, in children, 3931-3932
    of retroperitoneal fibrosis, 1216, 1216f
    of ureteral obstruction, 1210
    patient preparation for, 170
    technique of, 170, 170f
Pyelolithotomy
  concomitant, laparoscopic pyeloplasty with,
    for ureteropelvic junction obstruction,
    1253
  laparoscopic, 1776, 1778
Pyelonephritic hypertension, pediatric urinary
  tract infection and, 3259-3260
Pyelonephritis
  acute, 224, 267-271
    clinical manifestations of, 267
    definition of, 267
    diagnosis of, 267-268, 268f
    differential diagnosis of, 269
    management of, 269-271, 270f, 270t
      follow-up in, 271
      unfavorable response to, 271
    pathology of, 269
    radiologic findings in, 268-269, 269f
    vs. perinephric abscess, 278
  after augmentation cystoplasty, 3683
  after renal transplantation, 1321
  candidal, 462
  chronic, 224, 224f, 225f, 278-280
    clinical presentation of, 279
    management of, 279-280
    pathology of, 279
    radiologic findings in, 279, 279f
  definition of, 224
  during pregnancy, 289, 290
  emphysematous, 271-273
    clinical presentation of, 272
    management of, 273
    percutaneous treatment of, 1550-1551
    radiologic findings in, 272-273, 273f, 274f
  following ureterointestinal anastomosis, 2563
  in children, 3234-3236, 3235f
    radiologic findings in, 3245-3246
    sequelae of, 3256-3258, 3257f, 3259f
    signs and symptoms of, 3245
    xanthogranulomatous, 3258-3259
  infectious, scarring associated with, 4338. See
    also Renal scarring.
  signs and symptoms of, 238
  xanthogranulomatous, 280-283
    clinical presentation of, 281
    diagnosis of, 281
    differential diagnosis of, 283
    in children, 3258-3259
    management of, 283
    pathogenesis of, 281
    pathology of, 281, 282f
    radiologic findings in, 281-283, 282f
Pyeloplasty, for ureteropelvic junction
  obstruction
  Culp-DeWeerd spiral flap technique of, 1245,
    1246f
  dismembered, 1242-1243, 1243f, 1244f
    in children, 3370, 3372f, 3373
  flap procedures in, 1243-1245, 1245f

Pyeloplasty, for ureteropelvic junction
  obstruction (Continued)
  Foley Y-V plasty technique of, 1243-1245,
    1245f
    in children, 3370, 3370f
  historical aspects of, 1242
  laparoscopic, 1249-1253. See also
    Laparoscopic pyeloplasty.
    in children, 3375-3376, 3376f
  laparoscopic retroperitoneal, in children,
    3377-3378, 3378f, 3379f
  results of, 3380, 3380t
  Scardino-Prince vertical flap technique of,
    1245, 1246f
  surgical principles of, 1241-1242
Pyelovascular fistula, 2357
Pyoderma gangrenosum, 418
  of penis, 419f
Pyonephrosis, 276, 276f, 277f
  in children, 3246
  percutaneous treatment of, 1550-1551
Pyospermia, 625
Pyramid procedure, in hypospadias repair, 3725
Pyrazinamide, for genitourinary tuberculosis,
  444, 445t
Pyuria, 96
  definition of, 224, 3212
  in urinary tract infection, 239

Q

Quackels shunt, for priapism, 847f, 848
Quadratus lumborum muscle, 8, 9f, 9t, 10f
Quality of care, 147-149
  challenges in evaluation of, 148-149
  measurement approaches to, 149
  outcomes in, 148
  process of, 148
  structure in, 147-148
Quality of life
  after androgen deprivation, for locally
    advanced prostate cancer, 3066-3067
  after cryotherapy, 3050-3051
  after orthotopic urinary diversion, 2645-2647
  disease control and, in post-radiation prostate
    cancer patients, 3014-3031
    androgen suppression therapy and, 3027-
      3028
    brachytherapy and, 3021-3027, 3022f,
      3023f, 3024t, 3025t
    conformal radiation and, 3017-3018, 3018f
    gene therapy and, 3029-3031
    heavy particle beams and, 3020-3021, 3020f
    intensity modulation and, 3018-3020,
      3018f, 3019f
    palliation and, 3028-3029, 3029t
  health-related. See Health-related quality of
    life (HRQOL).
  urinary, radical prostatectomy vs. watchful
    waiting and, 2950t
Quality of life cost analysis, renal
  transplantation vs. renal dialysis in, 1296
Quality of life questionnaires, for incontinence
  and bladder overactivity, 2062, 2062t
Quality-adjusted life-years (QALY), 145
Quercetin, for prostatitis, clinical trial data on,
  323, 327t

R

Rabies immunization, for animal bite wounds,
  2651
Race
  germ cell tumor incidence and, 900
  pediatric urinary tract infection and, 3237-
    3238

Race *(Continued)*
  prostate cancer and, 2854-2855
  renal stones associated with, 1363-1364
  urothelial tumors and, 1638-1639
  vesicoureteral reflux and, 4324-4325
Radiation
  interstitial photon, 1818
  voiding dysfunction due to, 2043
Radiation injury, penile, 1052-1054
  cellulitis in, 1052
  lymphedema in, 1053
Radiation safety, for urologists, 1531t
Radiation therapy
  adjuvant
    after radical prostatectomy, 2941-2942
      for locally advanced cancer, 3061-3062,
        3061t
      side effects of, 2942
    for urothelial tumors, 1681-1682, 1682t
  for bladder cancer
    invasive, 2474
      interstitial, 2476
      preoperative, 2473
    non–muscle-invasive, refractory disease
      and, 2462
  for neuroblastoma, 3877
  for nonseminomatous germ cell tumors
    stage I and stage IIA, 915-916, 916t
    stage IIB, 920
  for paratesticular and testicular tumors, 933
  for penile cancer, 984-987
    disadvantages of, 985
    external beam, 984-985
    surgery after, 986, 986t
    to inguinal areas, 986-987
  for Peyronie's disease, 828
  for prostate adenocarcinoma, treatment
    effects of, 2880
  for prostate cancer, 2938-2943, 3006-3031
    adjuvant, after radical prostatectomy, 2941-
      2942
      for locally advanced disease, 3061-3062,
        3061t
      side effects of, 2942
    adjuvant androgen deprivation after, 3064-
      3065
    cryotherapy with, 3040
    disease control and quality of life following,
      3014-3031
      androgen suppression therapy and, 3027-
        3028
      brachytherapy and, 3021-3027, 3022f,
        3023f, 3024t, 3025t
      conformal radiation and, 3017-3018,
        3018f
      gene therapy and, 3029-3031
      heavy particle beams and, 3020-3021,
        3020f
      intensity-modulated radiotherapy and,
        3018-3020, 3018f, 3019f
      palliation and, 3028-3029, 3029t
    external beam, 2938-2941
      endpoints for, 2940
      hormone therapy with, 2939-2940
      localized disease and, 2940
      radiation dose and field of treatment in,
        2939
      results of, 2940-2941
      side effects of, 2939
    historical perspective of, 3006
    hormone therapy with, 3091-3092, 3093f,
      3093t
    hormone-refractory, palliative, 3113
    localized disease and, 3006-3014

Radiation therapy *(Continued)*
    posttreatment prognostic factors in,
      3009-3014, 3012t, 3013t
    pretreatment prognostic factors in, 3006-
      3009, 3007f-3011f
    locally advanced, 3063-3065
      adjuvant androgen deprivation after,
        3064-3065
      chemotherapy with, 3065
      neoadjuvant androgen deprivation
        before, 3063-3064
    rising PSA levels after, 3071
    salvage, 3048
    side effects of, 3015-3017, 3015t, 3016t
    vs. radical prostatectomy, 2942-2943
  for renal cell carcinoma, metastatic, 1626
  for seminomas
    stage I, 909-910, 911t
    stage IIA and stage IIB, 912
  for urethral cancer, in males, 1014
  for urothelial tumors, adjuvant, 1681-1682,
    1682t
  male infertility due to, 644
  pelvic
    bladder cancer associated with, 2416
    orthotopic urinary diversion with previous,
      2629-2630
  prior treatment with
    artificial sphincter placement and, 2402-
      2403
    perineal sling procedure and, 2396
    renal cell carcinoma related to, 1584
  rising PSA levels after, 3071
  vesicovaginal fistula due to, 2326
Radioactive seeds, deployment of, in
  brachytherapy, 3022-3023, 3022f, 3023f
Radiocontrast agent–induced nephropathy,
  1340
  prevention of, 1340-1341
Radiofrequency, delivery of, in transurethral
  needle ablation of prostate, 2809-2810
Radiofrequency ablation
  for adrenal lesions, 1887
  for localized renal cell carcinoma, 1618
  for renal tumor, 1814-1816
  laparoscopic, 1806, 1814-1815
    complications of, 1806-1807
    mode of action of, 1814, 1815f
  percutaneous, 1815-1816, 1816t
Radiofrequency interstitial tumor ablation, for
  prostate cancer, 2944-2945
Radiography
  contrast media in, 111, 113
  conventional, 111-118
  in infertility work-up, 627-630
  of bladder injury, 2656, 2656f
  of emphysematous pyelonephritis, 273, 273f,
    274f
  of fungal bezoars, 463, 463f
  of genitourinary tuberculosis, 437f, 441
  of germ cell tumors, 905
  of prostate cancer, localized vs. metastatic,
    3071
  of renal cell carcinoma, disease staging with,
    1602-1603, 1602f
  of sacral agenesis, 3646f
  of schistosomiasis, 453, 453f
  of staghorn calculus, 1405, 1405f, 1408f
  of thoracic kidney, 3282, 3282f
  of ureteropelvic junction obstruction, 1228,
    1229f, 1230f
  of urinary ascites, in infant, 3588, 3589f
  of urinary tract, 111, 112f, 113f, 242-243
  of urothelial tumors, 1644-1645

Radioimmunoscintigraphy, in staging of prostate
  cancer, 2930
Radiolabeled compounds
  in estimation of glomerular filtration rate,
    1132
  in renography, 1170
Radiolucent filling defects, urothelial tumors
  and, 1644, 1654
Radionuclide imaging. *See* Scintigraphy.
Radionuclide therapy, systemic, for bone
  metastases, 3029, 3029t
Radiosurgery, for renal tumors, 1818
RAND Medical Outcomes Study 36-Item Health
  Survey (SF-36), 150
Randall's plaques, in stone formation, 1368-
  1369, 1369f, 1370f
Randolph technique, in management of prune-
  belly syndrome, 3493
Raphe, median, cysts of, 431, 3760
Rapid eye movement (REM) sleep, nocturnal
  penile tumescence during, 763
Rapid screen methods, in diagnosis of urinary
  tract infection, 239-240
*RAS* gene, in bladder cancer, 2410
Ras pathway, in signal transduction, 483
Ras proteins, 483
Raz bladder neck suspension, for stress
  incontinence, 2213-2214, 2213f
Raz vaginal wall sling, for stress incontinence,
  2214
*RB* gene
  in bladder cancer, 2411-2412
  in prostate cancer, 524
Reactive oxygen species testing, of semen, 632
Realignment, primary, for urethral injury, 2659
Receptor(s), 538-539. *See also specific receptor.*
Receptor serine/threonine kinases, 539
Receptor tyrosine kinases, 539
Reconstructive surgery. *See also specific
    procedure.*
  for complex posterior urethral fisulas, 1086-
    1087, 1086f
  for penile curvature, 1087-1092. *See also
    Penile curvature.*
  for penile injury, 1049-1054. *See also Penile
    reconstruction.*
  for urethral injury, 1075-1084. *See also
    Urethral injury, distraction, repair of.*
  for urethral stricture, 1054-1074. *See also
    Urethral stricture, treatment of.*
  for vesicourethral distraction defects, 1084-
    1086, 1084f, 1085f
  generalities of, 1039-1040
  in female-to-male transsexualism, 1096-1097
  laparoscopic-assisted, in children, 3925-3926,
    3925f
  principles of, 1023-1026, 1028-1031, 1034-
    1036, 1039-1040
  selected processes in, 1040-1049
  tissue engineering for. *See* Tissue engineering.
Rectal artery, middle, 50f, 51
Rectal bladder, in continent urinary diversion,
  2582-2586, 2585f
Rectal injury
  after radical perineal prostatectomy, 2983
  after robotic-assisted laparoscopic radical
    prostatectomy, 3000
Rectal pain
  after cryotherapy, 3050
  in children, 3207
Rectal probe ejaculation, in spinal cord-injured
  men, 649
Rectal prolapse, in exstrophy patient, 3503
Rectal toxicity, of brachytherapy, 3026

Rectocele(s), 2200, 2200t, 2201f
  repair of, 2232, 2232f
  symptoms attributed to, 2204
Rectosigmoid bladder, folded, 2583
Rectosigmoid pouch, in laparoscopic-assisted
    urinary diversion, 2524, 2527
Rectourethral (urethrorectal) fistula, 2353-2357
  after cryotherapy, 3050
  etiology and presentation of, 2354-2355,
    2354f, 2355f
  management of, 2355-2357, 2356f
Rectouterine (Douglas) pouch, 56, 56f, 57
Rectovaginal fascia defect, repair of, 2232,
  2232f
Rectovaginal septum, 66f, 67
Rectovesical pouch, 56, 56f
Rectum. See also Bowel entries.
  anatomy of, 56, 56f
  examination of, 93-94. See also Digital rectal
    examination.
  valved
    augmented, 2583
    hemi-Kock and T-pouched procedures
      with, 2583-2584, 2585f
    sigma-rectum pouch (Mainz II) with, 2584,
      2586
Rectus abdominis muscle, 40, 41f
Rectus fascia, autologous, for slings, 2247
Recurrent (stuttering) priapism, 843. See also
    Priapism.
  natural history of, 841
  treatment of, 848-849
Red blood cell(s)
  in urinary sediment, 105-106, 106f, 107f
  production of, 1135-1136
5α-Reductase
  in benign prostatic hyperplasia, 2729
  type 1, 2729
  type 2, 2729
    immunohistochemical studies with,
      2729-2730
    polymorphisms in, 2730
  within prostate
    influence of, 2863-2864
    metabolism of, 2691-2693, 2691t, 2692f,
      2728, 2729f
5α-Reductase deficiency, 3825-3826, 3825f,
  3826f
5α-Reductase inhibitors
  for lowering PSA levels, 2916
  for prostate cancer, chemopreventive, 2870
Reduction cystoplasty, for prune-belly
    syndrome, 3491
Referrals, specialist, for erectile dysfunction,
  756-757
Reflex(es)
  bladder
    developmental changes of, 1948
    in urine storage phase, 1939-1941, 1940t,
      1942f, 1943f
    in voiding phase, 1940t, 1941-1943, 1944f,
      1945f
    promoting storage and emptying, 2149,
      2149f
    promotion or initiation of, 2299
  bladder-to-sphincter, 1941, 1943f
  bladder-to-urethra, 1942-1943, 1944f,
    1945f
  bulbocavernosus, 725, 726t
  cremasteric, absence of, 3790
  guarding, 1975
    in continence, 2049
  micturition. See Micturition reflex.
  sphincter-to-bladder, 1941, 1943f

Reflex(es) (Continued)
  spinal
    capsaicin-sensitive C-fiber, 1966
    in stimulation of penile dorsal nerve, 726t
    tendon, depression of, after sacral spinal cord
      injury, 2024
  urethra-to-bladder, 1942-1943, 1944f, 1945f
Reflex sympathetic dystrophy
  in painful bladder syndrome/interstitial
    cystitis, 346
  voiding dysfunction in, 2037
Reflux
  of urine
    intraprostatic, 308
    prevention of, orthotopic diversion and,
      2630-2633
  vesicoureteral. See Vesicoureteral reflux.
Refluxing megaureter. See also Megaureter(s).
  obstructive, 4371
    management of, 4375
  primary, 4370-4371
    management of, 4374
  secondary, 4370-4371
    management of, 4375
Refractory disease, in non–muscle-invasive
    bladder cancer, management of, 2460-2462
  alternative options in, 2462
  early cystectomy in, 2461-2462
  salvage intravesical therapy in, 2460-2461
Rehabilitation techniques
  for incontinence, 2071. See also Pelvic floor
    rehabilitation.
  for stress incontinence, 2074-2075
Reinfection, in recurrent urinary tract
    infections, 261-265
Reinke's crystals, in Leydig cell tumors, 3901
Reiter's syndrome, 1041
  in HIV patients, 397
  involving male genitalia, 411, 412f
  vs. psoriasis, 411f
Reliability, of HRQOL instruments, 152-154
  alternate-form, 153-154, 153f
  internal consistency, 152t, 154
  inter-observer, 152t, 154
  test-retest, 152-153, 152t
Reliance urethral insert, 2140, 2140f
Renal. See also Kidney(s); Neph- entries.
Renal abscess, 273-276
  clinical presentation of, 274
  diagnosis of, 274
  in children, 3246
  management of, 276
  radiologic findings in, 274-275, 275f
Renal access
  for pediatric laparoscopic surgery
    retroperitoneal - flank position, 3920,
      3922f, 3923f
    retroperitoneal - prone position, 3920,
      3922f, 3923f
    techniques of, 3919-3921
    transperitoneal, 3919, 3920f
  for percutaneous nephrolithotomy, 1487-
    1496. See also Nephrolithotomy,
    percutaneous, renal access for.
  in children, 3910
Renal adenoma, 1575-1576, 1576f
  in acquired renal cystic disease, 3352-3353
  malignant transformation of, 3353
Renal agenesis
  bilateral, 3269-3272, 3307
    associated anomalies in, 3270-3272, 3271f
    diagnosis of, 3272
    embryology of, 3270
    in females, 3271-3272

Renal agenesis (Continued)
  in males, 3271-3272
    incidence of, 3269-3270
    prenatal diagnosis of, 3184
    prognosis for, 3272
  in neonates, 3195
  unilateral, 3272-3276, 3307
    associated anomalies in, 3273-3275, 3274f,
      3275f
    diagnosis of, 3275-3276
    embryology of, 3273, 3273f
    incidence of, 3272-3273
    prognosis for, 3276
    syndromes associated with, 3275
  vesicoureteral reflux in, 4344
Renal angiomyolipoma, 1578-1580, 1579f
  in children, 3899-3900, 3900f
Renal aortic ratio, stenosis and, 1170
Renal artery(ies), 28-29, 28f, 29f
  aberrant, 3293, 3294, 3295f
  accessory, 3293-3294, 3295f
  anatomic variations of
    diagnosis of, 3294
    embryology of, 3293
    features of, 3293-3294, 3294f, 3294t
    incidence of, 3293
    prognosis for, 3294, 3296
    symptoms of, 3294, 3295f
  aneurysm of, 1187, 1188f, 1189, 3296-3297
    after renal bypass surgery, 1751-1752, 1752f
    dissecting, 1187, 1188f
    fusiform, 1187, 1188f
    intrarenal, 1187, 1188f
    saccular, 1187, 1188f
  atherosclerosis of, 1157-1159, 1157t, 1158f.
    See also Atherosclerosis, renal artery.
  embolism of, 1190, 1190t
    cholesterol, 1166
  extrinsic obstruction of, 1191
  fibromuscular hyperplasia of, 1157t, 1161
  in renal transplantation
    anastomoses of, 1310, 1311f, 1312
    multiple, preparation of, 1309, 1310f
  injury to, 1281
  intimal fibroplasia of, 1157t, 1159, 1159f,
    1160f
  ipsilateral, 24, 24f
  lacerations of, nephrostomy causing, 1546
  medial fibroplasia of, 1157t, 1159-1160, 1160f
  multiple, 3293, 3294, 3295f
  neurofibromatosis affecting, 1190-1191
  perimedial fibroplasia of, 1157t, 1160-1161,
    1160f, 1161f
  reconstruction of, 1733
    clinical results of, 1748-1749
    indications for, 1733-1734
    postoperative care in, 1748
    preoperative considerations in, 1734
  stenosis of. See also Renovascular
    hypertension.
    after renal bypass surgery, 1751
    after renal transplantation, 1318
    bilateral, 1165
    diagnosis of, 1168-1173
    endovascular stenting for, 1184-1187,
      1185t, 1186f, 1186t
    following renal revascularization, 1180
    in children, 1184
    in chronic renal failure, 1347
    ischemic nephropathy and, 1165-1166,
      1166f
    peak systolic velocity and, 1170
    percutaneous transluminal angioplasty for,
      1182, 1183f, 1183t, 1184, 1184f

Renal artery(ies) *(Continued)*
  renal aortic ratio and, 1170
  unilateral, 1165
  stenting of. *See under* Stent (stenting).
  thrombosis of, 1190, 1190t
    after renal bypass surgery, 1750-1751, 1750f
    in neonates, 3197
    PTA causing, 1181
Renal biopsy
  for chronic renal failure, 1349
  laparoscopic, 1770-1772
    indications for, 1770
    patient positioning for, 1770
    postoperative considerations in, 1771
    results of, 1771-1772
    technique of, 1770-1771, 1770f, 1771f
  open, 1753, 1754f
  percutaneous, 1551-1552
Renal blood flow
  fetal, 3149
  in neonate, 3151, 3152f
  regulation of, 1131
  triphasic pattern of, 1196, 1197f
  urinary tract obstruction and, 1195-1196
Renal blood vessels
  anomaly(ies) of, 3292-3297
    aberrant, accessory, or multiple vessels as,
      3292-3296, 3418
      diagnosis of, 3294
      embryology of, 3293
      features of, 3293-3294, 3294f, 3294t
      incidence of, 3293
      prognosis for, 3294, 3296
      symptoms of, 3294, 3295f
    arteriovenous fistula as, 3297
    renal artery aneurysm as, 3296-3297
  securing of, in laparoscopic nephrectomy,
      1763, 1768, 1768f
    hand-assisted, 1797, 1797f, 1798f
    transperitoneal approach to, 1783, 1784f
Renal calculi
  age and, 1364
  analysis of, in determination of metabolic
      abnormalities, 1408-1409, 1409t
  body mass index and weight associated with,
      1365
  calcium-based, 1374-1382, 1401-1405. *See also*
      Calcium calculi.
  classification of, 1373-1374, 1373t, 1401-1408,
      1402t
  composition of, treatment decisions
      regarding, 1439-1441, 1441f
  conduit urinary diversion and, 2575
  CT scan of, non–contrast-enhanced, 1441,
      1441f
  diagnostic evaluation of, 1393-1400
    economics of, 1409-1410
    extensive metabolic, 1397-1399, 1398t
    fast and calcium load test in, 1398-1399
    in low-risk single stone formers, 1395-1397,
      1395t, 1396f, 1397f, 1397t
    indications for, 1395t
    patient selection in, 1393-1394
    simplified metabolic, 1399-1400, 1401f,
      1402f
  drug-induced, 1388-1389, 1427, 1427t
  epidemiology of, 1363-1365
  gender associated with, 1363
  geographic distribution of, 1364, 1364f
  historical overview of, 1431-1432
  in anomalous kidney, ureteroscopic
      management of, 1521
  in autosomal dominant polycystic kidney
      disease, 3320

Renal calculi *(Continued)*
  in children, 1427, 3221-3224
    diagnostic approach to, 3224, 3224f, 3225t
    identifiable causes of, 3222t
    manipulation of, 3912
  in patients with primary
      hyperparathyroidism, parathyroidectomy
      for, 1420
  laparoscopic removal of, 1506-1507
  low urinary volume in, 1408
  medical management of
    allopurinol in, 1420
    chlorthalidone in, 1418
    conservative, 1410-1415
    dietary bran in, 1419
    dietary recommendations in, 1412-1413
    diuretics in, 1419, 1421t
    efficacy of outside academic center in, 1417
    fluid recommendations in, 1411-1412
    indapamide in, 1418
    magnesium salts in, 1423-1424
    obesity and, 1413-1414
    oral calcium in, 1422
    organophosphates in, 1419
    oxalate avoidance in, 1415
    physiochemical and physiologic effects of,
      1416t
    potassium citrate in, 1420, 1422, 1423
    prophylactic drug dosages in, 1416t
    role of dietary calcium in, 1414-1415
    selective therapies in, 1415-1427
    side effects of, 1416t
    simplified algorithm in, 1417f
    sodium cellulose phosphate in, 1416-1417
    sodium citrate in, 1423
    thiazides in, 1418
    trichlormethiazide in, 1418
  microscopic appearance of, 1395, 1396f, 1397t
  mineral metabolism of, 1371-1372
  mineralogic names of, 1408, 1409t
  occupation and, 1365
  open stone surgery for, 1505-1506, 1505t
  pathogenesis of, 1373-1391
    anatomic predisposition to stones in, 1389-
      1391
    calcium stones in, 1374-1382. *See also*
      Calcium calculi.
    calyceal diverticula in, 1390
    cystine stones in, 1385-1386, 1385f
    horseshoe kidneys in, 1390
    in pregnancy, 1391
    infection-based stones in, 1386-1387, 1386f,
      1387t. *See also* Infection-based calculi.
    medullary sponge kidney in, 1390-1391
    miscellaneous stones in, 1387-1389
    ureteropelvic junction obstruction in, 1389-
      1390
    uric acid stones in, 1382, 1383f, 1384-1385,
      1384f. *See also* Uric acid calculi.
  physiochemistry of, 1365-1371
    crystal aggregation and retention in, 1368-
      1369, 1369f, 1370f
    crystal formation in, inhibitors and
      promoters of, 1368, 1370-1371
    crystal growth in, 1367-1368
    crystal matrix in, 1371
    nucleation in, 1367
    saturation states in, 1366-1367, 1366f
  prevalence of, 1363
  race and ethnicity associated with, 1363-1364
  radiographic studies of, 111, 112f
  seasonal variation in, 1364-1365
  stone burden in, treatment decisions
      regarding, 1436-1439, 1437f

Renal calculi *(Continued)*
  surgical management of, 1434-1450
    adjunctive medical therapy with, 1449-1450
    anatomic factor(s) affecting, 1441-1447
      calyceal diverticula as, 1442-1443
      ectopic kidney as, 1443-1444, 1444f
      horseshoe kidney as, 1443
      lower pole stones as, 1444-1447, 1445t
      ureteropelvic junction obstruction as,
        1442
    calyceal stones and, 1435
    clinical factor(s) affecting
      morbid obesity as, 1447-1448
      spinal deformity and limb contractures
        as, 1448
      uncorrected coagulopathy as, 1448
      urinary tract infection as, 1447
    factors affecting, 1434, 1434t
    historical overview of, 1431-1432
    laparoscopic, 1506-1507
    open stone, 1505-1506, 1505t
    preoperative evaluation in, 1434-1435
    primary goal in, 1434
    residual fragments in, 1448-1449
    rise of endourology in, 1432-1434
    staghorn stones and, 1435-1436, 1436f
    stone burden and, treatment decisions
        regarding, 1436-1439, 1437f
    stone composition and, treatment decisions
        regarding, 1439-1441, 1441f
    stone factors in, 1436-1441
    techniques in, 1458-1507. *See also specific
        procedure.*
  urea-splitting bacteria causing, 261
  ureteroscopic management of, 1503-1505,
      1504t
    technique of, 1505
  uric acid-based, 1405, 1405f. *See also* Uric acid
      calculi.
  water intake and, 1365
Renal calyx (calyces)
  anatomy of, 26f, 32, 34f, 35f
  anomalies of, 3297-3303
  anomalous (pseudotumor of kidney), 3302,
      3302f
  diverticula of, 3297-3298, 3298f
    laparoscopic surgery for, 1778
    natural history of, 1552
    percutaneous nephrolithotomy into, 1496-
      1497, 1497f
    percutaneous treatment of
      complications of, 1554
      in children, 3913-3914
      results of, 1554
      technique of, 1552-1554, 1553f
    presentation of, 1552
    stone formation in, 1390
      natural history of, 1435
      surgical management of, 1442-1443
    ureteroscopic treatment of, 1521
  extrarenal, 3301, 3301f
  hydrocalycosis of, 3298-3299, 3299f
  maximal diameter of, according to gestational
      age, 1220t
  megacalycosis of, 3299-3301, 3300f
  urothelium of
    abnormal, 1642-1643
    normal, 1641, 1641f, 1642f
Renal carcinoids, 1635-1636
Renal cell carcinoma, 1582-1632
  adhesion in, 1591
  adoptive cell therapy for, 499
  angiogenesis in, 1589-1590, 1589f
  Bellini's duct (collecting duct), 1596

Renal cell carcinoma (*Continued*)
Birt-Hogg-Dubé syndrome associated with, 1584t, 1588
cell cycle regulation in, 1590-1591
chromophilic, 1593-1594, 1594f
cytogenetic abnormalities associated with, 1594-1595
chromophobic, 1595, 1595f
clear cell variant of, genetics in, 1584t, 1585-1587, 1585t, 1586f
clinical implications of, 1588-1591
clinical presentation of, 1597-1598, 1597t
collecting duct (Bellini's duct), 1596
conventional, 1592t, 1593, 1593f
cystic, 3339, 3340f
etiology of, 1583-1588
extracellular matrix in, 1591
familial
in von Hippel–Lindau disease, 1584t, 1585-1587, 1585t, 1586f
molecular genetics and, 1584-1585, 1585t
papillary, 1584t, 1587
genetics of, 1584-1585, 1584t, 1587
growth factors in, 1590
hereditary leiomyomatosis and, 1584t, 1587-1588
histologic classification of, 1592-1593, 1592t
immunobiology and immune tolerance of, 1588-1589
in acquired renal cystic disease, 3351-3352
in autosomal dominant polycystic kidney disease, 3323
screening for, 1599
in children, 1583, 3899
in horseshoe kidney, 3290
in tuberous sclerosis, 3332
in von Hippel–Lindau disease, 1584t, 1585-1587, 1586f, 3333-3334
nephron-sparing surgery for, 1615-1616, 1615f
screening for, 1599-1600
incidence of, 1582-1583
localized, treatment of, 1608-1619
nephron-sparing surgery in, 1609f, 1610-1616, 1611t, 1612t, 1613f
in von Hippel–Lindau disease, 1615-1616, 1615f
with normal opposite kidney, 1614-1615, 1614t
observation in, 1618-1619, 1618t
partial nephrectomy in. *See under* Nephrectomy, partial.
radical nephrectomy in, 1608-1610, 1609f, 1610t. *See also under* Nephrectomy, radical.
thermal ablative therapies in, 1616-1618, 1617t
locally advanced, treatment of, 1619-1623
adjuvant therapy in, 1622-1623, 1623t, 1624t
locally invasive, 1621-1622
recurrent, after radical or partial nephrectomy, 1622
with inferior vena caval involvement, 1619-1621, 1619f, 1620f
medullary-type, 1596
metastatic
prognosis of, 1628, 1629t
treatment of, 1623-1632
adoptive immunotherapy in, 1629
chemotherapy in, 1626
cytokines in, 1626-1628, 1626f, 1627t, 1628t
combination of, 1629

Renal cell carcinoma (*Continued*)
hormone therapy in, 1625-1626
multimodal therapy in, 1631-1632, 1631f
nephrectomy in, 1623-1625, 1624t, 1625f
radiation therapy in, 1626
targeted agents in, 1629-1631, 1630f, 1630t
vaccines in, 1629
multidrug resistance (MDR) proteins in, 1589
nuclear features of, Fuhrman's classification of, 1591, 1591t
papillary, 1594
hereditary, 515t, 518, 1584t, 1587
pathology of, 1591-1597, 1591t, 1592t
prognosis of, 1603-1607, 1607f, 1608f
inferior vena cava thrombosis and, 1605t
nuclear grade and histologic subtype and, 1606
Robson tumor stage and, 1604t
systemic metastasis and, 1605-1606
TNM stage and, 1604t
tumor size and, 1606
proteases in, 1591
sarcomatoid variants of, 1596, 1596f
screening for, 1598-1600
in autosomal dominant polycystic kidney disease, 1599
in target populations, 1599, 1599t
in tuberous sclerosis, 1599
in von Hippel–Lindau disease, 1599-1600
signal transduction in, 1590
staging of, 1600-1603
fine-needle aspiration, 1603
radiographic, 1602-1603, 1602f
Robson's, 1600, 1600f
TNM, 1600-1601, 1601t
syndromes associated with, 1597t
treatment of. *See also* Laparoscopic nephrectomy; Nephrectomy; Renal surgery.
adoptive cell therapy in, 499
for localized disease, 1608-1619
for locally advanced disease, 1619-1623
for metastatic disease, 1623-1632
tumor antigens of, 496
tumor biology in, 1588-1591
unclassified, 1596-1597
vs. renal oncocytoma, 1577-1578
Renal cholesterol embolism, 1166
Renal clear cell sarcoma, in children, 3898
Renal clearance, in glomerular filtration rate, 1132-1133
Renal colic
in medullary sponge kidney, 3349
management of, 1213
Renal collecting system, 31-32. *See also* Renal calyx (calyces); Renal papillae; Renal pelvis; Renal tubule(s).
anatomy of
microscopic, 31, 32f, 33f
pertinent, percutaneous nephrostomy and, 1528-1529, 1529f, 1530f
anomalies of, 3297-3303
cortical
intercalated cells in, 1146
principal cells in, 1144-1145, 1145f, 1146f
development of, 3126, 3127f
duplicated, heminephrectomy for, 1732-1733
medullary, 1145-1146
obstruction of, percutaneous treatment of, 1549-1550
opacification of, for percutaneous nephrolithotomy, 1486-1487, 1486f

Renal collecting system (*Continued*)
smooth muscle atony of, during pregnancy, 290
Renal corpuscle, 31, 32f
Renal cortex, 24f, 25, 33f
adenoma of, 1575-1576, 1576f
defects in, vesicoureteral reflux and, 4336-4341
scintigraphy of, 143, 143f
Renal cyst(s). *See also* Renal disease, cystic.
benign, 1575
category I, 3348, 3348t
category II, 1572-1573, 1573f, 3348, 3348t
category III, 1573, 1574f, 3348, 3348t
category IV, 1573, 1574f, 1575, 3348t
complex, Bosniak's classification of, 3348t
echinococcal, 285-286, 286f
fetal, 3177-3178
laparoscopic surgery for, 1772-1776
in autosomal dominant polycystic kidney disease, 1774-1775
indications for, 1772, 1772t
patient positioning for, 1773
patient preparation for, 1772-1773
results of, 1774
retroperitoneal approach to, 1774
transperitoneal approach to, 1773-1774, 1773f-1775f
multilocular, benign, 3339-3343, 3340f
characteristics of, 3314t
clinical features of, 3340
evaluation of, 3341, 3343
histopathology of, 3340-3341, 3342f
treatment of, 3343
multiple malformation syndromes with, 3329-3339, 3330t. *See also specific disorder.*
simple, 3343-3347
Bosniak's classification of, 3348t
characteristics of, 3314t
clinical features of, 3343
evaluation of, 3344-3346, 3344f-3347f
histopathology of, 3343
in autosomal dominant simple cyst disease, 3347-3348, 3348f, 3348t
in unilateral renal cystic disease, 3347
treatment and prognosis of, 3346-3347
upper pole, prenatal diagnosis of, 3185
variations of, 3347
Renal descensus, for ureteral stricture, 1264
Renal disease
congenital, implication of, adult renal function and, 3162
cystic, 3313-3315
acquired, 3351-3354, 3351f
characteristics of, 3314t
clinical features of, 3352
etiology of, 3352
evaluation of, 3353, 3354f
histopathology of, 3352-3353, 3353f
incidence of, 3351-3352
treatment of, 3353-3354, 3355f
uremic, 3351
autosomal dominant simple, 3347-3348, 3348f
bilateral, 3315, 3315t
classification of, 3313, 3313t, 3314t, 3315
heritable, 3315
sonographic differential diagnosis of, 3315t
unilateral, 3347
end-stage. *See* End-stage renal disease.
glomerulocystic
familial hypoplastic, 3329
characteristics of, 3314t

Renal disease (*Continued*)
  sporadic, 3350-3351
    characteristics of, 3314t
    conditions associated with, 3350t
  in children, 3217-3231. *See also under*
    Children; *specific disease.*
  multicystic dysplastic. *See* Multicystic
    dysplastic kidney.
  polycystic. *See also* Autosomal dominant
    polycystic kidney disease; Autosomal
    recessive polycystic kidney disease.
  surgery for, 1755
Renal dysgenesis
  definition of, 3307
  molecular genetics in, 3305-3307
  two-hit theory of, 3306-3307
Renal dysmorphism, reflux-associated, 4337,
  4337f, 4338f, 4338t
Renal dysplasia, 3307-3310
  critical determinants of, 3168
  cystic form of, 3308
  definition of, 3307
  familial, 3309-3310
  histologic hallmarks of, 3168-3169
  obstruction and, 3308, 3309f
  primitive ducts in, 3307-3308, 3308f
  with posterior urethral valves, 3587
Renal echinococcosis, 285-286, 286f
Renal ectopia
  cephalad, 3281
  crossed, 3283-3287
    associated anomalies with, 3286-3287
    bilaterally, 3283f
    diagnosis of, 3287
    embryology of, 3283-3284
    features of, 3284-3286, 3284f-3286f
    incidence of, 3283
    prognosis for, 3287
    solitary, 3283, 3283f
    symptoms of, 3287
    types of, 3283, 3283f
    with fusion, 3283, 3284f
    without fusion, 3283, 3283f
  lateral, 3312
  medial or caudal, 3312
  percutaneous nephrolithotomy into, 1498-
    1499
  simple, 3278-3281, 3278f
    associated anomalies with, 3279-3280
    diagnosis of, 3280-3281
    embryology of, 3279
    features of, 3279, 3280f
    incidence of, 3278-3279
    prognosis for, 3281
  stone formation in, surgical management of,
    1443-1444, 1444f
  superior, 3284f, 3286
Renal failure
  acute, 1325-1329
    acute glomerulonephritis in, 1327-1328,
     1328t
    acute interstitial nephritis in, 1328-1329,
     1328t
    acute tubular necrosis in, 1329-1332
     prevention of, 1339-1341
     prognosis of, 1339, 1340f
    after renal bypass surgery, 1753
    cardinal features of, 1325
    classification of, 1326
    complications of, 1335t
    definition of, 1325-1326
    differential diagnosis of, 1333-1335, 1334f,
     1334t, 1335t
    epidemiology of, 1326-1327

Renal failure (*Continued*)
    imaging of, 1335
    incidence and etiology of, 1329-1330, 1329t
    intrinsic causes of, 1327-1329, 1328t
    management of, 1335-1341
     conservative, 1337-1338, 1337t
     dialytic interventions in, 1338-1339
     pharmacologic, 1336-1337
    metabolic alterations in, 1338
    natural history of, 1330
    pathophysiology of, 1330-1332, 1331f-1333f
    postrenal causes of, 1327
    prerenal causes of, 1326-1327, 1326t
    urinary indices in, 1334-1335, 1334f,
     1335t
    urine sediment in, 1334, 1334t
  autosomal recessive polycystic kidney disease
    causing, 3318, 3320
  chronic, 1341-1359
    atherosclerotic risk factors in, 1352-1353
    autosomal dominant polycystic kidney
     disease in, 1346
    blood glucose control in, 1353-1354
    calcifications in, 1353
    cardiovascular complications associated
     with, 1353-1354
    clinical action plan for, 1342t
    clinical assessment of, 1348
    deterioration in, factors associated with,
     1346-1347, 1347t
    diabetes mellitus in, 1358-1359
    drug dosing in, 1352
    erectile dysfunction and, 748
    etiology of, 1345-1347, 1345t, 1346t,
     1347t
    function assessment of, 1348
    genetic factors in, 1344-1345
    hospitalization for, 1357-1359, 1358t
    kidney biopsy in, 1349
    malignancies in, 1346
    malnutrition in, 1353
    management of
     conservative, 1352-1354, 1352t, 1353f
     protective strategies in, 1349-1350,
      1351t
     renal replacement therapy in, 1354
      criteria for initiation of, 1358, 1358t
     treatment options in, 1354-1356, 1354t,
      1356t, 1357, 1357f, 1357t
    medullary cystic disease in, 1346
    membranoproliferative glomerulonephritis
     in, 1345-1346
    obstructive uropathy in, 1347
    preoperative evaluation of, 1350-1352
    progressive, 1341f
     causes of, 1346, 1346t
     mechanisms of, 1342-1344, 1343f
    proteinuria in, 1348
    radiographic assessment of, 1349
    renal artery stenosis in, 1347
    renal mass reduction and, 1342
    systemic diseases in, 1346, 1346t
    tubular interstitial disease in, 1346-1347
    urinalysis in, 1349
    urolithiasis in, 1347
  end-stage. *See* End-stage renal disease.
  vesicoureteral reflux causing, 4340-4341
Renal function
  alterations in, shockwave lithotripsy causing,
    1478-1479
  assessment of, prior to urinary tract
    reconstruction, 3659
  augmentation of, during pregnancy, 290-291,
    290t

Renal function (*Continued*)
  changes in
    shockwave lithotripsy causing, 1480
    urinary tract obstruction associated with,
     1195-1207
  deterioration of, after urinary diversion, 2563-
    2564
  evaluation of
    in fetus, 3150-3151, 3151f
    in infant/child, 3153-3156, 3155f, 3157f
    in neonate, 3151-3153, 3152f, 3153f
    prior to urinary tract reconstruction, 2616
  glomerular filtration in, 1131-1132. *See also*
    Glomerular filtration rate.
  hormonal control of, during development,
    3157-3159, 3158f
  impaired
    experimental treatment approaches to,
     1205-1206
    progression of
     in congenital urinary tract obstruction,
      3164, 3164f
     in pediatric urinary tract infection, 3260-
      3261
  level of, in renal artery atherosclerosis, 1175-
    1176, 1175f, 1176f
  with posterior urethral valves, prognostic
    indicators of, 3598-3599
Renal hemodynamics
  angiotensin II in, 1134
  in acute tubular necrosis, abnormalities of,
    1332
Renal hemorrhage, shockwave lithotripsy
  causing, 1477, 1478f
Renal hilum, identification of, in laparoscopic
  nephrectomy, 1763, 1767f
Renal hypercalciuria, 1375, 1402
  management of, 1419-1420, 1421t
Renal hypertension, trauma-induced, in
  children, 3935
Renal hypodysplasia, 3310
  associated with prune-belly syndrome, 3313
  classification of, 3310t
  with abnormal ureteral orifice, 3312
  with normal ureteral orifice, 3312, 3312f
  with urethral obstruction, 3312-3313
Renal hypoplasia, 3310-3312
  classification of, 3310t
  oligomeganephronia and, 3310, 3311f
  reflux associated with, 3310
  segmental (Ask-Upmark kidney), 1191, 3311-
    3312
Renal injury
  blunt, 1274
  classification of, 1275, 1275t, 1276f
  complications of, 1282
  hematuria with, 1275
  in children, 3929
    grading of, 3931t
    management of, 3932-3935
     consensus recommendations in, 3934t
     nonoperative, 3933-3934
     operative, 3934-3935
    radiographic and endoscopic assessment of,
     3930-3932
    vascular trauma and, 3935
  in developing kidney, functional response to,
    3159-3162, 3159t
  isolated, 1277-1278
  nonhemodynamic mechanisms of, 1343-1344
  nonoperative management of, 1277-1278,
    1278f
  pediatric urinary tract infections causing,
    factors affecting, 3236-3238

Renal injury (Continued)
  penetrating, 1274
  presentation of, 1274-1275
  recovery from, 3162
  shockwave lithotripsy causing
    acute trauma, 1477-1479, 1478f, 1479t
      animal studies of, 1480-1484, 1480t,
        1481f-1484f, 1482t
    chronic trauma, 1479-1480, 1479t
      animal studies of, 1484
  staging of, 1275-1277
    imaging indications in, 1275-1276, 1276f
    imaging studies in, 1276-1277, 1277f
  surgical management of, 1278-1282
    contraindications to, 1278
    damage control in, 1281
    exploration in, 1278-1279, 1279f
    nephrectomy in, indications for, 1282
    reconstruction in, 1279, 1280, 1281, 1281f
  with posterior urethral valves, management
    of, 3597-3598
Renal insufficiency
  after partial nephrectomy, 1730
  after radical nephrectomy, 1720
  chronic, in children, 3230, 3230t
  in benign prostatic hyperplasia, effects of
    medical therapy on, 2775
  posterior urethral valves causing, 3586t, 3588
  pregnancy and, 293, 3241
Renal ischemia
  intraoperative, 1689-1691
    mechanisms of, 1689-1690
    prevention of, 1690-1691
    warm, tolerance to, 1690
  perinatal, functional response to, 3161
Renal leiomyoma, 1582
Renal leiomyosarcoma, 1633, 1633f
Renal leukemia, 1634-1635
Renal lipoma, 1582
Renal liposarcoma, 1634
Renal lymphoma, 1634-1635, 1634t
Renal medulla, 24f, 25, 33f
Renal medullary carcinoma, 1596
Renal medullary fibroma, 1582
Renal oncocytoma, 1577-1578, 1577f
  vs. renal cell carcinoma, 1577-1578
Renal osteogenic sarcoma, 1634
Renal pain, patient history of, 82
Renal papillae
  anatomy of, 24f, 31-32
    renal scarring and, 4339, 4339f
  necrosis of, urinary tract infections in, 236-
    237, 237t
Renal parenchyma
  bacterial persistence in, relapse from, 280
  disease of, 1191
Renal pelvis. See also Ureteropelvic junction.
  anatomy of, 24f, 31-32, 34f, 35f
  injury to, percutaneous nephrostomy causing,
    1547
  transitional cell carcinoma of, in children,
    3900
  tumor of, renal surgery for, 1756, 1756f,
    1757f, 1758
  urothelium of
    abnormal, 1642-1643
    normal, 1641, 1641f, 1642f
    tumors of. See Urothelial tumor(s), of renal
      pelvis and ureters.
Renal phosphorus wasting, in neonate, 3156
Renal plasma flow, 1131
  increases in, 1132
  urinary tract obstruction and, 1195-1196
Renal pyramid, 24f, 25

Renal replacement therapy. See also
  Hemodialysis; Peritoneal dialysis; Renal
  transplantation.
  for acute renal failure, 1338
    continuous, 1339
  for chronic renal failure, 1354
    criteria for initiation of, 1358, 1358t
  mortality associated with, 1355
Renal rhabdoid tumor, in children, 3898
Renal sarcoma, 1632-1634, 1633f
Renal scarring
  pediatric urinary tract infection and, 3238
  vesicoureteral reflux and
    congenital, 4338t
      vs. acquired, 4336-4337
    pathophysiology of, 4338-4341, 4339f
Renal sinus cyst, 3356, 3356f, 3357f
  definition of, 3354, 3356
  parapelvic location of, 3354, 3355f
Renal small cell carcinoma, 1636
Renal surgery. See also Nephrectomy.
  anatomy pertinent to, 1686-1688, 1687f, 1688f
  approach(es) to, 1691-1703
    abdominal, 1695-1698, 1697f-1701f
    dorsal lumbotomy, 1695, 1696f
    flank, 1691-1694, 1691f-1695f
    pertinent renal anatomy in, 1527-1529,
      1527f-1530f, 1686-1688, 1687f, 1688f
    thoracoabdominal, 1698, 1701f-1702f, 1703
  bypass
    alternative techniques in, 1737-1748, 1738t,
      1739f
    aortorenal, 1734-1737, 1735f-1738f
      thoracic, 1742-1743, 1742f, 1743f
    clinical results of, 1748-1749
    complication(s) of, 1749-1753
      acute renal failure as, 1753
      aortic, 1752
      hemorrhage as, 1749-1750
      hypertension as, 1749
      operative mortality as, 1749
      renal artery aneurysm as, 1751-1752,
        1752f
      renal artery stenosis as, 1751
      renal artery thrombosis as, 1750-1751,
        1750f
      visceral, 1752-1753
    extracorporeal microvascular branch renal
      artery reconstruction in, 1745-1748,
      1745f-1748f
    hepatorenal, 1740-1741, 1741f, 1742f
    iliorenal, 1743-1744, 1743f
    mesenterorenal, 1744-1745, 1744f
    postoperative care in, 1748
    splenorenal, 1738-1740, 1739f, 1740f
    thoracic aortorenal, 1742-1743, 1742f,
      1743f
  for horseshoe kidney, 1755-1756
  for polycystic kidney disease, 1755
  for renal cell carcinoma. See under
    Nephrectomy.
  for renal cysts, 1753-1754, 1755f
  for renal pelvic tumor, 1756, 1756f, 1757f,
    1758
  historical aspects of, 1686
  laparoscopic, 1759-1809. See also Laparoscpic
    nephrectomy.
    ablative technique(s) in, 1804-1807
      complications of, 1806-1807
      cryosurgical, 1804-1806
      radiofrequency, 1806
    biopsy as, 1770-1772
      indications for, 1770
      patient positioning for, 1770

Renal surgery (Continued)
    postoperative considerations in, 1771
    results of, 1771-1772
    technique of, 1770-1771, 1770f, 1771f
    calyceal diverticulectomy as, 1778
    complications of, 1807-1808
    for cystic disease, 1772-1776. See also Renal
      cyst(s), laparoscopic surgery for.
    for malignancy, 1778-1781. See also
      Nephrectomy, partial, for malignancy.
      port site recurrence after, 1779, 1779f,
        1780t, 1781, 1781f
    hand-assisted approach to, 1761, 1761t
    historical background in, 1759
    in children, 3919-3924
      access for, 3919-3921
        retroperitoneal - flank position, 3920,
          3922f, 3923f
        retroperitoneal - prone position, 3920,
          3922f, 3923f
        transperitoneal, 3919, 3920f
      miscellaneous, 3923-3924
      nephrectomy as, 3921-3923, 3923f
      postoperative management of, 3923
      results of, 3924, 3924f
    nephron-sparing in, 1799-1804. See also
      Nephron-sparing surgery,
      laparoscopic.
    nephropexy as, 1776, 1777f
    patient evaluation and preparation for,
      1759-1760, 1760f
    pyelolithotomy as, 1776, 1778
    retroperitoneal approach to, 1761
    transperitoneal approach to, 1761
    ureterolithotomy as, 1776, 1778
  nephrostomy tube insertion in, 1754-1755,
    1756
  preoperative preparation for, 1688-1689
  renal arterial reconstruction in, 1733
    clinical results of, 1748-1749
    complications of, 1749-1753
    extracorporeal microvascular, 1745-1748,
      1745f-1748f
    indications for, 1733-1734
    postoperative care in, 1748
    preoperative considerations in, 1734
  renal ischemia during, 1689-1691
    mechanisms of, 1689-1690
    prevention of, 1690-1691
    warm, tolerance to, 1690
Renal thyroidization, 279
Renal tomography, of urinary tract infection,
  243
Renal toxicity, of contrast media, 113
Renal transplantation, 1295-1324
  anesthesia for, 1309t
  complication(s) associated with, 1318-1324
    allograft nephrectomy as, 1318-1319
    cancer as, 1323-1324
      bladder, 1324, 2416
    diabetes mellitus as, 1324
    erectile dysfunction as, 1321-1322, 1322t,
      1323f
    fluid collection as, 1319-1320, 1320f
    graft dysfunction as, 1318, 1319t
    hematuria as, 1319
    obstruction as, 1320, 1321f
    pregnancy and childbearing as, 1322-1323,
      1323t
    pulmonary infection as, 1323
    urinary calculi as, 1320
    urinary tract infection as, 1320-1321
    vascular, 1318, 1324
    vesicoureteral reflux as, 1321

Renal transplantation (Continued)
donor for
cadaver, 1296, 1303, 1305-1306
biopsy grading system in, 1305, 1305t
criteria for, 1303, 1305
goals of resuscitation in, 1305-1306
midline incisions in, 1306, 1307f-1308f
recipient selection for, 1308-1309
selection of, 1303, 1305-1306
living, 1296
evaluation of, 1302f
imaging techniques for, 1301t
selection of, 1301, 1303
nephrectomy in, 1301, 1303, 1304f-1305f
selection and preparation of, 1301-1303
for acquired renal cystic disease, 3354, 3355f
for end-stage renal disease, 1295-1296
in children, 1296
for valve patients, 3599
history of, 1296-1297
kidney graft in
early dysfunction of, 1318, 1319t
expanded criteria donor and, 1303, 1305
candidates for, 1309
definition of, 1303
preparation of, 1309, 1309f, 1310f
preservation of
cellular injury and, 1306
clinical, 1306-1308
cold storage in, 1306
rejection of, 1314-1317, 1315f-1317f, 1317t,
1318t
percutaneous nephrolithotomy after, 1498
postoperative care following, 1312-1314
autocoagulation in, 1314
fluid and electrolyte management in, 1312-
1313
tube and drain management in,
1313-1314
preoperative assessment in, 1309
primary, survival rates for, 1296t
recipients of
active malignancy in, 1298-1299
cadaver kidney for, allocation of,
1308-1309
compliance issues in, 1299
infection in, 1298
kidney disease recurrence in, 1297-1298
operation for, 1309-1310, 1309t, 1311f,
1312
perioperative morbidity and mortality in,
1299
preliminary screening of, 1297, 1298f
selection and preparation of, 1297-1301
unsuitable conditions for technical success
in, 1299-1301, 1299t, 1300t
rejection in, 1314-1317
classification of, 1315-1316
histocompatibility in, 1314-1315, 1315f,
1315t
immunosuppression in, 1316-1317, 1316f,
1317f, 1317t, 1318t
timing of, 1296
urinary tract reconstruction in, 1310, 1313f-
1314f
vascular anastomoses in, 1310, 1311f, 1312
waiting lists for, 1296
Renal tubular acidosis, 1153-1154
calcium stone formation associated with,
1380-1381
causes of, 1404t
in children, 3154-3155, 3155f, 3228-3229
in infants, 3154-3155, 3155f
management of, 1422

Renal tubular acidosis (Continued)
type 1, 1380, 1381f, 1403-1404, 1404f, 1404t
type 2, 1381
type 4, 1381
Renal tubular cells, in urinary sediment, 107
Renal tubule(s). See also Nephron(s).
atrophy and cell death in, mechanisms leading
to, 1205
collecting. See also Renal collecting system.
cortical, 1144-1145, 1145f, 1146f
medullary, 1145-1146
distal, 31, 33f
disorders of, in children, 3228-3229
function of, 1144
function of, 1138-1148, 1144-1148
basic, 1138, 1139f
congenital urinary tract obstruction and,
3172
effects of ureteral obstruction on, 1200
in infant and child, 3154-3156, 3155f
organization of, 1138, 1139f
proximal, 31, 33f
disorders of, in children, 3228
function of, 1138-1141, 1140f, 1141f
Renal tumor(s), 1567-1636
ablative therapy for, 1810-1818
cryoablation as, 1811-1814. See also
Cryoablation.
high-intensity focused ultrasonography as,
1817-1818
interstitial laser coagulation as, 1817
microwave ablation as, 1816-1817
radiofrequency ablation as, 1814-1816. See
also Radiofrequency ablation.
radiosurgery as, 1818
rationale in, 1810-1811
success of, 1811
benign, 1575-1582
adenomas as, 1575-1576, 1576f
angiomyolipoma as, 1578-1580, 1579f
cystic nephroma as, 1580, 1581f
cysts as. See Renal cyst(s).
distinctive features of, 1583
leiomyoma as, 1582
lipoma as, 1582
medullary fibroma as, 1582
mixed epithelial stomal tumor as, 1581-
1582
oncocytoma as, 1577-1578, 1577f
reninoma as, 1582
classification of, 1568-1569, 1568t
pathologic, 1569t
radiographic, 1570t
simplified, 1569t
CT scan of, 1571, 1571f, 1572f
fine-needle aspiration of, 1571-1572
functioning, reduced, 3159-3160
historical considerations in, 1567-1568
hypernephroid, 1567
malignant, 1582-1636. See also Renal cell
carcinoma.
carcinoids as, 1635-1636
in children, 3885-3900. See also specific
tumor, e.g., Wilms' tumor.
leiomyosarcoma as, 1633, 1633f
leukemia as, 1634-1635
liposarcoma as, 1634
lymphoma as, 1634-1635, 1634t
metastases of, 1635
osteogenic sarcoma as, 1634
peripheral neuroectodermal tumor as,
1636
sarcomas as, 1632-1634, 1633f
small cell carcinoma as, 1636

Renal tumor(s) (Continued)
MR imaging of, 1571, 1573f
prenatal diagnosis of, 3185
radiographic evaluation of, 1569, 1570f-1574f,
1571-1575
reduction of, in chronic renal failure, 1342
Renal vascular tone, control of, 1134, 1134t
vasoconstrictors in, 1134-1135, 1134f, 1134t
vasodilators in, 1134t, 1135
Renal vein(s), 11f, 13-14, 14f, 29, 30f
extension of, in renal transplantation, 1309,
1309f
injuries to, repair of, 1279, 1280f, 1281
lacerations of, nephrostomy causing, 1544-
1545, 1545f
renin levels in, renovascular hypertension
and, 1169-1170
thrombosis of, in neonates, 3196
Renin
in renin-angiotensin-aldosterone system,
1161-1162
renal vein levels of, in renovascular
hypertension, 1169-1170
secretion of
barorecptor mechanism in, 1162
macula densa mechanism in, 1162
neural control in, 1162
Renin-angiotensin system
changes in, congenital urinary tract
obstruction and, 3172
in kidney development, 3135
in male sexual function, 728
in renal development, 3157-3158, 3158f
Renin-angiotensin-aldosterone system
activation and inhibition of, factors in, 1826-
1827, 1826f, 1827f
CNS, 1163
gonadal, 1163
physiology of, 1161-1164
angiotensin II in, 1162-1163
angiotensin II receptor subtypes in, 1163-
1164
angiotensin-converting enzyme in, 1162
angiotensinogen in, 1161
baroreceptor mechanism in, 1162
endocrine/paraendocrine mechanisms in,
1162
intracellular mechanisms in, 1162
macula densa mechanism in, 1162
neural mechanism in, 1162
renin in, 1161-1162
Reninoma, 1582
Renography, radionuclide. See Scintigraphy,
renographic.
Renorrhaphy, technique of, 1279, 1280f
Renovascular fistula, 2357
Renovascular hypertension, 1156-1174
clinical features of, 1166-1167
definition of, 1157
diagnosis of, 1168-1173
captopril renography in, 1170
captopril test in, 1169
computed tomography angiography in, 1172
contrast arteriography in, 1172-1173
cost-effective approach to, 1173
duplex ultrasonography in, 1170-1171
intravenous urography in, 1169
magnetic resonance angiography in, 1171-
1172
peripheral plasma renin activity in, 1169
renal vein renin analysis on, 1169-1170
experimental
human correlates in, 1165
one-kidney, one-clip model in, 1164-1165

Renovascular hypertension (Continued)
  phases of, 1165t
  two-kidney, one-clip model in, 1164
  historical background of, 1156-1157
  laboratory investigations in, 1167
  natural history of, 1157t
  pathology of, 1157-1161
    atherosclerosis in, 1157-1159, 1157t, 1158f,
      1158t
    fibromuscular hyperplasia in, 1157t, 1161
    intimal fibroplasia in, 1157t, 1159, 1159f,
      1160f
    medial fibroplasia in, 1157t, 1159-1160,
      1160f
    perimedial fibroplasia in, 1157t, 1160-1161,
      1160f, 1161f
  pathophysiology of, 1164-1165
  renal artery reconstruction in, 1733
  renin-angiotensin-aldosterone system in,
    1161-1164
  symptoms of, 1167
  trauma-induced, in children, 3935
  treatment of
    endovascular stenting in, 1184-1187
      complications of, 1186-1187, 1186t
      indications for, 1185
      patient selection for, 1173-1174
      results of, 1185-1186, 1185t, 1186f
      technique of, 1185
    percutaneous transluminal angioplasty in,
      1180-1184
      atherosclerotic renal artery stenosis and,
        1182, 1183f, 1183t, 1184, 1184t
      children and, 1184
      complications of, 1181
      fibrous dysplasia and, 1181-1182, 1181t,
        1182f
      inflammatory renal artery stenosis and,
        1184
      mechanism of, 1181
      technique of, 1180-1181
    surgical, 1177-1180
      patient selection for, 1173-1174
      results of, 1179-1180, 1179t
      secondary revascularization in, 1180
      techniques in, 1177-1179
    vs. renal arterial disease, 1157
Renovascular injury, as complication of post-
  chemotherapy surgery, 956
Reproduction. See Fertility; Infertility;
  Pregnancy.
  assisted techniques in. See Assisted
    reproductive techniques (ART).
Reproductive axis, male, 577-580, 578f. See also
  specific reproductive organ.
  development of, 579
  physiology of, 577-607
  steroid feedback in, 578-579
  tiers of organization in, 577
Reproductive cloning, in tissue engineering, 571
"Rescue" therapy, with testosterone, for erectile
  dysfunction, 776
Resection
  endoscopic, of urothelial tumors, 1647-1648,
    1648f
    percutaneous approach to, 1648, 1648f
    results of, 1648, 1648t
  in partial nephrectomy
    transverse, 1724-1725, 1727f
    wedge, 1724, 1726f
  segmental, of urothelial tumors, 1649, 1649t
Resectoscope, spring-loaded, 2480-2481, 2481f
Reservoir insertion, safe, in penile prosthesis
    placement, 793-794, 794f

Residual mass, post-chemotherapy
  in nonseminomatous germ cell tumors,
    922
    indications for resection in, 922-923
  in seminomas, 912-913
Resiniferatoxin
  beneficial effects of, 2107
  for incontinence, 2072
  for painful bladder syndrome/interstitial
    cystitis, 362t, 364
  intravesical therapy with, 2106-2107
  uropharmacology of, 1958
Resistive index
  definition of, 3364
  in obstructed kidney, 3364-3365
Resorptive hypercalciuria, 1375-1377, 1402
Resource utilization, in health care, 145
Respiration, effects of, on pneumoperitoneum,
  200-201
Respiratory acidosis, 1154
Respiratory alkalosis, 1154
Respiratory distress syndrome, as complication
  of post-chemotherapy surgery, 956
Responsiveness, of HRQOL instruments, 155
Resting membrane potential, of ureteral smooth
  muscle, 1892-1893, 1893f
Retinitis pigmentosa, in juvenile
  nephronophthisis, 3327
Retinoblastoma, familial, 516t
Retinoblastoma gene. See RB gene.
Retinoblastoma protein, $G_1S$ checkpoint and,
  524
13-cis-Retinoic acid, for neuroblastoma, 3877
Retraction, in laparoscopy, 196-197, 197f
Retrocaval ureter. See Ureter(s), circumcaval
  (retrocaval).
Retrograde pyelography. See Pyelography,
  retrograde.
Retroperitoneal fibrosis
  causes of, 1215t
  diagnostic biopsy of, 1216-1217
  diagnostic imaging of, 1215-1216, 1216f,
    1217f
  drug-induced, 1270
  etiology of, 1270-1271
  evaluation of, 1271, 1271f
  gross appearance of, 1215, 1271
  idiopathic, 1270
  in ureteral obstruction, 1215-1218
  incidence of, 1215
  management of, 1271-1273
    initial, 1271
    laparoscopic ureterolysis in, 1273
    pharmacologic, 1217, 1271-1272
    ureterolysis in, 1217-1218, 1272-1273,
      1273f
  membranous glomerulonephritis associated
    with, 1270-1271
  presentation of, 1270
Retroperitoneal hemorrhage, during radical
  nephrectomy, management of, 1710-1712,
  1713f
Retroperitoneal ligation, for varicocele, 3796
Retroperitoneal lymph node dissection
  (RPLND)
  for testicular germ cell tumors
    anatomic considerations in, 939, 939f
    nonseminomatous
      stage I and stage IIA, 913, 915, 915f,
        916f, 948
      stage IIB, 919, 919t, 949
        adjuvant chemotherapy after, 919,
          949
    rationale for, 939

Retroperitoneal lymph node dissection
  (RPLND) (Continued)
    surgical technique of, 941-945
      intraoperative neurostimulation in, 945
      laparoscopic. See Laparoscopic
        retroperitoneal lymph node
        dissection.
      lymphadenectomy in, 943-944, 944f
      retroperitoneal exposure in, 941
      setting up for, 943
      thoracoabdominal approach in, 941-942
      transabdominal approach in, 942-943,
        942f, 943f
    surgical templates in, 940-941, 940f, 941f
  laparoscopic, 945-948. See also Laparoscopic
    retroperitoneal lymph node dissection.
  postchemotherapy, for testicular tumors, 954-
    955
Retroperitoneal space, access to, for
    ureteropelvic junction obstruction repair,
    in children, 3376-3378, 3376f-3379f
Retroperitoneoscopy
  closed (Veress) technique in, 183
  gasless assisted, 182
  limitations and advantages of, 219
  open (Hasson) technique in, 183, 183f, 184f
Retroperitoneum, 3-19, 4f-5f, 6f
  colon in, 19, 20f
  duodenum in, 19, 20f
  exposure of
    in left-sided laparoscopic RPLND, 946
    in retroperitoneal lymph node dissection, 941
  innervation of, 14-19
    autonomic, 15, 16f, 17, 17f
    somatic, 17-19, 17f, 18f, 19t
  lymphatics of, 14, 15f
  pancreas in, 19, 20f
  posterior abdominal wall of, 3, 6f-9f, 8-9, 9t
Retropubic suspension surgery, for female
    incontinence, 2168-2185, 2170, 2171f
  bladder drainage in, 2174
  bladder overactivity after, 2183
  choice of technique in, 2169-2170
  complications of, 2182-2184
  contraindications to, 2172-2173
  definition of cure in, 2172
  dissection in, 2174
  drains in, 2174
  duration of follow-up in, 2171
  hypermobility in, contribution of, 2170
  indications for, 2172-2174, 2173f
  intrinsic sphincter deficiency in
    contribution of, 2170
    issue of, 2171-2172
  laparoscopic, 2180, 2182
  options in, 2168-2169, 2169t
  outcomes of, 2170-2172
  paravaginal repair in
    results of, 2179-2180
    technique of, 2178-2179, 2179f
  patient's vs. physician's perspective in, 2172
  postoperative voiding difficulties after, 2183
  procedures for, 2170, 2171f. See also Burch
    colposuspension; Marshall-Marchetti-
    Krantz procedure.
    comparison of, 2184-2185
  suture material in, 2174
  vaginal prolapse after, 2184
  vagino-obturator shelf repair in, 2180, 2181f
  vs. vaginal surgery, 2173-2174
Retroviral agents, erectile dysfunction caused by,
  746
Retroviruses. See also specific virus or infection.
  RNA, 507

Revascularization
  penile. *See also* Penile vascular surgery.
    arterial, 802-812
    venous, 812-816
  renal, "no-reflow" phenomenon after, 1306
Reverse transcriptase inhibitors, for HIV
    infection, 401, 403t
Reverse transcriptase polymerase chain reaction
    (RT-PCR), in diagnosis of oncology, 548
Reverse transcription, of retroviruses, 389
Reye's syndrome, aspirin associated with, 3206
R-factor resistance, of bacteria, to antibiotics,
    244-245
Rhabdoid tumor, of kidney, in children, 3898
Rhabdomyolysis, after laparoscopic surgery, 218
Rhabdomyosarcoma, 3878-3885
  alveolar, 3879
  clinical grouping of, 3879, 3879t
  embryonal, 3879
  etiology, epidemiology, and genetics of, 3878-
    3879
  of bladder, 2446
  of prostate, 2881
  of testicular adnexa, 933
  of vagina, 3846, 3846f
  pathology of, 3879
  patterns of spread of, 3879
  staging of, 3879-3880, 3879t
  treatment of, 3880-3885
    for bladder tumors, 3880-3883, 3881f,
      3882f
    for nephrogenic adenoma, 3883
    for paratesticular tumors, 3883-3884
    for prostate tumors, 3880-3883, 3881f,
      3882f
    for transitional cell carcinoma of bladder,
      3883
    for uterine tumors, 3885
    for vaginal tumors, 3884-3885, 3884f
    for vulvar tumors, 3884-3885
    risk assignments in, 3880, 3881t
Rhizotomy, sacral
  for bladder denervation, 2289-2290
  for bladder storage disorders, 2152-2153
RhoA/Rho kinase, in penile smooth muscle, 732,
    732f
Rib cage, lower, 9, 11f
Ribonucleic acid. *See* RNA *entires.*
Rice bran, for nephrolithiasis, 1419
Rickets, hereditary hypophosphatemic, in
    hypercalciuria, 1375
Rifampin, for genitourinary tuberculosis, 443,
    445t
RigiScan studies, of nocturnal penile
    tumescence, 763-764, 764f
RNA
  interference, 510-512
  messenger, 509, 509f
  translation of, 511-512
  post-transcriptional modification of, 510
  ribosomal, 512
  transfer, 512
RNA viruses, 507
  oncogenes identified in, 513
*RNASEL* gene, in hereditary prostate cancer, 518
Robinson catheters, 161-162, 162f
Robotic-assisted laparoscopic surgery, 173-174
  for adrenalectomy, 1884
  for pyeloplasty, 1250
  for radical prostatectomy, 2985-3002. *See also*
    Laparoscopic radical prostatectomy,
    robotic-assisted.
  in children, 3927-3928, 3928f
  of seminal vesicles, 1124

Robson's staging, of renal cell carcinoma, 1600,
    1600f
  5-year survival and, 1604t
Rollerball, in transurethral vaporization of
    prostate, 2839
Rotating disk flowmeter, 1989
Rotoresection of prostate, for benign prostatic
    hyperplasia, 2843
Round cell(s), in semen, 625
Round ligament, of uterus, 3145
RPLND. *See* Retroperitoneal lymph node
    dissection (RPLND).
RT-PCR (reverse transcriptase polymerase chain
    reaction), in diagnosis of oncology, 548
Rubber bands, in penile strangulation injury,
    2652

**S**

S phase, of cell cycle, 524-525
Saccular aneurysm, of renal artery, 1187, 1188f
Sacher shunt, for priapism, 847f, 848
Sacral agenesis
  definition of, 3644
  diagnosis of, 3644-3645, 3645f, 3646f
  familial, Currarino triad associated with,
    3644
  findings in, 3645, 3647f
  management of, 3645, 3647
Sacral artery, 11f, 13, 13t
  middle, 46, 48t, 50f
Sacral colpopexy, in apical vaginal prolapse
    repair, 2228, 2229f
  laparoscopic, 2229-2230, 2230t
  vs. sacrospinous ligament fixation, 2190
Sacral evoked response-bulbocavernosus reflex
    latency test, in erectile dysfunction, 766
Sacral nerve electrostimulation
  for painful bladder syndrome/interstitial
    cystitis, 365
  responses to, 2148t
Sacral nerve neuromodulation
  complications of, 2160-2163
    published reports of, 2160-2162, 2161f,
      2162f
    troubleshooting algorithm for, 2162-2163,
      2163f
  for bladder emptying disorders, 2166-2167
  for bladder storage disorders, 2153-2158
    outcome of, 2155
    special populations and, 2155-2158
    technique of, 2153-2155, 2153f-2155f
  for incontinence, 2073
  mechanism of action of, 1947-1948, 1947f,
    1948f, 2149-2150
    in overactive bladder, 2150, 2150f
    in urinary retention, 2150, 2151f
Sacral plexus, 53
Sacral rhizotomy
  for bladder denervation, 2289
    selective, 2289
  for bladder storage disorders, 2152-2153
Sacral spinal cord injury, voiding dysfunction in,
    2012t, 2024, 2025f
Sacral vein, 13, 14f
Sacroiliac joint, defects of, in exstrophy patient,
    3501, 3501f
Sacrospinalis muscle, 8, 9t, 10f
Sacrospinous ligament, 38, 39f
  fixation of, in apical vaginal prolapse repair,
    2225-2226, 2226f
    vs. sacral colpopexy, 2229
Sacrum, 38, 39f
Safety, of injectable therapies, for incontinence,
    2284-2285

Safety guide wires, for ureteroscopy, 1515-1516
  cystoscopic placement of, 1515
*Salmonella* infection, in schistosomiasis, 453
Salvage chemotherapy. *See* Chemotherapy,
    salvage.
Salvage cryotherapy, for prostate cancer, 3039-
    3040
  outcomes after, 3047-3048, 3047t
Salvage metastasectomy, for renal cell
    carcinoma, 1632
Salvage procedure(s)
  for metastatic bladder cancer, 2478
  for penile prosthesis infections, 796
  for refractory disease, in non–muscle-invasive
    bladder cancer, 2460-2461
  for ureteropelvic junction obstruction, 1249
  tension-free vaginal taping in, 2256
Salvage radiation therapy, for prostate cancer,
    3048
Salvage radical prostatectomy, 2936, 2977-2978,
    3048-3049
  vs. other salvage therapies, 3047-3048
Salvage ureteroscopy, after failed shockwave
    lithotripsy, 1519
Sarcoidosis, hypercalcemia associated with, 1376
Sarcoma(s). *See also specific type, e.g.,* Kaposi's
    sarcoma.
  of kidney, 1632-1634, 1633f
  of penis, 990
  of prostate, 2881
    transrectal ultrasonography of, 2887
  of seminal vesicles, 1116
  of upper urinary tract, abnormal urothelium
    in, 1643
  renal clear cell, in children, 3898
Sarcomatoid variants, of renal cell carcinoma,
    1596, 1596f
*Sarcoptes scabiei*, 383, 425
Saturation states, in stone formation, 1366-1367,
    1366f
Saw palmetto berry. *See* Serenoa repens (saw
    palmetto berry).
S-bladder, for orthotopic urinary diversion,
    2634-2635
Scabies, 383, 383f, 425, 426f
Scalp, pediculosis of, 384
Scalpel, laparoscopic, 191
Scar, definition of, 4336
Scardino-Prince vertical flap technique, of
    pyeloplasty, 1245, 1246f
Scarpa's fascia, 38, 40, 40f, 1032f, 1036
Schafer nomogram, for outflow obstruction,
    1998-1999, 1999f
Schiller-Duvall bodies, in yolk sac tumors, 3901
*Schistosoma haematobium*, 448
  biology and life cycle of, 448-449, 448f
  in urinary sediment, 109
  infection with. *See also* Schistosomiasis.
    bladder cancer associated with, 2415, 2421
*Schistosoma japonicum*, 448
*Schistosoma mansoni*, 448
Schistosomal myelopathy, voiding dysfunction
    in, 2036-2037
Schistosomiasis, 448-455
  clinical manifestations of, 450, 452-453
  contracted bladder syndrome in, 452
  diagnosis of, 453-454, 453f
  epidemiology of, 449
  history of, 448
  hydronephrosis in, 450
  inactive, 450, 451f
  pathogenesis of, 449-450
  pathology of, 449-450, 450f, 451f
  prevention and control of, 455

Schistosomiasis (Continued)
  prognosis of, 455
  radiography of, 453, 453f
  risk of bladder cancer with, 450
  Salmonella infection associated with, 453
  treatment of
    medical, 454
    surgical, 454-455
  ultrasonography of, 453, 453f
Schizophrenia, voiding dysfunction in, 2041
Schwartz formula, estimation of glomerular
    filtration rate using, 3230t
Sciatic nerve, 19
Scintigraphy, 139-143
  diuretic, 141f-142f, 142-143
  in pediatric urologic patient, 3213-3214
  of acute renal failure, 1335
  of ectopic ureter, 3393
  of focal pyelonephritis, 3245-3246
  of megaureter, 4373, 4374f
  of pheochromocytoma, 1863, 1865f
  of posterior urethral valves, 3590
  of primary hyperaldosteronism, 1854
  of renal cortex, 143, 143f
  of renal injury, in children, 3932
  of scrotal cord torsion, 3791
  of urinary tract infections, 243
  of vesicoureteral reflux, 4336, 4336f
  of xanthogranulomatous pyelonephritis, 283
  renographic, 762-763
    of renovascular hypertension, 1170
    of ureteral obstruction, 1210-1211
    of ureteropelvic junction obstruction, 1229-
      1230, 1231f
      in children, 3365-3367, 3366f-3367f
    of urinary tract infection, in children,
      3255-3256
  Tc-99m-MAG3, 140f-142f, 142
  venographic, 1170
Scissors, laparoscopic, 191
Sclerosing lymphangitis
  of male genitalia, 431
  Zoon's, 431, 432f
Sclerosis
  diffuse mesangial, congenital nephrosis with,
    3328-3329
    characteristics of, 3314t
  multiple
    sacral neuromodulation for, 2156
    voiding dysfunction in, 2012t, 2019-2020
  systemic, voiding dysfunction in, 2042
  tuberous. See Tuberous sclerosis.
Sclerotherapy
  bismuth phosphate, for renal cysts, 3347
  for hydrocele, 1106
  for renal cysts, 1551-1552, 1552f
Screening
  for bladder cancer, 2432-2434
    carcinogen exposure and, 2436-2437
    DNA, 2432
  for prostate cancer, 2854, 2856, 2857f
    age to begin, 2923-2924
    age to discontinue, 2924-2925
    decreased mortality due to, 2854, 2857
    intervals between, 2924
    PSA-based, 2913
    simulations and population-based
      observations of, 2913-2914, 2914t
    specialty group and task force
      recommendations in, 2913
Screening questionnaires, for late-onset
    hypogonadism, 853-854, 854f, 854t
Scrotal ecchymosis, after laparoscopic surgery,
    217

Scrotal edema
  miscellaneous causes of, 3793
  testicular torsion causing, 3792
Scrotal elephantitis, 456, 456f, 457
  Onchocerca volvulus causing, 455
  treatment of, 458
Scrotal engulfment, 3758-3759, 3758f
Scrotal hypoplasia, 3759
Scrotal injury
  blunt, 2652, 2653f
  in children, 3945
  penetrating, 2654
  skin loss in, 2654, 2655f
    reconstruction following, 2655
Scrotal pain. See Orchialgia.
Scrotoplasty, for penoscrotal transposition,
    3758-3759, 3758f
Scrotum, 72-73, 73f, 1098-1108
  acute, 3790-3794
    differential diagnosis of, 3774t, 3790
    epididymal appendage torsion and, 3792
    spermatic cord torsion and, 3790-3791,
      3790f
      intermittent, 3791-3792
      perinatal, 3793-3794
    swelling in, miscellaneous causes of, 3793
    testicular torsion in, 3792
    vs. epididymitis, 3792-3793
  anatomy of, surgical, 1098, 1099t
  anomalies of, 3758-3759, 3758f, 3759f, 3790f
  bifid, 3759
  ectopic, 3759, 3759f
  examination of, 92-93, 92f
    infertility and, 613
  normal, in infant, 3208
  pain in. See Orchialgia.
  surgery of. See also specific procedure.
    lymphatic drainage following, 938
    patient preparation for, 1098
    postoperative care after, 1098
  ultrasonography of, 124, 126f, 127f
    in infertility work-up, 629-630
Sealants
  chemical-based, used in laparoscopy, 193, 193t
  used in percutaneous nephrostomy, 1561
Seasonal variation, in renal calculi, 1364-1365
Seattle procedure, of bladder exstrophy repair,
    3517
  results of, 3534-3535
Sebaceous glands, of male genitalia, ectopic, 431,
    432f
Seborrheic dermatitis, of male genitalia, 414-415
Seborrheic keratosis, of male genitalia, 433, 434f
Secale cereale, for benign prostatic hyperplasia,
    2800, 2800t
Second malignancy, chemotherapy causing, 923-
    924
Second messengers, in ureteral smooth muscle
    contractility, 1900-1902, 1900f-1902f
Sedative/hypnotics, causing geriatric
    incontinence, 2308, 2308t
Sedentary occupations, risk of stone formation
    associated with, 1365
Segmental resection, of urothelial tumors, 1649,
    1649t
Segmental ureterectomy, of urothelial tumors,
    1649
  results of, 1649, 1649t
Selective androgen receptor modulators, for late-
    onset hypogonadism, 858
Selective serotonin reuptake inhibitors (SSRIs)
  erectile dysfunction caused by, 744-745
  for depression, 770
  for premature ejaculation, 785-786, 786t

Selenium, for prostate cancer, chemopreventive,
    2870
Selenium with vitamin E, for prostate cancer,
    chemopreventive, 2871
Self-adhesive, skin patch electrode, 1989
Self-administered questionnaires, in erectile
    dysfunction, 751
Self-catheterization. See also Catheterization.
  clean intermittent, in renal transplant
    recipients, 1300
Self-mutilation, genital, 2651
Self-start intermittent therapy, for recurrent
    urinary tract infections, 264-265
Semen
  coagulation of, 2725
  collection of, 614
  culturing of, 625-626
  hyperviscosity of, 615
  leukocyte staining in, 625
  liquefaction of, 2725
  pH of, 617
    reference range for, 618
  physical characteristics of, 614-615
  processing, in assisted reproductive
    techniques, 651
  reactive oxygen species testing of, 632
  round cells in, 625
  volume of, reference range for, 618
  white blood cells in, 625
    reference range for, 618
Semen analysis, 614-618
  additional parameters in, 617
  computer-assisted, 617
  diagnostic algorithms for infertility based on,
    619, 620f, 620t, 621, 623
  interpretation of, 617-618
    reference ranges in, WHO definition of, 618
  methodology of, 614-615
  morphologic examination in, 615-617, 616f,
    617f
  physical characteristics in, 614-615
  post-vasectomy, 1102
  sample collection for, 614
  sperm count in, 615
  sperm motility in, 615
Semenogelins I and II, 2721
Seminal fluid, components of, 614-615
Seminal vesicles, 64-65, 1109-1126
  abscess of, 1114-1115
  agenesis of, 1113-1114, 1114f
  amyloid deposits in, 1116
  anatomy of, 1109-1110
  aspiration of, in assessment of ejaculatory
    duct obstruction, 710, 712f
  blood supply to, 1110
  calculi in, 1115, 2670
    endoscopic removal of, 1125
  computed tomography of, 133, 1112, 1112f
  congenital absence of, 617
  cysts of, 1115-1116, 1115f
    imaging of, 1112, 1112f
    laparoscopic surgery for, 2507-2509, 2509f
      in children, 3927
    medical-radiologic treatment of, 1125
  development of, 3137, 3139f
  dissection of, in robotic-assisted laparoscopic
    radical prostatectomy, 2989-2990, 2989f,
    2990f
  embryology of
    abnormalities in, 1109
    normal development in, 1109, 1110f
  excision of, in radical retropubic
    prostatectomy, 2969-2971, 2970f
  inflammation of, 1114-1115

Seminal vesicles *(Continued)*
  innervation of, 1110
  magnetic resonance imaging of, 1112-1113, 1113f
  obstruction of, 1114, 1115f
  pain in, patient history of, 82-83
  pathology of, 1113-1116
    congenital lesions in, 1113-1114, 1114f, 1115f
    infectious, 1114-1115
    masses in
      cystic, 1115-1116, 1115f
        medical-radiologic treatment of, 1125
      solid tumors in, 1116
    treatment of, 1116-1126. *See also* Seminal vesicles, surgical approaches to.
  physical examination of, 1110-1111
  physiology of, 1109
  secretions from, 1109
  secretory proteins of, 2724-2725
  sparing of, in radical retropubic prostatectomy, 2975-2976
  surgical approaches to, 1117-1126
    anterior, 1117
    endoscopic, 1125
    indications for, 1117
    laparoscopic technique in, 1120, 1122-1125. *See also* Laparoscopic surgery, of seminal vesicles.
    open techniques in, 1117-1120
    paravesical, 1119-1120
    preoperative preparation for, 1117
    retrovesical, 1120, 1121f
    transcoccygeal, 1120, 1122f
    transperitoneal, 1118, 1118f
    transvesical, 1118-1119, 1119f
  tumors of, 1115
    benign, 1116
    diagnosis of, 1110
    malignant, 1116
  ultrasonography of, 1111-1112, 1111f
  vasography of, 1113, 1114f
Seminal vesiculectomy, 1117. *See also* Seminal vesicles, surgical approaches to.
Seminal vesiculitis, 326-327
Seminal vesiculography, 710, 711f
Seminiferous tubules
  degeneration of, 3809
  dysgenesis of, 3808-3809. *See also* Klinefelter's syndrome.
  epithelium of, 592
  function of, 587
  peritubular tissue surrounding, 587-588, 588f
  structure of, 581
Seminoma(s)
  anaplastic, 895
  from cryptorchid testis, 3773
  histologic classification of, 893, 894t
  histopathologic characteristics of, 894
  incidence, pathology, and presentation of, 897t
  risk of, in complete androgen insensitivity syndrome, 3824
  spermatocytic, 895
  treatment of, 909-913
    algorithm in, 910f
    for stage I disease, 909-911, 910f, 911t
      surveillance studies after, 911-912, 911t
    for stage IIA and stage IIB disease, 910f, 912
    for stage IIC and stage III disease, 910f, 912, 913t
    postchemotherapy residual mass after, 912-913

Seminoma(s) *(Continued)*
  typical, 894-895
  vs. nonseminomatous germ cell tumors, 956-957
Senior-Loken syndrome, 3327
  characteristics of, 3314t
Sensorium, altered, conduit urinary diversion causing, 2573
Sensory nerves, role of, in ureteral function, 1906
Sentinel lymph node(s), biopsy of, in penile cancer, 979, 1003-1005, 1004f
Sepsis
  bacteriology of, 288
  BCG, 447
  characteristics of, 287t
  definition of, 287
  dental, treatment of, prior to renal transplantation, 1298
  due to intestinal anastomosis, 2549
  in neonate, 3196
  management of, 288-289
  percutaneous nephrostomy causing, 1548
Septic shock
  bacterial cell wall components in, 287-288
  bacteriology of, 288
  biologic effects of, 288
  clinical presentation of, 288
  definition of, 287
  diagnosis of, 288
  pathophysiology of, 287
Sequelae, delayed, in locally advanced prostate cancer, treatment of, 3067-3068
*Serenoa repens* (saw palmetto berry)
  for benign prostatic hyperplasia, 2799, 2799t
    dosage of, 2800t
  for prostatitis, 323
Seromuscular enteroplasty, in children, 3690, 3691f
Serotonin
  effect of
    on male sexual function, 729-730
    on ureteral function, 1918-1919
  uropharmacology of, 1957
Sertoli cell(s), 3136
  characteristics of, 588
  differentiation of, 3803-3804
  germ cells associated with, 588, 589f, 591-592, 591f
  in spermatogenesis, 579-580
  müllerian-inhibiting substance secretion by, 3804, 3805
  precursors of, 579
  secretion of müllerian-inhibiting substance by, 3144-3145
  secretory products of, 588-589
Sertoli cell tumor(s), 637, 927-928
  in children, 3901, 3904
  treatment of, 926t, 927
Sertoli cell–only syndrome
  infertility in, 642-643
  pure vs. acquired, 643t
Sertraline, for premature ejaculation, 785, 786t
Serum biomarkers. *See also* Tumor marker(s).
  for prostate cancer, molecular biology of, 2909-2910
Serum tests, for pediatric urinary tract infections, 3245
Sex
  chromosomal, 3799-3801, 3800f-3802f
  determination of, *SRY* gene in, 3146-3147, 3146f
  fetal, determination of, 3178, 3180f, 3573

Sex accessory gland(s). *See also* Bulbourethral glands; Prostate, Seminal vesicles.
  embryonic development of, 2678-2679
  in prune-belly syndrome, 3484
  secretions of, spermatozoal function and, 604-606
Sex cord–mesenchymal tumor(s), 925-928, 926t. *See also specific tumor.*
Sex hormone(s)
  fluctuations in, germ cell tumors due to, 901
  synthesis of, 1825, 1825f
Sex hormone–binding globulin, 767
  assessment of, in females, 872
Sex maturity stages, in boys, Tanner classification of, 3745, 3746t
Sex reversal syndrome, 639
Sex steroids. *See also specific steroid.*
  average plasma levels of, in males, 2686t
  uropharmacology of, 1956
Sextant biopsy, TRUS-guided, of prostate, 2890
Sexual abuse, of children, evaluation of, 3199, 3203, 3210
Sexual activity
  preoperative documentation of, in vesicovaginal fistula repair, 2332-2333
  prostate cancer associated with, 2862
  urinary tract infection and, in adolescents, 3240
Sexual arousal
  in females, disorders of, 864
  in males
    benign prostatic hyperplasia and, 2744, 2744f
    disorders of. *See specific disorder.*
    neural activation during, imaging of, 726-728
    release of neurotransmitters in, 723, 723f
    visual, brain activation with, 727t
Sexual aversion disorder, in females, 864
Sexual behaviors, HIV infection associated with, 388
Sexual desire
  in hypogonadal men, 859
  problems with, in females, 864
Sexual differentiation, 3799-3829. *See also* Genitalia; Gonad(s).
  abnormal, 3808-3827, 3808t
    evaluation and management of, 3827-3829, 3828f
    gender assignment in, 3829
    gonadal disorders in, 3808-3816
    gonadal dysgenesis syndromes as, 3809-3814. *See also specific syndrome.*
    hermaphroditism as, 3815-3816, 3815f
    Mayer-Rokitansky-Küster-Hauser syndrome as, 3827
    pseudohermaphroditism as, 3816-3827. *See also* Pseudohermaphroditism.
    seminiferous tubule dysgenesis as, 3808-3809
    testicular regression as, 3814-3815
    vanishing testes as, 3814-3815
    XX maleness as, 3809
  molecular mechanism of, 3146-3148, 3146f
  müllerian-inhibiting substance in, 2679, 3761-3762
  normal, 3799-3808
    chromosomal sex and, 3799-3801, 3800f-3802f
    genes involved in, 3802-3803, 3802f
    gonadal function in, 3804-3805, 3805f
    gonadal stage of, 3803-3804, 3803f
    psychosexual, 3805, 3808
    psychotypic, 3805, 3806f, 3807f

Sexual dimorphism, molecular basis of, in
    genital development, 3141
Sexual dysfunction
    androgen deprivation therapy causing, 3090
    depression and, 770
    female
        hemodynamic investigations in, 873-874,
            874f
        in pelvic organ prolapse, 2204-2205, 2204t
        in perimenopausal and postmenopausal
            women, hormonal therapy for, 878-
            881, 879f
        in premenopausal women, hormonal
            therapy for, 875-878
    male. See also Erectile dysfunction.
        benign prostatic hyperplasia and, 2744,
            2744f
        effects of testosterone therapy on, 859, 861
    patient history of, 86-87
    psychosocial history of, 755-756, 755t
    radiation-induced, 3016-3017, 3016t
Sexual function
    after hypospadias repair, 3742
    female, in exstrophy patient, 3552
        obstetric implications of, 3552-3553
    male
        brain centers involved in, 726t
        in exstrophy patient, 3550-3552
        neurotransmitters in, 728-730
            central, 729-730
            peripheral, 728-729
            release of, 723, 723f
Sexual health concerns, female, 863-889
    blood tests in, 872-873, 872f
    brain imaging in, 874
    classification of, 864
    diagnosis of, 865-875
    duplex Doppler ultrasonography in, 874,
        874f
    epidemiology of, 864
    laboratory testing in, 871-873
    medical history in, 865
    neurologic testing in, 875
    physical examination in, 866-867, 867f-871f,
        871
        bimanual, 867
        cotton swab test in, 866, 867f
        single-digit palpation in, 866, 868f
    psychosocial history in, 865-866
    sexual history in, 865
    specialized testing in, 873-875, 874f
    treatment of, 875-889
        hormonal therapy in
            for perimenopausal and postmenopausal
                women, 878-881, 879f
            for premenopausal women, 875-878
        medical, 883-886
        nonhormonal therapy in, 881-883
        surgical, 887-889, 887f, 888f
    vaginal pH testing in, 871
    wet mount testing in, 871
Sexual Medicine Society of North America
    report, on androgen therapy, 860
Sexual pain disorders, 883-889
    involving clitoris, prepuce, and frenulae, 883
    involving pelvic floor, 885-886
    involving Skene's glands, 884
    involving urethra, 883-884
    involving vagina, 885
    involving vestibule, 885
    involving vulva, 884
    medical management of, 883-886
    surgical management of, 886-889, 887f, 888f
Sexuality, myelodysplasia and, 3639-3640

Sexually transmitted disease, 371-385
    bacterial vaginosis as, 384
    causative agents in, 371
    chancroid as, 374-375, 375f, 420f
        in HIV patients, 395-396
    Chlamydia trachomatis infection as, 378-379
    circumcision and, 3747
    differential diagnosis of, 379t
    epidemiology of, 372
    genital ulcer as, 372, 373t
    genital warts as, 380-382, 380f, 381f, 420f
    gonorrhea as, 379
    HPV infection as, 372
        in HIV patients, 395, 395f
    HSV infection as, 373-374, 373f, 374f, 420f
        in HIV patients, 394-395, 394t
    in HIV patients, 387-388, 394-396, 394t. See
        also Human immunodeficiency virus
        (HIV) infection.
    in males, infertility due to, 611
    lymphogranuloma venereum as, 377-378,
        377f, 378f, 420f
    mollicutes in, 384
    molluscum contagiosum as, 382-383, 420f
        in HIV patients, 396
    partner notification of, 372
    pediculosis pubis as, 383-384
    proctitis as, 371
    risk of, 371
    scabies as, 383, 383f
    syphilis as, 375-377, 375f, 376f
        chancre with, 420f
        in HIV patients, 395
    trends associated with, 372
    trichomoniasis as, 380
    urinary tract infections and, 371
    vulvovaginal candidiasis as, 385
Sézary syndrome, 430
SF1 gene, in sex determination, 3802, 3802f
Sham control arms of device treatment trials, for
        benign prostatic hyperplasia, 2753
    natural history and disease progression in,
        2753-2754, 2754f, 2755f, 2756t
    sham/placebo effect in, 2753
        relationship between perception of
            improvement and, 2754, 2756
Sham procedure, vs. transurethral microwave
        therapy, 2818
Shear stress mechanism, of stone fragmentation,
        1475-1476
Shimada classification, of neuroblastoma,
        3871
Shock
    septic. See Septic shock.
    spinal, voiding dysfunction with, 2021-2022
Shockwave lithotripsy, 1465-1485
    anesthesia for, 1469, 1472
    antibiotic prophylaxis for, 252
    bioeffect(s) of, 1477-1484
        extrarenal damage as, 1477
        renal injury as
            acute, 1477-1479, 1478f, 1479t
                animal studies of, 1480-1484, 1480t,
                    1481f-1484f, 1482t
            chronic, 1479-1480, 1479t
                animal studies of, 1484
    comparison of lithotriptors in, 1472-1474,
        1472f, 1473t, 1474f
    failed, salvage ureteroscopy after, 1518-1519
    for bladder calculi, 2668
    for calyceal diverticular calculi, 1442
    for horseshoe kidney calculi, 1443
    for nonstaghorn calculi, 1436-1437, 1437f
    for Peyronie's disease, 828

Shockwave lithotripsy (Continued)
    for renal calculi
        ectopic, 1443
        lower pole, 1444-1447
            with associated urinary tract infection,
                1447
        for staghorn calculi, 1439
        for ureteral calculi
            distal, 1454-1455
            proximal, 1453-1454
            steinstrasse and, 1502-1503
            ureteral stent placement before, 1501-1502
    generator types for, 1465-1469
        electrohydraulic (spark gap), 1465, 1465f,
            1466t, 1470t
        electromagnetic, 1465, 1467t, 1468, 1468f,
            1470t-1471t
        other, 1469
        piezoelectric, 1467t, 1468, 1469f, 1471t
    imaging systems for, 1469
    outcomes of, 1473t
    overview of, 1433-1434
    physical principles of, 1465
    risk factors in, 1479, 1479t
    stone fragmentation in, mechanism of, 1474-
        1477, 1475f, 1476f
    stone recurrence rates after, 1480
    stone removal with, 1433-1434
    tissue injury in, mechanism of, 1484-1485
    vs. ureteroscopy, indications for, 1519t
Short stature, in Turner's syndrome, 3810,
    3810f
Shunt
    for priapism, 846, 847f-848f, 848, 3755
    vesicoamniotic, fetal placement of, 3188,
        3188f
Shy-Drager syndrome, voiding dysfunction in,
    2019
Siblings, vesicoureteral reflux in, 4325-4326
Sickle cell anemia, priapism associated with,
    3203
Sickle cell disease, priapism associated with, 840,
    3755
Sickness Impact Profile (SIP), 150
Side-firing laser, for benign prostatic
        hyperplasia, 2822
    clinical results of, 2824-2826
Sigma-rectum pouch (Mainz pouch II), for
        continent urinary diversion, with
        augmented valved rectum, 2584, 2586
Sigmoid cystoplasty, in children, 3677, 3677f
Sigmoid (S-shaped) kidney, 3284f, 3285
Sigmoid pouch, for orthotopic urinary
        diversion, 2642, 2643f
Sigmoid reservoir, stapled, for continent urinary
        diversion, 2609-2610, 2609f
Signal transduction, 1902
    aberrant activation of, in renal cell carcinoma,
        1590
    B cell receptor pathway in, 483-484
    intracellular calcium and protein kinase C in,
        activation of, 483
    Jak/STAT pathway in, 484
    Ras pathway in, 483
    T cell receptor pathway in, 482-483, 482f
Sildenafil
    adverse effects of, 776-777
    clinical response of, 776
    efficacy of, 775
    for erectile dysfunction, 773-775
    for premature ejaculation, 786
    onset of action of, 776
    patient satisfaction with, 776
    starting dose of, 777

Sildenafil (*Continued*)
structure of, 774f
vasodilator effects of, 778
vs. tadalafil and vardenafil, 774t
Silicate calculi, 1389
Silicone polymer injections, for incontinence, 2275
efficacy of, 2281-2282
Silicone prosthesis
for urinary incontinence, 553-554
penile, engineered, 565, 565f
Silicone stents, 1517
Silver nitrate, for painful bladder syndrome/interstitial cystitis, 362, 362t
Single nucleotide polymorphism, 519-520, 520f
Single-layer sutured anastomosis, 2541, 2541f
Sinovaginal bulb, 3831, 3831f
development failure of, 3833
Sinus of Guérin (lacuna magna), 3141
SIP (Sickness Impact Profile), 150
Sirolimus, as immunosuppressant, 1316, 1316f, 1316t
Six-corner bladder neck suspension, for vaginal wall prolapse, 2219-2221, 2219f, 2220t
Sjögren's syndrome, painful bladder syndrome/interstitial cystitis and, 337
Skeletal defects
in bladder exstrophy, 3500f, 3501f, 4326-4328
in cloacal exstrophy, 3539-3540
Skene's gland
abnormalities of, vs. urethral diverticula, 2383, 2383f
adenitis of, 884
sexual pain disorders involving, 884
Skin. See also Cutaneous *entries.*
neovagina creation from, 3835-3836, 3835f
of abdominal wall, anterior, 38
Skin bridges, penile, after circumcision, 3748-3749, 3750f
Skin disease(s). See also *specific disease.*
of genitalia
allergic dermatitis as, 407-410, 407f, 407t, 409f, 410f
benign, 430-431, 432f
examination of, 405, 406t
infectious, 419-425, 420f-425f
infestations as, 425, 425f, 426f
malignant, 426-430, 427f-431f
miscellaneous, 431, 433, 434f, 435f
noninfectious ulcers as, 417-419, 417t, 418f, 419f
papulosquamous disorders as, 410-415, 410t, 411f-414f
treatment of, 406-407, 407f
vesicobullous disorders as, 415-417, 415t, 416f, 417f
Skin flap. See also Flap(s).
in penile reconstruction, 994, 995f
Skin graft. See also Graft(s).
in penile curvature repair, 3714, 3715f
split-thickness
in penile reconstruction, 994, 996, 996f, 2654
in reoperative hypospadias repair, 3741
Skin lesions
of penis
benign, 960
premalignant, 960-961
types of, 406t
Skin loss, in male genital injury, 2654-2655, 2655f
Skin paddle flap(s), 1028. See also Flap(s).
Skin release and transfer, in penile curvature repair, 3713

Skin tags, 431, 433
hymenal, 3843, 3843f, 3844f
*SLC3A1 gene,* in cystinuria, 3223
*SLC7A9 gene,* in cystinuria, 3223
Sleep apnea, testosterone therapy causing, 859
Sleep arousal disturbance, nocturnal enuresis and, 3622, 3624
Sleep states, incidence of micturition during, 3608, 3608f
Sling procedures
allograft in, 2238
outcomes for, 2248t
anterior colporrhaphy with, 2220t, 2222
cadaveric dermis in, 2247, 2249
complication(s) of, 2245-2246
erosion as, 2235, 2236f, 2237f, 2246
pain syndromes as, 2246
sling failure as, 2246
sling release method as, 2246
transient retention as, 2245
eroded urethra reconstruction with, 2249
fascia lata
autologous, 2247
cadaveric, 2238, 2247
harvesting of, 2237-2238
for bladder filling/storage disorders, 2293
for bladder neck reconstruction, in children, 3665
for stress incontinence
in females, 2214
in males, 2077
materials for, 2237-2238
midurethral. See Transobturator sling; Vaginal tape procedure, tension-free.
operative, 2243-2244
outcome studies of, 2246-2249
definition of, 2246
endpoints in, 2246-2247
literature review in, 2247, 2248t, 2249
patient selection for, 2246
patient evaluation for, 2238-2242
pelvic organ prolapse and, 2249
perineal. See Perineal sling.
postoperative care following, 2245
previous, artificial sphincter placement and, 2403
pubovaginal, 2234-2249. See also Pubovaginal sling.
Raz vaginal wall, for stress incontinence, 2214
reconstructive procedures with, 2249
standard
crossover variety of, 2244
deliberate urethral closure in, with other reconstructive procedures, 2245
modifications of, 2244-2245
transobturator, 2266-2271. See also Transobturator sling.
urethral diverticula and, 2249
wound closure in, 2244
xenograft in, 2238
outcomes for, 2248t
Slow-twitch muscle fibers, of urethra, 1936-1937
Small bowel
anatomy of, 2534
submucosa of, in penile curvature repair, 3714
Small bowel anastomosis, 2557-2561
Bricker technique of, 2557, 2557f
hammock, 2559
Le Duc technique of, 2559, 2559f
split-nipple technique of, 2558-2559, 2559f
tunneled, 2558, 2558f
Wallace technique of, 2557-2558, 2558f
Small bowel obstruction, as complication of post-chemotherapy surgery, 956

Small cell carcinoma
of bladder, 2444
of kidney, 1636
of prostate, 2880
Small molecules, as inhibitors of angiogenesis, 545
Smoking
atherosclerotic disease associated with, 1167
benign prostatic hyperplasia and, 2745
bladder cancer associated with, 2413-2415
cessation of, in behavioral therapy for incontinence, 2128, 2128t
erectile dysfunction caused by, 746
incontinence associated with, 2190
patient history of, 88-89
penile cancer associated with, 965, 966
prostate cancer associated with, 2862
spermatogenesis and, 611, 645
urothelial tumors associated with, 1639
Smooth muscle
actin of, 1891
bladder, 1926-1931
atony of, during pregnancy, 290
cellular mechanics of, 1927-1931
contractile properties of, 1924
during filling, 1929
effect of drugs on, 1960-1962
electrical responses of, propagation of, 1929
excitation-contraction coupling in, 1928-1929, 1928t, 1929f
interstitial cells of, 1929-1930, 1930f
ion channels of, 1927-1928
length-tension relationships in, 1931
membrane electrical properties of, 1927-1928
morphology of, 1927, 1927f, 1928t
tone of, 1930, 1954
corporal, reconstruction of, 564-565, 564f
in benign prostatic hyperplasia, 2736-2737, 2736f
myosin of, 1891, 1898, 1899f
penile, 730-737
cavernous biopsy of, 763
changes in, erectile dysfunction associated with, 742
contraction and relaxation of
cross-activation in, 736
cyclic AMP-signaling pathway in, 732-734
cyclic GMP-signaling pathway in, 734-735
hyperpolarization of smooth muscle cells in, 737
intercellular communication in, 737
ion channels in, 736-737
molecular mechanism of, 731-737, 731f-733f
molecular oxygen modulation in, 737
phosphodiesterase in, 736, 736f
prostatic, adrenergic regulation of, 2737
relaxation of, nitric oxide in, 1954
troponin and tropomyosin of, 1898
tumors of. See *specific tumor.*
ureteral, 1891-1903. See also Ureter(s), muscle cells of.
contractile activity of, 1897-1902
electrical activity of, 1892-1897
mechanical properties of, 1902-1903
vs. striated muscle, 1928t
Smooth muscle cell(s), hyperpolarization, 737
Socioeconomic factors, in benign prostatic hyperplasia, 2743

Sodium
  fractional excretion of
    gestational age and, 3150
    in infant and child, 3154
    in preterm and term neonates, 3151, 3153f
  imbalance of, 1146-1149, 1147f, 1148f, 1149t,
    1150f
  in resting membrane potential, 1892-1893
  renal reabsorption of
    in cortical collecting tubules, 1144-1145,
      1145f
    in distal tubules, 1144
    in loop of Henle, 1142
    in medullary collecting tubules, 1146
    in proximal convoluted tubules, 1139, 1140f
  restriction of, for nephrolithiasis, 1413
  transport of
    across urothelium, 1935
    after bilateral ureteral obstruction, 1201-
      1202
Sodium cellulose phosphate, for absorptive
  hypercalciuria, 1416-1417
  guidelines in, 1418
Sodium citrate, for calcium oxalate
  nephrolithiasis, 1423
Sodium loading, in primary hyperaldosteronism,
  1853
Sodium pentosan polysulfate. See Pentosan
  polysulfate.
Soft tissues, of pelvis, 43-46
Solifenacin
  for incontinence, in elderly, 2316, 2317t
  for overactive bladder/detrusor overactivity,
    2093t, 2098-2099
  multinational trials of, 2099
Somatic mutations, associated with prostate
  cancer initiation and progression, 2865-
  2867
Somatic nervous system
  of lower urinary tract, pathways in, 1938
  of penis, pathways in, 725, 726t
  of retroperitoneum, 17-19, 17f, 18f, 19t
  testing of, in erectile dysfunction, 766
Sonohystography, in evaluation of fertility, 612
Sorafenib, for renal cell carcinoma, 1630t, 1631
Southwest Oncology Group (SWOG) study, of
  hormone-refractory prostate cancer, 3110,
  3110f, 3111f
SOX9 gene
  in sex determination, 3802-3803, 3802f
  male-determining, 3147
Soy, for prostate cancer, chemopreventive,
  2871
Space of Retzius, development of, in robotic-
  assisted laparoscopic radical prostatectomy,
  2991, 2991f
Spall fracture mechanism, of stone
  fragmentation, 1475
Spanner stent, 2807, 2807f
Spasm, bladder, after hypospadias repair, 3720
Spastic paraparesis, tropical, voiding dysfunction
  in, 2035-2036
Spastic paraplegia, hereditary, voiding
  dysfunction in, 2035
Specialist consultation, in erectile dysfunction,
  756-757
Specialized test(s), for sexual health problems, in
  females, 873-875, 874f
Specific gravity, of urine, 97
Spectrophotometry, infrared, 762
Sperm, 604-606
  biochemical changes in, during maturation,
    603
  capacitation of, 605

Sperm (Continued)
  concentration of
    in cryptorchidism, 640
    reference range for, 618
  delivery of, procedures to improve, 665-700.
    See also Vasectomy reversal;
    Vasoepididymostomy.
  disorders of
    delivery
      ductal obstruction in, 647-648
      ejaculatory problems in, 648-649
    function, 649-650
  epididymal reserves of, 606
  fertility of, maturation and, 602-603
  fine-needle aspiration of, 658
  function of
    accessory sex gland secretions and, 604-606
    testing of
      acrosome reaction in, 631
      hemizona assay in, 631
      penetration assay in, 631
      reactive oxygen species in, 632
      sperm-cervical mucus interaction in,
        630-631
      viability assay in, 631-632
  intracytoplasmic injection of, in vitro
    fertilization with, 717-718, 718f
  maturation of, 600-603
    arrest in, 634
    biochemical changes in, 603
    fertility in, 602-603
    motility in, 601-602, 601f
  morphologic examination of, 615-617, 616f,
    617f
  motility of, 615
    defects in, 621-623, 621f, 622f
    maturation and, 601-602, 601f
    reference range for, 618
  production of, procedures to improve, 658-665
  retrieval of, 700-707
    by electroejaculation, 716
    by microsurgical epididymal aspiration,
      700, 703f-704f
    by open testicular biopsy, 701
    by percutaneous epididymal aspiration,
      700, 702f-703f
    by testicular aspiration and needle biopsy,
      701, 703, 705-706, 705f-707f
    by testicular extraction, 706, 707f
      microsurgical, 705-706, 706f
    by vasal aspiration, 700, 701f
    for cyropreservation at time of
      vasovasostomy, 678
    in assisted reproductive techniques, 652-
      653
  storage of, 600
  structure of, 604, 605f
  transport of
    in epididymis, 600
    in vas deferens, 606-607
  ultrastructure of, abnormal, 627
  vas deferens reserves of, 606-607
  viability of
    assays of, 631-632
    reference range for, 618
Sperm count, 615, 617-618
  in exstrophy patient, 3551
Sperm granuloma, 1102, 1108
Sperm immobilization assay, for antisperm
  antibodies, 624t
Sperm penetration assay, 631
Spermatic cord
  examination of, 93, 613
  hydrocele of, 3789

Spermatic cord (Continued)
  internal, varicosities of. See Varicocele.
  leiomyosarcoma of, 934
  mesenchymal tumors of, miscellaneous, 934
  torsion of, in acute scrotum, 3790-3791,
    3790f
    intermittent, 3791-3792
    perinatal, 3793-3794
Spermatic fascia, 73
Spermatic nerve, to epididymis, 598
Spermatic vein
  internal, venography of, 629, 629f
  percutaneous embolization of, in varicocele
    repair, 662-663
Spermatic vessels, ligation of, in prune-belly
  syndrome, 3492-3493
Spermatid(s), radioresistance of, 644
Spermatocele, 3798
Spermatocelectomy, 1104
  complications of, 1104
Spermatocyte(s), 590, 590f
  radioresistance of, 644
Spermatocytic seminoma, 895
Spermatogenesis
  alcohol consumption affecting, 645
  blood-testis barrier and, 590, 590f, 591f
  caffeine and, 645
  cancer therapy and, 611, 643-644
  disorders of, 638-647
    chromosomal, 638-640
    gonadotropin therapy for, 636
    in Klinefelter's syndrome, 638-639
    in Noonan's syndrome, 639
    in XX male, 639
    in XYY syndrome, 639
    in Y chromosome microdeletions,
      639-640
  drugs affecting, 644-645
  environmental toxins and, 644
  febrile illness and, 611
  follicle-stimulating hormone in, 596
  genetic basis of, 596
  heat exposure and, 644
  hormonal regulation of, 595-596
  meiosis in, 593, 593f
  occupational exposures and, 644
  smoking and, 611, 645
  steps in, 592-595, 593f-595f
Spermatogonia, 589, 590
  development of, 592
  proliferation of, 592-593
  radioresistance of, 644
  type A, 592, 593f
  type B, 592, 593f
Spermatozoa. See Sperm.
Sperm-cervical mucus interaction, 630-631
Spermiogenesis, 593-595, 594f, 595f
Sphincter
  anal. See Anal sphincter.
  urinary. See Urethral sphincter.
    artificial. See Artificial urinary sphincter.
Sphincterotomy
  pharmacologic, 2301
  surgical, 2302-2303
Sphingolipids, in regulation of apoptosis, 533
Spina bifida cystica, 2029
Spinal cord
  adrenoreceptor action on, 1962-1963
  diseases distal to, voiding dysfunction with,
    2031-2031
  diseases involving, voiding dysfunction with,
    2019-2030
  glutamate in, 1964
  lesions of, classification of, 1984, 1984t

Spinal cord (*Continued*)
  tethering of
    definition of, 2030
    voiding dysfunction with, 2030
Spinal cord compression
  hormone-refractory prostate cancer and, palliative therapy for, 3112-3113, 3113t
  neuroblastoma with, treatment of, 3877-3878
  prostate cancer and, palliative therapy for, 3029
Spinal cord injury
  autonomic hyperreflexia with, 2026-2027
  bladder cancer with, 2028
  detrusor overactivity due to, 1966-1967, 1967f
  ejaculatory dysfunction in, 619, 649
    management of, 649
  epidemiology, morbidity, and general concepts of, 2020-2021
  erectile dysfunction in, 739
  follow-up in, 2028
  in children
    diagnosis of, 3651, 3651f
    findings in, 3652
    pathogenesis of, 3651
    recommendations for, 3653
    voiding dysfunction in, management of, 3652-3653
  in women, 2028
  infection with, 2027-2028
  neurologic and urodynamic correlations in, 2024-2026
  sacral neuromodulation for, 2156
  spinal shock with, 2021-2022
  urinary tract infection and
    clinical presentation of, 298
    diagnosis of, 298
    epidemiology of, 297
    management of, 298-299
    pathogenesis of, 297-298
  vesicoureteral reflux with, 2027
  voiding dysfunction in, 2012t, 2020-2028, 2022f, 2023f, 2025f
  with high-pressure bladders, 237-238
Spinal deformity(ies)
  affecting renal calculi surgery, 1448
  in bladder exstrophy, 3502
  in cloacal exstrophy, 3538-3539, 3539f
Spinal dysraphisms. *See also specific dysraphism.*
  emergent evaluation of, 3199
  types of, 3641t
Spinal nerves, in micturition reflex, pathways of, 1944-1945
Spinal reflexes, in stimulation of penile dorsal nerve, 726t
Spinal shock, voiding dysfunction with, 2021-2022
Spinal stenosis, voiding dysfunction with, 2031-2032
Spindle cell nodule, postoperative, of bladder, 2418
Spiral flap procedure, for ureteropelvic junction obstruction, in children, 3370, 3370f
Spiral stents, 1517
  for benign prostatic hyperplasia
    first-generation, 2804-2805
    second-generation, 2805-2806
Spironolactone, for primary hyperaldosteronism, 1856
Splanchnic nerve(s), of retroperitoneum, 15, 16f
Spleen
  function of, 475, 475f

Spleen (*Continued*)
  injury to
    in laparoscopic surgery, 215
    percutaneous nephrolithotomy causing, 1489
    percutaneous nephrostomy causing, 1548
Splenorenal bypass, 1738-1740, 1739f, 1740f
Split prepuce in-situ onlay technique, of hypospadias repair, 3725, 3728, 3730f-3731f, 3742
Split-nipple technique, of small bowel anastomosis, 2558-2559, 2559f
Split-thickness skin graft. *See also* Graft(s).
  in penile reconstruction, 994, 996, 996f, 2654
Sporadic glomerulocystic kidney disease, 3350-3351
  characteristics of, 3314t
  conditions associated with, 3350t
Squamous cell carcinoma
  genital, in AIDS patients, 399
  of bladder
    etiology of, 2421-2422
    histology of, 2422, 2422f
  of glans penis, 1012, 1012f
  of male genitalia, 427, 427f
    in situ, 426-427, 427f
  of penis, 964-972. *See also* Penile cancer, squamous cell.
  of upper urinary tract, abnormal urothelium in, 1643
  within bladder diverticula, 2366
  within urethral diverticula, 2389
*SRD5A2* gene, polymorphisms of, 2860-2861
*SRY* gene, 3800, 3800f
  absence of, ovarian organogenesis in, 3804
  in germ cell transformation, 3803
  in sex determination, 3146-3147, 3146f
  in testicular differentiation, 579, 3761
  in testis-determining factor, 3801
  in XX male, 3809
S-shaped kidney, 3284f, 3285
SSRIs. *See* Selective serotonin reuptake inhibitors (SSRIs).
Stab wounds
  to kidney, 1274
  to ureters, hematuria with, 1284-1285
Staghorn calculi, 1407-1408, 1407f, 1408f
  classification of, 1438-1439
  CT reconstruction of, 1436f
  struvite, 1435, 1438
  surgical management of, 1439
    natural history in, 1435-1436
  ureteroscopic management of, 1504-1505
Staging
  of bladder cancer, 2438-2441, 2441t
    invasive, laparoscopic, 2469
    non–muscle-invasive, 2447-2450, 2448f, 2448t, 2449f, 2450t
  of neuroblastoma, 3873, 3873t
  of prostate cancer, 2925-2931
    clinical system of, 2925-2926, 2927t
      vs. pathologic system, 2925, 2926f
    digital rectal examination in, 2929-2930
    imaging in, 2930
    molecular, 2930
    needle biopsy in, 2926-2927
    pelvic lymphadenectomy in, 2930-2931
    prediction of tumor extent in, 2926-2927, 2928t-2929t
    PSA levels in, 2929
    radioimmunoscintigraphy in, 2930
  of rhabdomyosarcoma, 3879-3880, 3879t
  of Wilms' tumor, 3892, 3892t
  TNM. *See* Tumor-node-metastasis (TNM) staging.

Stamey needle bladder neck suspension, for stress incontinence, 2212
Stamey percutaneous cystostomy, 164, 165f
*Staphylococcus*
  in prostatitis, 306
  in renal abscess, 3246
Stapled anastomosis, 2542-2544, 2543f, 2544f
  ileocolonic
    end-to-end, 2544, 2544f
    with circular stapling device, 2543-2544, 2543f
Stapled sigmoid reservoir, for continent urinary diversion, 2609-2610, 2609f
Stapling devices
  anastomotic, 2543
  circular, 2543-2544, 2543f
  in laparoscopy, 194-195, 194f
  linear, 2543
Stapling techniques, absorbable
  in continent urinary diversion
    with right colon pouch, 2607-2609, 2608f
    with sigmoid reservoir, 2609-2610, 2609f
    with W-stapled reservoir, 2610, 2610f
  in orthotopic urinary diversion, 2645
StAR (cholesterol side chain cleavage enzyme) deficiency, 3821
Starr plication, for megaureter, 4379, 4379f
Static urethral pressure profilometry, 2007
Statins, erectile dysfunction caused by, 745-746
Stauffer's syndrome, in renal cell carcinoma, 1597t, 1598
Steinstrasse, with ureteral calculi, 1501-1503
Stem cell(s)
  adult, 570
  bone marrow, differentiation of, 475. *See also* B cell(s); T cell(s).
  cancer and, 533-535
  embryonic, properties of, 569
  for tissue engineering, 569-570, 570f
  prostate, 2682-2683
    etiology and molecular genetics of, 2864-2865
    in benign prostatic hyperplasia, 2728
    renewal of, spermatogonial proliferation and, 592-593
Stem cell transplantation, chemotherapy with, for nonseminomatous germ cell tumors, 923
Stenosis. *See at specific anatomic site.*
Stent (stenting). *See also specific stent.*
  biomaterials used in, 1517-1518
  design of, 1517
  for urethral tears, 2659
  intraprostatic, for benign prostatic hyperplasia, 2804-2809. *See also* Intraprostatic stents.
  placement of, after ureteroscopy, 1516, 1517t
    technique of, 1518
  removal of, after orthotopic urinary diversion, 2633
  renal artery, 1184-1187
    complications of, 1186-1187, 1186t
    indications for, 1185
    patient selection for, 1173-1174
    results of, 1185-1186, 1185t, 1186f
    technique of, 1185
  ureteral
    after ureteroscopic stone manipulation, in children, 3908
    for contusions, 1286-1287
    for reimplanted ureters, in exstrophy patient, 3526
    for ureteral obstruction, 1212
    for ureteral stricture, 1255

Stent (stenting) *(Continued)*
  placement of, before shockwave lithotripsy, 1501-1502
  urethral
    for stress incontinence, 2140
    prosthetic, 2303-2304
Steroid(s)
  anabolic, abuse of, 611
  in regulation of prostate growth, protein growth factors and, 2689-2696
  natural and synthetic, half-life and biologic activity of, 1846t
Steroid feedback, on hypothalamus and pituitary, 578-579
Steroid receptor(s), in regulation of prostate growth, 2696-2705
Stevens-Johnson syndrome, 409-410, 410f
Stoma, abdominal, 2551-2553, 2552f, 2553f
Stomach. *See also* Gastric *entries.*
  anatomy of, 2533-2534, 2534f
  selection of, for urinary diversion, 2535-2536
Stomal stenosis, 2553
  after appendicovesicostomy, 42
Stone(s). *See* Calculus(i); *specific type.*
Straddle fractures, of pubic rami, 2658, 2658f
Straining, when voiding, 84
Strangulation injury, to penis, 2652
Strawberry hemangioma, of male genitalia, 3759
Streptococcal infection, glomerulonephritis after, 3226
Streptomycin, for genitourinary tuberculosis, 444, 445t
Stress, in painful bladder syndrome/interstitial cystitis, 348-349
Stress incontinence, 86. *See also* Incontinence.
  clinical evaluation of, 2202-2203
  clinical test for, 2206
  definition of, 2047, 2057
  diagnosis of, leak point pressures in, 2242
  female, 1977
    retropubic suspension surgery for, 2168-2185. *See also* Retropubic suspension surgery, for female incontinence.
  hammock theory of, 2051-2052, 2051f, 2052f
  in children, 3612
  in elderly, 2310
  in neurospinal dysraphism, 2029-2030
  integral theory of, 2052-2053
  male, 2314
    post-prostatectomy, sling for, 2392-2393. *See also* Perineal sling, for male incontinence.
  paraurethral tissue and, 1937
  risk factors for, 2128, 2128t, 2189-2190
  treatment of, 2074-2077, 2318
    behavioral therapy in, 2143
    injectable therapies in, 567-569, 2272-2287. *See also* Injection therapy, for incontinence.
    pelvic floor muscle in, 2142
    pharmacologic, 2075, 2109-2113, 2109t, 2110t
    rehabilitation techniques in, 2074-2075
    sling procedures in. *See* Sling procedures; *specific procedure.*
    surgical
      in females, 2076-2077, 2142-2143. *See also* Retropubic suspension surgery, for female incontinence; Stress incontinence, vaginal surgery for.
      in males, 2077
    tension-free transvaginal taping in, 2251-2266. *See also* Vaginal tape procedure, tension-free.

Stress incontinence *(Continued)*
  therapeutic options in, 2168-2169, 2169t
  urethral bulking agents in, 2075-2076
  urethral inserts in, 2138, 2140, 2140f
  urethral meatal occlusive devices in, 2138
  urethral stents in, 2140
  vaginal pessaries in, 2137-2138, 2138f, 2139f
  vaginal support prosthesis in, 2137, 2137f
  vaginal surgery for, 2212-2215
    complications of, 2214-2215
      intraoperative, 2214
      postoperative, 2214
    preoperative and intraoperative management in, 2212
    technique(s) of, 2212-2214
      Gittes bladder neck suspension, 2212-2213
      modified Pereyra, 2212
      Raz bladder neck suspension, 2213-2214, 2213f
      Raz vaginal wall sling, 2214
      Stamey needle bladder neck suspension, 2212
  vs. urgency incontinence, 2083
Stress relaxation, of ureter, 1902-1903, 1903f
Stress testing, 2313
Stress urethral pressure profilometry, 2007
Striated muscle
  fiber types in, 1936-1937
  vs. smooth muscle, 1928t
Strickler technique, of ureterocolonic anastomosis, 2556-2557, 2556f
Stricture. *See at anatomic site.*
String, in penile strangulation injury, 2652
Stroke
  after renal transplantation, 1324
  brain stem, voiding dysfunction after, 2016
  voiding dysfunction after, 2012t, 2014-2016
Stromal cell(s)
  epithelial cell interactions with, 2693-2694, 2706, 2707f
    in benign prostatic hyperplasia, 2731
  of bladder wall, 1931-1932
    nonfibrillar matrix of, 1932
  of prostate, 2683-2684, 2730
Stromal tumor(s), testicular, 927-928
  in children, 3904-3905
Strontium 89, clinical experience with, therapy, 3029
Struma lipomatodes aberrata renis, of tumors, 1567
Struvite calculi, 1407-1408, 1407f, 1408f
  in children, 3223
  urea-splitting bacteria causing, 261
Studer ileal bladder substitute, for orthotopic urinary diversion, 2635, 2636f
Sturge-Weber syndrome, pheochromocytoma associated with, 1861
SU11248, for renal cell carcinoma, 1630, 1630t
Subarachnoid block, for bladder denervation, 2289
Subcostal incisions, in adrenal surgery, 1874, 1875f
Subcostal nerve, 18, 18f
Subcutaneous fascia, of abdominal wall, anterior, 38, 40, 40f, 41f
Subcutaneous (dartos) flap. *See also* Flap(s).
  in hypospadias repair, 3716, 3716f
Subcutaneous (cavernous) hemangioma, of male genitalia, 3760
Subinguinal ligation, for varicocele, 3797

Substance P
  in pain transmission, 1959
  renal nerve activity responses to, 1906
Substitution cystoplasty, for painful bladder syndrome/interstitial cystitis, 367
Sulfisoxazole, prophylactic, for pediatric urinary tract infections, 3250t
Superfocusing mechanism, of stone fragmentation, 1476
Supernumerary kidney(s)
  associated anomalies with, 3277
  diagnosis of, 3278
  embryology of, 3277
  features of, 3277, 3277f, 3278f
  incidence of, 3276-3277
  symptoms of, 3277-3278
Supernumerary nipple(s), in children, 3207
Supernumerary ureter(s), 3417
Support devices, for bladder filling/storage disorders, 2291-2292
Supracostal puncture, for percutaneous nephrolithotomy, 1490, 1490f, 1490t, 1491f
Suprapubic cystostomy, for urethral injury, 2659
Suprapubic pain, patient history of, 82-92
Supraspinal pathways, in penile erection, 725-728, 726t, 727t
Supratrigonal cystectomy, for painful bladder syndrome/interstitial cystitis, 366-367
Suramin, for hormone-refractory prostate cancer, multidrug regimens with, 3107t
Surgery. *See also specific procedure.*
  antibiotic prophylaxis for, 253, 253t
  for genitourinary tuberculosis, 444-447
    reconstructive, 446-447
  for neuroblastoma, 3875-3877
    in high-risk disease, 3876-3877
    in low-risk disease, 3875-3876, 3876f
  for painful bladder syndrome/interstitial cystitis, 366-368
  for Peyronie's disease, 829-831, 831f-836f, 833, 836
    candidates for, 828-829
  for prostatitis, 325
    minimally invasive, 324
  for schistosomiasis, 454
  for sexual health problems, in females, 887-889, 887f, 888f
  for stress incontinence
    in females, 2076-2077
    in males, 2077
  laparoscopic. *See* Laparoscopic *entries.*
  organ-preserving, for testicular tumors, 908-909
  previous, patient history of, 88
  reconstructive. *See* Reconstructive surgery; *specific procedure.*
Surgical compression, for bladder filling/storage disorders, 2293-2294
Surgical templates, in retroperitoneal lymph node dissection, 915, 915f, 916f, 940-941, 940f, 941f
Surgical wounds, classification of, 253t
Surveillance studies
  after nonseminomatous germ cell tumor therapy, for stage I and stage IIA disease, 916-918, 917t
  after seminoma therapy, for stage I disease, 911-912, 911t
Survival pathways, in hormone-refractory prostate cancer, 3115-3116
Survivin, in bladder cancer, 2435-2436
Susceptibility gene(s), in prostate cancer, 2858, 2858t
Suspensory ligament, of clitoris, 67

Suture (suturing)
  in hypospadias repair, 3719
  in laparoscopy, 193-194
  material for, in retropubic suspension surgery, 2174
  sling, determination of tension in, 2244
  traction, 3372f, 3377, 3378f
Sutured anastomosis, 2540-2542, 2540f-2542f
  ileocolonic
    end-to-end, 2542, 2542f
    end-to-side, 2541-2542, 2541f, 2542f
    single-layer, 2541, 2541f
    two-layer, 2540-2541, 2540f
Sweeteners, artificial, bladder cancer associated with, 2415
Switch therapy, for pediatric urinary tract infection, 3249
Sympathectomy, for painful bladder syndrome/interstitial cystitis, 366
Sympathetic nervous system
  degeneration of, in transurethral microwave therapy, 2815
  increased activity of, in painful bladder syndrome/interstitial cystitis, 346-347, 346t
  of lower urinary tract, pathways in, 1938
  role of, in ureteral function, 1905-1906
Sympathetic skin response, in erectile dysfunction, 766-767
Sympatholytic agents, affecting lower urinary tract function, 3628t
Sympathomimetic agents
  affecting lower urinary tract function, 3628t
  for priapism, 845-846, 846t
Syndrome of inappropriate ADH secretion, 1147
  disorders associated with, 1149t
Synthetic grafts. See also Graft(s).
  in vaginal prolapse surgery, 2216, 2216t
Synthetic materials, injection of, for incontinence, 2274-2275, 2275f
Syphilis
  chancre with, 420f
  diagnosis of, 375-377, 375f, 376f
  in HIV patients, 395
  latent, 375
  rates of, 372
  secondary, 375-376, 376f
  tertiary, 376
  treatment of, 377
Syringomyelia, voiding dysfunction in, 2036
Systemic inflammatory response syndrome, 287
  biologic effects of, 288
  clinical presentation of, 288
Systemic lupus erythematosus
  painful bladder syndrome/interstitial cystitis and, 336
  renal manifestation of, in children, 3227
  voiding dysfunction in, 2037
Systemic sclerosis (scleroderma), voiding dysfunction in, 2042
Systemic therapy, for cutaneous diseases, of external genitalia, 406

**T**

T cell(s), 476-477
  activation of, 480-481, 480f
    NFAT in, 483
    signal 1 in, 480
    signal 2 in, 481
    signal 3 in, 481
    signaling events in, 482-483, 482f
    upregulated adhesion molecule expression in, 492-494, 493t

T cell(s) (*Continued*)
  antigen-specific
    activation of, 484-488
    clonal expansion in, 485, 485f
    cytokine production in, 486-487, 486f, 486t
    cytolysis of target cells in, 487-488, 487f
    development of memory cells in, 488
    phenotypic changes in, 488
  CD4+. See CD4+ T cell(s).
  CD8+. See CD8+ T cell(s).
  clonal anergy of, 491
  endothelial cell interaction with, 493, 493f
  in painful bladder syndrome/interstitial cystitis, 341
  induction of apoptosis of, mechanism of tumor escape in, 498-499
  memory, 488
  naive, trafficking of, 492
  peripheral deletion of, 491
  regulatory, 491-492
    in lymphocyte tolerance, 491-492
  role of, in tumor immunology, 495
  tumor antigens recognized by, 496t
T pouch ileal neobladder, for orthotopic urinary diversion, 2638, 2639f-2640f, 2640
Tabes dorsalis, voiding dysfunction with, 2030
Tachykinin(s), 1954-1955, 1954t
  effect of, on ureteral function, 1906
Tachykinin receptors, 1954-1955, 1954t
Tacrolimus
  as immunosuppressant, 1316, 1316f, 1316t
  drug interactions with, 1317, 1317t
Tadalafil
  adverse effects of, 776-777
  clinical response of, 776
  efficacy of, 775
  for erectile dysfunction, 773-775
  onset of action of, 776
  patient satisfaction with, 776
  starting dose of, 777
  structure of, 774f
  vasodilator effects of, 778
  vs. sildenafil and vardenafil, 774t
Tail stents, 1517
Takayasu's arteritis, in children, 1184
Tamm-Horsfall protein, 100, 3219, 3234, 3260
  as calcium oxalate crystal inhibitor, 1367, 1370
  in renal casts, 107
  renal excretion of, loop of Henle in, 1144
Tamoxifen
  for male infertility, 646
  for Peyronie's disease, 827
  for retroperitoneal fibrosis, 1217
Tamsulosin
  for benign prostatic hyperplasia, 2783-2784
    dosage of, 2778t, 2784
    efficacy of, 2784t
  for prostatitis, 321, 327t
  uropharmacology of, 2119
  vs. other α-adrenergic blockers, 2787
Tanagho technique, of bladder outlet reconstruction, 2294
Tanner classification, of sex maturity stages, in boys, 3745, 3746t
Tape erosion, intravesical, 2262-2263, 2262t
Tapering procedure, for megaureter, 4379, 4379f
Target cells, cytolysis of, 487-488, 487f
Target populations
  prostate cancer screening in, 2867-2868, 2868t
  renal cell carcinoma screening in, 1599, 1599t
Targeted agents, for metastatic renal cell carcinoma, 1629-1631, 1630f, 1630t

TATA box, 2703
Taxanes
  for bladder cancer, non–muscle-invasive, 2459-2460
  for locally advanced prostate cancer, before radical prostatectomy, 3060-3061
Taxol. See Paclitaxel.
Taxotere. See Docetaxel.
T-cell receptor
  in immune response, 479-480
  signaling events transmitted via, 482-483, 482f
Tea consumption, bladder cancer associated with, 2415
TEBS. See Transurethral electrical stimulation (TEBS).
Technetium-99m-mercaptoacetyltriglycine (Tc-99m-MAG3) scintigraphy, of kidneys, 140f-142f, 142, 1335
Technical process, in quality of health care, 148
TEF3 protein, overexpression of, in renal cell carcinoma, 1583
Telomere, 533, 534f, 2713
  in bladder cancer, 2435, 2465
  in renal cell carcinoma, 1590
  in urothelial tumors, 1644
  prostate cancer and, 2866
Telomerase reverse transcriptase, 2713
Telomerase RNA component, 2713
Telophase, in mitosis, 2712
Temperature, in transurethral microwave therapy, 2814-2815
Templates, brachytherapy-like, for cryotherapy, 3038, 3038f
Tendon reflexes, depression of, after sacral spinal cord injury, 2024
Tenesmus, 2204
Tenets of treatment, in cryptorchidism, 3775
TENS (transcutaneous electrical nerve stimulation), for painful bladder syndrome/interstitial cystitis, 364-365
Tension pneumothorax, laparoscopic renal surgery causing, 1808
Tension-free vaginal tape procedure. See Vaginal tape procedure, tension-free.
Teratoma(s), testicular, 895
  in children, 3901
    immature, 3903
    mature, 3902-3903
  incidence, pathology, and presentation of, 898t
  resection of, 951-952
Teratospermia, evaluation of, 623
Terazosin
  for autonomic hyperreflexia, 2027
  for benign prostatic hyperplasia, 2779-2780, 2779f, 2780t, 2781f
    dosage of, 2778t, 2780
    efficacy of, 2779t
  for prostatitis, 321, 327t
  uropharmacology of, 2119
  vs. other α-adrenergic blockers, 2787
Terbutaline, for overactive bladder/detrusor overactivity, 2093t, 2103-2104
Terfenadine, for Peyronie's disease, 827
Testicular adnexa tumor(s), 931-934, 932t
  adenomatoid, 931-933, 932t
  cystadenoma as, 933
  epithelial, 931
  mesothelioma as, 932
  paratesticular, 932t, 933-934
    leiomyosarcoma as, 934
    management of, 933-934
    rhabdomyosarcoma as, 933

Testicular appendage torsion, in acute scrotum, 3792
Testicular artery, 74, 75f, 581, 582-583, 583f
    injury to, varicocelectomy and, 665
Testicular cancer, 93, 893-934
    adenocarcinoma in, 929, 932t
    cryptorchidism associated with, 3772-3773
    germ cell tumors in, 893-925. *See also* Germ cell tumor(s), testicular.
    gonadoblastoma as, 926t, 928-929. *See also* Gonadoblastoma(s).
    in AIDS patients, 399-400
    leukemic infiltration in, 930-931
    lymphoma in, 930, 932t
    mesenchymal origin of, 929
    metastatic, 931
    sex cord–mesenchymal tumors in, 925-928, 926t
    surgery for, 936-957. *See also specific procedure.*
    teratoma as, 895. *See also* Teratoma(s).
Testicular cystic dysplasia, in children, 3905
Testicular dysfunction, pathology of, 3794-3795
Testicular failure, primary, micropenis due to, 3753
Testicular hormone replacement, 569, 569f
Testicular microlithiasis, in children, 3905
Testicular pain
    patient history of, 83
    post-hernia repair, 1108
Testicular regression, embryonic, 3814-3815
Testicular torsion, 93
    cryptorchidism and, 3773
    infertility with, 641
    intermittent, orchidopexy for, 1107
Testicular tumor(s)
    adenomatoid, 930
    adrenal rest tumors as, 929-930
    carcinoids as, 930
    epidermoid cysts as, 929
    in children, 3900-3905. *See also specific tumor.*
        classification of, 3900t
        diagnosis of, 3902
        etiology of, 3900-3901
        evaluation of, 3199
        genetics of, 3900
        pathology of, 3901-3902
        staging of, 3902, 3903t
    malignant. *See* Testicular cancer; *specific neoplasm.*
    surgery for, 936-957. *See also specific procedure.*
Testicular vein, 74, 75f, 583-584, 583f
    thrombophlebitis of, ureteral obstruction due to, 1223
    tortuosity and dilation of. *See* Varicocele.
Testis(es), 73-74, 74f, 75f, 77
    absent (vanishing), 3765
        laparoscopic assessment of, 3783-3784
    androgen production by, 2685-2686, 2686t, 2687f
    atrophy of, 621-622
        mumps-associated, germ cell tumors due to, 901
    biopsy of, 633-634, 633f
        complications of, 658
        indications for, 655
        open, 655-657, 656f, 657f
            sperm retrieval through, 701
        percutaneous, 657, 657f
    blood barrier of, 589-591, 590f, 591f
    blood supply to, 1099t
    cancer of. *See* Testicular cancer; *specific neoplasm.*

Testis(es) (*Continued*)
    cryoarchitecture of, 584-596
    delivery of, in varicocele repair, 662
    descent of, 3143-3145, 3144f
        calcitonin gene–related peptide in, 3769
        developmental defect in. *See* Cryptorchidism.
        endocrine factors in, 3766-3768
        epididymis related to, 3769-3770
        genitofemoral nerve in, 3769
        gubernaculum in, 3768-3769
        intra-abdominal pressure and, 3770
        normal, 3762-3763
            definition of, 3764
        theories of, 3766
    dimensions of, examination of, 613, 613t
    dysfunction of, tissue engineering for, 569, 569f
    ectopic, 3765
    embryology of, 3761-3763
    endocrinology of, 579-580
    end-stage, infertility and, 634
    fetal, endocrine function of, 3804, 3805f
    fine-needle aspiration of, sperm retrieval through, 701, 703, 705-706, 705f-707f
    function of, 584-596
    in prune-belly syndrome, 3485
    innervation of, 77, 581
    interstitium of, 581, 581f, 584-585, 585f-587f, 587
    intra-abdominal, 3765
        laparoscopic assessment of, 3784
        laparoscopic orchidopexy for, 3785-3786
    ipsilateral, varicocele associated with, 641
    lymphatic drainage of, 14, 583-584
    mumps-associated atrophy of, germ cell tumors due to, 901
    non-palpable, 3765
        diagnostic laparoscopy for, 3782
        laparoscopic assessment of, 3782-3784, 3783f
    normal, 633, 633f
    ovoid, 581
    prenatal development of, 592
    rete, 581, 582f
    retractile, 3765
        in adults, orchidopexy for, 1107
        in children, 3208
    seminiferous tubules of, 581, 587. *See also* Seminiferous tubules.
    structure of, 581-584, 581f-583f
    tissue extraction from, sperm retrieval through, 706, 707f
        microsurgical, 705-706, 706f
    torsion of. *See* Testicular torsion.
    tuberculosis of, 440
    tumors of. *See* Testicular tumor(s).
        malignant. *See* Testicular cancer.
    undescended, 3763-3787. *See also* Cryptorchidism.
        surgical management of. *See* Orchidopexy.
    vanishing (absent), 640, 3765, 3814-3815
        laparoscopic assessment of, 3783-3784
    vascularization of, 581-584, 583f
Testis cords, 3136
    in puberty, 3136-3137
Testis-determining factor, 3799-3800, 3800f, 3801f
    *SRY* gene in, 3801
Testis-sparing surgery, for teratomas, 3903
Testicular injury
    diagnosis of, 2652-2653, 2653f
    etiology of, 2652
    in children, 3945

Testicular injury (*Continued*)
    management of, 2653-2654, 2653f
    outcome and complications of, 2654
Testoderm gel, for erectile dysfunction, 772
Testoderm patch, for erectile dysfunction, 771-772
Testolactone, for male infertility, 646-647
Testosterone. *See also* Dihydrotestosterone.
    assays for, 855-856, 855t, 856f
    bioavailability of, measurement of, 767
    biosynthesis of
        disorders of, 3821-3823
        errors in, cryptorchidism associated with, 3767
    circulation of, 3084, 3085t
    commercial formulations of, 861
    fetal secretion of, 3761-3762, 3804
    for erectile dysfunction, 771-772, 771t
        injectable, 771
        oral, 772
        "rescue" therapy with, 776
        transdermal delivery of, 771-772
    for Kallmann syndrome, 635
    for late-onset hypogonadism, 857-858, 858t
        adverse effects of, 859-860
        body composition/strength changes with, 858-859
        bone mineral density changes with, 859
        buccal delivery of, 858, 858t
        cardiovascular changes with, 859
        intramuscular injections of, 857, 858t
        objective effects of, 858-859
        oral preparations of, 857-858, 858t
        sexual function changes with, 859
        transdermal delivery of, 858, 858t
    for micropenis, 3753
    for sexual dysfunction
        in perimenopausal and postmenopausal women, 880-881
        in premenopausal women, 876-878
    in regulation of spermatogenesis, 595-596
    in testicular descent, 3766-3767
    in utero deficiency of, 3767
    increased levels of, following varicocele repair, 664
    metabolism of, 851-852, 852-853, 852f
    plasma levels of, 2686, 2686t
    production of
        diurnal pattern in, 767
        luteinizing hormone in, 585, 586f
        regulation of, central mechanisms in, 851-852
    serum range of, 767-768
    synergism of, with PDE-5 inhibitors, 859
    synthesis and metabolism of, 2686, 2687f
    transport of, 851, 852f
Testosterone-secreting adrenal tumor, 1841-1842
Tetanus, for human and animal bite wounds, 2651
Tethered cord syndrome
    definition of, 2030
    voiding dysfunction with, 2030
Thalidomide
    as inhibitor of angiogenesis, 545
    for prostatitis, clinical trial data on, 322
Therapeutic cloning strategy, in tissue engineering, 570-572, 571f, 572f
Therapeutic observation, of renal cell carcinoma, 1618-1619, 1618t
Thermal ablative therapy, for localized renal cell carcinoma, 1616-1618, 1617t
Thermal mapping, in transurethral microwave therapy, 2814-2815

Thermal sensory testing, penile, in erectile dysfunction, 767
Thermocouples, for cryotherapy, 3038
   placement of, 3041, 3043f
Thermodynamic solubility product, 1366
Thermotherapy
   for prostatitis, 324-325
   transurethral microwave. See Transurethral microwave therapy (TUMT).
   water-induced, for benign prostatic hyperplasia, 2842
Thiamine, for Wernicke's encephalopathy, 2042
Thiazides. See also Diuretics.
   for absorptive hypercalciuria, 1418
   hypocitraturia due to, 1404
      management of, 1423
Thiosulfinate, for bladder cancer, non–muscle-invasive, 2458
Thiotepa, for bladder cancer, non–muscle-invasive, 2459
Thoracic aortorenal bypass, 1742-1743, 1742f, 1743f
Thoracic duct, formation of, 14
Thoracic kidney
   associated anomalies with, 3282
   diagnosis of, 3282
   embryology of, 3281-3282
   features of, 3282, 3282f
   incidence of, 3281
   prognosis for, 3282-3283
   symptoms of, 3282
Thoracoabdominal incisions
   in adrenal surgery, 1875-1876, 1876f
   in radical nephrectomy, 1709-1710, 1711f, 1712f
   in renal surgery, 1698, 1701f-1702f, 1703
Thrombophlebitis
   due to radical retropubic prostatectomy, 2973
   venous, ureteral obstruction due to, 1223
Thrombosis
   deep venous
      after laparoscopic surgery, 218
      after robotic-assisted laparoscopic radical prostatectomy, 3001
   in renal transplant recipients, 1299, 1318, 1324
   renal artery, 1190, 1190t
      after renal bypass surgery, 1750-1751, 1750f
      in neonates, 3197
      PTA causing, 1181
   renal vein, in neonates, 3196
Thrombospondin, as inhibitor of angiogenesis, 544
Thromboxane A₂, in male sexual function, 728
Thromboxanes, uropharmacology of, 1955
Thrombus
   inferior vena caval, 5-year survival for, 1605t
   infrahepatic, radical nephrectomy with, 1714, 1715f, 1716f
   intrahepatic or suprahepatic, radical nephrectomy with, 1714, 1716, 1718, 1718f-1720f
   treatment of, 1619-1621, 1619f, 1620f
Thrush. See Candidiasis.
Thyroid disorders, infertility associated with, 637-638
Thyroidization, renal, 279
Thyroid-stimulating hormone (TSH), secretion of, 578
Thyrotoxicosis. See also Hyperthyroidism.
   voiding dysfunction with, 2041
Thyroxin, affected by aging, 856t, 857
Ticarcillin, for pediatric urinary tract infections, 3248t

TIMP. See Tissue inhibitors of metalloproteinase (TIMP).
Tinea cruris (jock itch), 424-425, 425f
Tinea pedis (athlete's foot), 424
Tissue anastomosis, in laparoscopy, 193-194
Tissue cultures, in diagnosis of urinary tract infection, 241
Tissue destruction, cryotherapy causing, factors affecting, 3036-3037, 3036t
Tissue engineering, 553-573
   biomaterials for, 554-556
      design and selection of, 555
      types of, 555-556, 556f
   definition of, 553
   for testicular dysfunction, 569, 569f
   injectable therapies in, 567-569, 568f
   of bladder, 558-562, 559f
      artificial replacement by, 561-562, 562f, 563f
      matrices for, 559-560
      tissue expansion for bladder augmentation in, 558-559, 559f
      with cell transplantation, 561, 561f
   of fetal tissue, 566-567, 567f
   of genital tissue, 563-566
      female, 565-566
      male, corporal tissues reconstruction in, 564-565, 564f, 565f
   of renal structures, 566, 566f
   of ureters, 563
   of urethra, 557-558, 558f
   of urologic structures, 557-566
   stem cells for, 569-570, 570f
   strategies for, 554, 554f
   therapeutic cloning for, 570-572, 571f, 572f
   vascularization in, 556-557
Tissue expansion, for bladder augmentation, 558-559, 559f
Tissue (fasciocutaneous) flap. See also Flap(s).
   in hypospadias repair, 3716-3717
   in reoperative hypospadias repair, 3740-3741
Tissue inhibitors of metalloproteinase (TIMP), 544
   in ureteral obstruction, 1204
   in urothelial tumors, 2424
Tissue injury, mechanism for, in shockwave lithotripsy, 1484-1485
Tissue interposition techniques, in vesicovaginal fistula repair, 2337-2340
Tissue matrix, of prostate, 2683-2684, 2683f
Tissue response, to cryotherapy, 3035-3036, 3036f
Tissue sealants, in laparoscopy, 193, 193t
Tissue sloughing, urethral, after cryotherapy, 3050
TNF. See Tumor necrosis factor entries.
TNM staging. See Tumor-node-metastasis (TNM) staging.
Tobacco products. See also Smoking.
   exposure to, renal cell carcinoma associated with, 1583-1584
   penile cancer associated with, 966
Tobramycin, for pediatric urinary tract infections, 3248t
Toileting, 2127. See also Voiding.
Tolerodine
   for incontinence, in elderly, 2316, 2317t
   for overactive bladder/detrusor overactivity, 2093t, 2096-2097
Toll-like receptor(s)
   and ligands, 502t
   and microbial killing, 501-502
   identification of, 473
Tolterodine, uropharmacology of, 1950, 1950t

Tomography
   computed. See Computed tomography (CT).
   positron emission. See Positron emission tomography (PET).
   renal, of urinary tract infection, 243
Topical therapy. See also specific agent.
   for cutaneous diseases, of external genitalia, 406-407, 407f
Topiglan, transdermal delivery of, for erectile dysfunction, 781
Torcon deflatable catheter, 1053, 1535f
Torsion
   epididymal appendage, causing acute scrotum, 3792
   penile, 3754, 3754f
   spermatic cord, in acute scrotum, 3790-3791, 3790f
      intermittent, 3791-3792
      perinatal, 3793-3794
   testicular. See Testicular torsion.
Torulopsis glabrata, in pediatric urinary tract infections, 3265
Total urogenital mobilization
   for cloacal malformations, 3868
   for intersex conditions, 3859-3862, 3861f-3864f
Toxicity
   calcineurin inhibitor, vs. acute allograft rejection, 1319t
   of bacille Calmette-Guérin, Cleveland Clinic management of, 2458t
   of brachytherapy, 3025
      rectal, 3026
      urinary, 3026
   of chemotherapy, 923
   of contrast media, 113
   of immunosuppressant therapy, organ system targets for, 1317, 1318t
   pulmonary, bleomycin-induced, 924
   vascular, chemotherapy-induced, 924
Toxin(s)
   botulinum. See Botulinum toxin.
   environmental, male infertility due to, 644
TP53 gene
   G₁S checkpoint regulation by, 521-522, 522f
   in apoptosis induction, 530, 531f, 532
   in bladder cancer, 2411, 2414
   in urologic malignancies, 522-523
   mutational inactivation of, 522
TP53 protein, altered activity of, 522
T-pouch, for continent urinary diversion
   double, 2589, 2591, 2592f-2593f
   with augmented valved rectum, 2583-2584, 2585f
Traction sutures, in ureteropelvic junction obstruction repair, 3372f, 3377, 3378f
TRAF-1 gene, in apoptosis, 490
TRAF-2 gene, in apoptosis, 490
Transabdominal orchidopexy, for prune-belly syndrome, 3492, 3493f
Transcutaneous electrical nerve stimulation (TENS). See also Electrical stimulation.
   for bladder storage disorders, 2160
   for painful bladder syndrome/interstitial cystitis, 364-365
   for urethral sphincter dysfunction, in children, 3619
   for voiding dysfunction, in children, 2157
Transdermal delivery
   of Alprox-TD, for erectile dysfunction, 781-782
   of testosterone
      for erectile dysfunction, 771-772
      for late-onset hypogonadism, 858, 858t

Transducer, cystometry, 1988
Transferrin, in seminal plasma, 2724
Transforming growth factor-α, 2709
  properties of, 2706t
Transforming growth factor-β, 2709-2710
  accumulation of, in Peyronie's disease, 821,
    821f, 822f
  cancer and, 536-537
  in benign prostatic hyperplasia, 2731-2732,
    2731f
  in bladder cancer, 2428-2429
  in obstructive renal fibrosis, 3170
  in suppression of tumor immunity, 497
  in unilateral ureteral obstruction, 1204
  in ureteropelvic junction obstruction,
    measurement of, 3369-3370
  properties of, 2706t
  source and activity of, 486t
Transglomerular (hydraulic) pressure, in
  glomerular filtration rate, 1131-1132
Transglutaminases, prostate-specific, 2720-2721
Transillumination
  of kidneys, 90
  of scrotal mass, 93
Transit-amplifying cells, of prostate, 2680t,
  2681-2682, 2682f
Transitional cell carcinoma
  of bladder, 2419-2421
    high-grade urothelial tumors in, 2421, 2421f
    low-grade urothelial tumors in, 2420f, 2421
    metaplastic elements in, 2421
    papillary urothelial tumors in, 2420-2421,
      2420f
    treatment of, 3883
    tumor architecture in, 2419, 2419f-2421f
    tumor grading in, 2419-2421
  of prostate, 2881
  of renal pelvis, in children, 3900
  of upper urinary tract
    abnormal urothelium in, 1643
    postoperative BCG immunotherapy for,
      1523
    ureteroscopic management of, 1522-1524,
      1522f, 1523f
  of urethra, after cystectomy, 2623-2624
    in females, 2624-2628
    in males, 2624-2626
  within bladder diverticula, 2366
  within urethral diverticula, 2389
Translation, of ribonucleic acid, 511-512
Transmembrane potential, of ureteral muscle
  cells, 1893-1894, 1894f
Transobturator sling, 2266-2271
  complications of, 2269, 2271t
  efficacy of, 2269
  results of, 2269, 2270t
  surgical anatomy relative for, 2267
  technique of, 2267-2268, 2268f, 2268t
    transobturator inside out, 2268
    transobturator outside in, 2267-2268
Transperitoneal incision, in simple nephrectomy,
  1703, 1707, 1707f
Transperitoneal laparoscopic
  nephroureterectomy, 1665-1666, 1665f,
  1666f
Transplantation. See also Autotransplantation.
  bone marrow
    allogeneic, for hematologic malignancies,
      500
    autologous, chemotherapy with, for
      nonseminomatous germ cell tumors,
      923
  gene expression profiling in, 503, 504f
  renal. See Renal transplantation.

Transrectal ultrasonography (TRUS)
  gray-scale, 2885-2887
    technique of, 2885
    volume calculations in, 2885-2886
  in cryotherapy, 3037-3038, 3037f
    evaluation of, 3041
  in evaluation of prostatitis, 317
  in infertility work-up, 621, 628-629, 628f
  of ejaculatory duct obstruction, 707, 708f
  of locally advanced prostate cancer, 3054-
    3055, 3054f
  of prostate
    advanced techniques in, 2892-2895
    biopsy with, 2887-2891
      analgesia for, 2889
      antibiotic prophylaxis for, 251-252,
        2889
      cleansing enema for, 2889
      contraindications to, 2889
      indications for, 2887-2889, 2888t
      patient positioning for, 2889
      techniques of, 2889-2891, 2890f, 2890t,
        2891t
    color and power Doppler, 2892-2893,
      2893f, 2894f
    investigational techniques in, 2893, 2894f,
      2895
  of prostate basal cell carcinoma, 2887
  of prostate cancer, 2886-2887, 2887f
    after treatment, 2887
    biopsy with, 2923
    recommendations for, 2925
  of prostate lymphoid malignancy, 2887
  of prostate sarcoma, 2887
  of prostatic cystic lesions, 2886, 2886f
  of prostatitis, 317
  of seminal vesicles, 1111-1112, 1111f
Transsexualism, female-to-male, reassignment
  surgery in, 1096-1097
Transureteroureterostomy
  for ureteral stricture, 1264-1266
  in children, 3661-3662, 3661f
Transurethral electrical stimulation (TEBS)
  for bladder emptying disorders, 2165-2166
    results of, 2166
  for bladder storage disorders, 2152
Transurethral ethanol ablation of prostate, for
  benign prostatic hyperplasia, 2843
Transurethral incision of prostate (TUIP), for
  benign prostatic hyperplasia, 2841-2842,
  2842t
  clinical efficacy of, 2841
  comparative studies of, 2841-2842, 2842t
  complications of, 2841
  technique of, 2841, 2841f
Transurethral microwave therapy (TUMT), 324-
  325
  for benign prostatic hyperplasia, 2813-2820,
    2814f
    blood flow in, 2815
    clinical results of, 2816-2820
    induction of apoptosis in, 2815-2816
    mechanism of action of, 2814-2816
    open studies in, 2816-2818
    sympathetic nerve degeneration in, 2815
    temperature in, 2814-2815
    vs. sham procedure, 2818
    vs. transurethral resection of prostate,
      2818-2820
Transurethral needle ablation (TUNA), of
  prostate, 324, 2809-2813
  adverse effects of, 2813
  clinical results of, 2811-2813, 2811t, 2812t
  delivery of radiofrequency in, 2809-2810

Transurethral needle ablation (TUNA), of
  prostate (Continued)
  experimental studies in, 2810
  indications for, 2813
  instruments for, 2810, 2811f
  pressure-flow studies in, 2812-2813, 2812t
  reoperation in, 2813
  technique of, 2811
Transurethral procedures. See also specific
  procedure.
  antibiotic prophylaxis for, 252
Transurethral resection (TUR)
  of bladder, antibiotic prophylaxis for, 252
  of bladder cancer, 2479-2483
    complications of, 2482-2483, 2482f
    electrical currents used in, 2480
    indications for, 2479-2480
    invasive, 2468
      partial cystectomy with, 2474-2475
      chemotherapy and, 2475
      restaging, 2468-2469
    non–muscle-invasive, 2451
      complications of, 2451-2452
      repeat of, 2452
    panendoscopy in, 2480
    papillary lesions in, 2481
    postoperative management in, 2482
    preoperative preparation in, 2480
    sessile lesions in, 2481
    surgical technique of, 2480-2482, 2480f,
      2481f
    survival rates after, 2481-2482
  of bladder neck, 2300
  of ejaculatory duct obstruction, 708, 709f
  of Hunner's ulcer, 366
  of prostate cancer, specimens from, 2879
Transurethral resection of prostate (TURP)
  for benign prostatic hyperplasia, 2829-2838
    anesthesia for, 2831
    bipolar, 2838
    history of, 2829
    indications for, 2829-2831, 2830t
    intraoperative problems in, management
      of, 2833-2834, 2836
    mortality rate in, 2837-2838
    outcomes of, 2836-2838
    patient's symptoms in, 2836-2837
    perioperative antibiotics in, 2831
    surgical technique of, 2831-2836
      first stage in, 2832, 2832f
      second stage in, 2832-2833, 2833f,
        2834f
      third stage in, 2833-2834, 2834f, 2835f,
        2836
  radical, 325
  vs. transurethral microwave therapy, 2818-
    2820
Transurethral resection syndrome, management
  of, 2836
Transurethral vaporization of prostate
  (TUVP), for benign prostatic hyperplasia,
  2838-2841
  clinical experience with, 2839-2840
  comparative studies in, 2840
  electrode design in, 2839
  mechanism of action of, 2839
  vaporization-resection in, 2840
Transvaginal partial denervation, of bladder,
  2290
Transvaginal ultrasonography, in evaluation of
  fertility, 612
Transvenous occlusion, for varicocele, 3797
Transverse incision, in penile prosthesis
  placement, 790, 791f

Transverse preputial island flap. *See also* Flap(s).
in hypospadias repair, 3731-3732, 3732f-3733f, 3734
Transverse resection, in partial nephrectomy, 1724-1725, 1727f
Transversus abdominis muscle, 8-9, 9t, 10f
Transvesical infiltration, of pelvic plexus, 2291
Trapped penis, 3750f, 3751
resulting from circumcision, 3750f
Trauma. *See also at anatomic site; specific type of injury.*
germ cell tumors due to, 901
ulcerative, to genitalia, 418-419
Tray agglutination test, for antisperm antibodies, 624t
Trazodone, for erectile dysfunction, 782
Tremor, in early graft dysfunction, 1318
*Treponema pallidum,* in syphilis, 375. *See also* Syphilis.
Trestle stent, 2806
Triage, of pediatric urologic patient, 3198-3204, 3199t
emergent evaluations in, 3198-3200, 3200t-3201t, 3202t, 3203, 3203t
routine evaluations in, 3203-3204
semi-urgent evaluations in, 3203
urgent evaluations in, 3203
Triamterene calculi, 1389
Triazoles, 469
Trichlormethiazide
for absorptive hypercalciuria, 1418
for calcium oxalate stone prevention, 1421t
for calcium oxalate stones, 1421t
Trichloroacetic acid, for genital warts, 381
Trichloroethylene, exposure to, renal cell carcinoma associated with, 1584
*Trichomonas,* in prostatitis, 307
*Trichomonas vaginalis,* 380
in urinary sediment, 109, 109f
Trichomoniasis, 380
Trichomycosis axillaris, of male genitalia, 423-424, 424f
Tricyclic antidepressants. *See also* Antidepressants; *specific agent.*
erectile dysfunction caused by, 744
for urethral sphincter dysfunction, in children, 3620
Trigone, 59f, 60, 60f
formation of, 3132-3133, 3134f
Trigonosigmoidostomy, in exstrophy patient, 3537-3538
Trimethoprim, for pediatric urinary tract infections, prophylactic, 3250t, 3252
Trimethoprim-sulfamethoxazole
for cystitis, 256-257, 256t
for urinary tract infections, 245, 245t, 246t, 247t
in children, 3248t
prophylactic, 3250t, 3251, 3251t
low-dose prophylactic, for recurrent urinary tract infections, 262t, 263
prophylactic, for vesicoureteral reflux, 4348
Trimetrexate, for bladder cancer, metastatic, 2478
Trisphosphate, in ureteral smooth muscle contraction, 1901, 1902f
Trocar(s)
blind insertion of, 180
complications related to, 206-209, 207t, 208f
closure of, in hand-assisted laparoscopic nephrectomy, 1798

Trocar(s) *(Continued)*
configuration of, in robotic-assisted laparoscopic radical prostatectomy, 2986f, 2988-2989, 2989f
placement of
in laparoscopic antireflux surgery, 4366
in laparoscopic nephrectomy, 1762, 1764f, 1765f
hand-assisted, 1791, 1792f-1796f
retroperitoneal approach, 1788-1789, 1789f, 1790f
transperitoneal approach, 1781
initial, 187
secondary, 187-189, 188f, 189f
complications related to, 209-210, 209f, 210f
recurrence of, after laparoscopic surgery, 1779, 1779f, 1780t, 1781, 1781t
technology of, 185-187, 186f
types of, 185, 185f
Tropical pulmonary eosinophilia, in filariasis, 457
Tropical spastic paraparesis, voiding dysfunction in, 2035-2036
Tropomyosin, of smooth muscle, 1898
Troponin, of smooth muscle, 1898
Trospium
for incontinence, in elderly, 2316, 2317t
for overactive bladder/detrusor overactivity, 2093t, 2095-2096
TRUS. *See* Transrectal ultrasonography (TRUS).
*TSC1* gene, in tuberous sclerosis, 3306, 3330, 3331, 3899
*TSC2* gene, in tuberous sclerosis, 1599, 3306, 3330, 3331, 3899
TSH (thyroid-stimulating hormone), secretion of, 578
Tuberculin reaction, CDC definition of, 440, 441t
Tuberculin test, for genitourinary tuberculosis, 440, 441t
Tuberculosis, 436-447
arteriography of, 443
biopsy in, 443
clinical features of, 437-438, 440
computed tomography of, 442, 443f
cystoscopy of, 443
development of, 437
diagnosis of, 440-441
epidemiology of, 436-437
history of, 436
immunology of, 437
incidence of, 436-437, 437t
intravenous urography of, 441-442, 442f
magnetic resonance imaging of, 443
microbiology of, 440
multidrug-resistant, 444
of bladder, 438, 439f
of epididymis, 438, 440
of kidney, 438, 438f
in AIDS patients, 396
of penis, 440
of prostate, 440
of testis, 440
of ureter, 438, 439f, 440f
of urethra, 440
pathogenesis of, 437
pathology of, 437-438, 438f-440f, 440
percutaneous antegrade pyelography of, 443
radiography of, 437f, 441
retrograde pyelography of, 443
transmission of, 437

Tuberculosis *(Continued)*
treatment of
antituberculous drugs in, 443-444, 445t
excision of diseased tissue in, 444-446
intravesical BCG therapy in, 447
medical, regimens in, 444
reconstructive surgery in, 446-447
surgical, 444-447
vaccine prospects in, 447
tuberculin test for, 440, 441t
ultrasonography of, 442-443
urine examination in, 440-441
Tuberous sclerosis, 3329-3332, 3330t
angiomyolipoma in, 1578, 1579f, 1580, 3331
characteristics of, 3314t
clinical features of, 3331-3332
evaluation of, 3331
genes responsible for, 3306
genetics of, 3330-3331
histopathology of, 3331
pheochromocytoma associated with, 1861
renal angiomyolipoma with, 3899-3900, 3900f
renal cell carcinoma associated with, 3332
screening for, 1599
renal cysts in, 3329, 3329f, 3330t, 3331-3332, 3331f
Tubo-ovarian abscess, ureteral obstruction due to, 1220
Tubular interstitial disease, in chronic renal failure, 1346-1347
Tubularization techniques, of hypospadias repair, 3722-3723, 3724f, 3725, 3729, 3731-3732, 3732f-3733f, 3734
Tubularized flap technique, dismembered, of laparoscopic pyeloplasty, 1253
Tubularized incised plate (TIP) urethroplasty, in hypospadias repair, 3722, 3724f, 3725
Tubulogenesis, cell-cell interactions in, 3130-3131, 3130f
Tubuloglomerular feedback, 3172
in glomerular filtration rate, 1132
TUIP. *See* Transurethral incision of prostate (TUIP).
Tumor(s). *See also named tumor and at anatomic site.*
formation of, after augmentation cystoplasty, 3684
Tumor biology, of renal cell carcinoma, 1588-1591
Tumor DNA, somatic mutations in, 2865-2867
Tumor immunology, 495-500
adoptive cell therapy in, 499
allogeneic bone marrow transplantation in, 500
antigens in, 495-496, 496t
cancer vaccines in, 499-500
cytokines and interferons in, 499
immunotherapy in, 499-500
mechanism(s) of tumor escape in, 497-498, 498f
impaired antigen presentation as, 497
induction of apoptosis of T cells as, 498-499
secretion of immunosuppressive products as, 497-498, 498f
mechanisms of tumor evasion in, 496-497
monoclonal antibodies in, 500
role of NK cells in, 496
role of T cells in, 495
Tumor marker(s). *See also specific tumor marker.*
clinical applications of, 907
combination of, 2430
histologic subtype prediction with, 907-908
monitoring response of, 907

Tumor marker(s) *(Continued)*
  of bladder cancer
    combination studies in, 2436
    commercially available, 2464t
    non–muscle-invasive, 2464-2465, 2464t, 2465f
  of proliferation, 2429-2430
  of prostate cancer, 2896-2910
    epigenetic modifications of, 2908
    gene expression in, 2909
    genomic alterations and susceptibility of, 2908
    kallikrein(s) as, 2897-2907, 2897f
      hK2, 2906-2907
      hK3, 2897-2906. *See also* Prostate-specific antigen (PSA).
      KLK4, 2907
      KLK11, 2907
      KLK14, 2907
      KLK15, 2907
    prostate-specific membrane antigen as, 2907-2908
    proteomics in, 2909
  of testicular tumors, 893, 906-908
    prognostic value of, 908
Tumor necrosis factor-α
  in dendritic cell activation, 484
  in tubular apoptosis, 1205
  in ureteral obstruction, 1204
  source and activity of, 486t
Tumor necrosis factor-β, source and activity of, 486t
Tumor resection, of bladder cancer, 2438
Tumor suppressor gene(s), 514. *See also specific gene.*
  in bladder cancer, 2410-2411
  in von Hippel–Lindau disease, 517, 1585
  inactivation of, 515
  studies of, in knockout mice, 546
Tumor-associated antigens
  in bladder cancer, 2428
  in renal cell carcinoma, 496
Tumorigenesis, oncogene-induced, 546
Tumor-node-metastasis (TNM) staging
  of bladder cancer, 2441, 2441t
    non–muscle-invasive, 2448-2449, 2448f
  of germ cell tumors, 903-904, 904t, 938
  of penile cancer, 971-972, 971t, 972f, 972t
  of prostate cancer, 2927t
  of renal cell carcinoma, 1600-1601, 1601t
    5-year survival and, 1604t
  of rhabdomyosarcoma, 3879-3880, 3879t
  of urethral cancer, in males, 1012, 1012t
  of urothelial tumors, 1647
TUMT. *See* Transurethral microwave therapy (TUMT).
TUNA. *See* Transurethral needle ablation (TUNA).
Tunica albuginea, 3137, 3138f
  in penile curvature repair, 3714
  of penis, anatomy of, 70f, 72f
    functional, 719-720, 720f
  of testis, 73, 74f
    reconstruction of, 2653, 2653f
  transforming growth factor-β accumulation in, Peyronie's disease due to, 821, 821f, 822f
Tunica vaginalis
  in hypospadias repair, 3716, 3717f
  in penile curvature repair, 3714
  of testis, 73, 74f
Tunica vasculosa, of testis, 73
Tunneled technique, of small bowel anastomosis, 2558, 2558f
TUR. *See* Transurethral resection (TUR).

Turbidity, of urine, 96-97
Turner's syndrome, 3809-3811
  congenital anomalies associated with, 3810, 3810f
  contemporary treatment of, 3811
  gonadoblastoma in, 3810-3811
  horseshoe kidney in, 3811
  incidence of, 3810
TUVP. *See* Transurethral vaporization of prostate (TUVP).
TVUS. *See* Transvaginal ultrasonography (TVUS).
Two-hit theory, of renal dysgenesis, 3306-3307
Two-kidney, one-clip constriction, of renal artery, renovascular hypertension in, 1164
Two-layer sutured anastomosis, 2540-2541, 2540f
Two-stage proximal procedure, in hypospadias repair, 3734, 3735-3738, 3736f-3737f
  free-graft for neourethral formation in, 3734, 3736-3738, 3738f
Tyramine, effect of, on ureteral function, 1905
Tyrosine kinase receptor, in cell migration and proliferation, 1896
Tyrosine kinase-associated receptor(s), 539

**U**
Ubiquitin, 512
Ulcer(s)
  bladder, schistosomal, 453
  genital, 372, 373t
  Hunner's, 352, 353f
    transurethral resection of, 366
  of male genitalia
    aphthous, 417-418, 418f
    noninfectious, 417-419, 417t, 418f, 419f
    traumatic causes of, 418-419
Ultraflex stent, 2809
Ultrasonic lithotripsy, 1463-1465, 1464f
  advantages and disadvantages of, 1464
  technique of, 1464-1465
Ultrasonography, 118, 122-127
  Doppler. *See* Doppler ultrasonography.
  fetal
    of bladder exstrophy, 3507-3508, 3508f
    of cloacal exstrophy, 3541
    of hydronephrosis, 3176-3177, 3177f, 3179f
    of hydroureter, 3177, 3179f
    of normal kidney, 3176, 3177f
  high-intensity focused
    extracorporeal, 1817-1818
    for prostate cancer, 2945
    mode of action of, 1817
  in laparoscopy, 192
  in shockwave lithotripsy, 1469
    fluoroscopy with, 1469, 1470t-1471t
  intraoperative, in adrenal surgery, 1884
  of abdomen
    in children, blunt injury and, 3930
    in male infertility work-up, 630
  of acute pyelonephritis, 269
  of adrenals, 122, 124f
  of autosomal recessive polycystic kidney disease, 3317, 3317f
  of bacterial nephritis, 271, 272f
  of bladder, 122, 124, 125f
  of bladder cancer, 2440
  of blunt abdominal injury, in children, 3930
  of cloacal anomalies, 3852, 3852f
  of ectopic ureter, 3390-3391, 3391f
  of genitourinary tuberculosis, 442-443
  of kidneys, 122, 122f-124f
  of lipomeningocele, 3643, 3644f
  of medullary cystic disease, 3328f

Ultrasonography *(Continued)*
  of megaureter, 4373, 4373f
  of nephrostomy puncture, 1530-1531, 1531f
  of pediatric urologic patient, 3212-3213
  of pelvic organ prolapse, 2210
  of penile cancer, 969-970
  of posterior urethral valves, 3588-3589, 3590f
  of prostate, 124
  of prune belly syndrome, 3483f
    prenatal, 3487f
  of renal abscess, 274-275, 275f
  of renal cyst, 3344, 3344f
  of renal injury, 1277
  of schistosomiasis, 453, 453f
  of scrotum, 124, 126f, 127f
    for germ cell tumors, 903
    in infertility work-up, 729-630
  of testicular tumor, 3902, 3902f
  of ureteral obstruction, 1209
  of ureterocele, 3398-3399, 3399
  of ureteropelvic junction obstruction, 1228-1229
    in children, 3364-3365
  of urethra, 124, 127, 127f
  of urethral diverticula, 2380-2381
  of urethral sphincter dysfunction, in children, 3616
  of urinary tract infections, 243
    in children, 3255
  of varicocele, 658, 659f
  of vesicoureteral reflux, 4335-4336
  of xanthogranulomatous pyelonephritis, 282-283
  preoperative, of hypospadias, 3711
  transrectal. *See* Transrectal ultrasonography (TRUS).
  transvaginal, in evaluation of fertility, 612
Ultraviolet light therapy
  for cutaneous diseases, of external genitalia, 407
  penile cancer associated with, 966
Umbilical artery, single, in neonate, 3195
Umbilical folds, 43
Umbilical hernia, as contraindication to laparoscopy, 175
Umbilical-urachus sinus, 3577f, 3578
Umbrella cells, of urothelium, 1933-1934
Uncircumcised male infants, urinary tract infections in, increased risk of, 3238-3239
Unclassified renal cell carcinoma, 1592t, 1596-1597
Unconscious incontinence, 2046. *See also* Incontinence.
Unipapillary kidney, 3301
United Kingdom Children's Cancer Study Group, rhabdomyosarcoma clinical trials conducted by, 3895
University of Wisconsin Symptom Scale, for painful bladder syndrome/interstitial cystitis, 354-355, 354t
*UPK3* gene, in vesicoureteral reflux, 4326
Upper arm flap. *See also* Flap(s).
  in penile reconstruction, 1094-1095
Upper motor neuron lesion, voiding dysfunction after, classification of, 1983-1984, 1983t
Upper urinary tract. *See also* Urinary tract *entries.*
  anomaly(ies) of, 3269-3303
    of ascent, 3278-3283
      renal ectopia as, 3278-3281
      thoracic kidney as, 3281-3283
    of collecting system, 3297-3303
      calyx and infundibulum in, 3297-3303
      pelvis in, 3303

Upper urinary tract *(Continued)*
  of form and fusion, 3283-3291
    crossed renal ectopia with and without fusion as, 3283-3287
    harsh kidney as, 3287-3291
  of number, 3269-3278
    agenesis as, 3269-3276
    supernumerary kidney as, 3276-3278
  of renal vasculature, 3292-3297
    aberrant, accessory, or multiple vessels as, 3292-3296
    renal arteriovenous fistula as, 3297
    renal artery aneurysm as, 3296-3297
  of rotation, 3291-3292, 3292f, 3293f
  deterioration of, with benign prostatic hyperplasia, 2758
Urachus
  anchoring of, 57
  anomalies of, in children, 3576-3579, 3576f-3578f
  carcinoma of, 2422-2423
  cysts of, 3577f, 3578-3579
  diverticulum of, 3577f, 3579
  patent, 3576-3578, 3577f, 3578f
    laparoscopic management of, 3578
    surgical management of, 3577-3578
Urapidil, to facilitate bladder emptying, 2115
Urea
  plasma levels of, in glomerular filtration rate, 1133
  renal reabsorption of, in medullary collecting tubules, 1146
*Ureaplasma urealyticum*
  in genital tract, 384
  in painful bladder syndrome/interstitial cystitis, 339
  in prostatitis, 307
  in semen cultures, 625-626
Urease, organisms producing, 1387t, 1407t
Ureter(s), 32, 34-37. *See also* Ureteropelvic junction; Ureterovesical junction.
  accessory renal blood vessels and, 3417
  anastomosis of, in Politano-Leadbetter procedure, 4352
  anatomic relationships of, 34-35
  anatomy of
    cellular, 1891
    surgical, 1284, 1284f
  anomalies of
    embryology of, 3384-3387, 3385f-3388f
    of number, 3413-3417
    of position, 3417-3421
    of structure, 3397-3412
    of termination, 3387-3396
    terminology for, 3383-3384, 3384f, 3385f
    vascular, 3417-3421
  bifid, 3383, 3384f, 3416
    definition of, 3383
    duplex kidney with, 3386
  blood supply to, 36-37, 37f
  calculi in. *See* Ureteral calculi.
  caliper of, normal variations in, 36, 36f
  candidiasis of, 462
  circumcaval (retrocaval)
    bilateral vena cava associated with, 3419
    etiology of, 1253, 1254f
    surgical management of, 1253-1254, 1254f
    ureteral obstruction due to, 1223-1225, 1224f, 1225f, 1226f
  contractility of. *See* Ureter(s), peristalsis of.
  development of, 1891-1892
  dilation of, 1511t, 1512, 1512f. *See also* Megaureter(s).

Ureter(s) *(Continued)*
  dissection of. *See also* Ureteral injury.
    distal, 1666, 1667f
    in endoscopic cross-trigonal reimplantation, 4367
    in laparoscopic antireflux surgery, 4366
    in laparoscopic nephrectomy, 1763, 1767f
      hand-assisted, 1796-1797
      transperitoneal approach, 1783, 1783f
  distal, vascular obstruction of, 3420
  diverticulum of, 3411-3402, 3413f
  duplication of, 3413-3417
    and megaureter, surgical management of, 4380
    associated findings in, 3414, 3416
    blind-ending, 3416-3417, 3416f
    clinical, radiographic, and autopsy studies of, 3415t
    genetics of, 3413
    graduations of, 3413, 3414f
    incidence of, 3416
    inverted-Y, 3417
    position of orifices in, 3413-3414
    vesicoureteral reflux and, 4342, 4343f
  ectopic, 3383, 3384f, 3387-3396
    clinical presentation of, 3389, 3389f, 3390f
    covered, 3843, 3843f
    definition of, 3383
    diagnosis of, 3389-3393
    distribution of, 3387-3388, 3388t
    excretory urography of, 3391-3392, 3391f
    magnetic resonance imaging of, 3392-3393
    scintigraphy of, 3393
    single-system, bilateral, 3396, 3396f, 3397f
    treatment of, 3393-3396, 3393f
      alternative, 3395-3396
        laparoscopic nephrectomy in, 3395, 3395f
        upper pole nephrectomy in, 3393-3395, 3394f, 3395f
    ultrasonography of, 3390-3391, 3391f
    voiding cystourethrography of, 3392, 3392f
  embryology of, 3122f, 3133-3134, 3384-3387, 3385f-3388f
  endometriosis of, 1220-1221
  fetal
    congenital folds in, 3360, 3361f
    tortuous, ultrasound appearance of, 3178, 3179f
  frozen-section analysis of, after radical cystectomy, 2471
  herniation of, 3420-3421, 3421f
  ileal substitution of, in stricture repair, 1266, 1267f
    laparoscopic, 1266-1267
  in children, length and diameter of, 4328t
  in prune-belly syndrome, 3483, 3483f, 3484f
    reconstruction of, 3491
  injury to. *See* Ureteral injury.
  innervation of, 37, 1903-1907
    parasympathetic, 1904-1905
    purinergic, 1906-1907
    sensory, 1906
    sympathetic, 1905-1906
  intravesical mobilization of, in antireflux surgery, 4352
  ligation of, 1288
  lymphatic drainage of, 37
  muscle cells of
    action potential of, 1892-1895, 1894f, 1895f
    anatomy of, 1891
    contractile activity of, 1897-1902, 1898f. *See also* Ureter(s), peristalsis of.

Ureter(s) *(Continued)*
  excitation-contraction coupling in, 1899-1900
    proteins in, 1898-1899, 1898f, 1899f
    second messengers in, 1900-1902, 1900f-1902f
  electrical activity of, 1892-1897
    propagation of, 1897
  mechanical properties of, 1902-1903
    force-length relations in, 1902-1903, 1902f, 1903f
    force-velocity relations in, 1903, 1903f
    pressure-length-diameter relations in, 1903, 1904f
  pacemaker potentials and activity of, 1895-1897, 1896f, 1897f
  resting potential of, 1892-1893, 1893f
  normal urothelium of, 1641-1642, 1642f
  obstruction of. *See* Ureteral obstruction.
  pain in, patient history of, 82
  pathologic processes affecting, 1910-1916, 1910f-1915f
  pelvic, 56-57
  perforation of. *See also* Ureteral injury.
    in children, operative management of, 3937-3938
    management of, 1291
    ureteroscopy causing, 1503
  peristalsis of
    age and, 1916-1917, 1917f
    bladder filling and, 1909
    bolus propulsion in, 1907-1909, 1908f, 1909f
    calcium ions in, 1897-1898, 1898f
    calculi affecting, 1915-1916
    contractile proteins in, 1898-1899, 1898f, 1899f
    cyclic AMP in, 1900, 1900f
    cyclic GMP in, 1901
    diacylglycerol in, 1901-1902
    diuretic effects on, 1909
    drug effects on, 1918-1920
    excitation-contraction coupling in, 1899-1900
    infections and, 1915
    latent pacemaker activity in, 1896-1897
    nitric oxide synthase in, 1901, 1901f
    pacemaker for, 1895-1897, 1896f, 1897f
    pregnancy and, 1918
    trisphosphate in, 1901, 1902f
    vesical dysfunction and, 1909
    vesicoureteral reflux and, 1914-1915, 1915f
  preureteral vena cava and, 3408-3410, 3418f-3420f
  reflux into. *See* Vesicoureteral reflux.
  reimplantation of
    extravesical procedures in, 4357, 4358f, 4359-4360
      creation of tunnel in, 4359-4360
      laparoscopic, 4366
    infrahiatal tunnels in, 4356-4357, 4356f, 4357f
    intravesical procedures in, 4352
    laparoscopic, 2506-2507, 2507f, 2508f, 4366
    redo, psoas hitch in, 4362, 4362f
    single, in children, 3661-3662
    suprahiatal tunnels in, 4352, 4353f-4355f, 4356
  retrocaval. *See* Ureter(s), circumcaval (retrocaval).
  retroiliac, 3420, 3421f
  segmentation of, 36, 36f
  spiral twists and folds of, 3411, 3412f
  stenosis of, 3409-3410

Ureter(s) (*Continued*)
stricture of. *See* Ureteral stricture.
supernumerary, 3417
tapering of, 1914
tissue engineering of, 563
trifid, 3417
triplication of, 3417
tuberculosis of, 438, 439f, 440f
urine transport by, 1907-1910, 1908f, 1909f.
*See also* Ureter(s), peristalsis of.
urothelium of
abnormal, 1642-1643
tumors of. *See* Urothelial tumor(s), of renal
pelvis and ureters.
Ureteral access sheath, for ureteroscopy, 1511t,
1513
Ureteral calculi
distal, surgical management of, 1454-1455
effect of, on ureteral function, 1915-1916
historical overview of, 1432
lost, ureteroscopy and, 1503
medical management of, 1916
open stone surgery for, 1506
proximal, surgical management of, 1453-1454
radiographic studies of, 111, 113f
stricture associated with, 1503
submucosal, ureteroscopy and, 1503
surgical management of
ballistic lithotripsy in, 1462-1463, 1463t
clinical factor(s) in, 1450t
aberrant anatomy as, 1453
infection as, 1452-1453
pain as, 1452
patient's expectations as, 1453
solitary kidney as, 1453
electrohydraulic lithotripsy in, 1459-1460,
1460t
historical overview of, 1432
laparoscopic, 1455
laser lithotripsy in, 1461-1462, 1461t
natural history in, 1450-1451
of distal stones, 1454-1455
of proximal stones, 1453-1454
stone burden and, 1452
stone composition in, 1452
stone duration in, 1452
stone factors in, 1450t, 1451-1452
stone location in, 1451-1452
technical factors in, 1450t, 1453
techniques in, 1458-1507. *See also specific
procedure.*
treatment decisions in, 1451-1453
ureteroscopic management of, 1501-1503
complications of, 1503
in children, 3908
steinstrasse and, 1501-1503
Ureteral catheter(s)
commonly used, 170f
for ureteroscopy, 1511t, 1512, 1512f
Ureteral catheterization, in localizing site of
bacteriuria, 241, 241t
Ureteral injury, 1282-1292
avulsion
management of, 1289
stone removal causing, 1503
ureteroscopy causing, 1524
bladder diverticula causing, 2371
diagnosis of, 1284-1286, 1285f
algorithm in, 1290f-1291f
hematuria in, 1284-1285
imaging studies in, 1285-1286, 1285f
intraoperative recognition in, 1285
dissection as. *See* Ureter(s), dissection of.
etiology of, 1282-1284

Ureteral injury (*Continued*)
external, 1282-1283, 1282t, 1283f
surgical, 1283-1284, 1284f
ureteroscopic, 1284
external trauma resulting in, in children,
3937-3938
in children
after open, laparoscopic, and endoscopic
procedures, 3937
operative management of, 3937-3938
in laparoscopy, 214-215
management of, 1286-1291, 1286f
algorithm in, 1290f-1291f
for external ureteral trauma, 1286, 1286f,
1287f
for lower ureteral trauma, 1288
for mid-ureteral trauma, 1288
for upper ureteral trauma, 1287, 1287f
surgical
delayed recognition in, 1289
immediate recognition in, 1288-1289
perforation as. *See* Ureter(s), perforation of.
posterior urethral valves causing, 3586
ureteroscopic, management of, 1289, 1291
vesicovaginal fistula repair causing, 2336
Ureteral neocystostomy, in endoscopic cross-
trigonal reimplantation, 4367
Ureteral obstruction. *See also* Hydronephrosis;
Ureteropelvic junction obstruction.
after partial nephrectomy, 1730
antegrade pyelography in, 1210
assessment of
general, 1910-1913, 1910f-1913f
physiologic methodologies in, 1913-1914,
1914f
bilateral
atrial natriuretic peptide in, 1201
hemodynamic changes with, 1198, 1199f
hypertension with, 1211-1212, 1212t
potassium transport and, 1202
sodium transport in, 1201-1202
tubular function changes in, 1200
urinary concentrating ability after, 1200-
1201
diagnosis of, 1208-1211
antegrade pyelography in, 1210
computed tomography in, 1211
excretory urography in, 1209-1210
magnetic resonance imaging in, 1211
nuclear renography in, 1210-1211
retrograde pyelography in, 1210
ultrasonography in, 1209
Whitaker test in, 1210
effect of
on anion and cation transport, 1202-1203
on peptide and protein excretion, 1203
extrinsic cause(s) of, 1215-1225
abdominal aortic aneurysm as, 1221, 1222f
benign pelvic anomalies as, 1220-1221
circumcaval ureter as, 1223-1225, 1224f,
1225f, 1226f
endometriosis as, 1220-1221
iliac artery aneurysm as, 1222-1223, 1222f
ovarian lesions as, 1221
ovarian remnants as, 1221
pelvic lipomatosis as, 1218-1219, 1218f,
1219f
pregnancy as, 1219-1220, 1220t
puerperal ovarian vein thrombophlebitis as,
1223
retroperitoneal fibrosis as, 1215-1218,
1215t, 1216f, 1217f
testicular vein thrombophlebitis as, 1223
tubo-ovarian abscess as, 1220

Ureteral obstruction (*Continued*)
uterine lesions as, 1221
vascular, 1221-1225
vascular graft placement as, 1223
fetal, 1913
hydrogen ion transport and, 1202
management of, 1208-1214
diagnostic imaging in, 1208-1211
hypertension in, 1211-1212, 1212t
pain, 1213
postobstructive diuresis in, 1213-1214
renal drainage in, 1212
surgical intervention in, 1212-1213
partial, 1198-1200
pathologic changes in, 1207-1208, 1208f,
1209f
perfusion studies of, 1913-1914, 1914f
renal recovery after, 1207
resection causing, 2483
tissue inhibitors of metalloproteinase in, 1204
tumor necrosis factor-α in, 1204
unilateral
functional response to, 3160
hemodynamic changes with, 1196-1198,
1197f
in neonate, 3161
potassium transport and, 1202
sodium transport in, 1201-1202
transforming growth factor-β in, 1204
tubular function changes in, 1200
urinary acidification deficit in, 1202
Ureteral stent
after ureteroscopic stone manipulation, in
children, 3908
for contusions, 1286-1287
for reimplanted ureters, in exstrophy patient,
3526
for ureteral obstruction, 1212
for ureteral stricture, 1255
placement of, before shockwave lithotripsy,
1501-1502
Ureteral stricture, 1255-1267, 1503, 3409-3410
balloon dilatation for
antegrade approach to, 1256
results of, 1256-1257
retrograde approach to, 1255-1256, 1257f
diagnostic studies of, 1255
endoureterotomy for, 1257-1259
antegrade approach to, 1258
cautery wire balloon incision in,
1257-1258
combined approaches to, 1259
retrograde approach to, 1257, 1257f
etiology of, 1255, 1255t
from stone impaction, 1503
in tuberculosis, surgical management of, 446
intervention for
indications for, 1255
options for, 1255-1259
surgical repair of, 1259-1267, 1259t
autotransplantation in, 1267
Boari flap in, 1262, 1264, 1264f
laparoscopic, 1264
ileal ureteral substitution in, 1266, 1267f
laparoscopic, 1266-1267
intubated ureterotomy in, 1264
psoas hitch in, 1261, 1262f, 1263f
laparoscopic, 1261
renal descensus in, 1264
transureteroureterostomy in, 1264-1266
ureteroneocystostomy in, 1261
laparoscopic, 1261
ureteroureterostomy in, 1259-1261, 1260f
laparoscopic, 1261

Ureteral stricture (Continued)
  ureteral stent placement for, 1255
  ureteroscopic management of, 1521-1522
  ureteroscopy causing, 1524
Ureteral valves, 3410-3411, 3410f, 3411f
Ureterectomy
  distal, 1658-1662
    intussusception technique of, 1659,
      1662f
    laparoscopic ligation and detachment
      technique of, 1662, 1663f
    total laparoscopic, 1662, 1664f
    traditional open, 1659, 1660f, 1661f
    transurethral ureteral orifice resection in,
      1659, 1661f
    with bladder cuff excision, 1666
  open segmental, 1667-1672
    subtotal, 1671-1672, 1672t
    ureteroneocystostomy with Boari flap in
      indications for, 1667
      technique of, 1667-1668, 1669f-1671f,
        1671
    ureteroureterostomy in, 1667, 1668f
  segmental, 1649
    results of, 1649, 1649t
Ureteric bud, 3384-3387, 3385f-3387f
  dichotomous branching of, 3126, 3127f, 3129-
    3130
  division of, 3124-3125, 3125f
  interaction of metanephric mesenchyme with,
    3125, 3125f
  outgrowth of, toward metanephric
    mesenchyme, 3127, 3129, 3129f
Ureteritis, tuberculous, 438
Ureterocalycostomy, for ureteropelvic junction
  obstruction, 1247-1249, 1248f, 1253
Ureterocele, 3312, 3397-3412
  classification of, 3384
  diagnosis of, 3397-3401
  ectopic
    dilated, 3399
    prolapse of, 3194
  embryology of, 3397
  intravenous pyelography of, 3399-3400,
    3399f
  intravesical, 3384, 3385f
    definition of, 3384
    single-system, 3384, 3385f
  prenatal diagnosis of, 3181-3182, 3182f
  prolapsed, 3398, 3398f, 3409, 3845,
    3845f
  simple, definition of, 3383
  single-system, 3408-3409, 3409f
  sphincteric, 3383, 3384f
    definition of, 3383
  terminology for, 3383-3384
  treatment of, 3402-3404, 3406-3408
    cystoscopic incision in, 3407-3408, 3407f,
      3408f
    endoscopic, 3406
    excision in, 3404, 3405f, 3406
  ultrasonography of, 3398-3399, 3399f
  voiding cystourethrography of, 3400-3401,
    3401f, 3402f
Ureteroenteric fistula, 2353
Ureteroenteric stricture, anastomotic
  etiology of, 1267-1268
  evaluation of, 1268
  incidence of, 1267
  percutaneous treatment of, 1557
  radical cystectomy and, 2472
  surgical management of, 1269-1270
    indications for, 1268-1269
Ureterography, of ureteral injury, 1276

Ureterointestinal anastomosis, 2554-2563
  antireflux valves in, 2561-2562, 2561f, 2562f
  complications of, 2556t, 2562-2563
  ureterocolonic
    complications of, 2556t
    Cordonnier and Nesbit technique of, 2557
    Leadbetter and Clarke technique of, 2555-
      2556, 2556f
    Pagano technique of, 2557, 2557f
    Strickler technique of, 2556-2557, 2556f
    transcolonic Goodwin technique of, 2556,
      2556f
Ureterolithotomy, laparoscopic, 1776, 1778
  for ureteral calculi, 1455
Ureterolysis, for retroperitoneal fibrosis, 1217-
  1218, 1272-1273, 1273f
  laparoscopic, 1273
Ureteroneocystostomy
  antireflux, in renal transplantation, 1310,
    1313f-1314f
  for lower ureteral injuries, 1288
  for ureteral stricture, 1261
    laparoscopic, 1261
  laparoscopic
    extravesical, 2506, 2507f
    intravesical, 2506, 2508f
    results of, 2506-2507
  with psoas hitch or Boari flap
    indications for, 1667
    technique of, 1667-1668, 1669f-1671f, 1671
Ureteronephrectomy, proximal, laparoscopic,
  1665-1666, 1666f
Ureteropelvic junction
  disruption of, trauma-induced, 1283, 1283f
  in children, 3936
  kinking at, 3361, 3361f
  physiology of, 1907, 1908f
Ureteropelvic junction obstruction, 1227-1253
  acquired, 1228
  cautery wire balloon endopyelotomy for
    complications of, 1238-1239
    indications for and contraindications to,
      1237, 1237f
    postoperative care following, 1237
    results of, 1237-1238
    technique of, 1237, 1238f
  congenital, 1227. See also Urinary tract
    obstruction, congenital.
    progressive renal dysfunction in, 3164,
      3164f
  diagnosis of, 1228-1231
    computed tomography in, 1229, 1230f
    radiographic studies in, 1228, 1229f, 1230f
    radionuclide renography in, 1229-1230,
      1231f
    ultrasonography in, 1228-1229
  etiology of, aberrant vessels in, 1228
  in children, 3359-3382
    associated anomalies in, 3362, 3363f
    biochemical parameters in, 3369-3370
    diagnosis of, 3363-3370
    etiology of, 3359-3362
    evidence of, 3359
    extrinsic narrowing contributing to, 3361,
      3361f
    intrinsic narrowing contributing to, 3360,
      3360f, 3361f
    lower pole, 3361-3362, 3362f
    magnetic resonance imaging of, 3367-3368,
      3368f, 3369f
    presentation of, 3362-3363, 3364f
    pressure flow studies of, 3368-3369
    radionuclide renography of, 3365-3367,
      3366f-3367f

Ureteropelvic junction obstruction (Continued)
  secondary, 3361, 3362f
  surgical repair of, 3370-3380, 3370f-3372f
    Davis intubated ureterotomy in, 3370,
      3371f
    dismembered pyeloplasty in, 3370, 3372f,
      3373
      Anderson-Hynes modified, 3373-3374,
        3373f, 3374f
    endoscopic approaches to, 3374-3375,
      3375f
    flank approach to, 3374
    Foley Y-V plasty in, 3370, 3370f
    laparoscopic pyeloplasty in, 3375-3376,
      3376f
    minimally invasive techniques in, 3374-
      3376
    outcome of, 3380, 3380t, 3381f
    posterior lumbotomy in, 3374
    retroperitoneal access in, 3376-3378
      laparoscopic retroperitoneal
        pyeloplasty in, 3377-3378, 3378f,
        3379f
      lateral approach to, 3376-3377, 3376f,
        3377f
      prone posterior approach to, 3377
      transperitoneal approach to, 3377,
        3378f
    special situations in, 3378, 3380
    spiral flap technique in, 3370, 3371f
    traction sutures in, 3372f, 3377, 3378f
    vertical flap technique in, 3370, 3372f
  ultrasonography, 3364-3365
  in multicystic dysplastic kidney, 3335
  intervention in
    endourologic, 1232-1241
    indications for, 1231-1232
    laparoscopic, 1249-1253
    open operative, 1241-1249
    options for, 1232-1253
  intubated ureterotomy for, 1245, 1247, 1247f
  laparoscopic calicovesicostomy for, 1253
  laparoscopic dismembered tubularized flap
    pyeloplasty for, 1253
  laparoscopic pyeloplasty for, 1249-1252
    anterior extraperitoneal approach to, 1250
    complications of, 1252, 1252f
    indications for and contraindications to,
      1249-1250
    postoperative care following, 1250, 1252
    results of, 1252
    robotic-assisted approach to, 1250
    transperitoneal approach to, 1250, 1251f
    with concomitant pyelolithotomy, 1253
  laparoscopic ureterocalicostomy for, 1253
  pathogenesis of, 1227-1228
  percutaneous antegrade endopyelotomy for,
    1233-1237
    complications of, 1236-1237
    indications for and contraindications to,
      1233, 1233f
    patient preparation in, 1233
    postoperative care following, 1234, 1236
    results of, 1236
    simultaneous nephrolithotomy with,
      1234
    technique of, 1233-1234, 1235f, 1236f
  prenatal diagnosis of, 3180
  presentation of, 1228
  pyeloplasty for
    Culp-DeWeerd spiral flap technique of,
      1245, 1246f
    dismembered, 1242-1243, 1243f, 1244f
    flap procedures in, 1243-1245, 1245f

Ureteropelvic junction obstruction (Continued)
  Foley YV-plasty technique of, 1243-1245, 1245f
  historical aspects of, 1242
  laparoscopic, 1249-1253, 1251f, 1252f
  Scardino-Prince vertical flap technique of, 1245, 1246f
  surgical principles of, 1241-1242
  salvage procedures for, 1249
  secondary, 1232
  stone formation in, 1389-1390
    surgical management of, 1442
  ureterocalycostomy for, 1247-1249, 1248f
  ureteroscopic endopyelotomy for
    complications of, 1241
    indications for and contraindications to, 1239
    results of, 1241
    technique of, 1239, 1240f, 1241
  ureteroscopic management of, 1522
  vesicoureteral reflux and, 3361, 3362, 3362f, 4341, 4342f
Ureteroplasty, in children, 3687-3688, 3688f
Ureteropyeloscopy, 1672-1677
  results of, 1675, 1677
  steps in, 1674-1675, 1676f, 1677f
  technique and instrumentation in, 1673-1674, 1674f
Ureteroscope(s)
  damage caused by, 1524-1525
  flexible, 1433, 1509, 1511t
    characteristics of, 1509t
    insertion of, 1516, 1516t
  rigid, 1433
    insertion of, 1516
  semirigid, 1433, 1508-1509, 1511t
Ureteroscopic endopyelotomy. See Endopyelotomy, ureteroscopic.
Ureteroscopy, 1672-1677
  anesthesia for, 1501
  antibiotic prophylaxis for, 253
  complications of, 1284, 1523t, 1524
  in children, 1520, 3907-3909
    access in, 3908
    indications for, 3907-3908
    instruments for, 3907, 3908t
    postprocedure management for, 3908
    results of, 3909, 3909t
    stone manipulation and removal using, 3908
  in morbidly obese patient, 1520
  in patient with bleeding diatheses, 1520
  in pregnancy, 1519-1520
  in stone fragmentation and removal, 1432-1433
    from lower pole, 1447
    from ureter, 1501-1503
      complications of, 1503
      in children, 3908
      intrarenal, 1503-1505, 1504t
        technique of, 1505
      results of, 1518-1519
  indications for, 1508, 1509t
    in children, 3907-3908
    vs. shockwave lithotripsy, 1519t
  instrumentation for, 1508-1514, 1511t, 1673-1674, 1674f
    balloon dilators in, 1511t, 1512, 1512f
    endoscopes in, 1433, 1508-1509, 1509t, 1511t
    guide wires in, 1509, 1510f, 1511t, 1512, 1512f
    intracorporeal lithotriptors in, 1511t, 1513-1514

Ureteroscopy (Continued)
  irrigation devices in, 1511t, 1512-1513
  pediatric, 3907, 3908t
  ureteral access sheath in, 1511t, 1513
  ureteral catheters in, 1511t, 1512, 1512f
  of anomalous kidneys, 1521
  of calyceal diverticula, 1443, 1521
  of upper tract transitional cell carcinoma, 1522-1524, 1522f, 1523f
  of ureteral strictures, 1521-1522
  of ureteropelvic junction obstruction, 1522
  of urothelial tumors, 1645, 1646f
  overview of, 1432-1433
  postoperative care after, 1518
  results of, 1518-1519, 1675, 1677
  salvage, after failed shockwave lithotripsy, 1518-1519
  stent placement following, 1516, 1517t
    biomaterials used in, 1517-1518
    technique of, 1518
  step-by-step, 1514-1516
  steps in, 1674-1675, 1676f, 1677f
  technique in, 1673-1674, 1674f
  ureteral access in
    antibiotic prophylaxis for, 1514-1515
    endoscope insertion and, 1516, 1516t
    in children, 3908
    patient positioning for, 1515
    patient preparation for, 1514
    safety guide wires for, 1515-1516
      cystoscopic placement of, 1515
    video monitoring of, 1515
  ureteral avulsion due to, 1524
  ureteral injury due to, 1284
    management of, 1289, 1291
  ureteral stricture due to, 1524
  urosepsis due to, 1524
Ureterosigmoidostomy
  for continent urinary diversion, in children, 3693
  in exstrophy patient, 3537
  in urinary diversion, 2613
Ureterotomy, intubated
  for ureteral stricture, 1264
  for ureteropelvic junction obstruction, 1245, 1247, 1247f
Ureteroureterostomy
  for mid-ureteral injuries, 1288
  for upper ureteral injuries, 1287
  for ureteral contusion, 1286, 1287f
  for ureteral stricture, 1259-1261, 1260f
    laparoscopic, 1261
  technique of, 1667, 1668f
Ureterovaginal fistula, 2341-2345
  diagnosis of, 2341-2343, 2342f-2344f
  etiology and presentation of, 2341, 2342t
  management of, 2343-2345
Ureterovascular fistula, 2357-2359, 2358t
Ureterovesical junction, 58-59, 60f
  deficiency of, in epispadias, 3545, 3547
  embryology of, 4326-4327
  obstruction of, prenatal diagnosis of, 3180-3181
  opening of, 4328
  physiology of, 1909-1910
  refluxing, 4327-4328, 4327f, 4328t
  strictures of, tuberculosis-induced, surgical management of, 446
Ureter–small bowel anastomosis, 2559, 2560f, 2561
Urethra
  after cystectomy, management of, 1015-1018
  anatomy of, 1923-1924

Urethra (Continued)
  anterior, in prune-belly syndrome, 3484-3485, 3485f
  reconstruction in, 3491, 3491f, 3492f
  atrophy of
    after complete primary exstrophy repair, 3571
    artificial sphincter revision for, 2401
  bladder cancer recurrence in, after cystectomy, 2623-2628
    in female patient, 2626-2628
    in male patient, 2624-2626
  bladder neck, 1030, 1030f
  bulbous, 1029, 1030f
  cancer of. See Urethral cancer.
  catheterization of. See Urethral catheterization.
  cholinergic innervation of, gender differences in, 1954
  dilatation of. See Urethral dilatation.
  discharge from, patient history of, 87
  diverticulum of. See Urethral diverticulum(a).
  division of, in robotic-assisted laparoscopic radical prostatectomy, 2995, 2996f
  duplication of, 3601, 3602f, 3603
  dysfunction of
    acquired severe, 2235-2236, 2236f, 2237f
    incontinence associated with, 1922
    neuropathic, 2234-2235, 2235f
    sphincteric failure in, 2234
  embryology of
    ectodermal differentiation theory in, 3704
    endodermal differentiation theory in, 3704-3705
  erosion of
    after artificial sphincter placement, 2400
    sling and reconstruction procedures for, 2249
    vaginal tape–induced, 2260-2262, 2261t
  female, 67
    anatomy of, 1018-1019, 1019f, 2372-2374, 2373f, 2374f
    management of, after radical cystectomy, 2471
    prolapsed, 3844-3845, 3845f
  fetal, anomalies of, 3574
  fossa navicularis of, 1029, 1030f
  glandular, formation of, 3141
  hypermobility of, 1977
  in exstrophy repair
    closure of, 3510, 3511f-3512f, 3513
    reconstruction of, 3520
  injury to. See Urethral injury.
  innervation of, gender differences in, 1954
  instability of, 1977
  lengthening of, in children, 3668-3669
    results of, 3669
    technique of, 3669, 3670f
  magnetic resonance imaging of, 138
  male, 2053
    construction of, 1049
    management of, after radical cystectomy, 2470-2471
  membranous, 63-64, 64f, 1030, 1030f
  mobility of, observation of, 2205
  morphology of, 1935
  muscles of, 1935-1937
    fiber types in, 1936-1937
  natural defenses of, 234-235
  obstruction of, renal hypodysplasia with, 3312-3313
  overdilation of, therapeutic, 2303
  paraurethral tissue surrounding, 1937

Urethra (Continued)
  penile (pendulous), 1029, 1030f
    carcinoma of, 1012-1013, 1012f, 1013f
  perforation of, in penile prosthesis
      implantation, 797
  portions of, 1029-1030, 1030f
  posterior, complex fistulas of, surgical
      reconstruction for, 1086-1087, 1086f
  prostatic, 61, 62f, 1030, 1030f
    congenital diverticulum in, 1044. See also
      Urethral diverticulum(a).
  proximal closure of
    loss of, 2234-2236, 2235f
    weakness of, 2236-2237
  reconstruction of
    in epispadias, 3546
    in exstrophy patient, 3518-3524
  sensory aspects of, 1976
  sexual pain disorders involving, 883-884
  sphincter of. See Urethral sphincter.
  stricture of. See Urethral stricture.
  tissue engineering of, 557-558, 558f
  tone of, in women, 1953
  tuberculosis of, 440
  ultrasonography of, 124, 127, 127f
  valves of. See Urethral valves.
  wall of, passive properties of, 1975
Urethral bulking agents, for stress incontinence,
    2075-2076
Urethral calculi, 2670-2672
  management of, 2672
  migrant, 2672, 2672f
  native, 2671-2672, 2672f
Urethral cancer
  female, 1018-1022
    diagnosis of, 1019
    epidemiology, etiology, and presentation of,
        1018
    pathology of, 1019, 1019f
    staging of, 1019
    treatment of, 1019-1021
      for distal carcinomas, 1020-1021
      for proximal carcinomas, 1021
      results of, 1020t
  male, 1011-1018
    evaluation of, 1012
    general considerations in, 1011
    pathology of, 1011-1012, 1011f
    staging of, 1012, 1012t
    treatment of, 1012-1015
      chemotherapy in, 1014-1015
      for bulbomembranous urethral
          carcinoma, 1013-1014, 1014f
      for penile urethra carcinoma, 1012-1013,
          1012f, 1013f
      radiation therapy in, 1014
Urethral caruncle, vs. urethral diverticula, 2384-
    2385, 2384f
Urethral catheter
  dilating
    size of, 161
    types of, 161-162, 162f
  indwelling
    for underactive detrusor, 2319-2320
    long-term use of, carcinoma associated
        with, 2297
    principles of care of, 2320, 2320t
    removal of, 2319, 2319t
    urethral erosion due to, 2347, 2347f
Urethral catheterization, 161-164
  antibiotic prophylaxis for, 250
  difficulty of, 163-164, 163f
  for neurogenic bladder dysfunction, 2237,
      2237f

Urethral catheterization (Continued)
  indications for, 161
  patient preparation for, 162
  technique of, 162-163
  types of catheters used in, 161-162, 162f
Urethral continence, assessment of, 2240
Urethral cyst, parameatal, 3758
Urethral dilatation
  indications for, 165-166
  of stricture, 1057, 1059
  patient preparation for, 166
  technique of, 166, 166f, 167f
Urethral diverticulum(a)
  after hypospadias repair, 3739
  congenital, 1043-1044
  in females, 2372-2390, 2373f
    anatomy of, 2376-2377, 2377f
    classification of, 2385
    conditions associated with, 2389-2390,
        2389f
    cystourethroscopy of, 2378-2379, 2379f
    differential diagnosis of, 2382-2385
    during pregnancy, 2390
    imaging of, 2379-2382, 2380f-2382f
    morphology and characteristics of, 2376t
    pathophysiology of, 2374-2376, 2374f,
        2375f
    physical examination of, 2378, 2378f
    presentation of, 2377-2378, 2377t
    prevalence of, 2376
    sling procedures and, 2249
    surgical treatment of, 2385-2389
      complications of, 2388, 2388t, 2389f
      excision and reconstruction in, 2385-
          2386, 2385t
      indications for, 2385, 2386f
      postoperative care in, 2388
      preoperative preparation in, 2386
      symptoms persistence after, 2388-2389
      technique in, 2386-2388, 2387f
    urine studies in, 2378
    urodynamics of, 2379
    vs. Gartner's duct abnormalities, 2383,
        2383f
    vs. Skene's gland abnormalities, 2383, 2383f
    vs. urethral caruncle, 2384-2385, 2384f
    vs. urethral mucosal prolapse, 2384
    vs. vaginal leiomyoma, 2382-2383, 2382f
    vs. vaginal wall cysts, 2383-2384, 2385f
Urethral fistula, congenital, 3757-3758
Urethral fold, in male genital development,
    3141, 3143f
Urethral groove, 3141
  definitive, 3704
  primary, 3704
  secondary, 3704
Urethral hemangioma, 1040-1041
Urethral injury, 2658-2662
  anterior
    delayed reconstruction of, 2662
    in children, 3941-3942
    management of, 2661
  complex injuries in, management of, 2659
  distraction, 1075-1084
    evaluation of, 1076
    postoperative management of, 1079, 1082,
        1083f
    repair of, 1076-1079
      corporal rerouting in, 1079, 1082f
      division of triangular ligament in, 1077,
          1081f
      infrapubectomy in, 1079, 1081f
      patient position for, 1077, 1078f-1079f
      perineal approach to, 1077, 1080f

Urethral injury (Continued)
    timetable for reconstruction in, 1076
    urethroplasty in, 2661
  in children, 3939-3944
    anterior trauma and, 3941-3942
    diagnosis of, 3940, 3941f
    endoscopic repair of, 3942-3943
    erectile dysfunction after, 3944
    incontinence after, 3944
      pelvic fractures associated with, 3940
      posterior trauma and bladder neck
          incompetence after, Mitrofanoff
          principle in, 3944
      presentation of, 3940
    repair of, 3940-3941
    vs. adult trauma, 3939-3940
  in females, 3943-3944
  in penile gunshot wounds, 2651
  posterior
    complications of, 2661
    diagnosis of, 2658-2659, 2659f
    etiology of, 2658, 2658f
    in children
      bladder neck incompetence after,
          Mitrofanoff principle for, 3944
      pelvic fractures associated with, 3940
    management of, 2659
      complex trauma and, 2659
      delayed reconstruction in, 2659-2661
      endoscopic, 2660-2661
      Mitrofanoff principle in, 3944
      preoperative evaluation in, 2660, 2660f
      surgical reconstruction in, 2661
Urethral inserts, for stress incontinence, 2138,
    2140, 2140f
Urethral instrumentation, causing Peyronie's
    disease, 818
Urethral meatal occlusive devices, for stress
    incontinence, 2138
Urethral meatus stenosis, 1044
  in circumcised infant, 1044-1045, 1045f
Urethral mucosal prolapse, vs. urethral
    diverticula, 2384
Urethral muscles, 1935-1937
  fiber types of, 1936-1937
Urethral obstruction, congenital
  anterior, 3599-3600, 3600f, 3601f
  posterior. See Urethral valves, posterior.
Urethral plate, 3141
Urethral plugs, for bladder filling/storage
    disorders, 2292
Urethral polyps, 3845-3846, 3846f
  in children, 3601, 3601f
Urethral pressure profilometry, 2007-2008
  in children, 3626, 3626f, 3627f
  in incontinence, 2067
  micturitional, 2007-2008
  static, 2007
  stress, 2007
Urethral prolapse, 883-884
  in children, 3210
  in neonates, 3194
Urethral resistance factor, group-specific, 1999
Urethral sloughing, after cryotherapy, 3050
Urethral sphincter, 1030, 1031f, 1935, 1974
  configuration of, 1935-1936, 1936f
  dysfunction of
    conditions causing, 2057-2059
    contribution of, in retropubic suspension
        surgery, 2170
  in children
    categorization of, 3609-3611, 3610f
    during bladder emptying, 3612-3613
    during bladder filling, 3611-3612

Urethral sphincter (*Continued*)
  epidemiology and prevalence of, 3609
  history of, 3614
  laboratory investigations of, 3615
  management of, 3618-3620, 3619f, 3620f
  nocturnal enuresis and, 3621-3622, 3623f
  physical examination for, 3615
  recurrent urinary tract infections and, 3614
  ultrasonography of, 3616
  urodynamic studies of, 3616-3618, 3617f, 3618f
  vesicoureteral reflux and, 3614, 3615f
  voiding diary in, 3614-3615, 3616f
  in females, 2058-2059
  in incontinent patient, treatment of, 2074-2077
  in males, 2059
  intrinsic, 1977
  dyssynergia of. *See also* Detrusor-sphincter dyssynergia.
    definition of, 1981
  electromyographic studies of, 2002
  electromyography of, 2068
  evaluation of, prior to urinary tract reconstruction, 3660
  in females, 67
    abnormalities of, 2058-2059
    anatomic support of, 2050-2053, 2051f, 2052f
    incompetent, treatment of, 2401-2402
  in males, 61, 63-64, 64f
    abnormalities of, 2059
    anatomic support of, 2053
  in micturition
    in females, 2050-2053, 2051f, 2052f
    in males, 2053
  in retropubic suspension surgery, deficiency of, issue of, 2171-2172
  intrinsic deficiency of, 2053
    definition of, 2257
    tension-free vaginal taping for, 2257-2258
  reconstruction of, myoplasty in, 2294
  striated, 64, 64f
    decreased resistance of bladder outlet at, 2301-2304
    surgical anatomy of, 2958-2959, 2958f
Urethral stents
  for stress incontinence, 2140
  prosthetic, 2303-2304
Urethral stricture
  after cryotherapy, 3050
  after hypospadias repair, 3739-3740
  anatomic considerations in, 1054, 1056f
  congenital, 1056, 3600, 3601f
  diagnosis and evaluation of, 1056-1057, 1058f-1060f
  etiology of, 1055-1056
  in children
    assessment of, before delayed repair, 3942
    endoscopic repair of, 3942-3943
    spongiofibrosis in, 1054, 1055f
  treatment of, 1057, 1059-1074
    dilation in, 1057, 1059
    internal urethrotomy in, 1059-1061
    lasers in, 1061-1062
    open reconstruction in, 1062-1075
      excision and reanastomosis in, 1062, 1063f, 1064f
      flaps in, 1067, 1067f-1071f, 1073
      grafts in, 1062, 1064f-1066f, 1067

Urethral stricture (*Continued*)
      skin island onlay in, 1072f-1074f, 1073-1075
      success rate of, 1074
    urethrotomy for, 2660
Urethral syndrome, 368-370, 370t
  acute, 370
  chronic, 370
Urethral valves
  anterior, 3599-3600, 3600f, 3601f
  posterior
    clinical presentation of, 3588
    damage due to, 3586t
    diagnostic evaluation of, 3588-3591
    fetal, ultrasound appearance of, 3178, 3179f, 3180f
    hydronephrosis with
      fetal sonographic examination of, 3590f
      management of, 3596
    incidence of, 3583
    inheritance of, 3584-3585
    laboratory evaluation of, 3590-3591
    lower urinary tract injury due to, 3585-3586, 3586f
    management of, 3591-3595
      bladder drainage in, 3591
      cutaneous vesicostomy in, 3591-3592, 3593-3594f
      renal transplantation in, 3599
      urinary diversion in, 3592-3595, 3595f
      valve ablation in, 3591, 3592f
    pathophysiology of, 3585-3587, 3586t
    pulmonary hypoplasia due to, 3586t, 3588
    renal dysplasia with, 3587
    renal function with, prognostic indicators of, 3598-3599
    renal insufficiency due to, 3586t, 3588
    renal scintigraphy of, 3590
    type I, 3584, 3584f
    type II, 3584, 3584f
    type III, 3584, 3584f, 3585f
    ultrasonography of, 3588-3589, 3590f
    upper urinary tract injury due to, 3586-3587
    urinary ascites due to, 3586t, 3588
    vesicoureteral reflux with, 3587
      management of, 3595-3596, 3596f
    voiding cystourethrography of, 3589-3590, 3591f
    Young's classification of, 3583-3584, 3584f
Urethral warming device, for cryotherapy, 3038-3039
  placement of, 3041
Urethra-sparing surgery, in radical cystectomy, in females, 2498-2499, 2499f
Urethrectomy, 2489-2493
  anterior exenteration with, in female radical cystectomy, 2496-2498, 2497f-2499f
  complications of, 2493
  indications for, 2489
  postoperative management of, 2493
  surgical technique of, 2489-2492, 2490f-2493f
  total, for retained male urethra, after cystectomy, 1015, 1016f-1017f, 1018
Urethritis, 884
  atrophic, in geriatric incontinence, 2306-2308, 2307t
  causes of, 625
  in HIV patients, 397
Urethrocutaneous fistula, 1042-1043, 1043f
  after hypospadias repair, 3739
  of urinary tract, 2359
Urethrocystoscopy, in benign prostatic hyperplasia, 2772

Urethrography
  of urethral injury, 2658-2659, 2659f
  positive-pressure, of urethral diverticula, 2379, 2380f
  retrograde, 118, 121f. *See also* Cystourethrography.
Urethroplasty
  anastomotic, in children, 3943
  delayed, in children, 3942-3943
  in epispadias patient, results of, 3547
  in hypospadias repair, 3715-3718
    free grafts used in, 3716
    immediately advanced tissue used in, 3716
    local tissue flaps used in, 3716-3717
    neourethral coverage in, 3716-3718
      corpus spongiosum for, 3716, 3718
      subcutaneous (dartos) flap for, 3716, 3716f
      tunica vaginalis for, 3716, 3717f
    neourethral formation in, 3715-3716
    tubularized incised plate (TIP) technique of, 3722, 3724f, 3725
  in urethral distraction injuries, 2661
  patch, in children, 3943
Urethrorectal (rectourethral) fistula, 2353-2357
  after cryotherapy, 3050
  etiology and presentation of, 2354-2355, 2354f, 2355f
  management of, 2355-2357, 2356f
Urethroscopy, for urethral strictures, in children, 3942-3943
Urethrostomy, construction of, in total penectomy, 998, 999f-1001f
Urethrotomy
  for urethral strictures, 2660
    in children, 3943
  internal
    for prune-belly syndrome, 3490-3491
    for urethral stricture, 1059-1061
Urethrovaginal fistula, 2347-2351
  diagnosis of, 2348, 2348f, 2349f
  etiology and presentation of, 2347-2348, 2347f, 2348f
  management of, 2348-2351, 2350f
Urge inhibition, in behavioral therapy for incontinence, 2129
Urgency
  causes of, 370t
  definition of, 2079
    International Continence Society, 333, 2084
    patient explanation of, 2083-2084
  in overactive bladder, 2082
  measurement of, 2083
  vs. urge to void, 2082
Urgency incontinence, 86, 2046, 2082. *See also* Incontinence.
  definition of, 2079
  impact of, 2125
  in children, 3611
  integral theory of, 2052-2053
  medications for, 2316, 2317t
  vs. stress incontinence, 2083
Urgency percentage scale, 2083
Urgency Severity Scale, 2083
Urgency syndrome, in children, 3611
Uric acid, solubility of, urine pH in, 1382
Uric acid calculi, 1382, 1383f, 1384-1385, 1384f
  hyperuricosuria in, 1385
  low urinary pH in, 1382, 1384-1385
  low urinary volume in, 1385
  pathophysiologic mechanisms of, 1405, 1405f
Urinalysis
  abnormal, in HIV patients, 398
  chemical, 97-105

Urinalysis (*Continued*)
  bilirubin in, 104
  dipsticks in, 97
  glucose in, 103-104
  hematuria in, 97-100, 99f, 99t, 101f, 102f
  ketones in, 104
  leukocyte esterase activity in, 104-105
  nitrite tests in, 104-105
  proteinuria in, 100-103, 103f
  urobilinogen in, 104
  color in, 96, 96t
  dipsticks in, 97
  in acute renal failure, 1334-1335, 1334f, 1335t
  in benign prostatic hyperplasia, 2767-2768
  in chronic renal failure, 1349
  in incontinence, 2060
  in urinary tract infection, 239-240
    in childen, 3244
  osmolality in, 97
  pH in, 97
  physical, 96-97, 96t
  sediment microscopy in, 105-109
    bacteria in, 108, 108f, 109f
    casts in, 107, 107f, 108f
    cells in, 105-107, 105f-107f
    crystals in, 107-108, 108f. *See also* Crystals, urinary.
    expressed prostatic secretions in, 109, 109f
    parasites in, 109, 109f
    specimen preparation and technique of, 105
    yeast in, 106f, 109
  specific gravity in, 97
  specimen collection for. *See* Urine collection.
  turbidity in, 96-97
Urinary ascites
  in neonate, 3196
  posterior urethral valves causing, 3586t, 3588
Urinary bladder. *See* Bladder.
  artificial, for filling/storage disorders, 2297-2298
Urinary bolus, propulsion of, 1907-1909, 1909f
Urinary calculi
  after renal transplantation, 1320
  ammonium acid urate, 1387-1388
    management of, 1426-1427
  anatomic predisposition to, 1389-1391
  calcium-based
    hypercalciuria in, 1374-1377, 1376t
    hyperoxaluria in, 1377-1379, 1377f, 1378f
    hyperuricosuria in, 1379, 1385
    hypocitraturia in, 1379
    hypomagnesuria in, 1381-1382
    low urine pH in, 1379-1380
    pathogenesis of, 1374-1382
    renal tubular acidosis in, 1380-1381
  classification of, 1373-1374, 1373t
  CT evaluation of, 129, 130f, 1397, 1397f
  cystine, 1385-1386, 1385f
  dihydroxyadenine, 1387
  during pregnancy, 1455-1458
    evaluation of, 1457
    incidence of, 1456
    spontaneous passage of, 1457
    surgical management of, 1457-1458
  ephedrine, 1389
  guaifenesin, 1389
  in chronic renal failure, 1347
  in HIV patients, 397
  indinavir, 1388-1389
  infection-based, 1386-1387, 1386f, 1387t
    struvite, 1407-1408, 1407f, 1408f, 1408t
  matrix, 1388
  pathogenesis of, 1373-1391

Urinary calculi (*Continued*)
  anatomic predisposition to stones in, 1389-1391
  calcium stones in, 1374-1382
  caliceal diverticula in, 1390
  cystine stones in, 1385-1386, 1385f
  horseshoe kidneys in, 1390
  in pregnancy, 1391
  infection-related stones in, 1386-1387, 1386f, 1387t
  medullary sponge kidney in, 1390-1391
  miscellaneous stones in, 1387-1389
  ureteropelvic junction obstruction in, 1389-1390
  uric acid stones in, 1382, 1383f, 1384-1385, 1384f
  silicate, 1389
  surgical management of, techniques in, 1458-1507. *See also specific procedure.*
  triamterene, 1389
  uric acid, 1382, 1383f, 1384-1385, 1384f
    pathophysiologic mechanisms of, 1405, 1405f
  xanthine, 1387
Urinary diversion
  bladder calculi in, 2666-2667
    management of, 2669-2670, 2671f
  conduit (intestinal)
    colon conduit for
      complications of, 2568-2569, 2568t
      procedure in, 2567-2568, 2568f, 2569f
    ileal conduit for
      complications of, 2566, 2566f, 2566t
      procedure in, 2564, 2565f, 2566
    jejunal conduit for, 2566-2567
      complications of, 2567, 2567t
    management common to, 2570
    metabolic complication(s) of, 2570-2576
      abnormal drug absorption as, 2573-2574
      abnormal growth and development as, 2574
      altered sensorium as, 2573
      cancer as, 2576
      electrolyte abnormalities as, 2570-2573, 2571f, 2571t
      ileocecal valve loss as, 2575
      infection as, 2574-2575
      nutritional problems as, 2575
      osteomalacia as, 2574
      renal calculi as, 2575
      significant jejunal loss as, 2575-2576
    preparation for, 2564
  continent, in children
    continent vesicostomy for, 3697-3698, 3699f
    hydraulic valve for, 3696-3697
    ileocecal valve for, 3696
    mechanisms of, 3693-3699
    nipple valves for, 3693-3694, 3694f
    results of, 3698
    ureterosigmoidostomy for, 3693
    valve flaps for, 3694-3696
      alternatives to, 3696, 3697f
      Mitrofanoff principle in, 3694
      results of, 3695-3696
      technique of, 3694f, 3695
  cutaneous continent, 2579-2611
    cystectomy in, 2580-2581, 2581f
    patient preparation for, 2579-2580
    patient selection for, 2579
    postoperative care following, 2581-2582
    quality of life assessments of, 2606
    surgical technique variation(s) of, 2606-2610
      absorbable staples in, 2607

Urinary diversion (*Continued*)
    conduit conversion to continent reservoir in, 2607
    minimally invasive continent cutaneous diversion in, 2606-2607
    postoperative care in, 2610
    right colon pouch as, 2607-2609, 2608f
    stapled sigmoid reservoir as, 2609-2610, 2609f
    W-stapled reservoir as, 2610, 2610f
    with continent catheterizing pouches, 2586-2591, 2587f, 2590f-2592f
    with gastric pouches, 2604-2606, 2604f, 2605f
    with Indiana pouch, 2596-2597, 2599f-2601f, 2600-2602, 3696
    with Mainz pouch, 2591, 2593, 2594f, 2595-2596, 2596f-2599f
    with Penn pouch, 2602-2604, 2603f
    with rectal bladder, 2582-2586, 2585f
  for bladder filling/storage disorders, 2297
  for genitourinary tuberculosis, 446
  for painful bladder syndrome/interstitial cystitis, 367
  in exstrophy patient, 3537-3538
    continent, 3538
  in management of posterior urethral valves, 3592-3595, 3595f
  in vesicovaginal fistula repair, 2340
  intestinal anastomosis in, 2539-2551
    complications of, 2549-2551, 2550t, 2551f
    laparoscopic, 2542, 2545f-2547f
    postoperative care following, 2548-2549
    principles of, 2539-2540
    stapled, 2542-2544, 2543f, 2544f
    sutured, 2540-2542, 2540f-2542f
    types of, 2540-2544
    with biofragmentable rings, 2548
  intestinal segment(s) used in, 2533-2578
    abdominal stoma and, 2551-2553
      complications of, 2553-2554
      flush, 2552
      loop end ileostomy as, 2553, 2553f
      nipple "rosebud," 2552, 2552f
    colon as, surgical anatomy of, 2534-2535, 2535f
    complications of, 2551, 2551f
    neuromechanical aspects of, 2576-2578
    preparation of, 2536-2539
      antibiotic, 2538-2539, 2538t
      diarrhea and pseudomembranous enterocolitis following, 2539
      mechanical, 2537-2538, 2537t
    renal deterioration after, 2563-2564
    selection of, 2535-2536
    small bowel as, surgical anatomy of, 2534
    stomach as, surgical anatomy of, 2533-2534, 2534f
    volume-pressure considerations in, 2576-2577, 2577f
  laparoscopic-assisted, 2523-2527
    ileal conduit in, 2523-2524, 2524f, 2525f-2526f
    ileal orthotopic neobladder in, 2524, 2527f
    Mainz II pouch in, 2524, 2527
  orthotopic, 2613-2647
    absorbable stapling in, 2645
    antireflux mechanism in, 2630-2633
    bladder cancer recurrence after cystectomy in, 2623-2629
      pelvic, 2628-2629
      urethral, 2623-2628
        in female patient, 2626-2628
        in male patient, 2624-2626

Urinary diversion (Continued)
    continence mechanism in, 2618-2619
    continence preservation in, 2619-2623
        surgical technique of, 2621-2623
            anterior dissection in female patient, 2623
            anterior dissection in male patient, 2622-2623
    contraindications to, 2615
    evolution of, 2613-2615, 2614t, 2615f
    patient selection for, 2617-2618
    principles of, 2615-2617
    quality of life after, 2645-2647
    results of, 2642-2644, 2644t
    technique(s) of, 2633-2642
        Camey II, 2634, 2634f
        Hautmann ileal neobladder in, 2635, 2635f
        ileocolonic (Le Bag) pouch in, 2641-2642, 2642f
        orthotopic Kock ileal reservoir in, 2636, 2637f
        orthotopic Mainz pouch in, 2641, 2641f
        right colon pouch in, 2642
        S-bladder in, 2634-2635
        serous-lined extramural tunnel in, 2636, 2637f, 2638
        sigmoid pouch in, 2642, 2643f
        Studer ileal bladder substitute in, 2635, 2636f
        T pouch ileal neobladder in, 2638, 2639f-2640f, 2640
        vesical ileal pouch in, 2634
    with previous pelvic radiotherapy, 2629-2630
    renal deterioration after, 2563-2564
    small bowel anastomosis in, 2557-2561
        Bricker technique of, 2557, 2557f
        hammock, 2559
        Le Duc technique of, 2559, 2559f
        split-nipple technique of, 2558-2559, 2559f
        tunneled, 2558, 2558f
        Wallace technique of, 2557-2558, 2558f
    supravesical, for prune-belly syndrome, 3490
    ureterointestinal anastomosis in, 2554-2563
        antireflux valves in, 2552-2562, 2561f, 2562f
        complications of, 2556t, 2562-2563
        ureterocolonic
            complications of, 2556t
            Cordonnier and Nesbit technique of, 2557
            Leadbetter and Clarke technique of, 2555-2556, 2556f
            Pagano technique of, 2557, 2557f
            Strickler technique of, 2556-2557, 2556f
            transcolonic Goodwin technique of, 2556, 2556f
        ureter–small bowel anastomosis in, 2559, 2560f, 2561
Urinary fistula, after partial nephrectomy, 1730
Urinary frequency. See Frequency.
Urinary hesitancy, 84
Urinary incontinence. See Incontinence.
Urinary indices, in acute renal failure, 1334-1335, 1334f, 1335t
Urinary microorganisms, in vesicoureteral reflux, requirement for, 4337
Urinary pH, 97
    in uric acid solubility, 1382
    low
        in calcium stone formation, 1379-1380
        in uric acid stone formation, 1382, 1384-1385

Urinary retention
    after artificial sphincter placement, 2399-2409
    after orthotopic diversion, 2621
    anogenital HSV infection associated with, 2033
    in benign prostatic hyperplasia
        effects of α-adrenergic blockers on, 2785-2786
        effects of medical therapy on, 2774-2775
    in Fowler syndrome, voiding dysfunction with, 2040
    perineal sling procedure causing, 2395
    post-biopsy, 2892
    postoperative, voiding dysfunction with, 2040-2041
    sacral nerve neuromodulation for, mechanism of action of, 2150, 2151f
    with brain tumor, 2016-2017
Urinary sediment, 105-109
    analysis of. See Urinalysis, sediment microscopy in.
    crystals in, 107-108, 108f. See also Crystals, urinary.
    in acute renal failure, 1334, 1334t
Urinary sensation scale, 2083
Urinary sphincter. See Urethral sphincter.
    artificial. See Artificial urinary sphincter.
Urinary toxicity, of brachytherapy, 3026
Urinary tract. See also specific part.
    dynamics of, 3657-3658
    embryology of, 3384-3387, 3385f-3388f
    endometriosis of, 1220
    endoscopic procedures in. See also specific procedure.
        antibiotic prophylaxis for, 253
    fetal, anomalies of. See also specific anomaly.
        incidence of, 3186
    fistulas of, 2322-2359. See also Fistula(s).
    function of, 3657-3659
    imaging of, 111-143. See also under specific modality for details.
        computed tomographic, 127-135
        in benign prostatic hyperplasia, 2772-2773
        magnetic resonance, 135-139
        radiographic, 111-118
        scintigraphic, 139-143
        ultrasound, 118, 122-127
    in patient history. See also Patient history.
        chief complaint and present illness of, 81-88
        medical history of, 88-89
        overview of, 81
        physical examination of, 89-95. See also Physical examination.
        urinalysis and, 95-109. See also Urinalysis.
    infection of. See Urinary tract infection.
    injury to
        in laparoscopic surgery, 214-215
        posterior urethral valves causing, 3586-3587
        with trocar placement, 208-209
    lower. See Lower urinary tract.
    natural defenses of
        in bladder, 235-236
        in periurethral and urethral regions, 234-235
    obstruction of. See Urinary tract obstruction.
    pain perception patterns in, 37, 37f
    pediatric
        anomalies of, 3253-3254
        normal, urinary tract infection associated with, 3263. See also Urinary tract infection, in children.

Urinary tract (Continued)
    reconstruction of, 3656-3702. See also Urinary tract reconstruction, in children.
    percutaneous nephrolithotomy of, track dilation in, 1491-1494, 1492f-1494f
    percutaneous nephrostomy of
        blind access to, 1533-1534, 1533f
        innovations in, 1563
        tract cauterization in, 1561-1562
        tract dilation in, 1541-1544
            dilators in, 1542-1544, 1542f, 1543f
            guide wire entry in, 1541-1542
    reconstruction of. See also Urinary diversion; specific procedure.
        in children, 3656-3702. See also Urinary tract reconstruction, in children.
        in cloacal exstrophy
            modern staged, 3542-3543
            osteotomy in, 3543, 3543f
            single-staged, 3543
        in renal transplantation, 1310, 1313f-1314f
    transitional cell carcinoma of
        postoperative BCG immunotherapy for, 1523
        ureteroscopic management of, 1522-1524, 1522f, 1523f
    upper. See Upper urinary tract.
    urothelium of
        abnormal, 1642-1643
        normal, 1641-1642, 1641f, 1642f
        tumors of. See Urothelial tumor(s), of renal pelvis and ureters.
Urinary tract infection, 223-302. See also Hydronephrosis; Ureteral obstruction; Ureteropelvic junction obstruction.
    abdominal radiography of, 242-243
    after augmentation cystoplasty, 3683-3684
    after renal transplantation, 1320-1321
    antibiotic(s) for
        aminoglycosides as, 245t, 246t, 247t, 248, 248f, 249f
        aminopenicillins as, 245t, 246t, 247t, 248
        aztreonam as, 245t, 246t, 247t, 248
        bacterial resistance to, 244-245
        cephalosporins as, 245t, 246t, 247t, 248
        choice of, 249
        duration of, 249
        fluoroquinolones as, 245t, 246t, 247t, 248-249
        formulary of, 245-249
        mechanism of action of, 245t
        nitrofurantoin as, 245, 245t, 246t, 247t, 248
        principles of, 243-249, 244t
        prophylactic, 250-254
            cystoscopy and, 252
            endocarditis risk and, 253-254, 254t
            endoscopic procedures and, 253
            indwelling orthopedic hardware and, 254, 254t
            open and laparoscopic surgery and, 253, 253t
            principles of, 250, 250t, 251t
            shockwave lithotripsy and, 252
            transrectal prostate biopsy and, 251-252
            transurethral, procedures and, 252
            urethral catheterization and, 250
            urodynamics and, 251
        trimethoprim-sulfamethoxazole as, 245, 245t, 246t, 247t
    bacteria in. See Bacteremia; Bacteriuria.
    bacterial nephritis in, 265-271. See also Nephritis.
    candidal, 460. See also Candidiasis.

Urinary tract infection (*Continued*)
  local treatment of, 464
  systemic treatment of, 463-464
 catheter-induced, 238
 clinical manifestations of, 238-242
 complicated, 224, 224t
 computed tomography of, 243
 cystitis in. *See also* Cystitis.
  complicated, 258-259, 258t, 259t
  uncomplicated, 254-258
 definition of, 223-225
 diagnosis of, 238-242
  prostate localization in, 242
  rapid screen methods in, 239-240
  renal localization in, 240-241, 241t
  stone cultures in, 241
  suprapubic aspiration in, 238-239
  tissue cultures in, 241
  urinalysis in, 239-240
  urine collection in, 238-239
  urine culture in, 240, 240f
 epidemiology of, 226-227, 226f
 excretory urography of, 243
 granulomatous nephritis in, 280-286
 hydronephrosis in, 276
 imaging of, 242-243
  indications for, 242, 242t
 in benign prostatic hyperplasia, effects of
  medical therapy on, 2775
 in children, 3232-3268
  age and, 3236
  bacteria causing, 3234
  bacterial ecology and antimicrobial
   resistance in, 3266-3267
  bacteriuria in, factors affecting, 3236-3238,
   3236t, 3237f
  bowel-augmented bladder and, 3241
  catheter-associated, 3266
  classification of, 3233, 3233f, 3234t
  computed tomography of, 3256
  covert or asymptomatic, management of,
   3262-3263
  cystitis as, 3234-3236, 3235f. *See also*
   Cystitis.
   inflammatory hemorrhagic, 3263
   interstitial, 3263-3264
  definition of, 3233
  diagnosis of, 3242-3246
   criteria for, 3233t
   microscopic examination in, 3244
   serum tests in, 3245
   urinalysis in, 3244
   urinary cultures in, 3245
   urinary leukocyte esterase and nitrite in,
    3244, 3244t
   urinary specimens in, 3243-3244
  end-stage renal disease and, 3261
  epidemiology of, 3232-3234
  epididymitis and, 3264-3265
  febrile
   evaluation of, 3198, 3203
   management of, 3261
  fecal colonization in, 3239
  fungal, 3265
  gender and, 3237
  genetics and, 3236-3237
  genitourinary anomalies and, 3240-3241
  iatrogenic factors associated with, 3241-
   3242
  imaging of, 3252-3254, 3253f
   specific techniques in, 3254-3256
  immune status and, 3239
  in uncircumcised infants, 3747
  incontinence associated with, 3263

Urinary tract infection (*Continued*)
  intravenous urography of, 3256
  magnetic resonance imaging of, 3256
  management of, 3246-3249
   antibacterial agents in
    dosages of, 3248t
    prophylactic, 3249-3252. *See also*
     Urinary tract infection, in children,
     prophylactic treatment of.
    selection of, 3249
   considerations in, 3267-3268
   for specific infections and associated
    problems, 3261-3263
   future treatments in, 3252
   in infants, 3246-3247, 3248t
   outpatient, 3247-3249, 3248t
   switch therapy in, 3249
  neurogenic bladder and, 3241
  nonfebrile, 3203
  nosocomial, 3241-3242, 3242t, 3266
  nuclear renography of, 3255-3256
  pathogenesis of, 3234-3242
  periurethral colonization in, 3238
  physical examination for, 3243
  pregnancy and, 3241
  preputial colonization in, 3238-3239
  prophylactic treatment of, 3249-3252
   antimicrobial agents used in, 3250, 3250t
   cephalexin in, 3251
   indications for, 3250t
   nalidixic acid in, 3252
   nitrofurantoin in, 3251
   probiotic therapy in, 3252
   trimethoprim in, 3252
   trimethoprim-sulfamethoxazole in, 3251,
    3251t
  pyelonephritic hypertension and, 3259-
   3260
  pyelonephritis as, 3234-3236, 3235f. *See also*
   Pyelonephritis.
   sequelae of, 3256-3258, 3257f, 3259f
   xanthogranulomatous, 3258-3259
  race and ethnicity and, 3237-3238
  recurrent, management of, 3261-3262
  renal damage caused by, factors affecting,
   3236-3238
  renal dysfunction and, progressive, 3260-
   3261
  renal scarring and, 3238
  risk factors for, 3236-3238, 3236t, 3237f
  sequelae of, 3256-3261
  sexual activity and, 3240
  symptoms of, 3242-3243, 3243t
  ultrasonography of, 3255
  vesicoureteral reflux and, 3240
   persistent, in peripubertal girls, 3240-
    3241
  voiding cystourethrography of, 3254-3255,
   3255f
 in geriatric incontinence, 2306, 2307t
 in males, infertility due to, 611
 in medullary sponge kidney, 3349
 in spinal cord injury
  clinical presentation of, 298
  diagnosis of, 298
  epidemiology of, 297
  management of, 298-299
  pathogenesis of, 297-298
 incidence of, 225-226
 isolated, 225
 lower
  prostatitis and, evaluation of, 312-318,
   314f-316f
  vesicoureteral reflux and, 4329-4330

Urinary tract infection (*Continued*)
  assessment of, 4332-4335
   challenging assessment of reflux in,
    4333-4334
   confirmation of, 4331
   cystographic imaging of, 4332-4333,
    4334f
   evaluation of, 4331-4332
   PIC cystoscopy of, 4334-4335
   uroflowmetry of, 4334
  magnetic resonance imaging of, 243
  malacoplakia in, 283-285, 284f
  pathogenesis of, 227-238
   anaerobes in, 228
   bacterial adherence in, 229-230, 229f
   bacterial pili in vivo in, 230-231, 231f, 232f
   bacterial virulence factors in, 229
   *Chlamydia* in, 229
   epithelial cell receptivity in, 231-234, 233f
   fastidious organisms in, 228-229
   host defense mechanisms in, alterations of,
    236
   mycobacteria in, 228
   natural defenses in, 234-236
   pathogens in, 228
   route of infection in, 228
   vesicoureteral reflux in, 236-238
  perinephric abscess in, 276-278, 277f, 278f
  prevalence of, 226, 226f
  pyelonephritis in. *See also* Pyelonephritis.
   acute, 267-271, 268f-270f, 270t
   chronic, 278-280, 279f
   emphysematous, 271-273, 273f, 274f
   xanthogranulomatous, 280-283, 282f,
    283f
  pyonephrosis in, 276, 276f
  recurrent, 225, 260-265, 260f
   bacterial persistence in, 260-261
   in postmenopausal women, 262
   low-dose prophylaxis for, 262-265, 262t
    biologic basis in, 262-263
    cephalexin in, 264
    efficacy of, 264
    nitrofurantoin in, 263-264
    trimethoprim-sulfamethoxazole in, 263
   post-intercourse prophylaxis for, 265
   reinfection in, 261-265
   self-start intermittent therapy in, 264-265
   urethral sphincter dysfunction and, in
    children, 3614
  reinfection with, 227, 227f
  renal abscess in, 273-276, 275f
  renal calculi and, surgical management of,
   1447
  renal echinococcosis in, 285-286, 286f
  renal tomography of, 243
  routes of, 228
  scintigraphy of, 243
  sexually transmitted disease and, 371
  ultrasonography of, 243
  unresolved, 225, 259-260, 259t
  upper, vesicoureteral reflux and, assessment
   of, 4335-4336
   renal scintigraphy in, 4336, 4336f
   renal sonography in, 4335-4336
  voiding cystourethrography of, 243
  with benign prostatic hyperplasia,
   2757-2758
Urinary tract obstruction. *See also*
  Hydronephrosis; Ureteral obstruction;
  Ureteropelvic junction obstruction.
  after renal transplantation, 1320, 1321f
  cellular and molecular changes in, fibrosis due
   to, 1204

Urinary tract obstruction (Continued)
  congenital
    clinical challenge of, 3173
    clinical manifestations of, 3163-3164
    definition of, 3164-3165
    diagnosis of, 3173-3174
    effects of, on developing kidney, 3166
    fibrosis in, 3169-3171, 3170f
    functional response to, 3160-3161
    induction process in, 3168-3169
    inflammation in, 3171
    management strategies in, 3174-3175
    pathophysiology of, 3163-3175
    patterns of, 3165-3166, 3166f
    prognosis of, 3174
    progressive renal dysfunction in, 3164,
      3164f
    renal growth and, 3166-3167
      regulation of, 3167
    renal tubular function in, 3172
    renin-angiotensin system changes in,
      3172
    reversal of, 3172-3173
    role of vascular development in, 3171
  in acute renal failure, 1327
  pathologic findings in
    electron microscopic, 1208, 1209f
    gross, 1207
    microscopic, 1208, 1208f
  pathophysiology of, 1195-1226
  prevalence of, 1195, 1196t
  relief of, renal recovery after, 1207
  renal functional changes associated with,
    1195-1207
Urinary tract reconstruction. See also Urinary
    diversion; specific procedure.
  in children, 3656-3702
    antegrade continence enemas as, 3700-
      3701, 3700f
    antireflux, 3661-3663, 3661f, 3663f
    augmentation cystoplasty as, 3672-3691.
      See also Cystoplasty, augmentation, in
      children.
    bladder dysfunction and, 3657-3659
    bladder function and, 3657
    continent urinary diversion as, 3691-3699.
      See also Urinary diversion, continent,
      in children.
    of bladder neck, 3664-3672. See also
      Bladder neck reconstruction, in
      children.
    patient evaluation for, 3659-3660
    patient preparation for, 3660-3661
    urinary undiversion as, 3701-3702
  in cloacal exstrophy
    modern staged, 3542-3543
    osteotomy in, 3543, 3543f
    single-staged, 3543
  in renal transplantation, 1310, 1313f-1314f
Urinary undiversion, in children, 3701-3702
Urinary urgency. See Urgency.
Urinary values, for school-aged children,
    3225t
Urination. See Micturition.
Urine
  acidification of
    deficit in, ureteral obstruction and, 1202
    in infant and child, 3154-3155, 3155f
  bacteria in. See also Bacteriuria.
    growth of, 235
  bilirubin in, 104
  blood in. See Hematuria.
  collection of. See Urine collection.
  color of, 96, 96t

Urine (Continued)
  concentration of
    after ureteral obstruction, 1200-1201
    countercurrent mechanisms in, 1142-1144,
      1143f, 1144f
    in infant and child, 3155-3156
    in neonate, 3152
    normal, 1200
  culturing of. See Urine culture.
  diversion of. See Urinary diversion.
  egress of, from kidney, 1200
  excessive output of, in geriatric incontinence,
    2307f, 2309
  fetal production of, amniotic fluid as
    indicator of, 3573
  flow rate of
    in fetus, 3150
    in incontinent patient, 2063
  intraprostatic reflux of, 308
  leakage of
    after partial cystectomy, 2505
    with vesicovaginal fistula, 2326
  osmolality of, 97
  postvoid residual
    definition of, 1997
    in benign prostatic hyperplasia, assessment
      of, 2770-2771
    in incontinent patient, assessment of, 2060
  protein in. See Proteinuria.
  specific gravity of, 97
  stones in. See Urinary calculi.
  storage of, 2049
  toxicity of, in painful bladder
    syndrome/interstitial cystitis, 347
  transport of, 1907-1910. See also Ureter(s),
    peristalsis of.
    effect of bladder filling and vesical
      dysfunction on, 1909
    effect of diuresis on, 1909
    propulsion of bolus in, 1907-1909, 1909f
  turbidity of, 96-97
  urobilinogen in, 104
Urine collection
  by suprapubic aspiration, 238-239
  in endoscopic treatment of urothelial tumors,
    1674-1675
  in females, 96
  in males, 95-96
  in neonates and infants, 96
  instructions for, 1398
  24-hour, erroneous, causes of, 1408t
Urine culture, 240, 240f
  in genitourinary tuberculosis, 440-441
  in pediatric urinary tract infection, 3245
  in urethral diverticula, 2378
  in vesicovaginal fistula, 2329-2330
  preparation of and microscopic technique for,
    105
  prior to urinary tract reconstruction, in
    children, 3661
  techniques for, 314-315, 314f, 315f
Urine cytology, of non–muscle-invasive bladder
    cancer, for surveillance, 2463-2464
Urine tests, for urothelial tumors, 1644
Urinoma, perirenal, prenatal diagnosis of, 3178,
    3180f
Urobilinogen, in urine, 104
UROC28 gene, in prostate cancer, 2909
Urodynamic classification, of voiding
    dysfunction, 1981-1982, 1981t
Urodynamic equations, 1989t
Urodynamic evaluation
  ambulatory techniques of, 2008-2009
    in incontinent patient, 2069

Urodynamic evaluation (Continued)
  analysis and interpretation of, 2009
  antibiotics in, 1987
    prophylactic, 251
  artifacts in, 2004
  catheters in, 1988-1989
  conduction of, 1990-2008
    cystometrogram in, 1991-1995, 1992f,
      1993f, 1994t, 1995f
    electromyographic studies in, 2002
    kinesiologic studies in, 2002-2003, 2003f
    leak point pressures in, 2005-2007, 2005f,
      2006f
    multichannel urodynamics in, 2004-2005,
      2004f
    neurophysiologic studies in, 2003-2004,
      2004f
    pressure-flow studies in, 1995-2000, 1996f,
      1997f, 1999f, 2000f
    urethral pressure studies in, 2007-2008
    uroflow in, 1990-1991, 1990f
    videourodynamics in, 2000-2002, 2000f,
      2001f
  cystometry transducers in, 1988
  electrodes in, 1989-1990
  flowmeters in, 1989, 1989t
  indications for, 1986, 1987t
  of bladder capacity and compliance, prior
    to urinary tract reconstruction, 3659-
    3660
  of bladder diverticula, 2365
  of bladder emptying, prior to urinary tract
    reconstruction, 3660
  of lower urinary tract function
    drugs affecting, 3628t
    in children, 3625-3628, 3626f, 3628f
  of prostatitis, 316
  of urethral diverticula, 2379
  of urethral sphincter, prior to urinary tract
    reconstruction, 3660
  of voiding dysfunction, 1986-2009
  patient preparation for, 1987-1988
  preparation for, 1987
Urodynamic studies, of urethral sphincter
    dysfunction, in children, 3616-3618, 3617f,
    3618f
Urodynamic testing
  in geriatric incontinence, 2314
  in pelvic organ prolapse, 2209, 2210f
Urodynamics
  equipment for, 1988-1990, 1988t
    electromyographic, 1989-1990
  functional concept of, 1978-1979, 1979t
  in incontinent patient
    eyeball, 2064, 2064f
    multichannel, 2064-2068
      filling/storage phase of, 2065-2067,
        2065f-2067f
      indications for, 2065t
      voiding/emptying phase of, 2068
  parameters in, 1987-1988
  principles of, 1986
  room used for, 1987-1988, 1988f
Uroenteric fistula, 2351-2357. See also specific
    type.
Uroflow, 1990-1991, 1990f
  after hypospadias repair, 3742
  in females, 1991
  in males, 1991
Uroflowmeter, 1989, 1989t
Uroflowmetry
  in benign prostatic hyperplasia, preoperative,
    2769-2770
  in incontinence, 2063

Uroflowmetry (Continued)
  in urethral sphincter dysfunction, in children, 3616-3617
  in vesicoureteral reflux, 4334
Urogenital diaphragm, 68-69, 69f, 2192-2194, 2193f
Urogenital fold, 3141, 3142f
Urogenital hiatus, 46, 68
Urogenital mobilization, total
  for cloacal malformations, 3868
  for intersex conditions, 3859-3862, 3861f-3864f
Urogenital ridge, development of, *WT1*gene expression in, 3146, 3146f
Urogenital sinus
  anomalies of
    classification of, 3846, 3847f, 3848f
    evaluation of, 3848
    history and physical examination of, 3848-3849
    radiographic and endoscopic evaluation of, 3849, 3850f-3852f, 3851-3852
    surgical reconstruction of, 3853-3864. *See also* Intersex condition(s), surgical reconstruction of.
  embryology of, 3573
  formation of, 3131-3132, 3132f, 3133f
Urogenital system. *See also specific part.*
  development of, 3121-3148
  embryology of, 3830-3832, 3831f
Urogenital triangle, 46
  blood supply to, 69, 70f
  female, 76f, 77
  male, 68-69, 70f
Urography
  antegrade (nephrostography), 118
  computed tomographic, 133-134, 134f
  excretory
    of acute pyelonephritis, 268-269, 269f
    of bacterial nephritis, 271, 272f
    of bladder cancer, 2437
    of chronic pyelonephritis, 279, 279f
    of horseshoe kidney, 3290, 3290f
    of imperforate anus and duplicate vagina, 3275, 3275f
    of lumbar kidney, 3279, 3280f
    of prune belly syndrome, 3483f
    of renal injury, 1277
    of single-system ureterocele, 3408-3409, 3409f
    of unifocal malacoplakia, 285
    of ureteral injury, 1285, 1285f
    of ureteral obstruction, 1209-1210
    of urinary tract infections, 243
  intravenous, 113-114, 115f, 116f
    of autosomal dominant polycystic kidney disease, 3323
    of autosomal recessive polycystic kidney disease, 3317-3318, 3319f
    of bladder diverticula, 2364-2365, 2365f
    of genitourinary tuberculosis, 441-442, 442f
    of medullary sponge kidney, 3349f, 3350
    of pelvic lipomatosis, 1218, 1218f
    of renovascular hypertension, 1169
    of ureterovaginal fistula, 2342, 2343f
    of urinary tract infections, in children, 3256
  magnetic resonance. *See* Magnetic resonance urography.
Urogynecologic fistula, 2323-2351. *See also specific type.*
Urokinase plasminogen activator, 544
  inhibitors of, 544-545

Urolithiasis. *See* Urinary calculi.
Urologic anomalies, antenatal diagnosis and management of, 3598, 3598f
Urologic emergencies, neonatal, 3194-3196
  presenting signs of, 3194t
  specific diagnoses of, 3196-3197
Urologic office visit, pediatric, 3204-3215
  hematuria in, 3212
  history in, 3205
  laboratory examination in, 3211-3212
  outpatient procedures in, 3214-3215
  physical examination in, 3205-3210, 3206t, 3207t, 3208f, 3209f, 3211f, 3211t
  radiologic examination in, 3212-3214, 3214f
  surgical procedures performed in, 3215, 3215f
  voiding history in, 3205
Urologic oncology
  gene expression profiling in, 503
  pediatric, 3870-3905. *See also specific neoplasm.*
Urologic patient, pediatric, 3198-3216
  triage of, 3198-3204, 3199t
    emergent evaluations in, 3198-3200, 3200t-3201t, 3202t, 3203, 3203t
    routine evaluations in, 3203-3204
    semi-urgent evaluations in, 3203
    urgent evaluations in, 3203
Urologic procedures. *See also specific procedure.*
  antibiotic prophylaxis for, 250-254, 251t
Urologic structures, tissue engineering of, 557-566
Urologic studies. *See also specific study.*
  of renal transplant candidates, 1299-1300, 1300t
Urologist, perinatal, role of, 3186-3187
Urology team, pediatric, 3204-3205
UroLume permanent stent, for benign prostatic hyperplasia, 2808-2809
Uropathogens, in urinary tract, 228
Uropathy
  fetal
    appearance of, 3180-3185, 3181f-3184f
    diagnostic findings in, 3176-3178, 3177f, 3177t, 3179f, 3180f
    incidence of, 3186
    interventions for, 3187-3189, 3187t, 3188f
    management of, 3186-3189
    pathophysiology of, 3185-3186
    postnatal evaluation and management of, 3189-3194, 3190t
    screening for, timing of, 3589, 3590f
  obstructive, 1195
    congenital, 3163-3175. *See also* Urinary tract obstruction, congenital.
  in chronic renal failure, 1347
Uropharmacology, 1948-1966
  of adrenergic antagonists, 1952-1953
  of botulinum toxin, 1959-1960
  of calcium channel blockers, 1960-1961
  of duloxetine, 1963-1964
  of endothelins, 1956
  of glutamate, 1962, 1964-1965
  of hormones, 1956
  of inhibitory amino acids, 1962
  of muscarinic receptors, 1949-1951, 1949f, 1950t
    selectivity of, 1951
  of neuropeptides, 1954-1955
  of nitric oxide, 1953-1954, 1957
  of opioid peptides, 1964, 1965
  of potassium channel openers, 1961-1962
  of prostanoids, 1955
  of purinergic receptors, 1951-1952
  of serotonin, 1957

Uropharmacology (Continued)
  of tricyclic antidepressants, 1962
  of vanilloids, 1958-1959
  peripheral, 1948-1957
Uroplakin proteins, of urothelium, 1934
Uropontin, as calcium oxalate crystal inhibitor, 1367, 1371
Urosepsis, ureteroscopy causing, 1524
Urospiral stent, 2804-2805
Urothelial carcinoma, of bladder, 2418-2423
  adenocarcinoma as, 2422
  carcinoma in situ as, 2418-2419, 2418f
  dissemination of, 2423-2426
    histopathology and clinical correlates in, 2425
    implantation in, 2426
    lymphatic spread in, 2426
    metastatic spread in, 2426
    multicentric origin of, 2423-2424
    patterns of spread in, 2424-2425
    vascular spread in, 2426
  squamous cell carcinoma as
    etiology of, 2421-2422
    histology of, 2422, 2422f
  transitional cell carcinoma as, 2419-2421
    metaplastic elements in, 2421
    tumor architecture in, 2419, 2419f-2421f
    tumor grading in, 2419-2421
  urachal carcinoma as, 2422-2423
Urothelial cell(s), activated, in painful bladder syndrome/interstitial cystitis, 341
Urothelial dysplasia, in bladder cancer, 2417-2418, 2418f
Urothelial metaplasia, in bladder cancer, 2417
Urothelial tumor(s)
  of bladder, 2407-2446. *See also* Bladder cancer; Urothelial carcinoma, of bladder.
  of renal pelvis and ureters, 1638-1651
    after bladder cancer, 1639, 1654, 1655
      risk of, 1641
    antegrade endoscopy of, 1645
    biology of, 1638
    chromosome abnormalities in, 1639-1640
    cystoscopy of, 1645
    cytology of, 1645, 1647
    definition of, 1638
    diagnosis of, 1644-1647
    distribution of, 1640
    epidemiology of, 1638-1639
    etiology of, 1639
    follow-up procedures in, 1682-1684
      general, 1682
      issues in assessing recurrence in, 1682, 1683f
      metastatic restaging in, 1683-1684
      specific, 1682-1683
    frequency of, 1653
    grade of, 1643
    invasion of, into renal pelvis, 1640
    location of, 1640, 1643
    metastatic, 1640
      restaging of, 1683-1684
      treatment of, 1684, 1684f
    molecular markers of, 1643-1644
    mortality rates for, 1638
    natural history of, 1639-1641
    pathology of, 1641-1643, 1641f, 1642f
    prognostic factors of, 1643-1644
    radiographic evaluation of, 1644-1645
    recurrence of, issues in, 1682, 1683f
    risk factors for, 1639
    signs and symptoms of, 1644
    staging of, 1647, 1655, 1655t
    treatment of, 1647-1651, 1653-1684

Urothelial tumor(s) *(Continued)*
    adjuvant therapy in, 1681-1682, 1681f, 1682t
    brachytherapy in, 1681
    chemotherapy in, 1651, 1682
    endoscopic, 1672-1680. *See also* Endoscopy, of urothelial tumors.
    for metastatic disease, 1684, 1684f
    immunotherapy in, 1651, 1651t
    instillation therapy in, 1681, 1681f
    nephroureterectomy in. *See* Nephroureterectomy.
    open nephron-sparing surgery in
        adjuvant therapy after, 1681, 1681f
        indications for, 1656, 1656f
        results of, 1657
        technique of, 1656-1657
    radiation therapy in, 1681-1682, 1682t
    resection in
        adjuvant therapy after, 1681-1682, 1682t
        endoscopic, 1647-1648
            percutaneous approach to, 1648, 1648f
            results of, 1648, 1648t
            segmental, 1649, 1649tt
    ureterectomy in. *See* Ureterectomy.
    ureteroscopic evaluation of, 1645, 1646f
    urinary markers in, 1680-1681
    variatons of, by sex and race, 1638-1639
Urothelium
    abnormal anatomy of, 1642-1643
    glycosaminoglycan layer of, 1932-1933
    ionic transport across, 1934-1935
    normal anatomy of, 1641-1642, 1641f, 1642f
    of bladder
        dysplastic, 2417-2418, 2418f
        normal, 2417
    permeability of, 1934
    structure of, 1932-1934, 1933f
    transducer function of, 1956-1957
    umbrella cells of, 1933-1934
    uroplakin proteins of, 1934
Urotherapy, for urethral sphincter dysfunction, in children, 3618
Urovascular fistula, 2357-2359
*Urtica dioica,* for benign prostatic hyperplasia, 2800
    dosage of, 2800t
Uterine artery, 65, 65f
    middle, 49f, 51
Uterine cervix. *See* Cervix; Cervical *entries.*
Uterosacral ligament, 2197, 2198f
    suspension of, in apical vaginal prolapse repair, 2226-2227, 2227f
Uterus, 65, 65f, 66f
    anomalies of, in unilateral renal agenesis, 3274, 3274f
    development of, 3140, 3140f
    duplication of, with unilaterally imperforate vagina, 3839, 3839f, 3840f
    evaluation of, in female fertility, 612
    fibroids of, ureteral obstruction due to, 1221
    lesions of, ureteral obstruction due to, 1221
    prolapse of, 2200
    rhabdomyosarcoma of, treatment of, 3885
    sparing of, in laparoscopic radical cystectomy, 2521
UW solution, for kidney transplant preservation, 1306-1307

**V**

Vaccine(s)
    cancer, 499-500

Vaccine(s) *(Continued)*
    for genitourinary tuberculosis, prospective, 447
    for HIV infection, 403-404
    for HPV infection, 382
    for renal cell carcinoma, 1623, 1623t
        metastatic, 1629
VACTERL association, 3647
    vesicoureteral reflux and, 4344
Vacuum constriction device, for erectile dysfunction, 783
Vacuum erection device, for Peyronie's disease, 828
Vagina, 65, 65f-67f, 67. *See also* Neovagina.
    atrophy of, estrogen/progesterone therapy for, 880
    bacterial flora of, prophylactic antibiotic effect on, 262-263
    botryoid sarcomata of, in neonates, 3194-3195
    development of, 3140, 3140f, 3831, 3831f
    duplicate, in unilateral renal agenesis, 3275, 3275f
    epithelial cell receptivity of, in urinary tract infections, 231-233, 233f
    erosion of, vaginal tape–induced, 2259-2260, 2260t
    examination of, in incontinence, 2060-2061
    HSV infection of, 374f
    imperforate, cervix and uterine duplication with, 3839, 3839f, 3840f
    in exstrophy patient, 3505, 3505f
    leiomyoma of, vs. urethral diverticula, 2382-2383, 2382f
    pH testing in, 871
    prolapse of. *See also* Cystocele; Vaginal wall, prolapse of.
        after retropubic suspension surgery, 2184
    protrusion of, in pelvic organ prolapse, 2205
    rhabdomyosarcoma of, 3846, 3846f
        treatment of, 3884-3885, 3884f
    shortening of, vesicovaginal fistula repair causing, 2332, 2336
    stenosis of, vesicovaginal fistula repair causing, 2336
    supportive structures of, 2197-2198, 2198f
Vaginal agenesis, 3833-3838, 3834f
    associated findings with, 3833-3835
    incidence of, 3833
    management of, 3835-3839, 3835f-3838f
Vaginal atresia, 3833
Vaginal bleeding, in preadolescent, 3209
    tumors and, 3210
Vaginal cones, for incontinence, 2133, 2133f
    in elderly, 2318
Vaginal creams, antifungal, for vulvovaginal candidiasis, 385
Vaginal delivery, pelvic floor dysfunction associated with, 2189
Vaginal devices, for bladder filling/storage disorders, 2291-2292
Vaginal discharge, in children, 3209
Vaginal flap(s). *See also* Flap(s).
    in vesicovaginal fistula repair, splitting of, 2333-2335, 2334f, 2335f
Vaginal mass, in children, evaluation of, 3199
Vaginal pessaries, for pelvic organ prolapse, 2137-2138, 2138f, 2139f, 2215
Vaginal septum, transverse, 3832-3833, 3833f
Vaginal support prosthesis, for stress incontinence, 2137, 2137f
Vaginal surgery
    for prolapse, 2215-2232. *See also under* Vaginal wall, prolapse of.

Vaginal surgery *(Continued)*
    biologic and synthetic materials used in, 2216, 2216t
    glossary of terms in, 2215t
    principles of, 2215-2216, 2215t
    techniques of
        anterior compartment and, 2217-2222
        middle compartment and, 2222-2230
        posterior compartment and, 2230-2232
    for stress incontinence, 2212-2215
    complications of, 2214-2215
    preoperative and intraoperative management in, 2212
    techniques of, 2212-2214, 2213f
    vs. retropubic suspension surgery, for female incontinence, 2173-2174
Vaginal tape procedure, tension-free, 2251-2266
    anesthesia for, 2258
    complication(s) of, 2258-2266, 2259t
        hemorrhage as, 2258, 2259t
        infection-related, 2265-2266
        intravesical tape erosion as, 2262-2263, 2262t
        significant, 2266, 2266t
        urethral erosion as, 2260-2262, 2261t
        vaginal erosion as, 2259-2260, 2260t
        voiding dysfunction as, 2258, 2259t, 2263-2265, 2264t
        wound-related, 2266
    for bladder filling/storage disorders, 2293
    for concomitant pelvic organ prolapse, 2255-2256
    for intrinsic sphincteric deficiency, 2257-2258
    for mixed incontinence, 2256-2257
    in elderly patient, 2254
    in obese patient, 2254-2255
    midurethral sling device in, 2252, 2253f
    results of, 2252-2254, 2253t
    secondary or salvage, 2256
    type 1 mesh in, 2251-2252
    vs. colposuspension, 2185
    with prolapse repair, 2222
Vaginal wall
    anatomy of, 2199-2200, 2199f
    assessment of, 2205, 2206f
    cysts of, vs. urethral diverticula, 2383-2384, 2385f
    defects of, 2195, 2197f
    examination of, 2206-2207
    prolapse of
        anterior
            central defect in, anterior colporrhaphy for, 2217-2218, 2217f
            lateral and combined defects in abdominal repair for, 2218-2219, 2218t
            anterior colporrhaphy with needle bladder neck suspension for, 2220t, 2221-2222, 2221f
            anterior colporrhaphy with sling procedures for, 2220t, 2222
            four-corner bladder neck suspension for, 2219-2221, 2220t, 2221f
            grafts in vaginal repairs for, 2220t, 2222, 2223f
            paravaginal repair for, 2218t, 2219
            six-corner bladder neck suspension for, 2219-2221, 2219f, 2220t
        apical support defects in, 2222-2230
        abdominal approach to, 2224
        abdominal sacral colpopexy for, 2228, 2229f
        colpoclesis for, 2230

Vaginal wall *(Continued)*
 iliococcygeus ligament suspension for, 2227-2228, 2228t
 laparoscopic approach to, 2229-2230, 2230t
 sacrospinous ligament fixation for, 2225-2226, 2226f
 uterosacral ligament suspension for, 2226-2227, 2227f
 vaginal approach to, 2223-2224, 2224f, 2225f
 leak point pressure measurement in, 2007, 2240-2241, 2242f
 posterior, 2230-2232
  colporrhaphy and perineorrhaphy for, 2230-2232, 2231f
  rectovaginal fascia defect repair for, 2232, 2232f
 repair of, comparative trials in, 2229-2230
 sexual pain disorders involving, 885
Vaginal wall flap. *See also* Flap(s).
 in urethral diverticula repair, 2387f, 2388
Vaginal wall sling, Raz technique of, for stress incontinence, 2214
Vagina-sparing surgery, in radical cystectomy, 2498-2499, 2499f
Vaginismus, 864
Vaginitis, atrophic, 885
 in geriatric incontinence, 2306-2308, 2307t
Vagino-obturator shelf repair, for female incontinence, 2180, 2181f
Vaginoplasty
 for intersex conditions, 3854-3855
  flap, for low vaginal confluence with clitoral hypertrophy, 3856-3858, 3858f
  pull-through, for high vaginal confluence with or without clitoral hypertrophy, 3858-3859, 3859f-3861f
  results of, 3863-3864
  simultaneous clitoroplasty and labioplasty with, 3854
  technique of, 3855
  timing of, 3854, 3864
 laparoscopic, in children, 3927
Vaginosis, bacterial, 384
Valacyclovir, for herpes simplex virus infection, 374t
 in HIV patients, 394t
Validity, of HRQOL instruments, 154-155, 154t
Valsalva leak point pressure, measurement of, 2240-2242, 2241f, 2242f
Valsalva maneuver
 for bladder emptying disorders, 2298
 in evaluation of inguinal hernia, 93
 in examination of spermatic cords, 613
Valve ablation, in management of posterior urethral valves, 3591, 3592f
Valve bladder syndrome, 3596-3598
Valve flaps. *See also* Flap(s).
 for continent urinary diversion, 3694-3696
  alternatives to, 3696, 3697f
  Mitrofanoff principle in, 3694
  results of, 3695-3696
  technique of, 3694f, 3695
Vancomycin
 adverse reactions, precautions, and contraindications to, 247t
 for urinary tract infections, 246t
 mechanism of action of, 245t
 prophylactic, prior to pediatric genitourinary procedures, 3242t

Vanilloids. *See also* Capsaicin; Resiniferatoxin.
 biphasic effects of, 1959
 excitation and desensitizing effects of, 1959
 pharmacologic action of, at receptor level, 1958-1959
 uropharmacology of, 1958
Vanishing testis syndrome, 640, 3765, 3814-3815
 laparoscopic assessment of, 3783-3784
Vardenafil
 adverse effects of, 776-777
 clinical response of, 776
 efficacy of, 775
 for erectile dysfunction, 773-775
 onset of action of, 776
 patient satisfaction with, 776
 starting dose of, 777
 structure of, 774f
 vasodilator effects of, 778
 vs. sildenafil and tadalafil, 774t
Varicocele(s), 93, 1107, 3794-3797
 assessment of, adjunctive, 3795-3796
 clinical findings in, 3795
 diagnosis of, 658-659, 658t, 659f
 evaluation of, venography in, 629, 629f
 grading of, 658t
 identification of, 613-614, 1125
 in prepubertal boys, evaluation of, 3204, 3209
 infertility due to, 622-623, 641-642, 654
 pathophysiology of, 3794
 repair of, 642, 658-665. *See also* Varicocelectomy.
  ablation in, 3796
   outcome of, 3797t
  comparison of techniques in, 3797
  complication rates in, 3797
  inguinal ligation in, 3796-3797
  laparoscopic, 659-661, 660f, 1125-1126, 1126f
  laparoscopic ligation in, 3796
  retroperitoneal ligation in, 3796
  subinguinal ligation in, 3797
  transvenous occlusion in, 3797
  treatment alternatives in, 3796-3797
 subclinical, 658-659
 testicular dysfunction and, pathology of, 3794-3795
 ultrasonography of, 658, 659f
Varicocelectomy
 complications of, 665, 665t
 cost-effectiveness of, 665
 delivery of testis in, 662
 follow-up to, 665
 hydrocele formation following, 665
 indications for, 659
 inguinal approach to, 661-662, 661f-664f
 laparoscopic approach to, 659-661, 661f, 1125-1126, 1126f
 microsurgical vs. nonmicrosurgical approaches to, 662
 outcome of, 663-664
 percutaneous embolization in, 662-663
 recurrence of varicocele following, 665
 retroperitoneal approach to, 659, 660f
 scrotal approach to, 659
 subinguinal approach to, 662
 successful, prediction of, 664-665
Vas deferens, 64, 74f
 agenesis of, 3797-3798
 aspiration of mobile sperm from, 700
 blood supply to, 1099t
 congenital bilateral absence of, 611, 621, 647-648
 cryoarchitecture of, 606

Vas deferens *(Continued)*
 dissection of, in robotic-assisted laparoscopic radical prostatectomy, 2989-2990, 2989f, 2990f
 embryology of, 3124
 function of
  absorption and secretion in, 607
  spermatozoal transport in, 606-607
 innervation of, 606
 obstruction of
  after hernia repair, 676-678, 676f, 677f
  in sperm delivery, 647-648
  in vasectomy, 1101
 peristaltic dysfunction of, retrograde ejaculation and, 648-649
 preparation of, for anastomosis in vasectomy reversal, 667-669, 668f, 669f
 spermatozoal reserves in, 606-607
 vascularization of, 606
Vas deferens fixation clamp, ring-tipped, 1099f
Vascular endothelial cell(s), 477
Vascular endothelial growth factor
 in activation of angiogenesis, 542-543
 in urothelial tumors, 2424, 2425
 in Wilms' tumor, 3893
Vascular epithelial growth factor, in prostate cancer, 2866
Vascular erectile dysfunction, mechanisms of, 741-742
Vascular graft. *See also* Graft(s).
 placement of, ureteral obstruction due to, 1223
Vascular injury
 after adrenal surgery, 1885, 1885t
 in laparoscopic surgery, 213-214
 renal, in children, 3935
 with trocar placement, 207-208, 207t, 208f
 with Veress needle placement, 204
Vascular lesions, of male genitalia, 3759-3760
Vascular metastasis, of bladder cancer, 2426
Vascular surgery, penile, 802-816. *See also* Penile vascular surgery.
Vascular toxicity, chemotherapy-induced, 924
Vascularization
 in tissue engineering, 556-557
  approaches to, 557
 of epididymis, 598
 of testis, 581-584, 583f
Vasculogenesis, steps in, 556
Vasectomy, 1098-1103
 benign prostatic hyperplasia after, 2744
 complications of, 1102
 epididymal obstruction due to, 680
 failure of, vasal occlusion methods and, 1101-1102, 1101t
 incision techniques in, conventional, 1099
 local anesthesia for, 1099
 long-term effects of, 1102-1103
 no-scalpel, 1099-1101, 1099f-1101f
 open-ended, 1102
 pain after, 1102, 1108
 percutaneous, 1101
 prostate cancer associated with, 2862
 prostate cancer risk with, 1103
 semen analysis following, 1102
 vasitis nodosa after, 1102
Vasectomy reversal, 665-679
 anastomosis in, preparation of vas in, 667-669, 668f, 669f
 anesthetic considerations in, 667
 initial consultation for, 666
 microsurgical reconstruction in, instruments for, 666-667, 667f
 preparation of, 666

Vasectomy reversal (Continued)
    vasovasostomy in
        complications of, 678
        cyropreservation at time of, sperm retrieval
            for, 678
        inguinal, 669, 676-678, 676f-678f
        modified single-layer, 669, 674f, 676f
        multilayer, 669, 670f-673f
        patency and pregnancy rates after, 678-679,
            679t
        postoperative care following, 678
Vasitis nodosa, after vasectomy, 1102
Vasoactive intestinal peptide, in male sexual
    function, 734
Vasoconstrictors
    in erectile dysfunction, 741
    in renal hemodynamics, 1134-1135, 1134f,
        1134t
Vasodilators
    for erectile dysfunction, 741-742
    for female sexual dysfunction, 882-883
    in renal hemodynamics, 1134t, 1135
Vasoepididymostomy, 679-700
    anastomosis in
        end-to-end technique of, 683, 683f-685f
        end-to-side technique of, 683-684, 687f-
            693f, 690
        intussusception technique of, 690, 692-694,
            694f-698f
            two-suture modification in, 693-694,
                697f-698f
        methods of, 683-684, 690, 692-694
        side-to-side technique of, 679, 680f
    complications of, 694, 699
    Lepinasse single-tubule, 679, 681f
    microsurgical
        results of, 699t
        variations of, 679-680
    nonmicrosurgical, results of, 699t
    operative procedures in, 682-683, 682f, 683f
    postoperative care following, 699
    preoperative considerations in, 682
    results of, 699-700, 699t
Vasography
    complications of, 714
    in infertility work-up, 627-628, 628f
    of ejaculatory duct obstruction, 707-708
    of seminal vesicles, 1113, 1114f
    technique of, 710-711, 713f, 714, 714f
Vasopressin. See Antidiuretic hormone (ADH).
Vasovasostomy
    complications of, 678
    cyropreservation at time of, sperm retrieval
        for, 678
    inguinal, 669, 676-678, 676f-678f
    modified single-layer, 669, 674f, 676f
    multilayer, 669, 670f-673f
    patency and pregnancy rates after, 678-679,
        679t
    postoperative care following, 678
VATER association, 3647
    ureteropelvic junction obstruction in, in
        children, 3362
VBM chemotherapy regimen, for penile cancer,
    987-988, 988t
Vein(s). See specific vein.
Vena cava
    inferior. See Inferior vena cava.
    preureteral, 3417-3420
        anatomy of, 3417, 3418f
        diagnosis of, 3419
        embryology of, 3417-3419, 3419f, 3420f
        incidence of, 3419
        treatment of, 3419-3420

Venacavography
    of renal cell carcinoma, 1602
    of tumor involvement of inferior vena cava,
        1619-1620, 1619f, 1620f, 1621
Venography, in infertility work-up, 629, 629f
Veno-occlusive disease, in erectile dysfunction,
    742
    duplex ultrasound evaluation of, 760
Venous flow, pneumoperitoneum and, 200
Venous thrombophlebitis, ureteral obstruction
    due to, 1223
Venous thrombosis, deep
    after laparoscopic surgery, 218
    after robotic-assisted laparoscopic radical
        prostatectomy, 3001
Verapamil, for Peyronie's disease, 827-828
Veress needle, in laparoscopic surgery
    aspiration via, 180
    complications associated with, 204
    insertion of, 179-180, 179f
Veress technique, in retroperitoneoscopy, 183
Verrucous carcinoma (Buschke-Löwenstein
    tumor)
    of male genitalia, 427-428, 428f
    of penis, 963-964
Vertical flap technique, of pyeloplasty
    for ureteropelvic junction obstruction, in
        children, 3370, 3372f
    Scardino-Prince, 1245, 1246f
Vesical dysfunction, neurogenic, effect of, on
    ureteral function, 1909
Vesical fissure variant, of exstrophy complex,
    3550
Vesical ileal pouch, for orthotopic urinary
    diversion, 2634
Vesicle artery
    inferior, 50f
    superior, 50f, 51
Vesicle vein, inferior, 51, 51f
Vesicoamniotic shunt, fetal placement of, 3188,
    3188f
Vesicobullous disorders, of male genitalia, 415-
    417, 415t, 416f, 417f. See also specific
    disorder.
Vesicoenteric fistula, 2351-2353
    diagnosis of, 2352
    etiology and presentation of, 2351, 2351t
    management of, 2352-2353
Vesicostomy
    continent, for continent urinary diversion,
        3697-3698, 3699f
    cutaneous
        for prune-belly syndrome, 3490
        in management of posterior urethral valves,
            3591-3592, 3593-3594f
    ileal, 2570
Vesicourachal diverticulum, 3577f, 3579
Vesicoureteral reflux
    after renal transplantation, 1321
    age and, 4324, 4325t
        resolution according to, 4346-4347, 4346f
    as contraindication to Valsalva maneuver, 2298
    associated anomalies and conditions with,
        4341-4345
    associated with bladder diverticula, 2366-2367
    bladder diverticula and, 4343-4344, 4343f
    clinical correlates of, 4329
    contralateral, 4360-4361
    demographics of, 4324-4325, 4325t
    diagnosis of, 4331-4332
    etiology of, 4328-4329
    fetal, 4324
        postnatal evaluation and management of,
            3191

Vesicoureteral reflux (Continued)
    functional correlates in, 4327-4328, 4327f,
        4328t
    gender distribution of, 4324
    genes involved in, 4326
    genetics of, 4325-4326
    grading of, 4330-4331, 4330f, 4330t, 4331f
    historical perspective on, 4323-4324
    in CHARGE association, 4344
    in children
        landmark studies of, 3239
        persistent, 3240-3241
        risk of urinary tract infection and, 3240
        treatment of. See also Vesicoureteral reflux,
            management of.
        laparoscopic extravesical reimplantation
            in, 3926-3927
        outcomes of, 4347t
        patient positioning for, 4351
        recommendations in, 4349t
        urethral sphincter dysfunction and, 3614,
            3615f
    in exstrophy patient, 3507
    in megacystis-megaureter association, 4344
    in multicystic dysplastic kidney, 4344
    in pregnancy, 4344-4345
    in prune belly syndrome, 3483
    in renal agenesis, 4344
    in renal ectopia, 3279, 3280f
    in siblings, 4325-4326
    in spinal cord injury, voiding dysfunction
        with, 2027
    in ureteropelvic junction obstruction, 3361,
        3362, 3362f, 4341, 4342f
    in VACTERL association, 4344
    inheritance of, 4325-4326
    international classification of, 4330t
    low-grade, resolution of, 4345-4346
    management of
        endoscopic, 4348, 4362-4366
            follow-up of, 4363-4364
            materials for, 4364-4365, 4364t
            reflux recurrence after, 4365-4366
            STING technique of, 4362-4363, 4363f
        landmark studies in, 4350
        laparoscopic, 3926-3927, 4366-4367
        medical
            injectable therapies in, 567-569, 568f
            watchful waiting in, 4348, 4350
        principles of, 4347-4348, 4347t, 4349t
        redo reimplantation in, 4362, 4362f
        surgical, 4350-4360
            Cohen cross-trigonal technique in, 4356-
                4357, 4357f
            complications of
                early, 4360-4361
                long-term, 4361-4362
            cystoscopy in, 4351
            extravesical procedures in, 4357, 4358f,
                4359-4360
            Gil-Vernet procedure in, 4366
            Glenn-Anderson technique in, 4356,
                4356f
            incision in, 4351
            intravesical procedures in, 4352
            Paquin technique in, 4352, 4356
            patient positioning in, 4351
            Politano-Leadbetter technique in, 4352,
                4353f-4355f
            postoperative evaluation in, 4360
            principles of correction in, 4350-4351
    myelodysplasia with, management of, 3635-
        3636, 3637f
    natural history of, 4345-4347

Vesicoureteral reflux (Continued)
  persistent, 3240-3241, 4360, 4361-4362
    in peripubertal girls, 3240-3241
  prevalence of, 4324
  primary, 4328
    treatment recommendations for, 4349t
  racial distribution of, 4324-4325
  recurrence of
    after antireflux surgery, 4361-4362
    after endoscopic correction, 4365-4366
  renal cortical defects in, 4336-4341
  renal dysmorphism and, 4337, 4337f, 4338f, 4338t
  renal scarring in
    congenital vs. acquired, 4336-4337
    pathophysiology of, 4338-4341, 4339f
  resolution of
    by age, 4346-4347, 4346f
    by grade, 4345-4346
    spontaneous, 4345
  secondary, 4328-4329
  ureteral duplication and, 4342, 4343f
  ureteral peristaltic dysfunction and, 1914-1915, 1915f
  urinary microorganisms in, requirement for, 4337
  urinary tract infection and, 236-238
    lower, 4329-4330
      assessment of, 4332-4335
      challenging assessment of reflux in, 4333-4334
      confirmation of, 4331
      cystographic imaging of, 4332-4333, 4334f
      evaluation of, 4331-4332
      PIC cystoscopy of, 4334-4335
      uroflowmetry of, 4334
    upper, assessment of, 4335-4336
      renal scintigraphy in, 4336, 4336f
      renal sonography in, 4335-4336
  with posterior urethral valves, 3587
    management of, 3595-3596, 3596f
Vesicourethral anastomosis
  in radical perineal prostatectomy, 2982-2983, 2982f
  in robotic-assisted laparoscopic radical prostatectomy, 2995-2996, 2997f
Vesicourethral distraction defects, reconstructive surgery for, 1084-1086, 1084f, 1085f
Vesicourethral reflux, prenatal diagnosis of, 3181
Vesicourethral suspension, with prolapse repair, for bladder filling/storage disorders, 2293
Vesicouterine fistula, 2345-2347
  diagnosis of, 2345-2346, 2345f-2346f
  etiology and presentation of, 2345
  management of, 2346-2347
Vesicouterine pouch, 57
Vesicovaginal fistula, 2323-2340, 2323f
  clinical features of, 2326-2330
  cystoscopy for, 2327-2328, 2328f
  etiology and presentation of, 2323-2326, 2324f, 2325f, 2326t
  hysterectomy-related, 2323, 2323f, 2324f, 2326
  imaging of, 2328-2329, 2328f, 2329f
  physical examination of, 2327, 2327f
  presentation of, 2326-2327
  recurrence of, post-repair, 2336
  risk factors for, 2326
  treatment of, 2330-2340
    algorithm for, 2330f
    surgical
      abdominal approach to, 2336-2337, 2336f, 2337f

Vesicovaginal fistula (Continued)
      vs. transvaginal approach to, 2331, 2331t
      complications of, 2335-2336
      excision vs. no excision in, 2332
      flaps or grafts in, 2332, 2340
      greater omentum in, 2339-2340
      immediate vs. delayed repair in, 2330-2331
      indications for, 2333
      laparoscopic, 2512, 2513f
      Martius flap in, 2338-2339, 2338f
      other considerations in, 2332-2333
      outcomes of, 2340, 2342t
      peritoneal flap in, 2339, 2339f
      postoperative drainage following, 2333
      preoperative counseling in, 2333
      suprapubic intraperitoneal-extraperitoneal approach to, 2336-2337, 2336f, 2337f
      transvaginal approach to, 2331-2332, 2332t
        Latzko procedure in, 2336
        vs. abdominal approach, 2331, 2331t
      transvesical approach to, 2337
      vaginal techniques in, 2333-2336
        complications of, 2335-2336
        flap or flap-splitting, 2333-2335, 2334f, 2335f
      tissue interposition in, 2337-2340
      urinary diversion in, 2340
    urine cultures in, 2329-2330
Vesiculectomy, seminal, 1117. See also Seminal vesicles, surgical approaches to.
Vesiculitis, seminal, 325, 327, 1114
Vesiculodeferential artery, 65
Vesiculography, seminal, 710, 711f
Vestibular adenitis, 870f, 885
Vestibular glands
  abnormal and erythematous, 870f
  physical examination of, 866, 867f
Vestibule, sexual pain disorders involving, 885
  surgical treatment of, 889
Veterans Administration Cooperative Trial, for benign prostatic hyperplasia, 2763
Veterans Administration Cooperative Urological Research Group (VACURG) study, of locally advanced prostate cancer, 3056
Veterans Affairs Cooperative Study, of combination therapy for benign prostatic hyperplasia, 2793, 2793t, 2794f, 2795, 2795t, 2796f
VHL gene, in von Hippel–Lindau disease, 1585-1586, 3306, 3332
  mutations of, 1586, 1593, 1594
VHL protein
  as tumor suppressor, 3333
  biologic functions of, 1586, 1586f
Vibratory sexual stimulation, in erectile dysfunction, 764
Video monitor(ing)
  in laparoscopic surgery, 190
  of ureteroscopy, 1515
Video printers, in laparoscopic surgery, 190
Videocassette recorders, in laparoscopic surgery, 190
Video-cystoscopy unit, 168, 169f
Videourodynamics, 2000-2002, 2000f, 2001f
  equipment for, 2000-2001, 2001f
  in bladder neck dysfunction, 2001-2002
  in identification of pathology, 2002
  in incontinence, 2001

Videourodynamics (Continued)
  in neurogenic bladder dysfunction, 2002
  multichannel, in incontinence, 2068-2069, 2069f
Vincent's curtsey sign, 3611
Vincristine, for paratesticular and testicular tumors, 933
Viral infections. See also specific infection.
  immunity to, 501
Viral load, in HIV infection, monitoring of, 393-394
Virion, HIV, 388-389, 389f
  attachment, fusion, and uncoating of, 389
Virus(es). See also specific virus.
  DNA, 507-508
  RNA, 507
Visceral complications, after renal bypass surgery, 1752-1753
Visceral injury, with Veress needle placement, 204
Visualization, in laparoscopic surgery, instrumentation for, 189-190
Vitamin(s), in prevention of bladder cancer, 2442
Vitamin A
  in prevention of bladder cancer, 2442, 2467
  role of, in prostatic function, 2705
Vitamin $B_6$, in prevention of bladder cancer, 2442, 2467
Vitamin $B_{12}$ deficiency
  after augmentation cystoplasty, 3680
  due to conduit urinary diversion, 2575
Vitamin D
  active form of, in calcium absorption, 1371-1372
  activity of, 1137
  effect of, on calcium homeostasis, 1136, 1136f
  for metastatic prostate cancer, 3114
  in prostate cancer, epidemiologic studies of, 2861-2862
  regulation of, 1136-1137
  role of, in prostatic function, 2705
Vitamin D analogues, for hormone-refractory prostate cancer, 3116
Vitamin D receptors
  in hypercalciuria, 1374
  in prostate cancer, epidemiologic studies of, 2861-2862
Vitamin E
  for painful bladder syndrome/interstitial cystitis, 360t, 361
  for Peyronie's disease, 827
  for prostate cancer, chemopreventive, 2870-2871
  in prevention of bladder cancer, 2442
Vitamin E with selenium, for prostate cancer, chemopreventive, 2871
Vitiligo, of male genitalia, 433, 435
Void, urge to, vs. urgency, 2082
Voided volume, 3606-3607
Voiding. See also Micturition.
  absence of, in neonate, 3196
  active phase of, 3657
  detrusor pressure at, 3607, 3607f
  dysfunctional, 3612. See also Voiding dysfunction.
    during active bladder phase, 3659
  fractionated, 3612
  frequency of, 3606, 3606f
  infrequent, 3612
  involuntary, 1976
  low-pressure/low-flow, dysfunction associated with, 2039-2040
  mechanics of, 1925

Voiding (Continued)
  normal, 1990, 1990f
  prompted, 2127, 2315-2316
  scheduled, 2127
  staccato, 3612
  straining when, 84
  therapy to facilitate, 1980t, 2114-2122, 2298-
    2304. See also specific therapy.
  timed, in behavioral therapy for incontinence,
    2127-2128
  trigger, 2299
  types of, 1922, 1923f
  unphysiologic, 2298
  voluntary, 1976
  with normal bladder contraction, 1975
Voiding cystourethrography. See
  Cystourethrography, voiding.
Voiding diaries, 2203-2204, 2312, 2312f, 3614-
  3615, 3616f
Voiding dysfunction. See also Incontinence.
  classification of, 1978-1985
    Bors-Comarr, 1983-1984, 1983t
    Bradley, 1984-1985
    functional, 1978-1980, 1978t, 1979t, 1980t
    Hald-Bradley, 1984, 1984t
    International Continence Society, 1980-
      1981, 1981t
    Lapides, 1982-1983, 1982t
    urodynamic, 1981-1982, 1981t
  electrical stimulation for, 2148t. See also
    Electrical stimulation.
  in children
    neuropathic, 3625-3653
      central nervous system insults and, 3648-
        3653
      neurospinal dysraphisms and, 3628-3648
      urodynamic evaluation of, 3625-3628
    non-neuropathic. See also Urethral
      sphincter, dysfunction of.
      classification of, 3609-3611, 3610f
      epidemiology of, 3609
      evaluation of, 3614-3618
      management of, 3618-3620
      prevalence of, 3609
    sacral neuromodulation for, 2157-2158
    spinal cord injury and, management of,
      3652-3653
    urinary tract infections and, 3262
  in elderly, 2305-2320. See also Geriatric
    patient, incontinence in.
  in HIV patients, 397
  in pelvic organ prolapse, 2204
  in prostatitis, 308
  neurogenic/neuropathic
    aging and, 2043
    classification of, 1983-1984, 1983t, 2011-
      2012, 2012t
    defunctionalized bladder and, 2043
    in acute disseminated encephalomyelitis,
      2036
    in acute transverse myelitis, 2029
    in bashful bladder, 2039-2040
    in bladder neck dysfunction, 2038-2039
    in bladder outlet obstruction, 2039
    in brain stem stroke, 2016
    in brain tumor, 2016-2017
    in cerebellar ataxia, 2017
    in cerebral palsy, 2017
    in cerebrovascular disease, 2014-2016
    in cervical myelopathy, 2028-2029
    in children, 2038
    in dementia, 2016
    in detrusor sphincter dyssynergia, 2037-
      2038

Voiding dysfunction (Continued)
  in diabetes mellitus, 2033-2035
  in disease at or above brain stem, 2014-
    2019
  in disease distal to spinal cord, 2031-2031
  in disease involving spinal cord, 2019-2030
  in Ehlers-Danlos syndrome, 2042
  in Fowler syndrome, in young women,
    2040
  in gastroparesis, 2041
  in Guillain-Barré syndrome, 2035
  in hereditary spastic paraplegia, 2035
  in herpesvirus infections, 2033
  in HIV patients, 2036
  in hyperthyroidism, 2041
  in intervertebral disk disease, 2031
  in Isaac's syndrome, 2041-2042
  in Lyme disease, 2035
  in multiple sclerosis, 2019-2020
  in multiple system atrophy, 2018-2019
  in muscular dystrophy, 2042-2043
  in myasthenia gravis, 2041
  in neurospinal dysraphism, 2029-2030
  in normal pressure hydrocephalus, 2017
  in Parkinson's disease, 2017-2018
  in pelvic surgery, 2032
  in pernicious anemia, 2030
  in poliomyelitis, 2030
  in reflex sympathetic dystrophy, 2037
  in schistosomal myelopathy, 2036-2037
  in schizophrenia, 2041
  in Shy-Drager syndrome, 2019
  in spinal cord injury, 2020-2028
    autonomic hyperreflexia with, 2026-2027
    bladder cancer with, 2028
    epidemiology, morbidity and general
      concepts of, 2020-2021
    follow-up in, 2028
    in women, 2028
    infection with, 2027-2028
    neurologic and urodynamic correlations
      in, 2024-2026
    sacral, 2024, 2025f
    spinal shock with, 2021-2022
    suprasacral, 2022, 2022f, 2023f, 2024
    vesicoureteral reflux with, 2027
  in spinal stenosis, 2031-2032
  in syringomyelia, 2036
  in systemic lupus erythematosus, 2037
  in systemic sclerosis, 2042
  in tabes dorsalis, 2030
  in tethered cord syndrome, 2030
  in traumatic brain injury, 2016
  in tropical spastic paraparesis, 2035-2036
  in Wernicke's encephalopathy, 2042
  low-pressure/low-flow, in young men,
    2039-2040
  miscellaneous diseases causing, 2035-2044
  patterns of, 2012-2014, 2012t
  plasticity in, 2013-2014
  radiation-related, 2043
  treatment of, 2044, 2044t, 2118-2122
  urinary retention in, 2040
    postoperative, 2040-2041
  postoperative, after retropubic suspension
    surgery, 2183
  urodynamic evaluation of, 1986-2009. See also
    Urodynamic evaluation.
  vaginal tape–induced, 2258, 2259t, 2263-2265,
    2264t
Volume overload, intravascular, laparoscopic
  renal surgery causing, 1807
Volume-pressure considerations, in conduit
  urinary diversion, 2576-2577, 2577f

Von Brunn's nests, 1642-1643
Von Hippel–Lindau disease, 515t, 3330t, 3332-
  3334
  clinical features of, 3333-3334
  cystadenoma in, 933
  evaluation of, 3333
  gene mutations in, 3306
  genetics of, 3332-3333
  histopathology of, 3333
  inherited susceptibility to cancer in, 517-518
  manifestations of, 1585t
  pheochromocytoma associated with, 1861,
    1862t, 3334
  renal cell carcinoma associated with, 1584t,
    1585-1587, 1586f, 3333-3334
    nephron-sparing surgery for, 1615-1616,
      1615f
    screening for, 1599-1600
  renal cysts in, 3333-3334
  treatment of, 3334
Von Recklinghausen's disease,
  pheochromocytoma associated with, 1861
Voriconazole, 469
  cost of, 464t
  dosage of, 461t
Vulva
  basal cell carcinoma of, 428, 428f
  eczema of, 407, 407f
  HSV infection of, 374f
  injury to, in children, 3945
  Paget's disease of, 430, 430f
  rhabdomyosarcoma of, treatment of, 3884-
    3885
  sexual pain disorders involving, 884
  strawberry, trichomoniasis and, 380
Vulvar vestibulitis syndrome, 336-337, 885
  surgical treatment of, 887-889, 887f, 888f
Vulvitis, focal, painful bladder
  syndrome/interstitial cystitis and, 336-337
Vulvodynia, 885
Vulvovaginal candidiasis, 385, 460

W
WAGR syndrome, Wilms' tumor in, 519
Waldeyer's sheath, 59-60, 60f
Wallace technique, of small bowel anastomosis,
  2557-2558, 2558f
Warming probes, for cryotherapy, 3038
Warsaw procedure, of bladder exstrophy repair,
  3517
  results of, 3534
Warts, genital, 420f
  diagnosis of, 380-381, 380f, 381f
  treatment of, 381-382
Watchful waiting
  in prostate cancer, 2933-2934, 2948-2949,
    2949f, 2949t
    in low-risk men, 2950-2951
    vs. active surveillance, 2947-2948, 2948t
    vs. treatment, 2949-2950, 2949f, 2950t
  in untreated benign prostatic hyperplasia,
    2750-2752, 2751f, 2751t, 2752t, 2776-
    2777
    vs. placebo treatment, 2752t
  in vesicoureteral reflux, 4348, 4350
Water
  hardness of, nephrolithiasis and, 1411
  imbalance of, 1146, 1147f
  renal excretion of, medullary collecting
    tubules in, 1146
  renal reabsorption of
    in cortical collecting tubules, 1145
    in proximal convoluted tubules,
      1139-1140

Water jet dissectors, laparoscopic, 190-191
Water-induced thermotherapy, for benign prostatic hyperplasia, 2842
Webbed penis, 3749f, 3751
Wedge resection, in partial nephrectomy, 1724, 1726f
Weigert-Meyer rule
  of complete duplicated systems, 3387, 3388f
  of double ureters, 3413
    exceptions to, 3414
  of trigone formation, 3132
Weight reduction, in behavioral therapy for incontinence, 2129
Weiss criteria, of adrenal carcinoma, 1841t
Wernicke's encephalopathy, voiding dysfunction in, 2042
Western blot test, for schistosomiasis, 453
Wet mount test, for sexual health problems, in females, 871
Whitaker's test
  for megaureter, 4374
  of ureteral obstruction, 1210
White blood cell(s), in semen, 625
  reference range for, 618
Whitmore-Jewett staging, of prostate cancer, 2927t
Wilms' tumor, 515t, 1636, 3885-3898
  anaplastic, 3888-3889
  bilateral, treatment of, 3896-3897
  biology of, 3886-3888
  chromosomal abnormalities in, 3887-3888, 3892
  congenital anomalies in, incidence of, 3886t
  cystic, 3339, 3340f, 3341
  cystic partially differentiated, 3340, 3341, 3899
    multilocular cysts with, 3341, 3342f
      treatment of, 3343
  cytokines in, 3893
  DNA content of, 3892-3893
  epidemiology of, 3885-3886, 3886t
  familial, 3887
  favorable histology of, 3888
  imaging of, 3890-3892, 3891f
    recommended follow-up in, 3890t
  in horseshoe kidney, 3290-3291
  in mixed gonadal dysgenesis, 3812
  in multicystic dysplastic kidney, 3337
  inherited susceptibility to cancer in, 519
  inoperable, treatment of, 3896, 3896f
  multilocular cyst with nodules of, 3341
  nephrogenic rests in, 3889-3890, 3889f
    prevalence of, 3889t
  pathology of, 3888-3890
  preoperative evaluation of, 3890-3893
  prognostic factors for, 3892-3893
  staging of, 3892, 3892t
  treatment of, 3893-3898
    cooperative group trials of, 3893-3895, 3894t
    late effects of, 3897-3898
    preoperative chemotherapy vs. immediate nephrectomy in, 3895-3897, 3896f
    surgical considerations in, 3893
  unilateral, partial nephrectomy for, 3897

Wilms' tumor (Continued)
  WT1 gene in, identification and cloning of, 3887
  WT2 gene in, identification of, 3887
Wingspread classification, of anorectal malformations, 3647t
Wire electrode, 1989
  placement of, 2002
WNT4 gene
  in sex determination, 3802f, 3803
  protein product of, 3306
Wolffian duct, differentiation of, 3805, 3806f
Wolffian ducts, 2678
Women's Health Initiative (WHI) trial, of hormone therapy, 2307
World Health Organization (WHO) classification, of testicular tumors, 893, 894t
World Health Organization (WHO) definition, of reference ranges in semen analysis, 618
World Health Organization (WHO) estimate, of worldwide tuberculosis, 436
Wound(s)
  closure of, in sling procedures, 2244
  gunshot. See Gunshot wounds.
  stab. See Stab wounds.
  surgical, classification of, 253t
  vaginal tape–induced, 2266
Wound infections
  after laparoscopic surgery, 218
  as complication of post-chemotherapy surgery, 956
  post-circumcision, 3748
  radical cystectomy causing, 2488
W-stapled reservoir, for continent urinary diversion, 2610, 2610f
WT1 gene
  expression of, in urogenital ridge development, 3146, 3146f
  in sex determination, 3802, 3802f
  in Wilms' tumor, 519
Wuchereria bancrofti, 455. See also Filariasis.
  biology and life cycle of, 455
Wunderlich's syndrome, 1578

**X**

X chromosome, 3799
45,X/46,XX mosaicism, in Turner's syndrome, 3810
45,X/46,XY mosaicism, in Turner's syndrome, 3810
Xanthine calculi, 1387
Xanthogranulomatous pyelonephritis, 280-283, 282f, 283f
  in children, 3258-3259
Xenograft(s). See also Graft(s).
  for slings, 2238
    outcome of, 2248t, 2249
  in vaginal prolapse surgery, 2216
  mutagenesis and, 545-546
46,XX gonadal dysgenesis, pure, 3811
46,XX karyotype
  gender assignment in, 3829
  in hermaphrodites, 3815
46,XX male, 3800, 3809
  infertility associated with, 639

46,XX/46,XXY mosaicism, in hermaphrodites, 3815
46,XX/46,XY mosaicism, in hermaphrodites, 3815
46,XXY genotype, 3809. See also Klinefelter's syndrome.
46,XY gonadal dysgenesis. See also Pseudohermaphroditism.
  complete, 3813-3814, 3813f, 3814f
46,XY karyotype
  gender assignment in, 3829
  in hermaphrodites, 3815
  in pseudohermaphrodites, 3821, 3823, 3824, 3825
  in vanishing testis syndrome, 3814

**Y**

Y chromosome
  short arm of, genetic map of, 3800, 3800f
  study of, 3799-3800
    microdeletions of
      in oligospermia, 717
      infertility associated with, 632, 639-640
Yang-Monti technique, of continent urinary diversion, in children, 3696, 3697f
Yeast, in urinary sediment, 106f, 109
Yohimbine, for erectile dysfunction, 770t, 782
Yolk sac tumor
  of bladder, 2445
    Schiller-Duvall bodies in, 3901
  testicular, 895-896, 896f
    in children, 3903-3904
York-Mason procedure, in rectourethral fistula repair, 2355-2356, 2356f
Young-Dees-Leadbetter technique
  of bladder neck reconstruction
    in children, 3664-3665
    modified, in exstrophy patient, 3524, 3525f-3526f, 3526
  of bladder outlet reconstruction, 2294
Young's classification, of posterior urethral valves, 3583-3584, 3584f
Young's procedure, 68
Young's syndrome, 611
Youssef's syndrome, 2345
YV-plasty, of bladder neck, 2300

**Z**

Zantoterone, for benign prostatic hyperplasia, 2792
  dosage of, 2788t
ZEUS system, in laparoscopic surgery, 173-174
ZFY gene, 3800, 3800f
  infertility associated with, 639
Zidovudine, for HIV infection, 401
Zinc
  for erectile dysfunction, 770t
  in chronic pelvic pain syndrome, 318
  in prostatic secretions, 2718
Zipper injuries, to penis, 2652
Zirconium beads, carbon-coated, for stress incontinence, 2075
Zona pellucida, 631
Zoon's balanitis, 431, 432f
  of penis, 960
Zygomycosis, 466